Preface

Swimming in the 21st century

In his youth Nasreddin Hodja, the hero of so many folk tales of the Middle East, had a leaky ferry-boat, and used it to row people across the river. One day his passenger was a fussy schoolteacher who decided - on the way across - to give Nasreddin a test and see how much he knew.
- Tell me, Nasreddin, what are eight sixes?
- I've no idea, replied Nasreddin.
- How do you spell magnificence?
- I don't, replied Nasreddin.
- Didn't you study anything at school?
- No, replied Nasreddin.
- In that case, half your life is lost.
Just then a fierce storm blew up, and the boat began to sink.
- Tell me, schoolteacher, said Nasreddin. Did you ever learn to swim?
- No, replied the schoolteacher.
- In that case, your whole life is lost.

In our days, to learn how to swim, how to study, how to find one's way in life is increasingly recognized as more important than memorizing the capitals of the world. There are reference books for that. And this **World Guide** is one of them, but with much more on offer.

As in many other reference books, the reader will find here the names of all the capital cities and a wealth of other essential information about more than 200 countries and territories of the world. Unlike most other reference books with international reach, this one is written and edited in a developing country, Uruguay and most of its contributors are based in the South.

What difference does it make? Eight sixes are still 48, no matter where you live. But your concept of magnificence might be different if you are reminded that in 1520, when the first Spaniards took a glance at it floating in the lake of Tenochtitlan, Mexico City was 10 times bigger than any European city. Actually, for many guides and almanacs published from the North, there is no history at all in Africa or Latin America before the arrival of the Europeans.

And at the Third World Institute the team that put this **Guide** together feels that to ignore 'the other half' (the women, the indigenous peoples, the South or the East) is not a good way to learn to swim in the stormy waters of the 21st century.

Roberto Bissio
DIRECTOR, ITEM, URUGUAY

THE WORLD GUIDE

INSTITUTO DEL TERCER MUNDO

Executive Board 2001-2002
President:
Clara Píriz.
Secretary:
Luis Álvarez.

Executive Director:
Carlos Abín.
Director:
Roberto Bissio.

Adviser for current edition:
Andrés Alsina.

GUIA del MUNDO

Editors:
Roberto Elissalde and Amir Hamed.

Research and editing:
José Miguel Elosegui, Natalia Guelfi, Matteo Chiari, María Noel Reyes, Maribel Casas, Hersilia Fonseca, Sebastián Cobarrubias, Silvana Adami. Gonzalo Curbelo, Inés Bortagaray.

Statistics:
Daniel Macadar.

Translators:
Alvaro Queiruga, Sarah Mason, Linda Dorow and Beatriz Sosa.

Graphic Design:
OBRA

Layout Design:
Mara de Oliveira, Javier Santiago and Marta de Oliveira.

Information and communication technologies:
Pablo Cuadro and Red Telemática Chasque.

Marketing:
Hersilia Fonseca.

Administration:
Ana Claudia Ceballos, Lucía Rivero and Carmen Ridao.

NEW INTERNATIONALIST PUBLICATIONS LTD
(English language edition)

Editor:
Troth Wells.

Production:
Fran Harvey, Dean Ryan, Ian Nixon.

Marketing and Distribution:
Dexter Tiranti, Jo Lateu, Anthea Milnes.

This book is the result of documentation, research, writing, editing and design work done by the Instituto del Tercer Mundo (Third World Institute), a nonprofit institution devoted to information, communication and education, based in Montevideo, Uruguay

The World Guide 2003/2004 is an updated, corrected and expanded edition of the World Guide 2001/2002. This reference book was published for the first time in Mexico in 1979, on the initiative of Neiva Moreira, to complement the dissemination work of the Third World magazine he had begun publishing. In 1980 the first Portuguese version of the Guide was published. The first English version was published in 1984. New Internationalist Publications Ltd, in Oxford, England, has been in charge of the English version and its distribution in English-speaking countries since 1996. In 1999, SERMIS-EMI (Editrice Missionaria Italiana), from Bologna, launched the Italian version of The World Guide. Since 1992, The World Guide has been published on CD-ROM. Since 1997, through the Internet, the Spanish version of the World Guide has been available in Web Pages.

The World Guide is a cumulative work, building on the efforts of former staff members. We would like to mention the contributions of: Mohiuddin Ahmad, Claude Alvares, Iván Alves, Víctor Bacchetta, Juan José Argeriz, Maria Teresa Armas, Marcos Arruda, Iqbal Asaria, Gonzalo Abella, Susana de Avila, Edouard Balby, Artur Baptista, Roberto Bardini, Luis Barrios, Alicia Bidegaray, Beatriz Bissio, Ricardo de Bittencourt, Samuel Blixen, Gerardo Bocco, José Bottaro, José Cabral, Luis Caldera, Juan Cammá, Altair Campos, Paulo Cannabrava Filho, Carmen Canoura, Cristina Canoura, Gerónimo Cardozo, Diana Cariboni, Gustavo Carrier, Virgilio Caturra, Macário Costa, Carlos María Domínguez, Wáshington Estellano, Marta Etcheverrigaray, Carlos Fabião, Marcelo Falca, Helena Falcão, Wilson Fernández, Alejandro Flores, Lidia Freitas, Sonia Freitas, Marc Fried, Héctor García, José Carlos Gondim, Mario Handler, David Hathaway, Ann Heidenreich, Bill Hinchberger, Etevaldo Hipólito, Heraclio Labandera, Peter Lenny, Cecilia Lombardo, Linda Llosa, Geoffrey Lloyd Gilbert, Fernando López, Hakan Lundgren, Pablo Mazzini, Daniel Mazzone, Carol Milk, João Murteira, Abdul Naffey, Claudia Neiva, Ruben Olivera, Hattie Ortega, Pablo Piacentini, Ana Pérez, Christopher Peterson, Virginia Piera, Carlos Pinto Santos, Sieni C. Platino, Artur José Poerner, Graciela Pujol, Roberto Raposo, Felisberto Reigado, Maria da Gloria Rodrigues, Julio Rosiello, Ash Narain Roy, Ana Sadetzky, Alexandru Savulescu, John Sayer, Dieter Schonebohm, Irene Selser, Eunice H. Senna, Baptista da Silva, Yesse Jane V. de Souza, José Steinleger, Firiel Suijker, Carolina Trujillo, Pedro Velozo, Horacio Verbitsky, Amelia Villaverde, Anatoli Voronov and Asa Zatz.

We have received the help, encouragement and support of Carlos Afonso, Cedric Belfrage, Max van den Berg, Dirk-Jan Broertjes, Alberto Brusa, Anne-Pieter van Dijk, Rodrigo Egaña, Cecilia Ferraría, Goran Hammer, Mohammed Idris, Sytse Kujik, Arne Lindquist, Carlos Mañosa, Fernando Molina, Hans Poelgrom, Malva Rodríguez, John Schlanger, Gregorio Selser, Herbet de Souza, Sjef Theunis and Germán Wettstein. Leo van Grunsven gave us editorial suggestions, together with his confidence in the project.

The editorial staff acknowledges the valuable contributions made by the libraries of the following institutions: UNDE, UNESCO, CLASH, FE, the UN Information Center in Montevideo, Impala in Madrid and the UNCLAD in Geneva.

The Third World Network, Penang, Malaysia provided ideas, documents and links with many contributors.

To all of them we offer our thanks. Thanks also to the hundreds of readers who have given us their comments, suggestions and detailed information.

The judgements and values contained in this book are the exclusive responsibility of the editors and do not represent the opinion of any of the people or institutions listed, except for the Third World Institute. ∎

INSTITUTO DEL TERCER MUNDO
Juan D. Jackson 1136, Montevideo 11200, Uruguay
Phone: 598 2 419 6192; Fax: 598 2 411 9222.
E-mail: item@item.org.uy/
Website: http://www.item.org.uy/

NEW INTERNATIONALIST PUBLICATIONS LTD
55 Rectory Road, Oxford OX4 1BW, United Kingdom
Tel: (44) 1865 728181; Fax: (44) 1865 793152
E-mail: ni@newint.org
Website: http://www.newint.org/

© Copyright 2003 by Instituto del Tercer Mundo
ISBN: Hardback ISBN 0 9540499 6 9
Paperback ISBN 0 9540499 7 7

New Internationalist Publications Ltd has an exclusive license to publish and distribute the English language print and CD-Rom editions of The World Guide throughout the world.

Third World Guide (English language edition) 1984, 1985, 1986, 1988, 1990 and 1992.

The World Guide (English language edition) 1995, 1997, 1999, 2001 and 2003.

Global issues

A round-up of key topics

I. The earth and its peoples

Technological progress

WESTERN CIVILIZATION, as it drives globalization forward, has imposed its own narrative, its own approach to time and, with it, its own model for exploiting the planet. Globalization's narrative of history is the depletion of species and natural resources, and if this is not altered it will indeed be the end. To avert this threat, peoples of the South need to reassert their difference and provide alternatives to globalization.

History and what is hidden by globalization

Francis Fukuyama, adviser to the US government, coined the phrase 'the end of history' in a pamphlet in the early 1990s. His notion is that we are now witnessing this phenomenon, supposedly a time marking the end of eras and of nations, which will become a global community that has resolved its differences and, as such, its history.

Fukuyama's idea was intended to strengthen the modern Western narrative, generally known as 'History' with a capital 'H', with its central concept of evolution. This is primarily a legacy of the biblical narrative, in which time is linear and moves towards an end - in the case of the Bible, this end is the final judgement. This linear approach is a Western patriarchal notion, at odds with other notions of time such as menstrual cycles or those of many non-Christians who also prefer a cyclical concept. The thousands of peoples who lived on the continent that came to be known as the Americas by the Conquistadors conceived of time based on the cycles of nature. Similar approaches are found among the Africans, who were subjugated by Europe and Islam, while in several cultures the belief in the cycle of reincarnation remains strong.

Rewriting history

In the Western model, what marks the distinction between prehistory and history is an element that is both cultural and technological, such as writing. That is, the West has designated as prehistory the age in which humans lacked the written word, and history is humanity's capacity to document in writing its experience in the world. In the 15th and 16th centuries, the Spanish Conquistadors came upon peoples who preserved their traditions orally, not with the written word, and thus considered them 'peoples without a history'. This is effectively saying that most of the world's people are ahistoric, and that their conquest and subjugation into Western domi-

nance marked their entry into History and a world with 'a purpose'.

'Progress'

In the 16th century, the Italian statesman Nicollo Machiavelli formulated a change within the narrative of history. People, men, became its 'agents', the ones who decided its course. The course of history was no longer 'God-given' but was shaped by humans. With European expansion from the 15th century came wide-scale exploitation of natural resources that did not respect nature's cycles. Excavating the earth in search of precious metals or damming rivers to obtain gold were the 'natural' consequence of men's dominance over Nature; it became 'natural' therefore to exploit resources willy-nilly. Humans existed to be the architects of their destiny and that of the planet, or to create history. In the 18th century, the old Judeo-Christian model saw a new shift: protected by reason and technological progress, humanity now inevitably must reach happiness. A century later Carl Marx developed the concept of progress further to see the engine of history as class struggle. When that struggle reached its end, we would arrive finally, at his version of the end of history - a classless society and a withering away of the state.

From this brief review it seems obvious that Fukuyama's idea is nothing more than another turn of the phrase: the global community will have resolved its differences thanks to technological progress. In the philosopher Hegel's sense, the idea of the end of history reveals itself in the omnipresence of capitalism, and national histories dissolve in the limitless time of the globalized world. In short, with globalization we will have reached paradise, the never-ending era.

The lack of legitimacy

Looked at in this way, these perspectives on history and the conceptualization of trans-

formation are but branches growing from the same Judeo-Christian tree, a formulation that has been imposed on just about all inhabitants of the planet. The agency for this is technology. Globalization, more than a 'resolution of differences' and more than an era, is the technological imposition of one model, that of 'instantaneousness'. With satellites, modems and computers, all corners of the world have been subjugated and, to a large extent, made interdependent.

Globalization, which began in the 16th century with the European mercantilist ventures, is being completed through technology. Technology as the agent of Western advancement is not the same as the ideological alibis of the past such as 'civilization' and 'progress,' often wrought by conquest. Now the West no longer feels it is necessary to legitimize morally its global agenda. Technological expansion and interconnection in themselves are permeated with Western ideology because they were initiated within the parameters of the Western development ethos. The technological development of the West has connected the world, and the world can no longer live without technology.

We cannot however continue to endorse technology as a means to happiness because that is no longer credible. The measure of time, which was once - for many peoples - governed by the cycles of nature or the phases of the heavens, has been replaced by the moment, the latest newsflash or most recent computer software. It is the imposition of the linear model through technology, with no further debate. Paradoxically even critics cannot escape: the claims one could make in the name of national 'difference' and the means of proclaiming them are dependent on the model of technological development and its means of communication.

No way out

'Emancipation' from the West would seem to be an arduous and radical task as, for example, became evident in the efforts of the Taliban in Afghanistan to cut the country off from TVs, computers and communications. The rest of the world watched with horror and displeasure, but had done nothing until it finally consented to the 'war on terrorism' after the September 11 2001 attacks on the US. The Taliban's efforts were not a 'return to the Middle Ages' as the US insisted, during and after the bombings that overthrew the Taliban, but rather a rejection of the West and its worldview (even though the Taliban's own model was repressive and extreme).

Trying to steer clear of the West's linear, goal-oriented view of history is problematic as the Taliban example shows. To replace one form of dominance with another is no answer. We do not have to accept the West's idea of the end of history. The Western model of natural resource exploitation is seriously threatening the planet. The evidence of contemporary global struggles strongly suggests that people will fight to maintain cultural diversity and a sustainable use of their resources, despite the force of globalization. The wisdom of those peoples who learned to measure time with the cycles of Nature, and not simply as a means to a final purpose, is essential for preserving the planet. It is up to all of us to ensure that time and the passage of time are not swallowed up in the here and now. ∎

POPULATION DENSITY

People per SQ KM, 2002.

Afghanistan	35.7	East Timor	52.4	Libya	3.1	Samoa, American	360.9
Albania	115.5	Ecuador	47.4	Liechtenstein	208.6	San Marino	452.3
Algeria	13.2	Egypt	70.6	Lithuania	56.8	São Tomé and Príncipe	148.6
Andorra	207.9	El Salvador	314.7	Luxembourg	173.1	Saudi Arabia	10.1
Angola	11.2	Equatorial Guinea	17.2	Macedonia, TFYR	80.6	Senegal	51.5
Anguilla	125.3	Eritrea	39.5	Madagascar	29.1	Seychelles	183.4
Antigua	148.3	Estonia	32.2	Malawi	125.7	Sierra Leone	67.2
Aotearoa-New Zealand	14.3	Ethiopia	66.0	Malaysia	70.1	Singapore	6,866.0
Argentina	13.9	Faeroe Is.	33.8	Maldives	1,030.1	Slovakia	112.5
Armenia	134.4	Fiji	45.5	Mali	9.8	Slovenia	98.6
Aruba	566.8	Finland	17.0	Malta	1,229.3	Solomon Is.	17.1
Australia	2.5	France	108.5	Malvinas-Falklands	0.2	Somalia	15.2
Austria	97.5	French Guiana	2.0	Marshall Is.	291.8	South Africa	36.2
Azerbaijan	94.1	French Polynesia	169.6	Martinique	352.5	Spain	79.9
Bahamas	31.2	Gabon	5.0	Mauritania	2.8	Sri Lanka	298.4
Bahrain	961.4	Gambia	137.1	Mauritius	581.4	St Helena	30.5
Bangladesh	1,101.4	Georgia	74.8	Mexico	53.4	St Kitts-Nevis	105.4
Barbados	626.5	Germany	229.9	Micronesia	183.7	St Lucia	247.7
Belarus	48.7	Ghana	88.7	Moldova	129.9	St Pierre and Miquelon	28.7
Belgium	313.1	Gibraltar	2,653.4	Monaco	34,044.0	St Vincent	294.1
Belize	10.3	Greece	82.5	Mongolia	1.7	Sudan	13.7
Benin	59.9	Greenland	0.2	Montserrat	33.6	Suriname	2.7
Bermuda	1,275.3	Grenada	276.6	Morocco	69.4	Swaziland	55.1
Bhutan	46.8	Guadeloupe	254.4	Mozambique	24.2	Sweden	21.4
Bolivia	8.0	Guam	293.8	Myanmar-Burma	74.5	Switzerland	181.2
Bosnia-Herzegovina	80.9	Guatemala	110.6	Namibia	2.2	Syria	92.7
Botswana	2.8	Guinea	34.1	Nauru	640.9	Tajikistan	43.9
Brazil	20.7	Guinea-Bissau	44.7	Nepal	168.9	Tanzania	41.7
Brunei	64.7	Guyana	3.9	Netherlands	472.0	Thailand	125.9
Bulgaria	70.5	Haiti	304.8	Netherlands Antilles	273.8	Togo	87.9
Burkina Faso	44.6	Honduras	60.2	Nicaragua	44.0	Tokelau	144.6
Burundi	260.4	Hungary	106.9	Niger	9.2	Tonga	138.6
Cambodia	78.0	Iceland	2.8	Nigeria	131.8	Trinidad and Tobago	254.6
Cameroon	33.4	India	350.2	Niue	7.5	Tunisia	62.2
Canada	3.4	Indonesia	120.1	Northern Marianas	170.5	Turkey	89.1
Cape Verde	110.7	Iran	44.6	Norway	14.7	Turkmenistan	10.5
Cayman Is.	157.1	Iraq	55.4	Oman	12.8	Turks and Caicos	41.5
Central African Rep.	6.2	Ireland	56.3	Pakistan	192.9	Tuvalu	348.5
Chad	6.7	Israel	305.7	Palau	43.5	Uganda	125.7
Chile	20.8	Italy	195.3	Palestine	552.0	Ukraine	84.0
China	138.8	Jamaica	242.0	Panama	39.5	United Arab Emirates	32.3
Colombia	41.9	Japan	349.9	Papua New Guinea	11.1	United Kingdom	247.7
Comoros	335.7	Jordan	58.4	Paraguay	14.5	United States	31.5
Congo D.R.	22.5	Kanaky-New Caledonia	12.3	Peru	20.7	Uruguay	19.3
Congo R.	158.9	Kazakhstan	5.9	Philippines	263.6	Uzbekistan	61.8
Cook Is.	86.4	Kenya	56.1	Pitcairn	13.8	Vanuatu	17.0
Costa Rica	82.3	Kiribati	116.7	Poland	126.6	Vatican	1,768.2
Côte d'Ivoire	52.5	Korea, North	187.6	Portugal	109.8	Venezuela	28.4
Croatia	83.3	Korea, South	480.0	Puerto Rico	449.6	Vietnam	246.5
Cuba	102.6	Kuwait	113.5	Qatar	53.1	Virgin Is. (Am.)	363.6
Cyprus	86.2	Kyrgyzstan	26.3	Réunion	295.7	Virgin Is. (Br.)	166.0
Czech Republic	132.6	Laos	24.0	Romania	97.0	Wallis and Futuna Is.	73.1
Denmark	125.9	Latvia	38.6	Russia	8.5	Yemen	37.7
Djibouti	28.1	Lebanon	353.3	Rwanda	330.3	Yugoslavia Fed. Rep.	103.0
Dominica	93.9	Lesotho	68.4	Sahara, Western	1.0	Zambia	14.6
Dominican Republic	178.6	Liberia	34.2	Samoa	56.3	Zimbabwe	33.8

Source: World Population Prospects - The 2000 Revision. United Nations.

ALTHOUGH THE UNITED NATIONS was created under the motto 'We the Peoples', membership of the organization is based on representation of nation-states. This has meant that in the last half century numerous peoples have lacked a voice or representation within the international community.

State vs peoples

Since World War II, most violent conflicts have not been international but internal, the actors being groups polarized by religious and ethnic differences within borders. In the last decade of the 20th century, the United Nations (UN) recognized inter-community and inter-ethnic tensions as the greatest threat to peace in the regions where they occur, and that concern about them transcends the home country of the parties involved. But there is little awareness that these conflicts arise because many peoples have been 'left out' of the international pact.

The novelty of the nation-state

Nation-states are a legal conformation derived from nationalism, an ideology that took shape in the 18th century in the West. At the end of that century, civilization came to be seen as being determined by nationality and therefore, based on this principle each individual should be educated in his or her native language and not in those from other civilizations or eras (such as Greek or Latin). The first decisive manifestations of this ideology, in the political sphere, were the revolution of the colonies that signed the constitution of the United States of America and the French Revolution. After being an active agent in the emancipation of the rest of the colonies of the Americas at the beginning of the next century, nationalism penetrated Central Europe, and then Eastern Europe.

In the first half of the 20th century, this ideology fueled anti-colonial uprisings and struggles the breadth and width of Africa and Asia. In the context of global politics, nationalism implied the identification of the state and the nation with the people (or at least the desire to determine the size of the state according to ethnographic principles).

While this model, in search of legitimization, has attempted to uphold previous practices (in other words, to relate itself to the modes of political organization that preceded it), the fact is that nationalism was not important for the political administration of the West in the first 1,500 years of the Christian era. After the fall of the Roman Empire, the ideal government was the universal, earthly state, based on the Christian republic or community. Before the age of nationalism, political loyalties were determined by organizational approaches such as the city-state, vassal and lord, the dynasty, religious groups and sects. During the Middle Ages, for example, civilization was determined by religion for some people. Different nationalities referred to their communality in a civilization, whether Christianity or Islam, and to languages of civilization, such as Latin, Greek, Arabic or Farsi. Even in the neo-classical era, the culture or model of civilization of France for example was accepted across Europe as appropriate for all nationalities.

The people-excluding machine

The nationalist political and ideological projects, dating back to their first manifestations in the Americas - whether 'Anglo-Saxon' or 'Latin' - turned into exclusionary machines. The 'Creoles' (Americans born to European parents) modeled nation and state on European languages and cultures. Within this legal-political order, the loyalty and devotion of the individual to the nation-state transcended any other type of individual or group interests. And so in emerging as 'American', the dominant cultures achieved uniformity in all aspects of life, including dress, religion, language and music, shunning and fighting anything different. When the hegemonic groups did not attain their goals of establishing a uniform society through persuasion and propaganda, they imposed it by force.

It was on the basis of asymmetrical policies of exclusion and extermination of indigenous peoples that the definitive lines of the American states were drawn. The social tensions produced still exist today in the demands of indigenous peoples throughout the Americas. Examples include the Mapuche in Chile and the indigenous peoples' movements in Bolivia, Ecuador and Guatemala, which defend their cultural differences and demand better living conditions; and Lakota people in the US with their demand of self-determination. The tensions within this model can also be seen in other aspects of an integra-

Representation for the unrepresented

A total of 52 peoples and nations of varying levels of organization, but with the common denominator that all are stateless, are joined in the Unrepresented Nations and Peoples Organization (UNPO). UNPO receives assistance and support from professionals in assessment, education and training in the areas of diplomacy, international law and human rights, democratic processes, institution building, conflict management and resolution and environmental protection.

Based in The Hague, Netherlands, UNPO has helped five former members, Armenia, Palau, Estonia, Georgia and Latvia, achieve complete independence and they have now been admitted to the United Nations with full rights.

Within UNPO are representatives of more than 100 million people worldwide who are oppressed, persecuted and seriously harassed, to the point that their populations are diminishing day by day. The list includes the Greek minority in Albania, the Hungarians in Romania, the Turks and Assyrians in Iraq, the Kurds in Turkey, Iraq, Iran and Syria, the Moluccans in southern Indonesia, the Albanians in Macedonia, the Mapuche in Chile, the Aborigines of Australia, and the inhabitants of West Papua and Zanzibar, among others. ∎

tionist society. Despite the marginalization of its Native American peoples, the US - a multi-ethnic country whose motto *e pluribus unum* (one out of many) celebrates the integration of difference - continues to pressure its minorities to 'meld' with the dominant culture, adopting US patriotism and its global ambitions.

Violence and decolonization

The model of the nation-state was imposed in Europe, but not without trauma and genocide. With the decline of the different trans-European empires, from the Austro-Hungarian to the Ottoman, various nationalities claimed their right to self-determination and independence. Among other experiences, this led to independence movements in Ireland and Sardinia, the revitalization of Basque and Catalonian separatism. The violent fragmentation of the Balkans lit the fuse for World War I and more recently, following the collapse of the Soviet empire, was reignited by the conflict between the former Yugoslavia and Croatia, Bosnia and also the Kosovars of Albania. The violence of the process reached its nadir in Europe during World War II, with the genocide of Jews, homosexuals and gypsies (the Roma) - the latter could be considered the Native Americans of European nationalism.

After World War II, the process of 'decolonization' and withdrawal of the Europeans created divisions within Africa and Asia, with borders often arbitrarily drawn by the fleeing powers. The archetype of the nation-state was sufficiently secured, and the territories of those continents suddenly had to adapt to the model imposed by Western modernity. The breakdown of their traditional social structures and the imposition of the state organization led to many ethnic and religious conflicts that in Africa have nearly extinguished entire countries (Somalia, Sudan and Rwanda to name a few). When looking at certain conflicts in Asia it becomes evident that the imposition of the model has entailed violence above all. Examples can be seen in the separatist movements of Indonesia or Sri Lanka; the constant animosity of nuclear powers India and Pakistan; the displacement of Kurdistan into four countries in which the Kurds are the minority; or the increasingly explosive tensions between Burma and Thailand.

The nation-state, as a political model, implies the systematic creation of minorities, that is, those communities that are marginalized politically, economically or culturally. Nation-states are essentially mono-ethnic (in other words, they favor the culture of one ethnic group). The minorities, in many cases, are not demographically minorities. Sometimes the most populous group, as in Bosnia's case, are the banished ones. Those states that attempted to do away with a national ideology, at least superficially - as was the case of the Soviet Union which subscribed to a wider ideology: socialism - have done nothing more than temporarily paper over the ethnic tensions, which often arose out of the violence with which the model was imposed.

One language, one territory, one culture

This homogenization, which is at the basis of the nation-state and the root of much of the violence of the last two centuries, needs to be re-addressed. Perhaps today's new technologies are providing a fresh type of understanding. Take the case of virtual communities, organized in forums, chatrooms and discussion groups on the internet. The virtual world, which has no 'territory', encourages the co-participation of individuals who live in different places (providing of course that they have the access necessary), involving numerous languages and cultures. It could be that in the not-so-distant future, it will serve as the 'venue' or 'language of civilization' in which many of today's conflicts find resolution. ∎

Languages of the world: Endangered species

Since the dawn of time, languages have been born and died out. Thousands have already been lost. Many more are heading for extinction. To survive the test of time, languages need at least 100,000 speakers. Though there are an estimated 6,800 languages spoken in the world today, according to UNESCO half are currently spoken among communities of fewer than 2,500 people. According to the Worldwatch Institute, 50 to 90 per cent of the world's languages could disappear by the end of this century. Other estimates, such as the one included in the report presented by linguist Peter Ladefoged to the American Association for the Advancement of Science, predict that 40 per cent of the world's languages will be extinct within a hundred years. With each language that disappears, the world loses a culture. For some, the extinction of languages has its similarities to the extinction of species.

Why languages die out

War and genocide, natural disasters, the adoption of dominant languages, such as Mandarin Chinese and Russian, and the prohibitions imposed by some governments on the use of different languages, have contributed to their progressive disuse. Some people including Professor Ladefoged believe the reason for their accelerated disappearance lies not only in the economic system, government policies and educational systems, but fundamentally in the mass communications media, because they abandon local tongues in favor of the most widely spoken languages.

When a language dies, it does not die alone, because with it disappears rich sources of information about the people who spoke it. Today in Siberia approximately 100 people speak Udihe, while those who speak Arikapu number fewer than a half dozen. In 2001, 83-year-old Marie Smith was the only remaining speaker of Eyak, a language native to Alaska. In 1992, the death of a Turkish farmer meant the death of Ubykh, a language from the Caucasus that had a record number of consonants: 81. An earthquake can be enough to eliminate a large portion of a language's speakers, as occurred in western India in the late 20th century.

Some 30,000 speakers of Kutchi died in the disaster, leaving just 770,000 others to carry the language forward. Currently, eight countries - Papua New Guinea, Indonesia, Nigeria, India, Mexico, Cameroon, Australia and Brazil - are home to more than half of the world's languages.

Toward a uniform world

To a large extent, the disappearance of languages is occurring within the context of a movement toward cultural uniformity, brought about by globalization. An intrinsic role of languages is to serve as agents of diversity and differentiation.

There is a countercurrent, or a reaction, to the process of uniformity: some languages are making a comeback. In 1983, the people of Hawaii reintroduced into their schools the native Aha Punana Leo, which had almost become extinct. Its speakers did not number more than a thousand, the result of a ban on its teaching in schools imposed by the US when it annexed the country in 1898. Interestingly, the name means 'nest of languages'. Today, there are 7,000 to 10,000 Hawaiians who speak their native tongue.

For their part, the people of Cornwall in the UK are attempting to revive Cornish, a language believed to have died out in 1777. The same attempts are being made with the ancient Mayan languages of Mexico and Guatemala. Meanwhile, Hebrew evolved in the 20th century from a written language to a national language, spoken by some 5 million people. Other initiatives seek to revitalize Welsh, Navajo, Maori and several of Botswana's local languages.

This restoration of nearly extinct languages only serves to underscore the principal characteristic of language in general: that of distinguishing some speakers from others, the impetus of communities to differentiate themselves. Though the biblical legend portrays the diversity of languages as a punishment, the truth is that the more languages the world has, the richer, stronger and more complex it will be. The same applies to species of flora and fauna: the greater their diversity, the more resistant they are to catastrophe, and the more likely to survive. ∎

MORE THAN TWO DECADES since the first cases of AIDS appeared, the pandemic is depopulating Africa, expanding in Asia and remaining out of control in the rest of the world. Not only is there no vaccine available to eradicate the disease, but the social, institutional, cultural and economic suffering of those affected is often ignored. HIV/AIDS can destroy societies and ruin economies.

The spreading tentacles of HIV/AIDS

When AIDS first hit the headlines in the early 1980s it was seen largely as a disease of gay men. Increasingly though it has spread its tentacles around other groups of people and now - particularly in Africa - is mainly affecting women. In the period 1999 to 2001, the proportion of infected women grew from 41 to 47 per cent. This phenomenon has become known as the 'feminization of AIDS'. It results, at least in part, from the fact that many women do not have control over when or with whom they have sex, and that in many parts of the world they are not permitted or encouraged to understand their own bodies, which makes them more vulnerable.

In Africa, ten times more people are dying of AIDS than as a result of conflict. In 1998, 200,000 Africans died in wars; 2 million died from AIDS. In terms of gender, the pandemic produces the opposite effect of war. After an armed conflict, a country often sees a shortage of males - as did France after World War I, Russia after World War II and Paraguay after the War of the Triple Alliance. Conversely, HIV/AIDS leads to falling numbers of women in Africa, with forecasts that in the near future there will be 11 men for every 9 women.

According to Population Reports produced by Johns Hopkins University in the US, during a street theater AIDS-awareness performance in South Africa, an audience of 1,000 men applauded the male character when he struck his wife because she suggested that they use a condom. While female condoms can be purchased in some West African countries, they are relatively costly. In Senegal for example a female condom sells for nearly $1.7, 24 times more than a male condom - another form of discrimination against women.

Often the infected girls and women are victims of rape, by strangers, rampaging soldiers or their own relatives. Some 16 to 52 per cent of the women have suffered physical abuse from their partner at least once, and in many cases this abuse is sexual violation. Gender violence, and fear of it, often leads to women being submissive and therefore risking an increased possibility of HIV infection. Prostitution, sex trafficking and sex tourism, deeply rooted forms of exploitation worldwide, are also

factors that increase the feminization of the disease.

In epidemiological terms, women are also more vulnerable than men. Among infected individuals, semen has been found to have a much higher concentration of HIV than vaginal fluid. This means that women run a much greater risk of contracting the virus, even more so in cases in which sexual contact occurs at an age when the mucous membrane is still delicate or is damaged as a result of rituals like genital mutilation or traditional practices like early marriage.

AIDS orphans
Studies by the World Health Organization (WHO) in 11 African countries indicate that the incidence of HIV infection among women aged 20 to 24 is three times that of men, and is five times higher among female adolescents than among males of that age group. The AIDS pandemic in Africa, as well as reducing life expectancy, increasing mortality and curbing fertility rates, is both leaving fewer women and also producing millions of orphans: 90 per cent of the world's 11 million AIDS orphans are African.

According to a UNICEF report on Asia, the spread of the virus tripled the orphan population in 2000. Currently, the number of children with parents infected with HIV is much higher than the number of already orphaned children. AIDS orphans, says the report, are those under age 15 who have lost at least one parent to the disease.

The number of these orphans increased fourfold between 1994 and 1997 in Cambodia, Malaysia and India, and also in African countries including Botswana, Namibia, South Africa and Swaziland. In that period, the figure grew more than 300 per cent in Vietnam and Burma, more than 200 per cent in Pakistan, and more than 100 per cent in Papua New Guinea.

The growing incidence of HIV infection among the child population is an indicator of its rapid contagion. In Asia, the virus began to spread just over a decade ago. By late 1997, India had 48,000 infected children, three times more than in 1994. In China and Vietnam, which once had low HIV rates, the child infection rate quadrupled in the period between 1994 and 1997.

The growing epidemic among children indicates increased infection rates among the most vulnerable sectors of society. These children, often socially isolated because of the stigma of the disease, are less likely to be immunized and more likely to suffer malnutrition, remain illiterate and be victims of abuse.

Nearly 3 per cent of pregnant 15- to 19-year-olds treated in prenatal clinics in Cambodia's larger cities are HIV-positive. In Thailand, the figure is 2 per cent, in Burma, 1 per cent. According to data from UNAIDS (Joint United Nations Program on HIV/AIDS) and WHO, India is tenth on the list of countries (the rest are African) with the greatest number of children living with HIV/AIDS.

The virus reduces fertility. Once the symptoms appear, an infected woman is 70 per cent less likely to become pregnant than a woman free of the virus. Because older African men - who are also more likely to be infected with HIV - tend to have sex with younger women, these women contract the disease at an early age and die before their reproductive years are over.

Counting the cost of AIDS
Sub-Saharan Africa is home to 69 per cent of the world's HIV-positive population, but the fight against AIDS receives a maximum of 1 per cent of the health budget in those countries. There are just three developing countries that allocate more than 1 per cent of their health budgets to fight the pandemic. In sub-Saharan Africa, only Senegal, Zambia and Uganda have developed specific policies for combating the disease.

In Asia, HIV/AIDS is growing three times faster than the funds earmarked for handling the disease. Before the 1997 economic crisis, the budgets of Asian countries were barely sufficient to provide basic health services. Since the crisis, the situation has worsened.

In 2001, there were 3.4 million new HIV infections in sub-Saharan Africa, bringing the total infected population to 28.1 million. That year, some 2.3 million Africans died of AIDS.

Shorter lives
Life expectancy, a key indicator for economic growth, is falling rapidly in Africa. In

Zimbabwe, if HIV/AIDS had not intervened, life expectancy by 2010 would have been 70 years. Now, as a result of the virus, it is predicted to fall below 35 years. In South Africa, life expectancy will fall from 68 to 48 years, and in Zambia, from 60 to 30. 'These life expectancies are more akin to those of the Middle Ages than the modern age,' said Lester Brown, director of the Worldwatch Institute in Washington. He added that, unless there is a medical miracle, nearly all the 24 million Africans infected with the virus will die from the disease. For his part, UN Secretary-General Kofi Annan has said that, as a result of AIDS, a country like South Africa will lose $22 billion in national economic production by 2010.

Vicious circle

The disease and the pandemic form a vicious circle. The persistence of poverty in the least developed countries turns these into reservoirs of infection. The same occurs in terms of gender: households headed by women, generally poorer than male-headed households, are particularly vulnerable to the economic effects of HIV/AIDS and to the disease itself. Although indirect, there is a relationship between it and political instability. The severe social and economic impacts of the pandemic threaten to intensify the struggle for political power and control over state resources.

A threat to security

During the Clinton administration, Washington concluded that the pandemic could destabilize governments, for example those of Africa and Asia, which would turn HIV/AIDS into a security problem for the United States. A CIA report entitled 'The Global Infectious Disease Threat and Its Implications for the United States' argues that the expansion of HIV/AIDS in Africa, Asia and the countries of the former Soviet Union should be considered a 'security' problem. It is the first time that the CIA has overtly involved itself in health issues.

For the CIA, new diseases as well as outbreaks of older ones will be a growing global concern over the next 20 years. These epidemics will pose a threat to US troops abroad and will exacerbate political and social instability in 'key' countries and regions for Washington's interests. Furthermore, says the CIA with mounting hysteria, the fact that HIV/AIDS spreads rapidly among servicemen - often involved in cases of rape - would increase the likelihood of 'unstable individuals' (those who are infected) in command posts and with access to military arsenals, including nuclear weapons.

From the US perspective, AIDS - which is predicted soon to account for half the deaths caused by infectious diseases in non-industrialized countries - will be a threat both in the former Soviet Union and in Asia, where there is an abundance of nuclear weapons. This scenario, filled with those 'unstable, infected individuals' with access to nuclear arsenals, is already depicted in dozens of apocalyptic movies produced by Hollywood. However, since September 11 2001, the fear in Washington is far from virtual. According to analysts, HIV/AIDS is likely to become a source of political and economical friction between the US and the countries of the South, because the US could impose trade embargoes in order to seal itself off from any possible sources of infection. ∎

REGIONAL HIV/AIDS STATISTICS AND FEATURES, END OF 2001

Region	Epidemic started	Adults and children living with HIV/AIDS	Adults and children newly infected with HIV	Adult prevalence rate (/1)	% of HIV-positive adults who are women	Adult and child deaths due to HIV/AIDS during 2001	Main mode(s) of transmission (/2) for adults living with HIV/AIDS
Sub-Saharan Africa	late '70s early '80s	28,100,000	3,400,000	8.40%	55%	2,300,000	Hetero
North Africa & Middle East	late '80s	440,000	80,000	0.20%	40%	30,000	Hetero, IDU
South & South-East Asia	late '80s	6,100,000	800,000	0.60%	35%	400,000	Hetero, IDU
East Asia & Pacific	late '80s	1,000,000	270,000	0.10%	20%	35,000	IDU, hetero, MSM
Latin America	late '70s early '80s	1,400,000	130,000	0.50%	30%	80,000	MSM, IDU, hetero
Caribbean	late '70s early '80s	420,000	60,000	2.20%	50%	30,000	Hetero, MSM
Eastern Europe & Central Asia	early '90s	1,000,000	250,000	0.50%	20%	23,000	IDU
Western Europe	late '70s early '80s	560,000	30,000	0.30%	25%	6,800	MSM, IDU
North America	late '70s early '80s	940,000	45,000	0.60%	20%	20,000	MSM, IDU, hetero
Australia & New Zealand	late '70s early '80s	15,000	500	0.10%	10%	120	MSM
TOTAL		40,000,000	5,000,000	1.20%	48%	2,924,920	

/1 The proportion of adults (15 to 49 years of age) living with HIV/AIDS in 2001, using 2001 population numbers.

/2 Hetero (heterosexual transmission), IDU (transmission through injecting drug use), MSM (sexual transmission among men who have sex with men).

GLOBAL SUMMARY OF THE HIV/AIDS SITUATION, DECEMBER 2001.

Sex and age distribution

	Adults and children estimated to be living with HIV/AIDS at end of 2001	Estimated number of adults and children newly infected with HIV during 2001	Estimated adult and child deaths due to HIV/AIDS during 2001
Total	39,900,000	5,100,000	2,980,000
Adults	37,200,000	4,300,000	2,400,000
Children under 15 years	2,700,000	800,000	580,000
Women	17,600,000	1,800,000	1,100,000
Men	22,300,000	3,300,000	1,880,000

Source: UNAIDS Web site 2002

THE DEMOGRAPHIC EXPANSION of cities reached alarming levels in the 20th century and continues at an accelerated rate. Half of the world population lives in cities, and the forecast is that two-thirds will by 2025. The depletion of sources of potable water, and the contamination of air, soil and water are just some of the catastrophic consequences of this demographic trend.

Bailing out Europe's farmers

Migration from the countryside to the city, says the United Nations, will be the main demographic trend in the coming decades, just as it was in the past century. In European countries, policies give a lifeline to rural areas, often at the expense of exporters from the South.

According to the UN, most of the population growth for the period 2000-2030 will be concentrated in the cities, which will become home to more than three-fifths of the world's people.

The expansion of the urban population in the 20th century was dramatic. In 1900, approximately 86 per cent lived in rural areas, and just 14 per cent in towns, while in 2000 the rural population had dropped to 53 per cent of the total, with the remaining 47 per cent in the cities.

But now some countries, mainly in Europe, are seeking to address this trend and to help the rural population keep its unique lifestyle alive.

This is one reason European governments give for granting subsidies to farmers, protecting national production through tariffs, limiting imports of items that can be produced locally and implementing price intervention policies.

The Common Agricultural Policy (CAP) applied by the European Union (EU) absorbs more than 40 per cent of the bloc's budget. Its main aims have been to improve productivity in the agricultural sector and to ensure a stable food supply. For the 2000-2006 period, the CAP proposes to improve farm commodity prices through production assistance provided by the EU, thus enhancing their competitiveness on world markets.

The rich countries' support for agriculture has global repercussions: the price intervention policies practiced by the EU and US, which tend to improve income for their farmers and ensure their ability to compete at the local and international levels, is harmful to the farmers of poor countries.

The producers in developing nations have lower production costs and offer commodities that, if there were not policies that set the prices, would be cheaper than those of the industrialized countries. In addition the (often hidden) taxes imposed by some countries on imports of products that are also grown locally stands in the way of free competition. These measures prevent countries with lower production costs from gaining access to those markets.

Some nations of Central Europe, like Poland, Hungary, the Czech Republic and Slovenia, which are soon to join the EU, are also disturbed by the situation. The main cause of their concern is that, according to recent proposals, the direct payments the CAP makes to farmers of the countries entering the EU will begin at just 25 per cent of the subsidies made to farmers in existing member states. The farmers of the future EU members say this is discrimination - they would only receive the same subsidies as the others ten years after joining, which would make it impossible for them to compete.

Unlike other countries, the EU nations seem to have made it a priority to keep the countryside an active space with an economically active population. The EU has implemented a series of directives aimed at retaining the rural population, providing facilities to develop new enterprises or services. These measures try to attract young people into rural production and offer credit to those who want to develop activities that are not specifically agricultural, such as forestation or the creation of ecological reserves. Some local governments offer general, economic and technical training for the development and specialization of agriculture while also stimulating means of production that take into account care for the environment and natural resources.

Despite these efforts, some countries that practice protectionism, like the US and the UK, are unable to halt the decline of the rural economy and the loss of jobs in the countryside. Farmers criticize the lack of official support, which makes their survival difficult.

The outcomes are not always those expected, and the proof is that the proportion of people living in rural areas continues to decline. However, the emphasis placed on the economic, social and political aspects of a way of life, and the interest in preserving a unique culture stand out in a global panorama that is generally uninterested in the fate of the rural populations. ∎

Building sustainable cities

In 1992, the United Nations Conference on Environment and Development - the Earth Summit - took place in Rio de Janeiro. With the participation of heads of state from the world over, it approved Agenda 21, a document that analyzes and proposes policies for achieving the sustainable development of cities. This entails promoting changes in the modes of production and consumption to ensure that the population achieves a social and economic development that is not harmful to the environment on which it depends. However, five years later, the UN General Assembly recognized that 'the tendencies with respect to sustainable development are worse than in 1992,' stressing the importance of timely implementation of the Agenda 21 recommendations aimed at reversing this precarious situation.

Poverty and degradation of the environment are the main problems affecting cities, particularly those of the South. Although densely populated cities are in many cases a country's economic hub, as centers of commerce, services, industry and education, they are also agents of great social imbalances. In many cities, the basic needs of more than 60 per cent of the inhabitants are not met. While there are populations of urban areas that have been able to improve their quality of life, sustainable cities do not yet exist.

Built-in sustainability

A sustainable city would be one that possesses and provides quality services, a healthy environment, decent and adequate housing, security, parks, sports and recreation facilities, fruitful social coexistence, decent employment with decent wages, full sanitation, quality education and access to cultural activities for the entire population. Furthermore, making optimal use of the land is a fundamental aspect of urban planning, directly tied to sustainable development, both in the appropriate distribution of housing, commerce and industry, and in maximizing use of urban green spaces.

Sustainable urban development requires efficient services. The availability of water and sanitation in the cities - essential for the life and health of the population - must be handled in a way that ensures universal access and improves the level of safety in areas prone to disaster. In Latin America and the Caribbean, 79 million people lack water and sanitation services and, of that total, 50 million live in rural areas. But even where these services are available, quality is not assured due to the non-existence of monitoring systems. Another necessity is a healthy, safe and efficient public transportation system that is competitive with the automobile as a mode of transport for the individual. Related to this is urban traffic safety, which entails reducing speed limits and making streets, highways, vehicles and equipment safer.

Life cycle

Today's cities represent highly inefficient systems, with high volumes of waste and garbage. This is largely because they are organized according to a linear system that turns them into consumers of resources originating in the natural environment while depositing the waste they produce in that same environment. This leads to the depletion of resources and environmental contamination, given that the needs of the urban ecosystem far surpass the capacity of its zone of influence to reproduce the resources and recycle its waste.

Environmental degradation produces excessive waste that seriously compromises local resources, causing inequalities and threatening the sustainability of the development that has been achieved. As such, the challenge is to build urban systems with circular flows of materials and energy, in which most waste can be reused in the productive system, affecting the environment much less.

In most cities, treatment of solid waste is not carried out efficiently. The increased volume of garbage contaminates the water, land and air of extensive areas, constituting a threat to human health and the environ-

ment. The fact is that the inadequate elimination of waste contributes to the deaths of 5.2 million people annually (according to Agenda 21 studies), including 4 million children who die of preventable diseases. The way to end this tragedy lies in promoting the reuse, recycling, collection and safe elimination of waste.

A long road ahead

To achieve sustainable urban development, the political will of the authorities is not enough. It is also essential that the citizenry modify its pattern of consumption and incorporate new habits. Through the process of consultation and consensus-building, local governments and communities alike can learn from their own needs, accumulating information that allows them to formulate appropriate strategies. At the same time, the consultative process raises citizens' awareness about sustainable development. According to Agenda 21, these policies, implemented at the urban and regional levels, will be an important contribution towards the sustainability of urban centers. ∎

URBAN POPULATION

A = As % of total population, 2000. Source: World Development Indicators 2002, World Bank.

B = Estimates to 2015. Source: Human Development Report 2001, UNDP.

	A	B		A	B		A	B		A	B
Afghanistan	21.9		Djibouti	83.3	86.3	Laos	23.5	32.7	Samoa	21.5	26.7
Albania	39.1	50.8	Dominican Republic	65.0	72.6	Latvia	69.0	71.4	São Tomé and Príncipe	46.7	
Algeria	60.3	68.5	Ecuador	62.4	75.8	Lebanon	89.7	92.6	Saudi Arabia	85.7	89.7
Angola	34.2	44.1	Egypt	45.2	51.2	Lesotho	28.0	38.9	Senegal	47.4	57.4
Antigua	36.8		El Salvador	46.6	53.6	Liberia	44.9		Seychelles	58.5	
Aotearoa-New Zealand	86.9	87.7	Equatorial Guinea	48.2	61.4	Libya	87.6	90.3	Sierra Leone	36.6	
Argentina	89.4	92.6	Eritrea	18.7	26.2	Lithuania	68.4	71.4	Singapore	100.0	100.0
Armenia	70.0	75.0	Estonia	68.6	69.3	Luxembourg	91.5	95.0	Slovakia	57.4	62.1
Australia	84.7	86.0	Ethiopia	17.6		Macedonia, TFYR	62.0	68.5	Slovenia	50.4	55.2
Austria	64.7	68.5	Fiji	46.0	60.0	Madagascar	29.5	39.7	Solomon Is.	19.7	
Azerbaijan	57.3	64.0	Finland	67.3	74.2	Malawi	15.4		Somalia	27.5	
Bahamas	88.5	91.5	France	75.6	79.4	Malaysia	57.4	66.4	South Africa	55.0	56.3
Bahrain	92.2	95.0	French Polynesia	56.9		Maldives	26.1	31.4	Spain	77.6	81.3
Bangladesh	24.5	33.9	Gabon	81.4	88.9	Mali	30.0		Sri Lanka	23.6	32.0
Barbados	50.0	58.3	Gambia	32.5	42.5	Malta	90.5	92.6	St Kitts-Nevis	34.1	
Belarus	70.3	77.2	Georgia	60.7	67.7	Mauritania	57.7	68.6	St Lucia	37.8	
Belgium	97.3	98.0	Germany	87.5	89.9	Mauritius	41.3	48.5	St Vincent	54.8	
Belize	46.5	64.2	Ghana	38.4	47.8	Mexico	74.4	77.9	Sudan	36.1	48.7
Benin	42.3	53.0	Greece	60.1	65.1	Micronesia	29.7		Suriname	52.2	81.4
Bhutan	7.1	11.6	Grenada	37.9		Moldova	46.1	50.3	Swaziland	26.4	32.7
Bolivia	64.8	70.1	Guam	39.2		Mongolia	58.6	70.5	Sweden	83.3	85.2
Bosnia-Herzegovina	43.0		Guatemala	40.4	46.2	Morocco	56.1	65.6	Switzerland	67.7	70.9
Botswana	50.3	58.4	Guinea	32.8	42.9	Mozambique	40.2		Syria	54.5	62.1
Brazil	81.3	86.5	Guinea-Bissau	23.7		Myanmar-Burma	27.7	36.7	Tajikistan	27.5	29.5
Brunei	72.2	78.5	Guyana	38.2	48.0	Namibia	30.9	39.4	Tanzania	27.8	46.1
Bulgaria	69.6	74.5	Haiti	35.7	45.6	Nepal	11.9	18.1	Thailand	21.6	29.3
Burkina Faso	18.5		Honduras	46.9	64.3	Netherlands	89.4	90.8	Togo	33.3	42.5
Burundi	9.0		Hungary	64.0	68.5	Netherlands Antilles	70.4		Tonga	46.0	
Cambodia	15.9	22.8	Iceland	92.5	94.6	Nicaragua	64.7	62.6	Trinidad and Tobago	74.1	79.3
Cameroon	48.9	58.9	India	28.4	35.9	Niger	20.6		Tunisia	65.5	73.5
Canada	77.1	79.9	Indonesia	40.9	54.8	Nigeria	44.0	55.4	Turkey	75.3	84.5
Cape Verde	62.2	73.4	Iran	61.6	68.8	Norway	75.5	80.1	Turkmenistan	44.8	49.9
Central African Rep.	41.2		Iraq	76.8		Oman	84.0	92.7	Uganda	14.2	20.7
Chad	23.8		Ireland	59.0	64.0	Pakistan	37.0	46.7	Ukraine	68.0	71.5
Chile	84.6	88.7	Israel	91.2	92.5	Panama	57.7	61.7	United Arab Emirates	85.9	88.8
China	32.1	40.7	Italy	67.0	70.7	Papua New Guinea	17.4	23.7	United Kingdom	89.5	90.8
Colombia	74.9	79.1	Jamaica	56.1	63.5	Paraguay	56.0	65.0	United States	77.2	81.0
Comoros	33.2	42.6	Japan	78.8	81.5	Peru	72.8	77.9	Uruguay	91.3	93.6
Congo D.R.	30.3	39.3	Jordan	74.2	79.8	Philippines	58.6	67.8	Uzbekistan	36.9	38.
Congo R.	62.5	70.1	Kanaky-New Caledonia	64.1		Poland	65.6	71.4	Vanuatu	20.0	
Costa Rica	51.9	53.4	Kazakhstan	56.4	60.6	Portugal	64.4	77.5	Venezuela	87.4	90.0
Côte d'Ivoire	46.4	55.5	Kenya	33.1	44.5	Puerto Rico	75.2		Vietnam	24.0	24.3
Croatia	57.7	64.4	Kiribati	37.3		Qatar	92.5	94.3	Virgin Is. (Am.)	46.4	
Cuba	75.3		Korea, North	60.2		Romania	56.4	62.0	Yemen	24.7	31.2
Cyprus	56.8	64.5	Korea, South	81.9	88.2	Russia	73.1	82.0	Yugoslavia Fed. Rep.	52.2	
Czech Republic	74.7	77.4	Kuwait	97.6	98.2	Rwanda	6.2		Zambia	44.5	45.0
Denmark	85.1	86.8	Kyrgyzstan	33.3	35.0	Sahara, Western	34.4		Zimbabwe	35.3	45.9

A = Contraceptive prevalence, 1995-2001 /1. Source: The State of the World's Children 2002, UNICEF.
B = Crude death rate per 1,000 people, 2000-2005 /2. Source: World Population prospects - The 2000 Revision, United Nations.
C = Crude birth rate per 1,000 people, 2000-2005 /2. Source: World Population prospects - The 2000 Revision, United Nations.
D = Children per woman, 2000. Source: The State of the World's Children 2002, UNICEF.

	A	B	C	D
Afghanistan	2	21	47	6.9
Albania		5	18	2.5
Algeria	57	5	24	3.1
Angola	8	19	51	7.2
Antigua	53			
Aotearoa-New Zealand	75	8	14	2.0
Argentina	74	8	19	2.5
Armenia	61	7	9	1.3
Australia	76	7	13	1.8
Austria	51	10	8	1.3
Azerbaijan	55	6	13	1.7
Bahamas	62	7	20	2.4
Bahrain	62	4	16	2.5
Bangladesh	54	9	30	3.7
Barbados	55	8	12	1.5
Belarus	50	14	9	1.3
Belgium	78	10	10	1.5
Belize	56	4	25	3.2
Benin	37	12	41	5.9
Bhutan	31	9	35	5.3
Bolivia	48	8	30	4.2
Bosnia-Herzegovina	48	8	10	1.4
Botswana	48	24	31	4.2
Brazil	77	7	19	2.3
Brunei		3	19	2.7
Bulgaria	86	15	8	1.1
Burkina Faso	12	16	47	6.9
Burundi	9	21	43	6.8
Cambodia	24	11	35	5.1
Cameroon	26	15	36	4.9
Canada	75	8	11	1.6
Cape Verde	53	6	29	3.4
Central African Rep.	28	19	38	5.1
Chad	8	19	48	6.7
Chile	56	6	18	2.4
China	91	7	14	1.8
Colombia	77	6	22	2.7
Comoros	26	9	38	5.2
Congo D.R.	8	14	47	6.7
Congo R.		14	44	6.3
Cook Is.	50			
Costa Rica	75	4	22	2.8
Côte d'Ivoire	15	15	35	4.9
Croatia		11	12	1.7
Cuba	73	7	12	1.6
Cyprus		8	13	2.0
Czech Republic	69	11	9	1.2
Denmark	78	11	11	1.7
Djibouti		21	38	6.0
Dominica	50			
Dominican Republic	64	7	23	2.8
East Timor		13	25	4.2
Ecuador	66	6	23	3.0
Egypt	56	6	23	3.2
El Salvador	60	6	25	3.1
Equatorial Guinea		15	43	5.9
Eritrea	8	13	39	5.5
Estonia	70	13	9	1.2
Ethiopia	8	19	44	6.8
Fiji	32	5	24	3.1
Finland	77	10	10	1.7
France	75	9	12	1.8
French Guiana		4	28	
French Polynesia		5	20	
Gabon		15	38	5.4
Gambia	10	17	37	5.0

	A	B	C	D
Georgia	41	10	10	1.5
Germany	75	11	8	1.3
Ghana	22	10	33	4.4
Greece		10	9	1.3
Grenada	54			
Guadeloupe		6	16	
Guam		5	26	
Guatemala	38	7	34	4.7
Guinea	6	17	43	6.1
Guinea-Bissau	1	19	45	6.0
Guyana	41	9	22	2.4
Haiti	28	13	31	4.2
Honduras	50	7	30	4.0
Hungary	77	13	9	1.3
Iceland		7	14	2.0
India	48	8	24	3.2
Indonesia	55	7	20	2.5
Iran	73	5	22	3.0
Iraq	14	7	34	5.1
Ireland		8	15	2.0
Israel		6	20	2.8
Italy	78	11	9	1.2
Jamaica	66	6	20	2.5
Japan	59	8	9	1.4
Jordan	57	4	33	4.5
Kanaky-New Caledonia		5	20	
Kazakhstan	66	10	16	2.1
Kenya	39	14	34	4.4
Kiribati	28			
Korea, North				2.1
Korea, South	81	10	17	1.5
Kuwait	50	3	19	2.8
Kyrgyzstan	60	7	20	2.6
Laos	19	13	36	5.1
Latvia		13	8	1.1
Lebanon	63	5	19	2.3
Lesotho	23	22	33	4.7
Liberia	6	12	55	6.8
Libya	45	5	27	3.6
Lithuania		11	9	1.3
Luxembourg		9	12	1.8
Macedonia, TFYR		8	11	1.7
Madagascar	19	13	41	5.9
Malawi	31	23	45	6.6
Malaysia	55	5	22	3.1
Maldives	32	6	36	5.6
Mali	7	17	50	7.0
Malta		8	12	1.9
Marshall Is.	37			
Martinique		7	13	
Mauritania	8	14	44	6.0
Mauritius	26	7	16	2.0
Mexico	70	5	22	2.7
Micronesia			29	
Moldova	74	12	12	1.5
Mongolia	42	7	22	2.5
Morocco	59	6	25	3.2
Mozambique	10	24	42	6.1
Myanmar-Burma	33	12	23	3.1
Namibia	29	18	34	5.1
Nepal	39	10	34	4.7
Netherlands	79	9	11	1.5
Netherlands Antilles		6	15	
Nicaragua	60	5	32	4.1
Niger	14	19	55	8.0
Nigeria	15	13	39	5.7

	A	B	C	D
Norway	74	10	11	1.8
Oman	40	4	36	5.7
Pakistan	17	10	36	5.3
Palau	47			
Palestine		4	39	5.8
Panama	58	5	20	2.5
Papua New Guinea	26	10	32	4.5
Paraguay	57	5	30	4.0
Peru	64	6	23	2.8
Philippines	47	5	26	3.4
Poland	49	10	10	1.4
Portugal	66	11	11	1.5
Puerto Rico		8	15	
Qatar	43	4	17	3.5
Réunion		6	18	
Romania	64	13	10	1.3
Russia		15	9	1.2
Rwanda	21	21	42	6.0
Sahara, Western		9	40	
Samoa	30	6	28	4.4
São Tomé and Príncipe	10			
Saudi Arabia	32	4	34	5.9
Senegal	11	12	38	5.4
Sierra Leone	4	23	49	6.5
Singapore	74	5	11	1.6
Slovakia	74	10	10	1.4
Slovenia		10	8	1.2
Solomon Is.	25	5	38	5.5
Somalia	1	17	52	7.3
South Africa	56	17	25	3.0
Spain	81	10	9	1.2
Sri Lanka	69	6	17	2.1
St Kitts-Nevis	41			
St Lucia	47	5	23	2.6
St Vincent	58			
Sudan	10	11	34	4.7
Suriname	42	6	18	2.2
Swaziland	21	23	33	4.6
Sweden	78	11	8	1.4
Switzerland	82	10	9	1.5
Syria	46	4	30	3.9
Tajikistan	34	6	23	3.3
Tanzania	22	13	38	5.3
Thailand	72	6	18	2.1
Togo	24	13	39	5.6
Tonga	0			
Trinidad and Tobago	53	6	13	1.6
Tunisia	66	6	19	2.2
Turkey	64	6	20	2.5
Turkmenistan	62	7	25	3.4
Uganda	15	17	51	7.1
Ukraine	89	15	8	1.2
United Arab Emirates	28	4	16	3.1
United Kingdom	82	10	11	1.7
United States	76	8	13	2.0
Uruguay	84	9	17	2.4
Uzbekistan	67	6	20	2.6
Vanuatu	15	5	31	4.5
Venezuela	77	5	23	2.9
Vietnam	74	6	20	2.4
Yemen	21	8	49	7.6
Yugoslavia Fed. Rep.	58	11	11	1.7
Zambia	19	19	42	5.9
Zimbabwe	54	18	35	4.8

/1 Figures show the latest available data for the period.
/2 Figures show an estimate for the period.

DISTRIBUTION OF INCOME OR CONSUMPTION

The Gini index (see third column below) provides a convenient summary measure of the degree of inequality.
When the index is zero this represents perfect equality, while an index of 100 implies 'perfect' inequality.

COUNTRY	SURVEY YEAR	GINI INDEX	PERCENTAGE SHARE OF INCOME OR CONSUMPTION						
			Lowest 10%	Lowest 20%	Second 20%	Third 20%	Fourth 20%	Highest 20%	Highest 10%
Algeria	1995 a,b	35.3	2.8	7.0	11.6	16.1	22.7	42.6	26.8
Armenia	1996 a,b	44.4	2.3	5.5	9.4	13.9	20.6	50.6	35.2
Australia	1994 c,d	35.2	2.0	5.9	12.0	17.2	23.6	41.3	25.4
Austria	1987 c,d	23.1	4.4	10.4	14.8	18.5	22.9	33.3	19.3
Azerbaijan	1995 c,d	36.0	2.8	6.9	11.5	16.1	22.3	43.3	27.8
Bangladesh	1995-96 a,b	33.6	3.9	8.7	12.0	15.7	20.8	42.8	28.6
Belarus	1998 a,b	21.7	5.1	11.4	15.2	18.2	21.9	33.3	20.0
Belgium	1992 c,d	25.0	3.7	9.5	14.6	18.4	23.0	34.5	20.2
Bolivia	1997 c,d	58.9	0.5	1.9	5.9	11.1	19.3	61.8	45.7
Brazil	1997 c,d	59.1	1.0	2.6	5.7	10.3	18.5	63.0	46.7
Bulgaria	1997 c,d	26.4	4.5	10.1	13.9	17.4	21.9	36.8	22.8
Burkina Faso	1994 a,b	48.2	2.2	5.5	8.7	12.0	18.7	55.0	39.5
Burundi	1992 a,b	33.3	3.4	7.9	12.1	16.3	22.1	41.6	26.6
Cambodia	1997 a,b	40.4	2.9	6.9	10.7	14.7	20.1	47.6	33.8
Canada	1994 c,d	31.5	2.8	7.5	12.9	17.2	23.0	39.3	23.8
Central African Rep.	1993 a,b	61.3	0.7	2.0	4.9	9.6	18.5	65.0	47.7
Chile	1996 c,d	57.5	1.4	3.4	6.3	10.5	17.9	62.0	46.9
China	1998 c,d	40.3	2.4	5.9	10.2	15.1	22.2	46.6	30.4
Colombia	1996 c,d	57.1	1.1	3.0	6.6	11.1	18.4	60.9	46.1
Costa Rica	1997 c,d	45.9	1.7	4.5	8.9	14.1	21.6	51.0	34.6
Côte d'Ivoire	1995 a,b	36.7	3.1	7.1	11.2	15.6	21.9	44.3	28.8
Croatia	1998 c,d	29.0	3.7	8.8	13.3	17.4	22.6	38.0	23.3
Czech Republic	1996 c,d	25.4	4.3	10.3	14.5	17.7	21.7	35.9	22.4
Denmark	1992 c,d	24.7	3.6	9.6	14.9	18.3	22.7	34.5	20.5
Dominican Republic	1998 c,d	47.4	2.1	5.1	8.6	13.0	20.0	53.3	37.9
Ecuador	1995 a,b	43.7	2.2	5.4	9.4	14.2	21.3	49.7	33.8
Egypt	1995 a,b	28.9	4.4	9.8	13.2	16.6	21.4	39.0	25.0
El Salvador	1997 c,d	50.8	1.4	3.7	7.8	12.8	20.4	55.3	39.3
Estonia	1998 c,d	37.6	3.0	7.0	11.0	15.3	21.6	45.1	29.8
Ethiopia	1995 a,b	40.0	3.0	7.1	10.9	14.5	19.8	47.7	33.7
Finland	1991 c,d	25.6	4.2	10.0	14.2	17.6	22.3	35.8	21.6
France	1995 c,d	32.7	2.8	7.2	12.6	17.2	22.8	40.2	25.1
Gambia	1992 a,b	47.8	1.5	4.4	9.0	13.5	20.4	52.8	37.6
Georgia	1996 c,d	37.1	2.3	6.1	11.4	16.3	22.7	43.6	27.9
Germany	1994 c,d	30.0	3.3	8.2	13.2	17.5	22.7	38.5	23.7
Ghana	1998 a,b	39.6	2.4	5.9	10.4	15.3	22.5	45.9	29.5
Greece	1993 c,d	32.7	3.0	7.5	12.4	16.9	22.8	40.3	25.3
Guatemala	1998 c,d	55.8	1.6	3.8	6.8	10.9	17.9	60.6	46.0
Guinea	1994 a,b	40.3	2.6	6.4	10.4	14.8	21.2	47.2	32.0
Guinea-Bissau	1991 a,b	56.2	0.5	2.1	6.5	12.0	20.6	58.9	42.4
Guyana	1993 a,b	40.2	2.4	6.3	10.7	15.0	21.2	46.9	32.0
Honduras	1997 c,d	59.0	0.4	1.6	5.6	11.0	20.1	61.8	44.3
Hungary	1998 a,b	24.4	4.1	10.0	14.7	18.3	22.7	34.4	20.5
India	1997 a,b	37.8	3.5	8.1	11.6	15.0	19.3	46.1	33.5
Indonesia	1999 a,b	31.7	4.0	9.0	12.5	16.1	21.3	41.1	26.7
Ireland	1987 c,d	35.9	2.5	6.7	11.6	16.4	22.4	42.9	27.4
Israel	1992 c,d	35.5	2.8	6.9	11.4	16.3	22.9	42.5	26.9
Italy	1995 c,d	27.3	3.5	8.7	14.0	18.1	22.9	36.3	21.8
Jamaica	1996 a,b	36.4	2.9	7.0	11.5	15.8	21.8	43.9	28.9
Japan	1993 c,d	24.9	4.8	10.6	14.2	17.6	22.0	35.7	21.7
Jordan	1997 a,b	36.4	3.3	7.6	11.4	15.5	21.1	44.4	29.8
Kazakhstan	1996 a,b	35.4	2.7	6.7	11.5	16.4	23.1	42.3	26.3
Kenya	1994 a,b	44.5	1.8	5.0	9.7	14.2	20.9	50.2	34.9
Korea, South	1993 a,b	31.6	2.9	7.5	12.9	17.4	22.9	39.3	24.3
Kyrgyzstan	1997 c,d	40.5	2.7	6.3	10.2	14.7	21.4	47.4	31.7
Laos	1997 a,b	37.0	3.2	7.6	11.4	15.3	20.8	45.0	30.6
Latvia	1998 c,d	32.4	2.9	7.6	12.9	17.1	22.1	40.3	25.9

a. Refers to expenditure shares by percentiles of population.
b. Ranked by per capita expenditure.
c. Refers to income shares by percentiles of population.
d. Ranked by per capita income.

DISTRIBUTION OF INCOME OR CONSUMPTION

On this measure, Slovakia with 19.5 is most equal, and Sierra Leone with 62.9 has the widest discrepancies of income and consumption.

COUNTRY	SURVEY YEAR	GINI INDEX	PERCENTAGE SHARE OF INCOME OR CONSUMPTION						
			Lowest 10%	Lowest 20%	Second 20%	Third 20%	Fourth 20%	Highest 20%	Highest 10%
Lesotho	1986-87 a,b	56.0	0.9	2.8	6.5	11.2	19.4	60.1	43.4
Lithuania	1996 a,b	32.4	3.1	7.8	12.6	16.8	22.4	40.3	25.6
Luxembourg	1994 c,d	26.9	4.0	9.4	13.8	17.7	22.6	36.5	22.0
Madagascar	1997 a,b	46.0	2.2	5.4	9.2	13.4	19.9	52.0	37.3
Malaysia	1997 c,d	49.2	1.7	4.4	8.1	12.9	20.3	54.3	38.4
Mali	1994 a,b	50.5	1.8	4.6	8.0	11.9	19.3	56.2	40.4
Mauritania	1995 a,b	37.3	2.5	6.4	11.2	16	22.4	44.1	28.4
Mexico	1996 c,d	51.9	1.6	4.0	7.6	12.2	19.6	56.7	41.1
Moldova	1997 c,d	40.6	2.2	5.6	10.2	15.2	22.2	46.8	30.7
Mongolia	1995 a,b	33.2	2.9	7.3	12.2	16.6	23.0	40.9	24.5
Morocco	1998-99 a,b	39.5	2.6	6.5	10.6	14.8	21.3	46.6	30.9
Mozambique	1996-97 a,b	39.6	2.5	6.5	10.8	15.1	21.1	46.5	31.7
Nepal	1995-96 a,b	36.7	3.2	7.6	11.5	15.1	21.0	44.8	29.8
Netherlands	1994 c,d	32.6	2.8	7.3	12.7	17.2	22.8	40.1	25.1
Nicaragua	1998 a,b	60.3	0.7	2.3	5.9	10.4	17.9	63.6	48.8
Niger	1995 a,b	50.5	0.8	2.6	7.1	13.9	23.1	53.3	35.4
Nigeria	1996-97 a,b	50.6	1.6	4.4	8.2	12.5	19.3	55.7	40.8
Norway	1995 c,d	25.8	4.1	9.7	14.3	17.9	22.2	35.8	21.8
Pakistan	1996-97a,b	31.2	4.1	9.5	12.9	16.0	20.5	41.1	27.6
Panama	1997 a,b	48.5	1.2	3.6	8.1	13.6	21.9	52.8	35.7
Papua New Guinea	1996 a,b	50.9	1.7	4.5	7.9	11.9	19.2	56.5	40.5
Paraguay	1998 c,d	57.7	0.5	1.9	6.0	11.4	20.1	60.7	43.8
Peru	1996 c,d	46.2	1.6	4.4	9.1	14.1	21.3	51.2	35.4
Philippines	1997 a,b	46.2	2.3	5.4	8.8	13.2	20.3	52.3	36.6
Poland	1998 a,b	31.6	3.2	7.8	12.8	17.1	22.6	39.7	24.7
Portugal	1994-95c,d	35.6	3.1	7.3	11.6	15.9	21.8	43.4	28.4
Romania	1994 c,d	28.2	3.7	8.9	13.6	17.6	22.6	37.3	22.7
Russia	1998 a,b	48.7	1.7	4.4	8.6	13.3	20.1	53.7	38.7
Rwanda	1983-85 a,b	28.9	4.2	9.7	13.2	16.5	21.6	39.1	24.2
Senegal	1995 a,b	41.3	2.6	6.4	10.3	14.5	20.6	48.2	33.5
Sierra Leone	1989 a,b	62.9	0.5	1.1	2.0	9.8	23.7	63.4	43.6
Slovakia	1992 c,d	19.5	5.1	11.9	15.8	18.8	22.2	31.4	18.2
Slovenia	1998 c,d	28.4	3.9	9.1	13.4	17.3	22.5	37.7	23.0
South Africa	1993-94 a,b	59.3	1.1	2.9	5.5	9.2	17.7	64.8	45.9
Spain	1990 c,d	32.5	2.8	7.5	12.6	17.0	22.6	40.3	25.2
Sri Lanka	1995 a,b	34.4	3.5	8.0	11.8	15.8	21.5	42.8	28.0
St Lucia	1995 c,d	42.6	2.0	5.2	9.9	14.8	21.8	48.3	32.5
Swaziland	1994 c,d	60.9	1.0	2.7	5.8	10.0	17.1	64.4	50.2
Sweden	1992 c,d	25.0	3.7	9.6	14.5	18.1	23.2	34.5	20.1
Switzerland	1992 c,d	33.1	2.6	6.9	12.7	17.3	22.9	40.3	25.2
Tanzania	1993 a,b	38.2	2.8	6.8	11.0	15.1	21.6	45.5	30.1
Thailand	1998 a,b	41.4	2.8	6.4	9.8	14.2	21.2	48.4	32.4
Trinidad and Tobago	1992 c,d	40.3	2.1	5.5	10.3	15.5	22.7	45.9	29.9
Tunisia	1995 a,b	41.7	2.3	5.7	9.9	14.7	21.8	47.9	31.8
Turkey	1994 a,b	41.5	2.3	5.8	10.2	14.8	21.6	47.7	32.3
Turkmenistan	1998 a,b	40.8	2.6	6.1	10.2	14.7	21.5	47.5	31.7
Uganda	1996 a,b	37.4	3.0	7.1	11.1	15.4	21.5	44.9	29.8
Ukraine	1999 a,b	29.0	3.7	8.8	13.3	17.4	22.7	37.8	23.2
United Kingdom	1991 c,d	36.1	2.6	6.6	11.5	16.3	22.7	43.0	27.3
United States	1997 c,d	40.8	1.8	5.2	10.5	15.6	22.4	46.4	30.5
Uruguay	1989 c,d	42.3	2.1	5.4	10.0	14.8	21.5	48.3	32.7
Uzbekistan	1993 c,d	33.3	3.1	7.4	12.0	16.7	23.0	40.9	25.2
Venezuela	1997 a,b	48.8	1.6	4.1	8.3	13.2	20.7	53.7	37.6
Vietnam	1998 a,b	36.1	3.6	8.0	11.4	15.2	20.9	44.5	29.9
Yemen	1998 a,b	33.4	3.0	7.4	12.2	16.7	22.5	41.2	25.9
Zambia	1998 a,b	52.6	1.1	3.3	7.6	12.5	20.0	56.6	41.0
Zimbabwe	1990-91 a,b	56.8	1.8	4.0	6.3	10.0	17.4	62.3	46.9

a. Refers to expenditure shares by percentiles of population.

b. Ranked by per capita expenditure.

c. Refers to income shares by percentiles of population.

d. Ranked by per capita income.

Source: World Development Indicators 2001, World Bank, 2001.

Fundamentalisms

FUNDAMENTALISM HAS COME to mean any form of religious extremism. Its origins were much more specific, however, and the term did not always carry such negative connotations.

Politicized religion

Whenever you hear the word 'fundamentalism' today, invariably it is prefixed by the adjectives 'religious' or 'Islamic'. 'Islamic fundamentalism' has been blamed for terrorist attacks on the West; the Government of India has repeatedly been accused of being 'Hindu fundamentalist'; and books on 'Jewish fundamentalism' have been published.

Christian beginnings

Strictly speaking, the word *fundamentalist* has its origins in the Christian millennielist movement, born in the 19th century in the United States, when Protestant evangelists preached of the Second Coming of Christ, or the thousand years of the Kingdom of Christ. The name 'fundamentalism' itself first appeared in the early part of the 20th century, based on a series of the Movement's publications entitled 'The Fundamentals'. For the Fundamentalists, there were five foundations of the faith: the literal and infallible nature of the Scriptures, the virgin birth, atonement through good works, corporal resurrection and the authenticity of the miracles. Sparked in part by Charles Darwin's ideas, which directly contradicted the literal interpretations of the Bible's book of Genesis, Fundamentalism was institutionalized in 1919-1920. It had strong support and followers among the upper echelons of society and government, and was militant in its reaction to both secular and religious modernization. The Movement also opposed the atheism of the anarchist, socialist and communist thinkers and trade unionists of the day. The Movement still has a strong presence today in several church organizations, educational institutions and groups specializing in spreading the faith - evangelizing religions with some 30 million followers in the US alone.

Fundamentalism and the State

In the early 20th century, several Islamic movements arose in reaction to the modernization and Westernization of their culture and in resistance to colonialism. The preaching of the return to the splendor and power of Islamic civilization was intermixed with the conviction that its decline had been caused by the neglect of traditional customs. In the minority is the reformist or 'evolutionist' trend, known as *salafiyya*, which believes that the *sharia* (legal code of Islam) should be adapted according to contemporary reality through the effort of interpretation or *ijtihad*. The majority conservative or 'fundamentalist' trend advocates the return to Islam's roots and rejects the interpretation of the sharia, asserting it should be applied in its literal sense.

Several Muslim groups favor the creation of an Islamic state, though they disagree both about the structure of such a state and what strategies should be used to achieve it. There are those that advocate violence and believe, furthermore, that the sharia must be imposed from the pinnacle of power, over all society. There are others who believe it is necessary to wait for society to turn gradually to Islam. Some groups are open to political dialogue, others reject any compromise with the regimes of their respective countries.

A double-edged reaction to secularization is evident within the Jewish religion. The foundation of the Israeli state was based on a secular ideology, Zionism, which was born in the 19th century and consolidated in the 1896 book by Theodor Herzl, *The Jewish State*. In addition to advocating a state for the Jews, Zionism sought to culturally assimilate them with the European 'gentiles' (those who do not participate in the Jewish faith). In Israel as well as in the Jewish communities of the Diaspora, there are nationalist-religious groups and there are those who consider the state of Israel a new Diaspora - if not an occupation -, and they preach tranquility, given that the 'true' land of Israel will be granted with the coming of the Messiah. Alongside the Old Testament Commandments, the Talmud is the sacred code from which a large portion of fundamentalist Jews take the rules that govern their lives.

There is no question that, while some of these groups from the three religions of Abraham proclaim the literal truth of the sacred texts, this literalness is also governed by interpretation. The interpretations are the different translations produced by Protestantism (which broke off from Catholicism claiming the right to free interpretation), and those of the *mullahs* who claim the literal truth of the *Qur'an*, translations of which are not granted any authority. Although there are some literalists within Jewish fundamentalism, there are also those who have sought an alternative meaning for these texts to justify the colonization of Palestine.

While the applicability of the term 'fundamentalism' to Islamic and Jewish movements has been questioned repeatedly, it has come under greater doubt in its relevance to the movements that promote the revival and nationalization of the Brahmanic religions in India. In the first place, the *Vedas* (the sacred texts) are not canonized by any authority. The texts themselves encourage interpretation or the search for broader meanings. This has favored the development of Brahmanic cults of different extremes. From the perspective of this 'Hindu' diversity, one could even see Christianity, Islam and Judaism as sects of a single religion.

A broader meaning

In an attempt to define a phenomenon that has similar traits in different parts of the world, in the broad sense, the term *fundamentalism* could be a modern form of politicized religion in which the 'true believers' fight the marginalization of the religion within its respective societies. All variants share a resistance, if not outright hostility, to secularization and seek to restructure social and cultural relations and institutions according to the faith's traditional norms and precepts. Some seek to fight secularism through the schools, the press or academia, others do so within the political arena, and still others abandon conventional politics and legal institutions, turning to violence and religious war. There are those who draw a line between 'restorers of the faith' and 'fundamentalists'. The first would be devout but apolitical, and would not aim to force others to convert.

The latter would be those who intend to change the behavior of both those who share their faith and those who do not. In this sense, genuine 'fundamentalism' would have to be understood as being both religious and political, with adherents believing that circumstances require them to act politically (perhaps with violence) in order to meet their religious obligations.

Fundamentalism and globalization

Taken as a parameter of religious-political thought and conduct applicable to different cultures, and not as a specific set of religious beliefs, rituals or practices, fundamentalism can be found in all historic religions that have sacred scriptures and basic precepts. Fundamentalists, in this sense, are militant conservatives for whom the world is a battlefield between absolute good and absolute evil. They are warriors in spirit, and often in flesh, who oppose non-believers and doubters within their own religious communities. No matter what their origins, the different fundamentalisms may be considered united in their rejection of the replacement of divinity and divine law by human reason and by secular political principles as the basis for social and legal order. While this substitution occurred in the West - not without violence - based on Western ideas, in other regions, such as in the Muslim world, it occurred through colonization and the Empire. For example, Islamists believe that the foreigners and infidels converted their Muslim brothers, sisters and children to 'atheist' customs.

Fundamentalists are also united in considering their respective religions superior to the rest and in their rejection of pluralism. In their eyes, as messengers of the light or of revelation, they are obliged to take on a 'cosmic battle' against evil. There are some analysts who believe that the framework for this battle is globalization. According to this view, globalization (which to a great extent implies the exaltation of Western secular values) carries with it the seeds of reaction against the global process of secularization, a fight for a 're-sacralization', which in many cases takes fundamentalist forms.∎

EDUCATION IMBALANCES

Primary pupil-teacher ratio.
Too few schools, too few teachers – whatever the reason, there are around 58 kids per teacher at primary level in Malawi, compared with under six in the tiny state of San Marino or seven in Norway.

		year			year			year
Afghanistan	57.9	1994	French Polynesia	14.3	1995	Niger	41.1	1998
Albania	17.8	1995	Gabon	44.1	1998	Nigeria	33.8	1996
Algeria	28.2	1998	Gambia	32.9	1998	Oman	25.4	1998
Angola	27.2	1991	Georgia	17.4	1998	Pakistan	32.3	1998
Antigua	18.7	1998	Germany	17.0	1998	Panama	23.0	1990
Aotearoa-New Zealand	19.2	1996	Ghana	32.7	1996	Papua New Guinea	36.1	1998
Argentina	20.6	1998	Greece	13.5	1998	Paraguay	19.6	1998
Armenia	18.8	1996	Grenada	20.2	1998	Peru	25.3	1998
Aruba	19.2	1998	Guatemala	38.2	1999	Philippines	34.9	1996
Australia	18.1	1996	Guinea	46.8	1998	Poland	15.4	1996
Austria	13.5	1998	Guyana	26.7	1998	Portugal	12.2	1993
Azerbaijan	18.8	1998	Haiti	31.4	1998	Qatar	13.1	1998
Bahamas	22.2	1996	Honduras	33.0	1996	Romania	18.7	1998
Bahrain	21.2	1998	Hungary	10.7	1998	Russia	17.6	1998
Bangladesh	59.3	1998	Iceland	8.2	1998	Rwanda	54.3	1998
Barbados	18.7	1998	India	71.9	1998	Samoa	23.9	1996
Belarus	19.6	1998	Indonesia	22.0	1996	Samoa, American	15.1	1991
Belgium	22.2	1998	Iran	30.4	1996	San Marino	5.3	1996
Belize	26.5	1998	Iraq	22.1	1998	São Tomé and Príncipe	36.0	1998
Benin	53.4	1998	Ireland	21.6	1998	Saudi Arabia	12.2	1998
Bermuda	12.3	1996	Israel	13.4	1998	Senegal	48.6	1998
Bhutan	37.5	1998	Italy	11.3	1998	Seychelles	14.8	1998
Bolivia	26.4	1996	Jamaica	30.7	1998	Sierra Leone	33.9	1990
Botswana	27.6	1998	Japan	21.0	1998	Singapore	25.3	1998
Brazil	33.2	1998	Jordan	21.1	1996	Slovakia	18.8	1998
Brunei	14.6	1995	Kanaky-New Caledonia	20.4	1991	Slovenia	14.1	1998
Bulgaria	17.9	1998	Kazakhstan	18.4	1993	Solomon Is.	24.1	1994
Burkina Faso	49.0	1998	Kenya	28.5	1998	South Africa	37.0	1998
Burundi	46.1	1998	Kiribati	23.6	1996	Spain	15.0	1998
Cambodia	47.7	1998	Korea, South	31.2	1996	Sri Lanka	27.8	1996
Cameroon	51.9	1998	Kuwait	13.5	1998	St Kitts-Nevis	20.7	1991
Canada	18.0	1998	Kyrgyzstan	24.5	1998	St Lucia	25.8	1998
Cape Verde	28.7	1998	Laos	30.6	1998	St Vincent	19.8	1993
Cayman Is.	15.5	1998	Latvia	15.4	1998	Sudan	26.3	1998
Central African Rep.	99.4	1998	Lebanon	13.9	1998	Suriname	17.1	1998
Chad	67.9	1998	Lesotho	25.4	1998	Swaziland	33.0	1998
Chile	26.6	1998	Liberia	39.4	1998	Sweden	12.3	1998
China	21.5	1998	Libya	8.4	1998	Switzerland	13.4	1998
Colombia	23.0	1998	Lithuania	16.5	1998	Syria	22.9	1998
Comoros	34.8	1998	Luxembourg	13.0	1998	Tajikistan	23.5	1996
Congo D.R.	26.0	1998	Macedonia, TFYR	22.1	1998	Tanzania	38.0	1998
Congo R.	61.2	1998	Madagascar	47.2	1998	Thailand	20.6	1998
Costa Rica	29.5	1996	Malawi	58.8	1995	Togo	41.3	1998
Côte d'Ivoire	42.7	1998	Malaysia	21.8	1998	Tonga	21.9	1998
Croatia	19.2	1998	Maldives	24.3	1998	Trinidad and Tobago	21.3	1998
Cuba	13.1	1998	Mali	62.1	1998	Tunisia	23.9	1998
Cyprus	18.3	1998	Malta	19.6	1998	Turkey	27.8	1994
Czech Republic	18.3	1998	Marshall Is.	14.9	1998	Uganda	60.1	1998
Denmark	10.0	1998	Mauritania	47.0	1998	Ukraine	20.5	1998
Djibouti	39.5	1998	Mauritius	25.8	1998	United Arab Emirates	16.0	1998
Dominica	19.8	1998	Mexico	27.2	1998	United Kingdom	19.1	1998
Dominican Republic	37.2	1998	Moldova	22.8	1996	United States	15.4	1998
Ecuador	26.9	1998	Monaco	15.6	1998	Uruguay	20.6	1998
Egypt	23.4	1998	Mongolia	32.5	1998	Uzbekistan	20.6	1994
El Salvador	32.8	1996	Morocco	28.1	1998	Vanuatu	23.4	1998
Equatorial Guinea	56.7	1998	Mozambique	60.9	1998	Venezuela	21.1	1996
Eritrea	47.0	1998	Myanmar-Burma	30.6	1998	Vietnam	30.4	1998
Estonia	15.7	1998	Namibia	32.2	1998	Virgin Is. (Am.)	18.4	1992
Ethiopia	43.2	1996	Nepal	39.1	1998	Yemen	29.8	1998
Fiji	23.0	1998	Netherlands	7.3	1996	Yugoslavia Fed. Rep.	16.6	1998
Finland	17.3	1998	Netherlands Antilles	19.6	1998	Zambia	44.7	1998
France	18.9	1998	Nicaragua	36.3	1996	Zimbabwe	39.1	1996

Source: World Development Indicators 2002, World Bank.

IN ALMOST TOTAL SILENCE, their plight unknown, there are at least 27 million people around the world today living in slavery. Many believe this conservative figure falls far short of the reality. Until recently, the practice of slavery was thought to be largely exclusive to war-torn countries such as Angola, Sudan, Somalia and Chad. Today, even in relatively peaceful regions, slave trafficking is on the rise.

The traffic in human misery

A joint report in 2001 by the Shengen Commissions (which study free travel between the countries of the European Union) and the Anti-Mafia Commission of the Italian parliament estimates that the number of people living in a situation of forced servitude is in the region of 200 million. But even the most cautious figures show that today there are more people living in slavery-like conditions today than at any other moment in history. There is no doubt that there are millions of men, women and children, from the Philippines to Bangladesh, from Brazil to Italy and the Dominican Republic, who live in conditions of direct physical or economic submission. In Mauritania and Sudan, entire peoples are someone's property. The contemporary forms of slavery include forced labor and prostitution, debt servitude and child labor. Slaves today may be concubines, camel jockeys or sugarcane cutters, road construction workers, rug weavers or loggers. Though we do not see many images of whips and chains, and people are not sold at public auction, the slaves of today in many cases are subjected to treatment even more brutal, and conditions even more horrifying than their predecessors.

Slave trade at work

In 1926, the Slavery Convention, held under the auspices of the League of Nations, defined slavery as 'the status or condition of a person over whom any or all of the powers attaching to the right of ownership are exercised'. Slavery was thus recognized in the broad sense, paving the way for identifying it in its new variations. There are different mechanisms of subjugation, for the purposes of labor, for example: children forced to work in textile mills in India, in the mines in Congo or making cooking oil in the Philippines; women in the factories of Vietnam; Burmese emigrants in Thailand; and Haitians cutting sugarcane in the Dominican Republic. Or they could be slaves on the banana plantations of Honduras or the people subcontracted by shoe factories in Cambodia.

Sexual slavery is another major form of human subjugation. In addition to the prostitution networks and sexual exploitation involving women, children and immigrants over much of the world, a business with a turnover of $7-13 billion a year, there are also some forms of marriage in which women become slaves. In effect, while Article 1 of the Supplementary Convention on the Abolition of Slavery (1956) bans any practice or institution in which the woman, 'without the right to refuse, is promised or given in marriage on payment of a consideration in money or in kind to her parents, guardian, family or any other person or group', or in which 'the husband of a woman, his family, or his clan, has the right to transfer her to another person for value received or otherwise'. The reality is that practices remain in place around the world allowing marriages in exchange for money or some type of economic benefit. This practice often turns into the 'purchase' of the bride and her 'services'. In some places, it is the bride's family must pay a dowry to the groom or his family, and if that sum cannot be handed over in full before the marriage, the woman is 'retained' within the marriage and subjected to punishment, mistreatment and other forms of violence as long as the debt is not paid.

In many cases, modern slavery, particularly in rural areas, can be traced to the repayment of family debts through the sale of family members, usually children, or through servitude to the creditor. The widespread decline in the market for agricultural products and local natural disasters has forced small farmers to amass debt in order to survive; many have inherited debt several generations old. Such is the case of the Adivasi indigenous peoples in India, the peasant farmers in some areas of Brazil and the people of Bolivia's jungle regions who are forced to sell their harvests and their lands at rock-bottom prices. Debt also imprisons immigrants who cross borders illegally in search of work, and once at their destination find that their income must go to the networks that brought them there, to cover supposed expenses such as transport, food and lodging.

Like the children who are forcibly recruited into Sudan's army or by Somali warlords or Liberian guerrilla forces, many adults are forced, kidnapped or coerced into enlisting, whether in the regular army or with guerrillas, paramilitaries or other armed opposition groups.

Old-style slavery

There are an estimated 90,000 slaves in Sudan. The vast majority are black Christians captured by governmental militias and sold to Arabs in the country's north. According to some reports, there is not a village in the north where slaves bought from the military cannot be found. Although Islam bans the taking of Muslim slaves, the fact is that some of the black population of southern Mauritania for example, despite being Muslim are treated as slaves. There is no country nowadays in which slavery is legal, but in some places the ban has been merely a formal declaration without any effect in practice and no change in the economic, social, political or cultural conditions that force women, men and children into situations of slavery.

The industrialized world, which has carried high the banner of human rights, does not generally call attention to the phenomenon of slavery. Championing the human rights cause has its origins in the Cold War, when it concerned denouncing abuses committed by states, preferably - though not exclusively - within the socialist camp. The West defended prisoners of conscience, dissidents, intellectuals and victims of torture in order to exert pressure over governments. In other words, efforts were inspired by political motives.

Today's slavery is rooted in the absolute poverty of an ever-increasing portion of the world's population. It also emanates from the systematic exploitation of the weakest in society practiced by some individuals and companies with power. The causes of this misery are apparently not considered enemy enough to be fought by the powerful West. Denouncing slavery would be to denounce the hidden factors that foster it. For the slaves of the 21st century are children of wars, of the merciless competition of the markets, of the need to cut costs and of the desolation that corporate capital has created in all corners of the world. ■

WORKERS IN FIGURES

A = Labor force (% of total population), 2000. Source: World Development Indicators 2002, World Bank.
B = Unemployment (%). Source: KILM - Key Indicators of the Labour Market, ILO Web Site 2001-2002.
C = Female employment (% in agriculture), 1994/97. Source: Human Development Report 2001, UNDP.
D = Female employment (% in industry), 1994/97. Source: Human Development Report 2001, UNDP.
E = Female employment (% in services), 1994/97. Source: Human Development Report 2001, UNDP.
F = Male employment (% in agriculture), 1994/97. Source: Human Development Report 2001, UNDP.
G = Male employment (% in industry), 1994/97. Source: Human Development Report 2001, UNDP.
H = Male employment (% in services), 1994/97. Source: Human Development Report 2001, UNDP.

[1] 1999
[2] 1998
[3] 1997
[4] 1996
[5] 1995
[6] 1994
[7] 1993
[8] 1991

Country	A	B	female C	female D	female E	male F	male G	male H
Afghanistan	42.0							
Albania	49.9	9.1[8]						
Algeria	33.7	29.8						
Angola	45.9							
Aotearoa-New Zealand	50.1	6.0	6	13	81	11	33	56
Argentina	40.5	15.0		12	88	2	32	65
Armenia	50.3	36.4[3]						
Australia	51.0	6.6	4	11	85	6	31	63
Austria	46.8	3.6	8	14	78	6	42	52
Azerbaijan	44.7							
Bahamas	54.6	7.7[2]	1	6	93	8	22	69
Bahrain	45.2		32	67	1	57	41	
Belarus	52.6							
Belgium	41.6	7.0						
Belize	34.3	11.1[6]	5	10	84	38	20	40
Benin	45.1							
Bhutan	48.0							
Bolivia	40.7	7.4	2	16	82	2	40	58
Bosnia-Herzegovina	46.8							
Botswana	44.4							
Brazil	46.8	9.6[6]	22	9	68	28	26	45
Brunei	44.9							
Bulgaria	50.9	16.4						
Burkina Faso	49.3							
Burundi	54.5							
Cambodia	52.4							
Cameroon	40.7							
Canada	53.8	6.8	2	12	86	5	32	63
Cape Verde	41.1							
Central African Rep.	48.3							
Chad	48.4							
Chile	40.8	8.3	4	14	81	19	34	47
China	60.0	3.1						
Colombia	43.6	20.5						
Comoros	45.7							
Congo D.R.	41.2							
Congo R.	41.3							
Costa Rica	40.0	5.2	6	17	76	27	26	46
Côte d'Ivoire	40.0							
Croatia	47.3	16.1						
Cuba	49.6							
Cyprus	48.6	4.9	10	18	71	11	30	58
Czech Republic	56.2	8.3	4	29	66	7	50	43
Denmark	55.1	5.5[2]	2	15	83	5	36	58
Dominican Republic	44.0	15.9[3]						
Ecuador	39.1	11.5[2]	2	16	83	10	26	64
Egypt	38.1	8.1[1]	42	9	48	32	25	43
El Salvador	43.2	7.0	/1	7	21	72	38	25
Equatorial Guinea	41.7							
Eritrea	50.1							
Estonia	55.7	13.7	8	27	65	16	39	44
Ethiopia	42.9		88	2	11	89	2	9
Fiji	40.5	5.4[5]						
Finland	50.4	9.7	5	14	81	9	39	52
France	45.4	10.0						
Gabon	45.5							
Gambia	50.5							
Georgia	49.3	10.8						
Germany	49.8	7.9	3	19	79	3	46	51
Ghana	47.5							
Greece	43.3	11.1	23	13	63	18	28	54
Guam		5.5[7]						
Guatemala	36.9							
Guinea	47.4							
Guinea-Bissau	46.9							
Guyana	43.8							
Haiti	43.9							
Honduras	37.6	3.7[1]	7	27	66	53	19	28
Hungary	47.9	6.4	4	25	71	11	40	50
Iceland	56.4	2.3	4	15	81	12	35	53
India	44.4							
Indonesia	48.4	5.5[2]	42	16	42	41	21	39
Iran	30.9							
Iraq	27.7							
Ireland	42.5	5.7[1]	3	15	79	15	34	49
Israel	43.4	8.8	1	14	84	3	38	58
Italy	44.6	10.5	7	22	72	7	38	55
Jamaica	52.5	16.0[4]	11	12	77	31	27	42
Japan	53.8	4.7	6	24	69	5	39	55
Jordan	29.8							
Kazakhstan	48.9	13.7[2]						
Kenya	51.6							
Korea, North	52.4							
Korea, South	51.1	4.1	13	21	66	10	38	52
Kuwait	40.5							
Kyrgyzstan	43.2		48	7	38	48	12	31
Laos	47.6							
Latvia	54.7	14.6	18	20	62	23	33	44
Lebanon	35.1							
Lesotho	41.2							
Liberia	40.3							
Libya	28.6							
Lithuania	51.9	15.4	18	21	61	23	35	42
Luxembourg	42.7							
Macedonia, TFYR	46.8		6	41	51	10	53	32
Madagascar	47.2							
Malawi	48.1							
Malaysia	41.3	3.1	14	30	56	19	36	45
Maldives	40.5							
Mali	48.8							
Malta	38.0							
Mauritania	46.2							
Mauritius	43.2	9.8[5]	13	43	45	15	39	46
Mexico	41.2	1.6	13	19	68	30	24	46
Moldova	50.3	8.5						
Mongolia	50.1							
Morocco	40.0	22.0[1]						
Mozambique	51.9							
Myanmar-Burma	53.1							
Namibia	41.2							
Nepal	46.4							
Netherlands	46.5	3.3	2	9	85	4	31	62
Netherlands Antilles	45.3	14.0						
Nicaragua	40.5	9.8						
Niger	47.0							
Nigeria	39.6							
Norway	52.0	3.4	2	10	87	7	35	59
Oman	26.5							
Pakistan	37.5	5.9[2]	67	11	22	44	20	36
Panama	42.2	11.8[1]	3	11	86	29	21	49
Papua New Guinea	49.2							
Paraguay	37.8	8.2[1]	1	13	87	6	37	57
Peru	37.9	7.4	5	12	83	10	27	63
Philippines	42.2	10.1	28	13	59	48	19	33
Poland	51.4	16.1	20	21	59	21	41	38
Portugal	50.8	4.0	16	21	64	12	40	48
Puerto Rico	37.8	10.1						
Qatar	53.6							
Romania	47.9	7.1	43	24	33	35	36	29
Russia	53.4	13.4[1]						
Rwanda	54.2							
Saudi Arabia	32.9							
Senegal	44.7							
Sierra Leone	37.2							
Singapore	49.7	4.4		25	75		34	66
Slovakia	54.8	18.6	6	27	67	11	49	40
Slovenia	50.7	7.4[1]	13	31	57	12	49	38
Solomon Is.	51.3							
Somalia	42.8							
South Africa	39.7							
Spain	44.2	14.1	6	14	80	10	39	52
Sri Lanka	43.9	8.0	40	24	34	33	22	41
Sudan	39.9							
Suriname	37.9	14.0[1]	2	6	90	8	33	53
Swaziland	36.7							
Sweden	54.1	4.7	1	12	87	4	39	57
Switzerland	53.8	2.7	4	15	82	5	35	59
Syria	31.9							
Tajikistan	39.3							
Tanzania	51.4							
Thailand	60.6	2.4	51	17	32	49	22	28
Togo	41.4							
Trinidad and Tobago	44.8	13.1[1]	5	13	82	14	33	54
Tunisia	39.6	15.6	20	40	38	22	32	44
Turkey	47.9	7.3[1]	65	13	21	30	29	40
Turkmenistan	43.4							
Uganda	49.0							
Ukraine	50.7	11.7						
United Arab Emirates	49.4	2.3						
United Kingdom	50.1	5.5	1	13	86	3	38	59
United States	51.4	4.0	1	13	85	4	34	63
Uruguay	45.9	13.6	2	17	82	7	34	59
Uzbekistan	42.4							
Venezuela	40.9	14.9[1]	2	14	84	19	28	53
Vietnam	51.5		71	9	20	70	12	18
Yemen	31.5							
Yugoslavia Fed. Rep.	47.9							
Zambia	42.5							
Zimbabwe	46.2		38	10	52	22	32	46

The slave coast revisited

Far from being consigned to the history books, slavery is alive and flourishing in many parts of the world, and in Africa in particular.

The extreme poverty of several African countries is leading to the resurgence of slavery. During the height of the slave trade run by African kingdoms and the European powers from the 16th to the 19th centuries, the merchandise in highest demand was adult males. Today, although adult slaves are found - for example Malians on Côte d'Ivoire's cocoa plantations - it is the children who are the most sought after both for commercial work and sexual exploitation in West Africa (known as 'the slave coast' to the Europeans in the 17th century).

Until recently, the practice was thought to be largely exclusive to war-torn countries such as Angola, Sudan, Somalia and Chad - where girls as young as 10 years old served as slaves and concubines in rebel military camps. Today, even in relatively peaceful regions, slave trafficking is on the rise. Though their governments officially oppose this trade in humans, Benin, Burkina Faso, Cameroon, Côte d'Ivoire, Gabon, Nigeria and Togo are the countries where it is increasing.

In West Africa, the responsibility for educating children has traditionally rested with the extended family, which is an expression of community solidarity. But the increasing need for paid work is eroding the values of communities that once upon a time protected children from abuse.

Intermediaries crisscross between neighboring Benin and Togo, preying on the children of poor rural families. In some cases, they just wait outside their houses and kidnap them; at other times, traffickers pick up children who have traveled to urban areas in search of food. But much of the time, they can easily persuade the parents to surrender their offspring by telling them that the children will receive training or a good education if they go to work for a wealthy family. They also tend to sweeten the inducement with a small sum of cash (which is usually less than $15 and rarely more than $30).

The traffickers have to cover expenses - including food for the children during the journey and bribes to ensure the cooperation of the border guards. They recover their investment by exploiting the new slaves who, to pay off this debt in their new country, usually by working long hours for which they receive no money. They end up utterly dependent on the traffickers or whoever has bought them.

Children for sale
The girls from Benin and Togo are highly prized by rich families in Lagos, Nigeria or in Libreville, Gabon. But many of the girls travel much greater distances, for example to Bangui in the Central African Republic - an extremely poor country - or to Cameroon.

Another major supplier of child slaves is Mali. Here they are taken from their homes in rural areas and put to work on plantations. Salia Kante, director of Save the Children in Mali, said that 'Those who drink cocoa or coffee are drinking their blood, the blood of children who are not yet 10 years old.'

The declining price of coffee and chocolate over the last decade and the deregulation of the market have created hardship for the peasant farmers in West Africa. This has stimulated the new slave workforce; employers do not pay wages to the adults either. Big multinationals have not lifted a finger to end the trade in child slaves.

New slaves, ancient practice
Studies show that more than 30 children are brought across the border between Benin and Nigeria as slaves every two months. Some 95 per cent are girls, 50 per cent are under 15, and 45 per cent have never attended school. In Lagos and in Abidjan (Côte d'Ivoire), child slave markets have flourished. Traffickers occasionally take their merchandise for sale in Europe, traveling under the pretext that the boys are going to take part in sports tournaments or, as happened in one case, that the children were going to participate in an audience with the Pope.

In West African societies traditional community practises appear to have given way to others that are just as old. Today, as in the 15th to 19th centuries, the slave ships usually anchor in Cotonou, Benin. Some Africans continue hunting down others to sell them. In the past, some of the women and children were not put on the transatlantic ships, but were kept for the domestic market. Nowadays, although there is a global demand for the raw materials produced by adult slaves, there is no explicit demand for them; children have taken their place on the African market. ∎

Child labor

AROUND THE WORLD, some 400 million minors are working, either full- or part-time. Of these, over 250 million children between the ages of 5 and 14 are working in developing countries.

A complex issue

Around the world, some 400 million minors are working, either full- or part-time. Of these, over 250 million children between the ages of 5 and 14 are working in developing countries. Nearly two-thirds (61 per cent) of them are in Asia, most of the rest (32 per cent) are in Africa and the remainder - 7 per cent - in Latin America. At least a million children are forced to work in prostitution and 80 million in hazardous or life-threatening condition

In 1999, the member states of the International Labour Organization (ILO), which also make up the majority of United Nations members, signed the Convention on the Worst Forms of Child Labor. This has the goal of liberating millions of minors from slavery and debt servitude, prostitution, pornography, hazardous labor and forced recruitment into the armed forces.

Convention 182, which applies to all people under the age of 18, demands immediate and effective measures to secure the prohibition and elimination of the worst forms of child labor as a matter of urgency. According to the agreement, the ratifying states should design and implement programs of action to eliminate these forms of child labor and establish appropriate mechanisms to enforce the provisions of the Convention, implemented in consultation with relevant government institutions and employers' and workers' organizations. Furthermore, the ratifying countries should: provide direct assistance for the removal of children from the worst forms of child labor and for their rehabilitation and social reintegration; ensure that all such children have access to free basic education or vocational training; identify those children who are at special risk; and take account of the special situation of girls. The Convention also recommends that the worst forms of child labor be considered crimes by the ratifying states, which should impose criminal penalties against those responsible.

The view of many trade unions and non-governmental organizations (NGOs) is that although governments have made many official statements on the matter, they have so far done little or nothing to attack this global problem. Unions and NGOs are saying that the impact of publicity (especially awareness campaigns related to prostitution, slavery and trafficking in humans) is actually making it harder to get to the bottom of the problem. Raising awareness of child labor requires also raising awareness of the contributing factors and in order to attack the root causes it is necessary to deal with economic aspects, traditional and cultural influences, availability of school and so on.

If the underlying problems are disregarded, simply plucking a child from the work place and sticking it in school could do more harm than good in the short term. At a congress held in Mexico City in 1998, the Latin American Workers' Central (CLAT) stressed that to understand the magnitude of the problem, it was important to realize that the boys and girls who work are contributing additional income for their own survival and that of their families. It added that if child labor were to be eliminated, poverty would worsen for the lowest income families, deepening misery and marginalization. CLAT proposed to link efforts to eradicate child labor with the struggle for decent jobs, fair wages, quality education and effective professional training. ■

BREAST IS BEST

% of mothers who are breast feeding at 3 months, 1995-2000.
North Korea tops this table with nearly all mothers breastfeeding according to government figures – and with famine in the country maybe mothers will breastfeed for as long as possible.

Afghanistan	25	Georgia	18	Pakistan	16
Albania	9	Ghana	36	Palau	59
Algeria	16	Grenada	39	Palestine	29
Angola	12	Guatemala	47	Panama	32
Armenia	45	Guinea	12	Papua New Guinea	75
Azerbaijan	9	Guinea-Bissau	42	Paraguay	7
Bahrain	34	Haiti	32	Peru	63
Bangladesh	53	Honduras	42	Philippines	47
Belize	24	India	55	Qatar	12
Benin	15	Indonesia	52	Rwanda	81
Bolivia	61	Iran	66	Saudi Arabia	31
Botswana	29	Jordan	15	Senegal	24
Burkina Faso	5	Kazakhstan	47	Sierra Leone	2
Burundi	74	Kenya	16	Somalia	21
Cambodia	9	Korea, North	97	South Africa	10
Cameroon	16	Kuwait	12	Sri Lanka	24
Cape Verde	57	Kyrgyzstan	31	St Kitts-Nevis	56
Central African Rep.	22	Laos	28	Sudan	14
Chad	13	Lebanon	27	Suriname	13
Chile	73	Lesotho	54	Swaziland	37
China	67	Macedonia, TFYR	45	Tajikistan	19
Colombia	34	Madagascar	52	Tanzania	41
Comoros	24	Malawi	11	Thailand	4
Congo D.R.	32	Maldives	8	Togo	15
Congo R.	4	Mali	13	Trinidad and Tobago	10
Cook Is.	19	Mauritania	60	Tunisia	12
Costa Rica	35	Mauritius	16	Turkey	9
Côte d'Ivoire	11	Mexico	38	Turkmenistan	16
Croatia	24	Mongolia	64	Uganda	70
Cuba	46	Morocco	31	United Arab Emirates	34
Dominican Republic	16	Mozambique	38	Uzbekistan	22
Ecuador	29	Myanmar (Burma)	18	Venezuela	7
Egypt	68	Namibia	22	Vietnam	31
El Salvador	21	Nepal	83	Yemen	25
Eritrea	66	Nicaragua	29	Yugoslavia Fed. Rep.	11
Ethiopia	84	Niger	2	Zambia	11
Gabon	8	Nigeria	20	Zimbabwe	39
Gambia	35	Oman	31		

Source: The State of the World's Children 2002, UNICEF

Adult literacy rate (%), 2000.
A = Total
B = male
C = female

The adult literacy rate for women in Afghanistan increased from 16 per cent in 1995 to 21 per cent in 2000. This figure is worth watching to see how the effects of the lack of girls' education under the Taliban regime will work out. (see table School enrolment)
Overall in the world, the literacy rate continues to rise. The biggest discrepancies between male and female literacy rates occur in countries where women do not have equality with men.

	A	B	C		A	B	C		A	B	C
Afghanistan	36	51	21	Georgia	100	100	99	Nigeria	64	72	56
Algeria	63	75	51	Ghana	70	79	61	Oman	72	80	62
Antigua	82	80	83	Greece	97	99	96	Pakistan	43	58	28
Argentina	97	97	97	Guatemala	69	76	61	Panama	92	93	91
Armenia	99	100	99	Guinea	41	55	27	Papua New Guinea	76	84	68
Azerbaijan	97	99	96	Guinea-Bissau	37	53	21	Paraguay	93	94	92
Bahamas	96	95	97	Guyana	98	99	98	Peru	90	95	85
Bahrain	88	91	83	Haiti	49	51	46	Philippines	95	96	95
Bangladesh	41	52	29	Honduras	81	78	85	Poland	100	100	100
Barbados	98	98	97	Hungary	99	100	99	Portugal	92	95	90
Belarus	99	100	99	India	56	69	42	Qatar	81	80	83
Belize	80	80	80	Indonesia	87	92	82	Romania	98	99	97
Benin	37	52	24	Iran	77	84	70	Russia	99	100	99
Bhutan	47	61	34	Iraq	58	71	45	Rwanda	67	74	61
Bolivia	86	92	79	Israel	96	98	94	Saudi Arabia	77	84	67
Bosnia-Herzegovina	93	98	89	Italy	98	99	98	Senegal	37	47	28
Botswana	77	74	80	Jamaica	87	83	91	Seychelles	88	87	89
Brazil	85	85	85	Jordan	90	95	84	Sierra Leone	36	51	23
Brunei	92	95	88	Kazakhstan	98	98	98	Singapore	92	96	88
Bulgaria	99	99	98	Kenya	82	89	76	Slovakia	100	100	100
Burkina Faso	23	33	13	Korea, North	100	100	100	Slovenia	100	100	100
Burundi	48	56	41	Korea, South	98	99	96	South Africa	85	86	84
Cambodia	68	79	58	Kuwait	82	84	80	Spain	98	99	97
Cameroon	75	82	69	Kyrgyzstan	97	99	95	Sri Lanka	92	94	89
Cape Verde	73	84	65	Laos	62	74	50	Sudan	57	68	46
Central African Rep.	46	60	35	Latvia	100	100	100	Suriname	94	96	93
Chad	54	67	41	Lebanon	86	92	80	Swaziland	80	81	79
Chile	96	96	96	Lesotho	84	74	94	Syria	74	88	60
China	85	92	77	Liberia	53	70	37	Tajikistan	99	100	99
Colombia	92	92	92	Libya	80	91	68	Tanzania	75	84	67
Comoros	74	78	70	Lithuania	100	100	99	Thailand	96	97	94
Congo D.R.	67	83	54	Madagascar	47	50	44	Togo	57	72	43
Congo R.	81	88	74	Malawi	60	75	47	Tonga	99		
Costa Rica	96	95	96	Malaysia	88	91	84	Trinidad and Tobago	98	99	98
Côte d'Ivoire	47	55	38	Maldives	96	96	96	Tunisia	71	81	60
Croatia	98	99	97	Mali	40	48	33	Turkey	85	94	77
Cuba	96	96	96	Malta	92	91	93	Tuvalu	98	98	98
Cyprus	97	99	95	Mauritania	40	51	29	Uganda	67	78	57
Djibouti	51	65	38	Mauritius	84	88	81	Ukraine	99	98	99
Dominican Republic	84	84	84	Mexico	91	93	89	United Arab Emirates	87	85	93
Ecuador	92	94	90	Moldova	99	100	98	Uruguay	98	97	98
Egypt	55	67	44	Mongolia	99	99	99	Uzbekistan	99	99	99
El Salvador	79	82	76	Morocco	49	62	36	Venezuela	93	93	93
Equatorial Guinea	83	92	75	Mozambique	44	60	28	Vietnam	93	96	91
Eritrea	30			Myanmar-Burma	85	89	81	Yemen	46	67	25
Estonia	98	98	98	Namibia	82	83	81	Yugoslavia Fed. Rep.	98	99	97
Ethiopia	39	44	33	Nauru	95	93	96	Zambia	78	85	71
Fiji	93	95	91	Nepal	41	59	24	Zimbabwe	93	96	90
Gabon	71	80	62	Nicaragua	64	64	64				
Gambia	37	44	30	Niger	16	23	8				

Source: The State of the World's Children 2002, UNICEF.

UNDER FIVE MORTALITY

Under-5 mortality rate (per 1,000 live births), 2000.
Under-5 mortality is an important indicator that indirectly shows the end result of a country's development process.

1	Sierra Leone	316	65	South Africa	70	129	Belarus	20
2	Angola	295	66	Turkmenistan	70	130	Jamaica	20
3	Niger	270	67	Namibia	69	131	Libya	20
4	Afghanistan	257	68	Marshall Is.	68	132	Mauritius	20
5	Liberia	235	69	Uzbekistan	67	133	Trinidad and Tobago	20
6	Mali	233	70	Algeria	65	134	Yugoslavia Fed. Rep.	20
7	Somalia	225	71	Kyrgyzstan	63	135	Sri Lanka	19
8	Guinea-Bissau	215	72	Guatemala	59	136	St Lucia	19
9	Congo D.R.	207	73	Tuvalu	53	137	Bahamas	18
10	Zambia	202	74	Peru	50	138	Bosnia-Herzegovina	18
11	Mozambique	200	75	Dominican Republic	48	139	Seychelles	17
12	Burkina Faso	198	76	Indonesia	48	140	Uruguay	17
13	Chad	198	77	Morocco	46	141	Bahrain	16
14	Burundi	190	78	Nicaragua	45	142	Bulgaria	16
15	Malawi	188	79	Turkey	45	143	Dominica	16
16	Rwanda	187	80	Iran	44	144	Qatar	16
17	Nigeria	184	81	Vanuatu	44	145	Antigua	15
18	Mauritania	183	82	Egypt	43	146	Barbados	14
19	Central African Rep.	180	83	Belize	41	147	Oman	14
20	Guinea	175	84	Cape Verde	40	148	Chile	12
21	Ethiopia	174	85	China	40	149	Costa Rica	12
22	Côte d'Ivoire	173	86	El Salvador	40	150	Liechtenstein	11
23	Tanzania	165	87	Honduras	40	151	Kuwait	10
24	Equatorial Guinea	156	88	Philippines	40	152	Poland	10
25	Benin	154	89	Vietnam	39	153	Croatia	9
26	Cameroon	154	90	Brazil	38	154	Cuba	9
27	Djibouti	146	91	Jordan	34	155	Hungary	9
28	Swaziland	142	92	Moldova	33	156	Malaysia	9
29	Togo	142	93	Suriname	33	157	Slovakia	9
30	Madagascar	139	94	Ecuador	32	158	United Arab Emirates	9
31	Senegal	139	95	Lebanon	32	159	United States	8
32	Cambodia	135	96	Albania	31	160	Andorra	7
33	Lesotho	133	97	Paraguay	31	161	Brunei	7
34	Iraq	130	98	Armenia	30	162	Cyprus	7
35	Gambia	128	99	Colombia	30	163	Aotearoa-New Zealand	6
36	Uganda	127	100	Korea, North	30	164	Australia	6
37	Haiti	125	101	Mexico	30	165	Belgium	6
38	Kenya	120	102	Nauru	30	166	Canada	6
39	Yemen	117	103	Georgia	29	167	Greece	6
40	Zimbabwe	117	104	Palau	29	168	Ireland	6
41	Eritrea	114	105	Saudi Arabia	29	169	Israel	6
42	Papua New Guinea	112	106	Syria	29	170	Italy	6
43	Myanmar-Burma	110	107	Thailand	29	171	Malta	6
44	Pakistan	110	108	Tunisia	28	172	Portugal	6
45	Congo R.	108	109	Grenada	26	173	San Marino	6
46	Sudan	108	110	Macedonia, TFYR	26	174	United Kingdom	6
47	Azerbaijan	105	111	Panama	26	175	Austria	5
48	Laos	105	112	Samoa	26	176	Czech Republic	5
49	Ghana	102	113	Palestine	25	177	Denmark	5
50	Botswana	101	114	Solomon Is.	25	178	Finland	5
51	Bhutan	100	115	St Kitts-Nevis	25	179	France	5
52	Nepal	100	116	St Vincent	25	180	Germany	5
53	India	96	117	Cook Is.	24	181	Korea, South	5
54	Gabon	90	118	Micronesia	24	182	Luxembourg	5
55	Bangladesh	82	119	Venezuela	23	183	Monaco	5
56	Comoros	82	120	Fiji	22	184	Netherlands	5
57	Bolivia	80	121	Romania	22	185	Slovenia	5
58	Maldives	80	122	Russia	22	186	Spain	5
59	Mongolia	78	123	Argentina	21	187	Iceland	4
60	Kazakhstan	75	124	Estonia	21	188	Japan	4
61	São Tomé and Príncipe	75	125	Latvia	21	189	Norway	4
62	Guyana	74	126	Lithuania	21	190	Singapore	4
63	Tajikistan	73	127	Tonga	21	191	Sweden	4
64	Kiribati	70	128	Ukraine	21	192	Switzerland	4

Source: The State of the World's Children 2002, UNICEF.

MUSLIM WOMEN have their own perspective on feminism which can be overlooked by Western feminists whose own goals and experiences may have little relevance to the situation of women in Islam.

Feminism through the eyes of Islam

Some Western feminists are increasingly looking at issues that do not directly involve them, such as the place and role of women in Islam. For some time now the applicability of some aspects of Western feminism has been in question.

The modern feminist movement had its roots in England in the second half of the 19th century. It was promoted by women who sought property rights denied them under British law. Even after the British Parliament approved the first Married Women's Property Act in 1882, women continued to be denied property in their own right, independent of their husband's - a right that was granted Muslim women in the 7th century, in the time of the Prophet Muhammad.

Western feminism was conceived from the outset by middle-class white women who have tended to judge other cultures in a critical way. Today it is recognized within the feminist academy that, in many cases, their efforts to liberate their peers in the Third World have been marked by classist and ethnocentric prejudices. They also recognize that their standards for judging the rest of the world have ignored their own status and position of privilege as citizens of countries that were colonizing states (or which today are neo-colonialist).

As a counterweight, there are many female academics of the South, including Muslim women, who emphasize that the Northern feminists' critical perspective of patriarchy in the non-industrialized world often lacks contextualization. In the specific case of Islam, Muslim women academics say that the lens through which Westerners see them is colored by androcentric, ethnocentric and colonialist preconceptions, and also by the West's exoticization of Islam in general. In his book *Orientalism*, Palestinian academic Edward Said explains that this perspective denies Islam its historic reality, that it is perceived in the light of a past of splendor and a present that is invariably disappointing with respect to that history.

The battle over interpretation

In addition, Western feminists sometimes do not appear to perceive the existence of discourses within each culture that fall into socially constructed categories of man and woman and the status of women. These discourses are usually controlled by men or favor men. In the particular case of the ideological and activist struggle of women within the Muslim world, one discourse includes the interpretations of the Qur'an. A large part of the oppression of Muslim women is not the fault of the writings of the Qur'an, but of its interpretation. Because this sacred text also serves as a normative guide in the social and political spheres, it has been the ulemas (scholars of the Qur'an), over the centuries, who have jealously guarded its interpretation. They have imposed social norms that are not necessarily in keeping with what the Prophet said.

Taking Muhammad's words that the pursuit of knowledge is obligatory for every Muslim, male or female, Muslim women activists have made the sacred book a battlefield, claiming an interpretation of the text that favors the liberation of women. They have recalled the heroines named in the Qur'an, beginning with the wives and daughter of Muhammad, some of whom participated in battles and even led armies. They also point out that Qur'anic prescriptions are not limited to men; already in Muhammed's era women participated in the spheres of knowledge and education.

Many female Muslim academics have reacted to certain interpretations that they believe are too orthodox as examples of how the discourse is manipulated by men. These women cite the standard claims that the Prophet, by recognizing women's rights previously denied them (such as the right to property and the power to dissolve the marriage through *Khula'* - that is, by giving up some of her property to her husband) had completed the women's revolution in the 7th century. As a result some Muslim leaders believe that there is no need today to advocate new rights for women. Although many women agree that the Qur'an brought with it certain reforms, like the prohibition of infanticide, the payment of a dowry to the bride, female inheritance and women's property rights, nonetheless they point out that the Qur'an upholds divorce as an exclusively male prerogative. One reason for this is that the institution of Khula' - besides forcing women to give up property - specifies that a wife must dislike her husband enough to deny him conjugal rights which is virtually impossible for her to do.

Writer Leila Ahmed, for example, has said that the message of Islam, as instituted by the teachings and practices of Muhammaed, contained two strands that were at odds with each other. On the one hand, it preached patriarchal matrimony and the dominance of the man, while, on the other hand, it preached equality. This ambiguity casts doubt on what is Islamic and what is not. There are even some clothing-related institutions, such as the wearing of the veil, which should not be considered necessarily Muslim because it is not clear that this was obligatory in the Prophet's day.

Muslim women argue that times have changed. They say that scrutinizing the Qur'anic verses to evaluate their true or original meaning is no longer useful. The entry of some Muslim women into the workforce, which has enabled them to earn an income and a degree of independence, has made obsolete the prescriptive nature of the Islamic testament. In the face of such change, the repeated question about a woman's place in Islam would lose its relevance. New economic and social conditions, the dismantling of the traditional roles of men and women, would force a rethinking of the situation.

For them, this is a global problem. They insist that the horror expressed by Muslims, men and women alike, about the breakdown of the family caused by the impacts of industrialization is not exclusive to Islam. In their view, the entry of women into the labor market has begun to dismantle not the family, but the patriarchal system (and not just the Islamic one). This concern about the breakdown of patriarchy is also evident in the West, where some Christian groups continue to press for women to stay at home and forget about work. To sum up, for these activists the situation of Muslim women should be studied in two ways: on the one hand taking into account the specific Islamic context; and on the other, within the context of industrialization, where women's entry into the labor market has helped break up patriarchy. ∎

WOMEN IN POLITICAL AND ECONOMIC LIFE

A = % of women in labor force, 2000. Source: World Development Indicators 2002, World Bank.
B = % of professional and technical workers, 1990/99. Source: Human Development Report 2001, UNDP.
C = Female legislators, senior officials and managers (as % of total) 1990/99. Source: Human Development Report 2001, UNDP.
D = Women's earned income share (%), last available year. Source: Human Development Report 2001, UNDP.
E = % of ministerial posts occupied by women, 1999. Source: Human Development Report 2001, UNDP.
F = % of parliamentary seats occupied by women, 2001. Source: Human Development Report 2001, UNDP.

	A	B	C	D	E	F
Afghanistan	35.5					
Albania	41.3				15.0	5.2
Algeria	27.6				0.0	4.0
Angola	46.3				14.7	15.5
Aotearoa-New Zealand	45.0	52	37	65	44.0	30.8
Argentina	33.2				7.3	21.3
Armenia	48.6					3.1
Australia	43.7	47	25	67	19.5	25.4
Austria	40.3	49	26	48	31.3	25.1
Azerbaijan	44.6				2.6	10.5
Bahamas	47.3	51	31	66	16.7	19.6
Bahrain	20.8	20	9			
Bangladesh	42.4	35	5	58	9.5	9.1
Barbados	46.1	51	39	60	14.3	20.4
Belarus	49.0				25.7	18.4
Belgium	40.9	50	19	43	18.5	24.9
Belize	24.1	39	37	23	11.1	13.5
Benin	48.3				10.5	6.0
Bhutan	39.9					9.3
Bolivia	37.8	43	25	44		10.2
Bosnia-Herzegovina	38.1					
Botswana	45.3				26.7	17.0
Brazil	35.5	61			0.0	5.9
Brunei	35.6				0.0	
Bulgaria	48.2				18.8	10.8
Burkina Faso	46.5				8.6	11.0
Burundi	48.7				4.5	14.4
Cambodia	51.7				7.1	9.3
Cameroon	38.0				5.8	5.6
Canada	45.8	53	35	61	24.3	23.6
Cape Verde	38.9				35.0	11.1
Central African Rep.						7.3
Chad	44.7					2.4
Chile	33.6	51	22	36	25.6	8.9
China	45.2				5.1	21.8
Colombia	38.7	48	40	45	47.4	12.2
Comoros	42.3					
Congo D.R.	43.4					
Congo R.	43.5					12.0
Costa Rica	31.1	45	30	35	28.6	19.3
Côte d'Ivoire	33.4				9.1	8.5
Croatia	44.2	52	26	55	16.2	16.2
Cuba	39.5					
Cyprus	38.7					7.1
Czech Republic	47.3	54	23	64		14.2
Denmark	46.4	50	3	70	45.0	37.4
Djibouti					5.0	0.0
Dominican Republic	30.8	49	31	34		14.5
Ecuador	28.0	47	28	29	20.0	14.6
Egypt	30.4	29	11	37	6.1	2.4
El Salvador	36.5	47	28	38	15.4	9.5
Equatorial Guinea	35.6					5.0
Eritrea	47.4	30	17	52	11.8	14.7
Estonia	49.0	67	35	63	14.3	17.8
Ethiopia	40.9				22.2	7.8
Fiji	30.5	10	48		20.7	
Finland	48.1	62	29	66	44.4	36.5
France	45.1				37.9	9.1
Gabon	44.7				12.1	10.9
Gambia	45.1				30.8	2.0
Georgia	46.8				9.7	7.2
Germany	42.3	50	26	50	35.7	30.4
Ghana	50.5				8.6	9.0
Greece	37.8	46	25	44	7.1	8.7
Guatemala	28.9				7.1	8.8
Guinea	47.2				11.1	8.8
Guinea-Bissau	40.5				8.3	7.8
Guyana	34.0					18.5
Haiti	42.9					18.2
Honduras	31.8	51	36	35	33.3	9.4
Hungary	44.7	62	34	57	35.9	8.3
Iceland	45.3	53	25	62	33.3	34.9
India	32.3					10.1
Indonesia	40.8				5.9	8.0
Iran	27.1				9.4	3.4
Iraq	19.7					
Ireland	34.5	50	34	38	18.8	13.7
Israel	41.2	54	25	50	6.1	12.5
Italy	38.5	43	19	44	17.6	10.0
Jamaica	46.2				12.5	16.0
Japan	41.4	44	9	43	5.7	10.8
Jordan	24.6				0.0	2.5
Kazakhstan	47.1				17.5	11.2
Kenya	46.1				1.4	3.6
Korea, North	43.3					
Korea, South	41.4	31	5	45	6.5	5.9

	A	B	C	D	E	F
Kuwait	31.3				0.0	0.0
Kyrgyzstan	47.3					6.7
Laos					10.2	21.2
Latvia	50.5	65	39	65	6.7	17.0
Lebanon	29.6				0.0	2.3
Lesotho	36.9					10.7
Liberia	39.6					
Libya	23.1				12.5	
Lithuania	48.0	69	39	67	18.9	10.6
Luxembourg	36.6				28.6	16.7
Macedonia, TFYR	41.7				10.9	6.7
Madagascar	44.7				12.5	8.0
Malawi	48.6				11.8	9.3
Malaysia	37.9	44	21	46		14.5
Maldives	43.4					6.0
Mali	46.2				33.3	12.2
Malta	27.8				5.3	9.2
Mauritania	43.6				13.6	3.0
Mauritius	32.6	38	23	36	9.1	5.7
Mexico	33.2	40	23	37	11.1	15.9
Moldova	48.6					8.9
Mongolia	47.0				10.0	10.5
Morocco	34.7				4.9	0.7
Mozambique	48.4					30.0
Myanmar-Burma	43.4					
Namibia	40.9				16.3	20.4
Nepal	40.5				14.8	7.9
Netherlands	40.6	46	23	51	31.0	32.9
Netherlands Antilles	42.9					
Nicaragua	35.9				23.1	9.7
Niger	44.3				10.0	1.2
Nigeria	36.5				22.6	3.3
Norway	46.4	58	31	63	42.1	36.4
Oman	17.1					
Pakistan	28.6	25	8			
Panama	35.3	46	33	48	20.0	9.9
Papua New Guinea	42.2				0.0	1.8
Paraguay	30.0	54	23	32		8.0
Peru	31.3	41	23	25	16.2	20.0
Philippines	37.8	63	33	55		11.8
Poland	46.4	60	34	61	18.7	12.7
Portugal	44.0	51	32	52	9.7	18.7
Puerto Rico	37.2					
Qatar	15.0				0.0	
Romania	44.5	56	26	58	20.0	9.3
Russia	49.2	64	37	63		5.6
Rwanda	48.8				13.0	25.7
Samoa						7.7
Saudi Arabia	16.1					
Senegal	42.6				15.6	14.0
Sierra Leone	36.8				8.1	8.8
Singapore	39.1	42	21	49	5.7	6.5
Slovakia	47.8	60	32	65	19.0	14.0
Slovenia	46.5	51	31	61	15.0	12.2
Solomon Is.	46.5					
Somalia	43.4					
South Africa	37.8				38.1	27.9
Spain	37.2	44	31	42	17.6	26.6
Sri Lanka	36.6	50	50	51		4.0
Sudan	29.5				5.1	9.7
Suriname	33.7	69	13	36		17.6
Swaziland	37.7	61	24	43	12.5	6.3
Sweden	48.0	49	29	68	55.0	42.7
Switzerland	40.5	40	20	49	28.6	22.4
Syria	27.0				11.1	10.4
Tajikistan	44.9					12.4
Tanzania	49.1					22.2
Thailand	46.3	55	22		5.7	
Togo	40.0				7.4	4.9
Trinidad and Tobago	34.3	51	40	38	8.7	20.9
Tunisia	31.7				10.0	11.5
Turkey	37.6	36	9	45	0.0	4.2
Turkmenistan	45.9					26.0
Uganda	47.6				27.1	17.8
Ukraine	48.9	63	38	54		7.8
United Arab Emirates	14.8					0.0
United Kingdom	44.1	45	33	61	33.3	17.0
United States	46.0	53	45	61	31.8	13.8
Uruguay	41.8	61	28	50		11.5
Uzbekistan	46.9				4.4	7.2
Venezuela	34.8	58	24	40	0.0	9.7
Vietnam	48.9					26.0
Yemen	28.1					0.7
Yugoslavia Fed. Rep.	42.9					
Zambia	44.8				6.2	10.1
Zimbabwe	44.5				36.0	9.3

SOME WOMEN from Islamic countries and women converts to the faith who are born in the West insist that using/wearing the veil - which implies submission to the will of Allah - is truly an act of liberation.

What the veil reveals

The governments of the West systematically talk about the subjugation of women under Islam.

In the Western media, geopolitics wears the dress of haute couture and women covered by veils or burqas are cast as the symbol of tyranny and of Islam in general. When the Pentagon speaks, for example, about overthrowing some government in the Muslim world, the words are juxtaposed with the images of women with their heads covered - implying that, with bombs, freedom will arrive for the women and by extension, for the entire population.

From the Western perspective, modernization (and Westernization) tends to be confused with freedom. As a result, it is assumed that a woman living in an Islamic country who adopts styles of Western dress is thus more 'emancipated' than a woman who wears traditional clothes. But, as many women activists from the Islamic world point out, quite the opposite is true. For example, a woman working in a Palestinian factory and who wears traditional clothing,

including a head cover, may also be a political activist in the underground movement. Meanwhile, an Egyptian woman who wears fashions by an Italian designer may live in absolute submission to her husband, without a say in any sphere of her life. In that sense, it would seem that the veils shown so frequently by Western TV cameras may in some cases be stating the opposite of what appears to be the case.

Some women from Islamic countries and women converts to the faith who are born in the West insist that using/wearing the veil - which implies submission to the will of Allah that women be 'modest' - is truly an act of liberation. These women say the veil protects them from men's stares and harassment. Most of all, however, they are obeying the Qu'ran, because by covering their body they accentuate the individuality and wholeness of woman, which is otherwise overshadowed by the emphasis society places on appearance.

Activists also insist that the role of the veil varies depending on the time and the

place. Women activists in Saudi Arabia, for example, have resurrected the use of a special type of veil. Iranian women used the veil as a form of protest against the regime of the Shah, who was overthrown by the Islamic revolution of 1979. Within the Muslim world, women's dress can be a symbol of unity, but outside this world, it can mean just the opposite. The chador, the head covering worn by Muslim women in the West, can make them the target of discrimination - even those who are of Western descent.

The point is that outsiders should not seize on one aspect of other people's cultures and make judgments about what they see without understanding the full picture. But by the same token, no-one can sit back and assume that the struggle for women's true equality has been won, whether that woman wears a veil or not and whether that is her choice or not. The oppression of women whatever their color or creed is still a major factor holding back many countries from achieving their full potential. ■

Women of the Prophet: Gender and Islam

Islamic communities are expanding on both sides of the North Atlantic. Interestingly, the largest proportion of converts to Islam is among women. The number of British Muslims is estimated to be between 1 and 1.5 million. Of these, 10,000 to 20,000 are converts. According to current projections, within 20 years those who have converted to Islam in the United Kingdom will outnumber those who were born into the faith. Perhaps the most surprising fact is that almost all conversions to Islam involve women. Meanwhile, in the United States, for every male convert to Islam, there are four women converts.

The 'new eyes' of women converts
Both in the US and the UK, a large portion of the new female converts come from middle-class families. Many of them were

Christians, dissatisfied with the faith into which they were born, or with some of the dominant patterns in Western society, such as high crime rates, the breakdown of the family, alcoholism and drug abuse. However, this view disregards the fact that - although to a lesser degree - there is crime and drug abuse in Islamic countries, and some of the perpetrators get their limbs cut off.

There are other paths open to women converts: Some of them discover Islam through the study of comparative religions at university, but a large number do so through marriage. It is much more common for a woman of Christian background to marry a Muslim man than for a Christian man to marry a Muslim woman. Some of these new Western female converts say that they arrive at Islam with 'new eyes';

with an uncontaminated view in respect of the 'vices of interpretation' (and subsequent practices) that predominate in the 'East'.

British women converts argue that they are not 'betraying' their gender, as some think. Many Muslim women in the West interpret the Western idea of women's emancipation as 'women imitating men', an exercise, they say, in which femininity lacks intrinsic value. Unlike the Old Testament, which states that woman was created from man's rib, the Qur'an says that in the beginning God created both man and woman. In that sense, the sacred text of Islam implies both gender equality and gender difference (in which Muslim women interpret their biological destiny as different from that of men).

It is within this framework that

Qur'anic practices continue that do not concur with the Western scheme of things. Muslim women point out that Muhammed was the one who ended bridal dowry and female infanticide. They also stress that, of the Abrahamic testaments, it is the Qur'an that granted women 'equal' conditions, giving them the right to inheritance (even if a Muslim woman inherits only half what her male sibling does) and to keep their birth name in marriage.

Sisters in Islam

The concept of the Islamic family is one of an extended family: aunts, uncles, grandparents, cousins, in-laws and other relatives may live under the same roof as the immediate family or at least have a presence in day-to-day life. Since the time of the Prophet, this form of cohabitation has reinforced the role of the family, ensuring that all members are cared for, including widows and their children. The persistence of this order among Muslim families in Western industrialized countries has prompted more women to work outside the home because they know their children are well cared for. Many Muslim women assert that their biological fate grants them status and power within the household, which is their realm.

Traditional Muslim women are often intrigued that their non-Muslim counterparts may feel obliged to work outside the home for financial reasons. But 'modern' Muslim women, at least according to their British and US publications, say they do not consider that they are condemned to staying at home. They see the growing demand within the community for women professionals.

For many women converts, the notion of a 'sisterhood of women in Islam' demonstrates the failure of feminism as it is practiced in the West. The women new to Islam find support and reciprocity among Muslim women. They have the duty to assist others who use the *hijab* (the Muslim headdress) and who are in need or suffering. As Nuria, a British convert, said in an interview with *The Times* 'There's no such thing as a Muslim woman on her own or a single Muslim parent on her own. Nor a mentally ill woman on her own ... suffering'. That's unusual, she said, by Western standards. This can be understood within the concept of community, which is fundamental to Islam. Gender progress must take place, say Western Muslim women, within the context of family and community. Muslim women have 'everything the feminist movement is aiming for, except abortion and lesbianism' said Nuria. ∎

Polygamy and the Prophet

Polygamy - more precisely polygyny, or having more than one wife - is an ancient institution, practiced by numerous cultures, and still a hot subject of debate. The *Qur'an*, the sacred book of Islam, does not prohibit the practice but nor does it recommend it. The Qur'anic prescription that a Muslim man can have up to four wives - as long as each one, and their children, enjoy the same rights and living conditions - in practice turned out to be a limit imposed in Muhammad's time, when it was common for men to have a greater number of wives.

The practice of polygyny, in the original places of Islam as in many other parts of the world, could have been a response to the fact that women outnumbered men, usually as a result of the impacts of war. In Islam, the system was also meant to benefit widows who had been left on their own.

Today, the vast majority of Muslim men are monogamous (it is expensive to maintain four wives). However, with certain exceptions such as Tunisia or Turkey, polygyny is legal in most Muslim countries.

The Bible does not prohibit polygyny, although the Catholic Church always has. The lack of a biblical prohibition led Mormons, for example, to revive the practice. Islam's continued tolerance of polygyny is in part fueled by its unequivocal condemnation of adultery, whether by women or men. Polygyny is seen as an antidote to adultery within Islam. Despite this however there is still plenty of adultery, including some cases where under *sharia* law the woman has been stoned to death as a result, while the man has received no penalty. In defense of polygyny, Muslims point to the relative increase in adultery and divorce in Western societies. ∎

Female genital mutilation: 'Behind the Prophet's back'

One practice that causes particular horror among human rights activists is female genital mutilation. This term is used to describe the different types of ablations performed on young girls and women, such as the total or partial removal of the clitoris, of the labia minor or of all external genitalia; or different types of incisions, cauterizations and infibulation.

Female genital mutilation has been practiced for thousands of years. It continues today in some 30 countries in northeastern and sub-Saharan Africa, parts of the Middle East and, to a lesser extent, among Muslims in Asia, among some indigenous groups of South America, and among immigrant people in Europe and North America. While female genital mutilation is generally used to mark a girl's passage into adulthood, it is often carried out on 4-12 year olds. In some cases, even baby girls just days old are subjected to mutilation. In others, the custom is reserved for the moment prior to marriage or following the first pregnancy.

Though its exact origins remain unknown, studies show that the Egyptians in the 5th century BC knew of female genital mutilation, and that women underwent the procedure before marriage. The early Romans as well as the Arabs employed it for cosmetic reasons and, in some instances, applied it to indicate slavery or subordination. It is believed to have expanded throughout Africa through trade and the spread of Islam. But, in spite of such origins, and contrary to what is popularly believed, it is not a practice sanctioned by the Qur'an. The numerous variants of female genital mutilation are atavistic practices which, in each of the countries where it survives, are performed by groups consisting of Jews, Christians, Muslims and followers of African religions. Given that the Qur'an does not authorize it, one could say that, in the case of Islam, it is practiced 'behind the Prophet's back'. ∎

SCHOOL ENROLMENT IN FIGURES

Percentage of students across the school-age population. Gross enrolment rate (GER) is the number of children enrolled at a level - primary or secondary - regardless of age, divided by the population of that age group

A = GER, primary males, 1995-99. Source: The State of the World's Children 2002, UNICEF.
B = GER, primary females, 1995-99. Source: The State of the World's Children 2002, UNICEF.
C = GER, secondary males, 1995-97. Source: The State of the World's Children 2002, UNICEF.
D = GER, secondary females, 1995-97. Source: The State of the World's Children 2002, UNICEF.
E = GER, tertiary total, 1996-97. Source: World Development Indicators 2001, World Bank.

Country	A	B	C	D	E
Afghanistan	53	5	32	11	2
Albania	106	108	37	38	11
Algeria	97	93	65	62	15
Angola	95	88			1
Aotearoa-New Zealand	101	101	110	116	63
Argentina	110	108	73	81	47
Armenia	92	98	85	91	12
Australia	101	101	150	155	80
Austria	104	103	105	102	50
Azerbaijan	97	96	73	81	22
Bahamas	99	99	88	91	25
Bahrain	103	104	91	98	26
Bangladesh	98	95	25	13	5
Barbados	102	100	90	80	31
Belarus	101	96	91	95	45
Belgium	104	102	142	151	59
Belize	105	98	47	52	1
Benin	91	60	24	10	3
Bhutan	82	62	7	2	
Bolivia	99	95	40	34	25
Bosnia-Herzegovina	100	100			16
Botswana	119	118	61	68	4
Brazil	100	96	31	36	14
Brunei	109	104	71	82	11
Bulgaria	100	99	77	76	43
Burkina Faso	48	33	11	6	1
Burundi	68	55	9	5	1
Cambodia	95	84	30	18	1
Cameroon	88	74	32	22	5
Canada	103	101	105	105	58
Cape Verde	122	114	54	56	0
Central African Rep.	70	50	15	6	2
Chad	83	46	15	4	1
Chile	104	102	72	78	34
China	105	104	72	65	6
Colombia	103	103	70	75	20
Comoros	99	85	21	16	1
Congo D.R.	70	51	32	19	1
Congo R.	82	75	62	45	7
Cook Is.	113	110			
Costa Rica	109	108	47	50	31
Côte d'Ivoire	82	60	33	16	7
Croatia	94	97	81	83	29
Cuba	97	97	76	85	19
Cyprus	100	100	96	99	19
Czech Republic	105	103	97	100	26
Denmark	102	101	120	122	55
Djibouti	45	33	17	12	0
Dominica	93	105			
Dominican Republic	93	93	34	47	23
Ecuador	99	98	53	55	18
Egypt	103	96	80	70	39
El Salvador	94	94	30	35	18
Equatorial Guinea	139	118			
Eritrea	64	54	24	17	1
Estonia	95	93	100	108	47
Ethiopia	52	31	14	10	1
Fiji	111	110	64	65	14
Finland	98	99	110	125	83
France	106	104	112	111	51
French Polynesia					3
Gabon	134	130			8
Gambia	78	66	30	19	2
Georgia	95	95	78	76	34
Germany	104	104	105	103	46
Ghana	82	72	45	29	1
Greece	93	93	95	96	50
Grenada	133	118			
Guatemala	100	89	26	24	8
Guinea	68	40	20	7	1
Guinea-Bissau	85	52	9	4	1
Guyana	91	86	73	78	12
Haiti	128	124	21	20	1
Honduras	96	98	29	37	13
Hungary	104	102	96	99	34
Iceland	98	98	109	108	40
India	99	82	59	39	7
Indonesia	117	110	55	48	11
Iran	111	102	81	73	18
Iraq	110	95	51	32	13
Ireland	103	102	113	122	45
Israel	96	96	84	89	49
Italy	101	100	94	95	47
Jamaica	96	92	63	67	9
Japan	101	102	99	100	44
Jordan	93	93	52	54	19
Kanaky-New Caledonia					5
Kazakhstan	100	100	80	89	23
Kenya	89	88	26	22	1
Korea, North	108	101			
Korea, South	98	99	102	102	68
Kuwait	101	97	65	65	19
Kyrgyzstan	98	98	75	83	30
Laos	125	103	34	23	3
Latvia	101	100	82	85	51
Lebanon	113	108	78	85	38
Lesotho	96	92	25	36	2
Liberia	72	53	31	12	7
Libya	110	110	95	95	57
Lithuania	99	96	85	88	41
Luxembourg	88	94	72	76	10
Macedonia, TFYR	100	98	64	62	22
Madagascar	104	103	16	16	2
Malawi	142	128	21	12	0
Malaysia	95	96	58	66	11
Maldives	125	122	49	49	
Mali	60	40	14	7	2
Malta	108	107	86	82	20
Marshall Is.	134	133			
Mauritania	88	79	21	11	6
Mauritius	105	106	63	66	7
Mexico	107	117	64	64	18
Moldova	96	95	78	81	28
Mongolia	103	103	48	65	25
Morocco	94	76	44	34	9
Mozambique	86	65	9	5	1
Myanmar-Burma	102	99	29	30	6
Namibia	126	126	56	66	7
Nauru	104	98			
Nepal	140	104	49	25	3
Netherlands	109	107	134	129	49
Netherlands Antilles					14
Nicaragua	101	101	45	53	12
Niger	36	22	9	5	1
Nigeria	75	65	33	28	4
Niue	100	100			
Norway	100	100	121	116	65
Oman	100	95	68	65	8
Pakistan	99	69	33	17	4
Panama	106	102	60	65	33
Papua New Guinea	42	66	17	11	2
Paraguay	113	110	42	45	10
Peru	123	121	72	67	29
Philippines	118	119	71	75	28
Poland	97	95	98	97	44
Portugal	130	124	102	111	45
Puerto Rico					41
Qatar	106	100	81	79	26
Romania	101	99	79	78	24
Russia	108	107	83	91	41
Rwanda	88	88	12	9	1
Samoa	95	92	59	66	8
Saudi Arabia	97	90	65	57	19
Senegal	73	58	20	12	4
Seychelles	101	101			
Sierra Leone	59	41	22	13	1
Singapore	95	93	70	77	44
Slovakia	99	98	92	96	27
Slovenia	98	98	90	93	53
Solomon Is.	104	90	21	14	
Somalia	18	9	10	6	3
South Africa	98	86	76	91	17
Spain	110	108	116	128	56
Sri Lanka	103	101	71	78	5
St Kitts-Nevis	101	94			
St Lucia	121	119			
St Vincent	99	83			
Sudan	48	43	21	19	7
Suriname	129	125	50	58	7
Swaziland	119	112	55	54	5
Sweden	103	103	128	153	63
Switzerland	108	107	94	88	35
Syria	98	93	45	40	6
Tajikistan	96	94	81	72	20
Tanzania	77	76	6	5	1
Thailand	93	90	38	37	30
Togo	126	89	40	14	4
Tonga	124	120			
Trinidad and Tobago	99	98	72	75	6
Tunisia	119	112	66	63	17
Turkey	98	86	68	48	14
Turkmenistan					19
Tuvalu	100	100			
Uganda	129	114	15	9	2
Ukraine	87	86	88	94	42
United Arab Emirates	104	102	77	82	13
United Kingdom	114	114	120	139	58
United States	102	101	98	97	77
Uruguay	113	110	77	92	35
Uzbekistan	100	100	99	87	37
Vanuatu	105	107	23	18	0
Venezuela	90	93	33	46	28
Vietnam	110	107	44	41	11
Yemen	89	45	53	14	10
Yugoslavia Fed. Rep.	69	70	62	66	24
Zambia	102	100	34	21	3
Zimbabwe	111	105	52	44	7

Afghanistan's figure for girls in primary school is down from 32 per cent for the period 1990-97 (which was low enough) to just 5 per cent for the period 1995-99, presumably as a result of the Taliban regime's prohibition on girls' education.

HEALTH IN FIGURES

A = Doctors per 100,000 people.
B = Nurses per 100,000 people.

The number of doctors and nurses per population is a good indicator of the way healthcare is delivered (or not).
Within the overall figure, provision is often worse in rural areas. In addition, healthcare professionals may have few resources such as basic drugs or rehydration salts

Country	A	year	B	year
Afghanistan	11	1997	18	1997
Albania	129	1998	380	1998
Algeria	85	1995	298	1995
Andorra	253	1998	283	1998
Angola	8	1998	115	1997
Antigua	114	1996	330	1996
Aotearoa-New Zealand	218	1997	771	1997
Argentina	268	1992	77	1994
Armenia	316	1998	481	1998
Australia	240	1998	830	1998
Austria	302	1998	532	1998
Azerbaijan	360	1998	767	1998
Bahamas	152	1996	230	1996
Bahrain	100	1997	283	1997
Bangladesh	20	1997	11	1997
Barbados	125	1993	330	1993
Belarus	443	1998	1,182	1998
Belgium	395	1998	1,075	1996
Belize	55	1996	82	1996
Benin	6	1995	20	1995
Bhutan	16	1995	39	1995
Bolivia	130	1997	69	1997
Bosnia-Herzegovina	143	1998	452	1998
Botswana	24	1994	219	1994
Brazil	127	1996	41	1996
Brunei	85	1996	402	1996
Bulgaria	345	1998	713	1998
Burkina Faso	3	1995	20	1995
Cambodia	30	1998	74	1998
Cameroon	7	1996	37	1996
Canada	229	1995	897	1996
Cape Verde	17	1996	56	1996
Central African Rep.	4	1995	9	1995
Chad	3	1994	15	1994
Chile	110	1994	47	1996
China	162	1998	99	1998
Colombia	116	1997	48	1994
Comoros	7	1997	34	1997
Congo D.R.	7	1996	44	1996
Congo R.	25	1995	185	1995
Cook Is.	90	1997	200	1997
Costa Rica	141	1997	109	1997
Côte d'Ivoire	9	1996	31	1996
Croatia	229	1998	474	1998
Cuba	530	1997	678	1997
Cyprus	255	1996	447	1996
Czech Republic	303	1998	886	1998
Denmark	290	1994	722	1994
Djibouti	14	1996	74	1996
Dominica	49	1996	416	1996
Dominican Republic	216	1997	30	1997
Ecuador	170	1997	70	1997
Egypt	202	1996	233	1996
El Salvador	107	1997	35	1997
Equatorial Guinea	25	1996	40	1996
Eritrea	3	1996	16	1996
Estonia	297	1998	625	1998
Fiji	48	1997	195	1997
Finland	299	1998	2,162	1998
France	303	1997	497	1996
Gambia	4	1997	13	1997
Georgia	436	1998	474	1998
Germany	350	1998	957	1998
Ghana	6	1996	72	1996
Greece	392	1995	257	1992
Grenada	50	1997	368	1997
Guatemala	93	1997	27	1997
Guinea	13	1995	56	1995
Guinea-Bissau	17	1996	109	1996
Guyana	18	1997	84	1997
Haiti	8	1992	11	1997
Honduras	83	1997	26	1997
Hungary	357	1998	385	1998
Iceland	326	1997	865	1998
India	48	1992	45	1992
Indonesia	16	1994	50	1994
Iran	85	1996	259	1996
Iraq	55	1998	236	1995
Ireland	219	1998	497	1989
Israel	385	1998	613	1998
Italy	554	1997	296	1989
Jamaica	140	1996	65	1996
Japan	193	1996	745	1996
Jordan	166	1997	296	1997
Kazakhstan	353	1998	649	1998
Kenya	13	1995	90	1995
Kiribati	30	1998	236	1998
Korea, South	297	1995	180	1995
Kuwait	189	1997	475	1997
Kyrgyzstan	301	1998	750	1998
Laos	24	1996	108	1996
Latvia	282	1998	549	1998
Lebanon	210	1997	100	1997
Lesotho	5	1995	60	1995
Liberia	2	1997	6	1997
Libya	128	1997	360	1996
Lithuania	395	1998	884	1998
Luxembourg	272	1998	782	1998
Macedonia, TFYR	204	1998	488	1998
Madagascar	11	1996	22	1996
Malaysia	66	1997	113	1997
Maldives	40	1995	113	1995
Mali	5	1994	13	1994
Malta	261	1998	1,100	1993
Marshall Is.	42	1996	149	1996
Mauritania	14	1995	62	1995
Mauritius	85	1995	233	1995
Mexico	186	1990	87	1995
Micronesia	57	1999	279	1999
Moldova	350	1998	874	1998
Monaco	664	1995	1,621	1995
Mongolia	243	1998	307	1998
Morocco	46	1997	105	1997
Myanmar-Burma	30	1999	26	1999
Namibia	30	1997	168	1997
Nauru	157	1995	588	1995
Nepal	4	1995	5	1995
Netherlands	251	1990	902	1991
Nicaragua	86	1997	92	1997
Niger	4	1997	23	1997
Nigeria	19	1992	66	1992
Niue	130	1996	478	1996
Norway	413	1998	1,840	1998
Oman	133	1998	325	1998
Pakistan	57	1997	34	1996
Palau	110	1998	144	1998
Panama	167	1995	144	1997
Papua New Guinea	7	1998	67	1998
Paraguay	110	1997	24	1997
Peru	93	1997	115	1997
Philippines	123	1996	418	1996
Poland	236	1997	527	1990
Portugal	312	1998	379	1998
Qatar	126	1996	289	1996
Romania	184	1998	409	1998
Russia	421	1998	821	1998
Samoa	34	1996	155	1996
San Marino	252	1990	508	1990
São Tomé and Príncipe	47	1996	127	1996
Saudi Arabia	166	1997	330	1997
Senegal	8	1995	22	1995
Seychelles	132	1996	468	1996
Sierra Leone	7	1996	33	1996
Singapore	163	1998	492	1998
Slovakia	353	1998	708	1995
Slovenia	228	1998	681	1998
Solomon Is.	14	1995	119	1995
Somalia	4	1997	20	1997
South Africa	56	1996	472	1996
Spain	424	1997	458	1997
Sri Lanka	37	1999	103	1999
St Kitts-Nevis	117	1997	498	1997
St Lucia	47	1997	263	1997
St Vincent	88	1997	239	1997
Sudan	9	1996	58	1996
Suriname	25	1996	156	1996
Swaziland	15	1996		
Sweden	311	1997	821	1997
Switzerland	323	1998	779	1990
Syria	144	1998	189	1998
Tajikistan	201	1998	484	1998
Tanzania	4	1995	85	1995
Thailand	24	1995	87	1995
Togo	8	1995	30	1995
Tonga	44	1997	315	1997
Trinidad and Tobago	79	1994	287	1994
Tunisia	70	1997	286	1997
Turkey	121	1998	109	1998
Turkmenistan	300	1997	587	1997
Tuvalu	30	1999	300	1999
Uganda			19	1996
Ukraine	299	1998	736	1998
United Arab Emirates	181	1997	341	1996
United States	279	1995	972	1996
Uruguay	370	1996	70	1996
Uzbekistan	309	1998	1,011	1998
Vanuatu	12	1997	260	1997
Venezuela	236	1997	64	1997
Vietnam	48	1998	56	1998
Yemen	23	1996	51	1995
Zambia	7	1995	113	1995
Zimbabwe	14	1995	129	1995

Source: WHOSIS - WHO Statistical Information System, Web Site WHO 2002.

MANY PEOPLE feel that since the birth of modern democracy with the US revolution at the end of the 18th century, elections have fallen short of voter expectations in all parts of the world. How has this come about?

Poverty and democratic quality

Proof of the decline in voter expectations is evident in how regimes have been defended; changing from the 'government of the people, by the people and for the people' proclaimed by US president Abraham Lincoln in the 19th century, to the 'least bad of regimes,' in the words of Britain's premier Winston Churchill 100 years later.

However, the prestige of the term democracy has continued unabated. There has hardly existed a more prestigious (or promising) word in the modern period than 'democracy'. Hence, over the last two hundred years it has been refined by the addition of various adjectives like 'representative', 'popular' and 'participatory'. At all events, the collapse of the totalitarian regimes (all of which, ironically, claimed 'democratic' status) after the fall of the Berlin Wall appears to demonstrate that the longevity of democratic governments is not guaranteed by adjectives. Rather it is dependent on certain concrete democratic principles.

Electoral democracy became increasingly attractive over the last century. In 1900, monarchies and empires predominated and there were no states that could be called electoral democracies in terms of universal suffrage through multiparty elections. However, by the end of the 20th century 120 of the 189 countries in the United Nations formally defined themselves as electoral democracies. This process accelerated notably in the last 25 years: 28 per cent of countries had some form of democratic government in 1962, but the figure reached 62 per cent by 2000. As the main alternatives to democracy in the 20th century (communism, fascism and nazism) disappeared or were 'contained,' the dawn of the new millennium saw 58 per cent of the world's population living under regimes that, at least nominally, claimed to be electoral democracies.

However, the dominant model has shown few signs of alleviating poverty or guaranteeing rights and resources either within the countries ranked amongst the 'non-aligned' nations or in those that embraced electoral democracy following the fall of the Soviet bloc. Some 32 per cent of the Souths population live on less than one dollar a day. On a global level, the number of people subsisting on this amount increased from 1.2 billion in 1987 to 1.5 billion at present. If the trend persists, this figure will reach 1.9 billion by 2015. During the 1990s the number of poor people in the former Soviet Union and Eastern Europe increased by 150 million, outnumbering the total population of the western European nations - all of which have a high degree of human development. This situation has led to broad perception in the former communist countries of a direct link between the transition to democracy and an increase in poverty.

Meanwhile, poverty has also spread in the oldest of modern democracies, the US, where approximately 15 per cent of the population lives in severe deprivation and where child poverty rose from 15 per cent in 1970 to 22 per cent in 1993. Within this context, it is important to note that, on a world scale, inequality in income has corresponded almost exactly to the imposition of electoral democracy. Thus, during the last 200 years, the gap between the richest and poorest has multiplied hugely. While the relationship of poor to rich was 3 to 1 in 1820, 7 to 1 in 1870 and 11 to 1 in 1913, the chasm gaped over the next decades. It reached 35 to 1 in 1950, 44 to1 in 1973 and took another notable leap to hit 72 to 1 in 1992. It is impossible to not notice that it is in the latest period, when most countries have assumed electoral democracy that the rift between the rich and poor has widened most.

Democratic quality

Although there is no formula that the spread of electoral democracy leads to increased poverty and economic inequality, the relationship between those elements has become inescapable in recent years. This raises the question 'how much poverty can democracy tolerate?', which has become the leitmotiv of political analysis. It has been repeatedly stated that the failure of democratic-electoral systems to improve the wellbeing of the population in several regions is due to the fact that to a great extent these were governments with no 'real' democratic intention. Put another way, these were 'flawed democracies,' which ended in failure because they did not take on board the true principles of democracy for the wellbeing of their people. These principles include political representation, truly free elections, equal rights, individual freedoms, responsibility and peaceful resolution of conflicts and, above all, the protection of human rights, which must be at the very core. For it is this that guarantees that citizens may live without fear and in peace. It is clear that only by following these principles can a democratic environment be created where each individual can participate both in their own destiny and that of society, aspiring to a fair share of economic and social progress.

As a consequence of that, it is difficult to think of countries as real democracies when approximately 1 billion people are deprived of the right to education, drinking water or food world-wide. How can we attain the ideal of the sanctity of human rights when a quarter of the population in the South die before reaching the age of 40 and 110 million children, 80 per cent of them girls receive no schooling? How can we hope that starving, sick and illiterate populations will achieve any degree of meaningful political participation, or even have the will to make a considered judgment through the vote?

To a large extent, the widespread but flawed imposition of democratic systems (as in those referred to above, the superficially but not intrinsically democratic systems) has ultimately led to the development of variable 'democratic quality,' which measures the difference between the ideal of good government and real government. Good government is taken to be a regime that offers stable parameters to its citizens in terms of political, economic and social order, which increasingly incorporates citizens in the political and social systems and which guarantees citizens the protection of democratic law throughout national territory. The idea of democratic quality relates to the deficiencies identified in real democracies when compared to the democratic ideal of good government.

Democratic quality, however flawed, should not be used to question the presence of democracy; on the contrary, it must be understood as the result of governability, democratic depth and legality. While the first aspect implies the notion of order and stability, the second is reliant on the substantive incorporation of the citizenry and the third relates to civil rights. None of the three is in any way achievable whilst the respective democracies do not resolve poverty.

Poverty

The question of how to achieve good democratic government if democracy does not resolve the problem of poverty also needs to be addressed.

In 2000, the Institute for Democracy and Electoral Assistance (International IDEA) was created by 14 countries at a forum entitled 'Democracy and peace, a missing link?' The forum concluded that, even though there had been a huge increase in the adoption of the suffragist-democratic model globally, democracy will not be consolidated unless aid and economic policies simultaneously attack the problems created by poverty at the same time as building democracy.

According to International IDEA, rapprochement is vital not only to put poverty reduction and the attainment of democracy at the top of the international agenda but also to integrate these as twin elements in a plan of action. Within this combined focus, there would be better chances of achieving goals that result in achievements like peace, development, stability and economic growth. IDEA specifies that democracy is not a guarantee that these achievements will be made, although it could be considered a precondition that would contribute positively in the long term to these objectives being achieved.

There are a couple of other relevant points. In many cases, above all for loan and aid institutions, democracy is often mistakenly seen as being an end in itself - but it should not be seen this way. It was originally conceived as a means, firstly, for sovereignty to remain effectively with the people and thus for each citizen to gain respect for their rights, aspirations and dignity. Many believe that poverty is the greatest enemy of democracy. Be that as it may, it is certainly the case that if democracies do not tackle poverty (which does not only affect the economically poor countries) they will fail to fulfill their most basic responsibility: that of protecting human dignity. ∎

Representation

IN GIOVANNI SARTORI'S view, the word democracy is 'a pompous description of something that does not exist'. However, there is consensus on the founding principles of an electoral democratic regime.

An ideal of electoral democracy

Even though the term democracy originated in 5th century BC Athens, it is only in the last two hundred years that societies have really created political systems on the democratic model. Over the centuries the topic has been widely discussed by philosophers, politicians, historians and ordinary people. Down the years, democracy has been analyzed, defended, ignored, practiced, destroyed and restored, leading to the term itself meaning different things according to the provenance and perception of the speaker.

In Italian political expert Giovanni Sartori's view, the word democracy is 'a pompous description of something that does not exist'. However, despite the fact that the political ideal of pure democracy has, pretty much without exception, turned out to be impracticable there is consensus on the founding principles of an electoral democratic regime. These are directly derived from the definition that it is a 'government of the people, for the people, by the people.'

The notion of a 'government of the people' refers to the concept of popular or national sovereignty (of the nation taken as a whole). Power belongs to the people although they exercise this indirectly through the principle of representation.

The principle of representation, through universal suffrage, allows the sovereign people to delegate the right of leadership to a smaller number of leaders in their place. In order to be effective this principle implies that all citizens have free choice, and are broadly informed of the electoral options available.

The principle of the majority arises from the conflict of opinions and the conflict of ideas and interests. Unanimity is not only improbable but is suspect because it runs counter to the free debating of ideas which generates freedom of expression.

Democratically elected representatives must respect the 'social contract' (J J Rousseau), of a 'government for the people'. This implies the submission of government members to the law. This is the principle of the 'state of law', the establishment of a hierarchy of regulations with predominance of those enshrined by the 'constitutional' text of the State taking precedence over the others.

This state of law has to recognize two complementary principles: one relating to the operation of public authorities - the independence of the three authorities: executive, legislative and legal (as described by Montesquieu in *The Spirit of Laws*); and the other relating to the individual, guaranteeing 'human rights'.

These rights have evolved from the Declaration of the Rights of Man [sic] and of the Citizen, gradually broadening the content on the dignity of the human individual as the great economic and social events of the 19th and 20th centuries unfurled. This brought with it the right to peace, rights of children, consideration of gender, the status of the individual, conscientious objection, labor laws, and so on.

The right to freedom, which includes the freedom of association and expression, contains the seed of 'political pluralism', the freedom to dispose of your own body, of movement and of having and disposing of property. Elsewhere, the right to equality includes equality before the law and justice and equal opportunities.

This implies that, as all citizens are equal by law, democracy should guarantee an equal footing for everyone's expectations. This is contradictory to what often actually happens in societies that declare themselves democratic - that is, the majority of present democracies - where those who have access to education, health, and the most basic human rights are only the minority of the population. ∎

A = % of population with access to safe water, 2000. Source: The State of the World's Children 2002, UNICEF.
B = % of population with access to health services, 1990/96. Source: The State of the World's Children 1997, UNICEF [n].

	A	B		A	B		A	B
Afghanistan	13	29	Gambia	62	93	Palau	79	
Albania	97		Georgia	79		Palestine	86	
Algeria	89	98	Ghana	73	60	Panama	90	70
Andorra	100		Grenada	95		Papua New Guinea	42	96
Angola	38		Guatemala	92	57	Paraguay	78	63
Antigua	91		Guinea	48	80	Peru	80	44
Argentina		71	Guinea-Bissau	56	40	Philippines	86	71
Australia	100		Guyana	94		Romania	58	
Austria	100		Haiti	46	60	Russia	99	
Azerbaijan	78		Honduras	88	69	Rwanda	41	80
Bahamas	97		Hungary	99		Samoa	99	
Bangladesh	97	45	India	84	85	Saudi Arabia	95	97
Barbados	100		Indonesia	78	93	Senegal	78	90
Belarus	100		Iran	92	88	Sierra Leone	57	38
Belize	92		Iraq	85	93	Singapore	100	
Benin	63	18	Jamaica	92	90	Slovakia	100	
Bhutan	62	65	Jordan	96	97	Slovenia	100	
Bolivia	83	67	Kazakhstan	91		Solomon Is.	71	
Botswana	95		Kenya	57	77	Somalia	31	
Brazil	87		Kiribati	48		South Africa	86	
Bulgaria	100		Korea, North	100		Sri Lanka	77	
Burkina Faso	42	90	Korea, South	92	100	St Kitts-Nevis	98	
Burundi	78	80	Kuwait		100	St Lucia	98	
Cambodia	30	53	Kyrgyzstan	77		St Vincent	93	
Cameroon	58	80	Laos	37	67	Sudan	75	70
Canada	100		Lebanon	100	95	Suriname	82	
Cape Verde	74		Lesotho	78	80	Sweden	100	
Central African Rep.	70	52	Liberia		39	Switzerland	100	
Chad	27	30	Libya	72	95	Syria	80	90
Chile	93	97	Madagascar	47	38	Tajikistan	60	
China	75	88	Malawi	57	35	Tanzania	68	42
Colombia	91	81	Maldives	100		Thailand	84	90
Comoros	96		Mali	65	40	Togo	54	
Congo D.R.	45	26	Malta	100		Tonga	100	
Congo R.	51	83	Mauritania	37	63	Trinidad and Tobago	90	100
Cook Is.	100		Mauritius	100	100	Tunisia	80	
Costa Rica	95		Mexico	88	93	Turkey	82	
Côte d'Ivoire	81		Moldova	92		Turkmenistan		100
Cuba	91	100	Monaco	100		Tuvalu	100	
Cyprus	100		Mongolia	60	95	Uganda	52	49
Denmark	100		Morocco	80	70	Ukraine	98	
Djibouti	100		Mozambique	57	39	United Arab Emirates		99
Dominica	97		Myanmar-Burma	72	60	United Kingdom	100	
Dominican Republic	86	78	Namibia	77	59	United States	100	
Ecuador	85		Nepal	88		Uruguay	98	82
Egypt	97	99	Netherlands	100		Uzbekistan	85	
El Salvador	77	40	Nicaragua	77	83	Vanuatu	88	
Equatorial Guinea	44		Niger	59	99	Venezuela	83	
Eritrea	46		Nigeria	62	51	Vietnam	77	90
Ethiopia	24	46	Niue	100		Yemen	69	38
Fiji	47		Norway	100		Yugoslavia Fed. Rep.	98	
Finland	100		Oman	39	96	Zambia	64	
Gabon	86		Pakistan	90	55	Zimbabwe	83	85

[n] Last available data.

CHILDREN'S HEALTH

A = Births attended by health personnel (%), 1995-2000.
B = Life expectancy at birth (years), 2000.
C = % of low weight babies (2,500 g), 1995/2000.
D = Infant mortality (per 1,000 live births), 2000.
E = Underweight children under 5, (%), 1995-2000.
F = Maternal mortality (per 100,000 live births), 1985-1999.

Child health says a great deal about a country's social wellbeing. And of course, if the maternal mortality figure (F) is high, those babies and children will have less chance of survival. Central African Republic, Malawi and Mozambique are among the countries that have over 1,000 maternal deaths per 100,000 lives births, compared with 8 in the US and 41 in Malaysia.

	A	B	C	D	E	F
Afghanistan		43		165	48	
Albania		73	5	27	14	
Algeria	77	70	7	50	6	220
Andorra			6			
Angola	23	45		172		
Antigua	100		8	13	10	150
Aotearoa-New Zealand	95	78	6	6		15
Argentina	98	73	7	18		41
Armenia	97	73	9	25	3	35
Australia	100	79	7	5		
Austria	100	78	7	5		
Azerbaijan	88	72	10	74	17	80
Bahamas		69		15		
Bahrain	98	73	10	13	9	46
Bangladesh	13	59	30	54	48	350
Barbados	91	77	10	12	5	0
Belarus	100	69	5	17		20
Belgium	100	78	8	6		
Belize	77	74	4	34	6	140
Benin	60	54	15	98	29	500
Bhutan	15	62	15	77	19	380
Bolivia	59	62	8	62	10	390
Bosnia-Herzegovina	100	74	4	15	4	10
Botswana	99	40	11	74	13	330
Brazil	92	68	9	32	6	160
Brunei	98	76		6		0
Bulgaria		71	9	15		15
Burkina Faso	31	47	18	105	34	480
Burundi	19	41	16	114	45	
Cambodia	34	56	9	95	46	440
Cameroon	56	50	10	95	21	430
Canada	100	79	6	6		
Cape Verde	89	70	13	30	14	35
Central African Rep.	44	44	13	115	24	1,100
Chad	16	46	24	118	28	830
Chile	100	75	5	10	1	23
China	70	71	6	32	10	55
Colombia	86	71	7	25	7	80
Comoros	62	60	18	61	25	
Congo D.R.		51	15	128	34	
Congo R.		51		81	14	
Cook Is.	99		1	20		
Costa Rica	98	76	6	10	5	29
Côte d'Ivoire	47	48	17	102	21	600
Croatia	100	74	6	8	1	6
Cuba	100	76	6	7	4	33
Cyprus	100	78		6		0
Czech Republic	99	75	6	5	1	9
Denmark	100	76	6	4		10
Djibouti		43		102	18	
Dominica	100		8	14	5	65
Dominican Republic	99	67	13	42	5	230
East Timor		49				
Ecuador	99	70	16	25	15	160
Egypt	61	67	10	37	12	170
El Salvador	90	70	13	34	12	120
Equatorial Guinea	5	51		103		
Eritrea	21	52	14	73	44	1,000
Estonia		71	5	17		50
Ethiopia	10	44	12	117	47	
Fiji		69	12	18	8	38
Finland	100	78	6	4		6
France	99	79	6	4		10
Gabon		53		60		520
Gambia	44	46	14	92	17	

	A	B	C	D	E	F
Georgia	96	73	6	24	3	50
Germany	100	78	7	5		8
Ghana	44	57	9	58	25	210
Greece		78	7	5		1
Grenada	99		11	21		1
Guatemala	41	65	12	44	24	190
Guinea	35	48	10	112	23	530
Guinea-Bissau	25	45	20	132	23	910
Guyana		63	14	55	12	110
Haiti	27	53	28	81	28	520
Honduras	55	66	6	32	25	110
Hungary		71	9	8	2	15
Iceland		79	4	4		
India	42	63	26	69	47	540
Indonesia	56	66	9	35	26	380
Iran	86	69	7	36	11	37
Iraq	54	62	23	105	16	
Ireland	100	77	4	6		6
Israel	99	79	8	6		5
Italy		78	6	6		7
Jamaica	95	75	11	17	4	95
Japan	100	81	7	4		8
Jordan		70	10	28	5	41
Kazakhstan	99	65	6	60	4	65
Kenya	44	51	9	77	23	590
Kiribati	72		3	52	13	
Korea, North		64		23	60	110
Korea, South	98	75		5		20
Kuwait	98	76	7	9	10	5
Kyrgyzstan	98	68	6	53	11	65
Laos	21	53		90	40	650
Latvia	100	70	5	17		45
Lebanon	89	73	6	28	3	100
Lesotho	60	46		92	16	
Liberia		52		157	20	
Libya	94	70	7	17	5	75
Liechtenstein				10		
Lithuania		72	4	17		18
Luxembourg	100	77	4	5		0
Macedonia, TFYR	97	73	6	22	6	7
Madagascar	46	53	15	86	33	490
Malawi	55	40	13	117	25	1,100
Malaysia	96	72	9	8	18	41
Maldives	90	67	12	59	43	350
Mali	24	51	16	142	43	580
Malta	98	78	7	5		
Marshall Is.			14	55		
Mauritania	40	51		120	23	550
Mauritius	99	71	13	17	16	21
Mexico	86	73	9	25	8	55
Micronesia			9	20		
Moldova		67	7	27	3	28
Monaco				4		
Mongolia	93	63	6	62	13	150
Morocco	40	68	9	41	9	230
Mozambique	44	39	13	126	26	1,100
Myanmar-Burma	56	56	16	78	36	230
Namibia	76	45	15	56	26	230
Nauru				25		
Nepal	12	59	21	72	47	540
Netherlands	100	78		5		7
Nicaragua	65	68	13	37	12	150
Niger	16	45	12	159	40	590
Nigeria	42	52	9	110	27	
Niue	99					

	A	B	C	D	E	F
Norway	100	79	5	4		6
Oman	91	71	8	12	24	14
Pakistan	20	60	21	85	38	
Palau	99		8	24		
Palestine	97	72	9	0	4	
Panama	90	74	10	20	7	70
Papua New Guinea	53	57		79	35	370
Paraguay	71	70	9	26	5	190
Peru	56	69	10	40	8	270
Philippines	56	69	18	30	28	170
Poland	99	73	6	9		8
Portugal	98	76	7	6		8
Qatar	98	70	10	12	6	10
Romania	99	70	9	19	6	42
Russia	99	66	7	18	3	44
Rwanda	31	40	12	100	29	
Samoa	76	69		21		
San Marino				6		
São Tomé and Príncipe			7	58	16	
Saudi Arabia	91	72	3	24	14	
Senegal	51	53	12	80	18	560
Seychelles			10	13	6	
Sierra Leone	42	39	22	180	27	
Singapore		78	8	4	14	6
Slovakia		73	7	8		9
Slovenia	100	76	6	5		11
Solomon Is.	85	68		21	21	550
Somalia		48		133	26	
South Africa	84	52		55		
Spain		78	6	5		6
Sri Lanka	94	72	17	17	33	60
St Kitts-Nevis	99	70	13	21		130
St Lucia	100	73	8	17	14	30
St Vincent	99		10	21		43
Sudan	86	56		66	17	550
Suriname	95	71	11	27		110
Swaziland	56	44		101	10	230
Sweden	100	80	4	3		5
Switzerland		79	6	3		5
Syria	76	71	6	24	13	110
Tajikistan	71	68	13	54		65
Tanzania	36	51	11	104	29	530
Thailand		70	7	25	19	44
Togo	51	52	13	80	25	480
Tonga	92		2	17		
Trinidad and Tobago	99	74		17	7	70
Tunisia	90	70	5	22	4	70
Turkey	81	70	15	38	8	130
Turkmenistan	97	66	5	52		65
Tuvalu	100		3	38		
Uganda	38	44	13	81	26	510
Ukraine	100	68	6	17	3	25
United Arab Emirates	96	75		8	14	3
United Kingdom		78	8	6		7
United States	99	77	8	7	1	8
Uruguay	100	74		15	5	26
Uzbekistan	96	69	6	51	19	21
Vanuatu	87	68	7	35	20	
Venezuela	95	73	6	20	5	60
Vietnam	70	68	9	30	33	95
Yemen	22	61	26	85	46	350
Yugoslavia Fed. Rep.	99	73	5	17	2	9
Zambia	47	41	11	112	25	650
Zimbabwe	73	43	10	73	13	700

Source: The State of the World's Children 2002, UNICEF.

III. Science and technology

Deforestation

DEFORESTATION and the loss of biodiversity are common topics of conversation these days. Some 'experts' would have us believe that there is a 'green' solution to global warming: that the planting of thousands of hectares of trees will give the planet new lungs capable of absorbing carbon. The truth is somewhat different.

Ten myths about tree plantations

Large-scale plantations of rapid-growth species such as eucalyptus and pine have very negative impacts in both social and environmental terms. Because of this, resistance to these kinds of plantations is growing more widespread. The response of the firms responsible for these plantations and of the people who promote this model is to deny the harmful impacts and to devise and disseminate campaigns of disinformation designed to win support for their position amongst less well-informed sectors of the population. Below are ten of the most common misleading statements being disseminated about large-scale monoculture tree plantations:

Myth 1

Tree plantations are 'planted forests'

Forestry professionals and forestry firms insist on calling plantations 'planted forests'. This confusion between a crop (of trees) and a wood or forest is the starting point of all propaganda in favor of tree plantations. But a plantation is not a forest and the only thing the two have in common is that in both cases trees predominate. A real forest contains numerous species of trees and bushes at all stages of growth; a wide range of other types of vegetation, growing both on the forest floor and on the trees and bushes themselves; and a huge variety of fauna which find food and shelter and reproduce in the forest. This great diversity of plants and animals interacts with other elements such as soil nutrients, water, solar energy and climate in such a way as to ensure the forest's self-regeneration and the conservation of all its constituents. Human communities are also part of native forests, since many human beings live there, interacting with the flora and fauna and obtaining goods and services from them to ensure their survival. Unlike a native forest, a large-scale commercial plantation is composed of one or a few species of fast-growing trees, planted in homogenous blocks of the same age, and a scarce few species of flora and fauna that manage to survive in plantations.

Commercial tree plantations require preparation of the soil, and plants must be carefully selected for rapid growth and other technical characteristics needed by the industry. The plants must then be fertilized, 'weeds' must be removed using herbicides, and trees must be planted in regular lots and harvested after as short a growing period as possible.

As far as human communities are concerned, not only are they disallowed from inhabiting commercial plantations, but they are normally not even allowed access to them, since people are considered a threat to the plantations. At best, they are perceived as a source of cheap labor during planting and, later on, when the trees are harvested.

In short, a tree plantation is not a 'planted forest'. It is plainly impossible to 'plant' the enormous diversity of plants and animals that characterize a native forest, nor is it possible to obtain the overall series of interactions that occur between the living and inorganic elements that make up a forest.

Myth 2

Tree plantations improve the environment

It is claimed that these 'planted forests' are good for the environment. However, not only do large-scale tree plantations not benefit the environment, they also have a negative impact on soils and hydrological regulation. Plantations tend to degrade soils, because these remain exposed during the first two years following planting, as well as for two years after the harvest - thus facilitating the erosive action of water and wind. Harvesting large amounts of timber every few years causes loss of nutrients and the balance of components in the soil, while the use of heavy machinery that pre-vents good drainage and further facilitates soil erosion, produces soil compaction. Both the quantity and quality of water are affected. Fast-growing pine and eucalyptus trees have a particularly high water intake, depleting water resources. Meanwhile, soil erosion and the widespread use of agrochemicals contaminate what's left of it.

For the majority of species of local fauna, plantations are deserts in terms of food sources, so that these species tend to disappear. The few species that succeed in adapting are either exterminated (because they are considered 'pests') or lose their new habitat each time the plantation is harvested for the timber.

Myth 3

Plantations relieve pressure on indigenous forests

This argument goes thus: since plantations make more timber available, less timber will be extracted from native forests. Although this may seem logical, the reality is that plantations generally prove to be yet another factor in increased deforestation. This is because in many countries, plantations are established after previously eliminating indigenous forests. In some cases, this is done by setting forest fires. In other cases, timber is felled and then sold in order to finance the establishment of the plantation. Plantations have even been used to justify deforestation, since it is held that felling large areas of trees does not constitute deforestation if these areas are later replanted.

In many cases, the process described above leads either to voluntary or forced migration of local communities, who then settle in new forest areas which they need to clear for their own basic needs. In such cases, the deforestation resulting indirectly from the plantation is even greater than the one generated by the plantation itself.

The timber produced in plantations is no substitute for valuable species of tropical hardwoods, since the two have quite different markets. The wood from plantations is mainly destined for the production of paper pulp and other low-quality wood products, while most timber extracted from native tropical forests is transformed into high-quality wood products.

The need for wood is not the only cause of deforestation. Large areas of native forest are often cleared and then replaced by cash crops for export or by extensive cattle-ranching; other areas disappear beneath giant hydroelectric dams; mangroves are eliminated and replaced by industrial shrimp farming; drilling for oil and mining destroy vast areas of native forest; and so on. Monoculture plantations cannot lessen the forces behind these types of destruction.

Myth 4

Plantations enable degraded land to be improved and made more productive

This argument is absolutely untrue. Large-scale commercial tree-plantations are seldom established on degraded land, for the simple reason that they do not grow well there, and thus do not ensure a commercial return.

Myth 5

Plantations serve to counteract the greenhouse effect

It is said that as the trees grow, they absorb greater quantities of carbon dioxide (CO_2 - the principal gas producing the greenhouse effect) than they emit. However in general terms any area covered by a tree plantation, in the absence of proof to the contrary, should be considered a net source of carbon, not a sink. First, in many cases, these plantations replace native forests, which means that the volume of carbon released by deforestation is greater than that captured by a growing tree plantation, even over the long term. Even when they are not the product of deforestation, plantations are established in other ecosystems which also store carbon (such as prairies) and this is released into the atmosphere as a result of the plantation.

Moreover, there is a second crucial issue: are these plantations to be harvested or not? If they are, then at best they are only temporary sinks: the carbon is stored until they are harvested, then released in a matter of years (in some cases in a matter of months) when the paper or other products produced from the plantations are destroyed. If the trees are not to be harvested, then the plantations are occupying millions of hectares of land that could be employed for much more useful purposes - for example, for the production of food.

Myth 6

Plantations are necessary to supply the growing need for paper

Paper consumption is generally perceived as associated with literacy, access to written information and thus to a better quality of life. This perception is used by forestry firms to justify establishing their huge plantations of pine and eucalyptus. In fact, a large amount of the cellulose produced in the Southern Hemisphere is not used to supply the countries' own populations, but those of the Northern Hemisphere. Almost 40 per cent of world paper production is used for packaging and wrapping, while only 30 per cent is used for writing and printing paper. A huge part of the paper consumption for writing and printing purposes is used for advertising. In the US, 60 per cent of the space in magazines and newspapers is reserved for advertising, while 52,000 million units of different kinds of publicity material are produced each year, including 14,000 million mail-order catalogues, many of which go straight into the waste-basket.

Today's pattern of paper consumption is environmentally unsustainable and a great deal of it is socially unnecessary. It is difficult to justify plans for the expansion of tree plantations by saying that 'humanity' needs more paper.

Myth 7

Plantations are much more productive than indigenous forests

At first glance, this claim, which is based on the observation that eucalyptus and pine plantations grow very fast, may seem convincing. However, it depends what is meant by 'productive' and who benefits from this production. A commercial tree plantation produces, per hectare and per year, a large volume of wood for industry. But this is all it produces. The direct beneficiary of this production is the firm that owns the plantation. Like tree plantations, a native forest produces wood which can be sold, but it also produces many other kinds of products: other kinds of trees, vegetables, game, fruits, mushrooms, honey, fodder, compost, firewood, woods for local uses, vegetable fibers and natural medicines. It can also serve a number of other purposes such as conserving soils and water resources, protecting biodiversity and maintaining a micro-climate.

Myth 8

Plantations generate employment

In the vast majority of cases, this claim is totally false. Large-scale plantations generate employment mainly during planting and harvesting. After the trees have been planted, employment opportunities fall dramatically. When the trees are ready to be harvested, workers are hired once again but increasingly these jobs are tending to disappear because of the growing mechanization of this operation.

Myth 9

The eventual negative impacts of industrial monoculture plantations can be avoided or mitigated through good management

In the last count, the advocates of forestry plantations may accept that these are not really forests and can have negative impacts, but they add that these are caused by bad management and not by the plantations themselves. The solution, they claim, is therefore technical: good management methods must be applied.

With respect to the environmental impacts of commercial plantations, the view that they can be resolved through good management is utopian. The very characteristics of the model make it basically unsustainable, whether or not conservationist practices or monitoring techniques are used, which are in any case designed mainly to improve the image of the firm in the face of possible opposition by environmental activists.

Myth 10

Plantations cannot be judged in isolation

The proponents of plantations claim that there is a continuum between a primary forest and a 'planted forest'. That is to say that there exists a system, known as a 'forest' which includes protected primary forests, productive forests, protective forests - those that due to their position, protect soil, roads, shores, flora, fauna and so on - secondary forests and all kinds of plantations. Therefore, it is said, this 'forest' system must be analyzed as a whole, rather than isolating one of its components; in this case, the large-scale monoculture of tree plantations. Though intelligent, this argument is as false as the others. First, one cannot talk about a continuum between what are intrinsically different elements. One analogy would be to say that native fauna and dairy herds constitute a continuum and that therefore it is not possible to judge the impact of raising dairy cattle without analyzing its broader context.

Second, in general commercial tree plantations not only do not complement native forests but often constitute the direct or indirect causes of deforestation. The same can be said of the way they affect biodiversity, soils, water and in particular local populations.

Source: Ricardo Carrere, 'Ten replies to ten myths', World Rainforest Movement.

IT IS NO LONGER in dispute that levels of carbon dioxide in the atmosphere are rising dangerously and, if continued unchecked, could over time spell the end of life on earth. Agreeing on adequate and equitable solutions is proving more difficult.

Carbon fixing: Dodging obligations

In 1997, the governments of the industrialized countries committed themselves to curbing emissions of greenhouse gases by signing the Kyoto Protocol to the Convention on Climate Change.* At the same time, however, they invented what is known as the Clean Development Mechanism (CDM) in order to avoid having to comply with their promises. The idea behind the 'carbon emissions market' is elementary: some countries emit carbon dioxide (CO_2), some countries store it for you and charge for the service. How is it done? Quite simple: by planting trees. But that is where things get complicated.

The US subsequently did not ratify.

The role of CO_2 in regulating climate

Over the past 150 years, and especially since World War II, industrial activity has returned large quantities of CO_2, a formerly safely locked-up carbon, to the atmosphere. Before the Industrial Revolution, there were around 580 billion tons of CO_2 in the atmosphere. Today, the figure is more than 750 billion tons - the highest in 200,000 years - and a further 6 billion are being added each year. Up to 90 per cent of the increase in CO_2 and other global-warming gases has come from the countries in the Northern Hemisphere.

The world can only remain habitable if CO_2 levels neither fall too low nor rise too high. Without CO_2 and certain other gases, which help trap heat near the earth's surface, the average surface temperature would drop to -6°C. Too much CO_2, and the oceans would boil. At current levels, the earth's surface stays at the optimum average temperature of 15°C.

The world is heating up

Since the end of the last century, temperatures have drifted upward by 0.6°C. The 1990s were the hottest decade on record. Storms - a by-product of global warming - are becoming more frequent and more destructive. Asian monsoons are becoming less predictable. Unusually extreme droughts and floods are wreaking havoc in China, East Africa, the Middle East, Europe, North America, Aotearoa/New Zealand and the Indian subcontinent. Warmer, more CO_2-laden waters are killing coral reefs, which protect coastlines and nurture fish-eries. An area of Arctic ice the size of Texas has been lost over the past 20 years, with the ice over the Arctic Ocean thinning since the late 1950s from 3.1 to 1.8 meters, while Antarctica's Larsen Ice Shelf has broken away from the continent.

In short, the increase in atmospheric carbon levels cannot continue. Adding as little as another 200 billion tons will result in a 2° to 3°C rise in temperatures - a heat-wave unprecedented in human history. Adding 300 billion tons or more would be catastrophic, especially in that it might trigger runaway heating effects that could make the planet uninhabitable. Yet, more than 4,000 billion tons of carbon in fossil fuels is waiting to be recovered and burned, over three-quarters of it coal. It would seem that the vast bulk of this must be left in the ground.

Two ways to go

In the last few years it has become more difficult to deny that global warming has begun, and nearly impossible to pretend that consumption of remaining reserves of fossil fuels would not lead to disaster. That leaves only two approaches to the crisis.

The first is to reduce fossil fuel use dramatically and quickly. That means focusing first on reducing the 'luxury' emissions of those who have already used up more than their fair share of global carbon sinks and stocks (*), while promoting energy conservation and energy efficiency, worldwide use of solar and other renewable energy sources, and ecological instead of industrial agriculture. This approach treats inequality as a power imbalance and as a root of the ecological problem. It would move toward equalizing per capita emissions worldwide while contracting overall emissions, without forcing unnecessary hardship on any side. It acknowledges, moreover, that the 'carbon debt' that the North owes the South for its historical overuse of the atmosphere is still unpaid.

The second approach involves speculative programs to modify the Earth's biosphere and crust to allow them to absorb more CO_2, with the idea of making it 'safer' for richer nations and groups to continue rapid, high-level consumption of fossil fuels for as long as possible. This approach takes the impact on the carbon cycle of unequal use as a given. It assumes that because the rich industrialized countries have historically overused the atmosphere, they have a right to have done so, and to continue doing so. Not only does this approach ignore the history of unequal use of carbon stocks and sinks, it would actually worsen world inequalities in access to resources. The North's historic 'carbon debt' to the South is simply ignored.

The assumption of the second approach is that any CO_2 emissions are acceptable, no matter how extravagant, as long as they can be compensated for, or 'offset', by some activity that absorbs the CO_2. The leading example of such an activity is planting trees, which, through photosynthesis, convert CO_2 into wood carbon. Thus a utility company emitting a million tons of CO_2 a year can be just as 'carbon neutral' as a subsistence farmer emitting one ton a year - as long as the company plants thousands of trees.

The first approach is based on solid science. Thousands of years of experience have demonstrated the effectiveness of keeping hydrocarbons in the ground as a way of moderating CO_2 levels in the atmosphere. According to current scientific consensus, anything more than a doubling of atmospheric CO_2 concentrations over pre-industrial levels - 280 parts per million by volume - is likely to cause dangerous climate change. On current trends, this will happen by the middle of the 21st century; CO_2 levels already stand at 30 per cent above those of pre-industrial times. Although it is unclear exactly when CO_2 concentrations will threaten the habitability of the planet, the strategy of quick and drastic cuts is the approach to the problem that enjoys the most secure theoretical foundation. Ensuring that CO_2 levels do not double will require a reduction in emissions of 60 per cent or more over 1990 levels. What is required is not dazzling new technology so much as a more powerful political movement behind initiatives that already exist.

The second approach, by contrast, is based on science that nearly everyone acknowledges to be uncertain. No one is exactly sure even where the earth's current carbon 'sinks' are, or how they work. For example, no consensus exists today among scientists about how much carbon is moving into and out of temperate forests, or even how to go about finding out. Creating large, reliable new sinks with any degree of confidence would be far more daunting even than solving these recalcitrant puzzles. Still more difficult would be quantifying the effectiveness of each individual carbon sink separately in compensating for a given amount of industrial emissions.

The sink-plantations package

By comparison, the more familiar technique of using conventional tree plantations to 'fix' carbon emissions may seem straightforward and unproblematic. However, nobody has any idea how to calibrate a meaningful and reliable 'equivalence' between the carbon sequestered permanently in fossil fuel deposits, the transient CO_2 in the atmosphere and the carbon sequestered temporarily as a result of any particular tree plantation or national tree-planting program.

For now, at least, it is impossible to predict with the necessary certainty how much carbon any plantation project would remove from the atmosphere, and for how long. Unlike subterranean oil or coal or sea-floor carbonate, carbon stored in live or dead trees or in upper soil layers is 'fragile': it can quickly re-enter the atmosphere at any time.

In order to be able to claim credibly that a tree plantation 'equaled' or 'compensated for' a certain quantity of CO_2 emitted, carbon-plantation proponents would have to factor in a figure representing the degree to which their plantations destroyed existing carbon reservoirs, thus adding CO_2 to the air. According to satellite-image analysis, in the 1980s, 75 per cent of

new tree plantations in Southern countries in the tropics were established in places where, ten years earlier, natural forests had stood. The result was an estimated additional release of 725 million tons of CO_2 to the atmosphere. Replacing grasslands with plantations - another common practice - can be equally counterproductive. Recent studies show that the Andean Paramos ecosystem, for example, is more efficient than tree plantations in absorbing CO_2. In a recent study published in Nature, David Ellsworth, plant pathologist at the US Energy Department's Brookhaven National Laboratory, states that 'the key implication of this research is that, in response to elevated levels of CO_2 and nitrogen, ecosystems with high biodiversity will take up and sequester more carbon and nitrogen than do ecosystems with reduced biodiversity.'

In sum, the idea that a specified fragment of wooded land can 'offset' a specified amount of industrial CO_2 emissions depends on false assumptions about calculability. Rather than mitigating global warming, large-scale 'offset' plantations could make it even worse. In delaying the transition to a more equitable distribution of emissions and more sensible energy regimes, such plantations could result in an increased amount of avoidable carbon emissions both from industry and from the land.

Who owns the atmosphere?

Those who advocate creating a market in carbon 'offsets' - a universal 'carbon shop' - presuppose that the battle has already largely been won. This is far from being the case. One cannot, simply by waving a magic wand, turn the atmosphere - or the right to use it as a dump for CO_2 - into private property. One cannot, simply by waving a magic

wand, award the lion's share of that property to the rich. One cannot, simply by a further wave of the wand, empower the rich to buy up rights to pollute still more of the atmosphere on condition that they seize and degrade vast tracts of land with tree plantations. The defenders of the idea - oil companies, professional foresters, car companies, multilateral finance agencies, government officials of countries in the North, certain NGOs - will have to overcome many obstacles on the way. Among these are commonsense, science, and - by far the most important of all - the inevitable opposition of many who live or depend on that land, or who would otherwise lose out as a result of the redistribution of atmospheric rights from poor to rich.

Like the enclosure movement of early modern Europe, through which common lands were taken away from the rural poor and broken up, privatized and traded into the hands of the better-off, the movement for carbon-'offset' plantations is in essence a movement to extend and 'normalize' inequality. The movement critical of the unrestricted growth of a global carbon shop has an alternative solution, which is both scientifically sound and based on the principle that everyone should have equal rights to use of the atmosphere. This is the principle of 'contraction and convergence', under which countries would negotiate (and, if necessary, constantly renegotiate) a ceiling on CO_2 concentrations in the atmosphere in line with changing scientific estimates of the danger level. They would then agree to progressive cuts in emissions, which would allow the goal to be reached at the same time as emissions levels among rich and poor were gradually equalized.

Instead of enshrining and expanding inequalities in resource use while conceal-

Carbon emissions: Debtors and creditors

Decades of dubious global financial management by the multilateral banking institutions have made Africa and Latin America into debtors to the developed world. However, this familiar scenario of international relations (in which the creditor is invariably in the North) could change radically. The impacts of global climate change could invert the situation, with the creditors of the North becoming ecological debtors to the countries of the South.

In the Pacific Ocean, the archipelago of Tuvalu - a member of the United Nations since 2000 - may soon be considered the largest ecological creditor in the world. The rising sea levels caused by global warming threaten to erase this set of islands located between 6° and 11° latitude south. The Tuvalu authorities have already established an

evacuation plan with New Zealand and Australia. However, it is not just small islands that will suffer the effects of rising waters; in Bangladesh, some 20 million people could become environmental refugees.

The Canadian International Development Agency has proposed to cancel US$680,000 of Honduras' total $11 million debt to Canada if the Central American country sets up an office to promote reforestation and oversee forest conservation - a deal encouraged under the Kyoto Protocol. In exchange, Canada would obtain credits for 'reducing' its emissions of CO_2 and other greenhouse gases without having to alter any of its industrial practices at home.

Staking their bets on the Carbon Emissions Market, the wealthy countries are aiming to evade their historic debt incurred by their abusive use of shared natural resources. It is not an exclusively economic

debt, given that the disappearance of a country, in other words, a culture, cannot be compensated by any sum of money. Andrew Simms of the New Economics Foundation has stated that 'Third World debt pales into insignificance in the face of the ecological debts of industrialized countries.'

The ecological debt - incurred by the rich who have taken a larger share of the environmental wealth than a logical distribution would have granted them - gives the countries of the South a moral advantage in international negotiations. As Simms says, a realistic global solution to the ecological debt should include recognizing the right of all to share the common natural goods and the economic benefits they bring, as well as a plan for reducing greenhouse gas emissions. ∎

ing the pathologies of the current pattern of fossil-fuel exploitation - as the appeal to grand-scale carbon-'offset' plantations does - such an approach would go straight to the root of the climate crisis. Realistically, a livable climate can be promoted not through more monoculture plantations, more logging, more fossil-fuel plants and more automobiles, but only through a commitment to equality.

(*) 'Stocks' are understood to be the components of a climatic system that store greenhouse gases. 'Sinks' are any process, activity or mechanism that absorbs greenhouse gases. ∎

Source: Larry Lohmann, 'The carbon shop: planting new problems', published by the World Rainforest Movement.

George W Bush and global warming

While on the presidential campaign trail, George W Bush pledged to regulate carbon dioxide emissions in line with the Kyoto Protocol on climate change. But once he became president, it was a different story.

During his electoral campaign, Bush committed himself to regulating carbon dioxide emissions (a major cause of global warming), complying with the Kyoto Protocol that had been previously signed, though not ratified, by the US. According to this Protocol, the majority of industrialized countries must implement cutbacks in emissions of greenhouse gases. The UN's Intergovernmental Panel on Climate Change (IPCC) summary report had confirmed that human actions had contributed 'substantially to the warming observed in the last 50 years'. A previous IPCC report had predicted that, if present trends continue, the atmospheric temperature could increase between 1°C and 3.5 °C by 2100. The most recent report had upped the temperature range to between 1.5°C and 6°C.

When he was installed in the White House however, George Bush decided he didn't like the scientific results the IPCC reports relied upon. He requested a new study from the US National Academy of Science (NAS) in late 2001, seeking scientific support to justify his refusal to ratify the Kyoto agreement.

However, the NAS report did no more than confirm the IPCC 's conclusions. The first paragraph noted that 'greenhouse gases are accumulating in the earth's atmosphere as a result of human activity, causing an increase in air temperatures over the earth's surface and in the depths of the oceans. Temperatures are effectively increasing. Changes seen throughout recent decades are mainly a consequence of human activity, although we cannot exclude the possibility that some significant changes are due to natural variations. The increase in warming induced by humans and the consequent increase in sea levels are expected to continue throughout the 21st century.'

The NAS foresees a slightly less alarming increase in temperatures for this century than does the IPCC, and its conclusions add new forecasts and warnings to those made by the international panel. However, it states again that global warming should be taken seriously. On other issues, the NAS again endorsed the IPCC's findings: 'The conclusion of the Intergovernmental Panel on Climate Change that global warming observed in the last 50 years is, almost totally, due to the increase in concentrations of greenhouse gases, faithfully reflects current thinking of the scientific community on this issue.'

The NAS similarly rejected implications from members of the Bush team that the UN process was subject to political manipulation. Even though the NAS confirms the IPCC report, the latter puts more emphasis on human agency for climate change than on the other possibilities. The NAS authors suggest that 'this difference of emphasis appears to be the result of a summary process where the scientists work with those who draw up policies.'

For those like President Bush, who expected the NAS to reject IPCC conclusions, this second report could be seen as a major setback, forcing them to new heights of spin in order to justify this attempt to safeguard their interests. For although some NAS members state that their report in no way supports the Kyoto Protocol, the fact remains that there can be no further doubts as to the grave threat of global warming. The urgent question now is: when is the US going to act on what all the scientists say, and sign up to the Kyoto Protocol? ∎

The Royal Society

Founded in 1660, The Royal Society (RS) is the independent scientific academy in the UK devoted to promoting excellence in science. The RS has produced the following report on land carbon sinks.

There is still considerable uncertainty in the scientific understanding of the causes, magnitude and permanence of the land carbon sink. However, our current knowledge indicates that the potential to enhance the land carbon sink through changes in land management practices is finite in size and duration. The amount of CO_2 that can be sequestered in these sinks is small in comparison to the ever-increasing global emissions of greenhouse gases.

Projects designed to enhance land carbon sinks must therefore not be allowed to divert financial and political resources away from the restructuring of energy generation and use (eg increased use of renewable energy), technological innovation (eg increased fuel efficiency, sequestration of CO_2 at source) and technology transfer to less developed countries. It is these options that must provide the ultimate solution to the problem of reducing the concentration of greenhouse gases in the atmosphere.

The primary benefit of land carbon sinks is that they can be effective immediately (ie they do not require technological innovation) and can provide a financial incentive for the preservation and sustainable use of forests and agricultural land. However, due to their limited capacity and duration, land carbon sinks cannot be a major component of the long-term, 21st century solution to increasing levels of CO_2 in the atmosphere. The main means has to be cuts in emissions of CO_2 (and other greenhouse gases) primarily through energy-saving measures and a major replacement of fossil fuels by renewable or nuclear energy. Land carbon sinks must be seen as additional to these measures that can play a role in the next few decades while long-term measures are developed and implemented. Projects designed to enhance land carbon sinks must not divert financial and political resources away from long-term solutions to the problem of reducing the concentration of greenhouse gases in the atmosphere.

It is of concern to the Royal Society that measurement techniques available are not sufficiently accurate to permit the reliable monitoring of any land carbon sinks that may be designated as part of international agreements such as the Kyoto Protocol. ∎

COMMUNICATIONS IN FIGURES

A = Main telephone lines per 1,000 people, 2000.
B = Personal computers per 1,000 people, 2000.

The US, with 1 personal computer (pc) per 2 people, leads this table. China has quadrupled its number of pcs since 1996.

Country	A	B	Country	A	B	Country	A	B
Afghanistan	1.2		Gambia	25.5	11.5	Nigeria	4.3	6.6
Albania	39.0	6.4	Georgia	138.5		Northern Marianas	505.4	
Algeria	57.0	6.5	Germany	610.5	336.0	Norway	532.0	490.5
Andorra	438.6		Ghana	11.7	3.0	Oman	88.8	31.5
Angola	5.3	1.1	Greece	531.6	70.5	Pakistan	21.6	4.2
Antigua	499.4		Greenland	467.5	107.4	Panama	151.1	37.0
Aotearoa-New Zealand	499.8	360.2	Grenada	332.0	127.1	Papua New Guinea	13.4	
Argentina	213.1	51.3	Guam	477.9		Paraguay	50.0	12.7
Armenia	151.5	7.1	Guatemala	57.0	11.4	Peru	63.7	40.9
Aruba	371.5		Guinea	7.8	3.7	Philippines	40.0	19.4
Australia	524.6	464.6	Guinea-Bissau	9.2		Poland	282.3	68.9
Austria	466.8	276.5	Guyana	79.4	25.6	Portugal	430.3	299.3
Azerbaijan	103.5		Haiti	8.9		Puerto Rico	331.8	
Bahamas	375.8		Honduras	46.0	10.8	Qatar	267.6	150.4
Bahrain	249.7	138.7	Hungary	372.4	85.3	Romania	174.6	31.9
Bangladesh	3.5	1.5	Iceland	701.0	391.5	Russia	218.2	42.9
Barbados	437.3	82.2	India	32.0	4.5	Rwanda	2.2	
Belarus	268.8		Indonesia	31.4	9.9	Samoa	47.3	6.1
Belgium	498.0	344.5	Iran	149.0	62.8	Samoa, American	211.3	
Belize	148.8	124.9	Iraq	29.4		São Tomé and Príncipe	30.9	
Benin	8.4	1.6	Ireland	419.8	359.1	Saudi Arabia	137.2	60.2
Bermuda	869.8	465.4	Israel	481.8	253.6	Senegal	21.6	16.8
Bhutan	19.6	5.2	Italy	473.8	179.8	Seychelles	234.5	135.6
Bolivia	60.5	16.8	Jamaica	198.6	46.6	Sierra Leone	3.9	
Bosnia-Herzegovina	102.9		Japan	585.7	315.2	Singapore	484.4	483.1
Botswana	92.6	37.0	Jordan	92.9	22.5	Slovakia	314.1	136.9
Brazil	181.7	44.1	Kanaky-New Caledonia	236.9		Slovenia	386.3	275.9
Brunei	245.1	70.1	Kazakhstan	113.0		Solomon Is.	17.5	45.7
Bulgaria	350.3	43.9	Kenya	10.4	4.9	Somalia	1.5	
Burkina Faso	4.4	1.3	Kiribati	40.3	18.0	South Africa	113.5	61.8
Burundi	2.9		Korea, North	45.7		Spain	421.2	142.9
Cambodia	2.3	1.1	Korea, South	463.6	238.0	Sri Lanka	40.5	7.1
Cameroon	6.4	3.3	Kuwait	243.9	130.6	St Kitts-Nevis	568.7	181.7
Canada	676.5	390.2	Kyrgyzstan	77.0		St Lucia	313.4	141.0
Cape Verde	126.2		Laos	7.5	2.6	St Vincent	219.5	105.8
Cayman Is.	821.2		Latvia	303.0	140.3	Sudan	12.4	3.2
Central African Rep.	2.6	1.7	Lebanon	194.9	50.1	Suriname	173.5	
Chad	1.3	1.3	Lesotho	10.3		Swaziland	31.9	
Chile	221.3	82.3	Liberia	2.1		Sweden	682.0	506.7
China	111.8	15.9	Libya	107.9		Switzerland	726.6	499.7
Colombia	169.1	35.4	Liechtenstein	608.2		Syria	103.4	15.4
Comoros	10.0	4.3	Lithuania	321.1	64.9	Tajikistan	35.6	
Congo D.R.	0.3		Luxembourg	750.0	453.2	Tanzania	4.9	2.9
Congo R.	7.4	3.5	Macedonia, TFYR	254.9		Thailand	92.2	24.3
Costa Rica	249.4	149.1	Madagascar	3.4	2.2	Togo	9.2	21.6
Côte d'Ivoire	17.8	6.1	Malawi	4.3	1.2	Tonga	98.6	
Croatia	364.8	80.7	Malaysia	199.1	103.1	Trinidad and Tobago	231.0	61.8
Cuba	43.6	10.7	Maldives	90.8	20.5	Tunisia	89.8	22.9
Cyprus	647.1	220.6	Mali	3.4	1.2	Turkey	279.5	38.1
Czech Republic	377.9	122.0	Malta	521.6	204.4	Turkmenistan	81.8	
Denmark	719.5	431.5	Marshall Is.	58.7	47.0	Uganda	2.7	2.7
Djibouti	15.2	10.2	Mauritania	7.1	9.4	Ukraine	198.8	17.6
Dominica	294.2	71.3	Mauritius	235.3	100.5	United Arab Emirates	391.4	153.5
Dominican Republic	104.5		Mayotte Is.	72.6		United Kingdom	588.5	337.8
Ecuador	100.0	21.8	Mexico	124.7	50.6	United States	699.7	585.2
Egypt	86.3	22.1	Micronesia	81.4		Uruguay	278.4	104.9
El Salvador	99.7	19.1	Moldova	133.2	14.5	Uzbekistan	67.1	
Equatorial Guinea	13.4	2.3	Mongolia	55.6	12.6	Vanuatu	33.7	
Eritrea	7.9	1.6	Morocco	50.2	12.4	Venezuela	107.8	45.5
Estonia	363.2	152.9	Mozambique	4.3	3.1	Vietnam	31.8	8.8
Ethiopia	3.6	1.0	Myanmar-Burma	5.5	1.1	Virgin Is. (Am.)	569.6	
Faeroe Is.	554.4	67.1	Namibia	62.7	34.2	Yemen	18.8	1.9
Fiji	106.1	55.3	Nepal	11.5	3.0	Yugoslavia Fed. Rep.	226.1	22.6
Finland	550.2	396.1	Netherlands	617.9	394.1	Zambia	7.9	6.7
France	579.2	304.3	Netherlands Antilles	371.6		Zimbabwe	18.4	11.9
French Polynesia	220.7		Nicaragua	31.2	8.9			
Gabon	31.7	9.8	Niger	1.8	0.5			

Source: World Development Indicators 2002, World Bank.

IV. Ethics and economy

Neoliberalism

IN 1776, ECONOMIST ADAM SMITH'S *The Wealth of Nations* launched liberalism on the world as an economic and ideological model. Since then, it has had larger and smaller moments of success. Where Karl Marx saw 'a walking corpse', and other detractors a 'machine to generate injustices', supporters acclaimed 'the most successful ideology in the history of humanity' and above all a 'realistic', systematic, coherent vision. What is the view today?

Time for evaluation

Since the emergence of the global justice or anti-globalization movement in Seattle in December 1999 - a movement rooted in the 1994 Zapatista uprising in Mexico and the 1997 global economic crisis - increasing numbers of voices have been raised against the neoliberal economic model, the genetically modified grandchild of Smith's liberalism. One of the accusations that began to fly was of 'single-mindedness' or exclusivity and by extension, totalitarianism. Another was 'illegitimacy', where the only legitimacy was that of having claimed itself the 'only way' and the narrow focus of its outlook. These critics demanded a 'more human face of globalization'.

Whilst attempts were made to undermine the credibility of the Seattle movement by saying that the demonstrators were simply 'troublemakers', one key figure, Joseph Stiglitz, former chief economist of the World Bank, began to offer support for the protesters' arguments.

Professor Stiglitz had questioned the practices of the Bank and particularly the International Monetary Fund (IMF) since his time at the Bank. When he was awarded the Nobel Prize for Economics in 2001, he used his acceptance speech to call for greater state controls and regulation, restating objections to the neoliberal agenda that fed economic globalization from the Washington Consensus (US politicians, business and institutions).

The repeated economic crises affecting most of the nations of the South, especially in Asia and Latin America, were convincing evidence that the critics were right and that the neoliberal model had failed. Of course no single failing, nor even hundreds of these, necessarily imply the failure of the model; nor does the poor implementation of policies - indeed several of the criticisms voiced by Stiglitz pinpoint aspects in bureaucracy or application, and these do not negate the effectiveness of the model. However, the request for a 'more human face' is tantamount to demanding another model, although the nature of this replacement is not at all clear: neoliberalism, by definition, cannot have a human face.

Realism vs utopia

During the 20th century, defenders of liberalism considered it a 'realist' ideology, in opposition to the utopian visions of the socialists and Marxists in power behind the Iron Curtain and actively promoting political change all over the world. With the collapse of the socialist bloc in the early 1990s, the liberals proclaimed their age-old accusation that the utopian models give way to ones with their feet on the ground. In the last decade of the 20th century, neoliberalism - the Anglo-Saxon corporate version of liberalism - emerged for some as the only suitable model and, by implication the only one able to direct our political and economic destiny. It was not selling utopia, although supporters claimed there that the tools were there to manage the global economy in its current, transnationalized state.

It is worth pointing out here that neoliberalism did not need moral legitimacy. It was only claimed to be a 'suitable' tool and, where socialism promoted idealistic notions such as solidarity, happiness and equality, neoliberalism simply offered economic prosperity. It is essential to remember that in terms of a theoretical and 'scientific' model economic neoliberalism is not linked to any ethical or philosophical conditions. For although in the early stages capitalism underwent various interpretations by European Christian thinkers who posed questions about the links between the economy and moral issues, the two finally went their separate

AID IN FIGURES

Total net official development assistance (ODA) disbursed, 2000.

A= As % of GNP

B = Millions $

COUNTRY	A	B	COUNTRY	A	B	COUNTRY	A	B
Aotearoa-New Zealand	0.26	116	Germany	0.27	5,034	Portugal	0.26	261
Australia	0.27	995	Greece	0.19	216	Spain	0.24	1,321
Austria	0.25	461	Ireland	0.30	239	Sweden	0.81	1,813
Belgium	0.36	812	Italy	0.13	1,368	Switzerland	0.34	888
Canada	0.25	1,722	Japan	0.27	13,062	United Kingdom	0.31	4,458
Denmark	1.06	1,664	Luxembourg	0.70	116	United States	0.10	9,581
Finland	0.31	371	Netherlands	0.82	3,075			
France	0.33	4,221	Norway	0.80	1,264			

The US has halved the percentage of its contribution from 0.21 per cent in 1990 to 0.10 per cent of its GNP, remaining at the bottom of the table; although the actual cash is the second biggest after Japan. Denmark keeps its place at the top of the percentage chart having increased from 0.94 per cent in 1990 to 1.06. The UN's target for donors is 0.7 per cent of GNP – matched by only five of the main donor countries

Source: OECD - ODA figures from OECD 2000. OECD Web Site 2002.

ways, as did philosophy and science. In the end, as Adam Smith would note, the liberal doctrine established that 'it is not the benevolence of the butcher, brewer or baker which provides our food, but the consideration of his own interest. We do not invoke their humanitarian sentiments but their selfishness; nor do we speak of our needs, but of their advantages.'

Ethics versus economics

As neoliberalism is a 'driverless machine' and therefore amoral, its supporters claim there are no contradictions in the fact that, since its wide application in the world, the gap between poor and rich has currently widened to the extent that the wealth of the 10 richest people in the world is worth more than 1.5 times the income of all the least developed nations put together. Nor, for these advocates of neoliberalism, is it anomalous that a mere 4 per cent of the income of the 360 richest people - who together own more than the half the world's wealth - would be enough to solve the economic problems of the world's poor people. Three of the wealthiest people alone have assets equaling the GDP income of our 48 poorest nations.

However, for most religious, spiritual or 'humanitarian' institutions these discrepancies carry a moral contradiction that has led them to call for revision of the situation generated by this economic model. This is an ethical response that aims to return meaning to the world. Stiglitz' reaction, and his Nobel prize, are a response to a fear: that of awakening in a world ruled by 'driverless machines'. ∎

Debt and ecology

IN THE BIBLE, Jesus raged at the money-lenders and threw them out of the temple. Later, Shakespeare vilified the usurer Shylock in *The Merchant of Venice*. But today, lending money is big business. Global capital is pushing loans onto people and poor countries as never before, fueling the gap between rich and poor, accelerating the debt crisis and bringing economic and ecological chaos on a vast scale.

Live now, pay later

Today, lending money is big business. Global capital is pushing loans onto people and poor countries as never before, fueling the gap between rich and poor, accelerating the debt crisis and bringing economic and ecological chaos on a vast scale. In his Divine Comedy, Italian poet Dante placed usurers in the same category as criminals and those with 'unnatural vices'. Dante was responding to prohibitions and taboos that have their roots in ecology, the natural economy. A taboo arises from condemnation of an existing practice. Usury was seen, like incest, as an unnatural practice. It has been condemned since ancient times (see box 'Gods and Usury') because it seeks a benefit beyond the primary economic one. The transaction of usury - guaranteeing that the usurer gets something for nothing - was seen as a violation of the natural law, a design fault that would produce imbalance and disintegration.

The fact that usury had constantly to be outlawed shows just how deeply ingrained it was. But of course despite being illicit, money-lending never went away; the taboo was always broken. Since the Reformation in 16th century Europe, the practice spread rapidly. Today, usury - lending money at exorbitant interest rates - has conquered the world, lining up the rich world as lenders against the poor countries as borrowers.

Taboos are supposed to protect society. The taboo of incest for example arises from the need for healthy reproduction of the species and also to avoid confusion between the generations: children, who become parents, who become grandparents, great-grandparents, and so on. Whilst succession is also a way of dividing inheritance, both it and usury are economic forms of absorbing, locking up, future resources, denying them to others.

Usury and chaos

Several arguments back up the outlawing of usury. A main objection of the Christian Church was that earning income from the practice was immoral. The Bible's statement that bread must be earned 'by the sweat of the brow' led to the 1515 Council of Letran 'fair price doctrine' relating to a use or profit obtained without work, that is, something that is not gainful in itself, and at the expense or risk of the lender. In the Middle Ages people compared usury to 'selling a loaf of bread and then making a surcharge for its use' or, in the words of St Thomas, 'selling the same thing twice. In the same vein, a biographer quoted economist John Maynard Keynes as saying that the 'love of money' for its own was 'at the root of all the economic problems of the world. Usury, in this sense, marks the distinction between money as a means for negotiating supply and demand, and cash as an end in itself.

Exploitation of the most needy by usurers was condemned by most large religions. The Jains articulated it by saying that the poor live to pay the interest and not to enjoy the goods they bought with the loan: 'it is usury - this heartless extortion - which eats the bone-marrow of poor farmers and condemns them to a life of penury and slavery'. This thinking was given a contemporary dimension when Pope John Paul II said in his Solicitude Rei Socialis (1989) that 'the capital needed by the debtor nations to improve their standard of living ends up being used to pay the interest on their debts'. Elsewhere, today's economists have considered the loss in usefulness or utility of the loan suffered by the poor when paying their debts is much greater even than the profit made by the rich. Each unit of interest paid increases the loss in marginal utility, which leads to a reduction in utility in the economy (implying that those who justify this as an efficient economic tool should be made to prove that usury works in increasing utility - something they have so far been unable to do).

Finance versus ecology

Another argument against usury is the practice of discounting future values. Compound interest results in the growth of invested monetary capital, and tends to favor a definite in the now (present net value) rather than the same amount in the future. It has been noted that in an ecological context that this could lead to the 'economically rational' extinction of species, simply because the prevailing interest rate is greater than the reproduction rate of the exploited species. Meanwhile, the present net value leads toward maximizing utilities for the present generation at the expense of future ones. The financial economy operates on the basis of compound interest, whilst nature works in harmony with simple interest: money deposited in a bank becomes more (if capital of 100 becomes 110 in a year, interest in the second year is applied to this new amount), but it is difficult for an apple tree to produce a harvest with compound interest. In this way, there is disjuncture between the natural and financial economies, and the result is either the progressive destruction of nature or the absence of redistributive social justice, which has been at the root of financial crashes throughout history.

A cautionary note to end on: if Judas Iscariot had invested his 30 pieces of silver at a moderate rate of compound interest, his payment in silver today would be equal to the weight of the entire planet. ∎

DEBT IN FIGURES

A = Total external debt (million $), 2000.
B = Debt service as % of exports, 2000.
C = External debt $ per capita, 2000. (Calculated from total external debt and total population)
In the latest figures, Argentinians have the highest debt per person at $3,947 - contributing to the spectacular collapse of the country's economy at the end of the year 2001.

	A	B	C		A	B	C		A	B	C
Albania	784	3.7	250	Georgia	1,633	11.4	310	Papua New Guinea	2,604	9.6	541
Algeria	25,002	37.8	825	Ghana	6,657	19.9	345	Paraguay	3,091	6.6	562
Angola	10,146	21.1	772	Grenada	207		2,211	Peru	28,560	32.7	1,113
Argentina	146,172	75.9	3,947	Guatemala	4,622	10.3	406	Philippines	50,063	14.3	662
Armenia	898	11.9	237	Guinea	3,388	16.1	415	Poland	63,561	20.4	1,646
Azerbaijan	1,184	6.5	147	Guinea-Bissau	942	16.4	785	Romania	10,224	31.3	456
Bangladesh	15,609	10.1	114	Guyana	1,455		1,914	Russia	160,300	13.5	1,102
Belarus	851	3.2	84	Haiti	1,169	10.0	144	Rwanda	1,271	29.6	167
Belize	499		2,205	Honduras	5,487	13.5	855	Samoa	197		1,243
Benin	1,599	10.9	255	Hungary	29,415	26.6	2,951	São Tomé and Príncipe	316		2,294
Bhutan	198		95	India	100,367	15.0	99	Senegal	3,372	16.1	358
Bolivia	5,762	32.0	692	Indonesia	141,803	30.3	669	Seychelles	163		2,030
Bosnia-Herzegovina	2,828		711	Iran	7,953	22.6	113	Sierra Leone	1,273	29.9	289
Botswana	413	2.4	268	Jamaica	4,287	17.4	1,664	Slovakia	9,462	13.9	1,753
Brazil	237,953	110.9	1,396	Jordan	8,226	11.8	1,674	Solomon Is.	155		347
Bulgaria	10,026	19.1	1,261	Kazakhstan	6,664	19.4	412	Somalia	2,562		292
Burkina Faso	1,332	15.7	115	Kenya	6,295	26.7	205	South Africa	24,861	13.9	574
Burundi	1,100	45.6	173	Korea, South	134,417	24.6	2,876	Sri Lanka	9,066	7.9	479
Cambodia	2,357	2.9	180	Kyrgyzstan	1,829	21.8	372	St Kitts-Nevis	140		3,642
Cameroon	9,241	24.3	621	Laos	2,499	7.7	473	St Lucia	237		1,604
Cape Verde	327		766	Latvia	3,379	15.0	1,396	St Vincent	192		1,698
Central African Rep.	872	12.1	235	Lebanon	10,311		2,949	Sudan	15,741	6.5	506
Chad	1,116	10.3	142	Lesotho	716	9.4	352	Swaziland	262		283
Chile	36,978	25.4	2,431	Liberia	2,032		697	Syria	21,657	6.4	1,338
China	149,800	9.0	117	Lithuania	4,855	6.3	1,314	Tajikistan	1,170	6.5	192
Colombia	34,081	42.9	809	Macedonia, TFYR	1,465	29.9	720	Tanzania	7,445	15.6	212
Comoros	232		328	Madagascar	4,701	17.1	294	Thailand	79,675	22.0	1,269
Congo D.R.	11,645		229	Malawi	2,716	11.4	240	Togo	1,435	7.7	317
Congo R.	4,887	1.4	1,619	Malaysia	41,797	4.8	1,881	Tonga	58		588
Costa Rica	4,466	6.4	1,110	Maldives	207		710	Trinidad and Tobago	2,467	13.1	1,906
Côte d'Ivoire	12,138	26.2	758	Mali	2,956	14.3	260	Tunisia	10,610	15.9	1,122
Croatia	12,120	19.4	2,604	Mauritania	2,500	28.4	938	Turkey	116,209	26.2	1,743
Czech Republic	21,299	10.3	2,074	Mauritius	2,374	9.7	2,044	Turkmenistan	2,259	31.1	498
Djibouti	262		415	Mexico	150,288	25.1	1,520	Uganda	3,409	23.7	146
Dominica	108		1,533	Moldova	1,233	24.9	287	Ukraine	12,166	16.3	245
Dominican Republic	4,598	3.9	549	Mongolia	859	4.8	339	Uruguay	8,196	25.0	2,456
Ecuador	13,281	25.7	1,050	Morocco	17,944	24.3	601	Uzbekistan	4,340	17.9	174
Egypt	28,957	9.0	427	Mozambique	7,135	20.0	390	Vanuatu	69		349
El Salvador	4,023	7.6	641	Myanmar-Burma	6,046	7.9	127	Venezuela	38,196	23.2	1,580
Equatorial Guinea	248		543	Nepal	2,823	7.9	123	Vietnam	12,787	9.8	164
Eritrea	311	1.9	85	Nicaragua	7,019	16.1	1,384	Yemen	5,616	4.0	306
Estonia	3,280	13.2	2,354	Niger	1,638	16.8	151	Yugoslavia Fed. Rep.	11,960		1,133
Ethiopia	5,481	16.8	87	Nigeria	34,134	6.0	300	Zambia	5,730	46.6	550
Fiji	136		167	Oman	6,267	9.7	2,469	Zimbabwe	4,002	25.3	317
Gabon	3,995	19.3	3,248	Pakistan	32,091	28.3	227				
Gambia	471	8.5	361	Panama	7,056	8.7	2,471				

Source: World Development Indicators 2002, World Bank.

THE PRACTICE OF USURY - lending money and accumulating interest on the loan - can be traced back 4,000 years. But it has always been despised, condemned, restricted or banned by moral, ethical, legal or religious entities.

The morals of money-lending

The oldest references to usury are found in religious manuscripts of India, dating back to 2000-1400 BC where the 'usurer' is associated with any interest lender. In the Hindu Sutra (700-100 BC) as well as in the Buddhist Jatakas (600-400 BC) there are many references to the payment of interest, along with expressions of disdain for the practice.

Vasishtha, a prominent lawmaker of the era, drafted a law that banned the high caste Brahmans and Kshatryas from being usurers or money-lenders. In the second century AD, the term usury becomes relative, meaning that interest above the legal rate could not be charged; that would be a usurious loan. But usury in some form or other has continued to the present day, and although in principle it is condemned, the term 'usury' refers only to exorbitant interest, ie well above socially accepted rates. The practice operates in most parts of the world.

Usury in Western philosophy

Many of the early Western philosophers including Plato, Aristotle, Cato, Cicero, Seneca and Plutarch were critics of usury. In the legal reforms (Lex Genucia) of the Roman Republic (340 BC), usury and interest were banned. However, in the final period of the Republic, the practice was common. Under Julius Caesar, a limit of 12 per cent was imposed due to the great number of debtors, and under Justinian it was set at a mean between 4 per cent and 8 per cent.

Islam's view

During the prophet Muhammad's lifetime, criticism of usury became established. This stance was reinforced by his teachings in the Qur'an, around 600 AD. The original term for usury was riba, which literally means 'excess or addition' and referred just to interest on loans. For this reason, Muslim economists Choudhury and Malik maintain that, in the times of the Caliph Omar, the ban on interest was a principle established and integrated into the economic system of Islam. But that interpretation of usury was not universally applied nor universally accepted in the Muslim world. For instance, a school of Muslim thought that arose in the 18th century, led by Sir Sayyed, still maintains a distinction between usury - loans for consumption - and interest, which refers to loans for commercial investment. In modern times there

has been a gradual development of financial institutions that do not charge interest, for example in Iran, Pakistan and Saudi Arabia, the Dar-al-Mal-al-Islami in Geneva and Muslim banks in the United States.

'The dust of interest'

Judaism's criticisms of usury are rooted in several passages of the Old Testament in which charging interest is scorned, discouraged and prohibited. The Hebrew word for interest is neshekh, which means 'bite' (though in Leviticus tarbit and marbit are also used), and it is believed to refer to the charging of often exorbitant interest (from the debtor's perspective).

In the Hebrew books of Exodus and Leviticus the ban is thought to be applied exclusively to loans to the poor and the sick, while in Deuteronomy, it extends to all loans, excluding trade with foreigners. The word 'foreigner' is interpreted in general as 'enemy' and, armed with this text, Jews employed usury as a weapon, as other people's needs could be transformed into submission.

Beyond these biblical roots, there are several Talmudic extensions of the bans on interest, known as avak ribbit – literally 'the dust of interest', which is applied for example to certain types of sales, rent or work contracts. It is distinguished from the rubbit kezuzah, interest adjusted over a quantity or a rate agreed between the lender and borrower. The legal difference is that the latter, if the debtor pays the lender, is recoverable from the lender, while the former, once paid, is not recoverable, though it is recognized that a contract sullied by the dust of interest may not be fulfilled.

In spite of the ban, this rule does not appear to have been observed in biblical times. In addition to the various references in the Old Testament to lenders who are rigidly exacting high interest rates, it can be seen in the Elephantine Papyrus (dating to the reign of Tuthmosis III) that among the Jews of Egypt in the 5th century BC it was the norm for interest to be charged for loans. This suggests that the violation of the ban was not seen as a criminal offense with a penal sanction, but as a moral transgression.

This can also be partially explained by the change in economic conditions, beginning in the Amoraim period in Babylonia (200-500 AD), when the prohibition against

interest was agreed when usury became incompatible with the community's economic needs.

At the same time, a standard way of legalizing interest was established, known as hetter iska. This referred to the permission to create partnerships, which has become so common that today all transactions with interest are made openly according to Jewish law, simply adding to the corresponding note or contract the words al-pi hetter iskah.

Usury on the Cross

The prohibition of usury was adopted as a major campaign by the earliest Christian Church, following on from Jesus' expulsion of the money-lenders from the temple.

The decrees of the Hebrew Bible were revived and a new reference to usury in the New Testament was added. Based on the authority of those texts, the Catholic Church of the 4th century AD banned the clergy from charging interest, a rule that was later extended in the 5th century to the laity.

In the 8th century, under Charlemagne, usury was declared a criminal offense. The anti-usury movement gathered force in the late Middle Ages and reached its peak in 1311 when Pope Clement V totally banned the practice and declared null and void all secular law defending it.

In spite of subsequent papal and legislative bans, loopholes in the law and contradictions in the Church's arguments began to appear. Soon, on the rising tide of commerce, the pro-usury movement began to grow. The rise of Protestantism and its pro-capitalist slant strongly influenced change. However while both Luther and Calvin expressed reservations about the practice of usury, neither condemned it outright.

Calvin, for example, cited seven situations in which interest was 'sinful'. These were largely ignored however and his position interpreted as a general sanctioning of charging interest. As a result of these influences, around 1620, according to the theologian Ruston, 'usury passed from being an offense against public morality, which a Christian government was expected to suppress, to being a matter of private conscience, and a new generation of Christian moralists redefined usury as excessive interest'.

Nevertheless, the ancient criticisms continue to pervade the Church's modern thinking, as suggested by the viewpoint of the Church of Scotland (1988) when it released a report on the ethics of investment and banking.

'We accept that the practice of charging interest for business and personal loans is not in itself incompatible with Christian ethics. What is more difficult to determine is whether the interest imposed is just or excessive,' said the report.

In the same vein, it is interesting to contrast the clear moral mandate expressed through Pope Leo XIII's Rerum Novarum (634-644 AD) about 'ravenous usury' as 'a demon condemned by the Church but prac-

tized in a deceitful way by avaricious men,' with Pope John Paul II's encyclical Solicitude Rei Socialis (1987) which omits any explicit mention of usury, except for a vague reference to recognizing the Third World debt crisis.

This 'demon' governs current global relations, condemning most of the world population to living under the sign of debt: i.e., each person born in Latin America owes already $1,600 in foreign debt; each individual being conceived in Sub-Saharan Africa carries the burden of a $336 debt, for something that its ancestors have long ago paid-off. In 1980 the Southern countries'

debt amounted to $567 billion; since then, they have paid $3,450 billion in interests and write-offs, six times the original amount. In spite of this, that debt had quadrupled by the year 2000, reaching $2,070 billion. ∎

GROSS NATIONAL INCOME AS INDICATOR OF WEALTH

Gross National Income (per capita), 2000.
This is the ranking on income per head of the population used by the World Bank.
It takes no account of how that income is distributed.

	$	year		$	year		$	year
Luxembourg	42,060	2000	Brazil	3,580	2000	Ukraine	700	2000
Switzerland	38,140	2000	Estonia	3,580	2000	Georgia	630	2000
Japan	35,620	2000	Malaysia	3,380	2000	Solomon Is.	620	2000
Norway	34,530	2000	Botswana	3,300	2000	Azerbaijan	600	2000
United States	34,100	2000	Panama	3,260	2000	Côte d'Ivoire	600	2000
Denmark	32,280	2000	Gabon	3,190	2000	Bhutan	590	2000
Iceland	30,390	2000	Belize	3,110	2000	Cameroon	580	2000
Sweden	27,140	2000	Turkey	3,100	2000	Lesotho	580	2000
Austria	25,220	2000	South Africa	3,020	2000	Congo R.	570	2000
Finland	25,130	2000	Lithuania	2,930	2000	Indonesia	570	2000
Germany	25,120	2000	Latvia	2,920	2000	Armenia	520	2000
Netherlands	24,970	2000	Belarus	2,870	2000	Haiti	510	2000
Singapore	24,740	2000	St Vincent	2,720	2000	Senegal	490	2000
Belgium	24,540	2000	Jamaica	2,610	2000	Zimbabwe	460	2000
United Kingdom	24,430	2000	Iraq	2,170	1990	Guinea	450	2000
Brunei	24,100	1998	Dominican Republic	2,130	2000	India	450	2000
France	24,090	2000	Micronesia	2,110	2000	Pakistan	440	2000
Ireland	22,660	2000	Tunisia	2,100	2000	Moldova	400	2000
Canada	21,130	2000	Peru	2,080	2000	Nicaragua	400	2000
Australia	20,240	2000	Namibia	2,030	2000	Mongolia	390	2000
Italy	20,160	2000	Colombia	2,020	2000	Vietnam	390	2000
United Arab Emirates	18,060	1998	El Salvador	2,000	2000	Comoros	380	2000
Kuwait	18,030	2000	Thailand	2,000	2000	Bangladesh	370	2000
French Polynesia	17,290	2000	Maldives	1,960	2000	Benin	370	2000
Israel	16,710	2000	Suriname	1,890	2000	Mauritania	370	2000
Spain	15,080	2000	Fiji	1,820	2000	Yemen	370	2000
Kanaky-New Caledonia	15,060	2000	Macedonia, TFYR	1,820	2000	Uzbekistan	360	2000
Bahamas	14,960	2000	Jordan	1,710	2000	Kenya	350	2000
Aruba	14,920	1994	Guatemala	1,680	2000	Gambia	340	2000
Aotearoa-New Zealand	12,990	2000	Iran	1,680	2000	Ghana	340	2000
Cyprus	12,370	2000	Romania	1,670	2000	Sudan	310	2000
Greece	11,960	2000	Palestine	1,660	2000	Uganda	300	2000
Portugal	11,120	2000	Russia	1,660	2000	Zambia	300	2000
Slovenia	10,050	2000	Tonga	1,660	2000	Angola	290	2000
Antigua	9,440	2000	Algeria	1,580	2000	Laos	290	2000
Bahrain	9,370	1999	Bulgaria	1,520	2000	São Tomé and Príncipe	290	2000
Barbados	9,250	2000	Egypt	1,490	2000	Togo	290	2000
Malta	9,120	2000	Samoa	1,450	2000	Central African Rep.	280	2000
Korea, South	8,910	2000	Paraguay	1,440	2000	Kyrgyzstan	270	2000
Puerto Rico	8,230	1997	Swaziland	1,390	2000	Tanzania	270	2000
Argentina	7,460	2000	Cape Verde	1,330	2000	Cambodia	260	2000
Saudi Arabia	7,230	2000	Kazakhstan	1,260	2000	Nigeria	260	2000
Seychelles	7,050	2000	Bosnia-Herzegovina	1,230	2000	Madagascar	250	2000
St Kitts-Nevis	6,570	2000	Ecuador	1,210	2000	Mali	240	2000
Uruguay	6,000	2000	Morocco	1,180	2000	Nepal	240	2000
Czech Republic	5,250	2000	Vanuatu	1,150	2000	Rwanda	230	2000
Mexico	5,070	2000	Albania	1,120	2000	Burkina Faso	210	2000
Oman	5,050	1995	Philippines	1,040	2000	Mozambique	210	2000
Trinidad and Tobago	4,930	2000	Bolivia	990	2000	Chad	200	2000
Hungary	4,710	2000	Kiribati	950	2000	Guinea-Bissau	180	2000
Croatia	4,620	2000	Syria	940	2000	Niger	180	2000
Chile	4,590	2000	Yugoslavia Fed. Rep.	940	2000	Tajikistan	180	2000
Venezuela	4,310	2000	Djibouti	880	2000	Eritrea	170	2000
Poland	4,190	2000	Guyana	860	2000	Malawi	170	2000
St Lucia	4,120	2000	Honduras	860	2000	Sierra Leone	130	2000
Lebanon	4,010	2000	Sri Lanka	850	2000	Somalia	130	1990
Costa Rica	3,810	2000	China	840	2000	Burundi	110	2000
Grenada	3,770	2000	Equatorial Guinea	800	2000	Congo D.R.	100	1998
Mauritius	3,750	2000	Turkmenistan	750	2000	Ethiopia	100	2000
Slovakia	3,700	2000	Papua New Guinea	700	2000			

Source: World Development Indicators 2002, World Bank.

HUMAN DEVELOPMENT INDEX

The HDI value indicates how far a country has to go to attain certain goals: an average life expectancy of 85 years, access to education for all and a decent income. Methodical changes were made in the HDI calculation, thus HDI value from the 1999 Human Development Report is not comparable with previous years.

Countries ranked by HDI value, 1999.

Rank		HDI value	Rank		HDI value	Rank		HDI value
1	Norway	0.939	56	Malaysia	0.774	110	Equatorial Guinea	0.610
2	Australia	0.936	57	Bulgaria	0.772	111	Namibia	0.601
3	Canada	0.936	58	Romania	0.772	112	Morocco	0.596
4	Sweden	0.936	59	Libya	0.770	113	Swaziland	0.583
5	Belgium	0.935	60	Macedonia, TFYR	0.766	114	Botswana	0.577
6	United States	0.934	61	Venezuela	0.765	115	India	0.571
7	Iceland	0.932	62	Colombia	0.765	116	Mongolia	0.569
8	Netherlands	0.931	63	Mauritius	0.765	117	Zimbabwe	0.554
9	Japan	0.928	64	Suriname	0.758	118	Myanmar-Burma	0.551
10	Finland	0.925	65	Lebanon	0.758	119	Ghana	0.542
11	Switzerland	0.924	66	Thailand	0.757	120	Lesotho	0.541
12	Luxembourg	0.924	67	Fiji	0.757	121	Cambodia	0.541
13	France	0.924	68	Saudi Arabia	0.754	122	Papua New Guinea	0.534
14	United Kingdom	0.923	69	Brazil	0.750	123	Kenya	0.514
15	Denmark	0.921	70	Philippines	0.749	124	Comoros	0.510
16	Austria	0.921	71	Oman	0.747	125	Cameroon	0.506
17	Germany	0.921	72	Armenia	0.745	126	Congo R.	0.502
18	Ireland	0.916	73	Peru	0.743	127	Pakistan	0.498
19	Aotearoa-New Zealand	0.913	74	Ukraine	0.742	128	Togo	0.489
20	Italy	0.909	75	Kazakhstan	0.742	129	Nepal	0.480
21	Spain	0.908	76	Georgia	0.742	130	Bhutan	0.477
22	Israel	0.893	77	Maldives	0.739	131	Laos	0.476
23	Greece	0.881	78	Jamaica	0.738	132	Bangladesh	0.470
25	Cyprus	0.877	79	Azerbaijan	0.738	133	Yemen	0.468
26	Singapore	0.876	80	Paraguay	0.738	134	Haiti	0.467
27	Korea, South	0.875	81	Sri Lanka	0.735	135	Madagascar	0.462
28	Portugal	0.874	82	Turkey	0.735	136	Nigeria	0.455
29	Slovenia	0.874	83	Turkmenistan	0.730	137	Djibouti	0.447
30	Malta	0.866	84	Ecuador	0.726	138	Sudan	0.439
31	Barbados	0.864	85	Albania	0.725	139	Mauritania	0.437
32	Brunei	0.857	86	Dominican Republic	0.722	140	Tanzania	0.436
33	Czech Republic	0.844	87	China	0.718	141	Uganda	0.435
34	Argentina	0.842	88	Jordan	0.714	142	Congo D.R.	0.429
35	Slovakia	0.831	89	Tunisia	0.714	143	Zambia	0.427
36	Hungary	0.829	90	Iran	0.714	144	Côte d'Ivoire	0.426
37	Uruguay	0.828	91	Cape Verde	0.708	145	Senegal	0.423
38	Poland	0.828	92	Kyrgyzstan	0.707	146	Angola	0.422
39	Chile	0.825	93	Guyana	0.704	147	Benin	0.420
40	Bahrain	0.824	94	South Africa	0.702	148	Eritrea	0.416
41	Costa Rica	0.821	95	El Salvador	0.701	149	Gambia	0.398
42	Bahamas	0.820	96	Samoa	0.701	150	Guinea	0.397
43	Kuwait	0.818	97	Syria	0.700	151	Malawi	0.397
44	Estonia	0.812	98	Moldova	0.699	152	Rwanda	0.395
45	United Arab Emirates	0.809	99	Uzbekistan	0.698	153	Mali	0.378
46	Croatia	0.803	100	Algeria	0.693	154	Central African Rep.	0.372
47	Lithuania	0.803	101	Vietnam	0.682	155	Chad	0.359
48	Qatar	0.801	102	Indonesia	0.677	156	Guinea-Bissau	0.339
49	Trinidad and Tobago	0.798	103	Tajikistan	0.660	157	Mozambique	0.323
50	Latvia	0.791	104	Bolivia	0.648	158	Ethiopia	0.321
51	Mexico	0.790	105	Egypt	0.635	159	Burkina Faso	0.320
52	Panama	0.784	106	Nicaragua	0.635	160	Burundi	0.309
53	Belarus	0.782	107	Honduras	0.634	161	Niger	0.274
54	Belize	0.776	108	Guatemala	0.626	162	Sierra Leone	0.258
55	Russia	0.775	109	Gabon	0.617			

Source: Human Development Report 2001, UNDP.

FOOD IN FIGURES

A = Food production per capita index (1989-91=100), 2000. Source: World Development Indicators 2002, World Bank.

B = Food imports (as % of merchandise imports), 2000. Source: World Development Indicators 2002, World Bank.

C = Cereal imports (metric tons), 2000. Source: FAOSTAT - Statistical Database - FAO Web site 2001.

Country	A	B	C
Albania		22	403,083
Algeria	129	28	7,508,928
Andorra		20	
Angola	143		408,977
Antigua	99		4,817
Aotearoa-New Zealand	127	8	252,532
Argentina	139	5	47,730
Armenia	73	25	469,999
Aruba		19	8,135
Australia	139	5	54,331
Austria	104	6	443,936
Azerbaijan	63	19	765,748
Bahamas	146	16	19,060
Bahrain	119	10	28,040
Bangladesh	116	15	1,827,101
Barbados	99	15	68,352
Belarus	60	12	1,126,877
Belgium	116	9	5,967,860
Belize	159	17	15,104
Benin	154	25	184,959
Bermuda	78	20	2,315
Bhutan	114	18	42,910
Bolivia	143	14	459,675
Bosnia-Herzegovina			577,175
Botswana	99		133,198
Brazil	139	7	10,478,106
Brunei	179	17	57,299
Bulgaria	73	5	132,184
Burkina Faso	136		194,964
Burundi	88	23	30,088
Cambodia	142		65,475
Cameroon	127	19	308,622
Canada	131	5	1,933,326
Cape Verde	139	35	63,863
Cayman Is.	85		825
Central African Rep.	135	12	44,661
Chad	154	24	52,349
Chile	133	7	1,947,800
China	172	4	9,476,593
Colombia	121	12	2,263,009
Comoros	118	22	27,715
Congo D.R.	90		310,489
Congo R.	119	21	219,343
Cook Is.			2,062
Costa Rica	133	7	769,227
Côte d'Ivoire	135	17	735,532
Croatia	72	8	47,486
Cuba	59		1,582,711
Cyprus	110	19	655,134
Czech Republic	84	5	231,486
Denmark	109	11	702,263
Djibouti	88	27	167,414
Dominica	85	21	7,029
Dominican Republic	98		1,332,567
Ecuador	141	9	578,980
Egypt	154	23	10,144,538
El Salvador	123	16	681,076
Equatorial Guinea	96		12,045
Eritrea	127		79,613
Estonia	47	10	196,243
Ethiopia	120	7	148,851
Faeroe Is.	106	20	3,244
Fiji	82	16	128,290
Finland	96	5	329,631
France	107	8	1,664,242
French Polynesia	80	20	37,732
Gabon	115	19	91,948
Gambia	129	44	144,275
Georgia	79		853,272
Germany	94	7	3,446,125
Ghana	167	13	471,748
Greece	100	13	1,163,784
Greenland	106	15	2,284
Grenada	101	20	24,271
Guam	111		11,989
Guatemala	124	12	637,462
Guinea	143	24	224,217
Guinea-Bissau	120	44	47,169
Guyana	194	7	60,278
Haiti	96		512,179
Honduras	116	16	484,698
Hungary	70	3	104,386
Iceland	93	9	64,078
India	126	7	54,590
Indonesia	120	10	6,863,033
Iran	151	19	9,928,299
Iraq	61		4,229,169
Ireland	111	6	730,695
Israel	110	5	2,969,198
Italy	106	9	8,464,663
Jamaica	123	15	513,201
Japan	93	13	27,011,992
Jordan	145	21	1,536,663
Kanaky-New Caledonia	135	15	34,841
Kazakhstan	63	9	17,544
Kenya	104	14	753,113
Kiribati	115	39	10,812
Korea, South	106	5	1,466,817
Kuwait	199	17	700,695
Kyrgyzstan	119	14	245,761
Laos	150		15,467
Latvia	45	12	39,911
Lebanon	149		747,406
Lesotho	101		185,800
Liberia			130,669
Libya	165	23	1,602,846
Liechtenstein	91		
Lithuania	63	10	101,915
Luxembourg		10	53,808
Macedonia, TFYR	95	15	140,779
Madagascar	103	14	166,618
Malawi	158	20	120,332
Malaysia	137	4	4,150,602
Maldives	120	24	18,205
Mali	129	19	125,015
Malta	138	8	187,205
Mauritania	109	26	501,910
Mauritius	114	14	287,444
Mexico	133	5	14,064,500
Micronesia	18,866		13,973
Moldova	45	13	48,789
Mongolia	84	14	76,912
Montserrat			2,114
Morocco	92	14	5,215,045
Mozambique	114	22	381,271
Myanmar-Burma	158	15	100,774
Namibia	100		144,127
Nepal	124	17	195,417
Netherlands	102	10	4,905,796
Netherlands Antilles	158	9	21,089
Nicaragua	136	16	202,415
Niger	137	39	270,309
Nigeria	154	20	2,226,259
Norfolk Is.			167
Norway	96	6	313,774
Oman	115	22	387,328
Pakistan	144	14	1,054,474
Panama	117	12	382,365
Papua New Guinea	113	18	338,496
Paraguay	133	17	106,137
Peru	170	12	2,324,982
Philippines	134	8	3,798,848
Poland	86	6	1,864,175
Portugal	94	11	2,734,300
Puerto Rico	82		
Qatar	194	15	127,929
Romania	90	7	534,447
Russia	64	15	4,862,308
Rwanda	99		50,554
Sahara, Western		10	
Samoa	94	27	16,517
Samoa, American	96		4,784
São Tomé and Príncipe	167		9,306
Saudi Arabia	89	18	6,660,416
Senegal	121	24	793,589
Seychelles	135	20	15,079
Sierra Leone	81		275,592
Singapore	42	3	710,427
Slovakia	73	7	72,954
Slovenia	104	6	785,372
Solomon Is.	120	16	36,042
Somalia			133,659
South Africa	109	5	1,546,016
Spain	114	9	6,573,215
Sri Lanka	117	15	1,223,870
St Helena			388
St Kitts-Nevis	97	19	3,562
St Lucia	72	24	9,204
St Vincent	77	27	35,225
Sudan	157	15	635,957
Suriname	76	18	36,500
Swaziland	90		93,767
Sweden	105	6	182,362
Switzerland	98	6	544,249
Syria	151	19	1,730,716
Tajikistan	62		462,513
Tanzania	106	16	526,008
Thailand	114	4	1,099,955
Togo	145	18	304,522
Tonga	76	28	8,804
Trinidad and Tobago	110	8	205,174
Tunisia	127	8	2,490,344
Turkey	111	4	2,681,679
Turkmenistan	139	12	87,160
Tuvalu			1,411
Uganda	120	14	144,535
Ukraine	50		1,020,767
United Arab Emirates	256	10	1,910,577
United Kingdom	99	8	3,128,470
United States	126	4	5,091,040
Uruguay	133	11	79,453
Uzbekistan	118		706,931
Vanuatu	125	20	13,889
Venezuela	118	12	2,581,112
Vietnam	156		863,486
Virgin Is. (Am.)	103		
Wallis and Futuna Is.			1,042
Yemen	130	35	2,062,142
Yugoslavia Fed. Rep.	89	12	32,319
Zambia	103	10	84,608
Zimbabwe	119	9	243,664

Enron, the giant US energy company that crashed spectacularly in early 2002, is ranked 16 in this table compiled in 2000 and WorldCom is at 90. The top non-Western corporation is Venezuela's state-owned oil company PDVSA, the world's fourth largest oil exporter.

Corporation name	Revenues $ millions	Employees	HQ country
Exxon Mobil	210,392	123,000	United States
Wal-Mart Stores	193,295	1,244,000 [n]	United States
General Motors	184,632	365,000 [n]	United States
Ford Motor	180,598	345,991	United States
Daimler Chrysler	150,070	372,470 [n]	Germany
Royal Dutch/Shell Group	149,146	90,000	United Kingdom/Neth
BP	148,062	107,200	United Kingdom
General Electric	129,853	310,000 [n]	United States
Mitsubishi	126,579	10,230 [n]	Japan
Toyota Motor	121,416	215,648 [n]	Japan
Mitsui	118,014	10,337 [n]	Japan
Citigroup	111,826	272,000 [n]	United States.
Itochu	109,757	36,651	Japan
Total Fina Elf	105,870	123,300	France
Nippon Telegraph & Telephone	103,235	222,000 [n]	Japan
Enron	100,789	20,600	United States
AXA	92,782	90,357	France
Sumitomo	91,168	8,192	Japan
Intl. Business Machines	88,396	319,876 [n]	United States
Marubeni	85,351	7,073 [n]	Japan
Volkswagen	78,852	324,402	Germany
Hitachi	76,127	340,939 [n]	Japan
Siemens	74,858	450,000 [n]	Germany
ING Group	71,196	108,965	Netherlands
Allianz	71,022		Germany
Matsushita Electric Industrial	69,475	292,790	Japan
E. ON	68,433	186,788	Germany
Nippon Life Insurance	68,055	60,000 [n]	Japan
Deutsche Bank	67,133	98,311	Germany
Sony	66,158	181,800 [n]	Japan
AT&T	65,981	166,000	United States
Verizon Communications	64,707	260,000	United States
US Postal Service	64,540	797,795 [n]	United States
Philip Morris	63,276	178,000	United States
CGNU	61,499	72,749	United Kingdom
J.P. Morgan Chase	60,065	5,727	United States
Carrefour	59,888	330,247	France
Crédit Suisse	59,316	80,538	Switzerland
Nissho Iwai	58,557	4,563 [n]	Japan
Honda Motor	58,462	114,300 [n]	Japan
Bank of America Corp.	57,747	142,724	United States
BNP Paribas	57,612	80,464	France
Nissan Motor	55,077	133,833 [n]	Japan
Toshiba	53,827	188,042 [n]	Japan
PDVSA	53,680	45,520	Venezuela
Assicurazioni Generali	53,333	57,443	Italy
Fiat	53,190	223,953	Italy
Mizuho Holdings	52,069	31,378	Japan
SBC Communications	51,476	192,550 [n]	United States
Boeing	51,321	188,000 [n]	United States

Corporation name	Revenues $ millions	Employees	HQ country
Texaco	51,130	19,011	United States
Fujitsu	49,604	187,399 [n]	Japan
Duke Energy	49,318	23,000	United States
Kroger	49,000	312,000	United States
NEC	48,928	150,000 [n]	Japan
Hewlett-Packard	48,782	86,200 [n]	United States
HSBC Holdings	48,633	169,858	United Kingdom
Koninklijke Ahold	48,492	248,053	Netherlands
Nestlé	48,225	224,541	Switzerland
Chevron	48,069	34,610	United States
State Farm Insurance Cos.	47,863	79,300	United States
Tokyo Electric Power	47,556	43,000	Japan
UBS	47,316	71,000	Switzerland
Dai-ichi Mutual Life Insurance	46,436	59,922 [n]	Japan
American International Group	45,972	61,000	United States
Home Depot	45,738	230,000	United States
Morgan Stanley Dean Witter	45,413	61,000 [n]	United States
Sinopec	45,346	1,173,901	China
ENI	45,139	69,969	Italy
Merrill Lynch	44,872	72,000	United States
Fannie Mae	44,089	4,100	United States
Unilever	43,974	261,000	Britain/Netherlands
Fortis	43,831	62,881	Belgium
ABN AMRO Holding	43,390	115,098	Netherlands
Metro	43,371	179,561	Germany
Prudential	43,126	21,942	United Kingdom
State Power Corporation	42,549	1,137,025	China
Rwe Group	42,514	152,132	Germany
Compaq Computer	42,383	78,200 [n]	United States
Repsol YPF	42,273	37,387	Spain
Pemex	42,167	135,091	Mexico
McKesson HBOC	42,010	23,000	United States
China Petroleum	41,684	1,292,558	China
Lucent Technologies	41,420	77,000 [n]	United States
Sears Roebuck	40,937	323,000	United States
Peugeot	40,831	172,400	France
Munich Re Group	40,672	36,481	Germany
Merck	40,363	63,900	United States
Procter & Gamble	39,951	106,000 [n]	United States
WorldCom	39,090	90,000	United States
Vivendi Universal	38,628	290,000	France
Samsung Electronics	38,491	77,000	South Korea
TIAA-CREF	38,064	5,975	United States
Deutsche Telekom	37,834	227,015	Germany
Motorola	37,580	147,000	United States
Sumitomo Life Insurance	37,536	57,466 [n]	Japan
Zurich Financial Services	37,431	72,930	Switzerland
Mitsubishi Electric	37,349	116,715 [n]	Japan
Renault	37,128	166,114	France
Kmart	37,028	252,000	United States

Source: The Global 500, Fortune, 2002- [n] Employment from 2001

Armed conflicts

MODERN WAR is rarely a classic confrontation between the armed forces of two or more states. The huge imbalances in political and economic power and military might have led to the development of new forms of waging conflict that challenge the conventional view of war.

The changing face of war

The Cold War marked a change from the way war was conducted during World War I and II. The United States and the Soviet Union prepared their arsenals and armies less for combat than to ensure that the other side would be annihilated in the event of a military confrontation. The deadlock led to 'low intensity' conflicts in the nations of the South, in which the superpowers acted as hidden agents, arming, training and financing the adversary, such as occurred in Vietnam, where the USSR supported the Vietcong, and in Afghanistan, where the United States supported the mujahidin against the Red Army. Most of the conflicts since 1945 have been civil wars, and many of them involved guerrilla warfare, on a reduced scale, which diminished the strategic advantage that, a priori, the large national armies would enjoy.

The advent of asymmetric war
In the 1990s, the concept of 'asymmetric conflicts' began to gain favor among military analysts, who asserted that, when forces in confrontation do not possess the same level of military power, they adopt dissimilar tactics. In such cases, the military objectives are no longer the systematic pulverization of enemy lines but rather, in many cases, the erosion of popular support for the war within the society of the enemy. For analysts at the Pentagon, for example, the dividing line between governments and citizens, armies and civilians, public and private has dissipated.

Asymmetric war is basically a concept of conflict that eludes the rules of the international pact that entered into force with the League of Nations first, and then with the United Nations (UN). It is as old as war itself, because it is about a confrontation between the powerful and the weak. Since the Cold War, say analysts, examples of asymmetric war have included the struggles of the separatist Chechens against the Russian army and the Palestinians against the Israeli army, but also the use of terrorism. Today, they say, non-national and transnational groups, motivated by ideology, religion, cultural beliefs or 'illicit' eco-

nomic activities, have pushed 'a large portion of the world into anarchy'.

According to asymmetric war theorists, the use and management of publicity is usually part of the strategy of the David confronting the Goliath or the armed giant of the moment. For the theorists, in the asymmetric conflict not only can television news programs be turned into an operative weapon that is more powerful than the armed divisions, but also through them the distinction between war and peace begins to blur and the battlefields and frontlines become indefinable. At the same time, while terrorist tactics are perceived as crimes under international law, these are an almost privileged form of asymmetric war.

Marwan Bishara, professor of international relations at the American University of Paris, believes that the threat posed by terrorists has its departure point in the 'incredible quantitative difference in power and wealth between the North and South'. When people feel so militarily and economically inferior, he adds, they adopt asymmetric, not conventional, means to achieve their objective. There is agreement among Pentagon strategists that Iraqi President Saddam Hussein was the last to have the 'poor judgment' to engage a military superpower in non-asymmetric conflict, the 1991 Gulf War where the US deployed 'smart' technologies - but in many ways it was a conventional war with tanks and soldiers.

Privatization of war
While analysts were theorizing about the new type of war, the US army began to privatize, subcontracting out many of its military operations. This practice, known as outsourcing by its proponents, is described by its critics as the hiring of mercenaries. As a result of this privatization, the scale of US military intervention in other countries is often underestimated. Increasingly it is private citizens who carry out military actions, traveling internationally as if they were simply business executives or tourists. Democrat Congresswoman Jan Schakowsky said that

this process, in which military contractors are not held accountable, 'uses taxpayers' money to fund secret wars that could suck us into a Vietnam-like conflict'.

Currently, there are several private US firms that conduct Washington's military anti-drug policy in South America. DynCorp, a company based in Reston, Virginia, manages much of the air component of the anti-drug activities in the Andes, including spraying herbicides onto alleged plantations of coca and marijuana. According to Corporate Watch, DynCorp, with more than 20,000 employees and 550 offices worldwide, is the private company receiving by far the most money from the Pentagon, though it also gets funding from the FBI, CIA, the US departments of Justice and State, the Internal Revenue Service, the Drug Enforcement Agency, the Federal Communications Commission and others. In addition DynCorp assisted the UN forces in Angola. In 1999 it won a contract from the State Department to monitor the ceasefire in Kosovo, all the while training police forces in Panama, Somalia, El Salvador, Bosnia and Haiti.

The privatization of an army is, in itself, an asymmetrical practice that confuses the individual with the state.

Rewriting the rules
Within the current context, in which the US as the only true superpower categorizes other states as 'rogue' or 'criminal', denying them the sovereignty that defines the international pact embodied in the creation of the United Nations after World War II, it should come as no surprise that wars can be treated as abstractions - as occurred with the 'War on Terror' declared by US President George W Bush in 2001, following the attacks on the Pentagon and the World Trade Center. In effect, one can discern a declaration of the end of symmetric and international wars given that, by denying other states their sovereignty, the transnationalization - or globalization - of conflict prevails in the political-military practice of the US and its close allies.

In declaring other states 'rogues' or 'criminals', the US and its ally the United Kingdom have unilaterally taken on the policing role. They have made the sovereign state an individual, in many cases a criminal, and tried to convert themselves into the agents of an intangible, or at least non-judicial, order. Even that concept has been over-taken, however. If the US and the UK earlier attempted to turn themselves into the world's police force, through NATO and the bombings of former Yugoslavia, hiding behind an international tribunal, then the war on terror has transformed them into vigilantes who serve no law. The last rupture of the international pact was President Bush's branding terrorist Osama bin Laden a criminal with a price on his head. Any regulatory or legal framework - the true counterweight to asymmetric war - was abandoned. The US superpower certified the end of the international pact: there could be no trial, only an extra-judicial settling of accounts between private parties. ∎

'Rogue' states: Who is the real rogue?

Taking stock of 'threats' after the Gulf War, the then president of the United States, George Bush Snr, stated that the principal dangers to world peace would be the 'future Iraqs'. By this he meant the nations of the South that possessed weapons of mass destruction, sponsored terrorism and threatened US interests wherever they were in the world. In 1997, the US Secretary of State of the subsequent (Clinton) administration, Madeleine Albright, declared that the sole objective of the 'rogue state' was 'to destroy the international system'.

The terms 'pariah state' and 'criminal state' had been in vogue in Washington since the 1970s, but during the Clinton years the term 'rogue' was applied to the 'Iraqs of the future' (which were now in the present). This stance enabled the US to continue imposing itself as the arbiter of the 'international community'. The ambiguity of the term 'rogue' lends itself to many types of states seen as deviant in some way; whether they are considered 'criminals', 'misguided' or simply 'wayward'. If once the term was intended to refer to states that did not adhere to the rule of law, with the passage of time it became a flexible catchphrase

employed to demonize actions like organizing campaigns for political support.

The labeling of United Nations member states implies an overriding of the sovereignty of those on the 'black list'. The pact of sovereignty between member states, implied the egalitarian interaction of nations. But the list of 'rogue states' implies that, instead of the UN, it is the US that establishes the 'guidelines' (in other words, the framework) for the global agenda. A state is 'criminal' if it breaks a law, a 'boor' if it violates a moral code, 'astray' if it wanders from the herd, and 'wayward' if it leaves the desired path. The fact that Washington's list of rogue states includes Cuba, which is not breaking any of the international community's rules, is a clear indication that this state is being judged according to US interests and not those of the rest of the world.

Although the term 'rogue state' appears to refer to a country's supposed violations of accepted international norms, it lacks validity under international law. The concept leads to a political culture like that of the United States, which has traditionally seen international relations as a conflict between the forces of Good and Evil (with the US as the principal embodiment of the former). Given the scant analytical foundations and the fact that it is used in a political manner, the term 'rogue state' creates con-

tradictions, because states are added to the list of 'rogues' selectively, according to Washington's political interests, and not on 'merits'.

In terms of conduct, the international community is often confronted with the same wayward member. This is the US, a country that has unilaterally withdrawn from the Kyoto Protocol. It also - in solidarity with Israel - walked out of the World Conference against Racism, and ignored the requests of various national courts that have subpoenaed its former secretary of state, Henry Kissinger principally for his part in the downfall of Chile's democratically-elected President Allende in 1973.

In the same vague way that the term 'rogue state' is applied to Iran or North Korea, from the perspective of many countries of the world it would apply most aptly to the US. After all, since 1945 the US has attempted to overthrow more than 40 sovereign governments and quash over 30 popular nationalist movements that fought against intolerable regimes. In the process, the US has caused the deaths of millions of people, and condemned millions more to live in despair. ∎

Terrorism

THE THREAT OF VIOLENCE has always been an effective weapon used by individuals and groups of all persuasions. Some critics say that present-day terrorism can be understood as resistance to a 'definitive order', like the globalized and technocratic world that evolves into a single unit.

A brief archeology of the use of terror

Following the horror of the September 11 2001 attacks on the Twin Towers in New York and on the Pentagon in Washington, the world was shocked and began to speak of a new global crusade. In the words of US President George W Bush it became 'the war on terrorism', which has since become 'the war on terror'. Although the champions of this new war announced that it would be a wide-ranging exercise, perhaps the most significant problem - and one that widens its scope - is its lack of proper defini-

tion. Terror and terrorism are different things: the latter is the practice, the former the effect. The practice has been utilized since time immemorial, and the effect is also as old as time itself.

In the post-September 11 world, an

effort was made initially to distinguish between 'terrorist groups with a global reach' and 'freedom fighters' with territorial claims, such as the Tamil Tigers of Sri Lanka. But this distinction is confusing. The Arab countries for example have been quick to point out that Hamas, a group fighting for the creation of a Palestinian state, are 'freedom fighters', but have nonetheless been dubbed 'terrorists'. By contrast, the Al-Qaeda organization that is blamed for the attacks in New York and Washington, does not have national demands, but Islamic ones, and its reach is broad, global even.

A generic notion of terrorism is increasingly being applied, which is to equate terrorists with 'enemies of civilization'. By definition, this makes terrorism the enemy of a status quo, defined vaguely by Washington as 'civilization'. In doing so this repeats a commonplace, since terrorism has been identified with individuals or groups seeking to destabilize or overthrow the existing political institutions. However, terrorism has been used both by the colonial powers (such as France in Algeria or Indo-China, or the US in Vietnam) and by anti-colonialists (such as the Irish, the Algerians, Palestinians and Vietnamese). What is certain is that the systematic use of terror tactics, or of an unanticipated violence - whether against the government, the public or individuals - in order to achieve a political objective, is not only the conventional definition of 'terrorism', but also a practice as old as time. It has been used by political organizations of the right and left alike, by revolutionaries, by nationalist groups, by armies, by secret police and by governments.

Terrorists of the past
In ancient Greece, Xenophon (431-350 BC) wrote of the psychological effectiveness of using terror in the war against enemy populations. The Roman emperors Tiberius and Caligula used expropriation of property and executions as methods to protect their regimes. Precedents for political crimes can be found in the Old Testament, in the stories of Judith and Holofernes, of Jahel and Sisara, and in the reflections of classical theologians and philosophers, such as Seneca, who established that 'no sacrifice pleases the gods so much as the blood of a tyrant'. In Rome, and later also in Byzantium, the assassination of individuals in power became almost a tradition, seemingly endorsed by Cicero's idea that 'tyrants always bring a violent end upon themselves'. However, the assassination of individuals - even if it has existed throughout human history - differs from modern terrorism.

There are early examples of groups engaged in systematic terrorism, such as the Sicarians. They were one of the Jewish groups that fought the Roman occupation of Palestine and demanded an independent Jewish state. Historian Flavius Josephus considers the Sicarians (known as such for the daggers or siccas they carried) responsible for the catastrophe of the year 70AD, when the Second Temple was destroyed and the Jewish state came to an end in Jerusalem.

Another example is that of the Order of

the Assassins (hachichin), an offshoot of the Muslim sect of the Ismailis, which terrorized the Middle East in the 11th century. Its founder, Hassan I Sabah, ordered the capture of several forts in the mountains, though the Assassins soon moved their activities to the cities, killing enemies in Baghdad, Persia, Syria and Palestine. There were also secret societies in India and China, motivated more by religious creed than by politics, that made use of systematic violence.

Terror and the state
In Spain, the Inquisition used arbitrary arrests, torture and execution against what it perceived to be heresy, but the use of terror - along with the arrival of the word 'terrorism' - was the standard carried by the Jacobins during the French Revolution. In the period known as the Reign of Terror (1793-94) the revolutionary Robespierre advocated the practice and made use of it to encourage 'revolutionary virtue'. By 1798, the term was applied generally to any entity that sought to achieve political goals through violence and intimidation. The Jacobins were the only ones to use the term in a self-referential way, and with them was born what is currently known as 'modern terrorism'. From that time forward, the word 'terrorism' - initially linked to the concept of 'virtue' - took on negative connotations.

After the American Civil War (1861-65), some of the defeated but defiant southerners formed a terrorist organization, the Ku Klux Klan, to intimidate those who supported the Reconstruction. By the end of that century, terrorist tactics had been adopted by anarchists in Western Europe, Russia and the US. They believed that the most effective means for social and political change was to assassinate the individuals in power: in the period 1865-1905, anarchist bombs and bullets killed several kings, presidents and government officials.

In the 20th century, the practice of terrorism, by both the right and the left, came to be understood as the attempt by groups or individuals to use the power of terror to destabilize or overthrow the existing order. It was adopted as state policy by Adolf Hitler's Nazi Germany and by Joseph Stalin's Soviet Union. Without legal grounds or restrictions, they systematically used arrest, imprisonment, torture, executions and forced labor to fuel fear and encourage adherence to the national ideology and the state. This practice, whose origins lie with Robespierre, became known as state terrorism.

Following World War II, terrorism practiced by individuals or groups continued in Ireland and Spain, but largely disappeared from its modern home in Europe, shifting to Asia and the Middle East, where it was taken up by the Jews who demanded their own state in Palestine. It could be said that, in the 20th century, terrorism underwent a drastic change, as the main victims became random civilians rather than representatives of the state.

The Cold War and beyond
Some believe that what had been

considered 'ideological' terrorism (such as that practised in the late 1960s by the Red Army Faction in Germany, the Red Brigades of Italy or the Japanese Red Army) was more or less extinct by the end of the Cold War. They thought this mainly because the Soviet Union's role as an incubator for anti-capitalist or anti-democratic movements was not taken on by any other state. But supplanting the old ideological conflict are the ethno-religious conflicts. The increased US presence in the Middle East and the Pacific, as well as the fragile stability of Central Asia, leads some observers to believe that ethno-religious terrorism will continue to rise in those regions. Others believe that terrorism related to specific issues will undergo an inordinate expansion, utilized by groups such as the neo-Luddites that reject technology, or those opposed to abortion and taxes, like certain groups in the US.

Terror and media culture
The expanded reach both of weapons and media coverage has maximized the psychological effects - terror - of terrorism. If nuclear terrorism was for decades a dystopia (negative utopia) technological advances have made it a real possibility. Nowadays nuclear terrorism would entail the use of nuclear weapons by individuals or groups, not by states. The impact of terrorism has also been greatly magnified by the mass media: any act of violence attracts TV coverage and is beamed to millions of viewers. This extensive reach has led to the use of terror as a way of publicizing the demands, complaints or political objectives of a particular organization (see 'The changing face of war'). Although to date only one country, the US, has used nuclear weapons in war - against the civilians of two Japanese cities at the end of World War II - chemical weapons attacks have flourished during the last decades. They were not only used in international warfare (during the Iraq-Iran War in the 1980s) but also by a terrorist group. In March 1995 the Japanese religious cult Aum Shinrikyo carried out a nerve gas attack in the Tokyo subway, killing 12 people and injuring 5,000. Until then, an assault of that sort had been considered highly unlikely. An estimated 30 to 40 countries have the capability to produce chemical weapons. Germ warfare is another possibility. In the wake of the September 11 outrage, mail containing Anthrax spores brought more terror to US citizens.

Terrorism and globalization
It is commonly said that terrorism is 'the weapon of the weak'. Those who are overpowered by armies or economic means often resort to this practice. Powerful states nowadays fear that the new communication technologies, which encourage communication between groups and individuals worldwide, could foment global terrorism - aiming it beyond the realm of governments. Targets could include multinational corporations, international institutions and even non-governmental organizations (NGOs). Cyber-terrorism - attacks against computer networks - is a

threat that is currently manifest in the 'almost benign' actions of hackers and deliberately-spread computer viruses. In the midst of the globalization process, which erases borders, it seems that the current manifestations of terrorism whether political, religious or moral, have also become supranational. Occasionally, the terrorism may be apolitical, as in the case of Theodore Kaczynski, the Unabomber in the US, whose manifesto (made notorious through his bomb attacks) proclaimed a revolution, not against institutions, but against the 'economic and technological basis of present society'.

As some critics say, among them French philosopher Jean Baudrillard, present-day terrorism can be understood as resistance to a 'definitive order'. In that sense, the World Trade Center symbolized the world order that was imposed after the Cold War; the globalized and technocratic world sought to reflect its own image in the Twin Towers. This world is an interconnected system that evolves into a single unit that carries within it its own terror - insecurity. In that economic, political and technological web nobody is independent and no one can stand by her/himself. From this line of reasoning it follows that the formula can be reversed this time and that current global terrorism is just the effect, for terror is already embedded in the system. ∎

OFFICIAL AID: RECIPIENTS

Total net official development assistance (ODA) received (net disbursements).
A = As % of GNP, 1999.
B = Millions $, 1999.
C = Per capita $, 1999.

	A	B	C		A	B	C		A	B	C
Albania	13.0	480	142.1	Fiji	1.9	34	42.7	Nicaragua	29.8	675	137.2
Algeria	0.2	89	3.0	Gabon	1.1	48	39.3	Niger	9.3	187	17.8
Angola	4.5	388	31.4	Gambia	8.4	33	26.5	Nigeria	0.4	152	1.2
Argentina		91	2.5	Georgia	8.7	239	43.8	Oman		40	17.0
Armenia	11.3	209	54.7	Ghana	7.8	608	32.3	Pakistan	1.3	732	5.4
Azerbaijan	4.0	162	20.3	Guatemala	1.6	293	26.4	Panama	0.1	14	4.8
Bahamas		12	38.8	Guinea	6.8	238	32.8	Papua New Guinea	6.0	216	45.8
Bahrain		4	6.0	Guinea-Bissau	24.0	52	44.2	Paraguay	1.0	78	14.5
Bangladesh	2.6	1,203	9.4	Guyana	3.9	27	31.1	Peru	0.9	452	17.9
Barbados ⁿ	-0.1	-2	-7.9	Haiti	6.1	263	33.7	Philippines	0.9	690	9.3
Belarus	0.1	24	2.4	Honduras	15.2	817	129.3	Poland	0.6	984	25.5
Belize	6.3	46	186.3	Hungary	0.5	248	24.6	Qatar		5	8.7
Benin	8.9	211	34.5	India	0.3	1,484	1.5	Romania	1.1	373	16.6
Bhutan	15.1	67	85.2	Indonesia	1.5	2,206	10.7	Russia	0.5	1,816	12.4
Bolivia	6.8	569	69.9	Iran	0.1	161	2.6	Rwanda	19.1	373	44.9
Botswana	1.0	61	38.3	Israel	0.9	906	148.3	Samoa	13.0	23	136.1
Brazil		184	1.1	Jamaica ⁿ	-0.3	-23	-8.7	Saudi Arabia		29	1.4
Brunei		1	4.4	Jordan	5.3	430	90.7	Senegal	11.2	534	57.5
Bulgaria	2.1	265	32.3	Kazakhstan	1.0	161	10.8	Sierra Leone	11.0	74	14.9
Burkina Faso	15.4	398	36.2	Kenya	2.9	308	10.5	Singapore ⁿ		-1	-0.3
Burundi	10.4	74	11.1	Korea, South		-55	-1.2	Slovakia	1.6	318	59.0
Cambodia	8.9	279	23.7	Kuwait		7	3.8	Slovenia	0.2	31	15.6
Cameroon	4.7	434	29.5	Kyrgyzstan	21.3	267	54.8	South Africa	0.4	539	12.8
Cape Verde	23.5	136	318.8	Laos	20.5	294	57.7	Sri Lanka	1.6	251	13.2
Central African Rep.	11.1	117	33.1	Latvia	1.5	96	39.7	Sudan	2.5	243	8.4
Chad	12.3	188	25.1	Lebanon		194	45.4	Suriname		36	87.0
Chile	0.1	69	4.6	Lesotho	3.6	31	14.8	Swaziland	2.4	29	28.4
China	0.2	2,324	1.9	Libya		7	1.3	Syria	1.2	228	14.5
Colombia	0.3	301	7.3	Lithuania	1.2	129	34.9	Tajikistan	6.5	122	19.6
Comoros	11.1	22	39.4	Macedonia, TFYR	7.9	273	135.1	Tanzania	11.3	990	30.1
Congo D.R.		132	2.7	Madagascar	9.6	358	23.8	Thailand	0.8	1,003	16.7
Congo R.	6.3	140	49.1	Malawi	24.6	446	41.3	Togo	5.1	71	15.6
Costa Rica ⁿ	-0.1	-10	-2.7	Malaysia	0.2	143	6.3	Trinidad and Tobago	0.4	26	20.3
Côte d'Ivoire	4.0	447	28.8	Maldives		31	113.9	Tunisia	1.2	245	25.9
Croatia	0.2	48	10.8	Mali	13.8	354	33.4	Turkey ⁿ		-10	-0.2
Cyprus	0.6	50	65.6	Malta		25	66.2	Turkmenistan	0.7	21	4.4
Czech Republic	0.6	318	30.9	Mauritania	22.8	219	84.1	Uganda	9.2	590	27.5
Djibouti		75	115.8	Mauritius	1.0	42	35.3	Ukraine	1.2	480	9.6
Dominican Republic	1.1	195	23.2	Mexico		35	0.4	United Arab Emirates		4	1.5
Ecuador	0.8	146	11.7	Moldova	8.8	102	23.8	Uruguay	0.1	22	6.5
Egypt	1.8	1,579	25.2	Mongolia	23.9	219	91.9	Uzbekistan	0.8	134	5.5
El Salvador	1.5	183	29.7	Morocco	1.9	678	24.0	Venezuela		44	1.8
Equatorial Guinea	2.9	20	45.6	Mozambique	3.0	118	6.8	Vietnam	5.0	1,421	18.3
Eritrea	23.0	149	37.2	Myanmar-Burma		73	1.6	Yemen	6.7	456	26.8
Estonia	1.6	83	57.3	Namibia	5.8	178	104.4	Zambia	19.8	623	63.1
Ethiopia	9.8	633	10.1	Nepal	6.9	344	14.7	Zimbabwe	4.4	244	20.5

ⁿ- A negative value indicates that the repayment of ODA loans exceeds the amount of ODA received.

Source: Human Development Report 2001, UNDP.

A = Imports of conventional weapons ($ million, 1990 prices), 1999. Source: Human Development Report 2001, UNDP.

B = Military expenditure as % of GNI, 1998. Source: World Development Indicators 2002, World Bank.

In general, spending on arms has been going down since the end of the Cold War. But new worldwide operations, like the War on Terrorism, may stoke the fires again.

	A	B		A	B		A	B
Albania		1.3	Gabon		2.4	Nicaragua		1.2
Algeria		4.0	Gambia		1.3	Niger		1.2
Angola		21.2	Georgia	60	1.2	Nigeria		1.6
Aotearoa-New Zealand	337	1.2	Germany	126	1.6	Norway	170	2.2
Argentina	223	1.6	Ghana		0.8	Oman		15.3
Armenia		5.8	Greece	633	4.7	Pakistan	839	5.9
Australia	341	1.8	Guatemala		0.7	Panama		1.4
Austria	48	0.8	Guinea		1.6	Papua New Guinea		1.1
Azerbaijan		6.6	Guinea-Bissau		2.7	Paraguay		1.1
Bahamas	54		Guyana		0.8	Peru	108	2.4
Bahrain		8.1	Haiti		1.6	Philippines		1.4
Bangladesh	130	1.3	Honduras		0.7	Poland	1	2.1
Barbados		0.5	Hungary	56	1.7	Portugal	1	2.1
Belarus		1.3	Iceland		0.0	Qatar	117	10.0
Belgium	37	1.4	India	566	2.5	Romania	35	1.6
Belize		1.6	Indonesia	213	1.1	Russia		5.6
Benin		1.4	Iran	67	2.9	Rwanda	29	4.5
Bolivia		1.8	Iraq		5.5	São Tomé and Príncipe		1.0
Bosnia-Herzegovina		4.5	Ireland	30	1.0	Saudi Arabia	1,231	14.9
Botswana	34	4.7	Israel	1,205	8.8	Senegal		1.7
Brazil	221	1.9	Italy		2.0	Sierra Leone	6	3.0
Brunei		4.0	Jamaica	5	0.8	Singapore	163	4.8
Bulgaria	6	3.0	Japan	1,089	1.0	Slovakia		1.8
Burkina Faso		1.6	Jordan	44	9.2	Slovenia	19	1.4
Burundi		7.0	Kazakhstan	259	0.9	Somalia		0.9
Cambodia	2	4.0	Kenya		1.9	South Africa	14	1.5
Cameroon		1.8	Korea, North		18.8	Spain	289	1.3
Canada	33	1.4	Korea, South	1,245	2.9	Sri Lanka	26	4.7
Cape Verde		0.9	Kuwait	126	7.7	Sudan	10	4.8
Central African Rep.		2.8	Kyrgyzstan		2.4	Suriname	12	1.8
Chad		2.4	Laos		2.0	Swaziland		1.5
Chile	177	3.0	Latvia	4	0.9	Sweden	79	2.3
China	1,688	2.3	Lebanon		4.0	Switzerland	508	1.2
Colombia	40	3.2	Lesotho		2.6	Syria	20	7.0
Congo D.R.		14.4	Liberia		1.2	Tajikistan		1.3
Congo R.		3.5	Libya		6.1	Tanzania		1.4
Costa Rica		0.5	Lithuania	4	1.3	Thailand	185	1.7
Côte d'Ivoire		0.8	Luxembourg		0.8	Togo		1.8
Croatia		3.3	Macedonia, TFYR	95	2.5	Trinidad and Tobago		1.4
Cuba		1.9	Madagascar		1.2	Tunisia		1.8
Cyprus	242	3.4	Malawi		0.6	Turkey	1,134	5.3
Czech Republic		2.3	Malaysia	916	2.3	Turkmenistan		3.4
Denmark	137	1.6	Mali		2.3	Uganda	32	2.3
Djibouti		4.3	Malta		0.8	Ukraine		3.0
Dominican Republic	3	0.7	Mauritania		4.0	United Arab Emirates	595	4.1
Ecuador	24	3.7	Mauritius		0.2	United Kingdom	155	2.5
Egypt	748	2.7	Mexico	14	0.6	United States	111	3.0
El Salvador		0.9	Moldova		0.5	Uruguay	13	1.3
Equatorial Guinea		3.2	Mongolia		2.1	Uzbekistan		1.7
Eritrea		27.4	Morocco		4.3	Venezuela	142	1.4
Estonia		1.5	Mozambique		2.5	Vietnam	154	2.5
Ethiopia	8	8.8	Myanmar-Burma	27	7.8	Yemen	53	6.1
Fiji		2.0	Namibia		2.9	Yugoslavia Fed. Rep.		5.0
Finland	821	1.4	Nepal		0.8	Zambia		1.0
France	105	2.7	Netherlands	225	1.8	Zimbabwe		5.0

A = Exports (millions $), 2000.
B = Imports (millions $), 2000.

	A	B		A	B		A	B
Albania	709	1,516	Germany	624,742	617,521	Palestine	604	3,085
Algeria	22,579	11,709	Ghana	2,553	3,612	Panama	3,278	3,850
Angola	7,959	6,551	Greece	25,162/1	35,668/1	Papua New Guinea	1,611 [1]	1,503 [1]
Antigua	487	548	Grenada	250	309	Paraguay	1,525	2,660
Aotearoa-New Zealand	17,490 [1]	17,943 [1]	Guatemala	3,801	5,294	Peru	8,546	9,547
Argentina	30,731	32,552	Guinea	778	947	Philippines	42,076	37,493
Armenia	447	972	Guinea-Bissau	68	125	Poland	43,282	54,197
Australia	81,147 [1]	90,941 [1]	Guyana	687	792	Portugal	32,975	45,494
Austria	94,672 [1]	95,701 [1]	Haiti	506	1,109	Qatar	4,080 [3]	4,052 [3]
Azerbaijan	2,145	2,022	Honduras	2,512	3,344	Romania	12,506	14,640
Bahrain	6,530	5,056	Hungary	28,541	30,415	Russia	115,200	62,290
Bangladesh	6,585	9,057	Iceland	2,963 [1]	3,352 [1]	Rwanda	149	432
Barbados	1,317	1,456	India	63,764	75,656	Samoa	77	193
Belarus	20,309	20,768	Indonesia	59,075	47,045	São Tomé and Príncipe	15	38
Belgium	199,574	191,85	Iran	36,547	21,663	Saudi Arabia	85,891	44,579
Belize	385	523	Ireland	81,783 [1]	68,961 [1]	Senegal	1,335	1,729
Benin	334	627	Israel	44,147	51,813	Seychelles	481	530
Bhutan	144	292	Italy	304,553	292,458	Sierra Leone	110	212
Bolivia	1,453	2,078	Jamaica	3,262	4,076	Singapore	165,969	148,937
Bosnia-Herzegovina	1,192	2,543	Japan	448,994 [1]	379,706 [1]	Slovakia	14,060	14,537
Botswana	1,391 [1]	1,670 [1]	Jordan	3,534	5,720	Slovenia	10,719	11,363
Brazil	64,754	72,240	Kanaky-New Caledonia	400 [1]	1,008 [1]	Solomon Is.	99 [7]	154 [7]
Bulgaria	7,014	7,684	Kazakhstan	10,730	8,630	Somalia	90 [7]	346 [7]
Burkina Faso	235	649	Kenya	2,744	3,690	South Africa	36,572	32,842
Burundi	62	162	Kiribati	4 [6]	39 [6]	Spain	167,120	180,023
Cambodia	1,277	1,494	Korea, South	205,658	92,929	Sri Lanka	6,475	8,234
Cameroon	2,728	2,383	Kuwait	21,617	11,782	St Kitts-Nevis	163	250
Canada	277,551 [1]	258,892 [1]	Kyrgyzstan	567	719	St Lucia	394	464
Cape Verde	131	344	Laos	467 [2]	612 [2]	St Vincent	195	234
Central African Rep.	125	154	Latvia	3,273	3,883	Sudan	1,928	1,870
Chad	233	451	Lebanon	2,141	6,228	Suriname	145	148
Chile	22,468	21,718	Lesotho	256	794	Swaziland	969	1,194
China	279,558	250,685	Lithuania	5,109	5,833	Sweden	107,761	95,634
Colombia	17,762	16,596	Luxembourg	22,595	18,663	Switzerland	109,128 [1]	95,785 [1]
Comoros	52	64	Macedonia, TFYR	1,616	2,227	Syria	6,470	5,861
Congo D.R.	1,390 [3]	1,282 [3]	Madagascar	955	1,349	Tajikistan	800	839
Congo R.	2,526	1,345	Malawi	445	649	Tanzania	1,325	2,094
Costa Rica	7,651	7,304	Malaysia	112,513	93,565	Thailand	81,896	72,043
Côte d'Ivoire	4,298	3,698	Maldives	577	476	Togo	433	608
Croatia	8,56	9,635	Mali	575	927	Tonga	29 [6]	71 [6]
Cyprus	4,119 [1]	4,472 [1]	Malta	3,677	4,047	Trinidad and Tobago	4,783	3,834
Czech Republic	36,287	38,160	Marshall Is.	8 [1]	69 [1]	Tunisia	8,566	9,257
Denmark	68,894	60,123	Mauritania	387	528	Turkey	48,695	62,810
Djibouti	247	347	Mauritius	2,783	2,937	Turkmenistan	2,774	2,350
Dominica	137	173	Mexico	180,392	190,889	Uganda	626	1,587
Dominican Republic	5,862	7,736	Micronesia	62 [2]	115 [2]	Ukraine	19,522	18,116
Ecuador	5,774	4,191	Moldova	640	990	United Arab Emirates	25,225 [5]	25,034 [5]
Egypt	15,931	22,444	Mongolia	635	794	United Kingdom	384,833	411,853
El Salvador	3,646	5,642	Morocco	10,409	12,459	United States	990,500 [1]	1,244,200 [1]
Equatorial Guinea	1,272	782	Mozambique	5701,	476	Uruguay	3,805	4,082
Eritrea	95	523	Namibia	1,702 [1]	1,952 [1]	Uzbekistan	3,383	2,962
Estonia	4,158	4,397	Nepal	1,305	1,759	Vanuatu	96 [4]	116 [4]
Ethiopia	984	1,961	Netherlands	238,383 [1]	219,777 [1]	Venezuela	35,402	20,515
Fiji	1,028	940	Nicaragua	962	1,945	Vietnam	12,026 [3]	14,274 [3]
Finland	51,572	39,325	Niger	282	422	Yemen	4,305	3,537
France	370,902	352,622	Nigeria	21,499	16,861	Yugoslavia Fed. Rep.	2,666	4,256
French Polynesia	192	952	Norway	75,394	49,253	Zambia	890	1,333
Gabon	1,825	1,718	Oman	5,594 [5]	4,494 [5]	Zimbabwe	2,245	2,266
Gambia	202	257	Pakistan	9,575	11,762			
Georgia	1,136	1,410	Palau	12	87			

[1] 1999, [2] 1998, [3] 1997, [4] 1995, [5] 1994, [6] 1992, [7] 1990

Source: World Development Indicators 2002, World Bank.

INTERNATIONAL HUMAN RIGHTS law - a legal system that tries to protect people in times of war - became strengthened following World War II. Toward the end of the 19th century, Russian Czar Nicholas II had called a series of conferences within the framework of which the European powers subscribed to a conventional regulation of war. There was, however, never any thought of individual criminal responsibility being an issue.

Paving the way:
From impunity to responsibility

Before World War I, any legal action taken against people for 'war crimes' occurred under national jursidictions. The 1919 Treaty of Versailles at the end of World War I brought substantial changes, foreseeing the commitment to hand over war criminals and ordering that Germany's Kaiser Wilhelm be tried by an international court as 'guilty of a crime against peace,' that is: a 'supreme offense against international ethics and the sacred authority of treaties'. In any case, the court never came to session, because the Netherlands did not allow his extradition after he sought asylum there. The same treaty stipulated that those guilty of war crimes should be hand-

ed over to the Allies by Germany to be tried by military tribunal.

Although none of these provisions was ever applied, because the Allies gave up their jurisdiction to the German Court at Leipzig, the principle of international criminal responsibility of the individual - both leaders and troops - was established. International human rights law was no longer only applied to states and was no longer, at least in theory, exclusively a matter of national jurisdictions.

'Crimes against humanity'
If the idea of 'humanizing' war emerged over centuries, and the principle of crimi-

nal responsibility in human rights law was settled in Versailles, it took until after World War II - the most extensive conflict yet known - and the verification of Nazi genocide (killing six million Jews and more than a million Roma/gypsies, and homosexuals amongst others) for the victorious powers to procure a political and legal instrument to avoid the repetition of atrocities on such a scale. The defunct League of Nations was replaced by the United Nations in 1946, and the International Monetary Fund was founded in 1948.

Advances were made in international human rights law. The Nuremberg and

The International Criminal Court

The Rome Statute of the International Criminal Court (ICC) was adopted and opened for signature on 17 July 1998. It came into force when it was ratified by 60 states, in July 2002. How will it work?

The ICC is a permanent court with international jurisdiction. Its competence, according to the Rome Statute, is limited materially to trying crimes of genocide, crimes against humanity and war crimes. It tries individuals, not states. This differentiates it from the International Court of Justice, the principal judicial organ of the United Nations, which was set up to handle legal disputes submitted to it by states and does not have jurisdiction over matters involving the responsibility of an individual.

The ICC can exercise its jurisdiction in three areas:

1. In a specific case, where the state in whose territory the crime was committed or the state of the nationality of the accused, is party to the Statute.

2. The Court's Prosecutor can also initiate an investigation into a crime that has come to his or her attention.

3. The UN Security Council, acting under Chapter VII of the UN Charter, can also refer cases to the Court.

Only in a case referred by the Security Council is the jurisdiction of the ICC obligatorily and legally executable in all states, even in those that have not recognized its

legitimacy. This measure corresponds closely to the US proposals in the drafting of the Statute and reflects Washington's desire for the Security Council to have the definitive say. Given that the Security Council has the right of veto, it would be able to exercise this power over the Court.

In theory, the ICC will complement rather than replace national courts. The Court will act only when national courts are incapable of exercising their jurisdiction or prove reluctant to do so. If a national court is willing to exercise its jurisdiction and is capable of doing so, the ICC will not be able to intervene and no citizen of that country may be brought before it if not involved in the cases remitted by the Security Council. ∎

Tokyo courts were created and the principle of 'individual criminal responsibility' was extended, while a new category of 'crimes against humanity' was also created. These codes were written for the first time in the 1945 Treaty of London, signed by the four Allied powers - Britain, France, the Soviet Union and the United States - and they were declared 'unprescribable', another new element in international law. In order to try individuals and organizations accused of war crimes, the Statutes of the International Military Tribunal were co-opted. Thus in Nuremberg in 1945, an ad hoc Military Tribunal was able to try 24 Nazi leaders and six of their organizations, working on evidence provided by official documents.

End of the century: ICTFY and ICTR
Inspired by the Nuremberg and Tokyo Tribunals, and bolstered by increasingly developed international human rights law (Geneva Conventions 1949 and 1977), the UN revived the International Criminal Tribunals (ICT) when faced with the ethnic conflicts of the early 1990s in Yugoslavia and Rwanda. In 1993 the Security Council set up the ICT for the former Yugoslavia (ICTFY), backed by Chapter VII of the UN Charter, that is, in response to 'the threat that violations of international human rights law represent to peace and international security.' The International Criminal Tribunal for Rwanda (ICTR) followed in 1994.

These tribunals, in The Hague (the Netherlands) and Arusha (Tanzania) respectively, adopted similar structures, sharing the prosecutor and the Appeals Body, and benefiting from limited powers in material, temporal, geographical and personal terms. In material terms, both had jurisdiction over four types of crime: serious infractions of the 1949 and 1977 Geneva Conventions; violations of the laws and customs of war ('war crimes'); crimes against humanity and crimes of genocide. In territorial, temporal and personal terms, the jurisdiction of the ICTY extended to individuals, whatever their status, accused of committing crimes in former Yugoslavia since 1991; while the ICTR is exercised over individuals independent of their status, but in this case the Tribunal covers the territory of Rwanda and the neighboring countries, for the war which lasted from January to December 1994.

As well as having tried some of the most infamous, these ad hoc tribunals constituted a significant point of reference for the creation of a permanent International Criminal Court. The rulings made by judges in both tribunals, most confirmed by the Court of Appeals, contributed to the formation of a solid base of jurisprudence for future international jurisdiction. For example, clarifications were made on the application of the Geneva Conventions, the development of the doctrine of the responsibility of the superior rank, as well as the possible interpretation of certain acts, like rape, as crimes against humanity.

The US vs the permanent International Criminal Court (ICC)
Until the present, despite the progressive emergence of international human rights law and ad hoc jurisdictions, there has been a lack of a permanent global system of applying these regulations in order to make offenders answer for their crimes. In Rome, in July 1998, 160 States attended a Conference held under UN auspices where the Statute of the permanent ICC was approved. This would have neither spatial nor temporal restrictions and would judge, under the principle of universal justice, those accused of a certain category of crime when their own country could not or would not judge them under their own territorial jurisdiction.

However, 13 country ratifications are still needed to reach the milestone of 60 necessary for the Court to come into being. Although the figure may seem slight, a great deal of consolidation will be needed, as the US is not keen on the idea of a truly independent International Criminal Court able to judge anyone responsible of crimes against humanity - including US citizens. Washington has always considered this Court a threat to its sovereignty. Furthermore, the US, traditional defender of the ad hoc international Tribunals, when judging other countries, was the only Western country to vote against the ICC Statute. Not so long ago, then president of the Senate Foreign Relations Commission, Jesse Helms, classed it as a 'monster which must be destroyed before it matures and ends up eating us up'.

The US has alternatives to slow consolidation of the ICC: during debate in Rome, Washington pressed for a Statute considerably reducing the attributions of the ICC, transforming it into a complement subordinate to the UN Security Council where the US has a veto. Meanwhile, the American Servicepeople's Protection Act

The handover of Milosevic: A controversial precedent

June 28 2001, the date that former Yugoslav president Slobodan Milosevic was handed over to the International Criminal Tribunal for the Former Yugoslavia (ICTFY), will be recorded in the history of the Court - and undoubtedly in that of international criminal justice - as a controversial historic precedent. It was the first time that a former head of state had been brought before an international criminal court, an event applauded by most Western countries as progress in international justice. In addition, it has been stressed that the ICTFY has been a unique opportunity for the victims to be heard and to testify about the horrors they experienced.

However, there was plenty of criticism of the operations of the Court itself. Because the ICTFY depends on Western powers for its funding, for the documentation of its investigations, for the arrest and handover of the accused, the Court has been attacked for its lack of political independence. For, as much as the Northern countries and their media reiterate that it was the discovery of Milosevic's crimes that led the Serbian people to hand him over to the Court, the fact is that the then acting president Vojislav Kostunica - who did not recognize the authority of the ICTFY - had received heavy economic blackmail from Washington.

According to some critics, it is possible that the US desire to cover up its own war crimes is at the root of Washington's anxiety to bring Milosevic to justice. This was the man who, despite having been dubbed the butcher of the Balkans, was considered (until NATO openly attacked the Federal Republic of Yugoslavia) as the West's main contact in the region. It has also been asserted that the ICTFY is nothing more than an instrument of interference by the world's powers in the internal politics of others and that it is a violation of the principle of national sovereignty.

This kind of criticism reflects the inherent flaws of ad hoc tribunals such as the ICTFY and also demonstrates the urgent need for the setting up of the permanent International Criminal Court. ∎

(ASPA) - an initiative from the Republican Party 'hawks' - was well received by the Democrats and resoundingly approved by the US Senate. This Law would protect US citizens serving in various places around the world, both in the military and various state agencies. Amongst other measures, this law requires 'the suspension of military assistance to most of the countries ratifying the Rome Statute, until those countries reach an agreement with the US in respect of article 98 of said statute, whilst prohibiting the ICC from the persecution of US staff present in the respective country.' This law threatens the ratification and realization process of the ICC, as well as its later operation, creating an incoherent justice system offering global justice for some and not for others.

Steps toward the culture of responsibility

However, despite any obstacles which could delay the creation and operation of a permanent international criminal system, and beyond whether or not the ICC ever comes into operation, the world appears to be developing toward a culture of responsibility which would progressively substitute the culture of impunity.

One recent sign of sanctuary being increasingly scarce for despots and genocidal leaders was seen in British attempts to detain General Augusto Pinochet in order to have him tried in Spain for human rights violations committed during his dictatorship in Chile. Another sign lies in the multiplication of extradition demands by European courts on those accused of human rights crimes who have so far gone unpunished.

It is foreseeable that individuals like Israeli Prime Minister Ariel Sharon, accused in Belgian courts for his part in the

Rwanda: Tribunal for the influential

On November 28 1995, the International Criminal Tribunal for Rwanda (ICTR) issued its first indictment of eight suspects. In early 2002, there were more than 70 people facing charges, of whom 50 had been arrested and brought before the Tribunal. Nine cases have been tried, resulting in eight convictions (all upheld by the Appeals Court) and one acquittal. The number of cases tried represents more than half of the number arrested. The accused are all influential people: ministers, top officials, businessmen, religious leaders and journalists. The list includes Jean Kambada, Rwanda's prime minister during the genocide, who was found guilty and sentenced to life in prison. Kambada was the first head of government to be accused of the crime of genocide, which demonstrates that international penal law is applied, without exception, to the highest state authorities.

Given these encouraging results in international criminal justice, similar ad hoc tribunals have been requested in various parts of the world. It has also been suggested that the competence of the ICTR could be expanded to cover other conflict-affected countries in Africa.■

1982 Sabra and Chatila refugee campmassacres where thousands of Palestinians were killed, or Henry Kissinger, former secretary of State for US presidents Nixon and Ford, summonsed in various countries on charges of collaboration in the 1973 coup in Chile, will never appear in court or be extradited. However these extradition requests, the open cases, are creating a culture of responsibility. Even if it goes no further for Kissinger, the level of legal interest in his past - as the man behind a US foreign policy which spawned dictatorships and caused countless deaths - will contribute to changing the image of this man who was awarded a Nobel Peace Prize. ■

INDEX OF BRIBE-PAYERS

The Corruption Perception Index (see p 71) gives an indication of those countries whose officials may accept bribes or other inducements – but who offers these? Transparency International's Gallup Poll ranks the 19 top exporting countries of the world according to the degree their companies were perceived as paying bribes abroad. Of those countries, Sweden is seen as least likely to offer inducements and China the most likely.

Country Rank	Country	BPI	Country Rank	Country	BPI
1	Sweden	8.3	11	Singapore	5.7
2	Australia	8.1	12	Spain	5.3
2	Canada	8.1	13	France	5.2
4	Austria	7.8	14	Japan	5.1
5	Switzerland	7.7	15	Malaysia	3.9
6	Netherlands	7.4	16	Italy	3.7
7	United Kingdom	7.2	17	Taiwan	3.5
7	Belgium	6.8	18	Korea, South	3.4
9	Germany	6.2	19	China	3.1
9	United States	6.2			

Notes:
The survey asked: 'In the business sectors with which you are familiar, please indicate whether companies
from the following countries are very likely, quite likely, or unlikely to pay bribes to win or retain business in this country.'
The standard error in the results was 0.2 or less.

Source: Global Corruption Report 2001, Transparency International Web site.

CORRUPTION PERCEPTION INDEX (CPI)

Based on surveys by independent institutions, commissioned by Transparency International (TI), this charts the degree of corruption (for example in receiving bribes) perceived to exist among officials and politicians. TI requires at least three sources of information for a country to be included in the CPI; however there are many countries for which this information is not yet available. Therefore it should not be assumed that Bangladesh, with the lowest score in this table, is the most corrupt; it is the lowest of those for which the information is available. See also the Index of Bribe Payers.

Country Rank Score	Country	2001 CPI	Surveys Used	Standard Deviation	High-Low Range	Country Rank Score	Country	2001 CPI	Surveys Used	Standard Deviation	High-Low Range
1	Finland	9.9	7	0.6	9.2 -10.6	47	Bulgaria	3.9	6	0.6	3.2 - 5.0
2	Denmark	9.5	7	0.7	8.8 -10.6		Croatia	3.9	3	0.6	3.4 - 4.6
3	Aotearoa/New Zealand	9.4	7	0.6	8.6 -10.2		Czech Republic	3.9	10	0.9	2.6 - 5.6
4	Iceland	9.2	6	1.1	7.4 -10.1	50	Colombia	3.8	9	0.6	3.0 - 4.5
	Singapore	9.2	12	0.5	8.5 - 9.9	51	Mexico	3.7	9	0.6	2.5 - 5.0
6	Sweden	9	8	0.5	8.2 - 9.7		Panama	3.7	3	0.4	3.1 - 4.0
7	Canada	8.9	8	0.5	8.2 - 9.7		Slovakia	3.7	7	0.9	2.1 - 4.9
8	Netherlands	8.8	7	0.3	8.4 - 9.2	54	Egypt	3.6	7	1.5	1.2 - 6.2
9	Luxembourg	8.7	6	0.5	8.1 - 9.5		El Salvador	3.6	5	0.9	2.0 - 4.3
10	Norway	8.6	7	0.8	7.4 - 9.6		Turkey	3.6	9	0.8	2.0 - 4.5
11	Australia	8.5	9	0.9	6.8 - 9.4	57	Argentina	3.5	9	0.6	2.9 - 4.4
12	Switzerland	8.4	7	0.5	7.4 - 9.2		China	3.5	10	0.4	2.7 - 3.9
13	United Kingdom	8.3	9	0.5	7.4 - 8.8	59	Ghana	3.4	3	0.5	2.9 - 3.8
14	Hong Kong	7.9	11	0.5	7.2 - 8.7		Latvia	3.4	3	1.2	2.0 - 4.3
15	Austria	7.8	7	0.5	7.2 - 8.7	61	Malawi	3.2	3	1	2.0 - 3.9
16	Israel	7.6	8	0.3	7.3 - 8.1		Thailand	3.2	12	0.9	0.6 - 4.0
	United States	7.6	11	0.7	6.1 - 9.0	63	Dominican Republic	3.1	3	0.9	2.0 - 3.9
18	Chile	7.5	9	0.6	6.5 - 8.5		Moldova	3.1	3	0.9	2.1 - 3.8
	Ireland	7.5	7	0.3	6.8 - 7.9	65	Guatemala	2.9	4	0.9	2.0 - 4.2
20	Germany	7.4	8	0.8	5.8 - 8.6		Philippines	2.9	11	0.9	1.6 - 4.8
21	Japan	7.1	11	0.9	5.6 - 8.4		Senegal	2.9	3	0.8	2.2 - 3.8
22	Spain	7	8	0.7	5.8 - 8.1		Zimbabwe	2.9	6	1.1	1.6 - 4.7
23	France	6.7	8	0.8	5.6 - 7.8	69	Romania	2.8	5	0.5	2.0 - 3.4
24	Belgium	6.6	7	0.7	5.7 - 7.6		Venezuela	2.8	9	0.4	2.0 - 3.6
25	Portugal	6.3	8	0.8	5.3 - 7.4	71	Honduras	2.7	3	1.1	2.0 - 4.0
26	Botswana	6	3	0.5	5.6 - 6.6		India	2.7	12	0.5	2.1 - 3.8
27	Taiwan	5.9	11	1	4.6 - 7.3		Kazakhstan	2.7	3	1.3	1.8 - 4.3
28	Estonia	5.6	5	0.3	5.0 - 6.0		Uzbekistan	2.7	3	1.1	2.0 - 4.0
29	Italy	5.5	9	1	4.0 - 6.9	75	Vietnam	2.6	7	0.7	1.5 - 3.8
30	Namibia	5.4	3	1.4	3.8 - 6.7		Zambia	2.6	3	0.5	2.0 - 3.0
31	Hungary	5.3	10	0.8	4.0 - 6.2	77	Côte d'Ivoire	2.4	3	1	1.5 - 3.6
32	Trinidad and Tobago	5.3	3	1.5	3.8 - 6.9		Nicaragua	2.4	3	0.8	1.9 - 3.4
	Tunisia	5.3	3	1.3	3.8 - 6.5	79	Ecuador	2.3	6	0.3	1.8 - 2.6
34	Slovenia	5.2	7	1	4.1 - 7.1		Pakistan	2.3	3	1.7	0.8 - 4.2
35	Uruguay	5.1	4	0.7	4.4 - 5.8		Russia	2.3	10	1.2	0.3 - 4.2
36	Malaysia	5	11	0.7	3.8 - 5.9	82	Tanzania	2.2	3	0.6	1.6 - 2.9
37	Jordan	4.9	4	0.8	3.8 - 5.7	83	Ukraine	2.1	6	1.1	1.0 - 4.3
38	Lithuania	4.8	5	1.5	3.8 - 7.5	84	Azerbaijan	2	3	0.2	1.8 - 2.2
	South Africa	4.8	10	0.7	3.8 - 5.6		Bolivia	2	5	0.6	1.5 - 3.0
40	Costa Rica	4.5	5	0.7	3.7 - 5.6		Cameroon	2	3	0.8	1.2 - 2.9
	Mauritius	4.5	5	0.7	3.9 - 5.6		Kenya	2	4	0.7	0.9 - 2.6
42	Greece	4.2	8	0.6	3.6 - 5.6	88	Indonesia	1.9	12	0.8	0.2 - 3.1
	Korea, Rep. of	4.2	11	0.7	3.4 - 5.6		Uganda	1.9	3	0.6	1.3 - 2.4
44	Peru	4.1	6	1.1	2.0 - 5.3	90	Nigeria	1	4	0.9	- 2.1
	Poland	4.1	10	0.9	2.9 - 5.6	91	Bangladesh	0.4	3	2.9	- 5.5
46	Brazil	4	9	0.3	3.5 - 4.5						

2001 CPI Score relates to perceptions of the degree of corruption as seen by business people, academics and risk analysts, and ranges between 10 (most clean) and 0 (most corrupt).

Surveys Used refers to the number of surveys that assessed a country's performance. A total of 14 surveys were used, and at least three surveys were required for a country to be included in the CPI.

Standard Deviation indicates differences in the values of the sources: the greater the standard deviation, the greater the differences of perceptions of a country among the sources.

High-Low Range provides the highest and lowest values of the sources. Since each individual source has its own scaling system, scores are standardised around a common mean for the subset of countries featuring in the individual survey. As a result, it is possible in rare cases that the highest value exceeds 10.0 and the lowest can be lower than 0.0. Only the aggregate final country scores are restricted to the reported range between 0 and 10.

Source: Global Corruption Report 2001, Transparency International Web site.

TRIPS

BEFORE THE BIRTH of the World Trade Organization (WTO), intellectual property rights were absent from trade protocol and each country had its own legislation in the matter adapted to its ethical, social and economic conditions. But the implementation of the TRIPs agreement - aside from removing the prerogatives of various cultures in relation to their knowledge and increasing the obstacles to the South's development - is a major threat to biodiversity.

Intellectual property and biodiversity

The World Trade Organization (WTO) is imposing at a global level an agreement on intellectual property that forces the Southern countries especially to modify their legislation, according to the needs and conveniences of the Northern countries and multinationals. It must be recalled that the structure of the Agreement on Trade Related Intellectual Property Rights (known as TRIPs) was thought and formulated by corporate coalitions such as IPC (in the United States), Keidanren (in Japan), UNICE (in Europe), to impose values and interests of the Northern transnationals on the world's various cultures and societies, leaving aside any other type of interests, whether they were ethical, ecological or social. It can be asserted that the TRIPs are the final step on a series of fences encroaching on the South (which since colonialism have seen their lands and forests delimitated and turned from common goods into commodities) and which is now experiencing a delimitation of biodiversity and knowledge through intellectual property rights.

Biodiversity has always been a resource possessed and used in common by the inhabitants of a given territory, which generally take into account factors such as sustainability, combining their use with their preservation. The use of nature and the changes that take place in it both because of individual and collective efforts, are considered social and not individual phenomena. Thus, not only biodiversity but its use is a common good, freely exchanged within and among the communities.

Intellectual property, parcelling by the Empire

Innovations have been integrated into that common pool of knowledge on resources, which has been passed on throughout the centuries from generation to generation, and have been adopted for new uses, contributing immensely to the diversity of agricultural crops and medicinal plants existing today in our planet. But the concept of individual property over resources or knowledge - foreign to the producers of this knowledge - promotes the appropriation of indigenous peoples' knowledge, with serious consequences for them and the conservation of biodiversity.

More so, in the era of globalization, common lands are privatized and the power of communities is weakened by a delimitation in which life itself is turned into corporate private property, since the systems of intellectual property rights allow the 'encroachment' of both biodiversity and knowledge and, in law, the corporation is considered the only form of association with legal existence. Intellectual property rights have become the analogy of patents used by colonizers since 1492, when Christopher Columbus established the conquest of non-Christian peoples as a natural right for Europeans. Land deeds issued by the Pope through European monarchs - which were the first patents - for trade entrepreneurs were authorizations to 'discover, find and obtain lands, countries and remote, pagan and barbarian territories, not possessed by any Christian monarch or peoples.' The present possession of biologial diversity and ancestral knowledge is based on the strategy of separating land and biodiversity from any relationship with the peoples that do not belong to the developed world.

Commodities and piracy

The Euro-centered concept of property only considers as investment the use of capital, while it assumes the earnings it produces are the only right in need of protection. When this is applied to biodiversity, this restricted concept becomes a mechanism to deny the intrinsic value of diverse species, as well as the innovations and previous rights of the communities that use them. Based on the belief that knowledge is a product of individual creativity and on a Western system of creation and accumulation of knowledge, the basis of resources is considered - by the Western system - mere 'commodities'. According to this paradigm, intellectual property rights are property rights over products of the mind, therefore knowledge and creativity are so closely linked they ignore the creativity of nature and of non-Western systems of knowledge.

Intellectual property rights have a direct impact on previous rights of communities, since they allow for the appropriation of indigenous knowledge, which through a slight modification comes to be regarded as a Western invention. Thus, the piracy of cumulative innovation carried out by millions of people during thousands of years is accepted through the TRIPs. Countries such as the United States, which holds the largest number of patent applications for indigenous innovations, do not acknowledge the knowledge of other countries as a previous art, allowing for the appropriation - by scientists and businessmen - of biodiversity and other cultures' knowledge.

Those who actually lose

In the strictly economic field, the TRIPs force the economies of the Southern nations to open up to the Northern transnationals, which have pressed to protect intellectual property within the WTO framework 'to avoid great losses of world industry due to the inadequate and inefficient national protection on intellectual property'. However, having not taken into account the contribution of biodiversity from the Third World and the innovation of peasants and tribal peoples, these companies underestimate the scale of Southern losses. Once these contributions are taken into account, the roles are reversed and result, for example, in the United States owing Third World countries 202 million dollars in agriculture royalties and 5.097 billion dollars in pharmaceutical products. Ironically, the companies that created the TRIPs to stop 'piracy', take part in the piracy of biological wealth and the intellectual capital of the Third World on a large scale. Thus Pfizer, Bristol Myers and Merck - which form the IPC - have numerous patents on 'biomaterials' extracted from the Third World without permission and without having paid royalties to the original owners of that biological material.

TRIPs and pandemics

For the Southern countries, the TRIPs imply an

increase of payments for technology - such as royalties and licensing – to transnationals and enable the rise of prices of several products. By restricting competition, the rules on intellectual property rights will allow some companies to increase the prices of their products very much above their costs, and obtain revenues in terms of income and earnings in a monopoly context. The strengthening, and in other cases introduction, of patents, without the obligation of industrially exploiting the invention in the country it is registered (something allowed by the TRIPs, and not by the previous system of patent registration), will probably cause or widen trade deficits resulting from a larger volume and higher prices for imported finished products and/or their active components. This, which is evident in the case of software, can be disastrous for entire cultures in the case of pharmaceutical products, since it gives transnational companies the right to overprice their drugs. This puts those drugs out of reach for many Southern countries, - in Africa, for example - which are the ones that most suffer the HIV/AIDS pandemic and, in the cases that have the resources, are legally banned from producing their own medicines (the production of pharmaceutical articles by national firms would be limited to generic drugs.)

Intellectual property and unsustainability

Most of the developing countries are dependent on the agricultural sector. Although between 80 and 90 per cent of the seeds used in these countries are produced by farmers in an 'informal system of seed supply', the introduction of intellectual property rights in the vegetable realm could replace the better adapted varieties of farmers and reduce the diversity and sustainability of agriculture. For plant varieties, TRIPs do not allow countries to have the option of approving a system of alternative intellectual property protection, sui generis and effective. Also, it increases the threat of banning Third World farmers the traditional practice of storing the seed for the following season - if the seed used is intellectually protected by a company - and of forcing them to buy it each year. ∎

What you see and what you don't: the inner workings of the WTO

The World Trade Organization (WTO) is dominated by a few big industrial countries that negotiate and take decisions behind closed doors. They then attempt to win over selected 'influential' developing countries. This lack of democracy makes the WTO one of the least transparent of international organizations.

In theory, the World Trade Organization (WTO) consists of members that are equal in terms of formal decision-making rights. In reality however many developing countries have been unable to participate fully. Some do not even have a Mission in Geneva, where the WTO is headquartered; other Missions are understaffed and sometimes unable adequately to follow the twists and turns of discussions and negotiations and thus are unable to make an impact. The few officials may also have to cover UN agencies' meetings, they are often absent from those taking place simultaneously in the WTO. Unequal capacity compounds the unequal participation.

This problem of unequal capacity to participate is made more acute by the relative lack of transparency in some key aspects of WTO operations, which in turn has an adverse effect on participation. The WTO has been and remains one of the least transparent of international organizations. The main reason for this is its working methods and system of decision-making. Officially, decisions are made on the basis of 'one country, one vote' and by consensus, thus giving the WTO the appearance of an organization in which decision-making is democratic. Decisions are taken by the General Council (comprising diplomats of member states based in Geneva), or representatives in subsidiary bodies (such as the TRIP's Council or the Agriculture Committee). Major decisions are also made or endorsed by the members' Trade Ministers meeting at the Ministerial Conference, which normally takes place every two years.

The 'Green Room process'

But in practice, the WTO and its predecessor, GATT, have been dominated by a handful of industrial countries. Often, these countries negotiate and make decisions among themselves. Then, in informal meetings, they embark on an exercise of winning over (sometimes through intense pressure) a selected number of developing countries deemed to be more important or influential. Most WTO members may not be invited to these meetings and may not even know that they take place, or what happens there. When agreement is reached among a relatively small group, the decisions are rather easier to pass through the larger body. This process of decision-making by a limited number of countries is referred to in WTO jargon as the 'Green Room process', so named after the color of the room of the Director-General in which many such meetings took place during the GATT 'Uruguay Round' of trade negotiations. In the WTO era, this Green Room process has taken place particularly in the intense period prior to and at Ministerial Conferences, notably the first Ministerial (as they are called) in Singapore and the third Ministerial in Seattle.

The system of decision-making by 'consensus' is also implemented in an odd way. On issues where a majority of developing countries (which make up the bulk of WTO members) may agree, it is said that 'there is no consensus' even if a few developed countries disagree with the majority. The issue concerned is effectively killed or has no chance of being successfully dealt with. However, should the big powers (especially the US, the EU and Japan) agree on a particular issue, while a sizeable number of developing countries disagree and a large number remain silent, the major powers are likely to embark on a process they call 'building a consensus'. In reality, this means wearing down the resistance of the outspoken developing countries until only a few remain 'outside the consensus'. It is then relatively easy to pressure these few also to agree to 'join the consensus'.

No consensus

In 1996, developed countries lobbied very hard to get three topics (investment, competition and government procurement) introduced as new issues for WTO study (and eventual negotiation for agreements). In 1999, in the few months before the Seattle Ministerial Conference to launch a second round of negotiations, the 'Green Room process' was put into effect by the WTO Director-General. Several small groups were set up to discuss various contentious issues, but most countries of the South were not invited to attend. At Seattle itself, again these negotiating groups were set up, each with its own topic. Many developing countries were not invited onto any of the groups. And for those who were, their representatives were often unhappy with the way the meetings were conducted, and how conclusions were sought. Eventually, many countries of the South (especially members of the Africa Group and the Caribbean countries) made clear in statements on the eve of the Conference's closure that they would not join the consensus if a draft Declaration was put forward on the final day. This was a major factor in the collapse of the Seattle meeting, and fuelled the anti-globalization movement. ∎

Source:
The Multilateral Trading System:
A Development Perspective

The world according to...

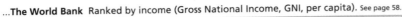

...The World Bank Ranked by income (Gross National Income, GNI, per capita). See page 58.

◼ LOW- INCOME ECONOMIES   ◼ UPPER-MIDDLE- INCOME ECONOMIES   ☐ NO DATA

◼ MIDDLE- INCOME ECONOMIES   ◻ HIGH- INCOME ECONOMIES

...UNDP (UN Development Program) Ranked by Human Development Index. See page 59.

◼ LOW "HUMAN DEVELOPMENT"   ◻ HIGH "HUMAN DEVELOPMENT"

◼ MEDIUM "HUMAN DEVELOPMENT"   ☐ NO DATA

...UNICEF (UN children's agency) Ranked by under-5 mortality rate. See page 36.

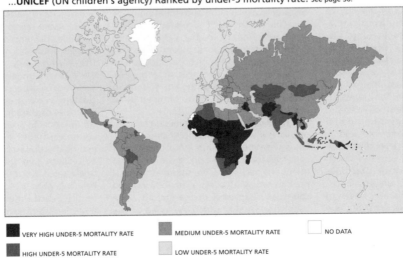

◼ VERY HIGH UNDER-5 MORTALITY RATE   ◼ MEDIUM UNDER-5 MORTALITY RATE   ☐ NO DATA

◼ HIGH UNDER-5 MORTALITY RATE   ◻ LOW UNDER-5 MORTALITY RATE

VI. International Organizations
Directory

UNITED NATIONS
First Avenue between 42nd Street and 48th Street, NY, New York, USA
http://www.un.org

Founded in 1945 by 51 countries after the Second World War, the UN is the legal successor of the League of Nations. The UN is an association of nations which signed the UN Charter, pledging to maintain international peace and security and to cooperate internationally to create the political, economic and social conditions to achieve these goals. The Charter does not authorize the organization to intervene in matters which are strictly the national concern of any state. Currently has 188 member states. Bodies: Security Council is the UN's principal organ for the enforcement of the organization's aims and principles. It is made up of five permanent members (China, France, Russia, United Kingdom and the United States) and 10 members elected by the General Assembly (currently are Bulgaria, Cameroon, Colombia, Guinea, Ireland, Mauritius, Mexico, Norway, Singapore and Syria. The Secretariat - an international staff working in duty stations around the world - carries out the diverse day-to-day work of the Organization. It services the other principal bodies of the United Nations and administers the programmes and policies laid down by them. At its head is the Secretary-General, who is appointed by the General Assembly on the recommendation of the Security Council for a five-year, renewable term. The International Court of Justice is the principal judicial organ of the United Nations. Its seat is at the Peace Palace in The Hague (Netherlands). It began work in 1946. The Court has a dual role: to settle in accordance with international law the legal disputes submitted to it by States, and to give advisory opinions on legal questions referred to it by duly authorized international organs and agencies. The Court is composed of 15 judges elected by the General Assembly and the Security Council; and the Trusteeship Council, created to protect the interests of those peoples who live in non-autonomous territories, that is, colonies placed under the trusteeship of an administrating state. The Trusteeship Council suspended operation on 1 November 1994, with the independence of Palau, the last remaining United Nations trust territory, on 1 October 1994. By a resolution adopted on 25 May 1994, the Council amended its rules of procedure to drop the obligation to meet annually and agreed to meet as occasion required - by its decision or the decision of its President, or at the request of a majority of its members or the General Assembly or the Security Council. The General Assembly is the main deliberative organ of the United Nations. It is composed of representatives of all Member States, each of which has one vote. Decisions on important questions, such as those on peace and security, admission of new members and budgetary matters, require a two-thirds majority. Decisions on other questions are reached by a simple majority. It does not, however, have the power to enforce its decisions. The Economic and Social Council (ECOSOC) was established by the Charter as the principal body, under the authority of the General Assembly, to promote higher standards of living, full employment, and conditions of economic and social progress and development; solutions of international economic, social, health, and related problems; and international cultural and educational cooperation; and universal respect for, and observance of, human rights and fundamental freedoms for all without distinction as to race, sex, language, or religion. The Council has 54 members who serve three-year terms. Voting in the Council is by simple majority; each member has one vote. ■

State and/or Governmental Organizations

AMAZON PACT
Founded July 3, 1978. Member countries: Bolivia, Brazil, Colombia, Ecuador, Guyana, Peru, Suriname and Venezuela. Designed to halt the 'internationalization' of the Amazon Basin and to restrict its exploration and economic exploitation to those countries sharing its territory.

ANDEAN COMMUNITY
Paseo de la República 3895, esq. Aramburú, San Isidro, Lima 27, Perú
http://www.comunidadandina.org
Founded May 25, 1969. Member countries: Bolivia, Ecuador, Peru, Venezuela (founding members), and Colombia (1973). Associate member: Panama. (Chile was a charter member but dropped out in 1976.) A sub-regional economic integration plan, the agreement establishes uniform customs tariffs for all the countries in the area. However, due to the state of crisis which besieged the region during the 1980s, the timetable for trade deregulation and introduction of a common external tariff has not been complied with.

ASIA PACIFIC ECONOMIC COOPERATION (APEC)
http://www.apec.org
Founded in November 7, 1989, established to promote economic integration around the Pacific Rim and to sustain economic growth. Its members are all the ASEAN members plus Aotearoa/New Zealand, Australia, Canada, Chile, China, Hong Kong (China), Japan, Mexico, South Korea, Papua New Guinea, Peru, Russia, Taiwan, USA and Vietnam.

ASSOCIATION OF SOUTHEAST ASIAN NATIONS (ASEAN)
Box 2072 - 70A Jalan Sisingamangaraja, Jakarta 12011, Indonesia
http://www.aseansec.org
Founded in 1967. Member countries: Brunei, Cambodia, Indonesia, Laos, Malaysia, Burma/Myanmar, Philippines, Singapore, Thailand and Vietnam. Its aim is 'to accelerate the economic growth, social progress and cultural development in the region through joint endeavors in the spirit of equality and partnership in order to strengthen the foundation for a prosperous and peaceful community of South-East Asian Nations.' (Bangkok Declaration, 1967).

BRITISH COMMONWEALTH
Marlborough House, Pall Mall, London, United Kingdom
http://thecommonwealth.org
Founded on December 31 1931. The British Commonwealth originated with the breakup of the British Empire. Member countries: the United Kingdom, Antigua and Barbuda, Australia, Bahamas, Bangladesh, Barbados, Belize, Botswana, Brunei Darussalam, Cameroon, Canada, Cyprus, Dominica, Fiji, Gambia, Ghana, Grenada, Guyana, India, Jamaica, Kenya, Kiribati, Lesotho, Malawi, Malaysia, Maldives, Malta, Mauritius, Mozambique, Namibia, Nauru, New Zealand/Aotearoa, Nigeria, Pakistan, Papua New Guinea, Samoa, Seychelles, Sierra Leone, Singapore, Solomon Islands, South Africa, Sri Lanka, St Kitts-Nevis, St Lucia, St Vincent and the Grenadines, Swaziland, Tanzania, Tonga, Trinidad and Tobago, Tuvalu, Uganda, Vanuatu, Zambia and Zimbabwe. The Commonwealth operates through informal meetings of heads of state and government, at which resolutions are reached by consensus. Queen Elizabeth II is seen as a symbol of association by all member countries and as the Commonwealth's highest authority, though she wields no legal power among them. She is also acknowledged as the formal head of state in Aotearoa (New Zealand), Australia, Bahamas, Barbados, Canada, Fiji, Grenada, Jamaica, Kiribati, Mauritius, Papua New Guinea, Solomon Islands and Tuvalu.

CARIBBEAN COMMUNITY AND COMMON MARKET (CARICOM)
Secretariat, P.O. Box 10827, Avenue of the Republic, Georgetown, Guyana
http://www.caricom.org
Founded in July 4,1973, to replace the Caribbean Free Trade Association (CARIFTA), founded in September 1966. Member countries: Antigua and Barbuda, Barbados and Guyana (charter members), Bahamas (member of the Community but not the Common Market), Belize, Haiti (full member in the near future), Dominica, Grenada, Jamaica, Montserrat, St Lucia, St Vincent and the Grenadines, St Kitts-Nevis, Suriname and Trinidad and Tobago. Associated states: Anguilla, British Virgin Islands and Turks and Caicos Islands. The free-trade zone was converted into a regional common market, on August 1st, 1973. Although CARICOM managed to increase intra-regional trade, the insular nature of the member States' economies, as well as their bilateral relations with countries outside the region, have prevented further progress. The aim is 'the attainment of a viable, internationally competitive and sustainable Community, with improved quality of life for all.'

COMMONWEALTH OF INDEPENDENT STATES (CIS)
Minsk, Belarus
http://www.cis.minsk.by
Founded in December 1991. Member states: Armenia,

Azerbaijan, Belarus, Georgia, Kazakhstan, Kyrgyzstan, Moldova, Russia, Tajikistan, Turkmenistan, Ukraine and Uzbekistan. Its aims are to maintain under new basis the economic, political and military relations of the republics of the former Soviet Union.

ECONOMIC COMMUNITY OF WEST AFRICAN STATES (ECOWAS)
Ouagadougou, Burkina Faso
http://www.ecowas.int

Founded on May 30, 1975. Member countries: Benin, Burkina Faso, Cape Verde, Côte d'Ivoire, Gambia, Ghana, Guinea-Bissau, Liberia, Mali, Mauritania, Niger, Nigeria, Senegal, Sierra Leone, Togo. Its aim is to lay the foundations for the economic integration of its member states.

EUROPEAN UNION
Rue de la Loi 200, B-1049, Brussels, Belgium
http://europa.eu.int

The idea of a united Europe first emerged in 1950. The European Union went into effect on January 1 1995, replacing the European Community that had been set up in 1967. Its key institutions are the Council of Ministers, the European Commission, the European Parliament, the Court of Justice and the European Council. Member countries: Belgium, France, Germany, The Netherlands, Italy and Luxembourg (charter members); Denmark, Ireland and the United Kingdom (since 1973); Greece (since 1981); Spain and Portugal (since 1986). In February 1992, in Maastricht, The Netherlands, the heads of state and of government of what was then the European Community ('The Twelve') signed treaties for political and monetary integration, leading to the formation of the European Union/EU. These treaties were ratified by referendum or by the parliaments of all the members of the EC, a process which was completed in mid-1994. That same year, treaties were signed admitting four countries: Austria, Finland, Norway and Sweden, but Norwegians rejected membership in a referendum. Further enlargement negotiations began in 1996 with some other countries. Turkey, Malta, Cyprus, Hungary and Poland have all applied for membership officially. Bulgaria, the Czech Republic, Estonia, Hungary, Latvia, Lithuania, Poland, Romania and Slovakia are invited as new candidate members to one meeting of the European Council every year. At the beginning of 2002, Euro coins and notes became legal tender and national currencies will become obsolete. Britain, Sweden and Denmark still use their own currencies.

GROUP OF 15 (G15)
54-56, rue de Montbrillant, case postale 2403, 1211 Geneva 2, Switzerland
http://www.sibexlink.com.my/g15

Established during the Ninth-Non-Aligned Summit in Belgrade in September 1989. Member countries: Algeria, Argentina, Brazil, Chile, Colombia, Egypt, India, Indonesia, Iran, Jamaica, Kenya, Malaysia, Mexico, Nigeria, Peru, Senegal, Sri Lanka and Venezuela, Yugoslavia, and Zimbabwe. Its aim is to harness the considerable potential for greater and mutually beneficial cooperation among developing countries and to serve as a forum for regular consultations among developing countries with a view to coordinating policies and actions.

GROUP OF SEVEN (G-7)
Founded in 1975, the first summit was held in France inaugurated by President Giscard of France and Chancellor Schmidt of Germany. Currently it brings together the world's seven most industrialized countries: Germany, Canada, US, France, Italy, Japan and the UK. Its initial goal was to coordinate economic, financial and trade policies, but in fact G-7 summit conferences dealt with all major international issues

(like arms, energy, foreign debt, technology. After the events of September 11 2001 in the US, G-8* leaders requested that their relevant Ministers develop measures to fight terrorism.

*In 1994, Russia was invited to participate in the Group of 7's meetings and the 1998 Birmingham Summit saw full Russian participation, giving birth to the G-8.

GROUP OF 77 (G-77)
http://www.g77.org

Established in June 1964 by seventy-seven Third World countries signatories of the Joint Declaration of the Seventy-Seven Countries issued at the end of the first session of the United Nations Conference on Trade and Development (UNCTAD) in Geneva. This resolution was to challenge the industrialized nations to be able to participate more equitably in world trade, dominated by the wealthy countries. In 2002, this association had 133 members.

INTER-PARLIAMENTARY UNION (IPU)
Place du Petit-Saconnex, 1209 Geneva, Switzerland
http://www.ipu.org

Founded in 1889 to promote 'world-wide parliamentary dialogue and works for peace and co-operation among peoples and for the firm establishment of representative democracy'. It holds a yearly Inter-Parliamentary Conference with representatives from the 142 national parliamentary groups affiliated with the Union.

LATIN AMERICAN ECONOMIC SYSTEM (SELA)
Av. Fr. de Miranda, Torre Europa, P. 4, Urb. Campo Alegre, Caracas 1060, Venezuela
http://sela2.sela.org

Founded in October 1975. Member countries: 28 Latin American and Caribbean states. Its aims are to promote a consultative and coordination system to agree common economic policies to improve cooperation between member countries.

LATIN AMERICAN INTEGRATION ASSOCIATION (ALADI)
Cebollatí 1461, Casilla de Correo 577, Montevideo, Uruguay
http://www.aladi.org

Founded in 1980 to replace the Latin American Free Trade Association (ALALC), created in 1962. Member countries: Argentina, Bolivia, Brazil, Colombia, Chile, Cuba, Ecuador, Mexico, Paraguay, Peru, Uruguay and Venezuela. ALADI establishes a regional, preferential tariff system and provides mechanisms for agreements to be made on a regional basis.

LATIN AMERICAN PARLIAMENT (PARLAMENTO LATINOAMERICANO)
Av. Auro Soares de Moura Andrade, n° 564, Barra Funda, São Paulo 01154-060, SP, Brazil
http://www.parlatino.org.br

Founded in 1965. Its purpose is to 'promote, harmonize and channel the movement towards the economic, political and cultural integration of Latin America'. In the period of the region's military dictatorships, the Latin American Parliament became a forum for reports of violations of human rights and granted membership to representatives of parliaments dissolved by these dictatorships. Member parliaments: Argentina, Aruba, Bolivia, Brazil, Chile, Colombia Costa Rica, Cuba, Dominican Republic, Ecuador, El Salvador, Guatemala, Honduras, Mexico, Netherlands Antilles, Nicaragua, Panama, Paraguay, Suriname, Uruguay and Venezuela.

LEAGUE OF ARAB STATES
www.leagueofarabstates.org

Founded March 22 1945. Member countries: Algeria, Bahrain, Comoros, Djibouti, Egypt, Iraq, Jordan, Kuwait,

Lebanon, Libya, Morocco, Mauritania, Oman, Palestine, Qatar, Saudi Arabia, Syria, Somalia, Sudan, Tunisia, United Arab Emirates and Yemen. The League's objectives include closer cooperation between member states and the coordination of their political action. It promotes close mutual understanding in economic, financial, trade, aviation, postal, telecommunication, sanitation, cultural and legal matters. The League created the Arab Bank for Economic Development in Africa (ABEDA-Sharaa el Baladia, PO Box 2640, Khartoum, Sudan) in 1973 with the purpose to finance development projects in sub-Saharan Africa and the Arab Monetary Fund (AMF-Box 2818, Abu Dhabi, United Arab Emirates) in 1976. 21 member countries. It is a regional financial institution with independent legal status. Its aim is to correct inequalities in the balances of payments of member states and to promote trade among them.

SOUTH CENTER
17-19 Chemin du Champ d'Anier 17, 1209 Petit Saconnex, Geneva, Switzerland
http://www.southcentre.org

Established July 30 1995. Evolved from the South Commission (founded in 1987), its aim is to give support to Third World countries' cooperation and to strengthen their capacity in North-South negotiations. Members: Algeria, Angola, Benin, Bolivia, Brazil, Burundi, Cambodia, Cape Verde, China, Colombia, Côte d'Ivoire, Cuba, North Korea, Egypt, Ghana, Guyana, Honduras, India, Indonesia, Iran, Jamaica, Jordan, Libya, Malawi, Malaysia, Mali, Micronesia, Morocco, Mozambique, Namibia, Nigeria, Pakistan, Panama, Philippines, Seychelles, Sierra Leone, South Africa, Sri Lanka, Sudan, Suriname, Uganda, Tanzania, Vietnam, Yugoslavia and Zimbabwe.

THE LOMÉ CONVENTIONS
Maison des ACP, Av. Georges Henri 451, 1040 Brussels, Belgium

The Lomé Conventions are agreements between the European Economic Community (EEC) and 78 African, Caribbean and Pacific (ACP) states on aid, trade and political cooperation, signed on February 28, 1975 and July 31, 1979 in Lomé, Togo. For the African countries, the Lomé Conventions replace the Arusha Agreement of 1968 and the Yaoundé Conventions of 1969. Unlike other similar agreements, the Lomé Conventions do not compel ACP countries to adhere to mutual preferences in their trade relations, requiring only that they apply the "most favored nation" clause. Under the Lomé Conventions, a free trade zone was established for all industrial products and for 96 percent of all agricultural products. In addition, the agreements established a system for stabilizing the exchange of exports, financial aid and technical cooperation, between members.

MERCOSUR (COMMON MARKET OF THE SOUTH)
Secretariat, Parque Hotel, Piera 1992, Montevideo, Uruguay
http://www.mercosur.org.uy

Founded on March 26 1991 by Argentina, Brazil, Paraguay and Uruguay, with the aim of establishing an economically integrated zone in which goods and services will circulate freely. In mid-1994 the four governments readjusted the timetable announced in 1991 in order for the common external tariff to go into effect in 2001. Chile and Bolivia effected a cooperation agreement with Mercosur, though not joining it as full members.

NON-ALIGNED MOVEMENT (NAM)
http://www.nam.gov.za

Founded in Belgrade, Yugoslavia in 1961, by 25 countries not identified with the blocs involved in the East-West conflict, to promote decolonization, disarmament, self-determination and to deter the use of force to resolve international controversies. At the 10th Summit, held in 1992 in Jakarta, Indonesia, the Non-Aligned Movement initiated a reformulation of its objectives, as a result of the new international situation. A series of conflicts between some member States, as well as the withdrawal of other countries, such as Argentina, have debilitated the Movement. Country members: 113 and 17 observers of the Movement.

NORTH AMERICAN FREE TRADE ASSOCIATION (NAFTA)
Mexican Section: Bv. A.López Mateos 3025, 2oP, Col.Héroes de Padierna, 10700, Mexico, D.F. Mexico
Canadian Section: 90 Sparks Street, Suite 705, Ottawa, Ontario, K1P 5B4, Canada
US Section: 14th Street & Constitution Av N.W. Room 2061, Washington, D.C. 20230, USA
http://www.nafta-sec-alena.org
In February 1991, the governments of Canada, Mexico and the US signed this agreement in order to create a free trade and economic integration zone in North America. There was opposition to the Agreement from both union and ecological quarters, especially in the US, which faced the threat of the loss of millions of jobs, due to the wage differential between that country and Mexico. The three countries created the North American Development Bank with funds totaling more than $3 billion.

ORGANIZATION FOR ECONOMIC COOPERATION AND DEVELOPMENT (OECD)
Chatêau de la Muette, 2 rue André Pascal, 75775 Paris Cedex 16, France
http://www.oecd.org
Founded December 14 1960, to replace the Organization for European Economic Cooperation (OEEC), established in 1948. Member countries: Aotearoa/New Zealand, Australia, Austria, Belgium, Canada, Czech Republic, Denmark, Finland, France, Germany, Greece, Hungary, Iceland, Ireland, Italy, Japan, South Korea, Luxembourg, Mexico, Netherlands, Norway, Poland, Portugal, Slovakia, Spain, Sweden, Switzerland, Turkey, UK and US. Its aim is to assist member governments in the formulation of their economic and social policies and coordinate the joint positions of the western capitalist nations.

AFRICAN UNION (AU)
http://www.africa-union.org
Founded in July 2002 with the aims of attracting foreign investment and spreading democracy in Africa, creating an African peacekeeping force. Its ultimate aim is to create a single African parliament, court of justice and central bank. It replaced the Organization of African Unity (OAU)

ORGANIZATION OF AMERICAN STATES (OAS)
17th Street and Constitution Avenue, NW, Washington DC 20006, USA
http://www.oas.org
Founded in May 1948, its charter went into effect in December 1951. The OAS replaced the Pan-American Union created in the 19th century. The charter was signed by 21 countries; Cuba was expelled in 1962. Currently 35 countries make up the organization that was created under the aegis of the US, which managed to mold the organization to suit Washington's policies in Latin American.

Financial Organizations

AFRICAN DEVELOPMENT BANK (AFDB)
1387, Abidjan, Côte d'Ivoire
http://www.afdb.org

Founded in November 1964. Member countries: 53 African countries and 24 non-regional countries. The bank was created on the initiative of the UN Economic Commission for Africa with the support of the Conference of African Heads of State and Government held in Addis Ababa in 1963. The Bank's mission is to 'contribute to the economic development and social progress of its regional members - individually and jointly'.

ASIAN DEVELOPMENT BANK (ASDB)
6 ADB Avenue, 0401 Mandaluyong City, Philippines
http://www.adb.org
Founded in 1966. It is currently made up of 61 countries of the region, as well as 17 non-Asian states. AsDB is a multilateral development finance institution dedicated to reducing poverty in Asia and the Pacific. Japan exerts a dominant influence within the Bank.

INTER-AMERICAN DEVELOPMENT BANK (IDB)
17th Street, NW, Washington, DC 20577, USA
http://www.iadb.org
Founded in December 1959. Member countries: all member states of the Organization of American States (OAS). The IDB's primary aim is to provide credits for infrastructure development projects and technical assistance in member countries. The US government is the main contributor to the bank's funds. Since 1976, non-American States may also be members of the IDB.

INTERNATIONAL MONETARY FUND (IMF)
Washington DC, USA
http://www.imf.org
A specialized agency of the UN, the IMF was created in 1944 by the Bretton Woods Accords. Its aim is to improve the international system of payments. It offers lines of credit to governments, subject to certain commitments in their economic and fiscal policies. Voting power in the IMF's decision-making process is determined by the member country's contribution of capital, which means that its policies are controlled by the world's richest nations. The IMF currently has 183 member States.

WORLD BANK (WB-IBRD)
Washington, DC, USA
http://www.worldbank.org
A specialized agency of the UN, the International Bank for Reconstruction and Development (IBRD) was created in 1944 by the Bretton Woods Accords. Its goals are to promote international trade and economic development by means of loans and technical assistance. Member countries: 183. Voting power (in the Bank's decisions) is determined by each country's contribution of capital to the Bank's funds, which in essence means that the Bank is controlled by the world's richest countries. Russia and 12 other republics belonging to the former Soviet Union joined on June 1 1992. WB group complementary organizations: the International Development Association (IDA), founded in 1960; the International Financial Corporation (IFC), created in 1956; and the Multilateral Investment Guarantee Agency (MIGA), which was established in 1985 and is autonomous with relation to the IBRD.

WORLD TRADE ORGANIZATION (WTO)
Rue de Lausanne 154, CH 1211, Geneva, Switzerland
http://www.wto.org
Created in 1994 to replace the General Agreement on Tariffs and Trade (GATT). Established on 1 January 1995, is the legal and institutional foundation of the multilateral trading system. WTO is a government-to-government organization. Member countries: 144. WTO members have agreed to enter into 'reciprocal and mutually advantageous arrangements directed to the

substantial reduction of tariffs and other barriers to trade and to the elimination of discriminatory treatment in international trade relations.' In fact, the implementation of WTO agreements and its mechanisms has shown that it is slanted in favor of big multinationals and global capital.

Military Organizations

THE INTER-AMERICAN TREATY OF RECIPROCAL ASSISTANCE (TIAR)
http://www.oas.org/juridico/english/Treaties/b-29.html
Founded in 1947 (in force in 1948) by the governments of American countries, it is also known as the Rio de Janeiro Treaty. Member countries: 35. Its original aim was to combat 'external threats', although it became increasingly concerned with halting 'subversion'. During the Falklands/Malvinas war in 1982, Argentina attempted to invoke the treaty against the UK, but the initiative was vetoed by the US. It was also invoked after September11 attacks in US in 2001: The Inter-American Treaty of Reciprocal Assistance states that 'an armed attack on one member is to be considered an attack on all' (Article 3.1).

NORTH ATLANTIC TREATY ORGANIZATION (NATO)
Brussels, Belgium
http://www.nato.int
Created April 4 1949. Its current members are: Belgium, Canada, Czech Republic, Denmark, France, Germany, Greece, Hungary, Iceland, Italy, Luxembourg, the Netherlands, Norway, Poland, Portugal, Spain, Turkey, UK and the US, plus 27 partner countries. NATO is currently promoting the incorporation of the countries of eastern and southeastern Europe - members of the defunct Warsaw Pact - although not as full members. NATO, and especially the armed forces of the US, France and Britain, has intervened in increasingly open fashion, in conflicts beyond the North Atlantic region which NATO was originally created to defend (such as Bosnia-Herzegovina, Kosovo and Afghanistan), acting more like a global police force, defending common interests, not territories. On 27 May 1997, Russia's President, Boris Yelstin, the then NATO Secretary-General, Javier Solana, and NATO Heads of State and Government signed the Founding Act on Mutual Relations, Cooperation and Security between NATO and the Russian Federation. The Founding Act acknowledged that NATO and Russia were no longer adversaries and marked the beginning of a new era in their relations. A new Summit meeting of NATO and Russia was held in Rome on 28 May 2002.

Non-Governmental Organizations (NGOs)

AMAZON BASIN INDIGENOUS ORGANIZATIONS COORDINATING COMMITTEE (COICA)
http://www.coica.org
Founded in Lima Peru in March 1984 by national indigenous organizations. Current member organizations: CIDOB (Bolivia), COIAB (Brazil), OPIAC (Colombia), CONFENIAE (Ecuador), FOAG (French Guiana), APA (Guyana), AIDESEP (Peru), OIS (Suriname) and CONIVE (Venezuela). Its aim is to strengthen local organizations and ties among indigenous peoples, in their struggle to defend their rights and their native lands. COICA is authorized to represent its members in international forums, before governments and intergovernmental organizations.

AMNESTY INTERNATIONAL (AI)
1 Easton Street, London, WC1X 8DJ, United Kingdom
http://www.amnesty.org

Founded in 1961, Amnesty International is a worldwide campaigning movement that works to promote all the human rights enshrined in the Universal Declaration of Human Rights and other internationally recognized human rights agreements. In particular, Amnesty International campaigns to free all prisoners of conscience; ensure fair and prompt trials for political prisoners; abolish the death penalty, torture and other cruel treatment of prisoners; and end political killings and 'disappearances'. AI has an active worldwide membership with more than 1,000,000 individual members, subscribers and supporters in over 140 countries and territories.

ATTAC (ASSOCIATION FOR THE TAXATION OF FINANCIAL TRANSACTIONS FOR THE AID OF CITIZENS)
International Office of Secretary, 6 rue Pinel, 75013, Paris, France
http://attac.org/ang/presentation.htm
Founded in France in 1998, now has about 40,000 members. It is an international network of independent national and local groups in more than 40 countries. It promotes the idea of an international tax on currency speculation (the Tobin Tax) and campaigns to outlaw tax havens, replace pension funds with state pensions, cancel Third World debt, reform or abolish the World Trade Organization (WTO) and recapture the democratic space that has been lost to the financial world.

FOCUS ON THE GLOBAL SOUTH
CUSRI, Chulalongkorn University, Wisit Prachuabmoh Building, Bangkok 10330, Thailand
http://www.focusweb.org
Bangkok-based research and advocacy group with wide-ranging contacts throughout the South. Focus aims to consciously and consistently articulate, link and develop greater coherence between local community-based and national, regional and global paradigms of change. Focus strives to create a distinct and cogent link between development at the grassroots and the "macro" levels.

INTERNATIONAL ALLIANCE OF THE INDIGENOUS-TRIBAL PEOPLES OF THE TROPICAL FORESTS
International Technical Secretariat, 14 Rudolf Place, Miles Street, London, SW8 1RP, England
http://iiaip.gn.apc.org
Founded in February 1992, in Penang, Malaysia, by 29 representatives of indigenous peoples of Asia, Africa and Latin America, with the aim of combating the destruction of their ancestral lands, defending their rights and presenting their case before international agencies involved in drawing up policies related to the tropical forests.

MÉDECINS SANS FRONTIÈRES (MSF)
8, rue Saint Sabin, 75011 Paris, France
http://www.msf.org
MSF is an international humanitarian aid organization created in 1971 in Paris by a group of doctors and journalists. MSF provides emergency medical assistance to populations in danger in more than 80 countries where health structures are insufficient or even non-existent. MSF has offices in 18 countries.

TRANSPARENCY INTERNATIONAL (TI)
International Secretariat, Otto-Suhr-Allee 97/99, 10585 Berlin, Germany
http://www.transparency.org
Founded in May 1993 as a global coalition against corruption. TI, through its International Secretariat and more than 80 independent national chapters around the world, works at both the national and international level to curb both the supply and demand of corruption. In an effort to make long-term gains against corruption, TI focuses on prevention and reforming systems, not in individual cases. TI annually publishes the Corruption Perception Index and the Bribe Payers Index.

WOMEN'S WORLD BANKING (WWB)
8 West 40th Street, 9th Floor, New York, NY 10018, USA
http://www.swwb.org
Established in 1980, WWB is the network of over 40 financial institutions in 34 countries managed by women. It provides lending, savings and/or business development services to hundreds of thousands of low income women entrepreneurs. Its aim is to increase the participation of women in the corporate world and in economic development.

Ecological Organizations

EARTH ACTION
5 Church Street, Wye, Kent, TN25 5BN, United Kingdom
http://www.earthaction.org
Created in 1992 Earth Summit (Rio de Janeiro). Its goal is to mobilize growing numbers of people around the world to press their governments (or sometimes corporations) for stronger action to solve global problems: environmental degradation, poverty, war and the abuse of human rights. Partners: 1,900 organizations in 161 countries. Around 1,000 of these groups are located in the Southern hemisphere.

ENVIRONMENT LIAISON CENTER INTERNATIONAL (ELCI)
Box 72461, Nairobi, Kenya
http://www.unep.org/unep/partners/global/elci/
Founded in 1975 in Nairobi as Environment Liaison Center. In 1987 changed to the current name. Is a global network of non-governmental organizations (NGOs) and community-based groups. Its aims are to facilitate the voice of the grassroots by: fostering communication and sharing information and skills between groups working at the grassroots level; developing mechanisms for greater and more effective communication between the NGO/grassroots sector and the governmental/intergovernmental sector; maintaining close contact with the United Nations Environment Program. Members: 850 organizations in 103.

FRIENDS OF THE EARTH (FOE)
26-28 Underwood Street, N1 7JQ, London, United Kingdom
http://www.foe.co.uk
Originally a Dutch organization, FoE is an international network that coordinates 68 environmental groups in the world. Its aim is to support policies and develop courses of action in defense of the environment, persuading governments, corporations or international agencies to change their programs and their plans or operations.

GREENPEACE INTERNATIONAL
Keizersgracht 176, 1016 DW Amsterdam, Netherlands
http://www.greenpeace.org
Founded in 1971. Its aims are to identify human activities that can affect the ecological balance, and to carry out campaigns in defense of the environment. It is a staunch protector of Antarctica, and has proposed that an 'international park' be created there. It operates in 40 countries, complemented by autonomous local organizations.

INTERNATIONAL FEDERATION OF ENVIRONMENTAL JOURNALISTS (IFEJ)
Grande Rue, Pierre d'Angle, F-26400 Beaufort sur Gervanne, France
http://www.ifej.org
Founded in October 1993 in Dresden Germany. IFEJ has members (individual members or national journalists' organizations) in 90 countries. The Federation's goal is the diffusion, through all forms, of exact information free from any pressures, in the fields of ecology, environmental management, nature conservation and sustainable development.

INTERGOVERNMENTAL PANEL ON CLIMATE CHANGE (IPCC)
World Meteorological Organization Building, 7bis Avenue de la Paix, CP 2300, CH-211 Geneva 2, Switzerland
http://www.ipcc.ch
Established in 1988. It is open to all members of the United Nations Environment Programme (UNEP) and World Meteorological Organization (WMO). Recognizing the problem of potential global climate change, the role of the IPCC is to assess the scientific, technical and socio-economic information relevant for the understanding of the risk of human-induced climate change. It does not carry out research nor does it monitor climate related data or other relevant parameters. It bases its assessment mainly on peer-reviewed and published scientific/technical literature. The Panel meets in plenary sessions about once a year. Its Second Assessment Report, Climate Change 1995, provided key input to the negotiations, which led to the adoption of the Kyoto Protocol in 1997.

UNITED NATIONS ENVIRONMENT PROGRAMME (UNEP)
United Nations Av, Gigiri, PO.Box 30552, Nairobi, Kenya
www.unep.org
Its mission is to provide leadership and encourage partnership in caring for the environment by inspiring, informing, and enabling nations and peoples to improve their quality of life without compromising that of future generations. In this, it makes a particular effort to nurture partnerships with other UN bodies possessing complementary skills and delivery capabilities and enhancing the participation of civil society - the private sector, scientific community, NGOs, youth, women, and sports organizations in the achievement of sustainable development.

WORLD RAINFOREST MOVEMENT (WRM)
International Secretariat, Maldonado 1858, 11200 Montevideo, Uruguay
http://www.wrm.org.uy
Established in 1986. The WRM is an international network of citizens' groups of North and South involved in efforts to defend the world's rainforests. It works to secure the lands and livelihoods of forest peoples and supports their efforts to defend the forests from commercial logging, dams, mining, plantations, shrimp farms, colonization, settlement and other projects that threaten them.

WORLDWIDE FUND FOR NATURE (WWF)
Avenue du Mont-Blanc, CH-1196 Gland, Switzerland
http://www.panda.org
World Wildlife Fund was founded in 1961. In 1989 changed its name to the Worldwide Fund for Nature. Originally concerned with the preservation of wildlife and natural habitats, current WWF aims are to conserve the world's biological diversity, ensure that the use of renewable natural resources is sustainable and tp promote the reduction of pollution and wasteful consumption. It coordinates 26 national organizations, 22 Program Offices and 5 Associates.

Countries of the world

Albania

Population: 3,164,000 (2002)
Land area: 27,400 SQ KM
Capital: Tirana (Tiranë)
Currency: New lek
Language: Albanian

Shqipëria

The Albanians are descendants of the ancient Illyrians, an Indo-European people who had migrated southward from Central Europe to the north of Greece by the beginning of the Iron Age. The southern Illyrians were much in contact with Greek colonies, while the northern Albanian tribes were united at various times under local kings. The most important of them was Argon, whose kingdom (second half of the 3rd century BC) expanded from Dalmatia in the north to the Vijose river in the south.

[2] By the year 168 BC the Romans conquered all of Illyria and then the Albanians became part of the prosperous Roman province of Illyricum. After 395 AD, with the decline of the Roman Empire, the area was administered from Constantinople (now Istanbul). Despite the Hun incursions during the 3rd to 5th centuries, and the Slavic invasions during the 6th and 7th centuries, the Albanians were one of the few peoples in the Balkans who kept their own language and customs. The passage of the years, the impact of the Roman, Byzantine and Slavic influences changed the old Illyrian culture into the new Albanian one. Between the 8th and 11th centuries AD, even the name of Illyria changed to Albania. When the Christian Church split in 1054, southern Albania maintained links with Constantinople, whilst the north fell under Roman jurisdiction, marking the first significant religious fragmentation of the country.

[3] When the Turks invaded in 1431, the Albanians put up stiff resistance, finally being occupied 47 years later. In the years that followed, the Ottoman Turks imposed Islam upon the country, and they kept up the Islamic pressure over the following century. By the early 18th century, two-thirds of the Albanian population had converted to Islam. More than 25 of the great Viziers of Turkey were of Albanian origin.

[4] The ideologists of the nationalist movement of the 19th century made great efforts to overcome the religious divisions and encourage national unity, adopting the slogan 'The religion of the Albanians is Albania'. The Albanian League - which had both political and cultural aims - was founded in 1878 in the Kosovan town of Pritzen. The League tried without success to bring the Albanian territories of Kosovo, Monastir, Shkodër and Jänina together as a single state within the framework of the Ottoman Empire. On a cultural front, the League worked hard to promote the language, literature and educational system which would foster nationalism.

[5] The Empire suppressed the League in 1881. In 1908, Albanian leaders met in Monastir (now in Macedonia) and adopted a national alphabet based mainly on Latin, which supplanted the Arabic and Greek versions that had been in use. Also that year, the 'Young Turks' who took power in Istanbul ignored their promises of bringing in democratic reforms and guaranteeing Albanian autonomy, which led to three years of armed conflict. Turkey finally accepted the Albanian demands in 1912, and independence was declared.

[6] Due to pressure from Albania's neighbors, the European powers ceded Kosovo and Serbia when drawing up the borders of the new country, allowing Greece the bulk of Sameria and a portion of Epirus. Half the Albanian population and territory was left beyond the Albanian borders.

[7] The international powers appointed German prince Wilhelm zu Wield as King of Albania. He arrived in the new nation in March 1914 but his lack of familiarity with the Albanians and the outset of World War I forced him to abandon the country six months later. During the War, Albania was occupied by the Austro-Hungarian, French, Italian, Greek, Montenegran and Serbian armies, and when the War ended the country would have disappeared had not US President Woodrow Wilson vetoed a plan by France, Britain and Italy, to divide the territory amongst its neighbors.

[8] A national congress, established in January 1920, set the bases for a new government. In December that year, Albania was admitted to the League of Nations. In 1927, Ahmed Zogu, who had become president in 1925, signed a treaty with Italy's leader Mussolini, turning the country into a virtual Italian protectorate. A year later, Zogu proclaimed the country a monarchy.

[9] In April 1939, Italy occupied and formally annexed Albania to the kingdom of Victor Emmanuel III. The Communists, under the leadership of Enver Hoxha, organized guerrilla resistance and a wide anti-Fascist front, receiving support from the Allies during World War II. The occupation forces withdrew on November 29 1944, and the People's Republic was declared on January 11 1945, with Hoxha at the helm.

[10] Despite its desire for independence, Albania matched its internal options to external events. When the neighboring Yugoslavian leader Tito and the Soviet Union's Joseph Stalin split in 1948 (see Yugoslavia), the Albanian Workers' Party sided with the KOMINFORM (communist parties allied with the Soviet Union). Albania broke with Moscow after the 'de-Stalinization' of the early 1960s. It established close ties with the People's Republic of China, with which it eventually broke in 1981, when the Cultural Revolution came to an end and the Maoists fell from power.

[11] The break with China became official at the Eighth Workers' Party Congress, where a party line was put forth 'against US imperialism, Soviet socialist-imperialism, Chinese and Yugoslavian revisionism, Euro-Communism and social democracy', whilst condemning the policies of non-alignment and European detente, as set out in the Helsinki accords.

[12] Until Albania's liberation from Italian Fascist occupation in 1944, 85 per cent of the population lived in the countryside, and 53 per cent lacked even a patch to grow their own vegetables. In 1967 collective farming was established. In 1977, Albania proclaimed self-sufficiency in wheat. According to official figures, between 1939 and 1992 industrial output increased over 100-fold, materials 250 times over, and electricity more than 300-fold.

[13] In 1989, Ramiz Alia, - head of state since Hoxha's death in April 1985 - initiated a process aimed at improving the economy, and breaking the country's international isolation. Border immigration procedures were simplified to encourage tourism and talks were initiated with the aim of resuming relations with both the US and the USSR. In addition, freedom of religion was declared; capital punishment was abolished for women and the number of crimes punishable by death was reduced from 34 to 11. Guidelines were established in the area of civil rights allowing home ownership, opening up to foreign investment and the

election of company directors by secret ballot.

[14] In February 1990, amnesty was granted to political and common prisoners. In November, Alia also announced that the constitution, in effect since 1976, would be revised. In December, independent political parties were authorized and general elections were announced - the first after 46 years of communist rule.

[15] The election had to be postponed due to the instability produced by a mass exodus of thousands of Albanians to Italy. However on 31 March almost 2 million voters chose from among one thousand candidates from 11 political parties, under the scrutiny of about 100 international observers and more than 250 foreign journalists. Amidst accusations of fraud the Communists won 156 of the 250 parliamentary seats.

[16] In May 1991, more than 300,000 workers went on strike demanding the resignation of the communist government, and also a 50 per cent salary increase. Prime Minister Fatos Nano dissolved his cabinet to form an alliance with the opposition. With a state of economic collapse in the country, the parliamentary elections of March 1992 gave the Democratic Party (DP) a spectacular triumph (65.6 per cent) over the Socialist Party (SP, 22.6 per cent). But 80 per cent of the two million voters abstained.

[17] In May, Sali Berisha, leader of the DP, replaced Ramiz Alia as president.

He won the parliamentary vote 96 to 35, becoming the first non-Marxist president since the end of World War II. The following year, the Government began trials of the main political figures of the previous regime. Naxhmija Hoxha, widow of the autocratic communist leader Enver Hoxha, ex-President Ramiz Alia and ex-Premier Fatos Nano among others, were sent to prison convicted of misuse of public funds.

[18] Throughout 1995 and 1996, various media complained of censorship and intimidation, and relations amongst the political parties remained difficult. The so-called Verification Bill allowed for government discretion on assigning certain public posts, in accordance with the reports of the Sigurimi, the communist regime's secret police. The Bill on Genocide and Communist Crimes barred notorious ex-political leaders from public office until the year 2002, and the new electoral law disallowed coalitions amongst the smaller parties.

[19] The parliamentary elections of 1996 took place but the main opposition leaders were not allowed to participate. The DP won 122 out of the 140 seats. In the following months, the legitimacy of the elections was challenged by the opposition, the US and several European countries interested in investing in Albania. In response to a recommendation by the European Council, Parliament formed an ad hoc commission to investigate

the accusations, particularly the violence against opposition leaders.

[20] In late January 1997, the collapse of a series of investment pyramid funds, guaranteed by the State, led to a bloody social and political uprising. One in six Albanians was left penniless and the biggest cities, including Tirana, rose in arms. This situation caused the virtual disintegration of the Albanian state. Eighty per cent of weapons fell into civilian hands, after people sacked forts and barracks abandoned by the army and the police, who had joined the rebels. Armed confrontations caused 1,500 deaths. President Berisha was forced to bring forward parliamentary elections to June 1997. The SP, led by Fatos Nano (now out of jail) won the elections.

[21] Berisha resigned in July and the government was headed by Nano as Prime Minister. In September, due to a disagreement with a Socialist MP, the National Council of the DP withdrew from Parliament. By the end of the year, the Nano administration had resumed control over the country and was able to reduce inflation. The socialist government pledged to carry out reforms that included the revitalization of the economy through an extensive privatization plan. In March 1998, the IMF praised Nano's management and promised funding for three years to support Albania's economic reforms.

[22] But in September that year an internal quarrel within the SP forced the Prime Minister to stand down. The administration was passed on to Pandeli Majko, who in turn had to hand over to Ilir Meta, also from the Socialist Party.

[23] As civil war erupted in Yugoslavia, Albania called for NATO intervention to protect Kosovan Albanians. Local mafias supplied weapons to the Kosovo Liberation Army (KLA). When NATO finally intervened, Albania accepted tens of thousands of refugees and served as a base for NATO troops

[24] Although the SP under Ilir Meta won a second term in the 2001 elections, stating that its priorities were joining the European Union and solving power shortages, new internal disputes paralyzed the Government, which was denounced by Nano as corrupt and incompetent. His followers blocked the appointment of new ministers.

[25] With both the Government and the economy crippled, the power shortage was compounded by a particularly harsh winter. Without funds for imports, the Government could only declare a state of emergency. Some areas spent 20 hours a day without electricity.

[26] Meta resigned and in February 2002 Pandeli Majko became Prime Minister for a second time. ∎

Algeria

Al Jaza'ir

Population:	31,403,000 (2002)
Land area:	2,381,740 SQ KM
Capital:	Algiers (Alger)
Currency:	Dinar
Language:	Arabic and Berber

The kingdoms that arose in Algeria dating back to antiquity were linked to the region's two power centers: Tunisia, from the Carthage era (10th century BC), and Morocco, following the Arab conquest of the Iberian Peninsula (711AD). Algeria's intermediate position facilitated the concentration there of dissent against the differentiated taxes imposed on born Muslims and recent converts. This dissent later led people to the Jariyite sect that promoted egalitarian principles and the belief that caliphs did not have to be descendants of Muhammad or his family: thus, any Muslim could ascend to the caliphate regardless of race, color or social status. This sect appealed especially to the Berbers (from the Romans' name for them: barbarians). They had resisted the Arab invasion in the 7th century AD but eventually converted to Islam and played a role in the Arab conquest of the Iberian Peninsula. Berbers remained subordinate to the Arabs who were politically dominant, though fewer in number. In the 12th century, invading Bedouin Arabs destroyed the Berbers' peasant economy in coastal North Africa; as a result, many became nomadic.

[2] With the downfall of the Almohad Empire in 1212, Yaglimorossen ibn Ziane founded a new state on the Algerian coast. Its borders were consolidated as economic prosperity and cultural development led nomadic peoples to settle. Ziane and his successors governed the country between 1235 and 1518. After the Christians had put an end to 7 centuries of Muslim domination, in 1492 the Zianids were confronted with a series of Spanish military incursions in which various strategic sites, like Oran, were taken.

[3] Algeria and Tunisia both became part of the Ottoman (Turkish) Empire in the 16th century.

The Arroudj and Kheireddine brothers drove the Spanish from the Algerian coast and expanded the state's authority over a sizeable territory. The Empire's mighty fleet won respect for the nation, and its sovereignty was acknowledged in a series of treaties (with the Low Countries in 1663, France in 1670, Britain in 1681 and the US in 1815).

[4] Wheat production gradually increased until it became an export crop once again, for the first time since the Hilalian invasion (see Mauritania). Wheat exports eventually became the indirect cause of European intervention. At the end of the 18th century, the French revolutionary government bought large amounts of wheat from Algeria but failed to pay. Napoleon, and later the Restoration monarchy, delayed payment until the Dey of Algiers demanded that the debt be paid. Reacting to further excuses and delays, he slapped a perplexed French official in the face - a show of temper that would cost the Turkish Pasha dearly. 36,000 French soldiers disembarked to 'avenge the offense', a pretext used by the French to carry out a long-standing project: to re-establish a colony on the African coast opposite their own shores. However, the French encountered heavy resistance, and were defeated.

WORKERS

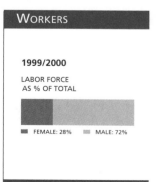

1999/2000

LABOR FORCE AS % OF TOTAL

- FEMALE: 28%   MALE: 72%

LAND USE

DEFORESTATION: 1.2% annual (1990/95)

1993

- FOREST & WOODLAND: 1.7%
- ARABLE: 3.1%
- OTHER: 95.2%

[5] In 1840, disembarking with 115,000 troops, the French set out once again to conquer Algeria. Successive rebellions were launched against the invaders. In the South the nomadic groups remained virtually independent and fought the French until well into the 20th century (see Western Sahara). In 1873, France decided to expropriate land for French settlers, or *pieds-noirs* as they were known, who wished to remain in the colonies (they numbered 500,000 by 1900, and over a million after World War II). As a result, the French pieds-noirs came to monopolize the fertile land, and the country's economy was restructured to meet French interests.

[6] Nationalist resistance grew stronger from the 1920s until in 1945 it exploded when the celebration of the victory over Nazi-Fascism turned into a popular rebellion. The French forces tried to put down the rebellion and according to official French reports, 45,000 Algerians and 108 Europeans were killed in the ensuing massacre.

[7] Shortly thereafter, the Algerian People's Party, founded in 1937, was restructured as the Movement for the Triumph of Democratic Liberties (MTLD) which participated in the 1948 and 1951 elections called by the colonialists.

[8] Convinced of the futility of elections under colonial control, nine leaders of the OS (Special Organization, the military wing of the MTLD) founded the Revolutionary Committee for Unity and Action (CRUA). In November 1954, this committee became the National Liberation Front (FLN) that led the armed rebellion. Franz Fanon, a doctor from Martinique, who had fought in the liberation of France during World War II, joined the FLN and came to exert great intellectual influence not only in Algeria but also throughout the sub-Saharan region.

[9] In order to maintain 'French Algeria'and the pieds-noirs, the French colonial regime destroyed 8,000 villages, killing more than a million civilians, made systematic use of torture and deployed more than 500,000 troops. Right-wing French residents of Algeria formed the Secret Army Organization (OAS), a terrorist group which blended Neo-Fascism with the demands of the French colonials, who resented the growing power of the Algerians. Finally, on March 18 1962, French

President De Gaulle signed the Evian Agreement, agreeing to a cease-fire and a plebiscite on the proposal for self-determination.

[10] Independence was declared on July 5 1962, and a Constituent Assembly was elected later that year. Ahmed Ben Bella was named Prime Minister. Almost all foreign companies were nationalized; 600,000 French nationals abandoned the country taking everything they could with them, and 500,000 Algerians returned, to share the lot of 150,000 landless and hungry peasants. A system of local agricultural and industrial operations was introduced by the new government.

[11] However, Ben Bella's self-management program came up against the reality of a government with little administrative expertise. In June 1965 a revolutionary council headed by Houari Boumedienne took power and jailed Ben Bella. A new emphasis on organization, centralization, and state power began to prevail over Ben Bella's self-management notions. Under Boumedienne, there was further nationalization and a program of rapid industrialization based on revenues from oil and liquid natural gas. The country entered a period of economic expansion, which was not reflected in the countryside. Population grew more rapidly than agricultural production, and Algeria went from exporting to importing food.

[12] Houari Boumedienne died in December 1978, after a long illness, just as the country's political institutions were beginning to consolidate. In 1976, a new National Charter was approved and, in 1977, the new members of the National People's Assembly were elected, with Colonel Chadli Ben Jedid appointed president.

[13] The new president initiated a policy of reconciliation by releasing Ahmed Ben Bella, who had been imprisoned for 14 years. Restrictions on travel abroad were lifted, taxes reduced and prohibitions removed on private housing. Over-large public enterprises gradually shrank and the restructuring of inefficient public enterprises gave an impetus to private companies.

[14] Ben Jedid was re-elected in January 1984. In October 1988, a

wave of protests broke out in several cities due to the lack of water and basic consumer goods; the legitimacy of the FLN and the military was called into question. Among the main groups participating in these mass protests were militant Islamists. Some mosques - especially in poorer neighborhoods - became sites of political demonstrations, particularly on Friday afternoons, when prayers ended in political declarations voicing economic and social demands.

[15] Some sectors of the most radical forms of Islam, influenced by Iran, began sending volunteers to fight in Afghanistan, to carry out the *jihad* or 'holy war' against the Soviet-backed Kabul regime. In mid-1989, against a background of protest and upheaval, Ben Jedid presented a new constitution which introduced a modified multiparty system, breaking the monopoly which the FLN had held.

[16] More than 20 opposition groups - including Muslims - openly expressed their views. The most significant were the Islamic Salvation Front (FIS), the Dawa Islamic League, the communist Socialist Avant Garde Party (PAGS) and the strongly Kabbyle (ethnic minority of Berber origin) Pro-Democracy and Culture Group (RDC). Mouloud Hamrouche, a leading reformer, was appointed Prime Minister. In the first multiparty elections since Algeria's independence from France in 1962, the FIS defeated the FLN in the June elections.

[17] Hamrouche and his cabinet resigned in June 1991, against a background of social agitation promoted by the mullahs (religious leaders). In early June, a state of siege was declared throughout the country in the face of massive protests. The country's military and police forces were pitted against FIS agitators who demanded that presidential elections be held ahead of schedule and that an Islamic state be proclaimed. Sid Ahmed Ghozali, an oil technician who had been Prime Minister during the previous administration, was designated as the new Prime Minister. Legislative and presidential elections were scheduled for later in the year, and the FIS suspended its campaign of social and political agitation.

[18] The country requested loans from the IMF in order to alleviate

MATERNAL MORTALITY 1985/99

Per 100,000 live births

220

LITERACY 2000

63%

PROFILE

ENVIRONMENT
South of the fertile lands on the Mediterranean coast lie the Tellian and Saharan Atlas mountain ranges, with a plateau extending between them. Further south is the Sahara desert, rich in oil, natural gas and iron deposits. Different altitudes and climates in the north make for agricultural diversity, with Mediterranean-type crops (vines, citrus fruits, olives and so on) predominating. The country's flora and fauna are seriously threatened. More than 30 mammal, 8 reptile and 70 bird species are in danger of extinction. Desertification affects primarily the peri-Saharan regions. However, erosion also poses a serious threat to 45 per cent of all agricultural land (12 million hectares). There is heavy pollution in the rivers and the coast due to oil industry.

SOCIETY
Peoples: Algerians are mostly Arab (80 per cent) and Berber (17 per cent). Nomadic groups linked to the Tuareg of Nigeria and Mali live in the south. Nearly a million Algerians live in France.
Religion: Islam
Languages: Arabic and Tamazight (Berber) are the official languages. Many people speak French, but Arabic has gradually been replacing it in education and public administration.
Political Parties: National Liberation Front (FLN); Vanguard Socialist Party (PAGS); Front for Socialist Forces (FFS); Movement for Democracy in Algeria (MDA); Reunion of Culture and Democracy (RCD); Islamic Salvation Front (FIS); Hamas; Movement for a Peaceful Society.
Social Organizations: General Union of Algerian Workers (UGTA), National Union of Algerian Peasants, National Union of Algerian Women, National Youth Union.

THE STATE
Official Name: Al-Jumjuriya al-Jazairia ash-Shaabiya.
Capital: Algiers (Alger) 1,840,000 people (1999).
Other cities: Oran 712,300 people; Constantine 501,900; Annaba 233,600 (2000).
Government: Abdel-Aziz Bouteflika, President since 1999. Ali Benflis, Prime Minister since August 2000.
National Holiday: November 1, Anniversary of the Revolution (1954).
Armed Forces: 121,700 (65,000 conscripts).
Other: 180,000 (Gendarmerie, National Security Forces, Republican Guard).

Lakes region has been exacerbated by endemic famine, malaria and cholera, and pandemics of tuberculosis and HIV-AIDS. The most manifest result of these conflicts is the hundreds of thousands of refugees who form yet another battle front maintained by various human rights organizations such as Medecins Sans Frontières and some UN agencies. In an attempt to mitigate these diseases, the aid agencies - some funded by the World Bank - involuntarily provided another source of conflict as the refugee camps were frequently moved by the Congolese authorities to serve as a human shield against attacks from rebel groups or the enemy of the moment.

And in addition, in both the DRC and the rest of the Great Lakes region is the legacy of the thousands of people killed and maimed by so many years of civil war. The battlegrounds are littered by myriad tiny undetectable plastic antipersonnel mines, whose presence is only revealed when someone treads on them and they explode.

THE CIVIL WAR

The start of the DRC's civil war is usually put at 1960, when this countrty gained independence. But the origins of this conflict – like the others in the region – harks back to the colonial legacy.

In 1884 at the Berlin Conference, the European powers partitioned Africa. Using a ruler, they mapped out 48 new states, and they imposed their governors or regents to ride roughshod over the empires, kingdoms and ancient civilizations which messily straddled or stood in the way of these completely new and national borders. The earlier civilizations and relations between the various cultures had never need such boundaries. Once the decolonization processes began in earnest in the mid-20th century - although the former Portuguese colonies in Africa only became independent after the Carnation Revolution in Lisbon in 1975 - the African nations were forced to adopt systems of government alien to their historical traditions and centuries-old cosmologies.

In today's DRC and the Great Lakes nations it became imperative that there be a President, a two-chamber parliament and a Prime Minister. This move came from the West which pressed the countries to modernize along the lines of Western-style democracy.

Since independence these countries have spilled blood in civil wars often fed by ethnic differences exploited by the colonizers. Faced with disease and structural poverty, aid to the region came initially from the International Monetary Fund (IMF) and the World Bank, as well as from US interests at the height of the Cold War. Then came the first structural adjustment plans which ensured the countries would continue to hand over their birthright (their minerals, commodities, etc.) and open up their markets.

MOBUTU AND THE ALLIANCES

When army commander Mobutu came to power in a coup in 1965, he renamed the country Zaire and began to form alliances in order to shore up his position.

For France, Belgium and the US (and its Central Intelligence Agency, the CIA), the dictator Mobutu was their best defense against the advance of "communist" forces such as the Congolese Liberation Front led by Laurent Kabila. With military aid for arms and training, Mobutu was able to repel rebel advances for years and also cultivate friends and enemies. However, when the rebel advance could no longer be contained, international aid began to fall off or to change. Mobutu played the leading role in this complex tapestry of alliances. He requested help from Uganda and Rwanda, countries fighting in Zairean territory against Burundian and Rwandan Hutu and Tutsi refugees. With the support of these countries, Mobutu created a new dimension by allowing these soldiers and refugees to exploit and sell gold from the mining areas close to their frontiers. Slowly, the foreign armies occupied more territory and nobody was now going to get them out. The conflict in Zaire became more international, and the country was disempowered.

CONGO AND THE END OF APARTHEID

The Congo Liberation Front meanwhile, also wove alliances. During the 1960s and 1970s Laurent Kabila was in exile in Dar es Salaam, capital of Tanzania, shaping his plans and directing his troops from there. His forces were armed and trained by Cuba, which had sent the famous guerrilla fighter Ernesto Che Guevara to lend his support to the Congo in 1965. From exile, Kabila cemented a friendship with Agostinho Neto of Angola. Neto appeared to be the leader of Angolan independence, and the People's Movement for the Liberation of Angola (MPLA) was formed under his leadership. Mobutu meanwhile supported Jonas Savimbi's National Union for the Total Independence of Angola (UNITA), and Uganda did the same. The civil wars in both countries were closely related.

Kabila's troops - with backing from Cuba and the MPLA - helped to expel the South African Army from Angolan territory. The turning point for the South Africans, and therefore also for Angola and its allies, was the battle of Cuito Cuanavale. Until this, whites had not died in combat; their relatives had not received their loved ones back in body bags. In December 1988 South Africa signed an agreement to withdraw its forces from Angola, and also from Namibia. In this way, the victory for the MPLA, helped by Laurent Kabila and Cuba, was also significant in the struggles to end apartheid in South Africa, and to achieve Namibian independence.∎

announcing it would not grant diplomatic recognition until after the 1992 elections. Consequently, the US companies in Angola were unable to get loans from banks in their own country.

[24] Following intense negotiations between the Government and UNITA, elections were set for September 1992. The ruling MPLA took nearly 50 per cent of the vote, to UNITA's 40 per cent. Savimbi refused to recognize defeat and hostilities resumed. In their advance, the UNITA troops occupied the diamond mines of the interior, leaving the Government with oil as the only stable source of income (between $1.6 and $1.7 billion per year).

[25] In November 1993, peace talks were re-started in Lusaka, the capital of Zambia. A year later in November 1994 a peace agreement was signed. The main points (a ceasefire and constitutional changes so that Savimbi could become Vice-President)

were not put into practice until late 1995 and the fighting continued.

[26] Some progress was seen during 1996. In May, an amnesty law was approved and UNITA soldiers began to be absorbed by the armed forces. Savimbi withdrew most of his troops to barracks and handed over some of the weapons. The civil war caused the most serious social and economic crisis in Angolan history. The adoption of IMF and World Bank economic liberalization measures did not improve matters for ordinary people.

[27] In April 1997, hard negotiating ended with UNITA accepting to join the government at executive, legislative and military levels. Even though its position in the capital was weak, UNITA's troops still controlled 40 per cent of the territory. The fall of Mobutu Sese Seko in Zaire (now DR Congo) in May weakened UNITA even further, and they were forced to abandon areas of the northern frontier. The

Angolans wanted to avoid the infiltration of Mobutu's troops - formerly allied to Savimbi - into their territory. Mobutu's soldiers were fleeing from the government of the new DR Congo leader Laurent Kabila, a former ally of dos Santos.

[28] In March 1998, thousands of demobilized soldiers mostly with little or no education encountered serious difficulties in returning to their home villages, given the scarce employment possibilities there and the slow arrival of economic aid. Since 1994, only 300,000 of the 4.5 million people uprooted by the civil war had been able to resettle according to the United Nations figures. The presence of large numbers of land mines across the country increased the insecurity of the population.

[29] Renewed hostilities in the DR Congo also affected UNITA members. The Government, which participated in the conflict by backing Kabila, recovered territories previously controlled by the opposition or their Congolese allies.

[30] In April 1999, the Government announced the formation of a self-defense front with Zimbabwe, Namibia and DR Congo. This reflected the interconnected nature of regional conflicts, which transcended frontiers established by former colonial powers. In late 1999, after winning back Andulo and Bailundo - the main cities under opposition control - and following a run of military victories the Government felt confident in announcing that the end of the war was in sight.

[31] However, after a period of relative peace, fighting between the Government and UNITA resumed in 2000. The UN Security Council decided to withdraw its peace mission from Angola, present since 1995 to mediate between the Government and UNITA.

[32] In 2001, in a new effort to stop the diamond trade that funds the war in Angola and other parts of Africa, the UN imposed new sanctions against the trade in precious stones.

[33] Jonas Savimbi, leader of UNITA since 1975, was killed in combat on 22 February 2002, in the central province of Moxico. Vice-President Antonio Dembo took over the organization's leadership. After the rebel chief had died, the Government called for the end of the civil war. President dos Santos then said the death of Savimbi had opened the way for general elections, but added that security had to be ensured first. In order to achieve it, he had begun to make contacts with Dembo. The ceasefire remained precarious. ∎

PROFILE

ENVIRONMENT

The 150 kilometer-wide strip of coastal plains is fertile and dry. The extensive inland plateaus, higher to the west, are covered by tropical rainforests in the north, grasslands at the center and dry plains in the south. In the more densely populated areas (the north and central west) diversified subsistence farming is practiced. Coffee, the main export crop, is grown in the north; sisal is cultivated on the Benguela and Huambo plateaus; sugarcane and oil palm along the coast. The country has abundant mineral reserves: diamonds in Luanda, petroleum in Cabinda and Luanda, iron ore in Cassinga and Cassala. The port of Lobito is linked by railway to the mining centers of Zaire and Zambia. There are a number of environmental problems aggravated by the civil war, the lack of drinking water (in 1987 there was a cholera epidemic in Luanda), soil erosion and especially deforestation of rainforests as a result of the export of valuable timber.

SOCIETY

Peoples: As a consequence of centuries of slave trade the population density is still very low. To maintain control over the country, the Portuguese colonizers fostered local divisions between the various ethnic groups; Bakondo (13 per cent), Kimbundu (25 per cent), Ovimbundu (37 per cent); others. Europeans (22 per cent) and Afro-European (2 per cent). **Religions:** The majority practice traditional African religions; 38 per cent are Catholic, and 15 per cent Protestant. However, there are forms of syncretism which make it impossible to establish clear boundaries between one religion and another. **Languages:** Portuguese (official) and 41 African languages including Ovidumbo, Kimbundu and Kikongo. **Political Parties:** The People's Movement for the Liberation of Angola (MPLA), founded by Agostinho Neto on December 10 1956; the Party for Social Renewal (PSR); Democratic Angolan Forum; the National Union for the Total Independence of Angola (UNITA); and the National Front for the Liberation of Angola (FNLA). In 1991 new parties were founded: Liberal Democratic Party; Alliance of Angolan Youth, Workers and Peasants. **Social Organizations:** National Union of Angolan Workers (UNTA); Organization of Angolan Women (OMA).

THE STATE

Official Name: República Popular de Angola. **Administrative Divisions:** 18 provinces. **Capital:** Luanda 2,555,000 people (1999). **Other cities:** Huambo (Nova Lisboa) 165,700 people; Lobito 133,100; Benguela 129,800 (2000). **Government:** José Eduardo dos Santos, President since September 1979, re-elected in 1992; Fernando Franca Van Dunem, Prime Minister up to January 1999 when the post was abolished. Unicameral legislature. 220-member National Assembly, elected by direct popular vote. **National Holiday:** November 11, Independence Day (1975). **Armed Forces:** 82,000. **Other:** 20,000 Internal Security Police.

STATISTICS

DEMOGRAPHY
Population: 13,936,000 (2002)
Annual growth: 3.0 % (1985-2000)
Estimates for year 2015: 20,795,000 (2000)
Annual growth to year 2015: 3.1 % (2000)
Urban population: 33.5 % (1999)
Urban growth: 4.8 % (2000)
Children per woman: 7.2 (2000)

HEALTH
Life expectancy at birth: 46 years (2000-2005)
male: 45 years (2000-2005)
female: 47 years (2000-2005)
Infant mortality: 172 per 1,000 (2000)
Under-5 child mortality: 295 per 1,000 (2000)
Daily calorie supply: 1,873 per capita (1999)
8 doctors per 100,000 people (1997)
Safe water: 38 % (2000)

EDUCATION
School enrolment (net): Primary total: 50 % (1994/2000)
Tertiary (gross): 1 % (1998)
Primary school teachers: one for every 27 pupils (1991)

COMMUNICATIONS
11 newspapers (1996), 74 radios (2000), 19 TV sets (2000) and 5 main telephone lines (2000) per 1,000 people

ECONOMY
Per capita, GDP: $ 2,187 (2000)
Annual growth: -0.8 % (2000)
Annual inflation: 325.0 % (2000)
Consumer price index: 415,713.0 (2000)
Currency: 31.6 new kwanzas = $ 1 (03/2002)
Cereal imports: 408,977 metric tons (2000)
Fertilizer use: 11 kg per ha (1999)
Exports: $ 7,959 million (2000)
Imports: $ 6,551 million (2000)
External debt: $ 10,146 million (2000); $ 772 per capita (2000)
Debt service: 21.1 % of exports (1999)
Development aid received: $ 388 million (1999); $ 31.4 per capita (1999); 4.50 % of GNP (1999)

ENERGY
Consumption: 595.3 Kgs of oil equivalent per capita yearly (1998); -474.9 % imported (1999)

HDI (ranking/value): 146 / 0.422 (1999)

Anguilla

Anguilla

Population: 12,000 (2002)
Land area: 96 SQ KM
Capital: The Valley
Currency: E.C. dollar
Language: English

Anguilla is the most northerly of the Leeward Islands. Its small size, barely 96 sq km including the neighboring Sombrero Island, and the lack of fresh water for agriculture, made the island unattractive to the British Empire. From 1816 to 1871 Anguilla, St Kitts-Nevis and the Virgin Islands were administered together as one colony. The Virgin Islands were split off in 1871, leaving the others as a colonial unit ruled from St Kitts.

² Colonialism lasted until the group became one of the five Caribbean 'States in Association with the United Kingdom'. Anguillans opposed the agreement and rebelled against the St Kitts government. Under the leadership of local entrepreneur Ronald Webster, Anguilla demanded a separate constitution. In March 1969, British troops disembarked on the island to supervise the installation of its colonial Commissioner, but the separatist movement continued its struggle.

³ In 1976 a new constitution was approved by Britain, establishing a parliamentary system of government under the patronage of the British Commissioner. But it was not until 1980 that Anguilla was able formally to withdraw from the Associated State arrangement with St Kitts-Nevis, gaining the status of 'British Dependent Territory'.

⁴ The 1976 constitution provided for a governor appointed by the British Crown, responsible for defense, foreign relations, internal security (including the police), utilities, justice and the public audit. The Governor presides over the Executive Council.

⁵ The first legislative elections held in March 1976 voted in the Anguilla United Party leader, Ronald Webster, as Chief Minister. A year later he failed to win a vote of confidence and was replaced by opposition leader Emile Gumbs. In the 1980 general elections, the United Party of Anguilla, led by Webster, won by a landslide majority, obtaining six out of the seven seats. A year later, the Government suffered internal divisions and Webster created the Popular Party of Anguilla (PPA). In the elections of June 1981, he won 5 seats, while the remaining 2 went to the Anguilla National Alliance (ANA), led by Emile Gumbs.

⁶ In September, the Constitution was changed leading to home rule on internal matters.

⁷ On March 9 1984 in accordance with the new constitution of 1982 requiring a parliamentary government, elections were held and Emile Gumbs became Chief Minister once more. The ANA received 53.8 per cent of the vote.

⁸ The new ANA government requested greater power for the Executive Council and an increase in British investment in the island's economic infrastructure. After the Council called for constitutional changes, particularly with reference to the situation of women and people born outside the island who had relatives there, the Governor appointed a Committee to review the Constitution.

⁹ Through the 1980s the building industry for tourism reduced unemployment from 26 per cent to 1 per cent, but at the beginning of the 1990s this trend stopped and the US recession brought a reduction of tourists.

¹⁰ In 1991 Prime Minister Gumbs tried to bring about closer cooperation between the British possessions and the Organization of East Caribbean States.

¹¹ Income generated from livestock, salt production, lobster fishing, boat-building and remittances from émigrés - mainly living in the US - was overtaken by the construction, tourism and international financial service sectors.

¹² In March 1994 the legislative elections were won by Hubert Hughes of the United Party of Anguilla. In November, the new legislative assembly proclaimed legislation to regulate the activity of transnational companies. In 1997 and part of 1998, there was an average annual growth of 7 per cent, as a result of increased tourism from the US and Britain.

¹³ The March 2000 parliamentary elections were won by a coalition formed between the ANA and the Democratic Party of Anguilla, known as the United Front. Osbourne Fleming became Chief Minister.

¹⁴ The Organization for Economic Co-operation and Development (OECD) listed Anguilla as a tax haven in November. According to OECD, the countries on this list were supposed to have adopted a program to eliminate practices allowing tax evasion by December 31 2001. ∎

PROFILE

ENVIRONMENT
Anguilla covers 91 sq km and its dependency, the island of Sombrero, is 5 sq km. They are part of the Leeward Islands of the Lesser Antilles. The climate is tropical with heavy rainfall. There are considerable salt deposits on the island. In some regions there are problems with the distribution of drinking water.

SOCIETY
Peoples: Most are descendants of African slaves integrated with European settlers. There is a British minority. Many Anguillans live permanently in the Virgin Islands or other US possessions.
Religions: Anglican 40 per cent; Methodist 33 per cent; Adventist 7 per cent; Baptist 5 per cent; Roman Catholic 3 per cent; other, 12 per cent (1996).
Languages: English (official).
Political Parties: The Anguillan National Alliance; The Anguilla United Party; The Democratic Party of Anguilla.

THE STATE
Official Name: Anguilla.
Capital: The Valley, 820 people (1999).
Government: Peter Johnstone, Governor-General appointed by the British Crown in February 2000. Osbourne Fleming, Chief Minister since March 2000. The single chamber Legislative Assembly has 11 members, 7 elected by direct vote.
Status: Overseas territory of the United Kingdom.

DEMOGRAPHY
Population: 12,000 (2002)
Annual growth: 3.0 % (1985-2000)
Estimates for year 2015: 16,000 (2000)
Annual growth to year 2015: 2.3 % (2000)

ECONOMY
Currency: 2.7 EC dollars = $ 1 (03/2002)

LAND USE
DEFORESTATION: 0.8% annual (1990/95)

1993

- FOREST & WOODLAND: 11.4%
- ARABLE: 18.2%
- OTHER: 70.4%

Antigua and Barbuda

Population:	65,000 (2002)
Land area:	440 SQ KM
Capital:	St John's
Currency:	E.C. dollar
Language:	English

Antigua and Barbuda

The Caribs inhabited most of the islands in the sea which took their name, but abandoned many of them, including Antigua, in the 16th century due to the lack of fresh water.

[2] In 1493 the name Antigua was given to one of the Antilles by Christopher Columbus in honor of a church in Seville. Other Europeans settled later (the Spanish in 1520, the French in 1629) but again left because of the scarcity of water. However, a few English were able to settle by using appropriate techniques to store rainwater. The nearby island of Barbuda was colonized in 1678 and granted by the crown to the Codrington family in 1685. Although it was planned as a slave-breeding colony, the slaves who were imported came to live self-reliantly in their own community.

[3] By 1640, the number of English families on Antigua had increased to 30. The few Indians who had dared to stay were eventually murdered by the settlers, who imported African slaves to work the tobacco plantations and later sugar plantations.

[4] In 1666, the French governor of Martinique invaded the island, kidnapping all the African slaves. When England regained control in 1676, a rich colonist from Barbuda,

Colonel Codrington, acquired large quantities of land and brought new African slaves. Thus sugar production was reinstated on the island.

[5] Slavery was abolished in the British colonies in 1838. The workers' situation did not noticeably change and quasi-slavery continued for many decades, until the early 20th century when trade unions began to appear.

[6] The first trade union, led by Vere Bird, was formed on January 16 1939. The Antigua Labor Party (ALP), the first political party, was originated within a trade union. It was also led by Vere Bird.

[7] In the elections of April 1960, Bird's party won and he became Prime Minister. In 1966, a new constitution introduced self-government with a Parliament elected by Antiguans and Barbudans. Britain remained responsible for defense and foreign relations. Bird was again successful in the 1967 elections.

[8] On November 1 1981, Antigua and Barbuda became independent as a 'sovereign, democratic and united state' and were admitted into the United Nations and the Caribbean Community (Caricom). Independence

also gave the islands the right to become indebted to the IMF and the World Bank. The foreign debt grew dramatically and reached almost half of the GDP by the end of that year.

[9] The Prime Minister maintained close relations with the US, who rented part of the island's territory for military purposes. The alliance with the US was further consolidated in 1983, when Antigua participated in the US invasion of Grenada. Parliamentary elections were held in April 1984, and despite accusations during the electoral campaign, Bird was re-elected. His victory was attributed to approval of his stance on the Grenada issue.

[10] Vere Bird retired from public life and his son Lester replaced him at the head of ALP in 1994. In the March elections, Labor lost 4 seats but retained an absolute majority at the Chamber of Representatives, with 11 seats out of 17.

[11] In September 1995, Hurricane Luis caused losses which amounted to $300 million, damaging 60 per cent of the country's buildings, whether partially or completely, including several main hotels, seriously affecting the country's tourism infrastructure.

[12] The US State Department categorized the country in 1999 as a major magnet in the Caribbean for money-launderers. It warned that controls over money-laundering and offshore commerce were so weakened by certain individuals in the government that this posed a threat to Antigua's democratic institutions.

[13] In the March 1999 general elections the ALP reaffirmed Bird as Prime Minister but his Government was damaged by a series of scandals, including arms trafficking and the case brought against his brother, Ivor, for cocaine smuggling.

[14] In February 2002, Parliament presented a constitutional reform bill that recommended reducing the legislative body to 17 Deputies and 12 Senators (the latter appointed directly by the President), giving greater representation to Barbuda, and establishing legislation to guarantee freedom of information. It also proposed several measures to give gender equality a constitutional base. ■

PROFILE

ENVIRONMENT

The islands - Antigua with 280 sq km and its dependencies Barbuda with 160 sq km and Redonda with 2 sq km - belong to the Leeward group of the Lesser Antilles. Antigua is endowed with beautiful coral reefs and large dunes. Its wide bays distinguish it from the rest of the Caribbean because they provide safe havens. Barbuda is a coral island with a large lagoon on the west side. It consists of a small volcano joined to a calcareous plain. Redonda is a small uninhabited rocky island, and is now a flora and fauna reserve. Sugar cane and cotton are grown along with tropical fruits; seafood is exported. The reduction of habitats due to the reforestation of native forests with imported species is the main environmental problem of most of the Caribbean islands.

SOCIETY

Peoples: The majority of Antiguans and Barbudans are of African origin (91.3 per cent); Europeans; Mestizo; Syrian-Lebanese; Indo-Pakistanis.
Religions: Protestants 73.7 per cent (Anglicans 32.1 per cent, Moravians 12 per cent; Methodists 9.1 per cent; Seventh Day Adventists 8.8 per cent; and others); Catholics 10.8 per cent; Jehovah Witnesses 1.2 per cent; Rastafarians 0.8 per cent.
Languages: English is the official language, but in daily life a local Patois dialect is spoken.
Political Parties: The Antigua Labor Party (ALP); The Antigua Caribbean Liberation Movement (ACLM); The United National Democratic Party (UNDP); The United Progressive Party (UPP).
Social Organizations: Antigua Workers' Union, linked to the UNDP;

Antigua Trades and Labor Union, with ALP leadership; People's Democratic Movement.

THE STATE

Official Name: Associated State of Antigua and Barbuda.
Capital: St John's 25,000 people (1999).
Other cities: Parham 1,400 people; Liberta 1,400 (2000).
Government: James Carlisle, Governor-General since June 1993, representative of Queen Elizabeth II (Head of State). Lester Bird, Prime Minister since March 1994, re-elected in 1999. Bicameral Legislative: House of Representatives, with 19 members, and the Senate, with 17 appointed members.
National Holiday: November 1, Independence Day (1981).
Armed Forces: 90 troops (1994).

Aotearoa/ New Zealand

Population: 3,837,000 (2002)
Land area: 267,990 SQ KM
Capital: Wellington
Currency: NZ dollar
Language: English and Maori

Aotearoa/New Zealand

Aotearoa, 'the land of the long white cloud', was settled around the 9th century by Maori, who arrived there from Polynesia (see box 'Melanesians and Polynesians: surviving cultures'). Over the years a distinct culture developed, based on tribal organization and a strong affinity with the land. Maori saw themselves as guardians of the land for future generations.

² In 1642 Abel Tasman, from Holland, reached the South Island, the larger of Aotearoa's two main islands. However, a misunderstanding with the indigenous population prevented him from going ashore. It was not until 1769 that James Cook from England surveyed the shores of the two larger islands. This opened the door for a growing colonization of the country which Abel Tasman had named 'New Zealand'. Whalers, sealers and traders, along with a few deserters from the navy and fugitives from Australian jails, established themselves on the islands.

³ In the early 19th century, colonization increased with the arrival of British immigrants and missionaries. They brought with them new diseases, values and beliefs, which affected the traditional Maori way of life. Trading with settlers initially brought wealth to many Maori communities, but these gains were reversed with interest once the settlers began to alienate significant amounts of Maori land.

⁴ In 1840 the territory of New Zealand was formally annexed by the British crown as a colony. The two larger islands were occupied under different legal arrangements: the South Island was incorporated by virtue of the right of 'discovery', and the North Island through the Treaty of Waitangi, signed in 1840 by Maori chiefs and representatives of the British Government. According to the text of the treaty - which is different in its English and Maori versions - Maori chiefs accepted the presence of British settlers and the establishment of a government by the Crown to rule the settlers. In exchange, Maori were assured absolute respect for their national sovereignty.

⁵ However, 20 years after the signing of the Treaty an extremely violent process of expropriation of Maori lands began. The so-called 'land wars' between Maori and the Europeans were essentially for sovereignty and guaranteed rights to the lands, forests, fisheries and other *taonga* (treasures).

⁶ Massive immigration, land confiscation and legal decisions led to the gradual annexation of Maori land. The magnitude of their loss becomes clearer if one considers that, out of the 27 million hectares they owned in 1840, they now have a little over a million left.

⁷ While the north of the country was involved in a series of wars, the South Island settlers went through a period of prosperity because of the discovery of gold. This discovery brought a massive flow of British, Chinese and Australian immigrants, which energized the region's economy.

⁸ After 1840 colonization increased. The Pakeha (non-Maori) usurped the right to fish in the area, thus depriving Maori of one of their main activities.

⁹ Maori opposition to Pakeha colonization found new expression by the end of the 19th century. They organized petitions, delegations and submitted their claims before local courts and even before the British Crown itself, demanding compliance with the Treaty of Waitangi. These efforts were fruitless. The lands that had once belonged to Maori were now used for farming, which had started to play a central role not only in the life of the settlers but also in the whole economy. New markets for dairy and meat products opened up in the 1880s, with the appearance of cold-storage systems which made long-distance shipping possible. These products constituted the basis of the country's economic development.

¹⁰ For Maori, British rule also meant the beginning of a process of cultural assimilation, through the arbitrary imposition of European language, religion, and customs. Thus, Maori language which was in theory protected by the Treaty of Waitangi, was given less and less importance.

¹¹ By the end of the century, the country's political scene was dominated by the Liberal government. They were the first in the world to grant the vote to women (including Pakeha and Maori women, in 1893) and to establish measures to protect the rights of industrial workers, a group which was growing parallel to the development of cities and manufacturing industries.

¹² In the 20th century new political movements appeared to oppose the power of the Liberals who had become a coherent, organized political party after 20 years in power. The Labor Party, with ample working-class and urban middle-class support, became one of the country's main political forces.

¹³ During the 1930s, Maori demands acquired new strength thanks to an alliance between the groups representing Maori interests and the Labor Party, which came to power for the first time in 1935 with Maori support. But there was still no legislative recognition of the Treaty of Waitangi.

¹⁴ World War II marked the beginning of a new era for the country. During the War Britain's inability to guarantee the security of its former colony led to closer ties between Aotearoa/New Zealand and the US. Through a series of political and military alliances, US presence was consolidated in the region. In the 1950s and 1960s Aotearoa had to pay the price for this relationship, particularly when it found itself involved in the Vietnam War, a conflict which touched the political life of the country very deeply.

¹⁵ Legislation in the 1950s forced many Maori from their land and the 1960s saw their increasing urbanization. In conditions of economic prosperity and labor shortages, New Zealand's monocultural education system served to direct Maori into mainly unskilled laboring jobs.

¹⁶ In the 1970s, Aotearoa/NZ's markets in the UK were shrinking as Britain moved closer to the (then) European Economic Community (EEC). It attempted, with limited success, to diversify its production and gain access to markets other than Britain and the US. Unemployment rose and inflation reached unprecedented levels due to the failure of the diversification scheme, the rise in the price of oil and massive external loans to finance 'think big' projects. 1975 saw a drastic fall in the purchasing power earned from primary exports. This fall, combined with the foreign

loans, provoked a period of rising foreign debt. After 12 years in opposition, the Labor Party held power from 1972 until it was defeated by the conservative National Party in the 1975 elections. The new government closed the doors on Pacific immigrants, whom it blamed for increasing unemployment.

[17] In 1975, growing Maori activism led to the formation of the Waitangi Tribunal to investigate Treaty claims. In 1986 the Labor Government gave it the power to hear claims dating back to the 1840 signing. The Tribunal had no binding powers over the Crown, and settlement of claims for compensation was slow and arbitrary.

[18] In 1984, the Labor Party regained office, and introduced a monetarist economic policy which included privatizating some public enterprises. These policies alienated many traditional Labor supporters. From 1986 to 1999, Aotearoa was an international showcase for neo-liberalism. Public spending was slashed and labor laws restricted trade union activity.

[19] A 1987 law prohibited the entry of nuclear arms or vessels to the nation's ports, thus questioning the military presence of France and the United States, which used the South Pacific as a nuclear weapons testing ground. This decision ended the defense treaties between the US and Aotearoa/New Zealand.

[20] The National Party won the October 1990 elections, but the change in administration did not change the economic model of the country. There was an increase in privatizations, protectionism was dismantled even further, and there were large cut-backs in funding for health, education and contributions to social benefits. Legislation neutralizing trade unions was also introduced. The result was falling inflation, but unemployment also rose.

[21] The diminished popularity of the government was not reflected in the electoral results of 1993, when the National Party (NP) took 50 of the 99 seats in p arliament and Jim Bolger was re-elected Prime Minister. The Labor Party (LP), the main opposition force, took 45 seats.

[22] Aotearoa achieved its first budget surplus in 17 years in 1994; the currency became more robust, unemployment fell and inflation settled at 2 per cent.

[23] Between 1994 and 1995, the Government compensated Tainui of North Island both with NZ$180 million and 15,400 hectares of land, for their claims over land colonized in the previous century. Even Britain's Queen Elizabeth apologized for the loss of life during the colonization of the islands. In 1997, the Government reached an agreement with Ngai Tahu of South Island to pay compensation of NZ$170 million and land.

[24] The general unemployment indices continued to fall, settling at 6 per cent in 1995. Young people, Maori and immigrants from other South Pacific islands constituted the bulk of the unemployed and nearly 10 per cent of the population received State subsidies. Citizen concern for the environment strengthened Bolger's position in the run-up to the October 1996 elections, as he was firmly opposed to the French nuclear trials on the Moruroa atoll.

[25] Bolger's NP beat the LP,

Niue

Population:	2,000 (2002)
Land area:	260 SQ KM
Capital:	Alofi
Currency:	NZ dollar
Language:	English

Niue was settled by Samoans and Tongans. Captain James Cook named it 'Savage Island' when he visited it in 1774. The indigenous peoples' reputation for fierceness kept missionaries away (the island's first permanent mission dates from 1861), and also the slave traders who caused much suffering in other areas of the Pacific. Emigration to the phosphate mines on other islands in the area initiated an outflow that has continued ever since. In 1900 the island was declared a British protectorate and was annexed by Aotearoa/New Zealand in 1901. It was administered along with the Cook Islands until 1904, when it separated to form a separate possession. In 1974 it became an Autonomous Associated State of Aotearoa/New Zealand. The United Nations recognized this as a legitimate decision and eliminated the 'Niue case' from the Decolonization Committee agenda. As well as economic support from Aotearoa, Niue also received help with defence and international affairs.

[2] In April 1989, questions arose over the management of economic aid received from Aotearoa by Prime Minister Robert Rex's government. Despite this, the opposition lacked the votes necessary to approve a parliamentary motion to censure Rex's administration.

[3] In 1991, Aotearoa announced a reduction of financial aid. Niue and Australia established diplomatic links during 1992. Prime Minister Roberto Rex died on December 12 and was replaced by Young Vivian, who was in turn defeated in the elections to be succeeded by Frank Lui in March 1993. In February 1996, Frank Lui was re-elected for a further three years.

[4] On March 26 1999 the new prime minister, Sani Lakatani, of the National Peoples' Party, took over. This year Niue requested entry to the United Nations Food and Agriculture Organization (FAO).

[5] As had happened before the elections, the Legislative Assembly was dissolved in 2002 and the country was administered by members of the cabinet. Elections were held on April 20, with Lakatani's Niue People's Action Party winning. In May, Young Vivian became the new premier.

DEMOGRAPHY

Population: 2,000 (2002)
Annual growth: -1.5 % (1985-2000)
Estimates for year 2015: 2,000 (2000)
Annual growth to year 2015: -1.0 % (2000)

HEALTH

130 doctors per 100,000 people (1996)
Safe water: 100 % (2000)

EDUCATION

School enrolment (net):
Primary total: 100 % (1994/2000)
male: 100 % (1995/99)
female: 100 % (1995/99)

ECONOMY

Currency: 2.4 NZ dollars = $ 1 (03/2002)

ENVIRONMENT

Aotearoa/New Zealand is situated in Oceania. Its two principal islands are relatively mountainous. The North Island is volcanic and has plateaus and geysers. The South Island is crossed by the Southern Alps, a mountain chain with peaks of over 3,000 meters. The climate is moderately rainy, with temperatures cooler in the south. The native rainforests have been devastated by early colonization, replaced by agricultural land and pastures. The economic base of the country is agricultural. Tourism is becoming increasingly important. The country suffers deforestation, erosion and disappearance of native species of flora and fauna.

SOCIETY

Peoples: Much of the population is descended from European settlers (71.8 per cent). 12.9 per cent are Maori (a figure rapidly increasing), and 5 per cent are from Pacific Islands descent. **Religions:** Anglican and other Protestant denominations dominate. There are also Catholic and various Maori church minorities. **Languages:** English and Maori are the official languages, with English dominant. **Political Parties:** A multi-party system since 1996 in change due to the adoption of a mixed member proportional representation voting system. Parties in government include Labour, National, New Zealand First, United Future New Zealand, Green Party, ACT and Progressive Coalition. Minority parties with no representation include the Alliance Party, Aotearoa Legalise Cannabis, Christian Heritage and Libertarianz. **Social Organizations:** The Trade Union Federation and the Council of Trade Unions (CTU), and several Maori organizations.

THE STATE

Official name: Aotearoa (Maori); New Zealand (English).
Administrative divisions: Divided into 15 town and 58 district authorities.
Capital: Wellington 341,000 people (1999).
Other cities: Auckland 1,119,000 people; Christchurch 343,300; Dunedin 111,400; Hamilton 172,400; Palmerston North 75,700 (2000).
Government: A parliamentary monarchy and member of the British Commonwealth. Governor-General: Silvia Cartwright since April 4 2001. Helen Clark, Prime Minister and Head of Government since November 1999. Aotearoa has a parliamentary system, with a unicameral legislative body of 120 members. The elected members of the Government form a cabinet chaired by the Prime Minister. On occasions this cabinet acts as the Executive Council presided over by the Governor-General. The Governor-General appoints cabinet on the recommendations of the Prime Minister, and has the power to dissolve Parliament.
National holiday: February 6, Waitangi Day (1840).
Armed forces: 9,611 (1996) **Dependencies:** Cook Islands, Niue, Tokelau.

although both majority parties lost seats to minority parties. The first proportionally representative parliament in 1996 increased the number of Maori representatives, and those of women grew from 14 to 21 out of the 120 seats. In 1999 parliament included 16 Maori deputies, 2 gay activists, a transsexual (the world's first transsexual MP). There were also 35 women, including current Prime Minister Helen Clark and the opposition leader, Jenny Shipley.

[26] Seeking to support consumers to make informed decisions, the Food Standards Australia-New Zealand Board agreed to the compulsory labeling of all genetically modified foods in August 1999, but a comprehensive system of enforcement has not yet materialized.

[27] In April 2000 the Government announced that the titles of Sir and Dame, issued by the British crown, would no longer be used but would be replaced by titles unique to NZ.

[28] That same month, to the alarm of consumers, environmentalist and Maori groups, which had organized a campaign to declare the country 'free from genetic engineering', the Aotearoa Royal Commission on Genetic Modification issued a report supporting the development and use of genetically modified organisms. To placate public concerns, the Government placed a moratorium on unauthorized GM field trials until October 2003.

[29] After being in private hands for 12 years, in October 2001, the Government re-nationalized the New Zealand airline, (Air New Zeland) after its bankruptcy. The capitalization agreement minimized participation of major private shareholders and will allow the initiation of a recovery process of the airline, of vital importance to the tourist sector, which employs 10 per cent of the population.

[30] In spite of the global recession, domestic consumption led to a 3.1 per cent economic growth as of March 31 2002, although the Treasury later estimated there would be a 1.9 per cent fall due to the international situation. Retail business employs some 300,000 people, approximately 17 per cent of the working population.

[31] Queen Elizabeth II visited New Zealand, commemorating her Golden Jubilee. Prime Minister Clark said it was 'inevitable that New Zealand shall become a republic and that this would reflect the reality that New Zealand is a 21st century state, completely sovereign and 20,000 kilometers away from the United Kingdom'. ∎

Cook Islands

Population: 20,000 (2002)
Land area: 230 SQ KM
Capital: Avarua
Currency: NZ dollar
Language: English

The islands, which had already been explored and settled by Polynesians and Spaniards, received their name from the English navigator Captain James Cook, who drew up the first map of the archipelago in 1770.

[2] In 1821, Tahitian missionaries were sent to the islands by the London Missionary Society; a Protestant theocracy was established and all 'pagan' structures were destroyed, as were many of the traditional forms of social organization. The islands were declared a British Protectorate in 1888 and became part of Aotearoa/New Zealand in 1901. The land rights of the indigenous Maori were recognized, and the sale of real estate to foreigners was prohibited. In 1965, the United Nations promoted and supervised a plebiscite, and the population voted against independence, and in favor of maintaining its ties to Aotearoa.

[3] Prime Minister Geoffrey Henry governed the country with an iron hand for 15 years before being replaced in 1978 by Thomas Davis, of the Democratic Party (DP), who gave incentives to private fruit planters. However he was dismissed from office by Parliament in 1987, being replaced by Pupuke Robati, also of the DP. In the 1990 elections, Geoffrey Henry's Cook Islands Party was returned to office, and re-elected in 1994.

[4] From 1991 on, when Aotearoa's economic injections to the Cook Islands fell to 17 per cent of the local budget, both governments decided that the auditors in the Cook Islands would take charge of the State finances in place of the Aotearoan office.

[5] The public debt stood at around $900 million as the second half of the 1990s began. Prime Minister Geoffrey Henry announced a series of drastic measures including a 50 per cent reduction in State employees, a 15 per cent pay reduction for the remaining personnel and a privatization plan. In late 1997, some ministries were closed due to the lack of funds and the budget of the remaining entities was reduced by 10 per cent.

[6] The islands' government created a whale sanctuary in 2001, the largest declared by a country in waters of its jurisdiction, to protect these sea mammals from being hunted to extinction.

ENVIRONMENT

Area: 236.6 sq km. Archipelago located in the South Pacific 2,700 km northeast of Aotearoa/New Zealand, made up of 15 islands which extend over an ocean area of 2 million sq km. They are divided into 2 groups. The northern group is made up of 6 small coral atolls, which are low and arid, with a total area of 25.5 sq km. The southern group comprises 8 larger and more fertile volcanic islands (211 sq km). The capital, Avarua, is located on Rarotonga, the largest of the islands. Every 5 years, for the past 2 decades, the islands have suffered terrible droughts.

SOCIETY

Peoples: The majority of the population is Maori. There are also some Europeans (2.4 per cent).
Religions: Christian (Cook Islands Church).
Languages: English (official), Cook Island Maori. Language and traditions similar to Maori in Aotearoa/New Zealand.
Political Parties: Democratic Alliance (DA); The Cook Islands Party (CIP); New Alliance (NA).

THE STATE

Official Name: The Cook Islands.
Capital: Avarua 11,600 people (1999).
Government: Autonomous associated state. Apenera Short, Representative of Aotearoa. Terepai Moate, Prime Minister since January 1999. Single-chamber legislature; there is a Legislative Assembly, with 25 members elected by direct vote every five years.

Tokelau

Tokelau Islands

Population: 1,000 (2002)
Land area: 10 SQ KM
Capital: Fakaofo
Currency: NZ dollar
Language: Tokelauan

From ancient times, the islands were inhabited by Polynesian peoples who lived by subsistence fishing and farming. The first European to set foot on the islands was English explorer John Byron, who arrived in 1765. However, the absence of great riches meant that the islands did not arouse the colonial interests of the British Crown.

[2] In 1877, the islands became a British protectorate. Britain annexed them in 1916, and included them as part of the colonial territory of the Gilbert and Ellice Islands (now Kiribati and Tuvalu). In 1925, Britain transferred administrative control of the islands to Aotearoa (New Zealand). In 1946, the group was officially designated the Tokelau Islands, and in 1958 full sovereignty passed to Aotearoa.

[3] The Government of Aotearoa adopted policies intended to maintain traditional customs, institutions and communal relations in Tokelau. The population lives in relative isolation; until 1990 there was only a single ship calling at the islands from Apia (Samoa) every two or three months. The ocean and lagoons provide fish and seafood which are the islanders' staple subsistence foods. The lack of adequate harbours that could facilitate access to the island has

been a major obstacle for the develpoment of tourism.

[4] In the 1980s, farming underwent a crisis due to a number of adverse climatic conditions. As a consequence, emigration to Aotearoa rose considerably. The New Zealand Government tried to encourage Tokelau immigrants to return to their homeland, but its policies have not been successful.

[5] In 1976 and 1981 the UN sent delegations to Tokelau. On both occasions the envoys reported that the inhabitants of the islands did not wish to change their relations with Aotearoa/NZ. In December 1984, the UN Assembly decided that Aotearoa should continue to administer the islands. However, in the report submitted to the UN Special Committee in June 1987, Tokelau

expressed a wish to achieve greater political autonomy, while maintaining unchanged relations with Aotearoa.

[6] A UN report on the consequences of the greenhouse effect (the warming of the atmosphere as a result of pollution) included Tokelau among the islands which could disappear under the sea in the 21st century, unless drastic measures are taken to halt pollution.

[7] In February 1990, the three groups of islands which make up the country's territory were devastated by Hurricane Ofa, which destroyed all the banana trees and 80 per cent of the coconut plantations, as well as hospitals, schools, houses, and bridges. As a result, emigration to Aotearoa/NZ increased once again.

[8] Aotearoa established the first regular maritime transport service between the three atolls during 1991.

[9] In May 1995, Aotearoa's Parliament approved extended powers for the local assembly.

[10] New Zealand Official Development Aid (NZODA) set aside a budget of NZ$7.5 million for Tokelau in 2000.

[11] The Minister of Pacific Islands from New Zealand implemented support programs in management and development of policies in 2001, to help Tokelau initiate its self-rule. ∎

PROFILE

ENVIRONMENT

A group of coral islands, comprising three atolls: Atafu 2.02 sq km and 577 people, Nakunono 5.46 sq km and 374 people, Fakaofo 2.63 sq km and 664 people. Geographically, Sivains atoll belongs to the group but is an administrative dependency of American Samoa. The group is located in Polynesia in the South Pacific, to the east of the Tuvalu islands. The islands are flat, with thin, not very fertile soil. Rainfall is erratic and there are frequent droughts. Fishing constitutes the traditional economic activity.

SOCIETY

Peoples: The population is of Polynesian origin. **Religions:** Mostly Protestant, 70 per cent. **Languages:** Tokelauan (official), English and local dialects. **Political Parties:** Rally of the Togolose People, (RPT,

authoritarian), the only legal party since 1969 until 1991; Coordination of New Forces, (CFN, centrist). The opposition parties are: Union of the Forces for Change; Action Committee for Renewal; Patriotic Pan-African Convergence; Party for Democracy and Renewal; Democratic Convention of African Peoples, (social-democratic) and Union of Independent Liberals.

THE STATE

Official Name: Tokelau.
Capital: Fakaofo 540 people (1999).
Other cities: Fenua Fala, and small villages on every island.
Government: All executive and administrative functions are in theory vested in the Administrator of Tokelau, responsible to the New Zealand Minister of Foreign Affairs and Trade. In 1994 these powers were formally delegated to Tokelau's Fono (Parliament with 45 members, representatives of the

three atolls), or to the Council of Faipule (cabinet) when the Fono is not in session. In 1996 the New Zealand Parliament amended the 1948 Act to confer limited legislative power on the Fono, giving Tokelau in practice, and in large measure, administrative and political autonomy. Pio Tuia, Head of Government since January 2002. Lindsay Watt, Administrator since March 1993. Each village has a Council of Elders (Taupulega) made up of the heads of family. There is currently a strong movement to develop self-government institutions and frameworks; work is being done on a draft Constitution, aiming for independence and free association with Aotearoa.
National Holiday: February 6, Waitangi Day (1840).
Armed Forces: The defense is responsibility of New Zealand.

Argentina

Population: 37,944,000 (2002)
Land area: 2,736,690 SQ KM
Capital: Buenos Aires
Currency: Peso
Language: Spanish

Argentina

The Patagonians and the Andeans were the two largest groups living in what is now Argentina at the beginning of the 16th century. Patagonians included Tehuelch, Rehuelche, Rampa, Mataco and Guaycure peoples. The latter two were stable,agrarian civilizations, while the others were nomadic hunters and gatherers. They settled in the south, center and north of the country. The principal Andean groups were the Ancient Rehuenche, Algarrobero Rehuelche, Huerpe, Diaguita, Capayane, Omahuaca and Patama. Through contact with the Incas, they perfected their agricultural system introducing terracing and artificial irrigation. They raised llamas, and traded in the northwest and west of the country.

[2] The Spanish explorations in the 16th century took Amerigo Vespuccio in 1502, and Juan Diaz de Solis in 1516, up the estuary they baptized the River Plate (Plata) in honor of the silver they were seeking - but did not find. In 1526, Sebastian Cabot founded a fort on the banks of the Carcarañá river which was the first European settlement of present-day Argentina.

[3] To check the Portuguese advance, Spain sent Pedro de Mendoza to the region on a contract granting the conquistador established political and economic privileges.In 1536, de Mendoza founded Santa Maria del Buen Ayre (Buenos Aires), a small town which was abandoned in 1541 after being besieged by the indigenous peoples.

[4] Using Asunción (in today's Paraguay) as a focus for colonization, the Spanish founded several cities in what is now Argentine territory (Santiago del Estero, Córdoba, Santa Fé), until they came to the second founding of Buenos Aires in 1580. Under colonial administration, the region was in principle subject to the Vice-Royalty of Peru. Three cities were predominant in succession. Tucumán, linked with gold exploitation in Upper Peru, was the centre during the 16th century. Córdoba, where the first university of the region was established in 1613, was the intellectual centre during the 17th and 18th centuries. And after the new administrative divisions in 1776, the port city of Buenos Aires became capital of the new Viceroyalty of the River Plate, which covered what are now Bolivia, Paraguay, Argentina and Uruguay.

[5] In the 17th and 18th centuries, the Spanish conquest pushed the Mapuche - named Araucans by the Europeans - from Chile into the centre and south-east of present-day Argentina with the ensuing 'Araucanisation' of the local inhabitants. The abundance of cattle, which provided the main product the viceroyalty sent to the metropolis, caused great ethnic and cultural changes. Outside the cities, vast plains of good pasture were ranged by horsemen, some of whom were indigenous people (who modified their diet to feed on beef). The rest were *gauchos* - mixed race cowboys who lived by working the cattle.

[6] The strong bourgeoisie of the port area who favored free trade initiated the revolutionary movement of 1810, which created the United Provinces of the River Plate and overthrew the Viceroy, accusing him of a lack of loyalty to Spain, at that time occupied by Napoleon's troops. Gauchos and Indians swelled the ranks of armies organized in Buenos Aires to fight the Spanish crown beyond the frontiers of the Viceroyalty. General José de San Martín led the armies which defeated the royalists and contributed decisively to the independence of Chile and Peru.

[7] Even though the Spanish were quickly expelled, discrepancies between Buenos Aires and the rest of the United Provinces of the River Plate (including the present-day Republic of Uruguay) kept the region in a permanent state of war. The Unionists defended the centralism of Buenos Aires, which threatened the economy of the interior, while the Federalists pursued a more equitable agreement for all the provinces.

[8] In 1829 Juan Manuel de Rosas, a land-owner from federal roots (opposed to Buenos Aires' centralism), took over as governor of

WORKERS

1990/2000

UNEMPLOYMENT: 15%
LABOR FORCE AS % OF TOTAL:

▬ FEMALE: 33%   ▬ MALE: 67%

1994/97

EMPLOYMENT DISTRIBUTION:

F
M

▬ SERVICES	F: 88%	M: 65%
▬ INDUSTRY	F: 12%	M: 32%
▬ AGRICULTURE	F: 0%	M: 2%

LAND USE

DEFORESTATION: 0.3% annual (1990/95)

1993

▬ FOREST & WOODLAND: 18.4%
▬ ARABLE: 9%
▬ OTHER: 72.6 %

PUBLIC EXPENDITURE

1999

DEFENSE 9.1%
SOCIAL 63.6%

Buenos Aires. Rosas, who had himself proclaimed Restorer of the Laws, gained fame in the 'Desert Campaign' where Buenos Aires expelled the indigenous peoples from its surroundings. He used political means and force to pacify the interior, bringing most of the governors together and deploying troops from Buenos Aires as far as the frontiers with Bolivia and Chile.

9 Since Buenos Aires was the gateway to the Paraná and Uruguay rivers - main arteries for French and British trade with the provinces of the interior and Paraguay - Rosas brought in a customs law which restricted access to foreign vessels and products. The Rosas government was attacked by armies from both powers, which blockaded the port of Buenos Aires intending to crush the government and support Rosas' more liberal rivals. During the campaign to put pressure on Rosas in 1833 Britain occupied the Malvinas (Falkland Islands).

10 The 'Great War' (waged in Argentina and Uruguay between 1839 and 1852) involved Argentina, Uruguay, Paraguay and Brazil, and saw direct intervention from Britain and France, bringing an end to Rosas' 20 years in power.

11 Justo José de Urquiza, Governor of Entre Rios, then presided over the Argentine Confederation with its capital in Paraná in accordance with the federal constitution. However, there was resistance from Buenos Aires, which proclaimed independence and declared itself a separate state, even having diplomatic representation abroad. After 10 years of fighting, in 1861 Buenos Aires got its own way.

12 Bartolomé Mitre (president from 1862 to 1868) made an alliance with Pedro II, Emperor of Brazil, and Venancio Flores, president of Uruguay, to wage the 'War of the Triple Alliance' on Paraguay. The fighting started in 1865 and ended in 1870 with the death of Paraguayan president Francisco Solano López and most of the Paraguayan population. By the time 'victory' came, Domingo Faustino Sarmiento had taken over from Mitre.

13 Once the war was over, the rest of what is now Argentina was occupied through successive incursions against the indigenous peoples of Patagonia, the Chaco and the Andean regions of Río Negro. In 1879, General Julio Roca (president from 1880-86 and 1898-1904) ended Argentina's 60-year military campaign to exterminate the indigenous peoples. The railway, symbol of modernization, ensured the Buenos Aires government's control over the territory. The mass immigration of European workers, above all Spaniards and Italians,

changed the face of the nation which underwent unprecedented industrial, agricultural and commercial growth. The population grew from less than a million people in 1869 to almost eight million in 1914.

14 Up until the electoral law of President Roque Sáenz Peña in 1912, which guaranteed universal, secret and obligatory suffrage for adult men, political power had never been a matter of democratic elections, rather the product of permanent fraud. This was the cause of the 1874, 1890, 1893 and 1905 rebellions led by Mitre, Leandro Alem, Aristóbulo del Valle and Hipólito Irigoyen, respectively.

15 The Sáenz Peña Law helped the Radical Party led by Irigoyen into power in 1916. During World War I, in which Argentina was neutral, the country experienced industrial growth. One result of this was that the unions became far stronger. In 1919, in the 'Tragic Week', army troops machine-gunned striking workers while far-right activists opposed to the Government attacked the Jewish quarter to root out 'Bolsheviks'.

16 Despite being re-elected by a margin of two to one in 1928, Irigoyen was unable to ride the consequences of the world economic crisis of 1929, which drastically undermined the agro-exporter model. Irigoyen was ousted a year later in a military coup led by General José Félix Uriburu. The coup marked the end of a period of constitutional continuity which had lasted 68 years, as well as a long period of economic expansion based on the export of raw materials which had doubled between 1913 and 1928.

17 During World War II, President Ramon S. Castillo maintained Argentina's neutrality, provoking opposition. Another military coup ousted Castillo in 1943. Ensuing dissent within the army - which wanted neither to restore democracy nor to prolong an indefinite dictatorship - together with pressure from political groups and the United States (which wanted Argentina to support the Allies) brought Colonel Juan Domingo Perón to the presidency from his post in the Employment Ministry.

18 Perón supported the unions and won the 1946 elections by a narrow margin. Backed by the General Labor Confederation (CGT), he declared a state of civil war, which allowed him to get round the opposition and extend his authoritarian power. He nationalized foreign trade, the banks, the railway, gas and telephones; extended the fleet and created the air force; increased the workers' share of the national income to 50 per cent and

framed advanced social legislation. Furthermore, he organized workers and bosses into national confederations with whom he negotiated the economic and social policy. His wife Eva ('Evita') formed an exceptionally charismatic nexus between Perón and the workers, whom she dubbed 'the Shirtless Ones'. It was Eva Perón who was largely responsible for Argentina giving women the vote in 1947. On a foreign front Perón took the 'Third Position' between the two superpowers of the Cold War, which

brought him into conflict with the US.

19 Re-elected in 1951, Perón lost army support by confronting the Church. He was ousted in a coup in 1955 and forced into exile. A dictatorship headed by Pedro Aramburu replaced him, embracing the National Security Doctrine which passed responsibility for defending the region against 'the enemies of democracy' to the US. The dictatorship imposed a regressive wealth distribution system and opponents from both

army and civilian ranks were executed in the 1956 'Operation Massacre', a precursor of decades of political violence.

[20] 'Peronism' was outlawed, but it was the Peronist vote which brought the pro-development government of Arturo Frondizi to power in 1958, opening the country to oil and automobile transnationals, and implanting a model of growth and wealth concentration which fed serious social confrontations. Frondizi legalized 'Peronism', and in the 1962 parliamentary elections the Peronists won in 10 provinces. This provoked another coup from the army which toppled Frondizi. Following two serious confrontations between separate factions of the army, General Juan Carlos Onganía emerged as the new strongman.

[21] With Peronism banned once again, the Radical Party's Arturo Illia was elected in 1963 in the first administration for 40 years not to apply a State of Emergency nor other special measures for repression or cultural censorship. His term in office was marked by friction with the Peronist unions who organized strikes, demonstrations and occupations of factories.

[22] In June 1966, Illia was overthrown by the 'Argentinian Revolution' of General Juan Carlos Onganía, who brought in a new authoritarian model, politically clerical and corporatist, economically liberal and defender of the 'ideological borders' in foreign policy. Ongania consecrated the country to the Sacred Heart, banned political parties, intervened in the universities and the CGT and denationalised the economy: bankrupted companies were bought up extremely cheaply by US, British and German consortia.

[23] A succession of social uprisings, like the 1969 'Cordobazo', and the emergence of a guerrilla force, threatened to split the army. General Agustín Lanusse took over the presidency in 1971 and in order to preserve the military institution he announced elections, although he banned Perón, exiled in Madrid, from taking part.

[24] Héctor Cámpora, the 'Justicialista' Liberation Front candidate - a Peronist electoral coalition - received 49 per cent of the vote in the March 1973 elections, taking office in May 1973, and resigning two months later to allow new elections after Perón's return to the country. On September 23, Perón was re-elected in a new contest with 62 per cent of the vote, and the vice-presidency went to María Estela 'Isabelita' Martínez de Perón, his third wife.

[25] Cámpora resumed diplomatic relations with Cuba, proposed a reorganization of the Organization of American States (OAS) to serve Latin America's interests, promoted Argentina's participation in the Non-Aligned Movement and increased trade with socialist countries. After the Ezeiza massacre on June 23 1973, the day Perón returned to Argentina, friction grew among various Peronist factions and a situation of open warfare broke out between the old-time labor leaders and the 'special squads', as Perón used to call the guerrillas.

[26] When Perón died in 1974, his widow Isabelita took office. Her Social Welfare Minister (Perón's former secretary), José López Rega, set up the 'Triple A' (Argentine Anticommunist Alliance), a paramilitary hit squad that murdered Marxist opponents and left-wing Peronists.

[27] On March 24 1976, a military coup put an end to Isabelita's inefficient and corrupt administration. A military junta led by General Jorge Videla suspended all civil liberties and set in motion a cycle of kidnapping, torture, betrayal and murder. The term 'missing person' became ominously commonplace, and government priorities were dictated by the newly adopted 'National Security' doctrine. Human rights organizations drew up a list of over 10,000 missing persons, 80 per cent of whom had been arrested by the police in front of witnesses. Their fate has never been determined with certainty, but a 1983 Armed Forces communiqué stated that the *desaparecidos* (disappeared) should be considered 'killed in action' by counter-insurgency troops.

[28] The Junta encouraged imports to the point of liquidating a third of the country's productive capacity. Fifty years of labor gains were wiped out, real wages lost half their purchasing power, and regional economies were choked by high interest rates. The country's cattle herds decreased by 10 million head and the foreign debt climbed to $60 billion, a quarter of which had been spent on arms. It was the era of what Argentines called the *patria financiera* (financial fatherland), when governmental economic policies encouraged most of the country's productive sector to turn to speculation. In 1980, a wave of bankruptcies hit banks and financial institutions.

[29] In 1981, General Leopoldo Galtieri became president and Army Commander-in-Chief. He agreed on Argentinean military participation in the US intervention in Nicaragua and El Salvador. Thinking that this was enough to secure US president Reagan's unconditional support, Galtieri decided to ward off the domestic crisis by recovering the Malvinas Islands, in British hands since 1833. His troops landed there on April 2 1982. Galtieri's error soon became evident. The UN Security Council opposed the invasion, Britain deployed a powerful fleet that included nuclear submarines, and the United States firmly supported its North Atlantic ally. After 45 days of fighting Argentina surrendered on June 15; 750 Argentineans and 250 British soldiers had been killed during the conflict. Two days later Galtieri was forced to resign from both his military and presidential posts.

[30] Soon after Galtieri resigned, the upper echelons of the Armed Forces underwent a series of purges. The junta set elections for October 30 1983 and the Army, without consulting the Navy and the Air Force, appointed retired General Reynaldo Bignone acting president until January 30 1984.

[31] The Radical Civic Union's new leader, Raul Alfonsín, won the election with 52 per cent of the vote, well ahead of the Peronists' 40 per cent. During his campaign, Alfonsín denounced the existence of a pact between the military and trade unions, and he offered himself as the candidate of law and life, standing against tyranny and death. This won him the election, even in the Greater Buenos Aires industrial belt, a traditional Peronist stronghold.

[32] The new government, which started well, ended with the complete discrediting of Alfonsín. On the political front, the Government wanted to try the military leaders who had taken part in the 'Dirty War', responsible for the disappearance of more than 30,000 people. On the economic front, it aimed to tackle inflation head on, as this had reached astronomical proportions - 688 per cent by the end of 1984 - by reducing public spending and launching the Austral Plan, which froze prices, fees for services and established a new currency, the Austral, initially worth more than the dollar.

[33] On the basis of revelations made in CONADEP (National Commission of Missing Persons) studies nine Commanders in Chief of the dictatorship were put on public trial accused of having ordered the crimes of that period. The sentences meted out to several high-ranking army leaders - including former president Videla - and the later extension of the trials to lower ranking officers caused strong pressures amongst the military and between 1987 and 1989, Alfonsín had to put down four military uprisings. In 1987, the President sent Congress the 'Due Obedience' bill, which was approved, exempting most military personnel accused of human rights violations, claiming they were simply obeying orders from above.

[34] The failure of the Austral Plan led to thousands of jobs being lost between December 1983 and April 1989, salaries were drastically reduced and some 10 million inhabitants - almost 30 per cent of the population - were virtually pushed out of the consumer market. In this period, the CGT organized 14 general strikes and shops were raided in various areas of the capital and some cities of the interior.

[35] The May 1989 presidential elections brought the Peronist Carlos Saúl Menem to power, the man who was to govern until 1999. The magnitude of the economic troubles resulted in the new president being asked to take office a couple of months early. Menem, who had been governor of La Rioja, established a program of privatizations based on the August 1989 State Reform Act. In his first year in power, the privatization of the state oil company was promoted. The economic liberalization policy caused a schism in the CGT between the sectors supporting the Government and those opposing them. The split in the Army was repeated in the main political parties.

[36] Menem re-established relations with the United Kingdom (leaving the key issue of sovereignty over the Malvinas under an ambiguous 'protective umbrella') and in two stages pardoned all the army officers responsible for the 'Dirty War'. In 1991, Argentina announced it would be leaving the Non-Aligned Movement and in early 1992 the country joined the US in condemning the human rights situation in Cuba, breaking its traditional stance of non-interference.

[37] Despite constant scandal and accusations of corruption, Menem maintained his image thanks to the economic stability achieved by the Convertibility Plan, which drastically reduced public spending and established parity between the new monetary unit - the peso - and the US dollar. Inflation fell and reached a historical low: in 1993 it was 7.4 per cent.

[38] Even though the Gross Domestic Product saw strong growth, industrial activity remained below 1987 indices. Unequal wealth distribution across the various regions worsened.

[39] The big surprise of the 1994 constituent elections was the performance of the leftist Frente Grande (Broad Front), which became the third strongest political force in the nation and triumphed in the Federal Capital with 37.6 per cent of the vote. It also won in the southern province of Neuquén. In Buenos Aires it became the second political force with 16.4 per cent of the vote. However, Peronists and

MATERNAL MORTALITY 1985/99

Per 100,000 live births

41

LITERACY 2000

97%

FOOD DEPENDENCY 2000

2000

5%

Radicals obtained the majority necessary to ensure the constitutional reform which allowed Menem to stand for re-election.

[40] Shortly before Menem won the elections with 50 per cent of the vote in May 1995, scandal struck at the heart of his family. When Menem's son, Carlos Menem Junior was killed in a helicopter crash, the President's former wife, Zulema Yoma, claimed her son had been murdered despite the federal police classing the crash as an accident.

[41] In August, Economy Minister Domingo Cavallo accused postal entrepreneur Alfredo Yabrán, a close ally of Menem, of being a 'Mafia chief' who aimed to monopolize the postal system and make million-dollar deals under cover of the State.

[42] In mid-1996, unemployment topped 2 million and underemployment 1.5 million, according to official figures. Foreign debt was up 57 per cent on its 1991 level, at the beginning of the anti-inflationary plan applied by the Government. In the first quarter of 1996, Menem sacked Cavallo. His replacement, Roque Fernández, a Chicago-school economist, kept Cavallo's policies in place and promised to reduce the fiscal deficit, unemployment and the recession.

[43] The murder of José Luis Cabezas, a photographer for a magazine critical of the government, added to the tension in late January 1997, as the media blamed Yabrán for the murder. The guilty parties, tried in late 1999, were members of Yabrán's security forces. Yabrán himself committed suicide in mid-1998, as the police net closed in on him. In the elections for the lower house in August, the ruling Justicialista Party was beaten nationally for the first time in 51 years. It was pushed out by the Electoral Alliance (made up of the Radical Party and Frepaso).

[44] In the 1999 presidential elections, the Alliance candidate, the radical Fernando de la Rúa, was victorious with almost 50 per cent of the vote in the first round. The Justicialist, Eduardo Duhalde was beaten, as was former minister Domingo Cavallo, in third place with around 10 per cent of the vote. In the Federal Capital, the biggest voting constituency in the

country, the former vice president, Justicialist Carlos Ruckauf won by a narrow margin.

[45] Economic recession deepened in 2000 and the new administration, which had promised to fight corruption, was involved in a scandal affecting relations among the Government branches. In September, Vice President Carlos 'Chacho' Álvarez denounced the Government had bribed several legislators in April, with money from expenses reserved for Intelligence services, so they would pass a new labor law. That month, senator Silvia Sapag, from Neuquen province, denounced that a Justicialist senator, chair of the Energy Commission, had offered her money, supplied by oil companies, for her to vote the new hydrocarbons bill. Álvarez requested the suspension of those involved, but De la Rúa, who modified the Cabinet, confirmed them, resulting in the Vice President's resignation in October.

[46] In late 2000, the IMF granted Argentina 40 billion dollars in aid to cover social needs, but these funds were spent amidst the country's difficulty to obtain funds from foreign private investors. Debt interests grew and Argentina found itself paying 2.7 billion dollars per year to the IMF, only one of its many creditors.

[47] After failing to reactivate the economy and once the country risk index reached 800 points, Economy Minister José Luis Machinea resigned in March 2001. The following day, De la Rúa requested his Cabinet's resignation. Liberal Ricardo López Murphy became the new Economy Minister and confirmed he would reach the goals agreed with the IMF. But when the new minister presented his plan, which implied a cut in government expenses to reduce the fiscal deficit, three ministers and six high officials resigned, in protest. To replace López Murphy, De la Rúa appointed Cavallo, who announced he would reduce the state deficit to zero, through expense cuts. The Senate passed a law binding the State to spend only what it had collected, and included a 13 per cent cut in state wages and pensions.

[48] Legislative elections were held on October 14, with 30 per cent abstention and 22 per cent of invalid or blank ballots (the so-called

bronca - anger - vote). Half the Chamber of Deputies (127 members) was renewed, as happens every two years, and all 72 members of the Senate were elected. Government candidates were defeated by the Peronists.

[49] In early December, the IMF denied Argentina a new loan, arguing that an economic policy that combined fiscal deficit, high debt and a fixed exchange-rate system (the convertibility that pegged the peso to the dollar) was unsustainable, and demanded more budget cuts. By then, Argentina owed international organizations more than $140 billion (54 per cent of its GDP) and, as a result of the crisis, had lost approximately $19 billion in investments.

[50] The massive withdrawal of deposits forced the Government to apply a series of temporary restrictions on accounts. The measure, announced on December 1 for an initial period of 90 days, came to be known as the *corralito* - little corral. Unemployment, which had reached 18.3 per cent, and social discontent were translated into a nationwide strike which paralyzed the country and ended with Cavallo's resignation.

[51] After failing to form a national unity government, De la Rúa resigned on December 20, amidst massive street protests. The demonstrations, which included looting in supermarkets and other businesses in downtown Buenos Aires, were severely repressed by security forces, which opened fire on the demonstrators, killing six and injuring dozens. Hundreds of people were detained.

[52] After De la Rúa resigned, Senate chairman Ramón Puerta, a Justicialist, first in the succession line due to the absence of a Vice-President, took office as President. Shortly after, the Legislative Assembly named another Justicialist, Adolfo Rodríguez Saá, who during the five days of his Presidency, announced the suspension of foreign debt payments and promised to create one million jobs. Rodríguez Saá resigned on December 30, pressured by his own party. Since Puerta rejected the Presidency, Eduardo Camaño, Chamber of Deputies

STATISTICS

DEMOGRAPHY
Population: 37,944,000 (2002)
Annual growth: 1.3 % (1985-2000)
Estimates for year 2015: 43,498,000 (2000)
Annual growth to year 2015: 1.1 % (2000)
Urban population: 89.4 % (2000)
Urban growth: 1.5 % (2000)
Children per woman: 2.5 (2000)

HEALTH
Life expectancy at birth: 74 years (2000-2005)
male: 71 years (2000-2005)
female: 78 years (2000-2005)
Maternal mortality: 41 per 100,000 live births (1985/99)
Infant mortality: 18 per 1,000 (2000)
Under-5 child mortality: 21 per 1,000 (2000)
Daily calorie supply: 3,176 per capita (1999)
268 doctors per 100,000 people (1992)

EDUCATION
Literacy: 97 % (2000)
male: 97 % (2000)
female: 97 % (2000)
School enrolment (net):
Primary total: 96 % (1994/2000)
male: 96 % (1995/99)
female: 96 % (1995/99)
Secondary (gross):
male: 73 % (1995/97)
female: 81 % (1995/97)
Tertiary (gross): 47 % (1998)
Primary school teachers: one for every 21 pupils (1998)

COMMUNICATIONS
37 newspapers (1998), 681 radios (1997), 293 TV sets (1998) and 213 main telephone lines (2000) per 1,000 people
Books: 26 new titles per 100,000 people (1992/94)

ECONOMY
Per capita, GDP: $ 12,377 (2000)
Annual growth: -1.7 % (2000)
Annual inflation: -0.9 % (2000)
Consumer price index: 99.5 (2000)
Currency: 2.1 pesos = $ 1 (03/2002)
Cereal imports: 47,730 metric tons (2000)
Food import dependency: 5 % (2000)
Fertilizer use: 329 kg per ha (1999)
Exports: $ 30,731 million (2000)
Imports: $ 32,552 million (2000)
External debt: $ 146,172 million (2000); $ 3,947 per capita (2000)
Debt service: 75.9 % of exports (1999)
Development aid received: $ 91 million (1999); $ 2.5 per capita (1999)

ENERGY
Consumption: 1,725.9 Kgs of oil equivalent per capita yearly (1998); -29.7 % imported (1999)

HDI (ranking/value): 34 / 0.842 (1999)

chairman and also from the PJ, was sworn in as interim President and called the Legislative Assembly. Finally, Duhalde - main Justicialist opposed to Menem - was chosen at a special session held on January 1 2002. Duhalde was allowed to preside over the Argentine Government until September 2003 and elections scheduled for March 3 were cancelled.

53 The Government announced in January 2002 that the corralito would be enforced until 2003 and people would only recover their money in installments. The Central Bank was forced to intervene in the exchange-rate market to avoid the peso from crashing. Protests continued throughout the country, causing destruction in banks and automatic bank tellers. Duhalde, who had undertaken in early January that those with deposits in dollars would get dollars in return, broke his promise and announced the blocked deposits would be returned only in devalued pesos. The total amount of savings in US currency, according to the Argentine Central Bank, reached $44.8 billion.

54 A massive nationwide *cacerolazo* (pot-banging protest carried out mostly by the middle class) took place on January 26 against corruption, the corralito and the Supreme Court of Justice. The population's discontent with the Court increased, among other things, after the judges freed former President Menem, who had been detained for arms smuggling to Croatia and Ecuador.

55 The Impeachment Commission of the Chamber of Deputies initiated in February impeachment proceedings against Supreme Court judges, charged with corruption. Duhalde denounced the judges for blackmail. After several months, the judges declared the corralito unconstitutional, to avoid going to trial.

56 In February the Government 'peso-ed' the economy and freed the dollar's flotation, while the Argentinian peso exceeded the 3-unit per dollar barrier. Without political backing from Congress to approve the Bonex plan - which aimed to turn dollar deposits, pesoed at 1.4 pesos in January, into a bond in pesos with 5-year expiry date - Economy Minister Jorge Remes Lenicov resigned in April. Duhalde replaced him with Roberto Lavagna, who started to devise a plan to avoid the dollar's uncontrollable rise. Reports indicated that 14 million Argentinians, almost half the total population, were living in poverty. ∎

Falklands/Malvinas

Islas Malvinas

Population:	2,000 (2002)
Land area:	12,170 SQ KM
Capital:	Port Stanley (Puerto Argentino)
Currency:	Pound sterling
Language:	English

When the islands were sighted for the first time in 1520 by a Spanish ship, they were uninhabited. In the 18th century, they were baptized the 'Malouines' in honor of Saint Malo, port of origin of the French fishermen and seal hunters who settled there. In 1764, Louis Antoine Bougainville founded Port Louis on Soledad Island. This move brought Spanish protests, and France recognized Spain's prior claim. That same year the British, who since 1690 had called the islands 'Falkland' (after the treasurer of the British Navy), founded Port Egmont. This was later returned to Spain in exchange for $24,000, and renamed Puerto Soledad.

2 In 1820, shortly after independence, Argentina appointed Daniel Jewit as first Governor of the Malvinas. In 1831, Governor Vernet impounded two US ships on charges of illegal fishing. A US fleet that was visiting South America avenged this act of 'piracy' by destroying houses and military facilities at Port Soledad. On January 3, 1833, the English corvette Clio landed a contingent of settlers, which the small local force was unable to repel.

3 After World War II, the United Nations Decolonization Committee included the Malvinas and their dependencies on the list of 'non-autonomous' territories and established that, as the inhabitants were British, the principle of self-determination was not applicable. The only juridically valid solution to the problem was to recognize Argentinian sovereignty.

4 On April 2 1982, Argentinian forces occupied the Malvinas. British Prime Minister Margaret Thatcher, whose popularity rating had been rock bottom before the conflict, responded by going to war. Two months later, at the cost of more than 1,000 lives, the Union Jack was once again hoisted over the islands.

5 Diplomatic relations between Britain and Argentina were placed on hold. At the beginning of his administration, Menem renewed relations with London, but the intractable issue of the Malvinas' sovereignty was left pending. During his first official visit to Malvinas, British Foreign Minister Douglas Hurd emphasized London's determination to maintain the islands under British sovereignty.

6 In November 1991 Britain authorized the Governor of the Malvinas to award contbacts for the exploration for and exploitation of possible underwater oil deposits around the islands.

7 In March 1994, the Argentinian Minister of Defense reported that in 1982, at least 9 Argentinian soldiers had died at the hands of British forces, in circumstances that violated the Geneva Convention on the treatment of prisoners of war. There were still some 15,000 live mines scattered across the islands.

8 Understanding agreed between President Carlos Menem and Prime Minister John Major at the United Nations, in September 1995, established that.Argentina and the United Kingdom will explore and exploit jointly the west of the islands, where border lines overlap.

9 The giant US oil company Amerada Hess announced on May 1998 the presence of 'minor hydrocarbons' while drilling a pilot well 120 miles off the north of the islands.

10 In October 1999, an Argentine contingent flew to the island, the first such visit since 1982. Members of the group, who were ex-combatants and journalists, paid tribute to those who died in the war. This historic trip was the result of talks between the Argentine and British governments.

11 On the 20th anniversary of the war, MPs and Eduardo Duhalde, interim president of Argentina since 2002, declared the government's intent to recover sovereignty of the islands, not through war but through 'patience and perseverance'.∎

PROFILE

ENVIRONMENT

An archipelago with nearly 100 islands located in the South Atlantic. It includes Georgia, Sandwich and Shetland Islands. There are two main islands - Soledad (East Malvina) and Gran Malvina (West Malvina) - separated by the San Carlos Channel. The coast is rough and mountainous. More than half of the population lives in the capital on Soledad. The main economic activity is sheep raising. The islands' territorial waters are believed to contain oil reserves. There is also hope that krill (a microscopic crustacean rich in protein) can be marketed. Its proximity to Antarctica also gives the archipelago strategic importance.

SOCIETY

Peoples: Since June 1982, the British have maintained a 4,000-strong garrison on the islands.
Language: English. **Religion:** Mostly Anglican; Catholics, other Protestant churches.

THE STATE

Capital: Port Stanley (Puerto Argentino) 2,000 people (1999).
Government: Donald Lamont, Governor since May 1999, appointed by Britain. The Legislative Assembly has 10 members, 8 members elected for a four year term and 2 members ex officio. At the last elections, 22 November 2001, only non-partisans have been elected in elections with a turnout of 68.7 %.
Armed Forces: 4,000 UK soldiers since June 1982.

Armenia

Population: 3,790,000 (2002)
Land area: 28,200 SQ KM
Capital: Yerevan
Currency: Dram
Language: Armenian

Hayastán

The first historical reference to the country 'Armina' (Armenia) was made in the cuneiform writings from the era of King Darius I of Persia (6th-5th centuries BC). But the name Hayk, as the Armenians are called, comes from the name of the country, Hayasa, mentioned in the Hittite writings from the 12th century BC. The Urartians, direct ancestors of the Armenians, founded a powerful state in the 9th to 6th centuries BC; its capital was the city of Tushpa (today Van, in Turkey). In the year 782 BC, they founded the fortress of Erebuni, in the north of the country (today Yerevan, capital of Armenia).

[2] With the collapse of Ur, the ancient Kingdom of Armenia emerged in its territory. The first rulers were the *satraps* (viceroys) of the shahs of Persia. This period was recorded in the works of Xenophon and Herodotus. In *Anabasis*, Xenophon described how the Armenians turned back 10,000 Greek mercenaries in 400 BC. His writings also describe Armenia's prosperous production, its wheat, fruit and delicious wines.

[3] After the expeditions of Alexander the Great and the rise of the Seleucid Empire, Armenia came under extensive Greek influence which had an important effect upon the cultural life of the country. The Seleucid State fell into the hands of the Romans in 190 BC, and Armenia became independent. The local government named Artashes (Artaxias) King of Greater Armenia.

[4] Armenia reached the pinnacle of its prosperity during the reign of Tigranes the Great (95-55 BC). King Tigranes united all Armenian-speaking regions and annexed several neighboring areas. Its borders extended as far as the Mediterranean to the south, the Black Sea to the north and the Caspian Sea to the east. Tigranes' empire soon fell, and Armenia was proclaimed 'friend and ally of the Roman people', a euphemism for the vassals of Rome.

[5] Armenia began to disintegrate over a 400-year period until it finally disappeared as a state in the year 428 AD, when the Roman Empire and the new kingdom of Persia divided it up between them.

[6] In 301, Armenia had become the first country in the world officially to adopt Christianity as a state religion. At that time, St Gregory the Illuminator, the first Armenian patriarch, founded the monastery at Echmiadzin, still extant as the headquarters for the patriarchs of the Armenian Church. Ever since the 4th century the Church has been identified with Armenian national feeling as religion made it possible to maintain the unity of the people over the long period during which the country lacked any actual state organization.

[7] In 405, the monk Mesrop Mashtots devised an alphabet that formed the basis of the Armenian writing system. The characters of this alphabet have remained unchanged, achieving a continuity which spans the centuries and links ancient, medieval and modern cultures. The 5th century was the golden age of religious and secular literature and of Armenian historiography; the natural sciences also developed during a later period. In the 7th century, Ananias Shirakatsi wrote that the world was round and formulated the hypothesis that there were several worlds inhabited by beings endowed with some form of intelligence.

[8] In the 5th and 6th centuries, Armenia was divided between Byzantium and Persia. The Persians tried to stamp out all traces of Christianity in the eastern Armenian regions triggering a massive rebellion. Prince Vartan Mamikonian, commander of the Armenian army, assumed the leadership of the rebellion. In the year 452, he led an army of 60,000 troops into battle against a vastly superior Persian force, in the Avaraev valley. The Armenians were defeated and Prince Vartan was killed, but the Persians also suffered heavy losses, and subsequently gave up their attempts to convert the Armenians to Islam. All those who lost their lives in this battle were later canonized by the Armenian Church.

[9] In the 7th century, Arab forces invaded Persia, bringing about the collapse of the Persian Empire. The new Muslim leaders also established control over the Armenian regions. The people resisted, fighting for their independence until the late 9th century, when Prince Ashot Bagratuni was named King of Armenia, and established an independent government. The epic novel *David of Sasun* describes this long struggle for independence.

[10] The prosperity of the Bagratids' reign was short-lived, for in the 11th century the Byzantines and Seleucids began bearing down on the Transcaucasian region from Central Asia. Many Armenian princes ceded their lands to the Byzantine Emperor, in exchange for lands in Cilicia (in modern-day Turkey). The inhabitants of other Armenian regions began flocking to Cilicia, fleeing the Turkish raids.

[11] At the end of the 11th century, the Rubenid dynasty founded a new Armenian state in Cilicia, which lasted 300 years. Cilicia had close ties to the western European states; Armenian troops took part in the Crusades, and intermarriage with other ruling dynasties introduced the Rubenids to the circle of European rulers. In 1375, Armenian Cilicia fell to the Mamelukes of Egypt, who retained Cilician science, culture and literature. In the meantime, the region that had originally been Armenia was devastated by invasions and wars.

[12] In the 13th century the Ottoman Turks replaced the Seleucids and began their conquest of Asia Minor. In 1453, they took Constantinople and marched eastwards, invading Persia. Armenia was the scene of numerous wars between Turkey and Persia, until the 17th century, when the country was divided between the two Islamic empires. During this period, the Church carried out secular functions and also called the attention of fellow-Christian European countries to the plight of the Armenians, who were forced to emigrate and settle far from their home country. Many of these expatriate Armenian 'colonies' exist to this day.

[13] In 1722, Russian troops sent an expedition to Transcaucasia, occupying the city of Baku and other territories belonging to Persia. Armenian princes in Nagorno-Karabakh and other neighboring areas seized the opportunity to join forces with the Russians, and organized a revolution against the Persians. The uprising was led by the Armenian national hero David-bek. However, Armenian hopes were dashed when the Russian Czar, Peter the Great, died. He had promised to support the Armenians, but on his death Russia signed a peace treaty with Persia. Another war between Russia and Persia, one hundred years later, ended in 1813 with the Treaty of Gulistan. According to the terms of this, Karabakh and other territories that had historically belonged to Armenia became part of the Russian Empire.

[14] Russia was at war with either Turkey or Persia during most of the 19th century; with each war, Russia annexed more and more Armenian territory. Finally, almost the entire eastern part - home to more than 2 million Armenians - was swallowed up. However, the major part of Armenia's historic lands - with a population of more than 4 million - belonged to Turkey.

[15] Protected by Russia against wars and invasions, Eastern Armenia prospered, while within the Ottoman Empire the Armenians were the objects of abuse and persecution. There were frequent disturbances and riots, which were cruelly suppressed by the Turks in 1915. During World War I, citing the Armenians' pro-Russian sympathies, the

'Young Turk' government perpetrated the massacre that killed between 800,000-1,000,000 Armenians. While the men were executed in the villages, the women and children were sent to the Syrian deserts, where they starved to death. Survivors of these atrocities sought refuge in Armenian expatriate communities.

[16] At the fall of the Russian Empire, Armenia's independence was proclaimed in Yerevan. Turkey attacked Armenia in 1918 and again in 1920. In spite of some resounding victories on the part of the Armenian troops, the young republic's economy suffered and it also lost a significant part of its territory. In late 1920, a coalition of communists and nationalists proclaimed the Soviet Republic of Armenia. The nationalists were eased out of power and in February 1921 the Communist government was brought down. However, with the help of the Red Army - which came into Armenia from Azerbaijan - the Communists were back in power after three months of fighting.

[17] In 1922, Armenia, Georgia and Azerbaijan formed the Transcaucasian Soviet Federated Socialist Republic, which became a part of the USSR at the end of the year. In order to avoid friction between Christian Armenians and Muslim Azeris, the Soviet regime adopted the policy of the separation of nationalities into different political/administrative entities, which implied the relocation of large segments of the population. In 1923, the Nakhichevan (Nachicevan) Autonomous Soviet Socialist Republic was created as a dependency of Azerbaijan, from which the entire Armenian population had been removed. Azerbaijan was also given Upper Nagorno-Karabakh, a region which had historically been Armenian and which Azerbaijan had previously relinquished in 1920. In 1936, the Transcaucasian Federation was dissolved, and the republics joined the Soviet Union as separate constituent republics.

[18] In 1965, Armenians around the world commemorated the 1915 genocide for the first time. In the Armenian capital, demonstrators clamored for the return of their lands, referring to the region of Upper Karabakh. The first petition for the reunification of Nagorno-Karabakh and Armenia - signed by 2,500 inhabitants of the former - was submitted to Nikita Krushchev, president of the USSR, in May 1963.

Since that time, there have been two diametrically opposed positions: Armenia, in favor of reunification, and Azerbaijan, against. In 1968, fighting broke out between Armenians and Azeris in Stepanakert, the capital of Nagorno-Karabakh (see Azerbaijan).

[19] In February 1988, within the framework of *perestroika* (restructuring) in the USSR, Nagorno-Karabakh Armenians (80 per cent of the local population) decided to join Armenia. Karabakh's Regional *Soviet* (Parliament) approved the resolution and in Armenia, the Karabakh petition for reunification was received enthusiastically. Moscow reacted violently and sent in troops to crush the demonstrations in Yerevan and Stepanakert.

[20] In the September 1991 referendum, 99.3 per cent of the electorate voted in favor of secession from the USSR. The Armenian Soviet proclaimed independence and in October Levon Ter-Petrosian was elected President with 83 per cent of the vote.

[21] That month Nagorno-Karabakh also declared independence after 99 per cent of the electorate approved separation. Azerbaijan responded with an economic and military blockade, sparking a war between the two republics. In December 1991 Armenia joined the Commonwealth of Independent States (CIS) and in February 1992 was admitted to the UN.

[22] From early 1993, while the pro-Armenian forces won important victories on the Nagorno-Karabakh front, Yerevan began to withdraw its unconditional support, at least officially.

[23] In May 1994 - when, according to Azerbaijan, the Armenian forces had taken over 12,000 square km of disputed territory - Russian pressure made a ceasefire possible. Some 20,000 people had been killed in the war and one million displaced from their homes.

[24] Ter-Petrosian started a second term as President after winning the September 1996 elections, but ongoing protests about the social situation - 20 per cent unemployment-forced him to resign in 1998. In the elections for the remaining term, Robert Kocharian, native of Nagorno-Karabakh defeated Karen Demirchian, leader of the Communist Party for 14 years during the Soviet era.

[25] Demirchian, now in the Miasnutiun (Unity) Alliance, was avenged in the June 1999 parliamentary elections, when he was elected president of the legislature with 43 per cent of the vote. But in October an armed group with no ties to political organizations entered Parliament and killed Prime Minister Vazgen Sarkisian, Demirchian and other lawmakers, including two ministers. As a result of negotiations with Kocharian, the attackers stepped down in exchange for guarantees of their personal safety.

[26] In February 2000 Armenia joined the Council of Europe as a full member. At mid-year, the European Parliament unanimously upheld a 1987 resolution establishing that Turkey could only enter the EU as a full member once it publicly recognized the 1915 Armenian genocide.

[27] That same year, Russian President Vladimir Putin inaugurated the visits of Russian leaders to independent Armenia. The treaty signed by both sides authorized the Russian army to defend Armenia's Turkish borders. Iran began setting up the Collective Security Committee, consisting of Armenia, Russia, Belarus, Kazakhstan, Kyrgyzstan and Tajikistan, which was strengthened a year later in Yerevan to include military cooperation against Islamic extremism.

[28] A thousand people gathered in Yerevan in October 2001, the second anniversary of the attack on Parliament, to demand the resignation of Kocharian, accusing him of hiding information about the crime and its organizers. ■

PROFILE

ENVIRONMENT

Armenia is a mountainous country, bounded to the north by Georgia, in the east by Azerbaijan and in the south, by Turkey and Iran. With an average altitude of 1,800 meters, high Caucasian peaks - like Mount Aragats (4,095 meters) - alternate with volcanic plateaus and deep river valleys. The most important river is the Aras, a tributary of the Kura, which forms a natural boundary with Turkey and Iran. The climate is dry and continental; the summers are long and hot and the winters extremely cold. On the plains, wheat, cotton, tobacco and sugar beet are grown. There are also vineyards, from which good quality wine is made. Cattle-raising is generally limited to the mountains. There are important copper, aluminum and molybdenum deposits. Environmental problems include soil contamination with highly toxic chemicals, such as DDT; overproduction of electricity resulting in pollution in Lake Sevan; problems at nuclear plant of Medzynor installed in a sismic region.

SOCIETY

Peoples: 93.3 per cent Armenian; 2.6 per cent Azeri; 2.3 per cent Russian; 1.7 per cent Kurd. **Religions:** Most belong to the Armenian Church (a branch of the Christian Orthodox Church). **Languages:** Armenian (official), Russian, Azerbaijani and Kurdish. **Political Parties:** Ruling government coalition of the Republican Party of Armenia and the People's Party of Armenia. Communist Party of Armenia (HKK); Law and Unity Party (IM); Armenian Revolutionary Federation (Dashnaktsutyun Party), social-democratic. Several minority parties (Armenian National Movement (HHS), Armenian Women's Party Shamiram, Democratic Party of Armenia (DPA) and others).

THE STATE

Official Name: Hayastani Hanrapetut'yun (Republic of Armenia). **Administrative divisions:** 10 provinces. **Capital:** Yerevan (Erevan) 1,281,000 people (1999). **Other cities:** Gyumri 130,400 people; Alaverdi 30,800; Dilijan 27,800; Goris 27,900 (2000).

Government: Robert Kocharian, President since February 1998; Andranik Markaryan, Prime Minister since May 2000. Single chamber National Assembly with 131 members. **National Holiday:** May 28, Independence (1918). **Armed Forces:** 57,400 (1996).

DEMOGRAPHY

Population: 3,790,000 (2002). **Estimates for year 2015:** 3,808,000 (2000). **Urban population:** 70 % (2000). **Urban growth:** 0.5 % (2000). **Children per woman:** 1.3 (2000)

HEALTH

Life expectancy at birth: 73 years (2000-2005). male: 70 years (2000-2005). female: 76 years (2000-2005) **Maternal mortality:** 35 per 100,000 live births (1985/99). **Infant mortality:** 25 per 1,000 (2000). **Under-5 child mortality:** 30 per 1,000 (2000). **Daily calorie supply:** 2,167 per capita (1999). 316 doctors per 100,000 people (1998).

EDUCATION

Literacy: 99 % (2000). **male:** 100 % (2000) **female:** 99 % (2000). **Secondary (gross):** **male:** 85 % (1995/97). **female:** 91 % (1995/97). **Tertiary (gross):** 12 % (1997). **Primary school teachers:** one for every 19 pupils (1996)

COMMUNICATIONS

6 newspapers (1998), 225 radios (1997), 244 TV sets (2000) and 152 main telephone lines (2000) per 1,000 people Books: 6 new titles per 100,000 people (1992/94)

ECONOMY

Per capita, GDP: $ 2,559 (2000). **Annual growth:** 5.9 % (2000). **Consumer price index:** 146.7 (2000). **Currency:** 567.0 dram = $ 1 (03/2002) **Exports:** $ 447 million (2000) **Imports:** $ 972 million (2000) **External debt:** $ 898 million (2000); $ 237 per capita (2000)

HDI (ranking/value): 72 / 0.745 (1999)

Aruba

Population: 108,000 (2002)
Land area: 190 SQ KM
Capital: Oranjestad
Currency: Aruban florin
Language: Dutch

Aruba

The Caiquetios, an Arawak nation originating in the Orinoco River basin, settled on the island now known as Aruba some 2,000 years ago (see box 'Arawaks and Caribs: Genocide in paradise'). Their culture and livelihood, based on intensive cultivation of manioc/cassava, sweet potato and maize, as well as hunting and gathering, underwent a dramatic change in 1499 when the island caught the attention of Spaniard Alonso de Ojeda. Within two decades, most of the population had been decimated by the diseases and slavery introduced by the Europeans.

[2] According to the Treaty of Westfalia (1648), the Netherlands ruled over Aruba, Curaçao and Bonaire. Aruba required little labor to support its horse and cattle-raising industry, which explains why only 12 per cent of the population was of African origin by the time slavery was abolished.

[3] The installation of large oil refineries on Aruba at the end of the 1920s generated a wave of immigration of specialized, high income workers, particularly from the US. Many Arubans began to resent the administrative dominance of Curaçao.

[4] In 1971, the Aruba People's Party (AVP), led by Prime Minister Henny Eman, an anti-Dutch, anti-

Curaçao nationalist, split into two separate parties. One was the Aruban Patriotic Party (PPA), which opposed the separation of Aruba. The other was the People's Electoral Movement (MEP), radical wing, led by Gilberto 'Betico' Croes, which supported each island's freedom to choose its own constitution and even become an autonomous republic. After the Netherlands' refusal to accept this proposal, Croes threatened a unilateral declaration of independence.

[5] In 1979 the Antiyas Nobo

Movement (MAN), active on 16 islands, won a significant electoral victory in Curaçao. With the MEP and the Bonaire Patriotic Union (UPB), it established a left-of-center coalition government. But while MAN favored a federation with broad autonomy for each island, the MEP insisted on the secession of Aruba. These differences led to the disintegration of the governmental alliance in 1981.

[6] In 1983, the Dutch Government granted Aruba separate status, effective from January 1986, establishing a governor appointed by

the Dutch queen, a single-chamber parliament with 21 members and its own national symbols. In the 1985 election, eight seats were won by the MEP, seven by the AVP and the remaining six by three minor parties who entered a coalition with the AVP. Henny Eman was Prime Minister. Croes died in 1986 in suspicious circumstances.

[7] In the 1989 elections the MEP won 10 seats, the AVP won 8, and each of the 3 remaining parties, National Democratic Action (ADN), New Patriotic Party (PPN), and Aruban Patriotic Party (PPA), gained one seat. The new Prime Minister Nelson Odaber, defended continued association with the Netherlands.

[8] The economy of Aruba has the support of Dutch credit. It exports rum and tobacco, but 98.9 per cent of its exports came from refining Venezuelan oil. In 1985 Exxon, the owners of the refinery, withdrew from the country, leaving the island's economy in serious difficulties. With unemployment at 20 per cent, the Government turned to the tourist industry, which has provided 35 per cent of GDP.

[9] In 1986 Aruba split off from the Netherlands Antilles as a first step towards what was to be total independence in 1996. The Netherlands revoked this resolution in 1990, but Aruba has autonomy over its internal affairs. After a faltering start, the economy grew at an average of 10 per cent annually between 1987 and 1993. Its strength was based on tourism, offshore finance and the resumption of oil refining.

[10] Henry Eman, of the AVP, was elected Prime Minister in 1994 and re-elected in 1997. That year, the Government of Aruba, along with those of the Netherlands and Netherlands Antilles, decided to postpone indefinitely transition to complete independence.

[11] Hurricane Lenny hit the island in November 1999, causing considerable destruction in its path. The port of Aruba suffered damage valued at $500,000.

[12] The MEP won the September 28 2001 elections, and for the first time since 1980 a single party had overall control of Parliament. The MEP obtained 12 of the 21 seats and its leader Nelson Oduber was named Prime Minister. ∎

PROFILE

ENVIRONMENT

Located off the coast of Venezuela, the island of Aruba was until January 1986 one of the 'ABC Islands', otherwise known as the Netherlands Antilles, together with Curaçao and Bonaire. The climate is tropical, moderated by ocean cur-rents. Oil refining, where Venezuelan petroleum is processed, and tourism are the main economic activities.

SOCIETY

Peoples: Predominantly of European and Carib origin, its inhabitants intermingled with Latin American and North American immigrants. **Religions:** Mainly Catholic (82 per cent). There is also a Protestant (8 per cent) minority and small Jewish, Muslim and Hindu communities. **Languages:** Dutch (official). The most widely spoken language, as on Curaçao and Bonaire, is Papiamento, a local dialect based on Spanish with elements of Dutch, Portuguese (spoken by the

Jewish community), English and some African languages. **Political Parties:** Aruba People's Party (AVP); People's Electoral Movement (MEP); Aruban Liberal Organization (OLA); National Democratic Action (ADN); Aruban Patriotic Party (PPA); Aruba Solidarity Movement (MAS); Awareness for the Liberation of Aruba. **Social Organizations:** The Aruba Workers' Federation.

THE STATE

Official Name: Aruba.
Capital: Oranjestad 21,000 people (1999). **Other cities:** St Nicolaas 17,400 people (2000). **Government:** Olindo Koolman, Governor appointed by Holland, since1992. Nelson Oduber, Prime Minister and Minister of General Affairs since 2001. Holland continues to be in charge of defense and foreign relations. Single-chamber legisla-ture; Parliament made up of 21 members elected for a 4-year term.
National Holiday: March 18, Flag Day (1976).

DEMOGRAPHY

Population: 108,000 (2002)
Annual growth: 3.3 % (1985-2000)
Estimates for year 2015: 157,000 (2000)
Annual growth to year 2015: 3.0 % (2000)

EDUCATION

Primary school teachers: one for every 19 pupils (1998)

COMMUNICATIONS

562 radios (1997), 224 TV sets (2000) and 372 main telephone lines (2000) per 1,000 people

ECONOMY

Annual growth: -0.1 % (1994)
Annual inflation: 4.0 % (2000)
Consumer price index: 115.3 (2000)
Currency: 1.8 Aruban florins = $ 1 (03/2002)
Cereal imports: 8,135 metric tons (2000)
Food import dependency: 19 % (1998)

Australia

Population: 19,536,000 (2002)
Land area: 7,682,300 SQ KM
Capital: Canberra
Currency: Australian dollar
Language: English

Australia

The first inhabitants of Australia came from Southeast Asia some 55,000 years ago, but whether or not they constituted one homogeneous ethnic group at the time of their arrival is not known.

2 These peoples, named 'Aborigines' by the Europeans, spoke over 260 different languages and had distinctive cultures, though they were all semi-nomadic hunters and gatherers. Their daily life was linked to a universal scheme through rituals which guaranteed the ordered changing of the seasons and the community's food supply.

3 Land was held in common, and there was no social stratification, other than the prestige gained by practising religious rites.

4 In 1606, the Spaniard Vaez de Torres explored the strait which today bears his name, located between Australia and Papua-New Guinea. Three years later, Fernández de Quirós, also Spanish, became the first European to set eyes on Australian territory. However, colonization did not begin until after the arrival of Captain James Cook from Britain in the late 18th century.

5 In 1788, the first British settlers arrived and established a penal colony. This was the beginning of an assault on the way of life and customs of the Aborigines. The two fundamental objectives were to take over the best lands and to obtain a supply of labor.

6 At first, the British settled in coastal areas, but the process of inland expansion soon began, with the settlers acting as though the land were uninhabited. While British and international law recognized the prior rights of indigenous peoples,

Australia was simply declared *terra nullius* (uninhabited).

7 The wars to gain control of the land claimed the lives of 80 per cent of the Aborigines. The 'Aboriginal problem' was dealt with by genocide. Entire families were poisoned and others were forcibly removed from their lands onto reservations administered by the British.

8 In 1830 more than 58,000 convicts were 'transported' to Australia, most of them petty thieves, deserters from the Royal Navy and members of Irish opposition groups. Known by the British as 'the human refuse of the Thames' most of them served out their sentences by providing inexpensive labor for European landowners.

9 Australia served as a safety valve for social tensions generated by Britain's rapid industrialization. Most of the wealth accumulated in the

colony returned to England, representing an important influx of capital. Finally, Australia's strategic location was important for British trade, in order to control its world-wide maritime network.

10 Australian society was marked by a strong authoritarian streak, a legacy of its original function as a penal colony. Local government was normally limited to a high-ranking military officer, appointed by the Crown to oversee the prison population and take charge of the defense against possible attack by other European powers.

11 The Aboriginal religion, based on a strong spiritual link between each person and the earth, was given no credence by the settlers. As a result, the religion and language were debased and the people persecuted. The Aborigines lost lands rich in natural resources, fishing areas

and any land that the settlers considered suitable for cultivation or grazing. Once the land was in the hands of settlers, it was stocked with sheep to provide the growing British textile industry with both an abundant supply of raw materials and a cheap source of food for the industry's workforce.

12 The development of the livestock industry and the subsequent discovery of gold and other precious metals boosted economic development between 1830 and 1860. The possibility of getting rich quickly led to increased European settlement. As resistance was broken, the Aborigines were progressively relegated to Australia's desert areas.

13 For many years, rural settlers had to deal with occasional armed Aboriginal resistance. Driven by their desire to free land from the Europeans, they fought the settlers and tried to disrupt their farming.

14 Once suppressed, Aborigines were forced to sign 'work contracts' written in English. These contracts committed them to the status of unpaid workers, household slaves or concubines, often subject to extremely severe disciplinary measures.

15 In the meantime, a dynamic labor movement was beginning to appear in the cities, and it soon had a significant following. From the mid-19th century onwards, the unions obtained important victories and concessions while Europe's working classes were still a long way from obtaining.

16 In the latter part of the 19th century, Australia's growing urbanization process went hand-in-hand with an accelerated rate of industrial development, especially in Sydney and Melbourne, which took on the characteristics of any large urban centre.

17 Successive waves of immigration also helped change the face of Australian society. The low cost of land and a demand for Australia's products on the world market provided large numbers of mostly British people with the means for achieving rapid social mobility. A vast middle class developed alongside a wealthy urban industrial bourgeoisie, utterly transforming Australian life. The liberal governments which dominated the country's political

WORKERS

1990/2000

UNEMPLOYMENT: 6.2%
LABOR FORCE AS % OF TOTAL:

▇ FEMALE: 44%   ▇ MALE: 56%

1994/97

EMPLOYMENT DISTRIBUTION:

F
M

▇ SERVICES   F: 85% M: 63%
▇ INDUSTRY   F: 11% M: 31%
▇ AGRICULTURE   F: 4%   M: 6%

LAND USE

DEFORESTATION: 0.0% annual (1990/95)

1993

▇ FOREST & WOODLAND: 18.8%
▇ ARABLE: 6%
▇ OTHER: 75.2%

PUBLIC EXPENDITURE

1999

60.7%

7.6%

DEFENSE   SOCIAL

scene between 1860 and 1900 accelerated this political, social and economic transformation.

[18] Confederation of the separate Australian colonies arrived after a constitution, drafted in 1897-1898, was approved by the British parliament. In 1901 the six colonies (New South Wales, Victoria, South Australia, Western Australia, Queensland and Tasmania), all of which by then had been granted self-government, were federated in the 'Commonwealth of Australia'. The Northern Territory and the Australian Capital Territory did not join until 1911.

[19] A prolonged period of economic prosperity made it possible for the country to finance a series of social reforms. Australia was a relatively open society, in which social mobility was possible for certain sectors of the population, and there was protective legislation for workers before most European countries. South Australia had granted women the right to vote in 1893; in 1902 Australia became one of the first countries to grant women the right to vote.

[20] World War II loosened the ties between Britain and Australia, as Britain was unable to guarantee the security of its former colonies, in the face of the threat of Japanese attack. The US assumed the role of guaranteeing the regions security, as it has done ever since.

[21] The Korean War triggered a sharp increase in the price of wool on the world market, reinforcing Australia's economic growth. It also helped to avoid creating a gap between urban prosperity and the relative stagnation of the rural areas.

[22] With the onset of the Cold War, the ANZUS military assistance treaty was signed in 1951 by Australia, Aotearoa/New Zealand and the US. The aim of the treaty was to guarantee the security of US and allied interests in the region.

This military alliance also committed the Australians to participate in the Vietnam War, which damaged the treaty's image internationally, and triggered an important anti-war movement.

[23] Japan became the main market for Australian minerals, financing coal exploration in Australia in the 1960s. The large coal deposits discovered have supplied local industry ever since, and have also met Japan's huge industrial needs.

[24] In the 1960s, the Labor Party became the platform for Aborigine groups, helping to publicize and sensitize public opinion to their grievances and demands.

[25] A plebiscite held in 1967 granted Australian Aborigines full citizenship rights. The Aboriginal issue was also placed under the jurisdiction of the federal government. However, the Aborigines still did not gain recognition of their land rights.

[26] There are currently around 200,000 Aborigines in Australia, many retaining their original languages. Two-thirds of them no longer live in tribal groups, living instead in urban areas. A minority continues to live in areas which Europeans consider to be inhospitable, like the central desert or the wetlands which lie in the northern part of the country, where they have managed to keep their own religious and social traditions alive.

[27] In 1983, powerful transnational corporations interested in developing mineral resources launched a campaign aimed at convincing the population that the Aborigines' defense of their territorial claims actually compromised the country's economic growth. As a result of this campaign, the Government's promise of passing federal legislation on territorial rights of the Aborigines was shelved.

[28] In many cases the Aborigines found themselves forced to give in to pressure from mining companies and sign land use agreements, even though they knew that it could well adversely affect their sacred sites, the environment, and their traditional life style.

[29] Although some aspects of the Aborigines' situation are uniform throughout the country, their legal status varies from one state to another. Tasmania, for example, put in practice proposals aimed at safeguarding some of the Aborigines' rights, as well as ways of combating the discrimination to which they were subjected.

[30] According to local and international human rights organizations, in 1987 the death rate of Aboriginal prisoners was two per month. In terms of the total prison population, this would be the equivalent of 100 deaths of

PROFILE

ENVIRONMENT

Australia occupies the continental part of Oceania and the island of Tasmania, and has a predominantly flat terrain. The Great Dividing Range runs along the eastern coast. Inland lies the Central Basin, a desert plateau surrounded by plains and savannas. The desert region runs west to the huge Western Plateau. Rainfall is greatest in the north where the climate is tropical, with dense rainforests. 75 per cent of the population is concentrated in the southeast, which has a temperate climate and year-round rainfall. Oats, rye, sugar cane and wheat are grown there; Australia is one of the world's largest producers of the latter. Australia has the largest number of sheep of any country in the world, located in the inland steppes and savannas, and is also the world's largest exporter of wool. It also exports meat and dairy products and is one of the world's largest producers of minerals: iron ore, bauxite, coal, lead, zinc, copper, nickel and uranium. It is self-sufficient in oil and has a large industrial zone concentrated in the southeast. The soil has undergone increasing salinization. Many unique species, both plant and animal, are in danger of extinction due to the destruction of their habitats.

SOCIETY

Peoples: When the British 'discovered' Australia in 1788, there were 250,000 Aborigines in approximately 500 different tribes. In 1901, only 66,000 of their descendents were still alive. Today, there are 410,000, representing just 2 per cent of the national population. Descendents of British immigrants make up two-thirds of the population. The rest are immigrants from Asia, Europe and Latin America, a process which continues today. **Religions:** Christians 74 per cent (Catholic 27 per cent, Anglican 24 per cent, Methodist 8 per cent). Buddhist, Muslim, Confucian and other, 13 per cent. **Languages:** English. **Political Parties:** Liberal (conservative) Party, a right-of-center power (aligned with the National Party (NP), which represents the interests of farmers); Labor Party, a center-left group; Australian Democrats (moderate); Party of the New Left, founded in 1989 after the dissolution of the Communist Party; Socialist Party; Marxist-Leninist Communist Party and Green Party. **Social Organizations:** The Australian Council of Trade Unions (ACTU) is the largest labor confederation, with 133 union affiliates.

THE STATE

Official Name: Commonwealth of Australia. **Administrative divisions:** 6 states and 2 territories. **Capital:** Canberra 368,000 people (1999). **Other cities:** Sydney 3,985,800 people; Melbourne 3,317,300; Brisbane 1,535,300; Perth 1,365,600; Adelaide 1,115,900 (2000). **Government:** Parliamentary monarchy. Peter Hollingworth, Governor General, appointed by the Queen of England in June 2001. John Howard, Prime Minister since March 1996, re-elected in 1998. Bicameral Legislature: the House of Representatives, with 150 members, and the Senate, with 76 members. **National Holiday:** January 26, Australia Day. **Armed Forces:** 56,100 (7,500 women included). **Dependencies:** Cocos Islands, Coral Sea Islands, Christmas Island, Norfolk Island.

prisoners of European descent, in the same amount of time.

[31] Australian Aborigines are probably the people with the largest prison population in the world. In 1981, the rate was 775 per 100,000 inhabitants. Among the population of European descent, the proportion

was 67 per 100,000. In Queensland, in the northeast of the country, Aborigines make up only 2 per cent of the population, yet account for 35 per cent of the prison population. In Western Australia, where they also make up 2 per cent of the population, 44 per cent of the prison population are Aborigines.

[32] In the area of health, the Aborigines are also at a clear disadvantage with relation to the rest of the population. They continue to contract diseases which have almost disappeared among the European population, and for which total immunization is available.

[33] In 1989 Australia proposed the creation of the Asian Pacific Economic Cooperation (APEC). The project proposed the formation of a common market among the countries of the region, with Australia taking a leading role. At the same time, Australia hoped to become the representative of food-exporting countries. To achieve this goal, it sponsored the creation of the so-called 'Cairns Group', to include Argentina, Colombia, Thailand, Uruguay and other countries within the Uruguay Round of the GATT.

[34] The social and economic crisis worsened, with unemployment figures totalling more than a million in 1991. This put pressure on Bob Hawke's Labor government, which found itself under growing opposition from other political parties, and from within the party as well.

[35] There was growing discontent among the population at large, and opposition to the government began to emerge within the Labor Party itself. In addition, a power struggle developed between Hawke and his former Treasurer (Economics Minister), Paul Keating. In December 1991, the Labor Government held internal elections to resolve these conflicts once and for all, and also to open up the possibility of improving the government's image. Keating obtained a slim majority and became Prime Minister.

[36] In 1992, unemployment reached 11.1 per cent. The Government approved legislation aimed at increasing employment, by reducing immigration by 27 per cent.

[37] In the 1993 general elections, Labor won by a narrow margin, with 50.5 per cent of the vote. One of Keating's campaign promises was to give the rights of Indigenous Australians a high priority.

[38] An important decision on native land rights was made by the Australian High Court in June 1993. Known as the Mabo decision, it effectively overturned the notion of *terra nullius*, which had assumed that when the British colonists arrived in 1788 the Aborigines had neither right of law nor ownership of the land. Mabo was one of Australia's most significant legal decisions since federation in 1901. The decision drew on the history of the Murray Island north of Queensland and to their Meriam people, whose rules of inheritance were crucial in the final judgement. Following the Mabo decision, the federal Labor government passed revised Native Title legislation. There are also concerns over other matters affecting

Cocos Island

Land area: 14 SQ KM
Capital: West Island
Currency: Australian dollar
Language: English

The Cocos were discovered in 1609 by captain William Keeling of the East Indies Company, but it was not until 1826 that a settlement was established by Alexander Hare from Britain.

[2] The Clunies-Ross Company, founded by Scotland's John Clunies-Ross in the early 1800s, established a second settlement as the real owner of the islands, in spite of their formal British status (since 1857). Queen Victoria ceded the islands to the Clunies-Ross family in 1886 in exchange for the right to use the land for public ends. Clunies-Ross brought in Malayan workers - in conditions that were close to slavery - to work the coconut groves.

[3] In 1978, after many years of negotiation, Australia bought the islands from the Company. However, the Company kept a monopoly on the production and commercialization of copra. The transfer was designed to give Home Island residents formal ownership of their plots of land in order to alleviate social tensions. On West Island, Australia also had a military base, purchased in 1951.

[4] In a 1984 referendum, the population voted in favor of Australian nationality for the islanders and full annexation of the territory to Australia. In December of that year the UN General Assembly validated the results of the plebiscite and Australia was freed from the obligation of reporting to the Decolonization Committee.

[5] An agreement was signed in 1991 in an effort to raise the standard of living on the islands to that of the continent. Australia purchased the remaining Clunies-Ross properties in 1993.

[6] In December 2001, West Island doubled its population by receiving illegal immigrants - mostly from Sri Lanka - arriving by sea. Tourism operators complain that this could end tourism to the islands.

ENVIRONMENT

A group of coral atolls in the Indian Ocean, southwest of Java, Indonesia. Of the 27 islets, only two are inhabited, West and Home. The climate is tropical and rainy, and the land is flat and covered with the coconut groves that give the islands their name. Direction Island has a military base.

SOCIETY

Peoples: The inhabitants of Home Island are descended from Malayan workers. Australians and Sri Lankans predominate on West Island.
Religions: Sunni Muslims (57 per cent). Christians (22 per cent). Other 21 per cent.
Languages: English and Malay.

THE STATE

Capital: West Island 250 people (1999).
Government: Bill Taylor, administrator appointed by the Australian Government, since February 1999.

Christmas Island

Land area: 135 SQ KM
Currency: Australian dollar

The island, formerly a dependency of the British colony of Singapore, was transferred to Australia on October 1 1958 and its residents were accepted as Australians as of 1981. In 1984, social benefits and political rights were granted, and in 1985 the income tax was imposed.

[2] Phosphate mining, the core economic activity and sole source of employment, was shut down in 1987 and reopened by private companies in 1990 under strict environmental conservation measures. Two-thirds of the island was declared a national park, and since 1991 the Government has attempted to promote tourism as an economic alternative. In 1993 a private casino was opened with state support and an investment of $34 million. Also under consideration is the possibility of building a space rocket launch site.

[3] In August 2001, some 460 illegal migrants, mostly Afghans, though also Sinhalese and Thais, were rescued by a Norwegian freighter when their boat foundered at sea. The ship tried to place the migrants on Christmas Island, but Australia refused them entry. A new Australian law excluded Christmas Island and other Australian dependencies from its migration zone. At the same time Canberra asked other Pacific islands - like Nauru, Palau, Fiji and Tuvalu - to install temporary camps for migrants seeking asylum, who were rejected by Australia.

ENVIRONMENT

An island in the Indian Ocean, 2,500 km northeast of Perth, Australia, and 380 km south of Java, Indonesia. Mountainous and arid, it has a dry climate.

SOCIETY

Peoples: Nearly two-thirds of the population are of Chinese origin. There are some Malays and a minority of Australians. There are no native inhabitants.
Religions: Christianity (Protestants), Confucianism and Taoism.
Languages: English, Malay, Mandarin and Cantonese.
Capital: Flying Fish Cove.
Government: Bill Taylor, Administrator appointed by the Australian Government, since February 1999. The assembly of 9 members is renewed every two years. There are no political parties.

Aborigines and Torres Strait Islanders, including infant mortality, health, education and the country's terrible record of black deaths in custody. Progress Australia had been making in multiculturalism also slowed, despite its being one of the most ethnically diverse countries in the world.

[39] The Government started to develop links with the Asian Pacific nations, through trade and dialogue with regional groups such as ASEAN. But its relations with Cambodia, North Korea, Vietnam, Indonesia, Malaysia and China advanced with greater difficulty.

[40] The French nuclear tests on Mururoa atoll caused public protests throughout Australia. The Keating and Chirac Governments were at loggerheads and broke off diplomatic relations. The Australian delegation which went to Europe with a South Pacific Representative did not gain the support of the British Government, which refused to confront France. The British decision strengthened Australia's pro-republican stance.

[41] In the general elections held in March 1996, Liberal Party leader John Howard defeated his Labor rival. Howard became Prime Minister after pledging the 'moralization' of his country's leadership.

[42] In early 1996, the High Court of Australia authorized Indigenous Australians to claim the use of land leased for grazing or mining activities. In August 1997, the start of new uranium mining activities in the north caused strong resentment among Aboriginal groups. The leaders of the protest, among them several women, claimed the mining

would contaminate their land and the money would devastate their culture. By the end of the year, several Aboriginal groups filed suits for the recognition of their property over vast coast and sea areas. The issue of Aboriginal land rights remains politically controversial and undecided.

[43] In 1997 Amnesty International reported an increase in the death rate of Aboriginal people held in jails or in police detention operations, as well as ill treatment and intimidation in the enforcement of the law.

[44] Despite government opposition to union activity, the unions struggled to retain bargaining power. In April 1998, the Patrick Stevedores company dismissed 1,400 dockers with the implicit support of the Government. This led the Maritime Union of Australia to call a strike which became one of the biggest in the 1990s and it ended with the rehiring of the fired workers.

[45] Australia took an active diplomatic role in the crisis between its two biggest neighbors, Indonesia and Papua-New Guinea. Australia headed the UN peacekeeping force that intervened in East Timor, supporting the former Portuguese colony on the route to independence and preventing violence between the Timorese and Indonesians.

[46] The November 1999 referendum on Australia becoming a republic was won by the monarchists, with 54 per cent of voters deciding in favor of Britain's Queen Elizabeth II remaining head of state. The opposition blamed this defeat on Prime Minister Howard, as his reform envisaged that the future head of state would be elected by the Prime

Minister, with the agreement of the leader of the opposition and parliamentary. Many voters would have preferred the head of State to be elected by direct vote.

[47] In September 2000 a United Nations report criticized Australia for its treatment of Aboriginal people and specifically for changes to land laws which threatened the reconciliation process between government and Aborigines. The Government resisted pressure from Aborigine groups for a national pardon in reparation for past mistreatment for fear of future requests for compensation. Instead, an official announcement of 'regret' was made.

[48] The World Economic Forum meeting in September 2001, in Melbourne, was boycotted when some 10,000 demonstrators prevented several delegates from entering the site of the forum in the Crown Casino. The police - under pressure from event organizers - used violence to put down the protest.

[49] In January 2002, 211 detainees went on hunger strike in the Woomera refugee camp - several of them sewing their mouths shut - in protest against the holding

conditions and difficulties in getting their asylum requests granted. The UN High Commissioner for Refugees (UNHCR) classed the policy of detaining undocumented asylum seekers as 'unacceptable'. Meanwhile, Howard defended obligatory detention as a clear statement 'that no one can come to this country illegally', maintaining that 'neither the condemnation of international bodies, nor strikes nor suicide attempts' would lead to any change in migration policies.

[50] A large proportion of the asylum seekers are Afghanis. Although the UN requested that all countries refrained from blocking asylum requests from Afghanis, Australia argued that the situation changed with the fall of the Taliban regime in Afghanistan in 2001. As an alternative solution it has offered economic aid for them to return to their country. In April 2002, several asylum seekers escaped from Woomera. Their escape had been assisted by hundreds of demonstrators who broke down the camp fence in protest at the treatment of the immigrants. ∎

Norfolk Island

Land area:	36 SQ KM
Capital:	Kingston
Currency:	Australian dollar
Language:	English

There are no records of the existence of an indigenous population before the arrival of the Europeans. British sailor Captain Cook arrived in 1774, and the island was used as a prison site between 1825 and 1855. It was transferred to Australia as an overseas territory in 1913. In November 1976, two thirds of the Norfolk Island electorate opposed annexation to Australia. Since 1979, the island has had autonomy.

[2] In December 1991, the local population rejected a proposal to become part of Australia's federal electorate.

ENVIRONMENT

The island is located in southern Melanesia, northwest of the North Island of Aotearoa/NZ. The subtropical climate is tempered by sea winds.

SOCIETY

Peoples: 3,000 inhabitants in 1994. A large part of the population is descended from the mutineers of the British vessel HMS Bounty, who came from Pitcairn Island in 1856.
Religions: Protestant.
Languages: English (official).
Political Parties: There are no political parties.

THE STATE

Official name: Norfolk Island.
Capital: Kingston 1,000 (1999).
Government: Anthony J Messner, Administrator appointed by the Governor-General of Australia in August 1997. Geoffrey Robert Gardner, Chief Minister since December 2001. Legislative Assembly with 9 members.

Coral Sea Islands

Created in 1969 as a separate administrative entity, the territory consists of several islets located east of Queensland (eastern Australia). The major ones are Cato and Chilcott in the Coringa group, and the Willis archipelago. With the exception of a weather station on one of the Willis islands and lighthouses in several islands, the rest of the islands are uninhabited.

[2] The Constitutional Act by which the territory was created did not provide for Australian administration of the islands, but only for control over foreign visitors by the Canberra Government. However the discovery of oil fields and the expanding fishing industry may change this situation.

[3] In 1997, the charter was amended in order to extend its boundaries and include the reefs of Elizabeth and Middletown, 160 km North of the Lord Howe island. At present, these reefs are considered part of the Australian continental shelf.

Austria

Österreich

Population: 8,069,000 (2002)
Land area: 82,730 SQ KM
Capital: Vienna (Wien)
Currency: Euro
Language: German

The first traces of human settlement in the Austrian Republic date back to the Early Paleolithic age. From then on, the territory was occupied by various ethnic groups. The Austrian region of Hallstat gave its name to the main culture in the Iron Age, from 800-450 BC.

[2] Celtic tribes moved into the Eastern Alps in the 5th century BC, and it is thought that they founded the kingdom of Noricum, comprising modern central Austria and parts of Bavaria. Later, the Romans also settled here, attracted by the iron in the area and by its strategic military importance.

[3] After peaceful invasion, the Roman troops conquered the whole of the country around the year 15 BC. Raetia, Noricum and Pannonia became Roman provinces, extending the Empire's dominions as far as the Danube. The provinces were subdivided into municipalities and a vast network of roads was built.

[4] The Pax Romana ended with the arrival of the Germanic tribes between 166 and 180 AD. This invasion was repulsed, but the region did not recover its prosperity. Between the 4th and 6th centuries, the Huns and the Germans raided the area pushing back the Empire's borders on the Danube.

[5] According to the only written records from the era, the Germanic tribes of the Rugii, Goths, Heruli and lastly the Langobardi (Lombards), settled in the territory and in the year 488 a part of the population of the devastated province of Noricum was forced to emigrate to Italy.

[6] Following the departure of the Lombards to Italy, after successive battles with Slavic tribes, the Bavarians - Germans under the political influence of the Franks - reached as far as the Avar frontiers in the 6th century. When the Frankish king Dagobert I died, the Bavarian dukes were left virtually independent. Christianity spread in the region and was also practised by the Romans who remained in the territory. Under the protection of the Christian churches of Salzburg and Passau, which resisted the missions of the east led by the Slav apostles Cyril and Methodius during the 8th century, the Bavarians expanded both militarily and economically.

[7] Toward the end of the 8th century, Charlemagne, king of the Franks, led various attacks which broke down Avar control in the south, annexing these lands to his kingdom. The surviving Avars were forced to settle in the eastern part of Low Austria, between the Fischa and Leitha rivers and soon disappeared from the historical record, probably mixing in with the native population.

[8] Charlemagne took over as Holy Roman Emperor in the year 800, becoming the model of Christian king and emperor. Even though the Empire disintegrated after his death, the German medieval monarchies - just like the French - derived their constitutional traditions from the Carolingian Empire.

[9] The final years of the 9th century witnessed Bulgar incursions and the Magyar invasion, taking control of the low lands to the Rivers Enns and Styria to Koralpe. However, the Germans and Slavs continued to settle and after the German king Otto started expelling the Magyars in 955, the territory was predominantly German again.

[10] Between the 10th and 13th centuries, during the period of Babenberg control, Austria was contested by the Pope and the Holy Roman Empire on several occasions in the battle for control of the German church. Meanwhile, the reformists gained ground, founding the monasteries of Gottweig, Lambach, and Admont in Styria.

[11] Apart from brief interruptions, the Babenbergs maintained their sovereignty over the duchies of Austria and Styria, expanding them north and south. New settlements were made by clearing the forests and moving into mountain areas. The colonization process changed the distribution of the German-speaking population and apart from some Alpine regions, the Slavs were gradually assimilated, as were the remnants of Roman population in Salzburg and the northern Tyrol.

[12] The expansion of the German language was also encouraged by the attraction the Babenburg court held for the leading German poets. Decorated texts proliferated in monasteries, and in the early 13th century, the saga of the Niebelungs was composed by and unknown Austrian poet. In this era Austria also saw the flowering of the best romanesque and early gothic architecture.

[13] Following the death of Frederick II, the Babenbergs' dominions were coveted by their neighbors. The main beneficiary was Premysl Otakar II of Bohemia, until Rodolfo IV of Hapsburg came to the German throne in 1273 and pushed him out with the help of the Hungarians.

[14] Even though they were initially rejected by the local nobility and their neighbors, the Hapsburgs managed to maintain control over their dominions. In 1322, the Hapsburgs' defeat by the Swiss, and in particular Frederick I at the hands of Louis IV of Bavaria, threatened the dominion of this royal house over the Rhine and Lake Constance. By passing the last years of his life on Austrian territory, and being buried in the Carthusian monastery of Mauerbach in 1330, Frederick was the first of his dynasty to consecrate Austria as a home for the Hapsburgs. From then on, the government and Hapsburg territories were known as dominium austriae, a term which would later be replaced by the concept of the House of Austria.

[15] The consolidation of the House of Austria was achieved through inheritance and marriage alliances. Even though in 1490 following several crises the Hapsburgs only controlled Lower Austria, Maximilian I on the death of Frederick III inherited the House of Austria and the German Empire. Similarly his son Phillip I, married in 1496 to the Infanta Juana, gained the throne of Spain. A famous saying of the time ran: 'Let others make wars: you, fortunate Austria, get married'.

[16] Martin Luther's reforming ideas penetrated Austria, supported by the noble families, especially in the south and centre of the country. In 1521, Protestant pamphlets were printed in Vienna, and bans on their dissemination had no practical effect. There were peasant revolts in Tyrol, Salzburg and Innerösterreich. Many peasants were joining the 'Anabaptists' rather than the Lutherans. The name Anabaptist came from the Greek meaning to baptize again, as they considered the christening of children ineffectual, and so subjected followers to a second christening. As they were more radical, and had no support from the powerful, they suffered greater persecution from the outset.

[17] In 1528, in Vienna, Balthasar Hubmaier, leader of the Anabaptists in the Danube valley and southern Moravia, was burned at the stake. In 1536, in Innsbruck, Jakob Hutter, a Tyrolian, was sentenced to the same fate after he had led his followers into Moravia.

[18] With the death of King Jagiellon of Bohemia and Hungary, Vienna took the chance to extend the power of the Hapsburgs. The union of Austria, Bohemia and Hungary became the driving idea behind Hapsburg policy. Ferdinand I was proclaimed King of Bohemia in 1526 but his troops were repelled with the help of the Turks when he tried to impose his choice on the Hungarians. The 1562 Constantinople Peace Treaty divided Hungary into

three possessions: the north and west which went to the Hapsburgs; the center held by the Turks; and Transylvannia, with its neighboring territories, to Hungary's Janos Zapolya and his successors.

[19] In Austria, the Counter-Reformation started with the Jesuits, strong in Vienna, Graz and Innsbruck, and mainly with the impetus of Melchior Klesl, apostolic administrator in Vienna, who was to become Bishop and Cardinal and a key figure in Austrian politics. Even if Maximilian II - who succeeded Ferdinand I as Emperor of Bohemia, a part of Hungary and the Austrian Danube - had Protestant inclinations, he promised his father he would keep the Catholic faith. His successor, Rudolf II, educated in Spain as a strict Catholic, expelled the Protestants from the court and put Klesl in charge of the conversion of the cities and markets. The implementation of the Counter-Reformation caused mass emigration, which included members of the nobility. Most of the emigrants headed to Protestant states and the imperial cities in southern Germany.

[20] The Catholic-Protestant controversy continued in the House of Hapsburg until the death of Emperor Matthias in 1619, and the accession of Ferdinand II, who had been recognized a year earlier as king of Bohemia and Hungary and who tried to impose Catholicism on his subjects. While the states of Lower Austria fruitlessly proposed religious concessions for themselves, the *Diet* (Legislature) of Bohemia - predominantly Protestant in 1619 - unilaterally deposed Ferdinand, choosing to replace him with Frederick V on the Bohemian throne. Two days after he was deposed, Ferdinand II was named Holy Roman Emperor; an investiture which gave him rights to that throne and committed him, as a secular branch of the church, to imposing Catholicism. The conflict, which ran beyond the borders of the Empire, led to a series of wars known as the Thirty Years War and changed the maps of Europe.

[21] Bavaria and Saxony joined Ferdinand II, as did Spain - then at war with the Low Countries to sustain Catholicism. After five years, the Bohemian army was defeated, an imperial edict reduced the Diet to powerlessness and Catholicism was imposed by force. Protestants emigrated en masse to Germany, which was then invaded by imperial troops. The reaction came from the King of Switzerland, Adolf II, who invaded Germany in 1630 and won over many German princes to his anti-Catholic and anti-Roman cause. Although Germany was from then on the Gordian knot of the war, no throne in Europe was free of the conflict which drew in France, Poland and Denmark.

[22] The Peace of Westfalia in 1648 brought an end to the war and marked a new order for Europe. Holland was recognized as an independent republic, and the member states of the Holy Roman Empire were granted complete sovereignty. The old notion of a Catholic empire of Europe, led spiritually by the Pope and secularly by the Emperor, was abandoned for good. The essential structure of the modern Europe was established as a community of sovereign states.

[23] Though reluctant to participate in new conflicts, Ferdinand II's heir Leopold was threatened by Hungarian rebels and frontier disputes with the Ottoman Turk Empire, which led to him form an alliance with Poland. In 1683, Vienna was besieged by the Turks, but the Austrians were rescued by Bavarian, Saxon, Frank and Polish forces, under the leadership of Polish king John III. Two years later a pact signed by the Emperor, Poland and the Republic of Venice established the Holy League.

[24] Between the 17th and 19th centuries, the Hapsburgs were involved in all the European conflicts. The Napoleonic Wars virtually dismantled the Austrian Empire, and it was only after Napoleon's abdication in 1814 that the House of Austria recovered most of its territory.

[25] The Austrian Chancellor Clemens Metternich was the creator of the Holy Alliance of the European powers in 1815. This upheld the principles of Christian authoritarianism and foreign intervention against the liberal and revolutionary movements of the time.

[26] In 1848, a revolt broke out in Vienna, led by crowds demanding the liberalization of the regime. Metternich's resignation, rather than bringing peace, unleashed a revolution throughout the Empire.

[27] In spite of their active presence in the street fights of Vienna, the workers had little muscle at that time due to Austria's lack of industrial development. The most important social consequence of the revolution was the liberation of the peasants, sanctioned by Emperor Franz Joseph in 1849.

[28] At the same time the liberal government of Hungary demanded independence. In Germany the revolution installed a National Assembly in Frankfurt, which incorporated Austro-German liberals and conservatives interested in separation from the Hapsburg Empire.

[29] The Emperor accepted the Budapest petitions, except on two key points: budget and military autonomy. The Hungarian Parliament declared the power of the Hapsburgs null and void, and proclaimed a republic in April 1849. The revolution was crushed four months later.

[30] Counter-revolution also annulled the Frankfurt Assembly, but the dispute persisted. From then on, the Hapsburg Empire weakened inexorably. It lost, ceded and decentralized its dominions until its final disintegration in 1918, at the end of World War I.

[31] In October of that year, a national assembly declared German Austria an independent state and, in November, following the abdication of the Emperor, the Austro-German republic was proclaimed a component of the Republic of Germany. The Socialist Karl Renner headed the first republican government, a coalition in which his deputy was the Social Democrat Otto Bauer.

[32] Amidst economic chaos and hunger inherited from the war, the new government - without consulting the old regime - decided to use its own forces to confront the social unease and increasing communist activism. The Communists had been inspired by the Russian revolution in 1917 and more especially by the Hungarian revolution of 1919. The personal prestige of Renner and Bauer helped them survive two attempted coups led by the communists.

[33] The Social Democrats had an indisputable majority in Vienna, where one-third of the population lived. Social Christians had guaranteed support among the peasants and the Conservatives, while German nationalism fed on popular discontent, with the support of the urban middle classes.

[34] The League of Nations supported Austrian economic recovery during the postwar period, on the condition that the country would remain independent and would not join Germany. In 1922, the Government was granted a loan which enabled the country's finances to stabilize.

[35] The great depression of 1929 brought the Austrian economy to the verge of collapse. The Government tried to arrange a customs agreement with Germany which was fiercely opposed by the rest of Europe. Together with the rise of Nazism under the leadership of Adolf Hitler, German nationalism in Austria was showing signs of strengthening.

[36] In 1932, the Social Christian government of Engelbert Dollfuss attempted to take an authoritarian stance against the Social Democrats and the Nazis simultaneously. The Social Democrats rebelled and were declared illegal and in 1934 the

PROFILE

ENVIRONMENT

Austria is a landlocked country in central Europe. The Alps stretch over most of its territory. Tourism, milk by-products and textiles are the main economic activities in the western mountain provinces of Vorarlberg and Tyrol. Rye and potatoes are farmed in the lower woodlands of the Eastern Alps. The rich agricultural basins of Klagenfurt and Styria, in the eastern Alps produce corn, wheat, fruit, cattle and poultry. Austria's iron ore and coal mines feed its large iron and steel industry. The Danube river valley runs across the northern foothills of the Alps and is a major route for river, highway and rail transportation. The gas emissions from industrial plants and cars in large cities, and the use of agrochemicals are the main causes of environmental degradation.

SOCIETY

Peoples: Mostly of Germanic origin. There are Slav, Polish, Hungarian and Roma minorities.
Religions: Mainly Catholic.
Languages: German (and various local dialects); Serbian; Croatian; Romani; Slovene and Hungarian.
Political Parties: The Austrian Social Democratic Party (SPÖ); the Freedom Party (FPÖ); the Austrian People's Party (ÖVP); the Green Alternative and the United Green Party of Austria; the Communist Party and the extreme-right National Democratic Party of Austria.
Social Movements: The Austrian Trade Union Federation; Österreichische Berbauernvereinigung (peasant organization).

THE STATE

Official Name: Republik Österreich.
Administrative Division: 9 states.
Capital: Vienna (Wien) 2,068,000 people (1999).
Other cities: Graz 240,500 people; Linz 188,200; Salzburg 143,300 (2000).
Government: Parliamentary Federal Republic. Thomas Klestil, President since July 1992, re-elected in 1998; Wolfgang Schüssel, Chancellor (Prime Minister) since February 2000. Bicameral Legislative: National Council, with 183 members; Federal Council, with 64 members elected by the provincial parliament.
National Holiday: October 26, National Day (1955).
Armed Forces: Around 52,000.

Nazis murdered Dollfuss in a failed coup.

[37] Taking advantage of the internal crisis and the government's weakness, German troops invaded Austria in 1938, unchallenged by the European powers. A plebiscite carried out that same year in greater Germany recorded a vote of more than 99 per cent in favor of Hitler.

[38] In 1945 after Hitler's defeat in World War II, Austria was divided into 4 zones, occupied by US, French, British and Soviet troops. In the November elections, out of the 165 seats in the National Council, the Conservatives obtained 85 and the Social Democrats 76 seats.

[39] The Austrian economy recovered with difficulty after the War, with the aid of the United Nations and the US, through the implementation of the Marshall Plan. Heavy industry and banking were nationalized in 1946, and inflation was controlled by price and salary agreements.

[40] Conservatives and Socialists shared the government of the Second Austrian Republic, which only recovered full independence in 1955, with the Treaty of State and the withdrawal of the allied troops. The coalition held until 1966, when the People's Party was elected to govern alone.

[41] In the postwar period, Austria did not become a member of international organizations. During the Cold War, the country was liberal in the acceptance of political refugees from Poland, and it was a transit station for Soviet Jewish émigrés.

[42] Austria became a member of the United Nations in 1955 and of the Council of Europe in 1956. Since then, Austrian foreign policy has centered on the dispute with Italy over Sudtirol (Bolzano), resolved in 1969, and its association with the European Economic Community (EEC).

[43] In 1958, Vienna joined the European Free Trade Association, establishing a special agreement with the EEC. It established negotiations with the neighboring countries belonging to the Common Economic Assistance Council. In this way it remained a neutral nation.

[44] The Socialist Party (SPÖ) won a narrow victory in 1970 forming a minority government led by Bruno Kreisky. In 1971 and 1975, the SPÖ obtained an absolute majority and monopolized government, supported by great economic stability and a policy of moderate social reforms.

[45] In 1978, the Government lost a referendum on the installation of a nuclear plant, but the SPÖ confirmed its support of the Prime Minister and maintained control in the 1979 election. Kreisky resigned when the SPÖ lost its majority in 1983. In coalition with the Liberal Party (FPÖ), the SPÖ maintained its social welfare policy and active neutrality in the international sphere.

[46] The political force which grew most in the last decade of the century was the ultra-nationalist Liberal Party (FPÖ) headed by Joerg Haider. Even though he was removed from his post as governor of Carinthia in June 1991 for praising the full employment policy of the Hitler's Third Reich, in the municipal elections of November that year - following a campaign in which he accused foreigners resident in Austria of 'stealing' jobs from the Austrians - the FPÖ gained 22.6 per cent of the vote, becoming the second political force in the country.

[47] In 1992, against a backdrop of increasing attacks on immigrants, the Government passed a law which punished neo-Nazi activities. In May, Thomas Klestil of the ÖVP was elected President with almost 57 per cent of the vote.

[48] A referendum in 1994 decided that Austria would join the European Union (EU), which in theory would not affect the country's neutrality, as stated by the Constitution. In the March regional elections, the FPÖ improved its electoral performance once again.

[49] Although Haider officially condemned a series of attacks on immigrants, in a widely circulated book, Hans Henning Scharsach highlighted the similarities between Haider and Hitler - who 'also came from populist origins'. The rise of the FPÖ leader coincided with a debate on the Austria's role in World War II.

[50] More than 1,600 companies went bust in the first nine months of 1996. This situation was associated with an increase in competitive pressure on the economy due to joining the EU. The ensuing discontent favored the growth of the ultra-nationalist Freedom Alliance which gained the same number of seats (six) as the SPÖ in the European Parliament in June 1996. This signaled the rise of the so-called Freedom Alliance, headed by the FPÖ, towards becoming the main right-wing party, overcoming the ÖVP.

[51] Foreign Minister Vranitsky resigned in January 1997 and was replaced by finance minister Viktor Klima, a sharp negotiator who masterminded an austerity plan for that year. On an official visit to Israel in March 1998, Klima promised to compensate Nazi victims and recognized the role of Austria in the massacre of millions of Jews. In April, a referendum called for the Government to end genetic modification of food.

[52] The October 1999 elections confirmed the decline of Social Democrats. Even though they came first with 33.4 per cent of the votes, it was their worst-ever turnout. Haider was re-elected in Carinthia and managed to transform the FPÖ into the second political force with 27.2 per cent of the votes, beating the conservative ÖVP party by 400 votes. The Greens increased their number of MPs from nine to 13 with 7 per cent of the votes, which proved to be inadequate for an alliance with the SPÖ.

[53] Klima's attempts to form a government failed and the President accepted a conservative-liberal alliance. Before the new government was constituted, the presidency of the European Union warned that giving power to Haider and his Freedom Party would cool relations with the whole bloc. Even though Haider was not in the cabinet, the 14 remaining EU members decided to restrict diplomatic contact and abstain from supporting Austrian candidates in the Union or other international bodies. Israel and other countries recalled their ambassadors from Vienna, accentuating the isolation of a government headed by the conservative Wolfgang Schüssel.

[54] In November 2000, the FPÖ faced accusations of corruption and suffered several defeats in provincial elections. Three of its ministers were forced to resign in 9 months, causing tensions within the governing coalitions.

[55] The first case of mad cow disease - bovine spongiform encephalopathy (BSE) - in Austrian cattle was detected in January 2001. It was a 7 year-old animal bred in Austria but sold to Germany.

[56] Chancellor Schüssel defended Austrian entry to NATO. However, he feared strong opposition from people who consider the politically neutral nature of Austria part of their national identity. Russian president, Vladimir Putin, also called on Austria to maintain neutrality on a visit in February 2001, stating this was good for Austria and Europe as a whole. The Russian ambassador in Vienna had previously declared that the end of neutrality would be seen by Russia as a violation of international law.

[57] Czech premier, Milos Zeman, fingered Haider as a pro-fascist populist charlatan after Haider called for a veto on Czech entry to the EU, claiming there were security problems in the Temelin nuclear power station - built by the former USSR 60 miles from the Austrian border. In January 2002, Schüssel spoke to Czech president Vaclav Havel to report his anger over Zeman's comments. This incident took relations between the two nations to their lowest point since the end of the Cold War, and the fragile governing coalition was rocked again.

[58] In April 2002, Austria began paying damages awarded to thousands of Russians who were used as slaves by the Nazis in their camps during the Second World War. Austria earmarked 53 million euros for the 30,000 or so victims. ∎

Azerbaijan

Azerbaijan

The Azeris came from the mix of ancient peoples of eastern Caucasus. In the 9th century BC, the States of Mana, Media, Caucasian Albania and Atropatene (the name 'Azerbaijan' being derived from the latter) emerged in the area corresponding to modern Azerbaijan. General Atropates proclaimed the independence of this province in the year 328 BC, when Persia was conquered by Alexander the Great.

[2] Later, these states were incorporated to the Persian Arsacid and Sassanid kingdoms. There were a number of anti-Sassanid revolts, such as the Mazdokite rebellion. In the year 642, the Arab caliphate conquered Azerbaijan, which was still inhabited by tribes of different ethnic groups. The Arabs united the country under Shi'a Islam, despite some resistance. Between 816 and 837, an anti-Arab revolt was led by Babek.

[3] Between the 7th and 10th centuries, an important trade route passed through Azerbaijan, united the Near East with Eastern Europe. From the 11th to the 14th centuries the Seleucid Turks occupied Transcaucasia and the north of Persia. All the peoples in the region adopted Turkish as their language, and the Azeris' ethnic identity was forged during this period. In the 15th and 16th centuries, the region of Sirvan in the north of Azerbaijan, became an independent State.

[4] Between the 15th and 16th centuries, the Setevid State emerged. Shah Ishmael I, founder of the dynasty, was supported by the nomadic Azeris who became the main power behind the State. In the late 16th century, Azeri nobility transferred its support to the Iranians.

[5] In the 16th to 18th centuries, East Transcaucasia was the scene of Iranian-Turkish rivalry. In the 18th century, the Russian Empire began its expansion toward Azerbaijan and by the middle of this century more than 15 Azerbaijani Khanates were dependent upon Iran. After several Russian wars against Turkey and Persia, the peace treaties of Gulistan (1813) and Turkmenchai (1828) were signed, granting Russia northern Azerbaijan (the provinces of Baku and Yelisavetpol, corresponding to modern Gyanja).

[6] The peasant reform carried out in Russia in 1879 accelerated the

Nagorno-Karabakh (Under Armenian control)

0   100 km

development of Azerbaijan, which was attractive because of the abundance of oil in the region. After the Russian Revolution of 1905, the nationalist Musavit (Equality) Party was founded in Baku in 1911. Its base was the country's bourgeoisie, and it had a pan-Turkish, and pan-Islamic platform. After the triumph of the Bolsheviks in October 1917, Soviet power was established in Azerbaijan by the Commune of Baku.

[7] In the summer of 1918, joint Turkish-British intervention ousted the Commune of Baku and brought the Musavatists to power. However, two years later the Red Army re-conquered Baku and re-established Soviet power throughout Azerbaijan. It was proclaimed the Soviet Socialist Republic (SSR) of Azerbaijan and in March 1922, became part of the Transcaucasian Federation of Soviet Socialist Republics, along with Armenia and Georgia.

[8] In the early 1920s, in an attempt to ease inter-ethnic tensions, Moscow decided to incorporate the regions of Upper Nagorno-Karabakh and Nakhichevan into Azerbaijan. These had previously belonged to Armenia as the ancient khanates of Karabakh and Nakhichevan. In July 1923, the Autonomous Region of Nagorno-Karabakh was founded, and in February of the following year, the Autonomous Region of Nakhichevan; both had formerly belonged to the SSR of Azerbaijan. In December 1936, the Transcaucasian Federation was dissolved, and the

SSR of Azerbaijan joined the USSR on its own. In 1929 an attempt was made to substitute the Latin alphabet for Azeri script, which used Arabic characters. In January 1940, the Cyrillic alphabet was introduced.

[9] Between 1969 and 1982, the leadership of the Communist Party of Azerbaijan was in the hands of Gueidar Aliev, a former KGB (Soviet secret police) agent who was known and trusted by the Secretary of the Soviet Communist Party, Leonid Brezhnev.

[10] By the end of the 1980s, socio-economic, political and ethnic problems exacerbated the feeling of discontent among the Azeris. In 1986, the new Soviet leader Mikhail Gorbachev initiated a period of economic reforms (perestroika) and openness (glasnost) in the administration of the country, which channeled popular discontent throughout the Soviet Union.

[11] In the republic of Azerbaijan, there was a wave of strikes, political rallies and demonstrations. New political movements came into being, like the leading People's Front of Azerbaijan (PFA) with a platform stressing civil rights, free elections and political and economic independence for the country. The PFA opposed the long-standing aspiration of the Armenian population of Nagorno-Karabakh (90 per cent of that region's inhabitants) to rejoin the Armenian republic.

[12] On September 25 1989, Azerbaijan was proclaimed a

sovereign state within the USSR. The worsening of ethnic conflicts between Azeris and Armenians led to the formation of extremist groups. In 1989, Armenians were massacred in Sumgait and in 1990, in Baku. After the events in Baku, the Communist Government decreed a state of emergency and called in troops from the USSR to re-establish order; a total of 100 people were killed in the ensuing violence.

[13] The Nagorno-Karabakh issue increased friction with Armenia, triggering an escalation of conflicts between Armenian and Azerbaijani guerrilla groups. The Autonomous Region of Nagorno-Karabakh proclaimed its independence from Azerbaijan. In December 1989, Armenia's Soviet (Council) approved reunification with Nagorno-Karabakh and Azerbaijan denounced this decision as interference in its internal affairs. In September 1991, the Republic of Nagorno-Karabakh declared independence from both Azerbaijan and Armenia. In November 1991, the Azerbaijani Soviet annulled the status of Nagorno-Karabakh as an 'autonomous region'.

[14] On August 30 1991, the USSR's Soviet Presidium approved Azerbaijan's declaration of independence. The state of emergency was lifted in Baku and on September 8, presidential elections were held. The Communist Party of Azerbaijan was dissolved. Former Azeri Communist leader, Ayaz Mutalibov, who had supported the aborted coup against Gorbachev, was the only candidate, and was elected President. The PFA called the elections 'undemocratic' because they were held under a state of emergency, and withdrew their candidate. The Autonomous Republic of Nakhichevan, with Gueidar Aliev, abstained from the voting.

[15] On December 22 1991, Azerbaijan joined the new Commonwealth of Independent States (CIS) which replaced the Soviet Union, and on February 2 1992 it was admitted to the UN as a new member.

[16] Besieged by Azeri troops and with bombs going off intermittently, the people of Nagorno-Karabakh participated on December 10 1991, in a plebiscite in which 99 per cent of

the electorate voted for independence. The Azeri minority abstained from voting. CIS troops began withdrawing from Nagorno-Karabakh, but fighting between Azeri and Armenian guerrillas intensified.

[17] The People's Front of Azerbaijan accused the Government of ineptitude in handling the Karabakh issue, and demanded that the Government speed up the creation of an Azeri national army. Baku, in turn, accused CIS troops of facilitating the union of Armenia and Nagorno-Karabakh. On March 6 1992, Ayaz Mutalibov resigned and Yuri Mamedov, the acting President of the Soviet, assumed presidential powers.

[18] In April, fighting between Armenians and Azeris extended to Nakhichevan. Turkey warned that it would not accept any changes in its borders, which have been in effect since 1921.

[19] On May 14 1992, Azerbaijan's Parliament, controlled by former communists, reinstated deposed President Ayaz Mutalibov. He subsequently suspended the June 7 presidential elections, banned all political activity, and imposed censorship of the press and a curfew. The leaders of the Popular Front, with the support of most of the leaders of the national militia, seized the Parliament building in Baku, declaring the reinstatement of Mutalibov illegal. After two days of street demonstrations and clashes in the capital between supporters of both factions, the opposition consolidated its position and ratified Mamedov as president. The Popular Front assumed key posts in the new government, such as the directorship of the security services and of the official media.

[20] In December 1992, President Mutalibov was forced to resign after the repeated defeat of Azeri troops and the forces of the Popular Front besieged Parliament. In the following weeks, Armenian attacks intensified and, in May 1993, an offensive was launched on Stepanakert, the administrative center of Nagorno-Karabakh.

[21] In mid-May, Parliament reinstated Mutalibov as President but the Popular Front ousted him once again in an armed uprising. The fighting extended beyond Nagorno-Karabakh and after occupying Stepanakert, Armenian forces fanned out to several other Azerbaijani regions.

[22] In June, Abulfez Elchibey, leader of the Popular Front, won the presidential elections, prompting the return to a senior post for Heydar Aliev, former leader of the Soviet Union Communist Party. However, a new Armenian offensive in Nagorno-Karabakh was followed by a coup. Led by Colonel Guseinov, the

rebels took immediate control of five regions. Elchibey fled when the offensive against Baku started, leaving Heydar Aliev as interim President.

[23] In September 1993, Azerbaijan joined the CIS. A month later, Aliev won the Presidential elections and launched a successful offensive against Karabakh. In May 1994, under Russian pressure, a ceasefire was declared and negotiations between the warring factions began.

[24] A coup by followers of Prime Minister Surat Husseynov failed in October. Parliamentary elections were held the following year, without participation of the powerful Musavit party, nor of communist or Islamic groups, being banned by the Government. Aliev's party, New Azerbaijan, won the elections.

[25] Main opposition leaders, among them former President Abulfez Elchibey, boycotted the 1998 Presidential elections. Aliev obtained 76 per cent of the vote, although the opposition took to the streets claiming the elections were rigged, while editors of 20 daily newspapers begun a hunger strike to press for the annulment of the elections.

[26] In late 1997 Azerbaijan celebrated the opening of its oil

fields in the Caspian Sea, made possible by a contract between the Government and a 12-company consortium, with a 40 per cent American stake. Azerbaijan, Kazakhstan and Turkmenistan possess the third largest oil reserves in the world. In December 1999 a Japanese company invested $2.3 billion to tap the resources, in a joint venture with Asian and Azerbaijani capital.

[27] Karabakh President Samvel Babayan was injured in a foiled assassination attempt in March 2000. Former Azerbaijani Defense Minister and army commander Arkady Gukasyan, accused of having planned the attack, was sentenced to 14 years in prison.

[28] Azerbaijan's lack of democracy was condemned again in 2001, this time by European Council officials. They criticized the lack of freedom of speech and the existence of political prisoners. Despite this however, Azerbaijan became a full member of the European Council that year.

[29] The terrorist attacks of September 11 2001 in Washington and New York, United States, gave Aliev breathing space. Since he supported Washington's anti-terrorist campaign, in exchange the US lifted the sanctions imposed on Azerbaijan

in 1992 because Baku had blocked a railroad to Armenia. Aliev allowed the US to use Azeri air space to mobilize troops and supplies for its bases in Central Asia. ■

PROFILE

ENVIRONMENT
Located in the eastern part of Transcaucasia, Azerbaijan is bordered by Iran to the south, Armenia to the west, Georgia to the northwest, Dagestan (an autonomous region of the Russian Federation) to the north, and the Caspian Sea to the east. The mountains of the Caucasus Range occupy half of its territory; the Kura-Araks river valley lies in the center of the country; and in the southeast, the Lenkoran Valley. The climate is moderate and subtropical, dry in the mountains and humid on the plains. The vegetation ranges from arid steppes and semi-deserts to Alpine-like meadows. The mountains are covered with forests. The country has important deposits of oil, gas, copper and iron. Like Armenia, Azerbaijan has problems with soil pollution from pesticide use. Highly toxic defoliants have been used extensively on cotton crops. Water pollution is another serious problem: approximately half the population lacks sewage facilities, while only a quarter of all water is treated. The Caspian Sea, near the Abseron Peninsula, is one of the areas ecologically more degradated of the world with high levels of drying.

SOCIETY
Peoples: Azeris, 90 per cent; Dagestanis, 3.2 per cent; Russians, 2.5 per cent; Armenians, 2.0 per cent; other 2,3 per cent
Religions: Muslim (majority Shi'ite, 93,4 per cent; minority Sunnite), orthodox Russian, orthodox Armenian. **Languages:** Azeri (official) and Russian. Armenian, Kurmanji, Talysh. **Political Parties:** New Azerbaijan Party; Popular Front of Azerbaijan; Citizens' Solidarity Party; Azerbaijan Communist Party; New Equality Party; Azerbaijan National Independence Party, Musavat Party, Vandat Party. **Social Organizations:** Sadval, movement of the Lezgian people; movement of the Talysh people; independent trade unions such as the journalists' union.

THE STATE
Official Name: Azerbayan Respublikasi. **Capital:** Baku 1,918,000 people (1999). **Other cities:** Gyanja (formerly Kirovabad) 299,300 people; Sumgait 277,300; Mingechaur 98,900; Nakhichevan 67,100 (2000). **Government:** Heydar Aliev, President since June 1993 (re-elected 1998); Artur Rasizade, Prime Minister since July 1996. **National Holiday:** May 28, Independence (1918). **Armed Forces:** 86,700. **Other:** Militia (Ministry of Internal Affairs): 20,000; Popular Front: Karabakh People's Defense 12,000 (est).

Bahamas

Population:	312,000 (2002)
Land area:	10,010 SQ KM
Capital:	Nassau
Currency:	Bahamian dollar
Language:	English

Bahamas

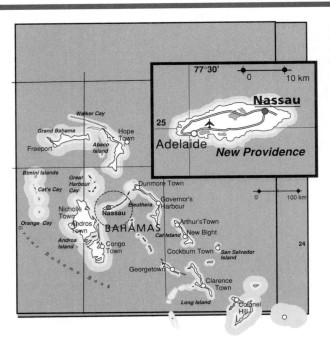

The Bahamian archipelago was one of the few areas of the Caribbean from which the Arawak Indians were not displaced by the Caribs. These Americans were probably the first to 'discover' the lost European navigators, on October 12 1492.

[2] Indeed Columbus probably first trod American soil on the Bahamian island of Guanahani or San Salvador, although he thought he was in Asia. 'The Arawaks opened their hearts to us', wrote the navigator to his Catholic sovereigns, 'We have become great friends'. Soon enough, the initial enthusiasm cooled to give way to less idealistic concerns: 'From here, in the name of the Holy Trinity we can send all the slaves that can be sold... If Your Majesties so commanded, the entire population could be shipped to Castile or be enslaved on the island... as these people are totally ignorant of warfare.'

[3] Only 300 out of 500 Indians lived through the first voyage to Spain. Moreover, most of the survivors died within a few years for they lacked immunity to European diseases. But Columbus had also set out to find gold for himself and the royal family. As Spanish historian Francisco de Gomara pointed out, 'over a period of 20 years, the Spaniards enslaved 40,000 Indians who were sent to work in mines on the other islands'.

[4] The Spaniards did not colonize the islands that lacked mineral resources. Instead, British privateers and pirates sought refuge in these islands after seizing 'Spanish' gold (or rather, gold appropriated by the Spanish with the heavy cost of Indian lives in different American territories). Both the Bahamas and the Bermudas were located in an area frequently hit by tropical storms, a fact that made buccaneers seek shelter in these islands. From 1640 the British began to settle the Bahamas. Sugarcane and other tropical crops were grown in plantations worked by African enslaved laborers whose descendants today make up most of the local population. In 1873, the Treaty of Madrid settled the dispute over control of the Bahamas in favor of the British.

[5] The British refused to accept the independence of this strategic archipelago, and it was not until 1973 that the Bahamas proclaimed their independence within the British Commonwealth. This change actually meant little to the islanders because in the meantime the country had become increasingly dependent on the United States.

[6] Most of the tourists who now visit the Bahamas come from the US, drawn to the beaches and casinos. The transnationals which use the Bahamas as their formal headquarters are also North American, taking advantage of the exemptions that make the country a 'tax-haven'. Also, US citizens are the chief buyers of lottery tickets, a source of fiscal revenues that contributes heavily to the state budget. In 1942, the US installed a naval base at Freeport, which helped control traffic from the Gulf of Mexico to the Atlantic, via the Florida Strait.

[7] While other Caribbean nations sought ways to bring about regional integration, the Bahamas preferred to take advantage of its proximity to the US, turning its back on regional co-operation. While other islands were founding regional organizations, the Bahamas did not join any of them.

[8] The first political party - the Progressive Liberal Party (PLP) - was formed in 1953, and in 1958 the United Party of the Bahamas was founded. In the 1954 elections the PLP obtained six seats out of a total 29. In 1956 the Assembly passed an anti-discriminatory resolution aimed at promoting ethnic equality. Thus, the Afro-Caribbean population was given access to places where they had never before been admitted.

[9] In the 1962 general elections the PLP won 8 of the 29 seats. Two years later the new Constitution was passed and a ministerial form of Government was established. The number of representatives to the Assembly was increased to 38. Sir Roland Symonette was elected prime minister and Lynden Pindling became the leader of the opposition. In the January 10 1967 election, each party obtained 18 seats, and the representatives who won the 2 remaining seats joined the PLP, thus enabling this party to form a Government. Lynden Pindling became Prime Minister.

[10] In 1977, when the economic and social crisis started to bite, the Government decided to give even greater incentives to foreign capital. It promoted the use of the Bahamian flag by foreign ships as a 'flag of convenience', to compete with Panama and Liberia. In an attempt to diminish the massive unemployment which threatened to create social tensions and changes in the archipelago, the Government opened an industrial estate of 1,200 hectares near a deep water port in Grand Bahama. It was meant to be used as a storage point for merchandise which was later to be re-exported after minimal local processing.

[11] During the 1977 electoral campaign the opposition parties - the Free National Movement, the Democratic Party of Bahamas, and the Vanguard Party - accused the Government of corruption and squandering public funds. Pindling promised to 'Bahamize' the economy, to give more participation to domestic capital, emphasizing that he would not damage the country's image as a tax haven. Both left and right criticized the Government's policy towards transnationals, the former because they considered it complacent, the latter because they thought that excessive taxation was driving foreign investment away. However, Pindling again won by a landslide and promised to lower unemployment. He opened the country's coasts to the 'seven sisters' (the seven companies controlling the world oil industry) which started oil prospecting in 1979.

[12] In 1984, the political scene was further upset when the US NBC Network News directly charged Prime Minister Pindling with receiving large sums of money for authorizing drug traffic through Bahamian territory. An investigation immediately confirmed that Government officials were involved in smuggling but cleared Pindling of any responsibility in the affair.

[13] In 1987, the unemployment rate was estimated to be above 18 per cent. With this figure in mind, public protests against the recruiting of Haitian refugees to the labor force became more understandable. Although they had strongly supported the Government in the past, labor unions now criticized the authorities for the lack of constructive, long-term programs aimed at solving the grave unemployment problem.

[14] After 20 years in office, Lynden Pindling won his sixth consecutive election on June 19 1987. His

Progressive Liberal Party obtained 31 out of 49 seats for a 5-year term. The opposition Free National Movement (FNM), led by Cecil Wallace Whitfield (after lawyer Kendal Isaac's resignation following the electoral defeat) repeatedly asked Pindling to step down, charging him with fraud, corruption, and being 'soft' towards drug dealers.

[15] In 1991, there was a sharp decrease in the number of tourists, estimated at three million per annum. This was attributed to the fact that there had been a rise in crime, compounded by the Bahamas' extremely high cocaine consumption rate. Although there had been a slow-down in inflation and a slight fiscal surplus, this did not prevent the people from taking to the streets, to voice discontent over economic conditions.

[16] US officials accused Pindling of allowing the Bahamas to be used as a transfer point for drugs. Testimony from the trial of the former Panamanian General, Manuel Antonio Noriega, alleged that Pindling had received at least $5 million in payments for this service.

[17] Tourism had generated over 65 per cent of the country's GDP, but in 1992 this fell by 10 per cent in relation to 1990 figures. Meanwhile the banking system lost customers to its competitors in the Cayman Islands. In addition, the Government was unable to increase agricultural production, making it necessary for the country to import 80 per cent of its food.

[18] Pindling's 25 years in office ended in 1992 when Hubert Ingraham, a former protegé of Pindling's and leader of the National Free Movement, won the parliamentary elections with 55 per cent of the vote. The new Government aimed to reduce unemployment through the liberalization of foreign investment laws and the re-establishment of the Bahamas as a major tourist destination.

[19] In February 1994, one of the prominent figures from Pindling's time, lawyer Nigel Bowe, was incarcerated in Miami for drug trafficking. That year, the Government appointed a commission to investigate Pindling, accused of having used the Hotel Corporation's funds to increase his wealth. Pindling denied the charges and sought protection in bank secrecy, which limited the Commission's progress.

[20] In 1995, foreign investors carried out the privatization of several hotels belonging to the Hotel Corporation. The most significant problems for the Government were unemployment and the presence of several thousands of Haitian and Cuban refugees. A repatriation agreement with Haiti was achieved, but the Cuban refugees refused to be sent back, and demanded to be transferred to the United States.

[21] In January the following year the conflict was resolved when the Bahamas signed an agreement with Cuba whereby Cubans living in Bahaman detention camps were returned to their home country. During 1996, 250 Cubans from the camps, and a further 70 living illegally with 'sympathisers' were returned to Cuba. Under the agreement, the Bahamas Government had the Cuban Government's commitment that the deportees would be treated 'fairly'.

[22] The death penalty was applied in March 1997 for the first time in 12 years when two prisoners were hanged. The National Free Movement won the Parliamentary elections held that month with 35 seats. The Progressive Liberal Party won five seats. Hubert Ingraham was reelected as Prime Minister.

[23] In February 1998, religious leaders in the country publicly demonstrated against visits from homosexual tourists, prompting a British Government representative to say the United Kingdom would oppose any type of discriminatory practices in the Bahamas.

[24] The Bahamas were ravaged in September 1999 by Hurricane Floyd, the worst storm in decades. Tens of thousands of people were evacuated, and the winds which came in 12-hour gusts reached speeds of 240 km per hour. They swept through whole villages, destroying boats and severing communications in Nassau. Prime Minister Hubert Ingraham, accompanied by US ambassador Arthur Schechter, flew over the affected areas.

[25] In spite of pleas for pardon from different human rights defense groups, a man was hanged in January 2000 for the murder of two German tourists. Amnesty International asked Bahamas Governor Orville Alton Turnquest to abide by international treaties, stop the executions and consider abolishing the death penalty.

[26] Late that year the Government enacted a series of laws to restructure the financial services sector and comply with certain demands of the Financial Action Task Force (FATF), the OECD and others that had included Bahamas in their 'black lists'. A package of nine laws came into effect which covered, among other things, a complete revision of the Central Bank and the Private Banks and Trust Funds Acts, revenues from illegal acts, reports of financial transactions and the creation of a Financial Intelligence Unit.

[27] In November 2001, Ivy Dumont took office as General Governor of Bahamas. ∎

PROFILE

ENVIRONMENT

The territory comprises over 750 islands, only 30 of them inhabited. The most important are: New Providence (where the capital is located), Grand Bahama and Andros. These islands, made of limestone and coral reefs, built up over a long period of time from the ocean floor. Despite the subtropical climate, the lack of rivers has prevented the favorable climatic conditions being fully exploited for agriculture. Farming is limited to small crops of cotton and sisal. The main economic activity is tourism, centered on New Providence. The effects of industrial development beyond their borders, the warming of the seas, the increasing frequency and intensity of tropical hurricanes and coastal erosion all pose a growing threat to the islands' environment.

SOCIETY

Peoples: Descendants of African slaves, 86 per cent, plus North Americans, Canadians and British (12 per cent) and Asian and Hispanic immigration (2 per cent).
Religions: Non-Anglican Protestants 55 per cent, of which 32 per cent are Baptists; Anglicans 20 per cent; Catholics 19 per cent.
Political Parties: Free National Movement (FNM); Progressive Liberal Party (PLP) founded in 1953; bringing together the population of African origin, under a pro-independence banner. The Vanguard Party, socialist. The People's Democratic Force.
Social Organizations: Trade Union Congress; trade unions such as the Bahamas Hotel Catering and Allied Workers Union, the Bahamas Union of Teachers, the Bahamas Public Service Union, the Airport & Allied Workers Union, the Musicians and Entertainers Union, the Taxi Cabs Union.
Languages: English (official) and Creole.

THE STATE

Official Name: Commonwealth of the Bahamas.
Capital: Nassau 214,000 people (1999), on New Providence Island.
Other islands: Freeport/Great Bahama 42,400 people; Eleuthera 3,300; Andros 2,800; Long Island 1,800 (2000).
Government: Queen Elizabeth II is Head of State, represented by Dame Ivy Dumont since 2001. Prime Minister Hubert Ingraham, since 1992, re-elected in 1997. There is a bicameral Legislative Power, with a 16-member Senate and a 40-member Assembly.
National Holiday: July 10, Independence (1973). **Armed Forces:** 2,550: Police (1,700); Defense Force (850).

Bahrain

Bahrayn

Population: 663,000 (2002)
Land area: 690 SQ KM
Capital: Manama (Al-Manamah)
Currency: Dinar
Language: Arabic

Since the time of the Sumerians, the area now called Bahrain was central to the intense maritime trade between Mesopotamia and India. This trade became particularly prosperous between the 11th and 15th centuries, as Islamic civilization expanded over all the territory from the Atlantic Ocean to the South Pacific.

2 Portuguese sailors occupied the island in 1507 and stayed there for a century until the Persians expelled them. Iran's claim to sovereignty over this part of the Persian or Arab Gulf dates from this period. Sheikh al-Khalifah took power in 1782, displacing the Persians the following year; his descendants are still in power. Independence lasted until 1861, when another Khalifah, afraid of Persian annexation, agreed to declare a 'protectorate' under the British.

3 During the two World Wars Bahrain was an important British military base. In 1932 the first oil wells were opened. Nationalist movements demanding labor rights, democracy and independence grew during the 1950s, as they did in other parts of the Arab world.

4 In 1954, a strike broke out in the oil fields and in 1956 colonial administrative offices were attacked. British troops were sent to quash the rebellion and opposition leaders were arrested and exiled. Slowly, some reforms were carried out and local participation in public administration increased.

5 Finally, beginning in the early 1970s, the British decided to withdraw from their last colonies 'east of Suez', though they maintained their economic and strategic interests in Bahrain. Bahrain and Qatar refused to join the United Arab Emirates, so in 1971 the country became independent under Sheikh Isa ibn-Sulman al-Khalifah.

6 The new nation authorized the US to set up naval bases in its ports. These were dismantled in 1973 following the Arab-Israeli conflict. Local elections were held the same year and the National Assembly came under the control of progressive candidates calling for freedom to organize political parties and greater electoral representation. The British felt their interests were being threatened, and, in August 1975,

they backed al-Khalifah's decision to dissolve Parliament.

7 In the 1970s, Iran managed to eclipse Saudi control of the Emirates, forcing a virtual protectorate over them. Meanwhile, heavy migration into Bahrain threatened to create an Iranian majority, or at least a large Iranian minority on the islands.

8 Shortly before his assassination in 1975, King Faisal of Saudi Arabia reacted against growing Iranian influence by embarking on a diplomatic campaign that his successors continued. He put pressure on Qatar, the only Emirate that was traditionally loyal to the Saudis, to solve its dispute with Bahrain over territorial waters. Faisal appealed to the 'Arab sentiment' that supposedly united them (Iran is Muslim but not Arab). This attempt at solidarity lost ground in 1976 when Saudi Arabia increased its oil prices less than the other OPEC countries, including Iran.

9 The fall of the Shah of Iran in 1979 made matters worse, as the unofficial representatives of the new Islamic Republic declared publicly that Iran maintained its claim to the Gulf islands. The Emir retaliated by cracking down even harder on both Iranian (or Shi'a) immigrants and on all progressive movements. At the

same time he drew closer to the other Arab governments, rejecting the Camp David agreement and signing mutual defense treaties with Kuwait and Saudi Arabia.

10 Bahrain is the 'least rich' oil producer in the Gulf. Its known total reserves (300 million barrels at the beginning of the 1990s) showed signs of exhaustion. Aware that dry oil wells, and competition to Bahrain's pearl-diving from Japanese oyster farms may leave the desert country with fishing as its only resource, the Government decided to slow down oil production in 1980 taking advantage of the islands' strategic location to turn them into a trade and financial center.

11 In May 1975, Bahrain had obtained a controlling interest in its oil industry and in 1978 announced that all concessions to transnational companies would be canceled.

12 The State also promoted the establishment of industries, especially for copper and aluminum production. Generous tax exemptions and unrestricted facilities for profit remittance encouraged transnational corporations to set up subsidiaries. The country became an entrepôt for re-exporting goods to other ports in the area. Bahrain also housed the

second largest refinery in the Middle East, BAPCO, which processed local as well as a large part of Saudi crude oil.

13 In 1981, the country joined the Gulf Cooperation Council (GCC). This was set up with US help to guarantee military and political control over the area, to counteract spreading Iranian influence, and to keep an eye on opposition groups in the member states.

14 One of the most closely watched movements was the Bahrain National Liberation Front, supported mainly by oil workers, students and professionals. This group was a member of the Gulf Liberation Front until 1981.

15 Toward the end of 1986, Bahrain bought ground-to-air missiles and warplanes from the US to defend itself in the event of Iranian aggression. In exchange, the US won authorization for the construction of a military airport and the right to use Bahrain's naval bases for its Gulf fleet, which patrolled the Gulf during the last few months of the Iran-Iraq war (1980-88).

16 In November 1986, a super-highway was opened between Saudi Arabia and Bahrain, making Bahrain no longer truly an island. During the first year alone, the highway was used by more than a million vehicles. The fall in world oil prices in the 1980s plunged the country into crisis and many of the grandiose building projects of the past were shelved.

17 In 1989, Bahrain was forced to seek credit in order to balance its budget. Kuwait and Saudi Arabia contributed $100 million per year to ensure the stability of the Manama government.

18 In March 1991, after the Iraqi defeat in the Gulf War, the foreign ministers of Egypt, Syria and the six Arab member States of the GCC signed an agreement with the US in Riyadh in order to 'preserve the regional security'.

19 In July 1991, the Government announced that it would allow foreign companies to have full control of the local businesses they bought. Previously, all business interests on the island had to have a minimum of 51 per cent of national capital. The change in policy was aimed at attracting foreign

MATERNAL MORTALITY

1985/99

Per 100,000
live births

46

investment to compensate for economic losses caused by the Gulf War.

[20] After Kuwait, Bahrain was the emirate most affected by the conflict. The country was threatened by the oil slick, and its skies were blackened for several months by Kuwait's burning oil wells. In the economic field, the effects of the invasion of Kuwait and the subsequent war against Iraq were also felt. For instance, private bank deposits dropped by 30 to 40 per cent. The number of foreign banks fell from 75 in 1981 to 51 by the end of 1991.

[21] As from 1992, foreign capital slowly began to return to Bahrain. Also that year, the country played an important role in the Middle East Peace Conference held in Moscow, which was attended by 10 Arab nations, as well as Israel.

[22] In October 1994, Israeli Minister Yoosi Sarid's visit to Manama - the first high level public contact between Israel and a Gulf State - was a clear indication of the economic liberalization policy of the regime.

[23] In December 1994, Shi'a leader Sheikh al-Jamri was arrested, after signing a claim for the restoration of the Constitution and Parliament, dissolved in 1975. His arrest provoked anti-government demonstrations, in which two students and a police officer died. In April 1995, Emir Isa ibn-Sulman al-Khalifah met with 20 opposition leaders in an attempt to put an end to growing violence. In August, both parties reached an agreement that concluded with the release of 1,000 political prisoners.

[24] In June, al-Jamri and another six opposition leaders denounced the lack of government commitment to the agreement and a hunger strike started which ended on November 1. A large opposition demonstration was countered by closing mosques, which only heightened the tension.

[25] In 1996, the demonstrations spread across the country, and some ended in violent confrontations with the police. The Government decided to use the death penalty to punish those 'responsible', a measure endorsed by the Courts. The UN

Working Group on Arbitrary Detentions issued three declarations on the situation of the inmates of Bahrain's prisons in September. The international organizations were not allowed to see the prisoners, who were in many cases denied the right to trial. In July, Amnesty International reported that many women and children suffered severe abuse in the nation's prisons.

[26] Due to the situation of social conflict, some financial bodies like the Core State Bank of the United States abandoned the country to set up in Dubai. In March 1998, Bahrain and the other five member nations of the Gulf Co-operation Council (Saudi Arabia, Oman, Kuwait, Qatar and the United Arab Emirates) looked into the possibility of freeing their currencies from the dollar to protect themselves from persistent fluctuations and to prevent greater losses in oil income.

[27] In December 1999, in his Independence Day address, Emir Sheik Hamad ibn Isa al-Khalifah spoke about democratic openness and promised to reinstate municipal councils. The following year, in addition to publicly promising to reinstate Parliament, the Emir for the first time named as members of the Consultative Council - a body created in 1992, made up of 40 people who monitor most of the government's policies - non-Muslim men and women, including a Jewish businessman and four women, one a Christian.

[28] In a February 2001 referendum, the Bahrainis overwhelmingly supported the proposals for political reforms proposed by the royal family. The reforms, which come into force in 2004, entail converting the State into a constitutional monarchy, pardoning more than 900 political prisoners and exiles and abolishing the State Security Law and the State Security Court, established in the wake of the 1995 anti-government protests.

[29] In December, the Ministry of Information tried journalist Hafez al-Shaikh for publishing articles critical of the Shi'a community. Al-Shaikh was accused of violating the country's press laws. He argued that the persecution was really due to his negative comments, published in a Lebanese daily, about Bahrain's collaboration with US incursions in Afghanistan, as part of Washington's War on Terror campaign after the September 11 2001 attacks.

[30] Moving up the deadlines set the year before, the State of Bahrain declared itself a constitutional monarchy on February 14 2002. The King (former Emir) moved the date for elections (the first in 27 years) to October 24 that same year. ■

PROFILE

ENVIRONMENT

This flat, sandy archipelago consists of 33 islands in the Persian Gulf between Saudi Arabia and the Qatar Peninsula. The largest island, also called Bahrain, is 48 km long and 15 km wide. The climate is warm, moderately humid in summer and slightly dry in winter. Manama, the capital and main trade center, is located on the island of Bahrain. Bahrain has the same environmental problems that are characteristic of all the Gulf countries. Industrialization led to the occupation of what few fertile lands there were, in the northern part of the main island. Bahrain is developing its petroleum industry; the refineries, the large storage tanks and transport pipelines have a major impact on the environment.

SOCIETY

Peoples: Bahrainis are Arab people. The petroleum industry has attracted a number of Iranian, Indian and Pakistani immigrants.
Religions: Islamic (85 per cent), predominantly of the Sunni sect in the urban areas and Shi'a in the rural areas. Christians 8.5 per cent. There are also Jews, Hindus, Baha'i and others.
Languages: Arabic, English, Farsi/Persian, Urdu.
Political Parties: There are neither legal political parties nor trade unions. Some opposition forces are the Liberation Front of Bahrain, the Ba'ath Arab Socialist Party and the Arab Nationalist Movement.

THE STATE

Official Name: Mamlakat al-Bahrayn.
Administrative divisions: 12 municipalities.
Capital: Manama (Al-Manamah) 162,000 people (1999).
Other cities: Al-Muharraq 81,800 people; Ar-Rifa' 82,000; Madinat'Isa 61,600. (2000).
Government: Sheikh Hamad ibn Isa al-Khalifah, Emir since March 1999 and King since February 2002; Sheikh Khalifah ibn Sulman al-Khalifah, Prime Minister since January 1970, assisted by an 11-member cabinet. The National Assembly, partially elected by popular vote, was dissolved in August 1975.
National Holidays: August 15, Independence (1971); December 16, National Day (1971). **Armed Forces:** 10,700. **Other:** (Ministry of Interior): Coast Guard: 400; Police: 9,000.

Bangladesh

Population:	143,364,000 (2002)
Land area:	130,170 SQ KM
Capital:	Dhaka (Dacca)
Currency:	Taka
Language:	Bengali

Bangladesh

The area comprising present-day Bangladesh and the Indian state of West Bengal was settled in about 1000 BC by Dravidian peoples who were later known as the Bang. The first Dravidian empire to spread over most of present-day India, Pakistan, and Bangladesh was the Mauryan Empire between the 3rd and 1st century BC. During the Mauryan Empire, a Buddhist chief named Gopala came to Bengal and conquered power becoming the first ruler of the Pala Dynasty (AD 750-1150). He and his successors provided stable government, security, and prosperity while spreading Buddhism throughout the state and into neighboring territories.

[2] The Senas, militant Hindus, replaced the Buddhist Palas as rulers of a united Bengal until the Turkish conquest in 1202. Opposed to the Brahmanic Hinduism of the Senas with its rigid caste system, vast numbers of Bengalis, especially those from the lower castes, would later convert to Islam.

[3] Turks ruled Bengal for several decades before the conquest of Dhaka by forces of the Mughal emperor Akbar the Great in 1576. The British East India Company, a private company formed in 1600 during the reign of Akbar and operating under a charter granted by Queen Elizabeth I, established a factory on the Hooghly River in Bengal in 1650 and founded the city of Calcutta in 1690.

[4] Although the initial aim of the East India Company (EIC) was to seek trade under concessions obtained from local governors, the steady collapse of the Mughal Empire (1526-1858) enticed the company to take a more direct involvement in the politics and military activities of the subcontinent. Siraj ud Daulah, governor of Bengal, provoked a military confrontation with the British at Plassey in 1757. He was defeated by Robert Clive, a young official of the Company. By 1815 the supremacy of the EIC was unchallengeable, and by the 1850s British control and influence had extended into territories that became the independent states of India and Pakistan in 1947.

[5] In 1905 the British governor general, Lord George Curzon, divided Bengal into eastern and western

sectors in order to improve administrative control of the huge and populous province. Curzon established a new province called Eastern Bengal and Assam, which had its capital at Dhaka. The new province of West Bengal (today's West Bengal in India) had its capital at Calcutta, which also was the capital of British India. Many Bengali Muslims viewed the partition as initial recognition of their cultural and political separation from the Hindu majority population. But Curzon's decision was hotly challenged by the Indian National Congress (INC), a Hindu-dominated political organization founded in 1885 and supported by the Calcutta élite. In 1912 the British voided the partition of Bengal, a decision that heightened the growing estrangement between the Muslims and Hindus in many parts of the country. The reunited province was reconstituted as a presidency and the capital of India was moved from Calcutta to the less politically electric atmosphere of New Delhi.

[6] In 1906 the All-India Muslim League (ML) declared its support for the partition of Bengal. In 1916 a INC-ML Pact was signed. It was a joint platform and call for national independence. But while the INC enthusiastically supported the war effort during World War I, in the hope that Britain would reward Indian loyalty with political concessions – possibly independence – after the war, the ML was more ambivalent. This was partly because many Muslims felt that the breaking up of the Ottoman Empire presaged the destruction of the last great Islamic power. Muslims in India were also alarmed over reports that the Allied Powers contemplated putting some of the holy places of Islam under non-Muslim jurisdiction. In response to the news of the breakup of the Ottoman Empire in 1920, the Khilafat Movement - a combined Indian nationalism and pan-Islamic sentiment with strong anti-British overtones - was launched.

[7] An agreement between the leaders of the Khilafat Movement

and Mahatma Gandhi, the leading figure in Congress, resulted in the joint advocacy of self-rule for India on the one hand and agitation for the protection of Islamic holy places and the restoration of the caliph of Turkey on the other hand.

[8] In 1922 the Hindu-Muslim accord suffered a double blow. First, their non-cooperation movement miscarried and then the Khilafat Movement lost its purpose when the postwar Turkish nationalists under the leadership of Atatürk abolished the Sultanate, proclaimed Turkey a secular republic. They also abolished the religious office of the caliph, and sent the last of the Ottoman ruling family into exile. After the eclipse of the Hindu-Muslim accord, the spirit of communal unity was never reestablished in the subcontinent.

[9] When the British partitioned India, transforming part of its territory into Pakistan in August 1947, Bengal was also partitioned. The Muslim majority areas, known as East Bengal, became part of Pakistan, and the Hindu majority areas became part of India. The people of East Pakistan became impatient when they became aware that many resources were being transferred from their part of the country to West Pakistan. They also lost patience with the bureaucratic military oligarchy in West Pakistan, and began to demand regional autonomy.

[10] As a result, East Pakistan elected its own political leadership in 1970. The Pakistani Government refused to recognize this secession; the military blocked all attempts to form a government and began campaigns of aggression against East Pakistani civilians on March 25, 1971.

[11] The people of East Pakistan declared independence on March 26 and launched an armed resistance movement. They formed a government-in-exile in India with Sheikh Mujibur Rahman as president, and finally succeeded in ousting the occupation forces. About 3 million lives were lost during the war and 10 million refugees were reported to have crossed the border into India.

[12] Bangladesh adopted a constitution providing for parliamentary democracy on December 16, 1972. Large industries, banks and insurance companies were

MATERNAL MORTALITY

1985/99

Per 100,000
live births

350

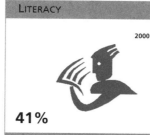

LITERACY

2000

41%

nationalized. Democracy, secularism, socialism and nationalism were declared as the states basic principles.

13 But the task of reviving the war-torn economy proved too great a challenge for the inexperienced leadership of the ruling party, the Awami League. Nationalist fervor soon died down, giving way to widespread feelings of disappointment. Bangladeshi politics degenerated into confusion as insurgency and armed political movements erupted throughout the country.

14 The Government declared a state of National Emergency in December 1974 and a month later fundamental civil rights were suspended. All opposition political parties and trade unions were banned leaving a single party, Bakshal, mainly made up of Awami League members and pro-Moscow communists. Newspapers were banned - except for four national dailies controlled by the Government - and a new press and publication law suppressed all opposition views. On August 15 1975, against this backdrop, a group of active and retired army officers assassinated President Sheikh Mujibur Rahman and his family, and declared martial law.

15 On November 7, 1975, General Zia ur Rahman emerged as the leading force in the opposition, following a series of coups and counter-coups. He founded the Bangladesh Nationalist Party (BNP) which included many members who had opposed Bangladesh's initial independence in 1971. The BNP won the 1978 and 1979 elections, and the Awami League went into opposition.

16 After two earlier attempts were blocked by Chinese vetoes, Bangladesh joined the UN in 1974. It was a founding member of the Non-Aligned Movement and also of the Organization of the Islamic Conference.

17 The country went through a brief period of relative stability. But in May 1981, Zia ur Rahman was killed in an abortive coup attempt. Almost a year later, on March 24 1982, the army engineered a successful coup, placing General Ershad in the presidency.

18 General Ershad formed the Jatiya Party (JP), going on to win the 1986 general election with what the opposition saw as widespread fraud. As a result of this, large popular uprisings forced Ershad to dissolve Parliament. Confidence in political integrity was so low that the 1988 elections were boycotted by all the major political parties as well as by a large percentage of the electorate.

19 Bangladesh has always been a predominantly rural society. Agriculture accounts for about half of the gross domestic product, compared to just 10 per cent from manufacturing. About four-fifths of the labor force is employed in agriculture or related activities. Participation by women in the formal labor market is small: only around seven per cent of the work force is female.

20 Prior to the 'green revolution' of the 1970s and 1980s, over 7,000 varieties of rice were grown in Bangladesh. More recently, only one is being widely cultivated. This new high-yield variety promised to meet all the country's rice needs, but the only real achievement was to open a new market for the manufacturers of chemical fertilizers, upon which the production of this new variety of rice depends.

21 Bangladesh also suffered from man-made disasters. The Asian Development Bank had $5 million in aid reserved to end the pollution of its waters. Leaks from oil tankers and the disposal of industrial waste along the coast are destroying the coastal ecosystem. Marine life has been decimated, and it is believed that the sea here will soon be completely dead. Bangladeshi fisherfolk are having to go further out to sea to obtain a satisfactory catch.

22 Under the Islamist-inspired constitution, a woman may inherit only half as much as her brother. In practice, this fraction goes to her husband or is saved as a dowry. Bengali feminists complain that women are treated as goods rather than individuals as they belong to their fathers in childhood, to their husbands in marriage (most marry at 13), and to their sons in old age. Their work in the home and the fields is not included in official production statistics, and divorce - a male prerogative under Islamic law - can be easily obtained if a woman's productivity drops. This frequently occurs as many women are seriously undernourished.

23 The gradual Islamization of politics led to a 1989 constitutional amendment that declared Islam the official religion.

24 Ershad was deposed in 1991, and elections were called, in which the Awami League (AL) opposed the Bangladesh Nationalist Party (BNP). Both political alliances had women as their major candidates; in both cases the widow of the former leader of the alliance.

25 Begum Khaleda Zia of the BNP was elected in March that year and declared that she supported the establishment of a parliamentary regime. Five months after her triumph in the general election, and with the unanimous approval of the legislative representatives of the two major parties, the Congress of Bangladesh replaced the country's presidential system with a parliamentary system.

26 On April 30, 1991, the worst storm to hit Bangladesh since 1970 killed nearly 100,000 people, caused several million dollars worth of damage and left millions of people homeless. The most devastated areas were along the coast and on islands of the Ganges delta.

27 The previous president, Hussain Muhammad Ershad, was sentenced that year to 10 years in prison for abuse of power, unlawful wealth and possession of illegal weapons. However, he was able to run for the 1996 elections after appealing against the sentence.

28 Bangladesh relies heavily upon international aid; in 1991, 95 per cent of its development programs were financed from abroad. 95 per cent of the country's budget was

PROFILE

ENVIRONMENT

Located on the Padma River Delta, formed by the confluence of the Meghna with the Ganges and the Brahmaputra, Bangladesh is a fertile, alluvial plain where rice, tea and jute are grown. There are vast rain forests and swamps. A tropical monsoon climate predominates, with heavy summer rains from June to September generally accompanied by hurricanes and floods of catastrophic consequences. Low-quality coal and natural gas are the only mineral resources. The increase in sea level poses a growing threat to the country. The coastal area along the Bay of Bengal has been severely affected by the discharge of sewage and industrial waste. This pollution, together with indiscriminate fishing to supply both internal and export markets, is leading to the destruction of one of the country's main resources with sea-borne pollution threatening to irreversibly damage the coastal ecosystem.

SOCIETY

Peoples: The people of Bangladesh are ethnically and culturally homogeneous, as a result of 25 centuries of integration between the local Bengali population and immigrants from Central Asia. There are small Urdu and Indian minorities. Of the present ethnic groups, the Chakma are known to have migrated from the hills of Chittagong to border states of India in 1981.
Religions: Mostly Islamic (83 per cent) and Hindu (16 per cent), with Buddhist and Christian minorities.
Languages: Bengali.
Political Parties: Bangladesh Awami League (AL), in favor of a socialist economy with the intervention of the private sector; Bangladesh Nationalist Party, right of center (Bangladesh Jatiyatabadi Dal, BNP); National Party (coalition), an Islamic-inspired alliance of five nationalist parties; Islamic Conference Bangladesh; Islamic Unity Front; National Socialist Party-Rob and other minor parties.
Social Organizations: Jana Sanghati Samiti, fighting for the rights of the tribal people; Women for Women.

THE STATE

Official Name: Gana Prajatantri Bangladesh.
Administrative divisions: 4 districts.
Capital: Dhaka (Dacca) 11,726,000 people (1999).
Other cities: Chittagong 2,500,900 people; Khulna 1,168,800; Rajshahi 687,300 (2000).
Government: Parliamentary republic. Badruddoza Chowdhury, President and Head of State since November 2001. Khaleda Zia, Prime Minister and Head of Government since October 2001. Single-chamber legislature: Parliament made up of 330 members (300 elected by direct vote and 30 reserved for women, nominated by Parliament, for 5-year term).
National Holidays: March 26, Independence Day (1971); December 16, Victory Day (1971).
Armed Forces: 115,500 (1995).
Other: Bangladesh Rifles: 30,000 (border guard); Ansars (Security Guards): 20,000.

taken up in interest payments on its foreign debt.

[29] In the early 1990s Bangladeshis had an average per capita annual income of $240. Fifty per cent of housing was of mud brick construction with no plumbing: one toilet may be shared by as many as 50 families. More than 13 million people lived in the shanties surrounding the cities, which continue to grow at a rapid rate.

[30] Among measures to shore up the fragile economy, the Government declared all-out war on smuggling, in December 1991. Smuggling became big business in Bangladesh, involving important financial institutions, the nouveau riche, and corrupt political and government officials.

[31] The IMF - and World Bank - launched a privatization scheme, which included the sale of 42 public enterprises, came to a standstill in 1991. Minister of Finance Saifur Rahman faced the opposition of organized labor, especially in the jute industry (one of the main sources of export earnings), as well as textile and railway unions that fear the loss of jobs. General strikes - demanding a national minimum wage - became commonplace.

[32] The Gulf War (1990-1991) prompted Bangladesh to reaffirm its identity as a Muslim community. This feeling was intensified in 1992, when the repatriation of Muslim refugees began. Early in that year, Bangladesh received several groups of some 250,000 Bihari Muslims, who had supported Pakistan in 1971. In June, another 270,000 Rohingya Muslims arrived, fleeing persecution in Burma, a predominantly Buddhist country. The repatriation agreements signed between the two countries in 1992 failed to stem the flow of refugees.

[33] Writer Taslima Nasrin became famous in 1994 for her book *Shame*, which condemned the alleged oppression of Hindus and other minorities by Muslims. Nasrin was detained for requesting a greater respect by Islamic law of women's rights: this was regarded as criticism against the *Qur'an*. Throughout that year, some 154 MPs opposed to the Khaleda Zia administration boycotted parliamentary activity and resigned en masse in December. Throughout 1994 and 1995 Sheikh Hasina, female leader of the Awami League (AL), led a series of protests by peasants demanding elections under a neutral administration: their protests paid off.

[34] In the 1996 general elections held on February 15, Prime Minister Khaleda Zia of the BNP kept her post but the elections, held under military supervision, were considered fraudulent. A general strike called

by the AL was followed by confrontations between the police and opposition activists. Violence did not end with Khaleda's fall on March 30. On June 23, the former head of the Supreme Court of Justice, Muhammad Habibur Rahman, who had led the neutral government before the June elections, handed over the administration to Prime Minister Sheikh Hasina Wajid, chosen in the second elections in a four-month period.

[35] Social unrest continued throughout 1997 and increased in December with a string of strikes called by opposition parties, after the agreement signed by the Government to put an end to armed rebels in the southeast. For several days, those who supported the strikes and those who were against them held marches in cities - Dhaka, Chittagong, Barisal, Syleht and Rajsani, among others - and in many small towns, which almost paralyzed the country.

[36] During 1988 it was discovered that 5 million people were at risk from polluted wells, the main source of water supply for the population. The wells, whose water contained naturally-occurring arsenic, had been dug in the last two decades after major mobilization campaigns. This contamination threatened to aggravate the situation of the poorest sectors of the population in a country where 50 per cent of newborn children were underweight.

[37] The Bangladesh Central Bank devaluated the taka by 3 per cent on November 1999 to improve competitiveness in the exporting sector. This had been recommended by the IMF, which considered the currency was overvalued. The BNP, now the main opposition party, warned that the measure went against the interests of the population, not least because it was the sixteenth currency devaluation since 1996. A month later, the Prime Minister extended her cabinet to 45 members, incorporating nine new Ministers. The only explanation Hasina Wajid gave for this move was that it gave representation to regions of the country forgotten up to that moment. However, she was also accused of nepotism since three of the new members were her relatives.

[38] In an official visit to southern Asia in March 2000, US President Clinton recognized the efforts Bangladesh was making to portray itself in a different light and for its battle against extreme poverty. However, this first visit of a US president in decades had its tense moments. As soon as he arrived in Bangladesh, Clinton declared it was 'the most dangerous country in the world' a reference to the strained

relations between India and Pakistan, as well as to the conflict in the separatist Indian province of Kashmir. Separatist rebels received military training in Bangladesh until 1996. The Minister of Internal Affairs, Muhammad Nasima, admitted this a month later, saying that military assistance had been given by the previous administration through a foreign network of intelligence operations. Although he did not elaborate, everything pointed to Pakistani intelligence services.

[39] In April 2000, two Supreme Court ministers rejected an appeal of sentences imposed on two former army officers who murdered then Prime Minister Sheikh Mujibur Rahman - independence leader and father of then Prime Minister Sheikh Hasina Wajed - in 1975. These officers were sentenced to death in 1998. Before carrying out the death sentence, the Supreme Court has to ratify it and hear the appeal.

[40] In September 2001, Bangladesh agreed the US could use its air space, ports and airports in the invasion of Afghanistan. In November chief of state Badruddoza Chowdhury traveled to Washington to meet US Secretary of State Colin Powell. While the US wanted to secure Bangladeshi support for its campaign against Afghanistan, as one of the biggest Muslim countries, Chowdhury hoped for economic benefits for the country in return for his backing.

[41] In March high-ranking officers in Bangladesh and India met for three day and announced new measures to reduce tension along the common 4,000 kilometer frontier. Policies included joint patrolling of the zone and periodical meetings between the commanders.

[42] Ekushey Television, the first and only Bangladeshi television network, faced possible closure when the Supreme Court ruled that its broadcasting license was illegal as the Hasina Government had not followed correct procedure in granting it. In turn, the anti-corruption bureau lodged accusations against Hasina and six of her ministers for bribery and the mismanagement of funds. Hasina - now an opposition leader - appealed to the international community for assistance against what she defined as religious and political persecution in her country.

[43] In April 2002, the Government announced the privatization of 21 state companies, mainly in the jute, textile, paper and oil sectors. The privatization process, announced years ago, had been delayed for many reasons; only a few of the 82 industries initially put up for sale were in fact sold. ■

Barbados

Population: 269,000 (2002)
Land area: 430 SQ KM
Capital: Bridgetown
Currency: Barbadian dollar
Language: English

Barbados

The peaceful and nomadic Arawak people expanded throughout the Caribbean region, and although they were dislodged from many islands by the Caribs, they remained on others - as in the case of Barbados.

2   The Spanish landed on the island early in the 16th century and christened it the 'island of the bearded fig tree'. Satisfied that there was no natural wealth they withdrew, but not before massacring the native population, taking a few survivors with them to amuse the Spanish court. In 1625 the British arrived and found a fertile, uninhabited territory.

3   Around 1640 the island had close to 30,000 inhabitants. The majority were farmers and their families, and some were political and religious dissidents from Britain. The settlers grew tobacco, cotton, pepper and fruit on small plots, raising cattle, pigs and poultry.

4   Sugarcane was introduced, with the support of the British, and caused extensive social change. Plantation owners purchased large plots, which were required in order to be profitable, and small landowners - most of them in debt - sold off their land to the plantation owners. The importation of slaves from Africa to work the sugar plantations began during this period.

5   In 1667, 12,000 farmers emigrated to other Caribbean islands or to the 13 colonies of North America. Nonetheless, the island had a commercial fleet of 600 vessels and, as recorded by a French traveler in 1696, was 'the most powerful island colony in America'.

6   Towards the end of the 18th century, the island was one huge

sugar-producing complex which included 745 plantations and over 80,000 African slaves. By that time there was no woodland left on an island described in a 16th century account as 'entirely covered with trees'. Its ecological balance seriously impaired, the island fell victim to drought in the early 19th century and parts of it suffered soil exhaustion.

7   The pursuit of increased profitability and an economy oriented toward foreign trade resulted in underdevelopment. A different approach might have led to development along the lines of the other North American colonies.

8   Slavery was abolished in 1834 but the plantation economy still dominated the islands fiscal system. European landowners controlled local politics until well into the 20th century.

9   In 1938, following the gradual extension of political rights, the Barbados Labor Party (BLP) led by Grantley Adams developed from within the existing labor unions. Universal suffrage was declared in 1951, and Adams became leader of the local government.

10   Internal autonomy was granted 1961, and in 1966 independence was proclaimed within the British Commonwealth. Errol Barrow was elected Prime Minister. Unlike the rest of the West Indies, Barbados never severed its links with the colonial capital in spite of its political independence.

11   After 1966, Errol Barrow's Democratic Labor Party (DLP) contributed to the creation of the Caribbean Free Trade Association which became CARICOM in 1973, involving 12 islands of the region. Barrow showed great interest in the Non-Aligned Countries movement.

12   Free education and new electoral laws were not followed by any significant change in DLP

policies towards the owners of sugar refining plants. The rise in unemployment diminished DLP support and resulted in the Party's electoral defeat. In 1970, the country became a member of the International Monetary Fund (IMF).

13   The BLP won 17 of the 24 available seats in 1976. Tom Adams, Grantley Adams' son, was elected Prime Minister. He promised to fight corruption and described himself as a social democrat (the BLP became a member of the Socialist International in 1978). However, the Government protected the interest of investors in sugar and tourism transnationals, while encouraging foreign investment.

14   Adams pressured Washington to withdraw from its naval base on nearby St Lucia, which it did in 1979. In 1981, Adams was re-elected and consolidated relations with Washington. Barbados supported the US invasion of Grenada.

15   In order to attract foreign capital, the Government passed new tax exemption laws and liberalized ship registration. In 1986, an agreement between the US and Barbados led to 650 new companies registering in the off-shore sector. Unemployment and inflation within Barbados continued to grow.

16   The 1986 election was won by the DLP. Prime Minister Errol Barrow committed the Government to changing the policy toward the US that had been followed by the BLP Government in the preceding 10 years. In 1987, Barrow died of a heart attack and was succeeded as Prime Minister by Erskine Sandiford. Two years later, as a result of a split within the DLP, a new opposition group was founded, the right-wing National Democratic Party (NDP), under the leadership of Richard Haynes.

17   Steadily falling sugar prices and rising interest rates fuelled inflation in 1989. The Government's resolve to cut its budget deficit roused fears of further unemployment and there were several strikes. Nonetheless, industry recovered, exchange reserves increased, and about a hundred Panamanian offshore concerns expressed interest in Barbados. Japan signed agreements to invest in tourism on the island.

WORKERS

1990/2000

UNEMPLOYMENT: 10.5%
LABOR FORCE AS % OF TOTAL:

■ FEMALE: 46%   ■ MALE: 54%

1994/97

EMPLOYMENT DISTRIBUTION:

F
M

■ SERVICES   F: 71%   M: 60%
■ INDUSTRY   F: 13%   M: 25%
■ AGRICULTURE F: 4%   M: 6%

LAND USE

DEFORESTATION: 0.0% annual (1990/95)

1993

■ FOREST & WOODLAND: 11.6%
■ ARABLE: 37.2%
■ OTHER: 56.1%

¹⁸ That same year, Barbados requested a review of the CARICOM charter as it was felt that the constraints were too limiting. In order to favor local agriculture, Government import restrictions were introduced, particularly on vegetables from Guyana.

¹⁹ In 1990, serious controversies arose over sugarcane prices between the sugar mills and the Government; demands from workers threatened to end in strike action. The tourist industry employed 15 per cent of the workforce of the island and 450,000 tourists had visited Barbados in 1988.

²⁰ In 1991, the DLP was re-elected with 49 per cent of the vote although it lost 2 of its 20 seats. In November, riots and protests due to an 8 per cent cutback on civil servants' wages led to a general strike. Despite this challenge, Sandiford remained in office.

²¹ In 1992 the Government obtained an IMF loan amounting to $64.9 million and the Prime Minister announced further wage reductions in the public sector, a rise in interest rates and cutbacks in the social system, as well as the privatization of oil and cement production and the tourism industry.

²² After two successive finance ministers resigned, Sandiford himself assumed the post in late 1992, attempting to transform the country into a financial center. Tourist activity has flourished since 1993. That year, tourism revenues reached $500 million, equivalent to one third of the country's GDP.

²³ In June 1994, the BLP withdrew its support for the Prime Minister and won the elections held on September 7. Owen Arthur, the new prime minister, canceled planned wage reductions, and this became law in February 1995.

²⁴ Arthur introduced a deficit budget in April, arguing that expenditure was needed to tackle unemployment, which had reached 21.2 per cent. The IMF had advised caution in the management of public funds, but Arthur chose to overlook their prescriptions.

²⁵ The island's Governor-General, Dame Nita Barrow, sister of former Prime Minister Errol Barrow, died on December 19 1995. She had held the post since June 1990.

²⁶ The legislative assembly voted in February 1996 for civil servants' salaries to be brought back up over a two-year period. The measure, promoted by the BLP, was a response to the salary reduction policy applied in 1994 by the Democratic Labor Party.

²⁷ In May, the Government signed a contract with a US company to explore possible offshore oil fields.

²⁸ Tourism continued to be the main source of income for Barbados in 1997. The Government managed to further increase that income, even though the infrastructure was not considered the most adequate for large-scale expansion of the sector.

²⁹ In April 1998, during the summit of American Presidents in Santiago, Chile, the Prime Minister of Barbados, Owen Arthur, said he was in favor of Cuba's inclusion at the next meeting.

³⁰ The January 1999 elections saw a broad victory for the BLP, which took 26 of the disputed seats, while the other two remained in DLP hands. Owen Arthur was returned to his post.

³¹ A Financial Intelligence Unit (FIU) was set up to fight money laundering. The new body was advised by members of the UN's International Drug Control Program (UNDCP).

³² In late 2000, the 20-year long fishing rights dispute between Barbados and Trinidad and Tobago peaked when two Barbadian fishers were arrested by maritime patrols from Port of Spain. Premier Arthur threatened Trinidad and Tobago with economic sanctions and warned he would apply the Immigration Act to expel illegal Trinidadian immigrants. He also suggested that free traffic rights granted to BWIA, the national Trinidad and Tobago airline, would be revised. The incident took place after Arthur and Trinidadian Prime Minister Basdeo Panday agreed on a plan to hold fishing talks. Exports from Barbados to Trinidad and Tobago fell from $39.5 million in 1982 to $30 million in 2000. Trinidad had exported $150 million in goods and services to Barbados in 1999. Bridgetown attacked Trinidad and Tobago for granting licenses to Taiwanese fishermen who would then export the fish to Barbados as a Trinidadian product, to benefit from the preferential treatment granted by the CARICOM agreements.

³³ Barbados enacted a law on international companies in 2001 in order to attract foreign investment. The law created a 2.5 per cent maximum income tax, exemptions on every other tax and on tariffs on the imports of materials for production, the exemption of foreign exchange controls, and a deduction of 150 per cent on the cost of research and development activities on exports.

³⁴ In June 2001, Barbados hosted the preparatory Regional Round Table for the World Summit on Sustainable Development, which was in Johannesburg, South Africa, in September 2002. The representatives gave their views on Agenda 21, an agreement reached in the Rio 1992 summit with the goal of promoting measures to reach a model for sustainable development. ∎

PROFILE

ENVIRONMENT
Of volcanic origin, Barbados is the eastern-most island of the Lesser Antilles. The fertile soil and rainy tropical climate favor intensive farming of sugarcane, rotated with cotton and corn. The most serious environmental problems are the disposal of sewage and refuse, water consumption, and soil and coastal erosion. The Caribbean Sea is increasingly contaminated and its resources are over-exploited.

SOCIETY
Peoples: Most are of African origin (92.5 per cent), with a minority of Europeans (3.2 per cent) and 2.8 per cent of mixed descent. It is one of the most densely populated countries in the world, with an average of 616 people per square kilometer.
Religions: 33 per cent Anglican. Methodists and Moravians (29.8 per cent). There are also Catholics (4.4 per cent).
Languages: English (official). Creole (Bajan) is also spoken.
Political Parties: The Barbados Labor Party (BLP), in power since 1994. The Democratic Labor Party (DLP); the right-wing National Democratic Party (NDP).
Social Organizations: Barbados Workers' Trade Union. National Women's Organization.

THE STATE
Official Name: Barbados.
Administrative divisions: 11 parishes.
Capital: Bridgetown 133,000 people (1999).
Other cities: Speightstown 820 people; Holetown 720; Bathsheba 720 (2000).
Government: Owen Arthur, Prime Minister since September 1994, re-elected in 1999; Sir Clifford Husband, Governor-General, appointed in 1996. The bicameral Parliament has been shaped on the British model. The Legislative power is constituted by a Parliament, with a Lower Chamber, Senate and the post of Governor General.
National Holiday: November 30, Independence Day (1966).
Armed Forces: 610 army (1995).

Belarus

Population: 10,106,000 (2002)
Land area: 207,480 SQ KM
Capital: Minsk (Mensk)
Currency: Ruble
Language: Belarusian

Belarus

The territory known today as Belarus (formerly Belorussia) was inhabited from the 1st century AD by the Krivich, Radimich and Dregovich Slavic peoples. The first principalities were those of Polotsk and Turov-Pinsk. In the 9th century, Eastern Slav tribes belonging to the Western Rus joined other Eastern Slav peoples to form the Kiev Rus, the ancient Russian State (see history of Russia) which gave rise to modern Russia, Ukraine and Belarus. The major cities of the area, Polotsk, Turov, Brest, Vitebsk, Orsha, Pinsk and Minsk date from the 9th and 10th centuries.

² In the 14th century, Lithuanian principalities annexed themselves to the Western Rus. As the Lithuanians lacked their own writing system, the language of the Belarusians (which was the only Russian language at the time) became the official language of the State. Between the 14th and 16th centuries, the Belarusian culture began to differentiate itself from that of the Russians and the Ukrainians.

³ In 1569, according to the terms of the Union Treaty between Poland and Lithuania, Belarus became a part of Poland. The Belarusians resisted domination by the Catholic Poles, and maintained their linguistic and cultural identity. With the first partition of Poland in 1772, Russia kept the eastern part of Belarus. Between 1793-95, the rest of Belarus became part of the Russian Empire. The abolition of serfdom in Russia in 1861 accelerated the development of Belarus. Important railways were built, including the Moscow-Brest and the Libava-Romni lines. By the end of the 19th century, Belarus had Russia's second most important railway system.

⁴ The Russian Czar's abolition of the serf system put an end to the peasants' feudal bondage to the landed nobility. However, this failed to solve the land tenure problem, as in Belarus only 35 per cent of the land was handed over to the peasants. This triggered a number of uprisings, the most important of which took place in 1863 under the leadership of Kalinovski.

⁵ In March 1899, the 1st Congress of the Social Democratic Workers' Party of Russia (SDWPR) was held secretly in Minsk. This group was inspired by Marxist socialism and was determined to bring down the Czar. Other sectors of the intelligentsia took their cue from the peasants' discontent, and founded an autonomous Belarusian movement in 1902, which sought to revive the nation's culture. During this period, the czarist regime deported Russian Jews to Belarus, where they came to account for a fifth of the local population.

⁶ During World War I (1914-1918) part of Belarus was occupied by German troops. After the Russian Revolution of February 1917, councils (soviets) made up of workers' representatives were formed in Minsk, Gomel, Vitebsk, Bobruisk and Orsha.

⁷ Soviet power began to be established at the end of 1917, and in February 1918 the large land holdings were nationalized. A few months later, land began to be distributed to the peasants. At the insistence of the Bolsheviks (socialist revolutionaries of the SDWPR), the first collective farms (*koljoses*) were set up. In reality, however, the land gradually went into State control.

⁸ The 6th Party Conference of the Russian Communists (Bolsheviks) - formerly the SDWPR - held in Smolensk, approved the decision to found the Soviet Socialist Republic of Belarus (SSRB). In January 1918, the decision to join Lithuania was made at the 1st Congress of the SSRB soviets. The Congress of the Soviets of Lithuania endorsed the same motion. On February 1919 in the city of Vilno (today Vilnius, the capital of Lithuania) the Government of the Soviet Socialist Republic of Lithuania and Belarus was elected, with Mickevicius-Kapsukas as head of state.

⁹ In the same month, Poland, which had become independent from Russia after the Bolsheviks had seized power in St Petersburg, occupied a large part of Belarus. According to the Treaty of Riga, signed between Soviet Russia and Poland (1921), Western Belarus became part of Poland.

¹⁰ On August 1 1920 the Assembly of representatives of the Lithuanian and Belarusian Communist Parties and of labor organizations in Minsk and its surrounding areas approved the foundation of the independent Belarusian republic.

¹¹ On December 30 1922, Belarus joined the Union of Soviet Socialist Republics (USSR) as one of its founders, along with the Russian Federation, Ukraine and the Transcaucasian Federation (Armenia, Georgia and Azerbaijan).

¹² The industrialization and collectivization of agriculture began in the second half of the 1920s. On February 19 1937 the 12th Congress of the Soviets of Belarus approved the new constitution. In November 1939, as a result of the Molotov-Ribbentrop Pact - signed between the USSR and Germany-Western Belarus was reincorporated into the Soviet Union.

¹³ In June 1941 the state became the first of the Soviet republics to suffer Hitler's aggression. The fortress at Brest offered fierce resistance, becoming a symbol of Belarus' heroic defense. Guerrilla warfare extended throughout the country for the duration of the War, a conflict in which more than 2 million Belarusians lost their lives.

¹⁴ After Germany's defeat in 1945, Belarus' current borders were established. It became a charter member of the United Nations that same year; like Ukraine it had its own delegation, independent of the USSR.

¹⁵ It took Belarus almost two decades to restore its economy, becoming in the process an important producer of heavy trucks, electrical appliances, radios and television sets. Between the 1920s and the 1980s, Belarus ceased to be a rural country in which 90 per cent of the population lived from traditional farming and livestock raising becoming an urban, industrialized country with nearly 70 per cent of its population living in cities.

¹⁶ Belarus is one of the few republics that managed to maintain a majority of its local population - more than 80 per cent - with minimal influence from Russian or other immigration.

¹⁷ Until 1985, the Communist Party and the Belarusian Government followed the course established by the Communist Party of the Soviet Union. Among the outstanding communist leaders of this period was Piotr Masherov.

[18] Because of the policies of *glasnost* (openness) and *perestroika* (restructuring) initiated by President Mikhail Gorbachev, there was no strong pressure within Belarus to secede immediately from the USSR, although there were movements favoring a multiparty political system, as well as protest demonstrations against high food prices.

[19] Belarus was the region outside Ukraine most affected by the 1986 catastrophe at the Chernobyl nuclear plant. According to foreign researchers, in the following years there was a rapid increase in cases of cancer, leukemia and birth defects in the areas affected by the disaster - Ukraine, Belarus and western Russia.

[20] In June 1991, Belarus declared independence and in October signed an economic integration agreement with Kazakhstan and Uzbekistan. On December 8, the presidents of the Russian Federation and Ukraine, Boris Yeltsin and Leonid Kravchuk, and of the Belarus Parliament, Stanislav Sushkevich, signed an historic agreement that effectively ended the USSR. Opposing President Gorbachev's idea of signing a new Union Treaty, the presidents decided to create an association of sovereign states. On June 21, in Alma-Ata (now Almaty, in Kazakhstan), 11 republics signed an agreement creating the Commonwealth of Independent States (CIS), whose members requested admission to the UN as separate countries. Belarus and 7 of the republics pledged to implement structural reforms which would convert them into market economies.

[21] In September 1993, tensions between the prime minister and the Parliamentary president came to a head amid rumors of a possible coup. In January 1994, Sushkevich was replaced by Mecheslav Grib. On March, Parliament passed the new Constitution, replacing the 1977 one when Belarus still belonged to the former USSR.

[22] The country became a presidential republic with a 260-seat Parliament. In July, Alexander Lukashenka obtained 80 per cent of the vote in the second round, after a campaign in which he lambasted the corruption of his predecessors.

[23] In spite of having criticized it in his electoral campaign, the President continued the policy of rapprochement which led to a monetary union with Russia on April 1994. In August, he met Russian President Boris Yeltsin and in November decreed a state of emergency, on the pretext of slowing down inflation.

[24] On February 1995, Minsk and Moscow signed a treaty of friendship and cooperation which enabled Russia to keep its troops deployed in the country. Insufficient participation in the May parliamentary elections, which Lukashenka held along with a referendum on his rapprochement policy toward Moscow, did not allow for the election of all deputies, which led to a second by-election in November.

[25] In April 1996, amid mass protests, Russia and Belarus strengthened their relations by signing a political and economic integration agreement. Several opposition leaders went into exile in the United States. By the end of the year, a constitutional reform granted more powers to Lukashenka. Among those arrested were the former Central Bank chairman and other senior officials. The opposition denounced the establishment of a dictatorship.

[26] The economy was in chaos in 1997. Over 70 per cent of the population was living below the poverty line. The value of the national currency, the rouble, fell against the dollar and inflation grew. Lukashenka dismissed foreign minister Vladimir Syanko and replaced him with Ivan Antanovich. Parliament confirmed the appointment of Syarhei Linh as prime minister.

[27] Amnesty International reported executions and arbitrary arrests and demanded the abolition of the death penalty. In February 1998, Belarus recalled its ambassador to Poland, amidst accusations of Polish interference in domestic affairs.

[28] In April 1999 Senate approval was given for integration with Russia. This caused some protest in the south of the country, but there was broad support in the north, where Russian influence is stronger. One issue agreed was that citizens of both countries would enjoy identical rights on either side of the border.

[29] Although the opposition, which had experienced the banning of several of its candidates, called a boycott of the parliamentary elections of October 2000, more than 60 per cent voted, according to the electoral commission, which was sufficient to validate the majority obtained by the government's party. According to European observers, the counting of the votes did not meet democratic international standards.

[30] As a reaction to the pressure, Lukashenka supported the re-run, in March 2001, of parliamentary elections in 13 districts which had had a very low turnout. The result was declared valid, and in Minsk police cracked down on a demonstration against Lukashenka by thousands of people.

[31] The September presidential elections were also condemned by the opposition and observers from Western countries. Lukashenka was re-elected for a second term. ∎

PROFILE

ENVIRONMENT

Belarus is located between the Dnepr (Dnieper), Western Dvina, Niemen and Western Bug rivers. It is bounded in the west by Poland, in the northwest by Latvia and Lithuania, in the northeast by Russia and in the south by Ukraine. It is a flat country, with many swamps and lakes, and forests covering a third of its territory. Its climate is continental and cool, with an average summer temperature of 17-19°, and 4-7° below zero in winter. Due to its proximity to Ukraine, Belarus received heavy radioactive fall-out following the disaster at the Chernobyl nuclear plant in 1986. A quarter of the country's arable land shows signs of chemical pollution from the overuse of pesticides.

SOCIETY

Peoples: Belarusians, 77.9 per cent; Russians, 13.2 per cent; Poles, 4.1 per cent; Ukrainians, 4.1 per cent; Jewish, 1.1 per cent (1989).
Religions: Christian Orthodox; in the west, Catholic.
Languages: Belarusian (official); Russian (second language for most of the population); Polish; Ukrainian; Yiddish and Tatar.
Political Parties: Communist Party; Agrarian Party; Republican Party of Labor and Justice; Belarusian People's Front-Revival; United Civic Party; Ecology Party.
Social Organizations: Labor Union Federation of Belarus; Free Union.

THE STATE

Official name: Respublika Belarus
Administrative divisions: Six regions (Brest, Gomel, Grodno, Mensk, Moguiliov and Vitebsk).
Capital: Minsk (Mensk) 1,758,000 people (1999).
Other cities: Gomel 503,400 people; Mogiliov 372,700; Vitebsk 356,000; Grodno 311,500; Brest 304,200 (2000).
Government: Aleksander Lukashenka, President since July 1994, re-elected in September 2001; Henadz Navitski, Prime Minister since October 2001. The National Assembly has two chambers: Representatives with 100 members and the Soviet with 64 seats.
National Holiday: June 27, Independence (1991).
Armed Forces: 102,600.
Other: Border Guards (Ministry of Interior): 8,000.

DEMOGRAPHY
Population: 10,106,000 (2002)
Annual growth: 0.1 % (1985-2000)
Estimates for year 2015: 9,664,000 (2000)
Annual growth to year 2015: -0.4 % (2000)
Urban population: 70.3 % (2000)
Urban growth: 0.6 % (2000)
Children per woman: 1.3 (2000)

HEALTH
Life expectancy at birth: 69 years (2000-2005)
male: 63 years (2000-2005)
female: 74 years (2000-2005)
Maternal mortality: 20 per 100,000 live births (1985/99)
Infant mortality: 17 per 1,000 (2000)
Under-5 child mortality: 20 per 1,000 (2000)
Daily calorie supply: 3,171 per capita (1999)
443 doctors per 100,000 people (1998)
Safe water: 100 % (2000)

EDUCATION
Literacy: 99 % (2000)
male: 100 % (2000)
female: 99 % (2000)
School enrolment (net):
Primary total: 85 % (1994/2000)
male: 87 % (1995/99)
female: 84 % (1995/99)
Secondary (gross):
male: 91 % (1995/97)
female: 95 % (1995/97)
Tertiary (gross): 45 % (1997)
Primary school teachers: one for every 20 pupils (1998)

COMMUNICATIONS
155 newspapers (1998), 299 radios (1997), 342 TV sets (2000) and 269 main telephone lines (2000) per 1,000 people
Books: 32 new titles per 100,000 people (1992/94)

ECONOMY
Per capita, GDP: $ 7,544 (2000)
Annual growth: 6.1 % (2000)
Annual inflation: 168.6 % (2000)
Consumer price index: 4,576.7 (2000)
Currency: 1,668.0 ruble = $ 1 (03/2002)
Cereal imports: 1,126,877 metric tons (2000)
Food import dependency: 12 % (2000)
Fertilizer use: 1,383 kg per ha (1999)
Exports: $ 20,309 million (2000)
Imports: $ 20,768 million (2000)
External debt: $ 851 million (2000); $ 84 per capita (2000)
Debt service: 3.2 % of exports (1999)
Development aid received: $ 24 million (1999); $ 2.4 per capita (1999); 0.10 % of GNP (1999)

ENERGY
Consumption: 2,614.3 Kgs of oil equivalent per capita yearly (1998); 85.5 % imported (1999)

HDI (ranking/value): 53 / 0.782 (1999)

Belgium

België / Belgique

Population: 10,276,000 (2002)
Land area: 32,820 SQ KM
Capital: Brussels (Bruxelles, Brussel)
Currency: Euro
Language: French, Dutch and German

Belgium, Holland, Luxembourg and a part of northern France make up the Low Countries, which had a common history until 1579 (see Netherlands). The linguistic separation which took place between the Roman and Germanic languages coincided with the borders of the Holy Roman Empire, which divided the Low Countries in two.

2 Between 1519 and 1814, the southern provinces were successively ruled by Spain (1519), Austria (1713) and France (1794). After the fall of Napoleon in 1814, the European powers enforced reunification with the north. The southern provinces had already forged an identity of their own, and were unwilling to accept Dutch authority.

3 The region's economy was based on the production of linen and textiles. Industrialization was facilitated by the fact that manufacturers and landowners were often one and the same, and that textile mills were concentrated in the hands of a few owners. Factories each employing more than 100 low-paid workers sprang up in Gent, Antwerp, and Tournai.

4 In 1830, the Belgian bourgeoisie, along with urban laborers from Brussels and Lièges, took up arms against the Dutch authorities. When the conflict spread and proved substantial, European powers recognized the independence of the southern provinces, which were henceforth known as Belgium. Congress adopted a parliamentary monarchy, with an electing body made up of property owners. Parliamentary monarchy, institutionalized in 1830, has survived until today.

5 By the end of the 19th century, workers forced the government to pass laws aimed at providing housing for working-class people, and improving conditions in the workplace, especially for women and children. At the same time, Parliament changed the constitution and in 1893, established limited male suffrage.

6 Between 1880 and 1885, Leopold II financed international expeditions to the Congo, making it effectively his 'private' colony. Substantial deficits and protests from several European nations against the severe repression and exploitation occurring in the Congo, forced the

Belgian Government to take it as a colony in 1908. With this, the worst excesses ended, but the Belgian Government, businesses and the Church increased their influence over the following years.

7 In the 20th century, the Belgian democratic system was threatened twice by a major world war, but each time democracy prevailed. In 1914, Germany wanted to cross Belgian territory, in order to invade France. Belgium refused to give way to the Germans and was drawn into war. The Treaty of Versailles (1918) granted the territories of Eupen and Malmedy to Belgium. In Africa, Belgium colonized the former German colonies of Rwanda and Burundi after the League of Nations granted them a mandate. But Belgium failed to realize any of its other territorial demands. In 1920 Belgium signed a military assistance treaty with France, and the following year, it formed an economic alliance with Luxembourg.

8 After the War, the Government established universal male suffrage. The parliament approved an 8-hour workday, a graduated income tax, and a retirement pension plan. From 1930, increased pressure was put on the government to tackle discrimination against the Flemish people and the

Dutch language. This resulted in several 'linguistic laws' and two regions: Flanders and Wallonia. In the former, Dutch is the official language, while in the latter it is French.

9 During World War II Belgium remained neutral, but was occupied by Germany in 1940, until liberation in 1944. The return of King Leopold III, who had been held prisoner by the Germans, unleashed a major controversy. In a plebiscite, 57 per cent of the population voted in favor of his return to the throne, but continuing tension in Wallonia forced Leopold to abdicate in favor of his son Baudouin (1950).

10 In 1947, Belgium, the Netherlands and Luxembourg formed an economic association known as the Benelux. This association can be considered as the cradle of the present European Union. Belgium also became a member of NATO in 1949. In 1960 the Belgian Congo became independent, but soon had to deal with secessionist movements in the southern province of Katanga. Belgian tacitly took side with the secessionists, but UN troops eventually restored national unity. Later on Belgium and the Western powers continued to intervene in the former colony (which became

Zaire, and is now the Democratic Republic of Congo). In 1962 Rwanda and Burundi became independent.

11 Female suffrage was granted in 1949. In 1975, Belgian women gained the right to equal pay.

12 During the 1960s and the 1970s questions about linguistic communities became increasingly important. In 1970, linguistic communities were granted autonomy in cultural matters. In 1980, a new federal structure was approved by Parliament, made up of Flanders, Wallonia, and Brussels as the bilingual capital district. This marked the beginning of a process of decentralization that would continue for the next 20 years.

13 In 1983, hundreds of thousands gathered in the streets of Brussels to protest against the installation of NATO nuclear missiles on Belgian soil. In no time, a movement of peace activists was born. The missiles were withdrawn in 1988, after an arms reduction agreement was signed between the US and the USSR. Together with the missiles the mass movement disappeared again.

14 In the elections held in November 1991, the Vlaams Blok (Flemish Bloc), a xenophobic group which had geared its campaign around the expulsion of immigrants, experienced a six-fold increase in its parliamentary representation.

15 In 1992, premier Dehaene, who had formed a government with the Christian Democrats and the Socialists, announced a plan to reduce the national deficit, in line with the requirements of the European Treaty of Maastricht. This included drastic curbs in public spending. The Government closed the 1997 budget with a national deficit of 2.7 per cent of the GDP. In spite of this enormous public dept, which clearly exceeded the criteria of the Maastricht Treaty, Belgium was allowed to join the European Monetary Union from its very beginning.

16 On July 31 1993, King Baudouin died after a reign of 42 years. He was succeeded by his brother Albert, who was crowned as Albert II.

17 The 1994 European elections reflected the population's lack of confidence in the governing Christian Democrats/Socialists coalition. After a corruption scandal in which three leading socialist politicians were

involved, the French-speaking Socialists went from 38.5 per cent of the vote in 1989 to 30.4 per cent in 1994. In the municipal elections of October, the Socialists lost votes again, while the Vlaams Blok became the second party in Antwerp, by winning 18 out of the 55 seats at stake on the city council.

[18] Meanwhile, the parliament had agreed on major constitutional changes that turned the country into a federal state. On May 21 1995, voters not only elected their members of parliament, but also three new regional assemblies of Brussels, Flanders and Wallonia. The government alliance led by premier Dehaene had a clear victory in the national elections, allowing him to continue as head of government.

[19] In 2001, the Lambermont agreements continued the reform of the state through decentralization. Federal powers concerning agriculture, foreign trade and development cooperation were transferred to Flanders and Wallonia. Food security however remained a federal issue. This measure was the result of the different food scandals that had threatened the country for years, including swine fever, mad cow disease, foot-and-mouth disease and the dioxin scandal. The scandal brought Dehaene down and allowed into the political arena a coalition headed by Guy Verhofstadt, leader of the Flemish Liberal Party (VLD). Verhofstadt formed a coalition with Socialists and Greens from both communities, leaving the Christian Democrats out of office for the first time in 41 years.

[20] On the basis of the genocide law of 1993, crimes against humanity, committed anywhere in the world, can be prosecuted in Belgium. This happened in 2001, when four Rwandan citizens were sentenced in Brussels for taking part in the 1994 genocide. In the same year, the existence of the genocide law prompted the Israeli premier Ariel Sharon to cancel his visit to Belgium: a case of genocide had been instigated against him by several Palestinians, survivors of the 1982 Sabra and Shatila massacre, for his alleged responsibility in those killings.

[21] In 2001, after several years of non-involvement, Belgium resumed diplomatic links with DR Congo. Premier Verhofstadt and Minister of Foreign Affairs Michel visited the former colony to further the peace negotiations that should end the civil war in the eastern part of the country. Verhofstadt also promised to put the Congolese problems on the European agenda.

[22] The flow of refugees from Third World and former communist states became a political issue in Europe. Most European countries introduced measures to shake off as many asylum seekers as possible. Belgium followed this trend by abolishing all financial support to refugees and by introducing a fast deportation procedure. The Belgian asylum policy was criticized by Amnesty International.

[23] In July 2001, Belgium took over the chair of the European Union. It put the Tobin Tax, the taxation of international financial transactions, on the European agenda. On January 1 2002, the Euro replaced the Belgian franc as the national currency.

[24] The Belgian section of the anti-globalization movement, consisting of trade unions, peace groups, ecological and Third World movements and several non-governmental organizations, occupied the streets of Gent and Brussels in the autumn of 2001, protesting against EU policy and other international organizations.

[25] In December, the autonomous Flemish government suspended relations with Israel protesting against the violence used on the Palestinian people. In early 2002, the council of the autonomous region of Brussels also decided to suspend a cooperation agreement signed with Israel two years previously.

[26] On April 1, 2002, a synagogue in the commune of Anderlecht in Brussels was petrol-bombed; there was slight damage which led to increased security measures. A large number of Arabs living in Brussels, along with human rights militants, demonstrated outside the Israeli embassy in Brussels.

[27] The Sharon case hit the news again in 2002. The Belgian court handling the Sharon trial postponed the verdict allowing lawyers to debate a new hearing on the ruling of the International Court to grant immunity to rulers currently in power.

[28] Similarly, on April 2 in Brussels, the European Union decided to continue with financial support to the Palestinian Authority, mainly for the maintenance of essential services. EU speaker, Emma Udwin, described the situation in Palestine as 'shattering' and called for compliance with UN Security Council resolution 1402. ■

PROFILE

ENVIRONMENT

Northwestern Belgium is a lowland, the Plains of Flanders, composed of sand and clay deposited by its rivers. In southern Belgium the southern highlands rise to 700 m on the Ardennes Plateau. One of the most densely populated European countries, its prosperity rests on trade, helped by its geography and by the transport network covering the northern plains, converging at the port of Antwerp. Belgium has highly intensive agriculture, and a major industrial center. Heavy industry was located near the coal fields of the Sambre-Meuse valley, and textiles were traditionally concentrated in Flanders, where new industries have developed since the late 1960s. Water protection laws were approved in 1971. However, the Meuse River, supplying 5 million people with drinking water, is contaminated by industrial waste. Pollution, by the excessive use of both animal wastes and chemical fertilizers, has increased the nitrate concentration in many rivers and accounts for the presence of algae. Belgian smokestack industries contribute to air pollution in Europe, and are responsible for acid rain in neighboring countries.

SOCIETY

Peoples: The country's two major language-based groups are the Flemish (55 per cent) and the Walloons (44 per cent). There is also a German minority (1 per cent). Many industrial workers are immigrants (Italian, Moroccan and, in lesser numbers, Turkish and African). Foreigners represent about 8 per cent of the whole population. **Religions:** Mainly Catholic. **Languages:** Dutch (58 per cent) and French (32 per cent) are the official languages. French is the main language spoken in the south and east, and Dutch in the north. German is spoken by about 0.6 per cent of the population. **Political Parties:** Flemish Christian Democrats (CD&V); French-speaking Social Christians (PSC); Flemish Socialists (SPA); Flemish Liberal party (VLD); French-speaking Liberal party (PRL); Green parties (AGALEV/ECOLO); Flemish nationalists (in September 2001 the VU was split into Spirit and NVA); and far right parties (Vlaams Blok, FN). **Social Organizations:** The General Labor Federation of Belgium (ABVV/FGTB), Confederation of Christian Labor Unions of Belgium (ACV/CSC).

THE STATE

Official Name: Royaume de Belgique/ Koninkrijk België. **Administrative Divisions:** 10 provinces. **Capital:** Brussels (Bruxelles/Brussel) 1,121,000 people (1999). Brussels is also the capital of the European Union. **Other cities:** Antwerpen 945,800 people; Liège 620,900; Charleroi 201,700; Gent 223,000 (2000). **Government:** Federal parliamentary state since 1993, under a constitutional monarch. It consists of the Flemish Region, the Walloon Region and the Brussels Capital Region. There are three official language communities: Flemish, French and German. King Albert II, Head of State since August 1993. Guy Verhofstadt, Prime Minister since July 1999. Bicameral Legislative: Chamber of People's Representatives, with 150 members; Senate, with 71 members. **National Holiday:** July 21, National Day (date King Leopold I came to the throne, 1831). **Armed Forces:** 53,000. Conscription was abolished in 1994. Belgium has now only a professional army.

Belize

Belize

ative American people known as the Itzae were the original occupants of what is now Belize (formerly British Honduras). Belize, together with Guatemala and southern Mexico, formed part of the Mayan Empire. In Belize, the Mayas built the cities of Lubaatún, Pusilhá, and a third which archaeologists call San José (its original name is unknown).

[2] In 1504 Columbus sailed into the bay naming it the Gulf of Honduras. Spain was nominally the colonial power in the region, but never pushed further into Belize, because of tough resistance from the local people. According to the terms of the Treaty of Paris (1763) Spain allowed the British to start exploiting timber in the area. This authorization was later confirmed in the Treaty of Versailles (1783). From the Captaincy-General of Yucatan (now Mexico) the Spaniards tried on several occasions to drive out the British, many of whom were involved in piracy. In 1798 the British gained control of the colony, although Spain retained sovereignty until it became a British colony in 1862. As of 1871 the Crown took charge of local government with the territory administered by the governor of Jamaica until 1884.

[3] By the second half of the 17th century, some British entrepreneurs attracted in particular by cedar, campeche wood, and timber, started establishing themselves in the depopulated coastal areas, importing African slaves to work their estates. Shortly afterwards, slaves outnumbered Europeans, and in 1784 only 10 per cent of the population was of European extraction, a ratio which has been steadily decreasing.

[4] The ethnic base became more heterogeneous in the early 19th century. By that time, Garifuna migrants had settled on the Southern coast of Belize. The War of Castes in Yucatan between 1847 and 1853 displaced thousands of Spanish-speaking inhabitants to the northern coast of Belize, while several Maya communities re-settled in the northern and western areas of the country. These immigrants introduced changes in agricultural techniques that set the pattern for subsistence farming and set the basis of sugar, banana and citrus production. During the 1860s and 1870s, sugarcane plantation owners sponsored the migration of several thousand workers from China and India. By the end of that century, Maya and Kekchi indigenous peoples, who had escaped oppression in Guatemala, established self-sufficient communities in the south and west of Belize.

[5] By the early 20th century, this ethnic mix had become settled. However, the economy was stagnant and the British colonial administration prevented any democratic participation. In 1931, a hurricane destroyed a large part of Belize City. Strikes and demonstrations by workers and the unemployed gave rise to unions and increasing demands for democracy. Eligibility for voting was legally introduced in 1936, but it was heavily restricted by level of literacy, land title and gender. In 1949 when the Governor devalued the national currency, union leaders and the local middle class joined in a People's Committee that demanded constitutional changes.

[6] In 1950 the People's United Party (PUP) was founded, led by George Price. First organized as a 'people's committee' to fight against arbitrary treatment by the colonial administration, the PUP won its first elections by a landslide majority. In 1954 universal suffrage was granted, and the majority of the legislative representatives were elected directly. In 1961 a ministerial system of government was established, and in 1964 the country was granted internal autonomy, with George Price becoming Prime Minister. On June 1 1973 the country changed its name from British Honduras to Belize.

[7] Guatemala claimed to have inherited sovereignty over Belize from Spain, and did not recognize the Guatemala-Belize border. In March 1981, Guatemala and Britain signed a 16-point agreement. Britain assured the future independence of Belize in exchange for some concessions to the Guatemalan regime, such as free and permanent access to the Atlantic, joint exploitation of the marine resources, the building of a pipeline, and an 'anti-terrorist' agreement.

[8] Price and the PUP were accused of partiality towards Cuba and Nicaragua, an issue exploited by the right-wing opposition, the United Democratic Party (UDP), which won 21 out of 28 seats in the December 1984 elections.

[9] The new Prime Minister, Manuel Esquivel, a US-educated physics professor, adopted a liberal economic policy and supported the private import-export sector, which was in the hands of inexperienced family business ventures. He also encouraged foreign investment and sought to attract US, Jamaican and Mexican investments in tourism, energy, and agriculture. The previous government had bequeathed Belize one of the most liberal set of laws concerning foreign investment in the Third World.

[10] Sugarcane generated 50 per cent of the country's revenue, but a fall in international prices badly affected the economy. The industry only survived because of import quotas guaranteed by the US and EEC markets, which took 60 per cent of the sugar output, with the remainder being sold at a loss.

[11] In March 1986, Prime Minister Esquivel proposed a plan for the sale of Belizean citizenship, aimed primarily at Hong Kong business people, as Hong Kong was due to revert to China in 1997. Anyone investing $25,000 in government bonds - really worth only $12,500 - would be granted instant citizenship of Belize.

[12] During the 1980s, the country received approximately 40,000 Salvadoran, Guatemalan, Honduran and Nicaraguan refugees. In spite of official tolerance, some officials blamed immigrants for the dramatic rise in marijuana trafficking and crime.

[13] When Vinicio Cerezo became President of Guatemala in 1986, relations between the countries changed substantially. In December 1986, Cerezo's government re-established diplomatic relations with Britain, broken off two decades earlier over Guatemalan claims to Belizean territory. A Permanent Joint Commission was formed with Belizean, Guatemalan and British representatives to find a peaceful solution to the issue.

[14] In spite of the existence of the Commission, Belize feared a Guatemalan invasion and kept a standing army of 1,800 British troops.

Esquivel declared in Mexico that he 'would not allow the installation of US military bases', stressing that he did not wish to become involved in the Central American crisis.

[15] However, the number of US embassy personnel grew sixfold after independence and the number of Peace Corps volunteers was ten times higher. Dean Barrow, Minister of Foreign Affairs and Economic Development, admitted that he was aware of the country's dependence upon the US. But he also stated that Belize could defend its territorial integrity through the Non-Aligned Movement.

[16] Drug-trafficking - or the sale of 'Belize breeze' as marijuana is known - showed spectacular growth. According to some foreign economists, it became the country's main export, and it was estimated that some 700 tons - worth at least $100 million had been taken into the US, where the resale price was at least ten times this sum. The area under cultivation increased by at least 20 per cent in spite of a US-sponsored herbicide-spraying campaign carried out with Mexican helicopters.

[17] George Price was returned to power when the PUP won the September 1989 elections with 15 of the 28 seats. The 13 remaining seats went to Esquivel's UDP.

[18] In September 1991, Guatemalan President Jorge Serrano Elias finally recognized Belize's sovereignty and right to self-determination. The Government of Belize in turn gave Guatemala free access to the Gulf of Honduras, thereby reducing its own territorial waters.

[19] At the end of the 1980s and early 1990s a large number of Haitians went to Belize as agricultural laborers, attracted by higher wages than at home. Lower inflation rates and more equal income distribution were incentives for immigration, and they also had access to health and education services. The social services consequently became overloaded, triggering a backlash from Belizeans who demanded that the Haitians be repatriated.

[20] A 1992 census revealed that the Spanish-speaking mestizo population had outgrown the English-speaking population of African origin who, together with the European descendants, had been the dominant group.

[21] Banana, sugar and citrus production increased, representing 40 per cent of the country's total production and four-fifths of its exports. Tourism became the sector with the greatest potential. Several environmental organizations cooperated in protecting nature reserves and attempts to improve the quality of the Caribbean waters.

Mayan archeological discoveries attracted many visitors.

[22] Hours after Guatemala's President Serrano was ousted on June 1 1993, Price brought the election date forward 15 months, counting on a new PUP victory to ratify agreements made with this neighbor. His opponent Manuel Esquivel questioned the validity of Price's concessions to Guatemala, and proposed that these be legitimized by a referendum.

[23] In the June 1993 elections the PUP was pushed out by the UDP, led by Esquivel. In March 1994, the UDP also won the elections for the nation's 7 local councils. The Government formed a group of economic advisors to look into establishing facilities for the capital and tourist markets, and the development of one or more free zones. The fear of new territorial demands from Guatemala and the withdrawal of British troops led to an increase in defense spending and new recruitment for the armed forces.

[24] Victory in the August 1998 general elections went to the PUP, which won 26 seats, and Said Wilbert Musa became the new Prime Minister. The UDP was reduced to just three seats.

[25] On February 24 2000 four members of the Belize security force where apprehended in Guatemala for allegedly entering that country's territory illegally. The incident intensified the border dispute between Belize and its neighbor. Almost immediately the Caribbean Community (Caricom) accused the Guatemalan Government of invading territory and kidnapping Belizeans.

[26] In October, Hurricane Keith caused widespread destruction. The storm left many dead, including tourists, and the subsequent floods severely damaged the country's infrastructure. The Government declared three coastal towns disaster areas.

[27] Another tragedy struck Belize in 2001 when Hurricane Iris buried entire towns and left at least 13,000 homeless. The hurricane, the most destructive in Central America in three years, flattened whole forests, destroyed the banana harvest and claimed around 20 lives. ∎

PROFILE

ENVIRONMENT

Belize covers the southeastern tip of the Yucatan Peninsula. The land is low, and the climate warm and rainy in the north. In southern Belize, the hillsides sustain a variety of crops. The northern coastline is marshy and flanked by low islands. In the south there are excellent natural harbors between reefs. Significant oil and gas deposits are believed to exist off the coast. The country shares many of the problems of the Caribbean region, including the deterioration of its water-quality and soil erosion. Close to the cities, the surface of the water is covered with residual wastes and by-products of sugarcane production. Industrial waste, dumped in the water, has generated public health problems and killed fish stocks.

SOCIETY

Peoples: Spanish-Indian descendants 43.6 per cent; Creole (predominantly black) 29.8 per cent; Mayan Indian 11.0 per cent; Garifuna (African-Carib Indian) 6.7 per cent; white 3.9 per cent; East Indian 3.5 per cent; other or not stated 1.5 per cent.
Religions: 60 per cent are Catholic, most of the rest are Protestant (Anglican, Methodist, Seventh-Day Adventist, Pentecostal, Jehovah's Witness).
Languages: English (official); common language is Creole. Spanish, Quiché, Yucatan Mayan and Garifuna are also spoken.
Political Parties: The People's United Party (PUP), founded in 1950; The United Democratic Party (UDP); the National Alliance for the Rights of Belize, founded in 1992 by members of the UDP opposed to compromise with Guatemala.
Social Organizations: The General Workers' Union, the Christian Workers' Union (CWU), the United General Federation, the General Federation of Workers and the Public Service Union of Belize.

THE STATE

Official Name: Belize.
Administrative divisions: 6 districts.
Capital: Belmopan 6,000 people (1999).
Other cities: Belize City 50,200 people; Orange Walk 13,800; San Ignacio 13,600; Dangriga (formerly known as Stann Creek) 9,000; Corozal 8,100 (2000).
Government: Parliamentary monarchy, Queen Elizabeth II of England is Head of State. Colville Young, Governor-General since November 1993. Said Wilbert Musa, Prime Minister since August 1998. Legislative power lies with the House of Representatives, which has 29 members and is elected by universal suffrage, and a 9-member Senate appointed by the Governor-General.
National Holidays: September 10, National Day; September 21, Independence Day (1981).
Armed Forces: 1,065 (1995).

Benin

Bénin

Population: 6,629,000 (2002)
Land area: 110,620 SQ KM
Capital: Porto Novo
Currency: CFA franc
Language: French

Benin (known as Dahomey until 1975) is among the poorest countries in the world. It lies in the region of the Yoruba culture, which developed at the ancient city of Ife. It was here that the Ewe peoples, who came from the same linguistic family, developed into two distinct kingdoms during the 17th century: Hogbonu (today known as Porto Novo) and Abomey, further inland. These states developed around the booming slave trade, serving as intermediaries.

2   The traditional rulers of Abomey, the Fon, built a centralized state that extended east and west beyond Benin's present-day frontiers. A well-disciplined army, with European rifles and a large contingent of female soldiers enabled them to end the patronage of the Alafin of Oyo (Nigeria) and capture various Yoruba cities. After the 17th century, Ouidah became the main port for British, French and Portuguese slave traders receiving their human cargo.

3   The ruling group of Abomey suffered a setback in 1818 when Britain banned the slave trade, although Ghezo who ruled between 1818 and 1856 maintained a thriving clandestine traffic to Brazil and Cuba. He also promoted the development of agriculture and established a strict state monopoly on foreign trade.

4   In 1889, Ghezo's grandson Benhanzin inherited a prosperous state, but one already threatened by colonialism. In 1891, Fon troops resisted the French invasion only to be defeated a year later. The King and his army retreated to the forests, where they held out until 1894. Benhanzin, who became a symbol of anti-colonial resistance, died in exile in Martinique in 1906.

5   The colonists destroyed the centralized political structure of the ancient Fon state. Traditional Fon society was dismantled and replaced with a system based on the exploitation of farm labor. The French also declared a monopoly on the palm-oil trade and ruined families that had resisted foreign penetration for nearly a century.

6   By the beginning of the 20th century, the colony of Dahomey (as the French called it), was no longer self-sufficient. When it gained

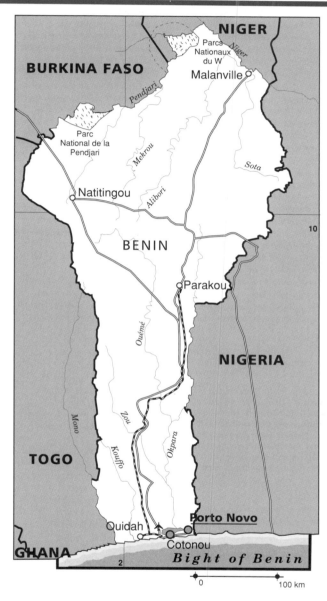

independence in August 1960, oil-seed exports stood at 1850 levels, while the population had tripled.

7   Independence came as a direct consequence both of France's weakness at the end of World War II and the activities of European-educated nationalists, led by Louis Hunkanrin, who waged a stubborn 20-year struggle against the compulsory labor imposed by the French. All forms of political organization were banned and in retaliation, Hunkanrin created the

Human Rights League. A period of ruthless repression followed: hundreds of villages were burned down, nearly 5,000 people were killed, and Hunkanrin took refuge in Mauritania.

8   By 1960, Dahomey had become an unbearable economic burden and France agreed to independence. The new Government inherited a bankrupt economy and a corrupt infrastructure. A series of 12 military and civilian governments marked a 16-year period of instability.

9   The neocolonial élite collapsed in 1972 when then-Major Mathieu Kérékou headed a coup by a group of young officers opposed to political corruption and official despotism. Two years later, a Marxist-Leninist state was proclaimed and its name changed to Benin, with a communitarian political and economic system. All foreign property was nationalized, and a single-party system was introduced with the creation of the People's Revolutionary Party.

10   The revolutionary government became the target of several conspiracies plotted abroad. There was an unsuccessful invasion in January 1977 with the participation of French mercenaries and the support of Gabon and Morocco.

11   In 1980, a new Revolutionary Assembly was elected through direct vote. The Government switched to a more pragmatic foreign policy and diplomatic relations with France were resumed. Although palm-oil production continued to fall as the trees grew older and were not replaced, cotton and sugar sales rose. High unemployment continued, but in 1982 offshore oil was discovered thus guaranteeing energy self-sufficiency. In addition large phosphate deposits were discovered in the northern Mekrou region.

12   Hopes of recovery dimmed as drought reached the northern provinces. Desertification was exacerbated, and the region was unable to supply its own food even in traditional subsistence crops such as cassava/manioc, yams, corn and sorghum.

13   To make matters worse, neighboring Nigeria cracked down on immigrants, expelling thousands back to Benin and closing the border.

14   The economic crisis forced the Government to accept the terms of the International Monetary Fund (IMF), including a 10 per cent income tax and a 50 per cent reduction in non-wage social benefits. In January 1989 students, teachers and other educational bodies staged a strike demanding back pay and scholarship payments that had not been honored.

15   On December 8 1989, disappointed with results and besieged by street demonstrations, President Kérékou announced that

he was abandoning his Marxist-Leninism. A new constitution was drawn up, providing for a series of political and economic reforms, especially the promotion of free enterprise.

[16] On March 24 1991 Prime Minister Nicéphore Soglo defeated President Kérékou with 68 per cent of the votes in the country's first presidential election in 30 years. In 1992, former president Kérékou, who had been prosecuted for his activities following the 1972 coup, was granted an amnesty, and political prisoners were released.

[17] Soglo continued the economic liberalization and privatization policy initiated by Kérékou in 1986. Debt servicing still represented a high percentage of the resources annually obtained (in 1992 debt service was equivalent to 27 per cent of the country's income).

[18] The 100 per cent devaluation of the CFA franc decreed by France in January 1994 provoked contradictory effects in Benin's economy. GDP continued to grow at a 4 per cent annual rate and cotton exports increased. However, public expenditure cuts - aimed among other things at curbing inflation after the devaluation - brought about drastic reductions in social spending schemes.

[19] In July 1994, Soglo assumed the leadership of the Renaissance Party of Benin (PRB), founded by his wife Rosine in 1992. The PRB was defeated in the legislative and municipal elections of March 1995 by the opposition Democratic Renewal Party (PRD). In May 1995 the Government banned food exports to reduce local prices and curb inflation, at the same time that it refused to increase salaries.

[20] Soglo's clannish style and his tendency to rule together with his family not only angered the political class in Benin. In the general elections held in March 1996, Soglo suffered a narrow defeat by Kérékou, the former leader of the Marxist regime.

[21] Between August and October 1997, disease killed around 60,000 pigs - 10 per cent of the country's stock of swine. The spread of HIV/AIDS was a factor in causing life expectancy in the country to drop by ten years.

[22] The country's five unions called for a strike in February 1998 against 'the antisocial budget for 1998, the dictates of the IMF, the World Bank and the European Union, as well as widespread corruption encouraged by Kérékou's government'. The Government answered with a $10 million increase in public spending, a move deemed insufficient by the unions, which now called for a general strike.

[23] The March 1998 parliamentary elections saw the presidential faction win over the other 55 parties. Prime Minister Adrien Houngdedji stood down and his role was taken on by Kérékou.

[24] In January 1999 the IMF offered the country a $14 million loan at the lowest rates of interest. In January 2000, the President denounced a conspiracy against his government by some of the military, particularly former members of regional peacekeeping forces. A group such as this had led a coup in Côte d'Ivoire in December 1999 and similar action in Mali had been narrowly avoided when another group attempted to claim outstanding pay.

[25] In July 2000, Benin qualified for the Broad Initiative for Heavily Indebted Poor Countries with a $460 million reduction in its foreign debt.

[26] A boat carrying dozens of children made Benin the center of an international search in April 2001, highlighting slave trafficking in that country and the region. In many cases the children are sold to work in cocoa and coffee plantations in the neighboring countries. In September, the Ministry of Family Affairs demanded international travel permit for all children under 15 years old in order to stem trafficking.

[27] Two months later, accusations of sorcery led to violence in Cotonou. A man declared that his penis had been stolen and raised a mob that attacked anyone they considered suspicious. Five people were set alight and burned to death, three of them foreigners. Belief that male sexual organs can mysteriously disappear following a handshake or from casting a spell is widespread in Benin, where some 60 per cent of the population follow traditional religions. ∎

PROFILE

ENVIRONMENT

Benin is a narrow strip of land that extends north from the Gulf of Guinea. Its 120-km sandy coast lacks natural ports. Several physical regions cut across the country from south to north: the coastal belt where oil palms are cultivated; the tropical wooded lowlands; and the plateau which rises gradually towards the headwaters of the Queme, Mekrou, Alibori and Pendjari rivers, in a region of tropical hills. The major environmental problems are deforestation and desertification, which has been made worse in recent years by a significant decrease in rainfall.

SOCIETY

Peoples: Benin's people stem from 60 ethnic groups. The Fon (47 per cent), Adja, Yoruba and Bariba groups are the most numerous and before French colonization they had already developed stable political institutions. There is a European minority.
Religion: Around 60 per cent practice traditional African religions, 15 per cent are Muslim and 15 per cent Catholic.
Languages: French (official). Other widely-spoken languages are Fon, Fulani, Mine, Yoruba and Massi.
Political parties: Renaissance Party of Benin (PRB), centrist; Democratic Renewal Party (PRD); Social Democratic Party (SDP); African Movement for Democracy and Progress (MADEP); Action Front for Renewal and Development (FARD); Impulse for Progress and Democracy (IPD); Benin Communist Party (PBC); Marxist-Leninist Party of Benin (a 1999 split from the PBC)
Social organizations: The Benin Workers' National Trade Union (UNSTB).

THE STATE

Official name: République Populaire du Bénin. **Capital:** Porto Novo 213,000 people (1999). **Other cities:** Cotonou 704,900 people; Djougou 177,300; Parakou 141,100; Abomey-Calavi 86,900 (2000). **Government:** Presidential republic. Mathieu Kérékou, President since April 1996. Since 1998 he has also taken the role of Prime Minister. Single chamber parliament. **National Holidays:** July 1, Independence (1960); November 30, Revolution Day (1974). **Armed Forces:** 4,800. **Other:** Gendarmerie: 2,000; People's Militia: 1,500-2,000.

STATISTICS

DEMOGRAPHY

Population: 6,629,000 (2002)
Annual growth: 3.0 % (1985-2000)
Estimates for year 2015: 9,448,000 (2000)
Annual growth to year 2015: 2.7 % (2000)
Urban population: 42.3 % (2000)
Urban growth: 4.5 % (2000)
Children per woman: 5.9 (2000)

HEALTH

Life expectancy at birth: 54 years (2000-2005)
male: 52 years (2000-2005)
female: 56 years (2000-2005)
Maternal mortality: 500 per 100,000 live births (1985/99)
Infant mortality: 98 per 1,000 (2000)
Under-5 child mortality: 154 per 1,000 (2000)
Daily calorie supply: 2,489 per capita (1999)
6 doctors per 100,000 people (1995)
Safe water: 63 % (2000)

EDUCATION

Literacy: 37 % (2000)
male: 52 % (2000)
female: 24 % (2000)
School enrolment (net):
Primary total: 63 % (1994/2000)
male: 75 % (1995/99)
female: 50 % (1995/99)
Secondary (gross):
male: 24 % (1995/97)
female: 10 % (1995/97)
Tertiary (gross): 3 % (1998)
Primary school teachers: one for every 53 pupils (1998)

COMMUNICATIONS

5 newspapers (1999), 439 radios (2000), 45 TV sets (2000) and 8 main telephone lines (2000) per 1,000 people
Books: 2 new titles per 100,000 people (1992/94)

ECONOMY

Per capita, GDP: $ 990 (2000)
Annual growth: 3.1 % (2000)
Annual inflation: 4.2 % (2000)
Consumer price index: 120.0 (2000)
Currency: 758.3 CFA francs = $ 1 (03/2002)
Cereal imports: 184,959 metric tons (2000)
Food import dependency: 25 % (1998)
Fertilizer use: 334 kg per ha (1999)
Exports: $ 334 million (2000)
Imports: $ 627 million (2000)
External debt: $ 1,599 million (2000); $ 255 per capita (2000)
Debt service: 10.9 % of exports (1999)
Development aid received: $ 211 million (1999); $ 34.5 per capita (1999); 8.90 % of GNP (1999)

ENERGY

Consumption: 376.5 Kgs of oil equivalent per capita yearly (1998); 21.1 % imported (1999)

HDI (ranking/value): 147 / 0.420 (1999)

Bermuda

Population: 64,000 (2002)
Land area: 50 SQ KM
Capital: Hamilton
Currency: Bermuda dollar
Language: English

Bermuda

The Bermuda archipelago was the first colony of the British Empire. Sighted by the Spanish navigator Juan Bermúdez in 1503, it was settled in 1609 when British emigrants on their way to America were shipwrecked nearby.

[2] From 1612, the colony welcomed religious and political dissidents. In 1684, it began to be administered by the British Crown, and the first parliament was installed. Even though African slaves formed the majority, only plantation owners could elect representatives.

[3] Agriculture almost disappeared in the 20th century, being replaced by tourism, gambling and transnational corporations lured by numerous tax exemptions. During the Prohibition (1919-1933) traffickers living in Bermuda smuggled rum into the United States. From 1941, Washington set up air and naval bases on the islands and has completely replaced the British military presence since 1957.

[4] After the creation of the Bermuda Industrial Union (BIU), in 1963 workers founded the Progessive Labor Party (PLP), which favored the country's total independence and the introduction of an income tax. The following year, the Right organized the United Bermuda Party (UBP).

[5] Britain granted the island's greater administrative autonomy in 1968, and the majority party was given the right to name the prime minister. The period leading up to the elections was marked by racial and political violence. The assassination of the governor led to intervention by British troops. When the election was held, the UBP won by a large margin.

[6] The PLP increased its number of seats in the 1976 election. From its position in opposition, the PLP continued to demand greater autonomy for the island.

[7] In 1977, two members of the 'Black Cadre' were sentenced to death, for participating in armed anti-colonial activities. Their execution unleashed a wave of protests, with British troops intervening once again. The Minister of Communal (Race) Relations was sacked, and his duties delegated to the Bermuda Regiment, responsible for putting down protest and discontent.

[8] In spite of charges of racism, the European population supported the Government, while the black population opted for the PLP or more radical organizations.

[9] The 1979 Bermuda Constitutional Convention failed to reach a consensus on representation and the minimum voting age. However, a reduction in the number of non-Bermudan voters went into effect that December.

[10] The UBP won both the 1980 and 1983 elections, although the opposition increased its representation. With the UBP in power, the country continued without self-determination as the Government claimed that the majority was against this.

[11] The island's strategic location along North Atlantic routes explained the continued presence of British, Canadian and US troops.

[12] Prime Minister John Swan of the UBP was re-elected in 1989 and his party gained 23 seats. The PLP obtained 15 seats; one seat went to the National Liberal Party (NLP), a center party, and the Environmental Party won one seat.

[13] During 1989 and 1990, unemployment rose by 0.5 per cent and 2 per cent, respectively. The US recession continued to affect tourism in the first few months of 1992. London rejected plans for independence.

[14] In 1992, Sir John Waddington was appointed Governor-General. Intense drug-trafficking in 1993 resulted in a major diversion of investment away from Bermuda. Measures also went into effect to control offshore banking operations.

[15] In August 1995 the question of independence was put to a referendum. The result was against independence, so the status of British colony was maintained.

[16] In March 1997, after then prime minister David Saul resigned, Pamela Gordon took over that post. In June, Thorold Masefield was named new governor.

[17] With winds up to 120 kilometers-per-hour, Hurricane Gert wreaked havoc in the Bermudas in September 1999. Floods caused by intense rains caused significant destruction in housing and infrastructure.

[18] Although capital punishment was on the statute book, nobody had been executed in Bermuda in 22 years. As a result, in December 1999, the authorities decided to put its practice into law and abolished capital punishment and physical punishment.

[19] Masefield left Bermuda on November 28 2001, thus ending his 4.5-year mandate on behalf of the British crown on the island. Tim Gurney was interim governor until Sir John Vereker took up the appointment in April 2002. ∎

PROFILE

ENVIRONMENT

This Atlantic archipelago is made up of 360 small coral islands, characterized by chalky, permeable soil. Bermuda includes 150 of these islands, of which 20 are uninhabited. The warm Gulf Stream current produces a mild climate which attracts tourists, mainly from the US. Pollution, especially from the US, caused by former military bases, is one of the country's main environmental problems.

SOCIETY

Peoples: Approximately 60 per cent are of African descent; there are also descendants of Portuguese from Madeira and the Azores; mixed European and Indian descendants and a minority of European origin.
Religions: Anglican majority (28 per cent), in addition to Methodists (12 per cent), Adventists (6 per cent), Catholics (15 per cent) and members of other religions. **Languages:** English (official): Portuguese.
Political parties: Progressive Labor Party (PLP); The United Bermuda Party (UBP); National Liberal Party of Bermuda; Environmental Party.
Social organizations: Bermuda Industrial Union (5,202 members); Bermuda Public Service Association (2,300 members). Audubon Society of Bermuda.

THE STATE

Official Name: Bermuda. **Administrative division:** 9 counties.
Capital: Hamilton 1,000 people (1999).
Other cities: St George's 1,800 people (2000).
Government: British dependency. John Vereker, Governor since April 2002; nominated by Queen Elizabeth II. Prime Minister Jennifer Smith since 1998. The Prime Minister appoints the cabinet on approval by the Governor. Bicameral parliament: Senate has 11 members, 5 elected by the Prime Minister, 3 by the opposition leader and 3 by the Governor. Assembly has 40 members elected for a 5-year term.
National Holiday: May 24, Bermuda Day.

Bhutan

Druk Yul

Population: 2,198,000 (2002)
Land area: 47,000 SQ KM
Capital: Thimbu
Currency: Ngultrum
Language: Dzongkha

Bhutan lies in the heart of the vast Himalayan mountains. Early explorers and envoys of the British colonial Government called it Bootan, land of the Booteas, or sometimes Bhotan. Wedged between giant neighbors China and India and cut off by some of the world's highest peaks, it was little known to the rest of the world. Even today, the origin of its name remains unknown. Perhaps it came from the Sanskrit *Bhot'ante* ('the end of Tibet') or from another Sanskrit word *Bhu'nthan* ('high land'). To the people of Bhutan it is Druk or Druk Yul, land of the Thunder Dragon. The name is derived from the Kargyud Sect of Mahayana Buddhism (Drukpa), now the state religion, which flourished in the 7th century.

[2] From the 12th century, the Drukpa Kargyud tradition became dominant. After a long period of rivalry among various groups, the country was united in the 17th century by a Drukpa Kargyud Lama named Ngawang Namgyal. Namgyal, popularly known as Shabdrung ('at whose feet one submits'), was both the country's spiritual and secular ruler. Factionalism gradually eroded the power of the subsequent Shabdrungs. On December 17 1907 Ugen Wangchuk reunified the country and established Bhutan's first hereditary monarchy.

[3] The British colonial administration in India signed important treaties with Bhutan in 1774 and 1865. The 1910 Treaty of Punakha stipulated that the British would not interfere in Bhutan's internal affairs, but made the country

a British protectorate in terms of external relations. Similar provisions were included in the 1949 treaty signed between Bhutan and independent India.

[4] Bhutan emerged from its isolation in the 1960s and joined the Colombo Plan for Cooperative, Economic, and Social Development in Asia and the Pacific in 1962. The creation of an economic infrastructure became a priority. A network of highways, especially

necessary since the closing of the Tibetan frontier by China in 1960, crosses the country, above all in a southerly direction toward the frontier with India.

[5] Bhutan is still one of the poorest countries in Asia, although the emergent industrialization and recent development make exploitation of its natural resources feasible. For example, the forests that cover 65 per cent of the territory could be used if Bhutan were to sell its 'pollution rights.' The country has one of the 10 most important protected areas of biodiversity on the planet.

[6] President-monarch, Jigme Singye Wangchuck, was crowned in 1972 and since ascending the throne the kingdom has begun a slow process of opening up to the world (it joined the UN and Non-Aligned Movement in 1970). Alongside this, a policy was initiated for the Bhutanization of the country, in a population made up of Tibetans (50 per cent) and geographically separated minorities: the Ngalong in the west, Sarchops

in the East and Nepalese (35 per cent) in the South.

[7] Since the Decree of Citizenship in 1985, many southerners were declared illegal immigrants. After the 1988 census, the monarch imposed the use of national dress and the Dzonga language in public places. Education in Nepalese was banned, as was tourist entry to sacred sites and television transmissions from India. Work permits for foreigners were stopped. The political crisis arising from these measures led to the displacement of 100,000 Nepalese to Nepal, where they lived in refugee camps. Since 1990, Bhutan has considered the refugees, known as Lhotsampas, as people of no nationality.

[8] The first chemical industry and the first financial company began to operate in 1988. The seventh five-year plan started in 1992, with the objective of increasing exports, environmental conservation, regional balance and the institutional promotion of women. The Government encouraged foreign investment and began a

WORKERS

1999/2000

LABOR FORCE AS % OF TOTAL

■ FEMALE: 40%   ■ MALE: 60%

LAND USE

DEFORESTATION: 0.3% annual (1990/95)

1993

■ FOREST & WOODLAND: 66%
■ ARABLE: 2.4%
■ OTHER: 31.6%

1985/99

Per 100,000
live births

380

2000

47%

cautious privatization program, aiming for the local public to acquire shares in State companies. Following the Rio Summit in Rio de Janeiro that year, Bhutan signed bilateral treaties with the Netherlands, promoting a form of co-operation for development based on equity, participation and reciprocity. Access to energy was one of the main issues in negotiations.

⁹ Although the Chukha hydroelectric project has a potential 8,000 megawatts to offer and will supply energy to neighboring areas of India, 80 per cent of Bhutanese have no electricity supply, although they are expected to have power by 2020. During the nineties, India, Norway, Kuwait, Japan and Switzerland (amongst others) provided funding for development programs in Bhutan.

¹⁰ In 1998, the king, who was also head of state, government and head of the Court of Appeals, appointed a prime minister and a cabinet, whilst also granting the Consultive Assembly the right to initiate ideas or veto his decisions, and even call for his abdication. The opposition accused him of planting his followers in key positions in the Assembly.

¹¹ The eighth plan, covering the 1997 to 2002 period, has prioritized decentralization of the decision making processes, taking them to the community level. The ninth plan will seek to implement new forms of decentralization, carrying district consultation to the 'village roots.' Singye Wangchuk set out his own philosophy of development in the document Bhutan 2020 Vision for Peace, Prosperity and Happiness, which states that economic growth and material progress are not the only way to achieve personal success, as equal emphasis must be placed on emotional and spiritual security. As State ideology, this implies the aim to be achieved is Gross National Happiness (GNH) above Gross Domestic Product.

¹² GNH formed the framework for an agreement signed in 2001 by Bhutan and the Asian Development Bank. The agreement prioritizes poverty reduction in the country and states that every measure to promote development must be translated into the Bhutanese context, whereby, 'the Bank must be sensitive to difficulties which, in translation to the national language of Bhutan, are presented by words like *poverty*, *vulnerable* and so on'. Furthermore, in procuring 'improvements', the Bank will attack objectives that do not reduce material wellbeing, in keeping with GNH. ∎

PROFILE

ENVIRONMENT

This Himalayan country is made up of three distinct climatic and geographical regions. The Duar plain in the south, humid and tropical, is densely wooded and ranges in height from 300 to 2,000 meters. At the center lies a temperate region with mountains of up to 3,000 meters. Finally, there are the great northern heights, with year-round snow and peaks that climb 8,000 meters high. Forests are the country's mainstay. Rivers and waterfalls have been exploited and they supply energy to the country and neighboring areas. There are graphite, marble, granite and limestone deposits. Approximately half of the arable land lies on steep slopes; of this nearly 15 per cent is merely topsoil. The combination of these two factors makes the terrain very susceptible to erosion.

SOCIETY

Peoples: Bhutia (Ngalops) 50 per cent; Nepalese (Gurung) 35 per cent; Sharchops 15 per cent. There are also Lepchas, indigenous people, and Santal, descended from Indian immigrants. 95 per cent of the teachers and 55 per cent of public servants are of Indian origin.
Religions: Buddhist 69.6 per cent; Hindu 24.6 per cent; Muslim 5.0 per cent; other 0.8 per cent (1980).
Languages: Dzongkha (official). Nepalese and other dialects are also spoken.
Political Parties: The Bhutan People's Party (BPP), founded in Nepal in 1990; the National Bhutanese Congress (DNC) founded in 1992, in Nepal and India; the People's Forum of Human Rights (PFHR), started in 1990, covering five refugee camps in Nepal; the United People's Liberation Front (UPLF), also founded in 1990.

THE STATE

Official Name: Druk Yul.
Administrative Divisions: 18 Districts.
Capital: Thimbu 28,000 people (1999).
Other cities: Phuntsholing 54,300 people; Punakha 20,700; Samdrup Jongkhar 13,200 (2000).
Government: Jigme Singye Wangchuk, King since July 1972; hereditary absolute monarchy. The monarch is assisted by a council of 9 members, of whom 5 are elected by the people, 2 are appointed by the monarch and 2 by the Buddhist religious dignitaries whose 6,000 lamas (monks) are headed by the Je Khempo. Lyonpo Khandu Wangchuk, Prime Minister since August 2001. There is also a consultative assembly (Tsogdu) of 150 members 101 of whom are elected and 49 appointed, most being Buddhist monks. The ruler also dispenses justice.
National Holidays: 8 August, Independence Day (1949, from India); December 17, National Day (1907); August 2, Buddhist Lent; October 30, end of Buddhist Lent.

DEMOGRAPHY
Population: 2,198,000 (2002)
Annual growth: 2.3 % (1985-2000)
Estimates for year 2015: 3,070,000 (2000)
Annual growth to year 2015: 2.6 % (2000)
Urban population: 7.1 % (2000)
Urban growth: 6.1 % (2000)
Children per woman: 5.3 (2000)

HEALTH
Life expectancy at birth: 63 years (2000-2005)
male: 62 years (2000-2005)
female: 65 years (2000-2005)
Maternal mortality: 380 per 100,000 live births (1985/99)
Infant mortality: 77 per 1,000 (2000)
Under-5 child mortality: 100 per 1,000 (2000)
16 doctors per 100,000 people (1995)
Safe water: 62 % (2000)

EDUCATION
Literacy: 47 % (2000)
male: 61 % (2000)
female: 34 % (2000)
School enrolment (net):
Primary total: 53 % (1994/2000)
male: 58 % (1995/99)
female: 47 % (1995/99)
Secondary (gross):
male: 7 % (1995/97)
female: 2 % (1995/97)
Primary school teachers: one for every 38 pupils (1998)

COMMUNICATIONS
50 radios (1997), 20 TV sets (2000) and 20 main telephone lines (2000) per 1,000 people

ECONOMY
Per capita, GDP: $ 1,412 (2000)
Annual growth: 3.9 % (2000)
Annual inflation: 6.8 % (1999)
Consumer price index: 136.8 (1999)
Currency: 48.7 Ngultrum = $ 1 (03/2002)
Cereal imports: 42,910 metric tons (2000)
Food import dependency: 18 % (1999)
Fertilizer use: 0 kg per ha (1999)
Exports: $ 144 million (2000)
Imports: $ 292 million (2000)
External debt: $ 198 million (2000); $ 95 per capita (2000)
Development aid received: $ 67 million (1999); $ 85.2 per capita (1999); 15.10 % of GNP (1999)

HDI (ranking/value): 130 / 0.477 (1999)

Bolivia

Population: 8,705,000 (2002)
Land area: 1,084,380 SQ KM
Capital: La Paz
Currency: Boliviano
Language: Spanish

Bolivia

In 2000 BC the region of modern-day Bolivia was inhabited by farmers in the Andes, and forest hunter-gatherers in the east. Their terrain ranged from high mountain areas, *puna*, to hot valleys and forests. They raised livestock and grew potatoes, cotton, maize, and coca; they also fished and mined. This region, rich in natural resources, sustained several kingdoms and fiefdoms around Lake Titicaca, with the Tiahuanaco-Huari (600 BC-1000 AC) civilization at their center.

[2]   The basic social unit was the *ayllu* kinship group, in which there was no private land ownership. The society was stratified into farmers, artisans and the ruling ayllu, of priests and warriors, who appointed the *malku* (chief).

[3]   By 800 AD, Tiahuanaco formed the first Pan-Andean empire. By 1100, the ayllu of the Incas, from the Cusco Valley in Peru, had colonized the other Andean peoples and formed a confederation of states called the Tahuantinsuyo. Also known as the Inca Empire, it adopted elements of Tiahuanaco culture, technology, religion and economics, particularly the ayllu social unit.

[4]   Through the *mita*, a mutual cooperation commitment between the different ayllus, each worker would render service to the centralized state; this system was later cruelly exploited by the Spaniards. The social structure was rigid: at the top was the *Inca* (son of the Sun), followed by the nobility and the priests. Then came the *capac*, governors of the regions into which the empire was divided, and lastly came the *curacas* (leaders of the ayllus) and the farmers. Social organization was based on self-sufficient, communal production.

[5]   When the Spanish arrived at the beginning of the 16th century, the Tahuantinsuyo extended from southern Colombia, through Ecuador and Peru, to northern Chile, and from Lake Titicaca and the *altiplano* highlands to northern Argentina, embracing the mountain valleys and the eastern plains. One million people were estimated to have been living within the area of the present Bolivia, and from 12 to 13 million in the Tahuantinsuyo as a whole, making it the most densely populated area of South America. This society included a number of ethnic groups, predominantly Aymara (around Lake Titicaca) and Quechua. The eastern plains were inhabited by dispersed groups of Tupi and Guaraní, with no central nucleus. To this day, Aymara and Quechua are the most widespread languages in Bolivia.

[6]   In 1545 the Spanish discovered silver at Potosi. They extracted immense quantities of the metal, which contributed to the capital accumulation of several European powers. Millions of Native Americans died there, cruelly exploited to the point of exhaustion. Potosi was one of the three largest cities of the 17th century, growing up at the foot of the hill. It became the economic nerve center for vast regions of Chile and Argentina, and nurtured a rich mining bourgeoisie, guilty of corruption, ostentation and wastefulness.

[7]   Decades of popular struggle against the Spanish reached their peak with the successive failed rebellions of Tupac Katari (1780-82), the Protective Board of La Paz (1809), headed by *mestizo* Pedro Domingo Murillo, and the 'independence guerrillas'. The pro-independence movement was subsequently taken up by the *criollos* (Spaniards born in America), who distorted it by advocating social, economic and political systems based not on indigenous models but on those of emerging European capitalist powers. A British blockade interrupted the supply of mercury, essential for treating the silver, and the Bolivian mining industry went into decline. The Buenos Aires based trading bourgeoisie soon lost interest in Upper Peru (Bolivia) and offered little resistance when it fell under the influence of the independence leader Simon Bolivar. The country was renamed after him when the Assembly of Representatives proclaimed independence in Chuquisaca, in 1825.

[8]   Peru exerted great influence over the independent Bolivia until 1841. Bolivian president Marshall Andrés de Santa Cruz tried to modernize Bolivia, founding universities and the Supreme Court of Justice, and compiling law codes.

[9]   A mine-owning oligarchy including Patiño, Aramayo and Hochschild worked with the politicians and generals, who were their associates, treating the Bolivian republic as if it were part of the tin business. British imperialist interests, initially in the saltpeter at Antofagasta and later in Bolivia's southern oil reserves, triggered two wars in South America: the Pacific War (Chile against Bolivia and Peru from 1879-83), and the Chaco War (Paraguay and Bolivia, from 1932-35). As a result of these conflicts, Bolivia lost its coast and three-quarters of its territory in the Chaco region. The ceding of Amazonian Acre to Brazil, in 1904, completed the country's dismemberment.

[10]   On July 21 1946 Bolivian president Gualberto Villarroel - accused by left and right parties as 'fascist'- was overthrown, assassinated, and his body hung from a lamp-post in downtown La Paz. Backed by a group of young army officials from RADEPA (Reason for the Fatherland) that were allied to the recently founded Nationalist Revolutionary Movement (MNR), Villarroel had overthrown elected-president General Enrique Peñaranda in 1943. Villarroel's government confronted the owner of the mines imposing taxes and organizing the miners' trade unions. He also mobilized peasants for the first time, gathered in the Indigenous Congress.

[11]   Nationwide frustration at these humiliations gave way to a powerful current of reformism and anti-

WORKERS

1990/2000

UNEMPLOYMENT: 7.4%
LABOR FORCE AS % OF TOTAL:

■ FEMALE: 38%   ■ MALE: 62%

1994/97

EMPLOYMENT DISTRIBUTION:

■ SERVICES   F: 82%   M: 58%
■ INDUSTRY   F: 16%   M: 40%
■ AGRICULTURE F: 2%   M: 2%

PUBLIC EXPENDITURE

1999

DEFENSE 8%
SOCIAL 53.6%

imperialism. The MNR grew up alongside progressive labor and peasant movements. After several uprisings, and a 1951 electoral victory thatwas not honored, the MNR led a popular insurrection in 1952. Civilians defeated seven regular army regiments in the streets, and they carried first Victor Paz Estenssoro, and then Hernan Siles Zuazo, to the presidency. The Bolivian revolution nationalized the tin mines, carried out agrarian reform and proclaimed universal suffrage. Workers' and peasants' militias were organized and together with the Bolivian Workers' Confederation (COB) formed a coalition with the MNR. The army was eliminated after the insurrection, but was later reorganized under US pressure.

[12] Troubled by internal divisions, the MNR gradually lost its drive and was defeated in November 1964 by a military junta led by René Barrientos. Ernesto 'Che' Guevara tried to establish a guerrilla nucleus in the Andes to spread revolutionary war throughout South America, but he was caught by US-trained counter-insurgency troops, and assassinated on October 8 1967.

[13] Division within the army coupled with pressure from the grassroots level led to an anti-imperialist faction taking over government in 1969, with General Juan José Torres as the leader. During his short time in office, there was a significant increase in the number of grassroots organizations. The People's Assembly was formed, with links to the COB and the parties of the Left. In August 1971 he was ousted by Colonel Hugo Bánzer Suárez, who formed a government with MNR support. The civilian-military coalition government remained in power until July 1978, with an authoritarian but development-oriented administration encouraging agribusiness and stressing infrastructure projects, bolstered by the high price of oil and other minerals.

[14] Military uprisings and disregard for election results occurred repeatedly between 1978 and 1980. Juan Pereda Asbun, David Padilla Arancibia, Walter Guevara Arce, Alberto Natusch Busch and Lidia Gueiler all had fleeting presidencies, ended either by coups or

parliamentary appointments. On June 29 1980, the elections were won by the Democratic Popular Union (UDP), a center-left coalition whose candidate, Hernan Siles Zuazo, was prevented from taking office by another bloody coup engineered by General Luis Garcia Meza. According to reports received by Amnesty International, thousands of people were killed or tortured, including Socialist leader Marcelo Quiroga Santa Cruz, Trotskyist parliamentary deputy Carlos Flores Bedregal, and miners' leader Gualberto Vega.

[15] By 1982, the army was seething with internal dissent. Government links with paramilitary groups and drug trafficking were eroding its international standing, and it was facing dogged popular resistance led by the Bolivian Workers' Confederation (COB), leading to its

destruction. In September, the military command decided to convene the government that had been democratically elected in 1980.

[16] On October 10, after 18 years of military rule, Hernan Siles Zuazo took office in a legal constitutional model that has continued ever since.

[17] Siles Zuazo, with a populist/nationalistic outlook, handed administration of the state-owned mines to the labor unions. He also announced the non-payment of Bolivia's foreign debt. The labor movement and the peasants exerted pressure on the government through demonstrations, and several laws passed by his administration allowed these groups to participate in the economic policy decisions of large businesses, and in local committees dealing with food, health and education issues. The Peasant Agricultural Corporation took partial control of the markets and set up collective machinery pools and work teams. In response to these measures, creditor banks, the IMF and the World Bank blocked credits to Bolivia placing an embargo on its international trade. These measures provoked a fiscal crisis and uncontrolled hyperinflation, with the average wage falling to $13 per month.

[18] Under heavy pressure from all social sectors, the Government cut short its term and called elections for July 14 1985. As neither candidate secured over 50 per cent of the vote, the decision was put to Congress, who elected Paz Estenssoro as constitutional president, though Hugo Banzer had marginally more votes.

[19] The Estenssoro Government decreed a program of neo-liberal measures to end subsidies and close down state enterprises. It eliminated price controls and the official listing of the dollar against the local currency. Mines were closed down, and others rented out, leaving thousands of miners jobless.

[20] There was a drastic cut in real wages, with high redundancies, while investment ground to a standstill. Inflation increased to four figures.

[21] In the 1989 national elections, Jaime Paz Zamora's Revolutionary Movement of the Left (MIR) proved itself a potent new political force, coming in third with 19 per cent of the votes (double that of previous elections). The MNR candidate, Gonzalo Sánchez de Losada, obtained 23 per cent and Banzer's Nationalist Democratic Action (ADN), 22.6 per cent. As no party had achieved a majority, an

PROFILE

ENVIRONMENT

A landlocked country with three geographic regions. 70 per cent of the population live in the cold, dry climate of the altiplano, an Andean highland plateau with an average altitude of 4,000 meters. This region holds the country's mineral resources: tin (second largest producer in the world), silver, zinc, lead and copper. The subtropical valleys (*yungas*) of the eastern slopes of the Andes form the country's main farming area, where coffee, citrics, cocoa, sugar-cane, coca and bananas are grown. The tropical plains of the East and North, a region of jungles and grasslands, produce cattle, rice, corn, and sugarcane. The area is also rich in oil. Bolivia is made up of three drainage basins: Lake Titicaca (closed basin), the Amazon in the north and the Río de la Plata in the south. Unconstrained exploitation of timber threatens the country's forest resources, as well as water supplies and fauna. In 'El Alto' (a high district of La Paz), air pollution has risen in direct proportion to the number of motor vehicles.

SOCIETY

Peoples: 57 per cent of Bolivians are Quechua and Aymara. *Mestizos* and *Cholos* account for 25 per cent of the population. A

minority of European descent has ruled the country since the Spanish conquest. The Tupí and Guaraní peoples live in the eastern forests.
Religions: Mainly Catholic (95 per cent). Syncretism in indigenous communities. Freedom of religion.
Languages: Spanish, Quechua and Aymara (officials). More than half the population speaks Quechua, Guarani and Aymara; there are 39 ethnic-linguistic groups.
Political Parties: The Nationalist Democratic Alliance (ADN); the Nationalist Revolutionary Movement (MNR); the Movement of Revolutionary Left (MIR); Citizens' Solidarity Union; Conscience of the Fatherland; the new Patriotic Conscience Party (CONDEPA); the Solidarity Civic Union (UCS); the Free Bolivia Movement; the Socialist Democratic Group (ASD); the Pachacuti-Axis, supported by peasants engaged in coca cultivation; and the MRTK-L (the political wing of the Tupac Katari Movement).
Social Organizations: The Bolivian Workers' Confederation (COB); the Sole Labor Union Confederation of Farm Workers of Bolivia (CSUTCB). There are also important ethnic and environmental organizations like the Indigenous Confederation of the

Eastern region, Chaco and Bolivian Amazon Area (CIDOB); the Guaraní People's Assembly (APG); the Federation of Campesino Women; the Federation of Neighborhood Commissions; and the Bolivian Forum on Environment and Development (FOBOMADE).

THE STATE

Official Name: República de Bolivia.
Administrative Divisions: 9 Departments.
Capital: La Paz 1,439,000 people (1999) - including El Alto (404,400 people) which became a separate city in 1988 - functions as the seat of the Government. Sucre is the constitutional capital, and seat of the judiciary.
Other cities: Santa Cruz de la Sierra 1,089,400 people; Cochabamba 558,500; Sucre 172,000 (2000).
Government: Gonzalo Sánchez de Lozada, President and Head of the Government since August 2002. Bicameral legislature: Chamber of Deputies, made up of 130 members; Senate with 27 members.
National Holiday: August 6, Independence Day (1825).
Armed Forces: 25,000 (1993).
Other: 23,000 Police.

agreement known as the Patriotic Accord (AP) between the MIR and the ADN made it possible for Paz Zamora to be nominated president by the National Congress.

[22] The Patriotic Accord continued Paz Estenssoro's neo-liberal economic policy. In 1991, the Government embarked upon a transformation of the State, which entailed privatization. Congress passed a law permitting the state to sell off 22 of the existing 64 public enterprises, though the Supreme Court ruled it unconstitutional. The Government promoted joint ventures between the state-owned Mining Corporation (COMIBOL) and private companies. The Federation of Mining Workers (FSTMB) launched a series of hunger strikes and threatened to occupy the mines, defending the principle of continued state ownership.

[23] In April 1991, Bolivia's Congress authorized US military officers to come and train local personnel in the war against drugs. Despite military action and the policy of crop substitution - a program called 'development in place of coca' - the area under coca cultivation increased. It was estimated that in 1992 there were some 463,000 people involved in coca-cocaine production, and that the national net earnings from this crop reached $950 million per year.

[24] The loss of power in the workers' movement was compensated for by new organizations of indigenous peoples and communities. In October 1991, the 9th Congress of the Confederation of Indigenous Peoples of the Eastern Region, the Chaco and the Bolivian Amazon Region (CIDOB) met in Santa Cruz. 340 representatives approved a series of demands, including claims to lands lost during the Spanish invasion and the use of their native languages in the educational system.

[25] At this time, the population of Bolivia's eastern region included 250,000 people of 10 linguistic groups and 35 ethnic groups. In September 1990, a group of peoples from this region carried out a 750 km march from the east to the capital with the slogan 'Land and Dignity'. Paz Zamora's government approved a National Plan for the Defense and Development of the Indigenous Peoples, and in August 1991, recognized the Santa Ana de Horachi Mosetana Community's right to 8,000 hectares of land, which they consider collective property. These resolutions were opposed by companies that were exploiting the region's vast forestry resources.

[26] In January 1992, Presidents Paz Zamora and Alberto Fujimori (of Peru) signed an agreement whereby Peru ceded an area of 327 hectares to Bolivia for it to develop a free

zone for commercial and touristic activities at the port of Ilo in southern Peru. In this way Bolivia gained access to the sea - a free port for its international trade.

[27] The MNR won the national elections of June 1993, with 36 per cent of the vote. Its presidential candidate was Gonzalo Sánchez Losada, and the vice-presidential candidate was Victor Hugo Cardenas, an Aymara sociologist and leader of the Tupac Katari Movement. While the ADN and MIR suffered significant losses, the new populist and nationalist movements, such as CONDEPA and UCS, led by Carlos Palenque and Max Fernandez retained their support among mestizos and the poorer neighborhoods.

[28] In its first year the Government established the right to education in the Indian languages (Aymara, Quecha, Guaraní). The Capitalization Bill aimed to privatize 50 per cent of the main public industries (telecommunications, electricity, oil, gas, railways, airlines) on the basis of transferring half the shares to the Bolivian citizens as pension funds. The aim was to attract foreign investment, reduce unemployment and increase GDP.

[29] Many local movements reacted against importing toxic waste from Europe and the environmental deterioration caused by mining, while others protested against the closure of mines and consequent job losses. The burning of coca plantations by the US led to continuous confrontations between the rural workers and the military. Meanwhile, the World Bank reported that 97 per cent of the rural population were living in poverty.

[30] In 1994, the YPBF oil corporation, on the brink of privatization, was made even more attractive by an agreement with Brazil for the construction of a $2 billion gas pipeline to join Santa Cruz de la Sierra with São Paulo. The Capitalization Bill, unpopular amongst workers fearful of losing their jobs, led to a series of strikes in 1995. The Government declared a state of emergency on two occasions, granting the police special powers and imposing a curfew. Public meetings were banned and more than 100 leaders were imprisoned.

[31] As part of its regional campaign to control the northward flow of cocaine, the US demanded that the Bolivian parliament approve a law against the drug-money laundering in February 1997. In January 1999 Washington stated that the plan had been a success and that Bolivian coca production had been reduced by 50 per cent.

[32] In the national elections in June, the ADN won with 22 per cent

of the vote, followed by the MNR, MIR, UCS and CONDEPA, with 18, 17, 16 and 16 per cent of the vote respectively. Hugo Banzer became president once again after complicated negotiation in Parliament between the parties, themselves divided.

[33] In the December 1999 local elections, ADN came third with 13 per cent of the vote, behind the opposition MNR which took 19.7 per cent, and the MIR with 14.7 per cent. But in general terms, the government alliance took all the major cities.

[34] While the 73-year-old Banzer was in the United States on a medical trip, Vice-President Jorge Quiroga called on Washington to supply more funds for the eradication of illegal coca plantations. The Government considered that having eliminated three-quarters of total plantations, the US should fulfil its part of the deal, by funding the changeover to legal produce for the farmers.

[35] According to Human Rights Watch (HRW), cocaine traffickers are very influential within the executive, Congress, armed forces, police, political parties and other public institutions. Drug trafficking and corruption prevent Bolivia from developing public institutions rooted within the law. HRW stated that the huge increase in Bolivia's coca production in recent decades reflects the growth in US demand for cocaine.

[36] Quiroga replaced Banzer as president in August 2001, the latter was suffering from cancer.

[37] The coca eradication plan hit another obstacle in December when poor farmers rejected a government offer of $900 per head per year to stop planting. The same month, rural farmers' leader Casimiro Huanca was shot dead by police when they dispersed a meeting in the coca planters' union headquarters.

[38] In the 1997-2002 period, Bolivia led the world in the certified management of tropical forests. This opened new markets for Bolivian timber in Europe and the United States. The lack of return in price terms for certified timber could be the weakest link in a business that aims to protect the bio-diversity of tropical forests.

[39] Two candidates topped the poll in the June 2002 national election. Sánchez de Lozada, with 22.46 per cent of the vote and Evo Morales, the Indian leader of the coca growers, who received 20.94 per cent. Since neither won an outright majority, Congress had to vote and Sánchez de Lozada was elected president in August. Sánchez - who was accused by Morales's supporters of 'selling the homeland' in a privatization program during his first presidency - called for cooperation among Bolivia's political factions. ■

Bosnia-Herzegovina

Population: 4,126,000 (2002)
Land area: 51,000 SQ KM
Capital: Sarajevo
Currency: Dinar
Language: Serb, Croat and Bosnian

Bosna I Hercegovina

The earliest inhabitants of what is now Bosnia-Herzegovina were Illyrians. After the Roman conquest in the mid-2nd century BC, this region became a part of the province of Illyria, although the Sava river basin remained within the province of Pannonia. Serbs settled in the area in the 7th century AD. Except for a brief interregnum (1081-1101), Bosnia remained politically separate from Serbia.

² Hungarian control over Bosnia began in the mid-12th century. The combined efforts of the papacy and of the Hungarians to impose their religious authority over Bosnia gave rise to strong national resistance. Although war was avoided, the region came under the jurisdiction of the Hungarian archbishop of Kalocsa.

³ During this period, Bosnia was seen as a bastion of the Bogomils (or Cathari), one of southern Europe's main heretical movements, who found support among the local population, and from the State, as well. Neighboring Christians - both Orthodox Serbs and Catholic Croats - organized several crusades against this heresy. The Bogomils defeated the crusaders, but some parts of Bosnia were converted to Christianity.

⁴ Ban Prijezda founded the Kotromanic dynasty (1254-1395) under which Bosnia conquered the province of Hum (Herzegovina). In 1377, Tvrtko crowned himself King of Serbia, Bosnia and the coastlands. With the Turkish invasion in 1386 the Serbs were defeated in Kosovo (1389), but Tvrtko carried out further conquests in the west, and in 1390 was crowned King of Rashka, Bosnia, Dalmatia, Croatia and the coastlands.

⁵ The Ottoman Empire occupied Serbia in 1459 and Bosnia became a province 1463. Hum resisted longer, but in 1482 the port of Novi fell, and Herzegovina too became a province of the Ottoman Empire.

⁶ After the Turkish conquest, a campaign began to convert Bosnian Bogomils to Islam. Thus, in addition to Catholic Slavs and Christian Orthodox Slavs, there were now Muslim Slavs. Ever since, relations between the three communities have been strained, and religion became the decisive social factor in the region.

⁷ At first, the Turkish governor (Pasha) had his headquarters in Banja Luka, but later transferred them to Sarajevo. In 1580, Bosnia was divided into 8 *sanjaks* (sub-regions), under the jurisdiction of 48 hereditary Kapetans, who exercised a feudal power over their territories. Mining and trade began to decline; only the manufacture of weapons and wrought metals survived.

⁸ In the 16th and 17th centuries, Bosnia played an important role in the Turkish wars against Austria and Venice. In 1697, Prince Eugene of Savoy captured Sarajevo. By the Treaty of Karlowitz (1699) the Sava river, which formed Bosnia's northern border, also became the northern boundary of the Ottoman Empire. Herzegovina and the part of Bosnia east of the Una river were ceded to Austria in 1718, and returned to Turkey in 1739.

⁹ In the 19th century, Bosnia's nobility resisted Turkish interference. In 1837, Herzegovina's regent declared independence. Uprisings became chronic, bringing Christians and Muslims together, despite their differences, against the bureaucracy and corruption of the Empire.

¹⁰ In 1875, a local Herzegovinian conflict unleashed a rebellion, which spilled over into Bosnia. Austria, Russia and Germany tried unsuccessfully to mediate between Turkey and the rebels. The Sultan's promise to reduce taxes, grant religious freedom and install a provincial assembly was also rejected.

¹¹ By a secret agreement in 1877, Russia authorized Austria-Hungary to occupy Bosnia-Herzegovina, in exchange for its neutrality in Russia's upcoming war against Turkey. After the Russo-Turkish War of 1877-78, the Congress of Berlin disregarded Serbian wishes, and assigned Bosnia and Herzegovina to the Austro-Hungarian Empire (although nominally they continued to be under Turkish control).

¹² In 1878, Vienna put down armed resistance from Bosnia-Herzegovina. The revolution launched by the Young Turks in 1908 brought on a crisis within the Ottoman Empire.

¹³ The Turkish Government asked Bosnia-Herzegovina to participate in the new parliament at Istanbul but Austria-Hungary annexed the two provinces in 1908, with Russian consent. Vienna established a provincial assembly (*Sabor*) and special laws of association, without representation in Vienna or Budapest.

¹⁴ The 1910 Constitution consolidated social and religious differences by establishing three electoral colleges - Orthodox, Catholic and Muslim - each with a fixed number of seats in the Sabor.

¹⁵ The influence of the Mlada Bosna (Young Bosnia) movement and other revolutionary groups led the Empire's authorities to close Bosnia's Sabor, and dissolve several Serbian political groups. The assassination of Archduke Francis Ferdinand and his wife the Duchess of Hohenberg in

Sarajevo in 1914 by a Bosnian Serb student triggered World War I.

[16] In 1915, emigrants in Peru founded the Yugoslav Committee (Yugoslav means 'southern Slavs'), which began an intense campaign in favor of independence and the unification of the 'Yugoslavs'. The kingdom of the Serbs, Croats and Slovenians was proclaimed on December 1 that year, and included Bosnia-Herzegovina.

[17] After the collapse of the Austro-Hungarian Empire in the Balkans in 1918, Bosnia-Herzegovina became a part of Serbia. In 1919 the Yugoslav Communist Party was founded, and won 14 per cent of the parliamentary seats. It was banned in 1920. The country was renamed the Kingdom of Yugoslavia in 1929, following an authoritarian coup that persecuted communists, trade unionists, and opponents of Serb dominance.

[18] The Nazis occupied Yugoslavia in 1941. Bosnia-Herzegovina was subjected to the puppet administration established in Croatia. In the two provinces, Croat *Ustashes* (Fascists) massacred the Serbs. The rivalry which had always existed between Muslim, Serb and Croat degenerated into deep hostility. The Communists, led by Tito, organized a guerrilla resistance movement with the support of the allies. At the end of World War II the country remained a federation of republics, one of which was Bosnia-Herzegovina. The slogan of the Yugoslav federated socialists was 'Brotherhood and Unity', but ethnic confrontation was visible in the arts, the humanities and literature.

[19] The federal system and Tito's leadership achieved a half-century of domestic peace. Development plans favored the poorer regions and diverse communities were successfully integrated. Following Tito's death in 1980, a collegial executive was established with representation from all the republics and a yearly rotation of the presidency among them. But instead of pacifying the rivalries between the federated entities, this mechanism seemed to exacerbate them.

[20] After the fall of the Berlin Wall in 1990, the Yugoslav Communist League withdrew its monopoly over the political system. Political demagogues incited discontent, stirring up local and ethnic demands. In April, in the post-war's first multi-party legislative elections, the Bosnian electorate chose candidates who were ethnic standard-bearers. The nationalist parties elected 73 Serbs and 44 Croats, while the candidates of the Democratic Reform Party (ex-Communist) and the liberal technocrats lost political ground.

[21] The Muslims were represented by the Democratic Action Party (DAP). Their leader, Alija Izetbegovic, who held a doctorate in theology, was elected president of the republic. The Bosnian Croat and Muslim leadership sought to follow the example of Slovenia and Croatia and secede from Yugoslavia, encouraged by Western Europe and fearful of the advance of Serbian nationalism. The Bosnian Serbs favored remaining within the Yugoslav federation.

[22] In October 1991, Bosnia-Herzegovina's Sabor approved a declaration of independence from the Yugoslav federation. In January 1992, Parliament agreed to hold a plebiscite on the issue of separation.

[23] Bosnian President Izetbegovic wanted to maintain the unity and integrity of the republic, promising that Bosnia-Herzegovina would not become a Muslim state, and guaranteeing that the rights of all nationalities would be respected. In early March, conflict broke out when the referendum was supported by 99.4 per cent of the Muslims and Croats, who ratified the republic's independence.

[24] On April 7, the European Community and the US recognized the independence of Bosnia-Herzegovina. The Bosnian republic was accepted as a member state in the Conference of Security and Cooperation in Europe; in May it became a member of the UN.

[25] At the same time, the Serb community proclaimed the independence of the 'Serb Republic of Bosnia-Herzegovina' in the areas under Serb control (Bosnian Krajina, with its center at Banja Luka). The conflict quickly extended throughout the entire region.

[26] Local Croat forces also controlled certain areas of the Republic; there were sporadic confrontations with Bosnian government troops. In late July, Croatia and Bosnia signed a mutual recognition pact.

[27] In January 1993, Serb troops killed Bosnian deputy prime minister, Hakija Turajlic, in Sarajevo. In March the UN decreed a cease-fire in that city, which was under siege. There were numerous reports on the existence of Serb concentration camps, as well as an 'ethnic cleansing' campaign. The latter involved the expulsion of all members of rival ethnic groups, especially from the smaller villages.

[28] According to Amnesty International, thousands of civilians, as well as soldiers that had been captured or wounded, were executed. In addition, prisoners were systematically submitted to torture and harsh treatment. According to UN figures, a total of 40,000 women had been raped. Although atrocities were committed by all sides, the Serbs bore the major responsibility, while the Muslims were the main victims.

[29] The UN Protection Forces (UNPROFOR) sent in some 20,000 peacekeeping troops. The US refused to send troops to Bosnia, despite pressure from the UN and European countries. Several security zones were decreed in such cities as Tuzla, Zepa, Gorazde, Bihac and Sarajevo. However, these were not always observed, just as successive ceasefires were consistently violated.

[30] In October, Serb occupation of Bosanki Brod opened up a corridor between Serbia and Bosnian Krajina. Serbs controlled 70 per cent of the territory, as a result of their superior artillery and armored vehicles, as well as their control of the bridges over the Drina river - on the border between Serbia and Bosnia - which allowed them to receive arms and other supplies from the Yugoslav Federation. As a result of the Federation's support for the Serbs, the UN called for an economic blockade on it, and an arms embargo aimed at Bosnians and Croats.

PROFILE

ENVIRONMENT

Bosnia-Herzegovina has a 20-kilometer coastline on the Adriatic Sea. In the west it is bordered by Croatia, Montenegro and Serbia. The major part of the country lies in the Dinaric Alps, with elevations of around 4,265 meters, making overland communication difficult. The country is drained by the Sava and Neretva rivers and their tributaries. The territory takes its name from the Bosna River, a tributary of the Sava. The main crops are grains, vegetables and grapes; there is also livestock rearing. There is a wealth of mineral resources, including coal, iron, copper and manganese. Because of air pollution, respiratory ailments are very common in urban areas. Barely half of the region's water supplies are considered safe, the Sava River being the most polluted of all.

SOCIETY

Peoples: From a common Slav origin, ethnic differences are historico-religious: for example Muslim Slavs (Bosnian), 49.2 per cent; Orthodox Serbs, 31.3; Catholic Croats, 17.3. Serbs are a majority in north-east Bosnia, with the center in Banja Luka; and the Croats in Herzegovina in the west, centered on Mostar. Ethnic distinctions are less clear in other regions. In the capital, Sarajevo, there are Muslims (majority), Croats and Serbs. Until 1992 there was a 1,200 strong Jewish community. There is also a large Roma (gypsy) minority.
Religions: The majority is Muslim. Other religions: Christian Orthodox and Roman Catholic.
Languages: Serb, Croat and Bosnian (all official) (very similar and previously known as Serbo-Croat).
Political Parties: Democratic Action Party (DAP - Muslim); Social Democratic Party (SDP - multiethnic); Democratic Serbian Party; Croat Democratic Community (CDC); Party for Bosnia Herzegovina (moderate Bosnian - Muslim).
Social Organizations: Currently in the process of being reorganized. Some ecologist groups operated even during the conflict.

THE STATE

Official Name: Republika Bosna I Hercegovina.
Administrative Division: 50 Districts.
Capital: Sarajevo 522,000 people (1999), reduced to less than 50,000 in September 1995.
Other cities: Banja Luka 175,700 people; Tuzla 111,900; Mostar 72,000 (2000).
Government: There are two administrative divisions: the Bosnia-Herzegovina Federation (the Croat and Muslim zones) and the Srpska Republic (mostly Serbians) although the city of Brcko is autonomous. Its President is Beriz Belkic, since February 2002. Prime Minister: Dragan Mikerevic since March 2002. Two-chamber parliament. International High Representative: Wolfgang Petritsch (Austria) since August 1999. Parliament: The House of Representatives has 42 members and the House of the People has 15 members. Safet Halilovic, President of the Bosnia-Herzegovina Federation since January 2002; Alija Behmen its Prime Minister since March 2001. Mirko Sarovic is the Srpska Republic's President since December 2000 and Mladen Ivanic its Prime Minister since January 2001. Sinisa Kisic is the Brcko Mayor since April 1999 and Henry Lee Clarke (US) is the international supervisor of the city (April 2001).
National Holiday: March 1, Independence Day (1992).
Armed Forces: approximately 60,000. 120,000 reserves (1993). Due to the conflict the United Nations Protection Force (UNPROFOR) deployed several thousand troops. As part of the peace agreements two separate armies are kept in the nation, one for the Federation and one of the Serb Republic. There are more than 150,000 troops from the Federal Yugoslav Army and Serb nationalist militias operating in the country.

1985/99

Per 100,000
live births

10

31 The Muslims found themselves cornered in Sarajevo and a few other minor sites, receiving what little financial and moral support they could from a few Islamic countries.

32 In June 1993, Serb President Slobodan Milosevic and his Croatian counterpart, Franjo Tudjman, announced the partition of Bosnia into three ethnic entities (Serb, Croatian and Muslim), within the framework of a federal state.

33 The Croats, faced with the partition of Bosnia, sought to gain the upper hand to negotiate from a position of strength. In July they launched an offensive against Mostar, capital of Herzegovina. The UN Human Rights Commission reported that 10,000 Muslims had been held in Croatian concentration camps, where they were submitted to torture and in some cases, to summary executions.

34 In the meantime, the situation in Sarajevo grew worse: there was a lack of electricity, water and food. Besieged by a series of epidemics, the city's estimated 300,000 inhabitants managed to survive on minimal rations, while international aid agencies tried to reach the city despite mounting difficulties. In early 1994, the UN appealed to the Serbs to stop their attacks on Sarajevo and withdraw the heavy artillery surrounding the city. Despite resistance from the Russians, NATO threatened to bomb Serb positions. When the formal deadline expired, the Serbs withdrew.

35 The peace conference sponsored by the UN and the EU in 1994 proposed the territory be divided into Bosnian, Muslim and Croatian areas as ethnically homogeneous republics. This option called for the transfer of people from one sector to another. The UN's Human Rights Commission for the former Yugoslavia criticized the creation of ethnic boundaries and defended a reform of the democratic system.

36 In 1994, the US and Russia exerted growing pressure upon the Serbs to accept the proposal. Croatians and Muslims approved a federal agreement between the two communities: 51 per cent of the territory would remain among Bosnians and Croatians while Serbs would be in control of 49 per cent,

without the need to divide Bosnia into three ethnically distinct states.

37 With support from the EU, Washington and Moscow, the federal agreement was signed by presidents Franjo Tudjman of Croatia and Alija Izetbegovic of Bosnia, but the Serbs rejected it. Negotiations were hampered because Serb president Slobodan Milosevic stated he had no authority over the self-proclaimed Bosnian-Serb Republic of Srpska.

38 In 1995, the Bosnian-Serbs held several UN troops hostage and took Bihac. In August, the situation was radically changed by NATO's bombing of Bosnian-Serb positions in the siege of Sarajevo. Almost at the same time, Croatia expelled Serb-Croat forces from the eastern side of the country forcing their delegates to negotiate.

39 The Dayton Accords of 1995 stipulated that elections were to be held in September 1996, with the aim of promoting more tolerant leaders among each of the nationalities in conflict. The agreement was carried out under US military pressure with - some said - the underlying objective of influencing US President Clinton's re-election campaign. The presence of American troops forced a peaceful settlement and, at the same time, froze the political situation.

40 The Dayton Accords acknowledged that the two ethnically based mini-states (the Bosnian-Serb Republic - Srpska - and the Croatian-Muslim Federation) resulted from the physical elimination or expulsion of ethnic minorities.

41 The International Criminal Tribunal for the Former Yugoslavia at the Hague convicted Radovan Karadzic, leader of the Srpska Republic and his military commander Ratko Mladic, for genocide. In spite of being convicted, neither was incarcerated. They retained great influence in the republic's political life even though the Dayton peace accords had banned the electoral participation of people accused of war crimes.

42 In June 1996, power, water and transport services began to be reinstated and Sarajevo regained some of its former vitality. The environment of political tranquillity considered necessary for the run-up to the September elections was hindered by the refugees' inability to return to their homes unless their fellow citizens ruled over the area, the limitations of journalists' movements and the difficulties imposed on the activities of several NGOs.

43 After the September 1996 elections, Bosnia had a three-member presidency ranked according to their share of the vote. Bosnia's Muslim President, Alija Izetbegovic, was first

chairman; the Serb nationalist Momcilo Krajisnik was second and the Croat leader, Kresimir Zubak was third. These three were the most nationalist among the candidates in each federated republic.

44 The Croatian and Bosnian presidents met in Split during August 1997 to relaunch the Muslim-Croatian federation, pledging once again to facilitate the return of the refugees. Karadzic questioned the December legislative elections, accusing Western representatives of having fixed the results in favor of the Muslim and Croatian parties.

45 High Commissioner for the republic, Carlos Westendorp, imposed some unification measures, like the creation of a common flag and national symbols for Bosnia-Herzegovina, but these issues produced fresh confrontation. Each group maintained their own armed forces and the federation between Croats and Muslims was shaped as a combination of both groups and not a unified identity.

46 The new currency, the mark, introduced in 1998, was widely accepted in the domestic market. However, it took until 2001 for the privatization of companies and the banks to pick up momentum, even though the process had been initiated two years earlier with a loan from the World Bank. By then, all the communist era payment offices had been closed. In the meantime, the country had depended on reconstruction and humanitarian aid from the international community, but this was expected to decline greatly in the following years.

47 The December 2000 parliamentary elections gave the nationalists a slight majority, but the process of forming a new government was paralyzed by the power struggle amongst the nationalist parties. The international High Commissioner, Wolfgang Petritsch, sacked the Croat president in the rotating presidency, Ante Jelavic, accusing him of diminishing the Daytona peace accords by supporting the creation of a Croat mini state. Meanwhile, in early 2001, the World Bank and the IMF warned that they would grant no more loans until the crisis was resolved. Finally, in February this year a new, non-nationalist government took power.

48 In August, Jelavic and other Croat officials were taken to court by Petritsch for diminishing the territorial integrity of the Muslim Croat Federation of Bosnia. Three hundred Bosnian-Croatian nationalists demonstrated outside the court in support of Jelavic. The persistent weight of the nationalist

parties continued to block the return of tens of thousands of internal refugees.

49 At the end of the war there had been 60,000 international peace-keepers, but by now barely 18,000 were left. The US proposed the withdrawal of its 3,000 blue helmets, causing Petritsch to state in February 2002 that Bosnia-Herzegovina was still far from being 'a viable state that can maintain itself alone' According to his estimations, a further three to four years are needed before the country can function independently, without an international administrator. ∎

Botswana

Population: 1,564,000 (2002)
Land area: 566,730 SQ KM
Capital: Gaborone
Currency: Pula
Language: Setswana

Botswana

The first inhabitants of what is now Botswana were probably the ancestors of the San (also known as Bushmen), hunters and gatherers who today inhabit the semi-arid plains of southwestern Botswana, and the Khoikhoi. Bantu-speaking populations reached the region in the first century BC. The ancestors of the Tswana, currently the country's majority group, settled in the 11th and 12th centuries in the plains of the Vaal River, in what was formerly the South African province of Transvaal. The Tswanas were divided among eight of the most powerful clans. Clan rivalry stood in the way of establishing a kingdom like those of other nations in southern Africa.

[2] In the course of its history 'Bechuanaland' (the English corruption of *ba'tswana* - Tswana people), was also known as the 'fatal crossroads' on account of its position in the heart of southern Africa, providing a passageway for pre-colonial movement and settlement. The territory served as a passageway for British, Dutch and Portuguese colonists since the 18th century. The region served as a crossroads not only for different colonial strategic interests, but also for their intersection with the Tswana people that had inhabited the area since the 17th century.

[3] Around 1830, the region was penetrated by Boer colonists (of Dutch origin), fleeing northward from the Cape to escape the British. These farmers fought with the local people for possession of the scant fertile lands, and the Tswana also clashed with Ndebele people who had been driven from Zululand by the Zulu kings (see South Africa). Tswanas and Boers united to

withstand the Ndebele invasion. In 1894, leaders of the three major kingdoms traveled to London to seek support. The British promptly complied, and Bechuanaland soon became a protectorate.

[4] British trusteeship prevented political absorption by South Africa but paved the way for white economic supremacy. Consequently, when the first nationalist movements arose they aimed at putting an end to both situations.

[5] Although Botswana has a large semi-arid area, it came to be one of southern Africa's major cattle and meat exporters. At the beginning of this century, 97 per cent of the population lived in rural areas, every family owned several cows, and the richest had oxen to plough their fields. By the 1960s, 15 per cent of the population had migrated to the cities and at least 40 per cent of the rural population had lost their cattle.

[6] The struggle for independence became entangled with the wedding of Seretse Khama, a leader of the major Bamagwato chiefdom who went to England to study law. He married Ruth Williams, a European white-collar worker. This upset both the British and the Afrikaners who prevented Seretse from returning home. He

withstood every pressure including offers of money from the British and, firmly supported by his people, he retained leadership of the country's main ethnic group. Seretse finally returned home in 1956, nine years before the general elections in which his Botswana Democratic Party (BDP) polled 80 per cent of the vote.

[7] In September 1966, Botswana gained independence and Seretse was elected first president. A year later he was knighted by the British. The BDP pursued a conciliatory policy towards Europeans, who controlled many of the country's economic resources, and Botswana continued to be highly dependent upon South Africa. Almost all its imports came through Cape Town, and 60 per cent of its exports were purchased by South Africa. Nevertheless, in the political arena, Seretse maintained his distance from South Africa, and supported the region's anti-racist movements. Botswana was one of the 'frontline nations' fighting apartheid, and a member of the SADCC (a grouping of the nine southern African countries seeking to end the economic dependence on South Africa).

[8] Seretse Khama died of cancer in July 1980 and was succeeded by the Vice-President, Quett Masire.

Strong pressures were exerted on Masire by revolutionary socialist groups to limit the concentration of arable land in Tswana and white hands and to increase the area allotted to cooperatives. The rural poor accused large landowners of overgrazing, causing a deterioration in the quality of the land, and threatening their future. A movement also arose demanding the nationalization of rich diamond, iron, copper and nickel deposits exploited by South African companies.

[9] Between 1978 and 1988, Botswana became the third largest diamond producer in the world. The national economy grew at a record rate of 12 per cent a year. Despite this, three-fifths of the population lived on subsistence crops or 'non-institutionalized' activities, that is in the informal economy, off the statistical record, beyond fiscal control and the commercial circuit.

[10] In 1985 there were repeated flare-ups along the frontier with South Africa due to the Botswana Government's support for the African National Congress (ANC) anti-apartheid campaign. In 1987, South Africa applied pressure blocking the roads to Gaborone.

[11] From 1989, the year Masire was re-elected President, the Government had to confront successive economic and political problems, fundamentally due to a fall in the international demand for diamonds. Increased unemployment and opposition criticism brought government corruption into the open, forcing several ministers to resign. During 1991, three of the seven opposition parties created the People's Progressive Front (PPF) in opposition to the ruling Botswana Democratic Party (BDP).

[12] That same year, Botswana witnessed the biggest strikes since independence. Public sector workers demanded a 154 per cent pay increase and the Government responded by sacking 18,000 state employees. Despite having maintained economic growth for decades, some studies showed Botswana had the most severe social inequalities in the world.

[13] In 1992, unemployment came close to 25 per cent. In an attempt

LAND USE

DEFORESTATION: 0.5% annual (1990/95)

1993

- FOREST & WOODLAND: 45.6%
- ARABLE: 0.7%
- OTHER: 53.7%

MATERNAL MORTALITY

1985/99

Per 100,000 live births

330

LITERACY

2000

77%

EXTERNAL DEBT

2000

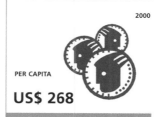

PER CAPITA

US$ 268

STATISTICS

DEMOGRAPHY
Population: 1,564,000 (2002)
Annual growth: 2.5 % (1985-2000)
Estimates for year 2015: 1,694,000 (2000)
Annual growth to year 2015: 0.6 % (2000)
Urban population: 50.3 % (2000)
Urban growth: 1.9 % (2000)
Children per woman: 4.2 (2000)

HEALTH
Life expectancy at birth: 36 years (2000-2005)
male: 37 years (2000-2005)
female: 36 years (2000-2005)
Maternal mortality: 330 per 100,000 live births (1985/99)
Infant mortality: 74 per 1,000 (2000)
Under-5 child mortality: 101 per 1,000 (2000)
Daily calorie supply: 2,288 per capita (1999)
24 doctors per 100,000 people (1994)
Safe water: 95 % (2000)

EDUCATION
Literacy: 77 % (2000)
male: 74 % (2000)
female: 80 % (2000)
School enrolment (net):
Primary total: 84 % (1994/2000)
male: 98 % (1995/99)
female: 99 % (1995/99)
Secondary (gross):
male: 61 % (1995/97)
female: 68 % (1995/97)
Tertiary (gross): 4 % (1998)
Primary school teachers: one for every 28 pupils (1998)

COMMUNICATIONS
27 newspapers (1996), 155 radios (1997), 25 TV sets (2000) and 93 main telephone lines (2000) per 1,000 people

ECONOMY
Per capita, GDP: $ 7,184 (2000)
Annual growth: 2.5 % (2000)
Annual inflation: 8.6 % (2000)
Consumer price index: 149.4 (2000)
Currency: 6.8 pula = $ 1 (03/2002)
Cereal imports: 133,198 metric tons (2000)
Fertilizer use: 134 kg per ha (1999)
Exports: $ 1,391 million (1999)
Imports: $ 1,670 million (1999)
External debt: $ 413 million (2000); $ 268 per capita (2000)
Debt service: 2.4 % of exports (1999)
Development aid received: $ 61 million (1999); $ 38.3 per capita (1999); 1.00 % of GNP (1999)

HDI (ranking/value): 114 / 0.577 (1999)

---

to increase employment and lift the flagging fortunes of the BDP, the Government initiated an incentive policy for non-mining industries. Severe drought forced the authorities to declare a state of emergency. Public spending was drastically reduced, which meant laying off more than a third of the workers employed directly or indirectly by the State.

[14] Despite the economic and social problems, the BDP kept its majority in the 1994 parliamentary elections, while losing nine seats. The country - now the second most important diamond exporter behind Russia - was still dependent on the export of its minerals. Tourism became the second largest foreign-exchange earner.

[15] Although the Government managed to keep the budget in the black, it failed to solve the most pressing problems of a population lacking, amongst other things, even the most basic medical attention. In 1998, 30 per cent of Botswana's adults were HIV-positive, according to the UN.

[16] In February of that year, an attempt by the Government to buy Belgian weapons brought German intervention to prevent the purchase. Two years previously, Germany had blocked Botswana's attempts to buy arms from the Netherlands. Despite these setbacks, Botswana appeared determined to acquire such weapons.

[17] Partly as a result of its diamond wealth, Botswana's economy has flourished over the last three decades. According to the World Bank, it had the fastest-growing economy in the world during the period 1965-1996, when per capita income grew at 9.2 per cent. The rapid growth led to increasing disparities between rich and poor people.

[18] The civil war in Namibia in the Caprivi Strip, a corridor 460 kilometers long and in some places 30 kilometers wide, affected Botswana's relations with its neighbor. In January 1999, some 2,000 residents of this area fled to Botswana. Many of them were separatists, and the decision to grant them asylum worsened relations with Windhoek. Both countries were also involved in a border dispute over an island in the Chobe river.

[19] The October 1999 elections once again gave victory to the BDP, which took 33 of the 40 seats open to direct vote. Its candidate, Festus Gontebanye Mogae was reconfirmed in the presidency he had held since Masire stood down in 1998.

[20] Following action taken by South Africa and Kenya to import generic - and therefore, cheaper - versions of AIDS drugs, corporations selling patented drugs began to sell them cheaper to Botswana. One in three Botswanans are infected with the HIV virus - the highest rate in the world.

[21] Meanwhile, Debeswana, the national diamond company, joint owned by national government and the South African De Beers corporation, began to subsidize the cost of AIDS medication for employees and their wives. However, the lack of infrastructure, doctors, nurses and trained advisers has made implementation of treatment difficult.

[22] In March 2002 the Government relocated the last 2,200 San people into settlements, having first deprived them of water and food, removing them from lands they had occupied for 30,000 years. In the last 17 years, 50,000 San have been settled into 63 camps to force them to give up their nomadic lifestyle. The Kalahari zone, the San ancestral lands, is rich in diamonds. ∎

PROFILE

ENVIRONMENT
An extensive and sparsely populated country, Botswana is divided into three large regions. In the center and southwest, the Kalahari basin is a desert steppe where grazing is only possible in certain seasons. The Okavango River basin in the northeast has a tropical climate suitable for agriculture. 80 per cent of the population lives within a strip in the east, stretching along the railroad. Traditionally pastoral, the country is beginning to exploit its mineral resources (manganese, copper, nickel and diamonds). Intensive cattle-raising has meant a reduction in the areas originally set aside for wildlife, and is also rapidly depleting the soil.

SOCIETY
Peoples: Tswana make up 90 per cent of the population; Kalanga, Basarwa and other.
Religions: Some are Catholic and Protestant, some follow African religions; sometimes the distinction between these and Christian practices is blurred. There are also Muslim and Hindu minorities.
Languages: Setswana (national) and English (official). There are diverse local languages, among them Kalanga, Mbukushu and Herero.
Political Parties: The Botswana Democratic Party (BDP), founded by Seretse Khama in 1961; the Botswana National Front (BNF) was founded in 1967 as a coalition of leftist and center-left parties; Botswana Congress Party (BCP). The latest attempts towards opposition unity were: PPF (People Progressive Front) in 1990; UDF (United Democratic Front) in 1994 and lately BAM (Botswana Alliance Movement) in 1999.
Social Organizations: 5 of the 13 local trade unions form the Botswana Federation of Trade Unions, founded in 1976. BOCONGO, Botswana's NGO Council, includes diverse groups as the Forum on Sustainable Agriculture, First People in the Kalahari; Task Force on Indigenous Minorities in the South of Africa.

THE STATE
Official Name: Republic of Botswana.
Administrative Divisions: 4 Districts.
Capital: Gaborone 254,000 people (1999).
Other cities: Francistown 101,700 people; Selebi-Phikwe 47,200 (2000).
Government: Festus Gontebanye Mogae, President since April 1998, confirmed in October 1999 elections. The single chamber National Assembly has 47 members.
National Holiday: September 30, Independence Day (1966).
Armed Forces: 7,500 (1997). **Other:** 1,000 Transport Police.

Brazil

Brasil

Population:	174,706,000 (2002)
Land area:	8,456,510 SQ KM
Capital:	Brasilia
Currency:	Real
Language:	Portuguese

Small bands belonging mainly to the Tupi Guarani, Carib and Arawak linguistic groups initially inhabited the huge tracts of land that were to become today's Brazil. The indigenous peoples from the Amazon basin fished and farmed while the inhabitants of the dry savanna lived by hunting and gathering. When the first Portuguese ships arrived at the coast of what today is Bahia de Todos os Santos in 1500, more than two million people inhabited these lands.

[2] Under the Tordesillas Treaty (1494) which divided the non-European world between Spain and Portugal, the latter was assured its rights over these lands. Sailing towards India, Pedro Alvarez Cabral landed at Bahia de todos os Santos in 1500 and christened the area the Island of Vera Cruz. Between 1501 and 1502 a naval expedition headed by Gaspar de Lemos charted the region between Rio Grande and the Río de la Plata. In this way Cabral's error (he thought he had reached an island) was corrected and the region came to be known by the Europeans as Santa Cruz Land.

[3] For the Portuguese, these lands were far less lucrative than Africa and India. The strip of coast did not reveal major deposits of precious metals. It was inhabited by semi-sedentary indigenous peoples, the Tupi, related to the Guaraní, whom the Spanish would also later find in Paraguay. At first the Portuguese crown only valued those lands as places to trade slaves or barter metals and trifles with the Indians in exchange for brazilwood. The pulp from this tree, used to make a fire-colored dye, would give the country

its final name - *brasa* in Portuguese means embers.

[4] Wood production was quite significant for a time although the industry did not lead to the creation of major cities or other signs of European development. Although the Indians were used to felling trees in order to clear the forests, they lacked a commercial tradition in wood and could not cut trees on a large scale. The Portuguese supplied axes and saws and trading agents had the timber ready for shipment. Trading posts were often established on islands on the Atlantic ocean and, shortly after, the first Portuguese settlements were also established on these islands. Only a few Portuguese exiles inhabited the continent by that time, together with the indigenous

communities. On several occasions, these exiles helped other mainland Portuguese make fruitful alliances with the natives.

[5] Around 1530, the Portuguese were forced to increase their involvement with Brazil. Other European traders, particularly the French, started to arrive. Commerce with India had slumped and the achievements of Spanish conquistadors in other parts of the continent represented both an incentive and a threat. The Portuguese sent an expedition to expel the French and establish its authority, along with some settlers. Thus in 1532 the first official Portuguese settlement, São Vicente, was established on an island close to São Paulo.

[6] The Spanish expanded their empire through the conquest of lands under the strict control of the Crown. The Portuguese however, in accordance with their maritime commercial tradition, divided the Brazilian coast into captaincies which were awarded to *donatarios*, prominent individuals who

supposedly had the wealth required to carry out the occupation and exploitation of the lands. The captaincies were hereditary, with extensive judicial and administrative powers, although several were never occupied and others survived for a brief time. However, four of them became permanent settlements and two (Pernambuco to the north and São Vicente to the south) turned out to be viable and lucrative.

[7] As happened in the Spanish colonial outposts, the first Portuguese settlements had to be fortified to defend them from Indian attacks. Procurement of supplies was difficult and for a while the Portuguese obtained most of their food by trading with the indigenous peoples and eating cassava instead of wheat, which was hard to grow in most of the region.

[8] Two agricultural systems developed, the *rozas* or farms and the large *fazendas*, given over to exports, mainly of sugarcane. In spite of favorable conditions, the fazendas took a long time to prosper, due to the lack of capital and labor. Agriculture and the discipline imposed on the plantations were foreign to the local peoples, whom the Portuguese forced to toil in exchange for European products. The settlers soon decided to obtain slave workers through expeditions which hunted for Indians or through other Indians acting as intermediaries.

[9] During the second half of the 16th century, many Indians of the region had been decimated by illnesses (influenza, smallpox, measles) or had fled to other areas. African slaves were then imported to grow sugar. This trade grew and it is estimated that from 3 to 4 million Africans arrived in Brazil between the 16th and 17th century. In 1848, as a result of pressures similar to those of 1530, the Crown appointed a general governor, who with 1,000 men carried out an expedition to Brazil, establishing the capital in Bahia on the northeastern coast. A bishopric was created in 1551. Only 50 years after the first contact, Brazil had reached the same degree of European institutionalization which characterized the Spanish territories.

[10] The Jesuits had started coming to the country by that time, and soon became the strongest branch of the

Workers

1990/2000
UNEMPLOYMENT: 9.6%
LABOR FORCE AS % OF TOTAL:

- FEMALE: 36%   MALE: 64%

1994/97
EMPLOYMENT DISTRIBUTION:

F
M

- SERVICES   F: 68%   M: 45%
- INDUSTRY   F: 9%   M: 26%
- AGRICULTURE   F: 22%   M: 28%

Land Use

DEFORESTATION: 0.5% annual (1990/95)

1993

- FOREST & WOODLAND: 57.3%
- ARABLE: 4.9%
- OTHER: 37.8%

Public Expenditure

Military expenditure (as % GNI):	**1.9%** (1999)
Defense expenditure (% of central government expenditure)	**5.5 %** (1997)

Catholic Church, unlike in Spanish America, where they arrived much later than other orders. The Jesuits were very active, learnt the Guaraní language to convert Indians to Catholicism and established villages very similar to the missions in the Spanish areas. The main contacts between Indians and Europeans (war, trade, slavery and missions) were the same as in the Spanish areas. Due to these contacts, Guaraní became the language used in that century for all kinds of exchanges.

[11] Brazil carried out major expansions towards the west of the Tordesillas line, whose meridian was drawn up 370 leagues to the west of Cape Verde. This expansion reached the slopes of the Andes mountain range and, from north to south, from the Amazon to the Río de la Plata. In the north, the movement was led by the Jesuits who established several missions along the Amazon. In the northeast, cattle farmers from the sugar areas of Pernambuco and Bahia ventured to the heart of the continent, looking for new grazing lands and reached today's Piauí, Goiás and Maranhao regions.

[12] The westward march was led by the *paulistas*, as São Paulo settlers were known. In the search for Indian slaves, gold and precious stones, the paulistas set up major expeditions to the interior, known as *bandeiras*. The incorporation of Portugal into the Spanish kingdom in 1580 facilitated the paulistas' incursions, since internal borders were broken and the Tordesillas division became ineffective. The bandeiras took the paulistas to Peru's mining regions and even to Bogota, Colombia. They also explored the region of Mato Grosso and to the south attacked local *reducciones* (missions), particularly those of Guaira. Here the Guaraní people were already relatively immune to disease and were accustomed to collective agricultural work. In most cases, the paulistas met resistance from the Indians and from the Jesuits who protected them. The human hunts were so devastating that the missions were gradually pushed further and further south until they reached the 'Seven Towns', in today's Rio Grande state.

[13] It was not just the paulistas who penetrated the dense forests. Thousands of Africans also sought refuge there, fleeing from the coastal plantations where they were kept as slaves. Africans, indigenous Americans and their mixed descendants joined forces in constant war against the colonial military expeditions. They also founded villages known by the African terms *quilombo* or *mokambo*, the most famous of which were at Palmares (1630-1695),

in northeastern Brazil, where the legendary Zumbi led the struggle. The Brazilian anti-racist movement still commemorates the date of Zumbi's death in battle, November 20, as Black Consciousness Day.

[14] Meanwhile, Brazil found itself involved in a war of independence between the Netherlands and Spain. Flanders and the Netherlands had been 'inherited' by the Spanish Crown. Between 1630 and 1654, the Dutch reasserted their control over Pernambuco after a failed attempt to conquer Bahia, which was repulsed by the joint efforts of native Americans, Africans and Portuguese.

[15] When Spain and Portugal were again separated in 1688, their colonial borders had shifted and the Tordesillas line could not be reinstated. In 1696, a bandeirantes expedition struck the first gold in what is now Minas Gerais. Gold mining peaked in the 18th century. The viceregal capital was transferred from Salvador to Rio de Janeiro in 1763 mostly due to the impact of these mines on the Brazilian economy.

[16] The local ruling class began to benefit from an expanding export economy and soon expressed a growing desire to dispense with the Portuguese role as intermediaries in their trade with Europe. The first moves towards independence came in the late 18th century and were rapidly crushed by the colonial power. Brazil's main freedom figure, Ensign Tiradentes, was executed in 1792 for his leading role in the Minas Conspiracy three years earlier.

[17] When Napoleon invaded the Iberian peninsula in 1808, Portuguese King Dom João VI had to transfer his court to Brazil, making the country semi-independent. Portugal ceased to be an intermediary and Brazil then dealt directly with its main customer, Britain. In this way, the Brazilian merchants prospered at the expense of other sectors linked to the Portuguese monopoly. The 1821 Oporto revolution in Portugal was an attempt to reinstate the old colonial system based on monopoly. When the King returned to Lisbon, the Brazilian merchants - determined to secure their gains - declared independence with British blessing. Brazil became an empire and Pedro I, formerly prince-regent, became its emperor in 1822.

[18] The following decade was one of the most turbulent in Brazilian history. From 1831 to 1835, a regency unsuccessfully tried to put an end to the civil war in the provinces and to the army's insubordination. In 1834, the Constitution was amended to decentralize the government, with the creation of provincial assemblies with considerable local powers, and to choose a regent for a period of

PROFILE

ENVIRONMENT

There are five major regions in Brazil. The Amazon Basin, in the North, is the largest tropical rainforest in the world. It consists of lowlands covered with rainforest and rivers. The Carajás mountain range contains one of the world's largest mineral reserves, rich in iron, manganese, copper, nickel and bauxite. The economy is mainly extractive. The northeastern *sertao* consists of rocky plateaus with a semi-arid climate and scrub vegetation. Raising cattle is the main economic activity. The more humid coastal strip, situated on the 'Serra do mar' (Coastal Sierra), has numerous sugarcane and cocoa plantations. In the southeast, the terrain consists of huge plateaus bordered in the east by the Serra do Mar mountain range. The main crops are coffee, cotton, corn and sugarcane. The southern plateau, with sub-tropical climate, is the country's main agricultural region, where coffee, soybeans, corn and wheat are grown. In the far south, on the Rio Grande do Sul plains, cattle raising is the main economic activity. Finally, the mid-west region is made up of vast plains where cattle-raising predominates. With the devastation of the Amazon region, caused by unrestrained felling of trees and forest fires, the habitats of many species have been destroyed.

SOCIETY

Peoples: Brazilians come from the ethnic and cultural integration of indigenous people (mainly Guaraní), African slaves and European (mostly Portuguese) immigrants. Arab and Japanese minorities have also settled in the Rio-São Paulo area. There are also many Indian peoples. Contrary to what is commonly admitted, racial discrimination does exist although the 1988 Constitution includes racism as a crime.

Religion: Most are baptized Catholic; but there is considerable merging into syncretic Afro-Brazilian cults (candomblé and umanda).

Language: Portuguese is the official and predominant language. Many Indian languages are spoken (ie Bariwa and Guajajára).

Political Parties: Party of the Brazil Social-Democracy (PSDB); Party of the Liberal Front; Party of the Brazilian Democratic Movement (PMDB); Brazilian Progressive Party; Workers' Party (PT); Brazilian Labor Party; Democratic Labor Party (PDT); Brazilian Socialist Party; Liberal Party; Communist Party of Brazil; Socialist People's Party; Social-Democratic Party; Party of National Mobilization; Christian Socialist Party. In addition, there are countless other minor national or provincial organizations.

Social Organizations: Workers are grouped together primarily in the Consolidated Union of Workers (CUT), the General Confederation of Workers (CGT) and the Labor Union Force. Many labor unions do not belong to any of these, preferring to remain independent. Landless Movement of Brazil (MST), an association of workers without land whose agenda is agrarian reform in rural areas, and land for the construction of housing in urban areas. National Union of Indigenous Peoples (UNI), an association of Brazil's different indigenous groups. Pastoral Commission of the Earth (CPT) and Indigenous Missionary Council (CIMI), pastoral groups of the Catholic Church involved in social action in defense. Defense Network of the Human Race (REDEH), an eco-feminist organization. 'Torture No More', state groups committed to the defense of human rights. There are serious pollution problems in the main cities.

THE STATE

Official Name: República Federativa do Brasil.
Administrative Divisions: 26 States, 1 Federal District.
Capital: Brasilia 1,949,000 people (1999).
Other cities: São Paulo 17,800,000 people; Rio de Janeiro 10,600,000; Belo Horizonte 4,310,000; Porto Alegre 3,576,500; Recife 3,377,600; Salvador 3,095,100 (2000).
Government: Fernando Henrique Cardoso, President since 1995, re-elected in 1998. Bicameral legislature: The National Congress has two chambers: the Chamber of Deputies has 513 members, and the Federal Senate has 81 members.
National Holiday: September 7, Independence Day (1822).
Armed Forces: 295,000 troops (1996). Other: 243,000 Public Security Forces.

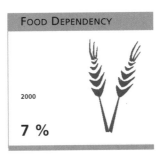
four years. In 1835, Diego Antonio Feijóo, a priest, was elected and fought against the break-up. The main revolt started in Rio Grande do Sul, called the *Guerra dos Farrapos* (War of the Ragged Ones) and was to last a decade. Feijóo was forced to resign in 1837. He was replaced by Pedro Araújo Lima. Impatient with the regency, Brazilians hoped to find in an Emperor the figurehead that would unite them. In 1840, Pedro de Alcántara - Pedro I's son - was declared of age and was enthroned with the name of Pedro II.

[19] The Empire lasted from 1822 to 1889. During this time Brazil consolidated its national unity and extended its borders over the areas settled by bandeirantes in the 17th and 18th centuries. This period of territorial expansion included the annexation of the Cisplatine Province (now Uruguay), the war of the Triple Alliance against Paraguay, in which Brazil annexed 90,000 square kilometers of Paraguayan territory; and, towards the end of the century, the annexation of Bolivia's Acre territory.

[20] Under the rule of Pedro II, the population grew from 4 to 14 million, but the economy continued to depend on large estates and the export of tropical agricultural products, mainly coffee. The abolition of slavery in 1888 accelerated the fall of the monarchy, but brought little change in the social and political conditions of blacks. As illiterate people, they were denied the right to vote and therefore political freedom.

[21] The gap between urban and rural areas widened in the last decades of the century. The urban middle class, the military and coffee growers pressed for the country's speedy modernization. For them, the monarchy was excessively linked to the old systems of production and to cattle-raising landowners. A republic was seen as a more convenient model for the modernization pursued by these three groups. In 1889, the army backed a conspiracy of modernists. Pedro II abdicated and was exiled in Europe.

[22] The consolidation and establishment of republican institutions was difficult. Prudente de Morais was elected first civilian President in 1894. The Federal

Republican Party had been founded in 1893, but the Navy rebelled both that year and the following. From 1893 to 1895, Brazil suffered a federalist rebellion in Rio Grande do Sul. From 1896 to 1897, the Canudos war, in which a religious community was wiped out by the republic's troops, took place in the northeastern provinces. This war was due to a clash between the interior - poor, illiterate and desperate - and the coast - literate, with a developed economy and seeking modernization.

[23] Uprisings, outbreaks of authoritarianism and fights among the regional oligarchies were frequent. Neither electoral justice nor the secret ballot was yet instituted and dissatisfaction with election results was widespread. Elections were rigged since the electoral rolls often included deceased voters.

[24] In the economic sphere, coffee remained the major export. Between 1914 and 1918, World War I brought an economic boom to Brazil, since the country was one of the main suppliers of commodities to the powers at war. Between 1920 and 1930, coffee prices tumbled as international competition reduced sales and, in 1929, due to that year's world slump, 29 million bags of coffee were left unsold.

[25] In 1930 a coup resulted in the appointment of Getulio Vargas as president. The Revolution of 1930 marked the end of the landowners' predominance, already weakened by the 1929 world economic lump that had destroyed the coffee industry.

[26] Getulio Vargas introduced the 'import substitution' model which gave priority to national industrial development, especially in iron and steel during World War II. Vargas held power from 1937 to 1945 as dictator of the New State and in 1950 was elected constitutional president. Nationalism and reformist defense of workers' rights, *trabalhismo* (laborism), the name of his movement, were the two outstanding features of his government.

[27] Fearing Vargas would attempt to retain power, the military forced him to resign in 1945. General Eurico Gaspar Dutra won the presidential election in December that year while Vargas was elected to a seat in the Senate. In reaction to the Vargas experience, the constitution promulgated in 1946 sought to prevent the rise of another all-powerful president. The three branches of government were separated, ensuring Congress of its independence and freedom in the election of its members. Also, this Constitution put in place restrictions to prevent abusive federal intervention in the internal affairs of the states.

[28] In 1953 the state oil monopoly was created and social security laws were passed. Vargas committed suicide in August 1954 leaving a letter accusing 'dark forces' (referring to imperialism and its local accomplices) of blocking his efforts to govern according to popular and national aspirations.

[29] Juscelino Kubitschek's administration (1956-61) promoted development and admitted transnationals to the Brazilian market, granting them exceptional privileges. Brasilia city was built during his term in office to mark a new era in the country's economic development. In 1960, the federal capital, previously at Rio de Janeiro, was transferred to the new city. Kubitschek's successor, Janio Quadros, initiated some changes in foreign policy but resigned in unclear circumstances barely seven months after taking office.

[30] In September 1961, Vice-President João Goulart, the Labor Party leader and Getulio Vargas' political heir, assumed the presidency. High-ranking military officers opposed his appointment but the new President was backed by a civilian/military movement which wanted a legal government, led by Leonel Brizola, governor of Rio Grande do Sul. A compromise parliamentary solution was adopted, with Tancredo Neves becoming Prime Minister. The presidential system was reinstated in January 1963 after a national plebiscite. Goulart then tried to introduce a series of 'basic reforms', including agrarian reform and legislation to regulate profit transfers abroad by foreign companies. A US-backed military coup deposed him on April 1 1964.

[31] The new government passed Institutional Act No. 1, which repealed the 1946 liberal constitution, allowing the revocation of parliamentary mandates and the suspension of political rights. A string of arrests all over the country forced major political leaders such as João Goulart, Leonel Brizola, Miguel Arraes and later even Juscelino Kubitschek into exile or to fight underground.

[32] The military junta appointed General Humberto de Alencar Castello Branco head of government for the remainder of the constitutional period, but his mandate was later extended until 1967. In the October 1965 state elections, opposition candidates won in Rio de Janeiro and Minas Gerais. The military retaliated with Institutional Act No. 2, stating that the President would henceforth be appointed by an electoral college and banning existing political parties. A two-party system was created guaranteeing a majority to

the pro-government National Renewal Alliance (ARENA), virtually excluding the opposition Party of the Brazilian Democratic Movement (PMDB) from power.

[33] In January 1967, a new Constitution came into effect and two months later General Arthur da Costa e Silva was appointed President. In December 1968, to confront growing electoral support for the popular opposition, Institutional Act No. 5 was passed, granting full autocratic powers to the military regime. In August 1969, Costa e Silva was replaced by a Military Junta that remained in power until the following October, when another army general, Emilio Garrastazú Médici, former head of the National Information Services (SNI), became President. The Médici administration was marked by extreme repression of both the legal and illegal opposition, while his economic ministers fed middle class consumerism. In 1974, General Ernesto Geisel was appointed President by the Junta. He put an end to the state oil monopoly, signed a controversial nuclear agreement with West Germany and granted further prerogatives to foreign investors. Its arms industry placed Brazil fifth among the world's main arms exporters.

[34] Under the Geisel administration there was a gradual relaxation of political controls, which allowed the democratic process to evolve. In 1974 and 1978, despite media censorship, the PMDB achieved significant victories at the polls. At the end of his mandate, Geisel delivered the reins of government to General João Baptista Figueiredo, also a former SNI head.

[35] Figueiredo came to power in March 1979, announcing that he intended to complete the softening of political restrictions. A month later, a strike by 180,000 metalworkers in Sao Paulo led by Luis Inácio 'Lula' da Silva was settled without violence, as a result of negotiations between the Labor Ministry and the Union. In November, the Brazilian Congress passed a bill granting a far broader amnesty to political opponents than the Executive had originally intended. As a result, political prisoners were released and exiles began to return.

[36] In the economic-financial arena, the after-effects of the monetary policies applied by successive military governments were felt during the Figueiredo administration. Foreign debt spiraled and in the early 1980s, Brazil became an early exporter rather than importer of capital in its efforts to find funds to pay off the interest on its $100 billion debt.

[37] In 1985, official statistics registered six million unemployed

and 13 million under-employed, out of a population of more than 130 million, of which over 50 per cent lived below the poverty line and outside the formal economy, in cities alone. In July 1985, Ministry of Labor officials stated that 'not even seven per cent growth per year for two consecutive decades would be enough to improve these peoples' living conditions'.

38   The opposition's electoral victory in 1983 reflected enormous popular discontent. The central government held only 12 states while the opposition won 10, including the economically decisive states of São Paulo, Rio de Janeiro and Minas Gerais which accounted for 59 per cent of the population and 75 per cent of the country's GDP.

39   Tancredo de Almeida Neves, governor of Minas Gerais, was the chief co-ordinator of the opposition front. A popular campaign for direct elections in 1984 failed, but the opposition won the Electoral College due to divisions within the ruling party. Tancredo Neves was elected President and José Sarney, who a few weeks earlier had been president of the Government party, became Vice President. Tancredo announced plans for a new social order: the New Republic.

40   In this context, agrarian reform, renegotiation of the foreign debt and economic growth were seen as the most effective means towards modernization and democratization. The day before his inauguration, Tancredo Neves was hospitalized and rushed into surgery. José Sarney was sworn in as interim President but stayed on after Tancredo died on April 21 1985. Sarney legalized the Communist Party and other left-wing organizations, some after 20 or even 40 years of illegal existence. Democratization began to take place with the approval of direct election for President of the Republic and mayors of state capitals. A national assembly was convened for January 1987 to draft a new constitution and illiterate people were granted the right to vote.

41   In 1986 Sarney declared a moratorium on the foreign debt and launched the Cruzado Plan to fight inflation. The plan produced impressive short-term results: a boom in consumption and economic growth. This startling prosperity coincided with the November 1987 parliamentary and state governmental elections which the PMDB won by a landslide. The new Congress faced the task of drafting a new constitution that would formally inaugurate the return to democratic government. It set Sarney's term at five years, after considerable pressure from the Executive to ignore the groups who wanted to honor

Tancredo's promise of reducing the term to four years.

42   But the Cruzado Plan could not be maintained without fighting financial speculation and halting pressure from the financial sector. Two days after the election, the price freeze came to an end and inflation leapt to a monthly rate in double figures. The planned agrarian reform was gradually reduced.

43   In the 1988 municipal elections, the left-wing and center-left PDT, PT, and PSDB parties began to make inroads on the PMDB's popularity.

44   In December 1988, landowners from the Acre region murdered Chico Mendes, leader of the *seringueiro* (rubber tappers) movement and the Amazonian indigenous peoples. They had organized an *empates* struggle (linking arms to stop trees being felled) to prevent the clearing of the forests, and proposed the creation of reserves, to guarantee their right to live and work in the forest without destroying it.

45   Direct presidential elections - the first in 29 years - were held in November and December 1989. Nearly 80 million people voted and the final round was fought between conservative candidate Fernando Collor de Mello and Workers' Party (PT) leader, Luiz Inacio 'Lula' da Silva. Collor de Mello, a young politician who had begun his career under the military regime, won the second round with 42.75 per cent to his opponent's 37.86 per cent of the vote.

46   On taking office, on March 16 1990, Collor de Mello announced the New Brazil Plan, an attempt to stem inflation by confiscating 80 per cent of the country's available financial assets.

47   Collor adopted the neo-liberal model of opening up the economy, with the privatization of state enterprises and the reduction of tariff barriers controlling the import of foreign products. However, he failed to control inflation, to hold off a recession and to reduce unemployment.

48   In this complex economic setting, the Government faced a critical social situation and the escalation of violence. In 1991, more than 350 street children were murdered in Rio de Janeiro. The parliamentary commission set up to investigate these murders estimated that over 5,000 children had been killed in this way over the past three years. The same commission reported that the persecution of homeless children - 7 million according to estimates of the Brazilian Center for Childhood and Adolescence - was carried out by paramilitary groups financed by shop owners.

49   The indigenous peoples remain under the constant threat of 'progress'. They have suffered

epidemics, the degradation or loss of natural resources, pollution and a systematic fall in their standard of living. They are being decimated by disease, high suicide rates, murders and other violence committed by miners and by the police.

50   The disappearance of indigenous cultures is linked to the accelerated destruction of the tropical forest in order to exploit its logging potential or to turn it into grassland or mining areas (especially for gold, whose processing pollutes the rivers with mercury). This predatory policy prevents the regeneration of natural resources and so they become depleted.

51   In September 1991, thousands of people belonging to the Landless Movement of Brazil (MST) staged a march in the state of Rio Grande do Sul, where there were 150,000 families of landless farmers alongside 9 million hectares of land not in production. The protesters demanded settlements to work and that the 4,700 million cruzeiros earmarked for agrarian reform should be spent. Up till then, only 800 million had actually been used.

52   Late in September 1991, a 400 per cent inflation rate and an increase in bank interest rates to almost 1,000 per cent a year, triggered wide-scale redundancies in the industrial sector which, in São Paulo alone, left more than one million jobless.

53   In May 1992, a Parliamentary Investigating Commission was set up to study government corruption which took the form of influence-peddling in exchange for deposits made to President Collor's personal account. Demonstrations against corruption and the discovery of evidence implicating other government figures in these schemes led all the political parties to vote for the President's impeachment.

54   In September, Congress voted to relieve Collor of his duties, so that he could be put on trial. Vice-President Itamar Franco became interim President. In December 1992, Collor was found guilty by the Senate of 'criminal responsibility' and sentenced. His presidential mandate was removed and his political rights suspended until the year 2000. Franco officially assumed the presidency until the end of that presidential term.

55   The new president tried to project an image of austerity and ethics onto the management of public affairs. After several changes in the Ministry of the Economy, Fernando Henrique Cardoso was appointed.

56   According to figures provided by the Pastoral Commission of the Earth, in 1992 there were 15,042 rural slaves - triple the number

recorded the previous year. According to data gathered by the Federal Bureau of Statistics, nearly four million people living in rural areas worked under conditions of virtual slavery. Collor's administration had zoned 20 million hectares as new land for indigenous peoples. This alleviated but did not fully solve the desperate situation of the indians.

57 The general outcry over these incidents led to some official response. In Rio de Janeiro, for the first time ever, a judge handed down prison sentences to the leaders of *jogo do bicho*, an illegal lottery linked to drug dealers and the police. In São Paulo, a police investigator received the maximum prison sentence (516 years) for causing the death of 18 prisoners who had died of asphyxiation in a police cell in 1992.

58 The Citizens' Action Against Hunger and for Life group, founded in 1993 by Herbert de Souza, organized tens of thousands of committees throughout the country to collect and distribute food and obtain more jobs. Two million people, mostly women, priests and trade unions joined this grassroots movement. By August 1994, over four million families had received food aid.

59 Towards the end of 1993, Economy Minister Cardoso presented the Plan Real, an economic stabilization project which ended index-linking and created a new currency, the Real, in July 1994. The success of this anti-inflationary policy rapidly made Cardoso the most popular candidate for the October elections. In the first round he beat the previous favorite Luis Ignacio 'Lula' da Silva, of the PT.

60 Cardoso began the privatization of state companies, including part of the operations of Petrobras and the telecommunications sector, but economic recession rose along with stabilization which led to the rise of unemployment, urban labor conflicts, crime and land seizures by poor peasants.

61 In September 1995, the President announced a government Multi-Year Plan with investments amounting to $153.39 billion, mainly focused on economic infrastructure. According to statistics, ten per cent of the population received 48 per cent of the income - four times the amount earned by the poor half of the country. World Bank figures showed that 43 per cent of fertile land belonged to 0.83 per cent of landowners in 1997. These figures placed Brazil among countries with extreme social inequality. In June, Parliament passed a constitutional

reform that permitted residential re-election.

62 In September, Cardoso issued a presidential decree which guaranteed indigenous peoples the exclusive use of 23 plots of land covering 8.4 million hectares, some 10 per cent of Brazilian territory. The marches and seizures by the MST received the implicit support of the Vatican's Pontifical Council of Justice and Peace in February 1998, in the document 'For better land distribution: the land reform challenge'.

63 In early 1999, former president Itamar Franco, then Governor of Minas Gerais, declared a moratorium on debt with the Federal Government. In the second week of January the Government freed the real against the dollar, resulting in a 10 per cent devaluation of the real. The president of the Central Bank resigned 'so that investors can regain confidence' but the real continued its slide with devaluation reaching 50 per cent in February. The real crisis hit consumption, industry working with imported resources and Brazil's relations with its Mercosur partners, but benefited the country's export sector.

64 To 'counter-commemorate' the fifth centennial of the Europeans' arrival in Brazil, 2,000 Indians met at a beach in northwest Bahia, carrying protest banners, on April 18 2000. The land had 5 million native inhabitants when the Portuguese arrived; now only 350,000 remained. Of the 1,000 groups that existed at the time of colonial contact, only around 200 are left (of which 50 have stayed beyond contact). The average life expectancy among Brazilian Indians is 42.6 years, compared to the country average of 67.

65 With the goal of reducing the discrepancy in land ownership, the Government suspended the property titles of some 1,900 landowners, since they were not able to justify the origin or legality of their property titles. Some 62 million hectares of land were involved - meaning that an area roughly the size of Central America was unlawfully held. The accumulation of lands with fake documents is an widescale and centuries-old practice in Brazil. In fact, it is estimated that a third of all landowners have built their estates with false papers. Nowadays, 90 per cent of all arable lands are in the hands of 20 per cent of the population, while 40 per cent of the poor population holds barely 1 per cent of land fit for agriculture.

66 The scandal caused by the embezzling of more than $90 million reserved for the construction of a court of justice, revealed in July 2000 and which involved government officials and a judge, weakened President Cardoso's position. In May

2001, he was forced to close two government development agencies, which were the focus of corruption allegations involving more than $1 billion. Federal police discovered that many of the projects promoted by these agencies, to develop the Amazon and poor areas in the northeast, were no more than façades to embezzle money. Both the Senate chairman, Jader Barbalho and his wife were investigated.

67 Also in May, José Nilson Pereira da Silva and Juliano Filipini Sabino were sentenced to 21 years in prison for the death of Edison Neris da Silva, a gay man who was beaten to death in early 2000 by a group of 18 skinheads in downtown São Paulo. The trial and sentence were considered landmark rulings by human rights and gay groups, since it was the first time individuals responsible for a sexual discrimination crime were sentenced in Brazil. According to Bahia's Grupo Gay, 299 homosexuals were murdered in Brazil between 1999 and 2000. Some 30 per cent of the victims were transvestites and 3 per cent were lesbians, while two thirds of the murders were committed in northeastern Brazil.

68 The following month, the Government, as part of its HIV/AIDS prevention program, hired a producer of pornographic films, Sexxy Videos, to show movies in which the actors wore condoms. Also, Sexxy Videos filmed a special AIDS prevention message to include at the beginning of its movies. This was the first compulsory measure affecting all adult films produced in the country. The AIDS program in Brazil includes lessons in school where teenagers are taught to how put on a condom using a clay model. According to international organization Médecins sans Frontières (MSF), AIDS-related deaths in Brazil fell more than 60 per cent since the introduction of such measures. The HIV and AIDS program in Brazil is renowned worldwide for its success: the State delivers free treatment to 90,000 patients at an individual cost of $5,000 dollars per year, less than half of what it would cost, for example, in the US.

69 Free access to the AIDS drugs-cocktail treatment is one of the main bases of the Brazilian program. A 1996 law states that, if foreign firms do not make their drugs locally, they will lose their patent in Brazil after a three-year period. Likewise, the law states that in situations of 'public interest', the local industry can break the patents. Currently, Brazil manufactures 8 out of the 12 drugs that are part of the drug-cocktail received freely by patients at state

clinics. Those opposing the program argued that poorer patients might not be able to follow the cocktail's complicated instructions. The Government solved the problem putting labels with suns, moons and drawings of food on each medication.

70 A study by the non-governmental organization Joint of Brazilian Women (AMB), published in July 2001, stated that African-Brazilian women die earlier than white men, in contrast with the world trend of longer life expectancy for women. Black women,who suffer both racial and gender discrimination, are the main victims of social inequity in Brazil. Their incomes are 55 per cent lower than those of white women, who also earn less than white men. Likewise, unemployment, illiteracy and domestic violence are worse among black women. Among the five million domestic employees, who generally do not enjoy the labor rights required by law, 56 per cent are black or *mestizas* (mixed parentage).

71 In Brazil, the average income per person among whites is 2.5 times that of black people. While 69 per cent of Brazil's poor people are black, only 45.3 per cent of the total population are African descendents. In 2001, unemployment amounted to 11 per cent among blacks and 7.5 per cent among whites. Only 2 per cent of blacks are university educated, compared to 11 per cent of whites.

72 With the title 'Towards a Globalization of the World Social Forum (WSF)', the second meeting of the WSF was held in Porto Alegre between January 31 and February 5 2002. The city had hosted the first of these global assemblies a year earlier. The WSF, which is held at the same time as the World Economic Forum in New York, was attended by 5,000 organizations to analyze, share ideas, debate and define parameters and alternatives in the anti-globalization struggle.

73 On March 30 some 500 activists from the Landless Movement (MST) invaded the estate of President Cardoso's children some 700 kilometers southeast of Brasilia. Their aim was to force the Government to free lands for redistribution in the region. The general coordinator of the MST, João Pedro Stédile, stressed the invasion was an 'extreme measure taken by landless workers due to a lack of solution to their demands'.The main demand, presented to the Government months before, was the delivery of lands to some 200 farmer families together with their property titles in the state of Minas Gerais. ∎

Brunei

Population: 341,000 (2002)
Land area: 5,270 SQ KM
Capital: Bandar Seri Begawan
Currency: Brunei dollar
Language: Malay

Brunei

Brunei was known to be trading with and paying tribute to China in the 6th century AD. Today's Sultanate is what remains of a 13th century Islamic empire that once covered most of the island of Borneo, from which it derives its name. Later it came under Hindu influence for a time through allegiance to the Majapahit kingdom in Java. When the ships of Ferdinand Magellan's expedition anchored off Brunei in 1521, the fifth sultan, the great Bolkiah, controlled practically the whole of Borneo, the Sulu Archipelago, and neighboring islands.

[2] Toward the end of the 16th century, Brunei was torn by internal strife. A gradual decline in power continued through the 19th century, notably in 1841. As payment for help in quelling a two-year long rebellion, the Sultan had to turn the province of Sarawak over to British adventurer James Brooke, who became a European *Rajah* over a Malayan state. In 1846 the British annexed the strategic island of Labuan, and in following years paved the way for the secession of the province of Sabah. In 1888, the British consolidated their position and established separate protectorates over Brunei, Sarawak and Sabah.

[3] Following World War II, despite Britain's efforts, the island began the decolonization process. An agreement signed with the incumbent Rajah Brooke in 1946 made Sarawak and Sabah into British colonies while Kalimantan (former Dutch Borneo) gained independence in 1954 as part of Indonesia.

[4] All that was left of the British

protectorate was the Sultanate of Brunei, reduced to a tiny enclave between two Malaysian provinces, scarcely 40 km from the border with Indonesia. In 1929, the transnational Shell discovered oil deposits in the area. In the following decades, drilling for oil and natural gas began, reaching production rates of 175,000 barrels a day.

[5] In 1962, Sultan Omar Ali Saiffudin accepted a proposal from Malaysian Premier Abdul Rahman to join the Federation of Malaysia, which at the time included Sabah, Sarawak, Singapore, and the provinces of the Malayan peninsula. The Brunei People's Party, (Rakyat) which held 16 seats in the 33-member Legislative Council, was not keen on the idea and opposed the move, proposing instead the creation of a unified state comprising Northern Borneo, Sarawak and Sabah, but excluding peninsular Malaya.

[6] A mass uprising broke out in December 1962, staged by the

Rakyat, backed by the Barisan Sosialis (Socialist Party) of Singapore, with support from the anticolonialist Sukarno regime in Indonesia. The rebels opposed integration to the Federation of Malaysia, demanding participation in administration and the end of the autocratic regime. The rebellion was rapidly stifled, the party outlawed and the leaders arrested or forced into exile.

[7] Finally, in spite of ethnic, historical, and cultural ties with Malaya, Sultan Omar decided to keep his sultanate out of the Federation. He was not satisfied with arrangements for power-sharing with the other Malayan rulers and least of all with Federation hopes of a share in his territory's oil resources.

[8] In 1976, with Malaysian prompting and UN support, an opportunity arose to renegotiate the anachronistic colonial statute, when the newly-elected Malaysian Prime Minister Datuk Hussain Onn promised to respect Brunei's independence. In 1977, Brunei finally

accepted independence, but postponed implementation until January 1 1984.

[9] Power was formally transferred on schedule but celebrations were postponed until February 23 1985, so that foreign guests could attend. One month later independence was formally proclaimed, and Hassanal Bokiah, son of Sultan Omar, who had abdicated in his favor in 1967, dissolved the Legislative Council and went on to govern by decree.

[10] Brunei embarked on independent existence in particularly favorable conditions for a Third World country. It had a relatively small population, a high per capita income, low unemployment, a generous social security system and considerable foreign exchange reserves. These reserves stood at $14 billion in 1984.

[11] The main sources of tension were the power struggle within the ruling family and the presence of foreigners in all the key positions of public office, the economy and the armed forces.

[12] Problems on the domestic front included poor basic education. In spite of advanced legislation for education, including a student transport allowance and free accommodation, the illiteracy rate kept climbing; it was estimated at 45 per cent in 1982, posing a serious obstacle to filling civil service posts with Brunei nationals.

[13] The Sultan was aware that the country depended on a non-renewable resource, and Brunei imported nearly 80 per cent of its food. Consequently, with a view to achieving self-sufficiency in food production, he attempted to diversify the economy and promote a new land-owning class. Only 10 per cent of the arable land was cultivated, and small farmers, especially rubber-tree growers, tended to emigrate to the city where they believed a higher standard of living awaited for them.

[14] Economically, Brunei depended upon the complex interplay of transnational interests. The Government's partnership in exploiting natural gas reserves with Brunei Shell Petroleum and Mitsubishi, a shipping contract with Royal Dutch Shell and oil field concessions to Woods Petroleum and Sunray Borneo, introduced powerful

WORKERS

1999/2000

LABOR FORCE AS % OF TOTAL

■ FEMALE: 36%   ■ MALE: 64%

new parties into the process of national decision-making.

[15] In March 1985, the Government announced the creation of an Energy Control Board to supervise the activities of the Brunei Shell Petroleum Company, a company funded equally by the Government and Shell.

[16] Membership of the Association of South East Asian Nations (ASEAN) and the UN, obtained in 1984, meant greater international support for the new nation.

[17] At this time 20 per cent of the population was living below the poverty line of $500 a month. Also, 90 per cent of all consumer goods - including basic foodstuffs - were still being imported, as the country produced little other than oil. The vast amount of imports explains the extremely high cost of living.

[18] In early 1987, it was reported that a request from US colonel Oliver North for 'non-lethal' aid to the Nicaraguan contras led the Sultan of Brunei to deposit a $10 million donation in a Swiss bank account.

[19] In early 1991, Sultan Hassanal Bolkiah freed 6 political prisoners who had been detained after the failed 1962 revolt. The release was ascribed to political pressure by the British Government. This same year Brunei signed a contract for almost $150 million with the United Kingdom in order to modernize its army.

[20] In mid-1992, Brunei joined the Non-Aligned Movement, together with Vietnam and India. The commemoration of the 25th anniversary of Hassanal Bolkiah's reign stressed the role of the monarchy in affirming Brunei's national identity. Brunei's sultan, the only absolute monarch in the Far East, is also one of the richest people in the world.

[21] In September 1992, Brunei together with other members of ASEAN - Indonesia, Singapore, Thailand, Malaysia and Philippines - signed an agreement to create the first integrated market in Asia in 2007. This project stipulated the creation of 'growth triangles' - association between some ASEAN members to deregulate trade in certain economic sectors, as a preparation for the overall liberalization planned for the year 2007.

[22] Thus, in March 1994, Brunei created - together with Philippines, Malaysia and Indonesia - a sub-regional market to intensify trade in tourism, fishing, and transport by sea and air.

[23] Negotiations with southeast Asian leaders were intensified following the regional stock market crisis in 1997, in order to co-ordinate policies to stabilize the regional economy and establish a recovery strategy. In the negotiations, the possibility was discussed of using local currencies instead of the US dollar for trade transactions within the area.

[24] In early 1998, uncontrollable fires in the Indonesian part of the island of Borneo caused dense smoke clouds over Brunei. These affected daily life in the Sultanate and spread to several other nations of the region, affecting tourism.

[25] In August of this year, the Sultan named his eldest son, Al-Muhtadee Billah his successor - next in line in a 600 year-old Islamic dynasty that is the oldest in the region. The announcement was made in the midst of the worst economic crisis since independence. Construction and the export sectors began a slow recovery during 1999.

[26] The Government announced plans to train a large part of the workforce in a period of five years, with the aim of diversifying the economy and developing other sectors, such as tourism.

[27] In 2000, the authorities indicted the Sultan's younger brother, Prince Jefri, for embezzling public funds during his terms as minister of Finance and president of the State Investment Agency, where he served until 1998. Jefri had been removed and forced to declare bankruptcy of his private company, to which he had transferred large sums of government funds during his 10 years in office. A year after the trial, an auction was held in which some 10,000 of the prince's belongings were sold.

[28] During the summit of the Association of Southeast Asian Nations (ASEAN) in Brunei in 2001, the leaders agreed to cooperate in the US-led war against international terrorism. They also postponed the launch date for the Asian Free Trade Area (AFTA), to be set for sometime between 2006 and 2010. ∎

PROFILE

ENVIRONMENT
Brunei comprises two tracts of land located on the northwestern coast of Borneo, in the Indonesian Archipelago. It has a tropical, rainy climate slightly tempered by the sea. Rubber is tapped in the dense forests. There are major petroleum deposits along the coast. The country is one of the world's main exporters of liquid gas.

SOCIETY
Peoples: Malay 67 per cent; Chinese 15 per cent; indigenous 6.0%; Indian and other 11.5 per cent.
Religions: Islam (official), Buddhism and Christianity.
Languages: Behasa Malay (official), Chinese, English, local languages.
Political Parties: The only authorized party is Brunei Solidarity National Party.

THE STATE
Official Name: Negara Brunei Darussalam.
Administrative divisions: 4 districts.
Capital: Bandar Seri Begawan 85,000 people (1999).
Other Cities: Kuala Belait 26,600 people; Seria 23,000; Tutong 16,300 (2000). Government: Hassanal Bolkiah Muizzaddin Waddaulah, Sultan and Prime Minister since 1967. Legislative Council is made up of 20 members and has only an advisory role.
National Holiday: January 1, Independence Day (1984); July 15, the Sultan's birthday.
Armed Forces: 4,900 (1995).

Bulgaria

Balgarija

Population: 7,790,000 (2002)
Land area: 110,550 SQ KM
Capital: Sofia (Sofija)
Currency: Leva
Language: Bulgarian

Evidence of human habitation in the Bulgarian area dates from the Middle Paleolithic period (100,000 to 40,000 BC). Agricultural communities appeared in the Neolithic Period, and Thracian peoples inhabited the lands in the Bronze Age. The Thracians were eventually expelled or absorbed by Greek, Persian, and Roman colonies, but traces of their culture remain in their monuments devoted to horse worship and in a mime-acting tradition that still survives in southwestern Bulgaria. In Roman times Bulgaria was divided between the provinces of Moesia and Thrace and was crossed by the main land route from the west to the Middle East.

[2] In the 6th and 7th centuries AD the region was occupied by the Slav people who spread across the area between the Danube and the Aegean Sea. Some of the old Thraco-Illyrian population were expelled, and the rest were assimilated by the invaders. The Slavs worked the land in small, organized communities.

[3] The Bulgarians were among the non-European groups who followed Attila, leader of the Huns. They were fierce warriors who lived by warfare and plunder. They first appeared in the region towards the end of the 5th century AD when they settled temporarily on the steppes north of the Black Sea and northeast of the Danube.

[4] Some peoples disappeared and others were enslaved by the Turks. Those led by Kubrat remained in this region until the mid-7th century when the Kazars bore down on them, forcing them into crossing the Danube. They reached as far as Moesia, at that time a province of the Byzantine Empire. Emperor Constantine IV formally recognized the State of Bulgaria in the year 681.

[5] Constant foreign invasions led the new state to consolidate its power in the center and southwest. Bulgarian leaders adopted the Slav language and culture. Prince Boris was initially baptized Roman Catholic, but in 870 he turned to the Orthodox Church.

[6] While the Patriarch of Byzantium recognized the independence of the Bulgarian Church, Rome refused to appoint a national patriarch. This support

helped to consolidate the Kingdom's power. Under Simeon (893-927), the Bulgarian State extended its domain as far as the Adriatic, subduing the Serbs, and becoming the most powerful kingdom of Eastern Europe.

[7] Bulgaria's power declined after Simeon's death. Internal disputes among the nobility, the opposition of the peasants and renewed attacks from abroad led to its downfall. In 1014, Bulgaria lost all its territory to the Byzantine Empire, which kept control for more than 150 years. After a large uprising in 1185, the northern part of Bulgaria recovered its independence.

[8] During the reign of Ivan Asen II (1218-41) Bulgaria regained power and territory, including Albania, Epirus, Macedonia and Thracia. However, none of Ivan's successors managed to impose a central authority over these diverse areas where feudalism was the norm. By 1393 the whole of Bulgaria had fallen under Turkish rule.

[9] In the 17th and 18th centuries, after the wars with Austria and the unsuccessful siege of Vienna, the Ottoman Empire began to decline, though it still retained much of its territory. The former Bulgarian State was twice invaded by Russia, in 1810 and 1828.

[10] Throughout the invasion period the Bulgarians maintained their cultural identity; keeping their language, music and folklore alive. Under Turkish domination, the Greek Orthodox Church assumed religious leadership, suppressing the independent patriarch. In this way Bulgarian monks were among

the precursors of the national liberation movement.

[11] The Bulgarian Church fought for 40 years to recover its independence. In 1870, the Sultan gave permission for the Church to create an exarchat (sub-Patriarchy) with 15 dioceses. The first exarch (deputy patriarch) and his successors were declared schismic and were excommunicated by the Greek patriarch; this further strengthened Bulgarian nationalism.

[12] From 1876 onwards, a series of revolts was cruelly put down. Some Bulgarian volunteers joined the ranks of the Serbian and Russian armies, who went to war against the Empire. One of Moscow's conditions for the Treaty of St Stephen (1878) was the creation of a Bulgarian state. The European powers feared the creation of a Russian satellite in the Balkans so they blocked the motion.

[13] In the 1878 Berlin Congress, the 'autonomous province' of Rumelia was created in the south, and the State of Bulgaria in the north. Rumelia was nominally under the Sultan's control, and Macedonia was to continue as part of the Ottoman Empire.

[14] The assembly approved a liberal Constitution, establishing a constitutional monarchy. Prince Alexander of Battenberg, grandson of Alexander II of Russia, was elected and assumed the Bulgarian throne in July 1878, swearing to uphold the Constitution. He suspended it two years later.

[15] The Prince set up a dictatorship, headed by Russian general LN Sobolev and other conservatives. The Russian Emperor's death modified

Alexander's behavior, making him more attuned to Bulgarian issues. In 1885, he supported the liberal rebellion in Rumelia, the governor there was replaced and union with Bulgaria was proclaimed.

[16] The treaties of Bucharest and Top-Khane, signed in 1886, recognized Prince Alexander as the ruler of Rumelia and Bulgaria. However, he was subsequently taken to Russia against his will and forced to abdicate. Looking for someone who would be acceptable to Russia, as well as the rest of Europe, the Bulgarians finally appointed Ferdinand of Saxe-Coburg-Gotha as his replacement.

[17] Although initially distrusted, Ferdinand was able to gain the support of Vienna, London, Rome and Russia. He then concentrated on the reunification of the Bulgarians whose territory had been divided under the Treaty of Berlin. Prince Ferdinand proclaimed Bulgaria's independence in 1908, thereby breaking its nominal dependence upon Turkey.

[18] In 1912, Bulgaria signed secret military agreements with Greece and Serbia. In October that year, Montenegro, accompanied by its Balkan allies, declared war on Istanbul. In May, Turkey ceded its European dominions, north of a line between Enos, in the Aegean Sea, and Midia on the Black Sea.

[19] The allies did not agree with the distribution; Bulgaria confronted Greece and Serbia over the issue and Romania joined Serbia as its ally. The Second Balkan War quickly ended in Bulgarian defeat. In Bucharest, in August 1913, Macedonia was divided between Greece and Serbia, and Romania gained an area of northern Bulgaria, rich in natural resources.

[20] In 1913, the Bulgarian Government abandoned its traditionally pro-Russian stance, seeking closer ties with Germany. When World War I broke out the Bulgarian people and the army disapproved of the official policy, even though Serbia was beaten. Ferdinand surrendered to the Allies in 1918 and abdicated in favor of his son Boris.

[21] Having lost much territory, Bulgaria was disarmed and forced to pay extensive war damages. With the restoration of the 1878 Constitution, elections were held in 1920. The anti-war reaction gave the Agrarian Party

a wide margin. Working on a Soviet model, the Government started radical agrarian reforms. The Government was not pro-Soviet, however, and local Communists were persecuted.

[22] Bulgaria joined the League of Nations and followed a conciliatory line of diplomacy for some time. However, its territorial losses and the pressure exerted by expatriots abroad soon led to new tensions with its neighbors. Aleksandur Stamboliyski, the leader of the Agrarian Party and head of the Government, was ousted and assassinated by a conspiracy of Macedonians and opposition figures in 1923.

[23] Aleksandur Tsankov assumed control of the Government, heading a multiparty alliance which excluded the Liberal, Communist and Agrarian parties. Uprisings and armed activity by the opposition led to hundreds of executions and assassinations. The Government declared martial law and reinforced the army in order to avoid outright rebellion.

[24] In 1926, Tsankov resigned in favor of Andrei Liapchev, leader of the Democratic Party, to make way for more liberal policies. The Government approved a partial amnesty, and permitted a reorganization of the Agrarian Party. In 1932, Liapchev's cabinet was made up of members of the Democratic, Liberal and Agrarian parties, known as the National Bloc.

[25] In 1934, fearing the effects of the worldwide economic depression and taking a cue from his neighbors, King Boris III supported the action of the conservative group, Zveno, which deposed Liapchev and set up a dictatorship. All political parties were proscribed, there was censorship of the press, the universities were closed and an ultra-right youth movement was established.

[26] Tension with Turkey eased and, in 1937, a peace and friendship treaty was signed with Yugoslavia. The following year, Bulgaria signed a non-aggression pact with the Balkan alliance, in exchange for the

rearmament of the Bulgarian army. While the King was once again seeking rapprochement with Germany, the Bulgarian dream of re-establishing its former borders was gathering strength.

[27] In 1940, Germany made Romania return the parts of Bulgaria which it had won in the second Balkan War. Bulgaria signed the Anti-Komintern pact and German troops set up bases aimed at Greece and Yugoslavia on Bulgarian soil. In exchange, Bulgarian troops were allowed to occupy the part of Thrace belonging to Greece, and the part of Macedonia belonging to Yugoslavia, and part of Serbia.

[28] When Bulgaria refused to declare war on the Soviet Union, King Boris was assassinated, and a new pro-German Government was formed. Growing anti-Nazi resistance, led by the Communists, contributed to the formation of the Patriotic Front in 1942. The Republicans, left-wing Agrarians, Democrats and independents all subsequently joined.

[29] In May 1944, paralyzed by the civil war, the pro-German Boshilov resigned, and was replaced by Bagrianov. While Soviet troops advanced toward the Danube, Bagrianov sought an agreement with the Allies. In August, Bulgaria proclaimed its neutrality, and ordered the disarmament of the German troops on its soil.

[30] Ignoring the Sofia Declaration, the Red Army entered Bulgarian territory. The resistance fanned local insurrection. On September 8, General Kyril Stanchev's troops took the capital, and the Patriotic Front formed a Government headed by the Republican Kimon Georgiev.

[31] Sofia signed a treaty with the allies in October 1944. Bulgarian troops, under Soviet command, collaborated in the defeat of the German forces in Hungary, Yugoslavia and Austria. During 1945, war trials led to the imprisonment of 6,870 people and the execution of 2,680 others.

[32] In March 1945, Communist leader Giorgi Dimitrov returned to Bulgaria after several years at the Komintern headquarters, in Moscow.

[33] In a referendum held in September 1946, 92 per cent of the electorate approved of the creation of the Republic of Bulgaria. In the October election, the Patriotic Front won 364 seats with 70.8 per cent of the vote, 277 seats went to the Communist Party (BCP). In November, Dimitrov became Prime Minister.

[34] In 1947, Britain and the US recognized the government. The National Assembly ratified the peace treaty with the Allies, the new Constitution went into effect and, at the end of the year, the Soviet troops withdrew from the country. After

PROFILE

ENVIRONMENT

Located in the Balkans, Bulgaria comprises four different natural regions. The fertile Danubian plains in the north are wheat and corn-producing areas. South of these lie the wooded Balkan Mountains, where cereals and potatoes are cultivated, cattle and sheep are raised, and the country's major mineral resources - iron ore, zinc and copper, are found. Cattle are also raised on the Rhodope Mountains in southern Bulgaria. South of the Balkan mountains there is a region of grassland, crossed by the Maritza River, where tobacco, cotton, rice, flowers and grapes are cultivated. Heavy metals, nitrates, petroleum derivatives and detergents have damaged the lower and mid-tributaries of the most important rivers. These flow into the Black Sea, which is highly polluted. About one quarter of the country's woodland is affected by air pollution, due to the emissions of metallurgical industries.

SOCIETY

People: The majority are Bulgars of Slav origin (85 per cent). There are also Turks (9.4) and Roma (gypsies, 3.6), plus immigrant communities of Macedonians, Armenians, Tatar, Gagauz, Circassians, Russians. **Religions:** Orthodox Christian Church of Bulgaria, 83 per cent, Muslim 13, Catholic 1.5, Jewish 0.8 and Protestants, Gregorian Armenians. **Languages:** Bulgarian (official and predominant); also spoken: Romani, Turkish, Macedonian, Gagauz and Armenian. **Political Parties:** There are many small parties, hence the formation of coalitions like the Union of Democratic Forces (UDF) (7 parties); Democratic Left, including the Bulgarian Socialist Party, the Ecologist Party, and the Rural Farmers' Union; National Movement Simeon the Second; National Salvation Union; Movement for Liberty and Human Rights (of the Turkish minority); the Euro-Left Coalition; the Bulgarian Businesses Bloc; the Communist Party; and the Union of the Monarchy. Ethnic parties are banned. **Social Organizations:** The Confederation of Independent Unions of Bulgaria was founded in 1990 and is the biggest (1.6 million members). Since January 1990 the Confederation of Labor Podkrepa has been legal, becoming a new union axis, headed by Constantin Trenchev. Importance of the agrarian movement led by the National Agrarian Union of Bulgaria and the national 'Nikola Petkov' union. There are many regional, ethnic and national groups with varied agendas, one of the most active is the Internal Macedonian Revolutionary Organization.

THE STATE

Official Name: Narodna Republika Balgarija. **Capital:** Sofia (Sofija) 1,192,000 people (1999). **Other cities:** Plovdiv 344,500 people; Varna 293,600; Burgas 192,900 (2000). **Government:** Georgi Parvanov, President since January 2002; Simeon Saxe-Cobourg, Prime Minister since July 2001. National Assembly has 240 members. **National Holiday:** March 3, National Liberation Day (1878). **Armed Forces:** 102,000. **Other:** Border Guards (Ministry of Interior): 12,000; Security Police: 4,000; Railway and Construction Troops: 18,000.

joining the BCP opposition, some of the Patriotic Fronts former leaders were arrested and sentenced to death for conspiracy.

35 Under the leadership of the BCP, the Bulgarian State adopted the Soviet socio-economic model. A process of accelerated economic growth was set in motion, without taking into account the lack of raw materials or the technical preparation of the labor force. In the countryside, collective farming was enforced.

36 Dimitrov resigned from the administration in March 1949, and died a few months later. Vulko Chervenkov succeeded him, first as leader of the government, and then as party premier. In March 1954, Todor Zhivkov was named First Secretary of the BCP, becoming Prime Minister in 1962. Bulgaria was the USSR's closest ally among the Warsaw Pact countries, and in 1968 Bulgarian troops accompanied Soviet troops in the invasion of Czechoslovakia.

37 In the 1980s Bulgaria was accused of imposing a policy of forced assimilation, on the country's 10 per cent Turkish minority. In 1986, Sofia refuted Amnesty International's accusation that more than 250 Turks had been detained or imprisoned for refusing to accept new identity cards.

38 In 1988, Bulgaria and Turkey signed a protocol governing bilateral economic relations. The dialogue was interrupted in the following year, when it was revealed that the Bulgarian militia had used violence to put down a protest by 30,000 Turks, who had been demonstrating against the Government's policy of assimilation.

39 In June 1989, more than 80,000 Turks were expelled from Bulgaria. Turkey promised to accommodate them all, but towards the end of August, after receiving 310,000 Bulgarian Turks, it closed its borders. 30,000 of these refugees subsequently returned to Bulgaria.

40 The largest protest meeting since the War was held in November in front of the National Assembly. A group known as 'Eco-glasnost' demonstrated against a proposed nuclear power plant on an island in the Danube, citing the fact that it lay in an earthquake-zone. They also protested against the construction of a reservoir in one of the country's largest nature reserves.

41 In December, some 6,000 members of the Pomak community - a Muslim minority group with an estimated 300,000 members - demanded religious and cultural freedom.

42 The Central Committee of the BCP replaced Zhivkov as Secretary General, a post he had held for 35 years. He was succeeded by Petur Mladenov, who had been Prime Minister since 1971 and was considered to be a proponent of liberalization of the regime. In December, Mladenov also replaced Zhivkov as president of the State Council.

43 The National Assembly lifted the ban on anti-government demonstrations, and granted amnesty to political prisoners. There was an immediate increase in the number of political demonstrations demanding reforms and elections.

44 In March 1990, the Union of Democratic Forces (UDF), made up of 16 opposition parties, and the BCP agreed to the election of a Constitutional Assembly. The July election was won by the Bulgarian Socialist Party, BSP (formerly BCP). In October, the BSP was forced to enter a new coalition, led by Yelio Yelev, a dissident during the 1970s and leader of the Social Democratic wing of the UDF.

45 The new coalition government adopted a program of economic reforms in consultation with the IMF and the World Bank. They reached an agreement with the labor unions for a 200-day 'social peace' until the reforms could go into effect.

46 In July 1991, the new Constitution was approved, establishing a parliamentary system, allowing personal property, and freedom of expression. After the October election, Parliament named Filip Dimitrov as Prime Minister. Virtually alienated from the Social Democrats and the 'Greens' - co-founders of the UDF - Dimitrov was chosen because of the support he had from the right-wing of the opposition coalition and the Movement for Freedom and Human Rights (of the Turkish minority).

47 In the January 1992 election, in which 75 per cent of registered voters participated, Yelev was elected President of the Republic. As leader of the political transition period and author of the rapprochement toward the West, he received 54.4 per cent of the vote in the second round of voting, defeating the BSP candidate, Velko Valkanov.

48 In June Bulgaria joined the Council of Europe. During that year, former Communist leader Todor Zhivkov, three former Prime Ministers and another former member of government prior to 1991, were arrested charged with corruption in the exercise of their duties. The economic situation led the Movement for Rights and Freedoms (MRF) to withdraw its support of Dimitrov, which caused the downfall of his cabinet.

49 Dimitrov was replaced by Liuben Berov from the MRF. The new Prime Minister stated he was willing to restore the lands confiscated by the Communists to the Turkish minority. Transition from a centralized planned economy to a free market economy continued to be difficult and caused paradoxical situations. For example, when agricultural cooperatives were dismantled, two million cattle were slaughtered as they could not be managed by the new private farms.

50 When the former Soviet Union stopped buying two-thirds of Bulgaria's exports, foreign trade was significantly reduced. UN sanctions imposed on neighboring former Yugoslavia caused losses of $1.5 million to Bulgaria. In 1993, Berov went on with the transition to a market economy at a rate considered excessively slow by the IMF, which caused a certain amount of tension between Sofia and the international organization.

51 However, Berov held on to power until mid 1994, thanks to the support of the MDL, the BSP and the New Union for Democracy, a breakaway group from the UDF. Members of this opposition coalition frequently accused the Prime Minister of wanting to 'restore socialism'. Disagreements between Berov and the MDL in matters related to human rights and the social condition of Bulgarians of Turkish background, further weakened the Government.

52 In June 1994, Berov was able to pass the privatization law and in September he presented his resignation. After three failed attempts to form a new Government, President Yelev dissolved Parliament and called new elections. The BSP won an absolute majority in the National Assembly in the December elections and the anti-Communist UDF came second.

53 In January 1995, socialist leader Zhan Videnov formed a new Government which included members from the BSP, the Bulgarian Agrarian National Union and the Eco-glasnost Political Club. His cabinet was the first in the history of post-Communist Bulgaria with an absolute majority at the National Assembly. Differences between the new Government and Yelev were frequent. In July, the President criticized the Government because he thought market reforms were not being implemented swiftly enough, suggesting the BSP was 'genetically connected' to organized crime.

54 Petar Stoyanov's Union of Democratic Forces won the first round of the Presidential elections in November 1996 and one month later beat the Socialist candidate, Ivan Marazov in the final round with 59.7 per cent of the vote. Hounded by his political rivals, Prime Minister Zhan Videnov resigned in December.

The conservative groups that supported Stoyanov called for the resignation of the Cabinet, bolstered by the parliamentary majority of Socialists and their allies. A series of large demonstrations in the capital and other cities pressed for new legislative elections. Stoyanov became President in January 1997, after vowing to bring forward the 1998 elections.

55 Legislative elections were won by the Union of Democratic Forces (UDF) in April 1997. The new government implemented a purely neo-liberal economic policy, following IMF guidelines, planning the privatization of state companies considered to be loss-making and the elimination of 60,000 jobs in the public sector. Services were liberalized with the aim of reducing inflation. In May 1998 agricultural subsidies were abolished and the State telecommunications company, several banks and the Bulgarian airline were privatized. The Government declared its objective would be fiscal balance. A few weeks later the IMF agreed an $800 million loan.

56 In November 1999 the EU announced it would seek solutions to replace the energy from the nuclear plant at Kozloduy, which produces 45 per cent of the nation's electricity. According to the agreement made, the Soviet-built reactors will close between 2003 and 2006.

57 Former king Simeon II - crowned at the age of six and reigning for three years from 1943 - launched the Simeon II National Movement in 2001. Simeon Saxe-Cobourg won the parliamentary elections and became Prime Minister in July, thus becoming the first former monarch of Eastern Europe to return to power. His campaign agenda did not include the restoration of the monarchy, but promised to end poverty, unemployment and other ills that plagued Bulgaria after the fall of Communism. However, 100 days later thousands thronged the streets of the capital protesting the promises had not been fulfilled.

58 Socialist Party leader, Georgi Parvanov, was elected president the same month, and the poor turnout - the worst since the fall of communism - was widely interpreted as a sign of public discontent.

59 Bulgaria, like Romania, hoped to be invited to join NATO at a summit to be held in November 2002. On a visit to Tirana, in April that year, Simeon Saxe-Cobourg discussed alliance to the pact with his counterpart Ion Iliescu, agreeing to a joint effort on non-competitive grounds in order to reach the goal. ∎

Burkina Faso

Population: 12,207,000 (2002)
Land area: 273,600 SQ KM
Capital: Ouagadougou
Currency: CFA franc
Language: French

Burkina Faso

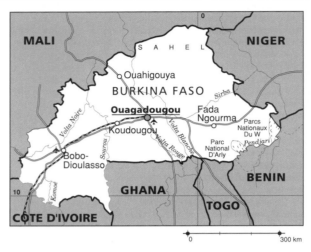

During the 11th century, indigenous peoples, ancestors of the Lobi and Bobo, settled in the western region of the Mouhoun River (or Volta Noire/Black Volta). Though they never developed a centralized political system, the populations that migrated from the Dagomba region (present-day Ghana) founded the Mossi dynasty in the north. The Mossi kings imposed their military aristocracy over the region of the Volta Rivers (Volta Noire, Volta Blanche and Volta Rouge - black, white and red).

[2] The Mossi and Mande resisted attempts at annexation by the Mali and Songhai empires (see Mali and Guinea) and remained independent throughout the Fulah invasions of the 18th and 19th centuries. In a series of military incursions between 1896 and 1904, the French laid waste the central plains, burning houses, and slaughtering people and animals. The ensuing reign of terror finally sparked off an insurrection in 1916, which met with such violent repression that millions were forced to emigrate, mostly to Ghana.

[3] By then the country had been incorporated into the colony of Haute Sénégal-Niger. It was reconstituted as the separate colony of Upper Volta in 1947.

[4] Upper Volta had no directly productive role in the international division of labor. Its task was to produce people: forced labor on plantations in Côte d'Ivoire, or cannon fodder for French armies at war in Europe or the colonies.

[5] Finally, in line with French neo-colonial strategy, the country was declared independent in 1960. That year's elections were won by the Voltanese Democratic Union (UDV),

a party backed by landowners and private enterprise. Maurice Yameogo was elected President and was re-elected in 1965 amidst intense trade-union agitation, which occurred in response to economic crisis, administrative chaos and austerity measures. Yameogo was overthrown a year later in a military coup led by army chief-of-staff, Colonel Sangoulé Lamizana.

[6] The 1970s witnessed a succession of elections, military coups, and more or less fraudulent re-elections orchestrated by Colonel Lamizana. Starvation was widespread, herds were dwindling and an estimated quarter of the population had emigrated to neighboring states. In 1980 Lamizana was ousted in a coup by another colonel, Saye Zerbo, and there were further coups in November 1982, May 1983 and on August 4 1983.

[7] The last of these changes was much more than just the latest game of musical chairs among the

military élite. The new leader, a young army captain called Thomas Sankara, saw it as a revolution. He launched into a program of radical change which aimed to chart an entirely new course for poor African countries, and this brought him to international notice. He was popular among soldiers and the rural poor as he brought in an anti-corruption campaign and organized brigades to assist victims of the prolonged drought and deforestation.

[8] In the first year of Sankara's government Upper Volta was renamed Burkina Faso - 'land of the incorruptible'; the national anthem was sung in African languages; land reform was carried out and popular courts were set up to dispense justice. Sankara set a target of two meals and 10 liters of water per person per day.

[9] The implementation of such measures presented a considerable challenge in a country where 82 per cent of adults were illiterate and absolute poverty was the norm. There were practically no bank accounts held within the country. Kerosene was the energy source for lighting. Cutting wood, the main fuel, contributed some 50,000 to 100,000 hectares to the total annual deforestation. Encroachment by the

Sahel arid area further aggravated the lack of firewood.

[10] On December 15 1987, Sankara was overthrown and executed along with 12 of his supporters in a coup led by his second-in-command, Blaise Compaoré, who pledged to continue the Popular Front and 'rectify' the regime internally.

[11] Contrasting with the image of Sankara, a man of austere habits who shunned personal property, Compaoré built a government palace and purchased a presidential plane. His economic strategy included encouragement of private enterprise and foreign capital, and consideration of denationalization, deregulation and agreements with international lending institutions.

[12] The 4th Republic adopted a new constitution, which was approved by referendum on June 2 1991 (90 per cent voting in favor, with 50 per cent of registered voters participating). The new constitution, which was put into effect by de facto President Compaoré, re-established a multiparty system and the division of powers, while reducing presidential powers. The office of Prime Minister was created, and general elections were to be held every seven years.

[13] In the May 1992 elections, the official party won 78 of the 107 National Assembly seats. The main opposition force, concentrated in the National Convention of Progressive Patriots-Social Democrats (CNPP-PSD) won 13 seats. Blaise Compaoré, who ran unopposed, became the first president of the 4th Republic, with 21.6 per cent of the vote.

[14] Prime Minister Yussuf Ouedraogo promised to prioritize agriculture and provide incentives for the creation of small and medium sized enterprises in order to create new jobs. International pressure made Ouedraogo pledge to reduce the country's bureaucracy; Burkina Faso had 36,000 public employees, most of them on pensions.

[15] In December 1992 and March 1993 there were two general strikes against the implementation of the structural- adjustment plan recommended by the IMF. Devaluation of the CFA franc in January 1994 led to Ouedraogo's resignation and his replacement by Marc-Christian Kabore in March that year. In July, in spite of protests from

WORKERS

1999/2000

LABOR FORCE
AS % OF TOTAL

■ FEMALE: 47%　■ MALE: 53%

LAND USE

DEFORESTATION: 0.7% annual (1990/95)

1993

■ FOREST & WOODLAND: 50.4%
■ ARABLE: 13%
■ OTHER: 36.6 %

PUBLIC EXPENDITURE

Military expenditure (as % GNI):	**1.6 %** (1999)
Defense expenditure (% of central government expenditure)	**5.9 %** (1999)

the opposition, Parliament passed a law that allowed the government to privatize 19 national companies.

[16] In February 1995, the opposition boycotted municipal elections since it considered these were being organized by a non-independent electoral commission. The ruling Organization for the People's Democracy-Workers' Movement won in 26 of the country's largest 33 cities. At a social level, conditions remained tense since indirect consequences from the 1994 devaluation led the cost of living to rise 30 per cent in the first half of 1995.

[17] The Government continued its policy of economic liberalization and officially took Burkina Faso into the World Trade Organization in June 1995. A project to restructure the recently privatized railways, resulting in 500 lay-offs, caused a new strike that led the country once again toward a tense situation, typical of the early 1990s.

[18] The economy grew 5 per cent in 1996. In June, the IMF approved a new $57 million loan to support the implementation of a structural-adjustment program in the subsequent three years. In 1997, a drought decimated food production and left the country in a critical situation. The deficit in food production, which added up to 32 per cent of the GDP and employed 90 per cent of the population, was estimated at 156,000 tonnes for the 1997-1998 period. In December 1997, Ouagadogou had to call on the international community for 67,000 tonnes of grain to tackle the crisis.

[19] Marijuana plantations grew swiftly in Burkina Faso, as well as in other countries of the region. It replaced some 'traditional' cash crops whose price had fallen. The devaluation of the CFA franc caused a reduction in the import of medicines, which further complicated the fight against the two major diseases that ravage the population: malaria and Aids. In 1998, there was only one doctor for every 25,000 people in Burkina Faso.

[20] The 1998 elections were boycotted by the opposition granting the president-candidate victory. A series of protests led to the resignation of Ouedraogo's cabinet, but the president confirmed most of the ministers in their posts in January 1999. Yussuf Ouedraogo, another former prime minister was appointed to the cabinet.

[21] The murder of journalist Norbert Zongo brought the government under suspicion, as an independent investigation pointed the finger at the upper echelons of power. Zongo had made important revelations about another murder, where the President's brother was the main suspect. In order to get round the crisis, Compaoré called on the Green Party leader and former presidential candidate to join the government, but demonstrations calling for justice for Zongo erupted again in December. The Government rejected the accusations and made no effort to prosecute the six presidential guards accused of the murder.

[22] In February 2000, the Commission for National Reconciliation requested the rehabilitation of former president Thomas Sankara, assassinated in 1987 in Compaoré's coup. The Commission had been formed by President Compaoré himself as a way of easing the tension caused by a lack of results in the Zongo case.

[23] A report by the UN stated in March 2000 that Compaoré acted as middleman in arms smuggling from the Soviet bloc to rebel groups such as UNITA in Angola and the RUF in Sierra Leone in violation of an international embargo on arms to these groups. His services were paid for with diamonds, whose trade for this purpose is also forbidden (see box 'Diamonds of war'). In December that year, the Government finally accepted the presence of a United Nations' supervisory committee to monitor the import of weapons.

[24] A meningitis epidemic killed more than 1,500 people in 2001. Meanwhile, it is estimated that more than 10 per cent of the population is HIV-positive, making Burkina Faso one of the countries most affected by the pandemic.

[25] There were legislative elections in 2002. These had been initially scheduled for April 28 2002, but were postponed to May 5 because of low voter registration. Some 3,540 candidates took part, competing for 111 Parliamentary seats and reflecting the largest number of political groups in the country's electoral history. This time, the opposition also took part, having boycotted the Presidential elections in 1998 and the local elections in 2000. The ruling CDP reduced its number of seats from 101 to 60, while the Alliance for Democracy and Federation (ADF) took

PROFILE

ENVIRONMENT

A landlocked country, Burkina Faso is one of the most densely populated areas of the African *Sahel* (the semi-arid southern rim of the Sahara). The Mossi plateau slopes gently southwards and is traversed by the valleys of the three Volta Rivers (Black Volta, White Volta and Red Volta). Though more fertile, these lands are plagued with tsetse flies. Like the rest of the Sahel region, Burkina suffers from desertification, caused by serious droughts and the intensive production of export crops such as peanuts and cotton.

SOCIETY

Peoples: Over half of the population are Mossi. Pouhi herders and the Tamajek clans with their vassals, the Bellah, amount to around 20 per cent. Djula peasants and traders are indigenous minorities. The language of these three population groups is the linguistic bridge among the various regions. Senufo and Bobo-Fing cultures inhabit the western plains where the savanna merges into the forest. In the south, the predominant Lebi, Bobo-Ule, Gurunsi and Bissa cultures extend into several states. The savanna to the east holds the great Gurmantehé civilization, while the Sampo, Rurumba and Marko cultures live in the desert regions to the north and northeast. **Religions:** 50 per cent are Muslims; traditional African religions, 40 per cent; Christian (mostly Catholic), 10 per cent. **Languages:** French (official); 71 languages from the Sudanic family, spoken by 90 per cent of the population (most common are Mossi, Bobo, Bissa and Gurma). **Political Parties:** Congress for Democracy and Progress (CDP-left-wing); Alliance for Democracy and Federation (ADF); Party for Democracy and Progress (PDP- social-democratic); National Convention of Progressive Patriots-Social-democratic Party (CNPP-PSD); African Democratic Rally (RDA); Party for African Independence (PIA) and Union of Greens for the Development of Burkina (UVDB). Social Forces Front, which continues former president Sankara's project. **Social organizations:** Voltanese Free Unions Organization, Confederation of Voltanese Unions.

THE STATE

Official Name: République de Burkina Faso. **Administrative division:** 45 provinces, 300 departments and 7,200 villages. **Capital:** Ouagadougou 1,062,000 people (1999). **Other cities:** Bobo-Dioulasso 474,300 people; Koudougou 124,400; Ouahigouya 74,000 (2000). Government: Republican parliamentary system, with a powerful head of state. Blaise Compaoré, President and Head of State, in power since October 1987 after a coup d'état; elected in 1991 and re-elected in 1998. Paramanga Ernest Yonli, Prime Minister and Head of Government since November 2000. Bicameral Parliament: the National Assembly, with 111 members, and the House of Representatives, with 178 members. **National Holiday:** August 5, Independence (1960). **Armed Forces:** 5,800 (1995). **Other:** Gendarmerie: 1,500; Security Company: 250; People's Militia: 45,000.

15, and the Party for Democracy and Progress (PDP) 10. On this occasion, and for the first time, a simple ballot was used, in reply to a request for cleaner elections made by the opposition for several years. ∎

Burundi

Population: 6,688,000 (2002)
Land area: 25,680 SQ KM
Capital: Bujumbura
Currency: Burundi franc
Language: Rundi, Kirundi and French

Burundi

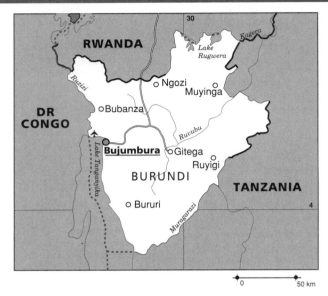

Burundi is one of the poorest countries in the world and one of the most densely populated in Africa. For five centuries it has been torn by ethnic and economic struggles involving the Hutu majority and the Tutsi (or Watusi). At least five major massacres affecting one or the other community have occurred since the 15th century.

² The Hutu, a Bantu group, were communal farmers. Five hundred years ago they were overrun by the Tutsi, who migrated south from Uganda and Ethiopia in search of fertile grazing land for their cattle. The Tutsis had more sophisticated weapons and were thus able to subdue the Hutus and enslave their people. Tutsi rulers held considerable power during the 17th and 18th centuries, but rivalry between the various local groups weakened the central power structure in the 19th century. This paved the way for German colonization around 1890. The Europeans upheld Tutsi domination and in turn forced the traditional ruler (Mwami) to accept German control. In 1899, Burundi and Rwanda (see Rwanda) were merged into a single colony, Rwanda-Urundi, which became famous for its ivory exports controled by a German trade monopoly.

³ Following the defeat of Germany in World War I, Belgium took over the colony and separated Burundi from Rwanda again only to merge the former with Zaire (now DR Congo). The Belgian system of indirect rule assigned Tutsi élites a privileged role and gave rise to nationalist movements in the 1950s. This process bred the Union for National Progress (UPRONA) led by Louis Rwagasore, elected Prime Minister in 1960. The Belgians feared that Rwagasore might become a Burundian Lumumba (see DR Congo) and he was therefore assassinated before independence was granted. Burundi gained independence on July 1 1962, governed by a puppet Tutsi ruler under Belgian control.

⁴ Violence marked the first four years of autonomous rule under five different Prime Ministers. Instability predominated until November 1966, when the Prime Minister Captain Michael Micombero, staged a coup and proclaimed the Republic of Burundi. The new president carried

out a massive purge of all Hutu government officials. In 1971, 350,000 Hutus were killed through government repression and an additional 70,000 went into exile.

⁵ In 1976, Lt-Col Jean Baptiste Bagaza took power promising to end ethnic persecution and set up a reformist government. Bagaza broadened UPRONA, put a land reform program into practice, and rehabilitated labor unions, all in blatant defiance of the Tutsi élite and their foreign capitalist allies. In foreign policy, the new government drew closer to Tanzania, and China sent aid to develop Burundi's mineral resources.

⁶ In 1979, the first post-independence congress of UPRONA was held and a new constitution drafted, effective in 1981. The new constitution prevented the exploitation of the Hutu majority by the Tutsi minority, prompted the modernization of the political structure, and gave women equal rights. Reforms stirred up strong feelings between the Government and the conservative Catholic hierarchy, leading to confiscation of properties and deportation of 63 missionaries.

⁷ Elections held in 1982, 20 years after independence, upheld President Bagaza's policies and brought about a swift stabilization of the young nation's political situation.

⁸ Despite Burundi's established political independence, the country

faced serious problems due mostly to economic dependence and its geographical location. Being a landlocked country raised the price of both imports and exports. Population density is high and unevenly distributed geographically; 70 per cent live in the north where overuse of the land has caused massive soil erosion. Wood is the main source of domestic fuel and unfortunately the high demand outstrips the forest production of the country. Ninety per cent of agricultural products were consumed by the domestic market. Burundi's economic hopes lay in the rich nickel deposits and in its hydroelectric potential. Belgian and US companies were developing the Musongati mines that also have large cobalt and uranium deposits.

⁹ In September 1987, while attending a summit meeting of French-speaking countries in Quebec, Bagaza was overthrown by army major Pierre Buyoya in a bloodless coup.

¹⁰ In August 1988, strife between Hutus and Tutsis broke out in Dtega and Marangana, in the north of the country. After this, 20,000 or more Hutus were massacred by the military. Over 60,000 Hutus sought refuge in Rwanda. The Government responded by appointing a Hutu Prime Minister, Adrien Sibomana, with a new cabinet in which half the ministers were Hutus.

¹¹ In 1989, most refugees returned and there was reconciliation between

the military government and the Catholic Church, who had regained their property. A structural adjustment program was initiated which included the privatization of public enterprises and the creation of a 'watchdog' tribunal to combat corruption.

¹² Burundi depended largely on the export of its main crop, coffee, and affected by its fluctuating prices. Poverty and high population density added to environmental degradation. The high rate of deforestation is partly due to the transformation of forests into farmland for landless peasants.

¹³ In 1992, Buyoya enacted a multiparty constitution and called elections in 1993. Buyoya, leading UPRONA - with a majority of Tutsis - was defeated by Melchior Ndadaye, from the opposing Front for Democracy in Burundi (FRODEBU) composed mainly of Hutus.

¹⁴ On October 24 1993, three months after he was elected, Ndadaye was assassinated during an attempted coup. Prime Minister Sylvie Kinigi, who sought asylum in the French embassy, managed to keep the situation under control. The leaders of the rebellion were either arrested or fled to Zaire (now DR Congo). Cyprien Ntaryamira - a Hutu like Ndadaye - was appointed President by Parliament.

¹⁵ Ndadaye's assassination led to one of the worst massacres in Burundi's history. Supporters of the former president attacked UPRONA members - Tutsis or Hutus - causing the death of tens of thousands of people and the flight of some 700,000. The so-called 'extremist armed militias' - hostile to living alongside the other ethnic groups - were consolidated by this time, as were the 'Undefeated' Tutsis and the Intagohekas ('those who never sleep') Hutus. Violence spread.

¹⁶ On April 6 1994, Ntaryamira died along with Rwandan president Juvenal Habyarimana when their plane was shot down over Kigali, capital of Rwanda. Another Hutu, Sylvestre Ntibantunganya, replaced the assassinated president. UPRONA joined the government in a coalition. Violence intensified, especially between militias in favor of Hutu power and the army, controlled by Tutsi officers.

[17] In February 1995, UPRONA left the government to force Prime Minister Anatole Kanyenkiko to resign. His resignation paved the way for nomination of Tutsi Antoine Nduwayo and UPRONA's return to the coalition government alongside FRODEBU.

[18] Fearing that the Burundian conflict would extend to neighboring countries, the UN and the Organization for African Unity decided to intervene. Pierre Buyoya, claiming the need to prevent an intervention by inter-African forces in the country, staged a successful coup in July 1996 and became the new president of Burundi. After this action, Ethiopia, Kenya, Rwanda, Tanzania, Uganda and Zaire (now DR Congo) imposed sanctions on Bujumbura. In mid-September, Hutu rebels reported the killing by the army of 10,000 civilians after the coup. A similar number was killed the following year, although Amnesty International considered it

was very difficult to distinguish between government and rebel responsibility in these massacres.

[19] In late 1997, special UN monitor Sergio Pinheiro confirmed that international sanctions had had devastating effects, significantly degrading the life conditions of poor Burundians and questioning the embargo's usefulness. Meanwhile, peace negotiations promoted by mediator Julius Nyerere, former Tanzanian president, had reached a stalemate. Relations between Burundi and Tanzania were significantly impaired and both accused each other of trespassing across their respective frontiers. In September, Buyoya accused Tanzania of protecting more than 200,000 Hutu rebels and of intending to 'annex' Burundi. In October, Bujumbura reported the attacks of Tanzanian forces in the southern towns of Kubonga and Mugina. In February 1998, the number of victims of the

civil war was estimated at more than 250,000.

[20] On July 16 1998, the National Assembly became the National Assembly in Transition (NAT) with the incorporation of 40 new representatives of the two political parties and the public. Until this point FRODEBU had 65 seats and UPRONA 16.

[21] Several initiatives were taken to restart peace negotiations throughout 1999. Despite some reticence on the part of Burundi's political leaders, on 1 December former South African president Nelson Mandela was chosen as mediator and Tanzania as host for the negotiations. The armed confrontations and massacres continued between Hutus and the (militarily superior) Tutsi minority, at war since 1994. Various leaders of eastern and southeastern Africa demanded the Government close down refugee camps within the conflict area. The nation's authorities stated these hundreds of thousands of people had been transferred to the camps for their own security. Meanwhile, the rebels stated the government camps prevented the civilian population from offering them help.

[22] In January 2000, US President Bill Clinton offered his personal support to Nelson Mandela in his role as mediator. On March 28, speaking from Arusha, Mandela's representative said peace talks for Burundi were 'progressing' and that the peace objectives had been 'written in a single text' for the first time since the 'peace negotiation' issue had been raised in mid-1998.

[23] In December 2001, Buyoya received loans of $764 million for reconstruction from the international financial bodies. In March 2002, some 45,000 Burundian refugees living in regroupment camps (likened by some to concentration camps, for their harsh conditions) in Tanzania agreed a plan with the UN for their return to their country.

[24] In January 2002, Tanzania protested over the bombardment of several Tanzanian villages by the Burundian army. In an official letter it demanded Burundi keep its conflict within its own borders.

[25] Buyoya visited Uganda and admitted to the press that a ceasefire had not yet been agreed, meaning that the Arusha accords could not be implemented. He called on President Museveni for support in achieving this objective. The UN Security Council called for an immediate end to hostilities, urging the armed groups to initiate negotiations 'in good faith with no delay'. In March 2002 the National Liberation Front (PALIPEHUTU-FNL

PROFILE

ENVIRONMENT

Most of the land is made up of flat plateaus and relatively low hills covered with natural pastures. Located in the African zone of the Great Lakes (Tanganyika, Victoria), the Ruvubu River valley stretches through the country from north to south. Tropical forests are found in the low, western regions. Most inhabitants engage in subsistence agriculture (corn, cassava, sorghum, beans). Coffee is the main export. Internal communications are hampered by natural barriers and the nearest sea outlet is 1,400 km beyond the border, a fact which makes foreign trade difficult. The forests are fundamental in maintaining climatic balance, and deforestation is one of the country's worst problems, aggravated by the growing incidence of farming on unsuitable lands.

SOCIETY

Peoples: Most Burundians (86 per cent) belong to the Hutu ethnic group, an agricultural people of Bantu origin. They were traditionally dominated by the Tutsi or Watusi (13 per cent), pastoralists of Hamitic descent; there are various subgroups including Hima. There is a small minority (1 per cent) of Twa pygmies.
Religions: 67 per cent Christian; 32 per cent follow traditional African religions and 1 per cent are Muslim.
Languages: Rundi, Kirundi and French, official, with Swahili the business language.
Political Parties: Front for Democracy in Burundi (FRODEBU); Union for National Progress (UPRONA), led by president Pierre Buyuya. Also there are approximately 17 parties that do not take part in government but which signed the peace document in Arusha. Rebel groups include the National Council for Defense of Democracy (CNDD), with its armed branch (FDD); and the National Liberation Forces (PALIPEHUTU-FNL - Parti pour la libération du peuple hutu-Forces nationales de libération).
Social Organizations: As a result of civil war, organizations are restructuring but there are many foreign non-governmental organizations (NGOs) and local NGOs like the Association for the Economic Promotion of Women.

THE STATE

Official Name: Republika y'u Burundi.
Administrative divisions: 16 Provinces.
Capital: Bujumbura 321,000 people (1999).
Other cities: Gitega 43,300 people; Muhinga 41,800 (2000).
Government: Pierre Buyoya, President since the July 1996 coup; in 1998 the Prime Minister was replaced by two vice-presidents, one Hutu, one Tutsi. The National Assembly has 81 members, elected for a five-year period, which proportionally represents the two parties. FRODEBU has 65 seats and UPRONA 16. On July 16, 1998, the Assembly was reformed into a Transitional National Assembly with the admission of forty new legislators, representing the political parties and the public.
National Holiday: July 1, Independence (1962). **Armed Forces:** 12,600.

Parti pour la libération du peuple hutu-Forces nationales de libération), which had earlier not taken part in peace negotiations, stated it was disposed to participate in dialogue under the auspices of mediators. ∎

Cambodia

Population:	13,776,000 (2002)
Land area:	176,520 SQ KM
Capital:	Phnom Penh (Phnum Pénh)
Currency:	Riel
Language:	Khmer

Kâmpuchéa

The land of Cambodia takes its name from a *rishi* (sage), for the first Cambodian kings proclaimed themselves descendants from the great sage Cambu Svayambhuva. The first kingdom of Cambodia was known in Chinese texts under the name of Funan and was founded by the Mon and Khmer peoples who migrated from the North in the first century AD. During these first centuries, there was strong Indian influence. By that time, Indian and Chinese pilgrims used to stop in today's Cambodian coasts to exchange silk and metals for spices and aromatic wood and gold.

[2] During the 2nd and 3rd century Khmer rulers used to offer presents to Chinese emperors. Chinese sources reveal the scope of Indian influence by the example of the sage Kaundimnya, who married princess Soma, of Nagi origin (that is, semi-divine) and transformed the Khmer institutions along Indian lines. One of the modifications was probably the introduction of large-scale irrigation, which allowed the production of up to three rice harvests a year. Also the worship of the Indian god Shiva, who was considered a guardian ancestor and the spirit of land by the Khmer.

[3] According to Chinese writings, the Funan created a centralized state machinery, headed by an absolute ruler. This ruler ran agricultural labor and used farming surpluses to maintain his lifestyle and that of a caste of priests, and also to build fortresses, palaces and temples.

[4] The first Sanskrit writings date from the 6th century and the first ones found in the Khmer language are from the 7th century. The developments between the decline of Funan and the foundation, three centuries later, of a new centralized state in the Cambodian north-eastern region (called Chenla in Chinese texts of that period) have not been fully documented as yet. Chinese sources

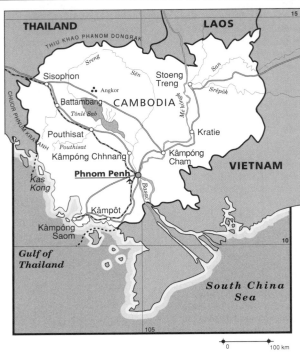

cite the existence of at least two Cambodian Kingdoms, which - under the sovereignty of the Java Kingdom - requested recognition from China. In the meantime, Sanskrit and Khmer sources cite the existence, during the 7th, 8th and 9th century, of multiple Kingdoms that paid homage and fealty to the Java Kingdom.

[5] In 790 AD, a Cambodian prince, born and raised in the Javanese court of the Sailendra dynasty, proclaimed himself descendant of the Funan rulers. He declared the Khmer territory independent from Java and was crowned Prince Jayavarman II. During the following decade, Jayavarman extended his

power north, controlling vassal states. In 802, he was named again, this time Chakravartin (a Sanskrit term meaning 'world ruler'). Jayavarman was the first 'national' king of Cambodia.

[6] In the year of 887 Indravarman I usurped the throne that belonged to his cousin Jayavarman III. During his reign, a large dam surrounding the capital city Roluos was built. This was the first of a vast system of dams, channels and irrigation canals that turned these lands productive and which would later allow the Khmer to maintain a densely populated and centralized State in the area, which otherwise would have resulted infertile. Two years later, Yasovarman I became king of Khmer and commenced the construction of Angkor city (then called Yasodharapura), which turned into the capital of the Khmer Empire. In 1002, Suryavarman I usurped the throne and extended the Kingdom of Angkor to parts of today's territories of Thailand and Laos. In 1080, after Angkor had been conquered by the Kingdom of Champa, a Khmer ruler of a northern province proclaimed himself king under the name of Javavarman VI, ruling the Kingdom from his home province rather than from Angkor.

[7] In 1177 Angkor was conquered once again by Champa forces. Jayavarman XII became king in 1181 and conquered Vijaya, capital of Champa (in present-day Vietnam). Under his rule, the Khmer Kingdom reached its height, virtually including the whole of today's Thailand and Laos and even reaching Myanmar/Burma, Malaysia and Vietnam. Jayavarman XII converted from Hinduism to Buddhism, which became the national religion.

[8] In 1200, work began on building the new capital city of Angkor Thom. This undertaking depleted the royal coffers and the Kingdom experienced economic problems during the subsequent decades. The decline of Angkor coincided with the rise of the Thai Kingdom to the west and the Vietnamese one to the east. Turned into a small buffer state between both, the Khmer Kingdom alternately depended on the power of the Thais or the Vietnamese.

[9] During more than 400 years, the Kingdom was alternately conquered by the Thai and Vietnamese forces. This changed in 1864, when Cambodian King Norodom accepted the status of French 'protectorate' for his country, in the hope that the French would prevent further annexations. The French were not able to prevent the Siamese (Thais) from temporarily annexing some west Cambodian areas, including the city of Battambang. However, by recognizing the French authority, King Norodom managed to prevent the country from being divided and distributed between Vietnamese and Siam (Thailand). During the previous centuries, Vietnam had taken control of large tracts of Cambodia. The Mekong Delta and the area around Ho Chi Minh City (formerly Saigon) had been inhabited by Cambodians until the 18th century.

[10] In 1884, with the consent of King Norodom, Cambodia became a French colony. France's political influence increased and, together with Vietnam and Laos, Cambodia became a part of the Indo-Chinese Union. During the following decades, the colonial empire installed a European administrative system in Cambodia and developed the country's infrastructure.

WORKERS

2000

LABOR FORCE AS % OF TOTAL

■ FEMALE: 52%   ■ MALE: 48%

LAND USE

DEFORESTATION: 1.6% annual (1990/95)

1993

■ FOREST & WOODLAND: 64.1%
■ ARABLE: 13%
■ OTHER: 22.9%

1985/99

2000

Per 100,000 live births

440

68%

However the economic development - or exploitation - of the French Indo-Chinese Union did not reach the levels attained by Burma or India under British rule.

[11] After France was invaded by Germany during World War II, Japanese forces occupied Indochina in September 1940. What this actually meant was that the Japanese were able to use the military facilities in exchange for allowing France to maintain administrative control. As a result Cambodia suffered less damage during the War than the South Pacific islands, which were fiercely disputed by opposing forces.

[12] In 1941, French authorities appointed the 18-year-old Prince Norodom Sihanouk as King of Cambodia, in the hope of controlling the politics of an inexperienced youngster. However,

when the Japanese invaders withdrew, on March 12 1945, Norodom Sihanouk declared independence. But the French occupied Indochina again. While Vietnam began an anti-colonial war, in Cambodia the King managed to gain greater autonomy from France.

[13] In 1947, a new constitution kept King Sihanouk on the throne. However his power was limited by parliament. In 1949, negotiations with France resulted in Cambodian independence 'within the French union', with Paris retaining control over military and foreign affairs. In 1953, the Vietnamese offensive forced French troops to withdraw from Cambodia, leaving the country fully independent. In 1955, Sihanouk abdicated in favor of his father, changing his name to Prince Sihanouk so that he could participate in political life. From

1960 onwards, Sihanouk became head of state.

[14] During the first years of US aggression against Vietnam, the Cambodian Government sought to maintain political and territorial neutrality. In 1965 however, following air raids by US-controlled South Vietnamese forces against North Vietnamese troop sanctuaries, Cambodia broke off relations with the US and moved closer towards the Chinese/Russian camp. Prince Sihanouk lost the 1966 elections to right-winger General Lon Nol who was later toppled during left-wing demonstrations. Sihanouk resumed power. In 1968 the US began launching regular air raids on the so-called Ho Chi Minh trail through Cambodian territory, allegedly supplying the Viet Cong from North Vietnam.

[15] While taking diplomatic action abroad to protect his country's sovereignty, Sihanouk was ousted in a coup and replaced again by Lon Nol. During his five-year rule, Lon Nol received $1.6 billion in aid from Washington. During that period, US forces intervened in Cambodia to bomb the Communist Khmer Rouge guerrillas and Vietnamese sanctuaries. In four years of bombing about 50,000 were killed. Sihanouk went into exile in China.

[16] From exile in Beijing, and supported by the Khmer Rouge, Sihanouk organized the National United Front of Kâmpuchéa (NUFK) using the name of the country in Khmer language. By 1972, the NUFK was in control of 85 per cent of Cambodian territory, and its forces closed in on the capital, Phnom Penh (Phnum Pénh).

[17] In 1975, the Khmer Rouge seized power. Lon Nol fled and the Kingdom became the Democratic Republic of Kâmpuchéa with Sihanouk as head of government. In 1976, while a new Constitution was being approved, the People's Congress confirmed Khieu Sampham as head of state with Pol Pot as Prime Minister. However, on his return from exile, Sihanouk was forced to resign and kept under house arrest, while Pol Pot rose to the fore as the regime's new leading force.

[18] Under Pol Pot, the country was completely sealed off from the outside world. Borders were closed and diplomats were not allowed to leave their embassies. Determined to build an unprecedented social system, Pol Pot set 1975 as Year Zero of a new era. He eliminated money and transferred large numbers of the urban population to the countryside, enforcing the return to an agricultural lifestyle. Mass purges and executions, hunger and illness, left at least a million people dead.

[19] The Pol Pot regime strengthened

ties with China, broke off diplomatic relations with Hanoi, refused to recognize borders 'established by colonialism' and sent Khmer Rouge troops to invade Vietnamese territory in late 1977. The disputed borders had been established in 1973 by agreement between Vietnam and Sihanouk, as historical records could provide no exact basis for establishing boundaries.

[20] The UN recognized the Khmer Rouge Government in 1978. The same year, Vietnam invaded to try and oust Pol Pot. In December 1978, when this border war was on the verge of being won by Vietnam, the United Front for the Salvation of Kâmpuchéa was created under the presidency of General Heng Samrin. On January 11 1979, the Vietnamese forces and those of the United Front entered Phnom Penh and proclaimed the People's Republic of Kâmpuchéa (PRK). A People's Revolutionary Council was established, and the Government began the enormous task of rebuilding a hungry and devastated nation.

[21] Heng Samrin's government defined its policy as being one of 'independence, non-alignment and democracy directed toward socialism'. Pol Pot was tried in absentia for war crimes, and his forces turned to guerrilla warfare. With the support of China and the US, the Khmer Rouge managed to maintain UN recognition as the country's legitimate government. In 1982, Sihanouk and the Khmer Serei, led by Son Sann, joined former head of state Khieu Samphan's opposition government-in-exile.

[22] One of the main goals of Heng Samrin's government was to reactivate the industrial, agricultural and transportation sectors. The Soviet Union, and other socialist countries gave aid which was focused on the reconstruction of power sources and the formation of a very basic industrial infrastructure.

[23] In March and April 1981 municipal and legislative elections were held, with many candidates for each post. The Non-Aligned Movement summit meeting at the time in New Delhi did not support any of the contending groups. Faced with a wide set of electoral options, Cambodia's seat in the movement was left vacant.

[24] In July 1985, the Vietnamese announced that their 150,000 troops would gradually be withdrawn from Cambodia over the following five years.

[25] Difficulties stemming from the war affected the Phnom Penh Government, and it was only officially recognized by some 30 countries. Still, it managed to bring about a steady increase in the production of rice, cattle, pigs and poultry.

PROFILE

ENVIRONMENT

The territory is mainly a plain surrounded by mountains, like the Cardamour Mountains in the southwest. In the north, the Dangrek range rises abruptly from the plain. The central basin of the country, occupied by the Tonle Sap (Great Lake) depression, is the point of confluence into the Mekong, one of the largest rivers in Asia. The country has a sub-tropical climate with monsoon rains. The population is concentrated in the central basin where rice, the mainstay of the diet and principal export crop, is grown. The country also exports rubber. The mineral reserves of phosphate, iron ore and limestone are as yet mainly unexploited. The main environmental problem is logging by foreign companies which if unchecked will destroy the remaining forests in under a decade. The country lost approximately 75 per cent of its fauna as a result of the war (1965-1975). Continued transportation of toxic waste from Taiwan has sparked uprisings in central populations affected by the health and environmental consequences.

SOCIETY

Peoples: Mostly Khmers. The Khmers inhabit an area that extends beyond the present boundaries of Cambodia. There are Vietnamese (5 per cent), Chinese (1 per cent) and Laotian minorities.
Religions: In 1986 Buddhism - the religion of the majority - became the country's official religion. There is an Islamic minority (Cham).
Languages: Khmer, official and predominant.
Political Parties: Cambodian People's Party United National Front for an Independent, Neutral, Peaceful and Cooperative Cambodia (Funcinpec); Sam Rainsy Party (centrist); Liberal Democratic Buddhist Party; National Liberation Movement of Cambodia.

THE STATE

Official Name: Preah Réaché'anachâkr Kâmpuchéa
Administrative divisions: 22 provinces.
Capital: Phnom Penh (Phnum Pénh) 938,000 people (1999).
Other cities: Battambang 183,600; Kompong Cham 53,800 (2000).
Government: Parliamentary monarchy. King Norodom Sihanouk since September 1993. Prime Minister, Hun Sen since November 1998. Bicameral Legislative: 122-member National Assembly; 61-member Senate.
National Holiday: November 9, Independence Day (1953).
Armed Forces: 88,500.

[26] In 1986 the Government made overtures to Sihanouk within the context of a general agreement, offering him the position of head of state in a government from which the Khmer Rouge would be excluded. From the end of 1987 to mid-1989, Hun Sen, who had become Prime Minister, met with Sihanouk on six occasions. The main disagreement each time was whether the Khmer Rouge would be admitted to a new provisional government or not.

[27] During the course of 1989, a curfew in effect since 1979 was lifted and private ownership of some 'non-strategic' enterprises was permitted. In addition, collective farms passed into the hands of peasant families, with the assurance that the land could henceforth be passed from generation to generation, and transportation services were privatized. On June 1 1989, to complete the diplomatic offensive and improve its image, the country changed its name to the State of Cambodia. After a meeting between Hun Sen and the new Thai Prime Minister, Chatichai Choonhavan, the possibilities of regional agreement and economic relations between the countries improved.

[28] The International Conference for Peace in Cambodia held in Paris in July 1989 ended in failure as the three factions of the armed opposition could not come to any agreement. The two main points of disagreement were UN monitoring of the Vietnamese withdrawal and Khmer Rouge participation in government. Even without this agreement, Vietnamese troops withdrew completely in September, as planned, followed by an advance in the position of rebel forces.

[29] In April 1990, after a military offensive by Heng Samrin and Hun Sen's government soldiers, the opposition forces retreated to the Thai border. With this development the Thai premier Chatichai Choonhavan sponsored a new meeting between Sihanouk and Hun Sen. In Bangkok, both leaders agreed to the installation of a supernational agency which would symbolize the sovereignty and national unity of Cambodia. An 'adequate' UN presence was also agreed to by both parties.

[30] In July 1990, the US announced they would recognize the State of Cambodia and would initiate negotiations with Vietnam over a peace settlement.

[31] In October 1991, a peace treaty was signed. The Supreme National Council was created, with representatives of the Phnom Penh government and part of the opposition, it was chaired by Sihanouk and was to govern the country until elections in 1993. In 1992, the UN sent a peacekeeping force consisting of

20,000 troops to enforce the cease-fire and organize the elections. To many observers' horror, the Khmer Rouge was included in the UN operation as a legitimate 'warring faction'. This enabled them to gain respectability over time, rehabilitating their reputation.

[32] In the constituent elections of May 1993, boycotted by the Khmer Rouge, the United National Front for an Independent, Neutral, Peaceful and Cooperative Cambodia (Funcinpec) party supporters led by Sihanouk's son Norodom Ranariddh won 58 seats. The former Cambodian People's Communist Party gained 51, the Liberal Democratic Party 10, and the National Liberation Movement of Cambodia, one. In the new government, Ranariddh and Hun Sen shared the post of Prime Minister.

[33] In September 1993, a new Constitution was enacted. It turned the National Assembly into a Parliament and established a parliamentary monarchy. Sihanouk was appointed King, 'independent' of all political parties. But he continued to advocate a 'national reconciliation' government, with the inclusion of the Khmer Rouge.

[34] In 1996, the Khmer Rouge began to show signs of weakness. The rumors of Pol Pot's death in June were construed as an indication of the existence of significant divisions within the guerrilla movement. Many defections - like Ieng Sary's (a leader of the armed group) in August - suggested that the government policy aim of splitting the Khmer Rouge was proving successful.

[35] Accused of treason and of planning a civil war alongside the Khmer Rouge, Prince Ranariddh was ousted in July 1997 by Cambodian army officials loyal to the second Prime Minister Hun Sen. From China, King Sihanouk approved Hun Sen's proposal to appoint foreign minister Ung Huot, from Funcinpec, to the position of first Prime Minister, in place of Ranariddh. In March, 1998 the monarch pardoned his son - who had been sentenced to a 30-year prison term - a decision regarded as an attempt to delay the political chaos which followed Ranariddh's expulsion and as a means to secure international financial aid which had been interrupted since the July 1997 coup.

[36] In spite of international efforts to rebuild Cambodian society, the lack of punishment of officials involved in serious human rights violations remained unchanged. Amnesty International reported the killing of hundreds of opposition members and the persistence of an incompetent, weak and corrupt judicial system.

[37] A month after the death of Pol Pot in Thailand in April 1998, Ranariddh returned to Cambodia to compete in the election, which was

won by Hun Sen. Both Ranariddh's Funcinpec and the other major opposition party, Sam Rainsy, denounced irregularities in the elections, including the disappearance of ballot papers, pressure on voters, errors in the count and an insufficient number of observers. According to the 600 international observers, however, there were no defects in the count.

[38] In May 1999, when the effects of the 1997 South East Asian economic crisis were at their worst, Cambodia joined ASEAN as its tenth member. Opposition leader Sam Rainsy was fearful that that ASEAN would destroy Cambodia's fragile industry, which found it hard to compete, leaving the country reduced to exporting raw materials.

[39] Spien Kizuna, the first bridge over the Cambodian stretch of the Mekong river, was opened. The 1.5 km bridge, built with Japanese money, lies 75 km north of the capital. The Government hoped it would stimulate domestic trade, connecting the west of the country and strengthening links with Laos and Vietnam, countries which border the river with Cambodia.

[40] In February 2002 the first local elections in many years were held. Hun Sen's Pracheachon won 1,597 of the 1,620 communes in the country and the opposition only 23 (10 for Funcinpec and 13 for Sam Rainsy's SRP). Although not totally free and held in a very violent atmosphere - at least 20 Funcinpec and SRP candidates were murdered during the campaign - it was hoped the long-term effect would be positive.

[41] In March, the Government imposed a three month deadline on UN attempts to restart negotiations on the trial of Khmer Rouge leaders. In April 1999, Cambodia had agreed with the UN for a tribunal to try former Khmer Rouge leaders for crimes against humanity committed under the Pol Pot regime. The UN had withdrawn its support for the special international court in February 2002 because it said the independence, impartiality and objectivity of the proposed court could not be guaranteed. The main sticking point appears to have been the Cambodian Government's insistence that national law would take precedence over the agreement with the UN in the trials.

[42] The Government accepted the repatriation of some 1,000 *Montagnards* - Moung people from the mountainous central region of Vietnam - who fled to Cambodia in 2001 after suffering persecution at the hands of the Vietnamese government (see Vietnam). Human rights groups have condemned a repatriation agreement between Phnom Penh and Hanoi, as they

consider it opens the way for forced expulsions of the Montagnards to Vietnam. A Vietnamese newspaper accused the Cambodian Government of forcibly repatriating the mountain people in February 2002. ■

Cameroon

Population: 15,535,000 (2002)
Land area: 465,400 SQ KM
Capital: Yaoundé
Currency: CFA franc
Language: French and English

Cameroun

The area known as Cameroon is the birthplace and original homeland of the Bantu ethnic group, which after 200 BC migrated east and south, spreading new crop varieties and methods for working iron. In 1472 Fernando Po named a river Camarones (Portuguese for shrimp) because of the crustaceans swarming at its mouth. The name eventually became Cameroon.

[2] The Fulah migration helped transform the local economies into part of a regional circuit which later gave rise to the Emirate of Adamaua in the north central region.

[3] German penetration began in June 1884 when German envoy Gustav Nachtigal signed an agreement with the ruler of the Doualas, a coastal group, making the region a protectorate. A year later, the Berlin Conference awarded Cameroon to Germany. But the Emirate of Adamaua, which the British wanted, was not given to the Germans until 1894.

[4] This protectorate did not survive very long. The Doualas dominated trade that the Germans wanted to control between the coast and Yaoundé, the trade center between Adamaua and the south. In 1897, the Doualas resisted German interference, and a bloody four-year war ensued.

[5] The Germans appropriated the most fertile lands, and the Africans began to die of hunger by the thousands, in an area where stable agriculture had existed for centuries. In 1918 France and Britain invaded Cameroon: the French taking three-fourths, and the English taking the rest. The pro-independence organizations found their cause was

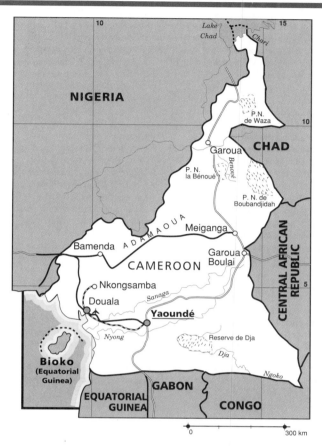

facilitated by the tensions between the colonial powers. In 1945, the People's Union of Cameroon (UPC) was founded, headed by Rubem Um Nyobé. The UPC earned popular support and launched a series of legal campaigns between 1948 and 1956, when it was outlawed.

[6] Nationalist leaders fled to the British-held western sector and organized a guerrilla movement. The UPC established liberated zones in the southern forests where they set up their own administration - a first for sub-Saharan Africa. The efficiency of the guerrillas made it possible for them to resist constant French attacks, until 1960. Two years later, Rubem Um Nyobé died, but the revolution continued.

[7] UPC resistance forced the French to adopt a new strategy, adding political maneuvers to their repressive tactics. Paris created the National Union of Cameroon (UNC), merging two conservative, predominantly Islamic, northern-based parties. UNC leader Alhaji Ahmadou Ahidjo gained power after the French granted the country independence, remaining so after a British plebiscite approved reunification. UPC nationalists were unable to help shape their long-held dream of an independent Cameroon as they were mostly underground or in exile.

[8] Ahidjo stepped up persecution of the opposition in the 1960s, developing one of sub-Saharan Africa's most efficient repressive systems. European human rights groups revealed the existence of thousands of political prisoners in the country. In 1982, Ahidjo suddenly resigned, and was succeeded by his former Prime Minister, Paul Biya.

[9] Biya maintained his predecessor's political and economic policies, though many of Adhidjo's followers supported a coup attempt by a group of military officers. Young people - especially students - resisted the coup attempt by taking to the streets.

[10] Growing unemployment and food shortages undermined Cameroon's traditionally prosperous image. Biya attempted to reinforce his control by calling early elections for April 1984. With democratic organizations prohibited, he was re-elected. Nevertheless, the overall instability of the country led to a new coup attempt, followed by a series of bloody incidents in which 200 people were killed.

[11] In the 1980s, the UNC changed its name to 'Democratic Group of the People of Cameroon' (RDPC), but its political line remained the same.

[12] The UPC later adopted a more flexible stance in order to broaden its social scope, and Biya created new northern provinces to give the Muslims greater economic and political power. Disagreements over oil revenues aggravated inter-ethnic and inter-regional friction. Economic problems stemming from a drop in world prices for coffee, rubber and cotton were exacerbated by Cameroon's dependence on French companies which controlled almost 44 per cent of the export market.

[13] Biya was re-elected in 1988. Censorship increased, journalists were arrested and the post of Prime Minister was abolished.

[14] Faced with the fall in oil prices on the world market and foreign debt payments, the Government sought World Bank and IMF support for a structural adjustment program to stabilize its finances. By reducing imports and state expenditure, privatizing public enterprises and reorganizing the banking system, the country's debts were renegotiated with the Paris Club.

[15] In 1990, social and political organizations reported an increase in government repression of hundreds of citizens.

[16] A few months later, the Government authorized the creation of political parties: some 70 political organizations were granted legal recognition.

LAND USE

DEFORESTATION: 0.6% annual (1990/95)

1993

- FOREST & WOODLAND: 75.5%
- ARABLE: 12.5%
- OTHER: 12%

PUBLIC EXPENDITURE

Military expenditure (as % GNI):	**18 %**	(1999)
Defense expenditure (% of central government expenditure)	**10.6 %**	(1999)

[17] In November 1991, opposition leaders demanded constitutional reform and a return to the federal system abolished in 1972. The political crisis deepened, strikes and pro-democracy demonstrations proliferated; 40 demonstrators were killed by the police.

[18] In December, the Government set the legislative elections for February 16 1992. The opposition wanted the constitution and electoral law be modified prior to the elections. Nonetheless, several parties participated in the elections on March 1 1992.

[19] The RDPC won 88 of the 180 parliamentary seats. The National Union for Democracy and Progress (UNDP) came in second, with 68 representatives. According to the official report, 61 per cent of the four million registered electorate voted.

[20] Biya brought forward the Presidential election to October 11 1992. Seven parties fielded candidates: among them, the Social Democratic Front (FSD) led by John Fru Ndi, the main opposition party representing the English-speaking community. Both the FSD and the Democratic Union of Cameroon, led by Adamu Ndam Njoya, had boycotted the March elections.

[21] Amid widespread accusations of fraud, the Government's narrow victory provoked incidents in the English-speaking Northwestern Province, Fru Ndi's territory.

[22] International observers confirmed the fraud, but the Supreme Court refused to annul the election. Fru Ndi proclaimed himself President, and the Government decreed a state of emergency in the Northwest. Fru Ndi and his supporters were immediately placed under house arrest.

[23] In November a 'coalition government' of the RDPC and minor groups was formed. Government repression intensified, bringing international condemnation, particularly when four members of the Bar Association were arrested in December for leading protest and one died as a result of torture. The United States suspended aid to the country; Biya ended the state of emergency and released Fru Ndi. In 1994, the division of the opposition facilitated Biya's 'iron fist' policy.

[24] In 1995, the opposition continued to suffer divisions. Siga Assanga, former secretary-general of Fru Ndi's Social Democratic Front (FSD), abandoned the party in May and founded the Social Democratic Movement. The UNDP also suffered a split following the expulsion of two of its members who had participated in Biya's governments.

[25] Biya was re-elected in 1997 in a poll challenged by the opposition parties, some of which had called for a boycott of the elections. Just three million of the six million people registered voters were called on to cast ballots. The rest were excluded by the Government, which insisted they were 'foreigners'.

[26] The economic crisis, exacerbated by the devaluation of the franc, unsettled Cameroon's society. In the 1990s, public beatings of petty offenders became widespread. Police corruption and the ineffective justice system led some sectors of the population to mete out punishment on their own: men and women were beaten and many innocent people killed.

[27] In the wake of the October 1999 publication of a Transparency International report that ranked Cameroon as the second most corrupt country in the world, Biya announced in January 2000 a campaign to fight corruption in his government as well as continued economic reforms. He promised to implement the constitutional changes that had been approved by Parliament in 1996, which included the creation of a Senate, of regional councils and of a constitutional council.

[28] In February, a trial of English-speaking secessionists ended with prison sentences for 33 of the defendants. Two of them, members of the RDPC, were also sentenced on embezzlement charges. Throughout the first half of 2000, the FSD continued its campaign in support of the separatist cause of the National Council of South Cameroon. That same year, the UN reported that torture and mistreatment are 'systematic and widespread' at Cameroon's police and gendarmerie stations.

[29] The International Court at The Hague was expected to issue a ruling in mid-2002 on the Cameroon-Nigeria border dispute. Both countries had presented petitions to the Court in 1998. The case, which began in 1994 with a sovereignty claim by Cameroon over the area, and about the presence of Nigerian troops in the Bakassi peninsula - which holds fishing and potential oil wealth - turned into a matter of defining the border between Cameroon and Nigeria, and also affected Equatorial Guinea. ∎

PROFILE

ENVIRONMENT

The country is divided into three regions: the plains of the Lake Chad basin in the northern region (savanna where cattle are raised and corn and cotton are grown); the central part, made up of humid grasslands; and the southern part, an area with rich volcanic soil where the main cash crops (coffee, bananas, cocoa and palm oil) are grown. It is in the latter that most of the population lives. Drought and desertification are the main concerns in the southern region, which covers 25 per cent of the nation's land area, and houses over a quarter of the population.

SOCIETY

Peoples: There are some 200 ethnic groups, the main ones being the Dualas, Bamilekes, Tikars and Bamauns in the south; the Euondos and Fulbes in the west, and the Fulanis in the north. In the southeast live the Baka Pygmies, who live by hunting and fishing. **Religions:** Half the population practice traditional African religions. Christians are a majority in the south while Muslims predominate in the north. **Languages:** French and English are the official languages. There are nearly two hundred African languages (Beti and Bulu being the most widely spoken). German is also spoken. **Political Parties:** Democratic Alliance of the People of Cameroon (RDPC, formerly the only party), Movement for the Defense of the Republic, Social Democratic Front (FSD), Social Democratic Movement, National Union for Democracy and Progress (UNDP), Democratic Union of Cameroon, Union of the Peoples of Cameroon. **Social Organizations:** In 1971, the Government banned the Workers' Union of Cameroon, heir to the labor movement from the previous century. The government-run National Workers' Union of Cameroon was created. Trade Union Confederation of Cameroon Workers. The US-based AFL-CIO trade union has committees in the local subsidiary companies of transnational corporations. There is a strong separatist movement in the English-speaking area of Cameroon. People's Conference of 'Southern Cameroons' (SCPC) unites several parties and organizations.

THE STATE

Official Name: République du Cameroun. **Capital:** Yaoundé 1,378,000 people (1999). **Other cities:** Douala 1,409,200 people; Garoua 180,900; Ncongsamba 106,800 (2000). **Government:** Parliamentary republic. Paul Biya, President since November 1982, re-elected in 1992 and 1997. Peter Musonge Mafani, Prime Minister since September 1996. Unicameral Legislature: National Assembly, with 180 members. **National Holidays:** January 1, Independence Day (1960); October 1, Reunification (1961); May 20, proclamation of the Republic (1972). **Armed Forces:** 14,600.

Canada

Population: 31,268,000 (2002)
Land area: 9,220,970 SQ KM
Capital: Ottawa
Currency: Canadian dollar
Language: English and French

Canada

Sometime between about 20,000 and 35,000 years ago, during the last Ice Age, the first humans to make their homes in North America migrated from Asia. Unknown numbers of people moved southward along the western edge of the North American ice cap. Archaeological evidence and oral traditions help rebuild the period that preceded contact with Europeans. There were 12 major language groups among the peoples living in what is now Canada: Algonquin, Iroquois, Siouan, Athabascan, Kootenaian, Salishan, Wakashan, Tsimshian, Haidan, Tlinglit, Inuktitut, and Beothukan. Within each language group there were usually political and cultural divisions. These subgroups were also divided; at the time of contact the Iroquois had organized themselves into a confederacy, the Iroquois League, consisting of the Mohawk, Oneida, Onondaga, Cayuga, and Seneca. A sixth group, the Tuscarora, joined later. The Inuit (Eskimo) who live in Canada's Arctic regions today were the last of the aboriginal peoples to reach Canada.

[2] The peoples of the Eastern Woodlands, such as the Huron, Iroquois, Petun, Neutral, Ottawa, and Algonquin, created a mixed subsistence economy of hunting and agriculture supplemented by trade. The Huron and the Iroquois formed political and religious confederacies and both created extensive trade systems and political alliances with other groups. Peoples living in the far north did not appear to have formed larger political communities, while those of the west coast and the Eastern Woodlands formed sophisticated political, social, and

cultural institutions. All the groups were self-governing and politically independent. The European colonists who came to North America in the 16th century estimated the indigenous population of the continent to be between 10 and 12 million.

[3] In AD 985 Norse (Viking) sailors sailing from Iceland to Greenland were blown far westward off their course and sighted the coast of Labrador. In AD 1000 Leif Ericson became the first European to land in North America. A colony was established in what the Vikings described as Vinland; the colony died out during the 14th and 15th centuries.

[4] Italian navigator Giovanni Caboto (Cabot) sailed from Bristol in 1497 under a commission from the English king to search for a short

route to Asia (what became known as the Northwest Passage). As Cabot and his sons explored the coasts of Labrador, Newfoundland, and possibly Nova Scotia they discovered that the cold northwest Atlantic waters were teeming with fish. Soon Portuguese, Spanish, and French fishing crews braved the Atlantic crossing to fish in the waters of the Grand Banks. Some began to land on the coast of Newfoundland to dry their catch before returning to Europe. The English paid little heed to the Atlantic fishery until 1583, when Sir Humphrey Gilbert laid claim to the lands around present-day St. John's in Newfoundland. The French also claimed parts of Newfoundland, primarily on the north and west coasts of the island. The initial period of contact between the Indians and the Europeans was ushered in by the fishery. Although each was deeply suspicious of the other, the fishing crews and the Indians carried on a sporadic trade in scattered locations. Chiefly as a sideline of the fishing industry, there continued an unorganized traffic in furs.

[5] Between the 17th and 19th centuries, these territories were colonized by Britain and France. Some areas changed hands several times until 1763 when the Peace of Paris which ended the Seven Years' War granted Canada to Britain. Colonization increased thanks to the profitable fur trade, with the local population growing to almost

half a million by the end of the 19th century.

[6] The British North America Act of 1867 determined that the Canadian constitution would be similar to Britain's, with executive power vested in the King and delegated to a Governor General and Council. The legislative function would, meanwhile, be carried out by a Parliament composed of a Senate and a House of Commons.

[7] In 1931, the Statute of Westminster released Britain's dominions from the colonial laws under which they had been governed, giving Canada legislative autonomy. That same year, Norway recognized Canadian sovereignty over the Arctic regions to the north of the main part of its territory.

[8] In 1981, the Canadian Government reached an agreement with the British Parliament over constitutional transition. The following year, the 1867 Constitution was replaced by the Act of Canada, which granted Canada the autonomy to reform the constitution.

[9] The Constitution Act of 1982 included a Charter of Rights and Freedoms, which recognized the country's pluralistic heritage and the rights of its indigenous peoples. It set forth the principle of equal benefits among the country's ten provinces, and the sovereignty of each province over its own natural resources, though Quebec did not sign the agreement.

[10] When Quebec was occupied by English Protestants in 1760, its predominantly French population sought to maintain a separate Quebecois identity, marked by both religious and political nationalism. Quebec assumed a special role as guardian of the Catholic faith, the French language and the French heritage in North America. It was a role which it performed well. From a French population of 6,000 in 1769, the number of Québécois had increased to 6 million by 1960.

[11] In Quebec, four-fifths of the population speak French as a first language and are fiercely proud of their cultural identity, and provincial autonomy has always been a delicate issue. In 1977, the ruling separatist Parti Québécois (PQ), led by René Lévèsque, adopted French as the official language of education,

WORKERS

2000
UNEMPLOYMENT: 6.8%
LABOR FORCE AS % OF TOTAL:

■ FEMALE: 46%   ■ MALE: 54%

1994/97
EMPLOYMENT DISTRIBUTION:

F
M

■ SERVICES   F: 86%   M: 63%
■ INDUSTRY   F: 12%   M: 32%
■ AGRICULTURE F: 2%   M: 5%

LAND USE

DEFORESTATION: 0.1% annual (1990/95)

1993

■ FOREST & WOODLAND: 49.5%
■ ARABLE: 4.6%
■ OTHER: 45.9%

business and local public administration.

[12] Lévèsque discarded the possibility of a unilateral separation proposing instead a concept of 'sovereignty-association' with a monetary and customs union. However, voters rejected this proposal by 59.5 to 40.5 per cent in a plebiscite held in 1980. Fifteen years later, in a new plebiscite favored by the Parti Québécois, the margin was narrowed with 50.4 per cent of voters opposing separation and 49.6 per cent approving it.

[13] Antiquated British law governed relations between the sexes in North America for a long time, and it was not until October 1929 that Canadian women obtained full legal rights, and it was only under the 1982 Constitution that true sexual equality in law was established.

[14] In addition to the federal law, each province has an equal rights law, guaranteeing access to housing, jobs, services and other facilities, without discrimination on the basis of race, religion, age, nationality or sex - though Quebec is the only province which prohibits discrimination on the basis of 'sexual inversion', its terminology for homosexuality. A supreme court decision extended protection against discrimination based on sexual preference.

[15] Nevertheless as in other Western countries women are still discriminated against. Between 1969 and 1979, there was a 62 per cent increase in the number of women working outside the home. By 1981, this figure represented 49 per cent of all women, and 39 per cent of the economically active population.

[16] Liberal governments, led by Pierre Trudeau, were elected in 1968, 1972, 1974 and again in 1980, after a brief Conservative interlude. Trudeau loosened Canada's traditional ties with Western Europe and the US, and strengthened those with the Far East, Africa and Latin America. In addition, he refused to participate in the economic blockade against Cuba.

[17] Economic difficulties stemming from the worldwide recession triggered a sharp drop in the Liberal Party's popularity, in favor of the Conservative Party. In 1983, Conservative leader Brian Mulroney, a labor relations lawyer and businessman from Quebec became Prime Minister, replacing John Turner, who had succeeded Trudeau as head of the Liberal Party.

[18] Mulroney re-established a 'special relationship' between Canada and the US, starting negotiations for a free trade agreement in 1985. This agreement, which went into effect in January 1989, provoked criticism from the Liberals and other members of the opposition, who claimed that the terms of the agreement were overly favorable to the US. Nevertheless, it received majority support from the voters in the 1988 election.

[19] The Conservative victory was made possible by the Québecois votes, reflecting the growing economic importance of French-speaking voters. The victory also reflected the impact of the Meech Lake Accord, initiated by Mulroney and signed in 1987, in which the Federal Government ceded important powers to the provinces, granting Quebec for the first time recognition of its unique cultural status, in order for it to accept the constitution and Charter of Rights and Freedoms.

[20] To be implemented, the Meech Lake Accord had to be ratified by the unanimous consent of each of the provinces, and it was blocked by Newfoundland and Manitoba. In Manitoba the one vote against came from a Native American who would not accept the 'distinct society' clause for Quebec, saying native people were every bit as distinct.

[21] The Northwest Territories (NWT) - which make up one-third of the country's land area with only 52,000 inhabitants, half of whom are Inuit or members of other indigenous groups - were considering the possibility of splitting into two regions, Nunavet and Denendeh, each with an autonomous government. While this plan was approved by the provincial legislature in 1987, it was subject to ratification by a plebiscite of its residents, and the Federal Government.

[22] The Federal Government declared its willingness to accept the right of the Inuit and other native peoples of the NWT to self-government, incorporating this right into the Constitution if approved by the provincial governments and by organizations representing the interests of these peoples. In 1988, it transferred 673,000 sq km to the other native peoples and the Inuit. In 1992, representatives from the Federal and provincial governments signed an agreement on the land claims of 17,500 native peoples from the Northwest Territories. The way was paved for the creation of Nunavut ('Our Land' in Inuit), approved in a referendum held on April 4. Nunavut, which includes the area west of Hudson Bay and the Arctic archipelago, covers an area of 2.2 million sq km, equal to one fifth of the country. The agreement also included the transference of 350,000 sq km to the Inuit and the payment of $580 million as a counterpart for the waiver of future land claims.

[23] The Inuit from northwestern Canada have been working with other indigenous groups of Greenland and Alaska to deal with ecological, cultural, social and political problems which affect their nation. The Fifth Circumpolar Conference of the Inuit (CCI) in 1989 reaffirmed Inuit rights to lands which Canada considered government property, and leased out to large mining interests.

[24] Canada's first trading partner is the US, and vice versa, but while the volume of Canada's sales to the US accounts for one-fifth of its total production, American exports to Canada represent less than 3 per cent. No other major Western economy maintains a trade

PROFILE

ENVIRONMENT

Canada is the second largest country in the world in land area, divided into five natural regions. The Maritime Provinces along the Atlantic coast are a mixture of rich agricultural land and forests. The Canadian Shield is a rocky region covered with woods and is rich in minerals. To the south, along the shores of the Great Lakes and the St Lawrence River, there is a large plain with fertile farmlands, where over 60 per cent of the population is concentrated, and the major urban centers are located. Farming (wheat, oats and rye), is the mainstay of the central prairie provinces. The Pacific Coast is a mountainous region with vast forests. The north is almost uninhabited, with very cold climate and tundra. There are ten provinces, and three territories; the Yukon, Northwest and Nunavut (the latter created in 1999 as land for Inuit people). These are working towards provincial status, but this is complicated by native land claims. Canada has immense mineral resources; it is the world's largest producer of asbestos, nickel, zinc and silver and the second largest of uranium. There are also major lead, copper, gold, iron ore, gas and oil deposits. Its industry is highly developed. Industrial emissions -together with those from vehicles - from Canadian and US plants contribute to the 'acid rain' which has affected thousands of lakes.

SOCIETY

Peoples: There are about 850,000 Native Americans, Métis (mixed race) and Inuit (Eskimos) ranging from highly acculturated city-dwellers to traditional hunters and trappers living in isolated northern communities. There are six distinct culture areas and ten language families; many native languages such as Cree and Ojibwa are still widely spoken. About 350,000 native people are classified as such: that is, they belong to one of 573 registered groups and can live on a federally protected reserve (though only about 70 per cent actually do so). Métis and those who do not have official status as 'native people' have historically enjoyed no separate legal recognition, but attempts are now being made to secure them special rights under the law. The original European settlers came from France, England and Scotland. Today Canada is multicultural with many people from Asia, the Caribbean and Europe (Germans 3.4 per cent; Italians 2.8 per cent; Chinese 2.2 per cent; Ukrainian 1.5 per cent, Dutch 1.3 per cent; also Portuguese, Polish, Pakistani, Filipino). **Languages:** English and French, both official. 13 per cent of the population is bilingual, 67 per cent speak only English, 18 per cent only French, and 2 per cent speak other languages (Italian, German and Ukrainian and indigenous languages).
Religions: Roman Catholic 45.7 per cent; Protestant 36.3 per cent; Eastern Orthodox 1.5 per cent; Jewish 1.2 per cent; Muslim 1.0 per cent; Buddhist 0.7 per cent; Hindu 0.6 per cent; no religion 12.4 per cent; other 0.6 per cent. 12.4 per cent of the population considers itself non religious. **Political Parties:** The Liberal Party; the Conservative Party; Bloque Québécois (BQ); Reform Party. New Democratic Party; Green Party. **Social Organizations:** Canadian Labour Congress, with more than 2.3 million members; Confédération des syndicats nationaux; Fédération de travailleurs et travailleuses du Québec; National Federation of Independent Trade Unions; Canadian Federation of Students. Non-union Assembly of First Nations; Council of Canadians.

THE STATE

Official Name: Canada. **Administrative Divisions:** 10 Provinces and 3 Territories. **Capital:** Ottawa 1,097,000 people (1999).
Other cities: Toronto 5,411,300 people; Montreal 3,490,600; Vancouver 1,922,000 (2000). **Government:** Adrienne Clarkson, Governor-General since October 1999. Jean Chrétien, Prime Minister and Head of Government since November 1993. Canada is a federation of ten provinces and a member of the British Commonwealth, with a parliamentary system of government. **National Holiday:** July 1, Canada Day (1867). **Armed Forces:** 70,500 (1996). **Others:** 6,400 (Coast Guard).

imbalance of such magnitude. It is comparable only to the dependence of Southern countries in relation to the industrialized countries.

[25] With the free trade agreement which went into effect in 1989, Canada's integration with the American economy has been accentuated. Through trade, the extension of credit, and investments in Canada, the US secured ever greater control over Canadian natural resources and majority control over shares in some Canadian industries.

[26] A recession in the US means recession in Canada; Ottawa's monetary policy is essentially defined by its neighbor's. This degree of dependence has been labeled 'colonial', despite the fact that Canada is the world's eighth largest industrial power, and that its standard of living is one of the highest in the world.

[27] The Canadian Armed Forces (CF) are charged with protecting national interests both inside and outside the country, with defending North America in cooperation with the US, and complying with its NATO commitments; in addition, it has participated in UN Peacekeeping Forces.

[28] The Canadian Forces supplied the NATO Supreme Command with troops which were permanently stationed in Germany, including four Mobile Command Brigades and an air division, all of which maintained maximum operational readiness. They also participated in the US intervention in Haiti in 1994.

[29] Relations between Canada and the US became tense in 1985, when a US Coast Guard vessel passed through the Northwest Passage without Canadian authorization. The US recognizes Canadian sovereignty over the Arctic islands but not over its waters; a similar dispute exists with relation to the waters surrounding the French islands of St Pierre and Miquelon.

[30] Canada made little headway in getting the US to control industrial gas emissions, which drift over Canadian territory, bringing with them acid rain; or in reaching agreement on catch limits for the shared west coast salmon fishery.

[31] The Canadian Government made a commitment to reduce its industrial emissions by half. This program anticipated a reduction in industrial pollution of 20 per cent by the year 2005.

[32] In 1991, Quebec's premier Robert Bourassa initiated the second phase of the huge James Bay Power Project, which involved damming or diverting nine rivers along 350,000 km of the northwestern part of the province, emptying into the James and Hudson Bays.

[33] The final capacity of 27,000 megawatts of hydro-electric power is far greater than the output of Itaipu Dam, in Brazil or that of Three Gorges Dam in China.

[34] The region affected by the projects is located in the hunting and fishing grounds of approximately 11,000 Cree and 7,000 Inuit, peoples who have lived in the area for over 5,000 years. This region contains the largest beluga whale population in the world, as well as the largest caribou herds and most of the world's fresh-water seals. Vast numbers of migratory birds make the extensive wetlands their home for several months each year.

[35] The second phase of the project involved flooding an additional 10,000 sq km of land. The dam enables Canada to sell electricity to the US, set up plants for aluminum production in Quebec and guarantee an energy supply for Canadian consumption, which is among the highest in the world. The ecological consequences of this project on the regional ecosystem are unforeseeable.

[36] In 1973, hunting and fishing provided two-thirds of the local population's food, with this percentage dropping to one-fourth, 20 years later. A 1975 treaty allowed local people to retain a small part of their lands, granting some economic compensation for the loss of the rest of their territory. Even so, the chances of the local indigenous culture surviving the nationalistic ecocide of Quebec are severely limited.

[37] The Inuit, who inhabit the Belcher Islands in the Hudson Bay and navigate the frozen waters in search of fish and game, were not taken into account in these agreements. The Dene, Innu and Inuit who still live from hunting and fishing, remain concerned about what effect these major changes will have upon their lands and livelihoods. The indigenous peoples are fighting for government respect of the treaties that affirm their rights to their land and resources.

[38] Canada's original inhabitants have now organized more and between the 1960s and 1970s this culminated in the creation of the National Indian Brotherhood (NIB). The aim of this organization is to represent indigenous peoples to the general public and also to make their grievances known to the federal government. The NIB was subsequently replaced by the Assembly of First Nations.

[39] In October 1991 Ottawa announced the decision to earmark some $700 million for the agricultural sector; however, farmers were not satisfied with this amount, considering it insufficient to

Quebec libre?

'Vive le Quebec libre!' exclaimed the French President, Charles de Gaulle, from the balcony of Montreal City Hall in 1967. His call was in open support of the province's separatists, awakening pro-independence demonstrations in the main cities.

French nationalism in Quebec had taken shape in the late 1960s. Intellectuals and workers blamed the economic crisis in Quebec on the Canadian Federation and they proposed two alternatives: better relations with the other provinces and central government, or the independence of Quebec and its constitution as a sovereign state. Supporters of the second stance gathered around the recently created Parti Quebecois (PQ), led by René Lévèsque and made up of former left-wing militants from the unionist Liberal Party.

However according to Canadian legislation, none of the provinces is allowed to separate and the pro-independence PQ would only be able to pursue the possibility by means of a referendum and the support of the international community.

Two important events then occurred in three years, which projected Quebec onto the national and international scene. The first was De Gaulle's call in 1967. And then in October 1970, the extremist Quebec Liberation Front kidnapped Quebec's employment minister, Pierre Laporte, and British Trade Comissioner James Cross. Laporte was found dead days later, and Cross was freed. As a result of these events, Canadian Prime Minister, Pierre Trudeau, declared a state of emergency, sent in the troops and suspended civil rights.

Once the economic problems were resolved, the separatist nationalists started to make other demands, like defending the French language from the Anglo and Protestant expansionism of the majority in Canada. To a certain degree, the separatists were running up the flag lost to Britain in 1759 when it took New France, the forerunner of Quebec, in the battle of the 'Plains of Abraham'.

In the September 1994 provincial elections, the PQ was returned to power again, and its leader, Jacques Parizeau - who was elected governor - promised a new referendum for independence - the first referendum had been held in 1980. The other separatist political force was the Bloque Quebecois (BQ), led by Lucien Bouchard, the current governor of Quebec. In the October 1995 referendum, the pro-independence parties just lost with 49 per cent of the vote, and certain things became clearer as a result.

Firstly, that independence required a prior phase of new economic, political and military relationships with Canada. The separatist leaders, had they won, were under instructions to schedule negotiations with Canada and only to declare independence if their proposals were rejected. Secondly, it became obvious there are increasing numbers of separatists in Quebec, or at least that growing numbers of Quebecois feel less Canadian (separatists had only received 40 per cent of the vote in 1980).

Since the failure of the most recent referendum on independence, many of the pro-independence movement have taken conservative stances - similar to those held by the Quebecois right in 1960. Today, Canada is structurally dependent on the US which does not want any split.

Things have not been easy for the Quebecois since then. The BQ majority has shown itself to be less demanding although - always within its nationalist framework - it has claimed greater powers for Quebec. In October 1999, US President Clinton said in Montreal, 'think twice before separating, in these times of globalization'. Of course, he would say that because 90 per cent of Canadian export earnings depend on the US. Bernard Landry became Chairman of the Parti Quebecois in March 2001 and became Quebec's Prime Minister later that month, after the resignation of Lucien Bouchard. ∎

compensate for the losses of the previous year. Farm subsidies by the governments of the US and European countries left Canadian farmers disadvantaged in operating its policy of liberalizing trade under the GATT agreement.

[40] In December 1991, the Canadian Minister of Finance stated that the country had registered its first trade deficit in 15 years (in September, the trade deficit was $275 million). The year was characterized by economic recession, high taxes, corruption scandals, increasing separatism and a decline in Mulroney's popularity.

[41] In early 1992, there was intense debate over Quebec's growing demands for autonomy. In August, the province rejected the Government's scheme for granting it 'special' status, as the terms were considered 'insufficient'.

[42] On August 12 1992, after 18 months of negotiations, Canada, the US and Mexico signed an agreement creating a free trade zone (North American Free Trade Agreement, NAFTA).

[43] In February 1993, Prime Minister Brian Mulroney resigned from the Conservative Party (and therefore from the Government) with the lowest popularity ratings ever. Earlier, in June, he had tried to take advantage of his 10-seat parliamentary majority to obtain ratification of NAFTA.

[44] Kim Campbell, former Defense Minister, became the first woman elected as Prime Minister in Canada. Campbell's first measure was to trim Cabinet to 25 members (10 less than the previous one).

[45] In June of the same year, Parliament ratified the NAFTA treaty. Two months later Campbell traveled the country promoting the adoption of austerity measures to combat the budget deficit. In the meantime, her rival, Liberal Jean Chrétien, promised to give high priority to the creation of new jobs.

[46] In the October 1993 general elections, the Liberal Party (opposition) regained power after 9 years, with a landslide victory over the Conservative Party, whose representation in the House of Commons dropped from 155 seats to 2. The Liberals won 178 seats, against 79 in the previous legislature. The separatist Bloque Québécois (54 seats) and the right-of-center Reform Party (52 seats) both made significant gains. This was the worst defeat for a governing party in Canada's 126-year history.

[47] The new Prime Minister, Jean Chrétien, took office on November 4 1993. The following month, former prime minister Kim Campbell resigned from her post as leader of the Conservative Party.

[48] The reduction in the public deficit and State spending, the increase in unemployment to more than 10 per cent and the separatist tendencies in Quebec were the main Government concerns during 1994 and 1995.

[49] The Parti Québecois (PQ) again brought up the possible secession of Quebec from Canada in 1994. The popularity of Prime Minister Chrétien had increased 13 per cent since the 1993 elections, but the PQ triumphed in the province of Quebec. The new provincial Premier, Jacques Parizeau, promised to do everything possible to make Quebec a sovereign state.

[50] The geopolitical context of NAFTA, which came into force on January 1 1994, meant that the Quebec issue was followed with great attention in Mexico and the US, even though the PQ had promised that the province would meet the obligations assumed by Canada. However on October 30 1995, separation was rejected by 50.6 per cent of the electorate.

[51] The Quebec secession threat faded in 1996, despite the high number of votes received by the separatist option. The Federal Government transferred some powers to the provinces in an attempt to calm the nationalist movement. Lucien Bouchard, leader of the separatist forces, replaced Parizeau as Premier of Quebec when the latter resigned following the referendum defeat. Unemployment continued to rise in 1996, despite the economic growth. Disagreements continued throughout the year with the US over Canadian companies dealing with Cuba.

[52] In June 1997, Chrétien's party won the parliamentary elections, gaining 155 of the 301 seats, followed by the Reform Party and the PQ, then the New Democratic Party with 21 and the Conservatives with 20.

[53] In 1998 the Supreme Court ruled that Quebec could not separate without the consent of Federal Government. The Prime Minister, a native of Quebec and ardent opponent of secession, said the ruling supported the principal arguments of federal government, by establishing that Quebec lacked authority, within Canadian law, to execute unilateral independence.

[54] In 1999, a study by the David Suzuki Foundation stated Canada had the greatest per capita oil and gas consumption and that 16,000 people there die each year from air pollution. Furthermore, the study named Canada as the leading per capita producer of greenhouse gases.

[55] After 50 years of Canadian government, the Inuit finally achieved that year the devolution of one-fifth of Canadian territory, with

the creation of the Nunavut territory, in the northwest. Given the lack of infrastructure to tap Nunavut's mineral resources, the 25,000 Inuit that live there are still dependent on Canadian government subsidies and welfare.

[56] The Jantzi Social Index (JSI) came in effect in the year 2000 in Canada, formed by 60 companies chosen among the country's largest, selected for their respect of environmental and social matters. It gave investors who do not wish their funds to contribute to the arms industry or companies that hire child labor at poverty wages the chance to select whom they support. The JSI also excludes those companies linked to nuclear power, alcohol, gambling and tobacco.

[57] In response to a wave of criticism against his government, Chrétien - against the opinion of members of his party - brought forward the elections to November 2000. He not only won an absolute majority in the House of Commons, but also received 17 more seats than four years earlier. Also, his Liberal Party won votes in Quebec, which weakened the separatists. The exceptional Canadian economy (according to the UN, at that time Canada ranked first in the Human Development Index) led voters to support the Prime Minister and his team.

[58] The Government passed new legislation in March 2001 against child pornography, stating that, not only is it a crime to produce or publish 'indecent' images of children, it is also an offense to access them in a website. Individuals who commit crimes described in this new law, regardless of where in the world they committed them, may be taken before the Canadian courts. Internet providers in Canada warned it would be very difficult to control everything that is published and seen in the worldwide web.

[59] In July Canada became the first country in the world to legalize the therapeutic use of marijuana. Likewise, the Government began to grow the drug for medicinal purposes. However, commercial production and its sale for non-medicinal purposes remain illegal.

[60] After secret negotiations between the Quebecois government and leaders of the Cree community, it was agreed the Cree would receive Can$2.2 billion in exchange for an environmental survey that would enable the construction of a hydroelectric dam. For most of the 12,000 Cree, which had struggled for decades against the project, the agreement amounted to a sell-out by their leaders and goes against their conviction that land is sacred and should not be harmed.

[61] After the September 11 attacks on the US, Canadian troops took part in US President Bush's war on terrorism. In April 2002 4 Canadian soldiers serving in Afghanistan were killed by US bombs. ∎

STATISTICS

DEMOGRAPHY
Population: 31,268,000 (2002)
Annual growth: 1.2 % (1985-2000)
Estimates for year 2015: 34,419,000 (2000)
Annual growth to year 2015: 0.8 % (2000)
Urban population: 77.1 % (2000)
Urban growth: 1.0 % (2000)
Children per woman: 1.6 (2000)

HEALTH
Life expectancy at birth: 79 years (2000-2005)
male: 76 years (2000-2005)
female: 82 years (2000-2005)
Infant mortality: 6 per 1,000 (2000)
Under-5 child mortality: 6 per 1,000 (2000)
Daily calorie supply: 3,161 per capita (1999)
229 doctors per 100,000 people (1995)
Safe water: 100 % (2000)

EDUCATION
School enrolment (net):
Primary total: 95 % (1994/2000)
male: 96 % (1995/99)
female: 94 % (1995/99)
Secondary (gross):
male: 105 % (1995/97)
female: 105 % (1995/97)
Tertiary (gross): 58 % (1998)
Primary school teachers: one for every 18 pupils (1998)

COMMUNICATIONS
159 newspapers (1996), 1,047 radios (1997), 715 TV sets (1997) and 677 main telephone lines (2000) per 1,000 people
Books: 76 new titles per 100,000 people (1992/94)

ECONOMY
Per capita, GDP: $ 27,840 (2000)
Annual growth: 3.6 % (2000)
Annual inflation: 2.8 % (2000)
Consumer price index: 109.0 (2000)
Currency: 1.6 Canadian dollars = $ 1 (03/2002)
Cereal imports: 1,933,326 metric tons (2000)
Food import dependency: 5 % (2000)
Fertilizer use: 567 kg per ha (1999)
Exports: $ 277,551 million (1999)
Imports: $ 258,892 million (1999)

ENERGY
Consumption: 7,747.1 Kgs of oil equivalent per capita yearly (1998); -51.6 % imported (1999)

HDI (ranking/value): 3 / 0.936 (1999)

Cape Verde

Population: 446,000 (2002)
Land area: 4,030 SQ KM
Capital: Praia
Currency: Escudo
Language: Portuguese and Creole

Cabo Verde

When the Portuguese settled on the Cape Verde archipelago in the 15th century, the islands were deserving of their descriptive name (Green Cape). They were covered by lush tropical vegetation that stood out against the black volcanic rock and the blue sea. Some 400 years later, Portuguese colonization had wrought devastation and transformed the islands into a 'floating desert' Most of the population emigrated to escape starvation, while those who stayed depended upon foreign aid.

[2] Cape Verde was a very important 16th century port of call for ships carrying slaves to America. Incursions by French, British and Dutch pirates were so frequent that Portugal brought farmers to the islands from the Alentejo region to ensure a more permanent presence. The agriculture practised by the new settlers quickly eroded the thin layer of fertile soil and periodic droughts have struck the country since the 18th century.

[3] Falling farm production caused massive emigration of Cape Verdeans; many went to Guinea-Bissau, another former Portuguese colony with close ties to the archipelago. In later years, there was further emigration to Angola, Mozambique, Senegal, Brazil, and the US.

[4] During the independence struggle, Cape Verde developed closer ties to Guinea-Bissau (see Guinea-Bissau). One major reason was the formation of the African Party for the Independence of Guinea and Cape Verde (PAIGC) in 1956, supported by both colonies. Amilcar Cabral, the PAIGC's founder and ideologist, planned that the two economically similar countries, could fight together for freedom and development, once independence was achieved.

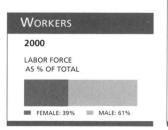

WORKERS

2000

LABOR FORCE
AS % OF TOTAL

FEMALE: 39%   MALE: 61%

[5] In 1961, guerrilla warfare broke out on the continent, and hundreds of Cape Verdean patriots joined the fight. Portugal's colonial government was overthrown in 1974, a transition government was installed and in 1975 the islands proclaimed independence. The PAIGC set an unusual precedent, as for the first time ever one political party took office in two different countries at the same time. Aristides Pereira was elected President and commander Pedro Pires became Prime Minister. The PAIGC leadership took the first steps toward establishing a federation between Cape Verde and Guinea-Bissau, and the national assemblies of the two countries sat together as the Council of the Union.

LAND USE

DEFORESTATION: 21.6% annual (1990/95)

1993

- FOREST & WOODLAND: 0.2%
- ARABLE: 10.7%
- OTHER: 89.1%

[6] In 1968 the Cape Verde Government faced the devastating effects of a drought that left 80 per cent of the population of the archipelago without food. However, the prudent action of civilian organizations supplemented by foreign assistance averted a major catastrophe.

[7] From 1975 onwards, the forested areas of Cape Verde increased from 3,000 to 45,000 hectares. The Government predicted that in the next 10 years a further 75,000 hectares would be planted making the islands self-sufficient in firewood. Early in the rainy season, the population of Cape Verde voluntarily spent a week planting trees.

[8] The Government implemented land reform, giving priority to subsistence farming to replace the export crops of the colonial period, when barely five per cent of food needs was met by local production. The drastic decline in agricultural production led the Government to invest in fisheries.

[9] Cape Verde supported Angola during its 'second liberation war' (see Angola) by allowing Cuban planes to land on the archipelago during the airlift that helped defeat the invasion of Angola by former Zaire and South Africa. Cape Verde adopted a policy of

non-alignment, declaring that no foreign military bases would be allowed in their territory.

[10] In 1981, while the PAIGC was negotiating a new constitution for Guinea-Bissau and Cape Verde, Guinea-Bissau's president Luis Cabral was overthrown. João Bernardo Vieira took office, and was initially hostile to integration with Cape Verde. An emergency meeting of PAIGC members in Cape Verde discussed the political developments in Guinea-Bissau. This reaffirmation of support for the principles of Amílcar Cabral led the party congress to adopt a new name 'the African Party for the Independence of Cape Verde' (PAICV) stressing their independence from Guinea.

[11] Relations between the two governments became tense, but mediation efforts, particularly by Angola and Mozambique paid off. Reconciliation came in August 1982 in Maputo when Mozambique's President Machel brought Aristides Pereira and João Bernardo Vieira together. Further progress was made at the Conference of Former Portuguese Colonies in Africa, held in Cape Verde in November 1982. In Praia, President João Bernardo Vieira met with colleagues from Angola, Mozambique, Cape Verde and São Tomé. Diplomatic relations returned to normal, but plans for reunification were abandoned.

[12] Political stability, defiance and perseverance helped Cape Verde avoid famine and the other drastic consequences of the drought which afflicted Africa. In 1984, crop yields fell by 25 per cent, the trade deficit stood at $70 million and the foreign debt reached $98 million. However the food distribution system and efficient state and resource management prevented famine, although the country has been ravaged by droughts for 19 years. Despite these positive factors, some sectors of the population are still severely undernourished.

[13] The paucity of resources made Cape Verde dependent upon foreign assistance, submitting to a number of projects which were doomed to failure, including the nation's First Development Plan.

[14] The Second Development Plan, launched in 1986, prioritized private enterprise especially in the informal

LITERACY

2000

73%

EXTERNAL DEBT

2000

PER CAPITA

US$ 766

sector. In agriculture, concentrated efforts were made in the fight against desertification. In 1990, the plan was to recover more than 500 sq km, and establish a centralized system of administering water reserves for the whole country. During the first phase of the plan, more than 15,000 dams were built to store rainwater, and 231 sq km were forested.

[15] Despite adverse climatic conditions, farm production gradually increased in the first half of the 1990s to make the country practically self-sufficient in meat and vegetables.

[16] Amidst the political decline linked to the crisis of socialism worldwide, the PAICV lost the first pluralist parliamentary elections, held in February 1991. The Movement for Democracy (MPD) led by Carlos Veiga won the elections with over 65 per

cent of the vote although 38 per cent of the electorate abstained from voting. Antonio Mascarenhas Monteiro, a legal expert educated at the University of Louvain, Belgium, and President of the Supreme Court of Cape Verde during the previous decade, was elected President.

[17] The new government began the transition to a free-market economy with the privatization of insurance companies, fishing and banking, in line with the requirements of international agencies on which the country greatly depended on. Foreign aid accounted for 46 per cent of the GDP, while remittances from the 700,000 Cape Verdeans residing abroad, constituted another 15 per cent of it.

[18] The liberal government, faced with a 25 per cent unemployment rate, declared its goal of restructuring the state. In the first

quarter of 1993, government authorities announced a 50 per cent reduction of the 12,000 civil servants and a gradual deregulation of prices.

[19] The 1994 budget, despite making cuts in public expenditure, included an increase of public investment from $80 million in 1993 to $138 million in 1994. The priority sectors for state investment were transport, telecommunications and rural development.

[20] In January 1995, Prime Minister Carlos Veiga introduced significant changes in government in order to 'facilitate the country's transition to a free-market economy' One of the most important changes was the merger of the Ministries of Finance, Economic Coordination and Tourism, and Industry and Commerce into one Ministry of Economic Coordination. Inflation in 1995 was 6 per cent and Cape Verdean economy is still greatly dependent upon foreign aid, particularly from the European Union.

[21] In 1997, unemployment remained at 25 per cent. Half way through the year, the Government announced more Italian investments in the tourism sector. The African Development Bank granted a $4.9 million loan for roadbuilding. Cape Verde also received economic support from China and created an association with Angola to invest in health and social welfare, amongst other sectors.

[22] Reports of police brutality to prisoners recurred throughout 1998 and 1999. The number of prisoners far exceeded the number of cells available, and most prisons offered way below minimum reasonable conditions.

[23] Opposition politicians criticized the pro-government media for its self-censorship. The authorities, using the law to suit themselves, try, fine and often imprison editors and journalists critical of government figures.

[24] Presidential elections were held February 12 2001 but no candidate won more than 50 per cent of the vote, forcing a run-off vote two weeks later. Amid accusations of irregularities by the two candidates, the Electoral Commission decided to halt the public recount and carry out another. In the end, Pedro Pires of the PAICV defeated Carlos Veiga by just 17 votes. Pires took office on March 22, becoming the third President since the country's independence.

[25] In February 2002 the Government began to step up efforts to decentralize and privatize its large public sector. To do so, it signed a cooperation agreement with France for 610 million euros. ■

PROFILE

ENVIRONMENT

An archipelago of volcanic origin, composed of Windward Islands Santo Antao, São Vicente, São Nicolau, Santa Luzia, Sal, Boa Vista, Branco and Raso; and Leeward Islands Fogo, Santiago, Maio, Rombo and Brava. The islands are mountainous (heights of up to 2,800 meters) without permanent rivers. The climate is arid, influenced by the cold Canary Islands current. Agriculture is poor; nonetheless it employs most of the population. Cape Verde lies within the Sahel region, which is undergoing increased desertification, with periodic droughts and deforestation. This phenomenon is aggravated by the islands' small size, topography of rolling hills and the prevalence of high winds.

SOCIETY

Peoples: Cape Verdeans descend from Africans, mainly from Bantu-speaking peoples, and from Europeans. Today the population is 71 per cent of mixed descent, 28 per cent African and 1 per cent European.
Religions: Roman Catholic 93.2 per cent (with influence of local practices); Protestant and other 6.8 per cent (mainly from the Nazareth Church).
Languages: Portuguese is the official language, but the national language is Creole, based on old Portuguese with African vocabulary and structures.
Political Parties: African Party of Independence of Cape Verde (PAICV); Movement for the Democracy (MPD); Democratic Alliance for Change.
Social Organizations: Organized workers belong to the National Cape Verde Workers' Union-Central Trade Union Committee (UNTC-CS); Cape Verde Confederation of Free Trade Unions.

THE STATE

Official Name: República do Cabo Verde.
Administrative divisions: 9 islands and 14 counties.
Capital: Praia 76,000 people (1999).
Other cities: Mindelo 64,000; Santa Maria 13,400 (2000).
Government: Parliamentary republic. Pedro Pires, President since March 2001. José Maria Neves, Prime Minister, since February 2001. National Assembly has 72 members.
National Holiday: July 5, Independence Day (1975).
Armed Forces: 1,100.

Cayman Islands

Population: 41,000 (2002)
Land area: 260 SQ KM
Capital: George Town
Currency: Cayman dollar
Language: English

Cayman Islands

In 1503, Christopher Columbus sighted the Cayman Islands and named them the 'Turtles' because of the vast numbers of turtles, iguanas and alligators which were their sole inhabitants. The Cayman Islands include Grand Cayman, which is the largest, Cayman Brac and Little Cayman, and all three are surrounded by coral reefs.

[2] Shortly afterwards, the islands came under French control or more accurately, under the control of buccaneers and privateers: 'the fathers of the French colonies in the West Indies'. For a good part of the 17th century, the Caymans were the pirate headquarters of the Antilles.

[3] The first permanent colonial settlement was established in Grand Cayman and most of the settlers came from Jamaica. It was not until around the year 1833 that they started to live on the other two islands. The Antilles were all affected by power struggles between the European colonialists. When Jamaica was ceded to the British Crown in 1670, under the Treaty of Madrid, the Cayman Islands became a Jamaican dependency. In 1959 they were given the status of British dependent territory.

[4] In 1972, a new constitution was passed granting some local autonomy on domestic matters. The Governor, appointed by the Crown, became responsible for defense, foreign affairs, internal security, and some social services. There was also an Executive Council and Legislative Assembly. The new Executive Council, created after the 1988 general elections, had two new members and two who were already appointed.

[5] The Cayman Islands have few natural resources other than the sea and sand, which make them popular tourist resorts. With the exception of turtle farming, local industry and agriculture only meet domestic needs. The Caymanese are renowned boat builders and sailors. One of the country's main sources of revenue is the money sent home by sailors.

[6] Their tax-exempt status has attracted a growing number of offshore banking and trust companies. In 1987, there were 515 banks in the Cayman Islands.

[7] By the end of the decade, a quarter of the economically active population worked in tourism. A large network of hotels was set up throughout the islands, with a total of 5,200 beds. The influx of visitors has produced considerable immigration, which currently accounts for 35 per cent of the population. In 1989, the Caymans were visited by 618,000 tourists. Fishing declined seriously in the 1970s and has not recovered. Turtle farming is being developed to replace traditional turtle fishing.

[8] In August 1991, McKeeva Bush, a member of the Assembly, founded the first political party in the Caymans. The DPP (Democratic Progressive Party) aimed to change the legal status of the islands from being British dependencies. The DPP promoted constitutional reform, seeking the creation of a party system, a rise in the number of members of the Executive Council, the creation of the post of Prime Minister, and an increase in the number of seats in the Legislative Assembly. The Governor would become the President of the extended Executive Council.

[9] In January 1996, the capture of a drug trafficker from Mexico - the third main country supplying cocaine to the United States - demonstrated the role of the Cayman Islands' banking system in a money-laundering circuit ranging from Texas to Switzerland.

[10] In 1998 the Government denied entry to the country to 910 gay tourists, mostly US citizens, alleging that they did not fulfill the 'appropriate behavior requirements'. The British Government distanced itself from this 'discriminatory' policy.

[11] In June 2000 concern about illegal financial practices led international monitors to categorize the Cayman Islands as 'reluctant' to collaborate in fighting money laundering. The country was removed from the blacklist in June 2001 after enacting regulations that banking authorities said were already being followed. Even so, anyone engaged in the finance industry, from banks to lawyers, must now verify the identity and source of income of each client.

[12] In February 2002 it was discovered that the US bankrupted power company Enron used some 700 partnerships registered in the archipelago to evade federal taxes. In April, the Cayman Islands signed an agreement with the US Government to share tax information in order to uncover offenders. ■

PROFILE

ENVIRONMENT

Located west of Jamaica and south of Cuba, this small archipelago is part of the Greater Antilles. It comprises the Grand Cayman islands, where most of the population live, Little Cayman, and Cayman Brac. The archipelago is of volcanic origin, and has rocky hills and considerable coral formations. The climate is tropical and rainy, tempered by oceanic influences. The shortage of freshwater is a problem for the inhabitants.

SOCIETY

Peoples: 50 per cent of the population are of mixed European and Indian descent; 25 per cent are of European descent; 25 per cent are of African origin. **Religions:** Protestant. **Languages:** English.
Political parties: Democratic Progressive Party (DPP). Groups of independent citizens are formed to elect the local government. In the last elections, only independent candidates were elected.

THE STATE

Official Name: Cayman Islands. **Administrative divisions:** There are eight districts (Creek, Eastern, Midland, South Rown, Spot Bay, Stake Bay, West End, Western). **Capital:** George Town 20,000 people (1999).
Other cities: West Bay 9,800 people; Bodden Town 5,900 (2000).
Government: Peter Smith, Governor since May 1999. There is an 18-member Legislative Assembly (15 elected by direct popular vote and 3 named by the Governor). **National holiday:** Constitution Day, first Monday in July. **Armed Forces:** The UK is responsible for the defense of the Islands. There is a civil guard for internal security.

STATISTICS

DEMOGRAPHY

Population: 41,000 (2002)
Estimates for year 2015: 59,000 (2000)

EDUCATION

Primary school teachers: one for every 15 pupils (1998)

COMMUNICATIONS

200 TV sets (1999) and 821 main telephone lines (2000) per 1,000 people

ECONOMY

Currency: 0.8 Cayman dollars = $ 1 (03/2002)
Cereal imports: 825 metric tons (2000)

Central African Republic

République Centrafricaine

Population:	3,844,000 (2002)
Land area:	622,980 SQ KM
Capital:	Bangui
Currency:	CFA franc
Language:	French

The old Oubangui-Chari empire, encompassing today's Central African Republic (CAR) was also associated with neighboring countries such as Chad, Gabon and Congo during the colonial period. The CAR has been ruled by chiefs, a sultan, colonial traders, French civil servants, a president, a military dictator, an emperor and corrupt politicians. This unstable leadership started late in the last century and has continued since the Central African Republic proclaimed independence in August 1960.

2   The region suffered one of the most savage and devastating colonial regimes ever imposed by European powers in Africa. France took an interest in the Central African highlands in the late 19th century, when the coast had already been colonized. Occupation of the interior was begun by three military expeditions directed against Sultan Rabah, the governor of the territory then known by the French as Soudan. The occupation provided an opening for about 40 trading companies which took over rubber and ivory operations in the region, later adding coffee, cotton and diamond mining to their production. This inaugurated a period of nearly 30 years in which the enslavement of Africans, killings and persecution were widely used by the companies which controlled 70 per cent of the colonized area, renamed Oubangui-Chari in 1908.

3   After World War II, France was short of the financial resources necessary for maintaining a full colonial administration, so it granted partial autonomy to the Bangui Government. The Europeanized local elite became an instrument of neocolonialism, by which the French retained control of foreign trade, defense and tax collection.

4   Violence and oppression were on the increase in 1949 when a former minister, Barthelemy Boganda, founded the Movement for the Social Evolution of Black Africa (MESAN) to fight for the independence of the Central

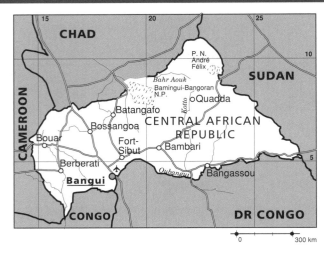

African Republic. Boganda's prestige grew enormously despite the French attempts to discredit him. In 1956, the French secret service infiltrated MESAN in an attempt to bribe two of Boganda's main advisers, David Dacko and Abel Goumba. Boganda died a year before independence in a suspicious airplane crash, in March 1959.

5   David Dacko took over the post vacated by MESAN's founder, becoming the independent country's first president in 1960. He used the position to purge the party's more progressive elements. He drew increasingly closer to the French as the US began to show an interest in exploiting the country's uranium and cobalt reserves. Dacko lost the support he had inherited from Boganda, and his government became increasingly corrupt, while the country plunged into deep economic crisis.

6   In December 1965, Dacko was ousted in a coup led by his cousin, Colonel Jean Bedel Bokassa who was pro-France, having served in the French Army for 22 years. Bokassa belonged to a small bourgeois group of M'Baka landowners from Lobaye, where France had recruited agents for its colonial administration. In 1972, he proclaimed himself president-for-life, later taking the rank of field marshal, and finally renaming the country the Central African Empire, crowning himself emperor. The coronation ceremony in December 1977 cost $28 million and was financed by France, Israel and South Africa.

7   In 1978, Bokassa gave 30,000 sq km rich in diamonds to the Israeli army, hiring a notorious international arms dealer as his military adviser. He sent troops to Zaire (now DR Congo) to help Mobutu put down a rebellion in the province of Shaba (see DR Congo).

8   Discontent finally erupted in a series of workers' and student rebellions, stifled with the help of Zairean troops. In April 1979, the students refused to comply with regulations specifying that uniforms had to be bought in stores owned by the emperor. In the ensuing demonstrations, 100 youths were arrested and taken to the infamous Ngaragba prison, where they were tortured and most of them killed under Bokassa's personal supervision.

9   Resorting to neocolonial maneuvering, France decided to depose the Emperor, attempting to erase the negative image it had created by supporting his crowning. On September 20 1979, while Bokassa was travelling in Libya, France sent a military plane to bring former president David Dacko back to Bangui. He took power, making no effort to hide his status as a colonial envoy, protected by 1,000 French troops. Dacko dissolved the Empire and reinstated a republic, granting France a 10-year lease on the big Bouar air base.

10   Dacko's return amounted to no more than a change of name as corruption and repression continued. In 1980, the CAR Government broke off relations with the USSR and Libya, expelling all their technical advisers

and diplomats. Political opposition was ruthlessly repressed and almost all opposition leaders were sent to prison or exiled. Amidst countless conspiracies, Dacko was overthrown by another military coup in September 1981, which brought General Kolingba to power.

11   The new government's first measures were to ask the French to pay the salaries of 24,000 civil servants, and to grant new economic concessions to the US, allowing them to exploit uranium resources. Meanwhile, the return to normality, initially set for 1982, was postponed until 1986. On November 21 of that year, in an election barred to the opposition, Kolingba was elected President with the support of his CAR Party of Democratic Recovery (PCRD). A constitution was passed establishing a one-party system, and on July 21 1987, the members of the General Assembly were chosen from PCRD members.

12   The Government launched a structural adjustment plan following IMF guidelines. Nevertheless, the economy as a whole showed no signs of recovery.

13   In 1986 Bokassa returned from exile in France. Sentenced to death during his absence the former 'emperor' was imprisoned.

14   Within the framework of the democratization process, direct municipal elections were held in May 1988, with universal suffrage. It was hoped that this would help to improve trade relations with the developed countries. Seeking popular support for a return to democratic institutions, the Government tried to address the question of self-sufficiency in food production, although the country still figures among the world's poorest.

15   In July 1991 a plan was approved for constitutional reform and for the adoption of a multiparty system. Elections were scheduled for October 1992, but shortly after the voting started Kolingba annulled the process claiming there had been irregularities. After the annulment a Provisional National Council of the Republic was formed, made up of the five presidential candidates. This council announced new elections for April 1993, but these were also postponed on several occasions.

PUBLIC EXPENDITURE

Military expenditure (as % GNI):	**2.8 %** (1999)
Defense expenditure (% of central government expenditure)	**15.4 %** (1999)

¹⁶ In May, a group of soldiers took the presidential palace and the Bangui radio station by force, demanding 8 months' backpay. They agreed to return to barracks after two months' salaries were paid. The first round of the presidential elections finally took place on August 11 1993. Kolingba, who came fourth, annulled the result by decree once again. However, France threatened to suspend its military and financial aid, forcing him to allow the second round to go ahead.

¹⁷ On September 1, Kolingba ordered the political prisoners to be freed, including former emperor Bokassa, who had been accused of cannibalism, murder and the misappropriation of public funds. On September 19, Ange-Felix Patassé, Bokassa's former Prime Minister, was returned as President with 52.47 per cent of the vote.

¹⁸ On December 28 1994, a new Constitution was approved by referendum. However, the opposition considered this a defeat for Patassé, as only 46 per cent of the electorate turned out to vote. The increase in international prices for cotton and diamonds produced economic growth, estimated at seven per cent for 1995. Nonetheless, inflation caused by the French imposed 100 per cent devaluation of the CFA continued to affect a large part of the population.

¹⁹ In May 1996, Patassé requested French military intervention to crush a new group of rebel soldiers. Direct involvement by French soldiers in street brawls led to a series of demonstrations against French intervention. Bangui was paralyzed after the rebellions, the looting and the French military action. The CAR economy became even more dependent on France.

²⁰ In June, the President announced a new government of national unity and named former ambassador in France, Jean Paul Ngoupande, Prime Minister. Social unrest was not appeased and caused the third rebellion in less than a year.

²¹ In spite of a truce, in early 1997, France launched an offensive against rebel troops in Bangui in retaliation for the death of two French soldiers. This led Patassé and the rebel leader Anicet Saulet to agree the replacement of French troops by a guard from African countries, although funded by Paris.

²² In January, Patassé appointed Michel Gbezera-Bria as Prime Minister. In February, a new Government was formed, including some opposition members. Most of the rebels returned to the barracks. In May, new armed confrontations caused a political crisis which led the opposition to leave the Government. New negotiations between the Government and rebel forces, with the mediation of foreign troops, settled the new crisis.

²³ Anti-French hostility was increasingly evident. In October, the CAR President demanded French withdrawal from the military bases. At the same time, he tried to strengthen links with the US, whose influence over the region had not stopped increasing at the expense of France.

²⁴ In March 1998, the UN Security Council authorized the deployment of the UN Mission in the Central African Republic (MINURCA), made up of some 1,400 troops. In April the Inter-African security force was replaced by 1,350 UN troops. The day the international force came in, France withdrew 1,400 troops. In May Patassé signed a mutual defense agreement with then President of the Democratic Republic of the Congo, Laurent Kabila. This same month the Government announced the elimination of customs subsidies, as a way to fulfil IMF-imposed conditions. In July, the IMF granted a $66-million loan to support the economic reform plan.

²⁵ In the legislative elections of November and December that year, the ruling National Liberation Movement (NLM), led by Patassé, and his allies took 49 of the 109 seats. But after some negotiations, five independents and an opposition dissident joined the government group making an NLM majority. However, the nomination of the new cabinet sparked violent street demonstrations in Bangui in January 1999.

²⁶ The September elections had to be delayed a week following requests from the opposition and the threat of disturbances. Finally Patassé took 51 per cent of the vote, but the opposition called for the elections to be annulled, accusing the Government of fraud. Former president Andre Kolingba came second, with 19 per cent of the vote.

²⁷ Shots between the presidential guard and a military squadron which had been loyal to President Patassé through the two previous coup attempts caused panic in the capital in January 2000. The presidential force finally managed to subdue the squadron, which accused the President of not keeping promises made during the previous uprisings.

²⁸ In December 2000, civil servants went on strike demanding back wages; some were owed for 30 months. In Bangui, the capital, most businesses and offices were closed and traffic was minimal. The police and army were on alert.

²⁹ Seeking an end of conflicts in the country, the leaders of Economic Community of Central African States (ECCAS), meeting in Cameroon in 2001, called for dialogue and respect of all parties for the constitution of the Central African Republic. Patassé also attended the meeting. However, a presidential spokesperson declared there was no conciliation possible with the leader of the uprising, François Bozize, former Chief of Staff of the Army.

³⁰ In February 2002, the population of Bangui began to tire of the presence of Libyan troops, ostensibly in the country to protect the President after the foiled coup. These troops controlled radio and TV stations and the airport. Their presence also caused difficulties with neighboring Chad, which has an oil pipeline to the south, near CAR's border. ∎

PROFILE

ENVIRONMENT

This is a landlocked country in the heart of Africa. It is located on a plateau irrigated by tributaries of the Congo River, like the Ubangui, the main export route, and of Lake Chad. The southwestern part of the country is covered by a dense tropical forest. Cotton, coffee and tobacco are the basic cash crops. Diamond mining is a major source of revenue. Inadequate methods of cultivation have increased soil erosion and led to a loss of fertility. The scarcity of water and pollution of important rivers pose a serious problem.

SOCIETY

Peoples: Baya (Gbaya) 23.7 per cent; Banda 23.4 per cent; Mandjia 14.7 per cent; Sara 6.5 per cent; Mbum 6.3 per cent; Mbaka 4.3 per cent; Kare 2.4 per cent; other 18.6 per cent. **Religions:** Protestant 25.0 per cent; Roman Catholic 25.0 per cent; traditional African religions 24.0 per cent; Muslim 15.0 per cent. **Languages:** French (official); Sango is the national language, used for communication between the various ethnic groups. **Political Parties:** Liberation Movement of the Central African People; Central African Democratic Rally; Movement for Democracy and Development; Patriotic Front for Progress; Social Democratic Party; Alliance for Democracy and Progress; Democratic Movement for the Rebirth and Evolution of the Central African Republic (MDRERC).

THE STATE

Official Name: République Centrafricaine. **Administrative Divisions:** 16 Prefectures, 52 Sub-prefectures. **Capital:** Bangui 622,000 people (1999). **Other cities:** Berberati 61,400 people; Bouar 53,800; Carnot 51,900; Bambari 49,900 (2000). **Government:** Ange-Félix Patassé, President since October 1993, re-elected in 1998. Martin Ziguélé, Prime Minister since April 2001. Parliament: National Assembly with 109 members, elected for a five-year term. **National Holiday:** December 1, Independence Day (1960). **Armed Forces:** 2,650 (1996). **Other:** 2,700 Gendarmes.

Chad

Tchad

Population: 8,390,000 (2002)
Land area: 1,259,200 SQ KM
Capital: N'Djamena
Currency: CFA franc
Language: Arabic and French

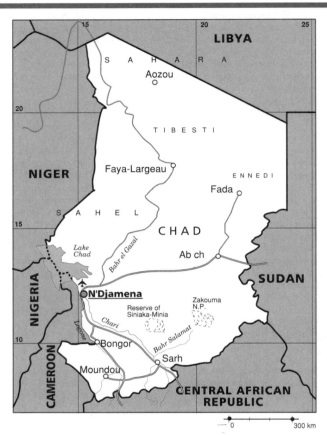

The Sahel region, of which the Republic of Chad is part, has been inhabited from time immemorial. Artifacts dating from 4,900 BC have been found in several tombs in the Tibesti mountain region, in the northern part of the country. The southern region around Chad has been under settlement since about 500 BC. In the 8th century AD, increased desiccation of Saharan borderlands stimulated Berber migrations into the area. At that time, the Kingdom of Kanem was founded; it converted to Islam in 1085. By the early 1200s, the borders of Kanem had been expanded to Fezzan in the north, Quaddaï in the west, and north of Lake Chad into the Bornu kingdom. The new Kingdom of Kanem-Bornu was established through merger, its power and prosperity peaking in the 16th century because of its command of the southern terminus of the trans-Sahara route to Tripoli.

2   At this point the rival kingdoms of Baguirmi and Ouaddaï evolved in the south. At the height of their power in the 17th century, the Baguirmi made an unsuccessful attempt to expand their territory into Kanem-Bornu. Eventually, in the years 1883-93, all three kingdoms (Ouaddaï, Kanem-Bornu and Baguirmi) were to fall to the Sudanese adventurer Rabih az-Zubayr during 1883-1893.

3   Towards the end of the 18th century, European missionaries converted some of the southern Sara to Christianity and gave them a European-style education. These converts subsequently sided with the Europeans against the native peoples of the north and by 1900 Rabih az-Zubayr was overthrown.

4   The French 'acquired' Chad in 1885 during the Berlin Conference, but did not establish themselves in the territory until a 1920 invasion by the notorious French Foreign Legion which defeated the northern Muslim groups.

5   The colonizers introduced cotton farming in 1930, and small parcels of land were distributed to peasants to grow this crop, while the French monopolized its trade. In the south, forced changes in the land tenure system replaced a communal practice of self-sufficient agriculture with large-scale farming. The result was a cotton surplus and a food shortage, accompanied by famine.

6   In August 1960 when France granted Chad its independence, southern leaders who had been negotiating with the colonizers since 1956 assumed power. However Chad's first president, François Tombalbaye, leader of the Chad Progressive Party, was unable to unite the country whose frontiers reflected the arbitrary colonial divisions.

7   The Chad Liberation Front (FROLINAT), founded in 1966, was crushed by the French troops. The Front had become fully active about the time that southern peasants rebelled against a cotton marketing system introduced by the French company Cotonfran which controlled the cotton industry. Northerners provided FROLINAT's main political support.

8   In 1970, the Front controlled two-thirds of the national territory, and by 1972 FROLINAT guerrillas were within range of N'Djamena, the capital. In 1975 Tombalbaye was ousted and killed in a French-staged coup that put General Felix Malloum in power. The guerrilla offensive

continued, and France began to take advantage of the split within the Front, which had divided into more than 10 groups.

9   Paris supported Hissene Habré's faction because he opposed Goukouni Oueddei, FROLINAT's president, who was receiving support from Muammar Khaddafi's government in Libya. At the time, Habré was at the helm of the Armed Forces of the North (AFN), and Oueddei was the leader of the People's Armed Forces (PAF). Two years later, France dispatched an additional force of 3,000 soldiers, along with fighter planes.

10   The French announced that their troops would maintain neutrality in the struggle between FROLINAT factions, while Hissene Habré accepted the post of Prime Minister in Malloum's government.

11   Towards the end of 1979 Chad's 11 major political groups formed a Provisional Government of National Unity (PGNU). Habré was named Minister of Defense. However, the French were displeased

with the make-up of the Cabinet because of their strategic interest in Chad - linked to the Maghreb and to the uranium and oil discoveries in the 1960s. In March 1980 Habré resigned, broke the alliance, and unleashed civil war that enabled him to consolidate his power in the south.

12   The ruling coalition split into three factions. In May 1980, Oueddei requested military aid from Libya, and Khaddafi sent 2,000 troops.

13   That same year, over 100,000 refugees fled the country, after the bombing of N'Djamena by Habré's forces. In October, Libyan troops reached the capital, mediation efforts by the Organization for African Unity (OAU) failed, and the defeated Habré fled to Cameroon in December 1980.

14   France led an international campaign against Libyan expansionism in Africa, with support from the United States, Egypt, Sudan, and other African countries, fearful that Khaddafi's revolutionary drive would eventually 'infect' poor Islamic populations of the Sahel region, south of the Sahara.

15   Habré was accused of being opportunistic and corrupt; however, Libyan support made it possible for France to divide Oueddei's allies. In April 1981, backed by France, Habré reorganized his followers in Sudan. In July, in Nairobi, the OAU decided to send a peacekeeping force to Chad, with the help of the French and troops from six African countries. Oueddei, yielding to foreign pressure and tensions within the PGNU, requested the withdrawal of Khaddafi's troops in November.

16   After his defeat by Habré's forces in June 1982, the exiled Oueddei set up a Provisional National Salvation Government in October with 8 of the 11 groups that had opposed Habré in the civil war. The new civil war practically split the country in two: northern Chad, under the control of a recently formed National Liberation Council with Libyan logistical support; and southern Chad, with the Habré Government dependent on French military support.

17   When Habré seized power, bringing this phase of the civil war to an end, the country was in ruins. The population of the capital, N'Djamena, had dropped to 40,000, and half of its businesses and small enterprises had closed. Outside the cities, 2,000 wells

and all the water towers had been destroyed, and the health and educational infrastructures were practically non-existent.

[18] An intense drought triggered widespread famine, despite French and American food aid. Massive protests and peasant uprisings occurred in the south. Repression by the Habré Government forced 25,000 Chadians to flee across the border into the Central African Republic.

[19] In 1987, the southern forces supported by France took Fada, Faya Largeau and the frontier strip of Aozou, claimed by Libya. In 1989, Chad and Libya signed an agreement on this 114,000 sq km territory, which included the return of prisoners and the presentation of a territorial lawsuit before the International Court in The Hague.

[20] In 1990, Idriss Déby (leader of the Patriotic Salvation Movement, supported by France) defeated Habré after a three-month military campaign. During the deposed president's term in office in the 1980s, some 40,000 people were executed or 'disappeared'.

[21] Habré fled to Senegal, where he planned a new insurrection. Some 5,000 of his rebel supporters assembled in the N'Guigmi region near Lake Chad, from where they launched several offensives. In 1992, 400 rebels died and 100 were captured when government forces put down an uprising by troops loyal to Habré with French support.

[22] Déby inaugurated a national conference in 1993 to 'democratize' Chad, with the participation of some 40 opposition parties, another 20 organizations and six armed rebel groups. Adoum Maurice El-Bongo was designated president of the conference. This meeting called a special court to judge Habré and selected Fidele Moungar as interim Premier during the transition period.

[23] In February 1994, the International Court in The Hague ruled that the Aozou strip belonged to Chad. In April, after Chad and the IMF signed an agreement to implement an annual growth program, the Transition High Council postponed the elections for one more year. In May, Libya officially returned the Aozou strip to N'Djamena.

[24] In March 1995, the Transition High Council once again postponed the elections for 12 months. At the same time, it considered as inadequate the Government measures to limit the impact of the devaluation of the CFA, decreed by France in 1994. In the Presidential elections, finally held in June and July 1996, Déby was elected constitutional President with 69 per cent of the vote.

[25] That was a year of 'reconciliation', as in January the Government had signed a peace agreement with the Action of Union and Development, which was legalized as a party once it abandoned the armed struggle. In a meeting in Gabon, in March, several rebel groups signed peace agreements with the Government and in August, Déby signed an agreement with the armed forces of the south to establish a federal republic, and the fighting was brought to a close.

[26] Southern Chad was at the heart of an international controversy in December 1997 when the Campaign for the Reform of the World Bank, supported by dozens of NGOs, opposed a megaproject planned by the Bank in this zone. The project included digging 300 oil wells and transporting oil to the Atlantic Ocean through Cameroon. The NGOs considered that funds for fighting poverty should not be used for this type of project.

[27] In March 1998, the director and editor of the *N'Djamena Hebdo* newspaper were sentenced to two years' imprisonment for 'slandering the President of Chad' in an article published in December of the previous year. However, the sentence remained suspended.

[28] In April, a new armed group of the opposition, the Renovated National Front of Chad kidnapped a French citizen and demanded the withdrawal of French troops and oil companies from the country.

[29] Since 1998, the most active guerrilla group had been the Movement for Democracy and Justice in Chad (MDJT), led by Youssouf Togoimi. The rebels were located in the mountainous area of Tibesti, in the country's desert north. In 1999, the MDJT decided to coordinate its activities with two other armed opposition groups, the Movement for Democracy and Development (MDD) and the Democratic Revolutionary Council (CDR).

[30] In the presidential elections of May 20 2001, Déby was re-elected with 67.4 per cent of the vote. The six defeated candidates claimed there was electoral fraud and called for the vote to be annulled, but international monitors stated they were mostly satisfied with the electoral process.

[31] In February 2002, the Government and the rebels of the MDJT signed a peace treaty, ending three years of civil war. The accord proclaimed an immediate ceasefire, the release of prisoners, and the incorporation of the rebels into the armed forces and the Government. Parliament passed a law guaranteeing amnesty for the guerrilla group, which planned to field candidates in the April 2002 parliamentary elections.

[32] In the parliamentary elections, President Déby's Patriotic Salvation Movement won 110 of 155 seats. ■

STATISTICS

DEMOGRAPHY
Population: 8,390,000 (2002)
Estimates for year 2015: 12,376,000 (2000)
Urban population: 23.8 % (2000)
Urban growth: 4.1 % (2000)
Children per woman: 6.7 (2000)

HEALTH
Life expectancy at birth: 46 years (2000-2005)
Maternal mortality: 830 per 100,000 live births (1985/99)
Infant mortality: 118 per 1,000 (2000)
Under-5 child mortality: 198 per 1,000 (2000)
Daily calorie supply: 2,206 per capita (1999)
3 doctors per 100,000 people (1994)
Safe water: 27 % (2000)

EDUCATION
Literacy: 54 % (2000)
male: 67 % (2000)
female: 41 % (2000)
School enrolment (net):
Primary total: 39 % (1994/2000)
male: 65 % (1995/99)
female: 39 % (1995/99)
Secondary (gross):
male: 15 % (1995/97)
female: 4 % (1995/97)
Tertiary (gross): 1 % (1997)
Primary school teachers: one for every 68 pupils (1998)

COMMUNICATIONS
0 newspapers (1996), 236 radios (1997), 1 TV set (2000) and 1 main telephone line (1999) per 1,000 people

ECONOMY
Per capita, GDP: $ 871 (2000)
Annual growth: -2.1 % (2000)
Annual inflation: 3.8 % (2000)
Cereal imports: 52,349 metric tons (2000)
Food import dependency: 24 % (1995)
Exports: $ 233 million (2000)
Imports: $ 451 million (2000)
External debt: $ 1,116 million (2000); $ 142 per capita (2000)
Debt service: 10.3 % of exports (1999)
Development aid received: $ 188 million (1999); $ 25.1 per capita (1999); 12.30 % of GNP (1999)

HDI (ranking/value): 155 / 0.359 (1999)

PROFILE

ENVIRONMENT
The northern part of Chad is desert, and 40 per cent of its territory is part of the Sahara Desert, with the great Tibesti volcanic highlands. The central region, the Sahel, which stretches to the banks of Lake Chad, is a transition plain where nomadic pastoralism is common. The lake, only half of which lies within Chad's borders, is shallow and mostly covered with swamps. Thought to be the remnant of an ancient inland sea, its waters are fed by the rivers Logane and Chari. The banks of these rivers, fertilized by flooding, contain the country's richest agricultural lands and are the most densely populated areas. In colonial times, economic activity was concentrated there. Cotton is the main export product but subsistence agriculture, though hampered by droughts, still predominates. In recent years, mineral reserves of uranium, tungsten and oil have attracted the attention of the transnationals. Desertification and drought are endemic to the region and affect all aspects of daily life.

SOCIETY
Peoples: Northern Chadians, mostly nomadic shepherds of Berber and Tuareg (Tubu, Quadainee, Kotoko, Maba) origins, have traditionally opposed the majority population of the south, where the farming Sara, Massa, Mundani and Hakka peoples predominate. Due to droughts in the Sahel region, there is a constant process of internal migration, from the north to the fertile regions of the south, which heightens conflicts.
Religions: An estimated 50 per cent of the population is Muslim, 27 per cent practice traditional African religions, 23 per cent Catholic. Muslims are mostly concentrated in the north, non-Muslims in the south.
Languages: Arabic and French are the official languages. There are more than 100 local languages, the most widely spoken being Sara (in the southern region). **Political Parties:** Patriotic Salvation Movement (MPS); National Union for Democracy and Socialism; Chad National Liberation Front (FROLINAT); National Front of Chad (FNT); Movement for Democracy and Development (MDD); National Union for Democracy and Renewal (URD); the Renovated National Front of Chad (RNFC), Movement for Democracy and Justice in Chad (MDJT), Democratic Revolutionary Council (CDR). **Social Organizations:** Chad Federation of Labor Unions, Chadian Human Rights League, Chad Non-violence.

THE STATE
Official Name: République du Tchad. **Administrative Divisions:** 14 Prefectures. **Capital:** N'Djamena 998,000 people (1999). **Other cities:** Moundou 111,200; Sarh 84,400 people; Abéché 61,100 (2000). Government: Idriss Déby, President since December 1990, re-elected in 2001. Nagoum Yamassoum, Prime Minister since December 1999. Council of the Republic with 31 members, appointed by the President. **National Holiday:** August 11, Independence Day (1960). **Armed Forces:** 25,200. **Other:** 4,500 Gendarmes.

Chile

Population: 15,589,000 (2002)
Land area: 748,800 SQ KM
Capital: Santiago
Currency: Peso
Language: Spanish

Chile

At the beginning of the 16th Century, the north of Chile formed the southernmost part of the Inca empire (see: Peru, Bolivia and Ecuador). The area between Copiapo to the north and Puerto Montt to the south was populated by the Mapuche, later called Araucanians by the Europeans. Further south lived the fishing peoples: the Yamana and the Alacalufe.

2 Diego de Almagro set off from Peru in 1536 to begin the conquest of Chile. With an expeditionary force of Spanish soldiers and enslaved native Americans he covered nearly 2,500 km, reaching central Chile when a mutiny in Lima forced him to turn back.

3 Between 1540 and 1558, Pedro de Valdivia settled in what is now the port of Valparaiso and founded several cities including Santiago. The Mapuche, led by chief Lautaro, a capable military strategist, beat the invaders on several occasions, adapting their military tactics to changing conditions in the region. Valdivia died in one of these battles. His successor, Francisco de Villagra, defeated and killed Lautaro in 1557. And in a case unique in colonial America, the Mapuche maintained an independent territory on the Bio-bio river for more than 300 years, officially recognized by Spain as Araucaria. Creole-Spanish dominion only spread to all the territory in the second half of the 19th century.

4 In 1811 the governing Junta headed by José Miguel Carrera instigated the independence process. General Bernardo O'Higgins, the son of a former viceroy in Peru, joined this movement. War broke out between the independence army and the royalist forces, with their strongholds in Valdivia and Concepción. Helped by the army of José de San Martín, which crossed the Andes to fight the royalists, the independence army finally defeated the Europeans on April 5 1818 in the Battle of Maipú.

5 In 1817, O'Higgins was designated Supreme Head of State, while the royalist troops still maintained pockets of resistance. He lay the political foundations of the country, which were reinforced in the 1833 Constitution, during the Presidential term of Diego Portales. This 'aristocratic republic', denied all forms of political expression to the new urban sectors, the middle class and the rising proletariat. English companies, in alliance with the creole oligarchy, organized an export economy based on the rich saltpeter deposits of the north along the maritime coast of then non-landlocked Bolivia to Peru. Soon the English controlled 49 per cent of Chile's foreign trade. Chilean and British capital also owned 33 per cent of Peru's saltpeter, but they wanted total control.

6 The 'Nitrate War' or Pacific War of 1879-1884 was caused by this Chilean-British alliance. Chilean territory increased by a third and left Bolivia in its present landlocked state. The victory brought about the rapid growth of the saltpeter industry and its labor force.

7 Jose Manuel Balmaceda was elected President in 1886 and tried to break the oligarchic order. The nationalism fostered by war, economic growth, social diversification and the education of the wealthy helped to gain him support. He encouraged protectionism to develop national industry. The oligarchy reacted violently, supported by the English. The army defeated the President's partisans, and Balmaceda committed suicide in the Argentine embassy in 1891.

8 In 1900, the first union was founded in Iquique. In 1904, 15 unions with 20,000 members joined to form a federation called the National Convention. That year the unions clashed with the military in Valparaíso and three years later automatic weapons supplied by the US were used to massacre 2,500 workers and their families in a school in Iquique.

9 Housing, railroads and new mines continued to expand, stimulating trade, new services and public administration. In 1920, populist politician Arturo Alessandri became the leader of the new social factions that sought to subvert the

WORKERS

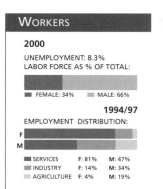

2000
UNEMPLOYMENT: 8.3%
LABOR FORCE AS % OF TOTAL:

■ FEMALE: 34%   ■ MALE: 66%

1994/97
EMPLOYMENT DISTRIBUTION:

F
M

■ SERVICES   F: 81%   M: 47%
■ INDUSTRY   F: 14%   M: 34%
■ AGRICULTURE   F: 4%   M: 19%

LAND USE

DEFORESTATION: 0.4% annual (1990/95)

1993

■ FOREST & WOODLAND: 21.8%
■ ARABLE: 5.3%
■ OTHER: 72.9%

PUBLIC EXPENDITURE

1999
66.2%

12.3%

DEFENSE   SOCIAL

oligarchic order and achieve representation in politics. Alessandri's government promoted constitutional reform and welfare legislation with electoral rights for literate men over 21, direct presidential elections, an 8-hour working day, social security, and labor regulations.

[10] Chile's economy, based on farm and mineral exports, was severely affected by the 1929-30 depression. Recovery did not come until the bourgeoisie was able to impose an industrialization program to produce previously imported goods. Their proposal served as a base for the 1936 Popular Front, which marshaled support from Communists and Socialists. The front was led by Pedro Aguirre Cerda who later became President. The armed forces were purged and withdrew from the political scene for almost 40 years. Although the oligarchy was weakened, it made a pact with the Government on agrarian policies and Aguirre Cerda never allowed land reform or the formation of rural workers' unions.

[11] The alliance worked out in the 1930s broke down during González Videla's term of office, 1946-1952. The climate created by the Cold War was used to legitimize the Law for the Permanent Defense of Democracy, which banned the Communist Party and deprived its members of the vote. On January 9 1949, to compensate for these measures, the Government brought in female suffrage. The Radical Party's repressive and de-nationalizing policies, and the disabling of the left enabled the Populist Carlos Ibáñez to win the 1952 election.

[12] Economic deterioration rapidly eroded the strength of the populist government. In 1957, offshoots from the National Falange (populist) and from the old Conservative Party (oligarchic), founded the Christian Democratic Party (PDC). The Communist Party was legalized and the Left rebuilt its alliances, forming the Popular Action Front. The people wanted change, but, sensitive to an aggressive anti-communist campaign, voted for Eduardo Frei's 'revolution in freedom', which initiated agrarian reform in 1964.

[13] The UP (Popular Unity) coalition led by Salvador Allende won the 1970 election, obtaining 35 per cent of the vote, while the rest of the electorate was split between the Christian Democrats and the conservative parties. The UP coalition included the Socialist Party, the Communist Party, the United Popular Action Movement (MAPU) and the Christian Left. The following year the UP won almost 50 per cent of the vote in the local elections, leading the right to fear a definitive loss of its majority.

[14] Allende nationalized copper and other strategic sectors, together with private banks and foreign trade. He increased land reform, promoted collective production and created a 'social sector' in the economy, managed by workers.

[15] The traditional élite, now out of power, conspired with the Pentagon, the CIA and transnational corporations, particularly ITT, to topple the Government. The Christian Democrats were indecisive, but finally supported the coup. Inflation, a shortage of goods and internal differences within Popular Unity contributed to the climate of instability.

[16] On September 11 1973 General Augusto Pinochet led a coup. The Presidential Palace at La Moneda was bombed by the air force, and President Allende died, possibly committing suicide, during the fighting. Violent repression ensued: people were shot without trial, sent to concentration camps, tortured, or simply 'disappeared'.

[17] The Chilean military dictatorship was one of many that ravaged the Southern Cone of South America during the 1970s, inspired by the National Security Doctrine. This was supported by the Chilean oligarchy and the middle classes, as well as by transnational corporations who recovered the companies which had escaped their control.

[18] After the coup, Chile's economic policy started to be based on neo-liberal doctrines. Inflation dropped below 10 per cent per year, unemployment practically disappeared and imported manufactured goods flooded the market. Alongside this ran a loss of earning power in workers' salaries and an overall impoverishment of the poorer classes.

[19] The detrimental influence of these neo-liberal economic policies became evident in 1983, two years after a constitution containing a mandate for 'continuity' was approved in a referendum by 60 per cent of the voters. Unemployment reached 30 per cent, 60 per cent of the population were malnourished, protein consumption had dropped by 30 per cent, real salaries had been reduced by 22 per cent in just two years and 55 per cent of all families were living below the poverty line. This situation provided the background for the violent popular uprising which took place in November 1983, led by the National Labor Co-ordination Board and the National Workers' Command.

[20] In 1984 the Church started talks. To participate in these, the opposition formed the Democratic Alliance, led by the PDC. The talks with Home Minister Sergio Onofre Jarpa failed and from September 1984, the break with the Church became evident. After this date, the Vicarate for Solidarity of the Archbishopric of Santiago played a key role in defending human rights.

[21] The political left joined together under the Popular Democratic Movement (MDP), vindicating all forms of struggle against the dictatorship. One faction formed the Manuel Rodriguez Patriotic Movement (MRPM), an armed group which carried out numerous attacks, the most important being an attempted assassination of Pinochet on September 7 1986.

[22] The international isolation of Chilean Government during the US Carter administration eased a little with the election of Ronald Reagan, and Margaret Thatcher in the UK. In August 1985 Chile authorized US space shuttle landings on Easter Island. At the beginning of 1986 a US delegation proposed that Chile be condemned before the UN Human Rights Commission, thereby avoiding having to take more drastic action against the country.

[23] On October 5 1988, an 8-year extension of Pinochet's rule was submitted to a referendum. Widespread opposition ended his government, bringing elections the following year.

[24] Facing up to the fact that change was inevitable, Pinochet negotiated constitutional reform. Proposed changes included further restrictions of the power of future governments, an increase in the number of senators, shortening the Presidential term from 8 years to 4 and a liberalization of left-wing parties. The reform was approved by referendum on July 30 1989.

PROFILE

ENVIRONMENT

Flanked by the Andes mountain range in the east and the Pacific in the west, the country is a thin strip of land 4,200 km long and never wider than 360 km. Its length explains its variety of climates and regions. Due to the cold ocean currents, the northern territory is a desert. The central region has a mild climate which makes it good for agriculture. The southern part of the country is colder and heavily wooded. The major salt and copper mines are located in northern Chile. 65 per cent of the population live in the central valleys. During the military regime, some 40 thousand hectares of native forests were cut down each year, and replaced by other tree species, causing the displacement and death of wildlife.

SOCIETY

Peoples: Chileans are descended from the native American population and European immigrants. 300,000 Mapuche Indians live mainly in southern Chile.
Religions: Mainly Catholic (77 per cent), Protestant 13 per cent.
Languages: Spanish, Mapudungun (Mapuche language), Rapa nui and other minority languages.
Political Parties: Concertación of Parties for Democracy (CPD), a coalition of the Christian Democratic Party (PDC), the Socialist Party (PS), the Democratic Party (PPD) and the Radical Party (RP). The National Renovation Party (RN); the Independent Democratic Union (UDI); Union of Center Center (UCC); Communist Party of Chile (PCCh); Revolutionary Movement of the Left (MIR); the Manuel Rodríguez Patriotic Movement (MPMR); Humanistic Party (PH); the Green Party.
Social Organizations: The Central Workers' Union (CUT), was the main labor organization until 1973, when it was forbidden. Legalized in 1990, it became the most important union again in the early 90s. Other trade unions are: the Copper Workers' Confederation (CTC) led by Rodolfo Seguel; the Confederation of Civil Servants of Chile (CEPCH) led by Federico Mujica; the National Association of Civil Servants; the United Workers' Front (FUT); the National Labor Co-ordination Board (CNS); the National Federation of Taxi Drivers; the Democratic Workers' Union (UDT), and unions representing artists, oil workers, professionals and truck drivers. El Surco (union of rural workers). The indigenous movement has independent organizations as the Action Group for the Bío Bío (GABB), the Mapuche Inter-regional Council (CIM) and the Mapuche Ad-Mapu Organization.

THE STATE

Official Name: República de Chile.
Administrative divisions: 12 numbered Regions and the unnumbered Metropolitan Region of Santiago.
Capital: Santiago 5,440,000 people (1999).
Other cities: Viña del Mar 356,800 people; Concepción 963,800; Valparaíso 888,300; Temuco 280,200 (2000).
Government: Ricardo Lagos, President since March 2000. Bicameral Legislative: the National Congress is formed by the Chamber of Deputies, with 117 members, and the Senate, with 48 members.
National Holiday: September 18, Independence Day (1810).
Armed Forces: 89,700 troops; 31,000 carabineros; 50,000 reservists (1996).

[25] Elections were held on December 14 1989. Patricio Aylwin, leader of the Christian Democrats, gained 55.2 per cent of the vote, taking office on March 11, 1990.

[26] In April, Aylwin appointed a Truth and Reconciliation Commission to investigate the issue of missing people. The Commission confirmed that there were at least 2,229 missing people, who were assumed dead. It also made a detailed study of repression during the dictatorship. When the facts were made public in March 1991 the President asked the nation for forgiveness in the name of the State. He announced that judicial procedures would follow and he requested the co-operation of the armed forces in these proceedings

[27] Official recognition virtually brought about an institutional crisis. The armed forces and the Supreme Court justified their conduct during the Pinochet dictatorship, and denied the validity of the Government report - thus discrediting the President. The crisis was defused when the Government accepted the prerequisites of 'Chilean transition', which included preserving the judicial system of the previous regime and guaranteeing impunity from charges of human rights violations.

[28] On April 2, Senator Jaime Guzmán, former adviser and ideologue of the military regime, was murdered and the assassination attributed to radical left wing groups. This enabled the Right to raise the issue of terrorism once more. Political life was slowly brought back to normal. On April 23, the MRPM announced its decision to abandon armed struggle.

[29] The Chilean economy maintained a 10-year expansion, with annual growth rates of over 6 per cent, mainly due to high levels of investment (especially fixed capital) and the expansion of the external sector. Direct foreign investment remained at significant levels: $3.5 and $2.9 billion in 1992 and 1993, respectively.

[30] During Aylwin's presidency, social indicators improved. In 1993, real salaries increaced 5 five per cent, the unemployment rate fell to 4.5 per cent, and social spending increased 14 per cent.

[31] In August 1993, the Special Commission on Indigenous Peoples (a government agency) proposed introducing indigenous language instruction in Mapuche, Aymara and Rapa Nui at primary school level. This was considered vital by Mapuche educators to reduce the loss of cultural identity indigenous children experienced when put into a school system where Spanish is the sole medium of instruction.

[32] In the 1993 elections, Eduardo Frei, candidate for the Christian Democratic Party and the Concertación (agreement) coalition, won the presidency with 58 per cent of the vote. However, he did not achieve the parliamentary majority required to do away completely with the old authoritarianism because of eight 'designated' seats in the Senate which were a legacy from the Pinochet regime.

[33] Shortly before handing over the presidency, President Aylwin pardoned four MRPM activists, sentenced to death for the assassination attempt against Pinochet in 1986.

[34] The Frei Government announced a plan to reduce the poverty which affected nearly a quarter of the population. In May 1995, the minimum salary was increased 13 per cent. Taxes were introduced on the sale of cigarettes and motor vehicles to fund a 10 per cent increase in the lowest pensions and a 5 per cent increase in the education budget. In June, Chile requested associate membership of the Mercosur market and negotiated entry into the North American Free Trade Association (NAFTA).

[35] Brigadier Pedro Espinoza and retired General Manuel Contreras were sentenced to imprisonment for their parts in the murder of former foreign minister Orlando Letelier in Washington in 1976. Pinochet reiterated his support for the sentenced officers, but then called for respect for the civil authorities. At the same time, the Government suspended investigations into corruption charges against the former dictator's son. In a later hearing, during February 1998, Contreras stated that the true leader of the DINA (the political police during the dictatorship) was Pinochet himself.

[36] The Chamber of Deputies approved the trade agreement with Mercosur member nations by 76 votes to 26. Two right-wing parties the UDI and RN, came out against the agreement. The signing of the free trade agreement took place on June 25 1996, establishing the 'four plus one' association between Argentina, Brazil, Paraguay, Uruguay and Chile. This formula was to remain in place until Chile became a full member of the agreement. The treaty with Mercosur came into operation on October 1 1996.

[37] A report from the National Society of Farmers (SNA) said the agreement would mean annual losses of $460 million for the Chilean agricultural sector, but, balancing this, the country would become integrated into a market of more than 200 million people.

[38] In the October municipal elections, the ruling Concertación Nacional took the majority of the votes. Representation of the Democratic Christians, the Socialist Party (PS), the Democratic Party (PPD) and the Radical Party (RP), increased in the municipal councils. However, the number of Concertación Nacional mayors fell compared with the previous elections in 1992.

[39] Within Concertación, the Democratic Christians lost support to the increasingly popular PS and PPD, who were more successful in local councils and mayoralties. This political advantage allowed them to strengthen their position within the coalition.

[40] Various studies in 1996 suggested the average economic growth of 6 per cent in the last 11 years had led to a reduction in 'extreme poverty' - but not in social inequality. Thus 20 per cent of the population still controlled 57 per cent of the national wealth, while the poorest 20 per cent handled only 3.9 per cent. During the first half of 1996, military and civil tribunals closed 21 cases of disappearances and extra-judicial killings involving 56 victims, without finding anyone responsible.

[41] In May 1997, demonstrations by the miners' union - a bastion of the union movement and the Communist Party - in central Santiago were put down violently.

[42] Concertación retained the majority in the December 11 legislative elections, but lost ground to the right. The government coalition took 50.6 per cent of the vote (compared with 56.1 per cent in the 1996 municipal elections), while the right took 39 per cent (35 per cent in 1996).

[43] After passing on the post of Commander-in-Chief of the armed forces to General Ricardo Izurieta, Pinochet entered the Senate on March 11 1998, amidst general indignation. During the former dictator's first appearance in the Senate, several senators carried photographs of people who had

DEMOGRAPHY
Population: 15,589,000 (2002)
Annual growth: 1.6 % (1985-2000)
Estimates for year 2015: 17,912,000 (2000)
Annual growth to year 2015: 1.1 % (2000)
Urban population: 84.6 % (2000)
Urban growth: 1.5 % (2000)
Children per woman: 2.4 (2000)

HEALTH
Life expectancy at birth: 76 years (2000-2005)
male: 73 years (2000-2005)
female: 79 years (2000-2005)
Maternal mortality: 23 per 100,000 live births (1985/99)
Infant mortality: 10 per 1,000 (2000)
Under-5 child mortality: 12 per 1,000 (2000)
Daily calorie supply: 2,858 per capita (1999)
110 doctors per 100,000 people (1994)
Safe water: 93 % (2000)

EDUCATION
Literacy: 96 % (2000)
male: 96 % (2000)
female: 96 % (2000)
School enrolment (net):
Primary total: 89 % (1994/2000)
male: 88 % (1995/99)
female: 88 % (1995/99)
Secondary (gross):
male: 72 % (1995/97)
female: 78 % (1995/97)
Tertiary (gross): 34 % (1998)
Primary school teachers: one for every 27 pupils (1998)

COMMUNICATIONS
98 newspapers (1996), 354 radios (1997), 242 TV sets (2000) and 221 main telephone lines (2000) per 1,000 people
Books: 13 new titles per 100,000 people (1992/94)

ECONOMY
Per capita, GDP: $ 9,417 (2000)
Annual growth: 4.0 % (2000)
Annual inflation: 3.8 % (2000)
Consumer price index: 128.5 (2000)
Currency: 674.3 pesos = $ 1 (03/2002)
Cereal imports: 1,947,800 metric tons (2000)
Food import dependency: 7 % (2000)
Fertilizer use: 2,398 kg per ha (1999)
Exports: $ 22,468 million (2000)
Imports: $ 21,718 million (2000)
External debt: $ 36,978 million (2000); $ 2,431 per capita (2000)
Debt service: 25.4 % of exports (1999)
Development aid received: $ 69 million (1999); $ 4.6 per capita (1999); 0.10 % of GNP (1999)

ENERGY
Consumption: 1,594.3 Kgs of oil equivalent per capita yearly (1998); 69.8 % imported (1999)

HDI (ranking/value): 39 / 0.825 (1999)

disappeared in the dictatorship. One member of Parliament hung a sign saying 'murderers not admitted' on the window of his office.

[44] Pinochet's arrest in Britain in October 1998, following an extradition bid by Spanish judge Baltasar Garzón, deeply shook the Chilean political process. The Government and opposition united in calls for the General to be returned to Chile. But while the Right accused the government of only making luke-warm efforts, Concertación suffered internally from having to defend the former dictator under the guise of defending national sovereignty. The legal comings and goings in London were accompanied by often violent demonstrations in Santiago both for and against the arrest.

[45] In November 1998, in a country where women only make up 32 per cent of the economically-active population, Mirella Pérez was appointed the first female general in Chile after being promoted throughout the ranks of the Carabineros.

[46] There were confrontations between Mapuche and forestry planters in southern Chile in October 1999. These led to the mobilization of a special armed group of 200 police officers with helicopter backing who surrounded the village of Temucuicui. The Government announced a plan

whereby Mapuche would receive $275 million for roads, technical agricultural aid, student grants, paying off the state agricultural agency debt and the establishment of bilingual schools. However, Mapuche leaders saw this as a collection of old unfulfilled promises dressed up as a new offer. The Chilean Constitution offers no special treatment to indigenous communities, unlike many other regional nations.

[47] Ricardo Lagos, the socialist Concertación candidate won a slim victory in the January 2000 presidential elections leaving the new government with very little room for maneuver. The Right, which took a moral victory with 49 per cent of the vote, promised an attitude of 'vigilant collaboration' with the president-elect.

[48] In an unprecedented ruling, the Supreme Court of Justice recognized the ancestral rights of a Mapuche indigenous community, against the interests of a powerful southern landowner who was occupying plots for commercial plantations. In its ruling, the Court recognized these were fiscal lands ancestrally held by the Huilliche. This case was significant because it was an exception to the government's customary treatment of the Mapuche people, often including conflicts over this very issue of indigenous peoples' land rights.

[49] Pinochet returned to Chile in March, after the British justice system

considered his 'bad health' exempted him from being tried in Spain. A week later, Chilean Congress approved a constitutional amendment guaranteeing immunity to former presidents. But, in a ruling published in May, the Court of Appeals requested Parliament to lift Pinochet's immunity. Two weeks later, representatives from the Government (including the army) and civil society formed a Human Rights Committee to find the remains of the 'disappeared'. In August, the Supreme Court ruled that Pinochet had lost his immunity. In early 2001, judge Juan Guzmán confirmed the charges of homicide and kidnapping against the former dictator and confined him to house arrest for his involvement with the 'Death Caravan', a military squad that traveled through Chile by helicopter, executing 75 political prisoners during the first weeks of the dictatorship.

[50] In July 2001, a Chilean court suspended the charges against Pinochet, claiming he was not able to stand trial since he was not 'in a state of mental capacity' enabling him to exercise 'efficiently the rights of due process'.

[51] Likewise, on September 11 of that year, a Washington DC (US) court began a trial against former Secretary of State Henry Kissinger for his involvement in the plan leading

to the murder of Chilean general René Schneider in 1970. The trial was started by Schneider's relatives, based on the contradictions between CIA reports and Kissinger's statements on the case. The Supreme Court of Chile approved a request from judge Guzmán to interrogate Kissinger about the death of American journalist Charles Horman.

[52] Parliamentary elections were held on December 16 2001 - the first test for the government coalition. Although having lost seats in the lower chamber, the government held on to an 8-deputy majority. In the Senate it lost the advantage it had over the Independent Democratic Union (UDI), and both were left with 24 representatives. This result further hampered the Government's plans to revoke Pinochet's 1981 Constitution.

[53] Although passing a divorce law was one of President Lagos' campaign priorities, the Government had not acted to bring in the law by March 2002 as promised, due to the Catholic Church's opposition and pressure on Chile as the only Catholic country without a divorce law.

[54] On February 21 2002, 25 members of the US Congress requested Attorney Roscoe Howard to present formal charges against Pinochet for terrorism and for his alleged responsibility in the 1976 murder of former Chilean Foreign Minister Letelier. ∎

The Mapuche and their struggle for land

The Mapuche of southern Chile have sought to democratize this country that has been in political transition since 1990, and where military prosecutors and courts still prevail.

For the last few years, the Mapuche communities living south of the Bío Bío River in Chile's Ninth region, have denounced the predation of their lands and destruction of their fields. They find especially galling the impunity with which the private logging and electricity help themselves to the 200,000 hectares plundered from the indigenous peoples during the military dictatorship of General Augusto Pinochet (1973-1989). Most of these companies are based on foreign capital, mainly from Spain.

The Mapuches staged peaceful demonstrations that were harshly repressed by the Carabineros - the military police force. The police force has increased its presence in the

region since then, ultimately creating greater awareness among the Chilean population about the Mapuche situation. The media has given wide coverage on the indigenous group's social and political organizations and its worldview – in sharp contrast to these South American native peoples' earlier separation. The Mapuches belong to the Araucano linguistic group, and currently number some 300,000 people who are primarily involved in farming.

As the neo-liberal economic model strengthened its grip on Chile in the 1980s, the Mapuche communities lost 60 per cent of their lands practically overnight. Lawsuits over land ownership in the region are still pending in the civil court system; the communities charge that the national governments have lacked the political will to resolve the conflict. In 1997, the Mapuches created the Association of Mapuche Communities, which

organized a march to Santiago in 1999, walking hundreds of kilometers to demand that the State return their lands and prevent the corporations from expanding activities in their territories.

Confrontations and repression led to the imprisonment of dozens of Mapuche leaders. They were tried by military prosecutors in military courts - which have jurisdiction over civilian issues - on charges of 'illegal association' and other crimes established under the dictatorship to fight the leftist national liberation movements of that time. According to legal observers and various human rights organizations, under international humanitarian law, the Chilean military justice system cannot try civilians and it did not provide the defendants with appropriate guarantees of due process.

For 350 years, the Mapuche have resisted invasions, first by the Spanish colo-

nists and later by successive Chilean governments and the army. Led by Chief Lautaro, these indigenous peoples won several battles against the Spanish Army and nearly invaded Santiago, the capital. When Chile achieved its independence, in the early 19th century, the Government and the dominant class decided that the 'Mapuche problem' must be resolved, but it was not until 1881 that the Chilean Army 'recovered' the indigenous Araucanía region by killing the native peoples. In 1883, after a series of treaties, the Mapuches were confined to 300,000 hectares. Previously they had held approximately five million hectares, and later under the Pinochet regime they lost the 200,000 hectares that are currently exploited by the Mininco forestry and Endesa hydroelectric firms. ∎

China

Zhong Ghuo

Population: 1,294,377,000 (2002)
Land area: 9,327,420 SQ KM
Capital: Beijing
Currency: Renminbi (Yuan)
Language: Chinese

China has one of the world's oldest civilizations, which achieved an unparalleled degree of cultural and social homogeneity several thousand years before most modern nations were formed.

2 Although the nation disintegrated into warring kingdoms at various points in its history, the development of Chinese civilization can be traced back 5,000 years to its emergence in the Yellow River (Huanghe) basin.

3 Territory was consolidated early on, and a single writing system was established by emperor Qin Shihuang some 2,200 years ago, in 221-206 BC; the same system is still in use today. In his determination to consolidate Chinese thinking he also ordered the burning of all previous books, and the execution of many scholars.

4 By the time of the Tang Dynasty, 618-907AD, China had developed a cultured civilization, and during the Song Dynasty, 960-1279 AD, the nation was more developed than Europe in every field.

5 Construction of the 5,000-km Great Wall of China was started in the third century BC in an attempt to repel invaders from the north. The wall ultimately failed, and China fell to Mongolian invaders; Genghis Khan and his grandson Kublai Khan ruled China from 1276 to 1368.

6 One of the most influential figures in Chinese culture was the scholar Confucius who lived about 2,500 years ago. As a philosopher, he emphasized respect for one's elders, the importance of unquestioning loyalty and responsibility to superiors in the social hierarchy and the central role of the family. Other philosophers such as Lao Zi emphasized a more imaginative role for individuals in society, but Confucian thinking is most accurately reflected in the partially surviving social structures of China, Korea, Japan and Vietnam.

~~~~ Great Wall

///// Area claimed by India

0   100 km

7 With their highly developed culture, the Chinese soon developed a disdain for the 'barbarians' beyond their borders. This attitude was often combined with the corruption of imperial dynasties, leading to eras of isolationism and social stagnation.

8 Regular contact with Europeans began when the Portuguese opened up maritime routes in the 15th century. The Chinese allowed Europeans to use a limited number of trading ports under strict conditions and granted the tiny enclave of Macau to the Portuguese in 1557. But the Chinese still refused to take foreign powers seriously.

9 The British eventually found a commodity that could be traded with China to pay for the Chinese silk, tea and porcelain products so fashionable in Europe. They began to import opium from India. When China tried to outlaw the drug trade, and later, to stop smuggling, Britain declared war in the name of free trade.

10 Modern European weapons easily defeated the Chinese imperial armies in the First Opium War, 1839-42. The victorious British demanded that five ports be opened to their trade, that low customs duties be imposed, and

that the territory of Xianggang (Hong Kong) be given to them

11 The tottering Chinese Empire suffered another type of defeat with the Taiping rebellion of 1851-64. The rebel empire controlled much of southern China for 11 years before being crushed with the help of Western troops.

12 Massive imports of opium were then being paid for in Chinese silver, impoverishing the nation as it was weakened by widespread drug addiction. Another war from 1856-1860, this time against Anglo-French forces, ended with the capture of Beijing and a new round of concessions, including the admission of missionaries.

13 In 1895, China suffered an even more humiliating defeat at the hands of its former tributary state Japan, which overran part of the Korean peninsula and the island of Taiwan.

14 An anti-Western rebellion broke out in 1898 led by the Boxers, a secret society that attempted to drive foreigners out of China and to force Chinese converts to renounce Christianity. A joint British, Russian, German, French, Japanese and US expedition intervened to put down the uprising. The victorious armies

WORKERS

2000

LABOR FORCE AS % OF TOTAL

■ FEMALE: 45%   ■ MALE: 55%

LAND USE

DEFORESTATION: 0.1% annual (1990/95)

1993

■ FOREST & WOODLAND: 13.5%
■ ARABLE: 9.6%
■ OTHER: 76.9%

PUBLIC EXPENDITURE

1999

22.2%   2.6%
DEFENSE   SOCIAL

divided the country into 'zones of influence' and demanded that the Chinese pay huge war reparations.

[15] The most spectacular example of foreign involvement in China was in Shanghai, where the port was developed for trading, and foreign companies invested in hundreds of factories, located within foreign 'concessions', to take advantage of cheap Chinese labor.

[16] Foreign exploitation also brought new ideas and concepts to China. The Government belatedly allowed small groups of students to study overseas. Nationalist groups emerged to focus and articulate the massive anti-foreign sentiment. In 1911, nationalists led by Sun Yat-sen, won the support of several imperial generals. A number of garrisons mutinied, and a Republic was proclaimed.

[17] Most of the generals who had joined the uprising wanted power and had no intention of instituting democratic reforms. Simmering rivalries soon burst into the open and China was thrust into an era of civil war as local 'warlords', backed by various foreign powers, fought over the fragmented country.

PROFILE

ENVIRONMENT

The terrain of the country is divided into three main areas. Central Asian China, comprising Lower Mongolia, Sin Kiang and Tibet, is made up of high plateaus, snow-covered in winter but with steppe and prairie vegetation in summer. North China holds the vast plains of Manchuria and Hoang-Ho, with extensive plantations of wheat, barley, sorghum, soybean and cotton (though no longer has a surplus in farm products and has become a net importer). The North also has coal and iron ore deposits (Manchuria is the country's leading mining region). South China is a hilly region crossed by the Yangtse Kian and Si-kiang Rivers and has a warm, humid, monsoon climate. The country holds great mineral wealth: coal, petroleum, iron and non-ferrous metals. The use of coal as the main source of energy produces acid rain, pollution and carbon dioxide emissions. Less than 13 percent of the land is forested. There is great potential for hydroelectric energy production, which is being sought through the construction of the Three Gorges dam on the Yangtse River. One of the largest such projects in the world, its environmental and social impacts are considered potentially catastrophic.

SOCIETY

Peoples: There are 56 official recognized nationalities. Han (91.96 per cent), Chuang (1.37 per cent), Manchu (0.87 per cent), Hui (0.76 per cent), Miao (0.65 per cent), Uighur (0.64 per cent), Yi (0.58 per cent), Tuchia (0.50 per cent), Mongol (0.42 per cent), Tibetan (0.41 per cent), Puyi (0.23 per cent), Tung (0.22 per cent), Yao (0.18 per cent), Korean (0.17 per cent), Pai (0.14 per cent), Hani (0.11 per cent), Kazak (0.1 per cent), Tai (0.09 per cent), Li (0.09 per cent), other (0.51 per cent).
Religions: No religion 59.2 per cent. Confucianism (a moral code, not a religion) combined with mystical elements from Taoism and Buddhism are what could be called the predominant 'beliefs'. Buddhist 6.0 per cent; Muslim 2.4 per cent; Christian 0.2 per cent; other 0.1 per cent.
Languages: Chinese (official) is a modernized version of northern Mandarin. Variants of this (many of which are mutually unintelligible) can be found in the rest of the country, the most widespread being Cantonese, in the south. Ethno-cultural diversity is reflected by the 205 registered languages. **Political Parties:** The Chinese Constitution states that the Communist Party is the 'leading nucleus of all the Chinese people'. There are eight minor parties that participate in political life, including the Democratic Party of Workers and Peasants, the Revolutionary Committee of the Kuomintang and the League for the self-governance of democratic Taiwan. Hong Kong and Macau also have their own parties. **Social Organizations:** Chinese Federation of Unions is the largest. Opposition groups of unknown size, based on ethnicity and religion, extending to the diaspora: movements in Tibet, Inner Mongolia, Xinjiang, as well as the Falungong group.

THE STATE

Official name: Zhonghua Renmin Gongheguo.
Administrative divisions: 23 provinces (including Taiwan), 5 autonomous regions, 4 municipalities and 2 special administrative regions (Macau and Hong Kong). **Capital:** Beijing 10,825,000 people (1999).
Other cities: Shanghai 12,900,000 people; Tianjin 9,200,000; Xianggang (Hong Kong) 8,087,700; Shenyang 6,326,000 (2000).
Government: Socialist Republic. Jiang Zemin, General Secretary of the Communist Party, President since March 1993, re-elected in 1998. Zhu Rongji, Prime Minister since March 1998. The 2,979-member National People's Congress (NPC) sits for about two weeks a year to ratify laws. NPC delegates are drawn from various geographical areas and social sectors (army, minorities, women, religious groups).
National Holiday: October 1 and 2, proclamation of the People's Republic of China. **Armed Forces:** 2,930,000 (1995).
Other: 1,200,000 Armed Peoples' Police, Defense Department.

[18] In 1915, young intellectuals, inspired by 'New Youth', a magazine edited by Ch'en Tu-hsiu, began agitating for the reform and strengthening of Chinese society. The New Youth attacked traditional Chinese ethics, philosophy, religion, and social and political institutions and exalted Western ideas, particularly science and democracy. On May 4 1919, more than 3,000 students held a mass demonstration in Beijing against the Chinese government's acquiescence to the decision of the Versailles Peace Conference to transfer the former German concessions in the Shantung Province to Japan. The students burned the house of the minister of communications and assaulted China's representative to Japan. Demonstrations occurred throughout the country and scores of students died in these incidents. More than 1,000 were arrested. Along the country and during more than two months students organized strikes and boycotts against Japanese assets.

[19] In 1921, 13 people from all over China gathered in a small house in the French concession of Shanghai to hold the first national congress of the Chinese Communist Party (CCP).

[20] The new party prioritized the organization of workers and it enjoyed considerable success. By 1926 it was involved with 700 trade unions representing 1.24 million members. They formed an alliance with Chiang Kai-Shek's Kuomintang (KMT) nationalist party to oppose the warlords. In 1927, the KMT turned on their allies and massacred some 40,000 communist labor leaders.

[21] In the face of such a defeat, a communist leader, Mao Zedong (Mao Tse Tung), argued that the Chinese peasantry should be mobilized as a revolutionary force. He led most of the Communist Party leadership into rural China, where they carried out political organizing and raised a peasant-based army.

[22] When the KMT armies tried to surround the CCP's remote bases in 1934, the communist army, their leaders and supporters began a march in search of an alternative site. They travelled for over a year, their numbers dwindling under frequent attacks and severe conditions, but they were eventually able to regroup. This legendary journey became known as the 'long march'.

[23] In 1937 a full-scale Japanese invasion of China forced the CCP and the KMT to set aside their differences and form a second United Front against the common enemy. While fighting against the Japanese, the Communists were also able to extend their influence among the workers in KMT-controlled areas. Chiang Kai-Shek showed more interest in fighting the Communists than the

Japanese and broke the pact on several occasions. On one occasion, his own generals arrested him and forced him to negotiate with the CCP to continue joint resistance to the Japanese.

[24] When the allies defeated the Japanese in 1945, the CCP-KMT front collapsed into civil war. The corrupt and autocratic KMT proved no match for the highly-motivated CCP armies and their supporters. On October 1 1949, the communist leadership declared the foundation of the People's Republic of China. An era of foreign control and humiliation went out and an era of social and economic reform came in.

[25] The remnants of the KMT Government and army fled to the island of Taiwan. There, under US protection, they claimed to represent all of China and laid plans to eventually 'reconquer' the mainland.

[26] The Chinese Communists instituted far-reaching land reforms, adding to those already carried out in their own liberated zones before the final victory. They also nationalized all foreign-controlled property and initiated widespread education and health programs.

[27] The first 5-year development plan incorporated many aspects of the Soviet model; the emphasis was on industrial investment rather than consumption, and heavy industry rather than light, all under a centralized economic plan. The creation of a strong industrial base could only be achieved by extracting a large surplus from rural areas, but by 1957 agricultural production was badly stagnating.

[28] In the name of open debate, and in search of solutions to the nation's problems, the party launched a campaign to 'let a hundred flowers bloom, let a hundred schools of thought contend', inviting people to criticize the system and suggest alternatives. When citizens began to complain about the lack of democracy and question party rule, the leadership turned about-face and cracked down on those who had spoken out.

[29] In 1958, Mao launched the Great Leap Forward, aimed at accelerating rural collectivization and urban industrialization. This heavy-handed, dogmatic and inflexible

85% 2000

2000

4%

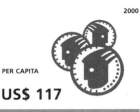

2000

PER CAPITA

US$ 117

Millions US$ 2000

IMPORTS
250,685

EXPORTS
279,558

plan led the country down a disastrous path, sparking widespread famine in the countryside. The official Chinese figure for deaths between 1959 and 1961 is 20 million; one of the greatest human tragedies of the century, and one of the least widely reported.

[30] In 1962, Mao was forced to deliver a public self-criticism of his economic policies and was replaced by Liu Shaoqi as state chairman. Mao still enjoyed support among many radicals and, most importantly, from the People's Liberation Army.

[31] During this period, relations with the Soviet Union were souring due to ideological differences. This was highlighted in a 1956 speech by Soviet leader Nikita Khruschev. The split came in 1963, and USSR advisors left China taking plans and blueprints with them.

[32] In 1966, the army and young people, the 'Red Guards', armed with the Little Red Book of Mao's thoughts, initiated campaigns throughout China attacking bureaucrats and university professors as reactionaries and 'capitalist followers'. The Great Proletarian Cultural Revolution had begun.

[33] At some stages during that period, with the internal 'struggle between two lines' attaining civil war proportions, production suffered severely with many factories and universities closing altogether. An estimated 10 million people died during the years of turmoil, including Liu Shaoqi, Mao's chief opponent.

[34] At the same time, China took a leading role in founding the Non-Aligned Movement, and sent large numbers of workers abroad on high-profile development projects such as the Tanzam railway in Africa, linking Zambia to the coast via Tanzania. Liberation movements in many countries were inspired by China, adopting the peasant war strategies outlined in the works of Mao Zedong and Lin Piao.

[35] In the early 1970s Prime Minister Zhou Enlai started talks with the US, and Liu Shaoqi's protégé, Deng Xiaoping, was returned to power.

[36] In 1971 the mainland communist Government won sufficient support to replace Taiwan as the representative of China in the United Nations. Unlike earlier

occasions, this time the US refrained from exercising its veto because it saw distinct advantages in improving relations with China. In 1976, the US and China re-established diplomatic relations.

[37] Internationally, China seemed to oppose all Soviet allies. This led to Chinese support for movements like UNITA in Angola and the PAC in South Africa. It also caused a growing rift with Vietnam after the defeat of the US in 1975. In 1979, China invaded Vietnam to 'teach it a lesson' over its military contribution to the Khmer Rouge defeat in Cambodia.

[38] In 1975, Zhou and revolutionary veteran Zhu De both died, with Mao following in 1976. The pragmatists and reformists prevailed, taking advantage of support among party bureaucrats.

[39] The leaders of the Maoist faction - Mao's widow Jiang Qing, Zhang Chunqiao, Yao Wenyuan and Wang Hongwen, dubbed the 'Gang of Four' - were arrested and charged with plotting to usurp state and party power. They became scapegoats for the failures and excesses of the Cultural Revolution. In 1981 they were put on public trial as a final symbolic gesture that the era of 'revolutionary struggle' was over.

[40] Deng Xiaoping was rehabilitated by the new leadership, and he was universally acknowledged as its leading authority.

[41] Government's acceptance of greater popular expression and criticism was apparent in 1978 and 1979. They knew that this would be directed against the turmoil of the Cultural Revolution and the radicals responsible for it. The 'Beijing Spring' was centered on the 'Democracy Wall', where ordinary citizens could display posters expressing their opinions. The wall also served as a spot where dissidents distributed unofficial magazines. When criticism began to focus on the country's core political structure, the leadership stopped the movement. The Democracy Wall, an institution throughout the Cultural Revolution, was discontinued. One dissident, Wei Jingshen, who published a magazine calling for a 'Fifth Modernization' - democracy - was tried and sentenced to a 15-year prison sentence.

[42] In December 1978, at the 3rd

plenary of the 11th Party Central Committee, Deng was fully rehabilitated and sweeping economic reforms were announced.

[43] In the countryside, the People's Communes were disbanded and land was redistributed into family-size units leased from the State. Production quotas were replaced by taxes, and peasants were permitted to sell their surpluses for cash in the towns and cities.

[44] China also announced a dramatic new openness to foreign trade, investment and borrowing. To attract foreign industry, Special Economic Zones were established near Hong Kong (Xianggang) and Macau, offering a range of incentives; such as tax breaks and cheap land and labor, similar to free trade zones elsewhere.

[45] In industry, a good deal of decision-making power was passed from the ministries to individual plant managers, who were now free to plan production and distribution, and choose the sources of their raw materials. Young workers were offered a contract system of employment instead of lifetime assignment to a production unit. Individuals and families were given permission to start small businesses such as restaurants and shops.

[46] The Government began a phased program of removing price subsidies on consumer goods, allowing the market to determine the price of such basics as food and clothing, to spur economic growth and encourage consumption.

[47] As the changes took hold, more goods and foodstuffs appeared in shops, and wages increased for several years. The long-standing problem of unemployment and underemployment diminished as more people became self-employed. Restrictions on the freedom of travel inside and outside China were loosened, greater artistic diversity and expression were tolerated and a greater diversity of information was made available.

[48] These economic reforms began to accelerate inflation, especially on such basic items as food and clothing, and in the late 1980s, workers found that their buying power was falling.

[49] In the countryside, peasants with easy access to urban centers

benefited as they were able to supply large markets. Those in more remote areas fell behind. The use of chemical pesticides and fertilizers soared, and production initially rose as well. But production levels began to fall, prompting farmers to apply greater quantities of chemicals, approaching danger levels. Pesticide and fertilizer prices rose sharply.

[50] Workers' welfare deteriorated, and the new employment systems generated insecurity. While managers were given more power, even to hire and fire workers and set production targets, trade unions were not granted any corresponding freedom to act.

[51] In 1986 students demonstrated in Shanghai, calling for freedom of the press and political reform. As a result, Hu Yaobang, then a relatively young Party General Secretary, was forced to step down, and a campaign against 'bourgeois liberalism' was launched by hard-liners. This aimed to root out what they called 'Western ideas'; most importantly political pluralism, though consumerism and corruption were also mentioned. Many viewed this campaign as a veiled attack on Deng's economic reform policies, given that Hu Yaobang was one of Deng's protégés.

[52] In March 1989, police in Central Asian China fired on Tibetan demonstrators who were protesting against cultural and religious persecution and demanding greater political rights. The shooting triggered three days of widespread rioting which resulted in the imposition of Martial Law, lifted only in April 1990. Tibetan exiles reported the detention of many dissidents and several executions. Tibet had been officially annexed to China in 1950 and converted into an autonomous region in 1965.

[53] In April, the death of Hu Yaobang served as a pretext for thousands of students to assemble in Tiananmen Square in downtown Beijing. In addition to mourning the death of the man who to them symbolized liberal reform, the students called for an end to corruption and changes in both society and the party.

[54] The students camped in the square and their numbers grew, as the time coincided with the anniversary of the student

Tibet: high plateau

According to 10th century Tang records in China, Tibetans were originally nomadic pastoral Chiang people from the great steppes of north eastern China. This region was a racial melting pot for hundreds of years, and Tibetans continued to mix with other peoples under conquests and alliances until at least the 7th century AD. In the farming valleys brachicephalic - round-headed - people predominate, possibly descending from the Huan Ho basin, coming from the same blood line as the first Chinese and Burmese. The dolicocephalic or long-headed people, were predominant among the nomads of the north and the noble families of Lhasa, and they would have links with the Turks. There are Dardic and Indian branches towards the west and along the Himalayan frontier.

[2] The first known religion in the region was Bon, which combined a belief in gods, demons, and ancestral spirits who were responsive to priests, or shamans. Chinese Buddhism was introduced in ancient times - the first scriptures date back to the 3rd century - but the mainstream Buddhist teachings came to Tibet from India in the 7th century. The blend of both produced the particular Lamaist Buddhism of the region and its many different sects. The principal monks of the many monasteries spread over the country became also temporal rulers and began to compete against each other. At different times the Mongols and Chinese took advantage of these conflicts, favouring one or another to suit their own purposes, setting up pendulum-like policy that lasted centuries.

[3] The Tibetans developed a phonetic alphabet about AD 600 and, after centuries of rivalry, a theocratic kind of feudal state was established in the early 10th century. Both political and religious power was conferred on the lamas, and monasteries who, along with the ruling class, controlled the peasants and the produce of the land.

[4] In 1240, the Mongols marched on central Tibet and attacked many important monasteries. In 1247, Köden, the younger brother of Güyük Khan, symbolically invested the Sa-skya lama with tempo-

ral authority over Tibet. Kublai Khan, grandson of Genghis Khan, appointed the lama Phags-pa as his çImperial preceptor'. The politico-religious relationship between Tibet and the Mongol Empire was characterized as a personal bond between the Emperor as patron and the lama as priest. During the century, many Sa-skya lamas, living at the Mongol court, became viceroys of Tibet on behalf of the Mongol emperors.

[5] The Dre-lugs-pa hierarchies set a new alliance with the Mongols in 1578. This re-established the framework that shared religious authority - assigned to Tibetan lamas - and political dominance - resting with Mongolian leaders. Atlan conferred on the Bsod-nams-rgya-mtsho - third in the lamas' hierarchy - the title of Dalai ('oceanwide') Lama. In 1640, the Mongols invaded Tibet and two years later the Güüshi Khan enthroned the fourth Dalai Lama as ruler of Tibet, keeping for himself the military protection of the region.

[6] The assassination of two Chinese high commissioners in 1751 - instigated by the Dalai Lama - brought an immediate and bloody response from the Manchu dynasty in power in Beijing: the Emperor sent in a military expedition to Lhasa. Since that time, the Dalai Lama's relationship with China became more difficult than that of the Panchens - the other leaders of the religious hierarchy. Worldly competition between the two heads of the Lamaist Buddhism often fostered division and sectarianism.

[7] In the 17th century, the fifth Dalai Lama declared that his tutor, Blo-bzang chos-kyi-rgyal-mtshan (1570-1662), who was the current Panchen Lama, would be reincarnated in a child.

[8] In 1904 a British military expedition headed by Colonel Younghusband invaded Tibet and forced the Tibetans into making a treaty.

[9] In 1910 Chinese troops entered Lhasa. The Dalai Lama appealed to the British to help expel them - and was refused. But the Chinese empire was in its death throes and fell to the Nationalists in 1911. Tibetans seized the chance to expel the invaders and in June 1912 the Dalai Lama proclaimed Tibetan independence.

About ten years later, disagreements between the Dalai Lama and the Panchen Lama ended in the flight of the latter to Beijing. A boy born of Tibetan parents about 1938 in Tsinghai province, China, Bskal-bzang Tshe-brtan, was recognized as his successor by the Chinese Government and brought to Tibet in 1952. Eventually, he entered Lhasa under Communist military escort and was enthroned as head monk of the Tashilhunpo Monastery.

[10] In 1949 the Communists came to power in China and the following year the Government declared its intention to 'liberate' Tibet from feudalism. Some 84,000 troops invaded Tibet's eastern province of Kham and met resistance from Tibetan Khampa horseriders, but they were crushed. In 1951 the present Dalai Lama, Tenzin Gyatso, then aged 15, signed an agreement with China.

[11] In 1959 Tibetan resistance exploded into an uprising which was put down by the Chinese. Chinese figures record 87,000 deaths; Tibetan sources suggest as many as 430,000 were killed. When the 1959 revolt collapsed, the Panchen Lama remained in Tibet, while the Dalai Lama fled into exile. The Panchen Lama's refusal to denounce the Dalai Lama as a traitor brought him into disfavour with the Chinese Government, which imprisoned him in Peking in 1964. He was released in the late 1970s and died in 1989.

[12] When the 1959 rising failed, the Panchen Lama remained in Tibet while the Dalai Lama left to exile in India where he spoke out against occupation in favour of a return to traditional society. The Panchen Lama refused to denounce the Dalai Lama as a traitor which set him at odds with the Chinese government, who imprisoned him in Peking in 1964. He was freed in the late seventies and died in 1989.

[13] In 1994 Chinese and Tibetan religious authorities declared a five-year old Tibetan child Panchen Lama, but the Dalai Lama did not recognise the nomination.

[14] In late 1999, the 14 year-old Buddhist leader Karmapa Lama managed to flee Tibet to India, meeting with the Dalai Lama. This heightened hopes abroad for independence in Tibet, and

India was concerned over possible confrontation with Beijing. The Karmapa Kagyupa, or 'black hat' sect was the most powerful in Tibet until it was supplanted by the Gelugpa school of the Dalai Lama.

[15] Tibet - presently one of the five Chinese autonomous regions - had a mostly Tibetan population until a large Han migration was encouraged by Beijing. The Han form the Chinese majority. Tibetans are no longer in a majority in the capital Lhasa. Furthermore, the region is settled by the Hui (Muslim Chinese), the Hu and the Monba, amongst others. It is estimated that 1.2 million Tibetans have fled the region since Chinese occupation. Beijing routinely denies any abuse of the population and highlights the construction of hospitals, highways and factories in Tibetan territory as signs of the 'benevolence' of its government.

[16] In November 2000, a delegation from the European Union proposed to Chinese chancellor Li Peng that the Dalai Lama be designated governor of Tibet. This idea was rejected, stating that he would have to renounce his Tibetan citizenship and become Chinese before this could happen. Beijing claims the Dalai Lama wants Tibetan independence, and has started to call for autonomous government 'jointly' with China. During a visit to Taiwan in April 2000, the Dalai Lama specified that he was not seeking the independence of either Tibet or Taiwan.

[17] In 2001, the Chinese government discovered the existence of an oil field 100 kilometers wide, estimated to hold 100 million tons of crude oil. In April of the following year, a monument was inaugurated opposite the Dalai Lama's traditional winter residence commemorating the 'peaceful liberation' of Tibet in 1951. Beijing also announced a plan for a hundred or so public works in Tibet at an initial cost of $3.8 billion, including the construction of a 1,000 km railway across the Himalayas, most of it at an altitude of 4000 metres, and a $14.4 million airport. ∎

demonstrations of 1919. Hundreds of thousands of citizens and workers in Beijing began to demonstrate support for the reform movement, bringing food and other supplies to the students, marching, and blockading intersections when it seemed likely that troops would move against the students.

[55] Students, citizens and workers began similar demonstrations in other cities, and the banners of groups of workers from the official media, trade unions, and various party sections began to appear in the daily demonstrations. Various autonomous bodies were set up by demonstrators, challenging four decades of complete party control over all social organizations.

[56] Finally, on June 4 1989, the Government moved decisively and violently, sending troops into downtown Beijing to clear out the citizens and students. Many hundreds were killed and thousands wounded. Many Beijing residents and students were killed as the troops forced their way past barricades in armored vehicles and opened fire on the crowds. The pro-democracy demonstrations were smashed. The assault on Tiananmen was followed by a nationwide hunt for leaders of the autonomous student and workers movements, thousands were arrested and badly beaten; many others were executed. There were important political changes and Li Peng became Prime Minister.

[57] The first Western government to send representatives to the capital after the Tiananmen massacre was Britain, in September 1991. They signed an agreement with Beijing on the construction of a new airport in Xianggang (Hong Kong), within the constraints of the negotiations to return the British colony to China in 1997.

[58] With one-third of all public enterprises operating at that time at a deficit, and less and less possibility of balancing the State budget, structural reforms seemed all but inevitable in state enterprises. The Chinese Communist Party was paving the way for a return to the economic liberalization program initiated by Deng Xiaoping, who had reappeared on the political scene at the age of 87. At the same time, there were other indicators of

changing attitudes: Jiang Zemin, Deng's successor as Communist Party Secretary, called for 'free thinking', and charges against former Secretary Zhao Zhiyang were reduced. Shortly afterwards, however, he was blamed for events leading to the Tiananmen massacre, rendering impossible his chances of rehabilitation.

[59] The Paris Accords on Cambodia (see Cambodia), signed in October 1991, and the end of the Soviet Union accelerated a rapprochement between China and Vietnam. In November 1991, diplomatic relations between the two countries were re-established.

[60] In late November 1991 the Government freed the student leaders from the Tiananmen demonstrations. However, there were an estimated 70,000 political prisoners in various provinces of the Xinjiang and Qinghai region.

[61] In 1992, China signed the Nuclear Non-Proliferation Treaty. At the annual session of the People's National Congress, Jiang Zemin was designated president of the republic, becoming the first person since Mao to combine the functions of head of state, the party and commander of the armed forces. Prime Minister Li Peng was confirmed in his post.

[62] In April 1992, the decision was made to build the giant Three Gorges dam on the Yangtse river. This controversial project was to be completed in 2009, flooding lands inhabited by 1.3 million people, drowning 10 cities and more than 800 towns. Ecologists immediately opposed the project, saying it would destroy the habitats of endangered species and would leave millions of people exposed to the danger of earthquakes, avalanches and floods. They also considered the dam would not be profitable. Hydrologists, seismologists, economists human rights defenders and activists against economic globalization opposed the project, saying it would destroy the habitats of endangered species and leave millions of people exposed to the dangers of earthquakes, avalanches and floods. Although the project's critics argue that it would not be profitable, CITIGROUP, one of the three most powerful financial bodies in the world (and which has supported environmentally destructive

enterprises like oil pipelines through the African rainforest and mining in the Amazon Basin), is providing major economic backing.

[63] In September, the Government said the pro-independence action in Tibet would be 'implacably repressed'. On the economic front, an austerity plan was launched in the State apparatus and taxes on the rural population were increased. However, a series of protests and demonstrations forced the Government to remove the new charge from a sector of the population which totaled around 800 million people.

[64] The GDP increased by 12.8 per cent in 1992, a figure unprecedented in the previous decade. However, this growth (the economy nearly doubled since 1990) had its first undesirable effects in 1993, when inflation hit 20 per cent in the first half year. In March 1994, Li Peng proposed limiting the economic expansion to 9 per cent in order to limit inflation despite protests from the coastal provinces like Guandong, the main beneficiaries of the Chinese 'boom'.

[65] The social inequalities between the new rich in the cities and the vast majority of the workers and rural population continued to increase along with the migration of millions of people from the countryside to the cities. This led the Government to be cautious in closing and privatizing unprofitable State enterprises, as a sharp rise in unemployment would only worsen an already tense and precarious social situation.

[66] However, another project which planned to limit the social effects of the economic reforms was postponed. The plan was to establish a redundancy payment for workers laid off from closed State companies, but the total lack of a State-run social security system in the nation - without so much as unemployment benefit - made the Government back off from launching excessively radical reforms.

[67] In 1995, Jiang Zemin consolidated his power to continue ruling the nation in the 'post-Deng' era. The authorities still concerned about the social effects of the reforms, maintained the large subsidies for state enterprises.

[68] In that year, inflation reached only 13 per cent, and the 1996-2000

DEMOGRAPHY
Population: 1,294,377,000 (2002)
Annual growth: 1.2 % (1985-2000)
Estimates for year 2015: 1,410,217,000 (2000)
Annual growth to year 2015: 0.7 % (2000)
Urban population: 32.1 % (2000)
Urban growth: 2.4 % (2000)
Children per woman: 1.8 (2000)

HEALTH
Life expectancy at birth: 71 years (2000-2005)
male: 69 years (2000-2005)
female: 74 years (2000-2005)
Maternal mortality: 55 per 100,000 live births (1985/99)
Infant mortality: 32 per 1,000 (2000)
Under-5 child mortality: 40 per 1,000 (2000)
Daily calorie supply: 3,045 per capita (1999)
162 doctors per 100,000 people (1998)
Safe water: 75 % (2000)

EDUCATION
Literacy: 85 % (2000)
male: 92 % (2000)
female: 77 % (2000)
School enrolment (net):
Primary total: 99 % (1994/2000)
male: 99 % (1995/99)
female: 99 % (1995/99)
Secondary (gross):
male: 72 % (1995/97)
female: 65 % (1995/97)
Tertiary (gross): 6 % (1998)
Primary school teachers: one for every 21 pupils (1998)

COMMUNICATIONS
42 newspapers (1990), 339 radios (1997), 293 TV sets (2000) and 112 main telephone lines (2000) per 1,000 people
Books: 8 new titles per 100,000 people (1992/94)

ECONOMY
Per capita, GDP: $ 3,976 (2000)
Annual growth: 7.2 % (2000)
Annual inflation: 0.3 % (2000)
Consumer price index: 109.2 (2000)
Currency: 8.3 renminbi (yuan) = $ 1 (03/2002)
Cereal imports: 9,476,593 metric tons (2000)
Food import dependency: 4 % (2000)
Fertilizer use: 2,954 kg per ha (1999)
Exports: $ 279,558 million (2000)
Imports: $ 250,685 million (2000)
External debt: $ 149,800 million (2000); $ 117 per capita (2000)
Debt service: 9.0 % of exports (1999)
Development aid received: $ 2,324 million (1999); $ 1.9 per capita (1999); 0.20 % of GNP (1999)

ENERGY
Consumption: 830.3 Kgs of oil equivalent per capita yearly (1998); 2.9 % imported (1999)

HDI (ranking/value): 87 / 0.718 (1999)

Hong Kong

Hong Kong (Xianggang) island was ceded to Britain 'in perpetuity' in 1842, when the British attacked China in the first Opium War. Eighteen years later, the British gained the rights over Kowloon, the mainland peninsula facing the island. In 1898, the British forced the Chinese to give them a 99-year lease on the rural zone north of Kowloon, known as the 'New Territories'.

[2] Hong Kong was initially used as a trade center, constituting a point of entry to China. But in the 1950s, following the Communist victory in China, the United States and Britain imposed a trade embargo. Deprived of its supplies, Hong Kong was forced to import all its basic goods from overseas, therefore having to develop exports, rapidly transforming itself into a light industry center, exporting textiles, clothing, plastic and electronic goods. Just as in Taiwan and South Korea, this development was generously supported by Western powers interested in these 'bastions' of the Cold War.

[3] Growth of trade and the export industry converted Hong Kong into a financial, communications and transport center. The Government policy also contributed, setting low taxes and minimal customs tariffs, offering trustworthiness and freedom in movements of capital.

[4] When China announced a stage of liberalization toward foreign trade and investment in the late 1970s, Hong Kong - armed with one of the best natural ports and port facilities in the world, sophisticated international investment and trade systems - was ready to take advantage of the situation. Between 30 and 50 per cent of China's foreign trade of was carried out through Hong Kong, which was also the source of nearly 90 per cent of foreign investment in the Chinese province of Kwangtung.

[5] Almost the entire population of Chinese origin had settled in the enclave following successive migratory waves resulting from political and economic events in their Communist neighbor.

[6] London and Beijing began negotiations on the future of the colony in the early 1980s, as the 99-year lease was due to end in 1997. The people of Hong Kong were not represented in these discussions.

[7] Agreement was reached in 1984, giving China sovereignty over the entire territory, but allowing Hong Kong 'a high degree of independence' as a Special Administrative Area.

[8] In September 1991, the people of Hong Kong elected the members of the Legislative Council for the first time in 150 years. The United Democrats of Hong Kong (UDHK), candidates - critical of the colonial government of Hong Kong and of China and supporting stronger democracy - won most of the seats.

[9] The last British Governor, Chris Patten, reformed the electoral system, totally separating the economic and legislative powers. China said this reform contradicted the principles of the Basic Law. In 1998, China appointed a Preparatory Committee for the Administrative Region of Hong Kong, made up of leading figures of Hong Kong, and consultants from the colonial government.

[10] In 1994, Patten proposed a plan to increase the number of voters in the 1995 elections, causing further confrontations with Beijing. In September 1995 the Democrat Party, opposed to the official Chinese interpretation of the Basic Law, triumphed in the Legislative Council elections. Beijing repeated its intention to dissolve the Council in 1997, alleging that it did not take the interests of all the social strata of Hong Kong into account.

[11] The British Governor publicly upbraided the Chinese authorities for only negotiating with 'multi-millionaires'. Patten referred to the alliance made in 1996 between leading Hong Kong business people and the Government in Beijing.

[12] At 00:00 hours, on Tuesday July 1 1997, China recovered control over Hong Kong after 155 years of British colonial dominion. Businessman Tung Chi Hua was appointed head of the new Executive with the support of a Legislative Council.

[13] According to the new law, Hong Kong retains its rights and liberties, its legal independence and nature as an international financial and trade center, along with its way of life, for 50 years. The zone mints its own currency and is ruled by its own immigration and customs laws. Beijing will only handle defense and foreign relations during this period.

[14] Reunification put China in a 'one country, two systems' situation, combining the free market economy of Hong Kong with rigid political control over the rest of the country, a totally unprecedented situation.

[15] The transferral took place against a backdrop of spectacular growth in the Chinese economy, which gave no signs of slowing. The Hong Kong economy, meanwhile, was considered the third most powerful in the world, and the former enclave was also the third most important international financial center behind New York and London.

[16] Hong Kong was much more severely hit by the Asian financial crisis than the rest of China. Both imports and exports declined, the economy shrank 7 per cent in the third quarter of 1997 and unemployment rose to its highest level in fifteen years. In a departure from previous laissez-faire practice, Hong Kong authorities intervened in currency markets to defend the Hong Kong dollar against currency speculators.

[17] For the first time since reunification, in June 1999 Beijing intervened in Hong Kong's judicial system to avoid an immigration 'influx' considered dangerous for the city's stability. The decision of the local Supreme Court had extended the right of citizenship to all Chinese children born of Hong Kong citizens. For the post-colonial Government, that decision put Hong Kong in risk of being 'invaded' by almost two million people (one third of its population).

[18] Between 2001 and 2002, the Hong Kong economy was affected by a deep recession. Unemployment peaked at 6.7 per cent in 2002, the highest in 20 years. To tackle this, one of the measures the Government adopted was an agreement with the Disney Corporation to the opening in 2005 of the Hong Kong Disneyland, which was expected to create new jobs. To that end, and to obtain the $40 billion the project would earn in 40 years (with a contribution of 0.3 per cent of the GDP per year), the Hong Kong authorities accepted an infrastructure cost of $1.75 billion and a direct or indirect/loan investment in the park itself of some $2.95 billion. ∎

five-year plan forecast annual growth of 'only' 8-9 per cent. The number of corruption scandals increased dramatically. The CCP first secretary in Beijing, Chen Xitong, was forced to leave his post when it became clear he had been misappropriating funds along with important communal leaders and a large municipal metallurgical company. In April, the deputy-mayor of Beijing, Wang Daosen committed suicide, accused of having embezzled $37 million of government funds.

[69] As in previous years, trade relations with the US strengthened, despite the constant public disagreements between the nations, like the situation provoked by military maneuvers in the waters around Taiwan (see Taiwan) or the nuclear tests carried out by Beijing. In November, Jiang made the first ever visit of a Chinese president to South Korea, in another demonstration of the commercial and political rapprochement of China with countries it had classed as anti-Communist during the Cold War.

[70] In May 1996 Amnesty International (AI) condemned the Chinese repression of Buddhist monks in Tibet. According to AI, 80 monks were injured for refusing to respect a ban on the public exhibition of pictures of the Dalai Lama.

[71] Two student leaders of the 1989 uprising were sentenced to prison sentences of 11 and 3 years, accused of promoting the overthrow of the Government. Another student gained political asylum in the United States. The regime continued the psychological harassment of Taiwan, carrying out large-scale military exercises around the island.

[72] Foreign investment, the dynamo of the great Chinese economic growth in these years, increased 20 per cent in 1996. Several foreign companies operating in the country were authorized to convert local money into dollars or yen.

[73] Following the death of Deng Xiaoping, in February 1997, the XV PC Congress confirmed Jiang Zemin as leader in October, reaffirming the present political system and reform policy, in particular with regard to the State companies.

[74] The 15th Communist Party Congress, in October of that year, consolidated reform policy, particularly as applied to the State companies, and reaffirmed the traditional political system.

[75] In March 1998, the People's National Congress ratified the changes decided by the Communist Party. Jiang Zemin was re-elected head of State and commander of the armed forces, with 98 per cent of the vote. Some 2,882 deputies voted in favor, 36 against and 29 abstained.

[76] Hu Jintao, mentioned as a possible successor to Zemin, was elected Vice-President, while outgoing Prime Minister, Li Peng, became Head of Parliament. The Constitution prevented him from serving a third term as Head of Government.

[77] Zhu Rongji, former deputy Prime Minister in charge of the economy, was elected Prime Minister. The new cabinet, made up mostly of economic experts, faced the preparation of the 370,000 State companies for free market rules, a process which had already cost between 20 and 30 million jobs.

[78] The Yangtse valley, home to some 400 million Chinese, suffered the worst flooding in decades in 1998, with a total of some 4,000 people killed and damage worth $25 billion. The authorities tried to reinforce and modernize dykes, dams and sluices in order to handle the large swells. However, heavy rains overwhelmed these barriers and, in August 1999, the government once again declared a state of emergency in the valley. More than two million people were evacuated while another 60 million were affected. Harvests and housing were ruined throughout the valley.

[79] In June 1999, the Government issued an arrest warrant on militants of the 'exercise and meditation movement' Falun Gong and asked Interpol to arrest Li Hongzhi, the man who founded the sect in 1992 before emigrating to the United States. At the same time, the authorities destroyed more than one and a half million books on the group's beliefs. This confrontation with Falun Gong - seen by the Chinese leadership as the greatest threat to the Government since the demonstrations in 1989 - started after the group staged a silent protests against government hostility in April when 25,000 of its supporters demonstrated opposite Jiang Zemin's residence.

[80] In a two pronged move in November, China called for a reduction in global deployment of missiles in order to create a 'favorable atmosphere' at the dawning of the new millennium. At the same time 100 new missiles were moved onto the south eastern coast facing Taiwan. This action aimed to pressure the US into limiting sales of advanced weapons to Formosa.

[81] In December 1999, for the first time in 442 years, China became whole once more, as Europe lost its last colonial possession in Asia when Portugal officially gave up Macao. On reunification, Macao, like Hong Kong, became a 'special administrative region' with considerable independence, at least for the next 50 years.

[82] In late 2000, the Government announced that 11 people had been sentenced to death, among them government officials and police, in the trial resulting from the country's worst corruption scandal. In total, 84 people were convicted for their involvement in a smuggling network that, through sexual favors and payoffs in billions of dollars, had bribed high officials. All were connected in some way with the Yuanhua Group, a mafia based in the port city of Xiamen, in the south. According to the official reports, one of the officials had received a payment of $960,000, a huge sum in any country, but particularly in China where per capita annual income is around $750 dollars.

[83] China made significant changes to its 'national minorities' law in March 2001, with new policies to accelerate economic development and integration in the country's west. The rights of the state were reinforced, opposing those of the autonomous peoples. While the 1984 law had centered on the structure, administration and exercise of national autonomy, at least superficially recognizing the right to retain some control over local affairs and to protect economic interests, the amendments did not address autonomy, but only the priorities of the central authorities.

[84] From 1996 to 2001, the Communist Party (CP) added 7.5 million members to its ranks, reaching a total of 64.5 million, or approximately five per cent of the population. Of the members, 11.2 million were women and four million belonged to ethnic minorities, and nearly half the membership was under age 45. Although Chinese leaders assert that these figures indicate that Marxism and revolutionary ideas continue to play an important role among Chinese youth, for some experts the CP's attraction is less related to ideology than to the connections the Party offers those who seek an entry into the business world.

[85] In June 2001, leaders from China, Russia, Kazakhstan, Uzbekistan, Tajikistan and Kyrgyzstan signed a treaty to fight ethnic and religious militancy, while at the same time promoting trade accords. A month later, in Moscow, Jiang Zemin signed a friendship treaty with Russian President Vladimir Putin. The 20-year agreement between China and Russia sought to counterbalance US hegemony at the international level. Because the treaty states explicitly that neither of the parties has territorial claims with the other, voices of concern were raised in Russia about the potential for Chinese immigrant incursions in Russia's far east, which is scarcely populated, and in the Siberian regions, which China claimed when it was a Moscow opponent during the Cold War.

[86] After 15 years of diplomatic disputes, China was formally admitted in November to the World Trade Organization (WTO). China's WTO membership implied that its state industries must be reformed, which could lead to a sharp increase in unemployment. Western companies were cleared to carry out joint ventures with the Government, even in 'sensitive' areas like cellular phones, banking and insurance. Given that the modifications would lead to greater foreign investment, it was assumed that China would improve its competitiveness in exports, a matter of concern to export powers like Japan and the southeast Asian countries. On joining the WTO, China threatened to become a major player in international trade negotiations. From the outset Beijing made clear its ambitions to lead the less industrialized countries by stressing that international rounds of trade talks would only be successful if the gap between rich and poor countries is addressed and all countries are assured of benefiting from economic globalization.

[87] The first direct commercial flight between China and India landed in Delhi on March 28 2002. The China Eastern Airlines flight, carrying top Beijing officials, was hailed as an improvement in bilateral relations. Later that week India's Foreign Minister Jaswant Singh flew to China. ∎

MATERNAL MORTALITY

1985/99

Per 100,000 live births

55

Taiwan

Population:	22,370,461 (2001)
Land area:	36,000 SQ KM
Capital:	Taipei
Currency:	New dollar
Language:	Chinese (Mandarin)

T'ai-wan

The island of Taiwan was originally inhabited by Australo-nesian populations, which also spread to the Polynesian archipelago and Aotearoa/New Zealand, and are still found among a dozen ethnic groups that have not assimilated into the Chinese culture.

[2] In 1590, the Portuguese landed on the island, renaming it Ilha Formosa. After a brief occupation by the Dutch in the early 17th century, the island was incorporated into the Chinese Empire during the Qing (Manchu) dynasty in 1683 and proclaimed a province of China in 1887. During this time, the political and administrative systems of mainland China were extended to Taiwan, and many people migrated there from the continent.

[3] After China's defeat in the 1895 Sino-Japanese war, Taiwan became a Japanese colony, but was returned to China after the defeat of Japan at the end of World War II. At first, the people of Taiwan rejoiced at the end of Japanese colonialism, but they soon discovered that life under the ruthlessly authoritarian, corrupt and vehemently anti-Communist Kuomintang (KMT) party led by Chiang Kai-Shek resembled nothing less than different kind of colonialism.

[4] On February 28 1947, there was a major demonstration against the KMT authorities. The KMT reacted at first by lifting martial law and inviting the opposition to form a Settlement Committee of politicians, trade unionists and student groups to discuss possible political reforms. Meanwhile, they drafted in 13,000 additional troops and when the opposition came forward, the KMT massacred large numbers of them, imprisoning others.

[5] In 1949, the entire KMT government, the remnants of its armies, and their relatives and supporters, fled to Taiwan after losing the mainland civil war to the Communist armies. From its refuge, backed by the United States, the KMT declared Taiwan to be the temporary base of the Republic of China pending recovery of the mainland. Most Western nations continued to recognize the KMT as the representatives of all China.

[6] When the Korean War erupted, with China supporting the North Koreans, the US redoubled its military and economic commitment to Taiwan, protecting it as a front-line state in the battle to defend the 'free world'.

[7] Democracy disappeared. Human rights were violated, demonstrations, strikes and political parties banned, and Martial Law imposed - all in the name of the battle to reconquer the mainland. The KMT set up a governmental system which claimed to represent the whole of China, with legislators representing each mainland province.

[8] Taiwan's remarkable industrialization began in the 1960s, when World Bank and US technocrats helped the Government apply an export-oriented development strategy. The era of Japanese colonialism had left Taiwan with only partially-developed transport and an education system. The US granted financial, trade and aid advantages to bolster an authoritarian political regime which, in turn, hectored Taiwan's disenfranchised, and politically disorganized workforce.

[9] Taiwanese output grew at an average of 8.6 per cent each year between 1953 and 1985, and became one of the four newly-industrialized 'tigers' of East Asia. Growth was entirely export-oriented, and the island developed the world's second-largest trade surplus with the US, following Japan. Today, Taiwan has highly developed plastics, chemical, ship-building, clothing and electronics industries.

[10] In 1971, the US decided to seek closer ties with China, no longer vetoing the latter's admission to the UN. Taiwan therefore lost its representation in that world body. A few years later in 1979 the US officially broke off diplomatic relations with Taiwan.

[11] The country found itself at an economic crossroads. It was over-dependent on a few export markets and labor-intensive industries, importing nations were pressuring for more balanced trade and Taiwan's labor was no longer as cheap as that of many of its Asian neighbors. Technocrats argued that in order to compete Taiwan should develop a more open political system. The KMT also faced an internal succession crisis as aging politicians from the civil war era clung precariously to power.

[12] In addition, a significant portion of the population did not consider their country to be a part of China, and rejected both the authoritarian policies of the KMT and Deng Xiaoping's unification proposal of 'one nation, two systems' with Taiwan becoming a Chinese dependency.

[13] In September 1986 the Democratic Progress Party (DPP) was formed as the first opposition party to challenge the KMT's political stranglehold. Although technically illegal, the party was allowed to survive, and Martial Law was formally lifted on July 15 1987.

[14] A huge upsurge in union activity took place in 1987. Strong independent sections were formed in the trade union system and supporters founded parallel political structures in the Labor Party and Worker's Party.

[15] While the KMT was resolutely opposed to independence, some DPP members formed the New Wave group proposing that Taiwan declare self-rule. Other groups advocated a referendum for self-determination.

[16] The National Assembly elections in December 1991 were regarded as a plebiscite on the independence issue. The DPP's electoral platform, favoring a definitive separation from China, was supported by just 21 per cent of the electorate, against the KMT's 71 per cent.

[17] From 1994, voices rose demanding an independent way for Taiwan, leaving behind the assumption of being a government representative of all Chinese. However, due to Beijing's opposition to any measure which could further lead the island toward independence, Taipei's efforts to be accepted into the United Nations were in vain.

[18] The first multiparty municipal elections were held in December. Most of the vote went to the ruling Kuomintang and the DPP. In spite of

opposition from environmentalists and anti-nuclear activists and DPP objections, the KMT supported the construction of a fourth nuclear plant on the island.

[19] In 1995, economic relations with Beijing intensified. Taiwan became the second 'foreign' investor in the People's Republic after Hong Kong, placing approximately $22 billion in China. In spite of this exchange, political relations between the two countries deteriorated after a private visit from Taiwanese president Lee Teng to the US in June. Heedless of US warnings, Beijing carried out a series of missile launchings in July and August on waters just 140 kilometers from Taiwan.

[20] In spite of losing ground in previous elections, the Kuomintang won the December legislative elections. In the campaign prior to the March 1996 presidential elections, new Chinese military maneuvers near the coast of Taiwan led Washington to send warships in defense of Taiwan's alleged threatened territorial integrity.

[21] Lee Teng, of the KMT, triumphed on March 20 in the first presidential elections with direct suffrage in the history of the island, taking 54 per cent of the vote.

[22] In July, China made a show of military force off the coast of Taiwan, timed to coincide with the return of Hong Kong to Chinese control.

[23] In August the Government announced the closure of its embassy on the island of St Lucia, following the Caribbean island's decision to strengthen links with China. The severing of diplomatic relations reduced the number of countries recognizing the Taipei Government to 30. Also that month, Prime Minister Lien Chan handed in his resignation and was replaced by Vincent Siew from September 1.

[24] In April 1998, China and Taiwan decided to reopen direct negotiations, having broken off relations in June 1995. The KMT victory in the municipal and legislative elections in December appeared to support possibilities of dialogue with Beijing. However the opposition DPP maintained a more openly nationalist posture. Internally, increased representation in the legislature finally allowed the KMT to pass cut backs in provincial government.

[25] In the weeks running up to the presidential elections of 2000, Beijing repeatedly announced it could resort to force if Taipei refused unification. The announcement was made as a response to the DPP election campaign where candidate Chen Shui-bian, had stated he would hold a referendum to decide the future status of the island were he to win.

[26] This external pressure did the KMT no good, and on March 18 it lost power on the island for the first time in its history. The DPP won, followed by an independent candidate, James Soong, a former KMT leader of who led a new faction which had split off. The KMT, which came in a poor third, immediately expelled more than 50 of its members, accusing them of supporting Soong instead of the ruling party candidate Lien Chan.

[27] In March 2000, shortly before the tightest Presidential election in Taiwan's history, Beijing threatened the Taiwanese people with resorting to force to achieve unification if they voted for opposition independence advocate Chen Shui-bian, who led the polls.

[28] The elections were held on March 18 and as predicted, Chen won, putting an end to 50 years of Kuomintang rule. He won with a slight margin of 39 per cent against 37 per cent of independent candidate James Soong. The greatest loser was Vice-President Lien Chan, who only obtained 23 per cent of the vote although he was supported by President Lee Teng Hui and was preferred by Beijing and Taiwan conservatives. Chen received more support thanks to his rejection of the Chinese formula 'one country, two systems' and for confirming that the island would remain independent.

[29] In response to the new Taiwanese President's actions - since taking office Chen sought rapprochement with Beijing - the Chinese Government ceased its threats and accepted Chen's victory. Kuomintang supporters did not react so patiently and blamed their leaders for their defeat, for having allowed the division of nationalist voters.

[30] In late 2000, Taipei allowed direct trade contacts between the Taiwanese islands of Qinmen and Matsu with the People's Republic. Until then, in spite of being separated by only a few miles from major cities such as Xianmen, business ties were indirect and, like the rest of Chinese-Taiwanese trade, went through Hong Kong or Macau. This detour was an obstacle to the expansion needs at a time of growing closeness between Asian economies. In early 2001, after more than 50 years of isolation, Taiwan and China inaugurated the first direct links between their territories. Beijing wanted greater access to Taiwan so that movement would be free from and to all entrance points in both territories.

[31] In 2001 Taiwanese exports and imports fell due to world recession, and unemployment reached an all time high of 5 per cent. That year Taiwan became the 144th member of the World Trade Organization, after China lifted its boycott.

[32] The Kuomintang lost its parliamentary majority in the December 2001 elections, putting an end to the political hegemony responsible for the 'Taiwanese miracle', which had ruled with an iron fist since 1949. The KMT did not resist the democratization process pushed by its own leaders.

[33] The Dalai Lama's visit to Taiwan in March 2002 irritated China, which claimed the trip of Tibet's spiritual leader had pro-independence political motives (China has occupied Tibet since the early 1950s). Taiwanese Government spokesperson, Su Cheng Ping, stated that the visit, the second of its type, would only foster the religious spirit of its citizens and promote traditional Tibetan culture.

[34] In January 2002, President Chen shuffled his economic team and for the first time, a woman, Christine Tsung, was appointed Economy Minister. Her mission was to lead the country out of recession, which would help the Taiwanese President's re-election prospects in 2004.

[35] On March 30 2002, a strong earthquake shook Taiwan, demolishing several buildings in Taipei, where people fled to the streets. The quake reached 6.8 points on the Richter scale, and its epicenter was located near Hualien, some 180 km to the east of the Taiwanese capital. At least 10 people died and some 200 were injured. ∎

PROFILE

ENVIRONMENT

Located 160 km southeast of continental China, Taiwan is part of a chain of volcanic islands in the West Pacific which also includes Japan. A mountain range stretches from north to south along the center of the country. A narrow plain along the island's western coast constitutes its main agricultural area where rice, sugar cane, bananas and tobacco are cultivated. More than two-thirds of the island's area is densely wooded. Taiwan has considerable mineral resources: coal, natural gas, marble, limestone and minor deposits of copper, gold, and oil. The country is suffering the consequences of its enormous industrial explosion, with high levels of water, air and land pollution.

SOCIETY

Peoples: Most are Chinese who have migrated from the mainland since the 17th century and are known as 'Taiwanese'. Hundreds of thousands of Kuomintang Chinese fled to Taiwan during 1949-50. The island's indigenous inhabitants are of Malayo-Polynesian origin, and make up about 1.7 per cent of the population. They are concentrated on the east coast, where they comprise 25 per cent of the population.
Religions: More than half are Chinese Buddhist. There are also Muslim and Christian minorities. Indigenous religions in some areas.
Languages: Chinese (Mandarin), official. Taiwanese, a derivative of the Chinese dialect from Fujian province, is the language of the majority. Hakka is the second Chinese dialect in Taiwan. There are several indigenous languages, such as Amis. **Political Parties:** Democratic Progressive Party (DPP), formed in 1986 with a very broad platform to restore political democracy in Taiwan; Kuomintang (Chinese Nationalist Party/KMT) founded in China in 1919, took political monopoly control of Taiwan when it fled from the continent in 1949 and ruled under Martial Law up to 1987; New Trend split from the DPP with claims for Taiwan independence; Labor Party, centrist, and Workers' Party, socialist, appeared after the resurgence of trade unions in 1987; Green Party Taiwan (GPT). Among the pro-independence groups there is the illegal World Union of Formosans for Independence; New Party (HT), pan-Chinese. **Social Organizations:** Every trade union has to be a member of the Chinese Federation of Labor, controlled by the Kuomintang, but in 1987 a few independent trade unions appeared. These are organized in several federations, including the National Federation of Independent Unions and Tao-Chu-Miao Brotherhood. There are several diaspora-based organizations; and groups campaigning for the rights of Taiwan's indigenous peoples.

THE STATE

Official name: Republic of China. **Administrative divisions:** 7 municipalities and 16 counties. **Capital:** Taipei (T'aipei) 7,423,000 people (1999). **Other cities:** Kaohsiung 2,478,600 people; Taichung 2,070,300; Tainan 770,100 (2000). **Government:** Chen Shui-bian, President since May 2000. Yu Shyi-kun, Prime Minister since February 2002. The National Assembly has 720 members; it is in charge of appointing the President for a six-year-period and is empowered to amend the Constitution. The President heads the legislative 'Yuan', with 225 members (including eight seats for indigenous representatives and eight for diaspora Chinese), and appoints the Prime Minister who heads the executive 'Yuan'. Internal affairs are under the control of a Provincial Assembly of 77 members, which deals with administrative matters.
National holiday: January 1, Day of the Republic; February 25, Constitution Day.
Armed Forces: 376,000 troops. **Other:** Military police 25,000.

Colombia

Population: 43,495,000 (2002)
Land area: 1,038,700 SQ KM
Capital: Bogotá
Currency: Peso
Language: Spanish

Colombia

The best known of Colombia's indigenous cultures is that of the Chibcha or 'Muisca' peoples. Living in northern Colombia and an area of what is now Panama, they were farmers and miners and developed a stratified society of feudal lords and vassals, with a matrilineal succession of power and patrilineal inheritance of property. The legend of *El Dorado* is attributed to a Chibcha ceremony in which a newly appointed chief was covered with gold dust and then bathed in a holy lake. The Chibcha culture and language remained isolated and, in spite of Spanish dominance, survive today in some areas of northern Colombia.

[2] In America, colonization resulted in the plundering of native wealth and the population was subjected to thinly disguised forms of slavery. After 300 years of colonialism, a large part of the indigenous population had disappeared.

[3] Spain conquered Colombia between 1536 and 1539. Gonzalo Giménez de Quesada decimated the Chibchas and founded the city of Santa Fé de Bogotá which became the center of the Viceroyalty of New Granada in 1718.

[4] Extensive, export-oriented agriculture (coffee, bananas, cotton and tobacco) replaced traditional crops (potatoes, cassava, corn, wood and medicinal plants) with African slaves replacing the more rebellious indigenous population.

[5] The Revolt of the Comuneros started the process leading to the declaration of independence in Cundinamarca, in 1813. The road to independence was marked by constant struggles between the advocates of centralized government and the federalists, headed by Camilo

WORKERS

2000

UNEMPLOYMENT: 20.5%
LABOR FORCE AS % OF TOTAL:

- ▮ FEMALE: 39%   ▮ MALE: 61%

1994/97

EMPLOYMENT DISTRIBUTION:

F
M

- ▮ SERVICES   F: 76%   M: 66%
- ▮ INDUSTRY   F: 21%   M: 32%
- ▯ AGRICULTURE F: 1%   M: 2%

Torres. Antonio Nariño (who had drafted the declaration of independence) represented the urban bourgeoisie, linked to European interests, while Torres presided over the Congress of the United Provinces, representing the less privileged.

[6] In 1816, Pablo Morillo reconquered this territory, executing Torres. Three years later, Simon Bolívar counter-attacked from Venezuela, liberated Colombia and founded the Republic of Greater Colombia, including Venezuela, Ecuador and the province of Panama. Regionalism and strong British pressure brought about the secession of Venezuela and Ecuador in 1829-30. The Republic of New Granada was then proclaimed and in 1886 Colombia adopted its current name.

[7] From 1830 to the early 20th century, the country went through civil wars, local wars (including two with Ecuador), three military uprisings and 11 constitutions. The Liberals and Conservatives have kept a permanent hold on the Colombian political situation, separated by a mutual hatred passed down from generation to generation, despite having similar platforms for governing the country.

[8] Between 1921 and 1957, over-production of the country's oil reserves led to a depletion of this resource, leaving American oil

companies with a profit of $1 billion, and Colombia with no oil. In those years American companies controlled 80 to 90 per cent of banana production and mining, and 98 per cent of energy production.

[9] In 1948, in Bogotá, Mayor Jorge Eliecer Gaitan of the Liberal Party was assassinated, and public indignation over his death triggered widespread riots, known as El Bogotázo. That same year, a Liberal mayor organized a guerrilla group, the first of 36 which were active during the presidencies of Ospina Pérez, Laureano Gómez and Rojas Pinilla. In 1957, a constitutional reform ensured the alternation of Liberals and Conservatives in the Government, every 12 years.

[10] The Revolutionary Armed Forces of Colombia (FARC), led by Manuel 'Tiro Fijo' (Sure Shot) Marulanda and Jacobo Arenas, appeared on the scene in 1964. Guerrilla strategists included Camilo Torres Restrepo, a priest and co-founder of the National Liberation Army (ELN), who was killed in combat in 1965.

[11] Large landowners organized, armed and paid 'self-defense' groups to fight these rural-based guerrilla movements. These were supported by members of the army and, in some cases, by foreign mercenaries. Closed out of official circles, the army also

created paramilitary groups, later condemned by Amnesty International.

[12] In 1974, President Alfonso López Michelsen, a Liberal, tried to give greater attention to popular demands, but vested economic interests led to the failure of this policy. Figures for 1978 reveal that only 30 per cent of industrial workers and 11 per cent of the rural workforce had social security benefits. Colombia is dependent on international coffee prices on the US and German markets for its foreign exchange, as these countries consumed 56 per cent of the Colombian product at that moment.

[13] Guerrilla movements, particularly FARC and the April 19 Revolutionary Movement (M-19), continued their activities into the late 1970s. Military repression grew during the Government of President Julio C Turbay Ayala (1978-82).

[14] In 1982, a divided Liberal Party nominated two candidates, thus handing the victory to the Conservative Party's Belisario Betancur, a journalist, poet and humanist, who had actively participated in the peace process in Central America. Betancur proposed that Colombia join the Non-Aligned Movement and reaffirmed the right of debtor nations to negotiate collectively with creditor banks. Also, in 1983 he entered into peace talks with leaders of the M-19.

[15] The M-19 had initiated the peace process in 1980, when guerrilla leader Jaime Bateman proposed a high-level meeting in Panama. Bateman subsequently died in a suspicious airline accident and talks were suspended. In the meantime, FARC and the Government reached an agreement which led to a ceasefire between them and to the adoption of political, social and economic reforms.

[16] Large landowners fiercely opposed talks between the Government and the guerrillas. The rural oligarchy, holding 67 per cent of the country's productive land, denounced the peace process as 'a concession to subversion' and proposed the creation of private armies. Paramilitary action started up again; subsequent investigations revealed the hand of the *Muerte a los Secuestradores* (MAS - 'death to the kidnappers'), which had opposed the withdrawal of the army from guerrilla-

controlled areas. A one-year truce went into effect but M-19 withdrew five months later, claiming that the army had violated the ceasefire.

[17] In January 1985, the Government passed a series of unpopular economic measures: drastic cuts in public spending, a salary freeze for civil servants, substantial fuel and transport price rises, increased taxes on over 200 products including some basic consumer goods, limited salary increases which lowered real purchasing power, and a currency devaluation. The object was to increase exports and reduce the $2 billion fiscal deficit by 30 per cent.

[18] Rejected by the labor unions and the parties of the Left, the plan also failed to satisfy the country's creditors. A commission of 14 banks, presided over by the Chemical Bank, stated that the Government would have to sign a letter of intent and reach a formal agreement with the IMF, two steps which Betancur had wanted to avoid.

[19] According to the Human Rights Commission, 80 prisoners had disappeared in one year, political prisoners had been tortured and 300 clandestine executions were confirmed. The number of political activists who had disappeared rose to 325.

[20] On November 6 1985, 35 guerrillas from M-19 took over the Palace of Justice in Bogotá. The army attacked, causing a massacre. All the guerrillas were killed, along with 53 civilians, including magistrates and employees. A guerrilla commander known as Alonso insisted that those who had been killed 'were deliberately sacrificed by the army'.

[21] Taking advantage of this panorama of violence, the drug lords and their traffickers have created a secure power base for themselves.

[22] Over 2,000 left-wing activists were killed by terrorists, and in 1987 Jaime Pardo Leal, a member of the Patriotic Union, was assassinated. Liberal senator and presidential candidate in the 1990 election, Luis Carlos Galán - who had promised to dismantle the paramilitary groups and fight drugs - was assassinated in August 1989. War broke out between the Government and the drug mafia. In March 1990, Bernardo Jaramillo, the Patriotic Union's presidential candidate, was assassinated, with Carlos Pizarro (replacing Jaramillo) also killed 20 days later.

[23] Official figures for the 1990s acknowledge the existence of more than 140 paramilitary groups, most financed by the drug mafia. Meanwhile, as part of its 'War on Drugs', the United States Drug Enforcement Agency allegedly bombarded coca plantations with chemical herbicides.

[24] Despite the huge profits generated by the planting, processing and export of drug products (which have given rise to an underground economy), agriculture continues to be the backbone of Colombia's legal economy. Despite using only 5 per cent of the land it represents 23 per cent of the GNP and in 1981 employed 21 per cent of the workforce.

[25] The presidential elections of May 27 1990 were won by Liberal Party candidate Cesar Gaviria, who received 48 per cent of the vote in an election where the abstention rate was 58 per cent.

[26] In December 1990, elections were held to form a constituent assembly; there was a 65 per cent abstention rate. The number of votes received by ADM-19 was significant as they won 19 seats, 4 fewer than the Liberal Party (the party in power).

[27] In June 1991, members of Gaviria's government met in Caracas with representatives of the Revolutionary Armed Forces of Colombia (FARC), the National Liberation Army (ELN) and the People's Liberation Army (EPL) - members of the Simón Bolívar Guerrilla Coordinating Committee, which controlled 35 per cent of the country. Talks dealt with the demobilization of guerrillas, the subordination of the armed forces to civilian authority, the dismantling of paramilitary groups and the reintegration of guerrilla fighters into areas where they could exert political influence.

[28] On July 5 1991, the new constitution created the office of vice-president, eliminated the possibility of presidential re-election and included some major gains: civil divorce for Catholic marriages, direct election of local authorities, autonomy for indigenous peoples, the democratic tools of referendum and grassroots legislative initiatives, and guarantees of equal opportunities for women.

[29] The Constitution met with criticism from the Left for failing to give civilian courts jurisdiction over members of the military accused of committing crimes against civilians and for granting judicial powers to State security agencies.

[30] On October 27, an agreement between the President and the three major political forces participating in the constituent assembly reduced the number of representatives. After the dissolution of Congress, parliamentary elections were held. The Liberal Party, split into several groups, obtained 60 per cent of the vote and support for the ADM-19 dropped to 10 per cent. In the March 1992 municipal elections, marked by a 70 per cent abstention rate, this trend was continued.

[31] The peace process reached a low point in 1992. After talks had been discontinued, the Government promoted its so-called 'Integral War', which authorized intervention in civilian organizations with suspected links to rebel groups.

[32] The Simón Bolívar Coordinating Committee resisted the army offensive, continuing its campaign. In response, paramilitary groups resumed their activities, primarily in the Mid-Magdalena (River Valley) region, Boyaca and Medellín. Violence caused massive population displacement from conflict areas to other regions in the interior.

[33] In November, the Government decreed a state of emergency after Pablo Escobar Gaviria - head of the Medellín Cartel, a powerful drug-trafficking ring - had escaped from prison in mid-1992, stepping up the Cartel's violent actions. In January 1993 a group appeared known as 'PEPES' - People Persecuted by Pablo Escobar. Within a two-month period, they killed 30 cartel members, destroyed several of Escobar's properties and harassed members of his family. The confrontation reached serious proportions, with car-bombs causing dozens of deaths.

[34] Finally, on December 2, Escobar was killed in a shoot-out with police forces in downtown Medellín. Although his death was a heavy blow to the political and social power of the Medellín Cartel, the drug-trafficking mafia still had many other operations, including the more discreet Cali Cartel, which emerged stronger.

[35] The Supreme Court of Justice decriminalized the use of cocaine, marijuana and other drugs, with the radical opposition of several political

PROFILE

ENVIRONMENT

The Andes cross the country from north to south, in three ranges: the western range on the Pacific coast, and further inland, the central and eastern ranges, separated by the large valleys of the Cauca and Magdalena Rivers. North of the Andes, the swampy delta of the Magdalena River opens up, leaving flat coastal lowlands to the west - along the Pacific coast - and to the east, plains covered by jungle and savannas extend downward to the Orinoco and Amazon Rivers. This diversity results in great climatic variety, from perpetual snows on Andean peaks to tropical Amazon rain forests. The country's Andean region houses most of the population. Coffee is the main export item, followed by bananas. Abundant mineral resources include petroleum, coal, gold, platinum, silver and emeralds. Intensive agriculture and mining have contributed to soil depletion. There is significant deforestation, and two-thirds of the country's bird species are in danger of extinction. Coca plantations in Colombia increased by almost 25 per cent in 2001, some 33,600 hectares out of a total of 169,800.

SOCIETY

Peoples: Colombians are descended from native Americans, Africans and Europeans.
Religions: 93 per cent are Catholic. Although this is the country's official religion, there is religious freedom.
Language: Spanish (official); there are dozens of Indian languages including wayuu, camsá and cuaiquer.
Political Parties: The New Democratic Force (NFD), conservative. The Liberal Party (LP); the Social Conservative Party (SCP); M-19 Democratic Alliance (ADM-19); National Conservative Movement; Movement Social Indigenous Alliance; National Salvation Movement (MSN), which broke away from the PSC; Patriotic Union, formed by the military. National Liberation Army (ELN) is the second insurgent group of Colombia; United Self-Defenses of Colombia (AUC) joins paramilitary groups.
Social Organizations: There are four major labor organizations: the Confederation of Colombian Workers; the Confederation of Workers' Unions of Colombia; and the General Labor Confederation. The Colombian United Labor Federation (CUT), founded on 26 September 1986, and 80 per cent of all salaried workers affiliated to trade unions are members.

THE STATE

Official Name: República de Colombia.
Administrative divisions: 32 departments and the capital district.
Capital: Bogotá 6,158,000 people (1999).
Other cities: Cali 1,718,900 people; Medellín 1,621,400; Barranquilla 1,064,300; Cartagena 745,700 (1995).
Government: Álvaro Uribe Vélez, President since August 2002. The Congress (Legislature) has two chambers: the Chamber of Representatives, with 161 members, and the Senate of the Republic, with 102 members.
National Holiday: July 20, Independence Day (1810).
Armed Forces: 146,300 troops; 40,400 conscripts (1996).
Other: National Police Force, with 85,000 members. Coast Guard: 1,500 (1993).

and religious circles, headed by President Gaviria.

[36] The coffee market crisis and the 1993 drought, as well as the reduction of banana quotas to the European Union, affected exports. However, with $2 billion per year from drug-trafficking and the discovery of oil in Casanare province, the country achieved a sustained growth of 2.8 per cent per capita. Construction grew 8 per cent in 1993, while both trade and transport increased by 5 per cent. Unemployment dipped below 9 per cent in the country's seven largest cities and wages maintained an upward trend. However, 45 per cent of the population were still living in abject poverty.

[37] President Gaviria was elected secretary-general of the Organization of American States (OAS), with the support of the United States, which welcomed the victory of Ernesto Samper, his party's candidate in the 1994 elections; defeating Conservative Andrés Pastrana by 50 per cent to 48.6 per cent of the vote. Support for the ADM-19 dropped to 4 per cent of the vote, with abstentions slightly decreased to 65 per cent.

[38] The Samper Government began with a series of successful blows to drug-trafficking, but in September 1995 political scandal broke out when the Cali Cartel revealed details of that organization's contributions to both the Samper and Pastrana campaigns. Defense Minister Fernando Botero, Samper's former campaign director, was sent to prison for embezzling.

[39] In August 1996, Samper decreed a state of emergency to curb a wave of violence and kidnappings, a move considered an attempt to protect himself from drug-linked scandals. However, the murders of several opposition leaders and actions by FARC and the ELN, which attacked high-tension power lines, oil pipes, police and military facilities, continued. With fighting in almost 100 places, these two groups controlled growing areas in the economically powerful coffee region, the Caribbean and even in the vicinity of Bogotá and Medellín.

[40] Efforts to eradicate coca and opium poppy plantations continued, as well as armed operations against the Cartel's bases. Some of the Cali Cartel's main leaders, responsible for 70 per cent of cocaine traffic worldwide, gave themselves up. In March 1996 the US took Colombia off its list of countries which co-operate in the war on drugs. This measure ended bilateral aid to Colombia and blocked its access to foreign financial sources. Washington denied an entry visa to Samper, in an attempt to corner him diplomatically.

[41] Some 1,900 candidates decided not to run for the October 26 local elections because 49 mayors and city councillors had been killed and more than 180 kidnapped since the beginning of the year. In spite of the traditionally low turnout, over 5 million people enclosed symbolic 'vote for peace' slogans onto their ballot papers.

[42] In November the Human Rights prosecutor revealed that since August 1995 his office had ordered disciplinary measures, including 50 dismissals, against 126 military and police officers for human rights abuses. In the same period, more than 600 cases were investigated against security forces members, related with 1,338 victims of murder, torture or disappearance. Some 500 kidnappings mainly by FARC and ELN were reported in the period.

[43] Several organizations estimated that since early 1997 one million Colombians had been displaced from their homes in conflict areas, mainly due to the activity of paramilitary groups. According to the Government, guerrilla groups obtained an annual net income $750 million, substantially more than that earned by coffee. The only sectors with higher earnings were the drug cartels of Medellín and Cali.

[44] In February 1998, US President Clinton decided, for 'national interest' reasons, to include Bogota as a cooperating state in the war on drugs. According to the World Bank, high murder rates reduced GDP growth by 2 per cent each year.

[45] The worst defeat suffered by the armed forces in their 35-year fight against the guerrillas took place in March 1998, in Caqueta. Between 60 and 80 soldiers died in confrontation with FARC. The Government's military inferiority was revealed, causing the administration's worst crisis.

[46] In June 1998, former Bogotá Mayor Andrés Pastrana was elected President. The winner, from the conservative New Democratic Force party, obtained 50.4 per cent of the vote, ending the Liberal Party's 12-year hold on the presidency.

[47] In August 2000, Pastrana announced the Plan Colombia, inspired by the US, which sought to eradicate, from the air, 60,000 hectares of coca crops. Plan Colombia encompassed the formation of three anti-narcotics battalions, trained and equipped by US special forces, backed by 60 helicopters. The US also promised to contribute with $1.3 billion, mostly in military aid. The objective was to weaken the guerrillas' and drug barons' finances, rather than facing them in the battlefield.

[48] After the September 11 2001 attacks in the US, Colombia was included by Washington among the targets in its 'war on terror', although the US Government did not spell out Plan Colombia's details. This enabled the US to overcome obstacles of its domestic legislation and cooperate actively - with more financial contributions, intelligence and a larger and non-specified number of military - in the Colombian Government's war on the guerrillas.

[49] Peace talks between the Government and FARC broke down on February 20 2002, after the guerrillas kidnapped politicians in order to influence electoral results and force a swap with jailed guerrillas. On March 10, when partial elections were being held, 12 politicians were held, including presidential candidate Ingrid Betancour. The Government lost in the elections and forces allied to right-wing candidate Álvaro Uribe Vélez took power. Uribe had been linked to paramilitary forces under the United Self-Defense Groups of Colombia (AUC). The candidate's father had died under torture by the FARC, and Uribe opposed any peace agreement with the guerrillas. On April 14, Uribe escaped the third attempt on his life in the last seven months - the 15th in total.

[50] After negotiations were broken off, FARC carried out attacks in several cities, claiming a high number of civilian lives. On May 4 2002, violence against civilians reached an all-time high when FARC mortar-bombed a church where the population of Bojaya was taking refuge, killing 117 people, at least 40 of them children.

[51] Washington approved $2.6 billion, twice the amount of Plan Colombia, in May 2002. Thus the US began a significant military intervention in the continent. At the same time, Pastrana held peace talks, in Cuba, with the ELN.

[52] The Government put the Democracy Plan into action in April, a strategy through which 212,000 members of the army, police, air force and secret services aimed to guarantee the presidential elections on May 26 across Colombia. The few voters who turned out did so in an atmosphere intensified by guerrilla sabotage attempts, which left at least 11 paramilitaries and guerrillas dead. Abstention ran at 55 per cent. Independent candidate Urube Vélez took the lead with 52.96 per cent of the vote to his rival Horacio Serpa's 31.77 per cent, breaking the traditional cycle of liberals and conservatives. Uribe's campaign promise had been 'security for all Colombians' even if this implied hardline policies against all those involved in violent and illegal activity - including guerrillas, paramilitaries and drug traffickers. However, Uribe's close links with paramilitaries and drug traffickers meant his policies would concentrate on FARC without touching other violent sectors. ∎

Comoros

Population: 749,000 (2002)
Land area: 2,230 SQ KM
Capital: Moroni
Currency: Comorian franc
Language: Arabic and French

Comores

Comoros was inhabited around the 5th century by one of the last Indonesian migrations (see Madagascar). The Comoros Islands remained isolated from the continent until the 12th century when Muslim traders from Kilwa settled on the islands, founded ports and reproduced the civilization of the eastern African coast (see Tanzania: The Zandj Culture in East Africa).

[2] In the 16th century Comoros had a prosperous economy but the Portuguese seized the islands and destroyed their active trade. When the Sultan of Oman finally drove the Portuguese from the region, Comoros came under the influence of Zanzibar. The Bantu-speaking population, originally brought from the continent to work on the islands, increased considerably as a result of the slave trade.

[3] In the 19th century, Zanzibar split from the sultanate of Oman and the French-occupied Mayotte in 1843. Colonial domination eventually spread to the entire archipelago as the islands' position on the Cape route gave them strategic value.

[4] The Comoros National Liberation Movement (MOLINACO) was created in the context of successful anti-colonial struggles throughout Africa. It joined forces with the local Socialist Party (PASOCO) to form the United National Front (FNU) which pressured the French Government into holding a plebiscite in 1974. A large majority, 154,182 people, voted in favor of the islands' independence, and only 8,854 voted against.

[5] Most of those who wished to remain under French rule were Mayotte residents (63 per cent of its voters). France had air and naval bases on Mayotte and the economy was controlled by a few dozen Catholic families, sympathetic to France and politically represented by the Mahorés People's Movement (MPM), led by Marcel Henry.

[6] Ahmed Abdallah, the archipelago's leading rice exporter and Prime Minister of the semi-autonomous local government, proclaimed the independence of Comoros in July 1975, before the French announced the result of the referendum. Abdallah was afraid that his Udzima (Unity) Party would lose out to the FNU in a future assembly to draft a new constitution. The MPM

took advantage of the situation to declare that Mayotte would continue under French rule. Paris supported the secession in order to maintain its military presence in the Indian Ocean, violating its previous commitment to respect the territorial integrity of Comoros and the result of the referendum. France did not oppose the islands' membership in the UN but vetoed specific Security Council resolutions to reincorporate Mayotte into the archipelago.

[7] Less than a month before the declaration of independence, a small group of FNU youths seized the national palace in Moroni and appointed their leader, the socialist Ali Soilih, as president, in place of Abdallah. France reacted by sending a task force of three warships and 10,000 soldiers to Mayotte; one soldier for every three inhabitants.

[8] In May 1978, a mercenary force, under the command of Ahmed Abdallah, in exile in Paris, landed on

Grand Comoro (now Ndjazidja) overthrowing Ali Soilih who was assassinated three days later. At the head of the operation was the notorious French mercenary Bob Denard, who had been tried in 1977 for mercenary acts of war against the Government of Benin. His presence in Comoros triggered international protests, to the point of the Comoros Islands' delegation being expelled from a meeting of the Organization for African Unity in Khartoum.

[9] From then on, Denard became a key figure in the archipelago's politics, and Abdallah's control of the Government came to depend on support from Denard and his 650 troops. On November 26 1989, a coup led by Denard ousted Abdallah, who was killed in the fighting. The European mercenaries were financed by South Africa. The Comoros were also said to have served as a supply base for RENAMO, South African-backed rebel group in Mozambique.

[10] In the days following this coup, the French Government suspended all economic aid to the islands and initiated negotiations designed to oust Denard and his mercenaries from the island. They left in mid-December, heading for South Africa,

[11] Restrictions on the formation of political parties ceased after Abdallah's death. A number of opposition groups returned from exile.

PROFILE

ENVIRONMENT

The Comoros Islands are located at the entrance of the strategic Mozambique Channel, on the oil tanker route between the Arab Gulf and western consumer nations. The four major islands of this volcanic archipelago are: Njazidja, formerly Grand Comoro; Nzwani, formerly Anjouan; Mwali, formerly Moheli; and Mahore, also known by its former name of Mayotte. Ndjazidja has an active volcano, Karthala, 2,500 meters in altitude. The mountainous island is covered by tropical forests. Only 37 per cent of the cultivated land (100,000 hectares) is used to grow cash crops - vanilla and other spices; the rest is devoted to subsistence farming which is carried out without permanent rivers. The rainwater, which is stored in reservoirs, is easily polluted.

SOCIETY

Peoples: The original Malay-Polynesian inhabitants were absorbed by waves of Bantu and Arab migrations. Today, the latter groups predominate, co-existing with minority Indian and Malagasy communities. **Religions:** Islam (official). There is one mosque for every 500 inhabitants. **Languages:** Arabic and

French are official. Most people speak Comoran, a Swahili dialect, and some groups speak Malagasy. **Political Parties:** Parliament is currently dissolved. The main parties out of Parliament are: Forum for National Renewal; National Front for Justice; National Union for Development; Republican Party of Comoros. **Social Organizations:** The main organization is the Comoran Workers' Union.

THE STATE

Official Name: République Féderal et Islamique des Comores. **Capital:** Moroni 44,000 people (1999). **Other cities:** Mutsamudu 25,400 people; Domoni 14,000; Fomboni 12,200 (2000). **Government:** Parliamentary federal Islamic republic. Colonel Azzali Assoumani seized power in April 1999 in a coup; in May 2002 he was elected President of Njazidja. Mohamed Bacar is President of Nzwani and Said Fazul of Mwali. Since the constitutional reform passed in 2002, Njazidja is in charge for the first term of the rotating Presidency of the Federation. The Chief of State is Hamada Madi since 2002. The Prime Minister is Bianrifi Tarmidi (1999). Legislature: General Assembly of 42 members. **National Holiday:** July 6, Independence Day (1975).

[12] In August 1991, the Supreme Court of the Islamic Federal Republic of the Comoros found President Said Mohammed Yohar unfit to govern and guilty of serious negligence. After a failed attempt to oust the President, the political parties and Yohar signed a national reconciliation pact. A new government was formed, headed by Mohammed Taki Abdoulkarim, leader of the National Union for Democracy in Comoros. At the same time, a National Conference drafted a new constitution, which was approved by referendum, in June 1992. In July, President Yohar dismissed Taki Abdoulkarim and his government, accusing him of appointing a former French mercenary to his cabinet.

[13] In September, there was a failed coup against Yohar, led by two sons of former president Ahmed Abdallah. Several opposition leaders accused of conspiring against the Government were arrested and at least six civilians were killed.

[14] In October 1993, when Yohar, aged about 80, had gone to Réunion to receive medical treatment, Prime Minister Caabi el Yachourtu Mohamed proclaimed himself 'interim President', refusing to up power on Yohar's return.

[15] Yohar recovered a 'symbolic' Presidency in January 1996, while Taki, leader of the National Union for Democracy in Comoros (UNDC), won the elections held on March 6-7.

[16] A month after taking office, in April, Taki dissolved the National Assembly and called for elections on October 6. The UNDC obtained 36 out of the 43 seats, in elections boycotted by the opposition.

[17] The October 1996 Constitution replaced the June 1992 one and included, among other innovations, the formation of a Council of Ulemas (Islamic teachers) to monitor the compliance of the laws with their interpretation of Islamic law. The death penalty, suspended in 1975, was reinstated.

[18] In August 1997, a separatist movement headed by Abdallah Ibrahim demanded the independence of Nzwani (Anjouan) island, where half the Comoran population lives. In March the following year, more than 99 per cent of Nzwani citizens voted for secession in a referendum, while Mwali (Mohéli) island also called for its independence. On April 23 1999, in Madagascar, an agreement was proposed to grant more autonomy to Nzwani and Mwali and to establish an interim Government and a rotating Presidency among the three islands. Nzwani delegates refused to sign it, alleging they had to consult their people first; this led to violent clashes both in Njazidja (Grand Comore) and Nzwani. Political instability led to a bloodless military coup on April 30. Colonel Azzali Assoumani became President, and promised to hold elections within 10 months.

[19] Neither the federal Government of Comoros nor the Organization of African Unity had recognized the independence of Nzwani. While the island's political leaders were in Mwali scrutinizing a constitutional draft with the goal of redefining the islands' relationships, a military committee, led by Major Mohamed Bacar, took over Nzwani in August 2001. The committee said it wanted to grant Nzwani 'regional autonomy regarding Comoros, but not total separation'.

[20] Two separatist coups within the military élite failed in Nzwani, and control was left in the hands of Bacar. Finally, a referendum in Njazidja supported the new constitution (already approved in the other two islands) that held the Federation, but granted more autonomy to each part. The Presidency would rotate among the three islands. The first four-year term went to Njazidja.

[21] After an election rife with protests of fraud, Assoumani was confirmed as President by a new ad hoc electoral body, the Commission of Ratification, in May. The Commission also declared Mohamed Fazul had won the elections in Mwali, which had also been denounced as fraudulent. Bacar had won Nzwani's presidential elections. ∎

Mayotte

Land area:	375 SQ KM
Currency:	Euro
Language:	French, Arabic, Swahili and Comoran

Known as the Island of Perfumes, Mayotte lies in the Indian Ocean, about half-way between Madagascar and the coast of Mozambique, 1,500 kilometers away from Réunion. Mahoré (Mayotte in Creole) comprises two main islands, Petite Terre and Grand Terre separated by two kilometers of sea and surrounded by a coral reef of 1,000 square kilometers.

[2] As a consequence of successive invasions since the 10th century, Mayotte is a combination of Arabic, Madgascan and French influence. After the treaty of April 25 1841, Mayotte became a French colony. In 1974, after pressure from independence movements, France agreed to a referendum in the Comoros islands, of which Mayotte was part. Nationalist forces won and in 1975 the independence of Comoros was proclaimed. However, those who wished to remain under French rule gathered in Mayotte and, supported by Paris, encouraged secession from the Comoros. Taking advantage of a movement that overthrew Ahmed Abdallah - prime minister of the semi-autonomous local government - 10,000 French troops occupied Mayotte.

[3] The policy statement of the Eighth Conference of Non-Aligned Countries, held in Harare (Zimbabwe) in September 1986, declared that 'the Comoran island of Mayotte, still under French occupation, is an integral part of the sovereign territory of the Federal Islamic Republic of the Comoros'. In October 1991, the UN General Assembly reaffirmed the sovereignty of the Comoros over Mayotte by an overwhelming majority.

[4] Today the island remains a French protectorate. France maintains an important air-naval base. In 1997, the islands of Nzwani (formerly Anjouan) and Mwali (formerly Moheli) declared their independence from Comoros' main island of Ndjazidja (formerly Grand Comoro), declaring their desire to return to French rule. Ndjazidja tried to recover them and in 1999 they arrived to a peace agreement sponsored by the Organization of African Unity. The islands were granted greater autonomy but voters on Nzwani rejected the peace agreement and endorsed independence in January 2000. The OAU imposed economic sanctions to the island.

[6] In July 2000, the people of Mayotte approved by referendum an offer by Paris to increase its autonomy. The agreement granted Mayotte a status similar to that of a department, instead of an overseas territory.

ENVIRONMENT
A mountainous island with tropical climate and heavy rainfall throughout the year. The island is of volcanic origin, has dense vegetation and is located at the entrance to the Mozambique Channel. Cyclones (hurricanes) are quite frequent.

SOCIETY
Peoples: Mayotte inhabitants are of the same origin as Comorans. There is an influential community of French origin that controls the island's commerce. **Religions:** 98 per cent Muslim. There is a Roman Catholic minority. **Languages:** Arabic, Swahili, Comoran, and French (official). **Political Parties:** The Mayotte Federation for the Organization of the Republic (RPR); the Mahoré People's Movement (MPM); the Party for the Democratic Organization of the Mahoré (PRDM), which seeks unification with the Comoros; the Union for French Democracy (UDF); the Social Democratic Center (CDS).

THE STATE
Official name: Collectivité Territoriale de Mayotte. **Capital:** Dzaoudzi 13,500 people (1999). **Other cities:** Mamoutzou 40,900 people (2000). **Government:** Philippe de Mester, Prefect since September 2001, appointed by the French Government. Unicameral Legislature: General Council, with 19 members. **National Holiday:** All French holidays. **Armed Forces:** The defense is responsibility of France; small contingent of French forces stationed on the island.

DR Congo

Population:	54,275,000 (2002)
Land area:	2,267,050 SQ KM
Capital:	Kinshasa
Currency:	New zaire
Language:	French

République Démocratique du Congo

The first known state to emerge in what is now DR Congo was the Luba kingdom, located in the Katanga (Shaba) region. The Luba Kingdom was created in the 16th century when a warrior named Kongolo subdued the small chiefdoms in the area and established a highly centralized state. To the northwest was the Kuba, a federation of numerous chiefdoms that reached its peak in the 18th century. Dr David Livingstone brought the region to the notice of the Western world through his explorations between 1840 and 1870. He met up with Henry Stanley, a journalist and adventurer sent to seek him, in Ujiji in 1871. In 1876, King Leopold II of Belgium founded the International African Association (later, the International Association of Congo), a private organization that financed Stanley's expeditions. Stanley succeeded in signing more than 400 trade and/or protectorate agreements with local leaders along the Congo River. These treaties, and the Belgian trading posts established at the mouth of the river, were used to devise a system for the economic exploitation of the Congo. The Berlin Conference, 1884-1885, decided that the 'Free State of Congo' was the Belgian King's personal property. Consequently, Leopold's 'Compagnie du Katanga' stopped British colonialist Cecil Rhodes' northward expansion.

[2] The Congolese population was subjected to extremely harsh working conditions, which did not change when they formally became a Belgian colony in 1908. Military force was systematically employed to suppress anticolonial opposition and to protect the flourishing copper mining industry in Katanga (now Shaba).

[3] In 1957, liberalizing measures permitted the formation of African political parties. This led countless tribal-based movements to enter the political arena, all trying to benefit from the general discontent. Only the National Congolese Movement led by Patrice Lumumba had a national outlook, opposing secessionist tendencies and supporting independence claims.

[4] In 1959, the police suppressed a peaceful political rally triggering a series of bloody confrontations. King Baudouin of Belgium tried to appease the demonstrators by promising independence in the near future, but European residents of the Congo reacted with more oppressive measures. Independence was finally achieved in 1960, with Joseph Kasavubu as President and Lumumba as Prime Minister. A few days later, Moise Tshombe, then Premier of the Province of Katanga, initiated a secessionist movement.

[5] Belgium sent in paratroopers and the United Nations, acting under US influence, intervened with a 'peacekeeping force'. Kasavubu staged a coup and arrested Lumumba, delivering him to Belgian mercenaries in Katanga who killed him. The civil war continued until 1963. Secessionist activity ceased when Tshombe, who represented the neo-colonial interests, was appointed Prime Minister. With the help of mercenaries, Belgian troops and US logistical support, the Tshombe regime was able to stifle the nationalist opposition movement. In 1965, he was forced to resign by Kasavubu who was in turn overthrown by army commander Joseph Desiré Mobutu. For the transnationals, Mobutu was the only person who could restore the conditions required for them to continue operating there.

[6] Under the doctrine of 'African authenticity', Mobutu changed the name of the country to Zaire and his own to Mobutu Sese Seko. However, his nationalism went little further than this, and the 'Zairization' of copper, which he declared in 1975, only benefited an already wealthy economic elite and the state bureaucracy.

[7] Although these measures caused some discomfort among US diplomats, Mobutu offered Washington his services in the region.

[8] Zaire sheltered and actively supported the so-called National Front for the Liberation of Angola (FNLA). Mobutu encouraged secessionist groups in the oil-rich Angolan province of Cabinda, and Zaire's troops effectively cooperated with the South African racist forces in their war against the Angolan nationalists.

[9] Meanwhile, in Zaire guerrillas continued the struggle in the interior. In 1978 and 1979, the major offensive launched by the Congolese Liberation Front was checked with the aid of French and Belgian paratroopers and Moroccan and Egyptian troops, again with US logistical support.

[10] At the end of 1977, international pressure led to parliamentary elections being held for an institution which had been given limited legislative functions. This helped to divert international attention from human rights violations against students and intellectuals in the cities, the establishment of concentration camps for Mobutu's opponents and the brutal reception given to refugees who returned under an 'amnesty' decreed in 1979.

[11] At this time Zaire was the world's largest cobalt exporter, the fourth biggest diamond exporter and ranked among the top ten world producers of uranium, copper, manganese and tin. But corruption was rampant throughout the country's administration, worsening the already unstable economic situation.

WORKERS

2000

LABOR FORCE AS % OF TOTAL

■ FEMALE: 43%　■ MALE: 57%

LAND USE

DEFORESTATION: 0.1% annual (1990/95)

1993

■ FOREST & WOODLAND: 74.1%
■ ARABLE: 3.1%
■ OTHER: 22.8%

PUBLIC EXPENDITURE

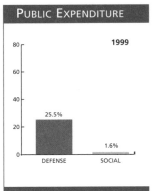

1999

25.5% DEFENSE
1.6% SOCIAL

12   During 1980 and 1981, the major Western powers decided to seize direct control of the strategic mineral reserves in the country. The International Monetary Fund (IMF) took special interest in Zaire's economy, facilitating the renegotiation of its foreign debt, while at the same time imposing drastic measures against corruption. Zaire's economy was under direct IMF control, and the Fund's representatives in Kinshasa began to supervise the country's accounts personally.

13   In April 1981, Prime Minister Nguza Karl I-Bond sought political asylum in Belgium; he presented himself to the western powers as a 'decent alternative' to the official corruption in Zaire.

14   The elections of June 1984 officially gave Mobutu 99.16 per cent of the vote.

15   In April 1990, anticipating the process of democratization which he considered imminent, Mobutu decided to take a bold step. He ended the one-party system, opened up the labor movement and promised to hold free elections within a year. A rapid process of political organization began. Hundreds of associations and political groups demanded legal recognition from the Government. The extent of the popular reaction frightened the authorities and on May 3, Mobutu issued a statement saying that no party had yet been legalized and that it would be necessary to modify the constitution before holding elections, because the head of state wished to 'preserve his authority without exposing himself to criticism'.

16   Students initiated demonstrations throughout the country, especially at the university in Lubumbashi, capital of the province of Shaba. The students began calling for the resignation of Mobutu, who reacted by sending in his presidential guard to stifle the protests.

17   The troops stormed the university campus at dawn on May 11. More than 100 students were killed and the terrified survivors fled to other provinces and Zambia, from where they condemned the massacre.

18   The massacre at Lubumbashi University generated an anti-Mobutu wave which led to a series of strikes, like that at state-owned Gecamina, the country's most important mining company. In the United States there were repeated calls to end aid to Mobutu.

19   In October 1990, under growing internal and external pressure, Mobutu decided to carry out a new political 'democratization' process and he authorized the unrestricted creation of new political parties. In December, the opposition - grouped together under the Holy Union, a front made up of nine parties (including the four largest) - demanded Mobutu's resignation and called for a National Conference to decide on the political future of Zaire without presidential intervention.

20   In November 1991, the Holy Union formed a 'shadow government', and appealed to the armed forces to depose Mobutu. The same month, the President appointed Nguza Karl I-Bond as his new Prime Minister - his fifth in that year. Nguza, a former opposition leader who had been Mobutu's head of government 10 years earlier, took office amidst a worsening economic crisis and growing international pressures, especially from the US.

21   Early in 1992, the National Conference was set up. The opposition had long awaited this opportunity to press for constitutional reform and transition to democracy. In February of the same year, Prime Minister Nguza Karl-I Bond suspended the Conference, causing a faction of the army to rebel, taking over a state-run radio station and demanding President Mobutu's resignation. Some hours later the rebels were defeated by troops loyal to the Government. Thousands of demonstrators demanding the president's resignation and the reopening of the Conference were harshly repressed by the army.

22   The European Community suspended financial aid to Zaire immediately, until the reinstatement of the National Conference. Meanwhile, representatives from the US, France and Belgium agreed to increase the pressure on the Mobutu government to speed up political change.

23   In March 1992, after meetings with Conference president Archbishop Monsegwo Pasinya, President Mobutu announced the reopening of the National Conference. Etienne Tshisekedi, leader of the Holy Union, was made Prime Minister, to replace Nguza Karl-I Bond.

24   Inter-ethnic strife erupted again in 1992. In Shaba there were outbreaks of violence after Karl-I Bond's dismissal. Lunda people, Karl-I Bond's group, attacked members of the Luba community, Tshisekedi's people. Some 2,000 people were killed, and thousands of Luba left Shaba as their homes had been destroyed. Security forces eventually intervened several weeks after the fighting broke out.

25   The 12 commercial banks operating in Zaire closed indefinitely in 1992, due to a lack of funds. Inflation reached 16,500 per cent. According to a report by the Washington-based Population Crisis Committee, in 1992 Zaire was among the 10 poorest countries in the world.

26   In December, galloping inflation prompted the Prime Minister to announce that the zaire would no longer be legal tender, placing a new currency in circulation. Regardless of this Mobutu ordered that troops receive their backpay in the old currency.

27   In early 1993, battles broke out between the soldiers, furious over having been paid in worthless bills, and Mobutu's personal guard. This confrontation caused over 1,000 deaths in Kinshasa.

28   On February 24, Mobutu's soldiers and tanks surrounded the building housing the High Council of the Republic, a transitional body formed by the National Conference, demanding that the 800 legislators approve the old currency which Mobutu had returned to circulation.

29   With the worsening situation, the US, Belgium and France sent a letter to Mobutu demanding that he resign in favor of a provisional government headed by Tshisekedi. Mobutu responded by dismissing Prime Minister Tshisekedi, in March 1993. Faustin Birindwa replaced him.

30   The economic and political uncertainty continued throughout 1994. The genocide in Rwanda and the arrival of masses of refugees - amongst whom were found thousands of members of the militias responsible for the massacre - created

PROFILE

ENVIRONMENT

Located in the heart of the African continent, DR Congo's territory covers most of the Congo River basin and has a narrow outlet into the Atlantic. The center and northern regions are covered with rainforests and are sparsely populated. Small plots of subsistence farming are found here. In the southeast, a plateau climbs to 1,000 meters in the Shaba region (former Katanga). Most of the nation's resources and population are located in the southern grasslands, where cotton, peanuts, coffee and sugarcane are grown. There are also large palm-oil and rubber plantations. The country's mineral wealth is concentrated in Shaba: copper, zinc, tin, gold, cobalt and uranium. Local industry is found in the mining areas too. In urban areas, polluted water is a source of infectious diseases. Once abundant forest resources have declined at a rapid rate. Wildlife is threatened by poaching and the lack of resources for protection of wildlife. Deforestation problems.

SOCIETY

Peoples: The people of Congo are made up of several major African ethnic groups. West African people live in the northwest, while Nilo-Hamitic descendants live in the northeast and a large pygmy minority lives in the eastern center. There are more than 200 ethnic groups, mainly: Luba (18 per cent), Mongo (13.5 per cent), Azande (6.1 per cent), Bangi and Ngale (5.8 per cent), Rundi (3.8 per cent), Teke (2.7 per cent), Boa (2.3 per cent), Chokwe (1.8 per cent), Lugbara (1.6 per cent), Banda (1.4 per cent), other (16.6 per cent).
Religions: It is difficult to pinpoint the religion of peoples in the DRC due to high levels of religious syncretism. There is a large Christian population, above all Catholic (41 to 50 per cent), a Muslim minority (1.2 to 10 per cent) and many traditional religions. Protestant 32 per cent.
Languages: French (official). The most widely-spoken local languages are Swahili, Shiluba, Kikongo and Lingala (the army's official language).
Political Parties: Parliament is currently dissolved, so these are non-parliamentary parties. Union for Democracy and Social Progress (UDPS, liberal); Union for the Republic and Democracy; Congolese Rally for Democracy; Congolese-Liberation Movement (RCD-ML).

THE STATE

Official Name: République Démocratique du Congo.
Administrative divisions: 10 provinces and a capital.
Capital: Kinshasa 4,885,000 people (1999).
Other cities: Lubumbashi 1,044,200 people; Mbuyi-Mayi 1,018,100; Kisangani 792,400; Kananga 521,900 (2000).
Government: Joseph Kabila, acting President since January 2001. There is a provisional 300-member government assembly appointed by former President Laurent Kabila in 2000.
National Holiday: June 30, Independence Day (1960).
Armed Forces: Between 20,000 and 40,000 of Kabila's troops constitute the new Armed Forces of the country.
Other: Gendarmerie: 21,000; Civil Guard: 19,000.

FOREIGN TRADE

Millions US$ 1997

IMPORTS

1,282

EXPORTS

1,390

STATISTICS

DEMOGRAPHY

Population: 54,275,000 (2002)
Annual growth: 3.2 % (1985-2000)
Estimates for year 2015: 84,045,000 (2000)
Annual growth to year 2015: 3.3 % (2000)
Urban population: 30.3 % (2000)
Urban growth: 3.8 % (2000)
Children per woman: 6.7 (2000)

HEALTH

Life expectancy at birth: 52 years (2000-2005)
male: 51 years (2000-2005)
female: 53 years (2000-2005)
Infant mortality: 128 per 1,000 (2000)
Under-5 child mortality: 207 per 1,000 (2000)
Daily calorie supply: 1,637 per capita (1999)
7 doctors per 100,000 people (1996)
Safe water: 45 % (2000)

EDUCATION

Literacy: 67 % (2000)
male: 83 % (2000)
female: 54 % (2000)
School enrolment (net):
Primary total: 59 % (1994/2000)
male: 66 % (1995/99)
female: 51 % (1995/99)
Secondary (gross):
male: 32 % (1995/97)
female: 19 % (1995/97)
Tertiary (gross): 1 % (1998)
Primary school teachers: one for every 26 pupils (1998)

COMMUNICATIONS

3 newspapers (1996), 386 radios (1997), 2 TV sets (1998) and 0 main telephone line (2000) per 1,000 people

ECONOMY

Per capita, GDP: $ 765 (1998)
Annual growth: -0.1 % (1998)
Annual inflation: 175.5 % (1997)
Consumer price index: 2,090.7 (1997)
Currency: 330.6 New zaires = $ 1 (03/2002)
Cereal imports: 310,489 metric tons (2000)
Fertilizer use: 1 kg per ha (1999)
Exports: $ 1,390 million (1997)
Imports: $ 1,282 million (1997)
External debt: $ 11,645 million (2000); $ 229 per capita (2000)
Development aid received: $ 132 million (1999); $ 2.7 per capita (1999)

ENERGY

Consumption: 284.4 Kgs of oil equivalent per capita yearly (1998); -2.3 % imported (1999)

HDI (ranking/value): 142 / 0.429 (1999)

great tension in eastern Zaire.

[31] When the Rwandan Patriotic Front (FPR) guerrillas came to power in Rwanda, several Western nations, including France, began to reduce the pressure on Mobutu - newly considered as a potential ally following the victory of 'the English-speaking Tutsis' in the neighboring country. This reinforced the President's power, facilitating the nomination of Léon Kengo Wa Dondo as prime minister, though this was immediately challenged by the opposition.

[32] The tension between Zaire and Rwanda increased in 1996, after the Rwandan Hutu militias, supported by members of the Zairian armed forces, began ethnic cleansing in the Masisi region, ousting and killing the Tutsis, the Banyamulenge, who had lived in this part of eastern Zaire for generations,.

[33] At the end of 1996, the conflict between armed Tutsi groups and the remnants of the Rwandan army (mostly Hutu), assumed civil war proportions. The confrontation spread with government forces participating to put a stop to the advance of the Tutsi rebels, who had taken several cities in the east of the country. The Mobutu regime became seriously threatened when various opposition forces formed an alliance led by the veteran guerrilla leader Laurent Kabila. After convalescing in Switzerland, Mobutu returned in December. After a short stay during which he declared a general increase in army salaries, Mobutu returned to Switzerland.

[34] In the first few months of 1997, opposition forces easily took over practically the whole country, and a group of states - South Africa, the US, France and Belgium included - attempted to mediate and seek a solution. South African president Nelson Mandela arranged a meeting between Mobutu and Kabila on a ship in international waters to negotiate the transition. However, the attempt was a failure, as Kabila demanded that Mobutu stand down as a pre-condition to the talks.

[35] In March, Parliament sacked Prime Minister Kengo Wa Dondo, and a month later Étienne Tshisekedi was appointed as a replacement for his third term in office, with

Mobutu's approval. Barely a week later, disagreements between the government parties led to Tshisekedi being replaced by Likulia Bolongo. Foreseeing the final outcome, the powerful mining companies began to negotiate with Kabila to protect their interests in Zaire.

[36] On May 16, Mobutu fled to Morocco and opposition troops entered Kinshasa the following day. Kabila declared himself President. Mobutu died in Rabat on September 7 and the new strongman took over as president that month with full military, legislative and administrative powers. The new government changed the name of Zaire to the Democratic Republic of Congo and announced a series of economic recovery measures. An investigation began into Mobutu's Swiss bank accounts, where he had put his personal fortune drawn from the Zaire's coffers.

[37] A study by Médecins Sans Frontières (MSF) in late 1997 exposed the massacres committed by Kabila's forces and the Rwandan troops that supported him in ousting Mobutu. Members of the Union for the Republic and Democracy (URD, former members of the AFDL founded by Kabila himself) accused Kabila of returning to tribalism, and under the leadership of Ernest Wamba dia Wamba - an intellectual - armed groups of Tutsi refugees and demobilised Congolese soldiers took half the country using weaponry and officers provided by the Rwandan and Ugandan governments. Kabila launched resistance under the slogan of a 'threat to the African civilization'.

[38] The conflict rapidly raised international concern and, in April 1999, in response to the attack, Kabila and the Angolan, Zimbabwean and Namibian leaders announced an alliance to provide a joint response if any of the members were attacked. Hence Angola, Zimbabwe and Namibia supplied Kabila with troops and weapons, while Uganda and Rwanda stepped up support of the rebels.

[39] Two years into the civil war which brought Kabila to power, whole provinces were under Ugandan and Rwandan control. The Congolese Parliament was dissolved in 2000, and

the President replaced it with a 300-member government assembly.

[40] Kabila was assassinated by one of his bodyguards in January 2001 while the Franco-African summit was meeting in the presidential palace. His son Joseph immediately replaced him in the presidency, while allies of the murdered man held an emergency meeting. All the dignitaries at the summit offered continued support for Joseph Kabila, but this situation was not expected to last for long, as the allies were expected to back out. One possible solution for the allies would be renewal of the 1999 peace agreements that called for United Nations military intervention, the withdrawal of foreign powers and transition to democracy.

[41] There was a withdrawal of troops monitored by the UN in May 2001. As troops were removed from combat, aid agencies discovered the full impact of the conflict which had pushed most of the population into remote areas where they lacked food, medicine or shelter. According to figures from the International Rescue Committee (IRC), five per cent of the Congolese population died during the war. In the eastern region of the country alone, two and a half million people had died, mostly due to malaria, diarrhea and violence.

[42] With a ceasefire in place, signed by all parties except the Congolese Rally for Democracy (CRD), it was hoped the various factions would negotiate a political agreement. This would, it was hoped, lead to a transition government and eventually to elections, but in August CRD rebels took the town of Lokandu from government forces. A United Nations report stated that both Rwanda and Uganda were prolonging their 'stay' in the country, partly to exploit the rich natural resources. Meanwhile, France accused Rwanda of re-lighting the fuse on the war, by sending 10,000 troops to help the rebels. By March 2002, rebels supported by Rwandan troops had taken the airport in Moliro, on the frontier between Rwanda and Zambia, on the shore of Lake Tanganika. ■

Congo

Population: 3,206,000 (2002)
Land area: 341,500 SQ KM
Capital: Brazzaville
Currency: CFA franc
Language: French

République du Congo

Today's Congo was originally populated by Pygmies and Bushmen (San). By the 16th century it comprised the Bantu states of Luango and Kacongo, for many years ruled by the Manicongo. These nations managed to stave off early Portuguese attempts at colonization. Instead, for three centuries, under the Batekes of Anzico, they acted as suppliers and intermediaries of British and French slave dealers.

[2] Towards the end of the 19th century, trade in rubber and palm oil replaced slave traffic. The new trade brought with it French colonization.

[3] In 1880 French troops led by Savorgnan de Brazza began to colonize the Congo by force, and by the 1920s two-thirds of the local population had been killed. This genocide, along with the use of forced labor to build the Brazzaville-Pointe Noire railroad, resulted in the early emergence of independence movements with strong religious beliefs, under the leadership of Matswa.

[4] After World War II, labor and student movements inspired by socialist ideas formed the backbone of resistance.

[5] Sponsored by the French, Friar Fulbert Youlou led the Democratic Union for the Defence of African Interests and was the first president of independent Congo in 1960. Mass participation grew however and Youlu's neo-colonialist policies were rejected. A wave of demonstrations against corruption and the banning of trade unions ended in a popular uprising during the 'three glorious days' (August 13-15) of 1963.

[6] Youlou resigned and the President of the National Assembly, socialist Alphonse Massemba-Debat, took office and forced the French troops stationed in the country to withdraw. He then founded the National Movement of the Revolution (MNR) as the country's sole party.

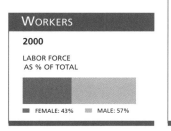

WORKERS

2000

LABOR FORCE
AS % OF TOTAL

■ FEMALE: 43%　■ MALE: 57%

LAND USE

DEFORESTATION: 0.2% annual (1990/95)

1993

■ FOREST & WOODLAND: 61.7%
■ ARABLE: 0.4%
■ OTHER: 37.9%

[7] This force could not coexist with the neo-colonial army, equipped and trained by the French, and the consequent crisis led Massemba-Debat to resign on January 1 1969. He was replaced by a young major, Marien N'Gouabi, backed by left-wing army officers. N'Gouabi founded a Marxist-Leninist party called the Congolese Workers' Party (PCT).

[8] In 1973, a new constitution was approved, proclaiming the Congo a people's republic, and the State took control of energy, water, major industrial firms, and petroleum.

[9] In December 1975, N'Gouabi made a public self-appraisal, issued a call to 'extend the revolution', and launched a general review of party structures, the state apparatus and mass organizations.

[10] To afford greater public participation in the running of the State, an ambitious educational reform was begun and the structure of the Government was reformed. Until then all the school textbooks had come from France and were Eurocentric.

[11] When Angola gained independence in 1975, Congo lost no time recognizing Agostinho Neto's government. His clear position on the problem of Cabinda was decisive in frustrating attempts to have this oil-rich province break away from Angola, a scheme which was being promoted by transnational companies with interests in the Congo.

[12] On March 18 1977, N'Gouabi was assassinated by followers of ex-president Massemba-Debat. The conspirators failed in their efforts to seize power, however, and Massemba-Debat was executed.

[13] The new president, Colonel Joachim Yombi Opango, did not maintain N'Gouabi's austere style and was forced to resign on February 6 1979, charged with corruption and abuse of power. Denis Sassou N'Guesso replaced him.

[14] N'Guesso launched a campaign against corruption in the public sector, as well as a broad administrative and ministerial reform. Toward the end of 1981, the Congo faced foreign trade difficulties directly linked to inefficiency in state enterprises which the Government refused to close.

[15] In 1982, the Congo's finances improved. Part of the recovery was attributed to oil exports, which financed 49.44 per cent of the budget.

[16] Congolese oil was exploited in partnership with French, US and Italian firms. Annual exports approached eight million tons of crude in 1988.

[17] President N'Guesso's foreign policy was pragmatic; he sought closer relations with Eastern Europe, while maintaining commercial ties with the United States and France. He played a leading role in negotiations between Angola, South Africa and Cuba, which culminated in the signing of a peace settlement for the region in December 1988, in Brazzaville, paving the way for Namibia's independence.

[18] The fall of the Berlin Wall and the demise of the Soviet Union precipitated political and economic changes. In December 1990, the country adopted a multiparty system. In July 1991, André Milongo took the post of Prime Minister until presidential elections could be held. This decision caused confrontation in the streets and the formation of a transition Government with army participation. Following elections in August 1992, Pascal Lissouba succeeded Sassou N'Guesso.

[19] In the early legislative elections of May 1993, the ruling party won 62 seats against the opposition coalition's 49. The opposition accused the Government of fraud and further clashes between demonstrators and the military left six people dead.

LITERACY

2000

81%

EXTERNAL DEBT

2000

PER CAPITA

US$ 1,619

FOREIGN TRADE

Millions US$ 2000

IMPORTS

1,345

EXPORTS

2,526

STATISTICS

DEMOGRAPHY

Population: 3,206,000 (2002)
Annual growth: 3.0 % (1985-2000)
Estimates for year 2015: 4,730,000 (2000)
Annual growth to year 2015: 3.0 % (2000)
Urban population: 62.5 % (2000)
Urban growth: 4.2 % (2000)
Children per woman: 6.3 (2000)

HEALTH

Life expectancy at birth: 52 years (2000-2005)
male: 50 years (2000-2005)
female: 54 years (2000-2005)
Infant mortality: 81 per 1,000 (2000)
Under-5 child mortality: 108 per 1,000 (2000)
Daily calorie supply: 2,212 per capita (1999)
25 doctors per 100,000 people (1995)
Safe water: 51 % (2000)

EDUCATION

Literacy: 81 % (2000)
male: 88 % (2000)
female: 74 % (2000)
School enrolment (net):
male: 99 % (1995/99)
female: 93 % (1995/99)
Secondary (gross):
male: 62 % (1995/97)
female: 45 % (1995/97)
Tertiary (gross): 7 % (1997)
Primary school teachers: one for every 61 pupils (1998)

COMMUNICATIONS

8 newspapers (1995), 123 radios (1997), 13 TV sets (1998) and 7 main telephone lines (2000) per 1,000 people

ECONOMY

Per capita, GDP: $ 825 (2000)
Annual growth: 4.9 % (2000)
Annual inflation: -0.9 % (2000)
Consumer price index: 129.7 (2000)
Currency: 758.3 CFA francs = $ 1 (03/2002)
Cereal imports: 219,343 metric tons (2000)
Food import dependency: 21 % (1995)
Fertilizer use: 286 kg per ha (1999)
Exports: $ 2,526 million (2000)
Imports: $ 1,345 million (2000)
External debt: $ 4,887 million (2000); $ 1,619 per capita (2000)
Debt service: 1.4 % of exports (1999)
Development aid received: $ 140 million (1999); $ 49.1 per capita (1999); 6.30 % of GNP (1999)

ENERGY

Consumption: 433.4 Kgs of oil equivalent per capita yearly (1998); -1,855.4 % imported (1999)

HDI (ranking/value): 126 / 0.502 (1999)

---

[20] President Lissouba named retired military officer, Jacques Yhombi-Opango, as Prime Minister, which led the opposition to form a parallel government led by Bernard Kolelas. In July and December, fresh disturbances caused the death of some 80 people. Meanwhile, the Government remained bankrupt and only paid civil servants 7 of their 12 pay packets in 1993.

[21] In January 1994, the army called in the artillery to counteract attacks from armed opposition groups. The disturbances caused the death of more than 100 people. An agreement between the opposition and the Government, in mid-March, marked the beginning of a cease-fire. Later, in July, the election of Kolelas

as mayor of Brazzaville further calmed the situation, allowing for a public reconciliation ceremony the following month.

[22] During 1994 Lissouba accepted the IMF structural adjustment program, including the reduction of the number of civil servants. Competition between various oil multinationals threatened the dominance of the French Elf in Congo, leading the company to increase the amount of profit reinvested in the country from 17 to 31 per cent.

[23] 1995 was dominated by the quest for a definitive agreement to disarm the anti-government urban militias and to eventually integrate them into the official army. On February 19 a general strike was

started calling for the payment of overdue salaries. On March 1, an agreement was made including a reduction in salaries in return for a drop in working hours, but this was rejected by the civil servants.

[24] Civil war began when the Government sought to disarm and arrest Denis Sassou N'Guesso and some of his followers in June 1997. In November, opposition forces defeated Lissouba, with the aid of Angolan troops. In many cases combat led to pillage against local communities. N'Guesso formed a new Government in Brazzaville and decided to wipe out 'ninja' militias, self-proclaimed resistance forces led by Kolelas.

[25] In January 1998, Brazzaville and Kinshasa initiated talks to demarcate both territories throughout their 2,410 km common border. That year, N'Guesso updated his army with weapons acquired from Russian organized crime, and put Israeli officers in charge of his personal guard.

[26] A cease-fire agreement was signed in November 1999 by N'Guesso and resistance forces, and was confirmed on December 29, with the mediation of Omar Bongo, President of Gabon. In compliance with the agreement, N'Guesso freed prisoners and during January 2000 thousands of rebels gave up their weapons. In February, Kolelas ratified his recognition N'Guesso as President.

[27] Eleven cases of Ebola were identified in December 2001, in spite of health controls in the borders. It is assumed that the virus was carried from Gabon by an infected woman. Medical teams tracked all people who had contact with those victims already identified; around 100 had been found.

[28] The first Presidential elections after the end of the civil war were held in February 2002, with an 80 per cent turnout (1.7 million voters out of a 2.9 million population). President Denis Sassou-N'Guesso obtained 74.7 per cent of the vote, enough to make a second electoral round unnecessary. Altough the elections were held in peace, the main opposition candidates were either in exile or withdrew their candidacy in the last minute, accusing the electoral process of being a 'charade' and demanding an independent electoral commission. ■

PROFILE

ENVIRONMENT

The country comprises four distinct regions: coastal plains; a central plateau (separated from the coast by a range of mountains rising to 800 meters); the Congo River basin in the northeast; and a large area of marshland. The central region is covered with dense rain forests and is sparsely populated. Two-thirds of the population live in the south, along the Brazzaville-Pointe Noire railroad. Lumber and agriculture employ more than one third of the population. The country has considerable mineral resources including oil, lead, gold, zinc, copper and diamonds. The environmental situation is characterized by haphazard urban development, the accumulation of refuse, a lack of sewage facilities, the proliferation of contagious diseases, pollution, deforestation and the disappearance of native fauna.

SOCIETY

Peoples: The Congolese are of Bantu origin; the Bakongo prevail in the South, the Teke (or Bateke) at the center; the Sanga and Vilil in the North. There is also a Pygmy minority.
Religions: The vast majority of the population practice traditional African cults. Christian elements are assimilated into these cults. There is a Muslim minority (2 per cent).
Languages: French (official), Kongo, Lingala, Téké.
Political Parties: Pan-African Union for Social Democracy; Congolese Workers' Party (PCT); Congolese Movement for Democracy and Integral Development.
Social Organizations: The four existing labor organizations merged in 1964 to form the Congolese Labor Confederation (CSC), Revolutionary Union of Congolese Women.

THE STATE

Official Name: République du Congo.
Administrative divisions: 8 regions and 6 communes.
Capital: Brazzaville 1,187,000 people (1999).
Other cities: Pointe Noire 765,300 people; Loubomo 84,500 people (2000).
Government: Parliamentary republic. Denis Sassou N'Guesso, President since October 1997, re-elected in March 2002. Parliament itself has been replaced by a National Transition Council made up of 75 members.
National Holiday: August 15, Independence Day (1960).
Armed Forces: 10,000.
Other: 6,100: Gendarmerie (1,400); People's Militia (4,700).

Slavery and sub-Saharan Africa

In the 13th century when the Europeans began to penetrate the region of Africa below the Sahara, lured by the promise of gold and ivory, they rediscovered slavery, which had become more or less obsolete in Catholic Europe. The practice, widespread in sub-Saharan Africa since pre-Islamic times, had expanded further with the arrival of Islam to the point that some 18 million black Africans were traded in the Islamic world between 865 and 1905. After this 'rediscovery', in the second half of the 15th century, the Portuguese began to trade slaves from the west coast of Africa, taking first European slaves and later Berber slaves to the kingdom of Ghana.

But the scale and nature of slavery underwent major changes as the first wave of what we now call globalization began. After Europeans conquered the Americas and circumnavigated the world, 'black Africa' was transformed by the wishes and needs of people living in far distant lands. The conquest of the Americas changed the status of slaves and how they were seen, as Europeans believed that Africans - like the Amerindians - were not 'fully human'. Once Spain sought African slaves in the early 16th century to replace the Amerindian workforce in its colonies, the 'denial of humanity' was transferred from the indigenous people to the African slaves, with some 10 million brought to the New World by 1867.

LINES ON A MAP

The Europeans' contempt towards the African 'savages' meant that they did not reach the interior of the continent until the mid-19th century, when the slave trade had already declined considerably. The European powers, requiring minerals and other raw materials to feed the industrial revolutions at home, parceled out the continent among themselves. In 1884 Africa was divided into 48 new states by the European powers at the Berlin Conference. The creation of this patchwork map did not respect local cultures or the geopolitical realities of the time: some peoples were divided and others, diverse and often ancestral enemies, were thrown together in order to meet the needs of the new European era.

The chaos and devastation that sub-Saharan Africa has suffered since the 'decolonization' process begun after World War II is undoubtedly a product of that partition. But it is also the result of an even greater conceit: the assumption that herders and hunters could or should adapt to the dictates of the European cultures. And nowadays the assumption is that these countries can be inserted into the most recent globalization process - one that no longer requires colonies as such but feeds institutions that encourage the development of an ever-more enslaving capitalism.

NATION STATES

The first modern nation-states were in the Americas, an achievement bought at the price of genocide perpetrated by the 'Creole' population (those of European origin) against the indigenous people who did not adapt to the demands of capitalism. Even among the European elite, this process sparked constant internal and external wars, both in 'Anglo' and 'Latin' America.

The sub-Saharan African countries were expected to become nation-states in a very short period of time. Lacking a European elite such as there had been in the Americas, the African countries had to establish states based on heterogeneous societies, while also taking on the demands of an interlinked world that called for modern and 'globalized' behavior of its citizens. Paradoxically, these nations are at an historic moment at the global level, but internally some have been cursed with genocide. In response we have witnessed the horror expressed by countries like the US - which reinforced its own territorial and material wealth through the systematic extermination of its native peoples - and also the European countries which built their strength on the exploitation of slaves and natural wealth from Africa.

The plundering and exploitation the West inflicted on sub-Saharan Africa throughout the centuries, most notoriously through the slave trade, has left painful problems for the continent. Some seem to have no solution: for example, how will herders, hunters and gatherers escape or survive the fast-spinning wheels of Western capitalism. ∎

Costa Rica

Population: 4,200,000 (2002)
Land area: 51,060 SQ KM
Capital: San José
Currency: Colón
Language: Spanish

Costa Rica

When the first Europeans arrived on its shores, the territory of present-day Costa Rica was populated by small groups of the Chorotega, Cobici, Carib and Boruca nations. Christopher Columbus reached the coast of Costa Rica - 'the rich coast' - on his last voyage in 1502. Although the first contact was friendly, the local people were not easily dominated by the Europeans, and it took nearly 60 years for a permanent settlement to be established in the region.

[2] Gaspar de Espinosa, Hernán Ponce de León and Juan de Castañeda traveled along the coast of the territory between 1514 and 1516. Between 1560 and 1564, they were followed by Juan de Cavallón, Juan de Estrada Rabago and Juan Vásquez de Coronado. The conquest of the territory was consolidated in the second half of the 16th century.

[3] The Spanish established the first permanent settlement, the town of Cartago, on the central plain in 1564. This was assigned to the political jurisdiction of the Captaincy-General of Guatemala, while remaining under the spiritual guidance of the bishop of Nicaragua.

[4] The indians' resistance kept the colonizers isolated for a long time. They were unable to establish a system of *encomiendas* - the virtual enslavement of the Indian work force. In this way a patriarchal society of small landowners was formed, with no powerful land-owning oligarchy as in the neighboring countries. This might explain how, instead of becoming a nation scourged by civil wars and military dictatorships, modern Costa

Rica maintained greater democratic stability and has not established a regular army like the other countries in the region.

[5] When Mexico declared independence from Spain in 1821, Costa Rica, along with other former Spanish colonies in Central America, formed part of the Mexican empire. In 1823, Costa Rica helped create the United Provinces of Central America and remained a part of this federation until its dissolution in 1840. A persistent opponent to the 'Balkanization' brought about by British imperialism, Costa Rica's territory was used as a base for operations by Francisco Morazán - an advocate of Central American unity - until 1848, when Costa Rica became an independent state.

[6] In the mid-19th century, William Walker - a US national who had taken control of Nicaragua - tried to extend his dominion over the Central American isthmus. He was defeated by forces commanded by the Costa Rican President Juan Rafael Mora. Material progress reached Costa Rica during the regime of General Tomás Guardia, who ruled the nation from 1870 to 1882. While his administration took away some liberties and increased foreign debt, coffee and sugar production rose and more schools were built. The constitution adopted in 1871 remained in place until 1949.

[7] The last decades of the 19th century were marked by a gradual reduction of Church influence in secular affairs. Cemeteries were

secularized and the Jesuits expelled from the country for a few years. Schools were founded, along with a museum and a national library. In 1886, primary education became obligatory and free In 1890, José Joaquín Rodríguez was elected President in what were considered the first free and fair elections in Central America, creating the Supreme Tribunal of Elections, still in force today, and establishing women's suffrage.

[8] In 1916, Nicaragua gave the US permission to use the San Juan river, which forms the frontier with Costa Rica. The San José Government protested that its rights had been overlooked and the complaint was taken to the Central American Court of Justice, which ruled in favor of Costa Rica. Nicaragua rejected the verdict and withdrew from the Court. This was one of the main reasons for the dissolution of the Court a year later.

[9] Costa Ricans had their first elections with direct voting in 1913. There was no outright winner and the Legislative Assembly designated Alfredo González Flores as President. General Federico Tinoco Granados, unhappy with the reforms proposed by González, led one of the few coups experienced by the nation, in 1917. But the lack of US recognition for his government and the threat of intervention forced Tinoco to resign in 1919.

[10] Between 1940 and 1948 the Government was backed by coffee plantation owners and bankers. However in 1948 opposition leader Otilio Ulate, nominated by the National Unity Party, won a presidential election which was annulled by Congress. This unleashed civil war which ended with a junta seizing power, presided over by José Figueres Ferrer. The junta issued a call for the election of new representatives, who in turn confirmed Ulate's victory.

[11] The new Constitution of 1949 was noteworthy because it abolished the army, which was replaced with a civil guard. The decision subsequently marked the country internationally as being pacifist and a promoter of demilitarization. Costa Rica stood apart from the other Central American countries because it did not suffer military coups and

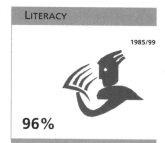

MATERNAL MORTALITY

2000

Per 100,000
live births

29

LITERACY

1985/99

96%

because it earmarked greater resources to areas key to the country's development, such as education and health.

[12] This opened the so-called 'Welfare State Capitalism'. Figueres was elected President in 1954 and during his administration Costa Rica became a strongly anti-communist welfare state. In 1958, the conservatives defeated Figueres and imposed an import-substitution development model.

[13] The traditional antagonism between liberals and conservatives gave way to new tensions between the National Liberation Party (PLN),

led by Figueres, and a heterogeneous group consisting of various small parties. In 1966, the opposition managed to form an electoral coalition, the United National Opposition which elected José Joaquín Trejos to the presidency.

[14] After the 1970 election, the PLN returned to power with Figueres, who remained in office until 1974, when Daniel Odúber Quirós, co-founder of the Party in 1950, was elected President.

[15] Odúber tried to restore unity to the Central American Common Market, left in a critical situation

after the 1969 war between El Salvador and Honduras. However, his obvious pro-democracy stance did not meet with the approval of Somoza's regime in Nicaragua. Costa Rica was constantly harassed by its neighbor and became a safe haven for thousands of political refugees.

[16] 1975 saw a rise in wages due to favorable conditions resulting from the nationalization of transnational oil companies and the rise in coffee prices on the world market.

[17] In 1978, contrary to all expectations, presidential elections gave the victory to a conservative coalition which had been critical of the previous government's administration. The leftist bloc, grouped in the United People's Coalition, increased considerably and became the third most important political force. However they remained isolated and unable to propose social changes within the democratic and pluralist system favored by the majority.

[18] The new President, Rodrigo Carazo Odio, imposed an unpopular economic policy prescribed by the International Monetary Fund (IMF), which resulted in growing confrontation with labor and left groups. In 1979 however, encouraged by popular sympathy towards the Sandinista rebels, and under threat of invasion by neighboring dictator Anastasio Somoza, the Costa Rican Government decided actively to support the Nicaraguan Sandinistas.

[19] A radically different attitude was taken in 1980 with regard to El Salvador's insurgency. In spite of grave and continuous human rights violations in that country, the San José Government supported the Salvadoran military junta. In 1981 President Carazo broke off diplomatic relations with Cuba.

[20] In January 1982, the US-backed Central American Democratic Community was set up in San José with the main objective of isolating revolutionary Nicaragua.

[21] Luis Alberto Monge, a right-wing PLN candidate, became President in February 1982. When he took office in May, Monge proclaimed his alignment with Western democracies, and announced economic austerity measures. At the same time, he

fostered closer ties with the governments of El Salvador, Guatemala and Honduras, thus aggravating relations with Nicaragua.

[22] Costa Rica's hostile attitude towards its neighbor was clearly demonstrated when the US declared a commercial embargo on Nicaragua's revolutionary Government. A series of border incidents brought relations between the two countries to breaking point during July and August 1985. However, prompt action taken by the Contadora Group (organization of Latin American countries - Mexico, Panama, Colombia and Venezuela - formed in 1983, at a meeting on Panama's Contadora island, to achieve a peace agreement for Central America) prevented mounting tension in the area; both governments agreed to place neutral observers along the common frontier to arbitrate any further border clashes.

[23] The winner of the February 1986 presidential election was Social Democrat Oscar Arias, who won a tight victory with 52 per cent of the vote.

[24] Arias devoted himself to the task of designing a policy that would break both the logic of war and the escalating tension within the region. In August 1987 he presented a peace plan at a summit meeting held in Esquipulas, Guatemala. This was accepted and signed by the Presidents of El Salvador, Nicaragua, Guatemala and Honduras. The focal points of the plan were: a simultaneous cease-fire in Nicaragua and El Salvador, an immediate end to American aid to the Nicaraguan *contras*, a democratization time-table for Nicaragua which included holding free elections and putting an end to the use of foreign territory as supply or attack bases.

[25] The signing of this peace plan, known as 'Esquipulas II', earned Costa Rica a special place in international relations, and constituted a personal triumph for President Arias, who received the Nobel Peace Prize in October 1987 in recognition of his efforts.

[26] During his term, Arias instituted the first phase, and later the second, of a structural adjustment program, with World Bank support. The objective of this

PROFILE

ENVIRONMENT

A mountain range with major volcanic peaks stretches across the country from northwest to southeast. Costa Rica has the highest rural population density in Latin America, with small and medium sized farmers who use modern agricultural techniques. Coffee is the main export crop. The lowlands along the Pacific and the Caribbean have different climate and vegetation. Along the Caribbean coast there is dense, tropical rainforest vegetation. Cocoa is grown in that region. The Pacific side is drier; extensive cattle raising is practiced along with artificially irrigated sugarcane and rice plantations. Deforestation has been partially responsible for soil erosion and reduced fertility.

SOCIETY

Peoples: Costa Ricans, usually called *ticos* in Central America, are descended from the integration between native Americans and European migrants, mainly Spanish. African descendants, who were brought in from Jamaica, make up 3 per cent of the population and are concentrated along the eastern coast. Indigenous peoples, 1 per cent.
Religions: 81.3 per cent of the population are Catholic; Evangelical Protestant 15 per cent.
Languages: Spanish is the official language, spoken by the majority. Mekaiteliu, a language derived from English, is spoken in the province of Limón (east coast). Several indigenous languages.
Political Parties: Social Christian Unity Party, President Rodríguez' Party (PUSC); National Liberation Party, social democrat (NLP); Citizens' Action Party (CAP); Libertarian Movement (LM); Costa Rica Renewal Party (CRRP); Democratic Force (DF).
Social Organizations: The Unitary Workers' Union (CUT); the 50,000-member CUT groups both workers and peasants from the National Federation of Civil Servants, the National Peasant Federation; the Federation of Industrial Workers, regional federations and smaller unions. 375 cooperatives.

THE STATE

Official Name: República de Costa Rica.
Administrative Divisions: 7 Provinces: Alajuela, Cartago, Guanacaste, Heredia, Limon, Puntarenas, San José.
Capital: San José 964,000 people (1999).
Other cities: Alajuela 663,800 people; Cartago 413,200; Limón 290,700 (2000).
Government: Abel Pacheco, President since May 2002. Unicameral Legislative: the Legislative Assembly, made up of 57 members, elected by proportional representation in each province for a four-year term. National Holiday: September 15, Independence Day (1821).
Armed Forces: Abolished in 1949.
Other: 7,500: Civil Guard (4,300), Rural Guard (3,200), (1995).

FOOD DEPENDENCY

2000

7%

EXTERNAL DEBT

2000

PER CAPITA

US$ 1,110

FOREIGN TRADE

Millions US$ 2000

IMPORTS

7,651

EXPORTS

7,304

STATISTICS

DEMOGRAPHY
Population: 4,200,000 (2002)
Annual growth: 2.8 % (1985-2000)
Estimates for year 2015: 5,233,000 (2000)
Annual growth to year 2015: 1.8 % (2000)
Urban population: 51.9 % (2000)
Urban growth: 3.1 % (2000)
Children per woman: 2.8 (2000)

HEALTH
Life expectancy at birth: 77 years (2000-2005)
male: 75 years (2000-2005)
female: 80 years (2000-2005)
Maternal mortality: 29 per 100,000 live births (1985/99)
Infant mortality: 10 per 1,000 (2000)
Under-5 child mortality: 12 per 1,000 (2000)
Daily calorie supply: 2,761 per capita (1999)
141 doctors per 100,000 people (1997)
Safe water: 95 % (2000)

EDUCATION
Literacy: 96 % (2000)
male: 95 % (2000)
female: 96 % (2000)
School enrolment (net):
Primary total: 91 % (1994/2000)
male: 93 % (1995/99)
female: 93 % (1995/99)
Secondary (gross):
male: 47 % (1995/97)
female: 50 % (1995/97)
Tertiary (gross): 31 % (1997)
Primary school teachers: one for every 30 pupils (1996)

COMMUNICATIONS
91 newspapers (1996), 816 radios (1999), 231 TV sets (2000) and 249 main telephone lines (2000) per 1,000 people
Books: 29 new titles per 100,000 people (1992/94)

ECONOMY
Per capita, GDP: $ 8,650 (2000)
Annual growth: -0.5 % (2000)
Annual inflation: 11.0 % (2000)
Consumer price index: 181.5 (2000)
Currency: 346.9 colones = $ 1 (03/2002)
Cereal imports: 769,227 metric tons (2000)
Food import dependency: 7 % (2000)
Fertilizer use: 7,680 kg per ha (1999)
Exports: $ 7,651 million (2000)
Imports: $ 7,304 million (2000)
External debt: $ 4,466 million (2000); $ 1,110 per capita (2000)
Debt service: 6.4 % of exports (1999)
Development aid received: $ -10 million (1999); $ -2.7 per capita (1999); -0.10 % of GNP (1999)

ENERGY
Consumption: 788.6 Kgs of oil equivalent per capita yearly (1998); 56.7 % imported (1999)

HDI (ranking/value): 41 / 0.821 (1999)

program was the transformation of industry through technological modernization, increased efficiency and greater productivity. Neo-liberal formulas were applied, following the dictates of international financial organizations. However, according to the labor unions, these 'prescriptions were formulated without looking at their social repercussions.

[27] In July 1989, an investigation into drug trafficking was carried out by a parliamentary commission. The report produced by the Commission found both of the main political parties (the PLN and the PUSC) guilty of receiving drug money during the 1986 electoral campaign. At the same time, another scandal broke out over the financing of electoral campaigns, with accusations that both parties - and Oscar Arias individually - had received money from Panamanian General Noriega in 1986.

[28] In 1990, women officially made up 29.9 per cent of the economically active population, but their number on the informal job market was estimated at 41 per cent. In the political arena women held only 15 per cent of posts. Women's organizations observed an increase in teenage through prostitution rings, which have become multi-million-dollar businesses for their owners.

[29] Under the slogan of 'change' and focusing specifically on low-income groups with lower educational levels, the social Christian candidate Rafael Angel Calderón won the election held in February 1990 by a wide margin. In addition, he obtained an absolute majority in the legislature.

[30] The application of a severe economic adjustment program led to a reduction in the State apparatus as well as in the fiscal deficit, which had reached 3.3 per cent of GDP. As a result of these cuts, unemployment rose and popular discontent increased.

[31] In the 1994 elections, social democrat candidate José María Figueres Olsen (José Figueres' son) defeated government candidate Miguel Rodriguez by a narrow margin, after a campaign with few differences in their political positions but with notably harsh speeches from the rival parties.

[32] A free trade agreement was signed with Mexico in January 1995. However, the deterioration of the economy, with rising inflation and a fiscal deficit led the Government to increase taxes in order to balance the budget. The World Bank rejected the economic plan and refused to finance the structural adjustment schedule.

[33] In 1996, the governing PLN agreed a budget plan with the opposition which limited the Government deficit to 1 per cent of the Gross Domestic Product. In late July, Hurricane Caesar struck Costa Rica, especially the south, causing some 30 deaths. The damage was estimated at around $100 million. The kidnappings of one German and another Swiss tourist dealt a blow to the tourist industry. Both were freed two and a half months later. Many tourist operators preferred not to run the risk and took Costa Rica off their list of destinations.

[34] In June 1997, San José ratified the Interamerican Convention on Forced Detentions. Amnesty International urged the Government to put an end to police abuse against prisoners and refugees, who were mostly Nicaraguans.

[35] In February 1998, Miguel Angel Rodríguez, the Social Christian Unity Party (PUSC) candidate was elected president, with the PUSC also gaining the majority of seats in the parliamentary elections. Rodríguez stressed that during his administration Costa Rica would not adhere to political integration mechanisms like the Central American Parliament, but to economic ones.

[36] In March, the US ambassador, Thomas Dodd, was accused by the Commission for the Defense of Human Rights in Central America (Codehuca) of interfering in the internal affairs of the country. Dodd had declared that his government might impose economic sanctions following the death of a US citizen in a private dispute.

[37] A nutrition survey in March 1999 revealed that 75 per cent of infants aged from one to two years old had some degree of anemia, a figure which fell to 26 per cent in pre-school children. Throughout the country, 33 per cent of people

living in rural areas and 16 per cent of urban dwellers suffered the same problem.

[38] In order to address the growing violence, and to avoid the country becoming a refuge for criminals operating in neighboring countries, in December the Government brought in the obligatory registration of weapons and offered a 12-month amnesty to those who gave up their arms.

[39] Jewish activists accused the government of protecting Bodhan Koziy, a Ukrainian Nazi convicted of war crimes who had resided in Costa Rica 15 years. In December, the Government initiated a review of Koziy's status and announced that it would consider extradition. In February 2000 San José broke off diplomatic relations with Vienna when the Austrian Freedom Party, with neo-Nazi tendencies, joined the government coalition.

[40] Costa Rica began construction in June 2001 of a wall along its border with Nicaragua, triggering a dispute between the two countries. Managua alleged that the wall was meant to halt immigration of Nicaraguans into Costa Rican territory, but the Rodríguez Government said the project was part of expanding the border customs infrastructure.

[41] For the first time in the country's electoral history, a run-off vote was necessary in the presidential elections because no candidate achieved the required 40 per cent of the vote. In April 2002 the PUSC candidate, Abel Pacheco, won 58.2 per cent, defeating his PLN rival, Rolando Araya, and became the new President. Another new factor in the elections was the rise of the Citizen Action Party (PAC), an independent movement that won 26 per cent of the vote, weakening the country's long-dominant two-party system. ∎

Côte d'Ivoire

Population: 16,691,000 (2002)
Land area: 318,000 SQ KM
Capital: Abidjan
Currency: CFA franc
Language: French

Côte d'Ivoire

According to Baulé tradition, in 1730 Queen Aura Poka (sister of a defeated pretender to the Ashanti throne) emigrated westwards with her people. They founded a new state in the center of a territory known to Europeans since the 15th century as the Côte d'Ivoire (or Ivory Coast) because of the active trade in elephant tusks. This Ashanti state soon grew and became a threat to the small states of Aigini, on the coast, and Atokpora, inland. In 1843, these states requested French protection, thus enabling France to obtain exclusive rights over the coastal trade centres.

[2] Fifty years later, French troops moved up the coast aiming to join Côte d'Ivoire to Guinea, Mali and Senegal. However, they met with stiff resistance from Samori Touré, a Fulani leader who had risen through the social ranks because of outstanding leadership ability. He had set up a state in the heart of the region which the Europeans were planning to unify under a central colonial administration (See Guinea).

[3] After three decades of bloody fighting (1870-1898), Touré was defeated and the leaders of the dominant Fulani groups were forced to sign colonial agreements with the French.

[4] In 1895 the area became known as French West Africa, comprising Senegal, French Sudan (now Mali), Guinea and Côte d'Ivoire. Later, what are now Chad, Burkina Faso and Mauritania were also annexed. The French hoped to balance the poorer regions of Chad and Burkina Faso with the better off Senegal and Côte d'Ivoire. This centralized administration failed after independence.

[5] Several attempts at economic integration were made, with different degrees of success, but real progress was made only recently with the creation of the Economic Community of West Africa, which includes 15 former colonies of France, Britain and Portugal.

[6] In French West Africa, modern political activities began in 1946 with the creation of the African Democratic Union (ADU), a political party with branches in Senegal, Mali and Guinea. The ADU promoted independence and unity for French colonies in the area. Felix Houphouët-Boigny, hereditary leader of the Baulé ethnic group, and also a physician and well-to-do farmer, was appointed party president, based on his experience leading a farmers' association which had fought against colonial policies.

[7] Tactically allied to the French Communist Party, the only anti-

colonial French party at the time, the ADU staged strikes, demonstrations and boycotts of European businesses. The nationalist cause was savagely suppressed, leaving dozens of activists dead and thousands imprisoned, giving Houphouët-Boigny grounds for ending his alliance with the French communists in 1950. He soon reached a new agreement with François Mitterrand, then Minister for Overseas Territories. This move undermined the ADU's standing, and Houphouët-Boigny was only just able to maintain his prestige in his own land.

[8] Between 1958 and 1960 all of French West Africa became independent and the new states joined the UN. Aware of their meager economic prospects, the political leaders proposed to form a federation. However Houphouët-Boigny, who became president in 1960, and confident in the relative prosperity of his country and his privileged neo-colonial relations with France, opposed the idea. 'We are not saying *goodbye* to France, but *see you later*', he had declared when announcing independence.

[9] As a major producer of cocoa, coffee, rubber and diamonds, Côte

d'Ivoire was able to attract transnational investors. In addition to the political stability produced by Houphouët-Boigny's paternalistic, authoritarian rule, the country offered extremely cheap labor, mostly supplied by neighboring countries. In the 10-year period (1966-76) the economic growth rate remained between 8 and 10 per cent a year. But prosperity withered as the West went into a recession after 1979. Agricultural exports fell from $4 billion to barely $1 billion between 1980 and 1983. Half the industries set up between 1966 and 1976 closed down, pushing unemployment figures up to 45 per cent of the active population. By 1985, the foreign debt was five times that of 1981.

[10] Following International Monetary Fund recommendations, President Houphouët-Boigny made severe budget cuts, paralyzed nearly all public projects and slashed food subsidies. These decisions did not spark social unrest immediately, but only because of the weakness of the labor unions and the lack of fresh political leadership. The only groups which retained potential for opposition were students and liberal professionals, and they organized mass demonstrations and strikes.

[11] In May 1984, following negotiations with the Paris Club and other sources of financing, Côte d'Ivoire was allowed to reschedule its foreign debt. The economy continued to deteriorate, particularly as coffee and cocoa export prices fell.

[12] In October 1985 the 8th congress of the Côte d'Ivoire Democratic Party (PDCI) presented octogenarian Houphouët-Boigny for a sixth presidential term, confirmed in elections that month by 99 per cent of the vote.

[13] The Government built the largest basilica in Africa in a country where only 12 per cent of the population is Christian.

[14] Côte d'Ivoire, the world's leading cocoa producer, suffered a blow to its main export product: from July to October 1987, cocoa prices plummeted 50 per cent on the international market.

[15] In 1991 the Government had failed to fully implement its three-year program to clean up public finances, privatize some of the state enterprises

LAND USE

DEFORESTATION: 0.6% annual (1990/95)

1993

- FOREST & WOODLAND: 22%
- ARABLE: 7.6%
- OTHER: 70.4%

PUBLIC EXPENDITURE

Military expenditure (as % GNI):	**0.8 %** (1999)
Defense expenditure (% of central government expenditure)	**3.4 %** (1999)

and stimulate the 'competitiveness' of private companies.

[16] The death of the President in December 1993 triggered a succession dispute. Henri Konan-Bédié, leader of the National Assembly, assumed the post and consolidated his power within the ruling Democratic Party in spite of opposition from former prime minister Ouattara.

[17] In 1994 the Government faced a strong labor movement demanding compensation after the 100-per cent devaluation of the CFA franc in January. In what was seen as a reward for having accepted the devaluation - imposed by France and the IMF - half of Côte d'Ivoire's debt to the Paris Club was cancelled. However, the country continued to have the world's highest per capita foreign debt.

[18] In October 1995, Bédié won a presidential election that the opposition boycotted. For the first time since the country's independence, residing foreigners were not allowed to vote, nor were Côte d'Ivoire citizens who had foreign parents. This permitted Bédié to dispose of Ouattara, whose father was from Burkina Faso. Prime Minister Daniel Kablan Duncan formed a new Cabinet in January 1996, making no significant changes.

[19] A December 1999 military coup led by General Robert Guéi overthrew Bédié, who fled the country. The US and the European Union urged the military junta to return to democracy. In January 2000, after declaring that the state coffers were empty, Guéi took over as interim president and announced a referendum that was approved in August. It modified the Constitution and set elections for October. The opposition candidates immediately began their electoral campaigns.

[20] The constitutional changes gave the right to vote to those age 18 and over (which Bédié had originally opposed, fearing that the younger segment of the population - affected by his social policies - would tend to vote against him). Last minute amendments stipulated that both parents of presidential candidates must be 'of Ivorian origin', a change that once again excluded Ouattara.

[21] The abstention rate was over 60 per cent in the October 22 2000 elections. Two days later, when the re-count gave the victory to the socialist candidate of the Ivorian People's Front (FPI), Laurent Gbagbo, with 51 per cent of the vote, Guéi declared himself President. The presidential guard took over the Electoral Commission and the director said errors had been made in the re-count and denounced fraud committed by Gbagbo's party. The streets filled with protesters, at Gbagbo's urging, but neither the army nor the police intervened. When the social chaos appeared to be uncontrollable, the Electoral Commission reappeared, but this time with the true results: Gbagbo 60 per cent; Guéi 32 per cent. Upon taking office, Gbagbo called for unity and peace, while Guéi left the country for Benin.

[22] Initially the three majority parties were united against Guéi, but after the official announcement of Gbagbo's victory, Ouattara's supporters demanded new elections. The dispute triggered an anti-North uprising. In the South, mosques were burned and some 500 Muslim northerners were massacred by FPI militants supported by the army and the police.

[23] Ouattara and Gbagbo met to seek a way out of the crisis and urged peace, but the new President refused to repeat the elections. The first actions of the Gbagbo administration included investigating the killings of the young Muslims linked to the Republican Regroupment (RdR) and punishing the perpetrators, and also creating a national reconciliation committee consisting of 29 representatives of the various sectors of civil society. Gbagbo assumed the responsibility of encouraging hope among a population that was tired of years of authoritarianism and anxious about the country's economic circumstances.

[24] Although economic development in 2001 was not as negative as in 2000 (after two years of international isolation resulting from the Guéi-led coup), there were few positive figures. GDP had declined 0.9 per cent in 2001, compared with a 2.3 per cent reduction in 2000. The main export industries, such as cocoa, coffee and petroleum, had suffered two years of recession, thus putting the country in an even more critical situation.

[25] The return to democracy improved international relations, and with them the expectation of economic growth. In April 2002, the European Union and the Paris Club cancelled $911 million of Côte d'Ivoire's debt. In exchange, the Government promised to implement broad structural reforms, which would include privatizing state companies, reducing subsidies and liberalizing trade.

[26] In September 2002 ex-military leader General Guéi was killed in Abidjan. ∎

PROFILE

ENVIRONMENT

Located on the Gulf of Guinea, the country is divided into two major natural regions: the South, with heavy rainfall and lush rainforests, where foreign investors have large plantations of cash crops like coffee, cocoa and bananas; and the North, a granite plain characterized by its savannas, where small landowners raise sorghum, corn and peanuts. Côte d'Ivoire currently has one of the fastest rates of deforestation in the world.

SOCIETY

Peoples: The population includes four major ethnic groups, the Kru, Akan, Voltaic speakers and Mande, some from the savannas and others from the rainforests, sub-divided into approximately 80 smaller groups. There are many 'non-Ivorians' living in the country, mostly from the neighboring countries **Religions:** Nearly two-thirds of the population practice traditional African religions, 23 per cent are Muslim and 12 per cent Christian. It is difficult to quantify the religions and mixture of beliefs of 'non-Ivorians'. They are divided more or less equally among traditional beliefs, Islam and Christianity. **Languages:** French (official). There are as many languages as ethnic groups; the most widely spoken are Diula, in the North; Baule, center and West; and Bete in the Southeast. **Political parties:** Ivorian People's Alliance (FPI); Côte d'Ivoire Democratic Party (PDCI); The Republican Rally (RDR); Côte d'Ivoire Workers' Party. **Social Organizations:** General Workers' Union.

THE STATE

Official Name: République de Côte d'Ivoire.
Administrative divisions: 49 departments.
Capital: Abidjan (economic center) 3,199,000 people; Yamoussoukro (political center since 1983) 165,000 (1999).
Other cities: Bouaké 741,100 people; Daloa 184,300; Korhogo 164,400 (2000).
Government: Parliamentary Republic. Laurent Gbagbo, President since October 2000. Affi N'Guessan, Prime Minister since October 2000. Unicameral Legislature: National Assembly, with 225 members. **National Holiday:** August 7, Independence (1960).
Armed Forces: 8,400.
Other: 7,800: Presidential Guard: 1,100; Gendarmerie: 4,400; Militia: 1,500; Military Fire Service: 800.

Croatia

Population: 4,657,000 (2002)
Land area: 55,920 SQ KM
Capital: Zagreb
Currency: Kuna
Language: Croatian

Hrvatska

The Croats, a Slav people, emigrated in the 6th century AD from White Croatia, a region today in the Ukraine, toward the lower Danube valley. They moved on toward the Adriatic Sea, where they conquered the Roman stronghold of Salona, in 614. Once established in the former Roman provinces of Pannonia and Dalmatia, the Croats freed themselves from the Avars - a people of undetermined origin and language who had built an empire in the area between the Adriatic and the Baltic Sea - and began developing independently. Even though the territory was under the Byzantine empire, the Croats accepted the Roman Catholic Church, whilst preserving the Slav liturgy.

2 The Croatians were a farming people, and maintained their old way of life, uniting under their tribal chieftains. In the 7th century, the Croats were converted to Roman Catholicism; a bishopric was established at Nin for this region, and the Croats obtained the right to use their own language in their religious services.

3 In the 9th century, an independent Croat State developed in Dalmatia. During the reign of Tomislav (910-928) this achieved great military development. Tomislav and his heirs defended themselves from the Bulgar Empire in Pannonia and the Venetian expansion along the Dalmatian coast. The Byzantine Empire helped King Stjepan Drzislav (969-997) to defend himself from the Venetians, but re-established its influence in the Adriatic. King Peter Kresimir (1058-1074) broke with Byzantium and strengthened links with the papacy. In that period, Croatia reached the peak of its power and territorial expansion.

4 However, during Kresimir's rule, the country split in two, with a Latin group favoring the king, and an opposition national group, backed up by broad popular support. When the Pope invited Dimitrije Zvonimir to involve the Kingdom in a war against the Seljuk Turks, the opposition accused him of being the Pope's vassal and assassinated him in 1089. The civil war which was then unleashed marked the beginning of the decline of the Croatian Kingdom.

5 The Byzantines recovered Dalmatia, and in the meantime, Lazlo

I of Hungary conquered Pannonia in 1091, laying claim to the Croatian crown. Lazlo founded a bishopric at Zagreb in 1094, which became the center of the Church's power in the region. Petar Svacic was crowned King by the Dalmatians, but the Pope considered him a rebel, and turned to King Kalman of Hungary to unseat him. Kalman invaded the country; Svacic - the last king of Croat blood - fell in 1097.

6 After an extended war Kalman signed a treaty, the Pacta Conventa, with the Croat representatives. Only Bosnia, then a part of the Croatian kingdom, refused to submit to a foreign monarch. For the next eight centuries, Croatia was linked to Hungary. In the 14th century, Dalmatia became a part of Venice, which ruled over it for 400 years.

7 After the defeat of the Croatian and Hungarian forces in the battles of Krbavsko Polje (1493) and Mohacs (1526), most of Pannonia and Hungary fell into Turkish hands.

8 Turkish domination altered the ethnic composition of Pannonia, as many Croats migrated northwards, some even going into Austria. In the meantime, the Turks brought in

German and Hungarian settlers, and gave incentives for Serbians fleeing the Balkans to settle in the Vojna Krajina.

9 When the Turks were driven back in the 17th century, Austria tried to limit Croatia and Hungary's state rights, to make them mere provinces of the Austrian Empire. The Croatian and Hungarian nobility conspired together to organize an independence movement, which failed. The Croatian leaders were executed and their lands were distributed among foreign nobles.

10 After the annexation of Rijeka (Fiume) in the 1770s, Hungary tried to impose its language, but this triggered a nationalist reaction among the Croatians. In the meantime, the French Revolution and the Napoleonic Wars which had incorporated Dalmatia, Pannonia and the area south of the Sava river to the French Empire, further stimulated Croatian nationalism. Upon the fall of Napoleon, relations between Hungary and Croatia rapidly deteriorated.

11 In April 1848, the Hungarian Parliament adopted a series of measures severely limiting Croatian

autonomy. The Croatian Diet (Parliament) declared its separation from Hungary, abolishing serfdom and approving equal rights for all its citizens. Hungary's troops were weakened by this conflict, making it easier for the Hapsburgs to put down the Hungarian Revolt and regain power later that year.

12 The Croatian Diet was dissolved in 1865, and two years later, with the division of the crown, Germany and Hungary became the major nations of the Austro-Hungarian Empire. In 1868, Hungary accepted the union of Croatia, Slavonia and Dalmatia as a separate political entity, though Austria refused to relinquish its claim to Dalmatia.

13 In the early 20th century, Croatian nationalist groups intensified their activity. An alliance of Croatian and Serbian leaders adopted the 'Rijeka resolution', a plan of action which enabled them to win the 1906 elections. In the meantime, the Croatian Peasant Party began political activity among the peasants. The Crown responded by increasing repression.

14 In 1915, Croatian, Serbian and Slovenian leaders organized the Yugoslav Committee in Paris to push for separation from the empire and union with an independent Serbia. Austria-Hungary's defeat in World War I accelerated the creation of the Yugoslav kingdom in 1918.

15 The Serbian dynasty's policy of amalgamating the regions immediately came into conflict with Croatian desires for independence. Croatia demanded the creation of a Yugoslav federation. As of 1920, the Peasant Party, led by Stjepan Radic headed the Croatian opposition. The assassination of Radic and other members of the opposition, in 1928 provoked a serious crisis.

16 When World War II broke out, Yugoslavia was divided internally, so it was easily occupied by Hitler in 1941. The German army set up a puppet regime made up of Croatia, Slavonia, parts of Dalmatia and Bosnia-Herzegovina. A racist campaign was launched in which Serbians, Jews, Gypsies and Croats opposed to Fascism were massacred in concentration camps or forced into exile.

17 After the anti-Nazi guerrillas had occupied Zagreb in May 1945, the Anti-Fascist Council of National

Liberation of Croatia assumed control of the Government. By the end of the year, Croatia was one of the constituent republics of the new People's Federated Republic of Yugoslavia.

[18] Within the Yugoslav socialist system (see Yugoslavia Federal Republic), Croatia maintained and strengthened its national independence, although this worked against its ethnic minorities. In 1972, a purge within the Croatian League of Communists led to the suspension of the Matica Hrvatska, the Croatian cultural organization.

[19] At the end of the 1980s, Yugoslavia modified its political system; the Yugoslav League of Communists (YLC) renounced the monopoly and leading role assigned to it by the constitution, and in April 1990, the first multiparty elections since World War II were held in the different regions.

[20] Following the collapse of Communism in Eastern Europe, Croatia saw the first free elections in 50 years. The Communists were defeated by the Democratic Croat Union (DCU), led by Franjo Tudjman. In June 1991, Croatia declared independence but the European Community and the US withheld recognition. The eastern Serbo-Croats expelled the Croats with help from the Yugoslav army. In late 1991, nearly a third of Croat territory was under Serb control. The Serbs declared the republic of Krajina (in southern Croatia) as a new member of the Yugoslav federation. In June 1992, EC mediation enabled Serbia and Croatia to accept a peace plan with the 15,000 UN peacekeepers in the conflict zone. In June 1992, EC mediation enabled Serbia and Croatia to accept a peace plan with the 15,000 UN peacekeepers in the conflict zone.

[21] Croatia initially supported the Bosnian Croats against the Bosnian Serbs, and then against the Muslims during the war in Bosnia-Herzegovina (1992-95).

[22] In May 1992 the UN accepted membership of former Yugoslavian republics Croatia, Slovenia and Bosnia-Herzegovina. In November that year, the Bosnian Serb leader Radovan Karadzic announced the formation of the Serb Republic of Bosnia-Herzegovina and the Serb Republic of Krajina (in Croatia), leading to renewed hostilities. Although less bloody than those in Bosnia, the conflict in Croatia caused tens of thousands of civilian deaths.

[23] In late 1993, Tudjman and President Izetbegovic of Bosnia-Herzegovnia signed a ceasefire agreement.

[24] In June 1994 Croatia re-established the Kuna, the currency issued in World War II by the Nazi-imposed government. This replaced the Dinar, which had been adopted after independence. Tudjman, re-elected president in 1992, signed the Dayton peace accords in 1995, putting an end to the war in Bosnia-Herzegovina. The following year, diplomatic relations were restored with Serbia. Even though the Croat re-occupation of Krajina was considered one of the biggest ethnic cleansing operations of the war in the former Yugoslavia, by May 1996 only eight Croats had been tried in absentia in the war crimes tribunal in The Hague.

[25] In April 1999 a court ruled there was not enough evidence to convict six former Croat soldiers of war crimes against Serbian rebels, even though one of the accused had admitted his guilt to the press. The court case was the first in which Croats, who generally saw themselves as victims of Serb aggression, were prepared to be judged for their own crimes.

[26] Tudjman died that year. In January 2000, his UDC party was defeated by a coalition led by the Social Democrats and the Social-Liberals. They promoted constitutional changes to avoid a concentration of power, as would have occurred under the single-party Tudjman government. In February, when Stjepan Mesic of the Croat Peoples Party became president, he announced Croatia's intention of joining NATO and the European Union. According to the new constitution, approved in 2000, parliament rather than the President had the power to appoint and dissolve government.

[27] In February 2001, hundreds of thousands of people, led by war veterans, marched through the port of Split on the Adriatic, protesting against attempts to arrest General Mirko Norac to face accusations of war crimes. This change in policy from the Social Democratic government led the Right to accuse them of treason with the intention of bringing down the Mesic government and Prime Minister Ivica Racan.

[28] The nationalist right accused Racan of treason in July 2001 because he decided to comply with the Hague Tribunal request for the extradition of generals Ademi and Gotovina. The parliamentary vote allowed the premier to continue in his post. On another issue, Croatia returned to Serbia some Orthodox icons which had been pillaged by its army following the fall of Vukovar, 10 years previously. ∎

PROFILE

ENVIRONMENT

Croatia is bounded to the north by Slovenia and Hungary, and to the east by Serbia. The Dalmatian coast - a 1,778-kilometer coastline on the Adriatic, with numerous ports and seaside resorts - lies in southern and western Croatia. The territory is made up of three regions with different landscapes: rolling hills in the north, around Zagreb; rocky mountains along the Adriatic coast and the inland valleys of the Pannonian Basin. The Pannonian Basin, under the influence of masses of continental air, is colder and not as rainy as the coast. The climate along the Dalmatian coast is Mediterranean, with an average temperature of 4°C in winter, and 24°C in summer. The country's traditional economic activities have been agriculture and cattle raising. After World War II, light industry was developed, and the discovery of rich deposits of oil changed the country's economy. The Government is in the process of reconstructing the country's productive capacity, as well as vast areas of the country which were devastated by the conflict. Likewise, it has begun to assess the impact of the civil war upon the environment.

SOCIETY

Peoples: 78.1 per cent Croats; 12.1 Serbs; Slav-Muslims 1.0; Hungarians 0.5; Slovenians 0.5. Czechs, Italians, Roma. Languages: Croatian (official). Istrian, Romani, Czech, Slovac, Italian. **Religions:** Roman Catholic 76 per cent; Orthodox 11 per cent; Muslims 1 per cent. Political Parties: The Croatian Democratic Union, right-of-center; the Croat Socio-Liberal Party (CSLP); the Croat Peasant Party; Istrian Democratic Assembly (IDS); Croatian Party of Rights (HSP) **Social Organizations:** Association of the Independent Trade Unions of Croatia, Union of Autonomous Trade Unions of Croatia, Railwaymen's Trade Union of Croatia, Metalworkers' Trade Union of Croatia, Croatian Journalists' Association.

THE STATE

Official Name: Republika Hrvatska. **Administrative Divisions:** 102 Districts. **Capital:** Zagreb 1,047,000 people (1999). **Other Cities:** Split 200,800 people; Rijeka 180,000 (2000). **Government:** Stipe Mesic, President since February 2000. Ivica Racan, Prime Minister since January 2000. The bicameral parliament (*Sabor*) is one of Europe's oldest: the Chamber of Deputies has 127 members and the Chamber of Districts has 68 members, elected for a 4-year term. **National Holiday:** June 25, Independence (1991). **Armed Forces:** 105,000 (1995). **Other:** 24,000 Police (1,000 deployed in Bosnia).

Cuba

Population: 11,273,000 (2002)
Land area: 109,820 SQ KM
Capital: Havana (La Habana)
Currency: Peso
Language: Spanish

Cuba

U ntil the 16th century the island of Cuba was inhabited by the Taino and Ciboney, a branch of the Arawak indians. In 1492, the Spanish emissary to the Indies arrived, but it was not until 1509 that a voyage was made around the coast proving that Cuba was an island. The conquest began in 1510 and Santiago de Cuba was founded in 1514 by Diego Velázquez. This was a violent period in the island's history, with a number of uprisings, like those led by chieftains Hatuey and Guama.

2   The Spanish expeditions which would subsequently conquer a large part of the Caribbean, Mexico and Central America, departed from Cuba. It was described in a mid-16th century document as 'high and mountainous' with small rivers 'rich in gold and fish'. In 1511, colonists from Santo Domingo started mining Cuban gold. It was a short-lived economic cycle, probably because the Indian population was rapidly exterminated. As the number of African enslaved workers on the island was insufficient, economic life soon declined and did not recover until the end of the 16th century, with the advent of sugar production.

3   As early as the 17th century, economic diversification was achieved through shipbuilding and the developing leather and copper industries. The economic center of the island gradually moved from Santiago, on the southern coast, to Havana, in the north, a port of great importance in the mid-17th century.

4   Sugarcane plantations in colonial America used slave labor and created economic dependence. There were periods, during 1840 for

example, when slave labor represented 77 per cent of the total Cuban workforce. There is also evidence that there were *palenques*, settlements of escaped slaves (see Brazil) on the island, and there was an abortive slave revolt in 1843. It took a long, complex process to change this situation, comparable only with that of Brazil, the last American country to abolish slavery. British pressure against the slave trade contributed decisively to abolition of slavery in 1886.

5   The struggle for independence began in the first few decades of the 19th century, but the decisive battle, with José Martí, Antonio Maceo and Máximo Gómez was not fought until 1895. In 1898, aware that the victory of the Cuban patriots was inevitable, the US declared war on Spain and invaded Cuba to guarantee their continued influence in the Caribbean.

6   US occupation forces ruled the country from 1899 to 1902, imposing a constitution including the so-called 'Platt Amendment'. This secured the US rights to intervene in Cuba and to retain a portion of its territory. Guantánamo became a powerful air and naval base that is still maintained. The 'right' to intervene has been exercised on various occasions, with US Marines remaining on Cuban soil for extended periods of time.

7   With the fall of the dictator Machado in 1933, Carlos Manuel de Céspedes came to power. Several months later there was a military coup and the rebelling sergeants established a short-lived 'Pentarchy'. A few days later, Grau formed the 'Government of a Hundred Days' with Fulgencio Batista and Antonio Guiteras, and several anti-imperialist measures were implemented. In January 1934, Batista led a reactionary counter-coup, and Guiteras was assassinated. Elections were held, ushering in a series of governments presided over by Batista's Authentic Party, dominating a period characterized by corruption and gangsterism under the auspices of the United States. On March 10 1952, Batista engineered yet another coup, establishing a dictatorial regime which was responsible for the death of 20,000 Cubans.

8   On July 26 1953, Fidel Castro and a group of revolutionaries attacked the Moncada Army Base in Santiago de Cuba. Although the attack itself failed, it marked the beginning of the revolution. After a short period of imprisonment, Castro went into exile in Mexico only to return in December 1956. Castro's revolutionary program had been defined during his trial after the failed initial uprising, ending with his well-known words: 'History will

absolve me'.

9   On December 31 1958, Batista fled from Cuba as guerrilla columns led by Ernesto 'Che' Guevara and Camilo Cienfuegos, closed on Havana. They were the vanguard of the Rebel Army. In just over two years, the guerrillas of the '26th of July' Movement, organized by Fidel Castro, broke the morale of Batista's corrupt army.

10   In 1961, counter-revolutionaries disembarked at Playa Giron (Giron Beach), in the Bay of Pigs, in an attempt to bring down the regime which had carried out agrarian reforms and expropriated various American enterprises. They had counted on a popular uprising against the revolutionary government, but this did not materialize. After 72 hours of fierce fighting, the Bay of Pigs invasion ended in the defeat of the invading forces. Two days before the invasion, on April 15, while the victims of the Havana Airport bombing were being buried, Castro proclaimed the socialist nature of the revolution.

11   Also in that year, all the pro-government organizations joined together in a common structure. This was initially known as the Integrated Revolutionary Organizations (ORI), and later became the United Party of the Socialist Cuban Revolution (PURSC). The US had Cuba excluded

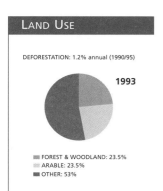

from the Organization of American States (OAS). It also put pressure on other countries to sever diplomatic relations, engineering an economic blockade of the island. That year the October Crisis made the possibility of a third World War into a near-probability. The US photographed Soviet nuclear missile launching sites on the island, and began preparations for another invasion. However, a peaceful solution was reached as the Soviet Union and the US came to an agreement. The US pledged not to invade Cuba, but disregarded the Cuban Government's demands for an end to the blockade, the withdrawal of US troops from Guantánamo and an end to US-managed terrorist activities.

12 The literacy campaign during these years soon bore fruit, and by 1964, Cuba was free of illiteracy.

Improvements in health were also one of the Government's priorities. In October 1965, the People's Socialist Party, the Revolutionary Directory and the 26 of July Movement (led by Castro himself) dropped the name PURSC and created the Cuban Communist Party (PCC). This was just one more step closer to the Soviet Union, a relationship which had been strengthened by the economic blockade.

13 With the consolidation of the socialist regime, Cuba began lending technical assistance to like-minded peoples and governments of the Third World. It sent troops to countries like Ethiopia and Angola, who requested help to resist invading forces. In October 1967 Che Guevara was captured and killed in Bolivia, where he had been attempting to extend the revolution.

14 The revolution began to be institutionalized after the first PCC congress in 1975. A new constitution was approved in 1976 and there were subsequent elections of representatives for the governing bodies at municipal, provincial and national levels. In 1979, Castro and the leaders of the PCC launched a campaign of revolutionary requirements to correct weaknesses in the administrative and political management areas of the revolutionary process.

15 Tension between Cuba and the US increased when Ronald Reagan came to the White House in 1979.

16 In the mid-1980s, some 120,000 people left Mariel port bound for Florida taking advantage of a clause offering automatic US residency to any Cuban arriving in the US - brought in when emigration from Cuba was practically impossible.

17 Cuba's relations with many Latin American countries improved as a consequence of the Cuban attitude during the Malvinas/Falklands war. Anxious to put a halt to Cuban-Latin American rapprochement, the US took a series of measures against Havana. In August 1982 the US Senate passed a resolution allowing its government to use the armed forces to halt 'Marxist-Leninist subversion' in Central America.

18 The results of the Third Congress were formalized in April 1986 and the so-called 'process of the rectification of errors and negative tendencies' was initiated. This coincided with the changes which were taking place in the Soviet Union, but the Cubans avoided adopting the eastern European model.

19 In June 1989, a high-ranking group of Army officers and officials of the Ministry of the Interior were brought to trial and executed for being involved in drug trafficking.

20 When George Bush became president there was an increase in US pressure on Cuba. In the first few months of 1990 there were military maneuvers at Guantánamo Base and in the Caribbean. The US also violated Cuban television airspace with transmissions by 'Televisión Martí', which was supported by 'The voice of America'. However, this broadcast was only picked up on the island for one day, after which it was jammed.

21 At this time, the last of Cuba's troops returned home from Zaire (now DR Congo) and Angola. More than 300,000 Cubans had served in Angola, with the loss of 2,016 lives.

22 After a seven-month delay, the 4th PCC congress took place in October 1991. It was decided to reform the Constitution so that members of the National Assembly

could be elected directly, a major ratification of the single-party system. People with religious beliefs were also admitted, and the Government recognized the need for joint ventures, especially with Latin American investors.

23 With the changes in Eastern Europe, and the disappearance of its former Council for Mutual Economic Assistance allies, some of Cuba's basic supplies dropped to critical levels. To ease this crisis, the Government strengthened its ties with China, Vietnam and North Korea, and looked for ways to capitalize on its recent technological advances.

24 The Government decided to ration fuel when the former USSR cut oil shipments by 25 per cent between 1989 and 1991. It also decided to strengthen the tourist industry. A further initiative was joint ventures with Spanish companies. The investors maintain 50 per cent ownership of the enterprise once it begins operation.

25 The loss of Cuba's main trading partners and the re-enforcement of the US blockade led to the creation of a Special Plan, aimed at distributing scarce resources equitably. In 1990, bread was rationed at 100 grams per person per day, three newspapers ceased publication, and the official newspaper, Granma, was forced to cut its circulation by more than two thirds. Alternative proposals included the possibility of offering more sugar, tobacco and coffee on the international market, an overall strengthening of the agricultural sector, and the possibility of oil purchase agreements with Mexico and Venezuela.

26 In early 1993, National Assembly (parliament) elections were held, and deputies were elected directly for the first time. Ricardo Alarcón, foreign minister, was designated president of the National Assembly, and Roberto Robaina, secretary-general of the Communist Youth organization, became foreign minister.

27 On July 26 1993, in his speech for the commemoration of the 40th anniversary of the attack on Moncada barracks, Castro announced that it would henceforth be legal for Cubans to possess and use foreign currency, and to be self-employed.

28 Towards the end of the same year, the National Assembly met to discuss the country's critical situation, especially its internal finances. The Assembly decided not to take any steps for the time being, but to discuss the issue and collect opinions and ideas in workplaces throughout the country. These 'Workers' Parliaments' were held during the first quarter of 1994.

PROFILE

ENVIRONMENT

The Cuban archipelago includes the island of Cuba, the Isle of Youth (formerly the Isle of Pines) and about 1,600 nearby keys and islets. Cuba, the largest island of the Antilles, has rainy, tropical climate. With the exception of the southeastern Sierra Maestra highlands, wide and fertile plains predominate in the country. Sugarcane farming takes up over 60 per cent of the cultivated land, particularly in the northern plains. Nickel is the main mineral resource. Cuba was chosen by the UN to celebrate World Environment Day 2001 in recognition of its advocacy in that area.

SOCIETY

Peoples: Cubans call themselves 'Afro-Latin Americans', because of the European and African influence in their heritage. Over half the population is of mixed descent; whites 37 per cent, blacks 11 per cent, Chinese and others 1 per cent.
Religions: Catholic 39.6 per cent; atheist 6.4 per cent; Protestant 3.3 per cent; and Afro-Cuban syncretists.
Languages: Spanish (official) and African languages used in Lucumi and Santeria (voodoo) rituals.
Political Parties: The Cuban Communist Party (PCC) is defined by the constitution as the 'supreme leading force of society and the state'. Illegal parties: Cuban Liberal Union; Christian Democrat Party; Democratic Solidarity Party.
Social Organizations: Cuban Workers' Union (CTC). The CTC had 2,984,393 members in 1988, and represented more than 80 per cent of the Cuban labor force; the National Association of Small Farmers, 167.461 members (1988) with 3,500 grass roots organizations; the Federation of Cuban Women (FMC), 2,420,000 members; the University Student Federation (FEU) and the Federation of Secondary School Students (FEEM), 450,000 student members; the José Martí Pioneers' Union, 2,200,000 children and young people; the Revolution Defense Committees.

THE STATE

Official Name: República de Cuba.
Administrative Divisions: 14 Provinces, 169 Municipalities including the special municipality of Isla de Pinos.
Capital: Havana (La Habana) 2,242,000 people (1999).
Other cities: Santiago de Cuba 534,600 people; Camaguey 342,900; Holguín 305,000; Guantánamo 264,100; Pinar del Río 172,300 (2000).
Government: Fidel Castro Ruiz, President of the Council of State and the Council of Ministers since December 1976, elected by the National Assembly of People's Power (with 601 members). The 1976 constitution states that the power is exercised through the Assemblies of People's Power. The local Assemblies delegate power to successively more encompassing representative bodies until a pyramid is formed which peaks in the National Assembly. Representatives are subject to recall by the voters.
National Holidays: January 1, Liberation Day (1959); July 26, Assault on the Moncada barracks (1953). **Armed Forces:** 105,000 (1995).
Other: 1,369,000 Civil Defense Force, Territorial Militia, State Security, Border Guard.

29   In April 1994, a meeting entitled 'The Nation and Emigration' was held in Havana on the initiative of Foreign Minister Robaina, and it was attended by some groups of Cubans living abroad. Shortly afterwards, there was a series of incidents in Havana involving people who wanted to leave the country illegally in frail boats. When Cuba announced it would not stop the 'boat people' from leaving, the US started official negotiations to regulate the illegal departure of the immigrants.

30   In July, Cuba entered the Association of Caribbean States (ACS) as a full member. Its participation in the ACS, a group emerging as a new economic bloc, encouraged greater integration of the Cuban economy in the region, offering tariff benefits and trade facilities.

31   In 1995, the fiscal deficit fell for the third year running, due to the reduction of public services and cutbacks in subsidies. A system of convertibility of the peso with the dollar was introduced and holding US currency was legalized. The Cuban parliament approved a new investment law, allowing for totally foreign-owned companies to be established, including by Cuban residents abroad. US Congress approved the Helms-Burton law which penalized companies dealing with Cuba through third-party countries. The international community, especially the EU, harshly criticized this measure for violating the WTO and GATT agreements on free trade.

32   The Helms-Burton law barred Cuban access to loans from international institutions like the World Bank or the IMF. However the foreign companies continued to invest in Cuba by using various subterfuges such as pseudonyms, and the economic reforms continued to be implemented. Banks were allowed to extend their offer of services and tax-free trading areas were created by a decree in June. In mid 1996, productivity was up 8 per cent on 1995 figures, while the GDP had increased 9.6 per cent.

33   In February 1996, the Cuban air force shot down two light aircraft flown by a group of Cuban exiles in Miami known as 'Brothers to the Rescue'. According to Havana, they had violated Cuban air space to drop anti-governmental leaflets on the island. Amnesty International denounced the imprisonment of several people linked to the Cuban Council. According to Amnesty, the Council included 140 groups of opponent journalists, professionals and union activists, while the Cuban government linked it with US intervention.

34   The Helms-Burton law barred Cuba from getting loans from the World Bank or the International Monetary Fund. However, foreign entrepreneurs continued to invest in Cuba, using various subterfuges, and the economic reforms continued. In mid-1996, productivity had grown 8 per cent on 1995 figures and the GDP had risen 9.6 per cent.

35   Cuban exiles in Miami suffered two setbacks in late 1997. The first was the death of its leader Más Canosa, on November 23, and second came with Castro's political coup with Pope John Paul II's visit to the island. Following the PCC meeting in 1991 and constitutional amendments of 1992, relations between Cuba and the Vatican improved considerably. As a run-up to the visit, the Pope condemned the US embargo on the island and Castro declared Christmas 1997 a national holiday.

36   In April 1998, Grenada and Cuba re-established diplomatic relations which had been suspended since the US invasion of the former in 1983. Grenada's prime minister Keith Mitchell made an official visit to Cuba where he signed an economic co-operation agreement.

37   In February, the UN Historical Verification Commission blamed the US for backing the Guatemalan army in massacres of the population, whilst pointing out that Cuba's government had supported the left-wing guerrillas here, even sending supplies of weapons.

38   Permanent tensions between Castro and successive US administrations were aggravated in November 1999, when a child was the only survivor of a Cuban boat that sank on its way to Miami. Cuba demanded the return of Elián González, while US political groups used the boy as a political banner for the 2000 elections. Ignoring the decisions of the US justice system and the Attorney General, which stated that Elián González had to be returned to his native country, they requested Congress to make the boy a US citizen. In Cuba, Elián also became a symbol of the struggle against the US and the blockade that country imposed on Cuba more than four decades ago. Finally, in June 2000, the boy returned to the island, after several months of judicial lawsuits and appeals.

39   In November 2001, Hurricane Michelle hit the island with up to 220 kilometer-per-hour winds, reaching category 4 in the Saffir-Simpson scale, killing 20 people and destroying homes and plots. More than 481,300 people were evacuated. The United States, for the first time in 40 years, exported food to the island to help overcome the disaster's effects.

40   Hundreds of Afghan prisoners were confined in the US military base at Guantanamo, in January 2002, awaiting interrogation as suspected members of terrorist Al-Qaeda network. The US hesitated in granting them prisoners of war status and called them 'illegal warriors', a legal term unknown in international law.

41   The Russian military base, Lourdes, was closed that month. Although Moscow claimed the decision was taken due to its high costs, Cuban authorities accused Russian President Vladimir Putin of closing it as a gesture to the US, part of a rapprochement policy adopted after the September 11 terrorist attacks in New York and Washington. In fact, the US Congress had voted in 2000 to restrict financial aid to Russia if the base was not closed. Located 20 kilometers from Havana, the base - which had radar and electronic equipment - had been set up in 1964 after the missile crisis, to monitor US movements and communications. Washington welcomed the closure and took it as a further sign of the Cold War's end.

42   On April 20 2002, the UN High Commissioner for Human Rights (UNHCR) passed a resolution against Cuba, urging its government to grant more individual liberties and political rights, and to allow the visit of a UN envoy to monitor progress in this area. The initiative was begun by Uruguay (see Uruguay) and is the first resolution of the Commissioner supported by Latin American countries. The official Cuban newspaper *Granma* reacted angrily against the resolution, saying that Washington - by exerting pressure and blackmail - and the 'humiliating subservience of some governments in the region', planned more trickery for Cuba. The resolution was supported by 23 countries and rejected by 21, while 9 abstained. Of the Latin American countries, Brazil and Ecuador abstained and Venezuela and Cuba voted against.

43   That month, Cuban President Fidel Castro released the tape of a phone call with Mexican president Vicente Fox to confirm the Mexican Government had asked Castro to cancel or cut short his stay at the March 2002 UN summit held in Monterrey (Mexico). He had also been told not to criticize the US in his speech. Likewise, Castro accused Mexican foreign minister Jorge Castaneda of being the main supporter of the change in Mexican policy toward Cuba, giving in to pressures from Washington. Mexico had been the only country in the region to maintain relations with Cuba after the blockade was imposed. ■

STATISTICS

DEMOGRAPHY
Population: 11,273,000 (2002)
Annual growth: 0.7 % (1985-2000)
Estimates for year 2015: 11,644,000 (2000)
Annual growth to year 2015: 0.3 % (2000)
Urban population: 75.3 % (2000)
Urban growth: 0.4 % (2000)
Children per woman: 1.6 (2000)

HEALTH
Life expectancy at birth: 76 years (2000-2005)
male: 75 years (2000-2005)
female: 79 years (2000-2005)
Maternal mortality: 33 per 100,000 live births (1985/99)
Infant mortality: 7 per 1,000 (2000)
Under-5 child mortality: 9 per 1,000 (2000)
Daily calorie supply: 2,490 per capita (1999)
530 doctors per 100,000 people (1997)
Safe water: 91 % (2000)

EDUCATION
Literacy: 96 % (2000)
male: 96 % (2000)
female: 96 % (2000)
School enrolment (net):
Primary total: 94 % (1994/2000)
male: 94 % (1995/99)
female: 95 % (1995/99)
Secondary (gross):
male: 76 % (1995/97)
female: 85 % (1995/97)
Tertiary (gross): 19 % (1998)
Primary school teachers: one for every 13 pupils (1998)

COMMUNICATIONS
118 newspapers (1996), 353 radios (1997), 250 TV sets (2000) and 44 main telephone lines (2000) per 1,000 people
Books: 9 new titles per 100,000 people (1992/94)

ECONOMY
Annual growth: 5.4 % (2000)
Currency: 1.0 pesos = $ 1 (03/2002)
Cereal imports: 1,582,711 metric tons (2000)
Fertilizer use: 404 kg per ha (1999)

ENERGY
Consumption: 1,066.1 Kgs of oil equivalent per capita yearly (1998); 57.9 % imported (1999)

Cyprus

Kipros Kibris

Population: 797,000 (2002)
Land area: 9,240 SQ KM
Capital: Nicosia (Levkosia)
Currency: Pound
Language: Greek and Turkish

The first civilization on Cyprus may be 3,000 years old. Hittites, Phoenicians, Greeks, Assyrians, Persians, Egyptians, Romans, Arabs and Turks trooped through its valleys and over its hills until 1878, when the British negotiated the island with Turkey in exchange for protection against Czarist Russia. Cyprus became a bridgehead of the British expansion eastward.

[2] In 1930, movements favoring *enosis* (annexation) by Greece, gained ground stimulated by the incorporation of Crete to Greece in 1913. Enosis was promoted by the Greek Orthodox Church, the spiritual guide of Greek-Cypriots, who make up the majority of the island's population. But Turkey, Greece's perennial rival, was averse to being completely surrounded by a hostile neighbor on its Mediterranean coast. The British sent many Greek-Cypriot priests into exile. After World War II the country's most important political figure was Archbishop Vaneziz Makarios, who led the Cypriot anti-colonial movement from exile.

[3] In 1959, representatives of the Greek and Turkish communities, of Makarios' Democratic Party and of British colonial interests, approved a plan whereby Cyprus was to become an independent republic with constitutional guarantees for the Turkish minority, and British sovereignty over the island's military bases. Independence was proclaimed on August 16 1960, and Makarios took office as president. An active supporter of anti-colonialism, the President played an important role in the Movement of Non-Aligned Countries. Makarios was re-elected in 1968 and 1973. Tensions between

Greece and Turkey persisted and had frequent repercussions in Cyprus where conflicts erupted between the Greek and Turkish communities.

[4] The US Government was not friendly toward Makarios, either, considering him the 'Fidel Castro of the Mediterranean'. In 1963 there was an unsuccessful coup attempt by members of the radical right, who supported enosis. On July 15 1974, the crisis came to a head when the Cypriot National Guard, under the command of Greek army officers, ousted the President-Archbishop, who fled to Britain. Nikos Sampson, who favored annexation by Greece was appointed. Five days later, Turkey invaded northern Cyprus, bombed Nicosia, and drove 200,000 Greek Cypriots southward, under the pretext of protecting the Turkish minority.

[5] Sampson turned the presidency over to the President of the Lower House, Glafkos Clerides, on July 23. That same day, the Greek military junta (in power since 1967) also stepped down, unable to face the prospect of a war with Turkey, domestic opposition, and world-wide repudiation.

[6] The Turkish forces, who were occupying 40 per cent of the island, refused to return to the situation which had prevailed prior to the coup, and continued to occupy the north of the country. On August 16 1974 a Turkish-Cypriot Federal state was proclaimed in the northern part of the island - the part under Turkish control - under the presidency of Rauf Denktash.

[7] Makarios returned to Cyprus in December 1974 and held the Presidential office until his death in 1977. Spyros Kyprianou succeeded Makarios and followed the same policy, refusing to recognize the division of Cyprus and retaining membership of the Non-Aligned Movement.

[8] A pact between Makarios and Denktash had set four basic conditions for a negotiated settlement: the establishment of a

communal, non-aligned, independent and federal republic; an exact delimitation of the territories that each community would administrate; the discussion of internal restrictions on travelling, ownership rights and other important issues within the frame of a federal system with equal rights for both communities; and sufficient federal power to ensure unity.

[9] The Turkish refusal to withdraw the troops meant that no substantial progress was made. On November 15 1983, the Turkish Republic of North Cyprus (TRNC) was proclaimed, but only Turkey recognized the new state.

[10] In the 1980s, Cyprus enjoyed a period of economic prosperity brought by tourism, foreign aid, and international business that made the island a financial center, replacing Beirut, whose money markets had been paralyzed by the Lebanese civil war. The main beneficiary of this was the Greek-Cypriot bourgeoisie.

[11] In the northern part of the island there had been an influx of 40,000 new Turkish immigrants. When added to the 35,000 Turkish soldiers stationed in the area, and the migration of 20,000 Turkish-Cypriots from the south, the Turkish population in the area tripled.

[12] On May 5 1985, in northern Cyprus, a constitution for the TRNC was submitted to a referendum. The turnout was 70 per cent, of which 65 percent voted in favor.

[13] In February 1987, the Greek premier cancelled a visit to the US, because the US had favorable relations with Turkey and installed US arms in the Turkish part of Cyprus.

[14] Giorgis Vassiliu was elected President of Cyprus in 1988. He re-established the negotiations with Denktash that had been stalled since 1985. Political leaders from both sides and representatives of the 350,000 Cypriots in exile called for 'constructive flexibility' on the part of the two leaders. The Greek community - buoyed by their economic prosperity and the fact that they were numerically the majority - wanted independence to be guaranteed by the UN. They also sought freedom of movement and property rights across the island. The Turkish Cypriots - based on the status quo and the superior strength of the

Map

TURKEY

Mediterranean Sea

Kyrenia

Morphou Bay

35

Morphou Bay

Trikomo
Famagusta Bay
Ammókhostos
(Famagusta)

**Levkosia
(Nicosia)**

CYPRUS

Solimi

T R O D O S

Lárnax
(Larnaca)

UK Sovereign
Base Area

Limassol

Paphos

UK Sovereign Base Area

34

///// TERRITORY UNDER TURKISH CONTROL

0   50 km

WORKERS

2000

UNEMPLOYMENT: 4.9%
LABOR FORCE AS % OF TOTAL:

■ FEMALE: 39%   ■ MALE: 61%

1994/97

EMPLOYMENT DISTRIBUTION:

F
M

■ SERVICES   F: 71%   M: 58%
■ INDUSTRY   F: 18%   M: 30%
■ AGRICULTURE   F: 11%   M: 12%

LAND USE

DEFORESTATION: 0.0% annual (1990/95)

1993

■ FOREST & WOODLAND: 13.3%
■ ARABLE: 11.9%
■ OTHER: 74.8%

PUBLIC EXPENDITURE

Military expenditure (as % GNI):	**3.4 %**	(1999)
Defense expenditure (% of central government expenditure)	**9.3 %**	(1999)

Turkish army - demanded a bi-national federation under Ankara's protection.

[15] The island's economy grew 6.9 per cent in 1988 and 6.0 per cent in 1989. Denktash was re-elected President of the 'Turkish Republic' in the north in April 1990. With the support of US President George Bush, in 1991 Turkey proposed a summit among representatives from Ankara, Athens and both Cypriot communities. Greece and the Greek-Cypriot authorities considered Washington's support for the initiative as compensation for the aid given to Turkey during the Gulf War.

[16] In April 1992, the UN declared Cyprus a bi-communal and bi-regional country, with equal political rights for both communities. In early 1993, Glafkos Klerides defeated Vassiliu in the presidential elections. The May 1996 elections, in which the Workers' Party won a third of the vote, reduced parliamentary support for the Klerides administration.

[17] In attempts to gain entry into the European Union (EU), Klerides and Denktash met throughout 1997. The meetings, backed by the UN, aimed for reunification of the island in the medium term, prior to EU admission. However, direct negotiations between the EU and Greek Cypriot authorities stalled dialogue within Cyprus and the drive for reunification broke down. The rivalry between Greece and Turkey on this issue also impeded the initiative.

[18] Given this impasse, the EU said if the island were not reunited, the Greek area could be admitted as if it were an independent state, leaving the Turkish area out. Denktash said that the former European Community should have recognized the political legitimacy of the Turkish-Cypriot region and admit the entire island to the Union.

[19] In March 1998, after three days of tough debate, the Foreign Ministers of the 15 EU member countries agreed to authorize the beginning of talks for incorporating the Greek zone (not the Turkish) into the EU.

[20] In 1999, Greece's decision to withdraw its veto on Turkey's entry to the EU, plus the aid it provided the Turkish Government after a devastating earthquake that year, marked a change in the political climate with regard to Cyprus. Within a UN framework, negotiations were renewed in February 2000 between Klerides and Denktash. These were held as 'proximity talks', avoiding direct contact between the parties.

[21] The third round of negotiations ended in August without making progress. In September, Klerides boycotted the launch of indirect talks in New York in protest against a statement by UN Secretary-General Kofi Annan in which he granted equal authority to the TRNC and the internationally recognized Cypriot Government. Annan modified his stance, stating that any accord involving Cyprus would be based on the premise of single sovereignty. The positions of the two sides continued to be irreconcilable on the future structure of Cyprus: the Greek-Cypriots advocated a reunified bi-communal federation, the Turkish-Cypriots wanted one based on equal sovereignty. In November, once the Geneva rounds ended, Denktash threatened to boycott the talks while the TRNC did not have international recognition.

[22] On December 3 2001, as an expression of its desire to overcome the differences with Greece, Turkey withdrew its veto - conditionally - on the agreement between the EU and NATO, which blocked the creation of a new European defense structure. Going on from this, just three days later the Cypriot heads of state held an historic meeting: for the first time in the 27 years that the country has been divided, Klerides crossed the 'green line' in Nicosia to meet with his Turkish-Cypriot colleague.

[23] The imminent entry of Cyprus into the EU breathed new life into the dialogue between the Greek and Turkish Cypriots. Until months later, under orders from Ankara - which made Northern Cyprus' entry to the EU conditional on it its own admission - the TRNC refused to negotiate entry alongside its southern neighbor, the Republic of Cyprus. But in early 2002, Turkey's intransigence exasperated the European Union, which then appeared to say it would accept only the southern (Greek) portion of the island, if no agreement was reached. ∎

PROFILE

ENVIRONMENT

Once part of continental Europe, the island of Cyprus is located in the eastern Mediterranean, close to Turkey. Two mountain ranges - the Troodos in the southwestern region, and the Kyrenia in northern Cyprus - enclose a fertile central plain. The temperate Mediterranean climate, with hot, dry summers and mild, rainy winters, is good for agriculture. The growing levels of atmospheric pollution rise even higher during peak hours of urban activity, with the combined effect of industrial pollution and traffic. However, though the quality of the air has been affected by pollution, it still lies within acceptable limits. Soil degradation is the result of natural causes and human abuse, particularly where there has been an excessive use of agrochemicals. The coastal ecosystem has felt the effects of tourism, particularly the construction of large hotels and high-rise apartment blocks. There are environmental problems related to freshwater, both for its scarcity and its contamination.

SOCIETY

Peoples: Cypriots are divided into Greek (80 per cent) and Turkish (18 per cent) communities, within which they have separate political, cultural and religious organizations. **Religions:** Greek Orthodox and Muslim. **Languages:** Greek and Turkish (official). English. **Political Parties:** Progressive Party of the Working People (AKEL-Anorthotikon Komma Ergazemenou Laou, socialist); Democratic Coalition (DISI-Dimokratikos Sinagermos, conservative); Democratic Party (DIKO-Dimokratikon Komma, liberal); National Unit (Turkish sector); Social Democrats Movement (KISOS-Kinima Sosialdimokraton); New Horizons (NEO-Neoi Orizontes); United Democrats (EDI-Enomeni Dimokrates); Fighting Democratic Movement (ADIK-Agonistiko Dimokratiko Kinima); Cyprus Green Party (KOP-Kinima Oikologoi Perivallontistoi). **Social Organizations:** There are two major labor organizations representing approximately 30 unions, the Pancyprian Federation of Labor, and the Cyprus Worker's Confederation.

THE STATE

Official Name: Kypriaki Dimokratia-Kibris Caemhuriyeti. **Capital:** Levkosia (Nicosia) 193,000 people (1999). **Other cities:** Limassol 137,000 people; Larnaca 61,000 (1992). **Government:** Greek sector: presidential republic, constitution in effect since August 16 1960. Glafkos Ioannou Klerides, Head of State and of the Government since January 28 1993, re-elected in February 1998. Single-chamber legislature: House of Representatives with 71 members (56 from the Greek community and 15 from the Turkish community). Turkish sector: parliamentary republic, constitution in effect since May 5 1985. Rauf Denktash, Head of State since February 13 1975. Single-chamber legislature: 50-member Assembly, elected every five years. The 'Turkish Republic of North Cyprus' based upon Turkish occupation and recognized only by Turkey, exercises an independent administration, including a judicial system and a Legislative Assembly.
National Holiday: October 1, Independence Day (1960). Turkish Cyprus celebrates November 16 as Independence Day. **Armed Forces:** 10,000. **Other:** Armed Police: 3,700.

Czech Republic

Population: 10,250,000 (2002)
Land area: 77,280 SQ KM
Capital: Prague
Currency: Koruny
Language: Czech

Ceska Republika

The exact origin of the first inhabitants of the Mid-Danube region remains uncertain, although there are signs left by the Boii, a Celtic people whose name gave rise to the Latin name 'Bohemia'. The Celts were displaced without major conflict by Germanic peoples and later, in the 6th century, by the Slavs, while the Germans continued their migration southward.

2 The inhabitants of mountain and forest areas had the natural protection of these areas. However, the lowlands were repeatedly invaded by the Avars. The Slavs were able to repel these invasions when they had leaders strong enough to unite the tribes. In the 8th century, peace was restored to Bohemia with the defeat of the Avars at the hands of Charlemagne.

3 In the early 9th century, three potential political centers emerged: the plains of Nitra, the Lower Morava Basin and Central Bohemia. The Slavs of Bohemia gained the upper hand in most of the region. The first Moravian King was Mojmir I, who extended his realm as far as Nitra. His successor, Rostislav I, institutionalized the State and consolidated political relations with the Eastern Frankish empire, as a way of maintaining his own sovereignty.

4 The Christian Franks organized the first missions at Nitra and in Bohemia, but Rostislav would not allow Latin to be taught, and asked the Byzantine emperor to send preachers who spoke the Slavic language. Religious texts were also translated into Slav. Constantine and Methodius arrived in 863, leading a group of Greek missionaries.

5 Methodius won recognition from Rome for his work in Moravia and in Panonia (Croatia), which became an ecclesiastical province linked to the Archbishop of Sirmium. The Franks came to consider Methodius an enemy; he was captured and kept prisoner until 873, when he returned to Moravia.

6 Rostislav was the founder of Great Moravia, uniting the territories inhabited by the Slavs of the region for the first time. Slovakia, bordered by the northern ring of the Carpathian Mountains and by the Morava River, was a natural member of Great Moravia.

7 Religious rivalry between the Latin and Slav languages continued throughout the period of expansion of the Bohemian principality. The death of Methodius in 885 strengthened the position of the Frankish Bishop Wiching, his life-long enemy. Wiching displaced Methodius's disciples, and convinced the new Pope to outlaw the Slavic liturgy.

8 Some years later the Czech expansion clashed with the kingdom of Germania. King Arnulf sent a military expedition to Moravia in 892, allying himself later with the Magyars to defeat the principality. Between 905 and 908, Great Moravia went through several foreign occupations, until an agreement was reached between Mojmir II and Arnulf.

9 In the 10th century, between the strengthening of Germania and the restoration of the Holy Roman Empire, Bohemia lost the major part of its possessions. When Bfetislav I ascended the throne in 1034, the principality recovered part of Moravia and invaded Poland in 1039. However, King Henry III of Germania forced a retreat, and the Hungarian Crown kept Slovakia.

10 In order to maintain its independence, Bohemia found it necessary to be actively involved in the campaigns of the Holy Roman Empire. Thus, the situation arose whereby the Bohemian princes were being crowned king by both the rival powers.

11 In the early 13th century the Church separated from the State, and the feudal lords began demanding greater political participation. At the same time, Germanic immigration increased the population. A series of incentives to build new urban centers and develop mineral resources gave rise to a new class of tradesmen and entrepreneurs.

12 Under the Przemysl dynasty, which lasted until 1306, Bohemia controlled part of Austria and the Alps; at one point a single king ruled over Bohemia and Poland. This dynasty was succeeded by the Luxembourgs in 1310. With the coronation of Emperor Charles I in 1455, Bohemia and the Holy Roman Empire were joined together. As the capital of the Kingdom and the Empire, this was Prague's greatest moment.

13 The high level of corruption among the clergy triggered a religious reform movement in the 14th century, which became even more radical under the influence of Father John Huss of Prague's Bethlehem Chapel. Excommunicated by the Pope, Huss was later tried for heresy and sedition by the Council of Constance, and was burned alive in 1415 after refusing to recant.

14 The anger which followed Huss' execution marked the birth of the Hussite movement in Bohemia and Moravia. The Germanic peoples remained faithful to Rome, however, and in addition to these religious differences, the ethnic issue remained, triggering political conflict between them. The Holy Roman Empire, allied with the German princes, launched several military campaigns in Bohemia, but they were repulsed by the Hussites.

15 Religious differences prevented political union between Bohemia and its former possessions for many years. Vladislav II reigned over Bohemia from 1471 but Moravia, Silesia and Lusacia were ruled by Mathias, of Hungary. Only when Vladislav II was elected king of Hungary, upon Mathias's death in 1490, were the territories reunited.

16 The death of Vladislav II's son Louis II in 1526, paved the way for the rise of the Hapsburgs. Ferdinand I, Louis' brother-in-law, became king

Workers

2000

UNEMPLOYMENT: 8.3%
LABOR FORCE AS % OF TOTAL:

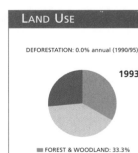

- FEMALE: 47%
- MALE: 53%

1994/97

EMPLOYMENT DISTRIBUTION:

F
M

- SERVICES   F: 66%   M: 43%
- INDUSTRY   F: 29%   M: 50%
- AGRICULTURE   F: 4%   M: 7%

Land Use

DEFORESTATION: 0.0% annual (1990/95)

1993

- FOREST & WOODLAND: 33.3%
- ARABLE: 40.2%
- OTHER: 26.5%

Public Expenditure

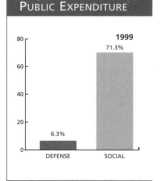

1999

DEFENSE 6.3%
SOCIAL 71.3%

MATERNAL MORTALITY

1985/99

Per 100,000
live births

9

FOOD DEPENDENCY

2000

5%

by currying favor with the nobility. Austria's victory over the Protestant Society of Schmalkaldica in 1547 permitted Ferdinand to impose the right of hereditary succession to the throne upon Bohemia and its states.

[17] The Hapsburgs strengthened the Counter-reformation throughout the region. Slovakia remained within its realm because the Hapsburgs had retained it when Hungary was invaded by the Ottoman Empire, in 1526.

[18] Rudolf II (1576-1612) transferred the seat of the empire to Prague, making it once again one of the continent's most important political and cultural centers. Many key positions of the kingdom were filled by Catholics during Rudolf's reign, as he himself was Catholic. However, this triggered a rebellion by the non-Catholic (Reformed church) majority, and the king was deposed in 1611.

[19] After a stormy succession, Ferdinand II of Styria, with the support of Maximilian I of Bavaria, defeated the Protestants and ruled with a strong hand. The Diet lost its power to initiate legislation, being reduced to merely approving the king's petitions. The Germanic language was added to the traditional use of Czech, and only the Catholic religion was authorized.

[20] Unlike Bohemia, Moravia did not become involved in the fight against the Hapsburgs and therefore did not suffer the effects of civil and religious strife as severely. In Moravia there was religious tolerance allowing the growth of Protestantism in the state, which remained separate from the Austrian Crown until 1848.

[21] Despite the hegemony of the Germans and the prohibition of political activity, the Czechs conserved their ethnic identity, their language and their culture. Something similar had also occurred in the Hungarian counties inhabited by Slovaks. This set the scene for a resurgence of nationalism in the early 19th century, which strengthened the traditional ties between these two peoples.

[22] Czechs and Slovaks, together with the inhabitants of the German republics, helped put a stop to the absolutist doctrine, amidst a revolutionary wave which swept Europe in 1848. In 1867, the empire split in two: Austria, where ethnic Germans outnumbered the Czechs, Poles and other nationalities; and Hungary, where the Magyars subdued the Slovaks.

[23] With World War I the fall of the Austro-Hungarian Empire finally brought about the recognition of the Republic of Czechoslovakia. The new state's borders established in 1919 by the victorious powers included parts of Poland, Hungary and the Sudetenland, all home to ethnic minorities, and all sources of potential conflict.

[24] Czech and Slovak leaders charged the National Assembly with drawing up a Constitution. The Assembly opted for a strict parliamentary system, in which the President and his cabinet would be responsible to two legislative chambers. Women's right to vote or to be elected was granted for the first time.

[25] The 1930s world-wide depression affected the Sudetenland intensely, as it was a highly industrialized region. It also accentuated nationalistic feeling among the German people there, who developed a separatist movement alongside Hitler's rise to power in 1933. Britain, France and Italy negotiated the ceding of the Sudetenland to Germany in 1938, thus paving the way for the German occupation of Czechoslovakia in 1939.

[26] After Hitler's defeat, Czechoslovakia recovered its 1919 borders, while the German population was almost entirely expelled from the country.

[27] The Communist Party (CKC) obtained 38 per cent of the vote in the 1946 election, increasing to 51 per cent in 1948. In June, a People's Republic was proclaimed, and the CKC applied the economic model in effect at the time in the USSR. Czechoslovakia joined the Council for Mutual Economic Assistance (CMEA) and the Warsaw Pact.

[28] In 1960, the People's Republic of Czechoslovakia added 'socialist' to its name. In political terms, this decade was a turning point. Slovak leaders, expelled from the party in the 1950s, were rehabilitated. The Slovak struggle for autonomy (which had been even further restricted by the new socialist constitution) together with the 1967 student strikes brought an end to Antony Novotny's leadership of the CKC.

[29] In early 1968, the election of Alexander Dubcek as Secretary of the CKC, and of Ludwik Svoboda as the country's president led to the implementation of a program to decentralize the economy, and affirm national sovereignty, against a background of broad popular support.

[30] Moscow viewed the possibility of Czechoslovakian reforms as a threat to the integrity of the socialist camp; in August 1968, it used Warsaw Pact Forces to intervene in the country and crush the movement. The leaders of the 'Prague Spring' were expelled from the CKC and political alignment with the USSR was re-established.

[31] Soviet Communist Party Secretary Mikhail Gorbechev's reform process brought about changes in Czechoslovakia, with the CKC trying to keep its hold on power. In 1989, despite violent repression, anti-Government protests continued, precipitating a crisis within the regime.

[32] The Government was forced to negotiate with the Civic Forum, an alliance of several opposition groups. Among other reforms, Parliament approved the elimination of the CKC's leadership role, issuing a condemnation of the 1968 Soviet intervention. In late 1989, a provisional Government was formed, with a non-communist majority.

[33] In December 1989, the Civic Forum declared that the CKC had redistributed cabinet positions in such a way as to keep its own people in the key positions. 200,000 people gathered in Prague to demand a greater opposition representation in the cabinet. Gustav Husak resigned

PROFILE

ENVIRONMENT

The Bohemian massif occupies the western region, bordered by the Moravian plains to the southeast. Cereals and sugar beet are cultivated in the lowlands of Bohemia and Moravia, where cattle and pigs are also raised. Rye and potatoes are grown in the Bohemian valleys. The country has rich mineral deposits: coal, lignite, graphite and uranium in the Bohemian massif; coal in Moravia. Sulfur dioxide emissions - produced in the generation of electrical energy - are very high, causing acid rain. Air pollution has destroyed or damaged large areas of forest. Approximately three-quarters of all the country's trees show a high degree of defoliation. Water pollution levels are also very high, especially in rural areas. Waste from industry, mining and intensive farms threatens the purity of the water, both above and below ground.

SOCIETY

Peoples: Czechs, 81.2 per cent; Moravians, 13.2 per cent; Slovaks, 3 per cent.
Religions: Catholic (39 per cent); Protestant (4.3 per cent); Orthodox (3 per cent). 40 per cent of the population are atheist.
Languages: Czech (official). Romani is spoken by the Roma (gypsy) community (200,000).
Political parties: Czech Social Democratic Party (SDP); Civic Democratic Party (CDP); Communist Party of Bohemia and Moravia, emerges from the reorganization of the former Communist Party of Czechoslovakia; Christian Democratic Union-Czechoslovakian People's Party (continued to exist after country's separation); Union of Liberty; Democratic Civic Alliance; Republican Party (extreme right). Minority parties: Socialist Party; Green Party.
Social Organizations: Czech and Moravian Confederation of Trade Unions; Autonomous Democracy Movement of Moravia and Silesia; groups of activists against economic globalization (INPEG).

THE STATE

Official Name: Ceska Republika. **Administrative divisions:** 8 regions, 73 districts and 4 municipalities. **Capital:** Prague 1,225,000 people (1999). **Other cities:** Brno 382,800 people; Ostrava 320,900; Olomouc 102,800 (2000). **Government:** Parliamentary republic. Vaclav Havel, President since February 1993, re-elected in 1998. Milos Zeman, Prime Minister since July 1998. The Parliament of the Czech Republic (Legislature) has two chambers: the Chamber of Representatives, with 200 members, and the Senate, with 81 members. **National holiday:** October 28, Czech Founding Day (1928); January 1, Independence (1993, from Czechoslovakia). **Armed Forces:** 44,000 (1996). **Other:** Border Guards: 7,000; Internal Security Forces: 2,000; Civil Defense Troops: 2,000.

the presidency of the federation and was replaced by Vaclav Havel, who immediately granted amnesty to all political prisoners and called elections for June 1990.

[34] In late 1989, the Soviet and Czech governments agreed on a gradual withdrawal of the 70,000 Red Army troops stationed within the country. In October 1991, after the dissolution of the Warsaw Pact, president Havel and his Hungarian and Polish counterparts requested some kind of association with the Atlantic alliance.

[35] After the June 1990 elections Havel was confirmed in the presidency and the Czech and Slovak Federal Republic was proclaimed. In September, the Republic joined the World Bank and the IMF.

[36] Following the elections, the Forum divided into the Civic Democratic Party, the self-proclaimed 'right with a conservative program', and the Civic Movement.

[37] In the June legislative elections, the Czech Civic Democratic Party and the Slovak group, Democratic Slovakia, won in their respective republics. When negotiations over the statutes of the new federation came to an impasse, Czech and Slovak leaders meeting in the Moravian city of Brno admitted that separation was inevitable.

[38] On July 17 1992, Czechoslovakian President Vaclav Havel announced his resignation after the declaration of sovereignty in the Slovakian National Assembly. Czechoslovakia disappeared from the world map, replaced by the Czech Republic, with its capital Prague (Praha), and the Republic of Slovakia, with its capital Bratislava.

[39] As soon as Slovakia became independent, in January 1993, the country began a rapid process of integration with Western Europe. On January 26, Vaclav Havel, the former president of Czechoslovakia, was elected President of the Czech Republic, with the support of a parliamentary majority led by the right wing Civic Democratic Party (CDP).

[40] As Prime Minister, the leader of the CDP, Vaclav Klaus, adopted a market economy with less negative results than the other former socialist republics. As for the rest of the region, the freeing of prices and the introduction of consumer taxes had limited inflationary effects: the price increase was 17 per cent in 1993. Unemployment remained at 2.5 per cent and per capita income continued to be one of the highest in Eastern Europe.

[41] The Czech Republic became the eleventh signatory of the Peace Association in March 1994, an organization which developed out of NATO to progressively include the nations of the former socialist bloc in the alliance.

[42] The national debt continued lower than that of other former communist countries of the region, while foreign investment was amongst the highest. Prime Minister Klaus planned an economic reform based on a rapid privatization. In 1995, the banking system saw a high number of deposits, many of which came from illegal economic activities. This same year, the Czech Republic became the first former Communist OECD member.

[43] In December 1996, the Czech Republic and Germany signed a reconciliation document, in which Germany asked forgiveness for the behavior of the Nazi regime during World War II, while the Czech Government apologized for the expulsion of three million Germans from the Sudetenland following the War.

[44] During 1997, the devaluation of the national currency, the crown, brought political chaos. Klaus' Civic Democratic Party led by Klaus was accused of encouraging financial groups which bribed several of its members with 'hidden commissions' during the privatization process. Havel publicly called for Klaus' resignation, which was received in November. Josef Tosovsky became the new Prime Minister.

[45] The economic crisis coincided with increasing in xenophobia, displayed in racist attacks against minority groups, like the Roma. This violence appeared to be supported by a large and increasing percentage of the population.

[46] In April 1998, the Czech Republic was admitted to NATO. The Social Democratic Party (SDP) won the June elections with 32.3 per cent of the vote. Given the difficulty in obtaining a majority, the Civic Democratic Party (CDP) agreed to give the SDP control in return for their leader, Klaus, being appointed parliamentary speaker. The Government, the first of the Left in the post-communist era, aimed to wipe out corruption, raise the national minimum wage and halt the 'devolving' of property to the Catholic Church. But it was unable to improve the economic situation, which by the end of the year had reached record levels of unemployment and inflation surpassing 11.5 per cent. In December 1999 protests of as many as 50,000 people demanded that the Government resign.

[47] In late September 2000, the World Bank and the International Monetary Fund - meeting for the first time in Prague - intended to show off the Czech Republic as their first economic success in a former Iron Curtain country. Its the poverty rate of 5 per cent was much lower

than other former socialist countries. But massive acts of civil disobedience and protest organized by international anti-globalization groups forced the meeting to end a day earlier than planned.

[48] Michal Zitkco, editor of the first complete Czech-language version of Adolf Hitler's *Mein Kampf*, received a three-year suspended sentence in December for promoting Nazism. The book, which in March of that year 100,000 copies were printed, was a sales success and immediately triggered protests by the Czech Jewish community, anti-fascist groups and several politicians. Unlike the partial re-edition in 1993, which included commentary against Nazism by former Czechoslovakian foreign minister Jiri Hajek, Zitko's complete version did not include critical comments by the editor.

[49] That month, journalists at the state-run media refused to accept the appointment of Jiri Hodac as director of the broadcast program of Parliament's lower house due to the close ties he maintained with Vaclav Klaus and the CDP. Klaus had been calling for the privatization of the channel and Hodac had fired 20 journalists who accused him of undermining editorial independence. They alleged that Hodac edited political news coverage to favor the CDP and the SDP as a result of a parliamentary 'back room' agreement. Havel declared his support for the journalists and, in January, after thousands of people engaged in the largest street protests since the fall of communism, Hodac resigned.

[50] The Temelin nuclear plant, built in the Soviet era and located 60 km from the Austrian border, became an obstacle to the Czech Republic's admission into the EU. Austria, which in a 1978 referendum had rejected the development of nuclear energy, had repeatedly expressed concern about the safety of the Czech plant and threatened to block its neighbor's entry into the EU. After negotiations in Brussels between Czech Prime Minister Milos Zeman and Austria's foreign minister, the dispute was settled. Prague promised to adopt a set of measures to improve the nuclear plant's security and to monitor its environmental impacts. In December, the European Summit put the Czech Republic on the list of 10 countries that might become members in January 2004.

[51] Zeman was caught up in a political storm after an Israeli newspaper published statements in which he compared Palestinian President Yasser Arafat with Hitler. The countries of the Arab world reacted sharply, and in February 2002 Egypt asked Zeman to postpone his visit to Cairo, which had been scheduled for that month. ∎

DEMOGRAPHY
Population: 10,250,000 (2002)
Annual growth: 0.0 % (1985-2000)
Estimates for year 2015: 10,028,000 (2000)
Annual growth to year 2015: -0.2 % (2000)
Urban population: 74.7 % (2000)
Urban growth: 0.0 % (2000)
Children per woman: 1.2 (2000)

HEALTH
Life expectancy at birth: 75 years (2000-2005)
male: 72 years (2000-2005)
female: 79 years (2000-2005)
Maternal mortality: 9 per 100,000 live births (1985/99)
Infant mortality: 5 per 1,000 (2000)
Under-5 child mortality: 5 per 1,000 (2000)
Daily calorie supply: 3,241 per capita (1999)
303 doctors per 100,000 people (1998)

EDUCATION
School enrolment (net):
Primary total: 91 % (1994/2000)
male: 87 % (1995/99)
female: 87 % (1995/99)
Secondary (gross):
male: 97 % (1995/97)
female: 100 % (1995/97)
Tertiary (gross): 26 % (1998)
Primary school teachers: one for every 18 pupils (1998)

COMMUNICATIONS
254 newspapers (1996), 803 radios (1997), 508 TV sets (2000) and 378 main telephone lines (2000) per 1,000 people
Books: 91 new titles per 100,000 people (1992/94)

ECONOMY
Per capita, GDP: $ 13,991 (2000)
Annual growth: 3.0 % (2000)
Annual inflation: 3.9 % (2000)
Consumer price index: 138.7 (2000)
Currency: 36.7 koruny = $ 1 (03/2002)
Cereal imports: 231,486 metric tons (2000)
Food import dependency: 5 % (2000)
Fertilizer use: 869 kg per ha (1999)
Exports: $ 36,287 million (2000)
Imports: $ 38,160 million (2000)
External debt: $ 21,299 million (2000); $ 2,074 per capita (2000)
Debt service: 10.3 % of exports (1999)
Development aid received: $ 318 million (1999); $ 30.9 per capita (1999); 0.60 % of GNP (1999)

ENERGY
Consumption: 3,985.9 Kgs of oil equivalent per capita yearly (1998); 27.6 % imported (1999)

HDI (ranking/value): 33 / 0.844 (1999)

Denmark

Danmark

Population: 5,343,000 (2002)
Land area: 42,430 SQ KM
Capital: Copenhagen
Currency: Kroner
Language: Danish

The first hunting peoples established themselves in Denmark in about 10,000 BC as the Neolithic period drew to a close. This was followed by a flourishing Bronze Age civilization, about 1000 BC. Around the year 500 AD, northern Germanic peoples began settling on the islands as fishers and navigators. Certain placenames bear witness to the worship of Scandinavian gods, such as Odin, Thor and Frey.

[2] The first evidence of hierarchical society in Denmark comes from the Viking age, mostly from cemeteries and settlement sites. The Vikings were Scandinavian farmers, navigators, merchants and above all raiders who ruled the northern seas between the 8th and 10th centuries AD.

[3] Archeological remains indicate that Roskilde on the island of Sealand, Hedeby, south of Jutland, and Jelling in the north, were the most intensely populated areas. After the Danish victory over the Germans the Eider River became the final southern border. A huge wall was built to the south and west of Hedeby.

[4] In the 10th century, after continuous conflict with rival kingdoms, the center of the kingdom's power was transferred to Jelling, where Gorm became king of Jutland. His son Harald Bluetooth (Blatand) is credited with uniting Denmark and conquering parts of Norway.

[5] Subsequent Viking reigns extended Danish possessions as far as modern-day England and Sweden. In 1397 Queen Margrethe managed to unite Denmark, Norway, Iceland, Greenland, Sweden and Finland in the 'Union of Kalmar'.

[6] The introduction and spread of Christianity and strengthening of the Hanseatic League went hand-in-hand with the weakening of Denmark's military power.

[7] The Danish kings were involved in successive wars between themselves, campaigns which were interspersed with peasant rebellions and bourgeois revolts; a large and powerful middle class had developed as a result of growing mercantile activity. These conflicts ceased in the 17th century, when a weakened nobility gave the King power as absolute sovereign. He was then able to create laws to be imposed throughout the land.

[8] During the 18th century, Denmark colonized the Virgin Islands. The Danish colonists organized local production using African slave labor and in 1917 the islands and their population were sold to the United States. (See US Virgin Islands)

[9] Peace existed in Denmark and Norway from 1720 until the Napoleonic Wars. After Napoleon's defeat, Sweden attacked Denmark and, under the Kiel Peace Treaty, annexed Norway in 1814.

[10] The loss of Norway, combined with British trading impositions brought on an economic collapse which worsened as a result of low wheat prices. The ensuing agricultural crisis forced land reform to a standstill. The situation later improved when agricultural prices stabilized, trade increased and industrialization began. In 1814 an educational reform made schooling obligatory.

[11] After the European revolutions of 1848, King Frederick VII called an assembly. A parliamentary monarchy was established and absolutism was abolished. The 1849 Constitution guaranteed freedom of the press, of religion and of association, as well as the right to hold public meetings. The main trends of the period were nationalism and liberalism.

[12] A territorial dispute with Germany over the Duchies of Schleswig and Holstein reinforced nationalistic sentiment. In 1864, when Denmark was defeated by Prussia and Austria, it lost its claim to these lands

and the national-liberal government was brought down.

[13] The 1866 Constitution maintained the monarchy. In 1871, Louis Pio, a former military officer, attempted to form a socialist party. A series of strikes and demonstrations organized by the socialists was put down by the army, and Pio was deported to the US. The Social Democratic Party, mainly supported by intellectuals and workers, was formed in 1876.

[14] The peasants and emerging middle class weakened the monarchy on three fronts: the farm co-operative movement, a liberal bourgeois party (popularly referred to as 'leftist') and the social democrat party.

[15] In 1901 the United Left (Liberal) came to power establishing a new government. The emergence of the UL and the Social Democrats as a leading force at the turn of the century was the result of agrarian reform, industrialization and the development of railroads. The growth of urbanization and overseas trade (accelerating the formation of labor unions throughout the country and the rise of co-operatives in the countryside) was the main reason for these changes.

[16] In 1915, the Constitution was revised. The voting age of 35 was maintained, but the right to vote was extended to women, servants and farm hands. There were judicial reforms, bringing in trial by jury, and land distribution in the largest states.

[17] Also in 1915 women were granted the right to stand for election. The first woman was appointed to the cabinet in 1924.

[18] After the 1870-71 Franco-German War, Denmark adopted a neutral international stance. World War I gave Copenhagen trading opportunities with the warring nations, but also affected its supplies. During World War II Denmark was invaded by Germany, although it officially maintained its independence until 1943.

[19] When Hitler attacked the USSR, Denmark created a volunteer army and outlawed communist activity. The 1943 election was an anti-Nazi plebiscite, with the electorate throwing its support behind the democratic parties. Resistance to the Nazi regime, strikes, and the Government's refusal to enforce Nazi rule, led the German occupation forces to declare a state of emergency dissolving Denmark's police and armed forces.

[20] In September 1943, the Danish Freedom Council was created to co-ordinate the anti-Nazi opposition. When Germany finally surrendered, a transition government was formed, with representatives from the Council and the traditional parties. The 1945 election was won by the liberals.

[21] The Faeroe Islands, under Danish control since 1380, were occupied by Britain during the war and subsequently returned to Denmark. The 1948 Constitution gave the islands greater autonomy, though the Danish Parliament retained control of defense and foreign affairs.

[22] Denmark was responsible for foreign policy and justice of Greenland, a territory controlled by the Danes since 1380. In 1979, the island obtained the right to have its own legislative assembly (Landsting), which has power over internal affairs. Other areas are dealt with by the Danish Parliament which has two representatives from the island.

[23] Since 1947, there has always been at least one woman in the cabinet. That same year, Protestant women achieved the right to be priests.

[24] In the post-war period, a proposed Nordic Defense Alliance did not come about, as Norway did not agree with Denmark and Sweden. Denmark joined NATO in 1949,

increasing its military power with the help of the US. A US proposal for setting up air bases on Danish soil was turned down.

25 The Constitution was amended in 1953, reducing the Legislature to a single chamber (*Folketing*). In 1954 the post of 'ombudsman' was created to ensure that municipal and national government complied with the law, and to protect 'ordinary' citizens from the misuse of power on the part of government officials or agencies.

26 Denmark became the founding member of the European Free Trade Association (EFTA) in 1959. In 1972, 63.7 per cent of the electorate voted yes in a referendum asking whether the country should join the European Economic Community. In 1973, the oil crisis seriously affected the Danish economy and unemployment rose to over 14 per cent.

27 In the 1973 election, the traditional parties were ousted in favor of two new parties; the extreme right Progressive Party and the Democratic Center, the right-wing of the Social Democratic Party. In 1975, the Social Democrats were voted back into power. They lost a significant number of votes in subsequent elections because of high unemployment and unpopular economic measures. In 1982 the Conservatives won office for the first time since 1894. Their victory was due to their alliance with the Liberals, the Democratic Center and the Christian People's Party.

28 By the 1980s, 23 per cent of the seats in Parliament were held by women.

29 In 1982, the Government appointed women as the ministers for Employment and Religious affairs. In that year 43.9 per cent of the economically-active population were women, and they were protected by specific legislation. Women can interrupt their careers for up to two years to raise their children.

30 Parliament approved a strict environmental protection law in 1986, which proved costly for both the industrial and agricultural sectors, in a country without nuclear plants.

31 Denmark has been one of the few countries to comply with the UN's recommendation to contribute at least 0.7 per cent of the GNP to development. The country recycles around 72 per cent of all paper used and recovers more than 100,000 tons of industrial waste per year.

32 Marriage between people of the same sex was authorized in 1989.

33 In 1993 the Danes finally approved the Maastricht Treaty, the formation of the European Union, after rejecting it the previous year, on condition that the country would not join the Economic and Monetary Union.

34 Social Democratic Prime Minister Poul Nyrup Rasmussen was reelected in 1994, after having been chosen for office the previous year as a result of the fall of the liberal-conservative government which broke refugee laws. Former Justice minister Erik Ninn Hansen was found guilty of having prevented the family reunion of Tamil refugees from Sri Lanka.

35 Rasmussen achieved the majority in Parliament through alliances with center and left-wing parties. Economic growth reached its peak in 1994, with 4.4 per cent GDP growth and a 2 per cent rise in inflation. Economic expansion slowed down in 1995 and 1996. Reduction of extended social benefits enabled unemployment to fall from 12.5 per cent to 10 per cent in two years

36 The country's domestic peace was disturbed by a conflict between motorcycle bands in 1996. The groups attacked bars where their rivals met

Faeroe Islands

Population:	47,000 (2002)
Land area:	1,400 SQ KM
Capital:	Torshavn
Language:	Danish

The climate is generally rainy and cloudy, with mild temperatures both in summer and winter. Only 6 per cent of the land is cultivated. Agricultural production mainly consists of vegetables as the land is not suitable for grain. Sheep are raised throughout the islands and there is mining in Suderoy. 20 per cent of the population are employed in handcraft production and 21 per cent in fisheries, which provide 90 per cent of the islands' exports. The Faeroe Islands are one of 10 largest salmon breeders in the world. To protect the fishing industry, a 200-mile zone was established in 1977. Modernization of the island's fishing fleet and methods was financed through a series of foreign loans, which totaled $839 million in 1990 - $18,000 per capita. Maritime oil prospecting was initiated.

SOCIETY

Peoples: The population is of Scandinavian origin.
Religions: Lutheran. There are a large number of Baptists and a small Catholic community.
Languages: Danish (official) and the Faeroese dialect.
Political Parties: Social Democratic and Union (liberal) parties, which favor ties with Denmark; the Republican 'Left', Popular and Progressive parties, favor independence.

THE STATE

Capital: Thorshavn 16,000 people (1999).

Other cities: Klaksvik 4,800 people; Runavík 2,500 (2000).
Government: The parliament (*Løgtinget*) has 32 members elected based on proportional representation. Parliament names a cabinet (*Landstyret*) of six ministers. The Prime Minister is Anfinn Kallsberg (1998). Birgit Kleis (since 2001) is the High Commissioner (*Rigsombudsman*) who represents the Crown. The islands send two representatives to the Danish Parliament.
Diplomacy: In January 1974 the Løgtinget resolved not to join the EEC and the aspiration for independence continues.
National Holiday: July 29, Olaifest (local holiday).
Armed Forces: Defense is responsibility of Denmark; no organized native military forces; only a small Police Force and Coast Guard are maintained.

DEMOGRAPHY

Population: 47,000 (2002)
Annual growth: 0.1 % (1985-2000)
Estimates for year 2015: 52,000 (2000)
Annual growth to year 2015: 0.8 % (2000)

COMMUNICATIONS

2,222 radios (2000), 1,022 TV sets (2000) and 554 main telephone lines (2000) per 1,000 people

ECONOMY

Cereal imports: 3,244 metric tons (2000)
Food import dependency: 20 % (1999)

ENVIRONMENT

With an average altitude of only 35 meters above sea level, Denmark is one of the lowest countries in Europe. The land is divided into the mainland - the Jutland peninsula - and the islands (including the islands of Sjaeland and Jelling) which represent one third of the territory. The continental summers are relatively warm and rainy. The land is intensely cultivated, in spite of cold winters. Denmark is a supplier of livestock products and has important maritime activity. Pollution in the North Sea, coming from the Central and Western European rivers, is serious due to the excess of nitrates and phosphates.

SOCIETY

Peoples: 95.5 per cent of the population is of Danish origin. A German minority lives in Jutland. There are immigrant communities from Turkey (1.5 per cent), Asia (1.6 per cent), Africa (0.3 per cent), former Yugoslavia (0.5 per cent) and other Scandinavian countries (0.4 per cent).
Religions: 96 per cent of the population belong to the Lutheran Church; minorities of Catholics and Jews.
Languages: Danish (official). English is spoken as a second language.
Political Parties: Liberal (Venstre); Social Democracy in Denmark; Danish People's Party; Conservative People's Party; Socialist People's Party; The Red Greens; Christian People's Party; Center-Democrats; Radical Left-Social Liberal Party (Venstre radical); Progress Party. Several parties out of Parliament are against joining the European Union.
Social Organizations: The powerful Danish Federation of Trade Unions has 1,200,000 members from 40 different unions. Organization of Technical Personnel and Employees (FTF), 360,000 members, and Central Organization of Academics (AC), 97,000 members.

THE STATE

Official Name: Kongeriget Danmark.
Administrative divisions: 14 departments (Amtskommuner), Frederiksberg, Copenhague.
Capital: Copenhagen 1,383,000 people (1999).
Other cities: Århus 645,300 people; Odense 145,200; Ålborg 119,800; Frederiksberg 91,200 (2000).
Government: A constitutional parliamentary monarchy. Queen Margrethe II, since January 1972. Prime Minister, Anders Fogh Rasmussen, elected by the parliament in November 2001. Unicameral Parliament: People's Diet, with 179 members, including 2 from Greenland and 2 from the Faeroe Islands.
National holiday: June 5, Constitution Day (1953); April 16, Queen's birthday (1940).
Armed forces: 33,100 (1995).

in urban areas with anti-tank missiles, causing panic and damage to private property. The Government decided to tackle the matter with emergency legislation. The same year, Denmark had a disagreement with Iceland over fishing rights in the strait located between Greenland and Iceland.

[37] The extreme right-wing Danish People's Party (DPP), an offshoot from the Progress Party, received more than 6 per cent of the vote in the local Copenhagen elections, in November 1997. Its leader, Pia Kjaersgaard, a 50-year old housewife, based her campaign on the 'danger' posed to her country by Third World immigrants. With a slightly 'softer' profile than other nationalist European parties, the DPP adapted its xenophobia to the liberal and tolerant Danish tradition. Their main target was Muslims, singled out with the slogan "Muslims are just as good as us, but they are a problem for a Christian country'.

[38] After 7,000 years of geographic isolation, a 16-kilometer long bridge and tunnel now joins Denmark and Sweden in 15 minutes. It connects the city of Malmo with the Danish capital and was opened by King Carl Gustav of Sweden and Queen Margrethe of Denmark, in July 2000.

[39] Denmark rejected, through a referendum in September 2000, the replacement of its currency by the Euro, revealing Danish skepticism and fear of the spirit of Brussels.

[40] In January 2001, Denmark reacted against the independence plan put forward by the Faroe islands, which would extend Danish subsidies until 2012. Oil prospects in the islands' sea platform had caused an upsurge of independence demands, but Copenhagen prefers shorter terms to put an end to the subsidies, if independence prevails.

[41] Jutland, the livestock region, is being 'invaded' by Dutch farmers, according to data from July 2001. Estimates point out there are already 600 farmers settled, while 60 more arrive each year. Danish farmers complain that the arrival of the Dutch - wealthier than the Danes - has increased the price of land, making it difficult for many to update and compete. Ten per cent of Danish milk is produced in Dutch farms and 60 per cent of the farms on sale are bought by Dutch farmers.

[42] The Liberal party won the general elections in November 2001, after 9 years of Social-Democrat Government. The centre-right coalition obtained 56 seats (90 are needed to form Government), with 52 for the Social-Democrats. It was the first time since 1920 that the Liberals received more seats than the Social-Democrats. The far-right DPP won 12 per cent of the vote and now has 22 seats in the country's 179-seat parliament. The Conservative People's Party obtained 16 seats. Although no more than 5 per cent of the population is made up of foreigners - fewer than several European countries - the Liberals had focused their campaign in the promise of passing tougher immigration laws. ■

Greenland

Population:	56,000 (2002)
Land area:	341,700 SQ KM
Capital:	Nuuk
Currency:	Kroner
Language:	Greenlandic, Danish and Inuit

Located in the Arctic Ocean, the island is the second largest tract of frozen land on the planet. Nearly four fifths of its surface is covered by an ice cap. In the month of June, soon after the rapid thaw, moss and lichen vegetation appears on certain parts of the coast. Most of the population is concentrated in the western region, where the climate is less severe. The country has lead, zinc, and tungsten deposits. Cryolite from the large reserves in Ivigtut is also exported. Fishing forms the basis of the economy, although fish stocks are approaching exhaustion in national waters, salted and frozen fish is exported, as well as whale oil. The island is encouraging tourism as an alternative source of income, with 35,000 visitors each year. There are highly protective policies on the nordic environment. Its ice covered coastlines are melting at a rate of more than a metre each year.

SOCIETY

Peoples: 80 per cent are Inuit. The remaining 20 per cent are Danish or other short-term European residents.
Religions: Lutheran. The Greenlandic Church comes under the jurisdiction of the Bishop of Copenhagen and the minister of ecclesiastical affairs.
Languages: Greenlandic Inuktitut (Inuit/Aleut language) and Danish (official). There are three linguistic groups amongst the Inuit population; Kalaallit (west coast), Inughuit (north) and Lit (east coast).
Political Parties: Siumut (Forward), social-democratic; Atássut (Feeling of Community), liberal; Inuit Atgatigiit (Eskimo Community), communist; Katusseqatigiit (Independents).

THE STATE

Official Name: Kalaallit Nunaat. Administrative Division: 3 districts: Avannaa, Tunu y Kitaa.
Capital: Nuuk (formerly Godhaab) 13,000 people (1999).
Other cities: Sisimiut 5,200 people; Ilulissat 4,100 (2000).
Government: Queen Margrethe II of Denmark, Head of State; Gunnar Martens, High Commissioner since 1995; Jonathan Motzfeldt, Prime Minister since September 1997, re-elected in 1999. Unicameral Legislative: The *Diet*, with 31 members elected by people for a four-year term. Greenland elects two representatives to the Danish *Folketing*, and has one representative on the Nordic Council.

Diplomacy: Greenland is not part of the European Union.
National Holiday: June 21, Longest Day; June 5, Danish Constitution (1953).
Armed Forces: Defense is responsibility of Denmark.

DEMOGRAPHY

Population: 56,000 (2002)
Annual growth: 0.4 % (1985-2000)
Estimates for year 2015: 58,000 (2000)
Annual growth to year 2015: 0.2 % (2000)

COMMUNICATIONS

18 newspapers (1996), 482 radios (1997), 410 TV sets (1998) and 468 main telephone lines (2000) per 1,000 people

ECONOMY

Currency: 8.6 kroner = $ 1 (03/2002)
Cereal imports: 2,284 metric tons (2000)
Food import dependency: 15 % (2000)

DEMOGRAPHY

Population: 5,343,000 (2002)
Annual growth: 0.3 % (1985-2000)
Estimates for year 2015: 5,372,000 (2000)
Annual growth to year 2015: 0.1 % (2000)
Urban population: 85.1 % (2000)
Urban growth: 0.3 % (2000)
Children per woman: 1.7 (2000)

HEALTH

Life expectancy at birth: 77 years (2000-2005)
male: 74 years (2000-2005)
female: 79 years (2000-2005)
Maternal mortality: 10 per 100,000 live births (1985/99)
Infant mortality: 4 per 1,000 (2000)
Under-5 child mortality: 5 per 1,000 (2000)
Daily calorie supply: 3,317 per capita (1999)
290 doctors per 100,000 people (1994)
Safe water: 100 % (2000)

EDUCATION

School enrolment (net):
Primary total: 99 % (1994/2000)
male: 99 % (1995/99)
female: 99 % (1995/99)
Secondary (gross):
male: 120 % (1995/97)
female: 122 % (1995/97)
Tertiary (gross): 55 % (1998)
Primary school teachers: one for every 10 pupils (1998)

COMMUNICATIONS

304 newspapers (1998), 1,349 radios (2000), 807 TV sets (2000) and 720 main telephone lines (2000) per 1,000 people
Books: 230 new titles per 100,000 people (1992/94)

ECONOMY

Per capita, GDP: $ 27,627 (2000)
Annual growth: 2.6 % (2000)
Annual inflation: 2.9 % (2000)
Consumer price index: 112.1 (2000)
Currency: 8.6 kroner = $ 1 (03/2002)
Cereal imports: 702,263 metric tons (2000)
Food import dependency: 11 % (2000)
Fertilizer use: 1,704 kg per ha (1999)
Exports: $ 68,894 million (2000)
Imports: $ 60,123 million (2000)

ENERGY

Consumption: 3,924.5 Kgs of oil equivalent per capita yearly (1998); -17.8 % imported (1999)

HDI (ranking/value): 15 / 0.921 (1999)

Djibouti

Population:	652,000 (2002)
Land area:	23,180 SQ KM
Capital:	Djibouti
Currency:	Franc
Language:	French

Djibouti

In about the 3rd century BC Ablé immigrants came from Arabia and settled in the north and parts of the south. The Afars, or Danakil, are descendants of these peoples. Later the Somali Issas pushed the Afars out of the south and settled in the coastal regions. In AD 825 Islam was brought to the area by missionaries. Arabs controlled the trade in this region until the 16th century, when the Portuguese competed for it. In 1862, Tadjoura, one of the Sultanates on the Somalian coast (see Somalia), sold the port of Obock and adjoining lands to the French for 52,000 francs and in 1888 French Somaliland (Côte Français des Somalis) was established.

[2] Djibouti became the official capital of this French territory in 1892. A treaty with Ethiopia in 1897 reduced the territory in size. A railway was built to connect Djibouti with the Ethiopian hinterland, reaching Dire Dawa in 1903 and Addis Ababa in 1917. The interior of the area was effectively opened up between 1924 and 1934 by the construction of roads and administrative posts. After World War II Djibouti port lost trade to the Ethiopian port of Asseb (now in Eritrea). In 1946 French Somaliland acquired the status of an overseas territory (from 1967 called the French Territory of the Afars and Issas), and in 1958 it voted to become an overseas territorial member of the French Community under the Fifth Republic.

[3] Independence and the reunification of neighboring Somalia stimulated the emergence of anti-colonialist movements such as the Somaliland Liberation Front and the African League for Independence, both of which used the legal and armed branches.

[4] During the 1970s, renewed resistance forced acting governor Ali Aref to resign. France called a plebiscite on May 8 1977, and 85 per cent of the population voted for independence. Hassan Gouled Aptidon, main leader of the African League for Independence, became President of the fledgling Republic.

[5] The Government of the new state had to deal with tension between the Afar and Issa peoples and with refugees from the war zones in Ethiopia and Somalia. In an attempt to overcome old ethnic

divisions, Gouled granted governmental participation to various groups. He even appointed several Afar ministers. Though French remained the official language, Djibouti was admitted into the Arab League.

[6] Ethiopia and Somalia, its two neighbors, both had territorial designs on Djibouti. Ethiopia's interest in Djibouti was basically geopolitical. In the event of Eritrean nationalists achieving independence, Ethiopia would become a landlocked territory - if an agreement could not be reached for the use of Eritrean ports, Djibouti would be their only available harbor. For Somalia it was mainly a historical aim to unify the Somali nation.

[7] In mid-1979, President Hassan Gouled resumed relations with Ethiopia and Somalia, signing trade and transportation agreements with them. The participation of Afars in the Government and in the newly-formed army was encouraged as a way of securing some semblance of national unity. A ruling party was organized and municipal administrations were created to encourage political participation. Foreign aid was basically used for irrigation works and to improve the situation of refugees from the Ogaden war.

[8] The Gouled administration received aid from Saudi Arabia, Kuwait, Iraq and Libya. Gouled skilfully administered his country, playing upon its only valuable resource: its strategic position at the mouth of the Red Sea. Contrary to expectations that foretold a rapid annexation by Ethiopia or Somalia, Djibouti stressed its determination to remain independent.

[9] In spite of a successful performance in diplomatic relations, Gouled faced serious domestic problems, particularly ethnic rivalries between Afars and Issas. Afars, 35 per cent of the population, complained of political and economic discrimination. The Issas, 60 per cent of the population and hold key positions in the Government, refuted all accusations of favoritism, and supported Gouled's radical policies to neutralize the opposition. After the prohibition of the Popular Liberation Movement in 1979, the Afars tried to reorganize as the Djibouti Popular Party in 1981, but this was also banned.

[10] In October 1981, President Gouled amended the Constitution to introduce a single-party system. The official Popular Association for Progress (RPP) became the sole legal party and the other groups were banned. It was argued that they had racial or religious aims and in

consequence were potentially harmful to national unity.

[11] During 1983, the first steps were taken in a project to radically alter Djibouti's economy. Incentives were to be given to transform the country into a financial center and free trading port, a sort of Middle Eastern Hong Kong. Six foreign banks opened offices in Djibouti, mainly attracted by a solid national currency backed by dollar deposits in the US.

[12] By the end of 1984, the first results were not encouraging: the number of passengers and goods in transit to Ethiopia and Somalia had dropped considerably and, therefore, customs revenues and bank activities had decreased. The continuing conflict in the area has been seen as the major cause for the withdrawal of European capital.

[13] With the support of the UN High Commissioner, Gouled's Government resumed the voluntary repatriation of more than a hundred thousand refugees, a process which had been interrupted in 1983.

[14] At the same time, bilateral agreements were signed with Ethiopia to combat contraband and promote peace in the border areas. These had been closed in 1977, at the outset of the conflict with Somalia over the Ogaden region.

[15] In August 1987, foreign military presence in Djibouti grew as French bases were also used by US and British forces participating in maneuvers in the Persian Gulf. Relations with the former colonial power were reinforced by President François Mitterand's visit, in December.

[16] Djibouti depended on French economic aid. Trying to avoid this dependence Prime Minister Barkad Gourad Hamadou signed an economic and technical aid agreement with Turkey in June 1989.

[17] In 1990 France wrote off Djibouti's debt by granting it $40,000,000 as public development aid. In 1991, confrontations between the Government and the Front for the Restoration of Unity and Democracy (FRUD) guerrillas were renewed. In November, Amnesty International accused the Government of the torture of 300 prisoners. Due to mounting pressure France pressed Gouled to begin talks with the opposition.

LITERACY

2000

51%

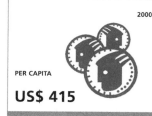

EXTERNAL DEBT

2000

PER CAPITA

US$ 415

FOREIGN TRADE

Millions US$ 2000

IMPORTS
347

EXPORTS
247

STATISTICS

DEMOGRAPHY
Population: 652,000 (2002)
Annual growth: 3.9 % (1985-2000)
Estimates for year 2015: 703,000 (2000)
Annual growth to year 2015: 0.7 % (2000)
Urban population: 83.3 % (200)
Urban growth: 2.3 % (2000)
Children per woman: 6.0 (2000)

HEALTH
Life expectancy at birth: 41 years (2000-2005)
male: 39 years (2000-2005)
female: 42 years (2000-2005)
Infant mortality: 102 per 1,000 (2000)
Under-5 child mortality: 146 per 1,000 (2000)
Daily calorie supply: 2,129 per capita (1999)
14 doctors per 100,000 people (1996)
Safe water: 100 % (2000)

EDUCATION
Literacy: 51 % (2000)
male: 65 % (2000)
female: 38 % (2000)
School enrolment (net):
Primary total: 33 % (1994/2000)
male: 39 % (1995/99)
female: 28 % (1995/99)
Secondary (gross):
male: 17 % (1995/97)
female: 12 % (1995/97)
Tertiary (gross): 0 % (1998)
Primary school teachers: one for every 40 pupils (1998)

COMMUNICATIONS
87 radios (2000), 71 TV sets (2000) and 15 main telephone lines (2000) per 1,000 people

ECONOMY
Annual growth: -1.3 % (2000)
Currency: 169.9 francs = $ 1 (03/2002)
Cereal imports: 167,414 metric tons (2000)
Food import dependency: 27 % (1992)
Exports: $ 247 million (2000)
Imports: $ 347 million (2000)
External debt: $ 262 million (2000); $ 415 per capita (2000)
Development aid received: $ 75 million (1999); $ 115.8 per capita (1999)

HDI (ranking/value): 137 / 0.447 (1999)

[18] In September 1992, amid combat against the FRUD, the Government introduced a constitutional reform that established a multiparty system. In the May 1993 presidential elections, Gouled was again re-elected, with over 60.8 per cent of the vote. However, encouraged by the FRUD, half of the electorate abstained from voting and the opposition considered the elections a 'fraud'.

[19] Armed confrontations between government troops and guerrillas escalated in the weeks following the elections, which led thousands to seek refuge in Ethiopia. Acting as mediator, the French Government sought a cease-fire and negotiations began. Meanwhile, Gouled believed the rebellion was part of a plan orchestrated by Ethiopia.

[20] In March 1994, the FRUD was divided due to a possible agreement with the Government. The movement's Politburo, led by Ahmad Dini Ahmad, who opposed the agreement, was replaced by an executive council headed by Ahmad Ougoureh Kible. In June, Gouled and the FRUD jointly decided to end the war.

[21] In June, a demonstration of mostly Afar residents from the Arhiba district, opposed to the demolition of their homes for 'security reasons', was quelled by government forces. Police intervention left four dead, 20 injured and 300 arrests, including that of Muhammad Ahmad Issa, United Opposition Front president.

[22] In October, dissent within the FRUD had grown and the movement's leaders banned Ahmad Dini Ahmad and Muhammad Adoyta Yussuf, another breakaway leader, from holding any 'activity or responsibility' in the FRUD. In 1995, after the Constitution was revised, a section of the FRUD formed an alliance with the ruling party. Ahmad Dini Ahmad said this alliance amounted to 'treason'.

[23] In mid-1995 under pressure from the IMF, the Government substantially reduced public spending and took a series of measures to increase fiscal income. The following year, the IMF granted Djibouti a $6.7 million credit to support the Government reform program. In March 1996, President Gouled dismissed two ministers: defense and justice post-holder, Ahmed Boulaleh Barreh and Moumin Bahon Farah, of prisons and Islamic affairs. The departure of these ministers consolidated the position of Prime Minister Barkat Gourad Hamadou and the Head of Cabinet Ismael Omar Guelleh, a close relative of Gouled.

[24] Farah, who had announced the formation of a new political party in April, was imprisoned for a month, accused of insulting Gouled. In August Farah began a hunger strike to protest his imprisonment. On September 26, in Addis Ababa, Ethiopia, 17 opponents of the Gouled regime were abducted and became prisoners of the Djibouti Government.

[25] In February 18 1998 in spite of Djibouti having signed the African Human Rights Charter, guaranteeing freedom of speech and information, the editor of the bimonthly *Al Wahda* publication, Ahmed Abdi Farah, and journalist Kamil Hassan Ali were arrested for an article published a year earlier in which the paper criticized the Government.

[26] April 1999 marked the first opportunity since independence for citizens to vote for a president, with Ismail Omar Guelleh elected by a wide margin. The electoral campaign of Guelleh, the second President in the history of the country, centered on promises to alleviate poverty. His political rivals accused him of having assassinated members of the opposition during two decades when he was a key advisor to and director of special police corps.

[27] General Yacin Yabeh Galab, chief of police, led a failed coup attempt in December 2000. For conspiring against the security of the State he spent a year in prison, and was released for medical attention due to his diabetes.

[28] The Government and the most radical faction of the FRUD signed a peace treaty in May 2001 that ended the civil war. Ahmad Dini returned to Djibouti after nine years in exile.

[29] As a first gesture toward the FRUD, Guelleh restructured the Government. However, in spite of previous speculation, no FRUD representative was named among the nine new Cabinet members. ■

PROFILE

ENVIRONMENT
Located in the Afar triangle, facing Yemen, Djibouti is one of the hottest countries in the world (average annual temperature 30° C). The land is mostly desert; its only green area is found in the basalt ranges of the northern region. Agriculture, confined to oases and to a few spots along the coast, satisfies only 25 per cent of the domestic food demand. Extensive cattle-raising is practised by nomads. Economic activity is concentrated around the port.

SOCIETY
Peoples: Djiboutians are divided into two major ethnic groups of equal size: the Afars, scattered throughout the country, and the Issas, of Somalian origin, who populate most of the southern territory and predominate in the capital. There are also French, Yemeni, Ethiopian, Italian, Greek and Pakistani minorities, among others.
Religions: Sunni Muslims. There is a small Christian minority (5 per cent).
Languages: Afar and Issa (Somali), French (official) and Arabic (religious).
Political Parties: People's Assembly for Progress (RPP), which emerged in 1979 from the African People's League for Independence, founded in 1975 by Hassan Gouled. Democratic Renovation Party (PRD); Democratic Front for the Liberation of Djibouti; Movement for the Liberation of Djibouti; Front for the Restoration of Unity and Democracy (FRUD). Movement for Djibouti's Liberation (MDL); Movement for Unity and Democracy (MUD).

THE STATE
Official Name: République de Djibouti.
Administrative divisions: 5 districts.
Capital: Djibouti 523,000 people (1999).
Other cities: Ali-Sabieh 12,200 people; Tajurah 11,500; Dikhil 9,900 (2000).
Government: Ismail Omar Guelleh, President since May 1999. Dileita Muhammad Dileita, Prime Minister since March 2001. The Prime Minister is traditionally Afar to counterbalance the power of Gouled, who is Issa. The National Assembly has 65 members.
National Holiday: June 27, Independence Day (1977).
Armed Forces: 9,000 (1997).
Other: Gendarmerie (Ministry of Defense): 600; National Security Force (Ministry of Interior): 3,000.

Dominica

Population: 70,000 (2002)
Land area: 750 SQ KM
Capital: Roseau
Currency: E.C. dollar
Language: English

Dominica

On Sunday, November 3 1493, Italian navigator Christopher Columbus reached an island, which he named Dominica. He planted a cross to claim Spanish sovereignty over the newly discovered territory in the name of Queen Isabella and King Ferdinand of Spain.

[2] This territory was actually already populated by Carib peoples, peaceful and friendly indigenous groups. They watched the claiming ceremony from a distance, but could not have fully understood its significance. Soon afterwards, the Spanish returned in a more aggressive frame of mind, searching for the vast stores of gold that they believed the Caribs were hiding from them. They rapidly exterminated all but a few of the island's people, a pattern of destruction and despoilment that would be repeated throughout the colonial possessions in the new continent.

[3] By 1632 there were only an estimated 1,000 Caribs on the island. Today, there are only 500 living in the reservations.

[4] The landscape of present-day Dominica has changed greatly since their ancestors' days. In colonial times, the forests were felled to clear the land for extensive sugar plantations. The Carib peoples could not provide a sufficiently robust and reliable workforce, so the plantations were worked by thousands of slaves transported from Africa.

[5] In the 17th century, the Spanish withdrew and the French took their place. They introduced cotton and coffee production to complement the sugar trade. In the following two centuries, frequent British attempts to seize the island from French hands culminated in Dominica becoming a British colony in 1805.

[6] French influence still persists. The Catholic religion predominates despite strong competition from well-financed Protestant sects, and Creole, the language spoken by the people, is based on French mixed with African languages.

[7] After five centuries of colonization, the Dominicans inherited a rudimentary agrarian economy based on the mono-cultivation of bananas for export. These are the only significant export item, because most of the land went over to banana production when

sugarcane became unprofitable at the end of the 19th century.

[8] The political system adopted on achieving internal autonomy in 1967 was a copy of the British model. The Constitution established the 'free association' of the Associated States of the West Indies with Britain. Britain retained responsibility for defense and foreign relations and each member island elected its own state government. The seat of the federal government was in Barbados.

[9] From 1975, independence was negotiated separately by each State. In the case of Dominica the negotiations were conducted by Labor Party premier, Patrick John. In 1978, the British Parliament approved a new statute for the island and on November 3 1978, exactly 485 years after the arrival of Columbus, Dominica became an independent country once more.

[10] The protest rallies that took place during the celebrations were an indication of the difficulties that lay ahead. Political division immediately became evident: a conservative group of veteran politicians opposed independence and a progressive sector supported by young people disagreed with the Labor Government which had done the negotiating.

[11] Since the island lacked the natural resources to attract transnationals and tourism, Dominica could not compete with its

neighbors. Vast numbers of young people emigrated to neighboring Guadeloupe, while others who were more radical found political inspiration in the 'black power' ideology of US black activists.

[12] In May 1979, the police fired at demonstrators protesting against two decrees limiting union activities and press freedom. At the same time, secret agreements between John and the South Africa were revealed. The Dominican premier had helped to plan a mercenary attack on Barbados and intended to supply Pretoria with oil refined in Dominica. Patrick John was forced to resign. His successor, Oliver Seraphine, from the progressive wing of the Labor Party, called elections and strengthened Dominica's ties with progressive neighboring governments. In September 1979, Hurricane David devastated the island. The Conservative opposition skillfully associated the catastrophe with the Labor administration and gained electoral support.

[13] In the July 1980 election, Mary Eugenia Charles won a landslide victory and became the first woman to head a Caribbean government. She was the daughter of a wealthy and influential landowner and described herself as 'liberal, democratic and anti-communist'.

[14] In the 1985 election, Charles' Dominican Freedom Party (DFP) obtained 15 of the 21 Parliamentary

seats; the Labor Party, led by Michael Douglas, won only 5 seats and the United Dominican Labor Party (UDLP) won the remaining seat for its leader. During the electoral campaign, the opposition called for an investigation into a $100,000 donation made to the Government. It was believed that the donation had been made by the CIA to confirm Dominican collaboration in the US invasion of Grenada.

[15] In August 1986, Air Force commander Frederick Newton was sentenced to death by hanging for his participation in a plot to topple the conservative government in 1981. Former Prime Minister Patrick John and Michael Reid, captain of the Defense Forces, were found guilty of similar charges, and of involvement in a minor Ku Klux Klan conspiracy. They were sentenced to 12 years in prison.

[16] After the May 28 1990 parliamentary election, the third government since independence took office. Of the 21 seats up for election, Charles's DFP won by a slim majority of 11 seats, while the Labor Party (led by Douglas) won 4 and the United Labor Party, a newcomer in the electoral process and led by Edison James, won 6 seats. Leonard Baptist's Progressive Force did not win any seats.

[17] The day after the election, which gave the 71-year-old lawyer Charles her third consecutive term, Patrick John and Michael Reid were freed.

[18] In 1990, Prime Minister Charles signed an agreement with her counterparts James Mitchell of St Vincent, John Compton of St Lucia and Nicholas Braithwaite of Grenada, for the four islands to form a new state.

[19] In the same year the Regional Constitutional Assembly of the Eastern Caribbean was set up. It comprised government officials, religious authorities and representatives from social organizations. In a second meeting, in St Lucia in April 1991, the Assembly studied various proposals for the establishment of the future State.

[20] This integration project was concordant with the Chaguaramas Treaty, which aimed at the unification of the entire English-

MATERNAL MORTALITY	FOOD DEPENDENCY	FOREIGN TRADE
1985/99		Millions US$ 2000
Per 100,000 live births	2000	IMPORTS 173
65	21%	EXPORTS 137

speaking Caribbean community, although the three islands of St Kitts, Montserrat and Antigua refused to commit themselves to the process. The opposition parties of Grenada and St Lucia also stated they were against it. The seven mini-States of the Eastern Caribbean have a common Central Bank, which coins their shared currency.

[21] In 1991, the Government decided on a series of measures to stimulate the national economy, centering its efforts on the development of agriculture and communications.

[22] The Prime Minister narrowly escaped censure in April through a motion presented by the United Workers' Party. At the end of 1991, Charles attempted to enact legislation making it illegal for civil servants to protest against the Government.

[23] In April 1994, the Government decision to increase the number of transport vehicle licenses caused protests and public disorder in Roseau. The Prime Minister accused the opposition of trying to bring forward the elections, and the crisis continued until an agreement was signed on May 6.

[24] In August and September 1995, Government plans were severely shaken as a succession of hurricanes and tropical storms destroyed the plantations and export projects. Houses, bridges, roads, hotels and public facilities were also destroyed and had to be rebuilt, absorbing vast amounts of resources.

[25] The external debt reached EC$ 320 million and the internal EC$ 80 million in January 1996. That year, the Government went ahead with a plan to privatize large public companies in an attempt to impose

order on the financial sector. The Companies that passed into private hands were: Dominican Electricity Services, the Industrial and Agricultural Development Bank, the Import-Export Agency of Dominica and other services at the port of Roseau.

[26] Cuban Foreign Minister Roberto Robaina visited the country in May 1996, marking the re-establishment of diplomatic relations between Dominica and Cuba.

[27] In early 1997, the opposition parties severely criticized the privatizations, especially the sale of the Dominican Electricity Services to a British company, claiming the reasons behind this had not been sufficiently explained. On top of the $5 million received from the British Government for development projects, Dominica was awarded another million in April for a project to protect its coasts from erosion.

[28] In October 1998 the Assembly appointed Vernon Lorden Shaw, a retired civil servant, seventh president of Dominica. Shaw promised recovery for the nation's sources of income which had been badly hit by climatic disasters and the global economic crisis.

[29] In February 2000, Rosie Douglas became Prime Minister. That same month, Dominica and Cuba signed a bilateral co-ordination and consultation agreement, including plans for annual meetings to strengthen cultural, social and political co-operation. Up until then, Cuban-Dominican co-operation had mainly concentrated on education, but now there were hopes for joint policies related to tourism.

[30] Douglas died unexpectedly on October 1, at age 58, and was succeeded by Pierre Charles.

[31] In 2000, Parliament passed amendments that allowed the state-owned National Commercial Bank to provide offshore services in the financial sector. This was the same Parliament that in February 2002, as a first step towards removal from an international black list, passed a law against money laundering aimed at allowing foreign investigators to review offshore bank accounts. ∎

PROFILE

ENVIRONMENT

The largest Windward Island of the Lesser Antilles, located between Guadeloupe to the north and Martinique to the south, Dominica is a volcanic island. Its highest peak is Morne Diablotin, at 2,000 meters. The climate is tropical with heavy summer rains. The volcanic soil allows for some agricultural activity, especially banana and cocoa plantations.

SOCIETY

Peoples: Descendants of Africans 89 per cent; descendants of Europeans and Africans 7.2 per cent; Caribs living in reservations 2.4 per cent; Europeans 0.4 per cent; Other 0.7 per cent.
Languages: English (official). Creole, a local French patois, with African elements, is widely spoken.
Religions: Roman Catholic 70.1 per cent; six largest Protestant groups 17.2 per cent.
Political parties: United Dominican Labor Party (UDLP); Dominica Revolutionary Party (PRD); Social Christian Reformist Party (PRSC); Dominican Liberation Party (PLD); Democratic Unity (UD); Dominican Freedom Party (DFP).
Social Organizations: National Workers' Union; Officials of Dominica Labor Union; Association for the Conservation of Dominica (environmentalist).

THE STATE

Official Name: Commonwealth of Dominica.
Administrative divisions: 10 parishes.
Capital: Roseau 24,000 people (1999).
Other cities: Portsmouth 3,600 people; Marigot 2,900; Atkinson 2,500 (2000).
Government: Vernon Lorden Shaw, President since October 1998; Pierre Charles, Prime Minister since October 2000.
National Holidays: November 3, Independence Day (1978) and Discovery by Christopher Columbus (1493).
Armed forces: Commonwealth of Dominica Police Force (includes Special Service Unit, Coast Guard).

STATISTICS

DEMOGRAPHY

Population: 70,000 (2002)
Annual growth: -0.2 % (1985-2000)
Estimates for year 2015: 70,000 (2000)
Annual growth to year 2015: 0.0 % (2000)

HEALTH

Maternal mortality: 65 per 100,000 live births (1985/99)
Infant mortality: 14 per 1,000 (2000)
Under-5 child mortality: 16 per 1,000 (2000)
Daily calorie supply: 2,947 per capita (1999)
49 doctors per 100,000 people (1996)
Safe water: 97 % (2000)

EDUCATION

School enrolment (net):
Primary total: 89 % (1994/2000)
male: 89 % (1995/99)
female: 89 % (1995/99)
Primary school teachers: one for every 20 pupils (1998)

COMMUNICATIONS

220 TV sets (2000) and 294 main telephone lines (2000) per 1,000 people

ECONOMY

Annual inflation: 0.9 % (2000)
Consumer price index: 107.3 (2000)
Currency: 2.7 E.C. dollars = $ 1 (03/2002)
Cereal imports: 7,029 metric tons (2000)
Food import dependency: 21 % (2000)
Fertilizer use: 10,000 kg per ha (1999)
Exports: $ 137 million (2000)
Imports: $ 173 million (2000)
External debt: $ 108 million (2000); $ 1,533 per capita (2000)

LAND USE

Forest & Woodland: 66.7 % of total (1993)
Arable: 9.3 % of total (1993)
Other: 24.0 % of total (1993)

Dominican Republic

Population: 8,639,000 (2002)
Land area: 48,380 SQ KM
Capital: Santo Domingo
Currency: Peso
Language: Spanish

República Dominicana

The island of Quisqueya is now two countries: Haiti and the Dominican Republic. The first inhabitants belonged to several ethnic groups: the Lucayo, the Ciguayo, the Taino and the Carib. They were fishers and gatherers who practiced basic agriculture. There was always a great deal of contact between the Caribbean islands and trade between the groups.

[2] In December 1492 Christopher Columbus reached the island of Quisqueya, which he renamed Hispaniola. With the wood from one of his vessels he built a fort, initiating the European colonization of America. Within a few years, the Europeans had appropriated the whole island, subduing the Carib population. The terrible living and working conditions imposed by the Spaniards nearly exterminated the indians. Faced with this shameful situation, Bishop Bartolomé de Las Casas proposed that they replace local slave labor with Africans, millions of whom were distributed throughout the American continent.

[3] Dominican historical records show that in 1523 a group of rebel African slave workers founded the first *quilombo* (former slave settlement) on the island. Subsequent rebel groups, in 1537 and 1548, set up their own quilombos. The replacement of native American labor with African labor accompanied a change in economic focus, from panning for gold to plantations of sugarcane and extensive cattle raising. As historian Pierre Vilar pointed out, the gold cycle in Hispaniola was 'destructive, not of raw materials, but rather, of the labor force'.

During the colonial period the extraordinary economic potential of the Dominican Republic was comparable only with that of Brazil. The island was successively the greatest gold producer in the Antilles; one of the largest producers of sugar in the New World between 1570 and 1630; and finally, such an important cattle producer that there were 40 cattle per person on the island.

[4] As a major sugar producer with a key position on the trade route from Mexico and Peru to Spain,

Hispaniola was coveted by the other colonial powers. In 1586, the English buccaneer Francis Drake raided the capital and in 1697 the French occupied the island's western half. When they were given official ownership under the Treaty of Ryswick, they renamed it Haiti. Later, the whole island fell under French rule but was partially recovered by Spain in 1809, after the first Afro-American republic had been established (in Haiti).

[5] Haiti's government regained control over the whole island in

1822. The Spanish descendants' (*criollo*) resistance came to a head after an uprising in Santo Domingo. The independence of the Dominican Republic was proclaimed, but in 1861 the Government asked Spain to reinstate colonial status, in an attempt to gain support for the criollos, whose dominance was threatened by the black and mulatto majorities.

[6] However, Spain did not defend its colony effectively and the Dominican Republic became independent again in 1865 after a mulatto uprising. The economic system remained unchanged.

[7] By that time the US, fully recovered from its civil war, began to gain influence in the West Indies (now called Caribbean). In 1907 the US imposed an economic and political treaty on the Dominican Republic prefiguring 'dollar diplomacy'. This treaty helped the US to invade the Dominican Republic and impose a protectorate that lasted until 1924.

[8] In 1930, when the country was autonomous again, Rafael Leónidas Trujillo seized power. He was Chief of Staff of the National Guard,

---

WORKERS

1999/2000

LABOR FORCE AS % OF TOTAL

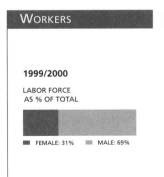

■ FEMALE: 31%   ■ MALE: 69%

LAND USE

DEFORESTATION: 1.6% annual (1990/95)

1993

■ FOREST & WOODLAND: 12.3%
■ ARABLE: 20.5%
■ OTHER: 67.2%

PUBLIC EXPENDITURE

1999

4.4%   41.5%
DEFENSE   SOCIAL

MATERNAL MORTALITY

1985/99

Per 100,000
live births

230

LITERACY

2000

84%

elected and trained by the American occupation forces. He set up a dictatorial regime, with US backing, without nominally occupying the presidency. His crimes were so numerous and so apparent that he finally became too embarrassing even for the US, and the CIA planned his assassination which was carried out in May 1961.

[9] On his death, Trujillo owned 71 per cent of the country's arable land and 90 per cent of its industry.

[10] In 1963, following a popular rebellion, the first democratic elections were held and writer Juan Bosch was elected president. Seven months later, he was overthrown by military officers from the Trujillo regime. In April 1965, Colonel Francisco Caamaño Deñó led a constitutional armed rebellion. Accusing the nationalists of having 'Pro-Castro /communist' sympathies, the US intervened once again,

sending in 35,000 Marines who suppressed the insurgency.

[11] Before leaving the country, the US occupation force paved the way for an unconditional Trujillo supporter, Joaquín Balaguer, to rise to power. In return, he opened the country to transnationals, especially Gulf and Western. The sugar industry fell under Gulf control. The corporation also bought shares in local banking, agro-industry, hotels and cattle raising, consequently, becoming very influential in Dominican Republic.

[12] The nationalist opposition kept up its resistance and in 1973 Francisco Cameo was killed while leading a guerrilla group. The Dominican Revolutionary Party (PRD), originally led by Juan Bosch, split with the right wing (led by landowner Antonio Guzmán) eliminating the main reformist measures from its program. This action made it acceptable to the

State Department and in 1978, when the PRD won the elections, the US used its influence - in the name of human rights - to ensure that the results would be respected.

[13] The PRD program promised to re-establish democratic freedoms and to follow an economic policy of income redistribution favoring the majority. The first promise was fulfilled and popular organizations took advantage of the new situation to reorganize their weakened structures after decades of harsh repression.

[14] New presidential elections were held on May 16 1981, and Salvador Jorge Blanco became president in the PRD's second successive victory. José Francisco Peña Gómez, one of the Latin American leaders in the Socialist International, was elected mayor of Santo Domingo. On July 4, departing president Antonio Guzmán killed himself, generating political tension which ended with the announcement of the electoral result.

[15] When President Blanco took office the trade deficit amounted to $562 million. In 1982, sugar prices fell and oil prices rose causing the foreign debt to climb to $2 billion. Unemployment affected 25 per cent of the active population.

[16] Blanco tried to tackle the situation by applying IMF-tailored austerity measures. But during 1983, the international price of sugar fell 50 per cent below the cost of production, and sugar accounted for 44 per cent of Dominican exports. In 1984, the Government withdrew the subsidies on several products, and imposed a 200 per cent price increase on staple and medical goods. These measures brought about protest rallies led by leftist organizations and labor unions. In return, the Union headquarters were occupied by soldiers leaving 100 dead, 400 injured and over 5,000 imprisoned.

[17] In 1985, the US reduced its Dominican sugar quota again, causing another decrease in exports. Unemployment rose abruptly, provoking yet another wave of social unrest. The Government continued to toe the IMF line, harshly repressing all the strikes and protests against its policies.

[18] In that year, the gravity of the economic crisis became evident. The judges went on strike and paralyzed

the courts for three months. In May, the powerful Dominican Republic Medical Association began a new round of disputes, backed by the nurses, the Association of Agriculture Professionals and the Veterinary Association. In August, the Association of Engineers followed suit, supported by the architects and surveyors, who demanded a minimum wage of $260. The Dominican Association of Economists wrote that since 1980 poverty had been 'initially limited to the low-income groups, (but) had spread to the point of affecting the middle classes'.

[19] For the poorer people, the situation was untenable. Committees for Popular Struggle began to appear and grass roots movements organized to resist price rises on basic goods and services. In April, dockworkers found 28 young Dominican Republic women asphyxiated in a ship's container. They could not find work and had expected to find a way of making a living on another island. It was disclosed that every two weeks a 'cargo' of young women from the Dominican Republic left for the Franco-Dutch island of St Martin, where a brothel manager sold them to other Caribbean islands for between 800 and 1,000 German marks.

[20] National elections were held May 16 1986, with three presidential candidates: Jacobo Majluta for the Dominican Revolutionary Party (PRD), Joaquín Balaguer for the Social Christian Reformist Party (PRSC) and Juan Bosch for the Marxist-inspired Dominican Liberation Party (PLD). In the chaotic climate that followed, which included an interruption of the vote count, the victory went to Balaguer's PRSC.

[21] Joaquín Balaguer of the Social Christians (SCRP) was elected president. The circumstances surrounding his inauguration were very difficult. Clearly a conservative, without a parliamentary majority and faced with highly organized social opposition, his hands were virtually tied. He did not even have the necessary power to impose a more restrictive economic program to get new loans from the IMF.

[22] Balaguer was re-elected in the May 16 1990 elections. His rival, Juan

PROFILE

ENVIRONMENT

The Dominican Republic comprises the eastern part of the island of Hispaniola, the second largest of the Antilles group. The Cordillera Central, the central mountain range, crosses the territory from northwest to southeast. Between the central and northern ranges, lies the fertile region of the Cibao. Sea winds and ocean currents contribute to the tropical, rainy climate. Between 1962 and 1990, the country lost a significant portion of its woodlands. Coral reefs are suffering the effects of pollution, which has harmed marine habitats and reduced fish populations. Hurricanes cause serious damages.

SOCIETY

Peoples: Most are of Spanish and African descent, with a small native American component.
Languages: Spanish.
Religions: Roman Catholic 91.3 per cent; other 8.7 per cent.
Political Parties: Dominican Revolutionary Party; Dominican Liberation Party; Social Christian Reformist Party. Minor parties: Strength of the Revolution; Quisqueyano Democrat Party.
Social Organizations: Most workers are represented by the General Workers' Union (CGT) and the Unity Workers' Union (CUT). In March 1991, 4 major labor groups, 57 federations and 366 labor unions merged within the CUT.

THE STATE

Official Name: República Dominicana.
Administrative Divisions: 26 Provinces, 1 National District.
Capital: Santo Domingo 3,523,000 people (1999).
Other cities: Santiago de Los Caballeros 446,800 people; La Vega 416,300: San Pedro de Marcorís 257,700 (2000).
Government: Rafael Hipólito Mejía Domínguez, President since August 2000. Presidential system with a bicameral legislature. Congress of the Republic: a 30-member House of senators and a 149-member House of Representatives, all elected by popular vote.
National Holiday: February 27, Independence Day (1844).
Armed forces: 24,500 (1995).
Other: National Police, 15,000.

Bosch, leader of the PLD, accused him of an electoral fraud. The third candidate, PRD's Peña Gómez, suggested a recount at the polling stations. This recount confirmed Balaguer's victory, with 35 per cent, to Bosch's 34 and Peña Gómez' 23.

[23] From 1990 to 1991 there were hundreds of thousands of Haitian immigrants working as cane-cutters in the Dominican Republic sugar industry. In June 1991, Balaguer expelled them as illegal immigrants.

[24] Negotiations by Balaguer made it possible to refinance the foreign debt. In 1993 tourism grew, making the country one of the most important tourist destinations in the Caribbean.

[25] As a result of the political crisis in neighboring Haiti, contraband goods were taken across the border from the Dominican Republic into Haiti. This practice foiled the international embargo against the Haitian regime. Oil was the main product smuggled into the country.

[26] Economic problems caused hundreds of Dominican Republicans to leave the country each year with forged visas and documents. Many sailed in unseaworthy vessels, bound for Puerto Rico, normally as a 'stopover' on their way to New York.

[27] More than a million expatriates live in the United States, and half are illegal. There are also an estimated 20,000 in Spain, half of them illegal. The majority are women who work as domestics, while another 25,000 women work as prostitutes throughout Europe, most of them lured by false promises of employment.

[28] Although he had announced his retirement, Balaguer sought re-election in 1994. His perennial opponent Juan Bosch also ran. According to opinion polls, José Francisco Peña Gómez, of the Dominican Revolutionary Party (PRD) held a slight lead over Balaguer. Intent upon avoiding another case of electoral fraud, four of the five participating parties signed a 'civility pact', with the Catholic Church acting as guarantor. In spite of this, the electoral campaign turned violent, with hundreds of people injured and 12 people killed.

[29] International observers were called in to supervise the elections. The PRD condemned the election stating that some 200,000 voters were unable to vote as a result of official party manipulation. According to official figures, Balaguer obtained 43 per cent of the vote, leading Peña Gómez by 1.5 per cent, while Juan Bosch obtained 31.2 per cent. Eventually, the Central Electoral Committee declared Balaguer the winner.

[30] On June 30 1996, Leonel Fernández Reyna of the PLDP won the elections after forming an alliance with the conservative PRSC. On August 18 he succeeded Joaquín Balaguer, who had served seven terms as president.

[31] After the election, the PRSC signed an agreement with the PRD giving them control of the Senate, and the PRD dominated the Chamber of Deputies. The PLD remained in a minority in both chambers, preventing the President from implementing several of the initiatives announced in his electoral campaign.

[32] Increasing prices, unemployment of more than 30 per cent, and the poverty that affected 70 per cent of the population led to an increase in social tension. There were demonstrations in the streets, some violent. Despite this, the overall economy saw exceptional growth of 6.9 per cent in the first half of the year.

[33] A law approved in June allowed private capital to invest in state companies, including the sugar and electricity sectors. The Government aimed to thus balance the state accounts.

[34] Towards the end of 1997, the Presidents of the Dominican Republic and Haiti agreed to stop the large-scale repatriation of Haitians and to respect human rights. The Haitians often worked in the worst conditions, and so the state sugar company had announced a plan to employ 16,000 Haitian cane-cutters. This cheap workforce was transported from the frontier to the various sugar plantations to work and then taken directly back to Haiti. However, pressure against the arrival of more Haitians did not stop: anti-immigrant protests led to the expulsion of some 2,500 undocumented Haitians and strengthened frontier controls.

[35] On April 16 1998, the Dominican Republic and Cuba restored diplomatic relations. The Government sent a consular representative to Havana, later followed by a delegation of ministers that formally inaugurated the diplomatic headquarters. The US protested against the measure, deeming it 'inappropriate'.

[36] The May 1998 legislative and municipal elections gave a clear advantage to the opposition DRP, which took 83 seats in Parliament and 24 in the Senate. The DLP retained just 49 seats in parliament and 4 in the Senate (120 and 30 members respectively). In June, Fernández Reyna made a 3-day visit to Haiti, the first official mission by a Dominican Republican president since 1936, in order to set up a more effective joint border initiative, in order to stop the trafficking of weapons, drugs and immigrants between the two countries.

[37] Fresh disturbances shook Santo Domingo in January 1999 following the outcome of voting for the new president of the municipal league, a body which handled a $100 million budget to aid local governments. In May, a general strike demanded changes in government economic policy, but these were refused. In January 2000, at the age of 93, Joaquín Balaguer announced he would again stand for the presidency with the official approval of his party, the SCRP.

[38] The May 2000 elections gave the Presidency to Hipólito Mejía, candidate of the PRD, who received a big enough margin to avoid a second round. Joaquín Balaguer ended up third. The new President took office in August, promising to create jobs and fight corruption and poverty. In November, a march held by Fernández Reyna to denounce the imprisonment of four members of his government was suppressed by the police. The former President, who was hospitalized as a result of police tear gas, claimed the prison sentences aimed to incriminate him in corruption cases.

[39] In October 2000, the Government refused to extradite seven Haitian police accused of taking part in a plot to destabilize the Haitian Government. Hugo Tolentino Dipp, Dominican Republic's Minister of Foreign Affairs, stated the seven would be held in his government's custody.

[40] The following year, in May, the Court of Appeals annulled a trial against former President Salvador Jorge Blanco on corruption charges.

[41] Since a wave of murders and kidnappings risked the arrival of tourists - one of the country's main sources of income - Mejía sent the army to patrol the streets, seeking to contain criminal escalation. ■

EXTERNAL DEBT

2000

PER CAPITA

US$ 549

FOREIGN TRADE

Millions US$ 2000

IMPORTS

7,736

EXPORTS

5,862

STATISTICS

DEMOGRAPHY
Population: 8,639,000 (2002)
Annual growth: 1.7 % (1985-2000)
Estimates for year 2015: 10,137,000 (2000)
Annual growth to year 2015: 1.3 % (2000)
Urban population: 65.0 % (2000)
Urban growth: 2.6 % (2000)
Children per woman: 2.8 (2000)

HEALTH
Life expectancy at birth: 67 years (2000-2005)
male: 64 years (2000-2005)
female: 70 years (2000-2005)
Maternal mortality: 230 per 100,000 live births (1985/99)
Infant mortality: 42 per 1,000 (2000)
Under-5 child mortality: 48 per 1,000 (2000)
Daily calorie supply: 2,333 per capita (1999)
216 doctors per 100,000 people (1997)
Safe water: 86 % (2000)

EDUCATION
Literacy: 84 % (2000)
male: 84 % (2000)
female: 84 % (2000)
School enrolment (net):
Primary total: 94 % (1994/2000)
male: 84 % (1995/99)
female: 85 % (1995/99)
Secondary (gross):
male: 34 % (1995/97)
female: 47 % (1995/97)
Tertiary (gross): 23 % (1997)
Primary school teachers: one for every 37 pupils (1998)

COMMUNICATIONS
156 newspapers (1998), 181 radios (1997), 97 TV sets (1998) and 105 main telephone lines (2000) per 1,000 people

ECONOMY
Per capita, GDP: $ 6,033 (2000)
Annual growth: 6.0 % (2000)
Annual inflation: 7.7 % (2000)
Consumer price index: 137.2 (2000)
Currency: 2.7 pesos = $ 1 (03/2002)
Cereal imports: 1,332,567 metric tons (2000)
Fertilizer use: 880 kg per ha (1999)
Exports: $ 5,862 million (2000)
Imports: $ 7,736 million (2000)
External debt: $ 4,598 million (2000); $ 549 per capita (2000)
Debt service: 3.9 % of exports (1999)
Development aid received: $ 195 million (1999); $ 23.2 per capita (1999); 1.10 % of GNP (1999)

ENERGY
Consumption: 676.4 Kgs of oil equivalent per capita yearly (1998); 80.0 % imported (1999)

HDI (ranking/value): 86 / 0.722 (1999)

East Timor

Timor Leste

Population: 779,000 (2002)
Land area: 14,870 SQ KM
Capital: Dili
Currency: Indonesian rupiah
Language: Tetum

Long before the arrival of the Portuguese, the Chinese and Arabs knew Timor as an 'inexhaustible' source of precious woods which were exchanged for axes, pottery, lead and other goods of use to the local inhabitants.

[2]   Timor's traditional Maubere society consisted of five major categories: the Liurari (kings and chiefs), the Dato (lesser nobles and warriors), the Ema-reino (freemen) the Ata (slaves) and the Lutum (nomadic shepherds).

[3]   In 1859, Portugal and the Netherlands agreed to divide the territory between them. The Portuguese kept the eastern part, under an accord ratified in 1904. Resistance to colonialism included armed insurrections in 1719, 1895 and 1959, all of which were put down. Passive resistance by the Maubere enabled their culture to survive five centuries of colonialism. It fared better than the forests of precious woods: species like sandalwood were exhausted very early, or replaced with coffee plantations which were Timor's economic mainstay.

[4]   The independence movement began later than in other Portuguese colonies, but in the mid-1970s a national liberation front was formed, bringing together nationalist forces and all sectors of society.

[5]   In April 1974, when the clandestine struggle against colonial rule had already grown and gained broad support, the 'Carnation Revolution' took place in Lisbon. With the fall of the fascist colonial regime in the metropolis the political scene in Timor changed and the patriotic movement was legalized. In September, the Revolutionary Front for the Independence of East Timor (FRETILIN) was created.

[6]   The new Portuguese Government promised independence but the colonial administration favored the creation of the Democratic Union of Timor (UDT), which supported the colonial status quo and 'federation' with Portugal. At the same time, the Indonesian consulate in Dili, Timor's capital, encouraged a group of Timorese to organize the Timor Popular Democratic Association (APODETI) which wanted full

independence from Portugal, and supported integration with Indonesia.

[7]   A period of conflict ensued between Portuguese neocolonial interests, Indonesian annexationists and the independence movement. In August, the UDT attempted a coup causing FRETILIN to issue a call for general armed insurrection, and the Portuguese administration withdrew from the country. FRETILIN achieved territorial control and declared independence on November 28 1975, proclaiming the Democratic Republic of East Timor. Portugal's withholding of official recognition had important diplomatic and political implications.

[8]   On December 7 1975, Indonesia invaded the new republic. A few hours earlier, US President Gerald Ford had visited Jakarta where he had probably learned of, and endorsed, Indonesian president General Suharto's expansionist plans. FRETILIN was forced to withdraw from the capital, Dili, and from the major ports. On June 2 1976, a so-called 'People's Assembly', made up of UDT and APODETI members, approved Timor's annexation as a province of Indonesia. However, this illegal resolution was not recognized by the United Nations Decolonization Committee, which still regards Portugal as the colonial power responsible for Timor.

[9]   Meanwhile, the Democratic Republic of East Timor established diplomatic relations with numerous former Portuguese colonies and socialist states.

[10]   In December 1978, Nicolás dos Reis Lobato, President of the Republic and FRETILIN leader died in combat. Despite this blow, the liberation forces reformed and resistance continued. Indonesian genocide on the island was claimed to have cost the lives of nearly a third of the population.

[11]   In an attempt to set the Maubere against each other, the Indonesian army recruited young Timorese. But the Timorese answered calls from the Front and mutinied to join FRETILIN. In 1983 a ceasefire was signed between FRETILIN commander in chief Xanana Gusmão and head of the expeditionary corps Colonel Purwanto. President Suharto did not recognize the agreement and guerrilla warfare continued.

[12]   In 1988, rapprochement between FRETILIN and the TDU culminated in the creation of a joint Nationalist Convergence and Gusmão was confirmed as commander in chief of the liberation army. This body was instrumental in Portugal, actively raising the Timorese question with the European Parliament and the European Commission (EC). Europe rejected Indonesian occupation and backed Maubere self-rule along with a negotiated solution to the conflict.

[13]   In October 1989 the UN Human Rights Sub-commission approved a motion condemning Indonesian occupation and repression in East Timor. When Pope John Paul II visited Dili that month a group of youths unrolled a FRETILIN banner 20 meters from the platform where he was leading Mass. Around 13,000 of the

80,000 people present at the open-air mass were members of the Indonesian security forces, and students shouting anti-occupation slogans were stopped immediately.

[14]   Timorese families were forced to hang a list of household members' names on their doors so that occupation forces could check who was present at any time of day or night. Thousands of Maubere women were given compulsory sterilization. Tetum, the national language, was banned from schools, and the Indonesian authorities applied transmigration policies, bringing in migrants, aimed at reducing the Maubere people to a minority within their own country. Mass graves proved that large-scale execution was another strategy used by the Indonesian occupiers.

[15]   On November 12 1991, a large peaceful funeral procession accompanying the remains of a young student who had been killed was turned into a bloodbath when the army machine-gunned the crowd, killing at least 50 and leaving countless people injured. When the Portuguese Government heard the news they called on the EC to cut trade with Indonesia - which had a preferential trade agreement - and call a UN Security Council meeting. Portugal produced veiled criticism of the body for not confronting Indonesia and acting as it had when Iraq invaded Kuwait in August 1990.

[16]   In late 1991, claims came to light in Portugal that Jakarta and Canberra had signed a contract with 12 companies for the extraction of a billion barrels of crude oil in the Timor Sea. This list of companies was headed by Royal Dutch Shell (British and Dutch capital) and the US Chevron company. These were followed by six Australian companies, Japan's Nippon Oil and the transnationals Phillips Petroleum, Marathon and the Enterprise Oil Company. Opposition leaders accused the companies' home countries of collaborating with Jakarta in playing down the genocide and silencing the international press for the benefit of their own economic interests.

[17]   In December 1996, exiled activist José Ramos Horta and Catholic bishop Carlos Filipe Ximenes Belo received the Nobel Peace Prize in Oslo. Indonesian authorities

planned to boycott the ceremony, but the problem of East Timor hit the headlines all around the world.

[18] Suharto's resignation in Jakarta, in June 1998 and his replacement by Bacharuddin Jusuf Habibie acted las a catalyst for instability on the island. Months of violence forced thousands of Timorese to leave the country, seeking refuge in the west of the island and hundreds died. Habibie announced a plan to give East Timor greater autonomy and a date was set for a referendum.

[19] The referendum was finally held on August 30 1999, amidst a campaign of violence by Indonesian paramilitaries, backed by some of the army. There was a 98 per cent turn out to vote, and 78.5 per cent of these wanted independence. This result was met by a fresh wave of paramilitary violence.

[20] Following discussion with Jakarta, the UN decided to send a peace mission headed by Australian troops. This force (known as Interfet) arrived in Dili two weeks after the referendum, ousting paramilitaries from the capital and surrounding areas, and setting up posts along the frontier. Interfet consisted of more than 3,000 troops, including British and New Zealand soldiers. Sovereignty was finally handed over on October 25.

[21] The UN made Sergio Vieira de Melo head of the Timor Transition Authority. Vieira created a 15-member Consultative Council, which included Gusmão. In February 2000, Interfet ceded control of large areas of the territory to the Transition Authority. Most of the troops remained the same, but they were put under Vieira's control.

[22] In March 2000, Indonesia and the UN stated that those responsible for the violence in August and September 1999 - which caused the death of around 1,000 people and the flight of 200,000 people to West Timor - must be tried for their crimes. In late February the Aitarak leaders- one of the pro-Indonesian paramilitary groups - had a meeting with military leaders and FALINTIL (Forças Armadas de Libertaçao Nacional de Timor Leste, pro independence guerrilla leaded by Xanana Gusmão) politicians in Singapore. The refugee issue was mentioned at the meeting - there are still some 90,000 in Indonesian territory - as were paths to reconciliation.

[23] The United Nations evacuated all human rights workers in August, after three of them were killed by pro-Jakarta militias. Meanwhile the Indonesian Red Cross office in Kupang said terrorist attacks were preventing it from providing aid to the 120,000 refugees in the western part of the island.

[24] In August 2001, FRETILIN won the parliamentary elections with 57 per cent of the vote, taking 55 of the 88 seats in the Assembly. This new body would draw up the Constitution and become the first parliament when East Timor proclaimed independence on May 20 2002. The Democratic Party came second with nine per cent of the vote and seven seats. There was a 91.3 per cent turn out. In September, Mari Alkatiri, of FRETILIN was sworn in as chief minister.

[25] In January 2002, East Timor inaugurated the Truth and Reconciliation Commission (TRC) to investigate atrocities committed by the Indonesian forces during the 25 years of occupation. In Vieira's words, the TRC would give an 'official hearing' to the population's complaints, recognizing past suffering and providing an opportunity for genuine and lasting reconciliation between victim and persecutors. However, no amnesty was offered to those admitting crimes like murder or rape. These cases would be transferred to the regular courts meaning the criminals could be tried. Between 100,000 and 200,000 Timorese were thought to have died in the first years of the occupation, many through starvation or disease.

[26] Also in January 2002, Jakarta officially inaugurated a human rights court to try military officers and others for atrocities committed in East Timor following the 1999 pro-independence vote there. Indonesia had been under international pressure to try at least 18 military and paramilitary leaders accused of encouraging pro-Indonesian forces in East Timor to commit murder.

[27] In February 2002, the assembly approved a draft Constitution for the country to adopt on formal independence. The project divided the authorities into executive, legislative and judicial bodies and stipulated that the military must be politically neutral. The document also stated that the predominantly Catholic nation would have no state religion, and press freedoms would be guaranteed. After long debate, Portuguese and Tetum were designated official languages, while English and Bahasa Indonesia would be used as working languages.

[28] The same month, Indonesia and the UN administration in East Timor signed two agreements - with a third expected to be settled soon - in order to 'smooth' relations between the two countries after East Timorese independence. The two parties reached agreement in a meeting in Bali, Indonesia, which included measures to facilitate the displacement of people across the frontier between East Timor and the western half of the island.

[29] Xanana Gusmão won the presidential elections in April with 82.7 per cent of the vote, while his only rival, Francisco Xavier do Amaral took 17.3 per cent of the vote. The turn-out totaled 86.3 per cent, and Gusmão was sworn in on May 20. Shortly after this, Gusmão met with Indonesian President Megawati Sukarnoputri in Jakarta, and offered her a personal invitation to the independence celebrations in East Timor.

[30] In early May, a UN Delopment Program report revealed that after independence East Timor would be the poorest country in Asia and that it would rank among the 20 poorest nations of the world. At present, most Timorese depend on subsistence fishing and agriculture. The country has no industry and practically no exportable products. Per capita GDP stood at $478 in early May and half the population earn less than 55 cents per day. According to the report, income from the gas fields in the Timor Sea could total $180 million per year from 2006, and the management of these funds will be enormously important in the nation achieving economic success.

[31] That same month, East Timor presented international lenders with a multimillion dollar development plan for its first years of independence. Timor wanted lenders to cover a budget deficit of $90 million over the next three years. The call for aid came at a conference hosted by the World Bank and the UN in Dili, with representatives from 27 countries and multilateral organizations. Gusmão, Alkatiri and Foreign Minister Ramos Horta attended the conference. ∎

PROFILE

ENVIRONMENT

Located between Australia and Indonesia, East Timor comprises the eastern portion of Timor Island, the dependency of Oecusse, located on the northwestern part of the island, the island of Atauro to the North, and the islet of Yaco to the East. Of volcanic origin, the island is mountainous and covered with dense rainforest. The climate is tropical with heavy rainfall, which accounts for the extensive river system. The southern region is flat and suitable for farming. Agriculture is the basis of its export-oriented economy, and copra, coffee, rice, cotton, tobacco and sandal are its main crops.

SOCIETY

Peoples: The Maubere people are descended from Melanesian and Malayan populations. In 1975 there was a Chinese minority of 20,000 as well as 4,000 Portuguese. Amnesty International estimates that 210,000 people have died as a result of the Indonesian occupation. There are 6,000 Maubere refugees in Australia and 1,500 in Portugal.
Religions: Most of the population follows traditional religions. 50-75 per cent are Catholic.
Languages: Tetum is the national language. There are some 40 dialects. Indonesian occupation had banned the use of these languages in education, and virtually all the teaching is done in Bahasa Indonesia, the main Indonesian language. This situation was reversed after Independence. A minority also speaks Portuguese.
Political Parties: Revolutionary Front for the Independence of East Timor (FRETILIN); Democratic Party; Social-Democratic Party; Timorese Social-Democratic Association; Timorese Democratic Union; Nationalist Timorese Party; Klibur Oan Timor Asuwain (KOTA); People's Party of Timor (PPT); Christian-Democratic Party (PDC); Socialist Party of Timor.

THE STATE

Official Name: República de Timor Leste.
Capital: Dili 65,000 people (1999).
Other cities: Dare 17,500 people; Baucau 14,500 (2000).
Government: Xanana Gusmão, President elected in April 2002, took office on 20 May that year, when the country became formally independent. That same day the Transitional Authority imposed by UN in 1999 ceased functioning. Mari Alkatiri, Chief Minister since September 2001. Legislature: 88-member Parliament.
National Holiday: November 28, Independence Day (1975).

Ecuador

Population:	13,112,000 (2002)
Land area:	276,840 SQ KM
Capital:	Quito
Currency:	US dollar
Language:	Spanish and Quechua

Ecuador

The territory now known as Ecuador has been inhabited at least since 2500 BC. The region was largely a border zone with influences of the Nazca, Tiahuanaco-Huari, Chibcha and also Mexica civilizations, among others. It has been suggested that there was contact with peoples of the Pacific, Japanese or Polynesians (see box 'Melanesians and Polynesians'), though there is still much debate on that point. It is known that by the 14th century AD the territory was divided among several warring states that spoke different languages. In the early 15th century, the Cara nation, led by the Shiri dynasty, expanded to the north and central Andean foothills. The Cara settled in the Quito kingdom, which was the largest unit of a confederation that left no historical records. In the same era, both the Chimu nation, originating in Peru's northern coastal zone, and the Inca empire began to exert pressure on the Cara and other peoples settled in the region.

[2]   In 1478, Inca Topa Yupanqui united the agricultural peoples who inhabited the territory within the Tahuantinsuyu (Inca empire). Within a few years the northern region of the Quechua territory, of which Quito was the center, acquired great economic importance and became the commercial and cultural center of a great civilization. But the rivalry for succession between Atahualpa (from Quito) and Huascar (from Cuzco) weakened the power of the Empire.

[3]   The Spanish conquistadors, under the command of Sebastián de Benalcázar, took advantage of the situation to usurp the kingdom of Quito in 1534. In the first era of the colonial period, the territory formed part of the Viceroyalty of Peru and was known as the Real Audiencia, or Royal District of Quito.

[4]   On the coastal plains the Spanish found very few indigenous peoples to serve as their slaves, and that, along with the undesirable climate, led the area to be left mostly uninhabited. It was a similar case in the Andean mountains, where the native South Americans were openly hostile to the Spanish authorities and where only missionaries ventured. The colonial administration wielded power over semi-autonomous indigenous communities and administrative and religious centers like Quito, Ambato and Cuenca. Crude textiles were the only industry of the Royal District of Quito at the time.

[5]   With the reorganization carried out by the Bourbons in 1717, Quito was transferred to the Viceroyalty of Nueva Granada, which comprised present-day Ecuador, Colombia, Panama and Venezuela. In 1809 there was an uprising against the authority of the Crown. In 1822, the armies of Simón Bolívar and Antonio José de Sucre invaded from Colombia, in support of the patriot rebels. On May 24 of that year, in Pichincha, near Quito, Sucre defeated the Spanish and won the emancipation of Ecuador, which was thus incorporated into Bolívar's Greater Colombia scheme.

[6]   In 1830, the Royal District of Quito seceded from Greater Colombia and adopted the name Republic of Ecuador.

[7]   In 1895, the Liberal Revolution nationalized Church property, but the large landowners were not affected. Leader Eloy Alfaro was assassinated in 1912 and the country came under the economic influence of the British Empire. In 1914 Ecuador ceded to Colombia the territory between river Caquetá and river Putumayo. In 1916, the elected president - the liberal Alfredo Baquerizo Moreno - promulgated the eight-hour working day.

[8]   A military coup led by young officers paved the way for a new reformist period in 1925, but the regime did not survive the world economic crisis of 1929. A period of instability began and saw 23 different presidents from 1925 to 1948.

[9]   In 1941, after a brief war with Peru, Ecuador was forced to renounce its claims to sovereignty over an extensive area of the Amazon. The Peace Protocol signed in 1942 in Rio de Janeiro, with Argentina, Brazil, Chile and the United States as guarantors, established the border between the two countries, but much of it was not demarcated because it crosses inaccessible areas.

[10]   A popular uprising in 1944 ousted President Carlos Arroyo, ushering in a populist government led by José María Velazco Ibarra and consisted of conservatives, communists and socialists, under the name of Democratic Alliance. The Cold War made it impossible for this alliance to continue and soon the left became the target of persecution. In 1962, under pressure from the United States, the government of Carlos Arosemena broke off diplomatic relations with Cuba.

[11]   In the early 1970s, bananas, coffee and cocoa exports represented 80 per cent of the country's revenues. In 1972, Ecuador began to export petroleum, which became the leading sector of the economy. That same year, the political situation changed, as veteran populist leader Velazco Ibarra was ousted for the fourth time by the armed forces. Under the government of General Guillermo Rodríguez Lara, the country joined OPEC, the state purchased 25 per cent of Texaco-Gulf shares and asserted its rights over the 200 miles of territorial waters when faced with US pressure for fishing interests, leading to what was dubbed the 'tuna war'.

[12]   Jaime Roldós, nominated by the Convergence of People's Forces (CPF) and the People's Democratic Party, became president in August 1979. Ecuador renewed diplomatic relations with Cuba, China and Albania. The Government also initiated a program aimed at integrating marginalized rural and urban populations into the

WORKERS

1998/2000

UNEMPLOYMENT: 11.5%
LABOR FORCE AS % OF TOTAL:

- FEMALE: 28%   MALE: 72%

1994/97

EMPLOYMENT DISTRIBUTION:

F
M

SERVICES	F: 83%	M: 64%
INDUSTRY	F: 16%	M: 26%
AGRICULTURE	F: 2%	M: 10%

LAND USE

DEFORESTATION: 1.6% annual (1990/95)

1993

- FOREST & WOODLAND: 55%
- ARABLE: 5.7%
- OTHER: 39.3%

economy. However, it encountered a hostile Congress, as well as opposition from the United States, which did not take kindly to its human rights policies and its antagonism to the dictatorships in the southern cone.

[13] Toward the end of January 1981, the Five Day War broke out between Ecuador and Peru, with skirmishes along borders which had not been clearly delineated by the 1942 Protocol.

[14] In May of the same year, Roldós died in a suspicious airplane accident, whereupon Vice President, Osvaldo Hurtado took office. The following year was marked by the most severe social crisis since the military had left power. It was triggered, on the one hand, by the application of IMF formulas, and on the other, by an overt drive to build up military power to achieve parity with the Peruvian armed forces.

[15] In the following decade, the Durán Ballén government promoted privatization of state companies and rigid structural adjustment; however, the economy did not improve, a factor which aided the populist Abdala Bucaram into power. He was later deposed following massive price rises on essential services (and after being declared 'insane' by parliament).

[16] In 1990 the indigenous people's movement erupted onto the political stage for the first time. The Confederation of Indigenous Nationalities of Ecuador (CONAIE) campaigned for the 1997 Constitution to recognize the pluri-cultural and multi-ethnic nature of the State (and, therefore, the right of indigenous people and Afro-Ecuadorians to participate in equality), and there were seven large demonstrations. The last of these ended in an uprising that ousted Bucaram's successor, economist Jamil Mahuad. In his fight to reduce inflation and public spending and to increase fiscal income, he had promoted measures which were widely opposed. Annual inflation reached 60 per cent and on January 5, 2000, the sucre fell to 26,000 to the dollar.

[17] Amidst nation-wide demonstrations, Mahuad announced the economy would be pegged to the dollar, precipitating an indigenous uprising. Parliament and Government buildings were invaded, with special troops deployed to guard the buildings joining the protesters. A government council formed by representatives of the army, judicial power, indigenous people and unions, was well received by the population. However, pressure from abroad, especially the United States, led to the arrest of the insurrectionist soldiers. Mahuad was replaced by Vice-President Gustavo Noboa, an Opus Dei (right-wing Catholic organization) militant, who implemented the dollarisation of the economy in April 2000.

[18] The Paris Club of rich countries did not recognize CONAIE as a valid voice when it requested that Ecuador's debt be cancelled in return for resources being spent on developing production, health and education, with public and local government participation.

[19] In 2000, the Government signed an agreement with UNICEF aiming to reduce the level of teenage pregnancy in the country - the highest in Latin America. For adolescents in rural areas, a poverty allowance of $10 is paid to single mothers. Some 49 per cent of women who reported having an abortion in 1999 had no subsequent medical attention.

[20] A year previously, also with UNESCO support, the Government had proposed modifications to the adult education system and a redefinition of training offered in the nation's 1,700 occupational training centers, aiming for the creation of small companies.

[21] Luis Maldonado, former CONAIE member, was appointed Social Welfare minister in 2001, becoming the first Indian to hold a cabinet post outside indigenous affairs. ■

PROFILE

ENVIRONMENT

The country is divided into three natural regions: the coast, the mountains and the rainforest. Due to the influence of the cold Humboldt current, the climate of the coastal region is mild. More than half of the population lives along the coast, where cash crops of bananas, cocoa, rice and coffee are grown. In the highlands, extending between two separate ranges of the Andes, the climate varies according to altitude, and subsistence crops are grown. In the eastern Amazon region, recent oil finds supply internal demand, leaving a small surplus for export. The Colón or Galapagos archipelago belongs to Ecuador. The country also lays claim to 200,000 sq km of Amazon territory presently controlled by Peru, as well as the air space over its territory, where communication satellites are stationed. In the coastal region, 95 per cent of the woodlands have been felled. Soil depletion has increased by 30 per cent over the past 25 years. Oil companies cause serious contamination.

SOCIETY

Peoples: Most Ecuadoreans are descended from the Quechua people who made up the kingdom of Quito. The current population is mainly mestizos, the result of inter-marriage with the Spaniards and their descendants, in addition to descendants of African slaves. There are nine indigenous nationalities: Huaorani, Shuar, Achar, Siona-Secoya, Cofan, Quechua, Tsachila and Chachi. There are over 1.5 million Quechua living in the inter-Andean valley.
Religions: Mainly Catholic.
Languages: Spanish (official), although 40 per cent of the population speaks Quechua; several indigenous languages.
Political Parties: The Social Christian Party (PSC); the United Republican Party (PUR), conservative; the Ecuadorean Roldosista Party; the Democratic Left, social democratic, affiliated to the Socialist International; the Conservative Party; People's Democracy (DP); the Christian Democratic Union; the Democratic People's Movement; the Ecuadorean Socialist Party; the Convergence of Popular Forces; the Radical Liberal Party; the Broad Front of the Left; the Radical Alfarista Front; the National Patriotic Front, of Frank Vargas; the Ecuadorean People's Revolutionary Action; the National Liberation Party.
Social Organizations: The major union federations are the Ecuadorean Central Organization of Class Unions (CEDOC), and the Central Organization of Ecuadorean Workers (CTE) coordinated with the United Workers' Front (FUT). In the last few years the Confederation of Indigenous Nationalities of Ecuador (CONAIE) has gained importance; the National Federation of Small Producers (FNPA), University Students Federation of Ecuador (FEUE).

THE STATE

Official Name: República del Ecuador.
Administrative divisions: 22 Provinces.
Capital: Quito 1,679,000 people (1999).
Other cities: Guayaquil 2,627,900 people; Cuenca 227,400; Machala 211,300 (2000).
Government: Gustavo Noboa Bejarano, President since January 2000. The Constitution approved by plebiscite in 1978 established a presidential system and granted the right to vote for illiterate people for the first time in 1984.
National Holiday: May 24, Independence (1822); August 10, First Shout of Independence of Quito (1809).
Armed Forces: 57,000 troops (conscripts). 100,000 reserves (1996).
Other: 200 Coast Guard and 6 coastal patrol units (1993).

Tahuantinsuyo: the Inca empire

The Tahuantinsuyo or Inca empire had a brilliant, if brief, life - its evolution being interrupted by the Spanish invasion of 1532, at a time when it was weakened by in-fighting. The empire once covered almost all of the Andes region.

The beginning of Tahuantinsuyo is estimated around the year 1300, its expansion around 1450 and its end in 1532. Its founders, probably emigrants from lake Titicaca led tribes from the Cuzco valley in order to unify all of the Andes region. If we refer to current political divisions, Tahuantinsuyo included a small part of southern Colombia, the high plateau and desert coast of Peru, the high plateau of Bolivia, northwest Argentina and all of the dry north and fertile lands of central Chile up to the Maule river.

The empire covered two major areas: the mountains or high plateau, where Tahuantinsuyo was founded, and the tropical, marshy and humid coast of Ecuador, as well as the deserted and rainless coast of Peru and Chile. The Incas failed to conquer the jungle.

Two north-south roads were the backbone of communications. The first, along the coast, measured 4,050 kilometers and the second, through the mountains, 5,180 kilometers. Estimates of the Empire's population vary. Most experts calculate it at between 10 and 16 million. Recent research has placed the figure at over 12 million inhabitants, which would give a population density of 13 inhabitants per square kilometer. By comparison, population density in the Roman Empire's Asian provinces under Augustus amounted to 30 and to 10 in the European provinces.

Some experts claim Tahuantinsuyo had organized armies of 200,000 to 300,000 soldiers, which does not seem far-fetched if we accept the 13 million population figure. The Roman empire had an army of 300,000 in the late second century.

QOSQO, THE CENTRE OF THE WORLD

Like other great empires, the Incas built upon knowledge acquired from previous cultures, such as the Chavin, Tiahuanaco-Huari, Nazca, Moche and Chimu. The Incas also stood out for their political and military efficiency, as well as their economic planning and social control. Cuzco (Qozqo to its founders), the capital of the Empire, had a population of 200,000 in 1532. At the time, only London and Naples in Europe were larger. Antwerp, Amsterdam, Lisbon, Rome and Seville had around 100,000 inhabitants each.

Located in an Andean valley blessed with fertile land and a beautiful landscape, Cuzco was specially developed to become a capital. With an area of some six square kilometers, the city had the shape of a puma, a sacred animal for the Incas. As centre of the empire, Cuzco was thought of as the intersection point of a sundial - Antisuyo was called the northeast quadrant, Contisuyo the southwest, Collasuyo the southeast and Chinchaysuyo the northwest, according to a tetramerous model.

A solar calendar was followed, which dictated agriculture and religious ceremonies, and which provided a mythical chronology.

It was believed history was ruled by a pattern of four pasts, each one with its own creation and a sudden violent end. The fifth age belonged to the time of Tahuantinsuyo and would also end in cosmic extermination.

SOCIAL STRUCTURE

The social structure of Tahuantinsuyo resembled a pyramid, with multiple rigid classes. Mobility from one class to another was exceptional and individual status was preordained. There were three distinct social classes.

The aristocracy included a reigning family group and descendants of monarchs, the clergy, military bosses, intellectuals and senior officials. At the summit was the *Sapainca*, Son of the Sun.

The middle class, the *Jatunrunakuna*, was a large mass of inhabitants which helped to support the state apparatus. Lastly, the *Yanakuna*, compared by some with Roman plebeians, who were relegated to menial jobs.

The monarch was not a mere autocrat, but a type of high priest and father, who had to conduct himself according to a code set down by tradition.

There were nine kinds of crimes: of status, high treason, against religion, against the administration and official duties, against taxes and property, and against life and health. Three principles were to be followed by everyone to prevent such crimes: *ama suwa*, *ama qella* and *ama llulla* (do not be a thief, a liar, or idle).

Everywhere, the empire was strictly organized. The population was ordered into communities (*ayllus*) according to the decimal system, ranging from smaller to larger units. Labour was divided into age categories, from childhood to old age, with an additional division for the disabled.

A TRULY AMERICAN ACHIEVEMENT

Capital was accumulated, mainly in the form of agricultural products, and its concentration enabled it to be used for social purposes. The system was based on the surplus production of the community.

The state and religious organization were maintained by this surplus. Planning was a key feature of the state.

One-third of arable land was allocated for religious purposes, another to the monarch and the rest to the community. The use of the land was distributed once a year among the members of the ayllu.

Artisanal production also had a significant role. The most important skills were looming, metallurgy, pottery and woodcarving. State, communal and private property co-existed in a unique way.

Western observers have classified Tahuantinsuyo in different ways: primitive communism, socialism, totalitarianism, collectivism, paternalism, a softer version of oriental despotism, a mix of theocracy, monarchy and socialism, etc.

However, a close analysis shows that the Inca empire did not fit in with Old World paradigms because, although certain features were similar on the surface to those European contexts, it did not wholly resemble any of them.

In spite of its short existence and of the efforts to underrate it, Tahuantinsuyo was a vast and original achievement of the South American peoples, and has earned its place amongst the major human cultures. ∎

Egypt

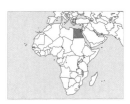

Population: 70,278,000 (2002)
Land area: 995,450 SQ KM
Capital: Cairo (Al-Qahirah)
Currency: Pound
Language: Arabic

Misr

Six thousand years ago, a civilization began to form in the Nile valley (Nahr-an-Nil) and, through its persistent struggle to control the river's periodic flooding, it developed into a centralized state. Around 6000 BC, Pharaoh Menes, from Upper Egypt, united the two kingdoms - Upper and Lower Egypt - that coexisted for some time.

[2] A powerful empire arose in the third millennium BC, though there were occasional lapses in the central control as other powers emerged and the territory was embroiled in civil war. The Ancient Empire saw its demise with the collapse of the central authority during the Sixth Dynasty, due in large part to widespread famine. During the period of the 12th Dynasty the model of the Ancient Empire was reinstated.

[3] The Third Dynasty developed the practice of constructing monumental tombs for the monarchs, the Pharaohs. These monuments or pyramids, also built for members of the élite, and the funeral ceremonies of the poor were closely linked to the belief in life after death, a notion inherited from the first Egyptian kingdoms. The pyramids and the decorated walls of the pharaonic tombs, the creation of a complex writing system and broad knowledge of medicine and agriculture are just a few examples of the level of civilization achieved by Egyptian society.

[4] Egypt reached its height of power, wealth and territorial dominance around 1500 BC. Reconverted into a military state, Egypt launched a series of campaigns to win control of Palestine, Syria and the north of the Euphrates. Territorial expansion led to the development of a complex diplomatic system of alliances and treaties.

[5] In the last millennium BC, the decline of this remarkable civilization opened the way to foreign Pharaohs (Libyan and Sudanese dynasties). Toward the end of the 20th dynasty, the weakening of the Pharaohs led to renewed division between Upper and Lower Egypt and, after the Persian Cambises deposed the Pharaoh, the territory formed part of other empires (Persian, Greek and Roman).

[6] During the period of Greco-Roman domination, Alexandria (Al-Iskandariyah) was one of the most influential cultural centers in the classical world, and its famous library was the largest until it was burned down under the Roman emperor Aurelian in the late 3rd century AD. It brought together the most outstanding philosophers, scientists and scholars of the era. In 642, when the Arabs conquered the country, little remained of its highly developed past and the Egyptians adopted Islam and the Arabian language.

[7] Three centuries later, under the government of the Fatimid Caliphs, the new capital, Cairo (Al-Qahirah), became one of the major intellectual centers in the Islamic world and scholars, particularly African Muslims, were attracted by its university.

[8] Between the 10th and 15th centuries, Egypt benefited from its geographic location, becoming the trade center between Asia and the Mediterranean. The Venetians and Genoese came to trade here, and even the constant warfare provoked by the European Crusades in Palestine, in the 11th to 13th centuries, did not stop active trade.

[9] Once the Crusaders were driven out, it seemed that Egypt would naturally become the center of the ancient Arab empire. However the Sultanate of the Ottoman Turks was the rising power in the Islamic world at the beginning of the 16th century, and it soon conquered Egypt. The opening of the sea route between Europe and the Far East had already put an end to Egypt's previous trade monopoly, reliant on its dominion over the Red Sea, and Egypt had begun its economic decline.

[10] Until the 19th century, Turkish domination was little more than nominal and the real power lay in the hands of Mameluke leaders. In 1805, Muhammad Ali, an Albanian military leader, took power. He forcibly eliminated local Mameluke leaders, established a centralized regime, reorganized the army, declared a state monopoly on foreign trade of sugarcane and cotton and achieved increasing autonomy from the Sultan of Istanbul laying the foundations of a modern economy.

[11] The economy was poorly managed by Muhammad Ali's successors, the crisis deepened and dependency on Europe increased. In 1874, Egypt was forced to sell all its shares in the Suez Canal, built as a joint Egyptian-French project between 1860 and 1870, to pay its debts to the British.

[12] The situation continued to deteriorate, loans piled up and in 1879 the creditors imposed a Bureau of Public Debt formed by three ministers, one English, one French and one Egyptian. This bureau assumed the management of the country's finances.

[13] This degree of interference awakened an intense nationalistic reaction, supported by the army. That year, the military overthrew Muhammad Ali's successor Khedive Ismail, forcing his son, Tawfiq, to expel the foreign ministers and appoint a nationalist cabinet. The colonial power reacted promptly: in 1882 an Anglo-French fleet landed English troops in Alexandria, seizing military control of the country.

[14] The occupation was 'legalized' in 1914, when Egypt was formally declared a protectorate. The British installed King Fuad II on the throne. This situation continued until 1922, when an Egyptian committee in London negotiated what turned out to be only nominal independence. More steps towards independence were taken in 1936 as Fuad's son Faruk took the throne on his father's death. But as before, the British retained control.

WORKERS

1990/2000
UNEMPLOYMENT: 8.1%
LABOR FORCE AS % OF TOTAL:

■ FEMALE: 30%   ■ MALE: 70%

1994/97
EMPLOYMENT DISTRIBUTION:

F
M

■ SERVICES	F: 48%	M: 43%
■ INDUSTRY	F: 9%	M: 25%
■ AGRICULTURE	F: 42%	M: 32%

PUBLIC EXPENDITURE

1999

DEFENSE 9.3%
SOCIAL 31.6%

MATERNAL MORTALITY

1985/99

Per 100,000 live births

170

LITERACY

2000

55%

FOOD DEPENDENCY

1999

23%

---

[15] During World War II, Egypt was used as a British military base again. Anti-colonial feeling reached its height in 1948, when the state of Israel was created in Palestine.

[16] Egypt and other Arab nations launched an unsuccessful war against the new state, and the frustration of defeat brought about massive demonstrations against the royal government.

[17] Against a background of widespread government corruption, a nationalist group known as the 'Free Officials' was formed within the Egyptian Army, led by General Mohammed Naguib and Colonel Gamal Abdel Nasser.

[18] On July 23 1952 this group ousted King Faruk and, in June 1953, proclaimed a Republic. Three years later, Nasser became President.

[19] The new regime declared itself nationalist and socialist, deciding to improve the living conditions of the *fellahin*, the country's impoverished peasants. Land reform was started, limiting the landowners' monopoly of the majority of the land.

[20] Nasser gave priority to the construction of the Aswan dam, one of the world's largest dam projects.

The construction was carried out by the Soviet Union, after the Western powers had refused to take it on. The dam, which had been hailed as the key to the country's industrialization and 'development', in fact caused serious environmental disruption.

[21] In 1955, Nasser was one of the leading organizers of the Bandung Conference, a forerunner neutralist Afro-Asian movement which preceded the Movement of Non-Aligned Countries. Twenty-nine Afro-Asian countries condemned colonialism, racial discrimination and nuclear armament.

[22] In October 1956, after the nationalization of the Suez Canal, French, British and Israeli troops invaded Egypt. The Government responded by distributing weapons to civilians. A diplomatic battle was also launched; as a result of UN intervention and joint US-Soviet disapproval, France, Britain and Israel were forced to withdraw and the Canal finally came under Egyptian control.

[23] On February 1 1958, the union of Egypt and Syria was officially announced, under the name of the United Arab Republic (UAR). This lasted until September 1961, when Syria decided to separate from Egypt, although Egypt continued to call itself the United Arab Republic.

[24] After Nasser's re-election in 1965, Egypt gave high priority to the conflict with Israel. However, its attempt to economically paralyze Israel by blockading the Gulf of Aqaba failed during the Arab-Israeli conflict, the 'Six-Day War' of June 1967. This ended in another defeat of the Arab countries - Egypt, Syria and Jordan - when Israeli forces occupied the Sinai Peninsula, the Gaza strip, the West Bank, and the Syrian Golan Heights. The cost of the war aggravated Egypt's financial problems and only Soviet aid prevented its total collapse.

[25] Nasser died in 1970, and Vice-President Anwar Sadat, a member of the right wing of Nasser's Arab Socialist Party, took his place. Sadat put the *infitah* into practice. This was a government plan that meant an opening to Western influence, the de-nationalization of the Egyptian economy and the end of the one-party system. Furthermore, the new Government broke off relations with

the Soviet Union and US economic and military aid flowed into Egypt.

[26] In 1973, Egyptian troops crossed the Suez Canal to bring to an end Israeli occupation of Sinai, beginning the fourth Arab-Israeli war. The Egyptians succeeded, and their success resulted in OPEC substantially increasing oil prices. This move did not produce the desired effect, and Israel retained the rest of the occupied territories.

[27] Substantial price rises and unemployment worsened the living conditions of workers and resulted in massive anti-government demonstrations in 1976 and 1977. Peasants rebelled against the land redistribution of 1952, and the Islamic parties began to conspire openly against Sadat, accusing him of paving the road for a new period of foreign domination.

[28] Sadat's visit to Jerusalem in November 1977 raised a wave of protest in the Arab world. The process of rapprochement with Israel reached its apex in March 1979, with the signing of the Camp David Agreement, wherein the US negotiated the return of Sinai to Egypt. From then on, Egypt became the main beneficiary of US military aid, aimed at turning the country into the new US watchdog in the Arab World, as Shah Pahlevi of Iran had recently been deposed.

[29] In October 1981, Sadat was killed in a conspiracy organized by sectors of the military opposed to infitah and the repression of fundamentalist Islamic movements. Vice-President Hosni Mubarak became President on October 14.

[30] Repression, corruption and increasing poverty led to widespread popular discontent. To distract public attention Mubarak ordered an inquiry into the wealth accumulated by the Sadat family. He also extended further concessions to foreign companies.

[31] There were some improvements in Egyptian foreign affairs during 1984. Egyptian diplomacy managed to overcome the most adverse reactions to the Camp David agreements. Their new position on the Palestinian question argued that any fair settlement of the Middle East crisis had to contemplate the rights of the Palestinian people and that Arab solidarity was 'the only way to recover the usurped rights'.

PROFILE

ENVIRONMENT

99 per cent of the population live in the Nile valley and the delta although this constitutes only 30 per cent of the land. The remaining land is covered by desert except for a few isolated oases. The floods of the Nile set a pattern for the country's economic life thousands of years ago. There are several dams, the major one being the Aswan dam in the south. This has enabled farmers to add new crops such as cotton and sugar cane to the traditional crops; wheat, rice and corn. The hydroelectric power supply, together with the northeastern oil wells, in the Sinai Peninsula, favored industrial development and the disproportionate growth of the cities. Problems which remain unsolved include the unchecked growth of the cities, which has swallowed up fertile lands; erosion of the soil and the use of fertilizers; and water pollution.

SOCIETY

Peoples: Egyptians are Arabs of Hamite origin with East Asian communities in the north and central regions and African groups in the Upper Nile area. The ethnic legacy of peoples that have passed through the territory are apparent, from the Romans and Greeks, to the Turks and Circasians, and more recently, to the English and French. The Berber minority lives mainly in the oases. The Coptic minority, are ethnically similar to the rest, but with a different religion. Armenian immigration and from other countries, including two million illegal refugees from southern Sudan.

Religions: Islamic, mostly Sunni. Orthodox Coptics (10 per cent) and other Christian churches.

Languages: Arab (official); English and French are used by an educated élite; Nobiin; Berber; Coptic (for religious matters).

Political Parties: National Democratic Party; Progressive National Unionist Party; New Delegation Party; Liberal Party; Nasserist Party. The Muslim Brotherhood is a social movement, but also a political party.

Social Organizations: The Egyptian Labor Federation is the only central labor organization, and the Union of Egyptian Students represents the university students.

THE STATE

Official Name: Jumhuriyah Misr al-'Arabiyah.

Administrative divisions: 26 provinces.

Capital: Cairo (Al-Qahirah) 10,345,000 people (1999).

Other cities: Alexandria (Al-Iskandariyah) 3,723,000 people; Al-Jizah 2,485,040; Subra al-Haymah 974,000 (2000).

Government: Presidentialist Republic. Hosni Mubarak, President since October 1981, re-elected in 1999. Atef Ebeid, Prime Minister since October 1999. Single-chamber Legislative: the Majlis (People's Assembly) has 454 members, of which 10 are named by the President.

National Holiday: July 23, Revolution Day (1952).

Armed Forces: 440,000 (incl. 270,000 conscripts).

Other: Coast Guard, National Guard and Border Guards, 74,000.

EXTERNAL DEBT

2000

PER CAPITA

US$ 427

FOREIGN TRADE

Millions US$ 2000

IMPORTS

22,444

EXPORTS

15,931

STATISTICS

DEMOGRAPHY
Population: 70,278,000 (2002)
Annual growth: 2.1 % (1985-2000)
Estimates for year 2015:
84,425,000 (2000)
Annual growth to year 2015:
1.5 % (2000)
Urban population: 45.2 % (2000)
Urban growth: 2.3 % (2000)
Children per woman: 3.2 (2000)

HEALTH
Life expectancy at birth: 68 years
(2000-2005)
male: 67 years (2000-2005)
female: 70 years (2000-2005)
Maternal mortality: 170 per
100,000 live births (1985/99)
Infant mortality: 37 per 1,000
(2000)
Under-5 child mortality: 43 per
1,000 (2000)
Daily calorie supply: 3,323 per
capita (1999)
202 doctors per 100,000 people
(1996)
Safe water: 97 % (2000)

EDUCATION
Literacy: 55 % (2000)
male: 67 % (2000)
female: 44 % (2000)
School enrolment (net):
Primary total: 86 % (1994/2000)
male: 94 % (1995/99)
female: 89 % (1995/99)
Secondary (gross):
male: 80 % (1995/97)
female: 70 % (1995/97)
Tertiary (gross): 39 % (1998)
Primary school teachers: one for
every 23 pupils (1998)

COMMUNICATIONS
35 newspapers (1997), 339 radios
(1997), 189 TV sets (2000) and 86
main telephone lines (2000) per
1,000 people
Books: 5 new titles per 100,000
people (1992/94)

ECONOMY
Per capita, GDP: $ 3,635 (2000)
Annual growth: 3.1 % (2000)
Annual inflation: 2.7 % (2000)
Consumer price index: 123.7
(2000)
Currency: 4.6 pounds = $ 1
(03/2002)
Cereal imports: 10,144,538 metric
tons (2000)
Food import dependency: 23 %
(1999)
Fertilizer use: 4,191 kg per ha
(1999)
Exports: $ 15,931 million (2000)
Imports: $ 22,444 million (2000)
External debt: $ 28,957 million
(2000); $ 427 per capita (2000)
Debt service: 9.0 % of exports
(1999)
Development aid received: $ 1,579
million (1999); $ 25.2 per capita
(1999); 1.80 % of GNP (1999)

ENERGY
Consumption: 679.4 Kgs of oil
equivalent per capita yearly
(1998); -31.4 % imported (1999)

HDI (ranking/value): 105 / 0.635
(1999)

[32] Between 1980 and 1986 there was a dramatic increase in the role of foreign capital in the national economy and US aid continued to be a very important source of income. The Government received almost $3 billion per year, $1.3 billion of which was spent on defense. The IMF granted a further $1.5 billion loan in October 1986.

[33] In August 1990 Iraqi troops invaded Kuwait; Egypt was among the first Arab countries to condemn the action, sending troops to the Gulf immediately.

[34] When the land offensive started in January 1991, the US announced the cancellation of the Egyptian military debt, which amounted to $7 billion.

[35] In May 1991, the IMF approved a stand-by loan of $372 million to Egypt, conditional on an economic 'structural adjustment plan'. Cairo committed itself to privatizing State-run companies, to eliminating controls on production and investment and to reducing the current fiscal deficit from 21 per cent to 6.5 per cent of the GNP. In order to achieve these goals the government decided to cut back subsidies on food and other staples and to reduce the program of aid for the needy.

[36] On May 15 1991, foreign minister and deputy minister Esmat Abdel Meguid was named the new secretary-general of the Arab League. Coming upon the heels of the return of Arab League headquarters to Cairo (from Tunis) this appointment signified Egypt's recovery of its leadership role within the Arab world.

[37] The escalation of violence from Islamic fundamentalists led the Government to enact an anti-terrorist law and extend for another three years the state of emergency which had been in effect for the past ten years. According to official statistics, this violence caused 175 deaths between February 1992 and August 1993. Thousands of Islamic followers were arrested and in June and July 1993, 15 people were executed.

[38] The ruling National Democratic Party won the 1995 parliamentary elections amidst violence and allegations of fraud.

[39] In July 1996 the Health Minister banned female circumcision - the removal of the clitoris or part of it and/or the sewing together of the vaginal labia - a practice common in some regions of the country.

[40] Attacks by armed Islamic groups continued throughout 1996 and 1997, along with government repression of all such groups, including those opposed to the use of violence, like the Muslim Brotherhood. In early 1998 an estimated 1,251 people had fallen victim to attacks and political killings, whilst the estimated number of political prisoners was between 10,000 and 30,000.

[41] There was heated parliamentary debate in March 1999 over decrees on female circumcision. Some argued that the present law protected the interests of circumcised women, for uncircumcised women have minimal chance of marriage. The ruling provoked resistance in the traditionalist sectors.

[42] In November 2000, the Supreme Court ruled unconstitutional a decree from the Home Ministry that allowed men to prevent their wives from traveling abroad. In March that year, the Government had authorized women to file for divorce, with or without their husband's approval, for reasons of incompatibility. Until then, divorce could only be requested for serious causes, such as domestic violence. However women, on filing for divorce, have to return all money, property and gifts that she received in the marriage and forgo alimony.

[43] Due to domestic and regional pressure, Egypt was forced to resume relations with Iraq, disrupted since the 1991 war. Anti-American and anti-Israeli sentiment had grown among the population after Israel responded violently to the second *intifada* (Palestinian uprising). The existing offices were raised to embassy status, paving the way for the restoration of full diplomatic relations. Likewise, Egypt withdrew its ambassador in Israel in protest for the escalation of violence against Palestinians.

[44] In December, Egypt, Lebanon and Syria signed an agreement to build a pipeline that would carry Egyptian natural gas under the Mediterranean to the Lebanese port of Tripoli, and also to Syria. Another pipeline would take gas to Turkey and the European markets. In March that year, Mubarak and the Presidents of Syria and Jordan had opened a line that connected the power grids of the three countries.

[45] In December 2001, the Cairo museum recovered from Germany - 80 years after it had been stolen - the lower half of Pharaoh Akenaton's sarcophagus, the husband of Nefertiti, who is said had led Egypt to monotheism. Completely covered in gold, the sarcophagus had been discovered in 1907 in the Valley of the Kings. Its base had been stolen and rediscovered 20 years ago, in the private collection of a Swiss collector. The Bavarian government reached an agreement with Cairo, by which the lower part would be returned if the upper part was loaned for exhibition; it attracted some 50,000 visitors.

[46] Although in March 2002 there were recovery signs, the influx of foreign exchange from tourism - one of the country's main sources of income - suffered a strong fall after the terrorist attacks of September 2001 against the US. Egypt had to resort to loans from international organizations to cover its losses.

[47] That same month, Mubarak visited Washington to inform President Bush of his own peace plan for Israel and Palestine. His goal was to promote a summit between the Israeli and Palestinian leaders in the Egyptian resort town of Sharm el-Sheikh. Before starting his trip, Mubarak spoke by phone with Israeli Prime Minister Ariel Sharon, to inform him of the idea. 'We will not solve all issues in a minute, but this meeting can help change the political climate... by showing both of you sitting together', said Mubarak. In the near future Egypt would receive more military assistance than Israel from the US. Egypt's role as a close friend of Palestinian President Yasser Arafat made it the ideal peace mediator.

[48] In April 2002 - a month that commemorates Israeli withdrawal from Egyptian territories in Sinai - Mubarak criticized Israel and accused it of resorting to state terrorism to crush Palestinians and abuse human rights. Likewise, it claimed Israel erased all traces of its crimes, for example in the Jenin refugee camp, and suggested that some international powers - referring to the US - did not honor their international responsibilities, losing all credibility. ∎

El Salvador

Population: 6,520,000 (2002)
Land area: 20,720 SQ KM
Capital: San Salvador
Currency: Dollar, colón
Language: Spanish

El Salvador

The region of El Salvador was inhabited from early times by Chibcha people (Muisca: see Colombia), most of whom were Pipile and Lenca. The Maya also lived within the region, but they were not very influential here.

[2] The Spaniards subdued the Aztecs in Mexico, and subsequently began the conquest of Central America under the leadership of Pedro de Alvarado. In 1525, Alvarado founded the city of El Salvador de Cuscatlan. The territory formed part of the Captaincy-General of Guatemala, a dependency of the Viceroyalty of Mexico. Central America became independent from Spain in 1821 and organized itself into a federation.

[3] In 1827, internal rivalries between 'imperialists' and 'republicans' led to civil war. In 1839, General Francisco Morazán, president of the Central American Republic, tried to prevent the break-up of the federation. From El Salvador, Morazán struggled to preserve the union with the support of some Nonulco natives, headed by Anastasio Aquino. Morazan was defeated in 1840 and sent into exile, and Anastasio Aquino was arrested and executed.

[4] When the federation was dissolved, Britain took advantage of the situation dominating the isthmus. In 1848, President Doroteo Vasconcelos refused to bow under British pressure, and the British blockaded Salvadoran ports. Over the last three decades of the 19th century, the US began to push the British out.

[5] At the end of the century, the invention of artificial coloring

0   100 km

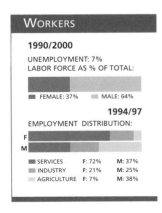

WORKERS

1990/2000

UNEMPLOYMENT: 7%
LABOR FORCE AS % OF TOTAL:

FEMALE: 37%   MALE: 64%

1994/97

EMPLOYMENT DISTRIBUTION:

SERVICES	F: 72%	M: 37%
INDUSTRY	F: 21%	M: 25%
AGRICULTURE	F: 7%	M: 38%

destroyed the demand for indigo - El Salvador's principal export product - and its price fell to rock bottom. Indigo was replaced with coffee. Coffee required larger and more extensive farming areas, and the Liberal Revolution of 1880 drove thousands of peasants from their communal lands, forming a rural working class and a countryside full of anger and conflict. The coffee plantation owners became the dominant oligarchy and the ruling class of El Salvador.

[6] The 1929 financial crash caused the coffee market to collapse, crops were left unharvested, and thousands of sharecroppers and poor peasants starved. This led to a mass uprising headed by the Communist Party of El Salvador and Farabundo Martí, a former secretary of Augusto C Sandino in his campaign against the US invasion of Nicaragua.

[7] The January 1932 rebellion was ruthlessly crushed, around 30,000 Salvadorans were massacred by the troops of General Maximiliano Hernández Martínez, who had taken power in 1931. This started a series of military regimes that lasted half a century. Twelve thousand people died as a consequence of the repression.

[8] In 1960, the Alliance for Progress sponsored an industrialization program, within the Central American Common Market.

High economic growth rates were attained without reducing the rampant unemployment that had caused 300,000 landless peasants to emigrate to neighboring Honduras. Population growth and competition between the local industrial interests, led to war between El Salvador and Honduras in June 1969. The regional common market collapsed after the 100-hour conflict, severely damaging Salvadoran industry.

[9] In the early 1970s unions and other civilian movements took on new life. Guerrilla fighters appeared in El Salvador and the legal opposition parties joined into a national front; the UNO, formed by the Christian Democrats (PDC), the Communists (UDN) and the Social Democrats (MNR). Colonel Arturo Molina, presidential candidate for the official National Conciliation Party, defeated the UNO's candidate Napoleón Duarte in a fixed election in 1972.

[10] In 1977, another fraudulent election made General Carlos Humberto Romero president. Mass riots broke out in protest but social unrest was suppressed leaving 7,000 dead.

[11] A civilian/military junta seized power on October 15 1979. It included representatives of the social democrats and the Christian democrats. The Junta lacked real power and had no control over the

ruthless repression campaigns carried out by police and military forces. Civilian members resigned and were replaced by right-wing Christian democrats from Duarte's party.

[12] On March 24 1980, the Archbishop of San Salvador, Monsignor Oscar A Romero, was assassinated while performing mass in a clear reprisal for his constant defence of human rights. The leading guerrilla organizations, democratic parties and mass organizations united under the policy of a common program of 'popular revolutionary democracy'.

[13] In October 1980, the five anti-regime political-military organizations agreed to form the Farabundo Martí Front for National Liberation (FMLN). On January 10 1981 the FMLN launched a 'general offensive' throughout most of the country. However, the Front was unable to seize power.

[14] In August 1981, the Mexican and French governments signed a joint agreement recognizing the FMLN and the Democratic Revolutionary Front (FDR) as 'a representative political force'.

[15] The US administration, led by President Ronald Reagan, saw the situation in El Salvador as a national security issue. The US became directly involved in the political and social conflict, and was the military and economic mainstay

MATERNAL MORTALITY 1985/99
Per 100,000 live births
120

LITERACY 2000
79%

FOOD DEPENDENCY 2000
16%

EXTERNAL DEBT 2000
PER CAPITA
US$ 641

of the 'counter-insurgency' war which the Salvadoran Army was unsuccessfully waging.

[16] On March 28 1982, as instructed by Washington, the regime held an election for a Constituent Assembly. In response, the rebels launched an offensive ending in a one-week siege of Usulatán, a provincial capital.

[17] After continuous internal tussling for power, the presidency of the constitutional convention went to Roberto D'Aubuisson, the main leader of the ultra-right Nationalist Republican Alliance (ARENA) and the power behind the assassination of Archbishop Romero.

[18] Against a background of an upsurge in fighting, general elections were held on March 25 1984. These were boycotted by the FDR-FMLN; the abstention rate by voters was 51 per cent. Ostensibly supported by the US, the PDC - led by Napoleon Duarte - obtained 43 per cent of the vote, against the 30 per cent won by ultra-right candidate Major Roberto D'Aubuisson.

[19] The extreme right parties disputed the election, but quick responses from the Minister of Defense and the High Command, in support of Duarte, quashed any further reaction. It was the first time that the armed forces had publicly supported the reformists.

[20] In October 1986, a strong earthquake brought about a virtual cease-fire, which eventually led to the renewal of negotiations in October 1987. These talks took place within the new framework of regional peace making. The Central American governments had signed the Esquipulas agreements in August 1987, agreeing to strive for peace.

[21] Elections were held in October 1989; these were boycotted by some of the guerrillas, but civilian sectors of the FDR (members of the social democratic and social Christian parties) participated, with Guillermo Ungo as their presidential candidate. Alfredo Cristiani, the ARENA (right-wing) party's candidate, won the election.

[22] In November 1989, the FMLN launched an offensive occupying several areas of the capital and surrounding regions. The Government responded by bombing several densely populated areas of the capital. Six Jesuits, including the rector of the University of Central America, Ignacio Ellacuria, were tortured and killed by heavily armed soldiers. This provoked a world-wide outcry, especially from the Catholic Church, and American economic aid was threatened.

[23] According to the El Salvador Human Rights Commission, women, students and members of labor unions were the people who suffered most from repression. During those years, the human rights movement was led by mothers, wives, daughters and relatives of the thousands of victims of repression, and by the National Union of Salvadoran Workers (UNTS).

[24] On March 10 1991, the legislative and local elections reflected a new spirit of negotiation. For the first time in 10 years the FMLN did not call for the boycott of the elections, instead they decreed a 3-day unilateral truce. Abstention was still above 50 per cent, and there were acts of paramilitary violence immediately prior to the polls. The ruling party won 43 out of 84 seats.

[25] In Mexico on April 4 1991 delegates of the Cristiani Government and the FMLN started negotiations for a cease-fire agreement. On April 19, 10,000 demonstrators, from 70 social organizations, gathered in the Permanent Committee for National Debate (CPDN), demanding that the Constitution be reformed.

[26] On April 27, after several attempts, representatives of the Government and the Farabundo Martí Front signed the 'Mexico Agreements' restricting the function of the armed forces to the defense of national sovereignty and territorial integrity. The formation of paramilitary groups was banned, and it was agreed to reform article 83 of the Constitution to say that sovereignty 'resides in the people, and that it is from the people that public power emerges'. In New York another agreement was reached in June. The Salvadoran Government committed itself to dismantling the National Guard and the Rural Police (Policía de Hacienda), replacing it with Civilian Police including FMLN-members.

[27] On November 16, new talks began in the UN headquarters. This time, the FMLN declared an indefinite unilateral truce until a new, definite, cease-fire was signed. A Spanish parliamentary delegation wrote a report on the murders of the six Spanish Jesuits from the Central American University (UCA). The report, submitted to the Spanish, European, Salvadoran, and US parliaments, accused the Salvadoran Government and the army of concealing evidence.

[28] On January 1 1992, after 21 weeks of negotiation and 12 years of civil war, both parties met in New York to sign agreements and covenants establishing peace in El Salvador. The war left 75,000 people dead, 8,000 missing, and nearly one million in exile.

[29] The final agreements were signed in the Mexican city of Chapultepec on January 16 1992. They included substantial modifications to the Constitution and to the armed forces. They guaranteed to change rural land tenure and to alter the terms of employee participation in the privatization of State companies; they established the creation of human-rights organizations, and guaranteed the legal status of the FMLN, which held its first official meeting in February 1992.

[30] According to the peace accords the Government was to reduce its troops by half by 1994, bringing the number down to 30,000; in addition, it was to disband its intelligence

PROFILE

ENVIRONMENT

It is the smallest and most densely populated country in Central America. A chain of volcanoes runs across the country from east to west and the altitude makes the climate mild. Coffee is the main cash crop in the highlands. Subsistence crops such as corn, beans and rice are also grown. Along the Pacific Coast, where the weather is warmer, there are sugarcane plantations. It is the country with the greatest problems of deforestation in Latin America.

SOCIETY

Peoples: 89 per cent of the Salvadoran population are mixed descendants of American natives and Spanish colonizers, 10 per cent are indigenous peoples, and 1 per cent are European.
Religions: Mainly Catholic (75 per cent), Protestant, Mormon, Jehovah's Witness.
Languages: Spanish is the official and predominant language. Indigenous minority groups speak Nahuatl and Kekchi.
Political Parties: The Nationalist Republican Alliance (ARENA); The Farabundo Martí National Liberation Front (FMLN), founded in October 1980, comprises five political-military organizations; the Party of National Conciliation (PCN); the Christian-Democratic Party; United Democratic Centre; National Action Party; the left-wing Democratic Convergence, the Farabundo Martí; People's Liberation Forces (FPL), the El Salvador Communist Party (PCS), the National Resistance Armed Forces (FARN), the People's Revolutionary Army (ERP) and the Central American Workers' Revolutionary Party (PRTC).
Social Organizations: National Union of Salvadoran Workers (UNTS); MUSYGES and the National Coordinator against Hunger and Repression (CNHR), formed in 1988. Coordinating Indigenous Salvadoran Council (CCNIS); Peasant Democratic Movement (ADC).

THE STATE

Official Name: República de El Salvador.
Administrative division: 14 Departments.
Capital: San Salvador 1,368,000 people (1999).
Other cities: Santa Ana 538,800 people; San Miguel 473,300; Soyapango 324,800; Mejicanos 152,900 (2000).
Government: Francisco Flores Pérez, President since June 1999.
Parliament: Legislative Assembly with 84 members.
National Holiday: September 15, Independence Day (1821).
Armed Forces: 30,700 troops (1994).
Other: National Civilian Police, made up of former guerrillas, soldiers and police.

service. As of March 3, a new civilian police was to be created, made up in part by former members of the FMLN. The UN verified the destruction of the arms in hands of the FMLN and enabled it to participate as a legal political party in the incoming elections. The FMLN held its first public meeting on February 1 1992. After years of being underground, it was presided over by guerrilla commanders Shafick Handal, Joaquín Villalobos, Fernán Cienfuegos, Francisco Jovel and Leonel González.

[31] In January 1992, the Law of National Reconciliation granted amnesty to all political prisoners. In addition, the Government pledged to turn over lands to the combatants and provide assistance to *campesinos* belonging to both bands.

[32] On February 15 1993, the last 1,700 armed rebels turned over their weapons in a ceremony which was attended by several Central American heads of state and by UN Secretary-General Boutros Boutros-Ghali. The National Civil Police was created, as well as a Human Rights Defense Commission and a Supreme Electoral Court.

[33] The result of the investigation of human-rights violations, carried out by the Truth Commission created by the UN, led to the resignation of Defense Minister General René Emilio Ponce, as being the one who ordered the assassination of six Jesuits in 1989. According to the Commission's final document, the military, the death squads linked to these and the State were responsible for 85 per cent of the civil rights violations committed during the war.

[34] The Truth Commission recommended the dismissal of 102 military leaders and that some former guerrilla leaders be deprived of their political rights. President Cristiani proposed a general amnesty for cases where excesses had been committed; this proposal was approved on March 20 1993, only 5 days after the Truth Commission document had been made public. With this measure, the most serious crimes committed during the war met with total impunity.

[35] A year later on March 20 1994, the first elections since the civil war were held. The candidate of the left coalition, Democratic Convergence - made up of the FMLN and other groups - won 25.5 per cent in the first round, against 49.2 per cent for the right-wing candidate, Armando Calderón Sol, from the ARENA party.

[36] According to UN the peace accords did not bring an end to the violence. In addition to the existence of intelligence activities within the armed forces, members of the military were linked to organized crime. And as there were few employment opportunities for discharged troops (from both sides), this led to an increase in petty crime.

[37] The long-promised award of land to demobilized fighters was slow and inefficient. By mid-1994, only one-third of the potential beneficiaries - 12,000 of a total 37,000 former members of the army or the guerrillas - had obtained plots. The rest remained inactive, living in substandard temporary housing and often drifting into organized crime.

[38] According to official studies, 90 per cent of El Salvador's vegetation was depleted, two-thirds of the land was deeply eroded and subjected to inadequate agricultural techniques and a mere 2 per cent of the virgin forests remained intact. Also, 90 per cent of the rivers were polluted by sewage and chemical waste and more than half the population drank untreated water. San Salvador is one of Central America's most polluted capitals.

[39] An agreement concluded on May 1995 between ARENA and the Democratic Party - split from the FMLN - enabled a 3 per cent rise of the valued added tax from 10 to 13 per cent. This raise was explained on the need to collect funds to finance land reform, infrastructure works and reconstruction of the country's electoral and judicial apparatus.

[40] In August 1996 demonstrators affected by the slowness of the land reform process, and the retribution to war veterans, occupied streets and government buildings in downtown San Salvador. In May, the Democratic Party withdrew from its deal with ARENA, which left the Government without a parliamentary majority.

[41] In March 1997, the opposition's FMLN obtained an important victory in municipal elections, after winning in the capital and dozens of provincial cities. In Parliament, ARENA, with 33.3 per cent of the vote, won 28 seats while FMLN with 32.1 per cent ended up with 27 MPs. The turnout was 40 per cent.

[42] A study by the InterAmerican Development Bank, issued in March 1998, estimated that 25 per cent of El Salvador's potential economic growth was lost every year due to political and criminal violence.

[43] In May 1998, the world recession also affected the textile *maquila* industry and 21 companies shut down in 1999, leaving some 9,000 Salvadorans jobless. Francisco Escobar, chairman of the textile industry, asked the Government to realign the national currency against the dollar, in order to revitalize the sector. According to Escobar, another cause of the crisis were the 'high wages' received by workers, which amount to $1.06 per hour of work, compared to 74 cents in Guatemala and 50 cents in Mexico. Likewise, the sugar sector requested the Legislative Assembly to lower interest rates from 12 to 6 per cent, and to be granted three years of grace. The request, according to the sugar workers, was rooted in the fact that the price of the sugar had fallen, in the last two harvests, from $14 to $4 per 100 kg, a price below production costs. In this country, the sugar sector employs 4 out of every 10 people in the rural sector.

[44] The March 1999 elections ratified ARENA's dominance. At the age of 39 Francisco Flores, a philosophy and political science graduate, became the youngest president in South America, providing an image of rejuvenation.

[45] The day after Flores was sworn in as president, peasant farmers and environmental leaders marched through the main streets of San Salvador, calling for a plan to overcome the disasters caused by Hurricane Mitch, in October 1998.

[46] Flores' government program, 'The New Alliance', had four priorities: work, social investment, citizen security and sustainable development. However the opposition, led by Schaffic Handal, thought the President would continue the policy of favoring the country's financial and business sectors.

[47] Dollarization of the economy was enforced as of January 1 2001, aiming to revitalize the economy and attract investors. Although the US currency was the new unit of the banking sector, citizens could carry out their transactions in colones.

[48] The earthquakes of January 13 and February 13 2001 left 1,159 dead, 8,122 injured and 1.5 million homeless (25 per cent of the population). It is estimated the earthquakes aggravated environmental deterioration and caused 225,000 new poor.

[49] The World Food Program began giving out food in August 2001, as a result of one of the worst droughts in the last years. Approximately 2 tons of corn, beans and cooking oil were distributed among 20,000 families who had lost all of their yearly harvest.

[50] US President George W Bush visited San Salvador in March 2002, on the same day Archbishop Romero had been murdered 22 years before. Bush promised to support free trade policies, as the only solution to the region's problems. Even though US intervention during the civil war years had been widely proven, US officials claimed the purpose of the visit was to celebrate a story with a 'happy ending', which had involved George Bush Snr, George W's father, as one of the signatories of the peace in 1992. George W Bush declared El Salvador had been 'a real bright light of Latin America'. ∎

DEMOGRAPHY

Population: 6,520,000 (2002)
Annual growth: 1.8 % (1985-2000)
Estimates for year 2015: 7,979,000 (2000)
Annual growth to year 2015: 1.6 % (2000)
Urban population: 46.6 % (2000)
Urban growth: 2.7 % (2000)
Children per woman: 3.1 (2000)

HEALTH

Life expectancy at birth: 70 years (2000-2005)
male: 68 years (2000-2005)
female: 74 years (2000-2005)
Maternal mortality: 120 per 100,000 live births (1985/99)
Infant mortality: 34 per 1,000 (2000)
Under-5 child mortality: 40 per 1,000 (2000)
Daily calorie supply: 2,463 per capita (1999)
107 doctors per 100,000 people (1997)
Safe water: 77 % (2000)

EDUCATION

Literacy: 79 % (2000)
male: 82 % (2000)
female: 76 % (2000)
School enrolment (net):
Primary total: 78 % (1994/2000)
male: 78 % (1995/99)
female: 78 % (1995/99)
Secondary (gross):
male: 30 % (1995/97)
female: 35 % (1995/97)
Tertiary (gross): 18 % (1998)
Primary school teachers: one for every 33 pupils (1996)

COMMUNICATIONS

28 newspapers (1998), 478 radios (1999), 201 TV sets (2000) and 100 main telephone lines (2000) per 1,000 people

ECONOMY

Per capita, GDP: $ 4,497 (2000)
Annual growth: 0.0 % (2000)
Annual inflation: 2.3 % (2000)
Consumer price index: 120.9 (2000)
Currency: 8.8 colones = $ 1 (03/2002)
Cereal imports: 681,076 metric tons (2000)
Food import dependency: 16 % (2000)
Fertilizer use: 1,536 kg per ha (1999)
Exports: $ 3,646 million (2000)
Imports: $ 5,642 million (2000)
External debt: $ 4,023 million (2000); $ 641 per capita (2000)
Debt service: 7.6 % of exports (1999)
Development aid received: $ 183 million (1999); $ 29.7 per capita (1999); 1.50 % of GNP (1999)

ENERGY

Consumption: 639.6 Kgs of oil equivalent per capita yearly (1998); 46.7 % imported (1999)

HDI (ranking/value): 95 / 0.701 (1999)

Equatorial Guinea

Population: 483,000 (2002)
Land area: 28,050 SQ KM
Capital: Malabo
Currency: CFA franc
Language: Spanish

Guinea Ecuatorial

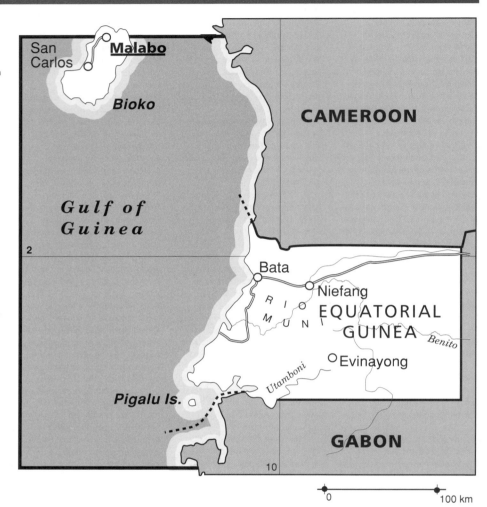

Around the 13th century, Fang and Ndowe people settled in the River Muni area, north of Gabon, subduing the Bayele pygmy population, who now only exist in a few isolated groups. From the continental coast, these nations expanded onto the nearby islands that were described as 'densely populated' in the 15th century. In the colonial division of Africa, the Rio Muni area and the islands received the name of Equatorial Guinea.

[2] The Ndowe became allies and intermediaries of Portuguese, Spanish, Dutch and English slave traders. Fang people, whose social organization did not include slavery, withdrew into the forests, convinced that the Europeans were cannibals.

[3] The kings of Portugal, proclaiming themselves the lords of Guinea, ceded the entire 'District of Biafra' to Spain under the treaties of San Ildefonso and Pardo in 1777 and 1778, in exchange for Spanish territory in southern Brazil. In 1778, an expedition sailed out from Montevideo to occupy the islands. They lost their commanding officer, Argelejos, in a battle against the Annaboneuses, and the survivors, under their new leader, Lieutenant Primo de Rivera, turned back. The French and British gradually took over sections of the territory, with the British finally occupying it, founding the first settlements. They used it as a base for their conquest of Nigeria and turned the freed slaves, or 'Fernandinos', into their agents, creating a ruling group that, in many aspects, still exists today.

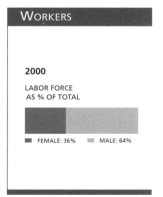

WORKERS

2000

LABOR FORCE
AS % OF TOTAL

■ FEMALE: 36%   ■ MALE: 64%

PUBLIC EXPENDITURE

Military expenditure (as % GNI):	**3.2 %** (1999)
Defense expenditure (% of central government expenditure)	**16.5 %** (1999)

[4] Between 1843 and 1858, the District was militarily re-conquered by Spain, re-establishing their 'rights' over the area. At that time, economic activity centered on cacao, coffee and timber, but the territory was ineffectively controlled from a distance.

[5] From 1963, the colony had a regime of internal autonomy which allowed for the legal existence of several political parties. Meanwhile, international pressure became so strong that Franco's Spain was forced to recognize the independence of Equatorial Guinea, with an official proclamation on October 12 1968.

[6] Francisco Macías Nguema took over the presidency a year later on the pretext of an alleged coup attempt. He instigated violent repression of the opposition, leaving a trail of thousands of political prisoners, killings, disappearances and 160,000 exiles.

[7] In August 1979, a coup led by Lieutenant Colonel Teodoro Obiang Mba Nzago, the President's nephew, brought an end to Macías's power, and he was executed for 'crimes against humanity'. Obiang set up the Supreme Military Council.

[8] The new regime continued the repression of its forerunner, and beneficiaries of the regime remained untouched, all now linked to the Democratic Party of Equatorial Guinea, the only legally authorized party. In elections held in 1984 and 1989 President Obiang was re-elected, unopposed. The National Alliance for the Recovery of Democracy formed in exile. Its attempts to negotiate with Obiang were fruitless. A coup attempt in 1986 sparked more arrests.

[9] Initial rapprochement with the Soviet Bloc was undone when Obiang took the nation into the Customs and Economic Union of Central Africa, linking the national currency - the ekwele - to central banks of the region. This measure led to a drastic reduction in facilities offered by the Soviets and East Germans. The United States,

LITERACY

2000

83%

EXTERNAL DEBT

2000

PER CAPITA

US$ 543

FOREIGN TRADE

Millions US$ 2000

IMPORTS

782

EXPORTS

1,272

France and Spain controlled iron, oil and timber production.

[10] Following his re-election in 1989, Obiang continued to apply IMF recipes in return for loans. The same year, he visited France and Equatorial Guinea later asked to join the French speaking African countries using the franc (CFA) as their currency.

[11] Ten political parties were legalized in early 1993. In late March, the freeing of all political prisoners was agreed with the Joint Opposition Platform (a 10-party coalition formed in November 1992 from legalized parties). In August the first multi-party elections were held but were boycotted by the opposition. The President's Partido Democrático de Guinea Ecuatorial (PDGE) took 68 of the 80 seats.

[12] Amidst accusations of arbitrary detentions and torture, the Government set presidential elections for early 1996. In February of that year, shortly before election day, the Government dissolved the Opposition Platform and detained several of its members. On February 25, Obiang romped home with 99 per cent of the vote in an election described as a farce by the oppositions. There was an 80 per cent abstention rate.

[13] The nation's fortunes changed that year, when giant oil deposits were found. Cacao, coffee and timber were replaced by oil at the head of the list leading to marked economic growth. In 1997 GDP grew by 71.2 per cent, by 22 per cent in 1998 and 15 per cent in 1999, doubling the size of the economy in less than three years.

[14] The US company Mobil handled oil extraction and production, and all income from this was controlled by the presidential entourage. According to the UN, 80 per cent of the wealth at this time was held by less than 5 per cent of the population. In 1999, the IMF itself complained that Obiang clan members had 'conserved' $96 million of the $ 130 million made from oil sales.

[15] Per capital income grew from $370 to $2,000 between 1995 and 2000. But these figures do not reveal the persistence of regressive distribution. It is the spectacular economic growth rather than fairer distribution that has allowed certain positive changes to occur in the social services, especially in the area of health and education.

[16] The discovery of natural gas deposits in 2001 caused a new leap in growth of over 50 per cent. Most local investment was poured into construction, and this dragged the other productive sectors in its wake, meaning some of the mineral wealth reached the worst-off sectors.

[17] That was a relatively turbulent year politically. In February, Cándido Muatetema Rivas was appointed Prime Minister, after Teodoro Obiang Nguema accused Ángel Serafín Seriche Dougan of causing a constitutional crisis and ousting him for 'not respecting the opinion of the people and the nation's interests'. The following month, eight opposition parties in exile formed a coalition in Spain to monitor the internal politics of the nation, stating that the Obiang government offered no more than a pretense of democracy.

[18] In July, while Obiang was named PDGE party candidate for the 2003 election, the exiled Florentino Ecomo Nsogo, leader of the Party for Reconstruction and Social Welfare, returned to the country. He was the first opposition figure to respond to the President's call for all opposition parties to register for the elections.

[19] Over the years of Obiang's rule, Amnesty International has repeatedly cited complaints of arrests, torture and murder. The Bubi minority have been regularly persecuted in their quest for self-determination for Bioko island. ∎

PROFILE

ENVIRONMENT

The country consists of mainland territory on the Gulf of Guinea (Río Muni, 26,017 sq km) and the islands of Bioko (formerly Fernando Po, and Macías Nguema) and Pigalu (formerly Annobon, Corisco, Greater Elobey and Lesser Elobey). The islands are of volcanic origin and extremely fertile; Río Muni is a coastal plain covered with tropical rainforests but without natural harbors. It is one of the most humid and rainy countries of the world, a characteristic that limits the variety of possible crops. The main exports are cocoa, wood and oil.

SOCIETY

Peoples: The population is mostly of Bantu-speaking origin. In the islands there are also Igbo and Efik peoples who migrated from Nigeria, subduing the local Bubi population. In Río Muni the inhabitants are mainly Fang and Ndowe. Nearly all of the Europeans and a third of the local population emigrated during the Macías regime.

Religions: Mainly Christian on the islands; traditional African beliefs in Rio Muni.

Languages: Spanish is official and predominant language. French is also official. In Rio Muni, Fang is also spoken, and on the islands, Bubi, Ibo and English.

Political Parties: Democratic Party of Equatorial Guinea (PDGE); People's Union; Convergence for Social Democracy.

Social Organizations: National Alliance for the Restoration of Democracy and other associations in exile (mainly in Spain) like the Platform for Peace and Human Rights in EG, Movement for the Self Determination of Bioko Island, Union of Workers of Equatorial Guinea.

THE STATE

Official Name: República de Guinea Ecuatorial.

Administrative divisions: 4 continental and 3 island regions.

Capital: Malabo 31,000 people (1999).

Other cities: Bata 43,000 people; Ela Nguema 14,700 (2000).

Government: Teodoro Obiang Nguema Mbasogo, President since August 1979. Cándido Muatetema Rivas, Prime Minister since March 2001. Parliament: Chamber of People's Representatives, with 80 members.

National Holiday: October 12, Independence Day (1968).

Armed Forces: 1,300.

DEMOGRAPHY

Population: 483,000 (2002)
Annual growth: 2.5 % (1985-2000)
Estimates for year 2015: 692,000 (2000)
Annual growth to year 2015: 2.8 % (2000)
Urban population: 48.2 % (2000)
Urban growth: 5.2 % (2000)
Children per woman: 5.9 (2000)

HEALTH

Life expectancy at birth: 52 years (2000-2005)
male: 50 years (2000-2005)
female: 54 years (2000-2005)
Infant mortality: 103 per 1,000 (2000)
Under-5 child mortality: 156 per 1,000 (2000)
25 doctors per 100,000 people (1996)
Safe water: 44 % (2000)

EDUCATION

Literacy: 83 % (2000)
male: 92 % (2000)
female: 75 % (2000)
School enrolment (net):
Primary total: 89 % (1994/2000)
male: 89 % (1995/99)
female: 89 % (1995/99)
Primary school teachers: one for every 57 pupils (1998)

COMMUNICATIONS

5 newspapers (1996), 427 radios (1997), 116 TV sets (1998) and 13 main telephone lines (2000) per 1,000 people

ECONOMY

Per capita, GDP: $ 15,073 (2000)
Annual growth: 13.8 % (2000)
Currency: 758.3 CFA francs = $ 1 (03/2002)
Cereal imports: 12,045 metric tons (2000)
Fertilizer use: 0 kg per ha (1999)
Exports: $ 1,272 million (2000)
Imports: $ 782 million (2000)
External debt: $ 248 million (2000); $ 543 per capita (2000)
Development aid received: $ 20 million (1999); $ 45.6 per capita (1999); 2.90 % of GNP (1999)

HDI (ranking/value): 110 / 0.610 (1999)

Eritrea

Population: 3,993,000 (2002)
Land area: 101,000 SQ KM
Capital: Asmara
Currency: Nafka
Language: Tigrinya

Ertra

As the site of the most important ports of the Aksumite empire (flourished 4th-6th century AD), Eritrea was linked to the beginnings of the Ethiopian kingdom, but it retained much of its independence until it fell under Ottoman rule in the 16th century. From the 17th to the 19th century control over the territory was disputed among Ethiopia, the Ottomans, the kingdom of Tigray, Egypt and Italy. In 1890, the Treaty of Wichale between Italy and Menilek II of Ethiopia recognized Italian possessions on the Red Sea, and the colony, created on January 1 1890, was named by the Italians for the Mare Erythraeum ('Red Sea' in Latin) of the Romans.

[2] Eritrea was used as the main base for the Italian invasions of Ethiopia (1896 and 1935-36) and it became one of the six provinces of Italian East Africa. During World War II, in 1941, the area came under British administration.

[3] The common struggle against the Italians had brought a reasonable degree of unity to almost one million Eritreans. On December 2 1950, the United Nations declared that Eritrea should become a federated state within the Ethiopian Empire. The resolution rejected Ethiopian demands for outright incorporation, but also left the process of Eritrean self-determination undefined.

[4] In Eritrea, a national assembly was elected which enjoyed some autonomy until 1962, when Ethiopian leader Haile Selassie forced a group of Eritrean politicians to vote for its complete incorporation into Ethiopia. The decision was contested by nationalist groups and immediately sparked a rebellion.

[5] The oldest anti-Ethiopian resistance movement is the Eritrean Liberation Front (ELF) founded in 1958, in Cairo, by journalist and union leader Idris Mohamed Adem. It began guerrilla activities in September 1961. In 1966, a split produced the Eritrean Popular Liberation Front (EPLF). In 1974, with Sudanese mediation, the two groups agreed to coordinate their actions and in the next few years, the EPLF imposed its leadership upon the rebel movement.

[6] During the pro-Soviet Mengistu government in Ethiopia, the Eritreans felt that the changes in Addis Ababa did not bring their self-determination closer, so they had no reason to stop fighting. The war against Ethiopia caused thousands of victims on both sides.

[7] In February 1990, the EPLF captured the port of Massawa and almost all of the Eritrean territory. The rebels took Asmara and, on the following day, the port city of Asseb. The road between Asseb and Addis Ababa was the only way supplies could reach the Ethiopian capital by land.

[8] Since 1991, Asmara and Addis Ababa started to relate as separate States. The Red Sea ports were opened again to enable the arrival of international aid.

[9] In the April 1993 referendum, 99.8 per cent of voters opted for independence. The EPLF formed a provisional government, led by Isaias Afwerki, which turned into a political party the following year, the People's Front for Democracy and Justice (PFDJ).

[10] Eritrea, which a year earlier had become a part of the UN, joined the IMF in February 1994.

[11] In late 1997, Eritrea introduced the *nafka*, replacing the Ethiopian *birr*. As a countermeasure, Ethiopia announced that transactions between both countries would be carried out exclusively in US dollars.

[12] Fighting with Ethiopia resumed in February 1999. The war sucked in Nigeria, which supplied weapons to Eritreans, and Kenya, which mobilized forces along its border with Ethiopia.

[13] In June, Afwerki and his Prime Minister Meles Zenawi accepted the OAU's proposal for an immediate ceasefire and withdrawal of troops from the area in dispute. In September, Eritrea accepted the peace plan proposed by the UN, while Ethiopia maintained minor differences.

[14] Eleven ruling party officials were arrested in September 2001, charged with 'defeatism' and 'treason' for criticizing the Government and demanding democratic reform. Likewise, the opposition press was closed and nine journalists were detained.

[15] The National Assembly - made up of Government followers - decided in February 2002 that the existence of political parties was not important at this stage in the country's life and postponed ratifying a law to allow them. However, the Assembly implicitly approved the electoral law by authorizing elections, although it did not set a date for these.

[16] In April 2002, the Permanent Court of Arbitration at The Hague decided on the border dispute between Eritrea and Ethiopia. The 1,000 km border was set by a court of five international specialists. The border cities of Zalembessa, Alitena and Bada were given over to Ethiopia, while Badme - with the symbolic value as the starting point for the war in 1998 - was apparently given to Eritrea, according to topographic maps used by the Soviets (see Ethiopia). According to experts, Ethiopia seems to have obtained a large part of its territorial demands. ∎

PROFILE

ENVIRONMENT

Eritrea is in the horn of Africa. The 1,000 km northeast coast is on the Red Sea; to the northeast lies Sudan; to the south, Ethiopia and to the southeast, Djibouti. The dry plains and extremely hot desert are inhabited by pastoralists. Deforestation and the consequent erosion are partly responsible for the frequent droughts.

SOCIETY

Peoples: The nine ethnic groups are the Tigrinya, Tigre, Bilen, Afar, Saho, Kunama, Nara, Hidareb and Rashaida. The majority are pastoralists or farmers; 20 per cent are urban workers. Half a million Eritrean refugees live in Sudan, 40,000 in Europe and 14,000 in the US.
Religions: Almost half of all Eritreans are Coptic Christians; most of the rest are Muslim, although there are Catholic and Protestant minorities.
Languages: Tigrinya; Afar, Beni-Amir, Tigré, Saho, Kunama, Arab and other local languages.
Political Parties: People's Front for Democracy and Justice (PFDJ) is the only party recognized by the Government. Formerly the Eritrean People's Liberation Front (EPLF), it adopted its new name in 1994.
Social organizations: Eritrean Liberation Front, split into several fractions; Eritrean Islamic Jihad.

THE STATE

Official Name: Hagere Ertra.
Administrative Division: 8 provinces.
Capital: Asmara 514,000 people (1999).
Other cities: Asseb 53,600 people; Keren 36,600; Mitsiwa 28,800 (2000).
Government: Parliamentary Republic. Isaias Afwerki, President since May 1993. Parliament: National Assembly with 104 members.
National Holiday: May 24, Independence (1993).
Armed Forces: 35,000 (1997).

Estonia

Population: 1,361,000 (2002)
Land area: 42,270 SQ KM
Capital: Tallinn
Currency: Krona
Language: Estonian

Eesti

Despite historical and political links with their southern neighbors, Lithuania and Latvia, the Estonian people have always been known for their spiritual and cultural independence. Belonging to a branch of the Finno-Ugric nations, Estonians have greater cultural and linguistic ties with the Finns to the north than with the Indo-European Balts to the south.

[2] The region was settled some 6,000 years ago. Around the year 400 AD, the semi-nomadic peoples' hunting and fishing activity began to be replaced by agriculture and cattle raising. At the same time, navigation and trade with neighboring countries along the Baltic Sea intensified. In the 11th and 12th centuries, combined Estonian forces successfully repelled Russia's attempts to invade the territory.

[3] The Germans, Russians and Danes, invading Estonia in the 13th century, found a federation of states with a high level of social development and a strong sense of independence, keeping them united against foreign conquerors.

[4] In the 13th century, the Knights of the Sword, a Germanic order which was created during the Crusades, conquered the southern part of Estonia and the north of Latvia, creating the kingdom of Livonia and converting the inhabitants to Christianity. German traders and landowners brought the Protestant Reformation to Estonia in the first half of the 16th century.

[5] The northern part of Estonia remained under Danish control. Livonia was much disputed between 1558 and 1583; it was repeatedly attacked by Russia before being broken up in 1561. Poland conquered Livonia in 1569; a hundred years later, it ceded the major part of the kingdom to Sweden. In the Nordic Wars (1700-1721), Russia took Livonia from Sweden, and kept these lands under the Treaty of Nystad.

[6] Russia received the Polish part of Livonia in 1772, with the first partition of Poland. The former kingdom of Livonia became a Russian province in 1783. Power was shared between the Czar of Russia and local German nobles, who owned most of the lands and the peasants lived in serfdom.

[7] The abolition of serfdom in Russia and peasant land ownership rights (1804), strengthened the Estonian national consciousness. During the second half of the 19th century, the Society of Estonian Literati developed the written language, and the preservation of national folklore, enabling the people to withstand the Czar's Russianisation campaigns.

[8] In 1904, Estonian nationalists seized control of Tallinn, ousting the German-Baltic rulers. After the fall of the Czar in February 1917, a demonstration by 40,000 Estonians in Petrograd forced the Provisional Government to grant them autonomy, maintained even after the Bolshevik Revolution.

[9] In November 1917, with the election of a constituent assembly, the Estonian Bolsheviks only obtained 35.5 per cent of the votes. On February 24 1918, Estonia declared its independence from the Soviet Union and set up a provisional government. The following day, German troops occupied Tallinn and the Estonian Government was forced to go into exile.

[10] After World War I, the Estonians successfully fought both the Red Army and the Germans. On February 2 1920, the Soviet Union recognized Estonia's independence.

[11] Estonia, Latvia and Lithuania, joined the League of Nations in 1921. Following the Swiss model, the Estonian constitution established a parliamentary democracy. The Government began the reconstruction of the country and initiated agrarian reform. In the 1920s, Estonia established the world's first shale-oil distillery.

[12] Estonia passed legislation guaranteeing the rights of minorities, and ensuring that all ethnic groups had access to schools in their own languages. The economic depression of the 1930s led to a modification of the Estonian constitution; in 1933, it became a virtual dictatorship before adopting a presidential-parliamentary system in 1937.

[13] The secret protocols of the Molotov-Ribbentrop pact, signed in 1939, determined that Estonia - like its two Baltic neighbors - would remain within the Soviet sphere of influence. At the same time, Tallinn signed a mutual assistance treaty with Moscow giving the USSR the right to install naval bases on Estonian soil.

[14] In June 1940, after demanding the right for his troops to enter Estonian territory under the pretext of searching for missing soldiers, Stalin deposed the Tallinn government and replaced it with members of the local Communist Party. Elections were held during the Soviet occupation, after which the Communist Party seized power.

[15] Following the examples of Latvia and Lithuania, the new government adopted the name 'Soviet Socialist Republic of Estonia', joining the USSR. According to the official record, all three Baltic States voluntarily became a part of the USSR. In 1941, around 60,000 Estonians were deported to Siberia.

[16] When the German offensive against the USSR began in 1941, Nazi troops invaded Estonia, establishing a reign of terror which was especially directed against Jews, gypsies and Estonian nationalists. The USSR recovered the Baltic States in 1944; Estonian groups began pro-independence guerrilla activity, but

had little impact against Soviet military might.

[17] Some 80,000 Estonians emigrated to the West, while Russian colonization gradually altered the traditional ethnic composition of the population. Around 20,000 Estonians were deported between 1945 and 1946. The third wave of mass deportations took place in 1949, when another 40,000 Estonians were sent to the farthest regions of the USSR, most of them farmers who refused to accept collectivization of the land, imposed by Soviet authorities.

[18] The reforms set in motion in 1985 by Soviet President, Mikhail Gorbachev stimulated social and political activity within Estonia. In August 1987, a demonstration in Tallinn demanded the publication of the Molotov-Ribbentrop pact. Latvians and Lithuanians also asked that the contents of the protocols be revealed.

[19] In January 1988, former Estonian political prisoners founded the Estonian Independence Party, defending the country's right to self-determination. In addition, this group called for the re-establishment of multiparty democracy, and the restoration of Estonian as the country's official language. Another group, the Estonian Heritage Society, began trying to locate and restore the country's historical monuments.

[20] The Popular Front of Estonia (FPE), founded in April by nationalists and communists, organized a rally in June 1988 which was attended by 150,000 people. The outlawed Estonian flag was displayed on this occasion. In September, some 300,000 Estonians held another rally; a few days later, the ban on the flag was lifted.

[21] In October, the first FPE congress reaffirmed Estonia's demand for autonomy, and asked Moscow for an admission of the fact that Estonia had been occupied against its will in 1940. The following month, Estonia's *soviet* (parliament) declared the country's sovereignty, and affirmed its right to veto laws imposed by Moscow without consent.

[22] In August 1989, some two million Estonians, Latvians and Lithuanians formed a 560-km human chain from Tallinn to Vilnius to demand the independence of the

Baltic States. In February 1990, a convention of Estonian representatives approved the Declaration of Independence, based on the 1920 Peace Treaty of Tartu between the Soviet Union and the newly independent Estonian republic.

[23] In the May 1990 elections, the FPE and other nationalist groups won an ample majority within parliament. Moderate nationalist leader Edgar Savisaar was named as the leader of the first elected government since 1940. In August, parliament proclaimed the independence of Estonia, but Moscow did not consider it to be valid.

[24] In late 1990 and early 1991, Moscow threatened to impede Estonia's separation from the USSR, by force, and skirmishes took place between Soviet troops and nationalist groups. In September, the USSR recognized the independence of the three Baltic States, and that same month, they were admitted to the United Nations.

[25] In January, Savisaar and his government resigned in the face of growing criticism over his economic policy. Parliament named former transportation minister Tiit Vahi to head the new government. Estonia had to ration food and fuel ever since the Russian Federation began restricting and raising the price of its products.

[26] On June 20 1992, the new constitution (based on the 1938 Constitution) was ratified by referendum.

[27] Lennart Meri, of the National Country Coalition Party, was elected President of Estonia by parliament on October 5 by 59 votes to 31.

[28] In 1992, Estonia became the first Eastern European country to abandon the rouble, and create its own currency, the krona.

[29] In June, a blatantly nationalistic law was approved, aimed at foreigners, especially those of Russian origin who make up 39 per cent of the total population. The law obliges foreigners to apply for a discretionary residence permit.

[30] The March 1995 elections led to the defeat of the coalition which had ruled Estonia since the former Soviet republic broke away from the USSR. The new Prime Minister, Tiit Vahi, caused a controversy when he named a 'disproportionate' number of former communist ministers in his government. In October his cabinet was forced to resign due to corruption charges against the Minister of the Interior. The new government was formed with the inclusion of Reform Party members.

[31] On September 20 1996, after a close vote from the Electoral College, Lennart Meri was re-elected as President. A report from the European Bank for Reconstruction and Development - created to help the transition of former Socialist countries toward a market economy - estimated on December 1997 that reforms carried out by Estonia in its financial sector, which led to the highest foreign investment per capita in the region, favored its swift incorporation into the European Union.

[32] In February 1998, Estonia, Latvia and Lithuania signed a Letter of Association with the US. In it, Washington committed itself to support the three states' integration into NATO. Russia announced it would normalize its relation with the Baltic countries, with the condition that they normalize the situation of Russian-speaking minorities.

[33] Mart Laar was appointed Prime Minister in March 1999. A program was launched in the Lake Peipus region, which covers a large part of the border with Russia and where 95 per cent of the residents speak Russian, for Estonian families in the city of Narva to lodge young people. This was one of the measures to compensate for the social impact caused by the lay-offs of Russian-speakers who did not speak Estonian.

[34] In Tallinn, the repatriation and ceremonial funeral of the remains of an Estonian officer who had led a Nazi unit in World War II was controversial, since the parties representing the Russian minority felt that this was supporing fascism.

[35] As of October 2001, 67 people had died and more than 100 had been hospitalized intoxicated with illegal vodka, laced with industrial methanol. Illegal sales of alcohol comprise between 40 and 60 per cent of total sales.

[36] Arnold Ruutel, former member of the Central Committee of the Soviet era, became President that month.

[37] Laar resigned in January 2002, alleging the 'betrayal' of the Reform Party, which had 'given up' the city of Tallinn to the opposition. During his term, Estonia, in addition to twice topping the group of former Soviet republics in the economic field, was included in the list of 10 candidates to join the European Union in 2004. Siim Kallas, who formed a new coalition government between the RP and the NCCP, was named Prime Minister.

[38] Russian speakers, two-thirds of the population, were helped when President Ruutel signed a law revoking the requirement for civil servants to be fluent in Estonian. ∎

PROFILE

ENVIRONMENT

Located on the northeastern coast of the Baltic Sea, Estonia is bounded by the Gulf of Finland in the north, the Russian Federation in the east and Latvia in the south. The Estonian landscape - with its numerous lakes and river - bears witness to its glacial origin. There are more than 1,500 lakes, the largest of which are Lake Peipsi (Europe's fourth largest) and Lake Vorts. Forests make up 38 per cent of Estonia's territory; the highest elevation is Mount Suur Muna Magi (317 m). The climate is temperate, with average temperatures of 28° C in summer and around –50° in winter. The Baltic coast is 1,240 km long and includes a number of fjords. Some 1,500 islands close to the Baltic coast make up around one-tenth of Estonia's territory. The Gulf of Finland has numerous ice-free bays, of which Tallinn is the largest. Estonia's most important mineral resources are bituminous shale (which meets most of Estonia's energy needs), and phosphates. Estonia also has an important fishing industry, although its fleet has had to begin fishing far from its coastal waters due to the polluted state of the Baltic Sea, which contains toxic waste dumped by industries in several countries with Baltic coastlines. Neither Tallinn nor other cities have satisfactory sewerage systems.

SOCIETY

Peoples: Estonians 64.2 per cent; Russians 28.7 per cent; Ukranians 2.6 per cent; Belarusians 1.5 per cent Finnish and others 3.3 per cent (1998).
Religions: Lutheran (majority), Orthodox, Baptist.
Languages: Estonian (official); Russian and others.
Political Parties: Estonian Center Party; Fatherland Union, conservative; Estonian Reform Party; People's Party Moderates, social-democratic; Estonian Coalition Party, liberal; Estonian Country People's Party, agrarian; Estonian United People's Party, pro-Russian minority.
Social organizations: Confederation of Estonian Trade Unions (EAKL)

THE STATE

Official Name: Eesti Vabariik.
Administrative Division: 15 counties.
Capital: Tallinn 397,000 people (1999).
Other cities: Tartu 98,400 people; Narva 72,100; Kohtla-Jarve 45,200; Pärnu 42,800 (2000).
Government: Parliamentary republic. Arnold Ruutel, President since October 2001. Siim Kallas, Primer Minister since January 2002. Unicameral Legislature: State Council (Riigikogu), with 101 members elected every 4 years.
National Holiday: February 24, Independence (1918).
Armed Forces: 2,500 (1993). **Other:** 2,000 (Coast Guard).

Ethiopia

Ityop'ya

Population:	66,040,000 (2002)
Land area:	1,000,000 SQ KM
Capital:	Addis Ababa
Currency:	Birr
Language:	Amharic

In ancient times, the term 'Ethiopian', meaning 'burnt face' in Greek, was applied indiscriminately to all Africans. Ethiopia's other name, Abyssinia, came from the Arabic 'Habbashat', which was the name of one of the groups that emigrated from Yemen to Africa around 2000 BC.

2 Axum, in the north of present-day Ethiopia, was the center of trade between the Upper Nile valley and the Red Sea ports which traded with Arabia and India, it reached its height in the first centuries AD. Ethiopia was a rich and prosperous state, which was able to subdue present-day Yemen, but which went through a crisis in the 7th century. Trade routes moved as Arab unification and expansion dominated the area, conquering Egypt.

3 The Ethiopian ruling elite had converted to Christianity in the 4th century, further contributing to their isolation. Expansion towards the south, excessive growth of the clergy, and declining trade led to a process of social and economic stratification similar to that in feudal western Europe. By the 16th century, one third of the land belonged to the 'king of kings'; another third belonged to the monasteries and the rest was divided among the nobility and the rest of the population.

4 The Muslim population that had developed a powerful trade economy on the coast of the Red Sea, instigated an insurrection, leading Ethiopia to resume its relations with Europe to request assistance. The aid took almost a century to arrive, but the Portuguese fleet, when it finally arrived in 1541, was decisive in destroying the Sultanate of Adal (See Somalia).

5 For 150 years, Ethiopian emperors focused their efforts on the coast, giving Oromo (a people akin to the Haussa) a chance to gradually penetrate from the west until they outnumbered the local population. Their influence grew so great that an Oromo became emperor, between 1755 and 1769; though the Amhara ruling elite took great pains to oust him.

6 This state of affairs continued until 1889 when Menelik II came to power. Designated heir to the throne in 1869, he spent the next 20 years training an army (with British and Italian assistance) and organizing the administration of his own territory, the state of Shoa. His efficiency was fortunate; in 1895 his former allies, the Italians, invaded the country claiming that previous commitments had not been honored. The final battle was fought in Adua in 1896 where, 4,000 of the 10,000 Italian soldiers were killed. It was the most devastating defeat suffered by European troops on African soil until the Algerian War. In the diplomatic negotiations that followed their defeat, the Italians succeeded in obtaining two territories that Ethiopia did not really control: Eritrea and the southern Somalian coast. In

1906, the world powers recognized the independence and territorial integrity of what was then known as Abyssinia, in exchange for certain economic privileges.

7 This arrangement saved Ethiopia from direct colonization until 1936, when Italian Fascist dictator Benito Mussolini invaded the country, taking advantage of internal strife among Menelik's would-be successors. Despite his pleas to the League of Nations, Haile Selassie, heir to the throne, got no concrete help. During the five-year occupation, several basic industries and coffee plantations were started, and a system of racial discrimination was installed, similar to that of apartheid in South Africa.

8 In 1948, Ethiopians won their autonomy back from Britain, which had taken over the country after Mussolini's defeat in 1941. When Selassie took the throne, his country was floundering in unprecedented crisis: foreign occupation had disrupted production; nationalist political movements had strengthened in the struggle for autonomy and rejected a return to feudalism; and poverty in the interior had grown considerably.

9 Selassie denounced colonialism, favored non-alignment and supported the creation of the Organization for African Unity, which finally set up headquarters in Addis Ababa. He also maintained close links with Israel. On the domestic front, the crisis deepened as his government was dominated by a corrupt oligarchy and the Orthodox Church, which between them held 80 percent of the country's fertile lands. The domestic crisis came to a head in 1956 when Eritrean separatist rebels intensified their attacks. In 1974, after a series of strikes, student rallies and widespread protests against absolutism and food shortages, Haile Selassie was overthrown.

10 In 1975, an Armed Forces Coordination Committee, the Dergue ('committee' in Amharic), headed by General Aman Andom abolished the monarchy and proclaimed a republic, suspending the Constitution and dissolving Parliament.

11 Popular movements became more radical, leading to a series of disputes among the military, and a subsequent crisis. Colonel Mengistu

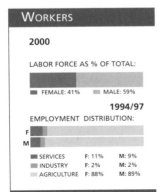

WORKERS

2000

LABOR FORCE AS % OF TOTAL:

- FEMALE: 41%   MALE: 59%

1994/97

EMPLOYMENT DISTRIBUTION:

F
M

- SERVICES   F: 11%   M: 9%
- INDUSTRY   F: 2%   M: 2%
- AGRICULTURE   F: 88%   M: 89%

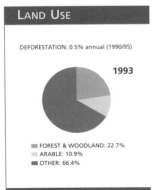

LAND USE

DEFORESTATION: 0.5% annual (1990/95)

1993

- FOREST & WOODLAND: 22.7%
- ARABLE: 10.9%
- OTHER: 66.4%

PUBLIC EXPENDITURE

1999

DEFENSE 29.1%   SOCIAL 30.8%

LITERACY
2000

39%

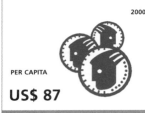

EXTERNAL DEBT
2000

PER CAPITA

US$ 87

FOREIGN TRADE

Millions US$
2000

IMPORTS
1,961
EXPORTS
984

Haile Mariam rose to power in December 1977. He managed to hold the Dergue together and put an end to the military's internal struggles.

[12] The military government succeeded in carrying out agrarian reform, and nationalizing foreign banks and heavy industry. US military bases were closed down. Right-wing groups carried out assassinations and bombings. Left-wing organizations retaliated by killing conspirators and monarchists on sight. Between December 1977 and April 1978, the violence left over 5,000 people dead.

[13] Once the military crisis was resolved, a struggle broke out for the control of grassroots organizations. At first the Dergue supported the Pan-Ethiopian Socialist Movement (Meison), which set up neighborhood committees (*kebeles*) as a basis for mass organization. The Meison grew stronger and proposed a system of self-controlled civilian units. This set them on a collision course with the Dergue, which rejected the creation of autonomous military groups.

[14] Mengistu declared the Meison illegal and backed the Revolutionary Flame, a group of officers and civilians who had studied in socialist Europe and were loyal to the president of the Dergue. After settling this latest crisis, the Government was able to confront the two separatist movements which had been gaining strength since 1977, in Eritrea and the Ogaden desert. The Eritrean rebels considered that their independence struggle was valid, regardless of the existence of a progressive government in Addis Ababa, and the Somali population of the Ogaden desert (claimed by Somalia) took advantage of the domestic crisis in Addis Ababa to further their own separatist cause.

[15] Mengistu rejected Eritrean separatist demands. He alleged that their struggle had only been reasonable when they had confronted the feudal monarchy, and not when they had opposed the pro-soviet regime.

[16] In 1979 the Government set up the Ethiopian Workers' Party Organization Committee (COPWE), and their first general congress was held in 1980. In that year, there was a 15 per cent increase in cultivated land, which raised the GNP by 6 per cent.

[17] In 1984, the country was struggling under the effects of a prolonged drought which had begun in 1982, causing thousands of deaths from starvation. The drought affected twelve provinces, threatened five million lives and killed over half a million people.

[18] The Ethiopian Workers' Party (PWE) held their founding congress in 1984, approving a program to transform the country into a socialist state.

[19] The newly-elected Assembly (the *Shengo*, or parliament) proclaimed the People's Democratic Republic of Ethiopia on September 12, ratifying Mengistu Haile Mariam as head of state. Separatists extended operations in Eritrea and Tigray, as well as in Wollo, Gondar and Oromo in the south.

[20] The new constitution provided for the creation of five autonomous regions and 25 administrative regions. Eritrea was able to legislate on all matters except defense, national security, foreign relations and its legal status in relation to central government. The separatists rejected the proposal, calling it 'colonial'.

[21] In December 1987, after a bloody battle, the Eritreans took Af Abed. 18,000 Ethiopian troops, three Soviet advisors and the army commander of the northern region were taken prisoner.

[22] The Tigray People's Liberation Front (TPLF) captured important cities like Wukro, a distribution center for international aid to drought victims. Building on these victories, the rebels from Eritrea and Tigray signed cooperation agreements and began to plan joint military strategies.

[23] Increased rebel activity took a heavy toll on the Ethiopian army and in 1989 12 divisions (150,000 troops) stationed in the front line attempted a coup. Mengistu returned hastily from West Germany and managed to abort the coup. He executed dozens of officers, among them Generals Amha Desta, airforce commander-in-chief, and Merrid Negusie, chief-of-staff of the armed forces.

[24] In September 1989, the last Cuban soldiers withdrew from Ethiopia. The Government had signed a peace agreement in April 1988, and no longer needed their services.

[25] In 1990, the Central Committee of the Ethiopian Workers' Party decided to restructure the party and change its name to the Ethiopian Democratic Union Party (EDUP. While excluding the possibility of a multiparty system, the changes sought to lay the basis of 'a party of all Ethiopians', open to 'opposition groups'. The Marxist-Leninist tag was dropped. The Government established a mixed economy, including state enterprises, cooperatives and private businesses.

[26] Within one month, the former USSR withdrew its military advisors from Eritrea, and the EPLF took the port of Massawa, thus controlling all of Eritrea, except Asmara, which was totally cut off from the rest of Ethiopia by occupied land.

[27] In May 1991, after overwhelming guerrilla victories in the north Mengistu Mariam's departure from Ethiopia was negotiated internationally. The

PROFILE

ENVIRONMENT

A mountainous country with altitudes of over 4,000 meters. Ethiopia is isolated from neighboring regions by its geography. In the North, the Eritrean plain, a desert steppe, extends alongside the Red Sea. In the mountains and plateaus, vegetation and climate vary with altitude. The Dega are cool, rainy highlands, above 2,500 meters, where grain is grown and cattle raised. The deep valleys which traverse the highlands are warm and rainy with tropical vegetation, known as the Kolla (up to 1,500 m). The drier, cooler, medium-range plateaus where coffee and cotton are grown (1,500 to 2,500 m) are the most densely populated parts of the country. To the East lies the Ogaden, a semi-desert plateau inhabited by nomadic shepherds of Somali origin. Many regions once rich in vegetation are now rocky, desert areas. Desertification and erosion have increased within the past decade. Ethiopia is the home of Arabica coffee, and coffee accounts for over 60 per cent of Ethiopia's export income. Other exports are skins, meat, oil seeds and pulses.

SOCIETY

Peoples: Two-thirds are Amhara or Oromo. There are many other ethnic groups including Tigrai who speak Tigrigna; Gurage, Niloti, Somali and Afar from Danaki region. At present there are 22 recognized minorities.
Religions: There are roughly equal numbers of Christians and Muslims. About 40 per cent of the population is Christian, 40 per cent Islamic, and the rest, mainly in the South and South-west, practice local religions.
Languages: Amharic is the language of government, with all parliamentary documents also written in English. The second major language is Oromigna (the language of the Oromo). There are at least 100 local languages.
Political Parties: Ethiopian People's Revolutionary Democratic Front (EPRDF) is made up of several members: Tigray People's Liberation Front; Oromo People's Democratic Organization; Southern Ethiopian People's Democratic Union; Ethiopian People's Democratic Movement. Others with Parliamentary representation: All Amhara People's Organization (AAPO); Ogaden National Liberation Front (ONLF).

THE STATE

Official Name: Federal Democratic Republic of Ethiopia.
Administrative Divisions: There are nine regional states (Tigray, Afar, Amhara, Oromia, Somali, Benishangul/Gumuz, Southern People's Region, Gambela and Harari) and two chartered cities (Addis Ababa and Dire Dawa).
Capital: Addis Ababa (Adis Abeba) 2,534,000 people (1999).
Other cities: Dire Dawa 202,700 people; Harar 93,900 (2000).
Government: Federal Republic. Girma Wolde-Giorgis, President since October 2001; Meles Zenawi, Prime Minister since August 1995, re-elected in 2000. Bicameral Legislature: the Federal Parliamentary Assembly is formed by the Council of People's Representatives, with 527 members, and Council of the Federation, with 117 members.
National Holiday: May 28, Overthrow of the Dergue (1991).
Armed Forces: 120,000 (1995).

Government was left in the hands of Vice-President Tesfaye Gabre Kidane, considered a moderate, who initiated his transitional government by negotiating a cease-fire with the Eritrean rebels.

[28] Kidane's government took part in peace talks, in London, presided over by the US, with the participation of the most important rebel groups. They aimed at reaching an agreement which would stave off civil war. Kidane resigned in late May, when the US advised the forces of the Ethiopian People's Revolutionary Democratic Front (EPRDF) to take control of Addis Ababa.

[29] Ata Meles Zenawi, the 36-year-old leader of the EPRDF became interim president, until a multi-party conference could be held. He promised to bring the civil war to an end, re-establish democracy and conquer the problem of hunger. Three months later, upon reopening Parliament and passing a new Constitution, Zenawi pledged to hold elections within a year.

[30] The interim president also promised to honor economic commitments assumed by the deposed government, and to respect the will of the Eritrean people. The Eritreans had announced the formation of an autonomous government, and scheduled a referendum to decide the issue of independence (see Eritrea).

[31] The new government confronted two practically insoluble problems: reconciling the various guerrilla groups, and hunger. Ethiopia became one of the poorest countries in the world. In recent years it has been simultaneously confronted with severe drought and civil war on at least four fronts.

[32] In March 1992, the minister of Insurance and Rehabilitation declared that if international aid did not arrive quickly, the transition to democracy would be jeopardized by the instability caused by the extreme poverty of a large number of Ethiopians. Population displacements and ethnic conflicts worsen the situation, events which are reminiscent of the 1984-85 famine.

[33] The transitional government promised to promote the market economy, stimulate agricultural production and reduce poverty, within a five year program coordinated by United Nations organizations and the World Bank. In January 1993, during a visit from the UN Secretary-General Boutros Boutros-Ghali, large student demonstrations once again reflected the tense social situation in the nation.

[34] In 1994, the delivery of the $1.2 billion in five years planned in the economic program, slowed down considerably as the international organizations decided the Ethiopian government was privatizing too slowly. In a criticism of the structural adjustment plan proposed by the IMF and the World Bank, humanitarian organizations supporting Ethiopia said there should be greater investment in seeds, tools and livestock in order to fight famine.

[35] Ten years after the 1984 famine, the situation became critical again in the first six months of 1994, with 5,000 deaths in the Wolayata district in the south of the country. In May, the Council of Representatives, a temporary 87-member body, approved a draft Constitution which created the Federal Democratic Republic of Ethiopia. This draft was based on the 'ethnic federalism' doctrine, which put an end to the previous official unified vision of the nation. According to the approved document, the 'sovereignty resides in the nations, nationalities and peoples of Ethiopia' and not the people as a whole.

[36] In June, elections were held for a Constituent Assembly, but were boycotted by main opposition parties, like the Oromo Liberation Front and the Ogaden National Liberation Front. In September, the police carried out mass arrests in the west of the country, a zone mainly inhabited by Oromos. Several human rights organizations, like Amnesty International, expressed concern over the situation of the country.

[37] In May and June 1995, parliamentary elections were held, also boycotted by most of the opposition parties. The new federal republic was officially established in August, when Negasso Gidada, a Christian Oromo from the Welega region in the west of Ethiopia, took over the presidency. The outgoing president, Meles Zenawi, became Prime Minister and the 17 members of government were carefully selected to reflect 'the ethnic balance' of the country.

[38] The Government went ahead with the privatization of state companies - 144 were sold in 1995 - and the annual grain deficit stood at around a million tons. In 1996, there was an abortive assassination attempt against Mengistu in Zimbabwe. Many of his former supporters were still in prison. The rainy season started well and increased expectations of food self-sufficiency. The World Bank announced a large reduction in the Ethiopian debt. In 1997, Amnesty repeated its plea for the liberation of members of the opposition and called for an end to arbitrary arrests, torture and disappearances.

[39] In early 1998, food shortages threatened millions of Ethiopians. Due to the price increases set by the Government (13 per cent between August and December 1997) the satisfaction of basic needs become increasingly difficult for the poorer people. The rains tailed off due to the climatic upset related to the El Niño phenomenon. The Ethiopian Disaster Prevention and Preparedness Commission (DPPC) formally called on international organizations for help to avoid another famine.

[40] Fighting against Eritrea began again in February 1999, following the short war that in May 1998 killed more than a thousand people. The UN Security Council called for an immediate cease-fire and a weapons and communications warfare embargo.

[41] In March 1999, US President Bill Clinton proposed the cancellation of $70 billion of foreign aid paid to 46 African countries in a meeting of ministers there. At this time, Clinton was under pressure from Congress to approve its 'Trade initiative with Africa'.

[42] In July 1999, the World Health Organization (WHO) announced that Ethiopia - as other African and Asian countries - would be offered a mass polio vaccination program, in an attempt to eradicate the disease by the year 2001.

[43] Thousands of people celebrated the decision of the Permanent Court of Arbitration at The Hague, in April 2002, to mark the boundaries of Ethiopia's 1,000 kilometer border with Eritrea. The government in Addis considered it a victory for its demands, although its claim over the port of Asseb was not taken into account by the commission. On April 29, experts began to take high-quality aerial photos to aid the setting of boundaries of some cities - especially Badme - whose inhabitants, mostly Ethiopians, lived amid uncertainty.

[44] In late April, Ethiopia decided to close its border with Eritrea to UN officials, accusing them of having taken journalists from Eritrea to the area without Ethiopian visas. The Eritrean Government accused Ethiopia of hampering the boundary setting process and of not complying with the recent border decision.

[45] The Ministry of Labor and Social Affairs revealed on April 30 that thousands of Ethiopian children end up living or working on the streets. Their number is estimated between 100,000 and 200,000, of which at least 50,000 - according to UNICEF figures - live on the capital's streets. Angela Walker, spokesperson from UNICEF, pointed out these children are exposed to multiple dangers, such as exploitation, sexual abuse, prostitution and HIV/Aids. Currently, another 500,000 run the risk of ending up as streetchildren. ■

Fiji

Fiji

Population: 832,000 (2002)
Land area: 18,270 SQ KM
Capital: Suva City
Currency: Fiji dollar
Language: English

Four thousand years ago the Fijian archipelago was already populated. Melanesian migrations first reached the islands in the 6th century BC, and the Fijians had one of the leading Pacific cultures. In 1789, British Captain William Bligh visited the islands, writing the first detailed account of Fijian life.

2   Social life on the islands was organized in families and clans which gradually formed larger communities. One of these, ruled by traditional leader Na Ulivau, extended its influence from Ngau over the rest of the islands, achieving unification.

3   Early in the 19th century, British adventurers and merchants exploited the forests of Fiji, rich in sandalwood and other aromatic species highly prized in China. To settle their rivalries, Europeans sought support from local leaders. In 1830, the first Christian missionaries arrived from Tonga and 24 years later achieved a major victory by christening ruler Thakombau, son of Na Ulivau. Contemporary accounts report a 'refined, courteous and honorable gentleman', and this 'king' (formerly reported to be a 'cannibal') became an enthusiastic admirer of the Western world. He offered to annex Fiji to the US, though this may have been more due to the Fijian ruler's heavy debts after prolonged wars with rival leaders. The White House, caught up in the turmoil of the Secession War, missed the opportunity to tack another star on the flag. The British, faced with a shortage of sugar, 'discovered' the archipelago's potential for growing cane and, with Thakombau's consent, officially annexed the islands on October 10 1874.

4   Fijian officials raised no objections to the purchase or expropriation of large tracts of land for the new crops, though the peasants were unwilling to leave their communal estates to work on the plantations. Consequently, a massive influx of bond workers were brought in, first from the Solomon islands, and then from India. Following the abolition of slavery, the British used this same system of transferring Indian workers to Africa and the Caribbean to curb the labor shortage and ease the population squeeze in India.

5   At the end of their contracts, the workers brought their families to Fiji and became small shop owners, craftspeople or bureaucrats in the colonial administration, and though far from India, they retained their language, religion and caste system. Colonial regulations meant that they were restricted from buying land from native Fijians; a law ostensibly designed to prevent inter-ethnic conflict.

6   Initial moves toward local autonomy resulted in a complicated electoral system securing political control by the 'natives' who were in the minority. Prime Minister Sir Kamisese Mara initiated an elaborate scheme of representation, where each electoral category was allotted a quota for governmental representation: Fijians 22; Indians 22 and General 8. The peculiar system nonetheless proved useful in preventing major disruptions during the transition to independence in 1970. His Alliance Party claimed to be multiracial, and marshaled support from some Indians and other minor groups, in addition to the Fijian electorate.

7   In 1976, the Government turned down a constitutional reform project which would have required multi-group cooperation in the country's administration.

8   The 1970s economic difficulties forced thousands of Fijians to emigrate to Aotearoa/New Zealand in search of jobs. Tourism, possibly the single industry which could improve the deficit balance of payments, required Melanesians to remain 'genuine' to satisfy Australian and Aotearoa's visitors' thirst for exoticism. Individualism and private land ownership were encouraged, seeking to bolster the economic situation of 'natives' over that of the Indians. However, under these conditions, the rural workers gained few improvements; urban income increased by 3.5 per cent in 1978, but rural income increased only 0.3 per cent.

9   The difficult economic situation swelled the number of 'racist' groups such as the Nationalist Party, militant against the Indian majority, though Indians have been on the islands for four or five generations.

10   Former Prime Minister Kamisese Mara's conservative administration was deeply marked by racial and ideological trends. His government was the only one in the Commonwealth to maintain relations with the racist Rhodesian and South African regimes and to welcome Chilean dictator Augusto Pinochet on an official visit in early 1980. Mass demonstrations during Pinochet's visit demonstrated the growing progressive movement in Fiji.

11   In the 1982 election, the incumbent Alliance Party retained office with a small margin over the opposition National Federation Party (NFP), which had united its two rival factions despite growing conflict within the party.

12   In the April 11 1987 election, the Indian majority won and Timoci Bavadra became premier, ending 16 years of government by Melanesians. In May, a few short weeks after the election, Bavadra's labor government was overthrown by a military coup led by Colonel Sitiveni Rabuka. The Colonel justified himself as 'attempting to solve the ethnic problem', though the real objective seemed to be the removal of the Indian Government, who believed in an independent foreign policy, and

planned to join the treaty of Rarotonga. The treaty promoted regional denuclearization; endorsed by Australia and Aotearoa, but criticized by Britain and the US.

13   In 1987 Bavadra, who had been imprisoned by the military during the coup, was freed. He rejected the idea of new elections proposed by the military for the end of 1988, ostensibly to draw up a new constitution. The main Indian and Melanesian political parties reached an agreement, with added pressure from the Commonwealth, which appeared to appease the military. However, on October 6 1987, Rabuka retaliated by proclaiming a Republic in a move intended to disavow the authority of the head of state, the British-appointed governor.

14   In December, Rabuka resigned as head of state in an attempt to create an image of a joint civilian-military government, aimed at improving its foreign image. Penaia Ganilau was named President and Kamisese Mara, Prime Minister - a regime never subjected to the approval of the electorate.

15   In July 1990 a new constitutional decree based on apartheid went into effect, assuring the indigenous people 37 of the Chamber of Representatives 70 seats and 24 of the Senate's 34 seats. A constitutional referendum announced for 1992 was finally cancelled. The following year, the apartheid model was denounced by the UN's General Assembly, as well as Mauritius and India. In November, the Association of Fijian Young People and Students organized a public burning of the new constitution's text. Demonstrators were harshly subdued.

16   Rabuka founded the Fijian Political Party (FPP/SVT) and in 1992, amid growing political and social strains, a military officer was named Prime Minister.

17   Fiji was not able to overcome its chronic balance of payments deficit: almost all of its fuel and manufactured products were imported and its main sources of income - sugar exports and tourism - were not enough to balance the budget.

18   In November 1993 six FPP/SVT members voted together with the opposition against the budget, forcing general elections. Rabuka retained power with 31 of the 37

Fijian seats and support from independent and General Vote Party members. Dissidents formed a Fijian Association obtaining only 5 seats.

[19] In November 1994, the Government began a timid revision of the racist constitution. In 1995, Rabuka had to reorganize his Cabinet several times due to internal divisions in the coalition. He took legal steps to challenge the findings of an independent prosecutor that which involved him in unlawful management linked to the Central Bank's deficit. The Government's plan to allow 28,000 Chinese from Hong Kong to settle in the country also led to criticism. According to the official plan, each one of the future immigrants would have to pay $130,000 to legally reside in the country.

[20] In September 1996, a Commission completed a report on the new constitution, which created a 'multiracial council' and reserved a certain number of seats in Parliament for certain ethnic groups. The document was approved in July 1997, coming into operation a year later.

[21] In September 1997, Fiji was readmitted into the British Commonwealth, 10 years after the coup which took it out.

[22] The Asian crisis forced the Government to devalue the currency 20 per cent against the dollar and to lower customs barriers.

[23] At the end of that year, a study revealed that 40 per cent of women on Suva suffered from sexually transmitted diseases. In early 1998, the Government launched a health plan to combat an outbreak of dengue fever (similar to malaria) which had killed four children.

[24] In the first truly democratic elections since the coup, in May 1999, the victor was Mahendra Chaudhry, of the Fiji Labor Party (FLP). The Fijian Political Party (FPP/SVT) headed by Rabuka, won just six of the 71 parliamentary seats. Its ally, the General Voters Party, which had been the minority, did not win any seats.

[25] Although tens of thousands of Indians had fled Fiji since the 1987 coup, they represented nearly half the population. Ethnic tensions exploded a year later, on May 19 2000, when an armed group led by Fijian businessman George Speight entered Parliament and abducted Prime Minister Mahendra along with 30 others (including the daughter of President Kamisese Mara). Speight was seeking a reform of the Constitution to instate Fijian supremacy and thereby prevent an Indian minority from holding power.

[26] President Mara deposed the abducted Prime Minister, believing it would undermine Speight's importance and force a change of attitude. Commodore Frank Bainarama led a new coup May 29 and overthrew the President, saying he had become weak and inoperative.

[27] The rebels were granted amnesty after releasing the hostages. In July, Ratu Josefa Iloilo was named interim President, while Laisenia Qarase was made Prime Minister, also interim. Because Speight had threatened to renew protests if the Cabinet did not include his supporters, the army arrested him and over 350 rebels.

[28] The coup left a deep wound in the country. Racial divisions intensified. In February 2001 the Fiji High Court ruled that the current military-backed government was illegal; the government announced elections would be held in August/September that year.

[29] Ilikini Naitini (commonly known as George Speight) of the Conservative Alliance (MV) was elected as an MP while he was in prison awaiting trial for treason. The United Fiji Party/SDL won 46 per cent of the vote, capping the 38 per cent of Mahendra Chaudhry's Fiji Labor party (FLP); the MV came third with 8 per cent. Although the 1997 Constitution gave the parties the right to occupy a number of seats in the Cabinet proportional to their representation in Parliament, Qarase, still chief of the interim government, excluded Chaudry's party from the Cabinet. The Supreme Court reversed the decision and ordered Qarase to include Indians in the Cabinet.

[30] In December, Speight was removed from office due to his inability to take part in sessions. Shortly after, he was sentenced to death, accused of treason. However, in February 2002, President Iloilo commuted his sentence to life imprisonment. ■

PROFILE

ENVIRONMENT

Fiji consists of nine large islands and 300 volcanic and coral islets and atolls, of which only 100 are inhabited. The group is located in Melanesia, in the Koro Sea, between Vanuatu (formerly New Hebrides) to the west and Tonga to the east, five degrees north of the Tropic of Capricorn. The largest islands are Viti Levu, where the capital is located, Vanua Levu, Taveuni, Lau, Kandavu, Asua, Karo, Ngau and Ovalau. The terrain is mainly mountainous. Fertile soils in flatland zones plus tropical rainy climate, mildly tempered by sea winds, make the islands suitable for plantation crops, sugarcane and copra. The marine environment is threatened by overfishing and the pollution of its coastal waters. Islands suffer a deforestation process.

SOCIETY

Peoples: Half of Fijians are of Melanesian origin with some Polynesian influence, the other are descendants of Indian workers who came to the archipelago early in the 20th century; plus those of European and Chinese origin. Banabans (see Kiribati) have bought the island of Rambi, between Vanua Levu and Taveuni, with the purpose of settling there since their own island was left uninhabitable by phosphate mining.
Religions: 53 per cent of Fijians are Christian (mainly Methodist and other Protestant sects) 38 per cent are Hindu and 8 per cent Muslim.
Languages: English (official), Urdu, Hindi, Fijian, Chinese. Rotuma and Kiribati (minority languages).
Political Parties: There are 26 registered political parties; 18 contested the 2001 elections. The main ones are: Soqosoqo Duavata Ni Lewenivanua/United Fiji Party (UFP/SDL), led by Laisenia Qarase; Fiji Labor Party (FLP), led by Mahendra Chaudry; Conservative Alliance/Matanitu Vanua (MV), members include George Speight; New Labor Unity Party (NLUP); United General Party (UGP); National Federation Party (NFP); Other/independent, including former major party Soqosoqo ni Vakavulewa ni Taukei/Fiji Political Party (FPP/SVT) of coup leader Sitiveni Rabuka; and the Fijian Association Party (FAP), founded by Native Land Trust Board head Josefata Kamikamica as an indigenous Fijian movement to oppose Rabuka. Since 1998, the party has been led by Adi Kuini Speed, a former Fiji Labor Party leader and widow of FLP founder,Timoci Bavadra. As Fiji's most prominent female politician, Adi Kuini has campaigned to attract the vote of women; its focus is on living conditions of the poor; it has also attempted to win the confidence of Indo-Fijians.
Social Organizations: The Association of Fijian Young People and Students, Fijian Trade Unions Congress (FTUC).

THE STATE

Official Name: Republic of the Fiji Islands.
Administrative Divisions: 5 Regions divided into 15 Provinces.
Capital: Suva City 196,000 people (1999).
Other cities: Lautoka 45,000 people; Nadi 32,100; Nausori 22,500 (2000).
Government: Ratu Josefa Iloilo, President since July 2000. Prime Minister, Laisenia Qarase caretaker since March 2001; elected September 2001. Parliament: House of Representatives (Vale) has 70 members and The Senate (Seniti) has 34 members.
National Holiday: October 10, Independence Day (1970).
Armed Forces: 3,900 (1995).

Finland

Population: 5,183,000 (2002)
Land area: 304,590 SQ KM
Capital: Helsinki
Currency: Euro
Language: Finnish

Suomi

Finland was inhabited from 7500 BC onwards, and the first settlers were the Sami (later also called 'Lapps' by other people). The Sami were hunters, fishers and gatherers. Over the centuries they began domesticating animals and practising subsistence agriculture, remaining isolated from the rest of Europe. Much later - in the 1st century AD - descendants of the Finno-Ugrics entered from the south, and they pushed the Sami to the north, taking control of the major part of the territory. By 1,000 years ago, the Finns had established many settlements in the south.

2   The ancestors of the tavastlanders came from the southwest across the Gulf of Finland, and the Carelians arrived from the southeast. Scandinavian peoples occupied the west coast, the archipelagos and also the Aland Islands (Ahvenanmaa).

3   From the 12th century onwards, Finland was claimed by both the Russian and Swedish empires. In 1172, the Pope advised the Swedes to control the Finns, to avoid their being proselytized by the Russian Orthodox Church. With the Protestant Reformation, Lutheranism became the official religion.

4   In 1809 Finland became a grand duchy of Imperial Russia, although it was allowed to maintain its own parliament, army and judicial system.

5   In 1889 the Social Democratic Party was founded, a party which was to play a leading role in Finnish political life from that moment onward. The presence of Lenin and other Bolshevik exiles also helped to strengthen the country's socialist leanings. In 1906 a single-chamber parliament was created, and universal suffrage was established. Finland became the third country in the world to recognize female suffrage.

6   Independence was declared in December 1917. Spurred on by the example of the Russian Revolution, Finnish Socialists tried to seize power by means of a revolution. In January 1918, the Social Democratic Party (SDP) took Helsinki and the major industrial centers. The Government counterattacked, backed by the White Army and German troops under the command of General Mannerheim. In May, the civil war came to an end and the Socialist leaders were tried and given harsh sentences.

7   The country became a monarchy, and German Prince Frederick Charles of Hessen was elected king. After Germany's defeat in World War I, the monarchy collapsed and General Mannerheim was appointed regent, while new republican institutions were established.

8   The 1919 Constitution established a parliamentary system with a strong presidential figure. In addition, it made the Prime Minister the head of the government, and the President head of state. Although the constitution recognized both Finnish and Swedish as official languages, nationalist youth groups later demanded that Finnish be given priority. This led to the creation of the Swedish People's Party. Subsequent constitutional reforms maintained the right of the Swedish minority to its own language.

9   In 1918, 70 per cent of all Finns depended upon agriculture and forestry for a living. The importance of this segment of the population led to the formation of the Rural Party, which became the Center Party.

10   The country was ruled almost uninterruptedly since independence by alliances between the Social Democrats and the Centrists. From 1920 to 1930, these two political forces backed an ambitious program of social and economic reforms. Agricultural production was modernized, and the exploitation of the country's lumber resources was intensified. Likewise, the Government fostered industrialization in the cities, and sponsored progressive legislation, aimed at protecting the emerging working class and agricultural workers.

11   The growth of the Communist Party (FCP) gave rise to the ultra-right-wing Lapua (Lappo) Movement, whose terrorist acts and mass protests were supported by conservative groups and by some Rural Party members. In 1930, the FCP was banned by law, with the support of these parties. In 1931 the Lappo movement began to carry out attacks against the Social Democrats. After an attempted coup the following year, they were finally arrested by the Government.

12   After the German invasion of Poland, the USSR demanded part of the Karelian Islands, a naval base on the Hanko peninsula and other islands of the Gulf of Finland, as a means of defending themselves against imminent German attack. Given the refusal of the Finns to cede the lands, the USSR seized them by force, giving rise to a brief conflict. The 1940 Treaty of Moscow forced Finland to cede these territories.

13   Finland had declared its neutrality at the beginning of World War I, but since it had become involved in a conflict with the USSR, it permitted German troops to use its territory to launch an attack against their mutual enemy. Thus, Finland was briefly able to recover the territories lost in 1940.

14   The 1944 Soviet counter-offensive and subsequent German retreat strengthened the Finnish peace movement. The Karelian Islands once again came under the control of the Red Army, causing the resignation of President Retie, the architect of the alliance with Germany. He was succeeded by General Mannerheim, who negotiated an armistice with Moscow, recognized the 1940 Treaty of Moscow and organized the fight to expel German troops from the country. During the war nearly 500,000 Finns had died.

15   When the War ended, the country's political life was once again controlled by the Social Democratic-Finnish Rural Party alliance, and the leader of the Finnish Rural Party, Urho Kekkonen, occupied the presidency from 1956-1982. The office of Prime Minister was also held by SDP figures for most of that same period.

16   During the post-war period, Finland was faced with a critical social and economic situation. Production had come to a standstill, there were thousands of unemployed and more than 300,000 refugees from the occupied areas.

17   Neutrality became the cornerstone of Finnish foreign policy. In 1948, Helsinki and Moscow signed the Finno-Soviet Pact of Friendship, Cooperation and Mutual Assistance. Seven years later, the USSR returned the naval base at Porkkala and the treaty was again ratified in 1970 and 1983. In 1955, Finland joined the European Free Trade Association (EFTA), the United Nations and the Nordic Council, but blocked the creation of a customs union within the framework of the Council. Finland was the only member of the

OECD which simultaneously maintained relations with the EC and the CMEA (organization established in January 1949 to facilitate and coordinate the economic development of the eastern European countries belonging to the Soviet bloc). This situation helps explain the country's relatively rapid economic recovery.

[18] The Finnish Government offered incentives to develop the lumber industry, axis of the economy. It promoted industrialization and took advantage of the profits generated by its lucrative foreign trade.

[19] However, with the disintegration of the USSR which had provided the market for over 25 per cent of Finland's exports, economic growth came to a standstill.

[20] In 1991, Prime Minister Esko Aho, politically moderate, launched a drastic structural adjustment program which was resisted by workers. Economic stagnation caused a decline in Finnish standards of living, and unemployment went from 3.5 to over 20 per cent.

[21] Finland requested European Union (EU) membership in 1992. A referendum in 1994 supported the initiative, which was confirmed in early 1995. The internal impact of this measure was softened by special subsidies for the farming sector, disadvantaged compared with its community partners, because of the cold climate. Part of the State monopoly on public health and the sale of alcoholic beverages was also maintained.

[22] Once the nation had effectively entered the EU, President Martti Ahtisaari declared Finland would not enter the Western European Union, which could have been a step toward NATO membership. The Finnish Government considered a common defense policy should be based on consensus and that their traditional neutrality was obsolete since the fall of the Iron Curtain. It also warned the West of the risk of isolating Russia and of the environmental danger posed by the nuclear plants and industries in that country.

[23] In the March elections the Social Democratic Party, led by Paavo Lipponen, pushed out the rural-based Center Party, which had been the ruling force in Parliament up until then. In October, the Government proposed a plan to reduce unemployment, which hovered at around 17 per cent. Lipponen was designated Prime Minister, replacing Esko Aho. The Finnish paper industry reduced its emissions of sulfur dioxide, but more than half the pollution continued to come from the neighboring countries.

[24] In 1996, the Government reiterated its policy of non-alliance on military matters, although it repeated its interest in the EU's economic and monetary union planned for 1999. Inflation stood at just under 1 per cent throughout 1997. The growth in industrial production was amongst the highest in the EU at 3.2 per cent. In October, unemployment fell to 12.6 per cent.

[25] The global Corruption Perception Index, issued by Transparency International in 1998 based on reports from investors, financial risk analysts and public opinion, rated Finland among the 5 countries whose commercial transactions are perceived to be relatively free of corruption.

[26] Social-Democrat Tarja Halonen won the January 1999 elections, becoming the first female head of state. The President, however, would carry out only representative functions, having no influence on the formation of government nor deciding foreign policy, since the latest constitutional reform had installed a parliamentary system in the country.

[27] Russian President Vladimir Putin visited Finland for the first time in September 2001. Meetings with Halonen and Prime Minister Paavo Lipponen focused on Russia's relations with the EU and the inclusion of new members in NATO, opposed by Russia. Putin became the first Russian leader to pay tribute at the grave of Marshal Carl Gustav Mannerheim, who led Finnish troops against the Red Army during the Second World War.

[28] In October 2001, Finland held first place in the economic competitiveness index made up by the World Economic Forum (WEF). The index analyzes the economies of 75 developed countries, based on surveys of 4,600 business people, and forecasts each country's potential growth. The improvement of Finland's competitiveness, from 4th place to 1st, was based on the electronics and telecommunications sector.

[29] In the midst of a lively public debate regarding the convenience of nuclear energy, and in order to meet the growing power needs, the Government decided in January 2002 to build a fifth nuclear reactor. The proposal has to be passed by Parliament. The opposition wanted Finland to buy the energy it required from neighbors, or to use Russian natural gas. Sinikka

PROFILE

ENVIRONMENT

Finland is a flat country (the average altitude is 150 meters above sea level) with vast marine clay plains, low plateaus, numerous hills and lakes formed by glaciers. The population is concentrated mainly on the coastal plains, the country's main farming area. Lumbering of coniferous forests is the central economic activity and provides the main export products: lumber, paper pulp and paper. Sulfur dioxide emissions and the dumping of contaminated water into the Baltic Sea pose serious threats to the environment. The population resides mainly along the coast, the main agricultural area. The economy's base is forest (coniferous) products and mobile phones. Main export products are from the energy (high technology in electronics and communications), metallurgy, wood (paper paste and paper) and chemicals sectors. Emissions of sulfur dioxide and polluted waters in the Baltic Sea are serious problems for the environment.

SOCIETY

Peoples: 92.1 per cent of the population is Finnish and 7.5 per cent Swedish. There are Roma and Sami minorities.
Religions: 86 per cent of the population are Lutherans and 1 per cent Finnish Orthodox Church (official churches). 12 per cent are non-religious.
Languages: Finnish (official and spoken by 93.2 per cent). Swedish, spoken by 6 per cent of the population, is also an official language. Sami/Lapp is spoken by a minority of around 1,700 people. **Political Parties:** The Social Democratic Party of Finland (SDP), center-left; Finnish Center; the People's Democratic League; the National Rally, moderate conservative; the Left Wing League; the Green League; the Swedish People's Party in Finland, liberal, represents interests of the Swedish-speaking minority; the Christian League of Finland; Reform Group; Rural Party. **Social Organizations:** Central Organization of Finnish Unions, with 1,086,000 members and 28 member unions. Finnish Confederation of Salaried Employees.

THE STATE

Official Name: Suomen Tasavalta. **Administrative divisions:** 6 provinces. **Capital:** Helsinki 1,150,000 people (1999). **Other cities:** Espoo 219,400 people; Tampere 197,200; Vantaa 182,700; Turku (Abo) 175,100 (2000). **Government:** Tarja Halonen, President since March 2000. Paavo Lipponen, Prime Minister since April 1995. Unicameral Legislature: the Diet, with 200 members. Since 1996 there is a Parliament for the Sami minority (the *samediggi*) with limited autonomy on cultural matters. **National Holiday:** December 6, Independence (1917, from Russia). **Armed Forces:** 31,200 (1994). **Other:** Border guards: 4,400.

Monkare, Minister of Industry and Trade, stated that the decision to increase nuclear power production was the cheapest of all options, both for the national economy and the Government's expenses. Finland was the only Western European country without research into the use of alternative energies. ∎

France

Population:	59,670,000 (2002)
Land area:	550,100 SQ KM
Capital:	Paris
Currency:	Euro
Language:	French

France

The two regions occupied by the Celts (see box 'The Celts') were known to the Romans as Gaul. The region between the Alps and Rome was Cisalpine Gaul, and beyond the Alps was Transalpine Gaul. With natural borders on all sides; the Alps, the Pyrénées, the Atlantic Ocean and the Rhine, Gaul occupied not only what is now France, but also Belgium, Switzerland and the western banks of the Rhine.

[2] Gallic society was essentially agricultural, with almost no urban life. The few cities, were used as fortresses, where the peasants sought refuge when under attack. Society was divided into the nobles (who were also warriors), the people and the Druids, keepers of Celtic wisdom and religious traditions.

[3] The Romans came to Gaul in 125 BC. They conquered the area along the Mediterranean, the Rhone valley and Languedoc, calling the combined area 'Provincia'. Caesar divided Gaul into two regions; Provincia and Free Gaul. Free Gaul was subdivided into Belgian Gaul in the north, between the Rhine and the Seine; Celtic Gaul in the center, between the Seine, the Garonne and the lower Rhine; and Aquitaine, in the southwest.

[4] In 27 BC, Augustus Caesar set up administrative centres in Gaul, to manage Rome's affairs encouraging urbanization. Bridges and an extensive road network were built throughout the region, facilitating an increase in trade. Wheat production was increased and vineyards were planted, with wine replacing beer as the traditional beverage. After a series of invasions by the Visigoths in the south and the Burgundians along the Saone and the Rhone, the northern Gauls conquered the rest of Gaul under the leadership of Clovis, adopting the name, 'Franks'.

[5] Between the 5th and the 9th centuries France emerged as the Merovingian and Carolingian dynasties brought the entire region under the influence of Christianity. With the Islamic expansion and the fall of the Roman Empire, trade ceased, urban civilization was almost completely wiped out, population decreased and the culture became decadent.

[6] By the 9th century, feudalism had become firmly established. Centralized authority practically disappeared, as local people were unable to repel the Scandinavians, Hungarians, Saracens, and other invaders of this era. By the end of the century, the previously united land was a conglomerate of more than 300 independent counties.

[7] From the 10th century onward, the royal dynasties slowly recovered their power. They established hereditary succession to the throne, they shared power with the Church and became the main feudal landowners.

[8] In the 13th century, an increase in commercial activity led to a remarkable rebirth of the cities, and agricultural techniques were improved, as the population increased. The Crusades led to a greater circulation of people and goods, and the gradual disappearance of serfdom gave rise to greater social mobility. This was the 'Golden Age' of the French Middle Ages, when France had great power over, and influence upon Western civilization.

[9] Paris was one of Europe's most important cities, and the prestige of its University was linked to its cultural

pre-eminence. The University trained lawyers in Roman law, and their influence helped form a new concept of the State where the king was no longer a feudal lord, but rather the embodiment of the law. Over a period of time, nationalistic feelings began to develop.

[10] Louis XIV, the 'Sun King', personified the concept of absolute monarchy. He came to the throne in 1661, and established the 'Divine Right of Kings'. He consolidated the unity of France, giving rise to the concept of the modern State. During his reign, French cultural influence reached its apogee.

[11] The 1789 Revolution opened up a new era in the history of France. The National Assembly, convened in July of that year, replaced the absolute monarch with a constitutional monarchy. The fall of the Bastille on July 14 and the Declaration of the Rights of Man, on August 27, brought the old regime to an end, thus paving the way for the rise of the bourgeoisie - the prevailing class of the towns - whose reforms came into direct conflict with the Church and the King. Finally, the Assembly overthrew the monarchy and proclaimed the First French Republic.

[12] The rest of Europe joined forces against revolutionary France. Danton and Robespierre declared the nation 'to be in peril' and formed a citizen army. This Committee of Public Salvation was able to forestall foreign invasion but internal confrontations resulted in the 'Reign of Terror'. Robespierre and his companions were overthrown and executed in July 1794.

[13] For the next five years, the revolutionaries tried to regain control of the country, which had fallen victim to corruption, internal strife and instability. Napoleon Bonaparte's coup (1799) brought an end to the dying regime. Seizing power, he had himself named Consul for Life in 1802 and then Emperor in 1804.

[14] Although Napoleon's reign represented a return to absolutism, it preserved the main achievements of the Revolution. Legal, administrative, religious, financial and educational reorganization changed the country irrevocably. Napoleon strove hard to bring the rest of Europe under his control and his armies occupied the whole of the continent from Madrid to the outskirts of Moscow. Finally, exhausted by war, France was defeated at Waterloo, in 1815.

[15] Rebellions in 1830, 1848 and 1871 rocked the country. In spite of this, the Industrial Revolution brought factories, railroads, large companies and credit institutions to France. The Third Republic, beginning in 1870, was to be France's longest-lasting regime in almost a century and a half.

[16] With the establishment of universal male suffrage in 1848, the peasants and the urban middle class had the greatest electoral power. The Government managed to win their support by protectionism and the establishment of free, secular and mandatory primary education, which raised aspirations of greater social mobility.

[17] Under the Republic, France had a period of colonial expansion, beginning with the conquest of Algeria in 1830, and continuing with other territories in Africa and the Far East. A large empire was built, with colonies in the Caribbean, Africa, the Middle East, the Indo-Chinese peninsula and the Pacific.

[18] World War I enabled France to recover Alsace and Lorraine, which

had been annexed by Germany in 1870. The War left France devastated. More than 1.5 million people had been killed. Property damage coupled with the internal and foreign debt added up to more than 150 billion gold francs, and the nation's currency lost its traditional stability. Neither the right-wing bloc nor the radical party was able to bring the economic and political situation under control.

[19] The world-wide recession reached France in 1931. In 1936, the parties of the left, who had joined together to form the Popular Front, had won the legislative elections. They had carried out important social reforms, such as paid vacations and the 40-hour working week, but they were unable to hold back unemployment or the looming economic crisis. Government became polarized between supporters of Italian Fascism and those of Communism. This split led to an impasse until 1939, when Germany invaded Poland.

[20] Germany went on to occupy almost one-third of France. In 1940, Marshall Pétain signed an armistice proclaiming the 'national revolution' transforming non-occupied France into a satellite of Berlin. From London, General de Gaulle urged the French people to continue the fight.

[21] France was liberated in 1944. The French participated in the liberation and the invasion of Germany, with the resistance movement (especially the communists and socialists), the Free French Forces (liberal nationalists) and French troops fighting alongside the Allies. In October 1946, the Fourth Republic was proclaimed. This period was characterized by political instability and bitter opposition between the French Communist Party (PCF) and General de Gaulle's party.

[22] Funds from the US Marshall Plan, led to the economic and social reconstruction of the country. Production reached a six per cent annual growth rate. Per capita income increased 47 per cent between 1949 and 1959; women were granted the right to vote; the banks were nationalized and a social security program went into effect. In 1957 France was one of the six signatories of the Treaty of Rome, which created the European Economic Community (EEC).

[23] After 1945, France was unable to re-establish its pre-war control over its colonies. The spirit of democracy and increasing awareness of universal human rights, was consolidated by the anti-Fascist alliance and the creation of the United Nations. Colonization had not allowed local identity to influence policy, so decolonization took place through fierce pro-independence movements, with little room for negotiation.

[24] In 1945, Syria and Libya were the first French colonies to become independent, followed by Morocco, Tunisia and Madagascar. Vietnam, Laos and Cambodia became independent only in 1954, after a long and bloody war. In May 1958, four years after the Algerian revolution began, the pieds-noirs - French people residing in the colony - revolted. They made the army promise not to leave the country. This dealt a mortal blow to the Fourth Republic, and the Government called in General de Gaulle to deal with the crisis.

[25] The establishment of the Fifth Republic in 1958 and the 1962 decision to elect the President by direct universal suffrage laid the foundation for a regime with strong presidential powers. After the independence of Algeria and the last remaining African colonies, the country sought to achieve greater stability. With national independence as the primary aim of their foreign policy, France made use of 'deterrent' atomic power and withdrew from the military structure of the North Atlantic Treaty Organization (NATO), in 1966.

[26] France continued to be a member of the Atlantic alliance, and maintained enormous economic, cultural and political influence over its former African colonies, south of the Sahara. Diplomatic relations with Algeria, Vietnam, and other countries that had fought bloody wars for independence were not restored until 1982.

[27] In May 1968, the greatest social and political crisis of the Fifth Republic took place. Huge student protests and labor strikes throughout the country were brought on by the regime's growing authoritarianism in the educational and social sectors. For a whole month, the Government seemed to be seriously threatened. Apart from the student leaders, however, there were no other political forces capable of toppling the government, and the general strike was called off when a salary increase was promised.

[28] The years which followed saw the birth of other groups based around social issues, such as the feminist, ecological and antinuclear movements. In 1972 the Socialist Party and the Communist Party created the Union of the Left, and François Mitterand, the Socialist candidate, was elected President in 1981 because of the Communist votes; his was the first left-wing cabinet since 1958.

[29] The new government carried out reforms: the nationalization of important industrial and banking groups, new labor rights for workers, the 39-hour working week, an increase in social benefits, retirement at the age of 60 and a decentralization of power. However, unemployment, the economic crisis and an increase in imports led the Government to enforce a harsh economic policy and to carry out restructuring of the industrial sector. This led communist ministers to resign from the Government, in 1984. In 1981, a Ministry of Women's Rights had been created, charged to enforce existing legislation.

[30] In 1986, expecting a defeat of the Left, Mitterand substituted the majority electoral system by a proportional system which gave more seats to the losers than the previous one. In March, a right-wing coalition made up mainly of the Group for the Republic (RPR), a party led by neo-Gaullist Jacques Chirac and by former president (1974-1981) Valery Giscard

PROFILE

ENVIRONMENT

In the north is the Paris Basin, which spreads out into fields and plains. The Massif Central, in the center of France, is made up of vast plateaus. The Alps rise in the south-east. The southern region includes the Mediterranean coast, with mountain ranges, such as the Pyrénées, and plains. Grain farming is the main agricultural activity; wheat is grown all over the country, especially in the north. Grapes are grown in the Mediterranean region for wine exports. The main mineral resources are coal, iron ore and bauxite. Dependence on nuclear energy poses a serious problem. Nuclear reactors operating in the country generate three-quarters of the national consumption of electricity, making France the second largest producer of nuclear energy, after the US. There is also a nuclear-reprocessing plant (Cap de la Hague), which generates plutonium, with serious sanitary and environmental risks.

SOCIETY

Peoples: Most of the population stem from the integration of three basic European groups: Nordic, Alpine and Mediterranean. Approximately 7 per cent of the population is of foreign descent. Portuguese 1.1 per cent; Algerian 1.1 per cent; Moroccan 1.0 per cent; Italian 0.4 per cent; Spanish 0.4 per cent; Turkish 0.3 per cent; other 2.1 per cent.
Religions: Mainly Catholic (76 per cent); Calvinist 2 per cent; Muslim 2 per cent, Jewish 1 per cent.
Languages: French is the official and predominant language. There are also regional languages: Breton in Brittany, a German dialect in Alsace and Lorraine, Flemish in the northeast, Catalan and Basque in the Southwest, Provençal in the south-east, Occitan in the central south, Corsican on the island of Corsica. Immigrants speak their own languages, mainly Portuguese, Arab, Berber, Spanish, Italian and African languages.
Political Parties: Socialist Party; Rally for the Republic (RPR); National Front; Union for the French Democracy (UDF); French Communist Party; the Greens; Revolutionary Communist League.
Social Organizations: General Labor Confederation (CGT); French Democratic Labor Confederation (CFDT); Workers' Force (FO); French Confederation of Christian Workers (CFTC). France has the lowest level of unionization in the European Community (8 per cent in 1990). Peasants' Confederation, one of whose founders is anti-globalization activist Jose Bové. ATTAC-France, the group that campaigns for a tax on financial transactions, was founded in France where it has its strongest backing. European Marches is the European movement of unemployed, but especially strong in France. SOS Racism, a group that began fighting against racism faced by immigrants and their descendants. National Students Union of France (UNEF). Political and social movements of several traditional minorities have grown: in Corsica, the National Liberation Front of Corsica (FLNC), and its multiple offshoots that practice armed struggle for the island's independence; Corsica Nation, a separatist political party. In the Basque Country there are Abertzaleen Batasuna (Patriotic Union), a separatist party, and Iparretarrak, a small armed group. Major independentist groups in some French overseas dependencies, especially in Kanaky (New Caledonia).

THE STATE

Official Name: République Française. **Administrative divisions:** 22 Regions with 96 Departments in France and 5 'Overseas Departments'. **Capital:** Paris 9,608,000 people (1999). **Other cities:** Lyon 1,660,000 people; Marseille 1,527,000; Toulouse 971,600; Nice 939,600 (2000). **Government:** Jacques Chirac, President since May 1995, re-elected in 2002. Jean-Pierre Raffarin, Prime Minister since May 2002. Bicameral Parliament: the National Assembly, with 577 members, and the Senate, with 321 members. **National Holiday:** July 14, Bastille Day (1789). **Armed Forces:** 409,000 (1995). **Other:** 96,300 Gendarmes.

MATERNAL MORTALITY	FOOD DEPENDENCY	FOREIGN TRADE
1985/99	2000	Millions US$ 2000
Per 100,000 live births **10**	**8%**	IMPORTS **352,622** EXPORTS **370,902**

D'Estaing's Union for the French Democracy (UDF), defeated the Left in the legislative elections. The elections confirmed a clear progress of Jean Marie Le Pen's ultra-right National Front. Chirac had to form a new government and for two years the country experienced its first 'cohabitation' between a left-wing president and a conservative council of ministers.

[31] Chirac's government wiped out some of the 1981 and 1982 reforms with the privatization of several companies nationalized by the left but kept most of the social gains. In the meantime, it continued a liberalization policy of the economy and finances begun in the socialist government's last years. In the field of individual liberties, the strong hand of Interior minister Charles Pasqua, especially regarding legislation concerning foreigners living in France, was criticized by several humanitarian organizations.

[32] In 1988, Mitterrand defeated Chirac in presidential elections. The elected President called for new legislative elections. After a new victory of the Socialist Party, socialist Michel Rocard was appointed Prime Minister.

[33] The Socialist economic policy did not differ substantially from that of the right. Unemployment kept on the rise, with a 9.5 per cent rate of the economically active population in 1991. That year,

Rocard was replaced by Edith Cresson, who was the first woman to become head of government in modern France. Nine months later, Mitterand replaced Cresson with former Economy minister Pierre Bérégovoy, with the backing of industrial and financial circles.

[34] In 1993, the Left was defeated in legislative elections once again and Mitterrand named conservative Edouard Balladur as Prime Minister. The corruption scandals, whose main targets had been socialist leaders, affected this time renowned right-wing politicians and caused three of Balladur's ministers to resign in 1994.

[35] In the April 1995 presidential elections Chirac defeated socialist Lionel Jospin and appointed conservative Alain Juppé as Prime Minister.

[36] In December, the largest civil servants' strike since 1968 paralyzed the country for over three weeks. The social situation remained tense in 1996, which some observers linked with unfair income distribution - 20 per cent of the population received 44 per cent of total personal income - and property distribution, since 20 per cent of the French owned 69 per cent of national wealth.

[37] The Juppé administration continued its austerity policy which caused confrontation with labor unions in 1996. A new law was passed in 1997 to restrict the entrance and residence of immigrants in the

country. In February there were demonstrations against the measure which mobilized over 150,000 people in one day.

[38] Unexpectedly, Chirac called for early legislative elections. In the second round, on May 25, the leftist opposition obtained an important victory after running united in the elections. The Socialist Party obtained 241 deputies and became the country's largest party once more. Together with the Communists, with 38 seats, the Greens, with seven, and other 33 deputies from the left, the Socialist Party achieved a comfortable majority in parliament. The right wing coalition obtained 256 deputies, while the National Front got only one seat.

[39] Lionel Jospin became the new Prime Minister and the Communists

had two ministries while former presidential candidate Dominique Voynet held one for the Greens.

[40] In 1997, in order to address unemployment, Jospin proposed the reduction of the working week to 35 hours. Many demonstrations, both by workers and unemployed, which continued through to 1998, demanded the immediate adoption of this measure.

[41] Several studies and surveys in 1998 published by *Le Monde*, showed that two out of every five French citizens openly admitted having racist sentiments. The country was top of the table for racism in the EU, closely followed by Belgium. These figures were surprising to the researchers due to the fact that, second to Luxembourg, France is the most ethnically mixed country in the EU.

OVERSEAS DEPARTMENTS AND TERRITORIES

Departments: Guadeloupe; Martinique; French Guiana; Réunion; St Pierre and Miquelon (see entries).

Territories: Mayotte; New Caledonia (see Kanaky); Wallis and Futuna (see entries); French Polynesia (see entry).

Southern and Antarctic Territories: Comprising two archipelagos: Kerguelen (7,000 sq km, with 80 people in Port-Aux-Francais) and Crozet (500 sq km, with 20 people); two islands: New Amsterdam (60 sq km, with 35 inhabitants.) and St Paul (7 sq km, uninhabited), located in the southern Indian Ocean; the Land of Adélie (500,000 sq km with 27 people at the Dumont Durville Base), in Antarctica. The Territories are governed by an Administrator-General advised by an even-member Consultative Council appointed by the French Government. Technical personnel at weather stations are the only inhabitants.

St Pierre and Miquelon

Population: 7,000 (2002)
Land area: 242 SQ KM
Capital: St Pierre
Currency: Euro
Language: French

ENVIRONMENT
Archipelago formed by two main islands: St Pierre (26 sq km) and Miquelon (which, with Langlade, amounts to 216 sq km) and some ten smaller islands off the Canadian coast in the North Atlantic. Economy almost exclusively depends on fishing.

SOCIETY
Peoples: The majority are descendants of French settlers.
Religion: Catholic.
Language: French.

THE STATE
Official name: Departément de Saint Pierre et Miquelon (Territorial Collectivity of Saint Pierre and Miquelon – conventional).
Capital: St Pierre 6,000 people (1999).
Other towns: Miquelon 1,100 people (2000).
Government: A French overseas

department. The Head of State is Jaques Chirac (French President). Administered by a Prefect, Jean-François Tallec (since January 2001), who represents the French state. Unicameral Legislature: the General Council, with 19 members elected for a six-year term in single-seat constituencies. The territory has one deputy and one senator in the French parliament and has representation in the European Parliament.

DEMOGRAPHY
Population: 7,000 (2002)
Annual growth: 0.9 % (1985-2000)
Estimates for year 2015: 8,000 (2000)
Annual growth to year 2015: 0.7 % (2000)

ECONOMY
Currency: 1.2 euro = $ 1 (03/2002)

42 In March 1999 the National Assembly approved a law giving legal status to unmarried couples, by 300 to 253 votes. Tens of thousands of citizens opposing the legislation demonstrated in the streets, fearing the law would allow gay couples to adopt children.

43 The 35-hour week law came into effect on February 1 2000. That day, truckers began a strike. This was organized by workers, and not by employers, who had organized a strike the previous month. While employers did not support a reduction of hours, most workers did, as long as it did not imply a cut in wages.

44 Scandal broke out in the political system when an illegal scheme of funding for political parties was revealed in August. Although the President was not directly implicated in the judicial investigation that analyzed the last six years of party funding, several of his collaborators were investigated for corruption. According to the public prosecutor, the focus of this fraudulent plan was the city of Paris, when Chirac was Mayor between 1990-1995. The investigations pointed to Michel Roussin, Chirac's assistant in the city government, as architect of a plan to give 'gifts' to the parties from businesspeople who were compensated with contracts to build or remodel schools in Paris' Ile de France region. According to statements by those investigated, the contracts amounted to $3.7 billion. A 1995 law banned companies from making donations to political parties, which are funded by public money.

45 In April 2002, in a presidential election with the lowest turnout in the 44 years of the Fifth Republic, the first round unexpectedly put the National Front's Le Pen in second place (17.02 per cent), leaving Jospin out (16.07 per cent). Jospin resigned as Prime Minister and left politics altogether, leaving the Socialist Party without a leader. He called on his followers to vote in the second round for Chirac, who had won the first round with 19.67 per cent of the vote. Le Pen's electoral platform was based on immigration and the crime rate, factors considered by many among the French population to be firmly linked. Immigrants made up 5.4 per cent (3.2 million) of French population, of which 44 per cent were African, mostly from the former French colonies. Approximately 47.5 per cent belonged to other European countries, 6.5 per cent were Asian and 2 per cent were from the Americas. Several demonstrations were held against Le Pen, with a strong participation of young people, who had previously been politically indifferent.

46 In the second round, on May 5 2002, Chirac obtained 82 per cent of the vote, while Le Pen held on to his 17 per cent. In his speech after winning, Chirac greeted 'those French people committed to solidarity and freedom, open to Europe and the world'. He added that the French people's vote had been a 'founding vote, a vote that renews our Republican pact'. European and world political leaders expressed their 'relief' at the results. However, the fact that Le Pen became Chirac's only rival in the second round made the far-right's agenda a focus for the European media, and also gave Chirac the opportunity to further his own right-wing program. ∎

Wallis and Futuna

Population:	15,000 (2002)
Land area:	200 SQ KM
Capital:	Mata-Utu
Currency:	CFP franc
Language:	French

Wallis was named after Samuel Wallis, a navigator who 'discovered' it in 1767. Marist missionaries arrived in the archipelago in 1837 and converted the inhabitants to Catholicism. It became a French protectorate in 1888, and in December 1959, after a referendum, the country adopted the status of French Overseas Territory.

2 Unlike other French dependencies in the Pacific, there are no independence movements on the islands. In 1983, the two kingdoms of Futuna achieved separation from Wallis, but maintained their relationship with France. The islands' economic prospects are poor: in addition to the devastating effect of cyclones that periodically hit the islands, the only bank on the islands was closed. Wallis and Futuna received FF55 million in aid from France in 1987 and still relies heavily on grants. Approximately 50 per cent of the economically active population has had to emigrate to other parts of Polynesia in search of work. Their remittances, together with public works projects, constitute the main source of income for the islands.

3 In the 1992 elections for the Territorial Assembly, the Left managed to defeat the neo-Gaullist Rassemblement pour la République (RPR), a party of the right, for the first time in 20 years. In 1997, the neo-Gaullist candidate Victor Brial gained the seat of deputy for Wallis in the French National Assembly.

4 On July 12 2000, President Chirac appointed Alain Waquet as new Chief-Administrator of the islands.

ENVIRONMENT

The territory consists of the Wallis archipelago (159 sq km), formed by Uvea Island - where the capital is located - and 22 islets, plus the Futuna (64 sq km) and Alofi Islands (51 sq km). This group is located in western Polynesia, surrounded by Tuvalu to the north, Fiji to the south and the Samoa archipelago to the east. With a rainy and tropical climate, the major commercial activities are copra and fishing.

SOCIETY

Peoples: Of Polynesian origin. Approximately two thirds of the population live on Wallis and the rest on Futuna. Nearly 12,000 inhabitants live in Kanaky and Vanuatu. **Religions:** Catholic. **Languages:** French (official) and Polynesian languages.

THE STATE

Official name: Territoire des îles de Wallis et Futuna. **Administrative divisions:** There are no defined administrative divisions, but there are three kingdoms: Wallis, Sigave and Alo. **Capital:** Mata-Utu (located on Uvea) 1,500 people (1999). **Other towns:** Utuofa 820 people; Vailala 800 (2000). **Government:** Overseas territory administered by a French-appointed Chief Administrator, Alain Waquet since July 2000, assisted by a 20-member Territorial Assembly elected for a 5-year term. The kingdoms of Wallis and Futuna (in Sigave and Alo) from which the country was formed, have very limited powers. They send one deputy to the French National Assembly, and another to the Senate. **Armed forces:** The defense is the responsibility of France.

DEMOGRAPHY

Population: 59,670,000 (2002)
Annual growth: 0.5 % (1985-2000)
Estimates for year 2015: 61,892,000 (2000)
Annual growth to year 2015: 0.3 % (2000)
Urban population: 75.6 % (2000)
Urban growth: 0.7 % (2000)
Children per woman: 1.8 (2000)

HEALTH

Life expectancy at birth: 79 years (2000-2005)
male: 75 years (2000-2005)
female: 83 years (2000-2005)
Maternal mortality: 10 per 100,000 live births (1985/99)
Infant mortality: 4 per 1,000 (2000)
Under-5 child mortality: 5 per 1,000 (2000)
Daily calorie supply: 3,575 per capita (1999)
303 doctors per 100,000 people (1997)

EDUCATION

School enrolment (net):
Primary total: 100 % (1994/2000)
male: 100 % (1995/99)
female: 100 % (1995/99)
Secondary (gross):
male: 112 % (1995/97)
female: 111 % (1995/97)
Tertiary (gross): 51 % (1998)
Primary school teachers: one for every 19 pupils (1998)

COMMUNICATIONS

201 newspapers (1997), 950 radios (1997), 628 TV sets (2000) and 579 main telephone lines (2000) per 1,000 people
Books: 78 new titles per 100,000 people (1992/94)

ECONOMY

Per capita, GDP: $ 24,223 (2000)
Annual growth: 2.6 % (2000)
Annual inflation: 1.7 % (2000)
Consumer price index: 106.3 (2000)
Currency: 1.2 euro = $ 1 (03/2002)
Cereal imports: 1,664,242 metric tons (2000)
Food import dependency: 8 % (2000)
Fertilizer use: 2,589 kg per ha (1999)
Exports: $ 370,902 million (2000)
Imports: $ 352,622 million (2000)

ENERGY

Consumption: 4,378.1 Kgs of oil equivalent per capita yearly (1998); 50.0 % imported (1999)

HDI (ranking/value): 13 / 0.924 (1999)

French Guiana

Population: 176,000 (2002)
Land area: 90,000 SQ KM
Capital: Cayenne
Currency: Euro
Language: French

Guyane française

The Arawaks were copper-skinned people with straight, black hair. They grew corn, cotton, yams and sweet potatoes. They built round huts with thatched, cone-shaped roofs, and slept in hammocks - an Arawak word which survived the culture which gave rise to it. The Caribs displaced them from the area and later resisted the Spaniards who began to arrive toward the beginning of the 16th century.

[2] In 1604 the French occupied Guiana, despite Carib resistance. The colony passed successively into Dutch, English and Portuguese hands, until the beginning of French domination in 1676. Towards the end of the 18th century, France sent more than 3,000 colonists to settle the interior. Few survived the tropical diseases, but those who did sought refuge in a group of islands off the coast, which they named Health Islands. After a brief period of prosperity brought about by the discovery of gold in the Appranage River basin, the colony gradually fell into decline.

[3] In 1946, Guiana became a French 'Overseas Department'. Nine-tenths of the country is covered by forests, and although the country is fertile, most of the food is imported. The creole (African and *mestizo*) 80 per cent of the population are limited to minor positions in the local bureaucracy or police. The country is heavily reliant on French funding which provided 70 per cent of the GNP in 1989. Imports are worth ten times the exports of wood, rum, coffee and gold.

[4] In 1967, the National Center for Space Studies was established. Over 1,300 foreign technicians work there, earning First World salaries, as well as 1,500 French Guyanan nationals. Thirty Ariane voyages have been launched from the base at Kourou, with all the satellites sent into space financed by European consortia.

[5] During the 1970s, the autonomist Socialist Party of Guiana (PSG) became the majority party at the local level. Early in the 1980s, armed groups attacked 'colonialist' targets, but tensions were defused with the victory in France of the French Socialist Party in 1981.

[6] At the 'First Conference of the Last French Colonies' held in Guadeloupe in 1985, there was severe criticism of the availability of French visas and citizenship for east Asians, while Haitians, Brazilians and Guyanans, with closer cultural ties, underwent persecution and discrimination.

[7] In 1986, Guyana's representation in the French National Assembly increased to two members. In the 1989 municipal elections, Cayenne and 12 other districts, out of the 19 at stake, were won by the Left. Georges Othily, a PSG dissident was elected for the French Senate.

[8] In 1992, the ongoing economic crisis led to a week-long general strike, called by unions and business leaders. As a result, Paris agreed to finance a plan to improve infrastructure and education. In 1994, French Guiana joined the Association of Caribbean States as an associate member.

[9] The French Government, after acknowledging the critical economic situation of its possession, announced a new 'development plan' for French Guiana in November 1997.

[10] The March 2000 visit by Jean-Jacques Queyranne, under-secretary of Overseas Territories, triggered protests that ended in clashes between the police and the demonstrators who demanded independence. The crowds looted businesses and set cars on fire, and several people were injured. The pro-independence Workers' Union of Guiana led a general strike.

[11] In December 2001, many French Guianan communities filed complaints with the French Government for its inaction in enforcing the environmental laws in the mining sector. Mercury, used in extracting gold from the ore, contaminates rivers and kills fish, the main source of food for the Wayana and Emerillon peoples. In June 2001, community leaders and activists from nine countries of the Amazon Basin including French Guiana, gathered in Washington under the auspices of the Amazon Alliance to discuss new environmental campaigns.

[12] Europe's largest and most expensive satellite was launched from the Kourou base in French Guiana in 2002, to monitor the health of the planet from outer space. ∎

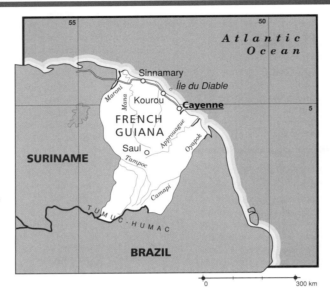

PROFILE

ENVIRONMENT

French Guiana is located slightly north of the Equator. Due to its hot and rainy climate, only the coastal alluvial lowlands are suitable for agriculture (cocoa, bananas, sugar cane, rice and corn). The hinterland mountains are covered with rainforests. The country has large reserves of bauxite and gold. Mining activities have polluted the Moroni River, the principal source of food for the indigenous peoples of the area

SOCIETY

Peoples: Mostly of mixed European and African slave roots. There are 4,000 indigenous peoples, including the Wayana, Oyami and Emerillon in the interior jungles, and the Arawak, Galibi and Palikur along the coast. There are minority groups from China, India and France. Also in the jungles there are *Cimarrones*, descendants of rebel or fugitive African slaves.
Religions: Mainly Roman Catholic, also Hindu and Islam.
Languages: French (official), local Creole. Some indigenous groups continue to speak their own languages, and Asian immigrant communities similarly.
Political Parties: Socialist Party of Guiana (PSG), Union for the Republic (RPR), Union for French Democracy (UDF), De-Colonization and Emancipation of Guiana Movement.
Social Organizations: Workers' Union of Guiana.

THE STATE

Official Name: Département d'Outre-Mer de la Guyane française.
Administrative Divisions: 2 Districts.
Capital: Cayenne 51,000 people (1999).
Other Cities: Kourou 21,000 people; St Laurent-du-Maroni 21,000 (2000).
Government: Jacques Chirac, Chief of State since May, 1995; re-elected May 2002. Henry Masse, Prefect appointed by France since August 1999. Regional parliament (consultative body): General Council, made up of 19 members, and Regional Council, with 31 members. The department has 2 representatives in the National Assembly and 2 in the French Senate.
National Holiday: All French holidays.
Armed Forces: 8,400 French troops.

French Polynesia

Population: 621,000 (2002)
Land area: 3,660 SQ KM
Capital: Papeete
Currency: CFP franc
Language: French

Polynésie française

Polynesia's first inhabitants either came from America or Indonesia, but the evidence is inconclusive.

[2] In 1840 the islands were occupied by France and in 1880, despite native resistance, the archipelago was officially made a colony under the name of 'the French Establishments of Oceania'. In 1958, they became an Overseas Territory.

[3] Except for some concessions on the domestic front, France continued to maintain its control over the islands, with a hard-line policy because of the strategic location of the islands and the atomic tests that have taken place on the Mururoa atoll since 1966. In 1975 France also carried out tests on the Fangataufa atoll for tests, despite strong opposition to the growing militarization of the islands from the population of the territory and other countries in the area, especially New Zealand.

[4] The 'nuclearization' of the area rapidly resulted in the destruction of French Polynesia's traditional economic base, as the island was currently dependent upon the French military budget. In less than one generation, the economy went from self-sufficiency to dependence upon imported goods. By the end of 1980, 80 per cent of basic foodstuffs were imported.

[5] Both the environment and the health of the islands' inhabitants has deteriorated over the last decades, and there were dramatic increases in the incidence of brain tumors, leukemia and thyroid cancer. The scale of these illnesses is hard to evaluate, as the French Government refused to divulge medical statistics in recent years.

[6] In 1985, the explosion of a bomb planted by two French secret agents killed an ecology activist and destroyed a Greenpeace ship that was heading for Mururoa in order to protest against nuclear testing. In 1992, French President François Mitterrand decided a temporary suspension of nuclear tests and Paris began negotiations with Papeete for an economic plan to be carried out after the permanent closure of the experiment centers in Mururoa and Fangataufa.

[7] The 'Progress Pact' between Paris and 'French' Polynesia was based on assumptions similar to those in structural adjustment programs advocated by the IMF, i.e. economic liberalization, privatization and 'major balancing' in public finance. However, the main pro-autonomy political party, Tavini Uiraatira (that means 'serving the people' in the Polynesian language) led by Oscar Temaru and representing 15 per cent of the voters, proposed nationalization and the extension of free services.

[8] French President Chirac carried out further nuclear tests in 1995. After the first one of these explosions, there were disturbances and fighting in French Polynesia. In January 1996, he announced the permanent suspension of nuclear tests.

[9] In February 1998, it was revealed that tourism, above all from Japan and Italy, had increased 35 per cent during 1997. This was partly due to the suspension of nuclear tests.

[10] Gaston Flosse, the President of Polynesia and a member of the French Senate, was prosecuted and found guilty of corruption by a French court of law. He received a two-year suspended prison sentence on November 1999 for having accepted tens of thousands of dollars in exchange for illegal gambling permits in Tahiti. Flosse refused to resign and stated he intended to appeal.

[11] In May 2001, The President's party, the Tahoeraa Huiraatira/Rally for the Republic (RPR), won Parliamentary elections obtaining 28 seats, compared to 13 obtained by the Tavini Huiraatira (TH). Flosse was re-elected President on May 18 that year with 29 votes, while the leader of the TH, Oscar Temaru, received 13.

[12] After the terrorist attacks of September 2001 in the United States, official data indicated that tourism had fallen by 9.7 per cent in early 2002. French Polynesia (after Fiji) is the second tourist destination in the region. ∎

PROFILE

ENVIRONMENT

The territory is located in the southeast portion of Polynesia. Most of the French Polynesian islands are of volcanic origin but they also have major coral formations. The islands are largely mountainous, with a tropical climate and heavy rainfall. Relatively fertile soils favor agricultural development. The Windward and Leeward Islands form the Society Islands archipelago. Nuclear tests on atolls such as Mururoa and Fangataufa carried out by France over a 26-year period have caused damage to the environment and people that is difficult to evaluate.

SOCIETY

Peoples: Polynesian 78 per cent, Chinese 12 per cent, French descendants 6 per cent.
Religions: Mostly Christian, 54 per cent Protestant, 30 per cent Catholic.
Languages: French (official), Tahitian (national).
Political Parties: Tahoeraa Huiraatira/People's Front-Rally for the Republic (RPR), conservative; Tavini Huiraatira/People's servant, an anti-nuclear and independence movement; Fetia Api/New Star.
Social Organizations: The Pacific Christian Workers' Central (CTCP), the Federation of French Polynesian Unions (FSPF) and the Territorial Union of the General Labor Confederation 'Workers' Force' (UTSCGT).

THE STATE

Official Name: Territoire d'Outre-Mer de la Polynésie française.
Administrative Divisions: Windward Islands, which include Tahiti, Murea, Maio; Papeete constitutes the center of the district. Leeward Islands, with the capital in Utoroa on Ralatea island. It also includes the islands of Huahine, Tahaa, Bora-Bora and Maupiti. Tuamotu and Gambier Archipelagos, the Austral Islands and the Marquesas Islands.
Capital: Papeete 121,000 people (1999).
Other cities: Punaauia 22,700 people; Pirae 16,200 (2000).
Government: The French Government is represented by a High Commissioner, who controls defense, foreign relations and justice, Michel Mathieu since October 2001. President: Gaston Flosse since April 1991 (re-elected in 2001). A local 49-member Territorial Assembly is elected by proportional representation for a 5-year term.
National Holiday: All French holidays.
Armed Forces: Defense is responsibility of the French Government. French Forces (includes Army, Navy, Air Force), Gendarmerie.

Gabon

Population: 1,293,000 (2002)
Land area: 257,670 SQ KM
Capital: Libreville
Currency: CFA franc
Language: French

Gabon

Tools found in the Gabon forests indicate that this region has been inhabited since the Palaeolithic age. Little else is known about life in the area until the 16th century, when the migrations that triggered the crisis in the ancient state of Congo brought the Myene and, in the 17th century, the Fang to Gabon. Thereafter, they monopolized the slave and ivory trade together with the Europeans.

[2] The Portuguese arrived in 1472. Around the middle of the 19th century, the French, Dutch and British established a permanent trade of ivory, precious woods and slaves. In 1849, Libreville was founded and established as a settlement for freed slaves from other French colonies. The territory was of little economic interest to the French, who used it as a base for expeditions into the heart of the continent.

[3] The quest for independence was relatively uneventful because the two local parties (the Joint Mixed Gabonese Movement of Leon M'Ba and the Democratic and Social Union of Jean-Hillaire Aubame) were willing to accept neo-colonialism.

[4] Gabon has abundant resources: iron ore, uranium, manganese, timber and oil. The transnational oil company Shell discovered oil in Rabikuna, near Port Gentil. These oil reserves contain enough crude to last for 40 years and the oil wells are already in operation. Shell holds an 80 per cent interest in the wells already in operation and French company ELF the remaining 20 per cent; Amoco (an American company) and Braspetro (Brazilian) have been authorized to continue oil exploration in the Port Gentil area.

[5] Until recently, timber mills were the only local industry of any size, but a few years ago, French and US transnationals discovered that Gabon could serve as a spearhead to penetrate the markets of central Africa, and they initiated its industrialization. This 'development', relying on foreign capital has only exacerbated social conflicts and the promise of jobs in the cities has encouraged urban migration. Gabon's social structure is changing as independent producers become suppliers of cheap labor for transnational industries. Economically, the breakdown of the rural economy has blocked the way to food self-sufficiency, destroying the only social sector which remained independent of foreign capital.

[6] The neo-colonial system was guaranteed by a military treaty signed between Libreville and Paris in 1960. Its effectiveness was proved in 1964 when M'Ba was deposed by a group of progressive officers.

[7] When M'Ba died in 1967, he was succeeded by Omar Bongo, head of cabinet, who faithfully followed and even refined his predecessor's style, becoming French President Giscard D'Estaing's 'privileged spokesman' in Africa. Applying the US thesis of 'sub-imperialisms' to French interests, Bongo became its watchdog in central Africa, with Gabon a base for aggression against neighboring progressive regimes. In January 1977, Gabon provided the planes and arms used by a mercenary group in an unsuccessful attack on Benin.

[8] Bongo's foreign policy maintained good relations with several states in the region, without altering the country's privileged relationship with France. Like Senegal, Ivory Coast, Chad, and the Central African Republic, Gabon also had French troops on its soil.

[9] In 1979 and again in 1986, Bongo was re-elected with 99 per cent of the vote, in presidential elections in which he was the only candidate.

[10] His squandering of the country's income led to violent protests in the early 1980s. The revolt spread to the police who in 1982 organized an unprecedented demonstration, demanding an increase in wages and the withdrawal of French advisors. The protests were brutally repressed by Gabon's secret police, officially known as the 'Documentation Center'.

[11] The Government repressed the National Reorientation Movement (MORENA), formed by intellectuals, workers, students and nationalist politicians. The movement was accused of having expropriated 30 tons of weapons in October 1982. At that time, the Bongo family and French military installations were the target of armed attacks. At least 28 top MORENA leaders were sentenced to 15 years' imprisonment. The French Socialist Party criticized the rulings, thus seriously upsetting Bongo's relations with French President Mitterrand.

[12] In late 1989 there were signs of democratic participation for Gabon's opposition forces. After violent confrontations in the streets the President had the constitution amended, introducing a multiparty system and lifting censorship of the press. In the meantime, he invited six opposition leaders to join the cabinet.

[13] There was a period of calm after all this social upheaval. However in May, Joseph Redjambe, president of the Gabonese Progressive Party was murdered in a Libreville hotel. His death provoked strong reactions against the Government, thought to be associated with the murder. A state of rebellion through the Port Gentil region lasted ten days and the French Government evacuated 5,000 French residents, charging the presidential

WORKERS

1999/2000

LABOR FORCE AS % OF TOTAL

- ■ FEMALE: 45%
- ■ MALE: 55%

LAND USE

DEFORESTATION: 0.3% annual (1990/95)

1993

- ■ FOREST & WOODLAND: 74.3%
- ■ ARABLE: 1.1%
- ■ OTHER: 24.6%

PUBLIC EXPENDITURE

Military expenditure (as % GNI):	**24 %** (1999)
Defense expenditure (% of central government expenditure)	**7.3 %** (1999)

guard with re-establishing order. According to information confirmed by Amnesty International, the incidents left a toll of six dead and a hundred wounded.

[14] Once calm had been restored, the political and social groups met on June 6, in a National Conference and an agreement was reached whereby presidential elections would be held. This was undoubtedly a major victory for the opposition, who extracted promises of multiparty elections from the President. But Bongo advanced the election date from 1992 to late 1990, so that he could use the power base he had built up over the past 20 years in office to carry out his campaign, while the opposition had no time to organize itself adequately or overcome its internal divisions.

[15] In September 1990, President Bongo's Gabonese Democratic Party (PDG), obtained a majority in the National Assembly. The new constitution, approved in March 1991, formally established a multiparty system.

[16] In 1991, the country was rocked by a new outbreak of political and social violence. The economic crisis continued to worsen. The stabilization program launched in September under IMF guidelines and the structural adjustment plan promoted by the World Bank failed to generate much hope.

[17] The presidential elections of December 1993, which returned Bongo to power, were questioned by the opposition. In February, the protests continued and were harshly repressed leaving 30 dead. In negotiations in Paris between September and November 1994, a coalition government was formed until new elections could be held.

[18] In July 1995, the President gained the support of 96 per cent of the voters in a referendum for constitutional reform in order for presidential and legislative elections to be held. The National Assembly elections in December 1996 gave the Democratic Party led by Bongo 47 of the 55 seats. Meanwhile, the opposition leader Paul Mba-Abessole,

scored a sizeable victory in the municipal elections, becoming mayor of the capital Libreville.

[19] Despite the fact Gabon had per capita income of $3,490 per year due to the oil income, the poverty indicators provided an alarming picture. In 1997, life expectancy was less than 55 years, literacy barely reached 63 per cent of adults and the infant mortality rate stood at 87 per thousand.

[20] Early in 1998, Mayor Mba-Abessole requested the United Nations to supervise presidential elections that were to be held later that year in order to avoid the 'fraudulent reelection of Omar Bongo'. The elections were in fact won by the president, who defeated Mba Abessole and Pierre-Andre Kombila, former deputy of Abessole in the Party of Timberworkers.

[21] The President appointed Jean-François Ntoutoume-Emane as Prime Minister on January 1999 in the midst of strong protests which led his government to close schools and the Libreville University to avoid demonstrations.

[22] The authorities sought the UN's humanitarian assistance due to the constant influx of refugees from the Republic of Congo. In October 1999, the international organization estimated the country had 10,000 refugees.

[23] In July 2000 two freighters, one Greek and one French, collided in Gabonese waters, causing a 400-ton oil spill. Bongo requested international aid to fund the clean-up costs, which amounted to $1.5 million.

[24] As other Central and Western African countries, Gabon also suffers from child smuggling, mostly coming from Nigeria. The children smuggled to Gabon work in plantations, as domestic employees, in the sexual trade, and are also sent to beg in the streets. The ratification of an agreement against child smuggling, signed by Gabon and three neighbors in the region, was expected for 2004. Once signed, the situation will be regulated and the children will be repatriated.

[25] In late 2001 Parliamentary elections were held, leading to a new and wide victory for the PDG, which obtained 84 out of the 120 seats of the National Assembly. In response to an invitation from Bongo to form a Government coalition, Abessole persuaded his followers to join the new administration in January 2002.

[26] Until March 2002, more than 60 per cent of deaths in the north were due to an ebola virus epidemic. The region of Mekambo and the border with the Republic of Congo were the most affected areas. ■

PROFILE

ENVIRONMENT

Irrigated by the Ogooué River basin, the country has an equatorial climate with year-round rainfall. The land is covered by dense rainforest. The timber industry - especially that of okoumé wood (used in plywood) - employs a large part of the population, together with the extractive industries (manganese, petroleum, uranium and iron), which make up 80 per cent of the country's exports The country has manganese, uranium, iron and petroleum reserves. Deforestation is one of the most serious environmental problems, together with the depredation of the country's wildlife.

SOCIETY

Peoples: Gabon was populated by Babinga (pygmies). In the 16th century it was invaded by Myene and other groups. Today over half of the population are Bantu-speaking peoples divided into more than 40 different groups including Galoa, Nkomi, and Irungu. One third of the population are Fang and Kwele, while in the northern and southern parts of Gabon there are Punu and Nzabi minorities; plus Baka and Babongo pygmy people.
Religions: Mainly Christian. More than one third practice traditional African religions and there is a small Muslim minority.
Languages: French (official). There are as many languages as ethnic groups. Bantu languages are predominant, divided into 10 main linguistic groups; pygmy languages also spoken.
Political Parties: Gabonese Democratic Party (PDG), pro-government; National Woodcutters' Rally, in the opposition; Gabonese Party of Progress; Social Democratic Party; Union of the People of Gabon.
Social organizations: Gabonese Confederation of Free Trade Unions (CGSL).

THE STATE

Official Name: République Gabonaise.
Administrative divisions: 9 provinces and 37 prefectures.
Capital: Libreville 523,000 people (1999).
Other cities: Port Gentil 99,300 people; Masuku 39,100; Oyem 28,100 (2000).
Government: Parliamentary republic with strong head of state. El Hadj Omar Bongo, President and head of State, since November 1967 and re-elected in 1998 for a seven-year term. Jean-François Ntoutoume-Emane, Prime Minister since January 1999 and re-elected in 2002.
Bicameral Legislative: National Assembly, with 120 members elected every five years, and the Senate, with 91 members.
National Holiday: August 17, Independence Day (1960).
Armed Forces: 4,700 (1995).
Other: Coast Guard: 2,800; Gendarmerie: 2,000.

Gambia

Population: 1,371,000 (2002)
Land area: 10,000 SQ KM
Capital: Banjul
Currency: Dalasi
Language: English

Gambia

The earliest settlers of the Gambia river valley came from what is now Senegal. Attracted by Gambia's coast, which lent itself to trade and navigation, they settled along the river, carrying out subsistence farming.

[2] In the 15th century, the region was colonized by the Mandingo who, together with the Mali Empire established their authority in the Gambia Valley. They also founded several kingdoms in the area, which controlled coastal trade and enabled them to develop economically and culturally.

[3] With the arrival of the Portuguese in 1455, most of the region's domestic trade was displaced toward the Atlantic coast, bringing about the decline of the local kingdoms which had prospered under this trade. For the Portuguese, Gambia became the point of departure for a large quantity of precious metals.

[4] Gambia was also important to them as a prosperous port of call on their route to the Orient. However, in 1618 the Portuguese Crown sold its commercial and territorial rights to the British Empire, which at the height of its naval prowess was trying to assert its dominance as a colonial power by acquiring a foothold in Africa.

[5] At that time, a war began between Britain and France (controlling all of what is now Senegal) which was to last for more than 200 years. From 1644, the British used this coastal area as a source of slaves, setting up alliances with inland tribal princes to provide them with human merchandise.

[6] Throughout the 17th century, Gambia was nothing more than a source of slave labor for Britain's colonies and for its slave trade with other colonial powers. The British therefore limited themselves to establishing a rudimentary trading post in the area, founded in 1660. Border disputes between the British and French increased during the 18th century.

[7] Throughout the 19th century a series of religious wars in the interior resulted in the complete Islamization of the country, with an increase in Muslim immigration from other parts of Africa. In the meantime, the region lost its international economic significance when the slave trade was abolished in Britain.

[8] It did however gain strategic importance by being a British enclave inserted into the heart of Senegal, a region instrumental in France's designs on sub-Saharan Africa. Slavery actually continued within the colony until the 20th century, not being outlawed until 1906.

[9] In 1889, France and Britain reached an agreement as to the boundaries of their respective colonies, ensuring peace in the region and the formal recognition of British sovereignty over Gambia by other European powers.

[10] Gambia's status as a British colony remained unchanged throughout the first half of the 20th century. Although the decolonization process in Africa began after World War II - resulting in the creation of a number of independent states in what had formerly been European colonies - Gambia did not receive administrative autonomy from Britain until 1963. Two years later, Gambia obtained full independence and joined the British Commonwealth. At the time of its independence, Gambia did not seem to constitute a nation as such because of its ethnic, cultural and economic complexity.

[11] After independence, the territory's social and economic structures remained unchanged. Exports continued to be based on a single crop, peanuts, while traditional social structures remained so unassailable that they were finally legitimized by the 1970 constitution. Thus, although some legislative seats were determined by the election of deputies, others were assigned to the 5 regional leaders.

[12] Dawda Jawara, founder of the People's Progressive Party (PPP), dominated Gambian politics since the 1960s. He won the 1962 elections, but failed to assume office because of a vote of no confidence from the opposition. However, he won the election in 1970 when the country was proclaimed a republic, with a presidential system of government.

[13] Around 1975, the success of Alex Haley's book 'Roots' turned Gambia into an important tourism center; but alongside this, prostitution and drug trafficking also increased while organized Islamic opposition emerged.

[14] The lack of border controls in Gambia led to it becoming a paradise for West African smuggling and a large part of Senegal's agricultural produce was illegally shipped through the port of Banjul.

[15] The close economic relationship between the countries led the Government of Dawda Jawara to accept a project for union with Senegal in 1973.

[16] In July 1981, Muslim dissidents attempted to overthrow Jawara, aiming to end official corruption through the establishment of a revolutionary Islamic regime. The revolt was crushed by Senegalese troops who entered Gambia at the request of President Dawda, who was in London at the time.

[17] The proposed union with Senegal had been planned for 1982, but the coup attempt against Gambia's government accelerated plans for creating the Senegambian federation.

[18] The 1980s were marked by a worsening of the country's economic situation, and a severe drought led to a sudden drop in the production of agricultural exports. The most obvious consequences were an increase in unemployment, migration from rural areas to the capital and increasing foreign debt to finance food imports.

[19] Senegambia was officially established in February 1982 with Abdou Diouf of Senegal as its first president, assisted by a council of ministers and a bi-national parliament. The federation did not totally unite Senegal and Gambia, as both states retained their autonomous character and internal organization. The treaty ensured that Dawda Jawara gained protection against internal rebellions and Senegal gained greater control over the leak of export tax revenues through smuggling.

[20] Gambia became unhappy with this alliance and its dissatisfaction became apparent in mid-1985, with its reluctance to sign the treaties aimed at strengthening ties with Senegal. Jawara subsequently failed to comply with the terms of the agreements promising Senegal military and diplomatic support in case of external or internal conflicts.

²¹ In late 1989 Gambia signed a mutual defense pact with Nigeria. Gambia sought to secure its defense through the agreement while recovering the autonomy lost in its relationship with Senegal. In practical terms, the measure meant the dissolution of Senegambia.

²² In May 1991, Gambia and Senegal took the first step toward reconciliation by signing a good-will and cooperation treaty. The agreement foresaw an annual meeting between the two heads of state and the creation of a joint commission presided over by the Foreign Ministers of both countries.

²³ In 1993, agriculture and tourism were hit by the consequences of the European economic crisis. Gambia's trade with Senegal was damaged when the Central Bank of the Western Africa States decided to stop financing trade based upon the African franc (CFA) outside the area comprised by countries using this monetary system.

²⁴ The Government took measures to initiate a national reconciliation process, including an amnesty granted to rebel movements fighting to oust the regime.

²⁵ In July 1994, a military coup overthrew President Dawda Jawara who sought asylum in Senegal after taking refuge in a US warship visiting the country. The presence of this ship in Banjul suggested complicity of the US with the military. The coup, headed by Yahya Jammeh, began with the protests of soldiers who demanded payment for their peace mission carried out in Liberia.

²⁶ Two members of the Provisional Armed Forces Council were arrested in January 1995 after trying to hand the Government over to civilians. In March, Jammeh also arrested the former Justice minister and general prosecutor for promoting the return of civilian rule. In November, the military junta expanded the powers of the security forces.

²⁷ The Government announced legislative and presidential elections would be held in June 1996, but the vote was postponed. In August, after a referendum, a new Constitution was approved. Jammeh described this event as the first step toward the restoration of national political life. In September 1996, Jammeh, up to then chief of the Armed Forces Government Junta, became Gambia's second elected President.

²⁸ In August 1997, the Government lifted other restrictions which limited political activity since the 1994 military coup. Arrests of Islamic leaders were common in 1998. In August, Jammeh traveled to Mauritania and met with president Moaouia Ould Sidi Mohammed Taya to 'find a solution to the two month conflict in Guinea-Bissau'.

²⁹ In May 1999, the opposition United Democratic Party (UDP) accused the Government of maintaining a democracy with 'untruthful' laws. On June 9, Jammeh accused Western 'donor' countries for making aid conditional on human rights and democracy. Days later, rebel leaders of Casamance, Senegal, met in Gambia to draw up a common strategy for peace talks.

³⁰ On September 25, before the UN in New York, Jammeh criticized 'the sloth and irresponsibility of this body in the conflicts facing Africa'. A month later, the Press Union denounced a new 'governmental measure to regulate press freedom', with annual raids on their buildings and the power of the minister of information to confiscate their records. The security forces prevented an 'attempted coup d'état' in January 2000 and arrested the two officers allegedly responsible for the uprising.

³¹ Gambia, in conjunction with another 44 countries - mostly African - lost its right to vote in the UN National Assembly on February 2000, for 'falling behind in debt payments'.

³² The Community of Sahelian-Saharan States (Comessa), meeting in Chad, on February 5, accepted Gambia, Senegal and Djibouti as new members. The 11 members agreed not to 'interfere in members' domestic affairs, not to allow the use of their territories to forces opposed to any member, and not to aid hostile forces in any of the countries'.

³³ The President decided to lift the ban on political parties for the coming elections. In October 2001, Jammeh won the presidential elections, receiving the approval of international observers that verified the transparency of the elections. However, months later, after the parliamentary elections that resulted in an overwhelming triumph for Jammeh's Alliance for Patriotic Reorientation and Construction (APRC), the opposition accused the Government of fraud.

³⁴ Gambia does not comply with international standards of respect for human rights. Journalists are arrested, there are extrajudicial executions and limitations of freedom of speech.

³⁵ Due to global warming and the fact that it is barely one meter above sea level, Banjul is in serious risk of going underwater in a few decades.

³⁶ Gambia hosts some 12,400 Senegalese refugees who escaped the conflict between the Government and separatist forces from that country. Since the Government of Gambia can not provide them with the bare necessities, some are held in UN camps, while the rest live outdoors. ■

PROFILE

ENVIRONMENT

One of the smallest African countries, Gambia stretches 320 km along the Gambia River, which is fully navigable and one of the main waterways in the area. The climate is tropical; there are rainforests along the river-banks and wooded savanna further inland. The economy is based on peanut exports and tourism. Because of the use of firewood as a main energy source and the production of export crops large areas of forest have been felled.

SOCIETY

Peoples: The majority of Gambians (40 per cent) are Mandingos; 14 per cent Futa, 13 per cent Wolof who belong to the same root, and 7 per cent are Diula. There are smaller groups inland (Serahuilis, Akus). Five to ten thousand laborers migrate from Mali, Senegal and Guinea-Bissau every year, returning home after the harvest.
Religions: The majority of Gambians are Muslims; a minority practice traditional religions and Christianity, mostly Protestant.
Languages: English (official); the most widespread local languages are Mandingo, Fulani and Wolof (the Wolof are a majority in the main trade center).
Political Parties: Alliance for Patriotic Reorientation and Construction (APRC); the United Democratic Party (UDP); the National Reconciliation Party (NRP); People's Democratic Organization for Independence and Socialism (PDOIS).
Social Organizations: There are three trade union federations: the Gambia Workers' Union; the Gambia Labor Union; and the Gambia Salesmen's and Merchants' Union.

THE STATE

Official Name: Republic of The Gambia.
Administrative Divisions: 5 Provinces and the Capital.
Capital: Banjul 229,000 people (1999).
Other cities: Serekunda 200,000 people; Brikama 56,100; Bakau 50,200 (2000).
Government: Presidential republic. Yahya Jammeh (former dictator), President since October 1996, re-elected in 2001. Single-chamber Legislature: National Assembly, with 45 members elected directly by people and 4 appointed members.
National Holiday: February 18, Independence (1965).
Armed Forces: 875 troops (1997).

Georgia

Population:	5,213,000 (2002)
Land area:	69,700 SQ KM
Capital:	Tbilisi
Currency:	Kupon
Language:	Georgian

Sak'art'velo

The peoples of the Caucasian Isthmus, thought to be the inventors of metallurgy, entered the Bronze Age around 2000 BC. The ancestors of modern Georgians are thought to have formed the first tribes in that region about this time. The kingdom of Kolkhida - which dates back to the 6th century BC - is mentioned in Homer's poems and in traditional Greek mythology.

[2] Two centuries later, legendary chieftain Farnavaz created the kingdom of Iberia, in what is now eastern Georgia. These two kingdoms were the first Georgian States, the result of a fusion of ancient agricultural and iron-smelting tribes of the region.

[3] Kolkhida and Iberia were subdued by Greece and then by Rome, as the result of Pompey's campaigns, in the 1st century BC. In the year 337 AD, King Mirian of Iberia adopted Christianity, making it the country's official religion. Like the Armenian church, the Georgian church separated from Rome in 506, to form the national Church of St George, with its headquarters at Tiflis (today Tbilisi).

[4] From a minor city, Tiflis became first the capital of Iberia, and later of all Georgia, after the unification of the 8th and 9th centuries. Both kingdoms fell under Iranian (Sasanid), then Byzantine and finally Arab control, between the 6th and 10th centuries. Feudal Georgia prospered under King David 'the Builder', 1089-1125 and Queen Tamara, 1184-1213.

[5] In the 13th and 14th centuries Georgia was invaded by the Tatars and Tamerlane. In the 15th century it dissolved into small fiefdoms, becoming the object of territorial disputes between Turkey and Iran from the 16th to the 18th centuries and there were a number of anti-Turkish and anti-Iranian revolts.

[6] Through the Treaty of Georgievsk (1783) Russia established its protection over eastern Georgia, annexing it in 1801. In the second half of the 19th century, Western Georgia (Tiblisi and Kutaisi) met the same fate. The Georgian provinces were incorporated into Transcaucasia, where the Government was in the hands of a viceroy designated by the Czar.

[7] Annexation to Russia had a number of negative effects on Georgian life. The local language was eliminated from administrative documents, and it was replaced by Russian in literature and in schools. The Catholic Church of St George was outlawed and its patriarchs deported, to be replaced by Russian Orthodox bishops and Russians were encouraged to come and settle in all of Georgia's cities, a fact which explains why the revolutionary movement was so strong in Georgia, in all of its Marxist, nationalist, populist and social democratic forms. It was here that Josef Dzhugashvili, known as Stalin, began his political career. After frequent rebellions during this period, Georgians played an important part in the revolution which shook the empire in 1905.

[8] When World War I broke out, the Caucasus saw fighting between Russia and Turkey. The Georgians formed a legion to fight alongside the Turks. In February 1917, a new wave of uprisings was unleashed by war policies and by hunger, and the peoples of the Caucasus brought down the czarist regime.

[9] In November, after the Bolshevik triumph in Petrograd, power in Transcaucasia fell into the hands of the Mensheviks (who wanted gradual change rather than revolution). Confronted with this situation, Stalin's group allowed the Caucasus to join the Bolsheviks led by Lenin. In April 1918, in Tbilisi, the United Government of Transcaucasia announced its separation from Soviet Russia. On May 26, 1918, Georgia proclaimed independence, which was recognized by Moscow two years later.

[10] Between 1918 and 1920, German, Turkish and British troops entered Georgia, all intent upon bringing down the socialist regime. In February 1921 the Red Army occupied Georgia and established Soviet power. On February 25, 1921, the Soviet Socialist Republic of Georgia was proclaimed, with the Abkhaz Autonomous Region as an administrative division of this republic. In March 1921, a peace treaty between the Russian Federation and Turkey was finalized, with the latter ceding Batumi and the northern part of Adzharistan, which became an autonomous republic within the Georgian SSR.

[11] In March 1922, Georgia, Azerbaijan and Armenia were reorganized as the Transcaucasian Federation. The following month, the South Ossetian Autonomous Region was formed, as a part of Georgia. On December 5 1936 the federation was dissolved and Georgia became one of the 15 republics of the Soviet Union (USSR).

[12] Stalin became Secretary General of the Communist Party of the Soviet Union in 1922, and after Lenin's death he became party leader. From 1928, he was leader of the USSR. Georgia witnessed many purges and suffered the effects of centralization and the repression of Stalinism, although to a lesser degree than other republics. In 1924, the Red Army intervened to put down a peasant uprising against forced land collectivization.

[13] Many Georgians - apart from Stalin - were in the leadership circle of the Soviet Union's CP, including Sergo Ordzhonikidzegv, the USSR's Minister of Heavy Industry, and Lavrenti Beria, head of the secret police (NKVD) who was executed after Stalin's death, in 1953. When Krushchev denounced his predecessor's crimes at the 20th Party Congress in 1956, it hurt Georgian national pride.

[14] In 1953, Moscow made Eduard Shevardnadze chief of police in Tbilisi. Implicated in cases of corruption and fraud, Mzhavanadze was replaced by Shevardnadze in 1972. A new nationalist feeling began to emerge with declarations in defense of the Georgian language and violent acts of sabotage.

[15] In 1978, the new constitution of the USSR triggered a wave of protest, as it made Russian the official language of the Soviet Union. However, Shevardnadze managed to have the measure abolished and allowed an anti-Stalin movie, 'Repent', to be screened. This marked the development of *glasnost* (openness) and *perestroika* (restructuring) process in Georgia.

[16] Shevardnadze remained at the head of Georgia's Communist Party and government until 1985, when he was made Foreign Minister of the Soviet Union. After the political changes made by Mikhail Gorbachev, several movements and parties emerged in Georgia, clamoring for the independence which Georgia claimed to have lost in 1921, with the establishment of Soviet power. On April 9 1989 in Tbilisi, Red Army units dispersed a crowd meeting in the main square to demand the secession of Georgia, citing Article 72 of the Constitution of the USSR. Nineteen people were killed, most of them women or adolescents.

[17] In the mid-1980s, a Green Party emerged in Georgia amid the first ever open debates on the country's ecological problems. The Greens combined their concern for the environment with a defense of non-violence, democracy and human rights. Georgia was the second former Soviet republic - after Estonia - to join the European 'Green' Parliament.

[18] On October 28 1990, elections were held for the Soviet (parliament) of the Georgian SSR, and the 'Free Georgia Round Table' coalition won. Zviad Gamsakhurdia, a well-known political dissident who had been proscribed during the Soviet regime, became the leader of the coalition. The Georgian Soviet decided to

change the country's name to the Republic of Georgia.

[19] Ethnic tensions increased, and the South Ossetian Autonomous Region claimed republican status. Georgia's Soviet annulled this decision, declared a state of emergency in South Ossetia and organized a blockade of this region. In April 1991, after fighting broke out between Ossetian guerrillas and Georgian troops, the Soviet approved the region's independence.

[20] On May 27, Gamsakhurdia was elected President. In September, a struggle began between Gamsakhurdia's supporters and the opposition, led by Dzhaba Ioseliani and Tenguiz Kitovani, commander of the National Guard. Repeated demonstrations ended in violence on January 6 1992, when government forces (following Kitovani's orders) stormed government headquarters. Gamsakhurdia fled first to Armenia, and then to the Chechen Autonomous Republic.

[21] A Military Council led by Kitovani seized power in Tbilisi and suspended the constitution. Gamsakhurdia loyalists continued to fight against the new regime's forces in western Georgia.

[22] In March, former USSR foreign minister, Eduard Shevardnadze, returned to Georgia to take charge of the presidency of the Council of State, the most powerful governing body. Chosen by the Military Council,

he held this post until democratic elections took place. Shevardnadze declared that his country would normalize relations with the international community, giving preference to relations with the former USSR republics, though for the moment not joining the Commonwealth of Independent States (CIS).

[23] On June 28 that year, a cease-fire was called in South Ossetia, supervised by a peacekeeping force of Russians, Georgians and Ossetians. From their capital in Sukhumi, the Abkhazian authorities resolved to limit the jurisdiction of Georgia's central government within the autonomous region. On August 14, government troops entered Abkhazia and occupied Sukhumi. Local authorities fled to the city of Gudauta, which became a center of resistance.

[24] In October, with the support of Russian volunteers and army regulars, they managed to extend their control over a large part of Abkhazia, coming close to Sukhumi.

[25] Early in 1993, the Russian air force began regular bombing of Sukhumi, and by March fighting had reached the outskirts of the city. On June 28, a Russian-mediated armistice went into effect, with both parties agreeing to demobilize their troops.

[26] In mid-September 1993, a strong Abkhazian offensive began, taking the Georgians by surprise and culminating in the capture of

Sukhumi by the Abkhazian army. Eduard Shevardnadze remained in Sukhumi, leaving on the last flight out of the city.

[27] In November, supporters of former president Gamsakhurdia launched a broad offensive, but were defeated with the help of Russian troops. In the same month, Georgia joined the CIS. In early 1994, Gamsakhurdia died in a suicide attempt, according to official reports. In February, Georgia signed a friendship treaty with Russia, and in April a peace treaty was signed with the Abkhazian rebels in Moscow.

[28] In spite of its rapprochement with Russia, Tbilisi joined the Association for Peace, sponsored by NATO. As a counter-measure and in spite of Tbilisi's protests, Moscow and Azerbaijan agreed to build an oil pipeline across Georgian territory to facilitate exports of Azerbaijani petroleum.

[29] In August 1995 Parliament approved a new Constitution defining Georgia as a presidential republic. Shevardnadze won the presidential elections in November and his party, the Union of Citizens of Georgia won an absolute majority in Parliament. In November 1997 the country became the first former Soviet republic to abolish the death penalty.

[30] Shevardnadze narrowly escaped two assassination attempts, in February 1998 and May 1999. In both cases there were rumors of Moscow's involvement, linked to the construction of the Azerbaijani pipeline.

[31] The Abkhaz parliament declared independence in October 1999. Tbilisi condemned the declaration as illegal and urged the world community not to recognize the new state. In March 2001, Georgia and Abkhazia signed an accord renouncing the use of force between them and agreeing to work towards the safe return of civilian refugees.

[32] After the security forces took over the private Rustavi-2 TV station, critical of the Prime Minister's policies and his failure to fight corruption, massive popular protests demanded the resignation of Shevardnadze and of several ministers. Shevardnadze sacked the entire administration. Nino Burdzhanadze was elected head of Parliament, and became the first woman to hold the country's second most important political post.

[33] The arrival in Georgia of five US military advisors in February 2002 - followed by an estimated 200 more - was criticized by Russian President Vladimir Putin, who said Tbilisi had not given warning of the plan, and from Foreign Minister Igor Ivanov, who warned that the presence of US troops would heighten tensions in the region. Washington's stated

objective was to support the local army in fighting an Islamic terrorist group with supposed ties to the al-Qaeda network and based in the Pankisi pass, on the Chechen border. The plan was widely seen as marking the beginning of a new front and that the US would extend its stay to 'protect' the Baku-Ceyhan gas pipeline connecting the Caspian Sea (in Azerbaijan) to the Mediterranean (in Turkey), via Georgia. Given the proximity of Iran and Iraq, it was believed that the United States planned to establish a permanent military base in the southern Caucasus. ■

PROFILE

ENVIRONMENT

Located in the central western part of Transcaucasia, Georgia is bordered in the north by Russia, in the east by Azerbaijan and in the south by Armenia and Turkey, with the Black Sea to the west. Most of its territory is occupied by mountains. Between the Little and the Great Caucasus lies the Kolkhida lowland and the Kartalinian Plain; the Alazan Valley lies to the east. Subtropical climate in the west, moderate in the east; there is heavy rainfall in the western area, along the shores of the Black Sea. Principal rivers are the Kura and Rioni. 40 per cent of the republic is covered by forests. Georgia is famous for its wine. Bacterial pollution of 70 per cent of the Black Sea constitutes a serious problem. Only 18 per cent of the residual waters in the main port of Batumi undergo adequate treatment. The abuse of pesticides has resulted a high level of chemical toxicity in the soil.

SOCIETY

Peoples: Georgians, 70 per cent; Armenians, 8.1 per cent; Russians, 6.3 per cent; Azeris, 5.7 per cent; Ossetians, Abkhazians and Adzharians.
Religions: Georgian Orthodox (65 per cent), Muslims (11 per cent), Russian Orthodox (10 per cent), and Armenian Orthodox (8 per cent).
Languages: Georgian (official), Russian, Abkhazian, Armenian, Azeri, Greek, Kurmanji, Turkish and various Caucasian languages. **Political Parties:** Citizens' Union of Georgia, All-Georgian Union for Revival; Industry will save Georgia; Georgian Labor Party; National-Democratic Alliance-Third Way; Communist Party, National Democratic Party, Aidguilara (national movement of the Abkhazians), Admon Nyjas (national movement of the South Ossetians). **Social Organizations:** the traditional trade unions have 2.6 million members. Currently, the Georgian Trade Union Association is the leading organization.

THE STATE

Official Name: Sakartvelos Respublika. **Capital:** Tbilisi 1,309,000 people (1999). **Other cities:** Batumi 143,800 people; Sukhumi 63,800; Kutaisi 264,600; Rustavi 178,900 (2000). **Government:** Eduard Shevardnadze, President of Parliament and Head of State 1992-1995 and President since 1995 (re-elected in 1999); Nino Burdzhanadze, first woman to chair the Parliament, since November 2001. Single-chamber parliament with 235 members. **National Holiday:** May 26, Independence (1991).
Armed Forces: 13,000.

STATISTICS

DEMOGRAPHY
Population: 5,213,000 (2002)
Estimates for year 2015: 4,775,000 (2000)
Urban population: 60.7 % (2000)
Urban growth: 0.8 % (2000)
Children per woman: 1.5 (2000)

HEALTH
Life expectancy at birth: 74 years (2000-2005)
male: 70 years (2000-2005)
female: 78 years (2000-2005)
Maternal mortality: 50 per 100,000 live births (1985/99)
Infant mortality: 24 per 1,000 (2000)
Under-5 child mortality: 29 per 1,000 (2000)
Daily calorie supply: 2,347 per capita (1999)
436 doctors per 100,000 people (1998)
Safe water: 79 % (2000)

EDUCATION
Literacy: 100 % (2000)
School enrolment (net):
Primary total: 98 % (1994/2000)
male: 95 % (1995/99)
female: 95 % (1995/99)
Secondary (gross):
male: 78 % (1995/97)
female: 76 % (1995/97)
Tertiary (gross): 34 % (1998)
Primary school teachers: one for every 17 pupils (1998)

COMMUNICATIONS
556 radios (1997), 474 TV sets (2000) and 139 main telephone lines (2000) per 1,000 people

ECONOMY
Per capita, GDP: $ 2,664 (2000)
Annual growth: 1.9 % (2000)
Exports: $ 1,136 million (2000)
Imports: $ 1,410 million (2000)
External debt: $ 1,633 million (2000); $ 310 per capita (2000)
Debt service: 11.4 % of exports (1999)
Development aid received: $ 239 million (1999); $ 43.8 per capita (1999); 8.70 % of GNP (1999)

ENERGY
Consumption: 464.2 Kgs of oil equivalent per capita yearly (1998); 71.3 % imported (1999)

HDI (ranking/value): 76 / 0.742 (1999)

Germany

Deutschland

Population: 81,990,000 (2002)
Land area: 356,680 SQ KM
Capital: Berlin
Currency: Euro
Language: German

The first reference to the Germanic peoples comes from between 58 and 51 BC when the Romans under Julius Caesar invaded a part of Gaul north of the Alps and west of the Rhine. The Germans descended from the Teutoni and the Cimbri, who had in turn descended from the Danes. Between 113 and 101 BC. Teutoni and Cimbri tribes invaded the Mediterranean regions including the Italian peninsula.

[2] In 9 AD Arminius, a Germanic chief and the earliest national hero, led a revolt which defeated three Roman legions in the Teutoburger Wald. By the second half of the 3rd century, the Germanic tribes had fused into larger political units; the Saxons, Franks and Germans.

[3] The Romans found it increasingly difficult to keep their dominion over the region and withdrew gradually. In the 4th century Attila's Huns invaded, and a long period of Migrations followed throughout Europe. In 455, the Germans defeated the Mongols at the battle of the river Nedao and the Mongol Empire subsequently collapsed. Clovis and Charlemagne later subjected the Germanic and Saxon tribes to the Frankish Empire.

[4] After the Treaty of Verdun and the division of the Carolingian Empire in 843, the first entirely Germanic kingdom was established under Louis the German. Under Otto I, crowned in Rome in 936, Germania became Europe's most powerful kingdom.

[5] During the 12th and 13th centuries Germany experienced a rapid growth in population, and continuous expansion.

[6] The instability of royal dynasties encouraged the strengthening of secular and religious principalities. Princes were free to build fortresses, exploit natural resources and administer justice in their dominions.

[7] In 1356, the authority of the king in relation to the papacy was consolidated in the Golden Bull of Charles IV (1346-1378) establishing the right to appoint the King without the Pope's approval, and strengthened the hand of the principalities, on whose support the king depended.

[8] During the 15th and 16th centuries internal instability persisted. In 1517 Martin Luther led

the Protestant Reformation, which, coupled with political rivalries, frustrated reunification efforts.

[9] The Reformation provided a forum for criticisms of secularization and corruption in the German Church, which had become an increasingly prosperous economic and financial institution. It owned a third of the land in some districts and profited from selling indulgences - one of the contributory factors to its downfall. After a succession of internal wars, including peasant uprisings, the Peace of Augsburg was reached in 1555, giving equal rights to both Catholics and Lutherans.

[10] Political and religious factions combined their strengths; in 1608 the Protestant Union was created, and the Catholic League a year later. The Bohemian rebellion triggered the Thirty Year War (1618-1648), which spread to the entire continent, and ultimately reduced the population of central Europe by around 30 per cent, ending with the Peace of Westfalia (1648).

[11] In the 18th century, the Kingdom of Prussia emerged as a economic and political unit, responsible for creating tensions among the German states. Napoleon's victories over Prussia in 1806 and the formation of the Confederation of the Rhine put an end to the Holy Roman Empire.

[12] In Central Europe during the 18th century, culture formed an outlet for intellectual energies which could not be expressed through politics, as political life itself was dominated by the autocratic rulers. Philosophers like Kant and Herder, and writers like Goethe and Schiller, expressed the idealism and spiritualism which characterized German art and literature of this time.

[13] When Napoleon fell, the German princes created a confederation of 39 states, which were independent except for foreign policy. Austrian and Prussian opposition to broader forms of representation increased popular unrest, leading to the 1830 revolts and increased repression.

[14] In 1834, Prussia threw its growing economic weight into the political realm, with the establishment of the German Customs Union, from which Austria was excluded. The main consequences of the Union were the duplication of trade among its members over the next ten years, as well as the formation of industrial centers and the emergence of a working class. Due to the rapid growth of the urban population, the supply of labor greatly exceeded the demand. The resulting impoverishment of industrial workers and artisans served as a

breeding ground for the rebellions of subsequent years, culminating in the revolutionary wave of 1848-49.

[15] A National Assembly first met in Frankfurt on May 18 1848; its representatives belonged mostly to liberal democratic sectors. They campaigned for German unity, and guarantees of political freedom. However, internal divisions facilitated the regrouping of the forces of the former regime, leading finally to the dissolution of Parliament in June 1849 and the repression of opposition organizations.

[16] With the revolutionary tendencies crushed, Austria and Prussia were free to dispute their respective roles in German unification. The issue was settled in 1866 with Prussia's victory in the Seven Weeks' War. The union was forged around the North German Confederation, a creation of the Prussian chancellor, Otto von Bismarck, that aimed to halt liberalism. The Parliament (Reichstag) was inaugurated in February 1867.

[17] Three years later, war broke out with France. Prussia's victory in 1871 was the last step in Bismarck's scheme to unite Germany under a single monarch, and Prussian domination.

[18] The Empire had to deal with opposing internal forces - the Church and social democracy. Bismarck passed the May Laws, secularizing education and some other activities. He later reversed this, securing the Church as an ally against socialism. Alarmed at the growth of social democracy, the regime used repression and social reform to neutralize the latter's potential.

[19] Bismarck's government introduced commercial protectionism to increase domestic income and foster national industry and the German economy grew substantially, especially in heavy industry, chemicals, the electro-technical area and production. The creation of the Triple Alliance with Austria and Italy, and the acquisition of colonies in Africa and Asia after 1884 made the German Empire a leading world power.

[20] German rivalry with France and Britain in the west, and Russia and Serbia in the east, triggered World War I. The capitulation of the Austro-Hungarian Empire and Turkey in November 1918 led to Germany's final defeat. The crisis was

aggravated by an internal revolution that led to the abdication of the Emperor. Government was handed over to the socialist Friedrich Ebert, who was to call a National Constituent Assembly.

[21] German social democracy split into a moderate tendency favoring a gradual evolution to socialism, and a radical tendency favoring revolutionary change. The radical group, the Spartacists, headed by Karl Liebknecht and Rosa Luxemburg, identified with the Russian revolution of October 1917 and wanted to set up a system similar to that of the Soviets. The Spartacist leaders were executed in January 1919 following a failed coup attempt. A few days later, the electorate returned a moderate socialist majority to power in the Constituent Assembly.

[22] Formally proclaimed in August of that year, the Weimar Constitution was welcomed as the most democratic of its time. The president elect had power to nominate the Chancellor, whose government needed approval of the lower chamber of parliament, or the Reichstag. It also provided for the constitution of an upper house or Länder, formed by delegates designate by the governments of the liberal states.

[23] The Weimar Republic had a short and hazardous life. Despite the virtues attributed to the Constitution, various factors came together to undermine it. One of the main destabilizing elements for the Republic was the conditions imposed on the country in Versailles by the victorious powers after World War I. These affected not only the economy but also the morale of the population which could not allow Germany to be considered 'guilty' of having caused the war in 1914 and was unable to accept the stipulations of the treaty that judged any German, from the Kaiser down, as a war criminal.

[24] Germany was declared bankrupt by the Commission of Reparations and in January 1923 Belgian and French troops occupied the industrial Ruhr region. Economic instability caused hyperinflation. Even though the Republican government managed to weather the serious economic crises, as in 1920-23 and events following the Wall Street crash in 1929, the destabilizing influence of the Communists and the National Socialist Party, led by Adolf Hitler were set to topple it. The National Socialist or Nazi party had attempted a coup in 1923. Although this failed, the Party saw a sustained increase in its popularity throughout the decade, with rocketing support after the crisis in 1929. While there were barely 170,000 members in 1929, the number grew to 1,378,000 by 1932.

[25] Marshall Paul Hindenburg, elected president in 1925, dissolved parliament in 1930. In the elections later that year, Communists and Nazis both saw a great increase in votes. The Nazis' promises to rebuild Greater Germany following the humiliation of the post-war treaties, and their campaign to blame the Jews and Communists for the economic crisis were ratified when the Nazi party doubled its share of the vote in the 1932 elections, gaining 37 per cent of the total.

[26] The rise of Hitler and the National Socialist Party proved unstoppable. Despite the fact that Hitler's demands to become head of government had been refused in principle, in January 1933 - as unemployment topped six million - Hindenberg was forced to hand him the reins of office. Hitler dissolved Parliament and called elections which his National Socialist Party won.

[27] In Potsdam in March 1933, the new parliament granted Hitler the power to issue decrees outside the Constitution without the approval of the legislative body or the President for four years. He had the power to set the budget, request loans and sign agreements with other countries, reorganize both his cabinet and the supreme ranks of the armed forces, and proclaim martial law. In July, Hitler abolished the German Federation and set up absolute central power. He outlawed trade unions, strikes and all parties except his own. Germany also withdrew from the Disarmament Conference and the League of Nations. The Nazis dubbed their government the *Third Reich* (Third Empire).

[28] After the death of President Hindenburg in August 1934, the cabinet was forced to swear personal allegiance to the Chancellor, Adolf Hitler. In 1935, in open violation of the Treaty of Versailles, he began to re-arm Germany. The European powers protested, but were unable to stop him. With the 1935 'Nuremberg Laws', the regime provided a legal framework for its racist ideology, laying the foundation for its subsequent policies of ethnic and religious persecution.

[29] Germany and Italy signed a co-operation agreement in October 1936 which included support for General Franco in the Spanish Civil War. The following month Germany and Japan (the Axis powers) agreed to set up a military exchange, and in November 1937 Germany, Italy and Japan signed the Anti-communist Pact in Rome.

[30] In March 1938, German troops invaded Austria, and Hitler annexed it. That same year, the pressure of Hitler and German nationalism on the Sudetenland forced the European powers to cede this Czechoslovakian region to Germany. On 'Kristallnacht', November 9-10, the Government carried out a systematic destruction of Jewish commercial property and religious and cultural institutions.

[31] In 1939, taking advantage of the disagreements between Czechs and Slovaks, German troops advanced into Prague; Bohemia, Moravia, and Slovakia became protectorates.

[32] Britain assured Poland, Romania, Greece and Turkey that it would protect their independence, and Britain and France attempted to establish an alliance with the Soviet Union. In August 1939, however, the USSR signed a non-aggression treaty with Germany. On September 1, German troops invaded Poland. Britain and France issued Germany an ultimatum which was disregarded. World War II broke out.

[33] By 1940, Germany had invaded Norway, Denmark, Belgium, the Netherlands, Luxembourg and France. In 1941 Hitler started his offensive against the USSR, but German troops were halted a few miles outside Moscow. They were finally defeated after the siege of Stalingrad (Volgograd) in 1943.

[34] From the outset, German aggression against its neighbors was accompanied by the systematic extermination of the Jewish population in concentration camps, primarily in Poland. Over six million Jews, and a million other people were killed.

35 The advance of the Red Army on the eastern front - culminating in the capture of Berlin - and the 1944 Allied landing in Normandy on the Western Front forced Germany to surrender in May 1945.

36 Four million Germans from neighboring countries, and from the territories annexed by Poland and the USSR, were forced to move to the four zones that Germany was now divided into. The country remained occupied by the United States, France, Britain and the USSR. In 1949, discord between the former Allies over the future governance of Germany led to the creation of the Federal Republic of Germany (FRG), in the West, and the German Democratic Republic (GDR), in the East. The issue of the two Germanies became a bone of contention in post-war relations between the USSR and the US.

37 In 1955, the sovereignty of both Germanies was recognized by their occupying forces. During the Cold War, West Germany became a member of NATO (the North Atlantic Treaty Organization) while East Germany joined the Warsaw Pact. Foreign forces continued to be based in their territories and the two republics were still subject to limitations on their armed forces and a ban on nuclear weapons.

38 The United Socialist Party (SED), formed from the union of Communists and Social Democrats in 1946, took over the government of East Germany. The USSR partly compensated them for war losses with money, equipment and cattle, and a social system similar to that of the USSR was set up. In 1953, the political and economic situation of East Germany led to a series of protests, which were put down by Soviet troops. In the meantime, emigration to the Federal Republic of Germany (FRG) increased.

39 Between the state's formation and 1961, when the East German Government forbade all emigration to the West, some three million East Germans emigrated to West Germany. To enforce their resolution, the East closed its borders and built the Berlin Wall between the eastern and the western sections of the city. In 1971, Erich Honecker took over the leadership of the SED party, and later the GDR Government.

40 Between 1949 and 1963, Chancellor Konrad Adenauer, a conservative Christian Democrat, oversaw the reconstruction of West Germany/FRG, under the slogan '[establishing] a social market economy'. With US support (the Marshall Plan) and huge amounts of foreign capital, the FRG became one of the most developed capitalist economies, playing a key role in the founding of the European Community (EC).

41 With the victory of the Social Democratic Party (SPD) in the 1969 elections, the government of Chancellor Willy Brandt launched a policy of rapprochement toward Eastern Europe and the German Democratic Republic. In 1970 the first formal talks between the FRG and the GDR began, and in 1971 the occupying powers agreed to free access of FRG citizens to the GDR. A Basic Treaty of bilateral relations was signed by both Germanies in 1973; in September they were admitted to the United Nations.

42 In the 1970s, the number of power stations producing nuclear energy increased. In response to this, a strong environmental movement was formed, with a network of hundreds of grassroots groups throughout the country.

43 In 1974, after the discovery that his private secretary was an East German spy, Brandt resigned as Chancellor and was succeeded by Helmut Schmidt. The modernization of Soviet medium-range missiles in East Germany, and the December 1979 NATO decision to do the same with its arsenal in West Germany, gave a strong impetus to the anti-nuclear movement in both states, with massive protests in the FRG.

44 In 1982, the Social Democratic Party (SPD) had to leave power when the Liberal Party withdrew from the government alliance after 13 years. It was succeeded by the liberal-conservative alliance (CDU/CSU, FDP) led by Chancellor Helmut Kohl of the Christian Democratic Union (CDU).

45 In mid-1989, Hungary liberalized regulations regarding transit across the border with Austria. Within a few weeks, some 350,000 Germans from the GDR had emigrated to the FRG. Street demonstrations demanding change brought on a crisis in the GDR. In August, Honecker resigned and was replaced by Egon Krenz. On November 9, the GDR opened up its borders and the Berlin Wall fell. Kohl immediately proposed the creation of a confederation of East and West Germany.

46 In February 1990, the East German Government agreed to German unification and the withdrawal of all foreign troops from its territory. The fusion of the two states was officially recognized in August 1990, as the Federal Republic of Germany. Political union was made possible when the USSR accepted the East German entry into NATO. The only important difference between the two Germanies over the next two years was the East's preservation of a more liberal abortion law.

47 In the first parliamentary elections of the new Federal Republic, in December 1990, the

governing coalition of Social Christians and Liberals obtained 54 per cent of the vote and stayed in power. From 1991, the extreme right made important gains at a local level, like in Bremen, where they increased their share of the vote by 7 per cent. During 1992, there were 2,280 attacks on foreigners and Jewish monuments, which left 17 people dead. After one incident which caused the death of a Turkish woman and two children, the Government outlawed three neo-Nazi organizations.

48 Throughout the following year, the closure of most of the industry in the east of the country and economic recession - the worst since 1945 - caused a constant increase in unemployment. In May 1994, the conservative, Roman Herzog, backed by Kohl, was designated president of Germany by a special electoral assembly, after defeating the Social Democrat Johannes Rau. In the second half of the year, a cycle of economic expansion began, which allowed a level of 2.8 per cent growth to be reached during the 1994 financial year. Kohl triumphed again in the October general elections, although his majority fell to only 10 seats of the 672 in play.

49 In 1995, the constant weakening of the Liberal Party (FDP) in various local elections prompted the resignation of Foreign Minister Klaus Kinkel. On the social front, Parliament adopted a new law which, despite again permitting abortion during the first 12 weeks of pregnancy, was more restrictive than the one annulled in 1993 for being unconstitutional.

50 The discontent of many foreigners resident in Germany led to the formation of the Democratic Party of Germany, which stood for greater access to the electoral role and citizenship - often restricted to people of German origin - for the children of immigrants.

51 In 1996, five years after unification and three years after the frontiers fell for workers of the European Union, unemployment stood at around 10.6 per cent on a national level, and up to 16 per cent in the states of the former East Germany. Five million people were out of work.

52 Racism and anti-Semitism continued to be issues for the Kohl administration. In October 1997, a television broadcast showed an army battalion giving Nazi salutes and shouting anti-Semitic and anti-US slogans. Amnesty International indicated that police abuse to foreigners could not be seen as isolated cases, due to the systematic repetition of the offences.

53 In early 1998, the Deutsche Bank paid back Jewish organizations

the money made from the sale of gold suspected to have been robbed from the Jews by the Nazis. At the same time, a Swiss foundation began to provide economic compensation - although with 'token' sums of money - to Roma (gypsy) residents in Germany who had survived the Nazi holocaust.

54 The September 1998 elections delivered an overwhelming victory for the Social Democrats and Gerhard Schröder was named Federal Chancellor. The SPD leader Oskar Lafontaine headed the Finance ministry. The former communists of former East Germany were well supported, winning 36 seats in the Federal Parliament.

[55] In March 1999, Lafontaine resigned from both posts following discrepancies with the political line of the head of government, in what became a party crisis. A series of defeats in the 1999 local elections put the squeeze on the SPD and it seemed the public had returned to the Christian Democrats.

[56] But the CDU was hit by a corruption scandal in November 1999. Initially, former chancellor Kohl was accused of authorizing the sale of armored vehicles to countries at war without parliament knowing, but later it was announced that he had accepted illegal contributions from private donors. Kohl had to stand down from honorary presidency of the CDU and he was was found guilty of illegal handling of funds. The former chancellor consistently refused to hand over the list of donors, in order to protect them.

[57] An historical fusion of Eastern and Western consumers' cooperatives took place in mid-June 2000, thus putting end to an old division, prior to the Cold War. The union of the new cooperative, which centralizes all consumers'

cooperative associations in Germany, was celebrated on June 27.

[58] Unemployment grew and, in November 2001, the number of unemployed reached 3,789,000, or 9.2 per cent of the working population.

[59] Following the Stability Pact of 1997, in which the EU member states agreed the economies of the Eurozone would act in concert, the European Commission warned Germany and Portugal in January 2002 that their budget deficit was nearing the 3 per cent maximum allowed by the organization. However, in February, both countries avoided the European sanction, assuring they would closely control their expenses in the future and would commit themselves to reaching a balanced budget for 2004.

[60] In March 2002 the lower chamber initiated the ratification process of the Kyoto Treaty, unanimously passing it into law. This commits the country to reduce its carbon dioxide emissions by one fifth by the year 2012.

[61] Defense Minister Rudolf Scharping rejected German participation in an attack against Iraq, in the context of the US war against terrorism.

[62] Schröder was re-elected by a narrow margin in September 2002. ∎

The Celts

Whether seen through the lens of Christianity, in the tales of King Arthur, the pagan standing stones of Stonehenge or the swirling musical rhythms, the traces of Celtic culture provide proof of past vigor. Today's interest contrasts with the somewhat elusive trail Celtic culture has followed for four thousand years. Thinking of runes, dolmen or bagpipes is to trace the footprints of a civilization that for a thousand years dominated a vast pan-European commonwealth. The importance of their place in European cultural, linguistic and artistic development is only now being rediscovered.

From Anatolia to the British Isles, from Transylvania to Northern Spain, the Celts have left traces of their passage. Archaeological evidence shows they originated 3,500 years ago at the source of the river Danube. Their generic name appears in Roman documents as *galatae*, *galli* or *celtae* (derived from *keltoi*, the name Herodotus in the 4th century BC and other Greek writers gave to this people). Etymologically the word 'Celt' appears to have originated in the syllable kal- also written as Gal or Cal - which evokes a certain condition of hardness. Calath means hard in old Irish, the same as calet in Breton.

The expansion of the Celts throughout Europe was a slow process, with broad phases of rise and decline. During the first millennium BC their influence extended progressively westward to what are now the British Isles, France and the Iberian Peninsula, to Romania and the Carpathians in the east and to Italy, Greece and Anatolia in the south. In 390 BC they sacked Rome and settled in northern Italy, creating Cisalpine Gaul. At the height of their civilisation (around 100 BC), the Celts controlled an extensive territory which covered almost all of Western Europe.

Dual pressure from Germanic groups and the Roman Empire began to make itself felt and 'Celtic civilization' started to break up. Most of Western Europe was Romanized, except for Ireland, where the Celts maintained a stable enclave. The language remained intact for centuries, protected from Roman invaders by the sea. Some Celtic communities in Britain were forced to flee to parts that were less accessible to the Romans: Cornwall, west Wales and the mountainous regions of Scotland.

PIECES OF A JIGSAW

The majority, however, settled in the north-east Iberian Peninsula (Galicia, Asturias, Tras os Montes, in Northern Portugal). In parts of western Iberia they mixed with the local population and were known as Celto-Iberians,. They practised guerrilla tactics which kept the Romans at bay for centuries. Finally, most of Spain and Portugal was Romanized and Latin replaced pre-Roman languages (apart from Basque).

The Celtic language is Indo-European in origin, and from the geographical-historical point of view it divides into two branches. Continental Celtic was represented exclusively by Gallic, and it disappeared completely from Gaul - the region where it was spoken - when the Romans conquered and imposed Latin. Insular Celtic was subdivided into English/British (which includes Breton, spoken in Brittany, Cornish and Welsh) and Gaelic, which covers the variants in Ireland, Scots-Gaelic and Manx (dialect of the Isle of Man).

The study of Celtic mythology and religion has been complicated by the scarcity of sources. Tales told by Greek historians including Herodotus, Hecataeo and Diodorus (5th century BC), and by Roman writers like Julius Caesar, Livy and Strabo (1st century BC) are an additional source of information. But these are not too reliable because of the problems associated with translation and interpretation, and also because many of the sources were local people who often provided incorrect data. According to classical histories, Celtic society was organised in small groups stratified into nobles, free farmers who were also warriors, craftspeople, manual laborers and slaves. People of various racial backgrounds - Indo-European, Nordic or Mediterranean and others indigenous to each region - participated in the Celtic culture. Even though the greatest authority figure was the king, decisions were not made without approval from the druids, or priestly healers whose functions included divination, making sacrifices, leading the rituals in religious festivals and the transmission of stories. Even when able to read and write Greek and Latin, the druids opted for the oral tradition to remember the chronicles of their people.

Celtic histories, laws and legends were kept alive in stories, songs and verse until the first transcriptions were made into written language in the Middle Ages. Although the oral tradition only dates back to the 6th century AD and bears the mark of a world that was being conquered by Christendom, insight into the mythological past of ancient Ireland and Britain can be found in the earliest writings of the insular Celts. In this literature scholars have found the traces of the Great Mother, a mighty Celtic goddess that was erased by the Christian patriarchal God and the 'son of Mary' (Jesus Christ). Even in the Christian tale of the Holy Grail contained in the legend of King Arthur, the decline of the cult of the Great Mother can be seen. This revisionist insight has been popularized by the 2001 film *The mists of Avalon*, based on a book by Marion Zimmer Bradley. ∎

Ghana

Population: 20,176,000 (2002)
Land area: 227,540 SQ KM
Capital: Accra
Currency: Cedi
Language: English

Ghana

In about 1300, the Akans or Ashantis moved into Ghana from the north. The powerful and organized Fanti State of Denkyira was already established on the coast so the Akans settled in the inland jungles. Here, they founded a series of small cities that paid tribute to the coastal nation.

2 In the 15th century the Ashantis began to trade in the markets of Begho, on the border of present-day Côte d'Ivoire. They traded slaves and gold for fabrics and other goods from North Africa and further afield. An ornate pitcher that had once belonged to Richard II, King of England between 1367 and 1400, was discovered in the treasure of a Kumasi ruler.

3 In the 17th century, new waves of migration threatened the existence of the small jungle states. This crisis forced the Akans to unite in confronting the Doma invaders. The Doma were defeated.

4 With the decline of the Songhai, the Moroccan incursions and the beginning of the Fulah expansion, the North African trade network collapsed with serious repercussions for the inland economy. The Ashanti were also deprived of access to the coastal trading posts as these were in Denkyira Territory. Instead of paying taxes, they declared war on the Denkyira and defeated them. They then organized a centralized state, ruled by the 'Ashantihene' (leader of the Ashanti nation) endowed with a powerful army. By 1700, the Ashanti had control of the slave trade to the coast and the flow of European goods to the interior.

5 When the British stopped trading in slaves, the Ashanti reacted by attempting to seize the shoreline from the Fanti, who had retained a significant share of the coastal trade. English backing of the Fanti led to the Anglo-Ashanti wars, 1806-1816, 1825-28 and 1874. After the last war, the British turned the Fanti territory into a colony. In 1895 under the pretext of defending the region from Samori Turé (see Guinea) they also proclaimed a protectorate over the northern territories.

6 While the coastal and northern regions were under British rule, the central region belonged to the autonomous Ashanti nation. It did not take long for friction to build up and another Anglo-Ashanti war broke out in 1896. The capital, Kumasi, was razed by cannon fire, and the ruler was deposed and exiled. The Ashanti were then told that they owed 50,000 ounces of gold in compensation for 'war damages'. An attempt to collect the debt coupled with the British Governor's culturally insensitive desire to sit on the gold throne, led to a general rebellion four years later. This was immediately put down with a great loss of lives. In 1902 the Ashanti state was formally annexed to the Gold Coast Colony.

7 During the first half of the 20th century, a strong nationalist current developed in spite of the ethnic and religious differences within Ghana. Economic opposition to the British also grew at this time both in the north, where the traditional structures had remained intact, and in the south, where a Westernized middle class and a relatively significant working class had developed.

8 Popular pressure on the colonial administration led to political concessions. In 1946, London admitted a few Africans into the colonial administration and in 1949 Kwame Nkrumah formed the Convention People's Party (CCP) to campaign for greater reform.

9 Nkrumah was one of the founding fathers of Pan-Africanism and African nationalism. He established a solid rural and urban party structure and, in 1952, he became Prime Minister of the colony. In his inaugural speech, he proclaimed himself a 'socialist, Marxist and Christian', promising to fight against imperialism.

10 Nkrumah represented Ghana at the Bandung Conference in 1955 which marked the birth of the Movement of Non-Aligned Countries. Together with Tito, Nasser, Nehru and Sukarno, Nkrumah played an important part. In 1957 he achieved a major victory and Ghana became the first country in West Africa to gain independence. Known as Osagyefo (redeemer), Nkrumah enthusiastically embraced the Pan-African anti-colonialism. He initiated a series of internal changes based on industrialization, agrarian reform and socialist education.

11 These new measures, however, did not suit everybody. Traditional and neo-colonial interests conspired against the Government and Nkrumah was overthrown. The coup leaders drew up a parliamentary constitution and in 1969 held elections for a civilian government. The CPP was not allowed to participate. Nkrumah died in exile in Bucharest in 1972.

12 In 1969, Colonel Ignatius

WORKERS

1999/2000

LABOR FORCE AS % OF TOTAL

- FEMALE: 51%
- MALE: 50%

LAND USE

DEFORESTATION: 1.3% annual (1990/95)

1993

- FOREST & WOODLAND: 33.1%
- ARABLE: 11.7%
- OTHER: 55.2%

PUBLIC EXPENDITURE

Military expenditure (as % GNI):	**0.8 %** (1999)	
Defense expenditure (% of central government expenditure)	**3.1 %** (1999)	

Acheampong led a coup replacing the Government of Dr Kofi Busia. Acheampong dropped the ambitious industrialization and development plans, substituting an essentially agrarian policy which favored the owners of large cocoa plantations.

[13] Acheampong survived eight coup attempts in five years, but his economic policy was not as successful. In 1977, Ghana had an inflation rate of 36 per cent, an oppressive foreign debt, a devalued currency and hundreds of imprisoned intellectuals and students, condemned for questioning government policy.

[14] In July 1977, the so-called revolt of the middle class occurred. The period of social unrest came to a head in July 1978 and Acheampong resigned. A new military regime was established, lead by General William Frederick Akuffo. The opposition claimed this was simply a continuation of the previous government under a different figurehead. On June 4 1979, a coup led by Lt Jerry Rawlings overthrew Akuffo and called fresh elections. The Convention People's Party, which included Nkrumah's followers, won a large majority. A transitional government took power promising an eventual return to a constitutional system.

[15] On October 1 1979, with the acquiescence of the Revolutionary Council of the Armed Forces, Hilla Limann, a PNP leader, took over the presidency. Limann abandoned many of Nkrumah's nationalistic economic policies, replacing them with International Monetary Fund policies, in an attempt to reduce the fiscal deficit. To attract foreign investors and overcome the sharp fall in cocoa export revenues, the Ghanaian Government drastically reduced all imports, including food. As a result, food prices escalated wildly while the purchasing power of workers fell drastically. This inevitably led to a series of strikes in 1980 and 1981.

[16] Support for Rawlings remained high among the poor. He accused the Government of being indecisive and preoccupied with foreign capital. Inflation exceeded 140 per cent and the unemployment rate was more than 25 per cent. This created an unstable situation which culminated in a further coup led by Rawlings on January 1 1982.

[17] The first concern of the new group of officers was to launch a campaign against corruption in the public sector. They committed themselves to nothing short of a revolution for social justice in the country. Within a few months they were able to increase the amount of taxes collected, and greatly reduce cocoa smuggling (kalabule) to neighboring countries. People's Courts were set up to pass judgement on irregularities committed by the authorities of the previous government.

[18] To deal with the economic crisis it was necessary to develop policy, and look for sources of foreign capital. Rawlings had already expressed his willingness to carry out an austerity program dictated by the IMF. He intensified relations with them in 1983, and generous loans were granted to Ghana on the basis that IMF prescriptions would be followed religiously and that Ghana would serve as a model for other countries in the region.

[19] To increase national income and bring contraband under control Ghana devalued its currency (the cedi). This went from 2.74 per $1 in 1982, to 183 per $1 in 1988. Taxes were increased, subsidies were removed, the Government salaries budget was reduced, financing for inefficient private enterprises was eliminated and the printing of currency was virtually suspended.

[20] However there were some positive results. Inflation fell from 200 to 25 per cent, the banking system improved and better prices were obtained for cocoa producers.

[21] By applying this economic policy Ghana obtained loans on extremely generous terms. The major drawback of this scheme was that Ghana's finances were under rigid IMF control. Ghana's foreign debt approached $4 billion and the servicing of the debt used up two-thirds of the country's export earnings.

[22] The social cost of this readjustment program was high. Consumer prices rose by some 30 per cent between 1983 and 1987; 45,000 public employees have lived under the constant threat of losing their jobs and there was a general loss of earning power leading to an increase in hunger, infant mortality and illiteracy.

[23] In 1900 there were only 8 urban centers in the whole of the country, but by 1984 the number had risen to 180. In recent years there has been a migration towards the major cities, resulting in the creation of shantytowns with no drinking water or sanitation. In the poorest quarters of Takoradi there were only 16 public toilets per 3,250 people. If current rates of rural exodus continue, by the year 2020 over half the population of Ghana will be living in urban centers.

[24] The economic upheaval had environmental costs as well. Tropical forest used to cover 34 per cent of the country's surface. This forest is now only a quarter of its original size; and 42 per cent of the area which is officially considered

PROFILE

ENVIRONMENT

The southern region is covered with dense rainforest, partially cleared to plant cocoa, coffee, banana and oil palm trees. Wide savannas extend to the north.
The rest of the territory is low-lying, with a few high points near the border with Togo. The Volta, Ghana's main river, has an artificial lake formed by the Akossombo dam. The climate is tropical, with summer rains. The subsoil is rich in gold, diamonds, manganese and bauxite. Desertification in the northwest and deforestation are the main environmental problems. Desertification, affecting the northwest, and deforestation, water pollution and a lack of drinking water are major environmental issues.

SOCIETY

Peoples: Ghanaians come from six main ethnic groups: the Akan (Ashanti and Fanti), 44 per cent, located in the mid southern part of the country; the Ewe, 13 per cent, and Ga-Adangbe, 8 per cent, on both sides of the Volta in southern and southeastern Ghana; the Mole-Dagbane, 16 per cent, in the northern savannas; the Guan, 4 per cent, and the Gurma, 3 per cent, in the valleys and plateaus of the northeastern territory.
Religions: 50 per cent Christian, 32 per cent traditional religions, 13 per cent Muslim.
Languages: English (official); Ga is the main local language, Fanti, Haussa, Fantéewe, Gaadanhe, Akan, Dagbandim and Mamprussi are also spoken.
Political Parties: New Patriotic Party (NPP), liberal; National Democratic Congress (NDC); People's National Convention (PNC); Convention People's Party (CPP).
Social Organizations: Ghana Trade Union Congress.

THE STATE

Official Name: Republic of Ghana.
Administrative divisions: 10 regions, subdivided into 110 districts.
Capital: Accra 1,904,000 people (1999).
Other cities: Kumasi 906,400 people; Tamale 259,200; Sekondi-Taloradi 164,400 (2000).
Government: John Agyekum Kufuor, President, Head of State and Government since January 2001. Alhaji Aliu Mahama, Vice-President since 2000. Unicameral Legislature, with 200 members elected for a four-year term.
National Holiday: March 6, Independence Day (1957).
Armed Forces: 7,000.
Other: People's Militia 5,000.

LITERACY

2000

70%

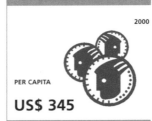

EXTERNAL DEBT

2000

PER CAPITA

US$ 345

FOREIGN TRADE

Millions US$ 2000

IMPORTS
3,612

EXPORTS
2,553

'forest', is in fact covered with timber plantations, secondary vegetation, or immature trees. For the people who live in the country, and for most of those who live in the cities, forest plants constitute the basis of their traditional medicine. 75 per cent of the population rely on bush meat for their basic source of protein and forests also provide firewood, a basic household necessity.

²⁵ All of these activities are ignored by official plans, which see the forest merely as a source of timber for export. In Ghana at present some 70,000 people are employed in the timber industry.

²⁶ A National Forestry Administration Program (NFAP) was established, supported by international bodies like USAID, the FAO and countries such as Canada and the UK. Such programs however lay the blame for deforestation, desertification and soil degradation on the poor population and its search for new areas of farmland. In this thinking the very people who are the victims of an economic model which encourages exports at any price are held responsible for environmental degradation.

²⁷ Ghana considerably increased its production of cocoa, gold, wood and bauxite, but the fall in the world market price of cocoa generated a loss of $200 million, and many industries were forced to close down. In meetings at the Paris Club in January and February of 1989, further loans of $900 million were granted.

²⁸ In 1990 in, spite of monetary infusions, the hopes of growth collapsed. GDP growth fell from 6.1 to 2.7 per cent. Inflation at 25 per cent in 1989, went up to 37 per cent. The current account deficit almost doubled and earnings for exports were lower than in 1988. Between 1988 and 1989, around 120 industries closed down because their products could not compete with cheaper and higher-quality goods from China, South Korea, and Taiwan.

²⁹ The Rawlings Government initiated a democratization program and a devolution plan, favoring local administrations. In June 1991, an advisory assembly of 260 members was elected to draft a new constitution. The National Council for Women and Development, a body with ministerial status, won 10 seats and the Organization of Graduate Nurses and Midwives was also represented.

³⁰ In December 1991, Amnesty International denounced the Ghanaian policy of silencing or intimidating its opponents. In view of such serious and constant human rights violations, the Ghana Committee for Human and Popular Rights was created in January 1992, the first such organization in the country.

³¹ In that year, a new constitution was approved and elections were held. Rawlings took 58.3 per cent of the vote in the November presidential elections and the three parties which supported him took 197 of the 200 seats in the December legislative elections.

³² In spite of alleged election irregularities, 80 countries and international organizations attended Rawlings' investiture in January 1993. This foreign support was attributed to the rigorous application of the IMF imposed structural adjustment plans in the previous decade and the prompt payment of servicing on the foreign debt, which represented some 35 per cent of export earnings.

³³ In February 1994, confrontations over land ownership caused the death of more than a thousand people and the migration of 150,000. The Government declared a state of emergency and in June an agreement was reached to bring an end to the violence. The budget for that year had a surplus of $80 million, following two years of deficit. In May, demonstrations against the new value-added tax left five people dead. Economy Minister, Kwesi Botchwey, withdrew the new tax from the budget, and after 13 years in the post - coinciding with the implementation of the IMF plans - resigned from his job.

³⁴ Despite the New Patriotic Party and the People's Convention trying to settle their differences and form an alliance to present a common electoral platform, Rawlings won the December 1996 elections with 57.2 per cent of the vote. A dramatic fall in the water level of the Akosombo dam produced a severe energy crisis. In March 1998, the Ministry of Science and Technology said Ghana could not pay the initial investment needed to develop a possible nuclear energy-based project. The crisis was partly resolved with help from Côte d'Ivoire, which increased the amount of electricity supplied to Ghana from 20 to 35 megawatts per day.

³⁵ The police harshly put down a student demonstration in August 1999. The students were protesting against an increase in fees and costs passed by the government. Finally, the authorities decided to close the University of Ghana temporarily until the demonstrators could be pacified.

³⁶ After winning the second electoral round in January 2001, beating Vice-President John Atta Mills (backed by Rawlings, but constitutionally barred from participating), John Kufuor from the NPP put an end to 20 years of NDC Government. The NPP also won the legislative elections, taking 97 of the 200 seats at stake, while the government party won only 86 seats. Kufuor assumed the Presidency, in the first occasion that a change of power took place through democratic means.

³⁷ Ghana remained an arena for clashes between different ethnic groups. In late 2001, violent confrontations took place between Mamprusis and Kusasis, leaving 50 dead. New clashes took place in March 2002, causing the death of KngYa-Na Yakubu Andani II, an Andani, and of 27 other people. The Government declared a state of emergency and deployed its troops in order to calm both groups. Historically, Mamprusi people tended to favor the NPP, while the Kusasis tend to support the NDC.

³⁸ Kufuor approved the creation of the National Reconciliation Commission, with the aim of investigating cases of human rights abuses that took place during the 22 years of military dictatorships. This Commission, similar to others implemented in several African countries, will grant immunity to those who testify and try to solve the 200 cases of disappeared persons, mostly during Rawlings' military regime. ∎

Greece

Population:	10,631,000 (2002)
Land area:	128,900 SQ KM
Capital:	Athens
Currency:	Euro
Language:	Greek

Ellás

0 — — — 300 km

Between 5000 and 3000 BC, the Greek peninsula was inhabited by maritime peoples from Asia. In Thessaly, central Greece and Crete traces have been found of previous inhabitants, nomadic and agricultural peoples. From the second millennium BC the Achaeans, an Indo-European people, started to expand throughout the peninsula.

2   The Achaeans founded Mycenae, Tyrins and Argos, later conquering Athens and the eastern Peloponnese, invading Crete and raiding Troy. They were warriors, with an economy based on agriculture and cattle-breeding. The hierarchical social organization had kings, nobles, and warriors dominating farmers, artisans and peasants.

3   By the first millennium BC, Mycenian civilization had succumbed to Dorian invasions. The Dorians used iron weapons, unknown to the Achaeans, and they soon mixed with the subject population, bringing linguistic unity to the region.

4   The peninsula's topography favored the appearance of city-states (polis), ruled by a king or tyrant, supported by the military aristocracy. The peasants were forced to pay tributes in kind, and if they could not produce sufficient crops they became serfs or their whole family was sold into slavery.

5   Despite the social differentiation, the Greeks had an original concept of the human being. All previous civilizations had seen humans as a mere instruments of the will of the gods or the monarchs, whereas in Greek philosophy they acquired the value of individuals. The concept of a citizen, as an individual who belongs to the polis regardless of nobility, was one Greek culture's main contributions to Western civilization.

6   The city states alternately established alliances and fought each other. However, Hellenic groups started to feel they belonged to a common nationality bound by factors like the Olympic games, and a common religion and language.

7   In the 8th century BC most city-states went through crises, due to the decline in power of the monarchs (who were progressively replaced by magistrates appointed by the nobility), to the lack of fertile soil, and to demographic growth. This produced great social tension spurring the Greeks to colonize the Mediterranean, creating active trade routes and expanding the use of Greek as the language of commerce.

8   Around 760 BC the Greeks established colonies in southern Italy, in the bay of Naples and in Sicily. The Phoenicians and the Etruscans prevented them from ruling the whole of Sicily and the south of Italy, but their culture was deeply influential in later developments on the Italian peninsula.

9   When colonization started, the social and political structure of the polis underwent transformations. Merchants, wealthy as a result of maritime expansion, were not ready to leave government to the nobility. They joined the peasants in pressing for political participation. Between the 7th and 6th centuries BC, Athens one of the most prosperous cities in the peninsula started a process of political transformations which led to the gradual democratization of its governmental structures. In 594 BC a reformer called Solon took the first steps in this direction with the establishment of written law, a court of justice and an assembly of 400 members, elected from among the wealthy, which was in charge of legislating on city matters.

10   Sparta, the other great city-state in the region, evolved in a completely different way. It consolidated an oligarchic state, with a strict social and political structure. Spartan society was completely militarized because of the central importance of the army, which had been a determining factor in expansion and annexation of neighboring territories.

11   In 540 BC the Persians started advancing on Asia Minor, conquering some Greek cities. These cities revolted, backed first by Athens and then by Sparta, resulting in several wars until the Persians were defeated around 449 BC. These wars served to consolidate Athenian power in the region, exerting its political and economic influence over the other city-states through the League of Delos.

12   The Athenian triremes (galleys) played a key role in the wars against the Persians. The oarsmen, who belonged to the lowest strata of Athenian society, became an indispensable tool in the defense of Athens, and were thus in a position to demand improvements in their living conditions and increased political rights. In 508 BC, after a period when the Athenian oligarchy had succeeded in recovering its political power, a reformer called Cleisthenes raised the number of assembly members to 500, turning this body into the main governmental structure. Participation in the Assembly was open to all free citizens in the polis. However, these constituted a minority of the population; Athenian prosperity was actually based on the exploitation of huge numbers of slaves. Athenian society of this period is therefore referred to as a 'slave holding democracy' by historians.

13   In 446 BC the archon or governor of Athens, Pericles, agreed the Thirty Years' Peace with Sparta, recognizing each city's areas of influence in the Athenian League and the League of the Peloponnese.

14   Under Pericles' rule, Athens became the trading, political, and cultural centre of the region. The domination of maritime trade and the prosperity this created enabled Pericles to start new democratic reforms. This was the period of scholars such as Anaxagoras, of dramatists such as Sophocles, Aeschylus, Euripides, Aristophanes, and of sculptors like Phidias. The Greeks achieved great scientific knowledge, much of which has now been altered, particularly in the fields of medicine or astronomy, but their contributions to geometry and mathematics are still indispensable for most of present-day science.

15   A long period of continuous struggles over who should control the region ensued between the Spartans and Athenians. This mutual attrition enabled the Macedonians to conquer this domain under the rule of Philip II, 359-336 BC. Philip's son, Alexander the Great, 336-323 BC, continued to spread Hellenic influence over the north of Africa and the Arabian Peninsula, through Mesopotamia, and as far as India. This empire, built over 11 years, contributed to the dissemination of Greek culture in the East. During the years of conquest, many trading cities were founded. Alexander promoted the fusion of Greek culture with that of the conquered peoples, giving rise to what is known as Hellenism. Upon his death, the Macedonian Empire collapsed and wars and rebellions continued to shake the peninsula.

16   These internal disputes resulted in a decline in the Greek civilization, leading to devastation and

impoverishment which enabled the Romans to move in. The Macedonian wars lasted from 215 to 168 BC, ending with the Romans establishing their rule over Greece by 146 BC.

[17] Under the Romans, Greece was acquainted with Christianity in the 3rd century, and it became a more rural society which was subjected to several invasions. From 395 to 1204, it belonged to the Eastern Empire, whose domination ended with the formation of the Eastern Roman Empire and the region's division into feudal possessions. In 1054, as a consequence of the Schism of the Roman Church, Greek Christians pledged obedience to the Orthodox Church in Constantinople.

[18] The Turks invaded and conquered in 1460, dividing Greece into six provinces which were forced to pay taxes. The Turks kept an army of occupation in the country for 400 years. External attempts to expel the Turks, in particular incursions led by Venice - eager to acquire this strategic territory for trade with the East - and internal revolts all failed. The Peace of Passarowitz incorporated Greece into the Ottoman Empire in 1718.

[19] In 1821 a Greek uprising succeeded in freeing Tripolitza, and a national assembly drafted a constitution, declaring independence. In 1825 the attempt ended in a bloodbath when the Turks, aided by Egypt, regained control of the city.

[20] In 1827 Russia, France and Britain, eager to keep the Turks away from their borders, signed the Treaty of London, which demanded Greek autonomy. The Turks refused it, and that year the allied fleet defeated the Turkish-Egyptian navy. In 1830, the London Convention declared the total independence of Greece, although the country had to sacrifice the region of Thessaly.

[21] In later years the European powers fought to control the peninsula, intervening in its domestic affairs and supporting kings who complied with their interests. Otto of Bavaria, 1831-1862, who favored the Russians, was followed by George I, 1864-1913, who was backed by the British.

[22] In 1910, a coup led by Eleutherios Vinizelos resulted in the enactment of a constitution (1911) establishing a parliamentary

monarchy. Throughout the two World Wars and the interwar years, subsequent military coups brought sympathizers of each side alternately to power.

[23] Once the German occupation was ended in 1944, an important part of the country remained under the control of communist guerrillas. They were led by Markos Vafiades, and had been crucial in resisting the Nazis. The British and Americans supported the Government in repressing the guerrillas until they were totally destroyed in 1949.

[24] Greece remained under American influence, becoming a member of the Council of Europe in 1949 and of NATO in 1951. In the 1956 elections women voted for the first time. After the War, Greece experienced political instability.

[25] In April 1967, a group of colonels staged a coup. Martial Law was enforced, the Constitution was suspended and democratic movements harshly repressed Socialist leader Andreas Papandreou was sentenced to nine years' imprisonment. In December the King attempted to oust the military junta, but he failed and fled to Rome. The military appointed General Zoitakis president, and Papadopoulos Prime Minister.

[26] The Colonels' regime, as it was known, was supported by the United States and by tycoons such as Onassis and Niarchos. Attempts were made to mask the dictatorship behind a unicameral Parliament in 1968, but in reality the military junta ruled by decree.

[27] Between 1973 and 1974 the military government grew weaker. In November, student demonstrations at the Polytechnic University of Athens were harshly repressed, leaving hundreds of casualties, and attracting international condemnation.

[28] In July 1974, the junta promoted a coup in Cyprus by collaborating with the Cypriot National Guard. The coup succeeded in deposing president Archbishop Vaneziz Makarios, who was forced into exile in London. A minister in favor of Greek annexation was appointed. The Turkish army immediately invaded Cyprus, allegedly defending the Turkish minority in the country. The Greek military government became even more discredited and internationally condemned, and they relinquished power immediately at the prospect of war with Turkey.

[29] In that month, former conservative Prime Minister Konstantin Karamanlis returned from exile and took over the government. In the 1974 elections his party won a parliamentary majority and a later referendum abolished the monarchy.

PROFILE

ENVIRONMENT
Located at the southeastern end of the Balkan peninsula, in the eastern Mediterranean, the country consists of a continental territory between the Aegean Sea and the Ionian Sea and numerous islands, including the island of Rhodes. Greece is a mountainous country, it has a Mediterranean climate with hot, dry summers. It is an essentially agricultural country (producing wine, olives, tobacco, wheat, barley); sheep and goats are raised in the mountains, where the soil is poor. Development is under way for salt-water fish farming. Greece produces lignite, bauxite, nickel and amianthus. The traditional manufacturing industries include food, beverages, apparel, leather and paper. Other major industries are cement, chemicals, petrochemicals and mining.

SOCIETY
Peoples: Most people are of Greek origin and there is a small Turkish minority (1 per cent), plus Albanian, Macedonian and Roma.
Religions: Greek Orthodox. There is a Muslim minority.
Languages: Greek.
Political Parties: Pan-Hellenic Socialist Movement (PASOK); New Democracy, conservative; Communist Party of Greece; Coalition of the Left and Progress, socialist; Democratic Socialist Movement.
Social Movements: The General Confederation of Greek Workers.

THE STATE
Official Name: Helleniké Demokratía.
Administrative divisions: 10 regions divided into 51 administrative units.
Capital: Athens/Piraeus 3,112,000 people (1999).
Other cities: Thessaloniki 793,900 people; Peiraías 188,500; Patras 172,100 (2000).
Government: Kostas Stephanopoulos, President since March 1995, re-elected in 2000. Kostas Simitis, Prime Minister since January 1996, re-elected in 2000. Unicameral Legislature: Greek Parliament (Vouli ton Ellinon), with 300 members.
National Holiday: March 25, Independence Day (1821).
Armed Forces: 159,300 (1994).
Other: Gendarmerie: 26,500; Coast Guard and customs: 4,000.

Per 100,000
live births
1

97%

1999
13%

IMPORTS
35,668
EXPORTS
25,162

In June 1975, Parliament adopted a new constitution and Konstantinos Tsatsos, a Karamanlis partisan, was elected first president of the republic.

[30] From 1974 Greece decided not to take part in NATO military exercises after conflict with Turkey, another member of the Organization.

[31] In the 1981 parliamentary elections, PASOK (Pan-Hellenic Socialist Movement) led by Papandreou gained an absolute majority, and the first socialist government in the history of Greece took office. The country also became the 10th member of the European Economic Community (EEC).

[32] The socialist government approached Third World countries, in particular the Arab nations, recognized the PLO and led a worldwide campaign in favor of handing back works of art that had been stolen during colonial domination.

[33] In 1983, salaries were frozen, provoking a wave of protests and strikes. Trade unions were granted greater participation in the public sector, but their right to strike was curtailed.

[34] The 1983 census revealed that women constituted one-third of the economically active population. Most of them worked in the service sector and their pay was lower than that of their male counterparts. Peasant women accounted for 40 per cent of the active female population, not counting the 400,000 women who worked unpaid on family plots.

[35] In the 1984 elections the PASOK won again, by an even greater margin than it had held in 1981. The 1986 constitutional amendment gave more power to the parliament at the expense of the President. Successive austerity plans and salary freezes fuelled new protests and strikes.

[36] In November 1988, details of embezzlement in the Bank of Crete, involving several government members were disclosed. This scandal caused several ministerial crises. In June of the following year, the Greek Left and the Communist Party formed the Left Alliance.

[37] In the 1989 elections PASOK lost its majority, and the conservative New Democracy party received a large part of the vote. As there was no adequate parliamentary majority and no agreement to form a government, the presidency went to the leader of the left-wing coalition, the communist Charilaos Florakis. He formed a temporary government with New Democracy, aiming to investigate the financial scandals.

[38] The results of the November 1989 and subsequent elections did not give any of the parties a significant majority. This led to coalition government.

[39] Between 1983 and 1989, Greece and the United States signed various co-operation agreements including the maintenance of four US military bases in the country, in return for economic and military assistance. This also guaranteed US diplomatic support for Greece in its disputes with Turkey, particularly over Cyprus.

[40] In January 1990, Washington and Athens publicized a new agreement, closing two military bases, as part of the US plan to reduce its military presence in the region.

[41] On March 7, a law was passed on collective work agreements for the private sector, public companies and services. The new law established free negotiations between workers and bosses, putting an end to 50 years of State intervention, and including norms for the organization of the company and union committees, as well as worker participation in company decisions.

[42] Following Karamanlis' triumph in the April presidential elections, a new government was formed headed by the conservative Constantinos Mitsotakis. In 1991, Mitsotakis promoted public spending cuts, price liberalization and privatizations.

[43] The social cost of these measures contributed to the defeat of the conservative government in the 1993 legislative elections. On October 12, Papandreou's PASOK gained the support of 47 per cent of the voters - compared with the 40 per cent of New Democracy - and the absolute majority in Parliament.

[44] The public debt and pressures from the European Union for a more 'rigorous' economic policy complicated Papandreou's leadership. In the 1994 European elections PASOK and above all New Democracy lost votes to the smaller parties like Political Spring, the Communist Party and the Progressive Left Coalition.

[45] Ill and increasingly criticized even within his own party, Papandreou resigned in January 1996. The famous leader of Greek socialism died in June. He was replaced by his former Industry Minister, Konstantinos Simitis. In September the Socialist Party, led by the new Prime Minister, won the legislative elections with 41.5 per cent of the vote.

[46] Backing its pro-regional integration position, Athens decided in January 1998 to abolish a discriminatory constitutional article allowing 'non-ethnic Greeks' seeking to leave the country to be stripped of citizenship. The article had been used mainly against the Muslim minority, mostly of Turkish origin. Some 60,000 people had lost their Greek nationality since this much-criticized measure was enacted during the so-called 'dictatorship of colonels'.

[47] Students engaged in three months of protests in early 1999 against the reform proposed by the Education Ministry. They took over schools and universities and erected roadblocks. The police retaliated with tear gas. The Government stated that reform was essential for modernizing education, while teachers and students perceived it as a requirement from Brussels for Greece's entry into the EU.

[48] A series of demonstrations and bomb attacks coincided with the visit of US president Bill Clinton in November, forcing him to cut short his stay to one day instead of three. Tensions with Washington had risen in proceeding months due to US leadership in the bombing campaign against Yugoslavia. Two earthquakes in 1999 a few weeks apart, one in Turkey and one in Greece, created solidarity between the two neighbors, which sent each other medical assistance and supplies. In November, under the auspices of the UN, the two countries for the first time backed a joint resolution that proposed the creation of an emergency aid unit.

[49] The closest elections in the country's history took place in April 2000, giving PASOK victory over the conservatives led by Costas Karamanlis. Greek electoral laws favor the winner, in spite of the 'technical draw', such that Prime Minister Kostas Simitis had 30 more seats that Karamanlis's defeated New Democracy. But the outcome was a reversal for Simitis, who had called early elections, confident that he could expand his parliamentary base, benefiting from what he thought would be strong public support in view of Greece's economic progress.

[50] The June assassination of the British defense attaché relaunched the 'November 17' terrorist group, which in 25 years had killed 17 people with not even one perpetrator arrested. International experts suggested that members of the current and previous Greek governments knew exactly who the November 17 members were and could be protecting them.

[51] In June 2000, the leader of the Orthodox Church, Archbishop Christodoulos, called on the faithful to take part in street protests against the government plan to exclude an individual's religion from the state-issued identification documents. 'The people's faith is opposed to this attempt to push religion to the sidelines,' said Christodoulos. The dispute exploded when Simitis declared that religion would be eliminated from identification documents in order to comply with laws protecting privacy. Also to be eliminated from the documents were fingerprints, profession and the name of the holder's spouse.

[52] Relations with Turkey significantly improved after the 1999 capture of the leader of the Kurdistan Workers' Party, Abdullah Ocalan, which news reports said was the result of cooperation between the intelligence services of Athens and Ankara.

[53] In April 2002, Greece and Turkey offered to mediate in the Israeli-Palestinian conflict. The fact that two former enemies joined forces was intended as proof that peace is possible. In March, the two countries signed an agreement to build a gas pipeline for Turkey to supply 500,000 cubic meters of natural gas daily to Greece. The Turkish energy minister Zeki Cakan said this cooperative effort in the energy sector would also improve bilateral political and economic relations. ∎

Grenada

Population: 94,000 (2002)
Land area: 340 SQ KM
Capital: St George's
Currency: EC dollar
Language: English

Grenada

The Carib Indians inhabited Grenada when Christopher Columbus arrived, around 1498, and named the island 'Concepción'. This European visit did not disrupt the island's peace but two centuries later in 1650 the governor of the French possession of Martinique, Du Parquet, decided to occupy the island. By 1674, France had established control over Grenada, despite fierce resistance from the Caribs.

[2] In 1753, French settlers from Martinique had around a 100 sugar mills and 12,000 slaves on Grenada. The indigenous population had been exterminated.

[3] The British took control of the island towards the end of the 18th century and cultivated cocoa, cotton and nutmeg, using slave labor. In 1788 there were 24,000 slaves, a number which remained stable until the abolition of slavery in the following century.

[4] The severe living conditions of workers resulted in the creation of the first union in the mid-20th century, the Grenada Manual and Metal Workers' Union. In 1951, a strike broke out and the labor struggle won considerable wage increases. Eric Matthew Gairy, a young adventurer who had lived away from the island most of his life, formed the first local political party, the Grenada United Labor Party (GULP) which favored independence. In 1951, GULP won a legislative election and Gairy became leader of the assembly.

[5] In 1958 Grenada joined the Federation of the British West Indies, which was dissolved in 1962. The country became part of the Associated State of the British Antilles in 1967. That year, Gairy was appointed Prime Minister when his party won the August elections. Their main objective was total independence from Britain.

[6] GULP soon obtained semi-independence, which gradually led to full independence. By that time, left-wing groups such as the New Jewel Movement (NJM) had appeared on the island, opposing separation from Britain. Though apparently paradoxical, many Grenadians considered that Gairy was seeking independence for his personal benefit, manipulating a politically unprepared population.

[7] In January 1974, an 'anti-independence' strike broke out to prevent Gairy from seizing power. After some weeks of total paralysis of the country, the Mongoose Squad - similar to the Haitian *Tonton-Macoutes* - appeared. Its paramilitaries were on the Prime Minister's payroll and brutal repression was used to end the strike. Independence was proclaimed the following week.

[8] As feared, Gairy exploited power for his own personal benefit. He distributed government jobs among the members of his party, while promoting the paramilitary squad to the level of a 'Defense Force', making it the only military body on the island. The 'Mongoose Squad' received military training from Chilean advisers and increased its numbers considerably by incorporating ex-inmates of St George's Prison.

[9] In the December 1976 election, the People's Alliance, made up of the NJM, the National Party of Grenada and the United Popular Party, gained new ground in Parliament, moving from one to six representatives in a total of 15 parliamentary seats. On March 13 1979, while Gairy was out of the country, the opposition carried out a bloodless coup and seized power. Thanks to widespread popular support, they were able to establish a provisional revolutionary government, under the leadership of Maurice Bishop, a lawyer.

[10] In four years, the People's Revolutionary Government (PRG) stimulated the formation of grass-roots organizations, and they created a mixed economy, expanding the public sector through agro-industries and state farms. Private enterprise was encouraged making Grenada more compatible with global economic policy.

[11] The Government based its foreign policy on the principles of anti-imperialism and non-alignment. Special attention was given to the development of ties with the socialist world. Cuba agreed to collaborate in the construction of an international airport. The project was conceived as a way to stimulate tourism, which employed 25 per cent of the country's work force.

[12] Prime Minister Bishop faced constant pressure from the NJM's extreme left wing. This faction, led by deputy Prime Minister Bernard Coard. On October 10 1983, on his return from a short state visit to Hungary, Czechoslovakia and Cuba, Bishop was placed under house arrest. General Hudson Austin, head of the army, seized power. Bishop was freed by a crowd of sympathizers, only to be shot dead by troops. A number of others were killed along with him, including his wife Jacqueline Creft - Minister of Education, the Foreign and Housing Ministers, two union leaders and 13 members of the crowd.

[13] The US took steps towards military intervention, a move which had been decided upon and planned for over a year; troop-landing had been rehearsed in maneuvers. Early in the morning of October 25 1983, 5,000 marines and Green Berets landed on the island. They were followed several hours later by a symbolic contingent of 300 police from six Caribbean countries: Antigua, Barbados, Dominica, Jamaica, St Lucia and St Vincent, who joined the farce of a 'multinational intervention for humanitarian reasons'.

[14] Resistance from the Grenadian militia and some Cuban technicians and workers, meant that the operation lasted much longer than expected. The US suffered combat casualties, and the press was barred from entering Grenada until all resistance had been eliminated. This made it impossible to verify how many civilians had been killed in attacks on a psychiatric hospital and other non-military targets.

[15] While strict US military control continued, Sir Paul Scoon, official British crown representative in Grenada, assumed the leadership of an interim government with the task of organizing an election within a period of 6 to 11 months. Under the discreet surveillance of the invaders, voting was held on December 3 1984 to elect the members of a unicameral parliament. In turn, the representatives appointed Herbert Blaize Prime Minister. Blaize led a coalition of parties that was presented to public opinion as the New National Party (NNP) and received support from the US.

[16] Neither NATO nor the OAS dared to condone the aggression. Twenty days later, Barbados was rewarded for its 'co-operation' in the invasion with a $18.5-million aid program.

[17] The new government reached a classic agreement with the International Monetary Fund including a reduction of the civil service, a wage-freeze and incentives to private enterprise.

[18] The Regional Security System (RSS) permitting the Prime Minister to call on troops from neighboring Caribbean islands if Grenada was threatened was established by Blaize in December 1986, under the pretext that the trial of those involved in the 1983 coup was coming to an end. Bernard Coard, his wife Phyllis, and former army commander Hudson Austin were sentenced to death, along with 11 soldiers. Three others

MATERNAL MORTALITY

1985/99

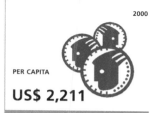

Per 100,000
live births

1

EXTERNAL DEBT

2000

PER CAPITA

US$ 2,211

FOREIGN TRADE

Millions US$ 2000

IMPORTS
250

EXPORTS
309

were tried, receiving prison sentences of 30 to 45 years.

[19] During his first years in government, Blaize achieved considerable economic growth, at between five and six per cent per year, basically from tourism. However, youth unemployment continued to increase, along with crime and drug addiction.

[20] Blaize died in 1989. He was replaced by Ben Jones of the National Party, who was backed by big business and the landowners. On March 13 1990 - the anniversary of the coup which overthrew Eric Gairy in 1979 - the general elections were won by Nicholas Braithwaite, member of the National Democratic Congress (NDC) and interim head of government after the invasion, and warmly regarded by the US.

[21] Studies carried out in 1994 revealed unemployment of 30 per cent and a clear pattern of emigration. The fall in international prices of bananas, coconuts, wood and nutmeg influenced this trend. Between March and April 1995, there were strikes in key sectors of the economy: hotels, sugar and cocoa production.

[22] In the June 1995 general elections, the governing NDC was pushed out by Keith Mitchell, former mathematics professor at the Howard University in Washington and leader of the New National Party (NNP). His victory was attributed to his promise to remove income tax, which had been revoked in 1986 and re-imposed by the NDC in 1994.

[23] Despite the 1994 agreement made between Indonesia and Grenada - the leading world nutmeg producer, the international prices continued to tumble in 1995.

[24] In early 1996, the ruling NNP objected against the privatization process in the State electricity company alleging 'misuse of funds'.

[25] The Government announced income on cocoa sales had fallen due to a leading US buyer suspending its imports from Grenada.

[26] In May, Grenada signed an extradition and legal co-operation agreement with the US. The treaties formed part of the campaign against drug-trafficking which Washington was implementing in the region.

[27] In March 1997, the Government rejected a request from the Grenada Council of Churches to free the two men serving life sentences for the 1993 murder of former Prime Minister Maurice Bishop, his wife and a group of ministers and union leaders.

[28] In April, Grenada and Cuba re-established diplomatic relations, broken off during the invasion of Grenada by US troops in 1983. Prime Minister Keith Mitchell made an official visit to Cuba, during which he signed an economic co-operation agreement.

[29] Mitchell swore he had cleaned up his image, but barely seven weeks later his government collapsed as its members of parliament defected in the face of repeated accusations of government corruption from the Grenada United Labor Party (GULP). In the January 1999 elections, Mitchell's New National Party won all the 15 seats in Parliament.

[30] In 2001 to 2002, Grenada was the Caribbean economy which showed the greatest growth, reaching a 6.5 per cent increase in GDP, mainly due to a larger number of tourists, greater foreign and public investment and growth in farming. Despite this, Grenada's policies have not been able to combat the high unemployment that mainly affects the youngest sector.

PROFILE

ENVIRONMENT

Grenada is the southernmost Windward island of the Lesser Antilles. The island is almost entirely volcanic. Lake Grand Etang and Lake Antoine are extinct volcanic craters. The rainy, tropical, climate, tempered by sea winds, is fit for agriculture, which constitutes the country's major source of income. It is famous for its spices, and is known as 'the Spice Island of the West'. The territory includes the islands of Carriacou (34 sq km) and Petite Martinique (2 sq km), which belong to the Grenadines.

SOCIETY

Peoples: Most are descended from African slaves (84 per cent); most of the others are of mixed descent (11 per cent) and European (0.7 per cent) and Indo-Pakistani (3 per cent) minorities.
Religions: Mainly Catholic (53.1 per cent); Protestant (38.1 per cent); other (7.4 per cent).
Languages: English (official and predominant). A patois dialect derived from French, and another from English are also spoken.
Political Parties: New National Party, conservative (NNP); National Democratic Congress, liberal (NDC); Grenada United Labor Party (GULP).
Social Organizations: Union Congress of Grenada; Rural Farmers' Association; National Council of Students of Grenada.

THE STATE

Official Name: Grenada.
Administrative divisions: 6 parishes and 1 dependency (Carricou and Petite Martinique).
Capital: St George's 35,000 people (1999).
Other cities: Gouyave 3,200 people; Grenville 2,300 (2000).
Government: Queen Elizabeth II, Head of State; Daniel Williams has been the representative of the British Crown since August 1996. Keith Mitchell, Prime Minister since January 1995, re-elected in 1999. Bicameral Legislative: a 15-member House of Representatives and a 13-member Senate. Representatives are elected by direct popular vote, while 7 of the senators are appointed by the governor, 3 by the prime minister and 3 by the leader of the opposition.
National Holiday: February 7, Independence (1974).
Armed Forces: Royal Grenada Police Force (includes Special Service Unit), Coastguards.

STATISTICS

DEMOGRAPHY

Population: 94,000 (2002)
Annual growth: 0.3 % (1985-2000)
Estimates for year 2015: 97,000 (2000)
Annual growth to year 2015: 0.3 % (2000)
Urban population: 37.9 % (2000)
Urban growth: 2.1 % (2000)

HEALTH

Maternal mortality: 1 per 100,000 live births (1985/99)
Infant mortality: 21 per 1,000 (2000)
Under-5 child mortality: 26 per 1,000 (2000)
Daily calorie supply: 2,685 per capita (1999)
50 doctors per 100,000 people (1997)
Safe water: 95 % (2000)

EDUCATION

School enrolment (net):
Primary total: 98 % (1994/2000)
male: 98 % (1995/99)
female: 97 % (1995/99)
Primary school teachers: one for every 20 pupils (1998)

COMMUNICATIONS

597 radios (1997), 375 TV sets (1999) and 332 main telephone lines (2000) per 1,000 people

ECONOMY

Per capita, GDP: $ 7,580 (2000)
Annual growth: 5.4 % (2000)
Annual inflation: 0.2 % (1999)
Consumer price index: 105.0 (1999)
Currency: 2.7 EC dollars = $ 1 (03/2002)
Cereal imports: 24,271 metric tons (2000)
Food import dependency: 20 % (1999)
Exports: $ 250 million (2000)
Imports: $ 309 million (2000)
External debt: $ 207 million (2000); $ 2,211 per capita (2000)

[31] The increase in tourism investment generated controversy between the Government and defenders of the island ecology, as the construction of large hotel complexes threatened to damage tropical forests and erode the beaches. ∎

Guadeloupe

Population: 435,000 (2002)
Land area: 1,710 SQ KM
Capital: Basse-Terre
Currency: Euro
Language: French

Guadeloupe

The entire archipelago of present-day Guadeloupe was inhabited by the Caribs. Originally from South America, they dispersed throughout the islands after overpowering the Arawak people. They resisted the Spanish invasion in 1493 but were defeated by the French two centuries later.

[2] The French colonizers built the first sugar mill on the island in 1633 and began importing African slave laborers. By the end of the 17th century, Guadeloupe had become one of the world's main sugar producers. The colonists killed the last of the archipelago's surviving Caribs in the early 18th century.

[3] With the abolition of the slave trade in 1815, France restructured its formal links with the Caribbean islands, giving them the status of colonies. In 1946, with the initiation of the new French constitution, Guadeloupe achieved greater political autonomy, as an Overseas Department.

[4] French Government subsidies increased per capita income and the consumption of imported goods, but ruined the local economy.

[5] Violent clashes between pro-independence groups and the police took place in 1985. Their violent attacks put members of the Caribbean Revolutionary Alliance (ARC) in prison. They benefited from an amnesty in 1989. The electoral defeat of the ARC - which for the first time took part in the elections - was taken as a sign of support for the situation.

[6] The European Union's decision in 1992 to reduce the import quota of bananas from the 'French' Antilles to benefit imports from Africa and Latin America caused strong protests in Guadeloupe.

[7] An important reduction in productive activities underlined the deficit in the trade balance. Exports, which amounted to barely 9.9 per cent of imports in 1995, were reduced to 5.2 per cent in 1996. The banana sector was also affected, since - due to the reduction in foreign demand and the competition from US-multinationals that managed plantations in Central America - it exported in 1996 less than half its exports of 1993.

[8] Banana workers began a strike in late 1997. Union representatives accused the plantation owners of creating private militias and threatening to kill the workers to make them lift the strike. In February 1998, in a country with 40 per cent of the working population unemployed and with growing social inequity, the strike had extended to other sectors.

[9] In September 1999, clashes broke out between the police and demonstrators protesting against the arrest of a labor activist accused of hurting two policemen. As a result, six police were hurt and 70 people arrested. That year Jean-Francois Carenco was appointed commissioner for the French Government.

[10] Jacques Chirac, President of France, visited the island in March 2000 to negotiate a special trade agreement between the European Union and its colonies in the Caribbean. Chirac's visit to the island coincided with a peak in independence protests in its colonies.

[11] In August 2001, Haitian immigrants complained to the public prosecutor about a TV show host for inciting hate and xenophobic racial violence against Haitian, Dominican and other residents. The accused, Ibo Simon, was also a Councillor on the Regional Council of Guadeloupe. ∎

PROFILE

ENVIRONMENT

Includes the dependencies of Marie Galante, La Désirade, Les Saintes, Petite-Terre, St Barthélemy and the French section of St Martin forming part of the Windward Islands of the Lesser Antilles. The tropical, rainy climate is tempered by sea winds, and sugarcane is grown.

SOCIETY

Peoples: 90 per cent of African descent. There is a small European minority. There are immigrants from Lebanon, China and India (5 per cent).
Religions: mostly Catholic. There are also African, Hindu and several Protestant religions.
Languages: French (official).
Political Parties: Guadeloupe Federation of the Rally for the Republic (RPR), and Guadeloupe Federation of the Union in French Democracy (UDF), are the local branches of the colonial parties; Guadeloupe Federation of the Socialist Party (PS); the Communist Party of Guadeloupe (PCG); the Guadeloupe Democrats; the Popular Union for the Liberation of Guadeloupe (UPLG), the largest of the radical pro-independence groups; the Revolutionary Caribbean Alliance (ARC), founded in Point-à-Pitre in 1983, has carried out several armed attacks. Also pro-independence is the Christian Movement for the Liberation of Guadeloupe.
Social Organizations: The Guadeloupe General Labor Confederation; the Department Organization of Trade Unions (CGT-FO), General Union of Guadeloupe Workers (UGTG).

THE STATE

Official Name: Département d'Outre-Mer de la Guadeloupe.
Administrative Divisions: 3 Arrondissements, 36 Cantons.
Capital: Basse-Terre 12,700 people (1999).
Other cities: Pointe-à-Pitre 21,400 people; Les Abymes 64,400 (2000).
Government: Jacques Chirac, Chief of State, represented by Jean-François Carenco, since July 1999. Legislative power: a 42-member General Council (chaired by Marcellin Lubeth since 1998), and 41-member regional Council (chaired by Lucette Michaux Chevry since 1992). Guadeloupe has 4 deputies and 2 senators in the French parliament.
National Holiday: July 14. Bastille Day (1789).

DEMOGRAPHY

Population: 435,000 (2002)
Annual growth: 1.2 % (1985-2000)
Estimates for year 2015: 471,000 (2000)
Annual growth to year 2015: 0.6 % (2000)

HEALTH

Life expectancy at birth: 78 years (2000-2005)
male: 75 years (2000-2005)
female: 82 years (2000-2005)

ECONOMY

Currency: 1.2 euro = $ 1 (03/2002)

Guam

Population: 162,000 (2002)
Land area: 550 SQ KM
Capital: Agaña
Currency: US dollar
Language: English

Guam

G uam shares a common history with the rest of the Micronesian archipelago (see Micronesia). The population, which settled on the island thousands of years ago, became the victim of extermination campaigns at the hands of Spanish colonizers, between 1668 and 1695.

[2] As a result of armed aggression and epidemics (the people lacked immunity against European illnesses) the population declined from 100,000 at the beginning of the 17th century to fewer than 5,000 in 1741.

[3] The few survivors intermarried with Spanish and Filipino immigrants, producing the Chamorro people who presently populate the island.

[4] For three centuries, Guam was a port of call on the Spanish galleon route between the Philippines and Acapulco (Mexico), a major depot on the trade route to Spain.

[5] Under the terms of the Treaty of Paris of 1898, Guam changed hands from Spain to the US, together with the Philippines. The island continued to serve as a stopover until it was invaded by the Japanese in 1941. Recovered in 1944, it became a US military base.

[6] Since 1973, the United Nations has unsuccessfully urged Washington to permit the islanders to exercise their right to self-determination. In January 1982, in a plebiscite on self-determination, 75 per cent of the electorate favored a system of association with the United States. As a result of this the UN General Assembly recommended that the US implement Guam's decolonization in December 1984.

The UN also reiterated its conviction that military bases are a major obstacle to self-determination and independence, two principles established in the UN Charter.

[7] In February 1987, former governor Ricardo Borballo, who had been elected in 1984, was found guilty of bribery, extortion and conspiracy.

[8] In November 1987, the High Commission initiated a self-determination referendum for Guam, and voters supported negotiation of a new relationship with the US. In February 1988 Guam received US economic aid, mainly as disaster relief for the damage done by a typhoon in January.

[9] Negotiations with the UN and US about the right to political self-determination and the creation of a Free Associated State were renewed in 1996. A landowners' organization demanded that the Government include the territory occupied by the US military in the talks. Washington considered Guam a key geo-strategic enclave.

[10] In September 1996, the island served as a base of operations for US bombers carrying out a 'limited attack' on Iraq.

[11] In early 1998 the economy was basically sustained by tourism. In 2000 the number of tourists was over one million, but the decline in visitors from Japan in 2001 had a sharp impact on Guam (the Japanese had comprised 80 per cent of tourists).

[12] The loss of civilian jobs as a result of restructuring and the closing of national bases - a process begun in the 1990s and largely involving naval installations - and the fiscal income deficit hurt the Guam economy, which is dominated by services. The major challenge is to build a civilian economy to reduce the impact of the declining military economy. Currently, to generate the same income, each job in the military sector would need to be replaced by 2.5 jobs elsewhere. ∎

PROFILE

ENVIRONMENT

Guam is the southernmost island of the Marianas archipelago, located east of the Philippines and south of Japan. Of volcanic origin, its contours are mountainous except for the coastal plain in the northern region. The climate is tropical, rainy from June to November (over 300 mm a month) and drier and colder from December to May. It has rainforest vegetation. One-third of the island is occupied by military installations.

SOCIETY

Peoples: Chamorro indigenous people account for approximately 47 per cent of the population; Filipino, 25 per cent. US troops and dependents, 10 per cent. Japanese, Chinese, Korean and other, 18 per cent.
Religions: 98 per cent of all Guamanians are Catholic. **Languages:** English (official), Chamorro (a dialect derived from Indonesian), and Japanese. **Political Parties:** Republican Party and Democratic party, as in the US.

THE STATE

Official Name: Territory of Guam. **Capital:** Agaña 2,000 people (1999).
Other cities: Tamuning 11,800 people; Mangilao 6,900 (2000).
Government: Carl TC Gutiérrez, Governor, elected in November 1994. His office reports to the US Interior Department and has less autonomy than the local military commander, as one-third of the island is under control of the US Navy and Air force. Although Guamanians formally possess US citizenship they have no representation in the US Congress nor do they participate in the presidential elections. Parliament: The Guam Legislature, with 15 members. **National Holiday:** First Monday in March, Discovery Day (1521). **Armed Forces:** Defense is responsibility of the US.

STATISTICS

DEMOGRAPHY

Population: 162,000 (2002)
Annual growth: 1.7 % (1985-2000)
Estimates for year 2015: 209,000 (2000)
Annual growth to year 2015: 2.0 % (2000)
Urban population: 39.2 % (2000)
Urban growth: 2.1 % (2000)

HEALTH

Life expectancy at birth: 75 years (2000-2005)
male: 72 years (2000-2005)
female: 77 years (2000-2005)

COMMUNICATIONS

193 newspapers (1996), 1,511 radios (1997), 669 TV sets (1999) and 478 main telephone lines (2000) per 1,000 people

Guatemala

Population:	11,995,000 (2002)
Land area:	108,430 SQ KM
Capital:	Guatemala
Currency:	Quetzal
Language:	Spanish

Guatemala

The Maya civilization flourished during the first ten centuries AD in what is now Guatemala and parts of Mexico, Honduras and El Salvador (see box 'Arawaks and Caribs: Genocide in Paradise').

[2] Spanish troops, under the command of Pedro de Alvarado, entered the country in 1524, founding the city of Guatemala and gaining total control over the country two years later. This process was facilitated by the fact that the country was undergoing a gradual transition and readjustment among its various ethnic groups - the K'iche', Kaqchi', Mam, Q'eqchi, Poqomchi', Q'anjob'al, Tz'utujiil and others - all of which stemmed from a common Mayan ancestry. Though the situation favored the invaders, there were nevertheless frequent incidents in which they faced stiff resistance.

[3] On September 15 1821, large landowners and local business interests joined forces with colonial officials, to peacefully proclaim the independence of the Viceroyalty of New Spain, including the five countries of Central America.

[4] The new political and administrative union, called the Federation of Central American States, was dissolved in 1839 as a result of internal struggles prompted by the British policy of 'divide and conquer'.

[5] In 1831, under tremendous debt pressure, the Government yielded large portions of territory to Britain for timber. This later became British Honduras, now the independent nation of Belize.

[6] The discovery of synthetic dyes in Europe in the mid-18th century caused a serious economic crisis in Guatemala, where the main export products were vegetable dyes. Coffee replaced dyes as the country's main cash crop, and plantation owners deprived the Indians of most of their communal lands through the Liberal Reform of 1871. During the late 19th century, Guatemalan politics were dominated by the antagonism between liberals and conservatives. German settlers in Guatemala developed ties with German companies and initiated an import-export business which damaged the interests of the incipient national bourgeoisie.

[7] Toward the end of the 19th century, Manuel Estrada Cabrera rose to power and governed Guatemala until 1920. He began an 'open door policy' for US transnationals, who eventually owned the railroads, ports, hydroelectric plants, shipping, international mailing services and the enormous banana plantations of the United Fruit Company (Unifruco).

[8] General Jorge Ubico Castañeda, the last of a generation of military leaders, was elected President in 1931. However, a popular uprising known as the 'October Revolution' toppled him in 1944 calling fresh elections. The winner was reformist Juan José Arévalo, who launched a process of economic and social reform.

[9] Arévalo's government heralded a climate of political and economic liberalization. In 1945, literate women were granted the right to vote. That same year the first campesino labor union was formed. The land reform program, under which extensive tracts of unused Unifruco land were expropriated, was considered 'a threat to US interests' by Washington. An aggressive anti-communist campaign was launched, with the sole aim of harassing Arévalo and his successor, President Jacobo Arbenz.

[10] John Foster Dulles, US Secretary of State, but also a United Fruit Company shareholder and company lawyer pressured the Organization of American States (OAS) to condemn the reforms being carried out by Jacobo Arbenz's government. Allen Dulles, director of the CIA and former president of the company organized an invasion carried out by Castillo Armas in June 1954. With the fall of Arbenz, UFCO managed to get back its lands, and subsequently changed its name to United Brands.

[11] Two decades of military regimes followed. Most Guatemalans felt that the four elections which followed, in 1970, 1974, 1978 and 1982, were rigged - with the top military candidates invariably elected.

[12] This kind of political atmosphere bred armed insurgency. The Rebel Armed Forces (FAR) entered the scene in 1962, followed by the Poor People's Guerrilla Army (EGP) and the Organization of the People in Arms (ORPA) in 1975 and 1979 respectively.

[13] According to estimates from several humanitarian organizations, official repression took some 80,000 lives between 1954 and 1982. The Guatemalan National Revolutionary Unity (URNG) was founded in February 1982, uniting the Poor People's Guerrilla Army, the Rebel Armed Forces, the Organization of the People in Arms, and the Guatemalan Labor Party (PGT, National Leadership Committee).

[14] On March 23 1982, only a few days after a rigged election which brought him to power, Lucas García was ousted in a military coup and replaced by General Efraín Ríos Montt.

[15] Ríos Montt's counter-insurgency campaign surpassed that of his predecessor's in terms of ferocity. Over 15,000 Guatemalans were killed in the first year of Ríos Montt's administration. 70,000 took refuge in neighboring countries, especially Mexico, and 500,000 fled to the mountains to escape the army. Hundreds of villages were razed, while the number of 'model hamlets' increased systematically. Peasants were taken by force to these hamlets, where they were required to produce cash crops for export, rather than growing subsistence crops.

[16] In August 1983, another coup staged by the CIA deposed Ríos Montt and General Oscar Mejía Víctores came into power, promising a quick return to a democratic system.

[17] An 88-seat Constituent Assembly was elected on July 18 1984, to replace the legal framework in effect since 1965, but annulled after the 1982 coup. The Assembly offered new constitutional guarantees, habeas corpus and electoral regulations. Seventeen parties ran candidates; however lack of guarantees forced the Left to abstain from running yet another time.

[18] The Constituent Assembly approved the right to strike for civil servants, authorized the return from exile of leaders of the Socialist Democratic Party and called for elections in November 1985.

[19] The election, boycotted by the URNG, gave a clear victory to the Christian Democratic candidate, Vinicio Cerezo. One of the first measures was the 'total and definitive' suspension of secret police activities.

[20] In October 1987, representatives of the URNG and Vinicio Cerezo's government met in Madrid, the first direct negotiations between the Government and guerrilla forces in 27 years of conflict. That year, the National Reconciliation Commission (CNR) played a decisive role in the rapprochement process. The commission was created as a result

of the Esquipulas II peace plan for Central America, signed by 6 countries in the region.

[21] On March 30, in Oslo, guerrillas and government agreed on an operational pattern for the meetings and the role of CNR and UN mediators. Despite the persistence of political persecution and assassination, on June 1 1990 a basic agreement was signed in Madrid by the National Commission for Reconciliation, the political parties and the URNG. The overall aim of the accord was to continue the search for peace in Guatemala.

[22] During the last few months of 1990, negotiations came to a standstill and a high degree of skepticism developed among voters, which led to a 70 per cent abstention rate in the November 11 1990 presidential elections. During the second round of the elections, held on January 6 1991, Jorge Serrano Elías, of the Solidarity Action Movement (MAS), was elected President.

[23] The Serrano Government and the URNG decided to take up peace negotiations. A fortnight later, in Cuernavaca, Mexico, a three-day meeting was held. After three decades of violence, during which over 100,000 people were murdered and 50,000 disappeared, the Government and the guerrillas committed themselves to the negotiation process, attended by top-level delegates and with the aim of achieving a firm and lasting peace agreement in the shortest possible time. The agenda included topics such as: democratization, human rights, the strengthening of civil groups, rights of the indigenous peoples, constitutional reforms, the resettlement of the landless, the incorporation of the URNG into legal political life.

[24] In July, the US Senate suspended military aid to Guatemala. The URNG demanded that human rights violations cease immediately. Human rights organizations found that in the first 9 months of Serrano's rule there had been 1,760 human rights violations, 650 of them executions without trial. Several deaths of street children below the age of six were also reported.

[25] Also in September 1991, the Guatemalan president recognized the sovereignty and self-determination of Belize, the former British colony which proclaimed its independence in 1981. The announcement caused the resignation of chancellor Alvaro Arzú, the leader of the National Advancement Party (PAN), and one of the ruling party's main allies.

[26] In 1992, a national debate began on the existence of government armed civilian groups, such as the Civilian Self-Defense Patrols (PAC). The Catholic Church criticized the Government's economic policy and spoke out in favor of agrarian reform. In the meantime, organizations representing the indigenous peoples demanded the ratification of ILO Agreement 169, dealing with indigenous and tribal peoples.

[27] The Government created the *Hunapú* force, made up of the Army, the National Police and the 'Hacienda Guard', replacing the former PACs. In April, members of the Hunapú provoked an incident during a student demonstration demanding improvements in the education policy. One student was killed and 7 injured. The World Bank, the US Government and the European Parliament urged the Guatemalan government to end political violence.

[28] In October, while the quincentenary of Columbus' arrival on the continent was celebrated by some, Rigoberta Menchú Tum, a leader from the Quiché people, won the Nobel Peace Prize. Menchú travelled world-wide, denouncing the situation of her country's indigenous peoples.

[29] On May 25 1993, President Serrano, backed by a group of military officers, carried out a coup themselves, revoking several articles of the constitution and dissolving Congress and the Supreme Court. On June 1, national and international rejection of this measure - including pressure from the United States - forced Serrano from office. On June 6, after several days of uncertainty, former Human Rights attorney Ramiro De León Carpio was elected head of the Executive, to finish Serrano's term.

[30] De León Carpio began by purging the officers that had supported Serrano, changing five military commands. Shortly afterwards, Jorge Carpio Nicolle, leader of the Union of the National Center and the president's cousin, was assassinated.

[31] Despite the intense campaign against the PACs and compulsory military service, President De León Carpio stated that he would maintain both institutions as long as the situation of armed conflict persisted, a U-turn on his previously stated opinion. On August 5, the Government announced that the 'Files' - records kept on citizens considered a 'danger' to State security - had disappeared. However, the loss of these papers also implied the elimination of evidence against those responsible for human-rights violations. In November, excavations in several clandestine cemeteries uncovered the remains of 177 women and children assassinated by the military in the 1982 'Rio Negro Massacre'.

[32] The 1994-95 Government Plan, presented in August, reaffirmed the structural adjustment program already in effect, prioritizing the end of state intervention in the economy, along with fiscal reform and the privatization of enterprises.

[33] De León Carpio's stated goal was to fight corruption in the public sector. On August 26, the President called for the resignation of legislative deputies and members of the Supreme Court, causing a confrontation between the President and Congress. This led to a clash of economic and political interests, culminating in the Executive and Congress agreeing on constitutional reform.

[34] A plebiscite was scheduled for January 30 1994, for nation's voters to decide on reforms to public administration and in the constitution.

[35] Following a 22-day occupation of the local OAS office by members of the Committee for Campesino Unity and the National Commission of Widows of Guatemala, some 5,000 members of indigenous groups carried out a march demanding the dissolution of the PACs.

[36] In January 1994, the Government and guerrillas signed agreements for the resettlement of the population displaced by the armed conflict, without a mediated cease fire. As a result of the accords 870 people were able to settle in the zones of Chacula, Nenton and Huehuetenango, but the majority of the resettlement areas were still under army control.

PROFILE

ENVIRONMENT

The Sierra Madre and the Cuchumatanes Mountains cross the country from east to west, and these are the areas of volcanic activity and earthquakes. Between the mountain ranges there is a high plateau with sandy soil and easily eroded slopes. Although the plateau occupies only 26 per cent of the country's territory, 53 per cent of the population is concentrated there. The long Atlantic coastline is covered with forests and is less populated. In the valleys along the Caribbean coast and in the Pacific lowlands there are banana and sugar plantations. In 1980, 41.9 per cent of the country's land area was covered by forests; in 1990, that figure had been reduced to 33.8 per cent, threatening the exceptionally diverse ecosystems.

SOCIETY

Peoples: Approximately 90 per cent are of Mayan descent. Amid the country's great cultural and linguistic diversity, four major peoples can be distinguished: the Ladino (descendants of Amerindians and Spaniards), the Maya, the Garifuna (of the Caribbean region) and the Xinca.
Religions: Mainly Catholic. In recent years a number of Protestant groups have appeared. The Mayan Religion has also survived.
Languages: Spanish is official but most of the population speak one of the 22 Maya dialects.
Political Parties: The Republican Guatemalan Front (FRG); the National Progress Party (NPP), conservative; the Guatemalan National Revolutionary Unity (UNRG), a coalition of different armed groups, extreme-left; the Guatemalan Christian Democracy (CDG). Non-parliamentary organizations: Solidarity Action Movement (MAS) and National Liberation Movement (MLN) of an authoritarian tendency; New Guatemala Democratic Front; National Centrist Union (UCN); Social Democratic Party (PSD); Democratic Union (UD); Civil Society Assembly.
Social Organizations: Union of Labor and Popular Associations; National Labor Union Alliance; National Workers' Coordinating Committee; Labor Union of Guatemalan Workers; Committee for Campesinos' Unity; National Coordinating Committee of Indigenous Campesinos; Communities of People's Resistance; Permanent Commissions of Refugees in Mexico; National Commission of Widows of Guatemala; Mutual Support Group; 'Runujel Junam' Council of Ethnic Communities; Office of Human Rights of the Archbishopric; Coordinating Committee of Mayan Women; Academy of Mayan Languages of Guatemala; 'Majawil Q'uij' Coordinating Committee and Council of Mayan Organizations of Guatemala.

THE STATE

Official Name: República de Guatemala.
Administrative Divisions: 22 Departments.
Capital: Guatemala 3,119,000 people (1999).
Other cities: Mixco 268,300 people; Villa Nueva 129,600; Quetzaltenango 115,900 (2000).
Government: Alfonso Portillo Cabrera, President since January 2000, elected for a four-year term. Unicameral Legislature: Congress of the Republic, with 113 members (91 members in departamental constituencies and 22 members elected by proportional representation).
National Holiday: September 15, Independence Day (1821).
Armed Forces: 44,200 troops (1994).
Other: 10,000 National Police, 2,500 Hacienda Guard; 500,000 Territorial Militia.

1985/99

Per 100,000
live births
190

2000

69%

2000

2000

12%

37 Monica Pinto, the UN Human Rights observer, recommended the demilitarization of society through the gradual reduction in size of the army, the disbanding of the PACs and the Presidential Staff, along with the creation of a Truth Commission.
38 Following a prolonged silence in early 1994, the Minister of Foreign Affairs recognized Belize as an independent State, but upheld Guatemala's territorial claim, meaning no frontier could be established.
39 In March, the Government and the URNG ratified an agreement related to the disbanding of the PACs and the international verification of human rights by the UN. Three days later the President of the Constitutional Court, Epaminondas González, was murdered.
40 In April, the police evicted 300 rural workers' families from an estate they had occupied in Escuintla. In May a new contingent of nearly 2,000 refugees returned, heading for the Quiche area, which was still occupied by the military.
41 The URNG and the Government signed a draft agreement for the 'Resettlement of the People Uprooted by the Armed Confrontation', in Oslo, Norway, in June. The Communities of Peoples were recognized as non-fighting civilians and the vital importance of land for these uprooted populations was explicitly stated. The second agreement in Oslo enshrined the principle of not individualizing responsibility for human rights violations as a way of neutralizing the action of sectors opposed to a negotiated outcome.
42 The peace negotiations between the guerrillas and the Government reached stalemate during 1995, due to the elections lack of interest by the army and landowners, and the Government weakness in face of them. The UN mission reported that impunity continued to be the main obstacle to the respect for human rights, and described hundreds of cases of torture, illegal detentions and extrajudicial executions.
43 In August 1995, Congress leader Efrain Rios Montt and another two members of the FRG lost their legal immunity and were tried by the

Supreme Court on charges of bugging telephones, falsifying documents and abuse of power.
44 In the November general elections, Alvaro Arzú, candidate for the National Progress Party (NPP), won over Alfonso Portillo Cabrera of the FRG. Abstention reached a record 63 per cent. In December - first in Europe and then in Mexico and Guatemala - the Government and the URNG signed a series of peace agreements which put an end to a civil war which had cost more than 100,000 lives. The cease-fire was respected and was followed by a large increase in crime. Around 80 per cent of the population were living below the poverty threshold at this time.
45 In December 1997, Guatemala was amongst the five Latin American countries most affected by climatic change resulting from El Niño. According to ECLAC preliminary figures Hurricane Mitch's passage through Central America in September 1998 caused damage in the region of $5.36 million and left around 24,000 dead, 256 of them Guatemalan. More than 100,000 people were made homeless and worsening health conditions left the country in a 'state of emergency'.
46 Investigation of human-rights violations during the war produced an avalanche of threats against investigators and members of the judiciary. After presenting a report condemning the armed forces for several massacres, Bishop Juan Gerardi was murdered in 1998. The public prosecutor working on the case fled to the US where he requested asylum, claiming he had been under heavy pressure and had received several death threats. In October that year, the Government ordered hundreds of bodies to be dug up in the grounds of an elite police unit in the capital. A UN report estimated this same year that 96 per cent of the deaths during the war were the responsibility of the army and armed forces.
47 In the second round of the elections held in late December 1999, Alfonso Portillo of the FRG took 68 per cent of the vote, defeating Oscar Berger of the ruling PAN. Abstention reached 59 per cent, while more than 50 per cent of registered voters had turned out in the first round ballot.
48 In early 2000, Guatemala lodged a claim for nearly half the territory of

neighboring Belize. The country recognized the independence of the former British colony in 1991, but still claimed this part of the territory. Representatives of both parties talked briefly in Miami in February and March 2000, under the auspices of the Organization of American States (OAS).
49 The drought in 2001 brought famine in its wake, killing 41 people by half way through the year. President Portillo declared a 'state of national disaster' for 30 days, and requested international aid. A UN report estimates that 80 per cent of Guatemalans live in extreme poverty.
50 Two public prosecutors and a judge investigating the murder of Bishop Gerardi exiled themselves after receiving death threats. Before Judge Yassim Barrios left for Spain she managed to solve the murder and send the three members of the armed forces and the bishop responsible for the murder to prison.
51 According to the president of the Supreme Court, in 2001, 23 judges had been on the receiving end of threats and intimidation by the time the UN Special Envoy for Judicial Independence, Param Cumaraswamy, came on his second visit. 'Impunity still reigns in Guatemala, and the Government has given no signs of political will to end this situation', said Cumaraswamy.
52 President Portillo was accused by Siglo XXI, a Guatemalan daily, of diverting public funds to personal accounts abroad. There are repeated reports in the press of officials involved in corruption and the intimidation of the legal establishment to impede the course of justice.
53 The Guatemalan Constitutional Court removed parliamentary immunity from Ríos Montt, bringing him nearer to being tried for changing the tax laws to favoring a company producing alcoholic drinks. As it has so far proved impossible to try him for murder, torture and other human rights violations, in his own country Nobel Peace Prizewinner, Rigoberta Menchú took the case to the Spanish courts in 2001. She sought an alternative route to try Ríos Montt and other members of the armed forces responsible for the deaths of 200,000 Guatemalans. ∎

DEMOGRAPHY
Population: 11,995,000 (2002)
Annual growth: 2.6 % (1985-2000)
Estimates for year 2015: 16,329,000 (2000)
Annual growth to year 2015: 2.4 % (2000)
Urban population: 40.4 % (2000)
Urban growth: 3.4 % (2000)
Children per woman: 4.7 (2000)

HEALTH
Life expectancy at birth: 66 years (2000-2005)
male: 63 years (2000-2005)
female: 69 years (2000-2005)
Maternal mortality: 190 per 100,000 live births (1985/99)
Infant mortality: 44 per 1,000 (2000)
Under-5 child mortality: 59 per 1,000 (2000)
Daily calorie supply: 2,331 per capita (1999)
93 doctors per 100,000 people (1997)
Safe water: 92 % (2000)

EDUCATION
Literacy: 69 % (2000)
male: 76 % (2000)
female: 61 % (2000)
School enrolment (net):
Primary total: 77 % (1994/2000)
male: 81 % (1995/99)
female: 75 % (1995/99)
Secondary (gross):
male: 26 % (1995/97)
female: 24 % (1995/97)
Tertiary (gross): 8 % (1997)
Primary school teachers: one for every 38 pupils (1999)

COMMUNICATIONS
33 newspapers (1996), 79 radios (1997), 61 TV sets (2000) and 57 main telephone lines (2000) per 1,000 people

ECONOMY
Per capita, GDP: $ 3,821 (2000)
Annual growth: 0.6 % (2000)
Annual inflation: 6.0 % (2000)
Consumer price index: 144.2 (2000)
Currency: 7.9 quetzales = $ 1 (03/2002)
Cereal imports: 637,462 metric tons (2000)
Food import dependency: 12 % (2000)
Fertilizer use: 1,332 kg per ha (1999)
Exports: $ 3,801 million (2000)
Imports: $ 5,294 million (2000)
External debt: $ 4,622 million (2000); $ 406 per capita (2000)
Debt service: 10.3 % of exports (1999)
Development aid received: $ 293 million (1999; $ 26.4 per capita (1999); 1.60 % of GNP (1999)

ENERGY
Consumption: 579.5 Kgs of oil equivalent per capita yearly (1998); 24.8 % imported (1999)
HDI (ranking/value): 108 / 0.626 (1999)

Arawaks and Caribs: genocide in Paradise

Before Christopher Columbus arrived in the Caribbean islands in 1492, the region had a large indigenous population. Today, virtually none of these people remain.

The story of Columbus's 'discovery' is well known: he thought he had reached the Garden of Eden, paradise, or at least the Spice Islands of southeast Asia by a new route. When his ships arrived, six million Americans (one-fifth of the current population of the zone) survived by hunting, fishing and waging war. Three groups of peoples inhabited the islands: the Ciboneys, in the western parts of present-day Cuba and Haiti; the Taino-Arawaks, in the Greater Antilles (now Cuba, Jamaica, Haiti, Dominican Republic, Puerto Rico and Trinidad); and the Caribs, who occupied the present-day Lesser Antilles (to the east of the Greater Antilles).

None of these peoples survive today, except for some 500 Caribs on reservations in the Dominican Republic, most of whom are of mixed African descent. The cultural impact, mass slavery and diseases that the Europeans brought to the area erased these peoples from the face of the islands that had been mistaken for the paradise of gold and spices.

The story of the Tainos is typical. They were of the same language group as the Arawaks who occupied an area extending from present-day Florida to Paraguay and northern Argentina. And although their history virtually ended with the arrival of the Europeans, it had begun many centuries before. Sometime around the 5th century BC the Arawaks set out from the Orinoco River Basin in the north of South America, settling on the island of Trinidad. From there they spread throughout the Antilles. Later they pushed the Ciboneys westwards, they became cultivators and traders. They were organized in communities run by religious chiefs, known as *caciques*, in a social hierarchy in which the lowest level was reserved for the slaves (for it was not only the Europeans who used slaves).

Before the Europeans arrived, the Tainos had been displaced from the Lesser Antilles by the Caribs, whose original name was Galibi, and who came from the north of South America, like the Arawaks.

The Caribs were mobile, warrior groups with a simple social structure dedicated primarily to warfare. The Carib women were mostly of Arawak origin, taken through military conquest.

In his first voyage, Columbus reached the Bahamas, and then Hispaniola (Cuba and the Dominican Republic) where he encountered the Taino. The Admiral, amazed by the islands, the climate, the vegetation and the nakedness of the Americans, thought he had found an earthly paradise. Columbus, who died believing he had reached Asia rather than a continent that the European maps did not show, had read both his bible and the travel writers, particularly Marco Polo's account of his journey to China. Columbus was ready to be fearful of such beasts as 'man-eaters' and 'man-dogs' recorded in the traveler's notebooks: he thought he had found them in the Carib peoples. According to what Columbus had understood from the stories of the Taino-Arawaks, the victims of the Caribs' actions, there were ferocious warring bands who ate humans (the word cannibal comes from their language; the Spaniards renamed them 'cannibals'). The tales of Columbus' voyage thus contributed to the creation of the New World myths: of *El Dorado*, the gilded man; of Seven Golden Cities of Cibola; or the riches of the Amazon.

The conquest of paradise meant hell for the Arawaks and Caribs. Within a century, the former declined from a population of 2-3 million people to just a few thousand. The high mortality rate was due to exposure to previously unknown diseases introduced by the Europeans and also to the brutality of the Conquistadors. The Caribs tried to resist the invaders, but this only postponed their extermination, which became final in the 17th century.

Though he never found it, Columbus searched obsessively for gold. In its place he brought back some Tainos as slaves, along with spices such as chilies and colorful birds. Queen Isabella, his patron, did not accept the Tainos, considering them subjects of the Spanish Empire. In practice, however, in their own land, the Tainos were subjects in name only. They were exploited as slaves and forced to work in conditions that accelerated their demise. As a result of wiping out the indigenous people, the Europeans had no labor force, so they began to import slaves from Africa. Finding paradise on earth meant re-introducing the practice of slavery, which had disappeared in Europe with the introduction of Christianity.

Today, the few surviving Arawaks are found in Guyana, Suriname, French Guiana, and Puerto Rico where they are organized in Confederations, Nations and Grand Councils that claim to speak for all the Taino People of the circum-Caribbean and United States diaspora. Among them, US authorities officially recognize only the Jatibonicu Taino Tribal Nation of Borikén. ∎

Guinea

Population: 8,381,000 (2002)
Land area: 245,720 SQ KM
Capital: Conakry
Currency: Franc
Language: French

Guinée

Guinea was first inhabited by pygmies who were then driven out by the Mande peoples towards the more inhospitable regions. The country was originally connected to the great states of Sudan and their trade system. The Bambuk gold mines that fed the Mediterranean economy for centuries were located on the ridges of the Futa Dyalon massif (see Mali and Morocco). The same region witnessed the rise and fall of the Fulah states between the 16th and 19th centuries.

[2] In 1870, against this background, Samor became the local political and spiritual leader (Almamy) of a state that included the greater part of Guinea and parts of present-day Mali and Côte d'Ivoire. He had first confronted the French troops in 1886, as they were advancing from Senegal, and he had continued to fight constantly until 1898 when he was taken prisoner and exiled to Gabon. He died there two years later.

[3] This episode had been kept alive in the people's memory until 1947 when a small group of activists led by Ahmed Sekou Touré founded the Guinea Democratic Party (GDP). Supported by labor unions, the GDP soon became a very influential political organization.

[4] Overwhelmed by the loss of Indochina in 1954, the independence of Tunisia and Morocco in 1956, and the uprising of Algeria which began in 1954, French President de Gaulle attempted to salvage his interests in West Africa by creating the French Community in 1958. Through agreements and covenants he attempted a neo-colonialist project, to guarantee continued French

hegemony in the area, in particular through its large monopolies. When the population of Guinea was consulted, 1,200,000 opposed de Gaulle's proposal for a French Community and only 57,000 supported it.

[5] Four days later, the country proclaimed independence. Sekou Touré stated: 'We'd rather be poor and free than rich and enslaved'. It was the first time that such a thing had happened in 'French' West Africa, and in retaliation, Paris withdrew its technical advisers, paralyzed the few industries that there were and blocked Guinean trade.

[6] In 1959, the State took over the main economic activities and Guinea immediately created its own currency, becoming independent from the French franc. Industry and farming were diversified in an attempt to attain self-sufficiency, and

aluminum production surpassed one million tons per year.

[7] French aggression mounted. In 1965, Guinea's bank accounts in Paris were blocked, large-scale smuggling was fostered and counterfeit currency introduced.

[8] In 1970, Portuguese mercenaries invaded the country in an attempt to overthrow the Government and destroy the PAIGC, which was fighting for the independence of neighboring 'Portuguese' Guinea-Bissau. In response to the ever more frequent destabilization campaigns, Local Revolutionary Powers (LRPs) were created in every neighborhood or village with the aim of fighting against corruption, mismanagement and contraband.

[9] In November 1978, the Congress decided to change the country's name to the People's and Revolutionary Republic of Guinea, and to re-open relations with France. After a long period of isolation, Sekou Touré visited African and Arab countries in search of new sources of foreign capital to exploit the country's mineral wealth and to attract investments which might help to pay the foreign debt.

[10] The rapprochement between France and Guinea brought new agreements. The exploitation of the Mount Nimba iron ore reserves was granted to a French firm while the French Oil Company started offshore oil prospecting and the exploitation of rich bauxite deposits discovered in the 1970s. Guinea became the world's second largest bauxite producer. At that time Guinea and Mali signed an agreement envisaging the merger of the two neighbors into an economic and political federation.

[11] At the end of March 1984, Sekou Touré died in a US hospital while undergoing treatment for an old ailment. A week later, Colonel Lansana Conté headed a military coup which overthrew interim president Louis Beavogui.

[12] The new regime dismantled the political structure, the grassroots organizations and the Assembly; the Constitution was abolished too. The Democratic Party of Guinea was banned and the name of the country was changed, eliminating the words 'People's' and 'Revolutionary'. The military government stimulated private enterprise, eliminated mixed companies and applied for economic aid to France, the US and the African States.

[13] Under the burden of an $800 million foreign debt, the Government decreed a 100 per cent devaluation of the syli (then the national currency), and reduced public expenditure, a precondition of Guinea's entry into the French franc monetary scheme.

[14] In December 1984, the number of cabinet members was reduced, as was the number serving on the Reconstruction Committee. In addition, Colonel Conté consolidated power by simultaneously taking on the positions of head of state, Prime Minister and minister of defense.

[15] In December 1985, an economic recovery program was introduced, where agriculture, especially the cultivation of rice, was given top priority. Industrial and agricultural enterprises were also to be privatized. Self-sufficiency in food is still an unattained goal.

[16] To meet the country's serious economic problems head-on, in 1987 there were mass dismissals of public

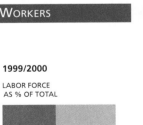

WORKERS

1999/2000

LABOR FORCE
AS % OF TOTAL

■ FEMALE: 47%   ■ MALE: 53%

LAND USE

DEFORESTATION: 1.1% annual (1990/95)

1993

■ FOREST & WOODLAND: 58.8%
■ ARABLE: 2.5%
■ OTHER: 38.7%

PUBLIC EXPENDITURE

Military expenditure (as % GNI):	**1.6 %** (1999)	
Defense expenditure (% of central government expenditure)	**7.4 %** (1999)	

officials. In 1988, Conté moved a group of military officers away from the capital, as their discontent over low salaries constituted a threat to his government. In January of the same year, the 80 per cent increase in all salaries caused a price explosion with prices tripling over a few days. The demonstrations that took place at the time forced the Government to freeze the prices of consumer good and rents.

[17] In February 1990 the Government announced an amnesty for political prisoners and exiles. In December, a referendum approved by a vast majority modified the Constitution and created a Temporary Council for National Development (CTDN) in charge of leading the transition to democracy. President Conté announced that legislative elections would be held in 1992, with the participation of several parties.

[18] When the multiparty system was approved, opposition leader Alpha Condé returned from exile and sponsored the creation of the National Democratic Forum (FND) which enclosed 30 opposition groups. However, tension and political persecution continued.

[19] Lansana Conté was re-elected in the December 1993 presidential elections with almost 51 per cent of the vote. Alpha Conde accused him of having staged a coup that led to confrontations between the police and opposition followers. In January 1994, dozens of people died in riots near the border with Liberia.

[20] In June 1995, the ruling parties won 76 seats out of 114 in parliamentary elections, which the opposition deemed fraudulent. Estimated annual GDP growth reached almost five per cent and, in recognition of what it considered to be good economic results, the Paris Club cancelled $85 million of Guinea's foreign debt, refinancing another $85 million still outstanding.

[21] In February 1996, a sector of the army rebelled when pay increases were not forthcoming. The mutiny ended in an attempt to overthrow the Government. The rebellion was put down in two days despite the fact that the mutineers, around 2,000 troops and some officers, had taken control of the urban center of the capital and used artillery to bombard the presidential palace. Several government officials were accused of encouraging the revolt, and were sent to prison. In July, the economist Sidia Touré was named Prime Minister. Touré announced the government priority would be reactivating the economy.

[22] The Government strengthened its health policy, one of its few successful areas. A Secretariat for the Promotion of Women had been formed two years earlier, which in 1996 became the Ministry of Social Affairs, Promotion of Women and Children, which planned the National Strategy of Women's Promotion. The Government had promised to comply with the commitments of the Cairo summit in 1994, focusing on family planning. The policy was revised in 1996, emphasizing on reproductive health and the gender gap, which was to be tackled through the education of mothers and children.

[23] The president of Sierra Leone, Ahmed Tejan Kabbah, was ousted in May 1997 and fled to Guinea with most of his government members. That country's political instability forced thousands of people to take refuge in Guinea, fearing attacks against their towns and villages.

[24] In September 1998, humanitarian organizations sent food to the country's northwest, where thousands of people had died after a lengthy drought. In November, Sierra Leone and Liberia signed a non-aggression treaty in Conakry, in a meeting mediated by US politician Jesse Jackson, special envoy of President Clinton. Both countries accused each other of harboring and aiding various rebel groups.

[25] In the December 1998 presidential elections, Lansana Conté was re-elected with 54.1 per cent of the vote, while the opposition complained of serious irregularities. A day later, opposition candidate Alpha Condé was arrested and held in prison until May 2001. Condé's release seemed a sign of Government flexibility.

[26] Organizations against female genital mutilation (FGM) stated that, after 14 years of fighting against this practice which is 'against human rights', they had persuaded doctors to use the proper instruments and avoid excessive bleeding and infections. But they had not succeeded in reducing or ending the practice.

[27] Taking advantage of sustained economic growth in the last years, the Government defined its goals in the document 'Guinea vision 2010', giving priority to education and health. With the support of several NGOs, the Ministry launched in 1999 a campaign against FGM. Infections caused by guinea worm fell 98 per cent in the last 12 years, while in countries such as Mali they rose 140 per cent between 2000 and 2001.

[28] On April 21 2001, in a meeting of the Economic Community of West African States (ECOWAS) held in the capital of Ghana, Accra, this country and Nigeria, Sierra Leone, Gambia and Liberia agreed to adopt a common currency by 2003.

[29] A meeting between the presidents of Guinea, Liberia and Sierra Leone on February 28 2002 calmed fears of an immediate regional conflict caused by the free movement of opposition members across these countries' borders. ∎

Guinea-Bissau

Population:	1,257,000 (2002)
Land area:	28,120 SQ KM
Capital:	Bissau
Currency:	Peso
Language:	Portuguese

Guiné-Bissau

Guinea-Bissau was the first Portuguese colony to gain independence in Africa. This was achieved even before the fall of the Portuguese dictatorship in Lisbon, in a successful political and military struggle led by Amilcar Cabral's African Party for the Independence of Guinea and Cape Verde (PAIGC).

[2] After belonging to the Mali and Songhai empires, the peoples in the Geba river valley became independent. This independence was soon threatened by the Portuguese, who had settled on the coast from the end of the 15th century, and by the Fulah, coming from the interior in the 16th century. Inland, the state of Gabu remained autonomous until the 19th century while the coastal population suffered the consequences of the slave trade and forced displacement to the Cape Verde Islands (see Cape Verde).

[3] Resistance against the European colonists began in 1500 when the Portuguese arrived in Guinea. At that time, the country was inhabited by several different groups, immigrants from the state of Mali along with the Fulah and Mandingo groups, who lived in organized autocratic societies in the savannas. During the 17th century Guineans made their first contact with the inhabitants of the Cape Verde islands, a mandatory stopover for the ships carrying slaves to Brazil.

[4] As the country was small and poor the monopoly on trade and agriculture was dealt with by a private company, the Unio Fabril. Guineans were forced to cultivate export crops while massively reducing the acreage available for subsistence farming. In the 1950s, infant mortality reached the remarkable rate of 600 deaths per 1,000 births. There were only 11 doctors in the country and only one per cent of the rural population was literate. In the early 1960s, only 11 Guineans had completed secondary education.

[5] It was against this setting of misery and exploitation that Amilcar Cabral founded the Athletics and Recreational Association in 1954. This organization developed into the African Party for the Independence of Guinea and Cape Verde (PAIGC) two years later. The Party called on all Guineans and inhabitants of Cape Verde to unite in anti-colonial

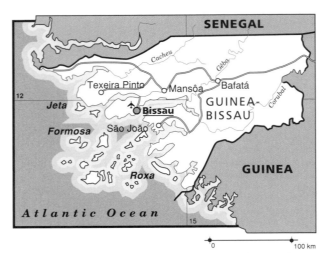

resistance, regardless of color, race or religion. In September 1959, after trying fruitlessly to engage the Portuguese in negotiations for three years, the PAIGC embarked upon guerrilla warfare. The fighting spread quickly and by 1968 the Portuguese were confined to the capital, Bissau, and a few coastal strongholds. Four years later, the PAIGC had taken two-thirds of the nation's territory under their control. In September and October 1972, the first free elections were held in the liberated areas. A Popular National Assembly was elected and a year later on September 24 1973, the 'democratic, anti-imperialist and anti-colonialist republic of Guinea' was proclaimed. Two months later the UN General Assembly recognized the independent state.

[6] Amilcar Cabral was assassinated in Conakry, Guinea, in February 1973, by Portuguese agents. He left many books and studies on the struggles for freedom in the African colonies. His successor, Luis Cabral, set up the Government Council of Guinea-Bissau in a small village called Madina do Boé, in the heart of the liberated area.

[7] The impact of the unilateral independence of Guinea-Bissau and its immediate recognition by the UN shook the infrastructure of Portuguese colonialism. General Spinola, commander of the 55,000 colonial soldiers, came to the realization that his army could not be successful in the war against the PAIGC and argued for political changes in Portugal. It was as a

result of these conditions in Bissau that the Captains' Movement was born. This movement later became the Armed Forces' Movement, the group which was responsible for the coup that overthrew the dictatorial regime in Portugal on April 25 1974. Four months after the coup, Portugal recognized the independence of Guinea-Bissau.

[8] The PAIGC Government diversified agriculture giving priority to feeding the population and reducing the emphasis on export crops. Foreign companies were nationalized, agrarian reform was implemented together with a mass literacy campaign. In foreign relations, the new government opted for non-alignment and unconditional support for the struggle against apartheid and colonialism in Africa. The PAIGC congress also gave top priority to economic integration with the archipelago of Cape Verde, with a view towards uniting the two countries.

[9] In 1980, a military conspiracy led by João Bernardino (Ninho) Vieira, a former guerrilla commander, overthrew Luis Cabral. Vieira replaced all the government bodies with a centralized Revolutionary Council, headed by himself.

[10] Talks with Cape Verde were cut short while the two countries were discussing a united constitution (See Cape Verde). The new government in Bissau was immediately recognized by the neighboring Republic of Guinea, which had been in despite with former president

Cabral over offshore oil rights in an area presumed to be rich in petroleum deposits.

[11] Contact between the two Guineas was intensified in September 1982, and in February 1983 diplomatic missions were exchanged.

[12] The first development plan of 1983-86 proposed an initial investment of $118.6 million, of which 75 per cent would be financed by international funds. In 1984, the construction of five ports was started at an estimated cost of $40 million, and the construction of the Bisalanca Airport was completed. The Government started a campaign against corruption and inefficiency in public administration, and as a result in 1984 Vice-President Victor Saude Maria was asked to resign. Shortly afterwards, the Popular Assembly eliminated the position of prime minister, and the Revolutionary Council became the Council of State.

[13] In November 1984, the vice-president of the Council of State, Colonel Paulo Correia, led an unsuccessful coup against President Vieira. Correia was executed on July 21 1986.

[14] The 1984 stabilization plan failed, causing further deterioration of the economic and financial situation. The international economic crisis increased, the price of Guinea-Bissau's oil exports lost market value. The Government adopted a 'corrective' policy, including freezing salaries and reducing public investment. This was an attempt to bring it into line with IMF conditions for refinancing the servicing of the foreign debt. The economy was subsequently opened up to foreign capital in the hope of attracting resources from Portugal and France, particularly in the high-priority areas of telecommunications. In 1989, Portugal participated in the creation of a commercial bank.

[15] In 1986, the Government granted an amnesty to political prisoners. Two years later, in June 1988, the Central Committee of the PAIGC began discussing a proposal for separating the executive and legislative powers. At that time Guinea-Bissau spent more on its military budget than on education and health combined.

[16] In February 1991, the PAIGC approved a political reform which

anticipated elections for 1992. The IMF cancelled several loans granted to Guinea-Bissau after the resignation of Economy Minister Manuel dos Santos.

[17] Dependence on agricultural exports - especially on peanuts, whose price had fallen abruptly - caused significant social and economic imbalances along with political tensions in 1992 and 1993. The 1992 elections were not held due to a government decision and after the murder in March 1993 of a high military commander they were delayed once more.

[18] Finally, in 1994 João Bernardo Vieira defeated Kumba Ialá of the Party for Social Renewal (PSR), obtaining 52 per cent of the vote in the second round. During the campaign, Ialá accused him of supporting tribalism and racism. In the parliamentary elections, Vieira's PAIGC took 64 of the 100 seats at stake. Believing that the ruling party had 'bought' votes, Ialá refused to take part in a national unity government. That same year, the West African Economic Monetary Union (WAEMU) was founded, with 8 member countries and a market of 72 million consumers, including Guinea-Bissau. This led to a progressive integration with a single currency and common rates.

[19] In January 1995, the IMF granted a new $14 million loan in support of economic reforms. In June, the visit of Senegalese president Abdou Diouf led to a rapprochement with Dakar after a period of relative hostility. Both countries agreed to exploit joint energy and mineral resources. In August, Ialá denounced Vieira's closer ties with France, the rise in the price of basic items like rice, and human rights violations by the government.

[20] In late 1995, Guinea-Bissau ratified the border agreement signed with Senegal in 1993, resetting its maritime frontiers and stipulating the joint exploitation of an area which was supposedly rich in oil.

[21] In August 1996, the Government accepted 44 illegal African immigrants expelled from Spain. The League of Human Rights of Guinea-Bissau said the Government had agreed to the Spanish request in return for payment.

[22] In 1998, Guinea-Bissau continued to house pro-independence rebels from the Senegalese Movement of Democratic Forces of Casamance (MFDC). However, Guinea-Bissau's military intervention against a refugee camp on the frontier with Senegal in January that year fed rumors of rapprochement between Bissau and Dakar, which led to a more hard-line attitude towards the Casamance refugees.

[23] On May 4 1998, the UN asked 'donor' countries to help Guinea-Bissau recover following eight months of civil war. Three days later, however General Mané who had earlier led a coup attempt rose up again and Vieira was defeated; he sought political asylum in Portugal. The army accused Vieira of corruption and treason. France condemned the coup and Mané was accused of violating the Abuja and Lomé agreements, signed three months earlier.

[24] In August, the FAO included Guinea-Bissau amongst the 16 African countries with the greatest poverty and food shortages, stating that it was facing a serious emergency.

[25] Five months after the coup, a mass grave was found containing 18 bodies in the town of Portogole, including former vice president Correira. Meanwhile, the military junta presented evidence to Portugal of the 'crimes' committed by Vieira in order to get him repatriated. On November 17, two weeks before the national elections, General Mané stated that 'any president who is elected and does not fulfil his promises will be immediately deposed'. Supporters of the General stated the military junta would be dissolved once the new president was in power.

[26] In the first round ballot on November 28, the populist PSR took 38 of the 102 seats in the National Assembly and the Resistance of Guinea-Bissau-Bafatá Movement came second with 28 seats. In the second round of presidential elections on January 16 2000, Kumba Ialá of the PSR was elected President with 72 per cent of the vote. The new government was made up of the two parties. Caetano N'Tchama was Prime Minister.

[27] In November, Mané proclaimed himself leader of the army and attempted a coup, but he was killed together with eight followers after cross-fire with government forces in Quinhamel, 30 kilometers from Bissau.

[28] The RGB abandoned the government coalition in January 2001, claiming it had not been consulted about a new design of the Cabinet. In March, against the opinion of several opposition parties, Ialá appointed Faustino Imbali as premier. According to observers, Imbali lacked political influence to address the economic problems and to recover political stability. In December of the same year, accused of lack of transparency, Imbali was removed from office and replaced by Minister of the Interior Alamara Nhassé.

[29] That same month, the UN Secretary General, Kofi Annan, called for political dialogue to temper the domestic tension, and warned that international aid was in jeopardy if

PROFILE

ENVIRONMENT
The land is flat with slight elevations in the southeast and abundant irrigation from rivers and canals. The coastal area is swampy, suitable for rice. Rice, peanuts, palm oil and cattle are produced in the drier eastern region. The need to increase exports led to over-cultivation of the soil; in addition, rice plantations are replacing part of the coastal woodlands. Slash-and-burn techniques, as well as numerous forest fires, have contributed to deforestation.

SOCIETY
Peoples: Balante 27.2 per cent; Fulani 22.9 per cent; Malinke 12.2 per cent; Mandyako 10.6 per cent; Pepel 10.0 per cent; other 17.1 per cent.
Religions: Two-thirds profess traditional African religions; nearly one-third are Muslim and there is a small Catholic minority.
Languages: Portuguese (official). The crioulo dialect, a mixture of Portuguese and African languages, is used as the lingua franca. The most widely spoken native languages are Mande and Fulah.
Political Parties: Multiparty republic with parliamentary groups: The Party for Social Renewal, progressive (PSR); the Resistance of Guinea-Bissau-Bafatá Movement (RGB); the African Independence Party of Guinea and Cape Verde (PAIGC); the Democratic Alliance; the Union for Change and the Social Democratic Party.
Social Organizations: National Workers' Union of Guinea-Bissau (UNTG).

THE STATE
Official Name: República da Guiné-Bissau.
Administrative Divisions: 8 Regions and 1 Autonomous Sector.
Capital: Bissau 274,000 people (1999).
Other cities: Bafatá 19,400 people; Gabu 12,200 (2000).
Government: Kumba Ialá, President since February 2000. Alamara Nhassé, Prime Minister since December 2001, appointed by the President with the agreement of the People's National Assembly (Legislature), which has 102 seats.
National Holiday: September 24, Independence declared unilaterally (1973). **Armed Forces:** 7,250 (1996).
Other: 2,000 Gendarmes.

DEMOGRAPHY
Population: 1,257,000 (2002)
Annual growth: 2.3 % (1985-2000)
Estimates for year 2015: 1,727,000 (2000)
Annual growth to year 2015: 2.4 % (2000)
Urban population: 23.7 % (2000)
Urban growth: 3.9 % (2000)
Children per woman: 6.0 (2000)

HEALTH
Life expectancy at birth: 45 years (2000-2005)
male: 44 years (2000-2005)
female: 47 years (2000-2005)
Maternal mortality: 910 per 100,000 live births (1985/99)
Infant mortality: 132 per 1,000 (2000)
Under-5 child mortality: 215 per 1,000 (2000)
Daily calorie supply: 2,245 per capita (1999)
17 doctors per 100,000 people (1996)
Safe water: 56 % (2000)

EDUCATION
Literacy: 37 % (2000)
male: 53 % (2000)
female: 21 % (2000)
School enrolment (net):
Primary total: 42 % (1994/2000)
male: 58 % (1995/99)
female: 32 % (1995/99)
Secondary (gross):
male: 9 % (1995/97)
female: 4 % (1995/97)
Tertiary (gross): 1 % (1997)

COMMUNICATIONS
5 newspapers (1996), 44 radios (1997) and 9 main telephone lines (2000) per 1,000 people

ECONOMY
Per capita, GDP: $ 755 (2000)
Annual growth: 5.2 % (2000)
Annual inflation: 8.6 % (2000)
Consumer price index: 258.2 (2000)
Currency: 761.6 pesos = $ 1 (03/2002)
Cereal imports: 47,169 metric tons (2000)
Food import dependency: 44 % (1995)
Fertilizer use: 20 kg per ha (1999)
Exports: $ 68 million (2000)
Imports: $ 125 million (2000)
External debt: $ 942 million (2000); $ 785 per capita (2000)
Debt service: 16.4 % of exports (1999)
Development aid received: $ 52 million (1999); $ 44.2 per capita (1999); 24.00 % of GNP (1999)

HDI (ranking/value): 156 / 0.339 (1999)

Guinea-Bissau did not reach the social and political stability imposed as a condition for grants. In May, both the IMF and the World Bank interrupted their monetary help due to the 'loss' of millions of dollars of aid for development. By the end of the year, the IMF praised the improvements of the country in terms of financial controls. ∎

Guyana

Population: 765,000 (2002)
Land area: 196,850 SQ KM
Capital: Georgetown
Currency: Guyana dollar
Language: English

Guyana

The original inhabitants of what is now Guyana, the Arawaks, were displaced from the area by the Caribs, warriors who dominated the region before moving on to the nearby islands which were later called after them.

[2] Both the Arawaks and the Caribs were nomads. Organized into families of 15 to 20 people, they lived by fishing and hunting. There are thought to have been half a million inhabitants at the time of the arrival of Europeans in Guyana. There are around 45,000 Indians, divided into nine ethnic groups, of which seven maintain their cultural identity and traditions.

[3] Led on by the legend of *El Dorado*, in 1616 the Dutch built the first fort. Guyana was made up of three colonies: Demerara, Berbice and Essequibo. But in 1796, the Dutch colony was taken over by the British, who had already begun a wide-scale introduction of slaves. A slave, Cuffy, led a rebellion in 1763 which was brutally put down. To this day, Cuffy is considered a national hero.

[4] Those slaves that escaped from the plantations went into the forests to live with the indigenous peoples, giving rise to the 'bush blacks'. The English brought in Chinese, Javanese and Indian workers as cheap labor. In the second half of the 20th century, Guyana's population managed to channel independence politics into a single movement, the People's Progressive Party (PPP), with policies of national independence and social improvements, with long-term aims for a socialist country. Cheddi Jagan, the first Prime Minister of the colony, was in power for three successive terms.

[5] After years of struggle and periods of great violence, Britain recognized Guyana's independence within the Commonwealth on May 26 1966. By that time, the PPP had split; most of the Afro-Guyanese population joined the People's National Congress (PNC), while indigenous people remained loyal to Jagan. Forbes Burnham, leader of the PNC took office, supported by other ethnic minorities.

[6] This process was influenced by ethnic conflict and by foreign interests, particularly from the US, which felt its hegemony in the

Caribbean threatened by Jagan's socialism.

[7] Even though Burnham came to power with Washington's blessing, he kept his distance. He declared himself in favor of non-alignment and proclaimed a Cooperative Republic in 1970. The bauxite, timber and sugar industries were nationalized in the first half of the 1970s, and by 1976 the State controlled 75 per cent of the country's economy. At the same time, regional integration was implemented through CARICOM (Caribbean Community), the Latin American Economic System (SELA), and the Caribbean Merchant Fleet. During the first decade after independence, Burnham and Jagan defended the same political platform.

[8] In May 1976, Cheddi Jagan stated the need to 'achieve national anti-imperialist unity', when disputes broke out with Brazil over the border. The PPP representatives returned to Parliament, from which they had withdrawn three years earlier to protest over electoral corruption. Shortly afterwards, Burnham announced the creation of a Popular Militia.

[9] Elections were postponed in order to hold a constitutional referendum, with Parliament drawing up a new constitution. This gave way to harsh criticism by the PPP, which withdrew from legislative activity for the second time. In 1980 Burnham was elected President. However, according to international observers, the election had been plagued by fraud. In 1980 Burnham granted authorization for transnational corporations to carry out oil and uranium operations. In addition, he turned to the IMF to obtain credit.

[10] In June of the same year, Walter Rodney, the famous Guyanese intellectual and founder of the opposition Working People's Alliance (WPA) was killed by a car bomb. The culprits were never found.

[11] In the post-election period, border disputes escalated. Venezuela claimed the Essequibo region, approximately 159,000 sq km (three quarters) of Guyanese territory, arguing that British imperialism illegally deprived Venezuela of that area in the 19th century.

[12] In 1983, both countries turned to the UN. In 1985 direct

negotiations started again to settle the dispute 'within a framework of cordiality and goodwill'. Negotiations were focused on an outlet to the Atlantic Ocean for Venezuela.

[13] While financial difficulties increased during 1984 and the Government faced a new crisis in its relations with labor unions, Burnham resumed contacts with the IMF to obtain a $150 million loan. Burnham considered the conditions on the loan 'unacceptable'. The American invasion of Grenada - and Guyana's criticism of this action - led to a deterioration of the relations between the two countries. Guyana made overtures to the socialist countries.

[14] Burnham died in August 1985 and was replaced by Desmond Hoyte. The PNC won the general elections that year with 78 per cent of the vote, but the opposition complained of alleged fraud. In 1986, five of the six opposition parties formed the Patriotic Coalition for Democracy, which boycotted the 1986 municipal elections, whereby all the seats went to the PNC. Hoyte, who was chosen President, announced in January 1987 his Government would return to 'Co-operative Socialism'.

[15] Parliament met on December 3 1991, five days after the Government declared a state of emergency in order to postpone the elections planned for that month. The Government ignored the opposition objections and extended the state of emergency until June 1992. On October 5 1992, Cheddi Jagan defeated President Desmond Hoyte (54 per cent to 41 per cent respectively) in the general elections. The Progressive People's Party took 32 seats in the National Assembly, while the PNC took 31.

[16] One of the first Latin American leaders to raise the flag of Marxism in the 1950s, Jagan returned to power, putting an end to 28 years of PNC dominion.

[17] In early 1993, unlike his neighbors including Brazil, President Jagan allowed US troops to be deployed for training in the forests. He accepted US military collaboration to combat drug-trafficking and aid to develop sanitation in the interior.

18 Guyana had frequent border disputes with neighboring Venezuela and Suriname, although it maintained good relations with Brazil, especially on the trade front.

19 Jagan intended to modify the adjustment plan launched by his predecessor, Desmond Hoyte, in agreement with the IMF. His government defended 'non-conventional' methods of problems solving in land distribution, transport, health, housing and education.

20 He proposed a market economy strategy to resolve the problem of the poverty of 80 per cent of the population. The emigration rate exceeded the demographic growth index, so that the population fell from 1,020,000 in 1989 to 808,000 in 1992.

21 The nation's wealth still remained nearly intact with large reserves of gold, diamonds, bauxite, forests and great agricultural potential. The fiscal deficit, which caused high inflation, was related to the smuggling of minerals, along with the price policy on exports of sugar, rice and other agricultural products.

22 The celebration of the first anniversary of Jagan's Government was tarnished by a strike in the national electricity company as the Government had failed to implement its promise to increase State workers' pay by 300 per cent. The Government claimed the conditions imposed by the IMF prevented it from being this generous.

23 In June 1994, Jagan rejected the ambassador to Georgetown nominated by the US, accusing him of 'subversive activities' during the last few years of British colonial administration.

24 In 1995, the worst environmental accident in the history of the country occurred, when four million cubic meters of cyanide-contaminated waste fell into the Omai river, a tributary of the Essequibo, the nations main river.

25 In February 1996, the human rights organization Amnesty International denounced the use of the death penalty by hanging in Guyana, the first such since 1990. That same year the Government had $500 million - nearly a quarter - of its foreign debt pardoned.

26 Following Jagan's death in 1997, his wife Janet took over as interim Prime Minister. In the December 15 elections, she was elected President with 55.5 per cent against the 40.6 per cent of Hoyte's PNC. Despite threats of civil disobedience incited by Hoyte, the 77 year-old, US-born Jagan took office on December 19. Sam Hinds was appointed Prime Minister.

27 In her first months in office, Jagan had to deal with a drought that affected the country's production (especially of gold), reduced trade, created transportation problems and facilitated forest fires. Rising prices triggered protests, the largest of which gathered outside the state telephone company to denounce rate increases of 400 to 1,000 per cent.

28 After serving just 20 months of her term, Jagan resigned for health reasons. Economy Minister Bharrat Jagdeo - a youngster at 35 - took her place. The National People's Party, mostly made up of Afro-Guyanans, criticized the way the power transition was handled.

29 In March 2000, Venezuelan President Hugo Chávez reiterated his country's claims to the Essequibo region, but affirmed that Venezuela would submit to UN arbitration. Chávez also criticized a US company planning to build a rocket-launching site in the area in question.

30 The permit granted by Guyana to a Canadian oil company for the exploitation of territorial waters caused conflict with Suriname. After a round of talks mediated by Jamaican Prime Minister Percival James Patterson, agreement was reached to hold future meetings between both parties to decide the future of the region.

31 In March 2001, the general election planned for 1997 was held, with international observers who confirmed that virtually everything was in good order, in spite of some irregularities due to the absence of some voters' names in the register. Finally, Jagdeo was re-elected. ∎

PROFILE

ENVIRONMENT

90 per cent of the population and most of the country's agriculture are concentrated on the coastal plain which ranges between 15 and 90 km in width. Rice and sugar cane are the main crops. As most of the shore is below sea level, dams and canals have been built to prevent flooding. The inner land consists of a 150 km-wide rainforest where the country's mineral resources are concentrated (bauxite, gold, and diamonds). To the west and south, the rest of the country is occupied by an ancient geological formation, the Guyana mountain range. Guyana is a native word meaning 'land of waters'. There are many rivers, as a result of the tropical climate and year-round rains. In terms of world-wide deforestation, Guyana has suffered little and until 1990, only a small fraction of the extensive forests had been felled. However, foreign companies are pressing for the intensification of lumber exploitation. In some areas, there has been no reforestation after logging, and this has led to soil erosion.

SOCIETY

Peoples: Half the population are descended from Indian indentured workers, one-third from African natives and the rest are native Americans, mixed European and Indian descendants, Chinese and Europeans.
Religions: Protestant 34 per cent; Catholic 18 per cent; Hindu 34 per cent; Muslim 9 per cent. Traditional religions are practiced by American Indian groups.
Languages: English, official. Hindi and Urdu are used in religious ceremonies.
Political Parties: People's Progressive Party, socialist (PPP); People's National Congress, socialist (PNC); coalition between: The Guyana Action Party and the Working People's Alliance; The United Force, conservative.
Social Organizations: Trade Union Congress (TUC with 22 member unions. Youth National Council; Amerindian Peoples Association of Guyana.

THE STATE

Official Name: Cooperative Republic of Guyana.
Administrative Divisions: 10 Regions.
Capital: Georgetown 275,000 people (1999).
Other cities: Linden 43,800 people; New Amsterdam 31,500 (2000).
Government: Bharrat Jagdeo, President since August 1999, re-elected in 2001. Samuel Hinds, Prime Minister since August 1999. Unicameral Legislature: National Assembly, with 65 members, of which 12 are regional representatives and 53 are elected through direct vote and proportional representation.
National Holiday: February 23, Proclamation of the Republic (1970).
Armed Forces: 1,600 (1995).
Other: 4,500 People's Militia, national service.

DEMOGRAPHY

Population: 765,000 (2002)
Annual growth: 0.1 % (1985-2000)
Estimates for year 2015: 749,000 (2000)
Annual growth to year 2015: -0.1 % (2000)
Urban population: 38.2 % (2000)
Urban growth: 2.1 % (2000)
Children per woman: 2.4 (2000)

HEALTH

Life expectancy at birth: 62 years (2000-2005)
male: 58 years (2000-2005)
female: 67 years (2000-2005)
Maternal mortality: 110 per 100,000 live births (1985/99)
Infant mortality: 55 per 1,000 (2000)
Under-5 child mortality: 74 per 1,000 (2000)
Daily calorie supply: 2,569 per capita (1999)
18 doctors per 100,000 people (1997)
Safe water: 94 % (2000)

EDUCATION

Literacy: 98 % (2000)
male: 99 % (2000)
female: 98 % (2000)
School enrolment (net):
Primary total: 95 % (1994/2000)
male: 89 % (1995/99)
female: 84 % (1995/99)
Secondary (gross):
male: 73 % (1995/97)
female: 78 % (1995/97)
Tertiary (gross): 12 % (1997)
Primary school teachers: one for every 27 pupils (1998)

COMMUNICATIONS

56 newspapers (1996), 558 radios (2000), 81 TV sets (2000) and 79 main telephone lines (2000) per 1,000 people
Books: 4 new titles per 100,000 people (1992/94)

ECONOMY

Per capita, GDP: $ 3,963 (2000)
Annual growth: -1.3 % (2000)
Annual inflation: 6.2 % (2000)
Consumer price index: 132.4 (2000)
Currency: 180.8 Guyana dollars = $ 1 (03/2002)
Cereal imports: 60,278 metric tons (2000)
Food import dependency: 7 % (1992)
Fertilizer use: 296 kg per ha (1999)
Exports: $ 687 million (2000)
Imports: $ 792 million (2000)
External debt: $ 1,455 million (2000); $ 1,914 per capita (2000)
Development aid received: $ 27 million (1999); $ 31.1 per capita (1999); 3.90 % of GNP (1999)

HDI (ranking/value): 93 / 0.704 (1999)

Haiti

Population:	8,400,000 (2002)
Land area:	27,560 SQ KM
Capital:	Port-au-Prince
Currency:	Gourde
Language:	French

Haïti

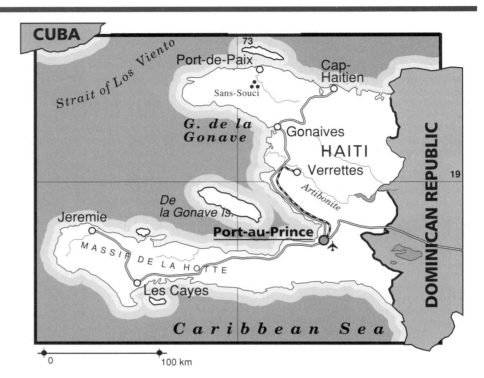

When Quisqueya, as the local population named it, was 'discovered' by Christopher Columbus in 1492, the island was inhabited by numerous Arawak peoples. The contact with Europeans was devastating for the Arawaks, who almost entirely disappeared from the island over the next few decades. Spanish colonists, supported by the Dominican missionaries, called the islands after their patron saint, St Dominic (Santo Domingo).

2 The island was later colonized by the French and other European settlers who were attracted by the sugar plantations. Disputes arose among the Europeans and in 1697 Spain ceded the west of the island to France, under the Treaty of Ryswick.

3 After gaining control of the island, France began to exploit it, introducing about 20,000 African slaves per year, leading to rapid racial mixing. Sugar soon became the principal export product of the region, and during the 18th century Haiti became the most important French possession in the Americas.

4 This prosperity was based on African slave labor. By 1789, the number of African slaves in the colony had reached 480,000. There were 60,000 mulattos and free 'colored' people, while the rich land-owning Europeans constituted a minority of no more than 20,000. The Haitians were influenced by the revolutionary movement that had started in the colonial capitals and they waged a revolutionary war, led by former slave Toussaint L'Ouverture. The war lasted from 1791 to 1803 and ended with the proclamation of the first black republic in the world.

5 Haiti's struggle for independence went through several stages. Initially, the large landowners joined the revolutionary movement, along with the slaves, merchants and poor Europeans (called petit blancs), forming a local Assembly to demand an end to colonial rule. In the second stage, the free mulattos supported the French revolution, under the assumption that it would give equal rights to all people, regardless of the color of their skin. However, in 1790 the European planters fiercely rejected the demands of the freed slaves, leaving them no alternative but to ally themselves with the marrons, two groups of rebel slaves, a year later.

6 It was L'Ouverture who gave the marrons their direction, rallying them to the call of 'general freedom for all', transforming the different groups into a disciplined army. On February 4 1794, taking advantage of the splits in the French colonial system, he succeeded in getting the French National Convention to ratify a decree abolishing slavery in Santo Domingo and appointing himself as a general.

7 After the coup of the Brumaire 18, Napoleon Bonaparte sent a large military expedition to reconquer the colony and re-establish slavery. L'Ouverture responded with a general uprising, but he was imprisoned and died in exile in France in 1803.

8 Jean-Jacques Dessalines took over leadership of the war of independence, aided by Henri Christophe and Alexandre Pétion, who together radicalized L'Ouvertures's legacy. They succeeded in uniting the Africans and mulattos and after a series of heroic campaigns, they forced the French troops to capitulate. Independence was proclaimed on November 28 1803, and Haiti became the first independent state in Latin America.

9 Dessalines gave his government a strong nationalist direction, trying to consolidate his personal power by creating an autocratic state, similar to the one emerging in France. Like Napoleon, Dessalines proclaimed himself emperor, calling himself Jacques I. Pétion and Christophe immediately started to plot against him, and he was murdered during a revolt in 1806.

10 The east of the island was recovered by the Spaniards under the Treaty of Paris in 1814, while in the west Christophe and Pétion fought for the leadership, dividing the territory. Henri Christophe established a republic in the north, later making it a kingdom with himself as King Henri I from 1811 to 1820. In the south, Alexandre Pétion ruled over a separate republic from 1808 to 1818, supporting Simon Bolívar with weapons and funding. Pétion was convinced that only total American independence could guarantee that of Haiti, as the country was being harassed by European powers and the US.

11 In 1818, JP Boyer was elected president instead of Pétion. Boyer recovered the north of the country in 1820, putting an end to Christophe's monarchic experiment. Two years

later he conquered Santo Domingo in the east of the island, thus achieving a fragile reunification, which lasted for a quarter of a century. In 1843, a revolution led by the Santo Domingan Creoles divided the island into two definite, independent States: the Dominican Republic in the east, and the Republic of Haiti in the west.

12 In spite of the permanent political violence throughout the 19th century, foreign investors gained access to the Haitian market by building ports and railways and by buying profitable plantations. The new transport and communications led to a faster and more effective extraction of the island's riches, with the profits going to the industrialized countries. The unfavorable trading exchange led the country into debt, until it became wholly dependent on its creditors, who were mostly American.

13 From 1867, a bloody civil war launched a period of political instability and economic crisis which lasted until 1915, when the country was occupied by US marines for non-compliance with 'its commitments'. A year later the US invaded the Dominican Republic, gaining control of the whole island.

[14] The invasion of Haiti was heroically resisted by Charlemagne Péralte's 'Revolutionary Army'. Péralte was treacherously murdered in 1919. The US troops finally defeated the resistance and controlled the country until 1934, turning it into a virtual colony. That year, President Vincent succeeded in getting the US troops to withdraw from the island, but he could not eliminate US influence from the country's domestic affairs.

[15] The national army, or Garde d'Haiti, took a central role in national politics, staging coups against presidents Lescot, 1941-1946; Estime, 1946-1950; and Magloire, 1950-1957. In 1957, François Duvalier,

a middle-class doctor, seized power supported by the army and the US.

[16] The elite *mestizo* group which was in power repressed the African-based culture until François Duvalier recognized the strategic power he could achieve by manipulating it. Over time he succeeded in building two great supports for his domination. The first was voodoo, the syncretic and distinctive religion of Haiti that combines African and Catholic rites. The second was the *Tontons-Macoutes*, a group of some 300,000 'national security volunteers'.

[17] The army, the commercial bourgeoisie, the ecclesiastic authorities, the state bureaucracy,

and the US State Department used Duvalier to control the country for over 30 years. With Washington's backing, Duvalier or 'Papa Doc' proclaimed himself President-for-life in 1964, passing on the title to his son Jean-Claude or 'Baby Doc' on his death in 1971.

[18] Assailed on the international level by continual condemnations of human rights violations, and on the domestic level by active opposition, Jean-Claude Duvalier's government called elections in 1984. Sixty-one per cent of the population abstained. Organizations opposed to Duvalier renewed their underground activities and the opposition grew, organizing itself into parties and trade unions, while the regime was becoming a burden to the US.

[19] Repression grew, and by 1985 it was estimated that Baby Doc's regime had been responsible for 40,000 murders. The country was enveloped by a growing wave of protests and strikes. Duvalier fled the country in a US airforce plane and received temporary asylum in France.

[20] A National Governing Council (CNG) led by General Henri Namphu assumed control of the government, promising 'free and direct' elections by the end of 1987.

[21] The dictator's flight did not end the mobilization of the people. Mass lynching by Tontons-Macoutes forced the National Governing Council to dissolve this repressive force and to free all the prisoners.

[22] In October 1986, the CNG called elections to elect a Constituent Assembly to draw up a new constitution. Less than 10 per cent of the 3 million Haitians participated in the election and, on March 29 1987 a referendum approved the new constitution with 99.8 per cent of the vote. The new constitution limited the presidential term to 5 years, prohibited re-election and divided the power with a prime minister chosen by Parliament.

[23] The elections were to be held in November 1987, but a few hours after the polling stations were opened, they were sabotaged by factions of the armed forces and by former Tontons-Macoutes, and the elections were suspended, finally taking place in January 1988. In a very volatile atmosphere, Leslie Manigat, the 'official' candidate, was

elected, only to be deposed in June, in a coup led by General Namphu.

[24] In September 1988, a movement of sergeants and soldiers deposed General Namphu, putting Prosper Avril, the *eminence grise* of the Duvalier period, into power.

[25] In March 1990, during a period of intense popular protest, General Avril was ousted by General Abraham, who relinquished control to a provisional civilian government headed by Judge Ertha Pascal-Trouillot, the first woman to occupy the presidency in Haiti. The provisional government created suitable conditions to put the Constitution into practice, and called elections for December 1990.

[26] These elections were won by a priest, Jean-Bertrand Aristide, who obtained 67 per cent of the vote as the leader of the National Front for Change and Democracy (FNCD). He was voted in mostly by the poor urban sectors, and he took office on February 7 1991.

[27] Aristide, a Liberation Theology activist, had been censured in 1988 by the church authorities and expelled from the Salesian order. His governmental program was based on a war against corruption and drug trafficking, including a thorough literacy campaign, and a project to move from 'extreme poverty to poverty with dignity'.

[28] On September 30, General Raoul Cédras staged a bloody coup. In protest the Organization of American States (OAS) declared a trade embargo, starting diplomatic negotiations in the region and in the UN. Meanwhile, the rebels tried to avoid international isolation by officially recognizing the sovereignty and operation of parliament.

[29] In February 1992, OAS representatives, Haitian members of parliament, and the deposed Aristide signed an agreement in Washington to re-establish democracy and reinstate the former president.

[30] In January 1993, the de facto government held legislative elections which many people considered illegitimate as they were designed only to partially replace Parliament. Less than 3 per cent of those registered to vote took part. Months later, Marc Bazin resigned as prime minister.

PROFILE

ENVIRONMENT

Haiti occupies the western third of the island of Hispaniola, the second largest of the Greater Antilles. Two main mountain ranges run from east to west, extending along the country's northern and southern peninsulas, contributing to their shape. The hills and river basins in between form the center of Haiti. The flatlands that open up to the sea in the west, are protected from the humid trade winds by the mountains to the north and east. Coffee is the main export product. Copper extraction ceased in 1976 and bauxite deposits are almost exhausted. The northern coastline has the heaviest rainfall and contains the country's most developed area, though the land there is suffering from serious erosion. Forests make up less than 2 per cent of the land area.

SOCIETY

Peoples: Nearly 95 per cent of Haitians are descendants of African slaves. There are also minorities of European and Asian origin, and integration has produced a small mestizo group. Thousands of Haitians have emigrated in recent years, especially to Colombia, Venezuela and the United States.
Religions: Voodoo, a mixture of Christianity and various African beliefs. Catholics (80 per cent); Protestants (16 per cent).
Languages: French and Creole (both official). French is spoken by less than 20 per cent of the population. Most people speak creole, a combination of Spanish, English, French and African languages.
Political Parties: National Front for Change and Democracy (FNCD); National Alliance for Democracy and Progress (ANDP); National Committee of the Democratic Movements (Konakom); National People's Assembly (APN); Agricultural Industrial Party (PAIN); Unified Party of Haitian Communists (PUCH); Union for National Reconciliation (UNR); Lavalas Political Organization (Organization of the Struggling Peoples (OPL).
Social Organizations: The 'Grassroots' Church groups, of Catholic origin; Movement in Favor of the Creole Language; Solidarity of the Women of Haiti (SOFA).

THE STATE

Official name: Repiblik Dayti.
Administrative divisions: 9 departments.
Capital: Port-au-Prince 1,699,000 people (1999).
Other Cities: Carrefour 356,400 people; Delmas 301,200; Cap-Haitien 119,400 (2000).
Government: Jean-Bertrand Aristide, President since February 2001. Yvon Neptune, Prime Minister since March 2002. The National Assembly (Legislature) has two chambers: the Chamber of Deputies, with 83 members, and the Senate, with 27 members.
National Holiday: January 1, Independence Day (1804).
Armed Forces: 1,500.

LITERACY

2000

49%

EXTERNAL DEBT

2000

PER CAPITA

US$ 144

FOREIGN TRADE

Millions US$ 2000

IMPORTS

1,109

EXPORTS

506

STATISTICS

DEMOGRAPHY

Population: 8,400,000 (2002)
Annual growth: 1.9 % (1985-2000)
Estimates for year 2015: 10,215,000 (2000)
Annual growth to year 2015: 1.5 % (2000)
Urban population: 35.7 % (2000)
Urban growth: 3.7 % (2000)
Children per woman: 4.2 (2000)

HEALTH

Life expectancy at birth: 53 years (2000-2005)
male: 50 years (2000-2005)
female: 56 years (2000-2005)
Maternal mortality: 520 per 100,000 live births (1985/99)
Infant mortality: 81 per 1,000 (2000)
Under-5 child mortality: 125 per 1,000 (2000)
Daily calorie supply: 1,977 per capita (1999)
8 doctors per 100,000 people (1992)
Safe water: 46 % (2000)

EDUCATION

Literacy: 49 % (2000)
male: 51 % (2000)
female: 46 % (2000)
School enrolment (net):
Primary total: 42 % (1994/2000)
male: 66 % (1995/99)
female: 66 % (1995/99)
Secondary (gross):
male: 21 % (1995/97)
female: 20 % (1995/97)
Tertiary (gross): 1 % (1997)
Primary school teachers: one for every 31 pupils (1998)

COMMUNICATIONS

3 newspapers (1996), 55 radios (1997), 5 TV sets (2000) and 9 main telephone lines (2000) per 1,000 people

ECONOMY

Per capita, GDP: $ 1,467 (2000)
Annual growth: -0.9 % (2000)
Annual inflation: 13.7 % (2000)
Consumer price index: 198.7 (2000)
Currency: 26.9 gourdes = $ 1 (03/2002)
Cereal imports: 512,179 metric tons (2000)
Fertilizer use: 156 kg per ha (1999)
Exports: $ 506 million (2000)
Imports: $ 1,109 million (2000)
External debt: $ 1,169 million (2000); $ 144 per capita (2000)
Debt service: 10.0 % of exports (1999)
Development aid received: $ 263 million (1999); $ 33.7 per capita (1999); 6.10 % of GNP (1999)

ENERGY

Consumption: 271.0 Kgs of oil equivalent per capita yearly (1998); 23.7 % imported (1999)

HDI (ranking/value): 134 / 0.467 (1999)

---

[31] On June 27, indirect talks began in New York between General Cédras and ousted president Aristide. Meanwhile, the UN Security Council imposed a financial, oil and arms embargo on Haiti. In July, Aristide and Cédras signed an agreement that guaranteed the return of the President as well as an amnesty for all military leaders involved in the coup. In accordance with the agreement, Aristide named Robert Malval prime minister.

[32] However, a new wave of violence soon broke out in Haiti, to prevent the agreement from going into effect. In October, a US warship patrolled the coast near the capital. An armed mob threatened the American troops, so US President Clinton ordered the ship back to US Guantanamo military base in Cuba. In the meantime, the Security Council reinstated the naval embargo.

[33] Malval's Justice Minister, Guy Malary, was assassinated. The attack was carried out almost in the same place where Antoine Izmery, a pro-Aristide businessman, had been killed a month earlier. Those responsible for the killings were members of the pro-military Front for the Advancement and Progress of Haiti, who used the same tactics as the Tontons-Macoutes.

[34] The UN embargo destroyed the formal economy and increased poverty, although it did not substantially affect the lifestyle of the country's wealthy families. Violence rose: according to a UN report, 426 Aristide supporters were murdered between May 1993 and February 1994.

[35] On October 15, Aristide returned after the coup leaders had gone into exile and the country was occupied by a multinational force led by the US. While in exile, the President had promised to implement a structural adjustment program prescribed by the IMF. In December, troops were demobilized in order to create a new national police force.

[36] In spite of meaning to punish those responsible for human rights abuses, Aristide - under sustained pressure from Washington - was forced to offer merely symbolic gestures in most cases, such as a gravestone in memory of the victims of death squads.

[37] In 1995, a contingent of UN troops replaced the multinational forces. In November, René Préval, an Aristide supporter, won the elections with 88 per cent of the vote and took office on February 7 1996. Préval requested the UN peace forces to remain for an additional period of time due to the numerous conflicts and acts of violence which involved national police. Kidnappings and murders - including those of eight policemen out of duty - did not stop, while popular uprisings were violently repressed.

[38] On July 16 1996, Claude Raymond, a general and minister in Duvalier's cabinet, was arrested for terrorist activities. Four days later, André Armand, former Army sergeant and leader of the retired soldiers lobby group, was killed by unknown assailants after publicly stating that retired army members were plotting to assassinate Préval and former president Aristide. The resignation of Prime Minister Rosny Smarth in 1997 and the Presidents decision to dissolve Parliament and govern by decree heightened political tensions and confrontation with the opposition. Jacques-Edouard Alexis, of the Lavalas political organization, was named in March 1999 to take over as Prime Minister.

[39] In 1997, UN peacekeeping troops were replaced by a 300-member civilian police force, which completed its withdrawal in January 2000. Elections slated for March of that year were postponed in order to resolve voter registration problems. A demonstration of Aristide supporters against election officials led to the deaths of four people in March 2000.

[40] In April that year the country's most noted journalist, Jean Dominique, owner of Radio Haiti Inter, was assassinated on arrival at work. The case, which had not been resolved two years later, became the best-financed and organized crime investigation in the country's history. A senator loyal to Aristide used his legislative immunity to avoid testimony, evidence for the case disappeared, and one of the witnesses was killed and his body vanished. Months later, another journalist was killed with a machete by presumed government allies.

[41] The opposition boycotted the February 2001 presidential elections, forcing their leading candidates not to participate. They appointed an 'alternative president'. Despite the boycott and the lack of international observers, the elections took place and gave an overwhelming victory to Aristide, who thus took office as President for a third time. Although the Electoral Council reported that 62 per cent of the electorate had voted, the foreign missions and the local and international media alike said that only 20 to 30 per cent had voted. Talks between Aristide's governing party and the opposition alliance failed in an attempt to establish a new Electoral Council to review the ballot. The motive of the dispute was the number of parliamentary seats belonging to each party. International economic aid had been suspended since the 2000 elections, which were as lacking in transparency as the subsequent elections.

[42] In December 2001, a group of heavily-armed former soldiers entered the presidential palace and opened fire on the security personnel in an attempted coup that left 12 people dead. Former policeman Guy Philippe was later arrested in the Dominican Republic after being fingered as the mastermind behind the failed coup.

[43] The economic crisis led Prime Minister Cherestal to resign in January 2002. In March, Parliament approved - by broad majority - the appointment of Yvon Neptune to the post. Neptune, a close friend of Aristide, promised to engage in dialogue with the opposition forces in order to pull the country out of political and socio-economic crisis.

[44] Most of Haiti's resources are in the hands of 15 per cent of the population (the one per cent of the population that is of European origin owns half of the country's wealth). The remaining 80 per cent live in poverty, most of them in extreme poverty, lacking access to sanitation, water, and electricity. Two-thirds of Haitians do not eat a proper meal a day, and most of the rest eat only once a day, usually a meal lacking basic nutrition requirements. These figures contribute to Haiti's ranking as the poorest country in the Western Hemisphere. ∎

Honduras

Population: 6,732,000 (2002)
Land area: 111,890 SQ KM
Capital: Tegucigalpa
Currency: Lempira
Language: Spanish

Honduras

Evidence shows the Copan valley, in the western part of present-day Honduras, has been occupied for about 4,000 years, by Maya people, although the city of Copan was inhabited for only about 500 years. Copan reached its peak around 500-800 AD during the Classic Period, when about 15,000 people lived in the area, but like other Maya city-states it was abandoned mysteriously around 900 AD. A variety of other peoples lived in the rest of the territory, including Chibcha (see Colombia) and Lenca.

2 Gold stimulated Spanish conquest of the area early in the 16th century. Despite strong resistance from the Indians led by Lempira, Pedro de Alvarado - who was in charge of the final Spanish conquest - joined the territory to the Captaincy-General of Guatemala. The initial mining centers were located near the Guatemalan border, around Gracias, but in the early 1540s the center for mining shifted eastward to the Río Guayape Valley, and silver joined gold as a major product. This change contributed to the rapid decline of Gracias and the rise of Comayagua as the center of colonial Honduras. The demand for labor led to revolts and accelerated the decimation of the native population. As a result, African slavery was introduced into Honduras, and by 1545 the province may have had as many as 2,000 slaves. In the 1570s, a silver strike in the highlands brought a rush of prospectors to Honduras, resulting in the rise of an important population center at Tegucigalpa, which competed thereafter, especially in the 18th century, with Comayagua. However, agriculture, the enduring economic base of Central America, was slow to develop in Honduras.

3 Development of Spanish society in the Honduras area was hindered by coastal attacks from the pirates and buccaneers endemic to the Caribbean and eventually by a concerted British effort to control the coastal areas. For long periods the Spanish utilized a soft defense against the Caribbean threat, falling back to the highlands and to the Pacific coast, which were generally closer to their network of communication and transportation. Thus, the British - counting on the

indispensable support of the Sambo-Miskito peoples - came to control the Caribbean's Mosquito coast. In the 18th century, however, the Spanish Bourbon kings made a sustained effort to recover these areas, and their success in the Gulf of Honduras was manifested by the completion of a fort at Omoa on the gulf by 1779.

4 In 1821, Honduras gained independence from Spain. Together with the other Central American provinces it joined the short-lived Mexican Empire of Iturbide, which collapsed two years later. Francisco Morazán and other Honduran leaders of the last century, sought in vain to set up an independent Central American federation. Their efforts were no match for Britain's 'Balkanization' tactics.

5 With the liberal reform of 1880, mining became the backbone of the economy. To encourage the development of this sector the country was opened to foreign investment and technology. In 1898, another 'empire' managed to penetrate Honduras: the notorious US United Fruit Company (Unifruco). The Company took over vast tracts of land. It produced almost the entire fruit output of the country, ruled railroads, ships and ports, and dictated many key political decisions.

6 US Marines invaded Honduras in 1924, imposing a formal democracy and allowing Unifruco to establish a monopoly in banana production by buying out its main competitor, the Cuyamel Fruit Company. Washington eventually

handed power over to Tiburcio Carias Andino, who governed Honduras from 1933 to 1949.

7 Border disputes with Guatemala led to US arbitration in 1930. In 1969, friction developed with El Salvador when the number of Salvadoran peasants emigrating to Honduras reached a critical level. This led to a further war, which was triggered by a soccer game, and was finally ended with mediation by the Organization of American States (see El Salvador).

8 In 1971, nationalists and liberals signed the Unity Pact. General Osvaldo López Arellano, in power since 1963, permitted elections and Ramón Ernesto Cruz of the National Party, was elected President.

9 However in 1972 López Arellano overthrew the Cruz administration. He demonstrated his sensitivity to peasant demands for land reform and began to impose controls upon United Brands (as Unifruco was now called). This resulted in López Arellano's resignation and his replacement by Colonel Juan A Melgar Castro.

10 The army commander-in-chief, General Policarpo Paz García, took power in August 1978. This regime became closely allied to that of the dictator Anastasio Somoza in neighboring Nicaragua. Nicaragua's Sandinista Revolution in 1979 hastened the election of a constituent assembly which promptly ratified Paz García as President. General elections were

held in 1981, but leftist parties were banned. Liberal Party candidate, Roberto Suazo Córdova, won the presidency and was inaugurated in January 1982.

11 The price of consumer goods immediately rose and an anti-terrorist law was passed forbidding strikes as intrinsically subversive. Death squads acted with impunity and opposition political figures disappeared daily.

12 Honduras tolerated the presence of US troops and Nicaraguan counter-revolutionary bases in its territory. It is estimated that, in 1983, the Pentagon had 1,200 soldiers in Honduras. Apart from intervening directly in armed operations, they gave military instruction, logistic support and built infrastructure works. The Nicaraguan 'contras' had some 15,000 fighters, together with some 30,000 Nicaraguan refugees.

13 Rafael Callejas, candidate for the National Party, had an easy victory in 1989 in elections that were considered fraudulent. Backed by the US and business circles, Callejas began a complete liberalization of the economy.

14 In 1990, after the Sandinistas were defeated in the Nicaraguan elections, the US Bush administration significantly reduced economic aid to Honduras. The Government decreed in December an amnesty for political prisoners and outlaws. The anti-terrorist law was abolished, and a climate of political consensus was created.

15 After eight years in exile, in January 1991, four leftist politicians returned to Honduras, announcing the end of the armed struggle.

16 Armed Forces commander, general Arnulfo Cantarera, accused of human rights violations, was dismissed and replaced by general Luis Discua, who headed a growing intervention of military power into political life. The murder of opposition members and other abuses committed by the military was denounced by the Committee in Defense of Human Rights.

17 The new agrarian laws authorized the sale of expropriated lands, which favoured the speculation of multinational agricultural companies. Popular discontent was expressed through

the ballots, when opposition candidate Carlos Roberto Reina triumphed in the 1993 elections.

[18] One of the Government's first resolutions was to abolish compulsory military service. But in August 1994, bowing in to military pressure, the Government accepted a temporary draft to fill 7,000 places in the Armed Forces. The Government dissolved the National Board of Investigations, accused of torturing prisoners.

[19] As a result in the decline of banana exports to the European Union, the US Tela Railroad Company, a banana firm, closed four of its factories and suspended 3,000 of its laborers. The Government forced the firm to reopen and take the workers back. The company negotiated with the trade union, taking back 1,200 employees, but keeping 1,000 women out.

[20] While the armed forces kept policing the cities, the Legislative Assembly began the process of constitutional reform which resulted in granting control of public security forces to the civilian power. The Unit of Criminal Investigation, led by civilians, began operating in January 1995, replacing of the secret police dissolved the previous year. The new body, formed initially with 1,500 agents, was trained by Israeli police and the US FBI. At the time, more than 50 people were murdered each day in Honduras.

[21] Senior government officials were jailed in 1995 for their involvement in the sale of official passports. The Supreme Court of Justice revoked former president Callejas' immunity so he could testify regarding the forged documents and misappropriation of public funds. President Reina was also investigated on the use of state funds for private purposes.

[22] The IMF imposed strict cuts on government spending. The Government cancelled military controls on the police and reduced the Army size.

[23] In October 1997 the police prevented some 400 people from putting a statue of Lempira, a leader of indigenous resistance against the Spanish conquest, in a public site in Tegucigalpa. A statue of Christopher Columbus was taken from its pedestal and destroyed by the demonstrators.

[24] On taking office in January 1998, President Carlos Flores was willing to form a national unity government and to reach a truce with the opposition linked to the military. With 80 per cent of the population living in extreme poverty, 228 landowners held more than 75 per cent of the country's lands.

[25] In October that year, the destruction wreaked by Hurricane Mitch amounted to over $5.36 billion. It killed 24,000 people throughout Central America, 14,000 of whom were Hondurans. Likewise, two million Hondurans lost their homes in the disaster. One year later floods killed 35 people and covered 14,000 hectares of arable land, causing $20 million in losses. The authorities said that, had they received the aid promised by developed countries after Mitch had struck, they could have dredged the rivers and avoided the new catastrophe.

[26] In 2001 the country suffered a drought which wiped out 90 per cent of the grain harvest, the staple food for the rural population. After declaring a state of emergency, the country received food assistance from the UN World Food Program.

[27] After 40 years of estrangement, and nearing the end of his mandate, Flores decided in January 2002 to reinstate diplomatic relations with Cuba. The decision was the outcome of a rapprochement policy initiated in 1998 with the establishment of an Honduran office in Havana, and which promptly resulted in medical and sanitation aid by the Cuban Government after Hurricane Mitch.

[28] That month, the National Party candidate, Ricardo Maduro, became the country's new President, after receiving 52.2 per cent of the vote. As a result of the economic crisis, the number of hold-ups rose, and kidnappings had become a common way to obtain money. Shortly after his coming to office, Maduro - who had promised he would put an end to this type of violence - formed a force of 10,000 soldiers to fight crime. ■

PROFILE

ENVIRONMENT

80 per cent of the land is covered by mountains and rainforests. Both population and economic activity are concentrated along the Caribbean coast and in the southern highlands, close to the border with El Salvador. The coastal plains have the largest banana plantations in Central America. Coffee, tobacco and corn are grown in the southern part of the country. Deforestation and uncontrolled development have led to soil depletion. Mining activity has caused water pollution, especially in Lake Yojo, the main source of fresh water.

SOCIETY

Peoples: Hondurans are of mixed Mayan and European descent. There is a 10 per cent minority of native Americans; 2 per cent are Afro-American. Garifunas, descendants of fugitive slaves and native Americans, live along the Caribbean coast and on the nearby islands, maintaining their traditional lifestyles.
Languages: Spanish is the official and most widely-spoken language; Garifuna, various Indian languages (eg Lenca and Miskito).
Religions: Roman Catholic 85 per cent; Protestant 10 per cent.
Political Parties: National Party (NP), conservative; Liberal Party of Honduras (LPH); Party for Innovation and Unity-Social-Democracy (PIU); Democratic Unification Party, left (DUP); Christian Democratic Party of Honduras (CDPH).
Social Organizations: The Confederation of Honduran Workers (CTH) founded in 1964 and affiliated to the ORIT (Regional Interamerican Labor Organization), is the only officially-recognized labor federation. The General Workers' Central Union (CGT), Social-Christian; the United Federation of Workers (FUT); the Federation of Honduran Workers' Unions (FESITRAH); the Independent Workers' Federation and the United National Peasants' Front of Honduras (FUNACAMPH). Coordinating Council of Honduran Peasant Organizations (COCOH); Honduran Indigenous Support Comittee; Committee in Defense of Human Rights (CODEH); Federation of University Students of Honduras.

THE STATE

Official Name: República de Honduras.
Administrative divisions: 18 Departments.
Capital: Tegucigalpa 919,000 people (1999).
Other cities: San Pedro Sula 616,500 people; La Ceiba 108,900; El Progreso 106,500; Choluteca 93,100 (2000).
Government: Ricardo Maduro, President since January 2002. Unicameral Legislature: National Congress, with 128 members.
National Holiday: September 15, Independence Day (1821).
Armed Forces: 18,800 troops, 13,200 conscripts (1995).
Other: 5,500 members of the Public Security Force.

DEMOGRAPHY
Population: 6,732,000 (2002)
Annual growth: 2.9 % (1985-2000)
Estimates for year 2015: 8,703,000 (2000)
Annual growth to year 2015: 2.0 % (2000)
Urban population: 46.9 % (2000)
Urban growth: 3.8 % (2000)
Children per woman: 4.0 (2000)

HEALTH
Life expectancy at birth: 66 years (2000-2005)
male: 63 years (2000-2005)
female: 69 years (2000-2005)
Maternal mortality: 110 per 100,000 live births (1985/99)
Infant mortality: 32 per 1,000 (2000)
Under-5 child mortality: 40 per 1,000 (2000)
Daily calorie supply: 2,396 per capita (1999)
83 doctors per 100,000 people (1997)
Safe water: 88 % (2000)

EDUCATION
Literacy: 81 % (2000)
male: 78 % (2000)
female: 85 % (2000)
School enrolment (net):
Primary total: 86 % (1994/2000)
male: 85 % (1995/99)
female: 86 % (1995/99)
Secondary (gross):
male: 29 % (1995/97)
female: 37 % (1995/97)
Tertiary (gross): 13 % (1998)
Primary school teachers: one for every 33 pupils (1996)

COMMUNICATIONS
55 newspapers (1996), 412 radios (1997), 96 TV sets (2000) and 46 main telephone lines (2000) per 1,000 people

ECONOMY
Per capita, GDP: $ 2,453 (2000)
Annual growth: 2.2 % (2000)
Annual inflation: -15.2 % (2000)
Consumer price index: 160.3 (2000)
Currency: 16.1 lempiras = $ 1 (03/2002)
Cereal imports: 484,698 metric tons (2000)
Food import dependency: 16 % (2000)
Fertilizer use: 1,082 kg per ha (1999)
Exports: $ 2,512 million (2000)
Imports: $ 3,344 million (2000)
External debt: $ 5,487 million (2000); $ 855 per capita (2000)
Debt service: 13.5 % of exports (1999)
Development aid received: $ 817 million (1999) ; $ 129.3 per capita (1999) ; 15.20 % of GNP (1999)

ENERGY
Consumption: 541.9 Kgs of oil equivalent per capita yearly (1998); 44.4 % imported (1999)

HDI (ranking/value): 107 / 0.634 (1999)

Hungary

Population: 9,867,000 (2002)
Land area: 92,340 SQ KM
Capital: Budapest
Currency: Forint
Language: Hungarian

Magyarország

The territory of Hungary belonged to the Roman provinces of Pannonia and Dacia. By the end of the 4th century Rome had lost Pannonia which had been occupied by Germans, Slavs, Huns and Avars. The latter ruled over the Danube basin during the 7th and 8th centuries, until they were conquered by Charlemagne.

[2] Charlemagne's successors set up a series of Duchies in the western and northern parts of the basin, while the southern and eastern parts were under the sphere of influence of the Byzantine Empire and Bulgaria. The Duchy of Croatia became independent in 869 and Moravia put up stiff resistance to the Carolingians until the appearance of the Magyars.

[3] The Magyars had organized a federation of tribes west of the lower Don. These were made up by several clans led by a hereditary chieftain. The federation was called On-Ogur (Ten Arrows); 'Hungarian' is a derivation of this term in the Slav language. In 982 Emperor Rudolf turned to the Magyars to break Moravian resistance.

[4] Led by Arpad, the prince elected by the chiefs of the seven groups Hungarians, the Magyars crossed the Carpathians and conquered the inhabitants of the central plateau. Moravia was defeated in 906 and Pannonia a year later. The Hungarians then expanded northwards and repeatedly raided the rest of Europe.

[5] The German Emperor Otto I defeated Arpad in 955 and halted Magyar expansion. Arpad's heirs reunified the tribes and adopted Western Christianity. Stephen I was crowned by Rome, subsequently laying the foundations of the Hungarian State.

[6] The question of succession upon Stephen's death triggered two centuries of instability, but Hungary consolidated its dominions as far as the Carpathian mountains and Transylvania in the north, and the region between the Sava and Drava rivers in the south. In addition, it ruled over Croatia, Bosnia, and Northern Dalmatia (although the latter remained a separate state).

[7] With the Mongol invasion of the 13th century, Hungary lost half of its population. This prompted the Kingdom to reorganize and open its doors to new settlers; however, it had to make important concessions to the Cuman overlords and immigrants, who further weakened the Kingdom. Finally, the succession of foreigner Charles Robert of Anjou to the throne, stabilized the country.

[8] As the struggles between the Holy Roman Empire and the Papacy did not involve Hungary, the 14th century was the country's golden age. The Kingdom established friendly relations with Austria, Bohemia and Poland, and strong links with Bosnia. However, during this period the country seized Dalmatia from Venice, and other territories from Serbia.

[9] Sigismund of Luxembourg (1387-1437) was both a German and Czech king. His long absences and arbitrary rule enabled the Hungarian Diet (parliament), which was made up of nobles, to expand its power. The Diet's consent was required in order for laws to be passed. Taxes were continually being exacted from the peasants, who started revolts in the north and in Transylvania.

[10] After another controversial succession, Matthias Corvinus of Prague was elected king of Hungary in 1458. He ruled over his country with an iron fist. With the help of the Black Army, an army of mercenaries, Matthias subdued his enemies inside the country and expanded his dominion over Bosnia, Serbia, Walachia, and Moldova. He also carried out a series of campaign against Bohemia and Austria.

[11] Upon Matthias' death in 1490 the magnates - the richest nobles - appointed Vladislav II, who was King of Bohemia and whose weak personality was well known. The Black Army was disbanded but the oppressed peasants rebelled again in 1514; the rebellion was ruthlessly put down. Meanwhile, Austria recovered the southern provinces and established its authority over Hungary.

[12] Hungary was conquered by the Ottoman empire in 1526. At first the Sultan supported Zapolya of Hapsburg to succeed the King who had been killed in battle. However, upon Zapoyla's death he occupied Budapest himself, and annexed a large portion to the south and center of the country. Croatia and the western and northern strip of the country remained under the rule of Ferdinand of Hapsburg, who had to pay tribute to the Turkish Empire.

[13] During the 17th and 18th centuries Hungary was under two empires whose only interest in the country lay in the tributes it paid. The situation became more volatile when the majority of the population embraced the Reformation, while Vienna attempted to re-establish Catholicism. Even the nobles began to react against absolutism, peasant oppression and stagnation.

[14] During the 1848 revolution, the Hungarian Diet passed the April Laws, which brought changes in agricultural and fiscal matters. They reorganized on a more representative basis and proposed the reunification of the country and the creation of a separate administration in Budapest. The reform was met with distrust on the part of large landowners and Serbian, Romanian, and Croatian minorities.

[15] When the revolution was defeated, Austria, aided by Russia, annulled all reforms and regained control over Hungary. When Austria was defeated by Prussia in 1866, Vienna decided to subdivide its empire and accepted Hungary's April Laws. A 'Nationalities Law' guaranteed respect for the rights of minorities, giving way to the establishment of the Austro-Hungarian Empire in 1867.

[16] In the early 20th century, Hungarian politics was still dominated by conservative landowners, as most business people were foreigners, Jewish or German, and the majority of the population remained excluded from political activity. Minorities continued to be oppressed and the country lacked a strong sense of autonomy.

[17] With the collapse of the Hapsburg empire during World War I, a provisional government took power and proclaimed the Republic of Hungary. But Serbians, Czechs and Romanians seized two-thirds of the country and the central government was paralyzed. In 1919 a communist rebellion was followed by the formation of a 'Soviet' republic.

[18] Bela Kun's Bolsheviks expected Moscow to support them, but they were forced to flee when the Romanian troops took over the capital. The European powers pushed Romania into withdrawing and installed a provisional government. The 1920 Parliament restored monarchy and appointed Admiral Milkos Horthy as provisional ruler.

[19] In the Trianon Treaty, the victorious allies recognized Hungarian independence, but Yugoslavia, Romania, and Czechoslovakia remained in possession of most of the country's territory and 60 per cent of its population. Austria, Poland, and Italy also benefited from the partition of Hungary.

[20] Hungary was forced to pay heavy reparations; its industry and production were left in a shambles. Unemployment rose to unprecedented figures and nearly 400,000 refugees arrived from the

territories it had lost. The middle classes and the refugees set up right-wing armed groups, blaming the left for their ruin.

[21] Funds granted by the League of Nations, followed by private investments and credits, alleviated domestic tension, but the depression of the 1930s had serious effects on Hungary. Horthy formed an extreme-right government which sided with Germany, while anti-Semitism grew within the country.

[22] The alliance with Berlin enabled Budapest to recover part of Slovakia, Ruthenia, and the north of Transylvania. Hungary cooperated in the German attacks on Romania, Yugoslavia and the USSR, but nothing could stop the Red Army counter-offensive. In the Treaty of Paris, Hungary was forced to retreat to the borders fixed in the Treaty of Trianon.

[23] In 1944 a provisional assembly formed a coalition government and took up a program proposed by communist leaders and backed by the USSR. This program included the expropriation of large estates, the nationalization of banking and

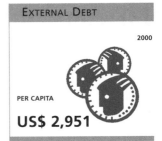
heavy industry, as well as guarantees for small landowners and private initiative, democratic rights and liberties.

[24] The Communists, at that time represented by the Workers' Socialist Party, assumed control of the government. In 1946 the Constitution of the Peoples' Republic of Hungary was established.

[25] In 1948, the Communist Government forcibly collectivized agriculture and started a series of development plans which stressed the development of heavy industry. Upon Stalin's death in 1953, Matyas Rakosi, head of government, was replaced by Imre Nagy, who promised political changes.

[26] In 1955, Nagy was deposed and expelled from the party. Rakosi returned for a short period, until 1956, when he handed power over to Erno Gero, who had similar political views to his own.

[27] Students staged a demonstration in Budapest, and were joined by the rest of the population. Gero reacted harshly: the police were instructed to shoot into the crowd, and the demonstration turned into a popular revolution, backed by the Army. The Government was handed back to Nagy, heading a broad national coalition.

[28] In November 1956, Nagy announced the withdrawal of Hungary from the Warsaw Pact, and requested that the United Nations recognize its neutrality. The Red Army, which had withdrawn during the revolution, occupied the country again and reinstated the communist government, led by Janos Kadar.

[29] Kadar followed Soviet guidelines, where foreign policy was concerned. As for domestic policy, central planning was partly liberalized from 1968 onwards, the standard of living rose, but bureaucracy and corruption increased.

[30] Sexual discrimination continued on all fronts. In 1981, while women made up 45 per cent of all workers, they were systematically paid less than men and their job opportunities were restricted to specific fields of traditionally female labor.

[31] Kadar was elected First Secretary of the Hungarian Workers' Socialist Party (WSP) and head of government, and he ruled without serious opposition until March 1986, when a youth protest march was heavily crushed. Two years later some 10,000 people demanded freedom and reforms in a demonstration in Budapest.

[32] The Government relaxed press censorship and permitted the formation of trade unions and independent political groups - such as the newly constituted Hungarian Democratic Forum (HDF) - to be formed.

[33] Between 1986 and 1988 Hungarian and Austrian environmentalists protested against the construction of a dam on the Danube; part of a Hungarian-

Czechoslovakian project supported by Austria. The Budapest Government resisted the pressure but in the end the project was shelved.

[34] In January 1989 Parliament passed a law legalizing strikes, public demonstrations and political associations. Meanwhile, it adopted an austerity plan which reduced subsidies and devalued the currency. Unemployment was expected to rise to 100,000 and annual inflation to 30 per cent.

[35] The WSP also approved the elimination of the single party system and agreed to celebrate Independence Day on March 15, the date of the 1848 revolt against Austria. In March 1989, 100,000 people demonstrated in Budapest, demanding elections and the withdrawal of Soviet troops.

[36] The opposition candidates won the provincial elections held in 1989. In August, two million workers went on strike, protesting against price increases. In October, after an agreement between the WSP and the opposition, Parliament proclaimed the Republic of Hungary and eliminated the single-party system.

[37] Hungary was the first country in the Warsaw Pact to break its Cold War alliances. Within two years, Budapest established relations with Israel, South Korea, and South Africa.

[38] By the end of the year, the Workers' Socialist Party had become the Hungarian Socialist Party, with one faction deciding to keep its old name. In the 1990 elections, the HDF obtained 43 per cent of the vote, forming a coalition government with two smaller parties: the Socialist Party and the WSP. These received 10.3 and 3.5 per cent of the vote, respectively.

[39] Hungary had a foreign debt of $21 billion, the largest in Europe. Its agricultural and industrial production fell by 10 per cent - a situation aggravated by IMF policies preventing domestic capital accumulation and favoring foreign investors. In 1990, inflation reached 30 per cent, with the average family spending 75 per cent of its income on basic consumer goods. The following year, the figure was 90 per cent, for the same goods. Of its 10

PROFILE

ENVIRONMENT

The country is a vast plain with a maximum altitude of 1,000 m partially ringed by the Carpathian Mountains. The mountainous region has abundant mineral resources (manganese, bauxite, coal). Between the Danube and its tributary, the Tisza, lies a very fertile plain, site of most of the country's farming activity. Cattle are raised on the grasslands east of the Tisza. In the past 30 years there has been rapid industrial expansion, particularly in the production of steel, non-ferrous metals, chemicals and railway equipment. Oil and natural gas deposits have been found in the Szegia and Zala river basins. 41 per cent of the population is exposed to sulfur dioxide and nitrogen dioxide in the air. The sulfurous emissions are greater than in most eastern European countries.

SOCIETY

Peoples: Hungarian 92 per cent; Croatian; German; Roma; Romanian; Serbian; Slovak and Slovene.
Religions: Roman Catholic 57.8 per cent, Protestant 21.6 per cent; no religious 18.5 per cent; other 1.9 per cent.
Languages: Hungarian (official), 98 per cent; German; Roma and Slovak.
Political Parties: Fidesz - Hungarian Civic Party; Hungarian Socialist Party; Independent Smallholders, Land Workers and Civic Party; Alliance of Free Democrats (SZDSZ); Hungarian Democratic Forum (HDF); Hungarian Truth and Life Party.
Social Organizations: Autonomous Union Confederation, Democratic Union Confederation, National Confederation of Hungarian Trade Unions; Hungarian Feminist Network.

THE STATE

Official Name: Magyar Koztarsasag (Hungarian Republic).
Administrative Divisions: 19 Counties and the capital.
Capital: Budapest 1,836,000 people (1999).
Other cities: Debrecen 209,600 people; Miskolc 181,900; Szeged 170,600 (2000).
Government: Ferenc Mádl, President since August 2000. Viktor Orbán, Prime Minister since July 1998. Both are elected by the single-chamber National Assembly (Legislature, 386 representatives elected for five-year terms). This Assembly is the supreme authority in the Republic. Eight seats in the Assembly are reserved for each of the country's minorities.
National Holiday: March 15, Independence Day (1848); October 23, Declaration of the Republic (1989).
Armed Forces: 64,300 (1996).
Other: Border Guard, 15,900. Civil Defense Troops, 2,000. Internal Security Troops, 2,500.

million inhabitants, 2 million were living below the poverty line.

⁴⁰ In this new era in Hungary, women's representation in politics declined. In the 1990 elections, women won 7.5 per cent of the seats, while in 1985 they had held 21 per cent. Women constitute 46 per cent of the active workforce, but this began to change with the increasingly popular ideological position of restoring the 'natural order'. The idea of women staying at home clashed with the new economic reality of the country, where two salaries were needed to cover even the most basic needs of a nuclear family.

⁴¹ The women's movement was also heavily involved in the abortion issue. Over 4 million legal abortions were carried out in Hungary in the past decades. However, in the early 1990s political parties, except for the Federation of Young Democrats and the Free Democrats, came out against the practice. Meanwhile, the Hungarian Women's Network campaigned against the criminalization of abortion and in defense of the living standards, working rights and health of women.

⁴² In January 1992, the Government decided to reduce the public deficit, which stood at a level in excess of $900 million in 1991. They hoped to achieve this by imposing a four per cent reduction in public spending. Growing popular discontent, which was reflected in a reduced turn-out for elections and in repeated union strikes, have forced Joszef Lantall's right-of-center government to take a more cautious position.

⁴³ The economic crisis encouraged nationalistic and xenophobic demonstrations, including the notorious publication of a manifesto signed by the writer and vice-president of the Democratic Forum, Istvan Csurka, blaming the ex-communists, the 'westernized' liberals, the Roma and the Jews for 'the deterioration of the social climate'.

⁴⁴ Horn was sworn in as Prime Minister and the electoral supremacy of the former communists was confirmed in local elections toward the end of the year. In March 1995, his

'honeymoon' with the electorate came to an end, when an unpopular package of economic measures was approved. The Government drastically reduced the education budget, funding for unemployment and maternity benefits, in order to cut back the fiscal deficit.

⁴⁵ Horn continued his rapprochement with the West and negotiation with neighboring countries in order to help the Hungarian minorities living abroad to 'preserve their cultural identity'. In May 1996, Hungary signed an agreement with Slovakia for the protection of ethnic minorities and, in September that year, a similar accord with Romania was signed.

⁴⁶ In early 1997, Hungary started negotiating NATO membership. Budapest accepted the installation of nuclear weapons and NATO troops in Hungarian territory as a pre-condition to joining the military alliance. In November, membership was approved in a referendum where 85 per cent of those who voted supported the integration. Half the electorate (around 4 million people) abstained.

⁴⁷ Bilateral relations with Romania, home to a large Hungarian minority, improved following former communist Ion Iliescu's defeat and the removal of the ultra-nationalist Romanian parties, which were hostile to the Hungarian and Gypsy/Roma minorities. In 1998, Hungary continued to focus its diplomatic efforts on admission into the European Union.

⁴⁸ Parliament voted overwhelmingly in February 1999 in favor of the country's joining NATO: 330 Deputies supported the decision, while 13 voted against and one abstained. The major force against entering the organization was the extreme right Party for Justice and Life. In March, Hungary, Poland and the Czech Republic were admitted into the alliance, one month before initially planned and just two weeks before the NATO bombings against Yugoslavia began.

⁴⁹ A 100,000 cubic meter cyanide spill - originating at a mining site in Romania - in the Tisza river valley in February 2000 resulted in the regions worst environmental disaster since the Chernobyl nuclear catastrophe in 1986. All life along a

40-km stretch of the river died, from microbes to fish and plants. The river, which flows into the Danube, contaminated an important source of potable water for Yugoslavia, as well as Romania and Hungary. Two smaller acid spills occurred in March 2000, prompting authorities to take legal action against the Romanian mining company, which had filed a bankruptcy claim almost immediately after the first accident.

⁵⁰ In June 2000, the National Assembly elected the independent Ferenc Mádl as president, the second democratically elected leader of the country. Three electoral rounds were necessary because in the first two rounds Mádl had not managed to reach the required two-thirds.

⁵¹ Like other Eastern European countries that wish to join the European Union, Hungary must solve the issue of the free movement of workers, as a part of the conditions of incorporation. So far, it has been the only candidate to conclude negotiations with the EU on this. This is a highly controversial topic for the 15 EU member countries because they fear a massive immigration of 'cheap' labor after Eastern European countries join the Union. If the remaining negotiations with Hungary about environmental, agricultural and employment issues continue at a fast pace, the country might enter the EU by 2004.

⁵² As a part of the 1,000 year celebration after Hungary's consolidation as a nation, a monument was re-erected, which had been first built in 1934. It commemorates four major national tragedies: the defeat by Tatars, Turkish and Hapsburgs and the Peace of Trianon, which caused the loss of two-thirds of the territory. During Communist times, it had been demolished, and finally it was restored in 2001 with the aim of remembering these events.

⁵³ In 2001, the Hungarian economy grew 4.2 per cent, with an important increase of the GDP and a slight but continuous decrease of unemployment, which positioned the country in the first place among the countries of Eastern Europe. ∎

STATISTICS

DEMOGRAPHY
Population: 9,867,000 (2002)
Annual growth: -0.4 % (1985-2000)
Estimates for year 2015: 9,254,000 (2000)
Annual growth to year 2015: -0.5 % (2000)
Urban population: 64.0 % (2000)
Urban growth: -0.1 % (2000)
Children per woman: 1.3 (2000)

HEALTH
Life expectancy at birth: 72 years (2000-2005)
male: 68 years (2000-2005)
female: 76 years (2000-2005)
Maternal mortality: 15 per 100,000 live births (1985/99)
Infant mortality: 8 per 1,000 (2000)
Under-5 child mortality: 9 per 1,000 (2000)
Daily calorie supply: 3,437 per capita (1999)
357 doctors per 100,000 people (1998)
Safe water: 99 % (2000)

EDUCATION
Literacy: 99 % (2000)
male: 100 % (2000)
female: 99 % (2000)
School enrolment (net):
Primary total: 97 % (1994/2000)
male: 97 % (1995/99)
female: 96 % (1995/99)
Secondary (gross):
male: 96 % (1995/97)
female: 99 % (1995/97)
Tertiary (gross): 34 % (1998)
Primary school teachers: one for every 11 pupils (1998)

COMMUNICATIONS
46 newspapers (1998), 690 radios (1997), 437 TV sets (2000) and 372 main telephone lines (2000) per 1,000 people
Books: 100 new titles per 100,000 people (1992/94)

ECONOMY
Per capita, GDP: $ 12,416 (2000)
Annual growth: 5.6 % (2000)
Annual inflation: 9.8 % (2000)
Consumer price index: 201.4 (2000)
Currency: 283.2 forint = $ 1 (03/2002)
Cereal imports: 104,386 metric tons (2000)
Food import dependency: 3 % (2000)
Fertilizer use: 804 kg per ha (1999)
Exports: $ 28,541 million (2000)
Imports: $ 30,415 million (2000)
External debt: $ 29,415 million (2000); $ 2,951 per capita (2000)
Debt service: 26.6 % of exports (1999)
Development aid received: $ 248 million (1999); $ 24.6 per capita (1999); 0.50 % of GNP (1999)

ENERGY
Consumption: 2,497.0 Kgs of oil equivalent per capita yearly (1998); 54.6 % imported (1999)

HDI (ranking/value): 36 / 0.829 (1999)

Iceland

Population: 283,000 (2002)
Land Area: 100,250 SQ KM
Capital: Reykjavik
Currency: Kronur
Language: Icelandic

Island

In 874, immigrants of European origin began settling in Iceland: Norwegians, Scots and Irish. Iceland was an independent state between 930 and 1264, but under the terms of the 'Old Treaty' of 1263, the country became part of the kingdom of Norway.

[2] In 1381, Iceland and Norway were conquered by Denmark, but when Norway separated from the Danish Crown in 1814, Iceland remained under its protection. In 1918, Iceland became an associated state of Denmark, until it recovered its independence and a republic was proclaimed in June 1944.

[3] Until the end of the 19th century, Iceland had no roads or bridges in the interior, and trade was entirely in the hands of Danish companies.

[4] In 1915, Icelandic women acquired equal rights with men, being granted the right to vote and to hold elected office. This was attained through the same legislation that granted these rights to Danish women, as at the time, the country was a Danish colony.

[5] After World War I, local agriculture was revitalized through a series of laws aimed at the agrarian sector, and the introduction of modern equipment. From 1920 onwards, the fishing industry grew steadily. In addition, communication throughout the island improved with the building of a new network of inland roads and bridges, and the creation of a coast guard.

[6] Iceland joined the Council of Europe and NATO in 1949. It had no army or navy, and the United States provided the country with defense forces, within NATO's strategic framework. Iceland had only three coast guard ships, one airplane and two helicopters to protect itself against illegal fishing in its territorial waters.

[7] In 1952, Iceland founded the Nordic Council, including Sweden, Norway, Finland and Denmark.

[8] Due to the importance of fishing for Iceland, and the fear of over-fishing near the island by foreign fleets, Reykjavik extended its territorial waters to 12 nautical miles in 1964, and in 1972 to 50 miles. This triggered two serious conflicts known as the 'cod wars' with the United Kingdom. They were resolved by a treaty signed in 1973.

[9] In October 1975, Iceland announced the extension of its territorial waters to 200 nautical miles, citing the protection of the environment and of its economic interests. The failure of the 1973 treaty with the UK, and the impossibility of reaching a new agreement led to the third and most serious 'cod war'.

[10] In February 1976, Iceland briefly broke off relations with the UK, the first breaking of diplomatic ties to occur between NATO members. In June, the two countries reached an agreement and in December, British trawlers withdrew from Icelandic waters. In July 1979, Iceland re-affirmed its 200-mile claim.

[11] NATO membership became a controversial issue in Iceland in the 1970s. In the 1978 election, the joint victory of the Popular Alliance, who favored renouncing the treaty, and the Social Democratic Party (SDP), who were more moderate, caused a two-month delay in the formation of a new government, which depended upon the alliance of the two political groups.

[12] In 1980, Vigdis Finnbogadottir, an independent candidate campaigning against the American military bases on the island, won the presidential election with the support of the Left, making her the country's first female head of state. This post did not confer the power for her significantly to alter government policy, so she was unable to carry out her campaign commitment. In 1984 she was re-elected with no opposition candidates.

[13] In May 1985, Parliament approved a resolution declaring Iceland a 'nuclear-free zone' thereby prohibiting nuclear weapons from being brought into the country. Iceland was chosen as the site for the important summit meeting between US president Ronald Reagan and his Soviet counterpart Mikhail Gorbachev in October 1986.

[14] Although Iceland's continuing NATO membership has not really been threatened, the air base at Keflavik continued to cause controversy. With 2,200 troops, the base is a part of the US 'early warning' system. In September 1988, Iceland's executive power formally declared that there would be no new military projects initiated in the country.

[15] That same year, relations between Reykjavik and Washington became tense. The US claimed that Iceland's decision to catch 80 fin whales and 40 sei whales violated the moratorium imposed by the International Whaling Commission. Iceland replied that it was a scientific program and did not modify its decision.

[16] The United States threatened to boycott Icelandic fish products and two Icelandic whaleboats were sunk by ecological activists in Reykjavik Bay. In 1987, Iceland announced the reduction of its catch to 20 whales. The threats of sanctions continued, and the following year it reduced this quota even further.

[17] In June 1988, President Finnbogadottir was re-elected for her third four-year term, with the backing of the main parties and a margin of over 90 per cent of the electorate. This victory was obtained in spite of the existence of an electoral rival, who had proposed increasing presidential power during the campaign.

[18] In September of 1988, Steingrimur Hermannsson became Prime Minister, as head of a coalition including center and left wing groups, made up of the SDP and the Popular Alliance. The new government promised to initiate an austerity program for Iceland's economy, which was suffering from high inflation and recession, accompanied by currency devaluations.

[19] In August 1989, as a result of growing international pressure, including an international boycott of Icelandic products organized by

WORKERS

1990/2000

UNEMPLOYMENT: 2.3%
LABOR FORCE AS % OF TOTAL:

- FEMALE: 45%
- MALE: 55%

1994/97

EMPLOYMENT DISTRIBUTION:

F
M

- SERVICES   F: 81%   M: 53%
- INDUSTRY   F: 15%   M: 35%
- AGRICULTURE F: 4%   M: 12%

LAND USE

DEFORESTATION: 0.0% annual (1990/95)

1993

- FOREST & WOODLAND: 1.2%
- ARABLE: 0.1%
- OTHER: 98.7%

Greenpeace, Reykjavik announced a two-year suspension of its whale hunting.

[20] In the parliamentary elections of April 1991, the majority again went to the center-left coalition of Prime Minister Hermannsson.

[21] From November 1992, discussion of the potential benefits of joining the European market, with its 380 million consumers, divided the political scene. The opposition Popular Alliance, including socialists and dissident Social Democrats, was against joining. Jon Baldvin Hannibalsson, foreign minister and minister of foreign trade, on the other hand, claimed that joining the EC would bring a flow of capital and new foreign investment to the island.

[22] Fishing, the most important source of employment, went into crisis as reserves of certain species, especially cod, suffered from over-fishing. This situation led to new laws restricting the foreign access to territorial waters, causing friction in commercial relations with other countries.

[23] The tourist industry expanded amid hopes that income from this will entail economic recovery for the island. A series of laws was passed in 1993 to protect polar bears which were being systematically exterminated.

[24] Iceland's entry into the EU was approved by the *Althing* (parliament) on January 1 1993. The preparations for unification caused excitement during that and the following year. There was a feeling that unification would not be achieved and a debate was triggered on whether joining the EU was beneficial or not. Iceland still has not joined the EU in spite of the initial support of its population.

[25] In 1994 a number of Iceland's fishing boats entered an area of the Barents Sea near Russian and Norwegian territorial waters, causing friction in relations with these two countries. Both nations had undertaken a process to recover fish reserves in the area by reducing capture. By the end of 1995, diplomatic negotiations were considered the only solution for the difference.

[26] In the parliamentary elections of April 8 1995, the Independence Party won 25 of the 63 seats and was forced to create an alliance with the Progress Party - with 15 seats - in order to reach a majority in the Althing. The representation of the Popular Alliance and the Women's Alliance dropped, while the new Popular Movement obtained 4 seats.

[27] Iceland's economy managed a slight recovery in 1995 after a slow growth in the previous years. The gross domestic product increased 3 per cent and inflation did not exceed 2 per cent. Unemployment - aggravated by redundancies at the NATO base - reached 5 per cent.

[28] After having governed the country for 16 years, President Vigdis Finnbogadottir did not stand in the June 29 elections in 1996. Olafur Ragnar Grimsson, former finance minister and member of the Popular Alliance, won the election with 41.4 per cent of the vote, taking office on August 1 of that year.

[29] In 1996, marine resources began to be exploited again and fishing quotas were increased after several years of restrictions imposed to preserve the species, and this stimulated economic growth. That year, the GDP increased 5.7 per cent, unemployment fell to 4 per cent and inflation stood at around 3 per cent.

[30] The economy continued to grow in 1997, partly due to expanding internal consumption, as exports increased only 3 per cent on the previous year's figures. The bulk of investments were aimed at aluminum production. Several foreign companies - mostly from Switzerland, the US and Norway - intensified exploitation of this mineral resource.

[31] At the end of that year, Iceland participated in the Kyoto negotiations for reductions in toxic gas emissions in. Because of its economic factors, Iceland, along with Australia and Norway, was authorized to increase emissions, unlike 'highly polluting' countries such as the US or the EU.

[32] Transparency International's 1998 Perception of Corruption index, based on the statements of investors, financial risk analysts and the public, ranked Iceland among the five least corrupt countries in the world.

[33] In May 1999 the Conservative Party won the Althing elections with 26 of the 63 seats, followed by the Alliance made up of feminists, socialists and social democrats, which obtained 17, the Liberal Party (12) and the Green Party (6).

[34] Four earthquakes of varying intensity shook the south-east of Reykjavik in the space of less than a week, in June 2000, leading to panic and causing some damage to homes and infrastructure, but no victims. The earthquake left a ravine 130 meters long and 1 meter wide near Selfoss.

[35] In 2000, as a member of FATF - the 29-nation working group for financial action against money laundering founded in 1989 - Iceland began general auditing to determine whether anti-laundering action was up to date and offered effective countermeasures. The process was to continue through 2001 and 2002.

[36] Iceland joined Japan and Norway in the crusade to suspend bans on whaling. Despite rejoining the International Whaling Commission (IWC) in June 2001 - having left in 1993 - Iceland announced it would be returning to commercial whaling, ignoring the IWC moratorium. ∎

PROFILE

ENVIRONMENT

Located between the North Atlantic and the Arctic Ocean, Iceland is an enormous plateau with an average altitude of 500 meters. A mountain range crosses the country from east to west passing through an extensive ice-covered region; source of the main rivers. The coastline falls sharply from the plateau forming fjords. Most of the population lives in the coastal area in the south and west, where ocean currents temper the climate. Reykjavik, the capital and economic center, is located in a fertile plain where the largest cities are found. The northern coast is much colder as a result of Arctic Ocean currents. Geysers and active volcanoes are used as a source of energy. Agricultural output is poor; fishing accounts for 80 per cent of all exports.

SOCIETY

Peoples: 96 per cent of Icelanders are descendants of Norwegian, Scottish and Irish immigrants.
Religions: Mainly Lutheran (91.5 per cent). Other: Protestants 4.3 per cent, Catholics 0.9 per cent.
Languages: Icelandic.
Political parties: Independence Party (conservative); People's Alliance (socialist); Progressive Party (center-left); Social Democratic Party; Liberal Party; Left-Green Alliance.
Social Organizations: Icelandic Workers Federation; Confederation of State and Municipal Employees of Iceland.

THE STATE

Official Name: Lydhveldid Island.
Administrative divisions: 7 districts.
Capital: Reykjavik 168,000 people (1999).
Other cities: Kopavogur 24,400 people; Hafnarfjordhur 19,800 (2000).
Government: Olafur Ragnar Grimsson, President and head of state since August 1996. David Oddson, Prime Minister and head of government since April 1991. Unicameral parliament composed of 63 members, elected by popular vote for a 4-year term.
National Holiday: June 17, Independence Day (1944).
Armed Forces: 120 coastguards (1996).
Other: 2,200 NATO troops (1996).

India

Population:	1,041,144,000 (2002)
Land area:	2,973,190 SQ KM
Capital:	New Delhi
Currency:	Rupee
Language:	Hindi

Bharat

1 Territory under Pakistan control 2 Territory under China's control 3 Territory claimed by Pakistan   0   300 km

Around 3000 BC, the Dravidian inhabitants of the Indus Valley, in present-day Pakistan, built about a hundred cities, erected huge temples in larger urban centers, like Harappa and Mohenjo Daro, created a written language that has yet to be deciphered, and carved cylindrical seals of rare perfection. With their irrigated agriculture they developed a prosperous economy and maintained active trade from the Indian Ocean to the spurs of the Himalayas, using the Indus River as their main means of communication. Little is known about their culture, their political organization or development except that, after five centuries of existence, invaders devastated the whole region, exterminating the population and destroying their civilization.

[2] Towards 1600 BC, waves of Indo-Europeans arrived from Afghanistan, gradually conquering the subcontinent. Armed with iron weapons, protected by armor and using war chariots, they subdued the local population and established numerous states. The civilization they created, later called Vedic, was based on a rigid caste system in which the conquerors constituted the dominant nobility. They were called the ariana or ayriana - nobility - giving rise to the term Aryan which was later generically used to designate all Indo-Europeans.

[3] The Iranian-Greek invasions of the 6th-4th centuries BC (see Iran) did not reach Magadha in the Ganges River valley, the most powerful state in India. Under the rule of Ashoka, 274-232 BC, Magadha occupied the entire subcontinent, except for the extreme south. Indian civilization proper dates from this period. Ashoka and his descendants were the driving force behind a cultural unification that included the organization and diffusion of Buddhism, based on the preaching of Gautama Siddhartha, who lived from 563 to 483 BC, and was later known as Buddha. Between the 1st and 3rd centuries AD, this civilization began to break up, fragmented by the development of the Seythian Kusana (see Afghanistan) and Ksatrapa states in the northeast.

[4] When the Guptas of Magadha seized power in the 3rd-6th centuries

AD, a new process of unification ushered in one of the most brilliant periods of Indian culture. The 8th century spread of Islam failed to take hold in India, but it was more successful four centuries later, when the Turks of Mahmud of Ghazni reintroduced the faith. Successive groups of Islamic migrants from central Asia invaded the subcontinent, ending with the Tatars of Timur Lenk (Tamburlaine). Between 1505 and 1525, one of their descendants, Babur, founded what later came to be known as the Empire of the Grand Mogul, with its capital in Delhi.

[5] Babur's descendants consolidated Islam, particularly in the northwest and northeast (see Pakistan and Bangladesh). Culture and the arts developed remarkably - the Taj Mahal was built around 1650 - but the European presence, which had been limited to coastal trading posts, began to make a deeper impression. In 1687, the British East India Company settled in Bombay. In 1696, it built Fort William in Calcutta, and throughout the 18th century, the Company's private army waged war against the French competition, emerging victorious in 1784. From

1798, Company troops led by Richard Wellesley, a brother of the Duke of Wellington, methodically conquered Indian territory in various campaigns. By 1820, the English were in control of almost all of India, except for the Punjab, Kashmir and Peshawar, which were governed by their Sikh ally, Ranjit Singh. After his death in 1849, the British annexed these territories. The 'loyal allies' retained nominal autonomy and were allowed to keep their courts, great palaces and immoderate luxury, much to the satisfaction of European visitors.

[6] The Indian economy was completely dismantled. Its textile industry, whose exports of high-quality cloth had reached half the globe, was an obstacle to the growth of the British cotton industry.

[7] The ruin of this industry, based on individual weavers, brought widespread impoverishment to the countryside. Peasants were also hard hit by the reorganization of agriculture for export crops. The early results of British domination were lower incomes and greater unemployment. Public accounts were conveniently arranged. All military spending, including the campaigns in

Afghanistan, Burma and Malaya, was covered by the Indian treasury, 70 per cent of whose budget was earmarked for these 'defense expenses'. All British spending, however remotely connected with India, was entered as expenditures of the 'Indian Empire'.

[8] 'Divide and rule' was a motto of British domination. Mercenaries recruited in one region were used to subdue others. Such was the case with Nepalese Gurkhas and Punjabi Sikhs. Religious strife was also fomented; an electoral reform at the beginning of the 20th century stated that Muslims, Hindus and Buddhists could each vote only for candidates of their own faiths. Throughout the colonial period all this manipulation generated innumerable uprisings, both large and small, on local and national levels.

[9] The most serious of these were the 1857-1858 rebellions by sepoys, Indian soldiers in the British army. These began as a barracks movement, eventually incorporating a range of grievances and growing into a nationwide revolt. Hindus and Muslims joined forces and even proposed the restoration of the ancient Moghul Empire. This movement demonstrated that the East India Company was incapable of administering such a large domain and led the British crown, after violent repression, to assume direct government of India.

[10] The educational system was based on the classic British model and was conceived to train 'natives' for colonial administration in the civil service. However, it did not exactly fulfill its purpose. What it did do was create an intellectual elite fully conversant with European culture and thinking. The British had certainly never planned that the first association of civil servants in India, created in 1876 by Surendranath Banerjee, would take the Italian revolutionary Giuseppe Mazzini as its patron and inspiration and not just quietly follow the Government line. Years later in 1885, it was this intelligentsia that formed the Indian National Congress which included British liberals and, for a long time, limited itself to proposing superficial reforms to improve British administration.

[11] When Mohandas K Gandhi, a lawyer educated in England with experience of colonial methods in

South Africa, returned to India in 1915, he became aware of the need to break out of the straitjacket of Anglo-Indian 'cooperation'. Gandhi tried to win Muslims over to the independence cause. He reintroduced Hindu teachings that Ram Mohan Roy had reinterpreted in the 19th century, giving particular importance to mass mobilization. His ties with the Indian National Congress strengthened the movement's most radical wing where young Jawaharlal Nehru was an activist. In 1919, the Amritsar massacre occurred; a demonstration was savagely repressed leaving, according to British sources, 380 dead and 1200 wounded.

[12] In 1920, in response to the Amritsar massacre, at Gandhi's urging, the Indian Congress launched a campaign which showed the effectiveness of unarmed civilian opposition. The campaign tactics included the boycotting of colonial institutions; non-participation in elections or administrative bodies, non-attendance at British schools, refusal to consume British products, and passive acceptance of the ensuing legal consequences. The movement spread nationwide at all levels. Gandhi came to be called Mahatma (Great Soul) in recognition of his leadership.

[13] A new campaign between 1930 and 1934 aimed to attain full independence denouncing the colony's Salt Act, which forbids citizens from collecting or selling the vital mineral. Gandhi sends a public letter to Lord Irwin announcing his intent to break the British salt monopoly at the conclusion of a long people's march to the sea - Salt March - where ordinary citizens will collect salt. This demonstrated Gandhi's ability to combine a key political goal with a specific demand affecting all the poor; one they would understand and support. For the first time the British saw women flocking to demonstrations. Jails overflowed with prisoners who did not resist arrest posing an immense problem to the colonial authorities. It was impossible not to negotiate with Gandhi, and after World War II the British were left with no option but to rapidly grant independence.

[14] With the British withdrawal in 1947, the subcontinent was divided into two states; the Indian Union, and Pakistan, which was created to concentrate the Muslim population into one area (see Pakistan and Bangladesh). This 'Partition' as it was called was a painful and often violent separation. The Indian Union brought together an enormous diversity of ethnic, linguistic, and cultural groups in a single federated state, consolidating the sentiment of national unity forged in the independence struggle that the British had never managed to stifle. The excitement of independence was clouded by the assassination of Gandhi less than a year later, on 30 January 1948.

[15] The division of Pakistan and India led to 562 principalities having to choose which state they would belong to in 1947. The local government in Kashmir - with a largely Muslim population - tried to avoid the question, but an invasion by Pakistani fighters led it to opt for India in return for military aid. After the Indo-Pakistan war in 1948-49, a third of Kashmir remained in Pakistani hands.

[16] After independence, Prime Minister Jawaharlal Nehru, along with Sukarno of Indonesia, Gamal Abdel Nasser of Egypt and Tito of Yugoslavia, advanced the concept of political non-alignment for newly decolonized countries. In India, he applied development policies based on the notion that the industrialization of the society would bring prosperity.

[17] In a few decades India made rapid technological progress, which enabled it to place satellites in orbit and, in 1974, to detonate an atom bomb, making India the first nuclear power in the non-aligned movement. However, the relevance of this kind of project to a country which had yet to feed all its people was widely questioned. Pakistan's civil war and conflict with India over East Pakistan eventually led to the independence of this portion as Bangladesh, in 1971.

[18] The Indian economy was severely hit by the oil crisis of the early 1970s as it was dependent on oil imports. Industrial exports could not grow fast enough to offset increases in import prices, nor to meet the demand for food from a population growing at a rate of 15 million per year. In 1975, the economic crisis, and popular resistance to the government's mass sterilization campaigns, led Indira Gandhi, Nehru's daughter, who had taken over as Prime Minister when her father died in 1966) to declare a state of emergency and impose press censorship.

[19] Abandoning the Congress Party's traditional populist policies, Mrs Gandhi followed World Bank economic guidelines, losing mass support for the government, without winning wholehearted backing from business sectors (particularly those linked to foreign capital), which demanded even greater concessions. The British tradition of respect for democratic freedoms instilled in mass organizations, big business and the middle class, led them (for different reasons) to close ranks in opposition and force the Government to call parliamentary elections for March 1977. The Congress Party was roundly defeated by the Janata Party, a heterogeneous coalition formed by a splinter group of rightwing Congress Party members, the Socialist Party headed by trade union leader George Fernandes, and the Congress for Democracy, led by Jagjivan Ram, leader of the Harijans (Children of God, as Gandhi had renamed the outcastes or 'untouchables') and former minister in Indira Gandhi's cabinet.

[20] India's foreign policy of non-alignment remained basically unchanged under ageing Prime Minister Morarji Desai. In his time in power he was also unable to fulfill his promises of full employment and economic improvement. By mid-1979, disagreements within the party caused groups led by Charan Singh and Jagjivan Ram to split from the Janata Party. Desai had to resign and, unable to form a cabinet with a stable parliamentary majority, the Prime Minister called early elections, which returned Indira Gandhi to power in January 1980.

[21] Indira's second term was marked by a growing concentration of power, and accusations of unnecessary bureaucracy and corruption in the government, which gradually blemished her image. The problems in the Punjab, where the Government faced increasingly strident demands from Sikh separatists, exemplified regionalism at its worst. Small groups of militant Sikhs harassed Hindus, to drive them out of the Punjab and create an absolute Sikh majority in the province. After that, the next step

PROFILE

ENVIRONMENT

The nation is divided into three large natural regions: the Himalayas, along the northern border; the fertile, densely populated Ganges plain immediately to the south, and the Deccan plateau in the center and south. The Himalayas shelter the country from cold north winds. The climate is subject to monsoon influence; hot and dry for eight months of the year, and raining heavily from June to September. Rice is widespread. Coal and iron ore are the main mineral resources. There is a long-standing territorial dispute with Pakistan over Kashmir in the northwest.

SOCIETY

Peoples: The population of India is a multitude of racial, cultural and ethnic groups. Most are descendants of the Aryan peoples who developed the Vedic civilization and created a caste system so robust that it has survived until the present. The influence of Arab invasions, in the 7th and 12th centuries, and Mongolian incursions, in the 13th century, is still felt in the north. Peoples of Dravidian origin still predominate on the Deccan plateau in the center and south of India. The north still bears the influence of Arab (7th and 13th centuries) and Mongol (12th century) invasions.
Religions: 83 per cent Hindu, 11 per cent Muslim, 2.5 per cent Sikh, 2 per cent Christian, 1 per cent Buddhist. **Languages:** 400 registered languages, of which 18 are officially recognized, like Hindi, Bengali, Tamil or Urdu. English is an associated language, widely used for administrative purposes. There are 16 official regional languages and an infinity of local variants. **Political Parties:** The Indian National Congress (INC), founded in 1885. Under the leadership of Mahatma Gandhi they fought for independence from Britain. The United Front, former National Front-Left Front. The Bharatiya Janata Party (BJP) is a rightwing nationalist party which supposedly has connections with the Rashtriya Swayan Sevak Sangh (RSSS), a paramilitary communal organization, considered responsible for a series of violent acts, especially against Muslims. The Communist Party of India-Marxist (CPI-M). The Lok Dal claims to be the party of the poor peasants and aims to have considerable influence in northern India. Its main support comes from the middle castes. Amongst the most important regional parties are the all-India Anna Dravida Munetva Kazhagam (AIA-DMK), the National Conference of Jammu and Kashmir, the Asom Ghana Parishad, ruling in Assam, the Telegu Desam, and the Akali Dal which leads a struggle for greater Punjabi autonomy.
Social Organizations: Foundation of Investigation in Science, Technology and Policies of Natural Resources, Chipko Movement, an eco-feminist movement which promotes protection of the forests. Organizations of the various separatist movements in Cashmere, Punjab, Assam and Tamils who support the Tamil Tigers (see Sri Lanka).

THE STATE

Official name: Bharat (Hindi).
Capital: Delhi and New Delhi 11,345,000 people (1999). Other cities: Greater Mumbai (Bombay) 18,100,000 people; Kolkata (Calcutta) 12,900,000; Hyderabad 6,300,000; Bangalore 6,200,000 (2000).
Government: Kocheril Raman Narayanan, President since July 1997. Atal Bihari Vajpayee, Prime Minister since March 1998.
National Holidays: August 15, Independence Day (1947); January 26, Day of the Republic (1950). **Armed Forces:** 1,145,000 troops (1996).
Other: 1,421,800: Army, Navy (including naval air arm), Air Force, various security or paramilitary forces (Border Security Force, Assam Rifles, Rashtriya Rifles, and National Security Guards).

would be secession and the formation of independent 'Khalistan'. Indira accused 'forces from abroad' (namely Pakistan and the US) of destabilizing the country.

22   On June 6 1984, the Prime Minister called in the army to evict hundreds of militant Sikhs from their most sacred shrine, the Golden Temple at Amritsar, which they had transformed into a command post for their separatist war. Hundreds of Sikh extremists were killed within the temple, including prominent Sikh leader, Jarnail Singh Bhindranwale. This bloody confrontation left moderate Sikh leaders with no room for negotiation. The atmosphere which prevailed throughout the region after the incident led to Indira Gandhi's assassination by two of her Sikh bodyguards, on October 31 1984.

23   After the assassination, thousands of Sikhs fell victim to indiscriminate retaliation by Hindu paramilitary groups. Bypassing party and institutional formalities, Indira's son Rajiv was rapidly promoted to the office of Prime Minister and leader of the Congress Party.

24   Elections in January 1985 gave him overwhelming support: he obtained 401 of Parliament's 508 seats. None of the other parties reached the 50 seats needed to be officially recognized as the opposition. Despite the landslide victory, some strongly regionalist areas such as the states of Karnataka and Andhra Pradesh were influenced by Rama Rao, a charismatic former actor, and turned their backs on Gandhi. Gandhi also lost in Sikkim, a Himalayan kingdom annexed to India in the 1970s, where the separatist Sikkim Sangram Parishad party won.

25   The new premier took several steps to deal with Punjab's problems. He appointed a conciliatory figure as governor of the area, released political prisoners including opposition leaders, and directed that militants within his own party who had participated in the anti-Sikh violence should be tried and punished. These measures paved the way for dialogue with Akali Dal, the regional majority party of Sikhs and other dissident groups. Some progress was made. The Punjab autonomists proposed that the Indian central government should keep responsibility for defense and foreign affairs, the issuing of currency, mail, highways and telecommunications. Meanwhile, the local government would have greater autonomy than in India's other states.

26   In 1987, India intervened in the conflict in Sri Lanka, by sending in troops pressing for a cease-fire and an agreement between Sinhalese and Tamils. Three years later, the Indian Peace Forces had to

discreetly withdraw, having suffered many casualties.

27   India's foreign policy remained loyal to non-alignment but some domestic changes were announced. Rajiv made the personal computer the symbol of his swift 'modernization' policy. He promised the private sector he would lift restrictions on imports and on the purchase of foreign technology, while relaxing fiscal controls. Labor unions feared that sophisticated technology would lead to unemployment and that Indian industry would not survive the competition from foreign products.

28   Elections in November 1989 were held amidst a violent atmosphere which left more than 100 dead and revealed the opposition's progress. The Congress Party's representation went down to 192 seats while Janata Dal's went up to 141. Although a minority, this party succeeded in forming a government coalition with the National Front which appointed Vishwanath Pratap Singh as Prime Minister. This was possible because of the unusual simultaneous support from the right-wing Bharatiya Janata Party (BJP) and several left-wing groups.

29   In March 1990, tensions between India and Pakistan mounted as Pakistan increased its support for the Kashmir independence movements. There were fears that, if both countries went to war, one of them could resort to nuclear weapons. In November, confrontations between Hindus and Muslims escalated amidst a general worsening of the economic crisis. Prime Minister Singh was replaced by Chandra Shekhar, also from the Janata Dal.

30   An election campaign which claimed over 280 lives gave way to parliamentary elections which started on May 20 1991. The following day, they were adjourned following the assassination of Rajiv Gandhi, attacked by one of the Tamil liberation movement. A week later, Narasimha Rao was appointed Gandhi's successor as leader of the Congress Party. The elections, in which only 53 per cent of those registered voted and which were to become the most violent in India's independent history, were resumed between June 12 and 16. The Congress Party obtained 225 seats followed by the Bharatiya Janata Party with 119.

31   In August 1991, the new government announced a drastic shift toward liberalism that would change the economic policy in force since independence. This change gave rise to criticism and protests. Already in September of the previous year, 70,000 representatives of tribal groups had met to halt dam constructions on the holy Narmada river, which threatened to flood ancient temples and ancestral lands belonging to the

region's peasants. Over 200,000 people driven from their lands by the dams protested in 1991.

32   Numerous acts of violence took place in 1992 by Hindu fundamentalists against the Islamic population in the northern cities of Bombay and Ayodhya. According to Hindu tradition, in the latter - which had a mosque that was built in 1528 - the god Rama had been born. In December, Lal Krishnan Advani, leader of the BJP, ordered his followers to destroy the temple. The following clashes between the two communities left approximately 1,300 dead in several Indian cities and reached neighboring countries such as Pakistan and Bangladesh. In 1995, the Supreme Court was consulted about the possible existence of a Hindu temple in Ayodhya, before the (ruined) Babri mosque was built. The members of the Court unanimously declined to issue an opinion on the matter.

33   The reforms planned by Prime Minister Rao, implemented by finance minister Manmohan Singh, included opening up India's market to foreign investment. The state gradually reduced its intervention in the economy, leaving the rupee to fluctuate freely against the dollar, and removing import controls.

34   Economic reforms triggered protests from several sectors, especially from agriculture. Resistance to multinationals involved in fertilizers and seeds was very strong. As part of the 'green revolution' and a capital-intensive agriculture, the World Bank had granted those subsidies following instructions from the World Bank's structural adjustment plan. The Farmers' Association of the State of Karnataka (KKRS) headed rural protests which were responsible for a number of direct attacks against representatives of multinational corporations since 1991.

35   At the International Conference on Rights of Third World Farmers held in Bangalore on October 3 and 4, 1993, farmers declared that the 'seeds, plants, biological material and wealth of the Third World form part of the Collective Intellectual Property of the peoples of the Third World'. They pledged to develop these rights in the face of the private patenting system which encourages the spread of monoculture and threatens biodiversity.

36   In 1994, the Supreme Court of India declared that state governments could lose some powers if they did not enforce religious freedom, which was stipulated in theConstitution. Conflicts between Hindus and Muslims continued in Karnataka. In December, three Cabinet members resigned after being involved in corruption cases related to public security.

37   That year India signed two agreements with China: the first one

DEMOGRAPHY

Population: 1,041,144,000 (2002)
Annual growth: 1.8 % (1985-2000)
Estimates for year 2015: 1,230,484,000 (2000)
Annual growth to year 2015: 1.3 % (2000)
Urban population: 28.4 % (2000)
Urban growth: 3.0 % (2000)
Children per woman: 3.2 (2000)

HEALTH

Life expectancy at birth: 64 years (2000-2005)
male: 64 years (2000-2005)
female: 65 years (2000-2005)
Maternal mortality: 540 per 100,000 live births (1985/99)
Infant mortality: 69 per 1,000 (2000)
Under-5 child mortality: 96 per 1,000 (2000)
Daily calorie supply: 2,417 per capita (1999)
48 doctors per 100,000 people (1992)
Safe water: 84 % (2000)

EDUCATION

Literacy: 56 % (2000)
male: 69 % (2000)
female: 42 % (2000)
School enrolment (net):
Primary total: 76 % (1994/2000)
male: 78 % (1995/99)
female: 64 % (1995/99)
Secondary (gross):
male: 59 % (1995/97)
female: 39 % (1995/97)
Tertiary (gross): 7 % (1997)
Primary school teachers: one for every 72 pupils (1998)

COMMUNICATIONS

48 newspapers (1997), 121 radios (1997), 78 TV sets (2000) and 32 main telephone lines (2000) per 1,000 people
Books: 1 new title per 100,000 people (1992/94)

ECONOMY

Per capita, GDP: $ 2,358 (2000)
Annual growth: 2.0 % (2000)
Annual inflation: 4.0 % (2000)
Consumer price index: 144.0 (2000)
Currency: 48.7 rupees = $ 1 (03/2002)
Cereal imports: 54,590 metric tons (2000)
Food import dependency: 7 % (1999)
Fertilizer use: 1,136 kg per ha (1999)
Exports: $ 63,764 million (2000)
Imports: $ 75,656 million (2000)
External debt: $ 100,367 million (2000); $ 99 per capita (2000)
Debt service: 15.0 % of exports (1999)
Development aid received: $ 1,484 million (1999); $ 1.5 per capita (1999); 0.30 % of GNP (1999)

ENERGY

Consumption: 485.7 Kgs of oil equivalent per capita yearly (1998); 14.7 % imported (1999)

HDI (ranking/value): 115 / 0.571 (1999)

stated a reduction of military troops stationed along the 4,000 km of common borders between the two countries while the other encouraged trade relations. When former Pakistani Prime Minister Nawaz Sharif claimed his country had nuclear weapons, relations between New Delhi and Islamabad were strained. Pakistan closed its consulate in Bombay.

[38] During 1995, Prime Minister Narasimha Rao changed his cabinet three times. Elections in several states revealed an increasingly weakened Congress Party, with several internal schisms, and growing support for the Hindu nationalist party Bharatiya Janata (BJP). The new BJP Government in the state of Maharashtra decided to change the name of Bombay to Mumbai.

[39] Economic stability and assistance schemes announced by Rao, which included a school dinners plan for 110 million children and the construction of 10 million rural homes, were not enough to stop his popularity from plummeting. Rao resigned on May 10 1996, following his party's defeat in the general elections held between April 27 and May 7. The BJP, in alliance with other minor parties, took 187 seats in the lower house, while the Congress Party took 138 and the National Front - Left Front, which changed its name to the United Front, took 117.

[40] The BJP did not get a big enough parliamentary majority to govern. The new Prime Minister, Atal Bihari Vajpayee, resigned on May 28, 12 days after taking office. President Shankar Dayal Sharma appointed HD Deve Gowda, leader of the United Front, to head the new Government, with Congress Party support.

[41] The Congress Party withdrew support from the Gowda Government, toppling the Prime Minister. Sitaram Kesri, the main force behind the break with the Left, was elected President of the Congress Party in June. Nearly a month after the fall of Gowda, Inder Kumar Gujral, also of the United Front, was appointed Prime Minister. In July, Vice-President KR Narayanan was elected President.

[42] The Congress Party withdrew its support from the Gujral Government in November when an official commission revealed alleged links between a governing coalition party, the Dravida Munnetra Kazagham (DMK), and Sri Lanka's Tamil guerrillas, a group involved in the murder of former Prime Minister Rajiv Gandhi. Gujral was forced to resign.

[43] The BJP triumphed in the February 1998 parliamentary elections. The BJP and its allies won 251 seats, followed by the Congress Party (166) and the United Front (96). For the second time in 22 months, Atal Biharia Vajpayee was designated Prime

Minister. In May, a series of nuclear tests in India heightened tensions with Pakistan, giving the neighboring country the pretext to carry out similar tests that same month.

[44] A legislative bill that would reserve one third of parliamentary seats for women was successively boycotted in Parliament throughout the month of July. The bill's opponents, led by two socialist parties, staged a protest outside the Parliament and repeatedly interrupted legislative proceedings. According to the opposition, the proposal was unacceptable because it did not include quotas for women from the lower castes. The bill's principal defenders were the ruling party and the major opposition force, the Indian National Congress Party in agreement for the first time.

[45] The Government coalition collapsed in April 1999 when Jayaram Jayalalitha, leader of the Tamil AIA-DMK party, forced two of his ministers to resign after Prime Minister Vajpayee rejected AIA-DMK demands that Defense Minister George Fernandes be removed from office and investigated for having sacked India's Navy Commander, Admiral Vishnu Bhagwat. After Jayalalitha retreated and the opposition parties were unable to put together a coalition to replace the collapsed government, President KR Narayanan dissolved the Lower House so that new elections would be called.

[46] Armed confrontations with Pakistan erupted in June after Pakistani forces crossed the border set by the United Nations. Some 1,000 people died in the conflicts. The international organization Human Rights Watch reported serious human rights violations on either side of the border, attributed to officials from both governments. India's security forces were accused of carrying out summary executions, rape and torture.

[47] In October, after five electoral rounds, the BJP once again led the administration after the alliance it led won 293 of the 545 parliamentary seats. Despite the coalition's victory, this election also marked a BJP decline that benefited leftist and regional parties. More than half of the legislative seats were no longer controlled by the two major national parties (the BJP and the Congress Party, which suffered the worst defeat of its history). The BJP's dependence on its minor partners foretold another difficult term for the Government.

[48] More than a million people were left homeless in Gujarat State in the west of the country when a huge earthquake struck the region in February 2001. At least 30,000 were killed and 55,000 injured. The region had been devastated by a cyclone in

1998 and was still suffering the after effects. A Muslim cleric, Mufti Imtiaz, blamed television and TV broadcasts for the earthquake, whereupon Muslim residents of Ahmadabad and Surat, towns in Gujarat, started to throw televisions off their roofs to smash and burn them in the streets, blaming 'immoral' television programs for the devastating earthquake. According to the Mufti 'the poisoning of minds produced by television had annoyed the almighty, and that was the reason for the earthquake.'

[49] The provisional outcome of the last official census, published in March, showed an increase of 180 million people during the last decade, even if the growth rate had diminished slightly. Two of every three Indians can now read and write, and the number of illiterate people fell for the first time since independence. The full results will only be available in 2004, and the Government hopes they will confirm how economic reforms have benefited the population. Some two million workers were involved in the census.

[50] The battle for control of world food supplies gave a legal victory to the less well off in a ruling on rights over Basmati rice - which had been produced on the Indian sub-continent for centuries. The 'rice battle' started in 1997, when RiceTech in the US patented 'Kasmati,' a type of Basmati rice, and ended in May 2001 when the US Patent Office rejected RiceTech's application. A ruling the other way would have meant an end to Indian rice exports to the US and also Asian farmers having to pay intellectual property rights for one of their traditional crops.

[51] The same month, the police arrested a group of men armed with machine-guns who had been hired to kill six Indian journalists. Those journalists had forced six politicians to resign following an undercover investigation into corruption in the government. The police accused the Pakistani Intelligence Services of contracting the gunmen in order to further undermine the image of the Indian Government.

[52] Due to growing controversy over its content, a report on AIDS funded by UNICEF and drawn up by the Human Rights Commission of Madhya Pradesh was withdrawn from circulation. Madhya Pradesh, a state in the heart of the country, considers prostitution to be an integral way of life for the Bedia caste - a fact rejected by non-governmental organizations (NGOs), UNICEF and the Bedia community of Madhya Pradesh, who demanded the report be withdrawn as it promoted suspicion and exacerbated caste discrimination. A year before, the founders of the NGO Sahyog, Abhijeet and

Yashodhara Das, barely escaped lynching in the Himalayan area of Almora, for producing a leaflet entitled 'AIDS and us,' which indicated that incest was widespread in the region.

[53] Chancellor, Jaswant Singh rejected caste as an issue for the World Conference against Racism, held between August and September in Durban, South Africa, alleging that this was 'an attempt to add racial connotations' to a problem of a different nature. However, the United Nations Committee on Civil and Political Rights indicated that the populations of indigenous people and lower castes 'continue to suffer serious discrimination' and suffer disproportionately from 'forced labor and inter-caste violence.' In cities like Haryana or several states in the north of India, some young people who marry outside their cast run the risk of being lynched by their own families.

[54] In July 2001, Prime Minister Vajpayee met Pakistani President Pervez Musharraf in the first summit between the neighbors for more than two years. The meeting ended with no resolution to the situation in Kashmir. Chancellor Singh accused Pakistan of having impeded agreement by making the Kashmir issue the main subject of the talks instead of advancing on other bilateral issues. Meanwhile, the Pakistani delegation responded that the root of the problems was the fact that the Indian officials insisted on changing the text of an agreement already approved by the rulers of both countries.

[55] Following the attacks on New York and Washington in September 2001, the US lifted sanctions it had imposed on India and Pakistan following the nuclear tests both nations held three years previously. This was a 'reward' for the support they offered Washington in its global war on terrorism.

[56] In October, Kashmir was once more the center of conflict when Indian troops fired on Pakistani military posts. Two months later, suicide squads attacked Parliament, in New Delhi, killing several police officers. Both countries made wide scale deployments of troops on the frontier, fearing a new war. In early 2002, India ran successful trials of the Agni, a missile with nuclear capacity.

[57] In June 2002 the situation was calmer due to the intervention by the US, Russia and other countries. Although Indian Defense Minister George Fernandes said Indian troops will remain along the border with Pakistan as long as necessary, there was a marked drop in incursions by militants fighting Indian rule in Kashmir. ∎

Indonesia

Population: 217,534,000 (2002)
Land area: 1,811,570 SQ KM
Capital: Jakarta
Currency: Rupiah
Language: Bahasa Indonesia

Indonesia

Indonesia has some of the world's earliest homo sapiens remains. The ancestors of the present-day population were Malay immigrants who arrived on the islands of Java and Sumatra around 400 BC. They brought with them the cultural and religious influences of India. Indonesian civilization reached its height in the 15th century when the state of Mojopahit extended far east - beyond Java, Bali, Sumatra, and Borneo - becoming commercially and culturally linked with China.

[2] At the end of the 13th century, through contact with Arab traders, Islam was introduced, rapidly flourishing in the archipelago. Islam was not imposed through conversion campaigns, but was freely adopted because it represented a simple, egalitarian faith suited to local conditions.

[3] When the Muslim traders sent spices from the Moluccas (now part of Indonesia) to Europe, the Europeans' interest was aroused, and they set their colonial sights on the region. In 1511, the Portuguese arrived in Melaka; in 1521, the Spanish reached the Moluccas and in 1595, private Dutch merchants organized their first expedition. The Netherlands had just won its independence from Spain and wanted to secure its own supply of spices. In 1602, the Dutch East India Company was founded, obtaining a trade monopoly, with a colonial

mandate from the Governor of the region.

[4] During the 17th and 18th centuries, Indonesia was fought over by Spain, Portugal, the Netherlands and Britain, the latter creating another private company. The Netherlands gained the upper hand and became the colonial power. Cash crops, coffee and sugar were introduced, yielding excellent profits for the European investors but seriously upsetting the local socio-economic organization. This had remained intact until then but was virtually destroyed by the export economy. Anti-colonial revolts broke out. Towards the end of the 19th century, rubber, palm oil and tin became the main export products, though industry only began to develop during World War II, when the Netherlands was unable to meet its production needs at home.

[5] In December 1916, nationalist pressure caused the formation of the Volksraad (People's Council), a body designed to defend the rights of the local population. Although its proposals were largely ignored, the Council encouraged political participation among the local population.

[6] In 1939, eight nationalist organizations formed a coalition called the Gabusan Politick Indonesia (GAPI), demanding democracy, autonomy and national unity within the framework of the anti Fascist

struggle. GAPI adopted the red and white flag and Bahasa Indonesia as the national language.

[7] After the outbreak of World War II, the Netherlands were invaded by Germany, and Indonesia by Japan in 1942. The Japanese, who claimed to be the 'Asiatic brothers' of the Indonesians, freed nationalist leaders like Achmed Sukarno and Muhammad Hatta who had been imprisoned under Dutch rule. On August 11 1945, just four days prior to the Japanese surrender, they invested Sukarno and Hatta with full powers to establish an autonomous Indonesian government.

[8] Indonesia proclaimed independence on August 17 1945. The Dutch tried to recover the archipelago, forcing the Indonesians to fight back. The Arab and Indian communities actively supported the pro-independence guerrillas, while Britain backed the Netherlands. The US pressed for a negotiated settlement.

[9] Unable to recover military control, the Netherlands was forced to surrender in 1949, although it retained partial control through a Dutch-Indonesian confederation.

[10] In 1954, the Dutch-Indonesian Union, which was never fully implemented, was renounced by the Sukarno Government and the archipelago became fully independent. Sukarno's government

soon began its own colonial policies in the region. In 1963, reacting to The Hague's refusal to withdraw from the island of New Guinea, Indonesia occupied West Irian (or Irian Jaya, now West Papua), the former Dutch colony whose territory took up half of the island. The Indonesian independence process offered an important example for the other Third World countries. Together with other major events of the period - Indian and Pakistani independence, the Cuban Revolution, the nationalization of the Suez Canal in Egypt, and the French defeats in Vietnam and Algeria - it heralded the arrival of the South onto the international political scene. Sukarno was one of the main leaders of the movement for Third World solidarity and in 1955 the Indonesian city of Bandung played host to a meeting of heads of government, giving rise to the Non-Aligned Movement.

[11] The three-million strong Communist Party - the second most powerful in Asia after the Chinese - supported Sukarno. He launched nationalist development programs, aimed at raising the living standards of a population with one of the world's lowest per capita incomes. The country had sizeable petroleum reserves, which provided a strong foundation on which to base economic development. Sukarno created a state petroleum company, PERTAMINA to break the domination

of the Anglo-Dutch transnational, Royal Dutch Shell.

[12] In 1965, Indonesian oil deposits were nationalized. In October of that year, a small force of soldiers led by General Suharto seized power under the pretext of stemming the 'communist penetration'. This bloody coup left nearly 700,000 dead, and some 200,000 political activists were imprisoned.

[13] Though deprived of any real power, Sukarno remained the nominal president until 1967, when Suharto was officially named head of state. Suharto opened the doors to foreign oil companies seeking drilling rights. But with the rise in oil prices, the influx of capital, and a liberal economic policy, the Government also widened the gap between those with the highest and lowest incomes. Living conditions did not improve for millions of rural dwellers, many of whom had to leave their lands joining the shantytowns in the large cities.

[14] In 1971, defying repression, students took to the streets in protest at the 'corrupt generals, Chinese merchants, and Japanese investors' controlling the nation. In an attempt to divert the attention of young officers and neutralize local dissent, Suharto invaded East Timor, on that country's independence from Portugal in 1975. US President Gerald Ford visited Jakarta a few hours before the invasion and apparently gave it his blessing. However, from the point of view of the Maubere people of Timor, the Indonesians were not seen as liberators but as new colonists. The unyielding resistance on the island only deepened Indonesia's internal problems.

[15] In May 1977, when elections were held for a portion of the seats in the House of Representatives, discontent surfaced once again. Despite repression, the banning of leftist parties and press censorship, the official Sekber Golkar (Golongan Karya) Party lost in Jakarta to a Muslim coalition which had campaigned against the rampant corruption. The governing party also lost ground in rural areas where it had always previously maintained effective political control.

[16] In the light of this setback, and to ensure victory in the election five years later, the regime clamped down on political activity and reorganized the electoral system, making it dependent on the Ministry of Home Affairs.

[17] On March 10 1983, in spite of growing opposition, the People's Consultative Assembly unanimously re-elected Suharto for a fourth 5-year presidential term.

[18] Indonesia adopted a birth control policy that led to a reduction in the population growth rate. While figures for the 1984 census revealed an annual increase of 2.34 per cent, the average rate of growth between 1980 and 1990 was only 1.8 per cent. Even so, demographic pressure, particularly on the island of Java, together with the radical reorientation of the country's economy and commerce toward a world market, coupled with rapid industrialization, have all led to a deterioration in the quality of the environment and the depletion of agricultural lands. From 1979, the Government reacted to this situation with a population transfer project known as Transmigrasi, which involved moving 2.5 million Javanese to other less populated islands, causing great social tension, and destroying the lifestyles of the peoples already on these islands.

[19] In the 1980s over 300 ethnic groups saw their standards of living drop sharply. The most energetic protests were those of the inhabitants of Irian Jaya (West Papua) who demanded self-determination and freedom of movement to and from the neighboring territory of Papua New Guinea, with which they had a high degree of cultural and historical affinity.

[20] In 1991 the fighting between the army and the Aceh liberation movements in Sumatra became more acute when the commander of the army called for the annihilation of the insurgents. At the beginning of March 1992, an armed offensive of several separatist groups was started in Irian Jaya province. At the same time the US Government asked Congress to approve $2,300,000 for the training of the official security forces of Indonesia.

[21] In March 1993 the Popular Consultative Assembly chose Suharto as President for the sixth time.

[22] During 1995 the technocrat middle class manifested a growing interest in political openness.

[23] Two years before the campaign for the parliamentary elections of mid-1997, Suharto's Minister of Information, Harmoko, toured Indonesia in support of Golkar, the major political party. The opposition accused the Government of interfering in its activities. Particularly vocal was the Indonesian Democratic Part (PDI), headed by Megawati Sukarnoputri, daughter of the still-respected independence leader, Sukarno.

[24] In 1996 the pre-election debates reached a new low when complaints about the illegal enrichment of the Suharto family and its circle grew. The military saw Islamic groups as well as Sukarnoputri and the PDI as the main threats to Suharto's power. The change of political climate is due partly to a wider circulation of information via the Internet as well as campaigning journalism and vigorous protest about arms sales to Indonesia.

[25] In spite of a climate of political uncertainty, the economy continued to prosper and inflation was kept at bay. However, the trade surplus fell due to the reduction of key exports, such as textiles. Suharto, then 75, had to travel to Germany for a medical check-up, which increased doubts over his government.

[26] In early 1997, the population reached 200 million. The Government announced it would continue its program to transfer the people from 'over-populated' regions to less populated areas.

[27] The ruling Golkar party won the May 1997 parliamentary elections, obtaining 74 per cent of the vote (325 out of 400 seats). The new parliament included 12 of President Suharto's relatives - six children, two wives, two son-in-laws, one brother and a cousin - as well as many of the leader's trade partners or cronies. On March 10 1998, parliament re-elected Suharto for a seventh 5-year term.

PROFILE

ENVIRONMENT

Indonesia is the largest archipelago-state in the world, made up of approximately 3,000 islands. The most important are Borneo (Kalimantan), Sumatra, Java, Celebes, Bali, the Moluccas, West Papua and Timor. Lying either side of the equator, the island group has a tropical, rainy climate and dense rainforest vegetation. The population, the fourth largest in the world, is unevenly distributed: Java has one of the highest population densities in the world (640 people per sq km), while Borneo has fewer than 10 people per sq km. Cash crops - mainly coffee, tea, rubber and palm oil - are cultivated, along with subsistence items, especially rice. Indonesia is the tenth largest oil producer and the third largest tin producer in the world. Like neighboring Malaysia, Indonesia suffers from widespread deforestation due to the expansion of the paper industry and lumber exports, which affects certain populations such as the indigenous people of West Papua (Irian Jaya). Air and water pollution are major problems, particularly in urban areas.

SOCIETY

Peoples: Principally Malay, Javanese, Sundanese, Madurese, Balinese, Ambon, Alfur, Toraja, Dayak, Batak, Minahasa and Papuan. There are also Chinese and Indian minorities.

Religions: 86 per cent of the population is Muslim, nearly 10 per cent Christian, 2 per cent Hindu (mostly in Bali), 1 per cent Buddhist, and small minorities that practice traditional beliefs. The State recognizes Islam, Protestant and Catholic Christianity, Hinduism and Buddhism.

Languages: Bahasa Indonesia (official), very similar to Bahasa Malaysia, official language of Malaysia. The governments of both countries have agreed to gradual unification, based on Melayu, the shared mother tongue. Javanese, language of 60 million inhabitants. English, language of business. There are hundreds of regional/local languages - more than 200 are concentrated in the province of West Papua (Irian Jaya).

Political Parties: National Awakening Party (PKB). Indonesian Democratic Party in Struggle (PDIP). The governing party during the Suharto era, Golongan Karya (Golkar) was founded in 1971. With the support of the armed forces, Golkar is an alliance of various professional groups and interests. Most civil servants are affiliated with the National Association of Civil Servants (KORPRI), which is part of Golkar. The United Party for Development (PPP) and the National Mandate Party (PAN), are both moderate Islamic groups. The Communist Party of Indonesia (PKI) was the world's third largest communist party until the 1965 military coup. Currently operating underground, it has lost its past influence. In 1990, the Free Aceh Movement and the Aceh National Liberation Front, made up of insurgents from that northern Sumatra region, launched attacks against the government but were virtually crushed by the army. Other separatist movements, particularly in West Papua (Irian Jaya), where there is an indigenous guerrilla group, the Free Papua Movement (OPM). There is a government-in-exile, in the Netherlands, of the Malukus islands.

Social Organizations: All-Indonesia Workers' Union (SPSI), since 1985, founded in 1973 under the name Labor Federation of Indonesia (FBSI).

THE STATE

Official Name: Republik Indonesia. **Administrative Divisions:** 26 Provinces. **Capital:** Jakarta 10,621,000 people (1999). **Other cities:** Bandung 3,834,300 people; Surabaya 3,683,200; Medan 2,977,000 (2000). **Government:** Megawati Sukarnoputri, President since July 2001. Legislature, single-chamber, made up of 500 members, 462 elected by direct popular vote, 38 appointed military representatives. **National Holiday:** August 17, Independence Day (1945). **Armed Forces:** 274,000 (1995). **Other:** Police, 215,000; Auxiliary Police, (Kamra), 1.5 million.

28 A severe stock market crisis in April increased inflation and caused a risk of hyperinflation. The currency had lost 50 per cent of its value since mid-1997. The price rise affected mostly basic goods. Two million workers lost their jobs between October 1997 and March 1998. Widespread social unrest followed, including the listing of shops and victimization of the Chinese community who were seen as wealthy and therefore supporters of the status quo. Student demonstrations calling for democracy met a brutal response, but Suharto stepped down on 21 May to be succeeded by his Vice-President Jusuf Habibie.

29 In October 1998, violent student protests to demand democracy and the removal of army chief Wiranto overwhelmed the capital. Five students were killed in confrontations with anti-insurrection forces. Also that month, two civilians died during armed conflicts between separatist rebels and police in Aceh province, the northernmost point of Indonesia, where the army had been accused of committing all kinds of abuses.

30 Inter-ethnic fighting intensified in Borneo, between the Malay, Bugi, Dayak and Chinese on one side and Maduran immigrants on the other, leading to the deaths of some 70 people in March 1999. In Jakarta the following month, hundreds of Muslims set fire to a community center in retaliation for a bomb explosion at a mosque in Ujung Pandang, the largest in Southeast Asia.

31 October elections gave the presidency to Abdurraman Wahid, who until that time had been leader of the Nahdlatul Ulama Muslim organization. A Sufi, and a pro-democracy activist during the Suharto regime, Wahid had repeatedly defended the rights of minorities in the country. Political analysts rejected the idea that he would establish a Government based on Islamic law.

32 One of Wahid's first acts as President was to offer Aceh broad autonomy and an increase in economic support if the province were to remain a part of Indonesia. He set a seven-month deadline to carry out a referendum, similar to the one held in August 1999 in East Timor (See East Timor). The plan to retain Aceh established that 75 per cent of all income produced there would remain in Aceh, one of the country's richest regions in natural resources. The news upset the army chiefs, who indicated that the referendum would lead to the disintegration of the whole country.

33 In spite of his public promise to eradicate corruption, Wahid immediately was implicated in financial scandals, which in August 2000 led Parliament to launch an unprecedented investigation. The first scandal emerged in May, when it was found that the President's personal masseur had obtained $4.1 million from the national food agency. The second entailed a personal donation to Wahid of $2 million from the Sultan of Brunei that Wahid failed to make public. In both cases - which the media dubbed Bulogate and Bruneigate - the money was to have been used for humanitarian programs in Aceh, where the separatist rebellion continued. Parliament moved to try Wahid and remove him from office, but abandoned the attempt in February 2001, after thousands of people took to the streets in support of the President and demanding that the opposition Golkar party be dismantled.

34 In Kalimantan, the following month, combatants of the Dayak peoples took over parts of the province in the worst outbreak of violence in the region since 1997. Within one week, at least 1,000 Madurese refugees were killed and tens of thousands were forced from their homes.

35 In May, the Parliament - the country's sole legislative body - voted 365 to 4 to begin impeachment proceedings against Wahid. Although before the vote Wahid's party and a small Christian party withdrew from Parliament, and the faction representing the army abstained, all the main parties voted in favor of censuring the President. It was the third vote of no confidence against him and facilitated the naming of a People's Consultative Assembly (MPR), made up of Parliament and 200 other members, with the authority to designate and remove presidents. The vote sparked a violent confrontation between the security forces and pro-Wahid groups outside Parliament and massive demonstrations in favor of the President in other parts of the country, particularly Java, his native province. Wahid, accused of corruption and incompetence, had addressed a letter to Parliament, before the vote, stating that he refused to resign and declared a state of emergency, which was not heeded by the police or the army.

36 Nearly two years after taking office, and after the Supreme Court ruled the decreed state of emergency unconstitutional, a vote by the MPR of 591-0 removed Wahid in July. Vice-President Megawati Sukarnoputri, Sukarno's daughter, assumed the presidency.

37 In an address on the eve of the 56th anniversary of Independence in August, the President issued an apology to the provinces of Aceh and West Papua (Irian Jaya) for the human rights abuses committed by previous governments. However she asserted that these provinces would never be allowed to secede as East Timor had done two years earlier. Megawati urged the two provinces - which Jakarta had exploited during decades for their natural resources: petroleum and natural gas in Aceh, minerals in West Papua (Irian Jaya) - to accept the new autonomy agreements the Government proposed. According to the President, these agreements would give them greater decision-making power over their own affairs.

38 The political will of the Government to hold the army responsible for the atrocities committed in East Timor after it had voted for independence in 1999 began to be tested when, in January 2002, Jakarta inaugurated the Human Rights Court. Three generals, including the military commander at the time of the massacres, Adam Damiri, appeared before the tribunal, which, according to its creators, 'is better than an International Court'. The following month, Indonesia and East Timor signed two agreements aimed at improving relations before East Timor assumed its complete independence in May.

39 In March 2002, Tommy Suharto, son of the former president, was accused of assassinating a Supreme Court judge who had sentenced him to prison on corruption charges. Analysts said the trial was a tough test of the country's legal and judicial system, still considered vulnerable to corruption. ∎

FOOD DEPENDENCY
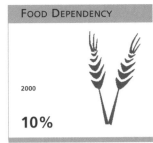
2000

10%

MATERNAL MORTALITY

1985/99

Per 100,000 live births

380

STATISTICS

DEMOGRAPHY
Population: 217,534,000 (2002)
Annual growth: 1.6 % (1985-2000)
Estimates for year 2015: 250,068,000 (2000)
Annual growth to year 2015: 1.1 % (2000)
Urban population: 40.9 % (2000)
Urban growth: 4.3 % (2000)
Children per woman: 2.5 (2000)

HEALTH
Life expectancy at birth: 67 years (2000-2005)
male: 65 years (2000-2005)
female: 69 years (2000-2005)
Maternal mortality: 380 per 100,000 live births (1985/99)
Infant mortality: 35 per 1,000 (2000)
Under-5 child mortality: 48 per 1,000 (2000)
Daily calorie supply: 2,931 per capita (1999)
16 doctors per 100,000 people (1994)
Safe water: 78 % (2000)

EDUCATION
Literacy: 87 % (2000)
male: 92 % (2000)
female: 82 % (2000)
School enrolment (net):
Primary total: 93 % (1994/2000)
male: 97 % (1995/99)
female: 93 % (1995/99)
Secondary (gross):
male: 55 % (1995/97)
female: 48 % (1995/97)
Tertiary (gross): 11 % (1997)
Primary school teachers: one for every 22 pupils (1996)

COMMUNICATIONS
23 newspapers (1998), 157 radios (1997), 149 TV sets (2000) and 31 main telephone lines (2000) per 1,000 people
Books: 3 new titles per 100,000 people (1992/94)

ECONOMY
Per capita, GDP: $ 3,043 (2000)
Annual growth: 3.1 % (2000)
Annual inflation: 3.7 % (2000)
Consumer price index: 227.0 (2000)
Currency: 10,190.0 rupiahs = $ 1 (03/2002)
Cereal imports: 6,863,033 metric tons (2000)
Food import dependency: 10 % (2000)
Fertilizer use: 1,482 kg per ha (1999)
Exports: $ 59,075 million (2000)
Imports: $ 47,045 million (2000)
External debt: $ 141,803 million (2000); $ 669 per capita (2000)
Debt service: 30.3 % of exports (1999)
Development aid received: $ 2,206 million (1999); $ 10.7 per capita (1999); 1.50 % of GNP (1999)

ENERGY
Consumption: 604.3 Kgs of oil equivalent per capita yearly (1998); -66.3 % imported (1999)

HDI (ranking/value): 102 / 0.677 (1999)

Iran

Population:	72,376,000 (2002)
Land area:	1,622,000 SQ KM
Capital:	Teheran (Tehran)
Currency:	Rial
Language:	Persian

Iran

Shortly before the 18th century BC, nations of the Indo-European area reached the plains of Iran, subduing the shepherds who inhabited the region. More of these people arrived up until the 10th century, contributing to the Mesopotamian cultural mix. They later became known by different names: Medes, from the name of the ruling group; Iranians, the name they adopted in Persia and India (from Sanskrit *ayriana* meaning nobles); Persians (a Greco-Latin term alluding to Perseus, the mythological ancestor that the Greeks foisted on Iranians), with its corrupted forms: Parsis, Farsis, Fars, or Parthians (according to the time and source). Whatever their names, they first won control of the mountainous region, then conquered the Mesopotamian plains under the reign of Ciaxares. During the rule of Ciro the Great (559-530 BC), this wave of expansion reached as far west as Asia Minor, and as far east as present-day Afghanistan. These borders were later extended as far as Greece, Egypt, Turkestan and part of India.

[2] Towards the end of the 4th century BC, this vast empire fell into the hands of Alexander of Macedonia. Alexander's successors, the Seleucides and Romans (see Syria) lost their hold on the eastern part of the empire to the Persians, who recovered their independence with the Arsacid dynasty (2nd century BC to 3rd AD). They remained independent under the Sassanids until the 7th century, though constantly at war with the Romans and Byzantines.

[3] After the Arab conquest reached the region in 641 (see Saudi Arabia), Islamic thought and

1 Neutral Zone ▨ Kurdistan   0   300 km

practices became dominant. Unlike the people in most other provinces of the Arab Empire, they retained their own language and distinctive styles in arts and literature. With the fall of the Caliphate of Baghdad, Persia attained virtual independence, first under the descendants of Tahir, the last Arab viceroy, and later under the Seleucidian Turks and the Persian dynasties. Despite political restlessness, the period was remarkably rich in cultural and scientific progress, personified by the poet, mathematician, philosopher and astronomer, Ummar al-Khayyam.

[4] The Mongol invasion led by Hulagu Khan that began in 1258 was an altogether different matter. Three centuries of Mongol domination brought dynastic strife between the descendants of Timur Lenk (Tamburlaine) and the Ottomans. The dispute paved the way for Persian Ismail Shah whose grandson Abbas I (1587-1629) succeeded in uniting the country. He expelled the Turks from the west, the Portuguese from the Ormuz region, and also conquered part of Afghanistan. For a short time Iran ruled a region extending from India to Syria.

[5] A 1909 treaty divided the country into two areas - one of Russian and the other of British economic influence. A British firm was given the opportunity to exploit Iranian petroleum fields. Military occupation by the two powers

during World War I, in addition to government corruption and inefficiency, led to the 1921 revolution headed by journalist Sayyid Tabatabai and Reza Khan, commander of the national guard.

[6] Reza, the revolution's war minister, became prime minister in 1923. Two years later, the National Assembly dismissed Tabatabai, and Reza ousted the Shah, occupying the throne himself. Reza repealed all treaties granting extra-territorial rights to foreign powers, abolished the obligatory use of the veil by women, reformed the education and health systems, and cancelled oil concessions that favored the British.

[7] His attempt to establish a militarily strong, internationally neutral modern state, that became known as Iran in 1935, met with strenuous resistance from European powers. Reza Shah insisted in maintaining strict neutrality, rejecting a July 1941 ultimatum demanding passage for allied arms to the Soviet Union through Iranian territory. In August, British and Soviet forces invaded, forcing the Iranian army to surrender in September. The Shah was overthrown and sent into exile after abdicating in favor of his son, Muhammad Reza Pahlevi. Educated in Europe and more amenable to European interests, the new ruler governed under Anglo-Soviet tutelage until the end of the war.

[8] A 1949 constitution curtailed the Shah's authority, and progressive, nationalist forces won seats in parliament. With their support, Prime Minister Muhammad Mossadegh attempted to nationalize oil reserves and expropriate the Anglo-Iranian Oil Company.

[9] Mossadegh maintained that it was 'better to be independent and produce only one ton of oil a year than produce 32 million tons and continue as slaves of England' - despite the fact that Britain had other sources of supply in the Arab states, Venezuela and the US, while Iran had no alternative market. Mossadegh's audacity was met in 1953 by an economic blockade and a coup backed by the US Central Intelligence Agency (CIA) which returned almost absolute power to the Shah. This chain of events was accompanied by the killing of nationalists and left-wing activists. Thousands were imprisoned. Mossadegh remained in prison until his death in 1967.

[10] The Shah's power depended principally on the oil economy. He encouraged multinational penetration of Iran, citing 'modernization' which effectively consisted of promoting Western consumer habits.

[11] Westernization was resisted by Islamic clergy who feared encroaching secularism, and by those social sectors most affected, notably small farmers and the urban poor. By the end of the 1970s, the growing power of foreign enterprises in the domestic market, plus rapidly changing consumption patterns, had lost the Shah the sympathies of the powerful commercial and industrial élites known locally as the 'bazaar'.

[12] Opposition groups included the National Front founded by Mossadegh, the Tudeh Communist Party, and Fedayin (Marxist) and Mujahedin (Islamic) guerrillas - each using a different strategy. The most effective opposition was centered around the Muslim leader Ayatollah Ruhollah Khomeini, exiled in 1964. Khomeini was resident in Iraq for many years until the Shah, irritated by political ferment in Iranian mosques, pressured the Iraqi Government into deporting him to France.

[13] The recordings of Khomeini's preaching in Paris became

WORKERS

2000

LABOR FORCE AS % OF TOTAL

■ FEMALE: 27%   ■ MALE: 73%

well-known and encouraged the masses to organize. During 1977, demonstrations began in secondary schools and by 1978 became generalized. The Shah was forced to flee in January 1979 and Khomeini made a triumphant return to Iran. On February 11 1979 crowds invaded the imperial palace; the Shah's prime minister resigned, and a divided army accepted the new state of affairs. The Islamic Revolution, seen as a successful alternative to both socialist and capitalist Western models, was welcomed enthusiastically, not only in Iran but throughout the Muslim world.

[14] Prime Minister Mehdi Bazargan of the National Front sought to reconcile Muslim traditions with a model of progressive development permitting broad participation. However he was supported neither by the revolutionary left nor by the Muslim fundamentalists. The latter, bolstered by the 'revolutionary guards' and Khomeini's popularity, first excluded their former left-wing and right-wing allies and then proceeded to suppress them harshly.

[15] In early November 1979, a student group stormed the US embassy in Tehran, taking the diplomatic personnel hostage. Documents found inside provided evidence of CIA involvement in Iranian politics. In April 1980, a US attempt to rescue the hostages was unsuccessful.

[16] On July 17 1980, the Shah died in Egypt and lengthy negotiations began for release of the hostages. This was finally accomplished on January 20 1981.

[17] In September 1980, Iran and Iraq began a war which lasted for eight years. Iraqi president Saddam Hussein wanted to reassert his country's sovereignty over both banks of the Shatt al-Arab river, which historically had been the

MATERNAL MORTALITY

1985/99x

Per 100,000 live births

37

LITERACY

2000

77%

border between the two countries. Hussein was also concerned over attempts by Iran's new Islamic revolutionary government to incite rebellion among Iraq's Shi'a majority.

[18] The Islamic Revolutionary Party (IRP) won the presidential elections with more than 90 per cent of the vote in 1981. On August 30, violent incidents and bombings caused the death of 72 political leaders, among them President Muhammad Ali Rajai and Prime Minister Muhammad Javad Bahonar. A new president, Ali Khamenei, former secretary-general of the IRP, was elected.

[19] The clergy held a favored position, and the Government made widespread use of imprisonment, exile and execution for both political opponents and common criminals. Government sources registered 500 executions in 1989 - mostly for drug trafficking.

[20] In 1985, the country made great commercial profits, despite the war with its neighbor. Iran's main clients were West Germany, Japan, Switzerland, Sweden, Italy and the Arab Emirates, with petroleum being the main export product, constituting 98 per cent of exports.

[21] Contrary to Western expectations, the death of Ayatollah Khomeini on June 3 1989 did not lead to widespread chaos and instability. As more than 8 million mostly poor mourners gathered to bury Khomeini, President Ali Sayed Khamenei was appointed Iran's spiritual leader by a vote of the Assembly of Experts.

[22] In August, new elections gave a landslide victory to Hojatoleslam Ali Akbar Hashemi Rafsanjani, ex-Speaker of Parliament, who became president. The new constitution enhanced the President's role and Rafsanjani took office as a fully empowered executive head of state rather than a ceremonial one. Iran's international image had deteriorated when Khomeini had issued a *fatwa* (death sentence) on Indo-British writer, Salman Rushdie, stating that the writer's book *The Satanic Verses* was blasphemous. Rushdie went into hiding, but in late 1990 he made a few public appearances, reconfirmed his Islamic faith and became reconciled with the main Islamic authorities.

[23] In 1990, Iran condemned the Iraqi invasion of Kuwait, taking advantage of the situation to negotiate previous border disputes. Iraq withdrew from 2,600 square kilometers of occupied Iranian territory, prisoners of war were exchanged, and the countries' sovereignty over the Shatt al-Arab canal was divided. Iran remained neutral when hostilities broke out in 1991.

[24] Rafsanjani's election as president meant a strengthening of the 'pro-Western' wing in the regime. According to the Iranian Constitution, religious and lay authorities share power. But, unlike his predecessor Ruholah Khomeini, the religious leader Ali Khamenei was appointed supreme leader but not Great Ayatollah. The old ayatollah, Araki, bore that responsibility.

[25] Sectors hostile to the West were pre-eminent, but did not have a two-thirds majority in the *Majlis* (Parliament), therefore having no power to change presidential resolutions. The Revolutionary Guards meanwhile were merged into the army, depriving the anti-West sectors of an important pressure group.

[26] Iranian neutrality during the Gulf War was designed to gain advantages over Baghdad, but also to gain acceptance in regional and international diplomacy. Diplomatic relations with Britain were renewed in 1990 and with Saudi Arabia in March 1991, during the Gulf War.

[27] This rapprochement with the West, and the refusal openly to support Iraq during the US offensive, affected relations with other Muslim groups in the region. Iran's lack of support to the Shi'a rebellion in Iraq at the end of the War disappointed those sectors which regarded Tehran as the capital of Shi'a expansion.

[28] The much-desired normalization of relations between Iran and the West was hindered by the use of violence by groups linked to Tehran. The secretary of Chaput Bakhtiar, Shah Reza Pahlevi's former prime minister, was assassinated in April 1991. Bakhtiar himself was killed in May.

[29] With the disintegration of the Soviet Union, a new area of influence lay open to Iran. In 1991, Tehran opened embassies in the Islamic

PROFILE

ENVIRONMENT

Central Iran is a steppe-like plateau with a hostile climate, surrounded by deserts and mountains (the Zagros on the western border and the Elburz to the north). Underground water irrigates the oases where several varieties of grain and fruit trees are cultivated. The shores of the Caspian Sea are more humid and suited to tropical and subtropical crops (cotton, sugar cane and rice). Modern industries (petrochemicals, textiles, building) expanded during the time of Shah Pahlevi, but the industry of hand-made rugs and other materials remains an important activity. Deforestation is occurring in the last remaining forested areas along the Caspian Sea and in the western mountain region, the sea was heavily polluted during the 1991 Gulf War, threatening marine life, and there is air pollution from automobile exhaust emissions, industry and oil refineries, especially in urban areas.

SOCIETY

Peoples: Persian 51 per cent; Azeris 24 per cent; Kurds 9 per cent; Gilaki and Mazandarani 8 per cent; Lur; Arab; Baloch; Bakhtar; Turkmen; Armenian.
Religions: Shi'a Muslims 93.4 per cent; Sunni Muslims 5.7 per cent; Bahai 0.6 per cent; Christians, Zoroastrians and Jews 0.1 per cent.
Languages: Persian (official) and minority languages (Kurds 9 per cent).
Political Parties: Reformist Coalition, whose main party is the Front of Islamic Participation; Islamic conservative parties: Assembly of the Followers of the Imam's Line, Islamic Solidarity of Iran Party, Association of Militant Clergy, and others. Out of Parliament: National Resistence Council; Kurdish Democratic Party; Communist Party; Party of the Masses (Tudeh).
Social organizations: People's Mojahedin is the largest and most active armed militant group, whose philosophy is a mix of Marxism and Islam. With it are the Iranian National Liberation Army and the Union of Islamic Student Societies. Student groups have a significant degree of involvement.

THE STATE

Official Name: Dshumhurije Islâmije Irân. **Administrative divisions:** 28 provinces, 472 towns and 499 municipalities. **Capital:** Teheran (Tehran) 7,158,000 people (1999). **Other cities:** Mashhad 2,020,400 people; Isfahan 2,535,000; Tabriz 1,207,600 (2000). **Government:** Presidential republic. Seyyed Muhammad Khatami, President since August 1997, re-elected in 2001. Religious power is exercised by Sayyed Ali Khamenei since June 1989. **Legislature:** Islamic Consultative Assembly (single-chamber), with 290 members elected by direct popular vote every four years. The members of parliament are elected by secret, universal ballot. **National Holiday:** April 1st, Revolution Day (1979). **Armed Forces:** 513,000 (1995). **Other:** BASIJ 'Popular Mobilization Army' volunteers, mostly youths: strength has been as high as 1 million during periods of offensive operations; Gendarmerie: (45,000 border guards).

republics of the Caucasus and Central Asia, signing trade and cultural agreements and opening new means of communications with its neighbors.

[30] On April 10 1992, legislative elections were held, with the 'moderates' who supported President Rafsanjani winning a clear victory over the 'radical' candidates.

[31] In July, Iran's spiritual leader Khamenei launched a campaign to 'eradicate Western influence', clashing with Rafsanjani and his more moderate vision of Islam to the extent that the President threatened to resign.

[32] However in June 1993, Rafsanjani was confirmed President by 63 per cent of the vote. The high rate of abstentions - 41 per cent of the country's 29 million voters - was read as a sign of discontent over corruption.

[33] In February 1994 - at a time of great tension among the different leading groups - a failed attempt was made on Rafsanjani's life during the celebration of the 15th anniversary of the Islamic Revolution. Disagreements with Saudi Arabia regarding the Muslims' annual pilgrimage to Mecca - Islam's main holy site, in Saudi territory - affected relations with the government of King Fahd and reflected once more the struggle between the two states for the world leadership of Islamic states.

[34] In the economic field, the results did not turn out as expected. Oil sales between March 1994 and March 1995 amounted to $10.5 billion, compared to $17.7 billion in the previous year. Meanwhile, the Government stopped subsidizing 23 imported products, mostly food and medicine, which led to rising prices .

[35] In July, the US toughened its sanctions against Iran, blaming the country for terrorist actions. The measure proposed was challenged by the international community. At the time, unemployment in Iran reached 10 per cent of the working people.

[36] In the May 23 1997 elections there was a 90 per cent turnout of voters. The winner with 69 per cent of the vote was Muhammad Khatami, regarded as the most pro-Western candidate. A new government took over in August and Khatami announced it would open up the country to the West.

[37] At the Islamic conference held in Tehran in December 1997, Israel was criticized for its 'expansionist policy'. The declaration also condemned 'terrorism', in what was considered a 'point in favor' of Khatami in the power struggle occurring within Iran.

[38] In March 1998, Masoume Ebtekar, Iran's deputy minister of Environmental Affairs, denounced the oppressive conditions in which the women of Afghanistan were living under the Islamic regime of the Taliban. In Iran, in contrast with other Muslim countries, women have the right to vote and are increasingly found in decision-making positions.

[39] In November of that year, a series of assassinations of writers and political dissidents began. Official investigations showed that members of the Intelligence Ministry were implicated in the murders. This intensified the struggle for power between reformists and the hardliners, and led President Khatami to propose Fiscal General Ali Yunesi as the new Intelligence Minister in February 1999.

[40] In July 1999, after six days of student protests demanding the reopening of a banned newspaper and greater liberalization, the orthodox sectors launched a counter-protest involving hundreds of thousands of people in support of the clerical authorities and 'revolutionary values'. Ali Khamenei sent a message to the demonstrators calling for strong sanctions against the opposition. Hasan Rowhani, a religious leader and parliamentary speaker, stated that those who were arrested in the student protests should face the death penalty. The orthodox sectors accused the United States of being behind the demonstrations.

[41] Days later, at various points on a tour through the nation's interior that he used as a counter-offensive against the orthodoxy, President Khatami affirmed he would keep his electoral promise to defend civil liberties, despite the attacks of the religious hierarchy, which accused him of having provoked the worst social disturbances since the beginning of the Islamic Revolution in 1979.

[42] The general elections of February 2000 gave an overwhelming victory to the reformists headed by Khatami, who won 226 of the 290 parliamentary seats. In March, the *Hammihan* newspaper printed an image of the US flag, something that had not occurred in this country since the 1979 revolution. Though there was no law prohibiting the publication of the flag, the *Hammihan* gesture was interpreted as the breaking of a taboo.

[43] After two years of negotiations, Iran and Saudi Arabia signed an agreement in April 2001 with measures to patrol the common border and of cooperation among both countries' police forces. Tehran and Riyadh committed themselves, to fighting terrorism, the drug trade and organized crime.

[44] A month later, with its approval of the change in name of Jaled Eslamboli street to Intifada Martyrs, Iran removed the main obstacle to re-establishing full diplomatic relations with Egypt. The street, which until then honored the assassin of Egyptian President Anwar Sadat (who had signed the peace with Israel), had been the seed of discord between both countries. The first contact between Iran and Egypt heads of state, after the Islamic Revolution, took place in June 2000, when Egyptian President Hosni Mubarak phoned Khatami to congratulate him on the incorporation of Iran to the Group of 15, formed by non-developed countries.

[45] In the June elections, which had a low turnout, Khatami was re-elected with 77 per cent of the vote, beating nine rivals, eight of them radicals and anti-reformist. The Government had been able to reduce dependence of the national economy regarding oil revenues and also lowered inflation, which in April that year had reached 12.6 per cent, the lowest in one decade. Notwithstanding, some social sectors were still unhappy with the economy's direction.

[46] The low electoral turnout (67 per cent) was explained mainly by the increase in poverty and economic troubles of the middle class, as well as by the President's failure to keep at bay the radicals, who controlled the powerful security services and justice system.

[47] Both reformists and radicals took to the streets when, in January 2002, the President of the US, George W Bush, described Iraq, Iran and North Korea as the 'axis of evil', sponsors of terrorism and wanting to obtain and develop mass destruction weapons. On a visit to Vienna in March, the first after Bush's statements, Khatami not only denied the allegations, but stressed that a country must not 'label' another with being 'evil'. On the contrary, he said, all countries must work jointly to attack the real 'evil in the world: poverty, injustice, terrorism and violence'.

[48] A month before, Tehran had rejected the new British ambassador, David Reddaway. For one week, Iranian radical journals had launched a campaign against Reddaway, calling him a Zionist Jew and spy. The decision was considered a severe blow to Iranian-British relations, which had improved considerably in the last years. Britain is considered a lackey of Washington by hardline authorities in Iran.

[49] Iranian and Chinese concerns about the growing influence of the US in the world, as well as about the reconstruction of Afghanistan, which borders both countries, led Chinese President Jiang Zemin, in April 2002, to make his first visit to Tehran since the Islamic Revolution. In the 1999-2001 period, trade between both countries had tripled. ∎

DEMOGRAPHY
Population: 72,376,000 (2002)
Annual growth: 2.5 % (1985-2000)
Estimates for year 2015: 87,103,000 (2000)
Annual growth to year 2015: 1.4 % (2000)
Urban population: 61.6 % (2000)
Urban growth: 2.3 % (2000)
Children per woman: 3.0 (2000)

HEALTH
Life expectancy at birth: 70 years (2000-2005)
male: 69 years (2000-2005)
female: 71 years (2000-2005)
Maternal mortality: 37 per 100,000 live births (1985/99)
Infant mortality: 36 per 1,000 (2000)
Under-5 child mortality: 44 per 1,000 (2000)
Daily calorie supply: 2,898 per capita (1999)
85 doctors per 100,000 people (1996)
Safe water: 92 % (2000)

EDUCATION
Literacy: 77 % (2000)
male: 84 % (2000)
female: 70 % (2000)
School enrolment (net):
Primary total: 97 % (1994/2000)
male: 99 % (1995/99)
female: 94 % (1995/99)
Secondary (gross):
male: 81 % (1995/97)
female: 73 % (1995/97)
Tertiary (gross): 18 % (1997)
Primary school teachers: one for every 30 pupils (1996)

COMMUNICATIONS
28 newspapers (1996), 281 radios (1998), 163 TV sets (2000) and 149 main telephone lines (2000) per 1,000 people
Books: 16 new titles per 100,000 people (1992/94)

ECONOMY
Per capita, GDP: $ 5,884 (2000)
Annual growth: 3.9 % (2000)
Annual inflation: 14.5 % (2000)
Consumer price index: 245.1 (2000)
Currency: 1,752.5 rials = $ 1 (03/2002)
Cereal imports: 9,928,299 metric tons (2000)
Food import dependency: 19 % (2000)
Fertilizer use: 652 kg per ha (1999)
Exports: $ 36,547 million (2000)
Imports: $ 21,663 million (2000)
External debt: $ 7,953 million (2000); $ 113 per capita (2000)
Debt service: 22.6 % of exports (1999)
Development aid received: $ 161 million (1999); $ 2.6 per capita (1999); 0.10 % of GNP (1999)

ENERGY
Consumption: 1,649.0 Kgs of oil equivalent per capita yearly (1998); -121.4 % imported (1999)

HDI (ranking/value): 90 / 0.714 (1999)

Iraq

Population:	24,246,000 (2002)
Land area:	437,370 SQ KM
Capital:	Baghdad
Currency:	Dinar
Language:	Arabic

Iraq

The territory of present-day Iraq is roughly equivalent to that of ancient Mesopotamia, where the world's 'classic' civilization developed. Around 5000 BC in the southern region of Iraq flourished the Sumerian civilization; in 2371 BC, King Sargon Of Akkad asserted control of the region and established the first Assyrian dynasty. The Assyrian empire expanded its dominion to include modern Turkey, Iran, Syria and Israel. The empire collapsed with the fall of its capital Nineveh (modern day Mosul) in 612 BC and was followed by the Babylonians. King Hammurabi (reigning circa 1792-50 BC), made Babylon the capital and established the first Code of Laws. King Nebuchadnezzar II (c. 605-562 B.C.), a splendid builder, developed hanging gardens that made Babylon the greatest city of the ancient world.

[2] The Babylonian era came to an end when the Persian ruler Cyrus the Great invaded in 539 BC. and Persia ruled until Alexander the Great's conquests in 331 BC. His successors, the Seleucids, ruled for 175 years, until new Persian invasions under the Parthi'ans and later the Sassanids established a new capital at Ctesiphon near the midpoint of the Tigris. Persians constructed many irrigation systems and canals.

[3] In the 7th century the Arab conquest transformed Mesopotamia into the center of an enormous empire (see Saudi Arabia). A century later, the new Abbas dynasty decided to move the capital east from Damascus. Caliph al-Mansur built the new capital, Baghdad, on the banks of the Tigris and for three centuries the city of the 'thousand and one nights' was the center of a new culture.

[4] This culture led to the greatest flourishing of the arts and sciences in the Mediterranean region since the days of the Greeks. The empire began to fall apart after the death of Harun al-Raschid. The African provinces were lost (see Tunisia: Islam in North Africa), and the region north and east of Persia won independence under the Tahiris (the Kingdom of Khorasan). The caliphs depended increasingly on armies of slaves or mercenaries (Sudanese or Turks) to retain their grip on an ever-shrinking empire. When the Mongols assassinated the last caliph in

Baghdad in 1258, the title had already lost its political meaning. The conquests of Genghis Khan devastated the region's agricultural economy, and the region was subsequently ruled in whole or part by Seleucids, Ottomans, Turks, Mongols, Turkomans, Tartars, and Kurds. The movement of steppe peoples (see Afghanistan), brought great instability to the fertile crescent, which finally achieved unification under the Ottoman Turks in the 16th century, having repelled an attack by Timur Lenk (Tamburlaine) in the 14th century.

[5] In the early 20th century, Arab Renaissance movements were active in Iraq, paving the way for the rebellion that rocked the Turkish realm during World War I (see Saudi Arabia, Jordan and Syria). The British already had a foothold in the region and were keen to expand their influence. With the defeat of the Turks, Iraq entertained hopes of independence. These however were dashed when the revolutionary Soviet government revealed the existence of the secret Sykes-Picot treaty (signed in 1916), whereby France and Britain divided the Arab territories between themselves. Faisal, son of the shereef Hussein, had proclaimed himself King of Syria and occupied Damascus. However, since this territory 'belonged' to the French, who had promised nothing

to the Arabs, (see Saudi Arabia, Jordan and Syria), he was forcibly evicted. In 1920, Britain was awarded a mandate over Mesopotamia by the League of Nations, triggering a pro-independence rebellion.

[6] In 1921, Emir Faisal ibn Hussain was appointed King of Iraq, in compensation for his previous bad treatment. In 1930, general Nuri as-Said was appointed Prime Minister, signing a treaty of alliance with the British, under which the country would become nominally independent on October 3 1932.

[7] That year, the Baghdad Pact was founded, making Iraq part of a military alliance with Turkey, Pakistan, Iran, Britain and the US. This pact was resisted by Iraqi nationalists. In July 1958, anti-imperialist agitation resulted in a military coup led by Abdul Karim Kassim, bringing about the execution of the royal family.

[8] In 1959 the regime tried to forge a union with Syria, but the Communist Party - one of the most important in the East - and the democrats, whose model was the European parliamentary system, opposed the move. In July, in an attempt to consolidate the regime, Kassim banned all political parties and proclaimed that the emirate of Kuwait belonged to Iraq. The Arab League, dominated by Egypt, authorized the deployment of British

troops to protect the oil rich enclave.

[9] Kassim's over-exaggerated ties with the Soviet Union and China fomented predictions that Iraq could become 'a new Cuba'. In the summer of 1960 the country suddenly moved towards the West. Steps toward economic change were taken, a land reform program was implemented, and the profits of the Iraq Petroleum Company were severely restricted. In 1963, Kassim was deposed by pan-Arabian sectors within the army. Several unstable governments ensued until July 17 1968, when a military coup placed the Ba'ath party in power.

[10] Founded in 1947, the Arab Ba'ath Socialist Party (ba'ath meaning renaissance) was inspired by the ideal of Pan-Arabism, regarding the Arab World as an indivisible political and economic unit where no country 'can be self-sufficient'. The Ba'athists proclaimed that 'socialism is a need which emerges from the very core of Arab nationalism. It is organized on a national (Arab) level, having several regional leaders in each country.'

[11] Iraq nationalized foreign companies, and Baghdad defended the use of oil as a 'political weapon in the struggle against imperialism and Zionism'. It insisted on protected prices and the consolidation of OPEC as an organization which would support the struggle of the Third World for the recovery and enhancement of its natural resources. A land reform program was decreed, and ambitious development plans encouraged the reinvestment of oil money into national industrialization.

[12] In 1970, the Baghdad Government gave the Kurdish language official status, and granted Kurdistan domestic autonomy. However, abetted by the Shah of Iran, and fearful of land reform, the traditional regional leaders rose in armed confrontation. In March 1975, the Iran-Iraq border agreement deprived the Kurds of their main foreign support and the rebels were defeated. The Baghdad Government decreed the teaching of Kurdish in local schools, greater state investment in the region, and the appointment of Kurds to key administrative positions.

[1] Neutral Zone　Kurdistan

0　300 km

¹³ On July 16 1979, President Ahmed Hassan al-Bakr resigned because of ill-health. He was replaced by Vice-President Saddam Hussein.

¹⁴ Saddam Hussein tried to establish himself as leader of the Arab world. He was one of the most outspoken critics of the 1979 Camp David agreements between Egypt, Israel and the US, but Iraqi relations with other Arab countries still worsened. A branch of the Ba'ath party took power in Syria in 1970, but its discrepancies with Baghdad led to rivalry and some border disputes.

¹⁵ Saddam wanted to reassert Iraq's sovereignty over both banks of the Shatt al-Arab waterway that historically had been the border with Iran. He was also concerned about attempts by Iran's new Islamic revolutionary government to incite rebellion among Iraq's Shi'a majority. These issues spurred Saddam to make a preemptive strike on Iran. By attacking when it did, Iraq took advantage of the apparent disorder of Iran's new government and demoralization of its regular armed forces. The Iraqis were confident of a quick victory but in the event the war lasted for 8 years.

¹⁶ During the war, the Saudis and Kuwaitis - like others who had benefited from Iraq acting as a bulwark against Iranian fundamentalism - granted Baghdad many loans which were used both in the conflict and for strengthening the country's infrastructure. An oil pipeline was built through Turkey as an alternative to the one which crossed Syria to the Mediterranean; Syria had closed this in sympathy with Iran. The roads to Jordan were also improved.

¹⁷ In November 1984, 17 years after they had broken off diplomatic relations, official links with the US were re-established.

¹⁸ The 1988 armistice meant that Iraq retained 2,600 square kilometers of Iranian territory with its powerful and skilful army. Neighboring Kuwait was extracting more oil than allowed from deposits under the border and refused to establish export quotas. As the US hinted that they would remain neutral in the event of conflict, Baghdad thought that it would be able to take the neighboring territory and exploit its wealth. On August 2, Iraq invaded Kuwait and took thousands of foreign hostages.

¹⁹ Four days later the UN decided on a total economic and military blockade until Iraq retreated unconditionally from the occupied territory. Withdrawal was rejected, but a proposal for an international conference to discuss the Middle East issue was submitted. When Iraq started to release the hostages and to make new attempts at negotiating, the US refused to talk and demanded an unconditional surrender.

²⁰ On January 17, 1991, an alliance of 32 countries led by the US started the attacks on Iraq. When the land offensive began in March, Saddam Hussein had already announced his unconditional withdrawal. The Iraqi army did not resist the offensive and hardly attempted to stage an organized withdrawal, yet it suffered great losses. The war ended early in March, with the total defeat of the Iraqis.

²¹ At the end of the offensive, the US encouraged an internal revolt of the southern Shi'a and of the northern Kurds so that Saddam Hussein would be deposed. However, the political differences between these factions made an alliance impossible, and Washington abandoned the rebels to their own fates, whereupon they were crushed by the still powerful Iraqi army. Over one million Kurds sought refuge in Iran and Turkey to escape the Baghdad forces, and thousands starved or froze to death when winter came.

²² Between 150,000 and 200,000 people, mostly civilians, died in the war. As a result of the blockade - still in force - some 70,000 more may have died in the first year, among them 20,000 children. At the end of 1991, both the Turkish and Iraqi armies were continuing to harass the Kurds in the border area.

²³ The conditions stipulated for lifting sanctions became even more demanding with the increased determination on the part of the US Government to bring down Hussein. In addition, The *New York Times* and the London *Sunday Telegraph* reported that the United States had introduced huge amounts of counterfeit dinars (Iraq's currency), smuggled across the Jordanian, Saudi Arabian, Turkish and Iranian borders. Baghdad established the death penalty for anyone participating in these operations.

²⁴ Toward the end of 1991, the Iraqi Government authorized UN inspections of military establishments. In 1992, Iraq was found to have a uranium enrichment project, which had been developed using German technology. UN inspection teams destroyed 460 x 122 mm warheads armed with sarin, a poisonous gas. They also dismantled the nuclear complex at

---

PROFILE

ENVIRONMENT

The Mesopotamian region, between the rivers Tigris (Dijlah) and Euphrates (Al-Furat) in the center of the country, is suitable for agriculture, and contains most of the population. In the mountainous areas in the north, in Kurdistan, there are important oil deposits. In Lower Mesopotamia, on the Shatt-al-Arab channel, where the Tigris and the Euphrates merge, 15 million palm trees produce 80 per cent of the world's dates sold worldwide, before the blockade. The war's devastation included the destruction of the major part of the country's infrastructure. Tank and troop movements caused major damage to road surfaces and soil, especially in the environmentally sensitive area along the Saudi Arabian border.

SOCIETY

Peoples: Three fourths of the population are Arabs. In the north there is a significant Kurd minority (20 per cent) and the rest are small minorities of Syrians, Armenians and others. **Religions:** Mostly Muslim. About 62 per cent of the population is Shi'a, concentrated in the south. Most of the political élite is Sunni. Northern Kurds also share this religious option (Sunnis amount to 35 per cent of the population), together with their traditional religion, Yezidi. There is a Christian minority. **Languages:** Arabic (official and predominant); in Kurdistan it is taught as a second language, after Kurdish. **Political Parties:** The Arab Ba'ath Socialist Party has been in power since 1968; Out of Parliament: Democratic Party of Kurdistan, Patriotic Union of Kurdistan and Christian Union. **Social Organizations:** General Federation of Trade Unions is the single labor confederation; General Union of Students of the Republic of Iraq; there are opposition groups among the 'swamp Arabs' in the south, such as the Supreme Council of the Islamic Revolution, a Shi'a resistance group.

THE STATE

Official Name: Al-Jumhuriyah al-'Iraqiyah.
Administrative divisions: 15 provinces and 3 autonomous regions.
Capital: Baghdad 4,689,000 people (1999). **Other cities:** Mosul 1,099,700 people; al-Basrah 1,004,800; Irbil 692,100; Karkuk (Kirkuk) 688,500 (2000).
Government: Saddam Hussein, President since July 1979, re-elected in 1995 and Prime Minister since May 1994. Parliament: The Majlis Watani (National Assembly) has 250 members but the 30 seats of the Kurdish region remained vacant. **National Holidays:** July 14, Proclamation of the Republic (1958); July 17, Revolution Day (1968).
Armed Forces: 380.000 troops (1997).

STATISTICS

DEMOGRAPHY
Population: 24,246,000 (2002)
Annual growth: 2.7 % (1985-2000)
Estimates for year 2015: 33,550,000 (2000)
Annual growth to year 2015: 2.5 % (2000)
Urban population: 76.8 % (2000)
Urban growth: 2.6 % (2000)
Children per woman: 5.1 (2000)

HEALTH
Life expectancy at birth: 65 years (2000-2005)
male: 63 years (2000-2005)
female: 66 years (2000-2005)
Infant mortality: 105 per 1,000 (2000)
Under-5 child mortality: 130 per 1,000 (2000)
Daily calorie supply: 2,446 per capita (1999)
55 doctors per 100,000 people (1998)
Safe water: 85 % (2000)

EDUCATION
Literacy: 58 % (2000)
male: 71 % (2000)
female: 45 % (2000)
School enrolment (net):
Primary total: 93 % (1994/2000)
male: 98 % (1995/99)
female: 88 % (1995/99)
Secondary (gross):
male: 51 % (1995/97)
female: 32 % (1995/97)
Tertiary (gross): 13 % (1998)
Primary school teachers: one for every 22 pupils (1998)

COMMUNICATIONS
19 newspapers (1996), 222 radios (1997), 83 TV sets (2000) and 29 main telephone lines (2000) per 1,000 people

ECONOMY
Annual growth: -52.1 % (1991)
Currency: 0.3 dinars = $ 1 (03/2002)
Cereal imports: 4,229,169 metric tons (2000)
Fertilizer use: 782 kg per ha (1999)

ENERGY
Consumption: 1,342.4 Kgs of oil equivalent per capita yearly (1998); -357.5 % imported (1999)

---

al-Athir, the uranium enrichment installations at Ash-Sharqat and Tarmiuah, and the chemical weapons plant at Muthana.

[25] In 1994 a frontier crossing was opened with Turkey to allow certain UN authorized foodstuffs and medicines to enter the country - the only exceptions to the trade embargo. However a few months later in March 1995, Turkish troops invaded Iraqi Kurdistan - under the military protection of 'allied' - basically US troops to repress members of the Kurdish Workers Party (PKK) which was launching attacks from there on Turkish troops stationed in Turkish Kurdistan.

[26] Baghdad's international isolation deepened in 1996, when Jordan distanced itself from Saddam's Government, having improved its relations with Kuwait and Saudi Arabia. However, the UN Security Council voted for the partial lifting of the blockade, allowing for a restricted sale of crude oil, in order to buy food and medicines for the Iraqi population.

[27] A UN report revealed in April 1997 that the number of dead due to hunger or lack of medicines arising from the embargo exceeded one million people, of which 570,000 were children. UNICEF claimed that '25 per cent of children below 5 had severe clinical malnutrition'.

[28] A new crisis unfolded in October concerning Iraq: the Security Council threatened to enforce new sanctions if a new inspection was not allowed to verify that the Saddam administration was not able to develop chemical and biological weapons. Iraq rejected the presence of US inspectors, which hardened US President Clinton's stance. Coinciding with the beginning of the debate leading to his impeachment by Congress (see US), Clinton, with the sole support of British Prime Minister Tony Blair, launched a missile attack on several Iraqi cities. From December 16, 'Operation Desert Fox' killed hundreds of civilian and military Iraqis. France, Russia and China - all of them members of the UN Security Council - denounced this British-US offensive and criticized the role played by Richard Butler, chief of UNSCOM, the UN commission in charge of supervising Iraq's chemical and nuclear disarmament.

[29] By a slight margin, in December 1999, the Security Council approved resumption of the weapons inspections in Iraq and the suspension of the economic sanctions in case Baghdad decided to cooperate. Russia, France, China and Malaysia abstained in the vote, which was a harsh blow to the interests of the US and UK. They had tried to send Saddam a clear signal but the resolution was a minority choice even among permanent members of the Security Council. Iraq, which had already announced it would reject the resolution, alleging it was an attempt by the US to impose its 'evil' will on the Security Council, refused to co-operate and demanded all sanctions be lifted.

[30] In July 2000 Communications Minister Ahmad Murtada opened the country's first internet center and promised three more would soon open in Baghdad. The Minister stated the center had been created in spite of obstacles brought about by US and British authorities in the UN Sanctions Committee, which had tried to prevent Iraqi acquisition of information technology, even though this had been approved under the oil-for-food program, which allowed Baghdad to export oil for food, medicines and basic products.

[31] Baghdad airport reopened in August, receiving several international flights which, in the guise of humanitarian missions, were supported by countries (some of them, like France, members of the anti-Iraq coalition during the Gulf War) and organizations that had campaigned against the sanctions. In November, for the first time in nine years, the Iraqi national airline operated within the country. That month, Iraqi deputy Prime Minister Tariq Aziz rejected a new proposal of weapons inspection.

[32] When George W Bush took office as US President in January 2001, he announced a tough policy and the 'fortification' of sanctions against Iraq. The attacks against Washington and New York in September put Iraq directly in the Pentagon's sights. The US tried to pressure - unsuccessfully - the alliance it had formed to fight global terrorism into making Baghdad its target. However, the allies' reluctance, including Britain's, led the White House to seek new ways of 'putting an end' to Saddam Hussein. Meanwhile Saddam regained popularity in the Arab world by supporting the second Palestinian intifada and proposing that Muslim countries pursue their common interests, foremost being the Palestine cause, through a control of oil prices.

[33] In January 2002, in his State of the Union speech, Bush aligned Iraq, Iran and North Korea as an 'axis of evil' which, he claimed, sought weapons of mass destruction and sponsors international terrorism. These statements were criticized by his global allies and democratic opposition. In April, *The New York Times* reported that the Bush administration was planning an attack on Iraq, which would involve 250,000 soldiers.

[34] In September President Bush sought a UN mandate for attacking Iraq. ∎

Kurds: from nomadism to nationalism

The Kurds are an ethnic and linguistic group living mostly in the mountains of Taurus, in eastern Anatolia, in the regions of Zagros and Khorasan (Iran), and in northern Iraq. It is estimated that, including the communities existing in Armenia, Georgia, Kazakhsztan, Lebanon and Syria, they number more than 15 million people. For centuries they have been nomads in the Mesopotamian plains and the mountain regions of Iran and Turkey, raising sheep and goats. Exceptionally, they have also been farmers. After World War I, many were forced to live in urban areas, leaving their traditions behind.

Although they have lived in the same geographic region for a long time, they have never had a national state. The Treaty of Sèvres, which was concluded in 1920 and granted autonomy to Kurdistan, was never ratified. It was followed in 1923 by the Lausanne Treaty, which no longer mentioned Kurdistan nor the Kurds. After the war, the region was engulfed by violence, with the appearance of armed separatist movements .

For centuries, the Kurds had a form of social government which followed the rules of the tribe. The sheik was the main authority. This holds true even today, although not as much in urban groups which have lost some of their tribal identity while adaptating to city life. In some cases, and even when the law does not allow it, as in Turkey, the Kurds practice polygamy.

In Turkey, Government discrimination against the Kurds is widespread. Their identity has been denied by calling them 'mountain Turks', their language is banned (and regarded as a dialect derived from Turkish) as are some of their most typical customs. The Government repressed their political activity in the Eastern provinces and also encouraged their migration to urban areas in the west, in order to disperse Kurds concentrated in mountain areas. In Iran they are subject to strong pressure by the Government to assimilate into the majority culture and religious persecution from the Shiite majority.

In Iraq, when the monarchy was defeated in 1958, the Kurds expected their linguistic status would be acknowledged and thought they would receive more social benefits and greater participation in development projects. However, these expectations were not fulfilled. Instead, the Iraqi Government implemented a policy of displacement, promoted armed conflicts and, in the 1980s, used lethal chemical weapons against whole communities. Over a period of 15 years, more than 400,000 Kurds died in Iraq.

Kurdish nationalism has begun to appear not just as a response to these discriminatory conditions. Its late emergence can perhaps be attributed to their ancient nomadic lifestyle. In a way, this nationalism is prompted by certain Western influences (such as private property), the partition of the Kurdistan region into states, and the appearance of an urban intellectual minority. The interests of some Western countries in the Persian Gulf have played a part as well. ∎

Ireland

Population:	3,878,000 (2002)
Land area:	68,890 SQ KM
Capital:	Dublin
Currency:	Euro
Language:	Irish and English

Eire

Ireland's original inhabitants were Middle Stone Age (Mesolithic) hunter-gatherers who used stone implements. Around 3000 BC, they evolved into Bronze Age (Neolithic) people who cultivated crops, raised domestic animals and (even though metals were extremely rare in Ireland) made weapons, tools and jewelry out of bronze. Starting about 2000 BC, they built the massive stone sanctuaries and tombs (megaliths) that still dot the Irish countryside. By the 1st Century BC, Ireland was under the control of the Picts, a Neolithic people described in Irish folklore as the 'Fir Bolg'.

[2] The first Celts (see box 'The Celts') arrived in Ireland about 600 BC, bringing Iron Age skills with them. A major migration arrived about 350 BC. The Celts dominated the island until 1170 AD and further dominated major parts of it until 1600 AD. Politically, the Celts divided Ireland into four provinces: Leinster, Munster, Ulster and Connaught. Before their arrival, the basic units of Irish society were the *tuatha*, or petty kingdoms; perhaps 150 tuatha for a population of less than 500,000. This societal structure suited the Celts, who were predisposed towards relatively small and autonomous units. A recurring theme throughout Irish history is popular resistance to centralized government under a strong monarch, and insistence upon a loose confederation of small and autonomous units of government.

[3] A bishop and missionary coming from England, St Patrick (c.389-461), arrived in Ireland to convert the inhabitants to Christianity. He was able to make important converts among the royal families and, through the monastery schools, introduced the written word in Latin. By the death of St. Patrick the Irish élite recorded their history in writing. Ireland became almost exclusively Christian, as well as a center of scholarship and culture, but most of this legacy was destroyed in the Viking raids of the 9th and 10th centuries.

[4] By the end of the 10th century Brian Boru, the king of a small state called Dal Cais, conquered his bigger neighbors and made himself the strongest king in the southern half of Ireland. But Mael Morda, King of Leinster, began to plot against him

and made an alliance with Sitric, the Viking king of Dublin, who got help from the Vikings of the Orkney Islands and the Isle of Man. The battle of Clontarf near Dublin in 1014 ended in victory for Boru's army, but Boru himself was killed in his tent by Vikings fleeing from the battle.

[5] In 1169, a party of Normans coming from England landed near Waterford. By 1300, the Normans controlled most of the country but they did not succeed in conquering Ireland because there was no central government that they could take control of. From about 1350, the Irish chieftains - who had acquired many of the weapons used by the Normans and had learnt some of their tactics - began to recover their territories. In 1534, Henry VIII of England refused to recognize the authority of the Pope. He persuaded the English Parliament to recognize him as head of the Church in England. He tried to impose a similar policy on Ireland and, in 1536, acts were passed forbidding people to appeal to Rome or to make payments to the Pope. Between 1537 and 1541, a number of monasteries were suppressed and their property confiscated. But, in areas under Irish rule, where the King had no real power, most of the people were unaware that any changes had taken place. Henry's daughter Mary, who succeeded to the throne in 1553, was a fervent

Roman Catholic who worked hard to restore the old religion. She believed that the best way to subdue Ireland was to introduce colonies of English people into the country and in 1556, she confiscated Irish land and sent English settlers there. The settlers were to take their English tenants and servants with them.

[6] Mary's half-sister, Elizabeth, who succeeded her in 1558, adopted a harsher attitude, and a number of Irish bishops and priests were executed. This persecution drove the Irish and those of the Anglo-Irish who had remained Roman Catholics closer together. A new national spirit developed that was both Roman Catholic and anti-English in outlook.

[7] By virtue of the 1800 Act of Union, Ireland was incorporated into the United Kingdom. During the 19th century most of the population outside the Protestant-dominated North-east supported independence, which led to the formation of a strong nationalist movement.

[8] In 1916, the republican Easter Rising in Dublin was crushed by the occupying forces but it marked the foundation of the Irish Republican Army (IRA) and the final stage of the long struggle for freedom.

[9] The IRA's campaign of guerrilla warfare forced the British in 1920 to grant independence to the 26 counties with Catholic majorities. Southern Ireland became a self-

governing region within the UK. The remaining six north-eastern counties became Northern Ireland, with a devolved government in Belfast and representation in the British parliament in Westminster. In 1922 Southern Ireland had declared independence and become the Irish Free State, a dominion under the British crown. In 1949 the Free State became the Irish Republic, formally breaking its final links with the British commonwealth.

[10] The 1937 Irish Constitution considered Ireland to be a single country, where all the inhabitants - North and South - have citizenship rights.

[11] Supported by the Protestant majority, the Ulster Unionist Party always managed to retain control of the Parliament in Belfast. For 50 years, Northern Ireland was ruled exclusively by Unionists, led by the Provincial Prime Minister and a Governor acting as a representative of the British Crown.

[12] The Catholic minority in Northern Ireland was thus excluded from domestic political affairs, and many other fields. This led to the creation of an active civil rights movement in the 1960s.

[13] Although it was non-violent, the civil rights movement was considered a threat to the region's status and their dominant position by Protestant extremists and they reacted to it with violence.

[14] In April 1969, amidst growing disturbances, the Northern Ireland government requested British troops to protect the region's strategic installations. In August, Belfast and London agreed that all the Province's security forces should come under British command.

[15] As a counterpart to the Provisional IRA, the 'loyalists' (loyal to the British crown) formed a number of paramilitary organizations, including the Ulster Volunteer Force and the Ulster Defence Association. Between 1969 and the middle of 1994, more than 3,100 people died at the hands of the Protestant and Catholic paramilitaries, the British army and the Ulster police force, the Royal Ulster Constabulary (RUC). In 1972 political status was given to paramilitary prisoners, but this amendment was abolished in 1976.

¹⁶ The growing violence provoked London to take over full responsibility for law and order in Northern Ireland. The Government in Belfast was abolished and a system of 'direct rule' from Westminster installed. In a plebiscite held in March 1973, 60 per cent of the population of Northern Ireland voted in favor of union with Britain.

¹⁷ At the end of 1973, a Northern Irish Assembly and Executive was created in Belfast in which Protestant and Catholic representatives were supposed to share power.

¹⁸ In December, the London and Dublin governments agreed on the establishment of an Irish Council. Both this agreement and the new power-sharing Assembly were bitterly opposed by most Protestants in Ulster. In 1974, the Protestant Ulster Workers' Council declared a general strike in Northern Ireland. This resulted in the resignation of the Executive and London took over direct rule once more.

¹⁹ In the 1973 election in the Irish Republic, Fianna Fáil - a conservative nationalist party which had been in power for 44 years - was defeated. A coalition between the conservative Fine Gael and the Labour Party took office. This new administration was committed to power-sharing between the two communities in Ulster, but it rejected the immediate withdrawal of British troops from the region.

²⁰ In 1976, after the IRA murdered the British ambassador in Dublin, the Irish Government took stricter anti-terrorist measures. Fianna Fáil was elected in 1977 and it maintained the friendly relations with London established by the previous administration. Prime Minister Jack Lynch supported the creation of a devolved parliament in the North, instead of total unification.

²¹ In August 1979, Dublin agreed to increase border security after the murders, on the same day, of Lord Mountbatten (a prominent British public figure related to the Royal Family) in the Irish Republic, and 18 British soldiers in Warrenpoint, Northern Ireland. In December, Lynch resigned and was replaced by former Prime Minister Charles Haughey, who went back to the old idea of reunification with some form of autonomy in Ulster.

²² The Irish Council on the Condition of Women had been created in 1972. Women of both parts of Ireland had to travel to England for abortion, which was banned, and the sale of contraceptives remained limited in the Irish Republic. A referendum held in 1983 approved a constitutional amendment affirming the ban on abortion. At the same time, a law prohibiting divorce - in place for 60 years and which the Government proposed to revoke - was maintained. It was estimated some 40,000 Irish women travel to the UK each year to have an abortion.

²³ Talks between the Irish and British heads of Government, in 1980, led to the signing of the Anglo-Irish Agreement in 1985. With it, the Dublin Government would have a say in political, judicial, security and border issues of Northern Ireland. Most of the Protestant population in Northern Ireland was strongly opposed, but the Agreement guaranteed that the Province's constitutional situation would be decided by its population.

²⁴ A new wave of violence broke out in the first months of 1989. In April, three members of the Ulster Defense Association (UDA) were arrested in Paris, together with a South African diplomat. It is presumed Pretoria gave them weapons to obtain secret technology from British missiles, stolen from a factory in Belfast.

²⁵ In September 1989, the Irish Government demanded a complete reorganization of the Ulster Defense Regiment (UDR), the largest volunteer Protestant regiment, to investigate its links with paramilitary groups, especially regarding the smuggling of secret intelligence documents. The United Kingdom accepted the Irish request and, in result, 94 soldiers from the UDR were arrested the following month.

²⁶ In the 1980s, the Irish economy suffered high unemployment levels (an average of 16.4 per cent between 1983 and 1988) and emigration levels, added to high inflation rates and industrial recession. Strict austerity measures, applied since 1987, allowed for growth in the second half of the decade. Irish women amounted to only 38.5 per cent of the working population, placing Ireland second-last in Western Europe.

²⁷ The General Synod of the Church of Ireland approved in 1990 the ordination of women, a decision which placed that church in a more progressive level than other Anglican churches.

²⁸ In November 1990, Mary Robinson, a lawyer who stood up for defending the rights of gays, women and the legal recognition of illegitimate children, became the first woman president of Ireland.

²⁹ Multi-party negotiations began in Belfast in April 1991, in another attempt to define Northern Ireland's political future. These were the first significant talks since 1974, with representatives from Ulster's constitutional parties (Protestant Unionists, Catholic Nationalists and the Alliance Party) and the London government. Sinn Féin, the political arm of the Provisional IRA, which supported the immediate withdrawal of British troops, the disarmament of the Royal Ulster Constabulary (RUC) police and Ireland's reunification, was excluded from the talks for having refused to condemn the IRA's acts of violence.

³⁰ Meanwhile, the IRA launched one of its largest military offensives, both in Ulster and England. In early 1992, in Ulster, independent Republicans were responsible for several acts of arson in businesses and shops. Since late 1991, Protestant paramilitary groups had reinforced their attacks on Catholics. These groups said they were willing to reply with 'an eye for an eye' to every IRA action.

³¹ During January 1993, Albert Reynolds, from Fianna Fáil, was confirmed as head of government, although his party and the Fine Gael lost seats to the Labor Party. At the same time, a referendum on abortion led two-thirds of voters to support the right to information on birth control and abortion to travel abroad to carry them out.

³² In January 1994, the Government lifted all restrictions on Sinn Féin's radio broadcasts. In

PROFILE

ENVIRONMENT

The country comprises most of the island of Ireland. The south is made up of rocky hills, none over 1,000 meters in height. The central plain extends from east to west and is irrigated by many rivers and lakes. With a humid ocean climate and poor soil, much of the country is covered with grazing land. Farming is concentrated mainly along the eastern slopes of the hills and the Shannon valleys. The main agricultural products are wheat, barley, oats, potatoes and beet. Meat and milk processing are among the major local industrial activities.

SOCIETY

Peoples: The Irish comprise 94 per cent of the population, with a small English minority. The great famines which struck the island over the last two centuries led to the emigration of about 4 million Irish people, especially to the US. **Religions:** 91.6 per cent Catholic, 2.3 per cent Anglican, 0.4 per cent Presbyterian (1991). **Languages:** Irish, English and Shelta (language of the Travelers/gypsies/Roma people). **Political Parties:** Fianna Fáil (FF), conservative; Fine Gael (FG), Christian democratic linked to the rural population; Labour Party; Progressive Democrats; Green Party; the Democratic Left and Sinn Féin, republican movement party based in Northern Ireland. **Social Organizations:** The Irish Congress of Trade Unions, with 600,000 members, amounts to 45 per cent of the economically active population.

THE STATE

Official Name: Poblacht na h'Eireann. **Administrative Divisions:** 26 Counties. **Capital:** Dublin 977,000 people (1999). **Other cities:** Cork 186,400 people; Limerick 82,000; Galway 59,400; Waterford 45,700 (2000). **Government:** Mary McAleese, President since November 1997. Bartholomew (Bertie) Ahern, Prime Minister since June 1997, re-elected in May 2002. Bicameral Parliament: the House of Representatives, with 166 members, and the Senate, with 60 members. **National Holiday:** March 17 (St Patrick's Day). **Armed Forces:** 11,450 (1999).

1985/99

Per 100,000
live births

6

August, the IRA declared it was ceasing all military operations, which paved the way for political talks.

33 The Reynolds administration fell in November, after the Labour Party withdrew its support due to the controversy on the delay of extradition to Northern Ireland of a priest accused of pedophilia. The new Prime Minister was John Bruton, from the Fine Gael, supported by the Labour Party and the democratic left.

34 There were more allegations of child abuse by priests. In Dublin, the archbishop publicly admitted he used church funds to pay-off a priest's victim. Meanwhile, the Supreme Court authorized doctors to inform women about abortion clinics abroad. In a referendum, the Irish approved (by 50 to 49 per cent of the vote) a constitutional reform authorizing divorce for couples separated for more than four years.

35 Bruton had excellent relations with British Prime Minister John Major. He also had close links with in Northern Ireland with John Hume of the Social Democratic and Labor party (SDLP) and Gerry Adams, Sinn Fein's leader. In the June 1996 round of talks held in Belfast, Bruton supported the British proposal to exclude Sinn Feín from the negotiating table, since both Governments regarded the IRA's attitude as unconstructive. In February the IRA ended its unilateral ceasefire (in place since August 1994) by setting off a bomb in London that killed two people and hurt several others.

36 In April 1997, several attacks announced by the IRA on streets, train stations and airports paralyzed the British transport system during the election campaign. Sinn Feín requested the IRA to declare a new cease-fire, which was decided in July. Negotiations were resumed in September, with the inclusion of Sinn Feín.

37 Bertie Ahern's Fianna Faíl won the June 1997 legislative elections with 77 out of 166 seats, Fine Gael, with 54 seats. The Labor Party obtained 17. The coalition formed by the Progressive Democrats (4 deputies) did not reach the majority needed to form a center-right Government. Sinn Feín obtained

one seat in a border county. On June 26, Parliament appointed Ahern as Prime Minister. Mary McAleese became President.

38 After tough negotiations, on April 10 1998, separatist Catholics and Unionist Protestants in Belfast reached a peace agreement known as the Good Friday Agreement. The text, negotiated by eight political parties, mediated by London, Dublin and Washington, included limited autonomy for Northern Ireland, with the creation of a legislative assembly and cross-border cooperation bodies. The plan also called for the disarmament of paramilitary organizations whose parties took part in the negotiation and gradual release of political prisoners.

39 Most political forces, including Sinn Feín, initially favored the Agreement, which overcame its first hurdle when Ulster Unionist leader David Trimble received the support of his party, the Ulster Unionist Party (UUP). Only two extremist Protestant parties were opposed: the Democratic Unionist Party (DUP), of Dr Ian Paisley, and Robert McCartney's United Kingdom Unionist Party (UKUP).

40 A referendum was held in late May, ratifying the Agreement with 95 per cent of the vote. A month later the first elections were held to form the Assembly as of February 1999. The new agreement paved the way for the people of Ulster to decide the Province's future, through a vote, to reunite with Ireland or to remain within the UK. In August, a bomb in Omagh, Northern Ireland, killed 30 people and endangered the fragile peace process. But the uproar caused by the attack in both sides of the border led the republican group responsible for the bomb (an offshoot of the IRA) to declare a unilateral ceasefire.

41 The establishment in December 1999 of the first Government of Northern Ireland in 25 years, although 'cross-border', confirmed the 'devolution' of sovereignty to the Province by the Westminster Parliament, in London. This new ruling body (Executive Council) was formed by the Prime Minister, David Trimble, from the UUP, with the deputy Prime Minister, Seamus Mallon, of the Social Democratic and Labor Party (SDLP). There were 10 ministers, three belonging to the pro-British UUP and the moderate Catholic SDLP, and two each from Sinn Feín and the radical Protestant Democratic Unionist Party (DUP), of Ian Paisley. It was the first time representatives from these parties had joint political responsibilities.

42 The DUP announced that,

although it rejected the inclusion of Sinn Feín in the Northern Ireland Assembly, it would take up its two seats in the Cabinet and would attempt to boycott the new Government's work. Ian Paisley's son, also in the DUP, declared: 'We do not plan to be a part of the Government, so if you think there is trouble now, wait until it gets to work. What is beginning is not the road to solutions, but the road to crisis'.

43 Coincidentally with the inauguration of the new Government, the Republic of Ireland withdrew its constitutional claim over Northern Ireland, present in the wording since Ireland's independence from the UK. The commitment was signed by Prime Minister Bertie Ahern while the cross-border bodies were being set up in which Northern and Southern Irish would take part. The elimination of articles 2 and 3 from the Constitution, although the result of a long debate, was seen as the only possible way to the reunification of the six Northern counties with the independent South.

44 Although the six Northern counties are mostly inhabited by Protestants, demographically the Catholics are in the ascendant. According to all estimates, in 10 years they would become the majority and a referendum could decide the reunification of the island.

45 Ireland has traditionally been a country of emigration, since its youngsters are constantly moving to Britain and further afield. But that situation has reversed to some degree in recent years. The country experienced significant economic growth, with practically no unemployment, making it an importer of skilled labor. Between 1995 and 2000 more than 250,000 foreigners entered the country. The Irish Government enacted equal opportunity laws, but some groups attack and insult people who are not descendants of the 'Celtic tiger'.

46 The Nice Treaty, which paved the way for 12 Eastern Europe countries to join the EU, was rejected by the Irish in a referendum held in June 2001. Unlike Britain, Ireland adopted the euro as its currency in January 2002.

47 By a margin of less than 2 per cent, a referendum in March 2002 rejected the Government's proposal to allow pregnant women who allegedly were at risk of suicide to have abortions.

48 Prime Minister Ahern was credited with the Northern Ireland Agreement and the strengthening of the economy. He was comfortably re-elected in the May elections. ∎

Israel

Yisra'el

Population: 6,303,000 (2002)
Land area: 20,620 SQ KM
Capital: Jerusalem/Tel Aviv
Currency: New shekel
Language: Hebrew and Arabic

By the 1800s, fewer than 25,000 Jews still lived in their ancient homeland, Palestine ('Land of the Philistines', the Latin name given to Judaea by the Romans). They were largely concentrated in Jerusalem, then a province of the Ottoman Empire. A rise in European anti-Semitism inspired a new wave of Jewish emigration to Palestine in the 1880s and agricultural colonies were financed by wealthy European Jewish families.

2 In 1896 Viennese journalist Theodor Herzl published *The Jewish State*. Influenced by the European nationalism that had engendered the unification of Germany and the Italian *Risorgimento*, Herzl envisaged a Jewish nation-state that would put an end to anti-Semitic acts, like the Russian pogroms. The name 'Palestine' inspired the Jews of Eastern Europe, who dreamed of the return to Zion, the land of the ancient kingdoms of Israel. Zion is the name of a hill in Jerusalem; by extension it became a synonym for Jerusalem itself and then for the whole of Palestine.

3 During World War I, Britain and France agreed to divide up the remains of the Ottoman Empire in the Middle East. In 1917, British Foreign Secretary Arthur Balfour declared his support for the establishment of a national homeland for the Jewish people in Palestine; when Prime Minister in 1905 he had opposed Jewish immigration into Britain. The Balfour Declaration stated 'that nothing shall be done which may prejudice the civil and religious rights of existing non-Jewish communities in Palestine'; these groups made up 90 per cent of the population.

4 The Zionist goal of Jewish statehood was violently opposed by the local Arab leaders, who saw the Ottoman Turks' defeat in World War I as an opportunity either to create their own state or to join a larger Arab entity and revive the old Arab empire of early Islamic times.

5 At the end of World War II, the French colonies of Syria and Lebanon and the British colonies of Iraq and Transjordan obtained their independence. But Britain retained control of Palestine, based on its commitment under the Balfour Declaration. Jewish militias grew,

the largest of them being the *Haganah* ('Defense'), a branch of the Jewish Agency, the organization most responsible for bringing Jews to Israel. These militias were associated with political factions from both the right and left of Zionist politics. The Irgun Zvai Leumi and its more violent splinter group, Lehi (also known as the Stern Gang), were affiliated with the ultra-conservative Revisionist Party, founded by Vladimir Zev Jabotinsky. The Palmach, though technically an elite arm of the Haganah, recruited many of its members from socialist-oriented

kibbutzim. Members of these militias - like Yigal Allon, Moshe Dayan, and Yitzhak Rabin - were to play an important role in Israeli politics for the next half century

6 Zionists regarded Jews the world over as exiles, and they organized migration to Israel from all corners of the globe. At the beginning of the 20th century there were 500,000 Arabs and 50,000 Jews living in Palestine. By the 1930s, the number of Jews had risen to 300,000. The anti-Semitic persecutions in Nazi Germany raised immigration above the legally permitted quotas, alarming the

British who saw their power in Palestine threatened. The Arabs of Palestine had also increased under the British mandate (through high birth rates and immigration) from about 440,000 to roughly 1,000,000 in 1940.

7 In 1939 London declared that its aim was not to set up a Jewish state but an independent, bi-national Palestinian state with both peoples sharing government. Ships bringing refugees from Hitler's Europe were turned back from Palestinian ports. The Zionists organized acts of sabotage and terrorism, using force to hold Britain to its promise.

8 Using donations from Jews all over the world, the Zionists purchased Arab lands from wealthy absentee owners living in Beirut or Paris, who cared little about the fate of their tenants, the Palestinian *fellahin* (peasants). The Jews then arrived, deeds in hand, to expel peasant families whose ancestors had lived there for generations. They set up agricultural colonies, kibbutzim, defended by armed Zionist militia.

9 In February 1947, in view of intensified anti-British attacks, London submitted the Palestinian problem to the United Nations. A special committee recommended partition of the territory into two independent states; one Arab, the other Jewish. Jerusalem would remain under international administration.

10 The Soviet Union preferred a Jewish state to continued British military presence, and its support was decisive in the creation of Israel. At the same time, London and Washington considered the partition unfeasible. US Secretary of Defense James Forrestal proposed that President Harry Truman send troops to impose a UN trusteeship over the territory of Palestine.

11 The UN General Assembly finally approved the partition plan in a 33 to 13 vote, there were 10 abstentions and the Arab countries and India voted against partition. Armed Zionist organizations seized control of major cities and towns and began to expel Palestinians en masse, alleging an imminent attack by Arab armies. This policy culminated in a massacre at the

---

OCCUPIED BY ISRAEL
1 Syria - Golan Heights - occupied in 1967
2 Southern Lebanon - occupied 1983-2000
3 West Bank - occupied in 1967
4 Gaza Strip - occupied 1967-1994
⊘ Recovered by Palestine from 1994: Gaza Strip, Jericho, Nablus, Ramallah
Israeli incursions into some areas, especially West Bank and Gaza, have resumed.

MATERNAL MORTALITY	LITERACY	FOOD DEPENDENCY	FOREIGN TRADE
1985/99	2000	2000	Millions US$ 2000
Per 100,000 live births			IMPORTS
5	**96%**	**5%**	**51,813**
	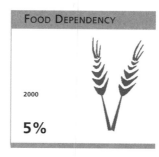		EXPORTS
			44,147

village of Deir Yasin in April 1948, when its entire population was murdered by the Irgun, an extremist group led by Menachem Begin.

[12] On May 14 1948, the British High Commissioner withdrew from Palestine, and David Ben Gurion proclaimed the state of Israel. The Jordanian, Egyptian, Syrian, Iraqi and Lebanese armies attacked immediately, and the governments of those countries urged the Palestinians to abandon their possessions and take refuge.

[13] The war ended with an armistice in January 1949, granting Israel 40 per cent more territory than it had been due under the partition plan. Soviet weapons and aircraft, purchased in Czechoslovakia, proved decisive in the Israeli victory.

[14] In 1956, when Israeli troops backed by France and Britain invaded Egypt in response to the nationalization of the Suez Canal, the United States and the Soviet Union both firmly opposed the move, and the expeditionary force had to be withdrawn.

[15] The diaries of former Prime Minister Moshe Sharett, published posthumously, revealed that Israel used Zionist agents to sabotage Western targets in Cairo, forcing US President Dwight Eisenhower to opt for Tel Aviv and not Cairo as its principal Middle East ally. The episode is known as the Lavon affair.

[16] In the 1960s, Egyptian President Gamal Abdel Nasser was deprived of US credit and arms, and he turned to the Soviet Union. This was enough to produce closer relations between Israel and Washington.

[17] In the 1967 Six Day War, Israel carried out a lightning strike, using North American weaponry, and seizing the whole of Palestine (the West Bank of the Jordan River), the Syrian Golan Heights and Egyptian Sinai .

[18] Resolution 242 of the UN Security Council, passed on November 22 1967, called on Israel to withdraw from the occupied territories. Israel refused, claiming that it needed 'secure borders' in order to resist Arab threats to its existence.

[19] Armed conflict broke out again in 1973, when Egyptian troops crossed the Suez Canal and ended the myth of Israeli military

invincibility. In truth, by the time armistice was decreed, battlefield positions had hardly changed.

[20] In 1977, Menachem Begin was elected Prime Minister, breaking with the political and ideological continuity of the previous governments. For the first time in the history of the Israeli state, the Labor Party was not in power.

[21] Begin's victory resulted partly from growing social tension between Ashkenazim (economically and culturally privileged Jews of European origin who were traditionally Labor supporters) and Sephardim (Eastern Jews from Arab countries).

[22] The oriental Jews, who culturally had more in common with the Arabs than with European Jews, made up 55 per cent of the population, but their average income was just two-thirds that of the Ashkenazis. Their resentment of the Ashkenazim, aggravated to the point of fanaticism, provided the electoral basis for the political right.

[23] Begin completely rejected the idea of negotiating with the Palestine Liberation Organization (PLO) and expressed his intention to annex the West Bank. Meanwhile in 1977, the US persuaded Egyptian President Anwar Sadat to sign the Camp David Agreement, leading to peace between Cairo and Tel Aviv and the return of Sinai to Egypt.

[24] From then on, international attention gradually shifted from the issue of secure borders for Israel to the plight of the Palestinians. Changing tactics, the PLO gained sympathy and allies, so that when Jerusalem was declared the capital of Israel in 1980, the move was condemned as an arrogant gesture by many of Israel's supporters.

[25] In June 1982, the Israelis launched 'Operation Peace for Galilee', invading Lebanon and devastating Beirut, under the pretext that these were maneuvers to stop infiltration by Palestinian guerrilla groups. PLO combatants agreed to evacuate the city in exchange for the deployment of a joint force of Italians, French, and North Americans to guarantee the security of Palestinian civilians.

[26] In spite of the agreement, hundreds of Palestinians in the Sabra and Shatila refugee camps, in

Israeli-controlled areas, were murdered by right-wing militia with Israeli complicity. The invasion of Lebanon fomented dissent in Israel, and 400,000 people attended a demonstration sponsored by the group Peace Now. Begin was forced to appoint a commission of inquiry, which found Defense Minister Ariel Sharon and other military leaders 'indirectly responsible' for the massacres.

[27] After the September 1984 elections, the Labor Party headed by Shimon Peres was able to form a government, though lacking an absolute majority. Its coalition included the right-wing Likud, and the agreement stipulated that the leader of that party, Yitzhak Shamir, would assume the prime minister's post in 1986.

[28] At the end of 1987, several young Palestinians were killed in a clash with Israeli military patrols in the occupied West Bank. The funerals turned into protest demonstrations and led to further confrontations, deaths, and general strikes - civil protests where people refuse to leave their homes. This marked the beginning of the *intifada* or uprising, and Middle Eastern politics were shaken from the least expected quarter - the unarmed grassroots.

[29] Images of young Palestinians armed with slingshots confronting the mighty Israeli army were televised worldwide, ruining Israel's international standing. This development came as a shock for a state founded on the basis of international solidarity.

[30] In Israel military service is mandatory for both women and men. All men up to the age of 51, and unmarried women up to age 24, belong to the Reserve. The militarization of society also resulted in a high level of State intervention in the economy and in an enormous weight of war industry on the country's production figures.

[31] In its search for markets, Israel became an arms exporter involved in dubious deals like the 'Iran-Contras' scandal, supplying arms to Iran. It also provided military training for Colombian drug militias.

[32] When Iraq invaded Kuwait on August 2 1990, Israel was excluded

from the anti-Iraq coalition led by the United States. This was done on the grounds that if it had participated, the Arab countries would not have joined. Israel made preparations for war regardless, and a state of siege was declared in the occupied territories.

[33] On January 17, in answer to the Allied bombing, Iraq launched several missile attacks against Israel. The aim was to try and force Israel to enter the war. However, Israel did not do so, leaving its defense to Patriot anti-missile units operated by American troops.

[34] When the war ended in March 1991, the US presented diplomatic circles with a 'land for peace' proposal. Two months later in Damascus, Syria and Lebanon signed a 'brotherhood, co-operation and co-ordination' treaty. To Israel, this treaty constituted a military threat to 'water tank' - a region in the north containing many important water sources.

[35] Israel asked the US to approve loans of $10 billion to ease its economic difficulties, caused by the resettling of between 250,000 and 400,000 Soviet Jews from 1989 to 1991.

[36] The Government began transferring immigrants to new settlements on the West Bank where in 1991 unemployment reached 11 per cent, despite efforts to create new jobs for immigrants.

[37] Wishing to launch peace negotiations in the region, the US government imposed the condition that loans granted would not be invested in settlements in occupied territories.

[38] The creation of Jewish settlements and the construction of new housing for Soviet Jews on the West Bank, became a double-edged sword for Shamir's government. The US loans and new settlements were vitally important, but Palestinians and other Arabs demanded that resettlement cease, in order for the peace talks to continue.

[39] On October 30 1991, a Middle-Eastern Peace Conference was held in Madrid, sponsored by the US and the former USSR. Shortly afterwards, hundreds of thousands of Israelis demonstrated, calling on their government to maintain a dialogue with the Palestinians and Israel's

Arab neighbors. Delegations from Jordan, Lebanon, Syria and Israel attended the conference; the Palestinians formed part of the Jordanian delegation, as Israel refused to negotiate directly with Palestinian representatives.

40   The Arab countries supported the 'land for peace' scheme, though it was rejected by Israel. Israel, in turn, showed itself willing to discuss limited self government by the Palestinian population in the occupied areas, as a provisional solution for a 5-year period. This offer triggered a crisis in the Likud's coalition government, when the Tehiya and Moladet (ultra-right-wing parties) walked out of the coalition, leaving Shamir without a parliamentary majority.

41   On June 23 1992, Labor won a decisive victory in the general

elections and Yitzhak Rabin was nominated prime minister. Construction of housing in the occupied territories came to a sudden standstill, and as a result, the United States removed the embargo on loan guarantees for Israel.

42   On September 13 1993, after months of secret negotiations in Oslo, Norway, Israeli authorities and PLO leaders signed the Declaration of the Principles of the Interim Self-government Agreement, in Washington. This agreement foresaw the installation of a limited autonomy system for Palestinians in the Gaza Strip and the city of Jericho for a five-year period. This agreement would subsequently be extended to include all of the West Bank.

43   Hamas and the pro-Iranian Hizbullah, two radical Islamist

movements active in many Arab countries, questioned the agreement. Meanwhile, Jewish settlers in the occupied territories - who had been supplied with arms by the Government - rejected the agreement out of hand, as it provided for the withdrawal of settlers and the Israeli army.

44   It was not long before this situation erupted in violence. On February 25 1994, Baruch Goldstein, a member of Kahane Kach's ultra-right-wing Jewish movement, entered the Tomb of the Patriarchs in Hebron, armed with an M-16 rifle and massacred several dozen Palestinians who were at prayer. He was subsequently beaten to death by Palestinians.

45   The official investigation of the Hebron massacre revealed that soldiers in the occupied territories had been under orders not to shoot against armed settlers under any circumstances. According to the investigation, several soldiers fired into the crowd, and doors were closed blocking the victims' escape. The PLO withdrew from the negotiations demanding that the settlers turn over their arms immediately, and that the United Nations issue an official condemnation. The latter approved a statement which categorically condemned the massacre and voted for a peacekeeping force to be sent to the occupied territories.

46   In early May 1994, Israeli Prime Minister Yitzhak Rabin and PLO leader Yasser Arafat signed an agreement in Cairo granting autonomy to Gaza and Jericho. Late that month, the Israeli army withdrew from Gaza, ending 27 years of occupation (see Palestine).

47   Negotiations with several Arab states progressed, especially with Jordan, which signed an agreement with Tel Aviv in July ending with the 'state of aggression' between the two countries. However, disagreements with Syria continued because, among other reasons, Israel refused to accept a full evacuation of the Golan Heights, occupied since 1967.

48   1995 was marked by a growing division of Israeli society regarding the peace process with the Palestinians. Anti-Rabin demonstrations were frequent and led to the Prime Minister's assassination by a young Israeli member of the far right. Shimon Peres, also from the Labor Party, took Rabin's place but was defeated in the general elections of May 1996 by right-wing leader Binyamin Netanyahu.

49   The return to power of the conservatives hindered negotiations with Palestine and heightened tensions, putting the country on the

brink of a new war in September. In the middle of that month the Government authorized the opening of a tunnel under the Al-Aqsa mosque, the third most sacred place of Islam, violating the status quo maintained since the signing of the peace agreements and provoking a Palestinian reaction. Several Israeli soldiers and dozens of Palestinians died during the disturbances.

50   Netanyahu, harshly critical of Rabin for having held talks with Arafat and the PLO, ended up meeting with the Palestinian leader on repeated occasions in late 1996 and early 1997 to negotiate the complete withdrawal of Israeli troops from the city of Hebron in the West Bank.

51   In March, the Government announced its plan to build a new settlement in the Har Homa hills, on the Palestinian outskirts of Jerusalem. The Palestine Authority and the United States rejected the project, considering it contrary to the spirit and letter of the Oslo agreements. Netanyahu's firm decision to go ahead with the settlements stalled the negotiations.

52   Ehud Barak, a retired general, replaced Peres as leader of the Labor Party and became leader of the opposition. Peres had been party to an agreement with the Likud to form a unity Government which would allow for the reopening of the peace process, suspended in the early months of 1997.

53   In November, the Israeli Supreme Court authorized the continued detention of 21 Lebanese prisoners (mostly members of Hizbullah) who had already completed their sentences, in retaliation for Israelis kidnapped in Lebanon. Earlier on, 'moderate physical force' had been authorized in the handling of prisoners during interrogation. Judge Aaron Barak even stated that the violation of human rights was 'obligatory' in these cases.

54   In February 1998, Israel tightened its anti-Syrian and Iraqi military alliance with Turkey. In the same month, Lebanon rejected an offer from Netanyahu to negotiate the withdrawal of Israeli troops from Lebanese territory, considering this withdrawal should be made totally unconditionally.

55   Mordechai Vanunu, the Israeli technician imprisoned for revealing Israel's nuclear secrets, was moved out of solitary confinement in March for the first time in 12 years. He was allowed to leave his cell and talk to other prisoners in the jail. The attitude was credited to international pressures in favor of Vanunu, who had been kidnapped

PROFILE

ENVIRONMENT

20,770 sq km, within the pre-1967 borders (see Palestine). These territories are currently occupied, both militarily and with settlements of Jewish colonists: Golan Heights (Syria) 1,150 sq km, West Bank 5,879 sq km, Greater Jerusalem 70 sq km. The land comprises four natural regions: the coastal plains, with a Mediterranean climate, the country's agricultural center; a central hilly and mountainous region, stretching from Galilee to Judea; the western lowlands, bound on the north by the Jordan River, which flows into the Dead Sea; and the Negev Desert, to the south, which covers half of the total territory. The main agricultural products are citrus fruits for export, grapes, vegetables, cotton, beet, potatoes and wheat. There is considerable livestock production. Industrial production is growing rapidly and there are serious difficulties with water; the country has over 2,000 sq km of irrigated land - part of the Negev has been reclaimed through irrigation. Pollution, caused by both industrial and domestic waste, as well as pesticides, is also an important problem.

SOCIETY

Peoples: Jews 81 per cent (of European, American, African and Asian descent); Arabs and others, 19 per cent.
Religions: Judaism (official). Arabs are Muslim (Sunni) or Christian; also Druze.
Languages: Hebrew and Arabic (official), several languages of the immigrants' countries of origin, especially English, Russian, Yiddish, Polish, Romanian, Hungarian. Also Sephardic (Judeo-Spanish).
Political Parties: The Zionist right is formed by Likud; Tehiya (Renaissance); Tsomet and Moledet. The Zionist left is formed by the Labor Party and the Meretz (Social Democrat). The non-Zionist left is made up of Hadash (formerly Communist) and the Democratic Arab Party. The religious parties are: the Shas; the Agudat-Israel (the League of Israel); the National Religious Party and the Degel Hatora. The non-Zionist left is made up of Hadash (formerly Communist) and the Democratic Arab Party. Parties of the Russian immigrants (Israel Baliyah) and minority parties (Socialist Struggle, Communist, Greens).
Social Organizations: The Histadrut Haoudim Haleumit (National Labor Federation) is the main trade union. Gush Emunim, nationalists demanding Jewish settlements in the Gaza Strip and West Bank; Peace Now supports territorial concessions in the West Bank.

THE STATE

Official Name: Medinat Yisrael (Hebrew); Israil (Arabic). Administrative divisions: 6 districts, 31 municipalities, 115 local councils and 49 regional councils. **Capital:** In 1980, Jerusalem (668,000 people in 1999) was proclaimed the 'sole and indivisible' capital of Israel. The UN condemned this decision and most diplomatic missions are in Tel Aviv. **Other cities:** Haifa 252,300 people; Tel Aviv-Jaffa 355,900; Holon 163,900 (1996). **Government:** Moshe Katzav, President since August 2000. Ariel Sharon, Prime Minister since March 2001. Parliamentary system, with 120 members. **National holiday:** May 14, Independence Day (1948; as the Jewish calendar is lunar the holiday may occur in April or May). **Armed Forces:** 175,000 (1996). **Other:** Border Police: 6,000; Coast Guard: 50.

by Israeli agents in London, in 1986, and condemned to 18 years of prison.

⁵⁶ The peace process appeared to reach its lowest point in June 1998, when Israel decided to boost the 'Civil Guard' in the occupied territories with Jewish settlers, who already armed themselves without any restriction. Labor leader Barak, alarmed both by Netanyahu's lack of political will to negotiate - he delayed a second withdrawal from occupied territories - and by the collapse of a mountain due to Israeli nuclear tests, warned that the entire region was on the verge of a blood bath. As the Prime Minister refused to hold a referendum to decide on the withdrawal of troops, President Ezer Weizman urged him to call early elections, a proposal Netanyahu rejected.

⁵⁷ However, as a result of strong international pressure, Netanyahu accepted the US proposal to seek an accord to restart the peace process. The Prime Minister met with US President Clinton and Arafat at the Wye River conference center in the US. After the meetings it was agreed that Israel would return Palestinian territory in exchange for Arafat's acceptance of supervision by US intelligence organizations in his fight against terrorism by Islamic groups. The accord, which weakened Arafat in the eyes of his internal enemies, also led to the fall of the Likud Government. Labor backed the signing of the accords, but the governing coalition dissolved and several Likud legislators abandoned the party. General elections were set for May 17 1999.

⁵⁸ In July, Barak was able to form a coalition government after the ultra-religious Shas, supported by Labor and its allies, agreed to take part in the new Cabinet. Shas participation complicated Labor's situation with its leftist allies, especially with Meretz, but also with the Central Party, an offshoot of Likud that had six deputies. Both groups demanded the definitive departure from the political scene by previous Shas leader, Aryeh Deri, who faced trial for fraud and accepting bribes. The acting Shas leader, Rabbi Ovadia Yosef, believed that ceding territory in exchange for peace guarantees was the only way to end violence in the region.

⁵⁹ Breaking with 50-year tradition, in November Israel decided to lift the state of emergency that had been in effect since 1948. The country held the world record: no other had maintained a longer continuous state of emergency. In late May 2000, Barak ordered the total withdrawal of troops from South Lebanon.

⁶⁰ Another summit was held at Camp David in the US from July 11-25, but failed in part because agreements on Israeli withdrawal did not materialize and the Palestinian territories were blockaded following a terrorist attack committed by extremist groups.

⁶¹ Likud leader Ariel Sharon's visit to the Al-Aqsa Mosque, a sacred site for Muslims and Jews, triggered a new Palestinian uprising on September 28. Hundreds of people, mostly Arab, died in clashes in the following months.

⁶² Barak resigned in December to hasten new elections. In balloting marked by high abstention rates, Sharon won 62 per cent of the vote and went on to negotiate a unity government with Barak. Sharon took office in March 2001 with Shimon Peres as Foreign Minister. Sharon's mandate turned into one of effective rupture with the Oslo Accords. Arafat tried to meet Israel's security demands by stepping up repression against Islamic extremist organizations, but the critical social situation (40 per cent unemployment, among other sever problems) breathed new life into the *intifada*. In the following months the armed clashes multiplied and all attempts to reach a truce were frustrated.

⁶³ The US and Israel withdrew their representatives from the UN-sponsored World Conference against Racism, held in the South African city of Durban in early September, when Arab delegations and a majority of the NGO Forum categorized the Jewish State as racist and blamed it for 'crimes of war, acts of genocide and ethnic cleansing.'

⁶⁴ In the wake of the terrorist attacks against Washington and New York on September 11 2001, Sharon thought that international public opinion and the attitudes of the Western governments would turn in favor of Israel and he stepped up the offensive against the Palestinian uprising. The effects of the war began to take a toll on the Israeli economy. Investment fell 65 per cent and some 200,000 people were left without jobs. International tourism dried up, worsening the situation. In just one year the tourism industry had fallen 51 per cent, particularly in Jerusalem and Bethlehem. The Sharon Government was not only left without cheap labor (when it barred entry to Israel for Palestinian workers), but also without consumers, as the Palestinian territories had been Israel's leading foreign market.

⁶⁵ Israel cut off ties with Arafat in December in response to a series of terrorist attacks by Palestinian groups against Jewish settlements.

The new Israeli strategy no longer considered the Palestinian leader a valid interlocutor and, with the rupture, any effort at negotiation was cut off.

⁶⁶ A Belgium court - in charge of the trial in which Sharon faced charges of genocide for the Shabra and Shatila massacres - was to issue its ruling on March 6 2002 but postponed the decision so that the attorneys could debate, in a new hearing, the International Court's ruling of granting immunity to heads of state while in power.

⁶⁷ The protests against the Israeli offensive spread around the world. Thousands of people demonstrated outside Israeli embassies, and in Brazil and Ecuador the supporters of the Palestinian cause burned Israeli flags and shouted slogans against the re-occupation of the West Bank cities. In Indonesia, hundreds of youths took to the streets to demand the creation of a Palestinian State.

⁶⁸ In January 2002, the violence shifted to Lebanon. Hizbullah repeatedly bombed Israeli army positions in the Shebaa Farms, and Israel responded with incursions into the south of that country. Sharon declared UN envoy Tarje Larsen *persona non grata* because he had described what occurred in Jenin, a Palestinian refugee camp that had been reduced to rubble after Israeli bombings, as 'a morally repugnant humanitarian disaster'. As a result of incursions into Jenin and other cities under relative control of the Palestinian Authority, Israel took some 5,000 Palestinians prisoner.

⁶⁹ In May, Likud voted against the creation of a Palestinian State at the request of Netanyahu, Sharon's main rival within the party. Netanyahu argued that a Palestinian State on the West Bank of the River Jordan would be a 'mortal threat' to Israel, while the top Palestinian negotiator, Saeb Erekat, responded that the vote undermined any attempt to reach a peace agreement. The Likud vote was a heavy blow to Sharon, who had publicly supported the creation of a Palestinian State in the area currently occupied by Israel. Israel continued its strikes on Palestinian towns on the West Bank, and its demands for Yasser Arafat to be replaced as PLO president. ∎

Italy

Population: 57,449,000 (2002)
Land area: 294,110 SQ KM
Capital: Rome (Roma)
Currency: Euro
Language: Italian

Italia

From 2000 to 1000 BC, the Italian peninsula received Indo-European peoples from Central Europe. In that period two homogenous cultural areas developed: one in the north, characterized by the construction of lake dwellings and the cremation of their dead; and the other, in the south, which was influenced by Mediterranean civilizations. At the end of the second millennium BC strong migratory currents weakened the northern and fragmented the southern cultures. Numerous regional cultures arose (Latin, Ligur, Veneta, Villanovan and Iliric, among others). The foundation of Greek colonies beginning in the 8th century BC was culturally significant. The cities on Sicily and the city of Cagliari, on Sardinia, were founded by the Phoenicians.

[2] With the fall of the Hittite empire around 900 BC the Etruscans established themselves to the north of the Tiber River. Their influence extended throughout the Po valley until the end of the 6th century, when the Celts bore down on them, destroying their territorial unity.

[3] According to legend, Romulus founded the city of Rome upon the Palatine hill in the year 753 BC. During the following century, this settlement was united with those on the Quirinal, Capitoline and Esquiline hills. The first form of government was an elective monarchy. Its powers were limited by a senate and a people's assembly of clans which held the power of imperium or mandate to govern.

[4] There were two social classes: the patricians, who could belong to the Senate, and the plebeians, who had to band together to protect themselves from the abuses of the large landowners.

[5] Under King Tarquinius Priscus (616-578), Rome entered the Latin League. The poverty of the plebeians and the system of debt-induced slavery led to the expulsion of the kings in 509. In the 5th century, the traditional laws were written down. This 'Law of the Twelve Tables' extended to the plebeians, who after a lengthy struggle had managed to win some rights.

[6] The Punic Wars against Carthage in the 3rd century allowed Rome to increase its possessions once again; in the early 2nd century,

after displacing the Macedonians, Greece became a 'protectorate'. Within a few years, Asia Minor, the northeast of Gaul, Spain, Macedonia and Carthage (including the northern part of Africa) had fallen into Roman hands.

[7] Toward the end of the 2nd century, the Gracchi brothers, Tiberius and Gaius - both Roman representatives - were assassinated by the nobles, along with 3,000 followers, for supporting the plebeians.

[8] The Roman Empire controlled the land from the Rhine in Germany to the north of Africa, and also included the entire Iberian Peninsula, France, Britain, Central Europe and the Middle East as far as Armenia. The 2nd century brought internal disputes which plunged Rome into chaos.

[9] In 330, the Emperor Constantine transferred the capital of the Empire to Byzantium - called New Rome - and converted to Christianity. In 364, the empire split into two parts: the Western and Eastern Roman Empires.

[10] The end of the 5th century was marked by the invasions of the

Mongols and other northern tribes, and by the attempts of the Byzantine Empire to recover its lost territories. In the mid-6th century, Italy became a province once again, but the Lombards conquered the northern part of the peninsula.

[11] When the capital of the empire had been transferred to Byzantium, the bishops of Rome had presented themselves as an alternative to Byzantine power with a separate power base in Rome. When the Lombard kings began taking up arms in defense of Christianity against Rome's enemies, the bishops broke the alliance, in order to maintain their temporal power.

[12] In 754, Pope Steven II asked for help from Pepin the Short, and in exchange, crowned him King of the Franks. After the defeat of the Lombards, Pepin turned over the center of the peninsula to the Pope. Charlemagne, Pepin's son, was crowned king and emperor of Rome in 800, but the Muslim invasions which took place mid-century once again left the region without government.

[13] Between the 9th and 10th centuries, the Church formed

Pontifical States in the central region, including Rome itself. In the 12th century, self-government arose in some cities because of the lack of a centralized power.

[14] In the 14th century, when the struggle intensified between the Guelfs (those who favored the Pope) and the Ghibellines (the defenders of the German Empire), the Holy See was transferred to Avignon, where it remained for the next seven papacies. Two centuries later, the prosperity and stability of cities like Venice, Genoa, Florence and Milan produced the intellectual and artistic flowering or the Renaissance.

[15] In the early 16th century, the peninsula was attacked by the French, the Spanish and the Austrians, who all craved control of Italy. In 1794, Napoleon Bonaparte entered the country expelling the Austrians. Four years later, he occupied Rome and created the Roman Republic and the Parthenopean Republic, in Naples. Only the two Italian states of Sicily and Sardinia were not under Napoleon's control, as they were governed by Victor Emmanuel I. The French Emperor rescinded the temporal power of the popes and deported Pius VII to Savona.

[16] Before the fall of Napoleon in 1815, Victor Emmanuel II named Camillo Benso di Cavour president of the council of ministers. Cavour was to be the architect of Italian unification, forging a single kingdom of Italy from those of Sardinia and Piedmont, with only Rome and Venice remaining outside the realm. In 1870, the Italians invaded Rome and, given Pope Pius IX's refusal to renounce his temporal power, they confined him to the Vatican, where his successors would remain until 1929. In 1878, the King, Humberto I, brought Italy into the Triple Alliance with Austria-Hungary and Germany. Italy's colonial conquest of Eritrea, Ethiopia and Somalia, in eastern Africa, also began.

[17] In 1872, influenced by the events of the Paris Commune, Italy's first socialist organization was formed, giving rise in 1892 to the Socialist Party (PSI). The encyclical Rerum Novarum (1891) oriented Catholics towards militant unionization and the union movement expanded rapidly. The

1985/99

Per 100,000
live births

7

Italian invasion of Ethiopia in 1896 ended in defeat for Italy.

[18] When World War I broke out, Italy proclaimed its neutrality; however, in the face of growing pressure from nationalist groups on the Left, it ended up declaring war against its former allies of the Triple Alliance.

[19] Benito Mussolini, who had been expelled from the PSI for supporting Italy's entry into the war, was able to manipulate resentment over the poor outcome. Through a blend of nationalism and pragmatism, he called for the unions to work towards collaboration between capital and labor, in the name of 'the interests of the nation'. In 1921, a group headed by Amadeo Bordiga and Antonio Gramsci split off from the PSI to form the Communist Party (PCI), leaving the PSI without its radical wing.

[20] Having confronted one government crisis after another, and following Mussolini's impressive march on Rome, Victor Emmanuel III turned over the government to Mussolini. An electoral reform, giving Mussolini's Fascist Party a majority, was denounced by socialist leader Giaccomo Matteotti, who was subsequently assassinated by followers of 'Il Duce' Mussolini in 1924. A new constitution established censorship of the press; in 1929 the Pact of Letran was signed with the Vatican, re-establishing the temporal power of the popes, and thereby gaining Catholic support for the Government.

[21] Mussolini's foreign policy was directed almost exclusively toward the acquisition of colonies. In 1936, Italy invaded Ethiopia, and a year later the Italian East African Empire was formed. During the Spanish Civil War, closer ties developed with Hitler's Germany, forming the basis for what was to become the Rome-Berlin axis. In April 1939, Italian troops took Albania.

[22] During World War II, Italy declared war on France and Britain. Its troops were not able to keep the war out of the country and the entire peninsula became a combat zone for Germans and Allies alike. In 1943, the latter defeated Hitler's troops, and Humberto II became king. Italy lost all of its colonies.

[23] Following a referendum at the end of the war (June 1946), the monarchy was abolished and the republic of Italy was formed. Under the leadership of Alcide de Gasperi, the Christian Democrats (DC) managed to form a minority government. These first elections marked the beginning of the Christian Democrats' hold on power. In May 1948, Luigi Einaudi, also of the DC, was elected Italy's first President.

[24] The 1946 International Conference authorized Italy to continue administrating Somalia (known as Italian Somaliland), a situation which continued until 1960. During the 1950s, Italy participated in the reconstruction of Europe. In 1957, it became one of the charter members of the Common Market.

[25] At the same time that the socialists were seeking closer links with the Christian Democrats, the Communist Party (PCI) embarked upon a revision of its political base under the leadership of Palmiro Togliatti. The PCI reaffirmed its belief in a democratic means toward a socialist end. During this period, the Party's influence extended into the labor unions, shaping the power structure of the General Union of Italian Workers (CGIL). The PCI, the country's second strongest electoral force, as well as the second largest Communist Party in the Western world, defined itself in terms of 'Eurocommunism' - Commusim with a European face.

[26] After successive victories at the polls, in 1961 the DC began opening up to the Left, seeking alliances with the Socialists and Social Democrats. The powerful Communist Party, in spite of its strong electoral presence, was permanently excluded from the Cabinet. The economic and institutional crises which took place during that decade led radical groups from the right and left alike to turn to violence as a means of bringing about change. The far right organized bombings to draw attention to its demands, while the Red Brigades of the Left used political kidnapping as their main tool. In 1978, the kidnapping and assassination of former Prime Minister Aldo Moro sealed their isolation from mainstream politics.

[27] Between 1952 and 1962, the average income of Italians doubled, as a result of the development of industry, which had come to employ 38 per cent of the national workforce. At the same time, agricultural employment dropped by 11 per cent, triggering migrations from the countryside to the cities, and from the south to the north. The industrial triangle of Milan, Turin and Genoa attracted a concentration of millions of people, living in overcrowded conditions inferior to those of the rest of Europe.

[28] According to the 1948 constitution the President of the republic, elected every seven years, is the head of state. One of their duties is to select a head of the government, the Prime Minister, who will have the support of the bicameral parliament. Until 1978, when socialist Sandro Pertini was elected, all presidents had belonged to the DC. Francesco Cossiga, elected in 1985, returned Italy to the tradition of Christian Democrat presidents.

[29] Cabinets which take lengthy negotiations to form generally only manage to last a few months. Charges against Christian Democrat Arnaldo Forlani's government - linking his supporters and allies to an organization called 'Propaganda Due' - brought the Government down in May 1981, giving way to just over a year of government led by Republican Giovanni Spadolini.

[30] The instability of the Government, coupled with astronomical fiscal deficits and the political influence of the Mafia and the 'Camorra' led many to consider the need for constitutional reform.

[31] In February 1991, the last secretary-general of the PCI proposed that the old name be changed to the Democratic Party of the Left (PDS). Immediately afterwards, the PDS sought admission into the Socialist International. The PDS also called for reunification with the PSI, hoping to heal the split which had taken place 70 years earlier. In December 1991, dissenters from the official party line decided to create the 'Reformed' Communist Party (PRC), using the red flag, hammer and sickle as its symbols.

[32] By the end of 1991, confrontations between DC's Cossiga and the PDS leader, Achille Occhetto worsened. In February

PROFILE

ENVIRONMENT

The northern region of the country consists of the Po River plains which extend as far as the Alps. It is the center of the country's economic activity, having the main concentration of industry and farming. Cattle are raised throughout the peninsula; important crops include olives and grapes, with vineyards extending along the southern coastal strip. The country includes not only the peninsula - which is divided by the Apennines - but also the islands of Sicily and Sardinia.

SOCIETY

Peoples: Italians 94 per cent. Others, particularly Sardinians and German in Alto Adige and immigrants from Africa.
Religions: Predominantly Catholic. Muslims are about 700,000.
Languages: Italian (official). Several regional languages, like Neapolitan and Sicilian, are widely spoken. French is spoken in Val d'Aosta and German in Alto Adige. Immigrants speak their own languages, particularly African languages.
Political Parties: House of Freedom (which includes: Forza Italia, led by Silvio Berlusconi; National Alliance; Northern League, a regional party; Christian Democratic Center; United Christian-Democrats and the New Italian Socialist Party); L'Ulivo (Olive Tree), center-left electoral coalition led by Romano Prodi, bringing together the Democrats of the Left (former Communist Italian Party); the Italian People's Party; Democrats; Italian Renewal; Democratic Union for Europe; Federation of Greens with the Socialist Italian Party (SIP) and the Party of Italian Communists); the Communist Refoundation.
Social Organizations: Italian workers are organized in three Union blocs: CGIL, a Left Democrat affiliate; CISL, centrist, and the UIL, of Social Democrat tendency, made up mostly of Socialists and Republicans. These three unions signed an agreement with the government and business people in 1993 to contract workers collectively. Other unions, smaller in size and power, have not adhered to this agreement.

THE STATE

Official Name: Repubblica Italiana.
Administrative Divisions: 20 Regions divided into 95 Provinces.
Capital: Rome (Roma) 2,685,000 people (1999).
Other cities: Milan (Milano) 4,047,500 people; Naples (Napoli) 3,620,300; Turin (Torino) 1,619,400; Palermo 947,300 (2000).
Government: Carlo Azeglio Ciampi, President since May 1999. Silvio Berlusconi, Prime Minister since June 2001. Bicameral parliamentary system: The Chamber of Deputies with 630 members and the Senate of the Republic with 326 members.
National holiday: June 2, Anniversary of the Republic (1946).
Armed Forces: 325,150 (1996).
Other: 111,800 Carabinieri; 80,400 Public Security Guard troops; 64,100 Treasure Security Guard.

1992, the President and the Prime Minister dissolved Parliament, bringing the legislative elections forward.

[33] In the April 1992 elections, the DC did not achieve a parliamentary majority, the first defeat of a Christian Democratic government since 1946. Days afterwards, Prime Minister Giulio Andreotti announced the dissolution of his government and President Cossiga resigned early. At the end of May, Judge Giovanni Falcone - number one enemy of the Mafia - was killed in Sicily. This allowed the election of former president of the chamber of deputies, Oscar Scalfaro.

[34] Two months after the assassination of Judge Falcone, the Mafia killed Paolo Borsellino who on Falcone's death had inherited the investigation against organized crime.

[35] In October 1992, the Government presented a series of economic adjustment measures. These gave rise to a general strike in protest against the measures, with 10 million workers participating.

[36] Attorney General Antonio di Pietro launched an investigation that revealed a complex system of illegal operations which included politicians of all persuasions, entrepreneurs and the mafia. During 1993, more than a thousand political and business leaders were tried under operation 'Clean Hands', including former Prime Ministers Bettino Craxi and Giulio Andreotti.

[37] Between 1980 and 1992, corruption deprived State coffers of some $20 billion. Because of illegal payments to officials and politicians, Italian public investments were 25 per cent more expensive than in the rest of the European Community.

[38] In April 1993, former Central Bank president, Carlo Azeglio Ciampi, was appointed Prime Minister. A few days later, a plebiscite was held on electoral reform according to which three quarters of the seats in the two chambers - Senate and Deputies - would be awarded by simple majority in the electoral districts. The remaining 25 per cent would be filled by proportional representation.

[39] For the March 1994 legislative elections, within a few months, media magnate, Silvio Berlusconi created the 'Forza Italia' party which, allied with Umberto Bossi's federalist Northern League and the Gianfranco Fini's neo-fascist National Alliance (NA), won an absolute majority in Parliament.

[40] Berlusconi was appointed Prime Minister in June and consolidated his popularity when 'Forza Italia' triumphed in the European elections. However, relations with the Northern League, which had persistently criticized Berlusconi, and the NA

'fascists', started to complicate government action.

[41] In October, the unions opposed retirement pension reforms proposed by the Prime Minister as, in their view, the reforms limited benefits, increased contributions and 'privatized' part of the system. Following a large demonstration in Rome, attended by more than a million people, Berlusconi withdrew his reform bill. In December, Bossi - who despite a poor show in the election had nearly a fifth of the deputies behind him - withdrew his support for the Government and Berlusconi resigned.

[42] In April 1996, the cener-left Olive Tree Coalition, led by former Democratic Christian, Romano Prodi and supported by the PDS, won the elections. Appointed Prime Minister, Prodi formed a government with prominent PDS leaders and leading conservative personalities like Ciampi and Fini. Having former communists in the cabinet and support from Communist Refoundation for the government formed the distinctive trait of the new period.

[43] A serious crisis shook the government in October 1997. The Communist Party threatened to withdraw support for Prodi and not approve the 1998 budget if the government did not accept the reduction of the working week to 35 hours. In October 1998 there were renewed disputes, and this time Prodi was forced to resign. In order to avoid calling new elections, which could have meant passing power to the right, the center-left alliance proposed Massimo D'Alema, former communist and leader of the PDS, as Prime Minister. D'Alema was confirmed in this post by president Scalfaro on October 21.

[44] Former premier Andreotti was accused by the public prosecutors in May 1999 of having used political influence to help the Mafia. This closed the case on a trial that had already run for four years. Public prosecutor Roberto Scarpinato also requested that the 80-year-old Andreotti be removed from public service (he was senator for life).

[45] Carlo Azeglio Ciampi, a 78-year-old banker and former economy minister, won the presidency with broad support from both right and left in May 1999. The presidency - which is to a large extent ceremonial in Italy - does carry some important powers as the President rules over political crises and decides on when to dissolve parliament and call new elections, while he also designates candidates to make up new governments.

[46] In June 2001, Berlusconi became Prime Minister again, leading a center-right coalition called

House of Freedom in the general elections. The new premier formed a new coalition government that included the two right-wing parties: Gianfranco Fini's National Alliance and Umberto Bossi's Northern League; the pro-European Renato Ruggiero was foreign minister.

[47] In October, a large majority of Italian people accepted constitutional changes, voting for greater autonomy for the 20 regions on matters of tax, education and environment. The Constitution had not been submitted to referendum since 1946.

[48] There was a resurgence of social movements in Italy and protests became more radical. For example the anti-globalization movement had several demonstrations in 2000-2001, in Bologna, Trieste and Naples, and in July 2001 a protestor was killed by the security forces in Genoa. Italian activists also played a significant part in anti-globalization protests in Prague and Nice in 2000, in Davos, 2001 and Porto Alegre, 2002.

[49] In January 2002, the euro replaced the lira, but Italy was the only country which did not celebrate its change of currency. In response to the unenthusiastic declarations of right wing colleagues in the cabinet, Chancellor Ruggiero resigned. While several European leaders regretted Ruggiero's departure, Berlusconi took over as Chancellor.

[50] Italian labor law was the most rigid in Europe, and the country was in the vanguard of the European economy. Claiming that continued economic growth was only sustainable with greater labor flexibility, the Government planned reforms to make it easier for employers to hire and fire staff. In March 2002, unemployment nationally stood at 9 per cent, and in the south one in five were out of work. On March 23, more than a million workers demonstrated at Rome's Coliseum protesting that the Government's labor, legal and social measures mainly benefited Berlusconi - the richest businessman in the country - and his peers.

[51] That same month, Interior Minister Claudio Scajola, declared there was evidence to suggest the militant leftist Red Brigades had reappeared and that a government aide had been killed by them. The murder only increased the breach between government and unions on labor law and made many fear a re-emergence of the political violence of the 1970s and 1980s.

[52] The country was paralyzed on April 16 when, in protest against labor laws, millions of workers across the country joined the first general strike to last more than one day in the last 20 years. ∎

Jamaica

Population: 2,621,000 (2002)
Land area: 10,830 SQ KM
Capital: Kingston
Currency: Jamaica dollar
Language: English

Jamaica

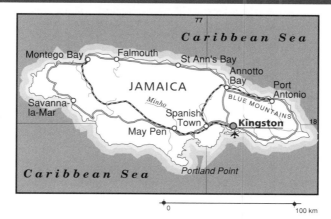

The name Jamaica apparently comes from the Arawak Indian name for the island - Xamayca. The Arawaks had pushed out the Guanahatabey, the original inhabitants, who had come from North America. The name Xamayca means 'land of springs', a reference to the abundant waters of its luxuriant forests. The Arawaks lived in villages of houses made from palm branches and carried out farming and fishing activities.

[2] Columbus reached Jamaica on his second voyage to the New World in May 1494, but it was his son, Diego Colon, who conquered the island in 1509. From then on, the number of Arawaks decreased dramatically. Around 1545, Spanish historian Francisco López de Gomara wrote that 'Jamaica resembles Haiti in all respects - here the Indians have also been wiped out'. Some sources believe that prior to the Spanish Conquest, there may have been as many as 60,000 Arawaks.

[3] The Spanish, now absolute rulers of the island, began to plant sugarcane and cotton, and to raise cattle. There were incursions by the British in 1596 and 1636, and in 1655, 6,500 British soldiers under the command of William Penn dislodged the 1,500 Spaniards and Portuguese. Jamaica rapidly became a haven for pirates who ravaged Spanish trade in the Caribbean. The last important enemies that the English had to face on the island were the enclaves of rebel slaves or *quilombos*, hidden in remote areas like the Blue Mountains. In 1760 a general rebellion in the colony was put down, and in 1795 a further revolution shook the island.

[4] By the late 19th century there were approximately 800 sugar mills and more than 1,000 cattle ranches in Jamaica. The economy was built on the labor of 200,000 slaves brought from Africa. Anti-slavery and anti-colonial rebellions of the 18th and 19th centuries were followed by labor union struggles in the first few decades of the 20th century. The two large contemporary political parties, the Labor Party and the People's National Party both grew out of workers' organizations. Independence was proclaimed in 1962, but successive Labor governments failed to rescue the economy from foreign hands.

[5] In 1942 rich deposits of bauxite were discovered, and the aluminum transnationals ALCOA, ALCAN, Reynolds and Kaiser quickly established themselves on the island. The sugar industry was virtually replaced by bauxite exploitation.

[6] The transnationals exploited Jamaica's bauxite by shipping the raw metal out of the country, making all the decisions on production, and paying minimal customs duties.

[7] After independence in 1962, a few plants were built to transform bauxite into aluminum, but the bulk of the mineral extracted continued to be shipped unprocessed to the US. In 1973, Jamaica was the second largest producer of bauxite in the world. The mineral accounted for half of the country's exports but employed only one per cent of the labor force. Transnationals' earnings were not reinvested in the country. Export and import duties were reduced as the transportation of the mineral was classified as an internal transfer, with preferential taxation rates.

[8] The People's National Party (PNP) won the 1972 elections and in 1974 the new Prime Minister, Michael Manley, raised the bauxite export tax. In addition, he began negotiations with the foreign companies to recover the third of the nation owned by them, and to assert greater control over their activities.

[9] At the same time, the PNP Government strongly supported Caribbean integration. A bi-national bauxite marketing company was created with Venezuela. Jamaica became a member of the Caribbean Multinational Merchant Fleet with Cuba and Costa Rica. Together, the associates devised ways to prevent penetration by US capital.

[10] These progressive measures were resisted by the mining companies and by local conservative forces who sought to upset the December 1976 elections. The PNP won anyway, with an overwhelming victory at the polls and an increased majority in parliament. Manley advocated socialism within the existing constitutional structure.

[11] Jamaica took active part in the Movement of Non-Aligned Countries. It also supported anti-colonial positions at all world forums and proclaimed its unconditional solidarity with all liberation movements, particularly those of southern Africa.

[12] This stand strained relations with the US. As a result, the transnational mining companies reduced their production, transferring operations to other countries. Export revenues fell, and with them, funding for government social programs.

[13] In 1979, the Government was forced to seek loans from the IMF which imposed harsh conditions. In February 1980, Manley announced that he was suspending negotiations with the Fund since meeting its requirements would mean a drastic reduction in living standards for the population. That year elections were held ahead of schedule, in a climate of destabilization generated by the right-wing opposition, which finally won a landslide victory. The new Labor government, headed by Edward Seaga, expelled the Cuban ambassador and imposed neo-liberal economic policies, opening the country to unconditional foreign investment and even suggesting that it might request Jamaica's admittance to the United States. The results were counterproductive: between 1981 and 1983, unemployment increased, bauxite production continued to decline, inflation rose and the foreign debt doubled.

[14] In November 1983, Jamaica was one of the small group of Caribbean countries that gave diplomatic support and symbolic military assistance to the invasion of Grenada. A month later, taking advantage of the favorable political atmosphere, Seaga decided to call early parliamentary elections. The PNP boycotted the elections, accusing the Government of not having fulfilled a previous commitment to update the electoral register and reorganize the system of voter identification, so as to avoid rigging. Only the governing party nominated candidates, thereby winning all 60 seats.

[15] In 1984 the need to negotiate new loans with the IMF and the consequent cuts in public spending aggravated an already critical situation. Inflation soared from 4.7 per cent in 1981 to 32 per cent in 1984. In addition, in 1985 revenues from bauxite production fell and there was a 50 per cent decrease in tourism. Union federations announced that workers' living conditions were being allowed to deteriorate deliberately in order to attract transnationals to the Kingston 'free zone' where workers' rights were not respected.

[16] 96 per cent of the workforce in the 'free zone' were women who bore long working days in unhealthy conditions, with no security and low pay. This affected the situation of the children of Kingston, as 52 per cent of the heads of household were women.

[17] Between 1985 and 1987, the Labor Government adopted a campaign against drug trafficking, in agreement with the United States. Some $750 million worth of marijuana was estimated to enter the United States via Jamaica each year.

[18] In 1989, Michael Manley's PNP came to power again,

1985/99

Per 100,000
live births

95

strengthened by its triumph in the June 1986 municipal elections. He presented a very different program from 1976, based on free enterprise and good relations with the United States. Manley re-established relations with Cuba and stated the agreements with the IMF would be respected, although he made it clear he would not accept conditions which would worsen the social inequalities. His aim was to maintain economic growth, but with better wealth distribution.

[19]   In April 1992, Percival Patterson replaced Manley as Prime Minister, as the latter resigned from this post and the presidency of the PNP, following a long period of illness. Patterson, a well-known politician, former senator and minister of several PNP governments, was also elected party president.

[20]   In 1992, promising labor guarantees, the Government started the privatization of around 300 State companies and public services classified as unproductive. This package included the entire sugar industry.

[21]   In March 1993, the PNP took more than 60 per cent of the vote, confirming Patterson in the post of Prime Minister. The Labor Party - led once again by Edward Seaga - refused to participate in the partial elections in 1994 in order to show their disagreement with the electoral system and lobby for modifications. In October 1995, a group of Seaga's opponents within the Labor Party abandoned the group to found the National Democratic Movement.

[22]   Prime Minister Patterson continued in 1995 with the economic and financial liberalization which, among other things, made Jamaica's financial sector one of the most prosperous in the country.

[23]   In 1997, a committee of political parties, religious representatives and community groups was formed to seek solutions to the internal violence. Pressure from this committee contributed to Jamaica becoming the first country to abandon an agreement, within the framework of the United Nations International Convention on Civil and Political Rights, which made the death penalty more difficult to apply.

[24]   The violence during the run-up to the December 18 1997 parliamentary elections led to the mass resignation of candidates. The National Democratic Movement had only 54 candidates for 60 seats. Following the election, the PNP retained the absolute majority, with 50 seats, while the Labor Party took 10.

[25]   Jamaica withdrew from the Inter-American Commission on Human Rights of the Organization of American States in 1998 due to the forum's opposition to the death penalty, still used by Jamaica and other Caribbean countries. In June, Jamaica, Barbados, Guyana and Trinidad - all independent nations but with various ties to Britain - announced plans to cut links with the House of Lords and form their own Caribbean Court of Justice.

[26]   After he was made president of the G-15 (a group of 15 developing countries), Prime Minister Patterson declared during the group's February 1999 meeting in Kingston that a lending organization would need to be created as a last resource. Patterson specified that in his opinion the IMF was not fit to play that role.

[27]   That same year, the army took to the streets to control violent riots caused by the price hike in for example fuel which had increased by 30 per cent. Over the last year, the island's murder rate had become the highest in the world. Up to December 2001, there had been a 30 per cent increase in crime, with 1,100 deaths in 12 months.

[28]   Some observers thought the country was at risk of falling into the hands of drug lords unless the Government finds a way to stop the groups that in 2001 had sold 100 tons of cocaine to the West. To add to the problem, some of the Jamaican police are in the pay of the drug cartels. The death toll by security forces in Jamaica is the highest in the world. ∎

PROFILE

ENVIRONMENT

Jamaica is the third largest of the Greater Antilles. A mountain range, occupying one third of the land area, runs across the island from East to West. A limestone plateau covered with tropical vegetation extends to the West. The plains are good for farming and the subsoil is rich in bauxite. The climate is rainy, tropical at sea level and temperate in the eastern highlands. Soil loss from deforestation and erosion reaches 80 million tons per year. In some metropolitan areas, the lack of sewerage and the dumping of industrial wastes have polluted drinking water supplies, threatening the urban population.

SOCIETY

Peoples: Most Jamaicans are of African descent. There are small Chinese, Indian, Arab and European minorities.
Religions: Protestants 56 per cent; Catholics 5 per cent, Rastafarians 5 per cent.
Languages: English (official). A dialect based on English is also spoken.
Political Parties: People's National Party (PNP), founded in 1938 by Norman Manley and led by Prime Minister Percival Patterson, a member of the Socialist International since 1975. The Jamaica Labor Party, founded in 1943 by Alexander Bustamante, is a private sector advocate and is led by Edward Seaga. National Democratic Movement, splintered from the latter. Natural Law Party.
Social Organizations: National Workers' Union of Jamaica (NWUJ); Bustamante Industrial Trade Union (BITU).

THE STATE

Official Name: Jamaica.
Administrative Divisions: 14 parishes.
Capital: Kingston 655,000 people (1999).
Other cities: Spanish Town 127,300 people; Montego Bay 90,500 (2000).
Government: Parliamentary monarchy. Head of State: Elizabeth II of Britain. Howard Cooke, Governor General, representing Britain since August 1991. Prime Minister, Percival J Patterson, since March 1992 and re-elected in 1997. Bicameral Legislature: House of Representatives, 60 members elected by direct popular vote every 5 years and the Senate, with 21 members appointed by the Governor General.
National Holiday: August 6, Independence Day (1962).
Armed Forces: 3,350 troops.

STATISTICS

DEMOGRAPHY

Population: 2,621,000 (2002)
Annual growth: 0.8 % (1985-2000)
Estimates for year 2015: 2,957,000 (2000)
Annual growth to year 2015: 0.9 % (2000)
Urban population: 56.1 % (2000)
Urban growth: 2.5 % (2000)
Children per woman: 2.5 (2000)

HEALTH

Life expectancy at birth: 76 years (2000-2005)
male: 74 years (2000-2005)
female: 78 years (2000-2005)
Maternal mortality: 95 per 100,000 live births (1985/99)
Infant mortality: 17 per 1,000 (2000)
Under-5 child mortality: 20 per 1,000 (2000)
Daily calorie supply: 2,708 per capita (1999)
140 doctors per 100,000 people (1996)
Safe water: 92 % (2000)

EDUCATION

Literacy: 87 % (2000)
male: 83 % (2000)
female: 91 % (2000)
School enrolment (net):
Primary total: 93 % (1994/2000)
male: 89 % (1995/99)
female: 87 % (1995/99)
Secondary (gross):
male: 63 % (1995/97)
female: 67 % (1995/97)
Tertiary (gross): 9 % (1998)
Primary school teachers: one for every 31 pupils (1998)

COMMUNICATIONS

62 newspapers (1996), 784 radios (1998), 194 TV sets (2000) and 199 main telephone lines (2000) per 1,000 people

ECONOMY

Per capita, GDP: $ 3,639 (2000)
Annual growth: -0.9 % (2000)
Annual inflation: 8.2 % (2000)
Consumer price index: 172.6 (2000)
Currency: 47.3 Jamaica dollars = $ 1 (03/2002)
Cereal imports: 513,201 metric tons (2000)
Food import dependency: 15 % (2000)
Fertilizer use: 1,324 kg per ha (1999)
Exports: $ 3,262 million (2000)
Imports: $ 4,076 million (2000)
External debt: $ 4,287 million (2000); $ 1,664 per capita (2000)
Debt service: 17.4 % of exports (1999)
Development aid received: $ -23 million (1999); $ -8.7 per capita (1999); -0.30 % of GNP (1999)

ENERGY

Consumption: 1,575.1 Kgs of oil equivalent per capita yearly (1998); 84.5 % imported (1999)

HDI (ranking/value): 78 / 0.738 (1999)

Japan

Population:	127,538,000 (2002)
Land area:	364,500 SQ KM
Capital:	Tokyo
Currency:	Yen
Language:	Japanese

Nihon

Earliest culture in Japan dates back 10,000 to 30,000 years ago to the Paleolithic Age, known as the Pre-Cambrian era. This was followed by the Jomon Neolithic culture, which lasted until 200-300 BC and extended throughout the Japanese archipelago.

[2] The Jomon culture was altered by the arrival of the Yayoi, who probably arrived from the continent at a time when Japan was still linked by land bridges across the straits of Korea, Tsushima, Soya and Tsugaru. The Yayoi introduced rice cultivation, horses and cows, the potter's wheel, weaving, and iron tools.

[3] According to Chinese chronicles, at the beginning of the Christian era the Wo region (Wa in Japanese) was divided into more than 100 states. During Himito's reign, some 30 of them were grouped together. The Wa people were divided into social classes and paid taxes, advanced building techniques were known and used, there were large markets and correspondence was exchanged with the continent.

[4] From the end of the civil war until Yamato's consolidation as emperor (266-413), the Wa territory was isolated. This led to the unification of the nation by the middle of the 4th century, a prerequisite for further expansion. In the year 369, Yamato subdued the Korean kingdoms of Paekche, Kaya and Sila and established military headquarters from which he could control the region.

[5] The Yamato empire suffered a rapid decline, due to both the resistance of its Korean subjects and to internal fighting within the court. During that period, between the years 538 and 552, Buddhism was introduced into the country, though initially it was merely an object of curiosity and admiration, due to its majestic temples and the magical powers that were attributed to it.

[6] The most important traces of Chinese presence in Japanese culture are the grid system for dividing the land, which dates back 1,500 years and is still visible today, the Chinese characters used in the writing system and the Buddhist religion.

[7] However, this cultural heritage underwent successive adaptations to the local weather, language, and habits, especially during the 17th

and 18th centuries. This was particularly apparent in the architecture and the language, each of which shows evidence of very different local influences.

[8] Japan's first permanent capital was Nara, established in the year 710. In the 9th century, tribal chieftains were replaced by a permanent court with a hereditary right to title. The aristocracy made Buddhism a controlling force, which served to reinforce the power of the state. After several conflicts, Kammu (781-806) re-established the empire's independence and transferred the capital to Heian (Kyoto).

[9] In the new capital, the power of the Fujiwara family was consolidated. The Fujiwaras established the regent as the ruling figure, above and beyond the power of the emperor. With imperial approval, two new Buddhist sects - Tendai and Shingon - developed in Heian. They were both seen to be more closely identified with Japanese culture than the previous Buddhist sects, a fact which brought an end to Nara's religious hegemony.

[10] The imperial land tenure system also fell increasingly into private hands. The members of the

aristocracy and the religious institutions began taking over large extensions of tax-free land (shoen). The nobility organized private armies for themselves, and a rural warrior class - the samurai - emerged.

[11] The Taira and Minamoto clans, who were prominent families and local leaders, became involved in a power struggle which led to a number of military confrontations between these two warlords. The Taira were in power from 1156 until their defeat in the Gempei War (1180-85). The shogun (general), Minamoto Yoritomo, founded the Kamakura shogunate, the first of a series of military regimes which ruled Japan until 1868.

[12] The Kamakura were put to the test during the Mongol invasions of 1274 and 1281. Aided by providential storms, which were called kamikaze (divine winds), the Japanese defeated the invaders. During this period, several new Buddhist sects emerged, such as Pure Land Buddhism, True Pure Land and Lotus.

[13] In the early 14th century, the Kamakura shogunate was destroyed, and Emperor Go-Daigo re-established his authority over the warlords in the Kemmu Restoration. However, a short

while later he was expelled from Kyoto and replaced by a puppet emperor, who was controlled by the military clans. Go-Daigo established his court in Yoshino, and for 56 years there were two imperial courts operating alongside each other.

[14] The Onin War (1467-77), over succession within the Ashikaga shogunate, became a civil war which lasted a hundred years. New military chiefs emerged, independent of imperial or shogun authority. They established themselves and their vassals within fortified cities, leaving the surrounding villages to run themselves, and to pay tribute.

[15] In the cities, trade and manufacturing ushered in a new way of life. Portugal began trading with Japan in 1545, and the missionary Francis Xavier introduced Catholicism to the Japanese in 1549. However, Christianity caused conflicts with feudal loyalties, and so it was proscribed in 1639. All of the Europeans in Japan, except for the Dutch, were banished from the country.

[16] Toward the end of the 16th century, the Japanese warlords isolated themselves from the rest of society, pacifying and uniting the country around a single national authority. To achieve these objectives, the warlords made use of firearms and of military fortresses; in addition, they disarmed the peasants and achieved greater control over the land.

[17] During the 17th century, the Tokugawa clan gained supremacy over the entire country. From the city-fortress of Edo (Tokyo), the Tokugawa shogunate governed Japan until 1867. A careful distribution of the land among their relatives and the local chieftains guaranteed them the control of the largest cities, Kyoto, Osaka and Nagasaki, as well as of the most important mines.

[18] Local chieftains were compelled to spend half their time on the shogun's affairs while their families remained behind, as hostages. Transformed into military bureaucrats, the samurai were the highest level of a four-class system, followed by the peasants, artisans and traders.

[19] A national market arose for textiles, food, handcrafts, books and other products. As of 1639, the Tokugawas implemented a policy of

almost total isolation from the outside world. Nagasaki was the only exception; here, the Chinese and the Dutch were allowed to open trading posts, although the latter were restricted to a nearby island.

20   In the 19th century, the old economic and social order went into a state of collapse. Peasant revolts became more and more frequent, and the samurai and local chieftains found themselves heavily in debt with the traders. In 1840, the government tried to carry out a series of reforms, but these failed and weakness allowed the United States to prize open its ports.

21   Japan was forced out of its isolation by Commodore Matthew Perry, using cannon to persuade the Japanese to cooperate with him. The signing of unfavorable trade agreements with the United States and several European countries simply deepened the crisis within the shogunate. The samurai carried out several attacks against the foreigners and then turned against the shogun, forcing him to resign in 1867.

22   Imperial authority was restored with the young Meiji emperor, in 1868. During the Meiji Restoration, Japan's modernization process began, following the Western model. The United States exerted its influence, as did England, France and Germany, in the fields of education, the sciences, communication and Japanese cultural expression.

23   Within less than 50 years, Japan was transformed from a closed, feudal society into an industrialized world power. Western advisers and technology were brought in, for education, trade and industry. An army based on the draft replaced the military authority of the samurai, who were defeated when they tried to rebel, in 1877.

24   In 1889, succumbing to internal political pressure, the emperor approved a constitution which established a constitutional monarchy, with a bicameral legislature (Diet). However, only one per cent of the population was eligible for office, and the prime minister and his cabinet were responsible to the emperor who continued to be seen as a divine figure.

25   Japan defeated China in the war of 1894-95, and maintained control over Korea. Japan's victory in the Russo-Japanese War (1904-05) enabled it to annex the Sajalin Peninsula, with Korea being annexed a few years later (1910). Japan entered World War I as a British ally, as a treaty had been signed to that effect in 1902.

26   The war allowed Japan to gain control of several German possessions in East Asia, including the Chinese territory of Kiaochow. In 1915, Japan forced China to accept the extension of its influence over Manchuria and Inner Mongolia. In

1918, Hara Takashi became the head of the first government to have a parliamentary majority.

27   In 1921-22 Japan signed a naval arms limitation treaty with the US in Washington, replacing an agreement with Britain, and establishing a new balance of power in the Pacific.

28   The economic difficulties caused by the international depression of the 1930s gave the militarists the excuse they were seeking to attack the government. They proposed that the country's problems could only be solved by expanding its military power, and through the conquest of new markets for their products and as sources of raw materials.

29   Within this context, Japanese officers occupied Manchuria in 1931, without government authorization. Unable to deter the military, the government accepted the creation of the puppet state of Manchukuo, in February 1932. Three months later, the country's political leaders were forced to turn the government over to the militarists, who retained power until 1945.

30   In 1940, Japan invaded Indochina hoping to open up a passage through to Southeast Asia. The United States and Britain reacted by imposing a total embargo upon Japanese merchandise. The Japanese attack on Pearl Harbor, in Hawaii, and of the Philippines, Hong Kong and Malaysia, unleashed the war with the United States and opened up a new phase of World War II.

31   Japan surrendered on August 14 1945, after the US had dropped two atomic bombs on Hiroshima and Nagasaki on August 6 and 9. Japan was subsequently occupied by US troops who remained in the country between 1945 and 1952, and was governed by the Supreme Command of the Allied Powers (SCAP) under the leadership of General Douglas MacArthur. SCAP forced Japan to abandon the Meiji institutions, to renounce the emperor's claim to divinity, and transfer the government to a parliament, which was charged with electing the prime minister and to establishing an independent judiciary.

32   Although imposed upon the Japanese from the outside, the principles laid down in the 1947 constitution were accepted by all sectors of society and in 1952 the country recovered its independence. Japanese sovereignty was restored over the Tokara archipelago in 1951, over the Amami islands in 1953, over the Bonin islands in 1968, and over the rest of the Ryukyu, including Okinawa, in 1972.

33   SCAP also took other measures to weaken the hierarchical model of the Meiji family-state. These ranged from giving tenants the right to

purchase the land they lived on, and laws aimed at strengthening free trade and preventing the return of monopolies. However, the Japanese financial system remained intact and provided the basis for economic recovery at the end of the occupation.

34   In 1955, opposing the country's conservative and nationalist sectors, which had supported the war policy, the Liberal Democratic Party (LDP) was formed. It was a center-right party, holding a majority in Parliament and has governed the country from its foundation to the present.

35   The 1947 Constitution established restrictions upon the development of Japanese military power. During the postwar period, Japan bowed to US strategy for the region forming alliances with Taiwan and South Korea. In 1956 it joined the UN and re-established relations with the USSR.

36   The return to independence found the Japanese economy in a state of growth and change. Farmers became unable to survive with the traditional methods of small-scale production and left the land in droves, leading to great urban migration. Industrialization and full employment triggered the need for technological innovation in the countryside to increase the food supply.

37   During the 1960s, Japan specialized in the production of high technology products, which made it necessary to establish stable trade relations with more industrialized countries instead of its previous Asian partners. The oil crisis of 1973 did not halt the growth of the Japanese industry, which led the world in steel, ship building, electronics, and automobile manufacturing.

38   Although Prime Minister Kakuei Tanaka's visit to Beijing in 1972 signaled Japanese recognition of the People's Republic of China, it damaged the country's relations with Taiwan. The scandal following the disclosure of the fact that Tanaka had been bribed by the Marubeni Corporation (a representative of the US Lockheed Aircraft Corporation), adversely affected the LDP's popularity and in 1976, for the first time in its history, it lost its absolute majority in parliament.

39   During the 1960s and 1970s, there was a large trade surplus in Japan's favor in its trade with the US. During this period, Japan began ranking first or second with all its trading partners. With direct investment and the establishment of subsidiaries of Japanese companies, Japan expanded worldwide.

40   The Japanese corporate world at the time dominated by the Sogo-Shosha system, huge conglomerates which commercialize virtually all

kinds of raw material in almost every country in the world, by means of state-of-the-art information systems capable of supplying data for instantaneous decision-making.

41   The organization of Japanese corporations maintains some principles which are the legacy of Japan's medieval tradition. The worker is bound to the corporation by an allegiance similar to that which bound the medieval peasant to his land and the local warlord. This often results in great company discipline and production efficiency.

42   The impressive development of the Japanese economy was due not only to this efficiency but also to a policy of foreign investment in projects which quickly deplete non-renewable natural resources. This policy has caused irreversible damage to rainforests and serious alterations to the Third World ecosystem.

43   At this time Japan was importing over 16 million cubic meters of tropical timber every year. This has caused a massive deforestation in Malaysia, Thailand, Indonesia, the Philippines, and Papua New Guinea. Japan has also become a consumer of endangered species and products derived from them, such as ivory and tortoise shells.

44   Japan makes direct investments in Third World countries and gives credits through its agencies to aid in building roads and in scientific research projects. As with all international aid this assistance is geared toward its own interest in gaining cheap, easy access to the raw materials of those countries.

45   The traditional full-employment situation in Japan was threatened by two factors: demographic growth and technological modernization which created a labor shortage. Japanese resistance to foreign immigrants and the progressively ageing profile of the population only intensified the problem. In June 1990, an immigration law went into effect opening up the Japanese labor market to foreign workers, for the first time ever.

46   Although the US at that time gave military support to Japan, Washington started exerting pressure in 1982 so that the country would increase its military expenditure (around 0.9 per cent of its GDP) and assume greater responsibility in regional security in the Western Pacific.

47   The death of Emperor Hirohito in January 1989 brought to an end the Showa era, which had begun in 1926. The coronation of his successor, Akihito, in the traditional Japanese style, marked the beginning of the Heisei era (achievement of universal peace). The coronation ceremony was

attended by more heads of state than had ever gathered together for any such event. The expense incurred generated internal protests.

[48] Japanese relations with the EC and the US have been strained at times, due to problems of protectionism and a trade imbalance (in Japan's favor). In 1987, Washington protested at Japan's sale of sophisticated submarine technology to the USSR, between 1982 and 1984. Nevertheless in 1989 Naboru Takeshita was the first head of government to be received by newly-elected US president, George Bush. Takeshita resigned in April, as a result of a real estate scandal. He was succeeded by Sosuke Uno, who was forced to resign after less than three months in office after admitting having sexual relations with a geisha woman.

[49] At the end of the Cold War, Japan emerged as one of the three main world economic powers, together with the US and the EC. At present, it is the country with the largest overseas investment. It is a key participant in the world financial system, and is influential in the exchange of Third World debt funds.

[50] On November 5 1991, Prime Minister Toshiki Kaifu presented his resignation, and was replaced by 72-year-old Kiichi Miyazawa who had been elected president of the Liberal Democratic Party nine days before. Kaifu had been elected in August 1989 because he was one of very few party members who had never been involved in a corruption scandal. His political career rapidly came to an end when he lost the support of the Takeshita clan, the most influential of the official party's five factions, and the one which had backed his election.

[51] The Takeshita clan also backed the next prime minister, Miyazawa, even though he had been forced to resign as minister of finance in December 1988, because of his involvement in the Recruit scandal. (Recruit was a Japanese telecommunications firm that had made large financial contributions to many politicians in the hope of obtaining governmental favors.) In his inaugural speech, Miyazawa outlined the objectives he had set for his administration: to expand relations with, and aid to China; to negotiate with the United States and to normalize relations with the USSR. In addition, he announced his willingness to liberalize the rice market, making concessions similar to those already made by the EC and the United States, to ward off a failure of the Uruguay Round of the GATT.

[52] On February 10 1992, it was revealed that the minister of postal services, Hideo Watanabe, had admitted to receiving a bribe greater than the $40,000 he had previously admitted to during the Recruit scandal of 1988. On February 14, four people were arrested with relation to another financial scandal, which involved more than 100 members of Miyazawa's government, as well as the mafia group known as Inagawagumi. It was revealed that billions of yen had been siphoned off from party donations making the new case, known as Kyubin, an even more serious breach of conduct than the Recruit scandal.

[53] Toward the middle of the year, after heated debate, a law was passed authorizing troops to be sent abroad for the first time since World War II.

[54] In early 1993, Miyazawa promised to broaden the scope of Japanese forces, both in terms of funding and personnel, within the framework of the UN peacekeeping missions.

[55] Also in 1993 the Prime Minister was censured by the Diet for failing to carry out electoral reforms needed to end the endemic corruption in Japanese political life. The official party split, losing 54 seats, and elections were moved up to July.

[56] The two dissident groups, led by Tsutomu Hata and Masayoshi Takemura, formed new parties; the Reformation Party and the Pioneer Party.

[57] Diplomatic relations with the Russian Government improved slightly when Japan announced that, while not relinquishing its claim to the Kuril Islands, it would not allow its claim to the islands to prevent economic aid to Russia.

[58] On July 18, general elections drew the lowest rate of voter participation since the war (67.3 per cent), a clear sign of the electorate's dissatisfaction with the corrupt state of Japan's political scene.

[59] The LDP, in power since 1955, lost its majority in the Kokkai (Diet), obtaining only 228 of the 512 disputed seats in the House of Representatives, compared with 275 in the 1990 election. This result was significant enough to alter the balance of power which had been in effect since World War II.

[60] Miyazawa, who had announced his decision to remain in office regardless of the election results, changed his mind. A few days later, he resigned the party presidency, and assumed responsibility for the LDP's defeat. Yohei Kono was named party President.

[61] In July, the 'new majority' of the Socialist, Reformation, Komeito (Buddhist), Democratic Socialist, Unified Democratic Socialist and Pioneer parties, agreed to form a new Government, based upon a limited platform which would not attempt any profound changes.

[62] Hosokawa, the former governor of the province of Kunamoto, was elected Prime Minister in August. Upon assuming office, he announced a far-reaching political-reform bill, aimed at fighting corruption, putting an end to the recession and modernizing the pension and health systems.

[63] In his first speech before the Diet, Hosokawa referred to the aggression with which Japan had treated its Asian neighbors, from the 1930s until the end of World War II. On August 15, the 48th anniversary of Japan's surrender, Hosokawa offered condolences and apologies to the victims of Japanese colonialism.

[64] In December 1993, the Japanese Government opened up the rice market, allowing up to 4 per cent of internal consumption, amounting to 10 million tons, to be imported. Many families tend to hoard domestic rice, and shopkeepers speculate with prices. The 'Rice Lord', or kome, is a sacred part in Japanese tradition, and is linked to the earth and the ancestors.

[65] A corruption scandal in top Government circles was revealed in 1992 when Shin Kanemaru, historic LDP leader, admitted he had received bribes. Kanemaru was arrested in March 1993 and was granted an amnesty shortly afterward. When Hosokawa succeeded Miyazawa, the Confederation of Industries announced it would discontinue its 'contributions' to the LDP. According to local press versions, these had amounted to $1 billion per year.

[66] In August, 165 political leaders and 445 business people were arrested for irregularities committed during the July 1993 election

PROFILE

ENVIRONMENT

The country is an archipelago made up of 3,400 islands, the most important being Hokkaido, Honshu and Kyushu. The terrain is mountainous, dominated by the so-called Japanese Alps, which are of volcanic origin. Since 85 per cent of the land is taken up by high, uninhabitable mountains, 40 per cent of the population lives on only 1 per cent of the land area, in the narrow Pacific coastal plains, where demographic density exceeds 1,000 inhabitants per sq km. The climate is sub-tropical in the south, temperate in the center and cold in the north. Located where cold and warm ocean currents converge, Japanese waters have excellent fishing, and this activity is important to the country's economy. Japan's intensive and highly mechanized farming is concentrated along the coastal plains (rice, soybeans and vegetables). There are few mineral resources. Highly industrialized, the country's economy revolves around foreign trade, exporting manufactured products and importing raw materials. The major environmental problems are air pollution, especially in the major urban areas of Tokyo, Osaka and Yokohama, and acid rain in many parts of the country. One of the world's largest heavy industries has polluted many coastal areas.

SOCIETY

Peoples: The Japanese are culturally and ethnically homogeneous, having their origin in the migration of peoples from the Asian continent. There are Korean, Chinese, Ainu and Brazilian minorities.
Religions: Buddhism and Shintoism 84 per cent.
Languages: Japanese.
Political Parties: The government coalition is made up of the Liberal Democratic Party (LDP), the Social Democratic Party of Japan (SPDJ) and the New Party Sakigake. The Shinshinto (Japan Renewal Party) has been in opposition since 1994.
Social Organizations: The General Council of Japanese Trade Unions has 4,500,000 members.

THE STATE

Official Name: Nihon-Koku
Capital: Tokyo 26,356,000 people (1999).
Other cities: Yokohama 3,518,000 people; Osaka 2,641,000; Nagoya 2,243,400; Kyoto 1,488,800 (2000). **Government:** Parliamentary constitutional monarchy. Emperor Akihito has been Head of State since January 1989, although his official coronation did not take place until November 12 1990. Junichiro Koizumi, Prime Minister and head of the Government since April 2001. Legislature (The Diet) is bicameral: House of Representatives, made up of 480 members; House of Counselors, with 252 members, elected by direct popular vote every 4 and 6 years, respectively.
National Holiday: December 23, Emperor's Birthday (1933). February 11, Founding of the Country (1889).
Armed Forces: 239,500 (including 8,000 women).
Other: 12,000 (non-combat Coast Guard, under the jurisdiction of the Ministry of Transport).

campaign. 5,500 cases were brought to court to deal with electoral fraud. In October, Shinji Kiyoyama - president of Kajima, the country's second largest construction firm - was arrested for paying a bribe in exchange for a building permit.

[67] Hosokawa's 'romance' with public opinion, after reaching record levels of popularity, started to cool off in early 1994 as press reports became critical, accusing him of having received huge amounts of money in exchange for favors.

[68] Already in February 1994, the Prime Minister had been forced to abandon a scheme which he himself had sponsored, aimed at keeping the Government coalition intact. Worn out by the pressure, he had to issue a self-critique - unpleasant for a head of Government - explaining the reckless manner in which he had handled the situation.

[69] A new $140 billion plan to reactivate the economy also drew criticism. Its feasibility was questioned and the press stressed the plan did not address the problems posed by a rapidly ageing population.

[70] In March 1994, a summit meeting between Japan and the US ended in failure. Although Hosokawa showed a willingness to accept opening up the Japanese automobile, telecommunications, medicine and insurance markets, he rejected the US scheme of mandatory quotas. Japanese businessmen disqualified Hosokawa and felt inclined to wage a commercial war with the US before yielding to its pressures. The automobile industry employs 11 per cent of Japan's labor and contributes 30 per cent of the GDP.

[71] A new corruption case involved LDP member of parliament Nakamura, who was arrested for accepting bribes from Kajima and other construction firms. Hosokawa was unable to shake off accusations from the opposition about his own involvement in illicit business deals. In April he resigned and asked 'sincerely for forgiveness from the people of Japan'.

[72] Tsutomu Hata was nominated Prime Minister and on April 28, Japan's first minority Government in four decades was formed. The socialists had walked out of the Government coalition leaving the Government with only 182 of the 512 seats in the lower house.

[73] Hata made official visits to Europe aiming to establish closer trade links with the European Community. He also admitted that Japan's trade surplus had caused the trade crisis with the United States. After an initial agreement was reached between the two countries, Hata launched a scheme to promote economic deregulation.

[74] Socialist Tomiichi Murayama was elected Prime Minister on June 29 1994 and took office on July 18. His party, the Social Democratic Party of Japan (SDPJ) did not obtain a majority in parliament but formed an alliance with its traditional rival, the LDP, and with a new party, the Sakigake.

[75] The opening of Kansai airport, located on an artificial island, led to a blossoming of island-city projects. The overpopulation of Japan's large cities has led to a permanent real estate development, taking up what little space is available for construction.

[76] On January 17 1995, an earthquake hit the area of Hanshin. Over 6,000 died, 100,000 buildings were destroyed in the city of Kobe and over 300,000 were left homeless. The Government's delayed response to the disaster was harshly criticized. The lower house added $10 billion to the budget for the area's recovery.

[77] In March, a series of attacks with poisonous Sarin gas killed 12 people and affected 12,000 others in Tokyo's subways. A similar attack had taken seven lives in Matsumoto in June 1994. Shoko Asahara, the leader of a religious sect called Aum Shinriyko (Supreme Truth), was charged with the attack and arrested along with 16 other leaders from the movement.

[78] Murayama was defeated when Independent Yukio Aoshima was elected governor of Tokyo in the April 9 1995 elections. The Socialists did not obtain favorable returns at the July elections either, which renewed half of the upper house's seats and in which opposition party Sakigake had a significant growth.

[79] In January 1996, Ryutaro Hashimoto (LDP president) replaced Murayama as Prime Minister. The new Head of Government called for general elections on October, in which his party won a relative majority in parliament. In November, Hashimoto formed a cabinet with only LDP members.

[80] In a referendum held in late 1997, slightly more than half of the Nago population, on Okinawa island, decided against the construction of a US heliport on the island. The United States had been stationed in Okinawa since the Japanese surrender in 1945 and had already built a sophisticated airbase with tens of thousands of soldiers. The Japanese and US governments claimed the construction of the heliport was a step towards the dismantling of the base which apparently did not convince the majority of Noga voters.

[81] The financial and economic crisis which struck Southeast Asia in 1997 also affected Japan, the second world power and first creditor of the world. On April 1998, the yen was at its lowest level in the last seven years and the Tokyo Stock Exchange had lost 6 per cent in three days. At an economic level, a reduction of the gross domestic product was expected. Hashimoto stated his country was facing an 'extremely severe' situation, not seen since World War II.

[82] Hashimoto resigned in early July after the bitter electoral results for his Liberal Democratic Party (LDP). On July 30, after being defeated in the Upper House of Parliament, former foreign minister Keizo Obuchi, also of the LDP, obtained the necessary votes in the Lower House and was named the new Prime Minister. The greatest challenges facing the new Government were to cut taxes in order to stimulate consumption and to take action against the bad loans that paralyzed the Japanese banking system.

[83] A major radioactive uranium leak at a JCO company reprocessing plant, just three kilometers from the Tokoaimura nuclear plant north of Tokyo, caused radiation levels to rise to 15,000 times higher than normal. The environmental organization Greenpeace denounced the accident as a symptom of the problems plaguing Japan's nuclear safety system. According to Greenpeace, Japan holds five tons of uranium within its territory, in addition to 30 tons it has purchased but which remain in Europe.

[84] Flourishing right-wing groups enthusiastically applauded the re-adoption, after a 50-year break, of the former imperial flag in August, while dozens of teachers who refused to salute the old imperial symbols of the military era were fired. Growing nationalism was also evident in the armed forces, which began to carry out maneuvers in Japanese waters and achieved their highest levels of recruitment in decades.

[85] Following yet another nuclear accident, this time at the Tokaimura plant in September, Obuchi ordered the inspection of all installations using nuclear fuel. The JCO firm, which recycled nuclear material, admitted that for years it had been using procedures that did not comply with the minimum safety requirements established by the Government. Despite the company's self-criticism, the Governor of Ibaraki province and the Mayor of Tokaimura presented complaints to the Prime Minister about the way authorities had responded to the emergency. Greenpeace claimed that the plant continued to emit radiation five times higher than recommended safety levels, while Government officials from the nuclear safety area were criticized for their slowness in measuring the

contamination. The Yomiuri newspaper reported that the three operators charged with negligence in the handling of radioactive materials did not even know what a nuclear chain reaction meant.

[86] Obuchi, who had worked hard to achieve his country's economic revival fell into a coma in early April 2000, and was immediately replaced

by Yoshiro Mori. In May, days before Obuchi's death, the new Prime Minister spoke at a meeting of Shintoist followers (who during World War II worshipped Emperor Hirohito as a living deity). Mori shocked national and international public opinion with his description of Japan as 'a divine nation that has the Emperor at its center'.

[87] Responding to demands for his resignation from the press, the opposition and factions within his own party, Mori - according to many the weakest prime minister in the history of the country - appointed a new cabinet and made administrative reductions. To prop up his eroded power base, Mori gave key positions to former prime ministers Kiichi Miyazawa and Ryutaro Hashimoto. In February 2001, however, Mori continued to play golf after hearing that a Japanese fishing vessel had collided with a US nuclear submarine, raising press calls for his resignation due to his 'lack of sensitivity.'

[88] Finally, in April, Mori admitted he had lost public confidence and resigned. He was replaced by Junichiro Koizumi who, as well as promising to revitalize the economy and clean up the government image, included 5 women in his cabinet, including Makiko Tanaka - daughter of former premier - who became the first female foreign minister. This government, with a record female contingent, was classed as a 'Hollywood' cabinet aiming chiefly for popularity. When he came to power, Koizumi had 90 per cent support.

[89] At the beginning of that month, China and South Korea condemned a history book approved by the Japanese authorities, due to its version of events of World War II. Seoul and Beijing said the text 'glossed over' atrocities by the Japanese army during the conflict. The book was written by a group of nationalist historians who felt the current texts went 'too far' in 'accommodating' the former enemies' viewpoints. By contrast the authors felt that during the War Tokyo benefited the South East Asian nations because it prepared them for independence. Amongst other things they stated that the Nanjing massacre of 1937 - where 300,000 civilians were killed - was 'very far from being a holocaust'. Following the protests, the Japanese Education Minister said 137 changes had been made to the text.

[90] Further friction with China and South Korea was caused by Koizumi's visit to the Shinto altar of Yasukuni in August. The 2.4 million soldiers honored there include some figures considered war criminals - for example, the executed prime minister Hideki Tojo - who led Japan during World War II. South Korea and China expressed unease over Koizumi's visit to what they considered 'a monument to militarism' and added that this caused untold damage to relations between the nations. Meanwhile, in a communiqué, the Chinese Government stated that the visit offended the sentiments of its people. In a park in Seoul, 20 Koreans cut off the end of their little fingers in protest. In October, Koizumi visited Seoul and offered apologies for the suffering of that country under the Japanese colonial government.

[91] Koizumi's popularity was hit by a series of scandals, and fell to 40 per cent in April 2002. In January he had sacked Chancellor Tanaka, whom he accused of lying in an argument with his bureaucrats. This was followed by resignations from allies and ministers, for various reasons, and in April, Yutaka Inoue, speaker of the ruling party in the upper house, also resigned.

[92] In May 2002 Japan, along with the European Union, ratified the 1997 Kyoto Protocol on climate change. This gave the Protocol the required number of signatories for it to come into force, despite the US' refusal to ratify it.

[93] Japan was co-host, along with South Korea, for the football World Cup in June 2002 - the first time the competition had been held in the region. ∎

Divine Shinto and Japanese life

Shinto, the national religion of Japan, is 2,500 years old and has no founder, no official sacred texts in the strict sense of the term, nor set dogmas. The word Shinto, which in the literal sense means 'the way of the *kami*' (kami means mystical, superior or divine and is applied to the beneficial and harmful principles of water, earth, water and deified people) used to differentiate Japanese indigenous beliefs from Buddhism, which was introduced to Japan in the 6th century AD.

Shinto is made up of traditional Japanese religious practices, beliefs and attitudes to life which harmonize with these practices. Today it subsists more as part of the social life of the Japanese and their motivations than as a formal pattern of beliefs or philosophy. It remains closely linked to the Japanese value system and their way of thinking and acting.

Its origins lie in a mixture of tribal religions, each one with its own kami; a system of faith and a stock of ethnic customs, festivals, myths, ancient writings and attitudes relating to the kami.

THE FOUR AFFIRMATIONS
There are four basic affirmations or beliefs to Shintoism:
1. The affirmation of family traditions: these are the vital rites like birth and marriage, and other traditions which have been passed down from generation to generation.
2. The affirmation of the love of nature: nature is sacred; hence contact with nature implies a person is in contact with the gods.
3. The affirmation of personal cleanliness: the worshipper must be clean in the presence of the spirits; anyone who is unclean is disrespectful.
4. Affirmation of the *matsuri*: the matsuri are festivals in honor of the spirits.

SANCTUARY, SECT AND POPULAR SHINTO
Shinto can be classified in three broad categories: Shinto of the sanctuary (jinja Shinto), Shinto of the sect (kyoha Shinto) and popular Shinto (minzoku Shinto). Jinja Shinto is one of the main currents and includes within its structure the now defunct state Shinto (kokka Shinto). Kyoha Shinto is relatively new and is made up of 13 main sects which originated in Japan in the 19th century as well as many others which arose after World War II. Each of these sects was organized, either by a founder, or a systematizer, as a body of doctrine. Minzoku Shinto is a strain of popular Japanese beliefs and is closely linked to other types of Shinto. It lacks a formal organizational structure and formulated doctrine, but is based on the veneration of small idols by the roadside and the farming rituals of rural families. These three variants are interrelated: popular Shinto exists as a substructure of the Shinto faith, as the follower of sect Shinto is usually a parishioner (*ujiko*) of a particular sanctuary.

SHINTO SANCTUARIES
There are more than 110,000 Shinto sanctuaries and temples for the kami in Japan. The sanctuaries usually owe their existence to a physical characteristic or historical event. Many are so big that they require a large well-organized staff to serve them. Many Japanese homes contain small house sanctuaries known as *kami-dana*.

SHINTO AND THE EMPEROR
Shintoists believe the kami created the islands of Japan and that the solar goddess Amaterasu was the mother of the first emperor, who was sent to Earth to found an imperial dynasty. This belief formed the basis of state Shinto. The Emperor became a symbol of the people and of the unity of the nation. This tradition fed respect for state authority, the employer and the family. During the Meiji dynasty (1868-1912), the Government decided to institutionalize Shinto, taking control of the sanctuaries, and it adopted a restrictive policy on other religions. The 1889 Constitution considers obedience to Shinto sanctuaries to be the patriotic duty of all Japanese, thus making Shinto the official religion and using it to justify the cult of the Emperor and Japanese militarism in the early 20th century. Even though the new Constitution drawn up after World War II reduced Shinto to the status of an ordinary sect, more than 80 per cent of Japanese are Shintoist today. As it is not an exclusive religion, people can practice Shinto alongside another faith: most Japanese are also Buddhists. ∎

Jordan

Population: 5,196,000 (2002)
Land area: 88,930 SQ KM
Capital: Amman
Currency: Dinar
Language: Arabic

Urdunn

By the 2000 BC large numbers of Semitic nomads, known as Amorites, had entered the region, which became known as Canaan (in present-day Jordan). By the middle of the second millennium the Amorities settled in the Jordan Valley, which became a Semitic language area. During the 15th to 13th centuries BC small tribal kingdoms with names familiar from the Old Testament developed: Edom, Moab, Bashan, Gilead. The conquest of Canaan by the Israelites was completed between 1220 and 1190 BC. In 722 BC Israel fell to the Assyrian king. The region of Judah preserved its political independence as a tribute state of Assyria, while the rest of the Jordan region was divided into Assyrian-controlled provinces.

2 Between the 3rd and 1st century BC, the history of Jordan was influenced by three peoples: Jews, Greeks, and Nabataeans. The Greeks were mainly veterans of Alexander's military campaigns who fought one another for regional hegemony. The Nabataeans were Arabs who had moved from the desert into Edom in the 7th century BC. By the 1st century BC, Roman legions removed the last remnants of the Seleucids from Syria, converting the area into a full Roman province.

3 In the face of the Muslim expansion, in the year 636 the Byzantine emperor Heraclius gathered a large army which met the Muslim army at the Yarmuk river. Hundreds of thousands met in ferocious combat, victory favoring the Arabs, who gained access to the fertile crescent (see Saudi Arabia).

OCCUPIED BY ISRAEL

1 Southern Lebanon - occupied 1983-2000
2 Syria - Golan Heights - occupied in 1967
3 West Bank - occupied in 1967 (some individual towns now have autonomy but Israeli incursions have continued).

0   100 km

During the Crusades, the western part of the Jordanian territory was used by Muslims as the operational base to initiate warfare against the European strongholds.

4 With Turkish domination in the 16th century, the territory was transformed into part of the district of Damascus and remained so until into the 20th century, when World War I broke out.

5 Jordanian peoples joined the widespread Arab rebellion against the Turks, forming a decisive element in defeating the Ottomans. Under the Sykes-Picot agreement - a secret document signed in 1916 - France was given Lebanon and Syria as protectorates, while Britain had the mandate over Iraq and Palestine - which was included in present-day Jordan. The British had promised Sherif Hussein of Mecca that they would form a single Arab kingdom with these territories and the Arab Peninsula.

6 The situation of Faisal - son of the Sherif - in Syria (see Syria) and his expulsion by the French in 1920, meant that Prince Abdullah - another of Hussein's sons - organized the Bedouin forces in Jordan to support his brother. The

British convinced him it was better to accept government from the Emirate of Transjordan.

7 The Emirate of Transjordan remained under British mandate until 1928, when the frontiers with Palestine were set and a law was passed giving Abdullah and his heirs the power to rule over and administer the State. However, foreign relations and the military remained under British control until May 1946, when the Emirate became the 'Hashemite Kingdom of Transjordan'. After the Arab-Israeli war in 1948, King Abdullah annexed the Palestinian territories on the West Bank. As a result of this annexation, the country became known as Jordan, but had new problems linked to the situation of Palestinian refugees, the legal status of Jerusalem, and the frontier with Israel almost doubling in length.

8 In 1951 Abdullah was assassinated and his son, Talal, succeeded him. He presented anti-British attitudes and promised a progressive government, but he was deposed a year later. In 1953 his son Hussein took over the throne at the age of 17.

9 Following Israeli occupation of Transjordan, the Kingdom received a great mass of Palestinians, initially robbed of their lands by the Jews in 1948 and then expelled from their refugee camps in 1967. Demographic pressure and Hussein's desire to replace the Palestine Liberation Organization (PLO) as the Palestinians' representative body, led to the Jordanian massacre of Palestinians known as 'black September' in Jordan in 1970.

10 After the Arab-Israeli war in 1973, the King re-established relations with the PLO, and in 1979 recognized it as the only legitimate representative of Palestine.

11 In 1985, King Hussein and Palestinian leader Yasser Arafat were reconciled; in July 1988 the King renounced all claim on Transjordan and passed the PLO responsibility for these Israeli-occupied territories.

12 Hussein was at the peak of his popularity when Iraq invaded Kuwait in August 1990. He was also in a difficult position. Militarily flanked by Israel and Iraq, a majority of Palestinian subjects who supported Iraq, and under pressure from the West, the country also depended on Saudi Arabia for finance and on Baghdad for oil. Jordan joined the trade blockade on Baghdad, but opposed the use of military force to get the Security Council resolutions fulfilled. The country lost $570 million due to the blockade. It also received 40,000 Kurdish refugees, more than 1,000,000 Iraqis and some 300,000 Jordanians of Palestinian origin who were expelled by Kuwait in response to Jordan's support of Iraq.

13 On June 9 1991, Hussein and political representatives signed a new Constitution, which legalized political parties and extended political rights for women.

14 The growth of fundamental Islam was less controlled than in other countries of the region. For example, the Muslim Brotherhood was allowed to operate, initially as a philanthropic organization. It gained prestige in the area of social welfare: it owns hospitals, schools and several Islamic study centers. Difficult relations between the fundamentalists and the throne put obstacles in the way of negotiations

LAND USE

DEFORESTATION: 2.5% annual (1990/95)

1993

- FOREST & WOODLAND: 0.8%
- ARABLE: 3.5%
- OTHER: 95.7%

MATERNAL MORTALITY

1985/99

Per 100,000 live births

41

LITERACY

2000

90%

EXTERNAL DEBT

2000

PER CAPITA

US$ 1,674

with Israel. In 1994, Hussein and Israeli premier Yitzhak Rabin signed a bilateral peace treaty. Israel handed over 300 square kilometers of desert to Jordan and the frontier was established, but more significance was give to the granting of custody of sacred Islamic sites in Jerusalem to the care of King Hussein. The Jordanian public was surprised by the speed of the peace agreement and the poor economic benefits for their country.
[15]   Despite its dependence on Iraqi oil, Jordan decided to cut back trade with Baghdad in 1996. Exports

to the country were reduced 50 per cent and the United States was authorized to use an air base within the territory.
[16]   Hussein died on February 7 1999 after a long illness, He had changed his heir, displacing his brother Hassan with Abdullah, the 37-year old son of his first marriage.
[17]   Abdullah II came to the throne to find Jordan involved in an Arab-Israeli peace process which had reached a stalemate, and with Iraq under US attacks. On the domestic front, the country was facing serious economic crisis while

the political parties demanded more openness from the government. Official unemployment rates exceeded 30 per cent, there were negligible foreign reserves and the fiscal deficit had gone from 2 per cent in 1997 to 6 per cent in 1998. Trade, the main activity in a country with few natural resources, was in free fall due to the combination of the embargo on Iraq and the effects of the 1997 Asian economic crisis.
[18]   The eruption of the second Palestinian *intifada* had a direct impact on Jordan. In October, following confrontations between the police and a crowd protesting against the Israeli government, the Government banned public demonstrations.
[19]   The death of an adolescent in police custody in the southern town of Maan gave rise to the worst violence in three years. According to the boy's family, he had been tortured by the police - who accused him of theft - after they found a photograph of terrorist Osama bin Laden in his pocket, along with others of Palestinians who had died during the intifada.
[20]   In February 2002, continuing the policy of alliance with the US, Abdullah supported Washington's description of Iran, Iraq and North Korea as 'the axis of terror.' The Government was pressured into taking a less cordial position in relation to Israel. Chancellor Marwan Muasher called the Israeli Ambassador to a meeting in March and threatened to take measures in protest against the attack on the Palestine Authority head quarters. Similarly, he asked the UN Security Council for immediate deployment of troops to the Palestinian territories.
[21]   Arafat declared in June 2002 that Palestinians 'must prepare for the local elections as well as presidential and legislative elections' and that the Government must 'quickly put in place and carry out plans that would bring back the ministries and institutions to make us more effective in carrying out our tasks.' He opened the cabinet meeting with the new ministers after the reorganization of the administration, that cut the number of cabinet posts from 31 to 21. ■

PROFILE

ENVIRONMENT

75 per cent of the country is a desert plateau, 600 to 900 meters in altitude. The western part of this plateau has a series of cleavages at the beginning of the great Rift Valley fault, which crosses the Red Sea and stretches into East Africa. In the past, these fissures widened the Jordan River valley and formed the steep depression that is now the Dead Sea. As most of the country is made up of dry plains, farming is limited to cereals (wheat and rye) and citrus fruits. Sheep and goats are also bred. The shortage of water is the chief environmental problem. Desertification and urban expansion have caused the loss of arable land near the Jordan River.

SOCIETY

Peoples: Most of the population is Palestinian, from Israeli post-war migrations. Native Jordanians are of the 20 large Bedouin ethnic groups of which about one third are still semi-nomadic. There is a Circassian minority from the Caucasus, who now play a major role in trade and administration.
Religions: 90 per cent of the population are Sunni Muslim but the Shi'a numbers are increasing rapidly.
Languages: Arabic (official). English is often used.
Political Parties: In 1991 political parties were legalized. The most important are: National Constitutional Party (nine party coalition) and the Jordan Socialist Arab Ba'ath Party. Extra parliamentary: Islamic Action Front, Shi'a; Jordan Democratic Popular Party; Democratic Arab Party of Jordan.
Social Organizations: The most important union body is the General Federation of Unions of Jordan. The Union of Jordanian Women has participated in the democratization process and in defense of the political rights of women. Others: National Union of Students of Jordan and the Muslim Brotherhood.

THE STATE

Official Name: al-Mamlakah al-Urdunniya al-Hashimiyah.
Administrative divisions: 12 provinces.
Capital: Amman 1,378,000 people (1999).
Other cities: Irbid 537,600 people; az-Zarqa 471,200; ar-Rusayfah 184,300; as-Salt 64,000 (2000).
Government: Abdullah II, King since February 1999. Ali Abu al-Ragheb, Prime Minister since June 2000. Legislative branch: National Assembly (bicameral), with a 40 member Senate appointed by the King, and an 80-member Chamber of Deputies elected by direct popular vote; the latter can be dissolved by the King. **National Holiday:** May 25, Independence Day (1946). **Armed Forces:** 98,650 troops (1996). **Other:** 6,000 soldiers under the authority of the Department of Public Security; 200,000 militia in the 'People's Army'; 3,000 Palestinians in the Palestinian Liberation Army, under the supervision of the Jordanian Army.

DEMOGRAPHY

Population: 5,196,000 (2002)
Annual growth: 4.0 % (1985-2000)
Estimates for year 2015: 7,191,000 (2000)
Annual growth to year 2015: 2.5 % (2000)
Urban population: 74.2 % (2000)
Urban growth: 3.8 % (2000)
Children per woman: 4.5 (2000)

HEALTH

Life expectancy at birth: 71 years (2000-2005)
male: 70 years (2000-2005)
female: 73 years (2000-2005)
Maternal mortality: 41 per 100,000 live births (1985/99)
Infant mortality: 28 per 1,000 (2000)
Under-5 child mortality: 34 per 1,000 (2000)
Daily calorie supply: 2,834 per capita (1999)
166 doctors per 100,000 people (1997)
Safe water: 96 % (2000)

EDUCATION

Literacy: 90 % (2000)
male: 95 % (2000)
female: 84 % (2000)
School enrolment (net):
Primary total: 95 % (1994/2000)
male: 86 % (1995/99)
female: 86 % (1995/99)
Secondary (gross):
male: 52 % (1995/97)
female: 54 % (1995/97)
Tertiary (gross): 19 % (1997)
Primary school teachers: one for every 21 pupils (1996)

COMMUNICATIONS

77 newspapers (1998), 372 radios (1997), 84 TV sets (2000) and 93 main telephone lines (2000) per 1,000 people
Books: 10 new titles per 100,000 people (1992/94)

ECONOMY

Per capita, GDP: $ 3,966 (2000)
Annual growth: 0.8 % (2000)
Annual inflation: 0.7 % (2000)
Consumer price index: 114.6 (2000)
Currency: 0.7 dinars = $ 1 (03/2002)
Cereal imports: 1,536,663 metric tons (2000)
Food import dependency: 21 % (2000)
Fertilizer use: 943 kg per ha (1999)
Exports: $ 3,534 million (2000)
Imports: $ 5,720 million (2000)
External debt: $ 8,226 million (2000); $ 1,674 per capita (2000)
Debt service: 11.8 % of exports (1999)
Development aid received: $ 430 million (1999); $ 90.7 per capita (1999); 5.30 % of GNP (1999)

ENERGY

Consumption: 1,063.1 Kgs of oil equivalent per capita yearly (1998); 94.1 % imported (1999)

HDI (ranking/value): 88 / 0.714 (1999)

Kanaky/
New Caledonia

Population:	224,000 (2002)
Land area:	18,280 SQ KM
Capital:	Nouméa
Currency:	CFP franc
Language:	French

Kanaky

New Caledonia (Kanaky) was populated by Melanesians (Kanaks) 3,000 years ago. The islands were named by Captain Cook in 1774, as the tree-covered hills reminded him of the Scottish - Caledonian - landscape.

[2] In 1853, the main island was occupied by the French Navy which organized a local guard to suppress frequent indigenous uprisings. Nickel and chrome mining attracted thousands of French settlers. The colonizers pushed out the original inhabitants, and traditional religions, crafts and social organizations were obliterated, and many landless natives were confined to 'reservations', and the system of terraced fields were trodden over by cattle. The last armed rebellion, stifled in 1917, only accelerated European land appropriation.

[3] After Algerian independence, in July 1962, colonization increased with the arrival of *pieds-noirs*, the former French colonists in Algeria. By 1946, New Caledonia had become a French Overseas Territory, but the resulting political autonomy did not favor the Kanaks, reduced to a minority group in relation to the *caldoches* (descendants of Europeans who had settled a century ago).

[4] Most of the Kanaks actively supported independence as the bulk of them lived in poverty, with high unemployment rates, and suffered educational discrimination.

[5] In the 1970s, discontent with the economic situation produced by colonial domination caused strikes, land invasions, experiments in cooperative work, and a powerful campaign to restore traditional lands to the local groups. These had been totally occupied by settlers and used mostly as cattle pastures. The rescue of *coutume* (cultural traditions) and the Kanak identity became a priority, and the proposed luxury tourist Club Méditerranée camps were firmly rejected.

[6] Kanak claims were supported by other independent Melanesian countries (Fiji, Solomon Islands, Papua New Guinea and above all Vanuatu), and were put forward at the South Pacific Forum in August 1981. A month later, pro-independence leader Pierre Declercq, a Catholic of European origin, was murdered at his home by right-wing extremists, changing the malaise to a full-blown political crisis.

[7] Another strong reason why France was hesitant to grant Kanaky independence is that it has the world's second largest nickel deposits, and extensive reserves of other minerals including chrome, iron, cobalt, manganese, and polymetallic nodules, discovered recently on the ocean floor within territorial waters.

[8] Furthermore, the islands' strategic position is of great military value. Its ports, facilities and bases house 6,000 troops and a small war fleet (including a nuclear submarine), considered by the military command as a 'vital point of support' for the French nuclear-testing site on Mururoa atoll.

[9] The election of President Mitterrand in 1981 rekindled the hopes of the pro-independence parties. The French socialist leader was supported by most Kanaks, who saw independence as a way to end the unfair income distribution on the island. This stood at $7,000 per capita (the highest in the Pacific except for Nauru) but the vast majority of the money was concentrated in the hands of European - mostly French - business people, the *métros*, who enjoyed incredible fiscal benefits, and the caldoches who monopolized the most important official positions.

[10] In July 1984, the French National Assembly passed special bills concerning the colony's autonomy, though it rejected amendments submitted by pro-independence parties, confirming Kanak fears that the socialist government of France had no intention of granting independence. In November, the main opposition force, the Socialist Kanak National Liberation Front (FLNKS) called for a boycott of local Territorial Assembly elections, which were sure to endorse the French government plan of postponing Kanak independence indefinitely.

[11] In December 1984, local government became fully controlled by the caldoches with no indigenous Kanak representation, therefore, the FLNKS unilaterally declared New Caledonia independent, proclaiming a Kanak state. The resulting election boycott involved 80 per cent of the Kanak population, forcing the Government to call off the election, and prepare for negotiations.

[12] In December 1986, the United Nations General Assembly proclaimed the right of the Kanak people to self-determination and independence, proposing that the FLNKS be recognized as their legitimate representative.

[13] One year later a referendum was held to determine whether or not ties with France should be maintained. Voting was open to all residents of the island, even Europeans and immigrants who arrived as recently as three years and, for this reason, the FLNKS boycotted the referendum. According to the opposition and the Australian and New Zealand/Aotearoan governments, the high abstention rate of around 41.5 per cent

PROFILE

ENVIRONMENT

The territory consists of the island of New Caledonia (16,700 sq km), the Loyauté/Loyalty Islands (Ouvea, Lifou, Maré and Walpole), the archipelagos of Chesterfield, Avon, Huon, Belep, and the island of Nouméa. The whole group is located in southern Melanesia, between the New Hebrides (Vanuatu) to the East and Australia to the West. Of volcanic origin, the islands are mountainous with coastal reefs. The climate is rainy, tropical, and suitable for agriculture. The vegetation is dense and the subsoil is rich in nickel deposits.

SOCIETY

Peoples: Indigenous Kanaks/New Caledonians are of Melanesian origin (the Kanaka group), 42.5 per cent; there are French and descendants of French (known as caldoches), 37.1 per cent; as well as Wallisian, 8.6 per cent, Vietnamese, Indonesian, Chinese and Polynesian minorities. **Religions:** Roughly 60 per cent Catholic, 16 per cent Protestant and around 5 per cent Muslim. **Languages:** French (official) and more than 30 Melanesian and Polynesian dialects. **Political Parties:** Rally for Caledonia within the Republic (RPCR), anti-separatist; Kanak and Socialist National Liberation Front (FLNKS); Federation of Committees for the Co-ordination of Independentists, separatist; National Front, nationalist; Socialist Kanak Liberation/Kanaky Future, extreme left separatist. **Social Organizations:** The Caledonian Workers' Confederation (CTC); the Federation of New Caledonian Miners' Unions (FSMNC); the New Caledonian Federation of Laborers' and Employees' Unions (USOENC); and the Union of Exploited Kanak Workers (USTKE).

THE STATE

Official Name: Territoire d'Outre-Mer de la Nouvelle-Calédonie et Dependances. **Administrative divisions:** Three provinces: Loyauté, Nord and Sud. **Capital:** Nouméa 129,900 people (1999). **Other Cities:** Mont-Doré 22,700 people; Dumbéa 15,200; Poindimié 4,700 (2000). **Government:** Head of State, French President Jacques Chirac. High Commissioner named by France, Thierry Lataste, since July 1999. Head of Government, Pierre Frogier, since April 2001. Legislature: 54-member Territorial Assembly. **National Holiday:** 14th July, Bastille Day (1789). **Armed Forces:** French troops 3,700 (1993).

invalidated any claim to legitimacy for continued colonial domination.

[14] When all attempts at negotiation failed for the Kanaks, the French attacked the island of Ouvéa, killing 19 people, most of whom were apparently executed rather than killed in combat.

[15] In June 1988, FLNKS leader, Jean-Marie Tjibaou, and Jacques Lafleur (leader of the Caledonian Popular Assembly for the Republic and strongly opposed to independence) signed Section 1 of the Matignon Accord, supported by the French prime minister Michel Rocard, in Paris. From July that year direct government over Kanaky was re-established from Paris. Section II of the Accord stipulated the adoption of preparatory measures for voting on self-determination in 1998 and the freezing of electoral roll, to prevent France increasing the number of voters by sending new colonists.

[16] The territory was divided into three regions, two with a majority of Kanak voters. One of the aims of this division was to create a Melanesian (Kanak) political and financial 'elite', taking over power from the pro-independence groups in most of the territory. Other clauses of the agreement planned greater financial support from Paris during the following ten years.

[17] In a first referendum that same year, the agreements were ratified.

In May 1989, Tjibaou and another independence leader who supported the Matignon agreements were assassinated in Ouvéa.

[18] In 1991, the trade balance was affected by the fall in international prices for nickel and fish. In the two provinces controlled by the pro-independence parties, a new generation of leaders appeared, but the situation worsened for most of the Melanesian population. The imbalance of income became pronounced amongst the Kanaks and greater access to material goods distanced many Melanesians from their community structures and traditions.

[19] In the caldoche areas, mainly covering the capital Nouméa, social inequalities also increased, partly due to the arrival of Melanesian farmers who built shanty towns on the outskirts of the city, but also due to the impoverishment of some caldoches. In a context of increasing social tension, disturbances like those in March 1992 became more common.

[20] The political repercussions of these new social contradictions were reflected in the 1995 provincial elections. The Palika, one of the FLNKS groups, registered separately, criticizing the leadership of the Front representatives in the two provinces controlled by the pro-

independence groups. Both political sectors obtained similar results.

[21] Nickel exploitation by the pro-independence groups in the northern province gave outstanding results in the first years of their leadership, allowing them to form an association with the Canadian Falconbridge company. However, the pro-independence groups' attempts to establish a processing plant with the Canadian company were complicated by similar plans in the French State mining company, SLN-Eramet. FLNKS sympathizers protested, blocking access to the French-controlled installations.

[22] Kanaky independence negotiations changed course in April 1998. The FLNKS and Paris established the basis for a general agreement, known as the Nouméa Accord. The coexistence of two different systems - one that follows Kanak traditions and the other imposed by France - proved to be the most difficult issue to resolve. The Kanaks wanted respect for their culture and their traditional civil organization. The Nouméa Accord allowed for the transference of powers that would assure a 'nearly sovereign' territory within 15 to 20 years. The Kanaks and the Caldoches agreed to share a common 'citizenship', while France acknowledged the

'shadows' remaining from the colonial period.

[23] In November, a referendum was held to ratify the Nouméa agreements. The Yes-vote was victorious with 69.14 per cent of the vote. In December, the text of the law defined the application of the Noumea Accord. On December 23, the National Assembly voted on the new country's legal foundations, which covered the implementation of new institutions as well as a 'progressive' transfer of state powers.

[24] Thierry Lataste was appointed new High Commissioner of the island in July 1999. Two years later, J Pierre Frogier was elected Head of Government. ∎

STATISTICS

DEMOGRAPHY
Urban population: 64.1 % (2000)
Urban growth: 2.4 % (2000)

HEALTH
Life expectancy at birth: 75 years (2000-2005)
male: 73 years (2000-2005)
female: 78 years (2000-2005)
Daily calorie supply: 2,772 per capita (1999)

ECONOMY
Per capita, GDP: $ 21,820 (2000)
Annual growth: 0.3 % (2000)
Currency: 758.3 CFP francs = $ 1 (03/2002)

Melanesians and Polynesians: Surviving cultures

Micronesia, Melanesia and Polynesia were originally inhabited by Melanesians and Polynesians. Melanesians (from the Greek *melas*, black and *nesio*, islands) live in a group of South Pacific islands which include New Guinea, Kanaky (New Caledonia), Vanuatu, Solomon islands, Fiji, the Santa Cruz islands and their smaller neighbors, as well as on the Bismarck and Louisiade archipelagos.

Because of the dark pigmentation of their skin and their hair type, Melanesians were classified in the past as a negroid group.

Their physical characteristics make them a homogeneous group although recent studies link them to the Papuans and even to Aboriginal communities in Australia. Polynesians, meanwhile, stem from the same

original ethnic groups, but are distinguished from the Melanesians by a more robust physical constitution, fair skin and straight hair. There are still common traits in language and physical appearance although their societies have taken different directions.

The first Melanesians arrived 40,000 years ago, probably from the south of the Asiatic continent. About 9,000 years ago, they began to domesticate indigenous root crops and organize their social life around agriculture. Later on, they also specialized in trade and maritime technology as well as fishing. They generally moved in small groups, with a stay in any one place limited by the duration of crop cycles.

Polynesians, by comparison, probably descended from Austronesians, ancient seafar-

ers who arrived on the Pacific archipelagos from South Asia around 4,000 BC, populating New Zealand/Aotearoa, the Samoan Islands, French Polynesia, Tonga, Tahiti, Hawaii and other smaller islands where they still live.

The range of languages spoken by Melanesians and Polynesians clearly displays the exceptional linguistic variation of Oceania, where one quarter of all world languages are spoken. Melanesian and Polynesian languages belong to the Malayo-Polynesian family - or more precisely to the eastern branch of this group - which includes more than 800 dialects spoken by approximately five million people. Melanesians speak more than 400 of the dialects in this group. In Fiji, the main dialect is spoken by nearly half the population - some 334,000 people -

and it is used in official journals and publications. Other dialects include Motu, Roviana, Bambatana, Tolai and Yabem.

Christianity has been gaining ground and progressively replacing traditional forms of religion, although some communities, Melanesian and Polynesian alike, continue to practice cosmic initiation rights and animism.

This great cultural, social and linguistic diversity suffered intense political upset with the arrival of the Europeans. Western culture has reached even the most remote villages, where some forms of business and capitalist organization can be seen, along with an increasing dependence on imported products. Traditional culture survives in marginal areas where there is greater resistance to the dominant culture. ∎

Kazakhstan

Population:	16,027,000 (2002)
Land area:	2,699,700 SQ KM
Capital:	Astana
Currency:	Tengue
Language:	Kazakh

Qazaqstan

In the Bronze Age (about 2000 BC), the territory of Kazakhstan was inhabited by people who lived by farming and raising livestock. Around 500 BC, an alliance was formed among the Saka peoples and in the 3rd century BC, the Usune and Kangli peoples - who lived near the Uighur, Chechen and Alan - subdued the other groups in the area. Later, Attila's Huns occupied the region until they were expelled by the Turks.

[2] In the mid-4th century, the Turkish Kaganate (*Khanate* or kingdom) was formed and later divided into Eastern and Western parts. In the 8th century two states emerged: a Turkish and a Karluk Kaganate. The Turkish conquerors built mosques and tried to impose Islam upon the local population. Over the following 300 years scholarship flourished in the area.

[3] Between the 9th and 12th centuries, the region was occupied by the Oghuz, Kimak, Kipchak and Karajanid groups. The Kipchaks never achieved political unity and remained outside the realm of Islamic influence, which was concentrated in the cities along the Caspian Sea. Until the 13th century, successive waves of Seleucid, Kidan and Tatar invasions swept across the great steppes. Kipchak chiefs and Muscovite princes joined together to resist foreign domination, but did not achieve independence until the fall of the Mongols.

[4] Most of these peoples were nomads but gradually, settled groups of farmers and artisans were organized, and cities like Otrar, Suyab, Balasagun, Yanguikent, Sauran and Kulan arose. The Silk Road, uniting Byzantium, Iran and China, passed through Kazakhstan. Trade relations developed between the nomads of the steppes and the inhabitants of the oases, which extended as far as Western Europe, Asia Minor and the Far East.

[5] By the late 15th century, the Khanate of Kazakh had been formed, disintegrating into three loosely allied but like-minded *yuzos* (hordes). By the 16th century, an ethnic identity had been forged among the Kazakhs. The khans of the Kazakh yuzos passed on their power to their heirs, who thought of themselves as descendants of

Juchi, the eldest son of Genghis Khan. Below them were the sultans, with administrative and judicial power, who governed through the *biy* and the local chieftains.

[6] In the 17th century, the Khanate of Dzhungar carried out successive raids in the Kazakh region, sometimes looting and other times remaining and occupying the area. Russian colonial expansion from the north began in the 18th century. The Russians built a line of forts and then began working their way southward, creating a line of defense against the Dzhungars. The two smaller hordes or yuzos fell under Russian protection eliminating their autonomy in the 1820s because of the frequent rebellions. With the defeat of the Great Horde, annexation of Kazakhstan to the Empire was completed.

[7] Russia installed its government institutions, collected taxes, established areas closed to the Kazakhs and built new cities, declaring the entire territory property of the State. As of 1868, there were six provinces under the control of governors general; the sultans and the biy became mere state officials. The conquest of Kazakhstan was a long process of wars against local tribes. The Cossack regiments were the vanguard of the Russian army and they overcame the khans of Khiva, Boukhara and Kokand, one by one, defeating the last of these in 1880.

[8] The Kazakhs were registered in the censuses as citizens of the State of Russia and were incorporated into the Russian army's foreign expeditions. Kazakhstan became a place to which Russian deportees were sent, including the Decembrists (aristocrats who had conspired against Czar Nikolai I in 1825), Polish and Ukrainian revolutionaries (including the Ukrainian hero, Taras Shevchenko) and the members of the St Petersburg 'Petrashevski circle', which included the writer Feodor Dostoyevsky.

[9] In the late 19th century and early 20th century, Russia built huge railroads (the Trans-Caspian, the Trans-Aralian and the Trans-Siberian), which crossed the region, uniting it with distant urban centers and facilitating the exploitation of Kazakhstan's fabulous mineral wealth. A third of Russia's coal reserves, half its copper, lead and zinc reserves; strategic metals like tungsten and molybdenum; iron, and oil were found in Kazakhstan. Agriculture remained stagnant and attempts to resettle farmers, after the abolition of feudal serfdom in Russia, met with limited success, although there was some development of cotton, wool and traditional Kazakh leather production.

[10] At the beginning of the 20th century, a small nationalist movement emerged in Kazakhstan, and after the Russian Revolution of

1905 the Kazakhs had their own representatives to the first and second *Duma* (parliament) convened by the Czar. In 1916, when the czarist regime ordered the mobilization of all men between the age of 19 and 43 for auxiliary military service, the Kazakhs rebelled, led by Abdulghaffar and Amangeldy Imanov. The revolt was brutally crushed, but in November 1917, after the triumph of the Soviet revolution in Petrograd, the Kazakh nationalists demanded total autonomy for their country. In the early decades of last century, Kazakhstan received massive waves of Ukrainian, Belorusian, German, Bulgarian, Polish, Jewish and Tatar immigrants. A nationalist government was installed in Alma-Ata (now Almaty) in 1918, but the country soon became a battleground.

[11] Fighting between the Red Army and the White Russians - the latter defending the overthrown regime - lasted until 1920, when the counter-revolution was defeated. The Autonomous Soviet Socialist Republic (ASSR) of Kirghiz was formed, as a part of the Russian Federation; it later became known as the ASSR of Kazakhstan. In 1925, the revision of the borders in Soviet central Asia was completed, and all Kazakh lands were unified. In 1936, Kazakhstan became one of the 15 republics of the USSR and the following year, the local Communist Party was founded.

[12] In addition to developing its industrial potential, the Soviet regime increased the amount of land under cultivation. Previously considered not very fertile (in 1913, only 4.2 million hectares were under cultivation), Kazakhstan increased the number of hectares of tilled land to 35.3 million, 15 per cent of all agricultural land in the USSR. Production included wheat, tobacco, mustard, fruit and cattle. Bringing virgin territory under cultivation was an achievement associated with Leonid Brezhnev, during his period as head of the Communist Party of Kazakhstan. Brezhnev replaced Nikita Khrushchev in 1964 as head of the Soviet Party until his death in 1982. Although he proclaimed an era of 'developed socialism', the country's

economic and political problems actually worsened during his administration.

[13] Until 1985, the person who wielded the power in Kazakhstan was Dinmujamed Kunaev, a member of the Politburo of the Soviet Communist Party Central Committee. In 1989, the forced resignation of Kunaev triggered student disturbances; the army resorted to violence in dealing with the demonstrators.

[14] After the transformations set in motion in the USSR by President Mikhail Gorbachev, the republic of Kazakhstan declared independence. During this period two social movements arose - Birlik and Zheltoksan - as well as the anti-nuclear movement Semipalatinsk-Nevada. The main test-sites for Soviet nuclear weapons were situated in Kazakhstan, as is the Baykonur cosmodrome for launching Soviet space vehicles. After the failed coup against the Soviet President in August 1991, Nursultan Nazarbayev resigned as head of the Soviet Communist Party, of which he had been a member, in his capacity as president of a Soviet republic.

[15] In September, Kazakhstan presented a seven-point plan for the creation of a new union treaty,

which was approved by Gorbachev and ten republics. On December 1 1991, Nazarbayev was elected the first president of an independent Kazakhstan. The Communist Party became the Socialist Party of Kazakhstan. On December 21, in Almaty (Kazakh form of Alma-Ata), 11 republics signed an agreement which formally dissolved the USSR and created the new Commonwealth of Independent States, whose members applied separately for admission to the UN. President Nazarbayev's foreign policy envisaged a privileged alliance with Russia and the Islamic republics of the region, as well as closer links with the West.

[16] Several political groups were formed in 1992, such as the Socialist Party, the People's Congress of Kazakhstan and the pro-government People's Unity Party. Nazarbayev's party won the first multiparty legislative elections, in March 1994.

[17] In April, the Government launched a vast privatizing plan, which included 3,500 state companies, 70 per cent of all state firms. The opening up of the economy and the country's natural resources attracted many foreign investors during 1995. The economic reforms also lowered living standards of many Kazakhs.

[18] A customs union between Kazakhstan, Kirgyzstan, Belarus and the Russian Federation was formed in March 1996, to promote a common market in goods, capitals and workers. A year later, Kazakhstan, together with Kyrgyzstan and Tajikistan, signed an agreement to reduce troops and demilitarize borders. This step followed the agreement signed by Russia and China, in the context of a Russian policy of rapprochement to Asian neighbors conceived in Gorbachev times.

[19] Nazarbayev won the January 1999 Presidential elections, having received 78 per cent of the vote. Although their fairness was questioned, the elections had an 80 per cent turnout.

[20] Eleven parties registered to take part in the elections for the Senate and the Mazhilis - lower chamber - which for the first time were held along party lines. Out of 77 seats in the Mazhilis, only 10 were disputed among the parties, while the remainder were contested by independent candidates.

[21] Prime Minister Nurlan Balgimbayev resigned in October, after having been censored by Parliament when he sought the approval of a very limited budget. Kasymzhomart Tokayev was appointed new premier.

[22] The economy had better prospects of growth with the inauguration, in May 2001, of its first large oil pipeline - built by Kazakh, Russian and American Governments - which will carry 20 million tons of crude oil from the Caspian to the Black sea, towards world markets.

[23] The country still suffers the environmental and health impact from the more than 500 nuclear tests carried out between 1949 and 1989 by Russia in Semipalatinsk. These caused the discharge of toxic waste and fuel into the sea by rockets launched from Baykonur. The country also suffers the droughts caused by the drying up of the Aral Sea.

[24] The Kazakh Parliament elected Imangali Tasmagambetov as new Prime Minister in February 2002, after Tokayev's resignation. The former Prime Minister had no other choice, due to constant inner strife among his Government team.

[25] In Kazakhstan, and other countries in the region, HIV incidence is growing at an alarming rate, with 3,500 cases in 2001, being mostly caused by intravenous drug use. The drugs have entered the country through the borders and foreigners working in the oil industry. ∎

PROFILE

ENVIRONMENT

Kazakhstan is bordered to the southeast by China; to the south by Kyrgyzstan; and to the north by the Russian Federation. In the western part of the country lie the Caspian and Turan plains; in the center, the Kazakh plateau; and in the eastern and southeastern regions, the Altai, Tarbagatay, Dzhungarian Alatau and Tien Shan mountains. It has a continental climate, with average January temperatures of -18°C in the north, and -3°C in the south. In July, the temperature varies from 19°C in the north, to 28°C in the south. Important rivers include the Ural, Irtysh, Syr Dar'ya, Chu and Ili. There is also Lake Balkhash and the Caspian and Aral Seas. The vegetation is characteristic of the steppes, but vast areas have come under cultivation (wheat, tobacco, etc) or are used for cattle-raising. The region's abundant mineral wealth includes coal, copper, semi-precious stones and gold. Toxic and radioactive waste (mainly from the weapons industry) has caused several health problems. A reduction in the water volume of the Aral Sea (due to the intensive cultivation of cotton in the riverbanks) has increased desertification in the area and caused environmental problems.

SOCIETY

Peoples: Kazakhs, 46.5 per cent, Russians, 35 per cent, Ukrainians 5 per cent, Uzbeks 2 per cent, Tatars 2 per cent. **Religions:** Muslim and Christian Orthodox. **Languages:** Kazakh (official), Russian, German, Ugric, Korean, Tatar. **Political Parties:** Republican Party of the Country (OTAN); Civil Party of Kazakhstan; Communist Party of Kazakhstan; Agrarian Party; National Co-operative Party of Kazakstan.
Social Organizations: Birlik Movement, Zheltokso and Semipalatinsk-Nevada, an anti-nuclear movement.

THE STATE

Official Name: Qazaqstan Respublikasy. **Administrative divisions:** 14 regions and 3 cities. **Capital:** Astana (formerly called Aqmola) 326,000 people (1999). **Other cities:** Almaty (formerly called Alma-Ata) 1,250,000 people (1995); Karaganda 420,500; Pavlodar 300,000; Kokchetav 123,000 (2000). **Government:** Nursultan Nazarbayev, President since April 1990, re-elected in 1999. Imangali Tasmagambetov, Prime Minister since January 2002. The legislative power has two chambers: the Mazhilis (Assembly) with 77 members and the Senate with 47 members.
National Holiday: December 16, Independence (1991); October 25, Republic Day (1991). **Armed Forces:** 40,000 troops (1996).

Kenya

Population: 31,904,000 (2002)
Land area: 569,140 SQ KM
Capital: Nairobi
Currency: Shilling
Language: English and Swahili

Kenya

B antu-speaking populations migrated toward the coast from the central African forests 3,000 years ago, settling along the shores of Lake Victoria. These communities also spread throughout West Africa, assimilating the existing populations. Around the 5th century AD, they reached the Indian Ocean and down as South Africa. Other migrations toward Kenya included the Nilotic-speaking people from Sudan, and the Cushitic, ancestors of the Oromo and Somali, which reached northern Kenya from the south of Ethiopia around 1000 AD.

[2] The Bantu people on the coast were mainly dedicated to the long-distance sea trade and established contact with the Arab merchants, many of whom began to settle on Africa's western seaboard. From this exchange arose the unique Swahili culture. The coastal cities, such as Malindi and Mombasa, were at their height from the 12th century until the arrival of the Portuguese in the 16th century, who destroyed the cities with cannon-fire. The inland peoples, mainly Bantu with some Nilotic and Somali groups, did not develop cultures or organized states comparable to those of the coast. It was not until the 19th century that the Masai, pastoralists of Nilotic origin, were able to establish a certain degree of authority over the other groups in the region. But a few decades later a bovine plague wiped out nearly all of their herds, and the collapse of their economic mainstay destroyed their political dominance.

[3] When the Portuguese were forced to withdraw in 1698 they left behind abandoned forts and economic ruin, ideal conditions for

the continuation of the slave and ivory trade managed by the Shirazi merchants from Zanzibar.

[4] At the end of the 19th century, the Berlin Conference and subsequent German-British agreements delimited spheres of European influence in East Africa. Zanzibar, Kenya and Uganda were assigned to the English who had already settled in Uganda, and who decided to build a railway line from this colony to the coast.

[5] White settlers occupied the lands that 'became available' along the railway line after half the local population died in an epidemic of

smallpox brought in with Indian laborers. As late as 1948, 4,200 sq km of the approximately 5,000 sq km of fertile land were held between 5,000 European planters, while one million Kikuyu (one of the larger groups) occupied fewer than 1,000 sq km. There was no indemnity or compensation for this theft.

[6] In 1944, the Kenya African Union (KAU) was created to defend Kikuyu interests. Under the leadership of Jomo Kenyatta, KAU organized strikes, farmers' rallies and mass demonstrations.

[7] At almost the same time the Mau-Mau, a political and religious

group organized as a secret society, launched its first offensive. The Mau-Mau program was both political and cultural. They demanded self-government, restitution of lands, and wage parity, while rejecting Christianity and other European influences in favor of traditional customs and beliefs.

[8] In 1952, in response to increased Mau-Mau attacks on settlers' lives and property, the colonial administration declared a state of emergency, arrested nationalist leaders (Kenyatta among them), dissolved political parties and imprisoned thousands of Kikuyu in concentration camps.

[9] After years of bitter repression and indiscriminate killing by colonial governments, KAU was legalized in 1960 as the Kenya African National Union (KANU).

[10] KANU found electoral support among leading urban and ethnic communities and, with British encouragement, was able to defeat tribal-based political movements. In 1961, Kenya was freed and in 1962 the Legislative Council was elected. After the May 1963 elections Kenya was granted autonomy. It achieved independence within the Commonwealth on December 12 1963. Kenyatta became Prime Minister, and when his country achieved full independence in 1964, he was elected first president.

[11] However, Jomo Kenyatta, a nom de guerre meaning 'Kenya's flaming spear', soon forgot his commitment to the nation as a whole, and began to favor his own ethnic group, the Kikuyu. His government encouraged private enterprise and transnational concerns. Farmers who had won back their lands lost them again under the burden of debt.

[12] A black bourgeoisie, largely Kenyatta's family and friends, took over where the former colonists had left off. KANU, once a model for other African parties in the struggle against foreign domination, succumbed to neo-colonialism. It even went so far as to admit British military forces to the port of Mombasa and in 1976 allowed its own military installations to be used for the notorious Israeli raid on Entebbe, Uganda.

WORKERS

2000

LABOR FORCE
AS % OF TOTAL

■ FEMALE: 46%   ■ MALE: 54%

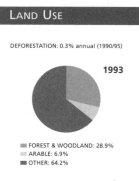

LAND USE

DEFORESTATION: 0.3% annual (1990/95)

1993

■ FOREST & WOODLAND: 28.9%
■ ARABLE: 6.9%
■ OTHER: 64.2%

PUBLIC EXPENDITURE

1999

80

60

40 — 29.6%

20

7.1%

0
DEFENSE   SOCIAL

MATERNAL MORTALITY	LITERACY	FOOD DEPENDENCY	EXTERNAL DEBT
1985/99	2000	2000	2000
Per 100,000 live births **590**	**82%**	**14%**	PER CAPITA **US$ 205**

[13] This led to a breach of relations between Kenya and Uganda, and tension with Tanzania grew over differences in economic policies. The three countries were unable to consolidate 1967 plans for an East African Economic Community, and this ambitious integration project was finally dropped in 1977.

[14] Kenyatta died at the age of 85 in September 1978. He was succeeded by his vice-president, Daniel Arap Moi, a member of the smaller Kalenjin ethnic group.

[15] This might have soothed ethnic conflict in Kenya, but penetration by transnationals produced structural imbalances, worsening an already difficult economic situation and aggravating social tensions. Even before Kenyatta's death there was growing distrust between the urban consumer bourgeoisie and the larger rural population. The country people's whole way of life was being steadily degraded, as the market for cash crops undermined traditional communal self-sufficiency.

PROFILE

ENVIRONMENT

Kenya is located on the east coast of central Africa. There are four main regions, from east to west: the coastal plains with regular rainfall and tropical vegetation; a sparsely populated inland strip with little rainfall which extends towards the north and northwest; a mountainous zone linked to the eastern end of the Rift valley, with a climate tempered by altitude, and volcanic soil fit for agriculture (most of the population and the main economic activities are concentrated here); and the west which is covered by an arid plateau, part of which benefits from the moderating influence of Lake Victoria. The principal environmental problems are soil exhaustion, erosion and desertification; deforestation; pollution of drinking water supplies, especially near such large cities as Nairobi and Mombasa.

SOCIETY

Peoples: Kenyans are descended from the main African ethnic groups: Bantu, Nilo-Hamitic, Sudanese and Cushitic. Numerically and culturally, the most significant groups are the Kikuyu, the Luyia and the Luo. Others include the Kamba, Meru, Gusii and Embu. There are Indian and Arab minorities.
Religions: 73 per cent of the population are Christian, 6 per cent are Muslim and 20 per cent practice traditional religions.
Languages: English and Swahili are the official ones. There are more than 50 languages spoken, such as Kikuyu and Kamba.
Political Parties: Kenya African National Union (KANU) founded in 1943 by Jomo Kenyatta. A Constitutional reform allowed the formation of new parties in 1991. Forum for the Restoration of Democracy (FORD), split into three branches in 1992 (FORD-Asili. FORD-Popular and FORD-Kenya).
Other parties: Democratic Party (DP); National Development Party; Kenya Social Congress (KSC); Social Democratic Party; the Safina and the Shirikisho. **Social Organizations:** Central Organization of Trade Unions (COTU), founded by the Government in 1965, is the only labor federation. Nairobi University Students Organization. Green Belt Movement, environmentalist.

THE STATE

Official Name: Jamhuri ya Kenya. Administrative Division: 7 provinces and 1 area.
Capital: Nairobi 2,205,000 people (1999).
Other cities: Mombasa 685,000 people; Kisumu 266,300; Nakuru 319,200; Machakos 173,700 (2000).
Government: Daniel Arap Moi, President since August 1978, elected in 1992 and re-elected in 1997. Unicameral Legislature: National Assembly, with 224 members. **National Holiday:** December 12, Independence Day (1963).
Armed Forces: 24,200 troops.
Other: 5,000.

[16] Arap Moi was interim president from September 1978 until the general election of November. KANU was the only party authorized to run candidates, and Moi was confirmed as President.

[17] In early 1979, President Moi declared an amnesty for political prisoners and launched a campaign against corruption. The first measures of the new administration revealed a technocratic approach which deflated hopes of radical change. One of the outstanding technocrats was Charles Njonjo, appointed minister of home affairs in June 1980.

[18] Njonjo played a key role in dissolving the ethnic-based organizations that arose in the early 1970s. The largest of these, GEMA (the Gikuyo, Embu and Meru Association), led by millionaire Karume Njenga, became a powerful pressure group for local leaders who were growing rich from business with British and US companies.

[19] GEMA opposed Moi's appointment, and after the death of Jomo Kenyatta had been indirectly involved in a conspiracy to assassinate all top government officials.

[20] Droughts and crop changes led to a drop in the production of corn and other basic consumer goods. Credits supplied by multinational companies encouraged Kenyan farmers to grow flowers and to plant sugarcane, coffee and tea for export under the control of large North American and British firms. As a result, the government had to import huge quantities of corn and wheat from the US and South Africa.

[21] These difficulties led President Moi to seek reconciliation with old political rivals who had been excluded from public life. It was a maneuver devised to neutralize potential opposition at a moment of great instability. Former vice-president Oginga Odinga, a veteran nationalist politician who had broken with Kenyatta in 1971 in disagreement with KANU's conciliatory policy, was one of the major beneficiaries of this relaxation of the regime. Odinga had lost his political rights after founding a dissident party, the Kenya Popular Union (KAPU). After

11 years of ostracism, he returned to parliament at the end of 1981.

[22] Despite all this reconciliation, the crisis erupted into violence in August 1982, in a military conspiracy that unleashed widespread rioting and looting of shops and public buildings in Nairobi. The coup attempt had been staged by members of the air force, leading to the disbanding of all airforce units after the army had suppressed the rebellion.

[23] Repression also affected the university, where dozens of professors and students were detained. Oginga Odinga was placed under house arrest and the university was closed down indefinitely. The frustrated coup precipitated profound changes in Kenyan politics and sowed distrust among the different political elements in KANU.

[24] In May 1983, President Moi denounced a conspiracy involving minister Charles Njonjo, supported by Israel and South Africa. In the midst of the confusion, President Moi decided to call general elections, in which his followers won a landslide victory, while Njonjo and his supporters were overwhelmingly defeated.

[25] Moi's administration reopened the border with Tanzania in November 1983, after a summit meeting in Arusha with Tanzania's Julius Nyerere and Uganda's Milton Obote. The meeting was a point of departure for gradually renewing economic co-operation between Kenya, Tanzania and Uganda after the failure of the East African Economic Community in 1977.

[26] President Arap Moi had extended the executive's jurisdiction to the detriment of the parliament. He made it compulsory for civil servants to join KANU, and replaced secret voting in internal party elections with a public vote making intimidation easier. The moderate women's opposition group, Mandeleo Ya Wanawake, was taken over by the Government in 1986.

[27] Reports backed by Amnesty International and other groups implicated the government in torture and the murder of opposition members, especially the 'subversive' Mwakenya group.

28 During October and November 1987, Muslim demonstrations in Mombasa served to justify a further wave of repression in which Nairobi University was once again closed. In December, a series of frontier skirmishes with Uganda, plus the expulsion of Libyan diplomats accused of encouraging civil disorder, seemed to herald new disturbances.

29 Despite harsh 'restructuring' policies imposed by the IMF and World Bank, elections in March 1988 consolidated the position of Moi's followers within both KANU and the Government. By August, Moi had completed his authoritarian reorganization by placing the judiciary directly under his command. He prolonged the period for which detainees may be held without notifying a judge from 24 hours to 14 days.

30 Robert Ouko, the Foreign Affairs minister and a harsh critic of corruption in the cabinet was murdered in February 1990. An inquest carried out by Scotland Yard disclosed that the culprits were close advisers of the President. This triggered a new wave of popular anti-government protests.

31 Kenya's diplomatic isolation became more marked during the 1980s, but it decreased after the Persian Gulf war. Kenya's strict alignment with the interests of the US-led coalition enabled the country to receive economic aid from Britain, and military support from Washington.

32 The permanent deterioration in the human rights situation, however, led to the severing of diplomatic relations with Norway in 1991, and relations with Sudan, Ethiopia, and Uganda also became tense. The governments of Kenya and Sudan accused each other of protecting rebel groups, hostile to Nairobi and Khartoum, operating in the neighboring country. Political differences between Uganda and Kenya have caused permanent conflict since 1986.

33 The economy was incapable of achieving growth rates like those of the past decade. According to official estimates, inflation in 1990 amounted to 15 per cent, but all independent sources indicate it was very near to 30 per cent. As a result of the Gulf war oil import expenditure was a great deal higher than expected, and this had a negative effect on the trade balance. Tourism dropped sharply, and the servicing of the foreign debt accounted for 30 per cent of 1990 exports. Like other countries in the region, Kenya has implemented cuts in public expenditure, which include privatizing state-run companies and not filling vacancies in the public sector. Kenya's economy is heavily dependent on foreign aid.

34 The KANU called the party Council to discuss the introduction of democratic reforms, including authorization for several national opposition parties. Lobbying groups such as the Forum for the Restoration of Democracy (FORD), led by Oginga Odinga, and the Moral Alliance for Peace (MAP), became fully-fledged parties.

35 In order to keep the situation under control, the Government continued to imprison opposition leaders. Early in 1992, lawyer James Orengo and environmentalist Wangari Maathai were arrested and accused of 'spreading malicious rumours' that President Moi planned to interrupt the democratization process started in 1991.

36 In February, 1992, the Democratic Party (PD) was created. It was a new opposition group which proposed the creation of a multiparty democratic system. Meanwhile, women's groups demanded greater participation in politics; they constituted 53 per cent of the electoral roll and 80 per cent of the work force in agriculture, the country's main production sector.

37 That same month a march organized by FORD rallied over 100,000 people in Nairobi demanding the end of repression and press censorship, and a definite date for elections. This was the first authorized anti-government march in the country's 22 years of independent life.

38 General elections were held in December. Moi was re-elected amidst accusations of fraud. His party obtained 95 seats with 36 per cent of the vote, while the opposition had only 88 seats with 60 per cent of the returns.

39 In February 1993, the Government prepared a privatization and trade liberalization plan, considered inadequate by the World Bank and the IMF. Talks were resumed and, in April, after a new devaluation of the currency (23.47 per cent), the World Bank released $350 million. In 1994 Nairobi eliminated exchange controls in order to attract Kenyan and foreign private investors.

40 In November 1997, the President dissolved Parliament and, on December 29, was re-elected with 40.1 per cent of the vote.

41 Environmentalist groups and fishing authorities warned that the environment in Lake Victoria region - one of the world's largest fishing reservoirs - would be seriously affected if the governments of Kenya, Uganda and Tanzania did not stop fish poisoning and pollution of the water sources. Kenyan fishermen, as well as Ugandan and Tanzanian, use chemicals to poison the fish and improve their catch.

42 Moi announced he would abolish female genital mutilation, but his words only intensified the practice. A non-government organization advocated as an alternative a ritual called Ntanira na Mugambo - or 'circumcision through words'. Ntanira na Mugambo started to displace the traditional mutilation of female genitalia, which is practiced in half the country's rural districts.

43 In August 1998 a bomb killed 213 people at the US Embassy in Nairobi, the work of Osama bin Laden's terrorist network.

44 In 2000, the worst drought in a century led to a loss of crops and a shortage of food, and a rationing of water and power cuts, both in the home and industry sectors.

45 Family planning programs funded by the US were cut back after President Bush - believing the money was being used for abortions - decided to withdraw. Many Kenyan women now run the risk of dying from illegal abortions as they do not have access to efficient contraception.

46 AIDS kills 700 Kenyans each day. Two million are HIV-positive and half the beds in state hospitals are taken by victims of the pandemic. As a measure to stop the disease from spreading, the Moi Government, with World Bank funding, bought condoms from a German company.

47 The Kenyan police allegedly are responsible for more than 60 per cent of the violent deaths taking place in the country in the last five years. The number increases every year, so in 2001 deaths caused by the police amounted to 90 per cent of the total.

48 Fighting increased between various groups in the south over land rights and the coast of the Tana river. A number of deaths and displacements of the population occurred after villages were burnt.

49 Approximately 4,000 people enter Kenya illegally each year to work in industrial areas set up in the border. Most are Somali and Ethiopian refugees, who have been subjected to abuse by Kenyan police: this forces them to return to their home countries, putting their lives at greater risk. In several occasions, the Moi Government banned the entrance of refugees, alleging they are a security risk for the country.

50 A law banning female circumcision in girls under 18 and penalizing those who practice it was passed in February 2002. In all, 40 per cent of Kenyan women have suffered the excision. Girls who have not been circumcised are social outcasts, since the rite is believed to reduce promiscuity. ∎

DEMOGRAPHY

Population: 31,904,000 (2002)
Annual growth: 2.9 % (1985-2000)
Estimates for year 2015: 40,001,000 (2000)
Annual growth to year 2015: 1.8 % (2000)
Urban population: 33.1 % (2000)
Urban growth: 5.0 % (2000)
Children per woman: 4.4 (2000)

HEALTH

Life expectancy at birth: 49 years (2000-2005)
male: 49 years (2000-2005)
female: 50 years (2000-2005)
Maternal mortality: 590 per 100,000 live births (1985/99)
Infant mortality: 77 per 1,000 (2000)
Under-5 child mortality: 120 per 1,000 (2000)
Daily calorie supply: 1,886 per capita (1999)
13 doctors per 100,000 people (1995)
Safe water: 57 % (2000)

EDUCATION

Literacy: 82 % (2000)
male: 89 % (2000)
female: 76 % (2000)
School enrolment (net):
Primary total: 74 % (1994/2000)
male: 92 % (1995/99)
female: 89 % (1995/99)
Secondary (gross):
male: 26 % (1995/97)
female: 22 % (1995/97)
Tertiary (gross): 1 % (1998)
Primary school teachers: one for every 29 pupils (1998)

COMMUNICATIONS

10 newspapers (1996), 223 radios (2000), 25 TV sets (2000) and 10 main telephone lines (2000) per 1,000 people

ECONOMY

Per capita, GDP: $ 1,022 (2000)
Annual growth: -2.5 % (2000)
Annual inflation: 5.9 % (2000)
Consumer price index: 140.1 (2000)
Currency: 78.1 shillings = $ 1 (03/2002)
Cereal imports: 753,113 metric tons (2000)
Food import dependency: 14 % (2000)
Fertilizer use: 383 kg per ha (1999)
Exports: $ 2,744 million (2000)
Imports: $ 3,690 million (2000)
External debt: $ 6,295 million (2000); $ 205 per capita (2000)
Debt service: 26.7 % of exports (1999)
Development aid received: $ 308 million (1999); $ 10.5 per capita (1999); 2.90 % of GNP (1999)

ENERGY

Consumption: 504.6 Kgs of oil equivalent per capita yearly (1998); 17.4 % imported (1999)

HDI (ranking/value): 123 / 0.514 (1999)

Kiribati

Population: 85,000 (2002)
Land area: 730 SQ KM
Capital: Bairiki on the island of Tarawa
Currency: Australian dollar
Language: English and Kiribati

Kiribati

The islands that make up the Republic of Kiribati (formerly known as Gilbert Islands) are inhabited by Micronesian people. In 1765 the British commodore John Byron discovered Nikunau; in 1788 Captain Thomas Gilbert sighted Tarawa, and Captain John Marshall, Aranuka. The islands - their respective native names being Makin, Butaritari, Marakei, Abaiang, Tarawa, Maiana, Abemama, Kuria, Aranuka, Nonouti, Tabiteuea, Beru, Nikunau - were named the Gilbert Islands in the 1820s.

[2] Missionaries arrived in 1857, and three years later, trade in palm oil and copra began. In 1892 the islands became a British protectorate. In 1915 the islands were annexed to the neighboring Ellice archipelago (now Tuvalu), to form the colony of the Gilbert and Ellice Islands.

[3] In 1916 Banaba Island became part of the colony. At that time, there were large deposits of guano (fertilizer from bird droppings) on the island which were exploited by the British Phosphate Commission from 1920, and exported to Australia and New Zealand. The Banabans were evacuated during World War II and resettled on the island of Rabi, 2,600 km from Fiji. They were unable to return to their island because the open-cast mining of guano had made the island uninhabitable.

[4] After discussing different alternatives in 1981 the Banabans

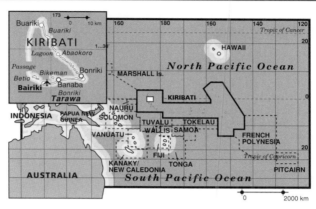

obtained an indemnity of £19 million from the British Government. In 1957 Britain, as part of its nuclear armament program, detonated three hydrogen bombs near Christmas Island.

[5] The Polynesian population of the Ellice Islands obtained administrative separation in 1975, arguing that the ethnic, historical and cultural differences between them and the Melanesian majority of the Gilbert Islands made secession necessary. Under the name of the Territory of Tuvalu these islands gained independence in 1978.

[6] The inhabitants of the Gilbert Islands proclaimed independence on July 12 1979 adopting the name: Republic of Kiribati (the equivalent of 'Gilbert' in Gilbertan).

[7] As the soil is not suitable for large-scale cultivation, copra and

fish are the main exports. Copra production is in the hands of small landowners, while its export is handled exclusively by the national trading company. Problems facing copra production include abrupt variations in price. Fishing is carried out primarily under agreements with Japanese, US, Korean and Taiwanese fishing fleets.

[8] Kiribati also hopes to exploit deep-sea mineral deposits. The manganese discovered is considered the highest-grade deposit of its kind in the world.

[9] In 1986 Kiribati began negotiations with the IMF and was recognized by the UN as one of the world's poorest countries, a fact which gives it access to certain credit and trade advantages.

[10] A 1989 UN report on global warming and the possible rise in sea level said that Kiribati could disappear under the rising sea.

[11] In the 1991 elections, Teatao Teannaki won with 46 per cent of the vote, producing the first change in president since independence.

[12] The Government of Teannaki, accused of misuse of state funds, was forced to resign in May 1994. In July, opposition coalition Maneaba Te Mauri won a Parliamentary majority and in September Teburoro Tito was elected President.

[13] In 1996, Kiribati signed an agreement with China, to increase trade between both countries. The following year Japan contributed $40 million to the construction of Port Betio, one of Kiribati's largest.

[14] Due to the low elevation of most of the islands - barely a couple of meters above sea level - there is a growing concern about the 'greenhouse effect' leading to a rise

in sea water levels. If the sea level were to rise, due to ice meltdowns among other things, the islands would be partially underwater and lose their sources of drinking water.

[15] Because of its position on the international date line, Kiribati was the first Pacific island group to see the dawn of the new millennium in 2000. One of its usually uninhabited territories, Millennium island, was the center of celebrations that included traditional dances, in the hours before sunrise.

[16] The country joined the United Nations in 1999 and the International Labour Organization the following year. The archipelago started the new millennium in the international field with an agreement to establish diplomatic relations with Morocco. ∎

PROFILE

ENVIRONMENT
33 islands and coral atolls, land area 810 sq km, scattered over 5,000 sq km in Micronesia in the Pacific. The climate is tropical and rainy, tempered by the effect of sea winds. The country's large phosphate deposits are now virtually exhausted. Fishing and underwater mineral deposits make up Kiribati's major economic potential.

SOCIETY
Peoples: The population is mostly of Micronesian descent. Kiribati 97.4 per cent; mixed (Kiribati and other) 1.5 per cent; Tuvaluan 0.5 per cent; European 0.2 per cent; other 0.4 per cent. **Languages:** English and Kiribati (Gilbertese). **Political Parties:** National Progressive Party and the Maneaban te Mauri. **Social Organizations:** Kiribati General Labor Confederation.

THE STATE
Official Name: Republic of Kiribati. **Capital:** Bairiki 25,100 people; (1999). **Other cities:** Bikenibeu 7,000; Abaiang 5,300 (2000). **Government:** Teburoro Tito, President since October 1994, re-elected in 1998. Parliament is made up of 39 members, elected by direct popular vote, plus one representative of Banaba Island. **National Holiday:** July 12, Independence Day (1979).

Korea

North Korea

South Korea

(see history and statistics on the following pages)

Korea

The Korean peninsula lies between China and Japan, and this position has shaped the nation's history, and the character of its people. The territory has frequently been the arena of struggles between armies from China, Mongolia and Japan. The peninsula was first inhabited by tribes of the Tungu language which emigrated to Siberia. Between the 10th and 8th centuries BC several tribal states were established, of which the most complex was the one known as Old Choson, in the Taedong river basin. Towards the 4th century BC, Choson developed into a league of tribes grouped between the basins of the Liao and Taedong rivers. At this time, Choson inhabitants used weapons made of iron, harnesses for horses and war carriages. In 108 BC, the Chinese empire defeated the kingdom of Choson and replaced it with four Chinese colonies. During the height of Old Choson, other tribal states flourished in the peninsula: Puyo, in the Manchurian region of the Sungari river basin, and Chin, which during the 2nd century BC appeared to the south of the Han river and was later divided into three tribal states (Mahan, Chinhan and Pyonhan).

[2] The different leagues expanded through the peninsula which, as of the 1st century BC, was divided into the rival kingdoms of Koguryo, Paekche and Silla. Koguryo (which in the 6th century covered an area similar to the present North Korea) was founded by Chu-mong in 37 BC. Paekche was founded by Onjo in 19 BC, and Silla by Pak Hyokkose in 57 BC. These three states were consolidated by King Taejo (53-146) in Koguryo, King Koi (204-286) in Paekche and King Naemul (356-402) in Silla. The three kingdoms developed into states through successive wars which led to the organization of centralized military and administrative systems. A powerful aristocracy grew up in all of them, comprised of tribal chiefs from the respective capitals. Another common feature of these kingdoms was that they developed highly sophisticated cultures and produced their own historiographies in order to strengthen the authority of the State.

[3] With the support of the T'ang Chinese dynasty, Silla conquered Paekche in the year 660 and Koguryo in 668. However, the survivors of the defeated Koguryo, led by General Tae Cho-yang, established the Kingdom of Perhae to the north of present Manchuria and soon, impeded by China from integrating with the other Korean kingdom, entered into direct confrontation with Silla. The peninsula was divided into two states, one in the north and one in the south, both paying taxes to China. Perhae became a very sophisticated state, called 'the prosperous state of the East' by the Chinese, but after it fell into the hands of the Khitan, a nomad people from the north, its territory no longer came into the history of Korea.

[4] United Silla became an absolute monarchy, which minimized the influence of the aristocracy. The Chinese variant of Avatamsaka Buddhism offered the ideological base for the monarchy and the aristocracy, while the underprivileged were attracted to Pure Land Buddhism, which promised redemption in the next world. In the capital (now Kwangju, in South Korea), the monarchs built giant palaces and royal tombs, while the State's administration was divided, following China's example, into provinces, prefectures and counties.

[5] The decline of Silla began towards the end of the 8th century, as a result of peasant uprisings and conflicts with the aristocracy, which had abolished royal despotism. A new system was established which increased the power of some landlords. Two provincial leaders, Konhwon and Kungye, established the kingdoms of Late Koguryo and Late Paechke respectively. During this period, known as the Three Late Kingdoms Period, Zen Buddhism was the most popular religion, with emphasis on individual fulfillment through contemplation. This doctrine was much less hierarchical

than that of Avatamsaka Buddhism, and favored individual autonomy.

[6] In 918, Wang Kong founded Songak (today's Kaesong, in North Korea) and in 936 he united the peninsula once more, incorporating the survivors of Late Paechke, devastated by the Khitan. Wang Kong proclaimed himself the legitimate succesor of Koguryo and repeatedly confronted the Khitan, expanding Koguryo's territory up to the Yalu river. Wang Kong was the founder of the Koryo dynasty, from which the western name Korea derives. The ruling class of Koryo was made up mainly of provincial lords, owners of castles, and by Silla's old aristocracy. Koryo was ruled by a Supreme State Council, formed by aristocrats, who adopted Buddhism as a religion to achieve spiritual goals and personal happiness, while they practiced the political principles and ethical value of Confucianism.

[7] In spite of the practical need to have a strong defensive system, the military were not well treated. This led to a coup in 1170 and, taking advantage of the subsequent chaos, one of the generals, Ch'oe Ch'ung-hon, established a military regime from 1197 to 1258. The Koryo dynasty stayed in power because the Ch'oe family preferred to rule behind the scenes and did not take over the throne. In the 13th. century, Koryo was repeatedly invaded by the Mongols who came to have great influence in the court. In 1392, Confucian master Yi song-gye overthrew the tottering dynasty and founded the Choson (Yi) dynasty, which would last until 1910. In 1394, Yi Song-gye founded Seoul and turned it into the capital of the Kingdom.

[8] The territory controlled by the Yi dynasty came to be known as Choson, with the approval of the Emperor of China. The Confucian ethical system was officially adopted and replaced Buddhism, which had become corrupt. Choson was dominated by an hereditary aristocratic class, called yangban, which devoted itself to the study of neo-Confucian doctrines. During the Kingdom of Sejo, the seventh monarch, a government structure emerged, led by the yangban ideology. The country was divided into eight provinces and the central

government appointed the administrative chiefs of the state. Legal codes were written and the State Council took charge of the administration. During the 15th century many teachers were recruited to serve the government. They criticized the bureaucracy and recommended several radical measures to implement the ideas of Confucius. However, these teachers had to leave the administration due to strong pressures.

9   In 1597, Toyotomi Hideyoshi, a Japanese military leader who had just reunited his country, invaded Shohon under the pretext of invading China. The national crisis made people from all spheres of life including Buddhist monks join in the struggle against the invaders. In 1598, with China's help, the Koreans forced the retreat of the aggressors, but most of Shohon was devastated. Many palaces, public buildings and homes were burnt, numerous national treasures destroyed and a large number of crafts people and experts were kidnapped and taken to Japan. In the beginning of the 17th century, nomad Manchurians invaded Shohon, took over the northern part of the territory, and captured Seoul in 1636, demanding the unconditional surrendering of the king. In 1640 the Manchurians overthrew the Ming dynasty in China and replaced it with the Ching dynasty. The taxes Korea paid to the Ming went to the Ch'ing.

10   During the second half of the 17th century and throughout the 18th century, Korean society underwent great changes. Rice became widespread and irrigation systems were improved. Agricultural production was increased and the peasants standard of living improved. Tobacco and ginseng crops encouraged domestic and foreign trade, thus intensifying contacts with European traders and Catholic priests. Meanwhile, radical ideological changes were taking place in Korea, since many teachers no longer concerned themselves only with theoretical speculation but also with matters of practical importance. This gave birth to *silhak* or education based on pragmatism, which urged the Government to undergo changes. Also, a school of

silhak devoted itself to the study of the Korean language and history and facilitated, jointly with the development of popular art, the access of the people to written texts. To the end of the 18th century some teachers of silhak had converted to Catholicism, followed by members of the aristocracy. Large sectors of the population, encouraged by the hope of finding equality before God after death, were seduced by the new religion which expanded itself rapidly.

11   The decline of the Yi dynasty was characterized by economic and religious factors, plus outside pressures. The yangban or aristocracy had appropriated public lands and did not pay taxes, which led the Government to increase the taxes on the poor, who could not pay and lost their lands. When the famines came, the Government did not have enough money to alleviate the situation. Also, the State banned Christianity, because of its incompatibility with Confucianism. During the persecutions of 1801, 1839 and 1866, the converted teachers were forced to die or fall into apostasy, while foreign missionaries were beheaded. At the same time, Japan pressed Korea to open its foreign trade and China increased its interference in the peninsula to counterbalance the Japanese influence. In 1860, the scholar Ch'oe-u founded a popular religion called Tonhak (oriental teachings) which combined elements of Confucianism, Christianity, Shamanism and Buddhism. Soon, these new teachings, in the name of resistance against foreigners and corruption, gained a large following among peasants and by 1893 had turned into a political movement. In May 1893, the Tonhak followers took the city of Chonju, in the southwest and the two intervening powers, China and Japan, sent troops to crush them.

12   To justify their military presence in the peninsula, Japan proposed that China carry out a joint reform in Korea, but China's negative reply led to a military conflict which ended with a Japanese victory in 1895. Emboldened by this victory, Japan occupied Korea in 1905 and in 1910

the country was formally annexed, putting an end to the Yi dynasty.

13   Under the Japanese, Korea was exploited as a supplier of foodstuffs and as a source of cheap labor. Japanese landlords and factory owners settled in Korea, with a developed infrastructure merely to extract the wealth of the country. In the 1930s, the northern part of Korea saw industrial development of war materials, to supply Japan's goal of expansion into China.

14   With the defeat of Japan in World War II, Korea was occupied on each side of the 38th parallel: the northern part by Soviet troops and the southern by the United States. Korean hopes for a united, independent country seemed on the verge of being realized but a complex struggle of interests between the two powers made it impossible. The Soviet Union maintained its influence and did not allow general elections in the north of the peninsula. In the south, under the supervision of a United Nations Temporary Commission, elections were held in May 1948 and Syngman Rhee was elected first president of the Republic of Korea, whose capital was established in Seoul. Meanwhile, the Supreme Assembly of the People of North Korea wrote a new constitution, which came into effect in August 1948. Kim Il-Sung was appointed Prime Minister and on September 9 the People's Republic of Korea was proclaimed, with its capital in Pyŏngyang.

15   On October 12, the Soviet Union recognized this state as the only legitimate government of Korea. In December, the General Assembly of the United Nations recognized the exclusive sovereignty of the southern Republic of Korea. Most foreign troops left both countries the following year but US troops remained in the south under the UN flag, then dominated by the United States.

16   In June 1950, North Korea launched a carefully planned offensive against South Korea. The United Nations convened its members, to put a stop to the invasion. In the meantime US President Truman called his army to assist South Korea, without asking Congress to declare war.

17   Likewise, Truman failed to seek UN permission before sending the US Fleet to the Strait of Formosa to protect one of the US Army's flanks, and also to come to the assistance of Chiang Kai Shek's anti-Communist Chinese regime, which had established itself on the island of Formosa (Taiwan). This in turn gave rise to fears in Peking of a nationalist invasion of 'continental' China.

18   In the meantime, the military campaign on the Korean peninsula was turning into a disaster for the South Koreans and US troops, who had arrived hurriedly and poorly equipped, and were forced to retreat nearly as far as Pusan, on the southern coast.

19   Defeat was narrowly avoided by the action of General Douglas MacArthur, who landed some 160 km south of the 38th parallel and managed to divide and defeat North Korean troops.

20   China, concerned over the advancing allied troops, warned that the presence of the US in North Korea would force it to enter the war. MacArthur ignored the warning and in November launched his 'Home by Christmas' offensive.

21   However, China sent 180,000 troops to Korea and by mid-December it had driven US troops back, south of the 38th parallel. On December 31 1951, China launched a second offensive against South Korea, subsequently taking up positions along the former border.

22   After differences of opinion on military strategy, MacArthur was relieved of his command by Truman. It was later revealed that MacArthur had outlined plans to use nuclear weapons against Chinese cities, advocating full-scale war with China.

23   The battle continued up and down the peninsula and the city of Seoul changed hands several times. Up to this point the conflict had left four million dead.

24   After renewed fighting in June 1953, an armistice went into effect the following month. From that time on, Korea was officially separated by the 38th parallel.

25   On August 8 1990, the UN Security Council unanimously approved the admission of both Koreas. On December 13 1991, Prime Ministers Yon Kyong Muk (North Korea) and Chong Won Shik (South Korea) signed a 'Reconciliation, Non-Aggression, Exchange, and Cooperation Agreement'. This has been the most important step towards reunification since 1972. The Korean peninsula is in a strategic region located between the three large powers of Russia, China and Japan. There are currently intense negotiations underway to solve the nuclear question. ∎

North Korea

Population: 22,586,000 (2002)
Land area: 120,410 SQ KM
Capital: P'yongyang
Currency: Won
Language: Korean

Choson

On September 3 1948, the People's Republic of Korea was proclaimed in Pyongyang and Kim Il Sung, leader of the Korean Workers Party was elected Prime Minister (see history of Korea).

[2] The Kingdom of Koguryo, the equivalent in the 7th century of the present North Korea, had a special way of treating foreign enemies. It avoided direct confrontation and maintained an impressive military capacity within the cities (see history of Korea). North Korea also had a similar strategy since it limited its outer contact and devoted its efforts to achieve considerable military strength. Despite its geographical proximity to the People's Republic of China, North Korea tried to remain neutral in the Sino-Soviet conflict.

[3] The Korean Workers' Party (KWP) enjoyed uninterrupted power for five decades. The party's philosophy is called Juche, a blend of self-reliance, nationalism and centralized control of the economy.

[4] With the establishment of a socialist regime, agrarian reform was carried out, with part of the country's agriculture being collectivized. Industrialization had begun during Japanese occupation, and large textile, chemical and hydroelectric plants were established.

[5] With the War behind it (1950-53, see Korea), and armistice signed in Panmunjon, North Korea devoted all its efforts to the reconstruction of the country, which had been devastated by the War. When Syngman Rhee was ousted from office in South Korea (1960), North Korea attempted rapprochement with its neighbor. However, when the military took power in Seoul these overtures were interrupted.

[6] Korea adopted a socialist economy with central planning; 90 per cent of the national industry was in the hands of the State with the remaining 10 per cent organized in cooperatives.

[7] Between 1954 and 1961, North Korea signed military assistance treaties with China and the USSR. In 1972, a new constitution was approved, making Kim Il Sung President as well as Prime Minister.

[8] Kim Jong Il, Kim Il Sung's son, was named head of the Government in 1980. In 1984, North Korea provided relief to flood victims in South Korea. That same year, the formation of mixed enterprises was authorized in the construction, technology and tourist sectors.

[9] In 1988, North Korea began 'ideological rectification' in direct contrast to the Soviet liberalization process introduced by Gorbachev.

[10] In 1990, there were massive demonstrations in support of the regime, on Kim Il Sung's 78th birthday. He was re-elected in May 1991.

[11] According to North Korea, any possibility of reunification was to be preceded by a formal peace treaty with the US and removal of their troops from Korean soil. In 1990, North Korea submitted a proposal for denuclearization to the International Agency for Atomic Energy, subject to guarantees from the US that it would not use the 1,000 nuclear bombs it has in South Korea against them.

[12] In 1991, the USSR cut Korea's oil quota by half. Signs of the regime's growing economic difficulties began to show. From 1992, Kim Jong Il assumed responsibility for the formulation of the country's foreign policy.

[13] Kim Il Sung's death at 82 - officially announced on July 7 1994 - once again complicated talks with the US and deferred the summit planned between the two Koreas. Kim Jong Il succeeded his father without having the same real power as the historical leader of North Korean communism, which gave way for a fight for power among leading cadres.

[14] In 1995, widespread floods affected some five million people. One consequence was the loss of the harvests. These losses were calculated at 1.9 million tons of crops, which led the North Korean Government to make an uncommon appeal for foreign aid. Japan, one of its main capitalist trade partners, donated 300,000 tons of rice and South Korea 150,000 tons.

[15] The US decided to lift the trade embargo and a delegation of US investors visited the country, while Pyongyang reported it no longer opposed the presence of US troops in South Korea.

[16] The defection of the Workers' Party secretary Huang Yang Yop in February 1997 triggered a new political crisis. Huang sought asylum in the South Korean embassy in Beijing as he returned from a tour of Japan and China. Two days later, Prime Minister Kang Song San was forced to step down and was replaced by Hong Song Nam. In October, Kim Jong Il, the de facto leader after his father's death, was officially appointed head of the Workers' Party. But due to internal rivalries he was not formally appointed President.

[17] In 1998, it was estimated that some 100,000 people had died of hunger, cold and lack of medical attention since 1995. The daily ration of rice per person was just 100 grams.

[18] In December 1999 Japan lifted sanctions against North Korea that had been in place since August 1998, the year when Pyongyang launched a ballistic missile over Japanese territory. A problem remaining between the two nations is that North Korea, as a precondition for full diplomatic relations, demands a formal apology from Japan for the atrocities committed before and during World War II.

[19] In June 2000, Pyongyang held an historic summit of the two Koreas. Kim Dae-Jung, South Korea's President, met with Kim Jong Il to discuss security issues, including the 37,000 US soldiers stationed in South Korea and missile programs. The two leaders signed an agreement to work together toward the reunification of the Korean peninsula.

[20] A delegation from the European Union, led by Swedish Prime Minister Göran Persson, visited the two Koreas in May 2001 in a mission aimed at supporting the process of peace and reconciliation between the countries.

[21] Pyongyang postponed the reunion of families planned for mid-October, stating that the intense security measures - the declaration of maximum alert - that South Korea implemented after the September 11 attacks in Washington and New York did not provide the best environment for carrying out the meetings.

[22] US President George W Bush stated in January 2002 that North Korea was part of the 'axis of evil', along with Iran and Iraq, dedicated to terrorism and developing long-range missile capabilities. Pyongyang responded saying the statement amounted to a declaration of war. Joint military operations involving the US and South Korea in March 2002 prompted North Korea to threaten to break the 1994 nuclear treaty in which Pyongyang had agreed to abandon its nuclear program. ∎

PROFILE

SOCIETY

Political Parties: The Korean Workers' Party (KWP), founded in 1945 with Marxist-Leninist orientation, is the dominant political organization. The Democratic People's Republic of Korea is a virtual one-party state, but smaller parties do exist: the Korean Social Democratic Party and the Chondokio Chong-u party, the first being affiliated to the KWP in a National Front for the Reunification of Korea, created in June 1945. Youth and women are organized into the Union of Young Socialist Workers and the Democratic Women's Union.

Social Organizations: The General Federation of Trade Unions is the only workers' organization, while the union of Agricultural Workers is a peasants' association.

THE STATE

Official Name: Choson Mintschutschui Inmin Konghwaguk.
Administrative Divisions: 9 Provinces, 1 District. **Capital:** Pyongyang 3,136,000 people (1999). **Other cities:** Hamhung 808,300 people; Chongjin 663,400; Sinuiju 371,300; Kaesong 195,300 (2000).
Government: Presidency is vacant since Kim Il Sung died in July 1994. His son, Kim Jong Il, de facto President of the Republic. Kim Yong Nam, Chairman of the Presidium of the Supreme People's Assembly since September 1998. Hong Song Nam, Premier since February 1997. The State's higher body is the Supreme People's Assembly, with 687 members. **National Holiday:** September 9, Republic Day (1948).
Armed Forces: 1,054,000 (1994). **Other:** 3,800,000 Peasant Red Guard, 115,000 Security Troops, of the Ministry of Public Security.

South Korea

Population: 47,389,000 (2002)
Land area: 98,730 SQ KM
Capital: Seoul
Currency: Won
Language: Korean

Taehaen - min 'guk

On August 15 1948, a Republic was established in the southern part of the Korean peninsula, with its capital in Seoul (see Korea). Syngman Rhee was named its first president and, supported by US military, economic and political advisors, he ruled the southern portion of Korea for 14 years. Through constitutional laws giving him indefinite power, he ruled as a constitutional dictator. All opposition forces were controlled by charging them with cooperating with the North at the first signs of dissent (see Korean War, in Korea).

[2] The US advisers convinced the Rhee regime of the need for a thorough land reform program. They were very much aware of events in China, where the nationalist Kuomintang had been defeated by the communists who promised rural peoples 'land to the tiller'. The US scheme in South Korea allowed for compensation, and land redistribution limited to three hectares per person; former Japanese-owned land was also redistributed. Many of the previous land-owners moved to the cities.

[3] Despite the introduction of a draconian National Security Law in 1958, when many political dissidents were jailed, the regime was unable to suppress opposition completely. Rhee was re-elected in 1952, 1956 and in 1960. The results of the last election were not accepted by the opposition, who claimed there had been fraud. There were protests in Seoul, which were repressed harshly by Government forces. Growing opposition and the danger of a revolution extending to the rest of the country, led Syngman Rhee to resign on April 27 1960. He was succeeded by Huh Chung Tok as interim President.

[4] New elections were held, and Po Sun Yun, a member of the Democratic Party, was elected President. John Chang, who had been named head of the government, attempted to lead the country toward effective economic development and put an end to the corruption and waste which had characterized the previous regime. Some members of his cabinet were in favor of warmer relations with North Korea.

[5] In May 1961 a military coup ousted Chang; a military junta was installed, presided over by General Chan Yung. In July, General Chung Hee Park took command of the junta and proceeded to suspend all democratic freedoms and imprison all members of the previous regime.

[6] The new regime initiated a National Reconciliation policy, including a planned strategy against communism and corruption, and promised a return to civilian government after completion of these 'revolutionary tasks'.

[7] In March 1962, Park took the presidency from Po Sun Yun. In late 1963, Park was confident of power and held elections. He won by a mere 1.4 per cent despite suppression of the opposition. The protests that followed led him to declare martial law, the military retained their political domination and a long, harsh dictatorship ensued.

[8] The military regime established strong centralized economic planning and, with the help of western technocrats, Korea became a prime example of export-oriented development. Imports and exports, domestic prices and access to credit were used as levers to control and guide the economy. Restrictive laws were established governing the right to strike, organize or allow collective bargaining.

[9] From a war-torn, mainly rural, indebted economy, South Korea developed into an industrial economy dominated by large, Korean-owned transnational corporations producing steel, ships, cars and electronics goods.

[10] Villagers, affected by low grain prices, were forced into cities and the urban labor pool, contributing to the 'Korean miracle'. Some of the world's lowest wages, longest hours and most unsafe working conditions are the norm for Korean workers.

[11] Eighteen years after taking power, Park was still president, having won four fraudulent elections.

[12] In October 1979, Park was killed: shot by the director of the hated Korean Central Intelligence Agency, Kim Jae Kiu, in murky circumstances.

[13] Before the end of 1979, General Chun Doo Hwan, head of military intelligence, decided to secure his position, arresting rivals. On May 17 1980, martial law was once again established and civilian politicians were arrested, dropping all pretense of civilian rule. Chun resigned from the army and on August 27 became President

[14] The following day, citizens in the southern city of Kwangju took control in protest against the military regime, and particularly the arrest of Kim Daw Jung, a leading opposition figure and a native of Kwangju. The Korean army suppressed the citizens with extreme brutality and hundreds lost their lives with the knowledge and agreement of US military commanders stationed in the country. Although the protest had been carried out as a public reaction to the arrest of Kim Daw Jung, this fact was ignored and Daw Jung was sentenced to life imprisonment, charged with 'instigating' the uprising. The Kwangju incident was used by the military as justification for seizing power and questions were raised as to whether the whole event had been deliberately provoked by the military.

[15] Chun launched a 'purification campaign' of public and private sectors, even setting quotas for singling out the corrupt and 'subversives'. In the same manner as his predecessor, Chun Doo Hwan held elections in an attempt to legitimize and civilianize his rule; he won the elections in 1981.

[16] In October 1983, several members of the South Korean cabinet were killed by a bomb at the Martyrs' Mausoleum in Burma during a state visit; arriving late, President Chun escaped the bomb blast. The Burmese, claiming proof of North Korean involvement, broke off diplomatic relations and rescinded their recognition of the North Korean Government.

[17] Opposition to Chun's regime continued to grow as repression escalated, reminiscent of Park's worst excesses. The US withdrew their support of the Marcos regime in the Philippines, after claims of election fraud and human rights abuses, and a worried Korean regime instituted some reforms.

Censorship was lifted somewhat and Kim Daw Jung released from house arrest.

[18] During 1987, hundreds of thousands of Korean workers joined in strikes and factory occupations in an unprecedented wave of protests. Korean workers demanded the right to form democratic unions independent of the government-run Federation of Korean Trade Unions, higher wages, an end to forced overtime and a larger share of the benefits of the nation's spectacular growth.

[19] In July 1987, Chun stepped down and appointed Roh Tae Woo both as his successor and as president of the official Democratic Justice Party. Demonstrations followed amid protests that Roh would continue the dictatorship as a close military colleague of Chun. Demands that Chun face trial for his part in the Kwangju massacre were also voiced.

[20] Faced with the possibility of larger street demonstrations and concern over its international image (South Korea was host of the Olympic Games in 1988) political restrictions were eased during the December, 1987 election campaign.

[21] In the elections, the newly-freed opposition together polled a majority, but failed to unite the two factions, led by Kim Yong Sam of the Reunification Democratic Party and Kim Dae Jung of the Party for Peace and Democracy. The split enabled the incumbent government, under Roh Tae Woo, to secure power with a majority of 42 per cent.

[22] In January 1990, the most conservative opposition groupings formed a merger with the official Democratic Justice Party, and became the Democratic Liberal Party, controlling 220 seats in the 298-member National Assembly. The Party for Peace and Democracy remained the only real parliamentary opposition.

[23] In the spring of 1990, a new offensive against independent trade unions and labor rights resulted in the arrest of the movement's leaders. In April, police stormed the Hyundai shipyards and arrested over 600 union activists, ending a 72-hour worker occupation protesting the arrest of union leaders. A few

days later, 400 striking workers occupying the Korean Broadcasting System's headquarters were also arrested. The resulting nationwide protests precipitated the biggest drop in the history of the Korean stock market.

[24] In September 1991, US President George Bush made the decision to withdraw tactical nuclear weapons from South Korea, and in November this was accomplished. This significant step met one of the requirements of North Korea and was necessary for inspections of their territory to be made.

[25] In December of that year, Seoul and Pyongyang signed a 'Reconciliation, Non-aggression, Exchange and Cooperation Accord', affecting bilateral relations (see Korea).

[26] In the legislative elections of March 1992, both the pro-government groups and the Left suffered a serious setback. The Democratic Liberal Party won 149 of the 299 seats, one short of the majority. The Democratic Party (DP, formerly the Party for Peace and Democracy) came in second with 30 per cent, followed by the Party of National Unification with 17.4 per cent and 31 seats, a new grouping led by a former corporate leader. The left-wing People's Party (PP) won 1.4 per cent of the vote and no seats.

[27] In May, President Roh Tae Woo named Kim Young Sam, who had obtained 41.4 per cent of the returns in the December presidential election, as his successor. Kim's election coincided with a weakening opposition, worsened by the resignation in February 1993 of Chung Ju-Yung, leader of the United People's Party, charged with having accepted illegal contributions from a major corporation during the electoral campaign.

[28] Corruption scandals also reached the Government. Choi Ki Son, a close aide of President Kim, admitted he had embezzled $1 million of public funds. Furthermore, Suh Eui Hyun, leader of the country's largest Buddhist order, was accused of accepting $10 million from a businessman to hand them over to Kim Young Sam. This accusation caused disputes among Buddhist monks, which led to 134 arrests.

[29] In 1995, two former presidents, Chun Doo Hwan (1979-1988) and Roh Tae Woo (1988-1993), were arrested for their role in the coup that put Chun in power in December 1997, and accused of treason and illicit enrichment. In June of that year the governing party was defeated in the first local and provincial elections not controlled by the government since 1961.

[30] In December 1996 the Seoul court sentenced former Defense Minister Lee Yanh-ho to four years in prison for accepting illegal commissions from Daewoo company, the country's third largest car manufacturer.

[31] In June 1997 the Kim Youn-sam Government requested an IMF loan, a move that prompted broad public rejection. Kim Dae Jung, of the opposition Democratic Party, won the December presidential elections. He agreed to the release of Chu Doo Hwan and Roh Tae

Woo, and announced amnesty for political prisoners. When the new President took office in March 1998, Kim Jong Pil became Prime Minister.

[32] A large crowd received Kim Dae Jung upon his return in June from a trip to Pyongyang for an historic summit between the two Koreas. He discussed with the North Korean leader Kim Jonh Il issues of security, including the 37,000 US soldiers stationed in South Korea, and missile programs. The two signed an agreement to work together toward the eventual reunification of the peninsula.

[33] In October 2000, Kim Dae Jung received the Nobel Peace Prize for his work for democracy, for human rights in South Korea and East Asia and for peace and reconciliation with North Korea.

[34] In November, the Daewoo car manufacturer declared bankruptcy. In prior months, billions of dollars from public coffers went toward bailing out the company, and in 1999 the company's president, Kim Woo Joong, had disappeared with a large portion of those funds. After the announcement that more employees would be laid off, in February 2001 the Daewoo workers went on strike. This was put down violently by the police, leaving hundreds injured and imprisoned.

[35] In November 2001, the Government refused to grant a visa to the Dalai Lama, who had been invited to visit the country by a South Korean Buddhist group. Ministry officials said they wanted to prevent a diplomatic misunderstanding with China, which considers the Dalai Lama a separatist.

[36] While most Asian countries continued in recession, the South Korean economy underwent a rapid recovery from the 1997-1998 financial crisis, growing 3.7 percent in the final quarter of 2001.

[37] The publication of a new Japanese textbook caused a hostile reaction from Seoul, which said the book distorted history and whitewashed the atrocities committed by the invading Japanese army in Korea in the early 20th century. In protest against Japan, 20 people gathered in a Seoul park and cut off the tips of their little fingers, and a South Korean civil society movement demanded that the book be withdrawn from circulation. In spite of these differences, the two countries agreed to jointly host the soccer World Cup in June 2002. Though the event was projected to generate 1.3 billion euros in profits, the excessive expenditures in preparing the sites in the two countries and the bankruptcy of ISL company, owner of all commercial rights, caused predicted income to plummet. ∎

PROFILE

SOCIETY
Political Parties: Democratic Liberal Part (DLP), in power. Democratic Party-Minjung Party is the only leftist party, Grand National Party, United Liberal Democrats.
Other parties: Republican Party, Unification Korea Party, People's Victory, New People's Party.
Social Organizations: Legally, all unions must belong to the Government-controlled Federation of Korean Trade Unions (FKTU). The Korean Confederation of Trade Unions (KCTU), founded in 1995-1996 with 600,000 members and a reputation for intervening against workers to end industrial action, sometimes violently. Federation of Student Associations, League of Korean Farmers, National Union of the Poor.

THE STATE
Official Name: Taehaen-min guk (Republic of Korea).
Administrative Divisions: 9 Provinces.
Capital: Seoul 9,935,000 people (1999).
Other cities: Pusan 4,266,100 people, Taegu 2,947,400; Incheon 2,403,700 (2000).
Government: Kim Dae Jung, President and Head of State since February 1998. Lee Han Dong, Prime Minister and Head of Government since May 2000. Single-chamber Legislature: National Assembly, with 273 members, elected every 4 years.
National Holiday: August 15, Liberation Day (1945).
Armed Forces: 633,000 (1995).
Other: 3,500, 000 Civil Defense Corps, 4,500 Coast Guard.

Kuwait

Population:	2,023,000 (2002)
Land area:	17,820 SQ KM
Capital:	Kuwait City
Currency:	Dinar
Language:	Arabic

Kuwayt

In the history of navigation, the voyage of Nearco, one of Alexander of Macedonia's admirals, was a milestone. He sailed from the Indo River to the farthest end of the Gulf of Arabia, ending his voyage in the port of Diridotis, in present-day Kuwait. This was not, however, the first contact between India and Kuwait, which had already been an active trade center for almost 2,000 years. The fate of the country was always intimately linked to that of the Mesopotamian civilizations (see Iraq) but, beginning in the 13th century, after the Mongol invasion caused collapse of the Caliphate, the region entered into a long period of isolation.

[2] After this, new Arab groups began to settle there. In the 18th century, although nominally subject to the Ottoman Empire, the settlements were virtually independent; they decided to elect a *shaij* (sheikh) to conduct sporadic negotiations with the Turks. In 1756, the leader of the Anaiza tribe, Abdul Rahim al-Sabah, founder of the reigning dynasty, was appointed to this task.

[3] At that time, the place, formerly known as the Qurain (horn) began to be called Kuwait, a diminutive for al-Kout, which is a local Arabic term to describe the fortified houses on the coast.

[4] The weakness of Turkish sultans and the growing British influence in the region were two fundamental factors that encouraged the formation of proto-states, of which the emirate of Najd (see Saudi Arabia) was the most dynamic.

[5] In order to avoid absorption by the Wahabites, the emirs of Kuwait requested support from the British who had moved the East India Company's overland mail terminal from Basra to Kuwait in 1779. The British sent Indian troops to guarantee the autonomy of the Emirate, an initiative which the Turks were helpless to stop. For decades Kuwait was the most prosperous and peaceful part of a region peppered by constant disputes.

[6] In 1892, with Turkish support, the Emir of Najd was deposed and was granted asylum in Kuwait. Sheikh Mubarak al Sabah allowed the territory to be used as a base for their raids against the pro-Turkish

Rashidis. Since this implied great risks, a treaty was signed with Britain in 1899, whereby the Sheikh undertook not to cede any part of the territory to another country without British consent; in exchange, Britain guaranteed Kuwait's territorial integrity. This treaty and the subsequent British military presence in the region frustrated Turkish attempts to expand the Berlin-Baghdad railway to reach the Gulf through Kuwaiti territory.

[7] At the end of World War I, France and Britain divided up the remains of the Ottoman Empire. Kuwait was now considered a British protectorate, separate from the newly-created kingdom of Iraq, which claimed it as a province, alleging the historical subjection of the region to the Government of Baghdad.

[8] In 1938, oil began to flow from the Burgan wells. Ahmad Jabir al-Sabah, the crown prince, opposed the exploitation of the extensive deposits, arguing that a high income and high salaries resulting from the new activity would ruin pearl fishing, until then the country's main economic activity, employing 10,000 sailors as deep-sea divers. After the impasse created by World War II, the emir granted the concession to the Kuwait Oil Company, owned by British BP and US Gulf, with oil first exported in 1946. The large-scale exploitation of

these reserves soon turned the small port into a large trading center.

[9] In 1961, independence was negotiated, within the British policy of gradual decolonization. Sheikh Sabah proclaimed himself Emir and took up full powers. Iraq refused to recognize the new state, claiming that it was an artificial creation of the British to maintain access to oil. Consequently, the British troops remained to defend the emirate until they were replaced by the troops of the Arab League.

[10] In 1962 a Constitution was enforced creating a National Assembly of 50 members, elected individually by male citizens aged over 21, whose fathers or grandfathers had resided in Kuwait before 1920. None of the candidates belonged to a political party, as these had been made illegal. Thus, out of the 826,500 Kuwaitis who lived in the country in 1990, a minority of the population - only 85,000 - would have been entitled to vote if elections had been called.

[11] In 1966, Kuwait and Saudi Arabia solved their ancient border disputes, and the 'neutral zone' which existed between both countries was divided equally. In 1969 the Central Bank of Kuwait was created, and in 1976 a Social Security Law and a Law of Reserves for Future Generations were passed. The latter established that 10 per

cent of the State revenue was to be earmarked for an investment fund.

[12] In a few years, oil entirely changed the country. The Bedouins replaced their camels with luxurious air-conditioned cars. Pearl fishing disappeared. The entire population settled in brand new cities, where the stylized mosque towers stood side-by-side with shopping centers which replaced the old *souks* (markets). The population's educational standards and life expectancy rose. All manual labor and work in the oil industry was done by immigrant workers. In 1970 the number of migrants equaled the local population, and by 1985 this figure had almost doubled.

[13] Kuwaiti rulers became concerned that despite so much prosperity in such a poor area its legitimacy could be questioned. In 1961 the Arab Fund for Economic Development was created, in order to channel 'soft' loans and donations to Third World countries. When the Organization of Petroleum Exporting Countries (OPEC) succeeded in raising prices in 1973, Kuwait increased its revenue immensely.

[14] Most of the Third World countries supported OPEC, hoping that they would receive help to establish a 'New International Economic Order', by asking for better prices for the other raw materials that they supply to the Northern countries. However, instead of investing their oil revenues in their own countries or in other Third World nations, the Gulf monarchs placed their fortunes in transnational banks. This further accentuated the excess of liquidity in transnational private banks, which started to grant loans to the Third World quite indiscriminately. This situation was one of the main factors that provoked the 'debt crisis' in 1982.

[15] Within the Gulf area, however, Kuwait was generous with its wealth. By the end of the 1980s, Kuwait had the highest rate of official development assistance in the world, proportional to its gross national product.

[16] Unfortunately, prosperity did not prevent political conflicts. In August 1976, the National Assembly was dissolved by Sheikh Jabir al-Sabah, arguing that it had acted against national interests. In

December 1977, the Emir died and the Crown of Kuwait passed to Jabir Al-Sabah, who called national elections in February 1981. Over 500 candidates ran for the 50 seats in the National Assembly and 40 were won by Sunni candidates, loyal to the ruling family. Shi'a candidates won four seats, and Islamic fundamentalists won six. Only 6.4 per cent of the population was permitted to vote.

[17] When the Iran-Iraq war broke out in 1979, Kuwait officially remained neutral, but in fact supported Iraq with large donations and loans. Kuwait considered Iraq to be a 'first line of defense' against the Iranian Islamic revolution.

[18] In 1985, the National Assembly began to disapprove of governmental measures such as press control, increases in the prices of public services and educational reforms, echoing other accusations that corruption existed within the ruling family. In August 1986, the Emir dissolved the Assembly and began to rule by decree.

[19] In the late 1980s, the Kuwait Investments Office (KIO) had capital assets outside the country estimated at $1 billion, which included hotels, art galleries, European and US real estate, and major shares in large transnational corporations: 10 per cent of British Petroleum, 23 per cent of Hoechst, 14 per cent of Daimler-Benz, and 11 per cent of the Midland Bank.

[20] In 1987, alleging that Iraq was using the port of Kuwait to export oil and import weapons, the Iranian navy attacked Kuwaiti merchant ships. In response, Kuwait requested and obtained permission from the major powers - US, France, Britain, and the USSR - to use their flags for the Kuwait merchant navy. The US and Britain sent their navies to protect Kuwaiti ships in the Gulf.

[21] Once the war between Iran and Iraq ended in 1988, tensions between Kuwait and Iraq started to mount. Kuwait demanded the payment of $15 billion on account of war loans, which Iraq refused to return, alleging that those sums had been used to protect Kuwait. Iraq accused Kuwait of 'stealing' their country's oil, by extracting large amounts of oil from the common deposits which stretch along the border. Iraq claimed that the Emirate was pumping out much more oil than its entitlement, and demanded $2.4 billion in compensation.

[22] On August 2 1990, Iraq invaded Kuwait quickly and decisively. Emir al-Sabah and his family took refuge in Saudi Arabia. Nearly 300,000 Kuwaitis fled the country, to join the other 100,000 who were abroad on their summer vacation. The occupation forces encouraged the exodus, perhaps to 'de-Kuwaitize' the country. A pro-Iraqi provisional government, led by Al Hussein Ali, requested the total fusion of Iraq and Kuwait. A few days later the Emirate was declared an Iraqi province.

[23] Iraq had expected understanding from the US, in exchange for assured oil supplies, but the US reacted very harshly to the invasion and promoted a series of extremely tough measures from the UN Security Council. On August 6, the trading, financial, and military boycott of Iraq was voted through, and on November 29, the use of force against Iraq was approved if the country refused to withdraw from Kuwait before January 15 1991. Only Cuba and Yemen abstained from voting.

[24] When the Emir went into exile in Saudi Arabia he was pressured by the US to promise democratic elections once the country was liberated.

[25] The ensuing Gulf War devastated the country, not so much in terms of lives lost, for most of the fighting was done on Iraqi territory, but the bombings and forced withdrawal of the occupation troops left most of Kuwait's oil wells burning and the country was unable to produce any oil until 1992.

[26] The War also turned Kuwait into an environmental disaster area. The black cloud formed by some 50 burning oil wells, and gigantic oil spills along the coast produced major degradation of the air, marine resources and soil. An enormous mass of oil lined the coasts, posing a threat to birds and other animals. The Gulf's ecosystem was seriously affected, especially fish species which form a staple of the local diet.

[27] It was estimated that the clean-up and reconstruction cost between $150 and 200 billion. On January 9 1991, Britain committed itself to grant a loan of $950 million for reconstruction. Kuwait's debts to allied countries, arising from war costs, rose to more than $22 billion.

[28] After the War was over more than 1,300 people were killed by mines which were laid during the conflict.

[29] On March 18 1991 Amnesty International in London denounced the arbitrary detention and torture of Palestinians residing in Kuwait,

Gypsies/Roma and the world

According to Iranian historiography, the true legend of the old Gypsy/Roma homeland was only known by Gypsies living on the island of Leinos in the Aegean Sea. The same sources claim the Gypsies - now known derogatively as 'Iurios' or 'nutters' in Iran - came to Persia in the third century AD and were known as 'Sindis' or 'Hindis' after the river which gave its name to India, the original homeland of the Gypsies.

They reached the Mediterranean and Greece in the 11th century, where they were known as 'Egyptians' - as they were believed to have come from Egypt - a term which later became 'Gypsies'. They have been present in Macedonia, Croatia and Romania since the 14th century and in Slovenia and Ireland since the 15th.

Dispersed across Asia, Europe and even South America (where their presence has been recorded since 1581), these nomadic peoples have been given endless names. In Turkey, Macedonia and Russia, they are known as 'Cigani', in Kurdistan as 'Luri' and in India as 'Banjar'.

Depending on the country or the tasks they carry out, they are also known as 'Farao Nerek', 'Bohemians', 'Gypsy', 'Roma', 'Manush', 'Sinti', 'Kale', 'Kalderash', 'Burugoti', and by several other names.

But despite the varied names, one common feature in Europe is that throughout history they have almost always been discriminated against and persecuted. This reached an extreme with the systematic extermination of Gypsies under the Nazi regime during World War II, but the limitation of the rights of Gypsies dates back much further. There was active persecution in France, Spain, the Netherlands and Germany in the 16th century. In the 17th century, a law was passed in England saying it was a serious crime to come into contact with Gypsies, and similar laws came into being in Switzerland at around the same time. In the first half of this century of 'enlightenment', in Austria and Germany alone, 68 laws were passed to persecute Gypsies. In Ireland, legal discrimination began in 1541 - in 1596, a group of 198 Gypsies were sentenced to death for being 'unemployed' - and the persecution continued without a break until the 18th century.

THE QUEST FOR RIGHTS
There are far too many examples of persecution to list, and even though active persecution has reduced, Gypsy rights have not improved greatly during the 20th century. The progress which has been made, however limited, has been the fruit of hard work by international organisations lobbying for the rights of Gypsies within countries in which they live or travel, and the efforts of the Gypsy communities themselves which, in recent decades have tried to recover their cultural values and identity.

In the 1970s, organizations came into being to defend the political rights of Gypsies. In London, the First Gypsy Congress in 1971 established a Gypsy anthem and flag. The first International Gypsy Festival took place in India in 1976. In 1977, following an Indian proposal, the United Nations commissions for the Prevention of Discrimination and the Protection of Minorities issued a call asking all countries with Gypsy populations to respect their rights.

In 1978, the Second Gypsy World Congress was held in Genoa (followed by a third in Sweden in 1981, and a fourth in Poland in 1990). Apart from strengthening the ethnic and cultural identity of the Gypsies in the countries where they live, these Congresses also tried to support their access to education. In present-day Europe, Gypsies have political parties in the Czech Republic, Croatia and Yugoslavia, and there are important institutions working to improve the legal, economic, cultural and social rights of Gypsies in other countries (like France, Britain, Hungary, Italy and India). In Macedonia, they have three political parties, two representatives in Parliament, one mayor, and radio and television channels in their language. ∎

carried out by Kuwaiti civilians and military.

[30] On April 1 1991 a group of Kuwaiti citizens demanded freedom of the press, independence of the judiciary, the legalization of political parties, and the implementation of measures to fight corruption.

[31] In June 1991, Sheikh Jabir al-Sabah called a National Council to discuss the elections, and female and foreign suffrage. The opposition was still demanding the re-establishment of the 1962 constitution and the formation of a democratically elected parliament, though no opposition leaders would be allowed in the Council. Over a thousand people demonstrated in the streets after the Emir made his announcement. Although street demonstrations are illegal in Kuwait, the Government made no attempt to stop the march.

[32] When the war ended, the Emir launched the slogan of 're-Kuwaitizing' Kuwait. The plan included a drastic reduction in the number of foreigners in the country. Over 800,000 people had to leave the country, to comply with the Sheikh's measure. A small number of foreigners were deported, but most have to leave when they fail to find jobs and schools for their children.

[33] In mid-December 1991, Saudi Arabia, the United Arab Emirates, Oman, Qatar, Bahrain, and Kuwait held a summit meeting aimed at creating a collective security mechanism, and establishing a new defensive framework for the region which holds 40 per cent of the world's oil reserves.

[34] After renewing oil production, Kuwait initially accepted the OPEC quota of two million barrels per day. However, in February, it confronted OPEC's other members and unilaterally decided to raise daily production to 2.16 million barrels. The Oil Minister explained that the country had confirmed the existence of new deposits of crude oil in what was formally a 'neutral zone' along the border with Saudi Arabia.

[35] In January, press censorship was lifted. Demonstrations were organized by women's groups demanding the right to vote. Elections for the National Assembly were finally held on October 5, with independent opposition groups winning 31 seats, the fundamentalists 19 and the liberals 12. For the first time ever, the cabinet contained several Members of Parliament elected by direct popular vote.

[36] In early 1993, a financial scandal broke involving the Kuwait Investment Office (KIO), and two members of the royal family were found to have been involved. The personal holdings of high-ranking KIO officials were frozen when $5 billion was discovered to be missing. $1 billion had been diverted to Torras, a Spanish business consortium.

[37] In 1993 the UN finally determined the frontier with Iraq, despite protests by Baghdad. As a response to supposed incursions by Iraqi troops, the US bombed Iraq repeatedly (see Iraq). Washington decided to install missiles in Kuwait and it began building a wall 130 kms long equipped with 1.3 million mines along the new frontier.

[38] In August the ex-chief of the Temporary Free Government imposed by Baghdad, Al-Hussein Ali, was condemned to death, as well as five Kuwaitis and 10 Jordanians accused of collaborating with the Iraqi occupation.

[39] The next year, the Government moved towards privatizing State companies and carried out major arms investments.

[40] In February 1996, Amnesty International denounced summary executions, torture and expulsions without trial occurred in Kuwait. In October, the Government won 30 of the National Assembly's 50 seats.

[41] After several legislators threatened to throw out the Minister of Islamic Affairs for errors printed in 120,000 copies of the Qur'an, the Emir dissolved Parliament in May 1999 and called legislative elections in July, 18 months earlier than scheduled.

[42] Although for decades Kuwaiti women had headed businesses and newspapers, led diplomatic missions and actively aided the petroleum industry, and made up approximately 30 per cent of the country's workforce, it was not until 1999 that, after years of lobbying, the Emir pushed through the Cabinet a law giving women the right to vote and to run for parliamentary seats. The law is to come into force in 2003, that is, after two parliamentary elections.

[43] In April 2001 there was another change of Cabinet. The burning of an oil refinery in early 2002 led to harsh criticisms of the new Petroleum Minister, who was forced to resign. In Parliament, a series of debates on the matter ended in denunciations of corruption, incompetence and nepotism, which for politicians and analysts alike underscored the Government's operational problems. Given the context, the candidates proposed for the ministerial seat refused the offer, paralyzing decision-making at the Petroleum Ministry. The Information minister, Sheikh Ahmad Fahd al-Sabah, was forced to take over the ministry until the 2003 elections.

[44] After the September 11 2001 attacks against the United States, the Emir expressed his support for the US led anti-terrorism coalition. The Islamists rejected that decision. Analysts say this could endanger Kuwait's social stability. ■

PROFILE

ENVIRONMENT
Nearly all the land is flat, except for a few ranges of dunes. The inland is desert with only one oasis, the al-Jahrah. The coast is low and uniform. The city and port of Kuwait is located in the only deep-water harbor. The hot climate is tempered by ocean currents but the temperature is high in summer. Winters are warm with frequent dust and sand storms. Petroleum is the main economic resource, with three refineries in Shuaiba, Mina al-Ahmadi and Mina Abdulla. Tremendous environmental damage was caused by burning oil wells, as a result of the Gulf War in 1991. The country also suffers from a lack of water.

SOCIETY
Peoples: Kuwaitis, of Arab descent, account for less than half of the population, 60 per cent of which is made up of immigrant workers from Palestine, Egypt, Iran, Pakistan, India, Bangladesh, the Philippines and other countries. **Religions:** Muslim 85 per cent, of which Sunni 45 per cent, Shi'a 30 per cent; other Muslim 10 per cent; other (mostly Christian and Hindu) 15 per cent. **Languages:** Arabic (official). **Political Parties:** There are no legal parties. In the National Assembly are represented: the Islamic Constitutional Movement, a moderate Sunni group; the Kuwaiti Democratic Forum, liberal; the Salafeen, a fundamentalist Sunni group. **Social Organizations:** Federation of Unions, founded in 1967 with 12,000 members. The Kuwait Students' National Union.

THE STATE
Official Name: Dawlat al-Kuwayt. (State of Kuwait). **Administrative divisions:** 5 governances. **Capital:** Kuwait City (Al-Kuwayt) 1,165,000 people (1999). **Other cities:** as-Salimiyah 142,700 people; Hawalli 90,100; al-Farwaniyah 58,100 al-Jahra 16,000 (2000). **Government:** Constitutional Monarchy. Jabir al-Ahmad al Sabah, Emir since December 1977; Saad al-Abdullah al-Salim al-Sabah, Prime Minister since February 1978. The National Assembly has 50 members, elected for a four-year term. **National Holiday:** February 25, National Day (1950). **Armed Forces:** 15,300 (1996).**Others:** The National Guard has 5,000 troops (Paramilitary).

DEMOGRAPHY
Population: 2,023,000 (2002)
Annual growth: 0.7 % (1985-2000)
Estimates for year 2015: 2,766,000 (2000)
Annual growth to year 2015: 2.5 % (2000)
Urban population: 97.6 % (2000)
Urban growth: 3.2 % (2000)
Children per woman: 2.8 (2000)

HEALTH
Life expectancy at birth: 76 years (2000-2005)
male: 75 years (2000-2005)
female: 79 years (2000-2005)
Maternal mortality: 5 per 100,000 live births (1985/99)
Infant mortality: 9 per 1,000 (2000)
Under-5 child mortality: 10 per 1,000 (2000)
Daily calorie supply: 3,167 per capita (1999)
189 doctors per 100,000 people (1997)

EDUCATION
Literacy: 82 % (2000)
male: 84 % (2000)
female: 80 % (2000)
School enrolment (net):
Primary total: 87 % (1994/2000)
male: 89 % (1995/99)
female: 85 % (1995/99)
Secondary (gross):
male: 65 % (1995/97)
female: 65 % (1995/97)
Tertiary (gross): 19 % (1997)
Primary school teachers: one for every 13 pupils (1998)

COMMUNICATIONS
374 newspapers (1996), 624 radios (1999), 486 TV sets (2000) and 244 main telephone lines (2000) per 1,000 people
Books: 11 new titles per 100,000 people (1992/94)

ECONOMY
Per capita, GDP: $ 15,799 (2000)
Annual growth: -1.4 % (2000)
Annual inflation: 1.8 % (2000)
Consumer price index: 109.5 (2000)
Currency: 0.3 dinars = $ 1 (03/2002)
Cereal imports: 700,695 metric tons (2000)
Food import dependency: 17 % (1999)
Fertilizer use: 1,833 kg per ha (1999)
Exports: $ 21,617 million (2000)
Imports: $ 11,782 million (2000)
Development aid received: $ 7 million (1999); $ 3.8 per capita (1999)

ENERGY
Consumption: 7,822.7 Kgs of oil equivalent per capita yearly (1998); -503.2 % imported (1999)

HDI (ranking/value): 43 / 0.818 (1999)

Kyrgyzstan

Population:	5,047,000 (2002)
Land area:	191,800 SQ KM
Capital:	Pishpek (Bishkek)
Currency:	Som
Language:	Kyrgyz

Kyrgyzstan

In the Bronze Age (2000 years BC), the present Kyrgyzstan was inhabited by tribes who farmed and raised livestock. Between the 7th and the 3rd centuries BC the Saks settled in the area, and between the 3rd and 2nd centuries BC, a group of Usun peoples.

[2] From the 1st century BC to the 4th century AD, Kyrgyzstan was a part of the state of Kushan, which disappeared after the nomadic Eufalites invaded. Toward the end of the 4th century, Kyrgyzstan became part of the western region of the Turkish Kaganate (Khanate), governed by the brothers Tumin and Istemi.

[3] In the 7th century, Kyrgyz territory was occupied by the Turguesh (under the chieftain Moje-Dajan). Between the 8th and 10th centuries it came under the Karluks who were replaced by the Karahanyds between the 10th and 12th centuries. From the 12th to the 14th century, the Turkish peoples of Kyrgyzstan were absorbed as part of the Mongol Empire, in the *ulus* (province) of the Chagatai khan.

[4] During this period, Kipchak-Kyrguish peoples in the area between the Irtysh and Yenisey rivers migrated to Tian Shan, where they mixed with the Mongols and local Turkish groups. In the 15th and 16th centuries, the Kyrgyz people were formed. The Kyrgyz Khanate was established in Tian Shan by Khan Ajmet.

[5] The distinguishing feature of Kyrgyz social organization was the lack of a ruling class of princes or nobles, with authority exercised instead by the *manaps* (elders), whose leadership depended on their

0   300 km

personal prestige. The groups maintained a high degree of cohesion because they were constantly at war against neighboring peoples.

[6] Between the 16th and 18th centuries, the Kyrgyz were subdued by the Oirat-Yungars. In the mid-18th century the Oirat-Yungar State was conquered by Chinese troops. Kyrgyzstan became a protectorate of the Tsin (Chin) Empire. In the early 19th century, Russia began to show interest in the region, which had been conquered by Khan Madali of Kokand.

[7] In 1862, Russian troops supported the Kyrgyz rebellion against the Khanate of Kokand, and took Pishpek. The following year, Kyrgyz representatives from central Tian Shan surrendered to Russia, in the city of Verni (today Almaty). In 1864, Northern Kyrgyzstan joined the Russian Empire, as part of the region of Semirechensk.

[8] In 1867, Czar Alexander II created the Regional Government of Turkistan. Russian colonists began arriving by the thousands, and the Kyrgyz saw their best lands confiscated, and turned over to immigrants for agricultural use.

[9] In 1875 there was an uprising against Khan Jodoyar of Kokand. The Russian Empire leapt in to annex the Khanate of Kokand and Southern Kyrgyzstan. Despite the fact that the major part of its population was Uzbek, the region of Fergana was formed as part of the Province of Turkistan. Kyrgyzstan was divided into three regions - Semirechensk, Syr Darya

and Fergana - within the province of Turkistan, with Tashkent as its center.

[10] Friction between the various ethnic groups periodically flared up over the issue of land ownership and mandatory military service, finally triggering a major revolt by the Kyrgyz, which was brutally put down by the czarist regime.

[11] Soviet power was established in the district of Bishkek in December 1917, though there was strong opposition from guerrilla groups in the rest of the country. In 1921 and 1922, agrarian and water reforms were carried out.

[12] In 1924 the Autonomous Region of Kara-Kirghiz was formed, as a part of the Russian Federation. In 1925, its name was changed to the Autonomous Region of Kirghizia, becoming, in 1926, an 'Autonomous Soviet Socialist Republic'. In December 1936, Kyrgyzstan became a federated republic of the Soviet Union (USSR).

[13] Under socialism the Kyrgyz had to change their nomadic way of life radically, joining the new agricultural cooperatives or working in the industries created by the State (textile, leather, tobacco, lumber, metal and hydroelectric power). They also had to change 'Bishkek' to 'Frunze', the name of a famous Red Army general, and the USSR continued to recruit a major part of its soldiers from among the Kyrgyz.

[14] As a part of the pre-World War II five-year development plans, the USSR built large plants in Kyrgyzstan for the extraction of antimony, as well as the processing

of its agricultural products. The first metal-processing plants and modern blast furnaces were set up during this period.

[15] During the War and in the decades that followed, the region's industry underwent further expansion, producing machinery, building materials and electric power.

[16] From 1961 until the end of the Brezhnev era, Turdakun Usubaliev was first secretary of the Kyrgyzstan Communist Party, which functioned as a branch of the CP of the Soviet Union. Kyrgyz writer Chingiz Aytmatov achieved international fame during the 1970s, as the author of a play dealing with the moral compromises made under Stalinism.

[17] From 1986, with the changes put in motion in the USSR by Mikhail Gorbachev, an independence movement developed in Kyrgyzstan. After the failed coup against Gorbachev in August 1991, the republic of Kyrgyzstan decided to separate from the USSR.

[18] On August 31 1991, Kyrgyzstan's Soviet declared the new republic a democratic and independent state. On that occasion, a statement was made in recognition of the three new Baltic states of Estonia, Latvia and Lithuania.

[19] In Kyrgyzstan's first presidential elections, held in October of that year, Askar Akayev, former president of the Academy of Sciences and a physicist of international renown, ran unopposed and was elected. Akayev was among the few leaders - along with Russian President, Boris Yeltsin - who had personally resisted the failed coup in August, at the Parliament in Moscow.

[20] Akayev was the first head of state in the former Soviet Union to ban the Communist Party and to proclaim the independence of his republic. In December, Kyrgyzstan signed the founding charter of the Commonwealth of Independent States (CIS) with 10 other ex-Soviet republics

[21] In December 1991, President Akayev had to exercise his veto power over a law approved by the Parliament, establishing the exclusive right of the Kyrgyz to the land. He thus avoided inflaming aggression between the native population and

WORKERS

2000

LABOUR FORCE
AS % OF TOTAL:

■ FEMALE: 47%   ■ MALE: 53%

1994/97

EMPLOYMENT DISTRIBUTION:

F

M

■ SERVICES   F: 38%   M: 31%
■ INDUSTRY   F: 7%   M: 12%
■ AGRICULTURE   F: 48%   M: 48%

the Uzbeks of Fergana, which could have turned into an even greater conflict with the neighboring republic of Uzbekistan. The previous year, in the region of Os, in the western part of the country, more than 200 Uzbeks were assassinated by bands of young Kyrgyz, manipulated, it was claimed at the time, by agents of the former Soviet secret police (KGB).

[22] Kyrgyzstan started to create a National Guard of a thousand troops, and asked CIS forces to remain in its territory. This military presence was justified, for 'security reasons', until the republic was ready for full membership of the international community.

[23] In March 1992, Akayev reaffirmed his intention to maintain a strict neutrality, in spite of the attempts of Muslim states like Pakistan, Saudi Arabia or Iran to have closer ties. However, the President of Kyrgyzstan stated he was willing to cultivate closer relations with Turkey.

[24] Kyrgyzstan's new Constitution was passed in May 1993. Akayev's struggle with Parliament - which opposed his reform policies - continued throughout the year. Russian residents, mostly

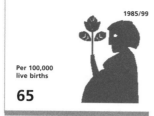

MATERNAL MORTALITY

1985/99

Per 100,000 live births

65

intellectuals and engineers, started to leave the country due to the growing tensions. The Government enacted the creation of a new currency, the som.

[25] In January 1994, Akayev won a referendum confirming the people's trust in the President and his political course. After the som was introduced, inflation went from 40 and 50 per cent per month to 4 per cent, one of the lowest in the former Soviet republics. But, along with falling inflation, came a fall in production by 19 per cent in 1992 and 16 per cent in 1993, while imports, particularly those from Turkey and China, grew at a staggering rate.

[26] The President tried to extend his term with a referendum in 1995, but Parliament forced him to take

part in elections held in December that year. Akayev was re-elected with more than 60 per cent of the vote.

[27] Approved by a wide majority through a referendum in February 1996, constitutional changes gave Akayev wider powers. As a result, opposition members and journalists that criticized the Government were persecuted, jailed for slander and even tortured.

[28] During 1997, Kyrgyzstan went from being a country of transit for the production and dealing of drugs in the region to hosting a growing number of drug processing labs. The private property of agricultural lands was approved through a referendum in 1998.

[29] The Government resigned in full in December 1999, after Akayev accused it of incompetence and not having improved the weakened economy. A high inflation rate, a trade balance deficit and a weakened national currency led Prime Minister Kubanychbek Zhumaliyev and all his Cabinet members to resign, after being criticized by the President and the Security Council.

[30] Akayev appointed Zhumabek Ibraimov as Prime Minister, but he died from cancer on April 4 1999. On April 12, Amangeldy Mursadykovich Muraliyev, former Governor of the southern region of Osh, was appointed premier.

[31] In the 2000 elections, Muraliyev was beaten by Kurmanbek Bakiyev, a Governor from the North. Bakiyev promised to reduce bureaucracy, restore Government order and continue the reforms toward a market economy. For the first time, none of the candidates were officially backed by Akayev.

[32] Tensions between Kyrgyz and Uzbeks for access to land, and ethnic discrimination, caused a constant exodus of Russians. This instability affected the economy, causing high unemployment, the closing of factories, a fall in the GDP, and an increase in malnourished population. According to a United Nations report, 88 per cent of the population lives on less than $4 per day.

[33] In June 2001 Kyrgyzstan signed an agreement with the Shangai Cooperation Organization countries, which it belongs to along with other Central Asian countries, that states their commitment to fight against ethnic and religious militant groups, promoting instead, trade and investment. Kyrgyzstan has been forced to increase military spending, since the presence of Uzbek Islamic guerrillas has increased in the country. According to the Kyrgyz Government, more than 50 soldiers and civilians died in armed attacks in the south between 1999 and 2000. ■

PROFILE

ENVIRONMENT

Located in the northeastern part of Central Asia, Kyrgyzstan lies in the heart of the Tian Shan mountain range. It is bounded by China and Tajikistan in the south, Kazakhstan in the north, Uzbekistan in the west, the Pamir and Altai mountain ranges in the southwest and the Tian Shan range in the northeast. It has plateaus and valleys: in the north, the Chu and Talas valley; in the south, the Alai Valley; and in the southwest, the Fergana Valley. The climate is continental, with sharp contrasts between day and night temperatures. The eastern part of Tian Shan is dry, while the southwestern slopes of the Fergana range are rainy. The main rivers are the Narym and the Kara-Suu. Lake Issyk-Kul is the most important of the country's lakes. In the mountains there are forests and meadows, while desert and semi-desert vegetation abounds at lower altitudes. Metal deposits include lead and zinc; in addition, there are large coal reserves and some oil and natural gas deposits. Water pollution is a serious problem, since one third of the population obtains its water from rivers, streams, or wells.

SOCIETY

Peoples: Kyrgyz, 52.4 per cent; Russians, 21.5 per cent; Uzbeks, 12.9 per cent; Ukrainians, 2.5 per cent, Germans 2.4 per cent. **Religions:** 75 per cent Muslim (Sunni); 6 per cent Christian (Russian Orthodox Church) and others. **Languages:** Kyrgyz (official); Russian (co-official); Uzbek; Dungan; Ukranian and others. **Political Parties:** Party of Communists of Kyrgyztan; Union of Democratic Forces; Women's Democratic Party of Kyrgyztan; Party of War Veterans in Afghanistan. **Social Organizations:** Council of Free Trade Unions, Kyrgyz Committee on Human Rights.

THE STATE

Official Name: Kyrgyz Respublikasy (Kyrgyz Republic)
Administrative division: 6 provinces and 1 city (Bishkek).
Capital: Bishkek 619,000 people (1999).
Other cities: Osh 217,000 people; Jalal-Abad 73,200; Kara-Köl 66,900; Tokmok 61,800; Narin 41,700 (2000).
Government: Askar Akayev, President since October 1990, re-elected in 1995 and 2000 by the people. Kurmanbek Bakiyev, Prime Minister since December 2000. There is a two-chamber Supreme Council: the Legislative Assembly (60 members) and the People's Representatives Assembly (45 members).
National Holiday: August 31, Independence Day (1991).
Armed Forces: 12,200 troops (1997).

Laos

Population: 5,530,000 (2002)
Land area: 230,800 SQ KM
Capital: Vientiane (Viangchan)
Currency: New kip
Language: Lao

Lao

The earliest inhabitants of Laos were migrants from southern China. From the 11th century onward, parts of Laos fell under the Khmer Empire (in the region now known as Cambodia), and later under Siamese influence from the Sukhothai dynasty. With the fall of Sukhothai in 1345, the first kingdom of Laos emerged under Fa Ngum, a Birmanian prince brought up in the court of Angkor Wat. As the Khmer Empire crumbled, Fa Ngum welded together a new empire, founding the flourishing state of Lang Xang, the 'Land of a Million Elephants'. In the late 18th century, the country split into three parts: Champassac, Vientiane and Luang Prabang.

[2] By the 19th century, the Thais had established dominion over the land and Tiao Anuvong, Prince of Vientiane, led an ill-fated nationalist rebellion in 1827. In 1892, the French invaded and by 1893 had established a protectorate over Luang Praband, with the rest of the country becoming part of French Indochina.

[3] During World War II, Japan occupied Laos and a pro-independence movement arose in Vientiane, led by three princes, Phetsarat, leader of the Free Laos government-in-exile, Suvana Fuma, leader of the National Progressive Party, and his half-brother, Tiao Sufanuvong, head of the Neo Lao Issara (Laos National United Front). In September 1945, Sufanuvong set up a provisional Pathet Lao government, declaring independence and promulgating the constitution of 'independent Laos', in spite of protests from King Sisavang Vong, reigning since 1904.

[4] In early 1946, the country was again under French occupation. The Pathet Lao provisional government sought refuge in Bangkok, where the Pathet leaders organized the anti-colonialist struggle through the Lao Issara or 'free Laos' movement.

[5] On July 19 1949, the Franco-Laotian Convention recognized Laotian independence 'as part of the French Union'. The Pathet Lao leaders saw this as mere formal independence and refused to recognize it. Suvana Fuma opted for negotiation, but the opposition coalition decided on active resistance; the military victories led to a new treaty in 1953.

[6] Differences between the Lao Issara, Suvana Fuma government, and the Pathet Lao were reconciled in November 1957. An agreement was reached, whereby the latter would participate in the political life of the country under the name 'Neo Lao Haksat' (Laotian Patriotic Front), led by Tiao Sufanuvong.

[7] The May 1958 elections were won by the Left, worrying the US. Suvana Fuma's ruling party joined forces with the Independent Party to form the so-called Laotian People's Demonstration, together achieving a small majority. They formed a center-left coalition government, led by 'neutralist' Suvana Fuma, with Sufanuvong as planning minister.

[8] The US was strongly opposed and threatened to cut economic aid. This destabilized the Government, and in August the leaders of the Committee for the Defense of National Interests took over. A military offensive against the Pathet Lao drove Sufanuvong from the capital, forcing him into guerrilla action in the forests.

[9] In 1959, the army gained control, while the Pathet Lao controlled the strategic northern provinces and the central plain of Jars.

[10] General Fumi Nosavang, the former defense minister, and his troops seized Vientiane on December 13 1960, driving out Pathet Lao troops. A massive air raid left 1,500 dead and forced Vientiane to surrender.

[11] The Thai and US supported Revolutionary Anti-Communist Committee, headed by Fumi Nosavang and Prince Bun Um claimed legitimacy to govern. On December 20 1960, however, Princes Suvana Fuma and Sufanuvong declared their intention of forming a national unity government.

[12] The 'neutralists' joined forces with the Pathet Lao and launched successful joint military campaigns.

[13] In 1961 in Geneva, Britain and the Soviet Union initiated negotiations for a peaceful solution, and on January 19 1962, a final agreement was signed for a national unity government.

[14] Growing US intervention resulted in the internationalization of the Vietnam War. Air raids on Laotian territory increased to 500 missions per day by 1970 and in nine years Laos was subjected to a greater number of bombings than the whole of Europe during World War II.

[15] The Pathet Lao declared an armistice in 1973, and the Vientiane Government formed a new cabinet, including Pathet Lao members, with a Council of Ministers headed by Suvana Fuma. After the US defeat in Vietnam, right-wing groups lost the support they had been getting from the US.

[16] In 1975, the national unity cabinet gave way to a majority of Neo Lao Haksat ministers, and on December 1, a peaceful movement put an end to the monarchy. A People's Democratic Republic was proclaimed with Sufanuvong as President, led by the Lao People's Revolutionary Party (PPRL). Entrepreneurs and state bureaucrats left the country en masse, ruining the economy and crippling public administration.

[17] The Government nationalized banks and reorganized the public sector. Rice production rose from 700,000 tons in 1976 to 1,200,000 in 1981, when grain self-sufficiency was achieved. For access to the sea and to reduce dependence on Thailand, a road was constructed to the Vietnamese port of Danang, and an oil pipeline to Vietnam's refineries.

[18] In 1986, Phumi Vengvichit became President. In November, Kaysone Phomvihane was re-elected secretary general of the PPRL, subsequently becoming Prime Minister.

[19] In 1988 diplomatic relations were renewed with China, and in early 1989 cooperation agreements were signed with the US, which granted a symbolic $10 million to combat the cultivation and trafficking of opium.

[20] In 1991, the poor economic situation was exacerbated by floods and pest infestations in a quarter of the country's farmlands. Consequently, over 200,000 tons of rice were imported to feed the population.

[21] Also in 1991, Thailand and Laos agreed to a repatriation plan for 60,000 Laotian refugees by 1994, also signing a Cooperation and Security Treaty. Thai investments were meanwhile concentrated in banking and trade. Laos has also put a lot of effort into establishing closer ties with China.

[22] In September 1991, 70-year-old Kaysone Phomvihane was named President. Upon his death a year later, Prime Minister Khamtay Sifandon assumed interim presidency of the country and the PPRL.

[23] In December 1992, legislative elections were called; only the PPRL

and a few independent government-authorized candidates took part. This essentially represented a continuation of the one-party system. Anti-government demonstrations were banned, and scores of government opponents were imprisoned.

24 The Supreme Assembly of the People met in February 1993, and named Nouhak Phumsavanh president of the republic, and Khamtai Siphandon leader of the PPRL.

25 Major free-market oriented reforms were introduced, but without drastically changing the political system. In 1993, Prince Suvana Fuma was authorized to return to the country in an unofficial capacity to represent foreign companies.

26 Following IMF-proposed strategies, the country managed to bring down the inflation rate - averaging 46 per cent in the 1980s - to an annual rate of 10 per cent, meanwhile the GDP grew by 7 per cent. It is estimated that part of that economic 'growth' resulted from products and activities previously not accounted for, and

not from an actual increase in production.

27 The US Agency for International Development (USAID) approved a $9.7 million loan to build roads in several regions of the country, arguing that access to markets would improve living conditions.

28 Deforestation became a serious environmental problem. The timber felled expanded from 6,000 cubic meters in 1964 to more than 600,000 in 1993. That year, the Government restricted lumber exports. In March 1994 the World Bank granted Laos a loan for reforestation worth $ 8.7 million. International environmental groups criticized the project because it gave the funds directly to the Government, with little input from local communities, and because of its emphasis on planting commercial tree species.

29 On April 6 1994 the 'Friendship Bridge' over the Mekong River was opened, uniting Laos and Thailand. This reconciliation represented a distancing from Vietnam and opened the way for economic and

cultural integration with Thailand, a more prosperous nation.

30 Soon Thailand-based capital dominated investment in Laos. A law passed in March eliminated the vestiges of the planned economy system. Another law updated labor legislation. However, the Government was determined to maintain its communist identity.

31 In December 1997 the PPRL retained its dominance, elected to 99 seats in the National Assembly. Just four of the 159 candidates were from outside the single party.

32 The stock crisis affecting several countries in the region hit the Laos economy. Imports and consumer prices increased, particularly for the basic food basket. From that time, the national currency, the kip, began an accelerated devaluation process that two years later showed a decline of more than 500 percent with respect to the dollar.

33 In February 1998, the National Assembly elected Prime Minister Siphandon as the new President. Sisavat Keobounphan became the new Prime Minister.

34 Burma/Myanmar, Thailand and Laos agreed in April 1999 to coordinate their fight against the production and export of drugs, especially opium, to other countries. Because of their opium production, the three countries are known as the 'Golden Triangle' - the area is the world's leading producer of that drug.

35 A wave of bomb attacks shook the country in 2000-2001. According to the Government they were the work of the guerrilla Chao Fa group, or of anticommunist groups based abroad. Chao Fa, consisting of members of the minority Hmong, was accused of receiving assistance from China. However, several analysts suspect that the violence could be linked to friction within the regime itself. There were no attacks during the December 2000 celebrations commemorating a quarter century of communist government. Laos is one of five communist regimes surviving in the world.

36 In his opening address before the PPRL congress in March 2001, President Siphandon said the party aimed to triple per capita income in Laos by the year 2020, though it recognized the failures in managing the country's fragile economy. He said it was necessary to strengthen the party, which has more than 100,000 members. A statute passed by the congress reaffirms the party's support for socialism and 'opposition to multiparty systems and political pluralism'.

37 The fight against drug trafficking intensified, and the death sentence was decreed for anyone found carrying more than 500 grams of heroin. ∎

PROFILE

ENVIRONMENT

Laos is the only landlocked country in Indochina. The territory is mountainous and covered with rainforests. The Mekong river valley, stretching down the country from north to south, is suited to agriculture, basically rice. It is estimated that 40 per cent of the arable land was left barren as a result of the 25-year war. The climate is tropical and the lowlands are prone to disasters such as the 1978 drought and the 1988 flood. The main environmental problem is intense logging and as a result of this, dwindling water supplies and a loss of 70 per cent of natural habitats. Less than 5 per cent of the land is suitable for agriculture, though farming generates 80 per cent of employment.

SOCIETY

Peoples: 60 per cent of Laotians are descendants of the Lao ethnic groups who inhabit the western valleys. The inhabitants of the mountains account for more than one-third of the total population, while 5 per cent are of Chinese and Vietnamese origin. **Religions:** Buddhist 57.8 per cent; traditional religions 33.6 per cent; Christian 1.8 per cent, of which Roman Catholic 0.8 per cent, Protestant 0.2 per cent; Muslim 1.0 per cent; atheist/no religion 4.8 per cent; Chinese folk-religions 0.9 per cent. **Languages:** Lao (official); French; English and many minor ethnic group languages. **Political Parties:** The Lao People's Revolutionary Party (PPRL), authoritarian communist, in power with 98 of the 99 National Assembly's seats. There are proscribed opponent parties as the Lao Democratic Party; the Lao Freedom Party and the Lao Nationalist Movement. **Social Organizations:** The Patriotic Youth and the Association of Patriotic Women. The National Liberation Front, based in the Meo ethnic minority, wages guerrilla warfare and is accused of receiving Chinese support.

THE STATE

Official Name: Sathalanalat Paxathipatai Paxaxon Lao (Lao People's Democratic Republic). **Administrative divisions:** 16 provinces, 1 special zone (Xaisomboun) and 1 municipality (Viangchan). **Capital:** Vientiane (Viangchan) 640,000 people (1999). **Other cities:** Savannakhét 154,900 people; Louangphrabang 116,000 (2000). **Government:** Khamtai Siphandon, President since February 1998, elected by the National Assembly for a five-year term. Boungnang Volachit, Prime Minister since March 2001, appointed by the President. Unicameral Legislature: National Assembly with 99 members. **National Holiday:** December 2, Proclamation of the Republic (1975). **Armed Forces:** 37,000 troops (conscripts), (1996). **Other:** 100,000 members of the Self-defense Militia Forces.

DEMOGRAPHY

Population: 5,530,000 (2002)
Annual growth: 2.5 % (1985-2000)
Estimates for year 2015: 7,334,000 (2000)
Annual growth to year 2015: 2.2 % (2000)
Urban population: 23.5 % (2000)
Urban growth: 4.7 % (2000)
Children per woman: 5.1 (2000)

HEALTH

Life expectancy at birth: 54 years (2000-2005)
male: 53 years (2000-2005)
female: 56 years (2000-2005)
Maternal mortality: 650 per 100,000 live births (1985/99)
Infant mortality: 90 per 1,000 (2000)
Under-5 child mortality: 105 per 1,000 (2000)
Daily calorie supply: 2,152 per capita (1999)
24 doctors per 100,000 people (1996)
Safe water: 37 % (2000)

EDUCATION

Literacy: 62 % (2000)
male: 74 % (2000)
female: 50 % (2000)
School enrolment (net):
Primary total: 69 % (1994/2000)
male: 80 % (1995/99)
female: 72 % (1995/99)
Secondary (gross):
male: 34 % (1995/97)
female: 23 % (1995/97)
Tertiary (gross): 3 % (1998)
Primary school teachers: one for every 31 pupils (1998)

COMMUNICATIONS

4 newspapers (1996), 148 radios (1997), 10 TV sets (2000) and 8 main telephone lines (2000) per 1,000 people
Books: 1 new title per 100,000 people (1992/94)

ECONOMY

Per capita, GDP: $ 1,575 (2000)
Annual growth: 3.3 % (2000)
Annual inflation: 25.1 % (2000)
Consumer price index: 786.4 (2000)
Currency: 7,593.9 new kips = $ 1 (03/2002)
Cereal imports: 15,467 metric tons (2000)
Fertilizer use: 93 kg per ha (1999)
Exports: $ 467 million (1998)
Imports: $ 612 million (1998)
External debt: $ 2,499 million (2000); $ 473 per capita (2000)
Debt service: 7.7 % of exports (1999)
Development aid received: $ 294 million (1999); $ 57.7 per capita (1999); 20.50 % of GNP (1999)

HDI (ranking/value): 131 / 0.476 (1999)

Latvia

Population: 2,392,000 (2002)
Land area: 62,050 SQ KM
Capital: Riga
Currency: Lat
Language: Latvian

Latvija

The first inhabitants of present-day Latvia were nomadic hunters, fishers and gatherers who migrated to the forests along the Baltic coast, after the last glaciers had retreated. Around 2,000 BC, these groups were replaced by the Baltic peoples, Indo-European tribes who began farming and established permanent settlements in Latvia, Lithuania and eastern Prussia.

[2] The ancient Baltic peoples had come into contact with the Roman Empire through the amber trade. This activity, which reached its peak during the first two centuries of the Christian era, was brought to a halt by Slav expansion toward central and eastern Europe. At this time, the Balts' trade and cultural relations turned northward, to their Scandinavian neighbors.

[3] The Danes used the Dvina and Dnepr rivers in their expansion toward the steppes north of the Black Sea, and therefore crossed Latvian territory. The Swedes and the Russians both claimed these lands during the 10th and 11th centuries and in the 12th century, German warriors and missionaries came to the Latvian coast. As it was inhabited at the time by the Livs, the Germans called it Livonia. In 1202, the bishop of the region, under authorization from Rome, established the Order of the Knights of the Sword.

[4] Before becoming the Knights of the Teutonic Order, in 1237, the Germans had subdued and converted the tribal groups of Latvia and Estonia to Christianity. The Teutonic Knights created the so-called Livonian Confederation, consisting of areas controlled by the Church, free cities and regions governed by knights. In the mid-16th century, rivalries within Livonia became more pronounced with the expansion of Protestantism and discontent among the peasants.

[5] During this period, Latvians benefited from Riga's participation in the Hanseatic League, a German mercantile society which attained a high level of prosperity. Nevertheless the Latvians were treated by the Germans like any vanquished people: the local nobility was abolished and the peasants were forced to pay tithes and taxes, paying with labor if they had no money. After being defeated by Lithuania and Poland,

the power of the Teutonic Order declined. However, as the knights' power diminished, their exploitation of the Latvians actually increased.

[6] When Russia invaded the region in 1558, to halt Polish-Lithuanian expansion, the Order fell apart and Livonia was partitioned. At the end of the Livonian War in 1583 Lithuania annexed the area north of the Dvina river; the south remained in Polish hands and Sweden kept the north of Estonia. In 1621, Sweden occupied Riga and Jelgava; Estonia and the northern part of Latvia were subsequently ceded to Sweden by the Truce of Altmark (1629).

[7] The region west of Riga, on the Baltic Sea, was organized into the Duchy of Courland, becoming a semi-independent vassal of Poland. In the mid-17th century, Courland became known as a major naval and trade center for northern Europe, and even had colonial aspirations. Duke Jacob led a brief Latvian occupation of Tobago, in the Caribbean, and of another island in the Gambia River delta in Africa. The name Great Courland Bay, in Tobago, dates back to this time.

[8] Sweden kept these territories until the Great Northern War, when it was forced to cede them to Russia under the Peace of Nystad. In 1795, after the three partitions of Poland, Livonia was finally subdivided into three regions within Russia: Estonia (the northern part of Estonia); Livonia (the south of Estonia and north of Latvia) and Courland. The Russian Revolution of 1905 gave rise to the first instances of Latvian national reaffirmation.

[9] The peasants revolted against their German feudal lords, and the Russian rulers. Although the

rebellion was put down by czarist troops, it set the stage for the war of independence 13 years later. After the Russian Revolution of 1917, the Latvian People's Council proclaimed the country's independence on November 18 1918. A government led by the leader of the Farmers' Union, Karlis Ulmanis, was formed.

[10] Far from having its desire for independence and sovereignty respected, Latvia was attacked by German troops and by the Red Army. Only in 1920 was Latvia able to sign a peace treaty with the USSR, in which the latter renounced its territorial ambitions. In 1922, a constituent assembly established a parliamentary republic. The international economic crisis of the 1930s, and the polarization of socialists and Nazi sympathizers led to the collapse of the Latvian Government. In 1934, Prime Minister Ulmanis suspended parliament and governed under a state of emergency until 1938.

[11] With the outbreak of World War II, according to the secret Russo-German pact, Latvia remained within the USSR's sphere of influence. In 1939, Latvia was forced to sign a treaty permitting the Soviets to install troops and bases on its soil. In 1940, it was invaded by the Red Army, and a new government was formed, which subsequently requested that the republic be admitted to the USSR.

[12] During the German offensive against the USSR, between 1940 and 1944, Latvia was annexed to the German province of Ostland, and its Jewish population was practically exterminated. The liberation of Latvia by the Red Army meant the re-establishment of Soviet Government. Before the Soviet

forces arrived, 65,000 Latvians fled to Western Europe.

[13] In 1945 and 1946, about 105,000 Latvians were deported to Russia, and the far northeastern corner of Latvia - with its predominantly Russian population - was taken away from Latvia to form part of the USSR. In 1949, forced collectivization of agriculture triggered a mass deportation of Latvians, with about 70,000 being sent to Russia and Siberia. In 1959 the President of Latvia's Supreme Soviet, Karlis Ozolins, was dismissed because of his nationalist tendencies.

[14] Armed Latvian resistance to the Soviet regime was finally put down, in 1952. All symbols of Latvian independence - the national anthem, the flag, and national monuments and history - were banned or adapted to the new regime. Russian became the official language, and massive immigration of Russians and other nationalities began. To the nationalists, this was taken to be a deliberate colonization policy, aimed at diminishing the influence of the indigenous population.

[15] Until the 1980s, Latvian resistance was expressed in isolated actions by political and religious dissidents, which were systematically repressed by the regime; in addition, some nationalist campaigns were carried out by exiles. From 1987, the policy of *glasnost* (openness) initiated by Mikhail Gorbachev in the USSR, gave hope to Latvian aspirations, permitting public political demonstrations, and the reinstatement of the national symbols.

[16] In June 1987 some 5,000 people gathered in front of the Monument to Liberty, in Riga, to honor the victims of the 1941 Soviet deportations. This marked the beginning of increasingly important political agitation, in which independence began to be discussed openly once again. In 1988, the National Independence Movement of Latvia (LNNK) demanded an end to the Russification of the country, and called for freedom of the press and for the formation of independent political parties.

[17] In October 1988, close to 150,000 people gathered to celebrate the founding of the Popular Front of

Latvia (LTF), which brought together all of Latvia's recently formed social and political groups, as well as militant communists. A month later, for the first time since Soviet occupation, hundreds of thousands of Latvians commemorated the anniversary of the 1918 declaration of independence. The LTF began to have influence with the local government, and with the Moscow authorities.

[18] A year later, the LTF Congress endorsed the country's political and economic independence from the Soviet Union. Despite Moscow's resistance to Latvia's secession, the LTF's policy of carrying out changes peacefully met with widespread popular support, from citizens of Russian or other origins. The LTF program for non-violent change included public demonstrations, free elections and change through parliamentary procedure. Latvia's 1938 constitution went into effect once again, for the first time since the 1940 Soviet occupation.

[19] May 4 1990 marked the Declaration of the Re-establishment of Independence, as well as the reinstatement of the 1922 constitution. In September 1991, the new Council of State of the USSR, in its inaugural session, formally recognized the independence of the Baltic republics. They were also immediately recognized by a number of countries, and admitted as new members to the UN in the General Assembly session held that same month. The three Baltic States initiated negotiations with the European Community (EC), in the areas of trade and financial assistance. In February 1992, Latvia and Russia signed an agreement on the withdrawal of the former USSR's troops, stationed within Latvian territory.

[20] A new parliament was selected in June 1993 which appointed Guntis Ulmanis as President. The beginning of an economic liberalization process caused a sharp rise of unemployment. In 1994, foreign investment grew but the economy was still dependant on Russia, its main supplier of fuel and its first exporting market. Also, in spite of the massive privatization of state companies, the budget and trade balance deficits persisted.

[21] In 1995, lack of controls over commercial banks led to the bankruptcy of several financial institutions. The September legislative elections did not reveal any clear winner since nine parties obtained between 5 per cent and 16 per cent of the vote. An agreement between the conservative National Block and two left-wing parties led to Andris Skele being appointed Prime Minister in December.

[23] In a new attempt to minimize tensions with the Russian minority, in February 1998 Latvia passed a law granting a passport to those foreigners living permanently in the country since 1991.

[24] Juris Dalbinsh, commander in chief of the Latvian Armed Forces, was discharged in April that year, after taking part in a rally of former Latvian SS members who had fought with German Third Reich forces against the USSR. That same week the police chief of Riga was dismissed for failing to protect a synagogue against bomb attacks.

[25] A referendum approved together with the October elections relaxed the requirement of obligatory fluency in Latvian in order to become a citizen, repealing a restrictive law passed in February. The People's Party, with 21.2 per cent of the vote, beat the Union Latvia's Way, which amounted to 18.1 per cent of the turnout. In April 1999 a Government commission proposed the payment of $2,000 to all those 'non Latvians' who would be willing to leave the country.

[26] Three Russians were sentenced to 15 years in prison for threatening to bomb an 800-year old church in Riga, the capital, in protest at a plan to join NATO. The sentence was criticized by Moscow, which referred to the lenient sentences received by some members of a Latvian nationalist group that had destroyed a Soviet war memorial in Russia.

[27] A week of commemoration for the victims of Stalin's deportations to Siberia, estimated at 15,000, was carried out in June 2001. The President stressed the need to remember those deportations.

[28] During the visit of the Prince of Wales to Riga in November 2001, a woman 'hit' him on the face with a flower. On being arrested she explained it was in protest for Latvia's incorporation into NATO. The 'attacker' claimed she had been against the war in Afghanistan and that the real 'enemy' was Britain.

[29] Foreign Minister Maris Riekstins stated at the March 2002 European Union summit in Barcelona that an increased integration of the least developed states into the international trade system should be sought, promoting a long-term development. He said Latvia had taken steps toward that goal, ensuring free access to the Latvian market for 49 industrially underdeveloped countries. ∎

PROFILE

ENVIRONMENT

Latvia's terrain is characterized by softly rolling hills (highest point: Gaizins, 310 m), and by the number of forests, lakes and rivers, which empty into the Baltic Sea and the Gulf of Riga, in the northeastern part of the country. Latvia has a 494 km coastline, with important ports and attractive beaches. The country's most fertile lands lie in the Zemgale Plain, which is known as the country's breadbasket. The plain is located in the south, extending as far as the Lithuanian border. The Highlands, which make up 40 per cent of the land, lie in the western and northern parts of the country, crossing over into Estonia. The climate is humid and cold, due to cold air masses coming from the Atlantic. Summers are short and rainy, with an average temperature of 17° C; winters last from December to March, with temperatures below zero, sometimes as low as -40° C. Two-thirds of all arable land is used for grain production, and the rest for pasture. The main industries are metal engineering (ships, automobiles, railway passenger cars and agricultural machinery), followed by the production of motorcycles, electrical appliances and scientific instruments. Industrial wastes and the pollution of the country's rivers and lakes are problems that remain to be solved.

SOCIETY

Peoples: Latvians and Lithuanians constitute the two main branches of the Baltic Indo-European peoples, with a distinct language and culture that sets them apart from the Germans and Slavs. Ethnic Latvians make up 52 per cent of the country's population, followed by Russians, 34 per cent; Poles, Belarusians, Ukrainians, Lithuanians and Estonians account for the remaining 14 per cent. **Religions:** The majority is Protestant (Lutheran), followed by Catholics. **Languages:** Latvian (official); Russian, Lithuanian and Polish. **Political Parties:** People's Party; Union Latvia's Way; Popular Concord Party; Alliance Fatherland and Freedom; Latvian Social Democratic Union; Latvian Farmers Union. **Social organizations:** Confederation of Free Trade Unions.

THE STATE

Official Name: Latvijas Respublika. **Capital:** Riga 783,000 people (1999). **Other cities:** Daugavpils 113,600 people; Liepaja 94,100; Jelgava 70,700; Jurmala 58,900 (2000). **Government:** Parliamentary republic. Vaira Vīke-Freiberga, President, elected in July 1999. Andris Berzins, Prime Minister since May 2000. Single-chamber parliament (Saeima), made up of 201 members, elected by direct vote. **National holiday:** November 18, Independence Day (1918). **Armed Forces:** 6,950 troops (1996).

Lebanon

Population:	3,614,000 (2002)
Land area:	10,230 SQ KM
Capital:	Beirut (Bayrut)
Currency:	Pound
Language:	Arabic

Lubnan

Much of present-day Lebanon corresponds to the ancient land of the Phoenicians, who probably arrived in the region in about 3000 BC. Commercial and religious connections were established with Egypt after about 2613 BC and continued until the end of the Egyptian Old Kingdom and the invasion of Phoenicia by the Amorites (c2200 BC). Other groups invading and periodically controlling Phoenicia included the Hyksos (18th century BC), the Egyptians of the New Kingdom (16th century BC), and the Hittites (14th century BC). Seti I (1290-79 BC) of the New Kingdom reconquered most of Phoenicia, but Ramses III (1187-56 BC) lost it to invaders from Asia Minor and Europe. Between the withdrawal of Egyptian rule and the western advance of Assyria (10th century BC), the history of Phoenicia is primarily the history of Tyre. This city-state rose to hegemony among Phoenician states and founded colonies throughout the Mediterranean region. The Achaemenians, an Iranian dynasty under the leadership of Cyrus II, conquered the area in 538 BC. Sidon, 20 miles (32 km) north of Tyre, became a principal coastal city of this empire. In 332 BC Tyre capitulated to the army of Alexander the Great after resisting for eight months. This event marked the demise of Tyre as a great commercial city, as its inhabitants were sold into slavery. In 64 BC Phoenicia was incorporated into the Roman province of Syria.

[2] Emperors embracing Christianity protected the area during the later Roman and

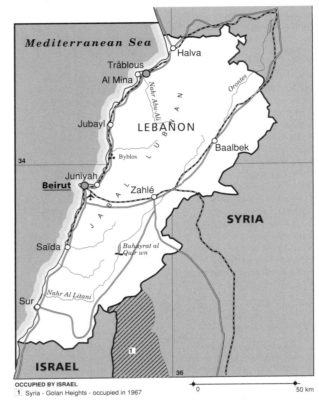

OCCUPIED BY ISRAEL
1 Syria - Golan Heights - occupied in 1967

0   50 km

Byzantine periods (c. AD 300-634). A 6th-century Christian group fleeing persecution in Syria settled in what is now northern Lebanon, absorbed the native population, and founded the Maronite Church. In the following century, Arab tribes settled in southern Lebanon after the Muslim conquest of Syria. Four hundred years later, many of this Arab group coalesced their beliefs into the Druze faith. In the coastal towns the population became mainly Sunni Muslim. By the end of the 11th century Lebanon had become part of the crusader states, and it later became part of the Mamluk state of Syria and Egypt. Lebanon was able to evolve a social and political system of its own between the 15th and the 18th century. Throughout this period European, particularly French, influence was growing. In 1516 the Ottoman Turks replaced the Mamluks. The social system came under severe strain as the Christian population grew.

[3] Around 1831 the vigorous Egypt of Muhammed Ali extended its influence northwards undermining the decadent Turkish empire. The European powers did not want the Turkish Empire to crumble until Europe was in a position to carry off the spoils. They conveniently decided that Christians anywhere in the world could be equated with Europeans, meriting their protection, and they began to support the Maronite Arab Christians against Egypt.

[4] Between 1831 and 1834, five powers intervened in the 'Syrian

question'. Russia and Austria devoted their efforts exclusively to the Balkans, and France and Britain were left to dispute domination of the Arab countries, laboriously shunting Prussia aside. The Ottoman Turks ended the local rule of the Druze Shihab princes in 1842, exacerbating already poor relations between the Maronites and the Druze. These relations reached a low ebb with the massacre of Maronites by Druze in 1860.

[5] The French intervened on behalf of the Christians, forcing the Ottoman Sultan to form an autonomous province within the Ottoman Empire for the mountainous Christian area, known as Mount Lebanon. In 1919, Syria and Lebanon became French protectorates, while Britain took Egypt, Jordan and Iraq. For administrative purposes, France separated Lebanon from Syria and when the army pulled out in 1947, they left behind two separate states.

[6] Camille Chamoun was elected President in 1952, following a clearly pro-Western foreign policy. The 1957 parliamentary elections were marked by Muslim demonstrations and riots, demanding closer alignment with Egypt and Syria, and rejecting re-election for the Maronite president.

[7] By the following year the rioting had grown into full scale insurrection, pitting Muslims against Christians in a bloody civil war. In July 1958, President Chamoun allowed 10,000 US Marines to disembark in order to 'pacify' the country. The foreign troops remained in Beirut (Bayrut) and in other strategically important Lebanese cities until October of that year.

[8] By the early 1970s, the population had become mostly Muslim, and they began to question the traditional political system which required a Christian president and a Sunni Muslim prime minister in order to maintain a balance between the two communities. The Shi'as had no specified role.

[9] Differences between the various religious and ethnic communities were combined with an eminently unjust social and economic system. Predatory colonial exploitation had exhausted the traditional cedars of Lebanon,

Workers

2000

LABOR FORCE AS % OF TOTAL

- FEMALE: 30%
- MALE: 70%

Land Use

DEFORESTATION: 8.1% annual (1990/95)

1993

- FOREST & WOODLAND: 7.7%
- ARABLE: 20.8%
- OTHER: 71.5%

leaving the land barren and farmers impoverished. The new distribution of labor and wealth kept trade control for the Maronites, while the Muslims worked as artisans, laborers and farm workers.

[10] These tensions erupted in civil war again, when the Christian right wing used the 'Palestinian problem' as a pretext for conflict in 1975. Lebanon, which had remained neutral in the 1973 Arab-Israeli War, granted refuge to 300,000 Palestinians in the southern part of its territory. Israel used this fact to justify frequent incursions and bombings against civilians. Meanwhile, the Lebanese Christian Phalange militia unleashed its might on the Palestinian refugee camps.

[11] In 1976, Syrian troops, part of an Arab-League peace force, put a stop to the fighting and guaranteed national unity. The underlying causes of the civil war persisted, and Israeli attacks continued. In 1981, Israeli artillery, together with a unit of the former Lebanese commander Saad Haddad, bombarded the cities of Tyre and Sidon (Saida), while Syrian troops installed anti-aircraft missiles in the Bekaa Valley. That July, Israeli jets launched a number of attacks against Palestinian positions, including a wave of air raids on West Beirut; they left 166 dead and 600 wounded.

[12] In June 1982, Israeli troops invaded Lebanon by land, sea and air. Tyre and Sidon were quickly overrun, and Nabataea and Tripoli (Trâblous) were devastated by bombings.

[13] Beirut, one of the most important political and cultural capitals in the Arab world, was virtually destroyed. Thousands of civilians were killed. Bridges, oil pipelines, airports, hospitals, schools, major buildings and modest homes, factories and museums were razed. Eight thousand Palestinians and Lebanese were interned in prison camps.

[14] The PLO finally agreed to pull out of Beirut, providing that the evacuation was carried out under international supervision. US, French and Italian soldiers provided the necessary protection, and the people of West Beirut gave a heroes' farewell to the freedom fighters, who went to seven other Arab countries.

[15] On August 23 1982, what was left of the Lebanese Congress named Israel's nominee, Maronite Bashir Gemayel - the sole candidate - to succeed President Elias Sarkis. The Maronite leader did not live to take office, however. He died on September 14 in a dynamite attack on the Phalange's east Beirut command headquarters. No one accepted responsibility for the act.

[16] The following day, Beirut was occupied by Israeli troops. On September 16 1982, a militia group led by former commander Haddad and Elie Hbaiqa burst into the Palestinian refugee camps of Sabra and Chatila and assassinated thousands of unarmed civilians, including old people, women and children.

[17] Later investigations left no doubt as to Israel's responsibility for the killings, as Israeli officers had encouraged the right-wing militia to act.

[18] While Israeli troops still held half of Lebanon, Amin Gemayel was elected president under the same conditions as his younger brother Bashir.

[19] The new president was unable to eliminate distrust among the various communities of Lebanon. A majority of the governing Phalange party sought to replace the 1943 National Alliance with a new constitutional decree to divide the state into districts under a central federal government. This raised the prospect of Lebanon's political division into several religious mini-states. Sunni and Shi'a leaders favored administrative (but not political) decentralization, and the Druze community wanted greater autonomy.

[20] In July 1984 the Lebanese currency, which had remained relatively stable since the beginning of the war in 1975, slumped abruptly, producing unprecedented inflation.

[21] Recession in the Gulf dealt a death blow to Beirut's economy which was already severely weakened by the withdrawal of foreign currency. This caused a balance of payments deficit of over $1.5 billion in 1984.

[22] Before the Israeli army officially withdrew from Lebanon in 1985, it ensured that the Christian militia had displaced the Muslims from southern Lebanon guaranteeing a 'friendly' civilian population in the 10-kilometre security zone they imposed.

[23] In September 1988, pro-Israeli Maronite General Michel Aoun took over the presidency, which had been vacant since Amin Gemayel's constitutional mandate was truncated in a palace coup. The country was now governed by two rival administrations - Aoun's, and that of Muslim Prime Minister Selim al-Hoss.

[24] In October 1989 Lebanon's single chamber parliament met, for the first time since independence, outside the country and under the auspices of the Arab League. The league includes Saudi Arabia, Algeria and Morocco, who acted as intermediaries in negotiations between the Lebanese factions. The meeting in Taif sealed the peace and laid down an alternative to the political system that had been in place since 1943. Under a new constitution, the next president would be elected indirectly by the parliament.

[25] Christian and Muslim Lebanese legislators announced a national reconciliation agreement on October 12, granting greater power to Muslims and providing for the withdrawal of Syrian troops from Lebanon. General Aoun rejected the agreement because it was instituted by Saudi Arabia, and he considered it a 'Syrian trap'.

[26] On November 5 1989, René Moawad, a Maronite Christian sympathetic to Muslim causes, was unanimously elected president. Moawad was killed by a car-bomb scarcely 17 days before taking office.

[27] Elias Hrawi, another Maronite Christian, was elected president on November 24 by a meeting of the parliament at Zahle, in Syrian-controlled territory. General Aoun immediately rejected the election of a new president in an area outside the Christian enclave under his control.

[28] Taking advantage of the new situation created by the Iraqi invasion of Kuwait, the Syrian-backed forces started an offensive against Aoun in October 1990. Lacking international support, as Syria belonged to the anti-Iraq coalition, Aoun was soon defeated and he sought asylum in France.

[29] In December 1990, a national unity government was formed, for the first time since the beginning of the war. It incorporated the Lebanese Forces (Christian), the Amal (Shi'a), the PSP (Druze), and the pro-Syrian parties.

[30] The presidents of Lebanon and Syria signed a Brotherhood, Co-operation and Co-ordination Agreement in Damascus, the Syrian capital on May 22 1991. Syria recognized Lebanon as a separate and independent state. The agreement established Syrian-

---

PROFILE

ENVIRONMENT

One of the smallest Middle East countries, Lebanon has a fertile coastal plain where most of the population lives, with a mild Mediterranean climate making it rainy in the winter; two parallel mountain ranges, the Lebanon Mountains (whose highest peak is Sauda, at 3,083 m) and the Anti-Lebanon Mountains, with temperate forests on their slopes, and between the ranges, the fertile Bekaa Valley. The soil is very fertile because of rich alluvial deposits. Along the coast, a dry bush known as *maquis* grows, while vineyards, and wheat, olives, and oranges are cultivated. Cedar has become a national symbol. This wood was used to build the Phoenician fleet and temples. Nowadays there are little over 400 cedars left, ranging in age between 200 and 800 years old. The war has had disastrous consequences, causing a loss of vegetation and soil erosion.

SOCIETY

Peoples: Mostly Arab. There are also small Armenian, European, Syrian and Kurdish minorities, and a large group of Palestinian refugees.
Religions: 55.3 per cent are Muslim, with the traditionally powerful Sunni (21.3 per cent) challenged by the militant Shi'a (34 per cent). Druze 7.1 per cent; Christian, 37.6 per cent (Maronites, 19 per cent; Catholics, 25.1 per cent and Orthodox Christians, 4.6 per cent); Orthodox, 11.7 per cent (Greek Orthodoxs, 6 per cent; Apostholic Armenians, 5.2 per cent) and Protestants, 0.5 per cent.
Languages: Arabic (official and predominant). French is widely spoken, Armenian and English are less common.
Political Parties: There are many political, political-military, political-religious factions and militias in Lebanon. The National Front is an alliance of groups from the left, especially Muslims. The Lebanese Phalange is the most important Maronite Christian party. The Progressive Socialist Party is primarily Druze. The political-military Shi'a organization Amal ('Hope') is pro-Syrian. Hizbullah ('party of God'), Shi'a guerrilla group, pro-Iranian.

THE STATE

Official Name: al-Jumhouriyah al-Lubnaniyah.
Administrative divisions: 6 governmental divisions.
Capital: Beirut (Bayrut) 2,012,000 people (1999).
Other cities: Tripoli (Trâblous) 206,500 people; Juniyah 77,400; Zahlah 74,300 (2000).
Government: Emile Lahoud, President since November 1998. Rafiq al-Hariri, Prime Minister since October 2000. Unicameral Legislature: Assembly of Representatives, with 128 members elected for a 4-year term by the religious communities.
National Holiday: November 22, Independence Day (1943); May 25, Resistance and Liberation Day (2000).
Armed Forces: 48,900 troops (1996). Syrian **occupation army:** 30,000 troops.
Other: Hizbullah 3,000.

Palestinian co-operation in military, security, cultural and economic matters, and it was ratified by the majority of the Lebanese parliament. The Israeli Government, the Phalangist party and the Lebanese Forces militia (both Christian and traditionally anti-Syrian), opposed the treaty as they believed that it gave Syria control over Lebanon's domestic matters.

31 Early in July, 6,000 soldiers of the Lebanese army took over the territories occupied by the PLO around the port of Sidon, in the south of the country. This offensive forced the PLO out of its main operations base for campaigns against Israel. On July 7, in spite of the apparent defeat of the PLO, Israel stated that it would not withdraw its forces from the security zone.

32 On February 16 1992 - eight days before peace talks between Arabs and Israelis were due to resume - an Israeli air raid killed Sheikh Abbas Mussawi, head of the Hizbullah (Iranian-backed Islamic group). Six days later, the Shi'a guerrillas suspended attacks against Israel as the result of an agreement between Hizbullah, Amal (another Islamic grouping) and the representatives of Syrian and Lebanese forces.

33 A general strike against the government's economic policy, accompanied by violent public demonstrations brought about the fall of the pro-Syrian Omar Karame government. President Elias Hrawi designated Rashid Al Sohl, a moderate Sunni, as the new head of government. He formed his cabinet with an equal number of Christians and Muslims. The August parliamentary elections were boycotted by the Christians. The new parliament included Hizbullah and Amal representatives. In October, Rafiq al-Hariri, a nationalized Saudi Arabian millionaire, was named prime minister.

34 In 1993, the World Bank granted a loan for reconstruction and education projects. The currency regained 10 per cent of its value and the country began receiving more foreign investment. The gap between rich and poor widened.

35 During 1995, government attention was focused on finding a solution to the armed conflict and the reconstruction of Beirut. In January, the UN Security Council decided to extend its intervention in the country. At the beginning of talks between Israel and Palestine in Oslo, Norway, Hizbullah and Southern Lebanon Army resumed their attacks in order to displace Israeli troops and defer negotiations with Syria.

36 On June 24, former Maronite leader Samir Geagea was sentenced to life imprisonment for the murders of his rival Dany Chamoun and his family. Political balance shifted toward the Muslims.

37 Prime Minister al-Hariri promoted the 'Horizon 2000' scheme to deal with Beirut's urban renovation and a constitutional reform which would extend the presidential term from 6 to 9 years to achieve the necessary stability to carry out his project. His goal of reinstating Lebanon as a central financial center in the Middle East made progress. A plan to reconstruct Beirut's business and residential area was delayed by the discovery of archaeological remains, which led to a debate about their rescue and effect on the costs of urban renovation.

38 The economic situation changed significantly from 1992 to 1996 with the reduction of annual inflation from 170 per cent to 10 per cent and in the 200-per-cent increase of foreign currency reserves.

39 In 1997, fighting was renewed between the Lebanese guerrillas and the Israeli army, which still occupied what Tel Aviv called a 'security zone', an area covering 850 square kilometers in southern Lebanon. Israel lost 39 soldiers that year, the highest number since 1985. The rise in the number of victims increased the pressure by Israeli public opinion on its government to put an end to the war.

40 On October 15, the National Assembly elected General Emile Lahoud president. Lahoud had the backing of the Syrian army. Municipal elections this year demonstrated a growth in support for Hizbullah. The Christians took 12 of the 24 seats in the council of Beirut. Salim al-Hoss was elected prime minister in December.

41 The change of government in Israel in July 1999 opened new perspectives for peace. Ehud Barak had promised a withdrawal from the south of Lebanon in his election campaign and in December offered a new plan to leave the Lebanese territory, but final negotiations remained pending on an agreement with Syria for the return of the Golan Heights.

42 Finally, in March 2000 the Israeli Government agreed it would withdraw from southern Lebanon before July that year, with or without a prior agreement with Lebanon or Syria. The Prime Minister initially welcomed the Israeli decision, but demanded that the withdrawal be made in the framework of a global peace agreement between both countries. President Lahoud stated that Israel

would not have the security it sought guaranteed until it returned the Golan Heights to Syria and resolved the problem of Palestinian refugees in southern Lebanon. The withdrawal of pro-Israeli militias brought worse confrontations with Hizbullah forces and led to al-Hoss criticizing Israeli reluctance to negotiate a global peace agreement in April 2000 during a trip to Damascus. A month later, under attack from Hizbullah forces, the Israeli troops abandoned the south of the country. The Lebanese Government declared May 25th an annual national holiday, the Day of Resistance and Liberation.

43 The Israeli withdrawal gave residents of the former occupied zone the chance to vote for the first time in nearly 30 years in the September parliamentary elections. During the electoral campaign, Christians and Muslims, Right and Left were joined by former premier Hariri, who protested against the role of the army in the national police and against the failure of the government to recover the economy. The multimillionaire and his allies won by a large margin, leaving President Lahoud (who had vehemently opposed Hariri) no other option than to appoint Hariri premier in October. Under the Lebanese constitution - which grants government posts according to religion in order to stem sectarian rivalry - the President, who belongs to the Maronite (Christian) church is chosen by Parliament for a six-year term and must consult parliament in the appointment of the new prime minister.

44 Lebanon began to pump water from the Hasbnani river - a tributary of the River Jordan - toward the town of Wazzani despite opposition from the Israeli Government which feared a reduced flow in the Jordan. Both town and river had been under Israeli control, and the pumping of water was celebrated by people and government alike as the 'liberation of the waters'.

45 In January 2002, Elie Hbaiqa was assassinated by a car bomb. The Lebanese Government accused Israel of the bombing, as Hbaiqa was a key witness in accusations raised in Brussels against Israeli premier Ariel Sharon - then defense minister - for the massacres in Sabra and Chatila.

46 The Syrian radar station in Lebanon was attacked by Israeli planes in April 2002, in revenge for a Hizbullah attack on three Israeli positions. There was increasing fear of a military escalation along the north Israeli-Lebanese frontier. ∎

Lesotho

Population:	2,076,000 (2002)
Land area:	30,350 SQ KM
Capital:	Maseru
Currency:	Loti
Language:	Sotho and English

Lesotho

For most African states, national unity is a task still to be accomplished. In some cases, however, the nation existed before the political state. Lesotho and Swaziland are both examples of this.

[2] The Zulu conquests, begun in 1818 by Shaka, affected a large number of Bantu-speaking nations, among them the North Sotho or Pedi who occupied a vast area in what became Transvaal. While some withdrew northwards, the head of the Bakwena tribe, Moshoeshoe, brought other Sotho tribes and groups of dissident Zulus together under his command, retreating with them towards the Drakensberg mountains. The lengthy war of resistance fought first against the Zulus, and then against the expansionist Boers, consolidated the bonds between these groups of diverse origin who gave Moshoeshoe the title of 'Great Leader of the Mountain', and called themselves Basothos.

[3] The Boers, the Dutch colonizers, tried to use the Basothos as labor. But they soon admitted defeat declaring that 'these savages prefer liberty to slavery'. Some Basothos refused to work on the Europeans' farms, saying 'God created animals to feed men and not men to feed animals'.

[4] Until 1867, Dutch colonization in South Africa was tenuous. Then diamonds were discovered. Soon afterwards gold was found, and along with its discovery the British came up from the Cape. In 1868, British missionaries persuaded the Basotho traditional leader Moshoeshoe, that only the 'protection' of the British Crown could save the people from subjection by the Boers. The territory became a protectorate, administered separately from South Africa even after the Boer War of 1899-1902, when the British took control of the whole country.

[5] Britain had promised the South African Government that Basotholand (Lesotho), Bechuanaland (Botswana) and Swaziland, which were all in similar situations, would eventually be integrated into South Africa. However, when the South African Union broke all ties with London in 1961, consolidating its racist policy of apartheid, the British

left those countries independent. In 1965, a constitution was promulgated in Basotholand and in 1966 the country proclaimed independence under the name of Lesotho.

[6] However, as an enclave within South Africa, Lesotho depended on the surrounding country as an outlet for its products of wheat, asbestos, cattle, and diamonds. The currency was the South African rand and South African companies controlled its economy and communications.

[7] Foreign trade was extremely unbalanced, with imports 10 times higher than exports. The difference was offset by money that the migrant workers sent home. At this time some 45 per cent of the labor force worked in the South African gold mines.

[8] The difficult economic situation enabled the opposition Congress Party to win a victory in the legislative elections of 1970. Prime Minister Leabua Jonathan engineered a coup, dissolved Parliament, and sent King Moshoeshoe into exile. He was allowed to return on the promise that he would refrain from any political activity.

[9] After the 1976 student uprising which took place in Soweto, South Africa, Lesotho opened its doors to thousands of young South African refugees despite the tremendous economic sacrifice this implied for such a poor country. When South Africa began its Bantustan policy, Lesotho, in compliance with the UN resolution condemning this new form

of apartheid, refused to recognize the puppet state in Transkei. In early 1977, South Africa closed the Lesotho border in retaliation. This economic aggression endangered the country's survival. Lesotho made dramatic appeals for international solidarity, requesting aid to resist the blockade.

[10] After Zimbabwean independence, Lesotho joined the economic integration project promoted by the Front Line states, strengthening relations with Mozambique.

[11] South Africa retaliated by supporting groups opposed to the Jonathan Government. This led the leader to seek help from the United Nations and the European Economic Community. The official Basotho National Party (BNP) also had to face the opposition of groups linked to the Basotho Congress Party (BCP), led by Ntsu Mokhele.

[12] Most of the incidents were really caused by South African military groups interested in preventing the anti-apartheid refugees of the African National Congress (ANC) from organizing in Maseru (see South Africa). The most important of these attacks took place in December 1982, when a South African military air raid killed 45 people, 12 of them children, in the outskirts of Maseru. During the attack, three ANC leaders were killed, but the other victims were all bystanders.

[13] In 1982, the Government imposed an emergency law allowing

the arrest of anyone suspected of illegal activities, without any previous judicial process. The army and the police were reinforced and a paramilitary group known as Koeko violently suppressed BCP supporters in the Drakensberg mountains.

[14] In March 1983, there was a border incident between Lesothan and South African troops, when saboteurs tried to enter the country to destroy the principal electric power plant. There was growing South African pressure to sign a non-aggression treaty with Pretoria, similar to the agreements that the apartheid regime had signed with Swaziland and Mozambique. The Prime Minister, Leabua Jonathan was against the treaty, but due to Lesotho's economic dependence on South Africa he was forced to be more flexible.

[15] Towards the end of 1984, the South African Government began to prevent products from getting to Lesotho, particularly weapons purchased in Europe, and to delay the remittances sent by almost 400,000 migrant workers. They also delayed plans to build a dam on the Sengu River, on the border between the two countries. South African pressures were directed at intimidating the Lesotho electorate and strengthening opposition to the BNP, the conservative Basotho Democratic Party (BDA) and the (ANC-aligned) BCP.

[16] But even these tough measures did not satisfy Pretoria and on January 20 1986, a military coup toppled Leabua Jonathan, and General Justin Lekhanya, head of Lesotho's paramilitary forces, led the Military Committee that replaced him.

[17] In 1988, workers residing in South Africa sent remittances totaling more than $350 million to Lesotho - 500 per cent of the total value of the country's exports.

[18] In March 1990, the military regime exiled King Moshoeshoe, accusing him of being a hindrance to the country's democratization program. His son Bereng Mohato Siisa replaced him as Letsie III. On April 30 1991, the armed forces went on strike for higher salaries, and a bloodless military coup deposed Lekhanya's government, setting up a Council chaired by Colonel Elias P Ramaema.

[19] The South African Government blocked remittances from migrant

workers in 1991. In May, a demonstration against foreign interference in the economy ended with 34 people dead and 425 arrests.

20 A new constitution designated the King head of state in 1993, without giving him either legal or executive powers. The July legislative elections gave all the seats to the BCP. In August the privatization of six state businesses was started with a loan from the IMF.

21 Erosion affected 58 per cent of the low lying soils. Two thirds of all farming land belonged to migrant laborers, but was worked by their wives and families. Plans were developed to make use of the water from the highlands - the main natural resource of the country - through a hydroelectric project which would change the course of several rivers to feed water to South Africa in return for electricity.

22 During 1994, the low salaries led to armed confrontations between rival military factions. The government plan to integrate the armed wing of the BCP into the army led to the kidnapping and murder of the finance minister by disgruntled soldiers.

23 The King dissolved the Government and Parliament. Protests outside the palace were put down by soldiers and police, with at least four people killed. The internal republican opposition and international pressure forced Letsie III to abdicate in favor of his father, King Moshoeshoe II, who was formally restored to the throne in January 1995.

24 During 1995, the tunnel under the mountains to supply water to the Vaal river valley in South Africa was completed.

25 In January 1996, the King died in a road accident. The Assembly designated his son Letsie III as his replacement.

26 The Government took up plans to use the water from the mountains again in 1998, and inaugurated the first stretch, including a dam, in April. The project had been suspended in 1997 following protests from the displaced local populations and accusations of corruption from the opposition. Non-governmental organizations accused the World Bank of violating the human rights of the communities and damaging the environment by funding the construction of hydroelectric dams in Lesotho.

27 In early 1998, the Catholic Church protested over the inclusion of courses in Islam, Hinduism, Buddhism and Judaism, in schools controlled by Catholics. The Government quashed their complaint saying the Constitution authorized religious diversity.

28 On March 8, hundreds of women demanded stiffer penalties for those guilty of rape. Official estimates pointed to an average of five women or girls being raped every day in Lesotho. A report from the Southern Africa Development Community stressed that in the majority of its 14 member nations - including Lesotho - the legislation on violence against women was not fulfilled. That same month, a new

political party, the Democratic Christian Party (DCP), was born of a split in the National Progress Party.

29 The May 1998 elections were won by the government, now called Lesotho Congress for Democracy (LCD). The opposition, which considered the elections fraudulent, organized demonstrations against the regime. According to electoral authorities, the opposition only won one of the 80 disputed seats. The Government asked South Africa for military assistance in September when a sector of the army joined the protests and the authorities considered the situation was out of control. The South African army calmed the situation through use of force. South Africa charged $1 million for the one-month intervention.

30 A 24-member body with government and opposition representatives was formed in December that year with the goal of organizing new elections and revising electoral legislation. South African troops, along with a small contingent from Botswana, pulled out of the territory by May 1999.

31 In mid-1999 a dozen foreign companies were accused of paying bribes to win the bids to build the largest infrastructure project in Africa. This was a joint Lesotho-South African venture to use the waters that come down from the Maloti mountains, flow into the Orange river and then into the Atlantic ocean. The project entails the construction of several hydroelectric dams, which would supply Lesotho with power and South Africa with water. Water is an important natural resource in Lesotho and South Africa has an industry with growing water needs.

32 It is estimated the project - backed by the World Bank - has displaced some 30,000 people who have lost their homes and lands. Although no full studies of environmental impact were made, the project planned for the affected population to 'keep their standard of living prior to the beginning of the works'. In fact, except for a few of the relocated, the situation worsened for the great majority, having been placed in plots without access to water. According to estimates the project will affect Lesotho's mountain water system and will endanger several animal and plant species in the region.

33 In February 2000 the King married a 23-year old science graduate. According to the king, she will be his only wife.

34 In April 2001, South African President, Thabo Mbeki, traveled to Lesotho to improve relations between the countries. He had to pay a fine of a cow - which the King of Lesotho has the right to impose on him since

Mbeki's mother was born in the kingdom - for not having attended the King's wedding party in 2000. The visit was not well received by the opposition due to the intervention of South African troops in 1998.

35 In March 2002, the King announced parliamentary elections which took place in May 25 and the Lesotho Congress for Democracy (LCD) obtained 54.9 per cent of the votes. ∎

PROFILE

ENVIRONMENT
This small country lies in the Drakensberg mountains in southern Africa, surrounded by South Africa. Landlocked and mountainous, its only fertile land is located in the west where corn, sorghum and wheat are grown. In the rest of the country cattle are raised. Except for small diamond deposits, there are no mineral resources. The problem of water scarcity is worsened by a hydroelectric project in the highlands that will divert water towards South Africa.

SOCIETY
Peoples: Ethnically homogeneous, the country is inhabited by the Basotho (Sotho) people (85 per cent) and a Zulu minority (15 per cent). There are small communities of Asian and European origin. **Religions:** Mainly Christian. Also traditional African beliefs. **Languages:** Sesotho (Southern Sotho) and English (officials), Zulu, Xhosa. **Political Parties:** Lesotho Congress for Democracy (LCD); Peoples' Congress; National Independent Party; the Lesotho Communist Party (LCP), founded in 1962; the Maremaltou Liberation Party, founded in 1962; the National Independence Party (NIP), Christian; and the People's Front for Democracy (PFD), which emerged from a split in the Lesotho Communist Party (LCP); the Kopanang of Basotho Party, Founded in 1992, leading campaigns for women's rights; Democratic Christian Party (DCP), resulting from a split in the National Progress Party (NPP). **Social Organizations:** The Lesotho General Workers' Union (LGWU), founded in 1954 is the only central labor organization. Representative Students' Council.

THE STATE
Official Name: Kingdom of Lesotho. **Administrative Divisions:** 10 Districts. **Capital:** Maseru 373,000 people (1999). **Other cities:** Maputsoe 32,800 people; Mafeteng 29,400 (2000). **Government:** King Letsie III, Chief of State since February 1996. Pakalitha Mosisili, Prime Minister since May 1998. Parliamentary Monarchy. Parliament has two chambers: the National Assembly has 120 members and the Senate 33 members. **National Holiday:** October 4, Independence Day (1966). **Armed Forces:** 2,000 troops (1996).

The Origins of Yoruba Culture

In the 5th century, iron working rural communities settled in the forest region of the coastal strip which stretches between Volta and Cameroon, establishing an organized agricultural economy with advanced and stable ways of life. Amongst the largest, and seemingly oldest, of these were the Yoruba communities, found in the Ife, Ilesha and Ekiti regions.

In around the 13th century, a movement outwards by the groups which imposed economic, political supremacy on the weaker communities led to the creation of the Yoruba kingdoms. But the idea of a 'kingdom' associated with the traditional African societies is far from the Western view of, for example, the 'kingdom of Louis XVI.'

THE YORUBA KINGDOMS OR STATES

The Yoruba kingdoms - south of modern-day Nigeria - owe their linguistic and cultural homogeneity to this ethnic group, recognizing their roots in these ancestors. The splendor accomplished by the Ife and Oyo kingdoms spread to the traditions of the other areas and overshadowed their own origins.

There is one belief structure which is based on the myth of Ife who created the world in the city of Ife-Ife, and another which attributes the creation to Oyo and says the Yoruba have their origins in a migration movement which came from the east. What is certain, however, is that the life of these kingdoms led to the spread of their institutions and practices amongst the local populations, and that the execution of complex functions - extensive agriculture, long-distance trade, tax systems, military expansion, citizen policies - were possible because of the well-planned and organized states.

Although each king aimed to leave his successor an even bigger kingdom, a policy of tolerance encouraged a certain level of interchange which led to the cultural enrichment of both the stronger communities and those they absorbed. It was this exchange which ultimately explained the heterogeneity of Yoruba civilization: a single culture expressed through differences.

THE ECONOMIC LIFE OF THE YORUBA KINGDOMS

The Yoruba states were generally of a modest size, sometimes covering only a single city and the surrounding villages. The kingdom of Oyo was one important exception, spreading over a vast area and acquiring imperial status in the 17th century. The more common kingdoms consisted of a compact town surrounding the compound of the kings and elders in an area contained by a wall marking the edge of the kingdom. Resources produced from agriculture, a certain amount of mining and craftwork were taken to local markets organized on alternate days in order to prevent competition between markets. However, luxury articles - like the gold paid in tax in the courts, marble, art objects, nuts and others- were the main object of long distance trade, like that with the Hausa states of the eastern zones, to the benefit of the richest strata of society -the kings and their courts, officials, merchants and professionals. In the more developed communities slave ownership was common as a result

of crimes or debts, and these people worked as domestic servants or agricultural laborers on the common lands.

There was no slave trade amongst the early traditional Yoruba societies. Historical reports tell of a slave trade which probably began in the 15th century under the kings of Benin, by which time this kingdom had become a powerful expansionist state.

THE YORUBA COSMOVISION

An ancient myth, revealing how mythical time is transposed over historical time, explains how the grandchildren of the mythical founder of Ife - the sacred city - spread out into the surrounding area establishing and naming the first generation of Yoruba states: Owu, Ketu, Benin, Illa, Dave, Popo and Oyo.

The Yoruba belief system is based on the idea of a superior entity made up of three divinities, Olofi, Oloddumare and Olorun. The first of these created the world, which was initially only populated by *orixas*, or saints. The power, or ache was later divided between the orixas, who from then on were empowered to intervene in human affairs and to represent people to Olofi through the mediation of the supreme judge or main messenger, Obbatala.

As in most of the languages of Black Africa, 'the power' is expressed amongst the Yoruba through the word 'ache' which means 'the force,' not in the sense of violence, but as a vital energy which creates a multiplicity of process and determines everything from physical and moral integrity to luck.

The Yoruba cosmovision is prevalent in all the cultural creations of this group of people. As is generally the case with peoples where every action is carried out, interpreted and lived as part of an organic belief system which is not precisely religious, this cosmology includes the idea that the order of the cosmic forces can be upset by immoral actions which have the effect of unbalancing and damaging humanity, nature and the perpetrators themselves.

The unity between nature and ethics in these cultures constitutes a cosmic determination, and along with it, a principle for the exercising of power, a condition for its beneficent application.

COMMUNITY LIFE

The community was of great value in the traditional Yoruba societies. It defined the conception of history -identified with the life of the group in continuous change - and time - conceived of as the social time, lived by the group, which transcends the time of the individual. It is, at the same time, the dimension where people can, and must, incessantly play out their fight against decadence and for the enrichment of their vital energy.

The Yoruba believed that throughout the history lived by the group a certain ache was accumulated incarnated in objects. These objects were sent from the ancestors down through the successive generations via their patriarchs or kings, who were intermediaries between the transcendental and visible worlds, as gifts from the orixas.

Although they were headed by kings, the communities were led by governing councils made up of men of varied standing, where the elders enjoyed their deserved dignity. The Yoruba, as in the majority of traditional African societies, were societies of public opinion, where the conduct of the authorities was monitored, spied on, and the violations of the principles which ruled the community life were always denounced through persistent verbal criticism and rumors which were so wearing that, in time, the subject of these was forced either to explain their actions or stand down.

Women also had a great deal of authority in other aspects of community life.

THE YORUBA RELIGION

The religion of the traditional Yoruba societies is characterized by the cult of God and a group of intermediary divinities, whose intervention and wills rule human life. The orixas were ancestors who accumulated power and knowledge over the forces of nature and humanity during their lifetimes, by virtue of which they one day changed from people into gods. Each one personifies certain forces of nature and is associated with a cult which obliges believers to offer food, sacrifices and prayers in order to escape their wrath and attract their favor.

The Yoruba gods and goddesses occasionally take possession of the faithful, and when this happens the god dances with his devotees in a friendly manner and sometimes speaks, offers advice or gives prophecies.

The most well known orixas include: Eleggua, the god who opens paths and is found behind the doors of Yoruba homes; Oggun, the inventor of the forge, god of the minerals and the mountains; Oxosi, the god of hunting; Xango, the god of fire and war; Oxun, the goddess of fresh water, love and all tenderness and Iemanya, the queen of the sea.

YORUBA ART

The art in the most ancient Yoruba communities was distinguished by its sculptures, metalwork and ceramics. Bas reliefs, woodworking, masks and human heads created by the lost-wax method were jealousy guarded as divine heirlooms. However, Yoruba art is definitely dominated by music. Though this has an autonomous and profane meaning as an art form, music is inseparably united to the Yoruba religious cults and liturgy.

The most characteristic musical tradition is the predominance of the drums and especially the presence of the *bata* (family) drums, an exclusive creation of the Yoruba people. This is an orchestra of three drums - *Iya* (the mother), *Itotele* and *Okongolo* played together by three drummers. For the Yoruba 'the batas speak' and each of their blows - be they of the sacred bata or the non sacred *bembe* - are inspired by legends attributed to the orixas.

The sound and symphonic integrity of the bata (the vegetable sound of the wood of the drums, the animal sound of the skins, and the mineral for the accompanying bells and rattles), along with human voices, obey a magical criteria through which the Yoruba evoke the integrity of the cosmic powers. ∎

Liberia

Population: 3,298,000 (2002)
Land area: 96,320 SQ KM
Capital: Monrovia
Currency: Liberian dollar
Language: English

Liberia

The present Liberia was formerly known as the Grain Coast, and was inhabited by 16 different ethnic groups. The Kru speakers lived in the southwest, and the Mande speaking peoples, including the Mandingo, lived in the east and northeast. After the arrival of the Portuguese, Mandingo traders and artisans played an important role as they spread throughout the territory, becoming the principal propagators of Islam.

2 Long before US President Abraham Lincoln freed the slaves in 1865, during the US civil war, emancipated blacks posed a social problem to US southern slaveholders. As a solution to the 'problem' some were 'repatriated' On the assumption that blacks would be at home in any part of Africa, it was planned to ship them to the British colony of Sierra Leone.

3 In 1821, the American Colonization Society purchased a portion of Sierra Leone and founded a city which was named Monrovia after James Monroe, President of the United States.

4 Only 20,000 US blacks returned to Africa. The native population distrusted these settlers whose language and religion were those of the colonizers. Supported by US Navy firepower, the newcomers settled on the coast and occupied the best lands. For a long time, they refused to mix with the 'junglemals', whom they considered 'savages'. Even today only 15 per cent of the population speak English and practice Christianity.

5 In 1841, the US Government approved a constitution for the African territory. It was written by Harvard academics, who called the country Liberia. Washington also appointed Liberia's first African governor: Joseph J Roberts. In July 1847, a Liberian Congress representing only the repatriates from the US, proclaimed independence. Roberts was appointed President and the Harvard-made constitution was kept, along with a flag which resembled that of the United States.

6 The emblem on the Liberian coat of arms reads: 'Love of liberty brought us here'. However, independence brought little freedom for the original

population. For a long time, only landowners were able to vote. Today, the 45,000 descendants of the former US slaves form the core of the local ruling class and are closely linked with transnational capital. One of the principal exports, rubber, is controlled by Firestone and Goodrich under 99-year concessions granted in 1926. The same is true of oil, iron ore and diamonds. Resistance to this situation has been suppressed on several occasions by US Marine interventions to 'defend democracy'.

7 The discovery of extensive mineral deposits, and the use of the Liberian flag by US ships, heralded a period of economic growth beginning in 1960. This was instantly dubbed an 'economic miracle', but this so-called miracle only reached the American-Liberian sector of the population, who secured significant increases in income during this period.

8 The political establishment was shaken in 1979, when the increase in the price of rice triggered demonstrations and unrest. A year later, Sergeant Samuel Doe overthrew the regime of William Tolbert, who was executed, along with other members of his government. These disturbances led to the suspension of the Constitution and the

banning of all political parties. In 1980, the beginning of a democratization process was announced, followed by the signing of the first agreement with the International Monetary Fund, that included a strong cut in public spending and the privatization of state-owned companies.

9 Falling exports, increasing unemployment, the reduction of salaries in both public and private sectors, and spiraling foreign debt threw the country into a crisis of substantial proportions.

10 Popular discontent increased. Between 1980 and 1989 Doe's administration uncovered many new anti-government conspiracies.

11 Elections were held in 1985. With any viable political opposition banned, and accusations of fraud and imprisonment of opposition leaders abounding, Doe obtained 50.9 per cent of the vote. The Liberian People's Party (LPP) and United People's Party (UPP), which represented the major opposition forces, were not allowed to participate.

12 In 1987, most of the funding obtained by the Government came directly from Washington. The US maintained valuable interests in Liberia, such as $450 million in capital goods, military bases, a radio station broadcasting the Voice of America for the region, as well as a

communications base for all US diplomatic services in Africa.

13 In June that year, the victory of the National Patriotic Front of Liberia (NPFL), led by Charles Taylor, seemed imminent. But in July, when the battle for Monrovia started, the rebel front split and an Independent Patriotic Front of Liberia (INPFL) was formed, led by Prince Johnson.

14 In September 1990, President Samuel Doe was murdered by Johnson's troops. In the confusion that ensued, several interim Presidents were announced simultaneously: Johnson, Taylor, Amos Sawyer and Raleigh Seekie, former head of Doe's presidential guard.

15 In November, Sawyer (LPP) formed a provisional government, supported by Côte d'Ivoire, Gambia, Nigeria, Burkina Faso and Togo. A peace force was formed, composed of 10,000 troops from Nigeria, 1,000 from Ghana and 600 from Guinea.

16 The United Liberation Movement for Democracy in Liberia (ULIMO) - formed in 1991 with followers of the former government of Doe - split in November 1992. Alhaji Kromah, accused of being aligned with Muslim groups and the Government of Libya, led the faction based in the liberian city of Tubmanburg (provincial capital). Raleigh Seekie led the faction in Sierra Leone.

17 US support to a more active role of the UN in the conflict gave the Security Council green light to demand a ceasefire and decree a blockade of weapons and other supplies. The standoff gave way to the signing of a peace agreement, on July 17 1993, in Geneva. The two main armed groups and the provisional Sawyer Government agreed a ceasefire in seven months' time and general elections.

18 In August, according to the schedule agreed in Geneva, was agreed the formation of the Council of State, a transitional body made up of representatives from the NPFL, ULIMO and the Sawyer administration.

19 In March 1994, the Council of State took office, but the new government's formation was delayed until May, due to disagreements between the NPFL, ULIMO and Sawyer's representatives. Meanwhile, battles

2000

53%

2000

PER CAPITA

US$ 697

DEMOGRAPHY

Population: 3,298,000 (2002)
Annual growth: 1.9 % (1985-2000)
Estimates for year 2015: 5,550,000 (2000)
Annual growth to year 2015: 4.3 % (2000)
Urban population: 44.9 % (2000)
Urban growth: 4.1 % (2000)
Children per woman: 6.8 (2000)

HEALTH

Life expectancy at birth: 56 years (2000-2005)
male: 55 years (2000-2005)
female: 57 years (2000-2005)
Infant mortality: 157 per 1,000 (2000)
Under-5 child mortality: 235 per 1,000 (2000)
Daily calorie supply: 2,089 per capita (1999)
2 doctors per 100,000 people (1997)

EDUCATION

Literacy: 53 % (2000)
male: 70 % (2000)
female: 37 % (2000)
School enrolment (net):
Primary total: 34 % (1994/2000)
male: 43 % (1995/99)
female: 31 % (1995/99)
Secondary (gross):
male: 31 % (1995/97)
female: 12 % (1995/97)
Tertiary (gross): 7 % (1998)
Primary school teachers: one for every 39 pupils (1998)

COMMUNICATIONS

12 newspapers (1996), 274 radios (1997), 25 TV sets (2000) and 2 main telephone lines (2000) per 1,000 people

ECONOMY

Currency: 1.0 Liberian dollars = $ 1 (03/2002)
Cereal imports: 130,669 metric tons (2000)
Fertilizer use: 0 kg per ha (1999)
External debt: $ 2,032 million (2000); $ 697 per capita (2000)

---

between rival armed groups and their skirmishes with the recently deployed peace forces of the Economic Community of Western African States (Ecomog) continued. Negotiations between the different parties continued in 1995, the composition of the Council of State was widened (Charles Taylor was incorporated), and a new Government was formed.

[20] The civil war was resumed in 1996 with violent combats, particularly in Monrovia. In September, Ruth Perry became the new head of the Council of State,

with the support of Ecomog. The war had seriously affected essential services.

[21] In November, peace forces began the disarmament of rival factions. The war had caused 200,000 dead; almost a million Liberians, out of a total population of 2.4 million, had been displaced from their homes or were living as refugees in neighboring countries.

[22] In July 1997, Charles Taylor won the Presidential and Parliamentary elections with 75.3 per cent of the vote. A month later he took office as President. Taylor's

National Patriotic Party obtained 21 of the 26 seats in the Senate and 49 of the 64 seats in the Chamber of Representatives.

[23] In March 1998, some 480,000 Liberian refugees, dispersed in several African countries, began to register for voluntary repatriation. However, the plan ran a serious risk of not being implemented because of the lack of funds promised by donor organizations. The aid also took into account some 220,000 internally displaced Liberians.

[24] Government relations with the opposition and the mass media were strained due to the closing of two radio stations in March 2000. After closing Veritas station, the Government allowed it to reopen in March 2000, but at the same time closed Star Radio, because it had broadcast statements criticizing Taylor by diplomats from the US and other countries.

[25] According to a report by Amnesty International, human rights abuses abounded in Liberia in 2001. In March, 40 university students, who had demonstrated peacefully within university grounds against the Government, were arbitrarily detained, tortured and raped by special security forces. Many students were forced to take refuge abroad.

[26] The conflict between the Government and the rebel movement Liberians United for Reconciliation and Democracy (LURD) caused the displacement of approximately 30,000 people to camps in other areas. The rebel movement, accused by President Taylor of being supported by Guinea, was trying to take control of the north of the country.

[27] According to reports by the UN High Commissioner for Refugees (UNHCR) and British aid agency Save the Children, girls and teenagers in the refugee camps of Liberia, Guinea and Sierra Leone were victims of sexual abuse by 67 officials belonging to more than 40 humanitarian organizations, including the UN, several national and international aid organizations as well as officials of the respective governments. The officials traded money or food for sex.

[28] In September, Taylor decided to reopen the borders with Guinea

PROFILE

ENVIRONMENT

The country is divided into three geographic regions: the coastal plain contains most of the population, and is low and swampy; the central plateau, crossed by numerous valleys and covered by dense tropical forests; and the mountainous inland along the border with Guinea. In the fertile coastal areas, rice, coffee, sugarcane, cocoa and palm oil are produced. American companies own large rubber plantations. Liberia is also the leading African iron-ore producer. War, the loss of biodiversity and erosion are the main threats to the environment.

SOCIETY

Peoples: Most Liberians belong to the Mende, Kwa and Vai groups, which are split into nearly 30 ethnic sub groups. Of these, the most significant are the Mandingo, Kpelle, Mendo, Kru, Gola and Bassa (the Vai are renowned for having created one of the few African written languages). The descendants of 'repatriated' US and Caribbean slaves control business and politics, though they constitute only 5 per cent of the population.
Religions: The majority profess traditional African religions. About 15 per cent are Muslim, and slightly fewer Christian. The State is officially Christian.
Languages: English (official), although it is only spoken by 15 per cent of the population. The rest speak African languages (some 30 are spoken throughout the country).
Political Parties: National Patriotic Party (NPP) Unity Paty; All Liberia Coalition Party; Alliance of Political Parties; United People's Party (UPP); Liberian People's Party (LPP); United Liberation Movement for Democracy in Liberia (ULIMO); Liberia Peace Council (LNC); Ulimo-J and Ulimo-K (both created after the division of the United Liberian Independence Movement).
Social organizations: Federation of Liberian Trade Unions; National Students Union of Liberia.

THE STATE

Official Name: Republic of Liberia.
Administrative divisions: 13 Counties.
Capital: Monrovia 479,000 people (1999).
Other cities: Buchanan 26,800 people; Yekepa 22,100; Harbel 17,300; Gbarnga 13,600 (2000).
Government: Charles Ghankay Taylor, President since August 1997. Bicameral Legislature: the House of Representatives with 64 members elected every six years, and the Senate integrated by 26 members elected every nine years.
National Holiday: July 26, Independence Day (1847).
Armed Forces: 3,000 (1996).

and Sierra Leone. These had been closed as a result of accusations by the neighboring governments that Liberia supported rebel movements within their borders. The UN had sanctioned Liberia because it had supported Sierra Leone's rebel forces, banning the export of diamonds and limiting officials' trips for one year.

[29] In February 2002, LURD forces entered the capital. They left Monrovia after clashes with security forces which left dozens of dead. Taylor declared a 'state of national emergency' and, in April, put a ban on any political meeting in the country until the rebels had been defeated, alleging that this was necessary to avoid any insurrection. ∎

Libya

Population: 5,529,000 (2002)
Land area: 1,759,540 SQ KM
Capital: Tripoli (Tarabulus)
Currency: Dinar
Language: Arabic

Libiya

The Socialist People's Libyan Arab Jamahiriya (known as Libya) has always been torn between the different political and economic centers of North Africa. Bordering pharaonic Egypt, Libya shared its culture and two Libyan dynasties ruled Egypt between the 10th and 8th centuries BC. However such influences did not lead to a unified state. The Carthaginian and Roman empires on the western border further stressed this division. After the Arab conquest in the 7th century, Tunisia, Morocco and Egypt became the new power centers.

[2] The development of maritime trade and the ensuing piracy turned Tripoli into one of the major Mediterranean ports, bringing European involvement which caused further intervention by the Turkish Sultan. In 1551, Suleiman the Magnificent annexed the region to the Ottoman Empire. A weakened central authority gave increasing autonomy to the governors precipitating independence movements. The beginning of the 19th century saw piracy again on Libya's shores; this was used as a pretext for US military intervention and in 1804 US forces attacked Tripoli.

[3] In 1837, Muhammad al-Sanussi founded a clandestine Muslim brotherhood (the Sanussi religious sect) which promoted resistance to Turkish domination, though the Italians really posed a greater threat. With the decline of the Ottoman Empire, Italy declared war on Turkey in 1911 and seized the Libyan coast, the northernmost Turkish possession in Africa. With the outbreak of World War I, the Italian presence was confined to Tripoli and Homs (Al-Khums) while the rest of the territory remained autonomous. At the end of the War Italy attempted to recover control of the territory but faced resistance for 20 years by Sidi Omar al-Mukhtar's forces. In 1931, al-Mukhtar was captured and executed and the Italians formally annexed the territory.

[4] From Egypt and Tunisia, the Sanussi brotherhood remained active and co-operated with the Allies in World War II. Muhammad Idris al-Sanussi, leader of the brotherhood, was recognized as

Emir of Cyrenaica by the British. At the end of the conflict, the country was divided into an British zone (Tripolitania and Cyrenaica) and a French (Fezzan) governed from Chad. In 1949, a UN resolution restored legitimate union to the region and established the independent nation of Libya, with Idris al-Sanussi as leader for his religious authority.

[5] Idris consolidated his position with support from the powerful Turkish-Libyan families, military advisers from the US and Britain and transnational oil companies. In 1960, foreigners settled in the country, as the oil began to flow in great quantities.

[6] In 1966, Muammar al-Khaddafi, the son of Bedouin nomads, founded the Union of Free Officials in London, where he was studying. He returned to Libya and on September 1 1969 he led an insurrection in Sabha overthrowing the King.

[7] Khaddafi's Revolutionary Council proclaimed itself Muslim, Nasserist and socialist, beginning to eliminate all US and British military bases in Libya, and imposing severe limitations on transnationals operating in the country. The production of petroleum and its derivatives was placed under state control but the Government kept

some ties with the foreign companies.

[8] Khaddafi began an ambitious modernization program, with special emphasis on agricultural development. Each rural family was allotted 10 hectares of land, a tractor, a house, tools, and irrigation facilities. Over 1,500 artesian wells were drilled and two million hectares of desert were irrigated and turned into fertile farmland.

[9] Rapid growth meant that immigrant workers and experienced technicians from other Arab countries were needed. In 1973 following publication of Khaddafi's Green Book a complex structure of popular participation was created through people's committees and a People's General Congress.

[10] In the cities, a social security system was created, with free medical assistance and family allowances to encourage large families. Industrial workers were granted 25 per cent participation in the profits of the companies. Industrial investment was 11 times greater than during the monarchy and agricultural investment was 30 times greater. This massive oil-financed reform transformed Libya into the North African Nation with the highest per-capita income on the continent, at $4,000 a year.

[11] In 1977, the country changed its name to the Socialist People's Libyan Arab Jamahiriya (meaning mass state in Arabic). But while Khaddafi achieved ample positive results internally, external relations were dismal. Attempts to unite with Syria and Egypt met with failure, and overtures towards Tunisia came to nothing. Khaddafi became the main critic of the diplomatic rapprochement between Egypt and Israel; he clashed with the Saudi monarchy and the Emirates, and maintained his long-standing antagonism with King Hassan of Morocco. In OPEC, Libya opposed the moderate stand of Saudi Arabia and the Emirates on oil prices, and firmly resisted the pressures and manoeuvres of transnational corporations.

[12] From 1980, Libya became diplomatically active in Sub-Saharan Africa and Latin America. The Government supported the Polisario Front in Western Sahara and participated directly in the civil war in Chad, defending the Transitional Government of National Union, led by Goukouni Oueddei.

[13] US President Reagan undertook a huge international campaign to link the Libyan leader with world terrorism. In August 1981 in the Gulf of Sidra, two Libyan planes were shot down by the US Sixth Fleet. Khaddafi skillfully avoided any violent response to the provocation, winning the sympathy of the conservative Arab regimes which had until then been hostile to his government.

[14] In 1983 Libya attempted to resume friendly relations with Morocco, a move which met with success in August 1984 when an agreement was signed. Most North African nations were surprised at the pact, for Moroccans and Libyans held opposite views on practically all political issues. However, the rapprochement could be regarded as a consequence of increasing cooperation between the Algerian, Tunisian and Mauritanian governments. Moreover, Morocco aimed at neutralizing Libyan support of the Polisario Front, while Libya sought to cut off Moroccan aid to Habre's regime in Chad.

[15] The US accused Libya of terrorism and, in 1986, in addition to imposing an economic blockade, bombed Tripoli and Benghazi, causing dozens of victims among the civilian population. Later it was revealed the real target had been Khaddafi.

[16] In November 1991, US and British courts charged the Libyan Government with two terrorist attacks in 1988 against commercial flights: one over Lockerbie, Scotland, involving a Pan Am airliner, which left 270 dead, 189 of whom were Americans. The second was over Nigeria, against a UTA plane, with 170 victims. Interpol issued an international detention warrant against two Libyan agents accused of both attacks. In January 1992, Libya announced it was willing to cooperate with the UN in investigating both attacks.

[17] Khaddafi rejected an extradition request from by the UN, and proposed, unsuccessfully, a trial in Tripoli. This hardened the UN's position. It demanded again the extradition of the accused and urged Khadaffi to renounce 'terrorism' before April 15 1992. After that day, the EU and the seven other industrialized countries adopted economic sanctions, and Khaddafi appealed - unsuccessfully - before the International Court of Justice. In 1994, the UN intensified the embargo.

[18] The isolation, however, did not impede the growth of the private sector nor of foreign investments, mainly in projects to tap oil resources. One section of the water pipeline designed to supply water to remote desert communities was re-opened in 1996.

[19] The Movement of Non-Aligned Countries and the Organization of African Unity supported in 1998 a Libyan request to try the two suspects of the Lockerbie bombing in a neutral country. After long multilateral negotiations, the UK and the US proposed that the two accused be tried in The Hague by Scottish judges under Scottish law. The proposal was finally accepted in March 1999, and in April, the UN Security Council lifted the sanctions in force since 1992. In September, more than 20 African and Arab leaders gathered in Tripoli to commemorate the 30th anniversary of the Libyan revolution. Fifteen years after having severed diplomatic relations, London sent its ambassador to Tripoli in December 1999.

[20] Libya took advantage of this to launch a diplomatic offensive in the region, offering itself as mediator in the Sudan conflict and resuming relations with Chad. In March 2000, Washington sent a high level delegation to study the lifting of obstacles to investments and trips to Libya, banned since 1981.

[21] According to the UN Development Program's 2001 report, Libya leads the human development index in Africa, mainly because of its oil wealth. Several incidents of violence took place between Libyans and illegal immigrants in recent years. In September 2000, the clashes left 50 dead. There are currently 1,000,000 immigrants from other parts of the continent.

[22] After the foiled coup in Central African Republic (CAR), in May 2001, the Khaddafi Government decided to deploy troops in that country, in order to protect President Patassé. In November, Patassé once again requested Libya's help. Once peace was restored, CAR demanded the withdrawal of Libyan soldiers for fear of a prolonged stay by the foreign army.

[23] The US extended sanctions imposed on Libya and Iran for five more years in August 2001, even though it lacked European support. It argued that the sanctions were aimed at stopping financing of terrorist groups in those countries. Any company that invested more than $20 million in the oil industry or set up in those countries would be sanctioned by Washington.

[24] In early 2001, the Scottish court absolved one of the Lockerbie suspects: Al Amin Khalifa Fhimah. The other, Abdelbaset al-Megrahi was sentenced to life imprisonment. In January 2002, Tripoli sought an appeal, but it was denied. Khaddafi accused the court of being under the influence of Washington and London and of lacking sufficient evidence. Meanwhile, a member of the Union of Arab Lawyers also announced his disagreement with the sentence, alleging it was a political pact which sought to condemn the Libyan political system.

[25] The Government had accused six Bulgarian and one Palestinian doctor of 'deliberately' infecting 400 children with HIV in 1999, as part of a conspiracy led by agencies - such as the CIA - against Libyan security. However no substantial evidence was found. By April 2002, Libyan justice had still not proved the doctors' involvement, nor decided whether the punishment, if they were guilty, should be life imprisonment. ∎

PROFILE

ENVIRONMENT

Most of the country is covered by desert. The only fertile lands are located along the temperate Mediterranean coast, where most of the population live. There are no perennial rivers and rain is scarce. The country has significant oil deposits. Water is scarce and most of it is pumped from underground deposits. One of the largest hydraulics development projects in the world has partially solved this problem. Atmospheric pollution is caused by gases from oil refining. Desertification and erosion are growing.

SOCIETY

Peoples: Arabs and Berbers account for 79 per cent of the population. There are Tunisian, Egyptian, Greek and Italian and Chadian minorities (21 per cent).
Religions: Islam (official), mainly Sunni. There is a small Christian minority.
Languages: Arabic (official); regional variations of Berber; languages of the immigrant communities; Italian and English.
Political Parties: Banned. According to Khaddafi's principles in his 'Green Book', Libya is headed toward a direct democracy, in which there are no intermediaries. The new political organization is structured on the Basic People's Congresses, directly elected, which elect the members of the 46 People's Congresses. These, in turn, choose those who will make up the General People's Congress, the supreme body. However, the Socialist Party of Libya is the party in power.
Social Organizations: There are mass organizations of workers, peasants, students and women.

THE STATE

Official Name: Jamahiriya Al-Arabiya Al-Libiya Al-Shabiya Al-Ishtirakiya Al-Uzma. (The Great Socialist People's Libyan Arab Jamahiriya)
Administrative divisions: 3 provinces, 10 counties and 1,500 communes.
Capital: Tripoli (Tarabulus) 1,773,000 people (1999).
Other cities: Benghazi 1,041,000 people; Misratah 179,100; az-Zawiyah 175,100 (2000).
Government: Muammar Khaddafi, leader of the Revolution and commander-in-chief of the People's Armed Forces, is the Head of State, since September 1969. He named Zintani Muhammad az-Zintani, Secretary of the General People's Congress in 1992 and Mubarak al-Shamikh as the Secretary of the People's Committee in 2000.
Unicameral Legislature: the General People's Congress is the highest Government body, with 2,700 representatives of the People's Congresses.
National Holiday: September 1, Revolution Day (1969).
Armed Forces: 65,000 actives (1996); 40,000 reservists, popular militia (1993). **Other:** Revolutionary Guards 3,000.

Liechtenstein

Population: 33,000 (2002)
Land area: 160 SQ KM
Capital: Vaduz
Currency: Swiss franc
Language: German

Liechtenstein

Research shows that the territory of the present principality of Liechtenstein (between Switzerland and Austria, under Lake Constance) was inhabited by neolithic times. The Romansch settled there in 800 BC, remaining until the Romans arrived in 15 BC. Excavations in Schaanwald and Nendeln revealed a Roman road crossing the country North to South. The Roman fortifications of Schaan were of special importance, as they protected the Alpine road against German incursions.

[2] In 4 AD, Saint Luke brought Christianity to the province of Churrhaetia. A century later, the Germans invaded the country and progressively eliminated the Romans. Years later, the region of the present principality then known as Retia Inferior passed into the hands of the Germanic Dukedom. This region was divided into two feudal estates of Vaduz and Schellenberg, ruled by the Counts of Werdenberg-Vaduz, the Barons of Brandis, the Counts of Sulz and the Counts of Hohenems. Prince Johann Adam of Liechtenstein, founder of the current principality, bought the Schellenberg estate in

1699 and that of Vaduz in 1712. By combining hereditary rights from these two estates - both dependencies of the Germanic authorities - he gained a seat and a vote in the Imperial Council of Princes.

[3] However, the Principality of Liechtenstein was really established on January 23 1719. That day, Emperor Charles VI of Germany converted the two estates of Vaduz and Schellenberg into a 'principality of the empire', naming it Liechtenstein for his servant Anton Florian de Liechtenstein.

[4] In 1806 Liechtenstein was included by Napoleon in the Renana Confederation, a league of 16 states belonging to the German Empire. Napoleon guaranteed them independence and they recognized him as a protector.

[5] The principality entered the Germanic Confederation under the Vienna Congress in 1815 and remained there until this was dissolved in 1866, breaking the last juridical links with Germany. Liechtenstein has had no army since 1868. Between 1852 and 1918 (end of the First World War) there was a tariff agreement between the principality and the Austro-Hungarian monarchy.

[6] With the modern period princes, beginning with the reign of Johann (1858-1929), Liechtenstein saw prosperity in all sectors. Modern development of the country really began with the Constitution in 1862 and was reinforced by the democratic-liberal magna carta of 1921, still in place today. Under Johann's leadership, Liechtenstein started to turn to Switzerland, with a tariff agreement signed in 1923. Since 1924, the Swiss franc has been legal currency in the nation.

[7] Prince Francis Joseph II was the first prince to establish his permanent residence in Liechtenstein. The monarch died on November 13 1989

after 51 years in power, and his eldest son Hans-Adam II took over from him.

[8] The neutrality of his country during the Second World War saved the noteworthy collection of works of art that the family held in its Vienna palace. Decades later, Liechtenstein - which is the only independent principality of the old Austro-Hungarian Empire - began to integrate with the rest of the continent and the world. The country entered the Council of Europe in 1978, the United Nations in 1990, the European Free Trade Area (EFTA) in 1991 and the European Economic Zone in 1995.

[9] The economy of the principality is tightly related to that of Switzerland, with no customs controls between the two countries. The combination of low tax levels, easy procedures and good protection from banking secrecy have made Liechtenstein a controversial fiscal paradise. It became involved in a money laundering scandal in the 1990s. New fiscal legislation allowed the principality to come off the Group's black list.

[10] Despite the new controls, Liechtenstein's European neighbors and international organizations have been pressing Prince Hans-Adam to modify legislation even further, as they believe the State still maintains openings for money laundering and tax evasion. The bankers - including the Prince himself, head of the LGT Bank, the biggest in Liechtenstein - said that further banking reform would endanger most of the $70.3 billion held in the principality.

[11] Hans-Adam does not control elected government nor fulfillment of the regulations, so he has threatened to move to Austria and take his family assets abroad, in case changes in tax regulations imposed from abroad should threaten his business. The royal family of Liechtenstein has the largest inherited fortune in Europe, followed by Luxembourg and Britain.

[12] Following the traditional way of life, many Liechtensteiners raise crops or herd cows. About half work in factories and make a wide variety of products, from computer components to sausage skins to dentures. Over 50 per cent of the country's workforce are foreigners who commute each day from Austria and Switzerland. ∎

PROFILE

ENVIRONMENT

This small principality lies between Switzerland and Austria, in the Rhine valley. Wheat, oats, rye, corn, grapes and fruit are produced. 38 per cent of the land is pasture. In recent years, the principality has been transformed into a highly industrialized country, producing textiles, pharmaceutical products, precision instruments and refrigerators among other items.

SOCIETY

Peoples: German 95 per cent; Italian and other 5 per cent. **Religions:** Catholic 80 per cent; Protestant 6.9 per cent; other 5.6 per cent. **Languages:** German (official). **Political Parties:** The Progressive Citizens Party (FBP); Patriotic Union (VU); Free List, green. **Social Organizations:** The Trades Union Association (artisans and traders), and the Agricultural Union.

THE STATE

Official Name: Fürstentum Liechtenstein. **Administrative divisions:** 11 communes. **Capital:** Vaduz 5,085 people (1996). **Other cities:** Schaan 5,143; Balzers 3,752; Triesen 3,586 (1995). **Government:** Liechtenstein is a constitutional monarchy. Prince Hans-Adam II, Head of State since November 13 1989. Otmar Hasler, Head of Government since April 2001. Government functions are carried out by a FBP and VU coalition. Single-chamber legislature: Parliament with 25 members elected every four years. **Diplomacy:** A member of the European Council, Liechtenstein has a customs and monetary alliance with Switzerland, which is its representative abroad. **National holiday:** February 14.

DEMOGRAPHY

Estimates for year 2015: 37,000 (2000)

HEALTH

Infant mortality: 10 per 1,000 (2000)
Under-5 child mortality: 11 per 1,000 (2000)

Lithuania

Population:	3,682,000 (2002)
Land area:	64,800 SQ KM
Capital:	Vilnius
Currency:	Lit
Language:	Lithuanian

Lietuva

L ithuanians have lived along the shores of the Baltic Sea since long before the Christian era. Protected by the forests, Lithuanian tribes fiercely resisted German efforts to subdue them in the 13th century, and united under the leadership of Mindaugas, who was crowned king by Pope Innocent IV in 1253.

[2] In the 14th century, Lithuania began its eastward and southern expansion, going into Belarusian lands. Gediminas built the Grand Duchy of Lithuania, which extended from the Baltic Sea to the Black Sea, with its capital at Vilnius. In 1386, Jagiello, Gediminas' grandson, married the Queen of Poland, thus uniting the two kingdoms.

[3] Lithuania withstood a series of attacks from the Teutonic Order, which continued to combat the Lithuanian-Polish union - despite the fact that the latter were Christian - until the Battle of Tannenberg in 1410, in which they suffered a crushing defeat. This defeat was a harsh blow to German supremacy in the Baltic region. A new pact between Lithuania and Poland, signed in 1413, reaffirmed the principle of union while respecting the autonomy of both States.

[4] With the coronation of Ivan III of Muscovy as the sovereign of all Russia, a new and greater threat emerged for historic Lithuania. Nevertheless, the Lithuanian-Polish union reached its peak in the 16th century, when it was unrivalled in Europe as a political system (see Poland), only to fall in the 17th century, in the course of a series of devastating wars with Sweden, Russia and Turkey and the peasant rebellions within.

[5] In the 1772 and 1793 partitions of Poland among Russia, Prussia and Austria, Russia kept only Belarus. But the Polish state disappeared in 1795, and all of Lithuania was in Russian hands by 1815. The Congress of Vienna granted the Russian Emperor the additional titles of King of Poland and Grand Prince of Lithuania.

[6] Lithuanians were harshly suppressed by the Russians. The czarist regime treated Lithuania as though it were a part of Russia, calling it the Northwest Territory after 1832. Between 1864 and 1905,

Russification extended to all aspects of life: books printed in Lithuanian had to use the Cyrillic alphabet, and Catholics were persecuted.

[7] With the Revolution of 1905, the peoples of the Russian Empire were granted freedom of speech. A congress with some 2,000 delegates called for the demarcation of Lithuania's borders, territorial autonomy and the election of a parliament by democratic means.

[8] During World War I, Germany occupied a major part of Lithuania. In 1915, a congress - authorized by the occupying Germans - elected the 20-member Council of Lithuania. The 214 delegates to the congress called for the creation of an independent Lithuanian state within its 'ethnic borders' and with Vilnius as its capital. On February 16 1918, the Council declared Lithuania's independence and terminated all political ties with other nations.

[9] In 1919, the Red Army entered Vilnius and formed a communist government, but the Allied powers forced it to withdraw. The new head of the Polish State, Josef Pilsudski, tried to re-establish the former union, but failed due to the resistance of the Lithuanians, Ukrainians and Belarusians. In the end, the League of Nations and the European powers agreed to the separation of Poland and Lithuania in 1923, but Lithuania refused to recognize the line of demarcation (with Poland) which had been established by these powers.

[10] In 1926, Lithuania and the Soviet Union signed a non-aggression treaty. A treaty of goodwill and cooperation was signed in Geneva in 1934 by

Lithuania, Latvia and Estonia. As of 1938, relations with Warsaw became tense, due to Poland's claim of sovereignty over Vilnius. Tension increased when a group of Nazis came to power in Klaipeda; they demanded the ceding of that city, which meant the loss of Lithuania's only port on the Baltic.

[11] In September 1939, a secret German-Soviet non-aggression treaty brought Lithuania within the USSR's sphere of influence. In October, a mutual assistance treaty was signed in Moscow; according to its terms, Lithuania was forced to accept the installation of Soviet garrisons and air bases on its soil. In 1940, the Soviet Army occupied Lithuania and a number of local political leaders were arrested and deported, while others fled toward Western Europe.

[12] The new Prime Minister, Justas Paleckis, and Parliament asked to be admitted to the USSR, a request which was immediately granted by the Supreme Soviet. Lithuania thereby became a constituent republic of the USSR in August 1940. After German occupation in 1941, the Baltic Sates and Belarus became the German province of Ostland.

[13] During German occupation, 190,000 Jews were sent to concentration camps. A hundred thousand residents of Vilnius - a third of that city's population, most of them Jews - were killed. Vilnius was known as the 'Jerusalem of Lithuania' and had been considered to be one of the most important centers of Jewish culture in the world. Many non-Jewish Lithuanians throughout the rest of the country were killed, and tens of thousands

of young people were sent to Germany to work.

[14] Vilnius was re-conquered by the Red Army in 1944. Lithuania was once again occupied by the Soviets and a new period of Sovietization began. This included religious persecution and wide-scale deportations to northern Russia and Siberia, amid the forced collectivization of agriculture.

[15] Religious persecution continued even after Stalin's death in 1953. Thus the resistance of the Catholic Church became identified with the nationalist movement. In 1972, the 'Lithuanian Catholic Church Chronicle' (banned by the Government) was published by the Lithuanian Movement for Human Rights. That year, a young man set fire to himself; his funeral triggered violent clashes in which 15 people were killed and 3,000 were arrested.

[16] With the democratization process initiated by Mikhail Gorbachev in the USSR, Lithuania began a period of intense political agitation. In June, the Lithuanian Movement to Support Perestroika (restructuring) was founded; its Executive Committee adopted the name *Sejm* - the name of the Lithuanian Parliament at the time of independence - also known as *Sajudis*. The Sajudis installed a kind of 'shadow' government, and demanded a return to the peace treaties which recognized the country's independence, stating that Lithuania's admission to the USSR was the result of a secret agreement and therefore had no legal value.

[17] In July, the Lithuanian Freedom League (LFL) emerged from underground activity. The LFL, which dates back to 1978, called for immediate withdrawal of Soviet troops from the country, and the independence of Lithuania. Police brutality toward participants of a demonstration sponsored by the LFL triggered joint protest actions by members of the League and the Sajudis, and led to a crisis within the Lithuanian Communist Party leadership.

[18] The Lithuanian Government opted not to follow the example set by Estonia's Supreme Soviet, which had made a unilateral decision on the question of sovereignty. Instead, Lithuanian authorities began

making concessions to local movements, legalizing the use of the flag and the national anthem, designating Independence Day as a holiday and authorizing public commemoration of that day. In addition, Lithuanian was adopted as the country's official language, and the Vilnius Cathedral and other churches were reopened.

[19] In February 1989, the first secretary of the CP and the Sajudis attended the official commemoration of the country's 1918 independence, side by side. In December, Lithuania's Supreme Soviet did away with the article of the constitution which assigned the CP a leading role; the first decision of its kind within the USSR.

[20] In January 1990, Gorbachev announced in Vilnius that the details of a future relation with the Union would be established through legislation. In March, the Lithuanian Parliament proclaimed the nation's independence, to be effected immediately. In September 1991, the new Council of State of the USSR accepted the independence of the three Baltic States, which were immediately recognized by several countries and by the UN.

[21] In August 1991, after the failed coup against Gorbachev in the USSR, the Lithuanian Parliament banned the Communist Party, the Democratic Workers' Party and the Lithuanian Communist Youth organization. The following month, President Vytautas Landsbergis issued a call, before the United Nations, for the withdrawal of 50,000 Soviet troops from Lithuania; they had been stationed in Vilnius since January of that year.

[22] The new constitution was approved by a referendum on October 25 1992. That year, the GNP diminished by 35 per cent and inflation soared to 1,150 per cent.

[23] On February 14 1993, the leader of the former Communist Party, Algirdas Brazauskas, was elected President with 60 per cent of the vote. In 1993 and 1994, Brazauskas continued with the transition policy toward a market economy.

[24] In 1995, around 80 per cent of Lithuanians were estimated to be 'poor', 15 per cent 'middle class', and 5 per cent 'rich'. The accentuation of social inequalities was seen as the key factor in the ruling party defeat in local elections this year.

[25] The opposition won the 1996 parliamentary elections. In 1998, Valdas Adamkus was elected President in the second round of voting, with a slight margin above his rival, the former Communist Arturas Paulauskas. Adamkus, 71, who lived more than 40 years in the US, had been a member of the Conservative Party. His campaign was based in achieving a market economy, improving relations with Washington and the incorporation of Lithuania into NATO.

[26] Finance minister Jonas Lionginas and Economy minister Eugenijus Maldeikis resigned in early October 1999, after the Government approved the sale of the state oil company to US firm Williams International. Massive demonstrations against the sale forced Prime Minister Rolandas Paksas to resign in October. The President then appointed Andrius Kubilius, formerly Vice-President, and went on with the sale.

[27] That month Parliament passed a border treaty with Russia, the first in the post-Soviet era, especially demarcating the accesses to Kaliningrad, a Russian enclave located in southwestern Lithuania and without any contact by land with the rest of the Russian Federation.

[28] Russian President Vladimir Putin held his first talks with President Adamkus in March 2001, in a show of approval for the Lithuanian integration process with NATO. According to figures from the statistics department, during January-February 2000, trade between both countries amounted to $237.8 million, 17.8 per cent of Lithuania's total trade. Imports from Russia were reduced to 26.8 per cent of total imports. It is estimated there are 1,054 companies with Russian capital registered in Lithuania.

[29] The New Union left the government coalition in mid 2001 in disagreement with privatization, taxes and pension plans. However, by a very slight margin in Parliament, the Government overcame a censure vote against its economic policy.

[30] Economic data from the National Statistics Bureau show a 5.7 per cent economic growth in 2001, thanks to the industrial, construction and commercial sectors, mainly in the last quarter of the year. ■

PROFILE

ENVIRONMENT

On the eastern coast of the Baltic Sea, Lithuania is characterized by gently rolling hills and flat plains. The largest of the Baltic 'mini-States', it has more than 700 rivers and streams, many forests and around 3,000 lakes. The Nemunas river, which crosses the country from east to west, is the country's largest river. It is lined with castles built centuries ago and it is still an important shipping route. Lithuania's climate is moderate because of its proximity to the sea: in summer, the average temperature is around 18° C and there is heavy rainfall; in the winter, it is often cold and foggy, with the temperature often falling below zero. 49 per cent of the land is arable; the chief crops are grain, potatoes and vegetables. There are large numbers of livestock. Among the country's most important industries are the food and machine manufacturing industries, as well as the export of energy. Most of the country's energy comes from Ignalina, a nuclear plant of the same type as the one in Chernobyl, Ukraine - site of the nuclear accident in 1986. Since the 1980s, there has been an increase in pollution, especially bacterial pollution of rivers and lakes; the latter has been linked to the increase in infectious childhood diseases, particularly in the first few years of life.

SOCIETY

Peoples: 83 per cent of the population is Lithuanian; the rest include Russians, 8.4 per cent; Poles, 7.0 per cent; Belarusians 1.5 per cent; Ukrainians 1.0 per cent and smaller populations of Germans, Jews, Latvians, Tatars, Armenians, Moldovans, Roma, Uzbeks, Azeris, Roma.
Religion: Catholic majority (80 per cent); there are Protestant minorities. There are also Orthodox Russians; some evangelist minorities; plus Muslims, Jews and people with no religion.
Languages: Lithuanian (official); Russian, Polish.
Political Parties: Lithuanian Democratic Labor Party; Homeland Union. Christian Democrat Party, Conservative Party, Social Democrat Party, Liberal Union, Young Lithuania National Party, Lithuanian Women.

THE STATE

Official Name: Lietuvos Respublika.
Administrative Division: 44 Districts.
Capital: Vilnius 579,000 people (1999).
Other cities: Kaunas 411,600 people; Klaipeda 202,400; Siauliai 146,300; Panevezys 133,600 (2000).
Government: Parliamentary republic. Valdas Adamkus, President since February 1998. Algirdas-Mykolas Brazauskas, Prime Minister since July 2001. Single-chamber parliament (*Seimas*) made up of 141 members.
National Holiday: February 16, Independence Day (1918).
Armed Forces: 5,100 (1996).
Other: Coast Guard, 5,000.

Luxembourg

Population:	448,000 (2002)
Land area	2,586 SQ KM
Capital:	Luxembourg
Currency:	Euro
Language:	French and German

Luxembourg

Luxembourg, Belgium, the Netherlands, and part of northern France constitute the Low Countries, and until 1579 they shared a common history (see the Netherlands).

[2] In the war of the Low Countries against Spain, Luxembourg sided with the southern provinces, acknowledging the authority of Philip II. Luxembourg was conquered by France in 1684, but returned to Spain 13 years later, under the Treaty of Rijswijk. In 1713, the Austrian Hapsburgs took control of the country until the Napoleonic invasion in 1795, when the country was annexed to the French Empire.

[3] In 1815, after the defeat of Napoleon, the Congress of Vienna handed over the Duchy of Luxembourg to William of Orange. William incorporated the Duchy as his kingdom's eighteenth province.

[4] After the Belgian revolt in 1831, Luxembourg was divided again: the largest section was given to Belgium, and the smallest was handed over to William as the Grand Duchy of Luxembourg, which he finally accepted in 1839. Thereafter the Duchy was administered independently until 1867. In 1866, the German Confederation was dissolved, the Treaty of London guaranteed the neutrality of the grand duchy giving control to the House of Nassau.

[5] Germany invaded the country twice, in 1914 and again during World War II. After the War productivity increased when the country formed an economic alliance with Belgium and the Netherlands called the Benelux, later becoming a member of the EEC.

[6] The Christian Social Party, a center-right party, maintained a majority in Parliament from 1919 until 1974. Afterwards a center-left coalition of the Socialist Workers' Party and the Democratic Party took office. The Christian Social Party recovered its majority in 1979, forming alliances with the Socialist Workers' Party and the Democratic Party.

[7] In 1949 Luxembourg became a founder member of NATO. In 1986, women were admitted to the armed forces.

[8] Women were granted the right to vote in 1919. The female presence in the registered

workforce was 25.2 per cent in 1979, increasing to 34 per cent by 1988. At that time, 74.8 per cent of all posts in education were held by women, the highest percentage in the European Community.

[9] The June 1989 legislative elections reaffirmed the dominance of the Social Christians and Socialists. The PCS took 22 seats, the POS 18 and the Democratic Party 11. The Action Committee, a group created to defend the pension rights of private sector workers, won four seats.

[10] In 1990, border controls were abolished with Belgium, France, Germany and the Netherlands.

[11] A new 'financial scandal' hit the headlines in 1991, when the International Bank of Credit and Commerce (BCCI) went bankrupt - an institution which was originally from Luxembourg with its headquarters in the Arab Emirates.

[12] In 1993, Josée Jacobs became the first woman to hold a cabinet position, becoming minister of agriculture and viniculture. In 1994, the PCS and the POS, who had governed the country together since 1984, were returned to power in the general elections, allowing Jacques Santer to continue as Prime Minister.

[13] In 1995, Santer became President of the European Commission and was replaced as Prime Minister by Jean-Claude Juncker. Luxembourg established itself as one of the main financial markets of the world, especially in the administration of social funds - like pension funds - with an estimated worth of $356 billion.

[14] As with the rest of the EU, unemployment rates increased in late 1997, although Luxembourg's continued to be the lowest of the 15 member states (3.7 per cent). In November, some 30,000 people from various European countries demonstrated in Luxembourg for a Europe 'serving employment'.

[15] In March 1998, the Government announced it would increase funding for the plan to extend the track for the high-speed train (TGV) - initially developed in France - to the east, in order to strengthen contact with Eastern Europe.

[16] In November 1999, along with Belgium and the Low Countries, Luxembourg proposed the European Union should authorize some of its members to join more closely, without expecting new members to reach such levels of harmony with the rest and without holding back those ready to continue advancing. Prime Minister Jean-Claude Juncker said the 'two speed operation' was a necessity.

[17] The Grand Duke Jean abdicated in September 2000, leaving his son Henri, 45, in his place, who took office in October. It was expected Henri would take a new and more active role than his father in matters of state.

[18] Hundreds of truckers blocked Luxembourg's border routes demanding a 48-hour week. The transport sector was excluded from the 1993 European Union guidelines, which limited the working week to 48 hours in most of the industries. The protest was supported by truckers from the Netherlands, France and Belgium.

[18] A report by a French Parliament commission accused Luxembourg in January 2002 of hindering the fight against money laundering and financial corruption. The report mentioned, among those obstacles imposed by the country, the strict banking secrecy and administrative delay any time the authorities' collaboration was required. ■

TFYR Macedonia

Population:	2,051,000 (2002)
Land area:	25,430 SQ KM
Capital:	Skopje
Currency:	TFYR Macedonian denar
Language:	Macedonian

Makedonija

Macedonia's ancient cultural history is linked to that of Greece and Anatolia. According to archaeological studies, the ancestors of the Macedonians can be identified in the early Bronze Age. In the year 700 BC, a people calling themselves 'Macedonian' migrated toward the east from their native lands on the banks of the Aliakmon River. Aegae was the capital of the kingdom which, during the reign of Amyntas I, extended to the Axios River and beyond, as far as the Chalcidice Peninsula.

[2] Macedonia reached a position of power and influence within Greece during the reign of Philip II (359-336 BC). Warriors had the power to choose a new king, and also to try cases of high treason. Alexander 'the Great', Philip's son and a student of Aristotle, defeated the Persian Empire and led the Macedonian armies to northern Africa and the Arabic peninsula, crossing Mesopotamia and reaching as far east as India.

[3] The Macedonian Empire, built up over 11 years, contributed to the propagation of Greek culture in the Orient. Alexander the Great founded a large number of cities and was responsible for the fusion of Greek culture with the cultures of the peoples he conquered, giving rise to what is known as Hellenism. His death in 323 BC was followed by a period of internal struggles, though Macedonia maintained the unity of the empire.

[4] Around the year 280 BC, groups of Galatian marauders invaded Macedonia, killing the King. Three years later, Antigonus II defeated the Galatians and was crowned king by an army from Macedonia. Most of the population were farmers, except in urban areas like Beroea and Pella, and the Greek settlements along the coast. The King held exclusive rights to the mines and forests.

[5] During the reign of Philip V (221-179 BC), Macedonia conquered Rome's client-states in Illyria and subsequently turned eastward and to the northeast, subduing the cities of Rhodes and Pergamum. Rome responded by going to war and defeated Philip in 197 BC adding Macedonia to its kingdom and taking Thessaly away from Macedonia. Philip collaborated with the Romans and consolidated his

power. This was a prosperous period for Macedonia, which also managed to recover Thessaly.

[6] From 168 to 146 BC, Macedonia was a Roman province, with four independent administrative sections. Macedonia supervised the Greeks for Rome, keeping watch for rebellions and invasion attempts across the northern border. In the year 27, Macedonia became a senatorial province separate from Greece. By the 4th century AD, most Macedonians had adopted Christianity.

[7] The ethnic composition of the Macedonians was not significantly affected by the Goth, Hun and Avar invasions. However, when Slavs arrived in the Balkans, they established permanent settlements throughout Macedonia.

[8] Between the 7th and the 14th centuries, Macedonia was successively subdued by the Bulgarian, Byzantine and Latin empires until they were almost completely dominated by the Serbs, except in the Greek region of Salonika.

[9] Towards the end of the 14th century, Turkey began invading the Balkans. By 1371, it had conquered most of Macedonia and in 1389, inflicted a decisive defeat upon the Serbian Empire at Kosovo. The Ottomans seized the best lands for themselves and established a feudal system. Christian peasants either became vassals of Muslim lords, to whom they paid a tithe, or were driven onto the less fertile lands.

[10] In 1864, the Ottoman Empire divided Macedonia into three provinces: Salonika, Monastir, including parts of Albania, and Kosovo, which extended into 'Old Serbia'. In 1878, Russia forced Turkey into accepting the creation of Bulgaria, which included most of Macedonia, but the other European powers returned this territory to the Ottomans. During the ensuing years, Bulgaria, Serbia and Greece all continued to lay claim to Macedonia.

[11] Towards the end of the 19th century, a strong nationalist movement emerged in Macedonia. Macedonian Slavs created the VMRO (Vatreshna Makedonska Revolutsionna Organizatsia) in 1893, with the slogan 'Macedonia for the Macedonians'. At the same time, Bulgaria and Greece began sending guerrillas into Macedonia, provoking the Greco-Turkish War of 1897. Turkey supported the Serbs to offset the influence of the VMRO and Bulgarians.

[12] By 1903, the increase in opposition activities by Bulgarians, Greeks, Serbs and Macedonians led Russia and Austria-Hungary to demand that an inspector general be appointed, and that the police force be reorganized. Turkey agreed to meet the demands, but in August there was a general uprising, apparently initiated by Bulgaria. It was ruthlessly put down by the Turks, who destroyed 105 Macedonian-Slav villages.

[13] In 1908, after the fall of the Ottoman Empire, with the 'Young Turks' rebellion, the clamor to divide

up Ottoman-Turkish territories in the region culminated in the two Balkan Wars of 1912 and 1913. Bulgaria and Serbia signed a Mutual Assistance Treaty, with Greece and Montenegro subsequently joining the alliance. Russia supported the Balkan League, because of its interest in halting the southeasterly advance of the Austro-Hungarian Empire.

[14] After defeating Turkey in the first war, the allies turned against each other. Bulgaria provoked the second Balkan War, confronting both Greece and Serbia. Romania and Turkey then allied themselves with Greece and Serbia to defeat Bulgaria. The Treaty of Bucharest gave Greece Salonika and most of the Macedonian coastal area, while Serbia was given the center and the northern parts of the territory.

[15] When World War I broke out, Bulgaria saw a chance to reassert its territorial claims over Macedonia. Sofia joined the Central Powers (Austria-Hungary, Germany and Turkey), and occupied all of Serbian Macedonia and also a part of Serbia. The victorious allied powers left the Greco-Macedonian borders as they were, and Yugoslav Macedonia was incorporated into the new Serbian, Croat and Slovenian kingdom.

[16] In the inter-war period, Serbian domination deepened Yugoslav inter-ethnic conflicts. King Alexander, who assumed dictatorial powers in 1929, was assassinated in Marseilles in 1934 by Croatian nationalists. At the beginning of World War II, when Germany invaded Yugoslavia, these internal divisions meant that the invaders met little resistance.

[17] The Yugoslav nationalist struggle intensified during the following years. Guerrillas led by the Yugoslav Communist League (YCL) seized power in May 1945, later proclaiming the Socialist Federal Republic of Macedonia. Yugoslav Macedonia joined the new state as one of its six constituent republics.

[18] In 1947, Yugoslavia declared that Macedonia was the country's least developed region. The federal government subsequently began earmarking funds for industrialization projects, especially in steel, chemical and textile production.

[19] In January, 1990, a special YCL Congress decided to adopt a

multiparty system, and eliminate the leadership role which the constitution assigned to the party. However, the motion to grant greater autonomy to YCL branches in the republics was not accepted. After the Congress, the Communist Leagues of Slovenia, Croatia and Macedonia decided to separate from the YCL and call themselves by a new name, the Democratic Renewal Party.

[20] On September 8 1991, in the midst of fighting between the new separate republics of Croatia and Slovenia and the federal army, a plebiscite was held in which Macedonians pronounced themselves in favor of separation from the former Yugoslav Federation. All Macedonian political parties, except for the Albanian ethnic minority, favored independence.

[21] On January 20 1992, Greek and Bulgarian representatives held an informal meeting. Sofia had recognized Macedonia five days previously. From Skopje, the newspaper *Nova Makedonika* accused the Greek and Bulgarian governments of entertaining territorial designs upon their country.

[22] On January 12, in a referendum, the Albanian minority of Macedonia had voted for the creation of their own independent state. On April 3, in the territory of Macedonia was proclaimed the Independent Republic of Illirida (republic of Albanians resident in Yugoslavia).

[23] The new Yugoslav Federation withdrew its troops from in the country. In July, the entire Cabinet resigned, after failing to achieve international recognition. Socialdemocrat Branko Crvenkovski took over as Prime Minister in August and was recognized by Russia, Albania, Bulgaria and Turkey.

[24] On April 1993, Macedonia was admitted as a member of the United Nations with the provisional name of The Former Yugoslav Republic (TFYR) of Macedonia.

[25] On February 16 1994, two and a half years after Macedonia's independence, Greece closed its northern border and Thessaloniki, the port of exit for 80 per cent of the country's production and all its oil. The Greek Government was taken before the European Court of Justice in April, but the economic blockade continued.

[26] On October 16, President Kiro Gligorov was re-elected with 52.4 per cent of the vote. Exactly one year later, a bomb exploded in the President's car. He survived, although his role became secondary to Crvenkovski's. That month, negotiations with Greece led to the lifting of the trade embargo and bilateral trade grew steadily.

[27] In 1996, a privatization plan led to the downfall of the ruling coalition. The October-November 1998 Parliamentary elections were won by a new coalition, called the Internal Macedonian Revolutionary Organization-Democratic Party for Macedonian National Unity (VMRO-DMPNE), which obtained 28.1 per cent of the vote. The Social-Democratic League took 25.1 per cent, while the Democratic Alternative, with slightly more than 10 per cent, joined the Government coalition. The Albanian Democratic Prosperity Party came in third, with 19.3 per cent of the vote.

[28] To avoid trouble with the Albanian minority, while tension soared in neighboring Yugoslavia, the Government asked NATO to station troops on the border. When the bombing of Yugoslavia began in March 1999, thousands of Albanian-Kosovars took refuge in Macedonia. Government authorities were inclined to encourage a swift return of refugees to Kosovo, or to expel them to Albania.

[29] The first round of the 1999 Presidential elections put Tito Petkovski, of the former Communist Social Democratic Party, in first place, with 38 per cent of the vote. But the second round was won by pro-government Boris Trajkovski, who had taken 25 per cent of the vote in the first round. The opposition and international observers said that elections were seriously flawed.

[30] A revolution broke out in March 2001 as people demanded more rights for the Albanian minority. This resulted in a wave of 100,000 refugees and the rebel National Liberation Army (NLA) took some territory. The violence stopped in August, after the international community intervened and demanded the rebels to hand over their weapons in exchange for the recognition of the Albanian minority.

[31] In November, after delays and breaks in the ceasefire, Parliament passed constitutional reforms which granted Albanians more rights. The constitutional charter would no longer mention the Albanian 'minority', but the 'Albanians that live in the territory of Macedonia'. The use of Albanian language was allowed in Parliament and state institutions -mainly the police- had to offer jobs to the Albanian population.

[32] A Human Rights Watch report, apart from denouncing several cases of human rights abuses committed by rebel and Macedonian troops, requested that the authorities not to give immunity to the perpetrators of serious abuses, despite the amnesty signed to end the conflict.

[33] The international community decided in early 2002 to send more

PROFILE

ENVIRONMENT

In the south-central part of the Balkan Peninsula, Macedonia, which is landlocked, is bordered in the north by Serbia and Kosovo, in the east by Bulgaria, in the south by Greece and in the west by Albania. Two mountain ranges cross the region, the Pindo (a continuation of the Alps) and the Rodope, in the center and the east. With a continental climate, the average temperature in the capital is 1° C in winter, and 24° C in summer. The country's main agricultural activity is centered in the Vardar River basin. In the mountain region, sheep and goats are raised. There are some copper, iron and lead deposits. The metal industry has caused environmental pollution.

SOCIETY

Peoples: Macedonians 66.4 per cent; Albanians 23.1 per cent; Turks 3.9 per cent; Roma 2.3 per cent; Serbs 1.9 per cent; other 2.3 per cent (1994).
Religions: Christian Orthodox (majority); Muslim and others.
Languages: Macedonian and Albanian (officials); Roma and Turk.
Political Parties: There is a coalition between the Internal Macedonian Revolutionary Organization, the Democratic Party for Macedonian National Unity and the Democratic Alternative; Social Democratic League of Macedonia; Albanian parties: the Democratic Prosperity Party and the Democratic Party of Albanians; a coalition between the Liberal-Democratic Party and the Democratic Party of Macedonia; the Socialist Party of Macedonia. There are also several parties of the Turk, Roma and Muslim minorities.
Social organizations: Union of Women's Organizations of the Republic of Macedonia.

THE STATE

Official Name: Republika Makedonija. **Administrative divisions:** 30 districts. **Capital:** Skopje 485,000 people (1999). **Other cities:** Bitolj (Bitola) 92,300 people; Prilep 81,600; Kumanovo 77,900; Tetovo 54,600 (2000). **Government:** Boris Trajkovski, President since December 1999. Ljubco Georgievski, Prime Minister since November 1998. Unicameral Legislative: the Sobranie (Assembly) integrated by 120 members elected for a four year term. **National Holiday:** September 8, Independence Day (1991). **Armed Forces:** 10,400 (8,000 conscripts). **Other:** 7,500 (police).

than 500 million euros, twice what was expected in first instance, for the reconstruction and economic reform of the country, in recognition of the stability achieved six months after the war had ended. ∎

Madagascar

Population:	16,913,000 (2002)
Land area:	581,540 SQ KM
Capital:	Antananarivo
Currency:	Franc
Language:	Malagasy and French

Madagasikara

About 2,000 years ago, Malay-Polynesian navigators reached the African coast in canoes, a voyage which was frequently repeated between the 1st and 5th centuries.

[2] Towards the 14th century, groups of Comoran traders established a series of ports in the northern region. These ports were destroyed by the Portuguese in 1506-1507.

[3] When the Portuguese found no gold, ivory or spices, they lost interest in the territory. By this time the Europeans had introduced firearms to the island in exchange for slaves.

[4] In the 16th century the Sakalawas on the west coast and the Betsilios on the east coast established the first monarchies. In the 17th century the state of Merina or Imerina came into being on the eastern edge of the central plateau. A century later it was the Merinas, under their leader Nampoina, who initiated the process of unification which was completed later by Nampoina's son Radama I (1810-1828).

[5] Contact with the Arabs and Europeans became more frequent. Radama adopted the Latin alphabet for the Malagasy language. He also used their help to create a modern army. However, the untimely death of the ruler and the ensuing conflicts over succession paved the way for European occupation of the island by the end of the century.

[6] The colonials cleared the virgin forests to make way for sugarcane, cotton, and coffee plantations. They seized the best lands and the peasants were forced to work in conditions of semi-slavery. The struggle for political rights and economic improvement led to a great uprising from 1947 to 1948, and this was ruthlessly put down by the French army with the loss of thousands of lives.

[7] The failure of the insurrection enabled the colonial administration to control the transition to autonomy. Independence was finally proclaimed in 1960. In the following September the country held it's first elections and the Social Democratic Party (PSD) won by a large margin. Its leader, Philibert Tsiranana, became the Republic's first President, an office to which he was re-elected in 1965 and 1972.

[8] In May 1972, after a series of serious disturbances, Tsiranana was forced to resign; he turned over full presidential powers to General Ramanantsoa, who suspended the National Assembly and the Senate. He also eliminated the presidency and abolished the 1959 Constitution, giving a military government both executive and legislative power, and creating Institutional and National Councils. In October, he had these measures approved by referendum.

[9] A year later, France decided to withdraw its troops, and the succeeding three years of instability ended in June 1975, when Cdr D Ratsiraka became Prime Minister. He adopted socialist policies, and called a referendum on December 21 1975. His nomination as head of state was overwhelmingly approved, and the Charter of the Madagascan Socialist Revolution was adopted as the basis for a new constitution. On December 30 1975 the State changed the country's name to the 'Democratic Republic of Madagascar'.

[10] In June 1976, the new power structure was put into operation, with a 12-member Supreme Council of the Revolution and the Government, which was presided over by Col J Rakotomalala. When he died in an airplane accident in July 1976, he was replaced by Justin Rakotoniaina. The legislative function was placed in the hands of a 144-member National Council.

[11] The progressive Malagasy parties joined together to form the National Revolutionary Front. AREMA (the Malagasy Revolutionary Vanguard) was the leading party of the Front, and was created in 1975 in support of Ratsiraka's renewal program. The Supreme Council of the Revolution was made up primarily of AREMA members, with members of five other parties ranging in their views from Marxist/Leninist to Christian Democrat. In 1977, Désiré Rakotoarijaona became Prime Minister.

[12] In 1982, the President was re-elected by 80 per cent of the vote while the radical sector - represented by MONIMA - obtained the remaining 20 per cent.

[13] In 1988, Lt-Col Victor Ramahatra succeeded Raotoarijaona as Prime Minister. AREMA, the party in power, won the 1989 elections; Didier Ratsiraka was re-elected President, with 67.2 per cent of the vote. His presidency was characterized by reform, with the restoration of a multiparty system and the inclusion in his cabinet of several opposition members by March 1990.

[14] In 1991, the opposition united around the Committee of Living Forces, made up of 16 organizations. A series of street demonstrations and the taking of the National Radio, led the Government to declare a state of emergency. The Committee called for Ratsiraka's resignation and, in July, nominated a transition government.

[15] In August, following the detention of two ministers from the transition cabinet, 400,000 people took to the streets and repeated the demand for Ratsiraka's resignation. The demonstration was brutally put down, with 31 people killed and more than 200 injured.

[16] In March 1992, a multiparty forum was created to draw up a new constitution and presidential elections were set for August. In this month, the new document was approved and Albert Zafy was elected President with 66.2 per cent of the vote to Ratsiraka's 33.8.

[17] The economic and social situation of the country, one of the poorest in the world, was considered disastrous. Per capita income barely increased between 1976 and 1992, going from $200 to $230 per year, while calorie consumption went from 108 per cent of those required in 1964-66, to 95 per cent in 1988-90.

[18] In March 1994, the Government introduced a series of austerity measures recommended by the International Monetary Fund, which increased the social tensions even further. At the end of that year, massive demonstrations were held in opposition to these policies. In January 1995, the governor of the Central Bank abandoned his post on request from the IMF and the World Bank.

[19] In September, the Malagasy people approved increased powers for Zafy in a referendum. The debate over structural adjustment coincided with disagreements over the use of the nation's natural resources, when the mining transnational RTZ proposed opening a mine on the southern coast of the island to extract titanium dioxide. This sparked strong protests by militant ecologists, convinced the project would destroy unique species of flora and fauna.

[20] In May 1996, the National Assembly approved a vote of no confidence in the Government,

leading to the formation of a new cabinet. The motion was partly caused by comments made by the IMF director, Michel Camdessus, who said the lack of governmental cohesion meant agreements with the body were not guaranteed.

[21] Accused of breaking the Constitution, Zafy resigned in September. In the subsequent presidential elections, Didier Ratsiraka was selected. A new Constitution, approved by referendum in March 1998, gave more power to the President and economic autonomy to the country's six provinces. The opposition Committee of Authorities boycotted the elections and accused the Government of authoritarian tendencies. After the May legislative elections, Tantely Andranarivo became the new Prime Minister in July, replacing Pascal Rakotomavo, both members of AREMA.

[22] The opposition, alleging that voters had not received adequate information, boycotted the December 2000 local elections - designed to give local governments control over their development, education and health programs. Seventy per cent of voters stayed at home and AREMA won in most cities. The exception was the capital, in control of Mark Ravalomanana who, from once being very poor and a yoghurt salesman, had become a tycoon and charismatic politician.

[23] The police used tear gas in Antananarivo, in February 2001, to break up demonstrators demanding freedom for Jean-Eugene Voninahitsy, Deputy Chairman of Parliament, who had been jailed for insulting Ratsiraka and for issuing bad cheques. After Voninahitsy's imprisonment, an opposition bloc was formed in Parliament, the Unit for Defense of Democracy in Crisis. In May, after 29 years, the Senate resumed operations, as had been agreed in the new Constitution, which included the Presidency, the National Assembly and the High Constitutional Court (HCC).

[24] Ravalomanana was a candidate in the December presidential elections and, once the count started, he claimed victory which made a second round unnecessary. This was rejected by Ratsiraka. In January, Ravalomanana and his followers organized a general strike in the capital and a series of protest demonstrations against what, according to them, had been a manipulation of votes by Ratsiraka.

[25] In the presence of thousands of followers, Ravalomanana proclaimed himself President in February 2002, and appointed the new ministers, who took office in the capital. Clashes took place between followers of the different candidates, and Ratsiraka declared martial law in Antananarivo. The country was at a standstill and, while Ratsiraka and his ministers left for Toamasina (previously Tamatave, second largest city and largest port in the country) - which they named the new capital - an economic blockade was imposed on Antananarivo. However, in March Ravalomanana took over the Home Ministry, last stronghold of Ratsiraka in Antananarivo, and also proclaimed himself Commander-in-Chief of the Armed Forces.

[26] In April, the HCC annuled the results of the December elections and asked for a recount, which was accepted by both candidates. The HCC, after finding that Ravalomanana had received 51.46 per cent of the vote, declared him the winner and new President. Ratsiraka - who obtained 35.9 per cent of the vote - did not accept the result, and alleged the HCC was 'prejudiced' against him.

[27] During the first week of May 2002, the province of Toamasina declared its independence. With this measure, Ratsiraka sought to enclose the capital and isolate it from the country's ports. But Ratsiraka experienced a series of military and diplomatic setbacks. After the US, Australia, Japan, Germany and former colonial power France recognized Ravalomanana's government, Ratsiraka flew to the Seychelles and then to France in July. Once the struggle was over and he was in control of the whole country, Ravalomanana ruled out any rerun of elections. ∎

PROFILE

ENVIRONMENT

Madagascar is one of the world's largest islands, separated from the African continent by the Mozambique Channel. The island has an extensive central plateau of volcanic origin which overhangs the hot and humid coastal plains. These are covered with dense rainforest to the east and grasslands to the west. The eastern side of the island is very rainy, but the rest has a dry, tropical climate. The population is concentrated on the high central plateau. Rice and export products (sugar, coffee, bananas, and vanilla) are cultivated on the coast. Cattle-raising is also important throughout the island. The major mineral resources are graphite, chrome and phosphate. Deforestation is one of the major environmental problems, it is estimated that the destruction of forests affects up to 75 per cent of the island. Only 10 per cent of the rural population has assured access to drinking water. The lack of sewage facilities and concentration of organic wastes have led to the pollution of many watercourses.

SOCIETY

Peoples: The Malgaches, 98.9 per cent of the population, are made up by different ethnic groups of Malagasy-Afro-Indonesian origin.
Immigrant communities: Indians and Pakistanis, 0.2 per cent; French, 0.2 per cent; Chinese, 0.1 per cent, and others.
Religions: Traditional beliefs 52.0 per cent; Christian 41 per cent (of which Roman Catholic 21 per cent, Protestant 19.0 per cent); Muslim 7 per cent.
Languages: Malagasy and French (official). Hovba and other local dialects are also spoken.
Political Parties: AREMA, socialist; Fanilo Group; Rally for Socialism and Democracy; Flower of Madagascar.
Social organizations: there are four trade union blocs: Confederation of Malgache Workers (FMM); Confederation of Christian Trade Unions of Madagascar (SEKRIMA); Union of Independent Trade Unions of Madagascar (USAM) and Union of Workers' Trade Unions of Madagascar (FISEMA). National Council of Christian Churches.

THE STATE

Official Name: Repoblikan'i Madagasikara. République Démocratique de Madagascar.
Administrative Divisions: 6 provinces, 10 districts, 1,252 sub-districts, and 11,333 towns.
Capital: Antananarivo 1,432,000 people (1999).
Other cities: Toamasina 166,000 people; Fianarantsoa 131,600; Mahajanga (Majunga) 128,600 (2000).
Government: Parliamentary republic. Mark Ravalomanana, President since April 2002; Jacques Silla, Prime Minister since February 2002. Unicameral Legislature: Senate (⅔ selected by an Electoral College and ⅓ selected by the president) and a National Assembly, whose members are directly elected.
National Holiday: July 26, Independence Day (1960).
Armed Forces: 21,000 (1996).
Other: 7,500 (Gendarmerie).

DEMOGRAPHY
Population: 16,913,000 (2002)
Annual growth: 2.9 % (1985-2000)
Estimates for year 2015: 24,072,000 (2000)
Annual growth to year 2015: 2.7 % (2000)
Urban population: 29.5 % (2000)
Urban growth: 5.2 % (2000)
Children per woman: 5.9 (2000)

HEALTH
Life expectancy at birth: 54 years (2000-2005)
male: 53 years (2000-2005)
female: 55 years (2000-2005)
Maternal mortality: 490 per 100,000 live births (1985/99)
Infant mortality: 86 per 1,000 (2000)
Under-5 child mortality: 139 per 1,000 (2000)
Daily calorie supply: 1,994 per capita (1999)
11 doctors per 100,000 people (1996)
Safe water: 47 % (2000)

EDUCATION
Literacy: 47 % (2000)
male: 50 % (2000)
female: 44 % (2000)
School enrolment (net):
Primary total: 57 % (1994/2000)
male: 67 % (1995/99)
female: 69 % (1995/99)
Secondary (gross):
male: 16 % (1995/97)
female: 16 % (1995/97)
Tertiary (gross): 2 % (1998)
Primary school teachers: one for every 47 pupils (1998)

COMMUNICATIONS
5 newspapers (1996), 216 radios (1997), 24 TV sets (2000) and 3 main telephone lines (2000) per 1,000 people
Books: 1 new title per 100,000 people (1992/94)

ECONOMY
Per capita, GDP: $ 840 (2000)
Annual growth: 1.6 % (2000)
Annual inflation: 12.0 % (2000)
Consumer price index: 163.7 (2000)
Currency: 6,656.3 francs = $ 1 (10/2000)
Cereal imports: 166,618 metric tons (2000)
Food import dependency: 14 % (1999)
Fertilizer use: 18 kg per ha (1999)
Exports: $ 955 million (2000)
Imports: $ 1,349 million (2000)
External debt: $ 4,701 million (2000); $ 294 per capita (2000)
Debt service: 17.1 % of exports (1999)
Development aid received: $ 358 million (1999); $ 23.8 per capita (1999); 9.60 % of GNP (1999)

HDI (ranking/value): 135 / 0.462 (1999)

Malawi

Population: 11,828,000 (2002)
Land area: 94,080 SQ KM
Capital: Lilongwe
Currency: Kwacha
Language: Chewa

Malawi

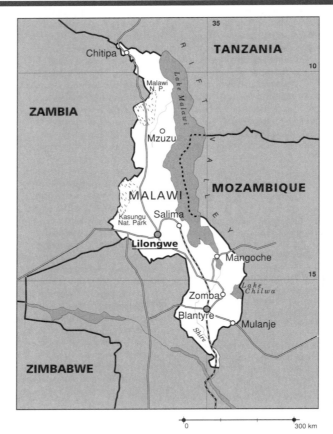

The state of Kitwara was part of a small country on the coast of Lake Malawi (previously Nyasa), and had been part of a series of nations related to gold production and ruled by the Monomotapa of Zimbabwe (see Zimbabwe). The decline of this power center allowed the Chewa to enlarge their territory, only to see it reduced again when the Changamira Rotsi restored the predominance of Zimbabwe. Around 1835, Zulu expansion (see South Africa) pushed the Ngoni-Ndwande to the shores of the lake, leading to 60 years of war between the Ngoni and the Chewa and Yao allies.

[2] The country was explored by Livingstone in 1859 and it suffered a Portuguese attempt at colonization in 1890 which was ended by an ultimatum from the British Government. Britain wanted to keep the territory which would eventually serve as a link in a continuous chain of colonies joining South Africa to Egypt. In 1891, Cecil Rhodes' British South African Company negotiated the Protectorate of what became Nyasaland.

[3] The British idea was to create a Central African Federation embracing present-day Zimbabwe, Malawi and Zambia - regions linked by similarities of people, climate, plains, plateaus and dry forests. Politically this would have meant the extension of a Rhodesian-style white-racist domination to the entire Federation.

[4] The Malawi Congress Party (MCP) and the UNIP of Zambia favored a pro-independence stance. They were strongly influenced by Dr Hastings Kamuzu Banda, a doctor who had studied in the US and who was presented as the 'nation's savior'.

[5] Banda's demands for greater power within the Party were granted to prevent internal division. When the colony became independent in 1964, Banda seized control of the MCP and the country. As President he established close economic and diplomatic relations with the racist governments of South Africa and Rhodesia, and with the colonial administration in Mozambique.

[6] South Africa became Malawi's main tea and tobacco purchaser while South African investors built roads, railways and a new capital city. South African managers took charge of the airline, information and development agencies and a large part of the state administration.

[7] In 1975, Mozambican independence radically changed Banda's situation. He had actively cooperated with the Portuguese in their struggle against FRELIMO. The closure of the Mozambique-Rhodesia border led to a drastic reduction in Malawi's trade with Rhodesia, depriving Ian Smith's racist government of an escape route from the international blockade.

[8] In June 1978, Banda held the first election in 17 years. All the candidates had to be MCP members and pass an English test, which immediately excluded the 90 per cent of the population who did not speak English.

[9] After 1980, Zimbabwe's independence changed the economic and political situation of Malawi. Banda lost direct communication with South Africa, and was therefore deprived of major support. Consequently the Government drew closer to the Front Line states, joining the SADCC association because of Malawi's dependence on the railway lines through Mozambique and Zimbabwe.

[10] The success of neighboring socialist governments strengthened the Socialist League of Malawi (LESOMA) which favored breaking economic and political ties with South Africa, putting an end to Banda's dictatorship and implementing full democracy in the country. In 1980 this party created a guerrilla force, the Malawi Freedom Movement (MAFREMO), led by Orton Chirwa, also gained strength.

[11] In 1983, Chirwa and Attati Mpakati, a LESOMA leader, were accused of conspiracy and sentenced to death. Shortly thereafter, Mpakati was assassinated by South African agents while visiting Harare. Chirwa and his wife were kidnapped in Zambia where they lived as exiles, and imprisoned in Blantyre.

[12] Banda created a secret police force, called the Special Branch, with South African and Israeli advisers. The president-for-life also personally controlled the economy, owning 33 per cent of all businesses.

[13] Between 1987 and 1988, the country received 600,000 refugees from Mozambique, in whose civil war Malawi had supported the counter-revolutionaries of the National Resistance Movement (Renamo). This support was discontinued in 1988, after the visit that Banda received from President Chissano of Mozambique.

[14] Also in 1988, Amnesty International denounced the imprisonment of well-known scholars and writers, among them Jack Mapanje, the country's foremost poet. The US announced the cancellation of $40 million of foreign debt in November 1989.

[15] The implementation of an IMF-adjustment program led to a reduction in inflation and in the balance of payments deficit, as well as an increase in investments. However, it also aggravated the situation faced by the poorest sectors of the population.

[16] In 1990 and 1991, earthquakes and floods exacerbated food shortages among the rural population, 90 per cent of the country's total population. The privatization of the maize/corn market benefited a few producers at the expense of the poorest rural sectors.

[17] For the first time since independence, the Catholic Church wrote a pastoral letter criticizing the human rights situation, and calling for greater political freedom. This letter was followed by a popular uprising in Blantyre, which was harshly repressed by government forces.

[18] In April 1992, opposition leader Chafuka Chihana of the Alliance for Democracy was caught trying to return to the country, and imprisoned. An international

campaign prevented him from being executed.

[19] In May 1992, a general strike called by textile workers was brutally put down, with 38 deaths and hundreds of injuries. In reprisal, the World Bank discontinued part of its financial aid.

[20] The ruling Congress Party of Malawi, the only party to participate in the June general elections, obtained 114 seats in the National Assembly.

[21] In late 1992, news was received of the death of Orton Chirwa of MAFREMO. He had been in prison since 1983, and died under torture. To keep popular indignation from turning violent, Banda announced that a referendum would be held on opening up the political system.

[22] The referendum took place in June 1993. Two thirds of voters chose a multiparty system. That month, Banda promised presidential elections would be held in 1994 and released Vera Chirwa, widow of the assassinated dissident.

[23] Opposition member Bakili Muluzi was elected President in May 1994. His party, the United Democratic Front (UDF), won 84 of the 177 seats at stake in the legislative elections. In September, having won only 55 seats,

Banda decided to retire from political activity.

[24] Malawi suffered the consequences of an intensive drought in 1994 that led to a food shortage. In the midst of a growing difficult social situation, the Government went ahead with its IMF-sponsored policy to cut public spending. In January 1995, ex-president Banda was arrested, charged with the murder of three former ministers. The alleged violation of human rights by Muluzi's government was frequently denounced by opposition members throughout the year.

[25] In January 1996, Malawi entered negotiations to form a free trade area, along with another 11 Southern African nations. The Government announced it would revoke the laws affecting foreign investors in rural areas.

[26] In 1997, the United States started to train Malawian troops with a view to creating an African peacekeeping force.

[27] The drought, which affected vast regions of Africa, almost totally dried up Malawi's Shire River, one of the main watercourses.

[28] International experts recommended a reduction in the amount of water used in agriculture through the importing of food, and

the progressive industrialization of the economy. In 1998, it was estimated the underground water reserves of the region would take 1,400 years to recover.

[29] The cholera epidemic which affected 15,000 people left 500 dead between 1998 and 1999. In April 1999 President Muluzi inaugurated the country's first television channel.

[30] After a questionable election process, Muluzi won the June elections, while his party, with 47.3 per cent of the vote, obtained 93 of the 192 seats at stake. In late February 2000, the President requested the resignation of his Cabinet. Some of his ministers, among them Economic Minister Cassim Chilumpha, were not considered trustworthy by donor countries of development aid.

[31] After the President criticized donor states for intervening in the country's domestic policy, Denmark cancelled its aid to Malawi in January 2002. This meant no new development or environmental programs would be initiated in Malawi. Denmark had assigned $87 million in aid for the period 2000-2004.

[32] A lack of food, especially in rural areas, caused a great death toll, leading the President to declare a state of national disaster in 2001. The Government was accused of having sold grain at low prices to Kenya, and of forcing the population to eat green grains. The famine ran the risk of spreading throughout the following year. Floods and the deterioration of roads and railways made food distribution more difficult. Children and the elderly were those at greater risk. It is estimated that 70 per cent of the population goes hungry.

[33] Using new instruments and tools, scientists began drilling in Lake Malawi, in order to obtain an annual log of weather and environmental variation with the hope of understanding the origin and evolution of humans. It is thought that the lake is 7 million years old.

[34] Fishing authorities declared in March 2002 that the Shire River, the longest in the country and one of its main power sources, could be obstructed and subverted by the quantity of vegetation affecting it. There were also fears that it could dry up in prolonged drought periods. The Shire, coming from Lake Malawi, flows into the Zambesi River and is an important source for transportation and food.

[35] Malawi, like its neighbors, was hit by famine in 2002. ∎

PROFILE

ENVIRONMENT

The terrain and the climate are extremely varied. The major geological feature is the great Rift fault that runs through the country from north to south. Part of this large depression is filled by Lake Malawi, which takes up one fifth of the land area. The rest is made up of plateaus of varying altitudes. The most temperate region is the southern part, which is also the highest, containing most of the population and economic activities (basically farming). The lowlands receive heavy rainfall and are covered by grasslands, forests or rainforests, depending on the amount of rainfall they receive. The degradation of the soil and deforestation are the main environmental problems.

SOCIETY

Peoples: Maravi (including Nyanja, Chewa, Tonga, and Tumbuka) 58.3 per cent; Lomwe 18.4 per cent; Yao 13.2 per cent; Ngoni 6.7 per cent.
Religions: Many people follow traditional religions, but they also belong to Christian (50 per cent) and Muslim (20 per cent) communities.
Languages: Chewa (official) and English; several Bantu languages - other than Chewa - are spoken by their respective ethnic groups.
Political Parties: United Democratic Front (UDF); Alliance for Democracy (Aford); Malawi Congress Party (MCP).
Social Organizations: Trade Union Congress of Malawi. Union of Malawian Students.

THE STATE

Official Name: Republic of Malawi.
Administrative divisions: 24 districts.
Capital: Lilongwe 765,000 people (1999).
Other cities: Blantyre 518,800 people; Mzuzu 94,400 (2000).
Government: Presidential republic. Bakili Muluzi, President since May 1994, re-elected in 1999. Legislature: single-chamber: National Assembly, made up of 177 members.
National Holiday: July 6, Independence Day (1964).
Armed Forces: 9,800 (1996).
Other: 1,500.

STATISTICS

DEMOGRAPHY

Population: 11,828,000 (2002)
Annual growth: 3.0 % (1985-2000)
Estimates for year 2015: 15,656,000 (2000)
Annual growth to year 2015: 2.2 % (2000)
Urban population: 15.4 % (2000)
Urban growth: 4.6 % (2000)
Children per woman: 6.6 (2000)

HEALTH

Life expectancy at birth: 39 years (2000-2005)
male: 40 years (2000-2005)
female: 39 years (2000-2005)
Maternal mortality: 1,100 per 100,000 live births (1985/99)
Infant mortality: 117 per 1,000 (2000)
Under-5 child mortality: 188 per 1,000 (2000)
Daily calorie supply: 2,164 per capita (1999)
Safe water: 57 % (2000)

EDUCATION

Literacy: 60 % (2000)
male: 75 % (2000)
female: 47 % (2000)
School enrolment (net):
Primary total: 83 % (1994/2000)
male: 100 % (1995/99)
female: 100 % (1995/99)
Secondary (gross):
male: 21 % (1995/97)
female: 12 % (1995/97)
Tertiary (gross): 0 % (1998)
Primary school teachers: one for every 59 pupils (1995)

COMMUNICATIONS

3 newspapers (1995), 499 radios (1998), 3 TV sets (2000) and 4 main telephone lines (2000) per 1,000 people
Books: 3 new titles per 100,000 people (1992/94)

ECONOMY

Per capita, GDP: $ 615 (2000)
Annual growth: -0.4 % (2000)
Annual inflation: 29.5 % (2000)
Consumer price index: 365.6 (2000)
Currency: 72.6 kwacha = $ 1 (03/2002)
Cereal imports: 120,332 metric tons (2000)
Food import dependency: 20 % (1998)
Fertilizer use: 242 kg per ha (1999)
Exports: $ 445 million (2000)
Imports: $ 649 million (2000)
External debt: $ 2,716 million (2000); $ 240 per capita (2000)
Debt service: 11.4 % of exports (1999)
Development aid received: $ 446 million (1999) ; $ 41.3 per capita (1999) ; 24.60 % of GNP (1999)

HDI (ranking/value): 151 /0.397 (1999)

Malaysia

Population:	23,036,000 (2002)
Land area:	328,550 SQ KM
Capital:	Kuala Lumpur
Currency:	Ringgit
Language:	Bahasa Melayu

Malaysia

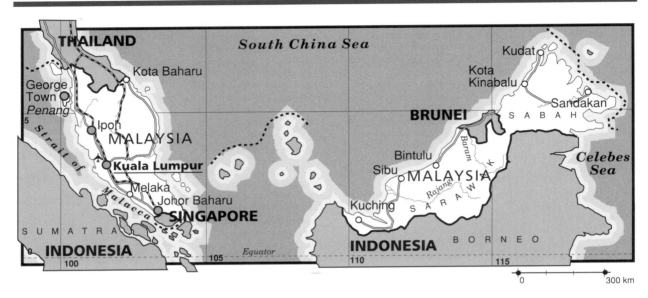

The Malay Peninsula and the Borneo states of Sarawak and Sabah were originally inhabited by native aboriginal peoples, living in the forests.

[2] In the second millennium BC, there was migration from the south of present-day China to present-day Malaysia, Indonesia and the Philippines. Over the millennia, metal-working techniques and agriculture were introduced. Rice farming was not developed until the first millennium AD. Indian influence was all-pervasive, bringing religion, political systems and the Sanskrit language.

[3] The Indianized kingdom of Funan was founded in the Mekong river area in the 1st century AD and Buddhist states eventually developed in the east, trading with China. In the 15th century, the port of Melaka (Malacca) was founded; its rulers were the first in the region to convert to Islam. Trade with Islamic merchants brought prosperity to Melaka. The new faith spread across the rest of present-day Malaysia and Indonesia, replacing Buddhism. At the beginning of the 16th century, Melaka attracted the Portuguese, who were competing with Arab merchants for the Indian Ocean trade routes.

[4] In 1511 the Portuguese viceroy of India, Alfonso de Albuquerque, seized the port by force. It was of vital strategic importance in the Portuguese struggle to maintain their monopoly on the spice-trade from the Moluccas Islands. These spices were exchanged for Indian textiles and Chinese silk and porcelain. In the 17th century, the Dutch formed an alliance with the Sultan of Johor to drive the Portuguese out of Melaka. This alliance between Johor and the Dutch was established in Batavia (present-day Jakarta) and it succeeded in eliminating European and Asian competition for a hundred years.

[5] Meanwhile, the British began to establish back-up points for their trade with China in northern Borneo (Kalimantan), and in 1786 founded the port of Georgetown, on the island of Penang (Pulau-Pinang), off the western coast. The British model of free trade proved more successful than the Dutch trade monopoly and Penang attracted a cosmopolitan population of Malays, Sumatrans, Indians and Chinese. In 1819, the British founded Singapore, but at the time they were more interested in safeguarding shipping than in the local spice trade, as their imports from China were being paid for with opium from India. Nevertheless, the Dutch and the British found it difficult to coexist in the region. A treaty drawn up in 1824 granted control of Indonesia to the Dutch, while Malaya was left in British hands.

[6] The colonies of Penang, Melaka and Singapore became the key points of the British colony. The British encouraged Chinese (and to a lesser degree, Indian) immigration to the ports along the Straits of Malacca, and large numbers of Chinese arrived to work the tin mines and service the urban ports. The Malay peasants and fishing people continued their traditional activities. From 1870, the British began to sign protectorate agreements with the sultans and in 1895 they encouraged them to form a federation, with Kuala Lumpur as its capital. The sultanates of northern Borneo (Brunei, Sabah and Sarawak, the latter ruled by James Brooke, and his heirs) also became British protectorates, administered from Singapore, but without any formal ties with the peninsula.

[7] Towards the end of the 19th century, the British introduced rubber with Hevea seeds smuggled from Brazil, so bringing about an end to the rubber boom in the South American Amazon. They encouraged Tamil immigration from southern India, to get workers for the rubber plantations which faced growing demand from the incipient automobile industries.

[8] The colonial administration set up a three band education system that differed for Malays, Indians and Chinese. In the economy, the Malays stayed mainly in rural agriculture, the Chinese worked in tin mines and the urban service sectors, and the Indians worked on the rubber estates. In the first decades of the 20th century, the Malays joined the Islamic reform movements of the Middle East, the Indians supported the struggles of Mahatma Gandhi, and the Chinese were ideologically influenced first by the nationalism of Sun Yat-Sen and then by the Communist Party.

[9] In 1942, during World War II, the country was occupied by the Japanese. The Japanese tried to form alliances with local Southeast Asian nationalist movements to gain support against the European powers. The greatest resistance came from the Chinese, especially the Malayan Communist Party, which organized guerrillas to oppose the invading forces.

[10] At the end of the war it was clear that British domination could not persist without changes, but the difficulties of diverse ethnic interests, 'protected' sultanates and ports under direct colonial administration, made it difficult to find a suitable political system. The British proposed a Malayan Union with equal citizenship for all. This threatened the position of the Malays, and Malay nationalists gathered around the symbolic figure of the sultans founding the United Malays' National Organization (UMNO), controlled by the dominant class but with popular support.

[11] In 1948, there was a communist-led insurrection that was

suppressed by British forces. Its failure was partly due to the view of many poor Malays and Indians that the revolt was a Chinese effort and not the action of a unifying, anti-colonial progressive movement. The Marxist parties were outlawed and their leaders jailed. From 1948 until 1960, the Communist Party waged guerrilla warfare in the northern Malayan Peninsula and in Borneo.

[12] Journalist and activist Dato Onn made a new attempt at creating a pan-ethnic party. He left UMNO to found the Malayan Independence Party. He was defeated in the 1952 municipal elections by an alliance of UMNO and the Malayan Chinese Association (MCA). The alliance was later broadened to include the Malayan Indian Congress (MIC), winning nationwide elections, except for Singapore, where Lee Kuan Yew's socialists were victorious.

[13] Faced with the threat of an armed communist insurrection, the British decided to negotiate. This resulted in Malayan independence in 1957. Tunku Abdul Rahman, a prince who led the independence movement, became the first prime minister. A federation of 11 states was established with a parliamentary system and a monarch chosen every five years from among nine state sultans. A constitutional bargain was struck by the three communities: citizenship was granted to the non-Malays, but the Malays were recognized as indigenous people. They were accorded special privileges in education and public-sector

MATERNAL MORTALITY

1985-99

Per 100,000 live births

41

LITERACY

2000

88%

employment and Malay would be the official language. The country adopted the free market system and a reliance on foreign capital, which had been established under colonialism, remained dominant. Malaya was politically pro-Western.

[14] In 1963, the British colonial states of Singapore (south of Malaya), Sabah and Sarawak obtained independence and joined Malaya to form the Federation of Malaysia. There were major disagreements over ethnic policy and Singapore was expelled from the federation in 1965 becoming an independent republic.

[15] The conservative Alliance Party ruled with a large majority from 1957, but in the 1969 elections it lost many seats to the Islamic PAS Party, Gerakan and - mostly - to the Chinese-based Democratic Action Party (DAP). Tensions escalated into widespread riots and unrest, largely blamed by the authorities on 'Communist Terrorists'.

[16] The parliamentary system was suspended and the country was ruled for two years by a National Operations Council. The Malay population were dissatisfied with their share of corporate equity, because in 1970 they made up over 50 per cent of the population, but had only one per cent of the income. A new economic policy was formulated to deal with this. It set targets to increase the Malay and other *Bumiputera* ('sons-of-the-soil' [sic] or indigenous people) share to 30 per cent by 1990, while the foreign share would drop from 70 to 30 per cent and the non-Bumiputera (mainly Chinese and Indian) share would be 40 per cent.

[17] This policy dominated internal economic policy for the next two decades. The Bumiputera equity share rose to almost 20 per cent by 1989 whilst foreign ownership fell below 40 per cent. Because of these policies, Malaysians of Chinese descent claimed that they faced discrimination at work, in education and elsewhere.

[18] The present prime minister, Mahathir Mohamad, took office in 1981, and started to develop Malaysia's industry. In the late 1980s he faced increasing challenges to his leadership from UMNO (the Front's main party). Some of his opponents

left to form a new opposition party, Semangat 46. In 1990 they formed a loose opposition coalition with the Islamic PAS, the DAP and the small left-wing People's Party.

[19] The Internal Security Act allowed detention without trial for two years. Under Mahathir at this time, the number of political prisoners declined from over 1,000 to a few hundred. In 1987 a major crackdown led to 150 more detentions, including opposition politicians and leaders of social groups, all of whom were released by 1990.

[20] Malaysian foreign policy moved from its pro-western position in the 1960s through non-alignment in the 1970s to a pro-Third World stance in the 1980s. In 1990, Kuala Lumpur hosted the inaugural summit meeting of 15 Third World countries (including India, Brazil, Indonesia, Mexico, Venezuela, Tanzania and Senegal) aimed at fostering concrete South-South co-operation projects and aiming to reduce Northern dominance of Southern economies. It played a major role in the South Commission and actively supported the Palestine Liberation Organization and South Africa's African National Congress in their nationalist and anti-racism struggles.

[21] Malaysia is a large tropical wood exporter and dealer, with a growing demand in the industrialized countries, especially Japan. In 1989 its timber exports earned $ 2.6 billion. More than 80 per cent of this timber came from Sarawak and Sabah, in Borneo. It is estimated that out of the previous 305,000 square kilometers (sq km) of tropical forests, only 157,000 sq km are left, and the country loses 5,000 sq km of tropical forest each year. Because of this Malaysia through its multinational companies shifted to logging in other countries (Brazil, RD Congo, Zimbabwe, Papua-New Guinea among others).

[22] Tuanku Ja'afar ibni al-Marhum Tuanku Abdul Rahman was elected sovereign in April 1994. Support for Prime Minister Mahathir was apparent in 1995 when his National Front coalition took 162 of the 192 seats in the Chamber of Representatives, and 84 per cent of the vote.

PROFILE

ENVIRONMENT

The Federation of Malaysia is made up of Peninsular Malaysia (131,588 sq km), and the states of Sarawak (124,450 sq km) and Sabah (73,711 sq km) in northern Borneo (Kalimantan), 640 km from the peninsula in the Indonesian archipelago. Thick tropical forests cover more than 70 per cent of the mainland area, and a mountain range stretches from north to south across the peninsula. Coastal plains border the hills on both sides. In Sabah and Sarawak, coastal plains ascend to the mountainous interior. There is heavy annual rainfall. Malaysia's economy is export orientated. Tin and rubber, the traditional export products have recently been replaced by petroleum and manufactured goods. Indiscriminate logging and the use of highly toxic herbicides worries ecologists who fear irreparable damage to native species, and the destruction of the few surviving native cultures.

SOCIETY

Peoples: Bumiputera (Malays and other indigenous peoples: Orang Asli, that includes the Negritos, Senoi and Proto-Malays) 60 per cent, Chinese 30 per cent, Indians 10 per cent.
Religions: Islam, the official religion, is practiced by 54 per cent of the population. Buddhist 17 per cent, Taoist 11 per cent, Hindu, 7 per cent, Christians 7 per cent.
Languages: Bahasa Melayu (Malay) is the official language. Chinese dialects, Tamil, English and dozens of Orang Asli languages.
Political parties: Barisan Nasional (National Front), including Pertubuhan Kebangsaan Melayu Bersatu (United Malays National Organisation) and smaller parties which represent Chinese and Indian minority groups; Barisan Alternatif (Alternative Front), including the Parti Tingkang Demokratik (Democratic Action Party), Parti Islam SeMalaysia PAS (Islamic Party of Malaysia) and Parti Keadilan Nasional (National Justice Party); Parti Rakyat Malaysia (Malaysian People's Party).
Social Organizations: The leading labor organization is the Congress of Malaysia's Unions. Network of Indigenous Peoples of Malaysia.

THE STATE

Official Name: Persekutan Tanah Malaysia.
Capital: Kuala Lumpur 1,348,000 people (1999).
Other cities: Johor Baharu 691,000; Ipoh 552,800 people; Petaling Jaya 474,600; Melaka 126,100 (2000).
Government: Constitutional, parliamentary and federal monarchy. Tuanku Salehuddin Abdul Aziz Shah ibn al-Marhum Hisamuddin Alam Shah is the current king or *yang di-pertuan agong*, since April 1999. The sovereign is elected every five years from among the nine regents (sultans), and only the sultans can vote. Datuk Seri Mahathir ibn Mohamad, Prime Minister since 1981. Central bicameral parliament, 69-member senate, 192-member chamber of deputies, with a constitution and a legislative assembly for every state.
National Holiday: August 31, Independence Day (1957).
Armed Forces: 114,500 (1995).
Other: 21,500 Police, Regular, Sea and Air, Auxiliaries.

FOOD DEPENDENCY

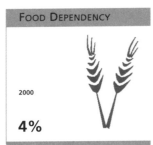

2000

4%

EXTERNAL DEBT

2000

PER CAPITA

US$ 1,881

FOREIGN TRADE

Millions US$ 2000

IMPORTS

93,565

EXPORTS

112,513

DEMOGRAPHY

Population: 23,036,000 (2002)
Annual growth: 2.3 % (1985-2000)
Estimates for year 2015: 27,911,000 (2000)
Annual growth to year 2015: 1.5 % (2000)
Urban population: 57.4 % (2000)
Urban growth: 3.7 % (2000)
Children per woman: 3.1 (2000)

HEALTH

Life expectancy at birth: 73 years (2000-2005)
male: 71 years (2000-2005)
female: 76 years (2000-2005)
Maternal mortality: 41 per 100,000 live births (1985/99)
Infant mortality: 8 per 1,000 (2000)
Under-5 child mortality: 9 per 1,000 (2000)
Daily calorie supply: 2,946 per capita (1999)
66 doctors per 100,000 people (1997)

EDUCATION

Literacy: 88 % (2000)
male: 91 % (2000)
female: 84 % (2000)
School enrolment (net):
Primary total: 94 % (1994/2000)
male: 95 % (1995/99)
female: 96 % (1995/99)
Secondary (gross):
male: 58 % (1995/97)
female: 66 % (1995/97)
Tertiary (gross): 11 % (1997)
Primary school teachers: one for every 22 pupils (1998)

COMMUNICATIONS

158 newspapers (1996), 420 radios (1997), 168 TV sets (2000) and 199 main telephone lines (2000) per 1,000 people
Books: 21 new titles per 100,000 people (1992/94)

ECONOMY

Per capita, GDP: $ 9,068 (2000)
Annual growth: 5.7 % (2000)
Annual inflation: 1.5 % (2000)
Consumer price index: 116.7 (2000)
Currency: 3.8 ringgits = $ 1 (03/2002)
Cereal imports: 4,150,602 metric tons (2000)
Food import dependency: 4 % (2000)
Fertilizer use: 8,359 kg per ha (1999)
Exports: $ 112,513 million (2000)
Imports: $ 93,565 million (2000)
External debt: $ 41,797 million (2000); $ 1,881 per capita (2000)
Debt service: 4.8 % of exports (1999)
Development aid received: $ 143 million (1999); $ 6.3 per capita (1999); 0.20 % of GNP (1999)

ENERGY

Consumption: 1,966.8 Kgs of oil equivalent per capita yearly (1998); -72.1 % imported (1999)

HDI (ranking/value): 56 / 0.774 (1999)

[23] In early September 1998, after months of debate on how to end the economic crisis, Prime Minister Mahathir removed Economy Minister Anwar Ibrahim from office, accusing him of 'sexual misconduct'. After his dismissal, Anwar led major protests against the Government and was arrested on September 20. The opposition could identify with Anwar, seeing him as a liberal and a champion of foreign investment, and showed its support in protests. After he was imprisoned, the opposition's leadership passed into the hands of his wife, Azizah Ismail. The economy suffered a 7 per cent recession compared to the previous year, and the new Economy Minister called for control over exchange rates and investment in order to stabilize the country.

[24] In April 1999, Anwar was sentenced to six years in prison, charged with 'sexual misconduct' and sodomy. Tens of thousands of demonstrators took to the streets of Kuala Lumpur to express solidarity for Anwar.

[25] The November 1999 legislative elections gave the absolute majority and more than two thirds of the seats to the governing party, allowing Mahathir to continue in power until 2005. The Alternative Front, led by Azizah Ismail, received less than 20 per cent of the vote and complained that the Government had permitted just nine days of political campaigning. Meanwhile, the party of the Prime Minister, UMNO, suffered internal divisions, losing ground to its Islamic partner, PAS.

[26] In January 2000, once the trial against Anwar resumed, the Government detained four opposition political leaders and the former Economy Minister's defense lawyer, unleashing a wave of protests within and outside the country. Charges against the opposition included sedition and inciting racial violence. In March that year, the Government limited the number of issues that *Harakah* could publish. *Harakah* had grown due to its extensive coverage of the Anwar case. In April, responding to criticism, the Government announced the formation of a National Commission of Human Rights, to take citizens' complaints.

[27] In a religious meeting held in October in Kota Baru, capital of Kelantan, a Kelantan leader, Nik Aziz Nik Mat, accused women of being the cause of 'social disease and moral decay'. Nik Aziz, religious teacher and spiritual advisor to the PAS, who governed both Kelantan and the neighboring state of Terengganu, had brought in separate cashiers for men and women in Kelantan's supermarkets. At this time there were several women in the Malaysian Government, among them two ministers and the Central Bank governor. Also, in December Mahathir appointed Ainum Mohamad Saaid as public prosecutor, the first time a woman held that office in the country's history. After the appointment, Mahathir stated his Government preferred to appoint women in high posts because they were better candidates than men.

[28] In spite of protests and complaints from environmentalists, in February 2001 the Government went ahead with a mega-dam project in Bakun, Borneo, planned to become the largest in South Asia. Apart from costing $5 billion, the dam would displace 10,000 people, log and flood large rainforest areas. A private company, jointly linked to the Government, began the logging.

[29] In March, dozens of people were arrested in a poor Kuala Lumpur suburb during the worst ethnic clashes between Indians and Malays since 1969. Defense minister Najib Tun Razak tried to minimize the ethnic causes and reduce it to a misunderstanding among neighbors. Kerk Kim Hock, Secretary General of the opposition Democratic Action Party, called for multi-party talks to ease the tension and the 'fragility of ethnic relations'. The Indian community, mostly descending from laborers who had come to work in rubber plantations during colonial times, is the poorest in the country.

[30] A tighter control over capital flows had enabled the Government to ease the effects of the financial crisis and avoid special loans and rules imposed by international financial institutions. On opening in June the yearly assembly of the UMNO, Mahathir lashed out at the West - as he had done before - the IMF and the World Bank, pointing out they 'hate Malaysia, and they hate it with a vengeance, especially its current Government'. With this he was alluding to the criticism he received for detaining opposition members. During the assembly, wives of jailed Anwar Ibrahim followers tried, unsuccessfully, to give Mahathir a petition of freedom for their husbands, jailed under the Security Decree, which allowed for imprisonment without trial for up to a two-year term. During the assembly, the Premier accused Anwar Ibrahim's opposition party, the Reformasi, of 'using Mafia-style strategies to reach its goals', and the PAS of being 'more interested in power than religious values', and that its members taught 'innocent children to hate the UMNO, so they may follow the PAS for life'.

[31] In April 2002 the Government gave illegal immigrants a certain period to 'give themselves up' and avoid punishments such as lashings, jail and fines, while Parliament passed amendments to the Immigration Act. After a conference in Bali, in which Asia-Pacific ministers agreed to take measures against human traffic, the authorities increased their actions against illegal residents, most of them Indonesian and Filipinos. Foreigners make up 20 per cent of the labor force in the country and are vital in areas such as construction and agriculture. More than half of the foreign workers are illegal residents.

[32] Before a visit by Mahathir to Washington, scheduled for May, the police arrested 14 people suspected of being Islamic militants, including the wife of a man accused of aiding hijackers who carried out the September 11 2001 attacks in the US. This police offensive was applauded by Washington, who thanked the support the Malaysian Government gave to the US 'war on terror'.

[33] In June 2002 Mahathir announced that he planned to resign in 2003. ∎

Maldives

Population:	309,000 (2002)
Land area:	300 SQ KM
Capital:	Male
Currency:	Rufiyaa
Language:	Dhivehi

Maldives

The Republic of the Maldives consists of an archipelago of more than 1,000 coral islands in the Indian Ocean, southwest of India and Sri Lanka, of which only 192 are permanently inhabited. Maldivans are skilled sailors and fishing people and have always had close contact with the mainland of Asia. It was through this connection that Arab and Muslim influence reached them in the 12th century; the islanders converted to Islam and their ruler took the title of Sultan.

[2] European colonizers came to the Maldives quite early on, as it was a compulsory stopover on the way to the Far East. The local peoples put up tenacious resistance to foreign domination, forcing the Portuguese to seek alternative harbors; hence the foundation of Goa on the west coast of India.

[3] Eventually, the Sultan of the Maldives gave in to the enticing offers of the agents of British imperialism and in 1887 he agreed to place his islands under British 'protection'. The economy was makeshift based on the production of coconut oil, fishing and the cultivation of tropical fruits. On the other hand, the Maldives possessed great strategic value, which was enhanced by the opening of the Suez Canal.

[4] A naval base was set up on Gan Island, on the equator, which became a link in the safety chain that protected navigation from Gibraltar to Hong Kong, via Aden and Singapore.

[5] The local population was of no interest to the authorities even as a source of labor, so very little was done for their education,

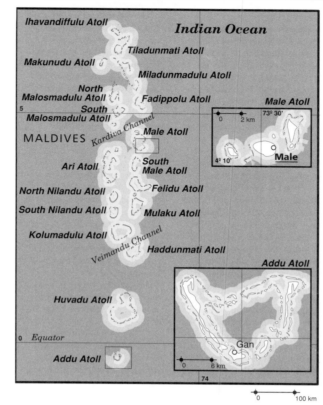

health or welfare.

[6] This neglect stimulated rebellion against the Sultan, whose position as an intermediary between his people and the colonial capital made him the only person to benefit from this contact. In 1952, a popular revolt overthrew the ruler and a republic was proclaimed. British troops intervened to 'restore order', putting the Sultan back on the throne two years later. In 1957, Britain requested permission to

enlarge the Gan naval base and install facilities for fighter planes to land there. The proposal aroused fierce opposition and pro-British Prime Minister Ibrahim Ali Didi was forced to resign. His successor, Amir Ibrahim Nasir, refused permission to build the new facilities claiming that such a project would violate the country's neutrality.

[7] In 1959, rebellion broke out in the southern Maldives, which decided to break away under the name of the Republic of Suvadiva. This autonomy was short-lived, and in 1960, the 20,000 Suvadivan republicans were restored to the sultanate with British help. The colonialists took the opportunity of signing a new agreement with the Sultan extending the protectorate, and maintaining and enlarging the bases.

[8] This time the British paid nothing towards them, only the pay due to the British soldiers and the cost of the ammunition used to stifle the rebellion in the south.

[9] The British Empire was by now in decline. During the 1960s, the

British finally decided to withdraw from their strategic positions 'east of Suez', making sure that their interests would continue to be defended by the United States.

[10] In 1965, the Maldives chose to become independent, receiving immediate recognition from the United Nations.

[11] The Sultan was unable to survive the withdrawal of foreign support and in 1968 a plebiscite was held which favored the establishment of a republic. Amir Ibrahim Nasir, the Prime Minister, now became President.

[12] The Gan naval base remained in British hands until 1975, when the building of modern US military installations on the neighboring island of Diego Garcia rendered it obsolete.

[13] In March 1975, President Nasir announced that he had uncovered a conspiracy led by Prime Minister Ahmed Zaki; Zaki was exiled to a desert island along with some of his supporters. Nasir's proposal to rent the unused installations on Gan Island to transnational enterprises was rejected by *the Majilis* (legislative council). Realizing that he had lost support, Nasir ended his second presidential term in 1978, without standing for re-election. The Majilis appointed Maumoon Gayoom, a Muslim intellectual of international prestige, to replace him.

[14] The new president concerned himself with the serious difficulties of the fishing community and set up a state fisheries corporation to control the country's main economic resource from catch to marketing. Gayoom founded schools in 19 of the major atolls and opened up the archipelago to the rest of the world, personally travelling to Europe, the Middle East and the Sixth Summit Conference of the Non-Aligned Movement.

[15] In May 1980, he officially announced that his government had crushed an attempted mercenary invasion of the islands, organized from abroad by Ibrahim Nasir. Nasir's extradition from Singapore was immediately requested.

[16] The Republic of Maldives supported Islamic solidarity, non-alignment, Palestine, the New International Economic Order,

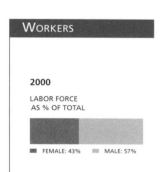

WORKERS

2000

LABOR FORCE
AS % OF TOTAL

- FEMALE: 43%
- MALE: 57%

LAND USE

DEFORESTATION: 0.8% annual (1990/95)

1993

- FOREST & WOODLAND: 3.3%
- ARABLE: 10%
- OTHER: 86.7%

96%

disarmament, African solidarity, and demilitarization of the Indian Ocean. In spite of its size, population and resources, its strategic location gave it considerable bargaining power for the country and an independent position in foreign policy. In addition, non-aligned foreign policy provided the basis for assistance and support from all, without sacrificing too much freedom of action.

[17] In April 1980, the Maldives signed a scientific and technological cooperation agreement with the Soviet Union, and in April 1981, a trade agreement with India, which is the country's closest cooperator in the region. In July, 1981, Chinese foreign minister Huang Hua visited Male and signed a technical cooperation agreement.

[18] In July 1982, the Government achieved a major diplomatic victory when the Maldives became the 47th member of the British Commonwealth. This was the second major achievement of Gayoom's government since 1979, when the Maldives had joined the Non-Aligned Movement. The Maldives have however refused to join ASEAN as this organization tends to act on bloc decisions agreed by a majority.

[19] In August 1988, three months before being elected President for the third time, Maumoon Gayoom frustrated another coup attempt, allegedly promoted by Amir Nasir. Seventy-five people were arrested, most of them Sri Lankans, of whom 16 were sentenced to death and 59 were given prison sentences.

[20] The environmental impact on the Maldives of industrial activity in developed countries, is a major issue. In March, 1990, thousands of schoolchildren demonstrated in the streets of the capital, voicing their concern over the rising sea levels around their tiny archipelago. This phenomenon is attributed to the 'greenhouse effect' which is producing global warming that will lead to the melting of the polar ice caps, causing the sea level to rise. According to scientific predictions, if present trends continue most of the islands will disappear over the next hundred years.

[21] In 1993 and 1994, the Maldives went through an economic crisis caused by the 1991 monsoons and a chronic trade deficit dating from 1992. The Government sold 25 per cent of the Bank of Maldives' shares and applied a free market economy to all sectors except frozen fish exports.

[22] President Gayoom began his fourth term of office in 1993 and remained as head of the ministries of defense, national security and finance. 27 per cent of the budget was turned over to education, health and social security. The fishing sector received 30 per cent since it employs one fourth of the working population.

[23] $113 million in tourism revenues from 1994 helped in the recovery of the archipelago's economy in 1995.

[24] Although no political parties or an organized opposition are allowed, young Maldivans educated abroad have shown signs of rejecting the system imposed by the President. The spread of religious radicalism throughout the islands was another reason for concern for Gayoom's government.

[25] The Maldives experienced slow but steady economic progress in 1996, and industrial production increased 10 per cent. Education spending increased to 9.2 per cent of the national budget.

[26] At a May 1997 meeting in Male, the Southeast Asian Co-operation Association approved poverty eradication initiatives and, based on studies confirming the rising sea level around Maldives, instituted environmental protection measures. A new Constitution was approved in November and went into effect January 1 1998, establishing that the legislature would elect the President. Choosing from among five candidates, legislators decided in September to re-elect Gayoom to a fifth term, which was confirmed by referendum in November with 90 per cent of the vote.

[27] Amnesty International (AI) accused the Government of arresting three legislative candidates in the November 1999 elections. According to AI's report, presented in January 2000, the candidates had been accused of 'inciting discontent', which could lead to their 15-year suspension from political activity. The Government had prohibited political parties from campaigning for their candidates, forcing all of them to run as individuals.

[28] In May Prime Minister of the Council of State of China, Zhu Rongji, visited Male aiming to develop a long term co-operation process with the Maldives.

PROFILE

ENVIRONMENT

There are nearly 1,200 coral islets in this archipelago, where the land is never more than 3.5 meters above sea level. Vegetation is sparse except for the plentiful coconut palms. A tropical monsoon climate prevails. There are no mineral or energy resources. Fishing is the economic mainstay.

SOCIETY

Peoples: The population of the archipelago came from migrations of Dravidian, Indo-Aryan and Sinhalese peoples from India, later followed by Arab peoples.
Religions: Muslim (official and proclaimed universal).
Languages: Dhivehi (official), an Indo-Aryan language related to Sinhalese; English and Arabic are also spoken.
Political Parties: There are no political parties. The *Majilis* or parliament is elected by direct vote and in turn proposes a president whose candidacy is submitted to a referendum.

THE STATE

Official Name: Dhivehi Jumhuriyya (Republic of the Maldives).
Administrative divisions: 20 districts.
Capital: Male 72,000 people (1999).
Other cities: Hithadhoo 10,800 people; Fuvahmulah 8,100 (2000).
Government: Presidential republic. Maumoon Abdul Gayoom, President since 1978, re-elected in 1998.
Legislative Power: the Citizens' Council, with 48 members, 8 of whom are elected by the President.
National Holiday: July 26, Independence Day (1965).
Armed forces: About 1,000. The force performs both army and police functions.

DEMOGRAPHY

Population: 309,000 (2002)
Annual growth: 3.1 % (1985-2000)
Estimates for year 2015: 453,000 (2000)
Annual growth to year 2015: 2.9 % (2000)
Urban population: 26.1 % (2000)
Urban growth: 2.8 % (2000)
Children per woman: 5.6 (2000)

HEALTH

Life expectancy at birth: 68 years (2000-2005)
male: 68 years (2000-2005)
female: 67 years (2000-2005)
Maternal mortality: 350 per 100,000 live births (1985/99)
Infant mortality: 59 per 1,000 (2000)
Under-5 child mortality: 80 per 1,000 (2000)
Daily calorie supply: 2,298 per capita (1999)
40 doctors per 100,000 people (1995)
Safe water: 100 % (2000)

EDUCATION

Literacy: 96 % (2000)
male: 96 % (2000)
female: 96 % (2000)
School enrolment (net):
Primary total: 98 % (1994/2000)
male: 93 % (1995/99)
female: 92 % (1995/99)
Secondary (gross):
male: 49 % (1995/97)
female: 49 % (1995/97)
Primary school teachers: one for every 24 pupils (1998)

COMMUNICATIONS

20 newspapers (1996), 133 radios (1997), 40 TV sets (2000) and 91 main telephone lines (2000) per 1,000 people

ECONOMY

Per capita, GDP: $ 4,485 (2000)
Annual growth: 2.3 % (2000)
Annual inflation: -1.1 % (2000)
Consumer price index: 114.7 (2000)
Currency: 11.8 rufiyaa = $ 1 (03/2002)
Cereal imports: 18,205 metric tons (2000)
Food import dependency: 24 % (2000)
Exports: $ 577 million (2000)
Imports: $ 476 million (2000)
External debt: $ 207 million (2000); $ 710 per capita (2000)
Development aid received: $ 31 million (1999); $ 113.9 per capita (1999)

HDI (ranking/value): 77 / 0.739 (1999)

[29] The global standstill in world tourism in 2001 also affected the Maldives, which despite achieving a strong 9 per cent growth in the first semester, ended the period with a loss of slightly more than 1 per cent. ∎

Mali

Population: 12,019,000 (2002)
Land area: 1,220,190 SQ KM
Capital: Bamako
Currency: CFA franc
Language: French

Mali

The territory of present-day Mali was formerly populated by groups of Berberand Arab origin in the north, and by the Bambara, Soninke, Malinke and Songhai, among others, in the west and south. In the 11th century the Malinke leader Allakoi Keita, king of Niani, converted to Islam and imposed that religion throughout his dominions. Two centuries later, after an invasion by the Soso, the only surviving Keita organized a confederation of Malinke tribes. The alliance proved powerful and in a few years had established its reign in the former kingdom of Ghana. In 1255, the new empire covered the area from the Atlantic coast to the curve of Niger and from the equatorial forests to the Sahara Desert, including present day Senegal, Gambia, Guinea-Bissau, part of Guinea, half of Mauritania, southern Algeria and all of Mali. The empire saw a great deal of trade, particularly in Djene (in the south) and Timbuktu (in the north), cities through which enormous quantities of gold passed. Timbuktu had a prestigious university that reached its peak of eminence in the 14th century.

[2] The empire of Mali was occupied by the French in 1850 and together with what are now Burkina Faso (Upper Volta), Benin and Senegal it was renamed the French Sudan and later French West Africa. Domination brought about considerable changes. Trade, which traditionally flowed towards the Mediterranean, was turned back towards the Atlantic where Dakar (in Senegal) had become the official trade center of the colony. This in turn caused the decline of the trans-Saharan trade routes. After 1945 the anti-colonial feelings of French Sudan were expressed in the formation of the African Democratic Assembly (RDA), at a conference in Bamako encouraged by the democratic atmosphere that prevailed after World War II. Under the impact of the Dien Bien Phu defeat of French colonialism in Vietnam and the Algerian revolution, Paris embarked on a policy of gradual concessions that would lead to Mali's independence in 1960.

[3] Aware of their limitations, the new states formed the Federation of Mali, but their differences soon caused it to collapse. French Sudan then severed its last remaining ties with France, becoming the Republic of Mali, with Modibo Keita as its first president.

[4] Together with presidents Senghor from Senegal and Houphouët-Boigny from Cote d'Ivoire, Keita belonged to a generation of African leaders educated in France and inspired by social democracy. Unlike his neighbors, the President of Mali did not accept neocolonialism. Instead he pushed for reforms and economic development under the banner of African socialism; moving closer to the views held by Guinea's Sekou Touré and Nkrumah of Ghana.

[5] The economy was nationalized, industrialization stimulated and the proportion of children in school rose from 4 to 20 per cent. His struggle for Pan-Africanism, non-alignment and independent foreign policy earned Keita a good reputation among progressive forces throughout the continent. He was however unable to build a strong political structure and there was a successful coup against him in November 1968.

[6] The Military Committee for National Liberation (CMLN) took over, headed by Moussa Traoré. The Committee promised to straighten out the economy and fight corruption, but the results were exactly the opposite. Grain, which had been produced in sufficient quantities to provide a surplus for export, began to be rationed in the 1970s.

[7] Economic dependence and agricultural intensification geared towards a world market created a large foreign debt for Mali during this decade.

[8] In 1974 seeking to gain political support, the CMLN held a referendum on a new constitution. With the opposition banned and the followers of Keita imprisoned, the Government won a 99.8 per cent majority, too large to be believed. On May 16 1977 Modibo Keita died somewhere in the desert where he had been held prisoner since 1968. The official cause of death was food poisoning, but this was commonly re-interpreted as simply poisoning. In the largest mass demonstration ever seen in Bamako, the people followed Keita's body to the cemetery in open defiance of the military regime.

[9] In 1979, President Moussa Traoré embarked upon an austerity program drawn up by the IMF and the international creditor banks. This stirred up social unrest. In November students and teachers took to the streets staging rallies and demonstrations which lasted for over a month. The Government reacted violently. Thirteen students were tortured to death and around 100 were arrested.

[10] In June 1985, President Traoré was re-elected for a further six years. As the official party's only candidate he received 99.94 per cent of the vote.

[11] In 1988 students, teachers and public employees took to the streets once again. The Government was reorganized and a Social and Economic Council was created, headed by General Amadou Baba Diarra.

[12] The Government faced a foreign debt which amounted to 125 per cent of its GDP, with the servicing of the debt exceeding a quarter of the income earned from exports. Negotiations for an economic adjustment program began with the IMF in 1988. The privatization of Mali's banking system was initiated, financed by an 8,000,000 CFA franc loan from France. At the same time the Government announced a reduction in their number of employees, and the decision to sell off state enterprises.

[13] On April 10 1991, a popular and military revolt against the Traoré regime carried Lt-Col Amadou Toumani Touré to power. He was the leader of the Council of Transition for the Salvation of the People (CTSP), which promised to transfer government to civilians early in 1992.

[14] Old political parties reorganized and new ones appeared. Social organizations demonstrated in favor of several issues, including pay increases, and against the privatization of public companies in the telecommunication, railroad, textile, pharmaceutical and cement sectors.

[15] In June, the rising of the Tuaregs in the north and the Moors in the east increased the state of social unrest. The new president met with his colleagues in Algeria and Mauritania to deal with the Tuareg question.

[16] An attempted coup by some of the armed forces initially led Toumani Touré to grant a salary increase of 70 per cent to the armed forces and civil servants in an effort to avert unrest.

[17] In March the next year, with Algerian mediation, the Government of Mali and the Tuaregs reached a new peace agreement. In April a final peace settlement was signed with the Azawad Unified Front and

Movements, an organization of four Tuareg opposition groups.

[18] The Malian Government and the Tuareg rebels in the north ratified a 'national peace pact' in April 1992, putting an end to almost two years of armed conflict.

[19] On April 26, Alpha Oumar Konaré, leader of the Alliance for Democracy in Mali (ADEMA), was elected President in the first multiparty elections since the country's independence in 1960. His main rival was Tieoule Mamadou Konaté, head of the Sudanese Union-African Democratic Group (US-RDA).

[20] Konaré and Konaté called for a second ballot, as neither had won an absolute majority in the initial round of voting on April 12, although seven candidates were eliminated in this first round. Both rounds of voting were characterized by a very low voter turnout (only 21 per cent of the voters participated in the second ballot).

[21] In its annual report for 1992, Amnesty International condemned the imprisonment of several opposition figures without charges or trial. Fourteen death sentences had also been passed, although

these were later commuted to life sentences. Finally, according to the report, several dozen members of the Tuareg community had been executed without trial by the army.

[22] With support from international financial organizations, Konaré consolidated the economic liberalization begun by Traoré. The President reformed the tax system, reduced public spending, privatized state companies and eliminated price controls.

[23] In 1995, the Government pursued negotiations with Tuareg rebel groups - likewise with neighboring countries - to organize the relocation of 120,000 Tuareg refugees from Algeria, Burkina Faso, Mauritania and Niger. A three year repatriation scheme was launched.

[24] A new peace agreement, signed on March 27 1996, put an end to the conflict with the Tuareg. The Government arranged the return of some 25,000 refugees from Niger. The agreement also included the demobilization of some 2,700 guerrillas.

[25] In May 1997, Alpha Oumar Konaré was re-elected President with 95.9 per cent of the valid votes. In the legislative elections of July

and August, the ruling ADEMA took 130 seats in the new parliament. In both cases, the opposition boycotted the elections and there was only a minimal turn-out.

[26] The opposition boycott coincided with increased violence in the streets, leading to the resignation of Prime Minister Ibrahim Boubacar Keita and his government in late 1997. A group of intellectuals called for the liberation of various opposition leaders to ease the situation. However, the President confirmed the Premier in his post and the latter designated a new government.

[27] In March 1998, the Government indefinitely postponed local elections planned for April 19. According to the Government, this measure was imposed to allow the political parties time to prepare, given the announcement of a further boycott by the opposition.

[28] Moussa Traore and his wife were charged with misappropriation and abuse of power, and were sentenced to death in January 1999, a sentence later changed to life imprisonment.

[29] A coup d'etat was foiled in January 2000, but few days later the President decided to include military officers in his Cabinet. Ibrahim Boubacar Keita resigned as Prime Minister in February 2000, accused by the press of being unable to eradicate poverty in the country. Mande Sidibe, an economist and former IMF official, was appointed to replace Keita.

[30] The official anti-corruption commission published its fourth report in July 2000, denouncing embezzlement and mismanagement in several private and state companies. Among those implied were the national tobacco company, pension funds, the Interior ministry and several state hospitals in Bamako, the capital. Legal actions were also lodged against the disappearance of great amounts of food donated by the United Nations.

[31] The first six Rwandan prisoners, tried and convicted of genocide by the International Criminal Court, arrived in Bamako, in December 2001, where they started serving their sentence. Among them was former Rwandan Prime Minister Jean Kambanda and the former mayor of Taba, Jean Paul Akayesu. The lack of security in Rwandan jails makes it impossible for the prisoners to serve their sentence in their homeland.

[32] After 13 years, the first turbine of the hydroelectric dam at Manantali, which Mali shares with Mauritania and Senegal, started operating. The delay of more than a decade was caused by haggling among the countries. It was finally agreed that 52 per cent of

PROFILE

ENVIRONMENT

There are three distinct regions: the northern region which is part of the Sahara desert; the central region which consists of the Sahel grasslands, subject to desertification, and finally, the southern region, with humid savannah vegetation, most of the population, and the two major rivers: the Senegal and the Niger. The shortage of water and the over use of forest resources have given rise to further aridity. There are significant gold resources. The desertification process is aggravated by the lack of water (compounded by its privatization) and the deforestation by fire in order to open the way for crops.

SOCIETY

Peoples: Among the many Malian ethnic groups, the largest are the Bambara. Other significant ethnic groups are the Malinke, Songhai, Senufo, Fulani, Dogon and Voltaic. In the north are located white and nomad populations, formed by the Tuareg and Moor, two Berber groups. **Religions:** 90 per cent, is Muslim, 9 per cent practice traditional African religions and there is a small Christian minority. **Languages:** French (official). Of the African languages, Bambara is the most widely spoken (80 per cent). Arabic and Tuareg are also spoken in the north. **Political Parties:** Alliance for Democracy in Mali (ADEMA); Party for National Renewal (PARENA); Democratic and Social Convention; Democracy and Justice Party. National Congress for Democratic Initiative (CNID); Sudanese Union-African Democratic Rally (US-RDA), a renovation of Modibo Keita's old party; Popular Movement for the Development and the United Republic of West Africa. Social organizations: National Workers Union of Mali (UNTM); Alumni and Students Association of Mali (AEEM); National Union of Women of Mali (UNFM) with 350,000 members; National Union of Mali Youth (UNJM); Movements and Unified Fronts of the Azawads (MFUA), opposition Tuareg groups. **Social Organizations:** Workers' Union of Mali; Union of Malian Women (UNFM); National Union of Malian Youth (UNJM); Association of Pupils and Students of Mali (AEEM).

THE STATE

Official Name: République du Mali. **Administrative divisions:** 8 regions and the district of Bamako. **Capital:** Bamako 1,083,000 people (1999). **Other cities:** Ségou 132,400 people; Mopti 114,400; Sikasso 125,400; Gao 104,700 (2000). **Government:** Parliamentary republic, with strong head of State. Alpha Oumar Konaré, President since June 1992, re-elected in 1997. Modibo Keita, Prime Minister since March 2002. Legislature: single-chamber: National Assembly, with 129 members, elected every 5 years. **National Holiday:** September 22, Independence Day (1960). **Armed Forces:** 7,350 (Gendarmes, Republican Guard, Militia and National Police).

production of the huge dam would go to Mali, 15 per cent to Mauritania, and 33 per cent to Senegal. More than 20,000 Malians were forcefully resettled, in 1986, in order to build the dam. ∎

Malta

Population: 393,000 (2002)
Land area: 320 SQ KM
Capital: Valletta
Currency: Liri
Language: Maltese and English

Malta

For territorial Expansionists, Malta's most valuable asset was probably its geographic location which made it the historical focus of every conflict for domination of the Mediterranean. In ancient times, Phoenicians, Greeks, Carthaginians, Romans and Saracens successively occupied the island.

² In 1090, the Normans conquered the island and 300 years later it fell to the Spanish Kingdom of Aragon. In the 16th century, the defense of the island was entrusted to the ancient order of the Knights of St John of the Hospital. Renamed the Knights of Malta, they remained there for another three centuries, until they were driven out by the French in 1798. The Congress of Vienna granted Britain sovereignty over the island, in 1815.

³ After a popular rebellion in 1921, London agreed to a certain degree of internal autonomy for the islands, which was revoked at the beginning of World War II.

⁴ During World War II, Malta suffered greatly; it was used as a base for the Allied counter-offensive against Italy. The heroic struggle of the Maltese raised their national

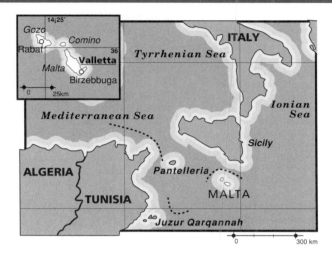

consciousness and in 1947, London restored autonomy to the island.

⁵ Independence was formally declared on September 8 1964, but Britain assumed responsibility for defense and financial support. In 1971, Dominic Mintoff's government established relations with Italy, Tunisia, the USSR and Libya, from whom it received substantial financial assistance. NATO forces left in 1971, and Malta joined the Movement of Non-Aligned Countries two years later. In December 1974, the Republic of Malta was proclaimed.

⁶ The construction of major port facilities - with financing from Libya- opened the way for new economic opportunities for the country.

⁷ In 1980, tensions developed in Malta's relations with Libya, primarily over oil explorations. The conflict was eventually turned over to the International Court of Justice in The Hague, and relations returned to normal.

⁸ From the beginning of the Labor administration, measures to reduce the Church's power had been introduced. The bishops owned 80 per cent of all real estate on the island and virtually controlled education. In July 1983, the Government expropriated all Church properties and made secular education obligatory in primary schools. In 1985, the Government and the Church signed an agreement providing for a gradual transition to secular education at the secondary level.

⁹ In May 1987, the Liberal Prime Minister, Dr Fenech Adami, initiated a policy of rapprochement towards US policies, favoring EEC membership.

¹⁰ In 1993 the European Community declared that Malta's democratic stability and its human rights policy rendered it acceptable for its incorporation into the Community. However, its economic structures were considered 'archaic' and the implementation of 'key economic reforms' was advised.

¹¹ In the elections of October 1996, the Labor Party obtained 50.7

per cent, while the National Party reached 47.8. Alfred Sant became Prime Minister.

¹² After the election, the new government withdrew the country from NATO. Sant asserted that Malta would use constitutional neutrality to promote stability and security in the Mediterranean region. The schedule for the incorporation into the European Union (EU) was also frozen, and Sant announced he would look for a more gradual entry through cooperation or free trade agreements.

¹³ A vote of censure by the opposition provoked the Sant's the government in March 1998. After the crisis, new elections were held in September. The National Party took 52 per cent of the vote. The first measure of the new head of state, Eddie Fenech Adami, was to revive the request to enter the EU.

¹⁴ On March 24 1999, the Minister of Foreign Affairs, Guido de Marco, was promoted to President by Parliament. That same year, the EU formally re-accepted Malta's application at its annual meeting in Brussels, and later authorized the start of final negotiations.

¹⁵ Malta was the first country in the new millennium to abolish the death penalty for all crimes when it passed the Law of the Armed Forces (Amendment) on March 21 2000. According to its provisions, life imprisonment replaced the death penalty for all crimes.

¹⁶ Pope John Paul II visited Malta in May 2001. Approximately 200,000 people - one half of the island population - attended the beatification by him of the three most celebrated Catholics (two priests and a nun). This open-air ceremony ended the Pope's visit to the island, where he was concluding his pilgrimage following the footsteps of St Paul. ∎

PROFILE

ENVIRONMENT
Includes five islands, two of which are uninhabited. The inhabited islands are the three largest ones: Malta, where the capital is located, 246 sq km; Gozo, 67 sq km; and Comino, 3 sq km. The archipelago is located in the Central Mediterranean Sea, south of Sicily, east of Tunis and north of Libya. The coast is high and rocky, with excellent natural harbors. The islands' environmental problems are concentrated precisely in these areas. The problems are caused by the encroachment of civilization, the development of tourism, the gradual abandonment of lands devoted to agriculture and the increase in waste. The coastal areas are also polluted by industrial activity.

SOCIETY
Peoples: The Maltese (95.7 per cent) come from numerous ethnic backgrounds, with strong Phoenician, Arab, Italian and British roots. There is a small British minority (2.1 per cent). **Religions:** Catholic (official); there are minorities of Anglicans and Muslims. **Languages:** Maltese and English, both official. Maltese is a Semitic language with Italian elements and Latin writing. **Political Parties:** The Nationalist Party; The Labor Party, Alternativa Demokratika/Alliance for Social Justice. **Social Organizations:** The Confederation of Trade Unions; the Movement of Young Students, the Graffiti Movement.

THE STATE
Official Name: Repubblika ta'Malta. **Capital:** Valletta 102,000 people (1999). **Other cities:** Birkirkara 21,700 people; Qormi 18,100; Sliema 11,800 (2000). **Government:** Parliamentary Republic. Guido de Marco, President since April 1999. Eddie Fenech Adami, Prime Minister since September 1998. Unicameral Legislature: House of Representatives has a minimum of 65 members, elected for a five-year term. The number of seats can increase if no party gets absolute majority in the parliament. **National Holiday:** September 21, Independence Day (1964). **Armed Forces:** 1,950 troops (1996).

Marshall Islands

Population: 53,000 (2002)
Land area: 180 SQ KM
Capital: Majuro
Currency: US dollar
Language: Marshallese and English

Marshall Islands

The Kwajalein and Bikini atolls of the Marshall Islands were thrust into modern history in February 1944 when heavy bombing by combined US naval and air force units hit the islands. This was followed by a prolonged and bloody battle which ended with the defeat of the Japanese and the occupation of the islands. Countless lives were lost but the military command considered it was a fair price to pay for the islands given their strategic position.

[2] In 1979, the US proposed to make an Associated Free State with the four administrative units of the region; the Kwajalein and Bikini atolls, plus the Mariana and Caroline islands which were also trust territories. The Marshall Islands were granted jurisdiction over local and foreign affairs but the US declared the islands military territory for specific use.

[3] In 1961, Kwajalein became the Pacific experimental missile target area, especially for intercontinental ballistic missiles launched from California, and early in the 1980s the US chose the atoll as a testing site for its new MX missiles. The local population was evicted and entry was forbidden to civilians.

[4] Twenty three nuclear tests were performed there between 1946 and 1958, including the detonation of the first H-bomb. Despite the legacy of cancer, thyroid diseases and leukemia left behind by the bomb, the inhabitants of the atoll insisted on returning to their homeland after having been transferred to the Rongerik atoll. In 1979, testing revealed that 139 of the total 600 inhabitants living on the Bikini atoll had extremely dangerous levels of plutonium in their bodies.

[5] The inhabitants of Bikini, together with those living on Rongelap (also exposed to the radioactivity of the H-bomb dropped on Bikini) sued the US Government for $450 million. Abnormalities already existed in children under 10 years of age and could not be eliminated. The charges were filed together with reports compiled by US Government agencies proving that local people had been intentionally exposed to radioactivity in 1954 in order to

study the effects of the bomb on humans. Reports revealed by the US Government in 1995 proved the dangers of exposure were known but this had never been passed on to the Marshall Islands population.

[6] In April 1990, the US announced that it would use the area to destroy all the nerve gas supplies which had been installed in Europe to date. Environmentalists denounced plans to dispose of 25 million tons of toxic waste on one

of the archipelago's atolls between 1989 and 1994.

[7] In October 1986, the US and the Marshall Islands signed a pact, whereby the latter became a Free Associated State, responsible for its own internal politics. According to the pact, the US would be responsible for the defense of the new state for a period of 15 years, which would enable the US to have an air base on the island, and entitle the island to US financial aid.

[8] In the first elections of the new state, held in 1986, Amata Kabua was elected President.

[9] On September 17 1990, during the 46th UN General Assembly, held in New York, the Marshall Islands were accepted as a member state of the organization.

[10] Chancellor Tony de Brun founded the Ralik Ratak Democratic Party in June 1991, after distancing himself from President Kabua who, after being re-elected for a fourth consecutive term, died in December 1996. In January 1997, Parliament appointed Imata Kabua, cousin of the deceased, as the new president.

[11] In June the opposition won a suspension of the storage of nuclear waste. The Government announced the construction of a large hotel and casino complex, funded with South Korean capital.

[12] In February 1998, the Asian banks expressed satisfaction with economic reforms which, according to the Government, related to the end of US aid. The Marshall Islands Government started talks with Washington to form a Free Association Agreement similar to that between the US and Micronesia. This would establish the sovereignty of the island, the right of the people to their own constitution and self-rule, and the possibility of withdrawing from the Agreement if either of the parties should so wish.

[13] In June the Government decided on a 12.5 per cent salary reduction for all state workers, which caused protests. The fiscal deficit, one of the Government's greatest economic problems, resisted reduction.

[14] In the legislative elections of November 15, 1999, the opposition United Democratic Party took 18 of the 33 seats. In January 2000, President Kessai Note was elected; he was previously speaker in the Nitigela (Legislature). Note announced that his aims were centered on anti-corruption policies, in response to denunciations made by the Money-Laundering Working Group, which pinpointed the island as amongst the states with most serious money-laundering problems. ∎

PROFILE

ENVIRONMENT

A total of 1,152 islands grouped in 34 atolls and 870 reefs. The land area covers 180 sq km, but the islands are scattered over a million sq km in the Pacific. The atolls of Mili, Majuro, Maloelap, Wotje and Likiep lie to the north-east. The south-west atolls are: Jaluit, Kwajalein, Rongelap, Bikini and Enewetak among others. The northern islands receive less rainfall than the southern atolls.

SOCIETY

Peoples: Sixty per cent of the population lives on Majuro and Kwajalein. A large number of Kwajalein's residents are US military personnel. Most inhabitants are of native descent (96.9 per cent), with minority communities of Filippino (0.5 per cent) and others (2.6 per cent).
Religions: Protestant 90.1 per cent; Roman Catholic 8.5 per cent; other 1.4 per cent.
Languages: Marshallese (kajin-majol), English.
Political Parties: Ralik Ratak Democratic Party; Kabua Party.

THE STATE

Official Name: Republic of the Marshall Islands.
Administrative divisions: 25 districts.
Capital: Majuro 33,000 people (1999).
Other cities: Ebeye 13,000 people; Jaluit 2,500 (2000).
Government: Parliamentary Republic. Kessai H Note, President of the islands' government since January 2000. High Commissioner Janet McCoy is the US Government delegate and handles security, defense and foreign affairs. The Constitution provides for a 33-member parliament which appoints the local President.
National holiday: May 1, Proclamation of the Republic (1979); October 26, Independence Day (1986).
Armed Forces: No regular military forces.

Martinique

Population: 388,000 (2002)
Land area: 1,100 SQ KM
Capital: Fort-de-France
Currency: Euro
Language: French

Martinique

The Carib Indians migrated throughout the central and northern parts of the South American continent, and from there to the nearby islands in the Caribbean. They called the largest of the Lesser Antilles 'Madinina', becoming known as Martinique in the colonial period.

[2] The Caribs were primarily hunter-gatherers and banded together to form a small group on the island. The French occupied it in 1635, but economic development did not occur until 150 years or so later.

[3] Late in the 17th century, sugar cultivation transformed the natural and economic landscape of the island, ending the Indians' lifestyle. The system of production changed on the sugarcane plantations. The indigenous population was replaced by African slaves, brought to the island by slave-traders. This monoculture dominated Martinique's economy, reinforcing the colonial ties with France.

[4] A minority of 12,000 European land, sugar mill and business owners controlled 93,000 slave laborers, an imbalance that gave rise to countless uprisings, known as Marronuage - meaning collective rebellions of slaves. Accounts written in those days recall the existence of *quilombos* (see Quilombos in Brazil) on the island in 1811, 1822 and 1833: years when rebellions shook Martinique.

[5] In the early 19th century, unprecedented social disturbances occurred as the traditional plantation system was abandoned and industrialization could not set off due to lack of investment.

[6] In 1937 the formation of Martinique's central labor union provided an organizational framework for social mobilization. Leftist Aimé Césaire was elected mayor of Fort-de-France in 1945 and, in 1946, Martinique's deputy in the National French Assembly. Césaire was co-founder, alongside Senegal's Léopold Sédar Senghor, of the *Négritude* (negritude) movement that protested the imposition of French cultural parameters.

[7] In 1946 the French Government revised its approach to colonial relations and in 1948 created the Overseas Department. Martinique's middle class at first aspired to have the same rights as the French, but opposition within the anti-colonialist movement blocked consensus support for that goal.

[8] While both emigration to France and French foreign aid had always been a palliative for Martinique's economic problems, demands for independence resulted only in the granting of greater autonomy. The visits of French President Charles de Gaulle (1956, 1960, and 1964) could not smooth over the political unrest and by the late 1970s the French government, in an apparent about-face, decided to help Martinique become economically self-sufficient in preparation for independence. Despite liberation groups being responsible for several bombings in Paris and the French Caribbean islands in the 1980s, there was little official movement toward independence.

[9] In the March 1986 elections, left-wing parties took 21 of a total of 41 seats in the regional Council. Aimé Césaire, representing the left coalition, was re-elected president of the Council. Rodolphe Désiré became the first left-wing Martinique representative in the French Senate, for the Martinique Progressive Party.

[10] The establishing of the single European market made the economic situation even worse in 1993. That year's elections resulted in a tie between the right on one side and pro-independence groups on the other. In the plebiscite to ratify the Maastricht treaty, three-quarters of the Martinique electorate abstained, showing hostility, or at least a passive attitude to deeper integration with the European Union.

[11] In 1997, US pressure encouraging banana production in Central America continued, damaging Caribbean exports. In early 1998, unemployment affected 40 per cent of the active population, a historical record in the country.

[12] French President Jacques Chirac visited the island in March 2000, where he was confronted by increasing demands from the people of Martinique, wanting greater trade with France, while demanding more autonomy from Paris in order to trade independently with its Caribbean neighbors.

[13] Michel Cadot became Commissioner, replacing Dominique Bellion in July 2000.

[14] The new European currency, the euro, became legal tender in Martinique in January 2001, as it did in France. ∎

PROFILE

ENVIRONMENT

Martinique is a volcanic island, one of the Windward Islands of the Lesser Antilles. Mount Pelée, whose eruption in 1902 destroyed the city of St Pierre is a dominant feature of the mountainous terrain. The fertile land is suitable for agriculture, especially sugarcane. The tropical, humid climate is tempered by sea winds.

SOCIETY

Peoples: Descendants of former enslaved Africans (90 per cent). There is a minority made up of people of European origin (5 per cent). Indian, Lebanese and Chinese (5 per cent).
Religions: Catholic (95 per cent) and traditional African religions (5 per cent).
Languages: French (official), and Creole.
Political Parties: Communist Party of Martinique, (PCM); Progressive Party of Martinique (PPM); Union of Martinican Democrats, (UDM); Socialist Party (SP); National Martinican Front for Autonomy; Democrat Union of Martinique (DUM); Socialist Revolution Group; Martinican Independence Movement (MIM).
Social Organizations: General Confederation of Workers.

THE STATE

Official Name: Département d'Outre-Mer de la Martinique.
Capital: Fort-de-France 107,000 people (1999).
Other cities: La Trinité 13,100 people; Le Marin 7,400 (2000).
Government: Michel Cadot, French-appointed prefect since June 2000. Claude Lise, re-elected in 1998 as General Council President. The Council's 36 members are elected through universal suffrage for a 6-year term.

Mauritania

Population: 2,830,000 (2002)
Land area: 1,025,220 SQ KM
Capital: Nouakchott
Currency: Ouguiya
Language: Arabic and French

Muritaniyah

The process of desertification that turned fertile plains into the Sahara desert would have separated southern Berbers from the Mediterranean coast if camels had not been introduced into the area. The groups that migrated southward in search of pastures kept in touch with their native culture, and later shared the benefits of the Islamic civilization which flourished along the Mediterranean coast.

[2] The southern part of present-day Mauritania was the setting for one of the most peculiar African civilizations. But the Almoravid conquest and later the Fulah migrations stimulated the integration and unification of the population.

[3] In the 14th century, the Beni Hilal, who had invaded North Africa three centuries before, reached Mauritania. For over 200 years, they plundered the region and fought with the Berbers throughout an area including present-day southern Algeria and Sahara. In 1644, all the Berber groups in the region joined to fight the Arabs, but the resulting conflict, the Cherr Baba War, ended 30 years later with the defeat of the Berbers. The Arabs became a warrior caste, known as the Hassani, monopolizing the use of weapons, while trade, education and other civilian activities were left in the hands of the local population. Beneath these two groups came the Haratan, African shepherds from the south, kept as semi-serfs. Though this rigid social stratification weakened with time, it is still intact among the Arab-Berbers, the Fulah and Soninke.

[4] Towards the end of the 17th century various emirates arose. These were unable to achieve the political organization of the country, due to their internal rivalries and dynastic quarrels. Nevertheless, they provided a minimal degree of order within the region that led in turn to a small revival of trade caravans. These efforts were supported by the cultural unification being carried out by the zuaias. These Berber-Marabouts devised a simple system of Arabic writing, propagating it along with their religious teachings.

[5] In the 19th century, growing trade coincided with a French project to transfer French-Sudanese (now Mali) commercial activities to Senegal, requiring the elimination of trans-Saharan trade and the frequent robberies in Senegal. The French therefore invaded Mauritania in 1858, under General Faidherbe, and the fighting continued until the 20th century. The resistance initially met in the emirates of Trarza and Brakna continued with the Sheikh Ma al-Aini (see Western Sahara), with his sons and later his cousin, Muhammad al-Mamun, the emir of Adrar. Pursued by the French almost one thousand kilometers into the Sahara, Muhammad al-Mamun died in combat in 1934.

[6] After World War II, Mauritania became a French Overseas Province, sending deputies to the French Parliament. Ten years later internal autonomy was granted and in 1960 independence was gained.

[7] A French transnational company, MIFERMA, was more powerful than the Government. MIFERMA's iron ore mines supplied 80 per cent of the country's exports and employed one in four salaried workers.

[8] In 1965 Mauritania withdrew from OCAM (the Common Afro-Mauritanian Organization), created to maintain French control over their former colonies.

[9] In 1966, the Government set up a state company, SOMITEX, with a monopoly on sugar, rice and tea imports, and a campaign was launched to rekindle the Arab culture. Mauritania set up its own customs system independent from Senegal; the Arab-Mauritanian Bank was granted the monopoly on foreign trade and the country began to issue its own currency.

[10] In 1974 the iron mines were nationalized. The country started to replace French influence by closer links with Muslim countries, and finally became a member of the Arab League. Saudi Arabia, Kuwait, and Morocco supplied economic assistance.

[11] In 1975 Mauritania, fulfilling an old ambition to annex part of 'Spanish' Sahara (now Western Sahara), joined Morocco in an attempt to divide the Spanish possession. With logistic and military support from France, 3,000 Mauritanian soldiers and 10,000 Moroccan troops occupied Western Sahara.

[12] Ould Haidalla's government paid an extremely high price for this aggression. Mauritania soon became the target of violent reprisals by the Polisario Front (see Western Sahara) and was virtually occupied by Moroccan troops.

[13] Economic hardship aroused widespread popular unrest leading to protest rallies and street fighting. Opposition groups condemned Mauritanian interference in the Western Sahara liberation war.

[14] The crisis exploded in 1978 and over the next six years there were five coups. An attempt was made to Arabize the whole population, ignoring the African population (20 per cent), living in the southern part of the country.

[15] Ould Haidalla's government stopped the Arabization process and relinquished Mauritania's claim to the Sahara, making peace with the Polisario Front in August 1979. Despite with the support of young officers and intellectuals from the

WORKERS

2000

LABOR FORCE
AS % OF TOTAL

■ FEMALE: 44%   ■ MALE: 56%

LAND USE

DEFORESTATION: 0.0% annual (1990/95)

1993

■ FOREST & WOODLAND: 4.3%
■ ARABLE: 0.2%
■ OTHER: 95.5%

PUBLIC EXPENDITURE

Military expenditure (as % GNI):	**4.0 %**	(1999)
Defense expenditure (% of central government expenditure)	**18.9%**	(1999)

MATERNAL MORTALITY 1985/99

Per 100,000 live births

550

LITERACY 2000

40%

EXTERNAL DEBT 2000

PER CAPITA

US$ 938

FOREIGN TRADE

Millions US$ 2000

IMPORTS
528
EXPORTS
387

Left a decree was signed abolishing slavery, there are still thousands of people living in slavery in Mauritania.

[16] A coup occurred on December 11 1984. Maawiya Ould Sid'Ahmed Taya, an army colonel and chief of staff, ousted Haidallah. The first measures of the new administration were the recognition of the Democratic Saharawi Arab Republic (Western Sahara) and steps to dismantle a growing 'clandestine economy' (only 50 per cent of the firms operating in the country kept legal accounting records).

[17] The economic and social outlook deteriorated; the southern farming and grazing lands reduced as the desert expanded, and the impoverished nomadic people were driven to the cities.

[18] In the fishing sector the Government adopted a long-term strategy, with two objectives: on the one hand, to save resources, and on the other, to integrate the fishing industry into the rest of the economy. No new licenses are being given to foreign fishing fleets.

[19] Since 1987, a number of incidents have occurred between farmers and cattle herders in the border area along the Senegal River. In Nouakchott, many angry Mauritanians attacked hundreds of unarmed Senegalese with sticks and stones in 1989. In Dakar, Senegalese returning from Mauritania reported assassinations and mutilations of their compatriots in Mauritania. Scores of furious Senegalese reacted by murdering Mauritanian

shopkeepers, and looting their shops. Within the country, there have been instances of violence between African Mauritanians from the south and Arabs and Berbers from the rest of the country. Throughout these events, the army supported the Arabs and Berbers, killing hundreds of African Mauritanians.

[20] Repeated border incidents with Senegal, leading to hundreds of victims on both sides, prompted Senegal to break off diplomatic relations in August 1989. Thousands of refugees returned to their country of origin: 170,000 returned to Mauritania.

[21] In July 1991, the Mauritanians approved a referendum that recognized a multiparty system and established a democratic government. The opposition, concentrated in the United Democratic Front (FDU) exerted pressure on the Government to achieve this objective, but by early 1991 the only response from the Government had been increased repression. In spite of the constitutional reform, social tensions caused by the crisis did not decrease. A period of great social conflict ensued, and the majority of the population went on strike.

[22] Six months later, in January 1992, President Maawiya Ould Sid Ahmed Taya was re-elected, in the first multiparty elections to be held. The opposition and numerous international observers suspected a fraud. Taya defeated his main rival, Ahmed Ould Daddah, winning 63 per cent of the vote to Daddah's 33. In March, after two rounds of voting in the legislative election, the DSRP (the official party) achieved an absolute majority in the National Assembly, winning 67 of the 79 disputed seats.

[23] Six opposition groups boycotted the voting and denounced there had been a fraud in the elections. In April, Mauritania re-established diplomatic relations with Senegal and Mali. This allowed to resume negotiations on pending border disputes and to find a possible solution for the situation of Mauritanian refugees in both neighboring countries.

[24] Foreign aid granted by China

and France gave new impetus to Taya's discredited government, accused of electoral fraud and of being responsible for the country's difficult social conditions. The application of an IMF-sponsored adjustment plan further aggravated mounting tensions, peaking in October when the prices of basic consumer goods were increased.

[25] Demonstrations were widespread and were harshly put down by the police. In early 1993, Interior minister Ba Aliu Ibra Hasni Uld Dudi was forced to resign and was replaced by a 'moderate'. In January 1994, the ruling party won the local elections, also considered a fraud by opposition members. In May, the Government tried to prevent *Le Calame* newspaper from appearing since it included a report on Mauritania by the Amnesty International, a human rights international association.

[26] Sixty Islamic leaders were arrested in October, on charges of creating an atmosphere of fear. Afterward, the Government ordered all 'fundamentalist' militants to cease political activity.

[27] In January 1995, thousands of demonstrators rocked Nouakchott, setting cars on fire and looting shops after a new valued added tax caused a rise in prices. In June, Mauritania's creditors accepted a re-negotiation of the public debt that was then partially cancelled.

[28] In January 1996, President Taya appointed fisheries minister El Afia Ould Mohamed Khouna as Prime Minister. Most of the opposition boycotted the April elections for a new Senate. The Democratic and Social Republican Party (PRSD), won the majority of the disputed seats in the Senate and, in the October legislative elections, took 71 of the 79 seats in the National Assembly.

[29] In June 1996, an agreement with the European Union gave Mauritania access to set figure credits for five years, in return for permission to fish its national waters, considered the richest in the world. International bodies said the nation's macroeconomic performance improved. However, it continued to rank amongst the poorest nations in its social indicators.

PROFILE

ENVIRONMENT

The Sahara Desert covers two-thirds of the country. The terrain consists of rocky, dry plateaus and vast expanses of dunes where extremely dry climate prevails. The desert region reaches into the southern part of the country, the Sahel grasslands, with some rainfall and sparse vegetation. The southwestern region receives slightly more rain and is irrigated by a tributary of the Senegal River. This region holds most of the population and the main economic activities. Nomadic shepherds are scattered throughout the country. Desertification is a serious problem for Mauritania.

SOCIETY

Peoples: Three-fourths of all Mauritanians are descendants of the Moors; a mixture of Arab, Berber and African peoples, nomadic shepherds of north-west Africa. The other 25 per cent are from African groups in the south, the most important being the Peul and the Soninke. There are small groups of Wolof and Bambara.
Religions: Muslim 99.5 per cent (official and predominant), Catholics 0.2 per cent.
Languages: Arabic and French (official). The Moors speak Bassanya, an Arab dialect. In southern Mauritania, Peul-Fulani and Sarakole (of the Soninke) are also spoken.
Political parties: Democratic and Social Republican Party; Action for Change; Assembly for Democracy and Unity; African Liberation Forces of Mauritania; Union of Democratic Forces - New Era (UDF-NE).
Social Organizations: Mauritanian Workers' Union; General Organization of Workers of Mauritania.

THE STATE

Official Name: al-Jumhuriyah al-Islamiyah al-Muritaniyah.
Administrative divisions: 12 regions and the district of Nouakchott.
Capital: Nouakchott 881,000 people (1999).
Other cities: Nouadhibou 103,100 people; Kaédi 50,200; Kiffa 61,400; Rosso 46,700 (2000).
Government: Maawiya Ould Sid'Ahmed Taya, President since 1984, re-elected in December 1997. El Afia Ould Mohamed Khouna, Prime Minister since November 1998.
National Holiday: November 28, Independence Day (1960).
Armed Forces: 15,600.
Other: 6,000 (National Guard and Gendarmes).

[30] In December 1997, President Taya was re-elected with nearly 90 per cent of the vote, with Mohamed Lemine Ould Guig as Prime Minister.

[31] Human-rights organizations appealed for an end to slavery in Mauritania in April 1998. Three human-rights activists were imprisoned for denouncing cases of slavery.

[32] In October, Taya called for Guig's resignation, as he had turned out to be extremely unpopular with Mauritanians, and designated Sheikh Mohamed Khouna the new prime Minister, and he partially reshuffled the cabinet.

[33] The Paris Club of creditor nations agreed to reduce Mauritania's debt by $620 million. The Club justified its decision by stating the country was making great efforts to reform its economy.

[34] After 12 years, hundreds of black Mauritanian refugees still live in Dagana (Senegal) and they claim to have been forgotten by both governments and the United Nations. They claim that Mauritania is a racist state and that they are treated as second class citizens.

[35] The Government announced it would divide the energy and water company for separate privatization. Communications Minister Rachid Ould Salah,

reported he would seek a majority partner for the former, whilst the water company would remain mostly state-owned. Mauritania had already privatized the telecommunications sector following World Bank recommendations.

[36] In October 2001 there were parliamentary and municipal elections that led to the ruling PRSD holding the majority in the National Assembly. The opposition increased its representation in municipal government and Parliament - from 1 to 10 seats in the latter. During the last 10 years, despite a nominally multi-party system, minorities were in fact barred from participation. The new proportional representation system makes for greater electoral transparency.

[37] The World Bank granted a loan of $119 million to improve living conditions in Mauritanian towns, especially in Nouakchott and Nouadhibou, and for improvements in the education sector.

[38] In January 2002 the Government dissolved the opposition Action for Change party, defender of the rights of slaves and black Mauritanians, accusing them of being a threat to national unity and of inciting intolerance. ■

STATISTICS

DEMOGRAPHY
Population: 2,830,000 (2002)
Annual growth: 2.7 % (1985-2000)
Estimates for year 2015: 4,105,000 (2000)
Annual growth to year 2015: 2.9 % (2000)
Urban population: 57.7 % (2000)
Urban growth: 5.7 % (2000)
Children per woman: 6.0 (2000)

HEALTH
Life expectancy at birth: 52 years (2000-2005)
male: 51 years (2000-2005)
female: 54 years (2000-2005)
Maternal mortality: 550 per 100,000 live births (1985/99)
Infant mortality: 120 per 1,000 (2000)
Under-5 child mortality: 183 per 1,000 (2000)
Daily calorie supply: 2,702 per capita (1999)
14 doctors per 100,000 people (1995)
Safe water: 37 % (2000)

EDUCATION
Literacy: 40 % (2000)
male: 51 % (2000)
female: 29 % (2000)
School enrolment (net):
Primary total: 54 % (1994/2000)
male: 61 % (1995/99)
female: 53 % (1995/99)
Secondary (gross):

male: 21 % (1995/97)
female: 11 % (1995/97)
Tertiary (gross): 6 % (1998)
Primary school teachers: one for every 47 pupils (1998)

COMMUNICATIONS
0 newspaper (1996), 149 radios (1997), 96 TV sets (1999) and 7 main telephone lines (2000) per 1,000 people

ECONOMY
Per capita, GDP: $ 1,677 (2000)
Annual growth: 1.7 % (2000)
Annual inflation: 3.3 % (2000)
Consumer price index: 127.2 (2000)
Currency: 273.7 ouguiyas = $ 1 (03/2002)
Cereal imports: 501,910 metric tons (2000)
Food import dependency: 26 % (1996)
Fertilizer use: 0 kg per ha (1999)
Exports: $ 387 million (2000)
Imports: $ 528 million (2000)
External debt: $ 2,500 million (2000); $ 938 per capita (2000)
Debt service: 28.4 % of exports (1999)
Development aid received: $ 219 million (1999); $ 84.1 per capita (1999); 22.80 % of GNP (1999)

HDI (ranking/value): 139 / 0.437 (1999)

Fishing: end of the line?

Four of the 15 main fishing regions of the world have already been decimated, and nine are well on the way to becoming exhausted. The Food and Agriculture Organization (FAO) warns that this crisis is a direct consequence of the over-exploitation of marine resources at the hands of the fishing industry Marine fishing has shot up in the last 50 years. In 1952, 18.5 million tons of fish were extracted, but by the late

1980s this figure had risen to 89 million tons.

The commercialization of sea products which has led to this over-exploitation, is threatening to do away with certain species, like Canadian cod, forever. Marine diversity is threatened by this relentless race to satisfy increasing world demand. In the United States alone, according to official figures, 80 per cent of the marine population (of more than 100 species) are in

danger of extinction.

Millions of people whose way of life depends on fishing (both commercialized and subsistence) are today up against the exhaustion of these resources and extremely unequal competition with an industry supplied by the great fishing fleets.

Commercial competition made the fishing industries increase the volume of catches using equipment so indiscriminate that it kills many

species which are not even eaten. Furthermore, enormous drag nets damage the sea bed, destroying marine habitats and coral reefs.

The FAO has forecasted that if this situation continues, marine resources will soon be insufficient to meet human needs. This threat is especially worrying for the millions of people living along the rivers of the Third World, for whom fish is the main source of protein. ■

Mauritius

Population: 1,180,000 (2002)
Land area: 2,030 SQ KM
Capital: Port Louis
Currency: Rupee
Language: English

Mauritius

According to Portuguese accounts, the island of Mauritius was deserted when they first explored it in the 16th century. The island was immediately coveted by the imperial powers, who fought over it ceaselessly by both diplomatic and military means. Between 1598 and 1710, the Dutch, attracted by the island's ebony, installed themselves and named it Mauritius. In 1715, it was recolonized by the French Bourbons, who renamed it Ile de France. When rivalry between France and Britain recurred over the control of India, the island of Mauritius constituted an important strategic base. The island was used in trade with India, and treaties were signed with Madagascar and Mozambique to use their coasts to expand sugarcane plantations.

[2] During the French Revolution, Mauritius acquired a certain degree of autonomy but in 1810, it fell into British hands. In 1815, after Napoleon's defeat, the Treaty of Paris recognized the status of the island as a British colony. The British introduced sugarcane, which became the island's main economic resource right up until the present.

[3] In the 19th century, sugar plantations expanded considerably, but in 1835 the emancipation of slaves, who constituted 70 per cent of the population, caused a serious labor shortage. Emancipation was opposed by the European landowners, who tried to alleviate the situation by importing over 450,000 Indian indentured 'hired' workers over the next 100 years. With the passage of time, the Indians became an increasingly important sector of the Mauritius social and economic structure, and today their descendants constitute the majority of the Mauritius population. Local culture however still bears the mark of French influence.

[4] In 1936, the Labor Party was organized but a series of strikes were brutally repressed, causing the death, imprisonment or exile of most party leaders. Seewooagur Ramgoolam, a doctor, started his political career as the leader of the Advance group. In the late 1940s, encouraged by the colonial administration, he became leader of the Labor Party of Mauritius (PLM).

[5] During World War II, the British were unable to guarantee the security of their colonial dominions, which encouraged the emergence of claims for independence. At the same time, US political and military influence increased. The inhabitants of Mauritius fought for and achieved representation within British colonial government. In 1957, a new government structure was created, giving Mauritius its own Prime Minister. In 1959, the first elections with universal suffrage brought the PLM to power, making Seewooagur Ramgoolam Prime Minister in 1961.

[6] From Mauritius, the British administration ran the islands of Rodrigues, Cargados-Carajos and the Chagos archipelago. In 1965, with the approval of Ramgoolam, Chagos and other islands became the British Indian Ocean Territories, and the United States established a major naval base on one of its islands, Diego García.

[7] Diego García's population was secretly transferred to Mauritius, a move that caused a scandal in Congress when it was later made public. However, the island was not returned to Mauritius and its inhabitants were not granted permission to return home.

[8] Mauritius became independent in 1968, after a long decolonization process. Britain expected it to end with the granting of a very limited autonomy for the island, allowing it merely to run its domestic affairs. The 1958 Constitution, still in force, was created by the Colonial Office following the usual model used in the Commonwealth. Mauritius was a monarchy, ruled by Elizabeth II, and the sovereign was represented by a Governor-General and a High Commissioner. In 1964, the Council of Ministers and the Legislative Assembly were created. The latter appointed the Prime Minister (head of government) and the rest of the ministerial cabinet.

[9] On independence, in 1968, there was an established two-party system in the country. The Labor Party, supported by the Indian population, was the majority party. That year, the French-Mauritians and Creoles gathered in the Social Democratic Party of Mauritius (PSDM), and Muslim groups founded the Muslim Action Committee. During the 1960s, the common struggle for independence drew the Indian Labor groups and Muslims together, and in 1967 they formed an alliance which took them to power. Sir Seegwooagur Ramgoolam was re-elected Prime Minister, and Gaetan Duval, the leader of the PSDM, led the group which opposed independence. In 1969, a coalition government was formed with the Labor Party and the PSDM. Duval, the representative of the French elite and the main opponent to independence, became foreign minister, showing that the British-granted independence was a mere formality.

[10] Internally, the Government was tainted by electoral fraud and trade union repression, and in foreign affairs, it established close links with Israel and South Africa. Pretoria had a free zone in Port Louis which enabled it to trade with the EEC, thus evading international sanctions.

[11] In the 1970s a new opposition group emerged, called the Militant Mauritius Movement (MMM). It denounced the alliance between the Labor Party and the former French settlers. The growth of the MMM and the general deterioration of the political environment led to the legislative elections scheduled for 1972, being postponed until 1976. The MMM was the best supported party in the 1976 elections, but the Labor party succeeded in forming weak alliances with certain minority groups, managing to stay in power. The workers' demonstrations and the social unrest caused by unemployment increased, reaching their peak in 1979.

[12] In the 1982 elections the MMM allied with the Socialist Party of Mauritius (PSM) and won with a landslide majority. This gave them 62 of the 66 seats and full control of the Government. Anerood Jugnauth became Prime Minister. The program of the MMM-PSM alliance promised to increase job opportunities and salaries, nationalize key sectors in the economy, reduce economic links with South Africa, and demand the return of Diego Garcia from the US.

[13] The increase in the price of oil, coupled with the drop in the world price of sugar, caused a deficit in the balance of payments equal to 12 percent of the gross domestic product. The Government was forced to turn to the IMF which approved five stand-by loans between 1979 and 1985.

[14] To receive these loans, the Government had to agree to conditions imposed by the IMF: to adopt austerity measures, to postpone part of the planned salary

MATERNAL MORTALITY

1985/99

Per 100,000 live births

21

LITERACY

2000

84%

FOOD DEPENDENCY

2000

14%

STATISTICS

DEMOGRAPHY
Population: 1,180,000 (2002)
Annual growth: 0.9 % (1985-2000)
Estimates for year 2015: 1,301,000 (2000)
Annual growth to year 2015: 0.8 % (2000)
Urban population: 41.3 % (2000)
Urban growth: 1.4 % (2000)
Children per woman: 2.0 (2000)

HEALTH
Life expectancy at birth: 72 years (2000-2005)
male: 68 years (2000-2005)
female: 76 years (2000-2005)
Maternal mortality: 21 per 100,000 live births (1985/99)
Infant mortality: 17 per 1,000 (2000)
Under-5 child mortality: 20 per 1,000 (2000)
Daily calorie supply: 2,972 per capita (1999)
85 doctors per 100,000 people (1995)
Safe water: 100 % (2000)

EDUCATION
Literacy: 84 % (2000)
male: 88 % (2000)
female: 81 % (2000)
School enrolment (net):
Primary total: 97 % (1994/2000)
male: 97 % (1995/99)
female: 99 % (1995/99)
Secondary (gross):
male: 63 % (1995/97)
female: 66 % (1995/97)
Tertiary (gross): 7 % (1998)
Primary school teachers: one for every 26 pupils (1998)

COMMUNICATIONS
71 newspapers (1998), 379 radios (2000), 268 TV sets (2000) and 235 main telephone lines (2000) per 1,000 people
Books: 8 new titles per 100,000 people (1992/94)

ECONOMY
Per capita, GDP: $ 10,017 (2000)
Annual growth: 7.0 % (2000)
Annual inflation: 4.2 % (2000)
Consumer price index: 135.4 (2000)
Currency: 30.3 rupee = $ 1 (03/2002)
Cereal imports: 287,444 metric tons (2000)
Food import dependency: 14 % (2000)
Fertilizer use: 3,300 kg per ha (1999)
Exports: $ 2,783 million (2000)
Imports: $ 2,937 million (2000)
External debt: $ 2,374 million (2000); $ 2,044 per capita (2000)
Debt service: 9.7 % of exports (1999)
Development aid received: $ 42 million (1999); $ 35.3 per capita (1999); 1.00 % of GNP (1999)

HDI (ranking/value): 63 / 0.765 (1999)

---

increase and job creation programs, to relinquish part of its control over public expenditure, to cut subsidies on basic foods and to devalue the Mauritian rupee.
[15] All these measures led to clashes between the MMM and the socialists, a situation which eventually led to a call for early elections, in August of that year. The MMM was defeated and a new coalition was formed including labor, socialists and Duval's social-democrats. However, this apparent political stability was very weak and was followed by a series of governmental alliances, which did not consolidate the coalition's position. Majority parties underwent serious divisions, giving

rise to new political groups such as the Mauritius Socialist Movement (MSM), a splinter of the PSM, led by Anerood Jugnauth.
[16] The main economic potential lay in manufacture, in particular in textiles. The industrial free zones employ 90,000 people, around 10 per cent of the population, and the per capita income of the population in Mauritius is three or four times higher than the average for other African countries, though inflation is increasing at an annual rate of 16 per cent. The lack of skilled labor on Mauritius could bring a new migratory wave from Madagascar, India, and Kenya.
[17] In 1988, in agreement with the Organization of African Unity

(OAU), Mauritius demanded the devolution of the island of Tromelin, administered by France, and of the Chagos archipelago, along with the demilitarization of the Indian Ocean, which is used for maneuvers by the superpowers. The claims were supported by environmentalist groups, because of the proliferation of nuclear weapons in the claimed territories.
[18] In the legislative elections of December, 1987, the coalition of MSM, PSDM and Labor won a very narrow victory, giving it a majority in parliament. Aneerood Jugnauth was re-elected Prime Minister, and the MMM became the main opposition force.
[19] In the legislative elections held in September 1991 the governing MSM succeeded in maintaining Jugnauth in the post of Prime Minister, by reinforcing the traditional alliance with the MMM. In March 1992, Mauritius changed from a constitutional monarchy to a republic, and in June Cassam Uteem became the first President of the country.
[20] In August 1993, the Foreign Minister Paul Bérenger of the MMM withdrew from the cabinet, leaving Jugnauth without an absolute majority. In 1994, the island's economic results were still regarded as satisfactory by international agencies such as the World Bank. The foreign debt accounted for 25 per cent of the GDP and the per capita income was $2,740.
[21] In January 1995, Jugnauth included representatives of the right-wing Social Democratic Party of Mauritius in his government. In the legislative elections of December, an opposition coalition (the Militant Mauritius Movement-Labor Party) led by Paul Bérenger and Nuvin Rangoolam took two thirds of the seats. Rangoolam became Prime Minister.
[22] The social indicators in Mauritius improved in 1996. Life expectancy reached an average of 70 years and literacy reached 81.7 per cent. Most of the population had access to healthcare, and 99 per cent to clean drinking water and drainage.
[23] In June 1997, the MMM left the governing coalition. Rangoolam

PROFILE

ENVIRONMENT
This island, located in the Indian Ocean, 800 sq km east of Madagascar, is 53 km wide and 72 km long. Mauritius also controls several dependencies: Rodrigues Island, 104 sq km with 23,000 inhabitants who farm and fish; Agalega, 69 sq km with 400 inhabitants, producing copra; and Saint Brandon, 22 small islands inhabited by people who fish and collect guano. The islands are of volcanic origin, surrounded by coral reefs. The terrain climbs from a coastal lowland to a central plain enclosed by mountains. Heavy rainfall contributes to the fertility of the red tropical soils. Sugarcane is the main crop. The degradation of the soil, due to monoculture and use of pesticides, and water pollution are the most serious environmental problems.

SOCIETY
Peoples: Indo-Pakistani 68.0 per cent; Creole (mixed Caucasian, Indo-Pakistani, and African) 27.0 per cent; Chinese 3.0 per cent; Illois.
Religions: 50.6 per cent Hindu; 27.2 per cent Christian (mostly Catholic, with an Anglican minority); 16.3 per cent Muslim; 0.3 per cent Buddhist; 2 per cent other.
Languages: English (official) 29.1 per cent. Creole 21.6 per cent. Hindi 18.6 per cent. Bhojpuri (a Hindi dialect), Urdu, Hakka, French, Chinese, Tamil, Arabic, Marati, Telegu, and other languages are also spoken.
Political Parties: Social Democratic Party of Mauritius (PSDM). Mauritius Socialist Movement (MSM); Militant Mauritian Movement - Labor Party (MMM); Mauritian Militant Renaissance (RMM).
Social Organizations: General Workers' Federation (GWF); Mauritian Women's Committee.

THE STATE
Official Name: State of Mauritius.
Administrative divisions: 4 islands and 9 districts.
Capital: Port Louis 172,000 people (1999).
Other cities: Curepipe 81,500 people; Quatre Bornes 78,900 (2000).
Government: Parliamentary republic. Karl Auguste Offmann, President since February 2002; Sir Anerood Jugnauth, Prime Minister since September 2000. Legislature: single-chamber: National Assembly, with 72 members, elected every 5 years.
National Holiday: March 12, Independence Day (1968).
Armed Forces: non-existent.
Other: 1,300 élite forces.

2000

PER CAPITA

US$ 2,044

took over the functions of foreign minister when Bérenger abandoned the post. A few days later, Parliament re-elected Cassam Uteem president.

[24] India's Prime Minister Vajpayee visited the island in March 2000. His visit coincided with Mauritius' celebration of 30 years of independence. Agreements were signed between the two countries on trade, IT and coastal patrols. In September that year, Jugnauth was returned to power.

[25] In January 2001, making the most of tariff advantages for the import of African textiles to the US under the African Growth and Opportunities Act (AGOA), China announced a textile factory in Mauritius that would produce 18,000 tons of cotton per year. Washington feared that these advantages could be exploited by other Asian countries in order to access the US textile market.

[26] In February, Arianga Pillay, third president to fill the post in one week, finally signed the new anti-terrorist law under consideration by Parliament. Amongst other changes, the law allowed for the detention of suspects for longer periods without firm charges. It also denied terrorism suspects the right to legal representation. Cassam Uteem and his successor Angidi Chettiar had stood down in disagreement with the law.

[27] Information, Technology and Telecommunications Minister Geehad Geelchand toured India, the UK, France and Ireland promoting Mauritius as a new pole for cyber-development. He was sure the fiber optic connection, from May 2002, linking Portugal to Malaysia via Mauritius would convince these countries to invest in the area. He announced that the nation could offer 80 gigabites of capacity on the information highway. In addition Geelchand stressed Mauritius' comparative advantages in location, tax incentives and the multilingual population - French, English, Chinese and Hindi - as well as low-cost electricity, facilities in acquiring property and permanent residency rights. ∎

Diego García

Land area: 52 SQ KM

Language: English

The settlement of Diego García began in 1776 when the French Viscount de Souillac sent a ship there from Mauritius, trying to establish a French presence before the English could get there. French entrepreneurs obtained permission to exploit all of the island's riches: coconuts (for coconut oil), giant tortoises, fish and birds. They also established a leper colony on the island. With the defeat of Napoleon in 1815, the island passed into the hands of the British Crown together with Mauritius' other dependencies. During the 19th century, many workers came from India and Africa.

[2] Around 1900, there were approximately 500 inhabitants but the population increased radically over the next decades, with the arrival of Africans, Madagascans and Indians. Once they had settled, they developed a culture of their own. They spoke creole, a mixture of their local languages and they took part in the Tamul rituals (of Madagascan origin) even though they were mostly Roman Catholic. The indigenous Chagos community, the Ilois, lived in their traditional manner more or less unchanged until the 1960s.

[3] In 1965, Britain decided to remove Diego García from Mauritius jurisdiction, annexing it to the BIOT (British Indian Ocean Territories). Although this change was condemned by the UN, the British and Mauritius governments made a deal where a large sum changed hands. Two years later, Britain ceded the island to the United States for 50 years in exchange for a discount on its purchase of nuclear arms. To make way for the construction of important US air and naval bases, the Ilois were deported to Mauritius in the early 1970s.

[4] The 2,000 or so Ilois were abandoned as soon as they arrived in Mauritius, finding themselves in a situation of total indigence. They had not been allowed to keep their belongings and they suffered the effects of being uprooted. Many died of despair or hunger, and until today are deprived of the right to nationality. The British Government does not recognize them as subjects, and the Mauritius Government does not consider them to be citizens. Ilois' attempts to return to their land became increasingly numerous, as did their demands for a solution to their problems, and they began to receive the support of international opinion. The situation reached the US Senate in 1975, but both the US and British governments have continued to ignore the problem, each blaming the other for the situation and both spending intermittent sums of money, which do nothing more than temporarily alleviate the severity of the problem. A report issued by the Mauritius Government in 1981 revealed that 77 per cent of the Ilois wished to return to their homeland.

[5] The Government of Mauritius stopped shipping foodstuffs and supplies to Diego García, as way of emphasizing its desire to recover the islands.

[6] Between 1992 and 1993, the Government issued repeated claims to the Chagos archipelago, including Diego García, before the UN and the International Court of Justice. In reprisal, Britain cut economic aid to the country.

[7] In July 1997, just as the UK returned Hong Kong to Chinese control, Mauritius demanded that the British Prime Minister Tony Blair return Diego García to Mauritius.

[8] In July 2000, the Ilois displaced from the Chagos archipelago brought a lawsuit against the British crown. The 500 or so remaining Ilois want to return to their lands.

[9] Since the 1960s, the UK has leased the island to the US as an air and naval base. As in the past - during the Cold War against the USSR, in the Gulf War for Operation Desert Fox - the US used the island for refuelling in the war on terror in Afghanistan in 2001. The US navy base has seriously degraded the coral reefs, due to large-scale dredging and the construction industry. ∎

PROFILE

ENVIRONMENT

The Chagos Archipelago is located some 1,600 km southwest of India, in the middle of the Indian Ocean. The main islands are Diego García (8 km long by 6 km wide), Chagos, Peros, Banhaus and Solomon. The islands are made up of coral formations and are flat; they have a large number of coconut trees, which grow well here because of the tropical climate and year-round rain.

SOCIETY

Peoples: All the inhabitants are US or British military personnel.
Social Organizations: Lalit, local movement that demands the de-militarization of all the archipelago's islands and the devolution of Diego García to Mauritius.

THE STATE

Government: Rule is nominally exercised by a Commissioner from the Foreign Office in London.
Armed Forces: 25-strong Royal Navy detachment.

Mexico

Population:	101,842,000 (2002)
Land area:	1,908,690 SQ KM
Capital:	Mexico City
Currency:	New peso
Language:	Spanish

México

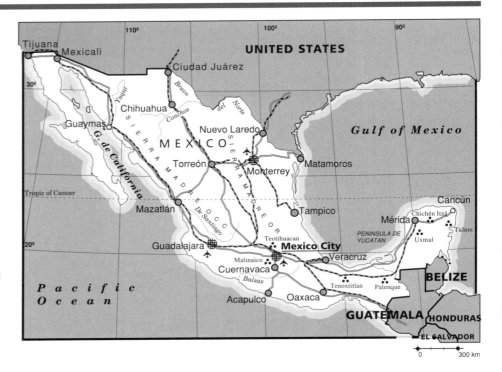

The 20,000-year history of what we know today as Mexico includes aver 2,000 years of urban life. Over this period, meso-American peoples developed advanced civilizations such as the Olmec, Teotihuacan, Maya and Mexica. These cultures had complex political and social organizations, and advanced artistic, scientific, and technological skills. The Olmecs (1200-200 BC), Mexico's first established culture, developed in the coastal states of Veracruz and Tabasco. Despite the absence of a local supply of stone, they developed massive buildings (La Venta, San Lorenzo, Tres Zapotes) and also created an advanced calendar. Around 1200 BC the Mayan culture emerged, most noted for its complex systems of mathematics and astrology, prolific city-building and complex architecture. By 1400 AD the Mayan state had splintered and almost disappeared, leaving an astonishing collection of ceremonial centers and ancient cities. In the valley of Oaxaca, around 900 BC rose the Zapotecs, who were great city builders and artisans; the Mixtec culture conquered the Zapotecs and developed around Mitla and Yagul. By the early 1400s the Mixtecs became vassals of the mighty Aztec empire. These two cultures continue their existence today in the State of Oaxaca, which is inhabited by some 2 million of their descendants.

[2] The Toltecs, a civilization of mighty warriors believed by some to have developed from the magnificent Teotihuacan culture, occupied the northern reaches of the Valley of Mexico from around 950-1300 AD. They built one of Mexico's most impressive cities (Tula), were master craftsmen, and strongly influenced later Mayan and Aztec cultures. The Aztec civilization dominated Mexico for nearly 200 years (1345-1521) and was flourishing when Spanish conquerors arrived in 1519. The Aztecs used an elaborate system of taxing and patronage to subjugate an enormous empire that stretched well into Central America. They borrowed heavily from their Olmec, Toltec, and Mayan predecessors to develop a complex linguistic,

religious, artistic, architectural and military heritage.

[3] The mighty empire came to a sudden end in 1521, when Spanish explorer Hernán Cortés took advantage of internal strife between the ruling Aztecs and other native peoples who paid them tribute. After killing Moctezuma II, Emperor of the Aztecs, Cortés put siege to the capital, Tenochtitlan, with the help of a huge native army led by the Tlazcaltecs. Once the city fell, Cortés initiated Christianization and Hispanization of the indigenous inhabitants.

[4] In the 17th century, the major economic structures of the so-called 'New Spain' were laid down. The hacienda, a landed estate, emerged as the basic production unit, and mining became the basis of a colonial economy conceived to meet the gold and silver needs of the Spanish homeland. The American Indian population was exploited and decimated by hard labor and disease. By 1800, Mexico had become one of the world's richest countries, but with great poverty also.

[5] After almost three centuries of colonial domination, the struggle for independence began in 1810,

led by *criollos* (Mexicans of Spanish descent) such as Miguel Hidalgo and José Maria Morelos, two priests. The struggle became a broad-based national movement as Indians and *Mestizos* (people of mixed European and Indian descent) joined its ranks, but the rebels were soon crushed by the royal army. The liberal revolution in Spain radically changed the situation. Afraid to lose their privileges, the Spanish residents and the conservative clergy came to an agreement with the surviving revolutionaries. This pact became known as the Iguala Plan, trading independence for a guaranteed continuation of Spanish dominance. In 1821 General Iturbide proclaimed himself Emperor, but was rapidly replaced by General Antonio López de Santa Anna.

[6] At the time, Mexico was the most extensive Spanish American country, covering 4.6 million square kilometers, including the Central American provinces, but it was also stricken by economic, political and social problems. In 1824, a Constitution was approved establishing a federal republic, made up of 19 states, four regions and a federal district. In 1836, Santa Anna, elected President three years

previously, passed a new Constitution which did away with all vestiges of federalism and the Mexican state of Texas, which had been settled by some 30,000 US citizens, called on the US for support and protection. Santa Anna led his army to victory against the Texans that year at the Alamo, but was defeated by US troops who took him prisoner later releasing him for a large ransom.

[7] In 1845, the US annexed Texas, which led to a break in diplomatic relations with Mexico. It also caused a frontier conflict, since the US claimed that the southern border of Texas was on the Rio Bravo, not the Rio Nueces (further north) as was commonly accepted. In 1846, the US president James Polk tried to force through a frontier agreement and buy the state of California - both moves rejected by Mexico. Polk ordered the US army to occupy the disputed lands between the two rivers, leading to a two-year war which was won by the US. The victors annexed all Mexican territory north of the Rio Bravo, paying $15 million and taking responsibility for a further $3.5 million to cover US citizens' claims against the Mexican government. More than half of the

Mexican territory was controlled by the US at the end of the war.

[8] Between 1821 and 1850, Mexico had 50 different governments. As with many other Latin American states, the Mexican bourgeoisie supported two political parties: the liberals and the conservatives. A minor conflict between Mexico and France (known as the Pastry War) arose in 1838-39 from the claim of a French pastry cook living in Tacubaya, near Mexico City, that some Mexican army officers had damaged his restaurant. A number of foreign powers had pressed the Mexican government without success to pay for losses that some of their nationals claimed they had suffered during several years of civil disturbances. France decided to back up its demand for $600,000 by sending a fleet to Veracruz. After occupying the city, the French won a guarantee of payment (with Britain's help) and withdrew their fleet. The main result of this conflict was the further enhancement of the prestige and influence of political dictator Antonio López de Santa Anna, who lost a leg in the fighting.

[9] After the Liberals' victory of 1857 Benito Juárez tried to strengthen the republic, instituting a free market economy, prescribing individual rights and guarantees, and expropriating the wealth of the clergy. Juárez - a Zapotec Indian educated as a middle-class liberal - and his party sought to give a juridical base for their reforms by drafting a new constitution. The Constitution of 1857 prohibited slavery and restrictions on freedom of speech or the press. It abolished special courts and prohibited civil and ecclesiastical corporations from owning property, except buildings in use; it eliminated monopolies and prescribed that Mexico was to be a representative, democratic, republican nation. Neither the religious community nor the military accepted this constitution, and both inveighed against the reform, calling for retention of 'religion and *fueros*' (privileges). The church excommunicated all civil officials who swore to support the constitution; civil war erupted and foreign powers became involved in the Mexican struggle. On April 6 1859, the United States recognized the Juárez government, permitted war supplies to be shipped to the liberal forces and encouraged its citizens to serve the liberal cause as volunteers; while Spain, Britain and France favored the conservatives.

[10] President Juárez was successful in re-establishing national unity in January 1861. He was however faced with many serious problems: the opposition's forces still remained intact, the new Congress distrusted its president, and the treasury was virtually empty. As a solution to this latter problem Juárez decided in July 1861 to suspend payment on all foreign debts for two years. France, Britain and Spain invaded Mexico in January, 1862, landing with their troops in Veracruz. But when Britain and Spain realized that Napoleon III intended to conquer Mexico and control it through a puppet, Maximilian of Austria, they withdrew their troops. Despite a major defeat at Puebla on May 5 1862, reinforcements enabled the French to occupy Mexico City in June 1863, and Maximilian - crowned Emperor of Mexico - soon followed to take control of the government. Forced to leave the capital again, Juárez kept himself and his government alive by a long series of retreats that ended only at Ciudad Juárez, on the Mexican-US border. Early in 1867, as a result of continued Mexican resistance, increased US pressure and criticism at home, Napoleon decided to withdraw his troops. Soon afterward, Mexican forces captured Maximilian and executed him.

[11] In 1871, Juan de Wata Rivera started the newspaper *The Socialist*. On September 10, this newspaper published the general statutes of the 1st Marxist International for the first time in Latin America. General Porfirio Díaz, who fought with the Liberals against French intervention, became president in 1876 and remained so until 1911. During the 35 years of his dictatorship, the country opened its doors to foreign investment, the economy was modernized and social inequalities increased.

[12] In 1910, Francisco Madero led the Mexican Revolution under the slogan 'effective suffrage, no re-election'. This was the first popular Latin American revolution of the century. In 1913, US ambassador Henry Lane Wilson participated in a conspiracy, resulting in the assassination of Madero. The people responded by taking up arms more vigorously than before. Peasants joined the revolt, led by Emiliano Zapata and Francisco (Pancho) Villa. The principles of this Revolution were set out in the Constitution of 1917, promulgated by Venustiano Carranza. It was the most socially-advanced constitution of its time and many of the principles are still in force today. However, conflict between the various revolutionary factions continued, resulting in the deaths of the major leaders.

[13] In 1929, under President Plutarco Elias Calles, these factions joined to form the National Revolutionary Party. In 1934, General Lázaro Cárdenas took office. He embodied the continuation of the revolutionary process, and was one of the main driving forces behind its accomplishments. The major reforms included land reform, the nationalization of oil (the founding of PEMEX), the expropriation of oil refineries, incentives for new industries, and a national education system. The 'No re-election' principle became lastingly inscribed in the Mexican Constitution. When Cárdenas was asked to amend the constitution for his own re-election, he refused. The National Revolutionary Party became the Institutional Revolutionary Party (PRI) and the deeply-rooted revolutionary socialist principles were gradually abandoned.

[14] Conditions created by World War II accelerated the first phase of Mexico's industrialization which reached its peak during Miguel Aleman's term of office (1946-1952). The changes that took place during this period altered the former social balance. Mexico's population remained predominantly rural, with only 40 per cent in the cities, but the rapid development was not able to absorb the quickly growing population. Communal land ownership, which had stimulated solidarity and revolutionary feeling among peasants in the 19th century, was gradually replaced by a new type of individual land tenure causing the formation of large estates or *latifundios*.

[15] During the following decade, Cardenas' successors, though not always loyal to his principles, stabilized the system by reinforcing those factors responsible for its success in a continent generally afflicted by underdevelopment and stagnation. Strong governmental influence, involving substantial public investment, kept the economy strong. A reasonable balance was maintained between heavy and light industry, tourism was encouraged and a stable government, seeming to satisfy the people's demands, was in power.

[16] Against the backdrop of the 1968 Mexico Olympics, the students' movement organized protests against the true social situation in the country. A student rally held on the Plaza de las Tres Culturas was dispersed by the army. The order to shoot to kill was given without warning, and hundreds of people died or were injured in the 'Tlatelolco Massacre'.

[17] During the presidency of José Lopez Portillo (1976-1982), important oil deposits were discovered. This bound Mexico, as the main oil supplier, more closely to the US.

[18] In 1982, Miguel de la Madrid assumed the presidency implementing an IMF economic adjustment plan. Cuts in subsidies and public spending, changes in the pattern of public investment, and a dual currency exchange rate caused public discontent and the PRI's first electoral defeat since its foundation.

[19] Under the pressure of foreign debt the trends of 1983 continued: growing inflation; losses in real wages; reductions of public spending; falls in production, and rising unemployment.

[20] In 1985, direct foreign investment increased by $1.5 billion, 66 per cent coming from US investors. However, export profits also increased, totaling $344 million in the first nine months. The $96 billion foreign debt continued to be the main problem, as it required an average annual servicing of $12 billion.

[21] The devastating earthquake of September 1986 which buried more than 20,000 people alive further aggravated an already critical situation. The reduction in the oil quota by the US made it necessary to generate alternative sources of income. One of these was tourism, and another was the *maquiladoras* - foreign companies on the border with the US which are exempt from taxes and from paying their workers social insurance, disposing of the products on the vast domestic market.

[22] The internal situation became more difficult for the PRI and it was accused of rigging the 1986 municipal elections. The formation of an independent Labor Union Negotiation Board posed a threat to the PRI's labor wing, which had traditionally formed a bloc within the Labor Congress, the largest coordinating board of labor federations.

[23] On July 6 1988, several parties gained a significant vote in the national elections, something which had not happened since 1910. Carlos Salinas de Gortari, the PRI candidate, won the ballot with - according to official figures - 50 per cent of the vote (the lowest percentage in party history). The Left emerged for the first time as a real alternative to the PRI. Cuauhtemoc Cárdenas, the son of President Cárdenas, led a coalition of groups operating as a single party, the FDN, representing the masses and opposing the Institutional Revolutionary Party. Cárdenas took second place in an election marked by accusations of fraud and irregularities, obtaining more votes than the conservative PAN (National Action Party). The abstention rate was 49.72 per cent.

[24] In 1989, the FDN split, and Cárdenas founded the Democratic Revolution Party, made up of former

members of the PRI, communists and members of smaller organizations. In the meantime, the People's Socialist Party (PPS), the Authentic Party of the Mexican Revolution (PARM) and the Party of the Cardenista Front for National Reconstruction (PFCRN) continued as autonomous organizations which voted with the PRI in Congress.

²⁵ The PRI administration resolved to open up the country to foreign investment, and also announced a series of measures aimed at controlling inflation. Both these decisions were welcomed by the US Government. Mexico made overtures to the US to sign a free trade agreement, coinciding with Mexico's entry into GATT (now the World Trade Organization - WTO) and the legal authorization for foreign investment in Mexican enterprises to go above the previously stipulated 49 per cent. In May 1990, President Salinas de Gortari privatized the banking system, which had been nationalized eight years earlier.

²⁶ In the elections of August 18 1991, the PRI proclaimed itself the winner with 61.4 per cent of the vote, amid accusation of fraud. It gained control of the Chamber of Deputies, and power to carry out constitutional reforms.

²⁷ The President presented an agrarian reform bill on November 8 1991. Approved in December, it granted property rights to *campesinos* (peasants) who farm state lands known as *ejidos* (co-operative farms ceded by the Zapata Revolution in 1917). According to the PRI, the new system was designed to reduce the annual 10 million tons of imported food. According to the opposition, the reform - which allowed campesinos to sell their lands - would bring about a transfer of small landholdings to larger investors.

²⁸ On December 17 1992, the Mexican, US and Canadian governments signed the North American Free Trade Association (NAFTA) Treaty.

²⁹ During the Salinas administration, inflation was reduced from three figures to a rate of 9 per cent in 1993. Between the end of 1988 and mid-1993, the State received some $21 billion from the privatization of state interests. Private foreign debt increased by $11 billion in 1993, to an accumulated total of $34.265 billion.

³⁰ In the first quarter of 1994 - as the NAFTA treaty went into effect - trade with the US increased at an unprecedented rate. Mexican sales increased by 22.5 per cent, while US exports to Mexico were up 15.7 per cent on the preceding quarter.

³¹ The high interest rates stifled the small and middle-sized businesses. Unemployment and under-employment affected 5 and 12 million people respectively, mostly indigenous people working as street vendors and domestic servants.

³² On January 1 1994, the previously unknown Zapatista National Liberation Army (EZLN) took three towns in the southern state of Chiapas, declaring them a freed zone. Chiapas was the region where the paramilitary guards contracted by the landowners to expel the indigenous people from their land acted with most impunity. It is one of the states with the largest Maya population, mostly from the Tzotzil group. It also has the highest level of Spanish language illiteracy and the lowest incomes. However, it also has large oil and gas reserves - 21 per cent of the nation's crude oil is extracted in Chiapas.

³³ The Government initially refused to accept the importance of the uprising which spread rapidly, increasing the size of the area under its control, with the rural public and workers of other areas taking up the cause. As a result, a fifth of the army was deployed to the region. When the number of dead rose above a thousand and the complaints of summary executions continued, the Government - at the insistence of Catholic Bishop Samuel Ruíz - agreed to negotiate.

³⁴ In February, a cease-fire was agreed and negotiations began in San Cristobal de las Casas - the city in the center of the Zapatista area - with the rebels demanding electoral reforms, the creation of new municipal areas, ethnic representation in Congress and the government of Chiapas, schooling in the native languages, health and education infrastructure, along with modifications to the Penal Code and land ownership. The Government accepted half the Zapatista claims, but after consulting with the indigenous communities, the rebels rejected the agreement.

³⁵ The PRI presidential candidate Luis Donaldo Colosio was murdered on March 23 in Tijuana. Three members of his bodyguard were involved. The PRI nominated Ernesto Zedillo as his replacement for the August 21 elections, and Zedillo was voted in by 49 per cent of the electorate. Both the PRD and the EZLN accused the Government of electoral fraud.

³⁶ In September, PRI secretary-general Jose Ruiz Massieu was assassinated, and in November his brother Mario resigned from his post as Attorney-General as he believed Party officials were blocking the criminal investigation. His brother's death increased suspicions that leading PRI figures, and perhaps the drug mafia, were also involved in the murders.

³⁷ The economy continued to grow until, on December 20, the new government abandoned the policy of gradually depreciating the currency because of the acceleration of capital flight. By the end of the year, the peso had lost 42 per cent of its value. Its fall caused the stock market to collapse in an event which came to be known as 'The Tequila effect'.

³⁸ The Zedillo Government took until March 1995 to put an austerity plan into action, gaining the support of the United States and the IMF, but provoking a deep recession.

³⁹ In January, Zedillo attempted to achieve a quick, peaceful solution to the situation in Chiapas. Following the failure of his

---

PROFILE

ENVIRONMENT

The country occupies the southern portion of North America. It is mostly mountainous, with the Western Sierra Madre range on the Pacific side, the Eastern Sierra Madre on the Gulf of Mexico, the Southern Sierra Madre and the Sierra Neovolcánica Transversal along the central part of the country. The climate varies from dry desert wasteland conditions in the north to rainy tropical conditions in southeastern Mexico, with a mild climate in the central plateau, where the majority of the population live. Due to its geological structure, Mexico has abundant hydrocarbon reserves, both on and off shore. The great climatic diversity leads to very varied vegetation. The rainforests in the southeastern zone and the temperate forests on the slopes of the Sierra Neovolcánica are strategic economic centers. The river system is scanty and unevenly distributed throughout the country. Air, water and land pollution is significant in industrial areas. Deforestation extends 6 thousand kilometers square per year. Mexico City and urban areas along the border with the US have high air pollution levels.

SOCIETY

Peoples: Mexicans are descended from Meso-American peoples and Spanish conquistadors. Indigenous peoples amount to 30 per cent of the national population. Out of the 56 indigenous groups, the most important are: Tarahumara, Nahua, Huichol, Purepecha, Mixteco, Zapoteca, Lacandon, Otomi, Totonaca, Maya and others. A significant number of Mexicans (32 million, in 2000) live in the United States.
Religions: Mainly Catholic.
Languages: Spanish (official). One million Mexicans speak indigenous languages.
Political Parties: National Action Party (PAN), conservative, founded in 1939, and the Green Party, joined in an electoral coalition; Institutional Revolutionary Party (PRI), was in Government since it was founded in 1929; Party of the Democratic Revolution (PRD), led by Cuauhtemoc Cárdenas, together with the Labor Party, Social Alliance Party, Nationalist Society Party and Convergence for Democracy in another electoral coalition. Minority parties: Authentic Party of the Mexican Revolution (PARM); Socialist People's Party (PPS); Democratic People's Revolutionary Party-Revolutionary People's Army (PDPR-EPR), illegal.
Social Organizations: The Labor Congress is a congregation of 34 large union organizations serving as a basic labor support for the PRI Government. Altogether they represent nearly 8 million workers. The National Peasants' Front, also official, was created in 1983 in a merger of the National Confederation of Farmers (CNC), the General Union of Workers and Farmers of Mexico (UGOCM), the National Confederation of Small Landowners (CNPP) and the Independent Farmers' Central Union (CCI). Authentic Labor Front (FAT); Mexican Network of Action against Free Trade (RMALC); National Coordinator of Mexican Students (CNEM); Zapatista National Liberation Front (FZLN) formed in 1995, as a civic-political group, promoted by the Zapatista National Liberation Army. Major indigenous groups: National Indigenous Congress, International Indigenous Press Agency, Plural National Indigenous Assembly for Autonomy.

THE STATE

Official Name: Estados Unidos Mexicanos. **Administrative Divisions:** 31 states and a federal district. **Capital:** Mexico City 17,900,000 people (1999). **Other cities:** Guadalajara 3,798,800 people; Netzahualcóyotl 1,401,300; Monterrey 3,409,100; Puebla 2,495,100 (2000). **Government:** The system is both federal and presidential. Vicente Fox Quesada, President since December 2000. The Congress of the Union (Legislature) has two chambers: the Chamber of Deputies, with 500 members, and the Chamber of Senators, with 128 members. **National Holiday:** September 16, Independence Day (1810). **Armed Forces:** 175,000 troops (include 60,000 conscripts), and 300,000 reserves (1996). **Other:** 14,000 Rural Defense Militia.

initiative, in February, he launched a military offensive. The investigations of the Colosio and Ruiz Massieu murders had still got nowhere.

[40] Raul Salinas de Gortari, brother of the former president, was arrested in February accused of masterminding the Ruiz Massieu killing. At the same time, the Government called for the extradition of Mario Ruiz Massieu from the United States, on charges of hampering the investigation into his brother's death. Raul Salinas' wife was arrested in Switzerland in November when using false documents to carry out a banking transaction. Mrs Salinas was attempting to transfer funds - presumably from the laundering of drug money - from her husband's account. The former president Carlos Salinas said he was astounded by his brother's illegal wealth.

[41] The PRI and the two leading opposition parties agreed an electoral reform in December, which included establishing an independent control commission and limiting campaign expenditure.

[42] In September 1996 the peace negotiations came to a halt after 16 months when the Zapatistas accused the Government of being arrogant and racist, and insensitive to their claims.

[43] Cuahutemoc Cárdenas was elected the new mayor of Mexico City in July 1997, while in the same elections the Democratic Revolution Party (PRD) became the opposition party with most seats in the chamber of deputies, outdoing the National Action Party (PAN). These two parties, along with the Greens and the Workers Party, announced the creation of an opposition alliance against the PRI, from September 1.

[44] On December 22, in Acteal, Chiapas, 45 Tzotzil indigenous people of the Las Abejas (the bees) pacifist group were massacred by paramilitaries with the compliance of the public security forces. Acting governor of the state, Julio Ruiz Ferro, and his secretary, Emilio Chuayffet were forced to resign.

[45] Even though investigators claimed that Mexico had overtaken Colombia as the main headquarters of the drug cartels, the US certified the nation - meaning it was still able to receive US loans and facilities.

[46] The number of deaths of people trying to cross the frontier with the United States increased four times in 1998 compared with the previous year. The crudeness of US anti-immigration forces and increased vigilance in places where illegal immigrants tended to cross forced people to attempt much more dangerous routes. Despite the obstacles, low pay and the lack of

work in Mexico make the effort worthwhile, and the number of illegals arriving in California, continued to rise.

[47] In August 1999, Cuauhtemoc Cárdenas's PDR and the right wing PAN led by Vicente Fox decided to form an alliance to confront PRI dominance, presenting a single candidate for the June 2000 elections.

[48] However, the coalition failed in December after the PAN rejected the proposal of a group of 'notables' on how to elect a common candidate for the coalition. The right had opposed 25 observations made in a proposal formulated by 14 independent personalities who suggested primary elections and four surveys in order to designate a candidate for the eight opposition parties. A survey published in La Reforma, the week the agreement failed stated that 63 per cent of Mexicans wanted the opposition alliance to challenge the PRI and that 60 per cent of those favored Fox as presidential candidate. Only 19 per cent supported Cárdenas.

[49] The PAN finally joined forces with the Green Party and in a landmark election, Fox was elected President in July, ending more than 70 years of PRI power. When he took office in December 2000, Fox promised to fight corruption and sought, among other things, to eradicate economic inequity and provide education and health services to the population. His first tour of the Southern Cone sought to open Mexican economy to foreign trade, especially with the Mercosur countries (Argentina, Brazil, Paraguay and Uruguay) and Chile.

[50] That month, Fox appointed former senator Luis Álvarez as commissioner for peace in Chiapas. By then, peace talks between the guerrillas and the Government were suspended. As he had promised in his campaign, a few hours before taking office Fox ordered the army to withdraw from indigenous communities. The President also ratified that the first bill he would send to the Legislative branch would refer to constitutional rights for the indigenous population. Subcommandante Marcos, rebel leader, agreed to resume negotiations with the Government.

[51] In February 2001, the newly-elected US President, George W Bush, chose Mexico as the first destination of his initial international tour, displaying his administration's foreign priorities. The three previous US Presidents had established a tradition to travel first to Canada, Washington's main trade partner.

[52] Fox announced he would lead a national offensive against drug

trafficking and organized crime. He also promised to dismantle a corrupt jail system, five days after one of the drugs barons of Sinaloa, Joaquín 'el Chapo' Guzmán, escaped from a maximum security prison in the western state of Jalisco, supposedly with the help of jail officials.

[53] Between February 24 and March 11, a caravan of 24 Zapatista delegates, followed by more than 60 vehicles, traveled from Chiapas to Mexico City to present its demands to Congress (legal guarantees, bilingual education, mass media that reflect indigenous cultures, autonomy in land use and customs, among others). After several discussions, legislators passed reforms on the Indigenous Act (Cocopa Law), but the EZLN rejected the new law because it did not take into account the indigenous peoples' demands, and announced it would not resume the peace talks.

[54] When the economic crisis worsened in late 2001, the President's popularity fell drastically. It was felt he had not fulfilled his promises - among them to create 1.5 million jobs. It was estimated 9 million people worked in the informal sector, ie one-fourth of the working population who, although they did not pay taxes, contributed with 12.7 per cent of the GDP. Thousands of peasants marched throughout the country in August, to demand solutions for their sector, one of the worst hit. In Mexico City alone, 30,000 peasants demonstrated on the ministries of Rural Development, Economy, Finance and Agriculture.

[55] In January 2002, the Supreme Court of Justice legalized abortion in cases of rape; when artificial insemination was applied without the woman's consent; and when the fetus had genetic or birth defects. This provoked different reactions in different sectors of society. The Mexican Bishops' Conference stated that the passing of a law does not imply its moral acceptance. Feminist groups considered the decision 'important for women's health and their dignity'.

[56] In April, Fox hosted a summit against poverty in Monterrey, attended by foreign ministers and presidents from several countries. It was later revealed that the sudden departure of Cuban president Fidel Castro, two days before the arrival of Bush, was as a consequence of Fox asking the Cuban President not meet his US colleague. At first, Fox denied this but Castro presented proof with the tape of a telephone conversation between them prior to the conference. ∎

Micronesia

Population: 129,000 (2002)
Land area: 702 SQ KM
Capital: Palikir
Currency: US dollar
Language: Kosrean, Yapese, Pohnpeian and Trukese

Micronesia

The name Micronesia is derived from the Greek meaning small islands. It refers to the Marshall Islands, the Marianas (including Guam) and the Caroline Islands.

[2] In 1531, Ferdinand Magellan named them the Islands of Thieves, but they were later renamed after Queen Mariana of Austria, Spanish regent.

[3] In 1885, the Germans tried to impose a protectorate on the islands, but the Spaniards appealed to the Vatican and managed to keep the islands. Guam was annexed to the United States by the Treaty of Paris of December 12 1898, and the rest of the Marianas were sold to Germany.

[4] In 1914 Micronesia was occupied by the Japanese who were negotiating the demilitarization of the region with the US. The accord was broken in 1935, and the Japanese launched the attack on Pearl Harbor from Micronesia on December 7 1941, bringing World War II to the Pacific.

[5] In 1947, when the fate of the Japanese and German possessions was decided, an agreement between the United Nations Security Council and the US

Government assigned the islands to Washington as a trust territory. Though located 13,000 km from the coast of the United States, they came under Washington's control.

[6] A UN mandate obliged the US to develop national consciousness and promote an economy enabling the native population to exercise their right to self-determination.

[7] In 1978, another plebiscite led to the creation of the Federated States of Micronesia. Four districts supported the motion, but Palau and the Marshall Islands decided to continue as autonomous states.

[8] Before World War II the major Micronesian economic activities were fishing and coconut plantations. After the War, the

population increase made this economic base insufficient.

[9] Bikini and Eniwetok atolls, where the first hydrogen bomb was tested in 1954, were used as sites for nuclear experiments and the people displaced from these islands have not been able to return. In 1968 the Bikini atoll and 34 neighboring islands were declared suitable for human habitation, but tests carried out in 1977 revealed that water, fruit, and vegetables were still too radioactive for consumption.

[10] In October 1982, the US signed a Free Association agreement with the Marshall Islands and the Federated States of Micronesia. This meant that all the islands, including the Northern Marianas would

manage their own internal affairs, while the US would be responsible for defense and security. In 1983 the agreement was approved in plebiscites, and in October 1986 President Reagan issued a proclamation, formally putting an end to the US administration of Micronesia. However, the US still controls Micronesian foreign affairs.

[11] On September 17 1990, the 46th UN General Assembly approved the admission of Micronesia and other six countries, increasing the number of member states from 159 to 166.

[12] In the March 1991 legislative elections, President John Haglelgam was defeated, and in May, Bailey Olter was elected President.

[13] In June 1993 Micronesia joined the IMF, which Olter saw as part of a scheme to solve the country's problems.

[14] Leo A Falcam was appointed President in May 1999. In September, Falcam issued a report repeating and confirming Micronesia's opposition to the transportation of plutonium through the region by nations such as Britain, France and Japan, especially in its own waters. Likewise, it criticized these countries' contempt for international maritime laws.

[15] In 1999, Micronesia and the US resumed negotiations started in 1965 leading to a Free Association Agreement, stating the island's sovereignty, its people's right to approve a Constitution and self-determination, and the possibility of revoking the agreement if any of the parties so desired. The agreement expired in 2001.

[16] Micronesia, together with 13 other nations from the Pacific Island Countries Trade Agreement (PICTA), met in August 2001 to negotiate trade agreements. They were required to lower their customs barriers and sought to commit Australia and Aotearoa (New Zealand), with whom they signed the Pacific Agreement on Closer Economic Relations (PACER), to offer their 'transitional assistance' (financial support) to the weaker economies of the PICTA group in their attempts at integration into a larger economy. ∎

PROFILE

ENVIRONMENT
Covers an area of 2,500 sq km, more than half of which is taken up by the island of Pohnpei (called Ponape until 1984). The terrain is mountainous, with tropical climate and heavy rainfall. The Federation is made up of four states, including the Caroline islands, except Palau: Yap,119 sq km; Chuuk, (called Truk before 1990), 127 sq km; Pohnpei, 345 sq km; and Kosrae, 100 sq km.

SOCIETY
Peoples: Trukese 41.1 per cent; Pohnpeian 25.9 per cent; Mortlockese 8.3 per cent; Kosraean 7.4 per cent; Yapese 6.0 per cent; Ulithian, or Woleaian, 4.0 per cent; Pingelapese, or Mokilese, 1.2 per cent; Western Trukese 1.0 per cent; Palauan 0.4 per cent; Filipino 0.2 per cent. **Religions:** Christianity is the predominant religious tradition, with the Kosraeans, Pohnpeians, and Trukese being mostly Protestant and the Yapese mostly Roman Catholic. **Languages:** Kosraean, Yapese, Pohnpeian and Trukese. English is a common language.

THE STATE
Official Name: Federated States of Micronesia.
Administrative Divisions: 4 states (Chuuk/Truk, Kosrae, Pohnpei, Yap). **Capital:** Palikir, on the island of Pohnpei 10,500 people (1999). **Other cities:** Weno (Moen) 23,900 people; Tol 10,000; Kolonia 5,800 (2000).
Government: Leo A Falcam, President since May 1999; Redley Killion, Vice President since 21 July 1999;

Legislature, single-chamber with 14 members (10 on 2-year terms, 4 on 4-year terms). **National Holiday:** May 10, Proclamation of the Federated States of Micronesia (1979); November 3, Independence (1986).
Armed Forces: Defense is guaranteed by the US.

STATISTICS
DEMOGRAPHY
Population: 129,000 (2002)
Annual growth: 2.6 % (1985-2000)
Estimates for year 2015: 172,000 (2000)
Annual growth to year 2015: 2.2 % (2000)
Urban population: 29.7 % (2000)
Urban growth: 3.2 % (2000)

HEALTH
Life expectancy at birth: 73 years (2000-2005)
male: 71 years (2000-2005)
female: 75 years (2000-2005)
Infant mortality: 20 per 1,000 (2000)
Under-5 child mortality: 24 per 1,000 (2000)
57 doctors per 100,000 people (1999)
COMMUNICATIONS
71 radios (1996), 20 TV sets (2000) and 81 main telephone lines (2000) per 1,000 people
ECONOMY
Annual growth: 1.2 % (2000)
Cereal imports: 13,973 metric tons (2000)
Exports: $ 62 million (1998)
Imports: $ 115 million (1998)

Moldova

Population: 4,273,000 (2002)
Land area: 32,910 SQ KM
Capital: Chisinau
Currency: Moldovan lei
Language: Moldovan

Moldova

Moldovans are descended from the peoples of the southern part of Eastern Europe who had been subdued, and culturally influenced, by the Roman Empire. The Vlachs were mentioned by Byzantine chronicler, John Skilitsa (976 AD) as the forebears of the Moldovan people. In the mid-14th century, Vlach tribes from the northeast formed their own state, independent of the Hungarian Kingdom, in the territory of South Bukovina. The first *gospodar* (governor) of the Moldovan Principality was Bogdan (1356-1374), although according to legend, it was Dragos who founded the principality.

[2] During the second half of the 14th century, the Moldovans freed themselves from Hungarian domination, and from the Tatar khans. By the early 15th century, Moldova's borders were the Dnestr River (to the west), the Black Sea and the Danube (to the south) and the Carpathian mountains (to the west).

[3] This small principality found itself subject to the influence and interest of the larger states: Hungary, Poland, Lithuania, Turkey and the Crimean Khanate. The principality was alternately a vassal of Hungary, Poland and the Ottoman Empire. The Christian Orthodox Church was the official church, and the language - known as Ecclesiastical Slav - was used for church liturgy, for official documents and education.

[4] The Moldovan Principality achieved its greatest political and economic success under the gospodars Alexander the Good (1400-1432) and Stephen the Great (1457-1504). During this period, Moldova warred against Hungary, Poland and the Crimean Khanate, but its main threat came from the Turks. In 1484 the Turks stripped Moldova of its territories. The Turks surrounded the fortresses at Kilia and Belgorod and gave them the Turkish name Akkerman; and the raya - enclaves ruled over by the Turks - were created.

[5] In the early 16th century, Moldova lost its independence as a state, being forced to recognize the power of the Turkish sultan (although still maintaining considerable autonomy within the Ottoman Empire). Turkish

domination over Bukovina lasted until 1775, when the latter was incorporated into the Austrian Empire. Bessarabia was under Turkish control until 1812, and the rest of the Moldovan Principality until 1878. Turkey seized one Moldovan territory after another; by the mid-18th century, Moldova had lost half of its lands between the Prut and the Dnestr rivers.

[6] Anti-Turkish sentiment increased because of Moldova's territorial losses, by the increase in the tributes paid to the sultans, and invasions by Turkish and Tatar troops, who devastated Moldovan cities and towns. Gospodars Petra Rares (1527-38, 1541-46), Ioann Voda Liuti (1572-74) and Dmitri Kantemir (1710-11) all turned against Turkey. In 1711, Dmitri Liuti and his Moldovan army joined forces with Russian czar, Peter the Great. In its struggle against the Ottomans, Moldova was forced to ally itself with the large powers that had opposed Turkey, signing pacts with Hungary, Austria and Poland. From the end of the 18th century, Moldova began developing closer relations with Russia.

[7] Under the Treaty of Jassy (1792), the Russians obtained the left bank of the Dnestr, south of the

Yagolik River. During the second partition of Poland between Russia, Prussia and Austria in 1793, Russia obtained the other part of the left bank of the Dnestr. After the Russo-Turkish War of 1806-1812 and the Peace of Bucharest, Russia seized the territory between the Prut and the Dnestr rivers calling it all Bessarabia. The Muslim population was deported, thus putting an end to the Turkish invasions of Bessarabia. At first, this territory was an autonomous region within Russia, with Chisinau as its capital. However, in 1873 it became a Russian province, subject to all the laws of the Russian Empire.

[8] All the wars between Russia and Turkey in the 18th and 19th centuries included Moldova in some way. The Prut expedition undertaken by Peter the Great in 1711 was a failure for Russia and its ally, Moldova, but it demonstrated Moldova's intention of achieving independence by relying upon Russian aid. Distrusting the Moldovans, the Ottomans began putting Greek Phanariotes (from Phanar, a suburb of Istanbul), on the Moldovan throne. They continued to rule over Bessarabia (a region bounded by the Prut and Dnestr rivers on the north and east, the

Black Sea on the southeast, and the Chilia arm of the Danube River delta on the south). It is until the beginning of the 19th century, and over the rest of the Moldovan Principality until 1821. There were bloody Russo-Turkish wars on Moldovan soil (1735-39; 1768-74; 1787-91), with a considerable number of Moldovan volunteers fighting against the Turks in Russian ranks.

[9] During the 19th century, the population of Bessarabia grew from 250,000 to 2,500,000 and by the end of the century, Moldovans made up half of the province's population. There were also a significant number of Ukrainians and Russians, as well as Bulgarians, Germans, Jews and Gagauz (Muslims). During the Russian-Turkish wars of 1828-29, 1877-78 and the Crimean War (1853-56), Bessarabia acted as a rearguard for the Russian army. Under the Treaty of Paris (1856), the part of Southern Bessarabia next to the Danube and the Black Sea was incorporated into the Moldovan Principality, which joined Walachia in 1859 to form the State of Romania. In 1878, the Treaty of Berlin returned this territory to Russia.

[10] Moldovan schools began to be closed in the 1840s, and as of 1866 the Moldovan language was no longer taught. After the Russian Revolution of 1905, the teaching of Moldovan was once again authorized. On December 2, 1917, the People's Republic of Moldova was proclaimed. Romanian troops entered Bessarabia and ousted local Soviet authorities. Between December 1917 and January 1918, first the Soviets and then the Romanians gained control over Moldova. Toward the end of January, the independent Moldovan Republic was proclaimed.

[11] In the 1920s and 1930s, the territory of modern Moldova was divided into two unequal parts. Bessarabia was part of the Romanian Kingdom, while the left bank of the Dnestr belonged to the USSR. On October 12 1924, the Autonomous Republic of Moldova was formed, in Ukraine. Its first capital was Balta, and after 1929, Tiraspol. Moldova made certain gains in industrial and cultural development, while Bessarabia, as part of Romania, remained at a standstill.

[12] On June 28 1940 - with World War II already underway - the Soviet Government issued an ultimatum whereby Romania was forced to accept Soviet annexation of Bessarabia. On August 2, the Federated Republic of Moldova was founded as a part of the USSR, uniting the central part of Bessarabia and the Autonomous Republic of Moldova. The northern and southern parts of Bessarabia, and the eastern region of the Autonomous Republic of Moldova, remained within Ukraine. In June 1941, Nazi troops invaded the USSR. Romania made an alliance with Hitler and recovered all of Bessarabia, as far as the Dnestr and Odessa. Three years later, the Red Army took on a weakened Germany, recovering Bessarabia and northern Bucovina.

[13] Soviet leader Leonid Brezhnev's political career began in Moldova, where he was leader of the local Communist Party. He was later to become Secretary General of the Communist Party of the Soviet Union (CPSU) and President of the USSR, positions which he held simultaneously until 1983.

[14] After the liberalization process initiated by Soviet president, Mikhail Gorbachev, in 1985, political and ethnic problems began to emerge in Moldova. In 1988, the Democratic Movement in Support of Perestroika (restructuring) began demanding the return to the use of the Latin alphabet instead of the Cyrillic alphabet for writing the Moldovan language. Moldovan nationalists called for an end to the political and economic privileges which Russian residents enjoyed, stating that if they could not do without them, they should return to their native land.

[15] On November 10 1989, Parliament approved the Official Language Law, which established Moldovan as the country's official language for political, economic, social and cultural affairs, with Russian to be used only in the press and other means of communication. There was an outbreak of nationalist protests and a strike by some 80,000 Russian workers. In the meantime, separatist activity increased in the Dnestr region, where a large proportion of the population is Russian, and the Gagauz Muslim region.

[16] On August 27 1991, Moldova declared its independence from the USSR. A month later, Dnestr and Gagauz - opposing both Moldova's independence and the possibility of union with Romania - declared themselves independent republics.

[17] After the failed coup against Gorbachev in Moscow in August 1991, the Moldovan Government arrested the leaders of the local separatist movements. In December, the country's first presidential elections were held, with Mircea Snegur winning. On March 2 1992, Moldova was admitted to the UN as a new member. Given the continued fighting in Dnestr, President Snegur declared a state of emergency on March 16, and ordered the elimination of the opposition forces fighting in the region.

[18] The political spectrum split into those supporting unification with Romania and groups preferring the sovereignty and independence of the State of Moldova. In parliamentary elections, pro-independence parties took an ample majority and in August the new Constitution declared Moldova an independent democratic state. Two months later an agreement was signed with Moscow for the withdrawal of Russian troops.

[19] In 1995, President Snegur accelerated the privatization of public companies and facilitated the inflow of foreign capital, but he failed to rally support and was defeated by Petru Lucinschi in the November 1996 elections. Economic reform continued.

[20] In 1999, Lucinschi began a new stage of privatizations with the aim of alleviating enormous recession and the pressure of both domestic and international debt. Sell-offs included the telecommunications monopoly and the electricity sector - the latter plagued by inefficiencies, shortages and appalling levels of non-payment. One part of the country had electricity for only two hours a day, while most were supplied through a Soviet-era network from Ukraine where the energy was purchased. The nation's tobacco and wine industries, a source of national pride, were also up for sale.

[21] After the Communist Party won the elections with 49.9 per cent of the vote, Vladimir Voronin became president in 2001. One of the first measures implemented by the Government was to introduce Russian as the compulsory language from the second grade in schools, sparking controversy in a nation where 70 per cent of the population are Romanian speakers. A month earlier, the Government had ratified a treaty with Russia as a strategic partner, leading to the measure being seen as one more step along the path to 'Russification'.

[22] Repeated anti-government protest marches organized by the Christian Democratic People's Party - which backed Moldova's unification with Romania - led to Education Minister Ilie Vancea being ousted in February 2002, despite earlier withdrawal of the obligatory Russian language ruling and changes to the history book texts. This was swiftly followed by the resignation of Interior Minister Vasile Dregenel who refused to halt the demonstrations.

[23] Moldova rejected financial aid from the IMF and the World Bank in March 2002. President Voronin pressed for independence from 'these organizations which ruled our country for 10 years with terrible results'. In one year the Voronin Government reduced inflation by two thirds to 6.3 per cent and economic growth trebled to 6.1 per cent.

[24] Relations with Romania deteriorated badly in early 2002, when Chisinau accused its neighbor of organizing protest demonstrations against the Moldovan government. Both countries ordered the expulsion of the military attachés. ■

Monaco

Population: 34,000 (2002)
Land area: 1.00 SQ KM
Currency: Euro
Language: French

Monaco

The present area of Monaco has been inhabited since the Stone Age. Monaco's Rock, located in the Mediterranean coast, was a refuge for numerous peoples. The first sedentary inhabitants of this region were the Ligurians. Monaco, less than two square kilometers in area, is mostly densely clustered hills looking southward over the Mediterranean. Monaco's coast and the harbor were the seaport for one of the Ligurian towns - Oratelli de Peille.

2   The region was first occupied by Phoenicians, Greeks and Carthaginians and then, by the end of the 2nd century BC, by Romans. Monaco became a part of the Alpes-Maritime area. During the occupation, the Romans built La Turbie, the trophy of Augustus celebrating the victory of his military campaigns. During that same period, Phoenician and Carthaginian sailors brought prosperity to the region. Monaco was annexed to Marseilles and converted to Christianity in the 1st century AD.

3   With the fall of the Roman Empire (5th century), the region was invaded at regular intervals by different peoples. During the 7th century it was a part of the Lombard kingdom and one hundred years later, of the kingdom of Arles. It was controlled by Muslims after the Saracen invasion of France. Since

the 10th century, after the expulsion of the Saracens by the Count of Provence, the coast gradually became inhabited.

4   In 1191, Monaco was ceded to Genoa as a colony. On January 8 1297 the Grimaldis, a Genoese family of exiles, held on to the fortress and placed the founding stone of their present palace. Emperor Henry VI gave control of the land around the Rock of Monaco to their chief, Fulco del Castello. In order to attract

population, Fulco granted several advantages such as the transfer of lands and tax exemptions. Since then, the Rock became an objective in the struggles between the two main parties of Genoa: the Ghibellines (sympathetic to the Emperor) and the Guelfs (sympathetic to the papacy) allied to the Grimaldis.

5   It was not until 1331 that Charles I Roquebrune - considered by many to have been the real founder of the Principality, and first lord of Monaco - recovered the control of the Rock and acquired control over Menton. His son Rainier II fought against the Genoese until 1489. Then the King of France and the Duke of Savoy recognized the sovereignty of Monaco.

6   In 1612 Honorato II takes the title of Prince and Lord of Monaco. In September 1641, after one decade of negotiations Honorato II and Louis XIII of France signed the Treaty of Peroné, by which the sovereign right of the Prince and his descendants over Monaco was recognized. The kingdom of France guaranteed then his protection to the prince of Monaco. The same year the Spanish were ejected of Monaco.

7   During the French Revolution in the late18th century, the principality was annexed to France. The Treaty of Vienna placed Monaco under the protection of Sardinia between 1815 until 1860. Monaco's

sovereignty was recognized by the Franco-Monegasque treaty of 1861.

8   Prince Charles III of Monaco decided to attract international high-society in order to contribute to the economic advancement of the Principality. In 1863 the first casino was opened and, in 1866, the Monte Carlo center.

9   Charles III ruled from 1856-1889; his son Albert promulgated the first constitution in 1911.

10   A treaty signed in 1918 contained provisions limiting French protection of Monaco. This agreement, written within the Treaty of Versailles, established that Monaco's aims and policies, including its military and economic interests, would be in line with those of France.

11   A new constitution, proclaimed in 1962, abolished the death penalty, authorized women to vote and appointed a Supreme Court in order to ensure civil liberties.

12   Its unusual characteristics made of Monaco one of the most luxurious and famous resorts of the world. Visitors are drawn by the beaches, sea, international automobile events, and the most famous Casino of the world in Monte Carlo.

13   In May 1993 Monaco became an official member of the UN.

14   Since there is no revenue tax, Monaco is now seen as a tax haven, which encourages money laundering. In 1998, an Israeli citizen was involved in a case of money laundering related to Latin American drug trafficking. A new investigation unit was set up because of suspicions that Russian mafia money might have entered the country.

15   Although not a European Union member, Monaco is about to join an economic mechanism of the EU through its customs union with France and its dependence on French currency.

16   Patrick Leclercq took over as head of government on January 5 2000, replacing Leveque. In October that year, France threatened to take parliamentary action against Monaco to pressure it to end the money laundering. Paris accused Monaco of hiding essential information through banking secrecy, and of weakening Europe's determination to stop illicit transfers of money, but Monaco ignored the criticism. ■

PROFILE

ENVIRONMENT

The Principality of Monaco is located at the foot of the Alps and bordering the Mediterranean sea. It shares borders with several French communities of the Alpes-Maritime département: Cap-d'Ail, La Turbie, Beausoleil and Roquebrune-Cap-Martin. Its territory covers an area of 195 hectares.

SOCIETY

Peoples: Only 15 per cent of Monacans are locals; French 47 per cent, Italian 15 per cent, others 12 per cent. **Religion:** The State is Catholic. There are also Anglicans, Baha'i, Jewish and Protestants. **Language:** French is the official language, also Monegasque, English and Italian. **Political Parties:** National and Democratic Union (UND); National Union for the Future of Monaco.

THE STATE

Official Name: Principality of Monaco **Administrative Divisions:** Four sections or *quartiers*, Monaco-Ville, the old town; La Condamine, the harbor area; Monte Carlo, residential area; Fontvielle, a newer zone taken from the sea. **Capital:** Monaco-Ville **Government:** Parliamentary monarchy. Constitution effective since December 17 1962. Prince Rainier III, sovereign since May 9 1949, Head of State. Patrick Leclercq, Minister of State and Head of Government since January 2000. Unicameral Legislature: National Council, with 18 members elected for a five-year term. **Armed Forces:** Defense is the responsibility of France.

Mongolia

Population:	2,587,000 (2002)
Land area:	1,566,500 SQ KM
Capital:	Ulaanbaatar (Ulan Bator)
Currency:	Tughrik
Language:	Khalkha Mongolian

Mongol Uls

The Mongols constitute one of the principal ethnic groups of northern and eastern Asia, linked by cultural ties and a common language. Dialects vary from one part of the region to another, but most can be understood by a Mongolian.

[2] Direct lineage from a male ancestor gives the family or clan its name, though there was an earlier tradition of female lineages. Intermarriage between members of the same clan was forbidden so there was great need for establishing alliances between clans, who formed tribal groups.

[3] The Mongols were mostly nomadic, with the movement of livestock and campsites determined by pasturage needs throughout the year. Animals were owned individually, while the grazing lands were collective property.

[4] The most powerful clans tended to control the tribal groups' activities. The weakest families maintained their own authority and their ownership of the animals, but they were obliged to pay tribute to the dominant clan. They moved, camped, grazed their livestock and went to war under that clan's orders.

[5] Political and military organization was adapted to the needs of each clan or tribe. A person capable of handling a weapon could be a chief or a soldier, according to the needs of the moment. Capturing livestock, women or prisoners from other tribes was a common means of acquiring wealth.

[6] When a tribal group became very powerful, as with that of

Genghis Khan in the 13th century, it organized itself in groups of 10, 100, 1,000 or 10,000 soldiers. The leaders of large units were assigned a territory where they could collect tribute and recruit warriors for the supreme leader.

[7] The Siung-nu, or Huns, were the earliest inhabitants of the Selenga valleys, joining Siberia to the heart of Asia, and they are thought to have been settled in this region by 400 BC.

[8] The Huns created a great empire in Mongolia when China was undergoing unification as an imperial state under the Ch'in and Han dynasties (221 BC-220 AD). The Hun Empire warred against China for centuries, until it disintegrated - perhaps due to internal conflicts - around the 4th century.

[9] Some of the southern tribes surrendered to China and settled in Chinese territory, where they were eventually absorbed by the Chinese, while others migrated westward. In the 5th century, Attila's Huns conquered almost all

of Europe, reaching Gaul and the Italian peninsula.

[10] The major Hun chieftains set up general headquarters, surrounded by cultivated lands where they bred larger, stronger horses, capable of carrying a warrior in armor.

[11] This led to a differentiation between aristocrats and traditional archers, who rode smaller horses. Agriculture also became more important to the economy. The Huns were subsequently displaced by the Turks who established themselves throughout the region. The Uigurs, who came to occupy the Orhon valley after the Turks, developed a settlement around an oasis, where agriculture was possible.

[12] The term 'Mongol' first appeared in records of different groups which were written during the T'ang Chinese dynasty. It then disappeared until the 11th century, when the Kidan became the rulers of Manchuria and northern China, controlling almost all of present-day Mongolia.

[13] The Kidan established the Liao dynasty in China (907-1125) and ruled Mongolia, fostering division between the different groups. Historical records mention the existence of a single Mongol nation, although it did not include all Mongolian-speaking peoples.

[14] The Kidan were succeeded by the Juchen, who were in turn succeeded by the Tatars, before the

era of Genghis Khan (Temujin). Born in 1162, Temujin was the grandson of Qabul (Kublai Khan), who had been the Mongols' greatest leader to date. Temujin inherited several fiefdoms that had been seized from his family.

[15] In 1206, because of his political and military prowess, Temujin was recognized as leader of all the Mongols, and given the title of Genghis Khan. His armies invaded northern China, reaching Beijing. By 1215, the Mongolian Empire extended as far as Tibet and Turkistan.

[16] Upon Genghis Khan's death in 1227 disputes among his successors caused the Mongolian Empire to disintegrate, until the Chinese throne was left in the hands of the Ming dynasty in 1368. China invaded Mongolia and destroyed Karakorum, the former imperial capital by fire, though it was unable to bring the territory under control.

[17] In the 15th and 16th centuries, controlling the areas beyond the Great Wall of China demanded military mobilization. In addition, cities were needed to act as centers of trade and serve as market places for food produced by local peasants.

[18] The Oyrat alliance made by groups living in western Mongolia began gaining control of the territory. They added their own mercantile and administrative expertise to the Mongols' tribal organization.

[19] The separation of the Oyrat from the Jaljas began during this period, with the latter forming the core of what was later to become Outer Mongolia. A tribal league was formed between the Khalkhas in the north and the Chahars in the south, while the leadership passed over to the Ordos, during the reign of Altan Khan (1543-83).

[20] To keep their hold on power, the Mongolian princes thought it useful to be backed up by a religious ideology. They adopted the Tibetan Buddhist religion as Tibet posed no cultural threat, and the Tibetan script was easy to use.

[21] Altan Khan proceeded to invite a Tibetan prelate, whom the Mongols called 'Dalai Lama' to lead the state religion. The merging of religious interests with those of the State was accomplished by claiming

WORKERS

2000

LABOR FORCE AS % OF TOTAL

■ FEMALE: 47%   ■ MALE: 53%

LAND USE

DEFORESTATION: 0.0% annual (1990/95)

1993

■ FOREST & WOODLAND: 8.8%
■ ARABLE: 0.9%
■ OTHER: 90.3%

PUBLIC EXPENDITURE

Military expenditure (as % GNI):	**2.1 %**	(1999)
Defense expenditure (% of central government expenditure)	**5.9 %**	(1999)

that an heir to the Khalkhas clan was the first 'reincarnation' of the Living Buddha of Urga.

22 In 1644, after consolidating their power in Manchuria, the Manchus seized the Chinese throne, with the help of Mongolian tribes from the far east. Before occupying Beijing, the Manchus took control of southern Mongolia, which was henceforth known as Inner Mongolia.

23 It took China almost a century to conquer Outer Mongolia. Meanwhile, Inner Mongolia became a part of China, and the Khalkhas' desire to retain power in the south prevented the Oyrats from attaining reunification.

24 This was the final stage of the great wars among the Mongols; ending in their overall dispersal. Several groups of Khalkhas remained in the south; some Chahars settled in Sinkiang and the Oyrat dispersed in different directions, including czarist Russia.

25 In the Russo-Japanese War of 1904-05, both armies used Mongolian troops and staff. This served Japanese interests well as a resurgence of Mongolian nationalism could weaken both Russia and China. At the end of the war, Russia secretly recognized Inner Mongolia as belonging to Japan's sphere of influence.

26 With the outbreak of the Chinese Revolution in 1911, there was a pervading malaise in Mongolia. Until then, the region had been the object of disputes between Russia and Japan. However, the Mongolians' social and political discontent was directed against the Manchus and the local government.

27 Led by their Buddhist leader, Mongolia proclaimed independence from China and sought Russian support. However, because of its secret treaties with Japan and England, Russia could offer nothing more than mere 'autonomy'. After lengthy negotiations, this status was granted to Outer Mongolia.

28 This situation continued until the Russian Revolution in 1917. China sent in troops and made the Mongolians sign a request for aid from Beijing. But the region was invaded by retreating czarist troops, who expelled the Chinese and mistreated the Mongolians.

29 With the traditional leaders discredited because of their poor handling of the Chinese and White Russian interventions, some groups of Mongolian revolutionaries sought help from the Bolsheviks. Russian and Mongolian troops took the capital, Urga, in July 1921.

30 This was the beginning of the republic, although the first monarchy had the Living Buddha as puppet king, only authorized to endorse the new regime's proposals. Upon his death in 1924, the People's Republic of Mongolia was proclaimed.

31 The People's Revolutionary Party (MPRP), made up of conservatives and revolutionary nationalists, wavered between Beijing and Moscow until the defeat of the Chinese Revolution, at the hands of Chiang Kai-shek. At this time, Mongolia began to fall increasingly under the influence of the USSR, and Joseph Stalin.

32 The new republic proclaimed the right for women to vote. The efforts to impose socialism upon Mongolia, which was still feudal in many ways, were marked by even greater excesses than those committed in other communist republics.

33 Following the Soviet model, the MPRP Government tried to collectivize the economy in order to break the power of the feudal lords and the Buddhist priests. Between 1936 and 1938, the Mongolian regime purged the party and the army, executing many leaders.

34 In the 1930s, the MPRP destroyed 750 monasteries and killed over a thousand monks. Mongolia's demographic level had been unchanged for hundreds of years, as a large part of the male population became Buddhist monks.

35 In 1939, Japan invaded northeastern Mongolia, along the Siberian border. With Soviet help Japan was defeated; a blow to the Axis powers in Berlin and Tokyo. Mongolia and the USSR fought together in the Inner Mongolian and Manchurian campaign, two weeks before the end of World War II.

36 As part of the Yalta agreement, Chiang Kai-shek agreed to hold a plebiscite in Mongolia. Although the result overwhelmingly favored independence, Mongolia failed to receive diplomatic recognition because of an unresolved territorial dispute. In 1961, Mongolia was admitted to the UN.

37 In 1960, Government officials in Ulaanbaatar accused the Chinese Government of mistreating Mongolian citizens and of seeking territorial expansion, at Mongolia's expense. In the early 1970s, there were a number of incidents along the border between the two countries, and 2,000 Chinese immigrants were expelled from Mongolia.

38 Friction continued until 1986, when the Chinese deputy minister of the Council of Ministers visited Mongolia and re-established consular and commercial relations. In 1987, the Soviet Government announced the withdrawal of part of its military forces, as a goodwill gesture aimed at stabilizing the region.

39 In March 1988, China and Mongolia signed the first treaty ever, aimed at defining the 4,655 km border between the two countries. A year later, during Mongolian premier Tserenpylium Gombasuren's visit, the first in 40 years, relations between the two countries were returned to normal.

40 In 1989, within the framework of Soviet perestroika (restructuring), Moscow announced that three-quarters of its troops would be withdrawn in 1990. Shortly afterwards, both governments agreed to the complete withdrawal of all Soviet military personnel and equipment from Mongolian territory by the end of 1992.

41 In 1989 and 1990, several opposition groups emerged. One of the most active, the Democratic Union of Mongolia, was officially recognized in January 1990. In March of that year, increasingly frequent public demonstrations against the Government triggered a new crisis within the MPRP.

42 The National Assembly approved a constitutional amendment withdrawing the reference to the MPRP as society's 'prime moving force' and approving new electoral legislation; however, no changes were made with relation to political party activity.

43 The legendary figure of Genghis Khan, whose name was forbidden for many years, has begun to be rehabilitated as an authentic expression of Mongolian pride and tradition, sentiments which until recently were condemned as being an expression of a narrow-minded 'nationalism'.

44 In spite of 65 years of Soviet aid, Mongolia's economy maintained vestiges of nomadism. In the early 1990s, urbanization was just beginning, and half of Ulaanbaatar's population lived in tents, with rudimentary electric and water supplies.

45 In the first months of 1991, Mongolia registered a substantial reduction in its foreign trade. Its balance of payments deficit reached $250 million. Shortages of food, medicine and fuel became more acute. The currency suffered devaluation, from 7.1 to 40 tughrik per US dollar, and government income declined sharply, while expenditure steadily increased.

46 Prime Minister Dashiun Byambasuren announced a new economic policy which included incentives to attract foreign investment, the establishment of a national stock exchange, the sale of two-thirds of the state's capital goods, deregulation of prices and changes in the banking system. The Government warned that the reform was complex and would take time to implement.

47 The life of most Mongolians, whose average income at this time

was $100, became harder than before. The population was not only anxious to see the results of the changes announced by the Government but was also worried about the scandals which affected the administration.

[48] After an official investigation, the President of the Central Bank of Mongolia, Zhargalsaikhan, together with a group of new investors, were arrested in December 1991, for a $82 million fraud, money which they had invested in business deals that went wrong. As a result, the country lost the major part of its reserves. At the same time, the deputy Prime Minister, Cabaadorjiyn Ganbold - the highest ranking reform figure in a government dominated by former communists - was accused of secretly authorizing the transfer of 4,400 kg of gold to a branch of Goldman Sachs - a British merchant bank. The gold was collateral for a $46 million loan, apparently earmarked for covering losses. The reform sector said that the minister of finance would try to cover the losses and accused the former communists of using such denunciations to try to discredit the transition toward a market economy.

[49] In January 1992, the National Assembly approved a proposed constitutional reform presented to the Government, adopting the official name 'Republic of Mongolia', and dropping the term 'People's'. The reform also established a pluralistic democratic system, replacing the socialist system.

[50] The governing People's Revolutionary Party gained more than 70 of the 76 Mongolian parliamentary seats in the June 1992 legislative elections. The opposition democratic coalition only obtained three or four seats according to the Electoral Commission which supervised the count. Over 90 per cent of the electorate voted.

[51] In October 1992, after being defeated in the June elections, the Mongolian National Democratic Party (MNDP) became an opposition party. The Social Democrats preferred to remain independent.

[52] A scheme implemented in November 1992 for privatizing 80 per cent of State enterprises involved distributing bonds for the purchase of shares to all of the country's inhabitants. However, it seems that the scheme was not explained fully enough to the largely nomadic population. They appeared not to understand it, and most of the bonds were sold on the black market.

[53] In 1992, the withdrawal of Russian troops - begun in 1987 - was completed. Meanwhile, Otchirbat had a rapprochement with the NMDP and the SDP to prepare the presidential elections in June 1993.

Thanks to the two groups, which had been previous members of the opposition, the President was re-elected with almost 58 per cent of the vote and announced the 'westernization' of economy.

[54] Disagreements between Otchirbat and the former communist majority in parliament were frequent. Poverty and unemployment kept growing and, according to official estimations, 26.5 per cent of the population did not earn the minimum income to subsist.

[55] Meanwhile, for the first time since the collapse of the Communist regime, Mongolia saw a 2.5 per cent economic growth in 1994. Differences between the parliament majority and the opposition NMDP and SDP groups diminished, which enabled a deal in 1995 to modify the election system. Thus, it was decided that 24 of the 76 members of parliament would be elected by proportional vote and the majority system would continue for the remaining seats.

[56] The June 1996 elections marked the end of communist dominion, with victory of the Democratic Union Coalition (DUC), a coalition formed by the Social Democratic party and the Mongolian National Democratic Party. The DA took 50 of the 76 seats, while the former communist bloc shrank from 70 to 25 seats. In July, Parliament accepted Mendsayhany Enkhsaikhan as Prime Minister.

[57] After the election, the Government went ahead with reforms to introduce the market economy as fast as possible. This process had a high social cost, increasing unemployment and poverty. This situation added to the damage caused by the lack of technical and economic assistance following the disappearance of the Soviet Union. Around 19.6 per cent of the population were living below the poverty line.

[58] In May 1997, Natsagiyn Bagabandi, of the Mongolian People's Revolutionary Party (MPRP), won the presidential election with 60.8 per cent of the vote. President Punsalmaagiyn Otchirbat, the DUC re-election candidate, took 29.8 per cent. The result was interpreted as a reaction against the 'shock therapy' applied in order to reach a liberal economy.

[59] A law introduced in June 1998 required the use of surnames in legal documents. The new legislation, which responded to demands for modernization and greater integration with the rest of the world, caused confusion and concern amongst the people. For centuries, most of the population had been made up of nomadic herders, living in small groups, and for whom surnames were irrelevant.

[60] The lack of capacity to confront the economic crisis and strong criticism caused the government to resign, and a new cabinet was established headed by Janlaviin Narantsatsralt. Seven months later, in July 1999, following a dispute related to the privatization of a copper mine co-owned between Mongolia and Russian, Narantsatsralt and his ten ministers all resigned. Parliament appointed a new member of the CUD, economist Rinchinnyamiin Amarjargal as premier.

[61] A report issued in January 2000 by non-governmental organizations estimated there were 4,000 street children, three quarters of whom were spending their days in the drains of the capital. According to the National Children's Center, when the country abandoned the Soviet model in 1992 there were only 300 street children. As factories and other workplaces closed, urban poverty increased compounding rural poverty. In a certain type of traditional family, when a family of Mongolian herders could not feed the whole group, it would send one or several children to live in the city. This system, which had worked for hundreds of years, became bankrupt as the urban relatives could not feed the children either. Ill-health is also a serious threat in the winter in Ulaanbataar, one of the coldest capital cities in the world.

[62] Living conditions became considerably worse after the winter of 2000 - the coldest in the country for 55 years. The Government declared more than half the country a disaster area. More than two million head of livestock were lost, the equivalent of $1.65 billion.

[63] In the July 2000 legislative elections the MPRP was elected with 72 of a total 76 seats.

[64] The winter of 2001 was even more severe than the previous one, with heavy blizzards and temperatures plunging below 50° C. More than six million head of livestock perished. China, the International Red Cross and the United Nations all appealed for support for the 75 thousand families affected, and especially for the thousands of herders whose survival depends almost exclusively on their animals.

[65] The IMF approved a $40 million low-interest loan over a three-year term. The loan was to be used in combatting poverty, boosting the economy and investing in social plans in Mongolia. ■

DEMOGRAPHY
Population: 2,587,000 (2002)
Annual growth: 1.9 % (1985-2000)
Estimates for year 2015: 3,085,000 (2000)
Annual growth to year 2015: 1.3 % (2000)
Urban population: 58.6 % (2000)
Urban growth: 1.0 % (2000)
Children per woman: 2.5 (2000)

HEALTH
Life expectancy at birth: 64 years (2000-2005)
male: 62 years (2000-2005)
female: 66 years (2000-2005)
Maternal mortality: 150 per 100,000 live births (1985/99)
Infant mortality: 62 per 1,000 (2000)
Under-5 child mortality: 78 per 1,000 (2000)
Daily calorie supply: 1,963 per capita (1999)
243 doctors per 100,000 people (1998)
Safe water: 60 % (2000)

EDUCATION
Literacy: 99 % (2000)
male: 99 % (2000)
female: 99 % (2000)
School enrolment (net):
Primary total: 90 % (1994/2000)
male: 93 % (1995/99)
female: 94 % (1995/99)
Secondary (gross):
male: 48 % (1995/97)
female: 65 % (1995/97)
Tertiary (gross): 25 % (1998)
Primary school teachers: one for every 32 pupils (1998)

COMMUNICATIONS
30 newspapers (1996), 154 radios (1997), 65 TV sets (2000) and 56 main telephone lines (2000) per 1,000 people
Books: 12 new titles per 100,000 people (1992/94)

ECONOMY
Per capita, GDP: $ 1,783 (2000)
Annual growth: 0.3 % (2000)
Annual inflation: 7.6 % (1999)
Consumer price index: 239.9 (1999)
Currency: 1,100.0 tughrik = $ 1 (03/2002)
Cereal imports: 76,912 metric tons (2000)
Food import dependency: 14 % (1996)
Fertilizer use: 21 kg per ha (1999)
Exports: $ 635 million (2000)
Imports: $ 794 million (2000)
External debt: $ 859 million (2000); $ 339 per capita (2000)
Debt service: 4.8 % of exports (1999)
Development aid received: $ 219 million (1999); $ 91.9 per capita (1999); 23.90 % of GNP (1999)

HDI (ranking/value): 116 / 0.569 (1999)

Montserrat

Population: 3,000 (2002)
Land area: 100 SQ KM
Capital: Plymouth
Currency: EC dollar
Language: English

Montserrat

The history of Montserrat is common to that of the rest of the Lesser Antilles. It was inhabited by the Caribs (see box 'Arawaks and Caribs'), who were wiped out by colonization. Large numbers of African slaves were imported to work on the sugar plantations, and France and Britain fought at length for the possession of the island, which was also a haven for pirates.

[2] Montserrat stands out in the region for being colonized by the Irish, after they were expelled from nearby St Kitts. Its poor land and inadequate coastline made it unattractive to European empires. The island was covered by sugar and cotton plantations. In mid-19th century the island had little more than 10,000 residents, of whom 9,000 were slaves.

[3] Montserrat has been a member of several Caribbean federations. The last was the West Indies Federation, dissolved in 1962. Since 1960 the island has been ruled by a colonial regime granting it wide autonomy in its domestic political organization. The Democratic Progressive Party (DPP), founded by William Bramble and later chaired by his son, Austin Bramble, refused to change that situation when the grouping West Indies Associate States was created in 1967, the step prior to complete independence.

[4] In spite of its isolation - only one weekly flight connects it with the neighboring island of Antigua - Montserrat was also affected by decolonization. The DPP lost all its seats in Parliament in November 1973 to the then recently created People's Liberation Movement (PLM). In 1979 the new chief minister, John Osborne, announced total independence for 1982 - but this has still not yet been achieved.

[5] Barely a fourth of the land is plowed and population density in cultivated lands is very high. Half of the island is suitable for livestock, a source of significant exports in recent years. Tourism - the island has two swimming pools per capita, one of the highest proportions in the world - has developed since 1979 due to US immigration. At present this residential tourism accounts for more than 20 per cent of Montserrat's GDP.

[6] Income from tourism and remittances of Montserrat nationals living abroad are not enough to cover the huge trade deficit, paid by the British crown. This deficiency is the main argument of those against independence.

[7] Relations between the local government and the UK are not good. Montserrat is known for having many offshore banks - 347 in early 1989 - that yield huge earnings to promoters and agents but not to the government, which received only 5 per cent from the sales of licenses granted. In 1992, a systematic investigation of banking operations led the UK to close 90 per cent of commercial and offshore banks dealing in illegal transactions and drug money laundering.

[8] Starting in 1995 and throughout 1996, the economy was seriously weakened by the constant expulsion of ashes from volcano Chances Peak. Bertrand Osborne, then Prime Minister, resigned in August 1997, after residents complained at the way their evacuation was carried out.

[9] The Soufriere Hills volcano erupted in mid-1997, killing more than 20 people and making the greater part of Montserrat uninhabitable. Tens of thousands of people were evacuated from areas in the north of the island to Britain and to other Caribbean countries. Prime Minister David Brandt requested a judicial investigation into the UK's responsibility. He accused Britain of systematically depopulating Montserrat, instead of aiding those who decided to stay on the island. The results of that investigation held both officials in Montserrat and the UK accountable for contributing to the death of nine farmers, for not having given them lands in which they would have found refuge.

[10] Presenting the 2001 budget, the new Prime Minister John Osborne listed the main causes for the economic crisis which affected the island. These included lack of capacity to create income, slow implementation of public sector projects, private sector hindrance of the government, and a -6.3% economic growth rate in fiscal year 2000, among other causes.

[11] That same year, some politicians voiced their concern that a bill proposed in the UK would grant British citizenship to its dependencies - something eagerly awaited by many residents - contradicting the pursuit of self-determination or independence of the island. The bill was passed in early 2002, after being endorsed by the British House of Lords. ∎

Morocco

Population: 30,988,000 (2002)
Land area: 446,300 SQ KM
Capital: Rabat
Currency: Dirham
Language: Arabic

Maghrib

Morocco was the cradle of the two North African empires that dominated the Iberian peninsula. It became one of the power centers of the region because of its geographic location: it was close to Spain, and at the northern end of the trans-Saharan trade routes. Although neither Fés nor Marrakech achieved the academic prestige of Cairo, their political influence was felt as far as Timbuktu and Valencia. Their close ties with Spain were culturally enriching during the Cordovan Caliphate, but they brought negative consequences to Morocco in the final stages of the 'Reconquest'. The war moved into Africa and the Spanish seized strongholds on the coast (Ceuta in 1415, and Tangier in 1471). European naval dominance blocked Mediterranean and Atlantic routes to Morocco causing a decline in trade.

[2] Unlike Algeria and Tunisia, Morocco was not formally annexed to the Ottoman Empire, but it did benefit from the presence of Turkish corsairs who hampered Luso-Spanish expansion. This precarious balance allowed the sultans to remain autonomous until the 20th century. France's policy of economic penetration meant that France was supervising Moroccan finances, aiming to guarantee repayment of the Moroccan foreign debt, while France argued with Germany over who should have political sway over the area. The French finally won, securing agreements with Spain over the borders of the Spanish Sahara, and Sultan Muley Hafid ended his support of the Saharan rebels (see Western Sahara). In 1912, an agreement between France, Spain and Britain transformed Morocco

into a French protectorate, giving Spain the Rif region, to the north (where Ceuta and Melilla are located), and the Ifni region to the south, near the Sahara. In exchange, Britain obtained French consent for its policies in Egypt and Sudan. The city of Tangier was declared an international free port and the sultan became a figurehead.

[3] The areas under Spanish control became sanctuaries for the nationalists who disagreed with European domination. In 1921, it was on Spanish territory that the Berber revolt led by Emir Abdel Krim (Abd al-Karim al-Khattab) began. Backed by the Third International and the Pan-Islamic Movement, he proclaimed the Republic of the Confederated Tribes of the Rif, induced the inland peoples to rebel, and put Spain on the defensive. The French intervened causing the rebellion to spread throughout the entire country. It took them until 1926 to force the Emir to surrender.

[4] In the south, Spanish rule was nominal, and French pressures to

WORKERS

2000

LABOR FORCE
AS % OF TOTAL

■ FEMALE: 35% ■ MALE: 65%

LAND USE

DEFORESTATION: 0.3% annual (1990/95)

1993

■ FOREST & WOODLAND: 20.1%
■ ARABLE: 20.7%
■ OTHER: 59.2%

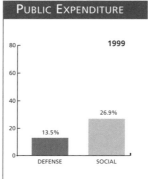

PUBLIC EXPENDITURE

1999

13.5% — DEFENSE
26.9% — SOCIAL

MATERNAL MORTALITY

1985/99

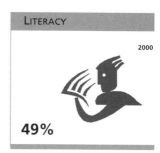

Per 100,000
live births
230

LITERACY

2000

49%

close down this 'sanctuary' for Algerian, Moroccan, Saharan and Mauritanian rebels failed (see Western Sahara).

[5] During World War II, there was sustained nationalist agitation. Demands for liberation were so pressing that Sultan Muhammad V himself became the spokesperson for the cause. To calm the people, the French thought they could rely on the prestige of the elderly Emir Abdel Krim who had been deported to Réunion. Unfortunately for them, the veteran fighter took advantage of a stopover in Egypt to escape from the ship, seeking refuge in Cairo where he died in 1963. Growing tension led the French to depose Muhammad V in 1953, but this only succeeded in making the nationalist movement more radical. The nationalists raised an army and fought until they achieved Muhammad's return to power. In 1956, the French were forced to acknowledge Morocco's independence.

[6] On April 7 1956, Morocco recovered Tangier, as well as the 'special zones' of Ceuta and Melilla, although the ports of these two cities still remain under Spanish control. Ifni was not returned to Morocco until 1969.

[7] The goal set by Muhammad V was 'to move forward slowly' gradually modernizing the country's economic and political structures. But his son, Hassan II, who succeeded him in 1961, had more conservative ideas. His family came from the lineage of Muhammad, the prophet, and his theocratic regime, based on a paternalistic system of favors and duties prevented the development of authentic national commerce. The King also encouraged foreign investment, especially from France, to exploit the nation's natural resources.

[8] In 1965, Ben Barka, leader of the powerful National Union of Popular Forces (NUPF) was assassinated on the orders of Hassan II. The NUPF worked for the social and economic welfare of workers and peasants.

[9] The death of Ben Barka in Paris was followed by a crackdown on popular organizations. The NUPF split and Ben Barka's followers were banned. Meanwhile, another NUPF faction, headed by Abderrahim Bouabid, changed its name to the Socialist Union and traded Ben Barka's principles for a minority place in parliament. The *Istiqlal*, who were originally anti-colonialist, became supporters of right-wing nationalist expansionism, fully backing Hassan's dream of restoring 'Greater Morocco' through the annexation of the Western Sahara and, if possible, Mauritania.

[10] In 1975, the conflicts underlying Moroccan society surfaced when King Hassan ordered the occupation of Sahara, unleashing a war that has brought about important political changes in North Africa (see Western Sahara).

[11] Funds for the military campaign, the fall in the price of phosphates on the international market, and the loss of financial aid from Saudi Arabia - in retaliation for Hassan's support of the Camp David agreements between Israel and Egypt - deepened the economic crisis. The political consequences of the crisis soon appeared. In 1979, students and workers held massive street demonstrations. The withdrawal of Mauritania from the Western Sahara war in July 1980 was a serious blow to the Moroccan Government, which then carried sole responsibility for continuing to fight.

[12] Severe drought in 1980 and 1981 drastically reduced food supplies, forcing the Government to increase food imports. This sent the country's foreign debt soaring to intolerable levels. The IMF assisted the monarchy with emergency loans which carried a condition eliminating subsidies on food and housing, a measure which increased the hardships faced by the working classes. The Government failed to achieve its ambitious development aims, and the export of unemployed workers was limited by French immigration restrictions.

[13] The situation worsened when several moderate opposition parties decided to break the tacit political truce. The Socialist Union of Popular Forces (USFP) staged anti-government street demonstrations. In June 1981, Casablanca was the scene of bloody repression which left 60 dead, according to official reports, or 637, according to the opposition. Two thousand people were arrested. This 'Casablanca massacre' led to an open conflict between the King and the leftist parties over the high cost of the Sahara, war which was swallowing more than $1 million a day.

[14] The stalemate on the battlefield caused conflict within the Moroccan armed forces, and in early 1983, they began to show signs of dissent. This tension became evident with the assassination of General Ahmed Dlimi, the supreme commander of the Royal Armed Forces, who was killed in mysterious circumstances after having secret meetings with European countries over ending the Sahara war.

[15] In 1984, the Saharan Arab Democratic Republic (RASD), proclaimed by the Polisario Front's fighters in the former Spanish Saharan colony, was recognized as a full member of the Organization of African Unity (OAU). Morocco reacted by withdrawing from the pan-African organization.

[16] In his capacity as religious leader, the Moroccan king became worried about the rise of Islamic

PROFILE

ENVIRONMENT

The country has an 800-km coastline influenced by the ocean. In the eastern part there are two mountain ranges (Atlas and Rif), covered with a barren plain and inhabited by nomadic Berbers. In the foothills lie irrigated lands where citrus fruit, vegetables and grain are cultivated. On the western slopes of the Atlas Mountains (Grand Atlas and Anti-Atlas), cattle are raised and there are phosphate, zinc and lead mines. Along the coastal plains, grapes and citrus fruit are grown. Fishing is important, though mainly exploited by foreign fleets. In the cities, many run-down neighborhoods have been occupied by the homeless, turning them into shantytowns. The lack of any kind of planned development in the countryside - which has a high agricultural potential - has led to depletion of the soil.

SOCIETY

Peoples: Arab 70 per cent; Berber 30 per cent.
Religions: Mainly Sunni Muslim (98.7 per cent). There are Christian (1.1 per cent) and Jewish minorities. (Many members of the Jewish community have emigrated since 1975).
Languages: Arab (official) and Berber variations. French and Spanish are also spoken.
Political Parties: Socialist Union of Popular Forces (progressive); Independence Party (*Istiqlal*), founded in 1943; National Rally of Independents (moderate); Popular Movement (Berber); Constitutional Union; Democratic and Social Movement; Organization of Action for Democracy and the People.
Social Organizations: General Union of Moroccan Workers (UGTM); Moroccan Workers Union; Democratic Labor Confederation; Organization of the Muslim Woman in Morocco; Islamic Educational Scientific and Cultural Organization (ISESCO).

THE STATE

Official Name: al-Mamlakah al-Maghribiyah.
Administrative divisions: 37 provinces and two municipalities, Casablanca and Rabat.
Capital: Rabat 1,453,000 people (1999).
Other cities: Casablanca (Dar-el-Beida) 3,292,100 people; Fés 900,900; Marrakech 736,500 (2000).
Government: Sayyidi Muhammad VI ibn al-Hasan, King since July 1999. Abederrahmane El Youssoufi, Prime Minister since February 1998. In September 1996, constitutional reform inaugurated a bicameral legislative regime. House of Deputies, Majkis an-Nawbab, with 325 members elected by direct vote for a 5-year term. The 270 members of the Senate, Majlis ash-Shura, an advisory body, are elected by non direct vote.
National Holiday: March 2, Independence Day (1956).
Armed Forces: 194,000 (1996).
Other: Gendarmerie Royale: 10,000; Force Auxiliaire: 30,000.

fundamentalism throughout the Arab world. For this reason, Hassan improved administrative measures for reinforcing the power of the *ulemas* (priests) and other religious representatives.

[17] In 1987, the Moroccan monarch suggested to King Juan Carlos of Spain that both governments form a study group designed to consider the future of Ceuta and Melilla (see boxes). The proposal was not well received in Spain, as there was an insistence on the 'historical nature' of Spain's presence in Ceuta and Melilla.

[18] In May 1988, after 12 years of tension, Morocco and Algeria re-established diplomatic relations, through the mediation of Saudi Arabia and Tunisia. The cause of the disruption in their relations had been the war in the Sahara, as Algeria had openly supported the Saharan nationalists from the beginning.

[19] Better relations between Algeria and Morocco meant that a gas pipeline was built across the Strait of Gibraltar joining the two countries to Europe. From 1995, an Algerian-Moroccan firm based in Rabat would transport between 10 and 15 billion cubic meters of Algerian gas via the line.

[20] Urban migration of a million people per year has exacerbated the urban housing situation, putting a strain on sanitation, water and other services. In October 1992, 800 Moroccans were arrested in Tarifa, in southern Spain, trying to enter the country illegally, while another 35 failed to make it to Spain, drowning in the Mediterranean.

[21] In March 1992, the Paris Club creditor countries agreed to

Ceuta

Population:	72,117 (1998)
Land area:	19 SQ KM
Currency:	Euro
Language:	Arabic and Spanish

This is an enclave on the Mediterranean coast of Morocco facing Gibraltar (Spain). The climate is Mediterranean with hot summers and moderate winters. There is sparse rainfall in winter.

[2] Occupied by troops of Portuguese King John in 1415, Ceuta was transferred to Spain in 1688 and retained by the Spanish after Moroccan independence in 1956. Despite many UN-backed claims and negotiations, before the United Nations Decolonization Committee, the port is still in Spanish hands. It is used as a harbor, but two thirds of the territory is reserved exclusively for military purposes.

[3] Estimates indicate that in the period 1995-1999 more than 3,000 people - seeking better work conditions - died while trying to cross the strait of Gibraltar to go to Europe.

[4] The continued flow of undocumented immigrants from Morocco entering Spain through Ceuta caused friction between Madrid and Rabat in 2001.

SOCIETY

Peoples: 80 per cent of the population is Spanish, born in Ceuta. Minorities include Hindu, Jews and others (according to 1996 census).
Religions: Catholic (majority), Muslim and others.
Languages: Arabic and Spanish.

THE STATE

Government: Civil authority is exercised by a representative of the Spanish Home Affairs Ministry, which administers it as part of Cádiz Province. Military authority lies in the hands of a General Commander. The territory has one representative in the Spanish parliament.

DEMOGRAPHY

Population: 72,117 (1998)

ECONOMY

Currency: 1.2 euro = $ 1 (03/2002)

Melilla

Population:	60,108 (1998)
Land area:	12 SQ KM
Currency:	Euro
Language:	Arabic and Spanish

Melilla is a small peninsula on the Mediterranean coast of Morocco with two adjacent island groups. The climate is similar to that of Ceuta. Melilla is an ancient walled town built upon a hill with a modern European-style city on the plain. It is an important port which, like Ceuta, hopes to be a tourist attraction.

[2] Founded by Phoenicians and successively held by Romans, Goths and Arabs, Melilla was occupied by Spain in 1495. It was repeatedly besieged by the Riffs, a Berber group that opposed French and Spanish domination, most recently in 1921. It has been claimed by Morocco and as Ceuta, is used for military purposes.

[3] On the northern Moroccan coast the Spanish also hold Peñón (rock) de Vélez de la Gomera, which had 60 inhabitants in 1982; Peñón de Alhucemas with 61 inhabitants in 1982, (with the islets of Mar and Tierra); and the Chafarinas Archipelago (Islands of Congreso, Isabel II and Rey), 1 sq km in area and with a population of 191 inhabitants in 1982.

[4] The Spanish Government approved a statute of autonomy for Melilla in 1995, replacing the city council with an assembly, similar to those of other autonomous regions of Spain.

[5] In 2000, Melilla received 16.95 per cent of the regional fund that Catalunya, the Balearic Islands, as well as Basque and Navarre provided to support other regions. Ceuta and Extremadura also benefited from this fund.

SOCIETY

Peoples: Languages, religions and other features of the population are similar to those of Ceuta.

THE STATE

Government: A representative of the Spanish Government is responsible for administrating the territory's civilian affairs. There is a military command in charge of military affairs. Like Ceuta, Melilla has a representative in the *Cortes*, the Spanish parliament.

DEMOGRAPHY

Population: 60,108 (1998)

ECONOMY

Currency: 1.2 euro = $ 1 (03/2002)

FOREIGN TRADE

Millions US$ 2000

IMPORTS
12,459
EXPORTS
10,409

EXTERNAL DEBT

2000

PER CAPITA

US$ 601

renegotiate the $21.3 billion foreign debt. Development loans were negotiated for 20 years, while other kinds of loans where extended to 15 years. The economy underwent an adjustment period and the Government deficit was reduced from 10 per cent in the early 1980s to 3.2 per cent in 1992. The balance of payments was re-balanced while the country's net reserves increased.

[22] The United Nations International Council for the Control of Narcotics condemned the fact that many farmers in countries like Morocco have been pressured into cultivating opium and coca, respectively the raw materials for the production of heroin and cocaine.

[23] In Western Sahara, a UN peace plan announced in 1991 led to a ceasefire and plans for a referendum that would give RASD inhabitants the option for independence or integration with Morocco. The Moroccan Government had delayed the referendum, hoping to defeat the Polisario Front (see Western Sahara).

[24] Torture and disappearances are common both in Western Sahara and Morocco. In February 1993, the Moroccan Human Rights Association announced the existence of 750 political prisoners - Nubier Amau, secretary general of the Democratic Confederation of Labor, was sentenced to two years imprisonment, for 'defaming' the regime. He was released a few months later, after the opposition's victory in Parliament.

[25] In June 1993, the opposition won in the first parliamentary elections following the 1992 reform of the constitution, taking 99 of the 222 seats, while the ruling party won only 74. Two months later, Hassan held a spectacular inauguration ceremony of one of the biggest mosques in the world, built in Casablanca at a cost of $536 million.

[26] Despite the constitutional reform, the King continued to dominate national politics, and in May 1994, he appointed one of his relations by marriage, Abd al-Latif Filali, as Prime Minister. In August, the King issued a surprise call for the integration of Berber culture and language into national life.

[27] In early 1996, the Government announced it would submit

proposals for constitutional reform to referendum. The changes, which basically aimed at the formation of a bicameral legislature, were approved in September. The King still had the right to dissolve the chambers. The privatization policies continued that year with the sale of several companies.

[28] In 1997 Morocco was forced by UN and US pressure to agree to a series of direct meetings with the Polisario Front which resulted in an agreement to relaunch the peace plan in Western Sahara (see Western Sahara). The long-postponed referendum offering self-determination for the Saharan people was set for December 1998 and a clear timetable laid down for the release of prisoners and return of refugees.

[29] The death of Hassan II in July 1999 and the succession of his son Muhammad VI as king brought significant political changes. The first move of the new monarch was to free some 800 political prisoners. In a television address in August, he pledged to fight social inequalities, domestic violence, unemployment and rural emigration. The Polisario Front welcomed the King's first measures and his decision to go ahead with the Western Sahara self-determination referendum. In November Muhammad VI announced his decision to make some form of self-rule possible for the occupied zone.

[30] That same month, the King dismissed Home Minister Driss Basri, who had served throughout King Hassan's reign of almost two decades. Muhammad VI announced the freeing of another 2,000 political prisoners as a goodwill gesture in January 2000, to celebrate the end of Ramadan. The Government's proposals to recognize some rights for women provoked demonstrations both for and against the measures during March 2000. The plans included the elimination of polygamy, raising the legal age of marriage for women from 14 to 18 and granting 50 per cent of marriage assets to wives in the case of divorce. This process would be handled by a judge and not by the husband, as traditionally had been the case.

[31] According to a report by the Moroccan Prison Observation Group,

published in May 2001, the country's jails were corrupt, violent, full of disease and child abuse (some of the victims as young as 12). In addition, 44 of the prisons were overpopulated and their health conditions deemed as 'belonging to a bygone era'. Moroccan prisons hold some 80,000 inmates in a system that was designed for less than half that number. According to the report, the only food the prisoners get is that taken to them by their relatives, who have previously had to bribe the guards.

[32] Tensions with Spain came to light after the September 11 2001 attacks in New York and Washington. Madrid tightened controls in its colonial enclaves of Ceuta and Melilla, and suggested Rabat 'do more' to limit the flow of illegal immigrants toward Spain. On October 27, days before Muhammad VI started an official visit to Western Sahara, Rabat called its ambassador in Madrid 'for consultations' and cancelled a bilateral summit with Spain, scheduled for December.

[33] Tourism, especially from the US, fell drastically after the September 11 attacks. In January 2002, authorities and influential individuals from Fés formed a delegation that traveled to New York in April to reassure the US people they would be warmly welcomed in Morocco.

[34] In a break with tradition, in January 2002 Muhammad VI announced his wedding, which took place in April, and also the name and image of the bride - Salma Bennani, a 24-year-old computer technician - appeared in the mass media. Commentators said the wedding marked the country's modernization, and it was expected the King's wife (who did not adopt the title of Queen) would encourage women's participation in public life.

[35] Disputes continued between Morocco and Spain over immigration, fishing rights and Spain's insistence on a UN sponsored referendum on Western Sahara. In July 2002 tension rose when Moroccan troops occupied the tiny island of Leile/Perijil (Parsley). Spanish troops reclaimed the island. ■

STATISTICS

DEMOGRAPHY
Population: 30,988,000 (2002)
Annual growth: 2.0 % (1985-2000)
Estimates for year 2015: 37,680,000 (2000)
Annual growth to year 2015: 1.5 % (2000)
Urban population: 56.1 % (2000)
Urban growth: 3.1 % (2000)
Children per woman: 3.2 (2000)

HEALTH
Life expectancy at birth: 69 years (2000-2005)
male: 67 years (2000-2005)
female: 71 years (2000-2005)
Maternal mortality: 230 per 100,000 live births (1985/99)
Infant mortality: 41 per 1,000 (2000)
Under-5 child mortality: 46 per 1,000 (2000)
Daily calorie supply: 3,010 per capita (1999)
46 doctors per 100,000 people (1997)
Safe water: 80 % (2000)

EDUCATION
Literacy: 49 % (2000)
male: 62 % (2000)
female: 36 % (2000)
School enrolment (net):
Primary total: 70 % (1994/2000)
male: 77 % (1995/99)
female: 64 % (1995/99)
Secondary (gross):
male: 44 % (1995/97)
female: 34 % (1995/97)
Tertiary (gross): 9 % (1998)
Primary school teachers: one for every 28 pupils (1998)

COMMUNICATIONS
26 newspapers (1998), 243 radios (1997), 166 TV sets (2000) and 50 main telephone lines (2000) per 1,000 people
Books: 1 new title per 100,000 people (1992/94)

ECONOMY
Per capita, GDP: $ 3,546 (2000)
Annual growth: -0.8 % (2000)
Annual inflation: 1.9 % (2000)
Consumer price index: 109.7 (2000)
Currency: 11.8 dirhams = $ 1 (03/2002)
Cereal imports: 5,215,045 metric tons (2000)
Food import dependency: 14 % (2000)
Fertilizer use: 386 kg per ha (1999)
Exports: $ 10,409 million (2000)
Imports: $ 12,459 million (2000)
External debt: $ 17,944 million (2000); $ 601 per capita (2000)
Debt service: 24.3 % of exports (1999)
Development aid received: $ 678 million (1999); $ 24.0 per capita (1999); 1.90 % of GNP (1999)

ENERGY
Consumption: 336.4 Kgs of oil equivalent per capita yearly (1998); 93.8 % imported (1999)

HDI (ranking/value): 112 / 0.596 (1999)

Mozambique

Population:	18,986,000 (2002)
Land area:	784,090 SQ KM
Capital:	Maputo
Currency:	Metical
Language:	Portuguese

Moçambique

The city of Sofa was founded by Shirazis towards the end of the 10th century. It became a point of contact between two of the most flourishing developed cultures in Africa: the commercial, Muslim cultures of the east coast and the metallurgical, animist culture of Zimbabwe. As with other civilizations on the continent, the Portuguese presence on the coast of present-day Mozambique was fatal; they planned to seize control of the Eastern trade which had nourished the two civilizations for centuries. This led to the destruction of the ports and the stifling of Zimbabwean gold exports.

[2] The Portuguese were never able to re-establish this trade to their own benefit, nor were they able to achieve their other goals. The Monomotapa (leaders of the Karanga) became Portuguese subjects in 1629, but these authorities were insignificant figureheads on the coast, and the way to the gold mines was still closed by the Changamiras of Zimbabwe.

[3] When Zanzibar expelled the Portuguese from their area of influence, the colonists turned to the slave trade as a profitable business. Attempts at connecting Mozambique and Angola by land failed repeatedly and European control was confined to a coastal strip where their entire 'administration' was limited to granting *prazos*, concessions of huge areas of land, to Portuguese and Indian adventurers who either plundered the land or searched for natives to enslave. These *prazeiros* became virtually independent of the Portuguese authorities.

[4] In 1890, the English questioned Portuguese control over these lands and threatened to

occupy them. The Portuguese Government underwent a long, hard struggle to forcibly subdue the prazeiros, and prove their authority over the region. The conquest of the interior, however, was only completed around 1920 when they finally defeated the ruler, Mokombe, in the Tete region.

[5] Mozambique started to supply South African gold mines with migrant workers (up to one million every year) and its ports were open

to South African and Rhodesian foreign trade.

[6] Portuguese colonialism controlled the country as an 'Overseas Province', encouraging local group rivalries to prevent nationalist feelings from developing. Split into several movements, the nationalists staged strikes and demonstrations in their struggle for independence.

[7] In 1960, a spontaneous and peaceful demonstration in Mueda was fiercely repressed, leaving over 500 people dead. This convinced many Mozambicans that any peaceful negotiations with colonialism were doomed to failure.

[8] The following year, Eduardo Mondlane, then a United Nations official, visited his home country and persuaded the struggling pro-

independence groups that their unity was essential. This was finally achieved on July 25 1962, in Tanzania, with the creation of FRELIMO (the Front for the Liberation of Mozambique). FRELIMO was made up of individuals and organizations from all regions and ethnic groups of Mozambique.

[9] On December 25 1964, after two years of underground activity, FRELIMO started guerrilla warfare to win 'total and complete independence'. By the end of 1965, FRELIMO controlled some areas in Mozambique and by 1969, one-fifth of the country's territory was under their control.

[10] In February of that year, Mondlane was assassinated by colonialist agents. Differences of opinion developed within FRELIMO about the desired form of independence; some wanting a mere 'Africanization' of the established system and others seeking to create a new popular democratic society.

[11] The second faction dominated FRELIMO's second congress, held in the liberated areas, and Samora Machel was elected president of the organization. From then on, the fighting intensified and spread to other areas. The impossibility of winning the colonial wars in Africa led to a military uprising in Lisbon on April 25 1974, ending the Salazar and Caetano's regimes.

[12] A transitional government was established in Mozambique and on June 25 1975, the People's Republic of Mozambique was formed, with new president Samora Machel announcing that 'the struggle will continue' in solidarity with the freedom fighters in Zimbabwe and South Africa.

[13] On the domestic front, the FRELIMO Government nationalized education, health care, foreign banks and several transnational corporations. The Government promoted communal villages, bringing together the scattered rural population and organizing collective production methods.

[14] In 1977, FRELIMO held its third congress in Maputo. Marxist-Leninism was announced as the Front's ideology.

[15] Mozambique supported Zimbabwe's independence struggle, blockading the imports and exports

WORKERS

2000

LABOR FORCE
AS % OF TOTAL

- FEMALE: 35%
- MALE: 65%

LAND USE

DEFORESTATION: 0.7% annual (1990/95)

1993

- FOREST & WOODLAND: 17.5%
- ARABLE: 3.7%
- OTHER: 78.8%

PUBLIC EXPENDITURE

Military expenditure (as % GNI):	**2.5 %**	(1999)
Defense expenditure (% of central government expenditure)	**9.1 %**	(1999)

of Ian Smith's racist regime despite severe repercussions on the Mozambican economy. Zimbabwean freedom fighters were given permission to set up bases within Mozambican territory; the white minority regimes retaliated with air raids and invasions.

[16] Zimbabwe finally gained independence in 1980, altering the political outlook of the region, tightening the circle around apartheid and allowing Mozambique to revitalize its economy through the economic integration of the Front-Line nations (Tanzania, Zambia, Angola and Botswana) and with Zimbabwe, Malawi, Lesotho and Swaziland.

[17] In March 1980 President Samora Machel launched a political campaign aimed at eliminating corruption, inefficiency and the increasing bureaucracy of state agencies and companies. A 10-year program for economic development was implemented, calling for investments of $1 billion in agriculture, transport and industry.

[18] All of these projects were affected by the increasing deterioration of relations with South Africa. In 1981 South African forces invaded Mozambican territory, attacking the Maputo suburb of Matola. They also backed the anti-government Movement of National Resistance (RENAMO), made up of former Salazar followers and mercenaries. South Africa's terrorism was aimed at their anti-racist refugees living in Mozambique, while RENAMO aimed to sabotage

economic objectives and intimidate the rural population.

[19] At the end of 1982, the Government cracked down on the black market and launched a major offensive against RENAMO in the Gorongoza region, where RENAMO's armed bands were attacking the communal villages of the interior.

[20] At the fourth congress of FRELIMO in April 1983, major changes in the Government's economic program were discussed. One of the main subjects under debate was a proposed reduction in the emphasis given to large agricultural projects, to provide greater incentives for smaller projects.

[21] Debate of the 'eight points' of the fourth congress resulted in the wider participation of party members who were called in to monitor the behavior of Government officials more directly. This initiative to refurbish the links between the party leadership and its rank and file, brought a complete change in the make-up of the delegation attending the congress. The overwhelming majority was rural workers and the number of women delegates had more than doubled since the third FRELIMO congress in 1977.

[22] The emphasis given to small-scale agriculture and industry was the result of a major reappraisal of all the large state-run farms. These were charged with excessive centralization, bureaucracy and economic inefficiency.

[23] 1985 marked the beginning of a critical period for Mozambique, with RENAMO terrorist attacks, on the one hand, and a severe drought, on the other. The drought decimated cattle, causing a 70 per cent drop in production, and was also responsible for a 25 per cent reduction in grain production.

[24] President Samora Machel denounced South Africa's covert support for RENAMO, saying that it was a violation of the Nkomati agreements of March 1984, when the two countries had signed a treaty of non-aggression.

[25] Already tense economic and defense situations were compounded by the death of President Samora Machel on October 19 1986. His plane crashed while returning from a high-level

conference in Zambia. At that conference, presidents Kenneth Kaunda of Zambia, Mobutu Sese Seko of Zaire (now DR Congo), José Eduardo Dos Santos of Angola and Machel had debated joining forces to confront South Africa's growing aggression toward the independent countries of southern Africa. They wanted to end South African support for UNITA and RENAMO in Angola and Mozambique. It has never been established whether the plane crash in which Machel died was an accident or an act of sabotage.

[26] On November 3, the FRELIMO Central Committee met in a special session where they elected Joaquim Chissano (minister of Foreign Relations) as the new president and Commander-in-Chief of the Armed Forces.

[27] In the following year, the Government began to reconsider the economic strategy it had followed since independence in 1975. A more flexible foreign investment policy was adopted and local producers were encouraged to invest more. This was the first step toward the establishment of a mixed economy, a concept adopted by the FRELIMO Congress in July 1989. The party dropped all references to its Marxist-Leninist orientation.

[28] Peace negotiations between RENAMO and the Government in Maputo began in 1990. These negotiations were made easier as the new constitution had recently brought in a multiparty system. The continuation of the single-party system had been one of the arguments used by the rebels to justify their terrorist activity.

[29] In October 1991 the authorities of Manica province, one of the most fertile regions of the country, declared a state of emergency because of the drought which destroyed most of the crops. It was considered the worst drought to have affected the area in the last 40 years causing enormous shortages for the 300,000 local inhabitants.

[30] In Rome, in November 1991, a peace protocol was signed by the Government of Mozambique and RENAMO. It foresaw the recognition of the rebel movement as a legal political party. This protocol was considered the forerunner to a peace agreement. In addition to the new

PROFILE

ENVIRONMENT

The wide coastal plain, wider in the south, gradually rises to relatively low inland plateaus. The Tropic of Capricorn runs across the country and the climate is hot and dry. Two major rivers cross the country: the Zambezi in the center and the Limpopo in the south. Due to its geographic location, the country's ports are the natural ocean outlets for Malawi, Zimbabwe and part of South Africa. However, trade has been hampered by wars during the past two decades. Mineral resources are important though scarcely exploited. The war devastated the country's entire productive structure, especially in the agricultural sector. The use of its mangrove forests for firewood has caused deforestation.

SOCIETY

Peoples: The Mozambican population is made up of a variety of ethnic groups, mainly of Bantu origin. The main groups are: Makua 47 per cent; Tsonga 23.3 per cent; Malawi 12 per cent; Shona 11.3 per cent; Swahili 9.8 per cent; Yao 3.8 per cent; Makonde 0.6 per cent.
Religions: The rural population practice traditional religions. Most of the urban population is Christian or Muslim. Islam prevails in the north.
Languages: Portuguese (official). Most of the population speaks Bantu languages, the main ones being Swahili and Macoa-Lomne.
Political Parties: Mozambique Liberation Front (FRELIMO); National Resistance of Mozambique (RENAMO); Liberal and Democratic Party of Mozambique (PALMO); National Union of Mozambique (UNAMO).
Social Organizations: Organization of Mozambican Women; Mozambican Youth Organization was formed.

THE STATE

Official Name: República de Moçambique.
Administrative divisions: 10 provinces and 1 city (Maputo).
Capital: Maputo-Matola 2,867,000 (1999).
Other cities: Matola 467,200 people; Beira 437,100; Napula 333,700 (2000).
Government: Joaquim Chissano, President since November 1986, re-elected in October 1994 and December 1999. Pascoal Mocumbi, Prime Minister since December 1994. The Assembly of the Republic is the main political body.
National Holiday: June 25, Independence Day (1975).
Armed Forces: 50,000 (1993).

2000

PER CAPITA

US$ 390

1996

22%

Population: 18,986,000 (2002)
Annual growth: 2.2 % (1985-2000)
Estimates for year 2015: 23,526,000 (2000)
Annual growth to year 2015: 1.7 % (2000)
Urban population: 40.2 % (2000)
Urban growth: 5.5 % (2000)
Children per woman: 6.1 (2000)

HEALTH

Life expectancy at birth: 38 years (2000-2005)
male: 37 years (2000-2005)
female: 39 years (2000-2005)
Maternal mortality: 1,100 per 100,000 live births (1985/99)
Infant mortality: 126 per 1,000 (2000)
Under-5 child mortality: 200 per 1,000 (2000)
Daily calorie supply: 1,939 per capita (1999)
Safe water: 57 % (2000)

EDUCATION

Literacy: 44 % (2000)
male: 60 % (2000)
female: 28 % (2000)
School enrolment (net):
Primary total: 44 % (1994/2000)
male: 47 % (1995/99)
female: 40 % (1995/99)
Secondary (gross):
male: 9 % (1995/97)
female: 5 % (1995/97)
Tertiary (gross): 1 % (1998)
Primary school teachers: one for every 61 pupils (1998)

COMMUNICATIONS

3 newspapers (1998), 44 radios (1997), 5 TV sets (2000) and 4 main telephone lines (2000) per 1,000 people

ECONOMY

Per capita, GDP: $ 854 (2000)
Annual growth: -0.7 % (2000)
Annual inflation: 2.0 % (1999)
Consumer price index: 160.3 (1999)
Currency: 22,750.0 meticals = $ 1 (03/2002)
Cereal imports: 381,271 metric tons (2000)
Food import dependency: 22 % (1996)
Fertilizer use: 26 kg per ha (1999)
Exports: $ 570 million (2000)
Imports: $ 1,476 million (2000)
External debt: $ 7,135 million (2000); $ 390 per capita (2000)
Debt service: 20.0 % of exports (1999)
Development aid received: $ 118 million (1999); $ 6.8 per capita (1999); 3.00 % of GNP (1999)

ENERGY

Consumption: 404.6 Kgs of oil equivalent per capita yearly (1998); -1.2 % imported (1999)

HDI (ranking/value): 157 / 0.323 (1999)

---

laws regulating the political parties, this agreement guaranteed freedom of information, expression and association, and pledged that elections would be held.

[31] The refinancing of the $1.6 billion foreign debt was contingent upon the success of the peace accord. Prime Minister Machungo explained that his country was suffering badly from the effects of the cessation of aid from the former USSR and the Eastern European countries.

[32] In May 1991, a new opposition party, the Liberal and Democratic Party of Mozambique, was created. The following month, a coup attempt by those opposed to peace negotiations ended in failure. In August, Chissano was re-elected during FRELIMO's 6th Congress, and Feliciano Salamao was named secretary general.

[33] In early 1992, the new political party regulations became one of the major hindrances to peace negotiations in Mozambique. The Chissano Government initially offered RENAMO a special status, guaranteeing their members political rights but the rebels turned down the offer. The armed opposition also refused to accept the terms which stated that they would have to have a minimum of a hundred registered members in each province, as well as in the capital, to qualify as a bona fide political party.

[34] On October 4 1992, with Italy as mediator, Chissano and Alfonso Dhlakama (of RENAMO) signed a peace agreement in Rome, putting an end to 16 years of conflict which had caused over a million deaths, and five million refugees.

[35] According to the terms of the agreement, RENAMO and Government troops were confined to pre-established areas, and weapons were to be turned over to UN soldiers charged with disarming both sides within a six-month period.

[36] Zimbabwean troops, who controlled the corridors linking that country with Mozambique's ports, were to be withdrawn. The agreement also provided for the creation of an army of both Government and guerrilla forces.

[37] Differences between the two parties led to direct UN Security Council intervention in December 1992. The Peace Plan approved civilian observers and 7,500 troops being sent into Mozambique.

[38] In February and March 1993, FRELIMO participated in joint military maneuvers with the United States. This change of attitude was interpreted as an attempt at rapprochement with the West, from whom Mozambique was seeking aid.

[39] The UN decided to postpone elections until October 1994, hoping to overcome the stalemate which was stalling the peace process. After negotiations, RENAMO agreed to take part in the elections. Chissano was re-elected with over 53 per cent of the vote. In the parliamentary elections FRELIMO won with 44.3 per cent, followed by RENAMO with 37.7 per cent.

[40] In March 1995, the Paris Club promised to give Maputo $780 billion for the country's reconstruction. Social conditions after the civil war were disastrous, not least because Mozambique - one of the poorest countries in the world - came out of the strife with a devastated agricultural sector and many fields ridden with landmines.

[41] During 1996, the Government managed to restore old trade links between Johannesburg and Maputo. Investment was needed to revive the ailing economy. An agreement between Chissano and his South African President Nelson Mandela allowed thousands of South African farmers to settle in 200,000 hectares in the North of the country, as part of a process resisted by the opposition.

[42] The heavy rains of 1997 displaced thousands of people, most of whom sought refuge in Malawi. This water, however, helped maintain cereal production, a family subsistence and main export crop.

[43] The Government privatization program went ahead. By mid-year, more than 900 of the 1,200 State companies had been sold. Inflation reached 5.8 per cent that year, the lowest figure since the World Bank and IMF began to oversee the national economy.

[44] In early 1998, a cholera epidemic killed more than 800 people. The disease spread mostly in the south and the central provinces.

[45] A report from the United Nations published in October established that life expectancy in Mozambique, one of the nine African countries hardest hit by the HIV virus, with more than 10 per cent of adults infected, would fall to 47 years. Had they not been afflicted with AIDS, Mozambicans would have had a life expectancy of 64 years in line with average global growth.

[46] The opening of trade relations with South Africa made economic growth possible, and in 1999 this was amongst the highest in the world (11 per cent). Expectations were not so high for the following year. The recession indicated that growth for 2000 would be below 10 per cent.

[47] The December legislative and presidential elections saw a FRELIMO win, with Chissano re-elected. The opposition RENAMO lodged complaints of electoral fraud.

[48] In February of the following year, several of the biggest creditors had approved an 18-month period of grace for the repayment of Mozambique's foreign debt of approximately $1.5 billion. However, after floods devastated the country in March 2000, Germany proposed canceling the debt. The catastrophe displaced more than a million people and killed more than 200.

[49] Journalist Carlos Cardoso, editor of independent daily *Metical*, who was investigating political and corporate corruption, was murdered in November. Months later, six people - among them two leading businessmen - were formally accused of the murder. The federal prosecutor accused the judicial system of incompetence, corruption and power abuse.

[50] Mozambique was ranked one of the lowest countries in the UNDP 2001 Report's Human Development Index (HDI). This indicator is calculated based on a combination of life expectancy at birth, income per capita, enrolment in the education system and adult literacy. Women in Mozambique account for 16 per cent of mass media jobs, one of the lowest proportions in the world.

[51] In early 2002, malaria turned into an epidemic and was the major cause of death in the country's hospitals, which received an average of 800 patients per day. Some of the main hospitals in Maputo had to place two patients on each bed.■

Myanmar (Burma)

Population: 48,956,000 (2002)
Land area: 657,550 SQ KM
Capital: Yangôn (Rangoon)
Currency: Kyat
Language: Burmese

Myanmar (Burma)

Inscriptions dating from the 6th century BC testify to the very early establishment of advanced civilizations in Burma. Migrations occurred frequently from north to south and from the mountains to the coast. The people intermingled and occasionally engaged in battles until the 11th century when Burmese conquered the southern Hmong and the northern Kadu, establishing the state of Pagan.

² The following two centuries were a golden age in Burmese thought and architecture. The Mongols attacked from the North, with aid from the Great Khan in Beijing. In 1283, the Mongol invasion ended the Pagan state and the Mongols remained in power until 1301. Marco Polo, in the service of Kublai Khan, participated in the invasion and may have been the first European to visit the country.

³ Burma remained divided into small ethnic states until the 16th century when Toungoo local leaders reunified the territory. The second of these rulers, Bayinnaung, extended his domain to parts of present-day Laos and Thailand.

⁴ Extravagance undermined the agricultural foundations of the economy, resulting in an exodus of peasants to neighboring states. The process of fragmentation was hastened by the presence of early European traders and their consequent rivalries.

⁵ In 1740, a Toungoo ruler again achieved unification, with the help of the British. But when his successors continued the project of national reconstruction, they clashed with British interests in Assam, India, and a confrontation resulted with their former European allies. The Burmese fought three wars against the British throughout the 19th century, in 1820-26, 1852-53 and 1885-86. During the last war, King Thibaw was taken prisoner and Burma was annexed to the British viceroyalty of India.

⁶ The 1930s began with a rising tide of nationalist movements; that of the Buddhist monk, U Ottama, inspired by Gandhi; Saya San's attempt to restore the monarchy; and uprisings organized by the University of Rangoon, bringing together Buddhists and Marxists. In 1936, a student demonstration became an anti-British national protest, led by Aung San.

⁷ The anti-colonial movement was not restricted to the urban élites. Heavy taxes and the collapse of the world rice market in 1930 forced thousands of small farmers into debt and ruin at the hands of British banks and Indian moneylenders. Discontent expressed itself as a generalized xenophobia, leading to popular rebellions in 1938 and 1939.

⁸ When World War II broke out, a group of militant anti-colonialists in Bangkok, known as 'the 30 comrades', including members from the newly-created Communist Party, formed the Burma Independence Army (BIA). They joined the Japanese against the British and invaded the capital on 7 March 1942. Minority groups of Karen, Kachin and Chin organized guerrilla groups to combat both the BIA and the Japanese.

⁹ The Japanese granted Burma independence on August 1 1943, appointing Ba Maw head of state. The 'national' army was placed under the command of General Ne Win. However, friction soon developed between the Japanese and the socialist wing that mustered thirty youths, who later came to be known as the '30 comrades'. On March 27 1945, the BIA declared war on Japan and was recognized by the British as the Patriotic Burmese Forces. On May 30, they captured Rangoon, this time with the help of the British. Aung San organized a transition government, and in 1947, a constitution was drafted. On July 19, a military commando assassinated Aung San and several aides in the palace, and U Nu stepped in as premier. On January 4 1948, independence was proclaimed.

¹⁰ Several challenges faced the new government: ethnic minorities rebelled; recently-defeated Chinese Kuomintang forces moved into Shan state, where they were also involved in drug trafficking, and Aung San's army, renamed the People's Volunteer Organization and linked to the Communist Party, mounted a further armed insurrection.

¹¹ On May 2 1962, General Ne Win overthrew U Nu, who had been very successful in the 1960 elections. Burma had peacefully settled its border conflicts with India and China, and throughout the war in Southeast Asia Rangoon maintained a policy of non-alignment. Ne Win nationalized the banks, the rice industry (which accounted for 70 per cent of foreign earnings), and the largely Indian-controlled trade.

¹² In 1972, a new constitution confirmed the governing Burma Socialist Program Party (BSSP) as the only legal political organization.

¹³ Ne Win's regime declined after the 1973 economic crisis and opponents emphasized the ambiguity of his 'Burmese Socialism'.

¹⁴ In 1979, Burma withdrew from the Non-Aligned Movement. In 1981, the National Congress named San Yu as successor to Ne Win, who resigned the presidency but continued as party chairperson and thus maintained control of the country.

¹⁵ The opposition organized for the multiparty elections scheduled for May 1990. The Government changed the country's name to Union of Myanmar and dropped the term 'Socialist'.

¹⁶ The National League for Democracy (NLD) won 80 per cent of the vote, while the ruling National Unity Party (ex-BSPP) retained only 10 of the 485 seats. The election results were ignored by the Government who banned opposition activities, imprisoned or banished its leaders, and harshly repressed street demonstrations.

¹⁷ In July 1989, the leader of the NLD, Aung San Suu Kyi, the daughter of anti-colonial hero Aung San, was sentenced to house arrest and held incommunicado. She received the Nobel Peace Prize in 1991.

¹⁸ The opposition was reinforced by agreements between students, Buddhist monks and some minorities. In March 1992, the UN High Commission for Refugees denounced the massacres carried out against ethnic minorities. All political parties were dissolved or banned.

¹⁹ In April, General Than Shwe took power releasing 200 dissidents and permitting 31 universities and

schools to reopen. Myanmar returned to the Movement of Non-Aligned Nations. In September, martial law was suspended, but Amnesty International reported the continued use of torture.

[20]	In January 1993, the military invoked a National Convention to draw up a new constitution. At the end of that year, Amnesty International denounced the imprisonment of over 1,550 opposition figures.

[21]	An article of the new 1994 constitution stipulated presidential candidates could neither be married to foreigners nor bear children under foreign citizenship and they should have been residing in Myanmar for the last 20 consecutive years. The regulation was custom-made for Suu Kyi who was married to a British subject and lived several years abroad. The military junta met with her in September 1994 for the first time since she was arrested. No agreement was reached regarding the new constitution.

[22]	In July 1995, Suu Kyi was released from house arrest and called on the State Law and Order Restoration Council (SLORC) to hold a dialogue. The SLORC refused, jailed dozens of dissidents and maintained the ban on political debates.

[23]	The fall early that year of Manerplaw, headquarters of the rebel minority, was a major blow to the opposition because it was also a base for activities of other groups. In January 1996, through a secret accord, the Government gained the surrender of Khun Sa, known as the 'opium king' and leader of a Shan force. Later that year the military junta ordered the arrest of 250 NLD members who had planned to celebrate the anniversary of their victory in the 1990 parliamentary elections. The regime also approved a law banning NLD political meetings and restricted Suu Kyi's freedom of movement, even prohibiting her from using the telephone.

[24]	Subjected to increasing international pressure, especially from the US and the EU, the SLORC made some concessions in 1997. In September it allowed the NLD to hold its first congress in seven years, though it authorized attendance for only half its 600 delegates. Towards the end of the year, the military junta dissolved itself, appointing a State Peace and Development Council (SPDC) in its place. In July, as a result of the influence of neighboring India and China, Myanmar became a member of the Association of Southeast Asian Nations (ASEAN).

[25]	In August 1998 the army launched a virulent press campaign against Suu Kyi, who had been arrested at a navy checkpoint when, for the fourth time, she tried to leave the capital to meet with supporters. The junta labeled Suu Kyi 'public enemy number one'. The government newspapers stated that anyone meeting with her in public 'would not live long'. The Government's intimidation policy continued and, in March 2000, Than Shwe warned in a military ceremony that the opposition would be 'eliminated'.

[26]	Intelligence chief Khin Nyunt visited Thailand in September 2001 in what was declared an improvement in bilateral relations and he announced that the anti-drug fight would pull his country out of the so-called 'Golden Triangle' of drug production (along the shared border with Thailand and Laos) by 2005. Earlier that year, Thai and Burmese troops had clashed along the border, with Bangkok and Rangoon accusing each other of supporting the narcotics-producing Shan militias. In May the tensions had reduced due to the growing presence of special US troops on the Thai side of the border. Their declared mission was to train the Thai army to fight drug trafficking.

[27]	There has been no tertiary-level education since the university was shut down in 1988 to prevent anti-government protests. At least a million people have HIV/AIDS and infant mortality is estimated at 33 per cent. Western sources charge that army personnel are paid in drugs, not money, and that the country's main source of revenues is the illegal trade in opium.

[28]	Jiang Zemin visited Burma in November, the first Chinese president to do so since the junta took power. In January 2002, the Government announced the construction of a nuclear power plant with Russian support. The US and EU said they were unwilling to lift the economic embargo until there are firm indications of a move toward democracy. After 19 months of house arrest, Suu Kyi was released May 6 and her right to participate in political activity was renewed, in what was seen as the beginning of a democratic transition process. The UN was an active mediator and proposed the immediate release of all prisoners of conscience, estimated at 1,500 to 2,000. Washington interpreted Suu Kyi's release as a direct result of the embargo, which had seriously hurt the country's tourism industry and international trade in oil, natural gas, wood and minerals. ∎

PROFILE

ENVIRONMENT

The country lies between the Tibetan plateau and the Malayan peninsula. Mountain ranges to the east, north and west surround a central valley where the Irrawaddy, Sittang and Salween rivers flow. Most of the population are concentrated in this area where rice is grown. The climate is tropical with monsoon rains between May and October. Rainforests extend over most of the country. Deforestation has been responsible for the destruction of two-thirds of the country's tropical forest.

SOCIETY

Peoples: Burmese 69 per cent; Shan 8.5 per cent; Karen 6.2 per cent; Rakhine 4.5 per cent; Mon 2.4 per cent; Chin 2.2 per cent; Kachin 1.4 per cent. **Religions:** Buddhist 89.1 per cent, Christian 4-9 per cent, Muslim 3.8 per cent; other 2.2 per cent. **Languages:** Burmese (official) and the languages of the ethnic groups. **Political Parties:** Political parties and their activities are generally illegal. The National League for Democracy (NLD) is the main opposition force. Military formed the dictatorial National Unity Party (Taingyintha Silonenyinyutye); the Government of the National Coalition of Burmese Unity is made up of parties that won the last elections but were not allowed to exercise power; it currently exists as a government in exile and as a leading opposition force. Karenni National Progressive Party; Arakan League for Democracy. **Social Organizations:** All Burma-Students Democratic Front; All Burma-Young Monks' Union; The Federation of Trade Unions-Kawthoolei (FTUK) was formed in October 1998 by The Karen Education Workers Union, the Karen Health Workers Union and the Karen Agriculture Unions.

THE STATE

Official Name: Pyidaungzu Myanma Naingngnandaw. **Capital:** Yangôn (Rangoon) 4,101,000 people (1999). **Other cities:** Mandalay 1,037,300 people; Mawlamyine 360,400; Bago 223,700; Akyab 161,200 (2000). **Government:** General Than Shwe, President, Head of State and Government since April 1992. Legislature: suspended since 1988. **National Holiday:** January 4, Independence Day (1948). **Armed Forces:** 286,000 (1995). **Other:** 85,000 (People's Police, People's Militia).

Namibia

Population: 1,819,000 (2002)
Land area: 823,290 SQ KM
Capital: Windhoek
Currency: Namibian dollar
Language: English

Namibia

Southwestern Africa was occupied first by San (Bushmen) and Khoikhoi peoples, Ovambo in the north and the Bantu-speaking Herero. Later the Nama, known as the Red Nation, set up lands in the southern part and maintained tight union between their clans and lived from grazing animals. Closely linked to this people were the Damara, coming from Central Africa, who combined herding with hunting and the smelting of copper. In the central and north eastern regions, the Herero built clan alliances, often led by a supreme chief. The Ovambo, farmers who developed several kingdoms along both banks of the Kunene river, were a constant threat for the unity of the Herero.

[2] Arid and scarcely populated, the territory of the Kalahari desert did not offer great attractions to European colonization. From 1670 onward German missionaries, European traders and Norwegian whalers began to arrive to the coast and some ventured into the hinterland. Traders stimulated conflict between the various clans, which became increasingly destructive and which encouraged the arrival, at the beginning of the 19th century, of the Oorlam-Nama, a tribe from The Cape whose military technology was inspired by that of the Afrikaners. Thanks to these strategies, which included horses, rifles and an organization model of small commands, they dominated the Nama and the Damara. Half way through the century, a kingdom was set up by Chief Jonker Afrikaner, of Oorlam and Herero lineage, who had the full backing of the Damara and the Red Nation.

[3] In 1870 the British made a treaty with the Herero and flew their flag on the port of Walvis Bay. However, the German Second Reich of Bismarck and William I, launched an occupation of the area through dubious treaties, plunder and the strategy of dividing the African peoples. In 1884, Germany annexed the territory under the name of South West Africa. In 1885, Herero resistance forced the Germans back to Walvis Bay, until the British arrived to support them.

[4] Toward the end of the century, German colonists arrived and started to build railways from Swakopmund and Luderitz. The country acquired strategic value for the Europeans with the discovery of large reserves of iron, lead, copper and diamonds, which were later augmented by metals of military interest: manganese, tungsten, vanadium, cadmium and great quantities of uranium.

[5] The great war of resistance from 1904-1907, led by the Herero, almost expelled the Germans, who reacted brutally with mass hangings and enforced detention in concentration camps, which led to a 90 per cent reduction in Herero numbers by 1910. The Nama, who had been slow to enter the conflict, were defeated in 1907. Only a third of the Nama population survived, confined in concentration camps. Despite the rigidity with which the Germans exercised their control, this did not extend northwards significantly to trouble the Ovambo.

0   300 km

WORKERS

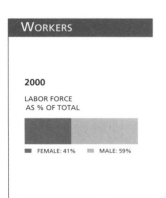

2000

LABOR FORCE
AS % OF TOTAL

■ FEMALE: 41%   ■ MALE: 59%

LAND USE

DEFORESTATION: 0.3% annual (1990/95)

1993

■ FOREST & WOODLAND: 21.8%
■ ARABLE: 0.8%
■ OTHER: 77.4%

PUBLIC EXPENDITURE

Military expenditure (as % GNI):	**2.9 %** (1999)	
Defense expenditure (% of central government expenditure)	**7.2 %** (1999)	

MATERNAL MORTALITY

1985/99

Per 100,000
live births

230

LITERACY

2000

82%

FOREIGN TRADE

Millions US$ 1999

IMPORTS

1,952

EXPORTS

1,702

[6] During World War I the British invaded the German colony from South Africa and took over. At the end of the War, the region became a League of Nations trust territory known as South West Africa, assigned to the Union of South Africa as 'a sacred charge of civilization' to 'promote to the maximum the material and moral well-being of its inhabitants'.

[7] The mandate did not help the local African population, who were exploited by the German colonists and South African boers. The territory was unofficially a 'fifth province' of South Africa. The railways were extended to Walvis Bay and Cape Town in order to link South West Africa's economy with South Africa.

[8] Local resistance there and elsewhere in South West Africa continued in a sustained and violent manner until the1930s. Through

trade union organizing, political and economic resistance began in the 1920s. Despite the efforts of the Afrikaners, the 'province' of South Western Africa was not productive until the end of World War II. Mining production was low and due to elevated export prices, there was only slight demand for minerals. Pretoria had to fund the survival of the colonists.

[9] From 1947, the Namibians started to ask the United Nations to free them from South African domination. On another front, the UN - which inherited responsibility for the colonies in trust from the League of Nations - ignored South African demands to officially annex the territory, arguing that 'the African inhabitants of South West Africa have still not achieved political independence'.

[10] Between 1961 and 1968, the United Nations tried to annul the

trust mandate and establish the independence of the country. Legal pressure was ineffective and the Namibian people, led by the South West Africa People's Organization (SWAPO) decided to fight for freedom. The fighting broke out on 26 August 1966.

[11] In 1968 the UN finally proclaimed that the South African occupation of the country now known as Namibia was illegal. However, attempts by most members of the UN General Assembly to follow this condemnation with economic sanctions systematically came up against the veto of the Western powers. A UN Council was set up as legal representative of the territory until sovereignty could be freely exercised by the people.

[12] Angolan independence, declared in 1975, gave SWAPO a supportive rearguard. The guerrilla war intensified despite South African pressure against Angola, and the Western powers started to put pressure on Pretoria to seek a 'moderate' solution before a revolutionary regime could take over the country.

[13] In December 1978, South Africa held elections in Namibia with a view to establishing an independent government, presented as a step toward independence. But the poll was carried out without UN observers, with the territory occupied by racist troops and with no SWAPO participation, leading to a total lack of credibility in the results.

[14] The economy had grown in a sustained manner since World War II, reaching a peak of $1,000 per head in the 1970s ($20,000 for Europeans and $150 for black Namibians). Even while incomes in the white enclave soared, the salary of black workers was barely enough to live on, at a level of minimal subsistence for one person. It took until half way through this decade for workers to be trained to any significant degree, in qualified tasks.

[15] The South African controlled administration in Windhoek operated along customary colonial lines of dependence. Ninety per cent of the goods consumed in Namibia came from South Africa. The Odendaal was a body established by

the colonial government to encourage growth along segregationist lines, favoring the elite of professional blacks in the 1980s. During this period the Government increased the salaries of professional blacks - teachers, nurses, administrators and army personnel. However, the vast majority of the black population, which at that time numbered two thirds of the total, were left in conditions of extreme poverty. On another front, employment contracts damaged the social and civil fabric, increasing the number of single female-headed households in rural areas and also in the outlying urban areas.

[16] According to the book *To be Born a Nation*, Namibian independence meant the loss of $240 million in exports and extra costs of $14 million of imports of foreign produce for South Africa. As a result, South Africa upped its military budget by 30 per cent for the conflict against the Namibian People's Liberation Army, SWAPO's armed wing. South Africa made any independence agreement conditional on the withdrawal of Cuban troops from Angola, whilst demanding guarantees that investments in Namibia would not be touched. SWAPO did not accept the privileges granted to the white population in the draft constitution, nor the limitations to possibilities of future reforms to this. It also insisted that the elections should be supervised by the UN, an idea not accepted by Pretoria.

[17] In February 1984, representatives of Angola and South Africa met in Zambia's capital, Lusaka, for peace negotiations. They agreed a planned withdrawal of South African troops from southern Angola, in return for a ceasefire. In May, delegates from SWAPO and other Namibian parties met a South African representative but negotiations failed due to South African intransigence. The South African withdrawal from Angola did not occur within the deadline and the situation was deadlocked again.

[18] In December 1988, after prolonged US-mediated negotiations, South Africa, Angola and Cuba reached an agreement whereby South African troops

PROFILE

ENVIRONMENT

Mainly made up of plateaus in the desert region along the Tropic of Capricorn. The Namib desert, along the coast, contains rich diamond deposits and is only populated because of mining activities. To the east, the country shares the Kalahari desert with Botswana, an area populated by herders and hunters. The population is densest in the north, and in the central plateau, where rainfall is heaviest. There is a coastal fishing industry which, together with cattle raising, was the mainstay of the economy before mining began in the 1960s. The country has important reserves of copper, lead, zinc, cadmium and uranium.

SOCIETY

Peoples: Ovambo 47.4 per cent; Kavango 8.8 per cent; Herero 7.1 per cent; Damara 7.1 per cent; Nama 4.6 per cent. There is a European minority (4.6 per cent).
Religions: Many people practice traditional African religions although there are a large number of Christians (Lutheran 51.2 per cent, Catholics 19.8 per cent, Anglican 5 per cent).
Languages: English (official), Khoisan, Bantu, German and Afrikaans.
Political Parties: Southwest African People's Organization (SWAPO); Congress of Democrats; Democratic Turnhalle Alliance (DTA); United Democratic Front.
Social Organizations: National Union of Workers of Namibia.

THE STATE

Official Name: Republic of Namibia.
Administrative divisions: 13 districts.
Capital: Windhoek 202,000 people (1999).
Other cities: Rehoboth 33,800 people; Rundu 28,500; Swakopmund 28,300; Walvis Bay 24,500; Keetmanshoop 20,000 (2000).
Government: Sam Nujoma, President since March 1990, re-elected in 1999. Hage Geingob, Prime Minister since 1990. The Constitution established a presidential regime and a multiparty system.
National holiday: March 21, Independence Day (1990).
Armed Forces: 8,100 (1996).

would leave Namibia and the Cubans would withdraw their 50,000 soldiers from Angola.

[19] In November 1989 more than 710,000 Namibians voted for members of the First Constituent Assembly. Ten political parties stood in the UN-supervised elections. SWAPO won a resounding victory with 60 per cent of the poll, and gained control of the Assembly. SWAPO leader, Sam Nujoma, became the first president of Namibia.

[20] Independence was proclaimed on 21 March 21 1990. The presidential guard of honor was made up of troops from SWAPO and the SWA Territory Force which had protected the South African regime; both to be integrated into the new National Army of Namibia.

[21] The new government had to face up to the inequalities inherited from the South African apartheid system, above all in health and education. Income inequality within the population led economic analysts to classify the nation as having a 'dual economy' as around 70 per cent of the population lived in Third World conditions, 25 per cent within a transition economy and only 5 per cent benefited from economic conditions linked to development.

[22] Namibia adopted English as its official language, replacing Afrikaans, at independence. The Government organized a Department of Informal Education to help women learn to read. In collaboration with UNICEF it decided Namibia's women should be taught to read first in their own languages in order to later learn English. As for health, the Government earmarked resources to develop a rehabilitation plan for some 40,000 unemployed - mostly the victims of 23 years of pro-independence guerrilla warfare.

[23] Prepared to play an important role in Southern Africa, Nujoma donated around $3 million in 1991 to the African National Congress (ANC), then the main black opposition to the minority white government in South Africa - a sum which was handed over to

ANC Nelson Mandela on a visit he made to Namibia on January 31.

[24] In 1992 Namibia and South Africa agreed to return the port of Walvis bay to Windhoek in 1994. One year later the National Council, the upper chamber of Parliament, came into operation. In 1994, the Government approved a land law, which aimed among other things to limit the concentration of wealth. It was estimated that 1 per cent of the population held 75 per cent of the nation's land.

[25] In December of that year, Nujoma was re-elected president with 70 per cent of popular support. However, in May 1995 his party, SWAPO, split - leading to the creation of the SWAPO for Justice group.

[26] In mid 1997, a SWAPO Congress proclaimed Nujoma for a third period as president of Namibia. Social protests, above all due to unemployment, were not heeded by the government. A large part of the former SWAPO army was still unemployed.

[27] The number of HIV-positive and people with AIDS increased alarmingly. In 1997, the illness caused 1,539 deaths, bringing the total registered since 1988 to 3,677. The number of those infected since the same year is 40,629.

[28] The fishing industry showed signs of recovery and recorded strong growth in 1998. Also that year, in search of new sources of income, the Government began promoting Namibia as a tourist destination, an industry that had not yet been developed in this country.

[29] After a small band of rebels attempted to take over the town of Katima Mulil in August 1999, some 200 people were detained and tortured until many 'confessed' to being supporters of Caprivi Strip independence, Namibia's panhandle territory that divides Botswana from Angola. Of the 200 detainees, at least 76 were tried for treason and other crimes, while the rest were released without charges. Some 100,000 people inhabit the Caprivi Strip, primarily the Iozi ethnic group, who refused to be led by the country's Ovambo majority, which also dominates SWAPO.

[30] Despite protests from the opposition, the Constitution was modified so that Nujoma could run for a third Presidential term in the 1999 elections, which he won with 76 per cent of the vote. On taking office in March 2000, apart from announcing he would not run again, Nujoma declared that the country's goals were to achieve a standard of living similar to the industrialized North by the year 2030, and in the immediate term, to fight HIV, which continued to decimate the population.

[31] Black community farmers urged the 4,000 commercial farmers, mainly white, to hasten the land reform to avoid what they called 'Zimbabwe-style invasions on their farms'. In their opinion, the Government policy of buying land from whites to hand over to blacks failed because whites refused to sell. Only some 35,000 Namibians have been relocated in fertile lands since 1990.

[32] In January 2002 the Herero community demanded compensation of $2 billion for war crimes that killed some 65,000 people and were committed between 1904-1907 under German rule. Several companies - the best known of which is Deutsche Bank - are accused of forming a 'brutal alliance' with imperial Germany to exterminate more than 65,000 Herero.

[33] In March 2002, in a speech at the University of Namibia Nujoma declared 'homosexuality or lesbianism are not allowed'. The record of human rights abuse by the Government includes extrajudicial executions, the killing of prisoners, disappearances, torture of inmates, atrocious prison conditions and detention of civilians in military centers. Journalists in government media are pressured not to criticize the Government; there are arbitrary deportations, state violence against women and children, including rape and other sexual abuse, and forced child labor.

[34] At the September 2002 Summit on Sustainable Development, Nujoma backed Zimbabwean President Mugabe's land appropriation measures. ∎

Nauru

Population: 13,000 (2002)
Land area: 20 SQ KM
Currency: Australian dollar
Language: English

Nauru

Nauru, which lies in the central Pacific, was originally populated by migrating Polynesian, Micronesian and Melanesian people. The British sailor John Fearn was the first European to visit the island, which he named Pleasant Island. Whaling ships often called at Nauru during the 19th century, until it was annexed by the German Second Reich in 1888.

[2] In 1899, Nauru was found to have phosphate-rich rock which made it one of the wealthiest territories in the world. In 1905, an Anglo-German company began mining on the island.

[3] At the beginning of World War I, Nauru came under Australian trusteeship and during World War II, under Japanese control with thousands of Nauruans sent to forced labor camps on the island of Truk (in present-day Micronesia). At the end of the War, only 700 came back alive. Australia recovered the island, and mining was continued by British, Australian and Aotearoan/New Zealand transnational consortia.

[4] The Nauruans did not adjust well to mining and were soon replaced by immigrants, mostly Chinese. Immigrant workers

became so numerous that in 1964, the Australian Government officially suggested that Nauruans should accept resettlement on a different island or elsewhere in Australia. Nauruans rejected this, deciding to stay on their island and seek autonomy.

[5] The mining sector was nationalized in 1967, which resulted in a large increase in per capita income. In 1992, the minimum annual salary was $6,500. Nauru declared independence on January 31 1968, rejecting Australian attempts at domination.

A year later it became a member of the Commonwealth.

[6] Government expenses and public investment were paid out of a huge legal fund fed by phosphate revenues. Education, medical care and housing are free.

[7] Hammer de Roburt dominated the political scene, and as the first President, he governed continuously until 1976 when he lost the majority to Bernard Dowiyogo, of the Nauru Party. Two years later, De Roburt once again obtained the majority, holding office from 1978 to 1986.

[8] Nauru established formal diplomatic relationship with the Republic of China on May 4 1980. Since then, both nations maintained close trade and friendship links.

[9] Bernard Dowiyogo's second administration sued the government of Australia for its indiscriminate exploitation of the phosphate mines for 50 years. In 1991, Australia acknowledged the right of Nauru to be indemnified. Britain and New Zealand agreed to collaborate with Australia in the payment of $100 million to Nauru.

[10] In December 1997 then president Godfrey Clodumar re-established diplomatic relations with France, broken off two years previously in protest against nuclear tests in French Polynesia. At the same time, Nauru demanded a drastic cut in the production of greenhouse gases which lead to global warming and the resultant rise in sea levels that would drown Nauru.

[11] Nauru citizens, who used to enjoy one of the highest per capita incomes in the world, suffered a sharp decrease in their standard of living due to bad investments of the government. Dowiyogo lost Parliament's confidence. In April, 1999, René Harris became President. On September 14, Nauru joined the United Nations.

[12] In August 2001, 460 illegal immigrants, most of them Afghans, and also Sinhalese and Thais, were rescued from a Norwegian cargo ship when the vessel was sinking. There was an attempt to land the immigrants on Australian territory at Christmas Island, but Australia refused to accept them. After several days of diplomatic negotiations, Aotearoa/New Zealand agreed to accept 150 refugees, while the rest went on to Nauru. Canberra offered to pay the expenses for the refugees heading for the island.

[13] That same year, IFAG (International Financial Action Group) applied countermeasures against Nauru because it had not complied with its commitment to strengthen the laws against money-laundering; it was put on its list of non-cooperative countries and territories. In 2002, the US deplored the fact that $70 billion taken from Russia in 1998 had entered Nauruan transnational accounts. ∎

PROFILE

ENVIRONMENT
Nauru is a coral island, 6 km long by 4 km wide, located near Micronesia just south of the Equator. With sandy beaches and a thin belt of fertile land (300 meters wide), the island has a 60-meter high central plateau of guano (bird droppings), rich in phosphoric acid and nitrogen.

SOCIETY
Peoples: Nauruans are descendants of Polynesian, Micronesian and Melanesian immigrants. There are also Australian, Aotearoan New Zealanders, Chinese, European minorities, and workers from Tuvalu, Kiribati and other neighboring islands. Men outnumber women two to one. **Religions:** Christian. **Languages:** English (official) and Nauruan. **Political Parties:** Nauru Party (NP); Democratic Party of Nauru. **Social Organizations:** There are two organizations: the Nauru Workers' Organization (NWO), founded in 1974 and affiliated to the NP; and the Phosphate Workers' Organization (PWO), founded in 1953.

THE STATE
Official Name: Republic of Nauru.
Administrative Divisions: 14 districts. **Capital:** There are no population centers and so the island has no formal capital. The Government buildings are located opposite the airport in the Yaren district.

Government: René Harris, President since March 2001, elected for a three-year term by the Legislature. It is unicameral and has 18 members. **National Holiday:** January 31, Independence Day (1968). **Armed Forces:** The defense is responsibility of Australia.

DEMOGRAPHY
Population: 13,000 (2002)
Annual growth: 2.7 % (1985-2000)
Estimates for year 2015: 17,000 (2000)
Annual growth to year 2015: 2.2 % (2000)

HEALTH
Infant mortality: 25 per 1,000 (2000)
Under-5 child mortality: 30 per 1,000 (2000)
157 doctors per 100,000 people (1995)

EDUCATION
Literacy: 95 % (2000) male: 93 % (2000)
female: 96 % (2000)
School enrolment (net):
Primary total: 98 % (1994/2000)
male: 99 % (1995/99)
female: 97 % (1995/99)

ECONOMY
Currency: 1.9 Australian dollars = $ 1 (03/2002)

Nepal

Population: 24,153,000 (2002)
Land area: 143,000 SQ KM
Capital: Kathmandu
Currency: Rupee
Language Nepali

Nepal

Nepal is a landlocked country in the central Himalayas between two of the world's most populated countries; India and China. References to Nepal Valley and Nepal's lower hill areas are found in the ancient Indian classics, suggesting that the Central Himalayan hills were closely connected culturally and politically to the Gangetic Plain at least 2,500 years ago. Lumbini, Gautama Buddha's birthplace in southern Nepal, and Nepal Valley also figure prominently in Buddhist accounts. There is substantial archaeological evidence of early Buddhist influence in Nepal, including a famous column inscribed by Ashoka (Emperor of India, 3rd century BC) at Lumbini and several shrines in the valley.

[2] Although there are gaps, the sequence of the Nepal Valley's history can be traced along with the rise of the Licchavi dynasty in the 4th or 5th century AD. While the earlier Kirati dynasty had claimed the status of the Kshatriya caste of rulers and warriors, the Licchavis were probably the first ruling family in that area of plain Indian origin. This set a precedent for what became the normal pattern thereafter (Hindu kings claiming high-caste Indian origin ruling over a population much of which was neither Indo-Aryan nor Hindu).

[3] The Licchavi dynastic chronicles, supplemented by numerous stone inscriptions, are particularly detailed from AD 500 to 700. A powerful, united kingdom also emerged in Tibet during this period, and the Himalayan passes to the north of the valley were opened. Extensive cultural, trade and political relations developed across the Himalayas, transforming the valley from a relatively remote backwater into the major intellectual and commercial center between South and Central Asia. Nepal's contacts with China began in the mid-7th century with the exchange of several missions. But intermittent warfare between Tibet and China terminated this relationship; and while there were briefly renewed contacts in subsequent centuries, these were re-established on a continuing basis only in the late 18th century.

[4] The middle period in Nepalese history roughly corresponds with the

rule of the Malla dynasty (10th-18th century) in Nepal Valley and surrounding areas. Although most of the Licchavi kings were devout Hindus, they did not impose Brahmanic social codes or values on their non-Hindu subjects. The Mallas perceived their responsibilities differently, however, and the Malla ruler Jaya Sthiti (reigned c. 1832-95) introduced the first legal and social code strongly influenced by contemporary Hindu principles. His successor Yaksa Malla (reigned 1429-1482) divided his kingdom among his three sons, thus creating the independent principalities of Kathmandu, Patan, and Bhaktpur (Bhagdaon) in the valley. Each of these states controlled territory in the surrounding hill areas, with particular importance attached to the trade routes northward to Tibet and southward to India that were vital to the valley's economy. There were also numerous small principalities in the western and eastern hill areas, whose independence was sustained through a delicate balance of power based upon traditional inter-relationships and in some cases common ancestral origins among the ruling families.

[5] In the 16th century virtually all these principalities were ruled by dynasties claiming high-caste Indian origin whose members had left the hills in the wake of Muslim invasions of Northern India. In the early 18th century the principality of Gorkha (or Gurkha) began to assert a predominant role in the hills and even to pose a challenge to Nepal Valley. The Mallas, weakened by familial dissent and

widespread social and economic discontent, were no match for the great Gorkha ruler Prithvi Narayan Shah, who conquered the valley in 1769 and moved his capital to Kathmandu shortly thereafter, providing the foundation of the modern state of Nepal.

[6] The Shah (or Saha) rulers faced persistent problems in trying to centralize an area long characterized by extreme diversity and ethnic and regional parochialism. They absorbed dominant regional and local élites into the central administration of Kathmandu, thus neutralizing potentially disintegrative political forces and involving them in national politics. However, this also severely limited the center's authority in outlying areas because local administration was based upon a compromise division of responsibilities between the local élites and the central administration.

[7] The British conquest of India in the 19th century posed a serious threat to Nepal and left the country with no real alternative but to seek an accommodation with the British to preserve its independence. This was accomplished by the Rana family regime after 1860. Under this de facto alliance, Kathmandu permitted the recruitment of highly valued Gurkha units for the British Indian Army and also accepted British 'guidance' on foreign policy. In exchange, the British guaranteed the Rana regime protection against both foreign and domestic enemies and allowed it virtual autonomy in domestic affairs. Nepal was also

careful to maintain a friendly relationship with China and Tibet, for economic reasons.

[8] When the British withdrew from India in 1947, the Ranas were deprived of a vital external source of support and the regime was exposed to new dangers. Anti-Rana forces, composed mainly of Nepalese residents in India who had served their political apprenticeship in the Indian nationalist movement, formed an alliance with the Nepalese royal family, led by the king. A tripartite agreement between Nepal, India and the UK was signed in Kathmandu in November 1947, and Gurkha troops were used by India in the war against China in 1961-62, Pakistan in 1965 and 1971, and by the UK against Argentina in 1982.

[9] In February 1951, the Nepalese Congress succeeded in overthrowing the Rana regime with support from King Tribhuvan Bir Bikram Shah Deva. From this time until December 1960 a series of democratic experiments took place in Nepal. Political parties were legalized and a general election was held in 1959, based on the Constitution approved by King Mahendra Bir Bikram Shah Deva. On December 15 1960, the first elected Prime Minister, B P Koirala, was arrested. Parliament was dissolved and most of the provisions of the Constitution were suspended. Political parties were outlawed and a non-party system or Panchayat was introduced in December 1962.

[10] Nepal became a member of the United Nations in 1955, and it has been an active member of the Non-Aligned Movement since the days of the Bandung Conference. By July 1986, some 75 countries, including the major powers, endorsed a proposal by King Birendra Bir Birkram Shah Deva that Nepal should be declared a peace zone. All of its neighbors except India and Bhutan endorsed the proposal.

[11] In 1979, student protest movements emerged in Kathmandu and other cities. Birendra responded by holding a plebiscite to choose between a multiparty system or a reformed Panchayat, the latter obtaining 55 per cent of the vote. The opposition considered the outcome the result of fraud.

[12] India is Nepal's leading trade partner. The two signed several trade and transit treaties since 1950, the last of which concluded in 1989 and locked them into an undeclared trade war. Nepal clashed with India on importing arms from China, leading India to halt trade with Nepal, closing 19 of the 21 transit routes in March 1989, seriously harming the Nepalese economy.

[13] The anti-Panchayat protests reached a peak . The King initiated talks with the opposition leaders and agreed to political pluralism. The transition to a parliamentary democracy with a constitutional monarchy was announced by royal decree in April 1990.

[14] On April 12 1991 the first free elections were held in Nepal after 32 years of semi-monarchic rule. The Communist Party of Nepal and the Nepalese Congress Party united for the elections, joining forces with other groups. The Communists won 4 of the 5 posts in the capital, but the national majority went to the Nepalese Congress Party.

[15] Prime Minister Bhattarai resigned on May 15. The new Government appointed Girija Prasad Koirala, member of the Nepalese Congress Party, in his place. Koirala promised to launch a mixed economy, earmarking 70 per cent of national income to rural regions and carrying out agrarian reform. He declared free primary education.

[16] In late 1991 the opposition harshly criticized Koirala for signing certain treaties with India, saying he had 'sold off national interests' given that India would benefit with five hydroelectric projects. To attract foreign investment, in 1993 Koirala promoted the total convertibility of the rupia (national currency) with foreign currencies, and signed new trade accords with India. The loss of parliamentary support and infighting in the monarchist Nepalese Congress Party (NCP) accelerated the demise of Koirala, who resigned in July 1994. In the November elections the United Communist Party (UCPN) won 88 seats in the Chamber of Representatives, surpassing the NCP's 83. Man Mohan Adhikari was named Prime Minister.

[17] Unable to gain majority political support for his leadership, the Communist Prime Minister handed over control in September 1995 to NCP leader Sher Bahadur Deuba.

[18] In early 1996, guerrilla groups describing themselves as Maoist launched campaigns to 'eradicate feudalism'. In March 1997 Bahadur Deuba resigned and Lokendra Bahadur Chand took over with support from an integrated coalition that included the pro-monarchy Nepalese Sadbhavana Party (NSP) and the United Communist Party (UCP). In October, Surya Bahadur Thapa took office as Prime Minister, with support from another fragile coalition, similar to the one that appointed his predecessor. In April 1998 the Nepalese Congress withdrew its support, forcing him to stand down and forcing the nomination of Koirala as the new Head of Government.

[19] In January 1999, King Birendra dissolved Parliament under the recommendation of Koirala and announced new elections for May, which he lost. However, following the resignation of Krishna Prasad Bhattarai, of the NCP, Koirala took power as Premier for a third time.

[20] On June 1 2001 King Birendra, Queen Aishwarya and other members of the royal family were shot to death by heir Prince Dipendra, 29, who was inebriated and later shot himself in a suicide attempt, but survived in a state of coma. The Royal Council appointed Dipendra King of Nepal and Prince Gyanendra, Birendra's brother, as his Regent. Dipendra died June 4 and Gyanendra became King. The population took to the streets in protest that they had not received full explanations of the events.

[21] After Koirala's resignation due to the growing violence between the insurgent Maoists and the security forces, Sher Bahadur Deuba took over as Prime Minister in July 2001 and declared a cease-fire. In the subsequent negotiations, the Maoists included among their 31 demands the abolition of the 1990 Constitution, the creating of an interim government and the election of a Constituent Assembly to draft a new national charter that would end the monarchy and create a republic. The government did not accept the demands and violence escalated. The King declared a state of emergency in November, categorizing the rebels as terrorists.

[22] With constitutional guarantees suspended, the death toll among civilians and rebels alike continued to rise. The conflict became civil war and by 2002 had claimed 2,100 lives, and 100,000 refugees fled to neighboring Bhutan.

[23] In spite of 5 per cent annual GDP growth, more than 40 per cent of the Nepalese population lives below the poverty line, 2.5 million children work, there is a serious energy crisis and lack of clean water. In order to facilitate a way out of the country's pressing economic situation, international agencies and several countries pledged a total of $2.5 billion in economic aid for Nepal. ∎

PROFILE

ENVIRONMENT

Nepal is a landlocked country in the Himalayas with three distinct geographical regions: the fertile, tropical plains of Terai, the central plateaus, covered with rainforest, and the Himalayan mountains, where the world's highest peaks are located. The climate varies according to altitude, from rainy and tropical, to cold in the high mountains. This diversity allows for the cultivation of rice, sugarcane, tobacco, jute and cereals. Livestock is also important; sheep and buffalo. Mineral and hydroelectric resources are as yet unexploited. Wood provides 90 per cent of the energy consumed, resulting in deforestation and soil erosion. Air and water pollution especially affect urban areas. The lack of sewerage systems in the most important cities has also contributed to the deterioration of the environment.

SOCIETY

Peoples: The Nepalese are descended from Indian, Tibetan and Mongolian migrants. Nepalese 53.2 per cent; Bihari (including Maithili and Bhojpuri) 18.4 per cent; Tharu 4.8 per cent; Tamang 4.7 per cent; Newar 3.4 per cent; Magar 2.2 per cent; Abadhi 1.7 per cent; other 11.6 per cent. **Religions:** Hinduism 86.2 per cent (official); Buddhism 7.8 per cent; Muslim 3.8 per cent; Christian 0.2 per cent; other 2 per cent. **Languages:** Nepali (official) is spoken by only half the population; many other languages are spoken, corresponding to the different cultural communities, Tibetan being the second most common in the country. **Political Parties:** The Nepalese Congress Party (NCP); the Communist Party of Nepal (Unified Marxist-Leninists); National Democratic Party (NDM); Nepalese Goodwill Party; National People's Front.

THE STATE

Official Name: Nepál Adhirajya. **Administrative divisions:** 5 regions, 14 zones and 75 districts. **Capital:** Kathmandu 669,000 people (1999). **Other cities:** Biratnagar 203,300 people; Pokhara 157,700; Lalitpur 153,900; Birganj 118,300 (2000). **Government:** Parliamentary Monarchy. Gyanendra Bir Bikram Shah Dev, King since June 2001. Sher Bahadur Deuba, Prime Minister and Chief of Government since July 2001. The Parliament has two chambers: The House of Representatives with 205 members and The House of the States which has 60 members. **National Holidays:** February 15, (Constitution) and February 18, (Fatherland); July 7, Birthday of King (1946). **Armed Forces:** 35,000 (1994). **Other:** 28,000 (Police Forces).

Netherlands

Population: 15,990,000 (2002)
Land area: 33,880 SQ KM
Capital: Amsterdam
Currency: Euro
Language: Dutch

Nederland

The Netherlands, Belgium, Luxembourg and the northern part of France constitute the region once known as the Low Countries. The first inhabitants of these lands arrived at the end of the last Ice Age, changing over thousands of years from hunter-gathering groups to the more elaborate and hierarchical cultures which the Romans encountered.

2   When the Romans reached the area in the 1st century BC it was inhabited by Celts and Germanic people. The Empire never managed to occupy the land of the Frisians, in the north above the Rhine, so the Romans settled in the southern delta, where they created the provinces of Belgica and lesser Germanica.

3   The Frisians lived by fishing and raising cattle, while in the south agriculture was carried on around the villages and towns. By the second half of the 3rd century, the encroaching sea had drastically altered the economic basis of the region.

4   The strengthening of the Germanic tribes forced Rome to grant them custody of the Empire's borders, as it did with the Franks in Toxandria and Brabant. The line between the Romance and Germanic languages ran across the middle of the Low Countries, coinciding with the borders of the Roman Empire.

5   The Frisians remained independent until the 7th century, when the Franks and the Catholic Church started a strong offensive. By the end of the century, the region had been subdued by the Franks, under the Pepin and Carolingian dynasties.

6   The decline of the Carolingian Empire led to a period of instability during the 10th century. Several principalities were formed, with feudal ties to the kingdoms of Germany and France. The Frisians still remained free of sovereign authorities.

7   The secular principalities of Flanders (Vlaanderen), Hainaut, Namur, Loon, Holland, Zeeland, Guelders, and the duchies of Brabant and Limburg were formed. In the principalities of Utrecht and Liege, the secular and ecclesiastic authorities shared power.

8   The principalities worked towards greater freedom from royal authority. Flanders was the first to establish an efficient administration, followed by Brabant, Hainaut, and Namur. The appointment of their own bishops marked the end of German influence, and the establishment of closer links between the principalities.

9   France tried to subdue Flanders but was defeated in the Battle of the Spurs in 1302. In general, France and Britain kept a balance of power, a situation that contributed to preserving the autonomy of the region.

10   Population pressure led to the creation of new farmlands. On the coast, the Cistercian and Premonstratensian monks (an order founded by St Norbert) constructed many dykes. These were initially built to defend people from the high tides, but they later served to reclaim land.

11   From the 11th century onwards, the Frisians developed a drainage system which removed the sea-water, providing land for pasturage and arable fields. During the 12th and 13th centuries, a vast peat bog in the Netherlands and Utrecht was reclaimed for agriculture.

12   This area of polders on the coast of Flanders and Friesland became economically very significant. Between the 12th and 14th centuries, the struggle against the sea and inland water became so important that water authorities were created to organize the

construction of dykes and the use of water.

13   This increase in arable land and population brought about growth, not only in agriculture but also in industry and commerce. The new towns gave birth to new social classes who sought autonomy. Merchants in the towns had to swear an oath of co-operation; promising that they would keep law and order.

14   The towns gradually became independent centers, having the power to sign commercial, political, and military agreements with other towns or with the Prince. The town owned the land within its boundaries and the inhabitants did not rely on any external authorities.

15   During the second half of the 14th century, the dukes of Burgundy from the French royal house of Valois ruled over most of the Low Countries, where they tried to create a centralized state. There was a movement to prevent this centralization, in 1477, but the accession of the Hapsburgs interrupted it.

16   By virtue of the Hapsburg marriage, the fate of the Low Countries depended on the outcome of the House of Austria's struggle for European domination. This situation intensified in 1504, when King Philip and his wife, Joan, inherited the Spanish Crown. Centralization was on the increase and the Church was no exception. A Papal Bull was issued, creating a Rome-based administration, with

three archbishops and 15 bishops. This was deeply resented by the local nobility.

17   The Lutheran and Anabaptist faiths had difficulty gaining converts in the Low Countries, while Calvinism quickly gained acceptance among the lower classes and the intellectuals. Repression drove many Calvinists into exile, but they still had influence in the 1567 anti-absolutism rebellion.

18   Popular unrest and the nobility and urban gentry's desire for autonomy led to a successful rebellion in Holland. After the defeat of the Spanish troops, the rebellion extended to all the provinces, ending with the Treaty of Ghent in 1576.

19   Three years later, for geographic, economic, political, and religious reasons, this union dissolved. The Union of Arras was founded in the south, and the Union of Utrecht in the north, both of these being within the boundaries of a larger unit led by the States-General.

20   The Utretcht Union became a unique state through the 1581 Abjuration Act, when the States-General seized King Felipe II's sovereignty. The Netherlands was the largest economic and political power within the Union, so all of the union's inhabitants became known as Netherlanders.

21   During the Twelve Years' Truce with Spain, 1609-21, controversies within the Union grew. The collaboration between the province of Holland and the House of Orange gave way to a growing rivalry. This situation was antagonized by the dispute over Church-State relations.

22   In 1618, Maurice of Orange, supported by the States-General, executed the leader of the main party in the Netherlands. When war against Spain resumed in 1621, the French and Dutch rivals were forced to reunite until the signing of the Treaty of Utrecht in 1713.

23   The 17th century is called the golden age in Dutch history. This was viewed as the birth of a great nation, one that rivaled the great powers of the time, a fact that was only called into question at the end of that century.

24   Dutch prosperity was not only the result of continental trade, but

also of its colonial power. In 1602, the Dutch East India Company was created, with bases in South Africa, Ceylon (Sri Lanka), India and Indonesia. The Netherlands had sovereign powers in these colonies, as did the British and French in theirs.

25 At first the Company only held coastal trading bases, but later on, it started to occupy the hinterland controlling the region and certain commodities. The colonial administration was autonomous, as the Dutch preferred governing through agreements with local leaders.

26 In 1621, the West Indies Company was founded. It made the bulk of its profits from the slave trade and privateering, it also operated outside Zeeland, a southwestern maritime province, especially against Spanish ships. The Netherlands dominated the slave trade during the 17th century.

27 In 1648, the Dutch had three large settlements in the Americas: one in the north, for the fur trade; another on the Atlantic coast, with outposts for the slave trade and smuggling with Spanish colonies; and another in what is now Brazil and Suriname (formerly Dutch Guyana). By 1700, they were left with only the trading outposts in Curaçao, St Eustacius and St Martin, the plantations in Guyana, and the slave port of Elmina.

28 Dutch maritime power weakened in the 18th century, especially after the war against Britain (1708-84). The country used up a portion of its capital to buy bonds in foreign governments. The bankers in Amsterdam were among the most powerful in Europe.

29 The 1750s saw the emergence of the Patriot movement, a group of factions who had been overlooked in governmental policies: they ranged from bankers and simple artisans, to dissident Protestants and Catholics, unhappy with monarchic abuse of power.

30 The Patriots went into exile during the Prussian invasion of 1786. Their hopes were rekindled with the French Revolution, but it was not until 1794 that France managed effective opposition to Britain and Prussia, who supported William V. They proclaimed the Republic and started the process of political modernization.

31 The new republic declared equality among its citizens and changed the institutional framework. It replaced the assembly of States-General for a National Assembly with direct electoral representation, and executive power was separated from the legislative and the judicial.

32 In 1806, France annexed the state to the Empire under the name of the Napoleonic Kingdom of the Netherlands. Five years later, Bonaparte incorporated the Netherlands into France, until the fall of the Empire. In 1814, King William I of Orange was chosen by the Dutch leaders, and he restored the monarchy.

33 In the Congress of Vienna, the victorious powers gave William I sovereignty over the whole of the Low Countries. The Belgian revolution of 1830 broke out during his reign.

34 The second half of the 19th century was marked by a liberalization of the government under the impact of the revolutions that had swept Europe during the 1840s. The constitution of 1848 became the foundation of Netherland's present-day democracy. Under its provisions arbitrary personal rule by the monarch was no longer possible and members of the first chamber of parliament, who had formerly been appointed by the King, were thereafter elected by the provincial states (assemblies). Members of the states and of the second chamber were chosen by voters who were enfranchised by paying taxes above a certain level.

35 In the late 19th century, suffrage was gradually extended, and agitation for social reform increased markedly. The rise of a strong Labor party and the organization of workers into labor unions resulted in further social reforms.

36 New political parties were founded, based on the religious ideas and ideologies of the time. To the Liberal, Protestant and Catholic parties were added the Protestant Conservative, the Socialist and the Communist parties. As none could obtain a majority, coalitions became commonplace. Universal male suffrage was approved in 1917; women were granted the vote in 1922. After decades of debate over the school system, Protestants and Catholics allied themselves against the liberals and, in 1888, the first private denominational schools were opened.

37 During World War I, the Netherlands declared its neutrality and political parties agreed on a truce in order to devote themselves to the domestic economy and trade. The merchant navy had recovered and industry grew, in particular textiles, electronics, and chemicals.

38 During the postwar period, the Netherlands was a member of the League of Nations, but it re-affirmed its neutrality. Symbolically, The Hague became the seat of the International Court of Justice. During the Versailles negotiations, Belgium tried unsuccessfully to revive an old territorial claim against the Netherlands.

39 During World War II, Hitler attacked France through the Netherlands, and Queen Wilhelmina formed a government-in-exile in London. All political factions took part in anti-Nazi resistance. German repression was harsh, and by the end of the war the country was on the verge of famine.

40 In 1945, an agreement was signed by the Government, companies and trade unions. It lasted 20 years and was aimed at controlling prices and salaries. Indonesia became independent in 1945 while Suriname had to wait until 1975. The Netherlands underwent rapid industrialization especially in steel production, electronics and petrochemicals.

41 Dutch capital controlled some large transnational corporations such as Shell (Royal Dutch Petroleum), the oil company (jointly a British company). Unilever, one of the world's largest food and soap manufacturer, had branches all over the world and its products were used by companies everywhere. Other Dutch transnationals included Philips (electronics), AKZO (chemical manufacturer), ABN AMRO (international banking), ING (international banking and insurance) and Heineken (beer).

42 In the postwar period, the Government was composed of Labor party (the former socialists) and Catholic coalitions. The Netherlands gave up neutrality, becoming a member of NATO and of the European Economic Community. Also, together with Belgium and Luxembourg it formed an economic alliance known as the Benelux.

43 During the 1960s, youth demonstrations developed into violent riots, the royal marriages also became the subject of public controversy and ideological and religious questioning occurred in all Dutch institutions.

44 In the 1970s, voters favored the center and the left, while the Government reformed the tax system and redistributed income. The most controversial subjects were the defense budget and the installation of NATO atomic missiles within the country.

45 The Netherlands was one of the few OECD countries giving over 0.7 per cent of its GNP for aid to the

PROFILE

ENVIRONMENT

The country is a large plain and 38 per cent of its territory is below sea level. Intensive agriculture and cattle raising produce high-quality milk products and crops (particularly flowers). Population density is amongst the highest in the world. Highly industrialized, the country is the world's third largest producer of natural gas, and is a dominant influence in petroleum activity. It has large refineries in the Netherlands Antilles and Rotterdam, the world center of the free, or 'spot', crude oil market. As a result of the heavy use of agrochemicals, underground water is polluted with high nitrate levels, and is also affected by a large quantity of heavy metals. The main rivers carry all types of organic and industrial wastes, especially from other European countries. Air pollution is significant, mainly from oil refining and automobiles. There are high levels of acid rain.

SOCIETY

Peoples: Dutch 91 per cent; Turks 1.3 per cent; Moroccans 1 per cent; Germans 0.3 per cent; and others. **Religions:** 31 per cent Catholic; Dutch Reformed Church 14 per cent; Calvinist 8 per cent; Muslim 3.9 per cent; other 4.1 per cent; no religion 39 per cent. **Languages:** Dutch (official); Frisian and Saxon; Turkish, Arab, Kurdish and from other immigrant communities. **Political Parties:** Labor Party (PvdA), social-democratic, affiliated to the Socialist International; People's Party for Freedom and Democracy (WD), conservative liberal; Christian-Democratic Appeal (CDA); List Pim Fortuyn, far right; Democrats 66 (D66), social-liberal; Political Reformed Party (SGP), Christian, Green Left (GL), ecologist and socialist; New Communist Party of the Netherlands (NCPN), Socialist Party (SP), extreme left, among other minority parties. **Social Organizations:** Federation of Netherlands Trade Union Movements, which includes Socialist and Catholic trade unions; National Confederation of Christian Trade Unions.

THE STATE

Official Name: Koninkrijk der Nederlanden. **Administrative Divisions:** 12 Provinces. **Capital:** Greater Amsterdam 1,137,000 people (1999). Although the Government has its seat in The Hague, Amsterdam is still considered the capital. **Other cities:** Rotterdam 1,125,500 people; The Hague (s'-Gravenhage) 443,700; Utrecht 232,900; Eindhoven 200,600 (2000). **Government:** Constitutional and parliamentary monarchy. Queen Beatrix, Head of State since April 1980. Prime Minister Jan Peter Balkenende, since July 2002. The Legislature (States-General) has two chambers: the First Chamber, with 75 members, and the Second Chamber, with 150 members. **National Holiday:** April 30, Queen's Day (1938). **Armed Forces:** 74,400 (1995). **Other:** 3,600 Royal Military Corps. **Dependencies:** See Netherlands Antilles and Aruba.

Third World. It had also maintained a coherent policy on the defense of human rights and against apartheid in South Africa, though links with Israel have tended to estrange it from some Arab countries.

46   In 1989 the Government approved a 0.6 per cent increase in the defense budget for 1990 and 1991, to be followed by a budget suspension until 1995 and the withdrawal of 750 Dutch soldiers posted in West Germany. This Dutch resolution caused much malaise within NATO.

47   In the Netherlands there were some 100,000 farms, with around 4,500,000 head of cattle. The cost to the country of raising and feeding each cow is $2,000 per year, a sum which is higher than the per capita income of many Third World countries. The Dutch export dairy products and flowers, but also import a great amount of raw materials for their agro-industry. Fifteen million hectares of land in other countries (including 5 million in the Third World) is under production for Dutch needs. This is mainly because much of the soy and tapioca that their farm animals eat comes from other countries, mainly Brazil and Thailand. Only 20 per cent of the vegetable protein fed to animals is converted to animal protein. The rest produces 110 million tons of manure a year, of which only half is used in agriculture. The other half ends up polluting the soil, drinking water and the air, where it adds to industrial emissions to cause acid rain. Over 40 per cent of Holland's trees have been irreversibly damaged by acid rain and the country has exceptionally high levels of contamination.

48   Due to the high level of consumption that characterizes Dutch society, each person produces an estimated 3,000 kg of refuse per year. In Amsterdam and other cities many apartment buildings are inhabited by people who live alone, a fact which increases the demand for housing.

49   Taking advantage of the fact that the Netherlands was occupying the EU presidency at the time, in December 1991 the Dutch Parliament pressed EU heads of state and governments to condemn all forms of racism in Maastricht. In addition, they urged the adoption of legislation prohibiting xenophobic acts throughout Europe.

50   Despite this official position, the country was beset by growing racism, although to a lesser degree than other European countries. In September 1993 the Netherlands adopted legislation restricting the admission of immigrants from outside the European Union.

51   Government agencies devised economic indicators capable of assessing environmental damage, and methods for calculating national income. In 1992, the Central Office of Statistics announced the 'green gross national product' (GGNP). This indicator evaluates losses in natural resources, according to the capacity for regeneration, and the effect on local communities.

52   The government coalition parties suffered a serious setback in the March 1994 local elections, which showed the growth of the anti-immigration far right. On August 22, Wim Kok became Prime Minister.

53   In 1995, for the second year running, the complex hydraulic system failed, causing flooding of vast areas in the south and center.

54   In late 1996, the unemployment rate fell to 6.6 per cent. The GDP grew 2.7 per cent as a result of, among other things, the rise of exports and the recovery of local demand.

55   The elections for the Second Chamber in May 1998 confirmed the ruling coalition's popularity. With 29 per cent and 27.7 per cent of the vote respectively, the Labor Party and People's Party for Freedom and Democracy maintained their dominance and reinforced the government alliance along with the Democrats 66. In the election for the First Chamber in March 1999, the Christian Democrats had the highest ranking as a single party, with 26 per cent of the vote, but the government coalition had a total of 50.6 per cent.

56   In December 2000 a bill was passed granting gay married couples the same legal status as that of heterosexual couples. Another law passed at the same time also granted gays rights to adopt children. Until then, a gay couple could only register its union, although since 1986 a Dutch church recognizes same-sex marriage. The law was passed by a large majority and its defenders claim it gives gays better rights than in any other European country.

57   Cattle were slaughtered after the first cases of foot and mouth disease were detected in March 2001. Although it was expected vaccination would be enough to keep the virus at bay, the number of independent cases forced the slaughter of some 80,000 animals, in order not to lose the status of 'country free from foot and mouth disease'. According to the official investigation, the infected animals had come from Ireland.

58   The International Criminal Tribunal for the former Yugoslavia (ICTY) marked an historic occasion in July 2001, when a sentence was upheld and thereby brought rape into the definition of a war crime. ICTY's Appeals Court upheld the December 1998 sentences passed on a Croatian paramilitary. Anto Furundzija was sentenced to 10 years in prison as a 'co-perpetrator of torture' and 8 years for 'aiding and abetting' rape and torture after he did not intervene to stop an assault by a soldier under his command.

59   In January 2002 a law legalizing euthanasia, passed by the Senate in April 2001, came into force. The law made the Netherlands the first country in the world to legalize mercy-killing. The new law permits ending a patient's life under certain criteria that must be strictly applied: the patient must suffer intolerable and constant pain, be of sound mind, and must have requested several times to be allowed to die. The supervising doctor must obtain a second medical opinion. Finally, the death must occur in an appropriate medical way.

60   The Government resigned on April 16 2002 after admitting its responsibility in the Srebrenica massacre, during the Bosnian war in 1995. The official report, 7,600 pages long, stated that Dutch security forces in the area - blue helmets under UN mandate - had not been able to prevent the killing of 7,000 Bosnian Muslims by Bosnian Serbs. The victims were 'evacuated' from the UN security area by Dutch troops, which allowed for their ultimate deaths. The report also accused the UN for not sending the troops with a clear mandate and the necessary weapons to defend the area. Dutch soldiers had their use of force and weapons limited to self-defense. The Government's resignation took place weeks before the Parliamentary elections set for May 15.

61   Far-right leader Pim Fortuyn was murdered in May 2002 in the city of Hilversum. Nevertheless, the Dutch Government decided to hold the elections on the date scheduled. The right-wing leader, riding high in the polls, had recently declared that Holland should close its borders to immigration and that Islam was a backward religion. Among his electoral proposals was the lay-off of 25 per cent of civil servants. The police detained a white man, 32, in whose home was found ammunition of a caliber matching that of the murder weapon.

62   The Christian Democrats (CDA) won the Parliamentary elections held that month, obtaining 43 seats. Its leader Jan Peter Balkenende became the new Prime Minister in July. Fortuyn's party - List Pim Fortuyn - came in second, with 26 seats. ■

DEMOGRAPHY

Population: 15,990,000 (2002)
Annual growth: 0.6 % (1985-2000)
Estimates for year 2015: 16,420,000 (2000)
Annual growth to year 2015: 0.2 % (2000)
Urban population: 89.4 % (2000)
Urban growth: 0.8 % (2000)
Children per woman: 1.5 (2000)

HEALTH

Life expectancy at birth: 78 years (2000-2005)
male: 76 years (2000-2005)
female: 81 years (2000-2005)
Maternal mortality: 7 per 100,000 live births (1985/99)
Infant mortality: 5 per 1,000 (2000)
Under-5 child mortality: 5 per 1,000 (2000)
Daily calorie supply: 3,243 per capita (1999)
251 doctors per 100,000 people (1990)
Safe water: 100 % (2000)

EDUCATION

School enrolment (net):
Primary total: 100 % (1994/2000)
male: 100 % (1995/99)
female: 99 % (1995/99)
Secondary (gross):
male: 134 % (1995/97)
female: 129 % (1995/97)
Tertiary (gross): 49 % (1998)
Primary school teachers: one for every 7 pupils (1996)

COMMUNICATIONS

306 newspapers (1996), 980 radios (1997), 538 TV sets (2000) and 618 main telephone lines (2000) per 1,000 people
Books: 222 new titles per 100,000 people (1992/94)

ECONOMY

Per capita, GDP: $ 25,657 (2000)
Annual growth: 2.8 % (2000)
Annual inflation: 2.5 % (2000)
Consumer price index: 111.4 (2000)
Currency: 1.2 euro = $ 1 (03/2002)
Cereal imports: 4,905,796 metric tons (2000)
Food import dependency: 10 % (2000)
Fertilizer use: 5,197 kg per ha (1999)
Exports: $ 238,383 million (1999)
Imports: $ 219,777 million (1999)

ENERGY

Consumption: 4,740.0 Kgs of oil equivalent per capita yearly (1998); 20.3 % imported (1999)

HDI (ranking/value): 8 / 0.931 (1999)

Netherlands Antilles

Population: 219,000 (2002)
Land area: 800 SQ KM
Capital: Willemstad
Currency: Netherlands Antillean guilder
Language: Dutch

Nederlandse Antillen

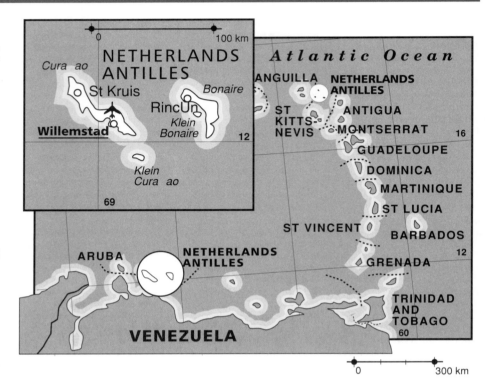

The Caiquetio, an Arawak nation, were the original inhabitants of what today are the islands of Aruba, Bonaire and Curaçao. Soon after the arrival of the Spaniard Alonso de Ojeda in 1499, these local people were enslaved and taken to Hispaniola (present-day Haiti and Dominican Republic). The Indians that Columbus found on the 'S Islands' (the Windward Islands) in 1493 met a similar fate.

[2] The conquistadors attached little importance to these islands because they lacked readily exploitable natural resources. However, the Windward Islands (particularly St Martin Island) acquired strategic importance as a port of entry into the Caribbean and also became important for their salt deposits. Ports on the Iberian Peninsula were closed to Holland after the war with Spain and Portugal, so the Dutch were forced to seek alternative sources of salt in the Antilles.

[3] In 1606, the Spanish Crown decided to put a halt to this intense traffic, and prohibited Dutch shipping in the Antilles. Holland retaliated by creating the West Indies Company, which was charged with establishing, managing and defending the colonies. Thus the theft of Spanish ships became one of the main sources of income.

[4] Although salt and Brazilwood were important products, the slave trade became the principal economic activity. In 1634, the stockholders of the Company in Amsterdam decided to invade Curaçao. The Spaniards offered no resistance and Curaçao became a major international slave-trading center.

[5] In 1648, after three centuries of conflict, the Treaty of Westphalia was signed, granting Holland control over these small islands in the Antilles. The native populations - particularly those of Curaçao and Bonaire - were replaced by African slaves to meet the needs of new agricultural operations, and thus became a minority on these islands. As in the rest of the Antilles, slave rebellions were frequent, culminating in the 18th century with a massacre at the hands of colonial troops.

[6] During the Napoleonic wars at the beginning of the 19th century, the three islands passed into British hands on two different occasions; however, the change failed to produce any improvement in the lives of the local inhabitants. Although the slave trade had been prohibited in 1814, it was not abolished in the Dutch colonies until 1863. Even then, although the slaves were 'free', their lives did not change substantially. Many migrated to the Dominican Republic, Panama, Venezuela and Cuba.

[7] Once slavery was abolished, interest in the islands waned. In 1876, the Dutch parliament proposed to sell them to Venezuela, but negotiations fell through. With the rise of the oil industry at the beginning of the 20th century, refineries were installed because of the proximity to Lake Maracaibo.

[8] From the 1920s onward, this new activity radically changed the colony. The plantations were abandoned and the demand for labor attracted thousands of immigrants from Venezuela, Suriname and the British West Indies.

[9] However, the boom dwindled over time, as automation significantly reduced the number of jobs. On May 30 1969, when unemployment stood at 20 per cent, police broke up a labor demonstration. This sparked large-scale riots which were quelled only by the joint intervention of 300 Dutch marines and some US marines from the American fleet, which happened to be anchored in the archipelago. As a result of these disturbances, Parliament was dissolved.

[10] The islands have been more politically active since 1937 when the first local parties were founded. However, they have only existed as states since 1948, when the new post-war Dutch constitution renamed what had been known as 'Curaçao and dependencies' as the 'Netherlands Antilles'.

[11] The issue of independence has long been at the center of local political life. In 1954, a new law established the islands' autonomy over their internal affairs. Nevertheless, the People's Electoral Movement (PEM), founded in 1971 in Aruba, maintained that, as the islands were no longer 'Dutch', they have nothing in common (not even a name, because 'Antilles' is the generic designation of the whole region) and each island should be free to choose its own constitution and set itself up as an autonomous republic. Secessionist feeling was strong in Aruba, where a referendum carried out in 1977 for consultation purposes only (ie, not politically binding), showed that the majority wished to separate from the other islands.

[12] The Netherlands however preferred to maintain the political unity of the islands, arguing that this would ensure better economic prospects for the whole group and, above all, more political stability in the turbulent Caribbean region. This difference of opinion, together with the diversity of views held by the local parties on the matter, delayed negotiations for independence.

[13] The delay radicalized the electorate and in 1979 the New Antilles Movement (MAN) achieved a parliamentary majority in Curaçao (7 out of 12 seats). In coalition with the PEM and the UPB (Bonaire Patriotic Union) it formed the first left-of-center government in the history of the islands. The MAN favored a federal formula with considerable autonomy for each of

the islands but the PEM insisted on the total separation of Aruba.

[14]   In 1980 it was agreed to set independence for 1990, on the condition that each of the six islands submitted the issue to a referendum as soon as possible. Aruba chose to become an individual associated state, breaking away from the federation in January 1986 (see Aruba).

[15]   The Netherlands Antilles became modern trading posts, totally dependent on transnational oil companies. Exxon and Royal Dutch Shell (an Anglo-Dutch consortium), maintained a monopoly on all oil refining and processing. They also controlled the petrochemical fertilizer industry and all transportation and sales. At this time, these powerful companies

- linked financially and commercially to branches of approximately 2,500 foreign firms registered on the islands - were responsible for 85 per cent of the total imports, 99 per cent of the exports and 50 per cent of the islands' net income.

[16]   Despite modest industrial growth and a booming tourist industry, the economy was fragile. This was clearly demonstrated towards the end of 1984, when the transnational oil companies announced their withdrawal from the islands, spreading panic among the people and local political leaders.

[17]   The conflict was partially resolved in October 1985 with the purchase of the Curaçao refinery by the Antilles Government, which in turn rented the facility to Petróleos de Venezuela SA., an oil company owned by the Venezuelan Government. The deal did not include the Exxon plant on Aruba which closed down.

[18]   The separation of Aruba favored the 1984 victory of a right-of-center coalition headed by María Liberia Peters of the National People's Party (PNP). This coalition was unable to sustain the minimum consensus necessary to stay in power. Therefore in January 1986, MAN leader, Domenico Martina, became Prime Minister once again. Two years later, María Liberia Peters returned to power.

[19]   In 1990 the Government renewed its contracts with the Venezuelan oil company and introduced a series of austerity measures designed to cover the deficit generated by the Aruban withdrawal from the federation.

[20]   The election of the Island Councils in 1991 was marked by the defeat of the Democratic Party as a result of internal divisions and financial irregularities committed by the administration.

[21]   The Netherlands requested that each island make a separate proposal for constitutional reform in 1993. Accordingly, Curaçao received special status, St Martin was made independent, while Bonaire, Saba and St Eustatius continued under Dutch control. The constitution also dictated that the Treaty of Strasburg, which predicted complete independence for 1999, would not

be applied in the islands.

[22]   In 1995 the Netherlands Antilles, with 233 AIDS cases, had the eighth highest infection rate of the 43 Latin American countries. The average rate for the region is 16 per 100,000, while that of the Netherlands Antilles is 117.

[23]   In November 1999 Miguel Pourier was elected Prime Minister for the third time.

[24]   The Netherlands announced a contribution equivalent to $6.24 million to subsidize the tourism industry, which suffered from the reduced air travel in the wake of the September 11 2001 terrorist attacks in the US. The tax reduction measures proposed by the local government proved insufficient to boost tourism, which led to the closing of hotels in the off-season.■

PROFILE

ENVIRONMENT

The Netherlands Antilles are made up of two Caribbean island groups. The main group is composed of Bonaire (288 sq km) and Curaçao (444 sq km). Located near the coast of Venezuela, they are known (together with Aruba) as the 'Dutch Leeward Islands' or the 'ABC Islands'. The smaller group is made up of three small islands of volcanic origin: St Eustatius (21 sq km), Saba (13 sq km) and St Martin (34 sq km - the southern part of which is a dependency of the French island of Guadeloupe). These are known as the 'S Islands' or the 'Dutch Windward Islands', although in fact they are part of the Leeward group of the Lesser Antilles. In general the climate is tropical, moderated by ocean currents. There is little farming. One of the largest oil refineries in the world is located on Curaçao; it is leased to a Venezuelan oil company. The coastal areas of the islands have suffered the consequences of economic development. The soil has been polluted, and waste disposal poses a serious problem. Curaçao is the most polluted of the islands.

SOCIETY

Peoples: Most of the population descend from African slaves. There are also Carib Indians and descendants of Europeans and Asians.
Religions: Mainly Catholic; some Protestants, Jews, Seventh-Day Adventists.
Languages: Dutch (official). The most widely spoken language - in Curaçao and Bonaire - is Papiamento, a local dialect based on Spanish with elements of Dutch, Portuguese, English and some African languages. In St Eustatius, Saba and St Martin, English is the main language. Spanish is also spoken and many claim that it should be taught as a second language (instead of English) to facilitate integration with Latin America.
Political Parties: Party Workers' Liberation Front (FOL); Party for the Restructured Antilles (PRA); National People's Party (PNP); Labor Party People's Crusade (PLKP); New Antilles Movement (MAN); Democratic Party (DP); Democratic Party of Bonaire (PDB).
Social Organizations: National Confederation of Curaçao Trade Unions (AVVC); General Workers' Union (CGT); Bonaire Labor Federation (FEDEBON); General Workers' Federation (GWF).

THE STATE

Capital: Willemstad 123,000 people (1999).
Other cities: Kralendijk 7,900 people; Philipsburg 6,300 (2000).
Government: Jaime M Saleh, Governor since October 1989, appointed by the Dutch Government. Miguel Pourier, Prime Minister since November 1999. Unicameral Legislature: the Staten (States), with 22 members elected every four years. There is an Advisory Council and a Council of Ministers, responsible to the Staten. Defense and foreign relations are handled by the Netherlands. Autonomy in internal affairs.
National Holiday: May 30, Anti-colonial Movement (1969).
Armed Forces: Royal Netherlands Navy, Marine Corps, Coast Guard, National Guard, Police Force.

Nicaragua

Population: 5,347,000 (2002)
Land area: 121,400 SQ KM
Capital: Managua
Currency: Córdoba
Language: Spanish

Nicaragua

Present-day Nicaragua was once a region of influence of the two great Central American cultures: the Chibcha (see Colombia) and the Maya. The Caribbean coast was inhabited by the Miskito, originally called 'Kiribi' - the oldest peoples in Nicaragua - and was visited by Christopher Columbus in 1502. By converting local leaders Nicoya and Nicarao to Christianity and crushing the resistance of Diriangen's armies, the conquistadors Gil Gonzales Dávila and Andrés Nino consolidated Spain's hold over the territory. In 1544 it was incorporated into the Captaincy-General of Guatemala.

[2] In 1821 Nicaragua became independent, together with the rest of Central America, joining the Mexican Empire but subsequently withdrawing in 1824 to form the Federation of the United Provinces of the Center of America.

[3] Nicaragua left the Federation in 1839, declaring itself an independent state. The country was divided between two groups: the coffee and sugar oligarchies, and the artisans and small landowners. The former would become the conservatives, and the latter, the liberals who favored free trade.

[4] In 1856, 120 soldiers landed in Nicaragua under the command of William Walker, an American mercenary. With Washington's tacit support, he proclaimed himself President of Nicaragua. His purpose was to find new territories for slavery which was on the point of being abolished in the Union. Walker was defeated by the allied armies of Central America in 1857, and later executed. Nicaragua's

ports were occupied by Germany in 1875 and Britain in 1895. Britain commandeered Nicaragua's Customs in order to collect on unpaid debts.

[5] After 30 years of conservative rule the Liberal Party came to power in 1893, and José Santos Zelaya became President. The liberals refused to comply with demands made by the United States, so in 1912 the US invaded. After killing the Liberal Party leader, Benjamín Zeledón, the US Marine force remained in Nicaragua until 1925. In 1926 they returned to protect president Adolfo Díaz, who was about to be overthrown.

[6] This second US occupation was resisted by Augusto C. Sandino, who raised and commanded a popular army of about 3,000 troops. For more than six years they held out against 12,000 US marines who were supported by the airforce and ground troops of the local oligarchy. Sandino promised that he would lay down arms when the last marine left Nicaragua. He carried out his promise in 1933, but was assassinated by US-backed Anastasio Somoza García who, after seizing power, ruled despotically until he

was killed by the patriot Rigoberto López Pérez in 1956.

[7] During two decades of dictatorship, Somoza had achieved almost absolute control of the nation's economy. He was succeeded by his son, engineer Luis Somoza Debayle, who in turn handed the Government on to his son, Anastasio, a West Point graduate.

[8] Anastasio Somoza outlawed all trade unions, massacred members of peasant movements and banned all opposition parties. In the 1960s the Sandinista National Liberation Front was founded. This organized and developed the guerrilla warfare which lasted for 17 years. When opposition leader Pedro Joaquín Chamorro, editor of the daily *La Prensa*, was assassinated on Somoza's orders in January 1978, a nationwide strike was called and there were massive protest demonstrations.

[9] By March 1979, the Sandinista Front had united its three factions and began to lead the political opposition, the 'Patriotic Front'. In May 1979 the Front launched the 'final offensive', combining a general strike, a popular uprising, armed

combat, and intense diplomatic activity abroad. On July 17, Somoza fled the country, bringing an end to a dynasty that had killed 50,000 people. The Junta for National Reconstruction, created a few weeks before in Costa Rica, was installed in Managua two days later.

[10] The victorious revolutionaries nationalized the Somoza's lands and industrial properties, which constituted 40 per cent of the economic resources of Nicaragua. They also replaced the defeated National Guard with the Sandinista Popular Army. The revolutionary government implemented a literacy campaign and began the reconstruction of the devastated economy. Other important policies were non-alignment, a mixed economy, political pluralism, and respect for individual rights and liberties.

[11] In May 1980 two non-Sandinista members of the Junta, Violeta Barrios de Chamorro and Alfonso Robelo, resigned. The Government avoided a crisis by replacing them with Rafael Córdoba and Arturo Cruz, two 'moderate' anti-Somoza activists.

LAND USE

DEFORESTATION: 2.5% annual (1990/95)

1993

- FOREST & WOODLAND: 24.6%
- ARABLE: 8.5%
- OTHER: 66.9%

[12] In 1981, US President Ronald Reagan announced his aim of destroying the Sandinistas. Between April and July 1982 deputy interior minister, Edén Pastora ('Commander Zero'), deserted and announced from Costa Rica that he would drive the Sandinista Front's National Directorate out 'at gunpoint'. Some 2,500 former National Guardsmen, supported by the US, invaded Nicaragua from Honduras. From then on Nicaragua was harassed without respite, forcing the authorities to extend the state of emergency, to institute compulsory military service and to ban pro-American political declarations.

[13] In 1983, President Reagan admitted the existence of secret funds destined for covert CIA operations against Nicaragua. The funds were also used to aid counter-revolutionaries or contras operating from Honduran territory. Reagan referred to the contras as 'freedom fighters'.

[14] Concerned at the serious threat of a war that might escalate throughout Central America, the governments of Colombia, Mexico, Panama and Venezuela began to seek a negotiated settlement to the conflict. As the 'Contadora Group', these countries' foreign ministers advanced peace plans which won great diplomatic support and prevented an invasion by US forces.

[15] Contra attacks intensified steadily with open US backing. Elections were held in November 1984. Candidates were drawn from the Sandinista National Liberation Front (FSLN), the Democratic Conservative Party, the Independent Liberal Party, the Popular Social Christian Party, the Communist Party, the Socialist Party and the Marxist-Leninist People's Action Movement. Over 80 per cent of Nicaragua's 1.5 million registered voters went to the polls and the Sandinista Front Government led by Daniel Ortega obtained 67 per cent of the vote. In November Reagan was re-elected and in April 1985 he declared a trade embargo against Nicaragua and seized its assets.

[16] In 1986, the Assembly discussed the details of a new Constitution, which went into effect in January 1987. It provided for a presidential system, with a president elected by direct vote for a six-year term. Legislators would be elected on the basis of proportional representation.

[17] In 1987, with UN and OAS participation, the Central American presidents met for negotiations in Esquipulas, Guatemala. The Esquipulas II accords stipulated an end to external support for armed opposition groups; the opening of internal dialogue in each of the countries, mediated by the Catholic Church; and an amnesty for those who lay down their arms, with guarantees of political representation.

[18] In Nicaragua a National Reconciliation Commission was formed. Among its most spectacular achievements was the return of contra leader Fernando Chamorro from exile. He was granted an amnesty after he renounced violence. Press censorship was lifted and Violeta Chamorro's opposition daily *La Prensa* reappeared. On October 7, a unilateral cease-fire went into effect in several parts of the country, although contra leaders announced that they would continue hostilities.

[19] Throughout 1988, as US pressure increased the economic situation worsened. A monetary reform and a 10 per cent reduction in the Government budget in February were insufficient to halt spiraling inflation.

[20] In July 1988, the US ambassador to Managua was expelled on the accusation of encouraging anti-Sandinista activities. The US Government responded by expelling Nicaragua's representative in Washington.

[21] The Esquipulas II accords seemed to be doomed, but when the five Central American presidents met at Costa del Sol, El Salvador, in February 1989, President Daniel Ortega embarked on fresh negotiations. The Sandinista proposal was to bring the elections forward to February 1990 and to accept proposed modifications to the 1988 electoral law. The condition was that the contras dismantle their bases in Honduras within three months of an agreement. The US however insisted that the contras continue in Honduras, and President George Bush persuaded Congress to award them $40 million in 'humanitarian aid'.

[22] Daniel Ortega was the FSLN presidential candidate. The National Opposition Union (UNO), a 14-party coalition, nominated Pedro Joaquin Chamorro's widow, Violeta Barrios de Chamorro. Unexpectedly, the UNO won the elections with 55 per cent of the vote against the FSLN's 41 per cent. The Sandinistas accepted defeat and ascribed it to the Nicaraguan people's desperate desire for peace, the dire state of the economy and FSLN overconfidence that victory was assured.

[23] On April 25, before she took office, the President and the FSLN signed a 'Transition Protocol'. This included respecting the standing Constitution and the social achievements of the revolution, and supporting disarmament of the contras. The new president announced that she would personally assume the defense portfolio and maintain the Sandinista General Humberto Ortega as commander of the armed forces. She also indefinitely suspended compulsory military service.

[24] The UNO's Vice-President, Virgilio Godoy, and other members of the coalition withdrew from the Government accusing Chamorro of betraying pre-election agreements by keeping Humberto Ortega in office.

[25] In May 1990, public employees went on strike for wage increases of up to 200 per cent. The Government declared the strike illegal, and revoked the civil service law (under which civil servants could not be fired without just cause) as well as the agrarian reform law passed by the Sandinista Government. Workers responded by extending the strike over the whole country. After a week, the Government partially gave in to the workers' demands, and the strike ended.

[26] In mid-1990, the Government received several offers from international consortia interested in carrying out projects in northern Nicaragua. This area comprises some 270,000 hectares of tropical rain forests, occupying more than half of the country's total land area. The proposals ranged from the creation of landfills for toxic waste, to the exploitation of the region's vast fishing, mineral and forestry resources.

[27] When the Government was accused of carrying out secret negotiations with a Taiwanese enterprise, the existence of large mineral deposits was inadvertently revealed. These included gold, silver, copper, tungsten and Central America's largest deposits of calcium carbonate, a raw material used in cement production.

[28] In 1991, President Chamorro agreed with the FSLN to recognize agrarian reform and to set aside for the workers at least 25 per cent of shares in state enterprises slated for privatization.

[29] Inflation fell from 7,000 per cent in 1990 to 3.8 per cent in 1992 due to an IMF and World Bank-sponsored adjustment program. Productive investments and spending in education and health were reduced. Unemployment rose to 60 per cent.

PROFILE

ENVIRONMENT

Nicaragua has both Pacific and Caribbean coastlines. It is crossed by two important mountain ranges: the Central American Andes, running from northwest to southeast, and a volcanic chain with several active volcanoes along the western coast. The Managua and Nicaragua lakes lie between the two ranges. On the eastern slopes, the climate is tropical with abundant rainfall, while it is drier on the western side where the population is concentrated. Cotton is the main cash crop in the mountain area, while bananas are grown along the Atlantic coast. Changes in water and soil have affected approximately 40 per cent of the country's territory.

SOCIETY

Peoples: 69 per cent of Nicaraguans are mixed descendants of American indians and Spanish colonizers; 17 per cent are of European descent; 9 per cent are African descendants and 5 per cent belong to Indian minorities (Miskitos, Sunos and Ramas).
Religion: Catholics (85 per cent); Protestants (15 per cent)
Languages: Spanish (official and predominant). Miskito, Suno, English and Garifuna are spoken on the Atlantic coast.
Political Parties: The Constitutional Liberal Party, conservative (CLP); Sandinista National Liberation Front (FSLN); Conservative Party of Nicaragua (CPN).
Social Organizations: The Nicaraguan Labor Confederation (CTN); the Labor Unity and Action Confederation (CAUS); the Rural Workers' Association (ATC); the Workers' Front (FO); the Unified Labor Confederation (CUS); the National Employees' Union (UNE); the National Confederation of Professionals (CONAPRO); National Union of Nicaraguan Students.

THE STATE

Official Name: República de Nicaragua.
Administrative Division: 9 regions, 15 departments, 143 municipalities.
Capital: Managua 930,000 people (1999).
Other cities: León 153,200 people; Chinandega 120,400; Masaya 110,000; Granada 88,800; Matagalpa 73,400 (2000).
Government: Enrique Bolaños Geyer, President since January 2002. Legislature: National Assembly, with 93 members.
National Holidays: September 15, Independence Day (1821); July 19, Sandinista Revolution Day (1979).
Armed Forces: 17,000 troops (1996).

30 Differences between the President and the UNO led them to break in 1993 after which Chamorro received support from the Sandinistas and the UNO's Center Group. The following month, the UNO expelled that group and changed its name to Political Opposition Alliance (APO).

31 Parliamentary debate on constitutional reform caused the FSLN's orthodox sector, led by former president Daniel Ortega, to exclude former Vice-President Sergio Ramírez, head of the Sandinista parliamentary bloc, from the Front. By-passing the party's leadership, the parliamentary bloc presented its own bill against nepotism which banned presidential re-election and prohibited relatives of the current president from running for president. This clause put an end to the political aspirations of Chamorro's son-in-law, minister Antonio Lacayo.

32 The economic crisis was intensified by a drought which led to the loss of 80,000 hectares of crops and left 200,000 farmers without food. Child malnutrition affected 300,000 children and some lost their sight through lack of vitamin A.

33 In January 1994, the UNO, with less than half its founders and unable to obtain the support to set up a constituent assembly, ended a year of boycotting the National Assembly. Violence continued between the army, gangs of criminals and small guerrilla groups.

34 General Humberto Ortega confirmed he would resign after a new military law had been passed. In August the Assembly passed the law which aimed at eliminating political involvement by the Sandinista Popular Army and increasing its dependence on civilian authority, although the power was actually left in the hands of a military council.

35 The Government signed a 3-year agreement with the IMF which opened the possibility of renegotiating public debt. Unemployment was estimated between 43 per cent and 60 per cent. The per capita GDP dropped for the eleventh year in a row.

36 Debate on constitutional reform prevailed in 1995. In February, the Assembly proposed to change the army's name, ban compulsory military service and grant guarantees to private property. These measures were supported by President Chamorro but she did not agree with the shift of power from the executive to the legislative branch, regarding the right to raise taxes. The Assembly published the reforms unilaterally in February and began to implement them.

37 In June, an agreement was reached on a general law for constitutional reforms which stated these had to be supported by a majority of 60 per cent in the Assembly before being signed by the President, who concluded the agreement in July. The National Assembly ratified its choice of judges for the Supreme Court of Justice and a new Supreme Electoral Tribunal was appointed.

38 The approval of the nepotism law was deferred. President Chamorro's son-in-law remained in the Government, although he announced he would not be standing as a presidential candidate.

39 Conservative Arnoldo Alemán, ex-mayor of Managua, obtained 49 per cent of the vote in the October 1996 elections. The electoral law established that if any of the candidates obtains more than 45 per cent of the vote, there is no need for a second vote, thus leaving Sandinista ex-President Daniel Ortega (with 39 per cent) out of the race. The FSLN suspected a fraud but the Supreme Electoral Court named Alemán president.

40 On assuming the presidency, Alemán promised to create 500,000 new jobs and launched a plan to relieve the debt of the agricultural sector, estimated at $150 million.

41 In April 1997, the Government and opposition accused each other of arming and training paramilitaries. Despite negotiations, no understanding was reached and relations between the ruling party and the Sandinistas remained tense.

42 In August, the Government announced it would not pass goods confiscated by the Sandinistas in 1979 on to Anastasio Somoza's heirs, in answer to a lawsuit filed by Lilian Somoza, the former dictator's daughter.

43 According to estimates made in early 1998, the US had once again become Managua's main trade partner. Nicaraguan exports to this country were worth $375 million in 1997, 30 per cent up on two years previously.

44 Hurricane Mitch struck in November 1998, leaving in its wake 3,000 dead, tens of thousands of people homeless and a devastated economy.

45 A dispute between Nicaragua and Honduras flared up in late 1999 when Tegucigalpa ratified a border treaty with Colombia on the possession of three island groups on the Caribbean and off the Nicaraguan coast which, according to Managua, meant a loss of 30,000 square kilometers of its maritime territory. After mediation by the OAS, Managua and Tegucigalpa agreed to suspend the deployment of troops on the land border and

to carry out joint patrolling while the dispute was legally solved at the International Court of Justice at The Hague.

46 In the area of industrial injuries, the Supreme Court of Justice concluded the first of nine cases and sentenced six US companies to pay $1 billion. This was to be distributed among 4,000 rural workers as compensation for the physical harm they suffered from highly toxic insecticides used between 1968 and 1983. The workers have suffered serious health problems, such as cancer, infertility and physical deformities.

47 After winning 53.3 per cent of the vote in the November 2001 elections, Liberal candidate Enrique Bolaños became President; Daniel Ortega received 46 per cent. However, the results were not translated into a majority of the Liberal Party or the FSLN in Parliament. Although Ortega contested the number of seats obtained in the Assembly - which did not tally with those counted by the FSLN - and the Electoral Council chairman received a death threat, OAS observers said the elections had been fair.

48 A week after Bolaños took office in January 2002, former president Alemán was elected chairman of the National Assembly. In protest, the FSLN bloc stayed away, regarding Alemán's election illegal since it was a result of constitutional reforms carried out during his administration. Shortly after, the Assembly approved the courts' request to lift Alemán's parliamentary immunity to try him for fraud against the state ($1.3 million), embezzlement and unlawful association.

49 In 2002, Nicaraguan justice absolved former president Ortega, ruling that the criminal action for sexual abuse and rape brought against him by his step-daughter Zoilamérica Narváez had lapsed. Narváez had pressed charges in 1998, but Ortega, then an MP, was protected by National Assembly immunity. A year later, the case was brought to the Inter-American Commission on Human Rights, which accepted Narváez' complaint of lack of justice in Nicaragua.

50 The number of homeless children and teenagers, who in many cases end up leading a life of crime, has grown in recent years. Some of them have been illegally arrested by the police, while citizens and other groups want to carry out 'social cleansing' - ie murder - as already happens in neighboring Honduras and Guatemala against street children. ■

Niger

Population: 11,641,000 (2002)
Land area: 1,266,700 SQ KM
Capital: Niamey
Currency: CFA franc
Language: French

Niger

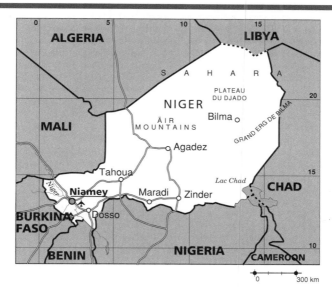

F ossil remains found in the Niger region indicate that it was inhabited in prehistoric times and later populated by many different nomadic and trading peoples. The Nok Empire, reaching its peak in present-day Nigeria between the 15th century BC and the 5th century AD (see Nigeria), left its mark on this neighboring region.

2   During the 7th century AD, the western side of the country became part of the Songhai Empire created by the Berber, who were important propagators of Islam from the 11th century onwards.

3   Between the 14th and 19th centuries the eastern part of the territory belonged to the Kanem-Bornu State, which had been founded by the Kurani in the 8th century. Meanwhile, during the 19th century, the Haussa states flourished in the south (see Nigeria), until conquered by the Fulani.

4   Throughout the 19th century, the French colonized the territory, making Niger a colony in 1922. Traditional subsistence crops were replaced by cash crops like peanuts and cotton, which were grown for export, causing food shortages in Niger.

5   In the 1950s, Niger launched its independence movement, led by Hamani Diori. In 1960, the country's first constitution was approved and Niger became an independent state.

6   When it broke its colonial ties, Niger was the poorest country in French West Africa, with 80 per cent of the population living in rural areas with persistent drought, soil erosion and population pressure which threaten the country's agriculture and ecology.

7   In the new republic's first election in 1960, the Progressive Party's candidate, Hamani Diori, was elected President. The new government maintained deep economic and political ties with France, to the point of allowing French troops to remain within its territory. In the first years of his presidency, Diori banned the opposition Sawaba party, forcing its leader, Djibo Bakari into exile. The Government was accused of corruption and of harsh repression of the growing political opposition.

8   In the early 1970s, the drought which hit the Sahel region meant

that the army was charged with distributing food among the peasants. This brought them into contact with the needs of the rural people for the first time. On April 13 1974, a Supreme Military Committee took power, naming Seyni Kuntche as President. Price controls were set on agricultural products, salaries were raised, nepotism was eliminated, investments were reoriented and education and health services were planned. An attempt was made to access underground water sources and incentives were given to set up farming cooperatives.

9   The new government tried out new ways of organizing the youth to establish the political base which the country lacked. It also expelled Djibo Bakari, who had returned from exile to lend his support to the regime, and signed bilateral agreements with France. These agreements allowed neocolonialism to focus greater attention on the exploitation of Niger's mineral wealth than on traditional colonial products.

10   During the 1970s the country experienced an economic boom, based on an increase in the international price of uranium. This mineral accounted for 90 per cent of the country's exports in 1980, when the so-called 'miracle' came to an abrupt end.

11   The foreign debt was $207 million in 1977 and by 1983 it had

increased to $1 billion, forcing Kuntch'e to introduce an IMF structural adjustment program, in an attempt to turn the economy around. The hoped-for return of favorable uranium prices did not materialize and, between 1984 and 1985, the perennial drought in the Sahel region worsened. The Government also confronted political challenges on different fronts: in 1983, it put down an attempted coup by former members of the secret police and it also engaged in combat with the Tuareg people who had resorted to guerrilla warfare.

12   The economic crisis worsened when Nigeria closed its borders between April 1984 and March 1986 halting traffic between the two countries, including the transportation of cattle and basic foodstuffs. The decision to close the borders was made by authorities in Lagos to carry out a readjustment of their monetary system. An exception was made in 1985, allowing fuel to be transported across the border.

13   In 1985 there was no change in the situation: the price of uranium fell an additional four points, there was a deficit of 400,000 tons of grain, a growing foreign debt and the increasing cost of servicing this debt.

14   In 1986 the Government tried changing its policies, but General Kuntche had a cerebral hemorrhage, dying in a Paris

military hospital 11 months later. The Supreme Military Committee appointed Ali Seibou as his successor. Among his first measures as President was the appointment of 10 new ministers, and the declaration of an amnesty which provided for the return of political exiles, including Djibo Bakari and Hamani Diori, who were personally welcomed by the President and were allowed to return to political activity. In April 1989, Diori died in Rabat, Morocco.

15   On August 1988 the National Movement for a Developing Society (MNSD) was formed as the only government authorized party, and the National Development Council drew up a new constitution, put to the vote and approved by plebiscite in 1989. In December, Seibou was elected President of the Republic by universal suffrage, in the first elections to be held since independence in 1960.

16   The drought in the Sahel forced the Government to give special attention to agricultural production and to the people in rural areas. During the 1980-90 period it invested 32 per cent of the national budget in agriculture. A major environmental problem was that 98 per cent of people used firewood for cooking. In a country facing deforestation and almost permanent drought, this almost exclusive use of wood for household energy is dangerously destructive. Facing the problem head-on, the Government had solar and wind-powered generators installed, developed electric energy and sponsored the manufacture of low-cost energy-saving stoves.

17   The new president had a favorable economic outlook on his side, as there was a grain surplus of 200,000 tons in 1989. He promised that he would initiate a true democratization process, but this did not occur and throughout 1990 there was intense opposition from the political sector, the labor unions and the students, demanding salary increases, the enactment of educational reforms, and the establishment of a multiparty system. Strikes and massive protest demonstrations were organized in support of

these demands and these were harshly suppressed by the police.

[18] In 1990, the country's agricultural production dropped by more than 70 per cent, while the population continued to increase at 3 per cent per year. Despite doubling the amount of arable land, food production rose by only one per cent, and the land has lost its fertility through phosphate and nitrogen depletion.

[19] To confront the crisis the Government launched another structural adjustment plan, imposed by the World Bank and the IMF. A two-year freeze on the salaries of public employees was announced as part of the plan. Workers and students reacted by calling a new series of strikes and holding more demonstrations. In late 1990, Seibou publicly announced his commitment to leading the country towards a multiparty democratic system and he created the National Conference, which was charged with organizing the political transformation.

[20] After four months, the National Conference decided to form a transitional government, headed by a new Prime Minister, Amadou Cheffou. André Salifou was named president of the High Council of the Republic, the body holding legislative power during the transition period. However, the country's situation had never been more critical. The State was bankrupt. There was no money to pay the salaries of the public

employees, and students did not receive money for their grants.

[21] The economic disaster and its accompanying social crisis could be traced back to the end of the uranium boom. In 1989, this mineral cost Fr 30,000,000 per kilo, dropping to Fr 19,000,000 per kilo in 1991.

[22] In February 1992, Tuareg guerrillas rose up against the Government once more. In December, the new constitution was approved with nearly 90 per cent of the votes in a referendum but two months later in February 1993 the ruling party was defeated in the legislative elections.

[23] In April, Mahamane Ousmane became President of Niger, with 55.4 per cent of the vote in the second round. The efforts to reach an agreement to end the insurrection of the Tuareg guerrillas in the north continued throughout 1993-1994.

[24] In May 1994, 40 people were killed in confrontations between the rebel and Government forces - but the main guerrilla group, the Coordination of Armed Resistance and the Government managed to seal an agreement. Thus, in June, Niamey granted autonomy to part of the country inhabited by some 750,000 Tuaregs.

[25] Amidst student protests calling for the payment of money owed in grants, amongst other things, the Government arrested 91 members of the opposition. In September, Prime Minister Mahamadou Issoufou resigned after his party, the Nigerien Party for Democracy and Socialism,

withdrew from the Government coalition, leaving it without an absolute majority in Parliament.

[26] In January 1995, an opposition coalition triumphed in the legislative elections and immediately replaced the Prime Minister, Amadou Cissé with Hama Amadou. The latter announced that his first move would be to bring in an economic austerity plan, reaching an agreement for settling the payment of overdue civil service salaries.

[27] Tension continued to mount between the new government and the President. In January 1996, a military coup toppled Ousmane, who was replaced by the National Salvation Council, headed by Colonel Ibrahim Baré Mainassara, who appointed Boukary Adji as Prime Minister. In July, Maïnassara was elected President with 52 per cent of the vote. The new 'strongman' dissolved the Independent National Electoral Commission, leading the main opposition parties to boycott the November elections. In December, following the victory of Baré's supporters, Amadou Cissé was made Prime Minister.

[28] In October 1997, Ali Sabo, campaign co-ordinator of the Front for the Restoration and Defense of Democracy was imprisoned. In November 1997, Ibrahim Hassane Mayaki was made Prime Minister, replacing Cissé. A month later in Algiers a ceasefire was agreed between the Government and the Tuareg guerrillas.

[29] In early 1998, Mainassara ordered the arrest of several members of the opposition, including Amadou, accused of an alleged conspiracy. Throughout the year, students, military personnel and public employees led a series of anti-government demonstrations. The Supreme Court annulled the March 1999 election results in some districts and called for a new round of balloting. On April 4, after a tension-filled week in which the opposition called on Baré to resign, the presidential guard assassinated him. Coup leader Daouda Malam Wanké was then named President and head of the National Reconciliation Council, which governed the country during the nine-month transition period. Prime Minister Ibrahim Hassane Mayaki dissolved the National Assembly, which was dominated by members of Baré's party, and political parties were temporarily suspended.

[30] The international community strongly pressured the country to return to democratic rule. In October Niger held the first round of general elections and, in the second round in November, retired

military officer Tandja Mamadou, of the MNSD, was victorious over his rival, former prime minister and parliamentary leader Mahamadou Issoufou.

STATISTICS

DEMOGRAPHY
Population: 11,641,000 (2002)
Annual growth: 3.3 % (1985-2000)
Estimates for year 2015: 18,482,000 (2000)
Annual growth to year 2015: 3.6 % (2000)
Urban population: 20.6 % (2000)
Urban growth: 5.7 % (2000)
Children per woman: 8.0 (2000)

HEALTH
Life expectancy at birth: 46 years (2000-2005)
male: 46 years (2000-2005)
female: 46 years (2000-2005)
Maternal mortality: 590 per 100,000 live births (1985/99)
Infant mortality: 159 per 1,000 (2000)
Under-5 child mortality: 270 per 1,000 (2000)
Daily calorie supply: 2,064 per capita (1999)
4 doctors per 100,000 people (1997)
Safe water: 59 % (2000)

EDUCATION
Literacy: 16 % (2000)
male: 23 % (2000)
female: 8 % (2000)
School enrolment (net):
Primary total: 37 % (1994/2000)
male: 30 % (1995/99)
female: 19 % (1995/99)
Secondary (gross):
male: 9 % (1995/97)
female: 5 % (1995/97)
Tertiary (gross): 1 % (1997)
Primary school teachers: one for every 41 pupils (1998)

COMMUNICATIONS
0 newspaper (1996), 121 radios (2000), 37 TV sets (2000) and 2 main telephone lines (2000) per 1,000 people

ECONOMY
Per capita, GDP: $ 746 (2000)
Annual growth: -3.2 % (2000)
Annual inflation: 2.9 % (2000)
Consumer price index: 113.9 (2000)
Currency: 758.3 CFA francs = $ 1 (03/2002)
Cereal imports: 270,309 metric tons (2000)
Food import dependency: 39 % (1998)
Fertilizer use: 6 kg per ha (1999)
Exports: $ 282 million (2000)
Imports: $ 422 million (2000)
External debt: $ 1,638 million (2000); $ 151 per capita (2000)
Debt service: 16.8 % of exports (1999)
Development aid received: $ 187 million (1999); $ 17.8 per capita (1999); 9.30 % of GNP (1999)
HDI (ranking/value): 161 / 0.274 (1999)

PROFILE

ENVIRONMENT
Most of this land-locked country is made up of a plateau at an average altitude of 350 m. The north is covered by the Sahara desert and the south by savannas. There are uranium, iron, coal and tin deposits, and possibly oil. 80 per cent of the population lives in rural areas. There are nomadic herders in the center of the country, and peanut, rice and cotton farming in the south. 85 per cent of all energy is provided by firewood. This region is affected by marked desertification. There is also considerable erosion, produced by strong winds. There is air and water pollution primarily in densely populated urban areas.

SOCIETY
Peoples: Among the herders of the central steppe, ethnic origins vary from the Berber Tuareg, to the Fulah, including the Tibu (Tubu). In the south there are west African ethnic groups; the Haussa, Djerma (Zarma), Songhai and Kamuri. **Religions:** mostly Muslim; in the south there are traditional African religions and a Christian minority. **Languages:** French (official) and several local languages. **Political Parties:** National Movement for the Developing Society (MNSD); Democratic and Social Convention (CDS); Nigerian Party for Democracy and Socialism; Rally for Democracy and Progress (RDP). **Social Organizations:** Nigerien National Workers' Union (UNTN).

THE STATE
Official Name: République du Niger. **Administrative Divisions:** 7 Départements. **Capital:** Niamey 731,000 people (1999). **Other cities:** Zinder 185,100 people; Maradi 172,900; Tahoua 87,700 (2000). **Government:** Tandja Mamadou, President since December 1999. Hama Amadou, Prime Minister since January 2000. **Parliament:** National Assembly, with 83 members elected every five years. **National Holiday:** August 3, Independence (1960). **Armed Forces:** 5,300. **Other:** 5,400 Gendarmes, Republican Guards and National Police.

President Tandja Mamadou took office December 1999.

[31] Aboubacar Oumarou Sandael, sultan of Zinder, a main chief in the country, was removed from office in July 2001, accused of murder, plotting to overthrow the Government, smuggling stolen cars and drug dealing. He was replaced by Elhadj Mamadou Moustapha, a former police agent. The title of sultan is not hereditary in Niger.

[32] Ten slaves were freed in December 2001 in Tahoua, a northern region. According to human rights group Timidria, slavery, although banned, is common in Niger's eight regions, and up to 20,000 people are subject to forced indenture. ∎

Diamonds of war

Africa, although a poor continent, has huge mineral wealth. But unregulated, illegal trafficking in diamonds and other precious stones exacerbates conflicts and worsens the poverty that affects the region.

The mineral wealth of some African countries is the direct cause of poverty for their people. While the diamond industry has benefited countries like Botswana - employing 10 per cent of the population and contributing two thirds of government income - it has had tragic consequences for others.

Hundreds of millions of dollars flow from the illegal diamond trade directly into the hands of rebels, corrupt governments and their armies who use the profits to buy arms. The illicit trade feeds war both local conflicts and across borders. The weapons are also used to gain or retain control of mines and the mineral wealth they bring, fueling a vicious cycle.

The result is systematic suffering and poverty of African people as the money from diamonds and minerals buys guns and pays mercenaries instead of being spent on social and development projects such as education and healthcare.

FUNDING THE REBELS

In Angola, Sierra Leone and the Democratic Republic of Congo (DRC), precious stones are the main source of funds for insurgent movements.

Diamond-generated wealth combines with racial and political motives to feed continuing confrontations between Hutu and Tutsi people in the DRC. Angola, Namibia and Zimbabwe support the Congolese government in return for mining rights in frontier zones. Burundi, Rwanda and Uganda support the rebels, trading diamonds for funds.

Laurent Kabila led his guerrilla force to victory in 1997, ending the long dictatorship of Mobutu Sese Seko and establishing the Democratic Republic of Congo (DRC). Since then the power struggle has been replaced by conflict over the control of mineral resources including oil, cobalt and diamonds.

Kabila was assassinated on January 6 2001, shortly after granting the Israel Diamond Industries exclusive rights over DRC's diamond trade. His son and successor Joseph Kabila revoked the move. He now presides over one of the worst diamond-fueled conflicts in Africa. Nearly half a million of the 48 million Congolese make a living directly or indirectly from contraband in precious metals.

In neighboring Angola for the last 30 years, the opposition National Union for the Total Independence of Angola (UNITA) has been fighting government forces for control of natural resources, a conflict which has already cost a million lives.

The 35,000-strong UNITA force, initially funded by the US to combat the left-wing Luanda government during the Cold War, survives on the profits of diamond smuggling. The death of UNITA leader Jonas Savimbi in February 2002 led to another ceasefire, but there have been many before.

Despite its rich and abundant natural resources of diamonds and oil, Angola ranks 160th out of the 174 nations in the UN Development Program's Human Development Index. War has become the spending priority: some 86 per cent of Angola's national budget is spent on defense. This has devastating effects on the people: nine out of ten people live below the poverty line, nearly one in three children die before the age of five, and only one third of the population have access to drinking water. More than three million internally displaced people do not have basic food, housing or health provision.

Over in West Africa, Sierra Leone's diamonds only make up one per cent of world supplies, but they are especially valued because of their quality. The country has suffered its own brutal conflict over control of its diamond fields in the north and east, where rebel Revolutionary United Front (RUF) militias fight for control of territory.

These guerrillas are infamous for their terror campaign against civilians and the use of child soldiers. Since the outbreak of conflict in 1991, rebel forces have killed, raped, mutilated and abducted tens of thousands of unarmed civilians. Sadly, it is the illegal diamond trafficking from the rebel-held zones that keeps the RUF in arms. Government allied forces and West African peace-keeping forces have also committed human rights abuses.

CONFLICT OF INTERESTS

There is a lack of transparency in the international trade in precious stones, and too few control mechanisms. Gems do not set off alarms at airports, sniffer dogs cannot detect them and the stones can be rapidly converted into cash. Networks of intermediaries and middlemen make the industry a difficult one to monitor.

Amberes is the Belgian city that handles two-thirds of all the world's diamonds. Diamond importers there receive packages of rough stones from African countries, and these are swiftly dispatched on to the rest of Belgium, Britain and India.

The International Committee of the Red Cross, the non-governmental organization Intermon/Oxfam and the United Nations have deplored the current situation and demanded regulation of diamond mining and trade. In July 2000, the UN Security Council imposed a ban on the illegal importation of diamonds from rebel-held zones of Sierra Leone, but the RUF dodged the embargo though weapons trading with Liberia, a nation that exported six million kilos of gems between 1994 and 1998.

Intermon/Oxfam, Global Witness, Medico International, Netherlands Institute for Southern Africa (NIZA) and the Dutch agency Novib foundation launched a 'Fatal Transactions' campaign which tried to persuade the industry and consumers to choose conflict-free diamonds and demanded the creation of an international certification system to testify the origin of stones.

The Belgian, Israeli and Ukrainian governments are being pressured into tighter controls on transactions taking place in Amberes, Tel Aviv and Kiev.

In mid-2001, a meeting in Moscow aimed to set up an international system to certify the source of diamonds and help find a solution to the wars in Angola, Sierra Leone and the Congo. Representatives of 34 governments, the European Commission, the international diamond industry, the World Diamond Council and non-governmental organizations met to discuss a system based on the Kimberley process - a certification system proposal initiated by the governments of South Africa, Botswana and Namibia in 2000.

The Diamond High Council (HRD), an organization representing the diamond industry in Belgium, is revising how diamonds are imported, valued and exported. But there are some 4,000 establishments in Amberes beyond its control, involving thousands of traders, jewelers and middlemen involved in the illegal trafficking of diamonds.

Rigorously applied international legislation could lead to some controls on the illicit trade, but there many interests in play.

Few want to threaten a business with an annual turnover of $50 billion, even though $5 billion goes directly to warring factions in Africa.

Some sectors of the industry have shown interest in clean diamond dealing, fearing that consumers will stop buying stones tainted by African blood. De Beers, the diamond giant that controls 75 per cent of the world trade, is now attempting to guarantee its diamonds come from war-free sources. In 2000, the company closed its offices in the Democratic Republic of Congo and Guinea and now demands its suppliers buy no diamonds from dubious sources. According to the company's director Nicky Oppenheimer, 'a diamond is forever' is a better motto than 'a diamond is for war'. ∎

Nigeria

Population: 120,047,000 (2002)
Land area: 910,770 SQ KM
Capital: Abuja
Currency: Naira
Language: English

Nigeria

As heirs to the ancient Nok civilization, the Yoruba lived in walled cities with broad avenues. As early as the 11th century they developed a democratic system of urban administration, also producing beautiful ceramics and bronze sculptures.

[2]   Between the 10th and 11th centuries, Ife, Oyo, Ilorin and Benin (not the present-day nation) were loosely confederated city-states extending their influence from the Niger River in the east to present-day Togo.

[3]   Ife always enjoyed a reputation as the main religious center of the nation, and the Oni of Ife is still the High Priest of all Yorubans, whether Nigerian or not.

[4]   The city of Oyo, strengthened since the 16th century by the slave trade, had a higher status as a political and economic center, through the *Alafin* (ruler). The dependence on slavery caused its downfall when that institution was abolished.

[5]   The northern part of the country held the Hausa states and was the center of a different culture. A similar group of active Igbo traders emerged in the southeast, but they did not develop urban civilizations like the Yoruba.

[6]   The British colonial system disregarded these differences, forcing all the territories under a single administration in 1914, creating an artificial state that has not attained national unity. British interests focused on the exploitation of tin and agricultural and timber resources.

[7]   British administration in northern Nigeria was indirect, based on traditional Muslim emirs who acted as go-betweens. Consequently this area, populated by Hausa and Peul, enjoyed greater political autonomy than the other regions.

[8]   Independence in 1960 brought the Northern People's Congress to power, in an alliance with the National Council of Nigerian Citizens, an Igbo organization. The country had been divided into a federal structure of four states, and a two-chamber parliament was established, based on the British model.

[9]   These political imports proved to be poorly suited to local conditions. Regional governors acquired more power than President Nnambi Azikiwe. Progressive parties were pushed aside in a succession of electoral frauds, while political leaders lost their national outlook, encouraging ethnic rivalries.

[10]   After months of infighting, the military chose General Yacubu Gowon as President in 1966. About this time the oil industry began to develop, just as France was inciting the separatist movement among the Igbo, provoking a secessionist civil war in Biafra that lasted from 1967 until 1970.

[11]   Nigeria became the world's 8th largest oil producer, and Gowon expropriated 55 per cent of the transnational petroleum operations, creating financing for local entrepreneurs.

[12]   Real power was vested in the nationalist Supreme Military Council, with different leaders acting as President. The council closed US military and espionage installations. During Olusegun Obasanjo's presidency, Barclays Bank and British Petroleum assets were nationalized as these companies were violating economic sanctions against apartheid South Africa.

[13]   In 1978, constitutional reform was proposed, calling for elections and a return to civilian government. The Federal Election Commission authorized only five parties, all representing the traditional financial and political elite. Parties with socialist or revolutionary perspectives were barred from the electoral process, under the pretext of avoiding political fragmentation.

[14]   The National Party of Nigeria (NPN) won the election with 25 per cent of the vote, and the Unity Party of Nigeria (UPN) came second, with 20 per cent.

[15]   The inauguration of Shagari, who lacked majorities in both legislative chambers, ended 13 years of military rule. He launched a capitalist development plan based exclusively on petrodollars, to transform Nigeria into the development hub of sub-Saharan Africa. His promises included constructing a new capital, doubling primary school attendance and achieving self-sufficiency in food production via controversial 'green revolution' methods.

[16]   None of these proposals came to anything. Contraband, large urban concentrations of immigrants and poor peasants, unemployment and poverty all increased.

[17]   The International Monetary Fund demanded the refinancing of

LITERACY	FOOD DEPENDENCY	FOREIGN TRADE	EXTERNAL DEBT

LITERACY

2000

64%

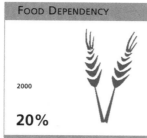

FOOD DEPENDENCY

2000

20%

FOREIGN TRADE

Millions US$ 2000

IMPORTS
16,861

EXPORTS
21,449

EXTERNAL DEBT

2000

PER CAPITA
US$ 300

the foreign debt, putting the country under further pressure. Shagari announced new elections, and took part as the NPN candidate. He was re-elected in December 1983, amidst accusations of electoral fraud and military conspiracies.

[18] On January 1 1984, Muhamad Buhari staged the fourth coup in the country's republican history. The new leaders accused their predecessors of corruption in the petroleum sector, accounting for 95 per cent of export earnings. Hundreds of people were arrested, and all civilian government officials were replaced by military personnel.

[19] However, the crisis was not checked, and the price of rice

quadrupled in a single year. Repression extended to foreigners and 600,000 were expelled, classed as illegal immigrants. These events set the stage for another coup, the countrys sixth, on August 26 1985. General Ibrahim Babangida became the new President. That year, the foreign debt reached $15 billion.

[20] In December 1987, local elections were held with 15,000 unaffiliated candidates taking part. A National Election Commission had been appointed to oversee the voting and ensure that the election was clean and free of coercion. The lack of proper preparation for the voting itself, however, led to acts of violence, confusion and subsequent

accusations of fraud. The election was finally annulled.

[21] On December 7 1989, the military government announced that the elections, originally scheduled for the end of the month, would be postponed until December 1990. Six months later, President Babangida announced that the ban on political activism had been lifted, in an attempt to monitor the transition from military to civilian government in 1992.

[22] Babangida visited Britain in May 1990. One outcome of the visit was a treaty between the two countries granting Nigeria $100 million in aid. Most of its trade is with the US, the UK and France, though it sought more balanced international relations by maintaining relations with all the countries in the world.

[23] Between August and October, the creation of nine new states to separate hostile ethnic groups generated protests which were repressed by the army, causing some 300 deaths according to unofficial figures. The Government imposed a curfew.

[24] Toward the end of 1991, the Government invalidated the allegedly fraudulent internal party elections, held to select government candidates. In November, a new census eliminated 20 million non-existent voters from the electoral register. On December 14, governmental elections were held; the Social Democratic Party (SDP) won in 16 states, and the National Republican Convention (NRC) in 14.

[25] The opposition groups were granted a general amnesty, and 11 dissidents were freed. A law prohibiting former Government officials from running for office was revoked.

[26] Early in 1992, the imprisonment of 263 Muslim militants caused protests in the state of Katsina. During this period, there was also an escalation of inter-ethnic conflict between Haussa and Kataj in the state of Kaduna, and territorial conflict between Tiv and Jukin in the Taraba.

[27] In July 1992, legislative elections were held, but the National Assembly did not convene until December. The SDP won 52 seats in the Senate, and 314 in the

Chamber of Representatives. Nigeria subsequently began the transition to civilian government, after 23 years of military regimes.

[28] In October, presidential primary elections were held, with candidates from the two main parties, the SDP (left-of-center) and the RNC (right-of-center). Both parties were created by the regime, with nearly identical manifestos. Another 23 candidates also took part. President Babangida invalidated the election, claiming fraud, stripped the candidates of their authority and ousted the leadership of the SDP and RNC. Later that month, the military government suspended all political activity. These developments halted the democratic transition process, jeopardizing the possibility of a transfer to civilian government in early 1993.

[29] In November Babangida announced that elections slated for January 1993 had been postponed until June. He also ratified the proscription of the 23 1992 presidential candidates. Finally, he postponed the transfer to a democratic regime until August.

[30] On June 12 1993, the first presidential elections since 1983 were held. The military government did not divulge election results until it had concluded an investigation of alleged fraud. The main contest was between the NCR and SDP candidates, who had been authorized to take part in the election, although the original candidates remained proscribed.

[31] Babangida invalidated the election results on June 23, accusing SDP and NCR candidates of 'buying votes'. Abiola, a wealthy Muslim who was the SDP candidate and who had apparently won the June election, left for London to campaign for international condemnation of the Babangida regime.

[32] The US and Britain suspended their economic aid and training of Nigerian military personnel. Abiola launched a civil disobedience campaign and large protests broke out in the streets of Lagos, where at least 25 people were killed by federal troops.

[33] Clashes continued and on August 26 Babangida resigned, leaving the provisional command of

ENVIRONMENT

The country's extensive river system includes the Niger and its main tributary, the Benue. In the north, the harmattan, a dry wind from the Sahara, creates a drier region made up of plateaus and grasslands where cotton and peanuts are grown for export. The central plains are also covered by grasslands, and are sparsely populated. The southern lowlands receive more rainfall, they have dense tropical forests and most of the country's population lives there. Cocoa and oil-palms are grown in this area. The massive delta of the Niger River divides the coast into two separate regions. In the east, oil production is concentrated around Port Harcourt, the homeland of the Igbo, who converted to Christianity and fought to establish an independent Biafra. To the west, the industrial area is concentrated around Lagos and Ibadan. Yoruba are the predominant western ethnic group, and some of them have converted to Islam. Nigeria has lost between 70 and 80 per cent of its original forests.

SOCIETY

Peoples: Nigeria has the largest population in Africa. The 250 or so ethnic groups fall into four main ones: the Hausa and Fulani in the north; the Yoruba in the southwest; and the Igbo in the southeast.
Religions: The north is predominantly Muslim, while Christians form the majority in the southeast. In the southwest are Muslims, Christians and followers of traditional African religions.
Languages: English (official). Each region has a main language depending on the predominant ethnic group, Hausa, Igbo or Yoruba.
Political Parties: People's Democratic Party; All People's Party; Alliance for Democracy.
Social Organizations: National Labor Congress; United Federation of Nigerian Unions.

THE STATE

Official Name: Federal Republic of Nigeria.
Administrative Divisions: 30 States.
Capital: Abuja 403,000 people (1999).
Other cities: Lagos 8,733,100 people; Ibadan 3,587,100; Kano 3,424,100; Ogbomosho 963,300 (2000).
Government: Olusegun Obasanjo, President since May 1999. Bicameral Legislature: the House of Representatives, with 360 members, and the Senate, with 109 members.
National Holiday: October 1, Independence Day (1960).
Armed Forces: 71,100 troops (1995).
Other: 7,000 National Guard, 2,000 Port Security Police.

the country in the hands of Ernest Shonekan, who promised to hold new elections.

[34] The following month, Abiola returned to London and labor unions called a general strike, demanding he be recognized as Nigerian president. Toward the end of 1993 the Minister of Defense, General Sani Abacha, overthrew Shonekan, dissolved Parliament and banned all political activity.

[35] This new 'strongman' had been a very influential member of the previous military regime and a key figure in the military coup that had ousted the Government in 1983. In one of his first statements, Abacha announced he would abandon some liberal economic reforms adopted in the 1980s.

[36] Interest rates fell and a new foreign exchange control was established, at a time when any possibility of reaching an agreement with the IMF was increasingly remote. Popular support for Abiola mounted; in June 1994, the political leader was arrested, which triggered a 10-day-strike by oil workers, the most important sector in the country.

[37] In November 1994, the execution of nine members of the Movement for the Survival of the Ogoni People, resulted in the isolation of the military regime. Several countries, including the United States, withdrew their ambassadors from Nigeria.

[38] In June 1996 on the basis of a register of political parties drawn up by the National Electoral Commission, Abacha and his military council legalized five political groups: the United Nigerian Congress Party, the Committee for National Consensus, the National Central Party of Nigeria, the Democratic Party of Nigeria and the 'Grassroots' Democratic Movement.

[39] An increase in oil prices stimulated economic growth in 1997. On several occasions, the Government confirmed that this increase had led to improvements in the difficult social situation of the country. However, official data indicated that 80 per cent of the population was living in poverty.

[40] In April 1998, Abacha announced that the August elections were to be replaced by a plebiscite that would determine whether he was to continue in power. The sudden death of the dictator on June 8 led to widespread expressions of happiness and generated expectations of political changes. General Abdusalam Abu-Bakar, appointed by the military junta as new President on June 9, promised to respect the democratic transition, but did not modify the referendum proposal.

[41] Local elections in February 1999 ended in victories for the Popular Democratic Party, of General Olusegun Obasanjo - a former military ruler - and the Alliance for Democracy. The Alliance, which primarily represents the Yoruba ethnic group, won the government of the former capital, Lagos, by a broad margin, while the All Peoples Party, led by supporters of former dictator Sani Abacha, won only the state of Jigawa. The Government set general elections for March 1999.

[42] Obasanjo won the March presidential elections. At first, the opposition attempted to appeal the results before the Electoral Court, but later backed down. The new President promised to re-evaluate the Government's investment policies and to reform the inefficient and corrupt public sector. Upon taking office in May, Obasanjo called upon Nigerians to join him in a three-day fast to seek divine intervention that would ensure his positive presidential performance. One of his first measures was to purge the army ranks, removing 30 military officers. At the same time, he confiscated millions of dollars which he said had been stolen from the public Treasury during previous administrations.

[43] The civilian-led Government improved the country's international image. In October, the US promised to quadruple its economic aid to Nigeria.

[44] Four days of ethnic fighting between Ijaw and Ilaje people in Lagos in December left 12 dead. The conflicts continued and by March 2000, when Obasanjo visited the area and established a peace committee made up of leaders from both communities, hundreds of people had been killed. The committee was able to put an end to the fighting, at least temporarily.

[45] The poor maintenance of oil pipelines by the government, and the public's vandalising of them to siphon off fuel, provoked serious accidents. In June, 700 people were killed when a pipeline exploded in the town of Jesse. Two weeks later, at a conference held in Stavanger, Norway, Obasanjo called for international aid to stop the 'huge' environmental threat caused by the oil industry.

[46] In June the following year, in the state of Nasarawa, neighbor of the capital, ethnic violence sparked off between the Azara and Tiv minorities after the death of an Azara community leader. 40,000 people fled because of the conflict.

[47] In 2001, Nigeria's telephone system was creaking. Phone lines were so regularly intercepted that

even international telephone calls by Cabinet members were interrupted without notice. At that time, the major mobile phone companies of the country, Johannesburg MTN and Wireless Econet promised a 'cable revolution'. However, due to frequent blackouts and excessive voltage, each company needed a generator for its transmission tower. In addition, each company must pay license fees of $285 million to the government. According to the 2001 Transparency International Index on perceptions of corruption in business, Nigeria was ranked second most corrupt after Bangladesh.

[48] In October, Obasanjo, together with the presidents of South Africa, Thabo Mbeki, and Algeria, Abdelaziz Bouteflika, formally launched the New Partnership for Africa's Development (NEPAD), which calls the rest of the world to become partners in the development of Africa. NEPAD is committed to institute clear and open governments in African states, respect human rights and stop war in exchange for more foreign aid, and break down trade barriers which hinder African exports.

[49] More than 1,500 people died in Lagos in January 2002 with the explosion of an army munitions arsenal in the area of Ikeja, near the airport. 15,000 were hurt and relocated in temporary camps.

[50] A radical version of the Islamic *Sharia* code covering crimes has been introduced in a dozen or so northern mainly Muslim states over the past two years, provoking much controversy and some violent protests. The law insists on stoning for adultery, amputation for theft and flogging for the lesser Islamic crimes of alcohol consumption and sex before marriage. In January 2002 a man was hanged in Katsina state for murder in the first execution since Islamic law was introduced. In the nearby state of Sokoto, a woman is facing death by stoning after being convicted of having sex outside marriage. Nigeria's federal government - under severe international pressure - has condemned the strict punishments handed down by Sharia courts.

[51] In June 2002, the African leaders presented their NEPAD initiative at the G-8 rich countries' meeting in Canada, but received less aid and trade concessions than had been hoped for. ∎

Northern Marianas

Population: 79,000 (2002)
Land area: 464 SQ KM
Capital: Saipan
Currency: US dollar
Language: English

Northern Marianas

In Saipan, the largest island of the Mariana archipelago, evidence has been found of human habitation from 1500 BC.

[2] During his first expedition around the world, Portuguese navigator Ferdinand Magellan sighted the islands in 1521 and claimed them for the Spanish Crown. They were held by the Spanish until ceded to Germany in 1899 as the Spanish empire declined.

[3] During World War I the islands came under the control of Japan, which had an alliance with Britain since 1902. The Japanese occupied the islands until World War II.

[4] In June 1944, after fierce fighting, the US took Saipan and Tinian from the Japanese. The islands were contested because of their strategic location in the North Pacific, on the route between Hawaii and the Philippines. They finally came to form part of the Trust Territory of the Pacific Islands in 1947.

[5] The islands held this status until they became a Free Associated State under a referendum held in 1975. In 1977, US President Jimmy Carter approved the constitution of the Northern Marianas islands.

[6] In 1978, the islands began to be administered autonomously. Washington developed a project to turn two-thirds of Tinian into a military air base and an alternative center for the storage of nuclear weapons.

[7] When news leaked out that cement deposits containing radioactive waste from Japanese nuclear plants had been dumped in this part of the Pacific, the alarm was sounded on similar US projects that would directly affect the Marianas Islands.

[8] In 1984 US President Reagan granted some civil and political rights to the islands' residents, such as equal employment opportunities in the federal government, the civil service and the US armed forces.

[9] The Northern Marianas were formally admitted to the Commonwealth of the United States in 1986. Marianas' inhabitants were granted US citizenship but not the right to vote in presidential elections. They have a representative in the US Congress with no voting rights.

[10] The main economic activities of the country are fishing, agriculture - concentrated in smallholdings - and tourism which employs about 10 per cent of the workforce. Some of these activities have been affected often by the typhoons that the islands suffer in the rainy season: in January 1988 Rota Island was devastated by a typhoon which forced the US to declare a state of emergency there. Two years later, the Koryn typhoon struck the archipelago in January 1990.

[11] In the local elections held in 1989, Republicans retained the governorship. Larry Guerrero was elected governor after Pedro P Tenorio had decided to stand down.

[12] The termination of UN Security Council trusteeship of the islands was approved in 1990. Thus, the Northern Marianas became an independent state, associated to the United States.

[13] In 1992, the US Supreme Court ratified the property ownership system, whereby only nationals could own land. In 1994, Froilan C Tenorio was elected governor.

[14] In 1995, there were some 22,600 foreign workers in the country, three times the number of Marianan workers. Unemployment amongst the latter stood at 15 per cent.

[15] In January 1998, Pedro P Tenorio was re-elected once more. His victory was questioned by opposition groups, as it was his third period in office following previous terms in 1982 and 1986.

[16] Throughout 1999 local officials, backed by key figures from the Republican Party in the US Congress, argued intensely with the Clinton (Democrat) administration, regarding the conditions of slavery and exploitation that immigrant workers were subjected to on the island. Tensions worsened when local Republican leaders told Clinton officials visiting the island that the Marianas would not relinquish the exemptions on Federal customs, immigration and labor laws that it enjoyed.

[17] Both human rights groups and Washington officials stated that this exemption allowed the growth of slavery in Saipan, as well as the terrible working conditions and salaries. In spite of these complaints, in practice Washington condones the conditions of slavery for workers on the island by allowing US capital to invest in Marianas' textile industries; there they avoid tariffs and use cheaper labor, while claiming US origin for their products.

[18] Since the 1960s, pollutants from the US Navy have affected the islands' environment. In Saipan, Tanapag locals protested in early 2002 together with activists from the non-governmental organization Greenpeace at the office of the US General Attorney, for what they considered a 'gross negligence and a crime against the environment'. ∎

Norway

Population: 4,505,000 (2002)
Land area: 306,830 SQ KM
Capital: Oslo
Currency: Kroner
Language: Norwegian

Norge

The earliest human traces in Norway correspond to the period between the 9th and the 7th millennia BC. Germanic tribes are thought to have emigrated to these areas when glaciers receded from the northern European coasts and mountains. Cave drawings show that navigation was already known to the peoples of the time, as were something like skis, designed for gliding over the snow.

[2] Historians believe that Norwegian nationality and conversion to Christianity began between 800 and 1030 AD. These dates also correspond to the rise of the Vikings, the name given to Scandinavian seafarers, merchants, and above all, raiders, who dominated the northern seas for 200 years. Harald Harfagre is considered to be the founder of the nation, a feat which he accomplished after defeating his rivals in a naval battle at Hafrsfjord, near the city of Stavanger. After this victory, a large part of the country came under his control.

[3] Viking expeditions expanded the Norwegian Empire, reaching Greenland to the west, and Ireland to the south. In 1002, Leif Erikson and his followers were the first Europeans to cross the Atlantic and reach North America, which they named Vinland.

[4] At the end of the Viking era, Norway was an independent kingdom in which four regional peasant assemblies (*lagting*) elected the monarch. Legitimate and illegitimate children of the king had equal rights to succession before the lagtings. In the 10th and 12th centuries it was common for two kings to govern simultaneously without any conflict arising between them.

[5] King Magnus III Barfot (1093-1103) conquered the Scottish Orkney and Hebrides Islands. His three sons governed together: they imposed a tithe, founded the first monasteries and built cathedrals. At the beginning of the 12th century, a hundred-year civil war broke out, as a result of the increased power of the monarchy and also of disputes between the monarchy and the church.

[6] This war continued until the coronation of Haakon IV in 1217. The new king reorganized public administration, imposing a hereditary monarchy. Haakon signed a treaty with Russia over the country's northern border. Greenland and Iceland agreed to a union with the King. With the Scottish islands and the Faeroes included the Norwegian Empire reached its maximum extent.

[7] The Black Death killed close to 50 per cent of Norway's population between 1349 and 1350. The upper classes were decimated; Danes and Swedes were hired to fill the positions left vacant in the higher levels of the Government and the church. However, the King lost control over his dominions and isolated regions organized autonomous administrations.

[8] The ascent of Queen Margrethe of Denmark to the throne in 1387 paved the way for the union of the Scandinavian countries. In 1389, she was crowned Queen of Sweden and in 1397 her adopted nephew Erik was elected king of all Scandinavia in Kalmar, Sweden. With the Kalmar union, Norway was gradually subordinated, ultimately becoming a province of Denmark, a situation which lasted for more than 400 years.

[9] After 1523, Norway's administrative council tried to obtain greater independence from Denmark. However, the fact that power lay in the hands of the Catholic bishops made it difficult to gain Swedish support. At the end of the civil war, between 1533 and 1536, the council was abolished. In 1537, the Danish King made the Lutheran religion the country's official religion; the Norwegian Church has been a State church ever since.

[10] During this period, social conditions in Norway were better than in Denmark. There was a class of rich landlords in the countryside which exploited the regional timber resources, as well as a large group of rural wage-earners. Most of Norway's population were peasants and fishing people. Cities were limited to fewer than 15,000 inhabitants.

[11] At the end of the Napoleonic wars, Denmark unilaterally surrendered control of Norway to Sweden. In 1814, Norway's constituent assembly proclaimed national independence. Sweden re-established its dominance over Norway by force, but this union was dissolved once again without bloodshed in 1905, with Norway regaining its sovereignty and with its full previous territories intact.

[12] In spite of its subordination to Sweden, the majority of the laws

WORKERS

2000
UNEMPLOYMENT: 3.4%
LABOR FORCE AS % OF TOTAL:

FEMALE: 46%   MALE: 54%

1994/97
EMPLOYMENT DISTRIBUTION:

F
M

SERVICES	F: 87%	M: 59%
INDUSTRY	F: 10%	M: 35%
AGRICULTURE	F: 2%	M: 7%

LAND USE

DEFORESTATION: 0.3% annual (1990/95)

1993

FOREST & WOODLAND: 25.7%
ARABLE: 2.7%
OTHER: 71.6%

PUBLIC EXPENDITURE

1999

DEFENSE 5%
SOCIAL 50.2%

MATERNAL MORTALITY

1985/99

Per 100,000
live births

6

FOOD DEPENDENCY

2000

6%

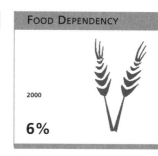

enacted in 1814 remained in force during this period. The Norwegian constitution is one of the oldest in the world, second only to that of the United States. It is based on the principles of national sovereignty, the separation of powers and the inviolability of human rights.

[13] Under a constitutional amendment in 1884, Norway adopted a parliamentary monarchy as its system of government. The Danish Prince Carl was elected king of Norway, under the name Haakon VII, in 1905. Up until 1914, the country experienced rapid economic expansion, with the hydroelectric wealth of the region allowing large-scale industrial development.

[14] The sale of a large number of Norwegian water courses with hydroelectric power-generating potential to foreigners, caused great concern among the population. In 1906, 75 per cent of Norway's hydroelectric dams belonged to foreign investors. In 1909, Parliament passed laws for the protection of the country's natural resources.

[15] Universal suffrage, a term which applied to men only when it was passed in 1898, was extended to women by reforms approved in 1907 and 1913. One consequence of industrialization and universal suffrage was the growth of the Labor Party (LP).

[16] During World War I, Norway tried to remain neutral, but was obliged by the other powers to cut trade with Germany. Anti-German feeling was strong, particularly because of the various accidents caused by German submarines. Price increases provoked by the conflict hit the workers hardest.

[17] Unlike other Western European social democracies, Norway's LP (in which the Left formed the majority) decided to join the Third Communist International in 1918. However, the Norwegian LP could not agree with the centralization applied by the Soviet Communist Party, and cut its ties with the Comintern in 1923.

[18] Despite economic difficulties and serious labor conflicts (with unemployment reaching 20 per cent in 1938), Norway underwent vigorous industrial expansion in the inter-war years. The Government extended social legislation to include pensions, mandatory leave for workers and unemployment benefits.

[19] In 1940, at the beginning of World War II, Norway was invaded by Germany, which seized control of the country after two months of fighting. King Haakon and the Government went into exile in London, co-ordinating the resistance from there. Norway was liberated in 1945. Haakon died in 1957 and was succeeded by his son Olaf V.

[20] The LP governed continuously between 1935 and 1965, except for a brief one-month period in 1963. In 1965, the LP lost its parliamentary majority and Per Borten, the leader of the Center Party, was named Prime Minister. However, he resigned in 1971 when it was revealed that he had leaked confidential information during EC negotiations.

[21] After the War, Norway abandoned its neutrality policy, joining NATO in 1949. This membership was encouraged by the fear of Soviet expansionism and the unsuccessful attempt to establish a Scandinavian military alliance between Norway, Denmark and Sweden. However, in 1952, the Scandinavian countries established the Nordic Council to deal with their common interests. Norway became a member of the Nordic Council in 1952, and of the European Free Trade Association (EFTA) in 1960. By 1972, the idea of joining the EC had been proposed. The issue divided the population and a plebiscite was held to decide the question; 53 per cent voted against, while 47 per cent were in favor.

[22] Trygve Bratteli, the Labor Prime Minister resigned and a new government was formed by Lars Korvald of the Christian People's Party, to negotiate a trade agreement with the EEC. After this the Labor Party formed a minority cabinet under Oddvar Nordli, who served until 1981, when the LP appointed Gro Harlem Brundtland, the first woman Prime Minister.

[23] In 1977, Norway extended its territorial waters to 200 miles and designated a protected fishing zone in its territory of Svalbard.

[24] In 1986, the Labor Party formed a minority government, once more under Gro Harlem Brundtland, who appointed 8 women to her 18-member cabinet.

[25] The vulnerability of the Norwegian environment to events beyond national borders was underscored in April 1986 when a fire broke out in the Chernobyl nuclear power plant, in the Ukraine. The high levels of radioactivity released into the atmosphere most seriously affected the Sami population in the northern part of the country, and over 70 per cent of all reindeer meat had to be destroyed.

[26] In the early 1970s, Norway and the former USSR were at odds over rights to large parts of the Barents Sea. A temporary agreement signed in 1978 defined a 'grey area' for the joint management of fishing. The unresolved questions continued to create tension until early 1989, when the USSR proposed that they begin negotiations.

[27] Protests were triggered by acid rain emanating from industries on the Kola Peninsula to the east of Norway. Since the fall of the communist regime this situation has changed, and there is growing trade across the border. Norway, Sweden and Finland have joined forces to help Russia solve the immense environmental problems in the area.

[28] Norway is the world's sixth largest producer of natural gas and crude oil, and the third largest

---

PROFILE

ENVIRONMENT

The Scandinavian mountain range runs north-south along the coast of the country. On the western side, glacier erosion has gouged out deep valleys that are way below actual sea level, resulting in the famous 'fjords', narrow, deep inlets walled in by steep cliffs. Maritime currents produce humid, mild winters and cool summers. The population is concentrated in the south, especially round Oslo. Nine-tenths of the territory is uninhabited.

SOCIETY

Peoples: Norwegians 96.3 per cent, Danish 0.4 per cent, British 0.3 per cent, Pakistani 0.2 per cent, Iranian 0.2 per cent, others (including 40,000 Sami, an indigenous people who live chiefly in the northern province of Finnmark) 1.9 per cent.
Religions: 88 per cent of the population belongs to the Church of Norway (Lutheran); there are Evangelical and Catholic minorities.
Languages: Two forms of Norwegian are officially recognized; 80 per cent of school children learn the old form 'Bokmal', and 20 per cent learn the neo-Norwegian 'Landsmal'. In the north, the Sami speak their own language.
Political Parties: Norwegian Labor Party, social-democratic; Right Party, conservative; Progress Party; Christian People's Party, christian-democratic; Socialist Left Party; Center Party, mainly agrarian; Venstre, left liberal party; Coastal Party, fishermens' party.
Social Organizations: Norwegian Federation of Unions; Organization of Academics (AF); Organization of Trades (YS).

THE STATE

Official Name: Kongeriket Norge.
Administrative divisions: 19 provinces (Fylker).
Capital: Oslo 959,000 people (1999).
Other cities: Bergen 200,200 people; Trondheim 140,700; Stavanger 109,900 (2000).
Government: Parliamentary constitutional monarchy. Harald V, King since January 1991. Prime Minister: Kjell Magne Bondevik, appointed by the King in October 2001. Legislative power resides in the Storting, the 165-member unicameral parliament.
National Holiday: May 17, Constitution Day (1814).
Armed Forces: 29,000 (1995).

FOREIGN TRADE

Millions US$ 2000

IMPORTS

49,253

EXPORTS

75,394

oil exporter. Operating outside the OPEC, oil concessions have always been handled as an economic and political weapon. Although drilling rights are granted to foreign companies, the State looks after its own interests by requiring 50 per cent participation by Statoil, the national oil company, in all operations.

[29] Norwegian diplomacy gained great prestige when the Minister of Foreign Affairs, Johan Juergen Holst served as an intermediary in the Israeli-PLO negotiations.

[30] Despite serious disagreements among Norwegians, Oslo sought entry to the European Union (EU) in late 1992. The unions considered that joining the former European Community would threaten national sovereignty, while many entrepreneurs - particularly in the export sector - wanted full access to the EU market.

[31] For entry to be effective it had to be approved by a referendum, and a date was set for November 1994. The campaign for this vote largely dominated political life for two years and revolved around three main issues: oil exploitation, the regional policy and the fishing policy.

[32] The social democrats and conservatives supported joining the EU, while all the others opposed the move, leading to an extremely close outcome: 52.4 per cent of the electorate voted against integration, blocking Norway's membership.

[33] In 1994, the economy continued to expand and unemployment to fall. In 1995, unemployment reached 4.8 per cent and the trend was expected to continue.

[34] In October 1996, the Labor Party's Thorbjorn Jagland became head of government after Gro Harlem Brundtland resigned.

[35] Following the September 1997 elections, Jagland was forced to stand down. The ruling Labor Party took 35 per cent of the votes and 65 seats out of the total 165 in play. The Prime Minister had announced he would stand down if the party could not equal the 36.9 per cent it had achieved in 1993.

[36] Christian Democrat, Kjell Magne Bondevik was appointed his successor. A coalition of three centrist parties took control but with only 43 votes in Parliament. Bondevik started by earmarking part of the oil income for investments in health and education.

[37] In 1997, the economy expanded for the fifth year running. However in early 1998, Norway began to suffer the consequences of falling international crude oil prices, following the stock exchange crash in Southeast Asia - the biggest oil-importing market in the world.

[38] A project to install the nation's first natural gas energy plants became the center of a controversy that led Bondevik to lose Parliament's vote of confidence. He resigned in March 2000. Bondevik's minority government maintained that the new energy plants would release too much carbon dioxide into the atmosphere, while the opposition parties insisted on avoiding increased spending on fuel imports at all costs.

[39] Labor leader Jens Stoltenberg took office as the new Prime Minister March 17 and named his Cabinet, primarily made up of his party's veterans. Women were designated to approximately half of the Cabinet posts.

[40] In early 2001, the Government decided to re-establish exports of whale meat and fat, thus lifting the ban imposed due to international pressures. Environmentalist organizations immediately protested, arguing endangered species would be affected. Also, due to the killing of grey wolves which the Government claimed were threatening its livestock, Oslo clashed with Sweden, who claimed the wolves were another endangered species. Meanwhile, the ministry, apart from promoting seal hunting as a tourist attraction, proposed the killing of dolphins for scientific research.

[41] Some 40,000 Norwegians demonstrated in the streets of Oslo against the first overtly racist murder in the country. Benjamin Hermansen, a young Norwegian-Ghanaian anti-racist activist was stabbed to death on January 26 2001, by six members of the neo-Nazi group Boot Boys, who were later arrested and tried.

[42] Crown Prince Haakon was married in August 2001 to a commoner, after having lived for a year with her. This caused controversy especially since the bride was a single mother. In a country where half the first-born children are from single mothers or non-married couples, their marriage was challenged mostly for legal and religious reason. The princess' son is banned by the Constitution from being an heir to the throne; and the Lutheran church, which the future king will preside over, is against unmarried couples living together.

[43] The Labor party did not gain enough votes for a majority in the 2001 general elections. A month later a 3-party coalition was formed: Conservative, Christian People's Party and Liberals, who jointly supported the right-wing Progress Party and Kjell Magne Bondevik as new Prime Minister.

[44] In September, the 'other Norwegian nation', the Sami, who for 20 years had tried to clarify their rights on the land, protested against a Government plan to tap a gold mine in the northern region of Pasvik. The Sami Parliament - a consultant, non executive organism - demanded its participation and said the use of the territory by the Government would endanger the community's survival, dependent on fishing and reindeer herds.

[45] For centuries the Sami were not allowed to claim any land rights, because the land was restricted to speakers of Norwegian. The Sami language started being taught in schools in 1960. It was expected that, by the year 2002, Sami television shows would be aired on a daily basis. ∎

STATISTICS

DEMOGRAPHY

Population: 4,505,000 (2002)
Annual growth: 0.5 % (1985-2000)
Estimates for year 2015: 4,670,000 (2000)
Annual growth to year 2015: 0.3 % (2000)
Urban population: 75.5 % (2000)
Urban growth: 1.2 % (2000)
Children per woman: 1.8 (2000)

HEALTH

Life expectancy at birth: 79 years (2000-2005)
male: 76 years (2000-2005)
female: 82 years (2000-2005)
Maternal mortality: 6 per 100,000 live births (1985/99)
Infant mortality: 4 per 1,000 (2000)
Under-5 child mortality: 4 per 1,000 (2000)
Daily calorie supply: 3,425 per capita (1999)
413 doctors per 100,000 people (1998)
Safe water: 100 % (2000)

EDUCATION

School enrolment (net):
Primary total: 100 % (1994/2000)
male: 100 % (1995/99)
female: 100 % (1995/99)
Secondary (gross):
male: 121 % (1995/97)
female: 116 % (1995/97)
Tertiary (gross): 65 % (1998)

COMMUNICATIONS

581 newspapers (1999), 915 radios (1997), 669 TV sets (2000) and 532 main telephone lines (2000) per 1,000 people
Books: 159 new titles per 100,000 people (1992/94)

ECONOMY

Per capita, GDP: $ 29,918 (2000)
Annual growth: 1.6 % (2000)
Annual inflation: 3.1 % (2000)
Consumer price index: 112.1 (2000)
Currency: 8.9 kroner = $ 1 (03/2002)
Cereal imports: 313,774 metric tons (2000)
Food import dependency: 6 % (2000)
Fertilizer use: 2,269 kg per ha (1999)
Exports: $ 75,394 million (2000)
Imports: $ 49,253 million (2000)

ENERGY

Consumption: 5,736.2 Kgs of oil equivalent per capita yearly (1998); -688.4 % imported (1999)

HDI (ranking/value): 1 / 0.939 (1999)

Oman

Population: 2,709,000 (2002)
Land area: 212,460 SQ KM
Capital: Muscat (Masqat)
Currency: Omani rial
Language: Arabic

Uman

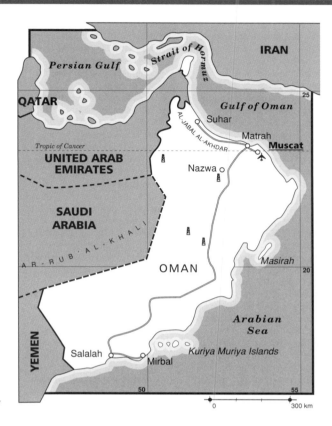

Sumerian clay tablets from the third century BC mention Oman as one of the outstanding markets in the economy of the Mesopotamian cities. Omani navigators became the lords of the Indian Ocean, connecting the Gulf to India, Indonesia and Indochina. In the 7th century they also played a major role in the peaceful propagation of Islam. Around 690 AD Abd Al-Malik decided to control the expansion of dissident sects. Consequently, some defeated leaders were forced to abandon the country. One of them, Prince Hamza, emigrated to Africa where he founded Zanzibar beginning a relationship between Oman and the African coast which would last until the 19th century.

2 Persecution only served to further reinforce Sharite 'heresy'. Towards 751, Oman took advantage of the dynastic strife in Damascus to elect an imam who gradually evolved from a spiritual leader to a temporal sovereign. Omani wealth gave the imam considerable power in the entire Gulf region, but also made Oman the object of successive invasions by the caliphs of Baghdad, the Persians, the Mongols and the local groups of central Arabia. The Portuguese arrived from 1507, destroying the fleet and coastal fortifications, opening the way for the occupation of the principal cities and the control of the Strait of Hormuz. The Portuguese held control of the region for almost 150 years, stifling the Gulf's trade.

3 In 1630, Imam Nasir ibn Murshid launched an inland struggle against the invaders. His

son, Said, concluded this endeavor in 1650 with the expulsion of the Portuguese from Muscat (Musqat) and the recovery of Zanzibar and the African coast of Mombasa in 1698. Thus a powerful state was created which obtained the political unification of the African and Asian territories where a common culture and economy had developed.

4 Sultan Said expanded the African territories and moved the capital to Zanzibar in 1832. At the time of his death in 1856, the British presence was already being strongly felt on both continents. Said's sons argued and as a result, the African and Asian parts of the state were separated: the elder son, Thuwaini, kept the sultanate of Oman while his brother Majid took control of Zanzibar. The 1891 Canning Agreement virtually made Oman a British protectorate.

5 In 1913, inland peoples elected their own imam in opposition to the sultan's hereditary rule. The struggle came to an end only in 1920, when a treaty was signed acknowledging

the country's division in two: the Sultanate of Muscat and the Imamate of Oman.

6 Muscat was an extremely poor country, where arable lands accounted for less than one per cent of the total territory. Between 1932 and 1970, it suffered the despotic rule of Sultan Said ibn Taimur, who fanatically opposed any foreign influence in the country, even in education and health. This did not prevent him from granting control over the country's oil deposits to Royal Dutch Shell.

7 Imam Ghaleb ibn Alim, elected in 1954, proclaimed independence and announced his intention to join the Arab League. In 1955 the British reunited Oman.

8 Taimur was overthrown by his own son Qabus on July 23 1970. Those who expected the young, Oxford-educated monarch to introduce modernizing changes soon realized that British domination was only being replaced by US domination. The US

became a net importer of oil and began to develop an active interest in the area.

9 Oil, produced commercially since 1967, provided more than half of the Gross Domestic Product. However more than half of Oman's labor force remained involved in agriculture, in the thin coastal strip that contains the country's only arable land.

10 With US assistance, Qabus organized a mercenary army but when this force proved incapable of smashing the Popular Front for the Liberation of the Gulf, he signed an agreement with Iran's Shah Reza Pahlevi to secure Iranian intervention in the conflict.

11 The guerrilla fighters were forced to retreat under the superior firepower of Iranian troops. Iranians also placed the Strait of Hormuz under their jurisdiction.

12 At the Shah's downfall, Iranian soldiers were quickly replaced by Egyptian commandos and troops. The Sultan decided to give the US the Masirah island air base, and later the air bases at Ihamrit and Sib and the naval bases at Matrah and Salalah. At that time, two-thirds of the national budget was committed to defense, while the people suffered acute poverty and widespread illiteracy.

13 Oman's strategic importance, with a geographic position giving the country full control over oil routes, led the US to concentrate on the sultanate in efforts to settle in the area.

14 In June 1989, the Petroleum Development of Oman announced the discovery of the most important natural gas deposits found within the last 20 years.

15 Following the Iraqi invasion of Kuwait in March 1991, a member of the Gulf Cooperation Council (GCC), Oman suspended aid to Jordan and to the PLO.

16 In 1991, the Foreign Ministers of Egypt, Syria and the six Arab member States of the Gulf Cooperation Council signed an agreement with the US in Riyadh, the capital of Saudi Arabia, aimed at maintaining the region's security.

17 Later that year, the Government announced that the democratization process was underway; this included the creation

WORKERS

2000

LABOR FORCE
AS % OF TOTAL

■ FEMALE: 17%   ■ MALE: 83%

MATERNAL MORTALITY
1985/99

Per 100,000
live births

14

LITERACY
2000

72%

FOOD DEPENDENCY
2000

2000

22%

STATISTICS

DEMOGRAPHY
Population: 2,709,000 (2002)
Annual growth: 3.8 % (1985-2000)
Estimates for year 2015: 4,110,000 (2000)
Annual growth to year 2015: 3.2 % (2000)
Urban population: 84.0 % (2000)
Urban growth: 4.0 % (2000)
Children per woman: 5.7 (2000)

HEALTH
Life expectancy at birth: 72 years (2000-2005)
male: 70 years (2000-2005)
female: 73 years (2000-2005)
Maternal mortality: 14 per 100,000 live births (1985/99)
Infant mortality: 12 per 1,000 (2000)
Under-5 child mortality: 14 per 1,000 (2000)
133 doctors per 100,000 people (1998)
Safe water: 39 % (2000)

EDUCATION
Literacy: 72 % (2000)
male: 80 % (2000)
female: 62 % (2000)
School enrolment (net):
Primary total: 89 % (1994/2000)
male: 86 % (1995/99)
female: 86 % (1995/99)
Secondary (gross):
male: 68 % (1995/97)
female: 65 % (1995/97)
Tertiary (gross): 8 % (1997)
Primary school teachers: one for every 25 pupils (1998)

COMMUNICATIONS
29 newspapers (1996), 621 radios (1997), 563 TV sets (2000) and 89 main telephone lines (2000) per 1,000 people
Books: 1 new title per 100,000 people (1992/94)

ECONOMY
Annual growth: 0.4 % (1995)
Annual inflation: -1.1 % (2000)
Consumer price index: 98.7 (2000)
Currency: 0.4 Omani rials = $ 1 (03/2002)
Cereal imports: 387,328 metric tons (2000)
Food import dependency: 22 % (2000)
Fertilizer use: 4,578 kg per ha (1999)
Exports: $ 5,594 million (1994)
Imports: $ 4,494 million (1994)
External debt: $ 6,267 million (2000); $ 2,469 per capita (2000)
Debt service: 9.7 % of exports (1999)
Development aid received: $ 40 million (1999); $ 17.0 per capita (1999)

ENERGY
Consumption: 3,164.8 Kgs of oil equivalent per capita yearly (1998); -543.6 % imported (1999)

HDI (ranking/value): 71 / 0.747

---

of a parliament directly elected by the country's citizens.

[18] During the summer of 1994, some 500 dissidents were arrested, including several senior officials and well-known business people, charged with trying to topple the Government 'using Islam as a cover'. The fiscal deficits accumulated by the Government since 1981, regarded as excessive, led the World Bank to warn that the level of State expenditure was 'unsustainable'.

[19] Taking heed of the international financial organization's stand, in 1995 the Sultan announced a program of reforms which included a reduction of state spending, a series of privatizations and measures to attract foreign investment.

[20] In 1996, the Government announced a five-year plan to balance the budget by 2000. The project, aiming to free the economy from oil dependence, included privatizations and stimuli to increase foreign investment.

[21] That same year, the Sultan established a new succession mechanism. This meant that, if the royal family could not reach agreement on the appointment of a successor within three days of his death, the candidate chosen by the Sultan himself would be accepted.

[22] Oman became one of the first Arab countries to establish diplomatic and trade relations with Israel in January 1997. A month later, the rapprochement process came to a halt, when the Arab League questioned the Israeli decision to build new settlements in eastern Jerusalem.

[23] In early 1998, Oman, along with all the other Gulf Cooperation Council (GCC) member nations, debated the possibility of freeing its currency from the dollar to prevent the loss of income on oil sales. The six GCC nations controlled 45 per cent of the world's crude oil reserves, but were losing millions of dollars per year due to falling international exchange rates of the US currency.

[24] Oman and the United Arab Emirates signed an accord in May 1999 that defined part of the common border with the Abu Dhabi Emirate. Both parties agreed that, eventually, they would have to delineate more exactly the borders between Oman and the other emirates.

[25] After an 18-year hiatus, the Government once again began to recruit young people for the Omani army in Makram, an area that belonged to Oman until the end of the 1950s, but which is currently part of Pakistan. Oman had abandoned recruitment measures in 1982 after a recruiting team was attacked by Pakistani troops.

[26] During the visit of US President Bill Clinton in March 2000, Sultan Qabus expressed his approval of the US announcement that it would lift some of its sanctions against Iran.

[27] In April 2001 the Government announced an amnesty for illegal workers. The amnesty allowed illegal residents not facing any criminal charge to leave Oman after paying a $125 fine at the Labor Ministry, rather than the normal penalty for over-stayers of $25 dollars a day.

[28] In July, three Pakistanis were executed at the prison in al-Manouwama a suburb in Muscat, convicted of smuggling illegal narcotics into the country.

[29] The Defense Ministry decided in January 2002 to buy 16 advanced combat helicopters from a British-Italian consortium Agusta Westland. Officials said these Super Lynx helicopters will contribute to the modernization of the Omani air defenses.

[30] A target date of 2003 has been set to have all government posts filled by Omanis. According to official figures, a quarter of the sultanate's population are foreigners. ∎

PROFILE

ENVIRONMENT
With its 2,600 km coastline, Oman occupies a strategic position on the southeastern edge of the Arabian Peninsula and flanking the Gulf of Oman, where oil tankers leave the Persian Gulf. It is separated from the rest of the peninsula by the Rub al Khali desert that stretches into the center of the country. Local nomadic groups now live with petroleum and natural gas exploitation. Favored by ocean currents, the coastal regions enjoy a better climate. Monsoon summer rains fall in the north.

SOCIETY
Peoples: Omani Arab 73.5 per cent; Pakistani (mostly Baluchi) 18.7 per cent; other 5.5 per cent.
Religions: Muslim 86 per cent; Hindu 13 per cent; other 1 per cent.
Languages: Arabic, official and predominant, English, Baluchi and Urdu are also spoken.
Political Parties: There are no legal political parties.

THE STATE
Official Name: Saltanat 'Uman (Sultanate of Oman).
Administrative divisions: 59 Districts.
Capital: Muscat (Masqat) 887,000 people (1999).
Other cities: Nizwa 74,400; Suma'il 42,700; Salalah 163,600 (2000).
Government: Absolute Monarchy. Qabus ibn Said, Sultan since July 1970 and Prime Minister since January 1972. Bicameral Legislature: the Consultative Assembly (Majlis al-Shura), with 82 elected members with only consultative tasks, and the Council of State (Majlis al-Dawla), with 40 appointed members.
National Holiday: November 19, The Sultan's birthday.
Armed Forces: 43,500 (1996).
Other: 3,900.

Pakistan

Population:	148,721,000 (2002)
Land area:	770,880 SQ KM
Capital:	Islamabad
Currency:	Rupee
Language:	Urdu

Pakistan

Pakistan means the land of the pure, as it was religion (Islam) that bound together the people of different ethnic communities and languages. Poet-philosopher Mohammed Iqbal articulated the concept of Pakistan in its basic form in 1931 when he proposed a separate state for the Muslims in India.

[2] The first Muslims to arrive in the Indian subcontinent were the traders from Arabia and Persia. A permanent Muslim foothold was achieved with Muhammad ibn Qasim's conquest of Sind in 711 AD. It was in the early 13th century that the foundations of Muslim rule in India were laid, establishing borders and a capital in Delhi. The region including the present territory of Pakistan was subsequently ruled by several Muslim dynasties, finishing with the Mughals.

[3] The question of Muslim identity emerged alongside the decline of Muslim power and the rise of the Hindu middle class during British colonialism. In the early years of the 20th century, Muslim leaders became convinced of the need for effective political organization. A delegation of Muslim leaders met the viceroy (the chief representative of the British imperial government in India) in October 1906, demanding the status of a separate electorate for the Muslims. The All India Muslim League (ML) was founded in Dhaka that year with the objective of defending the political rights and interests of Indian Muslims. The British conceded the status of a separate electorate in the Government of India Act of 1909, confirming the ML's status as the representative organization of Indian Muslims.

[4] In the 1930s there was a growing awareness of a separate Muslim identity and a greater desire to preserve it within separate territorial boundaries. Under the leadership of Muhammad Ali Jinnah, ML continued its campaign for Pakistan; a separate homeland in British India. After the general election of April 1946, ML called a convention of the newly-elected ML parliamentarians in Delhi. A motion by Hussain Shaheed Suhrawardi, then chief minister of Bengal, reiterated the demand for a separate state of Pakistan in no uncertain terms.

1   Claimed by India
2   Claimed by Pakistan

0   300 km

[5] The Hindu-Muslim relationship had been seriously affected by communal tensions and riots in different parts of India. This convinced the leadership of the Indian National Congress (representing mainly the nationalists) to accept Pakistan as a solution to the problems. A Partition Plan for transfer of power was announced on June 3 1947. Both the ML and the Congress accepted the Plan. On August 14 1947, the new state of Pakistan was born comprising West Punjab, Sind, Baluchistan, North-West Frontier Province and East Bengal. The process of partition was painful and often violent. In 1948-49 Pakistan waged a war with India and annexed one third of the border province, Kashmir. The territory, mostly Muslim, had been in control of India since 1947, after the local Kashmiri Government had chosen annexation to India in exchange for military support to fight an invasion of Pakistani fighters

[6] Pakistan has suffered numerous political crises. The first constitution was adopted on March 23 1956, but the civilian government was deposed in a coup on October 7 1958. Martial law was proclaimed and the constitution abrogated. On October 27 1958, General Ayub Khan emerged as the new leading force.

He introduced 'basic democracy', a system of local self-government and indirect presidential elections. Martial law was withdrawn in 1962 and a new constitution, granting absolute power to the president, was instituted, with Pakistan being declared an Islamic Republic. Ayub Khan was forced to resign on March 25, 1969, following a popular uprising. Martial law was promulgated again and General Yahya Khan became president.

[7] A general election was held at the end of 1970, the first ever in Pakistan under neutral administration. Two political parties, the Awami League (AL) and the Pakistan People's Party (PPP) emerged victorious in East and West Pakistan, respectively. However, the AL won an absolute majority in the parliamentary election on an all-Pakistan basis, forming the federal government. However, the parliamentary session was postponed, and the people of East Pakistan began the movement for an independent Bangladesh under the leadership of the AL in March 1971. The AL was banned and its leader Sheikh Mujibur Rahman was arrested. A civil war broke out, leading the AL to form a government in exile in India. The Indian army intervened and on

December 16 1971, Bangladesh's independence was granted.

[8] Zulfiqar Ali Bhutto, the leader of the PPP, formed a civilian government in 1972 following the resignation of General Yahya Khan. He encouraged strong public sector participation in the economy, followed a non-aligned foreign policy and approved radical land reforms. The PPP was victorious again in the general election of 1977, but the results were rejected by opposition political parties who accused the PPP of vote-rigging. Against this backdrop of political unrest, General Zia-ul Haq ousted the Bhutto government and proclaimed martial law. Bhutto was arrested and later sentenced to death on charge of conspiring to murder an opposition political leader.

[9] General Zia accelerated the process of Islamicization in all spheres of political and social life. Many political opponents were harassed and detained. A general election on a non-party basis was held in February 1985 under martial law, and a pro-Zia government was formed. Zia was killed in a mysterious air crash in August 1988. In the general election of November 1988, the PPP were victorious and a government was formed under the leadership of Bhutto's daughter Benazir Bhutto. The democratic system was brought back after an 11-year absence.

[10] Benazir Bhutto became the first woman to serve as head of state of a predominantly Islamic country. One of her first moves was to release all female prisoners charged with crimes other than murder. Many of these had been imprisoned under discriminatory 'Black Laws' passed during Zia's term in office. They included the law of evidence, under which the declaration of one man was given more weight than that of two women in legal proceedings. Zia left a legacy of such laws in the form of constitutional amendments, which required a virtually politically-impossible two-thirds majority to overturn.

[11] The army remained a strong institution in Pakistan. The country became a member of the Southeast Asian Treaty Organization (SEATO) in 1954 and the Central Treaty Organization (CENTO) in 1955, two strong military alliances led by the

United States. Although Pakistan later withdrew from these alliances, bilateral relations with the US remained cordial. Pakistan has received military and economic aid from the US.

[12] Relations with India have always been strained. Both countries have territorial claims over the state of Kashmir. India treats it as an integral part of the country, while Pakistan has been demanding a plebiscite there to allow the people of Kashmir to decide their own fate. After wars in 1948-49, 1965 and 1971, the two states agreed on a cease-fire zone on both sides of the Kashmir border. This meant not only a division of land, but also a separation of the local population. Since then, Kashmiri nationalist groups have demanded the creation of an independent state in the region.

[13] Throughout the 1980s, Pakistan was very vocal in its opposition to the Soviet intervention in Afghanistan (started in December 1979). Pakistan also supported the Mujahedin - Afghan resistance groups based in Pakistan - in their fight against the pro-Soviet regime in Kabul. During the Soviet intervention in Afghanistan, the US used Pakistani territory to supply arms to the rebel groups. This turned Pakistan into a key ally for the US

regional policy, and resulted in the granting of significant economic assistance to the country. There were about three million Afghan refugees living in Pakistan in mid-1990.

[14] On August 6 1990, President Ghulam Ishaq Khan dissolved the government of Prime Minister Benazir Bhutto, charging her administration with nepotism and corruption. The President suspended the National Assembly and named Ghulam Mustafa Jatoi, leader of the Combined Opposition Parties (COP) coalition, head of the interim government.

[15] Elections were held on October 24. Nawaz Sharif was elected Prime Minister, with the support of the Muslim League, the main party in the coalition opposing Benazir Bhutto. Benazir also put forward her candidacy.

[16] When the Gulf War broke out in January 1991, following the Iraqi invasion of Kuwait, Pakistan quickly aligned with the US and sent troops to Saudi Arabia. Surveys showed that the population had strong pro-Iraqi tendencies, but the Government announced that the country's forces would only defend Islamic holy places, and would not take part in combat or go into Iraqi territory.

[17] Shortly after taking office, Prime Minister Nawaz Sharif, who

came from a family of industrialists, implemented an economic reform plan, aimed at encouraging private investment. The plan included a far-reaching privatization process which was strongly resisted by the 300,000 workers in the state-run companies.

[18] Apart from the economic reforms, Sharif's government began a process of strengthening Islam which provoked wide hostility. The plan included the introduction of *Sharia* or Islamic law. In Sharif's opinion, Benazir Bhutto's term was a period of religious regression. The enforcement of Sharia immediately resulted in setbacks for women's social and legal status. The Government banned the media from making any reference to a woman's right to divorce. The main leaders of the women's movements, who demanded the end of discrimination against women, were harassed by security forces, and some were kidnapped and raped.

[19] On November 22 1990, a serious political and administrative scandal broke out. The opposition accused Nawaz Sharif of embezzling public funds. Sharif was responsible for the bankruptcy of several cooperative credit institutions. Only the unconditional support of President Ishaq Khan prevented the fall of the prime minister and the matter was referred to the judiciary. The scandal triggered a wave of demonstrations led by the PPP, and the Government responded with increased repression.

[20] Apart from the disputes between the government and the opposition, Pakistan has been periodically shaken by inter-ethnic violence, in particular between the Sindhis and the Muhajirs (former Indian refugees).

[21] In February 1992, the ancient dispute over the border territory of Kashmir brought Pakistan and India to the brink of a new armed conflict. The Jammu and Kashmir Liberation Front, a Muslim group demanding the creation of an independent state staged a protest march along the line that divides the country between Pakistan and India. The organizers encouraged thousands of demonstrators on both sides to cross the border. The Pakistan Government ordered the army to shoot at the demonstrators in order to stop the separatist march. Five people died and fifty were injured.

[22] Amid the tension created by the Kashmir border crisis, the differences between Washington and Islamabad became more obvious. When Pakistan announced their nuclear weapon construction project was well under way, the US began to exert pressure on the country. This resulted in the virtual suspension of US economic assistance and arms sales to Pakistan. As a

response to the US measures, Pakistan announced that China had guaranteed economic and technological support to continue the nuclear research program.

[23] President Ishaq Khan accused Prime Minister Nawaz Sharif of poor administration, corruption and nepotism, forcing him to resign in April 1993. The National Assembly was dissolved and elections were announced for July. Sharif appealed to the Supreme Court and was reinstated in May. The dissolution of the Assembly was revoked and the call for elections cancelled.

[24] Sharif's return aggravated the conflict with President Ishaq Khan. Both leaders resigned in July. The interim president, Moin Kureishi, a former World Bank and IMF official, took unprecedented measures: he abolished the old system whereby members of parliament had received funds for investment in their own districts, a source of endless corruption, and also taxed large property units.

[25] Traditionally, powerful landowners had dominated Pakistan's economy and political system and had exempted themselves from paying taxes. At that time, only one per cent of the country's Pakistani migrant workers, then 139 million inhabitants paid taxes, but charges of tax evasion had never been filed.

[26] Benazir Bhutto returned to power in the October 6 1993 elections. The PPP won 86 of the Assembly's 217 seats, against 72 obtained by Sharif. Bhutto received the support of minor parties and was confirmed with 121 votes. Her position was strengthened with the election of Faruk Ahmed Leghari (also from the PPP) as president in November.

[27] Bhutto's efforts to bring democracy and equal rights to her country were tainted by political and ethnic violence in 1994 and 1995, the bloodiest years since 1971 when Bangladesh was formed. Karachi and the northern separatist areas were the center of disputes. Over 3,500 people died in confrontations between August 1994 and October 1995.

[28] In June 1996, hundreds of people protesting against the proscription of pro-independence candidates in local elections in Azad, Jammu and Kashmir were arrested.

[29] One of Benazir Bhutto's main political rivals, her brother Murtaza, died in a confrontation with police on September 20 1996. Murtaza commanded a guerrilla group demanding the prime ministers resignation. The Bhuttos had been rivals since their father was overthrown in 1977.

[30] In November 1996, Benazir was forced to resign as Prime Minister, charged with corruption, and new

PROFILE

ENVIRONMENT

Pakistan is mountainous and semi-arid, with the exception of the Indus River basin in the east. This is virtually the only irrigated zone in the country, suitable for agriculture and vital to the local economy. The Indus rises in the Himalayas in the disputed province of Kashmir and flows into the Arabian Sea. The majority of the population live along its banks. The main agricultural products are wheat and cotton, grown under irrigation. The country's main industry is the manufacture of cotton goods. Pakistan suffers from water shortage, soil depletion and deforestation.

SOCIETY

Peoples: Pakistan has a complex ethnic and cultural composition, basically Indo-European combined with Persian, Greek and Arab in the Indus Valley, plus Turkish and Mongolian in the mountainous areas. Much Indian immigration has occurred in recent years. There are 5 main ethnic groups: Punjabi, Sindhi, Pashtun, Mujahir and Baluch. Pakistan is also host to some 3 million refugees, mainly from Afghanistan.
Religions: Islam is the official religion followed by 97 per cent of the population (most belong to the Sunni sect); 2 per cent are Christian;1.6 per cent are Hindu; the remainder belong to other smaller sects.
Languages: Urdu (official, although it is spoken by only 9 per cent of the population). Other languages are Punjabi, Sindhi, Pashto, Baluchi, English and several dialects.
Political Parties: Operating under the military regime. Pakistan People's Party (PPP); Awami National Party, Baluchistan National Party; Republican National Party; Jamaa-e-Islami (Islamic Assembly).
Social Organizations: The National Pakistan Federation of Unions.

THE STATE

Official Name: Islam-i Jamhuriya-e Pakistan. **Administrative divisions:** 4 provinces, 1 territory (Federally Administered Tribal Areas) and 1 capital territory (Islamabad). **Capital:** Islamabad 1,018,000 people (1999). **Other cities:** Karachi 11,800,000 people; Lahore 5,470,000; Faisalabad 2,136,000 (2000). **Government:** General Pervez Musharraf, Prime Minister since 1999 and self-appointed President since June 2001. After the 1999 military coup, Parliament was dissolved. **National Holidays:** August 14, Independence Day (1947); March 23, Proclamation of the Republic (1956). **Armed Forces:** 587,000 (1996). **Other:** 275,000 (National Guard, Border Corps, Maritime Security, Mounted Police).

parliamentary elections were held. The Pakistan People's Party was defeated, receiving only 19 seats out of the 217 at stake, compared to the 136 won by the followers of former prime minister Nawaz Sharif. Miraj Khalid led the Government as Deputy Prime Minister until Sharif came to office once again in early 1997.

[31] Armed confrontations between India and Pakistan continued in the Kashmir region. Negotiations between New Delhi and Islamabad were still at a halt: while India maintained the zone belonged to them and that its future was 'not negotiable', Sharif's government called for a referendum to be held on self-determination. Tension between the two countries worsened in May 1998, when India carried out a series of controlled nuclear explosions and Pakistan responded with its own atomic tests.

[32] On October 12 1999, General Pervez Musharraf, who had been in charge of the military operations in Kashmir, led a coup after Prime Minister Sharif ordered that the General be stripped of military power. Sharif was then imprisoned by the army, who accused him of kidnapping, terrorism and attempted murder for endangering the lives of people on board the airplane transporting Musharraf on his return to Islamabad. Pakistan became the first nuclear power to have a military leadership.

[33] The military government tried the former Prime Minister, and his lawyers received constant death threats. Leading defense lawyer, Iqbal Raad was murdered inside his own office. While Musharraf blamed the murder on terrorists, Sharif's supporters accused the Government of committing the murder.

[34] Sharif was freed on December 10 and, along with his family, was exiled in Saudi Arabia. The Government declared that the former Prime Minister had been granted a 'Presidential pardon' and had been allowed to leave the country to receive medical treatment. Sharif had renounced his personal and professional fortune, valued in 500 million rupees ($8 million) and promised not to return to Pakistan in the following decade nor to participate in the country's politics for 21 years.

[35] The first stage of the local elections was held in late December, in 18 of the 106 districts. Turnout had reached 43.5 per cent, according to official data, while the opposition claimed only 20 per cent had voted. Although officially the elections did not follow party lines, most of the candidates were supported by the LM and the PPP. Analysts observed a change in control of the electoral scene, which went from the political parties to

the local feudal families.

[36] In February, the Supreme Court ordered the military rulers to present a schedule to call new general elections. Musharraf, who had announced he would obey a previous decision by the Supreme Court to call elections within 3 years, this time declined to announce dates.

[37] By March, the second stage of local elections had been held in 20 districts, and the pressure had grown on the President to present a clear schedule to return to a democratic system in October 2002. Meanwhile, the police detained more than 2,000 activists from the Alliance for the Restoration of Democracy and 22 of its leaders, who were planning a demonstration.

[38] Musharraf became head of state and was appointed President on June 20 2001, announcing he would maintain the powers he had as head of the executive branch, and that he would remain as commander of the army. On October 6, Musharraf extended his mandate indefinitely as Supreme Commander of the Army, which he should leave after three years in the post, after having received the approval of the military and Cabinet members.

[39] A summit was held in mid July in Agra, (India) between Indian Prime Minister Bihari Vajpajee and Musharraf, but it did not solve the problems. India accused Pakistan of having impeded an agreement by making Kashmir the focus of the talks, instead of going on to other issues. Islamabad replied the disagreement was caused by the insistence of Indian officials in changing the text of an agreement already approved by the rulers of both countries.

[40] After the terrorist attacks on September 11 2001 against New York and Washington, the United States announced it would lift economic and military sanctions it had imposed on India and Pakistan after the nuclear tests of 1998. The measure was motivated by Musharraf's support for the US military operation in Afghanistan, against the Taliban regime that harbored Saudi-born terrorist Osama Bin Laden. The Taliban, which ruled in Kabul, had formerly received direct military, economic and ideological support from Pakistan. The Taliban's assumption of power in 1996 had been considered by members of the Pakistani army as their first 'victory'.

[41] The US bombings over Afghanistan caused extensive protests from Islamic Pakistani groups. Musharraf made changes in the army shortly before the US military operations began in the neighboring country, releasing some pro-Islamic generals from strategic posts.

[42] When US Secretary of State

Colin Powell visited Islamabad in October, Musharraf requested Washington's support in the Kashmir conflict, as well as aid for the economic consequences produced by the huge inflow of around Afghan refugees. Pakistan and Iran host together over 3 million refugees from Afghanistan, many from earlier conflicts in the war-torn country.

[43] After a suicide attack on the Indian Parliament in Delhi by Islamic activists on December 13, India blamed Pakistan for the action. Musharraf condemned the attack and denied that his government had supported those responsible for it. On December 26, India deployed troops and planes on its border with Pakistan, increasing the tension in Kashmir. While Indian and Pakistani troops exchanged fire along the border, on December 30 Pakistani authorities detained Mohammed Saeed, the leader of one of the militant groups blamed for the attack on Parliament. On January 4, during the summit of the South Asian Association for Regional Cooperation, Musharraf extended a 'hand of friendship' to Indian prime minister Vajpayee.

[44] On March 18, attackers threw grenades inside a Protestant church in Islamabad, killing five people and injuring over 45. No group claimed responsibility for the attack, but the Government blamed Islamic militants, in line with the terrorist hunt initiated by Musharraf under international pressure. A US journalist, Daniel Pearl, was kidnapped in January 2002 and later murdered by islamic militants.

[45] In early April 2002, Musharraf launched a referendum campaign to persuade the public to vote for him as President for 5 more years. The Constitution states the President of Pakistan must be chosen by Parliament, which would be elected in October that year. The opposition firmly opposed the call for a referendum, but the Supreme Court supported it and it was scheduled for April 30. Musharraf won it with 97 per cent of the vote, although human rights groups, and local and international observers denounced the elections as fraudulent.

[46] In June 2002 there was a marked drop in incursions by militants fighting Indian rule in Kashmir. Although Indian Defense Minister George Fernandes said Indian troops will remain along the border with Pakistan as long as necessary, tensions almost ended following the intervention by the US, Russia and other countries.

[47] In September a prominent al-Qaeda member was arrested in Karachi. ■

DEMOGRAPHY

Population: 148,721,000 (2002)
Annual growth: 2.6 % (1985-2000)
Estimates for year 2015: 204,267,000 (2000)
Annual growth to year 2015: 2.5 % (2000)
Urban population: 37.0 % (2000)
Urban growth: 3.9 % (2000)
Children per woman: 5.3 (2000)

HEALTH

Life expectancy at birth: 61 years (2000-2005)
male: 61 years (2000-2005)
female: 61 years (2000-2005)
Infant mortality: 85 per 1,000 (2000)
Under-5 child mortality: 110 per 1,000 (2000)
Daily calorie supply: 2,462 per capita (1999)
57 doctors per 100,000 people (1997)
Safe water: 90 % (2000)

EDUCATION

Literacy: 43 % (2000)
male: 58 % (2000)
female: 28 % (2000)
School enrolment (net):
Primary total: 46 % (1994/2000)
male: 84 % (1995/99)
female: 60 % (1995/99)
Secondary (gross):
male: 33 % (1995/97)
female: 17 % (1995/97)
Tertiary (gross): 4 % (1997)
Primary school teachers: one for every 32 pupils (1998)

COMMUNICATIONS

30 newspapers (1997), 105 radios (1997), 131 TV sets (2000) and 22 main telephone lines (2000) per 1,000 people

ECONOMY

Per capita, GDP: $ 1,928 (2000)
Annual growth: 1.9 % (2000)
Annual inflation: 4.4 % (2000)
Consumer price index: 141.9 (2000)
Currency: 60.1 rupees = $ 1 (03/2002)
Cereal imports: 1,054,474 metric tons (2000)
Food import dependency: 14 % (2000)
Fertilizer use: 1,330 kg per ha (1999)
Exports: $ 9,575 million (2000)
Imports: $ 11,762 million (2000)
External debt: $ 32,091 million (2000); $ 227 per capita (2000)
Debt service: 28.3 % of exports (1999)
Development aid received: $ 732 million (1999); $ 5.4 per capita (1999); 1.30 % of GNP (1999)

ENERGY

Consumption: 439.7 Kgs of oil equivalent per capita yearly (1998); 26.3 % imported (1999)

HDI (ranking/value): 127 / 0.498 (1999)

Palau

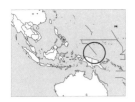

Population: 20,000 (2002)
Land area: 460 SQ KM
Capital: Koror
Currency: US dollar
Language: English

Belau

Five thousand years ago, sailors from China peopled the islands of Micronesia, forming highly stratified societies where age, sex and military prowess defined rank and wealth.

[2] European colonization in the 19th century, did not totally eliminate the indigenous peoples of Palau as it had on other islands.

[3] In 1914, the Japanese took the islands from Germany who had bought them from Spain in 1899. During World War II, Japan installed its main naval base in Palau and it soon became the scene of fierce combat when the US recognized its strategic position in relation to the Philippines.

[4] By the end of World War II, the indigenous population of Palau had been reduced from 45,000 to 6,000. Micronesia became a US trust territory. The US used the islands as nuclear testing grounds and reneged on promises of self-government, instead fostering economic dependence.

[5] In 1978, at the beginning of the transition to self-government, the archipelago opted for separation from Micronesia. In January 1979, the new constitution banned all nuclear weapons installations, nuclear waste storage, and foreign land ownership. A further amendment established a 200-mile area of territorial waters under the UN-approved Law of the Sea, which the US tried to veto.

[6] The new constitution received majority approval of assembly members, but the US put pressure on the local parliament to change provisions which would frustrate their attempts to use Palau as a military base. In July 1979, a referendum showed 92 per cent support for an unamended constitution. Bending to US pressure, the local Supreme Court annulled the referendum and entrusted Palau's parliament to draft a 'revised' constitution. In October 1979, this document was rejected by 70 per cent of the voters, and In July 1980, a third referendum ratified the original document by a 78 per cent majority.

[7] In 1981, International Power Systems (IPESCO) scheduled the installation of a 16-megawatt nuclear power plant in Palau; the scheme was to be financed by the US, subject to amendments to the anti-nuclear constitution.

[8] President Haruo Remliik was persuaded to hold another plebiscite to decide on the IPESCO plan and a 'Compact of Free Association' with the US. The Compact received majority support, but failed to achieve the 75 per cent needed to override the constitution. In 1983, despite this ambiguous ballot, the President signed agreements for a loan totaling $37.5 million. UN intervention was immediately called for by the opposition.

[9] In 1984, the power plant was built and the following year, Remliik refused to call a third referendum when the US proposed to revoke the historic anti-nuclear constitution. A few days later he was assassinated.

[10] The Palau Congress amended the Constitution by a referendum requiring a simple majority, and on August 21 1987, a further plebiscite approved the Compact. However, in April 1988, the constitutional amendment was invalidated by the Supreme Court, stating the 75 per cent majority requirement.

[11] In August 1988 President Salii was found dead from a gunshot wound. The official version was suicide.

[12] In early 1992 Palau requested Japanese aid to patrol its territorial waters and keep a check on illegal Indonesian vessels in return for fishing rights.

[13] The status of Free Associated State was approved by referendum in July 1993, with 68 per cent of the vote. The new regime came in a year later.

[14] In November 1996, Kuniwo Nakamura was made President in the first presidential elections since independence.

[15] Despite Chinese opposition, Palau slated diplomatic relations with Taiwan in 1999. This coincided with an aggressive Taiwanese policy of getting the recognition of small Pacific States in return for economic aid.

[16] In 2001, Tommy Remengesau, who had been Vice-President, was sworn in as leader after taking 52 per cent of the vote in the January general elections.

[17] Remengesau authorized US naval bases in Palau for personnel deployed in Okinawa, Japan.

[18] The Consultative Council, the parliamentary body advising on traditional law, urged the Government to authorize exploration rights to a Canadian oil company. President Tommy Remengesau, Jr. opposed to any exploration for oil and natural gas in the country. In November 2001 he said a referendum should be held to decide about this.

[19] In May 2002, Tommy Remengesau vetoed a bill that would have allowed the operation of slot machines, pachinko games and a casino. ■

Palestine

Population: 3,433,000 (2002)
Land area: 6,220 SQ KM
Capital: Jerusalem (Al-Quds Ash Sharif)
Language: Arabic

Filistin

Around 4000 BC, the Canaanites, a Semitic people from the inner Arabian peninsula, settled in the land which became known as Canaan and later, Palestine. The Jebusites, one of the Canaanite peoples, built a settlement that they called Urusalim (Jerusalem), meaning 'the city of peace'.

[2] The Egyptian Pharaohs occupied part of Canaan in 3200 BC, building fortresses to protect their trade routes, but the country kept its independence. Around 2000 BC, another Semitic people, Abraham's Hebrews, passed through Palestine on their way south. Seven centuries later, twelve Hebrew tribes returned from Egypt, following Moses. There was fierce fighting over possession of the land. The Bible records that 'The sons of Judah were unable to exterminate the Jebusites that dwell in Jerusalem' (Joshua 15, 63).

[3] Four centuries later, Isaac's son David managed to defeat the Jebusites and unite the Jewish nation. After the death of his son Solomon the Hebrews split into two states, Israel and Judah. These later fell into the hands of the Assyrians, in 721 BC, and Chaldeans, in 587 BC. It was in 587 that Nebuchadnezzar destroyed Jerusalem and took the Jews into captivity in Babylon.

[4] In 332 BC, Alexander the Great conquered Palestine, but the territory returned to the Egyptian Empire of the Ptolemies soon after his death. The country was subdued by the Seleucids from Syria before a rebellion, headed by Judas Maccabeus, restored the Jewish state in 67 BC.

[5] In 63 BC, the Roman Empire seized Jerusalem, placing the city under its domination. Maccabeans, Zealots and other Jewish tribes resisted the invaders but were fiercely subdued. Solomon's temple was demolished around 70 AD, and the Jews were expelled from Jerusalem around 135 AD.

[6] The Romans gave Palestine its present name, and Roman domination was followed by that of the Byzantine Empire (the Roman Empire in the East), which lasted until 611 when the province was invaded by the Persians. The Arabs, a Semitic people from the inner peninsula, conquered Palestine in 634, and, according to legend, it was

Jewish State, UN Plan, 1947
Arab State, UN Plan, 1947
1 West Bank

Jewish State, UN Plan, 1947
Annexed to Israel in the 1948 war
2 Gaza Strip

Israel's pre-1967 borders
Occupied by Israel in 1967
Recovered by Palestine from 1994: Gaza Strip, Jericho, Nablus, Ramallah
Israeli incursions into the West Bank and Gaza Strip have continued

in Jerusalem that the prophet Muhammad rose to the heavens. As a result, the city became a holy place for all three monotheistic religions.

[7] The Islamic faith and the Arabic language united all the Semitic peoples except for the Jews. With short intervals of partial domination by the Christian Crusaders and the Mongols in the 11th, 12th and 13th centuries, Palestine had Arab rulers for almost 1,000 years and Islamic governments for 15 centuries.

[8] In 1516, Jerusalem was conquered by the Ottoman Empire which maintained power until the end of World War I. During this conflict, the British promised Shereef Hussein the independence of the Arab lands in exchange for his cooperation in the struggle against the Turks. At the same time, in 1917, British Foreign Secretary Lord Balfour promised the Zionist Movement the establishment of a 'Jewish National Homeland' in Palestine.

[9] Britain had no power at all over the area, either *de facto* or *de jure*, but it soon obtained this right by defeating the Turks, with the

help of Arab allies, with a League of Nations mandate in 1922. Massive immigration raised the Jewish population of Palestine from 50,000 at the beginning of the century to 300,000 prior to World War II (see Israel).

[10] The Palestinians staged a general strike in April 1936 in protest against this immigration, which they saw as a threat to their rights. The British put forward a plan for the partition of Palestine into three states: Jewish in the north, Arab in the south, and a third section under British administration in the Jerusalem-Jaffa (Tel Aviv) corridor. The Arabs rejected the plan and rebellion broke out, lasting until 1939, when London gave up the idea and set limits to immigration.

[11] Once World War II was over, Britain handed the problem over to the newly-established United Nations.

[12] When the UN General Assembly approved a new partition plan (1947) 749,000 Arabs and 9,250 Jews lived in the territory where the Arab State would be set up, while 497,000 Arabs and 498,000 Jews lived

in the part which was to become the Jewish state.

[13] To drive the Palestinians from their land, a detachment of the Irgun organization commanded by Menachem Begin raided the village of Deir Yasin on April 9 1948, killing 254 civilians. 10,000 terrified Palestinians left the country.

[14] On May 14 1948, Israel unilaterally proclaimed itself an independent country. Neighboring Arab armies immediately attacked, but were unable to prevent the consolidation of the Jewish State. On the contrary, the latter emerged from the 1949 war with a land area larger than that proposed by the United Nations.

[15] More than half of Palestine's inhabitants had abandoned their homes: most of them lived as refugees on the West Bank, a territory which had been annexed by the Hashemite kingdom of Transjordan, and in the Gaza Strip, which was under Egyptian administration.

[16] In the eyes of the United Nations and therefore of

international law, the Palestinians were not a people but simply refugees, a 'problem' to be solved.

[17] Political decisions about the Palestinian cause were left entirely in the hands of the Arab governments, who even had the right to appoint the Palestinian representative to the Arab League. At the 1964 Arab summit, Egyptian leader, Gamal Abdel Nasser, asked the League to take on the task of forging a united Palestinian organization.

[18] In Jerusalem, on May 27, the Palestine National Council met for the first time. There were 422 participants, including personalities, business leaders, representatives of the refugee camps, the trade-union organizations, and the young people's and women's groups; they founded the Palestine Liberation Organization (PLO).

[19] Palestinian groups already operating secretly, such as Al Fatah, were wary of this Arab-promoted organization as they distrusted its emphasis on using diplomatic channels for its struggle. They were convinced that their land could only be recovered by military force.

[20] On January 1 1965, the first armed operation took place in Israel. The attacks intensified during the following months, until the outbreak of the Six Day War in 1967, when Israel occupied all of Jerusalem, Syria's Golan Heights, Egypt's Sinai Peninsula, the Palestinian territories of the West Bank and the Gaza strip. The defeat of the regular Arab armies strengthened the conviction that guerrilla warfare was the only path.

[21] In March 1968, during a battle in the village of Al-Karameh, Palestinians forced the Israelis to withdraw. The event passed into folk history as the first victory of the Palestinian force.

[22] With their prestige thus restored, the various armed groups joined the PLO and obtained the support of the Arab governments. In February 1969, Yasser Arafat was elected chairman of the organization.

[23] The growing political and military strength of the Palestinians was seen as a threat by King Hussein of Jordan, who had acted as their representative and spokesman. Tension mounted between the King and the Palestinians eventually reaching explosive proportions. In September 1970, after much bloody fighting, the PLO was expelled from Jordan to set up its headquarters in Beirut.

[24] This new exile reduced the possibility of armed attacks on targets inside Israel, and new radical groups such as 'Black September' directed their efforts towards Israeli institutions and businesses in Europe and other parts of the world. Palestinians, until then regarded by world opinion purely as refugees, quickly came to be identified by some as terrorists.

[25] PLO leaders promptly realized the need to change their tactics and, without abandoning armed struggle, launched a large-scale diplomatic offensive, starting to devote much of their energy to consolidating Palestinian unity and identity. The Algiers Conference of Non-Aligned Countries (1973) identified the Palestine problem, and not Arab-Israeli rivalry, as the key to the conflict in the Middle East for the first time.

[26] In 1974, an Arab League summit conference recognized the PLO as 'the only legitimate representative of the Palestinian people'. In October of the same year the PLO was granted observer status in the UN General Assembly, which recognized the right of the Palestinian people to self-determination and independence, and condemned Zionism as 'a form of racism'.

[27] The PLO program aimed to set up 'a secular and independent state in the whole of the Palestinian territory, where Muslims, Christians and Jews can live in peace, enjoying the same rights and duties'. This necessarily implied the end of the present state of Israel. Without giving up this ultimate goal, the PLO has gradually come to accept the 'temporary solution' of setting up an independent Palestinian state 'in any part of the territory that might be liberated by force of arms, or from which Israel may withdraw'.

PROFILE

ENVIRONMENT

In terms of international law 'Palestine' is the 27,000 sq km territory west of the Jordan River which the League of Nations handed over to Britain's 'mandatory' power in 1918. This territory comprises: the area occupied by Israel before 1967, 20,073 sq km; Jerusalem and its surroundings, 70 sq km; the West Bank area, 5,879 sq km and the Gaza Strip, 378 sq km. It is a land of temperate Mediterranean climate, fertile on the coast and in the Jordan Valley. It is surrounded in the south and the northeast by the Sinai and Syrian deserts respectively. The Gaza region suffers from a severe scarcity of water. The accumulation of waste water and refuse make the refugee camps highly contaminated. Soil erosion and deforestation are also serious problems.

SOCIETY

Peoples: Palestinians are an Arab people. In 1997 estimates put nearly seven million Palestinians living in Palestine and abroad. There are 700,000 in Israel; 1,500,000 on the West Bank; 800,000 in the Gaza Strip, and the rest spread in Middle Eastern (Jordan 2,170,000; Lebanon 395,000; Syria 360,000; other Arab countries 517,000) and European countries. 33 per cent of the inhabitants of the occupied territories live in refugee camps. There are large Palestinian populations in US, Chile, Brazil and other countries.
Religions: Muslim (mostly Sunni) 97 per cent; Christians of the Eastern Orthodox 3 per cent.
Languages: Palestinians speak Arabic and often also use Hebrew in the occupied territories, a language with the same Semitic root which is more similar to Arabic than to the European languages of immigrants.
Political Parties: The main political organization represented in the Palestine Liberation Organization (PLO) is the Al-Fatah National Liberation Movement, founded in 1965 by Yasser Arafat. The Popular Front for the Liberation of Palestine (PFLP), the second largest party, founded in 1967 by George Habash,

with a Marxist-Leninist orientation like the Democratic Front for the Liberation of Palestine (DFLP), led by Nayef Hawatmeth. Al-Saika (Sa'iqa), pan-Arabist, founded in 1966, led by 'Isam al-Qadi (Secretary General from 1979), has brought in the Palestinians who support the Syrian Ba'ath Party; the Arab Liberation Front, (Current Secretary General is Rakad Salem), pan-Arabist, have close links with the Iraqi Ba'ath Party; The General Command (al-Qiyada al-'amma)-DFLP, split from the DFLP, led by Talal Naji (Deputy secretary-general); The Palestinian People's Party (PPP-Hizb al-Sha'b, previously Palestine Communist Party) led by Mustafa Barghuthi, Hana Amira and 'Abd al-Majid Hamdan; The Palestinian Revolutionary Communist Party (al-Hizb al-Shuyu'i al-Thawri al-Filastini), led by 'Arabi 'Awwad. The Hamas group, very influential in Gaza and the West Bank, is opposed to Oslo process and autonomy agreements, led by Khalid Misha'al (president of Hamas Political Bureau), Abdel Aziz Rantisi (Hamas spokesman in Gaza), Abu Marzuq (member of Hamas Political Bureau), Ibrahim Ghousheh (Hamas spokesman), Jamal Mansour (Hamas leader in the West Bank). Islamic Jihad (Al-Jihad al-Islami), led by Jamal Amar, Ramadan Shallah, Ziyad Nahala, Ibrahim Shihada and Ahmad Muhana.
Social organizations: Palestinian Labor Federation; General Union of Palestine Women; Addamir (prisoners' association).

THE STATE

Official name: As-Sulta Al-Watania Al-Filistiniya.
Capital: Jerusalem (Al-Quds Ash Sharif), 668,000 people (1999), has traditionally been the capital of Palestine; the Palestine National Authority (PNA) is in Jericho, 14,744 people (1997).
Government: Yasser Arafat, President of the Palestine National Authority since July 1994, re-elected in January 1996. The Autonomous Council acts as a Parliament.
Armed Forces: there are no official data available.

28   In 1980, the Likud prime minister, Menachem Begin and Egyptian president Anwar Sadat signed a peace accord at Camp David, with US mediation. Shortly afterwards, Begin began officially to annex the Arab part of Jerusalem, proclaiming it the 'sole and indivisible capital' of Israel. Jewish settlements on the West Bank multiplied, using Palestinian lands and increasing tension in the occupied territories. Successive United Nations votes against these measures, or for any action against Israel, were stripped of any practical value by the US using its veto in the Security Council.

29   In July 1982, in an attempted 'final settlement' of the Palestine issue, Israeli forces invaded Lebanon. The intention, as it later became clear, was to destroy the PLO's military structure, capture the greatest possible number of its leaders and combatants, annex the southern part of Lebanon and set up a puppet government in Beirut. Surrounded in Beirut, the Palestinian forces only agreed to withdraw after receiving guarantees of protection for civilians under a French-Italian-North American international peace-keeping force.

30   The massacres that took place at the refugee camps of Sabra and Chatila by the Southern Lebanese Army under orders from Israeli Defense Minister Ariel Sharon, showed the ineffectiveness of international protection, but the PLO managed to transform what seemed a final defeat into a political and diplomatic victory. The headquarters of the organization were moved to Tunis and Yasser Arafat toured Europe receiving the honors due a head of state in various countries, most notably in the Vatican.

31   The PLO quietly initiated talks with Israeli leaders receptive to a negotiated settlement with the Palestinians. With the invasion of Lebanon, small but active peace groups emerged in Israel, demanding the initiation of a dialogue with the PLO. Palestinian radicals questioned these overtures, breaking with Yasser Arafats policies. This division of the PLO put its factions at odds with each other, sometimes causing violent confrontations.

32   In 1987, after several years of internal difficulties, the Palestine National Council met in Algiers with representatives from all Palestinian organizations, except those groups that favored direct action, and the internal structure of the PLO was rebuilt.

33   The official answer to the Arab protests was to increase the repression. But unlike what had happened on other occasions, this time the military intervention only managed to increase the number of women, elderly people and children taking part in the demonstrations. The more civilian casualties there were, the greater the hatred grew and the more demonstrations, strikes, and closures occurred. Funerals transformed into acts of open political defiance. This marked the beginning of the *intifada* or rebellion.

34   During the first few months of 1988 many Palestinians with Israeli citizenship participated in the strikes called by the so-called 'United Leadership of the Popular Uprising in the Occupied Territories'. This was the first instance of their joint political expression with Palestinians of the occupied territories.

35   In July 1988, King Hussein of Jordan announced that all economic and political links were being broken with the inhabitants of the West Bank. From that moment on, the PLO assumed sole responsibility for the territory's people.

36   At a meeting in Algeria on November 15 1988, the Palestine National Council proclaimed an independent Palestinian state in the occupied territories, citing Jerusalem as its capital. It also approved UN resolutions 181 and 242, which in effect meant accepting Israel's right to exist. Within the next 10 days, 54 countries around the world recognized the new state.

37   Arafat, elected president, was received in Geneva by the UN General Assembly, which had called a special session in order to hear him. The Palestinian leader repudiated terrorism, accepted the existence of Israel and asked that international forces be sent to the occupied territories. As a result of his speech, US president Ronald Reagan decided to initiate talks with the PLO.

38   When tensions began between Iraq and Kuwait in the second half of 1990, Arafat tried unsuccessfully to start negotiations between the countries. After the invasion, the Palestinian position seemed to strengthen when a parallel could be drawn between Kuwait and Palestine: if Iraq could be forced to submit to UN resolutions, then so could Israel.

39   When the war broke out, it was clear that the Palestine people were pro-Iraqi. This support deprived the PLO of the financial support of the rich Gulf emirates, who opposed the Iraqi regime.

40   In September 1991, in the closing session of the Palestine National Council, Yasser Arafat was confirmed as President of Palestine and of the PLO. The body accepted the resignation of Abu Abbas, the leader of the Palestine Liberation Front. Abbas had been given a life sentence in absentia by an Italian tribunal, for the hijacking of the *Achille Lauro* liner in 1985.

41   Between October 30 and November 4 1991, the first Peace Conference for the Middle East was held in Madrid, with support from the US and the former USSR. The Arab delegations unanimously demanded that the negotiations should be based on resolutions 242 and 338 of the UN Security Council. These resolutions forbade the acquisition of territories by force and recommended the granting of territories in exchange for peace agreements.

42   The Conference for the Middle East continued in Washington in December. No progress was made as far as the Palestinian issue was concerned, as Israel reaffirmed the validity of its own interpretations of the UN resolutions. At the end of the Conference, the Israeli delegation left satisfied because UN resolution 3379, defining Zionism as a form of racism, had been eliminated.

43   Following the Israeli elections of June 1992, the Labor leader and new prime minister Yitzak Rabin froze the settlement of new colonies in the Gaza strip and on the West Bank. However, it was difficult to restart negotiations that had been interrupted by the expulsion of 415 Palestinians from the Hamas group to Lebanon.

44   Secret negotiations between the PLO and Israel, with the active participation of Norwegian diplomats, resulted in mutual recognition in September 1993. The Declaration of Principles on the autonomy of the occupied territories granted limited autonomy to Palestinians in the Gaza strip and the city of Jericho in the West Bank. This autonomy was to be extended to the rest of the West Bank and, five years later, a definite status was to be negotiated for the occupied territories and the part of Jerusalem occupied by Israel since 1967.

45   Hamas and Hizbullah on the Palestinian side, as well as settlers in the occupied territories and far-right parties on the Israeli side, opposed the agreement. In a climate of hostility, Israeli military withdrawal from Gaza and Jericho anticipated for December 13 was postponed.

46   In May, 1994 Rabin and Arafat signed the 'Gaza and Jericho first' autonomy agreement, while Israeli withdrawal continued, enabling the return of several contingents of the Palestinian Liberation Army exiled in Egypt, Yemen, Libya, Jordan or Algeria.

47   Arafat arrived in Gaza in July and took office as head of the new

Palestine National Authority's Executive Council. The struggle between the PLO leader and his fundamentalist rivals became increasingly violent.

48 Once again, Gaza was on the brink of civil war in April 1995 when an explosion destroyed a building killing 7 people, including Kamal Kaheil, one of the leaders of the Ezzedin-El-Kassam brigades. In retaliation, suicide attacks by Hamas and Islamic Jihad caused the death of 7 Israeli soldiers and a US tourist, leaving 40 wounded. The Jihad's military wing said the attempt was a 'heroic suicide operation' and a 'gift for the soul of the criminal massacre's martyrs' - referring to the building explosion.

49 The tension continued, as did negotiations between Islamic fundamentalists and PLO leaders. Among other things, Arafat wanted Hamas to participate in the Palestinian general elections of January 1996, which would have legitimized his leadership. After negotiations, the fundamentalists decided to boycott the elections. Arafat was elected president with 87 per cent of the vote and government candidates won 66 out of the 88 seats.

50 Right-wing Likud leader Binyamin Netanyahu's election as Israeli Prime Minister (see Israel) in May 1996 aggravated tension between the countries.

51 The delicate negotiations which finally brought about the withdrawal of Israeli troops from the city of Hebron gave new support to the government led by Yasser Arafat. In January 1997, the Palestinian President highlighted again that the subject of Jerusalem's status was still pending and that, together with the formation of the Palestinian state, both were the next issues of the political agenda.

52 The Israeli decision to build a new settlement in the Har Homa hills, within the Palestinian sector in Jerusalem, was firmly rejected by the Palestine National Authority (PNA) and Western diplomats. The work started in March 1997, and led to fierce confrontations between Palestinians and the army, stalling the peace process. At the same time, the Israeli Government announced that it was going to return only 2 per cent of the West Bank to the PNA. Israeli President Ezer Weizman met Arafat as a gesture of good will, but he could not change Netanyahu's attitude nor the violent reaction of Palestinians. Soon afterwards, the PNA decided to apply capital punishment to those citizens who sold lands or houses to Israelis.

53 Israeli deferrals led Arafat to propose greater US participation in the negotiations. In April 2000, Ehud

Barak, Israel's new Prime Minister, accepted the suggestion, but Israel's position forced Arafat to postpone the declaration of a Palestinian State. Jerusalem, a holy city for Muslims and Jews, had become the biggest obstacle to the negotiations, since both parties wanted to install their capital in this city.

54 Violence broke out in September, after former Israeli Defense Minister Sharon visited a temple in Al Quds/Jerusalem, considered holy by Muslims and Jews. In the ongoing weeks, some 100 people died, mainly Palestinians. Arafat, Barak and US president Clinton, together with authorities from other countries, met in Egypt in October to try and salvage the peace process. However, the new intifada left Barak with a minority government, and he had to call new elections.

55 Sharon's victory in the Israeli elections of February 2001 was perceived as another blow to the weakened peace process. That month, the Secretary-General of the United Nations issued a document indicating that the economic blockade by Israel on the West Bank and Gaza Strip put Arafat's government on the verge of collapse for lack of income. The special UN envoy to the Middle East, Terje Road Larsen, warned that if other countries did not support Palestinians financially and urgently, violence would increase. According to the report, $1 billion was needed for the rest of the year.

56 Fighting increased during the following months. Israel's offensive and the stalled negotiations increased resistance to the occupation. Sharon replied with the selective murder of presumed terrorists, and extended his offensive to attacking Palestinian communities and towns with helicopters and gunships. These attacks were followed by night raids on Palestinian towns, which destroyed homes, airports and hospitals. Several hundred Palestinians died in the conflict, and military operations continued with the occupation of the territories that had been under relative Palestinian control.

57 After the attacks on the World Trade Center in New York and the Pentagon in Washington, on September 11 2001, Sharon believed international public opinion and Western governments could turn in his favor, and - counting on the support of the US - he increased the offensive against the Palestinian uprising. The new US President, George W Bush, needing to attract allies to his anti-terrorist campaign against the Taliban regime in Afghanistan, preferred to keep his

distance and avoid confrontations with the Arab world.

58 Numerous suicide attacks by radical Palestinian militants marked a new stage in the conflict. The suicide bombers of Hamas and Islamic Jihad, among other Islamic groups, chose places attended by Jewish young people to cause the greatest possible harm. To strengthen security, Sharon limited the traffic of goods and people through the borders of the West Bank and Gaza strip since the beginning of the uprising. The measure affected both Palestinian workers and businesses.

59 In December Sharon cut all his contacts with Arafat. The new Israeli strategy no longer acknowledged the Palestinian leader as a valid negotiator, and the break in relations also put an end to negotiation efforts. In early 2002, with the arrival of a new mediator from the US, Sharon lifted the restrictions imposed on Palestinians from the West Bank and Gaza, regions that were under the control of Jewish forces. On January 11, Islamic Jihad announced it would step up its actions, while Israel attacked PNA targets on land, sea and air in the largest offensive since the beginning of the second intifada.

60 Restrictions on the movement of goods and people in Israel and the occupied territories after 18 months of uprising placed the Palestinian economy on the verge of collapse. The continued closure of border checkpoints caused irreparable harm. Unemployment tripled, affecting almost 30 per cent of Palestinian labor. In spite of the relatively good financial performance of the PNA, the Government collected taxes that amounted to only one fifth of those collected in previous years. Donations from the Arab League and the European Union had increased in 2001, but not enough. The PNA had a budget deficit of $430 million and the estimated GDP in Gaza and the West Bank had fallen 12 per cent for the first quarter of 2002.

61 A summit of Arab countries was held in Beirut in March, to which Arafat could not attend because Sharon kept him cornered in his Ramallah bunker for more than a month. A group of 40 pacifists, 11 of them from the West, defied the Israeli army's siege and formed a 'human shield' to protect the Palestinian leader from a potential Israeli attack.

62 In spite of its initial chaos, the summit ended with the approval of a peace plan which included an historic decision. The signatory countries committed themselves to acknowledge the existence of the state of Israel, as long as it

withdrew to its pre-1967 borders and allowed the return of three million Palestinian refugees, as well as the creation of a Palestinian state with a sector of Jerusalem as its capital. Israel called the proposal 'unacceptable'.

63 In April, Al Fatah, Hamas, Islamic Jihad, People's Front and Democratic Front for the Liberation of Palestine, agreed for the first time a common fight plan 'to confront any Israeli attack'. Most of the 82 suicide bombers in Israel and the Jewish settlements since the beginning of the intifada were militants from those extremist organizations.

64 That month, Jenin refugee camp was the scene of bloody bombings from Israel, causing the death of hundreds of Palestinians. Terje Larsen, the UN envoy, called what happened in Jenin a 'morally repugnant humanitarian disaster', so Sharon declared him *persona non grata*. The Jenin camp was reduced to rubble. After the raids on this and other communities under the relative control of the PNA, Israel detained some 5,000 Palestinians.

65 After almost 40 days of siege, on May 10, 126 Palestinians who had taken refuge in the Church of the Nativity in Bethlehem, left the temple one by one. The first to leave - 13 men considered terrorists by Israel - were flown to Cyprus on a British plane, where they would remain until the European Union decided their final destination in several countries. Another 26 Palestinians, accused by Israel of minor offenses, were sent to the Gaza strip, while the rest were freed.

66 In mid-May Arafat declared that 'it was time for change', asserting he had made mistakes as a leader. In June 2002, Palestinian cabinet minister Saeb Erekat announced that presidential, parliamentary, and municipal elections would be held in January 2003. Erekat implied that the US position (falling in line with Sharon in saying they would not negotiate with Arafat) in Bush's speech was not a factor in the decision. 'Are we saying this in response to President Bush? We are saying this in response to Palestinian needs. We're saying this because we have been working on this reform for months', he said.

67 Israeli incursions continued in the West Bank and Gaza Strip. ∎

Panama

Population: 2,942,000 (2002)
Land area: 74,430 SQ KM
Capital: Panama City
Currency: Balboa
Language: Spanish

Panamá

The Chibcha civilization was one of America's great cultures, which developed in the Isthmus of Panama. They had a highly stratified society, developed elaborate architecture, crafted gold and had a wide scientific knowledge.

[2] In 1508, Diego de Nicuesa was given the task of colonizing what was known as the Gold Coast (present day Panama and Costa Rica). The enterprise ended in complete failure. In 1513, Vasco Nuñez de Balboa was sent to look for what was assumed to be a 'South Sea', and on the 25th of September he found the Pacific.

[3] The isthmus soon acquired great geopolitical significance. Panama became an important commercial center with merchandise distributed throughout America from San Francisco to Santiago. The Peruvian gold followed the opposite route, and the Ecuadorian straw hats are still called Panama hats because they were transported from there. The concentration of riches attracted English pirates and buccaneers; Francis Drake razed Portobelo in 1596 and Henry Morgan set fire to Panama in 1671.

[4] Panama was dependent upon the viceroyalty of Peru until 1717, when the Bourbons transferred it to the new viceroyalty of Granada, this was later to be a part of Greater Colombia when the country became independent from Spain in 1821.

[5] In 1826, Panama was selected by Simón Bolívar as the site of the Congressional Assembly which was to seal the continent's unity. But the economic decadence of the end of the 18th century, coupled with the change in commercial routes meant that Panama did not maintain its strategic importance after breaking with Spain, and did not become an independent nation with the disintegration of Greater Colombia in 1830.

[6] In 1831 Panama seceded from New Granada for a year, with the intention of forming a Colombian Confederation while maintaining autonomy. The state of Panama was created in 1855 within the Federation of New Granada (present-day Colombia).

[7] The first direct reference to the United States' 'right' of military intervention in Panama, is the Mallarino-Bidlak treaty of 1864 signed by the governments of Washington and Bogota. The document authorized the US to obtain a faster means of uniting the east coast with the west and to build a railroad across the isthmus; the Atlantic terminal was the Island of Manzanillo in the Bay of Limón. With the railway the US tried to offset British presence in the area, especially in Nicaragua.

[8] On January 1 1880, a French company started to build the Panama Canal. In 1891, the company was accused of fraud in its dealings, causing its eventual bankruptcy, though 33 km of the project had already been completed.

[9] In 1902, the US bought out the French company, and in January 1903, the Hay-Herran Treaty was signed with a representative of the Colombian Government. The treaty spelled out the terms of the construction and administration of the canal, granting the US the right to rent a 9.5 km-wide strip across the isthmus in perpetuity.

[10] The Colombian Senate rejected the treaty unanimously, considering it improper and an affront to Colombia's sovereignty. Only a revolution allowed the US to remain. The 'revolutionaries', supported by US marines, declared Panama's independence in November 1903, and the US recognized the new state within three days. While Theodore Roosevelt was President, the 'Big Stick' policy of sending troops into Central American states was common practice.

[11] A new treaty, the Hay-Buneau Varilla Treaty, granted the US full authority over a 16 km-wide strip and the waters at either end of the canal in perpetuity. Buneau Varilla, a former shareholder of the canal company and a French citizen, signed as the official representative of Panama. He received payment for his services in Washington, and did not return to Panama. The canal, covering a distance of 82 km, was officially dedicated on August 15 1914, and from then on was administrated and governed by the US.

[12] The Canal Zone brought incalculable wealth to the US, not so much in toll fees but in time and distance saved by vessels traveling between California and the East coast. US military bases in Panama functioned as an effective means of control over Latin America. Against the backdrop of the Cold War, American military instructors lectured Latin American military officers on the National Security Doctrine, a politico-military system which guaranteed loyalty to the US, including when necessary ousting legally constituted governments and replacing them with military dictators. Also, the financial center created in the isthmus became an initial foothold for the expansion of US transnational corporations and money laundering.

[13] In January 1964, 21 students died in an attempt to raise Panama's flag in the Canal Zone, still under US jurisdiction. The sacrifice of these young Panamanians transformed them into national martyrs.

[14] The demand for full sovereignty over the Zone was taken up by the Government of General Omar Torrijos. He rose to power in 1969, upon the dissolution of a three-member Military Junta which had overthrown President Arnulfo Arias in 1968. The diplomatic battle against the colonial enclave was waged in all the international forums and gained the support of the Latin American countries, the Movement of Non-Aligned Countries and the United Nations.

[15] The US finally agreed to open negotiations in favor of a new canal treaty, as the Panama issue was damaging its image in Latin America. The 1977 Torrijos-Carter Treaty (signed with US President Jimmy Carter) abrogated the previous one and provided for a Panamanian canal from the year 2,000. Amendments introduced by the US Senate, however, added provisions to the treaty that were contrary to Panamanian sovereignty. The US retained the right to intervene 'in defense of the Canal' even after expiration of the treaty, scheduled for December 31 1999.

[16] On July 31 1981 General Torrijos died in a suspicious airplane accident. Unconfirmed reports suggested that the plane's instruments were interfered with from the ground. President Aristides Royo, who succeeded Torrijos in 1978, lost the support of the National Guard and was forced to resign by his new commander-in-chief, Ruben Paredes. He started realigning the country's policies, adopting a pro-US stance.

[17] In 1983, Paredes was replaced as commander-in-chief of the National Guard by General Manuel Noriega. Presidential and legislative elections were narrowly won by Nicolas Barletta, the candidate of the Democratic Revolutionary Party, which was founded by Torrijos and supported by the armed forces. The opposition, led by veteran politician Arnulfo Arias brought accusations of fraud.

[18] Barletta encountered growing opposition to his economic policies, and resigned toward the end of 1985.

[19] He was succeeded by Eric del Valle, but the driving force continued to be General Noriega, whom the US targeted to overthrow.

A former protégé of the US Government, Noriega had not been forgiven by them for his unwillingness to collaborate in US plans to invade Sandinista-ruled Nicaragua. A 'settling of accounts' began, in which Noriega was accused of links with drug-traffickers and other crimes. The opposition united behind the National Civil Crusade, made up of parties of the right and center with broad support of the business community.

[20] In 1987 the US withdrew its economic and military aid. In 1988, it froze Panama's assets in the United States and imposed economic sanctions, including the cessation of payments for Canal operations. In March all the Panamanian banks closed for several weeks, provoking a financial crisis. American military presence increased. Del Valle overthrew Noriega, but the National Assembly backed the commander-in-chief and removed the President, replacing him with the Minister of Education, Manuel Solís Palma.

[21] Elections were called for May 5 1989. The official candidate was Carlos Duque and the opposition, the so-called Democratic Alliance of Civilian Opposition, put forward Guillermo Endara. Amid interference from the White House, which discredited the electoral process and its results even before it had taken place, the results of the ballot were kept secret for several days and, because they favored the opposition, the election was declared null and void.

[22] Solís declared that the US' objective was to set up a puppet government regardless of the election results and retain control of the Canal Zone, going back on the commitments it had assumed through the Torrijos-Carter treaty.

[23] An anti-Noriega uprising by a group of young officers failed in October 1989, and as the climax of a series of economic sanctions which destroyed the country's economy, the US invaded Panama. The attack began at dawn on December 20 1989 without prior declaration of war. Endara was installed as president at Fort Clayton, the American base, at the start of the invasion.

[24] This was the largest American military operation since the Vietnam War (1964-1973), with the mobilization of 26,000 troops. Indiscriminate bombing damaged heavily-populated neighborhoods. The invaders withheld all information concerning the number of people killed or injured, as well as figures for property damage. The number of dead is estimated at between 4,000 and 10,000, and the Chamber of Commerce estimated losses at more than $2 billion.

[25] The new government of Guillermo Endara abolished the National Defense Force and replaced it with a minor police agency, called the Public Force. In order to disarm the population, $150 was paid for each weapon that was turned in. American economic aid, which the new government had counted on, did not materialize and Endara himself began a hunger strike in order to obtain it. The Government had to accept the presence of US 'supervisors' in the ministries and the actions of the Southern Commando troops outside the canal zone in order to fight drug trafficking and Colombian guerrilla warfare.

[26] Washington's interest in the region waned after the defeat of the Sandinistas in Nicaragua, and so the economic crisis in Panama at the time of the invasion was never overcome. Independent sources put unemployment at 20 per cent in 1991.

[27] The Organization of American States called the invasion 'deplorable' and called for a vote on the withdrawal of troops; there were 20 votes in favor, one against (the US) and six abstentions. Britain supported the invasion and France vetoed the UN Security Council denunciation. In Latin America, only El Salvador supported the US invasion.

[28] In spite of this, control of the canal was given to Panama. In March 1991, a Panamanian took over the administration of the canal for the first time.

[29] In April 1991, Endara announced the end of his alliance with the Christian Democrat Party (PDC), dismissing five of their ministers. The Government's precarious stability was shaken by five coup attempts during its first two years. The Democratic Revolutionary Party (PRD), which won a significant victory in the by-elections of January 1991, called for general elections.

[30] In the course of General Noriega's trial, in 1991 in Miami, it was disclosed that the former leader had close connections with the US Drug Enforcement Agency (DEA) and the CIA. That same year it was discovered that President Endara's legal office had connections with 14 companies that laundered drug money. The DEA also disclosed that drug dealings had increased since the American invasion. In June 1992, Noriega was sentenced to 40 years in prison.

[31] The Government suffered a serious setback when, in a referendum on constitutional reform on November 15 1992, the people rejected the formal abolition of the Defense Force by 63.5 to 31.5 per cent. The Government was further weakened when the deputy vice-president, Christian Democrat Ricardo Arias Calderón, resigned on December 17 after accusing Endara of failing to deal with the social crisis.

[32] Foreign Minister Julio Linares was forced to resign in August 1993 as he had been involved in the sale of weapons to Serbian forces in Bosnia through the consulate in Barcelona.

[33] Economist Ernesto Pérez Balladares, former minister and admirer of Omar Torrijos, was

PROFILE

ENVIRONMENT

The country is bordered by the Caribbean in the north and the Pacific in the south. A high mountain range splits the country into two plains, a narrow one covered by rain-forests along the Atlantic slopes and a wider one with forests on the Pacific slopes. Panamanians generally say that their main resource is their geographic location, since the canal and the trade activities connected to it constitute the main economic resource of the country. Tropical products are cultivated and copper is mined at the large Cerro Colorado mines. Air and water pollution in both urban and rural areas is significant. 40 million tons of raw sewage are pumped into Panama Bay each year.

SOCIETY

Peoples: 64 per cent of the inhabitants are descendants from native Americans and European colonist immigrants. 14 per cent are of African descent. The three main indigenous groups are the Cunas on the island of San Blas in the Caribbean, the Chocoes in the province of Darien and the Guaymies, in the provinces of Chiriqui, Veraguas and Bocas del Toro.
Religions: 80 per cent Catholic, 10 per cent Protestant, 5 per cent Muslim, 1 per cent Baha'i, 0.3 per cent Jewish.
Languages: Spanish, official; several indigenous languages; most of the population speaks English.
Political Parties: the coalition New Nation integrated by the Revolutionary Democratic Party (RDP), founded by Omar Torrijos, the Solidarity Party and the National Liberal Party; the coalition Union for Panama integrated by the conservative Arnulfist Party, the Nationalist Republican Liberal Movement, the Democratic Party and the National Renewal Movement; and the Opposition Action coalition integrated by the Christian Democratic Party and the Civil Renewal Party.
Social Organizations: The National Council of Workers' Organizations (CONATO).

THE STATE

Official Name: República de Panamá.
Administrative divisions: 9 provinces and 4 indigenous territories.
Capital: Panama City 1,141,000 people (1999).
Other cities: San Miguelito 298,900 people; Colón 42,900; David 79,100 (2000).
Government: Mireya Moscoso, President since May 1999. Single-chamber parliament: Legislative Assembly, made up of 71 members, elected every 5 years by direct vote.
National Holiday: November 3, Independence (1903).
Armed Forces: The National Guard was declared illegal in June 1991.
Other: 11,000 National Police.

Millions US$ 2000

IMPORTS

3,850

EXPORTS

3,278

DEMOGRAPHY

Population: 2,942,000 (2002)
Annual growth: 1.8 % (1985-2000)
Estimates for year 2015: 3,451,000 (2000)
Annual growth to year 2015: 1.3 % (2000)
Urban population: 57.7 % (2000)
Urban growth: 2.3 % (2000)
Children per woman: 2.5 (2000)

HEALTH

Life expectancy at birth: 74 years (2000-2005)
male: 73 years (2000-2005)
female: 77 years (2000-2005)
Maternal mortality: 70 per 100,000 live births (1985/99)
Infant mortality: 20 per 1,000 (2000)
Under-5 child mortality: 26 per 1,000 (2000)
Daily calorie supply: 2,496 per capita (1999)
167 doctors per 100,000 people (1995)
Safe water: 90 % (2000)

EDUCATION

Literacy: 92 % (2000)
male: 93 % (2000)
female: 91 % (2000)
School enrolment (net):
Primary total: 91 % (1994/2000)
male: 91 % (1995/99)
female: 91 % (1995/99)
Secondary (gross):
male: 60 % (1995/97)
female: 65 % (1995/97)
Tertiary (gross): 33 % (1997)
Primary school teachers: one for every 23 pupils (1990)

COMMUNICATIONS

62 newspapers (1996), 300 radios (1997), 194 TV sets (2000) and 151 main telephone lines (2000) per 1,000 people

ECONOMY

Per capita, GDP: $ 6,000 (2000)
Annual growth: 1.0 % (2000)
Annual inflation: 1.5 % (2000)
Consumer price index: 106.0 (2000)
Currency: 1.0 balboas = $ 1 (03/2002)
Cereal imports: 382,365 metric tons (2000)
Food import dependency: 12 % (2000)
Fertilizer use: 668 kg per ha (1999)
Exports: $ 3,278 million (2000)
Imports: $ 3,850 million (2000)
External debt: $ 7,056 million (2000); $ 2,471 per capita (2000)
Debt service: 8.7 % of exports (1999)
Development aid received: $ 14 million (1999); $ 4.8 per capita (1999); 0.10 % of GNP (1999)

ENERGY

Consumption: 862.1 Kgs of oil equivalent per capita yearly (1998); 70.0 % imported (1999)

HDI (ranking/value): 52 / 0.784 (1999)

elected President in 1994 with 34 per cent of the vote. Balladares ran as candidate for the social democratic alliance Pueblo Unido (United People), made up of the PRD, the Liberal Republican Party and the Labor Party. Mireya Moscoso, from the right-wing Democratic Alliance, had 29 per cent and salsa singer Ruben Blades, from the Papa Egoro Movement, had 17 per cent. These were the first general elections held after the US invasion.

[34] In June 1994, the Kuna and Embera indigenous groups rejected the construction of a road through their autonomous territory. They were supported by environmentalist groups and the Catholic Church. The highway was to have crossed the 550,000 hectare rainforest called 'Darien's Barrier', declared a universal heritage by UNESCO. The 108-km highway would link Panama with Colombia. For years, this forest endured illegal logging of oak, cedar and mahogany. Likewise, the area has been devoted to coca cultivation and arms smuggling.

[35] A plan to assassinate Pérez Balladares and several cabinet members was uncovered in January 1995. Ten National Police members were arrested on charges of conspiracy but the investigation was shelved for lack of evidence.

[36] The country continued to have an active role in arms and drug traffic as well as money laundering. The explosion of a package during a routine drug inspection killed three officials and injured 25. The explosives, grenades and ammunitions, were being sent to Ecuador, supposedly to guerrilla groups. Two arms deposits were found in the capital, belonging to a Colombian citizen.

[37] The reform of the labor code, aimed at attracting foreign investment, led to an atmosphere of social violence and strikes, since it would reduce labor security and the freedom to unionize and negotiate collectively. Confrontations between workers and students with the police left 4 dead and 86 injured in August. However, the law was passed.

[38] Talks with the US over the transfer of the sovereignty of the Canal from 1999 seemed to point to the continuation of some form of US presence in Panama. In July 1996,

President Pérez Balladares announced that the Howard US Air Force Base would remain, in order to keep drug trafficking under control. The US army spent $319 million in Panama that year (5 per cent of the country's GDP).

[39] The announcement that US troops would remain in Panama was made after it became known Balladares had received money from the Colombian Cali cartel to fund his 1994 election campaign. The President admitted the fact but denied having known of the origin of the funds. This scandal was followed by the forced closure of the Agro-Industrial and Commercial Bank due to its excessive debts and drug money-laundering activities.

[40] In March 1997, the Government decreed price freezes on items like school books, milk, gas, sugar and medicines. The measure was designed to counteract the indiscriminate price increases complained of by the Free Competition Commission.

[41] In September, after 80 years' presence in Panama's territory, the Southern Command headquarters returned to the US, in Miami. The Government released statements guaranteeing that the operation of the Panama Canal would not be affected by its return to national ownership. It also announced plans for building a third set of lock gates in early 2000, due to the increase in traffic and the tonnage of the ships.

[42] After Balladares was defeated in a referendum in which he proposed to change the Constitution to allow for his re-election, the main candidates for the May 1999 elections were Mireya Moscoso, the widow of Arnulfo Arias, and Martín Torrijos, son of General Omar Torrijos. Moscoso won on a manifesto which proposed - as did her opponents - the avoidance of corruption and politicking in the administration of the Canal and also that both workers and ship owners were to be involved in decisions related to the Canal.

[43] On December 14, a ceremony was held to celebrate the return of the Canal to Panamanian jurisdiction. Moscoso and former US President Jimmy Carter - who had signed the treaty agreeing to return the Canal with Omar Torrijos in 1977

- put their seal on diplomatic addenda which ratified this. Carter stated it was 'one of the most important historic occasions in the hemisphere' and that with the vigorous development of trade, Panama now had the chance to 'become the Singapore of the region', making the most of the Canal, and the international financial center, which contained the offices of 120 banks of the world.

[44] The Government decided in November 2000 not to grant Vladimiro Montesinos, political asylum. He was a former Fujimori advisor accused in Peru of human rights abuses. Panama had been questioned by human rights groups for having granted asylum to two Haitian officers, living in the country since 1994 and who were accused of human rights violations and major crimes.

[45] Protests called in May 2001 by labor and student unions against the 66 per cent hike in public transport charges led to clashes with the police which left more than 100 injured and dozens arrested. The Government also raised taxes on essential services such as electricity, gasoline and telephones. Finally, after negotiations mediated by the Church, the measure was suspended.

[46] After the peace process with Colombian guerrillas ended, Panama increased its security forces along the border with Colombia, in case the conflict expanded to its territory. Panama also hosts hundreds of Colombian refugees escaping the guerrillas.

[47] In April 2002, the Truth Commission of Panama delivered its report. It had been formed by Moscoso to investigate what happened to the disappeared during the 1968-1989 military government, and clarified 110 of the 189 cases which had not been solved. During the investigation, the Commission carried out 35 excavations in old barracks and airports, finding 48 bodies. Some of the documents were supplied by the US Defense Department, which blamed the Defense Forces of the time for the crimes committed. ∎

Papua New Guinea

Population: 5,032,000 (2002)
Land area: 452,860 SQ KM
Capital: Port Moresby
Currency: Kina
Language: English

Papua New Guinea

apua New Guinea (PNG) has been inhabited by Melanesian peoples since 3,000-2,000 BC. Traditionally, its population lived in groups scattered throughout the dense tropical jungle, cut off from the outside world. As a result, over 700 dialects are spoken on New Guinea island and the smaller islands of the republic. One third of the population lives in the highlands, and many communities there were unfamiliar with the wheel, iron implements and Europeans until the 1930s.

[2] In a short time, PNG has passed from the stone age into the plastic age, and it currently faces an economic boom based on the exploitation of non-renewable natural resources (copper, gold, oil and hardwoods).

[3] The present state of Papua New Guinea was formed when the Territory of Papua, a British protectorate under Australian administration since 1906, was joined with New Guinea, a German colony until World War I. New Guinea was later administered by Australia under mandates, first from the League of Nations and then the United Nations.

[4] The process leading to self-government began in 1964 and culminated in the proclamation of independence in 1975. That same year, there was an unsuccessful attempt at secession by the island of Bougainville. This island has rich deposits of copper and gold and its population is ethnically closer to the Solomon Islanders than to the Papuans. Australia maintains a strong presence in PNG, providing considerable investment in business, and military and financial assistance.

[5] Papua New Guinea has strong links with Australia and in turn exercises a degree of leadership among South Pacific states. Its military contributed to suppressing a secession attempt by the island of Espiritu Santo (Vanuatu) in 1979, led by Jimmy Stevens, and backed by French authorities and US economic interests.

[6] In May 1988, Papua New Guinea together with Vanuatu and the Solomon Islands signed an agreement to defend and preserve traditional Melanesian cultures. It also expressed support for Kanaky's (New Caledonia) independence. Relations with the Government of Indonesia, which occupies the western portion of the island, West Papua, are troubled. The Free Papua independence movement operates in this province, and Indonesian military operations here in 1984 led 12,000 inhabitants to seek refuge in Papua New Guinea.

[7] In 1989, PNG strengthened its ties with Southeast Asia, signing a friendship and co-operation treaty with ASEAN and opening negotiations with Malaysia. At the same time, it granted the Soviets permission to open an embassy in Port Moresby. In December, a maritime agreement was signed with the Federated States of Micronesia that allowed PNG to take advantage of an existing multilateral fishing agreement between the South Pacific and the US.

[8] Two-thirds of the population are subsistence cultivators, and the 0.3 per cent that work with mining concerns generate 66 per cent of export earnings. Mines at Bougainville and Ok Tedi boasted the largest copper deposits in the world, as well as producing gold. The Porgera gold mine went into production in 1990, one of the largest in the world outside South Africa. Another on the island of Lihir may be even larger. The mines are exploited by transnationals, some of them Australian. Sizeable oil deposits have also been found and will be exploited only after a 175-mile oil pipeline is built, at a cost of $1 billion.

[9] Parliament reinstated the death penalty in August 1991, 34 years after it had been abolished. This move was denounced by Christian movements, feminists and human rights organizations. The National Council of Women feared that the reinstatement of the death penalty might lead to a return of 'bounty' payments in assassination cases, as has happened formerly.

[10] In June 1992, the Justice Department brought corruption charges against former Prime Minister Namaliu and his Finance Minister Paul Pora.

[11] The new Prime Minister, Palas Wingti pledged to increase the

WORKERS

2000

LABOR FORCE AS % OF TOTAL

■ FEMALE: 42% ■ MALE: 58%

LAND USE

DEFORESTATION: 0.4% annual (1990/95)

1993

■ FOREST & WOODLAND: 90.7%
■ ARABLE: 0.1%
■ OTHER: 9.2%

Per 100,000
live births

370

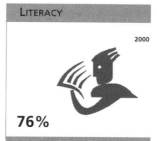

2000

76%

Millions US$ 1999

IMPORTS

1,503

EXPORTS

1,611

STATISTICS

DEMOGRAPHY

Population: 5,032,000 (2002)
Annual growth: 2.4 % (1985-2000)
Estimates for year 2015: 6,642,000 (2000)
Annual growth to year 2015: 2.2 % (2000)
Urban population: 17.4 % (2000)
Urban growth: 4.1 % (2000)
Children per woman: 4.5 (2000)

HEALTH

Life expectancy at birth: 58 years (2000-2005)
male: 57 years (2000-2005)
female: 59 years (2000-2005)
Maternal mortality: 370 per 100,000 live births (1985/99)
Infant mortality: 79 per 1,000 (2000)
Under-5 child mortality: 112 per 1,000 (2000)
Daily calorie supply: 2,186 per capita (1999)
7 doctors per 100,000 people (1998)
Safe water: 42 % (2000)

EDUCATION

Literacy: 76 % (2000)
male: 84 % (2000)
female: 68 % (2000)
School enrolment (net):
male: 79 % (1995/99)
female: 67 % (1995/99)
Secondary (gross):
male: 17 % (1995/97)
female: 11 % (1995/97)
Tertiary (gross): 2 % (1998)
Primary school teachers: one for every 36 pupils (1998)

COMMUNICATIONS

14 newspapers (1996), 86 radios (1997), 17 TV sets (2000) and 13 main telephone lines (2000) per 1,000 people

ECONOMY

Per capita, GDP: $ 2,280 (2000)
Annual growth: -2.1 % (2000)
Annual inflation: 15.6 % (2000)
Consumer price index: 175.1 (2000)
Currency: 3.6 kina = $ 1 (03/2002)
Cereal imports: 338,496 metric tons (2000)
Food import dependency: 18 % (2000)
Fertilizer use: 1,550 kg per ha (1999)
Exports: $ 1,611 million (1999)
Imports: $ 1,503 million (1999)
External debt: $ 2,604 million (2000); $ 541 per capita (2000)
Debt service: 9.6 % of exports (1999)
Development aid received: $ 216 million (1999); $ 45.8 per capita (1999); 6.00 % of GNP (1999)

HDI (ranking/value): 122 / 0.534 (1999)

---

country's participation in joint ventures with foreign capital. This triggered an angry reaction from PJV, an Anglo-Australo-Canadian consortium that controls 90 per cent of Porgera, the country's largest gold mine.

[12] Wingti was replaced in August 1994 by Julius Chan.

[13] Chan harshly denounced the French nuclear tests in the Pacific. After the second atomic test was carried out in October 1995, the Prime Minister of Papua New Guinea suspended talks between France and the South Pacific Forum, acting as president of the regional organization.

[14] The conflict in Bougainville worsened when Theodore Miriung was assassinated in 1996. He had been the main transitional authority on the island and had promoted a peace agreement. The Prime Minister was accused by a military leader of contracting international mercenaries to quell the secessionist forces . Consequently, representatives of the armed forces called for Chan to be sacked.

[15] Despite having parliamentary backing, the Prime Minister resigned in March 1997, and was replaced by an interim ruler, John Giheno. A few weeks later, Parliament appointed Bill Skate as Head of Government.

[16] In July 1997, in Aotearoa/New Zealand, the Government and secessionist rebels brought an end to the Bougainville crisis by signing a definitive peace agreement, including the demilitarization of the island and the deployment of UN peace-keeping troops. Australia promised funds for the rebuilding of Bougainville.

[17] The drought in other parts of the country caused extensive fires and also affected coffee production.

[18] In February 1998, 13 forestry companies closed down with the loss of 4,000 jobs as an indirect effect of the stock market and financial crisis in other Southeast Asian countries in 1997 and 1998.

[19] Skate's announcement of the opening of diplomatic relations with Taiwan, and that country's concession of a soft credit line worth $2.5 billion pushed Parliament into requesting the Prime Minister's resignation in July 1999.

[20] Mekere Morauta, leader of the opposition Popular Democratic Movement and former Central Bank governor, took a landslide majority of 99 votes to just 5 against and was appointed Prime Minister. Morauta immediately announced that the agreement with Taiwan, which had exasperated mainland China, would be invalidated.

[21] In order to make up for the loss of the Taiwanese loan, Morauta announced he would be appealing to the International Monetary Fund. The economic situation was becoming critical with inflation above 20 per cent per year and a large fiscal deficit.

[22] In November 2000, an earthquake measuring 8 on the Richter scale ravaged PNG. The cities of Rabaul and Kokopo were hit by giant waves or *tsunamis*, and a warning went out across the west Pacific region.

[23] Conversations between the Government and separatists ended in February 2001 without reaching a disarmament agreement. The talks, held in Australia, sought an autonomous government for Bougainville. It is thought that huge numbers of weapons remain hidden in Bougainville.

[24] In 2001, a group of soldiers rebelled in protest against government plans to downsize the army. Their outcry forced the Prime Minister to postpone his plans. However in March 2002, with the cuts on the horizon again, the rebels seized control of one of the largest barracks in the country, burning two of its facilities. ∎

PROFILE

ENVIRONMENT

Located east of Indonesia, just south of the Equator, the country is made up of the eastern portion of the island of New Guinea (the western part is the Indonesian territory of West Papua) plus a series of smaller islands; New Britain, New Ireland and Manus, in the Bismarck archipelago; Bougainville, Buka and Mussau, which form the northern part of the Solomon Islands group; the Louisiade and D'Entrecasteaux archipelagos; and the islands of Trobriand/Kiriwina and Woodlark, southeast of New Guinea.
The terrain is volcanic and mountainous, except for the narrow coastal plains. The climate is tropical and the vegetation is equatorial rainforest. The country suffers from deforestation, due to large-scale indiscriminate felling.

SOCIETY

Peoples: Papuans 85 per cent; Melanesians 15 per cent.
Religions: Many people follow local traditional religions but they also belong to Catholic (32.8 per cent) and Protestant (58.4 per cent) communities.
Languages: English (official). A local Pidgin, with many English words and Melanesian grammar is widely spoken, as well as 700 other local languages.
Political Parties: Popular Democratic Movement (PDM); Pangu Pati (PP); Popular Action Party; Popular Progressive Party (PPP).

THE STATE

Official Name: Independent State of Papua New Guinea.
Administrative Divisions: 20 Provinces.
Capital: Port Moresby 293,000 people (1999).
Other cities: Lae 112,400 people; Madang 33,900; Wewak 27,400; Goroka 17,900 (2000).
Government: Queen Elizabeth II, Head of State, represented since November 1997 by Governor General Silas Atopare. Mekere Morauta, Prime Minister and Head of the Government since July 1999. Single-chamber legislature: Parliament, with 109 members.
National Holiday: September 16, Independence Day (1975).
Armed Forces: 3,700 troops (1996).

Paraguay

Population:	5,778,000 (2002)
Land area:	397,300 SQ KM
Capital:	Asunción
Currency:	Guaraní
Language:	Spanish and Guaraní

Paraguay

There were three ethnic groups in the Paraguay River basin in the 16th century: the Guaranís in the center and the Guaycurús and Payaguás in the Chaco region to the south. The Guaranís cultivated cassava, squash, sweet potatoes and corn. They were settled agriculturalists, organized in villages headed by a *tubichá* (chief).

2 The Payaguás and Guaycurús were nomadic hunters and fishers. They periodically attacked the Guaraní plantations, leading the Guaranís to aid the Spaniards in the conquest of the Chaco area.

3 Spanish conquistadors sailed up the Paraná River in the mid-16th century, searching for the mythical silver mountains that gave the Río de la Plata (silver river) region its name. In 1537, Juan de Salazar founded the fort of Nuestra Señora de Asunción. This tiny settlement grew and became capital of the Río de la Plata Province for over a century.

4 Having failed to find precious metals in these 'worthless lands', it was only much later that Spanish colonizers were attracted by the wild cattle herds that prospered on the fertile plains of the Banda Oriental (today's Uruguay) and the humid Argentinian Pampas. A powerful oligarchy of trade merchants quickly developed in the ports of Buenos Aires (founded in 1580) and Montevideo (founded in 1726), and the former capital of the province, Asunción, declined.

5 A pre-capitalist system of large landed estates grew up around Buenos Aires and Montevideo. Meanwhile, in what is now Paraguay, the Jesuits organized a system of agricultural colonies in which the indigenous population worked the land and produced handicrafts on a communal basis. Private interests and the Spanish administration both resented this system, and the Jesuitas were finally expelled in 1767. The local people either became slaves on Brazilian sugarcane plantations or peasant laborers on large cattle ranches.

6 Although the Paraguayan province did not initially join the 1810 Liberal Revolution, the Asunción oligarchy ousted the Spanish Governor Velazco on May 14 1811, demanding free trade for *yerba mate* (a local tea) and tobacco.

7 This rebellion began a process which concentrated all the power in the hands of Gaspar Rodríguez de Francia, secretary to the junta that had overthrown Spanish rule and later appointed dictator. He was supported by the peasants, owners of small and medium-sized plots who wanted order and feared the 'anarchy' that was affecting the other provinces of the Río de la Plata Viceroyalty (that had been created in 1776). The oligarchy in Asunción, the new system's only enemy, was eliminated, and Paraguay withdrew into itself. Stimulated by public investment, industry began to develop, laying the foundations for Paraguay's future economic strength.

8 Paraguay continued to develop under the patriarchal governments of Gaspar Rodríguez de Francia (El Supremo), Carlos Antonio López and his son, Francisco Solano López. It remained cut off from the rest of the world for decades and was untouched by the British influence that was so greatly felt in the other newly independent Rio de la Plata provinces. Left to develop alone, the State assumed an important role in the country's economy, controlling agricultural production (yerba mate and high quality timber), and the

first railroads, telegraph system and steel furnaces in South America.

9 The leaders of Brazil, Argentina, and Uruguay - Pedro II, Bartolomé Mitre and Venancio Flores respectively - signed the Triple Alliance in 1865. With the support of the British Empire and the Baring Brothers' Bank, they began a 5-year war to eliminate Paraguay on the pretext of frontier disputes.

10 Sixty-two years later, Paraguay fought a second fratricidal war, this time against Bolivia, orchestrated by rival oil multinationals. The Chaco War (1932-1935) was won, but it cost Paraguay 50,000 lives.

11 In 31 years, there were 22 presidents, until the 1954 coup that brought General Alfredo Stroessner to power. Descended from Germans, and an admirer of Nazism, he gave refuge to war criminals fleeing Europe. Stroessner had himself re-elected seven times, the last time in February 1988. He allowed only a legal 'opposition', whose leaders he often appointed himself.

12 By the mid-1980s, the Stroessner regime was showing clear signs of weakening. Democratization processes elsewhere in Latin America doubtless contributed to this. Internal opposition was growing in a variety of forms: an Inter-Union

Labor Movement; a Permanent Assembly of Landless Rural Workers (APCT); indigenous people's organizations; and the Rural Women's Co-ordination Group. The Catholic church, through the Paraguayan clergy, began to voice the need for change.

13 On February 3 1989, General Stroessner was overthrown by a coup headed by his son's father-in-law, army commander General Andrés Rodríguez, who immediately called free elections for the following May to elect a government and legislators to see out Stroessner's term.

14 The elections, held on May 1 1989, were open to all political parties except the still-banned Communist Party. General Rodríguez was elected President with 68 per cent of the vote. The principal opposition group, the Authentic Radical Liberal Party led by Domingo Laíno, took 21 per cent. Despite the presence of foreign observers, voting was plagued by countless irregularities, attributed to the Colorado Party that was leaving power.

15 Nevertheless, opposition groups still considered the election to be the start of a democratization process, which was to be completed by 1993, with a Constituent Assembly convened, and a new constitution in place.

16 Transnationals became involved in the production of soybeans and cotton. At that time, 2 per cent of all landholders had 85 per cent of the land. Most of the companies and foreign settlers congregated along the border with Brazil on a strip of land 2000 km long and 65 km wide. The main language was Portuguese, and the Brazilian cruzeiro was common currency. Between 300,000 and 400,000 Brazilians lived in the border districts.

17 The World Bank-supported Caazapa and Caaguazu rural development projects involved the settlement and ranching of indigenous lands in eastern Paraguay. The Indians found themselves restricted to tiny pockets of their former territories. Twelve indigenous communities asked the Central United Workers (CUT) to represent them in the National Constitutional Assembly. In December 1991, in the first round

of elections to appoint representatives to this Assembly, the CUT gave its support to the 'Constitution for All' Movement.

[18] When the huge Itaipú hydroelectric plant on the border with Brazil went into operation, economic ties between the two countries increased.

[19] The first free municipal elections, held in June 1991, were marked by the emergence of the independent Asunción for All movement in the capital. Led by Carlos Filizzola, a 31 year-old doctor, the movement counted on the support of the United Workers' Center and various social groups, and was elected with more than 35 per cent of the vote.

[20] In the elections for the National Constituent Assembly in December, the Colorado Party took 60 per cent of the vote. The Authentic Radical Liberal Party (ARLP) of Domingo Laíno came second with 29 per cent and the Constitution for All Movement, led by Filizzola, came third.

[21] The Constitution of June 1992 replaced the one brought in by Stroessner in 1967. The presidents of the Republic, the Supreme Court and Congress did not take part in the public meeting held to announce the new constitution, which included broad dispensations for the protection of human rights and banned the death penalty for common crimes.

[22] The repeated accusations of widespread corruption within the armed forces, including drug trafficking, led to investigations. Warrants were issued for the arrest of leading generals, including the commander-in-chief of the army.

[23] In December 1992, Paraguay signed an agreement for the constitution of a common market: the Mercosur, which would come into operation in 1995, with Argentina, Brazil and Uruguay (see box in Brazil).

[24] In a climate influenced by threats of fraud and declarations from the military that they would keep the Colorado Party in power, ruling party candidate Juan Carlos Wasmosy took 40 per cent of the vote in the May 1993 elections. Some 75 per cent of the 1.7 million registered voters turned out. On taking up the post in August, Wasmosy became the first civilian president elected in the 182 years of independence. Congress granted control of the military to the civil authority.

[25] In May 1994, Parliament approved a law which banned the military from party politics. The Government (President and Ministers) and military high command took immediate action to have the law declared unconstitutional.

[26] Under pressure from the US, Wasmosy appointed General Ramón Rozas Rodríguez head of the anti-drugs campaign. Rozas was assassinated in 1994 when he was supposed to present a report on illegal activities involving the military leadership, including General Lino Oviedo.

[27] Violent confrontations between farmers and the police struck several regions of the country. A hundred protesters blocking roads into Asunción were injured by rubber bullets. The farmers were supported by church organizations, unions and opposition parties. A general strike was declared in May calling for salary increases and agrarian reform, and protesting about the privatization of state companies.

[28] In April 1996, the President retired eight high-ranking officers. General Oviedo resisted the order and holed up with a group of young officers. Wasmosy - refuged within the US embassy - made Oviedo Minister of Defense in order to overcome the crisis, and later revoked the decision. In May, the Colorado Party and the opposition agreed to ban the military from political activity.

[29] In Colorado Party internal elections in September 1997, Oviedo was elected presidential candidate with 36.8 per cent of the vote against 35 per cent for Luis María Argaña and 22.5 per cent for Wasmosy's candidate Carlos Facetti. In October, Oviedo was arrested on charges of sedition.

[30] Oviedo was sentenced to 10 years in prison by a military tribunal in April 1998. This provoked rumors of a coup attempt and delays to the presidential elections. Political uncertainty worsened the economic

PROFILE

ENVIRONMENT

A landlocked country in the heart of the Río de la Plata basin, Paraguay is divided into two distinct regions by the Paraguay River. To the east lie fertile plains irrigated by the tributaries of the Paraguay and Paraná rivers, and covered with rainforest. This is the main farming area, producing soybeans (the major export crop), wheat, corn and tobacco. The western region or Northern Chaco is dry savanna, producing cotton and cattle. Farmers, especially those linked to large agricultural operations, have felled wide areas of forest, destroying habitats in the process. Indiscriminate hunting and deforestation have resulted in 14 species of mammals, 11 birds and 2 reptiles now being in danger of extinction. Large amounts of industrial and domestic waste are dumped into watercourses, and untreated sewage from the capital city flows directly into the Bay of Asunción. Rapid deforestation is one of the most serious environmental problems facing the country.

SOCIETY

Peoples: Paraguayans are mostly mestizo (90 per cent), descending from the Spanish and indigenous peoples. The indigenous population belongs to the large Guaraní family, with linguistic and cultural variants. At present there are movements that defend the Guaraní ethnic identity. Immigration has produced German, Italian, Argentine and Brazilian minorities. Brazilians occupy a growing area in the border with their home country. A million Paraguayans live abroad, of whom approximately 200,000 emigrated for political reasons.
Religions: Mainly Catholic, official. Protestant groups.
Languages: Spanish and Guaraní (both official); most Paraguayans are bilingual.
Political Parties: Republican National Alliance/Colorado Party; Democratic Alliance, an electoral coalition made up of the parties led by Laíno and Filizzola (Authentic Radical Liberal Party/ARLP and National Agreement); White Party.
Social Organizations: The Paraguayan Labor Confederation; the Central United Workers (CUT) founded in 1990, uniting labor unions and the powerful Rural Workers' Movement; the Paraguayan Women's Union. Guaraní Ñanduti Rogue; Paraguayan Students Union.

THE STATE

Official Name: República del Paraguay.
Administrative Divisions: 17 departments and the capital city.
Capital: Asunción 1,224,000 people (1999).
Other cities: Ciudad del Este 254,300 people; San Lorenzo 224,900; Lambaré 167,900; Fernando de la Mora 160,300 (2000).
Government: Presidential republic. Luis González Macchi, President since March 1999, elected by popular vote for a five-year term. The National Congress (Legislature) has two chambers: the Chamber of Deputies, with 80 members, and the Chamber of Senators, with 45 members.
National Holiday: May 14, Independence Day (1811).
Armed Forces: 20,200 (1996).
Others: 8,000 (Police).

MATERNAL MORTALITY

1985/99

Per 100,000
live births

190

LITERACY

2000

93%

FOREIGN TRADE

Millions US$ 2000

IMPORTS

2,660

EXPORTS

1,525

crisis. Elections held on May 10, with Oviedo in prison, gave 46.8 per cent of the vote to the Colorado Party's Raúl Cubas and Luis María Argaña, against 38.2 per cent for Laíno and Filizzola's Democratic Alliance. One of the first measures taken by the new president was to release Oviedo, but in December, the Supreme Court ruled this action was unconstitutional and that Oviedo must return to prison, leading to a series of confrontations between Cubas's supporters and the opposition.

[31] Confrontation between State powers worsened and in March 1999 parliament prepared for a vote of no confidence in the president. However, on March 23, Vice President Argaña was assassinated by unknown troops. A week of street fighting in Asunción left nine dead. Cubas was forced to resign and flee to Brazil, meanwhile, Oviedo was granted safe pasage to Argentina. The head of Congress, Luis González Macchi, took over the presidency on March 28 and formed a cabinet made up of Colorado and opposition members. A ruling by the Supreme Court allowed González Macchi to replace Cubas for the full term left to run, meaning he would be president until 2003.

[32] The new president faced a wave of strikes and protests against the economic policy by sectors of workers, farmers and entrepreneurs. Meanwhile, state sector unions campaigned hard against the announced privatizations of telecommunications and electricity companies. Social tension worsened in March 2000, when groups of farmers demonstrated in the capital, demanding greater state aid, improvements in credit and higher prices for their produce. In the northern town of Santa Rosa, some farmers were killed and others seriously injured in clashes with the police.

[33] Elections were held in August to fill the gap left by Argaña. Julio César Franco, of the Liberal Party, was made Vice President, becoming the first opposition party candidate to be elected in 53 years.

[34] The ARLP demonstrated against government action and called for González Macchi to resign. This was not the first time González had been pressed to resign, given that the governing coalition split and in March 2001, a convention declared the president was not fulfilling his functions and that he should stand down.

[35] In September 2001, Brazil denied Oviedo refugee status, meaning Asunción could call for his extradition. Argaña's family pressed for this, wanting him tried for his part in the murder and for him to complete his sentence for the failed coup in 1996. Oviedo's political movement in Paraguay, the National Union of Ethical Colorados, was gaining ground rapidly at a local level, taking many seats in the municipal elections.

[36] Two left-wing activists were illegally detained for two weeks and tortured. They were considered fugitives from justice by the Paraguayan courts that accused them of kidnapping one of Stroessner's relatives who had been released following the payment of a million-dollar ransom. The pair claimed they were forced into confession and that they had been used as a smokescreen to hide the identities of the true culprits.

[37] In April 2002, Public Prosecutor, Javier Contreras accused Macchi of the illegal appropriation of funds after he siphoned off $16 million to an account in the US, and Contreras requested the right to start a political trial. The money came from the liquidation of two private Paraguayan banks in 2000 and from interest charged on two humanitarian foundations linked to the President. ■

The Archives of Terror and Operation Condor

The military dictatorships that governed South America's Southern Cone countries in the 1970s and 1980s coordinated and implemented transborder intelligence and repression through what they called Operation Condor.

For years, human rights organizations, left political parties and social movements in the region denounced the 'anti-subversive' atrocities committed by the armed forces and civilian collaborators in these countries under the National Security Doctrine implemented at the behest of the United States. But the charges - primarily based on testimony from witnesses who had suffered repression, torture or exile - did not take shape in civil society until 1992 because, for the most part, the claims could not be made through official channels.

It was in that year, at a police station in Asuncion, Paraguay, that a human rights lawyer discovered what would later become known as the 'Archives of Terror'. They consist of tens of thousands of documents created by Paraguayan dictator Alfredo Stroessner's staff . For the first time there was official proof of the covert operations carried out by the armed forces against leftist activists and politicians in Chile, Argentina, Paraguay, Brazil and Uruguay, often simply for being suspected of subversion.

The Archives of Terror identified when and how Operation Condor had originated and who was involved in orchestrating it: the military intelligence services in each of the participating countries. Once Operation Condor was exposed, political analysts, social activists and independent journalists began to put the facts together and come up with explanations or theories about the disappearances of thousands of people, as well as the attempted murders and international assassinations. The most notorious of these were the assassination of Chilean military official Carlos Pratts in Buenos Aires, that of Chile's ex-Foreign Affairs minister Orlando Lettelier in Washington DC, and of Uruguayan lawmakers Zelmar Michelini and Héctor Gutiérrez Ruiz in Buenos Aires.

The Archives of Terror cleared up other suspicions as well. One was that the authorities at the time, under Operation Condor, had designed a sinister plan to 'disappear' the children born to mothers in prison, changing the identities of the minors before they were 'adopted' by military personnel or civilian collaborators.

In recent years, some Argentine military officers have asked to be pardoned for the events of the past and others, members of the military Junta command, are facing trial for a second time. They had been released under an amnesty declared by then-President Carlos Menem. The military officials face charges of detention and disappearance of minors, a crime not covered by the amnesty laws. The discovery of the Archives of Terror and the information gleaned from them led to the arrest of former Chilean dictator, retired general Augusto Pinochet, in London in October 1998, as well as the charges of human rights' violations filed by Spanish judge Baltasar Garzón against Argentinian, Chilean and Uruguayan military officials – many of whom now hesitate to leave their home countries for fear of arrest. ■

Peru

Population: 26,523,000 (2002)
Land area: 1,280,000 SQ KM
Capital: Lima
Currency: New sol
Language: Spanish, Quechua and Aymara

Perú

Caves near Ayacucho revealed evidence that human beings had lived in Peru for more than 15 thousand years. For millennia complex cultures had settled in the Andean zone. The Chavin civilization excelled at urban planning, reaching its apogee between 1400 and 200 BC. The cultures which followed inherited its knowledge. The Paraca (700 to 100 BC) were the first to carry out brain surgery. The Mochica built great adobe temples in the Mocha valley, and it is thought their direct descendants were the Chimu (1000 to 1400 AD) who were great metalworkers. The Nazca culture (200 BC to 800 AD) developed agriculture with large-scale irrigation systems and built great calendars which can still be seen from the heights. The Tiahuanaco-Huari culture (600 BC to 1000 AD), based in what is now Bolivia, expanded into the Peruvian highlands.

[2] The 12th century marked the beginning of the rise of the Inca, who were united the various cultures and languages of the region. As with the rest of the Andean civilizations, the Incas' cultural legacy was preserved down the generations by oral tradition and texts written after the Spanish conquest. According to tradition, the founders of the Inca dynasty, Manco Capac and Mama Oclo, established their tribe in Cuzco, which remained the capital from then on. Up until the 14th century, little distinguished the Incas from the rest of the cultures dominating small territories in the Andes. It was during this century, under the reign of the fourth Emperor (or Inca) Mayta Capac, that the Inca began to attack the neighboring populations.

[3] Capac Yupanqui was the first to extend the influence of the Inca beyond the Cuzco valley. With the eighth emperor, Viracocha Inca, the Empire began a programme of permanent conquest, establishing garrisons amongst the settlements of the conquered peoples. In 1438, Pachacuti Inca Yupanqui, one of the sons of Viracocha Inca, usurped the throne from his brother Inca Urcon and the Tahuntinsuyu Empire - as it was known - expanded beyond lake Titicaca, subjugating powerful peoples like the Chanca, Quechua and the Chimu and taking over the kingdom of the Shiri in Quito.

[4] The Inca began a policy of forced resettlement, thereby assuring the political stability of the Empire. Large numbers of people were taken from their place of origin and redistributed to other points within the Empire. They were forced to live and work alongside other ethnic groups, in order to make the organization of uprisings against the seat of power in Cuzco difficult. Quechua was imposed as the common language across the Empire and during the reign of Topa Inca Yupanqui (1471-1493) the Inca extended their power southwards, towards what is now central Chile. On the death of Topa Inca a war of succession broke out, which was won by Huayna Capac (1493-1525). He extended the northern frontier up to the river Ancasmayo (the current frontier between Ecuador and Colombia) before dying. On his death, Tahuantisuyu, as the Inca state was known, imposed its government over more than 12 million people.

[5] The death of Huayna Capac caused a new war of succession

between Huascar, who governed in Cuzco, and his younger brother Atahualpa, a son of Huayna Capac and a Shiri princess, who ruled the northern part of the Empire from Quito. In 1532, the scales were tipped in favor of Atahualpa when a group of 180 Spaniards, led by Francisco Pizarro and his lieutenant Diego de Almagro disembarked in Tumbes. The Spanish intervened in the civil war, killing those loyal to Atahualpa but at the same time recognizing him as the legitimate governor of the Empire until they were able to meet him in Cajamarca, kidnap him and demand a large ransom in silver and gold. During his time in captivity, Atahualpa arranged for Huascar to be killed, before being strangled himself in 1533. The news of the death of Atahualpa paralysed the forces of the Empire, allowing the Spanish to reach Cuzco, where they crowned Topa Hualpa, an ally of Huascar. This put the Europeans, who wanted to reign through an Inca emperor, in a difficult situation, as they found themselves committed to the faction they initially did not want to support.

[6] Topa Hualpa died some months later and the Spanish reinforced their alliance with the pro-Huascar faction by putting his brother Manco Capac on the throne and helping him to disperse the last of Atahualpa's army. In 1535, Pizarro prohibited Manco Capac from re-establishing control over the dominions along the coast and in the north, which were either still loyal to Atahualpa or lacked central control. Manco Capac then understood that the Spanish were a far greater threat than any of Atahualpa's followers and in 1536 he besieged Cuzco for a year. But his forces were finally disbanded by Diego de Almagro, returning from an expedition to Chile.

[7] After his defeat, Manco Capac founded an independent Inca state in the Amazon regions which lasted until 1572, with the death by poisoning of Titu Cusi Yupanqui, the last Inca. The days of the Tahuantisuyu (the Inca Empire) were numbered from the moment Pizarro founded Lima in 1535 on the coast, operating as the center of Spanish power. The Spanish administration radically changed the property and land-use rules; the payment of tributes and forced labor broke up the bases of the old society and the old gods were officially replaced with Catholicism. Even though the official Inca religion was suppressed, an incalculable number of cults to minor deities survived amongst the people. Similarly, regions and cities of the old Empire survived beyond the reach of the Spanish Crown for centuries. The most notable example of this was the fortress of Macchu Pichu, 80 kilometres north-east of Cuzco which was only re-discovered in 1911 by Hiram Bingham, a Yale University professor.

[8] Conflicts between the *conquistadores* (the Spanish conquerors) meant that the Spanish Crown could not fully establish its authority for decades. Almagro, disillusioned by losing his chances to conquer lands in Chile, besieged Cuzco until he was beaten and executed in 1538. His allies continued conspiring with his son and they attacked Pizarro's palace. Pizarro died in 1541. The Spanish Crown refused to recognize the young Almagro, who was captured and executed in 1542. But the

conquistadores, led by Francisco Pizarro's brother Gonzalo, unhappy with the Spanish King's new laws (aiming to impede feudalism, and thereby threatening their wealth and power) rebelled again in 1542, remaining independent from Spanish control to all intents and purposes until 1544, when Gonzalo Pizarro was defeated and executed.

9   It was only with the appointment of Viceroy Francisco de Toledo in 1569 that Spain consolidated its dominion over the region. The Andeans' institutions were adapted to the ends of the Spanish authority and for a long time the chiefs of the various Andean nations administered the interests of their communities while taking on responsibility for the collection of tributes and the provision of an indigenous workforce for the mines. In any case, Toledo did not trust the Andeans and when the son of Manco Capac, Tupac Amaru, led the indigenous rural population in an uprising, the Spanish authority had him executed in 1571.

10   Once Toledo's administration was over, the Viceroyalty in Peru assumed the form it maintained until the 18th century, including all of South America except Venezuela and Brazil. The discovery of the silver mines in Potosí in 1545 was followed by those of Huancavelica in 1563. With the exception of the gold from New Granada (Colombia), mineral production was concentrated in Peru itself, or in Upper Peru (Bolivia). The Spanish Crown prioritized these areas, which became the most developed and rich parts of the continent.

11   During the 16th and 17th centuries, Lima was the center of power and wealth for all of Spanish-controlled South America. Based on the labor of the indigenous workforce, the Court of Lima - where the King's justice was meted out - attracted not only the rich and powerful but also religious orders, intellectuals and artists. It was in Lima that the tribunals of the Inquisition worked most avidly and cruelly. With the advent of the Bourbon dynasty in 1700, replacing the Hapsburgs as rulers of Spain, measures were taken to promote the development of the colonies and to achieve better government of the continent, something which severely affected Peru. The creation of the Viceroyalty of New Granada meant the Viceroyalty of Peru lost control over the port of Quito as well as the territory constituting modern day Colombia. The creation of the Viceroyalty of the River Plate in 1777 also removed control over Upper Peru and what are today Argentina, Paraguay and Uruguay. Chile, meanwhile, became an independent Captaincy of the Viceroy of Peru.

12   Reforms to the mercantile system, allowing the Pacific and Atlantic ports to trade directly with Spain, weakened the condition of the Viceroyalty even further. In 1780, the cacique (indigenous leader) José Gabriel Condorcanqui had a corregidor (chief magistrate) arrested on charges of cruelty. He led a general uprising of indigenous people against the authority of the Viceroyalty in 1781 under the name of Tupac Amaru II, even gaining the support of some criollos (descendants of the Spanish). The rebellion, which spread to Bolivia and Argentina lost support when it turned into a violent battle between the indigenous people and the whites. Tupac Amaru II was captured in 1781 and taken to Cuzco where, after being forced to witness the execution of his wife an children, he was quartered and beheaded. The revolution continued, however, until the Spanish Government approved a general pardon for the insurgents.

13   The effective suppression of the indigenous uprisings, the presence of numerous Spaniards, the concentration of the Crown's military power in Lima and the conservative attitude of the local oligarchy, meant that Peru remained loyal to Spain when the rest of the Hispanic colonies in South America began the fight for independence between 1810 and 1821. The forces which finally expelled the Spanish came from beyond Peruvian borders. General José de San Martín, an Argentinian criollo, freed Chile in 1818 and used it as a base to attack Peru by sea with the aim of securing control over the mines of Upper Peru and of assuring independence for the Argentine provinces. In September 1820, San Martín's forces occupied the port of Pisco and the Viceroy withdrew his troops into the interior of the country. San Martín entered Lima and declared independence on July 18 1821.

14   Lacking sufficient forces to attack the large Spanish contingents in the interior of Peru, San Martín asked for the help of Venezuela's Simón Bolívar, who had liberated the northern part of South America, but Bolívar would not agree to share the leadership. Hence, San Martín withdrew and Bolívar took over in Peru to continue the fight. In the battles of Junín and Ayacucho, in August and December 1824, the Spanish were defeated and effectively Peru became politically independent.

15   The first years of independence were spent in constant battles between the conservative oligarchy, yearning for the times of the viceroyalty, and the liberals. The wars with Colombia, in 1827, and Bolivia took place against that backdrop. The unification of Peru with Bolivia, attempted by Bolivian President Andrés Santa Cruz in 1835, failed both socially and economically

16   Marshal Ramón Castilla, who ruled the country from 1845 to 1862, shaped the modern Peru, after abolishing slavery and proclaiming the Constitution.

17   In 1864, Spain attempted to establish enclaves on the Peruvian coast. Peru, Chile, Bolivia and Ecuador declared war on the country. The Spanish fleet bombarded Valparaíso, Chile, and El Callao in Peru, before being defeated in 1866.

18   From 1845, with the silver mines exhausted, guano - bird faeces used as fertilizer - became Peru's main export product. When the guano 'boom' was over it was replaced by saltpeter from the southern deserts. The potential wealth to be made from this product brought about the Pacific War (1879-1883). Peru and Bolivia joined forces against Chile, which exploited the saltpeter, with the support of British companies. Peru and Bolivia lost the war and with it the provinces of Arica, Tarapac and Antofagasta.

19   The early decades of the 20th century marked the beginning of large-scale copper mining, particularly by the North American Cerro de Pasco Copper Corporation. Foreign capital was also involved in

ENVIRONMENT

The Andes divide the country into three regions. The desert coastal area, with large artificially irrigated plantations and some natural valleys has historically been the most modern and westernized. Half of the population live in the Sierra (highlands), between two ranges of the Andes. Numerous peasants here are still organized into ayllus (communities) with Incan roots.
Subsistence farming of corn and potatoes is practiced, the traditional raising of llamas and alpacas having been forced onto the higher slopes due to the incursions of mining and sheep rearing. The eastern region, comprising the Amazon lowlands, with tropical climate and rainforests, is sparsely populated. Peru is one of the largest producers of coca, a medicinal and energizing plant. Coca - traditionally consumed among Indians who chew its leaves - once chemically refined and developed into a different substance, becomes the basis of cocaine. The country suffers from soil depletion, on soils which are poor to begin with. Indiscriminate fishing has endangered some species. The coastal area has been polluted by both industrial and household waste.

SOCIETY

Peoples: Nearly half of all Peruvians are of indigenous American origin, mostly from the Quechua and Aymara ethnic groups living on the Sierra. Along the coast, most of the population are mixed descendants of native Indians and Spaniards. There are several indigenous groups in the East Amazon jungle. Also, there are Chinese and Japanese immigrant minorities. **Religions:** Catholic (official), with syncretic expressions related to Indian beliefs. **Languages:** Spanish, Quechua and Aymara (all official). **Political Parties:** Possible Peru; American Revolutionary People's Alliance (APRA); National Unity; Moralizing Independent Front; We are Peru; The Change 90-New Majority, founded in 1989 by Alberto Fujimori; People's Action (AP), led by Fernando Belaúnde Terry; Union for Peru; the Christian Popular Party; the United Left (IU), an alliance of the National Workers' and Campesinos' (Farmers) Front, the Peruvian Communist Party and the Union of the Revolutionary Left; the Socialist Left, a splinter group from the IU. The two main guerrilla organizations are the Peruvian Communist Revolutionary Party-Sendero Luminoso (Shining Path) and the Tupac Amaru Revolutionary Movement (MRTA). **Social Organizations:** The Peruvian Workers; General Central Union (CGTP), predominantly Communist. The Peruvian Workers' Central Union (CTP), linked to the APRA. The independent National Workers' Confederation (CNT). The Workers' Central of the Peruvian Revolution, founded in 1972 by Velasco backers. In March 1991, the four trade union federations (CGTP, CTP, CTRP, and CNT) created the National Coordinating Body of Trade Union Federations. There are two rural organizations: the National Agrarian Confederation (CNA), and the Peruvian Campesino Confederation (CCP).

THE STATE

Official Name: República del Perú. **Administrative divisions:** 25 Departments, 155 Provinces and 1,586 Districts. **Capital:** Lima 7,291,000 people (1999). **Other cities:** Arequipa 720,400 people; Trujillo 590,200; Chiclayo 481,100; Cusco 279,600 (2000). **Government:** Alejandro Toledo Manrique, President since July 2001. Roberto Dañino, Chairman of the Council of Ministers since July 2001. Unicameral Legislature: The Congress, with 120 members. **National Holiday:** July 28, Independence (1821). **Armed Forces:** 125,000 troops (65,000 conscripts). 188,000 reserves (1996). **Other:** National Police: 60,000 members. Coast Guard: 600 members. Campesino Rounds: the campesino self-defense forces, made up of 2,000 groups mobilized within emergency zones.

oil exploitation in the north, and sugarcane and cotton in the north and center. The anachronistic agrarian structures, however, continued unchanged.

20 Within this context, the APRA (American Popular Revolutionary Alliance), a Marxist-inspired party committed to Latin Americanism, achieved widespread support. Víctor Haya de la Torre, its main leader, was in favor of merging class boundaries and debated with José Carlos Maritegui, founder of the Peruvian Communist Party (PC). Triumphant in several elections, APRA never actually came to power as it was always prevented by military coups.

21 In 1968, a military faction headed by General Juan Velasco Alvarado ousted President Fernando Belaúnde Terry and started a process of change by nationalizing oil production. This also included recovery of the natural resources and fishing, co-operative based agrarian reform, worker participation in company ownership, the creation of socially-owned enterprises, the expropriation of the press - planning to hand this over to organized social sectors - and an independent non-aligned foreign policy.

22 An ailing Velasco gradually lost control over the process and the trust of his allies. He was overthrown by his Prime Minister, General Francisco Morales Bermúdez, in August 1975. Under pressure from the IMF and an oligarchy keen on regaining power, Morales called elections in 1978. Belaunde's Acción Popular (AP), which had boycotted the constituent elections, triumphed in 1980 presidential elections. Its economic policy followed IMF guidelines with disastrous results: unemployment grew, income became even more concentrated and an unregulated informal economy developed with no social benefits. The new outburst of armed violence led by the 'Shining Path' guerrilla in 1980 was escalated in 1984 with the emergence of the Tupac Amaru Revolutionary Movement (MRTA).

23 In the 1985 elections, the APRA candidate Alan García came in first with 46 per cent. When García took power, the foreign debt stood at $14 billion, with annual servicing of $3.5 billion. García announced he would limit payments to 10 per cent of the annual export income and would negotiate directly with the creditors, without IMF mediation.

24 The 1989 general elections were won by the unknown outsider, Alberto Fujimori, who was elected with 56.4 per cent of the vote. On assuming power in July 1990, Fujimori implemented a severe anti-inflationary plan which dropped the standard of living of all Peruvians, leaving more than half in extreme poverty. When parliamentary opposition got in his way, Fujimori began to govern by decree. On April 5 1992, Fujimori led a coup claiming that Parliament was corrupt and inoperative and that the judicial system was obstructing national reconstruction.

25 The imprisonment of Abimael Guzmán, founder and leader of 'Shining Path', dealt a major blow to the guerrilla group, which was willing to start peace talks.

26 In early 1995, Peru and Ecuador waged an undeclared war along their common border at the Condor mountain range. Peace talks were held under the Río Protocol, with Argentina, Brazil, Chile and the US as guarantors.

27 Re-elected by an overwhelming majority in the April elections, Fujimori amnestied members of the army and police convicted of human rights violations in the fight against the guerrillas since 1980. The so-called 'faceless judges', who remain anonymous during trials, convicted more than 2,000 people in 1992-1995.

28 On October 23 1998, three years after the armed conflict, Peru and Ecuador agreed on a peace treaty - to be signed a week later in Brasilia - based on new border lines proposed by the guarantor countries: Argentina, Brazil, Chile and the US.

29 Members of the Constitutional Court who had declared the Constitution did not allow for Fujimori's re-election were dismissed in 1997. In spite of the constitutional impediment, Fujimori stood. Peruvians took part in the April 9 2000 elections with amazement, since days before it had been revealed that Fujimori's political machine had presented one million forged signatures supporting his re-election. Once the primary results were known, the opposition candidate, economist Alejandro Toledo (with received 41 per cent of the vote) claimed Fujimori (which obtained 48.7 per cent) had misused state funds to finance his campaign and prevented the opposition's access to the media. That night, Toledo headed a protest by thousands of people in Lima, to force a second electoral round. Finally, days before this next vote, Toledo, a former shoeshine boy of indigenous origin, announced he would not take part in the elections until the necessary conditions were given to guarantee their fairness.

30 Finally, on May 28, without the presence of international observers and having been the only candidate, Fujimori was declared President by the Electoral Court. The number of ballots that were annulled - handwritten, on Toledo's request, with the words 'no to fraud' - and those in favor of the self-excluded candidate, showed that 54 per cent of the population had voted against Fujimori, who was strongly criticized by the OAS and the US. The OAS supported a schedule of institutional changes in the country, including reforms to guarantee freedom of the press, the independence of the courts, modifications in the electoral systema and civilian control of the army and intelligence services. In a meeting with US Secretary of State Madeleine Albright, held in early September, Fujimori promised to implement the changes.

31 In response to the scandal involving National Intelligence director Vladimiro Montesinos - according to many, the real 'power behind the throne' - Fujimori announced he would call new elections, in which he would not take part. A videotape had shown Montesinos bribing a legislator. Fujimori and opposition forces agreed in October to set the elections for April 2001.

32 Fujimori then fled to Japan, from where he resigned in November - at the same time as he was deposed by Parliament in Lima. Valentín Paniagua, of Popular Action, was appointed President of a Transition Constitutional Government. A Congress committee voted in February 2001 in favour of accusing Fujimori of abandoning his post, which put him on the verge of losing his political immunity.

33 Having won the cleanest elections in many years in Peru, Toledo became the first freely elected President of indigenous origin. On taking office on July 28 2001, he took over the reins of a country heavily indebted, with fiscal problems, a severe recession and 54 per cent of the population living in poverty. According to the forecast of Toledo's own economic team, poverty in the capital had increased from 35 to 45 per cent in 1997-2000.

34 In November, a Truth Commission began to analyze the thousands of cases of presumed human rights violations that had occurred in the last two decades. In December, the authorities issued a second international arrest warrant (the first had been issued three months earlier) against Fujimori, on charges of corruption and human rights violations.

35 Days before the visit of President George W Bush, in March 2002, nine people were killed when a bomb exploded near the US embassy in Lima. According to the Peruvian Government, the goal of Bush's visit - the first of a serving US President - was to support the Toledo administration and its plans for a free market economy. ■

Philippines

Population: 78,611,000 (2002)
Land area: 298,170 SQ KM
Capital: Manila
Currency: Peso
Language: Pilipino and English

Pilipinas

The Philippine archipelago was first inhabited in Palaeolithic times, and the Neolithic culture on the islands began around 900 BC with metal working beginning in about the 15th century. Native peoples, such as the Aeta and the Igorot, probably subsisted without being assimilated by the later groups of migrants.

[2] Between the 2nd and 15th centuries AD, migrants from Indonesia and Malaysia settled on the islands, gathering in clans. They were virtually uninfluenced by the classical Indian culture which had touched others in the region. Between the 11th and 13th centuries the coastal areas were raided by Muslim, Japanese, and Chinese merchant ships, bringing traders and craftspeople to the islands. The southern islands adopted Islam and sultanates soon appeared.

[3] The archipelago was only 'discovered' by Ferdinand Magellan in 1521 when it was named after the Spanish king Felipe. The explorer was killed on one of its beaches and Spanish possession of the islands, which were also coveted by the British and the Dutch, was not secured until 1564. The Igorot of the Cordillera region and the Islamic population of Mindanao were never fully incorporated by European colonization, and most of the rural population preserved their subsistence economy, never even paying tribute to the Europeans. Several uprisings by these communities and the Chinese were repressed by the Spaniards.

[4] Spanish colonization in the Philippines followed similar patterns to that in America. However, the

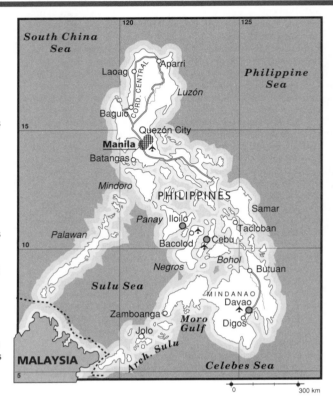

Philippines had two distinguishing features; they were located on the oceanic trading routes, in a position that received merchandise from all over Southeast Asia on its way to Europe, and they were ruled by the Viceroyalty of Mexico.

[5] Late in the 19th century, a local independence movement developed, led by the native bourgeoisie, who wanted the political power which was barred to them. They were soon followed by the other oppressed

sectors. Anti-colonial revolution erupted in 1896 and independence was proclaimed on July 12th. However, the US was attracted by the archipelago's strategic position and vulnerability, and it immediately stepped in to seize control. This resulted in the signing of the Treaty of Paris, on December 10 1898, ending the Spanish-US war (see history of Cuba and Puerto Rico). In meetings, which barred Filipino delegates, Spain decided to cede the

archipelago to the US in exchange for compensation.

[6] Between 1899 and 1911, more than 500,000 Filipinos died in the struggle against occupying troops commanded by US General Arthur MacArthur. During World War II, the archipelago was occupied by Japan and the Huk Movement, peasant-based and socialist inspired, emerged during the struggle against the invaders. In 1946, after the war had ended, occupation troops returned led by Douglas MacArthur, son of the earlier General MacArthur. The archipelago was eventually granted formal independence but the Philippines have remained under US economic domination ever since.

[7] Nor did independence bring about any social changes. The hacienda system persisted in the country, where large estates were farmed by sharecroppers. More than half the population were peasants, and 20 per cent of the population owned 60 per cent of the land. Although the sharecropper was supposed to receive half of the harvest, most of the peasant's actual income went to pay off the debts incurred with the *cacique*, the landowner. There was almost 9 per cent unemployment and the country suffered from the consequences of a balance of trade deficit, typical of a producer of agricultural commodities.

[8] The Nationalist Party, a conservative party of landowners, was in power until 1972 when Ferdinand Marcos, president since 1965, declared Martial Law. In 1986 a coalition of opposition forces rebelled against the continuous abuses of Ferdinand Marcos. During his presidency repression grew both against armed movements (the Muslim independent groups of Mindanao and the New People's Army led by the Maoist Communist Party), and against political and trade union opposition. This repression often had the military support of the US.

[9] Due to its long presence in the country, the Catholic Church is deeply rooted in Filipino society. This is reflected in the fact that 75 per cent of Filipinos over the age of 10 have learnt to read in institutions dependent on the Church. The Church played an active role in the

WORKERS

2000

UNEMPLOYMENT: 10.1%
LABOR FORCE AS % OF TOTAL:

FEMALE: 38%   MALE: 62%

1994/97
EMPLOYMENT DISTRIBUTION:

F
M

SERVICES   F: 59%   M: 33%
INDUSTRY   F: 13%   M: 19%
AGRICULTURE F: 28%   M: 48%

LAND USE

DEFORESTATION: 3.5% annual (1990/95)

1993

FOREST & WOODLAND: 45.3%
ARABLE: 18.4%
OTHER: 36.3%

PUBLIC EXPENDITURE

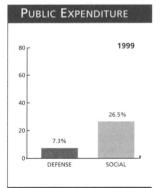

1999

DEFENSE 7.3%   SOCIAL 26.5%

MATERNAL MORTALITY	LITERACY	FOREIGN TRADE
1985/99	2000	Millions US$ 2000
Per 100,000 live births **170**	**95%**	IMPORTS **37,493** EXPORTS **42,076**

denunciation of fraud when the 1976 referendum supported the invocation of martial law. Five years later, 45 political and trade union organizations united to boycott the fraudulent and unconstitutional elections that Marcos used to stay in power. In September 1981 thousands of people demonstrated in Manila, demanding the end of dictatorship and the withdrawal of the US military bases. Since the 19th century, the US army has had its two largest foreign bases in the Philippines.

[10] On August 21 1983, opposition leader Benigno Aquino was murdered at Manila airport as he returned from the US. The murder was attributed to Marcos.

[11] Amidst a scenario of increased violence and repression, compared by the Church with the dirty war of Argentina in the 1970s, a large section of the population put pressure on Marcos, demanding early elections in 1986, and supporting the candidacy of Corazón Aquino, widow of the assassinated leader.

[12] Elections were held in February 1986, but widespread fraud prevented 'Cory' Aquino from winning, and she subsequently called for civil disobedience. Marcos' Minister of Defense, Juan Ponce Enrile, attempted a coup against the dictator, but failed. A million supporters surrounded the rebels, led by Enrile, in the field where they had taken refuge. The air force refused to bombard their comrades-in-arms and the people who supported them, so Marcos opted for exile and Corazon Aquino assumed the presidency with Enrile as her Minister of Defense.

[13] The new constitution was approved by a large majority in the February 1987 plebiscite. The charter granted autonomy to the Mindanao and Cordillera regions, thus paving the way for a truce with guerrilla groups operating in those areas. The New People's Army (NPA) representatives soon left the negotiating table, after several acts of provocation against mass organizations and attempts on the lives of civilian leaders. Agrarian reform, which should have been the cornerstone of the government's plan for social transformation, was diluted after going through a

legislature where many of the members are landowners. The debate over the future of the Clark and Subic Bay American military bases began in April 1988, as the contracts were due to expire in 1991.

[14] In 1990, 39 per cent of the Filipino population was under the age of 14, and in spite of NGO efforts, only a third of their basic needs were met. A number of government 'internal refugee' camps were created to provide basic assistance to some 1,250,000 homeless people.

[15] The UN has recorded a total of 110 regional and ethnic groups in the Philippines. During 1991

increasing pressure from these groups, the urgent need for better land and wealth distribution and, possibly, the approaching presidential elections of May 1992, led Corazon Aquino to create a Bureau of Northern Communities. The Bureau was concerned with the mountain tribes and ethnic groups, particularly in Luzon. There was also a Bureau of Southern Cultural Communities, excluding the Muslims. The staff of those bureaus were recruited from among the communities concerned.

[16] In June 1991, the eruption of Mount Pinatubo shook the country, claiming the lives of over 700

Filipinos, flattening entire villages, forcing the evacuation of over 300,000 people, and burying the evacuated Clark US airforce base under the ashes.

[17] With its airbase unusable, and swamped with difficult negotiations as the contract approached their expiry dates, the US opted to abandon the base of its own accord. On November 26 1991, Clark airbase was formally abandoned. It had employed over 6,000 US military, and over 40,000 Filipinos, most of whom had carried out the menial work. The Aetan people claimed the territory they had been deprived of when the base was installed, and

PROFILE

ENVIRONMENT

Of the 7,000 islands that make up the archipelago, spread over 1,600 km. from north to south, eleven account for 94 per cent of the total area and house most of the population. Luzon and Mindanao are the most important. The archipelago is of volcanic origin, forming part of the 'Ring of Fire of the Pacific'. The terrain is mountainous with large coastal plains where sugarcane, hemp, copra and tobacco are grown. The climate is tropical. Abundant rains favor the growth of dense forests. It is the main producer of iron ore in Southeast Asia, and also has oil, chromium, copper, nickel, cobalt, silver and gold. As other countries in the region, and due to its large lumber production, it has an accelerated deforestation. Manila has significant water and air pollution.

SOCIETY

Peoples: A wide majority of the population originates from the first migration waves from Malaysia and Indonesia. Some 200,000 Chinese traders were settled since the 11th century. Islamic communities from Borneo entered the territory in the 15th century, resisted the evangelization of the Spanish conquistadors - who arrived in 1521 - who had a significant cultural influence over the rest of the population. Some communities of Malaysian origin, in different evolution stages, were not Christianized either.
Religions: Catholics 83 per cent; Protestants 8 per cent, Muslims 5 per cent, Anglipayans (Independent Filipino Church), 3 per cent; Animists and Buddhists.
Languages: Fifty-five per cent of the population speaks Pilipino (official), based on the Tagalog language, of Malaysian origin. English, spoken by 45 per cent, is also official, and is compulsory in the education system. But 90 per cent of the population speaks one of the following languages: Cebuano (6 million); Hiligaynon (3 million); Bicolano (2 million); Waray-Waray (1 million). Spanish and Chinese are minority languages.
Political Parties: Lakas ñg Bansa (The People's Struggle); the Laban Party (The People's Power

Movement), founded in 1988 by Benigno Aquino, the Democratic Christian Party; the BISIG, socialist movement of Tagalog speakers; the People's Reform Party founded in 1991; the Liberal Party; the right-wing Nationalist Party. The main leftist opposition force is the National Democratic Front (NDF) which includes mass organizations, religious and cultural groups led by the Philippine Communist Party (PKP) and its military wing, the New Peoples Army (NPA). In the Cordillera region, an NPA splinter group, the Cordillera Peoples Liberation Army (CPLA) organized the Cordillera Bodong Association (CBA) which demands full autonomy for the north. In the southern Muslim areas, the Moro National Liberation Front also demands autonomy. Kababaihan Para Sa Inang Bayan (Women for the Motherland), created in 1986, the first party exclusively for women; the Mindanao Alliance, regional.
Social Organizations: Labor is divided between the left-wing Kihusan Mayo Uno (May Day Confederation) and the Trade Union Congress of the Philippines (TUCP), affiliated with AFL-CIO. The Philippines has over 700 voluntary organizations and church groups, gathered in the Green Forum.

THE STATE

Official Name: Republika ñg Pilipinas.
Administrative division: 3 regions, 73 provinces.
Capital: Metro Manila 10,546,000 people (1999).
Other cities: Cebu 1,172,800 people; Davao 1,145,600; Bacolod 739,600; Cagayan 407,800; Zamboanga 147,200 (2000).
Government: Presidentialist republic. Gloria Macapagal-Arroyo, President since January 2001. Teofisto Guingona, Vice President since January 2001. The Congress (Parliament) has two chambers: the House of Representatives 260 members, and the Senate, with 24 members.
National Holiday: July 4th, (from the US, 1946); July 12th, Independence Day (from Spain,1898).
Armed Forces: 107,500 troops (1996). **Others:** National police (Home Ministry): 40,500. Coast Guard: 2,000.

EXTERNAL DEBT

2000

PER CAPITA

US$ 662

the Philippines Government made plans to build an airport there.

[18] Of the 32 million Filipinos entitled to vote, 25 million took part in the May 1992 elections which were considered the calmest and cleanest in the country's history. The winner was Fidel Ramos, former Defense Minister in the Aquino administration. In September, the US left its naval base at Subic Bay with an infrastructure worth $8 billion. Thousands of rural women who had worked as prostitutes were left unemployed.

[19] In 1994, the Ramos Government had to turn to the opposition's support to control evasion of the 10 per cent VAT tax. This measure won him the IMF's support - including a loan - and enabled a five per cent growth of the GNP. The campaign against crime, now headed by Vice-President Estrada, implicated two per cent of police forces - who were discharged - in criminal activities, while another 5 per cent was kept under investigation. The NPA communist guerrillas lost strength due to an amnesty for its members and to internecine conflicts regarding the amnesty.

[20] In 1995 Imelda Marcos won the election to the Chamber of Deputies, in spite of being accused of many corruption charges. Swiss banks returned $475 million to the country deposited by her husand Ferdinand Marcos during the dictatorship, but the Government is convinced billions remain in other accounts.

[21] The elimination of restrictions to investments, the reduction in customs barriers and the presence of educated and cheap labor, attracted investors which led to a six-per-cent growth of the GNP. Remittances totaling $2 billion from 4.2 million workers living abroad - mainly domestics - came into the country in 1995.

[22] In late 1995, there was an unprecedented food crisis, with a 70 per cent increase in rice prices. More than two thirds of the population were estimated to be living below the poverty line. The farmers' organizations blamed the government for their incoherent and corrupt agricultural policy, calling for agrarian reform, including the industrialization of rural activity,

food self-sufficiency and protection of the environment.

[23] The Government and the Muslim guerrillas signed a peace agreement. Nur Misuari, leader of the Moro National Liberation Front (MNLF), became governor of Mindanao, an independent region which covers around a quarter of the national territory. The Christian opposition organized a referendum in 1998 against this agreement. President Ramos also started negotiations with the Communist Party, whose armed wing, the New People's Army, continued to operate in cities and rural towns. In August 1997, Ramos accepted the resignation of his Defense Minister Renato de Villa.

[24] In January 1998, thousands of children from various countries marched through the streets of Manila in protest against exploitative child labor. This sparked a worldwide campaign for better conditions for the worlds 250 million working children, employed despite international agreements banning this. 63 per cent of the exploited children are estimated to be living in Asia.

[25] In May, Vice-President Joseph Estrada was elected President with 37 per cent of the vote. In March 2000, Salamat Hashim, leader of the largest Islamic rebel group in the Philippines, called for a referendum on the self-determination of Muslims in the South, organized by the United Nations. Estrada promised not to budge on the separatist issue. The Moro Islamic Liberation Front (MILF) leader stated in an interview from Mindanao that 'if we want a real referendum, with real results, this must be carried out by a third party; ideally by the United Nations'. This island is the scene of a war between Islamic separatists and the army, which has lasted 28 years. Muslims make up 5 of the 70 million inhabitants of the Philippine archipelago, and live mostly in Mindanao.

[26] Tens of thousands of Filipinos took to the streets of Manila to demand Estrada's resignation in October, while the opposition requested the President's impeachment, after a former crony denounced Estrada for receiving

millions of dollars in kickbacks from an illegal gambling racket.

[27] Parliament started impeachment proceedings against the President. The process revealed that Estrada had hundreds of millions of dollars in bank accounts under false names. In the midst of massive mobilizations, which led to Estrada's fall, Vice-President Gloria Macapagal-Arroyo assumed the Presidency on January 20 2001.

[28] Since the start of her administration, the President denounced that, 'in spite of the Filipino people's victory and heroism, groups plotting against our Government still remain'. Referring to the different opinions on whether or not the former president should be exiled or remain in the country (the Government forbade him to leave Philippines), she stated it was for Estrada to decide, but that the criminal charges would stand.

[29] In April 2001, Estrada was finally accused by the prosecutor of having amassed a fortune of more than $80 million through corruption acts during his two and a half years as President. The 8 charges brought against him were: plundering, theft, bribery, embezzlement, perjury, illegal use of an alias, illegal gambling and infringement of the ethical standards act. Estrada's son and wife, Jinggoy and Luisa Ejército, as well as business partners of the former president, face similar charges. These were brought after the Supreme Court lifted Estrada's presidential immunity and rejected his request to be declared lawful President.

[30] Corruption charges touched the President when, in October 2001, her husband was accused of taking bribes. A former presidential palace employee accused lawyer José Miguel Arroyo of having accepted a bribe of more than $900,000 from a telecommunications firm, in exchange for lifting the presidential veto on a franchise agreement. Both the President and the suspect authorized a formal investigation on the case. 'The fact is that I vetoed the franchise agreement, I did not lift the veto and it will remain in place. However, I must be like the Caesar's wife and be above all suspicion', declared Macapagal-Arroyo.

[31] A state of emergency was declared in April 2002 in the city of General Santos, south of Mindanao, after several bombs killed 14 people. The police detained two suspects and concluded the attacks had been carried out by the MILF. ∎

Poland

Population: 38,542,000 (2002)
Land area: 304,420 SQ KM
Capital: Warsaw (Warzawa)
Currency: Zloty
Language: Polish

Polska

The name Poland comes from a Polanian tribe, the Poles, who tilled the soil in the Warta basin region, later known as Greater Poland. Their chiefs belonged to the Piast dynasty, descendants of a legendary ancestor, and they lived in the town of Gniezno.

2   During the 10th century, the Polanians subdued the Kujavians, the Mazovians, the Ledzians, the Pomeranians, the Vistulans, and the Silesians. Mieszko I (960-992) Duke of the Piast, founded the first Polish State when he united neighboring tribes under a common state structure. Mieszko was christened in the year 966 establishing the Christian influence in the area.

3   Poland was a hereditary monarchy until the 12th century. The duke and a group of nobles held power, supported by an army of elite warriors. Free peasants, who constituted the largest and poorest group, were mobilized as they were needed, and paid taxes to support the system.

4   The greatest dilemma for Poland was what stance to take towards the German Empire and the Pope. As the Empire expanded, Mieszko submitted - in exchange for an acknowledgment of his sovereignty. As compensation, he appealed for Papal protection and in 1,000 AD he founded the first Polish ecclesiastical city state.

5   From then on, the Roman Catholic Church became a crucial element in the political structure of the Polish State. Poland alternated phases of independence and annexation until the 12th century, when the State began to fragment.

6   During the feudal period, Poland was subdivided into several duchies, led by the Piasts and some 20 overlords. The nobility and the Church became increasingly autonomous as the central power and the dukes lost strength. This was also a period of great demographic growth.

7   The arrival of German settlers created a new ethnic situation in the country, for up to then the population had been of Slavic stock. From the 13th century, the population of the towns became increasingly German and Jewish. Immigrants brought in their own

legal systems, their capital, their crafts and their agricultural skills.

8   Under the reign of Casimir the Great (1333-70), Poland became a monarchy divided into estates, with the King acting as an arbiter between the nobility, the clergy, the bourgeoisie, and the peasants. The State ceased to be royal property and in 1399 the monarchy became elective.

9   Through a royal marriage in 1386, Poland joined with Lithuania, and they adopted an organization which respected the differences between the two countries. In 1409, the Teutonic Order attempted to stop Polish-Lithuanian expansion, but it was defeated at Grunwald. The Peace of Torun in 1411, did not end the conflict, and the power of the Order suffered a setback.

10   In 1466, after a new victory over the Teutons, Poland recovered Pomerania of Gdansk and Malbork, Elblag, and the Land of Chelm; it also gained the territory of Warmia. In recognition of their assistance during the war, Poland granted autonomy to Pomerania and some privileges to the towns. A period of economic prosperity and cultural renaissance began.

11   During the 15th century the General Diet (parliament) of Poland and Lithuania was created. It had two houses: a lower house,

constituted by members of the nobility, and an upper house, or royal council, presided over by the king. The two states shared the king, the diet, and the management of foreign affairs, while administration, justice, finance and the army remained separate.

12   The 16th or 'Golden' century is also known as the period of the Royal Republic, for the King had to consult the nobles before fixing taxes or declaring war. The reduction of the rights of the bourgeoisie and the peasantry in favor of the nobility and the clergy modified the original monarchy of divided estates.

13   In 1573, with the end of the Jagiellon dynasty, the Diet approved the free election of the King and guaranteed religious tolerance, which was exceptional in a time when Europe was being shaken by religious wars. King Stephen Bathory (1576-86) gave up his role as arbitrator and the nobility started to elect their own courts.

14   During the 17th century, international developments were unfavorable for Poland and Lithuania. Sweden fought Poland over the control of the Baltic, and Russia entered into conflict with Lithuania. Turkish and Austrian ambitions in central Europe also exerted pressure on Poland.

15   On the lower Dnepr, on the border with the Ukraine, free peasants and impoverished nobles became the first Cossacks, warriors who lived by pillaging. In 1648, the Cossacks and the Ukranian peasants started a national revolt. The King made unsuccessful attempts to reach an agreement with the rebels, whose victories weakened the Polish republic.

16   The Cossacks formed occasional alliances with the Turks and the Russians. In 1654, Russian troops entered Polish territory, and Sweden invaded the rest of the country a year later. King John Casimir fled to Silesia, and Poland was aided by Austria, while the peasants in the provinces organized the first large-scale armed resistance.

17   The Swedes and the Turks were expelled from the country and the Cossacks were defeated. Russia kept Smolensk and the Ukraine, the left bank of the Dnepr and the city of Kiev. The wars devastated the land, decimated the population and split the republic.

18   In 1772, Russia, Prussia, and Austria agreed on the territorial partition of Poland. A second partition followed in 1793, after a fresh Russian invasion annulled the 1791 Constitution and put an end to a new Polish attempt to reorganize the State.

19   A patriotic insurrection was crushed in 1794, and was followed a year later by the third partition of Poland. The Polish State disappeared from the map, but the Polish people retained a sense of national identity.

20   During the 19th century, the Poles made several attempts to free their homeland. National conscience and Catholicism, both under persecution, became stronger. New political parties appeared: a peasants', a workers', and a national party, and resistance was expressed through culture.

21   The consolidation of the Russian revolution in 1917 brought Poland the support of Western powers. In 1918 a provisional government was created, led by Jozef Pilsudski. It established an eight-hour working day and equal rights for men and women.

22   Boundaries could not be moved back, as a sense of national identity had emerged in the Ukraine, Lithuania and Belarus. The creation

of a federation failed as a result of the counter-offensive by the Soviet army. The Peace of Riga, signed in 1921, guaranteed the independence of the Baltic states and fixed the eastern border of Poland at Zbrucz.

23 The 1921 Constitution adopted a parliamentary system. During the years that followed, there was a series of coalition governments, generally between the National and Social Christian parties, which were both conservative, or the Peasants' party, which was moderate.

24 Political instability, a tariff war against Germany, unemployment and social unrest benefited the Communist Party, which had been banned in 1923. Its main military leader, Jozef Pilsudski, staged a coup in 1926 but the ensuing prosperity was ended by the effects of the 1929 Wall Street crash.

25 The growing power of Germany and the USSR became a threat to Poland, and Britain and France only gave the country formal support. In a secret agreement, the USSR and Germany divided the Polish territory once more. On September 1 1939, Germany invaded Poland.

26 Britain and France declared war on Germany. On September 17, the USSR also invaded Poland. In the occupied territories millions of Poles died, especially Jews, some of whom were taken to German concentration camps. Many others starved or were executed.

27 The Polish government-in-exile (most of them escaped to Romania and the rest of government members as well as miliary officers went to Hungary, crossing Slovakia) led the resistance. A military contingent fought on the western front, while the Home Army carried out subversive actions. After the German invasion, the USSR accepted the creation of a Polish army under its jurisdiction.

28 The Soviet counter-offensive modified relations with Poland. The government-in-exile demanded an inquiry into the murders of Polish officers, and the USSR broke diplomatic relations. The Red Army invaded Poland and re-established military occupation.

29 After the defeat of Germany, the allies gathered at Malta and agreed on a Provisional Polish Government of National Unity (made up by representatives from pro-Soviet and exiled groups) which was to call elections. The Government was dominated by the Polish Workers' Party.

30 In 1945 the provisional government and the USSR signed an agreement establishing the Polish eastern border, along the Curso line. The same year, the allies fixed the eastern border along the Oder-Neisse line of Lusetia.

31 The Polish Workers' Party and the Socialist Party of Poland constituted the Polish United Workers' Party (PUWP). The Polish Peasants' Party disintegrated, and elections were postponed.

32 The PUWP governed the country, modeling itself on the Soviet Communist Party (CPSU) in the USSR. Industry and commerce were nationalized, the State built great steel and metal works, and forcibly collectivized agriculture. Women were incorporated into the workforce.

33 The denunciation of Stalin's crimes during the 20th Congress of the CPSU in 1956 had repercussions on the PUWP. In November of that year Wladyslaw Gomulka was elected party first secretary and promised to take a 'Polish path towards socialism'. Gomulka freed Cardinal Stefan Wyszynski, who was the head of the Catholic Church, and stirred up popular expectations.

34 In 1968, action taken by an anti-Semitic group within the PUWP forced Jewish groups to leave the country. In a treaty signed in 1970, West Germany recognized the Polish borders established after the War. East Germany had done so in 1950.

35 In 1970, strikes broke out because of a huge increase in prices. The Government ordered the army to open fire on the workers and started another crisis within the PUWP. Gomulka was replaced by Edward Gierek, but the regime underwent renewed crises over corruption charges and internal fights within the party.

36 In 1976, new strikes broke out, and this time they were repressed not by the use of firearms but by long prison sentences. In 1979, the Polish Pope John Paul II visited his native land, rekindling the hopes of the population who welcomed him at massive gatherings.

37 The 1980 strike at Gdansk's Lenin Dockyard was led by trade unionist Lech Walesa. It turned into a general strike and the Government had to negotiate with the strikers. Two months later, the Government was forced to recognize Solidarity, a workers' union with 10 million members. Rural Solidarity was created, to represent three million peasants.

38 The PUWP suffered other crises that led to the appointment of Wojciech Jaruzelski, then prime minister, to the post of party first secretary. In December 1981, Jaruzelski declared martial law, Solidarity was banned and its leaders went underground.

39 Martial law was lifted in 1983, but the Constitution was modified to include a state of emergency. With the Catholic Church acting as a mediator, government and Solidarity representatives went back to negotiations in 1989, while the USSR was embarking on *perestroika* (restructuring).

40 In the elections in June that year, the PUWP only obtained the fixed number of representatives that had been agreed on during the negotiations with the opposition. Solidarity rejected General Jaruzelski's proposal to share government with the PUWP. Tadensz Mazowiecki, a journalist and a moderate member of Solidarity, was appointed the first president of a non-communist government in the East European bloc.

41 Poland re-established diplomatic relations with the Vatican and with Israel. The US and Germany committed themselves to financial assistance. German reunification caused some alarm, but the Four-Plus-Two negotiations (see Germany) ratified the postwar Polish borders.

42 In December 1989, the National Assembly approved reinstating the name, the Republic of Poland. In January 1990, the PUWP was dissolved to create another party, but it later split into the Social Democracy of the Republic of Poland and the Polish Social Democratic Union.

43 In January 1990, the Government started an economic adjustment program agreed with the International Monetary Fund (IMF). Poland requested its incorporation to the Council of Europe and established relations with the EU. The US and the Council of Europe made entry to NATO (the North Atlantic Treaty Organization) dependent on the results of the economic reforms under way and the upgrading of the military warfare to the Alliance's standards.

44 On May 10 1990, the first strike was held against Mazowiecki's government. This exercise of power hastened the fragmentation of Solidarity. The union became a political party in July 1990, and later divided into several factions.

45 In December 1990, the first direct presidential elections were held, and Lech Walesa was elected

---

PROFILE

ENVIRONMENT

On the extensive northern plains, crossed by the Vistula (Wisla), Warta and Oder (Odra) rivers, there are coniferous woodlands, rye, potato and linen plantations. The fertile soil of Central Poland's plains and highlands yield a considerable agricultural production of beet and cereals. The southern region, on the northern slopes of the Carpathian Mountains, is less fertile. Poland has large mineral resources: coal in Silesia (the world's fourth largest producer); sulfur in Tarnobrzeskie (the world's second largest producer); copper; zinc and lead. Major industries are steel, chemicals and shipbuilding. The country has high levels of air pollution; due to its geographical location in the center of Europe, it absorbs polluted water and air 'in transit' from other countries. Soil depletion has caused extensive erosion, due to the excessive deforestation that has accompanied intensive agriculture.

SOCIETY

Peoples: Polish, 96 per cent; Ukrainian, 0.8 per cent; other (Belarusian, 0.8 per cent; German, 0.5 per cent; Swedish, 0.5 per cent.
Religions: Catholic, 90.7 per cent; Orthodox, 1.4 per cent. Other (7.9 per cent).
Languages: Polish.
Political Parties: Democratic Left Alliance (SLD); Solidarity Electoral Action (AWS); Polish Peasants' Party (PPP), Freedom Union (UW); Self Defense Movement of the Polish Republic (SDM); League of Polish Families, Movement for the Reconstruction of Poland. The German minority has parliamentary representation.
Social Organizations: Union affiliation has descended greatly. Two main groups with political affiliation: Poland Trade Union Alliance and Solidarity. Independent unions like the Central Union of Agricultural Groups.

THE STATE

Official Name: Polska Rzeczpospolita.
Administrative Divisions: 49 provinces.
Capital: Warsaw (Warzawa) 2,260,000 people (1999).
Other cities: Lódz 1,017,300 people; Kraków 784,800; Wroclaw 634,600; Poznan 580,200 (2000).
Government: Aleksander Kwasniewski, President and Head of State since December 1995, re-elected in 2000. Leszek Miller, Chairman of the Council of Ministers (Premier) and Head of Government since October 2001. Bicameral Legislature: the *Diet*, with 460 members, and the Senate, with 100 members.
National Holiday: November 11, Independence Day (1918); May 3, Constitution Day (1791).
Armed Forces: 241,750 (1997).
Other: 23,400 Border Guard, Police, Coast Guard.

MATERNAL MORTALITY

1985/99

Per 100,000 live births

8

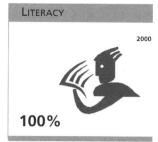

LITERACY

2000

100%

head of state with 75 per cent of the vote. In August 1991, new prime minister Jan Krysztof Bielecki resigned, upsetting the precarious balance of political transition. The former Communist Party and a small peasant party were ready to accept his resignation, but Walesa backed the prime minister and insisted on giving him special powers, by threatening to dissolve the Diet.

[46] In December 1991, the new Diet appointed Jan Olszewski as Prime Minister. He was accepted by President Walesa three days later, but the cabinet was not ratified by the Diet until December 23, and then only by a narrow margin of 17 votes.

[47] As of November 1991, Poland has been the twenty-sixth member country of the European Council, a Western European organization which also includes Turkey, the Czech Republic, and Hungary.

[48] At the end of May, President Walesa asked the *Sjem* (lower house) to form a new Government because of a lack of confidence in Olszewski. In mid-July Parliament accepted Walesa's proposal and appointed Hanna Suchocka Prime Minister, supported by a 7 party coalition.

[49] Suchocka applied strict monetary controls and promoted the privatization of approximately 600 state enterprises with a privatization act in August 1992. Meanwhile, in February 1993 Walesa, under pressure from the Church, made the controversial decision to revoke the law which instituted the right to abortion.

[50] Dissatisfied with Suchocka's social policies, Solidarity sponsored a motion censuring the Government, finally passed by a single-vote majority, forcing the Prime Minister to call early legislative elections.

[51] Elections were held in September and led to the return to power of those political sectors which had supported the communist regime: the Democratic Left Alliance (SLD) and the Polish Peasants' Party (PSL), winning 73 of the 100 seats.

[52] Initially refusing to acknowledge the defeat, Walesa appointed PSL leader Waldemar Pawlack as Prime Minister. Although 1994 featured constant conflicts between the President and the Government, the latter did not

significantly modify the economic liberalization policy, despite its attempt to slow the pace of some reforms in order to reduce their social impact.

[53] The former communists' return to power was concluded in November 1995 when Aleksander Kwasniewski defeated Walesa in the second round of presidential elections, with 52 per cent of the vote. The outgoing president had based his election campaign on anti-communism and the support of 'Christian values', insisting on the need to maintain the ban on abortion.

[54] At first, the government of Prime Minister Josef Olesky, who replaced Pawlak, was not altered. However in January 1996, Olesky (former Communist), was forced to resign after the Interior Minister accused him of having been a collaborator with the Soviet KGB. The following month, Olesky was replaced by Wlodzimierz Cimoszweicz.

[55] Right-wing factions of several parties, united by the notion of a conservative social policy and anti-communism, formed a coalition headed by Marian Krzaklewski, called Solidarity Electoral Action (SEA).

[56] In the 1997 parliamentary elections, the SEA defeated the ruling Democratic Left Alliance, with 33.8 per cent of the vote. Jerzy Buzek, a chemical engineer from Silesia, who designed the SEA's economic program, was named Prime Minister.

[57] Poland's entry to NATO was agreed upon in February 1999 by an overwhelming 409 to 7 in the Sjem.

[58] Economic reforms carried out by the government to prepare the nation for EU entry left thousands of people out of work and were extremely unpopular. In September, more than 30,000 farmers and workers held a protest march in Warsaw, accusing Buzek of ignoring the economic problems of the country and calling for elections to be brought forward.

[59] Despite Buzek declaring the country had met all the requisites and was ready to join the EU in April 2000, the ratification process implied Poland would have difficulty even in getting full membership before 2003.

[60] In October, Kwasniewski, leader of the Democratic Left Alliance (SLD) made up of former communists, became the first president to be re-elected since the transition to democracy, obtaining almost 54 per cent of the vote. The election also marked the withdrawal of Lech Walesa from politics, as he failed to get the necessary 1 per cent of the vote.

[61] The lowest voting levels in the brief democratic history of the country was seen a year later in the parliamentary elections where barely 41 per cent of the electorate turned out. Many corruption scandals under the Solidarity administration and the poor state of the economy, above all in rural areas, led to increased support for radical anti-Europeans, and Andrzej Lepper's Self Defense Movement of the Polish Republic (SDM) took an unexpected 10.2 per cent of the vote. The ultra-Catholic League of Polish Families also did well with 7.87 per cent. However, the SLD took the bulk of the vote with 41 per cent.

[62] A coalition government formed by the SLD and the Polish Peasants' Party (PPP) - which took 9 per cent of the vote - made Leszek Miller prime minister in October 2001. The greatest challenges facing the new Miller regime were to combat the budgetary crisis, boost economic growth and the negotiations to enter the EU. Miller promised the media they would 'not be bored under his administration'. The PPP - whose support at the polls was largely based on discontent with Europe in rural areas - threatened to block any action toward EU membership. In December, the EU Summit included Poland in the list of 10 countries hoping to become full members in January 2004.

[63] Scepticism about EU membership increased after Germany and Austria declared their fear of a flow of cheap foreign labor from the East and it was made clear that citizens of new member countries would have to wait seven years before being allowed to work in other EU countries. In rural areas, there were fears of an 'invasion' of people from other European countries, particularly Germany, as Polish land was 30 times cheaper than in many EU nations. In April 2002, Poland agreed with Brussels that foreigners would be barred from buying land in Poland for 12 years after it joins Europe.

[64] In May 2002 the first case of Bovine Spongiform Encephalopathy - Mad Cow Disease - was identified in the southern region of Malopolska. Poland exports beef to the EU and tested all animals over 30 months in order to detect the illness. ∎

Portugal

Population:	10,049,000 (2002)
Land area:	91,500 SQ KM
Capital:	Lisbon
Currency:	Euro
Language:	Portuguese

Portugal

In ancient times Portugal was inhabited by Lusitanians, an Iberian people whose cultural influence extended over a vast area including the whole western shore of the Iberian Peninsula. This area was successively conquered by several Middle Eastern peoples, who only occupied the coastal areas.

2   During the 2nd century BC the Romans settled in the territory, ruling over it until the fall of the Empire around the 5th century AD. Like the rest of Europe, Portugal was invaded by Northern European peoples (generically called Barbarians), who raided the Roman dominions. Among these peoples were the Visigoths. They had a developed culture and settled on the Iberian Peninsula dividing the territory into various kingdoms, and spreading the Christian faith. Their domination over the whole region lasted for nearly six centuries.

In the 8th century AD Arab peoples invaded the region imposing their political and cultural domination in spite of resistance from the earlier inhabitants.

4   During the 11th century the reconquest of the Lusitanian territory started, ending with the expulsion of the Arabs a hundred years later. With Muslim domination over, the territory was politically unified and Portugal entered a period of great economic prosperity. This reached its height during the 15th and 16th centuries, with great maritime expeditions and conquests of vast territories in America, Africa, and the Far East.

5   Its maritime superiority enabled Portugal to develop active worldwide trade and achieve a privileged economic position within Europe. A long time elapsed before

other nations like Britain and the Netherlands were in a position to threaten Portugal's naval supremacy.

6   Following a series of dynastic stuggles, in 1580 the country was made subject to Philip II, King of Spain. The two kingdoms remained united until 1688 when Portugal succeeded in having its independence recognized in the Treaty of Lisbon. Unity with Spain brought the decline of Portugal's power. Most of the maritime empire collapsed, besieged by the British and the Dutch, who

started to control most of the trading routes and outposts.

7   By the time Portugal recovered its independence, it had been devastated by three decades of war against Spain. The country was forced to look on while the new maritime powers seized most of its colonies in Africa and Asia. Brazil remained under Portuguese rule. The position of Britain as the leading maritime power became painfully obvious when Portugal was forced to sign the Treaty of Methuen, which established Portugal's political and economic dependence on the British. Pombal, an adviser of Jose I, carried out economic reforms. Like the Spanish Bourbons, Pombal had been influenced by the ideas of the French Enlightenment and he changed colonial management. The discovery and exploitation of gold mines in

Brazil enabled the country to enjoy a period of great economic prosperity. But in spite of Pombal, Portugal finally went into decline.

8   Dependence on Britain was further consolidated when Portugal was forced to seek support to end Napoleonic occupation, which lasted from 1807 to 1811. French domination led to the independence of Brazil; the Portuguese court had fled there in exile. Brazil had enjoyed a significant expansion in trade, in particular with Britain. At the end of the Napoleonic period in Europe, the rising Brazilian bourgeoisie was not ready to be displaced, so in 1821 Brazil declared independence. Meanwhile a civil war broke out in Portugal between those who wanted the restoration of absolutism and liberal groups preferring greater political participation.

9   The economy maintained its traditional agrarian structure. Other countries were embarking on an accelerated industrialization process which would quickly give them economic eminence. Portugal reached the end of the 19th century economically stagnant, deprived of the richest and largest part of its colonial empire, and suffering from acute internal political crisis.

10   The monarchy was incapable of ensuring the stability needed to start economic recovery, and was definitively overthrown by liberal opposition forces in 1910. This started the Republican period. Once they had attained their objective, the alliance of Liberal and Republican groups started to fragment and internal differences prevented them from achieving a common governmental agenda. One of the few things they shared was active opposition to the Church, which had been a traditional ally of the *ancien régime* and had had important privileges and powers, including the control of education. The inefficiency of the Liberals, together with the ruthless persecution of representatives of the ancien régime, encouraged the formation of a vast opposition movement.

11   Portugal sided with Britain in World War I. This only deepened the economic crisis and increased popular discontent. Political instability and economic stagnation were the most salient features of the period. In 1926

WORKERS

2000

UNEMPLOYMENT: 4%
LABOR FORCE AS % OF TOTAL:

■ FEMALE: 44%   ■ MALE: 56%

1994/97

EMPLOYMENT DISTRIBUTION:

F
M

■ SERVICES   F: 64%   M: 48%
■ INDUSTRY   F: 21%   M: 40%
■ AGRICULTURE   F: 16%   M: 12%

LAND USE

DEFORESTATION: 0.9% annual (1990/95)

1993

■ FOREST & WOODLAND: 35.7%
■ ARABLE: 25.5%
■ OTHER: 38.8%

PUBLIC EXPENDITURE

Military expenditure (as % GNI):	**2.1 %**	(1999)
Defense expenditure (% of central government expenditure)	**5.4 %**	(1999)

MATERNAL MORTALITY

1985/99

Per 100,000
live births

8

LITERACY

2000

92%

this led to a coup bringing a right-wing military group to power. They set up an authoritarian corporatist regime which they called the 'New State'. With a few changes, it was to rule the country for over 40 years. Political opposition was proscribed, with major figures imprisoned or exiled. Trade unions were dissolved and replaced by corporatist organizations similar to those in fascist Italy.

¹² The most significant figure of this period and the true ruler behind the military was economist Antonio de Oliveira Salazar, who occupied various positions and dominated Portuguese political and economic life. The country remained neutral during the Spanish Civil War and World War II which could both have jeopardized its barely stable economy.

¹³ The agricultural system remained unchanged throughout the whole period, causing much migration towards the major cities of Portugal and Europe. During the 1950s the decolonization movement started, and the country was faced with the possibility of losing its last dominions in Africa. From that moment on, Salazar's regime fought against the liberation movements emerging in the Portuguese colonies, becoming increasingly isolated from other countries and unpopular at home.

¹⁴ The human and economic cost of these colonial wars accelerated the internal attrition of Salazar's government. Repressive measures had to be increased to halt the growing opposition. Salazar's death in 1970 and the deepening of the economic crisis showed that the end of the regime was close at hand.

¹⁵ In 1974, amidst the opposition of many social groups and political parties, a significant number of dissatisfied army officers gathered under the Armed Forces Movement (*Movimento das Forças Armadas* - MFA). In April, they staged a coup intending to end the wars in Africa and start the democratization process.

¹⁶ The military government which emerged from this 'Carnation Revolution' or Captains' Revolution had vast popular support. This support came out as active encouragement of the progressive tendencies within the MFA. The new government quickly decolonized Angola, Mozambique, and Guinea-Bissau. Meanwhile it actively sought international recognition and attempted to improve the country's image abroad. It legalized left-wing political parties, decreed an amnesty for political prisoners and passed a series of land laws aiming at breaking up large rural estates and modernizing agricultural production.

¹⁷ The Socialist and Communist parties were the main supporters of the new regime, but after a year in office, their alliance began to break up. This slowed the democratization of the country, started in April 1974. In the 1976 general elections, the Socialist Party led by Mario Soares won the majority vote to become Portugal's first democratic constitutional government in the 20th century.

¹⁸ The continuing economic crisis, together with strong political and trade union opposition, wore the Socialist Government down very quickly. This situation was aggravated by Soares' harsh economic adjustment program.

¹⁹ During the 1980s the transition process continued. The electorate approved a new constitution and eliminated all the special bodies created under military rule. Portugal's foreign policy changed, and the country underwent speedy economic and political integration with Europe, including incorporation in NATO and the EEC, in 1986. That year, the Socialist Party lost power again, this time to its one-time ally the center-left Social Democratic Party (PSD).

²⁰ By the end of the 1980s Portugal was experiencing significant economic growth, but still far below the average level for the rest of Europe. Changes accelerated after the electoral victory of the PSD, which used its ample parliamentary majority to liberalize the economy. The new economic policy received strong opposition, particularly from the workers in the public sector, who make up 5 per cent of the country's active labor force and who saw the PSD's reforms as a threat to their jobs.

²¹ The trade union movement brought the country to a standstill on several occasions. It opposed the privatization of public companies, the elimination of labor legislation enacted during the 1974 revolution, and the attempt to repeal the 1974 land reform legislation. In 1984 an extreme left-wing group, called the Popular Forces of April 25 (FP-25), also started to take action against these measures. The group, which had been very active in recent years, demanded that the parties in power respect the achievements of the 'Carnation Revolution'.

²² In April 1987, the governments of Portugal and the People's Republic of China signed an agreement charging Portugal with the administration of Macau until 1999. Sovereignty is then transferred to China, under the 'one country, two systems' principle (see Macau).

²³ In 1988, after over a month of negotiations, the PSD and the Socialist Party agreed to modify the constitution to allow the re-privatization of various companies nationalized during the 'Carnation Revolution' and to further reduce presidential powers. President Mario Soares, former leader of the Socialist Party, opposed these reforms.

²⁴ Portuguese politics became polarized between the ruling PSD and the PS. The latter was a more viable left-wing alternative after the

PROFILE

ENVIRONMENT

The country includes the Iberian continental territory and the islands of the Azores and Madeira archipelagos. The Tagus, the country's largest river, divides the continental region into two separate areas. The northern region is mountainous, with abundant rains and intensive agriculture: wheat, corn, vines and olives are grown. In the valley of the Douro, the major wine-growing region in the country, large vineyards extend in terraces along the valley slopes. The city of Oporto is the northern economic center. The South, Alentejo, with extensive low plateaus and a very dry climate, has large wheat and olive plantations and sheep farming. The cork tree woods, which made Portugal a great cork producer, are found here. Fishing and shipbuilding are major contributors to the country's economy. Mineral resources include pyrite, tungsten, coal and iron. The effects of erosion are accentuated by the poor quality of the soil. Air pollution levels are significant in urban areas, or near cellulose and cement factories.

SOCIETY

Peoples: The Portuguese (99.5 per cent) came from the integration of various ethnic groups: Celts, Arabs, Berbers, Phoenicians, Carthaginians and others. Immigrants come from Africa (0.2 per cent) and America (Brazilians 0.1 per cent, US Americans 0.1 per cent). There is substantial migration by Portuguese towards richer countries in the continent.
Religions: Mainly Catholic. **Language:** Portuguese.
Political Parties: Socialist Party; Social Democrat Party (SDP); Unitarian Democratic Coalition (with the Portuguese Communist Party and the Greens); People's Party; Bloc of the Left; the Social Democratic Center Party, affiliated to the European Union of Christian Democrats. Other minor parties: the National Solidarity Party, the Revolutionary Socialist Party, the People's Monarchist Party; and the Democratic Renewal Party.
Social Organizations: The General Confederation of Portuguese Workers (CGTP), a nationwide multi-union organization with 287 union members (represents 80 per cent of the organized workers); the General Union of Portuguese Workers (UGTP), which combines 50 unions; National Agriculture Confederation (CNA).

THE STATE

Official Name: República Portuguesa.
Administrative Divisions: 18 districts, 2 autonomous regions.
Capital: Lisbon 3,754,000 people (1999). **Other cities:** Oporto 1,206,800 people; Amadora 123,400; Vila Nova de Gaia 74,800 (2000).
Government: Jorge Sampaio, President since March 1996, re-elected in 2001. Manuel Durão Barroso, Prime Minister since April 2002. Unicameral Legislature: Assembly of the Republic, with 230 members.
National Holidays: June 10, Portugal Day (1580); October 5, Independence Day (1910); April 25, Liberty Day (1975).
Armed Forces: 54,200 (1995). **Other:** 20,900 Republican National Guard; 20,000 Public Security Police; 8,900 Border Security Guard.

FOREIGN TRADE

Millions US$ 2000

IMPORTS
45,494
EXPORTS
32,975

FOOD DEPENDENCY

2000

11%

collapse of real socialism. However, in the October 1991 parliamentary elections, the PSD won over 50 per cent of the vote while the PS did not reach 30 per cent. Cavaco Silvas' political victory was due to the social democratic slant with which he disguised his orthodox liberal economic orientation. The right-wing Social Democratic Centre Party received a mere four per cent which led its leader Diego Freitas do Amaral to resign. Support for the Communist Party dropped 3 per cent since 1987.

[25] In January 1992, Portugal took over the presidency of the European Community. The new President, Luis Mira de Amaral, Portuguese minister of industry and energy, announced he would promote industrial cooperation with Latin America, Africa and central Europe. Another of his priorities was the signing of the Maastricht Treaty which entailed political, economic and monetary union between the members of the Community.

[26] In August 1993, the Assembly restricted the right to seek asylum and enabled the expulsion of foreigners from the country. The legislation was based on the defense of the job market and was opposed by President Soares. Unemployment reached eight per cent but it was set to increase with the privatization or closing of state-run airlines, shipyards and steel industries.

[27] Meanwhile a plan financed by the EU was approved for the 1993-1997 period for the poorest members, including Portugal, providing investment education, transport, industrial retrofitting and job creation.

[28] Portuguese politics were rocked by intense student protests against the cost and quality of education, and by strikes for higher wages in the public sector. The 50-per-cent increase in the toll charged at Lisbon's access bridge caused several blockades by transport workers. The Government justified the raise citing the need to finance a new bridge for the last World Expo of the century, held in 1998.

[29] The October 1995 general elections were won by the Socialist Party which gained an absolute majority at the Assembly. Antonio Guerres was appointed Prime Minister, replacing Anibal Cavaco.

After 10 years of PSD dominance, oriented toward European integration and economic liberalism, the PS capitalized on domestic discontent with education and health and assured the financial market it would not interfere with the goals regarding monetary union and privatization.

[30] The Socialist Jorge Sampaio took over the presidency of the country in March 1996, after winning the elections with 54 per cent of the vote, against the 46 per cent of former Prime Minister Cavaco Silva. The Government brought in an economic plan in line with EU demands, particularly regarding to the budget deficit.

[31] A successful campaign against tax evasion meant increased spending on health, education and social policies. The privatization program was intensified, selling shares in telecommunications, electricity and roads. Unemployment fell to 6.7 per cent of the active population.

[32] The Socialist Party triumphed in the December 1997 municipal elections, maintaining control over the main cities, Lisbon and Oporto/Porto, and beating the conservative Social Democratic Party by an overall margin of five points (38.2 to 33.1 per cent).

[33] In February 1998, Parliament approved a law legalizing abortion up to 10 weeks of pregnancy. Various estimates showed there were around 16,000 illegal abortions carried out each year.

[34] After 442 years' governing the island, Portugal handed Macao over to China on December 20 1999. President Sampaio was present at the ceremony, along with his Chinese counterpart Jiang Zemin. This act signified the end of the Portuguese empire, as well as the end of all European control in Asia. Portugal, which had been the first European power to control Asian territories, was also the last to withdraw.

[35] Sampaio visited Xanana Gusmao, East Timor's pro-independence leader, in February 2000 and promised to help the Timorese to restore their education system. This was the first visit of a Portuguese head of state since Portugal pulled out of Timor in 1974.

[36] Prime Minister Antonio Guterres took over as president of the EU until July 2000. His leadership led the EU to impose diplomatic isolation on Austria when the fascist-sympathizing Liberty Party, led by Jörg Haider, joined the Austrian governing coalition.

[37] In April 2001, Sampaio's presidential electoral victory confirmed his continuing popularity, consolidating the control of the Socialists led by Guterres.

[38] December saw the inauguration of the Alqueva hydroelectric project on the Guadiana river. It created the greatest artificial lake in Europe, and was condemned by several environmental groups as too big, destructive and unnecessary. Although the project would irrigate the southern wasteland of the country, it would also flood the habitat of its unusual wild life (including, eagles, wild boar, falcons and Iberian lynxes) as well as submerging 160 Stone Age period rocks. The Alqueva project dated from 1957, the time of Oliveira Salazar's dictatorship. The politicians endorsed the project arguing that it was essential for irrigating the wasteland areas of the country, but some environmentalists highlighted that only 48 per cent of the irrigated land would be useful for crops or pasture. The environmental group Quercus advocated the dam should be filled only to 139 meters and not to its maximum 152 meters in order to save the trees.

[39] The poor economic performance of Guterres' government led him to make repeated changes in the cabinet, which, together with charges of corruption within the Socialist Party, lost him popularity. In December 2001, after the drastic defeat in the local election, Guterres resigned and Parliament was dissolved.

[40] Elections were brought forward and, in March 2002, the social-democratic candidate Manuel Durão Barroso won. The new Prime Minister formed a center-right coalition government. At the time of his taking office he promised to cut corporate taxes and reduce public expenditure, as well as to privatize public services including health. ∎

Puerto Rico

Population: 3,988,000 (2002)
Land area: 8,870 SQ KM
Capital: San Juan
Currency: US dollar
Language: Spanish and English

Puerto Rico

In 1508, 15 years after Christopher Columbus's landfall, the island of Borinquen (as Puerto Rico was called by the Arawaks/Tainos who lived there) became a colony and has continued thus up to today. Puerto Rico is the easternmost of the Greater Antilles and because of its strategic location at the entrance of the Caribbean the island bore 400 years of Spanish rule. It also suffered the repeated attacks of pirates and regular naval forces, whether British, Dutch or French, plus US administration after the Spanish-American War of 1898.

[2] In the first few decades of the 16th century, a sugar-based economy began to take shape. By some estimates, by 1560 there were already 15,000 slaves on the island. The sugar economy however was a short-lived period in the island's history; in the latter part of the century leather became the principal product.

[3] As in neighboring islands, the local Taino people were exterminated by war, disease and overwork. African slaves were brought in to take their place in the fields where most food supplies for Spanish expeditions to the mainland were produced. Thus, Puerto Rican culture became a blend of its African and Spanish heritage.

[4] Spanish rule was continually challenged by attacks and rebellions by both the Tainos and enslaved African workers. The latter rebelled successively in 1822, 1826, 1843, and 1848. The struggle for independence in the rest of Latin America had its counterpart in Puerto Rico's struggle for administrative reform (1812-1840), but Spanish troops ruthlessly stifled the uprising.

[5] In 1868, five years before slavery was finally abolished, a group of patriots led by Ramón Emeterio Betances moved things nearer to liberation. In the town of Lares they proclaimed Puerto Rico's independence and took up arms to free the island. Despite their defeat, the Lares's revolt signaled the birth of the Puerto Rican nation.

[6] The independence movement continued to gain strength in the following years. The Cubans were already up in arms in 1897, led by José Martí in a movement that reached Puerto Rico. US military intervention in the war against Spain, in 1898, hastened Spain's defeat but for Puerto Rico it only meant the imposition of a new ruler.

[7] US colonial administrations, first military and then civilian, imposed English as the official language and attempted to turn the island into a sugar plantation and military base. Puerto Ricans were made US citizens in 1917, though they were given no participation in the island's government. As a result, resistance to colonial rule grew. In 1922 the pro-independence Nationalist Party (PN) was founded. PN-led uprisings in 1930 and 1950 were fiercely put down.

[8] The PN leader from 1930 until his death in 1965 was Pedro Albizu Campos, who suffered exile and imprisonment for his anti-colonial activities.

[9] In 1947, intense internal and international pressure forced the US to allow Puerto Rico to elect its own governor. The 1948 elections gave the post to Luis Muñoz Marín, leader of the Popular Democratic Party (PPD), who favored turning the country into a self-governing commonwealth or free associated state. The US Government authorized the drafting of a constitution in 1959, which was approved by a plebiscite and later ratified by the US. Muñoz Marín's program was thus sanctioned.

[10] With the institution of Commonwealth status, US administrations were freed from the obligation of reporting on Puerto Rico's status to the UN Decolonization Committee. Moreover, in this way the UN tacitly endorsed the arrangement declaring the 'end' of colonial rule. Nevertheless in September 1978 the Decolonization Committee reconsidered the situation. In December that year a UN General Assembly resolution once again defined Puerto Rico as a colony and demanded self-determination for its people.

[11] Muñoz Marín promoted industrialization on the island through massive US private investment enticed by government tax incentives. During the 1960s, Puerto Rican agriculture was destroyed by an influx of US products, resulting in over 50 per cent of the island's food being imported. The newly-formed labor reserve was more than enough to supply cheap hands for the growing US corporate community, and Puerto Ricans soon began migrating en masse to the US, and especially to New York in search of work. The 1980 US census registered over two million Puerto Ricans living in the United States.

[12] With the great social upheavals of the 1960s, the struggle for independence flowered anew on the island. Despite the revival of the independence movement, a 1967 plebiscite confirmed the Commonwealth status. Moreover, elections the following year gave the governorship to the New Progressive Party (PNP) which favored making the island the 51st state of the US. Nevertheless after the 1972 elections the PPD returned to power led by Rafael Hernández Colón. In 1976, supporters of the US statehood option returned to the governorship. Carlos Romero Barceló announced that if he were re-elected for a second term, he would call a pro-statehood referendum. Barceló went on to win in 1980, but by such a slim margin that plans for a statehood plebiscite were abandoned, despite encouragement from President Reagan.

[13] Puerto Rico has one representative in the US Congress, but with no voting rights other than in committees. US citizenship only gave Puerto Ricans the right to participate in the 1980 presidential elections, although residents in the US are able to vote in all elections.

[14] Rafael Hernández Colón was elected President on November 6 1984. He promised a 'four-year term of struggle against corruption and unemployment'. He renewed Puerto Rico's Commonwealth status thus rejecting his predecessor's intention to integrate into the Union.

[15] Hernández Colón was re-elected in November 1988, with 48.7 per cent of the vote, against 45.8 per cent for those in favor of annexation by the US, and 5.3 per cent for those who favored independence.

[16] In 1989 the Special United Nations Decolonization Committee expressed its wish that the people of Puerto Rico exercise their right to self-determination and independence. The resolution stressed the 'clearly Latin American character and identity of Puerto Rico's people and culture'.

[17] In April 1991, Governor Hernández Colón passed a law granting official status for the Spanish language. A few weeks later, the Puerto Rican people were granted the Prince of Asturias award by the Spanish crown, 'in recognition of the country's efforts to defend the Spanish language'.

[18] In the plebiscite carried out late in 1991, various strategies were proposed to promote development on the island. The governor succeeded in rallying moderate nationalists and supporters of

independence, who campaigned together. They were in favor of self-determination, the end of subjection to US jurisdiction, the affirmation of Puerto Rican identity, regardless of any future referendum decisions, and the maintenance of US citizenship. However, all this effort came to nothing in the polls, when 55 per cent of the voters supported the PNP's position that a break with Washington had to be avoided. Given this result, Hernández' position within his party was weakened, strengthening the hand of more pro-independence sectors and Hernández finally resigned the Popular Democratic Party leadership.

[19] Pedro Roselló, a supporter of Puerto Rico's integration into the United States, was elected governor in 1992. His plan to make English the only official language on the island - replacing Spanish - caused massive protest demonstrations. Finally in 1993 English was made an official language alongside Spanish.

[20] In November, a referendum was held to decide on the political future of the island. Those wanting to maintain the 'free associated state' status won a narrow victory, with 48.4 per cent of the vote, while the group supporting the transformation of Puerto Rico into the 51st US state took 46.2 per cent. Independence supporters had a mere 4 per cent.

[21] Some pro-independence supporters had agreed to collaborate - in sectors like culture - with the 'pro-annexation' cabinet led by the present governor. However, when Roselló sacked the director of the Puerto Rico Institute of Culture, Awilda Palau, in May 1995, the possibilities of collaboration were reduced.

[22] In 1996, opposition continued to the US Congress decision to grant tax exemptions to companies established in Puerto Rico, as this was the main fiscal instrument for development on the island.

[23] In January 1997, Roselló was elected for a second term. In a message for the occasion, US President Bill Clinton promised to promote legislation in Congress allowing Puerto Rico to hold a referendum on its future political status.

[24] In February 1998, Clinton went even further, openly supporting a referendum for Puerto Rico, allowing the nationals to choose between total incorporation to the US, independence or maintaining the island as an associated state.

[25] Seven Puerto Rican activists, imprisoned for setting off bombs in the US and pardoned by President Clinton, were received as heroes by crowds at San Juan airport on September 12 1999, waving flags and singing nationalist songs. The activists had carried out a terrorist campaign throughout the 1970s and 1980s.

[26] Tens of thousands of people protested in February 2000 against renewed military exercises by the US army on the Puerto Rican island of Vieques. This island had been used by the US for military exercises including bomb target practice for 50 years, but these had been suspended after the accidental death of a civilian in April 1999. Clinton and Governor Rosselló had made an agreement for training maneuvers until April 2000, but the church authorities organized a protest group to camp in the target area, thus interrupting the 'war games'.

[27] In August 2001, the Armed Forces committee of the US House of Representatives cancelled the referendum that Washington itself had called for on the future of exercises on Vieques. The wording of the referendum did not include the option of an immediate and permanent end to the target practice.

[28] Six months later, a US federal judge refused a Puerto Rico government petition for an immediate ending of the bombing on Vieques. According to Puerto Rico, the exercises infringe the 1972 Federal Noise Control Act, as well as Puerto Rican laws on noise pollution standards.

[29] On education, the goal of the Department of Education's Literacy Project is to eradicate illiteracy by 2008, which implies teaching 60,000 people to read and write. However by 2002 only a few people had enrolled, many courses were cancelled due to a lack of teachers or students, and many districts lacked the proper curricula. At that time, only 2,000 people had gained literacy skills as a result of the project. ∎

PROFILE

ENVIRONMENT
The smallest and easternmost island of the Greater Antilles. A central mountain range, covered with rainforests, runs across the island. In the highlands, subsistence crops are grown (corn, cassava/manioc); on the western slopes there are large coffee plantations and in the central region small tobacco farms. On the northern slopes citrus and pineapples are grown, exported to the US. The main crop is sugarcane, which uses the best farmlands along the coastline. The islands of Vieques (43 sq km), Mona (40 sq km) and Culebra also belong to Puerto Rico.

SOCIETY
Peoples: Most Puerto Ricans are descendants of African slaves (20 per cent) and Spanish colonizers (80 per cent). In addition, about 3 million Puerto Ricans have emigrated to the US to escape unemployment and poverty.
Religions: No official religion. Catholics (85.3 per cent), Protestants (4.7 per cent), others (10 per cent).
Languages: Spanish and English (both official).
Political Parties: The New Progressive Party (PNP), led by Pedro Rosselló, advocating total integration - or annexation - to the US as the 51st state of the Union; the Democratic People's Party (PPD), founded in 1938 by Luis Muñoz Marín, supports the current 'Commonwealth' status; the Puerto Rican Renewal Party (PRP), a split of the PNP; the Puerto Rican Independence Party (PI), founded in 1946 from a breakup of the PPD, social-democrat; the Communist Party (PC), founded in 1934, had intense activity which lost momentum following a strong repression in the 1950s; Puerto Rican Socialist Party (PSP), founded in 1971.

THE STATE
Official Name: Estado Libre Asociado de Puerto Rico.
Capital: San Juan 1,366,000 people (1999).
Other cities: Bayamon 205,400 people; Carolina 169,800; Ponce 156,500; Caguas 89,500 (2000).
Government: Sila María Calderón, since January 2001, the first woman Governor. Bicameral National Assembly: Chamber of Representatives with 51 members and the Senate with 28 members.
National Holiday: July 25, Constitution (1952); September 23, the Battle of Grito de Lares (start of the anti-colonial armed revolt in 1868); July 4, US Independence (1776).
Armed Forces: 3,518 troops of the US Army (1992).

Qatar

Population: 584,000 (2002)
Land area: 11,000 SQ KM
Capital: Doha (Ad-Dawhah)
Currency: Riyal
Language: Arabic

Qatar

In a small desert country without a single river, 400 farms produce almost all the foodstuffs required for domestic consumption. The miracle that changed the desert into a kitchen garden was the advent of oil revenues. Half a million barrels of oil per day, and the successful policies of Amir Khalifa ibn al-Thani's government, have helped bring about these achievements.

2 Like the neighboring island of Bahrain, since ancient times the Qatar peninsula participated in the Gulf trade between Mesopotamia and India. Islamicized in the 7th century (see Saudi Arabia), at the time of the Caliphate of Baghdad, Qatar had already obtained autonomy which was maintained until 1076 when it was conquered by the Emir of Bahrain.

3 From the 16th century, after a brief period of Portuguese occupation, the country lived in great prosperity due to the development of pearl fishing which attracted immigrants. Settled on the coasts, under the leadership of the al-Thani family, these settlers succeeded in politically uniting the country in the 18th century, though it remained subject to Bahrain's sovereignty. The process of independence, begun in 1815 by Sheikh Muhammad and his son Jassim, culminated in 1868 with the mediation of the English; the al-Thanis agreed to end the war in exchange for guaranteed territorial integrity.

4 The Turkish sultans, nominal sovereigns of the entire Arabian peninsula since the 16th century, did not look favorably upon increasing British penetration in the Gulf. Consequently, they named the reigning Sheikh (Jassim al-Thani) governor of the 'province' of Qatar as a pretext to establishing a small military garrison in Dawhah (Doha). Neither the Qataris nor the British concerned themselves over this formal affirmation of sovereignty and the garrison remained until World War I without the slightest effect on British influence in the region.

5 In 1930, the price of pearls dropped with the Japanese flooding the market with a cheaper version of cultivated pearls. Consequently Sheikh Abdullah sold all the country's oil prospecting and exploitation rights, and granted a 75-year lease on its territorial waters,

for £400,000. The Anglo-Iranian Oil Company discovered oil in 1939 but actual production only began after World War II, attracting other companies that purchased parts of the original concession. The immense wealth obtained by Royal Dutch Shell did not seem to concern Sheikh Ahmad ibn Ali al-Thani as oil and tariff revenues increased his personal fortune by £15 million.

6 Shortly thereafter, Ahmad was ousted by his own family. They replaced him with his cousin Khalifa, giving him the task of 'removing any elements that are opposed to progress and modernization'.

7 Sheikh Khalifa created a Council of Ministers and an Advisory Council to share the responsibilities of his absolute power and promised 'a new era of enlightened government, social justice and stability'. Redistributing the oil revenues, he exempted all inhabitants from taxation and provided free education and medical attention. His greatest achievement has perhaps been the subsidizing and promotion of productive activities nohe beginning of his mandate.

8 To reduce Qatar's dependency on a single product, the fishing industry was revitalized, industrialization was accelerated with new cement and fertilizer plants, plus iron and steel mills. The country took advantage of its strategic position to provide commercial and financial services to the economies of the entire region. In addition, a large part of the country's financial surplus was invested abroad (in Europe and the US). In 1980, it was estimated that income from this 'exportation of capital' would eventually equal all oil revenues. In this way Qatar sought to ensure its future when the oil wells ran dry.

9 As a tool of control, a state oil company - the Qatar Petroleum Producing Authority (QPPA) - was set up in 1972. By February 1977, all foreign oil installations had been expropriated.

10 Qatar's economic expansion required the large-scale immigration of foreign technical experts and workers - the former were mainly European and American; the latter Iranian, Pakistani, Indian and Palestinian. Estimates as to the actual

number of immigrant workers at this time varied widely, since surveys were not regularly taken. The figure was thought to be approximately 150,000 people, or about 60 per cent of the total population.

11 To avoid any profound transformation of the local culture, the Government preferred and promoted immigration from other Arab countries. Nevertheless, the advanced systems of social security also protect foreign workers. The local Iranian community lived in better conditions than in any other Gulf emirate and, because of this, Qatar had fewer conflicts with Iran's Khomeini regime than any other country in the region.

12 Adhering to OPEC policy, in 1982 the country cut crude oil production by 25 per cent. Consequently exports decreased, reflected in a considerable reduction in volume of petrodollars invested in the West, in public spending and in industrial expansion. Nevertheless, Qatar had the infrastructure to face the change. In the industrial center of Umm Said (Musay'id) the iron and steel plant was producing 450,000 tons a year at the beginning of the decade. A liquid gas plant was also set in full operation and the Government decided to go ahead with a $6 billion natural gas project for use in its energy and desalinization programs.

13 Qatar's geographical position brought the country both economic benefits and geopolitical worries. Israeli aggression against Lebanon, Syria and Iraq; the lack of solutions to the Palestinian problem; the war between Iran and Iraq, and the US Reagan administration's frightening interest in the region's 'military security' all helped to convince Qatar's rulers of the need to enter new alliances with their neighbors on the Arabian Gulf.

14 Since 1981, together with Bahrain, Kuwait, Oman, the United Arab Emirates and Saudi Arabia, Qatar has participated in the Gulf Cooperation Council (GCC), an organization designed to coordinate the area's policies in political, economic, social, cultural and military issues. Qatar strongly supported Saudi Arabia's stand regarding the need to reduce and if possible eliminate US troops stationed in the region, mainly in Oman.

¹⁵ In April 1986, tensions flared between Bahrain and Qatar over the artificial island of Fasht ad-Dibal. This conflict was resolved through negotiations sponsored by members of the GCC. In November 1987, the Government renewed diplomatic relations with Egypt.

¹⁶ In March 1991, after the Iraqi invasion of Kuwait, the GCC suspended all economic aid to Jordan and the Palestine Liberation Organization (PLO).

¹⁷ In the same month, the Foreign Ministers of Egypt, Syria, and the six Arab countries of the GCC gathered in the Saudi capital Riyadh to sign an agreement with the US to preserve security in the region. The plan included four points: a common military strategy between the US and the Arab countries in the anti-Iraqi coalition; mechanisms to avoid arms proliferation; acceptance of a peace treaty by Israel; and a new economic program for the development of the region.

¹⁸ In December, a group of 53 people including some government officials drew up and signed a petition to the Emir of Qatar asking for free parliamentary elections, a written constitution and increased personal and political freedoms. As a result, several citizens were arrested and detained in the Doha Central Prison; they were eventually released several months later.

¹⁹ In addition to this already difficult situation, toward the end of the year Qatar and Bahrain became involved in another territorial dispute over several small islands off the coast of the two emirates: Howard Island, and more especially underground rights to Dibval and Qitat, both potentially rich in oil. Growing tension between the two countries prompted Saudi Arabia to step in and mediate.

²⁰ In 1993, the fall in the price of oil on the international market triggered an almost 20 per cent decrease in fiscal income. Furthering his program to develop alternative income sources, in 1994 al-Thani negotiated new agreements with several Asian companies for the exploitation of natural gas.

²¹ In June 1995, heir to the throne Hamad ibn Khalifah al-Thani overthrew his father to become Emir of Qatar. The new sovereign promised to step up efforts to resolve the territorial disputes with Saudi Arabia and Bahrain. Qatar's membership of the Gulf Cooperation Council was thrown into doubt when its delegation withdrew from a Council meeting in December.

²² In April 1996, Qatar and Saudi Arabia resolved their territorial disputes on the basis of a previous treaty. A similar dispute between Qatar and Bahrain came to an end in March 1997, when both nations agreed to deal with the issue in the International Courts.

²³ In 1997, Qatar froze relations with Israel, applying the Arab League decision to reactivate the boycott on that country. However it offered its capital Doha as the venue for the Economic Conference of the Middle East and North Africa to be held in November, as part of the peace process. In October, Sheikh Abdullah ibn Khalifa al-Thani was appointed Prime Minister, a post previously occupied by Emir Hamad.

²⁴ On March 17 1998, the 25th Conference of Foreign Ministers of the Islamic Conference Organization (ICO) closed in Doha. Its resolutions included a call to the Arab states to reconsider relations with Israel. Qatar gratefully received the agreement between Saudi Arabia, Venezuela and Mexico to reduce their respective oil production limits, undertaking to do the same during that year.

²⁵ In the same month, Qatar and France held joint naval maneuvers under the title 'Pearl Collection II'. In April, the Emir signed a military co-operation agreement with Russia, including the exchange of specialists and military training projects.

²⁶ The ban on contracting Egyptian workers was lifted in June 1998 and in November that year a plan for constitutional reform was unveiled, with the goal of creating a parliament elected by direct vote. At this time the emirate was the only Gulf state with an elected parliament, but only men aged over 18 years old were eligible to vote. In the March 1999 local elections, women were allowed the vote for the first time. Despite the impact this created, none of the six female candidates was elected for local posts.

²⁷ The Emir was increasingly active on the diplomatic front, raising criticism for the US stance on Iraq and mediating in the dispute over agreements with Iran between the Saudi monarch and the United Arab Emirates. The UAE complained that Saudi Arabia and other members of the GCC had improved relations with Iran without considering that they had a territorial dispute with that country. Khalifah al-Thani's proposal led to consensus and the unity of the Council was re-launched.

²⁸ The 33 rebels responsible for a 1996 coup attempt against the Emir were sentenced to life imprisonment in February 2000. Amongst them was the Emir's cousin, Sheikh Hamad ibn Jassem al-Thani, an ally of the deposed father of the current monarch.

²⁹ In March 2001, Qatar solved its border conflicts with Bahrain and Saudi Arabia. In the first case, the International Court of Justice at The Hague found in favor of Bahrain's possession of Hawar islands, rich in oil and disputed since 1930. At the same time the Court acknowledged the rights of Qatar over the city of Zubarah, on the Qatari mainland. Both countries signed an agreement in Doha that comprises 15 maps and documents, which demarcate the 60 km common border of sea and land crossed by Bedouin. This dispute led both countries to armed conflicts in the past.

³⁰ In May 2001, the longest trial in Qatar's history came to an end. The court convicted 110 people for the failed coup in 1996. Among those sentenced to death by hanging or shooting was one of the Emir's cousins.

³¹ In September 2002 Qatar offered use of its land as bases for a possible US-led attack on Iraq. The US moved its air base to Qatar in 2002, from Saudi Arabia, in preparation for an attack on Iraq. ∎

PROFILE

ENVIRONMENT

The country consists of the Qatar Peninsula, on the eastern coast of the Arabian Peninsula in the Persian Gulf. The land is flat and the climate is hot and dry. Farming is possible only along the coastal strip. The country's main resource is its fabulous oil wealth on the western coast. Qatar suffered the negative effects of the burning oil wells during the 1991 Gulf War.

SOCIETY

Peoples: Qatari arabs make up 20 per cent of the population. Arabs however are a majority as a result of Palestinian, Egyptian and Yemeni immigrants, who account for 25 per cent of the population. The remaining 55 per cent are immigrants, mostly from Pakistan, India and Iran.
Religions: Muslim (official and predominant). The majority are Sunni, with mainly Shi'a Iranian immigrants. There are also Christian and Hindu minorities. **Languages:** Arabic (official and predominant). Urdu is spoken by Pakistani immigrants, and Farsi by Iranians. English is the business language. **Political Parties:** There are no organized political parties.

THE STATE

Official Name: Dawlat Qatar. **Capital:** Doha (Ad-Dawhah) 391,000 people (1999). **Other cities:** Rayyan 183,000 people; Wakrah 22,900; Umm Said (Musay'id)18,100 (2000). **Government:** Hamad ibn Khalifah al-Thani, Emir and Head of State since June 1995. Sheikh Abdullah ibn Khalifah al-Thani, Prime Minister since October 1996. Legislative Power: a Consultative Council with 30 members appointed by the Emir to 3 year-terms. **National Holiday:** September 3, Independence Day (1971). **Armed Forces:** 11,800 (1996).

Réunion

Population: 742,000 (2002)
Land area: 2,510 SQ KM
Capital: Saint Denis
Currency: Euro
Language: French

Réunion

The island of Réunion was uninhabited until the beginning of the 17th century when Arab explorers arrived and called it Diva Margabin. The Portuguese renamed it Ilha Santa Apolonia and the French settlers called it Bourbon. After the French Revolution it was given its current name of Réunion.

[2] The island's four renamings reflect the struggle between the colonial powers for possession of this strategically important point in the Indian Ocean. After decades of fighting, the French finally retained colonial rights over Réunion in 1638.

[3] The colonial regime replaced subsistence farming with the export commodities of sugarcane and coffee, and the island's fishing resources were depleted because of the over-exploitation of several species.

[4] Since March 1946, Réunion has been an Overseas Department by the French Government. The local middleclass and the French colonists supported the integration of the island into French territory. Later, conservative political changes in France brought realignment of political forces on the island.

[5] While sectors tied to colonial interests defended the Department status, the Réunion Communist Party (CPR) changed its stance, and in 1959 campaigned for partial autonomy and for ten years was the sole supporter of gradual independence.

[6] In 1978, the UN Decolonization Committee pronounced in favor of full independence for Réunion. The question of independence was transformed into an international issue.

[7] In 1978, the independence movement made important international contacts in a meeting with other anti-imperialist and anti-colonialist organizations in the Indian Ocean area. At this meeting, a Permanent Liaison Committee was formed in a joint effort against foreign domination. In June 1979, during elections for the European Parliament, Paul Vergés raised the issue of double colonialism, charging

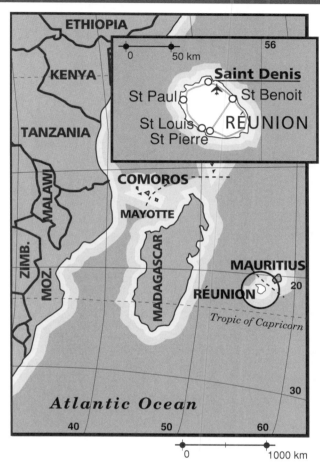

that Réunion Island was not only dominated by the French, but forced to serve the interests of the entire European Community.

[8] The production crisis and unemployment were not due to unfavorable climatic conditions (extensive drought, cyclones, etc.) but to the structure of the economy itself. The situation was worsened by the demographic explosion on the island, as the population had increased 20 per cent in the last decade.

[9] Disturbances became more frequent as the social situation deteriorated. In 1991, eight people died in clashes with police in protest over the closure of the pirate television station Tele Free-DOM, directed by the popular Camille Sudre. Sudre, a Frenchman settled in Réunion, formed a political list and won the regional elections in 1992. Support from the CPR enabled him to become leader of the Regional Council, one of the two main executive authorities of the island.

[10] However, the main French administrative tribunal annulled the elections for alleged irregularities and banned Sudre from standing again. In fresh elections in 1993, the Free-DOM party, led by Marguerite Sudre, Camille's wife, won again. The new leader formed links with the French Right and was appointed minister in the cabinet of the conservative, Edouard Balladur (in office 1993-1995), in Paris.

[11] Unemployment soared in 1996 to an all-time high of 40 per cent, and it was estimated to be even higher amongst the young. In 1997, the tension and social discontent erupted in constant demonstrations.

[12] In March 1998, Paul Vergés, the CPR leader was elected head of the Regional Council by 24 votes to the 20 of the right wing Union for French Democracy (UDF) candidate, Jean-Paul Virapoullé. The outcome was due to the support Marguerite Sudre gave Vergés, who had not achieved the 23 vote majority needed for him to stand in the first round.

[13] In June 2001 Gonthier Friederici took office on the island. In January 2002 he had to deal with the devastation wreaked by cyclone Dina, which ravaged the island for two days, causing huge losses in the agricultural sector and severely damaging housing infrastructure. ∎

PROFILE

ENVIRONMENT

Located in the Indian Ocean, 700 km east of Madagascar, Réunion is a volcanic, mountainous island with a tropical climate, heavy rainfall and numerous rivers. These conditions favor the growth of sugarcane, the main economic activity.

SOCIETY

Peoples: Mostly of African descent (63.5 per cent): Europeans 2.2 per cent; Chinese 2.2 per cent; Indian 28.3 per cent.
Religion: Mainly Catholic (94 per cent). Muslim, Hindu and Buddhist minorities.
Languages: French (official) and Creole.
Political Parties: Free-DOM Movement; Communist Party of Réunion (CPR); Rally for the Republic (RPR); Union for French Democracy (UFD); Socialist Party.

THE STATE

Official Name: Département d'Outre-Mer de la Réunion. Administrative Divisions: 5 Arrondisements.
Capital: Saint Denis 143,000 people (1999).
Other cities: St Paul 91,600 people; St Pierre 72,000; Le Tampon 63,000; St André 44,800 (2000).
Government: Gonthier Friederici, Prefect appointed by the French Government in June 2001. There are two local councils: the 47-member General Council, and the 45-member Regional Council. The island has 5 representatives and 3 senators in the French parliament.
National Holiday: December 20, Abolition of slavery (1848).
Armed Forces: 4,000 French troops (1995).

DEMOGRAPHY

Population: Estimates for year 2015: 845,000 (2000)

Romania

Population:	22,332,000 (2002)
Land area:	230,340 SQ KM
Capital:	Bucharest
Currency:	Lei
Language:	Romanian

România

The earliest inhabitants of Romania included the Thracians, whose descendants, known as the Getae, established contact with Greek colonies that appeared on the shore of the Black Sea in the 7th century BC. Together with the Dacians, a related people living in the Carpathian Mountains and in Transylvania, the Getae established a distinct society by the 4th century BC.

[2] In the first century BC, the Geto-Dacians bitterly resisted conquest by the Romans, who were interested in the region's mineral wealth. Rome finally triumphed over the powerful Dacian kingdom in 106 AD, putting its inhabitants to death or expelling them to the north. According to some Roman sources, most of the males of the conquered area who could not run were put to death or brought to Rome as slaves. However many Dacians ran away from the center of the former kingdom, into vast areas that belonged to the so-called free Dacians, in the north, east and north-east of the Roman province of Dacia.

[3] The province was then subdivided into Dacia Superior, Dacia Inferior and Dacia Porolissensis. Emperor Marcus Aurelius abandoned Dacia Superior and Inferior during the period between 271-275. Unwilling to acknowledge before the Senate that he withdrew from such important provinces, he reorganized the province of Moesia Superior at the south of Danube into Dacia Ripensis and Dacia Mediterranea (to keep the name Dacia). The center and east of present Walachia, southern Moldova and Dobrudja were at that time part of the Roman province of Moesia Inferior, which he still occupied. Roman rule left an enduring legacy on the Romanian language which is derived from Latin. This rule continued in the territory of present Romania until the 7th century, when the Byzantine Empire lost its last northern Danubian strongholds to the migratory peoples.

[4] Between the 3rd and the 12th centuries, the region underwent successive invasions by Germanic peoples, Slavs, Avars and others. Roman Christianity was brought by Romans during the 2nd and 3rd centuries and spread to the whole region by the 4th century. The Romanian-Bulgarian Empire, which

lasted over 200 years, introduced Greek Orthodox Christianity. The Romanian Church adopted the Slavonic language as a result of Bulgarian influence. Towards the end of the 9th century, the Bulgarians were expelled by the Magyars from the Pannonic plains (now Hungary) though they remained in what is today Romania.

[5] Transylvania, the cradle of the Romanian nation, was conquered by Hungary during the 10th-12th century. According to Hungarian sources the existing feudal states in Transylvania put up fierce resistance. The Vlachs from Transylvania reappeared in the 13th century to the south of the Carpathian Mountains, in two separate regions, Walachia and Moldova. Inlanders immediately accepted the newcomers as people with the same origins. The Tatar-Mongol invasion of 1241 produced big losses among the Romanians.

[6] The first Romanian state, Walachia, was established south of the Carpathians during the early 14th century and a second, Moldova, was founded in 1349 east of the Carpathians in the Spruth River valley.

[7] The principalities of Walachia and Moldova fought for their independence from Hungary, which after conquering Transylvania, tried unsuccessfully to conquer them also. This struggle ended in the first half of the 14th century, when Hungarian invaders were defeated in both areas. By the 15th century the Ottoman Empire began to be a greater threat.

[8] After defeating the Serbs in Kosovo in 1389, the Ottoman Empire began closing in on Walachia, with pressure intensifying after the fall of Bulgaria in 1393. Walachia became a vassal state of Sultan Mehmed I in 1417, though Prince Mircea maintained the claim to the throne and the Christian religion remained intact. In 1455 Moldova also became a vassal state.

[9] King Mircea's death in 1418 was followed by a rapid succession of princes, until the Turks appointed a Romanian prince of their choice to the throne. Walachia put up resistance, but after the Hungarian defeat at the battle of Mohacs in 1526, Turkish domination became inevitable. The Hungarian kingdom disappeared and was transformed by the Ottomans into a Pashalic. The three Romanian principalities, Walachia, Moldova and Transylvania entered into the sphere of influence of the Ottomans, but kept some indigence by paying a tribute in money.

[10] In 1594, the Turkish inhabitants of Walachia were massacred by Prince Michael in alliance with Moldova. He went on to invade Turkish territory, taking several key sites along the banks of the Danube. Faced with the collapse of his counter-offensive, the Sultan had no choice but to recognize the sovereignty of Walachia, which subsequently became linked to Transylvania.

[11] In 1600, Michael conquered Moldova, proclaiming himself regent. The Austrian Emperor Rudolf II recognized the claim, although he

later tried to take over Transylvania and Moldova. Michael the Brave was the first and the last to unite the Romanians until the modern reunification in 1918.

[12] In the 17th and 18th centuries, Walachia and Moldova fell under Turkish rule again. The sultans did not trust the Romanian princes, so they named either Greek princes from Romania, or Romanian princes from the Greek quarter in Istanbul, Fanar, to rule Walachia and Moldova. Russia occupied the region in 1769, but Austria forced Russia to return the principalities to the Sultan in 1774.

[13] Russia's power over the area gradually increased, until it included the right to appoint the princes. The Sultan ousted these princes, and in 1806, Russia retaliated by invading the region. Under the Treaty of Bucharest in 1812, Russia retained the southeastern part of Moldova - Bessarabia.

[14] Another war broke out between Russia and Turkey in 1828. The following year, the Treaty of Adrianopolis maintained the principalities as tributaries of the Sultan, but under Russian occupation. Russian troops remained in the region, and the princes began to be named for life.

[15] The local nobility drew up a constitution known as the 'Reglement organique', which was passed in Walachia in 1831 and in Moldova in 1832. This established administrative and legislative bodies made up of people of the principalities. In 1834, after the Sultan's approval of the 'Reglement', Russia withdrew.

[16] During the European revolutions of 1848, nationalist sentiment in Moldova and Walachia was stimulated by peasant rebellions. These reached a climax in May with the protests at Blaj, which were put down by Turkish and Russian troops, restoring the 'Reglement organique'. The revolutions were defeated with foreign aid, Ottoman in Walachia, Russian in Moldova, and Austrian and Russian in Transylvania.

[17] During the Crimean War 1854-1856, the three Romanian principalities were occupied alternately by Ottoman, Russian and Austrian troops. The Treaty of Paris, 1856, maintained the ancient

statutes of the principalities until its revision by a European commission in Bucharest in 1857, with delegates representing the sultan and both principalities.

[18] The local delegates made the following proposals: that the provinces be autonomous, joining together under the name 'Romania'; that a foreign king be elected, with the right to hereditary succession; and that the country be neutral. In August 1858, despite the Sultan's opposition, the Treaty of Paris created a commission to carry out the unification process.

[19] In 1859, the principalities elected a single prince, Alexandru Ion Cuza, who was recognized by the major powers and by the Sultan in 1861. The Constitution of 1864 established a bicameral legislative body, granting property holders greater electoral power.

[20] When the war between Russia and Turkey resumed in 1877, Romania authorized the transit of Russian troops through its territory in April. Romanian troops contributed to the Russian victory.

[21] The 1878 Treaty of Berlin respected Romania's independence, but failed to return Bessarabia to Romania, instead giving it Dobrudja - without its southern part - and the Danube Delta. In 1881 Romania became a kingdom.

[22] When the Balkan War broke out in 1912, tension from territorial disputes in past wars, persisted between Romania and its neighbors. After the first few battles, Bucharest demanded a ratification of its borders in Dobrudja. The St Petersburg Conference of 1913 gave Romania Silistra, much to Bulgaria's displeasure.

[23] Romania took advantage of the second Balkan War of 1913 to shore up its position. The Treaty of Bucharest gave Romania the southern part of Dobrudja, which was occupied by Romanian troops. At the beginning of World War I, Romania wavered between taking Bessarabia or Transylvania, finally opting for the latter.

[24] In 1916, Romania allied itself with Britain, France, Russia and Italy, declaring war on Austria and Hungary. After the occupation of Bucharest, King Ferdinand and the Romanian Government and army took refuge in Moldova. The defeat of the Central Powers in 1918 made it possible for Romania to double its size, since Transylvania, Bessarabia, Bucovina and Banat expressed their will to belong to Romania through referenda.

[25] In 1918 the King approved electoral reforms making voting obligatory for men over the age of 21, and introducing the secret ballot. At the time the peasants made up 80 per cent of the population, and they had their own political party. Social upheaval, and the landowner's fear of having their lands expropriated, led General Averescu (the hero of two wars and now the head of the government) to take harsh measures. The general strike of 1920 was put down and the Communist Party was declared illegal in 1924.

[26] In the 1928 election, the National Peasant Party (NPP) obtained 349 of 387 seats. The Government abolished martial law and press censorship, also decentralizing public administration, an issue supported by the ethnic minorities. It also authorized the sale of land and foreign investment in the country.

[27] The council of regency, which had been formed upon Ferdinand's death, was dissolved when King Carol assumed the throne in 1930, a succession agreed on by the major political parties. The economic crisis led to the displacement of the NPP, and the King took advantage of the emergence of the Iron Guard, a fascist Moldovan group similar to those that existed in Germany and Italy, to weaken the traditional parties.

[28] In 1938, after a fraudulent plebiscite, Carol passed a new corporative constitution. Seeking closer ties with Germany, he met Hitler in November 1938. Upon his return, he had 13 officials of the Iron Guard assassinated, along with its leader, and Carol founded his own party, the National Renaissance Front (NRF).

[29] Carol obtained French and German assurances of the country's territorial integrity. When Germany and the USSR invaded Poland in 1939, Romania not only renounced the mutual defense treaty which it had signed with Warsaw, but also detained Polish authorities as they fled across Romanian territory.

[30] Between June and September of 1940, Romania was forced to turn Bessarabia and Bucovina over to the USSR, north-east Transylvania over to Hungary, and southern Dobrudja to Bulgaria. Because of his disastrous foreign policy, Carol had no choice but to abdicate in September, leaving his son Michael on the throne and turning over the Government of the country to General Antonescu. Romania was occupied by 500,000 German troops, and was proclaimed a 'national legionary state'.

[31] Romanian troops cooperated with the abortive German offensive against the USSR, but when the counter-offensive was mounted by the Red Army, Bucharest abruptly changed sides. In June 1944, the Peasant, Liberal, Social Democratic and Communist Parties created the National Bloc and in August, King Michael ousted Antonescu and declared war on Germany.

[32] In September, with the major part of its territory occupied since mid-August by Soviet troops, Romania signed an armistice with the Allies. At the Potsdam Conference, the Allies decided to resume relations with Romania, provided its government was 'recognized and democratic'. The USSR granted it immediate recognition while the United States and Britain adopted a 'wait-and-see' attitude. The Government initiated a series of detentions, summary trials and life sentences against the leaders and members of the Social Democratic, the National Liberal and National Peasant parties. In 1947, King Michael was forced to abdicate.

[33] In 1948, the Communists and some Social Democrats formed the Romanian Workers' Party (RWP) which joined the Plougher's Front and the Hungarian People's Union to form the People's Democratic Front (PDF). In the March election that year, the PDF won 405 of the 414 seats of the National Assembly.

[34] On December 30 1947, the People's Republic of Romania was proclaimed, and a soviet style socialist constitution was adopted. In April, the Government adopted centralized economic planning.

[35] Between 1948 and 1949, Bucharest signed friendship and cooperation treaties with the European socialist bloc, and joined the Council for Mutual Economic Assistance. In 1955, Romania joined the Warsaw Pact, but in 1963 it began to drift away from the Soviet fold.

[36] In 1951 the First Five Year Plan was started, aimed at socialist industrialization of steel, coal, and oil. In 1952, the new regime started to consolidate under President Groza and Prime Minister Gheorghiu-Dej, head of state from 1961.

[37] Gheorghe Maurer was appointed Prime Minister in 1961, while Gheorghiu-Dej was President of the republic. Maurer tried to achieve greater economic and political independence, so Romania did not take sides in the Sino-Soviet dispute. In 1962 the economy underwent a series of reforms. The land collectivization policy was finished, and trade with the US, France, and Germany began.

PROFILE

ENVIRONMENT

The country is crossed from north to center by the Carpathian Mountains, the western ones are known as the Transylvanian Alps. The Transylvanian plateau is contained within the arc formed by the Carpathian Mountains. The Moldavian plains extend to the east, while the Walachian plains stretch to the south, crossed by the Danube, which flows into a large delta on the Black Sea. The mountain forests supply raw material for a well-developed timber industry. With abundant mineral resources (oil, natural gas, coal, iron ore and bauxite), Romania has begun extensive industrial development. Its economy still depends to a great extent on the export of raw materials and agricultural products. Romania defines itself as a 'developing country', and is attuned with Third World demands. It is also one of Europe's largest oil producers. Copsa Mica, in the center of Romania, is considered to be one of the areas with the highest levels of industrial pollution in Europe.

SOCIETY

Peoples: Romanian 89.4 per cent, Hungarian 9 per cent, German 0.5 per cent, Ukrainian, Turkish, Greek and Croatian. These data do not include Roma, which represented between 5 and 10 per cent of the population, but who usually are considered as Romanian in the census.
Religions: Mainly Romanian-Orthodox (86.8 per cent). There are Catholic (5 per cent) and Protestant (3.5 per cent) minorities.
Languages: Romanian (official language, spoken by the majority); ethnic minorities often speak their own languages, particularly Hungarian and Romany.
Political Parties: Democratic Convention, coalition led by the National Peasant Party and Christian Democrats (NPP-CD); Social Democratic Union; Democratic Union of Hungarians of Romania (UDMR); Party of Social Democracy in Romania (PDSR); Greater Romanian Party
Organizations: General Confederation of Trade Unions.

THE STATE

Official Name: România.
Administrative Divisions: 40 Districts and the Municipality of Bucharest.
Capital: Bucharest 2,054,000 people (1999).
Other cities: Timisoara 327,830 people; Constanza 348,000; Iasi 339,889 (1994).
Government: Ion Iliescu, President and Head of State since January 2001. Adrian Nastase, Prime Minister and Head of Government since January 2001. Legislature, bicameral: Senate, 143 members; Deputies, 341 members, 13 representing ethnic minorities.
National Holiday: December 1, Unification Day (1918)
Armed Forces: 228,400 (1996).
Other: 43,000 Border Guard, Gendarmes, Construction Troops.

³⁸ In 1965, when Gheorghiu-Dej died, Nicolae Ceausescu was elected First Secretary of the Romanian Workers Party (RWP), which subsequently changed its name to the Romanian Communist Party (RCP). The Constitution was reformed, and the name of the country was changed to the Socialist Republic of Romania, by the National Assembly. In 1967, Ceausescu was elected President of the State Council.

³⁹ Ceausescu placed some distance between Romania and the USSR. In 1966, he affirmed that his country was continuing its struggle for independence. Romania established diplomatic relations with West Germany and, unlike other members of the Warsaw Pact, it did not break off relations with Israel in 1967, nor intervene over the Soviet invasions of Czechoslovakia in 1968.

⁴⁰ In the 1970s and early 1980s, Ceausescu was re-elected several times, in apparently free elections, as secretary general of the RCP and as president of the country. Despite numerous government reorganizations, economic hardships, accentuated by administrative corruption, led to growing discontent.

⁴¹ From 1987, difficult living and labor conditions triggered marches and strikes. These were put down by the security forces. In 1988 and 1989, several government scandals broke out; various cabinet ministers and government authorities were subsequently tried and dismissed.

⁴² Towards the end of 1989, confrontations between civilians and the army in Timisoara left many dead or injured, the international press spoke of hundreds of deaths, and the news had strong repercussions within Romania.

⁴³ The Government declared a state of emergency, but a faction within the regime carried out a coup with massive popular support. Accused of 'genocide, corruption and destruction of the economy', Ceausescu and his wife were secretly executed by army soldiers. The National Salvation Front (NSF) assumed control of the government.

⁴⁴ Resistance towards the new government increased, leading to violent confrontations in the streets. In 1991, 77 per cent of the electorate approved the new consti-tution which turned Romania into a multiparty presidentialist democracy. In Transylvania, however, the new constitution received scant support.

⁴⁵ On January 1 1992, the cooperative farming system created by the Ceausescu regime ceased to exist legally, but in fact it was still operating. In the municipal elections of February 1992, incidents occurred in Transylvania when the Magyar Democratic Union candidate was barred from participation.

⁴⁶ Western countries and international financial organizations continued to voice their discontent to the Government for its alleged sluggishness in implementing economic reforms. One of the features criticized was land ownership, since 30 per cent still belonged to the State in 1994. After two years of deliberation, Bucharest passed in June 1995 the law to privatize state enterprises.

⁴⁷ Human rights organizations, such as Amnesty International, also criticized Romania especially for the violence and discrimination often practiced against the approximately 500,000 to 2,000,000 Romani (gypsies).

⁴⁸ After years of attempts, Bucharest and Budapest signed a treaty in September 1996 regarding the 1.6 million Hungarians living in Romania. Hungary had to agree to a commitment to 'guarantee the rights of the minority', leaving aside its demand of 'autonomy' for Transylvanian Hungarians. Although relations with Hungary (which opened a consulate in Cluj, capital of Transylvania) improved after ultranationalist tendencies diminished with the defeat of Iliescu in the November elections, problems arose again when the Romanian senate voted against a university education project for the minorities.

⁴⁹ The new government of Emil Constantinescu, the President elected in November 1996, announced it would attack corruption and organized crime. Prime Minister Victor Ciorbea implemented an economic and structural adjustment program based on IMF prescriptions: balanced state finance, increased privatizations and decentralization of the administration.

⁵⁰ Popular discontent with government policy led to a wave of protests that peaked in October 1997. After agreements were made among members of the government coalition, Ciorbea resigned in March 1998. He was replaced by Radu Vasile, who proposed accelerating the privatization of state enterprises, wiping out corruption and reducing bureaucracy. In the international sphere, sights were set on gaining admission into NATO and the European Union.

⁵¹ The new government coalition failed to achieve economic or political stability. In June, Daniel Daianu, Economy Minister, resigned after his recommendation against purchasing 96 helicopters from a foreign company was rejected. The refusal of the government majority to open a Hungarian-language university also destabilized the coalition. The party representing that minority threatened to withdraw from the government if the university project was not approved.

In the end they agreed to open a multicultural university that would operate in Hungarian and German.

⁵² In December 1999, a mining strike and internal disagreements in the coalition caused the Cabinet to collapse. Vasile attempted to resist the decree issued by the President but he was forced to resign Dec 14. His place was temporarily filled by Alexandru Athanasiu, and later by Mugur Isarescu.

⁵³ Tens of thousands of liters of cyanide spilled into the Somes River, a tributary of the Tisza and the Danube, killing flora and fauna along hundreds of km of the rivers in the worst water contamination catastrophe in Europe in a decade. The accident occurred at the Aurul gold mine, property of Australian and Romanian capital, located near Baia Maresobre. The contamination affected drinking water supplies in Hungary, Ukraine, Yugoslavia and Bulgaria. Hungary and Yugoslavia filed million-dollar lawsuits against Romania, but the country's authorities refused to accept official responsibility for the accident.

⁵⁴ Promising to speed up reforms that would help the country enter the European Union, Iliescu easily won the December presidential elections, beating ultra-nationalist and xenophobe Corneliu Vadim Tudor, of the Greater Romania Party. Adrian Nastase, also a Social Democrat, was appointed Prime Minister.

⁵⁵ In January 2001, the authorities of the town of Lepezi, 330 km northeast of Bucharest, went door to door confiscating and burning three tons of fish contaminated with cyanide. Since the spill, 72 people, including more than 50 children, had been hospitalized for gastritis and liver problems. The average income in Romania was just $100, and in the region where the spill occurred - one of the country's poorest - unemployment surpassed 20 per cent.

⁵⁶ That month, nearly 250,000 state buildings and properties, which had been nationalized during the Communist regime, were included on a reintegration list approved by Parliament. Numerous buildings, such as hospitals and schools, were exempt from the list. The property was to be returned to the original owners. The large Hungarian minority (est. 1,690,000 in the 1992 census and mostly Catholic and Calvinist) welcomed the measure because the law entitled them to reclaim several church-related buildings, lost in the secularization process that affected the churches of the Hungarian minority, particularly the Roman Catholic and Calvinist Churches, the two largest religious communities of this minority. The Romanian Orthodox Church has been a loyal servant of nationalist state policy. ■

Russia

Population: 143,752,000 (2002)
Land area: 16,888,500 SQ KM
Capital: Moscow (Moskva)
Currency: Ruble
Language: Russian

Rossiya

Before the Slavs appeared on the historical scene, the European territory of the present Russian Federation, Belarus and Ukraine was inhabited by different peoples, and underwent successive invasions by the Huns, Avars, Goths and Magyars. The first mention of the Slavs dates back to the 6th century. Byzantine writers wrote of several Slavic peoples: the Polians (based in Kiev), Drevlians, Dregoviches, Kriviches, Viatiches, Meria and others.

2   In the 9th century, the first Russian State was formed, known as the Ancient Rus or Kiev Rus. The latter emerged from the struggle against the Khazars of the south, and the Varangians (Scandinavians) of the north. In the 9th century, the route between the Baltic and Black seas, down the Dnepr river, 'the route of the Varangians and the Greeks', became important for European trade.

3   In 882, Prince Oleg of Novgorod conquered Kiev (in Ukraine) and transferred the center of the Russian State there. In the year 907, Oleg signed a treaty which was to be beneficial for the Rus. During the reign of Sviatoslav, Olegs grandson, the struggle between Byzantium and Bulgaria intensified. Vladimir (980-1015), Sviatoslav's son and successor, consolidated the judicial, dynastic and territorial organization of the Russian State. To overcome the isolation of the 'pagan' Rus vis-à-vis a monotheistic Europe, Vladimir made Christianity the state religion in 988, adopting the ornate Byzantine ritual.

4   At the end of Vladimir's reign, strong separatist tendencies were evident within the Principality of Novgorod. Svyatopolk, Vladimir's successor, killed three of his brothers in order to consolidate his own power, but Yaroslav, the fourth brother and prince of Novgorod, ousted Svyatopolk and assumed power in Kiev (now in Ukraine), granting Novgorod several benefices. After his death, the feudal republic of Novgorod was formed, along with the principalities of Vladimir-Suzdal, Galich-Volin and others. Muscovy (the principality of Rostov-Suzdal) is first mentioned in historical chronicles in 1147.

5   In 1237, the troops of the Tatar Khan Batu, the grandson of Genghis Khan, invaded the principalities of

Riazan and Vladimir, taking Moscow and other Russian cities. From 1239-40, the conquest of Russian principalities continued, followed by 250 centuries of Tatar rule. Apart from the Mongols in the East, the Teutons and the Swedes posed an additional danger in the West. In 1242, Prince Alexander of Novgorod defeated the Teutons in the famous 'battle on ice' on Lake Chudskoye, near the Neva River, obtaining the title 'Prince of Nevsky' as a result of this victory.

6   The Mongols governed through local princes or Turkish chieftains and Muslim merchants, who were given the authority (*yarlik*) to govern. In the early 14th century, Tver, Moscow, Riazan and Novgorod were the main principalities. Dmitry, grand prince of Moscow began uniting forces in order to expel the Tatars, but ran up against the opposition of the princes of Tver, Nizhni-Novgorod and Riazan. In 1378, the Mamai Khan led an expedition aimed at conquering Russia, but was defeated.

7   In 1380, Dmitry defeated Mamai in the battle of Kulikov, near the Don river, marking the beginning of Russian liberation from the Tatars. The struggle for liberation lasted a century, and ended in 1480, when Ajmat, the last of the Golden Horde's khans, retreated from a confrontation with the troops of Prince Ivan III, at the Ugra river.

8   In 1547, Ivan 'the Terrible' came to the throne. In 1552, Ivan IV took Kazan, and annexed the territory of the middle course of the Volga river, inhabited by Tatars, Chuvashes, Mari, Morduins and Udmurts. In 1556, he occupied Astrakhan, while the west continued to war against the Polish-Lithuanian State, trying to gain an outlet to the Baltic Sea. Serfdom was established, with peasants losing the right to leave without the feudal lord's permission. Ivan IV established absolute power by eliminating several upper nobility, the boyar clans.

9   Upon the death of Ivan IV, he was succeeded by his mentally ill son Fyodor in 1584 and power passed to the *boyar* (lord) Boris Godunov. Godunov conducted a short war against Sweden, signed an alliance with Georgia - which became a Russian protectorate - and annexed the principality of Siberia.

10   On Fyodor's death in 1598, the Council of Territories (*Zemski Sodor*) elected Boris Godunov as czar. However, the boyar clans of older lineage felt they had a greater claim to the throne, and a period of intrigue and conflict over succession began.

11   In 1601-2, in the Ukrainian territory - which belonged to Poland - an impostor calling himself 'Prince Dmitry' appeared, claiming to have escaped an attempt on his life by Boris Godunov. Amassing an army,

he moved towards Moscow, managing to gain a following among the disaffected members of the population, and eventually seizing the throne.

12   In 1606, the boyars killed the 'False Dmitry' but in 1607 another impostor - a second False Dmitry - appeared, supported by Poles, Lithuanians and Swedes. Polish troops occupied Moscow with the help of turncoat boyars. The Poles were finally expelled from Moscow, and in 1613 the Zemsky Sodor elected Michael Romanov as the new Czar. Between 1654 and 1667, Russia warred against the kingdoms of Sweden and Poland, managing in the process to annex eastern Ukraine.

13   Under the Romanovs, the Russian State became an absolute monarchy, administrated by an efficient bureaucracy and an oligarchy (made up of nobles, merchants and bishops) which was integrated into the Government structure. The church was reformed and the bible translated into Cyrillic script, causing a schism in the Russian church.

14   During the 17th century the economy grew rapidly, as a result of territorial expansion, and the exploitation of Siberia's natural resources. A market also developed for Russia's forest products and semi-manufactured goods, primarily in Britain and Holland.

¹⁵ In 1694, after the accession of Peter I, the Muscovite kingdom became known as the Russian Empire. Peter turned to the West to secure its scientific and technical advances, especially in order to develop the Russian Navy. Allied with Denmark and Poland, Russia successfully intervened in the Great Northern War against Sweden (1700-21). In 1703, he founded St Petersburg, transferring the capital of his empire there and organizing the Government along a set of strict regulations.

¹⁶ Peter established what amounted to a caste system, as well as an espionage network within his own administration, essential for maintaining his strict autocracy. He put down the boyars in Moscow, and had his own son, Alexei, tortured and executed for joining them.

¹⁷ In 1721, by the Treaty of Nystad, Russia obtained control of the Gulf of Finland and the provinces along the east coast of the Baltic Sea. After winning the war against Persia, Peter extended Russia's southern borders as far as the Caspian Sea. The territorial, economic and commercial expansion which characterized this period made Russia one of the major European powers but also created a mosaic of ethnic and cultural groups which could not easily be assimilated into a single unit.

¹⁸ Peter's sudden death in 1725 ushered in a period of instability, until the accession of Catherine II, in 1762. The Empire's conquests continued, with the occupation of Belarus and the part of Ukraine east of the Dnepr; the partition of Poland between Russia and Prussia; and the annexation of Lithuania and Crimea. Russia also gained control of the northern coast of the Black Sea, penetrating the steppes beyond the Urals and all along the coast, they began exercising an ever-increasing influence over the Balkans.

¹⁹ In the meantime, the impoverishment of the peasants increased. The military democracy of the Ukrainian Cossacks was abolished, and the nationalist sentiment of the subdued peoples began to cause friction.

²⁰ Toward the end of the 18th century the French Revolution and the fight against absolutism influenced the Russian intelligentsia, which began rebelling against existing social conditions. The accession of Alexander I to the throne brought with it radical changes in the policies of the Russian Empire.

²¹ Although Alexander sought peace, Napoleon declared war in 1805 and defeated Russia at Austerlitz. In 1812, Napoleon's troops invaded Russia. The 'War for

MATERNAL MORTALITY

1985/99

Per 100,000 live births

44

LITERACY

2000

99%

EXTERNAL DEBT

2000

PER CAPITA

US$ 1,102

the Motherland' in which peasant fighters were also involved, ended with the triumph of the Russian army commanded by Marshall Kutuzov. This victory transformed Russia into the continent's major power.

²² In December 1825, after the death of Alexander I, a group of aristocrats later known as 'the Decembrists' attempted a coup in the Senate Square in St Petersburg. When the 1848 revolutions shook Europe, Russia - governed by Nikolai I - remained untouched and used its army to subdue the Hungarians in Transylvania, though it was defeated in the Crimean War against Britain and France (1853-56).

²³ In 1861, Czar Alexander II abolished serfdom. However, freedom was not 'free', as the peasants had to pay their former landlords for the land which they farmed. A system of elected local assemblies was also established, with peasant representation, though the landowners maintained control.

²⁴ In the 1860s-70s, radical groups emerged whose aims ranged from demanding a constituent assembly to calling for insurrection. Socialist ideas influenced students and intellectuals, who saw in the peasants a revolutionary class. In 1861-62, several different revolutionary groups created an underground association in St Petersburg, called 'Land and Freedom', which existed until 1864. The Polish uprising of 1863 and a failed attempt on the Czar's life in 1866 deepened government repression.

²⁵ The intellectuals reached the conclusion that they would have to 'go to the people' in order to explain to them who their enemies were. In 1876, another 'Peace and Freedom' underground movement was established. Three years later the group split into three, including the 'People's Will', which assassinated Alexander II in 1881, and whose main leaders were hanged. Alexander III did away with his predecessor's reforms, and increased the power of the autocracy.

²⁶ In the early 20th century, Russian socialism had two main currents. The socialist revolutionaries promoted the socialization of the land in peasant communities, while the social

democrats based socialism upon industrialization and the working class. Within the Social Democratic Workers' Party of Russia (SDWPR), the Bolsheviks, led by Vladimir Ilich Ulyanov (known as 'Lenin') defended the idea of a workers' revolt, while the Mensheviks shared the idea of an evolutionary socialism, put forward by Europe's other social democratic parties.

²⁷ Russian expansionism in Eastern Asia led to a war with Japan in 1904. The violent repression of a demonstration in Moscow in 1905 unleashed a revolt in both capitals, which was only brought under control by the October 17 Manifesto: Czar Nicholas II's promise to convene a national parliament (*Duma*). The Bolsheviks boycotted the elections. The first Duma's majority was in the hands of constitutional democrats who were moderate liberals.

²⁸ The Duma's demands for agrarian reform, equal rights for members of all religions (Russian Orthodoxy was the official religion), an amnesty for political prisoners, and autonomy for Poland were unacceptable to the Czar. The Duma was dissolved and the regime put down the revolt after a long and bloody struggle. In 1907, the second Duma was elected, with the presence of the SDWPR. Both the left and the right wings were reinforced, and the main political issue continued to be land. Prime Minister Stolipin promoted an agrarian reform, in order to create a class of land-owning peasants and put an end to the traditional communal use of the land. However, he was unsuccessful and was assassinated. The second Duma was also dissolved. An electoral reform guaranteed that the Duma committees which followed also had a conservative majority.

²⁹ Russia's entry into World War I precipitated a crisis within the regime. The losses brought about by war, and the lack of food, simply deepened popular discontent. In January 1917, in Petrograd, a Council (*Soviet*) elected by workers, soldiers and members of the Duma formed a government. In February, Nicholas II abdicated and the Duma committee established a new Provisional Government, while local soviets multiplied. The German Government authorized a group of Bolsheviks, led

by Lenin, to pass through German territory, hoping to destabilize the enemy's internal situation. The Bolsheviks returned to Russia in a sealed railway car. Their influence within the soviets began to grow, and a power split emerged between the councils and Alexander Kerensky's Government.

³⁰ The Bolsheviks launched the slogans 'Peace, land and bread' and 'All power to the soviets', exhorting the people to 'turn the world war into a civil war'. On November 7, Lenin led the uprising which brought down the Government, and the first socialist republic was established. In early 1918, the Bolsheviks dissolved the Constituent Assembly, in which the revolutionary socialists held a majority.

³¹ The Soviet Government (Council of People's Commissars) approved a peace 'without annexation or indemnities', the abolition of private ownership of the land and its being turned over to the peasants and the nationalization of the banking system. Other measures were approved, including the control of factories by their workers, the creation of a militia and of revolutionary tribunals, the abolition of the privileges associated with class and of the right of inheritance, the separation of Church and State and equal rights for men and women.

³² Following Russia's unilateral peace settlement in 1918, Germany, France and Britain sent expeditionary forces to Russia (their former ally), to support the 'White Russians' - the former regime's army forces - and bring down the revolutionary government. This foreign intervention force was ousted in 1920, and two years later the civil war ceased, with the triumph of the Red Army. During this period, the Soviet Government's policy of 'war communism' resulted in a maximum centralization of power and a near-collapse of the monetary system.

³³ In December 1922, the Russian Federation, Ukraine, Belarus and the Transcaucasian Federation (Azerbaijan, Armenia and Georgia) established the Union of Soviet Socialist Republics (USSR). During the civil war, the regime had become the official preserve of the Russian (Bolshevik) Communist Party, or R(B)CP.

³⁴ In 1921, the R(B)CP - faced with the danger of an imminent economic collapse - was forced to do away with its 'war communism' policy, and adopt a New Economic Policy (NEP). This consisted of a return to the laws of a market system and private ownership of small business, while the State took care of infrastructure, heavy industry and general planning. In 1924, the NEP was interrupted by Lenin's death; internal disputes within the R(B)CP came to an end with the triumph of Joseph Stalin, who had become secretary general of the Party in 1922. Trotsky (Lenin's close associate) went into exile and was assassinated under Stalin's orders, in Mexico in 1940.

³⁵ Stalin re-established the system of centralized planning of the economy, and forcibly imposed the collectivization of agriculture. Opposition figures and dissidents were eliminated through summary trials. It is estimated that during the Great Purge of 1935-38 alone, nearly 10 million people died. The victims of the different waves of purges total at least 20 million. The secret police held almost absolute power.

³⁶ At the beginning of World War II, by means of a secret agreement with Germany (the Molotov-Ribbentrop Pact), the USSR occupied part of Poland, as well as Romania, Estonia, Latvia and Lithuania. In 1941, Hitler launched a large attack against Moscow, sending in thousands of troops, as well as German air power. The Nazis took control of many Russian cities; however, at a cost of some 20 million lives, the Soviets were able to repel the German attack. The Red Army liberated several countries, finally taking Berlin in May 1945.

³⁷ In 1945, at the Yalta conference, the Western powers and the USSR 'carved up' their respective areas of influence. In those countries occupied by the Red Army (Bulgaria, Hungary, Romania, Czechoslovakia, Poland and East Germany), the Communists took power and proclaimed first 'people's republics', then socialist republics, following the model of the Communist Party of the Soviet Union (CPSU).

³⁸ In 1956, at the 20th Party Congress of the CPSU, Nikita Krushchev began a de-Stalinization process, which abruptly came to an end when Leonid Brezhnev ousted Krushchev in October 1964. Despite difficulties of implementation, 'developed socialism' was proclaimed.

³⁹ The strategy of the Cold War devised by the US in the post-war period fuelled the arms race. A by-product of the Cold War was the creation of the Warsaw Pact between the USSR and its Eastern European allies in 1955. The East-West confrontation eventually included nuclear weapons and the control of outer space, where the US and the USSR actively pursued their own space programs in the 1960s and 1970s, with neither one actually taking a lead.

⁴⁰ In 1985, Mikhail Gorbachev became Secretary General of the CPSU and initiated drastic changes to avert a social and economic crisis. *glasnost* (transparency) and *perestroika* (restructuring) - geared to carrying out a series of transformations within the country - unleashed forces which had long been repressed, and brought out into the open the issue of the autonomy of different ethnic groups and nationalities. Changes within the USSR set in motion similar processes in other nations throughout Eastern Europe.

⁴¹ In April 1986, there was a serious accident in one of the reactors of the nuclear power plant at Chernobyl in the Ukraine. Some 135,000 people were evacuated and by 1993 7,000 people had died (see Ukraine).

⁴² Gorbachev initiated internal reforms and also made other initiatives in the area of foreign policy, such as the withdrawal of Soviet troops from Afghanistan (where the Soviet army had been involved in a war since 1979). In addition, he was responsible for accords leading to the reduction of nuclear weapons in Europe, and also accepted the reunification of Germany. In 1990, he proposed that the Warsaw Pact and NATO be phased out gradually.

⁴³ Economic reform, the opening of the country to foreign capital and a return to a free-market economy were all slow in being implemented due to the resistance of the CPSU leadership. After a failed coup, in August, the CPSU was dissolved after 70 years in power. Gorbachev resumed his duties as Soviet president, but his position had become irrevocably weakened. In June 1991, Boris Yeltsin was elected President of Russia.

⁴⁴ Trouble broke out in the Chechen-Ingush region (Northern Caucasia). Toward the end of October, parliamentary and presidential elections were held there. General Dzhojar Dudaev, leader of the Chechen nationalist movement, seized power. In early November he proclaimed the independence of the Chechen Republic. An economic embargo was promptly announced by Moscow.

⁴⁵ On October 6 1991, Yegor Gaidar was named Deputy Prime Minister, and he launched liberal economic reforms, dubbed 'shock therapy'. On December 8, Boris Yeltsin (Russia), Stanislav Shushkevich (Belarus) and Leonid Kravchuk (Ukraine) revoked the 1922 treaty under which the USSR had been founded, proclaiming the Commonwealth of Independent States (CIS) to take its place (see box on CIS). Russia assumed the formal representation of the former USSR in foreign affairs. Latvia, Estonia and Lithuania withdrew and were recognized as separate countries by the UN.

⁴⁶ In early 1992, there was a growing rivalry between the two most important members of the CIS, Russia and Ukraine, revolving around the issue of who controlled the nuclear weapons and navy which had belonged to the former USSR. Relations between them were further complicated by the issue of Crimea's sovereignty. President Yeltsin declared that the United States was no longer a 'strategic rival', and continued the reform of the economy that Gorbachev had begun, including the liberalization of prices, and the privatization of industry, agriculture and trade.

⁴⁷ On February 23 1992, violent confrontations broke out between communist and nationalist protesters, and the militia, with several people being killed by the police.

PROFILE

ENVIRONMENT

The largest country in the world, Russia is divided into five vast regions: the European region, the Ural area, Siberia, Caucasia and the Central Asian region. The European region is the richest of the Russian Federation, and lies between Russia's western border and the Ural Mountains (the conventional boundary between Europe and Asia); it is a vast plain crossed by the Volga, Don and Dnepr rivers. The Urals, which extend from north to south, have important mineral and oil deposits in their outlying areas. The third region, Siberia, lies between the Urals and the Pacific coast. It is rich in natural resources, but sparsely populated because of its harsh climate. Caucasia is an enormous steppe which extends northward from the mountains of the same name, between the Black and Caspian Seas. Finally, the Central Asian region is an enormous depression of land made up of deserts, steppes and mountains. Grain, potatoes and sugar beet are grown on the plains; cotton and fruit in Central Asia; tea, grapes and citrus fruit in the subtropical Caucasian and Black Sea regions. The country's vast mineral resources include oil, coal, iron, copper, zinc, lead, bauxite, manganese and tin, found in the Urals, Caucasia and Central Siberia. Chelyabinsk, a city which lies south of the Ural Mountains, has high levels of radioactivity, due to leaks in its plutonium plant. Pollution, caused by the dumping of industrial wastes, threatens Lake Baikal. Heavy industry and mining have contributed to increasing contamination of the country's main rivers, air and soil. Other contributing factors include the dependence upon coal in electrical generating plants, defects in nuclear reactors and the abuse of agrochemical products. Deforestation and soil erosion also threaten large areas of the countryside.

SOCIETY

Peoples: Russians, 81.5 per cent; Tatars, 3.8 per cent; Ukrainians, 3 per cent; over 100 other nationalities, including Chuvash (1.2 per cent), Bashkirs (0.9 per cent), Belarusians (0.8 per cent), Moldovans (0.7 per cent), Chechens (0.6 per cent) and Germans (0.6 per cent) (1996).
Religions: Christian Orthodox is predominant. There are also Muslim, Protestant and Jewish minorities.
Languages: Russian (official); there are almost as many languages as nationalities.
Political Parties: Russia Our Home and Option of Russia, both neo-liberal; the Liberal Democratic Party, Nationalist conservative; Communist Party; Democratic Agrarian Party; Yabloko; Congress of Russian Communities.
Social Organizations: Federation of Independent Labor Unions of Russia (FNPR), with more than 40 million workers; Sotsprof Labor Union Association, with one million affiliates.

THE STATE

Official Name: Rossiyskaya Federatsiya.
Administrative divisions: The federation is made up of 26 autonomous republics.
Capital: Moscow (Moskva) 9,314,000 people (1999).
Other cities: St Petersburg 4,656,900 people; Nizhnij Novgorod 1,351,800; Novosibirsk 1,397,800 (2000).
Government: Vladimir Vladimirovich Putin, President since December 1999; Mikhail Mikhaylovich Kasyanov, Prime Minister since May 2000. Parliamentary republic. Bicameral Legislature: the Federal Assembly is formed by the State Duma, with 450 members, and the Federation Council, with 178 members.
National Holiday: June 12, Russia Day (1990).
Armed Forces: 1,270,000 (1996).
Other: 220,000.

[48] In March 1993, Congress opposed a referendum proposed by Yeltsin and tried unsuccessfully to limit his powers. Following further disagreements, Yeltsin took all the power from Parliament, which then ousted the President and replaced him with Alexandr Rutskoi. On the same day, September 22, the police surrounded Parliament.

[49] The tension continued and on October 4 Parliament was taken by force. Several opposition leaders, like Rutskoi, vice-president of Congress, and its leader, Ruslan Khasbulatov, were arrested. A few days later, Yeltsin called for new elections and organized a referendum to increase his own powers.

[50] The December elections marked the defeat of those sectors faithful to Yeltsin, but 60 per cent of the voters approved the constitutional reform which granted him greater powers. In February 1994, a bilateral agreement was signed with the Russian republic of Tartarstan and a similar document was expected to be signed with Chechnya. However, the tension between Moscow and the pro-independence groups of this mostly Muslim republic, which had declared independence in 1991, became more serious and in December 1994, Yeltsin ordered military intervention.

[51] Despite protests both within Russia and abroad, the President maintained the military attacks on Grozny, the Chechen capital, which was almost totally destroyed in 1995. In December of that year, the Communist Party led by Zyuganov won the elections with 22.3 per cent, followed by the ultra-right and xenophobic Liberal Democratic Party of Vladimir Zhirinovski, with 11.8 per cent and the Russia Our Home of Prime Minister Viktor Chernomyrdin, with 10.1 per cent.

[52] Fearful of defeat in the July 1996 presidential elections, Yeltsin tried to modify his policies, stopping the privatizations and nominating Yevgeny Primakov - a diplomat from the Soviet era who was an ally of Gorbachev - as foreign minister. In the electoral campaign all the opposition candidates from Gorbachev to the Communists, criticized the unlimited financial speculation, corruption and 'clanishness' of Yeltsin and his allies.

[53] In the second round of the July elections, Yeltsin took 53.8 per cent of the vote and Zyuganov only 40 per cent (4.8 per cent of the voters voted against both). The outgoing president was able to win through an unexpected alliance with Alexandr Lebed, an opposition candidate who had received 11 million votes.

[54] Appointed State security adviser, Lebed immediately started action to end the war in Chechnya, which he stated had caused the deaths of 80,000 people. When it was announced Yeltsin would be undergoing surgery in September, Lebed and Prime Minister Chernomyrdin became the alternative, and opposed, choices should there be a power vacuum.

[55] Yeltsin returned in March 1997, following a long absence. He reformed his cabinet and launched a far-reaching plan to cut back State spending, and privatizations. The living conditions of the population continued to fall. The chaotic change to a market economy damaged the production mechanisms, dismantled the social protection systems, and fed the rise of the mafias. In that year 73 per cent of the banking sector was under mafia control, and one of their most lucrative lines was the trafficking of nuclear material.

[56] On May 12, Yeltsin signed an agreement with Chechnya granting it wide-ranging autonomy. The same day, the Russian Central Bank made an agreement with the Chechen bank according to which Chechnya would provisionally maintain the rouble as its currency, but Moscow would no longer control its banking system.

[57] With the vote of Communists, Nationalists and some Liberals, Eugeni Primakov was appointed Minister of Foreign Affairs in September 1998. Primakov, an economist, refinanced debts with international organizations, without promising concrete changes. Fiscal controls were reinstated and the Government began to intervene in the economy. In the international field, Primakov introduced a policy less dependent on Washington and stood up to US President Clinton and UK Prime Minister Blair after their attacks against Iraq in December 1998.

[58] Primakov's popularity, which outshone Yeltsin's, convinced the President that a change in the administration was needed. In May, during the bombing of Yugoslavia, he decided to replace Primakov with Sergei Stepashin. Stepashin was replaced in turn by Vladimir Putin in August.

[59] A guerrilla force crossed the Chechen border, entered Dagestan in August 1999 and took control of several cities. The Russian army expelled the rebels after several weeks of fighting. A series of bomb attacks against civilian buildings in Moscow, which caused dozens of deaths, were blamed on Chechen terrorists. Putin vowed to 'recover' Chechnya for the Russian Federation and used every possible means to conquer the territory, but even so, after eight months of fighting, he was barely able to control the captial Grozny and the central area, while the guerrillas remained strong in the mountains.

[60] On December 31 1999, Yeltsin resigned unexpectedly, leaving the Government in hands of Putin. Primakov, one of the main candidates to the Presidency, withdrew after being unable to form a coalition to oppose Yeltsin's protégé. The elections, held on March 26, were won in the first round by Putin, with 52.9 per cent of the vote. Second place went to Communist candidate Gennadi Zyuganov, with 29.2 per cent. Zyganov denounced a series of irregularities in the elections. After a six-month investigation, they were revealed by the Moscow Times.

[61] In August 2000, Russia's national pride took a knock when its flagship nuclear submarine Kursk sank after an explosion on board, killing all crew.

[62] In March 2001, during his first Cabinet re-shuffle, Putin appointed Sergei Ivanov as first civilian Defense Minister. Putin alleged that the changes would help to demilitarize Russian public life, tying in with his plan to reduce the army - one of the largest in the world - by one third and turn it into 'a compact and modern force'.

[63] Between 1992-2000, the Russian population fell by 2.8 million people. In 2001 it lost 700,000 more. Vladimir Zhirinovsky, far right leader who had in the past proposed an increase of population through polygamy, 'allowing men to have up to four women each', called for a halt to the 'reduction in population' and to make abortion illegal.

[64] According to official statistics, almost one in every three Russians lives in poverty, the average pension had fallen below the basic survival level and more than 60 per cent of pensioners were at risk. Minister of Labor and Social Development, Alexander Pochinok, admitted in July 2001 that civil servants were among those with lowest salaries, many of them unable to cover their families' basic needs. In some sectors, such as agriculture, health and education, the proportion of poor people again amounted to almost 60 per cent. The gap between the wealthy and the poorest - the highest and lowest 10 per cent in the scale of wealth - had widened year by year. If in 1992, when post-Soviet transition had begun, the income of the highest 10 per cent was eight times that of the lowest 10 per cent, in 2001 the proportion was 14 to 1.

[65] In December the *Duma* (Parliament) passed the first non-deficit budget since the demise of the Soviet Union. However, the fall in gas and oil prices after the September 2001 terrorist attacks in

DEMOGRAPHY

Population: 143,752,000 (2002)
Annual growth: 0.1 % (1985-2000)
Estimates for year 2015: 133,314,000 (2000)
Annual growth to year 2015: -0.6 % (2000)
Urban population: 73.1 % (2000)
Urban growth: -0.5 % (2000)
Children per woman: 1.2 (2000)

HEALTH

Life expectancy at birth: 66 years (2000-2005)
male: 60 years (2000-2005)
female: 73 years (2000-2005)
Maternal mortality: 44 per 100,000 live births (1985/99)
Infant mortality: 18 per 1,000 (2000)
Under-5 child mortality: 22 per 1,000 (2000)
Daily calorie supply: 2,879 per capita (1999)
421 doctors per 100,000 people (1998)
Safe water: 99 % (2000)

EDUCATION

Literacy: 99 % (2000)
male: 100 % (2000)
female: 99 % (2000)
School enrolment (net):
Primary total: 93 % (1994/2000)
male: 93 % (1995/99)
female: 93 % (1995/99)
Secondary (gross):
male: 83 % (1995/97)
female: 91 % (1995/97)
Tertiary (gross): 41 % (1997)
Primary school teachers: one for every 18 pupils (1998)

COMMUNICATIONS

105 newspapers (1996), 418 radios (1997), 421 TV sets (1998) and 218 main telephone lines (2000) per 1,000 people
Books: 20 new titles per 100,000 people (1992/94)

ECONOMY

Per capita, GDP: $ 8,377 (2000)
Annual growth: 8.9 % (2000)
Annual inflation: 20.8 % (2000)
Consumer price index: 485.2 (2000)
Currency: 31.0 rubles = $ 1 (03/2002)
Cereal imports: 4,862,308 metric tons (2000)
Food import dependency: 15 % (2000)
Fertilizer use: 114 kg per ha (1999)
Exports: $ 115,200 million (2000)
Imports: $ 62,290 million (2000)
External debt: $ 160,300 million (2000); $ 1,102 per capita (2000)
Debt service: 13.5 % of exports (1999)
Development aid received: $ 1,816 million (1999); $ 12.4 per capita (1999); 0.50 % of GNP (1999)

ENERGY

Consumption: 3,963.0 Kgs of oil equivalent per capita yearly (1998); -57.7 % imported (1999)
HDI (ranking/value): 55 / 0.775 (1999)

the US forced the Ministry of Finance to review its estimates, since the price of oil had fallen since then. Russia had become the second oil exporter in the world, after Saudi Arabia.

[66] In January 2002, the TV station TV-6, the last national independent station, was forced to shut down at the request of a minor stockholder. The Supreme Court of Moscow refused an appeal. The station's largest stockholder was Boris Berezovsky, a strong critic of Putin. Journalists and opposition politicians claimed it was another attempt by the President to gain control of the country's independent media.

[67] In June Putin attempted to mediate in the escalating tension between nuclear powers India and Pakistan over Kashmir.

[68] Putin opposed US plans to bomb Iraq in September 2002. ∎

National conflicts in the former USSR

Conflicts among different national groups in the former Soviet Union - that gained new strength by its dissolution - are the result, among other things, of the expansionist policy of the Tsarist regime begun in the 18th century and continued by its Soviet successors.

At the time of its break-up in October 1991 the USSR was a vast conglomerate of numerous ethnic groups. This was the result of a long historical process of Tsarist expansion which since the 18th century had transformed Russia. The Tsarist regime implemented a systematic policy of 'Russianisation', with the absolute pre-eminence of the Russian language and of the Orthodox Church, as well as obedience to a central power embodied in the Tsar. During the civil wars that followed the October 1917 revolution, the various republics were federated to form the Union of Soviet Socialist Republics.

Soviet policy, unlike the Tsarist one, sought, at least in name, to grant equal rights to the different ethnic groups and political divisions in the State. This implied giving primacy to the central power of the Soviet over land and ethnic conflicts between different regions, the forceful 'sedentarization' of nomadic peoples (such as in Kyrgysztan) and initiatives to fight ethnic divisions which consisted mostly of huge forced migrations from one region to another.

The Baltic republics were annexed to the USSR in 1940, in accordance with a secret agreement signed by Stalin and Hitler in 1939, jointly with the German-Soviet pact signed before World War II. Bukovina and Besarabia were confiscated from Romania in 1944, which, together with the Autonomous Republic of Moldavia, in Ukranian territory, made up the Socialist Republic of Moldavia (now Moldova).

The USSR consisted of 15 Soviet socialist republics, which were further subdivided into 20 autonomous Soviet socialist republics, 8 autonomous regions (smaller and less populated than the republics) and 10 autonomous districts (for small ethnic groups, mostly nomadic, from Siberia and the Far East).

In 1986, with Mikhail Gorbachev in the Presidential seat, it was clear that the tensions had only been muted (and in some cases increased) by the administrative initiatives of the Communist regime. Several republics demanded their independence, which led to the dissolution of the USSR.

Several regions and districts also demanded their autonomy, leading to armed conflicts. In 1998, some new republics which had declared their sovereignty had not yet resolved their status. These were the Transnitrian Republic of Moldavia (known as Transnitria), the Republic of South Ossetia, the Republic of Nagorno-Karabakh and the People's Republic of Abkhazia.

TRANSNITRIA
The 1989 census revealed that the population of Transnitria was still mostly Slavic (28 per cent Ukranians, 24 per cent Russians), while Moldavians amounted to 40 per cent. However, that year, the Government of Moldavia declared Moldavian as the Republic's sole official language, which led to strikes and social unrest. From January to October 1990, the population of Transnitria organized referenda which decided the creation of the Autonomous Republic of Transnitria. But the Supreme Soviet of the USSR declared these referenda illegal and refused to grant the territory autonomy. In December 1991, after the dissolution of the Soviet Union, Igor Smirnov was chosen first President of Transnitria and a new referendum declared independence. Moldavian police clashed with Transnitrian militias and, in 1992, the Russian Federation and Moldavia signed an agreement to re-establish peace in the region. In 1994, Transnitria and Moldavia re-established economic relations and 100,000 refugees returned to their homes, although in 1998 the political situation remained uncertain.

SOUTH OSSETIA
Ossetians came to the Caucasus territory in the 13th century. In 1774, Russia annexed the territories held by the Ossetians and, in 1918, created the Autonomous Republic of Ossetia (in the present Federated Republic of Russia). In 1922, the autonomous region of South Ossetia was created in Georgia. In the Eighties, when several movements for self-determination appeared in various parts of the Soviet Union, the idea of joining the Autonomous Republic of Ossetia started to grow in South Ossetia. In September 1990, South Ossetia proclaimed itself a sovereign republic. In December 1990, the parliament of Georgia repealed the status of autonomous region in South Ossetia and declared a state of emergency in the territory, which led to the beginning of armed confrontations. A Russian-Georgian-Ossetian peace force succeeded in putting an end to the fighting in 1992. In 1994, L. Chibirov was elected president of the parliament in South Ossetia and, in 1996, became President of the territory. Since then, several meetings between Georgian and Ossetians authorities failed to reach an agreement on the political status of South Ossetia.

NAGORNO-KARABAKH
Since May 1918, when Moscow's authority was established over Nagorno-Karabakh, it was discussed if the region, mostly populated by Armenians, should belong to Armenia or Azerbaidjan. In 1923 the territory became a province of Azerbaijan. The strikes of 1988 in Nagorno-Karabakh were one of the first signs of instability due to nationalist demands in the Soviet Union. In 1991, the Nagorno-Karabakh parliament not only declared the region's independence, but also annexed the district of Shaumia. Three months later, the majority of the population voted for independence. By then, a full-blown war had erupted between the Karabakhs (supported by Armenia) and Azerbaijan, in which 4,600 Karabakhs and some 30,000 Azerbaidjanis died. In 1994, Azerbaijan and Nagorno-Karabakh signed an armistice. The first elections of Nagorno-Karabakh elected Robert Kocharian President in December 1996. In 1997, Kocharian was appointed Prime Minister of Armenia and left Karabakh, being replaced by Arcady Gukassian. In 1998, the creation of Nagorno-Karabakh was still in process and negotiations with Azerbaijan progressed slowly. ∎

Rwanda

Population: 8,148,000 (2002)
Land area: 24,670 SQ KM
Capital: Kigali
Currency: Franc
Language: Kinyarwanda, English and French

Rwanda

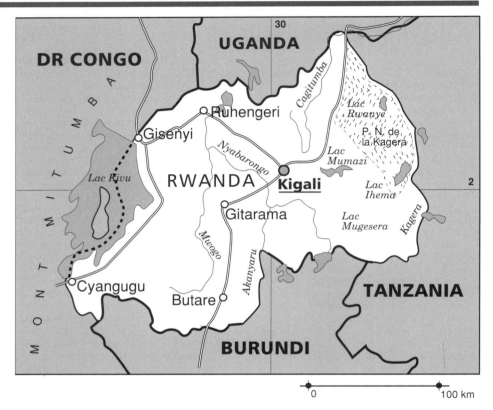

Inhabited since ancient times by the Hutu (Bantus) and Twa (pygmy) ethnic groups, Rwanda's highlands were invaded in the 15th century by the Tutsis (or Watutsis) from Ethiopia. After subduing the local population, the Tutsis set up a stratified society. This social and political organization remained basically unchanged even after German colonization started in the region in 1897. The territory became part of German East Africa, which also included Burundi.

[2] After World War I, the territory named Rwanda-Urundi was placed under Belgian custody and administered by them from the Congo (today's DR Congo, formerly Zaire). Of the three groups which inhabit the region, the minority - made up of the pastoralist and warrior Tutsis - consolidated its control over the agricultural Hutu and artisan Twa. In 1959, farm workers organized by the Parmehutu (Party of the Hutu Emancipation Movement) revolted against Tutsi rule.

[3] A bloody civil war ensued and the Belgian colonial government chose to abandon the territory. The Parmehutu won elections supervised by the United Nations in 1961 and proclaimed a Republic in 1962, autonomous from neighboring Burundi.

[4] The power structure favoring Tutsi rulers was abolished and land distributed on the capitalist basis of private ownership. However, this did not lead to true national unity, nor did it settle controversies between ethnic groups.

[5] The following year, civil war broke out again. Approximately 20,000 people died and 160,000 Tutsis were expelled from the country.

[6] Lacking other patterns, the Parmehutu reorganized society according to ethnic group interests: the Twa (40,000 in all) were assigned the crafts industry; the Tutsis, cattle-raising, and land ownership was reserved for the Hutus. The system virtually ignored the possibility of urban development, a fact evidenced by the tiny size of the capital city of Kigali. In order to set an example, President Gregory Kayibanda worked his own piece of land. As a result agriculture was almost entirely reduced to subsistence farming, with little surplus left over for the market.

[7] In the late 1960s, attempts to increase market production saw a revival of the coffee plantations, burnt down in 1959, in protest against colonial despotism.

[8] The new policy however did not solve Rwanda's economic problems but rather exacerbated social tensions as a new group of landowners arose, adding complexity to existing ethnic conflicts, and giving rise to new and violent outbreaks.

[9] Faced with the threat of a new civil war, Colonel Juvenal Habyarimana overthrew Kayibanda on July 5 1973. Habyarimana, previously defense minister, dissolved the Parmehutu, jailed Kayibanda (who died shortly afterwards) and launched a diplomatic offensive successfully dealing with conflicts which had arisen between Rwanda and neighboring countries during the previous regime.

[10] The close relationship between Habyarimana and France, and with Zaire's President Mobutu caused disagreements within the governing party, the National Revolutionary Movement for Development (MRND). Progressive factions criticized the situation and Habyarimana's liberal policies. During the 1980 party congress they were expelled. Their leader, labor minister Alexis Kanyarengwe, went into exile in Tanzania to escape prison. Resolutions by the party congress endorsed 'planned liberalism', which resulted in an open-door policy for foreign investments.

[11] In 1982, Uganda expelled large numbers of Rwandan exiles, who were not allowed back into their own country. Whole towns were burned down by Ugandan troops leaving at least 10,000 people homeless and without food.

[12] In 1986, the new president of Uganda, Yoweri Museveni, announced that Rwandans who had lived in the country for more than ten years would automatically receive citizenship. Relations improved between the two countries; in 1988, both presidents signed a declaration confirming progress in their international policies.

[13] President Habyarimana changed his policies and took firm steps towards establishing a democracy. Initially he set up a National Development Council in an attempt to draw up national policies taking into consideration the country's different social and economic realities. Later, he launched an austerity program, which yielded some positive economic results. He released more than 1,000 political prisoners, and implemented measures to ensure respect for human rights in the prisons.

[14] Habyarimana was re-elected in 1988. On December 26 that year, elections were held to renew one-third of the 70 deputies. Of these, 11 women but only 2 Tutsis were elected. 60,000 Hutu refugees from Burundi entered the country in the course of the year.

[15] On September 30 1990, Fred Rwigyema, a Tutsi, and government official, led an uprising, entering Rwanda from Uganda. President

Habyarimana requested help from Belgium, France and Zaire (now DR Congo), whose troops played a decisive role in repelling the rebel offensive, although there was also fighting in the capital. In October, a cease-fire was reached between the two parties, through the intervention of Belgian Prime Minister, Wilfried Martens.

[16] At the end of January 1991, some 600 troops belonging to the Rwandan People's Front (RPF) entered the country from Uganda. In March, a cease-fire was signed. Among its provisions were the liberation of political prisoners and prisoners of war, and a commitment by President Habyarimana to initiate negotiations establishing a more open political atmosphere.

[17] In June of that year, the President signed the new constitution, which provided for a multiparty system, creating the post of Prime Minister, guaranteeing freedom of the press, limiting the presidential term to two five-year periods with no further re-election, and establishing a separation of the powers of the state.

[18] In March 1992, at least 300 members of the Tutsi minority were assassinated, and another 15,000 were forcibly relocated to the region of Bugesera. The leaders of the two principal opposition parties, the Republican Democratic Movement (MDR) and the Liberal Party (PL), blamed the Government for the violence, and especially a militia made up of young Hutus belonging to the MRND.

[19] In early 1993, President Habyarimana rejected the agreement signed in Arusha between the Rwandan delegation - led by Prime Minister Dismas Nsengiyaremye of the Republican Democratic Movement - and the rebels of the Rwandan Patriotic Front (FPR), led by Alex Kanyarengue, made up of Tutsi exiles who had challenged the Hutu domination of their community.

[20] The President refused any form of power-sharing with the FPR, which had demanded five cabinet positions, the incorporation of its soldiers into the regular army and the repatriation of Tutsi refugees from Uganda and Tanzania.

[21] Although both bands had respected the cease-fire which had been in effect since August 1992, the FPR broke off negotiations in February, launching a new offensive which enabled them to gain control over most of the country's territory, and prepare an advance upon the capital.

[22] The death of Presidents of Rwanda, Juvenal Habyarimana, and Burundi, Cyprien Ntaryamira, in an attack on the aeroplane carrying them to Kigali after attending a peace conference in Tanzania on April 6 1994, initiated a new bloodbath which cost the lives of 800,000 mainly Tutsi people in three months. Both presidents were Hutus.

[23] Given the worsening of the civil war, France, the United States and Belgium decided in April to send in troops to 'guarantee security and evacuate the foreigners'. French troops took control of Kigali airport to oversee the repatriation of 600 French citizens resident in the capital.

[24] The new government tried to revive the Rwandan economy and organize trials for those guilty of what the UN described as 'genocide'. However, the Government did not receive the aid expected from the Western countries and many members of the militias responsible for the massacres continued to operate from their refuge in Zaire (now DR Congo).

[25] During 1995 and 1996 further mass graves were discovered nearly every week, while the violence of the new Rwandan army - formed around a core of FPR fighters - and the militias led to more deaths. Many of the victims of the militias had been witnesses of events in 1994, along with Hutu public officials, accused of 'collaboration'.

[26] Increasing tensions in eastern Zaire and the mass deportations of refugees made violations of human rights more serious. In February 1997, Amnesty International denounced the death of dozens of civilians, both Tutsis and Hutus, and the murder of four UN officials in the city of Cyangugu.

[27] In April 1998, despite the call for clemency made by Pope John Paul II and UN Secretary-General Kofi Annan, 22 of those responsible for the genocide were executed in strategically chosen places, where the largest massacres had taken place. The four executed in Kigali, included Silas Munyagishali (assistant district attorney in Kigali), Froduald Karamira (former vice president of the MDR) and Elie Nhimiyimana (organizer of the massacre in the Gikondo neighborhood of the capital). Amnesty International classed the executions as 'a brutal parody of justice which jeopardizes any hope of reconciliation in Rwanda following the genocide and which will perpetuate the cycle of violence'. Jean Kambanda, former Prime Minister of the Hutu government, decided to plead guilty and collaborate with the International Court, revealing information about his former government colleagues. Kambanda avoided the death penalty and was sentenced to life in prison.

[28] Clashes between government troops and Interahamwe Hutu rebel militias in the northwestern part of the country continued throughout the year causing hundreds of casualties.

[29] Prime Minister Pierre Celestin Rwigema, one of few Hutus in government, was accused in October 1999 of channeling hundreds of thousands of international relief dollars into personal projects such as the construction of schools in his home district. Government officials felt 'insulted' by the decision of the International Court to free one of the main suspects in the 1994 genocide. In November, the Government denied an entry visa to Carla del Ponte, the Court prosecutor. Del Ponte finally entered Rwanda in December. That month the UN asked Rwanda to pardon its inability to prevent the genocide.

[30] The allegations against Rwigema created a delicate situation by February 2000: both the press and public opinion accused him of misappropriation of funds and of allowing the dumping of toxic waste on the outskirts of Kigali. He was

PROFILE

ENVIRONMENT

Known as the country of a thousand hills on account of its geographical location between two mountain ranges, Rwanda lies in the heart of the African continent. The terrain is mountainous and well irrigated by numerous rivers and lakes supporting varied wild-life. Rwanda's forests are home to one of the few remaining populations of mountain gorillas. Most people live in the highlands where the economic mainstay is subsistence agriculture. The lowlands have been eroded and their natural vegetation is disappearing as a result of excessive grazing. 90 per cent of the energy consumed by Rwandans is derived from natural resources, consequently leading to deforestation and erosion.

SOCIETY

Peoples: 84 per cent are Hutu (Bantu-speaking people), 15 per cent Tutsi (Hamitic) and 1 per cent Twa (descendants of the pygmies). There is a minority of European origin most of whom are Belgian.
Religions: 69 per cent profess traditional African religions, 20 per cent are Catholic, 10 per cent Protestant and 1 per cent Muslim.
Languages: Rwanda, English and French (all official).
Political Parties: Rwandan Patriotic Front (FPR); National Revolutionary Movement for Development (MRND); Republican Democratic Movement (MDR); Liberal Party (PL).

THE STATE

Official Names: Repubulika y'u Rwanda; République Rwandaise; Republic of Rwanda.
Capital: Kigali 369,000 people (1999).
Other cities: Butare 32,400 people; Ruhengeri 33,500; Gisenyi 24,800 (2000).
Government: Paul Kagame, President since March 2000. Bernard Makuza, Prime Minister since March 2000. Legislature: National Transitory Assembly with 70 appointed members.
National Holiday: July 1, Independence Day (1962).
Armed Forces: 33,000 (1996).

EXTERNAL DEBT

2000

PER CAPITA

US$ 167

FOREIGN TRADE

Millions US$ 2000

IMPORTS

432

EXPORTS

149

replaced in March by Barnard Makuza, a Hutu from Rwigema's party. That month, president Bizimungu resigned office after some of his collaborators were not included in the new cabinet. With 81 out of 86 votes, Paul Kagame was elected President by parliament in March 2000.

[31] A United Nations report released in March 2000 accused Rwanda, Burkina Faso and Togo of assisting UNITA, the Angolan rebel organization. The report also accused Belgium of not to control the traffic of diamonds illegally extracted from Angola into its territory. The Government disagreed with the contents of the report and threatened to sue the UN.

[32] A UN memo claimed that the FPR, under orders from Kagame, had been responsible for the attack on the plane that killed Habyarimana on April 6 1994. Kagame rejected the charges, alleging the report tried to absolve the UN of its part of the guilt in the genocided that followed the events denounced.

[33] The conflicts in the region worsened in 2001, when the President of DR Congo (DRC), Laurent Kabila, was murdered by one of his bodyguards, and Kinshasa claimed that Rwanda and Uganda had masterminded the assassination. The tension led Kagame to consider, in May, the withdrawal of his troops from the DRC, but only on the condition that the UN sent in observers. The peace process was paralyzed after the DRC Government abandoned the talks, alleging that the constant attacks from Rwandan troops and Congolese rebels made any negotiation impossible.

[34] The International Criminal Tribunal for Rwanda (ICTR) announced its first verdicts in 2001. These set new standards in international law and justice for the cases of war crimes. Prosecutor Carla del Ponte had said that the investigation, which linked political, military and religious leaders to the genocide, could end in 2002.

[35] Seven years after the genocide, the survivors were the greatest

losers. Power was out of their hands, their country's economy was sinking, and AIDS was now decimating their youth more aggressively than the war had: in spite of its hundreds of thousands of dead, Rwanda's population had grown since the genocide. The problem of land tenure was unsolved; rural emigrants moved to the cities and increased the number of unemployed. Kigali went from 150,000 residents in 1995 to some 500,000 in 2002.

[36] The country started 2002 with a new national flag, anthem and coat of arms, presented in a ceremony in Kigali, replacing those designed in 1962. The new flag is blue, green and yellow. Blue to symbolize peace and calm; green for prosperity, work and productivity; and yellow (sun) a symbol of hope and transparency.

[37] Nyiragongo volcano erupted on January 20 in the DRC city of Goma, displacing some 500,000 people who sought refuge in the Rwandan city of Giseny. Kagame urged the international community to help the victims with aid. ∎

STATISTICS

DEMOGRAPHY
Population: 8,148,000 (2002)
Annual growth: 1.7 % (1985-2000)
Estimates for year 2015: 10,504,000 (2000)
Annual growth to year 2015: 2.1 % (2000)
Urban population: 6.2 % (2000)
Urban growth: 4.0 % (2000)
Children per woman: 6.0 (2000)

HEALTH
Life expectancy at birth: 41 years (2000-2005)
male: 40 years (2000-2005)
female: 42 years (2000-2005)
Infant mortality: 100 per 1,000 (2000)
Under-5 child mortality: 187 per 1,000 (2000)
Daily calorie supply: 2,011 per capita (1999)
Safe water: 41 % (2000)

EDUCATION
Literacy: 67 % (2000)
male: 74 % (2000)
female: 61 % (2000)
School enrolment (net):
Primary total: 66 % (1994/2000)
male: 67 % (1995/99)
female: 68 % (1995/99)
Secondary (gross):
male: 12 % (1995/97)
female: 9 % (1995/97)
Tertiary (gross): 1 % (1998)
Primary school teachers: one for every 54 pupils (1998)

COMMUNICATIONS
0 newspaper (1995), 76 radios (1997), 0 TV set (1998) and 2 main telephone lines (2000) per 1,000 people

ECONOMY
Per capita, GDP: $ 943 (2000)
Annual growth: 3.1 % (2000)
Annual inflation: 3.9 % (2000)
Consumer price index: 129.6 (2000)
Currency: 458.3 francs = $ 1 (03/2002)
Cereal imports: 50,554 metric tons (2000)
Fertilizer use: 3 kg per ha (1999)
Exports: $ 149 million (2000)
Imports: $ 432 million (2000)
External debt: $ 1,271 million (2000); $ 167 per capita (2000)
Debt service: 29.6 % of exports (1999)
Development aid received: $ 373 million (1999); $ 44.9 per capita (1999); 19.10 % of GNP (1999)

HDI (ranking/value): 152 / 0.395 (1999)

The hidden Twa

The Twa pygmies of Rwanda, Burundi and the Congo are largely overlooked. They were the first to occupy the region lapped by the water of Lake Kivu, as one member group of the Central African pygmy peoples. They are believed to have originated from deep in the forests and equatorial mountains, where they still live today.

The Twa lived more or less alone in this region until the 16th century. They were hunters and potters, with a varied and creative ceramic tradition. Their low numbers and height of just 1.5 meters left them at a disadvantage when Hutu farmers and Tutsi herders led successive invasions into their lands. The invaders swiftly made the Twa their slaves, considering them an inferior ethnic group. All three groups speak the same language.

Having neither livestock nor farms, the Twa go unregistered in the statistics of Rwanda and neighboring states, where 90 per cent of the population are farmers. In general

they suffer from very poor health, with a high incidence of malaria and various sexually-transmitted diseases. Rwanda is one of the Central African countries with the highest average infant mortality from malnutrition and parasites.

In recent decades, reports on Rwanda have also ignored these people, giving priority to the power struggle between the Hutus (85 per cent of the population) and Tutsis. In 1994 the Hutu Government unleashed a genocidal campaign against the Tutsis, killing over a million people, including some moderate Hutu that were against the slaughter. Eventually, a rebel Tutsi army dislodged the Hutus and formed a new Government.

While these two ethnic groups fight out their battles, the Twa live quietly away from the large towns, only coming down from the mountains to work as paid laborers in the potato, sorghum and corn plantations when they need supplies or when food is short. ∎

St Helena

Population:	6,000 (2002)
Land area:	210 SQ KM
Capital:	Jamestown
Currency:	Pound sterling
Language:	English

St Helena

St Helena was uninhabited when Portuguese navigators arrived in 1502. In 1659 an outpost of the British East India Company was established on the island, and since then St Helena has been an English colony. Of scant economic interest, the island acquired notoriety as the location of Napoleon's second exile, from 1815 until his death in 1821.

2	The Malvinas/Falklands War put it back on the map, a century and a half later. An English representative stated: 'It was only with the help of Ascension Island and the labor force provided by St Helena, that we could recover the Falklands'. This may justify the expensive maintenance of this British enclave through the Overseas Development Administration.

3	The UN supports all nations' rights to self-determination and independence. In December 1984, the UN General Assembly urged Britain to bolster the fishing industry, handcrafts and reforestation on the island and to foster awareness of the right to independence. Washington and London both voted against the resolution. The UN also questioned the existence of the military base on Ascension Island since there should not be any base in non-autonomous territories.

4	On January 1 1989 a new constitution was instituted conferring greater powers on the members of the Legislative Council and enabling civil servants to become election candidates with the approval of the governor. The new constitution also reduced the voting age to 18.

5	The island's only export is fish, but there has been a decline in the total catch: 27.2 tons in 1985, and a mere 9.2 tons in 1990.

6	St Helena is of scientific interest because of the its rare flora and fauna. The island has some 40 plant species unknown in the rest of the world.

7	In 1997 unemployment rose to 18 per cent. The announcement two years later that the UK would grant citizenship to the residents of the dependent territories was widely celebrated by the islanders.

8	The British Government had decades earlier acquired a ship to link the islands to the rest of the world, the RMS. It has been the only means for reaching St Helena. There has been more talk of building an airport, but the islanders are not all in accord with this, as it would harm the natural habitat.

9	St Helena is the only British Overseas Territory that receives period economic aid from the Crown to overcome the deficit generated by its limited economy.

10	In May 2002 the island celebrated the 500 years since discovery with a series of maritime and cultural events.■

PROFILE

ENVIRONMENT

Located in the South Atlantic some 2,000 km from the coast of Angola (Southern Africa), slightly west of the Greenwich meridian. Of volcanic origin, and 410 sq km in area, the island is mountainous, has no mineral reserves and industries and the only productive activities are subsistence agriculture and fishing.

SOCIETY

Peoples: The island's population is largely of African descent. Some 6,000 natives of St Helena have emigrated to South Africa and the UK.
Religions: Protestant, Anglican, Baptist, Seventh-Day Adventists, and also Roman Catholic.
Languages: English (official).
Political Parties: There are no parties in St Helena.

THE STATE

Official Name: St Helena.
Administrative division: one administrative division: St. Helena and two dependencies: Ascension and Tristan da Cunha.
Capital: Jamestown 2,000 people (1999). Inland is Longwood, where Napoleon Bonaparte was exiled.
Other cities: Georgetown 560 people; Edinburgh 270 (2000).
Government: Queen Elizabeth II, Head of State; David Hollamby, Governor, appointed by the British Crown in June 1999. There is a Legislative Council of 15 seats.
National Holiday: Second Saturday in June, Queen Elizabeth II's birthday (1926).
Armed Forces: Security is responsibility of the United Kingdom.

DEMOGRAPHY

Population: 6,000 (2002)

ECONOMY

Cereal imports: 388 metric tons (2000)

Tristan da Cunha

The most important of a group of South Atlantic islands 2,400 km west of Cape Town, South Africa, and under the administration of St Helena. The islands total 201 sq km (Tristan da Cunha 98 sq km; Inaccessible Island 10 sq km, 32 km west of the main island; Nightingale Islands 25 sq km, 32 km south of Tristan da Cunha, and Diego Alvarez or Gough Island 91 sq km, 350 km south of the main island).

2	The 300 inhabitants are concentrated on Tristan da Cunha, the majority employed by the Government and in a lobster-processing factory. There were volcanic eruptions in 1961 and the island was evacuated, though the population returned in 1963. On Diego Alvarez there is a small weather station run by the South African Government. The main religion is Protestant and the official language is English. There is an administrator, Brian P Baldwin, who represents the Government of St Helena and an advisory council with executive and legislative duties, comprising 8 elected and 3 appointed members.

3	A 10-year contract to operate Tristan da Cunha's lucrative lobster-fishing concession, which was awarded in 1996 to a South African firm, went into effect on January 1 1997. The residents of Tristan da Cunha - like those of St Helena - demanded British citizenship during the annual visit by St Helena's Governor.

4	In May 2001 the island was hit hard by a storm that destroyed the entire infrastructure. The British Crown earmarked $106,000 to begin reconstruction.

Ascension Island

Ascension Island is of volcanic origin, covering 88 sq km. Its importance derives from its strategic location in the South Atlantic, 1,200 km northwest of St Helena. It is a communication relay center between South Africa and Europe, and the United States maintains a missile tracking station - Wideawake Airfield - there under an accord with Britain. The island's naval installation and airbase were vital to Britain during the Malvinas Islands/Falklands Islands war (April-June 1982) and afterwards as a base for the ships and planes that supplied the British troops occupying the islands claimed by Argentina.

There is no indigenous population and the majority are employees of the St Helena Government. In 1988, out of the 1,099 inhabitants, 765 were from St Helena, 222 were British, 102 were American and 10 were of other nationalities. These figures do not include British military personnel. The main religion is Protestant and the official language is English. The island's administrator, Geoffrey Fairhurst, represents the Government of St Helena.

St Kitts-Nevis

Population: 38,000 (2002)
Land area: 360 SQ KM
Capital: Basseterre
Currency: EC dollar
Language: English

Saint Kitts-Nevis

The island of Liamuiga, or 'fertile land' in the language of the Carib Indians who originally lived there, was renamed St Christopher by Columbus on his second voyage to America, in 1493. It was not colonized by the Europeans until 1623, when adventurer Thomas Walker established the first English settlement in the Caribbean. The neighboring island of Nevis was colonized five years later. After the rapid extermination of the Caribs, the English started to grow plantation crops, especially sugarcane, for which they used slaves from Africa.

[2] After numerous clashes between France and Britain, St Kitts and Nevis became a British colony under the 1783 Treaty of Versailles, along with other Caribbean islands.

[3] In the 20th century, the decolonization process following World War II gave the islands total internal autonomy, while foreign relations and defense were left to the colonial capitals. These islands joined the Associate States of the West Indies. In 1980, Anguilla formally separated from St Kitts and Nevis (see Anguilla); after this the islands were governed by a Prime Minister and a parliament, both elected by universal suffrage.

[4] The Labor Party had been in office since 1967, but suffered a major defeat in the 1980 election, at the hands of an opposition coalition of the People's Action Movement (PAM) and the Nevis Reformation Party (NRP). Kennedy Alphonse Simmonds became Prime Minister. The opposition victory meant that independence, planned for June 1980, had to be postponed as the NRP was opposed to a post-independence federation with St

Kitts. The 1976 plebiscite showed that 99.4 per cent of the population of Nevis favored separation.

[5] In the 1984 elections, Kennedy Simmonds and his government increased their parliamentary representation. Simmonds was re-elected in March 1989, in line with the US interests in the region.

[6] In 1990, strikes broke out among agricultural workers who had been refused a 10 per cent wage increase. Sugar companies responded by hiring close to 1,000 workers from St Vincent and the Grenadines, to cut sugarcane.

[7] In June 1992, the Concerned Citizens' Movement won the election in Nevis, obtaining three seats in the Nevis Assembly, ousting the Nevis Reformation Party (NRP) led by Daniel Simeon. Together with the People's Action Movement, the NRP made up the main coalition. Weston Paris, Governor-General Sir Clement Athelston's representative on Nevis, died in unclarified circumstances.

[8] The November 1993 election was inconclusive. Further elections were held in July 1995 in which the St Kitts-Nevis Labor Party, led by Denzil Douglas, came to power.

[9] In 1998 the Concerned Citizens' Movement, led by Vance Amory, Prime Minister of Nevis, failed in its attempt to achieve independence for the island by not getting the necessary two-thirds of the vote. Delegations from Caricom member countries, the US and St Kitts came to Nevis to try to restore links damaged by the election campaign.

[10] Hurricane George, in September 1998, destroyed or seriously damaged 80 per cent of homes. Reconstruction on the islands, conducted jointly by residents and the Government with support from the international community, took many months.

[11] In October 2000, UNESCO declared the Fort of Brimston Hill National Park a Historic Heritage of Humanity site. The fort, located at the heart of the park, covers 40 acres and was built in 1690. It is a vivid reminder of the clashes between the Spanish and the French for control over the Caribbean islands.

[12] Prime Minister Douglas was awarded the Gandhi-King-Ikeda Peace Prize, by the International Martin Luther King Chapel at Morehouse College, for his work for unity and peace. ∎

PROFILE

ENVIRONMENT

The territory is divided between St Kitts, 168.4 sq km, and Nevis, 93.2 sq km. The two islands are in the Windward Islands of the Lesser Antilles. They are of volcanic origin, hilly, with a rainy tropical climate, tempered by sea winds which make the land fit for plantation crops, especially sugarcane.

SOCIETY

Peoples: 95 per cent of the population are people descended from African slaves and European colonizers (mulattos). There is a British minority. **Religions:** Mainly Protestant (76.4 per cent, of which Anglican 32.3 per cent, Methodist 32.3 per cent); Roman Catholic 10.7 per cent; other 12.9 per cent. **Languages:** English (official). **Political Parties:** St. Kitts and Nevis Labor Party (SKLP), the People's Action Movement (PAM); the Concerned Citizens' Movement and the Nevis Reformation Party (NRP).

THE STATE

Official Name: Federation of St Christopher (St Kitts) and Nevis. **Administrative division:** 14 parishes. **Capital:** Basseterre (St. Kitts) 12,000 people (1999). **Other cities:** Charlestown (Nevis) 1,300 people; Saint Paul's 1,200 (2000). **Government:** Cuthbert Montroville-Sebastian, Governor-General appointed by the British Crown in January 1996. Denzil Douglas, Prime Minister since July 1995, re-elected in 2000. There is a National Assembly with 15 members (11 representatives of St Kitts and 3 of Nevis) and 1 appointed ex-officio. **National holiday:** September 19, Independence (1983). **Armed forces:** Royal St Kitts and Nevis Police Force; Defense Force, and the Coast Guard.

St Lucia

Population: 151,000 (2002)
Land area: 610 SQ KM
Capital: Castries
Currency: EC dollar
Language: English

St Lucia

Before Christopher Columbus named it Santa Lucia in 1502, the island had already been conquered by the Caribs who had expelled the Arawak indians.

[2] Neither the Spaniards nor the British succeeded in defeating local resistance, and in 1660 the French settled on the island, starting a dispute with Britain which was to last for 150 years. Over this period, the flag of St Lucia changed 14 times.

[3] In 1814, the Treaty of Paris transferred the island from France to Britain, which kept it until 1978. France left the legacy of *patois*, a pidgin language of mixed African and French.

[4] Under British rule, St Lucia became one big sugarcane plantation populated by African slave laborers. Agriculture is still the main economic resource but 20 years ago sugar gave way to banana cultivation.

[5] The island was part of the Colony of the Windward Islands, and between 1959 and 1962 St Lucia belonged to the West Indies Federation. In 1967 the island became more autonomous and was granted a new constitution as one of the Federate States of the Antilles.

[6] In the first elections held as an independent nation, in July 1979, Prime Minister John G M Compton and his United Workers Party (UWP), who had governed the island since 1964, were beaten. The progressive St Lucia Labor Party (SLP) won.

[7] The new Prime Minister, Allen Louisy, promised to help workers and peasants and to encourage small business as a means of curbing unemployment. George Odlum was Deputy Prime Minister and minister of trade, industry, tourism and foreign affairs. He was also leader of the predominant SLP's 'new left' wing, and he promoted the country's entry to the Non-Aligned Movement and established diplomatic relations with Cuba and North Korea. He also adopted a policy of close collaboration with the neighboring island of Grenada, which had launched its own revolutionary process some months before.

[8] After repeated political crisis, the United Workers' Party won the 1982 and 1987 elections. Compton returned to power with a conservative platform, favoring a market economy and proposing adjustment measures recommended by the IMF. The increase in exports and tourism revenues was not enough to leave economic crisis behind, which continued through the 1990s.

[9] The years 1994 and 1995 were marked by protests from workers on banana plantations - the island's main export - and also by dock employees, demanding higher wages. In 1996, Vaughn Allen Lewis was elected President.

[10] In May 1997, the Labor Party won the elections with 61.3 per cent of the vote. Kenny Anthony took over as Prime Minister. One of his first measures was to form a commission to investigate corruption during the UWP administration.

[11] The summit of Caribbean nations in August 1998 decided to remove border tariffs between member countries to compensate for the reduction of US support. During the summit Kenny Anthony issued a statement which expressed 'deep discomfort' over the US policy of not including Caribbean textile industries into the North American Free Trade Agreement (NAFTA).

[12] St Lucia, supported by other countries, withdrew from the talks at the World Trade Organization in Geneva in January 1999. The withdrawal followed its refusal to discuss the sanctions proposed by the US against the European Union (EU) regarding the special treatment given by the EU to Caribbean banana exports, as against those from Latin America.

[13] On December 31 2000, churchgoers were attacked with machetes by a group who murdered a nun, injured 13 others and then set fire to the building. The attackers said that 'God had told them to carry out the attack, because of the corruption within the Catholic church'. More than 2,000 people attended the nun's funeral in Castries, the capital. ∎

STATISTICS

DEMOGRAPHY
Population: 151,000 (2002)
Estimates for year 2015: 169,000 (2000)
Urban population: 37.8 % (2000)
Children per woman: 2.6 (2000)

HEALTH
Life expectancy at birth: 74 years (2000-2005)
male: 71 years (2000-2005)
female: 76 years (2000-2005)
Maternal mortality: 30 per 100,000 live births (1985/99)
Infant mortality: 17 per 1,000 (2000)
Under-5 child mortality: 19 per 1,000 (2000)
47 doctors per 100,000 people (1997)
Safe water: 98 % (2000)

EDUCATION
Primary school teachers: one for every 26 pupils (1998)

ECONOMY
Per capita, GDP: $ 5,703 (2000)
Annual growth: 0.5 % (2000)
Currency: 2.7 EC dollars = $ 1 (03/2002)
Cereal imports: 9,204 metric tons (2000)
Food import dependency: 24 % (2000)
Exports: $ 394 million (2000)
Imports: $ 464 million (2000)

PROFILE

ENVIROMENT
One of the volcanic Windward Islands of the Lesser Antilles, south of Martinique and north of St Vincent. The climate is tropical with heavy rainfall, tempered by ocean currents. The soil is fertile, bananas, cocoa, sugarcane and coconuts are grown.

SOCIETY
Peoples: Most inhabitants are descended from the integration of African slave laborers and European colonists. **Religions:** Roman Catholic 79 per cent; Protestant 15.5 per cent, of which Seventh-Day Adventist 6.5 per cent, Pentecostal 3 per cent; other 5.5 per cent. **Languages:** English (official) and a local patois derived from French and African elements. **Political Parties:** The St Lucia Labor Party; The United Workers' Party (UWP); Progressive Labor Party (PLP); The Citizens' Democratic Party.

THE STATE
Official name: St Lucia. **Capital:** Castries 57,000 people (1999). **Other cities:** Vieux Fort 4,600 people; Micoud 3,700 (2000). **Government:** Queen Elizabeth II, Head of State; Calliopa Pearlette Louisy, Governor-General appointed by the British Crown in 1999. Kenny Anthony, Prime Minister since March 1997. **National Holiday:** 13 December, Independence Day (1978), and discovery by Christopher Columbus.

St Vincent and The Grenadines

Population: 115,000 (2002)
Land area: 390 SQ KM
Capital: Kingstown
Currency: EC dollar
Language: English

St Vincent

The first inhabitants were Arawaks who were displaced by the Caribs, the island's inhabitants when Columbus arrived in 1498.

[2] In 1783, St Vincent became a British colony. However, the local people resisted European conquest; the former slaves who had rebelled on the neighboring islands and those who took refuge in St Vincent joined the Caribs to oppose the invaders. In 1796, they were defeated and exterminated or deported.

[3] A plantation economy developed, using slave labor, the chief crops being sugarcane, cotton, coffee and cocoa. In 1833, St Vincent became part of the Windward Islands colony. In 1960, together with the Grenadine Islands, it was granted a new constitution with substantial internal autonomy. It also participated in the West Indies Federation until its dissolution in 1962.

[4] St Vincent became a self-governing state in association with the UK in 1969. The post of head minister - similar to that of Prime Minister, but with more limited powers - was held then by Milton Cato, together with the pro-US St Vincent Labor Party (SVLP). Defense and foreign relations continued to be controlled by Britain, but independence was declared in October 1979.

[5] The elections in December 1979 reinforced the predominance of the SVLP, and the opposition PPP received only 2.4 percent of the vote.

[6] The new government faced an armed rebellion of Rastafarians led by Lennox 'Bumba' Charles on Union Island. This rebellion was quickly put down by troops from Barbados.

[7] In the early 1980s, the Government faced a serious socio-economic crisis, enabling the popular movements to gain ground. In May 1981, the national Committee in Defense of Democracy was formed, supported by several opposition parties, the labor unions and other organizations. Several days later, the Government attempted to impose repressive legislation designed to maintain 'public order', triggering mass protests.

[8] Cato's government supported the US invasion in Grenada and sent a police detachment to join the occupation forces (see Grenada). Cato called early elections, but the economic crisis and the SVLP's tax policies meant the New Democratic Party (NDP) won the election, while the left found its vote reduced by half, to 7.2 per cent.

[9] In the May 1989 election, James Mitchell (NDP) was re-elected, going on to sign an agreement with the Prime Ministers of Dominica, St Lucia, and Grenada to create a new state of the four islands in 1990 (see Dominica).

[10] Given the Grenadians' secessionist feelings, which had already erupted in violence in 1980, Mitchell created a Ministry of Grenadine Affairs and named Herbert Young, a Grenadian, as Minister of Foreign Affairs.

[11] The SVLP took 3 of the 15 seats in Parliament in the early elections held in February 1994, becoming the official opposition to the NDP Government. In August, Mitchell survived a motion of no confidence. The opposition blamed him for the failure to fight the crisis and the fall in banana exports. This product brought in 80 per cent of the income of St Vincent.

[12] Pressure from Washington led to a flash operation in December 1998 lasting 10 days in which an army battalion wiped out marihuana crops. Cannabis growers complained the destruction left them without a source of income. More than 25,000 banana growers (bananas are the country's main crop) protested in 1999 against US attempts to pressure the World Trade Organization to revoke what the US considered European privileges for banana producers in the Caribbean.

[13] The situation did not improve in 2000, and the unemployment rate reached 30 per cent. Arnhim Eustace was appointed new Prime Minister in October that year, until the following elections were held, anticipated by protest demonstrations against the Mitchell Government.

[14] The March 2001 elections led to the defeat of the New Democratic Party (NDP) after 17 years in power, being replaced by the Unity Labor Party (ULP), led by Ralph Gonsalves.

[15] In March 2002 the island declared as its main national hero Caribbean leader Joseph Chatoyer, 200 years after his death. Chatoyer led the nationalist movement against English colonization and fought until his death. ∎

PROFILE

ENVIRONMENT
Comprises the island of St Vincent (345 sq km) and the northern part of the Grenadines (43 sq km) including Bequia, Canouan, Mustique, Matreau, Quatre, Savan and Union. They are part of the Windward Islands of the Lesser Antilles. Of volcanic origin, the islands have fertile rolling hills. The climate, tropical with heavy rainfall and tempered by ocean currents, is fit for plantation crops. St Vincent is a leading arrowroot producer, a plant with starch-rich rhizomes, used in the manufacture of a type of paper used in electronics. Bananas are the main export. The population is concentrated on the island of St Vincent. There are severe pollution problems in the coastal waters.

SOCIETY
Peoples: Descendants of African slaves 82 per cent, mixed 14 per cent; there are also European, Asian, and indigenous minorities.
Religions: Anglican and other Protestant; Catholic.
Languages: English (official); also a local dialect.
Political Parties: The New Democratic Party (NDP); the Unity Labor Party, social-democratic (ULP); the People's Independent Movement.

THE STATE
Official name: St Vincent and The Grenadines.
Capital: Kingstown 28,000 people (1999).
Other cities: Georgetown 1,600 people; Byera 1,300 (2000). **Government:** Head of State, Queen Elizabeth II. Charles Antrobus, Governor General appointed by Britain, since June 1996. Ralph Gonsalves, Prime Minister, elected in March 2001. There are 21 members in the House of Assembly. **National Holiday:** October 27, Independence Day (1979).

DEMOGRAPHY
Population: 115,000 (2002) **Annual growth:** 0.7 % (1985-2000) **Urban population:** 54.8 % (2000) **Urban growth:** 3.3 % (2000)

HEALTH
Maternal mortality: 43 per 100,000 live births (1985/99) **Infant mortality:** 21 per 1,000 (2000) **Under-5 child mortality:** 25 per 1,000 (2000) **Daily calorie supply:** 2,540 per capita (1999)

Samoa

Population: 159,000 (2002)
Land area: 2,830 SQ KM
Capital: Apia
Currency: Tala
Language: Samoan and English

Samoa

The archipelago of Samoa has been inhabited since at least 1000 BC. The people developed a complex social structure. Four of these local groups still hold a privileged position: the Malietoa, the Tamasese, the Mataafa and the Tuimalealiifano.

[2] The Dutch were the first Europeans to visit the islands in 1722, but colonization did not begin until the end of the 19th century.

[3] In 1855, Germany finally occupied the islands. German merchants bought copra with Bolivian and Chilean currency valued at 10 times its real worth. In 1889 a new treaty recognized the US rights over the part of Samoa located east of meridian 171; 'rights' which the US still retains. The western half remained under German rule.

[4] In 1914, upon the outbreak of World War I, New Zealand occupied the German part of the island, which was later granted to Aotearoa (New Zealand) by the League of Nations as a trust territory.

[5] In 1920, an influenza epidemic killed 25 per cent of the population. At about the same time, the 'Mau' movement began to spread throughout the archipelago, preaching resistance to the foreign governments. Samoans carried out a nine-year-long civil disobedience campaign, which eventually became a vigorous pro-independence movement.

[6] In 1961 after intense protests and pressure from the UN, a plebiscite was held for Samoans to vote on independence. This was achieved the following year, with a Constitution based largely on the traditional social structure and the executive power in the hands of two rulers, Tupua Tamasase Meoble and Malietoa Tanumafili. Only the leading group (*matai*), around 8,500 in all, were eligible to vote.

[7] After being elected Prime Minister in 1970, Tupua Tamasese Lealofi launched a battle against the matai. He also backed the establishment of foreign corporations on the archipelago, despite strong opposition.

[8] The 1976 elections were won by the opposition. Tupuola Tais became Prime Minister. In 1979 he retained office by only one vote in parliament. The price of cocoa and copra fell, further aggravating the economic and financial situation, making it necessary for 2,000 Samoans to emigrate each year.

[9] In February 1982, Va'al Kolone, leader of the Party for the Protection of Human Rights, became leader. In September he was removed from government, amid accusations of corruption and abuse of power.

[10] In April 1988, Tofilau Eti Alesana came to power. His political party won an absolute majority in the legislative in the 1985 elections when it obtained 31 of the 47 seats.

[11] The 1991 constitutional reform extended the parliamentary term from three to five years, and increased the number of seats from 47 to 49. Fiame Naomi became Minister of Education that year, the first woman to be appointed to the cabinet.

[12] In 1998 the partial burning of forests by farmers went out of control and destroyed 25 per cent of the natural forests. Prime Minister Tofilau Eti had to resign in November that year due to complications from cancer. He was replaced by Tuilaepa Sailele Malielegaoi.

[13] In April 2000, Leafa Vitale and Toi Aukuso, respectively Minister of Women's Affairs and former Minister of Communications, were sentenced to death by hanging for murdering a Cabinet colleague. According to the charges, they had killed the Minister of Public Works, Levaula Kamu, during a political rally held the previous year.

[14] After a tight electoral race, Malielegaoi was re-elected in March 2001 for a second term. Her political party, the HRPP, obtained 28 of the 49 seats in Parliament.

[15] During 2001, the Organization for Economic Cooperation and Development (OECD) intensified its pressure on Samoa to identify its banks' customers and to bring in financial controls. Samoa is one of the countries that the OECD considers 'black boxes' of the global finance system, so called because they hide illegal transactions that are evading taxes in their home countries. ■

PROFILE

ENVIRONMENT
Includes the islands of Savai'i, 1,690 sq km, 40,000 people; Upolu, 1,100 sq km, 110,000 people, Manono and Apolina, in Polynesia, northeast of Fiji. The eastern portion of the Samoa archipelago is under US administration. The islands are of volcanic origin, mountainous, with fertile soil in the lowland areas. The climate is tropical, tempered by sea winds.

SOCIETY
Peoples: Samoans are mostly Polynesian (92.6 per cent). 'Euronesians' (a result of European and Polynesian integration) make up 10 per cent of the population. There are Europeans and Pacific islanders.
Religions: Congregational 47.2 per cent; Roman Catholic 22.3 per cent; Methodist 15.1 per cent; Mormon 8.6 per cent; other 6.8 per cent.
Languages: Samoan and English are the official languages.
Political Parties: The Human Rights Protection Party (HRPP); the Samoa National Development Party.

THE STATE
Official Name: Samoa i Sisifo. **Capital:** Apia 38,000 people (1999).
Other cities: Falelatai 1,800 people; Safotulafai 1,800 (2000).
Government: Malietoa Tanumafili II, Head of State for life since April 1963. Tuilaepa Sailele Malielegaoi, Prime Minister since November 1998, re-elected in 2001. Unicameral Legislature: Legislative Assembly, with 49 members elected for a five-year term; 47 members out of the Matais (traditional heads of families) and two members by the non-Samoan nationals. According to the Constitution, after the death of Tanumafili II, the President will be elected for a five-year term by the parliament.
National Holiday: June 10, Independence Day (1962).

American Samoa

Population: 72,000 (2002)
Land area: 200 SQ KM
Capital: Pago Pago
Currency: US dollar
Language: Samoan and English

American Samoa

Inhabited since 7th century BC by Melanesians (see box: 'Melanesians and Polynesians'), the island was reached by Europeans in the 18th century. The colonial powers Germany, Britain and United States disputed the possession 150 years later. The 1899 treaty settled the conflict, granting the United States the seven islands east of Meridian 171. Traditional social structures were maintained but agriculture was not stimulated so the population became totally dependent on the external colonial economy. This situation resulted in an increasing number of emigrants; over half of the Samoan population currently lives in Hawaii and other parts of the United States.

[2] On December 5 1984, the UN General Assembly considered Eastern Samoa's right to self-determination and independence. A unanimous vote reiterated that factors such as territory, geographic location, population and meager resources should not hinder independence. The US, in its role as administrative power, was urged to implement an educational program to assure Samoans' full awareness of their rights, to hasten the decolonization

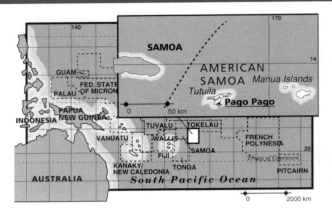

process. The islanders, however, seemed to be content with their existing status which allowed them to emigrate to the United States without restrictions. There were no organized pro-independence groups.

[3] In 1984, Governor Coleman (elected in the first elections for governor held in 1977) submitted proposals for a new Constitution in American Samoa for ratification by the US Congress. The proposals were withdrawn in May of the same year, because it was feared that they would be harmful to the interests of US citizens. In November, A P Lutali

was elected Governor and Faleomavaega Eni Hunkin became Vice-Governor.

[4] In July 1988, the delegate to the US House of Representatives, Fofo Sunia, announced that he would not stand for re-election because he was going to be subjected to official investigations after accusations of financial mismanagement. In October, he was sentenced to a 5 to 15 week term in prison for fraud. Hence, Eni Hunkin replaced Sunia. In November, Coleman was re-elected for his third term and Galeani Poumele replaced Hunkin as Vice-Governor.

[5] Despite reforms to the 1967 Constitution during the 1980s, proposed changes were not ratified by the United States Congress. According to the Constitution currently in effect, in addition to a governor, who is elected for a four-year term, there is also a legislature, or *Fono* with an 18-member Senate elected every four years by the *matai*, or clan heads. There is also a 20-member House of Representatives elected by direct popular vote for two-year terms. Women do not have the right to vote.

[6] After his re-election as governor in 1992, Lutali took measures to cut public spending, especially by reducing the number of government employees. The projected social security reform in the US and its dependencies led to a debate in the second half of 1996 about the consequences for the inhabitants of American Samoa.

[7] Figures from the archipelago expressed the concern for the reform's effects on American Samoan residents - regarded as US

'nationals' but with fewer rights than the 'citizens' of that country - and on immigrants, specifically those from other Polynesian territories.

[8] In November 1996, Tauese Pita Sunia was elected Governor with 51 per cent of the vote, to replace AP Lutali. Togiola Tulafano became Vice-Governor. Both took office in January 1997.

[9] Later that year, in November, the government in Pago Pago imposed a curfew between 9:00 pm and 6:00 am, after expressing concern over the apparent rise in crime rates. In February 1998, a senior official in the Education Ministry accused the Governor of diverting funds meant for school building improvements in order to install a sauna in his official residence. In September, the Opposition tried to challenge the Governor on the charges of 'abuse of power'. Republican Eni Faleomavaega was reelected senator to the US with 86 per cent of the vote during the month of November.

[10] The Government had to impose austerity measures in order to reduce the deficit, including a shortened work week, a rise in taxes and cost reductions.

[11] In November 2000, Governor Tauese P Sunia, from the Democrat Party, was elected with 50.7 per cent of the vote.■

PROFILE

ENVIRONMENT

The island occupies 197 sq km of the eastern part of the Samoan archipelago, located in Polynesia, slightly to the east of the International Date Line, northwest of the Fiji islands. The most important islands are Tutuila (where the capital is located), Tau, Olosega, Ofu, Annuu, Rose and Swains. Of volcanic origin, the islands are mountainous with fertile soil on the plains. The climate is rainy and tropical, tempered by sea winds. There is dense, woody vegetation and major streams of shallow waters. The main export product is fish, especially tuna. Bananas and crafts are also exported.

SOCIETY

Peoples: Samoans are mostly Polynesians (89 per cent); Tongans 4 per cent; other 5 per cent. **Religions:** Christian (Protestant 50 per cent, Catholic 20 per cent); others 30 per cent. **Languages:** Samoan, predominant, and English are the official languages. **Political parties:** Democratic Party; Republican Party

THE STATE

Official Name: Territory of American Samoa. **Capital:** Pago Pago (on Tutuila) 14,000 people (1999). **Other cities:** Tafuna 7,100 people; Nu'uuli 5,300; Fagatogo 3,800 (2000). **Government:** Head of State, President George W Bush. Tauese P Sunia, Governor since January 1997, re-elected in 2000. There is a bicameral Legislature: The House of Representatives with 21 members and the Senate integrated by 18 members. Samoans are considered US 'nationals', but without the right to vote in presidential elections while living on the islands. **National Holiday:** April 17, Territorial Flag Day (1900). **Armed Forces:** The defense is responsibility of the US.

San Marino

Population: 27,000 (2002)
Land area: 60 SQ KM
Capital: San Marino
Currency: Euro
Language: Italian

San Marino

According to archaeological evidence, the territory covering San Marino, located between the Italian provinces of Romana and Marca, was inhabited in prehistoric times. The city was founded in the year 301 AD, by a Dalmatian stonemason from the island of Arbe, called Marinus, who after converting to Christianity and escaping religious persecution by emperor Diocletian, took refuge with other Christians on Mount Titano, in the Apennines. Marinus built a community there that, in time, adopted the features of a small state. In memory of the stone cutter, the land was christened 'Land of San Marino', later to be called 'Community of San Marino', until it finally received its present-day name: Republic of San Marino.

3 The original government structure was made up of an assembly known as Arengo, consisting in the heads of each family. In 1243, the positions of Captains Regent (*Capitani Reggenti*) were created to be the joint heads of state. The lack of a central power after the fall of the Roman Empire (in the 5th century AD) favored, as of the 12th century, the self-rule of several Italian cities, and the development of trade, manufactures and crafts. The same happened in San Marino, with a difference being that it was the only city remaining independent until our days.

4 In the 15th century, the territory grew with the support of the Duke of Urbino and the participation of San Marino in an alliance against Sigismondo Pandolfo Malatesta, lord of Rimini. When the alliance won, Pope Pius II awarded San Marino the castles of Fiorentino, Montegiardino and Serravalle.

5 The Constitution of San Marino is from the year 1600, and the Sammarinese regard themselves as the oldest republic in the world.

6 In 1739 Cardinal Giulio Alberoni invaded the territory, as part of his campaign to recover Italian possessions, but civil disobedience acts and secret messages sent to the Pope seeking justice achieved from him the recognition of San Marino's autonomy and the re-establishment of its independence.

7 San Marino remained on the sidelines of Italian unification (1830-1870) and stayed independent; it even signed a Friendship Treaty with Italy in 1862.

8 The state did not take part in World War I (1914-1918) but the conflict affected the country's economy. At the end of the war, unemployment - already high - and inflation rose considerably.

9 In 1923, two years after Benito Mussolini came to power, the General Council was dissolved, giving way to the fascist Sovereign and Supreme Council. However, San Marino survived the expansion of Italian fascism and remained neutral during World War II (1939-1945). German troops bombed the republic in July 1944, but Nazi occupation ended after a massive demonstration, putting an end to the Supreme Council and enabling new elections. During the War, San Marino received more than 100,000 refugees.

10 After the War, the Communists took power. In 1945 the Communist Party and the San Marino Socialist Party (PSS) formed a coalition which held power for 12 years.

11 In 1957 a center alliance dominated by the San Marino Christian Democratic Party (PDCS) took office and led the nation until 1973.

12 An alliance between the PDCS and the PSS ruled during the following five years until in November 1977 the Socialists accused the Christian Democrats of not solving economic problems. They then formed a coalition with the Communists. Anticipated elections were held on May 28 1978, and since then the leftist coalition has ruled San Marino, applying advanced social protection measures.

13 San Marino reinforced its links with the West and joined the European Union (EU) and the European Council in 1988. In 1992 it became member state of the United Nations, and joined the IMF.

14 The Communist Party changed its name in 1990, calling itself Progressive Democratic Party, and remained in the coalition with the Christian Democrats. In 1992, the Christian Democrats formed a new coalition with the Socialists and this won the 1993 and 1998 elections.

15 One of the oldest sources of income in the tourist sector is the sale of its historic coins and stamps. San Marino issued its first commemorative stamps in 1894, which since then have become a feature of the country. San Marino's 10 postal offices sell the stamps and collectible credits, including currency in circulation. Today, agricultural activities are focused on cereals, grapes and fruit, as well as in livestock (cattle and pigs). Apart from the tourist industry, most of San Marino's income comes from the manufacture and export of ceramics, furniture, textile products, paintings and wines.

16 The growing number of young foreign women, most of them domestics, that married wealthier older men led the Government to recommend a minimum age of domestic employees at 50. Although many Italians seek jobs in San Marino, domestics generally come from Eastern European countries, such as Albania and Romania. Men in San Marino are particularly 'attractive', being the only ones that can pass on citizenship.

17 In 2000, San Marino had an enviable standard of living and medical system, considered one of the world's best. The Government sought to preserve its standard of living through an economic development program in support of traditional craftsmen and agriculture.

18 On April 1 2002, Antonio Lazzaro Volpinari and Giovanni Francesco Ugolini were elected the Captains-Regent. ∎

PROFILE

ENVIRONMENT

Located in Italy, San Marino is an independent enclave, south of the Rimini on the Adriatic coast. The hilly terrain is dominated by Appennine peak Mount Titano (738 m). The climate is Mediterranean. The scarce industrial activity (mostly in construction) is focused in the capital, San Marino, a population core which spreads across Titano's western slope. The main source of income is tourism, including crafts and stamps. Also significant are the remittances sent by the migrant population, settled mostly in Italy and in other neighboring countries.

SOCIETY

People: Sammarinese; Italians. **Language:** Italian (local) and a local dialect. **Religion:** Catholic 95 per cent. **Political parties:** Multiparty system. San Marino Christian Democrat Party (PDCS). San Marino Socialist Party (PSS). Progressive Democratic Party (PDP), formerly Communist, 11 seats. San Marino Popular Alliance of Democrats (APD). Socialists for Reform (SR), 2 seats. Communist Refoundation (RC). **Social organizations:** Unity Trade Union Central, Democratic General Confederation of Workers, General Confederation of Labor.

THE STATE

Official name: Serenisima Repubblica di San Marino. **Capital:** San Marino, 2,316 inhabitants (1996). **Administrative divisions:** 9 municipalities (castelli); Acquaviva, Borgo Maggiore, Chiesanuova, Domagnano, Faetano, Fiorentino, Monte Giardino, San Marino, Serravalle. **Other cities:** Serravalle/Dogano 4,726 inhabitants; Boego Maggiore 2,366 inhabitants (1996). **Government:** Presidential republic. The Executive Power lies within the Council of State, formed by 10 members, chaired by two Captains-Regent (Antonio Lazzaro Volpinari and Giovanni Francesco Ugolini since April 2002), elected from rival parties for mutual control. Unicameral Legislature: the Great General Council, with 60 members elected for a five-year term by proportional representation. **National holiday:** September 3, Foundation of the Republic (301 A.D.) **Armed Forces:** Volunteers. Military force is voluntary, but all citizens between 16 and 65 may be drafted if the State needs them for its defense. Police force.

São Tomé and Príncipe

São Tomé e Príncipe

Population: 143,000 (2002)
Land area: 960 SQ KM
Capital: São Tomé
Currency: Dobra
Language: Portuguese

These islands were probably uninhabited when first visited by European navigators in the 1470s. Thereafter, the Portuguese began to settle convicts and exiled Jews there and established sugar plantations, using slave labor from the African mainland. Strategically located 300 kilometers off the African coast, the islands' natural ports were used by the Portuguese as supply stops for ships in the 15th century. Dutch, French, Spanish, British and Portuguese slave traders bought enslaved African laborers to be sold in the American colonies. Some of those slaves remained on the islands, which later became the leading African producers of sugarcane.

[2] Rebellions broke out and after the failure of an insurrection headed by Yoan Gato, a slave named Amador led a revolt that succeeded in taking over two-thirds of the island of São Tomé, where he proclaimed himself ruler.

[3] Soon defeated, the rebels hid in *quilombos* (guerrilla shelters in the forest) after burning their crops. The Portuguese landlords who moved to Brazil took with them not only their

enslaved workers. The slaves carried the seed of insurrection with them, which quickly produced quilombos in Brazil, some of which - such as the Palmares quilombo - became true republics and held out for nearly a century.

[4] In São Tomé and Príncipe, agriculture virtually disappeared for three centuries. In the 17th century the island was briefly held by the Dutch. After a period of decline, the colony recovered its prosperity in the late 19th century with the cultivation of cocoa.

[5] Even after abolition was declared in 1869, slavery continued in a disguised manner ('free' workers signed contracts for nine years at fixed salaries), leading to revolts and an international boycott against the 'cocoa slavery' of the Portuguese colony in the early 20th century.

[6] This neo-slavery system continued until the mid-1900s. A Society for Immigration of São Tomé organized the modern slave trade, 'hiring' plantation workers in other Portuguese colonies: Angola, Cape Verde, Guinea and Mozambique. This flow 're-Africanized' the country

as the *filhos da terra* (sons of the earth), the result of several centuries of integration between the natives and the Portuguese, mixed with the African immigrants. During the colonial regimes of Salazar and Caetano, repression was particularly harsh. In February 1953, over 1,000 people were killed in Batepá in less than a week.

[7] This massacre revealed the need for the rebels to join forces, and in 1969 the Movement for the Liberation of São Tomé and Príncipe (MLSTP) was founded, with two main objectives: independence and land reform.

[8] Foreign companies owned 90 per cent of São Tomé land and despite the fertile soil, most food was imported due to the island's monoculture policy. Rural workers were one of the major pillars of the MLSTP, and held a 24-hour strike in August 1963, which paralyzed all the plantations.

[9] As the island's terrain did not favor guerrilla warfare, the MLSTP launched an intensive underground political campaign that resulted in its recognition by the OAU

(Organization of African Unity) and the Non-Aligned Nations. Together with the MPLA of Angola, the PAIGC of Guinea and Cape Verde, and FRELIMO of Mozambique, the MLSTP joined the Conference of National Organizations of the Portuguese Colonies. It was the only legitimate group in existence when, after the 1974 revolution, Portugal began to free its colonies.

[10] The MLSTP joined a transition government in 1974 and in the following year declared independence. Its accomplishments were impressive: banks and farms were nationalized, medicine was socialized, a national currency was created, a major administrative reform was launched to reorganize public administration, and numerous centers of popular culture, based on the culture-building educational methods of Brazilian Paulo Freire, were created as part of a literacy campaign.

[11] Opposing these reforms was a rightist faction led by Health Minister Carlos da Graça, who fled to Gabon to plot a mercenary invasion of the islands in early 1978.

MLSTP's first congress in August, aimed at strengthening the rank and file, eventually led to the formation of a People's Militia and the creation of mass organizations to 'defend the revolution'.

[12] In March 1986, two opposition groups based outside the country - the São Tomé e Príncipe Independent Democratic Union (UDISTP) and the more radical São Tomé e Príncipe National Resistance Front (FRNSTP), founded by Carlos da Graça - announced the formation of an alliance called the Democratic Opposition Coalition. Its aim was to put pressure on the Government to hold free elections. A month later, a fishing vessel with 76 members of the FRNSTP on board arrived in Walvis Bay, the South African enclave in Namibia. They asked the

Pretoria Government to supply military aid needed to destabilize the São Tomé Government. These events led to Carlos da Graça's resignation as president of the FRNSTP. In May, he announced his willingness to cooperate with the Government, on condition that Cuban and Angolan troops stationed in the country be withdrawn.

[13] In 1985, in the midst of the worst drought in the country's history, the Government sought to open up the economy: new legislation was designed to promote foreign investment and privatize the so-called 'people's stores'. Gradually, the State relinquished economic control, previously heavily dependent upon such key products as cocoa, coffee and bananas. The Government sought ways to attract

foreign capital to the agricultural, fishing and tourism sectors.

[14] Late in 1989, the MLSTP leadership discussed reform of the party statutes and of the national constitution. In March 1990, the People's National Assembly approved amendments to the Charter, later to be submitted to a referendum. These changes made possible a move to a multiparty system. Independent candidates were admitted in the legislative elections, and the tenure of the President was limited to no longer than two five-year terms.

[15] The first parliamentary elections after independence were held in January 1991. The opposition Democratic Convergence of Leonel d'Alva was voted into power. In March, the former prime minister Miguel Trovoada returned from exile and was unopposed in the presidential elections.

[16] The heads of state of São Tomé and Príncipe, Cape Verde, Guinea-Bissau, Mozambique and Angola - all former Portuguese colonies - met in February 1992. After being organized under single party systems, the five countries experienced rapid political change and economic liberalization processes.

[17] The social and economic situation of the country worsened in recent years as the result of an IMF and World Bank imposed austerity plan. Public sector salaries were frozen, a third of all civil servants were dismissed and the local currency was devalued by 80 per cent. While inflation fell, the price of basic foodstuffs quadrupled and unemployment reached 30 per cent.

[18] The island of Príncipe declared independence on April 29 1995 and established a five-member regional government.

[19] The São Tomé economy was sustained in 1997 by international assistance, largely from Europe, financing 60 per cent of the budget. The European Development Fund backed a program to create jobs and to set up and provide equipment for medical centers.

[20] The country's external debt in 1998 reached $270 million, more than five times its annual GDP, around $50 million.

[21] The November 1998 elections marked the MLSTP's return to the

government. Upon taking office in January 1999, Prime Minister Guilherme Posser da Costa stated that his center-left administration would have to implement an 'austerity package' while seeking to reactivate the economy through oil exploration and agricultural development.

[22] Overwhelmed by the national economic crisis, state employees launched a strike in December 2000 to demand payment of back-wages and a salary hike to compensate for the effects of inflation.

[23] In July 2001, businessman Fradique de Menezes, a wealthy cocoa exporter, won the presidential elections with 56.3 per cent of the vote, but in the legislative elections held in March 2002 the MLSTP narrowly won an overall majority in the National Assembly. ■

STATISTICS

DEMOGRAPHY
Population: 143,000 (2002)
Annual growth: 1.9 % (1985-2000)
Estimates for year 2015: 178,000 (2000)
Annual growth to year 2015: 1.7 % (2000)
Urban population: 46.7 % (2000)
Urban growth: 3.8 % (2000)

HEALTH
Infant mortality: 58 per 1,000 (2000)
Under-5 child mortality: 75 per 1,000 (2000)
Daily calorie supply: 2,269 per capita (1999)
47 doctors per 100,000 people (1996)

EDUCATION
School enrolment (net):
Primary total: 93 % (1994/2000)
Primary school teachers: one for every 36 pupils (1998)

COMMUNICATIONS
318 radios (1998), 228 TV sets (2000) and 31 main telephone lines (2000) per 1,000 people

ECONOMY
Annual growth: 0.7 % (2000)
Currency: 2,390.0 dobras = $ 1 (Dec-00)
Cereal imports: 9,306 metric tons (2000)
Exports: $ 15 million (2000)
Imports: $ 38 million (2000)
External debt: $ 316 million (2000); $ 2,294 per capita (2000)

PUBLIC EXPENDITURE
Military expenditure (as % GNI): 1.0 % (1999)
Defense expenditure as % of central government expenditure: 1.3 % (1999)

LAND USE
Deforestation: 0.0 % annual (1990/95)
Arable: 2.1 % of total (1993)

PROFILE

ENVIRONMENT
The country comprises the islands of São Tomé (857 sq km) and Príncipe (114 sq km), and the smaller islands of Rólas, Cabras, Bombom and Bone de Joquei in the Bay of Biafra of the Gulf of Guinea, facing the coast of Gabon. The islands are mountainous, of volcanic origin, with dense rainforests, a tropical climate and heavy rainfall. Cocoa, copra and coffee are the main export crops.

SOCIETY
Peoples: Most are Africans of Bantu origin traditionally classified in five groups formed as a result of different migratory waves: the *Filhos da terra* (sons of the earth), descendants of the first enslaved workers brought to the islands and intermingled with the Portuguese; the Angolares, thought to descend from Angolans who came to the islands in the 16th Century; the Fôrros, descendants of freed slaves when slavery was abolished; the Serviais, migrant workers from Mozambique, Angola and Cape Verde; and the native Tongans. Since independence, these categories have begun to disappear.
Religions: Roman Catholic, about 80.8 per cent; remainder mostly Protestant, predominantly Seventh-Day Adventist and an indigenous Evangelical Church.
Languages: Portuguese (official); Fôrro; Crioulo, a dialect with Portuguese and African elements, is widely spoken.
Political Parties: Movement for the Liberation of São Tomé and Príncipe-Social Democratic Party (MLSTP-PSD), in government; Democratic Convergence Party (PCD); Committee for the Liberation of São Tomé and Príncipe (CLSTP); Democratic Coalition, Christian Democratic Front.
Social Organizations: Women's, Youth and Pioneers Organizations linked to the MLSTP.

THE STATE
Official Name: República Democrática de São Tomé e Príncipe.
Administrative Divisions: 7 Districts.
Capital: São Tomé 66,000 people (1999).
Other cities: Trindade 11,388 people; Santana 6,190; Neves 5,919; Santo Amaro 5,878 (1991).
Government: Fradique de Menezes, President since September 2001. Gabriel Costa, Prime Minister since March 2002. Unicameral Legislature: National Assembly, with 55 members.
National Holiday: July 12, Independence Day (1975).

Saudi Arabia

Population:	21,701,000 (2002)
Land area:	2,149,690 SQ KM
Capital:	Riyadh (Ar-Riyad, royal capital)
Currency:	Saudi Arabian riyal
Language:	Arabic

Arabiyah as-Sa'udiyah

Arabia was drawn into the orbit of western Asiatic civilization toward the end of the 3rd millennium BC. Caravan trade between south Arabia and the Fertile Crescent began about the middle of the 2nd millennium BC. The domestication of the camel around the 12th century BC made desert travel easier and gave rise to a flourishing society in South Arabia, centered around the state of Saab (Sheila). In eastern Arabia the island of Dolman (Bahrain) had become a thriving entrepot between Mesopotamia, South Arabia, and India as early as the 24th century BC. The discovery by the Mediterranean peoples of the monsoon winds in the Indian Ocean made possible flourishing Roman and Byzantine seaborne trade between the northern Red Sea ports and South Arabia, extending to India and beyond. In the 5th and 6th centuries AD, successive invasions of the Christian Ethiopians and the counter-invasion of the Sasanian kings disrupted the states of South Arabia.

[2] In the 6th century Quraysh - the noble and holy house of the confederation of the Hejaz controlling the sacred enclave of Mecca - contrived a series of agreements with the northern and southern tribes. Under this aegis, caravans moved freely from the southern Yemen coast to Mecca and thence northward to Byzantium or eastward to Iraq. Furthermore, members of the Quraysh house of 'Abd Manaf concluded pacts with Byzantium, Persia, and rulers of Yemen and Ethiopia, promoting commerce outside Arabia. The 'Abd Manaf house could effect such agreements because of Quraysh's superior position with the tribes. Quraysh had some sanctity as lords of the Meccan temple (the Ka'bah) and were themselves known as the Protected Neighbors of Allah. The tribes on pilgrimage to Mecca were called the Guests of Allah.

[3] In its enclave Quraysh was secure from attack. It arbitrated in tribal disputes, attaining thereby at least a local pre-eminence and seemingly a loose hegemony over many Arabian tribes. The Ka'bah, through the additions of other cults, developed into a pantheon, the cult of other gods perhaps being linked with political agreements between Quraysh - worshippers of Allah - and the tribes.

[4] Muhammad, the prophet of Islam, was born in 570 of the Hashimite branch of the noble house of 'Abd Manaf; though orphaned at an early age and in consequence with little influence, he never lacked protection by his clan. Marriage to a wealthy widow improved his position as a merchant, but he began to make his mark in Mecca by preaching the oneness of Allah. Rejected by the Quraysh lords, Muhammad sought affiliation with other groups; he was unsuccessful until he managed to negotiate a pact with the tribal chiefs of Medina, whereby he obtained their protection and became theocratic head and arbiter of the Medina tribal confederation (*ummah*). Those Quraysh who joined him there were known as *muhajirun* (refugees or emigrants), while his Medina allies were called *ansar* (supporters). The Muslim era dates from the *hijrah* (hegira) - Muhammad's move to Medina in AD 622.

[5] Muhammad's supporters attacked a Quraysh caravan in AD 624, thus breaking the vital security system established by the Abd Manaf house, and hostilities broke out against his Mecca kin. In Medina two problems confronted him - the necessity to enforce his role as arbiter and to raise supplies for his moves against Quraysh. He overcame internal opposition, removing in the process three Jewish tribes, whose properties he distributed among his followers. Externally, his rising power was demonstrated following Quraysh's failure to overrun Medina, when he declared it his own sacred enclave. Muhammad foiled Quraysh offensives and marched back to Mecca. After taking Mecca in AD 630 he became lord of the two sacred enclaves; however, even though he broke the power of some Quraysh lords, his policy thenceforth was to conciliate his Quraysh kin.

[6] After Muhammad's entry into Mecca the groups linked with Quraysh came to negotiate with him and to accept Islam; this meant little more than giving up their local deities and worshipping Allah alone. They had to pay the tax, but this was not novel because the chiefs had already been taxed to protect the Meccan enclave. Many groups probably waited to join the winner. From then on Islam was destined for a world role.

[7] Under Muhammad's successors the expansionist urge of the different groups, temporarily united around the nucleus of the two sacred enclaves, coincided with the weakness of Byzantium and Sasanian Persia. Those summoned to the banners of Islam launched a career of conquest that promised to satisfy the mandate of their new faith as well as the desire for booty and lands. With families and flocks, they left the peninsula. Population movements of such magnitude affected all of Arabia; in Hadhramaut they possibly caused neglect of irrigation works, resulting in erosion of fertile lands. In Oman, too, when Arabs evicted the Persian ruling class, its complex irrigation system suffered. Many Omani Arabs about the mid-7th century left for Basra (in Iraq) and formed the influential Azd group there. Arabian Islam replaced Persian influence in the Bahrain district and Al-Hasa province in the northeast, and in Yemen.

[8] As the conquests far beyond Arabia poured loot into the Holy Cities (Mecca and Medina), they became wealthy centers of a sophisticated Arabian culture. Medina became a center for Qur'anic (Koranic) study, the evolution of Islamic law, and historical record. Under the caliphs - Muhammad's successors - Islam began to assume its characteristic shape. Paradoxically, outside the cities it made little difference to Arabian life for centuries. After the Prophet's death, the second caliph Omar led the Arab conquest. Within ten years the Arabs occupied Syria, Palestine, Egypt and Persia. With Muawiya the caliphate became hereditary in the family of the Ummaias and the Arabs became a privileged caste which ruled over the conquered nations.

[9] In the 8th century, the borders of the Arabian Empire reached from North Africa and Spain to the west, to Pakistan and Afghanistan in the east. Upon moving the capital to Damascus, Syria became the cultural, political and economic center of the Empire, and it was in Damascus that the foundations of a new culture were laid. Greco-Roman, Persian and Indian components blended into an original combination in which science played an important role. Contrary to Muhammad's expectations, the Arabian peninsula

was to remain on the sidelines within the enormous empire, except in religious matters. Mecca, although failing to match Baghdad or Damascus in socio-economic and cultural importance, continued to be the center of Islam and the destination for large pilgrimages from all over the world.

[10] This situation remained unchanged for centuries. The Empire split up; the capital moved to Baghdad and the power of the caliphs passed over to the viziers, while culturally Arabic civilization attained the highest standards in all fields of knowledge and artistic creation. Arabic became the language of scholars from Portugal to India. But little changed in the land that gave birth to all this civilization. Nomadic groups continued to shepherd their flocks,

the settled population kept up their commerce, and rivalries between the two were frequently settled through war. As in Muhammad's time, demographic growth was channeled towards conquest, with the emigration of whole communities, such as the Been Hills in the 11th century. Trading caravans carrying supplies to Mecca and stopping points along the way, became much more frequent, while the ports became more active as a result of trade with Africa. The peninsula was governed from Egypt, first by Saladin and later by the Mamelukes. The Turks ruled from the 16th century to the 20th century, without introducing any major changes in the socio-economic pattern of the Arab nation.

[11] Under Turkish rule the provinces of Hidjaz and Asir on the Red Sea

had a reasonable degree of autonomy due to the religious prestige of the shereefs of Mecca, descendants of Mohammed. The interior, with Riyadh as the main urban center, became the Emirate of Najd at the end of the 18th century, through the efforts of the Saud family supported by the Wahabite sect (known as the Islamic Puritans). In the 19th century, with Turkish assistance, the Rated clan forced Abd al-Rahman ibn Saud out of power; the ousted leader sought exile in Kuwait. In 1902, his son Abd al-Aziz, again with the support of the Wahabites, organized a religious-military sect, the Ikhwan, in which he enlisted nearly 50,000 Bedouins in order to reconquer Najd. Twelve years later the Saudis defeated the Rachidis and added the Al-Hasa region on the Gulf until then under direct control of the Turks, against whom the Saudi forces fought during World War I. At the end of the conflict, Britain - the predominant power in the area - faced a difficult situation. In exchange for Abd al-Aziz continued anti-Turk campaign, Britain had promised to guarantee the integrity of his state. But for the same reason it had also promised to make Hussein ibn Ali (the shereef of Mecca) king of a nation that would encompass Palestine, Jordan, Iraq and the Arabian peninsula.

[12] The Emir of Najd waited for some time. It seemed clear to him that Britain would not keep its word to Hussein: such a powerful kingdom, ruled by the Prophet's family with the capital in the holy city, would alter the regional balance of power. But in 1924 Hussein proclaimed himself caliph (see Jordan). Abd al-Aziz invaded his territory immediately, despite English opposition and in January 1926 was declared King of Hidjaz and Sultan of Nadj in the great mosque of Mecca. Six years later the 'Kingdom of Hidjaz, of Nedj and its dependencies' was formally unified under the name of Saudi Arabia.

[13] In 1930, the monarch gave US companies permission to drill for oil. When he died in 1953, his son Saud squandered all the revenues paid into the Kingdom's treasury by the Arab-American Oil Company (Aramco) on palaces, harems, fancy cars and casinos on the French Riviera. In 1964 the country was on the verge of bankruptcy when Saud was ousted by his brother Faisal, an able diplomat who had also proved a valiant soldier in the wars. Monogamous, deeply religious and austere to the point of asceticism, Faisal gave new life to the country's economy and began to invest petrodollars in ambitious development programs,

though maintaining the traditional feudal structure headed by the autocratic ruler.

[14] Faisal's religious views led him to bluntly reject the Soviet Union and any other system linked with atheism, including Nasser's nationalism in Egypt, as well as Iraqi or Syrian Ba'athism. His strategic alliance with the US was seen as 'natural', but was disturbed by US support of Israel after the war of 1967. Faisal used to say that his only dream was to be able to pray one day in Omar's mosque, in a freed Jerusalem and rivalries with neighboring Iran, which under the Shah Pahlevi also played watchdog for Washington's interests in the Gulf.

[15] During the 1973 Arab-Israeli war, Faisal supported an oil embargo on the countries backing Israel, including the US. The sudden oil shortage allowed the Organization of the Petroleum Exporting Countries (OPEC) to increase oil prices in a short space of time, heralding a new era in international relations. On March 25 1975, Faisal was murdered by an apparently insane nephew. His brother Khaled, almost paralyzed by a rheumatic illness, was named as his successor. However, due to his paralysis, the governing duties in an era of superabundance fell to his brother, Crown Prince Fahd ibn Abd al-Aziz.

[16] The oil revenue, which amounted to $500 million a year when Faisal was crowned in 1964, had gone up to almost $30 billion when he died. That same year the Bank of America closed its balance with assets of $57.5 billion, and West Germany's exports amounted to $90 billion. These figures revealed that, when compared with other major economic powers, Saudi economic power was overrated. But these were staggering figures for the Third World: three times the income of Egypt, whose population was eight times bigger.

[17] New cities, universities, hospitals, freeways and mosques sprouted up everywhere. Yet there was surplus money available. Instead of planning oil production to meet the country's needs, which would have avoided the fall in prices and the weakening of OPEC during the 1980s, fortunes accumulated in western banks. Thus, Saudi Arabia tied its future more closely with the industrialized capitalist world. In addition it created a surplus of money in circulation, which the banks lent to Third World countries in some irresponsible ventures. This gave rise to the 1984-85 foreign debt crisis, with a rise in interest rates.

[18] The Muslim fundamentalist groups denounced the Saudi dynasty for allegedly betraying Islam, leading

PROFILE

ENVIRONMENT

The land occupies up to 80 per cent of the Arabian peninsula. There are two major desert regions: the An Nefud in the north, and the Rub al-Khali in the south. Between the two lie the Nejd massif, of volcanic origin, and the plain of El Hasa, the country's only fertile region, where wheat and dates are cultivated. The country's cultivated land amounts to less than 0.3 per cent; 90 per cent of the agricultural products consumed, are imported. Oil extraction, concentrated along the Persian Gulf shores, is the source of its enormous wealth. The intense activity which revolves around the oil industry has raised levels of contamination in the water and along the coastline. (This situation was exacerbated during the Gulf War in the 1990s: 640 kilometers of beaches and swampland were affected by oil spillages totaling 4.5 million barrels of oil; thousands of fish and migratory birds were killed; the clean-up, carried out under the direction of the UN, cost the kingdom $450 million). The agricultural sector consumes huge quantities of water, through the vast system of artificial irrigation. Environmentalists have issued warnings on the shortage of water, made more acute by the slow rate at which water levels are replenished. Reports on this issue have estimated that, should the current rate of water use continue, this resource will be completely depleted in one or two decades.

SOCIETY

Peoples: Saudis are mainly of Arab origin. In recent years there has been large scale immigration of Iranians, Pakistanis and Palestinians who have settled in the new eastern industrial areas, bringing the number of foreigners to an estimated five million (1992).
Religions: Islam, Sunni orthodox Wahhabism (official) 95 per cent; Shi'a 3 per cent; Christians 1 per cent.
Languages: Arabic, with dialect variations; languages of other communities, particularly of foreign workers, include Farsi and Urdu.
Political Parties: Not permitted, but there exist opposition groups, most of them in the diaspora.
Social Organizations: Not permitted.

THE STATE

Official Name: al-Mamlakah al-'Arabiyah as-Saudiyah.
Administrative Divisions: 5 regions and 14 districts.
Capital: Riyadh (Ar-Riyad) (royal capital) 3,183,000 people (1999).
Other cities: Jeddah (administrative center) 2,604,500 people; Mecca (Makkah - religious center) 1,229,200 (2000).
Government: Absolute monarchy. King Fahd ibn Abd al-Aziz al-Saud, Head of State and of the Government since June 13 1982. Crown Prince and Regent Abdullah ibn Abd al-Aziz al Saud since 1996. Advisory Council, with advisory role to the King. The National Assembly (Majlis al-Umma) has two chambers: the Assembly of Deputies (Majlis al-Nuwaab) with 80 members elected by popular suffrage and the Assembly of Senators (Majlis al-Aayan) with 40 members appointed by the king.
National Holiday: September 23, National Unification (1932).
Armed Forces: 105,000 (plus 57,000 active National Guard).
Other: 10,500: Coast Guard, 4,500; Special Security Force, 500.

to several violent confrontations with government forces. The theological basis which legitimized the ruling autocracy was undermined by the progressive rise to power of new members of the ruling family, trained in European and US universities and military academies, rather than in the traditional desert-tent Quranic schools.

[19] After the overthrow of the Shah of Iran, the Saudi Government drew closer to the US. With King Khaled's death, on June 13 1982, his brother Fahd - the architect of Saudi Arabia's foreign policy - became king.

[20] The year before, the new monarch had created a peace plan for the Middle East which had been approved by several Arab countries, the PLO and the US, though the plan collapsed in August, 1981 due to Israeli opposition. This plan proposed the creation of a Palestinian State with Jerusalem as its capital, the withdrawal of Israel from the occupied Arab territories, and the dismantling of the Jewish colonies set up in 1967, as well as the recognition of the right of every state in the region to live peaceably. On September 26 1982, during the Haj or pilgrimage to Mecca, the King condemned Israeli intervention in Lebanon, which he called criminal aggression. He also criticized Soviet intervention in Afghanistan, accused Iran's Ayatollah Khomeini of attempting to destabilize the regime through sabotage, and generally condemned the 'influence of great powers' in the Muslim world.

[21] Naval bases in Jubail and Jeddah were built under the supervision of the US Army. Also, investments and bank deposits by the Saudi State and nobility were closely linked with the performance of the US economy: two-thirds of the huge amount of Saudi petrodollars invested abroad went into corporation stocks, treasury bonds and bank deposits in the US.

[22] The 1985-89 five-year plan promised a 'wide income redistribution'. Yet that intention coincided with the first signs of economic trouble in the Kingdom. In 1984, due to another drop in the price of crude, the official budget closed with a deficit for the first time. The Minister of Industry, Ghazi Al Gosaibi, was forced to resign after writing a poem which made reference to corruption.

[23] During the Iran-Iraq war in the 1980s, Saudi Arabia backed Iraq financially, afraid that the Iranian Islamic revolution might spread over the Gulf. Fahd changed his title of King to Guardian of the Holy Sites, but every year the pious pilgrims to Mecca protested more loudly, angry about the alliance between Riyadh and Washington and by what they

considered a commercialization and Westernization of the sacred places, surrounded today by shopping centers, highways and other symbols of transnational culture. On August 1 1987, a march by Iranian women and disabled war veterans in Mecca was fired upon by Saudi police. Hundreds of pilgrims were killed. In retaliation, the embassies of Saudi Arabia and Kuwait in Tehran were attacked and burned, and relations between both countries grew very tense.

[24] After the Iraqi invasion of Kuwait in August 1990 Saudi Arabia was the scene of a huge military deployment by a multinational coalition led by the US. Apart from the loss of human lives, the war caused a huge ecological disaster as oilfields burned.

[25] In March 1992, King Fahd issued several decrees called 'The Basic System of Government', aimed at decentralizing political power. It established an Advisory Council, with the right to review all matters of national policy. However, the ultimate decision-making power remained with the King. The royal decrees also created the *mutawein*, religious police, whose mandate was to ensure the observance of Islamic customs. The home was defined as a sacred place, and therefore the state (the religious police) may enter without legal authorization. This situation has led to the detention of several alleged violators of the law.

[26] Growing social inequalities aggravated tensions among the Saudis, even though they are privileged compared with the millions of foreign workers living in the country. An attack against the offices of US advisors in Riyadh in November 1992 killed at least 6 people and was seen as proof of those tensions.

[27] The hostility of one segment of the population toward the US grew stronger, reaching a critical point with the attack on the US El Khobar base in June 1996 that left 19 soldiers dead and hundreds injured.

[28] Due to his failing health, affected by diabetes, arthritis and obesity, in 1996 Fahd transferred power to his brother Abdullah bin Abd al-Aziz al Saud - who had been confirmed as heir to the throne four years earlier.

[29] In 1997 Saudi Arabia warned the US that its 'hardline' policy against Iraq, in contrast to its 'soft' policy with Israel, could inflame the region's Arab population.

[30] Riyadh signed an economic cooperation agreement with Iran in January 2000, thus ending years of poor diplomatic relations.

[31] In September 2001, the terrorist attacks in New York and Washington, perpetrated by several Saudi citizens (among others) cast the Saudi-US alliance into doubt. Interior Minister Prince Nayef disapproved of the US bombings of Afghanistan. Some of the leading US media suggested that Saudi Arabia had been hesitant to collaborate with the FBI in following up clues about those responsible for the September 11 attacks.

[32] In December, Saudi women won the right to their own identity documents (ID). Previously, they had been included in a family ID as dependents of the husband or father. In Saudi Arabia, women must have family permission to undergo surgical procedures. However, they are allowed to control their own money and to inherit wealth, as stated in Islamic law. It was businesswomen, some 1,500 throughout the country, who pressed for the right to their own IDs. This achievement is part of the struggle between the reform-minded Princes - where Abdullah plays a key role with his sights on the succession - and the religious hierarchy.

[33] In late March 2002, the Pentagon denied that the US had begun to transfer its air force base in Saudi Arabia to Qatar. However, The Guardian newspaper in the UK reported that most of the troops were being moved due to Riyadh's refusal to allow the base to be used in a military attack against Iraq.

[34] In April, petroleum prices fell, after Saudi Oil Minister Ali al-Naimi - in the wake of Iraq's reduction in output - attempted to calm the world markets by assuring that his country would not cut production or limit supplies. Iraq suspended oil exports to protest Israel's military siege in Palestinian territory. Baghdad had asked the other OPEC members to follow suit, or at least not to increase production. ■

LITERACY
2000

77%

FOOD DEPENDENCY
2000

2000

18%

STATISTICS

DEMOGRAPHY
Population: 21,701,000 (2002)
Annual growth: 3.4 % (1985-2000)
Estimates for year 2015: 31,748,000 (2000)
Annual growth to year 2015: 3.0 % (2000)
Urban population: 85.7 % (2000)
Urban growth: 3.3 % (2000)
Children per woman: 5.9 (2000)

HEALTH
Life expectancy at birth: 72 years (2000-2005)
male: 71 years (2000-2005)
female: 74 years (2000-2005)
Infant mortality: 24 per 1,000 (2000)
Under-5 child mortality: 29 per 1,000 (2000)
Daily calorie supply: 2,953 per capita (1999)
166 doctors per 100,000 people (1997)
Safe water: 95 % (2000)

EDUCATION
Literacy: 77 % (2000)
male: 84 % (2000)
female: 67 % (2000)
School enrolment (net):
Primary total: 76 % (1994/2000)
male: 81 % (1995/99)
female: 73 % (1995/99)
Secondary (gross):
male: 65 % (1995/97)
female: 57 % (1995/97)
Tertiary (gross): 19 % (1998)
Primary school teachers: one for every 12 pupils (1998)

COMMUNICATIONS
326 newspapers (1998), 326 radios (1997), 264 TV sets (2000) and 137 main telephone lines (2000) per 1,000 people

ECONOMY
Per capita, GDP: $ 11,367 (2000)
Annual growth: 1.9 % (2000)
Annual inflation: -0.9 % (2000)
Consumer price index: 98.5 (2000)
Currency: 3.8 saudi arabian riyals = $ 1 (03/2002)
Cereal imports: 6,660,416 metric tons (2000)
Food import dependency: 18 % (2000)
Fertilizer use: 985 kg per ha (1999)
Exports: $ 85,891 million (2000)
Imports: $ 44,579 million (2000)
Development aid received: $ 29 million (1999); $ 1.4 per capita (1999)

ENERGY
Consumption: 5,244.1 Kgs of oil equivalent per capita yearly (1998); -428.5 % imported (1999)

HDI (ranking/value): 68 / 0.754 (1999)

Senegal

Population: 9,908,000 (2002)
Land area: 192,530 SQ KM
Capital: Dakar
Currency: CFA franc
Language: French

Sénégal

The banks of the Senegal River have been inhabited for many centuries by peoples who had been Islamicized through contact with neighboring Arab countries. This group of countries make up the region known as the Sahel. The Wolof (who constitute more than a third of the population), Fulani, Pulaar and other peoples, all lived within the area of modern Senegal.

[2] When the French occupied the area during the 17th century, they incorporated it into the triangular world trade pattern of the time: European manufactured goods were exchanged for slaves, sold in the Antilles, where colonial European powers produced rum and sugar, which were sold back in Europe.

[3] After slavery was abolished by the French revolution of 1848, the Senegalese became 'second class citizens' of the French Empire, with one political representative in Paris. At this time Senegal exported thousands of tons of peanuts per year and supplied the French army with soldiers.

[4] During the second half of the 19th century, there were frequent rebellions among the Muslim leaders, and it was only in 1892 that the French managed to fully 'pacify' the country.

[5] The Pan-African movement inspired Senegalese Léopold Sédar Senghor and Martinique's Aimé Césaire, and together in Paris, they created the concept of négritude, an idea first presented to public opinion in 1933. Négritude stood against the imposition of French cultural patterns, which were enforced throughout the colonies. The concept was designed to serve as 'an effective liberation tool'. In Senghor's view, it had to escape 'peculiarism' and find a place within contemporary movements of solidarity, that is, to achieve a definite political profile.

[6] Senghor had been a member of the French *maquis* (resistance) during World War II, he had fought against fascism and was elected representative to the French National Assembly in 1945. Three years later, he brought about the foundation of the Senegalese Progressive Union, which demanded greater autonomy for the colonies, although not independence.

[7] Finally, on April 4 1960, Senegal declared independence, and on September 5 adopted a republican system. Senghor was elected President and through successive re-elections he stayed in power for two decades. He was finally replaced with Abdou Diouf on January 1 1981.

[8] The ideology of African socialism promoted by Senghor was based on the premise that traditional African agrarian society had always been essentially collectivist. Senghor believed that socialism already existed on the continent and therefore did not need to be imposed. This 'collectivism' actually mainly served to provide cheap labor for the export-oriented production of peanuts and cotton. 82 per cent of the nation's industry was French-controlled.

[9] In an effort to keep up with political changes in France, Senghor requested membership of the Socialist International. To this end he pushed through a constitutional reform restricting political representation to three political parties: a 'liberal democratic' party (the Senegalese Democratic Party), a Marxist-Leninist party (the African Party for Independence) and a 'social democratic' party (his own, renamed the Senegalese Socialist Party).

[10] In the 1980s Diouf brought flexibility to the rigid political system he inherited from his predecessor. This prevented the major political adversary Abdoulaye Wade's Democratic Party of Senegal (PDS),

from uniting all the Government opposition forces.

[11] In 1982, in the southern province of Casamance, on the border with Guinea-Bissau, there was a resurgence of separatist activity, leading to the creation of the Casamance Movement of Democratic Forces (MFDC) led by an abbot, Austin Diamacoune Senghor. The people of Casamance are primarily from the Diole ethnic group, animists who have prided themselves on their independence and resistance to the Islamic hierarchical societies of the north. In December 1983, after successive confrontations with the Senegalese police forces, many leaders of the MFDC were detained, among them Abbot Diamacoune.

[12] The country faced a series of serious droughts over the last 30 years. These were seen as part of the desertification process caused by climatic conditions and the French-imposed substitution of export crops for traditional food crops.

[13] In the early 1980s the Government gave in to pressure from the US, France, the World Bank and the IMF to accept a structural adjustment plan. The elimination of agricultural subsidies triggered a rise in production costs and the prices of basic consumer goods.

[14] In 1988 the Socialist Party (PS) won another victory in the national elections, obtaining 72.3 per cent of the vote, while the Senegalese Democratic Party (PDS) won only 25.8 per cent. After various groups questioned the legitimacy of the

election, government troops were mobilized to keep the peace. In the aftermath, hundreds of people were arrested, and the PDS candidate, Abdoulaye Wade, was forced to go into exile, only returning to Senegal in March 1989.

[15] A month later a border conflict broke out with Mauritania triggered by violent altercations between peasants and farmers, causing hundreds of casualties and forcing some 70,000 refugees to enter Senegal.

[16] Gambia's growing concern led to the dissolution in 1989 of the Senegambia Federation that had been agreed in 1981. In July 1991, Diouf was elected President of the ECOWAS (Economic Community of the Western African States), which included 16 countries of the region.

[17] In 1991, a series of political and institutional changes was launched. The office of Prime Minister was restored and members of opposition parties were named to two cabinet posts. In September 1991, after three months of negotiations with opposition parties, a consensus was reached to reform the electoral laws. The conflict with the Casamance separatist movement (MFDC) resumed in 1992, after a truce.

[18] On February 21 1993, amid denunciations of widespread fraud, President Diouf won the presidential elections on the first ballot, with 58.4 per cent of the vote. In the May legislative elections, his PSS party maintained control of the National Assembly, with 84 of the 120 seats. The main opposition party - the PDS - won 27 seats.

[19] The economic and financial situation of Senegal became more difficult during 1993, amongst other things because the international prices of the Senegalese export products fell considerably. This made the trade deficit worse, which was compensated by new loans which took the foreign debt to $3.5 billion, more than 60 per cent of the GDP.

[20] The 100 per cent devaluation of the CFA franc decided by France and the IMF accentuated the social tensions in early 1994. The opposition Coordination of Democratic Forces organized an anti-government demonstration on February 16, which ended in confrontations with the police. Six

MATERNAL MORTALITY

1985/99

Per 100,000
live births

560

LITERACY

2000

37%

[21] police officers died and dozens of people were injured.

[21] Some 180 people were arrested with supposed responsibility for the disturbances, including the opposition leaders, Abdoulaye Wade and Landing Savané, who were declared innocent and freed in July. The Government's repressive action was criticized by human rights organizations, the European Parliament and US Congress.

[22] Wade began negotiations with the Government, which led to him entering Diouf's cabinet in March 1995. The President received the clear support of the international funding organizations, when he announced legislative modifications to encourage foreign investment and accelerate privatization.

[23] Following relative calm, in 1997 fresh guerrilla action led to the mobilization of 2,500 soldiers against the MFDC bases, along the frontier with Guinea-Bissau.

[24] In March, Senegal extended its protocol with the European Union for four more years, under which it would receive nearly $11 million per year in compensation, an increase of 33 per cent.

[25] In early 1998, Amnesty International denounced the reigning 'terror' in Casamance, due to conflict which was decimating a population mainly made up of farmers and ruining an area considered prosperous before the outbreak of war.

[26] After 40 years of one-party rule, Wade won the March 2000 elections based on campaign promises denouncing the corruption and inefficiency of the Socialist government. He called for a change appealing to Senegalese youth, the most affected by unemployment.

The operation of new independent radio stations that monitored the voting made this one of the most transparent and peaceful elections the region had ever known.

[27] Upon his appointment in April, Wade appointed a former opposition veteran, Mustafa Niasse, as his Prime Minister. Although the new president promised that the main priority of his government would be to stop the separatist conflict by peaceful means, violence increased in Casamance that same month with successive attacks by some MFDC factions opposed to the conciliatory stance of some of their leaders.

[28] A referendum passed a new Constitution in 2001, limiting the president's period in office from seven to five years, reducing the presidency to a maximum of two consecutive periods and stating that any member of parliament who left their party would lose their seat. The President will also be able to dissolve the National Assembly (lower chamber) without the support of a majority of its members. A few days later, Wade announced he would dissolve the Assembly in early February, preparing for general elections in April.

[29] In these, 'Sopi' - or 'Change' - coalition, formed by parties loyal to Wade and led by the PDS, won by a landslide. In May, the new Senegalese Prime Minister - the first woman to hold that office in the country - Mame Madior Boye, announced the composition of her new government. Ten of the posts went to PDS members.

[30] In September 2001, Wade announced he would hand over Hissene Habré, former president of Chad facing war crime charges, if a third country would be willing to give him a fair trial. Human rights groups hold Habré responsible for some 40,000 executions and the torture of 200,000 people during his Government between 1982-1990.

[31] In November that year, Jean-Marie Francois Biagui resigned as Secretary-General of the MFDC, claiming lack of loyalty from its members. Biagui had been appointed in August, during a congress in which his movement tried to overcome its internal differences in order to resume the peace talks. However, those differences impeded the creation of a joint front and Biagui was never accepted by some factions, which remained loyal to Diamacoune.

[32] In January 2002 the CFA franc - the currency of the former French West African states - became pegged to the euro. ■

PROFILE

ENVIRONMENT

Located on the west coast of Africa, embracing Gambia, its northern border formed by the Senegal River, the country's population is concentrated in the less arid western part, close to Dakar. The Senegal Valley is still under-populated as a result of slave trade which was very intense in this region. There is acute deforestation and desertification. A project which is currently underway for building a hydroelectric dam in the Senegal River valley in the north poses a threat to the local environment.

SOCIETY

Peoples: Wolof 42 per cent; Peul (Fulani) Tukulor 9.3 per cent; Serer 14.9 per cent; Diola 5.3 per cent; Malinke (Mandingo) 3.6 per cent. Approximately 3 per cent are immigrants from non-African countries, mainly France, Lebanon and Syria.
Religions: 94 per cent Muslim, 5 per cent Christian, traditional African religions and others one per cent.
Languages: French (official). The most widely spoken indigenous languages are Wolof, Peul and Ful.
Political Parties: Coalition 'Sopi' or 'Change', headed by the Senegalese Democratic Party (PDS, liberal), of President Abdoulaye Wade; Alliance of Progress Forces (AFP); Socialist Party of Senegal (PSS), founded by Léopold Senghor; several other minority parties.
Social Organizations: National Federation of Senegalese Workers (CNTS); Union of Free Senegalese Workers (UTLS).

THE STATE

Official Name: République du Sénégal.
Administrative Divisions: 10 Districts.
Capital: Dakar 1,999,000 people (1999).
Other cities: Thies 255,200 people; Kaolack 221,400; Ziguinchor 200,700; Saint-Louis 144,100 (2000).
Government: Parliamentary Republic. Abdoulaye Wade, President and Chief of State since April 2000. Mame Madior Boye, Prime Minister and Head of Government since March 2001. Parliament: 120-member National Assembly and 60-member Senate.
National Holiday: April 4, Independence Day (1960).
Armed Forces: 13,400, and 1,200 French troops (1996).

STATISTICS

DEMOGRAPHY
Population: 9,908,000 (2002)
Annual growth: 2.6 % (1985-2000)
Estimates for year 2015: 13,516,000 (2000)
Annual growth to year 2015: 2.4 % (2000)
Urban population: 47.4 % (2000)
Urban growth: 4.1 % (2000)
Children per woman: 5.4 (2000)

HEALTH
Life expectancy at birth: 54 years (2000-2005)
male: 53 years (2000-2005)
female: 56 years (2000-2005)
Maternal mortality: 560 per 100,000 live births (1985/99)
Infant mortality: 80 per 1,000 (2000)
Under-5 child mortality: 139 per 1,000 (2000)
Daily calorie supply: 2,307 per capita (1999)
8 doctors per 100,000 people (1995)
Safe water: 78 % (2000)

EDUCATION
Literacy: 37 % (2000)
male: 47 % (2000)
female: 28 % (2000)
School enrolment (net):
Primary total: 49 % (1994/2000)
male: 65 % (1995/99)
female: 55 % (1995/99)
Secondary (gross):
male: 20 % (1995/97)
female: 12 % (1995/97)
Tertiary (gross): 4 % (1998)
Primary school teachers: one for every 49 pupils (1998)

COMMUNICATIONS
5 newspapers (1996), 141 radios (1997), 40 TV sets (2000) and 22 main telephone lines (2000) per 1,000 people

ECONOMY
Per capita, GDP: $ 1,510 (2000)
Annual growth: 2.9 % (2000)
Annual inflation: 0.7 % (2000)
Consumer price index: 107.2 (2000)
Currency: 758.3 CFA francs = $ 1 (03/2002)
Cereal imports: 793,589 metric tons (2000)
Food import dependency: 24 % (2000)
Fertilizer use: 126 kg per ha (1999)
Exports: $ 1,335 million (2000)
Imports: $ 1,729 million (2000)
External debt: $ 3,372 million (2000); $ 358 per capita (2000)
Debt service: 16.1 % of exports (1999)
Development aid received: $ 534 million (1999); $ 57.5 per capita (1999); 11.20 % of GNP (1999)

ENERGY
Consumption: 312.2 Kgs of oil equivalent per capita yearly (1998); 43.1 % imported (1999)

HDI (ranking/value): 145 / 0.423 (1999)

Cutting controversy: female genital mutilation

Reaching puberty is a challenging time. But for many young people, it is not simply their bodies changing as the hormones surge which marks the change to adulthood. There may also be circumcision. For girls, Female Genital Mutilation (FGM) is part of an initiation rite in which a girl or adolescent enters maturity. For the cultures that practice it, it means the passage from childhood to adulthood. For its detractors, usually from the West, it is an abuse of human rights.

There are many cultures of Africa, the Middle East and Asia that for centuries have performed clitoridectomy as it is known, which consists of removal of a woman's clitoris and often the inner labia and a major portion of the outer labia as well. Some of the countries where this procedure is done are Guinea, Senegal, Ethiopia, Egypt, Burkina Faso, Mali, Gambia, Eritrea, Sudan, Somalia, Nigeria, India, as well as some cultures in the Middle East.

It is the community that decides when a young woman can procreate. The initiation rite is a deeply rooted ceremony that serves to reinforce the social and political fabric of the community. Initially, FGM was practiced to protect virginity, and to prevent masturbation and pleasure during sex. It has also been reported that in some of these cultures girls grow up hearing that if they do not undergo circumcision all sorts of punishments will befall them.

In recent decades, various human rights groups, including some feminist organizations, put the issue on the Western agenda and began denouncing FGM while educating people about it and attempting to eradicate female circumcision. The reasons for fighting the practice are several. Firstly of course it is painful, requiring the cutting of flesh, and this produces excessive bleeding. Often infections such as tetanus arise from an unclean knife or the dirty water used to clean the wound. There can also be trauma and physical malformations leading to a life of health and reproductive problems. And the critics tend to target female 'surgeons', who are trusted members of society but generally not trained in medicine and hygiene.

Circumcision is also condemned because it can lead to the death of the initiates - a fairly common occurrence, usually as a result of infection. Other critics, such as some humanitarian organizations, maintain that the aim of female circumcision is to prevent women from feeling sexual pleasure. They argue that denying women enjoyment of sex is part of the continued subjugation of women to men and their power or supremacy in the political, social and cultural life of the community.

However Dr Nahid Toubia, from Sudan, an advisor to various UN agencies such as UNESCO which are studying the issue, feels that these societies circumcise women as part of a positive cultural rite. The intention is not to mutilate for the sake of mutilation, even though the practice causes injury. Toubia affirms that in 'the West they want to change things, but they will not be able to. Only African women can change their cultures'. And she points out that the only way to help them is through obtaining greater power within the community. Though testimonies about female genital mutilation have become increasingly common in recent years, no systematic study of the issue exists. There has been a veil of silence because the people affected must overcome several obstacles, including cultural issues, to come forward and tell their stories.

In May 2000 in Guinea, after years of effort and disseminating information, a group of women opposed to female circumcision scored a victory by convincing the 'surgeons' who perform the procedure to use appropriate medical instruments and disinfectants. But groups in Tanzania, meanwhile, reported that the practice has become more frequent since the government made it illegal and began prosecuting those who performed the circumcisions. Some Masai reached an agreement with their opponents so that they continue performing the ceremony but not the surgery.

New revelations about the female circumcision situation continue to shock. Certain women's groups in Guinea for example were charged with using funds from institutions which opposed the practice to continue circumcisions in secret, in a sort of private club. This shows how some were able to take advantage of the system that condemned and persecuted them and reveals the obstacles for human rights groups and their activists, who often are in conflict with the community and national authorities.

One important fact is that, in the series of national and international forums on the issue, those who have most vigorously defended the practice have been circumcised women. Some have stated, for example, that 'in our societies and in our lives there are tremendous problems and this, female circumcision, is not a priority issue for us'. Or they may say 'How can we leave our daughters uncircumcised? The Government can do what it wants, but we will continue to circumcise our daughters, we do not fear the punishment'. According to a study by the Egyptian Government, in 1997, 97 per cent of the 14,779 women surveyed were circumcised, and 80 per cent of them said they were content with the results. However, women internalize often the values of their male-dominated communities which ostracize uncircumcised women and make it impossible for them to marry and be part of the community.

Another issue is the criticism that most human rights groups fight FGM from the feminist perspective only. If the practice is to be condemned for the excessive bleeding, infections and deaths it causes, then male circumcision should be condemned as well, say FGM defenders. And there are many who would agree with them, arguing that both male and female circumcision is unnecessary and dangerous. But there is a qualitative difference between male and female circumcision. Male circumcision is not bound up with gender relations of dominance. Circumcised men do not lose sexual pleasure, nor are their reproductive capacities affected. ∎

Seychelles

Population: 83,000 (2002)
Land area: 450 SQ KM
Capital: Victoria
Currency: Rupee
Language: English and French

Seychelles

Prior to the exploration done by Portuguese sailors in the 16th century, the archipelago had already been visited by Persian Gulf merchants. French and British colonists fought violently over this Indian Ocean colony during the 18th century. After expelling the French in 1794, the British paid little attention to it, and it was governed from the island of Mauritius until 1903. During the World Wars, the Seychelles archipelago gained strategic significance.

[2] The Seychelles People's United Party (SPUP) founded in 1964 gave the local population - most of them descendants of enslaved Africans and Indian workers - a new sense of nationalism. The Party proved its strength during the general strikes of 1965 and 1966, and in the mass demonstrations of 1972. The colonial interests were opposed to the SPUP and independence, and they organized themselves into the Seychelles' Taxpayers Association. It was later renamed the Seychelles Democratic Party, led by James Mancham.

[3] In the legislative elections of April 1974, the SPUP won 47.6 per cent of the vote. However, the peculiar colonial 'democratic' system awarded the Party only 2 of the 15 seats and Mancham remained the Prime Minister. In spite of this, it was too late to stem the tide of nationalism and in 1976 Mancham agreed to the British Foreign Office's suggestion that he become the first president of the Republic of Seychelles. Shortly before independence, he had agreed to 'return' the strategic British Indian Ocean Territory (BIOT) islands to Britain; they had been administered from Mahé since 1967. The British in turn passed them on to the United States which built the important Diego Garcia naval base there.

[4] Aware that the people would not accept this deal, Mancham postponed the elections until 1979, arguing that they were not necessary as all of the parties were in favor of independence.

[5] Mancham's foreign policy was directed at cementing a strong alliance with South Africa, the source of most of the tourists, while domestic policy destroyed tea and coconut plantations to make room

for new five-star hotels, owned by foreign companies. Entire islands were sold off to foreigners like Harry Oppenheimer, the South African gold magnate, and the actor Peter Sellers.

[6] In 1977, while Mancham was manoeuvring to postpone the elections yet again, the SPUP took over the country 'with the collaboration of the local police force' while Mancham was out of the country. Accused of 'leading a wasteful life while his people worked hard', Mancham was replaced by SPUP leader Albert René.

[7] René renewed his support for the Non-Aligned Movement, which had recognized the SPUP as the country's sole legitimate liberation movement prior to independence. He also strengthened the Seychelles' ties with left-wing countries and movements around the Indian Ocean. The new government turned to socialism, promising to reorganize tourism, give priority to self-sufficiency in agriculture and fishing, increase education, and cut the high level of unemployment which was affecting nearly half of the working population.

[8] In mid-1978, in order to meet the new political situation, the SPUP became the People's Progressive Front of Seychelles (FPPS). In June 1979, the FPPS won the national elections with 98 per cent of the vote, in elections where the

abstention rate was a mere 5 per cent. After the victory, President René announced his decision to close down the American satellite tracking station on the archipelago and demanded that the US base on Diego Garcia be closed, with the island returning to Mauritius.

[9] In August 1978, he launched a land reform program calling for the expropriation of all uncultivated land. He also nationalized the water and electricity services, the construction industry and transportation. Controls were placed on food prices and an obligatory literacy program was introduced. These measures led to a rapid economic recovery in the Seychelles, and by 1979-80, on account of mineral and petroleum wealth, they had the largest per capita income of any of the islands in the region. The national currency was also revalued, something virtually unheard of in the Third World.

[10] This economic growth was encouraged and supported by tourism and effective administration. At this time the Seychelles received an average of 80,000 tourists a year. Under the Mancham Government, most of them were South Africans, but after René took over more Europeans came, especially British.

[11] The Seychelles received funding for the expansion of several quays from the African Development Bank,

aiming to increase the country's fishing activity.

[12] The opponents of Albert René, mainly the South African apartheid regime, did not give up their efforts to overthrow the socialist government of the Seychelles. In November 1981, a group of 45 mercenaries led by former colonel Mike Hoare tried to invade the island and oust the Government. The plot had been hatched in London by former president Mancham, with South African assistance. The attempted coup failed and the mercenaries had to hijack an Indian airliner to escape to South Africa. After the unsuccessful invasion, the Seychelles Government declared a state of emergency and imposed a curfew. The popular militia proved effective in neutralizing conspiracies and tightening controls on all foreigners.

[13] The failed invasion and the economic recession in Europe caused tourism to decline by approximately 10 per cent. In August 1982, the situation deteriorated further when military personnel plotted an unsuccessful rebellion, strengthening rumors of another approaching mercenary conspiracy, and European conservative groups organized a smear campaign to support these rumors. In June 1984, Albert René was re-elected with 93 per cent of the vote, and the last political prisoner was released immediately after the elections. The country's greater political stability allowed the President to adopt a more pragmatic policy.

[14] In 1986, the Seychelles and the US renegotiated their treaty, originally signed in 1976 and renewed in 1981, allowing a US satellite tracking station to be stationed on Mahé.

[15] In September 1986, there was another coup attempt. Albert René, who was in Zimbabwe participating in a Non-Aligned Countries summit conference, returned immediately and put down the rebellion. Most of those responsible for the coup were arrested, among them the main leader of the conspiracy, Minister of Defense Colonel Ogilvy Berlouis.

[16] The Seychelles Government promoted the creation of a peace zone in the Indian Ocean. It required

all warships wanting to call at its ports to be 'nuclear-free', and as a result the US and British naval fleets stopped calling at the archipelago. The Seychelles established diplomatic relations with Comoros and Mauritius in 1988, and with Morocco and Côte d'Ivoire in 1989.

[17] In the presidential elections of June 1989, Albert René was the only candidate and was re-elected for a third term, with 96 per cent of the vote, according to final election returns. After the election, the President announced that he was reorganizing his cabinet. He personally took charge of the ministry of industry and amalgamated the ministries of planning, foreign affairs, finance and tourism into a single cabinet post.

[18] In September 1989, Indian President Ramaswamy Venkataraman carried out a three-day visit to Victoria, signing a cultural exchange agreement. In January 1990, the Seychelles established diplomatic relations with Kenya.

[19] The opposition forced President René to accept a multiparty system. The first experiment was carried out in July 1992, when a commission was elected to draw up the new constitution. The People's Progressive Front of Seychelles (FPPS), the ruling party, took 13 of the 23 seats. The Democratic Party (PD) of former president Mancham won eight seats.

[20] The Government continued its authoritarian ways. The PD soon withdrew from the commission and the first draft constitution was rejected. The project was suspended until the PD returned to the commission in June 1993, and the text was written with support from both parties; 73.6 per cent of the voters approved the new constitution.

[21] This document made official the multiparty system, the 33-member National Assembly and a five year presidential term. The President can be re-elected twice. René won the July 1993 elections and his party took the absolute majority in the National Assembly.

[22] Tourism continued to be the main source of income for the nation. The annual number of visitors was higher than the national population in 1993 and 1994. Oil derivatives and tinned tuna made up more than 80 per cent of the islands' exports during this period. Despite unemployment running at 22 per cent, the gross national product of the Seychelles reached $6,680 per head in 1994. Nearly all have access to drinking water and 100 per cent can meet their basic nutritional needs.

[23] In 1997, only one per cent of the budget was dependent on international contributions, although some forms of technical assistance were maintained.

[24] Although according to the United Nations Development Program (UNDP) Seychelles ranked in 1998 as the African country with the highest human development index, it was only 56th in the world.

[25] With sights on proving the country's political stability to investors, René called for elections two years early. In September 2001, he was re-elected to his third consecutive term since the multiparty system was established. René won 54.2 per cent of the vote, while rival candidate Wavel Ramkalawan, of the Seychelles National Party, polled 44.9 per cent. Ramkalawan challenged the results saying voters had been intimidated or had received money to support the FPPS.

[26] Global warming is one of the pressing problems Seychelles faces today. Several plant and animal species, such as birds, giant turtles, coconut palms and others have already been affected by the increasing temperatures and rising sea levels. Most of the coral around the islands has died. The country's biodiversity makes it an important tourist destination, and tourism is among its leading sources of income. The Government has made environmental protection a top priority and the population is educated from a young age about the importance of preserving nature.

[27] In April 2002, the Consultative Council on Tourism, which has operated as a government advisory body since 1999, was reorganized and the number of representatives from the tourism industry was

increased. Simone de Comarmond, Minister of Tourism and Transportation, stated that the Government was committed to taking the necessary steps to develop tourism. She stated that in the wake of the September 11 terrorist attacks in the US it was more necessary than ever to ensure that the Seychelles tourism industry remained competitive. ■

STATISTICS

DEMOGRAPHY
Population: 83,000 (2002)
Annual growth: 1.4 % (1985-2000)
Estimates for year 2015: 97,000 (2000)
Annual growth to year 2015: 1.3 % (2000)
Urban population: 58.5 % (2000)
Urban growth: 2.9 % (2000)

HEALTH
Infant mortality: 13 per 1,000 (2000)
Under-5 child mortality: 17 per 1,000 (2000)
Daily calorie supply: 2,422 per capita (1999)
132 doctors per 100,000 people (1996)

EDUCATION
Literacy: 88 % (2000)
male: 87 % (2000)
female: 89 % (2000)
School enrolment (net):
Primary total: 100 % (1994/2000)
male: 100 % (1995/99)
female: 100 % (1995/99)
Primary school teachers: one for every 15 pupils (1998)

COMMUNICATIONS
39 newspapers (1996), 543 radios (1997), 203 TV sets (2000) and 235 main telephone lines (2000) per 1,000 people

ECONOMY
Annual growth: -0.3 % (2000)
Annual inflation: 6.3 % (2000)
Consumer price index: 115.4 (2000)
Currency: 5.6 rupees = $ 1 (03/2002)
Cereal imports: 15,079 metric tons (1996)
Food import dependency: 20 % (1996)
Fertilizer use: 0 kg per ha (1999)
Exports: $ 481 million (2000)
Imports: $ 530 million (2000)
External debt: $ 163 million (2000); $ 2,030 per capita (2000)

PROFILE

ENVIRONMENT
An archipelago of 92 islands: Mahé, Praslim, and La Digue are the largest islands, made of granite; the rest are of coral. The climate is tropical with plentiful vegetation and heavy rainfall. Only the largest islands are inhabited, but some economic use is made of the other islands.

SOCIETY
Peoples: Most residents of the Seychelles are mulattos, descendants of mixed African and European origin and most of them live on the island of Mahé. There are minorities of European, Chinese and Indian origin.
Religions: Roman Catholic 88.6 per cent; other Christian (mostly Anglican) 7.7 per cent; Hindu 0.7 per cent; other, 3 per cent (1996).
Languages: English and French (official); most of the population speak Creole, a local dialect with European and African influences.
Political Parties: People's Progressive Front of Seychelles (FPPS), extreme left; Seychelles National Party (SNP), continuation of the United Opposition (OU, centrist), in turn formed by the National Alliance Party, Seychelles Party and Seychelles National Movement; Democratic Party (PD), conservative.
Social Organizations: The National Workers' Union.

THE STATE
Official Name: Repiblik Sesel.
Capital: Victoria 28,000 people (1999).
Other cities: Anse Royal 3,700 people; Cascade 2,500 (2000).
Government: France-Albert René, President since June 1977, re-elected in 1993, 1998 and 2001. Legislature, single-chamber: National Assembly, with 34 members.
National Holiday: June 28, Independence Day (1976).
Armed Forces: 300 (1996).
Other: 1,300 National Guard.

Sierra Leone

Population: 4,814,000 (2002)
Land area: 71,620 SQ KM
Capital: Freetown
Currency: Leone
Language: English

Sierra Leone

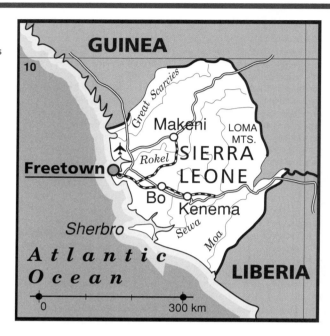

The Bulom (Sherbro), Temne, and Limba have been on the coast of present-day Sierra Leone for thousands of years. In the mid-16th century Mande-speaking people migrated from present-day Liberia, and they eventually established the states of Bullom, Loko, Boure, and Sherbro.

[2] In 1460 the Portuguese landed on the peninsula, naming it (Sierra Leone = lion mountains) after the mountains located there. In the opening of the 16th century, European traders stopped regularly on the peninsula, exchanging cloth and metal goods for ivory, timber, and small numbers of slaves. In the early 17th century British traders became increasingly active along the coast. In the early 18th century Fulani and Mande-speaking traders from the Fouta Djallon region of present-day Guinea converted numerous Temne to Islam, which became firmly established in the north and subsequently spread through the rest of the country.

[3] When Britain faced a 'demographic problem' with runaway slaves in the 1800s, the Government decided to 'return' them to Africa. They had come to London hoping to benefit from a court ruling that had abolished slavery in the city of London. Abolitionist leader Granville Sharp purchased an area of 250 sq km for £60 from the local rulers in 1792, organizing an agricultural society based on democratic principles. However, this society was quickly transformed into a colonial company involved in the British conquest of the entire country.

[4] Tossed into a land where they had no roots, the creoles sought to emulate European culture and considered themselves superior to the 'savage' of the interior, acting as brokers for British colonialism.

[5] Yet the 'savages' resisted strongly. In 1898 Bai Buré rallied most of the inland people, already angered by a British tax on their dwellings. However, after nearly a year of resistance, British military superiority overwhelmed and stifled the opposition.

[6] In 1960, the British wanted to withdraw from Sierra Leone, and an agreement was negotiated with the traditional leaders to protect their interests. In 1961, Sir Milton Margai,

secretary general of Sierra Leone People's Party (SLPP), became the first prime minister of an independent Sierra Leone.

[7] The creoles, together with British and Syrian-Lebanese merchants, held the colony's economic power. Although removed from political power, they maintained significant influence over the Margai Government.

[8] When Margai died in 1964, he was succeeded by his brother Albert and the situation quickly deteriorated. Corruption and gambling became so widespread that it was compared to the Batista period in Cuba. The diamond trade gave birth to a chain of smuggling operations and crime became a main source of income.

[9] In 1967 the All Peoples' Congress (APC) party led by Syaka Stevens won the elections, signaling the possibility for change; however, the conservative creoles, the traditional leaders, and the neo-colonialist British united to prevent Stevens from taking control of the country as they considered him 'dangerously progressive'. As a result, Stevens was overthrown by a military coup and forced into exile in Conakry (Guinea).

[10] In April 1968, a group of low-ranking officers took power through the so-called Sergeants' Revolt. They

brought back Stevens who in 1971 broke all ties with Britain and declared Sierra Leone a republic, becoming its first President.

[11] Important goals were achieved in the first years: the lumber industry was nationalized and the State seized majority control of the mining firm, which controlled the diamond trade. To protect the prices of iron ore and bauxite, Sierra Leone joined the associations of iron and bauxite producing countries.

[12] Stevens called for a plebiscite to establish a one-party system in 1978 in an attempt to appease the opposition. His proposal was approved and the APC incorporated prominent members of the SLPP within its ranks, granting them posts within the Government.

[13] In 1979, President Stevens' popularity began to ebb as a result of worsening living conditions, growing inflation, authoritarian measures, government corruption, a fall in exports and the increasing foreign debt.

[14] Popular unrest reached its climax in September 1981 when the Sierra Leone Labor Congress (SLLC) declared a general strike, demanding immediate changes in economic policy. The strike spread throughout the country and nearly toppled the Government, which had to make several concessions.

[15] In urban areas, the scarcity of staple foods - particularly rice - as well as periodic fuel shortages became chronic. Inflation and the high cost of living reduced the purchasing power of salaried workers by 60 per cent, and the late payment of salaries became normal. Members of parliament were paid with sacks of rice which were later sold on the black market at a large profit.

[16] The powerful Lebanese traders controlled the unofficial market and more than 70 per cent of the country's exports. Gold and diamond smuggling was estimated at nearly $150 million per year while official exports dropped from $80 million to barely $14 million between 1980 and 1984.

[17] In November 1985, Syaka Stevens handed over the presidency to Joseph Momoh, a member of his cabinet, changing nothing in the political and social condition of the country.

[18] The scale of the crisis culminated in the Government's declaration of a state of economic emergency in 1987. This measure included granting the State the sole right to commercialize gold and diamonds, a 15 per cent surcharge on imports, and the reduction of salaries of public employees.

[19] In March 1991, rebel forces operating from Liberia occupied two border towns. Guerrilla groups from Burkina Faso, Liberia, and Sierra Leone joined them, occupying one third of the country.

[20] A referendum approved held in August established a multiparty system. However, the economic crisis continued alongside ever increasing corruption.

[21] In 1992, the Government launched a structural adjustment program which had been imposed by the International Monetary Fund. James Funa, a former World Bank executive, was named minister of finance. He implemented monetary control, incentives for natural resource exploration by foreign companies, widespread privatization, an overhaul of the State apparatus, and a purge on the widespread corruption.

[22] On April 29, Captain Valentine Strasser seized power through a

coup. After suspending the constitution he created the National Provisional Governing Council, prohibiting all political activity, and confirmed the Minister of Finance in his post. In June, all civilian members of the Governing Council were expelled and its name was changed to 'Supreme Council of State'. Press censorship began.

23   The eastern part of the country was occupied at the time by the United Movement for Liberian Liberation and Democracy, which used Sierra Leone as a base from which to carry out attacks against Charles Taylor's forces (see Liberia). In the meantime, the Revolutionary United Front of Sierra Leone (RUF) was operating in the southeast.

24   The regions affected by warfare were also the country's richest, where gold and diamond deposits and the main agricultural production area were located. Guerrilla activity led to an abrupt decline in mining activity; the percentage represented by diamonds in the country's exports dropped from 54.7 per cent in 1987 to a mere 7 per cent in 1990. The per capita GDP dropped from $320 in 1980 to $210 in 1991.

25   The Government promise to organize elections did not convince the RUF, which continued with the armed struggle. The rebels had a series of military victories in early 1994, which left a total of 150 civilians dead.

26   In January 1996, following a bloodless coup, Strasser was replaced by a close former ally, Brigadier-General Julius Maada Bio. The presidential elections held in February as planned were won by Ahmad Tejan Kabbah of the Sierra Leone People's Party (SLPP) in the second round with nearly 60 per cent of the vote.

27   Rebel troops led by Major-General Johnny Paul Koroma ousted President Ahmad Tejan Kabbah on May 25 1997. The Organization of African Unity, meeting in Namibia, criticized the coup and began negotiations to make the leaders abandon power.

28   In September 1997, former president Tejan Kabbah asked the UN's General Assembly for help to re-establish his government. In March 1998, the UN ECOMOG troops - paradoxically mostly Nigerians who at that time were ruled by the dictator Sani Abacha (see Nigeria) - took the main cities and regions of Sierra Leone, forcing out Koroma and his military junta. Kabbah's return to government was not seen as a guarantee of the rapid re-establishment of peace in a country riddled with corruption.

29   The Kabbah administration achieved some stability and in March 1998 it ordered an end to gold and diamond mining which had been controlled by foreigners for the previous 60 years, allowing Sierra Leone citizens with valid licenses to mine these minerals. But the stability was short-lived, since in the last months of the year another rebel offensive took control of more than half of the capital. The arrival of Nigerian troops balanced the conflict which led to the signing of a cease fire by both sides in January 1999.

30   The new rebel leader, Foday Sankoh, signed a peace treaty with the Government in July to put an end to nine years of civil war. Under the treaty, Sankoh was appointed director of the Strategic Minerals Commission and Vice-President, though a 1998 UN resolution banned him from travel without its authorization.

31   The rebels reinitiated combat in May 2000, leading to Sankoh's imprisonment. Before that, in addition to frequent travelling - according to monitors, to sell diamonds - he accused the peacekeeping force of being 'a threat to the security of the people of Sierra Leone'. The UN estimated that only half of the 45,000 rebel soldiers had turned in their weapons. In August, the regional leaders replaced him, appointing field commander Issa Sesay as chief. Sankoh learned of the fact from Kabbah, who along with presidents Olusegun Obasanjo, of Nigeria, and Alfa Oumar Konare, of Mali, met with the imprisoned leader.

32   A splinter armed group 'West Side Boyz', previously loyal to Koroma, took seven British soldiers hostage in August. The next month, the British forces launched a mission to liberate the hostages and capture West Side Boyz' leader, Foday Kallay.

33   Claiming that the continued state of insecurity made free and fair elections impossible, in January 2001 the Government postponed parliamentary and presidential elections scheduled for February and March. For the first time, UN troops began a peaceful deployment in rebel territory in March, and in May initiated the disarmament of the 45,000 rebel soldiers, which according to UN mission reports was completed by January 2002. ■

LITERACY

2000

36%

EXTERNAL DEBT

2000

PER CAPITA

US$ 289

STATISTICS

DEMOGRAPHY
Population: 4,814,000 (2002)
Annual growth: 1.4 % (1985-2000)
Estimates for year 2015: 7,115,000 (2000)
Annual growth to year 2015: 3.2 % (2000)
Urban population: 36.6 % (2000)
Urban growth: 3.8 % (2000)
Children per woman: 6.5 (2000)

HEALTH
Life expectancy at birth: 41 years (2000-2005)
male: 39 years (2000-2005)
female: 42 years (2000-2005)
Infant mortality: 180 per 1,000 (2000)
Under-5 child mortality: 316 per 1,000 (2000)
Daily calorie supply: 2,017 per capita (1999)
7 doctors per 100,000 people (1996)
Safe water: 57 % (2000)

EDUCATION
Literacy: 36 % (2000)
male: 51 % (2000)
female: 23 % (2000)
School enrolment (net):
Primary total: 41 % (1994/2000)
Secondary (gross):
male: 22 % (1995/97)
female: 13 % (1995/97)
Tertiary (gross): 1 % (1997)
Primary school teachers: one for every 34 pupils (1990)

COMMUNICATIONS
4 newspapers (1996), 259 radios (1998), 13 TV sets (2000) and 4 main telephone lines (2000) per 1,000 people

ECONOMY
Per capita, GDP: $ 490 (2000)
Annual growth: 4.9 % (2000)
Annual inflation: -0.8 % (2000)
Consumer price index: 255.1 (2000)
Currency: 1,975.0 leones = $ 1 (03/2002)
Cereal imports: 275,592 metric tons (2000)
Fertilizer use: 0 kg per ha (1999)
Exports: $ 110 million (2000)
Imports: $ 212 million (2000)
External debt: $ 1,273 million (2000); $ 289 per capita (2000)
Debt service: 29.9 % of exports (1999)
Development aid received: $ 74 million (1999); $ 14.9 per capita (1999); 11.00 % of GNP (1999)

HDI (ranking/value): 162 / 0.258 (1999)

PROFILE

ENVIRONMENT
The country is divided into three regions. The coastal strip, nearly 100 kilometers long, is a swampy plain that includes the island of Sherbro. Several rivers drain the inner tropical forest, mostly cleared for agricultural exploitation. The eastern plateau contains the country's diamond mines. Deforestation is very severe, 85 per cent of all natural habitat has been destroyed.

SOCIETY
Peoples: The Temne and Mende account for nearly one-third of the population. Lokko, Sherbro, Limba, Sussu, Fulah, Kono and Krio are other important groups. The Krio - whose name is from the English word 'creole' - are descendants of African slaves freed in the 19th century who settled in Freetown. There is also an Arab minority.
Religions: Most of the people profess traditional African religions; nearly one third are Muslims, concentrated in the north; the Christian minority is located in the capital.
Languages: English (official). The most widely spoken native languages are Temne, Mende and Krio. The latter serves as the commercial language in the capital.
Political Parties: Sierra Leone People's Party (SLPP); All Peoples' Congress (APC); United Political Movements Front. The Revolutionary United Front (RUF).
Social Organizations: Sierra Leone Labor Congress.

THE STATE
Official Name: Republic of Sierra Leone.
Capital: Freetown 822,000 people (1999).
Other cities: Koidu 109,900 people; Bo 79,700; Kenema 69,900 (2000).
Government: Ahmad Tejan Kabbah, President elected in March 1996, re-elected in 2002; he was overthrown by Major Johnny Paul Koroma in May 1997, and re-installed when the UN-Ecomog forces took Sierra Leone in March 1998. Unicameral Legislature: House of Representatives, with 112 members.
National Holiday: April 19, Republic Day (1971).
Armed Forces: 13,000 troops (1995).

Singapore

Population: 4,188,000 (2002)
Land area: 610 SQ KM
Capital: Singapore
Currency: Singapore dollar
Language: Malay and English

Singapore

One of the earliest references to Singapore as Temasek, or Sea Town, was found in the Javanese 'Nagarakretagama' of 1365. The name was also mentioned in a Vietnamese source at around the same time. By the end of the 14th century, the Sanskrit name, Singapura (Lion City), became commonly used. By that time Singapore was caught in the struggles between Siam (now Thailand) and the Java-based Majapahit Empire for control over the Malay Peninsula. According to the Malay Annals, Singapore was defeated in one Majapahit attack, but Iskandar Shah, or Parameswara, a prince of Palembang, later killed the local chieftain and installed himself as the island's new ruler. Shortly after, he was driven out and fled north to Muar in the Malay Peninsula, where he founded the Malacca Sultanate.

[2] Singapore remained an important part of the Malacca Sultanate. From 1819 onwards, it became an extremely important base for the British; Sir Thomas Stamford Raffles established the local headquarters of the British East India Company there.

[3] In 1824, the island of Singapore and the adjacent islets were purchased as a single lot by Raffles from the Sultan of Johore (see Malaysia). The Company appointed Prince Hussein as the new ruler of Singapore. In gratitude, he granted the Company royal authorization to improve the port. Chinese immigrants soon constituted the majority of the local population.

[4] Singapore was part of the British colony called 'the Straits Settlements', together with the ports of Penang and Melaka (Malacca). In 1946, Penang and Melaka joined the Malayan Union and Singapore became a crown colony.

[5] At one point during World War II the Japanese dominated the whole of southeast Asia. They conquered Singapore in 1942 but were later defeated. Their defeat was partly due to a strong internal resistance group, organized by a revolutionary movement and led by the Communist Party of Malaya (CPM). The name Malaya included both Singapore and the Malay peninsula;

the separation of the latter was always questioned by the Left.

[6] Once the war was over, the Malay sultanates and the former Straits Settlements attempted to form a union or federation, with a view to attaining independence for the territory. However, the conflicting interests of the Chinese and Malay communities, and the conservative and progressive forces, made progress difficult. In January 1946, the Singapore Labor Union declared a general strike and in 1948 the Communist Party led an anti-colonial uprising which failed, as it failed to gain the support of the Malays and the poorer sectors of the Indian population. Marxist parties were outlawed and had to move into the forests, where they resorted to guerrilla warfare.

[7] As the first step towards the self-government of the city-state, municipal elections were held in 1949. Only English-speaking people were allowed to vote until 1954, when the People's Action Party (PAP) was founded. The anti-imperialism advocated by the PAP brought citizens of British and Chinese backgrounds together for the first time. In 1959, the Chinese were allowed to vote; full internal autonomy was granted, and the PAP obtained an overwhelming victory.

Lee Kuan Yew, founder of the party, became Prime Minister, campaigning on a platform of social reforms and independence. He planned a federation with Malaya, which had been independent since 1957.

[8] The PAP split into a socialist faction, led by Lim Chin Siong, and the 'moderates' of Lee Kuan Yew, who encouraged the promotion of private enterprise and foreign investment

[9] In 1961, the left wing of the PAP founded *Barisan Sosialis* (the Socialist Front), which opposed the prospect of uniting Singapore and Malaya under British control. In September 1963, the Federation of Malaysia, consisting of Singapore, the Malay peninsula, Sarawak and Sabah (both in the north and northeast of Borneo) was set up, after those opposed to the Federation had been conveniently purged.

[10] As a Federation member, Singapore depended heavily on the peninsula; even its water supply came from there. Integration at that time was not feasible because of profound disagreements between Singapore's Chinese community and the Malay community of the rest of the Federation. On August 9 1965, after several ethnic conflicts, Prime Minister Lee decided to withdraw from the Federation.

[11] In 1965, serious internal conflicts were caused by the mistreatment of the Malay population and other ethnic minorities. There were also intense struggles with the left-wing opposition, which the Government classified as 'communist subversives'. The island became an independent republic, and a Commonwealth member. A mutual assistance and defense treaty was signed with Malaysia, and on October 15 of the same year Singapore became a member of the United Nations.

[12] The first years of independence witnessed substantial economic growth. The island was turned into an 'enclave' for the export of products manufactured by transnationals, and into an international financial center which controlled the regional economy.

[13] The situation turned gloomy in 1974, when the oil crisis upset Singapore's export scheme. Singapore was the fourth largest port in the world, with the second highest per capita income in Asia, after Japan. The ensuing economic deterioration brought about public demonstrations by students and workers. These protests were fiercely controlled, reaching such proportions that the Socialist International expelled the PAP from its ranks in 1975.

[14] In order to placate criticism from the opposition, the regime approved a reform which allowed the entering of two representatives of the Workers' Party and the Democratic Party of Singapore, respectively.

[15] Despite the sustained economic growth since 1987, the Government expelled thousands of Thai and Filipino workers blaming them for taking over the jobs of the natural citizens.

[16] The decision to prohibit the circulation of foreign publications judged detrimental by the Government, the imprisonment of opposition members and a Security Law that allows indefinite imprisonment without trial for two renewable years each time, raised countless denunciations of violations of human rights.

[17] In the 1988 elections the opposition vote grew, but due to the mechanisms of the electoral system

its parliamentary representation diminished. In 1991, the PAP again won an overwhelming majority of seats. In November, Goh Chok Tong replaced Lee Kuan Yew as Prime Minister, but the latter nevertheless retained considerable political weight. At his initiative, Singapore offered Washington the possibility of installing bases in the country when the Filipino Congress decided to close US military bases in the Philippines.

[18] As an exporter of high technology goods, Singapore's industry was only marginally affected by the recession of its main partners, the US, Japan, and the European Union. In order to expand its activity, the Government started a policy of 'regionalization' increasing its investments in Indonesia and Malaysia. The investments in China surpassed $1 billion per year, and Singapore became the main commercial partner of Vietnam. From 1993 on, annual growth was over eight per cent.

[19] In 1994 and 1995 relations were strained between Singapore and the US, Philippines and Netherlands as a result of the hanging of a Dutch engineer on heroin trafficking charges, the imprisonment and sentencing of a young man from the US to a beating with a rattan cane for vandalism, and for executing a Filipina maid accused of murdering a colleague. In the case of the domestic worker, the crime was proved and diplomatic relations were re-established. As a result of a request from President Clinton, the US citizen's sentence was reduced by number of blows and months in prison.

[20] In June 1996 the 'Speak Mandarin' campaign was challenged by ethnic minorities, concerned that the language was becoming a requirement to obtain work. The Government - while urging the Chinese to have more children - responded that minorities have to be tolerant of the majority. The Government's concern shifted to the declining standard of English spoken by the population, and in 1999 launched a campaign against singlish, the local linguistic version with which the Singapore people adopted English. The 'Speak Proper English' campaign sought to reduce the use of that language, which reflects the multiracial nature of a country in combining colonial English with Malaysian, Tamil and Hokien.

[21] That year, Singapore played a key role in shoring up the region's faltering economy, dedicating part of its huge reserves and the trade surplus to support the baht and the rupiah, the Thai and Indonesian currencies, respectively.

[22] In the presidential elections of August 1999, only Sellapan Ramanthan Nathan, PAP candidate, was declared eligible to run. Nathan took office in September and the Government set out to transform the country into an 'Asian Silicon Valley'. During a trip to India in January 2000, Premier Goh Chok Tong urged Indian experts in technology and information to move to Singapore in an effort to boost the economy.

[23] Some 2,000 people engaged in an unprecedented political rally in April 2001 in protest against the Government and to collect funds for popular parliamentarian JB Jeyaretnam, who was on the verge of bankruptcy. It was the first legally sanctioned demonstration in Singapore outside of electoral periods. The organizers considered it an important step for human rights in the country. If Jeyaretnam had gone bankrupt, he would have been expelled from Parliament.

[24] Singapore's economy technically went into recession in the year's second quarter. The deceleration of the world economy had weakened global demand for high-tech equipment, a key industry for the country, contributing 25 per cent of its GDP. The authorities had predicted a recession since mid 2000 when the technology sector began to suffer, but the 0.9 per cent GDP decline was worse than expected. The recession however did not affect the Government's popularity, and the November elections gave an overwhelming victory to PAP, with 82 of the 84 seats in Parliament.

[25] The free trade accord signed by Singapore and Japan in January 2002 was seen as a 'milestone' by Singaporean authorities because it marked Japan's commitment to the region. Singaporean investors won access to the Japanese service market, valued at $6 billion annually. Under the terms of the agreement, companies based in Singapore could freely transfer investment in and out of Japan. ■

PROFILE

ENVIRONMENT

Singapore consists of one large island and 54 smaller adjacent islets. The country is connected to Malaysia by a causeway across the Johore Strait. The terrain, covered by swampy lowlands, is not conducive to farming and the population traditionally works in business and trade. The climate is tropical with heavy rainfall. In its strategic geographical location, central to the trade routes between Africa, Asia and Europe, the island has become a flourishing commercial center. Economically, the main resources of the country have been its port, the British naval base and, more recently, industrial activity; textiles, electronic goods and oil refining. Industrialization has caused severe air and water pollution.

SOCIETY

Peoples: 76 per cent of Singaporeans are of Chinese origin. Malaysians account for 15 per cent and 6 per cent are from India and Sri Lanka.
Religions: Buddhist 28 per cent; Christian 19 per cent; Islam 13 per cent; Taoist 13 per cent; Hindu 5 per cent. There are Sikh and Jewish minorities.
Languages: Malay, English, Chinese (Mandarin) and Tamil are the official languages. Malay is considered the national language but English is spoken in the public administration and serves as a unifying element for the communities. Various Chinese dialects are spoken, with Punjabi, Hindi, Bengali, Telegu and Malayalam in the Indian communities.
Political Parties: The People's Action Party (PAP); Singapore Democratic Party; the Workers' Party; Barisan Sosialis (the Socialist Front); the Singapore Justice Party; the United People's Front and the Singapore United Front.
Social Organizations: The major national trade union is the Congress of Singapore Labor Unions.

THE STATE

Official Name: Hsin-chia-p'o Kung-ho-kuo (Mandarin); Republik Singapura (Bahasa Malaysia); Singapore Kudiyarasu (Tamil); Republic of Singapore.
Capital: Singapore 3,522,000 people (1999).
Government: Parliamentary republic. Sellapan Ramanathan, president since September 1999; Goh Chok Tong, Prime Minister since November 1990. Unicameral Legislature, with 90 members.
National Holiday: August 9, Independence Day (1965).
Armed Forces: 55,500, inc. 34,800 conscripts.
Other: 11,600 Police and Maritime Police (estimate). 100,000 Civil Defense Force.

Slovakia

Population: 5,408,000 (2002)
Land area: 48,080 SQ KM
Capital: Bratislava
Currency: Koruny
Language: Slovak

Slovenska

Between the years 500 and 100 BC, a Celtic tribe from western Europe, the Cotini, settled in the territory of present-day Slovakia. Later, from the year 100 BC to 400 AD, the Quadi, a Germanic group, formed satellite states of the Roman Empire north of the Danube (the 'Limes Romanum'). Both the Hadi and the Marcomani, their Germanic neighbors in Bohemia, were pushed out by the Huns led by Attila.

[2] The Slovaks, Slavs from the eastern region of the Vistula and closely related to the Czechs, started to settle in the territory between the sixth and seventh centuries. They soon had to defend themselves from the Avars, nomads from lower Panonia, until the Frankish trader Samo united the Slavs and was chosen as their King. In 805, the Frankish King Charlemagne, expanding his Christian empire, formed an alliance with the Czech leaders of Bohemia and Moravia to defeat the Avars once and for all. In return for their help, Charlemagne distributed dukedoms amongst the Czechs, who took control over the regions of Moravia, Bohemia and Slovakia. The kingdom of Moravia, which included Bohemian and Slovakian territories, was thus established. The first Moravian monarch, Mojmir I, ruled from 830 to 846, and Christianity was adopted under his rule.

[3] The nephew who succeeded him, Rotislav I (ruling from 846 to 870), expanded the kingdom to include all of Bohemia and founded Great Moravia, unifying the Slav territories of the region for the first time. Rotislav consolidated relations with the Frankish Empire, which answered to Rome, and maintained constant contact with the Byzantine Empire. In 863, answering a request from Rotislav, the Byzantine Emperor sent Constantine and Methodius, leading a group of missionaries. The monks translated the gospels and designed the first Slav alphabet (see Czech Republic).

[4] During the reign of Svatopluc (870-894) the Moravian frontiers extended to include the western part of present-day Hungary and southern Poland. Svatopluc abandoned relations with the Byzantine Emperor, and Methodius' disciples were forced to abandon

the kingdom and take refuge in the Balkans.

[5] Great Moravia came to an end in 906, when it was destroyed by the German king Arnulf in alliance with the Magyars, a nomadic tribe from the Upper Volga who controlled most of the territories of modern-day Hungary. The western part of the old kingdom remained in the possession of the Czech dukes of Bohemia, while the area between the Carpathians and the Danube - the Slovakia of today - was occupied by the Magyars. Despite repeated attempts to take control of Slovak territory by the dukes of Bohemia, it continued as a dependency of the Hungarian Kings for ten centuries.

[6] The Slovaks never lost their language and cultural characteristics, retaining their links with the Czechs. During the 15th century, the University of Prague exercised considerable influence over the Slovaks. The Hussites of Bohemia repeatedly invaded Hungary, bringing the custom of reciting the liturgy in the national language instead of Latin to Slovakia.

[7] The Hussite incursions prepared the ground for the later reception of Protestantism, based on the teaching of the Kralice Bible translated by the Bohemian Brethren. In the early 16th century most of the Slovaks had adopted Calvinism. However, when Hungary was invaded by the Ottoman Empire in 1525, Slovakia was governed by the House of Austria, which strengthened the Counter-reformation throughout the region. This dependence on the House of

Austria Germanized Slovak culture to a large extent.

[8] In 1620, the Czech nobles were beaten by the Magyars, and Slovakia once again formed part of the Kingdom of Hungary. The conquest of central Hungary by the Ottoman Empire increased Magyar influence in Slovakia. Hungarian nobles fleeing Turkish power settled in Slovak villages and initiated Hungarian customs.

[9] In the 17th century Turkish dominion in Hungary was replaced by the House of Hapsburg. At the end of the 18th century the Emperor Joseph II changed the Kingdom of Hungary by Germanizing the bureaucracy and limited the power of the Hungarian authorities. This helped the Slovaks hark back to their Slav origin and their cultural links with the Czechs.

[10] The nationalist fever which ran across Europe following the Napoleonic Wars also reached the territories dominated by the Austrian Crown. Slovak and Hungarian nationalism came into conflict. In 1834, Magyar replaced Latin as the legal language. In 1848, the Slovaks, allied with Czechs and German Republicans rose up in arms against the Magyars, who had in turn rebelled against the Austrians. Within this period, the Slovaks took over control of their secondary education and founded their first scientific society, the Matica Slovaka.

[11] In the late 19th century, the Hungarian authorities banned the Slovak language from public life, replacing it with Magyar. Slovak leaders, especially editors of journals, were persecuted and many

were imprisoned. In 1907, the Appony law made Slovak-speaking primary schools adopt Magyar.

[12] In 1914, World War I gave the Slovaks with the chance to embrace the cause of the Allies fighting the Austro-Hungarian Empire. Tens of thousands of Slovak soldiers forced to serve in the Hungarian army joined the Allies. In 1915, the Czech Alliance and the Slovak League (in the U.S.) reached an agreement in Cleveland proclaiming the liberation of the Czech and Slovak nations and their federate union, with complete independence for Slovakia. It would have its own parliament and administration with Slovak as its official language.

[13] Once the War had ended with the Allied victory in 1918, the nationalist efforts of the Slovak doctor Thomas G Masaryk (the son of a Slovak coachman and a German-Moravian mother), the scientist Milan Stefanik (a Slovak living abroad), and the Czech Eduard Benes, working with the opposition forces in Czech and Slovak lands, led to the creation of the Republic of Czecho-Slovakia on October 28 of that year.

[14] In November, Masaryk, who had promised to respect the rights of the Germanic and Hungarian minorities, was elected President of the new Republic, a position he was to maintain until 1935 (see Czech Republic). During his term in government - and also that of his successor, Benes - the Slovaks felt they were relegated within a State controlled by the Czechs, without fair participation.

[15] The German occupation of the Sudetenland in 1938 forced Benes into exile in London, and the occupation of Czechoslovakia by Nazi troops in 1939 put the history of the Republic on hold. Czechoslovakia was dismembered. Bohemia became a German province and Carpathian Russia was taken by the Hungarians. In March 1939, Slovak independence was proclaimed, making it a free state on paper, with Hitler's puppet President Joseph Tiso in power.

[16] After the allied victory in 1945, with the support of Soviet presence in the territory, the Czecho-Slovak republic returned to its former shape. The exiled Eduard Benes returned

from abroad and continued in power. The integrity of the Republic was guaranteed by its membership of the Soviet bloc until, in 1991, with the fall of the Soviet regime and the system of alliances, the Czech and Slovak peoples divided to develop separate political lives.

[17] On February 15 1993 Michal Kovac was elected President of the new Republic of Slovakia. Vladimir Meciar, leader of the Movement for a Democratic Slovakia (MED) and the architect of Czechoslovakian separation, was named Prime Minister.

[18] Meciar's administration was marked by controversy and accusations of authoritarianism, from the opposition. He re-nationalized the newspaper Smena, and created a compulsory television slot for the broadcasting of government news and propaganda.

[19] Separation from the Czech Republic proved detrimental to the Slovakian economy, which lost nearly $1 billion in bilateral trade. The country suffered more severely than the Czech Republic, because of dependence upon the Socialist bloc. In the first half of 1993, according to the Organization for Economic Co-operation and Development, 500,000 jobs were lost and inflation rose by 18 per cent.

[20] Jozef Moravcik was appointed Prime Minister in March 1993. The new coalition government was formed with two main goals: to keep Meciar out of power and accept the general principles of European democracy. However, the coalition's inner differences weakened this project and, in the October 1994 elections, Meciar once again became Prime Minister (with 35 per cent of the vote) and cancelled the privatization policy begun by his predecessor.

[21] In late 1997 five opposition parties founded the Slovak Democratic Coalition (SDK) and signed an agreement with Coexistence, a coalition made up of the Hungarian Christian Democratic Movement the Hungarian People's Party and the group known as Coexistence. President Kovak, whose relations with Meciar were already strained, joined in criticizing the Prime Minister, urging him in January 1998 to improve relations with the US and the European Union. After his defeat in Parliamentary elections, Meciar resigned and the two main opposition parties, the Slovak Democratic Opposition and the Democratic Left, formed a new Government in October, with Mikulás Dzurinda as Prime Minister.

[22] Protesting against discrimination, some 1,000 Slovakian Roma people requested asylum in Finland in July 1999. President Schuster recognized the demand as legitimate. The Government, which adopted immediate measures to improve this minority's situation and avoid a large outflow, in July 2001 declared its 'deep regret' for the violent death of a Roma gypsy who was being held in a police station, and promised that those responsible would be tried.

[23] The Czech and Slovak Governments reached an agreement in November putting an end to financial differences arising from the separation. Prague promised to deliver 4.5 tons of gold to Bratislava and acknowledged having a $1.5 billion debt with Slovakia.

[24] In February 2001 Parliament approved important reforms to the constitution, preparatory to joining the EU and NATO, the Western countries' defense alliance. The new constitution decentralized power, granted more to the office that monitors and audits the Government, and strengthens the judicial system's autonomy. Russia immediately said it was against Slovakia's possible integration into NATO, seeking to keep that organization away from its borders.

[25] In April 2002, the European Union suspended financial aid to Slovakia, expressing its doubts as to how it was being used. The announcement was made after Roland Toth, Slovak official in charge of the funds, resigned amid accusations of corruption. The suspension dealt a serious blow to Slovakia's intentions of joining the EU.■

PROFILE

ENVIRONMENT

The terrain is mountainous, dominated by the Carpathian Mountain range. Mountainous areas are covered by forests which supply an important timber industry. Agriculture is concentrated in the fertile plains of the Danube and Uh rivers. There are abundant mineral resources, including copper, zinc, lead and mercury, as well as oil and natural gas deposits. Industrial pollution and sulfur emissions in the atmosphere constitute the country's main environmental problem.

SOCIETY

Peoples: Slovak 85.7 per cent; Hungarian 10.7 per cent; Roma 1.6 per cent; Czech 1.1 per cent; Ruthenia, 0.3 per cent; Ukrainian 0.3 per cent; German 0.1 per cent; other 0.3 per cent (1994).
Religions: Roman Catholic 60.3 per cent; non-religious and atheist 9.7 per cent; Protestant 7.9 per cent, of which Slovak Evangelical 6.2 per cent and Reformed Christian 1.6 per cent; Greek Catholic 3.4 per cent; Eastern Orthodox 0.7 per cent; other 18 per cent.
Languages: Slovak is the official language; Hungarian is also spoken.
Political parties: Movement for a Democratic Slovakia; Party of Democratic Left, including elements of the Communist Party of Slovakia, which still exists. Slovak Democratic Coalition; Party of the Hungarian Coalition; Party of Civic Understanding. Slovak Democratic Coalition (SDK); 'Coexistence' is a coalition made up of the Hungarian Christian Democratic Movement; the Hungarian People's Party and the group known as Coexistence.
Social Organizations: Confederation of Trade Unions of the Slovak Republic (KOZ-SR), Slovak Union of Nature and Landscape Protectors (environmentalist).

THE STATE

Official Name: Slovenska Republika.
Administrative divisions: 3 regions divided into 38 municipalities and the capital zone.
Capital: Bratislava 460,000 people (1999).
Other cities: Kosice 244,400 people; Presov 95,300; Zilina 87,600; Nitra 87,400; Banská Bystrica 84,400 (2000).
Government: Parliamentary republic, according to the constitution effective since January 1993. Rudolf Schuster, President since June 1999. Mikulás Dzurinda, Prime Minister since October 1998. Unicameral Legislature: National Council of the Slovak Republic, with 150 members elected for a four year term by proportional representation.
National Holiday: September 1, Constitution Day (1992).
Armed Forces: 47,000 (1995).
Other: Border Guards: 600; Internal Security Forces: 250; Civil Defense Troops: 3,100.

Slovenia

Population: 1,983,000 (2002)
Land area: 20,120 SQ KM
Capital: Ljubljana
Currency: Tolar
Language: Slovenian

Slovenija

One of the southern Slav groups, the Slovenes occupied what is now Slovenia and the land to the north of this region in the 6th century AD. Subdued by the Bavarians around the year 743, they were later incorporated into the Frankish Empire of the Carolingians.

[2] With the division of the Empire in the 9th century, the region was given to the Germans. The Slovenes were reduced to serfdom and the region north of the Drava River was completely dominated by the Germans.

[3] The Slovene people preserved their cultural identity because of the educational efforts of their native intelligentsia who were mostly Catholic monks and priests. The House of Austria gradually established itself in the region, from the latter part of the 13th century onwards.

[4] Between the 15th and 16th centuries, the Slovenes participated in several peasant revolts - some, like the 1573 revolt, in conjunction with the Croats - leading the Hapsburgs to improve the system of land tenure.

[5] After 1809, a large part of Slovene territory fell within the Napoleonic Empire's Illyrian provinces. After Napoleon's defeat in 1814, Hapsburg (House of Austria) rule was restored within the region. With the 1848 Revolution, the Slovenes called for the creation of a united Slovene province within the Austrian Empire. The first glimmer of hope for a union of southern Slavs (Slavs, Serbs and Croats) emerged in the 1870s.

[6] In the 1890s, the Slovene People's Party (Catholic), and the Progressive (Liberal) and Socialist parties were formed. Members of the Catholic clergy also promoted a large-scale organization of peasants and artisans into cooperatives.

[7] In 1917 the Austrian Parliament, representing Slovenes and other southern Slav peoples, defended the unification of these territories into a single autonomous political entity, within the Hapsburg realm.

[8] At the end of World War I, amid widespread enthusiasm over the fall of the Austro-Hungarian Empire, Slovene leaders supported the creation of a kingdom of Serbs, Croats and Slovenes. In 1919, the new state adopted the name Yugoslavia (land of the southern Slavs). Nevertheless at the Paris Peace Conference the victorious powers handed Gorica to Italy despite the presence of a large Slovene population.

[9] The St Germain Treaty, signed between the victorious powers and Austria, gave Yugoslavia only a small part of southern Carintia. Two plebiscites were announced, to define the future of the rest of Carintia. However, when the southern region opted to join Austria in 1920, the second plebiscite was not held, and both regions remained part of Austria.

[10] Serbian hegemony within the Yugoslav kingdom gave rise to a certain resentment among Slovenes. This feeling never reached the extremes that characterized Croat feelings and which led to a strong anti-Serbian movement there. In World War II, Slovenia was partitioned between Italy (the southwest), Germany (the northeast) and Hungary (a small area north of the Mura River). The most prominent group within the Slovene resistance movement was the Liberation Front, led by the Communists.

[11] The communist guerrillas fought on two fronts at the same time: against the foreign invaders and against their internal enemies (especially groups belonging to the Slovene People's Party). The occupiers, in turn, organized anti-communist military units, with the participation of the local population. After the defeat of the Axis (Germany, Italy and Japan), the major part of old Slovenia was returned to Yugoslavia.

[12] Upon the foundation of the Federated People's Republic of Yugoslavia, in 1945, Slovenia became one of the Federation's six republics, with its own governing and legislative bodies. Legislative power was made up of a republican council, elected by all citizens, and the council of producers, elected from among Slovenian industrial workers and officials.

[13] Although such entities did not add up to an autonomous government, Slovenia managed to maintain a high degree of cultural and economic independence through this self-management brand of socialism (led by the Yugoslav League of Communists). In 1974, changes in the Yugoslavian federal constitution made Slovenia a Socialist Republic.

[14] Slovenia became one of the most industrialized of the Federation's republics, especially in the area of steel production and the production of heavy equipment. Yugoslavia's first nuclear power plant was completed in 1981 in Krsko, with the assistance of a private US firm.

[15] During the socialist period, Slovenia was first or second among the Yugoslav republics with regard to family income, leading the table for economically active population outside the rural sector. Slovenia also produced both agricultural produce and cattle.

[16] In the late 1980s, influenced by the changes in Eastern Europe, Slovenia evolved toward a multiparty political system. In January 1989, the Slovene League of Social Democrats was founded, the country's first legal opposition party, and in October Slovenia's National Assembly approved a constitutional amendment permitting Slovenia to secede from Yugoslavia.

[17] The Slovene League of Communists left the Yugoslav League in January 1990, becoming the Democratic Renewal Party. In April, in the first multiparty elections to be held in Yugoslavia since World War II, the Demos coalition came out victorious. This coalition's members represented a broad political spectrum - including several communists - united in their aim of achieving Slovenian separation from the federation.

[18] Slovenia and Croatia declared their independence on June 25, 1991. In the hours that followed, central government tanks flocked to Slovenia's Austrian, Hungarian and Italian borders; 20,000 federal troops stationed within the republic were mobilized. After fierce fighting and the bombing of the Ljubljana airport, Belgrade announced that it controlled the federation's borders.

[19] A cease-fire went into effect on July 7 1991, following negotiations held on the Yugoslav island of Brioni between federal and Slovene authorities, with the mediation of the European Community. The agreement resulting from the negotiations reaffirmed the sovereignty of Yugoslav peoples and postponed Slovenian independence for a three-month period. At the same time, the federal president's authority over the army was recognized, and the Slovene police authority over Slovenia's borders.

[20] According to the Brioni compromise, customs tariffs along Slovenia's borders remained in the hands of Slovene police, although the income generated was to go into a joint account belonging to the various Yugoslav republics. The federal army was to remain in the green area (free of border controls) during the three-month period established for jurisdiction to be turned over to Slovene authorities.

[21] In order for the cease-fire to be enforced, the agreement established an unconditional return of federal army units to army barracks, and the demobilization of the Slovene territorial defense forces. Likewise, directives were established for clearing the highways and freeing prisoners on both sides.

[22] Between 1991 and January 1992, the EC countries recognized Slovenia and Croatia as independent states, although civil war continued in the latter. The EC threatened to apply economic sanctions to Belgrade unless fighting stopped. The homogeneity of the Slovenian population made its secession the least painful in the Yugoslavian dissolution process.

[23] Slovenia began to define itself as a 'European, not Balkan' State in 1993. Good trade relations with the European Union (EU) and the Slovenian authorities' willingness to open up markets led the country to seek association into the EU. The growth of tourism and the tolar's stability - convertible since September 1995 - enabled Slovenia's exports and gross domestic product to increase.

[24] Italy opposed Slovenia's association with the EU. Italian authorities demanded compensation for the nationalization of property belonging to 150,000 Italians between 1945 and 1972. The Catholic Church also demanded the return of property that had been nationalized by the communist regime.

[25] The European Commission approved Slovenia's request in May 1995 but Italian opposition continued. In late 1995, Croatia and Slovenia had not reached an agreement regarding the sovereignty of the waters of Piran bay. The destination of Croatian funds deposited in Slovenia's main bank, the Ljubljanska Banka, prior to the break-up of former Yugoslavia, was also discussed.

[26] In June 1996 Slovenia signed an agreement of association with the EU, a formal step in its incorporation as full member in 2001. One of the EU's conditions - emphasized by Italy - was the inclusion of an article in the Slovenian constitution authorizing foreigners to purchase property in the country.

[27] By 1998 the Slovenian economy was considered one of the most ready to join the EU. In November, however, a European Commission report stated the country had slackened its preparations to access the EU. During the bombings of Kosovo and Serbia in 1999, Slovenia allowed NATO the use of its airspace. In June, US President Clinton visited Ljubljana and stated Slovenia was a strong candidate to become a full member of NATO.

[28] According to a Slovenian research group, RIS, approximately 10 per cent of the working population - some 80,000 workers - work through the internet. Seventy per cent of them are highly qualified men, especially concentrated in Ljubljana, the capital.

[29] In June 2001, Presidents Putin, of Russia, and Bush, of the US, met for the first time in Slovenia, in what used to be the residence of President Tito, the former Yugoslavian leader. The reasons for the choice of venue were mainly strategic, since this is the only country in the region that neither shares borders with a former Soviet republic nor is a member of NATO. This summit - with the US missile shield and NATO's expansion on the agenda - took place two weeks before Slovenia and Croatia celebrated their 10 years of independence from Yugoslavia. ∎

PROFILE

ENVIRONMENT

Bordered in the west by Italy, in the north by Austria, in the northeast by Hungary and in the south and southeast by Croatia, Slovenia is characterized by mountains, forests and deep, fertile valleys. The Sava River flows from the Julian Alps (highest peak: Mt Triglav, 2,864 meters), in the northwest of the country, to the southeast, crossing the coal-mining region. The Karavanke mountain range is located along the northern border. The region lying between the Mura, Drava, Savinja and Sava rivers is known for its vineyards and wine production. To the west and southwest of Ljubljana, all along the Soca river (known as 'Isonzo' on the Italian side), the climate is less continental, and more Mediterranean. The capital has an average annual temperature of 9° C, with an average of − 1° C in the winter and 19° C in summer. The country's main mineral resources are coal and mercury, which contribute to the country's high level of industrialization. Metal and chemical plants have caused serious pollution in the Sava river and the coast with heavy metals and toxic products, as well as deforestation, caused by acid rain.

SOCIETY

Peoples: Slovenian, 87.8 per cent; Serbs, 2.4 per cent; Croats, 2.8 per cent; Bosnian, 1.4 per cent. The Hungarian (0.4 per cent) and Italian (0.1 per cent) minorities are officially recognized. Significant German presence.
Religions: Christian-Catholics are a majority (83.6 per cent), including followers of traditional Catholic church of Slovenia; Christians from the Eastern Orthodox Church (16.4 per cent).
Languages: Slovenian (official), Serbo-Croatian, Hungarian, Italian, German, Czech, Romani.
Political Parties: Liberal Democracy of Slovenia (center-left, originally Communist Youth); List of Social Democrats of Slovenia. People's Party (rightist conservative); New Slovenia Christian People's Party (previously Demos, first opposition party to the Communist Party); Social Democratic Party (rightist). Minority parties: Democratic Party of Retired People of Slovenia; Party of the Slovenia Youth; Greens; Slovenian Republicans, National Party (far-right).
Social organizations: Two large trade unions, and an independent one, successor of the communist trade union (Association of Free Trade Unions).

THE STATE

Official Name: Republika Slovenija.
Administrative Divisions: 62 Districts.
Capital: Ljubljana 295,000 people (1999).
Other cities: Maribor 97,800 people; Celje 38,300; Kranj 35,500; Velenje 26,400 (2000).
Government: Milan Kucan, President since May 1990, re-elected in November 1997. Janez Drnovsek, Prime Minister since November 2000. Bicameral Legislature: the Assembly of Slovenia is formed by a 90-member State Chamber (two members elected by ethnic minorities) and a 40-member State Council.
National Holiday: June 25, Independence Day (1991).
Armed Forces: 9,550 (1996).
Other: 4,500 Police (1994).

Solomon Islands

Population:	479,000 (2002)
Land area:	27,990 SQ KM
Capital:	Honiara
Currency:	Solomon Is. dollar
Language:	English

Solomon Islands

The earliest known occupation of the Solomon Islands is circa 28000 BC by Australoid hunter-gatherers. The islanders developed a complex social organization based on the *wantok* or extended family system.

[2] The Spaniard Alvaro de Mendaña arrived in 1567, searching for *El Dorado* - land of gold. In the 18th and 19th centuries, the islands were used as a source of slave labor for the sugar plantations of Fiji and Australia.

[3] Solomon Islands was declared a British Protectorate in 1893. It was taken over by the Japanese in 1942. After World War II, the archipelago was recovered and divided in two. The northern part, some 14,000 sq km, was placed under Australian administration, and later annexed to Papua New Guinea.

[4] On May 21 1975, Britain agreed to independence claims. The Islands were granted internal autonomy in 1976, and independence was finally declared on July 7 1978.

[5] Solomon Mamaloni was elected Prime Minister in August 1981, after the Islands' parliament censured Kenilorea. He banned nuclear-powered ships and planes,

or those carrying nuclear weapons, from the Islands' territorial waters and air space.

[6] In the 1984 election, a coalition worked together to achieve the re-election of Kenilorea as Prime Minister. He patched up relations with the United States and in 1986, named Ezequiel Alebua as his successor. After taking office, Alebua followed Kenilorea's policies faithfully.

[7] In 1989, Mamaloni was re-elected Prime Minister.

[8] Francis Billy Hilly was elected Prime Minister in June 1994 but on October 31 was forced to step down after a vote of no confidence from Parliament. Billy Hilly denounced accusations that the logging industry was a source of government corruption. The new Prime Minister, Mamaloni, did not pursue the conservationist policy. In 1995, the Government ordered the felling of all the trees on Pavuvu island and its inhabitants were transferred to other islands.

[9] In September 1997 Bartholomew Ulufa'alu was appointed Prime Minister. The new government announced the nationalization of the logging industry and ordered an investigation into the use of development funds by the previous administration. In December, the national currency was devalued by 20 per cent and commodity prices rose.

[10] In the first half of 1999, long simmering disputes over land ownership and access to education, employment and economic development erupted into armed conflict around Honiara on Guadalcanal.

[11] The Isatabu Freedom Movement (IFM) - representing Guadalcanal interests - demanded compensation for the use of their land for the national capital and extensive areas of plantations. When the compensation payment was not forthcoming, the IFM forcibly evicted people squatting on their land and forced businesses to close. The group most affected were islanders from Malaita, who hold most of the jobs and who control the power structures. The Malaitans retaliated by forming a private army, the Malaita Eagle Force (MEF), which seized arms and gunboats from the SI Police Force. Prime Minister Ulufa'alu, a Malaitan, offered to pay over $500,000 to the Guadalcanal Provincial Government as compensation. However counter-claims for compensation by Malaitans have further confused the dispute.

[12] In May 2000, the MEF, supported by some members of the SI Police Force, took Prime Minister Ulufa'alu and other government officials hostage. Months later a peace agreement was signed between both militias at the end of year 3000. Australia and Aotearoa/New Zealand were appointed as supervisors of its compliance.

[13] In December 2001, Allan Kemakeza became Prime Minister, after being elected by Parliament. Australia warned it would not grant any economic aid until the islands achieved significant political stability (compliance with the law, restoring order), budgetary and economic reforms. ∎

PROFILE

ENVIRONMENT
Comprises most of the island group of the same name, except for those in the northwest which belong to Papua-New Guinea, the archipelago of Ontong Java (Lord Howe Atoll), the Rennell Islands and the Santa Cruz Islands. The Solomon Islands are part of Melanesia, east of New Guinea. The major islands, of volcanic origin, are: Guadalcanal (with the capital Honiara), Malaita, Florida, New Georgia, Choiseul, Ysabel and Makira. The land is mountainous and there are several active volcanoes. Fishing and subsistence agriculture are the traditional economic activities. Ninety per cent of Solomon Islanders live as subsistence farmers in village communities of 100 to 1,000 people. Deforestation is severe. Heavy rains cause soil erosion, particularly in exposed areas.

SOCIETY
Peoples: Most of the population is of Melanesian origin (94 per cent). There are also Polynesians (4 per cent), Micronesians (1.4 per cent) and some Chinese and Europeans. **Religions:** Christian 96.7 per cent, of which Protestant account for 77.5 per cent and Roman Catholic for 19.2 per cent; Baha'i 0.4 per cent; traditional beliefs 0.2 per cent; other and no religion 2.7 per cent. **Languages:** English (official), pidgin (local language derived from English) and over 80 local languages and dialects. **Political Parties:** People's Action Party; Association of Independent Members; Solomon

Islands Alliance for Change; People's Progressive Party; Labor Party. **Social Organizations:** The Solomon Islands Council of Trade Unions (SICTU), formed in 1986, made up of 6 trade unions.

THE STATE
Official Name: Solomon Islands.
Administrative Divisions: 8 provinces and the capital.
Capital: Honiara 68,000 people (1999).
Other cities: Gizo 7,000 people; Auki 5,000; Kira Kira 3,800; Buala 3,000 (2000).
Government: Queen Elizabeth II, Head of State; John Lapli, Governor-General since July 1999, appointed by the British Government. Allan Kemakeza, Prime Minister since December 2001. The National Parliament, has 50 members for a four-year term.
National Holiday: July 7, Independence Day (1978).

DEMOGRAPHY
Urban population: 19.7 % (2000)
Children per woman: 5.5 (2000)

HEALTH
Life expectancy at birth: 69 years (2000-2005)
Maternal mortality: 550 per 100,000 live births (1985/99)
Infant mortality: 21 per 1,000 (2000)
Under-5 child mortality: 25 per 1,000 (2000)
Safe water: 71 % (2000)

Somalia

Population: 9,557,000 (2002)
Land area: 627,340 SQ KM
Capital: Mogadishu (Muqdisho)
Currency: Shilling
Language: Somali and Arabic

Soomaaliya

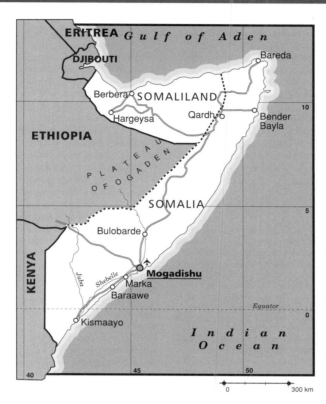

The region of Somalia, called 'Puntland' by the Egyptians thousands of years ago, was an Egyptian trading partner. Centuries later, the Romans called it 'the land of aroma' because of the incense produced there.

[2] This ancient commercial tradition took on new dimensions from the eighth century when Arab refugees founded a series of commercial settlements on the coast.

[3] In the 13th century, Islamicized and led by Yemeni immigrants, Somalis founded a state which they called Ifat, with its principal center in Zeila. Tribute was initially paid to the Ethiopian Empire but Ifat quickly entered into conflict with the Abyssinians and succeeded in consolidating its independence. New territories were annexed and a new name adopted: the Sultanate of Adal.

[4] Ties established with Arab markets and the southern part of the coast of Zandj contributed to develop intense commercial activity. At the same time, the sultans tried to enlarge their dominion, at the expense of unstable Ethiopian Empire.

[5] However, it was not until 1541 that the Portuguese Government, having acquired a clearer knowledge of Indian Ocean trade, sent its fleet. Backed up by the Ethiopian army, the latter razed the city of Zeila, going on to destroy Mogadishu (Muqdisho), Berbera and Brava.

[6] The Portuguese destroyed but did not occupy the area, though the presence of their armada hindered economic reconstruction. Adal declined, and was divided into a series of minor sultanates, the northern ones controlled by the Ottoman Empire, while the ones in the south accepted the sovereignty of the Sultan of Zanzibar after the expulsion of the Portuguese in 1698.

[7] The Suez Canal gave new strategic value to the region. In 1862, the French bought the port of Obock, leading to the creation of present-day Djibouti and in 1869 the Italians settled in Aseb and later extended their control over Eritrea. In 1885 the British, who had already occupied Aden on the Arabian peninsula, took the Egyptian settlements in Zeila and Berbera. In 1906, in compensation for their

defeat in Ethiopia, the Italians obtained Somalia's southern coast.

[8] The British colony was the leading center of resistance to foreign domination. Sheikh Muhammad bin Abdullah Hassan organized an Islamic revolutionary movement, which defeated the British troops on four occasions between 1900 and 1904. The British finally gained control of the territory in 1920.

[9] On July 1 1960, with decolonization in Africa underway, the British and Italian regions became independent and were merged as the Republic of Somalia. The new republic adopted a parliamentary system, until October 21 1969, when a group of officers led by General Said Barre seized power and proclaimed a socialist regime.

[10] In July 1976, the Front for the Liberation of Western Somalia initiated a military offensive in the Ogaden supported by the Somali Government. The invasion was repelled by the Ethiopian army, supported by Cuban troops and backed by most African nations

who opposed changes in colonial frontiers. The country broke off relations with Cuba and ended its military agreements with the Soviet Union.

[11] The war against Ethiopia caused serious difficulties to Somalia's fragile economy; prices of fuel and grain increased and a severe drought affected most of the country in 1978-79 bringing the Barre Government to the brink of collapse. A group of army officers unsuccessfully attempted to overthrow the government in April 1978. In October 1980 Barre declared a state of emergency and reinstated the Supreme Revolutionary Council, which had ceased functioning in 1976.

[12] Although the northeastern province of Kenya was historically been claimed by Somalia, relations with Kenya improved, through commercial and technical cooperation agreements.

[13] Problems with Ethiopia recurred sporadically because of the dispute over the Ogaden plains and the steady flow of Ethiopian

refugees into Somali camps. In 1988 alone the number of refugees was estimated at 840,000.

[14] Said Barre was re-elected in December 1986 by 99 per cent of the vote. In February 1989, he sent Prime Minister Ali Samater to London and Washington, to announce the amnesty and commuting of sentences for 400 political prisoners.

[15] Western credits and investments were drastically reduced and exports to Saudi Arabia, the principal market for its cattle, stopped almost completely.

[16] In January 1991, the opposition formed the United Somali Congress (USC) and ousted the President, replacing him with Ali Mahdi Mohammed, leader of the USC and representing business interests.

[17] After bloody confrontations between the two factions of the USC, President Mahdi fled Mogadishu in November 1991. The capital remained in the hands of General Mohamed Farah Aideed, leader of the military wing of the USC.

[18] The two rival factions of the United Somali Congress were made up of members of different sub-groups of the Hawiye clan, led by Farah Aideed and Ali Mahdi, respectively.

[19] Since the beginning of the war between the rival clans, 300,000 Somali children died, and 1.5 million inhabitants - a quarter of the total population - left the country.

[20] On March 9 1991, taking advantage of a cease-fire, 100,000 women and children held a peaceful march through Mogadishu. Nine leaders of the Hiraan region met to discuss how to bring about peace in their country. It was the first meeting of *ugas* or kings in more than a hundred years.

[21] In 1993, after two years of civil war and anarchy, Somalia still had no central governmental structures. The traditional authorities, unable to handle the unprecedented conditions, had abandoned their normal functions, leaving clans and sub-clans unrestrained. In some regions, though, the local population still respected the traditional authority of the tribal elders. However, in the vacuum created by the absence of central administration, power remained in

the hands of the warlords and of heavily armed bands of looters.

22 Under pressure from the US, in 1992 the UN sent 28,000 troops to assist. This was the first time the world organization had intervened militarily in the internal affairs of a nation.

23 The Republic of Somaliland broke away from Somalia and declared independence in 1992. The fledgling republic - comprising about 30 per cent of Somalia's territory - was not officially recognized. The port of Berbere, on the Gulf of Aden, formed its economic base. With the economy in ruins, it sheltered a million people displaced from the southern zone (Somalia).

24 Divided and without international recognition, the Republic of Somaliland continued to function in 1995. In the rest of the country the factions regrouped around the Somali Salvation Alliance

(SSA), led by Ali Mahdi Mohammed, and the SNA, led by Farah Aideed, both claiming the government. Farah Aidid died in August 1996 and was succeeded by his son, Hussein. Farah's former right-hand, Osman Hassan Ali ('Ato'), emerged as a new force, though associated with Ali Mahdi.

25 In January 1997 in Sodere, Ethiopia, 26 political leaders affiliated with the SSA, with the support of the Organization of African Unity, decided to establish a National Salvation Council with authority to organize a transition government. Hussein Aideed and Mohammed Ibrahim Egal, re-elected President of Somaliland in March, refused to recognize the decision.

26 With the aim of forming a new administration called Puntland, in June 1998 a conference of 300 northeastern leaders in the Garowe district elected Colonel Abdullah Yussuf Ahmed as President and

Mohammed Abdi Hashi as Vice-President. Puntland would include the Garowe, Bari and Galkayo areas, where the economies are based on cattle raising. The nominal founding leaders considered Garowe a possible capital.

27 In August 2000, a peace conference in Djibouti, involving several factions, elected the 245 members of Parliament, which continued functioning in exile, and chose Abdulkasim Salat Hassan - a minister in the Baré regime - as the new President. Hassan arrived in Mogadishu under heavy guard and was received by tens of thousands of people who gathered at a football stadium. In October, the new Prime Minister, Ali Khalif Galaydh, announced his Cabinet of 25 ministers, all men and representing the various Somali clans, which he called a 'reconciliation government'.

28 Like 17 other sub-Saharan African countries, Somalia faces repeated food emergencies caused by adverse climate conditions, the persistence of civil conflict and crime, according to a 2001 report by the UN Food and Agriculture Organization (FAO). Grain crops failed due to lack of rainfall, which caused prices to skyrocket, undermining the purchase power of much of the population.

29 In May a referendum on the separation of Somaliland resulted in overwhelming support for independence. Egal stated that Somaliland was no longer 'a group of clans, but rather a nation with its own laws'. The country still lacked recognition from the international community.

30 In late 2001, Barakaat, the largest corporation in Somalia, appeared on a list of businesses and individuals accused by the US of transferring money to the Bin Laden terrorist network. Washington was able to freeze a large portion of the telecommunications company's business in Somalia, Europe and the Arab world. A senior UN official warned the US in early 2002 that its efforts to shut down Somali companies allegedly linked to terrorism was aggravating Somalia's already desperate situation. The country is on the verge of total economic collapse due to conflict, prolonged drought and the ban on exporting livestock.

31 Eighteen months after taking power in Mogadishu, the provisional government had serious difficulty controlling the military warlords and their heavily-armed militias and confronting drought-related problems. The Government's attempts to establish its authority had disparate results due to the persistence of militarily powerful factions in various parts of the country and the ease with which the

warlords shifted loyalties. The central Government maintains authority in a few sectors of Mogadishu.

32 In March 2002, the UN Security Council began work on an initiative for launching an arms embargo against Somalia that had been signed a decade earlier. The proposal calls for the UN to appoint a panel of experts to monitor violations committed in the country.

33 Somaliland's leader Mohammed Egal had just had his term of office extended for another year in a final bid to secure the international recognition he craved when he died in a hospital in South Africa, in May. Dahir Riyale Kahin was sworn in as new president. Analysts and the government of Somaliland feared that after a decade of relative stability, the death of Egal could prompt old rivalries to re-emerge. ■

PROFILE

ENVIRONMENT

Somalia is a semi-desert country with a large population of nomads. The north is mountainous, descending gradually from the Galia-Somali plateau to the coastal strip bathed by the Gulf of Aden. The south is almost entirely desert with the exception of a fertile area crossed by two rivers originating in Ethiopia, the Juba and Shebeli. Drought, endemic in this region, has been exacerbated by overgrazing. Important banana, soy and maize production. Cyclical droughts, with the effects of the most recent worsened by over-grazing. A sharp increase in livestock triggered a desertification process. Fishing using explosives has damaged coral reefs and aquatic vegetation. The destruction of habitat of several fish species could threaten future catches. There are 74 threatened species in Somalia, including mammals, plants and birds. Serious levels of water contamination.

SOCIETY

Peoples: Somalis are Hamitic and their largest ethnic groups (Hawiye, Darod, Issaq, Dir and Digil-Mirifle) have a cultural and linguistic unity that is uncommon in Africa. Arabs and Bantu-speaking Africans (descendents of slaves). Italian minority.
Religions: Islam (official), mostly orthodox Sunni. There are a few Christians in Mogadishu.
Languages: Somali (a language without an alphabet until 1973, when it was adapted to the Latin alphabet) and Arabic, both official. English and Italian are spoken (a colonial legacy), as is Swahili.
Political Parties: There is confrontation between rival factions of the various clans. Major groupings of clans include the United Somali Congress (USC), the Somali Salvation Front (SSF) and the Somali National Alliance (SNA). The United Somali Congress (USC), created in 1991, led by Osman Ali Atto. The Somali National Alliance (SNA), made up of Said Barre's former troops, (formerly loyal to Farah Aideed, but ousted him in 1995). The USC and SNA then formed an alliance. The Somali Salvation Alliance (SSA), Ali Mahdi Mohammed's party. The Somali Patriotic Movement (SPM, Darod clan). The Somali Salvation Democratic Front (SSDF, Majertein clan) in the south. The Somali Democratic Alliance (SDA, Gadabursi clan) and the United Somali Front (USF, Issa clan) in the north.
Social Organizations: The General Federation of Somali Trade Unions, created in 1977 and controlled by the Government. Armed groups and also civil associations such as CEPADO (Somali Organization for the Defense of Nature and Against Deforestation).

THE STATE

Official Name: Jamhuriaydda Soomaaliya.
Administrative divisions: Somalia is divided into 18 regions or provinces. The northern part of the country declared itself independent as the Republic of Somaliland. **Capital:** Mogadishu 1,162,000 people (1999).
Government: Abdiqasim Salad Hassan, President and Hassan Abshir Farah, Prime Minister since November 2001. Since November 1991 there are no effective and recognized governmental structures.
National Holiday: July 1, Independence Day (1960).
Armed Forces: Regular armed forces have not existed since rebel forces ousted the Government in 1991.

South Africa

Population: 44,203,000 (2002)
Land area: 1,221,040 SQ KM
Capital: Pretoria
Currency: Rand
Language: Afrikaans, English + 9 African languages

South Africa

For most of the past 100,000 years, the territory of present-day South Africa has been occupied by the San, small mobile groups of hunting and gathering people who expressed their beliefs, rituals and activities in richly abundant rock art. They were gradually displaced by the Khoikhoi, agro-pastoralists whose presence goes back 2,000 years. About 1,500 years ago, immigrant Bantu-speakers began to work the soil, mainly in the river valleys of south-eastern Africa where summer rainfall predominates. Techniques first learnt further north came to be applied to the growing of edible crops such as millet and squash.

[2] Domestication of cattle created new possibilities as societal and political systems arose. The Bantu-speaking chiefs expanded their power through control of their women as producers, and the youth as workers and soldiers. Wealth in cattle made patronage possible, and was also used as *lobola*, bride-price, by the bridegroom's people to the father or guardian of the bride. Metallurgical skills gave the chiefs an additional valuable trading commodity and greater military potential.

[3] The first Dutch settlers arrived at Cape Town in 1652, more than 150 years after the Portuguese sailor Vasco de Gama rounded the Cape of Good Hope. The Portuguese, more interested in India, showed little desire to confront the Khoikhoi peoples who had been in the region for more than a thousand years and were hostile to the foreigners.

[4] Jan van Riebeeck was the first of the Dutch to challenge the Khoikhoi. He landed in Cape Town and established a colony providing crops and livestock to supply ships on their way to Indonesia. In 1688, nearly 600 farmers had settled there, dividing their energies between farming and the war against the Khoikhoi. Being such a small minority, the first Dutch colonists were fiercely united and aggressive, two characteristics which pervaded *boer* (farmer) society in southern Africa.

[5] The Dutch were not typical colonists. They worked for the Dutch East India Company (VOC), were not allowed to trade with the local people and had to deliver all their production to the Company's ships.

They gradually came into conflict with their overseas bosses, who would not loosen the grip of their monopoly. The Dutch won the dispute, and towards the end of the 17th century the so-called free colonists or burghers were in the majority. The population of European origin split: some continued to be linked to foreign trade and others moved inland in search of new lands.

[6] In 1806, with the Dutch colonial empire on the wane, the British settled in Cape Town. They moved ahead on agreements to trade goods, incorporated the African leaders into intermediaries and end slavery. This rapidly led to conflict with the intransigent Boers, who had begun calling themselves Afrikaners, to distinguish themselves from the more recent colonists. In 1834, nearly 14,000 of them emigrated to the interior, starting the Great Trek which would take them to what became Transvaal, the Orange Free State and Natal (now the provinces of Gauteng, Free State and KwaZulu-Natal). They established the state of Transvaal in 1852 and the Orange Free State in 1854. These regions were already occupied by African people who fiercely resisted the new settlers.

[7] The British recognized the independence of the two regions, as

the settling of new lands by Europeans contributed to Cape Town's security. In their expansion northward, the Afrikaners confronted Xhosas and Zulus. The latter had earlier been led by military genius Shaka, who died in 1828. The resistance blocked the colonists' advance over a period of 50 years. The great empire of the Zulus collapsed shortly before the Great Trek, due to internal strife over royal succession.

[8] Conflict between the Boers and the British Crown erupted in the late 19th century when rich gold and diamond fields were discovered in the interior. Realization that the region great economic and strategic value induced Britain to propose a federation between the Cape Colony the Transvaal (the South African Republic) and the Orange Free State. The Boers rejected the idea and war broke out in 1899. Britain was supported by most of its colonies, while the Boers had German backing. After three years of war, with nearly 50,000 Afrikaners dead and double that number confined to concentration camps, the Boers surrendered, accepting British domination, while maintaining a certain independence for its regions. The British victory in the Boer or South African War in 1902 signaled the end of the hegemony of landed

Boer farmers in the Orange Free State and Transvaal and the beginning of mining's importance in the economy.

[9] For some Boers, the African peoples were 'savages' who had to be forcibly tamed. White supremacy and racial segregation were established to justify the subjugation of the black population and to guarantee a supply of cheap farm labor from tenants. Boer farms in the interior were backward and unprofitable compared with the farming practiced in the Cape and Natal.

[10] The British focus on trade and liberalism led them to consider slavery a restraint on the creation of consumer markets. This did not prevent them from erecting rigid barriers to exclude black South Africans from economic and social advancement. The labor legislation from 1809 imposed severe controls on worker mobility. With the 1843 Master and Servant Act, along with later decrees, made it a criminal act to break a work contract.

[11] In the 19th century, the British also contracted black workers in the territories of present-day Mozambique, Lesotho, Botswana, as well as Indians and Chinese. These 'imported' workers were not allowed to bring their families; pay was poor and they had to return to their own countries if they lost their jobs.

[12] Both in the Cape and Natal hut and poll taxes were introduced, designed to force Africans to work for a salary far lower than that paid to those of European origin. Another law applied to peasants: an annual tax, paid in cash, which they could only get by selling their produce to the Europeans. This destroyed the traditional African ways of life and at the same time salaries could be kept low.

[13] When the gold and diamond mines began to be exploited, the European capitalists had to employ qualified white workers. Most of them were former Boer farmers who had lost everything in the war. Others came from Europe attracted by the 'gold fever'. Both of these groups, used to the workings of the industrial capitalist system, made demands for better pay and conditions. The mining companies promised benefits to these white

workers as long as they fell in with the exploitation of the black workforce.

[14] In 1896, the so-called color bar was in place in the mining sector and in the urban centers where the British were in the majority. In 1910, the Constitution of the Union of South Africa - a federation of Cape Province, Natal, the Orange Free State and Transvaal - deprived most black people of the right to vote or to own land.

[15] From 1910, the segregationist legislation increased. The Native Labor Act pushed urban workers into a system of submission similar to that operating on rural estates. The 1913 Native's Land Act, earmarked 7 per cent of national territory for the blacks as reserves which became home to 35-40 per cent of the population. Much of the remaining land was reserved for whites who only made up 20 per cent of the population. In the overcrowded black reservations subsistence agriculture was the main activity. The rest, under white control, was intensively farmed with the reserves providing a permanent source of cheap labor. The 1923 Native Urban Act, tightly regulated blacks' lives in cities which were considered white strongholds.

[16] Until 1984, political participation was limited very largely to whites. Most black Africans, almost two thirds of the population, were denied the right to vote. Constitutional Reform in 1984 extended the vote to the Asians - mainly Indians - and the 'Colored' or mixed race groups.

[17] At the outset of World War I, the white economy was based on mining and intensive agriculture. The post-war recession pushed the large mining companies into hiring blacks, which led to racial confrontations within the work force. The Rand strike in 1922 was harshly put down by the Government. Most of the strikers were poor whites, descendants of both English and Boers. Frustrated by their defeat in the war and the loss of their lands, with no easy way of entering the nascent industrial structure, Afrikaners were attracted by the ultra-nationalist propaganda of the far Right.

[18] The Nationalists, triumphant in the 1924 elections along with their English-speaking allies, broke with the traditional liberal economic policy and imposed protectionism. State capitalism promoted by the Nationalists - with steel works, railways and electricity - made rapid national growth possible, something many saw as an 'economic miracle'.

[19] Toward the end of the 1920s the falling gold price on the international market forced the

Nationalists into another alliance. They joined forces with traditionally despised foreign capital and maintained the racial segregation system which guaranteed cheap workers. The ensuing industrial take-off brought with it an increased number of blacks employed in industry and this led to racial conflict. A secret society, the Afrikaner Broeder Bond - Brotherhood - became the bastion of white right-wing politics.

[20] The recession following World War II led to a repeat of events: poor whites, threatened by unemployment, rebelled. Racism flourished under the slogan 'Gevaar KKK' (Beware blacks, Indians and communism - Kafir, Koelie, Komunism). In 1948, the Nationalists formed a government by themselves and imposed even harsher restrictions on the black population.

[21] The first national political organization of South African blacks had appeared in 1912. The African National Congress (ANC) was created by a group of former students from schools run by missionaries. Among its founders were also people who had studied or gained degrees in North American and European universities. They believed the Afrikaners could be persuaded of the unfairness of the racial segregation laws and that the Anglophile liberals would allow blacks to participate in politics. Their hopes were dashed in 1920 when the black mine workers strike was crushed and segregation entrenched.

[22] In the 1940s the ANC adopted a strategy of non-violent resistance to the race laws. In 1955, the anti-racist front was broadened with the Freedom Charter, proclaimed at a multiracial gathering in Kliptown. The Charter included a radical denunciation of *apartheid* (separateness) and called for its abolition, along with wealth redistribution.

[23] In 1958, sectors of the ANC that disagreed with the its multiracial policy created the Pan African Congress (PAC), which in 1960 held a demonstration in the city of Sharpeville to protest against the pass law that restricted the movement of black workers in areas reserved for whites. The march was brutally repressed, leaving 70 dead.

[24] Following this incident, the PAC, ANC and the Communist Party were all outlawed. The African National Congress (ANC) formed an armed group, the Umkhonto we Sizwe (Spear of the Nation), while the PAC set up another, Poqo (Only Us). In 1963, the main leaders of the ANC were arrested; Nelson Mandela was sentenced to life imprisonment and Oliver Tambo, in exile, took over leadership of the movement. The

Government's repressive violence and the lack of supply bases in neighboring countries - dominated by regimes allied to the Afrikaners - prevented the guerillas from making progress necessary to attract greater numbers of recruits.

[25] The racist system was largely upheld by the interests of international capitalism in the region, attracted by the great pool of cheap labor. Foreign investments, especially from the US, increased five times in value between 1958 and 1967. The Afrikaners' protectionist policies created the infrastructure necessary for large industries to be set up, with the aim of developing an industrial center capable of supplying all southern Africa.

[26] The 1960s saw an increasing flow of rural workers to the cities fuelled by the poverty of the 'Homelands' or Bantustans, some with poor quality soils, and the lack of social services. This population movement affected the expectations of other urban sectors, such as the Coloured people, who saw their hopes of integration into the white economy threatened.

[27] In 1976, the black community in the suburbs of Johannesburg erupted. The youth rebellion in Soweto - the South West Township - made the whites realize the crisis had reached their own cities where they had previously felt safe. In 1970, 75 per cent of workers in agriculture, mining or the services were black, and the participation of non-whites in specialized jobs had tripled over the last 20 years though blacks earned 5-10 times less than whites for the same work.

[28] The Pretoria regime declared four Bantustans - Transkei, Ciskei, Venda and Bophuthatswana - as 'independent states' in an effort to prevent the internal migration of the unemployed. Eight million people were thus deprived of their South African nationality and converted into foreigners by decree. However very few countries recognized these newly 'independent states'.

[29] The independence of Angola and Mozambique in 1975 and that of Zimbabwe in 1980 radically changed the situation in southern Africa. The ANC found in these countries the support bases it desperately needed - and in the other Frontline states of Botswana, Tanzania and Zambia. South Africa, with an economy three times bigger than that of those independent countries combined, initiated a destabilization campaign which included economic pressure, sabotage, support for rebel movements and invasion. All this to force the Frontline states to deny support to the anti-apartheid movement and the block attempts

by the newly independent countries to escape South African domination.

[30] One of the main arenas of the conflict in southern Africa was in Namibia, a former German colony which South Africa occupied during World War I and later annexed. In 1966, the UN ruled that South Africa had to grant Namibia its independence - a demand which the Organization of African Unity (OAU) and Frontline countries continued to make, despite the delaying tactics of South Africa and the Western powers. It took until March 21 1990 for Namibia to become independent.

[31] The support received from the US and Europe was crucial for South Africa in imposing its economic and military strength on southern Africa. Approximately 400 US companies had interests in the country, and US capital and technology were vital for the developing its industrial and military might.

[32] On the domestic front, PW Botha, Prime Minister from 1978 to 1989, began reforming to the apartheid system. Between 1982 and 1984, he brought in constitutional reform granting the vote to Indians and colored people and creating two more chambers in parliament for these groups. Blacks were still excluded, with their participation limited to a local level. Many non-whites boycotted the reform, abstaining from voting.

[33] The gradual liberalization of apartheid was widely opposed. Repression against blacks did not diminish; it was merely complicated by inter-ethnic confrontations. In July 1985, the Government declared a state of emergency in 36 districts. By the end of 1986, more than 750 had died and several thousands of the Government's opponents were in prison.

[34] Pressure from public opinion in the US and Europe forced Western governments and an increasing number of companies and banks to limit their activities in South Africa. The US Congress lifted the veto imposed by President Reagan on economic sanctions, forcing a change in its policy of constructive engagement. Within South Africa, political opposition led to the creation of the United Democratic Front (UDF) which brought together more than 600 organizations working together within the law.

[35] From early 1988 the Botha Government came down more heavily on the opposition, outlawing all the constituent groups and detaining religious leaders opposed to apartheid, including Archbishop Desmond Tutu, Nobel Peace Prize winner.

[36] In August 1989, cornered by an internal crisis in his party Botha resigned. He was replaced by FW De

Klerk, who was aware of the need to change South Africa's racist image. In September, parliamentary elections were held under the State of Emergency which had been operating since 1986.

[37] The Mass Democratic Movement (MDM), an anti-apartheid coalition of legal organizations, called a general strike. Despite police raids and threats, three million black South Africans stopped work in the largest protest ever held there. The growing momentum was accompanied by repression and killings. But by now an increasing number of the white minority was joining the protests.

[38] The opposition met in the University of the Witwatersrand (Johannesburg) for a Conference for a Democratic Future in December 1989, agreeing to establish the principle of 'one person, one vote' for any negotiations with the Government.

[39] In February 1990, De Klerk legalized the ANC and other opposition groups. Nelson Mandela was released on February 11 after 27 years in prison. A period of negotiations began. Mandela took back his role as leader of the black majority, a post not without its difficulties. Some were related to confrontations - which caused 5,000 deaths since 1986 - between the ANC and members of the Zulu Inkatha movement. Inkatha had government backing in arms, funds and training.

[40] In May, Mandela announced an agreement between the ANC and the Government in order to bring an end to the violence and bring political life back to normal. He called on the international community to maintain economic sanctions and other forms of pressure on the South African Government. The Government renounced its policy of creating Bantustans - it had set up ten so far - and abolished racial segregation in hospitals. In December ANC president Oliver Tambo returned to the country after more than 30 years of exile.

[41] In April 1991, the European Community (EC) considered lifting the economic blockade and set June 30 as the deadline for starting democratization. The same day, the Government abolished the Population Registration Act and the Land Acts, which had prevented blacks from owning land. De Klerk also promised to begin negotiations for a new Constitution. The US went ahead and lifted the blockade. The EC planned to do the same, but Denmark and Spain, which had received a visit from Mandela, vetoed the move.

[42] In 1993 the Inkatha Freedom Party (IFP), the Afrikaner National Front (NFA) and the Conservative Party left negotiations on the Constitution and decided to abandon boycott the electoral process. Bophuthatswana president Lucas Mangope - in the midst of a strike by public employees - declared he would join the boycott and received military support from the ultra-right Afrikaner Resistance Movement (AWB). The resistance of black civilians and local forces obliged them to withdraw. Mangope was deposed and the South African army took control.

[43] Meanwhile Inkatha boycotted ANC activities and clashed with Mandela's supporters. Buthelezi finally agreed to participate in the elections after the constitution finally recognized his nephew Goodwill Zwelethini as king of the Zulus.

[44] In October, the UN lifted sanctions against the South African regime. The United States immediately withdrew its financial restrictions.

[45] The provisional Constitution created a 400-seat National Assembly and a Senate with 90 members. The President would be elected by the Assembly for a 5-year term. The country was newly divided into nine provinces, each with a governor and legislature, absorbing the ten abolished Bantustans.

[46] The first multiracial elections in South Africa were held between April 26-29 1994. Some 87 per cent of registered voters turned out. The ANC won 63 per cent of the vote, De Klerk's NP 20 per cent and Inkatha 10 per cent. The right, the Freedom Front, came in with 2 per cent.

[47] The Government of National Unity (GNU) included members of the NP and IFP. The minister of finance and the governor of the South African Reserve Bank from the previous government kept their posts.

[48] Despite the removal of the barriers of apartheid, economic and cultural obstacles remained. Black workers earned nine times less than whites and unemployment was 33 per cent and 3 per cent respectively. The overall infant mortality is 50 per 1,000 lives births (1998) but the rate for blacks is far higher.

[49] The May 1994 constitution was radical in tone. Among the measures to be applied at the beginning of his term, Mandela proposed free health care for children aged under six and for pregnant women, a basic diet for schoolchildren and the provision of electricity to 350,000 homes. New legal education guidelines were established. In October it was announced that 3.5 million people would be given access to water services over the next 18 months. The first GNU budget gave 47 per cent to social services, education took 26 per cent, investment in housing doubled and military spending was reduced.

[50] Ambitious land reform was implemented by Land Affairs Minister Derek Hanekom, a farmer. A labor relations act was approved, guaranteeing the right to strike. There were far fewer strikes than in previous years.

[51] In January, the ANC withdrew immunity guaranteed before the elections to two former cabinet ministers and 3,500 police officers who were to be investigated by the Truth and Reconciliation Committee (TRC). The trial of a former police colonel for 121 murders, kidnappings and frauds, provided new evidence of police incitement of political violence during the former regime. Prominent Inkatha leaders appeared implicated in payments made to the security police. A report by the Goldstone Commission was presented to De Klerk in 1994, listing these charges. In June, the under-secretary of the IFP was arrested for murders committed in 1987.

[52] The local elections of November 1995 favored the ANC throughout the country. In May 1996, the NP left the Government to join the opposition, for the first time since 1948.

[53] The National Assembly approved a new Constitution which, in the Government's opinion consolidated the transition to democracy. During the production of the new text, demonstrations attended by thousands of workers and businesspeople led to the elimination of a clause in the final text which gave the bosses the right to close their factories.

PROFILE

ENVIRONMENT

Located on the southern tip of the African continent, with a coastline on the Indian and Atlantic Oceans, South Africa has several geographic zones. A narrow strip of lowland lies along the east coast, with a hot and humid climate, large sugarcane plantations. In the Cape region are vineyards and fynbos vegetation. The vast semi-arid and arid Karoo, with cattle and sheep ranching, makes up over 40 per cent of the total territory, extending inland. The Highveld extends to the north and is the richest arable area. It surrounds the Witwatersrand, a mining area in Gauteng (former Transvaal) where large cities and industries are found. The country's economic base lies in the exploitation of mineral resources: South Africa is the world's largest producer of gold and diamonds; the second largest producer of manganese; and the eighth largest producer of coal. The country's water resources are overtaxed, salinization is the main threat in dry areas. Soil erosion is a serious problem, particularly in the former Bantustans (homelands). High levels of acid rain.

SOCIETY

Peoples: Over 76 per cent of the population is of African origin, of which Zulu 22 per cent, Xhosa 18 per cent, Pedi 9 per cent, Sotho 7 per cent, Tswana 7 per cent, Tsonga 3.5 per cent, Swazi 3 per cent, Ndebele 2 per cent, and Venda 2 per cent. There are also descendants of whites, slaves and Khoisan, called 'Colored'. European descendants account for 13 per cent of the total. Asian groups, predominantly Hindu, make up less than 3 per cent.
Religions: Christianity predominant (68 per cent) including African independent churches. African beliefs (28 per cent); Islam (2 per cent).
Languages: 11 official languages: Afrikaans, English, isi Ndebele, Sepedi, Sesotho, siSwati, Xitsonga, Setswana, Tshivenda, isi Xhosa, isi Zulu.
Political Parties: African National Congress (ANC), which includes the South African Communist Party; Democratic Alliance (DA); United Democratic Movement (UDM); Inkatha Freedom Party (IFP); African Christian Democratic Party; New National Party (NNP); Pan African Congress of Azania (PAC), leftist; African Muslim Party (AMP); Dikwankwetla Party; Federal Party (FP); Minority Front (MF); Democratic Alliance.
Social Organizations: South African Students' Congress (SASCO), the Congress of South African Trade Unions (COSATU), the National Congress of Trade Unions. Azanian Peoples Organization, advocating black identity.

THE STATE

Official Name: Republic of South Africa.
Administrative Divisions: 9 provinces.
Capital: Pretoria (administrative) 1,475,000 people; Cape Town (legislative) 3,033,200 (1999); Bloemfontein (judicial).
Other cities: Johannesburg 4,927,200 people; Durban 2,314,100; Port Elizabeth 1,029,400 (2000).
Government: Thabo Mbeki, President since June 1999. Bicameral Legislature: the National Assembly, with 400 members, and the National Council of Provinces, with 90 members.
National Holiday: 27 April, Freedom Day (1994).
Armed Forces: 136,900 (1995).

54 In 1996 the Truth and Reconciliation Commission was set up, under the presidency of former Archbishop Desmond Tutu, and began to collect evidence of human rights violations committed between 1960 and 1993. The investigations uncovered many crimes. Several police officers admitted the use of torture in the 1980s and the hiring of mercenaries. Those responsible were offered an amnesty provided they clarified their part in the events.

55 The Government announced a new macro-economic strategy aimed at creating 800,000 jobs by the year 2000. Throughout 1996, GDP grew 3 per cent. By the end of November, some two million hectares of land had been redistributed under the Government agrarian reform program.

56 In October 1997, Mandela visited Libya to mediate in the conflict between Tripoli, Washington and London over the 1992 embargo against Libya resulting from the Lockerbie airplane bombing (see Libya). Mandela said he supported Libya's stance in calling for a trial in a neutral country, although he made it clear he did not back the unconditional lifting of the embargo.

57 During his June 1998 farewell message at the Organization of African Unity, Mandela demanded 'the right and the duty to intervene whenever behind sovereign borders people are being massacred to protect tyranny'. These statements contradicted the founding principle of the OAU of non-intervention in the internal affairs of member countries.

58 That year, during hearings of the Truth and Reconciliation Commission, it emerged that there had been a plan by apartheid scientists to undermine Mandela's health when he was imprisoned. The plan also included the development of fertility-inhibiting chemical agents and also diseases which would attack the black population.

59 Attacks against white farmers returned as the black population began to express its anger over the slow changes. During the ANC congress, Mandela and his deputy, Thabo Mbeki, warned that the formal reconciliation era would come to an end with the end of Mandela's term of office. A second ANC government would take tougher measures to improve the lives of the millions of black people marginalized by the apartheid regime.

60 Although the June 1999 elections gave the ANC solid control of Parliament, it did not reach the two-thirds needed to unilaterally amend the constitution. The opposition leadership in the National Assembly fell into the hands of the mainly white Democratic Party (DP). Thabo Mbeki became the new

President and appointed Jacob Zuma, also ANC, as deputy President.

61 Although main forms of discrimination had been constitutionally banned since 1994, a new law approved by Parliament on January 2000 implemented, for the first time, non-discrimination in relations between individuals. The law also prohibited all discrimination based on age, sexual orientation, culture, pregnancy, marital status, conscience and language.

62 Since 1994 South Africa had announced restriction policies in the export and import of weapons, and was one of the world leaders in the implementation of the Convention on the Ban, Use, Storage, Production and Transfer of anti-Personnel Mines and their Destruction in 1997. Despite this, a report by Human Rights Watch in October 2000 accused Pretoria of selling weapons to countries with human rights abuses and where the flow of arms could imply an increase of such abuse. In May 2001 a South African government panel began hearings to investigate accusations of corruption in a weapons deal which had involved Pretoria with British, German, French, Swedish and South African firms. The panel concluded its investigations in November and freed the government of any responsibility.

63 Reacting to an official who said the Indian community was unable to carry out certain responsibilities, in early 2001 Mandela accused members of the black majority of using his political power to frighten ethnic minorities and urged the ANC to take steps to change the situation.

64 In September 2001, the World Conference Against Racism took place in Durban. The meeting was marked by disagreements between those countries present and those that boycotted the event, such as the US and Israel, which refused to discuss whether the oppression by the Jewish state of the Palestinian people is discrimination or not. Another conflictual issue was the demand of African countries or economic reparation by the former colonizing countries. Most of the European states, which at first had been in favor of apologizing for the slave trade, later considered the demand 'unreasonable'.

65 Between 5 and 7 million South Africans will die of AIDS by 2010, according to a report issued by the South African Council of Medical Research, and life expectancy by then would fall to only 36 years. Mbeki disputed the research and pressed to delay its publication. South Africa has the one of the highest rates of HIV infection in the world at around 20 per cent, over 5 million people. In sub-Saharan Africa as a whole, there are more than 12 million AIDS orphans.

66 In March 2001 The leaders of the Democratic Alliance asked Mbeki to declare a state of emergency so HIV carriers could receive generic, ie cheaper, medicines. The South African law that allows the import of such drugs in case of emergency had not been invoked, due to a lawsuit filed by major multinational pharmaceutical firms, which make the drugs. However, international pressure led the 39 companies to withdraw their lawsuit - a decision hailed as an important precedent for poor countries needing to import cheap drugs to fight the pandemic.

67 South Africa was one of the initiators of the New Partnership for Africa's Development (NEPAD), launched in October 2001.

68 On April 11 2002, South African justice absolved Wouter Basson, known by the South African media as 'Doctor Death'. He was notorious for having developed a bacteriological war program against the black population in the apartheid era.

69 South Africa's economy continued to struggle, except for some exports which benefited from a weak rand. Political turmoil in neighboring Zimbabwe reduced foreign investment into the region. Drought in 2002 exacerbated food shortages in southern Africa, and poverty was compounded by HIV/AIDS.

70 In July 2002, the Constitutional Court ruled - in a case brought by the Treatment Action Campaign (TAC) started on the 1st of December 1998, Human Rights Day - that the Government is now legally obliged to implement a comprehensive nationwide program for the prevention of mother-to-child transmission of HIV. This must include the provision of anti-retroviral drug nevirapine.

71 July 2002 saw the inauguration, in Durban, of the African Union (AU), the brainchild of Libyan leader Colonel Muammar Khaddafi. The AU replaced the Organization of African Unity (OAU) which was seen as 'the dictators' club', whereas the focus of the AU is on people's progress and good governance. The 53-member Union was loosely modelled on the EU and will have the right to intervene in the affairs of its member states, in cases of genocide and war crimes. It will also have its own central bank and court of justice and will work towards creating a single currency. Mbeki was appointed as the AU's first chairman.

72 In September 2002 South Africa hosted the World Summit on Sustainable Development. ■

African cultures before colonization

Until a comparatively short time ago, Europeans knew little about Africa. Scholars of the 15th century summed up their knowledge of that continent writing on the maps 'Ibi sunt leones' (Here there are lions). The 19th century philosopher Hegel, described blacks as a childish race, and Africa as 'the unhistorical spirit, the non-developed spirit, still submerged in the conditions of the natural... situated on the threshold of the history of the world'.

[2]   Such notions corresponded with a lack of knowledge about the continent, and the subordination of its peoples to subjugation and slavery. But decolonization in the second half of the 20th century opened a period in which African peoples were confronted with the complex tasks of social and cultural change and development. Part of it consists of a reassessment and a revaluing of the African past. 'The history of Africa', Ki Zerbo has said, 'is the history of the awakening of its consciousness'.

[3]   The knowledge that the West has accumulated about Africa is littered with myths. Among them, the myth of the impossibility of a scientific history, or the myth of the inaccessibility of its past, or the myth of the absence of written testimonies and writing itself, or the myth of the stagnation of the black peoples - which reduced historical interest about Africa to its connections with the Mediterranean world and to isolated subjects, such as Egypt, the Maghreb, or Christian Ethiopia.

[4]   If these myths are not overturned, the true history of Africa cannot be born. The task involves the double operation of deconstructing traditional African history - written under the light of the prejudices of a domineering Eurocentric perspective - and of critically investigating an ample and ignored past.

[5]   In any case, the object of study should not be to wonder about the fate of Africa if colonialism had not existed, but to consider its autonomous contribution to the history of human culture and its promise for the future.

[6]   Charles Darwin wrote: 'It is likely that our first fathers had lived in Africa more than anywhere else'. This intuition is apparently being confirmed by contemporary science. Present research supports the view that conditions favourable for the essential phases in the evolution to the human form existed. Africa supposedly holds the most complete spectrum of prehistorical human remains.

[7]   Archaeological discoveries indicate the pre-eminence of African prehistory over the prehistory of other civilizations. Advanced techniques of toolmaking - quarries and workshops, manufacture of double-edged axes, the use of stones as heat accumulators, and pottery making - became differentiated as they extended over wider geographical areas, but 'the initiative, the great tradition, and the 'fashion' came from Africa'.

[8]   The Neolithic era began in Africa three thousand years earlier than in Europe. Not in Egypt as has been supposed, but in the Sahara, which was then an attractive area with wide rivers and abundant vegetation. The exchange of techniques between different communities made possible diversified agricultural activities. Corn, barley, sorghum, millet, palms, textile plants and so on, were cultivated. There were modest improvements in cattle-breeding. These practices evolved in an autonomous and parallel way to those of other Asian and Indo-American peoples.

[9]   Neolithic African peoples of the Sahara created one of the first technical revolutions through their agricultural practices. This allowed them to lead stable lives and to carry on technical and cultural exchanges with peoples from other areas. The development came from the south upwards through the communities living in the Sahara and then reached the north of Africa. The civilization which flourished later in the Nile valley cannot be accounted for solely as a result of the changes that were made possible there because of the extraordinary fertility of the land, and the population pressure which finally led to the desertification of the Sahara. The cultural riches created and transmitted by the black peoples of the South were also a factor in this process. The Egyptians recognized that those peoples shared their ancestry.

[10]   The Egyptians organized an agricultural civilization with artisanal skills and a consistent governing and military structure which triumphed over the neighbouring populations, among them the kingdoms of Nubia. They developed commercial relations along the river, and exported towards the south bronze manufactures and other products. They also invented their own writing. They drew hieroglyphs on papyrus, which evolved and became partly alphabetical.

[11]   Women had a significant role in Egyptian civilization. The mother figure was foremost in their culture. There was also a female clergy. Landed property was inherited by women, and a dowry was given to the parents of the wife. Their imposing works of art had a profound religious inspiration. Their worldview did not underline the value of progress but rather of equilibrium and peace in opposition to the forces of decay and chaos.

[12]   In the centuries immediately before and after the first century AD, migration and mingling took place among the peoples established south of the Sahara. Several languages were born then, and achievements include an indigenous iron culture which had a revolutionary impact. Iron was abundant in the region. The making of iron tools augmented the productive abilities and the military capabilities of those peoples, and allowed their expansion and their subjugation of less advanced groups. Ironsmiths and craftspeople gained the uppermost positions in these societies. This is the origin of a tradition which recognizes the king-smiths as the African ancestors. From the point of view of social organization, this era represents the passage from clan organization to the formation of kingdoms.

[13]   Between the 7th and the 12th Centuries the majority of the bigger African kingdoms were founded. The Arab-Muslim conquest of North Africa began in the 7th Century. From then on commerce through the Sahara became easier, as did commerce from the coasts towards the kingdoms of sub-Saharan Africa. The Arabs acted as intermediaries.

[14]   The empires of Ghana and Awdaghost to the west, and those of Nubia and Aksum to the north-east dominated several other kingdoms and won territories rich in gold mines. Thanks to the commerce in gold and slaves, they acquired considerable economic power. They created cities as market centres for agricultural products and cattle. Courts headed by black kings admitted civilian councils which, more frequently than not, included Muslim ministers, because of their technical competence. Powerful armies were organized for campaigns of expansion which led either to success, or the decline of those kingdoms.

[15]   Today it is recognized that the period between the 12th and the 16th centuries were the 'great centuries' of Black Africa. African countries reached well-balanced positions, were socio-politically well integrated and developed strong economies. The strongest were the empires of Mali, which at the time of Mahmud Ali had 400 cities in what is now west Sudan; the states of Hausa, Yoruba and Benin, respectively towards the south-east and the south-west of Nigeria; the Bantu Kingdom and the Kongo in Central Africa; and the Zimbabwe and Monomotapa in the South.

[16]   These empires derived revenue from taxes on harvests and cattle, from tributes, customs houses, gold nuggets (which were by law the property of the government), and war booty. They integrated politically different peoples through a government compounded of high officers whose competence was either functional - such as the ministers - or territorial - the chiefs who controlled the provinces - and whose mandates were revocable, not hereditary. Almost all of them had professional armies. Their lands were worked by peasants, compelled to pay a tribute, and by slaves. There was a distinction between war slaves and house slaves, who respectively served in the court and in households, and who had certain civil rights, and were eligible for eventual emancipation. But in some communities and ethnic groups, such as those of Equatorial Africa, there were no slaves.

[17]   Sometimes, as in Timbuktu, cities had centres of religious studies which evolved into universities of sorts. The empires fostered art and architecture, such as the prodigious buildings of Great Zimbabwe, which were heard about in Europe through reports by the Portuguese colonists.

[18]   From the 16th century onwards the independent life of the African empires began to be eroded. The Muslim states were not happy with being mere intermediaries anymore, and they launched expansionist policies which demolished the inner empires. In this they were gradually replaced by the Europeans who, after initial exploration, organized slave traffic in order to satisfy the needs of the New World for cheap manual labor. The slave trade was organized from coastal stations and involved a total of some 10-15 million slaves. Some African kings and leaders collaborated.

[19]   The economic involvement of Europe was not limited to the slave trade. An economy based on the export of grain was developed, but it did not include, at least at the beginning, direct political control, or the loss of sovereignty on the part of the African states.

[20]   These decisive historical changes entrenched a situation of general dependency and contributed to the later underdevelopment of Africa. In the 20 years between 1890 and 1910, the European powers conquered, occupied and finally subjugated a continent whose territory (or rather 80 per cent of it) had been previously governed by autonomous leaders. Most of them resisted this imposition in order to defend their sovereignty and independence, their religions, and their traditional lifestyles.

[21]   Despite this resistance, colonization destroyed the social and cultural balance of subjugated countries and established relationships of dependence. European capital and a world economy robbed African peoples of their resources through mining firms, commercial and financial institutions, compelling them to work for European development.

[22]   However, these cultures did not disappear. Today, African traditions have not only helped to shape the culture of the European countries which once subjugated them, but also have seen a renaissance in their own native soil over the last years. ∎

Spain

Population: 39,924,000 (2002)
Land area: 499,440 SQ KM
Capital: Madrid
Currency: Euro
Language: Spanish

España

The territoriy of present Spain has been inhabited by numerous cultures. Originally, the peninsula hosted peoples from northern Africa and western Europe. As of 1100 BC, the peninsula was an attraction pole for seafaring civilizations, such as Phoenicians, Greeks and Carthaginians, which founded settlements and trading posts, especially along the eastern and southern coasts. The seafarers found a diversity of peoples, collectively called Iberians (name probably derived from the Greek name for the river Ebro), without a common culture or language. Between the 9th and 7th centuries BC, the Celts had settled in the center and west of the peninsula (see box 'The Celts'). Later on, during the 6th and 5th centuries BC, the Iberian culture developed in the southern part of the territory and the fusion of these two cultures gave way to what is known as Celt-Iberian peoples. They were then colonized by the Carthaginians, who in the 3rd century BC took over most of the peninsula. The Carthaginians were expelled by the Romans, who by the 1st century BC had, for the first time, established a single political authority over Iberia. The Iberian élites adopted Roman culture and became citizens of Rome, especially in the south, where the imperial presence was stronger.

[2] The fall of the Roman Empire around 350 AD coincided with the spread of Christianity and, more importantly, with the invasion of the northern peoples who raided Europe. The Iberian peninsula was occupied by the Visigoths who ruled over the area for 300 years.

[3] In 700 AD the peninsula was invaded by Arabs who defeated Rodrigo, the last Visigoth king, thus starting a period of Muslim domination. The descendants of the Visigoths lived in the north of the territory and set up kingdoms like Castille, Catalonia, Navarre, Aragon, Leon and Portugal. Over the centuries they underwent a slow unification process, which consolidated when they started fighting against the Arabs.

[4] The Arabs called the lands in the south of the Iberian peninsula al-Andalus, a region that reached its peak during the 10th century. In contrast with the rest of impoverished rural Europe, its cities - and Cordoba in particular - prospered through active trade with the East. Religious tolerance enabled Muslims, Jews, and Christians to live side by side, and science, medicine, and philosophy developed. Copies and translations of the Greek classics were made, paving the way for the 15th century European Renaissance.

[5] In 1492, a triple process of national unification took place in Spain, through the marriage of Isabel of Castille and Fernando of Aragon, the expulsion of the Moors, and the conquest and subsequent colonization of the new American territories. The unification of the country's political power and the creation of the Kingdom of Spain were carried out at the expense of the Jews (and members of other cultures) who were expelled from Spain after having lived there for many centuries. Both the Inquisition and centralized power were institutionalized under the new system, while the new American colonies supplied precious metals, sustaining three centuries of economic bonanza. The indigenous people in America had Christianity imposed upon them by the Crown, and the exploitation they were subject to through forced labor was responsible for decimating many of their populations.

[6] The economic prosperity provided by the colonies was reflected in a period of great cultural development in Spain. Literature in particular developed extensively during the 16th and 17th centuries, which were dubbed the Spanish Golden Age. Portugal was joined to the Spanish Kingdom for the period 1580-1688.

[7] In the 18th century, the Bourbons came to the Spanish throne. They reorganized domestic and colonial administration, ruling in accordance with the principles of Enlightenment, as the liberal ideas of the French Revolution spread throughout Europe and America. Combined with Napoleonic expansion, this view contributed to the disintegration of the Spanish colonies after the wars of independence.

[8] At the end of the Napoleonic era, there was great conflict between the liberal sectors seeking political and economic modernization, and the absolutists who wished to preserve the traditional order. The disputes between groups weakened the power of the Empire, making way for revolutions in Spanish America.

[9] By the end of the 19th century Spain had renounced its last American territories and had come to terms with the loss of its privileges.

[10] At the beginning of the 20th century, Spain was plunged into a deep political, social, and economic crisis; this was exacerbated by World War I (1914-1918). In an atmosphere of extreme polarization, Primo de Rivera's dictatorship, which resulted from a coup in 1923, attempted to halt any further increase in demands from workers or regional groups seeking autonomy. The dictatorship, closely resembling the Italian fascist model, retained power until 1931. Its eventual loss of power was a result of existing contradictions within the Church, the armed forces and industry, who were all fascist supporters, and not to the continuous opposition from political and labor organizations. The end of the dictatorship marked the end of the monarchy, and the dawn of a new republican era.

[11] The 'Second Republic' was born in the midst of a series of extremely complex political and economic difficulties. In 1936, after two moderate governments, the People's Front, formed with socialists, republicans, communists and anarchists, gained a narrow electoral triumph, causing much friction with their political opponents.

[13] Franco's forces won the civil war in March 1939, assisted by internal divisions within the republican forces, the military superiority of his troops, and German and Italian support.

[14] When the Civil War ended, Franco became head of the new state. He set up an authoritarian regime along fascist lines, with a corporatist state, a personality cult, and extreme nationalism. Franco ruled over a deeply divided society and an economy that had been virtually devastated by the Civil War.

[15] From the beginning of the Cold War in the early 1950s, the US tried to secure Spanish support and Spain became a member of the United Nations in 1955, confirming a change in Franco's foreign policy, which was becoming preoccupied with improving the international image.

[16] In the 1960s, Franco opened Parliament to other groups and movements. During those years, key figures of Opus Dei, an ultra-conservative Catholic movement, occupied important posts in government and changed the country's economic policies.

¹⁷   Spain ended its economic isolation and liberalized its economy by eliminating many mechanisms of state control. The urban middle classes enjoyed a substantial improvement in their standard of living, which allowed a significant political relaxation. However, the peasants were still extremely poor and many emigrated to the major Spanish and European cities.

¹⁸   Franco died in 1975, and power was handed to his successor, the heir to the Spanish throne, Juan Carlos I of Bourbon. The new monarch immediately started negotiations with the political opposition to re-establish the democratic system overthrown in 1939.

¹⁹   Between 1976 and 1981 Adolfo Suarez, the leader of the Center Democratic Union (UCD), was Prime Minister. In December 1978 during his term in office, a plebiscite was held which turned Spain into a parliamentary monarchy, re-establishing political freedom, and guaranteeing the right of autonomy to some Spanish regions. Several politicians, intellectuals,and artists were able to return to the country after up to 40 years in exile.

²⁰   In February 1981, a group of Civil Guard officers took the *Cortes* (parliament) by force. The firm reaction of all the democratic political groups and in particular of King Juan Carlos, who had the support of the army, guaranteed the failure of the coup and the consolidation of the democratization process.

²¹   The Spanish Socialist Workers' Party (PSOE) won the October 1982 elections, with a solid majority in the Cortes. Felipe González became President of the Government, the equivalent of Prime Minister in other countries. He was subsequently re-elected in 1988 and 1993.

²²   Despite some setbacks, the parliamentary majority of the PSOE was able to enforce an ambitious adjustment and growth plan which deeply transformed the Spanish economy and gave vast social sectors access to unprecedented levels of consumption. However, this modernization resulted in high unemployment and tensions, which led to a split between the Government and the UGT, the trade union that had supported the PSOE.

²³   ETA, the Basque separatist group which many times has used violent means to achieve its political goals, suffered serious setbacks in 1993. Co-operation between French and Spanish security forces led to the arrest of some of its leaders, and the discovery in Bayonne, France, of the organization's main arsenal.

²⁴   The Spanish Government was active in international affairs, joining the European Economic Community and NATO in 1986. Membership of NATO had been opposed by the PSOE when in opposition, but once in power the party defended the decision and confirmed it through consultation with the people.

²⁵   Spain spent $10 billion in 1992 to celebrate the 500 years of the conquest of America, while it intensified its political shift toward Europe, having joined the European Union (EU) in January 1986.

²⁶   Due to a number of corruption scandals, the Socialist Government lost a key sector of its support in Parliament in 1995. While he defended his personal actions and those of his government, González brought forward the elections one year ahead of schedule.

²⁷   A former security chief and a socialist official were prosecuted in connection to the Anti-terrorist Liberation Groups (GAL), which judicial investigations linked to security forces. One of them testified before the court that Felipe González himself was responsible for the GAL, which killed 27 people along the border with France in the so-called 'dirty war' against ETA. A former Interior Minister was also investigated for having paid off French officials to collaborate in the persecution of ETA suspects.

²⁸   The conservative People's Party (PP) won the Parliamentary elections in March 1996 with 38.9 per cent of the vote. On April 5, the PP leader, José María Aznar, took office as Prime Minister.

²⁹   In August 1997, an ETA cell kidnapped Miguel Ángel Blanco, a PP activist and councilor at a small village in the Basque Country. The organization warned that it would execute him within 48 hours if the Spanish Government did not order the re-grouping of its prisoners in Basque jails. Once the deadline came, Blanco was murdered, sparking countrywide protest demonstrations, attended by more people than any other Spanish political event in the latter half of the century. The Government and the opposition, with the exception of Herri Batasuna (HB), a political group close to ETA, reached an agreement not to condone violence.

³⁰   ETA declared a ceasefire in September 1998. All of the Basque nationalist sectors, including the Basque Nationalist Party and former members of Herri Batasuna, signed the Estella Pact, an alliance of Basque nationalist parties that, under the slogan 'Basques rule themselves', won local elections in 1999. ETA resumed armed actions in September - blowing up several bombs and killing three people - which led to the breaking of the non-violence pact.

PROFILE

ENVIRONMENT

Spain comprises 82 per cent of the Iberian Peninsula and includes the Balearic and Canary Islands. The center of the country is a plateau which rises to the Pyrenees in the north, forming a natural border with France. The Betica mountain ranges extend to the South. Inland the Central Sierras separate the plateaus of Nueva and Vieja Castilla. In the Ebro River basin, to the north, lie the plains of Cataluña, Valencia, with Murcia in the south east. The Guadalquivir River basin, to the south, forms the plains of Andalucía. The climate is moderate and humid in the north and northwest, where there are many woodlands. In the interior, the climate is dry in the south and east. 40 per cent of the land is arable. Approximately 5 per cent of the total land area is under environmental protection. Natural resources include coal, some oil and natural gas, uranium and mercury. Industry is concentrated in Cataluña and the Basque Provinces. Per capita emissions of air and water pollutants exceed Western European averages. Since 1970, the use of nitrogen fertilizers has doubled. Nitrate concentrations in the Guadalquivir River are 25 per cent above 1975 levels.. The percentage of the population serviced by sewage systems rose from 14 per cent in 1975, to 48 per cent in the late 1980s. This fact, together with industrial wastes from oil refining plants and natural gas production, has increased the level of pollution of the Mediterranean. The Government has launched a reforestation plan to increase production and stop erosion. With more trees, there has been an exponential increase of forest fires. There is considerable mono-cropping, particularly of eucalyptus, that does not take biodiversity into account. Approximately 22 per cent of Spain's forests have suffered some degree of defoliation. The illegal proliferation of toxic and dangerous waste dumps nearby inhabited communities is a serious environmental concern, mainly in the rural areas of the peninsula.

SOCIETY

Peoples: Castillians, Asturians, Andalucians, Valencians, Catalans, Asturians, Aragonians, Andalucians, Extremenians, Basques and Galicians, descended from a fusion of the Iberian people of the Mediterranean, the Celts of Central Europe and the Arabs of North Africa. There is a Roma minority. Immigrant communities, especially Latin Americans, North Africans and Asians.
Religion: Catholicism is the religion of the vast majority of the Spanish people (95.2 per cent). Muslims 1.2 per cent.
Languages: Spanish or Castillian (official national); there are also official regional languages, such as Basque, Catalan, Valencian and Galician. Non official languages: Aragonian, Asturian, Castuo, Canarian,Caló, Romani.
Political Parties: People's Party (PP), in government; Spanish Socialist Workers' Party (PSOE); United Left. Political platforms of nationalist movements represented in Parliament: Convergence and Union, Basque Nationalist Party, Galician Nationalist Bloc, Canarian Coalition, Andalucian Party, Republican Left of Cataluña, Basque Solidarity, Aragonese Junta. Out of Parliament: Nationalist Bloc of Valencia, Beloved Land-Castilian Nationalist Party, Extremadura Coalition, Regionalist Party of Cantabria.
Social Organizations: Since the Franco era, the labor movement was organized into several central unions. The largest are the General Union of Workers (UGT) and Workers' Confederation (CCOO), along with anarchist organizations National Labor Confederation (CNT) and General Labor Confederation (CGT). There are also rural unions, such as the COAG.

THE STATE

Official Name: Estado Español.
Administrative Divisions: Spain is divided into 17 autonomous regions: the Basque Country, Cataluña, Galicia, Andalucia, the Principality of Asturias, Cantabria, La Rioja, Murcia, Valencia, Aragon, Castilla, La Mancha, the Canaries, Navarre, Extremadura, the Balearic Islands, Madrid and Castilla León. Each one has its own institutional system, a local leader in executive power and a unicameral legislative.
Capital: Madrid 4,070,000 people (1999).
Other cities: Barcelona 3,855,300 people; Valencia 1,406,600; Seville 1,130,600; Zaragoza 605,900 (2000).
Government: Hereditary monarchy, with King Juan Carlos I de Borbon y Borbon as Head of State. Prime Minister: José María Aznar, since May 1996, re-elected in March 2000. The parliament (*Cortes*) consists of two bodies: the Senate, with 255 members, and the Chamber of Deputies with 350 members elected by proportional representation.
National Holiday: October 12, Hispanic Day.
Armed Forces: 206,000 (1995).
Other: Civil Guard 66,000 (3,000 conscripts).

[31] The fall in unemployment achieved by the Aznar government's economic policy and Spain's entry into the European currency system, explain the support received by the PP in pre-election polls. Nevertheless, the results in March 2000 were surprising because the PP won an overall majority in Parliament, enabling it to govern without forming alliances.

[32] The Foreigners' Act, passed in August 2000, was strongly criticized by political parties and non-governmental organizations, and caused massive protest demonstrations. The law sought to regulate the rights and obligations of foreign residents. These include the right to freedom of movement, participation in the public realm, attendance at meetings and demonstrations; the right to education, employment and social security, to trade union organization and so on. The law's opponents claim that it specifically curtails the rights of immigrants. By January 2001,

according to different estimates, between 30,000-100,000-plus foreigners were left in inferior legal and labor conditions, unable to benefit from an additional legalization term.

[33] Inflation started rising in late 2000. Although unemployment fell during the Aznar administration, it remained around 14 per cent, the highest rate in the EU. In 2001, the Spanish economy was one of the fastest growing in the EU. Despite inflation of around 4 per cent, the strong economy helped Aznar face a difficult year in the political field. Problems stemmed from various financial scandals involving several officials, difficulties in the implementation of the Foreigners' Act, and the controversial university reforms that, late that year, caused strikes, demonstrations and sit-ins by students and faculty members.

[34] Tensions with Morocco came to the forefront as a result of Madrid's reaction to the September 11 2001

attacks in New York and Washington. Spain tightened its controls in the colonial enclaves of Ceuta and Melilla (on Morocco's coast), and suggestions to Rabat to 'do more' to limit the flow of illegal immigrants to Spain. Likewise, signs of agreement between Madrid and London regarding the future status of Gibraltar in 2002, intensified Morocco's unease: it claims sovereignty over Ceuta and Melilla. On October 27, days before Moroccan king Muhammad VI began an official visit to Western Sahara (annexed by Morocco in 1975), Rabat called its ambassador in Madrid 'for consultations' and cancelled a bilateral summit with Spain, scheduled for December.

[35] In spite of the economic growth, inequality persists between the coastal and interior areas in infrastructure, employment and other sectors. An example of this growing gap has been the project channel the waters of the Ebro, Spain's largest river, toward the golf courses and specialized agriculture of the coastal areas. In spite of Parliamentary opposition, the protests of Aragon region (for whom the Ebro is the only water source) and huge demonstrations in Zaragoza and Madrid, the Government has gone ahead with the project.

[36] Poverty in Spain affects 22.1 per cent of the population (7.5 points above the average in the EU); 44 per cent of the poor are aged below 25, which implies a relatively new phenomenon. It is estimated some 300,000 children below the legal working age work in Spain. In November 2001, the chairman of the Spanish Committee of UNICEF, Joaquín Ruiz-Giménez, stated there are some 100,000 children in Spain that 'labor for a wage in despicable conditions'.

[37] As of January 2002, the rotating presidency of the EU is held by Spain. Anti-terrorism became a priority of Aznar's European agenda, although the operation of the euro, the new European currency, and the expansion of the EU were touchy subjects that his administration had to also tackle. In March, the Spanish Government suggested that it would be inconvenient to hold the annual state of the nation debate during its European presidency. The PSOE demanded the immediate staging of the debate and its parliamentary spokesperson, Jesús Caldera, added that the Government should account for the economic, employment, educational and social state of the country, and the 'dangerous counter-reforms it is implementing, rather than just its anti-terrorist measures'. ■

Gibraltar

Population: 27,000 (2002)
Area: 10 SQ KM
Capital: Gibraltar
Currency: Gibraltar pound
Language: English and Spanish

A peninsula on the southern coast of Spain, only 32 km from Morocco, Gibraltar's strategic position allows it to control maritime trade between the Mediterranean and the Atlantic ocean.

[2] Gibraltar was occupied by England in 1704 and ceded by Spain in 1714, following the Treaty of Utrecht. Since 1964 Spain has tried to regain political control of the area. In 1967, a plebiscite opted for continued colonial dependency. In 1968 the UN voted in favor of the Spanish re-incorporation of Gibraltar. Since 1972, the two countries have started negotiations several times, but no significant progress has yet been made. The most recent attempt took place in May 2002 when president José María Aznar met Tony Blair in London.

[3] Gibraltar has been the door that immigrants without identification papers from North Africa use to arrive in Spain.

[4] In July 2002, Jack Straw - Foreign Secretary of Britain - declared that his country was disposed to share sovereignty with Spain. Gibraltar residents reacted unfavorably.

PROFILE

Peoples: Most of the permanent population is of British origin. The non-permanent population are mainly Spanish workers.
Religions: Anglican and Catholic.
Languages: English (official) and Spanish.
Official Name: Gibraltar.
Government: Non-autonomous territory under UN's control. General Governor named by the British crown: David Durie since April 2000. Chief minister: Peter Caruana, since May 1996- re-appointed in February 2000 by the 15-member advisory council. In the council's last election, held in February 2000, the Social Democrat Party obtained 58.3 per cent of the vote, while the second political force, the Socialist Labor Party, was supported by 41 per cent of the electorate. Britain has made Gibraltarian independence dependent upon an agreement with Spain. In September 1996, NATO Headquarters acknowledged that in the future military control over the peninsula would be exercised by Spain.

Sri Lanka

Population: 19,287,000 (2002)
Land area: 64,630 SQ KM
Capital: Colombo
Currency: Rupee
Language: Sinhalese

Sri Lanka

The island of Ceylon was populated by the indigenous Vedda in ancient times. It was then successively invaded by the Sinhalese, Indo-Europeans and Tamils, who laid the foundations of an advanced civilization. When the Portuguese arrived in 1505, the island was divided into seven autonomous local societies.

[2] The Dutch expelled the Portuguese from their coastal trading posts 150 years later, but it was the British - who had already taken possession of neighboring India - who finally made the island a colony in 1796. Even then, it took them until 1815 to subdue all the local governments who fought hard to remain autonomous. The British then introduced new export crops such as coffee and tea - products that gave Ceylon a worldwide reputation because of their excellent quality.

[3] In the 20th century, a strong nationalist movement developed. In 1948, Ceylon became independent and joined the British Commonwealth. Under the leadership of Sir John Kotelawala and Prime Minister Bandaranaike, the country pursued a vigorous anti-colonial foreign policy. In August 1954, Bandaranaike met in Colombo with India's Nehru, Muhammad Ali of Pakistan, U Nu of Burma and Indonesia's Sastroamidjojo. The meeting was of great political importance as it led to the 1955 summit conference of Afro-Asian countries in Bandung, heralding the Movement of Non-Aligned Countries.

[4] In the late 1950s, the Tamil minority staged a series of secessionist uprisings and in

September 1959 the Prime Minister was assassinated. His widow Sirimavo Bandaranaike led the Sri Lanka Freedom Party to electoral victory at the beginning of 1960, although she had no previous political experience.

[5] Bandaranaike became the first woman in the world to head a government. Governing in coalition the Communist and Trotskyist parties, in 1962 she nationalized various US oil and other companies. In 1965, she was defeated by a right-wing coalition but regained power in 1970, in a landslide election victory.

[6] She was faced with a 'Guevarist' (after Che Guevara) guerrilla uprising which she then had forcibly crushed. She never gave up her anti-imperialist stand and in 1972 declared Sri Lanka a republic, cutting all ties with the British Commonwealth

[7] A land reform program nationalized British-owned plantations but had little effect on the standard of living of the bulk of the rural population.

[8] Conflict between the Sinhalese majority and the Tamil minority, descended from the Dravidians of South India, has persisted throughout most of the island's history.

[9] The Sinhalese account for 74 per cent of the country's population, while the Tamils comprise 22 per cent and are divided into two groups: the Sri Lankan Tamils and the Indian Tamils. The Sri Lankan Tamils reached the island approximately 2,000 years ago and settled principally in the northern and eastern provinces, while the Indian Tamils are more recent immigrants. Both groups possess

common characteristics and seek regional autonomy or even the formation of a separate Tamil nation. The Tamil United Liberation Front (TULF) founded on May 4 1972, resulted from the fusion of three Tamil parties: the Federal Party, the Tamil Congress and the pro-Indian Ceylon Workers' Congress.

[10] Bandaranaike's main achievement was probably her appointment as president of the Non-Aligned Movement in 1976, at the Conference in Colombo. However, accusations of nepotism, and reaction from the country's intellectuals to the censorship of the press and to emergency measures in force since 1971, caused Bandaranaike to lose the July 1977 election.

[11] The United National Party (UNP), led by Junius Jayewardene, won a comfortable parliamentary majority, with the Tamil Liberation Front coming second. In spite of his socialist leanings, the new prime minister's economic policy exposed the country to transnational capital.

[12] A constitutional reform in 1978 made Jayewardene Sri Lanka's first president. In November 1980, a series of International Monetary Fund (IMF)-approved economic measures began to be applied, with disastrous consequences for the country.

[13] A month earlier, Bandaranaike had been expelled from Parliament and deprived of her political rights for seven years. A presidential commission had found her guilty of 'abuse of authority' during her coalition government, between 1970 and July 1977.

[14] An IMF package of measures went into effect. There was a general strike against these and the new economic policy, and 44,000 civil servants lost their jobs in the summer of 1980. In 1981 the Government received substantial US aid, supplied with the alleged purpose of stabilizing the region. The same argument was used to justify increasingly frequent visits by US naval ships to the port of Colombo.

[15] Sri Lanka's first presidential election in October 1982, gave Jayewardene a clear victory, with 52.5 per cent of the vote. His campaign was backed by the state apparatus and benefited from the division and internal strife of the

WORKERS

2000

UNEMPLOYMENT: 8%
LABOR FORCE AS % OF TOTAL:

■ FEMALE: 37%   ■ MALE: 63%

1994/97

EMPLOYMENT DISTRIBUTION:

F
M

■ SERVICES   F: 34%   M: 41%
■ INDUSTRY   F: 24%   M: 22%
■ AGRICULTURE F: 40%   M: 33%

LAND USE

DEFORESTATION: 1.1% annual (1990/95)

1993

■ FOREST & WOODLAND: 32%
■ ARABLE: 14.2%
■ OTHER: 53.8%

PUBLIC EXPENDITURE

1999

18.4% DEFENSE
33.6% SOCIAL

Freedom Party. In some parts of the country, the political upheaval meant that elections had to be held under state of emergency conditions.

[16] The project to turn Sri Lanka into an export center like Hong Kong or Taiwan led to the creation of a free zone in Latunyabe where foreign investment increased after 1978.

[17] In early 1982, in spite of earlier denials and the Government's outspoken commitment to non-alignment, the US Navy was granted permission to use Sri Lanka's refuelling facilities in Trincomalee, a vital spot linking eastern and western sea routes through the Suez Canal.

[18] Early in 1983, ethnic conflict worsened. It reached crisis point in July and August, leaving hundreds dead and wounded and thousands more homeless. More than 40,000 Sri Lankan Tamils fleeing the conflict sought refuge in Tamil Nadu. President Jayewardene's refusal to negotiate with the Tamil minority led the Indian Government to withdraw its attempts at mediation.

[19] The ethnic war became more bitter during 1985, discouraging foreign investors. However tourism remains one of the main sources of income of this 'fiscal paradise'.

[20] In late July 1987, presidents Rajiv Gandhi (of India) and Junius Jayewardene finally signed an accord in Colombo granting a certain autonomy to the Tamil minority of the northern and eastern provinces of Sri Lanka. The accord provided for the merger of the two provinces under a single government, and gave Tamil the status of a national language. India guaranteed the agreement and sent troops - the India Peace Keeping Force - to ensure that its terms were complied with. These terms were to be ratified by the parliaments of India and Sri Lanka, and approved by the main guerrilla group, the Liberation Tigers of Tamil Eelam (LTTE) known as the Tamil Tigers.

[21] These efforts did not succeed in pacifying the country, and the Indian military presence - far from

guaranteeing peace - became a further cause for irritation and renewed confrontations. Inter-ethnic violence worsened as the Tamil Tigers rejected the 1987 accords.

[22] In November 1988, the official party's hold on power was ratified by 50.4 per cent of the votes. Jayewardene, at the age of 82, ceded his post to the former prime minister Ranasinghe Premadasa. Political violence was so pervasive that only 53 per cent of the electorate actually voted. Elections were boycotted, by both the Tamil guerrillas and the Popular Liberation Front (made up of Sinhalese who were violently opposed to any kind of concessions to ethnic minorities). Political opposition to the Government increased, partly fuelled by a strong student movement which was eventually harshly repressed in early 1989.

[23] In early 1990, India withdrew the last of its 60,000 peacekeeping force, which had been stationed in Sri Lanka since 1987. More than 1,000 troops had died on the island. Amnesty International announced that, in 1990, the Sri Lankan Government had killed thousands of civilians in the region.

[24] In May 1991, the Tamil Tigers were accused of murdering Rajiv Gandhi in a suicide mission. Rajiv had become an enemy of the Tigers after the Indian peace forces in Sri Lanka had attacked the rebels. The Tigers denied any involvement in the attempt.

[25] In the November 1994 presidential elections, the Popular Alliance candidate Chandrika Bandaranaike Kumaratunga won with 63 per cent of the vote. Kumaratunga had been appointed Prime Minister following the parliamentary elections in August and it was the first time that two women have hold such high office together. Her mother, Sirimavo Bandaranaike succeeded her as Prime Minister.

[26] The Government and the Tigers agreed to start negotiations in January 1995, but the pact was broken by the Tamils. The guerrillas initiated a new series of attacks against government forces in April.

[27] Kumaratunga presented a plan for state reform in August. The proposal, supported by the Tamil parliamentarians, included transforming Sri Lanka into a federation of eight regions. The central government was to keep control over defense, foreign relations and international economic relations.

[28] This project required the support of two-thirds of Parliament followed by approval by referendum before it could come into action. The negotiations between the various

parties were slow and the inc reasing military action prevented it being completed.

[29] The city of Jaffna, on the peninsula of the same name, was at the center of the fighting from October 1995. Government forces occupied the city on December 5. Only 400 of the 140,000 people who lived there stayed throughout the fighting. By mid-1996, half the peninsula's Tamil population had returned to their homes.

[30] In early 1997, the Tigers destroyed an army garrison in Paranthan, in the north of the country. All the military personnel - an estimated 1,200 troops - were killed. Government forces' land and air reprisals led to great losses for the LTTE.

[31] In May, the army deployed some 20,000 troops in the biggest offensive since the outbreak of war. The government forces were able to capture strategic positions and roads, pushing the guerrilla into the jungle. The LTTE responded with a series of bomb attacks in the main tourist centers.

[32] The government offensive destroyed of a large proportion of Sri Lanka's paddy fields, affecting international rice prices and forcing the country to start importing rice. The social situation on the island worsened during the years of conflict. One example of this was the number of very young people involved in prostitution. According to United Nations estimates, around two thirds of all prostitutes were under the age of consent.

[32] The Government offered to suspend the military offensive and discuss proposals to increase the autonomy of regional councils administered by Tamils and Muslims. However, it continued to demand the surrender of the LTTE as a pre-condition for negotiations, something the guerrillas considered unacceptable. In April, the Government and the main opposition group, the United National Party, agreed to form a united front in any negotiations with the LTTE.

[33] Despite efforts at mediation, the civil war worsened in March 1998, with dozens killed on both sides. In April, the Government promised to publish the result of

PROFILE

ENVIRONMENT

An island in the Indian Ocean, southeast of India, separated from the continent by the Palk Channel. The land is flat, except for a central mountainous region. These mountains divide the island into two distinct regions and also block the monsoon winds which are responsible for the tropical climate. The southwest area receives abundant rainfall, and the remainder of the island is drier. Large tea plantations cover the southern mountain slopes, and other major crops are rice, for domestic consumption, and rubber, coconuts and cocoa, for export. Deforestation and soil erosion are important environmental problems. Likewise, air pollution is on the increase, due to industrial gas emissions.

SOCIETY

Peoples: 74 per cent of Sri Lankans are Sinhalese; Tamils are the largest minority group, 18 per cent, and there are Arab (7.7 per cent) and Vedda (1 per cent) minorities.
Religions: 70 per cent Buddhist; 15.5 per cent Hindu; 7.6 per cent Muslim; 7.5 per cent Christian; and 1 per cent other religions.
Languages: Sinhalese (official). Also Tamil and English.
Political Parties: Sri Lanka Freedom Party (SLFP); United National Party (UNP) (Siri Kotha); the United Democratic National Front; the Tamil United Liberation Front (TULF); the Communist Party; the Equal Society Party (Lanka Sama Samaja); the People's Democratic Party (Mahajana Prajathantra); the People's Liberation Front (Janata Vimuktui Peramuna); and the Popular Alliance coalition; Sri Lanka Muslim Congress (SLMC), Tamil Vimuktasi Peramuna (Tamil United Liberation Front, Tamil separatist); Eelam People's Democratic Party (Tamil regionalist).
Social Organizations: Workers' Congress, Trade Union Federation, Trade Union Council, Labor Federation of Workers. Pressure groups like the Buddhist clergy, the insurgent Liberation Tigers of Tamil Eelam/LTTE ('Tamil Tigers') and Sinhalese groups like the Nationalist Anti-Terrorism Movement.

THE STATE

Official Name: Sri Lanka Prajathanthrika Samajavadi Janarajaya.
Administrative Divisions: 9 Provinces, 24 Districts.
Capital: Colombo 2,381,000 people (1999).
Other cities: Dehiwala-Mount Lavinia 218,500 people; Moratuwa 204,500; Maha Nuwara 150,700; Kotte 127,000 (2000).
Government: Chandrika Kumaratunga, President since November 1994, re-elected in 1999. Ranil Wickremasinghe, Prime Minister since December 2001. Unicameral Legislature: National Assembly, with 225 members.
National Holiday: February 4, Independence Day (1948).
Armed Forces: 126,000 (1994).
Other: 70,000 Police Force, National Guard, Private Guard.

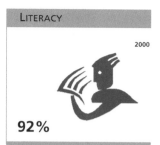

LITERACY 2000

92%

EXTERNAL DEBT 2000

PER CAPITA

US$ 479

FOREIGN TRADE

Millions US$ 2000

IMPORTS
8,234

EXPORTS
6,475

investigations into the disappearance of some 700 people reported in Jaffna. At that time an estimated 50,000 people had died since the war broke out.

³⁴ Government troops carried out a major offensive in December 1998, forcing the Tamil United Liberation Front (TULF) to retreat to inhospitable areas and abandon several Northern cities.

³⁵ Clashes between government troops and Tamil rebels intensified during the last quarter of 1999. The TULF took control of the important Northern city of Oddusudan in November, from which it had had to withdraw during the December 1998 government offensive.

³⁶ In December, President Chandrika Kumaratunga was reelected for a new term, just four days after escaping an assassination attempt. She beat her main rival, Ranil Wickremasinghe, from the UNP, by eight points. The high turnout (70 per cent of 11.5 million registered) surprised political analysts who expected a higher level of abstention due to the TULF attacks days before the election which had caused 33 dead and more than 130 injured one of them Kamaratunga herself.

³⁷ Both the President and Wickremasinghe promised during their campaign to put an end to the 16-year-old civil war that by then had caused more than 60,000 deaths. Although Tamil voters had supported Kamaratunga in her 1994 victory, this time they followed TULF's recommendation to vote for Wickremasinghe.

³⁸ Kumaratunga and Wickremasinghe met on March 2000 to discuss a possible political agreement to put an end to the ethnic conflict. While the talks were taking place, Tamil rebels captured a key government position on the Jaffna peninsula after a 12-hour battle.

³⁹ The TULF openly rejected the government peace plan, but agreed to take part in conversations if Norway acted as mediator. The Sri Lankan political class considered in turn that, before any negotiation with the rebels took place, a comprehensive agreement between the main political parties was needed to enact a new constitution.

⁴⁰ The rebels launched a new offensive in mid-April, and by May they had practically all Jaffna under control. Lack of commitment by government forces was one of the reasons cited for their repeated defeats in the peninsula a key area for the Tigers in their independence demands. The Tigers perceive the peninsula as their home and the right place to form their independent state.

⁴¹ In late December 2000 the LTTE declared a unilateral cease-fire that was to last until April 24 2001. But a radical commando unit, displeased with the way the agenda for the peace talks was being prepared, broke the cease-fire by attacking a navy vessel in Mullativu.

⁴² On July 11 2001, upon losing the majority in Parliament after the Muslim Alliance's withdrawal from her coalition, President Kumaratunga dissolved Parliament and called a referendum to reform the Constitution, which ultimately did not take place.

⁴³ Shortly after, the LTTE attacked again, killing 17 people at the Sri Lanka international airport. The suicide attack caused major losses for the national airline and the country's tourism industry.

⁴⁴ For the first time since the beginning of the civil war, in November 2001 the LTTE publicly renounced its demand for independence of the Tamil provinces. Velupillai Prabhakaran, leader of the rebels, said that autonomy allowing the Tamils to make political and economic decisions would be enough.

⁴⁵ The UN High Commissioner for Refugees (UNHCR) stated that in spite of the peace process the situation in Sri Lanka was still too delicate for any large-scale repatriation. The UNHCR said it was not yet prepared to promote the return of the 100,000 Tamil refugees living in southern India.

⁴⁶ The alliance led by Wickremasinghe won the December 19 2001 parliamentary elections with promises to try to negotiate an end to the conflict with the separatists and to reactivate the economy. Kumaratunga's Popular Alliance lost control of Parliament.

⁴⁷ The Government began a truce with the LTTE after the rebels

promised to comply with the strict cease-fire they had proposed. Prime Minister Wickremasinghe led efforts to develop a negotiation process to finally end the ethnic conflict.

⁴⁸ The Central Bank of Sri Lanka announced that the country began the year 2002 with the worst recession since independence. The war crippled the economy and reduced the nation's finances to a minimum. According to the National Peace Commission, over the last 20 years the Government's war expenditure reached $2.6 million and an additional $457,000 in refugee assistance. To cover those costs, the Government increased taxes, with a subsequent rise in inflation. The ones who have benefited from the conflict, according to the non-governmental organization Caritas of Sri Lanka, have been the arms traffickers and manufacturers and many young people - Sinhalese and Tamils alike - who have found work by joining the army.

⁴⁹ With the intention of strengthening the peace process, in January 2002 the Government eased the embargo on food, personal goods and medicine for the northern areas under rebel control, after a seven-year blockade. The measure was a condition the LTTE had imposed for the talks. The LTTE began its transition from guerrilla force to political organization. The negotiators expected to finalize a face-to-face meeting between the parties in July or August to take place in Thailand. Norway hoped that the parties would draw up an agenda for the negotiations in which they would focus on setting up an interim administration for northern and eastern Sri Lanka, the areas in conflict.

⁵⁰ Thousands of the opposition marched in Colombo in April in protest against the peace process. The rally, organized by the leftist People's Liberation Front and Kumaratunga's Popular Alliance, was the first major expression of discontent with the Government's efforts to reach a peace treaty. During the march, the President accused the Prime Minister of having made concessions that threatened Sri Lanka's sovereignty. ∎

STATISTICS

DEMOGRAPHY
Population: 19,287,000 (2002)
Annual growth: 1.2 % (1985-2000)
Estimates for year 2015: 21,451,000 (2000)
Annual growth to year 2015: 0.8 % (2000)
Urban population: 23.6 % (2000)
Urban growth: 2.9 % (2000)
Children per woman: 2.1 (2000)

HEALTH
Life expectancy at birth: 73 years (2000-2005)
male: 70 years (2000-2005)
female: 76 years (2000-2005)
Maternal mortality: 60 per 100,000 live births (1985/99)
Infant mortality: 17 per 1,000 (2000)
Under-5 child mortality: 19 per 1,000 (2000)
Daily calorie supply: 2,411 per capita (1999)
37 doctors per 100,000 people (1999)
Safe water: 77 % (2000)

EDUCATION
Literacy: 92 % (2000)
male: 94 % (2000)
female: 89 % (2000)
School enrolment (net):
Primary total: 90 % (1994/2000)
Secondary (gross):
male: 71 % (1995/97)
female: 78 % (1995/97)
Tertiary (gross): 5 % (1997)
Primary school teachers: one for every 28 pupils (1996)

COMMUNICATIONS
29 newspapers (1996), 208 radios (1997), 111 TV sets (2000) and 41 main telephone lines (2000) per 1,000 people
Books: 17 new titles per 100,000 people (1992/94)

ECONOMY
Per capita, GDP: $ 3,530 (2000)
Annual growth: 4.3 % (2000)
Annual inflation: 6.2 % (2000)
Consumer price index: 154.4 (2000)
Currency: 93.6 rupees = $ 1 (03/2002)
Cereal imports: 1,223,870 metric tons (2000)
Food import dependency: 15 % (1999)
Fertilizer use: 2,945 kg per ha (1999)
Exports: $ 6,475 million (2000)
Imports: $ 8,234 million (2000)
External debt: $ 9,066 million (2000); $ 479 per capita (2000)
Debt service: 7.9 % of exports (1999)
Development aid received: $ 251 million (1999); $ 13.2 per capita (1999); 1.60 % of GNP (1999)

ENERGY
Consumption: 388.8 Kgs of oil equivalent per capita yearly (1998); 41.2 % imported (1999)

HDI (ranking/value): 81 / 0.735 (1999)

Sudan

Population: 32,559,000 (2002)
Land area: 2,376,000 SQ KM
Capital: Khartoum (Al-Khartum)
Currency: Pound
Language: Arabic

Sudan

Around 3000 BC, the region called Kush by the Egyptians and Nubia by the Greeks was in the ambit of Pharaonic Egypt, a fact which considerably delayed the formation of an organized state. The Pharaohs favored disparate groups under their rule. Consequently, the state of Napata did not come into being until the 8th century when Egypt's decline gave foreign dynasties the opportunity to take over the country. The last of these was Sudanese. The rulers of Napata conquered Egypt in 730 BC and reigned as pharaohs until the Assyrian conquest in 663 BC, when the ruling family was ousted. The country disintegrated, though it was not occupied. Shortly afterwards, the three 'waterfall states', which would last over 20 centuries, rose in its place: Nobatia, Dongola and Alodia.

² While Egypt was ruled by Persians, Greeks, Romans and Arabs in succession, the waterfall states maintained their political and cultural autonomy. This was due to their position as trade intermediaries between the Mediterranean market and the sources of slaves, ivory, skins, and other goods in equatorial Africa. They were converted to Christianity in the 6th century under Ethiopian influence. A century later, the Arabs invaded, forcing the ruler of Dongola to give financial aid to Arab merchants and to allow Muslim preaching in exchange for preservation of the territorial integrity of Dongola and Alodia. This treaty remained in effect for over 600 years.

³ Egyptian Mamelukes destroyed Dongola and Alodia in the 14th century. Raids grew more frequent despite the emergence of new Islamic states: Sennar, on the Blue Nile; Kordofan to the west, and Darfur in the desert.

⁴ Intent on exterminating Egyptian soldiers, Pasha Muhammad Ali (see Egypt) entered Sudan in 1820. The Egyptian forces set up permanent quarters in Khartoum, controlling the entire country by 1876. Foreign military occupation brought radical changes: the country was united, limiting the autonomy of various small local governments; the introduction of foreign religious rites (even within the dominant Orthodox Sunni community) upset established

religious communities. Under British pressure, slavery was abolished, undermining the influence of powerful slave dealers. In addition, the burden of heavy taxes - particularly for farmers and cattle raisers - contributed to a general atmosphere of discontent.

⁵ In 1881 Muhammad Ahmad proclaimed himself Mahdi, meaning savior or redeemer, and launched a crusade to restore Islam. He rapidly gained support, especially among the Arabized population in the North. The British, having occupied Egypt in 1882, intervened militarily but were unable to change the course of the conflict. In 1885 Mahdi occupied Khartoum, defeated General Gordon's troops, and established the first national government, which was to last 13 years. The existence of the state threatened the British plan to unite all the territory from Cairo to Cape Town under their rule. In 1898, Egyptian troops moved in from Uganda and Kenya, attacking Mahdi on both fronts.

⁶ The French, with their own east-west transcontinental designs,

were also interested in Sudan, and sent troops into the area. This three-pronged attack defeated Mahdi, Khalifa Abdulahi, in September 1898. The colonial armies met in Fachoda, with small skirmishes between the French and British, but France finally recognized British predominance over the Nile basin. In 1899, Sudan was jointly administered by Britain and Egypt.

⁷ Egypt sought to achieve unity of the Nile by joining Cairo and Khartoum politically, and Britain was determined to prevent this. The British Empire threatened to grant 'federated independence' to the southern population, who were animists and Christians, but not to the Arabic and Muslim north. To make their threat effective, the British started a policy of 'closed districts', which prevented any contact between north and south.

⁸ A self-governing statute obtained by Sudan in 1953 was followed by the election of an all-Sudanese parliament in 1955 and the declaration of independence on January 1 1956. However, southerners charged that they had

been politically marginalized, and five months before independence a civil war broke out and lasted for 16 years.

⁹ In 1969, General Gaafar al-Nimeiry seized power through a coup. He dissolved Parliament, proclaimed the creation of the Sudanese Democratic Republic, and set up a one-party system, the Sudanese Socialist Union. The new government promised to support reconstruction and the development of the southern territories, offering them a certain degree of administrative autonomy.

¹⁰ After coming to power, Nimeiry changed course; he broke with the Sudanese Socialist Union and drew closer to conservative Arab regimes, never fulfilling his promise of greater autonomy for the South.

¹¹ Nimeiry was forced to sign an agreement with the guerrillas in 1972. This agreement granted autonomy to the southern provinces, while the guerrillas were incorporated into the regular army.

¹² In 1976, Sudan signed a mutual defense pact with Egypt and initially the Nimeiry government backed the Camp David accords signed by Egypt, Israel and the US. However when it became clear that this position would isolate Sudan from the Arab world, Nimeiry distanced himself from Cairo and drew closer to Saudi Arabia. Nimeiry stressed the Islamic nature of his regime, arousing opposition in the non-Muslim south.

¹³ In May 1977, Nimeiry was re-elected for a six-year term. Shortly afterwards the Government announced a 'national reconciliation' process which enabled exiled political leaders to return and paved the way for the rehabilitation of former opponents of the ruling Umma Party. However, the Sudanese Communist Party and former Finance Minister Shereef al-Hindi's National Front, were ignored.

¹⁴ Nimeiry was re-elected to a third six-year term in 1983, amid widespread accusations of electoral fraud. In September, he suddenly imposed Islamic law (the *Sharia*) on the whole country. This measure triggered a general protest among the animists and Christians in the South, and recharged the guerrilla movement.

¹⁵ A revolt broke out in the city of Bor, where the Sudanese Popular Liberation Movement (SPLM) arose. This political and military organization gave the southern guerrilla movement a new ideological foundation, with the objectives of achieving national unity and establishing socialism, while respecting southern autonomy and religious freedom.

¹⁶ In the north, Nimeiry was severely criticized by the Muslim Brotherhood and opposition parties for using Islamic law as a tool of repression against dissidents. The financial community also exerted pressure on the Sudanese president to limit the application of the Sharia in business as it stood in opposition to IMF policies.

¹⁷ Sudan's external debt rapidly rose to $8 billion. Debt servicing was systematically delayed until early 1984, with the country considered bankrupt on at least two occasions.

¹⁸ In 1985 the US suspended all credit and the IMF forced the Government to raise food prices. Rebellion broke out, quickly reaching the capital. Nimeiry visited the US in search of backing,

but was unable to return as Abdul Rahman Suwar al-Dahab, minister of defense and army chief of staff, had seized power in his absence.

¹⁹ The coup did not have much of an effect on the political scenario. The Islamic bourgeoisie in the north made deals with the Government, while the SPLM continued its activities in the south, as the political and economic discrimination against the region continued. Political parties were dissolved and the previous government's subdivision of the south was revoked. The new government promised to review the application of the Sharia, and Dahab promised elections in 1986.

²⁰ The elections were held in April 1986, and Sadiq al-Mahdi, from the Party of the People (UMMA), based on the Koran and on Islamic tradition, was elected Prime Minister.

²¹ Thirty-seven representatives were not elected because of the war in the southern provinces. The SPLM's 12,000 guerrillas besieged government garrisons in the southern provinces, practically splitting Sudan in two, and the south suffered from food shortages as a result of an insurgent blockade.

However, the guerrillas agreed to let through airborne food and medical supplies sent by the UN to besieged cities.

²² In June, 1989 the war between the SPLM and the army continued, the foreign debt reached $12 billion and the social tension increased, exacerbated by price increases. Also in June, Major-General Omar al-Bashir ousted the President, blaming his government for the political and economic crisis. Al-Bashir dissolved political parties and created a 15-member military junta, promising to bring the war to an end.

²³ Ten months after the military government took office, there was a coup attempt by a faction of army officials. Ethiopia, Kenya, Uganda, Zaire (now DR Congo), and the US all attempted mediation and all failed. Peace negotiations failed, and southern people continued to suffer at the hands of government troops and Arab paramilitary groups armed by al-Bashir's predecessors.

²⁴ On February 4 1991, the Government established a federal system in the country. According to the decree, Sudan would be divided into nine states, each administered by a governor and a ministerial cabinet. On January 31 of that year, General Omar al-Bashir's government had also signed a new criminal code based on the Sharia, only to be implemented in the north of the country, where Islam is predominant.

²⁵ With the Sudanese People's Liberation Army (SPLA), led by John Garang, operating in the south, and the Nasir rebel group - a splinter group of the SPLA led by Riak Mashar - operating in the north, the Government lost control. This led to violent government repression against its opponents in urban areas, and against rural communities which supported the guerrillas in the countryside.

²⁶ In May 1994, the Government signed a protocol for humanitarian aid with both rebel factions in order to provide relief for villages cut off by the conflict. Their situation continued to worsen and humanitarian organizations voiced their denunciations. In July 1995, the African Rights organization charged Khartoum of being responsible for the 'genocide' of the Nubian ethnic group.

²⁷ In the March 1996 elections, al-Bashir was re-elected with 76 per cent of the vote. The possibilities of coexistence between the 'theocrats' of the north and the rebels of the south appeared increasingly remote. The 12 years of war left a million dead and three million refugees.

²⁸ In November 1997, disputes with Egypt over administration of the Halaib triangle - rich in phosphates, manganese and,

supposedly, oil - led to Sudan asking for intervention from the Arab League. Under an agreement made in 1899, Halaib belonged to Egypt, but under a newer agreement of 1905, it had been awarded to Sudan.

²⁹ In January 1998, the U.S. announced an economic embargo on Sudan, alleging it had supported international terrorism, training opposition groups from neighboring countries in order to destabilize them, and lacking respect for human rights.

³⁰ A month later, the UN appealed to the international community for more than $100 million to aid 4 million victims of war and drought in Sudan.

³¹ The Sudanese guerrillas vindicated the air attack which had killed Vice-President Al Zubair Mohamed Saleh in February. According to observers, the Christian Sudanese People's Liberation Army (SPLA) rebels had been given US support in return for collaboration with Uganda, Ethiopia and Eritrea. The Catholic Church of Sudan decided to take part in peace talks between the Islamic Government and the military Sudanese Peoples Liberation Army faction prepared for dialogue.

³² In August 1998, the Shifa pharmaceutical plant was destroyed by US missiles in retaliation for the bombing of US embassies in Kenya and Tanzania. The factory was said to be linked with the World Islam Front led by Saudi millionaire and former US ally against communism, Osama bin Laden.

³³ A meningitis epidemic ravaged the country in March 1999. Thirty people died daily in Khartoum alone, the most affected areas being the outskirts of the city.

³⁴ With a $3 billion investment, Sudan managed to open a 1,500-km pipeline in June that would allow it to exploit vast reserves of petroleum, neglected as a result of the war and political problems. By late September, 150,000 barrels of oil a day were produced, and a target was set at 250,000. Because of the large investment, Sudan would only begin to see oil revenues after 2003. Meanwhile, hunger and war continued to haunt the country. Between 1,000 and 2,000 people displaced daily continued to arrive at refugee centers operated by international relief organizations.

³⁵ Dressed in uniform, al-Bashir took office once again in February 2001 in the presence of presidents from the region who were in Khartoum for a meeting of the group of Sahel and Saharan states. Al-Bashir was re-elected with 86.5 per cent of the votes in the December elections, which were boycotted by most of the opposition

---

PROFILE

ENVIRONMENT

The largest African country, Sudan has three distinct geographic regions: the barren deserts of the Sahara in the north, the flatlands of the central region and the dense rainforests of the south. Most of the population lives along the Nile, where cotton is grown. Port Sudan, on the Red Sea, handles all the country's foreign trade. Desertification has affected nearly 60 per cent of the territory. Industrial waste has contaminated coastal areas and some rivers.

SOCIETY

Peoples: The country has a wide ethnic spectrum with over 570 groups. Arabs, who live in the center and north of the country, together with Nubians, account for nearly half of the population. Among the other groups, the most important are the Nilote, Nilo-Hamitic and a few Bantu groups. In the south there are nearly 400,000 refugees from neighboring nations (Chad, Uganda, Ethiopia and Eritrea).
Religions: Islam is the predominant religion among Arabs and Nubians with a majority of Sunni Muslims. In the south, traditional African religions are practiced and there are Christian communities in both north and south.
Languages: Arabic (official and spoken by most of the population); the different ethnic groups speak over 100 different languages.
Political parties: Political parties were dissolved after the 1989 coup. Political associations have been allowed since 1999. National Congress Party, closely linked to the National Islamic Front; Alliance of the Labor Force. There are several extra-parliamentary parties: Umma Party; Democratic Unionist Party; Communist Party of Sudan. In the south, the predominant force is the Sudan People's Liberation Movement.

THE STATE

Official Name: Jumhuriyat as-Sudan.
Administrative Divisions: 9 states, 66 Provinces and 281 Local Government Areas.
Capital: Khartoum (Al-Khartum) 2,628,000 people (1999).
Other cities: Omdurman 1,599,300 people; Kassala 295,100; Port Sudan (Bur Sudan) 384,100 (2000).
Government: General Omar al-Bashir, President since June 30 1989, after overthrowing the civilian government (re-elected in 1996 and 2000). Unicameral Legislature: National Assembly, with 360 members.
National Holiday: January 1, Independence Day (1956).
Armed Forces: 118,500 (1995).
Other: 30,000-50,000 People's Defense Force.

parties. These organizations had called upon the President to establish full political and press freedoms and to end the civil war before holding elections.

36 After the Islamist National Congress Party (NCP) signed a protocol accord with the SPLA, its members began to be arrested. The first was leader Hassan al-Turabi, but the imprisonments continued until May, when Ali Ahmed el-Bashir died as a result of injuries during arrest. The police dispersed a protest by thousands of NCP militants with tear gas during Ahmed el-Bashir's funeral.

37 In June, the peace talks between President al-Bashir and rebel leader John Garang stagnated. A month later, both al-Bashir and the opposition agreed to an initiative by Egypt and Libya to put an end to the civil war, with plans for a national conference of reconciliation and constitutional reforms. The SPLA, meanwhile, was lukewarm on the proposal because it did not include a referendum on self-determination for the south. Furthermore, said the SPLA, any constitutional reform should include a separation of church and state.

38 The UN Security Council lifted the mostly symbolic sanctions against Sudan in September. These had included a ban on diplomatic travel as a result of charges that Khartoum had harbored suspects in the assassination attempt on Egyptian President Hosni Mubarak. The US however extended its unilateral sanctions for another year, alleging that the country had a history of protecting terrorists and violating human rights.

39 In response to a campaign by human rights activists, the Sudanese authorities reported that some 15,000 slaves, mostly from the south, had been released in December. That month, the SPLA accused the Government of violating the truce by bombing the Nuba mountains and killing 250 rebel soldiers during a mission to remove the population from parts of the south to open it up to oil drilling.

40 In January 2002 the SPLA signed a ceasefire agreement with Khartoum in the Nuba Mountains. But the battle for control over the oil fields led to clashes in May. The government forces, which had withdrawn from Nuba, were redeployed in the areas surrounding the Upper Nile oil fields, where they engaged in battles with a revitalized enemy: the Sudanese Popular Defense Force had joined forces with the SPLA. ■

Kanem-Bornu

Where the Bilma trade route neared Lake Chad, there lived, according to oral tradition, communities of 'small red men' who must have given rise, between the first and fifth centuries of our era, to the so-called Civilization of Chad, known for its high-quality artistic and metallurgical production. The Sao probably arrived towards the 10th century. They were a Nilotic nation, noted for their great size. They exterminated the 'little red men' and established a confederation of groups to the southeast of the lake. On the other side of the lake, communities of shepherds related to the Tibu (autochthonous nomads from the Tibesti mountains) had settled around the eighth century. These shepherds were the Kanuri who, after subduing the local population, set up the state of Kanema, ruled by a military caste. Converted to Islam in the 11th century, they cultivated close ties with the Arab world, based on the slave trade.

The capture of slaves frequently took the Kanuri to Sao territory which they eventually conquered. Thereafter, the Saif (Kanuri ruling family) came to be called 'the rulers of Kanem, the masters of Bornu' and their nation was known by this compound name.

The most outstanding period was during Dunama Dibalim's rule. Between 1220 and 1260 Dibalim ruled over the territory that extended from the banks of Lake Chad to Fezzan (Libya) in the north, and from the Haussa states in the west to Ouaddai (border of present-day Sudan) in the east.

The flourishing traffic allowed him to maintain a standing army of 30,000 horsemen. He also built a large residence in Cairo (Al Qahirah) for the young Kanuri who studied at the famous Al Azhar University.

However, total dominion over the other nations did not occur: the Sao, Tibu and Bulala (to the southeast) shook the 14th and 15th centuries with frequent rebellions, forcing the Saifs to leave Kanem and to move their capital.

Idris Alaoma (1571-1603) decided to solve these problems drastically; he bought muskets, hired instructors in Tunis and modernized the army to confront his enemies one by one.

The Sao, long considered rebellious, were completely exterminated in a campaign that razed all their towns. The Tibu were forced to abandon their mountains and settle in Bornu where they were easier to control. To subdue the Bulala he had to conquer the north of what is now Cameroon.

Paradoxically, this 'putting things in order' did not benefit the Kanuri economically. Although the Haussa merchants yielded to Idris' military drive, and eventually paid tribute to the Kanem - Bornu rulers, they succeeded in gaining control of the slave trade, thus benefitting from the 'peace' obtained with so much blood.

This situation remained more or less stable until the 19th century, when the Fulani invasion forced the king of Bornu to turn for help to Mahamad Al-Kanemi, a military chieftain. Al-Kanemi repulsed the invaders, but stayed and became the real power behing the throne, even though the crisis was over. This dual situation lasted until 1846, when the last of the Saifs, Ibrahim, was executed by Omar, al-Kanemi's son.

In 1893, Omar's successor was deposed by Rabah, a Sudanese guerrilla who had fought alongside the Mahdi (see Sudan). The new ruler extended the boundaries of Kanem-Bornu to Sudan. After several years of fighting against the French who wanted to seize control of the territory, Rabah was defeated by the joint action of three colonial armies coming from Algeria. Congo and Mali. His death signaled the end of resistance to colonial penetration. ■

Suriname

Population: 421,000 (2002)
Land area: 156,000 SQ KM
Capital: Paramaribo
Currency: Guilder
Language: Dutch, English and Sranang (creole)

Suriname

The Caribs settled along the Atlantic coasts of Central and South America. The original groups gradually dispersed; some inland, and others to the islands that lie off the coast of the continent. They lived in small communities where they existed by hunting, fishing and small-scale farming. They were also able warriors.

2 In the early 17th century Dutch colonists founded a settlement in Guyana and began to trade in slaves.

3 In 1863, when slavery was abolished in Dutch territories it was replaced by another source of cheap labor, Asian Indian and Javanese immigrants. This gave rise to a complex ethnic structure in the Guyana region. Asian Indians formed one of the largest groups, the most resistant to intermarriage and most strongly attached to their cultural heritage. Then came the Creoles or Afro-Americans, the Javanese, the 'bush people' whose ancestors had rebelled against slavery and fled the plantations, indigenous people and a small European minority.

4 These ethnic, cultural and linguistic differences hindered the development of a national identity. Political movements tended to represent individual ethnic communities, especially as these broadly corresponded to social divisions. The Creoles formed the NPK (National Party Combination), a coalition of four center-left parties, and they led the fight for independence after World War II. Jaggernauth Lachmon's Vatan Hitakarie represented the Indian population of shop owners and business people, and they sought to postpone independence.

5 In October 1973, the independence faction won the legislative elections. Liberal Hanck Arron, NPS (National Surinamese Party) leader was appointed Prime Minister.

6 Arron and Lachmon reached an agreement, and independence was finally proclaimed in 1975. Many middle-income Surinamese took advantage of their status as Dutch citizens to emigrate to the ex-colonial power. Nearly a third of the population, mostly Asian Indian, left and caused a serious shortage of technical, professional and

administrative personnel. The country lost much-needed qualified labor with only SURALCO and Billiton, the two transnationals which monopolized local bauxite mining, surviving the exodus. Economic activity decreased and agriculture declined to dangerous levels. In this difficult situation, Arron and his group of politicians were repeatedly accused of corruption and complicity with foreign companies.

7 On February 25 1980, the premier was overthrown by a coup which had begun as a protest by the sergeants' union for better working conditions. The National Military Council (NMC) summoned opposition leaders to form a government and several leftwing politicians accepted cabinet posts.

8 The Military Council, led by Lt-Colonel Desi Bouterse, took power from the politicians on February 4 1981, accusing the administration of corruption and underhand dealings with the Netherlands and the United States. This new government established relations with Cuba, in the face of opposition from the major internal parties, from the US and from the Netherlands. Brazil came to its aid on more than one occasion.

9 Labor unions, merchants and professional groups began to express their discontent in 1982. The conflict reached its peak in December of that year when 15 public figures were executed for allegedly organizing a 'counter-coup d'état'. The event is considered the most traumatic in the country's history.

10 In January 1983, Bouterse formed a new government, which appointed Errol Halibux, a nationalist and member of the Farmers and Labor Union, as Prime Minister. After the American invasion of Grenada, the Suriname Government did an about-face in its relations with Cuba, asking Havana to recall its ambassador and suspending all agreements for cooperation between the countries.

11 An effort was made to reduce Suriname's isolation and diversify its foreign relations, which were excessively dependent on Holland. To accelerate this process, the Government began to pursue a more aggressive foreign policy, joining CARICOM (Caribbean Community and Common Market) as an observer and establishing relations with Cuba, Grenada, Nicaragua, Brazil and Venezuela. It also became a member of SELA (Latin American

Economic System), the OAS (Organization of American States) and the Amazon Pact.

12 In mid-1986, former soldier Ronnie Brunswijk, aided by foreign mercenaries and funded by the Netherlands, began a campaign of harassment from bases in French Guyana.

13 In April 1987, the 33-member National Assembly (of whom 11 were labor union representatives) unanimously approved a draft constitution providing for a return to institutional government. The draft was supported by the three main political parties.

14 The coalition United Front for Democracy and Development won. On July 21 1989, President Ramsewak Shankar granted an amnesty to the still-active guerrilla movement, allowing them to hold on to their weapons as long as they were in the forests. Bouterse and the NDP opposed this agreement, arguing that it legalized an autonomous military force and encouraged the division.

15 In December 1990, another coup deposed Ramsewak Shankar, who had been the constitutional president since January 1988. Colonel Desi Bouterse, who had resigned a week prior to the coup, resumed his leadership of the army on December 30. The National Assembly, which had been set up in September 1987 for a period of five years appointed the NPS's Johan Draag as provisional president.

16 The May 1991 elections were held to choose the National Assembly, and the New Front (NF) won - a broad coalition of civilian parties and ethnic groups oppose to the military government. The NF proposed the re-establishment of relations with the Dutch Government and the tightening of economic and political links with the former colonizer.

17 In September, Ronald Venetiaan of the NF was elected President. The new head of state launched a 50 per cent cut in defense spending and a peace process, including a UN-sponsored guerrilla disarmament, under the supervision of Brazil and Guyana. In June 1992, a cooperation agreement was signed with the Netherlands, and a year later, a severe structural

adjustment program was adopted, which gave rise to discontent among the population.

[18] Poverty and unemployment in the rural agricultural communities formed the background for the occupation of the Afobakka dam, 100 kilometers south of Paramaribo, in March 1994. The rebels, who called for the resignation of the government, were expelled by government troops, after a four-day occupation. Another important movement took place in rural areas in 1995, when representatives of Indians and *Cimarrones* (runaway slaves living in the forest in their own communities) gathered to protest for the environmental damage caused by a Canadian mining company and an Indonesian timber company.

[19] In September 1996, Parliament elected Jules Wijdenbosch as President, thus blocking Venetiaan's re-election.

[20] The Netherlands issued an international warrant in April 1997 for former dictator Besi Bouterse, suspected of links with drug-trafficking. In response, Wijdenbosch appointed the former dictator State Councillor, granting him diplomatic immunity.

[21] Toward the end of that year, a failed coup ended in the arrest of 17 low-ranking officers. The army called for better pay and greater investment in equipment and weapons. The strength of the army had declined since the late 1980s when the Bouterse regime had fought the guerrilla groups. The coup attempt was related to the working conditions of the troops, which had deteriorated, with low salaries and outdated equipment.

[22] Price hikes, an 80-per-cent currency devaluation and demands in wage increases led to a difficult situation in Parliament which had voted itself salary increases both in February and November 1998. This caused deep social discontent. Teachers and civil servants carried out a series of strikes demanding salary increases which would enable them to regain their purchasing power.

[23] Social unrest and an unprecedented economic crisis intensified during the first months of 1999, leaving the country practically paralyzed. In February, several political groups had boycotted Parliament, preventing the necessary quorum for passage of any bill. The guilder, the national currency, suffered a 200-percent devaluation, inflation reached 20 per cent and the public health system was virtually bankrupt. There were ongoing protests by various social groups, particularly state employees, who represented 10 per cent of the population. Due to the state's large health system debts, doctors in private hospitals refused to treat patients who had state health insurance. The Government hired 52 doctors and nine health specialists in Cuba to serve in areas where Surinamese professionals refused to work.

[24] Parliament was shaken from its lethargy by the largest general strike in Suriname's history and massive protests endured for months in Paramaribo without a resolution in sight. Parliament deposed the Wijdenbosch Cabinet in June, blaming the officials for the country's economic collapse.

[25] In May 2000, Venetiaan's NF won the legislative elections with 47.3 per cent of the vote and in August he was elected President with 37 of the National Assembly's 51 votes. Jules Ajodhia was elected Vice-President and Prime Minister.

[26] Tensions between Suriname and Guyana, dating back decades due to disputes over territorial waters, reached a peak in June 2000 when a Surinamese vessel forced the withdrawal of the Canadian company CGX Energy, to which Guyana had granted oil exploration rights. In July, after the leaders of the two countries failed to reach an accord after several days of negotiations in Jamaica, the Canadian company called off the project.

[27] In November 2000, the High Court of Amsterdam ruled that coup leader Desi Bouterse - who had been condemned and sentenced in absentia by a court at the Hague for leading a cocaine-smuggling ring during and after his time in office - would be prosecuted, again in absentia, for charges implicating him in the December 1982 assassinations. Suriname had begun investigating the executions and asked the Netherlands for cooperation and assistance. Because there was no extradition treaty between the two countries, Suriname was not obliged to send Bouterse to Amsterdam for the trial.

[28] By 2001, Venetiaan had achieved greater fiscal and economic stability in the country. The currency had responded to corrective measures, inflation was reduced, the armed forces were largely depoliticized and the Government engaged in loan negotiations with the Netherlands and the Inter-American Development Bank for funding health, education and other social programs. ∎

PROFILE

ENVIRONMENT

The coastal plain, low and subject to floods, is suitable for agriculture. Rice, sugar and other crops are grown. Land has been reclaimed from the sea through drainage and dykes. Inland, the terrain is hilly with dense tropical vegetation, rich in bauxite deposits. Year-round heavy rainfall feeds an important system of rivers, some of which are used to generate hydro-electric power for the aluminum industry.

SOCIETY

Peoples: Suriname Creole 30 per cent; Indo-Pakistani 33 per cent; Javanese 16 per cent; 'Bush Negro' 10 per cent; Amerindian 3 per cent; other 3 per cent.
Religions: Christian 44 per cent (21.6 per cent Catholic, 18 per cent Protestant); Muslim 18.6 per cent; Hinduism 26 per cent; other 15.8 per cent.
Languages: Dutch (official). English (for business), Hindi, Javanese, and a form of Creole are spoken. This, called either Taki-Taki or Sranang-Tongo, is based on African languages mixed with Dutch, Spanish and English.
Political Parties: New Front for Democracy (NF) comprised of four parties: Suriname National Party, Progressive Reform Party, Pertjajah Luhur (Javanese minority) and the Suriname Labor Party; Millennium Combination (MC) comprises the National Democratic Party, Party for National Unity and Solidarity and the Democratic Alternative; Democratic National Platform 2000 (DNP2000); Democratic Alternative '91 (DA' 91).
Social Organizations: Suriname Trade Union Federation; Central Organization of Civil Servants.

THE STATE

Official Name: Republiek Suriname.
Administrative Divisions: 9 Districts.
Capital: Paramaribo 233,000 people (1999).
Other cities: Nieuw Nickerie 13,100 people; Meerzorg 6,400; Marienburg 4,300 (2000).
Government: Parliamentary Republic. President, Ronald Venetiaan since August 2000. Prime Minister, Jules Rattankoemar Ajodhia since August 2000. Unicameral Parliament: 51-member National Assembly.
National Holiday: November 25, Independence Day (1975).
Armed forces: 1,800 (1996).

Swaziland

Population: 948,000 (2002)
Land area: 17,200 SQ KM
Capital: Mbabane
Currency: Emalangeni
Language: English and Swazi

Swaziland

Like Lesotho, (see Lesotho) Swaziland achieved centralized administration when groups of very different origins joined to form a nation. The danger posed by Zulu expansion, (see South Africa) led Sobhuza, head of the Dlamini local groups, to bring together the remains of several peoples groups split apart by Shaka, including Zulu deserters and Bushmen or San who remained in the region. They became a powerful force in the northeastern part of the present-day South African province of Natal. Sobhuza died shortly after the Zulu defeat by the Boers (1839) leaving his son, Mswati, the task of keeping the nation together, in the face of constant threats from the Afrikaners. The nation was named after its king who led the nation in 30 years of resistance - aside from a period of alliance with the Boers against the Pedi - allying with the British shortly before his death so as to avoid defeat by the Boers.

[2] In 1867, Swaziland formally became a British protectorate, like Basutoland (Lesotho) and Bechuanaland (Botswana). When Britain defeated the Boers in 1902 and imposed its dominion over the whole of South Africa, these countries remained under separate colonial administrations. Native authorities were formally recognized according to British criterion of making use of 'local' intermediaries to facilitate colonial administration.

[3] In 1961, when the Union of South Africa broke off relations with Britain and toughened racial segregation policies, London accelerated the decolonization process in the region. Swaziland was granted internal autonomy in 1967 and formal independence the following year. Sobhuza II was recognized as head of state and governed with two legislative chambers. On April 12 1973, he dissolved Parliament, claiming that it contained 'destructive elements', suspended the constitution inherited from the British at independence in 1968, banned the action of all political parties and proclaimed himself absolute monarch. Sobhuza also announced a state of emergency that is still in place.

[4] On assuming power, Sobhuza II placed himself in the service of the

South African colonizers against whom his grandfather had fought. Communications, the postal service, transport, currency and the Bank of Swaziland all became dependent on South Africa. The big neighbor's companies exploited the country's asbestos and iron ore and South African experts ran the state's public administration - guaranteeing efficient control - and supervised agricultural production. Cotton, the main export product, was marketed by South African merchants and white South Africans opened brothels and cabarets which the strict official morality prohibited in their own country.

[5] At that time due to the lack of job opportunities, thousands of workers emigrated every year to work in the South African gold mines. The money they sent home to their families accounted for 25 per cent of Swaziland's foreign currency earnings.

[6] In 1978 the Swazi Liberation Movement (Swalimo) was founded, led by Dr Swane, who managed to escape from prison in the capital, Mbabane. The strengthening of the opposition was accompanied by a rapid growth of the armed forces, from 1,000 in 1975 to more than 5,000 in 1979, and the police force was considerably reinforced.

[7] Mounting opposition inside the country was encouraged by the

consolidation of a socialist regime in Mozambique, amongst other things. Increasing tension in Swaziland also led the Government to develop closer military relations with South Africa and Israel; Sobhuza II was one of only three African rulers who never severed diplomatic relations with the Government of Tel Aviv.

[8] The Constitution was suspended in 1973 and a reformed version was introduced in 1978 without approval from or consultation with the electorate. Following traditional customs, the process of approval consisted of consultation with the heads of the 40 clans a fortnight before the enactment of the new constitutional draft. It banned opposition parties and established a parliament with little decision-making power.

[9] After 1980, the economic situation in Swaziland was affected by the world recession. The post-independence boom period came to an end with an increase in the prices of imported goods and a drop in prices for corn, sugar and wood exports. Mineral exports fell from 40 per cent of total exports to only 10 per cent due to the depletion of iron ore reserves. Various new coal deposits were discovered in 1980 but their exploitation has been slow due to legal difficulties and the lack of adequate transport facilities.

[10] In August 1982, King Sobhuza died at the age of 83 when his successor, Prince Makhosetive was only 15 years old. The lack of effective government sparked a power struggle between several princes and Prince Mabandla Dlamini was deposed from his position as Prime Minister. He was succeeded by Bhekimpi Dlamini, a pro-South African conservative, who began his reign by persecuting South African refugees.

[11] In August 1983, Ntombi, one of Sobhuza's widows, overthrew the reigning Queen and took power, strengthening the conservative faction. Two months later, 200,000 of the country's 760,000 people voted for a new parliament through a complicated indirect electoral system called *tinkhundla*. As expected, Prince Bhekimpi Dlamini was successful in an electoral contest where no political parties participated.

[12] The election resulted in closer ties with South Africa. The repression of anti-apartheid militants increased in 1984, with detention and return to the Pretoria Government becoming the norm.

[13] During the second half of 1984, a student protest led the Government to close down the university. Prime Minister Bhekimpi Dlamini's authoritarianism stimulated the revival of the Swazi Liberation Movement, which resumed its activities in January 1985. This movement was led by Prince Clement Dumisa Dlamini, who was the former secretary-general of the Progressive Party and a well-known nationalist leader. He was later exiled to England.

[14] On April 25 1986, Prince Makhosetive was crowned, taking the name King Mswati III. His inaugural address reflected his conservative stance. In May he dissolved the *Liqoqo* (an assembly of local group leaders acting as Supreme State Council), consolidating his power and that of his ministers. Prime Minister Bhekimpi was relieved of his post and replaced by Sotsha Dlamini. In September 1987, King Mswati dissolved Parliament, announcing elections for November, a year ahead of schedule. The 40 members of Parliament and 10 senators were

elected by an electoral college. The King however disputed the election of the senators, demanding that the process be repeated in a more satisfactory manner.

[15] Since the late 1980s the country's economic situation had improved noticeably. The economy grew and foreign investment continued. A significant part of the food produced was sold to the European Community. This improvement, a direct consequence of trade sanctions against South Africa, allowed the manufacturing sector to increase - contributing 20 per cent of the GDP by 1991 - and helped the country raise its economic growth rate to 3.5 per cent per year.

[16] In 1992, a significant part of the opposition joined the Popular United Democratic Movement (PUDEMO) and lobbied for the King to accept a multiparty system. Discontent increased in 1993, as a prolonged drought destroyed the corn crop and generated further unemployment.

[17] According to some studies carried out in 1994, even though calorie consumption was slightly higher than the basic minimum, the country still had a high child mortality rate - 107 per 1,000 - and only 30 per cent of the population had access to drinking water. Moreover, Swaziland was still dependent on South Africa, the source of 90 per cent of imports.

[18] Protests against Mswati III

continued. After the deliberate fire of February 1995 in the seat of parliament, for which the Swaziland Youth Congress claimed responsibility, 40,000 people took part in a demonstration in support of a two-day general strike. Nelson Mandela's new government in Pretoria pressed the King, and in February 1996 he expressed his willingness to authorize political parties, amidst rumors of possible intervention from the South African army.

[19] The Swaziland Federation of Trade Unions called for an end to the absolute monarchy and the establishment of a multiparty regime. Violent clashes between demonstrators and the security forces caused at least three deaths.

[20] Mid-year, the King called for an end to the upheaval, repeating he would reconsider the banning of the political parties. He also said the citizens would be given the opportunity to participate in drawing up a new Constitution. In May, he sacked Prime Minister Mbilini Dlamini and appointed Barnabas Sibusiso Dlamini as his replacement in July.

[21] The political situation did not change substantially in 1997. In March the King let down the opposition by not sending delegates to the agreed negotiations. In July, he created a 30-member committee, charged with drafting a Constitution, asking for all related initiatives be referred to this body.

[22] These delaying tactics intensified the protests. The King reacted, ordering the security forces to fire live ammunition on demonstrators. The clashes produced large numbers of wounded and several union leaders were arrested. In October 1997, fresh strikes broke out in strategic areas, like the sugar sector. The unions also called for the Constitutional Revision Committee to be dissolved.

[23] In April 1998, the King put an 'environmental conservation' plan into action, with public and private sector participation. At the same time, bidding was opened on large-scale public works projects including bridges, the re-routing of major watercourses, and irrigation structures for vast areas hit by drought.

[24] In spite of the ban on political parties there were parliamentary elections in October. Few voters registered due to a boycott called by trade unions and the opposition. The Government raided the homes of many opposition union leaders in return.

[25] Several prominent lawyers and politicians, including the former justice minister who was one of the King's advisers, were accused of government fraud.

[26] A report from the Ministry of Economic Development indicated that the wrongful or poorly researched resettlement of farmers was the main cause of poverty in rural areas. The permanent displacements the citizens had to undergo were detrimental to farmers. As a result, public opinion swung in favor of changes in the administration of justice, royal rights and land resettlement policies. In October 2000, the Government evicted 40 families from their land in order to give it to the king's brother. The decision caused street demonstrations that paralyzed the country for two days.

[27] In mid 2001, Mswati declared a ban on any citizen imitating the king or making fun of him. The royal decree meant the monarch could ban any publication not in line with 'Swazi morality and ideals'. Two opposition publications were immediately banned.

[28] At least 19 per cent of the population of Swaziland are HIV-positive, one of the highest levels in the world. In early 2001, a law was passed banning the wearing of miniskirts in schools - supposedly to prevent sexual relationships between students and teachers. In March the following year, Parliament called for the reintroduction of brothels in order to reduce the incidence of rape and combat the spread of HIV and AIDS in the nation.

[29] The same month, Swaziland made an urgent appeal for food aid for 200,000 people at risk of dying

from hunger. Nearly 40 per cent of the population were threatened with death due to the poor harvest that year. Maize stocks had run out, and South Africa, the traditional supplier, did not have enough to export to Swaziland.

[30] The crisis deepened in 2002. ∎

PROFILE

ENVIRONMENT

The country is divided into three distinct geographical regions known as the high, middle and lowveld (plain) all approximately the same size. The western region is mountainous with a central plateau and flatlands to the east. The main crops are sugarcane, citrus fruits and rice (irrigated), cotton, corn (the basic foodstuff), sorghum and tobacco. In the lower veld, infections caused by polluted water are responsible for the high mortality rate. Wildlife was exterminated by European hunters in the first half of this century. Swaziland is suffering a serious problem of soil erosion due to overgrazing and also suffers a shortage of drinking water.

SOCIETY

Peoples: 84.3 per cent of the population belong to the Swazi ethnic group. Zulu account for 9.9 per cent; Tonga and Shangaan another 3 per cent; there are Indian (0.8 per cent), Pakistani (0.8 per cent) and Portuguese (0.2 per cent) minorities. **Religions:** 77 per cent of the population are Christian, the rest follow traditional African religions. **Languages:** Swazi and English (official); ethnic minorities speak their own languages. **Political Parties:** Popular United Democratic Movement (PUDEMO); Swaziland Progressive Party; Swaziland Democratic Alliance; National Congress of Ngwane Liberation. All political parties and activities were banned by King Sobhuza II in 1973.
Social Organizations: Swaziland Federation of Trade Unions (SFTU); Swaziland Youth Congress.

THE STATE

Official Name: Umbuso wakaNgwane. **Administrative Divisions:** 210 Tribal Areas, including 40 traditional communities. **Capital:** Mbabane 73,000 people (1999). **Other cities:** Manzini 22,500 people; Big Bend 14,300; Lobamba 14,000 (2000). **Government:** King Mswati III, crowned on April 25 1986. Barnabas Sibusiso Dlamini, Prime Minister since July 1996. Parliament has two chambers: The House of Assembly has 65 members and the Senate has 30 non-partisan members. **National holiday:** September 6, Independence Day (1968). **Armed Forces:** 2,657 (1983).

Sweden

Population: 8,823,000 (2002)
Land area: 411,620 SQ KM
Capital: Stockholm
Currency: Kronor
Language: Swedish

Sverige

According to archaeological research, the first inhabited area in Sweden is thought to have been the southern part of the country, with occupation dating back to 10000 years BC. Between 8000 and 6000 BC, the region was inhabited by peoples who made a living by hunting and fishing, using simple stone tools. The Bronze Age (1800-500 BC) brought with it cultural development, reflected in particular in the richness of the tombs of that period.

[2] In 500 AD, in Lake Malaren valley, the Sveas created the first important center of political power. From the 6th century BC until the year 800 the population went through a migration period, later becoming settled, with agriculture becoming the basis of economic and social activities.

[3] Between the 9th and 11th centuries, the Swedish Vikings reached the Baltic shores on trade expeditions as well as pirate raids and also went as far as what is now Russia, reaching the Black and Caspian Seas. There they established relations with the Byzantine and Arab empires.

[4] During the same period, Christian missions from the Carolingian empire (led by the missionary, Ansgar) converted most of Sweden. However, the gods of the ancient local mythologies survived into the 12th century. Sweden had its first archbishop in 1164.

[5] From the middle of the 12th century, Sverker and Erik's respective fiefdoms fought against each other to gain control of the Swedish kingdom, alternating in power between 1160 and 1250. The feudal

chieftains remained relatively autonomous until the second half of the 13th century, when the King enforced nationwide laws and annexed Finland.

[6] The Black Death brought the country's growth to a standstill in

1350, and it remained so until the second half of the 15th century. In that period the foundries in the central region became important. During the 15th and 16th centuries the German Hanseatic League dominated Swedish commerce and

encouraged the foundation of several cities.

[7] In 1397, the royal power of Norway, Sweden and Denmark was handed over to the Danish queen Margaret, who proclaimed the Union of Kalmar. The ensuing conflicts between the central Danish power and the rebellious Swedish nobility, townspeople and peasants ended in 1523, with the accession of Gustav Vasa to the throne of Sweden.

[8] Under the reign of Vasa, the monarchy ceased to be elected by the nobility and became hereditary. A German administrative model was adopted and the foundations were laid for a nation state. The possessions of the Church went to the state, with the Protestant Reformation following hot on its heels. From then on, Sweden aspired to becoming the main power in the Baltic region.

[9] In 1630, after intervening successfully in the Thirty Years' War, Sweden waged two more wars to conquer the Danish regions of Skane, Halland, Blekinge, and the Baltic island of Gotland, as well as the Norwegian islands of Bohuslan, Jamtland, and Harjedalen.

[10] Sweden thus became a great power in northern Europe, as it now ruled over Finland, several northern German provinces, and the Baltic provinces of Estonia, Latvia and Lithuania. However, the country was still basically rural and lacked resources to maintain its position or power indefinitely.

[11] After its defeat in the Great Northern War (1700-21), the Swedish Empire lost most of the provinces to the south and east of the Gulf of Finland. It was reduced to the territories roughly corresponding to modern Sweden and Finland, with Finland being ceded to Russia during the Napoleonic Wars.

[12] In 1718, after the death of Charles XII, a parliament (*Riksdag*) made up of nobles did away with the monarchy, assuming power itself. However, the new king Gustav II staged a coup in 1772, gradually claiming more and more power, and finally re-establishing full monarchic powers in 1789.

[13] In compensation for the losses incurred during the Napoleonic Wars, Norway was ceded to King Charles XIV, who had become king in

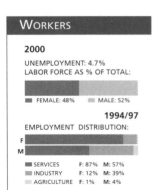

WORKERS

2000

UNEMPLOYMENT: 4.7%
LABOR FORCE AS % OF TOTAL:

- FEMALE: 48%
- MALE: 52%

1994/97

EMPLOYMENT DISTRIBUTION:

F
M

- SERVICES   F: 87%   M: 57%
- INDUSTRY   F: 12%   M: 39%
- AGRICULTURE F: 1%   M: 4%

LAND USE

DEFORESTATION: 0.0% annual (1990/95)

1993

- FOREST & WOODLAND: 62.2%
- ARABLE: 6.2%
- OTHER: 31.6%

PUBLIC EXPENDITURE

1999

DEFENSE: 5.5%
SOCIAL: 58.1%

1810. After a short war, it was forced to join Sweden in 1814. Nevertheless, after a series of conflicts, the union dissolved peacefully in 1905.

[14] In the second half of the 19th century, Sweden continued to be a poor country, with 90 per cent of the population engaged in agriculture. At this point, a great emigration movement began: one million out of a total of 5 million Swedes left, mainly for North America.

[15] During this period the liberal majority in parliament, supported by King Oscar I, established universal education (1842), the free enterprise system and the liberalization of foreign trade (1846). Legislation was also passed establishing sexual equality in inheritance law (1845), the rights of unmarried women (1858), and religious freedom (1860).

[16] Important social movements such as the temperance league, free churches, women's advancement, and especially the workers' movement emerged, growing with

industrialization and influencing the government through social democracy.

[17] From 1890 onwards, with the support of foreign capital, the process of industrialization accelerated in Sweden. The country had one of the most thriving economies in that part of Europe. Finished products using Swedish technical innovations quickly became the country's main exports.

[18] Universal male suffrage has been in force since 1908, a state old-age pension system was adopted in 1913, and in 1918 the 8-hour working day was established by law. That same year, the vote was extended to women.

[19] The parliamentary system has been in effect since 1918. The Social Democrats came to power in 1932; their policies fostered understanding between workers and industrialists, which was enshrined in the 1938 Pact of Salsboejaden.

[20] Sexual equality was achieved

earlier in Sweden than in other industrialized countries, through the efforts of feminists and state campaigns against social and sexual prejudice.

[21] The country's educational system - from primary onwards - sought to eliminate sexism by teaching both girls and boys housekeeping, babycare, woodwork and metalwork.

[22] Abortion is available on demand to women up to the third month of pregnancy. The law concerning rape states that there are no extenuating circumstances to be considered in the man's case, and there are also stiff sentences for rape within marriage.

[23] Women can take on any profession, with the exception of the army. However, the female population is still concentrated in the lowest income groups. In general their earnings are 20 per cent lower than those of their male counterparts for similar jobs. In 1981, over 50 per cent of all married women were economically active outside the home.

[24] Within the civil service, there is an official position of Ombudsman, whose role is to investigate cases of abuse of authority, breach of ethics, and ethnic or sexual discrimination in state agencies and private companies.

[25] Since World War I, Sweden has refused to take part in peacetime alliances in order to stay neutral in times of war. This policy relies on Sweden's strong defense system and compulsory national service for men.

[26] Trade routes were disrupted during World War II, which caused serious food shortages in the country. For security reasons Sweden is almost self-sufficient, with up to 80 per cent of its agricultural produce produced internally. The Government maintains a protectionist policy on agricultural imports, which means that food prices are higher than those on the international market.

[27] Sweden favored a thaw in East-West relations during the Cold War, and worked actively for international disarmament. One of the cornerstones of its foreign policy is its support for the UN.

[28] During four decades in power from 1932 to 1976, under the leadership of Tage Erlander, the

Social Democrats established conditions which made it possible to combine rapid economic and industrial growth with a redistribution of wealth through direct taxation. Thus, a costly social welfare system was established, using the framework of a capitalist economy with strong state intervention.

[29] In the 1970s there was a slow-down of economic growth, due partly to the increasing cost of oil imports to satisfy half the country's energy needs. Of the other 50 per cent 15 came from nuclear reactors and 7 per cent from coal and coke.

[30] After the 1976 elections, amid an incipient economic crisis, the moderate, liberal and conservative parties formed a coalition. Six years later, the Social Democrats returned to power. In 1986, charismatic leader Olof Palme was shot dead in a murder case that has still not been solved. Ingvar Carlsson succeeded him as prime minister.

[31] In the years that followed, Parliament investigated an alleged case of bribery - involving the Government and Bofors, an arms manufacturing company - in connection with to the sale of weapons to the Middle East and India. The country's laws forbade such conduct, as well as trade with areas where there are military tensions or with countries that are at war.

[32] The social service and welfare system established in Sweden by the Social Democrats was aimed at ensuring a minimum level of assistance and a more egalitarian wealth redistribution, through graduated taxation of the highest income groups.

[33] In spite of the important benefits obtained by the Swedish population, the largest taxpayers managed to evade taxation. On Carlsson's initiative, Parliament approved a fiscal reform in 1989, but it was considered too liberal and divided the Social Democrats.

[34] Under this new law, citizens with incomes below a certain level paid the same rate of tax, at 30 per cent. The rate for incomes above this limit went down from 72 to 50 per cent, while capital started to be taxed directly.

[35] In 1990 negotiations were held in order to create a 'European

PROFILE

ENVIRONMENT
Sweden lies on the eastern part of the Scandinavian Peninsula. In the wooded northern area are iron mines and paper mills. The central region has fertile plateaus and plains. The main industrial area is located in the southern part of the country that is also productive agriculturally with wheat, potatoes and sugar-beet as well as cattle. The southern area is also the most densely populated.

SOCIETY
Peoples: Swedes 89.4 per cent; Finn and Lapp minorities. There are refugees from Iran and former Yugoslavia.
Religion: Lutheran (official) 89 per cent; Catholics 1.8 per cent; Pentecostal Church 1.1 per cent. Other 10.6 per cent.
Languages: Swedish (official); Finnish and Lapp.
Political Parties: The left-of-center Social Democratic Workers' Party; the Center Party; the Moderate Rally Party (conservative); the Green Party; the right-wing Liberal Party; Christian Democratic Party (center-right) and the Leftwing-Party (formerly Communist Party).
Social Organizations: Confederation of Swedish Trade Unions, Confederation of Professional Associations, Central Wage Earners' Organization.

THE STATE
Official Name: Konungariket Sverige.
Administrative divisions: 24 provinces.
Capital: Stockholm 1,578,000 people (1999).
Other cities: Göteborg 744,300 people; Malmö 242,700; Uppsala 125,400 (2000).
Government: Hereditary constitutional monarchy. Sovereign: Carl XVI Gustaf, since September 15 1973. Goeran Persson, Prime Minister since March 1996, re-elected September 2002. Unicameral Legislature: the *Diet*, with 349 members.
National Holiday: June 6, Swedish Flag Day.
Armed Forces: 64,000 (1994).
Other: Coast Guard: 600 (1993).

FOOD DEPENDENCY

2000

6%

FOREIGN TRADE

Millions US$ 2000

IMPORTS
95,634

EXPORTS
107,761

STATISTICS

DEMOGRAPHY
Population: 8,823,000 (2002)
Annual growth: 0.4 % (1985-2000)
Estimates for year 2015: 8,625,000 (2000)
Annual growth to year 2015: -0.2 % (2000)
Urban population: 83.3 % (2000)
Urban growth: 0.2 % (2000)
Children per woman: 1.4 (2000)

HEALTH
Life expectancy at birth: 80 years (2000-2005)
male: 78 years (2000-2005)
female: 83 years (2000-2005)
Maternal mortality: 5 per 100,000 live births (1985/99)
Infant mortality: 3 per 1,000 (2000)
Under-5 child mortality: 4 per 1,000 (2000)
Daily calorie supply: 3,141 per capita (1999)
311 doctors per 100,000 people (1997)
Safe water: 100 % (2000)

EDUCATION
School enrolment (net):
Primary total: 100 % (1994/2000)
male: 100 % (1995/99)
female: 100 % (1995/99)
Secondary (gross):
male: 128 % (1995/97)
female: 153 % (1995/97)
Tertiary (gross): 63 % (1998)
Primary school teachers: one for every 12 pupils (1998)

COMMUNICATIONS
432 newspapers (1998), 932 radios (1997), 574 TV sets (2000) and 682 main telephone lines (2000) per 1,000 people
Books: 158 new titles per 100,000 people (1992/94)

ECONOMY
Per capita, GDP: $ 24,277 (2000)
Annual growth: 3.4 % (2000)
Annual inflation: 1.0 % (2000)
Consumer price index: 102.3 (2000)
Currency: 10.5 kronor = $ 1 (03/2002)
Cereal imports: 182,362 metric tons (2000)
Food import dependency: 6 % (2000)
Fertilizer use: 1,007 kg per ha (1999)
Exports: $ 107,761 million (2000)
Imports: $ 95,634 million (2000)

ENERGY
Consumption: 5,927.8 Kgs of oil equivalent per capita yearly (1998); 32.5 % imported (1999)

HDI (ranking/value): 4 / 0.936 (1999)

economic space' and in June 1991 Sweden - represented by the Carlsson Government - applied for entry to the EC.

[36] In the September 1991 elections, the Social Democrats lost their parliamentary majority. A coalition of the Moderate, Liberal, Center, and Christian Democratic parties appointed Carl Bildt, the leader of the Moderates, as Prime Minister. The new government promised to speed up Swedish membership of the EC, and the liberalization of the country's economy.

[37] By the end of 1991, unemployment in Sweden hit a record 160,000, doubling figures for the previous year. An additional 83,000 people were receiving vocational training, and 14,000 had been absorbed by government unemployment schemes.

[38] In 1991 and 92, the economic crisis served as the background for a wave of xenophobia and attacks against foreigners, phenomena which had previously been non-existent in a country that had had liberal immigration and asylum policies throughout the 1960s and 1970s.

[39] On August 26 1993, the King opened a new parliament for the Sami population of Samiland. At that time there were 17,000 Sami in that area of a total population of 60,000 living in Norway (40,000), Finland, Russia and Sweden. Most of the people by herded reindeer. A major dispute with the government arose over the abolition of the Sami's exclusive hunting rights over their lands.

[40] Sami children are given two weeks off in the autumn and spring in order for them to learn about pasturing reindeer. In 1971, the law regulating reindeer-raising recognized special Sami rights over the lands and watercourses where this is practiced.

[41] After a contentious electoral campaign, in a referendum held in November 1994, 52 per cent of voters approved Sweden's entry into the EU. A significant part of the political establishment and a number of entrepreneurs supported entry, while left-wing groups and environmentalists were against it. There were also 'geographical'

disagreements, since the majority of southern urban population voted for it and rural and northern inhabitants voted against it. Sweden joined the EU on January 1 1995.

[42] In September, the Prime Minister announced measures aimed at making the labor market more 'flexible'. The powerful Confederation of Swedish Unions considered the proposals an attack on worker security. Furthermore, it accused the Government of 'swerving to the right' and threatened to withhold its annual contribution to the Social Democratic Party funds.

[43] In August 1997 it was revealed that some 60,000 people, mostly women, had been sterilized between 1935 and 1976, as part of a government plan to prevent 'inferior human beings from multiplying'. The concept of the 'purity' of the Swedish race had been defined in 1922 by the Uppsala Institute of Racial Biology. The Government authorized a parliamentary investigation into the issue.

[44] At the end of the year, with a healthier economic situation - with lower unemployment (achieved, some believed, by government short-term programs which masked the real situation) the Government announced it would not be part of the monetary union with other EU nations, saying the project was 'highly dubious'.

[45] The Government issued a formal apology to the Sami population in August 1998 due to the 'injustices they had borne through the years' because of the colonization of Northern regions which expelled the Samis from their lands.

[46] Even though the Social Democrats had their worst election result in history at the September elections (with just 36.6 per cent of the vote), they managed to retain power due to a parliamentary majority supported by the Green Party and the former Socialist Party.

[47] This was not a comfortable majority for the Social Democrats, who considered the political platforms of the two other parties unrealistic, and the two other parties, in turn, opposed joining the European single currency system. Sweden, through Persson, assumed

the rotating European Union presidency for the first time in January 2001. Its objectives were focused on the expansion of the EU, new protocols for labor and environmental protection, leaving the currency issue aside.

[48] Opinion polls at the time showed that 50 per cent of the population opposed EU membership. Initially, the Government had agreed to join the euro regime, but did not set a date and was not convinced to carry out a referendum on the issue because it could not ensure an affirmative outcome. In August 2001, Persson said the Government would continue assessing the conditions and that if Sweden were to join the single currency it would not be until 2005.

[49] After a three-year-old Muslim boy died during circumcision, Parliament passed a law in October that the procedure must be conducted with anesthesia and medical assistance. Swedish Jews and Muslims alike protested the new law, saying it violated their religious rights. The Jewish community in Stockholm argued that it would be impossible to find doctors or nurses that would take part in the ceremony because Swedish health professionals considered circumcision a form of mutilation.

[50] The assassination of Fadime Sahendalen in January 2002 triggered demands for urgent action to protect young immigrants, who were victims of their own families. The young Kurdish woman had appeared in the media previously through a legal case. This had pitted her against her family, who wanted her to marry a Kurd and had threatened to kill her, because she was in a relationship with a Swedish man. In the end, her father, who had received a suspended sentence for the threats, killed her, which within the Kurdish community is considered an 'honor crime'. Fadime became a media symbol of the vulnerability of immigrant women. Her death led the Government to recognize that in some instances its integration policy had failed.

[51] Persson was re-elected in September 2002. His Social Democrats and leftist allies won an absolute majority. ■

Switzerland

Population: 7,167,000 (2002)
Land area: 39,550 SQ KM
Capital: Bern
Currency: Swiss franc
Languages: German, French and Italian

Schweiz / Suisse / Svizzera

Some Celtic tribes occupied the territory of Switzerland before Roman colonization. The most important of these were the Helvetians, who settled in the Alps and the Jura mountains. The area was strategically important for Rome, with access to its dominions. Consequently, the Alpine valleys north of the Italian peninsula were conquered by Julius Caesar in 58 BC.

[2] The Germanic tribes north of the Rhine invaded from the year 260 onwards. Between the 5th and 6th centuries the Germans established permanent settlements in the region east of the Aar river, together with Burgundian and Frankish groups. By 639 they had founded the kingdoms that would later become France.

[3] The Christian survivors from Roman times had completely disappeared when St Columba and St Gall arrived in the 6th century. These missionaries created the dioceses of Chur, Sion, Basel, Constance and Lausanne. Monasteries were built, in Saint-Gall, Zurich, Disentis and Romainmotier.

[4] Until the partition of Verdun in 843 these territories belonged to Charlemagne's empire. Thereafter, the region west of the Aar was allotted to Lothair, while the east remained in the hands of Louis the German. The French and German influence formed a peculiar blend with the Latin tradition of the Roman Catholic Church.

[5] Around 1033, for dynastic and political reasons, Helvetia became a part of the Holy Roman Empire, remaining so during the Middle Ages. In the 11th century the region was divided after the re-establishment of imperial authority

and its disputes with the Papacy. Dukes, counts, and bishops exerted virtually autonomous local power.

[6] Walled cities served as administrative and commercial centers, and protected powerful families seeking to expand their possessions through wars against other lords and kingdoms. In the 13th century, Rudolf IV of Hapsburg conquered most of the territories of Kyburg and became the most powerful lord in the region.

[7] In the cities independence gradually developed in opposition to the nobility. Meanwhile the peasant communities in the most inaccessible valleys practiced economic cooperation to survive the harsh conditions, rejecting forced labor and payment of tithes in cash or kind.

[8] In 1231 the canton (area) of Uri fell under the authority of the Holy Roman Empire, and in 1240 Schwyz and Nidwald were subjected to Emperor Frederick II, although retaining the right to choose their own magistrates.

[9] The Hapsburg overlords questioned this freedom and uncertainty remained until Rudolf of Hapsburg was crowned king of Germany in 1273. He exercised his imperial rights in Uri and inherited rights over Schwytz and Unterwald until his death in 1291. These regions thereafter constituted the Perpetual League.

[10] As with other circumstantial alliances among the regions, the Perpetual League constituted an agreement for dispute arbitration, putting law above armed strength.

The honorary magistrates had to be residents of those cantons.

[11] The league of the Uri, Schwyz, and Unterwald cantons was joined by the city of Zurich, constituting the first historic antecedent of the Swiss Confederation. This confederation was consolidated with the victory of Margarten in 1315, defeating an army of knights sent to impose imperial law in the region by the Hapsburgs.

[12] The Confederation was supported by new alliances. In 1302 the League signed a pact with the city of Luzern, previously dependent on Vienna. In 1315 Zurich reaffirmed its union and in 1353 it was joined by Bern. The Glarus and Zug cantons joined later, forming the core of an independent state within the Germanic Empire.

[13] During the second half of the 14th century, the rural oligarchy was defeated and their lands and laws given over to city councils. This democratic rural movement gave birth to the 'Landesgemeinde', a sovereign assembly of canton inhabitants and a similar movement was led by the city guilds.

[14] The Confederation soon launched into territorial conquest. During the 15th century the union grew to 13 cantons, it made alliances with other states, and the institution of government known as the *Diet* was formed where each canton was represented by two seats and one vote.

[15] In 1516, after the defeat of the Helvetians, the King of France forced a peace treaty with the cantons. In 1521 an alliance gave France the right to recruit Swiss soldiers. Only Zurich refused to sign this alliance, maintaining military and economic links with the Old Confederation until its end in 1798.

[16] The Reformation came to Switzerland with Huldrych Zwingli, a priest who preached against the mercenary service and the corruption and power of the clergy. Popular support for Zwingli strengthened the urban bourgeoisie. The Reformation became more radical in rural areas where harsh repression re-established the domination of cities over peasants.

[17] Zwingli's attempt to alter the federal alliance to benefit the reformed cities was frustrated by the

---

WORKERS

2000

UNEMPLOYMENT: 2.7%
LABOR FORCE AS % OF TOTAL:

■ FEMALE: 40%   ■ MALE: 60%

1994/97

EMPLOYMENT DISTRIBUTION:

F
M

■ SERVICES   F: 82%   M: 59%
■ INDUSTRY   F: 15%   M: 35%
■ AGRICULTURE F: 4%   M: 5%

LAND USE

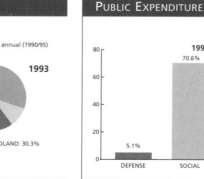

DEFORESTATION: 0.0% annual (1990/95)

1993

■ FOREST & WOODLAND: 30.3%
■ ARABLE: 9.6%
■ OTHER: 60.1%

PUBLIC EXPENDITURE

1999
70.6%

5.1%

DEFENSE   SOCIAL

---

military victory of the Catholic rural areas. The second national peace of Kappel, signed in 1531 gave the Catholic minority advantages over the Protestant majority.

[18] The areas where both religions coexisted were subject to constant tension, but cooperation was required to preserve the union of the federation. In Catholic regions agriculture prevailed, while in Protestant areas trade and industry flourished, aided by French, Italian and Dutch refugees.

[19] Popular consultation disappeared in the 17th century. The power of the cities caused uprisings, such as the great peasant revolt of 1653, which were harshly repressed. Three years later when a further war ensued the prerogatives of the Catholic cantons were re-established.

[20] During the European conflicts of the 17th and 18th centuries Switzerland remained neutral because of its religious division and its mercenary armies. Neutrality became a condition for the Confederations existence. The policy of armed neutrality, which still holds, was first formulated by the Diet in 1674.

[21] In 1712 the Protestant victory in the second battle of Villmergen ended religious struggles, ensuring the hegemony of cities which were undergoing industrial expansion. Switzerland became the most industrialized country in Europe. Industry was based on labor at home, completely transforming work in the countryside.

[22] Throughout the 18th century, a series of popular revolts against the urban oligarchy called for the reform of the Swiss Constitution. In March 1798, the Old Confederation fell under pressure from Napoleon's army. The Helvetic Republic was proclaimed 'whole and indivisible' with sovereignty for the people.

[23] Between the unitary Republic and the 1848 Federal Constitution, Switzerland was shaken by coups, popular revolts, and civil wars. The new federal pact marked a final victory for liberalism in the country. Two legislative bodies were established guaranteeing the rights of the small Catholic cantons.

[24] A state monopoly was created for custom duties and coin minting, while weights and measures were standardized, so satisfying the industrial and commercial bourgeoisie's economic requirements. The 1848 Constitution thus removed the obstacles to capitalist expansion.

[25] Nepotism and the concentration of capital benefited only the few and fuelled growing opposition to the institutional system. The 1874 Constitution partially addressed these issues, and introduced the mechanism of referendum as an element of direct democracy.

[26] Expansion of the home labor system delayed organization of the Swiss workers' movement in relation to the country's industrialization. The Swiss Workers' Federation, created in 1873 had only 3,000 members, and the Swiss Workers' Union, which replaced it in 1880, only exceeded this figure ten years later.

[27] The first achievement of the workers' movement was factory legislation, passed by parliament in 1877. The working day was limited to 11 hours with improved working conditions. In 1888 the Socialist Party was formed to give workers a political voice.

[28] In 1910, 15 per cent of the workers in Switzerland were foreign. Many were anarchists and socialists who had suffered persecution in their own countries and they consequently encouraged radical positions in the workers' movement. The Swiss Workers' Union took up a platform of 'proletarian class struggle', and the Socialist Party was inspired by the Second International's Marxism.

[29] World War I brought great internal tensions to Switzerland, especially between the French and German-speaking regions. Under the leadership of Ulrich Wile, the Swiss army cooperated with Germany. Tension only decreased after the French victory, when Switzerland formally approached the allies and became a member of the League of Nations.

[30] The 1918 general strike, although lifted three days later under pressure from the armed forces, led the bourgeoisie to form an anti-Socialist bloc. That year proportional representation was introduced.

[31] The elections in 1919 marked the end of the liberal hegemony, in place since 1848. The Socialists obtained 20 per cent of the vote, leading liberals to ally with the peasants who had 14 per cent, while the conservatives became the second power in the Federal Council.

[32] These changes produced noticeable consequences during the following years. The 48-hour week was included in factory legislation, while in 1925 an article on old-age pensions was added to the constitution. Assistance to the unemployed improved and collective work contracts became more common.

[33] During World War II, European powers recognized Swiss armed neutrality, but the country still suffered strong pressure from Nazi Germany. Throughout the war Switzerland maintained a delicate balance between accepting Hitler's advances and defending its independence; a strategy that kept them out of the conflict.

[34] After the War, the West resented Switzerland's relations with Germany, and the USSR refused to re-establish diplomatic relations, broken off since 1918. However, the country's financial power paved the way for its return to the international community. During the Cold War, Switzerland sided with the West but did not join the UN, in order to preserve its neutrality.

[35] The Swiss economy expanded greatly during the postwar period. The chemical, food, and machinery exporting industries became great transnational corporations. In 1973 Switzerland was placed fourth in direct foreign capital investments, after the US, France, and Britain.

[36] Switzerland's main transnational corporation, the food and babymilk manufacturer Nestlé AG, had 196,940 workers worldwide and sales worth $29.36 billion in 1989, operating through branches in Algeria, Bahamas, Brazil, Dominican Republic, Ecuador, Philippines, Ghana, Madagascar.

[37] The Swiss economic expansion attracted workers from Italy, Spain and other southern European countries. Between 1945 and 1974 the number of immigrants rose from 5 to 17 per cent. Several referenda called for an end to immigration forced thousands of people back to their countries.

[38] Due to its political neutrality, Switzerland did not join the European Economic Community in 1957. However, it has been a member of EFTA (European Free Trade Association) since 1960.

PROFILE

ENVIRONMENT

A small landlocked state in continental Europe, Switzerland is a mountainous country made up of three natural regions. To the northwest, on the French border, are the massive Jura mountains, an agricultural and industrial area. Industry is concentrated in the Mitteland, a sub-Alpine depression between the Jura and the Alps, with numerous lakes of glacial origin. It is also an agricultural and cattle-raising region. The Alps cover more than half of the territory and extend in a west-east direction with peaks of over 4,000 meters. The main activities of this region are dairy farming and tourism. The country's ecosystem is currently threatened by acid rain.

SOCIETY

Peoples: Two-thirds of the population are of German origin, while 18 per cent and 13 per cent are French and Italian, respectively. 17.1 per cent of the country's citizens or permanent residents are Italian, Yugoslav, Portuguese, German, Turkish or other nationalities.
Religions: 47.6 per cent Catholic, 44.3 per cent Protestant, 2.2 per cent Muslim, 1 per cent Orthodox Christian
Languages: German, French and Italian. A very small minority (0.4 per cent) in certain parts of the Grisons canton to the east speak Rhaeto-Romanic (or Romansch), of Latin origin.
Political Parties: Democratic Union of the Center (Swiss People's Party); Social Democratic Party; Free Democratic Party of Switzerland; Christian Democratic People's Party; Green Party of Switzerland (ecologist); Liberal Party of Switzerland; Swiss Democrats; Protestant People's Party; Federal Democratic Union; Swiss Labor Party; League of Ticinesians. There are several regional and Canton parties.
Social Organizations: The Swiss Federation of Trade Unions; the Confederation of Christian Trade Unions; the Federation of Swiss Employees' Societies.

THE STATE

Official Name: Confoederatio Helvetica (Romansche); Schweizerische Eidgenossenschaft (German); Confédération Suisse (French); Confederazione Svizzera (Italian).
Administrative Divisions: 20 Cantons, 6 Sub-Cantons.
Capital: Bern (administrative) 344,000 people; Lausanne (judicial) 114,600 (1999).
Other cities: Zurich 958,100 people; Geneva 172,900; Basel 163,600 (2000).
Government: Parliamentary republic with strong direct democracy. Kaspar Villiger, Federal President since January 2002. The Federal Assembly (Legislature) has two chambers: the National Council, with 200 members, and the Council of States, with 46 members. The Federal Council (executive collegiate), made of 7 members appointed by the United Federal Assembly for a 4-year term. The presidency rotates each year among the coalition in power's councilors.
National Holiday: August 1, Foundation of the Swiss Confederation (1291).
Armed Forces: 3,400 regular troops (1995) 28,000 annual conscripts (15-week courses).
Other: 480,000 Civil Defense.

MATERNAL MORTALITY		
	1985/99	

Per 100,000 live births

5

FOOD DEPENDENCY	

2000

6%

FOREIGN TRADE	
Millions US$	1999

IMPORTS

95,785

EXPORTS

109,128

DEMOGRAPHY
Population: 7,167,000 (2002)
Annual growth: 0.6 % (1985-2000)
Estimates for year 2015: 6,972,000 (2000)
Annual growth to year 2015: -0.2 % (2000)
Urban population: 67.7 % (2000)
Urban growth: 0.6 % (2000)
Children per woman: 1.5 (2000)

HEALTH
Life expectancy at birth: 79 years (2000-2005)
male: 76 years (2000-2005)
female: 82 years (2000-2005)
Maternal mortality: 5 per 100,000 live births (1985/99)
Infant mortality: 3 per 1,000 (2000)
Under-5 child mortality: 4 per 1,000 (2000)
Daily calorie supply: 3,258 per capita (1999)
323 doctors per 100,000 people (1998)
Safe water: 100 % (2000)

EDUCATION
School enrolment (net):
Primary total: 96 % (1994/2000)
male: 96 % (1995/99)
female: 96 % (1995/99)
Secondary (gross):
male: 94 % (1995/97)
female: 88 % (1995/97)
Tertiary (gross): 35 % (1998)
Primary school teachers: one for every 13 pupils (1998)

COMMUNICATIONS
369 newspapers (1998), 1,002 radios (1997), 548 TV sets (2000) and 727 main telephone lines (2000)
per 1,000 people
Books: 217 new titles per 100,000 people (1992/94)

ECONOMY
Per capita, GDP: $ 28,769 (2000)
Annual growth: 2.4 % (2000)
Annual inflation: 1.6 % (2000)
Consumer price index: 103.8 (2000)
Currency: 1.7 swiss francs = $ 1 (03/2002)
Cereal imports: 544,249 metric tons (2000)
Food import dependency: 6 % (2000)
Fertilizer use: 2,836 kg per ha (1999)
Exports: $ 109,128 million (1999)
Imports: $ 95,785 million (1999)

ENERGY
Consumption: 3,741.9 Kgs of oil equivalent per capita yearly (1998); 55.8 % imported (1999)

HDI (ranking/value): 11 / 0.924 (1999)

[39] In 1959, after 10 years of voluntary absence, the socialists joined the Federal Council with two representatives. The Executive consisted of two Radicals, two Christian Democrats, two Socialists, and a peasants' representative. This meant that 80 per cent of the electorate was represented in government.

[40] Women gained the right to vote in 1971, but some cantons retained male-only suffrage until 1985. In 1984, the first woman minister was elected when Elisabeth Kopp was made minister for justice and police.

[41] Increasing poverty amid the well being of the majority, and rising immigrant presence encouraged the growth of the extreme right. The small Swiss Democratic Party and the Party of Drivers, xenophobic and opposed to social policies, gained support in the early 1990s.

[42] In May 1992, a plebiscite approved Switzerland's integration into the IMF and World Bank. In June 1993, Parliament approved the idea of incorporating Swiss troops into the UN peacekeeping forces. This represented an important change in the traditional policy of Swiss neutrality. However, most of the Swiss voted against this proposal in a 1994 referendum.

[43] In July 1997, Swiss banks - the targets of international lawsuits filed by individuals - released a list of names of account-holders with funds untouched since World War II. Most of these were Jews who had been exterminated by Nazism. The World Jewish Congress, the main plaintiff, said the presentation was only a symbolic gesture as the banks had profited from the funds for over 50 years.

[44] A scandal that involved the embezzlement of millions of dollars by a former intelligence officer for organizing a clandestine army led the Government to suspend the military intelligence chief on charges of masterminding the operation. Defense Minister Adolf Ogi, who was in charge of the investigation, became a prominent political figure.

[45] Under Ogi's leadership, the Democratic Union of the Center (also known as the Swiss People's Party) won 22.5 per cent of the votes and 44 of the 200 parliamentary seats in the October 1999 elections. The Social Democratic Party also won 22.5 per cent of the votes and won 51 seats, the Freethinking-Democratic Party won 19.9 per cent and 43 seats, while the Christian Democrat People's Party won 15.8 per cent of the vote and 35 seats. The four parties formed the Confederation, which has an annual rotating presidency, held by Ogi beginning in January 2000.

[46] A 1998 government report established that anti-Semitism had re-emerged in Switzerland due to the controversy over its relations with Nazi Germany and also over the question of what Swiss banks had done with the accounts belonging to victims of the Holocaust. In January 2000, a study sponsored by the United States revealed that 16 per cent of the Swiss population had anti-Semitic views, marking an increase during the last decade.

[47] Immediately upon taking office as new President in January 2001, Social Democrat Moritz Leuenberger faced serious criticisms from the press and politicians. This was mainly because of the government's crack-down on anti-capitalist protesters who surrounded the World Economic Forum meeting of world economic and business leaders in Davos, a winter resort where the conference had been held annually since 1971.

[48] In March 2001, a referendum overwhelmingly rejected the 'Yes to Europe' proposal that had been presented by the Socialist Party and youth groups, with 77 per cent voting against. The governing coalition opposed the plan, saying that negotiations to become an EU member should not begin before the 2003-2007 legislative period.

[49] A new referendum in June narrowly approved a measure allowing Swiss soldiers to carry weapons during peace missions abroad. The electorate also decided that the armed forces could cooperate in military training exercises under NATO. That month, Swiss troops were serving in Kosovo and were themselves protected by Austrian troops because they were not allowed to carry weapons. The Government wanted its army to be able to work on equal footing with the other NATO forces.

[50] In 2001, after a promising start, the Swiss economy was shaken by restructuring measures, causing thousands of layoffs, with unemployment reaching 2 per cent. In October, Swissair, the country's flagship airline, filed for bankruptcy protection after an expansion plan failed. The Government, banks and several private companies launched a multi-million-dollar rescue package to create a new national airline, arising from Swissair regional subsidiary Crossair. Just 7 per cent of the population believed in January 2002 that the new airline, known simply as Swiss, could survive. That month, Kaspar Villiger, of the Freethinking-Democratic Party, took office as President.

[51] Citing efforts to show solidarity for New York after the September 2001 terrorist attacks, the World Economic Forum for 2002 was not held in Davos for the first time since 1971, but in the US city.

[52] In March 2002, a narrow majority of the electorate - around 55 per cent - voted in favor of joining the UN. Switzerland would be the 190th member of the organization. Foreign Minister Joseph Deiss called the vote a victory for the country and said it could now discuss its concerns within the UN and better defend its interests within the international community. However, voices of dissent argued the country would lose its neutrality.

[53] That month, the Bergier Commission (made up of nine members from Switzerland, UK, US and Israel) which had been established in 1996 by the Swiss Parliament to investigate the country's relationship with the Axis powers, reported that the Swiss authorities had held secret talks with Nazi Germany that helped prolong World War II. It further revealed that Switzerland had refused to give refuge to thousands of Jews - even though the authorities were aware of the existence of concentration camps - and that it had contributed to the expansion of the Nazi economy through commercial and financial agreements with Germany.

[54] In September 2002 Switzerland joined the UN as the 190th member state. ■

Syria

Population:	17,040,000 (2002)
Land area:	183,780 SQ KM
Capital:	Damascus (Dimashq)
Currency:	Pound
Language:	Arabic

Suriyah

S yria was once the name for the entire region between the peninsulas of Anatolia (Turkey) and Sinai, including the fertile crescent. Ancient civilizations coveted the territory: the Egyptians wanted it as a port, while the Persians considered the region a bridge to their plans of a universal empire.

[2] Between the 12th and 7th centuries BC, the Phoenician civilization developed on the central coastal stretch of the territory; a society of sailors and traders without expansionist aims. Phoenician cities were always independent, although some exercised temporary hegemony over others, and they developed the world's first commercial economy.

[3] The Phoenicians invented the alphabet, constructed ocean-going ships, practiced large-scale ceramic and textile manufacturing, expanded and systematized geography, sailing around the coast of Africa. The propagation of these throughout the Mediterranean helped form what would be later called 'Western civilization', of which the Greeks were the main exponents.

[4] The territory came under the control of Alexander of Macedonia (also known as Alexander the Great) during the 4th century BC. After Alexander's death, his vast empire was divided and Syria became the center of a Seleucidan state (named for Seleucus Nicator, one of Alexander's generals) that initially stretched as far as India. The eastern part was later lost to the Parthians. In the Roman era the province of Syria was a border zone constantly shaken by fierce local wars and resistance. One example of the latter was Queen Zenobia, whom the

Romans finally managed to defeat in 272 AD.

[5] The Arabization of the territory was carried out by the Ummaia Caliphs, who, between the years 650 and 750, turned Damascus (Dimashq) into the capital of the empire (see Saudi Arabia), and fostered a strong national spirit. When the Abbas defeated the Ummaias, the capital was transferred to Baghdad, where the new caliphs enjoyed greater support. Although still economically and culturally important, the loss of political power proved significant: in the 11th century when Europeans invaded during the Crusades, the caliphs of Baghdad reacted with indifference. Local emirs were left to their own resources, and disagreements among them allowed

a small Christian force to conquer the area, leading to 200-years of occupation.

[6] The Egyptians initiated the process to drive out the Europeans. One result was that Syria became a virtual Egyptian province and center stage for a confrontation with Mongol invaders. In the 16th century, the country became a part of the Ottoman Empire.

[7] The Crusaders left behind a significant Christian community, especially with the Maronites, serving as sufficient cause for European interference from the 17th century onwards. The Egyptian Khedive Muhammad (Mehemet) Ali conquered Syria in 1831, and heavy taxes and compulsory military service provoked revolt among both

Christian and Muslim communities. The European powers, concerned with propping up the Turkish Empire to stave off the emergence of a more aggressive power like Egypt, used the repression of Christians as an excuse for intervention. Ali's offensive was suppressed and the 'protection of Syrian Christians' was entrusted to the French. A withdrawal of Egyptian troops took place in 1840, along with the restoration of Ottoman domination and the establishment of Christian missions and schools subsidized by Europeans.

[8] However, the scene was set for confrontation and in 1858, Maronite Christians gathered in the mountainous region between Damascus and Jerusalem rebelled against the ruling class and eliminated the traditional system of land ownership. Their Muslim neighbors, particularly the Druze, moved to repress the movement before it spread further, triggering a conflict that culminated in the deaths of a large number of Christians in June 1860.

[9] A month later, French troops disembarked in Beirut, ostensibly to protect the Christian community, and forcing the Turkish Government to create a separate province called 'Little Lebanon'. This was to be governed by a Christian appointed by the Sultan but with the approval of the European powers, with its own police force, and traditional privileges were abolished in the territory. The social conflict thus became a confrontation between confessional groups with the Christians in 'Little Lebanon' placed in a position of superiority over the local Muslim population, providing firm roots for the politico-religious conflict that has marked Lebanese history ever since.

[10] When an Arab rebellion broke out during World War I (see Saudi Arabia, Jordan and Iraq), Emir Faisal was proclaimed king of Syria. At the time French and British intentions were unknown, but the Sykes-Picot agreement divided the fertile crescent giving Syria (with Lebanon) to France, and Palestine (including Jordan) and Iraq to Britain.

[11] Throughout 1932, Syria experienced a period of relative stability, and independence seemed

WORKERS

2000

LABOR FORCE
AS % OF TOTAL

- ■ FEMALE: 27%
- ■ MALE: 73%

LAND USE

DEFORESTATION: 2.2% annual (1990/95)

1993

- ■ FOREST & WOODLAND: 3.5%
- ■ ARABLE: 27.6%
- ■ OTHER: 68.9%

PUBLIC EXPENDITURE

1999

DEFENSE 25.1%
SOCIAL 18.2%

imminent. A Syrian president and parliament were elected that year, but France made it clear that autonomy was unacceptable. This attitude engendered political agitation and confrontation, which only ended with a 1936 agreement with the French. France recognized certain Syrian demands, chiefly reunification with Lebanon. However, the French Government never ratified the agreement, and this led to new waves of violence, which culminated in the 1939 resignation of the Syrian President and a French order to suspend the 1930 constitution that governed both Syria and Lebanon.

[12] In 1941, French and British troops occupied the region to flush out Nazi collaborators. In 1943 Chikri al-Quwatli was elected president of Syria and Bechara al-Kuri president of Lebanon. Bechara al-Kuri proposed elimination of the mandate provisions from the constitution; however, he and his cabinet members were imprisoned by the ever-present French troops. Violent demonstrations followed in

both Lebanon and Syria, and the British pressed for withdrawal of the French. In March 1946, the United Nations finally ordered the European forces to withdraw. This was completed in 1947 and the end of the French mandate was officially declared.

[13] In 1948 Syrian troops fought to prevent the partition of Palestine, and in 1956 joined Egypt in the battle against Israeli, French and British aggression. This aggression was the answer to Egyptian President Gamal Abdel Nasser's decision to nationalize the Suez Canal.

[14] In 1958, Syria joined Egypt in founding the United Arab Republic,

but Nasser's ambitious integration project collapsed in 1961. Ten years later the scheme was reactivated, with greater flexibility and the Federation of Arab Republics was created including Libya.

[15] In 1963, after a revolution, the Ba'ath Arab Socialist Party came to power. Its main tenet was that the Arab countries were merely 'regions' of a larger Arab Nation. In November 1970, General Hafez al-Assad became president. He launched a modernization campaign, including a series of social and economic changes. The subsequent party congress named Assad party leader and proposed 'accelerating the stages towards socialist transformation of different sectors'. This guideline was adopted and became part of the new constitution which was approved in 1973.

[16] Syria took an active part in the Arab-Israeli wars of 1967 and 1973, during which Israeli troops occupied the Golan Heights. Syria also resisted US efforts to impose a 'settlement' in the Middle East, together with Algeria, Iraq, Libya, Yemen and the Palestine Liberation Organization (PLO). They also opposed the Camp David agreement (see Egypt).

[17] In 1978, the Syrian and Iraqi branches of the Ba'ath Party drew closer, but negotiations for creation of a single state disintegrated. In late 1979, at the congress of the Syrian branch of the Ba'ath Party, the Muslim Brotherhood (a right-wing Islamic movement) was harshly censured and were labeled 'Zionist agents'.

[18] Brotherhood attacks continued. In 1982 the army launched a full offensive which resulted in thousands of casualties. The Syrian Government blamed Iraq for arming the rebels, and closed the border between the two countries in April 1982. Iraq retaliated by closing the oil pipeline connecting Kirkuk, Iraq, to the Syrian port of Banias.

[19] The virtual alliance formed in 1980 between Saudi Arabia, Iraq and Jordan and tensions between those three countries and Syria were exacerbated by the outbreak of the Iran-Iraq War. Assad charged Iraq as the aggressor and diverted attention from what he called the major regional issue - the Palestinian question. Toward the end of the

year, Syrian accusations of Jordanian support for the Brotherhood brought the two countries to the verge of war. The mediation of Saudi prince Abdalla ibn Abdul-Aziz averted armed conflict.

[20] In 1981 the 'missile crisis' broke out in Syria, when the Christian Phalangist Movement sought to extend their area of authority to include the area around the Lebanese city of Zahde. An Arab Deterrence Force, organized and commanded by Syria, attempted to prevent the advance. Syria installed Soviet surface-to-air SAM-9 missiles, triggering an Israeli reaction. The crisis was finally averted, but in 1983 Israel invaded Lebanon, and destroyed the bases of Syrian missiles.

[21] In mid-1983 there was a crisis between the Syrian authorities and the PLO leadership. This encouraged Syria to support the Palestinian groups opposed to Yasser Arafat's leadership, until the division ended in 1987. The fall in oil prices further aggravated the economic problems caused by the war and the Government set up strict austerity measures in 1984: financial activities were tightly controlled, borders were closed to the illegal trafficking of merchandise, previously tolerated, and public expenditure was substantially reduced.

[22] In 1985, President Assad won a new seven-year term. In 1987, Prime Minister Abdul Rauf al-Kassem was forced to resign amid charges of corruption, following the resignation of four other ministers. In November 1987, Mahmoud Az-Zoubi, president of the People's Assembly, was chosen as Prime Minister.

[23] In May 1990, Syria finally re-established diplomatic relations with Egypt.

[24] When Iraq invaded Kuwait, Syria immediately sided with the anti-Iraqi alliance and sent troops to Saudi Arabia. Diplomatic relations with the US improved noticeably. During the crisis Syria increased its influence over Lebanon and strengthened the allied government in that country; they were also successful in disarming most of the autonomous militias.

[25] In May 1991 Syria and Lebanon signed a cooperation agreement whereby Syria

PROFILE

ENVIRONMENT

To the west, near the sea, lies the Lebanon mountain range. To the south there are semi-desert plateaus and to the north low plateaus along the basin of the Euphrates River. Farming - grains, grapes and fruit - is concentrated in the western lowlands that receive adequate rainfall. In the south, the volcanic plateaus of the Djebel Druze are extremely fertile farmlands, some as the oases surrounding the desert, the main one being that of Damascus. Cotton and wool are exported. Exploitation of oil fields is the country's chief industry. The dumping of toxic substances from the extraction of crude is responsible for the high levels of pollution of Syria's waters.

SOCIETY

Peoples: Syrians are mostly Arabs, with minority ethnic groups in the north: Kurds, Turks and Armenians. There are few statistics on the number of Palestinian refugees (they were around 200,000 in 1977), and the Jewish population was authorized to emigrate in 1992.
Religions: Mainly Muslims, mostly Sunni, followed by Alamites, Shi'a and Ismailites. Also minor communities of eastern Christian religions.
Languages: Arabic (official). Minority groups speak their own languages.
Political Parties: The Ba'ath Arab Socialist Party, founded in Damascus in 1947 by Michel Aflaq, including the National Progressive Front and other minor parties. The armed political-religious opposition is represented by the Muslim Brotherhood, a fundamentalist Sunni sect. Communist Party of Syria, (government controlled); Arab Socialist Unity, (government controlled); Socialist Unity Movement, (government controlled); Arab Socialist Party, (government controlled); Socialist Unionist Democratic Party (government controlled).
Social Organizations: The General Federation of Labor Unions unites ten workers' federations representing different sectors of the economy.

THE STATE

Official Name: Al-Jumhouriya al Arabiya as-Suriya.
Administrative divisions: 14 Districts.
Capital: Damascus (Dimashq) 2,270,000 people (1999).
Other cities: Aleppo (Halab) 2,319,800 people; Homs (Hims) 698,800; Latakia 391,300; Hamah 350,900 (2000).
Government: Bashar al-Assad, President since July 2000. Muhammad Mustafa Miro, Prime Minister since March 2000. Unicameral Legislature: People's Assembly, with 250 members.
National Holidays: April 17, Independence Day (1946); November 16, Revolution Day (1978); May 25, Resistance and Liberation Day (2000).
Armed Forces: 421,000 troops (1996).
Other: 8,000 Gendarmes

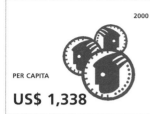

EXTERNAL DEBT

2000

PER CAPITA

US$ 1,338

FOREIGN TRADE

Millions US$ 2000

IMPORTS
5,861

EXPORTS
6,470

recognized Lebanon as an independent and separate state, for the first time since both countries gained independence from France.

[26] In December 1991, al-Assad was re-elected for the fourth time, by 99.98 per cent of the vote, in elections which had him as sole candidate. That month, the Government announced the pardon of 2,800 political prisoners, members of the Muslim Brotherhood.

[27] In 1992, the Government abolished the death penalty and allowed the emigration of 4,000 Jews. On the economic front GNP grew 7 per cent and exports of oil and its by-products amounted to $2 billion. New legislation favored investments in the private sector, which saw significant growth between 1991 and 1993.

[28] Syria stayed away from the first stages of the regional peace process, which facilitated the establishment of a limited autonomy for Palestine and the signing of agreements between Israel and Jordan in July 1994. In January, a 'historic' meeting took place between US President Clinton and Assad in Geneva and in September, the Syrian minister of foreign affairs was interviewed for the first time on Israeli television. However, Damascus maintained its refusal to negotiate officially with Israel, due to the murder of 29 Palestinians in Hebron committed by an Israeli settler in February.

[29] In June 1995, official negotiations with Israel failed to return the Golan Heights to Syria, as Tel Aviv wanted, to maintain limited military presence in the region indefinitely. In October, a Hizbullah ambush of Israeli troops in southern Lebanon complicated negotiations again. In mid 1996, al-Assad participated in a meeting of Arab countries to co-ordinate a common strategy for negotiation with Israel.

[30] As part of a policy to stimulate the Syrian economy private sector, key state sectors, including electricity generation, cement production and pharmaceuticals were opened up to private capital.

[31] In November 1997, Damascus unexpectedly strengthened relations with Baghdad at the threat of fresh US military intervention in Iraq - a strategy designed to work against the rapidly consolidating Turkish-

Israeli alliance. Given the situation of the Golan Heights, militarily Syria would remain in the middle of this new bloc. If Iraq were to be beaten, new states could emerge on the basis of linguistic or religious criteria, with Turkey possibly gaining control of the oil fields of Iraqi Kurdistan.

[32] The threat presented by the Turkish-Israeli military bloc - which planned to produce a thousand new tanks for its armed forces - forced Iran to join the Syrian-Iraqi negotiations on security issues in April 1998.

[33] Al-Assad was reelected for his seventh consecutive five-year presidential period in 1999. The President stated during his electoral speech that the Government needed 'new blood' to push ahead economic reforms.

[34] All 37 of Prime Minister Mahmoud el-Zouebi's cabinet members presented their resignation to the president in March 2000. Muhammad Mustafa Mero, a veteran leader of the Ba'ath party and governor of Aleppo province, was appointed the new Premier.

[35] Israel withdrew from Southern Lebanon in May 2000 but this was not matched by a parallel withdrawal from the Golan Heights.

[36] The sudden death of Assad on June 10 plunged the country into mourning for the only leader most Syrians had ever known. Moves to install his only living son, Bashar al-Assad, as president began immediately. After being named commander of the armed forces, he took office in July.

[37] Among the first measures of the new President was the April 2001 authorization to establish a private banking system and shortly after, a private radio station was granted broadcast rights for music only, no political content was allowed.

[38] In May, Pope John Paul II visited Syria, and at the reception ceremony al-Assad strongly criticized Israel, comparing the suffering of the Arabs to the persecution of Christ. He also asked the Pope to remember in his prayers the people of Golan Heights and Palestine. In response, John Paul II called upon all parties in the conflict to seek lasting peace and a new understanding, including respect among Christians, Muslims and Jews.

[39] With the unanimous support of Asian and African countries, Syria obtained a seat at the UN Security Council in October 2001. Neither Israel's opposition nor the request of 38 US lawmakers to their president to veto the election were successful, partly because of Washington's strategy after the September 11 attacks to convince the most influential Arab countries to join its global campaign against terrorism.

[40] Damascus engaged in intense international relations in 2001. After heavy pressure from the Lebanese government, Syrian troops withdrew from Beirut and were deployed in other parts of Lebanon. In August, Syria's Premier Miro visited Iraq in the first high-level visit to that country since relations had cooled as a result of Syrian support for Iran during the 1980-1988 Iran-Iraq war. British Prime Minister Tony Blair visited Damascus in November to try to rally Syrian support for the US-led anti-terrorism campaign. However, Blair and al-Assad could not reach agreement on the definition of 'terrorism' and the British leader returned to his country empty-handed.

[41] The November release of dozens of political prisoners belonging to the Muslim Brotherhood, after more than two decades behind bars, was applauded by Amnesty International as a 'satisfactory step towards respect for human rights in Syria'. Nearly all the prisoners had been kept incommunicado in degrading conditions and subjected to torture and mistreatment.

[42] In April 2002, the Syrian radar station in Lebanon was bombed by Israeli aircraft in response to an attack by Hezbollah guerrillas against three of the disputed sites in the region. The offensive raised fear of a military escalation along Israel's northern border. According to analysts, the Israeli offensive against Palestine and Syria's desire for Israel's withdrawal from the Golan Heights could precipitate a broad regional war. ∎

STATISTICS

DEMOGRAPHY
Population: 17,040,000 (2002)
Annual growth: 3.0 % (1985-2000)
Estimates for year 2015: 23,206,000 (2000)
Annual growth to year 2015: 2.4 % (2000)
Urban population: 54.5 % (2000)
Urban growth: 3.3 % (2000)
Children per woman: 3.9 (2000)

HEALTH
Life expectancy at birth: 72 years (2000-2005)
male: 71 years (2000-2005)
female: 73 years (2000-2005)
Maternal mortality: 110 per 100,000 live births (1985/99)
Infant mortality: 24 per 1,000 (2000)
Under-5 child mortality: 29 per 1,000 (2000)
Daily calorie supply: 3,272 per capita (1999)
144 doctors per 100,000 people (1998)
Safe water: 80 % (2000)

EDUCATION
Literacy: 74 % (2000)
male: 88 % (2000)
female: 60 % (2000)
School enrolment (net):
Primary total: 99 % (1994/2000)
male: 96 % (1995/99)
female: 92 % (1995/99)
Secondary (gross):
male: 45 % (1995/97)
female: 40 % (1995/97)
Tertiary (gross): 6 % (1998)
Primary school teachers: one for every 23 pupils (1998)

COMMUNICATIONS
20 newspapers (1996), 276 radios (1997), 67 TV sets (2000) and 103 main telephone lines (2000) per 1,000 people
Books: 4 new titles per 100,000 people (1992/94)

ECONOMY
Per capita, GDP: $ 3,556 (2000)
Annual growth: 0.0 % (2000)
Annual inflation: -0.5 % (2000)
Consumer price index: 106.8 (2000)
Currency: 51.1 pounds = $ 1 (03/2002)
Cereal imports: 1,730,716 metric tons (2000)
Food import dependency: 19 % (2000)
Fertilizer use: 790 kg per ha (1999)
Exports: $ 6,470 million (2000)
Imports: $ 5,861 million (2000)
External debt: $ 21,657 million (2000); $ 1,338 per capita (2000)
Debt service: 6.4 % of exports (1999)
Development aid received: $ 228 million (1999) ; $ 14.5 per capita (1999) ; 1.20 % of GNP (1999)

ENERGY
Consumption: 1,132.8 Kgs of oil equivalent per capita yearly (1998); -89.5 % imported (1999)

HDI (ranking/value): 97 /0.700 (1999)

Tajikistan

Tadzhikistan

Population: 6,177,000 (2002)
Land area: 140,600 SQ KM
Capital: Dushanbe (Dusanbe)
Currency: Ruble
Language: Tajik

Around 500 BC, Central Asia and southern Siberia's first centers of settled civilization arose in what is now Tajikistan. The Bactrian State was located in the upper tributaries of the Amu Darya. Likewise, in the Zeravshan river basin and the Kashkadarya river valley lay the nucleus of another State, Sogdiana. The inhabitants of these early civilizations built villages, with adobe and stone houses all along the rivers that they used for irrigating their crops. These included wheat, barley and millet, and a variety of fruits. Navigation was well developed and the cities that lay along the route of the caravans uniting Persia, China and India became important trading centers.

[2] In the 6th century BC these lands were annexed by the Persian Achaemenid Empire. In the 4th century BC, Alexander the Great conquered Bactria and Sogdiana. With the fall of his empire in the 3rd century, the Greco-Bactrian State and the Kingdom of Kushan emerged, and subsequently fell to the onslaught of the advancing Yuechzhi and Tojar steppe tribes. In the 4th and 5th centuries AD, Sogdiana and its surrounding regions were invaded by the Eftalites, and in the 6th and 7th centuries, by Central Asian Turkish peoples. In the 7th century, Tajikistan became a part of the Arab Caliphate, along with other Central Asian regions. After its demise, the region was incorporated into the Tahirid and Samanid kingdoms. In the 9th and 10th centuries, the Tajik people emerged as an identifiable ethnic group.

[3] From the 10th to the 13th centuries AD, Tajikistan formed part of the Gaznevid and Qarakhanid empires, as well as the realm of the Shah of Khwarezm. In the early 13th century, Tajikistan was conquered by Genghis Khan's Mongol Tatars. In 1238, Tarabi, a Tajik artisan, led a popular revolt. From the 14th to the 17th centuries, the Tajiks were under the control of the Timurids and the Uzbek Shaybanid dynasty. From the 17th to the 19th centuries, there were small fiefdoms throughout Tajikistan whose chieftains alternately submitted to or revolted against the khans of Bukhara.

[4] In the 1860s and 1870s, the Russian Empire conquered Central Asia, and the northern part of Tajikistan was annexed by Russia. The Khanate of Bukhara however maintained a relationship of sovereignty rather than annexation with Russia. The Tajik population of Kuliab, Guissar, Karateguin and Darvaz was incorporated into the Khanate as the province of Eastern Bukhara. Oppression by the Russian bureaucracy and the local feudal lords triggered a wave of peasant revolts toward the end of the 19th century and beginning of the 20th century. The most important of these was the 1885 uprising led by Vose.

[5] In 1916, during World War I, the local populations of Central Asia and Kazakhstan revolted over the mobilization of their people for rearguard duty with the retreating Russian army. After the triumph of the Bolshevik revolution in St Petersburg in October 1917, Soviet power was established in Northern Tajikistan. In April 1918, this territory became a part of the Autonomous Soviet Socialist Republic of Turkistan. Nevertheless, a large number of Tajiks remained under the power of the Emirate of Bukhara, which existed until 1921. In early 1921, the Red Army took Dushanbe, but in February it was forced to withdraw from Eastern Bukhara.

[6] Having broken Alim Khan's resistance in 1921-22, Soviet power was proclaimed throughout the entire territory of Tajikistan. In 1924, the Soviet Socialist Republic of Uzbekistan was formed, of which the Autonomous Soviet Socialist Republic of Tajikistan was a part. In January 1925, the Autonomous Region of Gorno-Badakhshan was established, high up in the Pamir range. On November 16 1929, Tajikistan became a federated republic of the Soviet Union. In the 1920s and 1930s, land and water reforms were carried out. The collectivization of agriculture was followed by industrialization, and the so-called 'cultural revolution' campaign.

[7] After World War II, the Soviet regime carried out a series of large construction projects, including a system of canals and reservoirs linking up with water projects in the neighboring republic of Uzbekistan. The purpose of this irrigation network was to develop the region's agricultural potential, especially for the cultivation of cotton. In the 1970s and 1980s, the effects of mismanagement and economic stagnation were felt in Tajikistan, one of the poorest regions in the USSR, with a high rate of unemployment, especially among the young, who made up most of the population.

[8] From 1985 onwards, the changes promoted by President Mikhail Gorbachev made the democratization process possible, which in turn gave way to the expression of long-suppressed ethnic and religious friction in Tajikistan. In February 1990, there were violent incidents between Tajiks and Russians in the capital,

with more than 30 people killed and scores injured. The Government decreed a state of emergency, which remained in effect during that year's Supreme Soviet (Parliament) elections, in which the Communist Party won 90 per cent of the available seats. The opposition attributed the February events to provocation by the former Soviet secret police (KGB), aimed at discrediting Gorbachev's reforms and suppressing nationalist tendencies. Muslims and Democrats called for the dissolution of the Soviet, because the elections had been held while a state of emergency was in effect.

[9] In August1990, Parliament passed a vote of no-confidence in President Majkamov, accusing him of supporting those responsible for the Moscow coup, and forcing him to resign. He was succeeded by Kadridin Aslonov as interim president of the republic.

[10] Tajikistan's religious revival has been stronger than in the rest of the former Soviet Union republics. In the early 1980s, there were 17 mosques; 10 years later, as a result of the liberalization promoted by Moscow, there were 128 large mosques, 2,800 places of prayer, an Islamic institute and five centers offering religious instruction. According to unofficial estimates, at this time between 60 and 80 per cent of the population were practising Muslims. The Islamic Renaissance Party proposed that the state allow political and religious freedom, but that it be based on Islam, with *Sharia* (Islamic law) as the law of the land. In 1991, the Tajik Government instituted the celebration of several important Muslim holy days.

[11] The mobilization of pro-Islamic forces, on the one hand, and mediation by Moscow, on the other, led to the state of emergency and the Communist Party ban being lifted in early October. Two months later, in the first presidential elections in November 1991, Nabiev was confirmed in his post by 58 per cent of the voters.

[12] On December 21 Tajikistan entered the Commonwealth of Independent States (CIS). At the same time, the Autonomous region of Gorno-Badakhshan requested the status of an autonomous province.

Like neighboring Afghanistan, the majority of this region's inhabitants are Shi'a Muslims.

[13] Outside Dushanbe there was violence from both pro-government and opposition forces, causing a conflict of civil-war proportions. Another protest demonstration against Nabiev led to his resignation on September 8. A private pro-communist army in the northern part of the country, far from accepting this state of affairs, launched a major offensive. The attack ended in December, with the fall of the capital and the formation of a new government controlled by the Popular Front (a paramilitary group).

[14] Some 300,000 people fled to other CIS republics and Afghanistan. As of February 1993, the persecution and massacre of members of the opposition began to diminish.

[15] Moscow recognized the new regime, led by Imomali Rakhmonov. In March bombing started from Afghanistan and there were incursions of opposition detachments across the frontier controlled by Russian troops. Rakhmonov proposed a draft for a new Constitution, approved by referendum in November. The President was re-elected at the same time, but the Fundamental Islamic opposition accused the government of fraud.

[16] The civil war officially ended on June 27 1997, with the signing of a peace agreement between the government and the opposition - grouped together in the United Tajik Opposition (UTO). The agreement guaranteed the opposition 30 per cent of posts in the cabinet, presence in the legal authorities and an amnesty for all those accused of war crimes.

[17] In February 1998, the Government announced acceleration of the privatization program. The war caused thousands of deaths and some 600,000 people were displaced within the country while another 300,000 fled to Afghanistan, Russia and other CIS countries. In 1997, cotton production - the main crop - reached only 60 per cent of the projected amount.

[18] Akbar Turayonzoda - second in command in the UTO - returned from exile to become the first deputy minister, giving new impulse to the peace process. One of his first proposals was to allow the Islamic Renaissance to enter political life with full rights, allowing it to participate in elections. Parliament voted for a law banning the creation of parties based on religious currents, and while the president vetoed the law, he made it clear he would not allow an Islamic government in the country.

[19] The elections slated for November 1999 went ahead despite strong protests from Usmon, the only opposition candidate. Other candidates could not raise the number of signatures required for their candidacy to go ahead, and the opposition blamed this on government pressure. Rakhmonov took 96 per cent of the vote, with a 98 per cent turnout of the 2.8 million registered voters.

[20] In January 2001, the minimum monthly salary in Tajikistan - one of the poorest states of the former Soviet Union – trebled. This was the first time that the authorities had increased the minimum salary in two years. Approximately 80 per cent of Tajiks live in poverty; annual GNP per capita is only around $300, with average monthly income about $25 dollars. Tajikistan was trying to overcome the effects of civil war and a devastating drought that had compounded the nation's difficulties in 2000.

[21] In September 2001, Tajikistan's culture minister, Abdurakhim Rakhimov, was assassinated in Dushanbe. Habib Sanginov, deputy Minister of the Interior, had also been killed in April.

[22] That same month, following the terrorist attacks in New York and Washington, Tajikistan offered its support for the anti-terrorism coalition created after the attacks and led by the US. In addition, Rakhmonov announced that the Tajik border with Afghanistan would be closed to all refugees in order to prevent Afghan refugee movement covering terrorist infiltration.

[23] In February 2002, Tajikistan became the last former soviet republic to join NATO for a peace program. According to Sharif Rahimov, Tajik ambassador in Brussels, joining the program would allow Tajikistan to modernize its armed forces.

[24] In April 2002, the governments of Tajikistan and Pakistan announced they were working together to seek regional security and to end terrorism. The two governments had supported opposite sides in Afghanistan - Pakistan backed the Taliban and Tajikistan the Northern Alliance. They added that they were also supporting the Afghan leader, Hamid Karzai, in order to extend peace and security throughout Afghanistan. ∎

Tanzania

Population: 36,820,000 (2002)
Land area: 883,590 SQ KM
Capital: Dodoma
Currency: Shilling
Language: Swahili and English

Tanzania

The oldest fossils of the human race were found in the Olduvai gorge, in the north of Tanzania. These remains date from millions of years ago, yet little is known about life on most of modern Tanzania's mainland before the 7th century.

[2] A mercantile civilization, heavily influenced by Arab culture, flourished in this region between 695 and 1550 but it was eventually destroyed by Portuguese invaders. One hundred and fifty years later, under the leadership of the Sultan of Oman, the Arabs succeeded in driving out the remaining Portuguese, but the rich cultural and commercial life of past times did not return. As the slave trade grew, Kilwa and Zanzibar became the leading trade centers.

[3] Between 1698 and 1830, Zanzibar and the coast were under the rule of the Oman Sultanate, with the Sultan living in Zanzibar. His sons, under British pressure, later split the inherited domain, dividing the old Sultanate in two.

[4] At the end of the 19th century a German adventurer, claiming rights over Tanzania, based on treaties signed by local Tanganyika leaders set up a company which immediately received imperial endorsement, leasing out the mainland coastal strip to the sultan of Zanzibar. The British had also made a similar deal, so the Berlin Conference, where the European powers distributed Africa among themselves, was obliged to recognize the claims of both powers. The European powers eventually agreed upon the 'cession of German rights' in favor of Britain.

[5] The areas of influence were delimited in 1886. Tanganyika, Rwanda and Burundi were recognized as German possessions while Zanzibar formally became a British protectorate in 1890. German troops and British warships joined efforts to stifle a Muslim rebellion on the coast of Tanganyika in 1905.

[6] After the defeat of Germany in World War I, the League of Nations placed Tanganyika under British mandate, while Rwanda and Burundi was handed over to the Belgians. Resistance to colonial and traditional tribal authority developed first among cooperative farmers, members of the colonial bureaucracy, and an emerging trade union movement. The Tanganyika African Association (TAA) was established in 1929 to give a forum to trade unionists and cooperative farmers who opposed British rule. In 1951 the British rulers began to implement a program to remove African homesteaders to make way for post-war British settlers, a policy that swelled an incipient nationalist movement.

[7] Nationalist feelings were later channeled into TANU (Tanganyika African National Union), a party founded in 1954 by Julius Nyerere, a primary school teacher known by the people as Mwalimu, the teacher.

[8] After seven years of organizing and fighting against racial discrimination and the appropriation of lands by European settlers, independence was achieved in 1961, and Nyerere became President, elected by an overwhelming majority.

[9] Meanwhile, in Zanzibar, two nationalist organizations, which had been active sporting and cultural institutions since the 1930s, merged to form the Afro-Shirazi Party in February 1957. In December 1963, the British transferred power to the Arab minority, and a month later this government was overthrown by the Afro-Shirazi. In April, Tanganyika and Zanzibar formed the United Republic of Tanzania, though the island maintained some autonomy.

[10] Under Nyerere's leadership, Tanzania based its foreign policy on non-alignment, standing for African unity, providing unconditional support to liberation movements, particularly FRELIMO in neighboring Mozambique.

[11] In February 1967, TANU issued the Arusha Declaration proclaiming socialism as its objective. The declaration laid down the principle of self-sufficiency and gave top priority to the development of agriculture, on the basis of communal land ownership, a traditional system known in Swahili as *ujamaa*, which means community.

[12] Ten years later TANU and the Afro-Shirazi Party merged into the Chama Cha Mapinduzi (CCM), which officially incorporated the aim of building socialism on the basis of self-sufficiency.

[13] In October 1978, Tanzania was invaded by Ugandan troops in an attempt by dictator Idi Amin to distract attention from his internal problems. At the same time he sought to divert Tanzanian energies from supporting the liberation struggles in Southern Africa. The aggression was repelled in a few weeks, and Tanzanian troops co-operated closely with the Ugandan National Liberation Front to overthrow Idi Amin.

[14] The cost of mobilizing the army and maintaining troops to prevent chaos in Uganda weighed heavily on the State budget, which was facing serious difficulties by the end of the 1970s. The falling price of Tanzania's main exports; coffee, spices, cotton, pyrethrum and cashew nuts, plus the growing cost of imported products, caused serious financial imbalances and forced cutbacks in the program to expand the ujamaa villages.

[15] These villages were conceived as the nucleus of the Tanzanian economy and were designed to be self-sufficient. To achieve autonomy, they received sizeable initial investments from the Government. Despite Nyerere's enormous efforts, various factors hindered the progress of ujamaa which grew slowly when compared with small and medium-sized private farms. They continued to depend upon imported foodstuffs and as the

WORKERS

2000

LABOR FORCE AS % OF TOTAL

- FEMALE: 49%
- MALE: 51%

LAND USE

DEFORESTATION: 1.0% annual (1990/95)

1993

- FOREST & WOODLAND: 35.4%
- ARABLE: 3.2%
- OTHER: 61.4%

PUBLIC EXPENDITURE

Military expenditure (as % GNI):	**21.2 %** (1999)
Defense expenditure (% of central government expenditure)	**41.1 %** (1999)

Government aid was cut, many of them collapsed.

[16] At the end of 1982 Edward Sokoine was appointed Prime Minister and immediately launched a campaign against corruption while adopting a more flexible policy towards foreign investment. Sokoine also arranged for Tanzania and Kenya to resume relations that had broken down in 1977 when the East African Economic Community of Tanzania, Kenya and Uganda was dissolved. After his death, his successor Salim Ahmed Salim from Zanzibar continued along the same lines.

[17] A national debate was organized to discuss constitutional reform to reorganize the executive power, grant greater political participation to women, strengthen democracy along CCM lines and prohibit more than two successive presidential terms.

[18] On November 5 1985, after 24 years as head of state, President Julius Nyerere passed power on to Ali Hassan Mwinyi, winner of the October 27 election, gaining 92.2 per cent of the vote. Nyerere took on a new post, presiding over the South-South Commission, an organization based in Geneva, working to strengthen Third World unity and its negotiating capacity with the North.

[19] In 1986, an economic recovery plan went into effect, following IMF and World Bank guidelines. The measures emphasized the reduction of tariff barriers and included incentives for private capital. Agricultural production improved and some industrial enterprises increased their profits.

[20] The development of private capital and incentives to create such capital caused new problems. According to UNICEF studies, half the children in the country at that time were malnourished. Tanzania remained among the 30 poorest countries in the world, although it managed to escape the famine that hit other Central African nations.

[21] Agricultural tasks have traditionally been carried out chiefly by women. While nearly half the workforce is made up of women, they do 85 per cent of all agricultural work. In the outlying areas around the major cities, the female population is increasingly opting for work in the underground economy.

[22] Economic data for 1989 revealed that the agricultural sector accounts for 51 per cent of the GDP, industry 10.2 per cent, trade 13.3 per cent and services 25 per cent. With only 10 per cent of the employed work force, the latter was the most competitive sector. Agriculture, in turn, was the least capital-intensive but the most labor-intensive, with 85.6 per cent of the total work force.

[23] At the beginning of 1990, former president Julius Nyerere said that he was not opposed to a multiparty democracy in his country. According to Nyerere, the absence of an opposition party contributed to the fact that the CCM had abandoned its program and its commitments, straying from its commitment to the masses.

[24] In February 1991, under the leadership of Abdullah Fundikira, a commission was formed to oversee the country's transition period.

[25] In its 1991 report, Amnesty International disclosed the existence of 120 prisoners on the island of Zanzibar, of which at least 40 were presumed to be political prisoners. Mwinyi's government denied that any political arrests had been made, and invited the human rights organization to prove its charges.

[26] In March 1991, the Tanzanian Workers' Organization (JUWATA) broke its ties with the CCM.

[27] In December, after a 23-year exile in England, opposition leader Oscar Kambona announced his plan to return to Tanzania and lead the fight for a multiparty system.

[28] The opposition leader announced the founding of the Democratic Alliance of Tanzania party. However, the national elections held in April 1993 confirmed yet again the predominance of the ruling CCM, which obtained 89 per cent of the vote.

[29] The Government pledged to the IMF it would implement a strict program of economic adjustment that included the elimination of 20,000 public sector jobs and a reduction of the budget deficit. It thus reduced education pending from 30 per cent in 1960 to 5 per cent of total public expenditure and in February 1994, authorized a 68 per cent raise in electricity bills and

PROFILE

ENVIRONMENT

The country is made up of the former territory of Tanganyika plus the islands of Zanzibar and Pemba. The offshore islands are made of coral. The coastal belt, where a large part of the population live, is a flat lowland along the Indian Ocean with a tropical climate and heavy rainfall. To the west lies the central plateau, dry and riddled with tsetse flies. The north is a mountainous region with slopes suited for agriculture. Around Lake Victoria, a heavily populated area, there are irrigated farmlands. Large plantations of sisal and sugarcane stretch along the coastal lowlands. Mount Kilimanjaro, the highest peak in Africa at 6,000 m, is located in the northern highlands. The need to increase exports has led to intensification of agricultural production in semi-arid areas, leading, in turn, to further soil erosion. Indiscriminate cutting of forests has continued.

SOCIETY

Peoples: Tanzanians are mostly of Bantu origin, subdivided into around 120 ethnic groups. On the mainland there are also Nilo-hamitic groups in the west; there is a Shirazi minority of Persian origin in Zanzibar. Both regions have groups of Arab, Indian and Pakistani and European immigrants.
Religions: Muslim 35 per cent; traditional religions 35 per cent; Christian 30 per cent. Zanzibar is 99 per cent Muslim, Shi'a and Sunni.
Languages: Swahili (official - the *lingua franca* of Central and Eastern Africa of Bantu origin). English (official), Arabic and more than 100 local languages.
Political Parties: Revolutionary Party of Tanzania (CCM-Chama Cha Mapinduzi), socialist orientation, emerged February 5 1977, from the fusion of the Tanganyika - later Tanzania - African National Union (TANU), founded by Julius K Nyerere in 1954, and the Afro-Shirazi Party of Zanzibar. Since 1992, a multiparty system that includes, amongst others: the Civic United Front (CUF, regionalist of Zanzibar); Party for Democracy and Progress (CHADEMA); Tanzania Labor Party; United Democratic Party.
Social Organizations: Organization of Tanzanian Trade Unions (OTTU); Union of Women of Tanzania (UWT); Co-operative Union of Tanzania (WASHIRICA); National Union of Students of Tanzania (MUWATA).

THE STATE

Official Name: Jamhuri ya Muungano wa Tanzania.
Administrative Divisions: 25 Divisions.
Capital: Dodoma 264,000 people (1999). Official capital since 1974, functions as seat of legislature.
Other cities: Dar es Salaam (former capital) 2,372,200 people; Mwanza 291,100; Zanzibar 247,500; Tanga 202,900 (2000).
Government: Benjamin Mkapa, President since November 1995, re-elected in 2000. Frederick Sumaye, Prime Minister since November 1995. The second Vice-President is also President of Zanzibar and Pemba. Unicameral Legislature: 274-member National Assembly.
National Holiday: April 26, Union Day (1964).
Armed Forces: 34,600 (1996).
Other: 1,400 Rural Police, 85,000 Militia.

AIDS in Africa: Pandemic of the poor

Of all the people in the world who are infected with HIV or have contracted AIDS - an estimated 33.4 million people - 63 per cent are found in Africa.

The statistics are chilling, the stories and images even more so. The future of African countries, which also face profound social, economic, political and military crises, is truly discouraging. According to the latest reports from the United Nations AIDS Program (UNAIDS), some 33.4 million people worldwide are infected with the virus that causes AIDS and of that total some 27.6 million were infected in 1999 alone.

But when these same studies show that 95 per cent of all infected people live in developing countries, and 63 per cent live in Africa, the problem shows its true character. The HIV-AIDS pandemic has hit hardest those countries which are extremely indebted. The economies of these nations depend structurally on international financial organizations, primarily the World Bank and the International Monetary Fund (IMF).

According to these organizations, the combined debt of all African countries amounts to some $350,000 million. This sum does not take into account the payments already made, in some form or another, and which far surpass this total, which is impossible for the African nations to pay. When it comes to AIDS, for example, the World Bank says it has already helped with $1,000 million for dozens of projects in various African countries since 1986. According to Dr Dorothy Logie, from a London-based medical organization, the 'AIDS crisis prospers amid poverty, with social disintegration and ignorance. The debt and adjustments have been instrumental in creating this situation, to the detriment of education and prevention'. In other words, some African nations earmark resources to refinance their debts rather than to directly combat HIV-AIDS and ensure access to health services and education for their citizens.

The sub-Saharan African countries are home to 63 per cent of all cases of HIV infection in the world, and are where 83 per cent of AIDS-related deaths have occurred since 1980 - at least 6 million people. In addition, 95 per cent of children who have lost one or both parents to the disease in the last 20 years live in this part of Africa. In Uganda alone, there are 1.7 million AIDS-orphaned children.

The HIV-AIDS epidemic has taken on new dimensions. In Zimbabwe, 26 per cent of adults are infected with the virus, and life expectancy has fallen by 23 years. The Zimbabwean Government estimates that within five years, 60 per cent of its health budget will be spent on HIV-AIDS research and prevention. In Botswana, 25 per cent of all adults are infected - a similar trend is found in Swaziland, Namibia and Zambia.

United Nations Secretary-General Kofi Annan made an illustrative comparison in May 2000 when he stated in London that more people have died in Africa from AIDS than from armed conflict there in the last two decades, citing the cases of Sierra Leone, Angola, Ethiopia, Eritrea, the Democratic Republic of the Congo, Congo and Somalia.

Yet this comparison gives only a limited perspective of the dimension of the HIV catastrophe in the region. The drastic reduction of life expectancy in these countries due to AIDS shows only too clearly that of all the misfortunes afflicting sub-Saharan Africa - poverty, starvation, war, various pandemics - none gets near the scale of destruction of this virus. ∎

---

233 per cent increase of several local taxes.

[30] In March, the World Bank praised Tanzania as it second-best African student after Ghana. The country's harsh social conditions were aggravated by an influx of Rwandan refugees, fleeing from massacres that killed over 500,000 in the neighboring country.

[31] 1995 was dominated by the multiparty legislative and presidential elections held in October, where the CCM triumphed again due to Nyerere's support. Benjamin Mkapa became the new President and appointed Frederick Sumaye Prime Minister.

[32] In December 1996, the Government decided to expel the majority of the 540,000 Rwandan refugees from the country. Most of them faced death, from the same conflicts they had fled three years previously. Tanzania still had 230,000 Hutu refugees from Burundi, and some 50,000 from DR Congo (formerly Zaire).

[33] In 1998, Tanzania's parliament began discussion of the Sexual Offences Law, proposing harsher sentences for sexual abuses committed against children aged under 18 years old. Poverty, child abuse and sex tourism were considered the main causes of the increase in child prostitution in the country.

[34] A bomb at the US embassy in Dar es Salaam killed 11 and injured 80 people in August. It was linked with the global terror network of Osama bin Laden, then based in Afghanistan.

[35] Political tensions between the capital and the Civic United Front of Zanzibar marked the first months of 1998. The opposition group protested about electoral fraud in 1995 and the subsequent repression of those who spoke out against the government.

[36] The death of Julius Nyerere in October that year brought tributes from dozens of political leaders all over the world. A draft plan for semi-autonomous local government on the mainland presented in December - to run alongside national government and Zanzibar's own semi-autonomous regime - unleashed another wave of attacks between the President and defenders of the project. The idea of a federation of autonomous regions had been criticized by Nyerere but his death paved the way for renewed discussion. Such a system would allow the mainland population equal rights to the islanders, who already had semi-autonomous government.

[37] Mkapa was re-elected with 72 per cent of the vote in the October elections. In Zanzibar the CCM candidate, Amani Karume was victorious, but flagrant irregularities in the monitoring on the island meant the opposition did not recognize the result. After violent protests where at least 30 people died, and a re-run of elections in two districts, Karume was sworn in as President of Zanzibar in November.

[38] In March 2001, the CCM signed an agreement with the main opposition party in Zanzibar, the United Civic Front, aiming to end the political violence in the semi-autonomous islands of Zanzibar. The parties agreed to form a joint committee to re-establish peace and encourage the 2,000 or so refugees in Kenya to return home. In April Dar es Salaam witnessed the first joint demonstration by opposition parties in decades. The opposition pressed for constitutional reform. The Labor Party demanded a new constitution and independent electoral commissions.

[39] An enormous new gold mine - the Bulyanhulu mine - opened in Tanzania in July 2001, which made the country the third biggest African producer. Bulyanhulu was taken over by the Canadian Barrick Gold Corporation and, after investing $280 million, production forecasts were made of 400,000 ounces of gold per year. It was estimated that some 300,000 smallscale miners and farmers had previously been evicted from the area.

[40] Mkapa founded an East African regional parliament and court with the presidents of Uganda and Kenya in Arusha, in November 2001. The agreement between Tanzania, Uganda and Kenya was seen as a step toward the creation of a common market across three countries with a total population of more than 80 million people.

[41] In December 2001 the UK press reported the sale of a £28 million military air traffic control system from Britain to Tanzania. Despite protests that the poverty-ridden country did not need such a system, the British Government said the sale would proceed. A leaked World Bank report in July the following year stated that a civilian system could be purchased for just an eighth of the cost.

[42] In early 2002, governor of the Central Bank, Doaud Ballali said there had been great progress in macroeconomic stability over the last seven years. According to Ballali, inflation had fallen from 30 per cent in 1995 to 4.7 per cent in 2002 and that by this date the economy was growing by more than 5 per cent per year (above the African average). In the financial sector there were an increasing number of banks - only one before 1993 and 20 by early 2002 - complemented by a further 12 non-banking financial institutions. ∎

Thailand

Population: 64,344,000 (2002)
Land area: 510,890 SQ KM
Capital: Bangkok (Krung Thep)
Currency: Baht
Language: Thai or Siamese

Thailand *Prathet Thai*

A rchaeological evidence indicates almost continuous human occupation of Thailand for the last 20,000 years. Thai-speaking peoples migrated southward from China around the 10th century AD. By the 13th century, the Thais emerged as a dominant force in the region, slowly absorbing the weakened empires of the Mons and Khmers. By 1238, the first Thai kingdom, Sukhothai, was established. King Ramkamhaeng the Great, noted as an administrator, legislator and statesman, is credited with the invention of the Thai script. The Sukhothai period saw the Thais for the first time developing a distinctive civilization with their own administrative institutions, art and architecture. Sukhothai Buddha images, characterized by refined facial features, lineal fluidity, and harmony of form, are considered to be the most beautiful and original of Thai artistic expression.

[2] In 1350 the more powerful state of Ayutthaya exerted its influence over Sukhothai, and from a former vassal status it usurped administrative power, leaving Sukhothai a deserted kingdom. The Ayutthaya kings became very powerful, moving east to take Lopburi - a former Khmer stronghold - and then in 1431 to Angkor, the capital of the Khmer Empire. The Aytthaya kings adopted Khmer court customs, language and culture. Unlike the paternal rulers of Sukhothai, Aytthaya's kings were absolute monarchs and assumed the title *devaraja* or God King. Aytthaya became one of the greatest and wealthiest cities in Asia. From the early 16th century the Portugese established trade, supplied mercenaries and taught the Thais cannon foundry and musketry.

[3] The Myanmar (Burmese) were the most powerful rival of the Aytthaya kingdom and in 1569 they defeated Aytthayan forces, occupied their capital, and ruled the kingdom for 15 years. The end of the Aytthayan rule arrived in 1767 when, after a siege of 14 months, a new Burmese invasion sacked the city, burning and looting and melting down the gold from Buddha images and took 90,000 captives. After expelling the Burmese occupying garrison in Aytthaya, Thai general Phya Taksin moved his capital to the

west bank of Bangkok, known as Thonburi, and was proclaimed king. During his reign Phya Taksin liberated Chiang Mai and the rest of northern Thailand from the Burmese.

[4] Rama I (1782–1809) founder of the Chakkri dynasty which still reigns in Thailand, moved his capital across the Chao Phraya River to Bangkok (Krung Thep), which at the time was still a small village. By the mid-19th century, Bangkok had become a city of some 400,000 people, swollen by the huge numbers of Chinese who had poured into Siam (as Thailand was then called) during these years. Rama II re-established relations with the West, allowing the Portuguese to construct the first Western embassy in Bangkok. His successor, Rama III, extended the Thai Empire south along the Malay Peninsula, north into Laos and southeast into

Cambodia while continued to reopen the country to foreigners, successfully promoting trade with China.

[5] The name Thailand means 'land of the free', and throughout the country's 800-year history, the Thai people was never colonized. While Rama IV (1851–68) opened the country to Western influence and initiated reforms and modern development, control of Siam was disputed by the French and the British. In 1896, the two powers agreed to leave the state formally independent. In World War I, Siam fought alongside the Allies and later joined the League of Nations.

[6] On June 24 1932, a coup curtailed the power of the monarchy, creating a parliament elected by universal suffrage. The country's name was changed to Thailand with

the advent of a democratic government in 1939, but the democratic experience was short-lived and in 1941, during World War II, the Bangkok Government allowed Japan to use its territory, becoming a virtual satellite of that country. During the conflict, Siamese troops occupied part of Malaysia, but were forced to abandon it in 1946, after the allied victory.

[7] In June that year, King Ananda Mahidol was assassinated in mysterious circumstances. US maneuvering succeeded in putting his brother, Rama IX, into power. Born in the US, the new king had never hidden his pro-US leanings. Since then, Thailand has remained under Washington's patronage.

[8] US interests in Thailand were essentially strategic as its geographical location and plans for a projected channel through the Kra Isthmus made the country critical to US military policy in the area. In 1954, the Southeast Asian Treaty Organization (SEATO), a military pact designed to counterbalance the growing power of revolutionary forces in the region, established its headquarters in Bangkok.

[9] In 1961, large numbers of US troops entered the country in reaction to an insurrection in Laos. The US military maintained its presence in Thailand for 14 years, resulting in strong ties being forged between the Thai and US armed forces. In exchange for their participation in the anti-communist struggle, the Thai military enjoyed greater political influence and impunity from their corrupt activities, which included control of the drug trade from the famous 'golden triangle' in the north.

[10] Between 1950 and 1975, US support of military regimes in Thailand cost it over $2 billion. On October 14 1973, a popular uprising by students brought down the government. As a result in 1975 the first civilian government in 20 years was formed. Elections brought Prince Seni Pramoj to power. He demanded the immediate withdrawal of US troops, the dismantling of military bases and an improvement of relations with neighboring revolutionary governments.

[11] The Thai military disagreed with the new government, and in October

1976 Pramoj was overthrown in a bloody coup planned by right-wing navy officers. Thousands of students and intellectuals joined a guerrilla struggle led by the Communist Party in the rural areas, and Thai relations with neighbors became extremely tense. Finally, in October 1977, a second coup brought the 'civilized right wing' of the military to power. They took a liberal line in policy-making as they were eager to attract new transnational investments. In 1979, Thailand granted asylum to Cambodian refugees. Refugee camps along the border became the rearguard of Cambodian strongman Pol Pot's Khmer Rouge guerrillas; a large part of international humanitarian aid was unwittingly channeled to them. Thailand thus served US interests in the region, as a base for new attacks against communist Vietnam which supported the anti-Khmer forces.

[12] On April 1 1981, another military coup shook Bangkok. This time it was led by General Sant Chitpatima with the support of young middle-ranking officers demanding institutional democracy and social change. The King and Prime Minister General Prem had been asked to lead the coup and had apparently accepted. However, they finally opposed the uprising, and it was put down after three days of great tension.

[13] The young officer's revolt, rooted within the military establishment, was at base a reaction to government measures bringing in forced retirement for certain senior generals. Nevertheless, the short-lived coup gained unusually strong support from trade unions and student groups - and this support in itself was extraordinary since the coup was instigated by the military.

[14] At the same time, the left-wing opposition was severely weakened by an internal split in the Communist Party into the pro-Vietnamese and pro-Chinese factions.

[15] On April 20 1983, elections were held and General Prem Tinsulanonda was appointed Prime Minister for a second successive term.

[16] Towards the end of 1984, the currency was sharply devalued, sparking discontent from General Arthit Kamlang-Ek and other hardline generals, who threatened to withdraw military support for Prem. Some timely political maneuvering by the prime minister, offering incentives to the officers for their support, allowed Prem to isolate Arthit.

[17] After a further coup attempt in September 1985, Prem relieved Arthit of his command and designated General Chaovalit Yongchaiyut as the head of the armed forces.

[18] Political instability continued in Bangkok, with several cabinet changes and requests for early legislative elections on two separate occasions. In May 1986, the Democrat Party obtained enough of a majority to form a coalition, presided over once again by General Prem as Prime Minister. While General Chaovalit's stature continued to grow, enhanced by his forceful attacks on corruption, the Government called for early elections in April 1988, to avoid the censure of Prem. The main criticisms of his administration were his questionable management of public funds and overall incompetence, particularly in the handling of the border war with Laos several months earlier, which had escalated from a dispute over the control of three villages.

[19] In the first general election since 1976, amid massive vote-buying campaigns (a practice considered normal by almost all candidates), the Thai Nation Party won the election. King Bhumibol Adulyahed asked General Chatichai Choonhavan to form a new government, which he did by arranging a six-party coalition.

[20] Thailand's new leading force and its successful entrepreneur, Chatichai, introduced important policy changes, breaking with the traditional focus on internal affairs and security. His main idea was to convert what had once been the Indochinese battlefield into a huge regional market. Tempted by the possibility of Cambodia and Laos opening up their markets, he invested considerably in those countries.

[21] This formula further fuelled the Thai economy, and in 1989 the growth rate exceeded 10 per cent. Thailand then challenged Western Europe and its subsidy policies for agricultural export products. There were also disagreements with the United States over Bangkok's refusal to accept North American trade criteria on intellectual property, especially with regard to computer programs.

[22] In 1989, rapid deforestation contributed to serious flooding as the regulatory effect of the forests on the water cycle was altered. Trees had been removed from river banks, where they had formed natural dikes.

[23] In March 1991, the military carried out another coup led by General Sunthorn Kongsompong, who presented King Bhumibol Adulyahed with a draft for a new constitution. The latter approved the draft, and justified the military coup on the grounds of 'growing corruption' within the civilian government. The King also agreed with the military on the need for calling new elections. As an indirect result of the military coup in Thailand, peace negotiations in

neighboring Cambodia came to a standstill, with the Cambodian Government denouncing Thailand for its renewed support of the Cambodian armed opposition.

[24] Throughout 1991, Thailand remained under the command of the Council for the Maintenance of National Peace (NPKC), a body of the military commanded by Sunthorn. In December, the King approved the new constitution which stipulated that elections to replace the NPKC Government would be held within 120 days. However, the military junta reserved the right to directly appoint 270 senators out of a total of 360, giving it total control over the new government.

[25] In elections held on March 22 1992, the majority of votes went to the opposition. There were 15 parties, with a total of 2,740 candidates, and 32 million out of 57 million Thais turned out to vote.

[26] In early April, General Suchinda Kraprayoon, commander-in-chief of the army at the time became Prime Minister, backed by a small majority made up of five pro-military parties. On his 49-member cabinet, Suchinda included 11 former ministers who had been accused of embezzlement during Chatichai's government.

[27] At the end of May, what began as an anti-government demonstration ended in a massacre, with hundreds of people killed and injured. Army troops fired into a crowd gathered at the Democracy Monument and political leaders such as Chamlong Srimuang were imprisoned. The protests continued until an unexpected television appeal for national reconciliation from the Thai king. Suchinda, in the meantime, announced his support of a constitutional amendment whereby the Prime Minister would have to be an elected member of Parliament, a clause which would disqualify even Suchinda from holding the post. Srimuang was subsequently freed, and an amnesty announced for those who had been arrested. With a curfew still in effect in Bangkok, Parliament initiated discussion of the constitutional amendment and the King appointed General Pren Tinsulanonda to supervise the process.

[28] On May 24, Suchinda resigned and his Vice President, Mitchai Ruchuphan, became interim president. Constitutional amendments approved in June reduced military participation in the government and King Bhumibol named Anand Panyarachun Prime Minister. Panyarachun, who enjoyed a great deal of prestige in Thailand, had been prime minister after the 1991 military coup.

[29] Parliament accepted the King's nomination of Panyarachun, who

---

ENVIRONMENT

Thailand is located in central Indochina. From the mountain ranges in the northern and western zones, the Ping and Nan Rivers flow down to the central valley through extensive deltas, into the Gulf of Thailand. The plains are fertile with large commercial rice plantations. The southern region occupies part of the Malay Peninsula. Severe deforestation of the area resulted in decreased production of rubber and timber, and has been responsible for migration of part of the native population. Pollution has increased dramatically through vehicle emissions, industrial pollution, lack of waste disposal and unrestricted industrial development.

SOCIETY

Peoples: The Thai group constitutes the majority of the population. The most important minority groups are the Chinese, 12 per cent and, in the south, the Malay, 13 per cent. Other groups are Khmer, Karen, Indians and Vietnamese. **Religions:** Most people (94 per cent) practice Buddhism. Muslims, concentrated in the south, make up about 4 per cent of the population. There is a Christian minority. **Languages:** Thai or Siamese (official). Minority groups speak their own languages. **Political Parties:** Phak Thai Rak Thai (TRT-Thais Love Thais Party); Democratic Party; Thai Nation Party; New Aspiration Party (NAP); National Development Party; Liberal Democratic Party.

THE STATE

Official Name: Muang Thai, or Prathet Thai (Kingdom of Thailand). **Administrative Division:** 5 regions and 73 provinces. **Capital:** Bangkok (Krung Thep) 7,133,000 people (1999). **Other cities:** Ratchasima 207,500 people; Chiang Mai 170,300; Khon Kaen 143,200; Nakhon Pathorn 122,500 Thanyaburi 115,500 (2000). **Government:** King Bhumibol Adulyadej, Head of State, since June 1946. Thaksin Shinawatra, Prime Minister and Head of Government since February 2001. The National Assembly (Parliament) has two chambers: the House of Representatives, with 438 members, and the Senate, with 200 members. **National Holiday:** December 5, the King's birthday (1927). **Armed Forces:** 254,000 troops (1996). **Other:** 141,700 (National Security Volunteer Force, Air Police, Frontier Police Patrols, Province Police and 'Hunter Soldiers').

---

appointed a number of technocrats to cabinet positions and requested the resignations of the 12 military officers responsible for the May massacre.

[30] On June 29, the Prime Minister dissolved Parliament and announced elections for September. The Democratic Party (DP) won the election, obtaining 79 seats in the Chamber of Representatives. On September 23, a parliamentary majority made up of the DP, the Palang Dharma (PD) and the New Aspiration Party (NAP) emerged, holding 177 seats, and anti-military political leader Chuan Leekpai was elected Prime Minister. Shortly afterwards, the pro-military New Aspiration Party joined the coalition.

[31] Several violent incidents motivated by religious sensitivities took place in 1993. Concerned with his country's role in the region, Chuan strengthened ties with China and Indonesia and in October officially terminated the support which Thailand had provided to Cambodia's Khmer Rouge since 1979. Cambodian authorities accused Thailand of supporting the 'Pol Potists' after 14 Thais were arrested during a thwarted coup attempt in Phnom Penh.

[32] The Government approved a reform to liberalize the banking system in January 1994. Among other things, the reform permitted the opening of branches of foreign banks in various Thai cities.

[33] Although in 1994 the economy of Thailand was among those that grew most, its economic stability did not spread to the political sphere. The first parliamentary session of 1995 brought an exchange of accusations and the tense political atmosphere led to the dissolution of Parliament. On July 2 early elections took place. The Thai Nation Party obtained 25 per cent of the seats and the Democrats 22 per cent. Banham Silapa-archa, leader of the winning party, formed a government supported by several small parties.

[34] In 1995, inflation reached 6.5 per cent. It was considered 'manageable' by the Central Bank. With an annual population growth rate of 1.5 per cent and a growth in the economy of over 8 per cent, Thailand remained on the list of countries with sustained economic success.

[35] In November 1996, Chavalit Yonchaiyudh (NAP) was elected Prime Minister, with 125 of the 393 seats in the Chamber of Representatives. Chuan Leekpai's DP, took 123 seats. A coalition with the Chart Pattana (52), Social Action (20), Prachakorn Thai (18) plus two minor parties, allowed Chavalit to obtain the majority weeks later.

[36] Thailand was hit by a financial crisis in 1997, exacerbated by scandals and attempts to salvage the banks - leading to the resignation of the economy minister and the closure of businesses - and by Chavalit's proposal for constitutional reform in order to lift a vote of no confidence lodged by the opposition.

[37] In August 1997, the constitutional reform project was completed. It aimed to limit corruption, put citizens' rights into the legislation and eliminate army influence from the Senate. Alarmed by the perceived loss of power, the governing parties initially rejected this project, but they were forced to accept it given the agreement between the army and King Bhumibol. The new Constitution was passed in a General Assembly on October 11.

[38] When the new prime minister Chuan Leekpai took office in November 1997, the Thai currency, the baht, had devaluated 37 per cent. The crisis lasted throughout the following year, which closed with an 8 per cent drop in Gross National Product. Unemployment affected 1.8 million people (6 per cent) of the population, while the Government proposed making 200,000 of its 1.5 million employees redundant. The $17.2-billion loan granted by the IMF involved a series of counterpart demands. As well as redundancies in the state sector, the Government put 59 state companies up for sale, including telecommunications, electricity, petrochemicals and finances.

[39] In March the Prime Minister survived a vote of no confidence and even extended his base of his alliance, by incorporating Chart Pattana, which had 51 votes in parliament, into the government. The Government decided not to renew the work permits of half a million immigrant workers, but finally gave in to pressure from rice-growers and other entrepreneurs who employ cheap labor, granting 95,000 new permits.

[40] After months of tension with political refugees from Burma (Myanmar), the Government demanded they register with the UN High Commissioner for Refugees' office in order to be relocated. Deportations continued throughout 1999, and in November of that year the Government reported it still hoped to expel another 700,000 foreign workers in order to give their jobs to unemployed Thais. In January 2000, under pressure from the business sector, the authorities once again allowed foreigners in as seasonal workers.

[41] The March 2000 elections for the direct appointment of senators were plagued with irregularities. The electoral authority disqualified 78 of the 200 legislators elected, accusing them of corruption and fraud. Two of the disqualified senators were the wives of the Interior and Justice ministers. It was the first time senators had been elected by popular vote.

[42] The Thais Love Thais Party (TRT), headed by media magnate Thaksin Shinawatra, won the January 2001 parliamentary elections but did not obtain an absolute majority. The TRT took 248 of the 500 seats in contention. Although the elections took place under a new Constitution, designed to reduce electoral fraud, accusations of irregularities forced the electoral commission to hold new balloting in 62 districts. In February, Parliament elected Shinawatra Prime Minister.

[43] In early 2001, Thai and Burmese troops clashed along the shared border - the Mae Sai-Tachilek crossing - and Bangkok and Rangoon accused each other of supporting drug-producing militias. Shinawatra had made combating drug-trafficking a government priority. In May 2001 the tensions escalated as the presence of special US troops increased on the Thai side of the border. Their stated mission was to train the Thai army in anti-drug trade techniques. That same month, near the border with Burma/Myanmar, more than 20,000 US and Thai soldiers carried out their annual joint maneuvers. In June, Shinawatra traveled to Rangoon to discuss the border problems, resulting in the reopening of Mae Sai-Tachilek.

[44] In August, a constitutional court absolved Shinawatra after a lower court had ruled against him in December 2000 for failing to declare his huge personal fortune when he was deputy prime minister in 1997. If the constitutional court had upheld the lower court's ruling, Shinawatra could have been banned from political activity for five years.

[45] The jewelry and precious stones industry suffered a major retraction in early 2002. US consumption, which represented 50 per cent of the global market for cut gems, had collapsed in the wake of the September 2001 terrorist attacks in New York and Washington. For Thailand, one of the leading world exporters, the consequences were severe. By March 2002, the recession in that market had left some 200,000 Thais without work.

[46] In April 2002, at a tripartite summit held in India, Rangoon and Bangkok agreed to a plan to repatriate more than 500,000 illegal Burmese immigrants living in Thailand. As part of the accord, the immigrants would undergo HIV testing. Those testing HIV-positive would be separated from the other illegal immigrants and treated as part of a special repatriation plan. ∎

Togo

Population: 4,779,000 (2002)
Land area: 54,390 SQ KM
Capital: Lomé
Currency: CFA franc
Language: French

Togo

Togo was peopled by the Ewe (of the same origin as the Igbo and Yoruba of Nigeria and the Ashanti of Ghana), who make up over a third of its population. The Ewe were a relatively poor and peaceful people with simple social structures like the Dagomba kingdoms in the north.

2 The slave trade gave the region the name of Slave Coast, and millions of people were shipped to slavery in the US between the 16th and 19th centuries.

3 Togo became a German colony in 1884 under 'treaties' signed with local chieftains. Occupied by Anglo-French troops during World War I, the territory was divided between the two powers with the endorsement of the League of Nations. The western part was annexed to Ghana in 1956, after a British-organized plebiscite, while the eastern part remained under French rule.

4 In 1958, Sylvanus Olympio, (a member of the Togolese Unity party) won the elections. His program was pro-independence, but moderate. The 1960 proclamation of independence seemed to overlook a contract signed in 1957 with the Benin Mines Company, in which the French consortium had seized control of Togo's phosphate reserves, its main natural resource, thus compromising independence. When Olympio confronted this situation in 1963, proposing a series of basic reforms - doubtlessly influenced by Nkrumah's radical pro-independence program in neighboring Ghana - he was assassinated in a military revolt, allegedly involving a young military officer, Eyadéma.

5 Olympio's successor, the neo-colonialist Nicholas Grunitzky, from the opposition Togolese Progress Party, was overthrown by a further coup in 1967, led by General Gnassingbé Eyadéma, who became the new head of state.

6 In 1969, Eyadéma's Togo People's Group (RPT) brought in a one-party system. In 1972 a law gave the state 35 per cent of shares of the mining company, which was raised to 51 per cent in 1975 and in 1976 the production and export of phosphate was nationalized.

7 On December 30 1979, a constitution was approved and Eyadéma was re-elected President for a 7-year term. His government was confident of improving the economy, basing its optimism on tourism, oil and a rise in world phosphate prices. However in 1981 phosphate prices dropped by 50 per cent and a worldwide economic recession reduced the number of European tourists. A serious balance of payments deficit increased the foreign debt to $1 billion.

8 In June 1984 a refinancing agreement with stringent conditions, was reached with the Paris Club and the IMF. Consequently, there were salary freezes, reduction of government investments and high taxes levied to increase government funds, including a so-called 'solidarity tax' which took 5 per cent of the population's incomes.

9 In January 1985 the Lomé III agreements were signed in Togo, regulating cooperation between ACP (Africa, Caribbean and Pacific) countries and the EEC.

10 In January 1986 Eyadéma was re-elected for 7 years, with 99.95 per cent of the vote. Consultation with the IMF resumed and new agreements were planned in 1988. In 1990, adjustment programs were initiated, including denationalization, on account of trade deficits and a public deficit of $1.27 billion. Meanwhile food production rose slightly.

11 In 1991, more than 10,000 peasants in the northern district of Keran Oti lost their lands to create an 80 sq km game reserve for hunting.

12 In early April 1991, there were pro-democracy demonstrations throughout the country, and on April 8 more than a thousand people took over one of Lomé's neighborhoods, setting up barricades and demanding Eyadéma's resignation. The police reacted violently, killing more than 30 people and injuring many more. However on April 12, opposition parties were legalized and Eyadéma announced an amnesty for political prisoners, and liberalization of the political system.

13 On August 28 1991, a National Conference named Kokou Koffigoh - president of Togo's Bar Association and a recognized human rights leader - as provisional Prime Minister. A legislative assembly was established which ousted Eyadéma as head of the armed forces and blocked his candidacy in the upcoming 1992 elections.

14 The dissolution of the RPT on November 26 1991, prompted a military coup. Two days later, the armed forces took over the government, dissolved the legislative assembly and kidnapped Koffigoh for several hours. The perpetrators of the coup claimed that the legislative assembly was made up of extremists, whose aim was to 'disrupt the army and discredit the military regime and its achievements'. Political parties and other opposition organizations cooperated together within the framework of the National Resistance Committee, and encouraged people to resist a return to dictatorship.

15 Togo's complicated political scenario was compounded by economic, social and ethnic problems. Eyadéma came from the southern Kabye group, which provided the majority of the country's 12,000 troops. Meanwhile, Koffigoh was a member of the Ewe tribe. Negotiations began between those who favored the military regime and the opposition, aimed at precipitating the transition to civilian government by 1992. That year, a timetable was established for a return to democracy, and all citizens were re-registered to vote.

16 In June, opposition leader Tavio Komlavi was assassinated. After an attempt upon the life of Mining Minister Joseph Yao Amefia, Eyadéma took advantage of the incident to have his powers restored by the High Council of the Republic (the interim legislature). Eyadéma proceeded to pack the cabinet with his supporters. In the face of widespread protests from the opposition, the Government

---

Map labels

BURKINA FASO
Dapango
Oti
Kara
BENIN
Lama-Kara
GHANA
Sokodé
Mono
CORDE DE TOGO
Blitta
Anié
Ogou
TOGO
L. Volta
Atakpamé
Palimé
Tabligbo
Anécho
Lomé
SLAVE COAST
Gulf of Guinea
0
0   100 km

MATERNAL MORTALITY	LITERACY	EXTERNAL DEBT

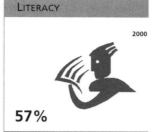

MATERNAL MORTALITY
1985/99
Per 100,000 live births
480

LITERACY
2000
57%

EXTERNAL DEBT
2000
PER CAPITA
US$ 317

postponed elections indefinitely. The unions, in reprisal, called a long-term general strike.

[17] The opposition split from Koffigoh in January 1993, after which they met in Benin and nominated a government in exile. In this same month the presidential guard killed some hundred demonstrators in Lomé, which led to thousands of people fleeing to Ghana and Benin.

[18] Eyadéma agreed to organize elections for August. In an atmosphere of civil war, he won with 96.5 per cent of the vote, in a poll denounced as fraudulent by the opposition. The protests in the streets intensified, and in January 1994, Eyadéma was unharmed in a foiled assassination attempt - carried out by around a hundred armed attackers - which left 67 people dead.

[19] The opposition triumphed in the February legislative elections, but Eyadéma barred Edem Kodjo from

forming a government without ruling party members. The Action Committee for Renewal, an alliance of opposition groups, decided to boycott parliament, paralyzing the government for almost a year.

[20] In July 1997 the opposition joined forces to defeat Eyadéma, who had been in power since 1967. Even the military applied pressure on him to liberalize the political system. The following year, the Legislative Assembly approved new press legislation, banning the arbitrary arrest of journalists, as well as other police abuse, for example night 'visits' with no legal justification. The June presidential elections were heavily criticized by the opposition, who saw them as fraudulent. The result was favorable for Eyadéma, who won with 52 per cent of the vote, beating Gilchrist Olympio, son of the assassinated president. The capital was shaken by constant opposition

demonstrations against the fraud over the following months.

[21] The meeting of Francophone nations of West Africa in March 2000 was a diplomatic success for the Eyadéma government, as Benin, Niger, Burkina Faso and Côte d'Ivoire all attended and the nation could open up to its neighbors. In September, Agbeyome Messan Kodjo was made Prime Minister.

[22] An international commission investigation published in February 2001 concluded there were systematic human rights violations in the country - including summary executions, the torture of prisoners, rapes and abductions - following the 1998 elections.

[23] In August 2001, the Government announced that Eyadéma would respect the constitution and end his term in 2003, the year after which he can no longer legally stand as president. Premier Kodjo controversially supported the possibility of constitutional change allowing Eyadéma to stand again.

[24] A month later, a group of 68 children aged from 18 months to 17 years old - thought to be victims of the child slave traffickers - were taken to Togo after the vessel they were on sank. Child trafficking, mainly in frontier regions with Benin, is one of the major problems facing the country. In mid-2001, the Togolese government was funding a child protection agency whilst increasing the number of police and army patrols to control the traffic.

[25] After planned legislative elections failed to be held in October, in March 2002 the Joint Commission of Inquiry - created from ruling party and opposition members to deal with the political crisis following the 1998 elections - came back into operation. The Commission met in Lomé to 'revive political dialogue' through the organization of elections. The opposition had refused to participate in the National Electoral Commission until attorney Yawovi Agboyibo - leader of the togolese opposition imprisoned since 3 August 2001 - was freed. On March 16 2001 Agboyibo was finally liberated and the main opposition parties declared they were ready to resume dialogue with government. ∎

PROFILE

ENVIRONMENT

The country is a long, narrow strip of land with distinct geographical regions. In the south, a low coastline with lakes, typical of the Gulf of Guinea; a highly populated plain where manioc, corn, banana and palm oil are grown. In the north, subsistence crops are gradually giving way to coffee and cocoa plantations. The Togo Mountains run through the country from northeast to southwest.

SOCIETY

Peoples: The main ethnic groups are the Ewe (43.1 per cent), Kabye (26.7 per cent), Gurma (16.1 per cent), Kebu (3.8 per cent) and Ana (Yoruba, 3.2 per cent). The descendants of formerly enslaved Africans who returned to Togo from Brazil are called Brazilians. They form a caste with great economic and political influence. The small European minority (0.3 per cent) is concentrated in the capital.
Religions: The majority follow traditional African religions (50 per cent). There are Christian (35 per cent) and Muslim (15 per cent) minorities.
Languages: French (official). The main local languages are Ewe, Kabye, Twi and Hausa.
Political Parties: Rally of the Togolese People (RTP), was the only legal party since 1969 until 1991; Coordination of New Forces (CFN); Union of the Forces for Change (UFC); Action Committee for Renewal (CAR).
Social Organizations: National Confederation of Togolese Workers (CNT).

THE STATE

Official Name: République Togolaise.
Administrative Divisions: 5 Regions and 21 Prefectures.
Capital: Lomé 790,000 people (1999).
Other cities: Sokodé 48,098 people; Kpalimé 27,700 (1983).
Government: Gnassingbé Eyadéma, President since April 1967, re-elected in 1998. Agbeyome Messan Kodjo, Prime Minister since August 2000. Unicameral Legislature: 81-member National Assembly.
National Holiday: April 27, Independence Day (1960).
Armed Forces: 6,950 (1997).
Other: 750 Gendarmes.

DEMOGRAPHY

Population: 4,779,000 (2002)
Annual growth: 2.8 % (1985-2000)
Estimates for year 2015: 6,576,000 (2000)
Annual growth to year 2015: 2.5 % (2000)
Urban population: 33.3 % (2000)
Urban growth: 4.7 % (2000)
Children per woman: 5.6 (2000)

HEALTH

Life expectancy at birth: 52 years (2000-2005)
male: 51 years (2000-2005)
female: 53 years (2000-2005)
Maternal mortality: 480 per 100,000 live births (1985/99)
Infant mortality: 80 per 1,000 (2000)
Under-5 child mortality: 142 per 1,000 (2000)
Daily calorie supply: 2,527 per capita (1999)
8 doctors per 100,000 people (1995)
Safe water: 54 % (2000)

EDUCATION

Literacy: 57 % (2000)
male: 72 % (2000)
female: 43 % (2000)
School enrolment (net):
Primary total: 69 % (1994/2000)
male: 85 % (1995/99)
female: 61 % (1995/99)
Secondary (gross):
male: 40 % (1995/97)
female: 14 % (1995/97)
Tertiary (gross): 4 % (1998)
Primary school teachers: one for every 41 pupils (1998)

COMMUNICATIONS

4 newspapers (1996), 265 radios (2000), 32 TV sets (2000) and 9 main telephone lines (2000) per 1,000 people

ECONOMY

Per capita, GDP: $ 1,442 (2000)
Annual growth: -3.7 % (2000)
Annual inflation: 1.9 % (2000)
Consumer price index: 116.5 (2000)
Currency: 758.3 CFA francs = $ 1 (03/2002)
Cereal imports: 304,522 metric tons (2000)
Food import dependency: 18 % (2000)
Fertilizer use: 77 kg per ha (1999)
Exports: $ 433 million (2000)
Imports: $ 608 million (2000)
External debt: $ 1,435 million (2000); $ 317 per capita (2000)
Debt service: 7.7 % of exports (1999)
Development aid received: $ 71 million (1999); $ 15.6 per capita (1999); 5.10 % of GNP (1999)

ENERGY

26.1 % imported (1999)

HDI (ranking/value): 128 / 0.489 (1999)

Tonga

Population: 100,000 (2002)
Land area: 720 SQ KM
Capital: Nuku'alofa
Currency: Pa'anga
Language: Tongan and English

Tonga

The original inhabitants of Tonga, which means 'south' in several Polynesian languages, immigrated from Fiji and Samoa over 1,000 years ago. Tongans developed a complex social organization, with a traditional leader in charge. According to oral tradition, the first *Tui Tonga* (ruler, Son of the Creator) of the islands was Aholitu in the second half of the 10th century. Towards the 15th century, religious and social roles were assigned to different leaders and this system of double leadership continued until the Dutch came to the islands in 1616. English explorer Captain James Cook, visited them in 1775 and named them the 'Friendly Islands'.

[2] The archipelago only achieved political reunification in the mid-19th century, in a civil war, under the leadership of Taufa'ahau Tupou, ruler of the island of Haapai from 1820 onwards. Converted to Christianity and subsequently backed by European missionaries, Taufa'ahau seized Vavau and Tongatopu, securing control over the whole of the territory which he ruled under the Christian name of George I until 1893. The King introduced a parliamentary system including the local leaders, and an agrarian reform which granted each adult male in the country 3.3 ha of arable land. This ensured social stability and agricultural self-sufficiency.

[3] In 1889, Britain and Germany signed a treaty which gave Britain a free hand in its relations with Tonga. The following year the archipelago was made a 'protectorate' of the British crown, though the monarchy was kept with limited powers.

[4] Queen Salote, great-granddaughter of George I was crowned in 1918 and in 1960, she gave women the right to vote in legislative elections.

[5] The British transformed the country's agriculture, which was reoriented towards the export crops of copra and bananas.

[6] Present King Taufa'ahau Tupou IV was crowned in 1967, and three years later Tonga obtained independence. The high international market prices for copra and bananas helped Tonga to develop a wide-ranging social security system which included free education and medical services for all the inhabitants of the islands.

[7] In the mid-1970s about 10,000 Tongans emigrated to Aotearoa/New Zealand. Tonga's economy suffers from serious inflation, with a high level of unemployment, despite emigration, and a substantial trade deficit.

[8] Opposition groups founded the Pro-Democracy Movement which won 6 of the 9 seats in the National Assembly in the February 1993 elections.

[9] However, power was retained by the King, who appointed government officers. In September 1994, the Pro-Democracy Movement became the Tonga Democratic Party, led by 'Akilisi Pohiva.

[10] The King continued to promote a multiparty system but did not modify his quasi-monopolistic grip on power.

[11] In January 1996, the People's Party (formerly Tonga Democratic Party) won six of the nine seats held by elected deputies in the Legislative Assembly.

[12] Demonstrations in favor of political liberalization continued in 1997. Several political leaders and journalists were arrested that year.

[13] In March 1998, Minister of Lands, the aristocrat Fakafanua (the King's brother-in-law) was arrested and charged with irregular management of public funds and of accepting bribes. A court overturned his imprisonment and he was released a few days later, though prohibited from leaving the country.

[14] The King of Tonga granted research rights to an Australian company in December 2000 to study the genes of the island's 108,000 inhabitants in exchange for the benefits of the research to be applied free of charge to the Tongans. Several companies specializing in gene research are interested in the island due to the unusual percentage of obese people among the population.

[15] In October 2001, a US businessman, Jesse Bogdonoff, who was appointed official Court Jester by the King, was involved in a financial scandal in which millions of dollars had been invested in a mysterious company that later disappeared. Two ministers, including the deputy Prime Minister, were forced to step down after the Government discovered that some $26 million could not be accounted for. ∎

PROFILE

ENVIRONMENT

The archipelago was known as the 'Friendly Isles' and is located in western Polynesia, east of the Fiji Islands, slightly north of the Tropic of Capricorn. It comprises approximately 169 islands, only 36 of which are permanently inhabited. It includes three main groups of islands: Tongatapu, the southernmost group where more than half of the population live; Vavau, to the north, and Haapai in between. The volcanic islands are mountainous while the coral ones are flat. The climate is mild and rainy with very hot summers. The fertile soil is suitable for growing banana, copra and coconut trees.

SOCIETY

Peoples: Tongans are Polynesian people. It is estimated that 20 per cent of them now live abroad.
Religions: Free Wesleyan, 43.6 per cent; Roman Catholic, 16.0 per cent; Mormon, 12.1 per cent; Free Church of Tonga, 11.0 per cent.
Languages: Tongan and English are official. **Political Parties:** People's Party (formerly Tonga Democratic Party).

THE STATE

Official Names: Pule'anga Fakatu'i o' Tonga. Kingdom of Tonga.
Administrative Divisions: 23 Districts. **Capital:** Nuku'alofa 37,000 people (1999).
Other cities: Neiafu 4,000 people; Haveloloto 3,200; Vaini 2,800; Tofoa-Koloua 2,400 (2000).
Government: Monarchy, limited by the power of the nobles (the five ministries are lifetime terms). Unicameral Legislative Assembly that includes the 5 ministers, governors of Háapai and Vavau, 7 nobles (elected by their 33 peers) and 7 deputies elected by the male taxpayers over age 21. Taufa'ahau Tupou IV, King since 1965; Prince Lavaka Ata 'Ulukalala, Prime Minister since January 2000. Legislative Assembly has 30 members.
National Holiday: June 4, Independence Day (1970).
Armed Forces: There is no army in Tonga. 300 National Police (1991).

HEALTH

Infant mortality: 17 per 1,000 (2000)
Under-5 child mortality: 21 per 1,000 (2000)
44 doctors per 100,000 people (1997)
Safe water: 100 % (2000)

EDUCATION

Literacy: 99 % (2000)

ECONOMY

Annual growth: 5.5 % (2000)
Cereal imports: 8,804 metric tons (2000)
Food import dependency: 28 % (1995)
Fertilizer use: 0 kg per ha (1999)
Exports: $ 29 million (1992)
Imports: $ 71 million (1992)
External debt: $ 58 million (2000); $ 588 per capita (2000)

Trinidad and Tobago

Population: 1,306,000 (2002)
Land area: 5,130 SQ KM
Capital: Port of Spain
Currency: Trinidad dollar
Language: English

Trinidad and Tobago

A lthough Trinidad and Tobago currently form a single nation, the two islands have different histories. Trinidad, 12 kilometers from the mouth of the Orinoco River, was claimed by Columbus in 1498 for Spain. Tobago had been inhabited by Carib Indians, but when the Dutch arrived in 1632, they found it apparently uninhabited. Shortly thereafter, Spanish troops invaded to prevent the Dutch from using Tobago as a base for exploring the Orinoco, where there was thought to be gold.

[2] The islands suffered a succession of invasions by the Dutch, French and British. In 1783, three centuries after the arrival of the first Europeans, the local population comprised 126 people of European origin, 605 of African origin including 310 slaves and 2,032 Amerindians. Trinidad finally became a British colony in 1802, and Tobago in 1814.

[3] The local economy was based on sugar. Once slavery was abolished in 1834, most Africans moved to the cities and were replaced on the plantations by workers from India and some Chinese. These changes defined the islands' current ethnic and social composition. The Africans were mostly urban workers, while the Indians constituted the large rural working class. Nonetheless, some African workers remained in the countryside, where they survived by a system of mutual aid called *gayap*.

[4] In 1924, the first moves towards autonomy were made and the colonial administration was reformed, allowing elections for certain secondary positions although suffrage was limited. The newly-organized trade unions also raised the issue of independence. In 1950 internal autonomy was granted, and the People's National Movement (PNM) won the elections. Dr Eric Williams became Prime Minister, a post which he held until his death in 1981. In 1962, after a brief period as part of the West Indies Federation (1958-62), Trinidad and Tobago became fully independent. On August 31 1976, a new constitution proclaimed the republic.

[5] In the early 1900s sugar production began to decline and was gradually replaced by oil; by 1940, the latter had become the principal

economic activity. Between 1972 and 1982, there was a five-fold increase in earnings from petroleum, as well as in government expenditure. Unemployment was reduced to less than 10 per cent and imports (primarily of luxury items) increased eleven-fold. Trinidad had the highest per capita income in Central and South America, and began to take on the aspect of a 'consumer society'. In the meantime, President Williams' PNM Government initiated nationalization of the oil industry and adapted pricing policies to those established by OPEC, while encouraging investment from transnational corporations.

[6] However, during the 1970s there was social unrest. In 1975, a number of strikes occurred and oil workers of African origin and Asian Indian plantation hands fought together for better conditions. The strike movement finally foundered when the PNM government called in the army and gave it the responsibility of gasoline distribution.

[7] The over-dependence on oil caused serious problems and instability from 1982. This was due to a number of reasons: the international recession and the fall in oil prices, as well as factors linked specifically to the oil industry; the decrease in the demand for heavy oil, competition from major refineries which had been installed along the southern and eastern coasts of the United States, and a decline in production rates.

[8] In 1983, the economy took a downturn. A 26-per-cent decrease in oil revenues was predicted, leading to an actual net loss of 5.2 per cent of the GNP. The Government was able to control this situation by eliminating subsidies, reducing public investment and holding down public salaries.

[9] In October 1983, the Government led by George Chambers opposed the US invasion of Grenada and did not provide troops for the expeditionary force from six Caribbean countries. Chambers' government faced growing social and political unrest. The opposition reformed as the National Alliance for Reconstruction (NAR) and won elections in December 1986, taking 33 of the 36 parliamentary seats to end 30 years of PNM government.

[10] Arthur Napoleon Robinson's new government proposed a five year 'readjustment' plan, effective as of December 1990, designed to accelerate the process of integration with other CARICOM members (Caribbean Community and Common Market). This project entailed eliminating protection for the textile industry, developing tourism and new industrial projects, such as methane and natural gas refineries.

[11] The Government applied austerity measures agreed with the IMF, from which it received $110 million in 1988, as well as a $128 million standby loan in 1989. There

were a number of strikes in the oil industry, including a general strike in March 1989.

[12] The Robinson administration committed itself to reducing inflation to 5 per cent a year, restructuring state-owned companies, limiting the number of public employees and further liberalizing the economy. To achieve these goals, the Government abolished export licenses, liberalized the national price system (while maintaining control over basic food products and pharmaceuticals), and decreed a 10 per cent reduction in the salaries in the public sector.

[13] On July 27 1990, Trinidad and Tobago suffered their first coup attempt since winning independence from Britain in 1962. One hundred Muslims of African origin occupied Parliament and took hostages. They demanded that Prime Minister Arthur Jay Robinson resign and call elections. On August 1, after freeing all the hostages, the group surrendered unconditionally.

[14] The 1990 balance-sheet showed a slight economic recovery, achieved through an increase in oil and petrochemical exports, which had increased as a result of the Gulf crisis. This enabled the Government to avoid enforcing the 10-per-cent reduction in salaries.

[15] In December 1991, the PNM won the general elections with 46 per cent of the vote, and obtained 20 of the 36 parliamentary seats. The United National Congress (UNC) obtained 26 per cent and Robinson's NAR, 20 per cent. Abstentions were considerably higher than before.

[16] The main obstacles facing the new government, led by Patrick Manning, were a foreign debt amounting to $2.51 billion, and 24 per cent unemployment in a 460,000-strong workforce.

[17] The Government's economic adjustment and privatization plans sparked protest demonstrations in January 1993. The civil servants also demanded the payment of overdue backpay. Manning called the army in to 'control' the situation given the increasing agitation.

[18] Partial parliamentary elections in 1994 showed the increasing unpopularity of Manning, as the governing PNM lost two of the three contested seats.

MATERNAL MORTALITY

1985/99

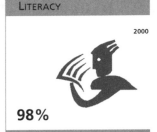

Per 100,000
live births

70

LITERACY

2000

98%

EXTERNAL DEBT

2000

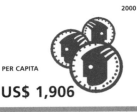

PER CAPITA

US$ 1,906

---

[19] On another front, the amnesty decreed by then Prime Minister Robinson on the 114 members of the Jamaat-al-Muslimeen Islamic group responsible for the July 1990 coup attempt was annulled. However, this was a symbolic measure, as the court decided the accused would be neither arrested nor taken to trial.

[20] Faced with what he considered a more favorable economic and political situation, Manning decided to call elections in November 1995, a year early. However, he had miscalculated, for the PNM took only 17 seats, as did the opposition UNC, led by Basdeo Panday.

[21] After making an alliance with the NAR, Panday became the first Asian to be a head of government in Trinidad and Tobago.

[22] In 1996, the governing coalition approved a balanced budget which reduced spending. The Government granted permission to a consortium, including a British company, to build a natural gas plant to supply the US and Spain, to come into operation in 1999.

[23] In early 1997, the opposition reduced its presence in the Chamber of Representatives even further, when two of its members joined the governing coalition as 'independents'. This desertion left it with only 15 seats to the ruling party's 21.

[24] On February 14, ruling party candidate and former Prime Minister AN Robinson was elected President, when he received 46 votes in the electoral college. The opposition candidate, Anthony Lucky, took 18. Robinson officially took office on March 19.

[25] In March 1998 new tensions emerged with the Jamaat-al-Muslimeen Islamic group. The Government reiterated its claims to a plot of land occupied by the fundamentalists. The group stated that it was their property, while the Government insisted it had been occupied illegally.

[26] In May, British legal authorities prevented the hanging of nine people accused of murders committed in 1996, causing discontent in the islands. Although Trinidad and Tobago have been independent since 1976, the Privy Council is the highest legal authority. According to local surveys, 80 per cent of the population supports execution in cases of murder and crimes related to drug-trafficking.

[27] In December 2001, general elections ended with an 18-seat tie between the UNC and the PNM in Parliament. Panday and Manning agreed that President Robinson could decide who would be Prime Minister. The President opted for Manning, but Panday called for new elections within six months. Panday had confirmed the governing party had the right to continue in power if another draw were to occur.

[28] Manning called on parliament - which had not met since the general elections of December 2001 - to choose a representative in order to break the deadlock that had paralyzed the nation's political system for nearly four months. But by April 2002, parliamentary representatives of the UNC and PNM had not managed to do this, as they could not outvote each other. Panday stated that if Manning could not show that he had a parliamentary majority, then new elections should be called. Manning meanwhile claimed that simply opening parliament would be sufficient to satisfy any constitutional requirements. ∎

PROFILE

ENVIRONMENT

The country is an archipelago located near the Orinoco River delta off the Venezuelan coast in the southern end of the Lesser Antilles in the Caribbean. Trinidad, the largest island (4,828 sq km), is crossed from East to West by a mountain range that is an extension of the Andes. One-third of the island is covered with sugar and cocoa plantations. Petroleum and asphalt are also produced. Tobago, 300 sq km with a small central volcanic mountain range, is flanked by Little Tobago (1 sq km), the islet of Goat and the Bucco Reef. In the archipelago the prevailing climate is tropical with rains from June to December, but tempered by the sea and east trade winds. Rivers are scarce, but dense forest vegetation covers the mountains. Its geographical proximity to the main sea route linking the Caribbean to the Atlantic, has led to pollution of the islands' coasts.

SOCIETY

Peoples: There is a large minority of African origin (43 per cent), and a slight majority descended from Asian Indians (40 per cent) brought during the 19th century as contract workers. Mestizo 14 per cent; Europeans (1 per cent) and Chinese (1 per cent) groups make up a small minority. **Religions:** There is no official religion. Catholic 29.4 per cent; Protestant 29.7 per cent; Hindu 23.7 per cent; Muslim 5.9 per cent; other 11.3 per cent. **Languages:** English (official). Hindi, Urdu, French and Spanish. **Political Parties:** The People's National Movement (PNM); United National Congress (UNC); Team Unity (TUN); National Alliance for Reconstruction (NAR). **Social Organizations:** Trinidad and Tobago Labor Congress (TTLC); Jamaat-al-Muslimeen.

THE STATE

Official Name: Republic of Trinidad and Tobago.
Administrative Divisions: 7 Counties, 4 Cities with own government, 1 semi-autonomous island, Tobago.
Capital: Port of Spain 53,000 people (1999). Scarborough is the main town on Tobago.
Other cities: San Fernando 29,600 people; Arima 26,400; Point Fortin 17,500 (2000).
Government: Arthur N R Robinson, President since March 1997. Patrick Manning, Prime Minister since December 2001. The Parliament of the Republic of Trinidad and Tobago (Legislature) has two chambers: the House of Representatives, with 36 members, and the Senate, with 31 members.
National Holiday: August 31, Independence Day (1962).
Armed Forces: 2,100 (1996). **Other:** 4,800 Police.

STATISTICS

DEMOGRAPHY

Population: 1,306,000 (2002)
Annual growth: 0.6 % (1985-2000)
Estimates for year 2015: 1,392,000 (2000)
Annual growth to year 2015: 0.5 % (2000)
Urban population: 74.1 % (2000)
Urban growth: 1.3 % (2000)
Children per woman: 1.6 (2000)

HEALTH

Life expectancy at birth: 75 years (2000-2005)
male: 73 years (2000-2005)
female: 77 years (2000-2005)
Maternal mortality: 70 per 100,000 live births (1985/99)
Infant mortality: 17 per 1,000 (2000)
Under-5 child mortality: 20 per 1,000 (2000)
Daily calorie supply: 2,703 per capita (1999)
79 doctors per 100,000 people (1994)
Safe water: 90 % (2000)

EDUCATION

Literacy: 98 % (2000)
male: 99 % (2000)
female: 98 % (2000)
School enrolment (net):
Primary total: 88 % (1994/2000)
male: 88 % (1995/99)
female: 88 % (1995/99)
Secondary (gross):
male: 72 % (1995/97)
female: 75 % (1995/97)
Tertiary (gross): 6 % (1998)
Primary school teachers: one for every 21 pupils (1998)

COMMUNICATIONS

123 newspapers (1996), 532 radios (1997), 340 TV sets (2000) and 231 main telephone lines (2000) per 1,000 people
Books: 2 new titles per 100,000 people (1992/94)

ECONOMY

Per capita, GDP: $ 8,964 (2000)
Annual growth: 4.1 % (2000)
Annual inflation: 3.6 % (2000)
Consumer price index: 121.2 (2000)
Currency: 6.1 Trinidad dollars = $ 1 (03/2002)
Cereal imports: 205,174 metric tons (2000)
Food import dependency: 8 % (2000)
Fertilizer use: 787 kg per ha (1999)
Exports: $ 4,783 million (2000)
Imports: $ 3,834 million (2000)
External debt: $ 2,467 million (2000); $ 1,906 per capita (2000)
Debt service: 13.1 % of exports (1999)
Development aid received: $ 26 million (1999); $ 20.3 per capita (1999); 0.40 % of GNP (1999)

ENERGY

Consumption: 6,964.2 Kgs of oil equivalent per capita yearly (1998); -100.4 % imported (1999)

HDI (ranking/value): 49 / 0.798 (1999)

Tunisia

Population: 9,670,000 (2002)
Land area: 155,360 SQ KM
Capital: Tunis
Currency: Dinar
Language: Arabic

Tunis

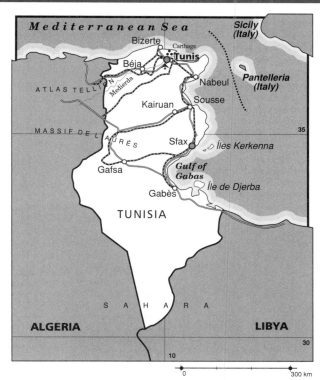

From the 12th century BC the Phoenicians had a series of trading posts and ports of call on the North African coast. Carthage was founded in the 8th century BC in the general vicinity of present-day Tunis, and by the 6th century the Carthaginian kingdom encompassed most of present-day Tunisia. Carthage became part of Rome's African province in 146 BC after the Punic Wars. Roman rule endured until the Muslim Arab invasions in the mid-7th century AD.

2   In Tunisia, the Arabs met the strongest resistance to their westward advance, but this region eventually became one of the best cultivated and developed of their cultural centers; the city of Kairuan is associated with some of the most outstanding names in Islamic architecture, medicine and historiography. During the dissolution of the Almohad Empire the region of Tunisia attained independence under the Berber dynasty of the Haffesides who, between the 13th century and the beginning of the 16th century, extended their power over the Algerian coast.

3   The development of European maritime trade attracted Turkish corsairs. The most famous, Khayr ad-Din (known as Red Beard), set up his headquarters in Tunisia, placing the Tunisian-Algerian coast under the domination of the Ottoman sultans. The inland regions, however, remained in the hands of the Berbers. The need to work with them, coupled with the distance from Istanbul, allowed the *Bey* (designated governor) to attain a large degree of autonomy and in practice, become a hereditary ruler. The Murad family ruled between 1612 and 1702, and from 1705 until after independence in 1957, this role was filled by the Husseinite family.

4   After the French occupation of Algeria, European economic penetration became increasingly evident and with it came increasing debts. In 1869 the burden of the foreign debt forced the Bey to allow an Anglo-French-Italian commission to supervise the country's finances. Foreign interference increased until 1882, when 30,000 French soldiers invaded the country, under an agreement whereby Britain, which

had just occupied Egypt, 'transferred its rights' to Tunisia, to compensate France for its loss of control over the Suez Canal.

5   In 1925, the Tunisians launched a campaign for a new Constitution (Destur 1), which would bring autonomy to the country. After World War II, the pro-independence Neo-Destur party grew considerably, and a series of demonstrations and anti-colonial uprisings led to armed struggle between 1952 and 1955. In March 1956, France recognized the sovereignty and independence of the country under the Bey's regime. The new ruler was a direct heir of the sovereign under whom the country had become a French Protectorate in 1882. However, the Bey was deposed on July 25 1957 by a constituent assembly controlled by 'Desturians'. A republic was proclaimed and the leader of the party, Habib Bourguiba, was elected President. Bourguiba started an energetic campaign against the French presence at the Bizerte naval base, finally dislodging them in 1964. Also in 1964 the New Destur Party became the Destur Socialist Party (PSD) and until 1981 was the only legal political organization.

6   Between 1963 and 1969, minister of finance Almed Ben Salah undertook a program of collectivization of small farms and trading companies, and nationalized foreign enterprises.

7   In 1969, following Ben Salah's arrest and subsequent deportation, government social and economic policy changed direction. The collectivization process was aborted and the economy thrown open to foreign investment. A 1972 law practically turned the whole country into a duty-free zone for export industries. Habib Bourguiba, the 'Supreme Combatant', was appointed president for life.

8   Towards the end of the 1970s, the economy suffered the effects of declining phosphate exports, and protectionist measures by the EEC against Tunisia's substantial textile industry. In January 1978, the UGTT (General Union of Tunisian Workers) called a general strike against wage controls and the repression of unions. The Government declared a state of emergency and street fighting left dozens dead. The union leaders, including the President Habib Achour, were arrested.

9   Appointed Prime Minister in 1980, Mohammed Mzali initiated a program of political liberalization. One year later, political parties were allowed to reorganize and trade union elections were held to renew the UGTT. General elections were held in November 1981 and, despite the vitality of the opposition parties, the ruling National Front won 94 per cent of the vote and all of the seats. Numerous irregularities were reported.

10   In January 1984, the Government decided to end several food subsidies. The price of bread rose 115 per cent and violent demonstrations left more than 100 dead. President Bourguiba cancelled the price increases. In 1985, there was further trade unrest and the UGTT was placed under government control. There were also violent confrontations with the emerging illegal Islamic fundamentalist movement that ended with hundreds of arrests and some death sentences.

11   During the period dominated by Bourguiba, Tunisia had developed as the most westernized of Arab societies. From 1986 onwards, the Fundamentalist reaction confronted the public with the issues of religion in the life of the individual and the community, and Tunisia's identity as an Arab-Muslim country. Female emancipation and European tourism were brought into question.

12   In 1985, Colonel (later General) Zine al-Abidene Ben Ali rose to power. In 1987, he was appointed Prime Minister and, in November, he dislodged president-for-life Bourguiba, whom a medical board declared mentally and physically unfit to govern. This marked the start of a period of national reconciliation, meaning greater press freedom and the liberation of hundreds of political prisoners and Islamic militants. The PSD was renamed the Democratic Constitutional Rally (RCD) without losing political dominance.

13   The presidential and legislative elections of April 2 1989, were considered by observers to be the most free and fair since independence, even though 1,300,000 citizens were not registered to vote. The electorate split between the Government RCD

MATERNAL MORTALITY

1985/99

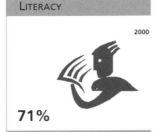

Per 100,000
live births

70

LITERACY

2000

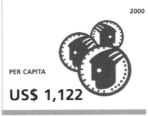

71%

EXTERNAL DEBT

2000

PER CAPITA

US$ 1,122

(with 80 per cent of the vote and all the seats) and the Hezb Ennahda Islamic movement, whose independent candidates won 15 per cent. Center and left-wing opposition parties trailed as tiny minorities. President Ben Ali was elected by 99 per cent of voters.

[14] Tunisia had opposed recognition of Israel by the Arab League in 1968 and broke off diplomatic relations with Egypt because of the 1979 Camp David accords. It received Palestinian militants expelled from Beirut in 1982 and also became the official headquarters of the PLO from that year on.

[15] Following a phase of openness to fundamental Islam in the early years of Ben Ali's leadership, the Government decided to crack down on the Hezb Ennahda movement and other opposition groups. In 1991, religious parties were banned. A restrictive law of association was adopted in March 1992 and, in July, members of Hezb Ennahda were

sentenced to life imprisonment. In November 1993, Ben Ali passed another law limiting 'basic freedoms'. In this political climate, the President was re-elected with 99 per cent of the vote in the March 1994 general elections, while the ruling party took control of 88 per cent of seats in parliament.

[16] The leader continued his plan for economic liberalization and hard-line political policy. One of the main opposition political leaders, Mohamed Moada, was sentenced to 11 years in prison in October 1995 for having published a document recounting the curtailment of freedoms in Tunisia and for maintaining secret relations with a 'foreign power' - Libya.

[17] The first multiparty elections, held in October 1999, gave an overwhelming victory to incumbent president al-Abidine Ben Ali, who took 99.4 per cent of the vote. His party, the DCR, took 148 of the 182 seats, while the other six parties

shared the 34 seats reserved for the opposition. One of the first measures passed by the new administration was the freeing of 600 political prisoners, mainly those from the al-Nahda Movement and the Workers' Communist Party.

[18] The death of Habib Bourguiba in April 2000 brought together political leaders from Europe and the Arab countries. Presidents Jacques Chirac of France, Abdelaziz Bouteflika of Algeria and Yasser Arafat of Palestine were present at the burial, held in the former president's home town of Monastir.

[19] In March 2001, human rights group Amnesty International (AI) called on Tunisian authorities to stop what it described as an escalation of harassment and pressure on human rights activists. In a new report, AI stated the pressure began when the Tunisian League of Human Rights was suspended in November 2000. From that time on, all League meetings were prevented by the security forces. The report also confirmed that legal action had been taken against the president of the Human Rights League, Moktar Trifi, and others.

[20] The constitution limited any president to three 5-year terms of office. But in September 2001 the DCR central committee again elected Ben Ali as presidential candidate for 2004. They hoped that DCR domination of the National Assembly would mean little or no opposition to the constitutional change they sought.

[21] In early April 2002 a massive explosion in the old Ghriba synagogue on the island of Djerba - center of a world-wide annual Jewish pilgrimage - left many dead and wounded including several German tourists. Although the Government initially claimed this was an accident, it was later confirmed as a deliberate explosion. The authorities blamed the attack on a Tunisian man living in the French city of Lyon, who planted the bomb with the help of a relation living in Tunisia. Attendance at the Lag B'Omer festival on the island of Djerba was expected to be lower than usual following the bombing and tension created in the Middle East. Damage left by the bomb in early April was quickly repaired. One third of Tunisia's 3,000 Jews live in Djerba. ∎

PROFILE

ENVIRONMENT
Tunisia is the northernmost African state. The eastern coastal plains are heavily populated and intensively cultivated with olives, citrus fruit and vineyards. The interior is dominated by the mountainous Tell and Aures regions populated by nomadic shepherds. The Sahara desert, in the south, has phosphate and iron deposits, while dates are cultivated in the oases.

SOCIETY
Peoples: 93 per cent of Tunisians are Arab, 5 per cent are Berber and 2 per cent European.
Religions: 99.4 per cent Islam, Sunni. There are also Jewish and Catholic groups.
Languages: Arabic (official). French, Berber.
Political Parties: Democratic Constitutional Rally (RCD); Movement of Socialist Democrats; Unionist Democratic Union; Party of People's Unity; Movement for Renewal; Social-Liberal Party.
Social Organizations: General Union of Tunisian Workers (UGTT).

THE STATE
Official Name: Al-Jumhuriyah at-Tunisiyah.
Administrative Divisions: 25 Government Regions.
Capital: Tunis 1,860,000 people (1999).
Other cities: Safaqis (Sfax) 262,000 people; Aryanah 203,500; Sousse 149,200 (2000).
Government: Zine al-Abidine Ben Ali, who became President after a bloodless coup in November 1987; he was elected as President in April 1989, re-elected in 1994 and 1999. Mohamed Ghannouchi, Prime Minister since November 1999. Unicameral Legislature: Chamber of Deputies, with 182 members.
National Holiday: March 20, Independence Day (1956).
Armed Forces: 35,500 (1997).
Other: 13,000, National Police; 10,000, National Guard.

STATISTICS

DEMOGRAPHY
Population: 9,670,000 (2002)
Annual growth: 1.7 % (1985-2000)
Estimates for year 2015: 11,257,000 (2000)
Annual growth to year 2015: 1.2 % (2000)
Urban population: 65.5 % (2000)
Urban growth: 2.2 % (2000)
Children per woman: 2.2 (2000)

HEALTH
Life expectancy at birth: 71 years (2000-2005)
male: 70 years (2000-2005)
female: 72 years (2000-2005)
Maternal mortality: 70 per 100,000 live births (1985/99)
Infant mortality: 22 per 1,000 (2000)
Under-5 child mortality: 28 per 1,000 (2000)
Daily calorie supply: 3,388 per capita (1999)
70 doctors per 100,000 people (1997)
Safe water: 80 % (2000)

EDUCATION
Literacy: 71 % (2000)
male: 81 % (2000)
female: 60 % (2000)
School enrolment (net):
Primary total: 94 % (1994/2000)
male: 97 % (1995/99)
female: 94 % (1995/99)
Secondary (gross):
male: 66 % (1995/97)
female: 63 % (1995/97)
Tertiary (gross): 17 % (1998)
Primary school teachers: one for every 24 pupils (1998)

COMMUNICATIONS
31 newspapers (1996), 158 radios (1999), 198 TV sets (2000) and 90 main telephone lines (1999) per 1,000 people
Books: 6 new titles per 100,000 people (1992/94)

ECONOMY
Per capita, GDP: $ 6,363 (2000)
Annual growth: 3.5 % (2000)
Annual inflation: 2.9 % (2000)
Consumer price index: 117.2 (2000)
Currency: 1.5 dinars = $ 1 (03/2002)
Cereal imports: 2,490,344 metric tons (2000)
Food import dependency: 8 % (2000)
Fertilizer use: 394 kg per ha (1999)
Exports: $ 8,566 million (2000)
Imports: $ 9,257 million (2000)
External debt: $ 10,610 million (2000); $ 1,122 per capita (2000)
Debt service: 15.9 % of exports (1999)
Development aid received: $ 245 million (1999); $ 25.9 per capita (1999); 1.20 % of GNP (1999)

ENERGY
Consumption: 812.3 Kgs of oil equivalent per capita yearly (1998); 7.2 % imported (1999)

HDI (ranking/value): 89 / 0.714 (1999)

Turkey

Population:	68,569,000 (2002)
Land area:	769,630 SQ KM
Capital:	Ankara
Currency:	Lire
Language:	Turkish

Türkiye

The region of Anatolia has been inhabited for thousands of years. In the 8th century BC the Greeks founded the city of Byzantium on the strategic strait of Bosphorus, controlling traffic between the Black Sea and the Mediterranean. The city was conquered by the Romans in 96 AD and Emperor Constantine had it rebuilt. Under the new name of Constantinople, it became the capital of the Eastern Roman Empire, which outlived the Barbarian destruction of Rome and the Western Roman Empire by a hundred years.

[2] Constantinople was seized by the Turks in 1453 and renamed Istanbul. It became the capital of the flourishing Ottoman Empire. In the 16th century, the domains of Suleyman the Magnificent reached from Algeria to the Caucasus and from Hungary to the southern end of the Arabian Peninsula, populated by 50 million people. Western visitors marveled at the efficiency and prosperity of the Government, and the respect shown for the rights of the peasants. This may explain why more than once the Christian peasants of the Balkans fought alongside the 'infidel' Muslim, against Christian nobles and clergy.

[3] From the 17th century, the Empire fell behind the impressive technological advance of western Europe and its aggressive trade expansion. The route to the East round the Cape of Good Hope, opened by the Portuguese, slowly deprived the Ottoman Empire of its trade monopoly between Europe and eastern Asia. The borders of the Empire gave way to the thrust of European traders, whose companies introduced French, British and Dutch products in the eastern Mediterranean region.

[4] The fate of Turkey foreshadowed the course of events that later affected the great civilizations of China and India. They all became peripheral markets where Europeans imposed the sale of their manufactured goods and collected the food and raw materials for their own workforce and industries. Turkish artisans went bankrupt, the local textile industry failed to compete with British technology and the peasants grew increasingly poor, having to pay the price of imported goods.

KURDISTAN

[5] In the 19th century, a modernizing movement known as Tanzimat tried to impose European patterns and to build a centralized state, using modern technology, the telegraph and railways. New accords were signed with Britain and Germany but the influx of capital and goods further deepened Turkish dependency on Europe. One of the outstanding consequences was a large external debt which turned Turkey into 'the sick man of Europe'.

[6] At the beginning of the 20th century, a clandestine organization started to emerge from the discontent with the autocratic government. The 'Young Turks' formed within the universities and military academies. In July 1908, they led a rebellion in Macedonia, and within a few days Sultan Abdul Hamid yielded to their demand for a constitution limiting his power. The following year he was forced to abdicate in favor of Muhammad V, who bestowed real power on the Young Turks. They followed a nationalistic policy opposed to foreign suppliers, and various ethnic minorities, in particular the Greeks and Armenians.

[7] In World War I, Turkey sided with the second German Empire and the Austro-Hungarian Empire, and it was defeated along with them. The Ottoman Empire was torn apart and many small autocratic states rose on the Arabian Peninsula and in the Balkan region. The ethnic minority groups which remained within Turkish borders were ruthlessly repressed. In 1915 some one million Armenians were killed in an episode that went down in history as 'the first genocide of the 20th century'.

[8] The conditions imposed on Turkey by the Treaty of Sèvres (1920) were so humiliating that military leader Mustafa Kemal (later known as Kemal Ataturk) deposed Sultan Muhammad VI, who had signed the accord, and launched a national liberation war. He finally succeeded in negotiating a new treaty, signed in Lausanne in 1923. Turkey was relieved of paying war reparations, and the privileges enjoyed by foreign traders (capitulations) were annulled. In exchange, the Bosphorus giving access to the Black Sea was declared international waters, open to all ships regardless of nationality in times of peace.

[9] Ataturk proclaimed a republic and had a new constitution approved. The Government initiated a process of rapid modernization. State and church separated, the Muslim Friday ceased to be the weekly holiday, replaced by Sunday, the Latin alphabet replaced Arab notation, and women were urged to stop wearing veils.

[10] After Ataturk's death in 1938, the military remained very influential in Turkish politics. The Government crushed the leftist groups which had grown under the influence of the neighboring Soviet revolution and during the fight against neo-colonialism. Eventually, Turkey signed a non-agression agreement with Nazi Germany in 1941 and kept neutrality until February 1945, when the Government decided to back the Allies.

[11] After World War II, Turkey now a US ally, became an anti-Soviet bastion. The growing influence of its northern neighbor led to stronger links with the US, which began to send military aid in 1947. The US built major military bases in Turkey and military doctrine was gradually replaced by the Pentagon's concept of 'national security'. With US influence Turkey adopted a multiparty system and gave incentives to foreign investors. Although the economy was still dependent upon agricultural exports, rural areas no longer provided enough jobs and young people emigrated to the cities or to western European countries, particularly West Germany. The country sent troops to Korea and in 1952 joined NATO.

[12] Turkish military intervention in Cyprus caused that island to split in 1974, provoking the resignation of Turkey's Prime Minister Bulent Ecevit, a social democrat. Conservative Suleyman Demirel succeeded Ecevit but the rivalry between these two leaders prevented the formation of a stable government for the rest of the decade.

[13] Demirel was ousted by the military in 1980 and General Kenan Evren became President. A new accord changed the conditions of the military bases, and Turkey started to receive US$1 billion per year for leasing them. Labor unions and political parties were banned and the Government was accused of systematic human rights violations.

[14] In 1983, a new constitution heralded a period of political liberalization designed to soothe western European critics. The new government program aimed at gaining access to the European Economic Community, giving new vigor to modernization, moving away from the old nationalistic policies and embracing economic liberalism.

[15] In 1987, rivalries between the main opposition groups, formed by the followers of Demirel and Ecevit, enabled the Motherland Party (ANAP) to win the elections.

[16] Prime Minister Turgut Ozal embarked enthusiastically on a policy of privatization, economic liberalization and promotion of exports, following IMF and World Bank guidelines. His willingness to adopt these policies was based on the assurance that they would lead

to prosperity and to admittance into the European Community, an undeniably popular goal in a country where nearly all families had at least one relative working in Western Europe. However, political freedoms were not liberalized to the same extent and the Community postponed considering the Turkish bid until 1993, alleging that its high rates of inflation and unemployment, the lack of a concrete social policy and Turkey's conflict with Greece made its incorporation into the Community untenable.

[17] Accused of nepotism, corruption and a lack of sensitivity over the social impact of his economic policy, Ozal suffered a total defeat in the March 1989 municipal elections. However, as a result of successful political maneuvering, he managed to get Parliament to name him President in October of the same year. In 1990, his government was confronted by the growing activism of the Kurd separatists in the southeast of the country, where the PKK (Kurkish Workers' Party) was taking military action.

[18] In August 1990, when Iraq was blockaded after the invasion of Kuwait, Turkey interrupted the flow of Iraqi oil to the Mediterranean by blocking the pipeline through the country. Although it did not send troops, Turkey authorized the use of its military airports and US bases for the massive bombings of Iraq. The opposition questioned these measures, arguing that they would affect relations with a neighboring country in an area already made unstable by Kurdish independence movements.

[19] Ankara feared that the independence of Iraqi Kurdistan might affect the Turkish Kurds. The 19 million Kurds live in a territory divided between four countries: Turkey, Syria, Iran, and Iraq. They are the world's largest ethnic minority without a territory of their own. For several decades, Turkey had a policy of virtual cultural annihilation against the Kurds, giving them few rights to use their language and express their identity.

[20] In October 1991, the Turkish army entered northern Iraq in order to attack PKK bases, supported by aircraft and helicopters. Kurdish representatives accused the Turkish Government of bombing the civilian population.

[21] The parliamentary elections of October 20 were won by Suleyman Demirel's True Path Party (DYP), which obtained 27 per cent of the vote, gaining 178 of the 450 parliamentary seats. This narrow majority forced Demirel to seek alliances with Erdal Inonu's Social Democratic Populist Party (SHP), which came in third with 21 per cent of the vote. The Motherland Party (ANAP), which obtained 24 per cent of the vote, formed the opposition.

[22] Demirel faced a budget deficit of US$6 billion, a foreign debt of US$44 billion, and an annual inflation rate of 70 per cent. Apart from the fundamentalist movements, all the other political parties agreed that Turkey's main priority was to gain entrance to the European Economic Community.

[23] In mid-March 1992, the banned PKK announced the formation of a war government and a national assembly in the territory which they claimed formed the core of Kurdistan, the internationally unrecognized Kurdish state. A few days later, coinciding with the Kurdish new year, there was an uprising in the southeastern provinces with violent action between the guerrillas and the Turkish security forces, especially in Cizre. In April, the Turkish Interior Minister, Ismet Sezgin, visited Damascus in Syria and Turkey announced an agreement to fight against the Kurdish 'terrorist organizations'. Under the agreement, the Syrian Government stated that it would close the PKK training camps and carry out stricter controls along its borders.

[24] In 1992, the Council of Europe urged the Government to reduce repression against the Kurdish community. The Turkish authorities subsequently granted an amnesty to 5,000 political prisoners and authorized the circulation of two Kurdish-language newspapers. In November, the EC set 1996 as the date for Turkish admission to the European Customs Union, a first step toward eventual membership of the EU.

[25] Upon the death of President Turgut Ozal in April 1993, Prime Minister Demirel was elected to be his successor. Tansu Ciller, minister of economic affairs, assumed the leadership of the DYP and was named Prime Minister. Ciller, the first woman to head a government in Turkey, presented her program which was approved by Parliament in July. It included an accelerated privatization program - to be carried out by decree - as well as fiscal reform. In order to stem the growing budget deficit, which stood at $9.4 billion, there would be a moratorium on public investment. In July, public employees carried out strikes and demonstrations to protest the massive loss of jobs which would be brought about by privatization. Some 700,000 people participated in the protests, which took place over a two-day period in Ankara, Istanbul and Izmir.

[26] The army extended its offensive during 1994, forcing the inhabitants of hundreds of Kurd villages to leave their homes while it bombed Iraqi Kurdistan to destroy PKK bases.

[27] The growth of Islamic fundamentalism in Turkey was apparent in 1995, in the run-up to the December elections. Its main representative, the Welfare Party, pledged during the election campaign to form Islamic organizations to compensate for the influence of NATO and the EU. The party became Turkey's main political group winning 158 of the 550 seats.

[28] Prime Minister Ciller's DYP and the ANAP, overcame their differences to prevent Islamic fundamentalists from coming to power and formed an unexpected government coalition, led by Mesul Yilmaz from the ANAP, who took office in March 1996. However, the alliance was swiftly dissolved and the DYP chose to rule with the fundamentalists. Necmettin Erbakan became head of government in June.

[29] At an international level, the signing of a military agreement with Israel in April further complicated Turkey's relations with several Arab countries, such as Syria. Tension mounted on the April 24, when Ankara decided temporarily to shut

---

PROFILE

ENVIRONMENT

The country is made up of a European part, Eastern Thrace, and an Asiatic part, the peninsula of Anatolia and Turkish Armenia, separated by the Dardanelles, the Sea of Marmara and the Bosphorus. Eastern Thrace, located in the southeast of the Balkan Peninsula, makes up less than one-thirtieth of the country's total land area, including an arid steppe plateau, the Istranca mountains to the east, and a group of hills suitable for farming. Anatolia is a mountainous area with many lakes and wetlands. The Ponticas range in the north and the Taurus range in the south form the natural boundaries for the Anatolian plateau, which extends eastward to form the Armenian plateaus. The east is taken up with the Armenian Massif, around the lake region of Van, where there is much volcanic activity and occasional earthquakes. Parallel to the Taurus there are a number of ranges known as Antitaurus, which run along the border of the Georgia, together with the Armenian mountains. The country is mainly agricultural. The lack of natural resources, and absence of capital and appropriate infrastructure, have been major obstacles to industrialization. The air around Istanbul contains high levels of sulfur dioxide and the Marmara Sea is contaminated with mercury.

SOCIETY

Peoples: Most are descendents of ethnic groups from Central Asia that began to settle in Anatolia in the 11th century. The largest minority are Kurdish (20 per cent), followed by Arabs (1.5 per cent), Jews, Greek, Georgians and Armenians (0.3 per cent). Their cultural autonomy (including the use and teaching in their languages) is severely limited.
Religions: Mainly Islamic (80 per cent Sunni, 20 per cent Shi'a, of which 14 per cent are Alevi, non-orthodox Shi'a); Christians (0.2 per cent).
Languages: Turkish (official) and some 30 languages of ethnic minorities, such as Kurmanji spoken by the Kurdish minority.
Political Parties: Party of the Democratic Left (DSP), center-left; Nationalist Action Party; Islamic Virtue Party (PIV, successor of the Welfare Party, Islamic); Motherland Party (ANAP); True Path Party (DYP); Social Democratic Populist Party (SHP); Republican People's Party; National Labor Movement; Socialist Party; Democracy Party (DEP), pro-Kurdish, outlawed in 1994. Largest underground political organization: Kurdistan Freedom and Democracy Congress (KADEK) since April 2002, former Kurdish Workers' Party (PKK), separatist guerrilla.
Social organizations: Confederation of Turkish Trade Unions (two million members); Confederation of Progressive Trade Unions of Turkey (500,000 members).

THE STATE

Official Name: Türkiye Cumhuriyeti.
Administrative Divisions: 74 Provinces.
Capital: Ankara 3,131,000 people (1999).
Other cities: Istanbul 9,500,000 people; Izmir (Smyrna) 2,272,500; Bursa 1,164,400; Adana 1,137,100; Gaziantep 778,200 (2000).
Government: Ahmet Necdet Sezer, President since May 2000. Bülent Ecevit, Prime Minister since January 1999. The Great National Assembly of Turkey has 550 members.
National Holiday: October 29, Republic's Day (1923).
Armed Forces: 639,000 troops (1996); 390,000 conscripts (1996).
Other: 70,000 Gendarmes-National Guard, 50,000 Reserves.

off the supply of water from its controversial dams on the Euphrates river for 'technical reasons', forcing Syrian authorities to ration water in Damascus, shortly before Muslim Aid el Adha (the sacrifice) festivities.

[30] The year 1997 was marked by the confrontation between the Erbakan administration and the army-backed secularist opposition. The army gave evidence linking the DYP with Islamic organizations made illegal by the previous government and now working underground, stating they were more dangerous than the PKK separatist Kurds. The President replaced Erbakan with Mesut Yilmaz in June, and the Constitutional Court - the most important Turkish legal entity - accused him of bringing the country 'to the brink of civil war and conspiring against the secular regime'.

[31] In September 1997, around 20,000 Turkish troops and 100 tanks crossed over the frontier with Iraq into Kurdistan to dismantle the military bases of the PKK. The Turkish soldiers, backed by Iraqi Kurds from the Democratic Party of Kurdistan (KDP), surrounded PKK bases close to the frontier with Iran.

[32] Although Turkey was one of the 11 countries on the EU waiting list, and had already been in the application process for 10 years, it did not attend the conference in London in March 1998 where the other 10 met up with the EU's 15 members. The Ankara Government said its absence was due to the veto imposed on its entry by Germany.

[33] In April that year Semdin Sakik, the best-known commander of the PKK, gave himself up to the forces of Iraqi Kurd leader Barzani, in northern Iraq. He alleged that he feared being killed by Abdullah Ocalan, leader of his party. Sakik had been relieved of his command in Southeastern Turkey, in the Tuncelli mountains region.

[34] The Government used the celebrations in October that year of the 75th anniversary of the Republic and the commemoration of the 60 years since the death of Kemal Atatürk to strengthen the centralized politics of the secular state. The offensive against Islamic forces had begun on January, when the Constitutional Court dissolved the Welfare Party and banned Nmettin Erbakan and other leaders from politics during five years. The Islamic Party of Virtue (PV) was immediately established to replace the banned Welfare Party. In September, an appeals court confirmed the ten month prison sentence to Recep Tayyip Erdogan, the Muslim mayor of Istanbul.

[35] The denial of political asylum to Kurd Abdullah Ocalan in late 1998 and his detention in February 1999 as he sought refuge at the Greek embassy in Kenya sparked fresh controversy. Kurds throughout Europe protested angrily at the extradition allowed to Turkey. Ocalan was sentenced to death in June.

[36] The Party of the Democratic Left (DSP) obtained a relative majority in the April 1999 elections, having won 22.3 per cent of the vote and 136 seats, ahead of the National Movement which received 18.1 per cent of the vote and 129 seats. The Islamic Party of Virtue was third with 15.5 per cent, defeating the Motherland Party, which had 13.3 per cent, and the True Path Party, with 12.1 per cent.

[37] By an overwhelming majority, in June Parliament approved the creation of a new government committed to crushing the Kurdish guerrillas in the Southeastern region of the country. The new administration included the DSP of Prime Minister Bulent Ecevit, the ultra-right Nationalist Movement Party and a small right of center party.

[38] Greek cooperation in the detention of Ocalan and the assistance received from Greece after the August 1999 earthquake served to improve relations between Athens and Ankara. The Greek Government lifted its veto on the incorporation of Turkey into the EU and on talks about the incorporation of Cyprus. After having waited for 36 years, Turkey was invited to join the EU in December 1999.

[39] Ocalan's death sentence was put on hold in January 2000 awaiting guidance from the European Human Rights Court. A PKK congress announced in February it was abandoning armed struggle and presented a seven-point plan to become a political party. During the third round of voting in May, Parliament elected Ahmet Necdet Sezer as president. Sezer, a well known democratic rights advocate, was expected to give momentum to the reforms demanded by the EU as a prerequisite to Turkey's membership.

[40] More than 1,000 political prisoners went on a hunger strike in October 2000, demanding the dissolution of the Security Tribunals of the State, the end of repression against inmates' families and the end of oppression against the Kurdish people. The Government launched a counter-propaganda and large-scale terror campaign leading to detentions and torture of strikers, leaving hundreds of injured. On the 60th day of the strike, government forces simultaneously raided 20 jails, killing at least 30 people, many of them burnt alive. The authorities, incapable of quelling resistance by violence, tried to sweeten the detainees with the promise of

release. Several were freed, but most remained in the PKK.

[41] A devastating financial crisis forced the devaluation of the national currency, the lira, which had fallen by some 50 per cent. Inflation rose 80 per cent and hundreds of thousands lost their jobs, leading the country to its worst recession in half a century. In February 2001 the IMF granted Turkey $12 billion in new and conditional loans, while freeing $4 billion of frozen loans.

[42] In April 2001 more than 200 people were injured in a huge demonstration about the economic crisis, which ended in clashes with the police. The demands made the Government postpone 32 modernization projects and announce a new economic plan. The measures included cutbacks in public spending, privatizations and reforms in the banking system. Fear of political instability caused panic in the markets, which made prices rise.

[43] In June, the Constitutional Court banned the Islamic Virtue Party (PIV) - the Government's main opposition - saying it had become a center of anti-secular activity. A month later, a new pro-Islamic party, called Saadet - translated as 'happiness' or 'prosperity' - was founded by members of the banned PIV.

[44] Parliament adopted a new series of reforms in October, including the abolition of the death penalty, except in war and for acts of terrorism. At the same time, it authorized radio and television campaigns to improve the possibility of joining the European Union (EU). Shortly after, at the EU's request, a debate was begun to decide on radio and television broadcasts in Kurdish, which had been banned for years.

[45] In January 2002, Turkish women obtained full legal equality with men, acquiring the same rights over family property in divorce. Parliament also approved a series of laws softening the restrictions on freedom of expression, but Kurdish human rights organizations claimed the measures were inadequate. Turkey is a long way from complying with political and institutional criteria of the EU, which considers the introduction of democratic reforms in Turkey excessively slow.

[46] Two years after ending its armed struggle, in April 2002, the banned PKK formally announced its change of name - Kurdistan Freedom and Democracy Congress (KADEK) - and strategy, stating its wish to initiate a peaceful campaign in favor of Kurdish people's rights. ∎

STATISTICS

DEMOGRAPHY
Population: 68,569,000 (2002)
Annual growth: 1.9 % (1985-2000)
Estimates for year 2015: 79,004,000 (2000)
Annual growth to year 2015: 1.1 % (2000)
Urban population: 75.3 % (2000)
Urban growth: 3.1 % (2000)
Children per woman: 2.5 (2000)

HEALTH
Life expectancy at birth: 71 years (2000-2005)
male: 68 years (2000-2005)
female: 73 years (2000-2005)
Maternal mortality: 130 per 100,000 live births (1985/99)
Infant mortality: 38 per 1,000 (2000)
Under-5 child mortality: 45 per 1,000 (2000)
Daily calorie supply: 3,469 per capita (1999)
121 doctors per 100,000 people (1998)
Safe water: 82 % (2000)

EDUCATION
Literacy: 85 % (2000)
male: 94 % (2000)
female: 77 % (2000)
School enrolment (net):
Primary total: 72 % (1994/2000)
male: 93 % (1995/99)
female: 82 % (1995/99)
Secondary (gross):
male: 68 % (1995/97)
female: 48 % (1995/97)
Tertiary (gross): 14 % (1998)
Primary school teachers: one for every 28 pupils (1994)

COMMUNICATIONS
111 newspapers (1996), 573 radios (2000), 449 TV sets (2000) and 280 main telephone lines (2000) per 1,000 people
Books: 8 new titles per 100,000 people (1992/94)

ECONOMY
Per capita, GDP: $ 6,974 (2000)
Annual growth: 5.7 % (2000)
Annual inflation: 54.9 % (2000)
Consumer price index: 1,579.6 (2000)
Currency: 1,410,500.0 lire = $ 1 (03/2002)
Cereal imports: 2,681,679 metric tons (2000)
Food import dependency: 4 % (2000)
Fertilizer use: 912 kg per ha (1999)
Exports: $ 48,695 million (2000)
Imports: $ 62,810 million (2000)
External debt: $ 116,209 million (2000); $ 1,743 per capita (2000)
Debt service: 26.2 % of exports (1999)
Development aid received: $ -10 million (1999); $ -0.2 per capita (1999)

ENERGY
Consumption: 1,144.2 Kgs of oil equivalent per capita yearly (1998); 61.8 % imported (1999)

HDI (ranking/value): 82 / 0.735 (1999)

Turkmenistan

Population: 4,930,000 (2002)
Land area: 469,930 SQ KM
Capital: Ashkhabad (Aschabad)
Currency: Manat
Language: Turkmen

Türkmenistan

From 1000 BC onwards, the area now known as Turkmenistan was part of several large states: the Persian Empire (controlled by the Achaemenid dynasty) and later, the empire of Alexander the Great. In the third century AD Turkmenistan was conquered by the Sassanids, an Iranian dynasty. Between the 5th and 8th centuries, there were successive invasions by the Eftalites, the Turks and the Arabs.

² From the 6th to the 8th century, the entire area adjacent to the Caspian Sea was under the Arab Caliphate, and when the latter dissolved in the 9th and 10th centuries, the territory became a part of the Tahirid and Sassanid states. In the mid-11th century, the Seljuk Empire was formed in Turkmenistan, and towards the end of the 12th century it was conquered by the dynasty of the Shah of Khwarezm (Anushteguinidas).

³ During the Seljuk period the Turkmens formed as an ethnic group through the fusion of Oguz Turks and local groups. This was a gradual process that was completed by the 15th century. In the early 13th century, Genghis Khan invaded Turkmenistan and his heirs divided it up. A large part of the territory was incorporated into the State of

Hulagidas, and the northern regions were overrun by the Golden Horde of the Mongol Tatars. In the 14th and 15th centuries, the country fell under the Timurids, who were succeeded by the Uzbek khans of the Shaybani dynasty. From the 16th to the 18th century, Turkmenistan belonged to the khanates of Khiva and Bukhara, and the Iranian state of the Safavids, successively.

⁴ In the 1880s, Turkmenia - as it was then known - was conquered by the Russian army. The major part of

its territory lay within the Trans-Caspian region and the province of Turkistan, but the lands inhabited by the Turkmens passed into the hands of Khiva and Bukhara, which were Russian protectorates.

⁵ There was strong resistance to Russian domination in Turkmenia until the Battle of Geok-Tepe in 1881, in which the last of the rebels were defeated. The Turkmens were active participants in the 1916 uprising against the Czar. The most violent revolt was in the city of

Tedzhen, where several Russian residents and government officials were executed by the local population.

⁶ The fall of the Czar in February 1917, led to the creation of soviets (councils of workers, peasants and soldiers) throughout the empire. The Trans-Caspian region fell under the control of the Russian Provisional Government. In December 1917, after the Bolshevik (socialists in favor of the revolution) take-over in St Petersburg, Soviet power was proclaimed.

⁷ In July 1918, the English expeditionary forces re-established the Provisional Government in Trans-Caspia. After two years of civil war, Soviet power was reinstated in 1920 and on February 14 1924, the Soviet Socialist Republic of Turkmenistan was founded (joining the USSR, at the same time).

⁸ Up until that time, Turkmenistan had never known even nominal national political unity. Tribal organization was the only form of social organization, and most of the population was nomadic. For this reason, the Soviet regime resorted to repressive techniques in order to impose industrialization and collective agriculture upon the local population.

⁹ After World War II, Turkmenistan entered a period of

PROFILE

ENVIRONMENT

Turkmenistan is in an arid zone, with dry continental climate, located in the southeastern part of Central Asia between the Caspian Sea to the west, the Amu Darya River to the east, the Ustiurt mountains to the north and the Kopet-Dag and Paropamiz mountain ranges to the south. The land is flat and most of the territory (80 per cent) lies within the Kara-Kum desert. Topographically, 90 per cent of Turkmenistan is sandy plain. On the eastern shore of the Caspian Sea lie the Major and Minor Balkan ranges, of relatively low altitude. The Amu Darya river crosses Turkmenistan from east to west. The Kara-Kum Canal diverts the waters of the Amu Darya to the irrigation systems of the Murgab and Tedzhen oases, as well as those of the Mary and Ashkhabad areas. Turkmenistan is bounded by Kazakhstan to the northwest, Uzbekistan to the east; and Afghanistan and Iran, to the south. There are rich mineral deposits, including natural gas and oil.

SOCIETY

Peoples: Turkmenis 77 per cent; Russians 6.7 per cent; Uzbeks 9.2 per cent, Kazakhs 2 per

cent; Tatars 0.8 per cent. Other 6.6 per cent. (1996).
Religions: Mainly Sunni Muslim (87 per cent); Russian Orthodox 6.4 per cent. Other 6.6 per cent. **Languages:** Turkmen (official), Russian.
Political Parties: Democratic Party (DP, split off from the former Communist Party); Party for Democratic Development; Agzibirlik (Unity). The only party allowed to put candidates forward for the December 1999 elections was the DP.
Social Organizations: Independent trade-unions in process of formation.

THE STATE

Official Name: Türkmenistan Jumhuriyäti.
Administrative divisions: 3 provinces and 1 Dependent Region (Ashkhabad). **Capital:** Ashkhabad (Aschabad) 525,000 people (1999).
Other cities: Chardzhou (Cardzou) 166,000 people. **Government:** Saparmurad Niyazov Turkmenbashi, President since October 1990. The Constitution adopted in 1992 gave the President the powers of Head of State and Head of Government. The epithet 'Turkmenbashi', which means 'Leader of the

Turkmen people', was conferred on the President in 1993. In 1999 Parliament decided that 'Turkmenbashi will be president for life'. Legislature: Parliament or Islamic Assembly, unicameral, with 50 members elected by direct election every five years. **National Holiday:** October 27, Independence Day (1991). **Armed Forces:** 18,000 (1997).

HEALTH

Life expectancy at birth: 67 years (2000-2005)
Maternal mortality: 65 per 100,000 live births (1985/99)
Infant mortality: 52 per 1,000 (2000)
Under-5 child mortality: 70 per 1,000 (2000)
300 doctors per 100,000 people (1997)

EDUCATION

School enrolment (net):
Primary total: 80 % (1994/2000)
Tertiary (gross): 19 % (1997)

ECONOMY

Per capita GDP: $ 3,956 (2000)
Annual growth: 15.3 % (2000)
Currency: 5,200 manat = $ 1 (03/2002)
HDI (ranking/value): 83 / 0.730 (1999)

economic growth, accompanied by increases in oil and gas production. In addition, gains were made in the area of cotton farming. But during Leonid Brezhnev's administration from 1963-83, political problems worsened and the economy entered a period of stagnation. In those republics where the Soviets had adopted a monocropping policy, as in the case of Turkmenistan with the cultivation of cotton, agriculture was more vulnerable to the effects of the recession.

[10] As of 1985, the changes promoted in the USSR by President Mikhail Gorbachev vitalized political life in Turkmenistan. There was also an Islamic religious rebirth, expressed through the construction of a number of mosques.

[11] After the coup attempt in the USSR in August 1991, the Communist Party of Turkmenistan lost its legitimacy to govern. Communist leader Saparmurad Niyazov declared the need to restore state sovereignty and in October, a plebiscite brought in a presidential system. In November, Turkmenistan joined the Commonwealth of Independent States (CIS), which replaced the former USSR, and the Communist Party changed its name to the Democratic Party. The sovereignty of Turkmenistan was internationally recognized.

[12] President Saparmurad Niyazov, former secretary of the Turkmen Communist Party stated that he would give priority to the country's relations with Turkey, given the cultural proximity between the two countries. Niyazov was re-elected in June 1992 and in 1994. Without distancing from Russia, Turkmenistan drew closer to Iran, through the construction of the Ashkhabad-Teheran railway, amongst other things. It also achieved the status of most favored nation with the US.

[13] The President continued with his 'hard handed' policy against the opposition. Several opposition leaders took refuge in Moscow.

[14] In December 1997, the first oil pipeline was opened between Turkmenistan and Iran, to export Turkmeni oil and gas to the countries of the Mediterranean and the Persian Gulf. The Government now had to negotiate with the United States over the non-application of the 1996 Iran Sanctions Act, which punished companies, subsidiaries and citizens investing more than $40 million per year in the Iranian oil or gas industries.

[15] In February 1998 Niyazov announced his plans to give Parliament more authority and less to the executive branch. However only the ruling DP party was allowed to field candidates in the parliamentary elections, causing the Organization for Security and Cooperation in Europe (OSCE) to withdraw its offer to supervise the elections. The Government claimed there were two or more candidates in almost all electoral areas. 95 per cent of the registered voters participated. In 1999 Parliament decided that Niyazov will be president for life but he announced that he will step down by 2010, when he is 70. He also passed a law abolishing the death penalty, making Turkmenistan the first of the five former USSR Asian republics to end capital punishment. The OSCE reported the February 2000 arrests of two opposition activists who were condemned to five years in prison.

[16] In October that year, Niyazov said that the country would not privatize the oil and gas industries for at least the next 10 to 15 years, adding that he expected the industry to continue as the economic mainstay of the country. In February 2001, one and half months after gas supplies to Russia had been stopped after disagreements on pricing, Turkmenistan agreed to supply the Russian company Itera with 10 billion cubic meters. The price was set at $40 per cubic meter – the price Turkmenistan had originally demanded.

[17] In May 2001 the exploitation of natural resources in the Caspian Sea led to conflict with Azerbaijan, which was working in oilfields claimed by Turkmenistan. Negotiations between experts from both nations could not resolve the dispute and in June, Turkmenistan withdrew its ambassador from Baku.

[18] After the September 2001 terrorist attacks on New York and Washington, and the warlike US response to Afghanistan, Turkmenistan stood by its neutrality and refused to allow its airspace to be used to carry out attacks. Niyazov did allow international humanitarian aid through to Afghanistan. The Imam-Nazar frontier crossing became a central point on transport routes. By the end of October, the United Nations World Food Program had already sent dozens of trucks of food through to be distributed in northern Afghanistan. The UNICEF operation for Northern Afghanistan also moved through Imam-Nazar.

[19] The turnover in government ministers that had begun in 2000 gathered pace in 2001. By the end of that year few office-holders had been in their jobs for more than a year. One of the most significant changes was the concentration of power in the hands of president of the National Security Committee, who was made deputy Prime Minister, responsible for defense, application of the law and foreign affairs, as well as special legal advisor to the President.

[20] In late 2001 and early 2002 the Turkmen Government had hopes that the new situation in Afghanistan would favor the expansion of their oil sales to other markets. Stability in Afghanistan could provide Turkmenistan with a pipeline route to the coast of Pakistan. The lack of economic development in the country is partly due to Russia's refusal to allow gas exports to more competitive markets. However, the Turkmen Government is careful to maintain good relations with Moscow.

[21] The strategic location of Turkmenistan - as well as its gas and oil - is another incentive for investors. Around 40 per cent of aid to Afghanistan comes through Turkmenistan and the country lies at the heart of the old 'silk route' between East and West. ∎

Chechnya and Abkhazia

Unlike former Soviet republics, which already had a degree of autonomy within the Soviet Union, the 'autonomous regions' such as Chechnya and Abkhazia did not obtain the independence demanded by some of their inhabitants.

[1] In 1922, Chechnya became an autonomous region (see Russia) of the Socialist Federate Soviet Republic of Russia. In 1936, along with Ingushetia, it became the Autonomous Republic of Checheno-Ingush. Chechens and Ingush were deported by Stalin in 1944 to Kazakhstan and Kyrgysztan and when Nikita Krushchev allowed them to return in 1957, the Autonomous Republic was re-established.

[2] In late 1990, the Chechnya National Congress declared the sovereignty of the Republic of Chechen-Ingush. The first presidential elections were held in November 1991 and Dzojar Dudayev was elected President. Dudayev declared the Chechnya Republic's independence from the Russian Federation. Russia launched a war against the Chechens to regain control over the territory and, after three months of fighting, took control of the devastated capital, Grozny. In 1995, the first Russian-Chechen armistice was signed, but fighting continued. In spite of the death of Dudayev, killed by a Russian missile, Chechen forces recovered the capital in August 1996. That same month, the first agreements between the Russian Federation and the Chechen Republic were signed. In January 1997, Aslan Mashadon was elected President.

[3] Early in 2000, the new Russian President Vladimir Putin proposed an end to the conflict which was crushing the Chechens with a massive deployment of Russian troops. However, just as it seemed Moscow would achieve its objective, the war appeared to veer off in a different direction when the Russian Government threatened to attack Afghanistan, on the understanding that the Taliban regime there was supporting the Chechen rebels. According to some analysts, Moscow's campaign was merely a front for a war 'against Islam'.

In 1810, Abkhazia, then under Ottoman rule, was annexed to Russia, followed by decades of dispute. In 1878, more than half the Abkhazian population was forcefully displaced to Turkey and Abkhazia became colonized by Armenians, Megrels and Russians. In 1921 the Socialist Soviet Republic of Abkhazia was proclaimed, but soon the region became a part of Georgia, as an autonomous province. In the early 1930s, Georgian settlers started to arrive in the region and would later become the largest ethnic group in Abkhazia. In the late 1980s, Abkhazian Georgians demanded secession, while the rest of the population preferred to continue within the Soviet Union. In August 1992, Georgia sent troops to control the region, with frequent armed conflicts. By October 1993, the Georgian forces had been defeated and most of the local Georgians had become refugees. In June 1994, a 24-kilometre border zone was established, patrolled by Russian peace forces. The Republic of Abkhazia was declared a sovereign and democratic state that same year. In 1997, the population of Abkhazia voted for a new parliament, but Georgia declared both the new constitution and the new parliament illegal. In 1998, a solution to the conflict was nowhere in sight, in spite of border restraints imposed by Russia in order 'to lead the Abkhazian Government towards peace'. ∎

Turks and Caicos

Population: 18,000 (2002)
Land area: 430 SQ KM
Capital: Cockburn Town
Currency: US dollar
Language: English

Turks and Caicos Islands

Turks and Caicos are two island chains separated by a deep water channel, lying approximately 150 km north of Haiti on the southernmost tip of the Bahamas chain. Like many of the smaller Caribbean islands, these were first inhabited by Arawak peoples. Some researchers claim it was on East Caicos or Grand Turk that Columbus first set foot on New World soil in 1492. The first Europeans to settle on the islands were salt-rakers from Bermuda in 1678.

2 During the following century, Turks and Caicos faced several invasions by both French and Spanish forces. The islands were a refuge during this period for both pirates and their merchant-vessel victims, Spanish galleons carrying American wealth to Europe. By 1787, colonial settlers had established cotton plantations and imported African slaves, and British domination was consolidated. Both archipelagos remained British colonies.

3 Turks and Caicos were administered from the Bahamas until the Separation Act of 1848. After 1874, the islands were annexed to Jamaica, remaining a dependency until independence in 1962, when they again became a separate colony.

During World War II, the United States built an airstrip on South Caicos and in 1951 the islands' authorities signed an agreement permitting the US to establish a missile base and a Navy base on Grand Turk island.

4 After the Bahamas' independence in 1972, Turks and Caicos received their own governor. Further autonomy achieved through the 1976 constitution, provided for a Governor, a

Legislative Council, a Supreme Court and a Court of Appeals.

5 In the 1976 elections, the pro-independence People's Democratic Movement (PDM), led by JAFS McCartney, won over the pro-US Progressive National Party (PNP). The PDM favored a new constitution that granted internal autonomy as a step towards eventual independence.

6 In 1980, election year, Britain showed an interest in granting independence to the islands, which receive $2 million a year in aid. The overwhelming electoral triumph of the PNP was attributed to the failure of the PDM to solve the country's economic crisis, including a 30 per cent unemployment rate and the local population's fears that the economy could worsen with independence.

7 The new head minister, entrepreneur Norman Saunders, convinced Britain to shelve the idea of independence. He concentrated on bringing new business to the islands: tourism talks with the French Club Mediterranée; the development of light industry and offshore banking; and finally an agreement with BCM Ltd, for construction of an oil refinery with a capacity of 125,000 barrels per day.

8 Internal differences arose within the Government with regard to economic policy. However, these differences were quickly forgotten when Saunders and Stafford Missik, his development minister and a key opposition figure within the government, were arrested in Miami. They were in the process of creating

an international drug network, using the islands as a bridge between the US and South America.

9 The British Government suspended the ministerial system until 1988, when a general election was held. PDM's Oswald Skippings won the election, with 11 of the 13 parliamentary seats going to his party. The election marked the end of direct British administration of the islands.

10 Unemployment reached 12 per cent of the active population in 1992. In 1993 imports cost $42.8 million and exports were worth $6.8 million.

11 Martin Bourke was appointed Governor in 1993, and Derek H Taylor became Prime Minister in 1995.

12 Tourism registered a 10 per cent increase in the first three months of 1995 compared with the same period of 1994. Some 70 per cent of the total 60,000 tourists were US citizens. The economy of the islands was also supported by fishing and international financial services.

13 Haitian refugee ships reaching the islands in 1998 and 1999 were systematically rejected by the archipelago's maritime authorities. One of these ships was sunk in June 1998 and six people died as a result of a confrontation with the coastguards. The survivors accused the coastguards of firing without warning.

14 The December 1999 Legislative Council elections resulted in a majority for the People's Democratic Movement. Mervyn Jones was appointed Governor in January 2000.

15 A new financial scandal arose in April that year when a lawyer disappeared leaving no trace of the money from a Christian foundation that he had managed. There are 7,000 offshore financial companies registered on the islands, which deal with business considered shady by other countries. The UK, the US and several European countries have complained that this financial system enables the laundering of millions of dollars produced daily by drug dealing and other criminal activities.

16 After the September 11 2001 attacks in the United States, tourism was significantly reduced on the islands, leading Governor Jones to implement a support plan for the islands' hotels and airlines. ∎

Tuvalu

Population: 10,000 (2002)
Land area: 30 SQ KM
Capital: Fongafale
Currency: Australian dollar
Language: Tuvaluan and English

Tuvalu

Around 30,000 BC, the peoples from Southeast Asia, ancestors of the Aboriginals, started their expansion toward the Pacific islands. By the 19th century AD, they had spread throughout practically all of Polynesia. The inhabitants of the archipelago then known as 'Funafuti' came there from the islands of Samoa and Tonga.

[2] In the 16th century the Europeans reported seeing the islands but did not settle on them due to the lack of exploitable resources. Years later, a European named the atolls the Ellice Islands.

[3] Between 1850 and 1875, thousands of islanders were captured by slave traders and sent to the phosphate (guano) works in Peru and the saltpeter mines in Chile. Within a few years, the population had shrunk from 20,000 to 3,000 inhabitants. As a source of slave labor, the Polynesian islands offered direct access to markets on the Pacific coast.

[4] A new wave of invasions began in 1865, with the arrival of British and North American missionaries. By 1892 the islands had become a British protectorate. In 1915, with their neighbors, the Gilbert Islands (see Kiribati), the British formed the Colony of the Gilbert and Ellice Islands.

[5] This arbitrary merger was decided on administrative grounds and had little to do with other factors. In a referendum of 1974, 90 per cent of the Ellice islanders voted in favor of separate administrations, after having attained relatively autonomous local government. The split became official in October 1975, and the first elections in independent Tuvalu were held in August 1977. Toaripi Lauti was named Prime Minister.

[6] The archipelago became independent on October 1 1978, adopting the name Tuvalu, which in the local language means 'united eight', symbolizing the eight inhabited islands which make up the country. The islands became autonomous from London, but they fell under the economic influence of Australia, which had already started to hold considerable sway on the economy.

[7] Under a friendship treaty of 1979 Washington relinquished its claim over the islands of Nurakita,

Nukulaelae, Funafuti, and Nukufetau.

[8] Tuvalu is the smallest of the Lesser Developed Countries, in both population and land area. One of its main sources of foreign exchange is the sale of stamps, which are valuable collectors' items, and the granting of fishing licenses to foreign fleets which earns some $100,000 per year.

[9] Faced with a lack of natural resources, a sparse population, and an almost total lack of internal sources of savings or investment, the country depends heavily on foreign aid, of which Australia is the principal source, to finance its regular budget and its development budget.

[10] In 1989, the State was able to meet about only 10 per cent of its expenses. Most of this money was sent home by the quarter of the islands' population, who lived on neighboring islands working in the phosphate mines. The situation of the archipelago worsened as citizens returning from abroad look for jobs, competing with young people just finishing school. Only 30 per cent of school-leavers were successful in finding employment at this period.

[11] In the Independence Day celebrations, in October 1995, a new flag was hoisted, replacing the British Union Flag. In 1996, the new Prime Minister, Bikenibeu Paeniu once again made the British flag official.

[12] A fire swept through a residential village for students in Vaitupu island, causing the death of 18 girls and their supervisor in March 2000.

[13] Prime Minister Ionatana, appointed in the April 1999 elections, died in December 2000. His deputy, Lagitupu Tuilimu, became the new Prime Minister.

[14] That same year the Government claimed that the money

it had collected through the sale of its website - identified by the letters 'tv' - to a Canadian television company for $50 million and a share in the company's future earnings would be used to improve education outside Funafuti, to rebuild deteriorating government buildings and to lengthen the capital's runway. Maritime communications within the archipelago and beyond are inadequate. Transportation between the islands runs by a ferry while an Australian defense ship patrols international waters and ensures the compliance of fishing rights.

[15] Foreign cultural trends accessed particularly through television and

video, have brought about changes in family and social life. Alcoholism and sexual offenses have increased in recent years.

[16] Some Tuvaluans are buying land in Fiji, Australia and Aotearoa/New Zealand, anticipating the moment when - as a result of the increase in seawater levels due to global warming - the water will no longer be fit to drink and they will be forced to abandon the archipelago.

[17] Koloa Talake, advisor to Prime Minister Faimalaga Luka, who had been appointed in February 2001, was elected Prime Minister by Parliament in December, after the downfall of Luka's Government.

[18] In August 2002 Tuvalu announced it was planning lawsuits against the US and Australia (both of whom had rejected the Kyoto Protocol on climate change). Tuvalu believes the polluters' contribution to global warming is causing the rising sea levels that threaten to flood the islands. ∎

PROFILE

ENVIRONMENT

Tuvalu is distributed over the coral atolls of Funafuti, Nanumanga, Nanumea, Niutao, Nui, Nukulaelae, Nukufetau, Nurakita and Vaitupu, known collectively as the Ellice Islands, within an ocean area of 1,060,000 sq km. The archipelago is situated slightly south of the equator, 4,000 km northeast of Australia, south of the Gilbert Islands, between Micronesia and Melanesia. The climate is tropical with heavy rainfall. The islands are completely flat with a thin layer of topsoil suffering from severe erosion. Fishing and coconut farming are traditional activities.

SOCIETY

Peoples: Tuvaluans are mainly Polynesians. **Religion:** Church of Tuvalu (Congregational) 96.9 per cent; Seventh-Day Adventist 1.4 per cent; Baha'i 1 per cent; Roman Catholic 1.4 per cent; other 0.5 per cent. **Languages:** Tuvaluan and English (spoken mostly on Funafuti). **Political Parties:** Prominent families control Tuvalu's politics. They are not formally organized in parties.

THE STATE

Official Name: Tuvalu. **Capital:** Fongafale on Funafuti's atoll 6,000 people (1999). **Other atolls:** Vaitupu 1,231 people; Niutao 904; Nanumea 879; Nukufetau 694 (1985). **Government:** Sir Tomasi Puapua, Governor-General and Chief of State, since June 1998; Koloa Talake, Prime Minister since December 2001. Tuvalu has a parliamentary government modeled on the British system. Parliament has 12 members. **National Holiday:** October 1, Independence Day (1978).

STATISTICS

Health: Infant mortality: 38 per 1,000 (2000). Under-5 child mortality: 53 per 1,000 (2000). Safe water: 100 % (2000) **Education:** Literacy: 98 % (2000) School enrolment (net): Primary total: 100 % (1994/2000).
Economy: Currency: 1.9 Australian dollars = $ 1 (2002).

Uganda

Population: 24,780,000 (2002)
Land area: 197,100 SQ KM
Capital: Kampala
Currency: Shilling
Language: Swahili

Uganda

In present-day Uganda the large mud walls of Bigo state are evidence of urban civilizations dating from the 10th century.

2 Various places in Uganda still bear the ruins of sizeable hilltop fortresses, overlooking the surrounding territory. Built with earthen walls, moats and trenches, these fortifications mark the lines of Bacwezi penetration. Around the 13th century, the Bacwezi, a nation of Nilotic herders, arrived from the north and subdued the Bantu inhabitants of the area. Their characteristic fortresses - in some cases up to 300 meters in diameter - were built to protect themselves and their cattle - their main source of wealth and status symbols. The fortresses were gradually abandoned, and the conquerors mixed with the conquered and adopted Bantu languages. The descendants of the Bacwezi, who preserved their nomadic herding lifestyle, intermingled less with the local population though they also adopted a Bantu language, and came to be called Bahima.

3 The peoples of Bunyoro, Buganda, Busoga and Ankole were connected to the eastern coast and the Swahili slave trade; they consolidated their national unity between the 17th and 18th centuries. A supremacy dispute arose between Bunyoro, supported by the Swahili traders, and Buganda, linked to the 'Shirazis' of Zanzibar. At the beginning of the 19th century, Bunyoro was already losing ground, and when some of their allies defected to form the independent state of Toro the predominance of Buganda became inevitable.

4 Buganda was governed by *Kabakas* or traditional leaders, who were in theory absolute rulers but in practice were limited by the *Lukiko*, a council representing the higher castes. In the mid-19th century, Buganda maintained a standing army which was enough to guarantee their autonomy from the regional powers: Egypt and Zanzibar. It had a balanced society in which caste privileges were more honorary and political than economic and a sound agricultural economy which allowed Buganda to overcome the decline of the slave trade.

5 The first contact with Europe occurred in 1862. The second contact had more far-reaching results. HM Stanley, adventurer and journalist, arrived in 1875. He vociferously denounced the spread of Islam in the region and announced an alleged 'request' made by Kabaka Mutesa I asking Europe to send missionaries to check Egyptian-Sudanese religious infiltration.

6 These missionaries soon arrived: English Protestants in 1877 and French Catholics in 1879. They quickly converted part of the Bugandese hierarchy, splitting the power elite into three parties. Two of these reflected the rivalry between missionaries, in local dialect the 'Franza' and 'Ingleza' parties, while the third took the role of defending national interests, as they were moderate and Islamic.

7 The main consequence of this conflict was the consolidation of European presence. The missionaries succeeded in deposing the Moslem Kabaka, Mwanga in 1888, and swift on their heels came the Imperial British East Africa Company (IBEA), a typical colonial trading company, followed by the British Government.

8 The 1886 Anglo-German agreements had delimited areas of influence and the states of the lakes area went to the British who established a Protectorate over them in 1893.

9 The other organized local groups did not have governmental institutions similar to those of Buganda's but these were imposed on them as the British thought that the Lukiko resembled their own parliamentary system.

10 With the intention of developing a ruling elite to serve as intermediaries to the colonial power, the British undertook 'land reform'. This consisted of distributing communally-owned land to select individuals, depriving the rural population of their legitimate property to benefit the bureaucracy that sat in the Lukiko.

11 The severe disruption of production caused by this confiscation was aggravated by the introduction of cash crops for export (including cotton, coffee and tea) in the post-World War II period. These crops were alien to the agricultural traditions of the region, and their production resulted in a deterioration in the living conditions of most of the inhabitants. There was no way of changing this state of affairs until the 1960s when the decolonization movement led to the independence of Uganda. Kabaka Mutesa II of Buganda was the first President of the new republic and the Prime Minister was Dr Milton Obote.

12 In 1965, Obote succeeded in reforming the Constitution and he assumed greater powers, eliminating the federal system imposed by the British, which had created various relatively autonomous territorial sub-divisions. He also adopted a policy that favored the most impoverished sectors. This aroused fierce opposition among the Asian bourgeoisie; a minority of 40,000 people who controlled almost all the commercial activity in the country. Since the Asians held British passports, they had resisted total integration into the new nation.

13 Obote decisively supported regional economic integration with Tanzania and Kenya to counterbalance the effects of Uganda's lack of access to the coast.

14 In January 1971, Obote was overthrown in a bloody coup led by former paratroop sergeant and boxing champion Idi Amin Dada. The economic base of the deposed government had been seriously shaken by a series of destabilization maneuvers by the Asian minority and interests connected to transnationals. Idi Amin quickly demonstrated his authoritarianism. In 1972 he ordered the extensive expulsion of the Asians.

15 Although he came to power with the support of the 'elite' of the business community, Amin's attitudes and measures were very controversial: he maintained commercial relations with the U.S. and Britain, also cultivating good relations with the socialist world. Similarly, while he supported several African liberation movements, he opposed Angola's bid for membership to the Organization of African Unity (OAU) and was permanently hostile to Nyerere's government in Tanzania. Finally, although he had been trained as a paratrooper in Israel, he expropriated the lands and other properties of members of the Jewish community and made overtures toward the Arab countries.

16 Amin declared himself President-for-Life. In 1978, he exacerbated tensions with Tanzania by annexing its northern territories. In April 1979, war between the two

LITERACY

2000

67%

FOOD DEPENDENCY

2000

14%

EXTERNAL DEBT

2000

PER CAPITA

US$ 146

FOREIGN TRADE

Millions US$ 2000

IMPORTS

1,587

EXPORTS

626

countries ended Amin's regime and he was forced to flee Kampala, after a joint offensive launched by Tanzanian troops and opposition activists united in the Ugandan National Liberation Front (FNLU).

[17] The new government's main body was a National Advisory Council led by Yusuf Lule, a politically inexperienced university professor with conservative tendencies. 68 days later, Lule was replaced by the FNLU's powerful Godfrey Binaisa. The Front was a frail, eclectic movement, founded merely on joint efforts aimed at ending the terror imposed by Idi Amin. As expected, Binaisa was unable to conciliate the conflicting tendencies within his movement. He

was even less capable of confronting the growing prestige of Milton Obote whose Uganda People's Congress party (UPC) continued to be very popular.

[18] The President brought forward the elections scheduled for 1981, and tried to ban Obote's candidacy. This fuelled a crisis that exploded in May 1980 when the army, on the pretext of preventing the implementation of the Government's policies, forced him to resign. The President was replaced by a Military Commission entrusted with maintaining the electoral schedule and enforcing the democratic principles of the movement that had overthrown Amin. The Commission, under the orders of General David Oyite Ojok,

supervised the elections in December 1980, and the UPC won the predicted overwhelming majority.

[19] Obote's party won 73 of the 126 seats in the new parliament. The legitimacy of the election was questioned, but an international commission of 60 members confirmed that, given the constraints of the country, minimum standards had been complied with.

[20] Obote inherited a bankrupt country. Copper mines had not been worked for several years and corruption and speculation were commonplace. Despite the reaffirmation support for Obote in the elections, in 1981 the defeated conservative groups initiated an intense destabilization campaign that gradually became an openly anti-government guerrilla movement.

[21] In spite of the guerrilla presence, Obote authorized the return of Asian businesses, regulated the participation of foreign capital and undertook the reorganization of the economy, fighting corruption and speculation. Despite the intensification of political violence in 1985, Obote requested and obtained the withdrawal of Tanzanian troops who had been in Uganda since the fall of Amin.

[22] Between 1981 and July 1985, 16 major military offensives were launched against the main strongholds of opposition guerrillas. These groups included; the National Resistance Army (NRA), the military wing of the National Resistance Movement (NRM) founded by former president Yusuf Lule and led by Yoweri Museveni; the Uganda National Rescue Front, led by retired Brigadier Moses Ali (one of Idi Amin's former associates); and Lt-Colonel George Nleawanga's Federal Democratic Movement (FEDEMU).

[23] Civil warfare displaced 100,000 people. In 1981, the Government took steps to prevent cattle smuggling by the nomadic peoples across the Kenyan border, causing starvation among thousands in the province of Karamoja.

[24] In spite of the guerrilla activity, Uganda's economy had grown an average 5 per cent yearly since 1982, and, according to the World Bank, exports had increased 45 per cent since 1983. Food was available and gasoline no longer rationed.

[25] General elections were scheduled for December 1985, and a UPC victory was expected. However, in late July 1985, General Bazilio Olara Okello led a military coup putting an end to Obote's government. General Tito Okello, not related to the rebel leader, was appointed President. Within 6 months, he called elections to form a broad-based government. The Okellos belonged to the northern Acholi ethnic group and Obote, member of the Lango, was accused of favoritism towards his own people.

[26] After the coup, the National Resistance Army intensified its action, occupying Kampala, the capital, in January 1986. After a bloody fight, Okello was ousted, and on January 30, NRA leader Yoweri Museveni assumed the presidency. The northern town of Gulu, the last bastion of forces loyal to Okello, finally fell in March of that year.

[27] Museveni was faced with the reconstruction of a country virtually destroyed by a series of authoritarian regimes which had left almost a million dead, two million refugees, 600,000 injured and incalculable property damage.

[28] Resources are scarce in a country with a fertility rate of 7.0 (1995) children per woman, and a life expectancy of not more than 41 years. This difficult situation has been aggravated by an extremely high incidence of AIDS, which is said to have achieved epidemic proportions in some parts of the country.

[29] Uganda's foreign debt rose to $1.2 billion in 1987. To solve this, Museveni resorted to exchange arrangements with other African countries. The country attempted to establish its economic independence, avoiding the International Monetary Fund (IMF). This led to some problems with Western countries, who did not approve of Uganda's relations with Cuba and Libya. The United States pressed Tanzania and Rwanda into ending the exchange operations which they had organized with Uganda.

[30] In February 1992, local human rights organizations accused Museveni of harassing his political opponents and of not allowing the establishment of a multiparty

PROFILE

ENVIRONMENT

The land is made up of a number of plateaus, gently rolling towards the northwest where the Nile River flows. There are volcanic ranges and numerous rivers, the largest of which is the Nile. Nearly 18 per cent of the territory is taken up with rivers, lakes and swamps. The climate is tropical, tempered by altitude. Lumber is taken from the rainforest that covers 6.2 per cent of the land. In addition to subsistence farming of rice and corn/maize, the cash crops are coffee, cotton, tea and tobacco. Lake Victoria is one of the largest fish reservoirs in the world. Swampland is being drained indiscriminately for agricultural use.

SOCIETY

Peoples: Most Ugandans come from the integration of various African ethnic groups, mainly the Baganda, Bunyoro and Batoro, and to a lesser extent, the San/Bushmen, Nilo-Hamitic, Sudanese, and Bantu-speakers. Some have the Hamitic features of the northern Nile, but they speak Bantu languages. There are also minorities of Indian and European origin.

Religions: More than half of the people are Christian (62 per cent), 19 per cent practice traditional religions and there are 15 per cent of Muslims. Others, 1 per cent.

Languages: English, the official language, is spoken by a minority. Of the native languages, Swahili and Luganda are the most widely spoken.

Political Parties: National Resistance Movement (NRM), led by President Museveni. All other parties have been disenfranchised by the Government; the most important among them are the Ugandan People's Congress (UPC); the Democratic Party (DP); the Ugandan Freedom Movement (UFM); the Conservative Party (CP); the Nationalist Liberal Party; the Ugandan Democratic Alliance; and the Ugandan Patriotic Movement.

Social Organizations: National Organization of Trade Unions (NOTU).

THE STATE

Official Name: Republic of Uganda.

Capital: Kampala 1,154,000 people (1999).

Other cities: Jinja 85,200 people; Mbale 70,600; Masaka 64,900 (2000).

Government: Yoweri Museveni, President since January 1986 (after the overthrow of Tito Okello), elected as President in 1996 and re-elected in 2001. Apolo Nsibambi (NRM), Prime Minister since April 1999.

Unicameral Legislature: National Parliament, with 292 members.

National Holiday: October 9, Independence Day (1962).

Armed Forces: 55,000 (1997).

democracy in the country. The Government replied that it preferred to build a democracy based on traditional tribal structures, and that political parties were therefore unnecessary.

[31] But pressure from the opposition and some international agencies led President Museveni to authorize the election of a Constituent Assembly, which would be announced in February 1993 and established in 1995, charged with studying a draft of the new constitution. Nevertheless, the text drafted by the Government was criticized by the opposition (Democratic Party and the UPC) for maintaining the partial ban on political parties for a seven-year period.

[32] In February, Pope John Paul II visited Uganda and urged the population to practice sexual abstinence, to prevent the spread of AIDS. This advice caused grave concern in a country where over 20 per cent of the population are HIV-carriers.

[33] As part of a policy aimed at winning the support of the Baganda people, Museveni authorized the restoration of the monarchy. During Prince Ronald Muenda Mutebi's coronation ceremony as Kabaka, on July 31, authorities returned all royal property, which had been confiscated during former president Obote's administration.

[34] On another front, Museveni was accused by the opposition of having ordered the assassination of opposition leader Amon Bazira in Kenya in August. In the March 1994 elections the supporters of the Ugandan President took around half the seats, but the direct appointment of some of the posts gave Museveni a broad majority in the new assembly.

[35] Continuing with his policy of restoring the local authorities, the leader once again authorized the Bunyoros, a people in the north of the country, to have their own kingdom, and this decision was implemented in June.

[36] The discussion of a multiparty system continued throughout 1995. Museveni continued to claim the authorization of several parties would only make the 'tribal divisions' more serious. On another front, the international funding organizations said they were satisfied with the economic performance of Uganda. Foreign investments grew, but budget cuts worsened the situation of most of the population as they already lived in poverty.

[37] On May 9 1996, Museveni was re-elected president by more than 75 per cent of the electorate, with a 72.6 per cent turnout, defeating Paul Semogerere and Muhammad

Mayanja. Museveni was victorious again in the May legislative elections, as his party took 156 of the 196 seats at stake. The new government was appointed in July, with Kintu Musoke as Prime Minister.

[38] The economic reforms carried out by Museveni with loans and aid from international creditors, meant Uganda topped the list in the World Bank project to help out 20 debtor countries in 1997. However, half the population was living below the poverty line, leading to estimates that $24 million would be needed to relieve the hunger in this country. The Franco-Australian LaSource company paid Uganda for the right to exploit its cobalt mines, and the nation received loans from the European Union and North Korea for the construction of a hydroelectric plant.

[39] In mid 1998, the Ugandan army entered neighboring Democratic Republic of Congo (DRC) and joined the rebels fighting President Laurent Kabila. On October 18 1999, Ugandan Defense Minister, Stephen Kavuma, stated that the troops would remain in DRC until peace was restored.

[40] On November 12 1999, 70 independent and state journalists marched through the streets of Kampala to denounce official persecution and the systematic abuse of freedom of speech. They also demanded the repeal of the so-called 'sedition act'. On November 30, in the Tanzanian city of Arusha, the presidents of Kenya, Tanzania, and Uganda signed a treaty which established the Economic Union of Eastern Africa.

[41] Hailed for the success, within the African context, of his fight against HIV/AIDS, Museveni hosted the African Development Forum 2000, held in Addis Ababa. Museveni referred there to the alarming statistics of the epidemic in sub-Saharan Africa, where by then there were 25 million people infected. The rate of infection in Uganda was one of the highest in the world, but through information and a press campaign called 'Loving with care', the Ugandan Government greatly reduced the epidemic.

[42] In compliance with the 1995 Constitution, a referendum was held on June 29 2000 to decide on the establishment of a multiparty system. In spite of the Democratic Party's (DP) and other political groups' boycott, the formula of 'democracy without parties', defended by Museveni in the campaign, was supported by 80 per cent of voters (50 per cent of those registered), leading Uganda to maintain a government ruling system unique in the continent. This did not mean that, in practice, the NRM (called the 'Movement') acted as a state party.

(see DRC)

MATERNAL MORTALITY

1985/99

Per 100,000 live births

510

The system put all power in the hands of its creator.

[43] Amnesty International warned that gays, lesbians, bisexuals and transsexuals in Uganda, among other countries, are at particular risk of suffering human rights abuses. As of 1999, Ugandan police had orders to localize and attack homosexuals. Since then, activists have been persecuted. In June 2000, the police murdered a member of Lesgabix, a group of lesbians and gays from Kampala.

[44] In the March 2001 presidential elections, Museveni was re-elected with 69.3 per cent of the vote, followed by 27.8 per cent for Kizza Besigye, former colonel of the NRM, who during the guerrilla war had been a medic and later on occupied senior government posts. International observers estimated there had been up to 15 per cent of electoral fraud, and confirmed that the elections had gone ahead in a climate of intimidation. Museveni stated that his support was were 'like Lake Victoria, which never dries up', and described his victory as an acclamation after 15 years of peaceful rule. On May 12 he took office for his new term until 2006, which, according to the Constitution, would be his last.

[45] On July 4 2001, Museveni held a bilateral meeting with Laurent Kabila's son, Joseph, now president of the DRC (see DRC) in Dar es Salaam, accelerating the withdrawal of the Ugandan army from that country and the stationing of UN soldiers along the front lines.

[46] A report by the World Trade Organization (WTO) indicated that the economic reforms carried out by the Museveni administration attracted foreign investment and contributed to the country's growth. The reforms included liberalization of the trade regime. The GDP had grown, until 2001, by about 6 per cent per year; fiscal deficit and inflation were reduced, improving the economic context. The agricultural sector amounted to 42 per cent of GDP and provided 80 per cent of jobs. The European Union was Uganda's main trade partner. As a consequence of regional integration, Uganda's trade with other sub-Sahara African countries developed. ■

DEMOGRAPHY
Population: 24,780,000 (2002)
Annual growth: 3.1 % (1985-2000)
Estimates for year 2015: 38,739,000 (2000)
Annual growth to year 2015: 3.4 % (2000)
Urban population: 14.2 % (2000)
Urban growth: 5.1 % (2000)
Children per woman: 7.1 (2000)

HEALTH
Life expectancy at birth: 46 years (2000-2005)
male: 45 years (2000-2005)
female: 47 years (2000-2005)
Maternal mortality: 510 per 100,000 live births (1985/99)
Infant mortality: 81 per 1,000 (2000)
Under-5 child mortality: 127 per 1,000 (2000)
Daily calorie supply: 2,238 per capita (1999)
Safe water: 52 % (2000)

EDUCATION
Literacy: 67 % (2000)
male: 78 % (2000)
female: 57 % (2000)
School enrolment (net):
Primary total: 87 % (1994/2000)
male: 92 % (1995/99)
female: 83 % (1995/99)
Secondary (gross):
male: 15 % (1995/97)
female: 9 % (1995/97)
Tertiary (gross): 2 % (1998)
Primary school teachers: one for every 60 pupils (1998)

COMMUNICATIONS
2 newspapers (1996), 127 radios (1997), 27 TV sets (2000) and 3 main telephone lines (2000) per 1,000 people
Books: 2 new titles per 100,000 people (1992/94)

ECONOMY
Per capita, GDP: $ 1,208 (2000)
Annual growth: 0.8 % (2000)
Annual inflation: 2.8 % (2000)
Consumer price index: 125.4 (2000)
Currency: 1,755.0 shillings = $ 1 (03/2002)
Cereal imports: 144,535 metric tons (2000)
Food import dependency: 14 % (2000)
Fertilizer use: 9 kg per ha (1999)
Exports: $ 626 million (2000)
Imports: $ 1,587 million (2000)
External debt: $ 3,409 million (2000); $ 146 per capita (2000)
Debt service: 23.7 % of exports (1999)
Development aid received: $ 590 million (1999); $ 27.5 per capita (1999); 9.20 % of GNP (1999)

HDI (ranking/value): 141 / 0.435 (1999)

Ukraine

Population: 48,652,000 (2002)
Land area: 579,350 SQ KM
Capital: Kiev (Kijef)
Currency: Grivna
Language: Ukranian

Ukrayina

Between the 9th and 12th centuries AD, most of the present Ukraine belonged to the Kievan (Kijef) Rus, which grouped together several alliances of Eastern Slavic peoples. Its nucleus was the Russian alliance, with its capital at Kiev. The ancient Russian people gave rise to the three main eastern Slav nations: Russia, Ukraine and Belarus. In the 12th century, the Kievan Rus separated into the principalities of Kiev, Chernigov, Galich and Vladimir-Volynski, all in what is now Ukrainian territory. In the 14th century, the Grand Principality of Lithuania annexed the territories of Chernigov and Novgorod-Severski, Podolia, Kiev and a large part of Volin. The Khanate of Crimea emerged in the southern part of Ukraine and Crimea, and expanded into Galicia and Podolia. After the 11th century, Hungary began seizing the Transcarpathian territories.

[2] The Ukrainians emerged, as an identifiable people, in the 15th century. Their name was derived from *krai*, meaning border, which in 1213 was the name given to the territories along the Polish border. In the 16th century, the use of the name was extended to the entire Ukrainian region. Historically, there were close ties between Ukrainians and Russians, they had fought together against the Polish and Lithuanian feudal kingdoms and against the Tatars in Crimea. The Ukrainian territories (Volin, eastern Podolia, Kiev and part of the left bank of the Dnepr) were incorporated into the Rzecz Pospolita (the union of Poland and Lithuania), which imposed Roman Catholicism.

[3] During the first half of the 17th century, the struggle for independence from Poland and Lithuania intensified. The Khmelnytsky insurrection (1648-1654) under Bohdan Khmelnytsky ended with the unification of Ukraine and Russia, approved by the Rada (council) of Pereyaslav. In March 1654, Ukrainian autonomy within the Russian Empire was ratified. The region along the right bank of the Dnepr and Galicia remained under Polish jurisdiction. Ukrainian colonization of what is now Kharkov (Char'cov) began in the 17th century.

[4] In 1783, the Khanate of Crimea

- home of the Tatars - was annexed by Russia. After the partition of Poland among Russia, Prussia and Austria (1793-95), the right bank of the Dnepr became a part of Russia and Ukraine's autonomy was abolished at the end of the 18th century. In 1796, the left bank of Ukraine became the Province of Malo-Rossiya (Little Russia).

[5] After the end of czarism in 1917, a dual system emerged in Ukraine, with power being divided between the Provisional Government of Saint Petersburg and the Ukrainian Central Rada (council) in Kiev. In December, after the Bolshevik Revolution, a Ukrainian Soviet government was formed in Kharkov. The Ukrainian Central Rada supported the Austro-German troops which invaded the country in the spring of 1918. In December, the Ukrainian Directorate, led by Symon Petlyura, seized power. Between 1918 and 1920, Ukraine was the scene of major fighting between the Soviets and their internal and external enemies. In December 1922, Ukraine attended the first All-Union Congress of the Soviets, held in Moscow, where the Treaty and Declaration of the Founding of the Union of Soviet Socialist Republics (USSR) was ratified.

[6] In the period between the world wars, the Soviet Government carried out rapid industrialization and collectivization of agriculture.

[7] The secret clauses of the 1939 Soviet-German non-aggression pact incorporated western Ukraine into the USSR. In 1940, the Ukrainian

Soviet Socialist Republic was enlarged through the addition of Bessarabia and Northern Bukovina. Germany attacked the Soviet Union in 1941, a strong guerrilla offensive began and by the end of World War II, all areas inhabited by ethnic Ukrainians became part of the USSR. Ukraine participated in the founding of the UN as a charter member.

[8] In 1954, Crimea - which had formerly belonged to the Russian Federation - was turned over to Ukraine, by the Soviet centralized authority. The leader of the Soviet Communist Party at the time was Nikita Krushchev, former first secretary of the Ukrainian CP.

[9] On April 26 1986, the nuclear plant at Chernobyl - 130 kilometers north of Kiev - was the scene of the worst nuclear accident in history when one of its reactors exploded. The explosion affected an area inhabited by 600,000 people; 135,000 were evacuated and by 1993, 7,000 had died of radiation-related diseases.

[10] In 1985 within the framework of the reforms in the USSR, Communist leaders and Ukrainian nationalists founded the Ukrainian People's Movement for *Perestroika* (restructuring) (RUKH), which demanded greater political and economic autonomy. In the March 1990 legislative elections, RUKH candidates received massive support from the population. On July 16 1990, the Ukrainian Supreme *Soviet* (Parliament) proclaimed the sovereignty of the republic. On August 24 1991, the

Ukrainian Parliament approved the republic's independence, and convened a plebiscite to ratify or reject the decision.

[11] Leonid Kravchuk, former first secretary of the Ukrainian Communist Party, was elected President. Russia, Canada, Poland and Hungary immediately recognized Ukrainian independence, underscoring the failure of Gorbachev's attempt to reach a new union treaty, within the USSR.

[12] On December 8 1991, the presidents of Ukraine, the Russian Federation and Belarus pronounced the end of the USSR, founding the Commonwealth of Independent States (CIS). Ukraine declared itself a neutral and nuclear-free country, and stated its willingness to participate in the process of European integration.

[13] In the first months of 1992, the Ukrainian Government declared the end of the fixed prices system; created a new currency, and called for bids to build arms factories, announcing incentives for attracting foreign investment.

[14] On May 5, the Crimea peninsula declared independence, but it was vetoed by the Ukrainian Parliament. Crimea yielded and withdrew the declaration. Russia reacted to the situation in June, annulling the 1954 decree by which it had ceded Crimea to Ukraine, demanding that it be returned. Kiev refused, but granted Crimea economic autonomy.

[15] Prime Minister Vitold Fokin resigned in September over the failure of his economic policies. He was replaced by Leonid Kuchma, former president of the Union of Industrialists and Entrepreneurs.

[16] The liberal policies of the new government and its privatization scheme soon came up against the dual obstacles of the Supreme Council - dominated by former communists - and worker resistance. Kuchma presented his resignation on May 21, but it was not accepted.

[17] In June, in a direct challenge to Kravchuk's moderate foreign policy, the Supreme Council announced the appropriation of the entire ex-USSR nuclear arsenal in Ukraine. With the disintegration of the Soviet Union, Ukraine became the world's third most important nuclear power.

[18] Finding himself politically vulnerable, in September 1993 Kravchuk agreed to cede Ukraine's Black Sea fleet to Russia, in compensation for debts incurred through oil and gas purchases from Moscow. In addition, he accepted help from Russia in dismantling the 46 intercontinental SS24 missiles which Ukraine had wanted to keep as a last bastion against any possible future expansionist schemes on the part of Russia. However, opposition in Kiev led to the invalidation of the settlement.

[19] In the meantime, the economy went out of control with inflation reaching 100 per cent per month and Kuchma resigned.

[20] The first presidential elections of the post-Soviet era took place in June and July 1994. Former Prime Minister Leonid Kuchma defeated Kravchuk with 52 per cent of the vote, after which he declared his intention to strengthen links with Russia and enter fully into the Commonwealth of Independent States (CIS).

[21] The Communist Party of Ukraine (KPU) obtained 113 seats (24.7 per cent) in the March 1998 Parliamentary elections, effectively becoming a left and center-left parliamentary majority. President Kuchma, an independent, was re-elected in the second round of the presidential elections on December 14 1999, with 56 per cent of the vote. Petro Symonenko, the KPU candidate, took 38 per cent of the vote. Kuchma promised to continue with market reforms and pro-Western policies, better ties with Eastern Europe, the US and NATO. Symonenko, on the other hand, based his campaign on deepening relations with Russia. International observers pointed out that the elections were far from free and fair.

[22] On November 26, and faithful to his promises, Kuchma urged the European Union (EU) to take Ukraine into account when the bloc discussed expansion plans in December. In late December, after striking a deal with the opposition, Kuchma appointed Viktor Yushchenko, then head of the National Bank of Ukraine, as Prime Minister. In February 2000, while on visit to London, Yushchenko announced Ukraine would restructure its foreign debt with tougher fiscal policies and a massive privatization plan. The President abolished the death penalty on March 22, following European Council demands. On April 16 in a referendum, 90 per cent of the population backed the alliance and reform initiatives proposed by Kuchma, who was now able to dissolve Parliament without a majority.

[23] After the disappearance of a journalist critical of the regime, opposition politicians alleged that there was a tape in which the President, prior to the journalist's disappearance, discussed the 'solution' to the problem with the journalist with security officials. In February 2001 the opposition's requests for Kuchma to resign were followed by massive demonstrations. Ukraine's rapprochement to the West was frozen with the finding of the journalist's decapitated body. Demonstrations against Kuchma continued and became even larger.

[24] In April 2001 Parliament removed Yushchenko, the best ally for the market reforms demanded by the West, causing a serious political crisis. This revealed the tensions among three sectors: pro-Russian forces who tried to return Kiev to the Kremlin's sphere, pro-Western forces that wanted to continue with the reforms and towards the EU and NATO, and organized crime, whose goal was to maintain the instability that benefited it. That month, Ukraine signed a technology and military cooperation agreement with Russia.

[25] Fourteen per cent of Ukrainian people were disabled, being either war veterans from Afghanistan or victims of the Chernobyl nuclear disaster or of the frequent accidents in the Donbass coal mining region. According to an ILO report, the death rate for that year amounted to 5 workers for every million tons of coal extracted, the highest in all Europe. Approximately 12,000 disabled veterans from the Afghanistan war and some 3.3 million Chernobyl victims lobbied the Government during 2001 to implement rehabilitation and job training programs for disabled people.

[26] In the eve of the March 2002 Parliamentary elections, the deputy governor of a western city, a member of the Social Democratic Party, was found dead, shot nine times in the back. The electoral campaign had been marked by pressure from the press, fraud and accusations between the Government and the opposition. The Viktor Yushchenko Bloc Our Ukraine won with 23.6 per cent of the vote, followed by the Communists, with 20 per cent. The pro-Government For United Ukraine took third place with 14.3 per cent of the vote. The Liberal opposition accused Ukrainian authorities of fraud. Yushchenko, leader of Our Ukraine Bloc, announced he would contest the results of several districts and said he had been robbed of 12 per cent of the vote. Analysts considered these elections as a step towards Presidential elections in 2004, crucial to decide the country's political system and its place between Russia and the West. ∎

PROFILE

ENVIRONMENT

Ukraine is bordered by Poland, Slovakia, Hungary, Romania and Moldova in the west and southwest; by Belarus in the north and Russia in the east and northeast. The Black Sea and the Sea of Azov (Acovsko More) are located in the south. Ukraine is mostly made up of flat plains and plateaus, with the Carpathian Mountains (max. altitude 2061 m) along the country's southwestern borders, and the Crimean Mountains (max. altitude 1545 m) in the south. The climate is moderate and mostly continental. There is black soil; both wooded and grassy steppes in the south. Much of the north is made up of mixed forest areas (such areas occupy 14 per cent of the republic's total land surface). Pollution of the country's rivers and air has reached significant levels. Approximately 2,800,000 people currently live in areas contaminated by the Chernobyl disaster.

SOCIETY

Peoples: Ukrainians, 72.7 per cent; Russians, 22.1 per cent; Belarusians, 0.9 per cent; Moldovans, 0.6 per cent, Poles, 0.4 per cent.
Religions: Mainly Christian Orthodox. Catholics, Protestants, Jews.
Languages: Ukrainian (official), Russian. **Political Parties:** Viktor Yushchenko Bloc Our Ukraine; Congress of Ukrainian Nationalists; Liberal Party; Youth Party of Ukraine; People's Movement of Ukraine; Party of Christian-Popular Union; Party Reforms and Order; Republican Christian Party; Forwards Ukraine; Communist Party of Ukraine (KPU); Agrarian Party of Ukraine; People's Democratic Party of Ukraine; Ukrainian People's Party Assembly; Ukrainian Social-Democratic Party; Socialist Party of Ukraine; Women for the Future; Ukrainian Green Party; Democratic Party of Ukraine. **Social Organizations:** Unions are being reorganized after recent institutional changes.

THE STATE

Official Name: Ukrayina. **Administrative Divisions:** 25 Regions, the Republic of Crimea has special status as well as great internal autonomy. **Capital:** Kiev (Kijef) 2,663,000 people (1999). **Other cities:** Kharkov (Char'cov) 1,692,700 people; Donetsk 1,764,000; Dnipropetrovsk 1,483,300; Odessa 1,121,500 (2000). **Government:** Leonid Kuchma, President and Head of State since July 1994, re-elected in 1999. Anatolii Kinakh, Prime Minister since May 2001. Legislature, single-chamber: Supreme Council, with 450 members. **National Holiday:** August 24, Independence (1991). **Armed Forces:** 387,400 (1997). **Other:** 72,000 National Guard and Border Guard.

United Arab Emirates

Population: 2,701,000 (2002)
Land area: 83,600 SQ KM
Capital: Abu Dhabi (Abu Zaby)
Currency: Dirham
Language: Arabic

al-Imarat al-'Arabiya al-Muttahida

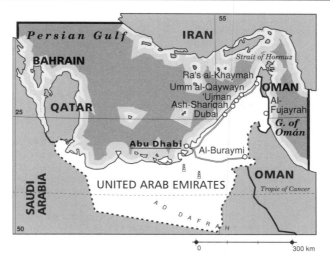

In the southeastern corner of the Arab peninsula, between the Jabal Ajdar mountain range in Oman and the rocky steppe of Najd extending from the center of the peninsula to the Gulf shores (al-Hasa), is the Rub al-Khali desert taking up part of the territory of present-day Saudi Arabia and almost the entire United Arab Emirates.

[2] By the 6th century the oases which were spread over the land supplied enough water to the small stable population, enabling them to farm regular crops. The residents of the area spoke different Arabian dialects and shared diverse lifestyles. Some were grain growers, others were merchants or craftspeople from small villages and others, still usually known as 'Bedouins' were nomads who raised camels, sheep and goats, making the most of the desert's scant water resources. Along with these activities, the coastal peoples also fished in Gulf waters.

[3] Despite being a minority, the nomads - taking advantage of their condition as a mobile and armed group - and together with the merchants, dominated farmers and craftspeople. Gathered around relatively stable family chiefs, they had a typically tribal organization.

[4] Among shepherds and farmers, religion had become another type of social control but it appeared not to have a defined form. Local gods were identified with the heavenly bodies and could incarnate into rocks, trees or animals. Some families, claiming they had the power to understand the language of the gods, managed to control the others.

[5] Until the 7th century, Byzantine and Sassanid empires waged a long war with constant comings and goings which involved the peninsula, although not directly the land of the present-day Emirates. Likewise, such activity and opening of trade routes brought immigrants (mostly merchants, dealers and craftspeople) who shared their culture and knowledge of the foreign world.

[6] Islam was peacefully adopted in the area during the prophet Muhammad's lifetime. Tribal chiefs secured their power but the lifestyle of the few inhabitants did not change significantly.

[7] Upon the Prophet's death, various groups appeared which disputed his spiritual inheritance. One of them, the Ibadis (who claimed to be his direct descendants), created the Uman (Oman) imanate in mid-8th century. It lasted to the 9th century when it was suppressed by the Abassids, caliphs who claimed a universal authority and whose main capital was in Baghdad.

[8] After the 11th century, the Sunni form of Islam gradually spread from being the ruling groups' religion to reach the population at large. The Ibadis' communities continued until the 15th century, exerting strong religious authority.

[9] The Gulf ports were already of significant importance for the traffic of commodities which came from China (textiles, glass, porcelain and spices), and were transported to the Red Sea through an oasis chain.

[10] During the 17th and 18th centuries, the Ottoman Empire occupied a large area of the peninsula but had not reached the Gulf coast in the southeastern region. The Ibadis had reinstated their imanate under a Yaribi dynasty. Further to the north, Bahrain was under Iranian domain.

[11] Beyond the reach of the Ottomans (occupied with constant wars in Europe, Africa and Asia), the southeastern region of the peninsula thrived on trade. Ruling families linked directly with merchants appeared and piracy developed, benefiting from the natural advantages of the indented coasts. The area came to be known as 'Pirate Coast'.

[12] An important change was introduced when European fleets increasingly used the maritime route round the Cape. British influence grew gradually, since they used the Gulf ports as a stop on the way to India, and helped to combat piracy.

[13] At the beginning of the 19th century, Britain held complete control over the region, obtained through agreements reached with the local chiefs and small governors of the ports. Since then, the Pirate Coast became the Trucial States, which included Abu Dhabi, Dubai and Sharjah. Relations with Britain continued in the same way until the first decades of the 20th century.

[14] Around 1914, the Saudi state re-emerged as a great force in Central Arabia, becoming a threat even for the Ottoman power. Russia, France and Germany also sought to intensify their presence in the area. This led the British to formalize relations with the Trucial States of Bahrain, Oman and Kuwait, which let the Government in London handle their affairs with the rest of the world.

[15] World War I, which led to the end of the Ottoman Empire and the independence of several Arab peninsula states, did not alter the relations between Britain and the Trucial States. London was the real power behind the puppet Abd al-Aziz in the new kingdom of Saudi Arabia, who controlled the southern and southeastern coasts of the peninsula. Furthermore, air routes were beginning to develop and the

Gulf's airfields along with those in Egypt, Palestine and Iraq had an important role in the Middle East.

[16] During the inter-war period, England focused its attention onto Egypt and Iraq (where oil fields were already being exploited). After World War II, relations among Arab countries changed. The League of Arab States was formed in 1945 by those countries which had some form of independence.

[17] At the beginning of the 1960s, the Middle East's oil deposits were known to be among the largest in the world. The United States joined Britain in keeping their control over the Gulf States, which received almost 100 per cent of their revenues from oil.

[18] The growing influence of Gamal Abdel Nasser in the Arab world led Britain to allow greater local participation in the governments of several states of the protectorate. In 1968, it decided to withdraw all its military forces from the region. That same year, the OPEAC - a branch of OPEC - was created, formed exclusively by oil-exporting Arab states.

[19] In 1971, upon Britain's withdrawal, Abu Dhabi began a large-scale exploitation of its oil wells. The clear establishment of borders within the territories became indispensable. Under British influence, the United Arab Emirates were created that year without participation of Qatar or Bahrain.

[20] Immediately after its formation, the new state had to face a conflict with Iran which, claiming historical rights, occupied the islands of Abu Mussa, Tunb al-Cubra and Tunb al-Sughra on the Strait of Hormuz. During the first decade, oil production rose mainly in the three most important emirates: Abu Dhabi with 79 per cent of the total, Dubai and Sharjah. National participation in the control of oil exploitation also grew.

[21] When the oil-exporting countries, through OPEC, decided in 1973 to raise the price of the barrel by 70 per cent and reduce supply by 5 per cent, a new era in the relations with the industrialized world began. The results of this policy were explosive. From the rock-bottom price of $1.50 a barrel of crude oil in the early 1960s, it rose to $10 in 1973

and to $34 between 1979 and 1980. The Emirates' annual growth rate in the 1970s was over 10 per cent due to oil revenues.

[22] This led to two immediate effects: a rapid growth of cities with state-of-the-art highways, oil pipelines and banks, and many immigrants attracted by the region's economic possibilities. Little was left of the ancient pursuits of fishing or collecting of pearls on the coast.

[23] The 1980s began with the Iran-Iraq war. Although the Emirates maintained an apparently neutral stand, they gave economic support to Iraq to avoid a possible 'Iranization' of the region. Once the conflict had ended, the Arab Emirates had become the Middle East's third biggest oil producer, after Saudi Arabia and Libya.

[24] Although since 1981 the Government has tried to develop other industrial fields, technological differences with other countries and a small domestic market limited possible industrial diversification which would reduce dependence on oil production.

[25] The UAE was a member of the Non-Aligned Movement and supported Palestinian claims. In late 1986, diplomatic relations were established with the Soviet Union and the People's Republic of Benin. In 1987, relations with Egypt were reinstated, broken after the Camp David agreements with Israel.

[26] During the Gulf War, the Emirates made financial contributions to the fight against Iraq. Once the conflict had ended, the policy to diversify the economy seemed to gather strength when the free port of Jabel Ali was opened to over 260 foreign companies.

[27] In March 1991, the Gulf Cooperation Council signed an agreement with the US to preserve security in the region, which included a common military strategy and mechanisms to prevent arms proliferation, among other items.

[28] In 1992, with Syrian mediation, Iran restricted the claims it had over the islands of the Strait of Hormuz, occupied since the 1970s. Tehran claimed sovereignty over Abu Mussa and has allowed expelled Arab residents to return. The conflict was, by pressure from the Emirates, under international arbitration.

[29] Waves of immigrants have formed a very heterogeneous population. According to 1993 figures, the Arab population in the country amounts to barely one quarter, half of it coming from other countries (mainly Egypt). The rest of

MATERNAL MORTALITY
1985/99

Per 100,000 live births
3

the population is made up by people from Bangladesh, Pakistan, Sri Lanka Iran and other Asian or African states.

[30] The influence of Islamic fundamentalism increased in the Emirates between 1993 and 1996. Sheikh Zayed, President of the Union, has often made it understood - as in a speech at the end of Ramadan in 1993 - that official circles were concerned about the spread of Muslim 'radicalism'. In February 1994, Zayed decided to extend Islamic law to many criminal cases which had previously been dealt with by civil courts.

[31] In 1995, new talks were held in an attempt to solve the dispute with Iran over the Strait of Hormuz islands, without any results. In 1997, in view of the US' threat of an armed intervention in Iraq, Sheik Zayed stated that the Iraqi people deserved a 'new chance'. Afterwards, he added that a measure of this type would be 'unacceptable and loathsome'.

[32] In the field of domestic policy, economic liberalization continued, leading, among other things, to the establishment of a free trade zone in 1998, in the city of Ra's al-Khaymah, being the first in the Middle East. In April 2000, the Emirates decided to reopen their embassy in Iraq, in spite of having broken relations with that country.

[33] The fall in oil prices was the main reason that GDP growth was reduced from 8 per cent in 2000 to 4 per cent in 2001. The country has tried to diversify its economic activity and, at present, sectors not related with oil - such as aluminum, tourism, telecommunications and aviation - make up two thirds of the GDP and 30 per cent of exports.

[34] As part of a policy of domestic 'embellishment', the Emirate of Ras al-Khaimah decided to fine companies whose advertisements in Arabic had spelling mistakes. The fine would amount to $135, which would be doubled in case of repetition of the mistake. A third mistake would result in the closure of the company.

[35] After an Iraqi boat with smuggled oil was shipwrecked in April 2002, the UAE decided to ban oil tankers belonging to 10 countries blacklisted by the International Maritime Organization from its territorial waters. ■

PROFILE

ENVIRONMENT

Located in the southeastern part of the Arabic peninsula, stretching from the Qatar peninsula toward the strait of Hormuz, the land is mostly desert with few oases and *wadis* (dry and rocky river beds). The coastal areas are very hilly lowlands with coral islands offshore and sand dunes. In this area lie most of the operating oilfields and, therefore, the biggest levels of coastal pollution. The country is one of the world's main oil producers.

SOCIETY

Peoples: Arabs 25 per cent, of which 13 per cent come from other Arab countries (mainly Egypt) and 12 per cent from the Emirates themselves. Population includes large immigrant component. From Bangladesh, India, Pakistan, Sri Lanka (45 per cent), Iran (17 per cent) and other Asian and African countries 8 per cent (1993). Europeans and US 5 per cent. 80 per cent live in Dubai, attracted by the oil wealth.
Religions: Muslim 94.9 per cent (Sunni 80 per cent, Shi'a 14.9 per cent); Christian 3.8 per cent; others 1.3 per cent.
Languages: Arabic (official); Persian, Hindi and Urdu are also spoken. English is spoken among immigrants and for business reasons.
Political Parties: No political parties or trade unions are allowed.

THE STATE

Official name: Daulat al-Imarat al-'Arabiya al-Muttahida.
Administrative divisions: 7 emirates: Abu Dhabi; Dubai; Sharjah; Ajman; Umm al-Qaiwain; Ras al-Khaimah and Fujairah. **Capital:** Abu Dhabi (Abu Zaby) 904,000 people (1999).
Other cities: Dubai 1,401,100 people; Ash-Shariqah 402,000; Al-'Ayn 283,800; Ajman 143,700 (2000).
Government: Parliamentary Republic with a president of the federation as a Head of State: Sheikh Zayed ibn Sultan al-Nahayan, Emir of Abu Dhabi, since December 1971. Vice President and Prime Minister: Sheikh Maktoum ibn Rashid al-Maktoum, Emir of Dubai, since November 1990. Unicameral Legislature: Federal National Council with 40 members appointed by the emirs.
National holiday: December 2, Independence Day and Proclamation of the Union (1971).
Armed forces: 64,500 (1997).

United Kingdom

Population: 59,657,000 (2002)
Land area: 240,880 SQ KM
Capital: London
Currency: Pound sterling
Language: English

United Kingdom

The first known inhabitants of what is now Britain were paleolithic hunters, following herds of wild animals. After the final ice age, agriculturalists began to settle on the island. Over thousands of years, these people and the many others who migrated from the continent, evolved increasingly complex social systems. By the final millennium BC, Britain was dominated by Celtic peoples who used iron tools and had extensive contact with the European mainland.

[2] In 44 AD the Romans invaded southern Britain. In 90 AD they created the province of Britannia, and founded London between 70 and 100 AD. In the early 5th century they abandoned the island, leaving it largely defenseless against the raids of Angles, Saxons and Jutes. These Germanic peoples pushed the Celts westwards, taking over the southern part of the island and establishing Anglo-Saxon kingdoms (see box 'The Celts').

[3] During the 5th century, the inhabitants of Ireland and Wales adopted Christianity. In the 7th century, the British church came under the power of Rome.

[4] During the 7th and 9th centuries Danish invaders overran the eastern part of England. In the 11th century, the Normans, led by William the Conqueror, invaded England and secured the throne. Successive Anglo-Norman kings maintained their power by establishing various forms of vassalage over the feudal lords.

[5] The prestige which Richard the Lion-Heart (1189-99), one of the leaders of the Third Crusade against the Muslims in the Holy Land (Middle East), had gained for the English Crown was lost under the reign of his successor, King John (1199-1216). Under John, England lost its French territories, and the barons, in alliance with the clergy, were able to restrict the power of the monarchy through the Magna Carta, signed in 1215.

[6] The Magna Carta laid the foundations for the British parliamentary system. It also marked the beginning of a continuous power struggle between the monarchy and the nobility. The growing power of the land-owning class and later the bourgeoisie eventually led to the consolidation of a parliamentary monarchy. The Welsh were taken under English control in 1382.

[7] Frequent dynastic conflicts, disputes over territories in France belonging to the English Crown, commercial rivalry between England and France in Flanders, and French aid to Scotland in its wars with England paved the way for the Hundred Years' War (1337-1453), which culminated in the loss of the English possessions on the continent. The Welsh came under English rule in 1382.

[8] The negative effects of the War increased the unpopularity of the monarchy which faced at the same time an anti-Papal movement led by the followers of Wycliffe (a precursor of Luther) and a peasant rebellion. The peasants, led by Wat Tyler, rose up against the payment of tribute and the power of the feudal lords. In 1381, Tyler and his followers managed to enter London and negotiate directly with the King. The Peasants' Revolt was unsuccessful however and Tyler was later executed.

[9] The period following the Hundred Years' War was dominated by a long struggle for control of the throne between the royal Houses of Lancaster and of York. This led to the War of the Roses which ended with the coming to power of the Welsh House of Tudor in 1485. The Tudor period is considered the beginning of the modern British state. One of the Tudor kings, Henry VIII (1509-47), broke away from the Church of Rome, confiscating all its monasteries and founding the Anglican Church. The desire to extend English authority and the religious Reformation to Ireland led to the subjugation of Ulster by Henry's successor Elizabeth I (1558-1603). Tudor involvement in Ireland laid the foundations of centuries of religious and political conflict in the country.

[10] Under the reign of Elizabeth I, poetry and the theatre flourished with playwrights such as Ben Jonson, Marlowe and Shakespeare. Industry and trade developed, and the country embarked upon its 'colonial adventure', the beginning of its future empire. After defeating the Spanish fleet - the 'Invincible Armada' - in 1588, the British Navy 'ruled the waves', with no other fleet capable of opposing it.

[11] British merchant ships involved in the slave trade, or laden with colonists or belonging to pirates and privateers sailed the oceans freely. Markets multiplied, demand grew rapidly, and producers were forced to seek new techniques in order to accelerate production. It was a prelude to the industrial revolution which was to arise in the country at the beginning of the 18th century.

[12] In 1603, the crowning of James I (James VI of Scotland) put an end to the independent Scottish monarchy. The religious intolerance of James' son Charles I, led to a Scottish uprising and increasing discontent in England. The deteriorating political situation led to the Puritans forming an army supported by Parliament; led by Oliver Cromwell, they defeated the royal forces in 1642. In 1649, Parliament sentenced the King to death and proclaimed Cromwell 'Lord Protector', establishing a republic known as the Commonwealth. After Cromwell's death, in 1658, the monarchy was restored with Charles II.

[13] The priorities of the new regime were the colonization of North America and trade with America, the Far East and the Mediterranean. The slave trade - the kidnapping, trafficking and selling of slaves from Africa to buyers in America and other places - which had started in the 16th century, became one of the main sources of income for the empire.

[14] The absolutism of Charles II's successor, James II and his espousal of Catholicism were opposed by the Protestant Parliament which deposed James through the 'Glorious Revolution'. Parliament invited the Dutch prince William of Orange to assume the English throne. William was forced to sign the Declaration of Rights (1689), limiting royal powers and guaranteeing the supremacy of Parliament.

[15] In this period John Locke summarized revolutionary ideals, proposing that people have basic natural rights: to property, life, liberty and personal security. Government, created by society to

protect these rights, must fulfil its mission; if it fails to do so, the people have the right to resist its authority.

[16] In 1707, the parliaments of Scotland and England were joined together, creating the United Kingdom of Great Britain. Britain intervened in the war of succession in Spain, obtaining Minorca, Gibraltar and Nova Scotia through the Treaty of Utrecht (1713). In 1765, increased taxes imposed by the Stamp Act triggered the rebellion and secession of the American colonies, which declared their independence in 1776.

[17] During this period, the two large political parties were formed: the Conservatives (Tories), representing the interests of the large landowners, and the Liberals (Whigs), representing the merchant class. The ideas forming the basis of economic liberalism were developed at this time by Adam Smith. The liberal doctrine provided the political ideology for British imperialism, which used the concept of 'free trade' as a justification for forcing open the ports and markets of the Third World, often with the use of naval force. Perhaps the most notorious examples of this were the Opium Wars fought against China in the mid-19th century.

[18] After the crushing of a nationalist rebellion in Ireland in 1798, the United Kingdom of Great Britain and Ireland was created in 1801 with the dissolution of the Irish Parliament.

[19] The 18th century gave rise to the agricultural 'revolution', which introduced important innovations in farming techniques, as well as major changes in land tenure. The large landowners enclosed their properties, eliminating communal lands which had hitherto been used by small farmers, and introducing a more capitalist agricultural economy.

[20] At the same time, the industrial revolution began, with the textile manufacturers being the first to confront the problem of meeting a growing demand for fabric overseas. The introduction of machinery changed the way in which work was done, and the medieval shop was replaced by the factory. On the heels of the textile industry came mining and metallurgy. The mechanization process was consolidated with the invention of the steam engine, the use of coal as a fuel and the substitution of first iron, then steel, for wood in construction.

[21] This period was characterized by population growth (up from 10,900,000 in 1801 to 21,000,000 in 1850), increasing demand and expanding trade, improvements in the transport system, capital accumulation, the creation of a vast colonial empire, scientific advances and the golden age of the bourgeoisie. Britain became the world's premier manufacturing nation. Its colonial policy helped to prevent competition for its factories; for example it established regulations which destroyed the Indian textile industry.

[22] The United Kingdom obtained new territories from its different wars with France, and its triumph over Napoleon at Waterloo (1815).

[23] One result of the industrial revolution was growing discontent among the rapidly increasing working class, due to low salaries, unhealthy working conditions, unsatisfactory housing, malnutrition, job insecurity and the long and tiring working days to which men, women and children were subjected. In many cases, popular uprisings were characterized by violence, and were met with equally violent repression.

[24] In the early stages of the industrial revolution, spontaneous movements arose, like the 'Luddites' - textile workers who destroyed machinery to prevent it from destroying their cottage industry. Trade unions began to appear later.

[25] In 1819 a demonstration in Manchester was ruthlessly put down, and repressive legislation followed, limiting the right of association and freedom of the press. Nevertheless, resistance movements continued their activity. One of the main movements of this period was the nationalist Irish Association led by Daniel O'Connell.

[26] The most important of the mass movements was the Chartist Movement, made up primarily of workers. It took its name from the People's Charter, published in 1838 at a mass assembly in Glasgow, Scotland. This movement brought a number of issues to the fore, both political - universal suffrage, use of the secret ballot, reform of voting registers - and social - better salaries and better working conditions. After its demonstrations and strikes, 'Chartism' faded away. However, it had a far-reaching influence and its grievances were subsequently taken up by some members of parliament.

[27] Robert Owen (1771-1858), considered to be the founder of socialism and the English co-operative movement, argued that the predominance of individual interests led to the impoverishment of the masses. From 1830 on, he devoted himself to the establishment of co-operatives and the organization of labor into trade unions.

[28] During the long reign of Queen Victoria (1837-1901), the traditional nobility strengthened its alliance with the industrial and mercantile bourgeoisie. Trade unions were legalized in 1871 and shortly afterwards some labor legislation was approved.

[29] Beginning in 1873, the rising population numbers led to a food shortage, making imports necessary. At the same time industry began to feel the competition from the US and Germany. Britain increased its imperial activities in Africa, Asia and Oceania, not only for economic reasons, but also because of the political ambition to build a great empire. The Boer or South African War (1899-1902), fought to secure control over southern Africa, was the most expensive regional conflict of the 19th century.

[30] The first quarter of the 20th century saw the birth of the women's liberation movement. The militancy of the suffragettes led to some women obtaining the right to vote in 1917. The most famous example of their militancy was the suicide of Emily Davison, who threw herself in front of the King's horse during a race in 1913.

[31] In Ireland, the majority Catholic population were stripped of their lands, restricted in their civil rights because of their religion, and deprived of their political autonomy. Millions emigrated, and political unrest periodically resulted in violent uprisings. Not until 1867 were the privileges of the Anglican Church eliminated; at the same time, measures were taken to improve the situation of the peasants. The 1916 Easter Rising in Dublin was ruthlessly put down by the British, but the Crown forces were unable to win the ensuing guerrilla war which began in 1918, and Britain finally granted Ireland independence in 1921. Six

PROFILE

ENVIRONMENT

The country consists of Britain (England, Scotland, Wales and Northern Ireland) and several smaller islands. The Pennines, a low mountain range, run down the northern center of England. The Grampian mountains are located in Scotland and the Cambrian mountains in Wales. The largest plains are in the southeast, around London. The climate is temperate. Farming is highly mechanized and is now a subsidiary activity. The service industry, especially insurance, finance and tourism are big income earners. The huge coal and iron ore deposits, which made the Industrial Revolution possible, have nearly run out, but gas and oil finds in the North Sea turned the UK into an exporter of these products. The country is very industrialized and environmental pollution, especially air pollution, poses a serious problem. The nuclear reprocessing plant at Seascale in the north west of England appeared to be linked to the high incidence of leukemia in surrounding areas.

SOCIETY

Peoples: English, Scots, Welsh and Irish. Minorities including Pakistanis, Indians, Bangladeshis and Afro-Caribbean people form about 6 per cent of the population. **Religions:** Protestant, 53.4 per cent (Anglican 43.5 per cent; Presbyterian 4.5 per cent; Methodist 2.2 per cent); Roman Catholic 9.8 per cent; Orthodox 1 per cent; other Christians 1.7 per cent); Muslim 2.6 per cent; Hindu 0.6 per cent, Sikh 0.5 per cent; Jewish 0.5 per cent; other/no religion 29.9 per cent. **Languages:** English (official), Welsh, Gaelic and the languages of various immigrant groups. **Political Parties:** Labor Party (social democrat), led by Tony Blair, in governement. Conservative Party, center-right; Liberal Democrat Party, center-left; Green Party; British National Party (extreme right); National Front (extreme right); Scottish Nationalist Party; Plaid Cymru (Welsh nationalist party). In Northern Ireland, Ulster Unionist Party (conservative); Social Democratic and Labor Party (SDLP), liberal-left; Democratic Unionist Party (DUP), ultra conservative; Sinn Féin (Irish nationalist) gained two seats in the last elections. **Social Organizations:** The Trade Union Congress has 12 million members. Scottish Crofters Union; Reclaim the Streets, a direct action citizen group.

THE STATE

Official Name: United Kingdom of Great Britain and Northern Ireland. **Administrative Divisions:** 39 Counties and 7 Metropolitan Districts. **Capital:** London 7,639,000 people (1999). **Other cities:** Birmingham 2,642,300 people; Leeds 1,502,100; Glasgow 1,083,600; Sheffield 1,106,400; Bristol 615,100; Liverpool 468,300 (2000). **Government:** Constitutional parliamentary monarchy. Elizabeth II, Queen and Head of State since February 1952. Tony Blair, Prime Minister since May 1997, re-elected in 2001. **Bicameral Legislature:** the House of Commons, with 659 members elected for a five-year term, and the unelected House of Lords, with 675 members, 557 life peers and 118 hereditary members (June 2001). **National Holiday:** Second Saturday in June, Queen Elizabeth II's birthday (1926). **Armed Forces:** 213,800 (1996). **Dependencies:** Anguilla, Bermuda, Gibraltar (contested by Spain), the Falkland Islands/Malvinas (contested by Argentina), British Virgin Islands, Montserrat, Cayman Islands, Channel Islands, Isle of Man, Turks and Caicos, St Helena, British Territories in the Indian Ocean (Mauritius) and Pitcairn (Oceania).

counties in the north-east, with Protestant majorities, remained under British control with a devolved administration in Belfast.

32 Economic and political rivalry between the European powers led to the outbreak of World War I (1914-18). The Central Powers of Austro-Hungary and Germany, joined subsequently by Turkey and Bulgaria, fought against the Allied powers of France, Britain, Russia, Serbia and Belgium, with Italy, Japan, Portugal, Romania, the United States and Greece joining during the course of the War.

33 Despite its victory, Britain emerged from the War weakened. It had invested $40 billion in military expenditure, mobilized 7,500,000 troops, suffered a loss of 1,200,000 soldiers and acquired an enormous foreign debt. The deep economic depression in the post-War years led to renewed unrest among workers, which reached its height in the General Strike of 1926. The Conservative Government declared the strike illegal, but did not take any measures to revive British industry. In the elections of 1929, the Labor Party (formed in 1924) came to power for the first time.

34 The UK supported the US proposal to create the League of Nations. In 1931, the British Community of Nations (Commonwealth) was established under the Statute of Westminster. This formally recognized the independence of Canada, Australia, New Zealand and South Africa.

35 On September 1 1939, Germany invaded Poland and two days later Britain declared war on Germany, marking the beginning of its participation in World War II (1939-45). In May 1940 a coalition cabinet was formed, with Winston Churchill as Prime Minister. From 1939 to 1941, Britain and France were ranged against Germany which was joined by Italy in 1940. Hungary, Romania, Bulgaria and Yugoslavia participated in the war as 'lesser' allies of the Nazis.

36 In 1941, the Soviet Union, Japan and the US entered the conflict. On May 8 1945, Germany surrendered. The UK, US and the USSR emerged as the major victors from the war. However, the British Empire was eclipsed by the rising power of the US, which became the undisputed economic, technological and military leader.

37 In May 1945, the Labor Government of Clement Attlee, who won the elections with the slogan 'We won the war, now we will win the peace', nationalized the coal mines, the Bank of England and the iron and steel industries.

38 Pakistan was formed and India became independent in 1947, although both remained members of

the British Commonwealth. During the following decade, most of Britain's overseas colonies obtained their independence. Britain was a founder member of NATO in 1949.

39 The Franco-British military intervention in the Suez Canal Zone in 1956, which failed due to a lack of US support, was met by strong criticism from both inside and outside Britain (see Egypt). The following year, the UK detonated its first hydrogen bomb in the Pacific Ocean.

40 The general election of 1964 was won by the Labor Party under the leadership of Harold Wilson. His government faced serious problems, such as the declaration of independence from Southern Rhodesia (today Zimbabwe), and the severing of diplomatic relations with nine other African countries.

41 In 1967, having been denied entry to the Common Market, and faced with rapidly increasing unemployment, Wilson withdrew British troops from South Yemen, evacuated all bases east of Suez except for Hong Kong, discontinued arms purchases from the US and implemented a savage austerity budget.

42 In Northern Ireland in 1969, the latent conflict erupted. A number of people were killed and wounded in riots between Catholics and Protestants. The Catholics demanded equal political rights, and better access to housing, schools and social security. The Protestant-controlled Northern Irish Government responded by sending in their armed police reserves against the Catholic demonstrators. The British Government sent in their troops to separate the two sides and took control of police and reserve forces away from the Belfast Government.

43 In August 1971, Prime Minister of Northern Ireland Brian Faulkner opened internment camps and authorized the detention of suspects without trial. Protests against these measures resulted in more than 25 deaths. On January 30 1972, 'Bloody Sunday', British soldiers opened fire on a peaceful protest march in Derry (Londonderry), killing 13 Catholics and injuring hundreds more. The Irish Republican Army (IRA) responded with numerous assassinations.

44 In March 1973, the people of Northern Ireland voted in a referendum to remain within the U.K. rather than join a united Ireland. There was a high abstention rate of 41.4 per cent, and the Protestant majority voted to stay in the UK.

45 In the 1970s, social conflict in Britain intensified, and Edward Heath's Conservative Government (1970-1974) was faced with strikes in

key public enterprises. The dockers, coal miners and railway workers all went on strike. Inability to deal with this labor unrest led to his resignation in 1974, and the Labor Party won the following elections. Amid a complex situation on the domestic front, in January 1973 a majority of the electorate voted in favor of entering the EEC. A policy of progressive integration with Europe began, as well as a search for new markets for ailing British industry.

46 A new divorce law was passed in 1975. The same year, feminists campaigned successfully against restrictions being added to the 1967 abortion law.

47 In 1979, voters in Scotland and Wales turned down autonomy for their regions in referenda organized by James Callaghan's Labor Government.

48 In May of that year, after the 'winter of discontent' characterized by strikes, the Conservative Party won the election, with Margaret Thatcher as its leader. The new Prime Minister brought in a severe monetarist policy to bring down inflation. She began to reverse the nationalization process carried out under Labor, and returned to a free market policy.

49 In 1981, a group of IRA prisoners began a hunger strike as part of their campaign to win recognition as political prisoners. The Government refused to accept the prisoners' demands. The strike resulted in 12 deaths.

50 In April 1982, Thatcher sent a Royal Navy force, including aircraft carriers and nuclear submarines, to the Malvinas islands (Falklands) which had been occupied by troops from the military junta in Argentina. After 45 days of fighting the British recovered the islands for the Crown (see Argentina).

51 In October 1983, the British Government decided to withdraw its troops from Belize. The following year, in agreement with a treaty dating back to the First Opium War, Britain ceded sovereignty over Hong Kong to the People's Republic of China, with effect from June 1997.

52 During the Thatcher administration, the trade union movement suffered serious setbacks, with the loss of local affiliates in the industrial sector, itself in decline. The 1984/85 miners' strike culminated in defeat for the union after a year of violent internal strife and confrontation with the police.

53 In 1987, Thatcher was elected to her third consecutive term in office. She continued her policies as before: radical economic liberalization, privatization of state corporations, and opposition to union demands. In foreign affairs, Britain opposed greater European

Community integration and continued to align itself closely with the US.

54 In mid-1989, after several years of growth, inflation reached high levels, unemployment continued to rise steeply, productive investments fell and the balance of payments deficit grew. At the same time, the introduction of a new Poll Tax and other projected reforms produced strong popular resistance.

55 In February 1990, the UK and Argentina renewed diplomatic relations and their representatives met in Madrid to negotiate the issue of the return of the Malvinas/Falklands.

56 In November 1990 Thatcher was replaced as head of the Government and Tory leader by her former minister, John Major. On taking office, Major declared himself to be in favor of capitalism with a human face, thus setting himself apart from the 'Iron Lady's' (Thatcher) harsh capitalism.

57 In 1991, Major announced that the Poll Tax would be replaced. However, Major continued most of Thatcher's reforms, including that of the health system and the selling-off of nationalized industries such as the railways.

58 In European affairs, the Prime Minister distanced himself from his predecessor. In 1991, London gave its backing to European agreements on monetary union. However, the fidelity which British diplomacy showed towards the US remained unaltered, as proven by British aid to the US in the Gulf War.

59 The Government managed to bring down inflation (which dropped from 10 per cent to 3.8 per cent between 1990 and 1991) and interest rates (which decreased from 15 per cent to 9.5 per cent), but economic activity remained stagnant. In 1991, industrial production declined and numerous small businesses failed. Unemployment continued to rise (over 9 per cent by late 1991), and now affected white-collar workers and professionals, groups which had supported Thatcher's neo-liberal policies.

60 Major's personal popularity (the highest in British history since Winston Churchill) did not translate itself into a similar level of support for his party. In the local elections

held at the end of April 1991, the Tories lost 800 council seats and several of its traditional districts, while Labor gained more than 400 council seats. In these elections, the Liberal Democratic Party also made important gains.

[61] From 1993 the Conservatives began to suffer a series of electoral defeats in local by elections against a backdrop of economic recession and three million unemployed. On December 15, London signed a joint declaration with Dublin on Northern Ireland, paving the way for peace talks (see Ireland). A series of scandals in 1994, like the illegal funding of a dam in Malaysia, further sullied the Tory image. Meanwhile, Parliament lowered the age of consent for homosexuals from 21 to 18, ignoring calls to match the legal age of 16 for heterosexual sex.

[62] Successive Labor local election victories in 1996 heralded the general election victory in May 1997, with Tony Blair becoming Prime Minister. The resounding defeat of the Conservatives, who took 30 per cent of the vote to Labor's 43.1 (an unprecedented rate this century) forced changes to the party leadership.

[63] Referenda in Wales and Scotland in 1997 supported greater devolution to the regions. In early 1998, talks on Northern Ireland brought a new peace plan. A referendum in Northern Ireland in May gave 70 per cent support for the plan. In London, that same month, people gave their approval for direct election to a new post, the Lord Mayor of London.

[64] Under the 'Good Friday' agreements, Northern Ireland would have its own legislative assembly, directly elected by the population, as in Wales and Scotland. A referendum in Ireland put an end to territorial claims over the North now that the people of Ulster were to be given a choice over their future. The nomination of Northern Ireland MPs David Trimble (Ulster Unionist) and John Hume (Social Democratic and Labor Party, sympathetic to the nationalists) for the Nobel Peace Prize in October 1998 helped create a feeling of a common goal between Protestant and Catholic communities.

[65] The Spanish courts called for Scotland Yard to arrest General Augusto Pinochet - the former Chilean dictator - as he recovered from a back operation in hospital in London. After a year and a half of legal wrangling, Pinochet was freed. Home Secretary Jack Straw said Pinochet's poor health meant he would be unable to stand the strain of extradition to Spain and the ensuing trial.

[66] During 1999 the Northern Irish unionist and nationalist parties made commitments on joint government, which culminated with the installation of the executive in December that year. The two-community cabinet operated under the leadership of David Trimble as Prime Minister, with the participation of Sinn Féin (nationalist). Gerry Adams and Martin McGuinness, of Sinn Féin, sat on the executive until February 2000 when Dr Ian Paisley's Democratic Unionist Party (DUP) withdrew, and the administration was suspended. Sovereignty, which had been devolved to the province in December, returned to London.

[67] Internal elections for Labor's candidate as Lord Mayor of London ended in a split between Ken Livingstone, the most popular candidate according to the surveys, and Tony Blair's preferred candidate, Frank Dobson. Livingstone - representative of the old Labor left - accused Blair and his followers of implementing an anti-democratic voting system that eliminated the 'one person, one vote' principle and weighed against his candidacy. The Labor Party finally expelled Livingstone in March 2000, but despite that he was elected Mayor in May 2000.

[68] A UNICEF report published in September revealed that one in three British children live in poverty. These figures rated the UK 20th out of the 23 countries examined by the report and implied that five million children and their families could not satisfy their basic needs. A year ago, the British Government had promised that 700,000 of the poorest children would have more money for better homes, clothes and food within two years.

[69] In February 2001 there was an outbreak of foot and mouth disease, the worst ever. The general election was postponed from May until June. Labor won again, with 41 per cent of the vote to the Conservatives' 32 per cent.

[70] By October, there were 2,030 outbreaks of foot and mouth disease in Britain. Slaughter had been used to stop the spread, and 3,914,000 animals were killed. This epidemic compounded the effects of the 'mad cow disease' (Bovine Spongiform Encephalopathy - BSE) from 1986 which peaked in 1996 and forced the health authorities to kill four and a half million cows. Exports to Europe were banned. BSE was thought to be transmitted through animal feed made from the remains of infected livestock, probably fed to cattle since the seventies. Creutzfeld Jakobs Disease, the human variant of BSE, has killed around 80 people so far. Exports of British beef dropped dramatically. Tourism was badly hit by the foot and mouth outbreak, as vast areas of the countryside were closed.

[71] Following the September 2001 attacks on Washington and New York, Britain offered support for the US-launched anti-terrorist campaign. Blair spearheaded the US offensive on Afghanistan, under the application of Article 5 of the NATO members' mutual defense clause, which stated that member states must support another member who comes under attack. Similarly, in March 2002, Blair declared jointly with US vice-president Dick Cheney that Iraq was a threat to world stability, making it a possible for Britain to support Washington in attacks on Iraq or Saddam Hussein - the Iraqi leader.

[72] In March 2002, Elizabeth the Queen Mother - mother of Queen Elizabeth II - died aged 101. She had gained wide popularity during World War II, mainly due to her determination to stay in London through the Nazi bombardment.

[73] In the May 2002 local elections, the far-right British National Party gained three seats, in Burnley and its overall showing was improved. The Conservatives took 34 per cent and Labor 32 per cent, with Liberal Democrats taking 27 per cent. Even though 5,889 seats had been up for election, BNP leader Nick Griffin saw the result as a 'triumph' and denied the party was using urban racial tension to its benefit, although he confirmed his Party's objective was to keep Britain white. Although local councils have lost power, they still manage education, refuse collection, roads and highways, libraries, leisure facilities, lighting, building regulations among others.

[74] Immigration and the issue of asylum-seekers continued to be at the forefront of national politics, with Labour wanting to tighten the rules. Campaigners protested over proposals to create new centers for immigrants whose applications were being processed; such places being seen as detention centers.

[75] In July 2002, Foreign Secretary Jack Straw announced that the UK was to supply parts to the US for its F-16 jet fighters destined for Israel. This outraged activists who saw the move as another nail in the coffin of Labour's so-called 'ethical' foreign policy. They also feared that the Government would give support to President Bush's plans to renew the attacks on Iraq.

[76] Also in that month, chancellor Gordon Brown announced a $95.93 billion package of new public spending over the next three years, including increases for housing, education and local government. The international aid budget saw a 35 per cent increase.

[77] In September, the US, backed by Britain, geared up for fresh attacks on Iraq. ■

STATISTICS

DEMOGRAPHY
Population: 59,657,000 (2002)
Annual growth: 0.3 % (1985-2000)
Estimates for year 2015: 60,566,000 (2000)
Annual growth to year 2015: 0.1 % (2000)
Urban population: 89.5 % (2000)
Urban growth: 0.5 % (2000)
Children per woman: 1.7 (2000)

HEALTH
Life expectancy at birth: 78 years (2000-2005)
male: 76 years (2000-2005)
female: 81 years (2000-2005)
Maternal mortality: 7 per 100,000 live births (1985/99)
Infant mortality: 6 per 1,000 (2000)
Under-5 child mortality: 6 per 1,000 (2000)
Daily calorie supply: 3,318 per capita (1999)
Safe water: 100 % (2000)

EDUCATION
School enrolment (net):
Primary total: 98 % (1994/2000)
male: 97 % (1995/99)
female: 98 % (1995/99)
Secondary (gross):
male: 120 % (1995/97)
female: 139 % (1995/97)
Tertiary (gross): 58 % (1998)
Primary school teachers: one for every 19 pupils (1998)

COMMUNICATIONS
329 newspapers (1996), 1,432 radios (1997), 1 TV set (2000) and 589 main telephone lines (2000) per 1,000 people
Books: 164 new titles per 100,000 people (1992/94)

ECONOMY
Per capita, GDP: $ 23,509 (2000)
Annual growth: 2.7 % (2000)
Annual inflation: 2.9 % (2000)
Consumer price index: 114.2 (2000)
Currency: 0.7 pounds sterling = $ 1 (03/2002)
Cereal imports: 3,128,470 metric tons (2000)
Food import dependency: 8 % (2000)
Fertilizer use: 3,458 kg per ha (1999)
Exports: $ 384,833 million (2000)
Imports: $ 411,853 million (2000)

ENERGY
Consumption: 3,930.1 Kgs of oil equivalent per capita yearly (1998); -22.3 % imported (1999)

HDI (ranking/value): 14 / 0.923 (1999)

United States

Population:	288,530,000 (2002)
Land area:	9,158,960 SQ KM
Capital:	Washington DC
Currency:	Dollar
Language:	English

United States

The continental territory occupied by the United States was inhabited 30,000 years before the arrival of the Europeans by peoples who came from the northwest, probably from Asia across the Bering Strait. Among the most significant were those who became the Apache, Arapaho, Cherokee, Cheyenne, Chippewa, Crow, Comanche, Hopi, Iroquois, Lakota, Navajo, Nez Percé, Oglala Sioux, Pawnee, Pueblo, Seminole, Shawnee, Shoshone and the Ute native Americans.

[2] In the deserts and on the plains, they were primarily hunters and gatherers, living in small tribes with a simple social structure. Where the lands were more fertile, agriculture developed and relatively large towns were established. The first and largest of these, Cahokia, close to what is now St Louis, is thought to have had a population of 40,000 in the year 1000 AD.

[3] The religious beliefs of these peoples were rooted in a cosmic conception of the Earth - that as it belongs to the Universe, it belongs to no one. The Earth is considered a living being, with both material and spiritual powers. American Indian religious leaders or shamans have the power to call upon the forces of this sacred Universe, either to foretell the future, to lead their people, or to heal the sick.

[4] The first Europeans to come to America were Viking sailors from Greenland, but they did not settle permanently in the region. After the voyage of Christopher Columbus in 1492, the Spaniards established the colonies of St Augustine in Florida, and Santa Fe in New Mexico; in addition, they explored both Texas

and California. After the Spanish came the British, French and Dutch, all bent on territorial conquest.

[5] In 1540, Hernando De Soto wrote in his journals of having found among the Cherokee an advanced agricultural society, linked to the peoples of the Ohio, the Mississippi and even the Aztecs. Europeans introduced firearms, which significantly altered life among the American peoples, and ultimately established domination by white people.

[6] There were an estimated 1,500,000 Native Americans in the 15th century. Two centuries later, the large plantations of the South began buying slaves, and by 1760 there was a total of 90,000 Africans - twice the number of whites in that part of the country. The total number of British settlers on the Atlantic coast at the time was 300,000, far outnumbering the French in the Mississippi Valley.

[7] Most British immigrants left their country fleeing from poverty, religious persecution and political

instability. Yet the birth of the colonies was marked by war against the native peoples, whose culture and way of life were systematically destroyed, and against other European colonists. By 1733, there were 13 English colonies, whose chief economic activities were agriculture, fishing and trade.

[8] In 1763, with the 17th and 18th century European imperial wars behind them, France ceded its colonies east of the Mississippi to Britain, while its possessions west of that river went to Spain.

[9] War with England broke out in 1775. The Declaration of Independence, which marked the birth of the United States, was signed on July 4 1776. The war continued, but in the end the United States won (aided by its ally, France), with American sovereignty finally being recognized by England in 1783.

[10] In 1787, the Philadelphia Constitutional Convention drew up the first federal constitution, which

went into effect the following year. George Washington, commander of the Continental Army, was elected President in April 1789. In 1791, ten amendments dealing with individual freedoms and 'states rights' were added to the original constitution.

[11] The prime attraction of the West was the possibility of acquiring land and wealth without previous ownership, simply by staking a claim. The presidents in power at the time justified this 'Empire of Freedom': it was the United States 'Manifest Destiny' to occupy the entire continent, in order to become a great nation.

[12] In 1803, the Louisiana purchase (from the French) doubled the size of the Union. Between 1810 and 1819, the US went to war against Spain in order to annex Florida. In 1836, the Texans rebelled against Mexico and set up a republic, subsequently joining the Union in 1845. The United States declared war on Mexico, taking over vast areas of Mexican territory. California became a state in 1850, and Oregon in 1853.

[13] Westward expansion meant not only a change of 'ownership', but also still another tragedy for the original inhabitants of the region, decimated by successive waves of land and gold fever. Treaties were signed then ignored as thousands of new settlers poured onto native lands. On occasion new treaties were imposed by force. In 1838, 14,000 Cherokee people were forced off their lands by the army, 4,000 perishing in a march to their new territory.

[14] The Civil War (or War of Secession),from 1861-65 revolved around the question of the preservation of slavery, but it was in fact a struggle between the two economic systems prevailing in the country. While the industrial North sought to free an important source of labor and protect the domestic market, the slave-owning and agricultural South's interest was to maintain its cheap force of labor and continue to enjoy free access to foreign markets.

[15] In 1850, of the six million inhabitants of European origin in the South, only 345,525 were slave owners. However, most whites were pro-slavery, remembering the slave rebellions which had taken place in

WORKERS

2000

UNEMPLOYMENT: 4%
LABOR FORCE AS % OF TOTAL:

■ FEMALE: 46%   ■ MALE: 54%

1994/97

EMPLOYMENT DISTRIBUTION:

F
M

■ SERVICES   F: 85%   M: 63%
■ INDUSTRY   F: 13%   M: 34%
■ AGRICULTURE F: 1%   M: 4%

LAND USE

DEFORESTATION: 0.3% annual (1990/95)

1993

■ FOREST & WOODLAND: 29.2%
■ ARABLE: 18.9%
■ OTHER: 51.9%

PUBLIC EXPENDITURE

1999

80

60 53.5%

40

20 15.7%

0
DEFENSE   SOCIAL

South Carolina (1822) and Virginia (1800 and 1831).

[16] The election of Abraham Lincoln in 1860 precipitated a conflict: before he had even been inaugurated as president, the Southern states seceded. Committed to preserving the Union, and with a superior industrial base and superior weapons, the North finally triumphed over the South in the Civil War, although a million people were killed on both sides. Slavery was abolished, but ill-feeling between the two regions continued to exist.

[17] After the War, the Native Americans of the Great Plains, especially the Sioux, launched repeated wars of defense. The treaties of 1851 and 1868, which had granted them sovereignty over their tribal lands were ignored after the discovery of gold in the area. The gradual occupation of their territory was completed by 1890, when the Sioux were defeated for the last time.

[18] In the 1880s, the remaining Native Americans were confined to reservations most of which were on arid, barren lands. Years later, when uranium, coal, oil, natural gas and other minerals were discovered on some of the reservations, mining companies became interested in developing these mineral resources. This triggered the question of 'rights' to the land on which the reservations were located.

[19] Between 1870 and 1920, the population of the United States grew from 38 to 106 million, and the number of states increased from 37 to 48. It was a period of rapid capitalist expansion, triggered by the growth of the railroads as huge companies. By the turn of the century, what had been essentially an agrarian country had been transformed into an industrial society.

[20] By the end of the 19th century, a two-party system of government had been established, with the Republican and Democratic parties alternately in power. Despite their different traditions, both parties have historically maintained a large degree of consensus on major national and international issues, a fact which led to a highly coherent foreign policy. The long struggle for women's suffrage began in 1889, being achieved in 1920.

[21] Having dealt with its principal domestic problems, the US ventured onto the international scene. The Spanish-American War in 1898, fought in Cuba and the Philippines, marked the beginning of a US imperial era. The occupation of Panama, and subsequent construction of the Panama Canal and a series of military bases turned Central America - an area of 'vital security interest' to the US - into a kind of protectorate.

[22] The US justified its interventions with the Monroe Doctrine, and former-President Monroe's slogan 'America for the Americans'. France was forced to withdraw its troops from Mexico (where they were protecting Emperor Maximilian) and Britain had to drop a territorial dispute with Venezuela. In 1890, the first Pan-American conference was held, paving the way for the inter-American system later set up.

[23] When World War I broke out in 1914, the United States declared its neutrality. However, in 1917 it declared war on Germany, Austria and Turkey. In 1918, President Woodrow Wilson was one of the architects of the Treaty of Versailles, which established the framework for a new European peace. However, in 1920 US entry into the League of Nations was blocked by Congress.

[24] The United States emerged from the War more powerful than ever, but the Great Crash on Wall Street (the US Stock Exchange) shook the country in 1929. In its wake, many banks failed, industry and trade were severely affected and unemployment figures rose to 11 million. Under Franklin Roosevelt's presidency (1933-45), the Government managed to bring the financial crisis under control.

[25] While Europe headed steadily toward another war, Congress passed a law in 1935 proclaiming US neutrality. However, when war broke out, Roosevelt introduced amendments to that law in order to allow arms shipments to France and Britain. In 1941, the Japanese attack on the US military base at Pearl Harbor in Hawaii precipitated the US entry into the World War II.

[26] The War acted as a dynamo for the entire American economy. With 15 million Americans at the Front, employment grew from 45,500,000 to 53,000,000, as workers churned out more supplies and arms for the war effort. To meet the demand for workers, six million people migrated from the countryside to the cities. On the labor front, in spite of a labor 'truce' in support of the war effort, there were 15,000 strikes during the War, a fact which led Congress to pass a law limiting the right to strike.

[27] With Germany defeated on the European front, President Harry Truman (who had assumed the presidency upon Roosevel's death) unleashed the United States' new military might upon Japan. On August 6 and 9, 1945 he gave the order for history's first atomic bombs to be dropped on the cities of Hiroshima and Nagasaki, wiping them out. That same year, at Yalta and Potsdam, Britain, the United States and the Soviet Union spelled out the terms for peace, and divided up the areas which would come under their respective spheres of influence.

[28] Truman presided over the opening of the United Nations in 1945, and was re-elected President in 1948. As the number one Western power, the US was in firm opposition to the USSR and its communist system. Soon a 'Cold War' developed as the two superpowers confronted each other in Eastern Europe and jousted for allies throughout the Third World. Within this framework, the Inter-American Treaty of Reciprocal Assistance was signed, and the North Atlantic Treaty Organization (NATO) was created.

PROFILE

ENVIRONMENT

There are four geo-economic regions. The East includes New England, the Appalachian Mountains and part of the Great Lakes and the Atlantic coast, a sedimentary plain which stretches from the mouth of the Hudson River to the peninsula of Florida. To the west are the Appalachian mountains, where mineral deposits (iron ore and coal) abound. This is the most densely populated and industrialized area, where the country's largest steel plants are located. A highly technological agriculture provides food for the large cities. The Midwest stretches from the western shores of Lake Erie to the Rocky Mountains, also including the middle Mississippi. Formed by the grasslands of the central plain, the Midwest is the country's largest agricultural area; horticulture and milk production predominate in the north, while wheat, corn and other cereals are cultivated in the south, side by side with cattle ranches where oxen and pigs are raised. Major industrial centers are located near the Great Lakes, near the area's agricultural production and large iron ore and coal deposits. The South is a subtropical flatland area, comprising the south of the Mississippi plain, the peninsula of Florida, Texas and Oklahoma. Large plantations, (cotton, sugarcane, rice) predominate here, while there is extensive cattle-raising in Texas. The region is also rich in mineral deposits (oil, coal, aluminum, etc.). The West is a mountainous, mineral-rich area (oil, copper, lead, zinc). A sizeable horticultural production exists along the fertile valleys of the Sacramento and San Joaquin rivers in California. Large industrial centers are located along the Pacific coast. In addition, the US has two states outside its original contiguous area: Alaska, on the continent's northwest where Mt McKinley is located (Mt 'Denali', in the indigenous Atabasco language), the highest peak in North America, and Hawaii, an archipelago in the Pacific Ocean. The US has desertification and deforestation problems and is the main producer of greenhouse gases - principally carbon dioxide - which are responsible for the global warming.

SOCIETY

Peoples: There are 1.9 million Native Americans, half of whom live in 300 reservations. The white population came originally from immigrant Europeans including English, Germans, Irish, Russian and Italian, now mixed with immigrants from all parts of the world. The largest minorities are of African origin, 11 per cent of the total population; Hispanic 10 per cent; and Asian 8 per cent. **Religions:** There is a Protestant majority (58 per cent), which encompasses several denominations. There are also a considerable number of Catholics (21 per cent). Other Christians 6.4 per cent; Jewish 2 per cent; Muslims 2 per cent. **Languages:** English; Spanish; Native American languages and those of each immigrant group. **Political Parties:** Republican Party, Democratic Party, Green Party, Reform Party, Libertarian Party (right-wing); other local/state parties. **Social Organizations:** The American Federation of Labor-Congress of Industrial Organizations (AFL-CIO) is the country's largest workers' organization, with 13,500,000 members. Teamsters Union (second-largest union); National Association for the Advancement of Colored People (NAAACP); Sierra Club (environmentalist); American Civil Liberties Union (ACLU). Many of the country's rural laborers, especially those of Mexican origin, are organized in the United Farm Workers (UFW) labor union, founded by César Chávez.

THE STATE

Official Name: United States of America.
Administrative Divisions: Federal State, 50 States and 1 Federal District, Columbia. **Capital:** Washington, DC 3,888,000 people (1999).
Other cities: Los Angeles 16,401,600 people; New York 8,056,200; Houston 4,596,000; Chicago 2,915,500; Philadelphia 1,520,300 (2000).
Government: Presidential government, federal system (50 states). George W Bush, President since January 2001. There is a bicameral Congress: the House of Representatives, with 435 members, and the Senate, with 100 members. **National Holiday:** July 4, Independence (1776). **Armed Forces:** 1,547,300 (1995). **Other:** 68,000 Civil Air Control.

²⁹ The US took it upon itself to safeguard the global capitalist system, with the support of such international institutions as the World Bank and the IMF, as well as armed intervention by its troops all around the world.

³⁰ In 1952, General Dwight Eisenhower, commander-in-chief of American forces in Europe during the War and head of NATO, was elected President. The events of this period - the Korean War (1950-53), the partition of Germany, popular uprisings in Poland and Hungary, the delicate balance of nuclear weapons between the superpowers and the space race - all served to maintain the tension in US-Soviet relations. In 1960, a summit meeting between Eisenhower and Soviet leader Khruschev was cancelled off when an American U-2 spy plane flying over Soviet territory was brought down.

³¹ In the 1950s, the US economy grew steadily, as did its population, leading to a sense of over-all prosperity and contentment. The 'American way of life' was exported to the rest of the world, hand-in-hand with American investments abroad. In 1956, the US offered South Vietnam's anti-communist puppet government military support. Labor conflict increased; in 1959, Congress passed a law aimed at curbing corruption in the labor unions.

³² The election of Democratic presidential candidate John F Kennedy in 1960 reflected the US people's desire for relief from domestic and foreign tensions. However, the President supported the abortive Bay of Pigs invasion of Cuba in 1961, initiated the economic blockade of Cuba and presided over the Cuban Missile Crisis. In 1963, the assassination of President Kennedy in Dallas, Texas, underscored the violence in American society.

³³ With regard to Latin America, President Kennedy had launched the Alliance for Progress in Uruguay in 1961, in an attempt to stem the influence of the Cuban Revolution throughout the hemisphere. However, the funds earmarked for this project were insufficient to effect real change, serving merely to expose the region's problems. Faced with growing guerrilla activity in the region, the United States decided to support official regional armies.

³⁴ Following the assassination of President Kennedy in 1963, Lyndon Johnson, also Democrat, was elected in 1964 and launched the 'Great Society'. However, the country was brought face to face with new frustrations. The war in Vietnam escalated and then became a stalemate, causing a wave of protests throughout the US. This led the Government to initiate a withdrawal from Vietnam, a blow to the American psyche. Racial segregation led to increasing confrontation. In 1968, violent protests in black neighborhoods in urban areas were sparked off by the assassination of black Civil Rights leader, Dr Martin Luther King.

³⁵ That same year, the American Indian Movement (AIM) was founded by two Chippewa leaders. In 1969, AIM occupied the abandoned prison on Alcatraz Island in San Francisco to call attention to its demands and denounce the mistreatment of their people, which was followed by similar actions elsewhere in the country.

³⁶ Richard Nixon was re-elected President in 1972 and visited Moscow and Beijing in 1973. In 1974, he signed the final withdrawal of US troops from Vietnam but was forced to resign that same year, after the discovery that Republicans had spied on Democrat election campaign headquarters located in the Watergate Hotel.

³⁷ In 1978, thousands of Native Americans demanding action on their grievances, carried out 'The Longest March', descending on Washington DC from the official 'Indian reservations' throughout the country. In 1982, AIM occupied the Black Hills in South Dakota, a site sacred to the Sioux, to protest against the mining operations of some 30 multinational companies, in that area.

³⁸ In the post-war period, the economy expanded as American transnational companies spread around the world. These companies included Ford and General Motors (with more than a million workers combined), the oil companies Exxon and Mobil Oil, International Business Machine (IBM), ITT, General Electric and Philip Morris, amongst others.

³⁹ The conservative Republican administration of Ronald Reagan (1980-88) reduced taxes on wealth and state social assistance, while increasing defense expenditure. The military-industrial complex energized the whole economy and partly made up for lagging behind Japan and Western Europe on other fronts.

⁴⁰ The Hispanic proportion of the population increased by 53 per cent in the 1980s, reaching more than 22 million in total. The proportion of Asian-Americans grew even more.

⁴¹ In the 1980s the US emitted 25 per cent of the world total of carbon dioxide, (compared with the 13 per cent for the European Community which had a similar sized industrial sector) and refused to establish a deadline for reducing this. In 1991, the United States was the biggest user of most forms of energy. It was also number one producer of nuclear energy and liquid gas, the number two producer of coal, hydroelectric power and natural gas, and the third largest oil producer. It was also the main consumer.

⁴² In February 1991, the US led the multinational force which confronted Iraq after its invasion of Kuwait. The Gulf War demonstrated US military supremacy and allowed Republican President George Bush to propose a new world order under the hegemony of his country.

⁴³ In 1991, 15 per cent of the population lived below the poverty line. Those most affected were the US citizens of African (33 per cent) and Latin American (29 per cent) origins.

⁴⁴ Bill Clinton, Democrat Governor of Arkansas, was elected President in November 1992, and the Democratic Party also gained the majority in the House of Representatives. Clinton promised to concentrate on domestic problems, to move the greatest income tax burden on to the richer sectors, and to meet the health needs of all citizens. The health system reform, conducted by the nation's First Lady Hillary Clinton in 1994, was rejected by Congress.

⁴⁵ The North American Free Trade Agreement (NAFTA) with Mexico and Canada went into operation in January 1994. The measures aiming at the globalization of the economy were criticized for giving other countries the jobs lost internally, both in the public and private sectors. The feeling of rejection grew amongst the immigrant workers, especially when California approved a state law reducing education rights for immigrants children.

⁴⁶ The economy recovered and unemployment fell. However, workers had to work five hours more per week to earn the same income. Consumption remained high, in spite of a rise in credit card interest rates, but fell late in the year. Social security reforms included benefit cuts and fewer programs for workers.

⁴⁷ For the first time in 40 years, the Democratic Party lost legislative elections in 1994. Discontent also expressed itself during 1995, through civil disobedience acts, such as those of right-wing paramilitary groups that did not acknowledge federal authority. An extreme example was the case of a Gulf War veteran who blew up a car-bomb in a federal building in Oklahoma.

⁴⁸ Aiming at a foreign policy to strengthen his image as world leader, in the year before the elections, Clinton led a military intervention in Bosnia-Herzegovina and imposed the Dayton (Ohio) agreements in November 1995. In October 1996, he supported talks between Israelis and

Palestinians in Washington. In November, he was re-elected with 49.2 per cent of the vote.

49 Clinton had to contest in 1998 the charge of perjury brought against him by Independent Counsel Kenneth Starr. Appointed to investigate a possible real estate fraud, Starr concluded that Clinton had lied under oath about having sex with a White House intern. The President's popularity was not affected by the charge and the Democratic Party obtained a significant victory in the mid-term elections of November 3. However, Starr showed evidence of Clinton's perjury, and the Senate decided in December to initiate impeachment proceedings.

50 Two days before the impeachment case was decided in the Senate, Clinton ordered the bombing of Baghdad and other Iraqi cities; he only had the backing of British Prime Minister Tony Blair. The attacks, in which more missiles were launched than during the Gulf War in 1991, caused hundreds of civilian victims.

51 In February 1999 the Senate voted against impeaching Clinton. Two-thirds of the votes were needed to impeach the President, but the Republicans did not even reach a simple majority. The perjury charge was rejected by 55 to 45 votes, and the obstruction of justice charge received 50 votes in favor and 50 votes against.

52 Presidential elections held on November 7 marked a critical point in the electoral system. One of the tightest elections ever, scarred with irregularities, pitched Republican candidate George W Bush, governor of Texas and son of the former president, against Democrat Vice-President Al Gore. The uncertainty went on for weeks after the state of Florida, which had had 6 million votes, ordered a recount. The fact that Florida's governor was George W Bush's brother was seen by some as playing a part in the proceedings.

53 Elections led to a succession of legal proceedings, initiated by both parties. The election was decided on December 12th 2000 when the US Supreme Court ruled in favour of Bush. He won 270 electoral votes although he obtained 50,456,062 of the popular vote. Gore obtained the majority of the popular vote, 50,996,582 but only 266 electoral votes. Analysts and observers, as well as President Clinton, stated the elections underlined the need to revise the country's electoral system.

54 On September 11 2001 the US suffered its most savage attack ever made on its territory. Four commercial airplanes were kidnapped by suicide bombers, and three of them reached their targets.

Two crashed into the World Trade Center twin towers in New York, which were destroyed, and another against the Pentagon building in Washington, causing in total more than 3,000 dead, a direct economic destruction estimated at $1 billion and a significant psychological impact on the population.

55 The Bush Government reacted by declaring a war on terror. Its target was not only the Islamic network al-Qaeda, blamed for the devastating attacks, but any organization deemed terrorist by Washington, be it linked to the attackers or not, the governments that harbored them and those countries that, according to the US, were able to develop or use weapons of mass destruction. Washington intensified the militaristic policy that had characterized Bush since the beginning of his administration when he increased the military budget by 20 per cent, adding some 15 per cent. The US military budget was thus larger than the total amount of all its 18 allies in NATO. The fate of private companies was no longer strictly determined by market laws, since the Government subsidized activities considered strategic, such as commercial aviation and the steel industry.

56 On October 7, the US initiated what would amount to 24,000 air raids against the Taliban Government in Afghanistan (see Afghanistan), accused by Washington of harboring al-Qaeda terrorists. The Taliban regime was deposed on November 13. Thousands of Afghans were killed and the fate of millions was worsened, aggravated by the cold winter. But Washington could not achieve its two main goals: to capture or kill al-Qaeda leader Osama Bin Laden and the leader of the Taliban, Mullah Muhammar Omar. The war in Afghanistan was used by the Pentagon to perfect technologies and techniques first used in the Gulf War, in 1991, such as precision bombing and long-distance command; indeed the commander of this campaign remained in the US.

57 The bankruptcy of energy giant Enron early in 2002 led to the collapse of a new business model promoted in the last 15 years. The fall-out took with it the auditing firm Andersen and called into question the accounting practices of big corporations. The lack of confidence of small investors due to the manipulation of their savings and of the price of stocks by Enron executives - who received part of their wages in stocks and, thus, speculated with them - challenged the US development finance system,

as well as auditing firms' regulation mechanisms. Enron had contributed $793,000 to the Republican party and $86,000 to the Democratic Party for the 2000 election campaigns. WorldCom, Xerox, Adelphia, Tyco, Global Crossing, Merrill Lynch and other huge companies were also investigated suspected of artificially inflating their profits.

58 In his State of the Union address in January 2002, Bush stated that North Korea, Iran and Iraq were enemy nations and members of an 'axis of evil', although only an attack on Iraq was anticipated. Anti-terrorist operations, or use of their territories as a base for these, were also initiated in Colombia, Philippines, Sudan, Somalia, Yemen, Uzbekistan, Tajikistan, Indonesia, Malaysia and possibly Pakistan. The September 11 attacks revealed major flaws in the intelligence service, whose restructuring was undertaken to return to Cold War

methods and anti-subversive fight, updated with agents in the realm of electronic espionage.

59 The Israeli occupation of the Gaza Strip initiated in April 2001 was condemned internationally, but in 2002 the US supported Israel adducing that it has the right to defend itself, to prevent further suicide bombings. The Bush administration realized that Israel's Prime Minister, Ariel Sharon, will not take orders after his refusal to leave Palestinian territory until suicide attacks come to an end.

60 The US temporarily vetoed the renewal of the UN peace mission in Bosnia hours ahead the International Criminal Court came into being in July 2002 in The Hague. Washington feared that US soldiers could be 'politically' prosecuted by the ICC.

61 In September, Bush appealed to the UN to back his planned campaign on Iraq. ∎

US DEPENDENCIES

JOHNSTON:
Coral atoll of 2.6 sq km, made up of the Johnston island and the Sand, East and North islets, located approximately 1,150 km west-southwest of Honolulu (Hawaii). With an Air Force base the population (all military) is approximately 1,000. The atoll was uninhabited when it was discovered by British Captain Johnston in 1807. In 1858, Hawaii claimed sovereignty, but that same year US companies started exploitation of phosphate. Since 1934, the atoll has been administered by the US Navy. Civilians are not admitted.

MIDWAY:
A round atoll which comprises two islands: Sand and Eastern, with 5 sq km of total area and 2,300 inhabitants (1985) almost exclusively military. In 1867, they were annexed by the US and are currently administered by its Navy. The islands are used for military purposes and operate as a refueling base for trans-Pacific flights. In 1942 during World War II, an important sea battle took place here.

WAKE:
Together with neighboring Wilkes and Peale, they make up an atoll with an area of 6.5 sq km and an estimated population of 1,600 inhabitants, mainly military personnel. Located between Midway and Guam, the island was seized by the United States during the 1898 war with Spain. It has a large airport which used to be a stopover for trans-Pacific flights, but nowadays it is not used for business purposes. Since 1972 it has been administered by the Air Force which now uses it as a missile testing station.

HOWLAND, JARVIS & BAKER:
Located in central Polynesia, in the Equatorial Pacific they were occupied by the US in the middle of the 19th century. The islands have been uninhabited since the end of World War II as major phosphate deposits had been depleted. There is a lighthouse in Howland. The islands are administered by the US Fishing and Wild Life Service.

PALMIRA & KINGMAN:
The northernmost islands of the Line archipelago. Palmira is an atoll surrounded by more than fifty coral islets covered with exuberant tropical vegetation. It was annexed in 1898 during the war with Spain and is now a private property, dependent on the US Department of the Interior. Kingman is a reef, located north of Palmira, annexed by the US in 1922. The total area of both islands is 7 sq km. Although uninhabited, the US-Japanese project to turn them into deposits of radioactive waste raised protests throughout the Pacific region in the 1980s.

Uruguay

Population: 3,385,000 (2002)
Land area: 175,020 SQ KM
Capital: Montevideo
Currency: Peso
Language: Spanish

Uruguay

The range lands and forests of the eastern shore of the Uruguay River have been inhabited for at least 10,000 years. By the beginning of the 16th century there were three major cultural groups: the Charrúa, the Chaná and the Guaraní. The Charrúa were hunters, while the Chaná developed a rudimentary form of agriculture along the banks of the Uruguay River. Eventually the Guaraní developed some agricultural skills, mastered ceramics and navigation of the river in canoes.

2 In 1517, Juan Díaz de Solís sailed into the Río de la Plata and was killed by Indians. Ten years later, Sebastian Cabot was the first European to sail up the rivers Paraná and Uruguay, where he established the first Spanish settlement in the territory. The settlers ignored the east bank of the Uruguay river for over a century, until cattle were brought in by the governor of Asunción, Hernando Arias de Saavedra (Hernandarias) in 1611.

3 Good pasture and a moderate climate were conducive to large-scale cattle rearing. This attracted the *faeneros*, the Río de la Plata equivalent of cowboys, from Brazil and Buenos Aires. The Indian culture was totally transformed by the introduction of beef in their diet, and the horse as a means of obtaining it. Through intermarriage with the Indians these 'cowboys' - hunters of wild cattle, not cattle tenders - gave rise to the *gaucho*. Not all the gauchos were *mestizos* (people of mixed European and Indian ancestry). Sometimes they were white, black or *mulato* (of mixed black and white ancestry).

4 In the 18th century, cattle-raising led to the extinction of some indigenous mammals, a reduction of plant diversity and soil degradation. By the mid-19th century the American Indians who could not adapt to this new life were killed or displaced and moved to the Jesuit missions further north.

5 In search of cattle and to gain control of the rivers which led to the interior regions of the Río de la Plata basin, the Portuguese advanced on the Banda Oriental (East Bank), an area approximately equivalent to that of present-day Uruguay, and founded Colonia del Sacramento on the shore opposite Buenos Aires in

1680. This settlement caused constant friction between Portugal and Spain. In 1724, Spain ordered the Governor of Buenos Aires, Bruno Mauricio de Zabala, to cross the Río de la Plata and establish a fort in the Bay of Montevideo.

6 Montevideo came under the Viceroyalty of Peru until 1776, as did Buenos Aires. That year, the Bourbon reforms decreed the creation of the Viceroyalty of the Río de la Plata, with Buenos Aires as the capital, and Montevideo as a naval station.

7 The May Revolution which broke out in Buenos Aires in 1810 was rejected by the Montevideans, who profited from the monopoly on trade with Spain. But it found support in the countryside among small and medium-scale producers and the landless people, led by the popular *caudillo* (leader) José Artigas. A Federal League was created with what is now Uruguay and the Argentine provinces of Cordoba, Corrientes, Entre Ríos, Misiones and Santa Fe.

8 Uruguay was invaded by the Portuguese in 1816, with the tacit approval of Buenos Aires, whose government was alarmed by events known as the 'Artigan chaos'. In

1820, Artigas fought his way to Paraguay, where he remained until his death in 1850. Portugal ruled over the Uruguayan territory until 1823 when Brazil became independent. Uruguay became the Brazilian Cisplatine Province. In 1825 the 'orientales' renewed their campaign against the Brazilian Empire, and one of its objectives was to return to the United Provinces of the Río de la Plata. On August 25 1825, independence was declared and the decision made to reunite with the territories of the former Viceroyalty.

9 The country was eventually granted independence in 1828, through an agreement between Buenos Aires and Brazil mediated by Britain. The 1830 Constitution created a republic for the elite: only independently wealthy males of European origin could vote or be eligible for office. The 19th century was riven by civil wars and witnessed the formation of two political parties: the *Blanco* (White) or National Party, linked to Argentine leader Juan Manuel de Rosas, and the *Colorado* (Red but not communist), linked to European capital and liberal ideas.

10 In 1865, Colorado dictator Venancio Flores signed an agreement with Brazil and Argentina and created the Triple Alliance, breaking Paraguayan isolation - with European support - and forcing the country to open its borders to foreign trade (see Paraguay).

11 Between 1876 and 1879, under the dictator Colonel Lorenzo Latorre, the countryside was enclosed by fences. The implications of this were far-reaching: the land was completely appropriated by the private sector, production was geared to the capitalist market (over which Britain held undisputed control) and the countryside was 'organized' leaving no space for the gaucho, who was transformed into a hired hand.

12 In 1903 the Colorado José Batlle y Ordoñez assumed the presidency. The following year he fought and defeated Aparicio Saravia - the last rural caudillo of the Blancos. With the ideological influence of European social-democracy, and the support of immigrants, Batlle laid the foundations for the modern Uruguayan state. The high rate of productivity of extensive cattle-raising generated such a surplus that, without changing the land ownership structure of large units in the hands of a few, the State was able to redistribute wealth in the form of welfare, education, and protection of local industry oriented toward domestic consumption.

13 The country underwent rapid urbanization. Commerce and services expanded quickly, with the State as the main employer. A large liberal middle-class developed, educated in State schools with Europeanized curricula.

14 The Church and the State were separated and divorce legalized. A collegiate system of government was introduced in 1917 to avoid power accumulation. This open legislation earned the country the title 'the Switzerland of South America'. Urban migration and European immigration enlarged the cities, but the birth-rate dropped. Abortion was the major birth-control technique, becoming so common that it was legal between 1933 and 1935, although made illegal again after political negotiations with Catholic authorities. In 1934, women were granted the right to vote.

[15] Uruguayan exports grew during both World Wars. Meat and its products were supplied first to the Allies, who were fighting against Nazism and Fascism in Europe, and later to US troops fighting in Korea.

[16] Trade balance surpluses secured the country large foreign currency reserves. The welfare policy of subsidies encouraged the emergence of relatively strong import-substitution industries. Meanwhile, a prosperous building industry helped maintain high employment.

[17] Instead of reinvesting their profits, land owners invested capital abroad, engaging in financial speculation and superfluous consumption. This inevitably led to inflation, corruption and the exacerbation of social conflict. In the mid-1950s, the industrial sector stagnated - a situation that proved impossible to reverse.

[18] The first Blanco Government of the century, which came to power in 1959, accepted IMF economic guidelines which accelerated the recession causing a strong reaction among workers. The situation became critical in 1968 when Jorge Pacheco Areco's government, yielding to IMF prescriptions, curtailed the purchasing power of wage-earners and aimed to eliminate the bargaining power of trade unions. The National Workers' Convention and the student organizations opposed such policies. At the same time the Tupamaro (MLN) guerrilla movement was active throughout the country. In 1971 the *Frente Amplio* (Broad Front), a left-wing coalition, was founded. It promoted a progressive government program, and nominated a retired general, Liber Seregni, in the presidential elections of that year.

[19] Juan María Bordaberry, the Colorado nominee, won the elections, which the Blanco National Party denounced as fraudulent. During that regime, the military took up the fight against the guerrilla movement, backed by parliament's declaration of a state of civil war. In 1972 the Tupamaros were defeated. A campaign including the systematic use of torture rapidly dismantled the clandestine organization. On June 27 1973, President Bordaberry and the armed forces staged a coup. Parliament was dissolved, and a civilian-military government was formed. Local trade unions resisted the coup with a 15-day strike.

[20] The Uruguayan military set up a regime based on the National Security Doctrine, a system learnt in US training academies. Economically, the neo-liberal theories of US Professor Milton Friedman were applied, favoring the concentration of wealth in transnational corporations. Salaries lost 50 per cent of their purchasing power, whilst foreign debt reached $5 billion. During this period, all public and private institutions, political parties and unions were banned, people disappeared and torture and arbitrary detentions were commonplace.

[21] The economic situation deteriorated and the civilian population systematically rebuffed efforts to legalize the police state, voting overwhelmingly against the draft of a new constitution that would support this. The Uruguayan generals had no alternative but to work out a timetable for reinstating an institutionally legitimate government.

[22] In April 1983, the Inter-union Plenary of Workers (PIT) was formed and May Day was celebrated for the first time since the coup. The three political parties recognized as legal by the military government took up the banner for the labor movement and the causes espoused prior to the dictatorship. They also demanded the release of all political prisoners. The Broad Front, whose president had been in prison since 1973, was excluded from political activity.

[23] Protests against the military regime intensified as a result of the break-down in negotiations. Women's groups defied the Government's prohibition of street demonstrations. After a successful 24-hour general strike called by the PIT, talks between the political parties and the military were resumed in January 1984, this time with the participation of representatives of the Broad Front.

[24] The Blanco Party leader Wilson Ferreira Aldunate was arrested on his return to the country after an 11-year exile. He was not permitted to run as a candidate in the 1984 election. General Liber Seregni and hundreds of others were also proscribed as candidates.

[25] Under the slogan of *cambio en paz* (peaceful change), the leader of the Colorado Party, Julio María Sanguinetti, won the national election. During the new government's first month in power, an amnesty law was approved whereby all political prisoners were freed.

[26] President Sanguinetti supported many international diplomatic moves in Latin America. The first two years of his term coincided with a favorable international situation, but he returned to the neo-liberal policies of the previous government, which were strongly resisted by the population.

[27] In 1986, under pressure from the President and the armed forces, Parliament approved an amnesty for military personnel accused of violations of human rights, by 3 to 1. A referendum in April 1988 ratified the law, with 56 per cent in favor, while 42 per cent wanted to try the military for their crimes.

[28] In May 1989, the Government signed a secret structural adjustment agreement with the World Bank, in exchange for rescheduling Uruguay's debt. The Government committed itself to reduce expenditure on social security; to privatize bankrupt banks absorbed by the State, and to reform public companies making them profitable and attractive for privatization.

[29] In the November 1989 election the Blanco/National Party under Luis Alberto Lacalle inflicted a severe electoral defeat upon the Colorado Party, taking 17 of the country's 19 departments. The Broad Front won in Montevideo with its candidate Tabaré Vázquez. The Left assumed responsibility for municipal administration for the first time in the history of the country. Six women were elected to the Chamber of Deputies and another seven to the Municipal Council (legislative) of the capital.

[30] Lacalle carried out his neo-liberal policy: taxes were increased and the privatization of state-run companies was encouraged. Salaries lost over 15 per cent of their purchasing power during the first year of his term, while inflation rose from 90 to 130 per cent at the end of his term. In March 1991, Argentina, Brazil and Paraguay approved the Mercosur agreement.

[31] A commission convened by the labor union movement, constituted by members of several parties, presented a petition requesting a plebiscite on a privatization law. In December 1992, 72 per cent of the population voted to repeal the law. However, the Government managed to privatize certain state enterprises, including the national airline, the gasworks and the sugarcane plantations in the north of the country.

[32] In the general and regional elections of November 27 1994, Colorado Party candidate Julio María Sanguinetti was elected once again by a small majority.

[33] The *Encuentro Progresista* (Progressive Encounter) - made up of the Broad Front, the Christian

PROFILE

ENVIRONMENT

Uruguay has a gently rolling terrain, crossed by characteristic low hills - an extension of Brazil's southern plateau - belonging to the old Guayanic-Brazilian massif. Its average altitude is 300 meters above sea level. This, together with its location and latitude, determines its temperate, subtropical, semi-humid weather, with rainfall throughout the year. The vegetation is made up almost entirely of natural grasslands, suitable for cattle and sheep raising. The territory is well irrigated by many rivers, and has over 1,100 km of navigable waterways, in particular on the rivers Negro and Uruguay, and on the Plata estuary. The coast is made up of many sandy beaches that attract tourists from the neighboring countries. There is increasing pollution in the northern regions as a result of emissions from a thermoelectric plant in Candiota (Brazil), while rivers and streams suffer from the use of poisonous agricultural chemicals. A growing loss of ecosystems on the plains and in the eastern wetlands has been observed, due to monoculture of wood and rice, respectively. Large infrastructure projects (eg the Buenos Aires-Colonia bridge, and connecting highway to São Paulo, Brazil) pose an additional threat to the environment.

SOCIETY

Peoples: Most Uruguayans are descendants of Spanish, Italian and other European immigrants. The indigenous population was annihilated in the mid-19th century. Afro-American descendants make up about 8 per cent of today's population. **Religions:** Catholics 66 per cent; Protestants 2 per cent. Afro-Brazilian cults are also practiced. **Languages:** Spanish.
Political Parties: Colorado Party (Red); National Party (Blanco/White); Broad Front/Progressive Encounter (Frente Amplio/Encuentro Progresista); Nuevo Espacio (New Space); Unión Cívica (Civic Union).
Social Organizations: PIT-CNT (Inter-Union Workers' Bureau - National Workers' Convention). FUCVAM (Uruguayan Federation of Housing Construction by Mutual Help). Federation of University Students (FEUU).

THE STATE

Official Name: República Oriental del Uruguay. **Administrative Divisions:** 19 Departments **Capital:** Montevideo 1,237,000 people (1999).
Other cities: Salto 86,600 people; Paysandú 76,400; Las Piedras 70,700; Rivera 69,400; Maldonado 40,600 (2000). **Government:** Presidential system. Jorge Batlle, President since March 2000. Luis Hierro López, Vice-President since March 2000. Bicameral Legislature: the Chamber of Senators, with 31 members, and the Chamber of Deputies, with 99 members. The Vice-President chairs the Senate. **National Holidays:** August 25, Independence Day (1825); July 18, Constitution Day (1830). **Armed Forces:** 25,600 (1997). **Other:** 700 Metropolitan Guard, 500 Republican Guard.

Democrats and other sectors which had split from the traditional parties - won the mayoralty of the capital for the second time

[34] In October, Uruguay became the first country for two decades officially to receive Cuban President Fidel Castro. Sanguinetti rejected Castro's invitation to visit Cuba in September 1996, considering the time was not right.

[35] The wife of former President Lacalle and several of his closest aides were accused of corruption which rocked the foundations of the political parties in mid-1996. A system of social security by savings accounts was implemented that year, in line with reforms previously carried out in Argentina and Chile.

[36] In 1996, Parliament discussed a constitutional reform which entailed difficult political negotiations. The main goal of the reform was the electoral system, establishing the ballot system to elect the president. The Broad Front voted against, arguing that it was conceived to prevent the left from winning the presidency, but the reform was approved with 50.6 per cent of the vote.

[37] Unemployment reached 11.5 per cent in early 1999, but inflation was driven down to 4 per cent, the lowest it had been for 30 years.

[38] In September that year, Uruguay rejected the extradition to Paraguay of former Paraguayan Defense Minister José Segovia. He was granted political asylum in Uruguay while being sought by the Paraguayan justice system on charges of fraud against the State. Segovia was a close associate of Lino Oviedo who had sought political asylum in Argentina following the murder of then vice-president José María Argaña.

[39] In October, Argentine poet Juan Gelman requested Sanguinetti to investigate the disappearance in Montevideo of his daughter-in-law María Claudia García in December 1976. Gelman also asked him to investigate the whereabouts of the child María Claudia had given birth to at the military hospital before 'disappearing' at the hands of identified army personnel. Days later, Sanguinetti told him no information could confirm nor deny Gelman's accusations, and that therefore the case was closed. In support of Gelman's case, hundreds of intellectuales, artists and journalists from both Uruguay and outisde sent letters to the President asking him to follow up the investigations in his role as 'Commander in Chief of the Armed Forces'.

[40] That month, in the Presidential and Parliamentary elections, the Encuentro Progresista became the majority political party with 40.1 per cent of the vote. To prevent a victory

of the left, the National Party allied itself with the Colorado Party and voted for the Colorado candidate, Jorge Batlle, who became President with 52 per cent of the vote in the November elections.

[41] During his inaugural speech on March 1 2000, Batlle declared that 'achieving peace between Uruguayans... belongs to all of us', clearly referring to the Gelman and other 'disappeared' cases. Forty days later, the President informed Gelman he had found his daughter-in-law's 'baby' (a 23-year old woman), much to the surprise of Gelman and national and international public opinion. The news confirmed the involvement of the armed forces in 'Operation Condor' and the kidnapping and disappearance in Uruguay of children born to mothers in detention, something denied by Sanguinetti during his last two terms of office. The Commission for Peace was set up in August to investigate the fate of 160 Uruguayans disappeared during the last military dictatorship.

[42] In early 2001, an outbreak of foot-and-mouth disease affected Uruguay's cattle and forced the country to lose its standing as country free from foot-and-mouth disease without vaccination. Among other measures, cattle transportation was banned throughout the country, except just before slaughter. Also, the rapid spread of the virus forced the authorities to launch a vaccination program for at least 500,000 animals, while 10,200 affected beasts were killed.

[43] At Colonia's cemetery in January 2002, a team of Argentine experts dug up the remains of three political activists murdered during the Argentinean military regime in the 1970s. Human rights organizations stated the activists had disappeared, thrown alive from planes over the sea, in the so-called 'death flights'. At the time, Uruguayan junta had identified the victims as Koreans who had died during a ship-board mutiny.

[44] That month, some 15,000 people from all over the country marched toward Punta del Este, the country's main sea resort during the summer season, to protest against the Government's economic policy. The demonstration paralyzed a large part of the country, and in some interior cities, several demonstrations were held in the context of a nation-wide strike, called for by the PIT-CNT. The Government banned the demonstrators from entering all the Atlantic seaside resorts and ordered special security measures with metal fences extending 5 km, which surrounded the Punta del Este peninsula.

[45] Into its third year of economic recession, Uruguay applied a 20 per cent tax on all products from Argentina. It feared that Uruguayan industry would not be able to compete with its neighbor's goods, whose prices had fallen more than 50 per cent due to the devaluation that took place in 2002. In March, the IMF approved a $443 million loan to help Uruguay out of the recession and to protect it from the Argentine economic crisis. The plan introduced by the Government had expected a fall in production of 1.7 per cent, and a 3 per cent growth in 2003. Uruguay agreed to reduce its general deficit to 2.5 per cent in 2002 and to 1.5 per cent in 2003, in order to reach a fiscal balance in 2004. The IMF urged Uruguay to privatize its state monopolies, such as electricity, oil, telecommunications and railroads.

[46] Argentine justice confirmed on March 19 2002 that a man living in that country was Simon Riquelo, son of Sara Mendez, a Uruguayan woman who had been detained by the Argentine junta. The news ended a 25-year search for the boy, who had been taken away from his mother in July 976, shortly after his birth. A huge crowd celebrated the reunion of mother and son. Mendez stated the Government had not cooperated with her in her long search.

[47] In April, Uruguay sponsored a UN resolution against Cuba regarding the human rights situation on the island. The proposal, entailing a UN inspector's visit to Cuba to investigate alleged abuses against individual rights by Fidel Castro's government, was passed by the UN Commission of Human Rights. The motion caused protests from Havana against the Batlle administration and against the President himself (Castro called him a 'wretched Judas'), resulting in the severing of diplomatic relations. In spite of this, Havana continued to supply Uruguay with free meningitis vaccine, as it had undertaken to do after an outbreak of the disease.

[48] For the first time in 20 years, employers and workers met on April 16 in a huge demonstration against the Government's economic policy. The national strike day, which paralyzed the health, education, transport and banking sectors, was called for by 20 associations which form the so-called Agreement for Growth and the PIT-CNT trade unions. Among the crowds were hundreds of men and women who had come from all over the country on horseback. The demonstrators protested against the bankruptcy filed by 35 per cent of businesses since 1998 and the closing of 15 agricultural concerns per day, overcome by debt. Over 75,000 workers had been laid off. ∎

Uzbekistan

Population: 25,618,000 (2002)
Land area: 414,240 SQ KM
Capital: Tashkent
Currency: Som-Kupon
Language: Uzbek

Uzbekistan

Several ancient agricultural centers developed in what is now Uzbekistan, including Khwarezm, Ma Wara an-Nahr and the Fergana Valley. The population and the languages of the first states to emerge in the 10th century BC were Indo-European. Between the 6th and 7th centuries AD, these states formed part of the Persian Achaemenid empire, the empire of Alexander the Great, the Greco-Bactrian kingdoms, and that of Kusha, the white Hun or Eftalite state.

[2] Turkish nomads defeated the Eftalites and brought the major part of Central Asia into their empire, the Turkish kaganate (Khanate), between the 6th and 8th centuries. During this period, Turkish-speaking peoples began coming to the region and integrating with the local population. In the mid-8th century the country was conquered by the Arabs. Islam spread quickly, particularly in the cities.

[3] When the power of the Arab caliphs declined, during the reign of the local Samanid and Karajanid dynasties, and under the shahs of Khwarezm (9th to early 13th centuries), an Islamic civilization developed. Agriculture was its main activity, made possible by a highly developed irrigation system. This culture was also noted for its artisans. The cities of Bukhara, Samarkand and Urgenca became prosperous trading centers for the caravans that crossed the Great Silk Route, from China to Byzantium.

[4] From 1219-1221, the state ruled over by the shahs of Khwarezm was overrun by the Tatars, and completely devastated. Khwarezm was turned over to the Golden Horde, under the leadership of Genghis Khan's oldest son. Ma Wara an-Nahr and Fergana went to the second son, Chagatai; the inhabitants of the area began calling themselves Chagatais. Turkish and Mongol tribes moved into the steppes, and in the second half of the 14th century, Timur, the head of one of these tribes, settled in Ma Wara an-Nahr, making Samarkand the capital of his empire.

[5] The union of nomad tribes who called themselves Uzbeks was achieved in the 15th century, in Central Kazakhstan. During the second half of the century, the great Uzbek poet and thinker Ali Shir Navai, who lived at the court

of one of Timur's descendants, became a world-renowned figure. The leader of the Uzbeks, Muhammad Shaybani, conquered Ma Wara an-Nahr at the beginning of the 16th century, and the Uzbek immigrants gave their name to all the country's inhabitants. After dissolving the State of Shaybani, Uzbek Khanates emerged in the region. In 1512, the Khanate of Khiva was formed; its military elite belonged to the Kungrats, an Uzbek people. In 1806 Muhammad Amin, head of the Kungrats, founded the dynasty which was to rule over Khiva until 1920.

[6] The Khanate of Bukhara was formed in the mid-16th century. Its military elite belonged to the Uzbek Manguite people. Muhammad Rajim, leader of the Manguites, founded his dynasty in 1753; it lasted in 1920. The Khanate of Bukhara reached its apogee at the time of Nasrula, a Khan who ruled from 1826-1860. In the early 19th century, the Emirs of Fergana (of the Ming dynasty) created the Khanate of Kokand. These feudal theocracies were populated by Uzbeks, Turkmens, Tajiks, Kyrgyz and Karakalpaks.

[7] None of these states had definite boundaries, nor were they capable of exacting absolute loyalty from their chieftains. The Emirs of Khiva and Bukhara exercised only nominal sovereignty over the Turkmen tribes of the Kara Kum Desert, who were slave traders in Iranian territory. Although the three Uzbek Khanates reached their highest level of organization during this period, they were not prepared to face the imminent European

expansion. In Central Asia, Russian and British colonial interests clashed over the cotton market.

[8] In 1860, the Russian offensive against the Khanates began, though it was impeded by their geographical isolation, particularly in the case of Khiva which was surrounded by desert. In 1867, the Czar created the province of Turkistan, with its center in Tashkent. Although it belonged to Kokand, it was officially annexed in 1875. By the end of the 19th century, the province included the regions of Samarkand, Syr Darya and Fergana. On August 12 1873, the Khan of Khiva signed a peace treaty with Russia, accepting protectorate status, as did the Khan of Bukhara in September of the same year. The difficult living conditions imposed on the people by czarist Russia triggered several uprisings including Andizhan in 1898 and Central Asia in 1916.

[9] With the fall of the Czar in February 1917, power was shared by the committee of the Provisional Government, and the *Soviets* (councils) of workers and soldiers. After the triumph of the October Revolution in St Petersburg power was concentrated in the hands of the Tashkent Soviet. In 1918, Red Army units crushed both the attempt to form an autonomous Muslim government in Kokand and an anti-Bolshevik uprising in Turkistan. The Red Army occupied Khiva in April 1920, and entered Bukhara in September. Land and water reform began in spring 1921, with military operations continuing until mid-1922, when the implementation of the reforms left the rebels without a cause.

[10] In 1924, the Soviet Government reorganized Central Asian borders along ethnic lines, and proclaimed the Soviet Socialist Republic (SSR) of Uzbekistan. In May 1925, Uzbekistan became a federated republic of the Soviet Union. The Autonomous Soviet Socialist Republic of Tajikistan was a part of Uzbekistan until 1929, when it joined the USSR. During the Great Purge of 1937-38, a number of Uzbeks including the prime minister, Fayzullah Khodzhayev and the first secretary of the Uzbek Communist Party, Akmal Ikramov, were sentenced to death. In Moscow in 1953, both leaders were rehabilitated.

[11] The socialist reforms were aimed primarily at taking advantage of the region's agricultural potential. Huge mechanized irrigation systems, including the Great Fergana, North Fergana and Tashkent canals, were constructed by the State, as were reservoirs like the Kattakurgan on the Zeravshan River (the Uzbek Sea), the Kuyumazar and the Akhangaran (the Tashkent Sea). Between 1956 and 1983 the Republic's economy revolved around cotton. National industry was geared toward producing machines and heavy equipment for cotton cultivation, harvesting and processing. Uzbekistan became the USSR's largest cotton producer and the third largest in the world.

[12] In the 1940s, the population increased; Kurds and Mesketian Turks, who had been deported from the Caucasus, came to Uzbekistan, and all was stable until the 1980s. When Leonid Brezhnev became head of the Communist Party of the USSR in 1983 he changed the Uzbek authorities. The new first secretary of the local CP, Inamjon Ousmankhodjaev, revealed that official cotton production statistics had been systematically falsified by his predecessor.

[13] The Uzbek corruption case was the biggest scandal in the Soviet Union at the time, and triggered many arrests, lawsuits against 4,000 civil servants and expulsions from the Party. However, this turned out to be just another political purge as it did not bring about any substantial changes.

[14] From 1985 onward, the changes initiated by President Mikhail Gorbachev, the deterioration of the economic situation and the

weakening of the Soviet Communist Party's centralized authority gave rise to increased ethnic and religious conflicts in Uzbekistan. The Uzbeks, predominantly Sunni Muslims, resisted the Party's anti-clerical campaigns.

[15] The USSR's intervention in Afghanistan against fellow-Sunni Muslims only worsened the situation, and all these factors combined to create a hostile climate toward Moscow and the Russian minority residing in Uzbekistan. The most serious consequence was the conflict in the region of Fergana in June 1989, and conflicts in Namangan, in December 1990.

[16] Islam Karimov had come to power as First Secretary of the Communist Party of Uzbekistan in 1989 and was named president of the Uzbek Soviet Socialist Republic in 1990. In August 1991, the Uzbek Soviet (Parliament) approved the Law of Independence. On December 12, in Almaty, (Kazakhstan), the Uzbek delegation signed the agreement creating the Commonwealth of Independent States (CIS), which marked the end of the USSR. In a direct ballot in which most opposition groups were not allowed to field candidates, Karimov was elected president in December.

[17] Karimov imposed an authoritarian style and defined a new course for Uzbekistan based upon the development model of Southeast Asia: elimination of dissidence and modernization of the economy, adapting it to the market. Karimov approved a privatization plan in January 1994 and announced 300 per cent price hikes in food and electric power.

[18] From 1995 the country's foreign policy was geared towards containing Russian and Iranian influences in the region. Karimov actively supported the US embargo on Iran and called for the creation of a 'common Turkestan' among its neighbors, making it understood that he was threatened by 'imperialist' temptations from Russia. It was one of three countries - together with Israel and the United States - that, in late 1997, voted against lifting the economic embargo on Cuba at the UN General Assembly (a majority of 143 countries voted in favor of the resolution).

[19] During early 1998, Tashkent was concerned about the spread of fundamentalist Islam in neighboring Tajikistan. It was also wary of the actions of members of the Wahhabi sect, backed by the Taliban regime in Afghanistan, who had settled in the Fergana valley, a densely populated area shared by Uzbekistan, Tajikistan and Kyrgyzstan. In November, Karimov backed Russia in its war against Chechnya. The Islamic Movement of Uzbekistan (IMU), led by a Taliban commander, had launched an offensive to try and create an Islamic state in the north of the country. The Government stated that the IMU had been responsible in 1999 of placing a series of car bombs in the country.

[20] On January 9 2000, Karimov was re-elected with 92 per cent of the vote. Although Washington stated the elections had neither been 'free nor fair', since the population had had no 'alternatives', in March, a visit from US secretary of State Madeleine Albright offered a $3 million 'package' to fight drug trafficking and terrorism. The Organization for the Cooperation and Security of Europe (OCSE) did not send observers, for similar reasons. Human Rights Watch condemned the Government for carrying out a 'brutal campaign' against religious activists. With this support, Karimov asked India for its cooperation to fight against international terrorism in Afghanistan and other Central Asian countries.

[21] In June 2001 when Uzbekistan joined the Shanghai Five group - China, Russia, Kazakhstan, Kyrgyzstan and Tajikistan - the six countries became the Shanghai Cooperation Organization (CSO), which signed an agreement to fight against ethnic and religious militants. Other CSO goals are the promotion of trade and investment.

[22] Karimov became a key ally for the US in its attacks on Afghanistan. Tashkent wanted to use Afghan territory to build a railroad to the Indian ocean (until then it only had access to the sea in the north, via Russia). Karimov signed an agreement offering its air space and military base to US troops. After international pressure, in December 2001 Karimov decided to open the border with Afghanistan with the goal of transporting international aid from the UN and humanitarian organizations. In response to the assistance offered by Uzbekistan, the US promised economic aid of $160 million.

[23] In January 2002, Karimov's proposal to extend the presidential term from 5 to 7 years was passed by a large majority in a referendum. This was criticized by the West, who believed that Karimov wanted to remain indefinitely in power.

[24] In March 2002, the Human Rights Society of Uzbekistan (HRSU) was officially recognized as the first independent human rights organization in the country, after five years in operation. According to its activists, the Uzbek Government's decision was taken after international pressure and was prior to President Karimov's visit to the US. ■

PROFILE

ENVIRONMENT
Uzbekistan is bordered in the north and northwest by Kazakhstan, in the southeast by Tajikistan, in the northeast by Kyrgyzstan and in the south by Afghanistan. Part of its terrain is flat, while the rest is mountainous. There are two main rivers and more than 600 streams, some of which are diverted for irrigation, while others are utilized for hydroelectric projects. The plains are located in the northwest and the center (the Ustyurt Plateau, the Amu Darya Valley and the Kyzylkum desert), while the mountains are in the southeast (the Tien-Shan and Gissar and Alay ranges). It has a hot, dry climate on the plains, and is more humid in the mountains. There are large deposits of natural gas, oil and coal. Among the most pressing environmental problems are the salinization of the soil as a result of monoculture, desertification, drinking water and air contamination.

SOCIETY
Peoples: Uzbeks 75.8 per cent; Russians 6 per cent; Tajiks 4.8 per cent; Kazakhs 4.1 per cent, Kyrgyz 0.9 per cent; Ukranians 0.6 per cent; Turks 0.6 per cent; other 7.2 per cent (1995).
Religions: Muslim (Sunni), 88 per cent; Orthodox, 1 per cent. Other (mostly non-religious), 11 per cent.
Languages: Uzbek (official), Russian, Tajik.
Political Parties: Democratic People's Party, communist; Fidokorlar (Self Sacrifice); Progress of the Fatherland Party; Adolat (Justice); National Renaissance.
Social organizations: There are no independent trade unions. All workers of state-owned enterprises belong to Uzbekistan Federation of Trade Unions.

THE STATE
Official Name: Uzbekistan Jumhuriyati.
Administrative divisions: 12 regions, 1 capital city and 1 autonomous republic (Qoraqalpoghiston).
Capital: Tashkent 2,140,000 people (1999).
Other cities: Samarkand 362,000 people; Namangan 333,000; Andizhan 313,000; Bukhara 235,000 (1995).
Government: Islam Karimov, President since March 1990, elected in 1991 (shortly after the independence of Uzbekistan) and re-elected in 2000. Otkir Sultonov, Prime Minister since December 1995, re-elected in 2000.
Unicameral Legislature: National Assembly, with 250 members.
National Holiday: September 1, Independence Day (1991).
Armed Forces: 65,000 (1995).
Other: (National Guard) 700.

Vanuatu

Population: 207,000 (2002)
Land area: 12,190 SQ KM
Capital: Vila
Currency: Vatu
Language: Bislama, English and French

Vanuatu

The first colonization of Polynesia is still a mystery to anthropologists and historians (see box 'Melanesians and Polynesians').

[2] Sailing westwards, Polynesians reached Vanuatu around 1400 BC. These navigators crossed and populated the entire Pacific Ocean from Antarctica to Hawaii and as far as Easter Island on the eastern edge of the Pacific Ocean. Their culture was highly developed, Polynesians domesticated animals and developed some subsistence crops; they manufactured ceramics and textiles, organized their societies with a caste system and, in some cases, possessed a historical knowledge which had been orally transmitted down the generations for centuries.

[3] On April 29 1605 the Portuguese-Spanish navigator, Pedro Fernández de Quiros, was the first European to sight mountains which he believed to be part of the Great Southern Continent for which he was searching; he named the place 'Tierra del Espíritu Santo' (Land of the Holy Spirit). A century and a half later, Frenchman Louis Antoine de Bougainville, sailed around the region and demonstrated that it was not part of Australia but rather a series of islands. In 1774, James Cook drew the first map of the archipelago, calling it the New Hebrides.

[4] Shortly thereafter traders arrived and felled the forests and the islands became the source of a semi-enslaved labor force. The workers were either taken by force or purchased from local leaders in exchange for tobacco, mirrors and firearms.

[5] During almost all of the 19th century, the archipelago was on the dividing line between the French (in New Caledonia) and British (in the Solomon Islands) zones of influence, and the two nations finally decided to share the islands instead of fighting over them. In 1887, a Joint Naval Commission was established, and in 1906, the Condominium was formalized. The formula of shared domination envisaged the joint provisions of some basic services; the post, radio, customs, public works, but left each power free to develop other services. Consequently, there were two police forces, two monetary systems, two health services and two school systems ruled by two representatives on the islands.

[6] Melanesians were relegated to being 'stateless' in their own country, and they were not considered citizens until a legislative assembly was established in the territory in 1974. Until then only British or French people were entitled to citizenship or land ownership.

[7] Most of the neighboring archipelagos achieved independence in the 1970s. This encouraged the foundation of the National Party of the New Hebrides (the Vanuatu Party, VP) in 1971. The Party organized grassroots groups on all of the islands on the basis of the Protestant parochial structure. The Party became the country's leading political force and demanded total independence, in opposition to various 'moderate' pro-French parties that preferred to maintain the colonial status. When the Party won two-thirds of the vote in 1979 this convinced the British that independence could no longer be postponed.

[8] Vanuatan independence was declared on July 30 1980. Measures were immediately taken to return the land held by foreigners to the Melanesians; the school system was unified and a national army was created.

[9] At this time government revenues depended heavily on foreign aid and the country's exports covered only half of the cost of its imports. Since the country was a tax haven with more than 60 banks established in Vila there was no firm strategy raise taxes.

[10] In early 1998, the Court of Appeals confirmed the dissolution of the Parliament of the Republic, requested by the president Jean-Marie Leye. In the ensuing elections, held in March, the Vanua'aku Unity Front (UF) won 18 of the 52 seats in play, followed by the Union of Moderate Parties (UMP), with 12.

[11] Growing corruption in government spheres was cited by Ombudsman Marie-Noelle Ferrieux-Patterson, who presented reports denouncing the diversion of funds meant for cyclone victim aid, the issuing of false passports and the misappropriation of monies from pensions funds. These accusations provoked street demonstrations and the Government declared a state of emergency to bring the disturbances under control.

[12] In early 2002, an earthquake measuring 7.2 on the Richter scale, with an epicenter in the ocean some 50 km west of the capital, cut the power and water supply in most neighborhoods. Several houses, an administrative building and bridges were destroyed, and many people injured. ∎

PROFILE

ENVIRONMENT

Vanuatu is a Melanesian archipelago of volcanic origin, comprising more than 70 islands and islets, many of them uninhabited. It stretches for 800 km, in a north-south direction in the South Pacific about 1,200 km east of Australia. Major islands are: Espiritu Santo, Malekula, Epi, Pentecost, Aoba, Maewa, Paama, Ambrym, Efate, Erromango, Tanna and Aneityum. Active volcanoes are found in Tanna, Ambrym and Lopevi and the area is subject to earthquakes. The land is mountainous and covered with dense tropical forests. The climate is tropical with heavy rainfall. The subsoil of Efate is rich in manganese and the soil is suitable for farming. Fishing is a traditional economic activity. The land tenure system has contributed to general soil depletion (deforestation, erosion). Rising sea levels will affect both inhabited and uninhabited coastal areas. There is also a risk that rising tides will seep into ground water, threatening water supplies.

SOCIETY

Peoples: Most people are Melanesian (98 per cent), with 1 per cent European (British and French) and smaller groups from Vietnam, China and other Pacific islands. **Religions:** Mainly Christian (77 per cent). **Languages:** Bislama, English and French are official. Other Melanesian languages are also spoken. **Political Parties:** Party of Our Land; Union of Moderate Parties; Vanuatu National United Party; Melanesian Progressive Party; Vanuatu Republican Party; People's Democratic Party. **Social Organizations:** Vanuatu Trade Union Congress.

THE STATE

Official Name: Ripablik blong Vanuatu. République de Vanuatu, Republic of Vanuatu.
Administrative Divisions: 11 Government Regions, 2 Municipalities.
Capital: Vila, on Efate Island, 26,000 people (1999).
Other cities: Luganville (Santo) 6,900 people; Port Olry 884; Isangel 752 (1989). Government: John Bernard Bani, President since March 1999. Edward Natapei, Prime Minister since April 2001. Unicameral Legislature, with 52 members elected for a four-year term.
National Holiday: July 30, Independence Day (1980).

Vatican City

Population: 778 (2002)
Land area: 0.44 SQ KM
Currency: Euro
Language: Italian and Latin

Città del Vaticano

In ancient times, the territory now known as the Vatican City, to the west of the Tiber river, was known as the Ager Vaticanus (Vatican fields). Some sources say the name Vatican comes from a former Etruscan town on the site called Vaticum. However, others say it derives from the Latin *vates* (seer), and that in ancient times there used to be a hill called Vatican inhabited by sooth-sayers and fortune tellers who predicted the fate of passers-by.

[2] Due to the persecution of Christians and the destruction in Rome of all documents of the Church by Emperor Diocletian in 303, today there are very few traces of the presence in the area of the first Christians.

[3] This changed with the arrival of emperor Constantine the Great (307-337), who forged peace with the Church, allowing Christianity to abandon its clandestine status and hold a privileged juridical standing.

[4] In the 4th century the construction began, at the foot of Vatican Hill, of what would later be known as St Peter's Basilica. According to archaeological evidence, the first pope was buried there. Medieval pontiffs purchased the territory and built a bridge, the Pons Aelius, to link the lands with Rome. Although by then Rome was beginning to decline, the first Christian basilicas were built in this period, including St Peter's.

[5] The landscape and building architecture of the time were developed throughout different ages and criteria according to the taste and sensibility of each pope. In the 7th century, landscape architects such as Antonio Tempesta, Giovanni Maggi and Giambattista Faldi gave shape to the lawn from behind the great basilica and up to one of the seven hills that surround Rome. The popes became rulers of the city of Rome and the surrounding areas.

[6] In the year 756 this domain was officially granted to pontiff Stephen II by Pippin the Short, King of the Franks, in appreciation for having named him king. Papal possessions increased through donations, acquisitions and conquest and in this way the future Papal States, legally established by Charlemagne in the IX century, covered almost all of the central zone of Italy.

[7] In the year 847, Pope Leon IV erected a large wall, named Leonine, virtually around the whole territory, to defend the Vatican against the Saracens. Starting at Castel Sant'Angelo, the wall extends behind the Vatican Basilica and reaches down to the Tiber shore. This wall turned the St Peter's area into walled grounds and turned the city into a sui generis district, different from the rest of Rome.

[8] During 1309-77, the popes lived mostly in Avignon, due to constant conflicts in Rome. Pressed by Philip IV of France, Pope Clement V moved the pontiff's capital to Avignon, then belonging to the pope's vassals and which in 1348 became property of the pontiffs. The seven popes of that period were French, as well as 111 of the 134 cardinals.

[9] After Gregory XI re-established the pontifical capital in Rome, Clement VII led the cardinals that in 1378 declared invalid the election of Urban VI, and was elected anti-pope in 1378, occupying the empty throne in Avignon. Europe was divided in its support for both pontiffs: while France backed Clement, England supported Urban, a dispute that would continue throughout the 100 years War (1337-1453). The conflict between both Sees launched the period known as the Great Schism, in which several anti-popes were named, and which would finally end in 1417.

[10] Most of the annexations to the Vatican territory were kept under pontifical rule until 1797, when the French troops of Napoleon Bonaparte took the territory, creating the Roman Republic.

[11] In 1801 pope Pius VII recovered some of his power and in 1815 after the fall of Napoleon, the Congress of Vienna returned almost all of the papacy's possessions.

[12] The first Vatican Council was held in 1869 and decreed the dogma of papal infallibility. A year later, the Papal States were finally dissolved when Victor Emmanuel II annexed them to the unified kingdom of Italy, including Rome. The papacy's jurisdiction was limited to the Vatican, in which each of the successive pontiffs remained, in protest, as self-imposed prisoner. This voluntary reclusion continued until 1929 when, after the Lateran Treaty, signed between the Holy See and the Kingdom of Italy - ruled then by Benito Mussolini - acknowledged the sovereignty and international status of the State of the Vatican City. This state is different from the Holy See, since the former is the executive organ of the Catholic Church, and the latter is the physical territory over which that Government rules. Thus, the pontiff's political authority was consolidated.

[13] The chairman of the German Bishops' Conference, Monsignor Karl Lehmann, shocked the Catholic world in January 2000, the year of the Jubilee, declaring he was convinced the Pope, aged 79, would resign if it were resolved he was not fit to continue his pontificate. Lehmann broke the unwritten rule of not talking about papal resignations, an event authorized by the Code of Canonic Law, but extremely rare in the Vatican's history. The closest precedent is found a thousand years ago, when Benedict IX and Gregory VI resigned.

[14] During the last decade of the 20th century, scandals of allegations against pedophile priests rocked the Vatican. The victims received a total of $119.6 million in damages, the largest compensation awarded in the history of sexual abuse cases. In November 2001, the Pope published for the first time on the internet a 120-page document in which, indirectly, he apologized to the victims ofthese crimes committed by members of the Catholic clergy. ∎

PROFILE

ENVIRONMENT

Located within the city of Rome, next to the Tiber river, it includes St Peter's basilica and square, Vatican palaces and gardens, the church and palace of St John in Lateran, the papal 'villa' of Castelgandolfo, and 13 buildings outside this area, which are considered extraterritorial.

SOCIETY

People: Vatican citizens are members of the Papal and Catholic Church administration that live there because of their work. Most of the permanent officials are Italians, a large number are Swiss and the rest come from different countries. **Religion:** Catholic. **Languages:** Italian (the state) and Latin (official).

THE STATE

Official name: Stato della Città del Vaticano. **Administrative divisions:** Two parallel administrations: Holy See (supreme organ of the Catholic Church); Vatican City (See of the church) Capital: Vatican City, 778 residents (est 2002). **Government:** monarchy elected for life. Pope John Paul II (Karol Wojtyla, Polish), sovereign elected on October 16 1978 by the College of Cardinals (in secret meeting). He is the first non-Italian Pope in 456 years. The equivalent of the head of government is the Secretary of State, Cardinal Angelo Sodano, since 1991, who chairs a commission of five cardinals. The Pope is also the Bishop of Rome and supreme head of the Catholic Church. The Church administration is advised by the College of Cardinals and the Bishops' Synods, who meet when the pontiff wishes. The Church's administrative bodies are 9 Holy Congregations, 3 Secretariats and several commissions, prefectures or courts, which are jointly known as the Roman Curia.

DEMOGRAPHY

Population: 778 (2002) **Annual growth:** -1.7 % (1985-2000)
Estimates for year 2015: 780 (2000) **Annual growth to year 2015:** 0.0 % (2000)

ECONOMY

Currency: 1.2 euro = $ 1 (03/2002)

Venezuela

Population: 25,093,000 (2002)
Land area: 882,050 SQ KM
Capital: Caracas
Currency: Bolívar
Language: Spanish

Venezuela

Cumanagotos, Tamaques, Maquiritares, Arecunas, and other Carib groups inhabited the northern tip of South America when the Spanish arrived on these shores in 1498. Local buildings, constructed on poles, reminded the Spaniards of the appearance of Venice, so they named the country Venezuela.

[2] During the colonial period, Venezuela was organized as a Captaincy General of the Viceroyalty of New Granada, and in the 18th century it became the most important farming colony, producing mainly cocoa. A local aristocracy of *mantuanos* developed, a landowning class of European extraction, who used African slave labor on their plantations. The *pardos* (blacks) who constitute the overwhelming majority of the population are descended from the slaves.

[3] Two of the greatest leaders of the Latin American independence movement were born in the Captaincy: Francisco de Miranda and Simón Bolívar. On April 19 1810, the wars of independence broke out after the constitution of a Cabildo or Assembly. Miranda became the commander of the army, envisaging a vast American Confederacy to be known as Colombia, which would crown an Inca emperor. His dreams did not however come to fruition as he was captured by the Spaniards in 1811 and later died in prison.

[4] Bolívar took up Miranda's project for American liberation and was backed, in principle, by the mantuano oligarchy. In a swift campaign (1812-13) he took over the country, and was able to install a government in Caracas. His plans for independence did not include changes in social structure, and he was not supported by the masses who lived in the plains (*llaneros*), most of whom were mulattos living under the severe repression of white creoles whom they hated. Their liberation movement was led by the Spanish loyalist General José Tomás Boves, who defeated Bolívar in 1814. Boves abolished slavery and redistributed the land among the people.

[5] Having lost the first republic, Bolívar went into exile, working closely with the Haitian President, Alexandre Sabés Petión, who helped him add a social dimension to his

American revolutionary project. Bolívar returned to Venezuela and, championing popular demands, he won mass support.

[6] Accompanied by other important military leaders like Antonio José de Sucre, Mariño, José A Páez and Arismendi, he carried out successful military campaigns in the northern half of the continent. He subsequently founded Bolivia in what had hitherto been known as 'Upperu'.

[7] In 1819, the Angostura Congress created the new republic of 'Gran Colombia', uniting Colombia, Ecuador, Panama and Venezuela. In 1830, after Bolívar's death, General José Antonio Páez declared Venezuela's secession from Gran Colombia, establishing it as an independent nation.

[8] For decades, Venezuelan politics revolved around the caudillo or leader, Páez. His political successor, Antonio Guzmán Blanco, was determined to modernize Venezuela. He succeeded to a certain extent, introducing new technology, new means of communication, and reforming the country's legal code.

[9] Juan Vicente Gómez took power in 1908 ruling for 17 years, and his government made an attempt to eliminate the caudillo system. He gave free access to the multinational oil companies, which set up oil extracting

operations primarily on the Lake Maracaibo oil fields.

[10] In 1935 Gómez' former aide, General Eleazar López Contreras, took office. He was succeeded in 1941 by General Isaías Medina Angarita, who laid the foundations for greater political activity by legalizing the Democratic Action Party (AD).

[11] It was a long time before majority demands were met, however, and this situation was aggravated by the unrest within the army. A civilian-military movement took power, led by Rómulo Betancourt, the leader of AD, and General Marcos Pérez Jiménez, and they held the country's first free elections in 1947. The writer Rómulo Gallegos of AD was elected President only to be overthrown in 1948 by yet another military coup, installing the harsh dictatorship of Marcos Pérez Jiménez.

[12] Ten years later, in January 1958, Pérez Jiménez was overthrown by a popular revolt and he fled the country. Venezuela then entered a stable democratic period under a coalition government formed by Democratic Action, COPEI (the Christian Democrats) and the Republican Democratic Union (URD). This stability was largely achieved because of massive oil revenues, improved relations with the US, and expanded political rights.

[13] Unfortunately, the ensuing economic growth brought little change to the lives of the poor majority. Popular discontent resulted in guerrilla warfare led by the Communist Party, the Movement of the Revolutionary Left (which split from AD), and other groups.

[14] In 1960, Venezuela sponsored the formation of the Organization of Petroleum Exporting Countries (OPEC). Sixteen years later, during the presidency of social democrat Carlos Andrés Pérez, Venezuelan reserves of oil and iron were nationalized. Pérez also supported the creation of the Latin American Economic System (SELA) and argued in favor of a New International Economic Order.

[15] At this time, Venezuela was the world's third largest oil exporter and received its highest prices during the governments of Pérez and Christian Democrat Luis Herrera Campins. It had the highest per capita income in Latin America, but the Government was unable to manage the enormous amounts of money coming into the country. Huge state-run companies were created for the manufacture of iron ore, aluminum, cement, and for hydroelectric power, while most private companies were being subsidized. The Venezuelan state obtained 95 per cent of the country's revenues from oil exports and was by far its largest business owner.

[16] In 1982, a sharp decrease in oil revenues, foreign debt, and a flight of private capital abroad, forced the Government to take control of exchange rates and foreign trade. The foreign debt grew while inflation, unemployment, and housing shortages started to rise, and critical poverty rose.

[17] Charges of government corruption contributed to the victory of the AD's Jaime Lusinchi in the December 1983 elections where he gained 56 per cent of the vote, defeating COPEI's Rafael Caldera.

[18] The population continued to support Lusinchi for some time, but when the June 1983 economic collapse proved impossible to halt, Venezuela had to suspend $5 billion in service payments on its $37 billion debt, and the ensuing difficulties resulted in a drop in his popularity.

[19] In response to the economic problems, Lusinchi's policy

comprised an austerity plan which gave meagre results, and a flawed 'social pact' between employers and unions and, towards the end of his term, increasing state control over the economy.

20   The AD's candidate for the December 1988 elections was former president Carlos Andrés Pérez. Backed by the Confederation of Venezuelan Workers (CTV), he took 54.5 per cent of the vote, and Eduardo Fernández, the COPEI candidate, took 41.7 per cent.

21   Social tension increased and 25 days later the most underprivileged sectors responded with a wave of riots and looting. Police repression left more than 1,000 dead (246 according to the government), and 2,000 wounded or jailed.

22   The populist tone was dropped, and IMF-backed economic restructuring measures were initiated. In December 1989, these policies were blamed for abstention rates of nearly 70 per cent and broad gains by the Christian Democrats and left-wing parties, when Venezuelans elected their 20 state governors and 369 mayors for the first time.

23   Ten AD governors were elected, and COPEI had four, with the AD losing seats in many of its traditional strongholds. Most remarkable were the left-wing victories in three states: in Bolívar, the trade union leader Andrés Velázquez of the Popular Cause party was elected; in Aragua, the Movement Toward Socialism (MAS) won; and Anzoátegui elected a leader of the People's Electoral Movement (MEP).

24   In the early 1990s, Venezuela's indigenous population totaled around 200,000 - approximately one per cent of the population - but their future survival was threatened.

Despite the fact that the Government has clearly recognized Yanomami land rights, there has not been adequate protection of the indigenous population. They suffer persecution from landowners, farmers and government officials, while Brazilian miners continue to invade their land prospecting for gold within Venezuelan territory.

25   Early in 1992, the popularity of the Pérez Government was at its lowest, with the AD party distancing itself from imposing further economic measures. Congress exercised its controlling function by investigating crimes, but due to the corruption and inefficiency of the Judiciary these investigations very rarely led to prosecutions.

26   On February 4 1992, a group of colonels staged a coup against the President. The group was led by Francisco Arias and while the attempt failed, it re-emphasized the fact that administrative corruption and the economic crisis were the causes of instability. Arias and parachute commander Hugo Chávez, both belonging to the Bolívar-200 Military Movement, were arrested. This coup attempt caused several dozen civilian and military casualties.

27   On the day of the attempted coup, the Venezuelan President suspended all constitutional rights. This emergency measure - ratified by Congress - banned meetings, limited the freedom of press and movement and made it possible to arrest citizens without a warrant. An agreement was reached with the teachers' trade unions, putting an end to a fortnight of strikes and police repression of students and teachers.

28   Another coup attempt took place on November 27 1992. The air force played a key role in controlling the rebels. The ruling party only won in 7 of the 22 states where elections for governors, mayors, regional legislative assemblies and municipal councils were held.

29   President Pérez was suspended from office on May 21 1993, charged with the misappropriation of funds. He was provisionally replaced by Ramón Velázquez.

30   Rafael Caldera, President between 1969 and 1974 from the Social Christian Party, won the general elections on December 5 1993. He was supported by a wide range of sectors and political parties, with the backing of Convergencia and MAS being the most important factors in his success. Abstention reached 40 per cent as only around 5 million voted.

31   Another source of social unrest was the repeated violation of human rights, both of ethnic minorities and of inmates in several prisons. On August 21 the murder of 16

Yanomami close to the Brazilian border at the hands of the garimpeiros - Brazilian gold prospectors - was reported. Several members of the Yupca people were murdered by landowners in the state of Zulia.

32   Because of his age - over 75 - former president Pérez was sentenced to house arrest. In his opulent residence overlooking Caracas, Pérez concluded his sentence in September 1996 and returned to the political scene, affirming he would be president once more. During his 'confinement', Pérez was accused of having traveled abroad.

33   At the end of the 1980s, Caracas had become one of Latin America's most violent cities. A feeling of insecurity prevailed as the number of murders rose. In 1995 it was estimated that 10 per cent of Caracas residents carried a weapon.

34   The economic crisis worsened after 1994. The banks' collapse began in February 1993 with the fall of the Banco Latino, the country's second commercial bank. In August 1995, 18 out of the 41 private banks had been investigated and 70 per cent of the deposits were being managed by the Government.

35   President Caldera suspended constitutional guarantees regarding real estate, private property and business. He also restricted trips abroad, meetings and the immunity against arbitrary arrests. Despite Congress' vote to reinstate these rights, the President restricted them once more to prevent speculation and capital flight.

36   In 1997 the divisions both between and within the political parties interrupted parliamentary analysis of the 'Agenda Venezuela' reform project promoted by the government. This was to include privatization of the electricity, aluminum and iron industries; reform of the judicial system and the reorganization of public finances. With less than 10 per cent of the seats, Caldera's party had to seek alliances in various sectors in order to get the reforms approved. Democratic Action demanded a greater economic liberalization in return for its support.

37   On December 6 1998, the leader of the 1992 coup attempts, Hugo Chávez, was elected constitutional president with 56.5 per cent of the vote. In his inaugural speech, he announced he would replace what he described as a 'dead' constitution through a 'peaceful revolution' to reduce poverty and restructure foreign debt, standing at more than $23 billion. In order to do this there would be a National Constituent

PROFILE

ENVIRONMENT

The country comprises three main regions. In the north and west, the Andes and other mountain chains, and high mountains to the south. The central Orinoco Plains are a livestock farming area. In the southeast, highlands of ancient rock and sandstone extend to the borders with Brazil and Guyana, forming Venezuelan Guyana. It is a sparsely inhabited area with thick forests, savannas, rivers, and some peculiar features: the tepuyes or plateau mountains, and the rare Sarisarinama depths. Most of the population lives in the hilly north. The main oil basins are: Lake Maracaibo (Zulia), Orinoco River Basin (Delta Amacuro, Monagas, Guárico), Falcón Basin (Falcón), Apuré-Barinas Basin (Apure and Barinas states) and Cariacó Basin (Sucre). In the Gulf of Paria and the center of the State of Anzoátegui there are natural gas reserves. The country produces iron ore, manganese, bauxite, tungsten and chrome, gold and diamonds. Among the country's most important environmental problems are deforestation and the degradation of the soil. In addition, the lack of sewage treatment facilities in the main urban and industrial centers has increased pollution in the country's rivers and the Caribbean Sea.

SOCIETY

Peoples: Venezuelans are descended from the integration of indigenous peoples, Afro-Caribbean and European settlers. Today, indigenous peoples and Afro-Caribbeans each account for less than 7 per cent of the population. In recent times, Venezuela has received more immigrants than any other South American country. **Religions:** Mainly Catholic, 92.7 per cent. **Languages:** Spanish, official and predominant; 31 local languages are spoken. **Political Parties:** Movement for the Fifth Republic, led by Hugo Chávez. Democratic Action (AD), member of the Socialist International; the Movement Towards Socialism (MAS), founded in 1970; Project Venezuela; the Social Christian Party of Venezuela (COPEI), a member of the Christian Democrat International; First Justice; Radical Cause; New Time; National Convergence, created in 1993 by Christian Democratic splinter groups; The Fatherland for Everybody; People's Electoral Movement (MEP); the Venezuelan Communist Party (PCV); the New Democratic Generation, linked to the Liberal International; Integration, Representation, New Hope (IRENE), founded in 1997 by independent mayor of Chacao, Irene Saez. **Social Organizations:** The Venezuelan Confederation of Workers (CTV) is the main trade union, and is controlled by AD. There are other trade unions which are clearly linked to political parties.

THE STATE

Official Name: República Bolivariana de Venezuela. **Administrative divisions:** 21 states with partial autonomy (including the Federal District), 2 Federal territories. **Capital:** Caracas 3,127,000 people (1999). **Other cities:** Maracaibo 1,847,000 people; Valencia 1,719,500; Barquisimeto 1,027,700; Guyana City 748,200 (2000). **Government:** Presidential System. Hugo Rafael Chávez Frías, President since February 1999, re-elected in 2000. Unicameral Legislature: National Assembly, with 165 members. **National Holiday:** July 5, Independence Day (1811). **Armed Forces:** 79,000, including 18,000 conscripts (1997). **Other:** Cooperation Army 23,000.

Assembly (NCA) which would draw up a new constitution in six months.

[38] In early 1999, Chávez publicized his 'peaceful revolution' through his diplomatic corps and through a television program which received and directly 'resolved' the concerns of the public. On July 25, in elections for the NCA, 75 per cent of the population voted for the Chávez' Movement for the Fifth Republic , giving it the absolute majority in the body.

[39] In September, the country hosted the second meeting between Colombia's National Liberation Army (ELN) and the Colombian governmental authorities. Chávez, who started to play an important role in the Colombian conflict turned down a US request to use his air bases to 'combat drug trafficking' there. It was widely believed the US aimed to invade Colombia and do away with insurgent groups.

[40] In a referendum on December 15, 70 per cent of the Venezuelans who turned out to vote - half the electoral roll - approved a new constitution which named the country the 'Bolivarian Republic of Venezuela' and dissolved Congress. The high abstention rate was due, amongst other factors, to floods which plagued the country and killed 50,000 people.

[41] On January 30 2000, the National Constituent Assembly was dissolved - as stipulated - after new presidential and parliamentary elections were slated for May 28. With neither NCA nor Parliament, in the face of the national elections, Claudio Fermin (National Meeting) and Francisco Arias (independent) presented candidacies on a 'get Chávez out' ticket.

[42] The elections were finally held in June and Chávez was re-elected by an overwhelming majority for a term ending in 2006. In August, he met the leaders of the main oil exporting countries. The re-elected President faced harsh criticism from the US for meeting Iraqi president Saddam Hussein in Baghdad. Chávez was the first democratically elected head of state to visit Iraq since the Gulf War.

[43] The President announced a series of measures in early 2002 aimed at stimulating the economy. These included a reform of the Lands Law that would give the Government expropriation powers, as well as reforms of fossil fuels legislation, which included taxes on flexible revenues of the companies operating state oil wells. A law that doubled the royalty taxes paid by ExxonMobil - the number-one extractor of Venezuelan oil - and other oil operators from about 16 per cent to roughly 30 per cent on new finds was passed by the Government.

[44] The announcement triggered unrest in the middle-income and business sectors, and the support that the Chávez administration enjoyed at the beginning of his term turned into a frail social base and scant political support. His personalist view of politics and the long list of unkept promises led him into conflict with many social sectors: trade unionists, entrepreneurs, the communications media and the Catholic Church.

[45] The Gross Domestic Product grew by 2.8 per cent and economic activity - excluding crude oil - jumped by about 4 per cent in 2001. However Chávez was unable to capitalize on the high oil prices to shift revenues to development programs for the most vulnerable strata of the population. His bold statements led to an increase in capital flight that in just the first three months of his term had reached nearly $3 billion.

[46] In February 2002, to confront the crisis, Chávez enacted a strict adjustment package that was applauded by the IMF. He announced that the currency exchange rate would be floated, after parity with the dollar had been anchored at a 10-per cent annual depreciation of the bolívar, which represented a devaluation of more than 25 per cent. The budget was reduced by 22 per cent and public spending by 7 points. Furthermore, he ratified additional taxes. Many Venezuelans reacted against the price hikes, especially on items of mass consumption. The successive cases of military officers publicly speaking out against Chávez undermined his prestige in the armed forces and created further tension in the political climate.

[47] As a result of his ties with Cuba, Iraq and Libya, and his hesitation to condemn the September 2001 attacks against New York and Washington, Chávez ended up in direct confrontation with the US. He had almost single-handedly rebuilt OPEC by committing Venezuela to adhere to its OPEC sales quotas, causing world oil prices to double to over $20 per barrel. Venezuela is one of the most important oil suppliers to the US.

[48] The President moved to take control of the state oil company Petróleos de Venezuela (PDVSA)- nominally owned by the government, but in fact in thrall to the foreign operators - and removed several of its managers. This move unleashed a new crisis. A general strike, begun on April 9 by PDVSA executives against the imposition of a new Chávez-named board of directors, ended three days later with a massive demonstration that pitted anti-Chávez protesters against his supporters. Business interests also decried Chávez' new land law which promised to give unused land to the landless.

[49] An opposition group made up of military and business leaders, removed Chávez from office, took him to an island base and kept him prisoner and incommunicado. A coup put Pedro Carmona, head of the country's main business association, into the presidency. He was sworn in on April 12 and immediately dissolved Parliament and the Supreme Court, annulled the Constitution, called presidential elections to take place in a year and convened legislative elections for December, under a decree of 'reorganizing the public powers'. These announcements came with the figures on the previous day's violence: 15 dead and 350 injured, according to the fire department. And massive demonstrations continued despite the new government's attempts to control the situation.

[50] Two rumors circulated in the media during the two days Chávez was held captive: one was that he had never agreed to resign and had been deposed by force, while the other indicated that he had stepped down willingly. On April 14, at midnight, troops loyal to Venezuela's legitimate government entered the Miraflores presidential palace, took up positions and waited for another operation that would rescue Chávez and return him to power. Carmona was forced to step down and was arrested.

[51] After Venezuela had regained a level of stability, the Organization of American States applauded its return to constitutional order and backed Chávez's initiative to convene a national dialogue.

[52] US Assistant Secretary of State for Western Hemisphere Affairs, Otto Reich - one of the architects and managers of the 'Reagan Doctrine' in Central America two decades earlier - had been in contact with Carmona the same day the latter had seized power. Reich apparently phoned Carmona to urge him against dissolving the National Assembly. The US did not condemn the coup against Chávez until he returned to power. The British *Guardian* newspaper reported that US intelligence had been studying the possibility of removing Chávez from office for over a year; also that on the day of the coup, the US navy on the Venezuelan coast had tuned in to communications in Caracas. Washington's stance on Venezuela fed fears of 'coup contagion' throughout the region. ∎

STATISTICS

DEMOGRAPHY
Population: 25,093,000 (2002)
Annual growth: 2.3 % (1985-2000)
Estimates for year 2015: 30,877,000 (2000)
Annual growth to year 2015: 1.6 % (2000)
Urban population: 87.4 % (2000)
Urban growth: 2.3 % (2000)
Children per woman: 2.9 (2000)

HEALTH
Life expectancy at birth: 73 years (2000-2005)
male: 71 years (2000-2005)
female: 77 years (2000-2005)
Maternal mortality: 60 per 100,000 live births (1985/99)
Infant mortality: 20 per 1,000 (2000)
Under-5 child mortality: 23 per 1,000 (2000)
Daily calorie supply: 2,229 per capita (1999)
236 doctors per 100,000 people (1997)
Safe water: 83 % (2000)

EDUCATION
Literacy: 93 % (2000)
male: 93 % (2000)
female: 93 % (2000)
School enrolment (net):
Primary total: 84 % (1994/2000)
male: 83 % (1995/99)
female: 85 % (1995/99)
Secondary (gross):
male: 33 % (1995/97)
female: 46 % (1995/97)
Tertiary (gross): 28 % (1997)
Primary school teachers: one for every 21 pupils (1996)

COMMUNICATIONS
206 newspapers (1996), 294 radios (2000), 185 TV sets (2000) and 108 main telephone lines (2000) per 1,000 people
Books: 17 new titles per 100,000 people (1992/94)

ECONOMY
Per capita, GDP: $ 5,794 (2000)
Annual growth: 1.2 % (2000)
Annual inflation: -98.8 % (2000)
Consumer price index: 5.8 (2000)
Currency: 1,053.3 bolívares = $ 1 (03/2002)
Cereal imports: 2,581,112 metric tons (2000)
Food import dependency: 12 % (2000)
Fertilizer use: 859 kg per ha (1999)
Exports: $ 35,402 million (2000)
Imports: $ 20,515 million (2000)
External debt: $ 38,196 million (2000); $ 1,580 per capita (2000)
Debt service: 23.2 % of exports (1999)
Development aid received: $ 44 million (1999); $ 1.8 per capita (1999)

ENERGY
Consumption: 2,432.8 Kgs of oil equivalent per capita yearly (1998); -292.7 % imported (1999)

HDI (ranking/value): 61 / 0.765 (1999)

Vietnam

Population: 80,226,000 (2002)
Land area: 325,490 SQ KM
Capital: Hanoi
Currency: Dong
Language: Vietnamese

Viêt-nam

The Vietnamese nation was established after centuries of struggle against more powerful peoples. In the ninth century, they defeated the Chinese Han dynasty, ending nearly a thousand years of subjugation. In the 11th and 12th centuries, the Vietnamese succeeded in fighting off the Chams. They repulsed Genghis Khan, his Mongol hordes, and later his grandson Kublai Khan, when these were conquering the Asian world in the 18th century. In the 15th and 18th centuries the Vietnamese were victorious over the Ming and Ching Chinese dynasties, and in the 18th century they drove back the Khmers.

[2] In 1860, the French began to occupy Indochina, meeting with spontaneous, disorganized and badly armed resistance which, nonetheless, took them three decades to overcome. By 1900 the French had consolidated their domination over the region. Vietnam was divided into three parts: Tonkin in the north, Annam in the center and Cochinchina in the south. To eliminate Chinese cultural influence, the French taught Quoc Ngu, a Romanized writing script of the Vietnamese language. The French did not intend to help Vietnam's nationalists in the renewal and dissemination of national culture, but this system of notation facilitated reading and lowered printing costs when compared with the formerly used Chinese ideograms.

[3] In the 1920s, the first nationalist organizations were created. Marxist-Leninist parties appeared in different parts of Vietnam in 1929, achieving unity as the Indochina Communist Party the following year. This was founded by a patriot called Nguyen Ai Quoc, who adopted the name Ho Chi Minh. The Party later decided that it would be more effective if it was split into three different national sections, for Cambodia, Laos and Vietnam respectively. The latter was known as the Workers' Party until its 4th Congress in 1976, when it became the Communist Party of Vietnam once again.

[4] During World War II, the country was occupied by Japan. Vietnam's communists organized the resistance from the start,

cooperating with the allies but staying true to their intent to defeat colonialism. In 1941, Ho Chi Minh founded the communist Viet Minh or League for the Independence of Viet Nam, conceived as a broad unity front to include workers, peasants, the petit-bourgeoisie and the nationalist bourgeoisie. By the time of the Japanese surrender, the Viet Minh army had become a powerful force with widespread popular support in the northern part of the country. On August 18 1945, Ho Chi Minh launched a general insurrection in the north. Within two weeks the revolutionary forces took control of the entire country, and an independent republic was declared. Emperor Bao Dao abdicated and offered to cooperate in advising the new regime.

[5] Negotiations between the French - who seized the southern part known as Cochinchina - and Ho Chi Minh led to an agreement in March 1946 that appeared to promise a peaceful solution. Under the agreement France would recognize the Viet Minh government and give Vietnam the status of a free state within the French Union. However, the French aimed to re-establish colonial rule, while Hanoi wanted total independence. Georges-Thierry d'Angelieu, the High Commissioner for Indochina, proclaimed Cochinchina an autonomous republic in June 1946. The French reunited Cochinchina with the rest of Vietnam in 1949 and proclaimed the Associated State of Vietnam, appointing former emperor Bao Dao as chief of state. The Viet

Minh did not surrender and waged an increasingly successful guerrilla war, aided after 1949 by the new Communist Government of China. After nine years of fighting, the Vietnamese were finally victorious when they captured the garrison of Dien Bien Phu, in the north, on May 7 1954.

[6] The 1954 Geneva Agreements stipulated the withdrawal of the French and directed the Vietnamese to hold general elections in 1956. Viet Minh troops were to withdraw north of the 17th parallel. The United States set up the Ngo Dinh Diem regime in Saigon (now Ho Chi Minh City), dividing the country and violating the Geneva agreements, as elections were prevented. In 1960, the organizations hostile to Diem's regime (democratic, socialist, nationalist and Marxist forces) became the National Liberation Front, led by lawyer Nguyen Huu Tho. The 'second resistance' was then launched, this time against the successive military governments based in Saigon and above all against the United States, the true supporter, arms-supplier and policy-maker. US aid was initially limited to a handful of advisors. Then troops were sent to bolster the Diem regime - a process that escalated until, by 1969, 580,000 US troops were in Vietnam. A larger tonnage of bombs was dropped in Vietnam than during the whole of World War II, and terrible chemical and biological weapons were used. In that year, Ho Chi Minh died at the age of 79.

[7] The US spent $150 billion in Vietnam, destroyed 70 per cent of the northern villages and left 10 million hectares of productive land barren. Despite their efforts, Saigon - renamed Ho Chi Minh - was finally liberated by the Viet Cong on April 30 1975. On July 2 1976, Vietnam was reunited under the name of the Socialist Republic of Vietnam.

[8] Since then Vietnam has not enjoyed stable peace. In January 1979, it went to war against Pol Pot's regime in Cambodia. Pol Pot had claimed vast portions of Vietnamese territory. No sooner had the Cambodian regime been overthrown, than China invaded Vietnam on its northern border as a punitive measure. China had been a

MATERNAL MORTALITY

1985-99

Per 100,000
live births

95

LITERACY

2000

93%

FOREIGN TRADE

Millions US$ 1997

IMPORTS
14,274
EXPORTS
12,026

EXTERNAL DEBT

2000

PER CAPITA
US$ 164

---

staunch ally of the ousted Cambodian regime. Subsequent clashes along the border in 1980 underscored the military superiority of the Vietnamese, but the border between the two countries remained unchanged.

9   Vietnam considered Cambodia's union with the other regional states to be essential for its security. Vietnam's support of the Heng Samrin Government against the Khmer Rouge, Prince Sihanouk, and the National Liberation Front

entailed costly military efforts and a drain on Vietnam's resources, particularly in terms of food, which was already scarce. Also, from 1978 to 1981, Vietnam suffered floods, typhoons and droughts.

10   After 1981, Vietnam faced active hostility from the Reagan administration in the US, which stopped grain shipments provided by an American charity and blocked a Vietnamese aid program organized by the United Nations Development Program (UNDP).

11   In April 1985, several political prisoners were freed, and diplomatic ties with ASEAN countries and the US were intensified in an effort to reach negotiated settlements for Indochina. Arrangements were made to cooperate with the US to search for the corpses of missing soldiers as well as to allow people loyal to the former government to leave the country, and to permit the exit of children of US servicemen.

12   Le Duan, Secretary-General of the Communist Party of Vietnam since 1969 and a close collaborator of Ho Chi Minh, died on July 11 1986. The Congress designated 71 year-old Nguyen Van Linh, a former Viet Cong strategist, as the new Secretary-General.

13   The political changes in Eastern Europe at the end of the 1980s were not well received by Vietnamese communists since these had local repercussions, specifically growing demands for a multiparty political system. In the absence of such a system, dissenting voices sought expression within the Vietnamese Communist Party (VCP) itself. Some sectors of the Party demanded change toward a multiparty, parliamentary political system.

14   In August, the Central Committee of the VCP accused the West of trying to destroy the socialist world. Nguyen Van Linh urged his fellow-citizens to reject bourgeois liberalization, multiparty politics and opposition parties, whose aims were to make them renounce socialism. Even so, the participation of non-communist candidates was authorized in the 1989 National Assembly elections, and a year later, the Government authorized the formation of the Vietnam Veterans Association. However, this liberalization was accompanied by a

reaffirmation of the dominant role of the VCP, with the arrest of a number of campaigners for multiparty politics, and the dismissal of 18,000 public employees accused of corruption.

15   During the 1980s, 'illegal emigration' - the flight of Vietnamese toward neighboring countries - continued. The reluctance of Western countries to receive them has indefinitely prolonged their stays in overpopulated refugee centers. This was especially true in Hong Kong; the British Government began deporting them from there in December 1989, though this operation was later suspended because of international pressure.

16   The 7th VCP Congress held in June 1991 agreed to continue the process of building socialism, a path considered to be 'the only correct choice'. Van Linh was replaced as the party's general secretary by Du Muoi, who continued with the renewal process (*Doi Moi*) that had been initiated in 1986. Tron My Moa, the first woman member of the country's new leadership, became a member of the 9-member Secretariat of the Central Committee.

17   The VCP confirmed the continuance of a single-party system. The first step toward renewal and reform was a more flexible economic policy - specifically a change to a mixed economy. This implied allowing private enterprise and foreign investment within pre-determined parameters.

18   In October 1991, the initiation of negotiations between the four Cambodian factions opened the way for the normalization of Sino-Vietnamese relations.

19   In November 1991, the British Government with the support of the US began the forcible repatriation of 64,000 Vietnamese exiles from refugee camps within Hong Kong, a British dependency.

20   The new Constitution approved in April 1992 authorized independent candidates to run for election, but in the July legislative elections 90 per cent of the candidates belonged to the VCP. In September the new Assembly elected General Le Duc Anh president, known ally of Prime Minister Vo Van Kiet. In November, a commission of US senators visited the country to

---

PROFILE

ENVIRONMENT

A long narrow country covering the eastern portion of Indochina along the Gulf of Tongkin and the South China Sea. The monsoon-influenced climate is hot and rainy. Rainforests predominate and there is a well-supplied river system. The northern region is comparatively higher. There are two river deltas: the Song Koi in the north, and the Mekong in the south. Most of the people are farmers, and rice is the main crop. The north is rich in anthracite, lignite, coal, iron ore, manganese, bauxite and titanium. Textile manufacture, food products and mining are the major economic activities. The felling of trees for domestic use (firewood) and construction have contributed to deforestation. However, the most significant losses - particularly in the northern part of the country - are a result of the Vietnam War, specifically from the use of such chemical defoliants like 'Agent Orange'. Vietnamese Government policy - started after 1975 and reaching its peak in the mid-1980s - that moved millions of former North Vietnamese to what was thought to be the relatively under-populated central highlands took a heavy toll on the environment, including wide-scale deforestation on the highlands.

SOCIETY

Peoples: Most are Vietnamese (90 per cent). Mountain groups of different ethnic origins from southern Asia - Tho, Hoa, Tai, Khmer, Muong, Nung - and descendants of the Chinese form the rest of the population.
Religions: Mainly Buddhist; traditional religions. There are some 2 million Catholics and 3 million followers of the Hoa-Hao and Cao-Dai sects.
Languages: Vietnamese (official) and languages of the ethnic minorities.
Political Parties: The Vietnamese Communist Party (DCSV-Dan Cong San Vietnam), according to the Constitution 'the leading organization of society', founded by Ho Chi Minh in 1931; the Democratic Party and the Socialist Party of Vietnam, founded respectively in 1944 and 1946, organized intellectuals and the national bourgeoisie for the anti-colonialist struggle. Coalition of Vietnamese National Parties; Vietnamese Nationalist Party.
Social Organizations: The Federation of Unions of Vietnam (Tong Cong Doan Vietnam), founded in 1946, is the only union confederation and a WFTU member; the Vietnamese Women's Union, founded in 1930.

THE STATE

Official Name: Cộng hòa xã hôi chu' nghî'a Viêt Nam.
Administrative Divisions: 39 Provinces, including the urban areas of Hanoi, Haiphong and Ho Chi Minh City.
Capital: Hanoi 3,671,000 people (1999).
Other cities: Ho Chi Minh City (formerly Saigon) 5,566,900 people; Haiphong 1,763,300; Da-Nang 762,800 (2000).
Government: Tran Duc Luong, President and Head of State since September 1997. Phan Van Khai, Prime Minister and Head of Government since September 1997. Nong Duc Manh, General Secretary of the Communist Party since April 2001. Unicameral Legislature: National Assembly, with 498 members. The Executive Power is exercised by a Council of Ministers.
National Holiday: September 2, Independence Day (1945).
Armed Forces: 572,000 troops (1995).
Other: 5,000,000 (Urban Defense Units, Rural Defense Units).

discuss the issue of the missing remains of over 2,000 US military killed in action.

[21] At the beginning of the 1990s Vietnam decided to follow the example of its neighbors, the so-called 'Asian tigers'. Privatization and the liberalization of foreign investment led to an 8.3 per cent increase in the GDP in 1992. The volume of exports rose 20 per cent per year. However, the 'economic takeoff' also brought a number of negative results. Vietnamese workers were among the lowest paid in Asia, while economic growth put growing pressure on the environment, particularly in the cities.

[22] As for foreign trade, Vietnam depended primarily on two products: rice and, to a lesser extent, oil. In 1989, Vietnam became the world's third largest exporter of rice, after Thailand and the United States.

[23] According to Vietnamese standards at that time, a poor family was one that could not afford 13 kg of rice per person each month. A hungry family was one that could not afford 8 kg of rice per person each month.

[24] The south was the main beneficiary of the rice production and export boom in the Mekong delta. This underscored the structural inequality between the two parts of the country. With more than 5 million inhabitants - almost double the size of Hanoi, the capital city - Ho Chi Minh City (formerly Saigon) is the country's economic capital, adapting itself far better to the new era than the north.

[25] The Government granted a number of benefits to farmers, such as loans and long-term land leases, tax cuts and the right to inherit up to three hectares of land. However, total private land ownership has not yet been authorized (for instance, farmers enjoy what is called Land Use Rights, under which they can sell, transfer or will land).

[26] The effects of several decades of war are still evident, especially in the economic structure which was tailored to the demands of war. The devastation remains visible in a large part of the country, as a result of the use of lethal weapons like napalm or Agent Orange, a powerful defoliant. The country's infrastructure, in general - telecommunications,

highways and energy production - slowly began to recover as a result of projects financed by the World Bank and Asian Development Bank loans.

[27] Vietnam and the US established formal diplomatic relations in August 1995. President Clinton stated his concern for the 2,200 US soldiers still considered to be lost in action in Southeast Asia.

[28] The rapprochement between Hanoi and Washington did not lead to a rush of US firms, although many multinational corporations showed interest in the liberalization of the Vietnamese economy.

[29] In September, Tran Duc Luong and Phan Van Khai, were elected as new President and Prime Minister, respectively. Observers said the former would maintain his predecessor's economic policy and 'rejuvenate' the party leadership. In December, the VCP Central Committee decided to replace three of its leading figures. Former president Le Duc Anh and former Prime Minister Vo Van Kiet went and the civilian Le Kha Phieu was appointed Secretary-General, replacing veteran leader Du Muoi.

[30] In April 1998, the drought that had affected the southern province since January destroyed some 7,000 hectares of coffee plantations, while a further 40,000 (out of a total of 160,000) were threatened. Vietnam had increased its plantations from 15,000 to 260,000 hectares since the economic liberalization of the 1980s, exporting the product mainly to Europe and the US.

[31] The economic crisis which affected the region in 1998 barely touched Vietnamese growth, which fell from 8.8 per cent in 1997 to 6.1 per cent. But in order to maintain competitive edge as an exporter, the government devalued the currency twice. Direct foreign investment fell 70 per cent in respect to the previous year. In September Vietnam joined as a full member of the Asia-Pacific Economic Co-operation (APEC).

[32] Corruption was recognized as a national problem in 1998 and identified as an undesirable by-product of economic liberalization. In January, three Tamexco company employees, with close ties to the VCP, were executed for corruption. They included director the Pham Huy

Phuoc, who had appropriated $26 million of the $50 million embezzled. In 1999, the VCP demanded the resignation of one of the deputy prime ministers, Ngo Xuan Loc - who re-entered the Cabinet five months later - and sanctions against the former governor of the Central Bank, Cao Sy Kiem, for acts of corruption and misappropriation of funds.

[33] The VCP politburo acknowledged that relatives of its own members were involved in corruption and later recognized that this was a problem throughout party ranks. It was established that leaders must declare their wealth. An independent monitoring body was created to travel the country gathering complaints, reporting to a national leader. The party identified the lack of judicial autonomy, the need for information about current legislation and the need for independence in the legislative process, giving Parliament a true voice in politics. In April 2001, reformist Nong Duc Manh - previously president of the National Assembly - was appointed the new secretary-general of the VCP.

[34] US President Bill Clinton made an official three-day visit to the country in November 2000, marking a new era of normal relations between the two countries. He committed more US assistance for clearing the country of unexploded landmines, which had caused 40,000 deaths in the last quarter century. In June 2001, Tran Duc Luong signed an historic agreement with the US in Hanoi, during a donors' meeting. There, the World Bank expressed satisfaction with 'the progress of reforms in Vietnam.' In December, the trade agreement that normalized relations with the United States entered into force.

[35] In April 2002, 59 people faced charges of bank fraud for a total of $100 million in Ho Chi Minh City. Hundreds of people and organizations were expected to be caught up in the criminal case, including those who had been victims of fraud. The trial was seen as another effort by the Government to fight corruption in a country ranked among the most corrupt in the world. ∎

Virgins Is (US)

Population: 124,000 (2002)
Land area: 340 SQ KM
Capital: Charlotte Amalie
Currency: US dollar
Language: English

Virgin Islands

As is the case in other Caribbean islands, the Virgin Islands were originally inhabited by Carib and Arawak indians. The only gold on the islands was seen in the ornaments worn by the inhabitants and was of little economic interest. From the time of Columbus' arrival in 1493 onwards, the local population was persecuted and massacred and also was destroyed by the second half of the 16th century.

[2] The western part of the archipelago was claimed by other countries after the departure of the Spaniards. The Netherlands gained control in the 18th century and organized crop cultivation; first of sugar cane and then of cotton. They imported African slave workers as in many other parts of Latin America and the Caribbean. At the height of Dutch colonization, there were 40,000 African slaves on the islands.

[3] During Abraham Lincoln's second presidential term, the United States failed to acquire the islands. But in 1917, after World War 1 when the US wanted to consolidate its presence in the area, $25 million was paid to the Dutch for the islands and the 26,000 African former slaves who inhabited them.

[4] From that time on, the US initiated a series of changes in the territorial administration, ranging from the continuation of the legislation established by the Dutch, to the new law approved in 1969. This instituted the election of a Governor and Vice-Governor, the election of a non-voting Congressional delegate and the right of its inhabitants to vote in American elections. In a 1981 referendum, a proposed Constitution was voted against by 50 per cent of the registered voters. In December 1984, the UN General Assembly reiterated the right of the islands to self-determination, and urged the local population to exercise their right to independence.

[5] The local economy depended on the US. It largely revolved around an oil refinery owned by US-Ameranda Hess Corporation on the island of St Croix. The company's influence on local politics was very important, as it had 1,300 permanent and 1,700 temporary employees. The Corporation also supplied all the islands' energy needs. In spite of this,

ENVIRONMENT

It comprises the western part of the Virgin Islands group, east of Puerto Rico. The territory includes three main islands - St Thomas, St John and St Croix - and approximately 50 uninhabited small islands. The mountainous terrain is of volcanic origin. The climate is tropical, but irregular rainfall makes farming difficult. A small amount of fruit and vegetables are grown in St Croix and St Thomas. Tourism is an important economic activity. There is a large oil refinery in St Croix, supplying the US market.

SOCIETY

Peoples: Most of the population is English-speaking and of African origin with a small Spanish-speaking Puerto Rican minority. 35 to 40 per cent of the inhabitants are from other Caribbean islands; 10 per cent from the US.
Religions: Protestant and Catholic.
Languages: English, official; also Spanish and Creole.
Political Parties: There are local representatives of the US Republican and Democrat parties and an Independent Citizens Movement (ICM).

THE STATE

Official Name: Virgin Islands of the United States.
Capital: Charlotte Amalie 12,000 people (1999).
Other cities: Anna's Retreat 13,500 people; Charlotte Amalie West 8,000 (2000).
Government: Charles Turnbull, Governor since January 1999. The unicameral legislature is made up of 15 representatives (7 from St Thomas, 7 from St Croix and 1 from St John).
National Holiday: March 27, Transfer Day (from Denmark to the US, 1917).
Armed Forces: The US is responsible for the defense of the islands. The naval bases have been under local jurisdiction since 1967, but the US retains the right to occupy them at any moment, as well as to recruit local residents for US armed forces.

DEMOGRAPHY
Population: 124,000 (2002)

EDUCATION
Primary school teachers: one for every 18 pupils (1992)

ECONOMY
Fertilizer use: 1,500 kg per ha (1999)

tourism was still the island's main source of income.

[6] A referendum scheduled for November 1989 was to decide the future status of the islands. However, it was not held because in September 1989 the islands were severely damaged by Hurricane Hugo. According to official estimates, 80 per cent of the buildings were destroyed. The disaster caused an outbreak of looting and unrest. Armed bands wandered the streets; some members of the police and National Guard also took part in the pillaging. The US sent more than 1,000 troops to the area, but the disturbances had virtually ceased by the time they arrived. In the words of local people, there was nothing left to steal.

[7] The US Government declared the islands a disaster area and granted $500 million in humanitarian aid. However, damages were estimated at $1 billion.

[8] An aluminum oxide plant, which had been closed in 1985, was purchased in 1989 by an international group trading in raw materials. The plant has a capacity for an annual production of 700,000 metric tons. Shipments to the US and Europe began in 1990.

[9] Alexander A Farrelly, who had governed the islands since 1987, abandoned his post in 1995 and was replaced by Roy L Schneider. In the following elections, in November 1998 Charles Turnbull won with 58.9 per cent of the vote, while Schneider took the remaining 41.1 per cent. In elections for the senate, Turnbull's Democrat Party took 6 seats while the Republicans kept 2 and the pro-region Independent Citizens' Movement took one seat. The independents drew even with the Democrats, holding six seats.

[10] Hurricane Lenny lashed the islands in November 1999 causing four deaths in St Croix and serious damage to buildings and roads.

[11] Fourteen counts of embezzlement, fraud and falsifying documents against former Governor Schneider and three top officials of his administration were dismissed by Judge Ive Swan in March 2000. ∎

Virgins Is (British)

Population: 25,000 (2002)
Land area: 150 SQ KM
Capital: Road Town
Currency: US dollar
Language: English

British Virgin Islands

The Virgin Islands, were named by Christopher Columbus in 1493 in honour of St Ursula. At that time the islands were inhabited by Caribs and Arawaks, but by the mid-16th century they had all been exterminated by the Europeans.

[2] In the 18th century, the English gained control of the easternmost islands of the archipelago and, using African slave labor, they began cultivating sugarcane, indigo and cotton. By the mid-18th century, the islands' slave population had reached 7,000, outnumbering the European colonists 6 to 1. Slavery was eventually abolished there in the 1830s.

[3] From 1872 the islands joined the British colony of the Leeward Islands, which were administered under a federal system. This federation was dissolved in July 1956, but the Governor of the Leeward Islands continued to be responsible for the administration of the Virgin Islands until 1960. In that year direct control over the islands passed into the hands of an administrator designated by the British Crown. Unlike the Leeward Islands, the British Virgin Islands did not belong to the East Indies Federation, which existed between 1958 and 1962, preferring to develop links with the American Virgin Islands, under US control.

[4] Constitutional reform required elections to fill the seats of the Legislative Council. They were held in November 1979. Independent candidates won five of the nine seats and the Virgin Islands Party (VIP) won the remaining four. Five years later, the independent candidates only retained one seat; however, by forming an alliance with the United Party (UP), they managed to have one of their members appointed Prime Minister.

[5] The colony was governed under several constitutions during the 20th century, and the ministerial form of government began in 1967 with the first open elections. In 1977 the Constitution was modified, granting greater autonomy and carrying out changes in the electoral system. The responsibility for defense, internal security and foreign affairs remained in the hands of the British-appointed governor.

[6] In the 1980s tourism accounted for 45 per cent of the national income, while fishing was the traditional economic activity. Gravel and sand were important exports, and a 'tax-haven' banking facility has been established.

[7] In August 1986, the British Government dissolved the Legislative Council, calling a new election several days after the opposition presented a vote of no-confidence in the Prime Minister. In September the VIP won 5 of the 9 seats and the UP won 2. Lavity Stott, the VIP leader, was named chief minister.

[8] In March 1988, Chief Minister Omar Hodge resigned under accusations of corruption, and was replaced by Ralph O'Neal. Hodge denied the charges against him, and in March 1989 he created a new party, the Independent People's Movement and in early 1990 was cleared of the charges against him.

[9] In the November elections, the VIP increased its majority to 6 seats, while the IPM obtained 1 seat, and the independents 2. Stoutt maintained his post as chief minister, and O'Neal was re-elected Chief Minister.

[10] Due to the increase in drug trafficking, and following recommendations by the British Government, legislation was introduced to control the operations of international financial companies. These would need a license to operate on the islands and their activities would be subject to periodic inspections, as the authorities believed most of the investments were coming from the drug trade.

[11] In October 1991, Peter Alfred Penfold was named Governor.

[12] In the legislative elections of February 1995, the VIP took 6 seats, the IPM 3, the Movement of Concerned Citizens (CCM) took 2, as did the UP. On May 15 1995, following the death of H Lavity Stoutt, Ralph O'Neal took over as Chief Minister. In June 1995, David Mackilligin was appointed Governor.

[13] In July 1997, the Government approved a three-year development plan, which included a $2 million plan to extend the port and the construction of two tourist centers.

[14] The British crown appointed Frank Savage governor in 1998, and in the May 1999 elections the VIP took 8 seats with 38 per cent of the vote. The National Democratic Party took 5 with 36.9 per cent of the vote, while the remainder went to the Concerned Citizens' Movement (4 per cent). Independent candidates took 13.4 per cent of the vote, but none had enough support to get into the Legislative Council.

[15] The Government started road works and other infrastructural projects on the outer islands . In December 2001 Chief Minister Ralph T. O'Neal presented the 2002 budget and underscored the importance of this infrastructural works for developing tourism in Virgin Gorda, Anegada and Jost Van Dyke ∎

PROFILE

ENVIRONMENT

The eastern portion of the Virgin Islands comprises 36 islands and reefs, 16 of which are inhabited. The larger ones are Tortola, Anegada, Virgin Gorda and Jost Van Dyke, which hold most of the population. The islands' rolling terrain is of volcanic origin. Agricultural production is limited to fruit and vegetables as a result of erratic rainfall. The major economic activities are fishing and tourism. The coral reefs are threatened by tourist activities.

SOCIETY

Peoples: Most are descendants of African slaves. There is also a small British minority. 86 per cent of the population are concentrated on Tortola Island, 9 per cent live on Virgin Gorda, 3 per cent on Anegada and 2 per cent on Jost Van Dyke. **Religions:** Mainly Protestant (45 per cent Methodist, 21 per cent Anglican, 7 per cent Church of God, 5 per cent Seventh-Day Adventists, 4 per cent Baptist, 2 per cent Jehovah's Witnesses, 2 per cent others); 6 per cent Roman Catholic; 6 per cent others (1981). **Languages:** English (official). **Political Parties:** The Virgin Islands Party (VIP), of Ralph T O'Neal; National Democratic Party; the Independent People's Movement (IPM), of Omar Hodge and Allen O'Neal; the United Party (UP), of Conrad Maduro; the Concerned Citizens' Movement (CCM), of E Walwyln Brewley.

THE STATE

Official Name: British Virgin Islands. **Capital:** Road Town 8,500 people (1999). **Other cities:** East End-Long Look 4,900 people (2000).
Government: Frank Savage, British-appointed Governor since 1998. Ralph O'Neal is the Chief Minister since May 1995. There is a Legislative Council of 9 elected and 4 appointed members.
National Holiday: July 1, Territory Day.
Armed Forces: The defense is responsibility of the United Kingdom.

Western Sahara

Population: 268,000 (2002)
Land area: 266,000 SQ KM
Capital: L'ayoun
Currency: Moroccan dirham
Language: Arabic and Spanish

Sahara Occidental

From the 5th century, the far west of the Sahara has been populated by Moors, Tuaregs and Tubus. These populations originated as a result of the desertification the area has undergone since the Neolithic Era. Their presence is documented by the Tassili stone carvings and other relics. In the 9th century, waves of migrants arrived from Yemen and intermarried with the local population. Four hundred years on, the first confederation of Saharawi peoples appeared.

[2] The main motivation for the Spanish occupation of this coast was strategic: to cover the flank of the Canary Islands. Colonization was mostly limited to Villa Cisneros (present-day Dakhla) until 1886, when, as a result of the Berlin Conference (see box in Congo Republic), Madrid resolved not to let an 'empty space' fall to another power. However, after an agreement with France was reached in 1904, establishing the borders of Spanish Sahara, the situation returned to what it had been. The nomadic ethnic groups lived completely independently in a territory that colonialism divided into four countries, effectively untouched by the Europeans' agreements.

[3] In 1895, Sheikh Ma al-Aini founded the Smara citadel and fought the Franco-Spanish presence with the support of the Sultan of Morocco until 1910, when the latter gave in to European pressure and suspended assistance to the rebels, who expanded their actions into Morocco and even threatened Marrakesh. The French counter-attack consisted of an invasion of 'Spanish' territory and the conquest of Smara in 1913, though resistance continued until 1920.

[4] The French pressed Spain to increase its control over the territory, and in 1932 L'ayoun was founded. In 1933, the victory of the forces under Mohammed al Mamun, cousin to Ma al-Aini and Emir of Adrad, forced a change in colonialist tactics. France occupied the rebel base at Tindouf oasis and advanced into Algeria, Mauritania and Morocco, while Spanish troops took Smara, overcoming the insurgents in 1934.

[5] When the French deposed Sultan Mohammed V, the National

Liberation Army (ALN) was created in Morocco, and its Southern Division operated in close cooperation with the Saharawi people. Following Morocco's independence in 1956, and the dissolution of the ALN, the Saharawis were left to face Spain and the French air force on their own, leading to a withdrawal of resistance in 1958.

[6] At that time, exploitation of the phosphates discovered at Boucraa began. Transnational capital, with the consent of Spain's fascist Franco regime, invested more than $160 million, transforming the country, particularly its population

distribution. In 1959, L'ayoun had 6,000 residents, but had reached 28,000 by 1974, while the nomadic population dropped from 90 percent to 16 percent of the country's total in that same period.

[7] With the progressive abandonment of the traditional nomadic way of life, ties and relationships began to weaken, though the colonial administration maintained latent divisions through political recognition of the *shiuj* (clan chiefs) and notables of the different groups. The system of individual identification contributed to that end, given that the nationally issued documents specified which people or faction the holder belonged to. However, a new national identity slowly developed, transcending traditional divisions.

[8] The Saharawis founded the Al Muslim movement in 1967, and the Sahara Liberation Front a year later. In 1973, the revolutionary leadership decided to pursue armed struggle, creating the Polisario Front, which was led by Mustafa Seyid El Uali until he died in combat. The war and the resolutions of the UN, which favored the independence movement, prompted the Franco government to recognize the right of self-determination, but in order to maintain control it created the Party of Saharawi National Union (PUNS).

[9] Spain withdrew under an agreement that gave it 33.7 per cent of the phosphate mines, and allowed Spanish ships to continue fishing Saharan seas over the next 10 years. It further won a commitment from Morocco not to reclaim Ceuta or Melilla, its enclaves on the Mediterranean coast of Morocco.

[10] In 1974, the World Bank defined Western Sahara as the richest territory of the Magreb region for its leading fisheries and for its phosphate reserves. The latter reached 1.7 billion tons in the Boucraa area, but the entire region is believed to hold another 10 billions tons.

[11] In 1975, Morocco claimed sovereignty over Western Sahara, but the International Court of Justice at The Hague overruled its claims and ordered decolonization. King Hassan II of Morocco organized what was dubbed the 'Green March' on the Sahara, a

PROFILE

ENVIRONMENT

The country is almost completely desert and is divided into two regions: Saguia el Hamra in the north and Río de Oro in the south. It has one of the world's largest fishing reserves, but the principal source of wealth is mining, especially phosphate deposits.

SOCIETY

Peoples: The Polisario Front estimates the dispersed Saharawi population at one million. These are traditionally nomadic groups that differ from the Tuaregs and Berbers in their social and cultural organization.
Religion: Islam. **Languages:** Arabic and Spanish (official). Many Saharans also speak Hassania. **Political Parties:** The People's Liberation Front of Saguia al-Hamra and Rio de Oro (Polisario Front) founded on May 10 1973 by Elwali Mustafa Sayed. **Social Movements:** The Saguia al-Hamra and Rio de Oro General Workers' Union (UGTSARIO).

THE STATE

Official name: Saharawi Arab Democratic Republic.
Capital: L'ayoun (Layoune) 195,000 people (1999).
Other cities: Ad Dakhla 40,200 people; Semara 36,100; Bu-Craa 27,800 (2000).
Government: Muhammad Abdelaziz, President of the Republic since 1982, is also Secretary-General of the Polisario Front. Bouchraya Hammoudi Bayoune, Prime Minister since 1999. The National Assembly (parliament) has 101 members, elected by local and regional conferences and acts as a check on the executive branch. Polisario is committed to multiparty democracy when it gains independence.
National Holiday: February 27, Proclamation of the Republic (1976).

propaganda move that mobilized 350,000 Moroccans to head south, crossing the border, to press for a reversal of The Hague ruling.

[12] The Spanish Government ceded possession of the Sahara to Morocco and Mauritania in 1975, but the Saharawi proclaimed the Saharawi Arab Democratic Republic (SADR) on February 27 of the following year. The new African republic was born in Bir Lahlu, a desert post in Saguia El Hamra, a few kilometers from the Mauritania border. Just hours earlier, in L'ayoun, the last representative of the colonial administration had officially announced the end of Spanish presence.

[13] Several countries recognized the new nation, but it triggered a war against Moroccans and Mauritanians. In 1979, Mauritania, on the verge of collapse, decided to halt fighting and sign a peace treaty with the Polisario Front. Hassan's troops, however, stepped up attacks with French and US support.

[14] The Polisario Front's military victories led to a diplomatic success in July 1980 at the conference of the Organization of African Unity (OAU) in Freetown, where 26 African countries announced official recognition of SADR as legitimate representative of the Saharawi people. Four months later the UN issued a resolution requesting Morocco's withdrawal. In 1980 and 1981, 50 countries maintained diplomatic ties with SADR. The military offensive continued in March 1981 with the takeover of the city of Guelta Zemmur.

[15] SADR was accepted in November 1984 as a full member of the OAU. Morocco withdrew from the organization, as it had announced it would. On November 14 1985 the UN Decolonization Committee recognized the Saharawi people's right to self-determination.

[16] In July 1990, representatives from Morocco and the Polisario Front debated in Geneva a procedural code for holding a referendum to allow the Saharawis to decide their own future. The greatest challenge was how to define who could vote. The most recent census of the Saharan population dated to 1974, and Morocco wanted its people in the occupied zone to be authorized to vote. Both sides agreed on giving the UN 'sole and exclusive' control over the voting procedures, ballot count and announcement of the results.

[17] The parties also agreed on an end to hostilities for the referendum, the gradual reduction of Moroccan troops in the territory - estimated at 160,000 - to 25,000, and the withdrawal of the remaining forces 24 hours after the announcement of the referendum results. The

Polisario Front, meanwhile, would withdraw its forces to an area near Tindouf, in Algeria.

[18] The UN Security Council approved a peace plan on April 29 1991 that called for a ceasefire to come into force on September 6 , and the creation of the UN Mission for the Referendum in Western Sahara (MINURSO). The plebiscite was scheduled to take place in January 1992.

[19] In the following months, the Moroccan Government settled thousands of Moroccan citizens in Saharawi territory to make them eligible voters, repeatedly violated the ceasefire and obstructed the work of international journalists. It also banned international observers from entering the area, whilst repression against the Saharawis mounted, and launched an intensive propaganda campaign that claimed the referendum was a confirmation of Morocco's ownership of the Sahara.

[20] MINURSO was entrusted with drawing up the electoral roster based on the 1974 census. This implied that an undetermined number of Saharawis could not vote in the referendum, but nor could the Moroccans who immigrated after 1976. The Saharawis of voting age who were living in refugee camps in Algeria would be transported back to their towns of origin.

[21] By January 1992, when the referendum was slated to take place, MINURSO was far from completing its program for identifying voters and the Saharawi repatriation plan could not be finalized. Meanwhile, 60,000 Moroccan soldiers remained in Western Sahara. Brahim Hakim, member of the Polisario Front's directorate, ended his exile in Algeria in 1992 and returned to Morocco. Hakim stated that armed struggle had become futile and ordered his followers to lay down their weapons. In recent years, a growing number of rebels had distanced themselves from the Front as military defeats continued.

[22] September 4 1992 marked the third time that Western Sahara residents voted in Moroccan elections as they took part in a referendum on a constitutional reform proposed by King Hassan (see Morocco). Members of diplomatic circles interpreted this as an attempt by Moroccan authorities to incorporate the disputed territory before the referendum on its political status took place.

[23] Morocco continued to obstruct moves towards the referendum, apparently convinced that time was on its side. After several postponements of the vote over the next few years, the Polisario Front threatened to return to war. At the pace it was going at the time, the

identification of voters would not be complete until 2005, according to Polisario president Muhammad Abdelaziz in May 1996.

[24] In 1996, 170,000 Saharawis remained in refugee camps in the Tindouf region of Algeria, near Western Sahara. The Polisario Front had established schools and other services there.

[25] Morocco and the Polisario Front agreed September 16 1997 to reactivate the peace plan for Western Sahara, exchange prisoners and release political prisoners. The referendum date was set for December 7 1998.

[26] Polisario Defense Minister, Brahim Gali, and Foreign Minister, Bachir Mustafa Sayed (head of diplomacy for the last 15 years) were replaced in January 1998. The move was attributed to the Front's need to keep its hands free for negotiating the last phase of the referendum.

[27] President Abdelaziz announced that if the Polisario Front won, the Moroccan citizens could remain in the territory provided they were not 'related to the occupation and annexation'.

[28] Under the UN plan, Morocco and the Polisario agreed to accept that if Morocco won, the UN would disarm the Saharawi combatants, while if the Polisario won, it would supervise the withdrawal of Moroccan troops and administration from Western Sahara. The resettlement of the 200,000 Saharawis exiled since the 1970s, mostly in Tindouf, was a matter left pending.

[29] The 10th Congress of the Polisario Front was held in Tindouf in August 1999, and Abdelaziz was re-elected as president of the SADR. In his inaugural speech, Abdelaziz admitted 'deficient management and inadmissible practices' in the Saharan administration, but insisted there were no internal differences over the quest for independence. The President also expressed the hope that the new Moroccan king, Muhammad VI, would respect agreements made before the UN.

[30] In March 2000 at a meeting of the Polisario Front National Secretariat, in the Saharan government-controlled zone, the Secretariat called on the European Union countries for a firm hand in meeting the official schedule. Before threats of further delays, which would stall the referendum set for July 2000, the Polisario Front National Secretariat expressed its support for UN Secretary-General Kofi Annan's special envoy, US official James Baker, who negotiated compliance with the agreements. The referendum, which had already been suspended in 1998 due to difficulties in drawing up the draft document, was delayed once again.

After growing international pressure to reach an alternative solution after more than 10 years of discussions on who was entitled to vote, talks were resumed in London in June. However these failed once again when the Polisario Front rejected the terms of the autonomy proposal, instead of independence, and threatened to resume armed struggle.

[31] A new informal meeting, sponsored by James Baker, took place at his Wyoming ranch in August 2001, attended by the Polisario Front, Algeria and Mauritania. Morocco did not take part.

[32] In October 2001, king Muhammad VI made his first trip to the Western Sahara region since coming to the throne. This trip coincided with an agreement between Morocco and French and US oil companies to explore along the Sahara coast. President Abdelaziz described this trip - which coincided with a new anniversary of the Green March - as a provocation and announced the peace process would deteriorate.

[33] French President Chirac, visiting Morocco, declared that the disputed territory was part of that country. His statements, made in late 2001, were heavily criticized by Abdelaziz and also upset Algeria - a traditional advocate of Western Saharan independence - and Spain, which had lately withdrawn its support for Morocco. Chirac's words were the first of a major power in support of Moroccan rights, against the UN resolution.

[34] The Polisario Front freed 115 Moroccan prisoners of war. A second trip through Western Sahara by King Muhammad VI took place in March 2002, in a new attempt to consolidate the sovereignty of Morocco over the territory. ∎

West Papua

Population: 2,100,000
Land area: 421,918 SQ KM
Capital: Jayapura
Currency: Indonesian rupiah
Language: Bahasa Indonesian

Papua

Humans first settled New Guinea at least 50,000 years ago, which was connected to Australia by a land bridge until about 10,000 before the present. There is evidence of agriculture from possibly as early 9,000 years ago, which makes the island one of the earliest independent centers for the domestication of several varieties of sweet potato and fruit-bearing tree.

[2] The British were the first Europeans who attempted to settle the western part of the island (which the indigenous people now call West Papua). In 1793 a short-lived British colony was set up near present-day Manokwari but it was evacuated within two years. A unilateral proclamation was made by the Dutch on the 24th of August 1828 at the newly founded Fort du Bus on West Papua's south coast: the natives of the western half of New Guinea were to be subjects of the King of the Netherlands from this point forward.

[3] The Dutch were not initially concerned with colonizing West Papua, but opened Fort du Bus to protect their lucrative trade in the surrounding spice islands (the Dutch East Indies) from other European powers. Fort du Bus was abandoned after only ten years. Until the turn of the twentieth century, the Dutch governed West Papua indirectly through the Sultan of Tidore, who

regularly made raiding expeditions to West Papua and demanded tribute in the form of bird of paradise plumes, sea cucumbers, and slaves. The Dutch did not establish a continuous settlement in West Papua until 1897, and did not engage in any substantial development within the country until the 1950s. Organized resistance to foreign control was clearly demonstrated when people in the province (the West Papuans) refused to both pay taxes and to engage in forced labour.

[4] On 27 November 1949 the Dutch ceded sovereignty of the Dutch East Indies to Indonesia, but excluded Dutch New Guinea (West Papua).

Throughout the 1950s, the Dutch argued that West Papua was geographically and ethnically different from Indonesia and the Papuans should (over time) be given self-determination. By contrast, the Indonesians argued that Dutch New Guinea had already been transferred to them in 1949, and had achieved independence then. In 1962, 1,500 Indonesians 'invaded'.

[5] Under the auspices of the UN, the US urged Indonesia and the Netherlands to the negotiating table. Retired US diplomat Ellsworth Bunker drew up a plan to transfer the administrative authority for West Papua from the Netherlands to a

neutral administrator, and thence to Indonesia. No West Papuans were involved in these negotiations. This 'New York Agreement' was signed by the Indonesians and the Dutch at UN headquarters on 15 August 1962. It fell well short of guaranteeing a referendum on independence, instead requiring Indonesia to make vague arrangements for West Papuans to 'exercise freedom of choice'.

[6] In 1968, a UN team arrived to 'assist, advise and participate' in the 'Act of Free Choice', which took place the following year. Only 1,025 West Papuans were chosen (many handpicked and intimidated by Indonesian troops) to vote in open meetings. UN Secretary-General U Thant later reported that without dissent the West Papuans had pronounced themselves in favor of remaining with Indonesia.

[7] More than 100,000 have been killed by the Indonesian forces since then. Political leaders in Sentani and Jayapura and local leaders in Wamena estimate an 800,000 death-toll.

[8] Indonesian mining company PT Freeport has paid a yearly average of $180 million in taxes and royalties to Indonesia from its activities in West Papua (where it operates the world's biggest gold mine and the third biggest copper deposit). Only a fifth of this revenue has been returned to West Papua.

[9] In February 2000, 400 delegates including representatives of the armed wing of West Papua's most long-standing separatist movement (the OPM) met in Sentani and openly discussed a strategy to take West Papua towards independence. This meeting rejected the 1969 Act of Free Choice as fraudulent and illegal.

[10] Later in 2000 a Papua People's Congress attracted 3,000 delegates. The Papua Council and its Presidium (Executive) emerged from these two meetings. Throughout these developments, Jakarta has consistently opposed independence but supported greater 'autonomy' for the 'province'. Legislation implemented in January 2002 hands back much of the tax and royalties previously sent to Jakarta and spent elsewhere. Nevertheless, the Papuans oppose autonomy because it fails to deliver self-determination and allows continued military and police intervention. ∎

PROFILE

ENVIRONMENT

Located in the Pacific Ocean directly north of Australia, West Papua, taken with the eastern half of its island landmass, Papua New Guinea, comprises the second largest island in the world and contains rainforests second only in size to those of the Amazon. West Papua has an abundance of natural resource wealth such as oil, gold, copper and wood. Most indigenous people live in a traditional subsistence economy based on agriculture (taros, yams, cassava) and the breeding of animals.

SOCIETY

Peoples: Melanesians 62 per cent. (60 per cent). Migrants and transmigrants born in other parts of Indonesia (called 'Javanese'): 17 per cent (40 per cent). **Religion:** Christianity is threaded through the belief system of many indigenous West Papuans. Indonesian migrants and transmigrants are predominantly Muslim **Languages:** Bahasa Indonesian (official). There are 253 tribal languages. West Papua and its neighbor, Papua New Guinea, contain 15 per cent of all the world's known languages.

THE STATE

Official name: Papua, (West Papua) formerly Irian Jaya. **Capital:** Jayapura **Government:** Indonesian President Megawati Sukarnoputri. In February 2000 a Papua People's Congress was held where 3,000 delegates came together. The Papua Council (currently led by Tom Beanal) and its Presidium (Executive). The source of their continuing legitimacy relies on a loose consensus of all the organizations advocating independence in West Papua. The local legislature with native Papuan upper house has limited real power. **National Holiday:** West Papuans celebrate their Independence Day on 1 December, Independence Day (1961). **Indonesian armed forces in the country:** Between 15,000 to 20,000.

STATISTICS

NOTE: *The information from Indonesia often differs from that from West Papuans. Where there are discrepancies, the Indonesian version is given first, then the West Papuan version in brackets.*
Urban population: 6.8 % **Health:** children per woman: 2.5 (2000). Life expectancy at birth: 64 (40 depending on locality). Infant mortality: 49 per 1,000 (70-200 depending on locality). **Education:** Literacy: 71.5 %. **Economy:** Per capita, GDP: $ 450

Yemen

Population: 19,912,000 (2002)
Land area: 527,970 SQ KM
Capital: Sana´a
Currency: Rial
Language: French

Yaman

When the Cretan civilization reached its highest point, another trade culture was flourishing on the Arabian peninsula which rapidly led to the appearance of numerous cities. Ma'in, Marib, Timna, and Najzan were the principle cities of the interior, along the caravan routes that brought aromatic fragrances from Dhufar (presently part of Oman) and Punt (Somalia). These extensive trade routes continued along the coast of the Red Sea as far as the Mediterranean markets, and from Taima on towards Mesopotamia.

2   These cities were united and ruled by whichever trade center held greatest power at the time, first Mina and later the better-known Saba, cited in the Bible. The latter's ties with the African coast dated from the founding of the Ethiopian state of Axum (see Ethiopia).

3   In spite of the rudimentary state of their fleet, Saban merchants kept close links with Africa for centuries, and as a result Christianity was propagated among the Yemenis through the teachings of Ethiopian preachers during the fourth century. Shortly thereafter, the Himyarites (a Hebrew sect) took control in Southern Arabia, establishing Judaism as the official religion and provoking a series of conflicts between the groups.

4   Ethiopians conquered the country in 525 AD and were driven out by the Persians in 570. At this time the Persians established their first contact with southern African trade, which was renewed centuries later when the Persians settled in Africa.

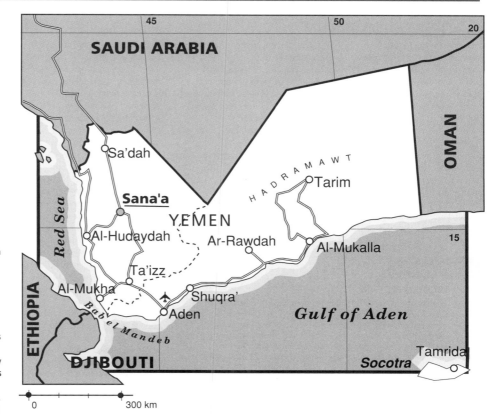

5   By the time of Muhammad and the ensuing Arab unification, the region had suffered almost three centuries of conflict and invasions, resulting in the loss of much of its splendor. Even the Marib Dam, a monumental construction forming the center of the agricultural irrigation system, had collapsed from lack of maintenance. The downfall of this civilization triggered great population migrations towards Africa and the eastern part of the peninsula.

6   By the end of the 8th century the borders of the Arabian Empire reached from north Africa and Spain in the west, to Pakistan and Afghanistan in the east. Damascus in Syria became the capital of the empire, where the foundations of a new culture were laid. Greco-Roman, Persian and Indian components blended to form the new dominant culture, with the Arabs reaching high levels of scholarship and philosophy. The Arabs formed the social elite, the ruling class, though little changed in

the lives of the Yemenis and other subject peoples.

7   Then, in the 16th century, the Ottoman expansion started. The Turks occupied a few of the coastal areas of the Red Sea, leaving inland areas and the southern coast independent, governed by an *imam* (priest).

8   In 1618, the British arrived in the area and established the East India Company in the port of Mukha (Mocha: origin of the name for a type of coffee).

9   In the 19th century they expanded their presence. As a consequence of Muhammad Ali's conquest of the country, the British occupied the entire extreme south-western region (see Egypt) and took Aden, the best harbor in the region, to discreetly monitor Turkish activities. Meanwhile the Turks consolidated their inland dominion, which was finally achieved in 1872. Concessions were made to allow the imam to retain his position and also make the post hereditary rather than elective.

10   Towards 1870, with the opening of the Suez Canal and the

consolidation of Turkish domination over the northern part of Yemen, the Aden settlement acquired new importance in British global strategy; it was a key port on the Red Sea and ultimately gave them access to the new canal.

11   Friendship and protectorate treaties were gradually signed with local leaders, but it was a slow process, only completed in 1934 when the British gained control of the entire territory, as far as the border with Oman.

12   In 1911, Imam Yahya Hamid ad-Din led a nationalist rebellion; and two years later the Turks recognized the imam's full authority over the territory in exchange for the formal acceptance of Turkish sovereignty. After World War I Yahya proclaimed himself independent sovereign of the whole of Yemen, and conflicts arose with the Saudi Emir of Najd and with the British, in Aden.

13   After uniting Hidjaz with his nation, leader ibn Saud launched a rapid military offensive against Yahya. In the 1934 peace treaty,

LAND USE

DEFORESTATION: 0.0% annual (1990/95)

1993

- FOREST & WOODLAND: 3.8%
- ARABLE: 2.6%
- OTHER: 93.6%

1985-99

Per 100,000
live births

350

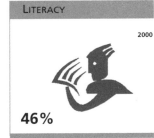

2000

46%

FOREIGN TRADE

Millions US$ 2000

IMPORTS
3,537

EXPORTS
4,305

1998

35%

Yahya accepted the loss of territory in the northern part of the country, in return for the cessation of aggression. The British stopped before the actual declaration of war, but internal rivalries were fuelled and groups actively opposed to the imam were encouraged; the imam was assassinated in 1948.

[14] In 1958, his successor Ahmad ash-Shams joined the United Arab Republic formed by Egypt and Syria but he later withdrew in 1961. He was succeeded in 1962 by his son Muhammad al-Badr, who was later deposed by the Nasserist military in September of that year. The former imam received both Saudi and British support, initiating a long civil war against the republican government, which lasted until 1970.

[15] The new People's Democratic Republic of Yemen closed all the British bases in 1969, nationalized the banking system, took charge of foreign trade and the shipbuilding industry and initiated agrarian reform.

[16] In October 1972, despite ideological and political differences between North and South Yemen, Rahman al-Iriani signed a treaty with the revolutionary government of the People's Democratic Republic of Yemen (South Yemen) for a future merger of the two states.

[17] This ran counter to Saudi strategy and, in June 1974 Colonel Ibrahim al-Hamadi forced al-Iriani to resign and installed himself as ruler in Sana'a. Although initially accepted by Saudi's King Faisal, the young officer made a powerful enemy when he challenged the landlords of the north in an effort to centralize power. He survived three assassination attempts, but was finally killed on October 11, 1977 together with his brother, Lt-Colonel Muhammad al-Hamadi.

[18] A junta led by Lt-Colonel Ahmed al-Gashmi, with Prime Minister Aziz Abdel Ghani and Major Abdul al-Abdel Aalim, took power vowing to continue their predecessor's policies. This action cost al-Gashmi his life as he died in a bomb attack in June 1978.

[19] Major Ali Abdullah Saleh was appointed President in 1978 but was unable to prevent internal dissent leading to armed conflict in January 1979. The National Democratic Front, which included the nation's progressive sectors, was on the brink of taking power, so with Saudi provocation the conflict was diverted into a war with Democratic Yemen. Syria, Iraq and Jordan intervened and their mediation led to a cease-fire and negotiations for the unification of the two Yemeni states, which had been suspended since 1972.

[20] In February 1985, the People's Supreme Council made President Ali Nasser Muhammad step down as prime minister, appointing Haider Abu Bakr Al-Atlas as his successor. Nasser Muhammad resented the loss of power and conspired to recover his position. On January 13, a counter-coup led to a brief but intense armed confrontation leaving 10,000 dead. Nasser Muhammad was ousted and Haider Abu Bakr Al-Atlas was appointed president. The new head of state pledged to maintain the alliance with Ethiopia and Syria.

[21] President Saleh's successful efforts to balance internal and external pressures resulted in more favorable conditions for rapid reunification.

[22] Finally, on May 22 1990, the Republic of Yemen was proclaimed, with the political capital in Sana'a (former capital of the Arab Republic of Yemen) and the economic capital in Aden (former capital of the Democratic Republic of Yemen).

[23] In a joint session of the Legislative Assemblies of the two states, held in Aden, a Presidential Council was elected, made up of General Ali Abdullah Saleh (ex-president of North Yemen), Abdel Karim Abdullah al-Arashi, Salem Saleh Mohammed and Abdul Aziz Abdel Ghani. The members of the Council elected Ali Abdullah Saleh president of the united republic. Ali Al Beid was vice-president and General Haidar Abu Bakr Al-Atlas, ex-president of South Yemen, was also given a post in the new government.

[24] In May 1991, the Constitution was ratified in a national referendum: an overwhelming majority voted for freedom of expression and political pluralism. Islamic fundamentalist groups opposed to unification called for a boycott, finding the absence of the principles of *sharia* (Islamic law) unacceptable, including, among other things, the introduction of voting rights for women.

[25] As a consequence of the Gulf War in 1991, a million Yemeni migrant workers were expelled from Saudi Arabia and other countries of the region in retaliation for Yemen's pro-Iraqi stance during the Gulf War. However, Yemen made proposals to Saudi Arabia to settle border disputes, which had existed since 1930 when Saudi Arabia had annexed three Yemeni provinces.

[26] At the same time, another million Yemenis returned to the country from Africa, mainly from Somalia. The sudden arrival of such a large number of people from abroad had a negative impact on the economic situation within Yemen. Unemployment at this time stood at over two million in a total population 10.5 million. The returning workers, especially from Saudi Arabia, also deprived Yemen of an important source of foreign currency that came from their remittances.

[27] Thirty-six per cent unemployment and price increases in basic consumer goods led to a series

PROFILE

ENVIRONMENT

The Republic of Yemen is formed by the union of Democratic Yemen (South) and Arab Yemen (North). North Yemen has the most fertile lands of the Arabian Peninsula. For that reason the country, together with the Hadhramaut Valley, used to be called 'Happy Arabia'. Beyond a semi-desert coastal strip along the Red Sea, lies a more humid mountainous region where the agricultural lands are found (sorghum is grown for internal consumption and cotton for export). The traditional coffee crop has been replaced by *qat*, a narcotic herb. The climate is tropical with high temperatures especially in Tihmah - where rainfall is heavy - and in the eastern region. The country has no mineral resources. The southern territory is dry, mountainous and lacks permanent rivers. Two-thirds of its land area is either desert or semi-desert. Agriculture is concentrated in the valleys and oases (1.2 per cent of the territory). Fishing is an important commercial activity. The country's boundaries include the island of Socotra, which due to its location at the entrance to the Gulf of Aden, has important strategic value. This island, which became part of South Yemen in 1967, has 17,000 inhabitants spread over 3,626 sq km. The use of ground water beyond its capacity to regenerate has caused a decline in its levels.

SOCIETY

Peoples: Nearly all Arab. A small Persian minority lives along the coast.
Religions: Islam, official (Shi'a, 53 per cent and Sunni, 46.9 per cent).
Languages: Arabic, official.
Political Parties: General People's Congress (GCP); Yemeni Congregation for Reform; Nasserite Unionist People's Organization; Arab Socialist Rebirth Party; the Yemenite Socialist Party; the Islah Party.

THE STATE

Official Name: al-Jumhuriya al-Yamaniya.
Administrative Divisions: 16 Provinces.
Political Capital: Sana'a 1,231,000 people (1999).
Other cities: Aden 562,000 people; Al-Hudaydah (Hodeida) 246,000; Taiz 290,107 (1995).
Government: Ali Abdullah Saleh, President since May 1990, re-elected in 1994 and 1999. Abdel Qadir Bajamal, Prime Minister since March 2001. Since unification of the Yemen Arab Republic (North) and the People's Democratic Republic of Yemen (South) in May 1990, Presidential Council made up of 5 members (3 from the North, 2 from the South).
Unicameral Legislature: Assembly of Representatives, with 301 members.
National Holiday: May 22, unification (1990).
Armed Forces: 66,300 (1997).
Other: 20,000 (Central Organization for Security); 20,000 (tribal forces).

of demonstrations in late 1992 and early 1993. At the same time, Islamic fundamentalism - strongly supported by the poorest sectors of the population - was blamed for a series of attacks against politicians from South Yemen.

[28] In March 1993, Saleh's General Congress of the People (GCP) won the elections and obtained 122 seats, followed by the fundamentalist Reform (Islah) Party, with 62. The Socialist Party of then vice-president Salem al-Baidh came in third place, with 56 seats. In order to weaken unified Yemen, a hypothetical 'bad example' to the region's monarchies, Saudi Arabia supported the fight for secession led by al-Baidh.

[29] In May 1994, once again secessionists proclaimed the creation of a southern Yemen democratic republic and requested diplomatic support from Saudi Arabia and the Gulf states. However they were defeated by forces loyal to the Government. In July, the council of ministers adopted a plan of general amnesty in order to protect political pluralism. Furthermore, the Government named Aden as the country's economic capital, which was regarded as a gesture towards southern Yemenites.

[30] In September, Socialist Party members were forced to leave the government, while Islah obtained six new places in the cabinet. The Constitution was modified, stating that sharia law would be the source of all Yemenite legislation.

[31] In February 1995, 11 parties formed a new alliance, the Opposing Democratic Coalition, seeking to obtain the power. The Government signed an agreement draft with Saudi Arabia in which both states express their will to set permanent common borders and promote bilateral relations.

[32] The landing of Eritrean forces on the Hanish Islands in the Red Sea in December was considered an act of aggression by the Yemeni Government, causing a war. Egypt's President Hosni Mubarak offered to mediate and in March 1996 Yemen and Eritrea accepted international arbitration to resolve the disagreement. At the end of that year, however, the key points had still not been resolved.

[33] On April 27 1997, the GCP won the parliamentary elections, taking 187 of the 301 seats, followed by the Islamic Islah party, with 53. The Socialist Party, after extensive internal debate, boycotted the elections.

[34] On May 15, the new Prime Minister, Faraj Said ibn Ghanem formed a 28-member government, including 24 GCP representatives. That year the Government implemented a structural adjustment plan to revive an economy suffering the effects of civil war and the reduction of aid from many Western and Arab nations. The economic reforms, especially the privatizations, earned the Government funding from the World Bank and the International Monetary Fund.

[35] According to Amnesty International, Yemen was one of the five countries still applying the death penalty to offending minors in 1998, along with Iran, Pakistan, Saudi Arabia and the US.

[36] Abdel Karim al-Iriani took over as Prime Minister in May 1998, a post he had held from 1980 to 1983 in the north. A Saudi attack on a Yemeni detachment on the island of Duwaima, in the Red Sea, in July, further worsened relations between the two neighbors. In October the international court in The Hague ruled in favor of Yemeni ownership of the Hanish islands, also claimed by Eritrea.

[37] The September 1999 elections gave a clear victory to Ali Abdullah Saleh, who was re-elected with 96.3 per cent of the vote.

[38] The abduction of 28 mostly British tourists in December 1998 raised controversy over the method used by some clans to make their claims known to the central authorities. Kidnapping was becoming a common practice in order to get government attention and to force it to give in to local petitioners. In the 1990s some 200 tourists or executives from European or US companies were taken in this manner. In February 2000, a new law was introduced making the abduction of foreigners a capital offence. A month later a group kidnapped the Polish ambassador in Yemen, freeing him four days later.

[39] In October 2000, 17 US soldiers were killed in Aden in a suicide attack on the USS Cole. The radical Islamist Osama bin Laden, a Saudi of Yemeni descent, was blamed for masterminding the attack. That same month, a bomb exploded at the British embassy. Four Yemenis were imprisoned after declaring they had carried out the attack in solidarity with the Palestinian cause.

[40] Violence marked the municipal elections of February 2001, which were accompanied by a referendum on extending the presidential term to seven years. Clashes among factions and with the police, as a result of the vote recount, left 30 people dead. The recount resulted approval for the constitutional reform and Saleh's term in office was extended.

[41] In May, without explanation, the President restructured the Cabinet and deposed Premier Abdul-Karim al-Iryani, naming former foreign minister Abdul Kader Bajammal in his place. The new Cabinet had 23 new members, including Wahiba Fare, who took over the Human Rights portfolio and became the first woman in Yemen to head a ministry.

[42] In November, Saleh traveled to Washington to reassure his US counterpart that Yemen would participate in the coalition of nations that Washington was organizing to fight terrorism. In March 2002, the Government expelled more than 100 Islamic students, including French and British citizens, as part of its campaign against terrorism and against members of the al-Qaeda network, headed by Bin Laden. In March, the US agreed to send military advisers to train Yemeni forces in anti-terrorism tactics. According to Washington, Yemen, like Afghanistan, could favor al-Qaeda's growth.

[43] At least 5,000 people staged a protest in April, burning Israeli and US flags and effigies of US President George W Bush and Israel's Prime Minister Ariel Sharon, and demanding the closure of the US embassy. An explosion and a grenade attack had recently occurred at the embassy compound. ∎

Yugoslavia

Population:	10,522,000 (2002)
Land area:	102,170 SQ KM
Capital:	Belgrade
Currency:	New dinar
Language:	Serb

Jugoslavija

In the 4th century BC, the Balkan Peninsula and the Adriatic coast were inhabited by Illyrian, Thracian and Panonian groups, and they were also the site of Greek colonies. In the mid-2nd century, Rome defeated the alliance of the Illyrian peoples and began colonizing the new province of Illyria. Important Roman cities developed, such as Emona (now Ljubljana), Mursa (Osijek) and Singidunum (Belgrade). When the Roman Empire split into Eastern and Western regions, the border between the two ran straight through what is now Yugoslavian territory. Towards the end of Roman domination, Christianity was established in the region.

[2] In the 5th and 6th centuries AD, these territories were invaded by a number of nomadic tribes: Visigoths, Huns, Ostrogoths, Avars, Bulgars and Slavs. They imposed their own religious beliefs upon the people, but Christianity gradually took hold again between the 9th and 11th centuries. From the 7th to the 13th centuries there were several feudal states. The Serbs were separate from these states, although they were unable to resist external pressure. Bosnia was subdued by Hungary, and the rest of the territory, as far as the state of Ducla, by Byzantium. Macedonia was divided up between Byzantium and Bulgaria (see Bosnia and Herzegovina, and Croatia).

[3] In the mid-11th century, under the reign of Stephen Nemanja (1168-1196), Serbia freed itself from Byzantine domination. The Serbian rulers of the Nemanja dynasty fought against the non-Christian religions which had been spread by the Bulgars. They received a royal title from the Pope in 1217, but the hoped-for propagation of the Catholic faith did not follow. In 1219, the Serbian Orthodox Church was founded, and mass began to be celebrated in Serbian. Under the reign of Stefan Dusan (1331-1355) the medieval Serbian State reached its apogee when it occupied Albania and Macedonia.

[4] The Ottoman Empire began its conquest of the Balkans in the mid-14th century, after the Battle of Kosovo in 1389. In the 14th and 15th centuries, the first of a series of migrations began from Serbia and Bosnia to neighboring Slav regions and ultimately to Russia. In 1395, all of Macedonia came under the Ottoman Empire. Bosnia which had been a part of the Hungarian kingdom since the 12th century was conquered in 1463. The Slav population of Bosnia became Muslim within a relatively short period of time. In 1465, the Turks occupied Herzegovina. By this time, Venetia had annexed the territories of Neretva and Zetina, along the coast. The city-state of Dubrovnik came under Hungarian control, and then, after 1526, became a part of the Ottoman Empire for 489 years.

[5] Between the 16th and 18th centuries, all of Yugoslavia's territories had been divided up. Serbia, Bosnia, Herzegovina, Montenegro and Macedonia belonged to the Ottoman Empire; Croatia, Slovenia, Slavonia, part of Dalmatia and Vaivodina belonged to the Hapsburgs; and Istria and Dalmatia belonged to the Venetian Republic. After the 1690 revolution was put down in Old Serbia, some 70,000 people took refuge in the Hapsburg Empire. The Ottoman Empire transferred Albanian Muslims to the abandoned territories of Kosovo and Motojia.

[6] After the Russo-Turkish war of 1768-74, Russia obtained the right to sponsor the Orthodox population of the Ottoman Empire, through the Treaty of Kuchuk-Kainardzhi. Austria seized the Balkans in 1797, as a result of the Napoleonic Wars, The Balkan *pashalik* (the north of Serbia), which belonged to the Ottoman Empire after the first Serbian uprising (1804-13), the Russo-Turkish war (1806-12) and the second Serbian uprising (1815), was granted internal autonomy. The political and military leaders Gueorgui Cherny (Karadjordje) and Milos Obrenovic founded Serbia's ruling dynasties. In 1829, Serbia became an independent principality within the Ottoman Empire, with Milos Obrenovic as its prince.

[7] In the 1878 Congress of Berlin, the Great Powers recognized the full independence of Serbia and Montenegro, which became kingdoms in 1882 and 1905 respectively. In the first Balkan war in 1912, Serbia, Montenegro, Greece, Romania and Bulgaria formed an alliance. In the second, in 1913, they warred against each other over the Ottoman Empire's domains. The end result was Macedonia's partition between Serbia, Greece and Bulgaria, while Serbia and Montenegro expanded their territories.

[8] Serbian resistance to the Austro-Hungarian Empire led to the assassination of the Austrian archduke Franz Ferdinand in 1914, in Sarajevo, the event that marked the beginning of World War I. After the War, which saw an end to Austria-Hungary's empire, a kingdom of Serbs, Croats and Slovenes was founded, including Serbia, Montenegro and the territories of Slovenia, Croatia, Slavonia, Bosnia and Herzegovina.

[9] In 1929, the nation began to be called Yugoslavia: the land of the southern Slavs. The Government remained in the hands of Serbians, and under the reign of Alexandr Karagueorgevich, it became an absolute monarchy. The regime's exclusivist policies gave rise to a strong anti-Serbian movement among Croats and other ethnic minorities, which led to the King's assassination in Marseilles in 1934.

[10] At the beginning of World War II, Yugoslavia was neutral. In 1941, when Hitler attacked Yugoslavia, the country was so divided internally that it was easily subdued within a few days. The King and the members of the government fled the country, and the German Command carried out a policy of extermination against the Serbian and Muslim population.

[11] Two groups which were hostile towards each other launched the resistance movement: the nationalists loyal to the King - called *chetniks* - led by Draza Mihajlovic, and the partisans under the leadership of Josip Brozxz, a Croat better known by his nom de guerre, Tito. This group was made up of communists in favor of a united Yugoslavia, and anti-Nazi forces from all the republics with the exception of Serbia; it later became the Yugoslav League of Communists (YLC).

[12] After bloody fighting against occupation troops and the Croatian *ustasha* (fascist) movement allied to the Germans, Tito emerged victorious. After the liberation of the country in May 1945, a Provisional Government was formed led by Tito and supported by the Soviet Union and Britain.

[13] During the War 2,000,000 Yugoslavians were killed and 3,500,000 were left homeless. When the War finally ended, the country was in ruins.

MATERNAL MORTALITY	LITERACY	FOOD DEPENDENCY	FOREIGN TRADE

MATERNAL MORTALITY 1985-99

Per 100,000 live births
9

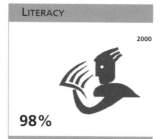

LITERACY 2000

98%

FOOD DEPENDENCY

1990

12%

FOREIGN TRADE

Millions US$ 2000

IMPORTS
4,256

EXPORTS
2,666

[14] On November 29 1945, a Constituent Assembly abolished the monarchy, proclaiming a federation of six republics: Slovenia and Croatia in the North, Serbia in the East, Bosnia-Herzegovina and Montenegro at the center, and Macedonia in the South. It also founded two autonomous provinces: Voyvodina and Kosovo, to the northeast and southeast of Serbia, respectively.

[15] The YLC joined the Cominform (Communist and Workers' Parties' Information Bureau) in 1947, but withdrew in the Spring of 1948 over disagreements with the Soviet CP leadership. The USSR initiated an embargo against Yugoslavia, which led to the strengthening of its ties with the West and the Third World.

[16] After a phase of economic centralization including the forced collectivization of agriculture in 1950, Tito introduced the concept of 'self-management'. Its goals were to ensure workers direct, democratic participation in all decision-making processes concerning their living and working conditions, and to protect social democracy against the distortions and abuses of 'statism' - bureaucracy and technocracy. The system was based on social (not state) ownership of the means of production and natural resources, managed directly by workers in their own and the community's interest. Similar forms of self-management were developed for trade and services.

[17] Tito was one of the founders of the Non-Aligned Movement. The Yugoslav leader defined non-alignment as the process whereby countries which were not linked to political or military blocs could take part in international issues, without being satellites of the major powers.

[18] The Yugoslavian leadership was charged with revisionism and isolated from the international Communist movement because of its neutral foreign policy and heterodox model of social and economic organization. Relations with the USSR slowly returned to normal after Stalin's death in 1953.

[19] That same year, an Agrarian Reform Law was approved authorizing private farming, and 80 per cent of the land returned to private hands. The combination of private economic activity and the self-management system led to average annual GNP growth rates of 8.1 per cent, between 1953 and 1965. In 1968, industrial production was 12 times greater than in 1950, the year in which the self-management system was first introduced. Likewise, industrial production was three times as important as agricultural production, in its impact upon the national economy. As a result, Yugoslavia's social and economic model was of great interest to the European left.

[20] The country's growth rate declined slightly toward the end of the 1960s. Even so, until the end of the 1970s, the annual growth rate exceeded 5 per cent.

[21] President Tito was aware of the inter-ethnic tensions in the Yugoslavia of his day, as well as the sharp contrasts between the socio-economic situation of the industrialized north and that of the underdeveloped south. In 1970, he announced that after he stepped down, the country's leadership should be exercised by a body made up of the federated republics and the autonomous provinces.

[22] In 1971 and 1972, ethnic conflicts worsened especially between Serbs and Croats, and Croatia presented a formal complaint against the confederated system. After 1974, there was an increase in separatist activity by Kosovo's Albanian majority.

[23] After Tito's death in April 1980, the executive power was vested in a collective presidential body, made up of a representative of each republic and autonomous province, and the president of the YLC with a rotating annual presidency. The new regime ratified Tito's policies of self-management socialism and non-alignment.

[24] Despite a strong economic position during the 1960s, both Serbia and Croatia became exporters of labor. Yugoslavia continued to export labor, and cash remittances from Yugoslavian workers in Western Europe together with revenues from tourism constituted an essential source of foreign currency to improve the balance of payments. This became more important in 1980 when the economic situation worsened.

[25] In March and April 1981, there were riots in the autonomous province of Kosovo (bordering on Albania) and these recurred in 1988 and 1990. In Kosovo, 90 per cent of the population (1.9 million) at this time was of Albanian origin. It was the poorest region of Yugoslavia, with unemployment reaching 50 per cent in 1990, with a per capita GNP of $730 while Serbia's was $2,200.

[26] According to the federal government, Kosovo housed nationalist forces and separatist extremists inspired and instigated from abroad, whose final objective was secession from Serbia and Yugoslavia. Many Serbs and Montenegrins left the area. Repression of the uprisings in Kosovo, which left a number of people dead and injured, led to mutual diplomatic recrimination between Belgrade and Tirana (the Albanian capital) and the resignation of Kosovo's governor, Jusuf Zejnullahu, in March 1990. There was also tension in other republics due to the growth of militant Muslim and Catholic groups.

PROFILE

ENVIRONMENT

Most of the country is taken up by mountain ranges, leaving one important plain north of the Sava River, a tributary of the Danube, where agricultural activities are concentrated. The climate is continental in this area, and Mediterranean along the coast. Rich deposits of bauxite, coal, lead, copper and zinc in the mountains, together with tourism in the Adriatic coast of Montenegro are major sources of income. There are several environmental problems as a result of the war, particularly the NATO bombings. The most notorious is contamination from the depleted uranium used in the NATO missiles.

SOCIETY

Peoples: Serb 62.6 per cent; Albanian 16.5 per cent; Montenegrin 5.0 per cent; multiethnic 3.4 per cent; Hungarian 3.3 per cent; Muslim 3.3 per cent; Romany (Gypsy) 1.3 per cent; Croat 1.1 per cent; other 3.5 per cent. In Kosovo - under international protectorate - up to 90 per cent of the population is of Albanian origin. These rates are subject to error because of the exceptional political situation.
Religions: 65 per cent Serb-Orthodox, 19 per cent Muslim, 4 per cent Catholic.
Languages: Serb (official), Albanian, Montenegran, Hungarian, Slovakian and Roma.
Political Parties: Socialist Party of Serbia (SPS); Serbian Radical Party; Reformist Party, neo-liberal; Democratic Movement of Serbia; Socialist Party of Voivodina; Hungarian Democratic League of Voivodina; Green Party, among others.
Social Organizations: League of Unions.

THE STATE

Official name: Savezna Republika Jugoslavija (Federal Republic of Yugoslavia).
Capital: Belgrade 1,697,800 people (1999).
Other cities: Pristina 190,500 people; Nis 184,400; Novi Sad 176,100 (2000).
Government: Serbia and Montenegro agreed in March 2002 to create a new federal state in which the members would each have their own president, foreign ministry and defense ministry. After three years, their respective populations are to be asked by referendum whether they want to continue membership in this new, looser federation, or opt for independence. President, Vojislav Kostunica, since October 2000. Prime Minister, Dragisa Pesic, since July 2001. Bicameral Parliament: 183-member Citizens' Council (Serbia: 108, Montenegro: 30), and Council of the Republics, with 40 members (20 from each). President of Serbia, Milan Milutinovic, since December 1997. President of Montenegro, Milo Djukanovic, since January 1998; Prime Minister Filip Vujanovic. Kosovo and Voivodina are provinces within Serbia, autonomous until 1990 and 1989, respectively. Kosovo is under an international protectorate presided over by Danish diplomat Hans Haekkerup, in office since January 2001.
National Holiday: November 29, Proclamation of the Republic (1945).
Armed Forces: 126,500 (60,000 recruits) (1995).

[27] Ethnic conflicts - coupled with inflation, which reached 90 per cent in 1986 and four figures in 1989 - were considered by the central committee of the Communist League to be rooted in deeper contradictions. During these years, several lawsuits dealing with government corruption exposed the fact that the system was crumbling. The Communist parties of Slovenia and Croatia announced their withdrawal from the YLC. In its January 1990 congress, the Yugoslavian League of Communists renounced its constitutional single-party role, and called on parliament to draft a new constitution, eliminating the leading role assigned to the League in all spheres of Yugoslav life.

[28] In April of the same year, in the first multiparty elections to be held in Yugoslavia since World War II, nationalist groups demanding either secession or a confederated structure won in all of the republics except Serbia and Montenegro.

[29] In 1989, Yugoslavia's last socialist prime minister, Ante Markovic - a Croat and a neo-liberal - launched a series of structural reforms in order to put an end to the crisis.

[30] As of 1990, the situation began to deteriorate even further, with the exception of foreign trade which began registering negative figures a year later. Industrial production fell by 18-20 per cent in Serbia and 13 per cent in Montenegro - while the gross foreign debt of the Federation as a whole reached $16.295 million. Of this, more than $5.5 million arose from Serbia and Montenegro.

[31] With mounting social pressures because of the economic situation and the disintegrating state, Yugoslavian politics were polarized by two fundamentally opposed concepts. Kucan in Slovenia argued for decentralization to relieve the wealthier regions of the obligation to subsidize the more backward areas, while Slobodan Milosevic, charismatic president of the Serbian Communist League, proposed greater centralization and solidarity in the Federation.

[32] In December 1990, the Croatian Parliament adopted a new constitution which established the right to withdraw from the Federation. At the same time, a referendum in Slovenia endorsed independence. In the following months, there was disagreement over the reform of the federal system and the appointment of the President.

[33] On September 8 1991, Croatia and Slovenia declared their independence from the Federation, and the Serbian population within Croatia declared its intention of separating from Croatia. The federal army, whose officials answered primarily to Serbia, intervened in Slovenia and Croatia, stating that separation was a threat to Yugoslavia's integrity. War broke out, with many victims on both sides (see Croatia).

[34] War led to the destruction by federal troops of entire cities - like Osijek, Vukovar and Karlovac - as well as the occupation of nearly a fourth of Croat's total land area. Areas affected included the territories of West and East Slavonia, as well as the area known as Krajina, which toward the end of 1991 proclaimed itself the 'Republic of Serbian Krajina'.

[35] In December, both the president of the governing council, Stjepan Mesic, and Prime Minister Markovic resigned, the last representatives of a united government. Markovic - like Mesic, a Croat - was unwilling to present the preliminary legislation for the 1992 budget, believing it to be biased against Croatia (81 per cent of the projected budget was earmarked for the federal army). By the end of 1991, there was a total of 550,000 refugees, 300,000 of them from occupied areas of Croatia.

[36] In 1992, within the territory which still defined itself as Yugoslavia, Serbian president Milosevic shored up his position by retiring 70 generals and admirals of the federal armed forces whose loyalty to him was in question. He also won Montenegrin support for his plan to establish a unified Yugoslavia with its capital in Belgrade, through a plebiscite in that republic. The March 1 referendum was boycotted by the opposition.

[37] On January 15 1992, the European Community recognized Croatia and Slovenia as sovereign states. On April 27, the parliament of Serbian and Montenegrin deputies announced the foundation of the new Federal Republic of Yugoslavia, a federation between Serbia and Montenegro with a parliamentary system of government.

[38] In the meantime, fighting continued in the regions characterized by inter-ethnic strife. Since April 1992, the heart of the fighting had been the republic of Bosnia-Herzegovina, which was recognized by the EC on April 7. In order to divest itself of responsibility for the aggression in Croatia and Bosnia-Herzegovina, in early May Belgrade announced that it was no longer in control of troops from what had formerly been the federal army, now fighting in the independent republics. Far from having the desired effect, Serbia's position led the EC to declare a trade embargo against Yugoslavia on May 28.

[39] However, the general elections held in the new federation on May 31 served to further strengthen Milosevic's position. His Socialist Party of Serbia (SPS) won 70.6 per cent of the vote in Serbia, while the Socialist Democratic Party of Montenegro won 76.6 per cent. The democratic opposition, as well as the Albanian minorities and the Muslims of Sandchak, boycotted the elections; only 56 per cent of the electorate participated.

[40] With the election of Dobrica Cosic, a writer, as federal president on June 15, and Milan Panic, a businessman, as prime minister on July 14 Serbia's leaders projected an image of a greater willingness to negotiate. Unlike Milosevic, Panic agreed with the London peace proposals of August 26 and 27. Nevertheless, this new development did not prevent the intensification of Serbian aggression in Bosnia.

[41] In the presidential elections held in Serbia on December 20, Panic was defeated by Milosevic, and Radoje Kontic succeeded Panic as prime minister on February 9. A series of purges began within Serbian government institutions, in which more than a thousand state radio and television employees - as well as dissident intellectuals and professors - lost their jobs. Finally, on June 25 federal president Cosic was replaced by Zoran Lilic, a member of Milosevic's inner circle.

[42] The intransigence of the Serbian government was evident in Kosovo, where any attempt at independence, even in the cultural scene, was met with repression.

[43] As Milosevic and the ruling SPS party grew more authoritarian, international pressure increased and the social and economic crisis deepened. In 1993, 80 per cent of the federal budget was earmarked for the armed forces, and 20 per cent of the country's GNP went to supporting the Serbs in Bosnia and Croatia.

[44] The power of Milosevic's SPS party increased from 1994 onwards. After the parliamentary elections of December 1993 they held 123 of the 250 seats in the Assembly and had formalized alliances with eight opposition deputies, gaining the majority in the chamber. Milosevic imprisoned his most important political rivals and tried to take a less central role in the war. This line of action included selective collaboration with the war crimes trials in The Hague.

[45] Milosevic's main aim was that the UN should suspend its sanctions on Yugoslavia from May 1992. On September 24 1994, the international organization decided to partially lift the measures for 100 days, allowing international flights, and cultural and sporting exchanges. This diplomatic coup by Milosevic - who was previously accused of being the main instigator of the war in the Balkans - contributed to his increasing popularity in the Federation.

[46] The Yugoslav President Zoran Lilic continued to play an important role in the peace process in Bosnia-Herzegovina during 1995. The political distancing between Yugoslavia and the Bosnian Serb leaders Radovan Karadzic and Ratko Mladic was at odds with the attitude adopted on the military front.

[47] Milosevic's popularity soared again following the signing of the peace agreement in Dayton, Ohio, though his major triumph came on December 14 1995 when the US suspended the sanctions on Yugoslavia as a result of the signing of the Paris agreement. During the embargo, per capita income had fallen to half the previous amount and more than one and a half million people were unemployed.

[48] The year 1997 was marked by confrontations between the federal army and the population of Kosovo (90 per cent of Albanian origin). Milosevic called a referendum, in all of Serbia, on the need for foreign mediation on this conflict. This move was rejected by 75 per cent of the voters (with a boycott by the Albanian-speaking population of Kosovo).

[49] In April 1998, Yugoslav army soldiers killed two Albanian citizens trying to enter the Federation, claiming they were 'terrorists'. This aggravated tension between Yugoslavia and Albania - accused by Belgrade of arming the Kosovan Liberation Army (KLA). A week later, members of the 'contact group', the US, France, Italy, Germany, Russia and Britain, meeting in Rome to agree a common stance, confirmed they would seek dialogue between the parts. The US stated its support for a fresh embargo on Belgrade if Milosevic refused dialogue, including a ban on weapons deliveries and a ban on investments. This proposal was not accepted by Russia.

[50] Later confrontations in Kosovo in June 1998 led Britain and other NATO member countries to issue a call for intervention in the region. After a brief truce in the second half of this year, which the KLA forces used to establish an independent policy of persecuting the Serb minority, the Yugoslav army re-entered the territory. The failure of a round of negotiations held in Rambouillet, France, through which the European countries and the US wanted to make Yugoslavia a protectorate, paved the way for war. Yugoslavia, presented as the party guilty of failing to agree the accords in Rambouillet, remained under NATO observation and isolated from its old ally, Russia.

[51] In March, 1999 the Alliance launched a series of air raids against Yugoslav targets in Serbia, Montenegro and the province of Kosovo. The United Kingdom and the United States, the main military forces, also had air, naval and logistical support from Germany, Italy, France and Turkey amongst others. Bombardments, practiced at a height beyond the reach of anti-aircraft fire, caused hundreds of deaths amongst Kosovans and Serbs.

The air attack unleashed a campaign of revenge attacks against Kosovars, who had to flee in tens of thousands to neighboring countries and Montenegro. NATO air attacks with 'intelligent' bombs destroyed hundreds of civilian buildings, including a State TV station, schools, a hospital and the Chinese embassy in Belgrade. The violence between Serb and Kosovan civilians grew from the initiation of the bombardments.

[52] At the beginning of June, the Group of Eight richest countries sent former Russian prime minister Viktor Chernomyrdin and former Finnish president Martti Ahtisaari to negotiate conditions for a cease fire. The proposal was less severe than that of Rambouillet, but implied the creation of a NATO protectorate, with the symbolic presence of Russian troops in the province. The bombardment ended on June 10 and after negotiating with NATO commanders, the Yugoslav forces accepted the stationing of a UN force, KFOR, made up of some 35,000 troops. According to the agreement, Yugoslav sovereignty was recognized over the province, but in practice it was a protectorate under NATO military control and the political coverage of the UN.

[53] Ethnic cleansing of Serbs and Gypsies led to dozens of deaths after KFOR arrived, and the force was unable to totally disarm the KLA, integrating this into the police force. Several thousand members of these communities had to move from their homes, while a large number of Kosovan refugees returned to the province.

[54] The Serb opposition was unable to unite against Milosevic, and despite demonstrations after the arrival of KFOR troops in which up to 10,000 people demanded his resignation, the movement split and then disappeared.

[55] The railway from Montenegro to Serbia was reopened in October 1999, while the ban on commercial flights between third countries and Yugoslavia was lifted in February 2000. In November, Montenegro adopted the German mark as its currency, while it continued at loggerheads with Belgrade.

[56] Arkan - real name Zeljko Raznjatovic - one of the Serb paramilitary leaders and president of the Serbian Unity Party, was assassinated in January 2000 in a hotel in Belgrade. This prompted a cycle of political killings that also took the Defense Minister, the Montenegran Pavle Bulatovic in February that year.

[57] In June the Yugoslav legislature approved constitutional changes in which the President would be elected by popular vote instead of by the assembly.

Previously, a president elected by Parliament could not serve a second term, but the reform gave Milosevic the opportunity for re-election in the September elections.

[58] After the elections, the opposition claimed that their candidate, Vojislav Kostunica, had won by a majority and that a second-round election was not needed. But after several days of silence, the electoral commission gave Kostunica 48.22 per cent of the vote, to Milosevic's 40.23 per cent, making a run-off vote necessary. The US and the EU denounced the election as fraudulent, charged that the electoral commission lacked credibility, and demanded that Milosevic acknowledge defeat.

[59] A popular uprising, organized by the opposition, joined by the police and army, forced Milosevic to flee. After intense negotiations with the former president's supporters, Kostunica was finally sworn in as President. A new Parliament, elected in early November, appointed a Milosevic supporter, Zoran Zizic, as Prime Minister.

[60] After the Socialist Party lost the parliamentary elections by a broad margin to the Democratic Opposition of Serbia (DOS) coalition, in January 2001 Milosevic was placed under house arrest. In April he was transferred to a prison in Belgrade. Prosecutors announced there would charges brought against him. The following month, US President George W Bush said economic aid to Yugoslavia was conditional upon Milosevic being handing over to the International Criminal Tribunal for the Former Yugoslavia (ICTFY) at The Hague. On June 28 the former president was extradited, prompting Premier Zizic to resign in protest. In his first appearance before the ICTFY, Milosevic refused to recognize the legitimacy of the court and said that the objective of the trial was 'to produce false justifications for the war crimes that NATO committed in Yugoslavia'.

[61] As part of the reforms intended to revitalize the economy, the first large layoff in 50 years took place in Serbia in August. Since the end of World War II lifetime employment had been guaranteed, but that ended when, after several weeks of talks between the Government and the trade unions of the Zastava car factory in the city of Kragujevac, an agreement was reached to lay off 8,000 of its 12,000 workers. Economy and Privatization Minister Aleksandar Vlahovic announced that the Government would invest $60 million to restart production at the Zastava plant to produce 11,000 automobiles annually. Prior to the disintegration of the former Yugoslavia in 1991, the factory had

produced 230,000 cars per year, and the 45 companies of the Zastava group were the pride of the Serbian economy. The two rounds of international sanctions imposed by the UN, which cut off trade with the rest of the world, led the Zastava factory to ruin, and it became a symbol of the economic catastrophe the country experienced in the final decade of the 20th century. The Milosevic regime had never retrenched workers, but had ensured that they had received a minimum salary of $10 a month, even during the war.

[62] Vuk Obradovic, one of Serbia's five deputy prime ministers, who ran the investigative commission on the 10 years of the Milosevic regime, was ousted in May by the new Prime Minister Zoran Djindjic, after reports of sexual harassment filed by dozens of women, including secretaries, legislators and journalists. Obradovic refused to step down and denied the charges, saying that the 'remnants' of the Milosevic government were using the plaintiffs as political pawns.

[63] Although the GDP of the Yugoslav Federation had grown an estimated five per cent in 2001, it was just half the growth recorded in 1989. The Paris Club - rich world creditor nations - had canceled $3 billion, two-thirds, of Yugoslavia's official debt. This opened possibilities of recovery for the economy - which continued to be one of the most devastated on the continent. The Government's highest expectations were placed on an increase in foreign capital investment, in hopes that it would accelerate recovery.

[64] Fear in Europe about new fragmentation in the Balkans prompted the EU to draft an interim plan for the dissolution of the Federal Republic of Yugoslavia, but declarations of independence were postponed. In March 2002 Yugoslavia, Montenegro and Serbia signed an accord under which the name 'Yugoslavia' would disappear, provisionally creating a new state called 'Serbia and Montenegro'. At the end of the year, each would vote on new Constitutions and each would have its own President, Defense Minister and Foreign Minister. These semi-independent states would also take charge of their own economies. After three years, each would hold a referendum to decide whether or not to seek independence. ∎

Zambia

Population: 10,872,000 (2002)
Land area: 743,390 SQ KM
Capital: Lusaka
Currency: Kwacha
Language: English

Zambia

Archaeological evidence suggests that early humans roamed present-day Zambia between 2,000,000 and 1,000,000 years ago. Stone Age sites and artifacts are found in many areas. Early Iron Age peoples settled in the region with their agriculture and domesticated animals about 2,000 years ago. Ancestors of the modern Tonga people reached the region early in the 2nd millennium AD, but other groups reached the country only in the 17th and 18th centuries from Zaire (DR Congo) and Angola.

[2] Portuguese trading missions were established early in the 18th century at the confluence of the Zambezi and Luangwa rivers. The mighty state of Lunda began to lose power towards the end of the 18th century. The slave trade declined in the 19th century, weakening the authority of the Mwata Yambo (traditional Lunda leaders). This, coupled with the growing autonomy of Kazembes (provincial governors), gave rise to small local autocratic states. In 1835 a group of Bantu-speaking Ngoni settled in the Lake Nyasa-Luangwa watershed. The Sotho people, the Kololo (Makololo), crossed the upper Zambezi and in 1835 took control of what became Barotseland.

[3] In 1851, David Livingstone, a British missionary, followed the Zambezi river as far as Victoria Falls. Later came merchants and explorers in the service of British-born millionaire Cecil Rhodes, who owned a vast fortune in South Africa and wanted to expand northwards.

[4] In 1889 the British Crown granted Rhodes, and his British-South Africa Company exclusive rights to establish a mining and trade monopoly in the Katanga area in present-day DR Congo (formerly Zaire). A year later Cecil Rhodes signed a treaty with the Barotse ruler Lewanika and this protectorate was soon followed by colonial domination which created Northern Rhodesia (Zambia).

[5] The British-South Africa Company kept control of this territory in order to prevent the Portuguese from achieving their plan of joining Angola and Mozambique. In 1909, a railway line was built to the coast of the Indian Ocean and in 1924, Britain assumed direct control of the region, developing arable and livestock farms along the railway. South African and US mining companies increased their investment in copper, and 13 years later nearly 40,000 Africans worked in the mines which made massive profits as the labor was cheap. The miserable conditions of the miners led to protest campaigns and stimulated the formation of workers unions; the Northern Rhodesia African National Congress (NRANC), linked to South Africa's African National Congress (ANC), was born in this era. In 1952, Kenneth Kaunda, a primary school teacher, became NRANC secretary-general with Harry Nkumbula as president. Kaunda was to be Zambia's main leader in the independence struggle.

[6] In 1953, the British engineered a federation which threatened to serve white settler interests alone. The Federation comprised Northern Rhodesia (Zambia), Southern Rhodesia (Zimbabwe) and Nyasaland (Malawi), assigning Zambia mining production and Zimbabwe, agricultural. The ANC had just launched its struggle for independence and against racial discrimination. When Nkumbula hesitated before a constitutional project designed to institutionalize European domination, Kaunda chose to leave the NRANC, founding the African National Council of Zambia (ANCZ) and boycotting the elections.

[7] The ANCZ was promptly outlawed and Kaunda was arrested in 1959. Undaunted, his followers created the United National Independence Party (UNIP), which Kaunda chaired when he was released in 1960.

[8] The UNIP was outlawed a few months later when the British recognized the existence of popular support for the Party's nationalist platform. In 1961, repression and marginalization of the majority led to an outbreak of violence in Zambia. By October 1964, the Federation was dissolved, UNIP candidates had won the general election and proclaimed independence.

[9] Zambia actively supported liberation movements in Angola and Mozambique. It nationalized its copper reserves, acted as a founding member of OCEC (Organization of Copper Exporting Countries), sometimes referred to as the 'copper OPEC', and served as host for the 3rd Summit Meeting of the Non-Aligned Countries Movement in 1970.

[10] In 1974, with the inauguration of the Tan-Zam Railway, Zambia gained access to an ocean outlet not dominated by colonial forces. In the same year, Angolan and Mozambican independence brought about a complete turnaround in the regional balance of power.

[11] Zimbabwean independence in 1980 was welcomed by Zambia. However, forces from the South African army made incursions into Zambia, attacking Namibian refugee camps. In October, a coup against Kaunda, supported by the South African regime, failed.

[12] President Kaunda tried to surround himself with former comrades-at-arms, generating friction with the younger sectors, who felt that after Zimbabwe's independence, they no longer needed to live in a climate of war. They even questioned the one-party system. This inter-generational conflict diminished after the October 1983 election, where President Kenneth Kaunda won 93 per cent of the votes, 10 per cent more than in 1978.

[13] With 45 per cent abstention, Kaunda was re-elected in 1988. The following elections were brought forward 2 years to 1991, because of the critical economic situation. That time, Kaunda was defeated by Frederick Chiluba, a former union leader who gained 81 per cent of the vote, and 125 of the 150 seats in Parliament. Kaunda resigned as UNIP party leader in January 1992.

[14] The new government restructured the economy, privatized state enterprises and doubled the price of corn meal and other basic consumer goods. In December 1992, the Government adopted the IMF and the World Bank recommendations, devaluing the country's currency by 29 per cent, freeing the exchange market and deregulating foreign trade. In early 1992, Southern Africa experienced the worst drought of the century, resulting in widespread food shortages.

[15] A meeting of Western countries called by the World Bank granted $400 million of food aid to Zambia, and the Paris Club - rich world creditor nations -agreed to restructure its debt.

[16] Chiluba declared Christianity the official religion and banned the creation of a fundamentalist party. Muslim religious leaders estimated there were 1.2 million Shi'as and more than a million Sunnis in the country.

[17] Accusations of corruption and the lack of an agricultural policy led

MATERNAL MORTALITY

1985-99

Per 100,000
live births

650

LITERACY

2000

78%

FOREIGN TRADE

Millions US$ 2000

IMPORTS
1,333

EXPORTS
890

STATISTICS

DEMOGRAPHY
Population: 10,872,000 (2002)
Annual growth: 2.8 % (1985-2000)
Estimates for year 2015: 14,796,000 (2000)
Annual growth to year 2015: 2.3 % (2000)
Urban population: 44.5 % (2000)
Urban growth: 2.8 % (2000)
Children per woman: 5.9 (2000)

HEALTH
Life expectancy at birth: 42 years (2000-2005)
male: 43 years (2000-2005)
female: 42 years (2000-2005)
Maternal mortality: 650 per 100,000 live births (1985/99)
Infant mortality: 112 per 1,000 (2000)
Under-5 child mortality: 202 per 1,000 (2000)
Daily calorie supply: 1,934 per capita (1999)
7 doctors per 100,000 people (1995)
Safe water: 64 % (2000)

EDUCATION
Literacy: 78 % (2000)
male: 85 % (2000)
female: 71 % (2000)
School enrolment (net):
Primary total: 67 % (1994/2000)
male: 85 % (1995/99)
female: 86 % (1995/99)
Secondary (gross):
male: 34 % (1995/97)
female: 21 % (1995/97)
Tertiary (gross): 3 % (1998)
Primary school teachers: one for every 45 pupils (1998)

COMMUNICATIONS
12 newspapers (1996), 145 radios (1999), 134 TV sets (2000) and 8 main telephone lines (2000) per 1,000 people

ECONOMY
Per capita, GDP: $ 780 (2000)
Annual growth: 1.3 % (2000)
Annual inflation: 24.8 % (1997)
Consumer price index: 182.6 (1997)
Currency: 4,650.0 kwacha = $ 1 (03/2002)
Cereal imports: 84,608 metric tons (2000)
Food import dependency: 10 % (1995)
Fertilizer use: 101 kg per ha (1999)
Exports: $ 890 million (2000)
Imports: $ 1,333 million (2000)
External debt: $ 5,730 million (2000); $ 550 per capita (2000)
Debt service: 46.6 % of exports (1999)
Development aid received: $ 623 million (1999); $ 63.1 per capita (1999); 19.80 % of GNP (1999)

ENERGY
Consumption: 629.8 Kgs of oil equivalent per capita yearly (1998); 6.6 % imported (1999)

HDI (ranking/value): 143 / 0.427 (1999)

---

the President to ask his Lands Minister to step down and the others to declare their incomes. Shortly after, he removed the director of the Bank of Zambia for suddenly devaluing the currency, the kwacha, by more than 20 per cent. Chiluba blamed the crisis on the foreign debt payments, which ate 40 per cent of the country's GDP, while 5.5 million of the 9.5 million population lived in extreme poverty.

[18] In March 1996 the Paris Club cancelled 67 per cent of Zambia's debt. The implementation of the IMF/World Bank structural adjustment program in 1997 brought increased poverty among the rural population and, as a result of the privatization of state enterprises, layoffs of at least 150,000 workers.

[19] In November 1997, a month after a failed coup, dozens of people - including Kaunda, disqualified from possible re-election by a constitutional amendment - were arrested for alleged ties to rebel troops. The Government declared a three-month state of emergency, extended to March 1998. Kaunda was released from house arrest in June and the charges against him were withdrawn.

[20] The decline of international copper prices blocked the sale of the Nkana and Nchanga mines demanded by potential aid donors, complicating things for the Government. Drought and floods combined at the end of the year, causing the economy to fall apart. The UN World Food Program sent $17 million in aid. In November, just

months after being forced to resign, former Economy Minister Ronald Penza was assassinated.

[21] In May 2001, political divisions prompted the creation of a new party to challenge Chiluba's Movement for a Multiparty Democracy (MMD). Some 80 MMD members quit the party's national executive committee and created the Forum for Democracy and Development (FDD). The division of the MMD was the result of a debate about whether Chiluba should run for a third term as president, something the dissidents opposed.

[22] In July 2001, Paul Tembo, previously Chiluba's campaign manager and a recent recruit to the FDD, was murdered shortly before he was to testify against three ministers in a high-level corruption case. Tembo's legal team and party representatives suspected it was a political assassination.

[23] Also in July, Zambia issued an urgent appeal for food aid to feed some two million people in the wake of poor harvests caused by flooding and drought in different parts of the country. Vice-President Enock Kavindele stated that some 100,000 tons of corn was needed to fill the food deficit.

[24] MMD candidate Levy Mwanawasa was declared President in January 2002 amid controversy arising from the close presidential and parliamentary elections of December 2001. Ten opposition parties charged that fraud and ballot manipulation had skewed the outcome. Mwanawasa won 28.7 per cent of the vote, while Anderson Mazoka, of the United Party of National Development (UPND), won 26.7 percent.

[25] In April, the partial privatization of the deeply indebted Zambia National Commercial Bank (Zanaco) - a condition for the IMF and World Bank to cancel $3.8 billion of Zambia's foreign debt - was in danger of failing because there were no potential buyers.

[26] Like its southern African neighbors, Zambia was hit by famine in 2002. ∎

PROFILE

ENVIRONMENT
A high plateau extends from Malawi in the east to the swamp region along the border with Angola in the west. The Zambezi River flows from north to south and provides hydroelectric power at the Kariba Dam. The climate is tropical, tempered by altitude. Mining is the main economic activity, as there are large copper deposits. Mining has had a bad effect upon the environment. Soil erosion and loss of fertility are associated with the overuse of fertilizers. Shanty towns account for 45 per cent of the housing in Lusaka, linked with problems like the lack of drinking water and adequate health care, factors which contributed to the 1990 and 1991 cholera epidemics. Wildlife is threatened by poaching, and a lack of resources with which to maintain wildlife reserves.

SOCIETY
Peoples: 98 per cent of Zambians are descendants of successive waves of Bantu migrants, in some 70 ethnic groups. There are approximately 70,000 inhabitants of European descent and 15,000 Asians.
Religions: Traditional African religions are practiced. There are Christians and Muslim and Hindu minorities.
Languages: English (official). Of the many Bantu languages, five are officially used in education and administration; Nyanja, Bemba, Lozi, Luvale and Tonga.
Political Parties: Movement for Multiparty Democracy (MMD); United Party for National Development (UPND); United National Independence Party (UNIP); Forum for Democracy and Development (FDD); Heritage Party (HP).
Social organizations: The Trade Union Congress of Zambia comprises 16 unions. The newly-created Workers Trade Union has 2 million members.

THE STATE
Official Name: Republic of Zambia.
Capital: Lusaka 1,577,000 people (1999).
Other cities: Ndola 346,500 people; Kitwe 762,700; Mufulira 130,400 (2000).
Government: Levy Mwanawasa, President since January 2002. Unicameral Legislature: National Assembly, with 159 members.
National Holiday: October 24, Independence Day (1964).
Armed Forces: 21,600 (1997).
Other: Police Mobile Unit (PMU): 700; Police Paramilitary Unit (PPMU): 700.

Zimbabwe

Population: 13,076,000 (2002)
Land area: 386,850 SQ KM
Capital: Harare
Currency: Zimbabwe dollar
Language: English

Zimbabwe

B etween the Zambezi and Limpopo rivers one can find, in the words of French historian Pierre Bertaux, 'thousands of abandoned mines; cultivated terraces that covered entire mountains, irrigation canals, paths, and wells 12 meters deep wells excavated in rock.'

² Among the ruins scattered over an extensive region including nearly 300 archaeological sites, the most important cities were Khami, Naletali, DhloDhlo, Mapungubwe and the better known Zimbabwe with its high-walled enclosure. The Karangas, members of the present-day Shona people built these walls in the 10th century.

³ The Bantu ironworkers who settled in the region in the 5th century also discovered gold, copper and tin deposits. In a few centuries they developed sophisticated techniques for working these metals. In the 8th century, the rise of Arab-influenced trade centers on the coast provided a market for their goods, and the growth of trade resulted in a great expansion of this culture. When the Shirazis founded Sofala (in present-day Mozambique) in the 10th century, the Karanga state acquired an export market for its mining production. The 'Monomotapa', the Karanga leader, imposed a tributary relation on the neighboring Muslim nation as he had done with other minor cultures of the area. Thus, Karangan supremacy was established over a region including parts of present-day Malawi.

⁴ This civilization established important trading connections with Asia and continued to develop until the mid-15th century when the Rotsi, a southern people belonging to the Shona, the same ethnic group as the Karanga, forced the Monomotapa to withdraw towards the north and the coast. The Zimbabwe citadel and palace were taken over by the Rotsi, whose *Changamira* (king) extended his control over the mining area. He did not however succeed in controlling an area as vast as the ancient Karanga had done.

⁵ Portuguese presence brought about the end of the prosperous trade with the east and a consequent economic decline. Also, in reaction to the Europeans greed' for gold, the Shona miners filled in

their mines, keeping only their ironworks functioning.

⁶ In 1834, the Zulus devastated the region. The Rotsi emigrated westwards; cities and farmlands, palaces and irrigation canals were abandoned and grass began to grow over the ancient walls of Zimbabwe. In the first half of the 19th century, the territory was divided between the Shona peoples in the northeast, and the Zulu kingdom of Ndebele in the southeast. In 1889, Lobenguela, the Ndebele ruler, received a visit from Charles Rudd, envoy of the wealthy English adventurer-entrepreneur Cecil Rhodes. In exchange for arms and a life pension, Lobenguela granted exclusive rights for the exploitation of the country's mineral resources to Rhodes's British-South Africa Company (BSA).

⁷ The British Government gave the BSA control over trade, immigration, communications and the police in the Ndebele territory. Since Matabeleland, as the British called it, was an independent state, the concession of these privileges granted by a foreign government, needed 'formal and free' approval from ruler Lobenguela who lived in Bulawayo. After Rhodes took control, British settlers were established in the Shona territory. They were protected by 700 police officers and were authorized to live

there, founding a fortified camp which they called Salisbury. The settlers had no legal title deeds to the land, just the backing of the British Government.

⁸ Lobenguela withheld his approval for the BSA's activities. So Rhodes' agents created conflictual situations with him to provide a 'reason' to depose him. In 1895, under the pretext of arresting some Ndebele who had stolen cattle from the Shona, Rhodes's 'police' attacked Bulawayo, Lobenguela's central town. The ruler was driven into the bush and his nation and the Shona territory fell under BSA domination, under the name of Southern Rhodesia.

⁹ In 1960, settlers of European origin accounted for barely five per cent of the population but owned more than 70 per cent of the arable land. When the decolonization process began in Africa, Zambia and Malawi, formerly part of a federation with Southern Rhodesia, resisted further European domination and gained independence in 1964. In Rhodesia, the African National Congress (ANC) also intensified the struggle for independence. The colonial government of Prime Minister Ian Smith reacted declaring a 'state of emergency' in November 1965. The British Government urged Southern Rhodesia to transfer power gradually to the African native

majority. Smith flatly refused and proclaimed independence unilaterally on November 11 1965 in order to remain in power with his segregationist Rhodesian Front.

¹⁰ The rebel regime faced an embargo declared by the United Nations, though the blockade was systematically violated by the western powers. Guerrilla warfare organized by ZAPU (Zimbabwe African Peoples Union) and ZANU (Zimbabwe African National Union), was launched. The armed struggle grew increasingly intense and the Smith regime bombarded Zambia and Mozambique. These countries together with Angola, Botswana and Tanzania, formed the group of Front Line Countries to fight racism. In Zimbabwe, ZAPU and ZANU joined to form the Patriotic Front under the joint leadership of Joshua Nkomo and Robert Mugabe.

¹¹ In 1978 Smith and some African leaders opposed to the Patriotic Front signed an 'internal agreement', which legalized their own political parties. In 1979, after fraudulent elections, Bishop Abel Muzorewa became premier and changed the name of the country to ZimbabweRhodesia. With the majority of parliamentary seats, the racist minority had the power to control the socio-economic and political system.

¹² However, guerrilla pressure was mounting, and finally the white government and its African allies were forced to negotiate. The British Government agreed to supervise free elections arranged for February 1980, when Robert Mugabe's ZANU party won a landslide victory. By the Lancaster House agreements, signed on April 18 1980, Britain held power temporarily before transferring to the ZANU Party. Although the white Zimbabweans maintained some economic and political privileges, they lost their veto over possible constitutional changes.

¹³ Meanwhile, because of war, the country's cattle herd had shrunk to a third of its previous size; many roads had been rendered useless, and some schools had remained closed for seven years. The medical and sanitary systems were also in serious disrepair and diseases such as malaria were increasingly in evidence among the population.

MATERNAL MORTALITY	LITERACY	FOOD DEPENDENCY	FOREIGN TRADE
1985-99 Per 100,000 live births **700**	2000 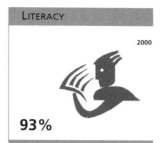 **93%**	1999 **9%**	Millions US$ 2000 IMPORTS **2,266** EXPORTS **2,245**

[14] Prime Minister Robert Mugabe offered generous cabinet participation to the ZAPU leadership, also calling in segregationist politicians to form the government team. These steps were aimed at preventing old rivalries from interfering with national reconstruction, especially the ambitious National Development Plan. The gross national product grew by seven per cent, farm production broke all records, and consumption reached higher levels than expected. However, Robert Mugabe had to face two major difficulties: South Africa's blockade on Zimbabwes agricultural exports and political dissent between ZANU and ZAPU. In 1981 this led the Prime Minister to remove Nkomo from the home affairs ministry, though maintaining his ministerial rank.

[15] Political differences intensified. In 1982, Nkomo's followers created an armed movement called 'Super-ZAPU'. Growing political tension coincided with the start of the great drought which was responsible for a drop in agricultural production.

[16] Pressure from African farmers, who had hoped for a true agrarian reform after independence, clashed with the limitations imposed by the Lancaster House agreement. This treaty impeded the expropriation of European land-holdings and the British and Americans avoided giving Zimbabwe the resources promised for the purchase and distribution of land. In Matabeleland, Nkomo's followers explained that the difficulties stemming from the drought and lack of funds were anti-Ndebele schemes of Mugabe's, aimed at repressing the country's second largest ethnic group after the Shona, and that they were all elements designed to create inter-tribal animosity.

[17] Towards the end of June 1985, Mugabe's ZANU-PF obtained a comfortable victory in parliamentary elections throughout the country, except in Matabeleland, while the majority of whites voted for the Rhodesian Front, created by Ian Smith, a fact which led the President to remind them that the privileges granted to former colonists under the Lancaster House agreement should not be considered unalterable.

[18] The political privileges enjoyed by whites were subsequently eliminated, though there were extensive privileges in other areas. These were evident by figures in a technical report on Zimbabwe's land-tenure system: 4,500 farmers (most of them white) owned 50 per cent of the country's productive land while the 4.5 million peasants lived in communally-owned rural areas - known as 'tribal lands', where the black population were moved to during the colonial era.

[19] The Commercial Farmers Union (CFU) of white farmers blocked many initiatives for rural relocation. They controlled 90 per cent of all agricultural production, paid a third of Zimbabwe's salaries and exported 40 per cent of the country's goods. This situation existed despite the fact that a third of the properties belonging to members were not exploitable, and that productivity could be increased, and that the great efficiency of the farmers was due to state support rather than the managerial talent of the farmers themselves.

[20] Two constitutional reforms were carried out in September 1987. Previously, 20 seats of the Assembly and 10 in the Senate had been reserved for whites, but this practice was abolished. In addition, an executive authority was assigned to the President, elected by Parliament for a six-year period.

[21] Mugabe played an important role in the summit of the Movement of Non-Aligned Countries held in September in Harare, where he enthusiastically promoted the widespread adoption of sanctions against South Africa. In addition, Zimbabwe supported the Government of Mozambique against the counter-revolutionaries of the National Resistance of Mozambique (RENAMO). In May 1987, some 12,000 Zimbabwean troops were stationed in Mozambique, while RENAMO led incursions into Zimbabwean territory during 1987 and 1988.

[22] In December 1987, Mugabe and Nkomo reached reconciliation, and the two major political parties agree to unification. This agreement was ratified in April 1988 creating the Patriotic Front of the Zimbabwe African National Union (ZANU-PF). Subsequently, with the help of the alliance of several white deputies within ZANU, the country oriented itself, against the general trend in Africa, toward a one-party system.

[23] In the March 1990 elections, ZANU-PF obtained 116 of the 119 parliamentary seats. Mugabe interpreted the results as a mandate in favor of a one-party system. Nevertheless, only 54 per cent of the people went to the polls and the newly organized Zimbabwe Unity Movement obtained 15 per cent of the votes. In Harare and other urban centers, the opposition obtained almost 30 per cent of the votes, while ZAPU held its ground in rural areas.

[24] In an economy with an average annual growth of 4 per cent, the share of agriculture in the GNP was 14 per cent in 1980, and rose to 20 per cent in 1990. That same year, Parliament approved land reform authorizing the Government to expropriate land held by Europeans, at a price fixed by the State, and to redistribute it among the poor. The majority of the African population supported the law, deeming it an act of racial and economic justice. The white farmers, on the other hand, supported by legal experts, criticized it as a violation of the civil and human rights established under the Constitution.

[25] In June 1991, the ruling ZANU-PF decided to relinquish its Marxist-Leninist doctrine,

PROFILE

ENVIRONMENT

The country consists mainly of a high rolling plateau. Most of the urban population live in the High Veld, an area of fertile land, with moderate rainfall and mineral wealth. The climate is tropical, tempered by altitude. Soil depletion is very severe, above all on communal farms, where subsistence agriculture is practised.

SOCIETY

Peoples: The majority of Zimbabweans, 94 per cent, are of Bantu origin from the Shona (founders of the first nation in the region) and the Ndebele group (a Zulu people that arrived in the 19th century).
Religions: African traditional beliefs 55 per cent; Christian 45 per cent, predominantly Anglican.
Languages: English, official. Most of the people speak their own Bantu languages.
Political Parties: Zimbabwe African National Union-Patriotic Front (ZANU-PF), authoritarian, emerged in December 1987 from the fusion of the Zimbabwe African National Union (ZANU), led by Robert Mugabe, and the Zimbabwe People's Union (ZAPU), led by Joshua Nkomo; Zimbabwe Congress of Trade Union, ZCTU; Zimbabwe Unity Movement (ZUM), of Edgar Tekere; Movement for Democratic Change (MDC); Zimbabwe African National Union-Ndonga, conservative; Regional ZANU-Ndonga party, of right-wing nationalist Ndabaningi Sithole; Emmanuel Magoche's Democratic Party split from the ZUM in 1991.
Social Organizations: Organization of Rural Associations for Progress; Council of Trade Unions of Zimbabwe, National Students Union of Zimbabwe.

THE STATE

Official Name: Republic of Zimbabwe.
Administrative Divisions: 8 Provinces.
Capital: Harare 1,686,000 people (1999).
Other cities: Bulawayo 794,600 people; Chitungwiza 390,600; Mutare 168,100 (2000).
Government: Robert Mugabe, President since December 1987, re-elected in 1990, 1996 and 2002.
Unicameral Legislature: the House of Assembly, with 150 members.
National Holiday: April 18, Independence Day (1980).
Armed Forces: 39,000 (1997).
Other: 15,000 Republican Police Force, 2,000 Police Support Unit, 4,000 National Militia.

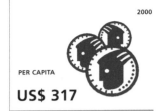

2000

PER CAPITA

US$ 317

eliminating all references to this and scientific socialism from its program. Mugabe appealed for the doctrine of pure socialism to be abandoned, in favor of social democracy and a mixed economy.

[26] In October 1991, the Zimbabwean Unity Movement (ZUM) split, creating the Democratic Party led by Emmanuel Magoche, the former president of the ZUM.

[27] In January 1992, the Government announced that a five-year reform plan would be implemented. Its aim would be to liberalize the economy, bring the budget deficit down to 5 per cent of the GNP, and to substantially increase job opportunities.

[28] In October 1995, Ndabaningi Sithole, leader of the ZANU-Ndonga, and one of the two members of the Assembly not belonging to the ZANU-PF, was arrested for allegedly planning the assassination of the President. Mugabe's opponents attributed the arrest to Sithole's announcement of his candidacy for the presidency.

[29] With the abstention of 68 per cent of the voters, the April 1996 elections resulted in Mugabe's victory with 93 per cent of the votes. Several opposition parties boycotted the elections since they questioned the electoral procedures.

[30] Due to pressure from his supporters on one side and from the European Union and IMF - which threatened to block the loans agreed with Zimbabwe - on the other, the Government vacillated in its plan to confiscate farms from some 1,500 white owners. From January to March, the policy was repeatedly suspended then reimposed. In June some landless war veterans took over six farms east of Harare and in July the Government announced a new plan to settle 100,000 families on five million hectares to be purchased from white farmers. The IMF and EU, although recognizing the need for land reform, rejected the plan, saying it was too ambitious, and agreed only to support a two-year pilot project. Mugabe changed his mind yet again in November, ordering the expropriation of 841 white-owned farms. Some 4,000 landowners, mostly descendants of British colonists, held

approximately a third of Zimbabwe's productive land.

[31] In October 1999 a special 3-per cent tax was imposed on salaries. The Government said the new revenues would be used to treat people with HIV/AIDS, at least 20 per cent of the country's adult population. However, the measure was seen by many as a scheme to finance the 11,000 troops that Mugabe had sent to back the Laurent Kabila regime in the Democratic Republic of the Congo (former Zaire).

[32] In March 2000, 420 white-owned farms were occupied by black war veterans. The Commercial Farmers Union accused Mugabe of orchestrating the occupations as a smokescreen to hide the failure of the land distribution projects, pointing out that the Government owned nearly two million acres of farmland that had not been used for resettlement and were kept fallow. Mugabe responded that the country could not pay for the division of land into smaller plots or to provide minimal infrastructure, such as waterworks and roads. In May, as a platform for the June parliamentary elections, Mugabe launched a manifesto stating that he would not give in to international pressure and that he would not block the land invasions. 'It is our land and we will take it,' said the President.

[33] Weeks before the elections, the Government decided to slash the number of local observers from the Electoral Supervisory Commission, from 16,000 to 4,000: in other words, just one local observer for each of the 4,000 electoral colleges in the country. Among the foreign observers, just 200 of the nearly 500 who arrived in the country were authorized to complete their mission. ZANU won only five more seats than the opposition Movement for Democratic Change (MDC). A small independent party won a single seat. Mugabe and his party had governed practically without opposition since 1980.

[34] Djibouti, Egypt, Kenya, Madagascar, Malawi, Mauricio, Sudan, Zambia and Zimbabwe established a free trade zone in October known as the Common Market for Eastern and Southern Africa (COMESA). The participating governments committed to allowing the free circulation of qualified labor by 2004, free circulation of people by 2014 and monetary union by 2025.

[35] In 2001, Mugabe was the target of numerous charges of human rights violations in his country, including the right to information. The British media and several NGOs reported that judges and journalists had been forced to

leave Zimbabwe and that several opposition leaders had been assassinated. The Congolese Commission that was investigating the assassination of Laurent Kabila (in January that year) pointed to Zimbabwe and Angola as the masterminds behind the murder.

[36] Pressured again by Western countries and also by his southern African neighbors, who were concerned about the repercussions of Zimbabwe's crisis on their economies, Mugabe decided to halt the illegal land occupations in exchange for major financial aid from Britain to compensate the white farmers whose land had been expropriated. The reticence of companies to invest in the country had further boosted the unemployment rate, and inflation reached 70 per cent by year end.

[37] The Government, which had banned televised debates in order to prevent criticism of the administration, presented a bill before Parliament in January 2002 for a law known as the Information Access and Privacy Protection Act. This sought to silence the independent press and prevent foreign journalists from working in Zimbabwe before the upcoming presidential elections. National and international pressure led the government to withdraw the bill, promptly amending it and returning it to Parliament. According to some analysts, the move meant that Mugabe had given in to the US, the British Commonwealth - of which Zimbabwe was a member - and the EU, which threatened to impose sanctions against Zimbabwe.

[38] Mugabe won the March 2002 presidential elections with 56.2 per cent of the vote, beating Morgan Tsvangirai of the MDC, which garnered 41.9 per cent of the vote. The opposition, independent election observers and the international community declared the vote fraudulent. After the elections, the Commonwealth expelled Zimbabwe for one year. This followed recommendations by its electoral observers that the voting had been obstructed by government-inspired violence. The expulsion would be reviewed in 12 months. after studies of the 'progress made in the country'. The EU and the US announced that they would impose severe sanctions against Zimbabwe throughout 2002. Denmark closed its embassy in Harare and Switzerland decided to block the bank accounts of any Harare official and to refuse them entry into the country.

[39] Despite the pressure – and the growing famine in Zimbabwe and the region – Mugabe continued his land appropriation policies. ■

Bibliography

ABDEL-MALEK, A., ed.- Contemporary Arab Political Thought. London, Zed, 1983.

AGUILAR DERPICH, J.- Guyana: Otra vía al socialismo. Caracas, El ojo del camello, 1973.

ALGERIE: Guide economique et social. Dely, ANEP, 1987.

ALIANZAS políticas y procesos revolucionarios. Mexico, SEPLA, 1979.

ALMANAQUE BRASIL 1995/1996. Editora Terceiro Mundo, Rio de Janeiro, 1995.

AMARASINGAM, SP.- The Industrialized Nations of the West and the Third World. Colombo, Tribune, 1982.

AMIN, S., et al.- Nuevo Orden Internacional. Mexico, Nueva Política, 1977.

AMNESTY INTERNATIONAL.- Contra la pena de muerte. Madrid, 1992.

AMNESTY INTERNATIONAL.- Guía de la Carta Africana de los derechos humanos y de los pueblos. Madrid, 1991.

AMNESTY INTERNATIONAL.- Informes 1984-1996. Madrid, 1996.

AMNESTY INTERNATIONAL.- Reino Unido: desigualdad ante la ley. Madrid, 1991.

ANUARIO del Centro de Investigaciones para la Paz 1988/1989: Paz, militarización y conflictos. Madrid, IEPALA, 1989.

ANNUAIRE Geopolitique Mondial. Paris, Hachette, 1989. (Suppl. de Politique International.)

ARNOLD, M.- The Testimony of Steve Biko. Suffolk, Granada Publ., 1979.

ARRUDA, M., et al.- Transnational Corporations: A Challenge for Churches and Christians. Geneva, World Council of Churches, 1982.

ASIA 1990 Yearbook. Hong Kong, Dai Nippon, 1990.

ATLAS Barsa. Rio de Janeiro, Encyclopaedia Britannica, 1980.

ATLASECO du Monde 1997. Paris, Les Editions EOC, 1996.

ATLAS de L'humanité. Paris, Solar, 1983.

AZIZ, T.- Reflexions sur les relations Arabo-Iraniennes. Baghdad, 1980.

BARDINI, R.- Belice:historia de una nación en movimiento. Tegucigalpa, Universitaria, 1978.

BARDINI, R.- El Frente Polisario y la lucha del pueblo saharaui. Tegucigalpa, CIPAAL, 1979.

BARRACLOUGH, G.- Introducción a la Historia Contemporánea. Barcelona, Anagrama, 1975.

BASSOLS BATALLA, A.- Geografía, subdesarrollo y regionalización. Mexico, Nuestro Tiempo, 1976.

BASSOLS BATALLA, A.- Los recursos naturales. Mexico, Nuestro Tiempo, 1974.

BASTIDE, R.- Las Américas negras. Madrid, Alianza, 1969.

BECKFORD, G.- Persistent Poverty, Underdevelopment in Plantations of the Third World. 2a.ed. London, 1983.

BEDJAQUI, M.- Towards a new International Economic Order. Paris, UNESCO, 1979.

BELFRACE, C & ARONSON, J.- Something to Guard. New York, Columbia Univ. Press, 1978.

BELLER, WS., ed.- Environmental and Economic Growth in the Smaller Caribbean Island. Washington, Department of State, 1979.

BENOT, I.- Ideologías de las independencias africanas. Barcelona, 1973.

BENZ, W.- El siglo XX: Problemas mundiales entre los dos bloques de poder. Madrid, Siglo XXI, 1984.

BERGER, J. & MOHR, J.- A seventh man. Middlesex, 1975.

BIANCO , L.- Asia contemporánea. Mexico, Siglo XXI, 1980.

BILAN Economique et Social 1984-1989-1991. Le Monde; Dossiers et Documents; Paris, 1992.

BOUSTANI, R & FARGUES, P.- Atlas du Monde Arabe. Géopolitique et Société. Paris, Bordas, 1990.

BRANDT, W.et al.- Das Ueberleben sichern. Kiepenheur y Witsch, Koln, 1980.

BRITTAIN, V., & SIMMONS, M.- Third World Review. London, Guardian, 1987.

BROWN, L.- Food or Fuel: New Competition for the Worlds Cropland. Washington, Worldwatch Institute, 1980.

BRUBAKER, S.- Para vivir en la tierra. Mexico, Pax, 1973.

BRUHAT, J.- Historia de Indonesia. Buenos Aires, EUDEBA, 1964.

BUETTNER, T., et al.- Afrika: Geschichte von den Anfaengen bis zur Gegenwart. Koln, Pahl-Rugenstein, 1979.

BURCHETT, WG.- Otra vez Corea. Mexico, ERA, 1968.

BURGER, J.- The Gaia Atlas of first peoples. A future for the indigenous world. London, Gaia, 1990.

CALCAGNO, AE & JAKOBOWICZ, JM.- El monólogo Norte-Sur y la explotación de los países subdesarrollados. México, Siglo XXI, 1981.

CALCHI NOVATI, G.- La revolución argelina. Barcelona, Bruguera, 1970.

CALDWELL, M.- The Wealth of Some Nations. London, Zed, 1977.

CARATINI, R.- Dictionnaire des nationalités et des minorités en URSS. Paris, Larousse, 1990.

CARRERAS, J.- Historia de Jamaica. Havana, Ed.Ciencias Sociales, 1984.

CARTA africana de Derechos Humanos y de los pueblos. Nairobi, 1981. Adoptada por la Decimoctava Conferencia de Jefes de Estado y de Gobierno de la Organización de la Unidad Africana.

CASTRO, F.- La crisis económica y social del mundo. Havana, OPCE, 1983.

CAVALLA, A.- Geopolítica y Seguridad Nacional en América. Mexico, UNAM, 1979.

CEPAL.- Anuario estadístico de América Latina. Santiago de Chile, 1981.

CEPAL.- Estudio económico de América Latina y el Caribe. Santiago de Chile, 1984.

CEPAL.- Notas sobre la economía y el desarrollo. Santiago de Chile, 1985.

CEPAL.- La evolución de la economía de América Latina en 1983. Santiago de Chile, 1984.

CHALIAND, G.- Revolution in the Third World. Middlesex, Penguin, 1979.

CHEE, Y.- How big powers dominate the Third World. Penang, Third World Network, 1987.

CHOMSKY, N., STEELE, J. & GITTINGS, J. Super Powers in Collision. Penguin, 1984.

CHRISTENSEN, Ch.- The Right to Food: how to guarantee. New York, 1978.

CINCO conferencias Cumbres de los Países No Alineados. Havana, 1979.

CIPOLLA, C.- La explosión demográfica (entrevista). Barcelona, Salvat, 1973.

CLAIRMONTE, FF & CAVANAGH, H.- Transnational Corporations and Services: The final frontier. Geneva, UNCTAD, 1984.

CLARK, C.- Crecimiento demográfico y utilización del suelo. Madrid, 1968.

COLCHESTER, M & LOHMANN, L.- The tropical forestry action plan;what progress? 1990.

COMANDANTE de los pobres: testimonios sobre Omar Torrijos. Madrid, Centro de Estudios Torrijistas, 1984.

COMISION INTERNACIONAL SOBRE PROBLEMAS DE LA COMUNICACION.-Un solo mundo, voces múltiples. Mexico, Fondo de Cultura, 1980.

CONNELL-SMITH, G.- Los Estados Unidos y la América Latina. Mexico, 1977.

CONSTANTINO, R.- The Philippines:A past revisited. Manila, 1975.

CONTRERAS, M.& SOSA, I.-Latinoamérica en el siglo XX. Mexico, UNAM, 1973.

CORDOVA, A., et alii.- El Imperialismo. Mexico, Nuestro Tiempo, 1979.

CORM, G.- Le Proche-Orient éclaté. Paris, La Découverte, 1983. Le COURIER des Pays de l'est. Paris, 1986.

CUEVA, A.- El proceso de dominación política en el Ecuador. Quito, Critica, 1973.

DAVIDSON, B.- The Liberation of Guiné. Middlesex, Penguin, 1971.

DAWISHA, K.- Eastern Europe, Gorbachev and reform: the great challenge. 2a.ed. New York, Cambridge Univ., 1990.

DEBRAY, R.-La crítica de las armas. Madrid, Siglo XXI, 1975.

DECRAENE, P.- El Panafricanismo. Bs.As., EUDEBA, 1962.

DEGENHARDT, H, comp.- Political dissention international guide to dissent, extraparliamentary, guerrillas and illegal political movements. London, Longman, 1983.

DE LA COURT, T; PICK, D & NORDQUIST, D.- The nuclear fix. A guide to nuclear activities in the Third World. Amsterdam, Wise, 1982.

DENVERS, A.- Points choc:l'environnement dans tous ses états. Editions 1, 1990.

DE SOUZA, H.- El capital mundial. Montevideo, CUI, 1987. v.1.

DER FISCHER WELT ALMANACH 1993. Fischer Taschenbuch Verlag. Bonn, 1992.

DIFRIERI, H., et al.- Geografía Universal. Bs.As., ANESA, 1971.

DORE, F.- Los regímenes políticos en Asia. Mexico, Siglo XXI, 1976.

DRECHSLER, H.-Africa del Sudoeste bajo la dominación colonial alemana. Berlin, Verlag, 1986.

DREIFUSS, R.-A Internacional capitalista. Rio de Janeiro, Espaço e Tempo, 1986.

ECE.- Economic Bulletin for Europe. New York, 1991.

ECE.- Economic Survey of Europe in 1988-1989. New York, 1989.

ECE.- Economic Survey of Europe in 1989-1990. New York, 1990.

ECE.- Economic Survey of Europe in 1990-1991. New York, 1991.

ECKHOLM, E.- The dispossessed of the earth: Land reform and Sustainable Development. Washington, Worldwatch Institute, 1979.

L'ECONOMIE de la drogue. Le Monde; Dossiers et Documents; Paris, feb.1990.

L'ECONOMIE de l'Espagne. Le Monde; Dossiers et Documents; Paris, Jan.1990.

ELLIOT, F.- A Dictionary of Politics. Middlesex, Penguin, 1974.

EMMANUEL, A., AMIN, S, et al.- Imperialismo y comercio Internacional.(El intercambio desigual). Madrid, Siglo XXI, 1977.

El EMPUJE del Islam. Madrid, IEPALA, 1989. (Africa Internacional, 7)

El SALVADOR. Alianzas políticas y proceso revolucionario. Mexico, SEPLA, 1979.

ENTRALGO, A., ed.- Africa. Havana, Ed.Ciencias Sociales, 1979.

ENZENSBERG, H.-Zur Kritik der politischen Okologie. Berlin, Kursbuch, 1973.

L'ETAT du Monde 1989-1990. Annuaire économique et géopolitique mondial. Paris, La Découverte, 1989.

L'ETAT des religions dans le Monde. Paris, La Découverte, 1987.

L'ETAT du Monde. Paris, La Découverte, 1996 and 1997.

L'ETAT du Tiers Monde. Paris, La Découverte, 1989. The EUROPA Yearbook. London, Europa Pub., 1984.

FABER, G.- The Third World and the EEC. Netherlands, 1982.

FAHRNI, D.- Historia de Suiza. Ojeada a la evolución de un peque–o país desde sus orígenes hasta nuestros días. 2a.ed. Zurich, Pro Helvetia, 1984.

FALK, R & WAHL, P.- Befreiungsbewegungen in Afrika. Pahl-Rugenstein, Koln, 1980.

FANON, F.- Os condenados da Terra. Rio de Janeiro, Civilizaçao Brasileira, 1979.

FAO.- Estado mundial de la agricultura y la alimentación. Rome, 1983.

FAO.- Production Yearbook. Rome, 1993.

FERNANDEZ, W.- El gran culpable.La responsabilidad de los Estados Unidos en el proceso militar uruguayo. Montevideo, Atenea, 1986.

FIELDHOUSE, DK.- The Colonial Empires.A comparative survey from the eighteenth century. 2a.ed. London, MacMillan1982.

FIGUEROA ALCACES, E, ed.- Antología de geografía histórica moderna y contemporánea. Mexico, UNAM, 1974.

FISHLOW, A, et al.- Rich and Poor Nations in the World Economy. New York, McGraw Hill, 1978.

FORDHAM, P.- The geography of African Affairs. Middlesex, Penguin.

FOREST Resources crisis in the Third World, Malaysia, Sep.1986. Proceeding. Malaysia, 1987.

FRENTE POLISARIO.-VII Anniversaire du Declenchement de la Lutte de Liberation nationale. Dep. Informations, 1980.

FRETLIN Conquers the Right to Dialogue. London, 1978.

GALEANO, E.- As Véias Abertas de América Latina. Rio de Janeiro, Vozes, 1979.

GALTUNG, J. & O'BRIEN, P, et al.- Self-reliance. A Strategy for development. London, IDS, 1980.

GANDHI, MK.- An autobiography. Boston, Beacon Press, 1957.

GATT International trade 1981-1982. New York, 1982.

GAZOL SANTAGE, A.- Los países pobres. México, FCE, 1987.

GENOUD, R.- Sobre las revoluciones parciales del Tercer Mundo. Barcelona, Anagrama, 1974.

GEORGE, P.- Geografía económica. Barcelona, Ariel, 1976.

GEORGE, P.- Panorama del mundo actual. Barcelona, Ariel, 1970.

GEORGE, P.- Geografía y medio ambiente, población y economía. Mexico, UNAM, 1979.

GEORGE, S.- How the Other Half Dies. Middlesex, Penguin, 1980.

GEZE, F., et al.- L'Etat du Monde-1982. Paris, Maspero, 1982.

GOUROU, P.- L'Afrique. Paris, Hachette,

1970.

GRANT, JP.- Situaçao Mundial da Infancia. New York, UNICEF, 1984.

GREENBERG, S, ed.- Guinness book of Olympic Records. Bantam, 1988.

GREINER, B.- Amerikanische Aussenpolitik von Truman bis heute. Koln, Pahl-Rugenstein, 1980.

GROUSSET, R.- Historia de Asia. Buenos Aires, EUDEBA, 1962.

GUIA CIUDADANA sobre el Banco Mundial y el Banco Interamericano de Desarrollo, Red Bancos, Instituto del Tercer Mundo, Montevideo, 1996.

GRUNEBAM, GE, ed.- El Islam. Desde la caída de Constantinopla hasta neus-tros días. Mexico, Siglo XXI, 1975.

GUIM, JB.- Compendio de geografía Universal. Mexico, Bouret, 1875.

HALLIDAY, F.- Arabia without Sultans. Middlesex, Penguin, 1974.

HALPERIN DONGHI, T.- Historia contemporánea de América Latina. Madrid, Alianza, 1983.

HAMELINK, C.- The Corporate Village. Rome, IDOC, 1977.

HANDWÖRTERBUCH INTERNATIONALE POLITIK. Wichard Woyke (Hrsg.). Leske Budrich. 1993.

HAYES, MD.- Dimensiones de seguridad de los intereses de Estados Unidos en América Latina. Mexico, CIDE, 1981.

HERRERA, L & VAYRYNEN, R, ed.- Pace, development and New International Economic Order. Tampere, IPRA, 1979.

HUIZER, G.- El potencial revolucionario del campesino en América Latina. Mexico, Siglo XXI, 1974.

HUMAN Rights Newsletter. 1991.

HUMANN, K. & BRODERSEN, I.- Welt Aktuell'86. Hamburg, Roro, 1985.

IBGE.- Tabulaçoes Avançadas do Censo Demográfico. Rio de Janeiro, 1982.

IDB.- External Debt and Economic Development in Latin America. Washington, 1984.

IDB.- Progreso económico y social en América Latina. Washington, 1984.

ILO.- Yearbook of Labour Statistics/Anuario de Estadísticas del Trabajo. Geneva, 1997.

IIED.- World Resources 1986. New York, 1986.

INDEX on Censorship. London. 1991-1992

INSTITUTE OF RACE RELATIONS.- Patterns of Racism. London, 1982.

INSTITUTO GEOGRAFICO DE AGOSTINI.- Atlas

Universal Geo-económico. Barcelona, Teide, 1977.

INTERNATIONAL INSTITUTE FOR STRATEGIC STUDIES.- The Military Balance 1993-94. London, Brassey's, 1993.

INTERNATIONAL INSTITUTE FOR STRATEGIC STUDIES.- Strategic Survey 1982-1983. London, 1983.

INTERNATIONAL COMMISSION OF JURISTS AND CONSUMERS'ASSOCIATION OF PENANG.- Rural development and Human Rights in South East Asia. Penang, 1982.

INTERNATIONAL MONETARY FUND.- Directory of Regional Economic Organizations and Intergovernmental Commodity Organizations. Washington, 1979.

INTERNATIONAL MONETARY FUND.- Estadísticas Financieras Internacionales. Washington, 1985.

JALEE, P.- El Tercer Mundo en la economía Mundial. Mexico, Siglo XXI, 1980.

JAULIN, R.- La des-civilization. Política y práctica del etnocidio. Mexico, Nueva Imagen, 1979.

JONAS, S.& TOBIS, D.-Guatemala. New York, NACLA, 1974.

JOYAUX, F.- L'année internationale 1990. Paris, Hachete, 1989. Annuaire géo-politique de la Revue Politique Internationale.

KAPLAN, L.- Revoluciones. Mexico, Extemporáneos, 1973.

K+K...NEN, J.- The Mechanics of Neo-Colonialism. M+ntt+, Finnish Peace Research Association, 1974.

KENT, G.- Food Trade: The Poor Feed the Rich en the Ecologist Ecosystem. United Kingdom, 1985.

KETTANI, M.- Ali, the Muslim Minorities. Leicester, Islamic Foundation, 1979.

KHADAFI, M.- O livro verde. Tripoli, EPO-EPD.

KHOR, K.P.- Recession and the Malaysian Economy. Penang, Masyarakat, 1983.

KIDROM, M & SEGAL, R.- The State of the World Atlas. London, Pan Books, 1981.

KINDER, H. & HILGEMANN, W.- The Penguin Atlas of World History. New York, 1978.

KI-ZERBO, J.- Historia del Africa Negra. Madrid, Alianza, 1980.

KLAINER, R, LOPEZ, D & PIERA, V.- Aprender con los chicos:propuesta para una tarea docente fundada en los Derechos Humanos. Buenos Aires, MEDH, 1988.

KLARE, M, et al.- Supplying Repression. Washington, IPS, 1981.

KUPER, L.- Genocide: Its political use in the Twentieth Century. Middlesex, Penguin, 1981.

LACOSTE, Y.-Geografía del subdesarrollo. Barcelona, Ariel, 1978.

LACOSTE, Y.-Los países subdesarrollados. Buenos Aires, EUDEBA, 1965.

LAINO, D.- Paraguai: Fronteiras e penetra-çao brasileira. Sao Paulo, Global, 1979.

LEBEDEV, N.- La URSS en la política mun-dial. Moscow, Progreso, 1983.

LEGER SIVARD, R.- World Military and Social Expenditures 1986. Washington, 1986.

LEGER SIVARD, R.- World Military and Social Expenditures 1989. Washington, 1989.

LEWIS, DE.- Reform and revolution in Grenada:1950-1981. Havana, Casa de las Américas, 1984.

LEWYCKY, D.& WHITE, S.- An African abs-tract;Council for International Cooperation. Manitoba, 1979.

LICHTHEIM, G.- Imperialism. Middlesex, Penguin, 1974.

LINHARES, MY.- A luta contra a metrópole (Asia e Africa). Sao Paulo, Brasilense, 1981.

LINIGER GOUMAZ, M.- Guinée Equatorial: de la dictadure des Colons á la Dictadure des Colonels. Geneva, Ed.Temps, 1982.

LINIGER GOUMAZ, M.- De la Guinée Equatorial Nguemiste. Geneva, Ed.Temps, 1982.

LINTER, B.- OUTRAGE: Burma's struggle for democracy. Hong Kong, Review Publ., 1989.

LIPSCHUTZ, A.-El problema racial en la con-quista de América. Mexico, Siglo XXI, 1963.

LUNA, J.-Granada, la nueva joya del Caribe. Havana, Ciencias Sociales, 1982.

McCOY, A.& JESUS, EDC.- Philippine Social History. Manila, ASSA, 1982.

McEVEDY, C.& JONES, R.-Atlas of world Population History. Kerala, 1986. Middlesex, Penguin, 1978

MAGDOFF, H.- La empresa multinacional en una perspectiva histórica. Barcelona, 1980.

MAHATHIR BIN MOHAMED.- The Malay dilema. Selangor, 1982.

MANORAMA Yearbook 1986. Kerala, 1986.

MASUREL, E.- L'année 1989 dans le Monde:les principaux evénements en France et a la l'etranger. Paris, Gallinard, 1990.

MAX-NEEF, M.- La economía descalza. Lima, 1985.

MAYOBRE MACHADO, J.- Información dependencia y desarrollo;la prensa y el nuevo orden económico interna-cional. Caracas, Monte Avila, 1978.

MEILE, P.- Historia de la India. Buenos

Aires, EUDEBA, 1962.

MEJIA RICART, T.- Breve historia dominica-na. Santa Dominica, 1982.

MENENDEZ DEL VALLE, E.- Angola, impe-rialismo y guerra civil. Barcelona, Akal, 1976.

MICHELINI, Z.- Uruguay vencerá. Barcelona, Laja, 1978.

MOITA, L. Os Congressos da Frelimo do PAIGC e do MPLA, CIDAC. Lisbon, 1979.

MOORE LAPPE, F & COLLINS, J.-El hambre en el mundo. Diez mitos. Mexico, COPIDER/FONAPAS, 1980.

MOREIRA, N.- Modelo peruano. Rio de Janeiro, Paz e Terra, 1975.

MOREIRA, N.- El Nasserrismo y la revolu-ción del Tercer Mundo. Montevideo, EBO, 1975.

MPLA.- Historia de Angola. Porto, Afrontamento, 1975.

MYERS, N., ed.- The Gaia Atlas of Planet Management. London, Pan Books, 1985.

MYERS, N.- The Gaia Atlas of future worlds: challenge and opportunity in age of change. London, Gaia, 1990.

MYLLYMAKI, E.& DILLINGER, B.- Dependency and Latin American Development. Finnish Peace Research Association. Tampere, 1977.

El NACIMIENTO de una nación: la lucha por la liberación de Namibia. London, Zed, 1985.

NKRUMAH, K.- I Speak of Freedom. New York, Praeger, 1961.

NKRUMAH, K.- Africa debe unirse. Buenos Aires, EUDEBA, 1965

NEARING, S & FREEMAN, J.- La diplomacia del dólar. Mexico, SELFA, 1926.

NEDJATIGIL, ZM.- The Cyprus Conflict. Nicosia, A-Z Publ., 1981.

NYERERE, JK.- El reto del Sur; informe de la Comisión sur.

NYERERE, JK.- Freedom and Socialism. London, Oxford Univ.Press, 1968.

NEWLAND, K.- The Sisterhood of Man. New York, WW Norton, 1979.

OECD.- Geographical Distribution of Financial Flows to Developing Countries. Paris, 1982.

OMAR TORRIJOS imágenes y voz. Panama, CET, 1985.

O MUNDO HOJE/93. Anuario Economico e Geopolitico Mundial. Ensaio, Sao Paulo, 1993.

ORTIZ MENA, A.-América Latina en des-arrollo. Washington, IDB, 1980.

ORTIZ QUESADA, F.- Salud en la pobreza. Mexico, CEESTEM-Nueva Imagen, 1982.

OSBORNE, M.- Region of Revolt. Focus of Southeast Asia. Middlesex, Penguin, 1970.

OSMANCZYK, EJ.-Enciclopedia Mundial de relaciones internacionales y Naciones Unidas. Madrid, Fondo de Cultura, 1976.

PAIGC.- História da Guiné e Ilhas de Cabo Verde. Porto, Afrontamento, 1974.

PAISES NO ALINEADOS, Los. Mexico, Diogenes, 1976.

PAISES NO ALINEADOS, Los. Prague, Prensa Latina-Orbis, 1979.

PALOMINO, E.- Qosqo, Centro del Mundo, Perú, Municipalidad Provincial del Qosqo, 1993.

PAQUE, R., ed.- Afrika antwortet Europa. Berlin, Ullstein, 1976.

PEASE GARCIA, H., ed.- América Latina 80: Democracia y movimiento popular. Lima, DESCO, 1981.

PERROT, D.& PREISWEK, R.- Etnocentrismo e Historia. Mexico, Nueva Imagen, 1979.

Le PETROLE, les matières de base et le développment. Algeria, Sonatrach, 1974.

PIACENTINI, P.- O Mundo do petróleo. Lisbon, Tricontinental, 1984.

PONCE SANGINES, C.- La cultura nativa en

Bolivia, La Paz, Ed. Amigos del Libro, 1992.

PIERRE-CHARLES, G.- El caribe contemporá-neo. Mexico, Siglo XXI, 1981.

PUTZGER, FW.- Historicher Weltatlas. Berlin, Velhagen, 1961. Quality of Life, from a common people's point of view, by PapyRossa Verlags GmbH & Co. KG, K+ln & World Data Research Center, Ernst Fidel FŸrntratt-Kloep, 1995, Hackús, Sweden.

QUIROGA SANTA CRUZ, M.- El saqueo de Bolivia. Buenos Aires, Crisis, 1973.

RAGHAVAN, Ch.- Un GATT sin cascabel. La Ronda Uruguay, una sigilosa recon-quista del tercer Mundo. Montevideo, Red del Tercer Mundo, 1990

RAGHAVAN, Ch.- Recolonization. GATT, the Uruguay round and the Third World. Penang, Third World Network, 1990

RAHMAN, MA.- Grass-Roots Participation and self-reliance: experiences in South and South East. Asia, ILO, 1984.

RAMA, C.- Historia de América Latina. Barcelona, Bruguera, 1978.

REFORMS in foreigns economic relations of Eastern Europe and the Soviet Union. Proceedings. New York, ECE, 1991. (Economic Studies, 2)

RETURN to the good earth. Third World Network Dossier, Penang, 1983.

REYES MATTA, F, ed.- La noticia internacio-nal. Mexico, ILET, 1977.

RIBEIRO, D.- Las Américas y la civilización. Buenos Aires, Centro Editor, 1973.

RIBEIRO, S.- Sobre a unidade no pensamen-to de Amilcar Cabral. Lisbon, Tricontinental, 1983.

RODNEY, W.- How Europe Underdeveloped Africa. Washington, Howard Univ., 1974.

RODRIGUEZ, M.- Haití, un pueblo rebela-do. Mexico, 1982.

ROGER, M.- Timor - hier la colonisation portugaise, aujourd'hui la résistance. Paris, L'Harmattan, 1977.

SAID, E.- Orientalism. Middlesex, Penguin, 1985.

SALAS, RM.- Estado de la población mun-dial. Barcelona, FNUA, 1983.

SARKAR, S, - Modern India 1885-1947. Madras, McMillan India, 1985.

SCHLESINGER, R.-La Internacional Comunista y el Problema Colonial. Mexico, Pasado y Presente, 1974.

SCHMIEDER, O.- Geografía de América Latina. Mexico, FCE, 1975.

SCHUON, F.- Understanding Islam. London, Mandala Books, 1979.

SEAGER, J & OLSON, A.- Women in the world. An International Atlas. London, Pan Books, 1986.

SECRETARIA DE AGRICULTURA (MEXICO).- El desarrollo Agroindustrial y la Economía Internacional. 1979.

SEGAL, G.- The world affairs companion. New York, Touchstone, 1991.

SELSER, G.- Apuntes sobre Nicaragua. Mexico, CESTEM, 1981.

SERRYN, P.- le Monde d'aujourd'hui. Paris, Bordas, 1981.

SHINNIE, P.- Ancient African Kingdoms. New York, Mentor, 1980.

SHIVA, V.- The violence of the green revolu-tion, ecological degradation and poli-tical conflict in Punjab. India, 1989.

SITUACION en el mundo 1991, La. Buenos Aires, Sudamericana, 1991.

SIVARD, RL.- World Military and Social Expeditures. Virginia, World Priorities, 1979.

SOCIAL WATCH - The Starting Point, Nº 1 and Nº 2, Instituto del Tercer Mundo, Montevideo, 1996, 1997 and 1998.

SOMALIA.MINISTRY OF INFORMATION.-The Arab World. Magdishn, 1975. SOY un soldado de América Latina. Panama, CET, 1981.

STANLEY, D.- Eastern Europe on a shoestring. Australia, Lonely Planet, 1989.

STANLEY, D.- South Pacific Handbook. Hong Kong, Moon Publ., 1982.

STATE OF THE WORLD 1991-1996. World Watch Institute, New York, Norton & Company, 1996.

STAVRIANOS, LS.- Global Rift.The Third World Comes of Age. New York, William Morow, 1981.

SUAREZ, L.- Los Países No Alineados. Mexico, FCE, 1975.

SUB-SHARAN AFRICA: From crisis to sustainable growth, a long-term perspective study. Washington, World Bank, 1989.

SUTER, K.- West Irian, East Timor and Indonesia. London, 1979.

SWEEZY, P.- Teoria do Desenvolvimento Capitalista. Sao Paulo, Abril, 1983.

TERRE DES FEMMES. Panorama de la situation des femmes dans le monde. Paris, La Découverte, 1982.

THE STATE of the World's Refugees 1995, United Nations High Commissioner for Refugees-UNHCR, New York, 1995.

THE UNIVERSAL ALMANAC 1994. Wright, John W. USA, 1993.

THIRD WORLD FOUNDATION.- Third World Affairs 1987. London, 1987.

THOMAS, EJ., ed.- Les travailleurs immigrés en Europe: quel status? Paris, UNESCO, 1981.

TIMERMAN, J.- Israel: La Guerra más larga. Madrid, Mochnik, 1983.

TITO, JB.- La misión histórica del Movimiento de No Alineación. Beograd, CAS, 1979.

TOMLINSON, A. & WHANNEL, G., ed.- Five-ring circus: Money, power and politics at the Olympic Games. London, Pluto Press, 1984.

TORRIELLO GARRIDO, G.- Tras la Cortina de Banano. Havana, Ciencias Sociales, 1979.

TORRIJOS, O.- La quinta frontera. Costa Rica, Ed.Univ.Centroamericana, 1981.

TORRIJOS, O.- Figura, tiempo, faena. Panama, Lotería Nacional, 1981.

TOWARDS Socialist Planning. Tanzania, UCHEMI, 1980.

TRIBUNAL PERMANENTE DOS POVOS. Sessao sobre Timor-Leste. Lisbon, 1981.

TUNBULL, M.- A Short History of Malaysia, Singapore and Brunei. Singapore, Graham Brash, 1980.

UL HAQ, M.- La cortina de la pobreza. Mexico, FCE, 1978.

UN.- ABC das Nacoes Unidas. New York, 1982.

UN.- Concise Report on the World Population situation. New York, 1979.

UN.- Demographic Yearbook. New York, 1984.

UN.- Efectos de la empresas multinacionales en el desarrollo. New York, 1974.

UN.- Final documents of the Eighth Conference of Heads of States or Government of Non-Aligned Countries. New York, 1986.

UN.- A guide to the New Law of the Sea. New York, 1979.

UN.- Informe del Comité Especial sobre descolonización. New York, 1975.

UN.- Monthly Bulletin of Statistics. New York.

UN.- Resolutions and Decisions. General Assembly. New York, 1995.

UN.- Resolutions on the Palestine question. Beirut

UN.- Statistical Yearbook, 41st issue. New York, 1997.

UN.- Statistical Yearbook for Asia and the Pacific. New York, 1980.

UN.- Terminology Bulletin. New York, 1979.

UN.- A trust betrayed: Namibia. New York, 1974.

UN.- UNCTAD VII. Actas. Geneva 1987.

UNCTAD.- Handbook of International Trade and Development Statistics

1995. New York, 1997.

UNESCO.- Geografía de América Latina. Barcelona, 1975.

UNESCO.- Historia General de Africa.

UNESCO-Tecnos, 1987.

UNESCO.- Recherches en matière du relations raciales. Paris, 1965.

UNESCO.- Résumé statistique. Paris, 1982.

UNESCO.- Yearbook 1984. Paris, 1985.

UNDP.- Human Development Reports 1980-2001. New York, 2001.

UNICEF.- The State of the World's Children Report 2000. New York 2000.

URSS Anuario 1991. Moscow, Novosti.

US ARMS CONTROL AND DISARMAMENT-TAGENCY.- World Military Expenditure and Arms Transfer 1972-1982. Washington, 1982.

VALDES VIVO, R.- Etiopía: la Revolución desconocida. Havana, Ciencias Sociales, 1977.

VARELA BARRAZA, H.- Africa:Crisis del poder político. Mexico, CEESTEM, 1981.

VARGAS, JA.- Terminología sobre Derecho del Mar. Mexico, CEESTEM, 1979.

VENTURA, J.- El Poder Popular en El Salvador. Mexico, SALPRESS, 1983.

VERDIEU, E & BWATSHIA, K.- Les Eglises face au Nouvel Ordre Economique National e International. Quebec, CECI, 1980.

VERDIEU, E & BWATSHIA, K.- Cooperation Technique des Pays en Development;est-ce Possible? Quebec, CECI, 1980.

VERDIEU, E & BWATSHIA, K.- Liberation et Autonomie Collectives. Québec, CECI, 1980.

VERLAG DIE WIRTSHAFT.- L+nder der Erde. Koln, Pahl- Rugenstein, 1982.

VIEL, B.- La explosión demográfica. Mexico, PAX, 1974.

VILLALOBOS, J.- Por qué lucha el FMLN. Radio Venceremos, 1983.

VILLEGAS QUIROGA, C & AGUIRRE BADANI, A.- Estudio de la crisis y la nueva política económica en Bolivia. Bolivia, Centro de Estudios para el Desarrollo Laboral y Agrario.

VISION de Belice. Havana, Casa de las América, 1982.

VIVO ESCOTO, JA.- Geografía Humana y Económica. Mexico, Patria, 1975.

WEISSMAN, S. et al.- The Trojan Horse. A radical Look at Foreign Aid. San Francisco, Ramparts, 1974.

WETTSTEIN, G.- Subdesarrollo y geografía. Mérida, Universida de los Andes, 1978.

WHANNEL, G.- Blowing the whistle: The politics of sport. London, Pluto, 1983.

WIENER, D.- Shalom, Israels Friedensbewegung. Hamburg, Rowohlt, 1984.

WILLIAMS, N.- Chronology of the modern World 1763-1965. Middlesex, Penguin, 1975.

WOLFE, A.et al.- La cuestión de la Democracia. Mexico, UILA, 1980.

WORLD DEBT TABLES 1996. External debt of developing countries. Washington, 1996.

WORLD BANK.- Atlas 1996. New York, 1996.

WORLD BANK.- Energy in the Developing Countries. Washington, 1980.

WORLD BANK.- World Development Indicators 2002. Washington, 2002.

WORLD FACTS and MAPS. Rand McNally. USA, 1994.

WORLD OF INFORMATION: The Africa Review 2001; The Americas Review 2001; The Asia and Pacific Review 2001; The Europe Review 2001; The Middle East Review 2001 - Walden Publishing Ltd, Saffron Walden, UK, 2001.

WORLD Military Expenditure and Arms Transfer 1972-1982. Washington,1984.

WORLD RESOURCES INSTITUTE.- The Environmental Almanac 1993.

Houghton Mifflin Company, Boston & New York, 1992.

WORLD RESOURCES INSTITUTE.- World Resources 1990-91. A guide to the global environment. New York, Oxford Univ., 1991.

WORLD RESOURCE INSTITUTE.- World Resources 1986. New York, Basic Books, 1986.

WORSLEY, P.- El tercer Mundo: una nueva fuerza en los asuntos internacionales. Mexico, Siglo XXI, 1978.

ZERAOUI, Z.- El mundo arabe: imperialismo y nacionalismo. Mexico, CEESTEM-Nueva Imágen, 1981.

ZERAOUI, Z.- Irán-Iraq: guerra política y sociedad. Mexico, Nueva Imágen, 1982.

ZIEGLER, J.- Main Basse sur l'Afrique. Paris, Du Seuil, 1978.

PERIODICALS

Africa News, Durham, NC, EUA

Afrique Mass-Media, Budapest, Hungary

Afrique Nouvelle, Dakar, Senegal

Afrique-Asie, Paris, France

ALAI, Montreal, Canada

ALDHU, Quito, Ecuador

Altercom, Mexico,

AMPO Japan-Asia Quarterly Review,Tokyo,

Análisis, Santiago de Chile,

APSI, Santiago de Chile, Chile

AQUI, La Paz, Bolivia

Barricada Internacional, Managua, Nicaragua

Bohemia, La Habana, Cuba

Boletín de Namibia, UNITED NATIONS, New York

Bulletin of Concerned African Scholars, Charlemont, MA, EUA

Caribbean Monthly, Río Piedras, Puerto Rico

CEAL, Brussels, Belgium

Central America Update, Toronto, Canada

CERES, Rome, Italy

CILA, Mexico

Comercio Exterior, Mexico,

Contextos, Mexico,

Counterspy, Washington, DC, EUA

CovertAction, Washington, EUA

CRIE, Mexico,

Cuadernos del Tercer Mundo, Brasil,

Descolonización, UNITED NATIONS, New York

Diálogo Social, Panama,

Documentos FIPAD, Ginebra, Switzerland

Economie et Politique, Paris, France

El Caribe Contemporáneo, Mexico,

Eritrea in Struggle, New York, EUA

Facts & Reports, Amsterdam, Netherlands

Far Eastern Economic Review, Asia 1990, Yearbook. Japan

Fortune International, Los Angeles, CA, EUA

Freedomways, New York, EUA

Gombay, Belize

IFDA, Nyon, Switzerland

Informe R - CEDOIN , Bolivia.

Indian and Foreign Review, New Delhi, India

Internews, Berkeley, EUA

Isis, Rome, Italy

Ko-Eyú, Caracas, Venezuela

L'Economiste du Tiers Monde, Paris, France

Lateinamerika Nachrichten, Berlin

Latin America Weekly Report, London, United Kingdom

Le Monde Diplomatique, Paris, France

Monthly Review, New York, US

Mujer-Fempress, Santiago, Chile.

Multinational Monitor, Washington, US

NACLA Report on the Americas, New York, US

New Outlook, Dar-es-Salaam, Tanzania

New Internationalist, Oxford, UK

Newsfront International, Oakland, US

Noticias Aliadas, Lima, Peru

Novembro, Luanda, Angola

O Correio da UNESCO, Paris-Rio de Janeiro,

Onze Wereld, Den Haag, Netherlands

Palestine, Beirut, Lebanon

Pensamiento Propio, Managua, Nicaragua

Philippine Liberation Courier, Oakland, US

Política Internazionale, Rome, Italy

Política Internacional, Belgrade, Yugoslavia

Resister (Bulletin of the Committee on South African War Resistance), London, UK

Revista del Centro de Estudios del Tercer Mundo, Mexico.

Revista del Sur, ITeM, Montevideo, Uruguay.

Sharing, Geneva, Switzerland

SIAL, Italy

Soberanía, Managua, Nicaragua

Southern Africa, New York, US

Statesman's Yearbook, 1988-1989.

Tempo, Maputo, Mozambique

Tercer Mundo Económico, ITeM, Montevideo, Uruguay

The Black Scholar, Sausalito, CA, US

The Ecologist, United Kingdom.

The CTC Reporter, UNITED NATIONS, New York.

Third World Quarterly, London, United Kingdom.

Third World Resurgence, Penang, Malaysia.

Tiempos Nuevos, Moscow

Tigris, Madrid, Spain

Tribune, Sri Lanka

Tricontinental, Havana, Cuba

Two Thirds, A journal of underdeveloment studies, Toronto, Canada

WISE (World Information Service on Energy), Netherlands

YEKATIT Quarterly, Addis Ababa, Ethiopia

NEWS AGENCIES

Interpress – IPS, INA, WAFA, SALPRESS, ANN, Prensa Latina, Angop, AIM, Shihata.

ALAI (Agencia Latinoamericana de Información).

SEM (Servicio Especial de la Mujer).

ELECTRONIC SOURCES

Rulers: http://www.geocities.com/Athens/1058/rulers.html

Le Monde Diplomatique online: http://www.ina.fr/CP/MondeDiplo/Thesaurus/thesaurus.fr.html

Folha de São Paulo: http://www.uol.com.br/fsp/

OneWorld News Service: http:// www.one-world.org/news/index.html

Fourth World Documentation Project: http://www.halcyon.com/FWDP/fwdp.html

Banco Interamericano de Desarrollo: http://www.iadb.org/

OMRI Daily Digest: http://www.omri.cz/Publications/Digests/DigestIndex.html

Il Manifesto in Rete: http://www.mir.it/mani/index.html

Electric Library: http://www.elibrary.com/id/2525/

United Nations: http://www.un.org/

The Washington Report's Resources Page: http://www.washington-report.org/links.html

Foundation for Middle East Peace: http://www2.ari.net/fmep/

Institute of Latin American Studies: http://lanic.utexas.edu/

New Internationalist magazine: http://www.newint.org

Index

Fernandes, George 295, 297, 433
Fernández de Quiros, Pedro 572
Fernandez, Max 140
Fernández, Roque 104
Fernando of Aragon 508
Ferreira Aldunate, Wilson 568
Ferrieux-Patterson, Marie-Noelle 572
Figueres Ferrer, José 200
Figueres Olsen, José María 202
Fiji 244, 253
Fijian archipelago 244
Financial Intelligence Unit (FIU) 126
Finland 246
Finnbogadottir, Vigdis 292
Finno-Ugric peoples 239, 246
First Gypsy Congress 340
FIS 88, 89
Five Day War 228
Fleming, Osbourne 95
FLN 88, 89
flora 48
Florakis, Charilaos 269
Flores Bedregal, Carlos 139
Flores Pérez, Francisco 234
Flores, Carlos 288
Flores, Venancio 102
Flosse, Gaston 253
FNLA 91
Fogh Rasmussen, Anders 216
Fokin, Vitold 555
Fon society 133
Food and Agriculture Organization (FAO) 380
forced labor 32
forced servitude 32
Ford, Gerald 225, 299
forestation 25
forests 48, 52
Forlani, Arnaldo 315
Formosa 335
Forné, Marc 90
Forza Italia 316
fossil fuels 50, 51, 52
Fox Quesada, Vicente 209, 386, 387
FPÖ 115
France 102, 129, 213, 248, 249, 252, 260, 340
Francisco de Miranda 574
Franco, Francisco 508, 509
Franco, Itamar 149, 150
Franco, Julio César 446
Franco-German War 215
Franco-Laotian Convention 344
freedom 40, 45
freedom fighter 64
Freetown 493
Frei, Eduardo 178
FRELIMO 400, 402
French Foreign Legion 174
French Guiana 252
French Polynesia 250, 253
French Revolution 90, 205, 248
French Somaliland 218
Frepaso 102, 104
Frey 215
Friederici, Gonthier 463
Frogier, Pierre 326, 327
FROLINAT 174
Frondizi, Arturo 103
Front for the Liberation of Mozambique 400
Fru Ndi, John 164
Frunze 342
FSLN 417, 418
Fujimori, Alberto 140

Fukuyama, Francis 19
Fulah 378
Fundamentalism 30, 31
Futa people 257

G

Gabon 172, 236, 254, 278
Gabu, state of 280
Gabusan Politick Indonesia 298
Gagauz 154
Gairy, Eric Matthew 270
Galab, Yacin Yabeh 219
Galaydh, Ali Khalif 502
Galtieri, Leopoldo 103
Gambia 256, 489
Gambia River 256, 346
Gamsakhurdia, Zviad 258
Gandhi, Indira 295
Gandhi, Mohandas K (Mahatma) 122, 294, 295
Gandhi, Rajiv 296, 297
Gandhi-King-Ikeda Peace Prize 476
Ganges River 294
Ganilau, Penaia 244
Garang, John 516
garbage 26
Garcia Meza, Luis 139
Gardner, Geoffrey Robert 112
Garifuna 132
Garrastazú Médici, Emilio 148
Garzón, Baltasar 179, 446
gases 50
Gaspar Dutra, Eurico 148
GATT agreements 73, 111, 209
Gauchos 101
Gaul region 248
Gaviria, Cesar 190, 191
Gayoom, Maumoon Abdul 372
Gaza strip 231
Gbagbo, Laurent 204
Gbezera-Bria, Michel 173
Geagea, Samir 350
Geelchand, Geehad 383
Geingob, Hage 406
Geisel, Ernesto 148
Gemayel, Amin 349
Gemayel, Bashir 349
Gempei War 319
Gender violence 23
General Union of Italian Workers 315
generic drugs 73
Geneva Conventions 69
Genghis Khan 81, 180, 183, 304, 328, 392, 467, 577
genital mutilation 41
genocide 68, 199, 277
Georgia 258, 471
German Court at Leipzig 68
German Customs Union 260
German Empire 314, 358
German-Soviet pact 471
Germania 260
Germanic peoples 260
Germany 213, 249, 260, 314
Ghana 264, 507
Ghezo 133
Ghibellines 314, 391
Ghozali, Sid Ahmed 88
Ghulam Ishaq Khan 432
Ghulam Mustafa Jatoi 432
GIA 89
Gibraltar 510
Gilbert Islands 333
Gilbert, Humphrey 165
Gilbert, Thomas 333

Gilead kingdom 324
Giménez de Quesada, Gonzalo 189
Giscard D'Estaing, Valery 249, 254
glasnost 116, 128
Gligorov, Kiro 363
global community 19
global justice 70
global warming 48, 50, 52
globalization 19, 20, 22, 31, 54, 199
Go-Daigo 319
Golan Heights 231, 311, 350, 529
gold 92, 199, 507
Goldstein, Baruch 312
Golkar, Sekber 299
Gombasuren, Tserenpylium 393
Gómez, Laureano 189
Gorkha 409
Gonsalves, Ralph 478
Gontebanye Mogae, Festus 145
González Macchi, Luis 446
González, Elián 209
González, Epaminondas 276
Gopala 122
Gorbachev, Mikhail 116, 128, 292, 329, 342, 346, 469, 471, 549, 570
Gordon, Pamela 135
Gore, Al 566
Goths 398
Goulart, João 148
Goumba, Abel 172
Gourad Hamadou, Barkad 218, 219
Gowda, Deve 297
Gramsci, Antonio 315
Grand Comoro 192
Grand Duchy of Lithuania 359
Grand Duke Henri 361
Great Ayatollah 302
Great Lakes 92
Great Moravia 212
Great Northern War 346
Great Wall of China 392
Greater Colombia 227
Greco-Turkish War 362
Greece 210, 258, 261, 267
Greek Empire 230
Greek Orthodox Church 210
Greek-Cypriot 2101
greenhouse effect 49, 50, 51, 52
Greenpeace 293, 322
Greenland 217
Gregorian 154
Gregory VI 573
Grenada 125, 221, 270
Grib, Mecheslav 128
Grimaldis 391
Grimsson, Olafur Ragnar 293
Guadeloupe 250, 272
Guam 273
Guama 207
Guantanamo military base 209
Guaraní 147, 444, 567
Guardia, Tomás 200
Guatemala 131, 274
Guaycurús 444
Gudauta city 259
Guéi, Robert 204
Gueiler, Lidia 139
Guelfs 314, 391
Guelleh, Omar 219
Guerrero, Larry 425
Guevara Arce, Walter 139
Guevara, Ernesto 'Che' 93, 139
Guiana 252

Guinea 203, 278, 489
Guinea-Bissau 169, 257, 280
Guingona, Teofisto 451
Guiteras, Antonio 207
Gujral, Inder Kumar 297
Gukassian, Arkady 117, 471
Gulbuddin 82
Gulf Cooperation Council 429, 430
Gulf of Arabia 339
Gulf of Finland 246
Gulf War 62, 63, 120, 121, 124, 302, 306, 332, 340, 383, 432, 462, 566
Gumbs, Emile 95
Guptas 294
Gurion, David Ben 311
Gurkha 409
Gurma 157
Gurmantehé 157
Gurney, Tim 135
Gurunsi 157
Gusmão, Xanana 225, 226
Gutiérrez Ruiz, Héctor 446
Gutiérrez, Carl TC 273
Guyana 282
Guzmán, Abimael 449
Guzmán, Antonio 223
Guzmán, Jaime 178
Guzmán, Joaquín 'el Chapo' 387
Guzmán, Juan 179
gypsies 154, 340

H

H-bomb 376
Haakon IV 426
Haakon VII 427
Habib Souaidia 89
Habib, Bourguiba 544
Habibie, Jusuf 226, 300
Habré, Hissene 174, 488
Habyarimana, Juvenal 158
Hachani, Abdelkader 89
Haddad, Saad 349
Haekkerup, Hans 589
Hafez al-Shaikh 121
Haganah 310
Haidalla, Ould 378
Haidan 165
Haider, Joerg 115
Haiti 284
Hakim, Brahim 583
Hakka 175
Halilovic, Safet 142
Halonen, Tarja 247
Hamani Diori 419
Hamas 312, 438
Han 392
Han Dong, Lee 338
Hannibalsson, Jon Baldvin 293
Hanseatic League 346
Hapsburg Empire 114, 411
Harakat-e Islami 82
Harappa 294
hardwoods 49
Harijans 295
Harris, René 408
Hashemite Kingdom of Transjordan 324
Hashi, Mohammed Abdi 502
Hashim, Salamat 452
Hashimoto, Ryutaro 322, 323
Hasler, Otmar 358
Hassan Ali, Kamil 219
Hassan I Sabah 64
Hassan II 397, 399, 582

L

M

Meri, Lennart 240
MESAN 172
Mesic, Stipe 206
Mesolithic 307
Mesopotamia 585
Mesopotamian civilization 339
Messner, Anthony J 112
Meta, Ilir 86
Methodius 212
Metro Manila 451
Metternich, Clemens 114
Mexica 384
Mexica civilization 227
Mexico 200, 233, 234, 274, 384
Michelini, Zelmar 446
Micombero, Michael 158
Micronesia 388, 408
Micronesian archipelago 273
Middle Age 20, 21, 55, 57
Middle East 310, 311, 438, 462, 489
Middle Stone Age 307
Midway Island 566
Migration 25
Mikerevic, Dragan 142
Militant Mauritius Movement 381
military tribunal 68, 69
Millennium Island 333
Miller, Leszek 454, 455
millet 507
Milongo, André 197
Milosevic, Slobodan 69, 590, 591
Milutinovic, Milan 589
Mindaugas 359
Ming dynasty 335, 392
minority 22, 45, 114
Mintoff, Dominic 375
Miskito 416
Mitchell, James 220
Mitchell, Keith 271
Mitla 384
Mitre, Bartolomé 102
Mitsotakis, Constantinos 269
Mitterrand, François 203, 218, 249, 253
Mixtec culture 384
Miyazawa, Kiichi 321, 323
Mladenov, Petur 155
Mladic, Ratko 143
MMM 381
MNR 139
MNSD 419, 420
Moab kingdom 324
Moada, Mohamed 544
Moate, Terepai 99
Moawad, René 349
Moctezuma II 384
Mocumbi, Pascoal 401
modern democracies 44
modern war 62
Mogadishu 502
Moghul Empire 294
Mohamad Saaid, Ainum 370
Mohamad, Mahathir 369
Mohammad Qasem Fahim 84
Mohammed Asif Mohseni 82
Mohan Adhikari, Man 410
Moheli 192
Mohenjo Daro 294
Moi, Daniel Arap 331
Moje-Dajan 342
Moldova 289, 389
Molotov-Ribbentrop pact 239
Moluccans 21
Moluccas 298
Mombasa 332
Monaco 391

Moncada Army Base 207
Money Laundering Working Group 376
money-laundering 96
money-lending 55, 57
Mongol Empire 260, 342, 392
Mongolia 392
Mongolian National Democratic Party 394
Mongoose Squad 270
Monkare, Sinikka 247
monoculture plantations 49
Monomotapa 400, 507
Monroe, James 354
Monsignor Karl Lehmann 573
Monsignor Oscar A Romero 233
Monte Carlo center 391
Monteiro, Antonio Mascarenhas 170
Montenegro 590, 591
Montesinos, Vladimiro 441, 449
Montesquieu 45
Montevideo 236, 567, 568, 569
Montroville-Sebastian, Cuthbert 476
Montserrat 221, 395
Moor 582
Moors 90
Morales, Evo 140
Moravcik, Jozef 497
Moravia 212, 213, 261
Morazán, Francisco 200, 233, 287
Morda, Mael 307
Morillo, Pablo 189
Mormons 41
Moro, Aldo 315
Morocco 249, 396, 582, 583
Moruroa atoll 98
Moscoso, Mireya 440, 441
Moscow 469
Moshoeshoe 351
Mosquito coast 287
Mossadegh 301
Mothers of Plaza de Mayo 102
Motzfeldt, Jonathan 217
Mouhoun River 156
Mount Lebanon 348
Movement of National Resistance 401
Movement of Non-Aligned Countries 317, 357, 375, 404
Mozambique 169, 400
MST 149,150
MPLA 91, 92, 93
Muashe, Marwan 325
Muatetema Rivas, Cándido 237
Mubarak, Hosni 231, 232, 303, 516, 587
Mugabe, Robert 595
Mughal 122
Mughal Empire 122
Muhamad Buhari 423
Muhammad Ali Jinnah 431
mujahedin 62, 83, 301
Mullah Muhammar Omar 566
Mullah Omar 82, 84
Mulroney, Brian 166
multinationals 34
multiparty elections 44
Muluzi, Bakili 367
Mundani 175
Mundigak 81
Muraliyev, Amangeldy Mursadykovich 343
Murayama, Tomiichi 322
Murillo, Pedro Domingo 138
Murtada, Ahmad 306

Murtaza 432
Mururoa atoll 112, 253, 326
Musa, Said Wilbert 132
Muscat 429, 430
Museveni, Yoweri 472, 553
Musharraf, Pervez 297, 432, 433
Muslim women 38, 40
Muslim world 30, 31, 32, 38, 40, 41, 82, 87, 88, 89, 90, 106, 107, 108, 110, 111, 117, 154
Muslims 38, 41, 122, 157, 206, 294, 350, 523, 528
Mussolini, Benito 85, 241, 315, 481, 573
Mutalibov, Ayaz 117
Mwakenya group 331
Mwanawasa, Levy 593
Myanmar see Burma
Mycenae 267

N

N'Guessan, Affi 204
Nabataea 349
Nabataeans 324
NAFTA 168, 178
Nagasaki 320
Nagorno-Karabakh 106, 107, 116, 117, 471
Naguib, Mohammed 231
Nahnah, Mahfoud 89
Nairobi 331
Naitini, Ilikini 245
Najibullah, Mohammed 83
Nakamura, Kuniwo 434
Nama people 405
Namgyal, Ngawang 136
Namibia 92, 405, 421, 534
Nano, Fatos 86
Napoleonic Wars 205, 215, 496, 521, 588
Narayanan, Kocheril Raman 295
Nariño, Antonio 189
Nasrin, Taslima 124
Nasser Muhammad, Ali 586
Nasser, Gamal Abdel 231, 295, 311, 436, 528
Nastase, Adrian 465
Natapei, Edward 572
Nathan, Sellapan Ramanthan 495
nation-states 21, 22
National Congolese Movement 194
National Independence Movement of Latvia 346
National Security Doctrine 446
National Union for the Total Independence of Angola 93, 421
nationalism 21
native forest 48, 49
NATO 115, 129, 143, 155, 167, 292, 347, 360, 375, 413, 427, 469, 499, 509, 510, 526, 545, 546, 556, 562, 564, 565, 566, 589, 591
natural environment 25, 26
Natusch Busch, Alberto 139
Nauru 408
Nauru Party 408
Nauruan people 408
Navajo 22, 563
Navitski, Henadz 128
Nawaz Sharif 432, 433
Nazarbayev, Nursultan 329
Nazca civilization 227
Nazi genocide 68
Nazi Germany 214, 340, 526

nazism 44
Ndabaningi Sithole 595, 596
Ndadaye, Melchior 158
Ndowe peoples 236
Nearco 339
Nehru, Jawaharlal 295
Neo Lao Haksat 344
Neo Lao Issara 344
neo-classical era 21
neo-colonialism 254
neo-Confucian doctrine 334
neoliberal economic model 54
Neoliberalism 54, 55
Neolithic era 81, 307, 507
NEPAD 506
Nepal 409
Neptune, Yvon 286
Netanyahu, Binyamin 312, 313
Netherlands 261, 361
Neto, Agostinho 92, 93, 197
Neves, Tancredo 148, 149
New Caledonia/Kanaky 250, 326
New Partnership for Africa's Development (NEPAD) 506
New Testament 57
New Zealand see Aotearoa 253
Nez Percé 563
Ngale people 195
Ngalong 136
Ngoni-Ndwande 366
Nhassé, Alamara 281
Niamey 420
Niasse, Mustafa 488
Nicaragua 103, 131, 201
Nicholas II 468
Nicosia 211
Nigeria 91, 133, 255, 257, 422, 489, 507
Nikunau Island 333
Nile valley 230, 507
Nilotic people 330
Niue 98
Nixon, Richard 565
Niyazov Turkmenbashi, Saparmurad 548, 549
Njenga, Karume 331
Njonjo, Charles 331
Njoya, Adamu Ndam 164
Nkomati agreements 401
Nkrumah, Kwame 264
Nkumbula, Harry 592
Nobel Peace Prize 70, 338
Nobel Prize for Economics 54
Noboa Bejarano, Gustavo 228
Noboa, Gustavo 228
non-aligned 44
Non-Aligned Movement 132, 161, 189, 298, 403
Nonouti Island 333
Norac, Mirko 206
Nordic Council 292
Nordli, Oddvar 427
Norfolk Island 112
Noriega, Manuel Antonio 119, 439, 440
North Korea 208, 334, 336
Northern Alliance 82
Northern Marianas 425
Norway 215, 261, 292, 350, 426
Nosavang, Fumi 344
Note, Kessai H 376
Nouméa Accord 327
Novotny, Antony 213
Ntanira na Mugambo 332
Ntaryamira, Cyprien 158, 473
Ntoutoume-Emane, Jean-François 255